The Daily Walk® BIBLE

BRUCE H. WILKINSON
Executive Editor

PAULA A. KIRK
General Editor

JOHN W. HOOVER
Editor

Walk Thru the Bible Ministries, Inc.
Atlanta, Georgia

Tyndale House Publishers, Inc.
Wheaton, Illinois

03   02   01   00
10   9   8   7   6   5   4   3   2

THE DAILY WALK® BIBLE

Index
to the books of the Bible

Alphabetical Index
to the books of the Bible

Introduction

You are holding in your hands a book designed to help you in your spiritual walk with God. *The Daily Walk Bible* brings together the insightful devotionals from Walk Thru the Bible's *Daily Walk* reading guide and the popular New International Version.

As a result, you can spend a fruitful time each day in God's Word by gaining practical devotional insights related to the Scripture you've read. At the end of one year you will have read the Bible from cover to cover at an easy, manageable pace . . . and you will have enjoyed it! But more than that, you will find your relationship with the Lord deepening as you spend time reading and meditating on his Word.

Not only is *The Daily Walk Bible* appropriate for personal devotions, you can also use it with your children as a family devotional. And churches can use it in Bible study groups or simply to encourage congregational reading of God's Word.

As a result of using *The Daily Walk Bible,* you will see the Scriptures from Genesis to Revelation in a new light and be able to understand how they all fit together. You will experience firsthand how practical God's Word is as you find the answers to the perplexing problems you face each day. You will learn from great men and women of faith how to express your innermost thoughts to God . . . how to handle disappointments and heartaches . . . how to express joy and praise . . . how to draw on the unlimited power of God moment by moment . . . and so much more. And you will delight in sharing your newfound knowledge with others, helping them to cope in their chaotic world by turning to the life-changing Word of God.

The Daily Walk Bible will help transform your attitudes and energize you with confidence in your loving God by giving you new insight into his Scriptures. With the Bible as your foundation for living, you will never be the same again.

We at Walk Thru the Bible Ministries are thrilled to join together with Tyndale House Publishers to make this Bible-reading devotional tool available to you. The common purpose of our ministries is to help more Christians become rooted and grounded in the Scriptures.

And now, prepare yourself for the walk of your lifetime!

Bruce H. Wilkinson
President and Executive Editor
Walk Thru the Bible Ministries

How to Get the Most out of *The Daily Walk Bible*

The Daily Walk Bible is conveniently arranged for daily Bible reading 365 days of the year. Each section is dated with the month and the day; however, if you would like to start reading through the Bible at some time in the year other than January, simply use the optional reading track ("Day 231"), and put a check mark in the box to help you keep your place.

 Overview provides a foretaste for your Bible reading of the day. A convenient chart also summarizes the main ideas of the Scripture section.

 Your Daily Walk encourages you to think carefully about one scriptural insight from the day's reading and offers you specific ways to put the truths you will read into action in your own life. Principles from God's Word are explained practically to help you successfully cope with life today.

 Insight brings to light a fascinating scriptural or historical fact to build your total Bible knowledge.

Every seventh day, four times a month, you'll have the opportunity to pause and rest in your walk through the Bible with a special devotional reviewing the past several days' readings. After you *Look Back* at the broad sweep of your reading for the previous week, you can *Look Up* at God and consider what he wants to say to you through his Word and *Look Ahead* at what's to come. You can also use this seventh day to catch up on any reading from the past few days.

You will also find in *The Daily Walk Bible* a helpful introductory page for each of the sixty-six books of the Bible. A concise overview of the background and purpose of each book is followed by a useful chart summarizing its content and flow.

Every feature of *The Daily Walk Bible* is designed to help you get the most out of your devotional times with the Lord. It's the tool you have been looking for to bring the Bible alive for you!

Walk Thru the Bible Ministries

Walk Thru the Bible Ministries (WTB) unofficially began in the early 1970s in Portland, Oregon. A young teacher named Bruce Wilkinson developed an innovative way of teaching Old and New Testament surveys of the Bible.

From these small beginnings emerged the multifaceted Bible-teaching outreach that Dr. Wilkinson officially founded as a nonprofit ministry in 1976. WTB has grown into one of the leading Christian organizations in America with an international ministry extending to more than fifty countries representing some thirty-five languages. International branch offices are located in Australia, Great Britain, Singapore, New Zealand, South Africa and Ukraine.

By focusing on the central themes of Scripture and their practical application, WTB has been able to develop and maintain wide acceptance in denominations and fellowships around the world. In addition, it has carefully initiated strategic ministry alliances with more than one hundred Christian organizations and missions of wide diversity and background.

WTB has four major outreach ministries: seminars, publishing, leadership training and video.

Seminars Since it began its seminar ministry more than two decades ago, WTB has instructed more than 2 million people worldwide through seminars taught by more than 1,600 certified teachers. People of all ages and religious persuasions have developed a deeper understanding of the Bible through these unique Old and New Testament surveys, and many have come to know Christ in a new and more personal way.

Publishing WTB's publishing ministry began in 1978 with the launching of *The Daily Walk* magazine. Since then, WTB Publishing has continued to develop additional publications that enable individuals and families to maintain a meaningful habit of daily devotional time in the Word of God. The publications include *Closer Walk, Family Walk, LifeWalk, Quiet Walk, Youthwalk* and *Tapestry*.

Leadership Training WTB's Leadership Training ministry goes into the secular marketplace as well as churches and organizations to communicate biblical principles of leadership. There are several leadership modules available to fit the unique needs of each group. Each training module provides practical tools that make biblical truth relevant in both personal relationships and in the marketplace.

Video Training The newest ministry of WTB is the video-training curriculum. In just a few short years, the WTB creative team has developed a number of leading video courses that have enjoyed widespread distribution. Video makes it possible to bring WTB's life-changing Bible teaching into churches and homes throughout the world.

WTB has had a consistent history of strategic ministry from the beginning. The organization strives to help fulfill the Great Commission in obedience to the Lord's call. With this mission in mind, WTB lives out its commitment to excellence with the highest standards of ethical conduct and integrity, not only in ministry, but also in its internal operational policies and procedures. No matter what the ministry, no matter where the ministry, WTB focuses on the Word of God and encourages people of all nations to grow in their knowledge of God and in unreserved obedience and service to him.

For more information about Walk Thru the Bible's publications, videos or seminars in your area, write to *Walk Thru the Bible Ministries, P.O. Box 80587, Atlanta, GA 30366 or call (770) 458-9300.*

God's Word in Our Language

Do you speak Hebrew . . . or Aramaic . . . or Greek . . . or Latin . . . or German? Most Americans don't.

And that is why the copy of the Bible you can pick up and read today is such a remarkable accomplishment—and such a priceless treasure. You have many dedicated people to thank for the privilege of reading God's Word in your mother tongue.

The story of how we got the English Bible begins many centuries ago and many miles away. Written translations of the entire Hebrew (Old) Testament have existed since the third century B.C., when Jews living in Egypt discovered that their children could no longer understand the Hebrew Scriptures. The Greek translation that resulted has been given the name "Septuagint" (Latin for *seventy*), which reflects the tradition that it was translated by seventy elders in seventy sessions.

When Jesus lived in Israel, Aramaic was the language of the common people. But the four Gospel accounts, as well as Paul's letters and the rest of the New Testament, were written in Greek—the language of the Mediterranean world.

By the late fourth century, the spoken language of the Roman Empire was Latin. Few people could read or write Greek any longer, and a Latin translation was needed. About 382 the bishop of Rome asked a learned Bible scholar named Jerome to undertake the task, and the Vulgate or "common" Bible was produced. When Latin became the liturgical language of the church and the Bible became associated with the liturgy, it continued to be written and read in Latin.

After the conversion of the British Isles to Christianity, various monks attempted to translate the Vulgate into English. No complete English translation was available for many years, and Bible stories were commonly taught through pictures, carvings and drama.

The first complete English Bible did not appear until the end of the fourteenth century. John Wycliffe, an English priest, began to preach in the *vernacular* language (English), rather than the *liturgical* language (Latin). Under his leadership the first translation of the entire Bible from Latin to English was completed in 1384.

As with all copies of the Bible up to this time, duplication was only possible by hand—a process that was slow, tedious and expensive. With the invention of movable type in Mainz, Germany, production and distribution of the Bible entered a new era. The Latin Vulgate was the first Bible to appear in printed form. Produced by Johannes Gutenberg, it soon became known as the *Gutenberg Bible*.

The Reformation brought a renewed demand for the Bible in the language of the people. Martin Luther translated the Bible from Hebrew and Greek into German. When church authorities in England prohibited a similar English translation, Luther's counterpart, William Tyndale, went to Germany, where he translated the New Testament from the original Greek in 1526. Miles Coverdale, an

English bishop, prepared the first complete English Bible from the original languages in 1535. His work was later revised, and portions can still be found today in the *Book of Common Prayer.*

English refugees living in France made the first Roman Catholic translation of the Bible from Latin into English, publishing the New Testament in Rheims, France, in 1582, and the Old Testament in Douay, France, in 1610. This translation is known today as the *Douay-Rheims* or *Douay Bible.*

In 1604, King James of England commissioned a group of fifty scholars to prepare a revision of earlier English translations of the Bible. The resulting King James (or Authorized) Version of 1611 was warmly and widely received. Acclaimed for its accuracy, readability and poetic beauty, it soon became the most popular English Bible—a tribute held for more than 350 years.

God never changes (James 1:17), and God's Word never changes (Matthew 5:18). But human language—the vehicle for communicating God's changeless message—undergoes constant metamorphosis. In the twentieth century this has given impetus to numerous revisions and translations—the product of scholarly committees employing the most recent findings from archaeology and linguistics. Contemporary translations include:

American Standard Version (1901)
Revised Standard Version (1952)
Jerusalem Bible (1966)
New English Bible (1966)
New American Bible (1970)
New American Standard Bible (1971)
Good News Bible: Today's English Version (1976)
New International Version (1978)
New King James Version (1982)
New Jewish Publications Society Translation (1982)
Revised English Bible (1989)
New Revised Standard Version (1989)
Contemporary English Version (1995)
New Living Translation (1996)

In addition, popular paraphrases such as *The Living Bible* (1971), J. B. Phillips's *New Testament in Modern English* (1960) and Eugene Peterson's *The Message* (1993) have provided fresh, easy-to-read versions.

The English Bible—God's Word in our language. It is a priceless treasure in any generation, especially when millions of people today still do not have a single verse of Scripture in their mother tongue.

Take time to read a portion of your Bible each day, for God has something to say to you!

Seven Benefits from Reading Your Bible

Bible reading is more than a pleasant pastime. It can become a daily habit that will change your life.

God's Word holds out the promise of rich benefits for those who spend time reading it and taking its truths to heart. Here are just seven of the many ways your life can be better as you make the Bible your daily reading companion. All seven come from Psalm 119—a magnificent song of praise for God's Word.

1. **The Bible will help keep you from sin.** "I have hidden your word in my heart that I might not sin against you" (verse 11).

2. **The Bible will lift your burdens.** "My soul is weary with sorrow; strengthen me according to your word" (verse 28).

3. **The Bible will guide your steps.** "Your word is a lamp to my feet and a light for my path" (verse 105).

4. **The Bible will bring you joy.** "Your statutes are my heritage forever; they are the joy of my heart" (verse 111).

5. **The Bible will lead you to wisdom.** "The unfolding of your words gives light; it gives understanding to the simple" (verse 130).

6. **The Bible will give you peace.** "Great peace have they who love your law, and nothing can make them stumble" (verse 165).

7. **The Bible will bring you back to God.** "I have strayed like a lost sheep. Seek your servant, for I have not forgotten your commands" (verse 176).

Preface

The New International Version is a completely new translation of the Holy Bible made by over a hundred scholars working directly from the best available Hebrew, Aramaic and Greek texts. It had its beginning in 1965 when, after several years of exploratory study by committees from the Christian Reformed Church and the National Association of Evangelicals, a group of scholars met at Palos Heights, Illinois, and concurred in the need for a new translation of the Bible in contemporary English. This group, though not made up of official church representatives, was transdenominational. Its conclusion was endorsed by a large number of leaders from many denominations who met in Chicago in 1966.

Responsibility for the new version was delegated by the Palos Heights group to a self-governing body of fifteen, the Committee on Bible Translation, composed for the most part of biblical scholars from colleges, universities and seminaries. In 1967 the New York Bible Society (now the International Bible Society) generously undertook the financial sponsorship of the project—a sponsorship that made it possible to enlist the help of many distinguished scholars. The fact that participants from the United States, Great Britain, Canada, Australia and New Zealand worked together gave the project its international scope. That they were from many denominations—including Anglican, Assemblies of God, Baptist, Brethren, Christian Reformed, Church of Christ, Evangelical Free, Lutheran, Mennonite, Methodist, Nazarene, Presbyterian, Wesleyan and other churches—helped to safeguard the translation from sectarian bias.

How it was made helps to give the New International Version its distinctiveness. The translation of each book was assigned to a team of scholars. Next, one of the Intermediate Editorial Committees revised the initial translation, with constant reference to the Hebrew, Aramaic or Greek. Their work then went to one of the General Editorial Committees, which checked it in detail and made another thorough revision. This revision in turn was carefully reviewed by the Committee on Bible Translation, which made further changes and then released the final version for publication. In this way the entire Bible underwent three revisions, during each of which the translation was examined for its faithfulness to the original languages and for its English style.

All this involved many thousands of hours of research and discussion regarding the meaning of the texts and the precise way of putting them into English. It may well be that no other translation has been made by a more thorough process of review and revision from committee to committee than this one.

From the beginning of the project, the Committee on Bible Translation held to certain goals for the New International Version: that it would be an accurate translation and one that would have clarity and literary quality and so prove suitable for public and private reading, teaching, preaching, memorizing and liturgical use. The Committee also sought to preserve some measure of continuity with the long tradition of translating the Scriptures into English.

In working toward these goals, the translators were united in their commitment to the authority and infallibility of the Bible as God's Word in written form. They believe that it contains the divine answer to the deepest needs of humanity, that it sheds unique light on our path in a dark world, and that it sets forth the way to our eternal well-being.

The first concern of the translators has been the accuracy of the translation and its fidelity to the thought of the biblical writers. They have weighed the significance of the lexical and grammatical details of the Hebrew, Aramaic and Greek texts. At the same time, they have striven for more than a word-for-word translation. Because thought patterns and syntax differ from language to language, faithful communication of the meaning of the writers of the Bible demands frequent modifications in sentence structure and constant regard for the contextual meanings of words.

A sensitive feeling for style does not always accompany scholarship. Accordingly the Committee on Bible Translation submitted the developing version to a number of stylistic consultants. Two of them read every book of both Old and New Testaments twice—once before and once after the last major revision—and made invaluable suggestions. Samples of the translation were tested for clarity and ease of reading by various kinds of people—young and old, highly educated and less well educated, ministers and laymen.

Concern for clear and natural English—that the New International Version should be idiomatic but not idiosyncratic, contemporary but not dated—motivated the translators and consultants. At the same time, they tried to reflect the differing styles of the biblical writers. In view of the international use of English, the translators sought to avoid obvious Americanisms on the one hand and obvious Anglicisms on the other. A British edition reflects the comparatively few differences of significant idiom and of spelling.

As for the traditional pronouns "thou," "thee" and "thine" in reference to the Deity, the translators judged that to use these archaisms (along with the old verb forms such as "doest," "wouldest" and "hadst" would violate accuracy in translation. Neither Hebrew, Aramaic nor Greek uses special pronouns for the persons of the Godhead. A present-day translation is not enhanced by forms that in the time of the King James Version were used in everyday speech, whether referring to God or man.

For the Old Testament the standard Hebrew text, the Masoretic Text as published in the latest editions of *Biblia Hebraica*, was used throughout. The Dead Sea Scrolls contain material bearing on an earlier stage of the Hebrew text. They were consulted, as were the Samaritan Pentateuch and the ancient scribal traditions relating to textual changes. Sometimes a variant Hebrew reading in the margin of the Masoretic Text was followed instead of the text itself. Such instances, being variants within the Masoretic tradition, are not specified by footnotes. In rare cases, words in the consonantal text were divided differently from the way they appear in the Masoretic Text. Footnotes indicate this. The translators also consulted the more important early versions—the Septuagint; Aquila, Symmachus and Theodotion; the Vulgate; the Syriac Peshitta; the Targums; and for the Psalms the *Juxta Hebraica* of Jerome. Readings from these versions were occasionally followed where the Masoretic Text seemed doubtful and where accepted principles of textual criticism showed that one or more of these textual witnesses appeared to provide the correct reading. Such instances are footnoted. Sometimes vowel letters and vowel signs did not, in the judgment of the translators, represent the correct vowels for the original consonantal text. Accordingly some words were read with a different set of vowels. These instances are usually not indicated by footnotes.

The Greek text used in translating the New Testament was an eclectic one. No other piece of ancient literature has such an abundance of manuscript witnesses as does the New Testament. Where existing manuscripts differ, the translators made their choice of readings according to accepted principles of New Testament textual criticism. Footnotes call attention to places where there was uncertainty about what the original text was. The best current printed texts of the Greek New Testament were used.

There is a sense in which the work of translation is never wholly finished. This applies to all great literature and uniquely so to the Bible. In 1973 the New Testament in the New International Version was published. Since then, suggestions for corrections and revisions have been received from various sources. The Committee on Bible Translation carefully considered the suggestions and adopted a number of them. These were incorporated in the first printing of the entire Bible in 1978. Additional revisions were made by the Committee on Bible Translation in 1983 and appear in printings after that date.

As in other ancient documents, the precise meaning of the biblical texts is sometimes uncertain. This is more often the case with the Hebrew and Aramaic texts than with the Greek text. Although archaeological and linguistic discoveries in this century aid in understanding difficult passages, some uncertainties remain. The more significant of these have been called to the reader's attention in the footnotes.

In regard to the divine name *YHWH*, commonly referred to as the *Tetragrammaton*, the translators adopted the device used in most English versions of rendering that name as "Lord" in capital letters to distinguish it from *Adonai*, another Hebrew word rendered "Lord," for which small letters are used. Wherever the two names stand together in the Old Testament as a compound name of God, they are rendered "Sovereign Lord."

Because for most readers today the phrases "the Lord of hosts" and "God of hosts" have little meaning, this version renders them "the Lord Almighty" and "God Almighty." These renderings convey the sense of the Hebrew, namely, "he who is sovereign over all the 'hosts' (powers) in heaven and on earth, especially over the 'hosts' (armies) of Israel." For readers unacquainted with Hebrew this does not make clear the distinction between *Sabaoth* ("hosts" or "Almighty") and *Shaddai* (which can also be translated "Almighty"), but the latter occurs infrequently and is always footnoted. When *Adonai* and *YHWH Sabaoth* occur together, they are rendered "the Lord, the Lord Almighty."

As for other proper nouns, the familiar spellings of the King James Version are generally retained. Names traditionally spelled with "ch," except where it is final, are usually spelled in this translation with "k" or "c," since the biblical languages do not have the sound that "ch" frequently indicates in English—for example, in *chant*. For well-known names such as Zechariah, however, the traditional spelling has been retained. Variation in the spelling of names in the original languages has usually not been indicated. Where a person or place has two or more different names in the Hebrew, Aramaic or Greek texts, the more familiar one has generally been used, with footnotes where needed.

To achieve clarity the translators sometimes supplied words not in the original texts but required by the context. If there was uncertainty about such material, it is enclosed in brackets. Also for the sake of clarity or style, nouns, including some proper nouns, are sometimes substituted for pronouns, and vice versa. And though the Hebrew writers often shifted back and forth between first, second and third personal pronouns without change of antecedent, this translation often makes them uniform, in accordance with English style and without the use of footnotes.

Poetical passages are printed as poetry, that is, with indentation of lines and with separate stanzas. These are generally designed to reflect the structure of Hebrew poetry. This poetry is normally characterized by parallelism in balanced lines. Most of the poetry in the Bible is in the Old Testament, and scholars differ regarding the scansion of Hebrew lines. The translators determined the stanza divisions for the most part by analysis of the subject matter. The stanzas therefore serve as poetic paragraphs.

The footnotes in this version are of several kinds, most of which need no explanation. Those giving alternative translations begin with "Or" and generally introduce the alternative with the last word preceding it in the text, except when it is a single-word alternative; in poetry quoted in a footnote a slant mark indicates a line division. Footnotes introduced by "Or" do not have uniform significance. In some cases two possible translations were considered to have about equal validity. In other cases, though the translators were convinced that the translation in the text was correct, they judged that another interpretation was possible and of sufficient importance to be represented in a footnote.

In the New Testament, footnotes that refer to uncertainty regarding the original text are introduced by "Some manuscripts" or similar expressions. In the Old Testament, evidence for the reading chosen is given first and evidence for the alternative is added after a semicolon (for example: Septuagint; Hebrew *father*). In such notes the term "Hebrew" refers to the Masoretic Text.

It should be noted that minerals, flora and fauna, architectural details, articles of clothing and jewelry, musical instruments and other articles cannot always be identified with precision. Also measures of capacity in the biblical period are particularly uncertain (see the table of weights and measures following the text).

Like all translations of the Bible, made as they are by imperfect man, this one undoubtedly falls short of its goals. Yet we are grateful to God for the extent to which he has enabled us to realize these goals and for the strength he has given us and our colleagues to complete our task. We offer this version of the Bible to him in whose name and for whose glory it has been made. We pray that it will lead many into a better understanding of the Holy Scriptures and a fuller knowledge of Jesus Christ the incarnate Word, of whom the Scriptures so faithfully testify.

The Committee on Bible Translation

June 1978
(Revised August 1983)

Names of the translators and editors may be secured
from the International Bible Society,
translation sponsors of the New International Version
1820 Jet Stream Drive, Colorado Springs,
Colorado 80921-3696 USA.

Table of Weights and Measures

BIBLICAL UNIT		APPROXIMATE AMERICAN EQUIVALENT		APPROXIMATE METRIC EQUIVALENT	
WEIGHTS					
talent	(60 minas)	75	pounds	34	kilograms
mina	(50 shekels)	1¼	pounds	0.6	kilogram
shekel	(2 bekas)	²/₅	pounds	11.5	grams
pim	(²/₃ shekel)	¹/₃	ounce	7.6	grams
beka	(10 gerahs)	¹/₅	ounce	5.5	grams
gerah		¹/₅₀	ounce	0.6	gram
LENGTH					
cubit		18	inches	0.5	meter
span		9	inches	23	centimeters
handbreadth		3	inches	8	centimeters
CAPACITY *Dry Measure*					
cor [homer]	(10 ephahs)	6	bushels	220	liters
lethek	(5 ephahs)	3	bushels	110	liters
ephah	(10 omers)	³/₅	bushels	22	liters
seah	(¹/₃ ephah)	7	quarts	7.3	liters
omer	(¹/₁₀ ephah)	2	quarts	2	liters
cab	(¹/₁₈ ephah)	1	quart	1	liter
Liquid Measure					
bath	(1 ephah)	6	gallons	22	liters
hin	(¹/₆ bath)	4	quarts	4	liters
log	(¹/₇₂ bath)	¹/₃	quart	0.3	liter

The figures of the table are calculated on the basis of a shekel equaling 11.5 grams, a cubit equaling 18 inches and an ephah equaling 22 liters. The quart referred to is either a dry quart (slightly smaller than a liter) or a liquid quart (slightly larger than a liter), whichever is applicable. The ton referred to in the footnotes is the American ton of 2,000 pounds.

This table is based upon the best available information, but it is not intended to be mathematically precise; like the measurement equivalents in the footnotes, it merely gives approximate amounts and distances. Weights and measures differed somewhat at various times and places in the ancient world. There is uncertainty particularly about the ephah and the bath; further discoveries may give more light on these units of capacity.

Old Testament

The Old Testament traces the plan of God from the creation of the world to about 400 B.C. The historical books portray the birth, growth, development and discipline of God's covenant people, Israel. Following their four hundred years of captivity in Egypt, God plants them in the land of Canaan, where they eventually establish a kingdom. The poetical books capture the emotions and heartbeat of men and women living during this historical period. And the prophetical books record God's repeated attempts to call his people back to the godly behavior they abandoned.

THE OLD TESTAMENT

HISTORICAL (17)		POETICAL (5)	PROPHETICAL (17)	
PENTATEUCH (5)	Genesis Exodus Leviticus Numbers Deuteronomy	Job Psalms Proverbs Ecclesiastes Song of Songs	Isaiah Jeremiah Lamentations Ezekiel Daniel	MAJOR (5)
HISTORICAL (12)	Joshua Judges Ruth 1 Samuel 2 Samuel 1 Kings 2 Kings 1 Chronicles 2 Chronicles Ezra Nehemiah Esther		Hosea Joel Amos Obadiah Jonah Micah Nahum Habakkuk Zephaniah Haggai Zechariah Malachi	MINOR (12)

New Testament

The New Testament continues to unfold the program of God from the birth of Jesus to about the end of the first century A.D. The record of Jesus' incomparable words and works is preserved in the four Gospels (Matthew—John). After his ascension, Jesus' followers spread the Good News of his message (Acts). One of these followers, Paul of Tarsus, penned many letters to churches and individuals, providing much-needed encouragement and instruction. The final nine books contain practical help for the followers of Jesus Christ.

THE NEW TESTAMENT

PAULINE EPISTLES: INDIVIDUALS				
1 Timothy	2 Timothy	Titus	Philemon	
PAULINE EPISTLES: CHURCHES — 2 Thessalonians / 1 Thessalonians / Colossians / Philippians / Ephesians / Galatians / 2 Corinthians / 1 Corinthians / Romans			Hebrews / James / 1 Peter / 2 Peter / 1 John / 2 John / 3 John / Jude / Revelation	**NON-PAULINE EPISTLES AND REVELATIONS**
Matthew	Mark	Luke	John	Acts
HISTORICAL BOOKS				

Genesis

GENESIS begins "in the beginning." Its fifty chapters sketch human history from Creation to Babel (Genesis 1–11) and from Abraham to Joseph (Genesis 12–50). The first eleven chapters introduce the Creator God and the beginnings of life, sin, judgment, family, worship and salvation. The remainder of the book focuses on the lives of the four patriarchs of the faith—Abraham, Isaac, Jacob and Joseph—from whom will come the nation Israel . . . and ultimately the Savior, Jesus Christ.

Focus	Four Great Events				Four Great People			
Divisions	Creation	Fall	Flood	Nations	Abraham	Isaac	Jacob	Joseph
	1 2 3	5 6	9 10	11	12 24	25 26	27 36	37 50
Topics	Primeval History				Patriarchal History			
	Beginning of the Human Race				Beginning of the Hebrew Race			
Place	East (Eden to Ur)				West (Canaan to Egypt)			
Time	Over 2,000 Years (20% of Genesis)				About 350 Years (80% of Genesis)			

JANUARY 1 □ DAY 1
GENESIS 1-2
"In the Beginning . . ."

OVERVIEW Genesis opens with two accounts of creation. The first (1:1–2:3) describes the events in chronological order; the second (2:4–25) considers the events topically, in order to focus on one aspect of creation. The first provides a wide-angle view of the creation of the universe; the second takes a zoom-lens look at man and woman, the climax of creation—for they are the ones who will bear God's image and enjoy God's fellowship in the garden prepared especially for them.

Chapter 1	Chapter 2
Six Days of Creation Summarized	Sixth Day of Creation Scrutinized
Chronological	Topical

YOUR DAILY WALK

That God created us from dust is no reason to treat another person like dirt.

- What is the longest book you ever read?
- What is the greatest distance you ever walked?
- What is the biggest meal you ever ate?
- And what could these three curious questions possibly have in common?

In case you haven't guessed, they are all examples of big projects completed in small stages. You read that book one page at a time . . . covered that distance one step at a time . . . ate that meal one bite at a time. One page, one step, one bite might not seem like much when compared to the whole, but each brings you closer to your goal.

This year, with the help of the *New Daily Walk Bible,* you'll be fulfilling what for many people has been a lifelong dream: to read through the Bible—all 1,189 chapters of it! And like thousands of other "daily walkers," you'll discover you *can* reach your goal—one day at a time! Are you ready to launch your exciting expedition through the Bible? It starts with the first words of Genesis: "In the beginning God created . . ."

INSIGHT The Days of Creation
If the days of Creation are arranged in two columns of three days each, you'll discover an interesting fact!

First God created the realm	Then God created the ruler
Day 1—Light	Day 4—Sun, Moon, & Stars
Day 2—Sky & Oceans	Day 5—Birds & Fish
Day 3—Dry Land	Day 6—Animals & Man

CHAPTER 1

In the beginning God created the heavens and the earth. ²Now the earth was[a] formless and empty, darkness was over the surface of the deep, and

[a]2 Or possibly *became*

the Spirit of God was hovering over the waters.

[3]And God said, "Let there be light," and there was light. [4]God saw that the light was good, and he separated the light from the darkness. [5]God called the light "day," and the darkness he called "night." And there was evening, and there was morning—the first day.

[6]And God said, "Let there be an expanse between the waters to separate water from water." [7]So God made the expanse and separated the water under the expanse from the water above it. And it was so. [8]God called the expanse "sky." And there was evening, and there was morning—the second day.

[9]And God said, "Let the water under the sky be gathered to one place, and let dry ground appear." And it was so. [10]God called the dry ground "land," and the gathered waters he called "seas." And God saw that it was good.

[11]Then God said, "Let the land produce vegetation: seed-bearing plants and trees on the land that bear fruit with seed in it, according to their various kinds." And it was so. [12]The land produced vegetation: plants bearing seed according to their kinds and trees bearing fruit with seed in it according to their kinds. And God saw that it was good. [13]And there was evening, and there was morning—the third day.

[14]And God said, "Let there be lights in the expanse of the sky to separate the day from the night, and let them serve as signs to mark seasons and days and years, [15]and let them be lights in the expanse of the sky to give light on the earth." And it was so. [16]God made two great lights—the greater light to govern the day and the lesser light to govern the night. He also made the stars. [17]God set them in the expanse of the sky to give light on the earth, [18]to govern the day and the night, and to separate light from darkness. And God saw that it was good. [19]And there was evening, and there was morning—the fourth day.

[20]And God said, "Let the water teem with living creatures, and let birds fly above the earth across the expanse of the sky." [21]So God created the great creatures of the sea and every living and moving thing with which the water teems, according to their kinds, and every winged bird according to its kind. And God saw that it was good. [22]God blessed them and said, "Be fruitful and increase in number and fill the water in the seas, and let the birds increase on the earth." [23]And there was evening, and there was morning—the fifth day.

[24]And God said, "Let the land produce living creatures according to their kinds: livestock, creatures that move along the ground, and wild animals, each according to its kind." And it was so. [25]God made the wild animals according to their kinds, the livestock according to their kinds, and all the creatures that move along the ground according to their kinds. And God saw that it was good.

[26]Then God said, "Let us make man in our image, in our likeness, and let them rule over the fish of the sea and the birds of the air, over the livestock, over all the earth,[b] and over all the creatures that move along the ground."

[27]So God created man in his own image,
in the image of God he created him;
male and female he created them.

[28]God blessed them and said to them, "Be fruitful and increase in number; fill the earth and subdue it. Rule over the fish of the sea and the birds of the air and over every living creature that moves on the ground." [29]Then God said, "I give you every seed-bearing plant on the face of the whole earth and every tree that has fruit with seed in it. They will be yours for food. [30]And to all the beasts of the earth and all the birds of the air and all the creatures that move on the ground—everything that has the breath of life in it—I give every green plant for food." And it was so. [31]God saw all that he had made, and it was very good. And there was

[b]26 Hebrew; Syriac *all the wild animals*

evening, and there was morning—the sixth day.

CHAPTER 2

Thus the heavens and the earth were completed in all their vast array.

2By the seventh day God had finished the work he had been doing; so on the seventh day he rested[c] from all his work. 3And God blessed the seventh day and made it holy, because on it he rested from all the work of creating that he had done.

4This is the account of the heavens and the earth when they were created.

When the LORD God made the earth and the heavens— 5and no shrub of the field had yet appeared on the earth[d] and no plant of the field had yet sprung up, for the LORD God had not sent rain on the earth[d] and there was no man to work the ground, 6but streams[e] came up from the earth and watered the whole surface of the ground— 7the LORD God formed the man[f] from the dust of the ground and breathed into his nostrils the breath of life, and the man became a living being.

8Now the LORD God had planted a garden in the east, in Eden; and there he put the man he had formed. 9And the LORD God made all kinds of trees grow out of the ground—trees that were pleasing to the eye and good for food. In the middle of the garden were the tree of life and the tree of the knowledge of good and evil.

10A river watering the garden flowed from Eden; from there it was separated into four headwaters. 11The name of the first is the Pishon; it winds through the entire land of Havilah, where there is gold. 12(The gold of that land is good; aromatic resin[g] and onyx are also there.) 13The name of the second river is the Gi-

hon; it winds through the entire land of Cush.[h] 14The name of the third river is the Tigris; it runs along the east side of Asshur. And the fourth river is the Euphrates.

15The LORD God took the man and put him in the Garden of Eden to work it and take care of it. 16And the LORD God commanded the man, "You are free to eat from any tree in the garden; 17but you must not eat from the tree of the knowledge of good and evil, for when you eat of it you will surely die."

18The LORD God said, "It is not good for the man to be alone. I will make a helper suitable for him."

19Now the LORD God had formed out of the ground all the beasts of the field and all the birds of the air. He brought them to the man to see what he would name them; and whatever the man called each living creature, that was its name. 20So the man gave names to all the livestock, the birds of the air and all the beasts of the field.

But for Adam[i] no suitable helper was found. 21So the LORD God caused the man to fall into a deep sleep; and while he was sleeping, he took one of the man's ribs[j] and closed up the place with flesh. 22Then the LORD God made a woman from the rib[k] he had taken out of the man, and he brought her to the man.

23The man said,

"This is now bone of my bones
   and flesh of my flesh;
she shall be called 'woman,'[l]
   for she was taken out of man."

24For this reason a man will leave his father and mother and be united to his wife, and they will become one flesh.

25The man and his wife were both naked, and they felt no shame.

c2 Or ceased; also in verse 3   d5 Or land; also in verse 6   e6 Or mist   f7 The Hebrew for man (adam) sounds like and may be related to the Hebrew for ground (adamah); it is also the name Adam (see Gen. 2:20).   g12 Or good; pearls   h13 Possibly southeast Mesopotamia   i20 Or the man   j21 Or took part of the man's side   k22 Or part   l23 The Hebrew for woman sounds like the Hebrew for man.

JANUARY 2 □ DAY 2
GENESIS 3–5
From Paradise to Pain

OVERVIEW What began as paradise is soon spoiled by sin. Satan, disguised as a serpent, tempts the woman by turning her gaze from God's bountiful provision (the many trees) to God's one prohibition (the single tree of the knowledge of good and evil). Adam and Eve's disobedience in eating from the forbidden tree results in their expulsion from the garden. The seeds of their sin quickly grow as their first son (Cain) commits the first murder. For generation after generation the spiral continues, setting the stage for God's judgment.

Chapter 3	Chapter 4	Chapter 5
The First Sin	The First Murder	The First Family Tree
Adam and Eve	Cain and Abel	Seth

YOUR DAILY WALK Satan is a master at taking the blessings of God and turning them into something that brings a curse instead. If given the chance, he'll convince you to seek the pleasures of sex outside the bonds of marriage . . . to exchange the worship of the Creator for the worship of the creation . . . to substitute what is convenient for what is obedient. The temptation will be cunning, the promise inviting. But as Adam and Eve discovered, the painful consequences will far outweigh the temporary pleasures.

Satan, like a fisherman, baits his hook according to the appetite of the fish.

For many Christians, resisting temptation is difficult because they don't want to discourage it completely. God has promised to provide an avenue of escape (1 Corinthians 10:13), but that doesn't help if you keep leaving a forwarding address! Write the references of James 4:7 and 2 Timothy 2:22 in the margin next to Genesis 3. Look them up; read them twice; take them to heart!

INSIGHT Cataloging a Curse
Genesis 3 introduces more than the beginning of sin. There you'll also find some of its consequences: crabgrass, labor pains, slithering snakes, and perspiration! After reading chapter 3, try to summarize each part of the curse as it relates to the following:
- the serpent (3:14)
- Satan (3:15)
- the woman (3:15–16)
- the man (3:17–19)

CHAPTER 3
Now the serpent was more crafty than any of the wild animals the LORD God had made. He said to the woman, "Did God really say, 'You must not eat from any tree in the garden'?"

²The woman said to the serpent, "We may eat fruit from the trees in the garden, ³but God did say, 'You must not eat fruit from the tree that is in the middle of the garden, and you must not touch it, or you will die.' "

⁴"You will not surely die," the serpent said to the woman. ⁵"For God knows that when you eat of it your eyes will be opened, and you will be like God, knowing good and evil."

⁶When the woman saw that the fruit of the tree was good for food and pleasing to the eye, and also desirable for gaining wisdom, she took some and ate it. She also gave some to her husband, who was with her, and he ate it. ⁷Then the eyes of both of them were opened, and they

realized they were naked; so they sewed fig leaves together and made coverings for themselves.

8Then the man and his wife heard the sound of the LORD God as he was walking in the garden in the cool of the day, and they hid from the LORD God among the trees of the garden. 9But the LORD God called to the man, "Where are you?"

10He answered, "I heard you in the garden, and I was afraid because I was naked; so I hid."

11And he said, "Who told you that you were naked? Have you eaten from the tree that I commanded you not to eat from?"

12The man said, "The woman you put here with me—she gave me some fruit from the tree, and I ate it."

13Then the LORD God said to the woman, "What is this you have done?"

The woman said, "The serpent deceived me, and I ate."

14So the LORD God said to the serpent, "Because you have done this,

"Cursed are you above all the livestock
    and all the wild animals!
You will crawl on your belly
    and you will eat dust
    all the days of your life.
15And I will put enmity
    between you and the woman,
    and between your offspring*m* and
        hers;
he will crush*n* your head,
    and you will strike his heel."

16To the woman he said,

"I will greatly increase your pains in
        childbearing;
    with pain you will give birth to
        children.
Your desire will be for your husband,
    and he will rule over you."

17To Adam he said, "Because you listened to your wife and ate from the tree about which I commanded you, 'You must not eat of it,'

"Cursed is the ground because of you;
    through painful toil you will eat of
        it
    all the days of your life.

18It will produce thorns and thistles for
        you,
    and you will eat the plants of the
        field.
19By the sweat of your brow
    you will eat your food
until you return to the ground,
    since from it you were taken;
for dust you are
    and to dust you will return."

20Adam*o* named his wife Eve,*p* because she would become the mother of all the living.

21The LORD God made garments of skin for Adam and his wife and clothed them. 22And the LORD God said, "The man has now become like one of us, knowing good and evil. He must not be allowed to reach out his hand and take also from the tree of life and eat, and live forever." 23So the LORD God banished him from the Garden of Eden to work the ground from which he had been taken. 24After he drove the man out, he placed on the east side*q* of the Garden of Eden cherubim and a flaming sword flashing back and forth to guard the way to the tree of life.

CHAPTER 4

Adam*o* lay with his wife Eve, and she became pregnant and gave birth to Cain.*r* She said, "With the help of the LORD I have brought forth*s* a man." 2Later she gave birth to his brother Abel.

Now Abel kept flocks, and Cain worked the soil. 3In the course of time Cain brought some of the fruits of the soil as an offering to the LORD. 4But Abel brought fat portions from some of the firstborn of his flock. The LORD looked with favor on Abel and his offering, 5but on Cain and his offering he did not look with favor. So Cain was very angry, and his face was downcast.

6Then the LORD said to Cain, "Why are you angry? Why is your face downcast? 7If you do what is right, will you not be accepted? But if you do not do what is right, sin is crouching at your door; it desires to have you, but you must master it."

8Now Cain said to his brother Abel, "Let's go out to the field."*t* And while they were in the field, Cain attacked his brother Abel and killed him.

m15 Or seed   n15 Or strike   o20,1 Or The man   p20 Eve probably means *living.   q24 Or placed in front   r1 Cain* sounds like the Hebrew for *brought forth* or *acquired.   s1 Or have acquired   t8* Samaritan Pentateuch, Septuagint, Vulgate and Syriac; Masoretic Text does not have "Let's go out to the field."

⁹Then the LORD said to Cain, "Where is your brother Abel?"

"I don't know," he replied. "Am I my brother's keeper?"

¹⁰The LORD said, "What have you done? Listen! Your brother's blood cries out to me from the ground. ¹¹Now you are under a curse and driven from the ground, which opened its mouth to receive your brother's blood from your hand. ¹²When you work the ground, it will no longer yield its crops for you. You will be a restless wanderer on the earth."

¹³Cain said to the LORD, "My punishment is more than I can bear. ¹⁴Today you are driving me from the land, and I will be hidden from your presence; I will be a restless wanderer on the earth, and whoever finds me will kill me."

¹⁵But the LORD said to him, "Not so[u]; if anyone kills Cain, he will suffer vengeance seven times over." Then the LORD put a mark on Cain so that no one who found him would kill him. ¹⁶So Cain went out from the LORD's presence and lived in the land of Nod,[v] east of Eden.

¹⁷Cain lay with his wife, and she became pregnant and gave birth to Enoch. Cain was then building a city, and he named it after his son Enoch. ¹⁸To Enoch was born Irad, and Irad was the father of Mehujael, and Mehujael was the father of Methushael, and Methushael was the father of Lamech.

¹⁹Lamech married two women, one named Adah and the other Zillah. ²⁰Adah gave birth to Jabal; he was the father of those who live in tents and raise livestock. ²¹His brother's name was Jubal; he was the father of all who play the harp and flute. ²²Zillah also had a son, Tubal-Cain, who forged all kinds of tools out of[w] bronze and iron. Tubal-Cain's sister was Naamah.

²³Lamech said to his wives,

"Adah and Zillah, listen to me;
    wives of Lamech, hear my words.
I have killed[x] a man for wounding
    me,
    a young man for injuring me.
²⁴If Cain is avenged seven times,
    then Lamech seventy-seven times."

²⁵Adam lay with his wife again, and she gave birth to a son and named him Seth,[y] saying, "God has granted me another child in place of Abel, since Cain killed him." ²⁶Seth also had a son, and he named him Enosh.

At that time men began to call on[z] the name of the LORD.

CHAPTER 5

This is the written account of Adam's line.

When God created man, he made him in the likeness of God. ²He created them male and female and blessed them. And when they were created, he called them "man.[a]"

³When Adam had lived 130 years, he had a son in his own likeness, in his own image; and he named him Seth. ⁴After Seth was born, Adam lived 800 years and had other sons and daughters. ⁵Altogether, Adam lived 930 years, and then he died.

⁶When Seth had lived 105 years, he became the father[b] of Enosh. ⁷And after he became the father of Enosh, Seth lived 807 years and had other sons and daughters. ⁸Altogether, Seth lived 912 years, and then he died.

⁹When Enosh had lived 90 years, he became the father of Kenan. ¹⁰And after he became the father of Kenan, Enosh lived 815 years and had other sons and daughters. ¹¹Altogether, Enosh lived 905 years, and then he died.

¹²When Kenan had lived 70 years, he became the father of Mahalalel. ¹³And after he became the father of Mahalalel, Kenan lived 840 years and had other sons and daughters. ¹⁴Altogether, Kenan lived 910 years, and then he died.

¹⁵When Mahalalel had lived 65 years, he became the father of Jared. ¹⁶And after he became the father of Jared, Mahalalel lived 830 years and had other sons and daughters. ¹⁷Altogether, Mahalalel lived 895 years, and then he died.

¹⁸When Jared had lived 162 years, he became the father of Enoch. ¹⁹And after he became the father of Enoch, Jared lived

---

u15 Septuagint, Vulgate and Syriac; Hebrew Very well   v16 Nod means wandering (see verses 12 and 14).   w22 Or who instructed all who work in   x23 Or I will kill   y25 Seth probably means granted.   z26 Or to proclaim   a2 Hebrew adam
b6 Father may mean ancestor; also in verses 7-26.

800 years and had other sons and daughters. [20]Altogether, Jared lived 962 years, and then he died.

[21]When Enoch had lived 65 years, he became the father of Methuselah. [22]And after he became the father of Methuselah, Enoch walked with God 300 years and had other sons and daughters. [23]Altogether, Enoch lived 365 years. [24]Enoch walked with God; then he was no more, because God took him away.

[25]When Methuselah had lived 187 years, he became the father of Lamech. [26]And after he became the father of Lamech, Methuselah lived 782 years and

[c]29 *Noah* sounds like the Hebrew for *comfort.*

had other sons and daughters. [27]Altogether, Methuselah lived 969 years, and then he died.

[28]When Lamech had lived 182 years, he had a son. [29]He named him Noah[c] and said, "He will comfort us in the labor and painful toil of our hands caused by the ground the LORD has cursed." [30]After Noah was born, Lamech lived 595 years and had other sons and daughters. [31]Altogether, Lamech lived 777 years, and then he died.

[32]After Noah was 500 years old, he became the father of Shem, Ham and Japheth.

JANUARY 3 ☐ DAY 3
GENESIS 6–9
Noah's Ark and God's Judgment

 OVERVIEW As the generations begin to multiply on the face of the earth, the world's population greatly increases . . . and so does the world's wickedness (6:5). At last, God prepares to destroy mankind with a judgment of water. But one man and his family receive God's commendation, while the rest of humanity faces God's condemnation. Noah obediently undertakes a century-long shipbuilding project in preparation for saving his believing family. As the floodwaters rise, Noah's eight-member family rides high in God's loving protection.

Chapter 6	Chapter 7	Chapter 8	Chapter 9
Mankind's Corruption	God's Condemnation Executed	Ended	God's Covenant
Building the Ark	Riding in the Ark		Rainbow in the Sky

 YOUR DAILY WALK When a man repeats a promise over and over, you can be pretty sure that he must have a problem keeping it. When God repeats a promise over and over, you can be absolutely sure that he doesn't!

God may not promise a comfortable journey, but he does guarantee a safe landing.

Is God trustworthy? Does he keep his word? When he makes a promise, is there an 80 . . . 90 . . . 100 percent chance it will come true? The ancient shipbuilder named Noah must have wrestled with such questions, for his very life and the lives of his family were totally bound up in the promises of God. Spend a few minutes evaluating God's "scorecard" on how well he kept his promises to Noah:

"I will send rain on the earth" (7:4). Yes or no?

"I will wipe from the face of the earth every living creature I have made" (7:4). Yes or no?

"Never again will I curse the ground" (8:21). Yes or no?

"I will remember my covenant" (9:15). Yes or no?

The rainbow in the sky (9:12–16) is God's eternal reminder that he will never repeat the watery horror of Noah's day. Keep an eye out for rainbows today in photographs and drawings—or even real ones! Let each one remind you (as it did Noah) that when you're resting on a promise from God, you needn't worry how deep the water gets!

 INSIGHT Water, Water, Everywhere . . . and Very Little Else!
Three times in the space of three verses (7:18–20) it is said "the waters rose." God wanted to make it clear that this was no ordinary flood and that his promise—to destroy "every living creature I have made"—was no idle threat.

CHAPTER 6

When men began to increase in number on the earth and daughters were born to them, ²the sons of God saw that the daughters of men were beautiful, and they married any of them they chose. ³Then the LORD said, "My Spirit will not contend with*d* man forever, for he is mortal*e*; his days will be a hundred and twenty years."

⁴The Nephilim were on the earth in those days—and also afterward—when the sons of God went to the daughters of men and had children by them. They were the heroes of old, men of renown.

⁵The LORD saw how great man's wickedness on the earth had become, and that every inclination of the thoughts of his heart was only evil all the time. ⁶The LORD was grieved that he had made man on the earth, and his heart was filled with pain. ⁷So the LORD said, "I will wipe mankind, whom I have created, from the face of the earth—men and animals, and creatures that move along the ground, and birds of the air—for I am grieved that I have made them." ⁸But Noah found favor in the eyes of the LORD.

⁹This is the account of Noah.

Noah was a righteous man, blameless among the people of his time, and he walked with God. ¹⁰Noah had three sons: Shem, Ham and Japheth.

¹¹Now the earth was corrupt in God's sight and was full of violence. ¹²God saw how corrupt the earth had become, for all the people on earth had corrupted their ways. ¹³So God said to Noah, "I am going to put an end to all people, for the earth is filled with violence because of them. I am surely going to destroy both them and the earth. ¹⁴So make yourself an ark of cypress*f* wood; make rooms in it and coat it with pitch inside and out. ¹⁵This is how

you are to build it: The ark is to be 450 feet long, 75 feet wide and 45 feet high.*g* ¹⁶Make a roof for it and finish*h* the ark to within 18 inches*i* of the top. Put a door in the side of the ark and make lower, middle and upper decks. ¹⁷I am going to bring floodwaters on the earth to destroy all life under the heavens, every creature that has the breath of life in it. Everything on earth will perish. ¹⁸But I will establish my covenant with you, and you will enter the ark—you and your sons and your wife and your sons' wives with you. ¹⁹You are to bring into the ark two of all living creatures, male and female, to keep them alive with you. ²⁰Two of every kind of bird, of every kind of animal and of every kind of creature that moves along the ground will come to you to be kept alive. ²¹You are to take every kind of food that is to be eaten and store it away as food for you and for them."

²²Noah did everything just as God commanded him.

CHAPTER 7

The LORD then said to Noah, "Go into the ark, you and your whole family, because I have found you righteous in this generation. ²Take with you seven*j* of every kind of clean animal, a male and its mate, and two of every kind of unclean animal, a male and its mate, ³and also seven of every kind of bird, male and female, to keep their various kinds alive throughout the earth. ⁴Seven days from now I will send rain on the earth for forty days and forty nights, and I will wipe from the face of the earth every living creature I have made."

⁵And Noah did all that the LORD commanded him.

⁶Noah was six hundred years old when the floodwaters came on the earth. ⁷And Noah and his sons and his wife and his

---

d3 Or *My spirit will not remain in*   *e3* Or *corrupt*   *f14* The meaning of the Hebrew for this word is uncertain.   *g15* Hebrew *300 cubits long, 50 cubits wide and 30 cubits high (about 140 meters long, 23 meters wide and 13.5 meters high)*   *h16* Or *Make an opening for light by finishing*   *i16* Hebrew *a cubit (about 0.5 meter)*   *j2* Or *seven pairs; also in verse 3* sons' wives entered the ark to escape the waters of the flood. [8]Pairs of clean and unclean animals, of birds and of all creatures that move along the ground, [9]male and female, came to Noah and entered the ark, as God had commanded Noah. [10]And after the seven days the floodwaters came on the earth.

[11]In the six hundredth year of Noah's life, on the seventeenth day of the second month—on that day all the springs of the great deep burst forth, and the floodgates of the heavens were opened. [12]And rain fell on the earth forty days and forty nights.

[13]On that very day Noah and his sons, Shem, Ham and Japheth, together with his wife and the wives of his three sons, entered the ark. [14]They had with them every wild animal according to its kind, all livestock according to their kinds, every creature that moves along the ground according to its kind and every bird according to its kind, everything with wings. [15]Pairs of all creatures that have the breath of life in them came to Noah and entered the ark. [16]The animals going in were male and female of every living thing, as God had commanded Noah. Then the LORD shut him in.

[17]For forty days the flood kept coming on the earth, and as the waters increased they lifted the ark high above the earth. [18]The waters rose and increased greatly on the earth, and the ark floated on the surface of the water. [19]They rose greatly on the earth, and all the high mountains under the entire heavens were covered. [20]The waters rose and covered the mountains to a depth of more than twenty feet.[k,l] [21]Every living thing that moved on the earth perished—birds, livestock, wild animals, all the creatures that swarm over the earth, and all mankind. [22]Everything on dry land that had the breath of life in its nostrils died. [23]Every living thing on the face of the earth was wiped out; men and animals and the creatures that move along the ground and the birds of the air were wiped from the earth. Only Noah was left, and those with him in the ark.

[24]The waters flooded the earth for a hundred and fifty days.

CHAPTER 8

But God remembered Noah and all the wild animals and the livestock that were with him in the ark, and he sent a wind over the earth, and the waters receded. [2]Now the springs of the deep and the floodgates of the heavens had been closed, and the rain had stopped falling from the sky. [3]The water receded steadily from the earth. At the end of the hundred and fifty days the water had gone down, [4]and on the seventeenth day of the seventh month the ark came to rest on the mountains of Ararat. [5]The waters continued to recede until the tenth month, and on the first day of the tenth month the tops of the mountains became visible.

[6]After forty days Noah opened the window he had made in the ark [7]and sent out a raven, and it kept flying back and forth until the water had dried up from the earth. [8]Then he sent out a dove to see if the water had receded from the surface of the ground. [9]But the dove could find no place to set its feet because there was water over all the surface of the earth; so it returned to Noah in the ark. He reached out his hand and took the dove and brought it back to himself in the ark. [10]He waited seven more days and again sent out the dove from the ark. [11]When the dove returned to him in the evening, there in its beak was a freshly plucked olive leaf! Then Noah knew that the water had receded from the earth. [12]He waited seven more days and sent the dove out again, but this time it did not return to him.

[13]By the first day of the first month of Noah's six hundred and first year, the water had dried up from the earth. Noah then removed the covering from the ark and saw that the surface of the ground was dry. [14]By the twenty-seventh day of the second month the earth was completely dry.

[15]Then God said to Noah, [16]"Come out of the ark, you and your wife and your sons and their wives. [17]Bring out every kind of living creature that is with you—the birds, the animals, and all the creatures that move along the ground—so they can multiply on the earth and be fruitful and increase in number upon it."

[18]So Noah came out, together with his

---

[k]20 Hebrew *fifteen cubits* (about 6.9 meters)   [l]20 Or *rose more than twenty feet, and the mountains were covered*

sons and his wife and his sons' wives. [19]All the animals and all the creatures that move along the ground and all the birds—everything that moves on the earth—came out of the ark, one kind after another.

[20]Then Noah built an altar to the LORD and, taking some of all the clean animals and clean birds, he sacrificed burnt offerings on it. [21]The LORD smelled the pleasing aroma and said in his heart: "Never again will I curse the ground because of man, even though[m] every inclination of his heart is evil from childhood. And never again will I destroy all living creatures, as I have done.

[22]"As long as the earth endures,
    seedtime and harvest,
    cold and heat,
    summer and winter,
    day and night
    will never cease."

CHAPTER 9

Then God blessed Noah and his sons, saying to them, "Be fruitful and increase in number and fill the earth. [2]The fear and dread of you will fall upon all the beasts of the earth and all the birds of the air, upon every creature that moves along the ground, and upon all the fish of the sea; they are given into your hands. [3]Everything that lives and moves will be food for you. Just as I gave you the green plants, I now give you everything.

[4]"But you must not eat meat that has its lifeblood still in it. [5]And for your lifeblood I will surely demand an accounting. I will demand an accounting from every animal. And from each man, too, I will demand an accounting for the life of his fellow man.

[6]"Whoever sheds the blood of man,
    by man shall his blood be shed;
    for in the image of God
    has God made man.

[7]As for you, be fruitful and increase in number; multiply on the earth and increase upon it."

[8]Then God said to Noah and to his sons with him: [9]"I now establish my covenant with you and with your descendants after you [10]and with every living creature that was with you—the birds, the livestock and all the wild animals, all those that came out of the ark with you—every living creature on earth. [11]I establish my covenant with you: Never again will all life be cut off by the waters of a flood; never again will there be a flood to destroy the earth."

[12]And God said, "This is the sign of the covenant I am making between me and you and every living creature with you, a covenant for all generations to come: [13]I have set my rainbow in the clouds, and it will be the sign of the covenant between me and the earth. [14]Whenever I bring clouds over the earth and the rainbow appears in the clouds, [15]I will remember my covenant between me and you and all living creatures of every kind. Never again will the waters become a flood to destroy all life. [16]Whenever the rainbow appears in the clouds, I will see it and remember the everlasting covenant between God and all living creatures of every kind on the earth."

[17]So God said to Noah, "This is the sign of the covenant I have established between me and all life on the earth."

[18]The sons of Noah who came out of the ark were Shem, Ham and Japheth. (Ham was the father of Canaan.) [19]These were the three sons of Noah, and from them came the people who were scattered over the earth.

[20]Noah, a man of the soil, proceeded[n] to plant a vineyard. [21]When he drank some of its wine, he became drunk and lay uncovered inside his tent. [22]Ham, the father of Canaan, saw his father's nakedness and told his two brothers outside. [23]But Shem and Japheth took a garment and laid it across their shoulders; then they walked in backward and covered their father's nakedness. Their faces were turned the other way so that they would not see their father's nakedness.

[24]When Noah awoke from his wine and found out what his youngest son had done to him, [25]he said,

"Cursed be Canaan!
    The lowest of slaves
    will he be to his brothers."

[26]He also said,

"Blessed be the LORD, the God of
    Shem!

---

m 21 Or *man, for*   *n* 20 Or *soil, was the first*

May Canaan be the slave of Shem.ᵒ
²⁷May God extend the territory of
    Japhethᵖ;
may Japheth live in the tents of
    Shem,

and may Canaan be his�q slave."

²⁸After the flood Noah lived 350 years. ²⁹Altogether, Noah lived 950 years, and then he died.

ᵒ26 Or be his slave   ᵖ27 Japheth sounds like the Hebrew for extend.   q27 Or their

JANUARY 4 □ DAY 4
GENESIS 10–11
Construction and Confusion

OVERVIEW Starting with Noah and his three sons, God begins to repopulate the world. But since the root of sin has not been removed, the fruit of sin soon becomes apparent again in proud, disobedient actions. As Noah's descendants seek to build "a city, with a tower that reaches to the heavens" (11:4), God brings the project to a halt by confusing their speech, causing them to disperse over the face of the earth—precisely as God had originally commanded (9:1).

Chapter 10			Chapter 11	
Table of Nations			Tower of Babel	
Japheth	Ham	Shem	God's Judgment	Shem's Genealogy
1	5 | 6 20 | 21	32	1 9 | 10	32
Origin of the Nations			Dispersion of the Nations	

YOUR DAILY WALK Even on television the sight is impressive. Delegates from around the world meet in the General Assembly of the United Nations to discuss world problems and seek solutions to international tensions. Most wear headsets—an eloquent reminder of the barriers that divide humanity—as they labor together to make the nations united in more than name alone.

The best way to put an idea across is to wrap it up in a person.

Centuries ago, mankind turned from God in rebellion. The result was confusion. Genesis 11 paints a pathetic picture of disoriented people separating from one another in distrust and bewilderment. And yet that scene is not so far removed from today's world. The Babel of antiquity foreshadows the "babble" of the late twentieth century. Languages still divide; people are still perplexed. And God's solution for humanity's chaos is still the same: divine truth communicated through individuals who have experienced that truth. It's a message that is timeless: the good news of sins forgiven in Jesus Christ. No doubt you've shared this with someone in English; have you ever shared it with someone who speaks a different language? Your local Christian bookstore would be a good source of gospel tracts and Scripture portions in other languages. Today would be a great day to look for someone who needs to know that God speaks his or her language.

INSIGHT Looking Down from Above
The Babel builders were proud of the mighty tower they thought would reach up to heaven (11:4). But from God's viewpoint (11:5), he had to come down to view their puny pinnacle far below!

CHAPTER 10

This is the account of Shem, Ham and Japheth, Noah's sons, who themselves had sons after the flood.

²The sons[r] of Japheth:

Gomer, Magog, Madai, Javan, Tubal, Meshech and Tiras.

³The sons of Gomer:

Ashkenaz, Riphath and Togarmah.

⁴The sons of Javan:

Elishah, Tarshish, the Kittim and the Rodanim.[s] ⁵(From these the maritime peoples spread out into their territories by their clans within their nations, each with its own language.)

⁶The sons of Ham:

Cush, Mizraim,[t] Put and Canaan.

⁷The sons of Cush:

Seba, Havilah, Sabtah, Raamah and Sabteca.

The sons of Raamah:

Sheba and Dedan.

⁸Cush was the father[u] of Nimrod, who grew to be a mighty warrior on the earth. ⁹He was a mighty hunter before the LORD; that is why it is said, "Like Nimrod, a mighty hunter before the LORD." ¹⁰The first centers of his kingdom were Babylon, Erech, Akkad and Calneh, in[v] Shinar.[w] ¹¹From that land he went to Assyria, where he built Nineveh, Rehoboth Ir,[x] Calah ¹²and Resen, which is between Nineveh and Calah; that is the great city.

¹³Mizraim was the father of

the Ludites, Anamites, Lehabites, Naphtuhites, ¹⁴Pathrusites, Casluhites (from whom the Philistines came) and Caphtorites.

¹⁵Canaan was the father of

Sidon his firstborn,[y] and of the Hittites, ¹⁶Jebusites, Amorites, Girgashites, ¹⁷Hivites, Arkites, Sinites, ¹⁸Arvadites, Zemarites and Hamathites.

Later the Canaanite clans scattered ¹⁹and the borders of Canaan reached from Sidon toward Gerar as far as Gaza, and then toward Sodom, Gomorrah, Admah and Zeboiim, as far as Lasha.

²⁰These are the sons of Ham by their clans and languages, in their territories and nations.

²¹Sons were also born to Shem, whose older brother was[z] Japheth; Shem was the ancestor of all the sons of Eber.

²²The sons of Shem:

Elam, Asshur, Arphaxad, Lud and Aram.

²³The sons of Aram:

Uz, Hul, Gether and Meshech.[a]

²⁴Arphaxad was the father of[b] Shelah,

and Shelah the father of Eber.

²⁵Two sons were born to Eber:

One was named Peleg,[c] because in his time the earth was divided; his brother was named Joktan.

²⁶Joktan was the father of

Almodad, Sheleph, Hazarmaveth, Jerah, ²⁷Hadoram, Uzal, Diklah, ²⁸Obal, Abimael, Sheba, ²⁹Ophir, Havilah and Jobab. All these were sons of Joktan.

³⁰The region where they lived stretched from Mesha toward Sephar, in the eastern hill country.

³¹These are the sons of Shem by their clans and languages, in their territories and nations.

³²These are the clans of Noah's sons, according to their lines of descent, within their nations. From these the nations spread out over the earth after the flood.

CHAPTER 11

Now the whole world had one language and a common speech. ²As men moved eastward,[d] they found a plain in Shinar[w] and settled there.

³They said to each other, "Come, let's make bricks and bake them thoroughly." They used brick instead of stone, and tar for mortar. ⁴Then they said, "Come, let us build ourselves a city, with a tower that reaches to the heavens, so that we may make a name for ourselves and not be

r2 Sons may mean descendants or successors or nations; also in verses 3, 4, 6, 7, 20-23, 29 and 31.   s4 Some manuscripts of the Masoretic Text and Samaritan Pentateuch (see also Septuagint and 1 Chron. 1:7); most manuscripts of the Masoretic Text Dodanim   t6 That is, Egypt; also in verse 13   u8 Father may mean ancestor or predecessor or founder; also in verses 13, 15, 24 and 26.   v10 Or Erech and Akkad—all of them in   w10,2 That is, Babylonia   x11 Or Nineveh with its city squares   y15 Or of the Sidonians, the foremost   z21 Or Shem, the older brother of   a23 See Septuagint and 1 Chron. 1:17; Hebrew Mash   b24 Hebrew; Septuagint father of Cainan, and Cainan was the father of   c25 Peleg means division.   d2 Or from the east; or in the east scattered over the face of the whole earth."

⁵But the LORD came down to see the city and the tower that the men were building. ⁶The LORD said, "If as one people speaking the same language they have begun to do this, then nothing they plan to do will be impossible for them. ⁷Come, let us go down and confuse their language so they will not understand each other."

⁸So the LORD scattered them from there over all the earth, and they stopped building the city. ⁹That is why it was called Babel*e*—because there the LORD confused the language of the whole world. From there the LORD scattered them over the face of the whole earth.

¹⁰This is the account of Shem.

Two years after the flood, when Shem was 100 years old, he became the father*f* of Arphaxad. ¹¹And after he became the father of Arphaxad, Shem lived 500 years and had other sons and daughters.

¹²When Arphaxad had lived 35 years, he became the father of Shelah. ¹³And after he became the father of Shelah, Arphaxad lived 403 years and had other sons and daughters.*g*

¹⁴When Shelah had lived 30 years, he became the father of Eber. ¹⁵And after he became the father of Eber, Shelah lived 403 years and had other sons and daughters.

¹⁶When Eber had lived 34 years, he became the father of Peleg. ¹⁷And after he became the father of Peleg, Eber lived 430 years and had other sons and daughters.

¹⁸When Peleg had lived 30 years, he became the father of Reu. ¹⁹And after he be-

came the father of Reu, Peleg lived 209 years and had other sons and daughters.

²⁰When Reu had lived 32 years, he became the father of Serug. ²¹And after he became the father of Serug, Reu lived 207 years and had other sons and daughters.

²²When Serug had lived 30 years, he became the father of Nahor. ²³And after he became the father of Nahor, Serug lived 200 years and had other sons and daughters.

²⁴When Nahor had lived 29 years, he became the father of Terah. ²⁵And after he became the father of Terah, Nahor lived 119 years and had other sons and daughters.

²⁶After Terah had lived 70 years, he became the father of Abram, Nahor and Haran.

²⁷This is the account of Terah.

Terah became the father of Abram, Nahor and Haran. And Haran became the father of Lot. ²⁸While his father Terah was still alive, Haran died in Ur of the Chaldeans, in the land of his birth. ²⁹Abram and Nahor both married. The name of Abram's wife was Sarai, and the name of Nahor's wife was Milcah; she was the daughter of Haran, the father of both Milcah and Iscah. ³⁰Now Sarai was barren; she had no children.

³¹Terah took his son Abram, his grandson Lot son of Haran, and his daughter-in-law Sarai, the wife of his son Abram, and together they set out from Ur of the Chaldeans to go to Canaan. But when they came to Haran, they settled there. ³²Terah lived 205 years, and he died in Haran.

e9 That is, Babylon; *Babel* sounds like the Hebrew for *confused.* *f10* *Father* may mean *ancestor;* also in verses 11-25.
g12,13 Hebrew; Septuagint (see also Luke 3:35, 36 and note at Gen. 10:24) *35 years, he became the father of Cainan.* *13And after he became the father of Cainan, Arphaxad lived 430 years and had other sons and daughters, and then he died. When Cainan had lived 130 years, he became the father of Shelah. And after he became the father of Shelah, Cainan lived 330 years and had other sons and daughters*

JANUARY 5 □ DAY 5
GENESIS 12–14
Abram's Call and God's Promises

OVERVIEW Having dealt with rebellious mankind for generations, God now begins to unfold his great plan of redemption—a plan beginning with one man, Abram. God calls Abram to leave his home in Ur of the Chaldeans and travel to a distant but unspecified new land.

Responding in faith, Abram obeys with nothing to cling to but the promises of God—promises of a great name, a great nation and a great blessing for all mankind. The journey is not without its moments of danger, as seen in the life of Lot. But through it all, Abram dares to believe God for what seems impossible, given his childless condition.

Chapter 12		Chapter 13	Chapter 14
Abram in Ur	Abram in Egypt	Abram in Canaan	Lot in Danger
1 9	10 20		
Calling	Compromising	Choosing	Conquering

The evidence of knowing God is obeying God.

YOUR DAILY WALK How long have you lived in your present home? If your answer is less than three years, you are typical! The average American family moves about once every three years.

Genesis 12:1-4 describes a similar "moving experience"—a God-fearing family obeying the voice of God, pulling up stakes in Ur, and heading for a new home more than a thousand miles away. But Hebrews 11:8 explains why this was no ordinary move! "Abraham . . . obeyed and went, even though he did not know where he was going." The command of God was clear, but the destination was not! That's faith—the kind that pleases God (Hebrews 11:6) and the kind God wants you to exercise today as you face similar situations in which his will may be clear . . . though the way he wants you to accomplish it is not. Abram found that you don't always need to know where you're going, provided you know whom you're following!

Call a family council this evening to discuss a decision you are facing involving career, home or finances—and the way Abram's example can make your decision easier. Then memorize together this verse from tomorrow's reading about the basis for Abram's obedience, his faith in God: "Abram believed the LORD, and he credited it to him as righteousness" (15:6).

INSIGHT The True Test of Values

Lot's choice of the well-watered plains of Jordan was the beginning of his downfall, for it caused him to pitch his tent toward the wicked city of Sodom. By contrast, Abram was building his life on the promises of God. Lot chose for *himself* (13:11); Abram allowed *God* to choose for him (13:14–15). Which do you think was the better choice?

CHAPTER 12

The LORD had said to Abram, "Leave your country, your people and your father's household and go to the land I will show you.

2"I will make you into a great nation
  and I will bless you;
 I will make your name great,
  and you will be a blessing.
3I will bless those who bless you,
  and whoever curses you I will curse;
and all peoples on earth
  will be blessed through you."

4So Abram left, as the LORD had told him; and Lot went with him. Abram was

seventy-five years old when he set out from Haran. 5He took his wife Sarai, his nephew Lot, all the possessions they had accumulated and the people they had acquired in Haran, and they set out for the land of Canaan, and they arrived there.

6Abram traveled through the land as far as the site of the great tree of Moreh at Shechem. At that time the Canaanites were in the land. 7The LORD appeared to Abram and said, "To your offspring[h] I will give this land." So he built an altar there to the LORD, who had appeared to him.

8From there he went on toward the hills east of Bethel and pitched his tent, with

[h]7 Or *seed*

Bethel on the west and Ai on the east. There he built an altar to the LORD and called on the name of the LORD. ⁹Then Abram set out and continued toward the Negev.

¹⁰Now there was a famine in the land, and Abram went down to Egypt to live there for a while because the famine was severe. ¹¹As he was about to enter Egypt, he said to his wife Sarai, "I know what a beautiful woman you are. ¹²When the Egyptians see you, they will say, 'This is his wife.' Then they will kill me but will let you live. ¹³Say you are my sister, so that I will be treated well for your sake and my life will be spared because of you."

¹⁴When Abram came to Egypt, the Egyptians saw that she was a very beautiful woman. ¹⁵And when Pharaoh's officials saw her, they praised her to Pharaoh, and she was taken into his palace. ¹⁶He treated Abram well for her sake, and Abram acquired sheep and cattle, male and female donkeys, menservants and maidservants, and camels.

¹⁷But the LORD inflicted serious diseases on Pharaoh and his household because of Abram's wife Sarai. ¹⁸So Pharaoh summoned Abram. "What have you done to me?" he said. "Why didn't you tell me she was your wife? ¹⁹Why did you say, 'She is my sister,' so that I took her to be my wife? Now then, here is your wife. Take her and go!" ²⁰Then Pharaoh gave orders about Abram to his men, and they sent him on his way, with his wife and everything he had.

CHAPTER 13

So Abram went up from Egypt to the Negev, with his wife and everything he had, and Lot went with him. ²Abram had become very wealthy in livestock and in silver and gold.

³From the Negev he went from place to place until he came to Bethel, to the place between Bethel and Ai where his tent had been earlier ⁴and where he had first built an altar. There Abram called on the name of the LORD.

⁵Now Lot, who was moving about with Abram, also had flocks and herds and tents. ⁶But the land could not support them while they stayed together, for their possessions were so great that they were not able to stay together. ⁷And quarreling arose between Abram's herdsmen and the herdsmen of Lot. The Canaanites and Perizzites were also living in the land at that time.

⁸So Abram said to Lot, "Let's not have any quarreling between you and me, or between your herdsmen and mine, for we are brothers. ⁹Is not the whole land before you? Let's part company. If you go to the left, I'll go to the right; if you go to the right, I'll go to the left."

¹⁰Lot looked up and saw that the whole plain of the Jordan was well watered, like the garden of the LORD, like the land of Egypt, toward Zoar. (This was before the LORD destroyed Sodom and Gomorrah.) ¹¹So Lot chose for himself the whole plain of the Jordan and set out toward the east. The two men parted company: ¹²Abram lived in the land of Canaan, while Lot lived among the cities of the plain and pitched his tents near Sodom. ¹³Now the men of Sodom were wicked and were sinning greatly against the LORD.

¹⁴The LORD said to Abram after Lot had parted from him, "Lift up your eyes from where you are and look north and south, east and west. ¹⁵All the land that you see I will give to you and your offspringⁱ forever. ¹⁶I will make your offspring like the dust of the earth, so that if anyone could count the dust, then your offspring could be counted. ¹⁷Go, walk through the length and breadth of the land, for I am giving it to you."

¹⁸So Abram moved his tents and went to live near the great trees of Mamre at Hebron, where he built an altar to the LORD.

CHAPTER 14

At this time Amraphel king of Shinar,ʲ Arioch king of Ellasar, Kedorlaomer king of Elam and Tidal king of Goiim ²went to war against Bera king of Sodom, Birsha king of Gomorrah, Shinab king of Admah, Shemeber king of Zeboiim, and the king of Bela (that is, Zoar). ³All these latter kings joined forces in the Valley of Siddim (the Salt Seaᵏ). ⁴For twelve years they had been subject to Kedorlaomer, but in the thirteenth year they rebelled.

⁵In the fourteenth year, Kedorlaomer

ⁱ15 Or *seed*; also in verse 16   ʲ1 That is, Babylonia; also in verse 9   ᵏ3 That is, the Dead Sea and the kings allied with him went out and defeated the Rephaites in Ashteroth Karnaim, the Zuzites in Ham, the Emites in Shaveh Kiriathaim [6]and the Horites in the hill country of Seir, as far as El Paran near the desert. [7]Then they turned back and went to En Mishpat (that is, Kadesh), and they conquered the whole territory of the Amalekites, as well as the Amorites who were living in Hazazon Tamar.

[8]Then the king of Sodom, the king of Gomorrah, the king of Admah, the king of Zeboiim and the king of Bela (that is, Zoar) marched out and drew up their battle lines in the Valley of Siddim [9]against Kedorlaomer king of Elam, Tidal king of Goiim, Amraphel king of Shinar and Arioch king of Ellasar—four kings against five. [10]Now the Valley of Siddim was full of tar pits, and when the kings of Sodom and Gomorrah fled, some of the men fell into them and the rest fled to the hills. [11]The four kings seized all the goods of Sodom and Gomorrah and all their food; then they went away. [12]They also carried off Abram's nephew Lot and his possessions, since he was living in Sodom.

[13]One who had escaped came and reported this to Abram the Hebrew. Now Abram was living near the great trees of Mamre the Amorite, a brother[l] of Eshcol and Aner, all of whom were allied with Abram. [14]When Abram heard that his relative had been taken captive, he called out the 318 trained men born in his household and went in pursuit as far as Dan. [15]During the night Abram divided

his men to attack them and he routed them, pursuing them as far as Hobah, north of Damascus. [16]He recovered all the goods and brought back his relative Lot and his possessions, together with the women and the other people.

[17]After Abram returned from defeating Kedorlaomer and the kings allied with him, the king of Sodom came out to meet him in the Valley of Shaveh (that is, the King's Valley).

[18]Then Melchizedek king of Salem[m] brought out bread and wine. He was priest of God Most High, [19]and he blessed Abram, saying,

"Blessed be Abram by God Most High,
    Creator[n] of heaven and earth.
[20]And blessed be[o] God Most High,
    who delivered your enemies into
    your hand."

Then Abram gave him a tenth of everything.

[21]The king of Sodom said to Abram, "Give me the people and keep the goods for yourself."

[22]But Abram said to the king of Sodom, "I have raised my hand to the LORD, God Most High, Creator of heaven and earth, and have taken an oath [23]that I will accept nothing belonging to you, not even a thread or the thong of a sandal, so that you will never be able to say, 'I made Abram rich.' [24]I will accept nothing but what my men have eaten and the share that belongs to the men who went with me—to Aner, Eshcol and Mamre. Let them have their share."

---

[l]13 Or *a relative; or an ally*   [m]18 That is, Jerusalem   [n]19 Or *Possessor*; also in verse 22   [o]20 Or *And praise be to*

JANUARY 6 ☐ DAY 6
GENESIS 15–17
God's Covenant with Abram

 OVERVIEW It is one thing to walk with God; it is something else to run ahead of God. God's promise to Abram of many descendants is amply repeated (12:2; 13:16; 15:4–5). But as the years pass with no evidence of fulfillment, Abram acts in foolish impatience. The result is a son, Ishmael, who becomes the heartbreak of his father and a constant reminder of the high price of unbelief. But God's promise stands sure! Though his promise is biologically impossible, Abram and Sarai will yet give birth to a son—a promise confirmed by new names for the parents-to-be: Abraham ("father of many") and Sarah ("princess").

Chapter 15	Chapter 16	Chapter 17
Abram's Covenant of Faith	Abram's Child of Impatience	Abram's Covenant Confirmed
Promise	Presumption	Prescribed Rite

YOUR DAILY WALK Hindsight may be a harsh teacher, but its vision is always 20/20! The book of Genesis does not seek to cover up the frailties of Abraham and Sarah but includes them right along with the moments of shining faith and obedience. Why? So that we might learn from their example, good or bad!

Many a man has turned and left the dock just before his ship came in.

In hindsight, what can you learn from Abraham's life about the danger of running ahead of God? Here are two lessons worth noting:

(1) Abraham's God was too small. Abraham assumed that Sarah's barrenness was a permanent obstacle to God's promise, forgetting that ". . . nothing is impossible with God" (Luke 1:37).

(2) Abraham's patience was too short. He got in a hurry. He decided to fulfill a promise that God was responsible to fulfill.

Write out one of God's timeless promises to you (Philippians 4:19 would do nicely), and attach it to a clock you glance at regularly. This is a great way to remind yourself throughout the day that there's no better time of day to take God at his word!

INSIGHT Who Gets the Estate?
In the ancient Near East, the heirs to a man's property on his death would be in this order: (1) the son of his first wife; (2) the son of another wife; (3) the son of a slave girl; (4) the highest ranking servant in his house. Using this "law of the land," who would have received the estate in 15:2–3? in 16:15?

CHAPTER 15

After this, the word of the LORD came to Abram in a vision:

"Do not be afraid, Abram.
I am your shield,*p*
your very great reward.*q*"

²But Abram said, "O Sovereign LORD, what can you give me since I remain childless and the one who will inherit*r* my estate is Eliezer of Damascus?" ³And Abram said, "You have given me no children; so a servant in my household will be my heir."

⁴Then the word of the LORD came to him: "This man will not be your heir, but a son coming from your own body will be your heir." ⁵He took him outside and said, "Look up at the heavens and count the stars—if indeed you can count them." Then he said to him, "So shall your offspring be."

⁶Abram believed the LORD, and he credited it to him as righteousness.

⁷He also said to him, "I am the LORD, who brought you out of Ur of the Chaldeans to give you this land to take possession of it."

⁸But Abram said, "O Sovereign LORD, how can I know that I will gain possession of it?"

⁹So the LORD said to him, "Bring me a heifer, a goat and a ram, each three years old, along with a dove and a young pigeon."

¹⁰Abram brought all these to him, cut them in two and arranged the halves opposite each other; the birds, however, he did not cut in half. ¹¹Then birds of prey came down on the carcasses, but Abram drove them away.

¹²As the sun was setting, Abram fell into a deep sleep, and a thick and dreadful darkness came over him. ¹³Then the LORD said to him, "Know for certain that

p1 Or sovereign   *q1 Or shield; / your reward will be very great*   *r2 The meaning of the Hebrew for this phrase is uncertain.*

your descendants will be strangers in a country not their own, and they will be enslaved and mistreated four hundred years. ¹⁴But I will punish the nation they serve as slaves, and afterward they will come out with great possessions. ¹⁵You, however, will go to your fathers in peace and be buried at a good old age. ¹⁶In the fourth generation your descendants will come back here, for the sin of the Amorites has not yet reached its full measure."

¹⁷When the sun had set and darkness had fallen, a smoking firepot with a blazing torch appeared and passed between the pieces. ¹⁸On that day the LORD made a covenant with Abram and said, "To your descendants I give this land, from the river^s of Egypt to the great river, the Euphrates— ¹⁹the land of the Kenites, Kenizzites, Kadmonites, ²⁰Hittites, Perizzites, Rephaites, ²¹Amorites, Canaanites, Girgashites and Jebusites."

CHAPTER 16

Now Sarai, Abram's wife, had borne him no children. But she had an Egyptian maidservant named Hagar; ²so she said to Abram, "The LORD has kept me from having children. Go, sleep with my maidservant; perhaps I can build a family through her."

Abram agreed to what Sarai said. ³So after Abram had been living in Canaan ten years, Sarai his wife took her Egyptian maidservant Hagar and gave her to her husband to be his wife. ⁴He slept with Hagar, and she conceived.

When she knew she was pregnant, she began to despise her mistress. ⁵Then Sarai said to Abram, "You are responsible for the wrong I am suffering. I put my servant in your arms, and now that she knows she is pregnant, she despises me. May the LORD judge between you and me."

⁶"Your servant is in your hands," Abram said. "Do with her whatever you think best." Then Sarai mistreated Hagar; so she fled from her.

⁷The angel of the LORD found Hagar near a spring in the desert; it was the spring that is beside the road to Shur. ⁸And he said, "Hagar, servant of Sarai, where have you come from, and where are you going?"

"I'm running away from my mistress Sarai," she answered.

⁹Then the angel of the LORD told her, "Go back to your mistress and submit to her." ¹⁰The angel added, "I will so increase your descendants that they will be too numerous to count."

¹¹The angel of the LORD also said to her:

"You are now with child
 and you will have a son.
You shall name him Ishmael,^{t}
 for the LORD has heard of your
 misery.
¹²He will be a wild donkey of a man;
 his hand will be against everyone
 and everyone's hand against him,
and he will live in hostility
 toward^u all his brothers."

¹³She gave this name to the LORD who spoke to her: "You are the God who sees me," for she said, "I have now seen^v the One who sees me." ¹⁴That is why the well was called Beer Lahai Roi^w; it is still there, between Kadesh and Bered.

¹⁵So Hagar bore Abram a son, and Abram gave the name Ishmael to the son she had borne. ¹⁶Abram was eighty-six years old when Hagar bore him Ishmael.

CHAPTER 17

When Abram was ninety-nine years old, the LORD appeared to him and said, "I am God Almighty^x; walk before me and be blameless. ²I will confirm my covenant between me and you and will greatly increase your numbers."

³Abram fell facedown, and God said to him, ⁴"As for me, this is my covenant with you: You will be the father of many nations. ⁵No longer will you be called Abram^y; your name will be Abraham,^{z} for I have made you a father of many nations. ⁶I will make you very fruitful; I will make nations of you, and kings will come from you. ⁷I will establish my covenant as an everlasting covenant between me and you and your descendants after you for the generations to come, to be your God and the God of your descendants after you. ⁸The whole land of Canaan, where you are now an alien, I will give as an

everlasting possession to you and your descendants after you; and I will be their God."

⁹Then God said to Abraham, "As for you, you must keep my covenant, you and your descendants after you for the generations to come. ¹⁰This is my covenant with you and your descendants after you, the covenant you are to keep: Every male among you shall be circumcised. ¹¹You are to undergo circumcision, and it will be the sign of the covenant between me and you. ¹²For the generations to come every male among you who is eight days old must be circumcised, including those born in your household or bought with money from a foreigner—those who are not your offspring. ¹³Whether born in your household or bought with your money, they must be circumcised. My covenant in your flesh is to be an everlasting covenant. ¹⁴Any uncircumcised male, who has not been circumcised in the flesh, will be cut off from his people; he has broken my covenant."

¹⁵God also said to Abraham, "As for Sarai your wife, you are no longer to call her Sarai; her name will be Sarah. ¹⁶I will bless her and will surely give you a son by her. I will bless her so that she will be the mother of nations; kings of peoples will come from her."

¹⁷Abraham fell facedown; he laughed

ᵃ 19 *Isaac* means *he laughs.*

and said to himself, "Will a son be born to a man a hundred years old? Will Sarah bear a child at the age of ninety?" ¹⁸And Abraham said to God, "If only Ishmael might live under your blessing!"

¹⁹Then God said, "Yes, but your wife Sarah will bear you a son, and you will call him Isaac.ᵃ I will establish my covenant with him as an everlasting covenant for his descendants after him. ²⁰And as for Ishmael, I have heard you: I will surely bless him; I will make him fruitful and will greatly increase his numbers. He will be the father of twelve rulers, and I will make him into a great nation. ²¹But my covenant I will establish with Isaac, whom Sarah will bear to you by this time next year." ²²When he had finished speaking with Abraham, God went up from him.

²³On that very day Abraham took his son Ishmael and all those born in his household or bought with his money, every male in his household, and circumcised them, as God told him. ²⁴Abraham was ninety-nine years old when he was circumcised, ²⁵and his son Ishmael was thirteen; ²⁶Abraham and his son Ishmael were both circumcised on that same day. ²⁷And every male in Abraham's household, including those born in his household or bought from a foreigner, was circumcised with him.

JANUARY 7 □ DAY 7
The God You Can Know

 LOOK BACK Congratulations! You've taken an exciting step in your spiritual walk through God's Word. Already you've read about God's masterful creation of the universe, the first sin and its spread throughout humanity, Noah and his ark, the tower of Babel and the scattering of the nations and God's promise to Abraham to make him a father of a nation special to him.

But now let's pause and refresh ourselves as we walk through the pages of Scripture. About every seventh day you'll have the opportunity to catch up on your reading from the week if you need to. But more than that, you'll have a chance to *look back* at what you've been reading, *look up* at God and consider what he wants to say to you through his Word, and *look ahead* at what's to come.

Don't hurry through these seventh-day devotionals. Instead, take the opportunity to rest in God's presence because you're not just reading through the Bible this year—you're beginning a walk with God himself . . . a walk that will last forever!

LOOK UP Believe what you hear on the radio, and you might conclude that "God is watching us from a distance." Believe what you read in the book of Genesis, and you'll most certainly conclude that "God is close by, and he takes a personal interest in my life." And you'll be right!

The best way to face life's changes is to look to the unchanging God.

After all, look at the divine fingerprints clearly visible on the lives of Adam (who walked with God in the cool of the evening), Noah (who rode high above the floodwaters in an ark built with the aid of a blueprint from heaven—and notice in Genesis 7:16 who shut the door!), and Abram (selected by God to be the father of nations and the channel of blessing to the entire world). Not the picture of a distant, detached deity, but the portrait of a powerful yet personal God of creation, who not only made you but wants to guide and provide for you each day of your life.

LOOK AHEAD Even though you have only just begun to read through the Old Testament, pause for a moment to read an important verse from the New Testament. In it you will find one of the most compelling reasons to keep reading each and every day.

In Hebrews 11 you'll find enshrined the names of many of the heroes of faith you will be meeting "up close and personal" over the next few months. But notice the last half of verse 6: "And without faith it is impossible to please God, because anyone who comes to him must believe that he exists and that he rewards those who earnestly seek him."

The God of creation is not an impersonal cosmic force but a personal, promise-keeping friend and guide. At times when God may seem far away and it feels as if he is watching you from a distance, you can be confident it was you, not he, that moved. The one who put the galaxies in space and is big enough to rule the universe is looking for men and women, boys and girls who earnestly desire to seek and find him.

The God who showed himself strong to Adam, Noah and Abram thousands of years ago is still alive and well today, and he is the same God you will meet each day in the pages of his Word as you journey through the *New Daily Walk Bible.* If you're not in the habit of doing so, why not begin keeping a journal to record your observations, insights and action points? By the end of the year, you'll have a treasure chest of memories about your daily time with God—whether in the cool of the evening or the quiet of the morning, or sometime in between.

JANUARY 8 ☐ DAY 8
GENESIS 18–20
God's Judgment on Sodom

OVERVIEW Three heavenly messengers arrive with both good news and bad news for Abraham's family. The good news: Abraham and Sarah's long-awaited dream is about to come true! They will soon experience the joys of parenthood. The bad news: Sodom and Gomorrah will soon experience the full fury of God's judgment for their grievous sins. In response to Abraham's intercession, God spares Lot's family during Sodom's destruction, though their grudging departure reflects their lukewarm spiritual condition.

Chapter 18	Chapter 19	Chapter 20
Sodom's Doom Declared	Sodom and Gomorrah Destroyed	Abraham's Deceit
	Saving Lot	Saving Sarah

YOUR DAILY WALK One day a man named Lot sat down at his desk, pulled out a sheet of paper, and wrote across the top: "Goals for My Life." Then he began to compile the goals that would shape the direction of his life:

Many people have the right aims in life; they just never get around to pulling the trigger.

1. To lose all sense of moral values.
2. To forfeit all spiritual authority in my home.
3. To exert no influence for good in my community.
4. To lose everyone and everything dear to me.

Ridiculous, you say? Then consider this: Lot set no such goals, yet he accomplished everything on that list! Those unwritten goals simply became the consequences of his worldly choices.

Lot had no spiritual goals in his life, but you should. Written goals help prevent the kind of purposeless drift that set Lot up for disaster. What do you want to accomplish specifically this year in the areas of Scripture memorization . . . time in God's Word . . . reading good Christian books . . . sharing your faith? Write them down; hang them up; pray them through; and with God's help watch them happen!

INSIGHT Where Are They Today?
From the offspring resulting from Lot's incest with his daughters came the forerunners of the Moabites and Ammonites (19:37–38), who—though related to them—were the Israelites' constant enemies. For their gross idolatry, both Moab and Ammon would later be destroyed (Amos 2:1–3; Ezekiel 25:1–7).

CHAPTER 18

The LORD appeared to Abraham near the great trees of Mamre while he was sitting at the entrance to his tent in the heat of the day. ²Abraham looked up and saw three men standing nearby. When he saw them, he hurried from the entrance of his tent to meet them and bowed low to the ground.

³He said, "If I have found favor in your eyes, my lord,ᵇ do not pass your servant by. ⁴Let a little water be brought, and then you may all wash your feet and rest under this tree. ⁵Let me get you something to eat, so you can be refreshed and then go on your way—now that you have come to your servant."

"Very well," they answered, "do as you say."

⁶So Abraham hurried into the tent to Sarah. "Quick," he said, "get three seahsᶜ of fine flour and knead it and bake some bread."

⁷Then he ran to the herd and selected a choice, tender calf and gave it to a ser-

vant, who hurried to prepare it. ⁸He then brought some curds and milk and the calf that had been prepared, and set these before them. While they ate, he stood near them under a tree.

⁹"Where is your wife Sarah?" they asked him.

"There, in the tent," he said.

¹⁰Then the LORDᵈ said, "I will surely return to you about this time next year, and Sarah your wife will have a son."

Now Sarah was listening at the entrance to the tent, which was behind him. ¹¹Abraham and Sarah were already old and well advanced in years, and Sarah was past the age of childbearing. ¹²So Sarah laughed to herself as she thought, "After I am worn out and my masterᵉ is old, will I now have this pleasure?"

¹³Then the LORD said to Abraham, "Why did Sarah laugh and say, 'Will I really have a child, now that I am old?' ¹⁴Is anything too hard for the LORD? I will return to you at the appointed time next year and Sarah will have a son."

ᵇ3 Or O Lord   ᶜ6 That is, probably about 20 quarts (about 22 liters)   ᵈ10 Hebrew *Then he*   ᵉ12 Or *husband*

¹⁵Sarah was afraid, so she lied and said, "I did not laugh."

But he said, "Yes, you did laugh."

¹⁶When the men got up to leave, they looked down toward Sodom, and Abraham walked along with them to see them on their way. ¹⁷Then the LORD said, "Shall I hide from Abraham what I am about to do? ¹⁸Abraham will surely become a great and powerful nation, and all nations on earth will be blessed through him. ¹⁹For I have chosen him, so that he will direct his children and his household after him to keep the way of the LORD by doing what is right and just, so that the LORD will bring about for Abraham what he has promised him."

²⁰Then the LORD said, "The outcry against Sodom and Gomorrah is so great and their sin so grievous ²¹that I will go down and see if what they have done is as bad as the outcry that has reached me. If not, I will know."

²²The men turned away and went toward Sodom, but Abraham remained standing before the LORD.ᶠ ²³Then Abraham approached him and said: "Will you sweep away the righteous with the wicked? ²⁴What if there are fifty righteous people in the city? Will you really sweep it away and not spareᵍ the place for the sake of the fifty righteous people in it? ²⁵Far be it from you to do such a thing—to kill the righteous with the wicked, treating the righteous and the wicked alike. Far be it from you! Will not the Judgeʰ of all the earth do right?"

²⁶The LORD said, "If I find fifty righteous people in the city of Sodom, I will spare the whole place for their sake."

²⁷Then Abraham spoke up again: "Now that I have been so bold as to speak to the Lord, though I am nothing but dust and ashes, ²⁸what if the number of the righteous is five less than fifty? Will you destroy the whole city because of five people?"

"If I find forty-five there," he said, "I will not destroy it."

²⁹Once again he spoke to him, "What if only forty are found there?"

He said, "For the sake of forty, I will not do it."

³⁰Then he said, "May the Lord not be angry, but let me speak. What if only thirty can be found there?"

He answered, "I will not do it if I find thirty there."

³¹Abraham said, "Now that I have been so bold as to speak to the Lord, what if only twenty can be found there?"

He said, "For the sake of twenty, I will not destroy it."

³²Then he said, "May the Lord not be angry, but let me speak just once more. What if only ten can be found there?"

He answered, "For the sake of ten, I will not destroy it."

³³When the LORD had finished speaking with Abraham, he left, and Abraham returned home.

CHAPTER 19

The two angels arrived at Sodom in the evening, and Lot was sitting in the gateway of the city. When he saw them, he got up to meet them and bowed down with his face to the ground. ²"My lords," he said, "please turn aside to your servant's house. You can wash your feet and spend the night and then go on your way early in the morning."

"No," they answered, "we will spend the night in the square."

³But he insisted so strongly that they did go with him and entered his house. He prepared a meal for them, baking bread without yeast, and they ate. ⁴Before they had gone to bed, all the men from every part of the city of Sodom—both young and old—surrounded the house. ⁵They called to Lot, "Where are the men who came to you tonight? Bring them out to us so that we can have sex with them."

⁶Lot went outside to meet them and shut the door behind him ⁷and said, "No, my friends. Don't do this wicked thing. ⁸Look, I have two daughters who have never slept with a man. Let me bring them out to you, and you can do what you like with them. But don't do anything to these men, for they have come under the protection of my roof."

⁹"Get out of our way," they replied. And they said, "This fellow came here as an alien, and now he wants to play the judge! We'll treat you worse than them." They kept bringing pressure on Lot and moved forward to break down the door.

ᶠ22 Masoretic Text; an ancient Hebrew scribal tradition *but the* LORD *remained standing before Abraham*   ᵍ24 Or *forgive*; also in verse 26   ʰ25 Or *Ruler*

¹⁰But the men inside reached out and pulled Lot back into the house and shut the door. ¹¹Then they struck the men who were at the door of the house, young and old, with blindness so that they could not find the door.

¹²The two men said to Lot, "Do you have anyone else here—sons-in-law, sons or daughters, or anyone else in the city who belongs to you? Get them out of here, ¹³because we are going to destroy this place. The outcry to the LORD against its people is so great that he has sent us to destroy it."

¹⁴So Lot went out and spoke to his sons-in-law, who were pledged to marry*i* his daughters. He said, "Hurry and get out of this place, because the LORD is about to destroy the city!" But his sons-in-law thought he was joking.

¹⁵With the coming of dawn, the angels urged Lot, saying, "Hurry! Take your wife and your two daughters who are here, or you will be swept away when the city is punished."

¹⁶When he hesitated, the men grasped his hand and the hands of his wife and of his two daughters and led them safely out of the city, for the LORD was merciful to them. ¹⁷As soon as they had brought them out, one of them said, "Flee for your lives! Don't look back, and don't stop anywhere in the plain! Flee to the mountains or you will be swept away!"

¹⁸But Lot said to them, "No, my lords,*j* please! ¹⁹Your*k* servant has found favor in your*k* eyes, and you*k* have shown great kindness to me in sparing my life. But I can't flee to the mountains; this disaster will overtake me, and I'll die. ²⁰Look, here is a town near enough to run to, and it is small. Let me flee to it—it is very small, isn't it? Then my life will be spared."

²¹He said to him, "Very well, I will grant this request too; I will not overthrow the town you speak of. ²²But flee there quickly, because I cannot do anything until you reach it." (That is why the town was called Zoar.*l*)

²³By the time Lot reached Zoar, the sun had risen over the land. ²⁴Then the LORD rained down burning sulfur on Sodom and Gomorrah—from the LORD out of the heavens. ²⁵Thus he overthrew those cities and the entire plain, including all those living in the cities—and also the vegetation in the land. ²⁶But Lot's wife looked back, and she became a pillar of salt.

²⁷Early the next morning Abraham got up and returned to the place where he had stood before the LORD. ²⁸He looked down toward Sodom and Gomorrah, toward all the land of the plain, and he saw dense smoke rising from the land, like smoke from a furnace.

²⁹So when God destroyed the cities of the plain, he remembered Abraham, and he brought Lot out of the catastrophe that overthrew the cities where Lot had lived.

³⁰Lot and his two daughters left Zoar and settled in the mountains, for he was afraid to stay in Zoar. He and his two daughters lived in a cave. ³¹One day the older daughter said to the younger, "Our father is old, and there is no man around here to lie with us, as is the custom all over the earth. ³²Let's get our father to drink wine and then lie with him and preserve our family line through our father."

³³That night they got their father to drink wine, and the older daughter went in and lay with him. He was not aware of it when she lay down or when she got up.

³⁴The next day the older daughter said to the younger, "Last night I lay with my father. Let's get him to drink wine again tonight, and you go in and lie with him so we can preserve our family line through our father." ³⁵So they got their father to drink wine that night also, and the younger daughter went and lay with him. Again he was not aware of it when she lay down or when she got up.

³⁶So both of Lot's daughters became pregnant by their father. ³⁷The older daughter had a son, and she named him Moab*m*; he is the father of the Moabites of today. ³⁸The younger daughter also had a son, and she named him Ben-Ammi*n*; he is the father of the Ammonites of today.

CHAPTER 20

Now Abraham moved on from there into the region of the Negev and lived between Kadesh and Shur. For a while he stayed in Gerar, ²and there Abraham said of his wife Sarah, "She is my sister." Then

---

i14 Or *were married to*   *j18* Or *No, Lord*; or *No, my lord*   *k19* The Hebrew is singular.   *l22* Zoar means small.
m37 Moab sounds like the Hebrew for *from father*.   *n38* Ben-Ammi means son of my people.

Abimelech king of Gerar sent for Sarah and took her.

³But God came to Abimelech in a dream one night and said to him, "You are as good as dead because of the woman you have taken; she is a married woman."

⁴Now Abimelech had not gone near her, so he said, "Lord, will you destroy an innocent nation? ⁵Did he not say to me, 'She is my sister,' and didn't she also say, 'He is my brother'? I have done this with a clear conscience and clean hands."

⁶Then God said to him in the dream, "Yes, I know you did this with a clear conscience, and so I have kept you from sinning against me. That is why I did not let you touch her. ⁷Now return the man's wife, for he is a prophet, and he will pray for you and you will live. But if you do not return her, you may be sure that you and all yours will die."

⁸Early the next morning Abimelech summoned all his officials, and when he told them all that had happened, they were very much afraid. ⁹Then Abimelech called Abraham in and said, "What have you done to us? How have I wronged you that you have brought such great guilt upon me and my kingdom? You have done things to me that should not be done." ¹⁰And Abimelech asked Abraham, "What was your reason for doing this?"

¹¹Abraham replied, "I said to myself, 'There is surely no fear of God in this place, and they will kill me because of my wife.' ¹²Besides, she really is my sister, the daughter of my father though not of my mother; and she became my wife. ¹³And when God had me wander from my father's household, I said to her, 'This is how you can show your love to me: Everywhere we go, say of me, "He is my brother." ' "

¹⁴Then Abimelech brought sheep and cattle and male and female slaves and gave them to Abraham, and he returned Sarah his wife to him. ¹⁵And Abimelech said, "My land is before you; live wherever you like."

¹⁶To Sarah he said, "I am giving your brother a thousand shekels° of silver. This is to cover the offense against you before all who are with you; you are completely vindicated."

¹⁷Then Abraham prayed to God, and God healed Abimelech, his wife and his slave girls so they could have children again, ¹⁸for the LORD had closed up every womb in Abimelech's household because of Abraham's wife Sarah.

°16 That is, about 25 pounds (about 11.5 kilograms)

JANUARY 9 □ DAY 9
GENESIS 21–24
Isaac—God's Promise in Flesh and Blood

OVERVIEW Today's reading describes the birth and early years of Isaac, the long-awaited son God had promised Abraham. After many years of learning to walk by faith, Abraham and Sarah experience the greatest joy of their lives: the miraculous birth of a son and heir and the one through whom God would form a great nation! The stage is set for Abraham's severest test—the command to sacrifice his treasured son as a burnt offering to God. Drawing upon a faith in God that has grown with the years, Abraham obeys, thereby learning another lesson about God's faithfulness. Sarah, who sees her son reach manhood, does not live to see him marry.

Chapter 21	Chapter 22	Chapter 23	Chapter 24
Birth of Isaac	Offering of Isaac	Death of Sarah	Marriage of Isaac
Isaac's Childhood		Isaac's Early Adulthood	

YOUR DAILY WALK "There is no such thing as an *accident*, only *incidents* in the perfect will of God." That's not just a glib maxim. It was spoken by a father whose teenage daughter had just undergone brain surgery after a car and bus collision. He meant that both the *type* and the *timing* of "accidents" are under God's wise control.

The best measure of a spiritual life is not its ecstasies but its obedience.

It is no coincidence that chapter 22, the offering of Isaac, begins with these words: "Some time later God tested Abraham." Why did God choose to test Abraham at this point in time? Abraham had endured many faith-stretching lessons, which are recorded in chapters 12–21. Only after these lessons did God put Abraham through the extreme test with Isaac.

Are you learning the lessons today that will help you handle the tests God has for you tomorrow? Think of one faith-stretching situation you are facing today (a grumpy neighbor, a difficult boss, a houseful of kids). How might God use it to prepare you for tomorrow? Pause right now and ask him to make you teachable in today's tests so you'll be prepared for the bigger ones tomorrow.

INSIGHT Ephron's Generosity . . . or Was It?
As a burial place for Sarah, Abraham purchased the cave of Machpelah at Hebron from a Hittite named Ephron (23:3–16). In Hittite law, a property owner was subject to military duty. Abraham only wanted to buy the cave; Ephron urged him to take the whole field. In this way, Ephron freed himself from military obligation.

CHAPTER 21

Now the LORD was gracious to Sarah as he had said, and the LORD did for Sarah what he had promised. ²Sarah became pregnant and bore a son to Abraham in his old age, at the very time God had promised him. ³Abraham gave the name Isaac[p] to the son Sarah bore him. ⁴When his son Isaac was eight days old, Abraham circumcised him, as God commanded him. ⁵Abraham was a hundred years old when his son Isaac was born to him.

⁶Sarah said, "God has brought me laughter, and everyone who hears about this will laugh with me." ⁷And she added, "Who would have said to Abraham that Sarah would nurse children? Yet I have borne him a son in his old age."

⁸The child grew and was weaned, and on the day Isaac was weaned Abraham held a great feast. ⁹But Sarah saw that the son whom Hagar the Egyptian had borne to Abraham was mocking, ¹⁰and she said to Abraham, "Get rid of that slave woman and her son, for that slave woman's son will never share in the inheritance with my son Isaac."

¹¹The matter distressed Abraham greatly because it concerned his son. ¹²But God said to him, "Do not be so distressed about the boy and your maidservant. Lis-

ten to whatever Sarah tells you, because it is through Isaac that your offspring[q] will be reckoned. ¹³I will make the son of the maidservant into a nation also, because he is your offspring."

¹⁴Early the next morning Abraham took some food and a skin of water and gave them to Hagar. He set them on her shoulders and then sent her off with the boy. She went on her way and wandered in the desert of Beersheba.

¹⁵When the water in the skin was gone, she put the boy under one of the bushes. ¹⁶Then she went off and sat down nearby, about a bowshot away, for she thought, "I cannot watch the boy die." And as she sat there nearby, she[r] began to sob.

¹⁷God heard the boy crying, and the angel of God called to Hagar from heaven and said to her, "What is the matter, Hagar? Do not be afraid; God has heard the boy crying as he lies there. ¹⁸Lift the boy up and take him by the hand, for I will make him into a great nation."

¹⁹Then God opened her eyes and she saw a well of water. So she went and filled the skin with water and gave the boy a drink.

²⁰God was with the boy as he grew up. He lived in the desert and became an archer. ²¹While he was living in the Desert

p3 *Isaac* means *he laughs.*   q12 Or *seed*   r16 Hebrew; Septuagint *the child* of Paran, his mother got a wife for him from Egypt.

²²At that time Abimelech and Phicol the commander of his forces said to Abraham, "God is with you in everything you do. ²³Now swear to me here before God that you will not deal falsely with me or my children or my descendants. Show to me and the country where you are living as an alien the same kindness I have shown to you."

²⁴Abraham said, "I swear it."

²⁵Then Abraham complained to Abimelech about a well of water that Abimelech's servants had seized. ²⁶But Abimelech said, "I don't know who has done this. You did not tell me, and I heard about it only today."

²⁷So Abraham brought sheep and cattle and gave them to Abimelech, and the two men made a treaty. ²⁸Abraham set apart seven ewe lambs from the flock, ²⁹and Abimelech asked Abraham, "What is the meaning of these seven ewe lambs you have set apart by themselves?"

³⁰He replied, "Accept these seven lambs from my hand as a witness that I dug this well."

³¹So that place was called Beersheba,ˢ because the two men swore an oath there.

³²After the treaty had been made at Beersheba, Abimelech and Phicol the commander of his forces returned to the land of the Philistines. ³³Abraham planted a tamarisk tree in Beersheba, and there he called upon the name of the LORD, the Eternal God. ³⁴And Abraham stayed in the land of the Philistines for a long time.

CHAPTER 22

Some time later God tested Abraham. He said to him, "Abraham!"

"Here I am," he replied.

²Then God said, "Take your son, your only son, Isaac, whom you love, and go to the region of Moriah. Sacrifice him there as a burnt offering on one of the mountains I will tell you about."

³Early the next morning Abraham got up and saddled his donkey. He took with him two of his servants and his son Isaac. When he had cut enough wood for the burnt offering, he set out for the place God had told him about. ⁴On the third day Abraham looked up and saw the place in the distance. ⁵He said to his servants, "Stay here with the donkey while I and the boy go over there. We will worship and then we will come back to you."

⁶Abraham took the wood for the burnt offering and placed it on his son Isaac, and he himself carried the fire and the knife. As the two of them went on together, ⁷Isaac spoke up and said to his father Abraham, "Father?"

"Yes, my son?" Abraham replied.

"The fire and wood are here," Isaac said, "but where is the lamb for the burnt offering?"

⁸Abraham answered, "God himself will provide the lamb for the burnt offering, my son." And the two of them went on together.

⁹When they reached the place God had told him about, Abraham built an altar there and arranged the wood on it. He bound his son Isaac and laid him on the altar, on top of the wood. ¹⁰Then he reached out his hand and took the knife to slay his son. ¹¹But the angel of the LORD called out to him from heaven, "Abraham! Abraham!"

"Here I am," he replied.

¹²"Do not lay a hand on the boy," he said. "Do not do anything to him. Now I know that you fear God, because you have not withheld from me your son, your only son."

¹³Abraham looked up and there in a thicket he saw a ramᵗ caught by its horns. He went over and took the ram and sacrificed it as a burnt offering instead of his son. ¹⁴So Abraham called that place The LORD Will Provide. And to this day it is said, "On the mountain of the LORD it will be provided."

¹⁵The angel of the LORD called to Abraham from heaven a second time ¹⁶and said, "I swear by myself, declares the LORD, that because you have done this and have not withheld your son, your only son, ¹⁷I will surely bless you and make your descendants as numerous as the stars in the sky and as the sand on the seashore. Your descendants will take possession of the cities of their enemies, ¹⁸and through your offspringᵘ all nations on earth will be blessed, because you have obeyed me."

ˢ31 *Beersheba* can mean *well of seven* or *well of the oath.*   ᵗ13 Many manuscripts of the Masoretic Text, Samaritan Pentateuch, Septuagint and Syriac; most manuscripts of the Masoretic Text *a ram behind ⌐him⌐*   ᵘ18 Or *seed*

¹⁹Then Abraham returned to his servants, and they set off together for Beersheba. And Abraham stayed in Beersheba.

²⁰Some time later Abraham was told, "Milcah is also a mother; she has borne sons to your brother Nahor: ²¹Uz the firstborn, Buz his brother, Kemuel (the father of Aram), ²²Kesed, Hazo, Pildash, Jidlaph and Bethuel." ²³Bethuel became the father of Rebekah. Milcah bore these eight sons to Abraham's brother Nahor. ²⁴His concubine, whose name was Reumah, also had sons: Tebah, Gaham, Tahash and Maacah.

CHAPTER 23

Sarah lived to be a hundred and twenty-seven years old. ²She died at Kiriath Arba (that is, Hebron) in the land of Canaan, and Abraham went to mourn for Sarah and to weep over her.

³Then Abraham rose from beside his dead wife and spoke to the Hittites.ᵛ He said, ⁴"I am an alien and a stranger among you. Sell me some property for a burial site here so I can bury my dead."

⁵The Hittites replied to Abraham, ⁶"Sir, listen to us. You are a mighty prince among us. Bury your dead in the choicest of our tombs. None of us will refuse you his tomb for burying your dead."

⁷Then Abraham rose and bowed down before the people of the land, the Hittites. ⁸He said to them, "If you are willing to let me bury my dead, then listen to me and intercede with Ephron son of Zohar on my behalf ⁹so he will sell me the cave of Machpelah, which belongs to him and is at the end of his field. Ask him to sell it to me for the full price as a burial site among you."

¹⁰Ephron the Hittite was sitting among his people and he replied to Abraham in the hearing of all the Hittites who had come to the gate of his city. ¹¹"No, my lord," he said. "Listen to me; I giveʷ you the field, and I giveʷ you the cave that is in it. I giveʷ it to you in the presence of my people. Bury your dead."

¹²Again Abraham bowed down before the people of the land ¹³and he said to Ephron in their hearing, "Listen to me, if you will. I will pay the price of the field. Accept it from me so I can bury my dead there."

¹⁴Ephron answered Abraham, ¹⁵"Listen to me, my lord; the land is worth four hundred shekelsˣ of silver, but what is that between me and you? Bury your dead."

¹⁶Abraham agreed to Ephron's terms and weighed out for him the price he had named in the hearing of the Hittites: four hundred shekels of silver, according to the weight current among the merchants.

¹⁷So Ephron's field in Machpelah near Mamre—both the field and the cave in it, and all the trees within the borders of the field—was deeded ¹⁸to Abraham as his property in the presence of all the Hittites who had come to the gate of the city. ¹⁹Afterward Abraham buried his wife Sarah in the cave in the field of Machpelah near Mamre (which is at Hebron) in the land of Canaan. ²⁰So the field and the cave in it were deeded to Abraham by the Hittites as a burial site.

CHAPTER 24

Abraham was now old and well advanced in years, and the LORD had blessed him in every way. ²He said to the chiefʸ servant in his household, the one in charge of all that he had, "Put your hand under my thigh. ³I want you to swear by the LORD, the God of heaven and the God of earth, that you will not get a wife for my son from the daughters of the Canaanites, among whom I am living, ⁴but will go to my country and my own relatives and get a wife for my son Isaac."

⁵The servant asked him, "What if the woman is unwilling to come back with me to this land? Shall I then take your son back to the country you came from?"

⁶"Make sure that you do not take my son back there," Abraham said. ⁷"The LORD, the God of heaven, who brought me out of my father's household and my native land and who spoke to me and promised me on oath, saying, 'To your offspringᶻ I will give this land'—he will send his angel before you so that you can get a wife for my son from there. ⁸If the woman is unwilling to come back with you, then you will be released from this oath of mine. Only do not take my son back there." ⁹So the servant put his hand under the thigh of his master Abraham

ᵛ3 Or the sons of Heth; also in verses 5, 7, 10, 16, 18 and 20   ʷ11 Or sell   ˣ15 That is, about 10 pounds (about 4.5 kilograms)   ʸ2 Or oldest   ᶻ7 Or seed and swore an oath to him concerning this matter.

¹⁰Then the servant took ten of his master's camels and left, taking with him all kinds of good things from his master. He set out for Aram Naharaim*ᵃ* and made his way to the town of Nahor. ¹¹He had the camels kneel down near the well outside the town; it was toward evening, the time the women go out to draw water.

¹²Then he prayed, "O LORD, God of my master Abraham, give me success today, and show kindness to my master Abraham. ¹³See, I am standing beside this spring, and the daughters of the townspeople are coming out to draw water. ¹⁴May it be that when I say to a girl, 'Please let down your jar that I may have a drink,' and she says, 'Drink, and I'll water your camels too'—let her be the one you have chosen for your servant Isaac. By this I will know that you have shown kindness to my master."

¹⁵Before he had finished praying, Rebekah came out with her jar on her shoulder. She was the daughter of Bethuel son of Milcah, who was the wife of Abraham's brother Nahor. ¹⁶The girl was very beautiful, a virgin; no man had ever lain with her. She went down to the spring, filled her jar and came up again.

¹⁷The servant hurried to meet her and said, "Please give me a little water from your jar."

¹⁸"Drink, my lord," she said, and quickly lowered the jar to her hands and gave him a drink.

¹⁹After she had given him a drink, she said, "I'll draw water for your camels too, until they have finished drinking." ²⁰So she quickly emptied her jar into the trough, ran back to the well to draw more water, and drew enough for all his camels. ²¹Without saying a word, the man watched her closely to learn whether or not the LORD had made his journey successful.

²²When the camels had finished drinking, the man took out a gold nose ring weighing a beka*ᵇ* and two gold bracelets weighing ten shekels.*ᶜ* ²³Then he asked, "Whose daughter are you? Please tell me, is there room in your father's house for us to spend the night?"

²⁴She answered him, "I am the daughter of Bethuel, the son that Milcah bore to Nahor." ²⁵And she added, "We have plenty of straw and fodder, as well as room for you to spend the night."

²⁶Then the man bowed down and worshiped the LORD, ²⁷saying, "Praise be to the LORD, the God of my master Abraham, who has not abandoned his kindness and faithfulness to my master. As for me, the LORD has led me on the journey to the house of my master's relatives."

²⁸The girl ran and told her mother's household about these things. ²⁹Now Rebekah had a brother named Laban, and he hurried out to the man at the spring. ³⁰As soon as he had seen the nose ring, and the bracelets on his sister's arms, and had heard Rebekah tell what the man said to her, he went out to the man and found him standing by the camels near the spring. ³¹"Come, you who are blessed by the LORD," he said. "Why are you standing out here? I have prepared the house and a place for the camels."

³²So the man went to the house, and the camels were unloaded. Straw and fodder were brought for the camels, and water for him and his men to wash their feet. ³³Then food was set before him, but he said, "I will not eat until I have told you what I have to say."

"Then tell us," ⌊Laban⌋ said.

³⁴So he said, "I am Abraham's servant. ³⁵The LORD has blessed my master abundantly, and he has become wealthy. He has given him sheep and cattle, silver and gold, menservants and maidservants, and camels and donkeys. ³⁶My master's wife Sarah has borne him a son in her*ᵈ* old age, and he has given him everything he owns. ³⁷And my master made me swear an oath, and said, 'You must not get a wife for my son from the daughters of the Canaanites, in whose land I live, ³⁸but go to my father's family and to my own clan, and get a wife for my son.'

³⁹"Then I asked my master, 'What if the woman will not come back with me?'

⁴⁰"He replied, 'The LORD, before whom I have walked, will send his angel with you and make your journey a success, so that you can get a wife for my son from my own clan and from my father's family. ⁴¹Then, when you go to my clan, you will be released from my oath even if they

*ᵃ*10 That is, Northwest Mesopotamia   *ᵇ*22 That is, about 1/5 ounce (about 5.5 grams)   *ᶜ*22 That is, about 4 ounces (about 110 grams)   *ᵈ*36 Or *his* refuse to give her to you—you will be released from my oath.'

⁴²"When I came to the spring today, I said, 'O Lord, God of my master Abraham, if you will, please grant success to the journey on which I have come. ⁴³See, I am standing beside this spring; if a maiden comes out to draw water and I say to her, "Please let me drink a little water from your jar," ⁴⁴and if she says to me, "Drink, and I'll draw water for your camels too," let her be the one the Lord has chosen for my master's son.'

⁴⁵"Before I finished praying in my heart, Rebekah came out, with her jar on her shoulder. She went down to the spring and drew water, and I said to her, 'Please give me a drink.'

⁴⁶"She quickly lowered her jar from her shoulder and said, 'Drink, and I'll water your camels too.' So I drank, and she watered the camels also.

⁴⁷"I asked her, 'Whose daughter are you?'

"She said, 'The daughter of Bethuel son of Nahor, whom Milcah bore to him.'

"Then I put the ring in her nose and the bracelets on her arms, ⁴⁸and I bowed down and worshiped the Lord. I praised the Lord, the God of my master Abraham, who had led me on the right road to get the granddaughter of my master's brother for his son. ⁴⁹Now if you will show kindness and faithfulness to my master, tell me; and if not, tell me, so I may know which way to turn."

⁵⁰Laban and Bethuel answered, "This is from the Lord; we can say nothing to you one way or the other. ⁵¹Here is Rebekah; take her and go, and let her become the wife of your master's son, as the Lord has directed."

⁵²When Abraham's servant heard what they said, he bowed down to the ground before the Lord. ⁵³Then the servant brought out gold and silver jewelry and articles of clothing and gave them to Rebekah; he also gave costly gifts to her

brother and to her mother. ⁵⁴Then he and the men who were with him ate and drank and spent the night there.

When they got up the next morning, he said, "Send me on my way to my master."

⁵⁵But her brother and her mother replied, "Let the girl remain with us ten days or so; then youᵉ may go."

⁵⁶But he said to them, "Do not detain me, now that the Lord has granted success to my journey. Send me on my way so I may go to my master."

⁵⁷Then they said, "Let's call the girl and ask her about it." ⁵⁸So they called Rebekah and asked her, "Will you go with this man?"

"I will go," she said.

⁵⁹So they sent their sister Rebekah on her way, along with her nurse and Abraham's servant and his men. ⁶⁰And they blessed Rebekah and said to her,

"Our sister, may you increase
    to thousands upon thousands;
may your offspring possess
    the gates of their enemies."

⁶¹Then Rebekah and her maids got ready and mounted their camels and went back with the man. So the servant took Rebekah and left.

⁶²Now Isaac had come from Beer Lahai Roi, for he was living in the Negev. ⁶³He went out to the field one evening to meditate,ᶠ and as he looked up, he saw camels approaching. ⁶⁴Rebekah also looked up and saw Isaac. She got down from her camel ⁶⁵and asked the servant, "Who is that man in the field coming to meet us?"

"He is my master," the servant answered. So she took her veil and covered herself.

⁶⁶Then the servant told Isaac all he had done. ⁶⁷Isaac brought her into the tent of his mother Sarah, and he married Rebekah. So she became his wife, and he loved her; and Isaac was comforted after his mother's death.

ᵉ55 Or she ᶠ63 The meaning of the Hebrew for this word is uncertain.

JANUARY 10 □ DAY 10
GENESIS 25–26
Isaac's Family and Fortune

OVERVIEW Isaac's family, though presented only briefly in the book of Genesis, is immensely significant. Born to Isaac are twin sons who would later be the fathers of twin nations: Jacob (Israel) and Esau (Edom). Isaac repeats one of his father's most memorable mistakes (26:6–16), but in spite of his failures, he hears the reassuring promise from God: "For to you and your descendants I will . . . confirm the oath I swore to your father Abraham" (26:3).

Chapter 25		Chapter 26	
Birth of Twins	Battle for a Birthright	Deception in Gerar	Dispute in Gerar
1 28	29 34	1 16	17 35
Isaac's Family		Isaac's Faith and Failures	

Faithfulness in little things is a big thing.

YOUR DAILY WALK Take a piece of paper and list everything you know about the life of Isaac. Then compare it with the following paragraph.

Isaac was Abraham's son, Rebekah's husband, and Jacob and Esau's father. He imitated his father and got tricked by his son. He dug a few wells and fathered a set of twins. In short, he generally did what God told him to do without much fanfare.

How would you like your epitaph to read: "He generally did what God told him to do"? There's not a lot of glamour in quiet faithfulness, but as far as God is concerned, it's more important than just about anything else. Maybe that's one reason Isaac gets equal billing with his father and son every time God identifies himself as "the God of Abraham, the God of Isaac and the God of Jacob."

Has the Lord assigned you a supporting role that escapes the notice of the crowd? Not everyone can function without applause, but apparently God knows that you can by his grace. Thank God right now for the privilege of serving in the "Isaac Brigade," and ask him for that same steadfastness of spirit that produced God's commendation for Isaac!

INSIGHT Abraham's Life—Filled to the Brim
The original Hebrew text of 25:8 reads, "Then Abraham . . . died at a good old age, an old man and *full*." When Abraham breathed his last, he was full, not only of years, but also of trials and temptations . . . victories and rewards . . . reminders and reassurances that God's promises to his posterity would surely come to pass.

CHAPTER 25
Abraham took⁸ another wife, whose name was Keturah. ²She bore him Zimran, Jokshan, Medan, Midian, Ishbak and Shuah. ³Jokshan was the father of Sheba and Dedan; the descendants of Dedan were the Asshurites, the Letushites and the Leummites. ⁴The sons of Midian were Ephah, Epher, Hanoch, Abida and El-

daah. All these were descendants of Keturah.

⁵Abraham left everything he owned to Isaac. ⁶But while he was still living, he gave gifts to the sons of his concubines and sent them away from his son Isaac to the land of the east.

⁷Altogether, Abraham lived a hundred and seventy-five years. ⁸Then Abraham

8 1 Or had taken

breathed his last and died at a good old age, an old man and full of years; and he was gathered to his people. [9]His sons Isaac and Ishmael buried him in the cave of Machpelah near Mamre, in the field of Ephron son of Zohar the Hittite, [10]the field Abraham had bought from the Hittites.[h] There Abraham was buried with his wife Sarah. [11]After Abraham's death, God blessed his son Isaac, who then lived near Beer Lahai Roi.

[12]This is the account of Abraham's son Ishmael, whom Sarah's maidservant, Hagar the Egyptian, bore to Abraham.

[13]These are the names of the sons of Ishmael, listed in the order of their birth: Nebaioth the firstborn of Ishmael, Kedar, Adbeel, Mibsam, [14]Mishma, Dumah, Massa, [15]Hadad, Tema, Jetur, Naphish and Kedemah. [16]These were the sons of Ishmael, and these are the names of the twelve tribal rulers according to their settlements and camps. [17]Altogether, Ishmael lived a hundred and thirty-seven years. He breathed his last and died, and he was gathered to his people. [18]His descendants settled in the area from Havilah to Shur, near the border of Egypt, as you go toward Asshur. And they lived in hostility toward[i] all their brothers.

[19]This is the account of Abraham's son Isaac.

Abraham became the father of Isaac, [20]and Isaac was forty years old when he married Rebekah daughter of Bethuel the Aramean from Paddan Aram[j] and sister of Laban the Aramean.
[21]Isaac prayed to the LORD on behalf of his wife, because she was barren. The LORD answered his prayer, and his wife Rebekah became pregnant. [22]The babies jostled each other within her, and she said, "Why is this happening to me?" So she went to inquire of the LORD.
[23]The LORD said to her,

"Two nations are in your womb,
  and two peoples from within you
    will be separated;
one people will be stronger than the
    other,
  and the older will serve the younger."

[24]When the time came for her to give birth, there were twin boys in her womb. [25]The first to come out was red, and his whole body was like a hairy garment; so they named him Esau.[k] [26]After this, his brother came out, with his hand grasping Esau's heel; so he was named Jacob.[l] Isaac was sixty years old when Rebekah gave birth to them.

[27]The boys grew up, and Esau became a skillful hunter, a man of the open country, while Jacob was a quiet man, staying among the tents. [28]Isaac, who had a taste for wild game, loved Esau, but Rebekah loved Jacob.

[29]Once when Jacob was cooking some stew, Esau came in from the open country, famished. [30]He said to Jacob, "Quick, let me have some of that red stew! I'm famished!" (That is why he was also called Edom.[m])

[31]Jacob replied, "First sell me your birthright."

[32]"Look, I am about to die," Esau said. "What good is the birthright to me?"

[33]But Jacob said, "Swear to me first." So he swore an oath to him, selling his birthright to Jacob.

[34]Then Jacob gave Esau some bread and some lentil stew. He ate and drank, and then got up and left.

So Esau despised his birthright.

CHAPTER 26
Now there was a famine in the land—besides the earlier famine of Abraham's time—and Isaac went to Abimelech king of the Philistines in Gerar. [2]The LORD appeared to Isaac and said, "Do not go down to Egypt; live in the land where I tell you to live. [3]Stay in this land for a while, and I will be with you and will bless you. For to you and your descendants I will give all these lands and will confirm the oath I swore to your father Abraham. [4]I will make your descendants as numerous as the stars in the sky and will give them all these lands, and through your offspring[n] all nations on earth will be blessed, [5]because Abraham obeyed me and kept my requirements, my commands, my decrees and my laws." [6]So Isaac stayed in Gerar.

[7]When the men of that place asked him about his wife, he said, "She is my sister,"

h10 Or the sons of Heth   i18 Or lived to the east of   j20 That is, Northwest Mesopotamia   k25 Esau may mean hairy; he was also called Edom, which means red.   l26 Jacob means he grasps the heel (figuratively, he deceives).   m30 Edom means red.
n4 Or seed

because he was afraid to say, "She is my wife." He thought, "The men of this place might kill me on account of Rebekah, because she is beautiful."

8When Isaac had been there a long time, Abimelech king of the Philistines looked down from a window and saw Isaac caressing his wife Rebekah. 9So Abimelech summoned Isaac and said, "She is really your wife! Why did you say, 'She is my sister'?"

Isaac answered him, "Because I thought I might lose my life on account of her."

10Then Abimelech said, "What is this you have done to us? One of the men might well have slept with your wife, and you would have brought guilt upon us."

11So Abimelech gave orders to all the people: "Anyone who molests this man or his wife shall surely be put to death."

12Isaac planted crops in that land and the same year reaped a hundredfold, because the LORD blessed him. 13The man became rich, and his wealth continued to grow until he became very wealthy. 14He had so many flocks and herds and servants that the Philistines envied him. 15So all the wells that his father's servants had dug in the time of his father Abraham, the Philistines stopped up, filling them with earth.

16Then Abimelech said to Isaac, "Move away from us; you have become too powerful for us."

17So Isaac moved away from there and encamped in the Valley of Gerar and settled there. 18Isaac reopened the wells that had been dug in the time of his father Abraham, which the Philistines had stopped up after Abraham died, and he gave them the same names his father had given them.

19Isaac's servants dug in the valley and discovered a well of fresh water there. 20But the herdsmen of Gerar quarreled with Isaac's herdsmen and said, "The water is ours!" So he named the well Esek,o because they disputed with him. 21Then they dug another well, but they quarreled over that one also; so he named it Sitnah.p 22He moved on from there and dug another well, and no one quarreled over it. He named it Rehoboth,q saying, "Now the LORD has given us room and we will flourish in the land."

23From there he went up to Beersheba. 24That night the LORD appeared to him and said, "I am the God of your father Abraham. Do not be afraid, for I am with you; I will bless you and will increase the number of your descendants for the sake of my servant Abraham."

25Isaac built an altar there and called on the name of the LORD. There he pitched his tent, and there his servants dug a well.

26Meanwhile, Abimelech had come to him from Gerar, with Ahuzzath his personal adviser and Phicol the commander of his forces. 27Isaac asked them, "Why have you come to me, since you were hostile to me and sent me away?"

28They answered, "We saw clearly that the LORD was with you; so we said, 'There ought to be a sworn agreement between us'—between us and you. Let us make a treaty with you 29that you will do us no harm, just as we did not molest you but always treated you well and sent you away in peace. And now you are blessed by the LORD."

30Isaac then made a feast for them, and they ate and drank. 31Early the next morning the men swore an oath to each other. Then Isaac sent them on their way, and they left him in peace.

32That day Isaac's servants came and told him about the well they had dug. They said, "We've found water!" 33He called it Shibah,r and to this day the name of the town has been Beersheba.s

34When Esau was forty years old, he married Judith daughter of Beeri the Hittite, and also Basemath daughter of Elon the Hittite. 35They were a source of grief to Isaac and Rebekah.

---

o20 Esek means dispute.   p21 Sitnah means opposition.   q22 Rehoboth means room.   r33 Shibah can mean oath or seven.
s33 Beersheba can mean well of the oath or well of seven.

JANUARY 11 ☐ DAY 11
GENESIS 27–31
Jacob's Dream and Flight from Esau

OVERVIEW The conflict that began in their mother's womb carries over into the adult lives of Esau and Jacob. After following Rebekah's plan to trick Isaac into giving him the patriarchal blessing, Jacob flees to Haran for safety. En route, he receives assurance from God in a dream that he is indeed the heir to the covenant promises. After twenty years in Haran learning painful lessons from his uncle Laban, Jacob returns to Canaan with his livestock, servants and family—the nucleus from which God will fashion a new nation: Israel.

Chapter 27	Chapter 28	Chapters 29–30	Chapter 31
Jacob's Stolen Blessing	Jacob's Dream at Bethel	Jacob's Family	Jacob's Flight
Leaving Home		Longing for Home	

Satan's primary tool is not an active sinner but an inactive saint.

YOUR DAILY WALK The first important experience of a new Hebrew baby was receiving a name. Often the name given would describe the parents' hopes for the child or picture the child's personality. So an infant would tend to live up to his name!

You as a child of God bear the name *Christian*. And that raises a penetrating question: Are you living up to your name? Talk to your heavenly Father about it right now. If you are willing to be a Christian today in more than name alone, tell him so!

INSIGHT You Can't Tell the Patriarchs without a Program!

Order	Name	Meaning	Mother (Son)
1	Reuben	"See, a son"	Leah (1)
2	Simeon	"One who hears"	Leah (2)
3	Levi	"Attached"	Leah (3)
4	Judah	"Praised"	Leah (4)
5	Dan	"He has vindicated"	Bilhah (1)
6	Naphtali	"My struggle"	Bilhah (2)
7	Gad	"Good fortune"	Zilpah (1)
8	Asher	"Happy"	Zilpah (2)
9	Issachar	"Reward"	Leah (5)
10	Zebulun	"Honor"	Leah (6)
11	Joseph	"May he add"	Rachel (1)
12	Benjamin	"Son of my right hand"	Rachel (2)

CHAPTER 27

When Isaac was old and his eyes were so weak that he could no longer see, he called for Esau his older son and said to him, "My son."

"Here I am," he answered.

²Isaac said, "I am now an old man and don't know the day of my death. ³Now then, get your weapons—your quiver and bow—and go out to the open country to hunt some wild game for me. ⁴Prepare me the kind of tasty food I like and bring it to me to eat, so that I

may give you my blessing before I die."

⁵Now Rebekah was listening as Isaac spoke to his son Esau. When Esau left for the open country to hunt game and bring it back, ⁶Rebekah said to her son Jacob, "Look, I overheard your father say to your brother Esau, ⁷'Bring me some game and prepare me some tasty food to eat, so that I may give you my blessing in the presence of the LORD before I die.' ⁸Now, my son, listen carefully and do what I tell you: ⁹Go out to the flock and bring me two choice young goats, so I can prepare

some tasty food for your father, just the way he likes it. ¹⁰Then take it to your father to eat, so that he may give you his blessing before he dies."

¹¹Jacob said to Rebekah his mother, "But my brother Esau is a hairy man, and I'm a man with smooth skin. ¹²What if my father touches me? I would appear to be tricking him and would bring down a curse on myself rather than a blessing."

¹³His mother said to him, "My son, let the curse fall on me. Just do what I say; go and get them for me."

¹⁴So he went and got them and brought them to his mother, and she prepared some tasty food, just the way his father liked it. ¹⁵Then Rebekah took the best clothes of Esau her older son, which she had in the house, and put them on her younger son Jacob. ¹⁶She also covered his hands and the smooth part of his neck with the goatskins. ¹⁷Then she handed to her son Jacob the tasty food and the bread she had made.

¹⁸He went to his father and said, "My father."

"Yes, my son," he answered. "Who is it?"

¹⁹Jacob said to his father, "I am Esau your firstborn. I have done as you told me. Please sit up and eat some of my game so that you may give me your blessing."

²⁰Isaac asked his son, "How did you find it so quickly, my son?"

"The LORD your God gave me success," he replied.

²¹Then Isaac said to Jacob, "Come near so I can touch you, my son, to know whether you really are my son Esau or not."

²²Jacob went close to his father Isaac, who touched him and said, "The voice is the voice of Jacob, but the hands are the hands of Esau." ²³He did not recognize him, for his hands were hairy like those of his brother Esau; so he blessed him. ²⁴"Are you really my son Esau?" he asked.

"I am," he replied.

²⁵Then he said, "My son, bring me some of your game to eat, so that I may give you my blessing."

Jacob brought it to him and he ate; and he brought some wine and he drank.

²⁶Then his father Isaac said to him, "Come here, my son, and kiss me."

²⁷So he went to him and kissed him. When Isaac caught the smell of his clothes, he blessed him and said,

"Ah, the smell of my son
    is like the smell of a field
    that the LORD has blessed.
²⁸May God give you of heaven's dew
    and of earth's richness—
    an abundance of grain and new
        wine.
²⁹May nations serve you
    and peoples bow down to you.
Be lord over your brothers,
    and may the sons of your mother
        bow down to you.
May those who curse you be cursed
    and those who bless you be blessed."

³⁰After Isaac finished blessing him and Jacob had scarcely left his father's presence, his brother Esau came in from hunting. ³¹He too prepared some tasty food and brought it to his father. Then he said to him, "My father, sit up and eat some of my game, so that you may give me your blessing."

³²His father Isaac asked him, "Who are you?"

"I am your son," he answered, "your firstborn, Esau."

³³Isaac trembled violently and said, "Who was it, then, that hunted game and brought it to me? I ate it just before you came and I blessed him—and indeed he will be blessed!"

³⁴When Esau heard his father's words, he burst out with a loud and bitter cry and said to his father, "Bless me—me too, my father!"

³⁵But he said, "Your brother came deceitfully and took your blessing."

³⁶Esau said, "Isn't he rightly named Jacobᵗ? He has deceived me these two times: He took my birthright, and now he's taken my blessing!" Then he asked, "Haven't you reserved any blessing for me?"

³⁷Isaac answered Esau, "I have made him lord over you and have made all his relatives his servants, and I have sustained him with grain and new wine. So what can I possibly do for you, my son?"

³⁸Esau said to his father, "Do you have

ᵗ36 *Jacob* means *he grasps the heel* (figuratively, *he deceives*).

only one blessing, my father? Bless me too, my father!" Then Esau wept aloud. ³⁹His father Isaac answered him,

"Your dwelling will be
  away from the earth's richness,
  away from the dew of heaven
    above.
⁴⁰You will live by the sword
  and you will serve your brother.
But when you grow restless,
  you will throw his yoke
  from off your neck."

⁴¹Esau held a grudge against Jacob because of the blessing his father had given him. He said to himself, "The days of mourning for my father are near; then I will kill my brother Jacob."

⁴²When Rebekah was told what her older son Esau had said, she sent for her younger son Jacob and said to him, "Your brother Esau is consoling himself with the thought of killing you. ⁴³Now then, my son, do what I say: Flee at once to my brother Laban in Haran. ⁴⁴Stay with him for a while until your brother's fury subsides. ⁴⁵When your brother is no longer angry with you and forgets what you did to him, I'll send word for you to come back from there. Why should I lose both of you in one day?"

⁴⁶Then Rebekah said to Isaac, "I'm disgusted with living because of these Hittite women. If Jacob takes a wife from among the women of this land, from Hittite women like these, my life will not be worth living."

CHAPTER 28

So Isaac called for Jacob and blessed[u] him and commanded him: "Do not marry a Canaanite woman. ²Go at once to Paddan Aram,[v] to the house of your mother's father Bethuel. Take a wife for yourself there, from among the daughters of Laban, your mother's brother. ³May God Almighty[w] bless you and make you fruitful and increase your numbers until you become a community of peoples. ⁴May he give you and your descendants the blessing given to Abraham, so that you may take possession of the land where you now live as an alien, the land God gave to Abraham." ⁵Then Isaac sent Jacob on his way, and he went to Paddan

Aram, to Laban son of Bethuel the Aramean, the brother of Rebekah, who was the mother of Jacob and Esau.

⁶Now Esau learned that Isaac had blessed Jacob and had sent him to Paddan Aram to take a wife from there, and that when he blessed him he commanded him, "Do not marry a Canaanite woman," ⁷and that Jacob had obeyed his father and mother and had gone to Paddan Aram. ⁸Esau then realized how displeasing the Canaanite women were to his father Isaac; ⁹so he went to Ishmael and married Mahalath, the sister of Nebaioth and daughter of Ishmael son of Abraham, in addition to the wives he already had.

¹⁰Jacob left Beersheba and set out for Haran. ¹¹When he reached a certain place, he stopped for the night because the sun had set. Taking one of the stones there, he put it under his head and lay down to sleep. ¹²He had a dream in which he saw a stairway[x] resting on the earth, with its top reaching to heaven, and the angels of God were ascending and descending on it. ¹³There above it[y] stood the LORD, and he said: "I am the LORD, the God of your father Abraham and the God of Isaac. I will give you and your descendants the land on which you are lying. ¹⁴Your descendants will be like the dust of the earth, and you will spread out to the west and to the east, to the north and to the south. All peoples on earth will be blessed through you and your offspring. ¹⁵I am with you and will watch over you wherever you go, and I will bring you back to this land. I will not leave you until I have done what I have promised you."

¹⁶When Jacob awoke from his sleep, he thought, "Surely the LORD is in this place, and I was not aware of it." ¹⁷He was afraid and said, "How awesome is this place! This is none other than the house of God; this is the gate of heaven."

¹⁸Early the next morning Jacob took the stone he had placed under his head and set it up as a pillar and poured oil on top of it. ¹⁹He called that place Bethel,[z] though the city used to be called Luz. ²⁰Then Jacob made a vow, saying, "If God will be with me and will watch over me on this journey I am taking and will give me food to eat and clothes to wear ²¹so that I return safely to my father's

---

[u]1 Or greeted   [v]2 That is, Northwest Mesopotamia; also in verses 5, 6 and 7   [w]3 Hebrew El-Shaddai   [x]12 Or ladder
[y]13 Or There beside him   [z]19 Bethel means house of God.

house, then the LORD*a* will be my God ²²and*b* this stone that I have set up as a pillar will be God's house, and of all that you give me I will give you a tenth."

CHAPTER 29
Then Jacob continued on his journey and came to the land of the eastern peoples. ²There he saw a well in the field, with three flocks of sheep lying near it because the flocks were watered from that well. The stone over the mouth of the well was large. ³When all the flocks were gathered there, the shepherds would roll the stone away from the well's mouth and water the sheep. Then they would return the stone to its place over the mouth of the well.

⁴Jacob asked the shepherds, "My brothers, where are you from?"

"We're from Haran," they replied.

⁵He said to them, "Do you know Laban, Nahor's grandson?"

"Yes, we know him," they answered.

⁶Then Jacob asked them, "Is he well?"

"Yes, he is," they said, "and here comes his daughter Rachel with the sheep."

⁷"Look," he said, "the sun is still high; it is not time for the flocks to be gathered. Water the sheep and take them back to pasture."

⁸"We can't," they replied, "until all the flocks are gathered and the stone has been rolled away from the mouth of the well. Then we will water the sheep."

⁹While he was still talking with them, Rachel came with her father's sheep, for she was a shepherdess. ¹⁰When Jacob saw Rachel daughter of Laban, his mother's brother, and Laban's sheep, he went over and rolled the stone away from the mouth of the well and watered his uncle's sheep. ¹¹Then Jacob kissed Rachel and began to weep aloud. ¹²He had told Rachel that he was a relative of her father and a son of Rebekah. So she ran and told her father.

¹³As soon as Laban heard the news about Jacob, his sister's son, he hurried to meet him. He embraced him and kissed him and brought him to his home, and there Jacob told him all these things. ¹⁴Then Laban said to him, "You are my own flesh and blood."

After Jacob had stayed with him for a whole month, ¹⁵Laban said to him, "Just

because you are a relative of mine, should you work for me for nothing? Tell me what your wages should be."

¹⁶Now Laban had two daughters; the name of the older was Leah, and the name of the younger was Rachel. ¹⁷Leah had weak*c* eyes, but Rachel was lovely in form, and beautiful. ¹⁸Jacob was in love with Rachel and said, "I'll work for you seven years in return for your younger daughter Rachel."

¹⁹Laban said, "It's better that I give her to you than to some other man. Stay here with me." ²⁰So Jacob served seven years to get Rachel, but they seemed like only a few days to him because of his love for her.

²¹Then Jacob said to Laban, "Give me my wife. My time is completed, and I want to lie with her."

²²So Laban brought together all the people of the place and gave a feast. ²³But when evening came, he took his daughter Leah and gave her to Jacob, and Jacob lay with her. ²⁴And Laban gave his servant girl Zilpah to his daughter as her maidservant.

²⁵When morning came, there was Leah! So Jacob said to Laban, "What is this you have done to me? I served you for Rachel, didn't I? Why have you deceived me?"

²⁶Laban replied, "It is not our custom here to give the younger daughter in marriage before the older one. ²⁷Finish this daughter's bridal week; then we will give you the younger one also, in return for another seven years of work."

²⁸And Jacob did so. He finished the week with Leah, and then Laban gave him his daughter Rachel to be his wife. ²⁹Laban gave his servant girl Bilhah to his daughter Rachel as her maidservant. ³⁰Jacob lay with Rachel also, and he loved Rachel more than Leah. And he worked for Laban another seven years.

³¹When the LORD saw that Leah was not loved, he opened her womb, but Rachel was barren. ³²Leah became pregnant and gave birth to a son. She named him Reuben,*d* for she said, "It is because the LORD has seen my misery. Surely my husband will love me now."

³³She conceived again, and when she gave birth to a son she said, "Because the LORD heard that I am not loved, he gave

---

a 20,21 Or *Since God . . . father's house, the* LORD   *b 21,22* Or *house, and the* LORD *will be my God,* ²²*then*   *c 17* Or *delicate*
d 32 *Reuben* sounds like the Hebrew for *he has seen my misery;* the name means *see, a son.*

me this one too." So she named him Simeon.*

³⁴Again she conceived, and when she
gave birth to a son she said, "Now at last
my husband will become attached to me,
because I have borne him three sons." So
he was named Levi.ᶠ

³⁵She conceived again, and when she
gave birth to a son she said, "This time I
will praise the LORD." So she named him
Judah.ᵍ Then she stopped having children.

CHAPTER 30
When Rachel saw that she was not bearing Jacob any children, she became jealous of her sister. So she said to Jacob,
"Give me children, or I'll die!"

²Jacob became angry with her and said,
"Am I in the place of God, who has kept
you from having children?"

³Then she said, "Here is Bilhah, my
maidservant. Sleep with her so that she
can bear children for me and that through
her I too can build a family."

⁴So she gave him her servant Bilhah as
a wife. Jacob slept with her, ⁵and she became pregnant and bore him a son. ⁶Then
Rachel said, "God has vindicated me; he
has listened to my plea and given me a
son." Because of this she named him
Dan.ʰ

⁷Rachel's servant Bilhah conceived
again and bore Jacob a second son. ⁸Then
Rachel said, "I have had a great struggle
with my sister, and I have won." So she
named him Naphtali.ⁱ

⁹When Leah saw that she had stopped
having children, she took her maidservant Zilpah and gave her to Jacob as a
wife. ¹⁰Leah's servant Zilpah bore Jacob a
son. ¹¹Then Leah said, "What good fortune!"ʲ So she named him Gad.ᵏ

¹²Leah's servant Zilpah bore Jacob a
second son. ¹³Then Leah said, "How
happy I am! The women will call me
happy." So she named him Asher.ˡ

¹⁴During wheat harvest, Reuben went
out into the fields and found some man-
drake plants, which he brought to his
mother Leah. Rachel said to Leah, "Please
give me some of your son's mandrakes."

¹⁵But she said to her, "Wasn't it enough

that you took away my husband? Will
you take my son's mandrakes too?"

"Very well," Rachel said, "he can sleep
with you tonight in return for your son's
mandrakes."

¹⁶So when Jacob came in from the fields
that evening, Leah went out to meet him.
"You must sleep with me," she said. "I
have hired you with my son's mandrakes." So he slept with her that night.

¹⁷God listened to Leah, and she became
pregnant and bore Jacob a fifth son.
¹⁸Then Leah said, "God has rewarded me
for giving my maidservant to my husband." So she named him Issachar.ᵐ

¹⁹Leah conceived again and bore Jacob
a sixth son. ²⁰Then Leah said, "God has
presented me with a precious gift. This
time my husband will treat me with
honor, because I have borne him six sons."
So she named him Zebulun.ⁿ

²¹Some time later she gave birth to a
daughter and named her Dinah.

²²Then God remembered Rachel; he listened to her and opened her womb. ²³She
became pregnant and gave birth to a son
and said, "God has taken away my disgrace." ²⁴She named him Joseph,ᵒ and
said, "May the LORD add to me another
son."

²⁵After Rachel gave birth to Joseph, Jacob said to Laban, "Send me on my way
so I can go back to my own homeland.
²⁶Give me my wives and children, for
whom I have served you, and I will be on
my way. You know how much work I've
done for you."

²⁷But Laban said to him, "If I have
found favor in your eyes, please stay. I
have learned by divination thatᵖ the LORD
has blessed me because of you." ²⁸He
added, "Name your wages, and I will pay
them."

²⁹Jacob said to him, "You know how I
have worked for you and how your livestock has fared under my care. ³⁰The little
you had before I came has increased
greatly, and the LORD has blessed you
wherever I have been. But now, when
may I do something for my own household?"

³¹"What shall I give you?" he asked.

---

*33 Simeon probably means one who hears.   ᶠ34 Levi sounds like and may be derived from the Hebrew for attached.
ᵍ35 Judah sounds like and may be derived from the Hebrew for praise.   ʰ6 Dan here means he has vindicated.   ⁱ8 Naphtali
means my struggle.   ʲ11 Or "A troop is coming!"   ᵏ11 Gad can mean good fortune or a troop.   ˡ13 Asher means happy.
ᵐ18 Issachar sounds like the Hebrew for reward.   ⁿ20 Zebulun probably means honor.   ᵒ24 Joseph means may he add.
ᵖ27 Or possibly have become rich and

"Don't give me anything," Jacob replied. "But if you will do this one thing for me, I will go on tending your flocks and watching over them: 32Let me go through all your flocks today and remove from them every speckled or spotted sheep, every dark-colored lamb and every spotted or speckled goat. They will be my wages. 33And my honesty will testify for me in the future, whenever you check on the wages you have paid me. Any goat in my possession that is not speckled or spotted, or any lamb that is not dark-colored, will be considered stolen."

34"Agreed," said Laban. "Let it be as you have said." 35That same day he removed all the male goats that were streaked or spotted, and all the speckled or spotted female goats (all that had white on them) and all the dark-colored lambs, and he placed them in the care of his sons. 36Then he put a three-day journey between himself and Jacob, while Jacob continued to tend the rest of Laban's flocks.

37Jacob, however, took fresh-cut branches from poplar, almond and plane trees and made white stripes on them by peeling the bark and exposing the white inner wood of the branches. 38Then he placed the peeled branches in all the watering troughs, so that they would be directly in front of the flocks when they came to drink. When the flocks were in heat and came to drink, 39they mated in front of the branches. And they bore young that were streaked or speckled or spotted. 40Jacob set apart the young of the flock by themselves, but made the rest face the streaked and dark-colored animals that belonged to Laban. Thus he made separate flocks for himself and did not put them with Laban's animals. 41Whenever the stronger females were in heat, Jacob would place the branches in the troughs in front of the animals so they would mate near the branches, 42but if the animals were weak, he would not place them there. So the weak animals went to Laban and the strong ones to Jacob. 43In this way the man grew exceedingly prosperous and came to own large flocks, and maidservants and menservants, and camels and donkeys.

CHAPTER 31

Jacob heard that Laban's sons were saying, "Jacob has taken everything our father owned and has gained all this wealth from what belonged to our father." 2And Jacob noticed that Laban's attitude toward him was not what it had been.

3Then the LORD said to Jacob, "Go back to the land of your fathers and to your relatives, and I will be with you."

4So Jacob sent word to Rachel and Leah to come out to the fields where his flocks were. 5He said to them, "I see that your father's attitude toward me is not what it was before, but the God of my father has been with me. 6You know that I've worked for your father with all my strength, 7yet your father has cheated me by changing my wages ten times. However, God has not allowed him to harm me. 8If he said, 'The speckled ones will be your wages,' then all the flocks gave birth to speckled young; and if he said, 'The streaked ones will be your wages,' then all the flocks bore streaked young. 9So God has taken away your father's livestock and has given them to me.

10"In breeding season I once had a dream in which I looked up and saw that the male goats mating with the flock were streaked, speckled or spotted. 11The angel of God said to me in the dream, 'Jacob.' I answered, 'Here I am.' 12And he said, 'Look up and see that all the male goats mating with the flock are streaked, speckled or spotted, for I have seen all that Laban has been doing to you. 13I am the God of Bethel, where you anointed a pillar and where you made a vow to me. Now leave this land at once and go back to your native land.' "

14Then Rachel and Leah replied, "Do we still have any share in the inheritance of our father's estate? 15Does he not regard us as foreigners? Not only has he sold us, but he has used up what was paid for us. 16Surely all the wealth that God took away from our father belongs to us and our children. So do whatever God has told you."

17Then Jacob put his children and his wives on camels, 18and he drove all his livestock ahead of him, along with all the goods he had accumulated in Paddan

Aram,^q to go to his father Isaac in the land of Canaan.

¹⁹When Laban had gone to shear his sheep, Rachel stole her father's household gods. ²⁰Moreover, Jacob deceived Laban the Aramean by not telling him he was running away. ²¹So he fled with all he had, and crossing the River,^r he headed for the hill country of Gilead.

²²On the third day Laban was told that Jacob had fled. ²³Taking his relatives with him, he pursued Jacob for seven days and caught up with him in the hill country of Gilead. ²⁴Then God came to Laban the Aramean in a dream at night and said to him, "Be careful not to say anything to Jacob, either good or bad."

²⁵Jacob had pitched his tent in the hill country of Gilead when Laban overtook him, and Laban and his relatives camped there too. ²⁶Then Laban said to Jacob, "What have you done? You've deceived me, and you've carried off my daughters like captives in war. ²⁷Why did you run off secretly and deceive me? Why didn't you tell me, so I could send you away with joy and singing to the music of tambourines and harps? ²⁸You didn't even let me kiss my grandchildren and my daughters good-by. You have done a foolish thing. ²⁹I have the power to harm you; but last night the God of your father said to me, 'Be careful not to say anything to Jacob, either good or bad.' ³⁰Now you have gone off because you longed to return to your father's house. But why did you steal my gods?"

³¹Jacob answered Laban, "I was afraid, because I thought you would take your daughters away from me by force. ³²But if you find anyone who has your gods, he shall not live. In the presence of our relatives, see for yourself whether there is anything of yours here with me; and if so, take it." Now Jacob did not know that Rachel had stolen the gods.

³³So Laban went into Jacob's tent and into Leah's tent and into the tent of the two maidservants, but he found nothing. After he came out of Leah's tent, he entered Rachel's tent. ³⁴Now Rachel had taken the household gods and put them inside her camel's saddle and was sitting on them. Laban searched through everything in the tent but found nothing.

³⁵Rachel said to her father, "Don't be angry, my lord, that I cannot stand up in your presence; I'm having my period." So he searched but could not find the household gods.

³⁶Jacob was angry and took Laban to task. "What is my crime?" he asked Laban. "What sin have I committed that you hunt me down? ³⁷Now that you have searched through all my goods, what have you found that belongs to your household? Put it here in front of your relatives and mine, and let them judge between the two of us.

³⁸"I have been with you for twenty years now. Your sheep and goats have not miscarried, nor have I eaten rams from your flocks. ³⁹I did not bring you animals torn by wild beasts; I bore the loss myself. And you demanded payment from me for whatever was stolen by day or night. ⁴⁰This was my situation: The heat consumed me in the daytime and the cold at night, and sleep fled from my eyes. ⁴¹It was like this for the twenty years I was in your household. I worked for you fourteen years for your two daughters and six years for your flocks, and you changed my wages ten times. ⁴²If the God of my father, the God of Abraham and the Fear of Isaac, had not been with me, you would surely have sent me away empty-handed. But God has seen my hardship and the toil of my hands, and last night he rebuked you."

⁴³Laban answered Jacob, "The women are my daughters, the children are my children, and the flocks are my flocks. All you see is mine. Yet what can I do today about these daughters of mine, or about the children they have borne? ⁴⁴Come now, let's make a covenant, you and I, and let it serve as a witness between us."

⁴⁵So Jacob took a stone and set it up as a pillar. ⁴⁶He said to his relatives, "Gather some stones." So they took stones and piled them in a heap, and they ate there by the heap. ⁴⁷Laban called it Jegar Sahadutha,^s and Jacob called it Galeed.^t

⁴⁸Laban said, "This heap is a witness between you and me today." That is why it was called Galeed. ⁴⁹It was also called Mizpah,^u because he said, "May the LORD keep watch between you and me when

^q18 That is, Northwest Mesopotamia   ^r21 That is, the Euphrates   ^s47 The Aramaic Jegar Sahadutha means witness heap.
^t47 The Hebrew Galeed means witness heap.   ^u49 Mizpah means watchtower.

we are away from each other. ⁵⁰If you mistreat my daughters or if you take any wives besides my daughters, even though no one is with us, remember that God is a witness between you and me."

⁵¹Laban also said to Jacob, "Here is this heap, and here is this pillar I have set up between you and me. ⁵²This heap is a witness, and this pillar is a witness, that I will not go past this heap to your side to harm you and that you will not go past this heap and pillar to my side to harm

me. ⁵³May the God of Abraham and the God of Nahor, the God of their father, judge between us."

So Jacob took an oath in the name of the Fear of his father Isaac. ⁵⁴He offered a sacrifice there in the hill country and invited his relatives to a meal. After they had eaten, they spent the night there.

⁵⁵Early the next morning Laban kissed his grandchildren and his daughters and blessed them. Then he left and returned home.

JANUARY 12 □ DAY 12
GENESIS 32–36
Jacob's Encounter with Esau

 OVERVIEW Having survived the pursuit of his jealous uncle, Laban, Jacob now faces an even greater danger from his estranged brother, Esau. After sending his family across the Jabbok River, Jacob wrestles with God, who appeared as a man, until daybreak. God assures him of his continued presence and leaves Jacob with both a new name—Israel ("he struggles with God")—and a permanent limp as reminders of the encounter. Once reconciled to God, Jacob is ready to be reconciled to Esau and to return to Canaan as the vital link in God's continuing promises.

Chapter 32	Chapter 33	Chapter 34	Chapter 35	Chapter 36
Meeting God	Meeting Esau	Avenging Dinah	Returning to Bethel	Recounting Esau's Line
Jacob's Reconciliation		Jacob's Rededication		

 YOUR DAILY WALK David, Jabez and Jacob. A more unlikely trio you will never meet! David, the mighty king of Israel . . . Jabez, an obscure figure from the pages of 1 Chronicles . . . Jacob, the schemer-turned-servant. Yet they shared a common experience. Do you know what it was?

All blessings carry responsibility, so don't pray for the first if you're not ready for the second.

David prayed, "May God be gracious to us and bless us" (Psalm 67:1). Jabez "cried out to the God of Israel, 'Oh, that you would bless me' " (1 Chronicles 4:10). Jacob wrestled with God, not willing to let go "unless you bless me!" (32:26). And in each case, God did precisely that! David's kingdom enjoyed unprecedented peace and prosperity; Jabez received from God what he had requested; and in response to Jacob's petition, God "blessed him there" (32:29).

Is it possible God has a blessing in store for you—in the form of protection (like David), expanded responsibility (like Jabez) or renewed promises (like Jacob)—but that "you do not have, because you do not ask" (James 4:2)? Use the prayer of David, Jabez or Jacob to express the desire of your heart. And don't be surprised if God answers! He's in the business of blessing.

INSIGHT Three Spiritual Milestones in Jacob's Life
Three times Jacob encountered the God of his forefathers. At Haran he
was *redirected* by God (31:1–16); at Peniel he was *restored* by God
(32:24–32); at Bethel he was *reassured* by God (35:1–15).

CHAPTER 32

Jacob also went on his way, and the angels of God met him. ²When Jacob saw them, he said, "This is the camp of God!" So he named that place Mahanaim.ᵛ

³Jacob sent messengers ahead of him to his brother Esau in the land of Seir, the country of Edom. ⁴He instructed them: "This is what you are to say to my master Esau: 'Your servant Jacob says, I have been staying with Laban and have remained there till now. ⁵I have cattle and donkeys, sheep and goats, menservants and maidservants. Now I am sending this message to my lord, that I may find favor in your eyes.'"

⁶When the messengers returned to Jacob, they said, "We went to your brother Esau, and now he is coming to meet you, and four hundred men are with him."

⁷In great fear and distress Jacob divided the people who were with him into two groups,ʷ and the flocks and herds and camels as well. ⁸He thought, "If Esau comes and attacks one group,ˣ the groupˣ that is left may escape."

⁹Then Jacob prayed, "O God of my father Abraham, God of my father Isaac, O LORD, who said to me, 'Go back to your country and your relatives, and I will make you prosper,' ¹⁰I am unworthy of all the kindness and faithfulness you have shown your servant. I had only my staff when I crossed this Jordan, but now I have become two groups. ¹¹Save me, I pray, from the hand of my brother Esau, for I am afraid he will come and attack me, and also the mothers with their children. ¹²But you have said, 'I will surely make you prosper and will make your descendants like the sand of the sea, which cannot be counted.'"

¹³He spent the night there, and from what he had with him he selected a gift for his brother Esau: ¹⁴two hundred female goats and twenty male goats, two hundred ewes and twenty rams, ¹⁵thirty female camels with their young, forty cows and ten bulls, and twenty female donkeys and ten male donkeys. ¹⁶He put them in the care of his servants, each herd by itself, and said to his servants, "Go ahead of me, and keep some space between the herds."

¹⁷He instructed the one in the lead: "When my brother Esau meets you and asks, 'To whom do you belong, and where are you going, and who owns all these animals in front of you?' ¹⁸then you are to say, 'They belong to your servant Jacob. They are a gift sent to my lord Esau, and he is coming behind us.'"

¹⁹He also instructed the second, the third and all the others who followed the herds: "You are to say the same thing to Esau when you meet him. ²⁰And be sure to say, 'Your servant Jacob is coming behind us.'" For he thought, "I will pacify him with these gifts I am sending on ahead; later, when I see him, perhaps he will receive me." ²¹So Jacob's gifts went on ahead of him, but he himself spent the night in the camp.

²²That night Jacob got up and took his two wives, his two maidservants and his eleven sons and crossed the ford of the Jabbok. ²³After he had sent them across the stream, he sent over all his possessions. ²⁴So Jacob was left alone, and a man wrestled with him till daybreak. ²⁵When the man saw that he could not overpower him, he touched the socket of Jacob's hip so that his hip was wrenched as he wrestled with the man. ²⁶Then the man said, "Let me go, for it is daybreak."

But Jacob replied, "I will not let you go unless you bless me."

²⁷The man asked him, "What is your name?"

"Jacob," he answered.

²⁸Then the man said, "Your name will no longer be Jacob, but Israel,ʸ because you have struggled with God and with men and have overcome."

²⁹Jacob said, "Please tell me your name." But he replied, "Why do you ask my name?" Then he blessed him there.

³⁰So Jacob called the place Peniel,ᶻ

ᵛ2 *Mahanaim* means *two camps*.   ʷ7 Or *camps*; also in verse 10   ˣ8 Or *camp*   ʸ28 *Israel* means *he struggles with God*.
ᶻ30 *Peniel* means *face of God*.

saying, "It is because I saw God face to face, and yet my life was spared."

[31]The sun rose above him as he passed Peniel,[a] and he was limping because of his hip. [32]Therefore to this day the Israelites do not eat the tendon attached to the socket of the hip, because the socket of Jacob's hip was touched near the tendon.

CHAPTER 33

Jacob looked up and there was Esau, coming with his four hundred men; so he divided the children among Leah, Rachel and the two maidservants. [2]He put the maidservants and their children in front, Leah and her children next, and Rachel and Joseph in the rear. [3]He himself went on ahead and bowed down to the ground seven times as he approached his brother.

[4]But Esau ran to meet Jacob and embraced him; he threw his arms around his neck and kissed him. And they wept. [5]Then Esau looked up and saw the women and children. "Who are these with you?" he asked.

Jacob answered, "They are the children God has graciously given your servant."

[6]Then the maidservants and their children approached and bowed down. [7]Next, Leah and her children came and bowed down. Last of all came Joseph and Rachel, and they too bowed down.

[8]Esau asked, "What do you mean by all these droves I met?"

"To find favor in your eyes, my lord," he said.

[9]But Esau said, "I already have plenty, my brother. Keep what you have for yourself."

[10]"No, please!" said Jacob. "If I have found favor in your eyes, accept this gift from me. For to see your face is like seeing the face of God, now that you have received me favorably. [11]Please accept the present that was brought to you, for God has been gracious to me and I have all I need." And because Jacob insisted, Esau accepted it.

[12]Then Esau said, "Let us be on our way; I'll accompany you."

[13]But Jacob said to him, "My lord knows that the children are tender and that I must care for the ewes and cows that are nursing their young. If they are driven hard just one day, all the animals will die. [14]So let my lord go on ahead of his servant, while I move along slowly at the pace of the droves before me and that of the children, until I come to my lord in Seir."

[15]Esau said, "Then let me leave some of my men with you."

"But why do that?" Jacob asked. "Just let me find favor in the eyes of my lord."

[16]So that day Esau started on his way back to Seir. [17]Jacob, however, went to Succoth, where he built a place for himself and made shelters for his livestock. That is why the place is called Succoth.[b]

[18]After Jacob came from Paddan Aram,[c] he arrived safely at the[d] city of Shechem in Canaan and camped within sight of the city. [19]For a hundred pieces of silver,[e] he bought from the sons of Hamor, the father of Shechem, the plot of ground where he pitched his tent. [20]There he set up an altar and called it El Elohe Israel.[f]

CHAPTER 34

Now Dinah, the daughter Leah had borne to Jacob, went out to visit the women of the land. [2]When Shechem son of Hamor the Hivite, the ruler of that area, saw her, he took her and violated her. [3]His heart was drawn to Dinah daughter of Jacob, and he loved the girl and spoke tenderly to her. [4]And Shechem said to his father Hamor, "Get me this girl as my wife."

[5]When Jacob heard that his daughter Dinah had been defiled, his sons were in the fields with his livestock; so he kept quiet about it until they came home.

[6]Then Shechem's father Hamor went out to talk with Jacob. [7]Now Jacob's sons had come in from the fields as soon as they heard what had happened. They were filled with grief and fury, because Shechem had done a disgraceful thing in[g] Israel by lying with Jacob's daughter—a thing that should not be done.

[8]But Hamor said to them, "My son Shechem has his heart set on your daughter. Please give her to him as his wife. [9]Intermarry with us; give us your daughters and take our daughters for yourselves. [10]You can settle among us; the land is

---

[a]31 Hebrew Penuel, a variant of Peniel   [b]17 Succoth means shelters.   [c]18 That is, Northwest Mesopotamia   [d]18 Or arrived at Shalem, a   [e]19 Hebrew hundred kesitahs; a kesitah was a unit of money of unknown weight and value.   [f]20 El Elohe Israel can mean God, the God of Israel or mighty is the God of Israel.   [g]7 Or against

open to you. Live in it, trade*h* in it, and acquire property in it."

[11]Then Shechem said to Dinah's father and brothers, "Let me find favor in your eyes, and I will give you whatever you ask. [12]Make the price for the bride and the gift I am to bring as great as you like, and I'll pay whatever you ask me. Only give me the girl as my wife."

[13]Because their sister Dinah had been defiled, Jacob's sons replied deceitfully as they spoke to Shechem and his father Hamor. [14]They said to them, "We can't do such a thing; we can't give our sister to a man who is not circumcised. That would be a disgrace to us. [15]We will give our consent to you on one condition only: that you become like us by circumcising all your males. [16]Then we will give you our daughters and take your daughters for ourselves. We'll settle among you and become one people with you. [17]But if you will not agree to be circumcised, we'll take our sister*i* and go."

[18]Their proposal seemed good to Hamor and his son Shechem. [19]The young man, who was the most honored of all his father's household, lost no time in doing what they said, because he was delighted with Jacob's daughter. [20]So Hamor and his son Shechem went to the gate of their city to speak to their fellow townsmen. [21]"These men are friendly toward us," they said. "Let them live in our land and trade in it; the land has plenty of room for them. We can marry their daughters and they can marry ours. [22]But the men will consent to live with us as one people only on the condition that our males be circumcised, as they themselves are. [23]Won't their livestock, their property and all their other animals become ours? So let us give our consent to them, and they will settle among us."

[24]All the men who went out of the city gate agreed with Hamor and his son Shechem, and every male in the city was circumcised.

[25]Three days later, while all of them were still in pain, two of Jacob's sons, Simeon and Levi, Dinah's brothers, took their swords and attacked the unsuspecting city, killing every male. [26]They put Hamor and his son Shechem to the sword

and took Dinah from Shechem's house and left. [27]The sons of Jacob came upon the dead bodies and looted the city where*j* their sister had been defiled. [28]They seized their flocks and herds and donkeys and everything else of theirs in the city and out in the fields. [29]They carried off all their wealth and all their women and children, taking as plunder everything in the houses.

[30]Then Jacob said to Simeon and Levi, "You have brought trouble on me by making me a stench to the Canaanites and Perizzites, the people living in this land. We are few in number, and if they join forces against me and attack me, I and my household will be destroyed."

[31]But they replied, "Should he have treated our sister like a prostitute?"

CHAPTER 35
Then God said to Jacob, "Go up to Bethel and settle there, and build an altar there to God, who appeared to you when you were fleeing from your brother Esau."

[2]So Jacob said to his household and to all who were with him, "Get rid of the foreign gods you have with you, and purify yourselves and change your clothes. [3]Then come, let us go up to Bethel, where I will build an altar to God, who answered me in the day of my distress and who has been with me wherever I have gone." [4]So they gave Jacob all the foreign gods they had and the rings in their ears, and Jacob buried them under the oak at Shechem. [5]Then they set out, and the terror of God fell upon the towns all around them so that no one pursued them.

[6]Jacob and all the people with him came to Luz (that is, Bethel) in the land of Canaan. [7]There he built an altar, and he called the place El Bethel,*k* because it was there that God revealed himself to him when he was fleeing from his brother.

[8]Now Deborah, Rebekah's nurse, died and was buried under the oak below Bethel. So it was named Allon Bacuth.*l*

[9]After Jacob returned from Paddan Aram,*m* God appeared to him again and blessed him. [10]God said to him, "Your name is Jacob,*n* but you will no longer be called Jacob; your name will be Israel.*o*" So he named him Israel.

---

*h*10 Or *move about freely*; also in verse 21   *i*17 Hebrew *daughter*   *j*27 Or *because*   *k*7 *El Bethel* means *God of Bethel*.
*l*8 *Allon Bacuth* means *oak of weeping*.   *m*9 That is, Northwest Mesopotamia; also in verse 26   *n*10 *Jacob* means *he grasps the heel* (figuratively, *he deceives*).   *o*10 *Israel* means *he struggles with God*.

[11]And God said to him, "I am God Almighty[p]; be fruitful and increase in number. A nation and a community of nations will come from you, and kings will come from your body. [12]The land I gave to Abraham and Isaac I also give to you, and I will give this land to your descendants after you." [13]Then God went up from him at the place where he had talked with him.

[14]Jacob set up a stone pillar at the place where God had talked with him, and he poured out a drink offering on it; he also poured oil on it. [15]Jacob called the place where God had talked with him Bethel.[q]

[16]Then they moved on from Bethel. While they were still some distance from Ephrath, Rachel began to give birth and had great difficulty. [17]And as she was having great difficulty in childbirth, the midwife said to her, "Don't be afraid, for you have another son." [18]As she breathed her last—for she was dying—she named her son Ben-Oni.[r] But his father named him Benjamin.[s]

[19]So Rachel died and was buried on the way to Ephrath (that is, Bethlehem). [20]Over her tomb Jacob set up a pillar, and to this day that pillar marks Rachel's tomb.

[21]Israel moved on again and pitched his tent beyond Migdal Eder. [22]While Israel was living in that region, Reuben went in and slept with his father's concubine Bilhah, and Israel heard of it.

Jacob had twelve sons:

[23]The sons of Leah:
  Reuben the firstborn of Jacob,
  Simeon, Levi, Judah, Issachar and
  Zebulun.
[24]The sons of Rachel:
  Joseph and Benjamin.
[25]The sons of Rachel's maidservant
  Bilhah:
  Dan and Naphtali.
[26]The sons of Leah's maidservant Zilpah:
  Gad and Asher.
  These were the sons of Jacob, who were born to him in Paddan Aram.

[27]Jacob came home to his father Isaac in Mamre, near Kiriath Arba (that is, Hebron), where Abraham and Isaac had stayed. [28]Isaac lived a hundred and eighty

years. [29]Then he breathed his last and died and was gathered to his people, old and full of years. And his sons Esau and Jacob buried him.

CHAPTER 36

This is the account of Esau (that is, Edom).

[2]Esau took his wives from the women of Canaan: Adah daughter of Elon the Hittite, and Oholibamah daughter of Anah and granddaughter of Zibeon the Hivite— [3]also Basemath daughter of Ishmael and sister of Nebaioth.

[4]Adah bore Eliphaz to Esau, Basemath bore Reuel, [5]and Oholibamah bore Jeush, Jalam and Korah. These were the sons of Esau, who were born to him in Canaan.

[6]Esau took his wives and sons and daughters and all the members of his household, as well as his livestock and all his other animals and all the goods he had acquired in Canaan, and moved to a land some distance from his brother Jacob. [7]Their possessions were too great for them to remain together; the land where they were staying could not support them both because of their livestock. [8]So Esau (that is, Edom) settled in the hill country of Seir.

[9]This is the account of Esau the father of the Edomites in the hill country of Seir.

[10]These are the names of Esau's sons:
  Eliphaz, the son of Esau's wife
  Adah, and Reuel, the son of Esau's
  wife Basemath.
[11]The sons of Eliphaz:
  Teman, Omar, Zepho, Gatam and
  Kenaz.
[12]Esau's son Eliphaz also had a
  concubine named Timna, who
  bore him Amalek. These were
  grandsons of Esau's wife Adah.
[13]The sons of Reuel:
  Nahath, Zerah, Shammah and
  Mizzah. These were grandsons of
  Esau's wife Basemath.
[14]The sons of Esau's wife Oholibamah
  daughter of Anah and granddaughter of Zibeon, whom she bore to
  Esau:

[p]11 Hebrew *El-Shaddai*   [q]15 *Bethel* means *house of God.*   [r]18 *Ben-Oni* means *son of my trouble.*   [s]18 *Benjamin* means *son of my right hand.*

Jeush, Jalam and Korah.

¹⁵These were the chiefs among Esau's descendants:

The sons of Eliphaz the firstborn of Esau:
Chiefs Teman, Omar, Zepho, Kenaz, ¹⁶Korah,^t Gatam and Amalek. These were the chiefs descended from Eliphaz in Edom; they were grandsons of Adah.

¹⁷The sons of Esau's son Reuel:
Chiefs Nahath, Zerah, Shammah and Mizzah. These were the chiefs descended from Reuel in Edom; they were grandsons of Esau's wife Basemath.

¹⁸The sons of Esau's wife Oholibamah:
Chiefs Jeush, Jalam and Korah. These were the chiefs descended from Esau's wife Oholibamah daughter of Anah.

¹⁹These were the sons of Esau (that is, Edom), and these were their chiefs.

²⁰These were the sons of Seir the Horite, who were living in the region:
Lotan, Shobal, Zibeon, Anah, ²¹Dishon, Ezer and Dishan. These sons of Seir in Edom were Horite chiefs.

²²The sons of Lotan:
Hori and Homam.^u Timna was Lotan's sister.

²³The sons of Shobal:
Alvan, Manahath, Ebal, Shepho and Onam.

²⁴The sons of Zibeon:
Aiah and Anah. This is the Anah who discovered the hot springs^v in the desert while he was grazing the donkeys of his father Zibeon.

²⁵The children of Anah:
Dishon and Oholibamah daughter of Anah.

²⁶The sons of Dishon^w:
Hemdan, Eshban, Ithran and Keran.

²⁷The sons of Ezer:
Bilhan, Zaavan and Akan.

²⁸The sons of Dishan:

Uz and Aran.

²⁹These were the Horite chiefs:
Lotan, Shobal, Zibeon, Anah, ³⁰Dishon, Ezer and Dishan. These were the Horite chiefs, according to their divisions, in the land of Seir.

³¹These were the kings who reigned in Edom before any Israelite king reigned^x:
³²Bela son of Beor became king of Edom. His city was named Dinhabah.

³³When Bela died, Jobab son of Zerah from Bozrah succeeded him as king.

³⁴When Jobab died, Husham from the land of the Temanites succeeded him as king.

³⁵When Husham died, Hadad son of Bedad, who defeated Midian in the country of Moab, succeeded him as king. His city was named Avith.

³⁶When Hadad died, Samlah from Masrekah succeeded him as king.

³⁷When Samlah died, Shaul from Rehoboth on the river^y succeeded him as king.

³⁸When Shaul died, Baal-Hanan son of Acbor succeeded him as king.

³⁹When Baal-Hanan son of Acbor died, Hadad^z succeeded him as king. His city was named Pau, and his wife's name was Mehetabel daughter of Matred, the daughter of Me-Zahab.

⁴⁰These were the chiefs descended from Esau, by name, according to their clans and regions:
Timna, Alvah, Jetheth, ⁴¹Oholibamah, Elah, Pinon, ⁴²Kenaz, Teman, Mibzar, ⁴³Magdiel and Iram. These were the chiefs of Edom, according to their settlements in the land they occupied.

This was Esau the father of the Edomites.

---

^t16 Masoretic Text; Samaritan Pentateuch (see also Gen. 36:11 and 1 Chron. 1:36) does not have *Korah*.   ^u22 Hebrew *Hemam*, a variant of *Homam* (see 1 Chron. 1:39)   ^v24 Vulgate; Syriac *discovered water*; the meaning of the Hebrew for this word is uncertain.   ^w26 Hebrew *Dishan*, a variant of *Dishon*   ^x31 Or *before an Israelite king reigned over them*   ^y37 Possibly the Euphrates   ^z39 Many manuscripts of the Masoretic Text, Samaritan Pentateuch and Syriac (see also 1 Chron. 1:50); most manuscripts of the Masoretic Text *Hadar*

JANUARY 13 □ DAY 13
GENESIS 37–40
Joseph's Bondage in Egypt

 OVERVIEW Abraham . . . Isaac . . . Jacob . . . and now comes Joseph, the fourth major character in the Genesis account of the patriarchs (fathers of the faith). Favored by his father but alienated by his brothers, Joseph is sold into Egyptian slavery. Imprisoned for a crime he did not commit and ignored by the forgetful chief cupbearer, Joseph finds his faith—and his integrity—sorely tested. Though Joseph doesn't realize it, through it all God is preparing him for an important role that will bring fruition to his childhood dreams.

Chapter 37	Chapter 38	Chapter 39	Chapter 40
Joseph's Slavery	Judah's Shame	Joseph's Integrity	Joseph's Imprisonment
Life in Jacob's Family		Life in Pharaoh's Prison	

 YOUR DAILY WALK "God, why did you let this happen to me?"

Have you ever felt the urge to ask that question? The average Christian does . . . about every twenty minutes or so! *Why* is a question Christians frequently ask—and God often leaves unanswered. Joseph must have been tempted often to ask for a heavenly explanation for his earthly troubles. Though God did not answer all of Joseph's questions, he did meet all of Joseph's needs (39:21)—and he has promised to do the same for you (Philippians 4:13, 19). That means giving you power over discouragement when you're down in the pits (37:24) . . . power over temptation from lustful thoughts (39:12) . . . purpose for living even when you're mistreated or ignored (39:20–21).

It is better to go straight than to move in the best of circles.

Joseph's faith in God fortified him to face the pit of Canaan, the prison of Egypt, and everything in between. You can develop a faith like that, too! Read about it in James 1:2–4. Then make a little sign that reads, Another Joseph under Construction, and put it by your telephone. That way every ring can provide a comforting reminder!

 INSIGHT Brothers in the Business

The members of the Ishmaelite caravan who bought Joseph from his brothers and sold him in Egypt were called Midianites (37:28, 36). Midian and Medan were two sons of Abraham and his second wife, Keturah (25:2). From them developed a nomadic people who, while blood brothers of the Jews, became their constant enemies (Judges 6:1).

CHAPTER 37

Jacob lived in the land where his father had stayed, the land of Canaan.

²This is the account of Jacob.

Joseph, a young man of seventeen, was tending the flocks with his brothers, the sons of Bilhah and the sons of Zilpah, his father's wives, and he brought their father a bad report about them.

³Now Israel loved Joseph more than any of his other sons, because he had been born to him in his old age; and he made a richly ornamented[a] robe for him. ⁴When his brothers saw that their father loved him more than any of them, they hated him and could not speak a kind word to him.

⁵Joseph had a dream, and when he told it to his brothers, they hated him all the more. ⁶He said to them, "Listen to this dream I had: ⁷We were binding sheaves

[a]3 The meaning of the Hebrew for *richly ornamented* is uncertain; also in verses 23 and 32.

of grain out in the field when suddenly my sheaf rose and stood upright, while your sheaves gathered around mine and bowed down to it."

[8]His brothers said to him, "Do you intend to reign over us? Will you actually rule us?" And they hated him all the more because of his dream and what he had said.

[9]Then he had another dream, and he told it to his brothers. "Listen," he said, "I had another dream, and this time the sun and moon and eleven stars were bowing down to me."

[10]When he told his father as well as his brothers, his father rebuked him and said, "What is this dream you had? Will your mother and I and your brothers actually come and bow down to the ground before you?" [11]His brothers were jealous of him, but his father kept the matter in mind.

[12]Now his brothers had gone to graze their father's flocks near Shechem, [13]and Israel said to Joseph, "As you know, your brothers are grazing the flocks near Shechem. Come, I am going to send you to them."

"Very well," he replied.

[14]So he said to him, "Go and see if all is well with your brothers and with the flocks, and bring word back to me." Then he sent him off from the Valley of Hebron.

When Joseph arrived at Shechem, [15]a man found him wandering around in the fields and asked him, "What are you looking for?"

[16]He replied, "I'm looking for my brothers. Can you tell me where they are grazing their flocks?"

[17]"They have moved on from here," the man answered. "I heard them say, 'Let's go to Dothan.'"

So Joseph went after his brothers and found them near Dothan. [18]But they saw him in the distance, and before he reached them, they plotted to kill him.

[19]"Here comes that dreamer!" they said to each other. [20]"Come now, let's kill him and throw him into one of these cisterns and say that a ferocious animal devoured him. Then we'll see what comes of his dreams."

[21]When Reuben heard this, he tried to rescue him from their hands. "Let's not take his life," he said. [22]"Don't shed any blood. Throw him into this cistern here in the desert, but don't lay a hand on him." Reuben said this to rescue him from them and take him back to his father.

[23]So when Joseph came to his brothers, they stripped him of his robe—the richly ornamented robe he was wearing— [24]and they took him and threw him into the cistern. Now the cistern was empty; there was no water in it.

[25]As they sat down to eat their meal, they looked up and saw a caravan of Ishmaelites coming from Gilead. Their camels were loaded with spices, balm and myrrh, and they were on their way to take them down to Egypt.

[26]Judah said to his brothers, "What will we gain if we kill our brother and cover up his blood? [27]Come, let's sell him to the Ishmaelites and not lay our hands on him; after all, he is our brother, our own flesh and blood." His brothers agreed.

[28]So when the Midianite merchants came by, his brothers pulled Joseph up out of the cistern and sold him for twenty shekels[b] of silver to the Ishmaelites, who took him to Egypt.

[29]When Reuben returned to the cistern and saw that Joseph was not there, he tore his clothes. [30]He went back to his brothers and said, "The boy isn't there! Where can I turn now?"

[31]Then they got Joseph's robe, slaughtered a goat and dipped the robe in the blood. [32]They took the ornamented robe back to their father and said, "We found this. Examine it to see whether it is your son's robe."

[33]He recognized it and said, "It is my son's robe! Some ferocious animal has devoured him. Joseph has surely been torn to pieces."

[34]Then Jacob tore his clothes, put on sackcloth and mourned for his son many days. [35]All his sons and daughters came to comfort him, but he refused to be comforted. "No," he said, "in mourning will I go down to the grave[c] to my son." So his father wept for him.

[36]Meanwhile, the Midianites[d] sold Joseph in Egypt to Potiphar, one of Pharaoh's officials, the captain of the guard.

[b]28 That is, about 8 ounces (about 0.2 kilogram)   [c]35 Hebrew *Sheol*   [d]36 Samaritan Pentateuch, Septuagint, Vulgate and Syriac (see also verse 28); Masoretic Text *Medanites*

CHAPTER 38
At that time, Judah left his brothers and went down to stay with a man of Adullam named Hirah. ²There Judah met the daughter of a Canaanite man named Shua. He married her and lay with her; ³she became pregnant and gave birth to a son, who was named Er. ⁴She conceived again and gave birth to a son and named him Onan. ⁵She gave birth to still another son and named him Shelah. It was at Kezib that she gave birth to him.

⁶Judah got a wife for Er, his firstborn, and her name was Tamar. ⁷But Er, Judah's firstborn, was wicked in the LORD's sight; so the LORD put him to death. ⁸Then Judah said to Onan, "Lie with your brother's wife and fulfill your duty to her as a brother-in-law to produce offspring for your brother." ⁹But Onan knew that the offspring would not be his; so whenever he lay with his brother's wife, he spilled his semen on the ground to keep from producing offspring for his brother. ¹⁰What he did was wicked in the LORD's sight; so he put him to death also.

¹¹Judah then said to his daughter-in-law Tamar, "Live as a widow in your father's house until my son Shelah grows up." For he thought, "He may die too, just like his brothers." So Tamar went to live in her father's house.

¹²After a long time Judah's wife, the daughter of Shua, died. When Judah had recovered from his grief, he went up to Timnah, to the men who were shearing his sheep, and his friend Hirah the Adullamite went with him.

¹³When Tamar was told, "Your father-in-law is on his way to Timnah to shear his sheep," ¹⁴she took off her widow's clothes, covered herself with a veil to disguise herself, and then sat down at the entrance to Enaim, which is on the road to Timnah. For she saw that, though Shelah had now grown up, she had not been given to him as his wife.

¹⁵When Judah saw her, he thought she was a prostitute, for she had covered her face. ¹⁶Not realizing that she was his daughter-in-law, he went over to her by the roadside and said, "Come now, let me sleep with you."

"And what will you give me to sleep with you?" she asked.

¹⁷"I'll send you a young goat from my flock," he said.

"Will you give me something as a pledge until you send it?" she asked.

¹⁸He said, "What pledge should I give you?"

"Your seal and its cord, and the staff in your hand," she answered. So he gave them to her and slept with her, and she became pregnant by him. ¹⁹After she left, she took off her veil and put on her widow's clothes again.

²⁰Meanwhile Judah sent the young goat by his friend the Adullamite in order to get his pledge back from the woman, but he did not find her. ²¹He asked the men who lived there, "Where is the shrine prostitute who was beside the road at Enaim?"

"There hasn't been any shrine prostitute here," they said.

²²So he went back to Judah and said, "I didn't find her. Besides, the men who lived there said, 'There hasn't been any shrine prostitute here.'"

²³Then Judah said, "Let her keep what she has, or we will become a laughingstock. After all, I did send her this young goat, but you didn't find her."

²⁴About three months later Judah was told, "Your daughter-in-law Tamar is guilty of prostitution, and as a result she is now pregnant."

Judah said, "Bring her out and have her burned to death!"

²⁵As she was being brought out, she sent a message to her father-in-law. "I am pregnant by the man who owns these," she said. And she added, "See if you recognize whose seal and cord and staff these are."

²⁶Judah recognized them and said, "She is more righteous than I, since I wouldn't give her to my son Shelah." And he did not sleep with her again.

²⁷When the time came for her to give birth, there were twin boys in her womb. ²⁸As she was giving birth, one of them put out his hand; so the midwife took a scarlet thread and tied it on his wrist and said, "This one came out first." ²⁹But when he drew back his hand, his brother came out, and she said, "So this is how you have broken out!" And he was named Perez.ᵉ ³⁰Then his brother, who had the scarlet

ᵉ29 *Perez* means *breaking out.*

thread on his wrist, came out and he was given the name Zerah.*f*

CHAPTER 39

Now Joseph had been taken down to Egypt. Potiphar, an Egyptian who was one of Pharaoh's officials, the captain of the guard, bought him from the Ishmaelites who had taken him there.

²The LORD was with Joseph and he prospered, and he lived in the house of his Egyptian master. ³When his master saw that the LORD was with him and that the LORD gave him success in everything he did, ⁴Joseph found favor in his eyes and became his attendant. Potiphar put him in charge of his household, and he entrusted to his care everything he owned. ⁵From the time he put him in charge of his household and of all that he owned, the LORD blessed the household of the Egyptian because of Joseph. The blessing of the LORD was on everything Potiphar had, both in the house and in the field. ⁶So he left in Joseph's care everything he had; with Joseph in charge, he did not concern himself with anything except the food he ate.

Now Joseph was well-built and handsome, ⁷and after a while his master's wife took notice of Joseph and said, "Come to bed with me!"

⁸But he refused. "With me in charge," he told her, "my master does not concern himself with anything in the house; everything he owns he has entrusted to my care. ⁹No one is greater in this house than I am. My master has withheld nothing from me except you, because you are his wife. How then could I do such a wicked thing and sin against God?" ¹⁰And though she spoke to Joseph day after day, he refused to go to bed with her or even be with her.

¹¹One day he went into the house to attend to his duties, and none of the household servants was inside. ¹²She caught him by his cloak and said, "Come to bed with me!" But he left his cloak in her hand and ran out of the house.

¹³When she saw that he had left his cloak in her hand and had run out of the house, ¹⁴she called her household servants. "Look," she said to them, "this Hebrew has been brought to us to make

sport of us! He came in here to sleep with me, but I screamed. ¹⁵When he heard me scream for help, he left his cloak beside me and ran out of the house."

¹⁶She kept his cloak beside her until his master came home. ¹⁷Then she told him this story: "That Hebrew slave you brought us came to me to make sport of me. ¹⁸But as soon as I screamed for help, he left his cloak beside me and ran out of the house."

¹⁹When his master heard the story his wife told him, saying, "This is how your slave treated me," he burned with anger. ²⁰Joseph's master took him and put him in prison, the place where the king's prisoners were confined.

But while Joseph was there in the prison, ²¹the LORD was with him; he showed him kindness and granted him favor in the eyes of the prison warden. ²²So the warden put Joseph in charge of all those held in the prison, and he was made responsible for all that was done there. ²³The warden paid no attention to anything under Joseph's care, because the LORD was with Joseph and gave him success in whatever he did.

CHAPTER 40

Some time later, the cupbearer and the baker of the king of Egypt offended their master, the king of Egypt. ²Pharaoh was angry with his two officials, the chief cupbearer and the chief baker, ³and put them in custody in the house of the captain of the guard, in the same prison where Joseph was confined. ⁴The captain of the guard assigned them to Joseph, and he attended them.

After they had been in custody for some time, ⁵each of the two men—the cupbearer and the baker of the king of Egypt, who were being held in prison—had a dream the same night, and each dream had a meaning of its own.

⁶When Joseph came to them the next morning, he saw that they were dejected. ⁷So he asked Pharaoh's officials who were in custody with him in his master's house, "Why are your faces so sad today?"

⁸"We both had dreams," they answered, "but there is no one to interpret them."

Then Joseph said to them, "Do not in-

f30 Zerah can mean *scarlet* or *brightness.*

terpretations belong to God? Tell me your dreams."

⁹So the chief cupbearer told Joseph his dream. He said to him, "In my dream I saw a vine in front of me, ¹⁰and on the vine were three branches. As soon as it budded, it blossomed, and its clusters ripened into grapes. ¹¹Pharaoh's cup was in my hand, and I took the grapes, squeezed them into Pharaoh's cup and put the cup in his hand."

¹²"This is what it means," Joseph said to him. "The three branches are three days. ¹³Within three days Pharaoh will lift up your head and restore you to your position, and you will put Pharaoh's cup in his hand, just as you used to do when you were his cupbearer. ¹⁴But when all goes well with you, remember me and show me kindness; mention me to Pharaoh and get me out of this prison. ¹⁵For I was forcibly carried off from the land of the Hebrews, and even here I have done nothing to deserve being put in a dungeon."

¹⁶When the chief baker saw that Joseph had given a favorable interpretation, he said to Joseph, "I too had a dream: On my head were three baskets of bread.ᵍ ¹⁷In the top basket were all kinds of baked goods for Pharaoh, but the birds were eating them out of the basket on my head."

¹⁸"This is what it means," Joseph said. "The three baskets are three days. ¹⁹Within three days Pharaoh will lift off your head and hang you on a tree.ʰ And the birds will eat away your flesh."

²⁰Now the third day was Pharaoh's birthday, and he gave a feast for all his officials. He lifted up the heads of the chief cupbearer and the chief baker in the presence of his officials: ²¹He restored the chief cupbearer to his position, so that he once again put the cup into Pharaoh's hand, ²²but he hangedⁱ the chief baker, just as Joseph had said to them in his interpretation.

²³The chief cupbearer, however, did not remember Joseph; he forgot him.

ᵍ16 Or *three wicker baskets*   ʰ19 Or *and impale you on a pole*   ⁱ22 Or *impaled*

JANUARY 14 □ DAY 14
A Faith That Stands the Test of Time

LOOK BACK Buy a new appliance, and you'll be lucky to get a warranty with it that protects your purchase for ninety days. Buy a new car, and you might do a little better: five years or fifty thousand miles. But get ahold of the faith of Abraham, Isaac, Jacob and Joseph, and you just might discover the genuine item that will endure for generations!

Over the past week you have read about the courageous faith of Abraham, who clung to the promises of God against all odds; the quiet faith of Isaac, who built altars, dug wells and proclaimed the name of the Lord wherever he went; the struggling faith of Jacob, who wasn't content until he experienced God's blessing firsthand; and the patient faith of Joseph, whose confidence in God carried him literally from the pit to the palace. Four different men, four different sets of circumstances, but one thing in common: a faith in God that grew with the years.

LOOK UP Definitions of faith are plentiful and at times helpful. Here are just a few. Faith is

A faith that falters before the finish was faulty from the first.

- "Forsaking All, I Trust Him,"
- taking God at his Word,
- seeing the promises of God as present realities,
- living your life in such a way that it does not make sense unless God exists.

Genesis does more than define the faith of Abraham, Isaac, Jacob and Joseph—it paints a portrait of faith in brush strokes of everyday living. Did you find yourself identifying with the struggles of Jacob? yearning to know the God of Isaac? wishing your faith was as strong as Abraham's? Then wait till you read the rest of Joseph's amazing story! His faith in God will carry him through more than a decade in prison.

Faith is like a muscle that grows stronger through exercise. And the exercise that builds a vibrant faith is the stress of facing daily trials with confidence in God.

Learning patience and persistence (like ninety-nine-year-old Abraham waiting for God to keep his promise); leaning on God to resolve a bitter family feud (like Jacob seeking to be reunited with his estranged brother, Esau); following God and doing what's right regardless of the consequences (like Joseph, who ended up in the pit and in prison through no fault of his own)—that's how to build a faith that stands the test of time!

 AHEAD Perhaps you have been blessed with other models of faith in your lifetime: a parent or family member who walked with God for decades, a spiritual leader who practiced what he or she preached, a friend or coworker who talked to God in prayer as if God were in the same room. Have you ever shared with that person what his or her model of faith has meant to you? A note or phone call today would be an excellent way to do so.

Models of faith are in short supply today, just as they were in the days of the patriarchs. You can't get physically fit in a day, nor can you develop the faith of a Jacob or a Joseph overnight. But you can see your faith grow and deepen each day as you face life's challenges in the strength of the Lord. Take one of those faith-stretching circumstances or decisions you're facing right now, and talk to your ever faithful God about it. Tell him that Abraham, Isaac, Jacob and Joseph sent you!

JANUARY 15 ☐ DAY 15
GENESIS 41–44
Joseph's Brothers in Egypt

 OVERVIEW During his imprisonment, Joseph gains a reputation as an accurate interpreter of dreams. He is now called upon to use his God-given ability to interpret the disturbing dreams of Pharaoh. Though the interpretation is ominous, Pharaoh's response is overwhelming: Joseph becomes prime minister of the land, with power second only to Pharaoh himself! With a worldwide famine coming, Joseph becomes Pharaoh's choice to administer a relief program to meet the challenge. Joseph's new position allows him to confront his brothers with their carefully concealed crime.

Chapter 41	Chapter 42	Chapter 43	Chapter 44
Joseph's Promotion	Jacob's Problem	Benjamin's Visit	Joseph's Vengeance
Faithfulness	Famine	Fear	Confession

YOUR DAILY WALK There are many skills you can learn in an afternoon: how to ride a bicycle, how to change the oil in your car, or how to bake a batch of cookies. Other skills take weeks to master: how to read a thousand words a minute, how to sing harmony, or how

It is possible to learn from an enemy things we can't learn from a friend.

to drive a car. And then there are skills you will hone and develop for the rest of your life: how to work with people, how to study God's Word, or how to draw upon God's promises even when the circumstances aren't too promising.

Thirteen years of Joseph's life were spent in obscurity in Egypt. But they were not wasted years. God in his infinite wisdom knew that the man who emerged in chapter 41 would be different from the man who submerged in chapter 37.

It takes a world with trouble in it to train men and women for their high calling as children of God. Faced with trouble, some people (like Joseph) grow wings; others buy crutches. Which kind are you? Read Isaiah 40:31, and wherever you encounter the word *they*, substitute your own name. It's a promise aimed at you!

INSIGHT From Prison to Palace in One Day
At the tender age of seventeen, Joseph was sold into Egyptian slavery (37:28). Thirteen years later he was still in prison (41:46). But when the time was right, God promoted him from the prison to the palace . . . overnight! That's a much-needed reminder that God's "Graduate School of Growing" is seldom a one-year curriculum!

CHAPTER 41

When two full years had passed, Pharaoh had a dream: He was standing by the Nile, ²when out of the river there came up seven cows, sleek and fat, and they grazed among the reeds. ³After them, seven other cows, ugly and gaunt, came up out of the Nile and stood beside those on the riverbank. ⁴And the cows that were ugly and gaunt ate up the seven sleek, fat cows. Then Pharaoh woke up.

⁵He fell asleep again and had a second dream: Seven heads of grain, healthy and good, were growing on a single stalk. ⁶After them, seven other heads of grain sprouted—thin and scorched by the east wind. ⁷The thin heads of grain swallowed up the seven healthy, full heads. Then Pharaoh woke up; it had been a dream.

⁸In the morning his mind was troubled, so he sent for all the magicians and wise men of Egypt. Pharaoh told them his dreams, but no one could interpret them for him.

⁹Then the chief cupbearer said to Pharaoh, "Today I am reminded of my shortcomings. ¹⁰Pharaoh was once angry with his servants, and he imprisoned me and the chief baker in the house of the captain of the guard. ¹¹Each of us had a dream the same night, and each dream had a mean-

ing of its own. ¹²Now a young Hebrew was there with us, a servant of the captain of the guard. We told him our dreams, and he interpreted them for us, giving each man the interpretation of his dream. ¹³And things turned out exactly as he interpreted them to us: I was restored to my position, and the other man was hanged.'"

¹⁴So Pharaoh sent for Joseph, and he was quickly brought from the dungeon. When he had shaved and changed his clothes, he came before Pharaoh.

¹⁵Pharaoh said to Joseph, "I had a dream, and no one can interpret it. But I have heard it said of you that when you hear a dream you can interpret it."

¹⁶"I cannot do it," Joseph replied to Pharaoh, "but God will give Pharaoh the answer he desires."

¹⁷Then Pharaoh said to Joseph, "In my dream I was standing on the bank of the Nile, ¹⁸when out of the river there came up seven cows, fat and sleek, and they grazed among the reeds. ¹⁹After them, seven other cows came up—scrawny and very ugly and lean. I had never seen such ugly cows in all the land of Egypt. ²⁰The lean, ugly cows ate up the seven fat cows that came up first. ²¹But even after they ate them, no one could tell that they had

j13 Or impaled

done so; they looked just as ugly as before. Then I woke up.

22"In my dreams I also saw seven heads of grain, full and good, growing on a single stalk. 23After them, seven other heads sprouted—withered and thin and scorched by the east wind. 24The thin heads of grain swallowed up the seven good heads. I told this to the magicians, but none could explain it to me."

25Then Joseph said to Pharaoh, "The dreams of Pharaoh are one and the same. God has revealed to Pharaoh what he is about to do. 26The seven good cows are seven years, and the seven good heads of grain are seven years; it is one and the same dream. 27The seven lean, ugly cows that came up afterward are seven years, and so are the seven worthless heads of grain scorched by the east wind: They are seven years of famine.

28"It is just as I said to Pharaoh: God has shown Pharaoh what he is about to do. 29Seven years of great abundance are coming throughout the land of Egypt, 30but seven years of famine will follow them. Then all the abundance in Egypt will be forgotten, and the famine will ravage the land. 31The abundance in the land will not be remembered, because the famine that follows it will be so severe. 32The reason the dream was given to Pharaoh in two forms is that the matter has been firmly decided by God, and God will do it soon.

33"And now let Pharaoh look for a discerning and wise man and put him in charge of the land of Egypt. 34Let Pharaoh appoint commissioners over the land to take a fifth of the harvest of Egypt during the seven years of abundance. 35They should collect all the food of these good years that are coming and store up the grain under the authority of Pharaoh, to be kept in the cities for food. 36This food should be held in reserve for the country, to be used during the seven years of famine that will come upon Egypt, so that the country may not be ruined by the famine."

37The plan seemed good to Pharaoh and to all his officials. 38So Pharaoh asked them, "Can we find anyone like this man, one in whom is the spirit of God[k]?"

39Then Pharaoh said to Joseph, "Since God has made all this known to you, there is no one so discerning and wise as you. 40You shall be in charge of my palace, and all my people are to submit to your orders. Only with respect to the throne will I be greater than you."

41So Pharaoh said to Joseph, "I hereby put you in charge of the whole land of Egypt." 42Then Pharaoh took his signet ring from his finger and put it on Joseph's finger. He dressed him in robes of fine linen and put a gold chain around his neck. 43He had him ride in a chariot as his second-in-command,[l] and men shouted before him, "Make way[m]!" Thus he put him in charge of the whole land of Egypt.

44Then Pharaoh said to Joseph, "I am Pharaoh, but without your word no one will lift hand or foot in all Egypt." 45Pharaoh gave Joseph the name Zaphenath-Paneah and gave him Asenath daughter of Potiphera, priest of On,[n] to be his wife. And Joseph went throughout the land of Egypt.

46Joseph was thirty years old when he entered the service of Pharaoh king of Egypt. And Joseph went out from Pharaoh's presence and traveled throughout Egypt. 47During the seven years of abundance the land produced plentifully. 48Joseph collected all the food produced in those seven years of abundance in Egypt and stored it in the cities. In each city he put the food grown in the fields surrounding it. 49Joseph stored up huge quantities of grain, like the sand of the sea; it was so much that he stopped keeping records because it was beyond measure.

50Before the years of famine came, two sons were born to Joseph by Asenath daughter of Potiphera, priest of On. 51Joseph named his firstborn Manasseh[o] and said, "It is because God has made me forget all my trouble and all my father's household." 52The second son he named Ephraim[p] and said, "It is because God has made me fruitful in the land of my suffering."

53The seven years of abundance in Egypt came to an end, 54and the seven years of famine began, just as Joseph had said. There was famine in all the other

k38 Or of the gods   l43 Or in the chariot of his second-in-command; or in his second chariot   m43 Or Bow down   n45 That is, Heliopolis; also in verse 50   o51 Manasseh sounds like and may be derived from the Hebrew for forget.   p52 Ephraim sounds like the Hebrew for twice fruitful.

lands, but in the whole land of Egypt there was food. ⁵⁵When all Egypt began to feel the famine, the people cried to Pharaoh for food. Then Pharaoh told all the Egyptians, "Go to Joseph and do what he tells you."

⁵⁶When the famine had spread over the whole country, Joseph opened the storehouses and sold grain to the Egyptians, for the famine was severe throughout Egypt. ⁵⁷And all the countries came to Egypt to buy grain from Joseph, because the famine was severe in all the world.

CHAPTER 42

When Jacob learned that there was grain in Egypt, he said to his sons, "Why do you just keep looking at each other?" ²He continued, "I have heard that there is grain in Egypt. Go down there and buy some for us, so that we may live and not die."

³Then ten of Joseph's brothers went down to buy grain from Egypt. ⁴But Jacob did not send Benjamin, Joseph's brother, with the others, because he was afraid that harm might come to him. ⁵So Israel's sons were among those who went to buy grain, for the famine was in the land of Canaan also.

⁶Now Joseph was the governor of the land, the one who sold grain to all its people. So when Joseph's brothers arrived, they bowed down to him with their faces to the ground. ⁷As soon as Joseph saw his brothers, he recognized them, but he pretended to be a stranger and spoke harshly to them. "Where do you come from?" he asked.

"From the land of Canaan," they replied, "to buy food."

⁸Although Joseph recognized his brothers, they did not recognize him. ⁹Then he remembered his dreams about them and said to them, "You are spies! You have come to see where our land is unprotected."

¹⁰"No, my lord," they answered. "Your servants have come to buy food. ¹¹We are all the sons of one man. Your servants are honest men, not spies."

¹²"No!" he said to them. "You have come to see where our land is unprotected."

¹³But they replied, "Your servants were twelve brothers, the sons of one man, who lives in the land of Canaan. The youngest is now with our father, and one is no more."

¹⁴Joseph said to them, "It is just as I told you: You are spies! ¹⁵And this is how you will be tested: As surely as Pharaoh lives, you will not leave this place unless your youngest brother comes here. ¹⁶Send one of your number to get your brother; the rest of you will be kept in prison, so that your words may be tested to see if you are telling the truth. If you are not, then as surely as Pharaoh lives, you are spies!" ¹⁷And he put them all in custody for three days.

¹⁸On the third day, Joseph said to them, "Do this and you will live, for I fear God: ¹⁹If you are honest men, let one of your brothers stay here in prison, while the rest of you go and take grain back for your starving households. ²⁰But you must bring your youngest brother to me, so that your words may be verified and that you may not die." This they proceeded to do.

²¹They said to one another, "Surely we are being punished because of our brother. We saw how distressed he was when he pleaded with us for his life, but we would not listen; that's why this distress has come upon us."

²²Reuben replied, "Didn't I tell you not to sin against the boy? But you wouldn't listen! Now we must give an accounting for his blood." ²³They did not realize that Joseph could understand them, since he was using an interpreter.

²⁴He turned away from them and began to weep, but then turned back and spoke to them again. He had Simeon taken from them and bound before their eyes.

²⁵Joseph gave orders to fill their bags with grain, to put each man's silver back in his sack, and to give them provisions for their journey. After this was done for them, ²⁶they loaded their grain on their donkeys and left.

²⁷At the place where they stopped for the night one of them opened his sack to get feed for his donkey, and he saw his silver in the mouth of his sack. ²⁸"My silver has been returned," he said to his brothers. "Here it is in my sack."

Their hearts sank and they turned to each other trembling and said, "What is this that God has done to us?"

²⁹When they came to their father Jacob in the land of Canaan, they told him all that had happened to them. They said, ³⁰"The man who is lord over the land

spoke harshly to us and treated us as though we were spying on the land. ³¹But we said to him, 'We are honest men; we are not spies. ³²We were twelve brothers, sons of one father. One is no more, and the youngest is now with our father in Canaan.'

³³"Then the man who is lord over the land said to us, 'This is how I will know whether you are honest men: Leave one of your brothers here with me, and take food for your starving households and go. ³⁴But bring your youngest brother to me so I will know that you are not spies but honest men. Then I will give your brother back to you, and you can trade*q* in the land.' "

³⁵As they were emptying their sacks, there in each man's sack was his pouch of silver! When they and their father saw the money pouches, they were frightened. ³⁶Their father Jacob said to them, "You have deprived me of my children. Joseph is no more and Simeon is no more, and now you want to take Benjamin. Everything is against me!"

³⁷Then Reuben said to his father, "You may put both of my sons to death if I do not bring him back to you. Entrust him to my care, and I will bring him back."

³⁸But Jacob said, "My son will not go down there with you; his brother is dead and he is the only one left. If harm comes to him on the journey you are taking, you will bring my gray head down to the grave*r* in sorrow."

C H A P T E R   4 3

Now the famine was still severe in the land. ²So when they had eaten all the grain they had brought from Egypt, their father said to them, "Go back and buy us a little more food."

³But Judah said to him, "The man warned us solemnly, 'You will not see my face again unless your brother is with you.' ⁴If you will send our brother along with us, we will go down and buy food for you. ⁵But if you will not send him, we will not go down, because the man said to us, 'You will not see my face again unless your brother is with you.' "

⁶Israel asked, "Why did you bring this trouble on me by telling the man you had another brother?"

⁷They replied, "The man questioned us closely about ourselves and our family. 'Is your father still living?' he asked us. 'Do you have another brother?' We simply answered his questions. How were we to know he would say, 'Bring your brother down here'?"

⁸Then Judah said to Israel his father, "Send the boy along with me and we will go at once, so that we and you and our children may live and not die. ⁹I myself will guarantee his safety; you can hold me personally responsible for him. If I do not bring him back to you and set him here before you, I will bear the blame before you all my life. ¹⁰As it is, if we had not delayed, we could have gone and returned twice."

¹¹Then their father Israel said to them, "If it must be, then do this: Put some of the best products of the land in your bags and take them down to the man as a gift— a little balm and a little honey, some spices and myrrh, some pistachio nuts and almonds. ¹²Take double the amount of silver with you, for you must return the silver that was put back into the mouths of your sacks. Perhaps it was a mistake. ¹³Take your brother also and go back to the man at once. ¹⁴And may God Almighty*s* grant you mercy before the man so that he will let your other brother and Benjamin come back with you. As for me, if I am bereaved, I am bereaved."

¹⁵So the men took the gifts and double the amount of silver, and Benjamin also. They hurried down to Egypt and presented themselves to Joseph. ¹⁶When Joseph saw Benjamin with them, he said to the steward of his house, "Take these men to my house, slaughter an animal and prepare dinner; they are to eat with me at noon."

¹⁷The man did as Joseph told him and took the men to Joseph's house. ¹⁸Now the men were frightened when they were taken to his house. They thought, "We were brought here because of the silver that was put back into our sacks the first time. He wants to attack us and overpower us and seize us as slaves and take our donkeys."

¹⁹So they went up to Joseph's steward and spoke to him at the entrance to the house. ²⁰"Please, sir," they said, "we came

q34 Or move about freely   r38 Hebrew Sheol   s14 Hebrew El-Shaddai down here the first time to buy food. [21]But at the place where we stopped for the night we opened our sacks and each of us found his silver—the exact weight—in the mouth of his sack. So we have brought it back with us. [22]We have also brought additional silver with us to buy food. We don't know who put our silver in our sacks."

[23]"It's all right," he said. "Don't be afraid. Your God, the God of your father, has given you treasure in your sacks; I received your silver." Then he brought Simeon out to them.

[24]The steward took the men into Joseph's house, gave them water to wash their feet and provided fodder for their donkeys. [25]They prepared their gifts for Joseph's arrival at noon, because they had heard that they were to eat there.

[26]When Joseph came home, they presented to him the gifts they had brought into the house, and they bowed down before him to the ground. [27]He asked them how they were, and then he said, "How is your aged father you told me about? Is he still living?"

[28]They replied, "Your servant our father is still alive and well." And they bowed low to pay him honor.

[29]As he looked about and saw his brother Benjamin, his own mother's son, he asked, "Is this your youngest brother, the one you told me about?" And he said, "God be gracious to you, my son." [30]Deeply moved at the sight of his brother, Joseph hurried out and looked for a place to weep. He went into his private room and wept there.

[31]After he had washed his face, he came out and, controlling himself, said, "Serve the food."

[32]They served him by himself, the brothers by themselves, and the Egyptians who ate with him by themselves, because Egyptians could not eat with Hebrews, for that is detestable to Egyptians. [33]The men had been seated before him in the order of their ages, from the firstborn to the youngest; and they looked at each other in astonishment. [34]When portions were served to them from Joseph's table, Benjamin's portion was five times as much as anyone else's. So they feasted and drank freely with him.

CHAPTER 44

Now Joseph gave these instructions to the steward of his house: "Fill the men's sacks with as much food as they can carry, and put each man's silver in the mouth of his sack. [2]Then put my cup, the silver one, in the mouth of the youngest one's sack, along with the silver for his grain." And he did as Joseph said.

[3]As morning dawned, the men were sent on their way with their donkeys. [4]They had not gone far from the city when Joseph said to his steward, "Go after those men at once, and when you catch up with them, say to them, 'Why have you repaid good with evil? [5]Isn't this the cup my master drinks from and also uses for divination? This is a wicked thing you have done.'"

[6]When he caught up with them, he repeated these words to them. [7]But they said to him, "Why does my lord say such things? Far be it from your servants to do anything like that! [8]We even brought back to you from the land of Canaan the silver we found inside the mouths of our sacks. So why would we steal silver or gold from your master's house? [9]If any of your servants is found to have it, he will die; and the rest of us will become my lord's slaves."

[10]"Very well, then," he said, "let it be as you say. Whoever is found to have it will become my slave; the rest of you will be free from blame."

[11]Each of them quickly lowered his sack to the ground and opened it. [12]Then the steward proceeded to search, beginning with the oldest and ending with the youngest. And the cup was found in Benjamin's sack. [13]At this, they tore their clothes. Then they all loaded their donkeys and returned to the city.

[14]Joseph was still in the house when Judah and his brothers came in, and they threw themselves to the ground before him. [15]Joseph said to them, "What is this you have done? Don't you know that a man like me can find things out by divination?"

[16]"What can we say to my lord?" Judah replied. "What can we say? How can we prove our innocence? God has uncovered your servants' guilt. We are now my lord's slaves—we ourselves and the one who was found to have the cup."

[17]But Joseph said, "Far be it from me to

do such a thing! Only the man who was found to have the cup will become my slave. The rest of you, go back to your father in peace."

¹⁸Then Judah went up to him and said: "Please, my lord, let your servant speak a word to my lord. Do not be angry with your servant, though you are equal to Pharaoh himself. ¹⁹My lord asked his servants, 'Do you have a father or a brother?' ²⁰And we answered, 'We have an aged father, and there is a young son born to him in his old age. His brother is dead, and he is the only one of his mother's sons left, and his father loves him.'

²¹"Then you said to your servants, 'Bring him down to me so I can see him for myself.' ²²And we said to my lord, 'The boy cannot leave his father; if he leaves him, his father will die.' ²³But you told your servants, 'Unless your youngest brother comes down with you, you will not see my face again.' ²⁴When we went back to your servant my father, we told him what my lord had said.

²⁵"Then our father said, 'Go back and buy a little more food.' ²⁶But we said, 'We cannot go down. Only if our youngest brother is with us will we go. We cannot

ᵗ29 Hebrew *Sheol*; also in verse 31

see the man's face unless our youngest brother is with us.'

²⁷"Your servant my father said to us, 'You know that my wife bore me two sons. ²⁸One of them went away from me, and I said, "He has surely been torn to pieces." And I have not seen him since. ²⁹If you take this one from me too and harm comes to him, you will bring my gray head down to the graveᵗ in misery.'

³⁰"So now, if the boy is not with us when I go back to your servant my father and if my father, whose life is closely bound up with the boy's life, ³¹sees that the boy isn't there, he will die. Your servants will bring the gray head of our father down to the grave in sorrow. ³²Your servant guaranteed the boy's safety to my father. I said, 'If I do not bring him back to you, I will bear the blame before you, my father, all my life!'

³³"Now then, please let your servant remain here as my lord's slave in place of the boy, and let the boy return with his brothers. ³⁴How can I go back to my father if the boy is not with me? No! Do not let me see the misery that would come upon my father."

JANUARY 16 ☐ DAY 16
GENESIS 45–47
Joseph's Family United in Egypt

 OVERVIEW Today's reading contains the exciting conclusion to the story of Joseph and his unsuspecting brothers. After twice planting evidence on his brothers that would ensure their return to Egypt, Joseph can contain his secret no longer. In an emotion-packed scene, he reveals that he is the brother they sold into slavery and left for dead. At last in a position to avenge his ill treatment, Joseph instead shows kindness, acknowledging that God was behind it all to bring much good out of his difficult circumstances. Jacob moves to Egypt to spend his remaining years with his united family.

Chapter 45	Chapter 46	Chapter 47
Joseph's Surprise Announcement	Jacob's Move to Egypt	Jacob's Exaltation in Egypt
Joseph's Family Reunited	Joseph's Family Treated Kindly	

YOUR DAILY WALK *Sovereignty* is a big word, but it is also a biblical concept that touches your life every day. God is sovereign. That means nothing takes him by surprise. Every experience in life, from the most pleasant to the most painful, has been allowed by God for a very special purpose. Joseph learned this important truth, although it took years of mistreatment to drive the point home. Addressing his brothers who sold him, he declared, "It was not you who sent me here, but God" (45:8). God was at work even then.

We should be thankful that God always turns out to be bigger than we thought.

Think back over your life and select one event that stands out as a time when it appeared that God had lost control of the situation. Perhaps it was a death in the family or the loss of a job or an unexpected accident. Now across that painful memory, mentally write the words, "God was there." Write out a definition of sovereignty in your own words, and make it speak to your own situation. (For example: "Sovereignty means that God had a purpose when I lost my job. He hasn't forgotten about me; he just has something better in store!")

INSIGHT Why God Moved the Jews to Egypt
It is not difficult to see the divine wisdom in moving Jacob's family to Egypt. In Egypt the Jews would have to remain a separate, distinct people, for Jacob and his sons were shepherds, an abominable occupation to Egyptians and thus a natural barrier to intermarriage. For four hundred years the Jews would multiply under these ideal conditions.

CHAPTER 45

Then Joseph could no longer control himself before all his attendants, and he cried out, "Have everyone leave my presence!" So there was no one with Joseph when he made himself known to his brothers. ²And he wept so loudly that the Egyptians heard him, and Pharaoh's household heard about it.

³Joseph said to his brothers, "I am Joseph! Is my father still living?" But his brothers were not able to answer him, because they were terrified at his presence.

⁴Then Joseph said to his brothers, "Come close to me." When they had done so, he said, "I am your brother Joseph, the one you sold into Egypt! ⁵And now, do not be distressed and do not be angry with yourselves for selling me here, because it was to save lives that God sent me ahead of you. ⁶For two years now there has been famine in the land, and for the next five years there will not be plowing and reaping. ⁷But God sent me ahead of you to preserve for you a remnant on earth and to save your lives by a great deliverance.ᵘ

⁸"So then, it was not you who sent me here, but God. He made me father to Pharaoh, lord of his entire household and ruler of all Egypt. ⁹Now hurry back to my father and say to him, 'This is what your son Joseph says: God has made me lord of all Egypt. Come down to me; don't delay. ¹⁰You shall live in the region of Goshen and be near me—you, your children and grandchildren, your flocks and herds, and all you have. ¹¹I will provide for you there, because five years of famine are still to come. Otherwise you and your household and all who belong to you will become destitute.'

¹²"You can see for yourselves, and so can my brother Benjamin, that it is really I who am speaking to you. ¹³Tell my father about all the honor accorded me in Egypt and about everything you have seen. And bring my father down here quickly."

¹⁴Then he threw his arms around his brother Benjamin and wept, and Benjamin embraced him, weeping. ¹⁵And he kissed all his brothers and wept over them. Afterward his brothers talked with him.

¹⁶When the news reached Pharaoh's palace that Joseph's brothers had come, Pharaoh and all his officials were pleased. ¹⁷Pharaoh said to Joseph, "Tell your brothers, 'Do this: Load your animals and return to the land of Canaan, ¹⁸and bring your father and your families back to me.

ᵘ7 Or *save you as a great band of survivors*

I will give you the best of the land of Egypt and you can enjoy the fat of the land.'

19"You are also directed to tell them, 'Do this: Take some carts from Egypt for your children and your wives, and get your father and come. 20Never mind about your belongings, because the best of all Egypt will be yours.' "

21So the sons of Israel did this. Joseph gave them carts, as Pharaoh had commanded, and he also gave them provisions for their journey. 22To each of them he gave new clothing, but to Benjamin he gave three hundred shekels*v* of silver and five sets of clothes. 23And this is what he sent to his father: ten donkeys loaded with the best things of Egypt, and ten female donkeys loaded with grain and bread and other provisions for his journey. 24Then he sent his brothers away, and as they were leaving he said to them, "Don't quarrel on the way!"

25So they went up out of Egypt and came to their father Jacob in the land of Canaan. 26They told him, "Joseph is still alive! In fact, he is ruler of all Egypt." Jacob was stunned; he did not believe them. 27But when they told him everything Joseph had said to them, and when he saw the carts Joseph had sent to carry him back, the spirit of their father Jacob revived. 28And Israel said, "I'm convinced! My son Joseph is still alive. I will go and see him before I die."

CHAPTER 46

So Israel set out with all that was his, and when he reached Beersheba, he offered sacrifices to the God of his father Isaac. 2And God spoke to Israel in a vision at night and said, "Jacob! Jacob!"

"Here I am," he replied.

3"I am God, the God of your father," he said. "Do not be afraid to go down to Egypt, for I will make you into a great nation there. 4I will go down to Egypt with you, and I will surely bring you back again. And Joseph's own hand will close your eyes."

5Then Jacob left Beersheba, and Israel's sons took their father Jacob and their children and their wives in the carts that Pharaoh had sent to transport him. 6They also took with them their livestock and the possessions they had acquired in Canaan, and Jacob and all his offspring went to Egypt. 7He took with him to Egypt his sons and grandsons and his daughters and granddaughters—all his offspring.

8These are the names of the sons of Israel (Jacob and his descendants) who went to Egypt:

Reuben the firstborn of Jacob.
9The sons of Reuben:
  Hanoch, Pallu, Hezron and Carmi.
10The sons of Simeon:
  Jemuel, Jamin, Ohad, Jakin, Zohar and Shaul the son of a Canaanite woman.
11The sons of Levi:
  Gershon, Kohath and Merari.
12The sons of Judah:
  Er, Onan, Shelah, Perez and Zerah (but Er and Onan had died in the land of Canaan).
  The sons of Perez:
    Hezron and Hamul.
13The sons of Issachar:
  Tola, Puah,*w* Jashub*x* and Shimron.
14The sons of Zebulun:
  Sered, Elon and Jahleel.
15These were the sons Leah bore to Jacob in Paddan Aram,*y* besides his daughter Dinah. These sons and daughters of his were thirty-three in all.

16The sons of Gad:
  Zephon,*z* Haggi, Shuni, Ezbon, Eri, Arodi and Areli.
17The sons of Asher:
  Imnah, Ishvah, Ishvi and Beriah.
  Their sister was Serah.
  The sons of Beriah:
    Heber and Malkiel.
18These were the children born to Jacob by Zilpah, whom Laban had given to his daughter Leah—sixteen in all.

19The sons of Jacob's wife Rachel:
  Joseph and Benjamin. 20In Egypt, Manasseh and Ephraim were born to Joseph by Asenath daughter of Potiphera, priest of On.*a*
21The sons of Benjamin:

*v*22 That is, about 7 1/2 pounds (about 3.5 kilograms)   *w*13 Samaritan Pentateuch and Syriac (see also 1 Chron. 7:1); Masoretic Text *Puvah*   *x*13 Samaritan Pentateuch and some Septuagint manuscripts (see also Num. 26:24 and 1 Chron. 7:1); Masoretic Text *Iob*   *y*15 That is, Northwest Mesopotamia   *z*16 Samaritan Pentateuch and Septuagint (see also Num. 26:15); Masoretic Text *Ziphion*   *a*20 That is, Heliopolis

Bela, Beker, Ashbel, Gera, Naaman, Ehi, Rosh, Muppim, Huppim and Ard.

22These were the sons of Rachel who were born to Jacob—fourteen in all.

23The son of Dan:
Hushim.

24The sons of Naphtali:
Jahziel, Guni, Jezer and Shillem.

25These were the sons born to Jacob by Bilhah, whom Laban had given to his daughter Rachel—seven in all.

26All those who went to Egypt with Jacob—those who were his direct descendants, not counting his sons' wives—numbered sixty-six persons. 27With the two sons[b] who had been born to Joseph in Egypt, the members of Jacob's family, which went to Egypt, were seventy[c] in all.

28Now Jacob sent Judah ahead of him to Joseph to get directions to Goshen. When they arrived in the region of Goshen, 29Joseph had his chariot made ready and went to Goshen to meet his father Israel. As soon as Joseph appeared before him, he threw his arms around his father[d] and wept for a long time.

30Israel said to Joseph, "Now I am ready to die, since I have seen for myself that you are still alive."

31Then Joseph said to his brothers and to his father's household, "I will go up and speak to Pharaoh and will say to him, 'My brothers and my father's household, who were living in the land of Canaan, have come to me. 32The men are shepherds; they tend livestock, and they have brought along their flocks and herds and everything they own.' 33When Pharaoh calls you in and asks, 'What is your occupation?' 34you should answer, 'Your servants have tended livestock from our boyhood on, just as our fathers did.' Then you will be allowed to settle in the region of Goshen, for all shepherds are detestable to the Egyptians."

CHAPTER 47
Joseph went and told Pharaoh, "My father and brothers, with their flocks and herds and everything they own, have come from the land of Canaan and are now in Goshen." 2He chose five of his brothers and presented them before Pharaoh.

3Pharaoh asked the brothers, "What is your occupation?"

"Your servants are shepherds," they replied to Pharaoh, "just as our fathers were." 4They also said to him, "We have come to live here awhile, because the famine is severe in Canaan and your servants' flocks have no pasture. So now, please let your servants settle in Goshen."

5Pharaoh said to Joseph, "Your father and your brothers have come to you, 6and the land of Egypt is before you; settle your father and your brothers in the best part of the land. Let them live in Goshen. And if you know of any among them with special ability, put them in charge of my own livestock."

7Then Joseph brought his father Jacob in and presented him before Pharaoh. After Jacob blessed[e] Pharaoh, 8Pharaoh asked him, "How old are you?"

9And Jacob said to Pharaoh, "The years of my pilgrimage are a hundred and thirty. My years have been few and difficult, and they do not equal the years of the pilgrimage of my fathers." 10Then Jacob blessed[f] Pharaoh and went out from his presence.

11So Joseph settled his father and his brothers in Egypt and gave them property in the best part of the land, the district of Rameses, as Pharaoh directed. 12Joseph also provided his father and his brothers and all his father's household with food, according to the number of their children.

13There was no food, however, in the whole region because the famine was severe; both Egypt and Canaan wasted away because of the famine. 14Joseph collected all the money that was to be found in Egypt and Canaan in payment for the grain they were buying, and he brought it to Pharaoh's palace. 15When the money of the people of Egypt and Canaan was gone, all Egypt came to Joseph and said, "Give us food. Why should we die before your eyes? Our money is used up."

16"Then bring your livestock," said Joseph. "I will sell you food in exchange for your livestock, since your money is gone." 17So they brought their livestock to Joseph, and he gave them food in exchange for their horses, their sheep and goats,

---

b27 Hebrew; Septuagint *the nine children*   *c27* Hebrew (see also Exodus 1:5 and footnote); Septuagint (see also Acts 7:14) *seventy-five*   *d29* Hebrew *around him*   *e7* Or *greeted*   *f10* Or *said farewell to* their cattle and donkeys. And he brought them through that year with food in exchange for all their livestock.

¹⁸When that year was over, they came to him the following year and said, "We cannot hide from our lord the fact that since our money is gone and our livestock belongs to you, there is nothing left for our lord except our bodies and our land. ¹⁹Why should we perish before your eyes—we and our land as well? Buy us and our land in exchange for food, and we with our land will be in bondage to Pharaoh. Give us seed so that we may live and not die, and that the land may not become desolate."

²⁰So Joseph bought all the land in Egypt for Pharaoh. The Egyptians, one and all, sold their fields, because the famine was too severe for them. The land became Pharaoh's, ²¹and Joseph reduced the people to servitude,ᵍ from one end of Egypt to the other. ²²However, he did not buy the land of the priests, because they received a regular allotment from Pharaoh and had food enough from the allotment Pharaoh gave them. That is why they did not sell their land.

²³Joseph said to the people, "Now that I have bought you and your land today for Pharaoh, here is seed for you so you can plant the ground. ²⁴But when the crop comes in, give a fifth of it to Pharaoh. The other four-fifths you may keep as seed for the fields and as food for yourselves and your households and your children."

²⁵"You have saved our lives," they said. "May we find favor in the eyes of our lord; we will be in bondage to Pharaoh."

²⁶So Joseph established it as a law concerning land in Egypt—still in force today—that a fifth of the produce belongs to Pharaoh. It was only the land of the priests that did not become Pharaoh's.

²⁷Now the Israelites settled in Egypt in the region of Goshen. They acquired property there and were fruitful and increased greatly in number.

²⁸Jacob lived in Egypt seventeen years, and the years of his life were a hundred and forty-seven. ²⁹When the time drew near for Israel to die, he called for his son Joseph and said to him, "If I have found favor in your eyes, put your hand under my thigh and promise that you will show me kindness and faithfulness. Do not bury me in Egypt, ³⁰but when I rest with my fathers, carry me out of Egypt and bury me where they are buried."

"I will do as you say," he said.

³¹"Swear to me," he said. Then Joseph swore to him, and Israel worshiped as he leaned on the top of his staff.ʰ

ᵍ21 Samaritan Pentateuch and Septuagint (see also Vulgate); Masoretic Text and he moved the people into the cities
ʰ31 Or Israel bowed down at the head of his bed

JANUARY 17 □ DAY 17
GENESIS 48–50
The Last Days of Jacob and Joseph

 OVERVIEW As Jacob's life in Egypt draws to a close, he summons Joseph's two sons and blesses them, exalting the younger, Ephraim, over the older, Manasseh. As his final act, Jacob prophetically outlines the future of his twelve sons. His desire for burial in Canaan testifies that the destiny of the nation still lies in the promised land. Joseph also dies after a faithful and prosperous life and adds his testimony that God will one day liberate his people.

Chapter 48		Chapter 49	Chapter 50	
Blessing the Sons of			Death and Burial of	
Joseph		Jacob	Jacob	Joseph
			1 21	22 26
Last Words			Last Resting Place	

YOUR DAILY WALK On a scale of one to ten (with one being low and ten high), rate yourself on the following two statements:
- I am a forgiving person.
- I am quick to forget offenses against me.

For most of us, forgiveness comes easily... after we've gotten even.

You've probably heard the phrase "I'll forgive, but I won't forget." That's really just another way of saying, "I won't forgive," for true forgiveness involves totally putting out of our mind the wrong suffered. That's the way God forgives (Ephesians 4:32), and his brand of forgiveness is the model he expects us to follow as well.

Joseph exhibited the quality of full forgiveness with his brothers. After Jacob's death, the brothers feared revenge (50:15) even though Joseph had already forgiven them. Their pleas for mercy moved him to tears as he reassured his brothers that he had totally forgiven them.

If you have experienced God's forgiveness in Christ, you have the greatest motivation possible for forgiving others. In what relationships have you *forgiven* but not *forgotten* an offense against you? Talk to God about it right now. Thank him for the peace that only total forgiveness can bring. Then phone, write or visit the offending party and share your newfound victory.

INSIGHT "A Moving Epitaph" for Jacob and Joseph

Joseph's care in honoring his father Jacob's dying request to be buried in Canaan (49:29–30) was duplicated by Moses hundreds of years later. Moses carried out Joseph's last wish by transporting his remains back to Canaan (Exodus 13:19).

CHAPTER 48

Some time later Joseph was told, "Your father is ill." So he took his two sons Manasseh and Ephraim along with him. ²When Jacob was told, "Your son Joseph has come to you," Israel rallied his strength and sat up on the bed.

³Jacob said to Joseph, "God Almighty[i] appeared to me at Luz in the land of Canaan, and there he blessed me ⁴and said to me, 'I am going to make you fruitful and will increase your numbers. I will make you a community of peoples, and I will give this land as an everlasting possession to your descendants after you.'

⁵"Now then, your two sons born to you in Egypt before I came to you here will be reckoned as mine; Ephraim and Manasseh will be mine, just as Reuben and Simeon are mine. ⁶Any children born to you after them will be yours; in the territory they inherit they will be reckoned under the names of their brothers. ⁷As I was returning from Paddan,[j] to my sorrow Rachel died in the land of Canaan while we were still on the way, a little distance from Ephrath. So I buried her there beside the road to Ephrath" (that is, Bethlehem).

⁸When Israel saw the sons of Joseph, he asked, "Who are these?"

⁹"They are the sons God has given me here," Joseph said to his father.

Then Israel said, "Bring them to me so I may bless them."

¹⁰Now Israel's eyes were failing because of old age, and he could hardly see. So Joseph brought his sons close to him, and his father kissed them and embraced them.

¹¹Israel said to Joseph, "I never expected to see your face again, and now God has allowed me to see your children too."

¹²Then Joseph removed them from Israel's knees and bowed down with his face to the ground. ¹³And Joseph took both of them, Ephraim on his right toward Israel's left hand and Manasseh on his left toward Israel's right hand, and brought them close to him. ¹⁴But Israel reached out his right hand and put it on Ephraim's head, though he was the younger, and crossing his arms, he put his left hand on Manasseh's head, even though Manasseh was the firstborn.

¹⁵Then he blessed Joseph and said,

"May the God before whom my fathers
  Abraham and Isaac walked,
the God who has been my shepherd
  all my life to this day,

i3 Hebrew El-Shaddai   j7 That is, Northwest Mesopotamia

[16]the Angel who has delivered me from
all harm
—may he bless these boys.
May they be called by my name
and the names of my fathers
Abraham and Isaac,
and may they increase greatly
upon the earth."

[17]When Joseph saw his father placing his right hand on Ephraim's head he was displeased; so he took hold of his father's hand to move it from Ephraim's head to Manasseh's head. [18]Joseph said to him, "No, my father, this one is the firstborn; put your right hand on his head."

[19]But his father refused and said, "I know, my son, I know. He too will become a people, and he too will become great. Nevertheless, his younger brother will be greater than he, and his descendants will become a group of nations." [20]He blessed them that day and said,

"In your[k] name will Israel pronounce
this blessing:
'May God make you like Ephraim
and Manasseh.' "

So he put Ephraim ahead of Manasseh.

[21]Then Israel said to Joseph, "I am about to die, but God will be with you[l] and take you[l] back to the land of your[l] fathers. [22]And to you, as one who is over your brothers, I give the ridge of land[m] I took from the Amorites with my sword and my bow."

CHAPTER 49

Then Jacob called for his sons and said: "Gather around so I can tell you what will happen to you in days to come.

[2]"Assemble and listen, sons of Jacob;
listen to your father Israel.

[3]"Reuben, you are my firstborn,
my might, the first sign of my
strength,
excelling in honor, excelling in
power.
[4]Turbulent as the waters, you will no
longer excel,
for you went up onto your father's
bed,
onto my couch and defiled it.

[5]"Simeon and Levi are brothers—
their swords[n] are weapons of
violence.
[6]Let me not enter their council,
let me not join their assembly,
for they have killed men in their anger
and hamstrung oxen as they
pleased.
[7]Cursed be their anger, so fierce,
and their fury, so cruel!
I will scatter them in Jacob
and disperse them in Israel.

[8]"Judah,[o] your brothers will praise
you;
your hand will be on the neck of
your enemies;
your father's sons will bow down to
you.
[9]You are a lion's cub, O Judah;
you return from the prey, my son.
Like a lion he crouches and lies down,
like a lioness—who dares to rouse
him?
[10]The scepter will not depart from
Judah,
nor the ruler's staff from between
his feet,
until he comes to whom it belongs[p]
and the obedience of the nations is
his.
[11]He will tether his donkey to a vine,
his colt to the choicest branch;
he will wash his garments in wine,
his robes in the blood of grapes.
[12]His eyes will be darker than wine,
his teeth whiter than milk.[q]

[13]"Zebulun will live by the seashore
and become a haven for ships;
his border will extend toward Sidon.

[14]"Issachar is a rawboned[r] donkey
lying down between two
saddlebags.[s]
[15]When he sees how good is his resting
place
and how pleasant is his land,
he will bend his shoulder to the
burden
and submit to forced labor.

[16]"Dan[t] will provide justice for his
people
as one of the tribes of Israel.

[k]20 The Hebrew is singular.   [l]21 The Hebrew is plural.   [m]22 Or And to you I give one portion more than to your brothers—the portion   [n]5 The meaning of the Hebrew for this word is uncertain.   [o]8 Judah sounds like and may be derived from the Hebrew for praise.   [p]10 Or until Shiloh comes; or until he comes to whom tribute belongs   [q]12 Or will be dull from wine, / his teeth white from milk   [r]14 Or strong   [s]14 Or campfires   [t]16 Dan here means he provides justice.

¹⁷Dan will be a serpent by the roadside,
   a viper along the path,
that bites the horse's heels
   so that its rider tumbles backward.

¹⁸"I look for your deliverance, O LORD.

¹⁹"Gad ᵘ will be attacked by a band of
      raiders,
   but he will attack them at their
      heels.

²⁰"Asher's food will be rich;
   he will provide delicacies fit for a
      king.

²¹"Naphtali is a doe set free
   that bears beautiful fawns.ᵛ

²²"Joseph is a fruitful vine,
   a fruitful vine near a spring,
   whose branches climb over a wall.ʷ

²³With bitterness archers attacked him;
   they shot at him with hostility.

²⁴But his bow remained steady,
   his strong arms stayedˣ limber,
because of the hand of the Mighty One
   of Jacob,
   because of the Shepherd, the Rock of
      Israel,

²⁵because of your father's God, who
      helps you,
   because of the Almighty,ʸ who
      blesses you
with blessings of the heavens above,
   blessings of the deep that lies below,
   blessings of the breast and womb.

²⁶Your father's blessings are greater
   than the blessings of the ancient
      mountains,
   thanᶻ the bounty of the age-old
      hills.
Let all these rest on the head of
   Joseph,
   on the brow of the prince amongᵃ
      his brothers.

²⁷"Benjamin is a ravenous wolf;
   in the morning he devours the prey,
   in the evening he divides the
      plunder."

²⁸All these are the twelve tribes of Israel, and this is what their father said to them when he blessed them, giving each the blessing appropriate to him.

²⁹Then he gave them these instructions: "I am about to be gathered to my people. Bury me with my fathers in the cave in the field of Ephron the Hittite, ³⁰the cave in the field of Machpelah, near Mamre in Canaan, which Abraham bought as a burial place from Ephron the Hittite, along with the field. ³¹There Abraham and his wife Sarah were buried, there Isaac and his wife Rebekah were buried, and there I buried Leah. ³²The field and the cave in it were bought from the Hittites.ᵇ"

³³When Jacob had finished giving instructions to his sons, he drew his feet up into the bed, breathed his last and was gathered to his people.

CHAPTER 50

Joseph threw himself upon his father and wept over him and kissed him. ²Then Joseph directed the physicians in his service to embalm his father Israel. So the physicians embalmed him, ³taking a full forty days, for that was the time required for embalming. And the Egyptians mourned for him seventy days.

⁴When the days of mourning had passed, Joseph said to Pharaoh's court, "If I have found favor in your eyes, speak to Pharaoh for me. Tell him, ⁵'My father made me swear an oath and said, "I am about to die; bury me in the tomb I dug for myself in the land of Canaan." Now let me go up and bury my father; then I will return.' "

⁶Pharaoh said, "Go up and bury your father, as he made you swear to do."

⁷So Joseph went up to bury his father. All Pharaoh's officials accompanied him— the dignitaries of his court and all the dignitaries of Egypt— ⁸besides all the members of Joseph's household and his brothers and those belonging to his father's household. Only their children and their flocks and herds were left in Goshen. ⁹Chariots and horsemenᶜ also went up with him. It was a very large company.

¹⁰When they reached the threshing floor of Atad, near the Jordan, they lamented loudly and bitterly; and there Joseph observed a seven-day period of mourning for his father. ¹¹When the Canaanites who lived there saw the mourning at the

---

ᵘ19 Gad can mean attack and band of raiders.   ᵛ21 Or free; / he utters beautiful words   ʷ22 Or Joseph is a wild colt, / a wild colt near a spring, / a wild donkey on a terraced hill   ˣ23,24 Or archers will attack . . . will shoot . . . will remain . . . will stay   ʸ25 Hebrew Shaddai   ᶻ26 Or of my progenitors, / as great as   ᵃ26 Or the one separated from   ᵇ32 Or the sons of Heth   ᶜ9 Or charioteers threshing floor of Atad, they said, "The Egyptians are holding a solemn ceremony of mourning." That is why that place near the Jordan is called Abel Mizraim.*d*

¹²So Jacob's sons did as he had commanded them: ¹³They carried him to the land of Canaan and buried him in the cave in the field of Machpelah, near Mamre, which Abraham had bought as a burial place from Ephron the Hittite, along with the field. ¹⁴After burying his father, Joseph returned to Egypt, together with his brothers and all the others who had gone with him to bury his father.

¹⁵When Joseph's brothers saw that their father was dead, they said, "What if Joseph holds a grudge against us and pays us back for all the wrongs we did to him?" ¹⁶So they sent word to Joseph, saying, "Your father left these instructions before he died: ¹⁷'This is what you are to say to Joseph: I ask you to forgive your brothers the sins and the wrongs they committed in treating you so badly.' Now please forgive the sins of the servants of the God of your father." When their message came to him, Joseph wept.

¹⁸His brothers then came and threw

themselves down before him. "We are your slaves," they said.

¹⁹But Joseph said to them, "Don't be afraid. Am I in the place of God? ²⁰You intended to harm me, but God intended it for good to accomplish what is now being done, the saving of many lives. ²¹So then, don't be afraid. I will provide for you and your children." And he reassured them and spoke kindly to them.

²²Joseph stayed in Egypt, along with all his father's family. He lived a hundred and ten years ²³and saw the third generation of Ephraim's children. Also the children of Makir son of Manasseh were placed at birth on Joseph's knees.*e*

²⁴Then Joseph said to his brothers, "I am about to die. But God will surely come to your aid and take you up out of this land to the land he promised on oath to Abraham, Isaac and Jacob." ²⁵And Joseph made the sons of Israel swear an oath and said, "God will surely come to your aid, and then you must carry my bones up from this place."

²⁶So Joseph died at the age of a hundred and ten. And after they embalmed him, he was placed in a coffin in Egypt.

d11 Abel Mizraim means *mourning of the Egyptians.* *e23* That is, were counted as his

Exodus

DURING the nearly four hundred years since the close of Genesis, the descendants of the patriarchal family have experienced good news and bad news. The good news: They have grown into a nation numbering several million. The bad news: They have become oppressed slaves in the land of Egypt. Exodus is thus the story of redemption from bondage to Pharaoh through a covenant relationship with God. From Egypt to Sinai, Israel learns of the might and power of God and of the importance of national worship.

Focus	Slavery		Salvation				Sanctification			
Divisions	Birth of Moses	Call of Moses	Conflict with Pharaoh	Exodus from Egypt	Red Sea Crossing	Journey to Sinai	Laws and Ceremonies	Tabernacle Blueprint	Golden Calf	Tabernacle Dedication
	1　2	3　　6	7　10	11 12	13 15	16 18	19 24	25 31	32 34	35 40
Topics	Deliverance from Oppression						Preparation for Worship			
	Getting Israel Out of Egypt						Getting Egypt Out of Israel			
Place	In Egypt		On the March				At Sinai			
Time	430 Years (15% of Exodus)		2 Months (30% of Exodus)				10 Months (55% of Exodus)			

JANUARY 18 □ DAY 18
EXODUS 1–2
Birth of Moses

OVERVIEW Exodus opens where Genesis leaves off: with Jacob's descendants multiplying in Egypt. A new ruler emerges who respects neither Joseph's memory nor the Israelites' human rights. Though Pharaoh attempts to kill all newborn Hebrew males, the infant Moses is providentially spared and raised in the very palace of the one who sought his death! At the age of forty, Moses seeks to bring about the right thing (deliverance) in the wrong way (murder) and spends the next four decades of his life in exile, tending sheep in the Midian wilderness.

Chapter 1		Chapter 2		
Israel's Multiplication	Pharaoh's Mistreatment	Faith of Parents	Failure of Moses	Faithfulness of God
1 7	8 22	1 10	11 22	23 25
People Prepared for Deliverance		Deliverer Prepared for People		

YOUR DAILY WALK The man sitting by the desert well was lost in his thoughts. Dejection on every line of his face, he felt much older than his forty years. Moses was miserable—and with good reason.

Our God has a big eraser.

He had been the one man in all of Egypt who might have had a chance to bring relief to his people. He had position, training, natural ability and the desire to help. But in one foolish act, he killed a man and forfeited all the advantages he had hoped to use.

Satan delights in convincing believers that they are of no use to God. And God delights in building cathedrals out of rubble. Moses' life needed reconstruction, to be sure! But when that rebuilding process was complete, he was a monument to God's grace.

Where in your life have you nearly given up hope that God could ever salvage the situation: your job? schooling? marriage? ministry? Before you throw in the towel, walk a mile in Moses' sandals. Study his failures. Learn about God's patience with him.

Then find your own "desert well" to sit by, and meditate on the encouraging words for discouraged disciples found in Exodus 4:11–12.

INSIGHT The Ark Revisited
The same Hebrew word for *ark* (as in Noah's) describes the vessel used by Moses' mother to hide him in the reeds. Once again we see God delivering his chosen from destruction by water after an obedient act of the faithful.

CHAPTER 1

These are the names of the sons of Israel who went to Egypt with Jacob, each with his family: ²Reuben, Simeon, Levi and Judah; ³Issachar, Zebulun and Benjamin; ⁴Dan and Naphtali; Gad and Asher. ⁵The descendants of Jacob numbered seventy*a* in all; Joseph was already in Egypt.

⁶Now Joseph and all his brothers and all that generation died, ⁷but the Israelites

*a*5 Masoretic Text (see also Gen. 46:27); Dead Sea Scrolls and Septuagint (see also Acts 7:14 and note at Gen. 46:27) *seventy-five* were fruitful and multiplied greatly and became exceedingly numerous, so that the land was filled with them.

⁸Then a new king, who did not know about Joseph, came to power in Egypt. ⁹"Look," he said to his people, "the Israelites have become much too numerous for us. ¹⁰Come, we must deal shrewdly with them or they will become even more numerous and, if war breaks out, will join our enemies, fight against us and leave the country."

¹¹So they put slave masters over them to oppress them with forced labor, and they built Pithom and Rameses as store cities for Pharaoh. ¹²But the more they were oppressed, the more they multiplied and spread; so the Egyptians came to dread the Israelites ¹³and worked them ruthlessly. ¹⁴They made their lives bitter with hard labor in brick and mortar and with all kinds of work in the fields; in all their hard labor the Egyptians used them ruthlessly.

¹⁵The king of Egypt said to the Hebrew midwives, whose names were Shiphrah and Puah, ¹⁶"When you help the Hebrew women in childbirth and observe them on the delivery stool, if it is a boy, kill him; but if it is a girl, let her live." ¹⁷The midwives, however, feared God and did not do what the king of Egypt had told them to do; they let the boys live. ¹⁸Then the king of Egypt summoned the midwives and asked them, "Why have you done this? Why have you let the boys live?"

¹⁹The midwives answered Pharaoh, "Hebrew women are not like Egyptian women; they are vigorous and give birth before the midwives arrive."

²⁰So God was kind to the midwives and the people increased and became even more numerous. ²¹And because the midwives feared God, he gave them families of their own.

²²Then Pharaoh gave this order to all his people: "Every boy that is born^b you must throw into the Nile, but let every girl live."

CHAPTER 2

Now a man of the house of Levi married a Levite woman, ²and she became pregnant and gave birth to a son. When she saw that he was a fine child, she hid him

for three months. ³But when she could hide him no longer, she got a papyrus basket for him and coated it with tar and pitch. Then she placed the child in it and put it among the reeds along the bank of the Nile. ⁴His sister stood at a distance to see what would happen to him.

⁵Then Pharaoh's daughter went down to the Nile to bathe, and her attendants were walking along the river bank. She saw the basket among the reeds and sent her slave girl to get it. ⁶She opened it and saw the baby. He was crying, and she felt sorry for him. "This is one of the Hebrew babies," she said.

⁷Then his sister asked Pharaoh's daughter, "Shall I go and get one of the Hebrew women to nurse the baby for you?"

⁸"Yes, go," she answered. And the girl went and got the baby's mother. ⁹Pharaoh's daughter said to her, "Take this baby and nurse him for me, and I will pay you." So the woman took the baby and nursed him. ¹⁰When the child grew older, she took him to Pharaoh's daughter and he became her son. She named him Moses,^c saying, "I drew him out of the water."

¹¹One day, after Moses had grown up, he went out to where his own people were and watched them at their hard labor. He saw an Egyptian beating a Hebrew, one of his own people. ¹²Glancing this way and that and seeing no one, he killed the Egyptian and hid him in the sand. ¹³The next day he went out and saw two Hebrews fighting. He asked the one in the wrong, "Why are you hitting your fellow Hebrew?"

¹⁴The man said, "Who made you ruler and judge over us? Are you thinking of killing me as you killed the Egyptian?" Then Moses was afraid and thought, "What I did must have become known."

¹⁵When Pharaoh heard of this, he tried to kill Moses, but Moses fled from Pharaoh and went to live in Midian, where he sat down by a well. ¹⁶Now a priest of Midian had seven daughters, and they came to draw water and fill the troughs to water their father's flock. ¹⁷Some shepherds came along and drove them away, but Moses got up and came to their rescue and watered their flock.

^b22 Masoretic Text; Samaritan Pentateuch, Septuagint and Targums *born to the Hebrews*   ^c10 *Moses* sounds like the Hebrew for *draw out.*

¹⁸When the girls returned to Reuel their father, he asked them, "Why have you returned so early today?"

¹⁹They answered, "An Egyptian rescued us from the shepherds. He even drew water for us and watered the flock."

²⁰"And where is he?" he asked his daughters. "Why did you leave him? Invite him to have something to eat."

²¹Moses agreed to stay with the man, who gave his daughter Zipporah to Moses in marriage. ²²Zipporah gave birth to a son, and Moses named him Gershom,ᵈ saying, "I have become an alien in a foreign land."

²³During that long period, the king of Egypt died. The Israelites groaned in their slavery and cried out, and their cry for help because of their slavery went up to God. ²⁴God heard their groaning and he remembered his covenant with Abraham, with Isaac and with Jacob. ²⁵So God looked on the Israelites and was concerned about them.

ᵈ22 *Gershom* sounds like the Hebrew for *an alien there.*

JANUARY 19 □ DAY 19
EXODUS 3–6
Confrontation with Pharaoh

 OVERVIEW After forty years of reflection, Moses concludes he is permanently disqualified from God's service. In a remarkable debate with the living God, Moses offers four excuses and begs the Lord to send someone else as his spokesman. Finally, when God provides Aaron as a mouthpiece, Moses confronts Pharaoh with God's message. As predicted, Pharaoh not only denies God's demand but increases the miseries of the Hebrews. Moses' popularity with his people plummets, but God assures Moses that he will keep his promise of deliverance.

Chapters 3–4		Chapter 5	Chapter 6
Moses' Call by God	Moses' Excuses to God	Pharaoh's Response to Moses	God's Reassurance to Moses
3:1 3:10	3:11 4:31		
God Confronts Moses		Moses Confronts Pharaoh	

 YOUR DAILY WALK The church has been likened to a football game in which thousands of spectators desperately in need of exercise are watching a handful of players desperately in need of rest.

Are you a spectator or a player?

In God's strategy for successful living, character is more important than intelligence. Before you can pull out your list of reasons excusing you from active duty in your local church, eavesdrop on an eighty-year-old shepherd as he argues with a burning bush. With good reason Moses anticipated resistance and rejection from his own people—to say nothing of Pharaoh. Besides, he had a speech impediment and an inferiority complex! Surely God was showing poor judgment (so Moses thought) in his choice of a deliverer for his people.

Patiently, thoroughly, God gave his rebuttal: I can use this bush, that staff in your hand, or even your stammering lips—whatever is available—to accomplish my plan and fulfill my promises. For all that you lack and everything you are not, I AM.

God probably isn't recruiting you to lead a nation out of bondage. But he definitely wants to show what he can accomplish through you. In response to his promise that "I AM all you need," will you answer, "I am available"?

INSIGHT Speak Softly and Carry a Big Stick
Moses' staff was subsequently used by God to turn water into blood, bring hail and lightning, summon locusts, divide the Red Sea, bring water out of rocks and signal victory in battle.

CHAPTER 3

Now Moses was tending the flock of Jethro his father-in-law, the priest of Midian, and he led the flock to the far side of the desert and came to Horeb, the mountain of God. ²There the angel of the LORD appeared to him in flames of fire from within a bush. Moses saw that though the bush was on fire it did not burn up. ³So Moses thought, "I will go over and see this strange sight—why the bush does not burn up."

⁴When the LORD saw that he had gone over to look, God called to him from within the bush, "Moses! Moses!"

And Moses said, "Here I am."

⁵"Do not come any closer," God said. "Take off your sandals, for the place where you are standing is holy ground." ⁶Then he said, "I am the God of your father, the God of Abraham, the God of Isaac and the God of Jacob." At this, Moses hid his face, because he was afraid to look at God.

⁷The LORD said, "I have indeed seen the misery of my people in Egypt. I have heard them crying out because of their slave drivers, and I am concerned about their suffering. ⁸So I have come down to rescue them from the hand of the Egyptians and to bring them up out of that land into a good and spacious land, a land flowing with milk and honey—the home of the Canaanites, Hittites, Amorites, Perizzites, Hivites and Jebusites. ⁹And now the cry of the Israelites has reached me, and I have seen the way the Egyptians are oppressing them. ¹⁰So now, go. I am sending you to Pharaoh to bring my people the Israelites out of Egypt."

¹¹But Moses said to God, "Who am I, that I should go to Pharaoh and bring the Israelites out of Egypt?"

¹²And God said, "I will be with you. And this will be the sign to you that it is I who have sent you: When you have brought the people out of Egypt, you*ᵉ* will worship God on this mountain."

¹³Moses said to God, "Suppose I go to the Israelites and say to them, 'The God of your fathers has sent me to you,' and they ask me, 'What is his name?' Then what shall I tell them?"

¹⁴God said to Moses, "I AM WHO I AM.*ᶠ* This is what you are to say to the Israelites: 'I AM has sent me to you.' "

¹⁵God also said to Moses, "Say to the Israelites, 'The LORD,*ᵍ* the God of your fathers—the God of Abraham, the God of Isaac and the God of Jacob—has sent me to you.' This is my name forever, the name by which I am to be remembered from generation to generation.

¹⁶"Go, assemble the elders of Israel and say to them, 'The LORD, the God of your fathers—the God of Abraham, Isaac and Jacob—appeared to me and said: I have watched over you and have seen what has been done to you in Egypt. ¹⁷And I have promised to bring you up out of your misery in Egypt into the land of the Canaanites, Hittites, Amorites, Perizzites, Hivites and Jebusites—a land flowing with milk and honey.'

¹⁸"The elders of Israel will listen to you. Then you and the elders are to go to the king of Egypt and say to him, 'The LORD, the God of the Hebrews, has met with us. Let us take a three-day journey into the desert to offer sacrifices to the LORD our God.' ¹⁹But I know that the king of Egypt will not let you go unless a mighty hand compels him. ²⁰So I will stretch out my hand and strike the Egyptians with all the wonders that I will perform among them. After that, he will let you go.

²¹"And I will make the Egyptians favorably disposed toward this people, so that when you leave you will not go empty-handed. ²²Every woman is to ask her neighbor and any woman living in her house for articles of silver and gold and for clothing, which you will put on your sons and daughters. And so you will plunder the Egyptians."

ᵉ12 The Hebrew is plural.   *ᶠ14* Or *I WILL BE WHAT I WILL BE*   *ᵍ15* The Hebrew for LORD sounds like and may be derived from the Hebrew for *I AM* in verse 14.

CHAPTER 4

Moses answered, "What if they do not believe me or listen to me and say, 'The LORD did not appear to you'?"

²Then the LORD said to him, "What is that in your hand?"

"A staff," he replied.

³The LORD said, "Throw it on the ground."

Moses threw it on the ground and it became a snake, and he ran from it. ⁴Then the LORD said to him, "Reach out your hand and take it by the tail." So Moses reached out and took hold of the snake and it turned back into a staff in his hand. ⁵"This," said the LORD, "is so that they may believe that the LORD, the God of their fathers—the God of Abraham, the God of Isaac and the God of Jacob—has appeared to you."

⁶Then the LORD said, "Put your hand inside your cloak." So Moses put his hand into his cloak, and when he took it out, it was leprous,^h like snow.

⁷"Now put it back into your cloak," he said. So Moses put his hand back into his cloak, and when he took it out, it was restored, like the rest of his flesh.

⁸Then the LORD said, "If they do not believe you or pay attention to the first miraculous sign, they may believe the second. ⁹But if they do not believe these two signs or listen to you, take some water from the Nile and pour it on the dry ground. The water you take from the river will become blood on the ground."

¹⁰Moses said to the LORD, "O Lord, I have never been eloquent, neither in the past nor since you have spoken to your servant. I am slow of speech and tongue."

¹¹The LORD said to him, "Who gave man his mouth? Who makes him deaf or mute? Who gives him sight or makes him blind? Is it not I, the LORD? ¹²Now go; I will help you speak and will teach you what to say."

¹³But Moses said, "O Lord, please send someone else to do it."

¹⁴Then the LORD's anger burned against Moses and he said, "What about your brother, Aaron the Levite? I know he can speak well. He is already on his way to meet you, and his heart will be glad when he sees you. ¹⁵You shall speak to him and

put words in his mouth; I will help both of you speak and will teach you what to do. ¹⁶He will speak to the people for you, and it will be as if he were your mouth and as if you were God to him. ¹⁷But take this staff in your hand so you can perform miraculous signs with it."

¹⁸Then Moses went back to Jethro his father-in-law and said to him, "Let me go back to my own people in Egypt to see if any of them are still alive."

Jethro said, "Go, and I wish you well."

¹⁹Now the LORD had said to Moses in Midian, "Go back to Egypt, for all the men who wanted to kill you are dead." ²⁰So Moses took his wife and sons, put them on a donkey and started back to Egypt. And he took the staff of God in his hand.

²¹The LORD said to Moses, "When you return to Egypt, see that you perform before Pharaoh all the wonders I have given you the power to do. But I will harden his heart so that he will not let the people go. ²²Then say to Pharaoh, 'This is what the LORD says: Israel is my firstborn son, ²³and I told you, "Let my son go, so he may worship me." But you refused to let him go; so I will kill your firstborn son.' "

²⁴At a lodging place on the way, the LORD met ⌊Moses⌋ⁱ and was about to kill him. ²⁵But Zipporah took a flint knife, cut off her son's foreskin and touched ⌊Moses'⌋ feet with it.^j "Surely you are a bridegroom of blood to me," she said. ²⁶So the LORD let him alone. (At that time she said "bridegroom of blood," referring to circumcision.)

²⁷The LORD said to Aaron, "Go into the desert to meet Moses." So he met Moses at the mountain of God and kissed him. ²⁸Then Moses told Aaron everything the LORD had sent him to say, and also about all the miraculous signs he had commanded him to perform.

²⁹Moses and Aaron brought together all the elders of the Israelites, ³⁰and Aaron told them everything the LORD had said to Moses. He also performed the signs before the people, ³¹and they believed. And when they heard that the LORD was concerned about them and had seen their misery, they bowed down and worshiped.

---

^h6 The Hebrew word was used for various diseases affecting the skin—not necessarily leprosy.   ⁱ24 Or ⌊Moses' son⌋; Hebrew him   ^j25 Or and drew near ⌊Moses'⌋ feet

CHAPTER 5

Afterward Moses and Aaron went to Pharaoh and said, "This is what the LORD, the God of Israel, says: 'Let my people go, so that they may hold a festival to me in the desert.'"

²Pharaoh said, "Who is the LORD, that I should obey him and let Israel go? I do not know the LORD and I will not let Israel go."

³Then they said, "The God of the Hebrews has met with us. Now let us take a three-day journey into the desert to offer sacrifices to the LORD our God, or he may strike us with plagues or with the sword."

⁴But the king of Egypt said, "Moses and Aaron, why are you taking the people away from their labor? Get back to your work!" ⁵Then Pharaoh said, "Look, the people of the land are now numerous, and you are stopping them from working."

⁶That same day Pharaoh gave this order to the slave drivers and foremen in charge of the people: ⁷"You are no longer to supply the people with straw for making bricks; let them go and gather their own straw. ⁸But require them to make the same number of bricks as before; don't reduce the quota. They are lazy; that is why they are crying out, 'Let us go and sacrifice to our God.' ⁹Make the work harder for the men so that they keep working and pay no attention to lies."

¹⁰Then the slave drivers and the foremen went out and said to the people, "This is what Pharaoh says: 'I will not give you any more straw. ¹¹Go and get your own straw wherever you can find it, but your work will not be reduced at all.'" ¹²So the people scattered all over Egypt to gather stubble to use for straw. ¹³The slave drivers kept pressing them, saying, "Complete the work required of you for each day, just as when you had straw." ¹⁴The Israelite foremen appointed by Pharaoh's slave drivers were beaten and were asked, "Why didn't you meet your quota of bricks yesterday or today, as before?"

¹⁵Then the Israelite foremen went and appealed to Pharaoh: "Why have you treated your servants this way? ¹⁶Your servants are given no straw, yet we are told, 'Make bricks!' Your servants are being beaten, but the fault is with your own people."

¹⁷Pharaoh said, "Lazy, that's what you are—lazy! That is why you keep saying, 'Let us go and sacrifice to the LORD.' ¹⁸Now get to work. You will not be given any straw, yet you must produce your full quota of bricks."

¹⁹The Israelite foremen realized they were in trouble when they were told, "You are not to reduce the number of bricks required of you for each day." ²⁰When they left Pharaoh, they found Moses and Aaron waiting to meet them, ²¹and they said, "May the LORD look upon you and judge you! You have made us a stench to Pharaoh and his officials and have put a sword in their hand to kill us."

²²Moses returned to the LORD and said, "O Lord, why have you brought trouble upon this people? Is this why you sent me? ²³Ever since I went to Pharaoh to speak in your name, he has brought trouble upon this people, and you have not rescued your people at all."

CHAPTER 6

Then the LORD said to Moses, "Now you will see what I will do to Pharaoh: Because of my mighty hand he will let them go; because of my mighty hand he will drive them out of his country."

²God also said to Moses, "I am the LORD. ³I appeared to Abraham, to Isaac and to Jacob as God Almighty,ᵏ but by my name the LORDˡ I did not make myself known to them.ᵐ ⁴I also established my covenant with them to give them the land of Canaan, where they lived as aliens. ⁵Moreover, I have heard the groaning of the Israelites, whom the Egyptians are enslaving, and I have remembered my covenant.

⁶"Therefore, say to the Israelites: 'I am the LORD, and I will bring you out from under the yoke of the Egyptians. I will free you from being slaves to them, and I will redeem you with an outstretched arm and with mighty acts of judgment. ⁷I will take you as my own people, and I will be your God. Then you will know that I am the LORD your God, who brought you out from under the yoke of the Egyptians. ⁸And I will bring you to the land I swore with uplifted hand to give to Abraham, to

ᵏ3 Hebrew *El-Shaddai*   ˡ3 See note at Exodus 3:15.   ᵐ3 Or *Almighty, and by my name the LORD did I not let myself be known to them?*

Isaac and to Jacob. I will give it to you as a possession. I am the LORD.' "

⁹Moses reported this to the Israelites, but they did not listen to him because of their discouragement and cruel bondage.

¹⁰Then the LORD said to Moses, ¹¹"Go, tell Pharaoh king of Egypt to let the Israelites go out of his country."

¹²But Moses said to the LORD, "If the Israelites will not listen to me, why would Pharaoh listen to me, since I speak with faltering lips[n]?"

¹³Now the LORD spoke to Moses and Aaron about the Israelites and Pharaoh king of Egypt, and he commanded them to bring the Israelites out of Egypt.

¹⁴These were the heads of their families[o]:

The sons of Reuben the firstborn son of Israel were Hanoch and Pallu, Hezron and Carmi. These were the clans of Reuben.

¹⁵The sons of Simeon were Jemuel, Jamin, Ohad, Jakin, Zohar and Shaul the son of a Canaanite woman. These were the clans of Simeon.

¹⁶These were the names of the sons of Levi according to their records: Gershon, Kohath and Merari. Levi lived 137 years.

¹⁷The sons of Gershon, by clans, were Libni and Shimei.

¹⁸The sons of Kohath were Amram, Izhar, Hebron and Uzziel. Kohath lived 133 years.

¹⁹The sons of Merari were Mahli and Mushi.

These were the clans of Levi according to their records.

²⁰Amram married his father's sister Jochebed, who bore him Aaron and Moses. Amram lived 137 years.

²¹The sons of Izhar were Korah, Nepheg and Zicri.

²²The sons of Uzziel were Mishael, Elzaphan and Sithri.

²³Aaron married Elisheba, daughter of Amminadab and sister of Nahshon, and she bore him Nadab and Abihu, Eleazar and Ithamar.

²⁴The sons of Korah were Assir, Elkanah and Abiasaph. These were the Korahite clans.

²⁵Eleazar son of Aaron married one of the daughters of Putiel, and she bore him Phinehas.

These were the heads of the Levite families, clan by clan.

²⁶It was this same Aaron and Moses to whom the LORD said, "Bring the Israelites out of Egypt by their divisions." ²⁷They were the ones who spoke to Pharaoh king of Egypt about bringing the Israelites out of Egypt. It was the same Moses and Aaron.

²⁸Now when the LORD spoke to Moses in Egypt, ²⁹he said to him, "I am the LORD. Tell Pharaoh king of Egypt everything I tell you."

³⁰But Moses said to the LORD, "Since I speak with faltering lips, why would Pharaoh listen to me?"

---

[n] 12 Hebrew *I am uncircumcised of lips*; also in verse 30   [o] 14 The Hebrew for *families* here and in verse 25 refers to units larger than clans.

JANUARY 20 □ DAY 20
EXODUS 7–10
First Nine Plagues in Egypt

OVERVIEW Pharaoh's stubborn refusal to release the people prompts God to unleash nine devastating plagues against Egypt. Moved by this display of God's power, Pharaoh repeatedly promises to release the nation. But when the time arrives, his heart is hardened, and he breaks his word. To shatter Pharaoh's unyielding will, God prepares one last plague—the visit of the death angel to every unprepared home in the land.

Ch. 7	Chapter 8				Chapter 9			Chapter 10	
First Nine Plagues upon Egypt									
Blood	Frogs	Gnats	Flies	Dead Livestock	Boils	Hail	Locusts	Darkness	
1	15	16 19	20 32	1 7	8 12	13 35	1 20	21 29	
The gods of Egypt vs. the God of Israel									

YOUR DAILY WALK While on a trip, have you ever yielded to the temptation to take what you thought was a shortcut, only to find yourself hopelessly lost? Maybe you've experienced the same thing in your spiritual life as you looked for a shortcut to accomplish God's will.

One Almighty is more than all mighties.

"Alternate routes" may look very attractive, but they can often have unexpected consequences. Pharaoh offered Moses four shortcuts to releasing the people from bondage (8:25, 28; 10:11, 24). None of the four conformed to God's specific instructions. They were only attempts by Pharaoh to hide his refusal to obey God. Moses detected Pharaoh's motives, for he knew that *anything short of obedience is disobedience.*

That principle is still true today. There is no safe "alternate route" when the Bible clearly states, "This is what the LORD says." Nothing short of doing God's will in God's way will guarantee that you arrive at your intended destination! Look up the following verses to discover how God wants to guide you from the pages of his Word:
- The Bible is a _____ and a _____ (Psalm 119:105).
- The entrance of God's Word gives _____ (Psalm 119:130).
- The best place to hide God's Word is _____ (Psalm 119:11).

Now map out God's route to one of *your* destinations today!

INSIGHT Terror in the Sky
The locust, tool of divine judgment upon Egypt (Exodus 10) and numerous other nations in the pages of Scripture, is one of nature's most destructive creatures. A swarm of locusts may number more than one hundred thousand insects per square mile and can eat thousands of acres of vegetation in a single day.

CHAPTER 7
Then the LORD said to Moses, "See, I have made you like God to Pharaoh, and your brother Aaron will be your prophet. ²You are to say everything I command you, and your brother Aaron is to tell Pharaoh to let the Israelites go out of his country. ³But I will harden Pharaoh's heart, and though I multiply my miraculous signs and wonders in Egypt, ⁴he will not listen to you. Then I will lay my hand on Egypt and with mighty acts of judgment I will bring out my divisions, my people the Israelites. ⁵And the Egyptians will know that I am the LORD when I stretch out my hand against Egypt and bring the Israelites out of it."

⁶Moses and Aaron did just as the LORD commanded them. ⁷Moses was eighty years old and Aaron eighty-three when they spoke to Pharaoh.

⁸The LORD said to Moses and Aaron,

⁹"When Pharaoh says to you, 'Perform a miracle,' then say to Aaron, 'Take your staff and throw it down before Pharaoh,' and it will become a snake."

¹⁰So Moses and Aaron went to Pharaoh and did just as the LORD commanded. Aaron threw his staff down in front of Pharaoh and his officials, and it became a snake. ¹¹Pharaoh then summoned wise men and sorcerers, and the Egyptian magicians also did the same things by their secret arts: ¹²Each one threw down his staff and it became a snake. But Aaron's staff swallowed up their staffs. ¹³Yet Pharaoh's heart became hard and he would not listen to them, just as the LORD had said.

¹⁴Then the LORD said to Moses, "Pharaoh's heart is unyielding; he refuses to let the people go. ¹⁵Go to Pharaoh in the morning as he goes out to the water. Wait on the bank of the Nile to meet him, and

take in your hand the staff that was changed into a snake. [16]Then say to him, 'The LORD, the God of the Hebrews, has sent me to say to you: Let my people go, so that they may worship me in the desert. But until now you have not listened. [17]This is what the LORD says: By this you will know that I am the LORD: With the staff that is in my hand I will strike the water of the Nile, and it will be changed into blood. [18]The fish in the Nile will die, and the river will stink; the Egyptians will not be able to drink its water.' "

[19]The LORD said to Moses, "Tell Aaron, 'Take your staff and stretch out your hand over the waters of Egypt—over the streams and canals, over the ponds and all the reservoirs'—and they will turn to blood. Blood will be everywhere in Egypt, even in the wooden buckets and stone jars."

[20]Moses and Aaron did just as the LORD had commanded. He raised his staff in the presence of Pharaoh and his officials and struck the water of the Nile, and all the water was changed into blood. [21]The fish in the Nile died, and the river smelled so bad that the Egyptians could not drink its water. Blood was everywhere in Egypt.

[22]But the Egyptian magicians did the same things by their secret arts, and Pharaoh's heart became hard; he would not listen to Moses and Aaron, just as the LORD had said. [23]Instead, he turned and went into his palace, and did not take even this to heart. [24]And all the Egyptians dug along the Nile to get drinking water, because they could not drink the water of the river.

[25]Seven days passed after the LORD struck the Nile.

CHAPTER 8 [1]Then the LORD said to Moses, "Go to Pharaoh and say to him, 'This is what the LORD says: Let my people go, so that they may worship me. [2]If you refuse to let them go, I will plague your whole country with frogs. [3]The Nile will teem with frogs. They will come up into your palace and your bedroom and onto your bed, into the houses of your officials and on your people, and into your ovens and kneading troughs. [4]The frogs will go up on you and your people and all your officials.' "

[5]Then the LORD said to Moses, "Tell Aaron, 'Stretch out your hand with your staff over the streams and canals and ponds, and make frogs come up on the land of Egypt.' "

[6]So Aaron stretched out his hand over the waters of Egypt, and the frogs came up and covered the land. [7]But the magicians did the same things by their secret arts; they also made frogs come up on the land of Egypt.

[8]Pharaoh summoned Moses and Aaron and said, "Pray to the LORD to take the frogs away from me and my people, and I will let your people go to offer sacrifices to the LORD."

[9]Moses said to Pharaoh, "I leave to you the honor of setting the time for me to pray for you and your officials and your people that you and your houses may be rid of the frogs, except for those that remain in the Nile."

[10]"Tomorrow," Pharaoh said.

Moses replied, "It will be as you say, so that you may know there is no one like the LORD our God. [11]The frogs will leave you and your houses, your officials and your people; they will remain only in the Nile."

[12]After Moses and Aaron left Pharaoh, Moses cried out to the LORD about the frogs he had brought on Pharaoh. [13]And the LORD did what Moses asked. The frogs died in the houses, in the courtyards and in the fields. [14]They were piled into heaps, and the land reeked of them. [15]But when Pharaoh saw that there was relief, he hardened his heart and would not listen to Moses and Aaron, just as the LORD had said.

[16]Then the LORD said to Moses, "Tell Aaron, 'Stretch out your staff and strike the dust of the ground,' and throughout the land of Egypt the dust will become gnats." [17]They did this, and when Aaron stretched out his hand with the staff and struck the dust of the ground, gnats came upon men and animals. All the dust throughout the land of Egypt became gnats. [18]But when the magicians tried to produce gnats by their secret arts, they could not. And the gnats were on men and animals.

[19]The magicians said to Pharaoh, "This is the finger of God." But Pharaoh's heart was hard and he would not listen, just as the LORD had said.

[20]Then the LORD said to Moses, "Get up early in the morning and confront Pharaoh as he goes to the water and say to

him, 'This is what the LORD says: Let my people go, so that they may worship me. ²¹If you do not let my people go, I will send swarms of flies on you and your officials, on your people and into your houses. The houses of the Egyptians will be full of flies, and even the ground where they are.

²²" 'But on that day I will deal differently with the land of Goshen, where my people live; no swarms of flies will be there, so that you will know that I, the LORD, am in this land. ²³I will make a distinction[p] between my people and your people. This miraculous sign will occur tomorrow.' "

²⁴And the LORD did this. Dense swarms of flies poured into Pharaoh's palace and into the houses of his officials, and throughout Egypt the land was ruined by the flies.

²⁵Then Pharaoh summoned Moses and Aaron and said, "Go, sacrifice to your God here in the land."

²⁶But Moses said, "That would not be right. The sacrifices we offer the LORD our God would be detestable to the Egyptians. And if we offer sacrifices that are detestable in their eyes, will they not stone us? ²⁷We must take a three-day journey into the desert to offer sacrifices to the LORD our God, as he commands us."

²⁸Pharaoh said, "I will let you go to offer sacrifices to the LORD your God in the desert, but you must not go very far. Now pray for me."

²⁹Moses answered, "As soon as I leave you, I will pray to the LORD, and tomorrow the flies will leave Pharaoh and his officials and his people. Only be sure that Pharaoh does not act deceitfully again by not letting the people go to offer sacrifices to the LORD."

³⁰Then Moses left Pharaoh and prayed to the LORD, ³¹and the LORD did what Moses asked: The flies left Pharaoh and his officials and his people; not a fly remained. ³²But this time also Pharaoh hardened his heart and would not let the people go.

CHAPTER 9
Then the LORD said to Moses, "Go to Pharaoh and say to him, 'This is what the LORD, the God of the Hebrews, says: "Let my people go, so that they may worship me." ²If you refuse to let them go and continue to hold them back, ³the hand of the LORD will bring a terrible plague on your livestock in the field—on your horses and donkeys and camels and on your cattle and sheep and goats. ⁴But the LORD will make a distinction between the livestock of Israel and that of Egypt, so that no animal belonging to the Israelites will die.' "

⁵The LORD set a time and said, "Tomorrow the LORD will do this in the land." ⁶And the next day the LORD did it: All the livestock of the Egyptians died, but not one animal belonging to the Israelites died. ⁷Pharaoh sent men to investigate and found that not even one of the animals of the Israelites had died. Yet his heart was unyielding and he would not let the people go.

⁸Then the LORD said to Moses and Aaron, "Take handfuls of soot from a furnace and have Moses toss it into the air in the presence of Pharaoh. ⁹It will become fine dust over the whole land of Egypt, and festering boils will break out on men and animals throughout the land."

¹⁰So they took soot from a furnace and stood before Pharaoh. Moses tossed it into the air, and festering boils broke out on men and animals. ¹¹The magicians could not stand before Moses because of the boils that were on them and on all the Egyptians. ¹²But the LORD hardened Pharaoh's heart and he would not listen to Moses and Aaron, just as the LORD had said to Moses.

¹³Then the LORD said to Moses, "Get up early in the morning, confront Pharaoh and say to him, 'This is what the LORD, the God of the Hebrews, says: Let my people go, so that they may worship me, ¹⁴or this time I will send the full force of my plagues against you and against your officials and your people, so you may know that there is no one like me in all the earth. ¹⁵For by now I could have stretched out my hand and struck you and your people with a plague that would have wiped you off the earth. ¹⁶But I have raised you up[q] for this very purpose, that I might show you my power and that my name might be proclaimed in all the earth. ¹⁷You still set yourself against my

p23 Septuagint and Vulgate; Hebrew *will put a deliverance*   q16 Or *have spared you* people and will not let them go. ¹⁸There-fore, at this time tomorrow I will send the worst hailstorm that has ever fallen on Egypt, from the day it was founded till now. ¹⁹Give an order now to bring your livestock and everything you have in the field to a place of shelter, because the hail will fall on every man and animal that has not been brought in and is still out in the field, and they will die.' "

²⁰Those officials of Pharaoh who feared the word of the LORD hurried to bring their slaves and their livestock inside. ²¹But those who ignored the word of the LORD left their slaves and livestock in the field.

²²Then the LORD said to Moses, "Stretch out your hand toward the sky so that hail will fall all over Egypt—on men and ani-mals and on everything growing in the fields of Egypt." ²³When Moses stretched out his staff toward the sky, the LORD sent thunder and hail, and lightning flashed down to the ground. So the LORD rained hail on the land of Egypt; ²⁴hail fell and lightning flashed back and forth. It was the worst storm in all the land of Egypt since it had become a nation. ²⁵Throughout Egypt hail struck every-thing in the fields—both men and ani-mals; it beat down everything growing in the fields and stripped every tree. ²⁶The only place it did not hail was the land of Goshen, where the Israelites were.

²⁷Then Pharaoh summoned Moses and Aaron. "This time I have sinned," he said to them. "The LORD is in the right, and I and my people are in the wrong. ²⁸Pray to the LORD, for we have had enough thun-der and hail. I will let you go; you don't have to stay any longer."

²⁹Moses replied, "When I have gone out of the city, I will spread out my hands in prayer to the LORD. The thunder will stop and there will be no more hail, so you may know that the earth is the LORD's. ³⁰But I know that you and your officials still do not fear the LORD God."

³¹(The flax and barley were destroyed, since the barley had headed and the flax was in bloom. ³²The wheat and spelt, however, were not destroyed, because they ripen later.)

³³Then Moses left Pharaoh and went out of the city. He spread out his hands

toward the LORD; the thunder and hail stopped, and the rain no longer poured down on the land. ³⁴When Pharaoh saw that the rain and hail and thunder had stopped, he sinned again: He and his offi-cials hardened their hearts. ³⁵So Pharaoh's heart was hard and he would not let the Israelites go, just as the LORD had said through Moses.

CHAPTER 10

Then the LORD said to Moses, "Go to Phar-aoh, for I have hardened his heart and the hearts of his officials so that I may per-form these miraculous signs of mine among them ²that you may tell your children and grandchildren how I dealt harshly with the Egyptians and how I performed my signs among them, and that you may know that I am the LORD."

³So Moses and Aaron went to Pharaoh and said to him, "This is what the LORD, the God of the Hebrews, says: 'How long will you refuse to humble yourself before me? Let my people go, so that they may worship me. ⁴If you refuse to let them go, I will bring locusts into your country to-morrow. ⁵They will cover the face of the ground so that it cannot be seen. They will devour what little you have left after the hail, including every tree that is growing in your fields. ⁶They will fill your houses and those of all your officials and all the Egyptians—something neither your fathers nor your forefathers have ever seen from the day they settled in this land till now.' " Then Moses turned and left Pharaoh.

⁷Pharaoh's officials said to him, "How long will this man be a snare to us? Let the people go, so that they may worship the LORD their God. Do you not yet realize that Egypt is ruined?"

⁸Then Moses and Aaron were brought back to Pharaoh. "Go, worship the LORD your God," he said. "But just who will be going?"

⁹Moses answered, "We will go with our young and old, with our sons and daugh-ters, and with our flocks and herds, be-cause we are to celebrate a festival to the LORD."

¹⁰Pharaoh said, "The LORD be with you— if I let you go, along with your women and children! Clearly you are bent on

evil.*r* ¹¹No! Have only the men go; and worship the LORD, since that's what you have been asking for." Then Moses and Aaron were driven out of Pharaoh's presence.

¹²And the LORD said to Moses, "Stretch out your hand over Egypt so that locusts will swarm over the land and devour everything growing in the fields, everything left by the hail."

¹³So Moses stretched out his staff over Egypt, and the LORD made an east wind blow across the land all that day and all that night. By morning the wind had brought the locusts; ¹⁴they invaded all Egypt and settled down in every area of the country in great numbers. Never before had there been such a plague of locusts, nor will there ever be again. ¹⁵They covered all the ground until it was black. They devoured all that was left after the hail—everything growing in the fields and the fruit on the trees. Nothing green remained on tree or plant in all the land of Egypt.

¹⁶Pharaoh quickly summoned Moses and Aaron and said, "I have sinned against the LORD your God and against you. ¹⁷Now forgive my sin once more and pray to the LORD your God to take this deadly plague away from me."

¹⁸Moses then left Pharaoh and prayed to the LORD. ¹⁹And the LORD changed the wind to a very strong west wind, which caught up the locusts and carried them into the Red Sea.*s* Not a locust was left anywhere in Egypt. ²⁰But the LORD hardened Pharaoh's heart, and he would not let the Israelites go.

²¹Then the LORD said to Moses, "Stretch out your hand toward the sky so that darkness will spread over Egypt—darkness that can be felt." ²²So Moses stretched out his hand toward the sky, and total darkness covered all Egypt for three days. ²³No one could see anyone else or leave his place for three days. Yet all the Israelites had light in the places where they lived.

²⁴Then Pharaoh summoned Moses and said, "Go, worship the LORD. Even your women and children may go with you; only leave your flocks and herds behind."

²⁵But Moses said, "You must allow us to have sacrifices and burnt offerings to present to the LORD our God. ²⁶Our livestock too must go with us; not a hoof is to be left behind. We have to use some of them in worshiping the LORD our God, and until we get there we will not know what we are to use to worship the LORD."

²⁷But the LORD hardened Pharaoh's heart, and he was not willing to let them go. ²⁸Pharaoh said to Moses, "Get out of my sight! Make sure you do not appear before me again! The day you see my face you will die."

²⁹"Just as you say," Moses replied, "I will never appear before you again."

*r*10 Or *Be careful, trouble is in store for you!*   *s*19 Hebrew *Yam Suph;* that is, Sea of Reeds

JANUARY 21 ☐ DAY 21
Choices That Affect Your Destiny

 LOOK BACK Joseph and Moses, a study in contrasts. Joseph grew up in a typical Hebrew household; Moses was raised with an Egyptian silver spoon in his mouth. Joseph spent his early years in prison; Moses spent his early years in the palace. Joseph was nearly a murder victim; Moses fled as a fugitive because of a murder he had committed. Joseph was promoted to the position of prime minister in Egypt; Moses was demoted from a similar position!

And yet in many ways these two men were similar. Both encountered God under miraculous circumstances (Joseph in visions, Moses at the burning bush). Both were used by God in a remarkable way (Joseph to administer famine relief in Egypt, Moses to lead God's people

out of Egyptian bondage). And both were faced with crucial decisions at pivotal moments in their lives—decisions that affected their destiny.

LOOK UP Life is a series of choices and consequences. Decide today to step in front of a speeding car, and you will face the consequences of that choice for the rest of your life (as brief as that life may be!). Decide to harbor bitterness in your heart for something someone said or did to you, and you will experience the byproduct of that bitterness. Decide to leave God out of your plans, and you will soon discover that life without God is foolish and unfulfilling (Psalm 14:1).

He who provides for this life but takes no care for the next is wise for a moment but a fool forever.

Consider for a moment some of the "could haves" from the lives of Joseph and Moses. Joseph could have been bitter and unforgiving for what his brothers did to him—and with good reason. He could have shaken his fist at God for the injustice he experienced in the pit and in prison. He could have been angry with God for the years that were wasted because of other people's cruelty and lies. He could have taken the credit for being able to interpret Pharaoh's dreams. But in each case he chose to do something else.

Moses could have chosen to keep his true identity hidden. He could have ignored the plight of his countrymen. He could have settled down in Midian and nurtured a grudge against God for the rest of his life. He could have ignored the burning bush and the commission he received from God. He could have allowed his past mistakes and present feelings of inadequacy to keep him from obeying God. But in each case he chose to do something else.

In each case, Joseph and Moses were faced with a choice. And the path they chose determined the destination they reached.

LOOK AHEAD Life is a matter of choices, not chances. And the choices you face today may be remarkably similar to those that confronted Joseph and Moses:
- Bitterness or forgiveness
- Anger or acceptance
- Self-promotion or seeking God's kingdom
- Self-pity over the past or putting the past behind you
- Comfortable compromise or painful obedience

Chances are good you won't find yourself standing before the world's most powerful leader. But then again, when you dare to choose wisely like a Joseph or a Moses, you never know.

JANUARY 22 ☐ DAY 22
EXODUS 11–12
Tenth Plague, Passover and Exodus

OVERVIEW In the end, it's no contest. Death touches every Egyptian family as the final plague brings destruction to every firstborn child and beast. But the Israelite homes escape death because their households are protected by the blood of a sacrificial animal slain as a substitute for the firstborn. Pharaoh, the stubborn monarch, commands the Hebrews to leave, and the long-awaited exodus begins. The holiday called *Passover* thereafter becomes an annual memorial of the salvation of God's people from their Egyptian homes of bondage.

Chapter 11		Chapter 12		
Tenth Plague Announced	Passover Observed	Firstborn Destroyed	Exodus Begun	
	1 28	29 36	37 51	
Packing Up		Moving Out		

YOUR DAILY WALK "One generation will commend your works to another; they will tell of your mighty acts" (Psalm 145:4).

If everyone turned gossip into prayer, there would be no more reason for gossip.

If someone were to write an article entitled "What to Do between God's Miracles," it might consist of a single word: *Remember.* The mighty supernatural acts of God on behalf of his people have been relatively few and far between. One of God's purposes for such spectacular demonstrations has been to reveal his power quietly at work behind the scenes. Because miracles like the ten plagues occurred infrequently, God's people were instructed to recall the past as a basis for faith in the present. And as an aid to feeble memories, God instituted memorials—such as the Passover—to be observed on a regular basis by his people throughout the generations.

What was a good idea then is a good idea now. Are there objects in your home that can serve to remind you of God's faithfulness in the past: a picture on the wall . . . a cancelled check . . . a scrapbook? Are there certain dates you could designate "Memorial Anniversaries" to recall special provisions of God? Select your own memorial today, and plan now to recall a mighty act of God in your life. Like Passover, let it become a yearly habit to recall God's goodness!

INSIGHT Israel's Severance Pay for Forced Labor
In their eagerness to remove the Israelites (and the plagues) from their land, the Egyptians turned over vast quantities of jewelry, gold and clothing—fair payment for years of slave labor!

CHAPTER 11

Now the LORD had said to Moses, "I will bring one more plague on Pharaoh and on Egypt. After that, he will let you go from here, and when he does, he will drive you out completely. ²Tell the people that men and women alike are to ask their neighbors for articles of silver and gold." ³(The LORD made the Egyptians favorably disposed toward the people, and Moses himself was highly regarded in Egypt by Pharaoh's officials and by the people.)

⁴So Moses said, "This is what the LORD says: 'About midnight I will go throughout Egypt. ⁵Every firstborn son in Egypt will die, from the firstborn son of Pharaoh, who sits on the throne, to the firstborn son of the slave girl, who is at her hand mill, and all the firstborn of the cattle as well. ⁶There will be loud wailing throughout Egypt—worse than there has ever been or ever will be again. ⁷But among the Israelites not a dog will bark at any man or animal.' Then you will know that the LORD makes a distinction between

Egypt and Israel. ⁸All these officials of yours will come to me, bowing down before me and saying, 'Go, you and all the people who follow you!' After that I will leave." Then Moses, hot with anger, left Pharaoh.

⁹The LORD had said to Moses, "Pharaoh will refuse to listen to you—so that my wonders may be multiplied in Egypt." ¹⁰Moses and Aaron performed all these wonders before Pharaoh, but the LORD hardened Pharaoh's heart, and he would not let the Israelites go out of his country.

CHAPTER 12

The LORD said to Moses and Aaron in Egypt, ²"This month is to be for you the first month, the first month of your year. ³Tell the whole community of Israel that on the tenth day of this month each man is to take a lamb^t for his family, one for each household. ⁴If any household is too small for a whole lamb, they must share one with their nearest neighbor, having taken into account the number of people

---

^t3 The Hebrew word can mean *lamb* or *kid*; also in verse 4.

there are. You are to determine the amount of lamb needed in accordance with what each person will eat. ⁵The animals you choose must be year-old males without defect, and you may take them from the sheep or the goats. ⁶Take care of them until the fourteenth day of the month, when all the people of the community of Israel must slaughter them at twilight. ⁷Then they are to take some of the blood and put it on the sides and tops of the doorframes of the houses where they eat the lambs. ⁸That same night they are to eat the meat roasted over the fire, along with bitter herbs, and bread made without yeast. ⁹Do not eat the meat raw or cooked in water, but roast it over the fire—head, legs and inner parts. ¹⁰Do not leave any of it till morning; if some is left till morning, you must burn it. ¹¹This is how you are to eat it: with your cloak tucked into your belt, your sandals on your feet and your staff in your hand. Eat it in haste; it is the LORD's Passover.

¹²"On that same night I will pass through Egypt and strike down every firstborn—both men and animals—and I will bring judgment on all the gods of Egypt. I am the LORD. ¹³The blood will be a sign for you on the houses where you are; and when I see the blood, I will pass over you. No destructive plague will touch you when I strike Egypt.

¹⁴"This is a day you are to commemorate; for the generations to come you shall celebrate it as a festival to the LORD—a lasting ordinance. ¹⁵For seven days you are to eat bread made without yeast. On the first day remove the yeast from your houses, for whoever eats anything with yeast in it from the first day through the seventh must be cut off from Israel. ¹⁶On the first day hold a sacred assembly, and another one on the seventh day. Do no work at all on these days, except to prepare food for everyone to eat—that is all you may do.

¹⁷"Celebrate the Feast of Unleavened Bread, because it was on this very day that I brought your divisions out of Egypt. Celebrate this day as a lasting ordinance for the generations to come. ¹⁸In the first month you are to eat bread made without yeast, from the evening of the fourteenth day until the evening of the twenty-first day. ¹⁹For seven days no yeast is to be found in your houses. And whoever eats anything with yeast in it must be cut off from the community of Israel, whether he is an alien or native-born. ²⁰Eat nothing made with yeast. Wherever you live, you must eat unleavened bread."

²¹Then Moses summoned all the elders of Israel and said to them, "Go at once and select the animals for your families and slaughter the Passover lamb. ²²Take a bunch of hyssop, dip it into the blood in the basin and put some of the blood on the top and on both sides of the doorframe. Not one of you shall go out the door of his house until morning. ²³When the LORD goes through the land to strike down the Egyptians, he will see the blood on the top and sides of the doorframe and will pass over that doorway, and he will not permit the destroyer to enter your houses and strike you down.

²⁴"Obey these instructions as a lasting ordinance for you and your descendants. ²⁵When you enter the land that the LORD will give you as he promised, observe this ceremony. ²⁶And when your children ask you, 'What does this ceremony mean to you?' ²⁷then tell them, 'It is the Passover sacrifice to the LORD, who passed over the houses of the Israelites in Egypt and spared our homes when he struck down the Egyptians.' " Then the people bowed down and worshiped. ²⁸The Israelites did just what the LORD commanded Moses and Aaron.

²⁹At midnight the LORD struck down all the firstborn in Egypt, from the firstborn of Pharaoh, who sat on the throne, to the firstborn of the prisoner, who was in the dungeon, and the firstborn of all the livestock as well. ³⁰Pharaoh and all his officials and all the Egyptians got up during the night, and there was loud wailing in Egypt, for there was not a house without someone dead.

³¹During the night Pharaoh summoned Moses and Aaron and said, "Up! Leave my people, you and the Israelites! Go, worship the LORD as you have requested. ³²Take your flocks and herds, as you have said, and go. And also bless me."

³³The Egyptians urged the people to hurry and leave the country. "For otherwise," they said, "we will all die!" ³⁴So the people took their dough before the yeast was added, and carried it on their shoulders in kneading troughs wrapped in

clothing. ³⁵The Israelites did as Moses in-structed and asked the Egyptians for arti-cles of silver and gold and for clothing. ³⁶The LORD had made the Egyptians fa-vorably disposed toward the people, and they gave them what they asked for; so they plundered the Egyptians.

³⁷The Israelites journeyed from Rame-ses to Succoth. There were about six hun-dred thousand men on foot, besides women and children. ³⁸Many other peo-ple went up with them, as well as large droves of livestock, both flocks and herds. ³⁹With the dough they had brought from Egypt, they baked cakes of unleavened bread. The dough was without yeast be-cause they had been driven out of Egypt and did not have time to prepare food for themselves.

⁴⁰Now the length of time the Israelite people lived in Egypt" was 430 years. ⁴¹At the end of the 430 years, to the very day, all the LORD's divisions left Egypt. ⁴²Because the LORD kept vigil that night to bring them out of Egypt, on this night all the Israelites are to keep vigil to honor the LORD for the generations to come.

ᵘ40 Masoretic Text; Samaritan Pentateuch and Septuagint *Egypt and Canaan*

⁴³The LORD said to Moses and Aaron, "These are the regulations for the Pass-over:

"No foreigner is to eat of it. ⁴⁴Any slave you have bought may eat of it after you have circumcised him, ⁴⁵but a temporary resident and a hired worker may not eat of it.

⁴⁶"It must be eaten inside one house; take none of the meat outside the house. Do not break any of the bones. ⁴⁷The whole community of Israel must cele-brate it.

⁴⁸"An alien living among you who wants to celebrate the LORD's Passover must have all the males in his household circumcised; then he may take part like one born in the land. No uncircumcised male may eat of it. ⁴⁹The same law applies to the native-born and to the alien living among you."

⁵⁰All the Israelites did just what the LORD had commanded Moses and Aaron. ⁵¹And on that very day the LORD brought the Israelites out of Egypt by their divi-sions.

JANUARY 23 □ DAY 23
EXODUS 13–15
Crossing the Red Sea

OVERVIEW Things get worse for the Israelites before they get better. God leads his band of 3 million refugees to the intersection of Baal Zephon and the Red Sea—a seemingly inescapable dead end. Pharaoh, experiencing yet another change of heart, dispatches a crack chariot division to bring the Israelite exodus to an end. Instead, the Egyptian army meets its end in the swirling waters of the Red Sea. Moses watches the people's panic turn to praise as they cross the sea bed dry-shod and sing a great song of jubilation to God their Savior.

Chapter 13	Chapter 14	Chapter 15
God's Guiding Cloud	Israel's Great Crossing	Moses' Grateful Chorus
Direction	Protection	Jubilation

YOUR DAILY WALK You are seated in church when you hear the words, "Please bow your head and worship the Lord in the quietness of your own heart." You put aside your bulletin and close your eyes. Then you think to yourself, *What am I supposed to do now?*

The miraculous is absolutely basic to Christianity. Worshiping God is a skill seldom taught . . . and infrequently practiced. The root meaning of *worship* involves recognizing the "worthship" of another. It is a response to the greatness of God. People in the Bible worshiped God for who he was (his person) and what he did (his works), for his actions are always consistent with his character.

If you had been standing with the Israelites on the far banks of the Red Sea as the waters swallowed up the Egyptian army, you would have had no trouble responding in an attitude of worship! Even today you can join in their chorus of praise. Read through their song in chapter 15 again, making one list of God's *actions* (conduct), which prompted worship from his people, and a second list of what is proclaimed about God's *attributes* (character). Now you, too, should be ready to "sing the praises" of your God and Savior today!

 INSIGHT Taking the Scenic Route
Israel's God and guide (in the form of a cloudy pillar) steered the travelers away from the most direct route to Canaan for at least two reasons: (1) to avoid certain warfare, and (2) to take Israel to the mountain of God (3:12). The nation needed to learn to walk with God before learning to fight for God.

CHAPTER 13

The Lord said to Moses, ²"Consecrate to me every firstborn male. The first offspring of every womb among the Israelites belongs to me, whether man or animal."

³Then Moses said to the people, "Commemorate this day, the day you came out of Egypt, out of the land of slavery, because the Lord brought you out of it with a mighty hand. Eat nothing containing yeast. ⁴Today, in the month of Abib, you are leaving. ⁵When the Lord brings you into the land of the Canaanites, Hittites, Amorites, Hivites and Jebusites—the land he swore to your forefathers to give you, a land flowing with milk and honey—you are to observe this ceremony in this month: ⁶For seven days eat bread made without yeast and on the seventh day hold a festival to the Lord. ⁷Eat unleavened bread during those seven days; nothing with yeast in it is to be seen among you, nor shall any yeast be seen anywhere within your borders. ⁸On that day tell your son, 'I do this because of what the Lord did for me when I came out of Egypt.' ⁹This observance will be for you like a sign on your hand and a reminder on your forehead that the law of the Lord is to be on your lips. For the Lord brought you out of Egypt with his mighty hand. ¹⁰You must keep this ordinance at the appointed time year after year.

¹¹"After the Lord brings you into the land of the Canaanites and gives it to you, as he promised on oath to you and your forefathers, ¹²you are to give over to the Lord the first offspring of every womb. All the firstborn males of your livestock belong to the Lord. ¹³Redeem with a lamb every firstborn donkey, but if you do not redeem it, break its neck. Redeem every firstborn among your sons.

¹⁴"In days to come, when your son asks you, 'What does this mean?' say to him, 'With a mighty hand the Lord brought us out of Egypt, out of the land of slavery. ¹⁵When Pharaoh stubbornly refused to let us go, the Lord killed every firstborn in Egypt, both man and animal. This is why I sacrifice to the Lord the first male offspring of every womb and redeem each of my firstborn sons.' ¹⁶And it will be like a sign on your hand and a symbol on your forehead that the Lord brought us out of Egypt with his mighty hand."

¹⁷When Pharaoh let the people go, God did not lead them on the road through the Philistine country, though that was shorter. For God said, "If they face war, they might change their minds and return to Egypt." ¹⁸So God led the people around by the desert road toward the Red Sea.ᵛ The Israelites went up out of Egypt armed for battle.

¹⁹Moses took the bones of Joseph with him because Joseph had made the sons of Israel swear an oath. He had said, "God will surely come to your aid, and then

ᵛ 18 Hebrew *Yam Suph;* that is, Sea of Reeds

you must carry my bones up with you from this place."[w]

[20]After leaving Succoth they camped at Etham on the edge of the desert. [21]By day the LORD went ahead of them in a pillar of cloud to guide them on their way and by night in a pillar of fire to give them light, so that they could travel by day or night. [22]Neither the pillar of cloud by day nor the pillar of fire by night left its place in front of the people.

CHAPTER 14

Then the LORD said to Moses, [2]"Tell the Israelites to turn back and encamp near Pi Hahiroth, between Migdol and the sea. They are to encamp by the sea, directly opposite Baal Zephon. [3]Pharaoh will think, 'The Israelites are wandering around the land in confusion, hemmed in by the desert.' [4]And I will harden Pharaoh's heart, and he will pursue them. But I will gain glory for myself through Pharaoh and all his army, and the Egyptians will know that I am the LORD." So the Israelites did this.

[5]When the king of Egypt was told that the people had fled, Pharaoh and his officials changed their minds about them and said, "What have we done? We have let the Israelites go and have lost their services!" [6]So he had his chariot made ready and took his army with him. [7]He took six hundred of the best chariots, along with all the other chariots of Egypt, with officers over all of them. [8]The LORD hardened the heart of Pharaoh king of Egypt, so that he pursued the Israelites, who were marching out boldly. [9]The Egyptians—all Pharaoh's horses and chariots, horsemen[x] and troops—pursued the Israelites and overtook them as they camped by the sea near Pi Hahiroth, opposite Baal Zephon.

[10]As Pharaoh approached, the Israelites looked up, and there were the Egyptians, marching after them. They were terrified and cried out to the LORD. [11]They said to Moses, "Was it because there were no graves in Egypt that you brought us to the desert to die? What have you done to us by bringing us out of Egypt? [12]Didn't we say to you in Egypt, 'Leave us alone; let us serve the Egyptians'? It would have

been better for us to serve the Egyptians than to die in the desert!"

[13]Moses answered the people, "Do not be afraid. Stand firm and you will see the deliverance the LORD will bring you today. The Egyptians you see today you will never see again. [14]The LORD will fight for you; you need only to be still."

[15]Then the LORD said to Moses, "Why are you crying out to me? Tell the Israelites to move on. [16]Raise your staff and stretch out your hand over the sea to divide the water so that the Israelites can go through the sea on dry ground. [17]I will harden the hearts of the Egyptians so that they will go in after them. And I will gain glory through Pharaoh and all his army, through his chariots and his horsemen. [18]The Egyptians will know that I am the LORD when I gain glory through Pharaoh, his chariots and his horsemen."

[19]Then the angel of God, who had been traveling in front of Israel's army, withdrew and went behind them. The pillar of cloud also moved from in front and stood behind them, [20]coming between the armies of Egypt and Israel. Throughout the night the cloud brought darkness to the one side and light to the other side; so neither went near the other all night long.

[21]Then Moses stretched out his hand over the sea, and all that night the LORD drove the sea back with a strong east wind and turned it into dry land. The waters were divided, [22]and the Israelites went through the sea on dry ground, with a wall of water on their right and on their left.

[23]The Egyptians pursued them, and all Pharaoh's horses and chariots and horsemen followed them into the sea. [24]During the last watch of the night the LORD looked down from the pillar of fire and cloud at the Egyptian army and threw it into confusion. [25]He made the wheels of their chariots come off[y] so that they had difficulty driving. And the Egyptians said, "Let's get away from the Israelites! The LORD is fighting for them against Egypt."

[26]Then the LORD said to Moses, "Stretch out your hand over the sea so that the waters may flow back over the Egyptians and their chariots and horsemen." [27]Moses stretched out his hand over the sea, and at daybreak the sea went back to its place.

---

w19 See Gen. 50:25.   *x9* Or *charioteers; also in verses 17, 18, 23, 26 and 28*   *y25* Or *He jammed the wheels of their chariots* (see Samaritan Pentateuch, Septuagint and Syriac)

The Egyptians were fleeing toward² it, and the LORD swept them into the sea. ²⁸The water flowed back and covered the chariots and horsemen—the entire army of Pharaoh that had followed the Israelites into the sea. Not one of them survived.

²⁹But the Israelites went through the sea on dry ground, with a wall of water on their right and on their left. ³⁰That day the LORD saved Israel from the hands of the Egyptians, and Israel saw the Egyptians lying dead on the shore. ³¹And when the Israelites saw the great power the LORD displayed against the Egyptians, the people feared the LORD and put their trust in him and in Moses his servant.

CHAPTER 15

Then Moses and the Israelites sang this song to the LORD:

"I will sing to the LORD,
  for he is highly exalted.
The horse and its rider
  he has hurled into the sea.
²The LORD is my strength and my song;
  he has become my salvation.
He is my God, and I will praise him,
  my father's God, and I will exalt
    him.
³The LORD is a warrior;
  the LORD is his name.
⁴Pharaoh's chariots and his army
  he has hurled into the sea.
The best of Pharaoh's officers
  are drowned in the Red Sea.ᵃ
⁵The deep waters have covered them;
  they sank to the depths like a stone.

⁶"Your right hand, O LORD,
  was majestic in power.
Your right hand, O LORD,
  shattered the enemy.
⁷In the greatness of your majesty
  you threw down those who opposed
    you.
You unleashed your burning anger;
  it consumed them like stubble.
⁸By the blast of your nostrils
  the waters piled up.
The surging waters stood firm like a
    wall;
  the deep waters congealed in the
    heart of the sea.

⁹"The enemy boasted,
  'I will pursue, I will overtake them.
I will divide the spoils;
  I will gorge myself on them.
I will draw my sword
  and my hand will destroy them.'
¹⁰But you blew with your breath,
  and the sea covered them.
They sank like lead
  in the mighty waters.

¹¹"Who among the gods is like you,
    O LORD?
Who is like you—
    majestic in holiness,
    awesome in glory,
    working wonders?
¹²You stretched out your right hand
  and the earth swallowed them.

¹³"In your unfailing love you will lead
  the people you have redeemed.
In your strength you will guide them
  to your holy dwelling.
¹⁴The nations will hear and tremble;
  anguish will grip the people of
    Philistia.
¹⁵The chiefs of Edom will be terrified,
  the leaders of Moab will be seized
    with trembling,
the peopleᵇ of Canaan will melt
    away;
¹⁶ terror and dread will fall upon
    them.
By the power of your arm
  they will be as still as a stone—
until your people pass by, O LORD,
  until the people you boughtᶜ pass
    by.
¹⁷You will bring them in and plant them
  on the mountain of your
    inheritance—
the place, O LORD, you made for your
    dwelling,
  the sanctuary, O Lord, your hands
    established.
¹⁸The LORD will reign
  for ever and ever."

¹⁹When Pharaoh's horses, chariots and horsemenᵈ went into the sea, the LORD brought the waters of the sea back over them, but the Israelites walked through the sea on dry ground. ²⁰Then Miriam the prophetess, Aaron's sister, took a tambourine in her hand, and all the women

---

²27 Or *from*   ᵃ4 Hebrew *Yam Suph*; that is, Sea of Reeds; also in verse 22   ᵇ15 Or *rulers*   ᶜ16 Or *created*
ᵈ19 Or *charioteers*

followed her, with tambourines and dancing. ²¹Miriam sang to them:

> "Sing to the LORD,
>   for he is highly exalted.
> The horse and its rider
>   he has hurled into the sea."

²²Then Moses led Israel from the Red Sea and they went into the Desert of Shur. For three days they traveled in the desert without finding water. ²³When they came to Marah, they could not drink its water because it was bitter. (That is why the place is called Marah.ᵉ) ²⁴So the people grumbled against Moses, saying, "What are we to drink?"

ᵉ23 *Marah* means *bitter.*

²⁵Then Moses cried out to the LORD, and the LORD showed him a piece of wood. He threw it into the water, and the water became sweet.

There the LORD made a decree and a law for them, and there he tested them. ²⁶He said, "If you listen carefully to the voice of the LORD your God and do what is right in his eyes, if you pay attention to his commands and keep all his decrees, I will not bring on you any of the diseases I brought on the Egyptians, for I am the LORD, who heals you."

²⁷Then they came to Elim, where there were twelve springs and seventy palm trees, and they camped there near the water.

JANUARY 24 ☐ DAY 24
EXODUS 16–18
Israel's Journey to Mount Sinai

 OVERVIEW Only days after the miracle of the Red Sea, grumbling and discontent begin to surface among the people on the march. The nation God delivered by faith must now learn to walk by faith, and they have much to learn! Of prime concern is finding sufficient water and food to sustain a caravan of 3 million people in the desolate desert. A month into the journey, when food and water supplies are exhausted, the people cry out anxiously to Moses. Miraculously, God provides manna, quail and water in abundance to remind them that he is the source of their supply. Even Moses must learn this lesson. Exhausted from attempting to administer the nation single-handedly, Moses follows the advice of his father-in-law and selects seventy assistants to help him with the work.

Chapter 16	Chapter 17	Chapter 18
Famine in the Desert	Thirst at Rephidim	Exhaustion in Moses' Office
Israel's Complaints		Moses' Coworkers

 YOUR DAILY WALK Have you found that your *blessings* are also your biggest *problems*? The things you thought would bring you the greatest joy are in fact the things that cause you the most headaches; for instance, the new car (which spends more time in the shop than on the road), the long-awaited child (who now has the house in a state of siege), the unexpected promotion (which produced those equally unexpected ulcers).

God gives us the ingredients for our daily bread, but he expects us to do the baking.

Israel learned the hard way that *blessings bring responsibility.* Daily manna was a wonderful provision from God, but it had to be collected and eaten in a particular way. God's presence in the pillar of cloud and fire was comforting, but it meant unquestioned obedience. When the pillar moved, Israel moved.

Make a list of some of God's recent blessings to you, including the ones that seem to give you grief. Next to each, put an obligation that is yours if you enjoy the blessing as God intended.

INSIGHT A Subtle Prophecy
The water from the rock at Rephidim beautifully symbolizes Christ, our life-giver. The apostle Paul wrote that the rock from which the Israelites drank was Christ (1 Corinthians 10:4). The life—and living water— that Jesus offers is available to you today! "If anyone is thirsty, let him come to me and drink. Whoever believes in me, as the Scripture has said, streams of living water will flow from within him" (John 7:37–38).

CHAPTER 16

The whole Israelite community set out from Elim and came to the Desert of Sin, which is between Elim and Sinai, on the fifteenth day of the second month after they had come out of Egypt. ²In the desert the whole community grumbled against Moses and Aaron. ³The Israelites said to them, "If only we had died by the LORD's hand in Egypt! There we sat around pots of meat and ate all the food we wanted, but you have brought us out into this desert to starve this entire assembly to death."

⁴Then the LORD said to Moses, "I will rain down bread from heaven for you. The people are to go out each day and gather enough for that day. In this way I will test them and see whether they will follow my instructions. ⁵On the sixth day they are to prepare what they bring in, and that is to be twice as much as they gather on the other days."

⁶So Moses and Aaron said to all the Israelites, "In the evening you will know that it was the LORD who brought you out of Egypt, ⁷and in the morning you will see the glory of the LORD, because he has heard your grumbling against him. Who are we, that you should grumble against us?" ⁸Moses also said, "You will know that it was the LORD when he gives you meat to eat in the evening and all the bread you want in the morning, because he has heard your grumbling against him. Who are we? You are not grumbling against us, but against the LORD."

⁹Then Moses told Aaron, "Say to the entire Israelite community, 'Come before the LORD, for he has heard your grumbling.' "

¹⁰While Aaron was speaking to the whole Israelite community, they looked toward the desert, and there was the glory of the LORD appearing in the cloud.

¹¹The LORD said to Moses, ¹²"I have heard the grumbling of the Israelites. Tell them, 'At twilight you will eat meat, and in the morning you will be filled with bread. Then you will know that I am the LORD your God.' "

¹³That evening quail came and covered the camp, and in the morning there was a layer of dew around the camp. ¹⁴When the dew was gone, thin flakes like frost on the ground appeared on the desert floor. ¹⁵When the Israelites saw it, they said to each other, "What is it?" For they did not know what it was.

Moses said to them, "It is the bread the LORD has given you to eat. ¹⁶This is what the LORD has commanded: 'Each one is to gather as much as he needs. Take an omer^f for each person you have in your tent.' "

¹⁷The Israelites did as they were told; some gathered much, some little. ¹⁸And when they measured it by the omer, he who gathered much did not have too much, and he who gathered little did not have too little. Each one gathered as much as he needed.

¹⁹Then Moses said to them, "No one is to keep any of it until morning."

²⁰However, some of them paid no attention to Moses; they kept part of it until morning, but it was full of maggots and began to smell. So Moses was angry with them.

²¹Each morning everyone gathered as much as he needed, and when the sun grew hot, it melted away. ²²On the sixth day, they gathered twice as much—two

f16 That is, probably about 2 quarts (about 2 liters); also in verses 18, 32, 33 and 36 omers⁸ for each person—and the leaders of the community came and reported this to Moses. ²³He said to them, "This is what the LORD commanded: 'Tomorrow is to be a day of rest, a holy Sabbath to the LORD. So bake what you want to bake and boil what you want to boil. Save whatever is left and keep it until morning.' "

²⁴So they saved it until morning, as Moses commanded, and it did not stink or get maggots in it. ²⁵"Eat it today," Moses said, "because today is a Sabbath to the LORD. You will not find any of it on the ground today. ²⁶Six days you are to gather it, but on the seventh day, the Sabbath, there will not be any."

²⁷Nevertheless, some of the people went out on the seventh day to gather it, but they found none. ²⁸Then the LORD said to Moses, "How long will youʰ refuse to keep my commands and my instructions? ²⁹Bear in mind that the LORD has given you the Sabbath; that is why on the sixth day he gives you bread for two days. Everyone is to stay where he is on the seventh day; no one is to go out." ³⁰So the people rested on the seventh day.

³¹The people of Israel called the bread manna.ⁱ It was white like coriander seed and tasted like wafers made with honey. ³²Moses said, "This is what the LORD has commanded: 'Take an omer of manna and keep it for the generations to come, so they can see the bread I gave you to eat in the desert when I brought you out of Egypt.' "

³³So Moses said to Aaron, "Take a jar and put an omer of manna in it. Then place it before the LORD to be kept for the generations to come."

³⁴As the LORD commanded Moses, Aaron put the manna in front of the Testimony, that it might be kept. ³⁵The Israelites ate manna forty years, until they came to a land that was settled; they ate manna until they reached the border of Canaan.

³⁶(An omer is one tenth of an ephah.)

CHAPTER 17
The whole Israelite community set out from the Desert of Sin, traveling from place to place as the LORD commanded. They camped at Rephidim, but there was no water for the people to drink. ²So they quarreled with Moses and said, "Give us water to drink."

Moses replied, "Why do you quarrel with me? Why do you put the LORD to the test?"

³But the people were thirsty for water there, and they grumbled against Moses. They said, "Why did you bring us up out of Egypt to make us and our children and livestock die of thirst?"

⁴Then Moses cried out to the LORD, "What am I to do with these people? They are almost ready to stone me."

⁵The LORD answered Moses, "Walk on ahead of the people. Take with you some of the elders of Israel and take in your hand the staff with which you struck the Nile, and go. ⁶I will stand there before you by the rock at Horeb. Strike the rock, and water will come out of it for the people to drink." So Moses did this in the sight of the elders of Israel. ⁷And he called the place Massahʲ and Meribahᵏ because the Israelites quarreled and because they tested the LORD saying, "Is the LORD among us or not?"

⁸The Amalekites came and attacked the Israelites at Rephidim. ⁹Moses said to Joshua, "Choose some of our men and go out to fight the Amalekites. Tomorrow I will stand on top of the hill with the staff of God in my hands."

¹⁰So Joshua fought the Amalekites as Moses had ordered, and Moses, Aaron and Hur went to the top of the hill. ¹¹As long as Moses held up his hands, the Israelites were winning, but whenever he lowered his hands, the Amalekites were winning. ¹²When Moses' hands grew tired, they took a stone and put it under him and he sat on it. Aaron and Hur held his hands up—one on one side, one on the other—so that his hands remained steady till sunset. ¹³So Joshua overcame the Amalekite army with the sword.

¹⁴Then the LORD said to Moses, "Write this on a scroll as something to be remembered and make sure that Joshua hears it, because I will completely blot out the memory of Amalek from under heaven."

¹⁵Moses built an altar and called it The LORD is my Banner. ¹⁶He said, "For hands were lifted up to the throne of the LORD.

⁸22 That is, probably about 4 quarts (about 4.5 liters)   ʰ28 The Hebrew is plural.   ⁱ31 *Manna* means *What is it?* (see verse 15).   ʲ7 *Massah* means *testing*.   ᵏ7 *Meribah* means *quarreling*.

The[l] LORD will be at war against the Amalekites from generation to generation."

CHAPTER 18

Now Jethro, the priest of Midian and father-in-law of Moses, heard of everything God had done for Moses and for his people Israel, and how the LORD had brought Israel out of Egypt.

[2]After Moses had sent away his wife Zipporah, his father-in-law Jethro received her [3]and her two sons. One son was named Gershom,[m] for Moses said, "I have become an alien in a foreign land"; [4]and the other was named Eliezer,[n] for he said, "My father's God was my helper; he saved me from the sword of Pharaoh."

[5]Jethro, Moses' father-in-law, together with Moses' sons and wife, came to him in the desert, where he was camped near the mountain of God. [6]Jethro had sent word to him, "I, your father-in-law Jethro, am coming to you with your wife and her two sons."

[7]So Moses went out to meet his father-in-law and bowed down and kissed him. They greeted each other and then went into the tent. [8]Moses told his father-in-law about everything the LORD had done to Pharaoh and the Egyptians for Israel's sake and about all the hardships they had met along the way and how the LORD had saved them.

[9]Jethro was delighted to hear about all the good things the LORD had done for Israel in rescuing them from the hand of the Egyptians. [10]He said, "Praise be to the LORD, who rescued you from the hand of the Egyptians and of Pharaoh, and who rescued the people from the hand of the Egyptians. [11]Now I know that the LORD is greater than all other gods, for he did this to those who had treated Israel arrogantly." [12]Then Jethro, Moses' father-in-law, brought a burnt offering and other sacrifices to God, and Aaron came with all the elders of Israel to eat bread with Moses' father-in-law in the presence of God.

[13]The next day Moses took his seat to serve as judge for the people, and they stood around him from morning till evening. [14]When his father-in-law saw all that Moses was doing for the people, he said, "What is this you are doing for the people? Why do you alone sit as judge, while all these people stand around you from morning till evening?"

[15]Moses answered him, "Because the people come to me to seek God's will. [16]Whenever they have a dispute, it is brought to me, and I decide between the parties and inform them of God's decrees and laws."

[17]Moses' father-in-law replied, "What you are doing is not good. [18]You and these people who come to you will only wear yourselves out. The work is too heavy for you; you cannot handle it alone. [19]Listen now to me and I will give you some advice, and may God be with you. You must be the people's representative before God and bring their disputes to him. [20]Teach them the decrees and laws, and show them the way to live and the duties they are to perform. [21]But select capable men from all the people—men who fear God, trustworthy men who hate dishonest gain—and appoint them as officials over thousands, hundreds, fifties and tens. [22]Have them serve as judges for the people at all times, but have them bring every difficult case to you; the simple cases they can decide themselves. That will make your load lighter, because they will share it with you. [23]If you do this and God so commands, you will be able to stand the strain, and all these people will go home satisfied."

[24]Moses listened to his father-in-law and did everything he said. [25]He chose capable men from all Israel and made them leaders of the people, officials over thousands, hundreds, fifties and tens. [26]They served as judges for the people at all times. The difficult cases they brought to Moses, but the simple ones they decided themselves.

[27]Then Moses sent his father-in-law on his way, and Jethro returned to his own country.

[l]16 Or "Because a hand was against the throne of the LORD, the   [m]3 Gershom sounds like the Hebrew for an alien there.
[n]4 Eliezer means my God is helper.

JANUARY 25 □ DAY 25
EXODUS 19–20
The Ten Commandments

OVERVIEW Except for its size, Israel could scarcely be called a nation. Up to this point it was just a vast group of unorganized people. Self-government was impossible in Egypt, and as yet there are still no laws. But at Mount Sinai, in a setting designed to remove distractions and focus attention on God, the people receive their charter as God's chosen nation. After declaring their willingness to obey the commands they are about to receive, the Israelites spend two days preparing themselves to hear God. On the third day, beginning with an awe-inspiring display on Mount Sinai, God delivers the broad moral principles on which the nation's social and religious life will be based.

Chapter 19			Chapter 20	
A Promised Blessing 1 6	A Prepared People 7 15	A Powerful God 16 25	Four Commands Godward 1 11	Six Commands Manward 12 26
The Setting			The Ten Commandments	

YOUR DAILY WALK "The Christian life is a bunch of do's and don'ts!" "The Christian life is liberty to do as I please!"

Stop! You're both wrong. To be sure, in Christ there is freedom from bondage to sin and release from the guilt of past failures. But *liberty* does not mean *license* to live as you please. Just because the Israelites were free from Egyptian slavery did not mean they were free to follow their every desire. God still wanted them to live as his chosen people, so he gave them rules for their daily conduct—not a list of do's and don'ts to spoil their fun, but a series of commands for their protection and profit.

The tablets at Sinai were given to show the need for the cross at Calvary.

Imagine what a football game would be like without rules: no boundaries, no clock, no referees, no time limit. Probably no fun! Rules are essential for the enjoyment of life.

As you read your way through the list of commandments in today's reading, try to think of at least one way in which each command would make your life happier or safer if you kept it unquestioningly. Is there one you need to work on today?

INSIGHT What Was the Hike Up Sinai Like?

Mount Sinai is best identified with Jebel Musa, a 7,363-foot peak on the southern end of a granite mountain ridge two miles long and one mile wide. Before it stretches a plain adequate to hold Israel's camp.

CHAPTER 19

In the third month after the Israelites left Egypt—on the very day—they came to the Desert of Sinai. ²After they set out from Rephidim, they entered the Desert of Sinai, and Israel camped there in the desert in front of the mountain.

³Then Moses went up to God, and the LORD called to him from the mountain and said, "This is what you are to say to the house of Jacob and what you are to tell the people of Israel: ⁴'You yourselves have seen what I did to Egypt, and how I carried you on eagles' wings and brought you to myself. ⁵Now if you obey me fully and keep my covenant, then out of all nations you will be my treasured possession. Although the whole earth is mine, ⁶you⁰ will be for me a kingdom of priests and a holy nation.' These are the words you are to speak to the Israelites."

⁷So Moses went back and summoned

⁰5,6 Or *possession, for the whole earth is mine.* ⁶*You*

the elders of the people and set before them all the words the Lord had commanded him to speak. ⁸The people all responded together, "We will do everything the Lord has said." So Moses brought their answer back to the Lord.

⁹The Lord said to Moses, "I am going to come to you in a dense cloud, so that the people will hear me speaking with you and will always put their trust in you." Then Moses told the Lord what the people had said.

¹⁰And the Lord said to Moses, "Go to the people and consecrate them today and tomorrow. Have them wash their clothes ¹¹and be ready by the third day, because on that day the Lord will come down on Mount Sinai in the sight of all the people. ¹²Put limits for the people around the mountain and tell them, 'Be careful that you do not go up the mountain or touch the foot of it. Whoever touches the mountain shall surely be put to death. ¹³He shall surely be stoned or shot with arrows; not a hand is to be laid on him. Whether man or animal, he shall not be permitted to live.' Only when the ram's horn sounds a long blast may they go up to the mountain."

¹⁴After Moses had gone down the mountain to the people, he consecrated them, and they washed their clothes. ¹⁵Then he said to the people, "Prepare yourselves for the third day. Abstain from sexual relations."

¹⁶On the morning of the third day there was thunder and lightning, with a thick cloud over the mountain, and a very loud trumpet blast. Everyone in the camp trembled. ¹⁷Then Moses led the people out of the camp to meet with God, and they stood at the foot of the mountain. ¹⁸Mount Sinai was covered with smoke, because the Lord descended on it in fire. The smoke billowed up from it like smoke from a furnace, the whole mountainᵖ trembled violently, ¹⁹and the sound of the trumpet grew louder and louder. Then Moses spoke and the voice of God answered him.�q

²⁰The Lord descended to the top of Mount Sinai and called Moses to the top of the mountain. So Moses went up ²¹and the Lord said to him, "Go down and warn the people so they do not force their way

through to see the Lord and many of them perish. ²²Even the priests, who approach the Lord, must consecrate themselves, or the Lord will break out against them."

²³Moses said to the Lord, "The people cannot come up Mount Sinai, because you yourself warned us, 'Put limits around the mountain and set it apart as holy.' "

²⁴The Lord replied, "Go down and bring Aaron up with you. But the priests and the people must not force their way through to come up to the Lord, or he will break out against them."

²⁵So Moses went down to the people and told them.

CHAPTER 20
And God spoke all these words:

²"I am the Lord your God, who brought you out of Egypt, out of the land of slavery.

³"You shall have no other gods beforeʳ me.

⁴"You shall not make for yourself an idol in the form of anything in heaven above or on the earth beneath or in the waters below. ⁵You shall not bow down to them or worship them; for I, the Lord your God, am a jealous God, punishing the children for the sin of the fathers to the third and fourth generation of those who hate me, ⁶but showing love to a thousand ˌgenerationsˌ of those who love me and keep my commandments.

⁷"You shall not misuse the name of the Lord your God, for the Lord will not hold anyone guiltless who misuses his name.

⁸"Remember the Sabbath day by keeping it holy. ⁹Six days you shall labor and do all your work, ¹⁰but the seventh day is a Sabbath to the Lord your God. On it you shall not do any work, neither you, nor your son or daughter, nor your manservant or maidservant, nor your animals, nor the alien within your gates. ¹¹For in six days the Lord made the heavens and the earth, the sea, and all that is in them,

---

ᵖ18 Most Hebrew manuscripts; a few Hebrew manuscripts and Septuagint *all the people*   q19 Or *and God answered him with thunder*   ʳ3 Or *besides* but he rested on the seventh day. Therefore the LORD blessed the Sabbath day and made it holy.

¹²"Honor your father and your mother, so that you may live long in the land the LORD your God is giving you.

¹³"You shall not murder.

¹⁴"You shall not commit adultery.

¹⁵"You shall not steal.

¹⁶"You shall not give false testimony against your neighbor.

¹⁷"You shall not covet your neighbor's house. You shall not covet your neighbor's wife, or his manservant or maidservant, his ox or donkey, or anything that belongs to your neighbor."

¹⁸When the people saw the thunder and lightning and heard the trumpet and saw the mountain in smoke, they trembled with fear. They stayed at a distance ¹⁹and said to Moses, "Speak to us yourself and we will listen. But do not have God speak to us or we will die."

²⁰Moses said to the people, "Do not be afraid. God has come to test you, so that the fear of God will be with you to keep you from sinning."

²¹The people remained at a distance, while Moses approached the thick darkness where God was.

²²Then the LORD said to Moses, "Tell the Israelites this: 'You have seen for yourselves that I have spoken to you from heaven: ²³Do not make any gods to be alongside me; do not make for yourselves gods of silver or gods of gold.

²⁴" 'Make an altar of earth for me and sacrifice on it your burnt offerings and fellowship offerings,ˢ your sheep and goats and your cattle. Wherever I cause my name to be honored, I will come to you and bless you. ²⁵If you make an altar of stones for me, do not build it with dressed stones, for you will defile it if you use a tool on it. ²⁶And do not go up to my altar on steps, lest your nakedness be exposed on it.'

ˢ24 Traditionally *peace offerings*

JANUARY 26 □ DAY 26
EXODUS 21–24
Civil and Ceremonial Laws

 OVERVIEW The law given by God to Israel at Sinai falls into three categories: moral laws (Exodus 20), civil and social laws (Exodus 21–23) and religious laws (Exodus 24—Leviticus). Today's reading contains the laws that comprise the Book of the Covenant (24:7) given along with the Ten Commandments. Following a formal ceremony ratifying the covenant, Moses is called again by God to Mount Sinai to receive further revelation.

Chapters 21–22	Chapter 23	Chapter 24
Relationships under the Law	Relgious Observances under the Law	Ratification of the Law
Civil Laws	Ceremonial Laws	Compulsory Laws

 YOUR DAILY WALK "If I've told you once, I've told you *a hundred times . . . !*"

Some things bear repeating, and even then they don't always sink in. God's word to Israel in the first two commandments could hardly have been clearer: No other gods . . . no idols. Yet he would later repeat those same warnings again and again. He wanted to impress upon his people the seriousness of his lordship and to make certain

Where law ends, tyranny begins.

they understood the necessity for exclusive devotion to the God of Israel.

God knew full well the principle that you eventually worship what you serve. Therefore, whatever or whoever commands your attention becomes your god. Recognizing that fact can help you guard against idolatry. Here are two questions that may point to the real "lord" of your life:

1. What do you think about when your mind is in neutral?
2. What do you do during your idle moments?

Review your own loyalties, and then fill in the blank: "An objective observer of my life over the past week would conclude that _____ is my god." Is there something that needs to change so that you, like Israel, have "no other gods" besides the Lord?

INSIGHT A Forbidden Recipe
The prohibition against cooking a young goat in its mother's milk (23:19) made little sense to modern scholars until archaeological discoveries revealed that the practice was current in Canaan as a pagan magic spell connected with fertility rites.

CHAPTER 21

"These are the laws you are to set before them:

2"If you buy a Hebrew servant, he is to serve you for six years. But in the seventh year, he shall go free, without paying anything. 3If he comes alone, he is to go free alone; but if he has a wife when he comes, she is to go with him. 4If his master gives him a wife and she bears him sons or daughters, the woman and her children shall belong to her master, and only the man shall go free.

5"But if the servant declares, 'I love my master and my wife and children and do not want to go free,' 6then his master must take him before the judges.ᵗ He shall take him to the door or the doorpost and pierce his ear with an awl. Then he will be his servant for life.

7"If a man sells his daughter as a servant, she is not to go free as menservants do. 8If she does not please the master who has selected her for himself,ᵘ he must let her be redeemed. He has no right to sell her to foreigners, because he has broken faith with her. 9If he selects her for his son, he must grant her the rights of a daughter. 10If he marries another woman, he must not deprive the first one of her food, clothing and marital rights. 11If he does not provide her with these three things, she is to go free, without any payment of money.

12"Anyone who strikes a man and kills him shall surely be put to death. 13However, if he does not do it intentionally, but God lets it happen, he is to flee to a place I will designate. 14But if a man schemes and kills another man deliberately, take him away from my altar and put him to death.

15"Anyone who attacksᵛ his father or his mother must be put to death.

16"Anyone who kidnaps another and either sells him or still has him when he is caught must be put to death.

17"Anyone who curses his father or mother must be put to death.

18"If men quarrel and one hits the other with a stone or with his fistʷ and he does not die but is confined to bed, 19the one who struck the blow will not be held responsible if the other gets up and walks around outside with his staff; however, he must pay the injured man for the loss of his time and see that he is completely healed.

20"If a man beats his male or female slave with a rod and the slave dies as a direct result, he must be punished, 21but he is not to be punished if the slave gets up after a day or two, since the slave is his property.

22"If men who are fighting hit a pregnant woman and she gives birth prematurelyˣ but there is no serious injury, the offender must be fined whatever the woman's husband demands and the court allows. 23But if there is serious injury, you are to take life for life, 24eye for eye, tooth for tooth, hand for hand, foot for foot,

ᵗ6 Or before God   ᵘ8 Or master so that he does not choose her   ᵛ15 Or kills   ʷ18 Or with a tool   ˣ22 Or she has a miscarriage

²⁵burn for burn, wound for wound, bruise for bruise.

²⁶"If a man hits a manservant or maidservant in the eye and destroys it, he must let the servant go free to compensate for the eye. ²⁷And if he knocks out the tooth of a manservant or maidservant, he must let the servant go free to compensate for the tooth.

²⁸"If a bull gores a man or a woman to death, the bull must be stoned to death, and its meat must not be eaten. But the owner of the bull will not be held responsible. ²⁹If, however, the bull has had the habit of goring and the owner has been warned but has not kept it penned up and it kills a man or woman, the bull must be stoned and the owner also must be put to death. ³⁰However, if payment is demanded of him, he may redeem his life by paying whatever is demanded. ³¹This law also applies if the bull gores a son or daughter. ³²If the bull gores a male or female slave, the owner must pay thirty shekels*y* of silver to the master of the slave, and the bull must be stoned.

³³"If a man uncovers a pit or digs one and fails to cover it and an ox or a donkey falls into it, ³⁴the owner of the pit must pay for the loss; he must pay its owner, and the dead animal will be his.

³⁵"If a man's bull injures the bull of another and it dies, they are to sell the live one and divide both the money and the dead animal equally. ³⁶However, if it was known that the bull had the habit of goring, yet the owner did not keep it penned up, the owner must pay, animal for animal, and the dead animal will be his.

CHAPTER 22

"If a man steals an ox or a sheep and slaughters it or sells it, he must pay back five head of cattle for the ox and four sheep for the sheep.

²"If a thief is caught breaking in and is struck so that he dies, the defender is not guilty of bloodshed; ³but if it happens*z* after sunrise, he is guilty of bloodshed.

"A thief must certainly make restitution, but if he has nothing, he must be sold to pay for his theft.

⁴"If the stolen animal is found alive in his possession—whether ox or donkey or sheep—he must pay back double.

⁵"If a man grazes his livestock in a field or vineyard and lets them stray and they graze in another man's field, he must make restitution from the best of his own field or vineyard.

⁶"If a fire breaks out and spreads into thornbushes so that it burns shocks of grain or standing grain or the whole field, the one who started the fire must make restitution.

⁷"If a man gives his neighbor silver or goods for safekeeping and they are stolen from the neighbor's house, the thief, if he is caught, must pay back double. ⁸But if the thief is not found, the owner of the house must appear before the judges*a* to determine whether he has laid his hands on the other man's property. ⁹In all cases of illegal possession of an ox, a donkey, a sheep, a garment, or any other lost property about which somebody says, 'This is mine,' both parties are to bring their cases before the judges. The one whom the judges declare*b* guilty must pay back double to his neighbor.

¹⁰"If a man gives a donkey, an ox, a sheep or any other animal to his neighbor for safekeeping and it dies or is injured or is taken away while no one is looking, ¹¹the issue between them will be settled by the taking of an oath before the Lᴏʀᴅ that the neighbor did not lay hands on the other person's property. The owner is to accept this, and no restitution is required. ¹²But if the animal was stolen from the neighbor, he must make restitution to the owner. ¹³If it was torn to pieces by a wild animal, he shall bring in the remains as evidence and he will not be required to pay for the torn animal.

¹⁴"If a man borrows an animal from his neighbor and it is injured or dies while the owner is not present, he must make restitution. ¹⁵But if the owner is with the animal, the borrower will not have to pay. If the animal was hired, the money paid for the hire covers the loss.

¹⁶"If a man seduces a virgin who is not pledged to be married and sleeps with her, he must pay the bride-price, and she shall be his wife. ¹⁷If her father absolutely refuses to give her to him, he must still pay the bride-price for virgins.

¹⁸"Do not allow a sorceress to live.

y32 That is, about 12 ounces (about 0.3 kilogram)　　*z3* Or *if he strikes him*　　*a8* Or *before God*; also in verse 9　　*b9* Or *whom God declares*

¹⁹"Anyone who has sexual relations with an animal must be put to death.

²⁰"Whoever sacrifices to any god other than the LORD must be destroyed.ᶜ

²¹"Do not mistreat an alien or oppress him, for you were aliens in Egypt.

²²"Do not take advantage of a widow or an orphan. ²³If you do and they cry out to me, I will certainly hear their cry. ²⁴My anger will be aroused, and I will kill you with the sword; your wives will become widows and your children fatherless.

²⁵"If you lend money to one of my people among you who is needy, do not be like a moneylender; charge him no interest.ᵈ ²⁶If you take your neighbor's cloak as a pledge, return it to him by sunset, ²⁷because his cloak is the only covering he has for his body. What else will he sleep in? When he cries out to me, I will hear, for I am compassionate.

²⁸"Do not blaspheme Godᵉ or curse the ruler of your people.

²⁹"Do not hold back offerings from your granaries or your vats.ᶠ

"You must give me the firstborn of your sons. ³⁰Do the same with your cattle and your sheep. Let them stay with their mothers for seven days, but give them to me on the eighth day.

³¹"You are to be my holy people. So do not eat the meat of an animal torn by wild beasts; throw it to the dogs.

CHAPTER 23

"Do not spread false reports. Do not help a wicked man by being a malicious witness.

²"Do not follow the crowd in doing wrong. When you give testimony in a lawsuit, do not pervert justice by siding with the crowd, ³and do not show favoritism to a poor man in his lawsuit.

⁴"If you come across your enemy's ox or donkey wandering off, be sure to take it back to him. ⁵If you see the donkey of someone who hates you fallen down under its load, do not leave it there; be sure you help him with it.

⁶"Do not deny justice to your poor people in their lawsuits. ⁷Have nothing to do with a false charge and do not put an innocent or honest person to death, for I will not acquit the guilty.

⁸"Do not accept a bribe, for a bribe blinds those who see and twists the words of the righteous.

⁹"Do not oppress an alien; you yourselves know how it feels to be aliens, because you were aliens in Egypt.

¹⁰"For six years you are to sow your fields and harvest the crops, ¹¹but during the seventh year let the land lie unplowed and unused. Then the poor among your people may get food from it, and the wild animals may eat what they leave. Do the same with your vineyard and your olive grove.

¹²"Six days do your work, but on the seventh day do not work, so that your ox and your donkey may rest and the slave born in your household, and the alien as well, may be refreshed.

¹³"Be careful to do everything I have said to you. Do not invoke the names of other gods; do not let them be heard on your lips.

¹⁴"Three times a year you are to celebrate a festival to me.

¹⁵"Celebrate the Feast of Unleavened Bread; for seven days eat bread made without yeast, as I commanded you. Do this at the appointed time in the month of Abib, for in that month you came out of Egypt.

"No one is to appear before me empty-handed.

¹⁶"Celebrate the Feast of Harvest with the firstfruits of the crops you sow in your field.

"Celebrate the Feast of Ingathering at the end of the year, when you gather in your crops from the field.

¹⁷"Three times a year all the men are to appear before the Sovereign LORD.

¹⁸"Do not offer the blood of a sacrifice to me along with anything containing yeast.

"The fat of my festival offerings must not be kept until morning.

¹⁹"Bring the best of the firstfruits of your soil to the house of the LORD your God.

"Do not cook a young goat in its mother's milk.

²⁰"See, I am sending an angel ahead of you to guard you along the way and to bring you to the place I have prepared. ²¹Pay attention to him and listen to what he says. Do not rebel against him; he will not forgive your rebellion, since my

---

ᶜ20 The Hebrew term refers to the irrevocable giving over of things or persons to the LORD, often by totally destroying them. ᵈ25 Or excessive interest ᵉ28 Or Do not revile the judges ᶠ29 The meaning of the Hebrew for this phrase is uncertain.

Name is in him. ²²If you listen carefully to what he says and do all that I say, I will be an enemy to your enemies and will oppose those who oppose you. ²³My angel will go ahead of you and bring you into the land of the Amorites, Hittites, Perizzites, Canaanites, Hivites and Jebusites, and I will wipe them out. ²⁴Do not bow down before their gods or worship them or follow their practices. You must demolish them and break their sacred stones to pieces. ²⁵Worship the LORD your God, and his blessing will be on your food and water. I will take away sickness from among you, ²⁶and none will miscarry or be barren in your land. I will give you a full life span.

²⁷"I will send my terror ahead of you and throw into confusion every nation you encounter. I will make all your enemies turn their backs and run. ²⁸I will send the hornet ahead of you to drive the Hivites, Canaanites and Hittites out of your way. ²⁹But I will not drive them out in a single year, because the land would become desolate and the wild animals too numerous for you. ³⁰Little by little I will drive them out before you, until you have increased enough to take possession of the land.

³¹"I will establish your borders from the Red Sea^g to the Sea of the Philistines,^{h} and from the desert to the River.^{i} I will hand over to you the people who live in the land and you will drive them out before you. ³²Do not make a covenant with them or with their gods. ³³Do not let them live in your land, or they will cause you to sin against me, because the worship of their gods will certainly be a snare to you."

CHAPTER 24

Then he said to Moses, "Come up to the LORD, you and Aaron, Nadab and Abihu, and seventy of the elders of Israel. You are to worship at a distance, ²but Moses alone is to approach the LORD; the others must not come near. And the people may not come up with him."

³When Moses went and told the people all the LORD's words and laws, they responded with one voice, "Everything the LORD has said we will do." ⁴Moses then wrote down everything the LORD had said.

He got up early the next morning and built an altar at the foot of the mountain and set up twelve stone pillars representing the twelve tribes of Israel. ⁵Then he sent young Israelite men, and they offered burnt offerings and sacrificed young bulls as fellowship offerings^j to the LORD. ⁶Moses took half of the blood and put it in bowls, and the other half he sprinkled on the altar. ⁷Then he took the Book of the Covenant and read it to the people. They responded, "We will do everything the LORD has said; we will obey."

⁸Moses then took the blood, sprinkled it on the people and said, "This is the blood of the covenant that the LORD has made with you in accordance with all these words."

⁹Moses and Aaron, Nadab and Abihu, and the seventy elders of Israel went up ¹⁰and saw the God of Israel. Under his feet was something like a pavement made of sapphire,^{k} clear as the sky itself. ¹¹But God did not raise his hand against these leaders of the Israelites; they saw God, and they ate and drank.

¹²The LORD said to Moses, "Come up to me on the mountain and stay here, and I will give you the tablets of stone, with the law and commands I have written for their instruction."

¹³Then Moses set out with Joshua his aide, and Moses went up on the mountain of God. ¹⁴He said to the elders, "Wait here for us until we come back to you. Aaron and Hur are with you, and anyone involved in a dispute can go to them."

¹⁵When Moses went up on the mountain, the cloud covered it, ¹⁶and the glory of the LORD settled on Mount Sinai. For six days the cloud covered the mountain, and on the seventh day the LORD called to Moses from within the cloud. ¹⁷To the Israelites the glory of the LORD looked like a consuming fire on top of the mountain. ¹⁸Then Moses entered the cloud as he went on up the mountain. And he stayed on the mountain forty days and forty nights.

---

^{g}31 Hebrew *Yam Suph;* that is, Sea of Reeds　　^{h}31 That is, the Mediterranean　　^{i}31 That is, the Euphrates　　^{j}5 Traditionally *peace offerings*　　^{k}10 Or *lapis lazuli*

JANUARY 27 □ DAY 27
EXODUS 25–27
Design of the Tabernacle

OVERVIEW During Moses' stay on the mountain, God reveals his detailed plans for the tabernacle in which he will dwell and receive his people's worship. No item is overlooked in God's design of this portable tent of worship. Everything is to be done "according to the plan shown you on the mountain" (26:30). The place of God's abode with Israel will be the central structure in the camp and the focus of the nation's attention and activities.

Chapter 25	Chapter 26	Chapter 27
Tabernacle Interior	Tabernacle Structure	Tabernacle Exterior
Items of Worship	Place of Worship	

YOUR DAILY WALK How big is *your* God?

After you have studied the tabernacle in detail, keep in mind this was a portable building, capable of being dismantled and carried about as Israel journeyed. Though God's presence uniquely inhabited the tabernacle, the fact that it could be disassembled for travel served to remind the Israelites that their God could not be confined to four walls! He was with them in the fire and cloud; he could divide great seas and drown mighty armies; he could provide water from rocks and manna from the morning dew. Contrast this with the pagan gods of neighboring nations—powerless idols that had to be carried on their worshipers' shoulders (Isaiah 46:5–7). Israel's priests carried God's temporary *house* on their shoulders, but Israel's God carried *them!*

God is neither shut up nor shut out of any place.

If at times you find yourself wishing your God were a little more flexible, yielding more to your own desires and expectations, consider this fact: If God were small enough for you to control, he would be too small to help you in time of need.

If you can, pay a visit to your church sometime today, and in the quiet, worshipful atmosphere of the silent sanctuary, spend a few minutes praising the God you serve—a God no building can contain!

INSIGHT How Would You Like to Hang These Drapes?

The Jewish historian Josephus explained that the veil that separated the Holy Place from the Most Holy Place was *four inches thick!* It was so strong that it could not be torn apart by horses tied to it, pulling in opposite directions.

CHAPTER 25
The LORD said to Moses, 2"Tell the Israelites to bring me an offering. You are to receive the offering for me from each man whose heart prompts him to give. 3These are the offerings you are to receive from them: gold, silver and bronze; 4blue, purple and scarlet yarn and fine linen; goat hair; 5ram skins dyed red and hides of sea cows*l*; acacia wood; 6olive oil for the light; spices for the anointing oil and for

the fragrant incense; 7and onyx stones and other gems to be mounted on the ephod and breastpiece.

8"Then have them make a sanctuary for me, and I will dwell among them. 9Make this tabernacle and all its furnishings exactly like the pattern I will show you.

10"Have them make a chest of acacia wood—two and a half cubits long, a cubit and a half wide, and a cubit and a half high.*m* 11Overlay it with pure gold, both

l 5 That is, dugongs   *m* 10 That is, about 3 3/4 feet (about 1.1 meters) long and 2 1/4 feet (about 0.7 meter) wide and high inside and out, and make a gold molding around it. ¹²Cast four gold rings for it and fasten them to its four feet, with two rings on one side and two rings on the other. ¹³Then make poles of acacia wood and overlay them with gold. ¹⁴Insert the poles into the rings on the sides of the chest to carry it. ¹⁵The poles are to remain in the rings of this ark; they are not to be removed. ¹⁶Then put in the ark the Testimony, which I will give you.

¹⁷"Make an atonement cover[n] of pure gold—two and a half cubits long and a cubit and a half wide.[o] ¹⁸And make two cherubim out of hammered gold at the ends of the cover. ¹⁹Make one cherub on one end and the second cherub on the other; make the cherubim of one piece with the cover, at the two ends. ²⁰The cherubim are to have their wings spread upward, overshadowing the cover with them. The cherubim are to face each other, looking toward the cover. ²¹Place the cover on top of the ark and put in the ark the Testimony, which I will give you. ²²There, above the cover between the two cherubim that are over the ark of the Testimony, I will meet with you and give you all my commands for the Israelites.

²³"Make a table of acacia wood—two cubits long, a cubit wide and a cubit and a half high.[p] ²⁴Overlay it with pure gold and make a gold molding around it. ²⁵Also make around it a rim a handbreadth[q] wide and put a gold molding on the rim. ²⁶Make four gold rings for the table and fasten them to the four corners, where the four legs are. ²⁷The rings are to be close to the rim to hold the poles used in carrying the table. ²⁸Make the poles of acacia wood, overlay them with gold and carry the table with them. ²⁹And make its plates and dishes of pure gold, as well as its pitchers and bowls for the pouring out of offerings. ³⁰Put the bread of the Presence on this table to be before me at all times.

³¹"Make a lampstand of pure gold and hammer it out, base and shaft; its flower-like cups, buds and blossoms shall be of one piece with it. ³²Six branches are to extend from the sides of the lampstand—three on one side and three on the other.

³³Three cups shaped like almond flowers with buds and blossoms are to be on one branch, three on the next branch, and the same for all six branches extending from the lampstand. ³⁴And on the lampstand there are to be four cups shaped like almond flowers with buds and blossoms. ³⁵One bud shall be under the first pair of branches extending from the lampstand, a second bud under the second pair, and a third bud under the third pair—six branches in all. ³⁶The buds and branches shall all be of one piece with the lampstand, hammered out of pure gold.

³⁷"Then make its seven lamps and set them up on it so that they light the space in front of it. ³⁸Its wick trimmers and trays are to be of pure gold. ³⁹A talent[r] of pure gold is to be used for the lampstand and all these accessories. ⁴⁰See that you make them according to the pattern shown you on the mountain.

CHAPTER 26

"Make the tabernacle with ten curtains of finely twisted linen and blue, purple and scarlet yarn, with cherubim worked into them by a skilled craftsman. ²All the curtains are to be the same size—twenty-eight cubits long and four cubits wide.[s] ³Join five of the curtains together, and do the same with the other five. ⁴Make loops of blue material along the edge of the end curtain in one set, and do the same with the end curtain in the other set. ⁵Make fifty loops on one curtain and fifty loops on the end curtain of the other set, with the loops opposite each other. ⁶Then make fifty gold clasps and use them to fasten the curtains together so that the tabernacle is a unit.

⁷"Make curtains of goat hair for the tent over the tabernacle—eleven altogether. ⁸All eleven curtains are to be the same size—thirty cubits long and four cubits wide.[t] ⁹Join five of the curtains together into one set and the other six into another set. Fold the sixth curtain double at the front of the tent. ¹⁰Make fifty loops along the edge of the end curtain in one set and also along the edge of the end curtain in the other set. ¹¹Then make fifty bronze clasps and put them in the loops to fasten

---

[n] **17** Traditionally *a mercy seat*   [o] **17** That is, about 3 3/4 feet (about 1.1 meters) long and 2 1/4 feet (about 0.7 meter) wide
[p] **23** That is, about 3 feet (about 0.9 meter) long and 1 1/2 feet (about 0.5 meter) wide and 2 1/4 feet (about 0.7 meter) high
[q] **25** That is, about 3 inches (about 8 centimeters)   [r] **39** That is, about 75 pounds (about 34 kilograms)   [s] **2** That is, about 42 feet (about 12.5 meters) long and 6 feet (about 1.8 meters) wide   [t] **8** That is, about 45 feet (about 13.5 meters) long and 6 feet (about 1.8 meters) wide

the tent together as a unit. [12]As for the additional length of the tent curtains, the half curtain that is left over is to hang down at the rear of the tabernacle. [13]The tent curtains will be a cubit[u] longer on both sides; what is left will hang over the sides of the tabernacle so as to cover it. [14]Make for the tent a covering of ram skins dyed red, and over that a covering of hides of sea cows.[v]

[15]"Make upright frames of acacia wood for the tabernacle. [16]Each frame is to be ten cubits long and a cubit and a half wide,[w] [17]with two projections set parallel to each other. Make all the frames of the tabernacle in this way. [18]Make twenty frames for the south side of the tabernacle [19]and make forty silver bases to go under them—two bases for each frame, one under each projection. [20]For the other side, the north side of the tabernacle, make twenty frames [21]and forty silver bases—two under each frame. [22]Make six frames for the far end, that is, the west end of the tabernacle, [23]and make two frames for the corners at the far end. [24]At these two corners they must be double from the bottom all the way to the top, and fitted into a single ring; both shall be like that. [25]So there will be eight frames and sixteen silver bases—two under each frame.

[26]"Also make crossbars of acacia wood: five for the frames on one side of the tabernacle, [27]five for those on the other side, and five for the frames on the west, at the far end of the tabernacle. [28]The center crossbar is to extend from end to end at the middle of the frames. [29]Overlay the frames with gold and make gold rings to hold the crossbars. Also overlay the crossbars with gold.

[30]"Set up the tabernacle according to the plan shown you on the mountain.

[31]"Make a curtain of blue, purple and scarlet yarn and finely twisted linen, with cherubim worked into it by a skilled craftsman. [32]Hang it with gold hooks on four posts of acacia wood overlaid with gold and standing on four silver bases. [33]Hang the curtain from the clasps and place the ark of the Testimony behind the curtain. The curtain will separate the Holy Place from the Most Holy Place.

[34]Put the atonement cover on the ark of the Testimony in the Most Holy Place. [35]Place the table outside the curtain on the north side of the tabernacle and put the lampstand opposite it on the south side.

[36]"For the entrance to the tent make a curtain of blue, purple and scarlet yarn and finely twisted linen—the work of an embroiderer. [37]Make gold hooks for this curtain and five posts of acacia wood overlaid with gold. And cast five bronze bases for them.

C H A P T E R   2 7

"Build an altar of acacia wood, three cubits[x] high; it is to be square, five cubits long and five cubits wide.[y] [2]Make a horn at each of the four corners, so that the horns and the altar are of one piece, and overlay the altar with bronze. [3]Make all its utensils of bronze—its pots to remove the ashes, and its shovels, sprinkling bowls, meat forks and firepans. [4]Make a grating for it, a bronze network, and make a bronze ring at each of the four corners of the network. [5]Put it under the ledge of the altar so that it is halfway up the altar. [6]Make poles of acacia wood for the altar and overlay them with bronze. [7]The poles are to be inserted into the rings so they will be on two sides of the altar when it is carried. [8]Make the altar hollow, out of boards. It is to be made just as you were shown on the mountain.

[9]"Make a courtyard for the tabernacle. The south side shall be a hundred cubits[z] long and is to have curtains of finely twisted linen, [10]with twenty posts and twenty bronze bases and with silver hooks and bands on the posts. [11]The north side shall also be a hundred cubits long and is to have curtains, with twenty posts and twenty bronze bases and with silver hooks and bands on the posts.

[12]"The west end of the courtyard shall be fifty cubits[a] wide and have curtains, with ten posts and ten bases. [13]On the east end, toward the sunrise, the courtyard shall also be fifty cubits wide. [14]Curtains fifteen cubits[b] long are to be on one side of the entrance, with three posts and three bases, [15]and curtains fifteen cubits long

[u]13 That is, about 1 1/2 feet (about 0.5 meter)   [v]14 That is, dugongs   [w]16 That is, about 15 feet (about 4.5 meters) long and 2 1/4 feet (about 0.7 meter) wide   [x]1 That is, about 4 1/2 feet (about 1.3 meters)   [y]1 That is, about 7 1/2 feet (about 2.3 meters) long and wide   [z]9 That is, about 150 feet (about 46 meters); also in verse 11   [a]12 That is, about 75 feet (about 23 meters); also in verse 13   [b]14 That is, about 22 1/2 feet (about 6.9 meters); also in verse 15

are to be on the other side, with three posts and three bases.

¹⁶"For the entrance to the courtyard, provide a curtain twenty cubits^c long, of blue, purple and scarlet yarn and finely twisted linen—the work of an embroiderer—with four posts and four bases. ¹⁷All the posts around the courtyard are to have silver bands and hooks, and bronze bases. ¹⁸The courtyard shall be a hundred cubits long and fifty cubits wide,^{d} with curtains of finely twisted linen five cubits^e high, and with bronze bases. ¹⁹All the other articles used in the

service of the tabernacle, whatever their function, including all the tent pegs for it and those for the courtyard, are to be of bronze.

²⁰"Command the Israelites to bring you clear oil of pressed olives for the light so that the lamps may be kept burning. ²¹In the Tent of Meeting, outside the curtain that is in front of the Testimony, Aaron and his sons are to keep the lamps burning before the LORD from evening till morning. This is to be a lasting ordinance among the Israelites for the generations to come.

^{c}16 That is, about 30 feet (about 9 meters) ^{d}18 That is, about 150 feet (about 46 meters) long and 75 feet (about 23 meters) wide ^{e}18 That is, about 7 1/2 feet (about 2.3 meters)

JANUARY 28 ☐ DAY 28
Father Knows Best

LOOK BACK On center stage for the entire week of reading from the book of Exodus has been Moses, the humble servant-leader of the Hebrew people. Whether calling down plagues upon hard-hearted Pharaoh, leading God's people through the Red Sea and the wilderness, or receiving God's law at Mount Sinai, Moses demonstrates the attitudes of humility and authority. Entrusted with a high visibility role, Moses never flaunts his position or exploits his countrymen for personal gain. Rather, he leads them in the fear of the Lord. That's not to say Moses' patience isn't severely tried by God's stiff-necked people. (You have already read about six encounters between Moses and his rebellious countrymen, and four more confrontations lie just ahead.) But Moses' leadership is consistently marked by 20/20 vision—Exodus 20:20, that is: "Do not be afraid. God has come to test you, so that the fear of God will be with you to keep you from sinning."

LOOK UP Which is the longest word in the English language? The one that follows the announcement "And now a word from our sponsor."

Words communicate thoughts. If you want to know what someone is thinking, listen carefully to what he or she is saying. And if you want to know the most important thought on a person's heart, ask that person to express his or her thoughts in just ten words. Try it yourself! In the space provided, take ten words (or less) to capture the most important thought on your mind right now.

More than 35,000 laws have been written trying to improve upon what God said in the Ten Commandments.

_____

_____

The Ten Commandments that Moses received on Mount Sinai contain more than ten words. But in them you will find ten thoughts that are near and dear to the heart of God. Think back over what you read this past week (or turn to Exodus 20 if you need a quick review), and summarize what God said about each of the following:

- Other gods (20:3)
- Idols (20:4–6)
- Cursing (20:7)

- Murder (20:13)
- Adultery (20:14)
- Stealing (20:15)

- Sabbath (20:8–11)   • Lying (20:16)
- Parents (20:12)   • Coveting (20:17)

And lest you conclude that the Ten Commandments are only found in the Old Testament, notice what Jesus said to the rich young ruler in Mark 10:19!

LOOK AHEAD It might be easy to conclude that God as described in the pages of the Old Testament is a God of do's and don'ts. After all, look at all the rules and regulations that the people of God were required to observe. But God often goes beyond telling his people *what* to do and tells them *why* they should do it. (Watch for the telltale words *for, because,* or *that,* which signal that God is about to include the *why* along with the *what*.) He wants his people to learn that "Father knows best."

As you continue your reading in the books of Exodus and Leviticus, don't get lost in the maze of statutes and ordinances. Remember to use Exodus 20:20 vision as you read. And if you're curious to know which of the hundreds of commandments is nearest and dearest to the heart of God, take a look at Matthew 22:34–40 and Mark 12:28–34!

JANUARY 29 ☐ DAY 29
EXODUS 28–31
Special Instructions for Priests

OVERVIEW No center of worship is complete without people to minister in it and utensils to use in the worship services. Exodus 28–31 describes the priests, Israel's representatives before God, who are chosen to lead the worship in the tabernacle. Everything about them is special, from the clothing they wear to the elaborate sacrifices needed to prepare them for ministry, as well as the supplies and furnishings they use (such as incense, perfumes, oil, the altar and the basin) in the tabernacle worship. Even the designers and construction workers for the tabernacle are handpicked by God.

Chapter 28	Chapter 29	Chapter 30	Chapter 31
Clothing for the Priests	Consecration of the Priests	Commands for the Priests	Craftsmen for the Tabernacle
Priestly Ministry			Priestly Carpenters

YOUR DAILY WALK Preparing the priest for service in the tabernacle was no small chore (Exodus 29). The most curious part of the ceremony involved killing a ram and applying the blood to the tip of the priest's right ear, the thumb of his right hand, and the big toe of his right foot.

God deserves to be served with all the energy of which we are capable.

The blood was a picture of cleansing. Before the priest could minister before the Lord, he had to be clean from the sin that polluted him. Then he needed to be dedicated to the Lord from the top of his head to the bottom of his feet. Every part of him, from his ear (which listens to God's law) to his hand (which does God's will) to his foot (which follows in God's steps) had to be surrendered to the will of God.

Does God have that kind of control over your whole life? If not, starting with your head, give each part of your body to him in a prayer of dedication: "Lord, take my eyes; help me to look only at those things that please you. Take my ears; help me to listen only to those things that build up, not those that tear down . . ." Then you, like Israel's priest, will be ready to do his will—from head to toe!

INSIGHT Urim, You Win; Thummim, You Lose
The Urim and Thummim were used to determine the will of God. Scholars have been unable to determine exactly what they were or how they were used. One theory is that the Urim and Thummim were two flat stones kept in the breastplate of the high priest. Each had one dark side and one light. They were tossed into the air and allowed to fall to the ground. Two dark sides showing meant yes, two light sides meant no, and one of each meant no reply.

CHAPTER 28

"Have Aaron your brother brought to you from among the Israelites, along with his sons Nadab and Abihu, Eleazar and Ithamar, so they may serve me as priests. ²Make sacred garments for your brother Aaron, to give him dignity and honor. ³Tell all the skilled men to whom I have given wisdom in such matters that they are to make garments for Aaron, for his consecration, so he may serve me as priest. ⁴These are the garments they are to make: a breastpiece, an ephod, a robe, a woven tunic, a turban and a sash. They are to make these sacred garments for your brother Aaron and his sons, so they may serve me as priests. ⁵Have them use gold, and blue, purple and scarlet yarn, and fine linen.

⁶"Make the ephod of gold, and of blue, purple and scarlet yarn, and of finely twisted linen—the work of a skilled craftsman. ⁷It is to have two shoulder pieces attached to two of its corners, so it can be fastened. ⁸Its skillfully woven waistband is to be like it—of one piece with the ephod and made with gold, and with blue, purple and scarlet yarn, and with finely twisted linen.

⁹"Take two onyx stones and engrave on them the names of the sons of Israel ¹⁰in the order of their birth—six names on one stone and the remaining six on the other. ¹¹Engrave the names of the sons of Israel on the two stones the way a gem cutter engraves a seal. Then mount the stones in gold filigree settings ¹²and fasten them on the shoulder pieces of the ephod as memorial stones for the sons of Israel. Aaron

is to bear the names on his shoulders as a memorial before the LORD. ¹³Make gold filigree settings ¹⁴and two braided chains of pure gold, like a rope, and attach the chains to the settings.

¹⁵"Fashion a breastpiece for making decisions—the work of a skilled craftsman. Make it like the ephod: of gold, and of blue, purple and scarlet yarn, and of finely twisted linen. ¹⁶It is to be square—a span *f* long and a span wide—and folded double. ¹⁷Then mount four rows of precious stones on it. In the first row there shall be a ruby, a topaz and a beryl; ¹⁸in the second row a turquoise, a sapphire *g* and an emerald; ¹⁹in the third row a jacinth, an agate and an amethyst; ²⁰in the fourth row a chrysolite, an onyx and a jasper. *h* Mount them in gold filigree settings. ²¹There are to be twelve stones, one for each of the names of the sons of Israel, each engraved like a seal with the name of one of the twelve tribes.

²²"For the breastpiece make braided chains of pure gold, like a rope. ²³Make two gold rings for it and fasten them to two corners of the breastpiece. ²⁴Fasten the two gold chains to the rings at the corners of the breastpiece, ²⁵and the other ends of the chains to the two settings, attaching them to the shoulder pieces of the ephod at the front. ²⁶Make two gold rings and attach them to the other two corners of the breastpiece on the inside edge next to the ephod. ²⁷Make two more gold rings and attach them to the bottom of the shoulder pieces on the front of the ephod, close to the seam just above the waistband of the ephod. ²⁸The rings of the

f16 That is, about 9 inches (about 22 centimeters)   *g18* Or *lapis lazuli*   *h20* The precise identification of some of these precious stones is uncertain.

breastpiece are to be tied to the rings of the ephod with blue cord, connecting it to the waistband, so that the breastpiece will not swing out from the ephod.

[29]"Whenever Aaron enters the Holy Place, he will bear the names of the sons of Israel over his heart on the breastpiece of decision as a continuing memorial before the LORD. [30]Also put the Urim and the Thummim in the breastpiece, so they may be over Aaron's heart whenever he enters the presence of the LORD. Thus Aaron will always bear the means of making decisions for the Israelites over his heart before the LORD.

[31]"Make the robe of the ephod entirely of blue cloth, [32]with an opening for the head in its center. There shall be a woven edge like a collar[i] around this opening, so that it will not tear. [33]Make pomegranates of blue, purple and scarlet yarn around the hem of the robe, with gold bells between them. [34]The gold bells and the pomegranates are to alternate around the hem of the robe. [35]Aaron must wear it when he ministers. The sound of the bells will be heard when he enters the Holy Place before the LORD and when he comes out, so that he will not die.

[36]"Make a plate of pure gold and engrave on it as on a seal: HOLY TO THE LORD. [37]Fasten a blue cord to it to attach it to the turban; it is to be on the front of the turban. [38]It will be on Aaron's forehead, and he will bear the guilt involved in the sacred gifts the Israelites consecrate, whatever their gifts may be. It will be on Aaron's forehead continually so that they will be acceptable to the LORD.

[39]"Weave the tunic of fine linen and make the turban of fine linen. The sash is to be the work of an embroiderer. [40]Make tunics, sashes and headbands for Aaron's sons, to give them dignity and honor. [41]After you put these clothes on your brother Aaron and his sons, anoint and ordain them. Consecrate them so they may serve me as priests.

[42]"Make linen undergarments as a covering for the body, reaching from the waist to the thigh. [43]Aaron and his sons must wear them whenever they enter the Tent of Meeting or approach the altar to minister in the Holy Place, so that they will not incur guilt and die.

"This is to be a lasting ordinance for Aaron and his descendants.

CHAPTER 29

"This is what you are to do to consecrate them, so they may serve me as priests: Take a young bull and two rams without defect. [2]And from fine wheat flour, without yeast, make bread, and cakes mixed with oil, and wafers spread with oil. [3]Put them in a basket and present them in it— along with the bull and the two rams. [4]Then bring Aaron and his sons to the entrance to the Tent of Meeting and wash them with water. [5]Take the garments and dress Aaron with the tunic, the robe of the ephod, the ephod itself and the breastpiece. Fasten the ephod on him by its skillfully woven waistband. [6]Put the turban on his head and attach the sacred diadem to the turban. [7]Take the anointing oil and anoint him by pouring it on his head. [8]Bring his sons and dress them in tunics [9]and put headbands on them. Then tie sashes on Aaron and his sons.[j] The priesthood is theirs by a lasting ordinance. In this way you shall ordain Aaron and his sons.

[10]"Bring the bull to the front of the Tent of Meeting, and Aaron and his sons shall lay their hands on its head. [11]Slaughter it in the LORD's presence at the entrance to the Tent of Meeting. [12]Take some of the bull's blood and put it on the horns of the altar with your finger, and pour out the rest of it at the base of the altar. [13]Then take all the fat around the inner parts, the covering of the liver, and both kidneys with the fat on them, and burn them on the altar. [14]But burn the bull's flesh and its hide and its offal outside the camp. It is a sin offering.

[15]"Take one of the rams, and Aaron and his sons shall lay their hands on its head. [16]Slaughter it and take the blood and sprinkle it against the altar on all sides. [17]Cut the ram into pieces and wash the inner parts and the legs, putting them with the head and the other pieces. [18]Then burn the entire ram on the altar. It is a burnt offering to the LORD, a pleasing aroma, an offering made to the LORD by fire.

[19]"Take the other ram, and Aaron and his sons shall lay their hands on its head.

---

i32 The meaning of the Hebrew for this word is uncertain.   j9 Hebrew; Septuagint on them

²⁰Slaughter it, take some of its blood and put it on the lobes of the right ears of Aaron and his sons, on the thumbs of their right hands, and on the big toes of their right feet. Then sprinkle blood against the altar on all sides. ²¹And take some of the blood on the altar and some of the anointing oil and sprinkle it on Aaron and his garments and on his sons and their garments. Then he and his sons and their garments will be consecrated.

²²"Take from this ram the fat, the fat tail, the fat around the inner parts, the covering of the liver, both kidneys with the fat on them, and the right thigh. (This is the ram for the ordination.) ²³From the basket of bread made without yeast, which is before the LORD, take a loaf, and a cake made with oil, and a wafer. ²⁴Put all these in the hands of Aaron and his sons and wave them before the LORD as a wave offering. ²⁵Then take them from their hands and burn them on the altar along with the burnt offering for a pleasing aroma to the LORD, an offering made to the LORD by fire. ²⁶After you take the breast of the ram for Aaron's ordination, wave it before the LORD as a wave offering, and it will be your share.

²⁷"Consecrate those parts of the ordination ram that belong to Aaron and his sons: the breast that was waved and the thigh that was presented. ²⁸This is always to be the regular share from the Israelites for Aaron and his sons. It is the contribution the Israelites are to make to the LORD from their fellowship offerings.ᵏ

²⁹"Aaron's sacred garments will belong to his descendants so that they can be anointed and ordained in them. ³⁰The son who succeeds him as priest and comes to the Tent of Meeting to minister in the Holy Place is to wear them seven days.

³¹"Take the ram for the ordination and cook the meat in a sacred place. ³²At the entrance to the Tent of Meeting, Aaron and his sons are to eat the meat of the ram and the bread that is in the basket. ³³They are to eat these offerings by which atonement was made for their ordination and consecration. But no one else may eat them, because they are sacred. ³⁴And if any of the meat of the ordination ram or any bread is left over till morning, burn it

up. It must not be eaten, because it is sacred.

³⁵"Do for Aaron and his sons everything I have commanded you, taking seven days to ordain them. ³⁶Sacrifice a bull each day as a sin offering to make atonement. Purify the altar by making atonement for it, and anoint it to consecrate it. ³⁷For seven days make atonement for the altar and consecrate it. Then the altar will be most holy, and whatever touches it will be holy.

³⁸"This is what you are to offer on the altar regularly each day: two lambs a year old. ³⁹Offer one in the morning and the other at twilight. ⁴⁰With the first lamb offer a tenth of an ephahˡ of fine flour mixed with a quarter of a hinᵐ of oil from pressed olives, and a quarter of a hin of wine as a drink offering. ⁴¹Sacrifice the other lamb at twilight with the same grain offering and its drink offering as in the morning—a pleasing aroma, an offering made to the LORD by fire.

⁴²"For the generations to come this burnt offering is to be made regularly at the entrance to the Tent of Meeting before the LORD. There I will meet you and speak to you; ⁴³there also I will meet with the Israelites, and the place will be consecrated by my glory.

⁴⁴"So I will consecrate the Tent of Meeting and the altar and will consecrate Aaron and his sons to serve me as priests. ⁴⁵Then I will dwell among the Israelites and be their God. ⁴⁶They will know that I am the LORD their God, who brought them out of Egypt so that I might dwell among them. I am the LORD their God.

C H A P T E R   3 0

"Make an altar of acacia wood for burning incense. ²It is to be square, a cubit long and a cubit wide, and two cubits highⁿ— its horns of one piece with it. ³Overlay the top and all the sides and the horns with pure gold, and make a gold molding around it. ⁴Make two gold rings for the altar below the molding—two on opposite sides—to hold the poles used to carry it. ⁵Make the poles of acacia wood and overlay them with gold. ⁶Put the altar in front of the curtain that is before the ark of the Testimony—before the atonement cover

ᵏ*28* Traditionally *peace offerings*   ˡ*40* That is, probably about 2 quarts (about 2 liters)   ᵐ*40* That is, probably about 1 quart (about 1 liter)   ⁿ*2* That is, about 1 1/2 feet (about 0.5 meter) long and wide and about 3 feet (about 0.9 meter) high that is over the Testimony—where I will meet with you.

⁷"Aaron must burn fragrant incense on the altar every morning when he tends the lamps. ⁸He must burn incense again when he lights the lamps at twilight so incense will burn regularly before the LORD for the generations to come. ⁹Do not offer on this altar any other incense or any burnt offering or grain offering, and do not pour a drink offering on it. ¹⁰Once a year Aaron shall make atonement on its horns. This annual atonement must be made with the blood of the atoning sin offering for the generations to come. It is most holy to the LORD."

¹¹Then the LORD said to Moses, ¹²"When you take a census of the Israelites to count them, each one must pay the LORD a ransom for his life at the time he is counted. Then no plague will come on them when you number them. ¹³Each one who crosses over to those already counted is to give a half shekel,ᵒ according to the sanctuary shekel, which weighs twenty gerahs. This half shekel is an offering to the LORD. ¹⁴All who cross over, those twenty years old or more, are to give an offering to the LORD. ¹⁵The rich are not to give more than a half shekel and the poor are not to give less when you make the offering to the LORD to atone for your lives. ¹⁶Receive the atonement money from the Israelites and use it for the service of the Tent of Meeting. It will be a memorial for the Israelites before the LORD, making atonement for your lives."

¹⁷Then the LORD said to Moses, ¹⁸"Make a bronze basin, with its bronze stand, for washing. Place it between the Tent of Meeting and the altar, and put water in it. ¹⁹Aaron and his sons are to wash their hands and feet with water from it. ²⁰Whenever they enter the Tent of Meeting, they shall wash with water so that they will not die. Also, when they approach the altar to minister by presenting an offering made to the LORD by fire, ²¹they shall wash their hands and feet so that they will not die. This is to be a lasting ordinance for Aaron and his descendants for the generations to come."

²²Then the LORD said to Moses, ²³"Take the following fine spices: 500 shekelsᵖ of liquid myrrh, half as much (that is, 250 shekels) of fragrant cinnamon, 250 shekels of fragrant cane, ²⁴500 shekels of cassia—all according to the sanctuary shekel—and a hinᵍ of olive oil. ²⁵Make these into a sacred anointing oil, a fragrant blend, the work of a perfumer. It will be the sacred anointing oil. ²⁶Then use it to anoint the Tent of Meeting, the ark of the Testimony, ²⁷the table and all its articles, the lampstand and its accessories, the altar of incense, ²⁸the altar of burnt offering and all its utensils, and the basin with its stand. ²⁹You shall consecrate them so they will be most holy, and whatever touches them will be holy.

³⁰"Anoint Aaron and his sons and consecrate them so they may serve me as priests. ³¹Say to the Israelites, 'This is to be my sacred anointing oil for the generations to come. ³²Do not pour it on men's bodies and do not make any oil with the same formula. It is sacred, and you are to consider it sacred. ³³Whoever makes perfume like it and whoever puts it on anyone other than a priest must be cut off from his people.' "

³⁴Then the LORD said to Moses, "Take fragrant spices—gum resin, onycha and galbanum—and pure frankincense, all in equal amounts, ³⁵and make a fragrant blend of incense, the work of a perfumer. It is to be salted and pure and sacred. ³⁶Grind some of it to powder and place it in front of the Testimony in the Tent of Meeting, where I will meet with you. It shall be most holy to you. ³⁷Do not make any incense with this formula for yourselves; consider it holy to the LORD. ³⁸Whoever makes any like it to enjoy its fragrance must be cut off from his people."

CHAPTER 31

Then the LORD said to Moses, ²"See, I have chosen Bezalel son of Uri, the son of Hur, of the tribe of Judah, ³and I have filled him with the Spirit of God, with skill, ability and knowledge in all kinds of crafts— ⁴to make artistic designs for work in gold, silver and bronze, ⁵to cut and set stones, to work in wood, and to engage in all kinds of craftsmanship. ⁶Moreover, I have appointed Oholiab son of Ahisa-

ᵒ13 That is, about 1/5 ounce (about 6 grams); also in verse 15   ᵖ23 That is, about 12 1/2 pounds (about 6 kilograms)
ᵍ24 That is, probably about 4 quarts (about 4 liters)

mach, of the tribe of Dan, to help him. Also I have given skill to all the craftsmen to make everything I have commanded you: [7]the Tent of Meeting, the ark of the Testimony with the atonement cover on it, and all the other furnishings of the tent— [8]the table and its articles, the pure gold lampstand and all its accessories, the altar of burnt offering and all its utensils, the basin with its stand— [10]and also the woven garments, both the sacred garments for Aaron the priest and the garments for his sons when they serve as priests, [11]and the anointing oil and fragrant incense for the Holy Place. They are to make them just as I commanded you."

[12]Then the LORD said to Moses, [13]"Say to the Israelites, 'You must observe my Sabbaths. This will be a sign between me and you for the generations to come, so you

[r]13 Or *who sanctifies you;* or *who sets you apart as holy*

may know that I am the LORD, who makes you holy.[r]

[14]" 'Observe the Sabbath, because it is holy to you. Anyone who desecrates it must be put to death; whoever does any work on that day must be cut off from his people. [15]For six days, work is to be done, but the seventh day is a Sabbath of rest, holy to the LORD. Whoever does any work on the Sabbath day must be put to death. [16]The Israelites are to observe the Sabbath, celebrating it for the generations to come as a lasting covenant. [17]It will be a sign between me and the Israelites forever, for in six days the LORD made the heavens and the earth, and on the seventh day he abstained from work and rested.' "

[18]When the LORD finished speaking to Moses on Mount Sinai, he gave him the two tablets of the Testimony, the tablets of stone inscribed by the finger of God.

JANUARY 30 □ DAY 30
EXODUS 32–34
Incident of the Golden Calf

OVERVIEW Six weeks have passed since the people made their solemn vow of fidelity to God. Concluding that Moses has died on the mountain, they insist on creating a replica of an Egyptian god and worshiping it. Coming upon this grotesque scene, Moses dashes the newly inscribed tablets to pieces, dramatically illustrating the broken covenant. He destroys the golden calf and orders the Levites to slay the guilty Israelites. Israel's repentance, Moses' selfless intercession and God's faithfulness to his promises lead to a renewal of the covenant. New tablets are engraved, and Moses experiences yet another encounter with God on Mount Sinai.

Chapter 32		Chapter 33		Chapter 34
Covenant's Interruption	Moses' Intercession	Israel's Repentance	Moses' Request	Covenant's Renewal
1 6	7 35	1 17	18 23	
Israel's Rebellion		God's Restoration		

YOUR DAILY WALK "I just can't understand teenagers. One minute they want to be treated like adults; the next minute they act like children."

Never look back unless you want to go that way.

This oft-voiced exasperation of many a parent illustrates a fact about growth. The process of maturation does not proceed at a consistent pace. Everyone at one time or another reverts to former patterns of behavior.

The incident of the golden calf is but one of many cases of backsliding in Israel's history. One lesson is clear: Believers are not immune from reverting to old habits and patterns of living. It may occur in an unguarded moment, such as an outburst of temper. Or it may be the result of impatience, when God's timetable seems agonizingly slow.

Take a personal inventory of your spiritual life. Have you made a commitment to the Lord in recent weeks? If so, have you followed through on it or reverted to your previous behavior? If you see a "golden calf" in your life, deal with it now! You'll discover that "golden calves" make terrible "sacred cows"—but excellent hamburger!

 INSIGHT The Golden Calf: A Lingering Legacy
Calf worship—or worshiping idols of any kind—was expressly forbidden in the law (20:4–6). Yet, at least once more in Israel's history, a golden calf spelled destruction for the people (see 1 Kings 12:28).

CHAPTER 32

When the people saw that Moses was so long in coming down from the mountain, they gathered around Aaron and said, "Come, make us gods^s who will go before us. As for this fellow Moses who brought us up out of Egypt, we don't know what has happened to him."

^{2}Aaron answered them, "Take off the gold earrings that your wives, your sons and your daughters are wearing, and bring them to me." ^{3}So all the people took off their earrings and brought them to Aaron. ^{4}He took what they handed him and made it into an idol cast in the shape of a calf, fashioning it with a tool. Then they said, "These are your gods,^{t} O Israel, who brought you up out of Egypt."

^{5}When Aaron saw this, he built an altar in front of the calf and announced, "Tomorrow there will be a festival to the LORD." ^{6}So the next day the people rose early and sacrificed burnt offerings and presented fellowship offerings.^{u} Afterward they sat down to eat and drink and got up to indulge in revelry.

^{7}Then the LORD said to Moses, "Go down, because your people, whom you brought up out of Egypt, have become corrupt. ^{8}They have been quick to turn away from what I commanded them and have made themselves an idol cast in the shape of a calf. They have bowed down to it and sacrificed to it and have said, 'These are your gods, O Israel, who brought you up out of Egypt.'

^{9}"I have seen these people," the LORD said to Moses, "and they are a stiff-necked people. ^{10}Now leave me alone so that my anger may burn against them and

that I may destroy them. Then I will make you into a great nation."

^{11}But Moses sought the favor of the LORD his God. "O LORD," he said, "why should your anger burn against your people, whom you brought out of Egypt with great power and a mighty hand? ^{12}Why should the Egyptians say, 'It was with evil intent that he brought them out, to kill them in the mountains and to wipe them off the face of the earth'? Turn from your fierce anger; relent and do not bring disaster on your people. ^{13}Remember your servants Abraham, Isaac and Israel, to whom you swore by your own self: 'I will make your descendants as numerous as the stars in the sky and I will give your descendants all this land I promised them, and it will be their inheritance forever.' " ^{14}Then the LORD relented and did not bring on his people the disaster he had threatened.

^{15}Moses turned and went down the mountain with the two tablets of the Testimony in his hands. They were inscribed on both sides, front and back. ^{16}The tablets were the work of God; the writing was the writing of God, engraved on the tablets.

^{17}When Joshua heard the noise of the people shouting, he said to Moses, "There is the sound of war in the camp."

^{18}Moses replied:

"It is not the sound of victory,
    it is not the sound of defeat;
    it is the sound of singing that I
        hear."

^{19}When Moses approached the camp and saw the calf and the dancing, his anger burned and he threw the tablets out of his hands, breaking them to pieces at the

---

^{s}1 Or *a god*; also in verses 23 and 31 ^{t}4 Or *This is your god*; also in verse 8 ^{u}6 Traditionally *peace offerings* foot of the mountain. ²⁰And he took the calf they had made and burned it in the fire; then he ground it to powder, scattered it on the water and made the Israelites drink it.

²¹He said to Aaron, "What did these people do to you, that you led them into such great sin?"

²²"Do not be angry, my lord," Aaron answered. "You know how prone these people are to evil. ²³They said to me, 'Make us gods who will go before us. As for this fellow Moses who brought us up out of Egypt, we don't know what has happened to him.' ²⁴So I told them, 'Whoever has any gold jewelry, take it off.' Then they gave me the gold, and I threw it into the fire, and out came this calf!"

²⁵Moses saw that the people were running wild and that Aaron had let them get out of control and so become a laughingstock to their enemies. ²⁶So he stood at the entrance to the camp and said, "Whoever is for the LORD, come to me." And all the Levites rallied to him.

²⁷Then he said to them, "This is what the LORD, the God of Israel, says: 'Each man strap a sword to his side. Go back and forth through the camp from one end to the other, each killing his brother and friend and neighbor.' " ²⁸The Levites did as Moses commanded, and that day about three thousand of the people died. ²⁹Then Moses said, "You have been set apart to the LORD today, for you were against your own sons and brothers, and he has blessed you this day."

³⁰The next day Moses said to the people, "You have committed a great sin. But now I will go up to the LORD; perhaps I can make atonement for your sin."

³¹So Moses went back to the LORD and said, "Oh, what a great sin these people have committed! They have made themselves gods of gold. ³²But now, please forgive their sin—but if not, then blot me out of the book you have written."

³³The LORD replied to Moses, "Whoever has sinned against me I will blot out of my book. ³⁴Now go, lead the people to the place I spoke of, and my angel will go before you. However, when the time comes for me to punish, I will punish them for their sin."

³⁵And the LORD struck the people with a plague because of what they did with the calf Aaron had made.

CHAPTER 33

Then the LORD said to Moses, "Leave this place, you and the people you brought up out of Egypt, and go up to the land I promised on oath to Abraham, Isaac and Jacob, saying, 'I will give it to your descendants.' ²I will send an angel before you and drive out the Canaanites, Amorites, Hittites, Perizzites, Hivites and Jebusites. ³Go up to the land flowing with milk and honey. But I will not go with you, because you are a stiff-necked people and I might destroy you on the way."

⁴When the people heard these distressing words, they began to mourn and no one put on any ornaments. ⁵For the LORD had said to Moses, "Tell the Israelites, 'You are a stiff-necked people. If I were to go with you even for a moment, I might destroy you. Now take off your ornaments and I will decide what to do with you.' " ⁶So the Israelites stripped off their ornaments at Mount Horeb.

⁷Now Moses used to take a tent and pitch it outside the camp some distance away, calling it the "tent of meeting." Anyone inquiring of the LORD would go to the tent of meeting outside the camp. ⁸And whenever Moses went out to the tent, all the people rose and stood at the entrances to their tents, watching Moses until he entered the tent. ⁹As Moses went into the tent, the pillar of cloud would come down and stay at the entrance, while the LORD spoke with Moses. ¹⁰Whenever the people saw the pillar of cloud standing at the entrance to the tent, they all stood and worshiped, each at the entrance to his tent. ¹¹The LORD would speak to Moses face to face, as a man speaks with his friend. Then Moses would return to the camp, but his young aide Joshua son of Nun did not leave the tent.

¹²Moses said to the LORD, "You have been telling me, 'Lead these people,' but you have not let me know whom you will send with me. You have said, 'I know you by name and you have found favor with me.' ¹³If you are pleased with me, teach me your ways so I may know you and continue to find favor with you. Remember that this nation is your people."

¹⁴The LORD replied, "My Presence will go with you, and I will give you rest."

¹⁵Then Moses said to him, "If your Presence does not go with us, do not send us up from here. ¹⁶How will anyone know that you are pleased with me and with your people unless you go with us? What else will distinguish me and your people from all the other people on the face of the earth?"

¹⁷And the LORD said to Moses, "I will do the very thing you have asked, because I am pleased with you and I know you by name."

¹⁸Then Moses said, "Now show me your glory."

¹⁹And the LORD said, "I will cause all my goodness to pass in front of you, and I will proclaim my name, the LORD, in your presence. I will have mercy on whom I will have mercy, and I will have compassion on whom I will have compassion. ²⁰But," he said, "you cannot see my face, for no one may see me and live."

²¹Then the LORD said, "There is a place near me where you may stand on a rock. ²²When my glory passes by, I will put you in a cleft in the rock and cover you with my hand until I have passed by. ²³Then I will remove my hand and you will see my back; but my face must not be seen."

CHAPTER 34

The LORD said to Moses, "Chisel out two stone tablets like the first ones, and I will write on them the words that were on the first tablets, which you broke. ²Be ready in the morning, and then come up on Mount Sinai. Present yourself to me there on top of the mountain. ³No one is to come with you or be seen anywhere on the mountain; not even the flocks and herds may graze in front of the mountain."

⁴So Moses chiseled out two stone tablets like the first ones and went up Mount Sinai early in the morning, as the LORD had commanded him; and he carried the two stone tablets in his hands. ⁵Then the LORD came down in the cloud and stood there with him and proclaimed his name, the LORD. ⁶And he passed in front of Moses, proclaiming, "The LORD, the LORD, the compassionate and gracious God, slow to anger, abounding in love and faithfulness, ⁷maintaining love to thousands, and forgiving wickedness, rebellion and sin. Yet

he does not leave the guilty unpunished; he punishes the children and their children for the sin of the fathers to the third and fourth generation."

⁸Moses bowed to the ground at once and worshiped. ⁹"O Lord, if I have found favor in your eyes," he said, "then let the Lord go with us. Although this is a stiff-necked people, forgive our wickedness and our sin, and take us as your inheritance."

¹⁰Then the LORD said: "I am making a covenant with you. Before all your people I will do wonders never before done in any nation in all the world. The people you live among will see how awesome is the work that I, the LORD, will do for you. ¹¹Obey what I command you today. I will drive out before you the Amorites, Canaanites, Hittites, Perizzites, Hivites and Jebusites. ¹²Be careful not to make a treaty with those who live in the land where you are going, or they will be a snare among you. ¹³Break down their altars, smash their sacred stones and cut down their Asherah poles.ᵛ ¹⁴Do not worship any other god, for the LORD, whose name is Jealous, is a jealous God.

¹⁵"Be careful not to make a treaty with those who live in the land; for when they prostitute themselves to their gods and sacrifice to them, they will invite you and you will eat their sacrifices. ¹⁶And when you choose some of their daughters as wives for your sons and those daughters prostitute themselves to their gods, they will lead your sons to do the same.

¹⁷"Do not make cast idols.

¹⁸"Celebrate the Feast of Unleavened Bread. For seven days eat bread made without yeast, as I commanded you. Do this at the appointed time in the month of Abib, for in that month you came out of Egypt.

¹⁹"The first offspring of every womb belongs to me, including all the firstborn males of your livestock, whether from herd or flock. ²⁰Redeem the firstborn donkey with a lamb, but if you do not redeem it, break its neck. Redeem all your firstborn sons.

"No one is to appear before me empty-handed.

²¹"Six days you shall labor, but on the seventh day you shall rest; even during

ᵛ13 That is, symbols of the goddess Asherah

the plowing season and harvest you must rest.

22"Celebrate the Feast of Weeks with the firstfruits of the wheat harvest, and the Feast of Ingathering at the turn of the year.ʷ 23Three times a year all your men are to appear before the Sovereign LORD, the God of Israel. 24I will drive out nations before you and enlarge your territory, and no one will covet your land when you go up three times each year to appear before the LORD your God.

25"Do not offer the blood of a sacrifice to me along with anything containing yeast, and do not let any of the sacrifice from the Passover Feast remain until morning.

26"Bring the best of the firstfruits of your soil to the house of the LORD your God.

"Do not cook a young goat in its mother's milk."

27Then the LORD said to Moses, "Write down these words, for in accordance with these words I have made a covenant with you and with Israel." 28Moses was there with the LORD forty days and forty nights

ʷ22 That is, in the fall

without eating bread or drinking water. And he wrote on the tablets the words of the covenant—the Ten Commandments.

29When Moses came down from Mount Sinai with the two tablets of the Testimony in his hands, he was not aware that his face was radiant because he had spoken with the LORD. 30When Aaron and all the Israelites saw Moses, his face was radiant, and they were afraid to come near him. 31But Moses called to them; so Aaron and all the leaders of the community came back to him, and he spoke to them. 32Afterward all the Israelites came near him, and he gave them all the commands the LORD had given him on Mount Sinai.

33When Moses finished speaking to them, he put a veil over his face. 34But whenever he entered the LORD's presence to speak with him, he removed the veil until he came out. And when he came out and told the Israelites what he had been commanded, 35they saw that his face was radiant. Then Moses would put the veil back over his face until he went in to speak with the LORD.

JANUARY 31 ☐ DAY 31
EXODUS 35–40
Tabernacle Erected and Occupied

 OVERVIEW The book of Exodus closes with a detailed account of the construction of the tabernacle, the new place of residence for the God of Israel as he accompanies his people to Canaan. Notice the many steps involved in the project: Moses organizes the needed workers and materials; skilled artisans do the actual construction; Moses inspects the finished work; the tabernacle is erected and the furniture set in place; and finally the glory of the Lord fills the tabernacle, showing God's pleasure with the structure. From start to finish, the entire project is done "just as the Lord commanded [Moses]."

Chapter 35	Chapters 36–39		Chapter 40	
Step 1: Preparation	Step 2: Construction 36:1 39:31	Step 3: Inspection 39:32 39:43	Step 4: Erection 1 33	Step 5: Occupation 34 38
Tabernacle Completed		Tabernacle Occupied		

 YOUR DAILY WALK God has always sought to dwell in the midst of his people. Think back to the opening chapters of Genesis, and what do you find? Adam and Eve in the garden. And in the cool of the

How many friends would you have left if you started spending as much time with them as you do with God?

evening God walks through the garden, seeking face-to-face fellowship with his creation.

In today's reading, God's glory takes up residence in the tabernacle in order to accompany the Israelites on their journey to Canaan. Later in Israel's history, God's presence will reside in Solomon's magnificent temple. And today God's Holy Spirit indwells every child of God (1 Corinthians 6:19–20). The lesson is clear: God wants to identify himself with those who are truly his. More specifically, God wants to identify himself with *you*, fellowship with *you*, spend time with *you*, help *you* get to know him better.

How do you go about building a relationship like that? Jot down the first five things that come to mind. Now use your list to help you organize your day and assign priorities to your activities. Place "Time with God" at the top of the list. After all, that's *his* greatest desire: to walk and talk with you! If that's *your* greatest desire, tell him so right now.

 INSIGHT "We've Come a Long Way, Baby"
Exodus begins with a mob of miserable slaves held captive in Egypt, yet ends with an emancipated nation in fellowship with God and on its way to Canaan. No wonder Exodus is called the "book of redemption"!

CHAPTER 35

Moses assembled the whole Israelite community and said to them, "These are the things the LORD has commanded you to do: ²For six days, work is to be done, but the seventh day shall be your holy day, a Sabbath of rest to the LORD. Whoever does any work on it must be put to death. ³Do not light a fire in any of your dwellings on the Sabbath day."

⁴Moses said to the whole Israelite community, "This is what the LORD has commanded: ⁵From what you have, take an offering for the LORD. Everyone who is willing is to bring to the LORD an offering of gold, silver and bronze; ⁶blue, purple and scarlet yarn and fine linen; goat hair; ⁷ram skins dyed red and hides of sea cowsˣ; acacia wood; ⁸olive oil for the light; spices for the anointing oil and for the fragrant incense; ⁹and onyx stones and other gems to be mounted on the ephod and breastpiece.

¹⁰"All who are skilled among you are to come and make everything the LORD has commanded: ¹¹the tabernacle with its tent and its covering, clasps, frames, crossbars, posts and bases; ¹²the ark with its poles and the atonement cover and the curtain that shields it; ¹³the table with its poles and all its articles and the bread of the Presence; ¹⁴the lampstand that is for light with its accessories, lamps and oil for the

light; ¹⁵the altar of incense with its poles, the anointing oil and the fragrant incense; the curtain for the doorway at the entrance to the tabernacle; ¹⁶the altar of burnt offering with its bronze grating, its poles and all its utensils; the bronze basin with its stand; ¹⁷the curtains of the courtyard with its posts and bases, and the curtain for the entrance to the courtyard; ¹⁸the tent pegs for the tabernacle and for the courtyard, and their ropes; ¹⁹the woven garments worn for ministering in the sanctuary—both the sacred garments for Aaron the priest and the garments for his sons when they serve as priests."

²⁰Then the whole Israelite community withdrew from Moses' presence, ²¹and everyone who was willing and whose heart moved him came and brought an offering to the LORD for the work on the Tent of Meeting, for all its service, and for the sacred garments. ²²All who were willing, men and women alike, came and brought gold jewelry of all kinds: brooches, earrings, rings and ornaments. They all presented their gold as a wave offering to the LORD. ²³Everyone who had blue, purple or scarlet yarn or fine linen, or goat hair, ram skins dyed red or hides of sea cows brought them. ²⁴Those presenting an offering of silver or bronze brought it as an offering to the LORD, and everyone who had acacia wood for any

ˣ7 That is, dugongs; also in verse 23

part of the work brought it. ²⁵Every skilled woman spun with her hands and brought what she had spun—blue, purple or scarlet yarn or fine linen. ²⁶And all the women who were willing and had the skill spun the goat hair. ²⁷The leaders brought onyx stones and other gems to be mounted on the ephod and breastpiece. ²⁸They also brought spices and olive oil for the light and for the anointing oil and for the fragrant incense. ²⁹All the Israelite men and women who were willing brought to the LORD freewill offerings for all the work the LORD through Moses had commanded them to do.

³⁰Then Moses said to the Israelites, "See, the LORD has chosen Bezalel son of Uri, the son of Hur, of the tribe of Judah, ³¹and he has filled him with the Spirit of God, with skill, ability and knowledge in all kinds of crafts— ³²to make artistic designs for work in gold, silver and bronze, ³³to cut and set stones, to work in wood and to engage in all kinds of artistic craftsmanship. ³⁴And he has given both him and Oholiab son of Ahisamach, of the tribe of Dan, the ability to teach others. ³⁵He has filled them with skill to do all kinds of work as craftsmen, designers, embroiderers in blue, purple and scarlet yarn and fine linen, and weavers—all of them master craftsmen and C H A P T E R   3 6 designers. ¹So Bezalel, Oholiab and every skilled person to whom the LORD has given skill and ability to know how to carry out all the work of constructing the sanctuary are to do the work just as the Lord has commanded."

²Then Moses summoned Bezalel and Oholiab and every skilled person to whom the LORD had given ability and who was willing to come and do the work. ³They received from Moses all the offerings the Israelites had brought to carry out the work of constructing the sanctuary. And the people continued to bring freewill offerings morning after morning. ⁴So all the skilled craftsmen who were doing all the work on the sanctuary left their work ⁵and said to Moses, "The people are bringing more than enough for doing the work the LORD commanded to be done."

⁶Then Moses gave an order and they sent this word throughout the camp: "No man or woman is to make anything else as an offering for the sanctuary." And so the people were restrained from bringing more, ⁷because what they already had was more than enough to do all the work.

⁸All the skilled men among the workmen made the tabernacle with ten curtains of finely twisted linen and blue, purple and scarlet yarn, with cherubim worked into them by a skilled craftsman. ⁹All the curtains were the same size—twenty-eight cubits long and four cubits wide.ʸ ¹⁰They joined five of the curtains together and did the same with the other five. ¹¹Then they made loops of blue material along the edge of the end curtain in one set, and the same was done with the end curtain in the other set. ¹²They also made fifty loops on one curtain and fifty loops on the end curtain of the other set, with the loops opposite each other. ¹³Then they made fifty gold clasps and used them to fasten the two sets of curtains together so that the tabernacle was a unit.

¹⁴They made curtains of goat hair for the tent over the tabernacle—eleven altogether. ¹⁵All eleven curtains were the same size—thirty cubits long and four cubits wide.ᶻ ¹⁶They joined five of the curtains into one set and the other six into another set. ¹⁷Then they made fifty loops along the edge of the end curtain in one set and also along the edge of the end curtain in the other set. ¹⁸They made fifty bronze clasps to fasten the tent together as a unit. ¹⁹Then they made for the tent a covering of ram skins dyed red, and over that a covering of hides of sea cows.ᵃ

²⁰They made upright frames of acacia wood for the tabernacle. ²¹Each frame was ten cubits long and a cubit and a half wide,ᵇ ²²with two projections set parallel to each other. They made all the frames of the tabernacle in this way. ²³They made twenty frames for the south side of the tabernacle ²⁴and made forty silver bases to go under them—two bases for each frame, one under each projection. ²⁵For the other side, the north side of the tabernacle, they made twenty frames ²⁶and forty silver bases—two under each frame. ²⁷They made six frames for the far end, that is, the west end of the tabernacle,

y9 That is, about 42 feet (about 12.5 meters) long and 6 feet (about 1.8 meters) long and 6 feet (about 1.8 meters) wide   z15 That is, about 45 feet (about 13.5 meters) long and 6 feet (about 1.8 meters) wide   ª19 That is, dugongs   b21 That is, about 15 feet (about 4.5 meters) long and 2 1/4 feet (about 0.7 meter) wide

[28]and two frames were made for the corners of the tabernacle at the far end. [29]At these two corners the frames were double from the bottom all the way to the top and fitted into a single ring; both were made alike. [30]So there were eight frames and sixteen silver bases—two under each frame.

[31]They also made crossbars of acacia wood: five for the frames on one side of the tabernacle, [32]five for those on the other side, and five for the frames on the west, at the far end of the tabernacle. [33]They made the center crossbar so that it extended from end to end at the middle of the frames. [34]They overlaid the frames with gold and made gold rings to hold the crossbars. They also overlaid the crossbars with gold.

[35]They made the curtain of blue, purple and scarlet yarn and finely twisted linen, with cherubim worked into it by a skilled craftsman. [36]They made four posts of acacia wood for it and overlaid them with gold. They made gold hooks for them and cast their four silver bases. [37]For the entrance to the tent they made a curtain of blue, purple and scarlet yarn and finely twisted linen—the work of an embroiderer; [38]and they made five posts with hooks for them. They overlaid the tops of the posts and their bands with gold and made their five bases of bronze.

CHAPTER 37

Bezalel made the ark of acacia wood—two and a half cubits long, a cubit and a half wide, and a cubit and a half high.[c] [2]He overlaid it with pure gold, both inside and out, and made a gold molding around it. [3]He cast four gold rings for it and fastened them to its four feet, with two rings on one side and two rings on the other. [4]Then he made poles of acacia wood and overlaid them with gold. [5]And he inserted the poles into the rings on the sides of the ark to carry it.

[6]He made the atonement cover of pure gold—two and a half cubits long and a cubit and a half wide.[d] [7]Then he made two cherubim out of hammered gold at the ends of the cover. [8]He made one cherub on one end and the second cherub on the other; at the two ends he made them of one piece with the cover. [9]The cherubim had their wings spread upward, overshadowing the cover with them. The cherubim faced each other, looking toward the cover.

[10]They[e] made the table of acacia wood—two cubits long, a cubit wide, and a cubit and a half high.[f] [11]Then they overlaid it with pure gold and made a gold molding around it. [12]They also made around it a rim a handbreadth[g] wide and put a gold molding on the rim. [13]They cast four gold rings for the table and fastened them to the four corners, where the four legs were. [14]The rings were put close to the rim to hold the poles used in carrying the table. [15]The poles for carrying the table were made of acacia wood and were overlaid with gold. [16]And they made from pure gold the articles for the table—its plates and dishes and bowls and its pitchers for the pouring out of drink offerings.

[17]They made the lampstand of pure gold and hammered it out, base and shaft; its flowerlike cups, buds and blossoms were of one piece with it. [18]Six branches extended from the sides of the lampstand—three on one side and three on the other. [19]Three cups shaped like almond flowers with buds and blossoms were on one branch, three on the next branch and the same for all six branches extending from the lampstand. [20]And on the lampstand were four cups shaped like almond flowers with buds and blossoms. [21]One bud was under the first pair of branches extending from the lampstand, a second bud under the second pair, and a third bud under the third pair—six branches in all. [22]The buds and the branches were all of one piece with the lampstand, hammered out of pure gold.

[23]They made its seven lamps, as well as its wick trimmers and trays, of pure gold. [24]They made the lampstand and all its accessories from one talent[h] of pure gold.

[25]They made the altar of incense out of acacia wood. It was square, a cubit long and a cubit wide, and two cubits high[i]—its horns of one piece with it. [26]They overlaid the top and all the sides and the

---

[c]1 That is, about 3 3/4 feet (about 1.1 meters) long and 2 1/4 feet (about 0.7 meter) wide and high   [d]6 That is, about 3 3/4 feet (about 1.1 meters) long and 2 1/4 feet (about 0.7 meter) wide   [e]10 Or *He*; also in verses 11-29   [f]10 That is, about 3 feet (about 0.9 meter) long, 1 1/2 feet (about 0.5 meter) wide, and 2 1/4 feet (about 0.7 meter) high   [g]12 That is, about 3 inches (about 8 centimeters)   [h]24 That is, about 75 pounds (about 34 kilograms)   [i]25 That is, about 1 1/2 feet (about 0.5 meter) long and wide, and about 3 feet (about 0.9 meter) high

horns with pure gold, and made a gold molding around it. 27They made two gold rings below the molding—two on opposite sides—to hold the poles used to carry it. 28They made the poles of acacia wood and overlaid them with gold.

29They also made the sacred anointing oil and the pure, fragrant incense—the work of a perfumer.

CHAPTER 38

They[j] built the altar of burnt offering of acacia wood, three cubits[k] high; it was square, five cubits long and five cubits wide.[l] 2They made a horn at each of the four corners, so that the horns and the altar were of one piece, and they overlaid the altar with bronze. 3They made all its utensils of bronze—its pots, shovels, sprinkling bowls, meat forks and firepans. 4They made a grating for the altar, a bronze network, to be under its ledge, halfway up the altar. 5They cast bronze rings to hold the poles for the four corners of the bronze grating. 6They made the poles of acacia wood and overlaid them with bronze. 7They inserted the poles into the rings so they would be on the sides of the altar for carrying it. They made it hollow, out of boards.

8They made the bronze basin and its bronze stand from the mirrors of the women who served at the entrance to the Tent of Meeting.

9Next they made the courtyard. The south side was a hundred cubits[m] long and had curtains of finely twisted linen, 10with twenty posts and twenty bronze bases, and with silver hooks and bands on the posts. 11The north side was also a hundred cubits long and had twenty posts and twenty bronze bases, with silver hooks and bands on the posts.

12The west end was fifty cubits[n] wide and had curtains, with ten posts and ten bases, with silver hooks and bands on the posts. 13The east end, toward the sunrise, was also fifty cubits wide. 14Curtains fifteen cubits[o] long were on one side of the entrance, with three posts and three bases, 15and curtains fifteen cubits long were on the other side of the entrance to

the courtyard, with three posts and three bases. 16All the curtains around the courtyard were of finely twisted linen. 17The bases for the posts were bronze. The hooks and bands on the posts were silver, and their tops were overlaid with silver; so all the posts of the courtyard had silver bands.

18The curtain for the entrance to the courtyard was of blue, purple and scarlet yarn and finely twisted linen—the work of an embroiderer. It was twenty cubits[p] long and, like the curtains of the courtyard, five cubits[q] high, 19with four posts and four bronze bases. Their hooks and bands were silver, and their tops were overlaid with silver. 20All the tent pegs of the tabernacle and of the surrounding courtyard were bronze.

21These are the amounts of the materials used for the tabernacle, the tabernacle of the Testimony, which were recorded at Moses' command by the Levites under the direction of Ithamar son of Aaron, the priest. 22(Bezalel son of Uri, the son of Hur, of the tribe of Judah, made everything the LORD commanded Moses; 23with him was Oholiab son of Ahisamach, of the tribe of Dan—a craftsman and designer, and an embroiderer in blue, purple and scarlet yarn and fine linen.) 24The total amount of the gold from the wave offering used for all the work on the sanctuary was 29 talents and 730 shekels,[r] according to the sanctuary shekel.

25The silver obtained from those of the community who were counted in the census was 100 talents and 1,775 shekels,[s] according to the sanctuary shekel— 26one beka per person, that is, half a shekel,[t] according to the sanctuary shekel, from everyone who had crossed over to those counted, twenty years old or more, a total of 603,550 men. 27The 100 talents[u] of silver were used to cast the bases for the sanctuary and for the curtain—100 bases from the 100 talents, one talent for each base. 28They used the 1,775 shekels[v] to make the hooks for the posts, to overlay the tops of the posts, and to make their bands.

29The bronze from the wave offering

j1 Or He; also in verses 2-9   k1 That is, about 4 1/2 feet (about 1.3 meters)   l1 That is, about 7 1/2 feet (about 2.3 meters) long and wide   m9 That is, about 150 feet (about 46 meters)   n12 That is, about 75 feet (about 23 meters)   o14 That is, about 22 1/2 feet (about 6.9 meters)   p18 That is, about 30 feet (about 9 meters)   q18 That is, about 7 1/2 feet (about 2.3 meters)   r24 The weight of the gold was a little over one ton (about 1 metric ton).   s25 The weight of the silver was a little over 3 3/4 tons (about 3.4 metric tons).   t26 That is, about 1/5 ounce (about 5.5 grams)   u27 That is about 3 3/4 tons (about 3.4 metric tons)   v28 That is, about 45 pounds (about 20 kilograms) was 70 talents and 2,400 shekels. [w] [30]They used it to make the bases for the entrance to the Tent of Meeting, the bronze altar with its bronze grating and all its utensils, [31]the bases for the surrounding courtyard and those for its entrance and all the tent pegs for the tabernacle and those for the surrounding courtyard.

CHAPTER 39

From the blue, purple and scarlet yarn they made woven garments for ministering in the sanctuary. They also made sacred garments for Aaron, as the LORD commanded Moses.

[2]They[x] made the ephod of gold, and of blue, purple and scarlet yarn, and of finely twisted linen. [3]They hammered out thin sheets of gold and cut strands to be worked into the blue, purple and scarlet yarn and fine linen—the work of a skilled craftsman. [4]They made shoulder pieces for the ephod, which were attached to two of its corners, so it could be fastened. [5]Its skillfully woven waistband was like it—of one piece with the ephod and made with gold, and with blue, purple and scarlet yarn, and with finely twisted linen, as the LORD commanded Moses.

[6]They mounted the onyx stones in gold filigree settings and engraved them like a seal with the names of the sons of Israel. [7]Then they fastened them on the shoulder pieces of the ephod as memorial stones for the sons of Israel, as the LORD commanded Moses.

[8]They fashioned the breastpiece—the work of a skilled craftsman. They made it like the ephod: of gold, and of blue, purple and scarlet yarn, and of finely twisted linen. [9]It was square—a span[y] long and a span wide—and folded double. [10]Then they mounted four rows of precious stones on it. In the first row there was a ruby, a topaz and a beryl; [11]in the second row a turquoise, a sapphire[z] and an emerald; [12]in the third row a jacinth, an agate and an amethyst; [13]in the fourth row a chrysolite, an onyx and a jasper.[a] They were mounted in gold filigree settings. [14]There were twelve stones, one for each of the names of the sons of Israel, each engraved like a seal with the name of one of the twelve tribes.

[15]For the breastpiece they made braided chains of pure gold, like a rope. [16]They made two gold filigree settings and two gold rings, and fastened the rings to two of the corners of the breastpiece. [17]They fastened the two gold chains to the rings at the corners of the breastpiece, [18]and the other ends of the chains to the two settings, attaching them to the shoulder pieces of the ephod at the front. [19]They made two gold rings and attached them to the other two corners of the breastpiece on the inside edge next to the ephod. [20]Then they made two more gold rings and attached them to the bottom of the shoulder pieces on the front of the ephod, close to the seam just above the waistband of the ephod. [21]They tied the rings of the breastpiece to the rings of the ephod with blue cord, connecting it to the waistband so that the breastpiece would not swing out from the ephod—as the LORD commanded Moses.

[22]They made the robe of the ephod entirely of blue cloth—the work of a weaver— [23]with an opening in the center of the robe like the opening of a collar,[b] and a band around this opening, so that it would not tear. [24]They made pomegranates of blue, purple and scarlet yarn and finely twisted linen around the hem of the robe. [25]And they made bells of pure gold and attached them around the hem between the pomegranates. [26]The bells and pomegranates alternated around the hem of the robe to be worn for ministering, as the LORD commanded Moses.

[27]For Aaron and his sons, they made tunics of fine linen—the work of a weaver— [28]and the turban of fine linen, the linen headbands and the undergarments of finely twisted linen. [29]The sash was of finely twisted linen and blue, purple and scarlet yarn—the work of an embroiderer—as the LORD commanded Moses.

[30]They made the plate, the sacred diadem, out of pure gold and engraved on it, like an inscription on a seal: HOLY TO THE LORD. [31]Then they fastened a blue cord to it to attach it to the turban, as the LORD commanded Moses.

[32]So all the work on the tabernacle, the Tent of Meeting, was completed. The Is-

---

[w]29 The weight of the bronze was about 2 1/2 tons (about 2.4 metric tons).   [x]2 Or *He*; also in verses 7, 8 and 22   [y]9 That is, about 9 inches (about 22 centimeters)   [z]11 Or *lapis lazuli*   [a]13 The precise identification of some of these precious stones is uncertain.   [b]23 The meaning of the Hebrew for this word is uncertain.

raelites did everything just as the LORD commanded Moses. ³³Then they brought the tabernacle to Moses: the tent and all its furnishings, its clasps, frames, crossbars, posts and bases; ³⁴the covering of ram skins dyed red, the covering of hides of sea cowsᶜ and the shielding curtain; ³⁵the ark of the Testimony with its poles and the atonement cover; ³⁶the table with all its articles and the bread of the Presence; ³⁷the pure gold lampstand with its row of lamps and all its accessories, and the oil for the light; ³⁸the gold altar, the anointing oil, the fragrant incense, and the curtain for the entrance to the tent; ³⁹the bronze altar with its bronze grating, its poles and all its utensils; the basin with its stand; ⁴⁰the curtains of the courtyard with its posts and bases, and the curtain for the entrance to the courtyard; the ropes and tent pegs for the courtyard; all the furnishings for the tabernacle, the Tent of Meeting; ⁴¹and the woven garments worn for ministering in the sanctuary, both the sacred garments for Aaron the priest and the garments for his sons when serving as priests.

⁴²The Israelites had done all the work just as the LORD had commanded Moses. ⁴³Moses inspected the work and saw that they had done it just as the LORD had commanded. So Moses blessed them.

CHAPTER 40

Then the LORD said to Moses: ²"Set up the tabernacle, the Tent of Meeting, on the first day of the first month. ³Place the ark of the Testimony in it and shield the ark with the curtain. ⁴Bring in the table and set out what belongs on it. Then bring in the lampstand and set up its lamps. ⁵Place the gold altar of incense in front of the ark of the Testimony and put the curtain at the entrance to the tabernacle.

⁶"Place the altar of burnt offering in front of the entrance to the tabernacle, the Tent of Meeting; ⁷place the basin between the Tent of Meeting and the altar and put water in it. ⁸Set up the courtyard around it and put the curtain at the entrance to the courtyard.

⁹"Take the anointing oil and anoint the tabernacle and everything in it; consecrate it and all its furnishings, and it will be holy. ¹⁰Then anoint the altar of burnt offering and all its utensils; consecrate the altar, and it will be most holy. ¹¹Anoint the basin and its stand and consecrate them.

¹²"Bring Aaron and his sons to the entrance to the Tent of Meeting and wash them with water. ¹³Then dress Aaron in the sacred garments, anoint him and consecrate him so he may serve me as priest. ¹⁴Bring his sons and dress them in tunics. ¹⁵Anoint them just as you anointed their father, so they may serve me as priests. Their anointing will be to a priesthood that will continue for all generations to come." ¹⁶Moses did everything just as the LORD commanded him.

¹⁷So the tabernacle was set up on the first day of the first month in the second year. ¹⁸When Moses set up the tabernacle, he put the bases in place, erected the frames, inserted the crossbars and set up the posts. ¹⁹Then he spread the tent over the tabernacle and put the covering over the tent, as the LORD commanded him.

²⁰He took the Testimony and placed it in the ark, attached the poles to the ark and put the atonement cover over it. ²¹Then he brought the ark into the tabernacle and hung the shielding curtain and shielded the ark of the Testimony, as the LORD commanded him.

²²Moses placed the table in the Tent of Meeting on the north side of the tabernacle outside the curtain ²³and set out the bread on it before the LORD, as the LORD commanded him.

²⁴He placed the lampstand in the Tent of Meeting opposite the table on the south side of the tabernacle ²⁵and set up the lamps before the LORD, as the LORD commanded him.

²⁶Moses placed the gold altar in the Tent of Meeting in front of the curtain ²⁷and burned fragrant incense on it, as the LORD commanded him. ²⁸Then he put up the curtain at the entrance to the tabernacle.

²⁹He set the altar of burnt offering near the entrance to the tabernacle, the Tent of Meeting, and offered on it burnt offerings and grain offerings, as the LORD commanded him.

³⁰He placed the basin between the Tent of Meeting and the altar and put water in

it for washing, [31]and Moses and Aaron and his sons used it to wash their hands and feet. [32]They washed whenever they entered the Tent of Meeting or approached the altar, as the LORD commanded Moses.

[33]Then Moses set up the courtyard around the tabernacle and altar and put up the curtain at the entrance to the courtyard. And so Moses finished the work.

[34]Then the cloud covered the Tent of Meeting, and the glory of the LORD filled the tabernacle. [35]Moses could not enter the Tent of Meeting because the cloud had settled upon it, and the glory of the LORD filled the tabernacle.

[36]In all the travels of the Israelites, whenever the cloud lifted from above the tabernacle, they would set out; [37]but if the cloud did not lift, they did not set out—until the day it lifted. [38]So the cloud of the LORD was over the tabernacle by day, and fire was in the cloud by night, in the sight of all the house of Israel during all their travels.

Leviticus

DELIVERED by God to Moses on Mount Sinai, the instructions of Leviticus pertain to Israel's personal and national life. Leviticus—the new nation's book of worship—derives its name from the tribe of Levi, which was entrusted with the ceremonial worship of God and the physical care of the tabernacle. Leviticus solves the twin dilemmas of how a sinful people can achieve access to God (through animal sacrifices) and maintain fellowship with God (through obedience to his Word).

Focus	Sacrifice			Sanctification			
Divisions	Voluntary Offerings	Compulsory Offerings	Priestly Orders	Personal Purity	National Purity	Priestly Purity	Future Purity
	1 3	4 7	8 10	11 15	16 20	21 23	24 27
Topics	Access to God by Sacrifice			Fellowship with God by Obedience			
	Priests			Feasts			
Place	Mount Sinai						
Time	About One Month						

FEBRUARY 1 □ DAY 32
LEVITICUS 1–3
Three Voluntary Offerings

OVERVIEW Leviticus opens with a description of the five different sacrifices an Israelite could offer: three for those in fellowship with God and two for those out of fellowship with God. The first three offerings were tailored to the person's ability to give, and each had a special significance. The burnt offering signified the devotion of the worshiper to God, the grain offering pointed to God's provision in life and the fellowship offering pictured the thankful worshiper's friendship with God.

Chapter 1	Chapter 2	Chapter 3
Burnt Offering	Grain Offering	Fellowship Offering
Worship Offerings		

YOUR DAILY WALK During a visit to Korea two American business-men were highly amused to see a young farmer hitched to a plow that was guided by his father. Later they learned that both father and son were Christians who sold their only ox to provide money for a new church building.

A drop of praise is unsuitable acknowledgment for an ocean of mercy.

"What a stupendous sacrifice!" exclaimed one of the businessmen.

"Not really," replied a missionary accompanying them. "They were only sorry they had but one ox to give to the Lord's work."

On one occasion Jesus was dining with a Pharisee named Simon when a woman of the streets interrupted the dinner in a most star-tling way. Breaking an alabaster jar of perfume, she anointed the feet of Jesus, prompting the Lord to respond, "Therefore, I tell you, her many sins have been forgiven—for she loved much. But he who has been forgiven little loves little" (Luke 7:47).

What is one tangible way in which you can show your gratitude to-day for God's great love and forgiveness? Select a twentieth-century sacrifice of praise you can offer him—perhaps in the form of a special offering or act of kindness—to say thank you to your heavenly Father who so richly deserves it!

INSIGHT Exodus and Leviticus: A Study in Contrasts

Exodus emphasizes:	*Leviticus emphasizes:*
Pardon	Purity
God's approach to mankind	Mankind's approach to God
Salvation	Sanctification
"Let my people go"	"Be holy because I, the LORD your God, am holy"

CHAPTER 1

The LORD called to Moses and spoke to him from the Tent of Meeting. He said, ²"Speak to the Israelites and say to them: 'When any of you brings an offering to the LORD, bring as your offering an animal from either the herd or the flock.

³"'If the offering is a burnt offering from the herd, he is to offer a male with-out defect. He must present it at the

entrance to the Tent of Meeting so that it[a] will be acceptable to the LORD. [4]He is to lay his hand on the head of the burnt offering, and it will be accepted on his behalf to make atonement for him. [5]He is to slaughter the young bull before the LORD, and then Aaron's sons the priests shall bring the blood and sprinkle it against the altar on all sides at the entrance to the Tent of Meeting. [6]He is to skin the burnt offering and cut it into pieces. [7]The sons of Aaron the priest are to put fire on the altar and arrange wood on the fire. [8]Then Aaron's sons the priests shall arrange the pieces, including the head and the fat, on the burning wood that is on the altar. [9]He is to wash the inner parts and the legs with water, and the priest is to burn all of it on the altar. It is a burnt offering, an offering made by fire, an aroma pleasing to the LORD.

[10]" 'If the offering is a burnt offering from the flock, from either the sheep or the goats, he is to offer a male without defect. [11]He is to slaughter it at the north side of the altar before the LORD, and Aaron's sons the priests shall sprinkle its blood against the altar on all sides. [12]He is to cut it into pieces, and the priest shall arrange them, including the head and the fat, on the burning wood that is on the altar. [13]He is to wash the inner parts and the legs with water, and the priest is to bring all of it and burn it on the altar. It is a burnt offering, an offering made by fire, an aroma pleasing to the LORD.

[14]" 'If the offering to the LORD is a burnt offering of birds, he is to offer a dove or a young pigeon. [15]The priest shall bring it to the altar, wring off the head and burn it on the altar; its blood shall be drained out on the side of the altar. [16]He is to remove the crop with its contents[b] and throw it to the east side of the altar, where the ashes are. [17]He shall tear it open by the wings, not severing it completely, and then the priest shall burn it on the wood that is on the fire on the altar. It is a burnt offering, an offering made by fire, an aroma pleasing to the LORD.

CHAPTER 2

" 'When someone brings a grain offering to the LORD, his offering is to be of fine flour. He is to pour oil on it, put incense on it [2]and take it to Aaron's sons the priests. The priest shall take a handful of the fine flour and oil, together with all the incense, and burn this as a memorial portion on the altar, an offering made by fire, an aroma pleasing to the LORD. [3]The rest of the grain offering belongs to Aaron and his sons; it is a most holy part of the offerings made to the LORD by fire.

[4]" 'If you bring a grain offering baked in an oven, it is to consist of fine flour: cakes made without yeast and mixed with oil, or[c] wafers made without yeast and spread with oil. [5]If your grain offering is prepared on a griddle, it is to be made of fine flour mixed with oil, and without yeast. [6]Crumble it and pour oil on it; it is a grain offering. [7]If your grain offering is cooked in a pan, it is to be made of fine flour and oil. [8]Bring the grain offering made of these things to the LORD; present it to the priest, who shall take it to the altar. [9]He shall take out the memorial portion from the grain offering and burn it on the altar as an offering made by fire, an aroma pleasing to the LORD. [10]The rest of the grain offering belongs to Aaron and his sons; it is a most holy part of the offerings made to the LORD by fire.

[11]" 'Every grain offering you bring to the LORD must be made without yeast, for you are not to burn any yeast or honey in an offering made to the LORD by fire. [12]You may bring them to the LORD as an offering of the firstfruits, but they are not to be offered on the altar as a pleasing aroma. [13]Season all your grain offerings with salt. Do not leave the salt of the covenant of your God out of your grain offerings; add salt to all your offerings.

[14]" 'If you bring a grain offering of firstfruits to the LORD, offer crushed heads of new grain roasted in the fire. [15]Put oil and incense on it; it is a grain offering. [16]The priest shall burn the memorial portion of the crushed grain and the oil, together with all the incense, as an offering made to the LORD by fire.

CHAPTER 3

" 'If someone's offering is a fellowship offering,[d] and he offers an animal from the herd, whether male or female, he is to present before the LORD an animal without defect. [2]He is to lay his hand on the head

---

[a]3 Or he   [b]16 Or crop and the feathers; the meaning of the Hebrew for this word is uncertain.   [c]4 Or and   [d]1 Traditionally peace offering; also in verses 3, 6 and 9

of his offering and slaughter it at the entrance to the Tent of Meeting. Then Aaron's sons the priests shall sprinkle the blood against the altar on all sides. ³From the fellowship offering he is to bring a sacrifice made to the LORD by fire: all the fat that covers the inner parts or is connected to them, ⁴both kidneys with the fat on them near the loins, and the covering of the liver, which he will remove with the kidneys. ⁵Then Aaron's sons are to burn it on the altar on top of the burnt offering that is on the burning wood, as an offering made by fire, an aroma pleasing to the LORD.

⁶" 'If he offers an animal from the flock as a fellowship offering to the LORD, he is to offer a male or female without defect. ⁷If he offers a lamb, he is to present it before the LORD. ⁸He is to lay his hand on the head of his offering and slaughter it in front of the Tent of Meeting. Then Aaron's sons shall sprinkle its blood against the altar on all sides. ⁹From the fellowship offering he is to bring a sacrifice made to the LORD by fire: its fat, the entire fat tail cut off close to the backbone, all the fat that covers the inner parts or is connected to them, ¹⁰both kidneys with the fat on them near the loins, and the covering of the liver, which he will remove with the kidneys. ¹¹The priest shall burn them on the altar as food, an offering made to the LORD by fire.

¹²" 'If his offering is a goat, he is to present it before the LORD. ¹³He is to lay his hand on its head and slaughter it in front of the Tent of Meeting. Then Aaron's sons shall sprinkle its blood against the altar on all sides. ¹⁴From what he offers he is to make this offering to the LORD by fire: all the fat that covers the inner parts or is connected to them, ¹⁵both kidneys with the fat on them near the loins, and the covering of the liver, which he will remove with the kidneys. ¹⁶The priest shall burn them on the altar as food, an offering made by fire, a pleasing aroma. All the fat is the LORD's.

¹⁷" 'This is a lasting ordinance for the generations to come, wherever you live: You must not eat any fat or any blood.' "

FEBRUARY 2 ☐ DAY 33
LEVITICUS 4–7
Two Compulsory Offerings

 OVERVIEW In addition to the three fellowship offerings, God gives instruction regarding two compulsory offerings—both required when sin had interrupted fellowship with him. The sin offering, which covered sins of uncleanness, neglect or thoughtlessness, provided restoration for the sinner while reinforcing the seriousness of sin. The guilt offering, which covered sins of injury to God and others, provided compensation for the injured or offended party.

Chapter 4	Chapter 5	Chapters 6–7
Sin Offering	Guilt Offering	Law of the Offerings
Compulsory Offerings		Reviewing the Offerings

 YOUR DAILY WALK What do a dented fender, a facial scar and a stain on the carpet all have in common? (Hint: It has nothing to do with your teenage son!) Give up? They are all constant reminders of unpleasant experiences: the fire hydrant that ran into your car, the razor that "gotcha," the spill that ruined the rug.

For the Israelites there was another collection of reminders: the bleating of a lamb, the smell of fresh blood, the sight of rising smoke.

Sin is so big that it takes Christ with a cross to measure it. All served to remind them that they were sinners. Every new sin, even an unintentional one, demanded that another animal be slain.

Doesn't that make you appreciate all the more the death of Jesus Christ for you? The fact that he died to set you free from the endless requirement of additional sacrifices is indeed a great reason for rejoicing. Remind yourself often today of Christ's once-for-all-time sacrifice for you, and let that reminder bear the fruit of praise on your lips and in your life.

INSIGHT Sweet and Sour Offerings
Unlike the other three offerings, neither the sin nor the guilt offering was a sweet fragrance to God because sin is never sweet to God. Those two offerings foreshadowed many details of Christ's sacrificial death on the cross:
- The sacrifice was without defect.
- Sin was transferred from the offerer to the sacrifice.
- The sacrifice died in the sinner's place.
- The sin sacrifice was offered outside the camp.

CHAPTER 4

The LORD said to Moses, ²"Say to the Israelites: 'When anyone sins unintentionally and does what is forbidden in any of the LORD's commands—

³" 'If the anointed priest sins, bringing guilt on the people, he must bring to the LORD a young bull without defect as a sin offering for the sin he has committed. ⁴He is to present the bull at the entrance to the Tent of Meeting before the LORD. He is to lay his hand on its head and slaughter it before the LORD. ⁵Then the anointed priest shall take some of the bull's blood and carry it into the Tent of Meeting. ⁶He is to dip his finger into the blood and sprinkle some of it seven times before the LORD, in front of the curtain of the sanctuary. ⁷The priest shall then put some of the blood on the horns of the altar of fragrant incense that is before the LORD in the Tent of Meeting. The rest of the bull's blood he shall pour out at the base of the altar of burnt offering at the entrance to the Tent of Meeting. ⁸He shall remove all the fat from the bull of the sin offering—the fat that covers the inner parts or is connected to them, ⁹both kidneys with the fat on them near the loins, and the covering of the liver, which he will remove with the kidneys— ¹⁰just as the fat is removed from the ox^e sacrificed as a fellowship offering.^f Then the priest shall burn them on the altar of burnt offering. ¹¹But the hide of the bull and all its flesh, as well as the head and legs, the inner parts and offal— ¹²that is, all the rest of the bull—he must take outside the camp to a place ceremonially clean, where the ashes are thrown, and burn it in a wood fire on the ash heap.

¹³" 'If the whole Israelite community sins unintentionally and does what is forbidden in any of the LORD's commands, even though the community is unaware of the matter, they are guilty. ¹⁴When they become aware of the sin they committed, the assembly must bring a young bull as a sin offering and present it before the Tent of Meeting. ¹⁵The elders of the community are to lay their hands on the bull's head before the LORD, and the bull shall be slaughtered before the LORD. ¹⁶Then the anointed priest is to take some of the bull's blood into the Tent of Meeting. ¹⁷He shall dip his finger into the blood and sprinkle it before the LORD seven times in front of the curtain. ¹⁸He is to put some of the blood on the horns of the altar that is before the LORD in the Tent of Meeting. The rest of the blood he shall pour out at the base of the altar of burnt offering at the entrance to the Tent of Meeting. ¹⁹He shall remove all the fat from it and burn it on the altar, ²⁰and do with this bull just as he did with the bull for the sin offering. In this way the priest will make atonement for them, and they will be forgiven. ²¹Then he shall take the bull outside the camp and burn it as he burned the first bull. This is the sin offering for the community.

²²" 'When a leader sins unintentionally

^e10 The Hebrew word can include both male and female.   ^f10 Traditionally *peace offering*; also in verses 26, 31 and 35 and does what is forbidden in any of the commands of the LORD his God, he is guilty. ²³When he is made aware of the sin he committed, he must bring as his offering a male goat without defect. ²⁴He is to lay his hand on the goat's head and slaughter it at the place where the burnt offering is slaughtered before the LORD. It is a sin offering. ²⁵Then the priest shall take some of the blood of the sin offering with his finger and put it on the horns of the altar of burnt offering and pour out the rest of the blood at the base of the altar. ²⁶He shall burn all the fat on the altar as he burned the fat of the fellowship offering. In this way the priest will make atonement for the man's sin, and he will be forgiven.

²⁷" 'If a member of the community sins unintentionally and does what is forbidden in any of the LORD's commands, he is guilty. ²⁸When he is made aware of the sin he committed, he must bring as his offering for the sin he committed a female goat without defect. ²⁹He is to lay his hand on the head of the sin offering and slaughter it at the place of the burnt offering. ³⁰Then the priest is to take some of the blood with his finger and put it on the horns of the altar of burnt offering and pour out the rest of the blood at the base of the altar. ³¹He shall remove all the fat, just as the fat is removed from the fellowship offering, and the priest shall burn it on the altar as an aroma pleasing to the LORD. In this way the priest will make atonement for him, and he will be forgiven.

³²" 'If he brings a lamb as his sin offering, he is to bring a female without defect. ³³He is to lay his hand on its head and slaughter it for a sin offering at the place where the burnt offering is slaughtered. ³⁴Then the priest shall take some of the blood of the sin offering with his finger and put it on the horns of the altar of burnt offering and pour out the rest of the blood at the base of the altar. ³⁵He shall remove all the fat, just as the fat is removed from the lamb of the fellowship offering, and the priest shall burn it on the altar on top of the offerings made to the LORD by fire. In this way the priest will make atonement for him for the sin he has committed, and he will be forgiven.

CHAPTER 5

" 'If a person sins because he does not speak up when he hears a public charge to testify regarding something he has seen or learned about, he will be held responsible.

²" 'Or if a person touches anything ceremonially unclean—whether the carcasses of unclean wild animals or of unclean livestock or of unclean creatures that move along the ground—even though he is unaware of it, he has become unclean and is guilty.

³" 'Or if he touches human uncleanness—anything that would make him unclean—even though he is unaware of it, when he learns of it he will be guilty.

⁴" 'Or if a person thoughtlessly takes an oath to do anything, whether good or evil—in any matter one might carelessly swear about—even though he is unaware of it, in any case when he learns of it he will be guilty.

⁵" 'When anyone is guilty in any of these ways, he must confess in what way he has sinned ⁶and, as a penalty for the sin he has committed, he must bring to the LORD a female lamb or goat from the flock as a sin offering; and the priest shall make atonement for him for his sin.

⁷" 'If he cannot afford a lamb, he is to bring two doves or two young pigeons to the LORD as a penalty for his sin—one for a sin offering and the other for a burnt offering. ⁸He is to bring them to the priest, who shall first offer the one for the sin offering. He is to wring its head from its neck, not severing it completely, ⁹and is to sprinkle some of the blood of the sin offering against the side of the altar; the rest of the blood must be drained out at the base of the altar. It is a sin offering. ¹⁰The priest shall then offer the other as a burnt offering in the prescribed way and make atonement for him for the sin he has committed, and he will be forgiven.

¹¹" 'If, however, he cannot afford two doves or two young pigeons, he is to bring as an offering for his sin a tenth of an ephahᵍ of fine flour for a sin offering. He must not put oil or incense on it, because it is a sin offering. ¹²He is to bring it to the priest, who shall take a handful of it as a memorial portion and burn it on the altar on top of the offerings made to the

---

g 11 That is, probably about 2 quarts (about 2 liters)

LORD by fire. It is a sin offering. ¹³In this way the priest will make atonement for him for any of these sins he has committed, and he will be forgiven. The rest of the offering will belong to the priest, as in the case of the grain offering.' "

¹⁴The LORD said to Moses: ¹⁵"When a person commits a violation and sins unintentionally in regard to any of the LORD's holy things, he is to bring to the LORD as a penalty a ram from the flock, one without defect and of the proper value in silver, according to the sanctuary shekel.ʰ It is a guilt offering. ¹⁶He must make restitution for what he has failed to do in regard to the holy things, add a fifth of the value to that and give it all to the priest, who will make atonement for him with the ram as a guilt offering, and he will be forgiven.

¹⁷"If a person sins and does what is forbidden in any of the LORD's commands, even though he does not know it, he is guilty and will be held responsible. ¹⁸He is to bring to the priest as a guilt offering a ram from the flock, one without defect and of the proper value. In this way the priest will make atonement for him for the wrong he has committed unintentionally, and he will be forgiven. ¹⁹It is a guilt offering; he has been guilty ofⁱ wrongdoing against the LORD."

CHAPTER 6

The LORD said to Moses: ²"If anyone sins and is unfaithful to the LORD by deceiving his neighbor about something entrusted to him or left in his care or stolen, or if he cheats him, ³or if he finds lost property and lies about it, or if he swears falsely, or if he commits any such sin that people may do— ⁴when he thus sins and becomes guilty, he must return what he has stolen or taken by extortion, or what was entrusted to him, or the lost property he found, ⁵or whatever it was he swore falsely about. He must make restitution in full, add a fifth of the value to it and give it all to the owner on the day he presents his guilt offering. ⁶And as a penalty he must bring to the priest, that is, to the LORD, his guilt offering, a ram from the flock, one without defect and of the proper value. ⁷In this way the priest

will make atonement for him before the LORD, and he will be forgiven for any of these things he did that made him guilty."

⁸The LORD said to Moses: ⁹"Give Aaron and his sons this command: 'These are the regulations for the burnt offering: The burnt offering is to remain on the altar hearth throughout the night, till morning, and the fire must be kept burning on the altar. ¹⁰The priest shall then put on his linen clothes, with linen undergarments next to his body, and shall remove the ashes of the burnt offering that the fire has consumed on the altar and place them beside the altar. ¹¹Then he is to take off these clothes and put on others, and carry the ashes outside the camp to a place that is ceremonially clean. ¹²The fire on the altar must be kept burning; it must not go out. Every morning the priest is to add firewood and arrange the burnt offering on the fire and burn the fat of the fellowship offeringsʲ on it. ¹³The fire must be kept burning on the altar continuously; it must not go out.

¹⁴" 'These are the regulations for the grain offering: Aaron's sons are to bring it before the LORD, in front of the altar. ¹⁵The priest is to take a handful of fine flour and oil, together with all the incense on the grain offering, and burn the memorial portion on the altar as an aroma pleasing to the LORD. ¹⁶Aaron and his sons shall eat the rest of it, but it is to be eaten without yeast in a holy place; they are to eat it in the courtyard of the Tent of Meeting. ¹⁷It must not be baked with yeast; I have given it as their share of the offerings made to me by fire. Like the sin offering and the guilt offering, it is most holy. ¹⁸Any male descendant of Aaron may eat it. It is his regular share of the offerings made to the LORD by fire for the generations to come. Whatever touches them will become holy.ᵏ' "

¹⁹The LORD also said to Moses, ²⁰"This is the offering Aaron and his sons are to bring to the LORD on the day heˡ is anointed: a tenth of an ephahᵐ of fine flour as a regular grain offering, half of it in the morning and half in the evening. ²¹Prepare it with oil on a griddle; bring it well-mixed and present the grain offering brokenⁿ in pieces as an aroma

---

ʰ15 That is, about 2/5 ounce (about 11.5 grams)   ⁱ19 Or has made full expiation for his   ʲ12 Traditionally peace offerings
ᵏ18 Or Whoever touches them must be holy; similarly in verse 27   ˡ20 Or each   ᵐ20 That is, probably about 2 quarts (about 2 liters)   ⁿ21 The meaning of the Hebrew for this word is uncertain.

pleasing to the LORD. ²²The son who is to succeed him as anointed priest shall prepare it. It is the LORD's regular share and is to be burned completely. ²³Every grain offering of a priest shall be burned completely; it must not be eaten."

²⁴The LORD said to Moses, ²⁵"Say to Aaron and his sons: 'These are the regulations for the sin offering: The sin offering is to be slaughtered before the LORD in the place the burnt offering is slaughtered; it is most holy. ²⁶The priest who offers it shall eat it; it is to be eaten in a holy place, in the courtyard of the Tent of Meeting. ²⁷Whatever touches any of the flesh will become holy, and if any of the blood is spattered on a garment, you must wash it in a holy place. ²⁸The clay pot the meat is cooked in must be broken; but if it is cooked in a bronze pot, the pot is to be scoured and rinsed with water. ²⁹Any male in a priest's family may eat it; it is most holy. ³⁰But any sin offering whose blood is brought into the Tent of Meeting to make atonement in the Holy Place must not be eaten; it must be burned.

CHAPTER 7

" 'These are the regulations for the guilt offering, which is most holy: ²The guilt offering is to be slaughtered in the place where the burnt offering is slaughtered, and its blood is to be sprinkled against the altar on all sides. ³All its fat shall be offered: the fat tail and the fat that covers the inner parts, ⁴both kidneys with the fat on them near the loins, and the covering of the liver, which is to be removed with the kidneys. ⁵The priest shall burn them on the altar as an offering made to the LORD by fire. It is a guilt offering. ⁶Any male in a priest's family may eat it, but it must be eaten in a holy place; it is most holy.

⁷" 'The same law applies to both the sin offering and the guilt offering: They belong to the priest who makes atonement with them. ⁸The priest who offers a burnt offering for anyone may keep its hide for himself. ⁹Every grain offering baked in an oven or cooked in a pan or on a griddle belongs to the priest who offers it, ¹⁰and every grain offering, whether mixed with oil or dry, belongs equally to all the sons of Aaron.

¹¹" 'These are the regulations for the fellowship offering^o a person may present to the LORD:

¹²" 'If he offers it as an expression of thankfulness, then along with this thank offering he is to offer cakes of bread made without yeast and mixed with oil, wafers made without yeast and spread with oil, and cakes of fine flour well-kneaded and mixed with oil. ¹³Along with his fellowship offering of thanksgiving he is to present an offering with cakes of bread made with yeast. ¹⁴He is to bring one of each kind as an offering, a contribution to the LORD; it belongs to the priest who sprinkles the blood of the fellowship offerings. ¹⁵The meat of his fellowship offering of thanksgiving must be eaten on the day it is offered; he must leave none of it till morning.

¹⁶" 'If, however, his offering is the result of a vow or is a freewill offering, the sacrifice shall be eaten on the day he offers it, but anything left over may be eaten on the next day. ¹⁷Any meat of the sacrifice left over till the third day must be burned up. ¹⁸If any meat of the fellowship offering is eaten on the third day, it will not be accepted. It will not be credited to the one who offered it, for it is impure; the person who eats any of it will be held responsible.

¹⁹" 'Meat that touches anything ceremonially unclean must not be eaten; it must be burned up. As for other meat, anyone ceremonially clean may eat it. ²⁰But if anyone who is unclean eats any meat of the fellowship offering belonging to the LORD, that person must be cut off from his people. ²¹If anyone touches something unclean—whether human uncleanness or an unclean animal or any unclean, detestable thing—and then eats any of the meat of the fellowship offering belonging to the LORD, that person must be cut off from his people.' "

²²The LORD said to Moses, ²³"Say to the Israelites: 'Do not eat any of the fat of cattle, sheep or goats. ²⁴The fat of an animal found dead or torn by wild animals may be used for any other purpose, but you must not eat it. ²⁵Anyone who eats the fat of an animal from which an offering by fire may be^p made to the LORD must be cut off from his people. ²⁶And wherever

---

^o11 Traditionally *peace offering*; also in verses 13-37   ^p25 Or *fire is*

you live, you must not eat the blood of any bird or animal. ²⁷If anyone eats blood, that person must be cut off from his people.' "

²⁸The LORD said to Moses, ²⁹"Say to the Israelites: 'Anyone who brings a fellowship offering to the LORD is to bring part of it as his sacrifice to the LORD. ³⁰With his own hands he is to bring the offering made to the LORD by fire; he is to bring the fat, together with the breast, and wave the breast before the LORD as a wave offering. ³¹The priest shall burn the fat on the altar, but the breast belongs to Aaron and his sons. ³²You are to give the right thigh of your fellowship offerings to the priest as a contribution. ³³The son of Aaron who offers the blood and the fat of the fellowship offering shall have the right thigh as his share. ³⁴From the fellowship offerings of the Israelites, I have taken the breast that

is waved and the thigh that is presented and have given them to Aaron the priest and his sons as their regular share from the Israelites.' "

³⁵This is the portion of the offerings made to the LORD by fire that were allotted to Aaron and his sons on the day they were presented to serve the LORD as priests. ³⁶On the day they were anointed, the LORD commanded that the Israelites give this to them as their regular share for the generations to come.

³⁷These, then, are the regulations for the burnt offering, the grain offering, the sin offering, the guilt offering, the ordination offering and the fellowship offering, ³⁸which the LORD gave Moses on Mount Sinai on the day he commanded the Israelites to bring their offerings to the LORD, in the Desert of Sinai.

FEBRUARY 3 ☐ DAY 34
LEVITICUS 8–10
Priestly Orders and Offense

OVERVIEW After the sacrifices come the divine requirements for the priests who are to offer them. Moses consecrates Aaron and his four sons to minister in the tabernacle. Sacrifices and ceremonies take place for seven consecutive days, after which Aaron begins his duties. The joyous inaugural week abruptly ends, however, with the disobedience and death of two of Aaron's sons, which leads to a divine announcement of restrictions concerning the priests' conduct.

Chapter 8	Chapter 9	Chapter 10
Consecration of the Priests	Ministry of the Priests	Restrictions on the Priests
Dedication	Duty	Disqualification

YOUR DAILY WALK Has this ever happened to you? You are late for an appointment and pushing the speed limit—from the wrong direction. Suddenly you catch a glimpse of flashing lights in your rearview mirror. You watch in numb despair as a police car draws ever closer and finally pulls over . . . the car next to you! Would that experience change your driving habits (at least for the next few miles)?

If you go against the grain of God's law, you get splinters!

One of the reasons God gave you the Old Testament was to provide flashing lights to warn you of dangerous situations. Others learned the hard way, but you don't have to—if you take their painful example to heart. Nadab and Abihu met an untimely death because they took God's holiness lightly. In a moment of proud disobedience they offered the wrong kind of fire in the wrong place and paid for that act with their lives.

At the dinner table this evening, read aloud 1 Corinthians 10:11. Then, beginning with the story of Nadab and Abihu, share "Lessons from the Lives of Old Testament People" from which you can benefit today. After all, you'll never live long enough to duplicate all the mistakes of others—nor do you have to!

 INSIGHT The High Priest's Wardrobe—Fit for One! There would be many priests, but only one high priest—only one who would represent the people before God by entering the Most Holy Place to make atonement. To signify this unique role, only the high priest wore the *ephod*—a sacred garment of gold, blue, purple, and scarlet yarn, and finely twined linen (8:6–13; see also Exodus 28:4–14).

CHAPTER 8

The LORD said to Moses, ²"Bring Aaron and his sons, their garments, the anointing oil, the bull for the sin offering, the two rams and the basket containing bread made without yeast, ³and gather the entire assembly at the entrance to the Tent of Meeting." ⁴Moses did as the LORD commanded him, and the assembly gathered at the entrance to the Tent of Meeting.

⁵Moses said to the assembly, "This is what the LORD has commanded to be done." ⁶Then Moses brought Aaron and his sons forward and washed them with water. ⁷He put the tunic on Aaron, tied the sash around him, clothed him with the robe and put the ephod on him. He also tied the ephod to him by its skillfully woven waistband; so it was fastened on him. ⁸He placed the breastpiece on him and put the Urim and Thummim in the breastpiece. ⁹Then he placed the turban on Aaron's head and set the gold plate, the sacred diadem, on the front of it, as the LORD commanded Moses.

¹⁰Then Moses took the anointing oil and anointed the tabernacle and everything in it, and so consecrated them. ¹¹He sprinkled some of the oil on the altar seven times, anointing the altar and all its utensils and the basin with its stand, to consecrate them. ¹²He poured some of the anointing oil on Aaron's head and anointed him to consecrate him. ¹³Then he brought Aaron's sons forward, put tunics on them, tied sashes around them and put headbands on them, as the LORD commanded Moses.

¹⁴He then presented the bull for the sin offering, and Aaron and his sons laid their hands on its head. ¹⁵Moses slaughtered the bull and took some of the blood, and with his finger he put it on all the horns of the altar to purify the altar. He poured out the rest of the blood at the base of the altar. So he consecrated it to make atonement for it. ¹⁶Moses also took all the fat around the inner parts, the covering of the liver, and both kidneys and their fat, and burned it on the altar. ¹⁷But the bull with its hide and its flesh and its offal he burned up outside the camp, as the LORD commanded Moses.

¹⁸He then presented the ram for the burnt offering, and Aaron and his sons laid their hands on its head. ¹⁹Then Moses slaughtered the ram and sprinkled the blood against the altar on all sides. ²⁰He cut the ram into pieces and burned the head, the pieces and the fat. ²¹He washed the inner parts and the legs with water and burned the whole ram on the altar as a burnt offering, a pleasing aroma, an offering made to the LORD by fire, as the LORD commanded Moses.

²²He then presented the other ram, the ram for the ordination, and Aaron and his sons laid their hands on its head. ²³Moses slaughtered the ram and took some of its blood and put it on the lobe of Aaron's right ear, on the thumb of his right hand and on the big toe of his right foot. ²⁴Moses also brought Aaron's sons forward and put some of the blood on the lobes of their right ears, on the thumbs of their right hands and on the big toes of their right feet. Then he sprinkled blood against the altar on all sides. ²⁵He took the fat, the fat tail, all the fat around the inner parts, the covering of the liver, both kidneys and their fat and the right thigh. ²⁶Then from the basket of bread made without yeast, which was before the LORD, he took a cake of bread, and one made with oil, and a wafer; he put these on the fat portions and on the right thigh. ²⁷He

put all these in the hands of Aaron and his sons and waved them before the LORD as a wave offering. 28Then Moses took them from their hands and burned them on the altar on top of the burnt offering as an ordination offering, a pleasing aroma, an offering made to the LORD by fire. 29He also took the breast—Moses' share of the ordination ram—and waved it before the LORD as a wave offering, as the LORD commanded Moses.

30Then Moses took some of the anointing oil and some of the blood from the altar and sprinkled them on Aaron and his garments and on his sons and their garments. So he consecrated Aaron and his garments and his sons and their garments.

31Moses then said to Aaron and his sons, "Cook the meat at the entrance to the Tent of Meeting and eat it there with the bread from the basket of ordination offerings, as I commanded, saying,q 'Aaron and his sons are to eat it.' 32Then burn up the rest of the meat and the bread. 33Do not leave the entrance to the Tent of Meeting for seven days, until the days of your ordination are completed, for your ordination will last seven days. 34What has been done today was commanded by the LORD to make atonement for you. 35You must stay at the entrance to the Tent of Meeting day and night for seven days and do what the LORD requires, so you will not die; for that is what I have been commanded." 36So Aaron and his sons did everything the LORD commanded through Moses.

CHAPTER 9
On the eighth day Moses summoned Aaron and his sons and the elders of Israel. 2He said to Aaron, "Take a bull calf for your sin offering and a ram for your burnt offering, both without defect, and present them before the LORD. 3Then say to the Israelites: 'Take a male goat for a sin offering, a calf and a lamb—both a year old and without defect—for a burnt offering, 4and an oxr and a ram for a fellowship offerings to sacrifice before the LORD, together with a grain offering mixed with oil. For today the LORD will appear to you.' "

5They took the things Moses com-manded to the front of the Tent of Meeting, and the entire assembly came near and stood before the LORD. 6Then Moses said, "This is what the LORD has commanded you to do, so that the glory of the LORD may appear to you."

7Moses said to Aaron, "Come to the altar and sacrifice your sin offering and your burnt offering and make atonement for yourself and the people; sacrifice the offering that is for the people and make atonement for them, as the LORD has commanded."

8So Aaron came to the altar and slaughtered the calf as a sin offering for himself. 9His sons brought the blood to him, and he dipped his finger into the blood and put it on the horns of the altar; the rest of the blood he poured out at the base of the altar. 10On the altar he burned the fat, the kidneys and the covering of the liver from the sin offering, as the LORD commanded Moses; 11the flesh and the hide he burned up outside the camp.

12Then he slaughtered the burnt offering. His sons handed him the blood, and he sprinkled it against the altar on all sides. 13They handed him the burnt offering piece by piece, including the head, and he burned them on the altar. 14He washed the inner parts and the legs and burned them on top of the burnt offering on the altar.

15Aaron then brought the offering that was for the people. He took the goat for the people's sin offering and slaughtered it and offered it for a sin offering as he did with the first one.

16He brought the burnt offering and offered it in the prescribed way. 17He also brought the grain offering, took a handful of it and burned it on the altar in addition to the morning's burnt offering.

18He slaughtered the ox and the ram as the fellowship offering for the people. His sons handed him the blood, and he sprinkled it against the altar on all sides. 19But the fat portions of the ox and the ram—the fat tail, the layer of fat, the kidneys and the covering of the liver— 20these they laid on the breasts, and then Aaron burned the fat on the altar. 21Aaron waved the breasts and the right thigh before the LORD as a wave offering, as Moses commanded.

q31 Or I was commanded: r4 The Hebrew word can include both male and female; also in verses 18 and 19.
s4 Traditionally peace offering; also in verses 18 and 22

[22]Then Aaron lifted his hands toward the people and blessed them. And having sacrificed the sin offering, the burnt offering and the fellowship offering, he stepped down.

[23]Moses and Aaron then went into the Tent of Meeting. When they came out, they blessed the people; and the glory of the LORD appeared to all the people. [24]Fire came out from the presence of the LORD and consumed the burnt offering and the fat portions on the altar. And when all the people saw it, they shouted for joy and fell facedown.

CHAPTER 10

Aaron's sons Nadab and Abihu took their censers, put fire in them and added incense; and they offered unauthorized fire before the LORD, contrary to his command. [2]So fire came out from the presence of the LORD and consumed them, and they died before the LORD. [3]Moses then said to Aaron, "This is what the LORD spoke of when he said:

" 'Among those who approach me
    I will show myself holy;
in the sight of all the people
    I will be honored.' "

Aaron remained silent.

[4]Moses summoned Mishael and Elzaphan, sons of Aaron's uncle Uzziel, and said to them, "Come here; carry your cousins outside the camp, away from the front of the sanctuary." [5]So they came and carried them, still in their tunics, outside the camp, as Moses ordered.

[6]Then Moses said to Aaron and his sons Eleazar and Ithamar, "Do not let your hair become unkempt,[f] and do not tear your clothes, or you will die and the LORD will be angry with the whole community. But your relatives, all the house of Israel, may mourn for those the LORD has destroyed by fire. [7]Do not leave the entrance to the Tent of Meeting or you will die, because the LORD's anointing oil is on you." So they did as Moses said.

[8]Then the LORD said to Aaron, [9]"You and your sons are not to drink wine or other fermented drink whenever you go into the Tent of Meeting, or you will die. This is a lasting ordinance for the generations to come. [10]You must distinguish between the holy and the common, between the unclean and the clean, [11]and you must teach the Israelites all the decrees the LORD has given them through Moses."

[12]Moses said to Aaron and his remaining sons, Eleazar and Ithamar, "Take the grain offering left over from the offerings made to the LORD by fire and eat it prepared without yeast beside the altar, for it is most holy. [13]Eat it in a holy place, because it is your share and your sons' share of the offerings made to the LORD by fire; for so I have been commanded. [14]But you and your sons and your daughters may eat the breast that was waved and the thigh that was presented. Eat them in a ceremonially clean place; they have been given to you and your children as your share of the Israelites' fellowship offerings.[u] [15]The thigh that was presented and the breast that was waved must be brought with the fat portions of the offerings made by fire, to be waved before the LORD as a wave offering. This will be the regular share for you and your children, as the LORD has commanded."

[16]When Moses inquired about the goat of the sin offering and found that it had been burned up, he was angry with Eleazar and Ithamar, Aaron's remaining sons, and asked, [17]"Why didn't you eat the sin offering in the sanctuary area? It is most holy; it was given to you to take away the guilt of the community by making atonement for them before the LORD. [18]Since its blood was not taken into the Holy Place, you should have eaten the goat in the sanctuary area, as I commanded."

[19]Aaron replied to Moses, "Today they sacrificed their sin offering and their burnt offering before the LORD, but such things as this have happened to me. Would the LORD have been pleased if I had eaten the sin offering today?" [20]When Moses heard this, he was satisfied.

---

[f]6 Or Do not uncover your heads   [u]14 Traditionally peace offerings

FEBRUARY 4 □ DAY 35
LEVITICUS 11–15
Personal Purity in Daily Life

OVERVIEW Today's reading sets forth laws regarding clean and un-clean food, childbirth, leprosy and other skin diseases, and discharges. Being a holy people demands a holy lifestyle. Ceremonial purity is an indispensable part of worshiping a holy God, though it imposes re-strictions on one's conduct. For the Israelites this meant dietary laws, strict health requirements, and temporary quarantines after contact with potentially harmful substances. The word *unclean* occurs more than a hundred times in these chapters, showing that ceremonial un-cleanness (which is, in fact, disobedience) is no small matter with God.

Chapter 11	Chapter 12	Chapters 13–14	Chapter 15
Rules Regarding Food	Rules Regarding Childbirth	Rules Regarding Skin Diseases	Rules Regarding Discharges
Home Matters		Health Matters	

YOUR DAILY WALK Rules and restrictions bring out the absolute worst in people! There is something about seeing a sign that says Wet Paint—Do Not Touch that makes us a little bit touchy. Signs such as Keep Off the Grass or Don't Feed the Chimps or Speed Limit 55 seem to whisper in our ears, "I dare you . . ."

What man uncovers, God will cover; what man covers, God will uncover.

But did you ever stop to think why those rules are there? Someone is trying to look out for the best interests of you and others. They know that fresh paint looks better on park benches than on dresses; that grass stays prettier when a horde of people isn't trampling it to death; that chimps don't survive well on a diet of Chee-tos; and that gas—and people—last longer if you drive moderately. Such rules are for your own good.

The same was true for many of Israel's laws. God gave them for his people's protection. So no scavenger animals for dinner, no contact with leprous people and plenty of baths! In today's passage look for ways God protected his people through the laws he gave.

INSIGHT A Holy People, a Horrible Disease
Leprosy in Old Testament times was regarded as hereditary and incur-able. The leper was excluded from the camp, and only after quaran-tine and careful inspection would that person be declared "clean" once again. Leprosy is often used in the New Testament as a picture of sin. Like leprosy, sin's treatment demands cleansing and constant alertness (1 Corinthians 11:31). The forgiveness of sin, like the healing of lep-rosy, can be effected by God alone.

CHAPTER 11
The LORD said to Moses and Aaron, ²"Say to the Israelites: 'Of all the animals that live on land, these are the ones you may eat: ³You may eat any animal that has a split hoof completely divided and that chews the cud.

⁴" 'There are some that only chew the cud or only have a split hoof, but you must not eat them. The camel, though it chews the cud, does not have a split hoof; it is ceremonially unclean for you. ⁵The coney,ᵛ though it chews the cud, does not have a split hoof; it is unclean for you. ⁶The rabbit, though it chews the cud, does not have a split hoof; it is unclean for you. ⁷And the pig, though it has a split hoof completely divided, does not chew the

ᵛ5 That is, the hyrax or rock badger

cud; it is unclean for you. [8]You must not eat their meat or touch their carcasses; they are unclean for you.

[9]" 'Of all the creatures living in the water of the seas and the streams, you may eat any that have fins and scales. [10]But all creatures in the seas or streams that do not have fins and scales—whether among all the swarming things or among all the other living creatures in the water—you are to detest. [11]And since you are to detest them, you must not eat their meat and you must detest their carcasses. [12]Anything living in the water that does not have fins and scales is to be detestable to you.

[13]" 'These are the birds you are to detest and not eat because they are detestable: the eagle, the vulture, the black vulture, [14]the red kite, any kind of black kite, [15]any kind of raven, [16]the horned owl, the screech owl, the gull, any kind of hawk, [17]the little owl, the cormorant, the great owl, [18]the white owl, the desert owl, the osprey, [19]the stork, any kind of heron, the hoopoe and the bat.[w]

[20]" 'All flying insects that walk on all fours are to be detestable to you. [21]There are, however, some winged creatures that walk on all fours that you may eat: those that have jointed legs for hopping on the ground. [22]Of these you may eat any kind of locust, katydid, cricket or grasshopper. [23]But all other winged creatures that have four legs you are to detest.

[24]" 'You will make yourselves unclean by these; whoever touches their carcasses will be unclean till evening. [25]Whoever picks up one of their carcasses must wash his clothes, and he will be unclean till evening.

[26]" 'Every animal that has a split hoof not completely divided or that does not chew the cud is unclean for you; whoever touches ˌthe carcass ofˌ any of them will be unclean. [27]Of all the animals that walk on all fours, those that walk on their paws are unclean for you; whoever touches their carcasses will be unclean till evening. [28]Anyone who picks up their carcasses must wash his clothes, and he will be unclean till evening. They are unclean for you.

[29]" 'Of the animals that move about on the ground, these are unclean for you: the weasel, the rat, any kind of great lizard, [30]the gecko, the monitor lizard, the wall lizard, the skink and the chameleon. [31]Of all those that move along the ground, these are unclean for you. Whoever touches them when they are dead will be unclean till evening. [32]When one of them dies and falls on something, that article, whatever its use, will be unclean, whether it is made of wood, cloth, hide or sackcloth. Put it in water; it will be unclean till evening, and then it will be clean. [33]If one of them falls into a clay pot, everything in it will be unclean, and you must break the pot. [34]Any food that could be eaten but has water on it from such a pot is unclean, and any liquid that could be drunk from it is unclean. [35]Anything that one of their carcasses falls on becomes unclean; an oven or cooking pot must be broken up. They are unclean, and you are to regard them as unclean. [36]A spring, however, or a cistern for collecting water remains clean, but anyone who touches one of these carcasses is unclean. [37]If a carcass falls on any seeds that are to be planted, they remain clean. [38]But if water has been put on the seed and a carcass falls on it, it is unclean for you.

[39]" 'If an animal that you are allowed to eat dies, anyone who touches the carcass will be unclean till evening. [40]Anyone who eats some of the carcass must wash his clothes, and he will be unclean till evening. Anyone who picks up the carcass must wash his clothes, and he will be unclean till evening.

[41]" 'Every creature that moves about on the ground is detestable; it is not to be eaten. [42]You are not to eat any creature that moves about on the ground, whether it moves on its belly or walks on all fours or on many feet; it is detestable. [43]Do not defile yourselves by any of these creatures. Do not make yourselves unclean by means of them or be made unclean by them. [44]I am the LORD your God; consecrate yourselves and be holy, because I am holy. Do not make yourselves unclean by any creature that moves about on the ground. [45]I am the LORD who brought you up out of Egypt to be your God; therefore be holy, because I am holy.

[46]" 'These are the regulations concerning animals, birds, every living thing that

[w]19 The precise identification of some of the birds, insects and animals in this chapter is uncertain.

moves in the water and every creature that moves about on the ground. ⁴⁷You must distinguish between the unclean and the clean, between living creatures that may be eaten and those that may not be eaten.' "

CHAPTER 12

The LORD said to Moses, ²"Say to the Israelites: 'A woman who becomes pregnant and gives birth to a son will be ceremonially unclean for seven days, just as she is unclean during her monthly period. ³On the eighth day the boy is to be circumcised. ⁴Then the woman must wait thirty-three days to be purified from her bleeding. She must not touch anything sacred or go to the sanctuary until the days of her purification are over. ⁵If she gives birth to a daughter, for two weeks the woman will be unclean, as during her period. Then she must wait sixty-six days to be purified from her bleeding.

⁶" 'When the days of her purification for a son or daughter are over, she is to bring to the priest at the entrance to the Tent of Meeting a year-old lamb for a burnt offering and a young pigeon or a dove for a sin offering. ⁷He shall offer them before the LORD to make atonement for her, and then she will be ceremonially clean from her flow of blood.

" 'These are the regulations for the woman who gives birth to a boy or a girl. ⁸If she cannot afford a lamb, she is to bring two doves or two young pigeons, one for a burnt offering and the other for a sin offering. In this way the priest will make atonement for her, and she will be clean.' "

CHAPTER 13

The LORD said to Moses and Aaron, ²"When anyone has a swelling or a rash or a bright spot on his skin that may become an infectious skin disease,ˣ he must be brought to Aaron the priest or to one of his sonsʸ who is a priest. ³The priest is to examine the sore on his skin, and if the hair in the sore has turned white and the sore appears to be more than skin deep,ᶻ it is an infectious skin disease. When the priest examines him, he shall pronounce him ceremonially unclean. ⁴If the spot on his skin is white but does not appear to be

more than skin deep and the hair in it has not turned white, the priest is to put the infected person in isolation for seven days. ⁵On the seventh day the priest is to examine him, and if he sees that the sore is unchanged and has not spread in the skin, he is to keep him in isolation another seven days. ⁶On the seventh day the priest is to examine him again, and if the sore has faded and has not spread in the skin, the priest shall pronounce him clean; it is only a rash. The man must wash his clothes, and he will be clean. ⁷But if the rash does spread in his skin after he has shown himself to the priest to be pronounced clean, he must appear before the priest again. ⁸The priest is to examine him, and if the rash has spread in the skin, he shall pronounce him unclean; it is an infectious disease.

⁹"When anyone has an infectious skin disease, he must be brought to the priest. ¹⁰The priest is to examine him, and if there is a white swelling in the skin that has turned the hair white and if there is raw flesh in the swelling, ¹¹it is a chronic skin disease and the priest shall pronounce him unclean. He is not to put him in isolation, because he is already unclean.

¹²"If the disease breaks out all over his skin and, so far as the priest can see, it covers all the skin of the infected person from head to foot, ¹³the priest is to examine him, and if the disease has covered his whole body, he shall pronounce that person clean. Since it has all turned white, he is clean. ¹⁴But whenever raw flesh appears on him, he will be unclean. ¹⁵When the priest sees the raw flesh, he shall pronounce him unclean. The raw flesh is unclean; he has an infectious disease. ¹⁶Should the raw flesh change and turn white, he must go to the priest. ¹⁷The priest is to examine him, and if the sores have turned white, the priest shall pronounce the infected person clean; then he will be clean.

¹⁸"When someone has a boil on his skin and it heals, ¹⁹and in the place where the boil was, a white swelling or reddish-white spot appears, he must present himself to the priest. ²⁰The priest is to examine it, and if it appears to be more than skin deep and the hair in it has turned white, the priest shall pronounce

him unclean. It is an infectious skin disease that has broken out where the boil was. [21]But if, when the priest examines it, there is no white hair in it and it is not more than skin deep and has faded, then the priest is to put him in isolation for seven days. [22]If it is spreading in the skin, the priest shall pronounce him unclean; it is infectious. [23]But if the spot is unchanged and has not spread, it is only a scar from the boil, and the priest shall pronounce him clean.

[24]"When someone has a burn on his skin and a reddish-white or white spot appears in the raw flesh of the burn, [25]the priest is to examine the spot, and if the hair in it has turned white, and it appears to be more than skin deep, it is an infectious disease that has broken out in the burn. The priest shall pronounce him unclean; it is an infectious skin disease. [26]But if the priest examines it and there is no white hair in the spot and if it is not more than skin deep and has faded, then the priest is to put him in isolation for seven days. [27]On the seventh day the priest is to examine him, and if it is spreading in the skin, the priest shall pronounce him unclean; it is an infectious skin disease. [28]If, however, the spot is unchanged and has not spread in the skin but has faded, it is a swelling from the burn, and the priest shall pronounce him clean; it is only a scar from the burn.

[29]"If a man or woman has a sore on the head or on the chin, [30]the priest is to examine the sore, and if it appears to be more than skin deep and the hair in it is yellow and thin, the priest shall pronounce that person unclean; it is an itch, an infectious disease of the head or chin. [31]But if, when the priest examines this kind of sore, it does not seem to be more than skin deep and there is no black hair in it, then the priest is to put the infected person in isolation for seven days. [32]On the seventh day the priest is to examine the sore, and if the itch has not spread and there is no yellow hair in it and it does not appear to be more than skin deep, [33]he must be shaved except for the diseased area, and the priest is to keep him in isolation another seven days. [34]On the seventh day the priest is to examine the itch, and if it has not spread in the skin and

appears to be no more than skin deep, the priest shall pronounce him clean. He must wash his clothes, and he will be clean. [35]But if the itch does spread in the skin after he is pronounced clean, [36]the priest is to examine him, and if the itch has spread in the skin, the priest does not need to look for yellow hair; the person is unclean. [37]If, however, in his judgment it is unchanged and black hair has grown in it, the itch is healed. He is clean, and the priest shall pronounce him clean.

[38]"When a man or woman has white spots on the skin, [39]the priest is to examine them, and if the spots are dull white, it is a harmless rash that has broken out on the skin; that person is clean.

[40]"When a man has lost his hair and is bald, he is clean. [41]If he has lost his hair from the front of his scalp and has a bald forehead, he is clean. [42]But if he has a reddish-white sore on his bald head or forehead, it is an infectious disease breaking out on his head or forehead. [43]The priest is to examine him, and if the swollen sore on his head or forehead is reddish-white like an infectious skin disease, [44]the man is diseased and is unclean. The priest shall pronounce him unclean because of the sore on his head.

[45]"The person with such an infectious disease must wear torn clothes, let his hair be unkempt,[a] cover the lower part of his face and cry out, 'Unclean! Unclean!' [46]As long as he has the infection he remains unclean. He must live alone; he must live outside the camp.

[47]"If any clothing is contaminated with mildew—any woolen or linen clothing, [48]any woven or knitted material of linen or wool, any leather or anything made of leather— [49]and if the contamination in the clothing, or leather, or woven or knitted material, or any leather article, is greenish or reddish, it is a spreading mildew and must be shown to the priest. [50]The priest is to examine the mildew and isolate the affected article for seven days. [51]On the seventh day he is to examine it, and if the mildew has spread in the clothing, or the woven or knitted material, or the leather, whatever its use, it is a destructive mildew; the article is unclean. [52]He must burn up the clothing, or the woven or knitted material of wool or linen, or

a45 Or clothes, uncover his head

any leather article that has the contamination in it, because the mildew is destructive; the article must be burned up.

⁵³"But if, when the priest examines it, the mildew has not spread in the clothing, or the woven or knitted material, or the leather article, ⁵⁴he shall order that the contaminated article be washed. Then he is to isolate it for another seven days. ⁵⁵After the affected article has been washed, the priest is to examine it, and if the mildew has not changed its appearance, even though it has not spread, it is unclean. Burn it with fire, whether the mildew has affected one side or the other. ⁵⁶If, when the priest examines it, the mildew has faded after the article has been washed, he is to tear the contaminated part out of the clothing, or the leather, or the woven or knitted material. ⁵⁷But if it reappears in the clothing, or in the woven or knitted material, or in the leather article, it is spreading, and whatever has the mildew must be burned with fire. ⁵⁸The clothing, or the woven or knitted material, or any leather article that has been washed and is rid of the mildew, must be washed again, and it will be clean."

⁵⁹These are the regulations concerning contamination by mildew in woolen or linen clothing, woven or knitted material, or any leather article, for pronouncing them clean or unclean.

CHAPTER 14

The LORD said to Moses, ²"These are the regulations for the diseased person at the time of his ceremonial cleansing, when he is brought to the priest: ³The priest is to go outside the camp and examine him. If the person has been healed of his infectious skin disease,^b ⁴the priest shall order that two live clean birds and some cedar wood, scarlet yarn and hyssop be brought for the one to be cleansed. ⁵Then the priest shall order that one of the birds be killed over fresh water in a clay pot. ⁶He is then to take the live bird and dip it, together with the cedar wood, the scarlet yarn and the hyssop, into the blood of the bird that was killed over the fresh water. ⁷Seven times he shall sprinkle the one to be cleansed of the infectious disease and

pronounce him clean. Then he is to release the live bird in the open fields.

⁸"The person to be cleansed must wash his clothes, shave off all his hair and bathe with water; then he will be ceremonially clean. After this he may come into the camp, but he must stay outside his tent for seven days. ⁹On the seventh day he must shave off all his hair; he must shave his head, his beard, his eyebrows and the rest of his hair. He must wash his clothes and bathe himself with water, and he will be clean.

¹⁰"On the eighth day he must bring two male lambs and one ewe lamb a year old, each without defect, along with three-tenths of an ephah^c of fine flour mixed with oil for a grain offering, and one log^d of oil. ¹¹The priest who pronounces him clean shall present both the one to be cleansed and his offerings before the LORD at the entrance to the Tent of Meeting.

¹²"Then the priest is to take one of the male lambs and offer it as a guilt offering, along with the log of oil; he shall wave them before the LORD as a wave offering. ¹³He is to slaughter the lamb in the holy place where the sin offering and the burnt offering are slaughtered. Like the sin offering, the guilt offering belongs to the priest; it is most holy. ¹⁴The priest is to take some of the blood of the guilt offering and put it on the lobe of the right ear of the one to be cleansed, on the thumb of his right hand and on the big toe of his right foot. ¹⁵The priest shall then take some of the log of oil, pour it in the palm of his own left hand, ¹⁶dip his right forefinger into the oil in his palm, and with his finger sprinkle some of it before the LORD seven times. ¹⁷The priest is to put some of the oil remaining in his palm on the lobe of the right ear of the one to be cleansed, on the thumb of his right hand and on the big toe of his right foot, on top of the blood of the guilt offering. ¹⁸The rest of the oil in his palm the priest shall put on the head of the one to be cleansed and make atonement for him before the LORD.

¹⁹"Then the priest is to sacrifice the sin offering and make atonement for the one to be cleansed from his uncleanness. After that, the priest shall slaughter the burnt

---

^b3 Traditionally *leprosy*; the Hebrew word was used for various diseases affecting the skin—not necessarily leprosy; also elsewhere in this chapter.   ^c10 That is, probably about 6 quarts (about 6.5 liters)   ^d10 That is, probably about 2/3 pint (about 0.3 liter); also in verses 12, 15, 21 and 24

offering ²⁰and offer it on the altar, together with the grain offering, and make atonement for him, and he will be clean.

²¹"If, however, he is poor and cannot afford these, he must take one male lamb as a guilt offering to be waved to make atonement for him, together with a tenth of an ephah^e of fine flour mixed with oil for a grain offering, a log of oil, ²²and two doves or two young pigeons, which he can afford, one for a sin offering and the other for a burnt offering.

²³"On the eighth day he must bring them for his cleansing to the priest at the entrance to the Tent of Meeting, before the LORD. ²⁴The priest is to take the lamb for the guilt offering, together with the log of oil, and wave them before the LORD as a wave offering. ²⁵He shall slaughter the lamb for the guilt offering and take some of its blood and put it on the lobe of the right ear of the one to be cleansed, on the thumb of his right hand and on the big toe of his right foot. ²⁶The priest is to pour some of the oil into the palm of his own left hand, ²⁷and with his right forefinger sprinkle some of the oil from his palm seven times before the LORD. ²⁸Some of the oil in his palm he is to put on the same places he put the blood of the guilt offering—on the lobe of the right ear of the one to be cleansed, on the thumb of his right hand and on the big toe of his right foot. ²⁹The rest of the oil in his palm the priest shall put on the head of the one to be cleansed, to make atonement for him before the LORD. ³⁰Then he shall sacrifice the doves or the young pigeons, which the person can afford, ³¹one^f as a sin offering and the other as a burnt offering, together with the grain offering. In this way the priest will make atonement before the LORD on behalf of the one to be cleansed."

³²These are the regulations for anyone who has an infectious skin disease and who cannot afford the regular offerings for his cleansing.

³³The LORD said to Moses and Aaron, ³⁴"When you enter the land of Canaan, which I am giving you as your possession, and I put a spreading mildew in a house in that land, ³⁵the owner of the house must go and tell the priest, 'I have seen something that looks like mildew in

my house.' ³⁶The priest is to order the house to be emptied before he goes in to examine the mildew, so that nothing in the house will be pronounced unclean. After this the priest is to go in and inspect the house. ³⁷He is to examine the mildew on the walls, and if it has greenish or reddish depressions that appear to be deeper than the surface of the wall, ³⁸the priest shall go out the doorway of the house and close it up for seven days. ³⁹On the seventh day the priest shall return to inspect the house. If the mildew has spread on the walls, ⁴⁰he is to order that the contaminated stones be torn out and thrown into an unclean place outside the town. ⁴¹He must have all the inside walls of the house scraped and the material that is scraped off dumped into an unclean place outside the town. ⁴²Then they are to take other stones to replace these and take new clay and plaster the house.

⁴³"If the mildew reappears in the house after the stones have been torn out and the house scraped and plastered, ⁴⁴the priest is to go and examine it and, if the mildew has spread in the house, it is a destructive mildew; the house is unclean. ⁴⁵It must be torn down—its stones, timbers and all the plaster—and taken out of the town to an unclean place.

⁴⁶"Anyone who goes into the house while it is closed up will be unclean till evening. ⁴⁷Anyone who sleeps or eats in the house must wash his clothes.

⁴⁸"But if the priest comes to examine it and the mildew has not spread after the house has been plastered, he shall pronounce the house clean, because the mildew is gone. ⁴⁹To purify the house he is to take two birds and some cedar wood, scarlet yarn and hyssop. ⁵⁰He shall kill one of the birds over fresh water in a clay pot. ⁵¹Then he is to take the cedar wood, the hyssop, the scarlet yarn and the live bird, dip them into the blood of the dead bird and the fresh water, and sprinkle the house seven times. ⁵²He shall purify the house with the bird's blood, the fresh water, the live bird, the cedar wood, the hyssop and the scarlet yarn. ⁵³Then he is to release the live bird in the open fields outside the town. In this way he will make atonement for the house, and it will be clean."

⁵⁴These are the regulations for any infectious skin disease, for an itch, ⁵⁵for mildew in clothing or in a house, ⁵⁶and for a swelling, a rash or a bright spot, ⁵⁷to determine when something is clean or unclean.

These are the regulations for infectious skin diseases and mildew.

CHAPTER 15

The LORD said to Moses and Aaron, ²"Speak to the Israelites and say to them: 'When any man has a bodily discharge, the discharge is unclean. ³Whether it continues flowing from his body or is blocked, it will make him unclean. This is how his discharge will bring about uncleanness:

⁴" 'Any bed the man with a discharge lies on will be unclean, and anything he sits on will be unclean. ⁵Anyone who touches his bed must wash his clothes and bathe with water, and he will be unclean till evening. ⁶Whoever sits on anything that the man with a discharge sat on must wash his clothes and bathe with water, and he will be unclean till evening.

⁷" 'Whoever touches the man who has a discharge must wash his clothes and bathe with water, and he will be unclean till evening.

⁸" 'If the man with the discharge spits on someone who is clean, that person must wash his clothes and bathe with water, and he will be unclean till evening.

⁹" 'Everything the man sits on when riding will be unclean, ¹⁰and whoever touches any of the things that were under him will be unclean till evening; whoever picks up those things must wash his clothes and bathe with water, and he will be unclean till evening.

¹¹" 'Anyone the man with a discharge touches without rinsing his hands with water must wash his clothes and bathe with water, and he will be unclean till evening.

¹²" 'A clay pot that the man touches must be broken, and any wooden article is to be rinsed with water.

¹³" 'When a man is cleansed from his discharge, he is to count off seven days for his ceremonial cleansing; he must wash his clothes and bathe himself with fresh water, and he will be clean. ¹⁴On the eighth day he must take two doves or two

young pigeons and come before the LORD to the entrance to the Tent of Meeting and give them to the priest. ¹⁵The priest is to sacrifice them, the one for a sin offering and the other for a burnt offering. In this way he will make atonement before the LORD for the man because of his discharge.

¹⁶" 'When a man has an emission of semen, he must bathe his whole body with water, and he will be unclean till evening. ¹⁷Any clothing or leather that has semen on it must be washed with water, and it will be unclean till evening. ¹⁸When a man lies with a woman and there is an emission of semen, both must bathe with water, and they will be unclean till evening.

¹⁹" 'When a woman has her regular flow of blood, the impurity of her monthly period will last seven days, and anyone who touches her will be unclean till evening.

²⁰" 'Anything she lies on during her period will be unclean, and anything she sits on will be unclean. ²¹Whoever touches her bed must wash his clothes and bathe with water, and he will be unclean till evening. ²²Whoever touches anything she sits on must wash his clothes and bathe with water, and he will be unclean till evening. ²³Whether it is the bed or anything she was sitting on, when anyone touches it, he will be unclean till evening.

²⁴" 'If a man lies with her and her monthly flow touches him, he will be unclean for seven days; any bed he lies on will be unclean.

²⁵" 'When a woman has a discharge of blood for many days at a time other than her monthly period or has a discharge that continues beyond her period, she will be unclean as long as she has the discharge, just as in the days of her period. ²⁶Any bed she lies on while her discharge continues will be unclean, as is her bed during her monthly period, and anything she sits on will be unclean, as during her period. ²⁷Whoever touches them will be unclean; he must wash his clothes and bathe with water, and he will be unclean till evening.

²⁸" 'When she is cleansed from her discharge, she must count off seven days, and after that she will be ceremonially clean. ²⁹On the eighth day she must take two doves or two young pigeons and

bring them to the priest at the entrance to the Tent of Meeting. ³⁰The priest is to sacrifice one for a sin offering and the other for a burnt offering. In this way he will make atonement for her before the LORD for the uncleanness of her discharge.

³¹" 'You must keep the Israelites separate from things that make them unclean, so they will not die in their uncleanness

g31 Or my tabernacle

for defiling my dwelling place,ᵍ which is among them.' "

³²These are the regulations for a man with a discharge, for anyone made unclean by an emission of semen, ³³for a woman in her monthly period, for a man or a woman with a discharge, and for a man who lies with a woman who is ceremonially unclean.

FEBRUARY 5 □ DAY 36
LEVITICUS 16–17
The Holiest Day of the Year

OVERVIEW The great Day of Atonement observed each year was Israel's most significant act of worship. On that day the nation gathered to watch expectantly as the high priest entered the Most Holy Place with the blood of atonement to cover the sins of the nation for another year. Because blood was the central ingredient in Israel's national and personal forgiveness, God prohibited its use for any purpose except sacrifice to him, for "it is the blood that makes atonement" (17:11).

Chapter 16	Chapter 17
Atonement by Blood	Abstaining from Blood
Life of the Nation	Life of the Flesh

YOUR DAILY WALK Have you ever had to live with a gnawing uncertainty? a recurring illness? an overdue bill? a threat of legal action? The emotions of facing situations like those are intensely painful.

The wonder of the cross is not the blood, but whose blood.

In Old Testament times the emotions that charged the air on every Day of Atonement were just as intense. As the high priest cautiously entered the Most Holy Place to make atonement for the sins of the nation, one question was uppermost in everyone's mind: Will God pass over our sins for another year?

The awful reality of the Day of Atonement was this: Sins were never fully *cleansed.* They were only temporarily *covered* and sent away on the head of the scapegoat. The debt of sin remained unpaid, like a promissory note deferred from year to year.

Aren't you glad Jesus Christ ended that uncertainty for all time? By his death the long-standing debt of sin was paid in full (Colossians 2:14). When you pay your bills this month, remind yourself—and one other person—of the price Jesus paid.

INSIGHT Covered and Protected for Another Year
The words *atone, appease* and *pacify* all come from the same Hebrew root meaning "to cover," which appears more than one hundred times in the Old Testament. The same root occurs in Genesis 6:14, where Noah is commanded to "coat it [the ark] with pitch inside and out." Just as the pitch covered the ark and protected the ark's passengers, so the shed blood of the sacrifice stood between sinful humanity and the holy God whose law had been violated.

CHAPTER 16

The LORD spoke to Moses after the death of the two sons of Aaron who died when they approached the LORD. [2]The LORD said to Moses: "Tell your brother Aaron not to come whenever he chooses into the Most Holy Place behind the curtain in front of the atonement cover on the ark, or else he will die, because I appear in the cloud over the atonement cover.

[3]"This is how Aaron is to enter the sanctuary area: with a young bull for a sin offering and a ram for a burnt offering. [4]He is to put on the sacred linen tunic, with linen undergarments next to his body; he is to tie the linen sash around him and put on the linen turban. These are sacred garments; so he must bathe himself with water before he puts them on. [5]From the Israelite community he is to take two male goats for a sin offering and a ram for a burnt offering.

[6]"Aaron is to offer the bull for his own sin offering to make atonement for himself and his household. [7]Then he is to take the two goats and present them before the LORD at the entrance to the Tent of Meeting. [8]He is to cast lots for the two goats— one lot for the LORD and the other for the scapegoat.[h] [9]Aaron shall bring the goat whose lot falls to the LORD and sacrifice it for a sin offering. [10]But the goat chosen by lot as the scapegoat shall be presented alive before the LORD to be used for making atonement by sending it into the desert as a scapegoat.

[11]"Aaron shall bring the bull for his own sin offering to make atonement for himself and his household, and he is to slaughter the bull for his own sin offering. [12]He is to take a censer full of burning coals from the altar before the LORD and two handfuls of finely ground fragrant incense and take them behind the curtain. [13]He is to put the incense on the fire before the LORD, and the smoke of the incense will conceal the atonement cover above the Testimony, so that he will not die. [14]He is to take some of the bull's blood and with his finger sprinkle it on the front of the atonement cover; then he shall sprinkle some of it with his finger seven times before the atonement cover. [15]"He shall then slaughter the goat for the sin offering for the people and take its

blood behind the curtain and do with it as he did with the bull's blood: He shall sprinkle it on the atonement cover and in front of it. [16]In this way he will make atonement for the Most Holy Place because of the uncleanness and rebellion of the Israelites, whatever their sins have been. He is to do the same for the Tent of Meeting, which is among them in the midst of their uncleanness. [17]No one is to be in the Tent of Meeting from the time Aaron goes in to make atonement in the Most Holy Place until he comes out, having made atonement for himself, his household and the whole community of Israel.

[18]"Then he shall come out to the altar that is before the LORD and make atonement for it. He shall take some of the bull's blood and some of the goat's blood and put it on all the horns of the altar. [19]He shall sprinkle some of the blood on it with his finger seven times to cleanse it and to consecrate it from the uncleanness of the Israelites.

[20]"When Aaron has finished making atonement for the Most Holy Place, the Tent of Meeting and the altar, he shall bring forward the live goat. [21]He is to lay both hands on the head of the live goat and confess over it all the wickedness and rebellion of the Israelites—all their sins— and put them on the goat's head. He shall send the goat away into the desert in the care of a man appointed for the task. [22]The goat will carry on itself all their sins to a solitary place; and the man shall release it in the desert.

[23]"Then Aaron is to go into the Tent of Meeting and take off the linen garments he put on before he entered the Most Holy Place, and he is to leave them there. [24]He shall bathe himself with water in a holy place and put on his regular garments. Then he shall come out and sacrifice the burnt offering for himself and the burnt offering for the people, to make atonement for himself and for the people. [25]He shall also burn the fat of the sin offering on the altar.

[26]"The man who releases the goat as a scapegoat must wash his clothes and bathe himself with water; afterward he may come into the camp. [27]The bull and the goat for the sin offerings, whose blood

---

[h]8 That is, the goat of removal; Hebrew *azazel*; also in verses 10 and 26

was brought into the Most Holy Place to make atonement, must be taken outside the camp; their hides, flesh and offal are to be burned up. ²⁸The man who burns them must wash his clothes and bathe himself with water; afterward he may come into the camp.

²⁹"This is to be a lasting ordinance for you: On the tenth day of the seventh month you must deny yourselves* and not do any work—whether native-born or an alien living among you— ³⁰because on this day atonement will be made for you, to cleanse you. Then, before the LORD, you will be clean from all your sins. ³¹It is a sabbath of rest, and you must deny yourselves; it is a lasting ordinance. ³²The priest who is anointed and ordained to succeed his father as high priest is to make atonement. He is to put on the sacred linen garments ³³and make atonement for the Most Holy Place, for the Tent of Meeting and the altar, and for the priests and all the people of the community.

³⁴"This is to be a lasting ordinance for you: Atonement is to be made once a year for all the sins of the Israelites."

And it was done, as the LORD commanded Moses.

CHAPTER 17

The LORD said to Moses, ²"Speak to Aaron and his sons and to all the Israelites and say to them: 'This is what the LORD has commanded: ³Any Israelite who sacrifices an ox,ʲ a lamb or a goat in the camp or outside of it ⁴instead of bringing it to the entrance to the Tent of Meeting to present it as an offering to the LORD in front of the tabernacle of the LORD—that man shall be considered guilty of bloodshed; he has shed blood and must be cut off from his people. ⁵This is so the Israelites will bring to the LORD the sacrifices they are now making in the open fields. They must bring them to the priest, that is, to the

LORD, at the entrance to the Tent of Meeting and sacrifice them as fellowship offerings.ᵏ ⁶The priest is to sprinkle the blood against the altar of the LORD at the entrance to the Tent of Meeting and burn the fat as an aroma pleasing to the LORD. ⁷They must no longer offer any of their sacrifices to the goat idolsˡ to whom they prostitute themselves. This is to be a lasting ordinance for them and for the generations to come.'

⁸"Say to them: 'Any Israelite or any alien living among them who offers a burnt offering or sacrifice ⁹and does not bring it to the entrance to the Tent of Meeting to sacrifice it to the LORD—that man must be cut off from his people.

¹⁰" 'Any Israelite or any alien living among them who eats any blood—I will set my face against that person who eats blood and will cut him off from his people. ¹¹For the life of a creature is in the blood, and I have given it to you to make atonement for yourselves on the altar; it is the blood that makes atonement for one's life. ¹²Therefore I say to the Israelites, "None of you may eat blood, nor may an alien living among you eat blood."

¹³" 'Any Israelite or any alien living among you who hunts any animal or bird that may be eaten must drain out the blood and cover it with earth, ¹⁴because the life of every creature is its blood. That is why I have said to the Israelites, "You must not eat the blood of any creature, because the life of every creature is its blood; anyone who eats it must be cut off."

¹⁵" 'Anyone, whether native-born or alien, who eats anything found dead or torn by wild animals must wash his clothes and bathe with water, and he will be ceremonially unclean till evening; then he will be clean. ¹⁶But if he does not wash his clothes and bathe himself, he will be held responsible.' "

ⁱ29 Or must fast; also in verse 31   ʲ3 The Hebrew word can include both male and female.   ᵏ5 Traditionally peace offerings
ˡ7 Or demons

FEBRUARY 6 ☐ DAY 37
LEVITICUS 18–20
A Holy People Uniquely His

OVERVIEW In addition to the regulations governing national holiness, God provides Israel with laws governing personal conduct and purity in matters pertaining to the family, community and society in general. Because of the central importance of obedience, God requires that violators be punished promptly and in a manner appropriate to the crime committed. God's strict guidelines for living reflect his desire that his people be holy and uniquely his.

Chapter 18	Chapter 19	Chapter 20
Abstaining from Sexual Sins	Abstaining from Social Sins	Avoiding the Penalty for Sins
Holy People		Holy God

A Christian's spiritual health is exactly proportional to his devotion to God.

YOUR DAILY WALK The chapters you read today are not pleasant, for in them you will discover the depths to which fallen human nature is capable of sinking: incest, child sacrifice, prostitution, bestiality, homosexuality.

More than fourteen hundred years later, Paul would describe human nature in these dismaying words: "godlessness . . . shameful lusts . . . depraved mind . . . filled with every kind of wickedness . . . envy, murder, strife, deceit . . . they invent ways of doing evil . . . faithless, heartless" (Romans 1:18–31). Perhaps these lists look like today's headlines, for human nature has not changed over the generations.

With so many ways to go astray, is it any wonder that God must lay down so many rules for his children to follow before he can turn them loose in pagan Canaan? God desires that his people be transformed by their relationships with him—not conformed to their world.

How about you? Are you *transformed* by godliness or *conformed* to worldliness? (Or are you *deformed* by trying to be both?) Take a strip of paper and write down those areas of your life in which you may be too much of a conformist (dress, activities, personal life, speech). Use it as a bookmark in your Bible to remind you that "living what you read" is the transformation God desires.

INSIGHT Ten Familiar Commands in an Unfamiliar Place
Last month you read Exodus 20:1–17, the passage containing the familiar Ten Commandments. But did you know most of the ten are also contained in Leviticus 19? Go prospecting through the chapter to see how many you can find. Happy hunting!

CHAPTER 18
The LORD said to Moses, ²"Speak to the Israelites and say to them: 'I am the LORD your God. ³You must not do as they do in Egypt, where you used to live, and you must not do as they do in the land of Canaan, where I am bringing you. Do not follow their practices. ⁴You must obey my laws and be careful to follow my decrees. I am the LORD your God. ⁵Keep my decrees and laws, for the man who obeys them will live by them. I am the LORD.

⁶" 'No one is to approach any close relative to have sexual relations. I am the LORD.

⁷" 'Do not dishonor your father by having sexual relations with your mother. She is your mother; do not have relations with her.

⁸" 'Do not have sexual relations with your father's wife; that would dishonor your father.

⁹" 'Do not have sexual relations with your sister, either your father's daughter

or your mother's daughter, whether she was born in the same home or elsewhere.

[10] 'Do not have sexual relations with your son's daughter or your daughter's daughter; that would dishonor you.

[11] 'Do not have sexual relations with the daughter of your father's wife, born to your father; she is your sister.

[12] 'Do not have sexual relations with your father's sister; she is your father's close relative.

[13] 'Do not have sexual relations with your mother's sister, because she is your mother's close relative.

[14] 'Do not dishonor your father's brother by approaching his wife to have sexual relations; she is your aunt.

[15] 'Do not have sexual relations with your daughter-in-law. She is your son's wife; do not have relations with her.

[16] 'Do not have sexual relations with your brother's wife; that would dishonor your brother.

[17] 'Do not have sexual relations with both a woman and her daughter. Do not have sexual relations with either her son's daughter or her daughter's daughter; they are her close relatives. That is wickedness.

[18] 'Do not take your wife's sister as a rival wife and have sexual relations with her while your wife is living.

[19] 'Do not approach a woman to have sexual relations during the uncleanness of her monthly period.

[20] 'Do not have sexual relations with your neighbor's wife and defile yourself with her.

[21] 'Do not give any of your children to be sacrificed[m] to Molech, for you must not profane the name of your God. I am the LORD.

[22] 'Do not lie with a man as one lies with a woman; that is detestable.

[23] 'Do not have sexual relations with an animal and defile yourself with it. A woman must not present herself to an animal to have sexual relations with it; that is a perversion.

[24] 'Do not defile yourselves in any of these ways, because this is how the nations that I am going to drive out before you became defiled. [25]Even the land was defiled; so I punished it for its sin, and the land vomited out its inhabitants. [26]But you must keep my decrees and my laws. The native-born and the aliens living among you must not do any of these detestable things, [27]for all these things were done by the people who lived in the land before you, and the land became defiled. [28]And if you defile the land, it will vomit you out as it vomited out the nations that were before you.

[29] 'Everyone who does any of these detestable things—such persons must be cut off from their people. [30]Keep my requirements and do not follow any of the detestable customs that were practiced before you came and do not defile yourselves with them. I am the LORD your God.' "

CHAPTER 19

The LORD said to Moses, [2]"Speak to the entire assembly of Israel and say to them: 'Be holy because I, the LORD your God, am holy.

[3] 'Each of you must respect his mother and father, and you must observe my Sabbaths. I am the LORD your God.

[4] 'Do not turn to idols or make gods of cast metal for yourselves. I am the LORD your God.

[5] 'When you sacrifice a fellowship offering[n] to the LORD, sacrifice it in such a way that it will be accepted on your behalf. [6]It shall be eaten on the day you sacrifice it or on the next day; anything left over until the third day must be burned up. [7]If any of it is eaten on the third day, it is impure and will not be accepted. [8]Whoever eats it will be held responsible because he has desecrated what is holy to the LORD; that person must be cut off from his people.

[9] 'When you reap the harvest of your land, do not reap to the very edges of your field or gather the gleanings of your harvest. [10]Do not go over your vineyard a second time or pick up the grapes that have fallen. Leave them for the poor and the alien. I am the LORD your God.

[11] 'Do not steal.

'Do not lie.

'Do not deceive one another.

[12] 'Do not swear falsely by my name

---

m 21 Or *to be passed through the fire.*   n 5 Traditionally *peace offering* and so profane the name of your God. I am the LORD.

¹³" 'Do not defraud your neighbor or rob him.

" 'Do not hold back the wages of a hired man overnight.

¹⁴" 'Do not curse the deaf or put a stumbling block in front of the blind, but fear your God. I am the LORD.

¹⁵" 'Do not pervert justice; do not show partiality to the poor or favoritism to the great, but judge your neighbor fairly.

¹⁶" 'Do not go about spreading slander among your people.

" 'Do not do anything that endangers your neighbor's life. I am the LORD.

¹⁷" 'Do not hate your brother in your heart. Rebuke your neighbor frankly so you will not share in his guilt.

¹⁸" 'Do not seek revenge or bear a grudge against one of your people, but love your neighbor as yourself. I am the LORD.

¹⁹" 'Keep my decrees.

" 'Do not mate different kinds of animals.

" 'Do not plant your field with two kinds of seed.

" 'Do not wear clothing woven of two kinds of material.

²⁰" 'If a man sleeps with a woman who is a slave girl promised to another man but who has not been ransomed or given her freedom, there must be due punishment. Yet they are not to be put to death, because she had not been freed. ²¹The man, however, must bring a ram to the entrance to the Tent of Meeting for a guilt offering to the LORD. ²²With the ram of the guilt offering the priest is to make atonement for him before the LORD for the sin he has committed, and his sin will be forgiven.

²³" 'When you enter the land and plant any kind of fruit tree, regard its fruit as forbidden.ᵒ For three years you are to consider it forbiddenᵒ; it must not be eaten. ²⁴In the fourth year all its fruit will be holy, an offering of praise to the LORD. ²⁵But in the fifth year you may eat its fruit. In this way your harvest will be increased. I am the LORD your God.

²⁶" 'Do not eat any meat with the blood still in it.

" 'Do not practice divination or sorcery.

²⁷" 'Do not cut the hair at the sides of your head or clip off the edges of your beard.

²⁸" 'Do not cut your bodies for the dead or put tattoo marks on yourselves. I am the LORD.

²⁹" 'Do not degrade your daughter by making her a prostitute, or the land will turn to prostitution and be filled with wickedness.

³⁰" 'Observe my Sabbaths and have reverence for my sanctuary. I am the LORD.

³¹" 'Do not turn to mediums or seek out spiritists, for you will be defiled by them. I am the LORD your God.

³²" 'Rise in the presence of the aged, show respect for the elderly and revere your God. I am the LORD.

³³" 'When an alien lives with you in your land, do not mistreat him. ³⁴The alien living with you must be treated as one of your native-born. Love him as yourself, for you were aliens in Egypt. I am the LORD your God.

³⁵" 'Do not use dishonest standards when measuring length, weight or quantity. ³⁶Use honest scales and honest weights, an honest ephahᵖ and an honest hin.�q I am the LORD your God, who brought you out of Egypt.

³⁷" 'Keep all my decrees and all my laws and follow them. I am the LORD.' "

CHAPTER 20

The LORD said to Moses, ²"Say to the Israelites: 'Any Israelite or any alien living in Israel who givesʳ any of his children to Molech must be put to death. The people of the community are to stone him. ³I will set my face against that man and I will cut him off from his people; for by giving his children to Molech, he has defiled my sanctuary and profaned my holy name. ⁴If the people of the community close their eyes when that man gives one of his children to Molech and they fail to put him to death, ⁵I will set my face against that man and his family and will cut off from their people both him and all who follow him in prostituting themselves to Molech.

⁶" 'I will set my face against the person who turns to mediums and spiritists to

---

ᵒ23 Hebrew *uncircumcised*   ᵖ36 An ephah was a dry measure. in verses 3 and 4   q36 A hin was a liquid measure.   ʳ2 Or *sacrifices*; also prostitute himself by following them, and I will cut him off from his people.

[7] "'Consecrate yourselves and be holy, because I am the LORD your God. [8]Keep my decrees and follow them. I am the LORD, who makes you holy.[s]

[9] "'If anyone curses his father or mother, he must be put to death. He has cursed his father or his mother, and his blood will be on his own head.

[10] "'If a man commits adultery with another man's wife—with the wife of his neighbor—both the adulterer and the adulteress must be put to death.

[11] "'If a man sleeps with his father's wife, he has dishonored his father. Both the man and the woman must be put to death; their blood will be on their own heads.

[12] "'If a man sleeps with his daughter-in-law, both of them must be put to death. What they have done is a perversion; their blood will be on their own heads.

[13] "'If a man lies with a man as one lies with a woman, both of them have done what is detestable. They must be put to death; their blood will be on their own heads.

[14] "'If a man marries both a woman and her mother, it is wicked. Both he and they must be burned in the fire, so that no wickedness will be among you.

[15] "'If a man has sexual relations with an animal, he must be put to death, and you must kill the animal.

[16] "'If a woman approaches an animal to have sexual relations with it, kill both the woman and the animal. They must be put to death; their blood will be on their own heads.

[17] "'If a man marries his sister, the daughter of either his father or his mother, and they have sexual relations, it is a disgrace. They must be cut off before the eyes of their people. He has dishon-

ored his sister and will be held responsible.

[18] "'If a man lies with a woman during her monthly period and has sexual relations with her, he has exposed the source of her flow, and she has also uncovered it. Both of them must be cut off from their people.

[19] "'Do not have sexual relations with the sister of either your mother or your father, for that would dishonor a close relative; both of you would be held responsible.

[20] "'If a man sleeps with his aunt, he has dishonored his uncle. They will be held responsible; they will die childless.

[21] "'If a man marries his brother's wife, it is an act of impurity; he has dishonored his brother. They will be childless.

[22] "'Keep all my decrees and laws and follow them, so that the land where I am bringing you to live may not vomit you out. [23]You must not live according to the customs of the nations I am going to drive out before you. Because they did all these things, I abhorred them. [24]But I said to you, "You will possess their land; I will give it to you as an inheritance, a land flowing with milk and honey." I am the LORD your God, who has set you apart from the nations.

[25] "'You must therefore make a distinction between clean and unclean animals and between unclean and clean birds. Do not defile yourselves by any animal or bird or anything that moves along the ground—those which I have set apart as unclean for you. [26]You are to be holy to me[t] because I, the LORD, am holy, and I have set you apart from the nations to be my own.

[27] "'A man or woman who is a medium or spiritist among you must be put to death. You are to stone them; their blood will be on their own heads.'"

---

[s]8 Or who sanctifies you; or who sets you apart as holy   [t]26 Or be my holy ones

FEBRUARY 7 ☐ DAY 38
A Blueprint for Worship

 LOOK BACK If you have safely navigated through the Scripture readings for this past week, congratulations! Many who begin with great enthusiasm in January to read all the way through the Bible wonder if they are going to falter and fall by the wayside in February when they get to the book of Leviticus. It needn't be that way if you understand the intention of the author!

In Exodus 25–30 you read about the divine blueprint for the tabernacle, the ornate traveling tent that would be Israel's place of worship on the march to the promised land. In exquisite detail God set forth the plan, and Moses—assisted by skillful, Spirit-filled workmen—followed the plan to the last detail. Only when the job was done "as the Lord commanded [Moses]" did the glory of God fill the tabernacle.

But who would assist those who came to the tabernacle to worship? And how would they know how to offer acceptable sacrifices on behalf of the people? Leviticus provides a helpful handbook for the Levites and priests who carried the awesome responsibility of leading the nation in corporate and private worship.

 LOOK UP What would you think of a restaurant chef who decided that the weights and measures in a recipe were "a needless bother" and ignored them in preparing your dinner?

You cannot walk with God and run with the devil.

What would you think of an auto mechanic who decided that a sledgehammer and machete were just as good as metric tools when it came to servicing your car?

What would you think of a surgeon who used hedge clippers because "I never was much good with a scalpel"?

Probably you would use someone else's services. Why? Because *how* you do something is as important as *what* you do. Well-meaning, inept chefs, mechanics and surgeons just don't get the job done.

Think of worship the same way. It's not enough to *want* to worship God—you must consider carefully *how* you worship God. You cannot approach a holy God with soiled hands or an unclean heart. You cannot expect to please God by offering him what is unacceptable to him. You cannot call something insignificant when God has called it indispensable.

 LOOK AHEAD Chuck Swindoll has commented that we in America are guilty of playing at our worship, worshiping our work and working at our play. Worship, done properly, is hard work. It involves the entire person in an attitude of humility and dependence upon God, acknowledging the "worth-ship" of our Creator and Sustainer. Begin now to prepare for the next visit you will make to your local house of worship. Here are some verses to look up and meditate upon as you prepare to give God the honor and adoration he so richly deserves: 1 Chronicles 16:29; Psalm 95:6; John 4:24; Revelation 15:4.

And if you find that you just can't wait, feel free to worship him for a few minutes right now! You might want to read the words of Psalm 100 out loud as the expression of your heart.

FEBRUARY 8 ☐ DAY 39
LEVITICUS 21–23
Priestly Purity

OVERVIEW Ministry to and for a holy people requires a holy priest-hood. Because of their high calling, the priests accepted extra restrictions on their conduct and privileges. They had to be physically perfect and willing to avoid defilements that were permissible for others. The sacrifices they offered had to be without defect. They were required to carry out their duties with meticulous attention to detail. Their busiest times of the year came during the holy convocations—joyous times of feasting and reflecting on God's goodness in dealing with Israel.

Chapter 21		Chapter 22	Chapter 23
Priestly Defilements	Priestly Defects	Priestly Duties	Important Days
1 15	16 24		
Holy Priests			Yearly Feasts

YOUR DAILY WALK Here is a statement worth considering, especially if you are the hard-driving kind of person commonly labeled as a workaholic: Seven days without relaxation makes one weak.

Jesus knows we must come apart and rest awhile or else we may just plain come apart.

On the seventh day of each week the Israelites were commanded to rest from their labors. Seven times each year they enjoyed a "holy holiday" to commemorate important days in their nation's history. These were no mere business meetings but were times of feasting and festivity.

How long has it been since you set aside your work to spend time alone or with your family enjoying a leisurely activity? If your mind is constantly focused on your job, it will seldom be focused on God. In contrast, periodic times of refreshment and reflection will help to improve your attitude toward your work.

Look at your personal or family calendar, and prayerfully consider whether a vacation is long overdue. It needn't be long to be refreshing. But it does need to be a priority in your schedule if it is ever to become more than just a good idea.

INSIGHT How about This for a Vacation Schedule?
Life in the nation of Israel was not all work, work, work. There were nineteen days of national holiday: Passover, Unleavened Bread (seven days), Firstfruits, Pentecost, Trumpets, Day of Atonement, and Tabernacles (seven days). Counting the weekly Sabbath days of rest, that makes ten weeks of vacation a year!

CHAPTER 21
The LORD said to Moses, "Speak to the priests, the sons of Aaron, and say to them: 'A priest must not make himself ceremonially unclean for any of his people who die, ²except for a close relative, such as his mother or father, his son or daughter, his brother, ³or an unmarried sister who is dependent on him since she has no husband—for her he may make himself unclean. ⁴He must not make himself unclean for people related to him by marriage,ᵘ and so defile himself.

⁵" 'Priests must not shave their heads or shave off the edges of their beards or cut their bodies. ⁶They must be holy to their God and must not profane the name of their God. Because they present the offerings made to the LORD by fire, the food of their God, they are to be holy.

ᵘ4 Or *unclean as a leader among his people*

⁷" 'They must not marry women defiled by prostitution or divorced from their husbands, because priests are holy to their God. ⁸Regard them as holy, because they offer up the food of your God. Consider them holy, because I the LORD am holy—I who make you holy.ᵛ

⁹" 'If a priest's daughter defiles herself by becoming a prostitute, she disgraces her father; she must be burned in the fire.

¹⁰" 'The high priest, the one among his brothers who has had the anointing oil poured on his head and who has been ordained to wear the priestly garments, must not let his hair become unkemptʷ or tear his clothes. ¹¹He must not enter a place where there is a dead body. He must not make himself unclean, even for his father or mother, ¹²nor leave the sanctuary of his God or desecrate it, because he has been dedicated by the anointing oil of his God. I am the LORD.

¹³" 'The woman he marries must be a virgin. ¹⁴He must not marry a widow, a divorced woman, or a woman defiled by prostitution, but only a virgin from his own people, ¹⁵so he will not defile his offspring among his people. I am the LORD, who makes him holy.ˣ' "

¹⁶The LORD said to Moses, ¹⁷"Say to Aaron: 'For the generations to come none of your descendants who has a defect may come near to offer the food of his God. ¹⁸No man who has any defect may come near: no man who is blind or lame, disfigured or deformed; ¹⁹no man with a crippled foot or hand, ²⁰or who is hunchbacked or dwarfed, or who has any eye defect, or who has festering or running sores or damaged testicles. ²¹No descendant of Aaron the priest who has any defect is to come near to present the offerings made to the LORD by fire. He has a defect; he must not come near to offer the food of his God. ²²He may eat the most holy food of his God, as well as the holy food; ²³yet because of his defect, he must not go near the curtain or approach the altar, and so desecrate my sanctuary. I am the LORD, who makes them holy.ʸ' "

²⁴So Moses told this to Aaron and his sons and to all the Israelites.

CHAPTER 22

The LORD said to Moses, ²"Tell Aaron and his sons to treat with respect the sacred offerings the Israelites consecrate to me, so they will not profane my holy name. I am the LORD.

³"Say to them: 'For the generations to come, if any of your descendants is ceremonially unclean and yet comes near the sacred offerings that the Israelites consecrate to the LORD, that person must be cut off from my presence. I am the LORD.

⁴" 'If a descendant of Aaron has an infectious skin diseaseᶻ or a bodily discharge, he may not eat the sacred offerings until he is cleansed. He will also be unclean if he touches something defiled by a corpse or by anyone who has an emission of semen, ⁵or if he touches any crawling thing that makes him unclean, or any person who makes him unclean, whatever the uncleanness may be. ⁶The one who touches any such thing will be unclean till evening. He must not eat any of the sacred offerings unless he has bathed himself with water. ⁷When the sun goes down, he will be clean, and after that he may eat the sacred offerings, for they are his food. ⁸He must not eat anything found dead or torn by wild animals, and so become unclean through it. I am the LORD.

⁹" 'The priests are to keep my requirements so that they do not become guilty and die for treating them with contempt. I am the LORD, who makes them holy.ᵃ

¹⁰" 'No one outside a priest's family may eat the sacred offering, nor may the guest of a priest or his hired worker eat it. ¹¹But if a priest buys a slave with money, or if a slave is born in his household, that slave may eat his food. ¹²If a priest's daughter marries anyone other than a priest, she may not eat any of the sacred contributions. ¹³But if a priest's daughter becomes a widow or is divorced, yet has no children, and she returns to live in her father's house as in her youth, she may eat of her father's food. No unauthorized person, however, may eat any of it.

¹⁴" 'If anyone eats a sacred offering by mistake, he must make restitution to the priest for the offering and add a fifth of

the value to it. ¹⁵The priests must not desecrate the sacred offerings the Israelites present to the LORD ¹⁶by allowing them to eat the sacred offerings and so bring upon them guilt requiring payment. I am the LORD, who makes them holy.' "

¹⁷The LORD said to Moses, ¹⁸"Speak to Aaron and his sons and to all the Israelites and say to them: 'If any of you—either an Israelite or an alien living in Israel—presents a gift for a burnt offering to the LORD, either to fulfill a vow or as a freewill offering, ¹⁹you must present a male without defect from the cattle, sheep or goats in order that it may be accepted on your behalf. ²⁰Do not bring anything with a defect, because it will not be accepted on your behalf. ²¹When anyone brings from the herd or flock a fellowship offering^b to the LORD to fulfill a special vow or as a freewill offering, it must be without defect or blemish to be acceptable. ²²Do not offer to the LORD the blind, the injured or the maimed, or anything with warts or festering or running sores. Do not place any of these on the altar as an offering made to the LORD by fire. ²³You may, however, present as a freewill offering an ox^c or a sheep that is deformed or stunted, but it will not be accepted in fulfillment of a vow. ²⁴You must not offer to the LORD an animal whose testicles are bruised, crushed, torn or cut. You must not do this in your own land, ²⁵and you must not accept such animals from the hand of a foreigner and offer them as the food of your God. They will not be accepted on your behalf, because they are deformed and have defects.' "

²⁶The LORD said to Moses, ²⁷"When a calf, a lamb or a goat is born, it is to remain with its mother for seven days. From the eighth day on, it will be acceptable as an offering made to the LORD by fire. ²⁸Do not slaughter a cow or a sheep and its young on the same day.

²⁹"When you sacrifice a thank offering to the LORD, sacrifice it in such a way that it will be accepted on your behalf. ³⁰It must be eaten that same day; leave none of it till morning. I am the LORD.

³¹"Keep my commands and follow them. I am the LORD. ³²Do not profane my holy name. I must be acknowledged as

holy by the Israelites. I am the LORD, who makes^d you holy^e ³³and who brought you out of Egypt to be your God. I am the LORD."

CHAPTER 23

The LORD said to Moses, ²"Speak to the Israelites and say to them: 'These are my appointed feasts, the appointed feasts of the LORD, which you are to proclaim as sacred assemblies.

³" 'There are six days when you may work, but the seventh day is a Sabbath of rest, a day of sacred assembly. You are not to do any work; wherever you live, it is a Sabbath to the LORD.

⁴" 'These are the LORD's appointed feasts, the sacred assemblies you are to proclaim at their appointed times: ⁵The LORD's Passover begins at twilight on the fourteenth day of the first month. ⁶On the fifteenth day of that month the LORD's Feast of Unleavened Bread begins; for seven days you must eat bread made without yeast. ⁷On the first day hold a sacred assembly and do no regular work. ⁸For seven days present an offering made to the LORD by fire. And on the seventh day hold a sacred assembly and do no regular work.' "

⁹The LORD said to Moses, ¹⁰"Speak to the Israelites and say to them: 'When you enter the land I am going to give you and you reap its harvest, bring to the priest a sheaf of the first grain you harvest. ¹¹He is to wave the sheaf before the LORD so it will be accepted on your behalf; the priest is to wave it on the day after the Sabbath. ¹²On the day you wave the sheaf, you must sacrifice as a burnt offering to the LORD a lamb a year old without defect, ¹³together with its grain offering of two-tenths of an ephah^f of fine flour mixed with oil—an offering made to the LORD by fire, a pleasing aroma—and its drink offering of a quarter of a hin^g of wine. ¹⁴You must not eat any bread, or roasted or new grain, until the very day you bring this offering to your God. This is to be a lasting ordinance for the generations to come, wherever you live.

¹⁵" 'From the day after the Sabbath, the day you brought the sheaf of the wave offering, count off seven full weeks.

^b21 Traditionally *peace offering*   ^c23 The Hebrew word can include both male and female.   ^d32 Or *made*   ^e32 Or *who sanctifies you; or who sets you apart as holy*   ^f13 That is, probably about 4 quarts (about 4.5 liters); also in verse 17   ^g13 That is, probably about 1 quart (about 1 liter)

¹⁶Count off fifty days up to the day after the seventh Sabbath, and then present an offering of new grain to the LORD. ¹⁷From wherever you live, bring two loaves made of two-tenths of an ephah of fine flour, baked with yeast, as a wave offering of firstfruits to the LORD. ¹⁸Present with this bread seven male lambs, each a year old and without defect, one young bull and two rams. They will be a burnt offering to the LORD, together with their grain offerings and drink offerings—an offering made by fire, an aroma pleasing to the LORD. ¹⁹Then sacrifice one male goat for a sin offering and two lambs, each a year old, for a fellowship offering.ʰ ²⁰The priest is to wave the two lambs before the LORD as a wave offering, together with the bread of the firstfruits. They are a sacred offering to the LORD for the priest. ²¹On that same day you are to proclaim a sacred assembly and do no regular work. This is to be a lasting ordinance for the generations to come, wherever you live.

²²" 'When you reap the harvest of your land, do not reap to the very edges of your field or gather the gleanings of your harvest. Leave them for the poor and the alien. I am the LORD your God.' "

²³The LORD said to Moses, ²⁴"Say to the Israelites: 'On the first day of the seventh month you are to have a day of rest, a sacred assembly commemorated with trumpet blasts. ²⁵Do no regular work, but present an offering made to the LORD by fire.' "

²⁶The LORD said to Moses, ²⁷"The tenth day of this seventh month is the Day of Atonement. Hold a sacred assembly and deny yourselves,ⁱ and present an offering made to the LORD by fire. ²⁸Do no work on that day, because it is the Day of Atonement, when atonement is made for you before the LORD your God. ²⁹Anyone who does not deny himself on that day must be cut off from his people. ³⁰I will destroy from among his people anyone who does any work on that day. ³¹You shall do no work at all. This is to be a lasting ordinance for the generations to come, wherever you live. ³²It is a sabbath of rest for you, and you must deny yourselves. From the evening of the ninth day of the month until the following evening you are to observe your sabbath."

³³The LORD said to Moses, ³⁴"Say to the Israelites: 'On the fifteenth day of the seventh month the LORD's Feast of Tabernacles begins, and it lasts for seven days. ³⁵The first day is a sacred assembly; do no regular work. ³⁶For seven days present offerings made to the LORD by fire, and on the eighth day hold a sacred assembly and present an offering made to the LORD by fire. It is the closing assembly; do no regular work.

³⁷(" 'These are the LORD's appointed feasts, which you are to proclaim as sacred assemblies for bringing offerings made to the LORD by fire—the burnt offerings and grain offerings, sacrifices and drink offerings required for each day. ³⁸These offerings are in addition to those for the LORD's Sabbaths andʲ in addition to your gifts and whatever you have vowed and all the freewill offerings you give to the LORD.)

³⁹" 'So beginning with the fifteenth day of the seventh month, after you have gathered the crops of the land, celebrate the festival to the LORD for seven days; the first day is a day of rest, and the eighth day also is a day of rest. ⁴⁰On the first day you are to take choice fruit from the trees, and palm fronds, leafy branches and poplars, and rejoice before the LORD your God for seven days. ⁴¹Celebrate this as a festival to the LORD for seven days each year. This is to be a lasting ordinance for the generations to come; celebrate it in the seventh month. ⁴²Live in booths for seven days: All native-born Israelites are to live in booths ⁴³so your descendants will know that I had the Israelites live in booths when I brought them out of Egypt. I am the LORD your God.' "

⁴⁴So Moses announced to the Israelites the appointed feasts of the LORD.

ʰ19 Traditionally *peace offering*   ⁱ27 Or *and fast*; also in verses 29 and 32   ʲ38 Or *These feasts are in addition to the LORD's Sabbaths, and these offerings are*

Sabbath after Sabbath, on behalf of the Israelites, as a lasting covenant. [9]It belongs to Aaron and his sons, who are to eat it in a holy place, because it is a most holy part of their regular share of the offerings made to the LORD by fire."

[10]Now the son of an Israelite mother and an Egyptian father went out among the Israelites, and a fight broke out in the camp between him and an Israelite. [11]The son of the Israelite woman blasphemed the Name with a curse; so they brought him to Moses. (His mother's name was Shelomith, the daughter of Dibri the Danite.) [12]They put him in custody until the will of the LORD should be made clear to them.

[13]Then the LORD said to Moses: [14]"Take the blasphemer outside the camp. All those who heard him are to lay their hands on his head, and the entire assembly is to stone him. [15]Say to the Israelites: 'If anyone curses his God, he will be held responsible; [16]anyone who blasphemes the name of the LORD must be put to death. The entire assembly must stone him. Whether an alien or native-born, when he blasphemes the Name, he must be put to death.

[17]" 'If anyone takes the life of a human being, he must be put to death. [18]Anyone who takes the life of someone's animal must make restitution—life for life. [19]If anyone injures his neighbor, whatever he has done must be done to him: [20]fracture for fracture, eye for eye, tooth for tooth. As he has injured the other, so he is to be injured. [21]Whoever kills an animal must make restitution, but whoever kills a man must be put to death. [22]You are to have the same law for the alien and the native-born. I am the LORD your God.' "

[23]Then Moses spoke to the Israelites, and they took the blasphemer outside the camp and stoned him. The Israelites did as the LORD commanded Moses.

CHAPTER 25

The LORD said to Moses on Mount Sinai, [2]"Speak to the Israelites and say to them: 'When you enter the land I am going to give you, the land itself must observe a sabbath to the LORD. [3]For six years sow your fields, and for six years prune your vineyards and gather their crops. [4]But in the seventh year the land is to have a sabbath of rest, a sabbath to the LORD. Do not sow your fields or prune your vineyards. [5]Do not reap what grows of itself or harvest the grapes of your untended vines. The land is to have a year of rest. [6]Whatever the land yields during the sabbath year will be food for you—for yourself, your manservant and maidservant, and the hired worker and temporary resident who live among you, [7]as well as for your livestock and the wild animals in your land. Whatever the land produces may be eaten.

[8]" 'Count off seven sabbaths of years—seven times seven years—so that the seven sabbaths of years amount to a period of forty-nine years. [9]Then have the trumpet sounded everywhere on the tenth day of the seventh month; on the Day of Atonement sound the trumpet throughout your land. [10]Consecrate the fiftieth year and proclaim liberty throughout the land to all its inhabitants. It shall be a jubilee for you; each one of you is to return to his family property and each to his own clan. [11]The fiftieth year shall be a jubilee for you; do not sow and do not reap what grows of itself or harvest the untended vines. [12]For it is a jubilee and is to be holy for you; eat only what is taken directly from the fields.

[13]" 'In this Year of Jubilee everyone is to return to his own property.

[14]" 'If you sell land to one of your countrymen or buy any from him, do not take advantage of each other. [15]You are to buy from your countryman on the basis of the number of years since the Jubilee. And he is to sell to you on the basis of the number of years left for harvesting crops. [16]When the years are many, you are to increase the price, and when the years are few, you are to decrease the price, because what he is really selling you is the number of crops. [17]Do not take advantage of each other, but fear your God. I am the LORD your God.

[18]" 'Follow my decrees and be careful to obey my laws, and you will live safely in the land. [19]Then the land will yield its fruit, and you will eat your fill and live there in safety. [20]You may ask, "What will we eat in the seventh year if we do not plant or harvest our crops?" [21]I will send you such a blessing in the sixth year that the land will yield enough for three years. [22]While you plant during the eighth year, you will eat from the old crop and will

continue to eat from it until the harvest of the ninth year comes in.

23" 'The land must not be sold permanently, because the land is mine and you are but aliens and my tenants. 24Throughout the country that you hold as a possession, you must provide for the redemption of the land.

25" 'If one of your countrymen becomes poor and sells some of his property, his nearest relative is to come and redeem what his countryman has sold. 26If, however, a man has no one to redeem it for him but he himself prospers and acquires sufficient means to redeem it, 27he is to determine the value for the years since he sold it and refund the balance to the man to whom he sold it; he can then go back to his own property. 28But if he does not acquire the means to repay him, what he sold will remain in the possession of the buyer until the Year of Jubilee. It will be returned in the Jubilee, and he can then go back to his property.

29" 'If a man sells a house in a walled city, he retains the right of redemption a full year after its sale. During that time he may redeem it. 30If it is not redeemed before a full year has passed, the house in the walled city shall belong permanently to the buyer and his descendants. It is not to be returned in the Jubilee. 31But houses in villages without walls around them are to be considered as open country. They can be redeemed, and they are to be returned in the Jubilee.

32" 'The Levites always have the right to redeem their houses in the Levitical towns, which they possess. 33So the property of the Levites is redeemable—that is, a house sold in any town they hold—and is to be returned in the Jubilee, because the houses in the towns of the Levites are their property among the Israelites. 34But the pastureland belonging to their towns must not be sold; it is their permanent possession.

35" 'If one of your countrymen becomes poor and is unable to support himself among you, help him as you would an alien or a temporary resident, so he can continue to live among you. 36Do not take interest of any kind[l] from him, but fear your God, so that your countryman may continue to live among you. 37You must

not lend him money at interest or sell him food at a profit. 38I am the LORD your God, who brought you out of Egypt to give you the land of Canaan and to be your God.

39" 'If one of your countrymen becomes poor among you and sells himself to you, do not make him work as a slave. 40He is to be treated as a hired worker or a temporary resident among you; he is to work for you until the Year of Jubilee. 41Then he and his children are to be released, and he will go back to his own clan and to the property of his forefathers. 42Because the Israelites are my servants, whom I brought out of Egypt, they must not be sold as slaves. 43Do not rule over them ruthlessly, but fear your God.

44" 'Your male and female slaves are to come from the nations around you; from them you may buy slaves. 45You may also buy some of the temporary residents living among you and members of their clans born in your country, and they will become your property. 46You can will them to your children as inherited property and can make them slaves for life, but you must not rule over your fellow Israelites ruthlessly.

47" 'If an alien or a temporary resident among you becomes rich and one of your countrymen becomes poor and sells himself to the alien living among you or to a member of the alien's clan, 48he retains the right of redemption after he has sold himself. One of his relatives may redeem him: 49An uncle or a cousin or any blood relative in his clan may redeem him. Or if he prospers, he may redeem himself. 50He and his buyer are to count the time from the year he sold himself up to the Year of Jubilee. The price for his release is to be based on the rate paid to a hired man for that number of years. 51If many years remain, he must pay for his redemption a larger share of the price paid for him. 52If only a few years remain until the Year of Jubilee, he is to compute that and pay for his redemption accordingly. 53He is to be treated as a man hired from year to year; you must see to it that his owner does not rule over him ruthlessly.

54" 'Even if he is not redeemed in any of these ways, he and his children are to be released in the Year of Jubilee, 55for the Israelites belong to me as servants. They

l36 Or take excessive interest; similarly in verse 37

are my servants, whom I brought out of Egypt. I am the LORD your God.

CHAPTER 26

ⁱ" 'Do not make idols or set up an image or a sacred stone for yourselves, and do not place a carved stone in your land to bow down before it. I am the LORD your God.

²" 'Observe my Sabbaths and have reverence for my sanctuary. I am the LORD.

³" 'If you follow my decrees and are careful to obey my commands, ⁴I will send you rain in its season, and the ground will yield its crops and the trees of the field their fruit. ⁵Your threshing will continue until grape harvest and the grape harvest will continue until planting, and you will eat all the food you want and live in safety in your land.

⁶" 'I will grant peace in the land, and you will lie down and no one will make you afraid. I will remove savage beasts from the land, and the sword will not pass through your country. ⁷You will pursue your enemies, and they will fall by the sword before you. ⁸Five of you will chase a hundred, and a hundred of you will chase ten thousand, and your enemies will fall by the sword before you.

⁹" 'I will look on you with favor and make you fruitful and increase your numbers, and I will keep my covenant with you. ¹⁰You will still be eating last year's harvest when you will have to move it out to make room for the new. ¹¹I will put my dwelling place*m* among you, and I will not abhor you. ¹²I will walk among you and be your God, and you will be my people. ¹³I am the LORD your God, who brought you out of Egypt so that you would no longer be slaves to the Egyptians; I broke the bars of your yoke and enabled you to walk with heads held high.

¹⁴" 'But if you will not listen to me and carry out all these commands, ¹⁵and if you reject my decrees and abhor my laws and fail to carry out all my commands and so violate my covenant, ¹⁶then I will do this to you: I will bring upon you sudden terror, wasting diseases and fever that will destroy your sight and drain away your life. You will plant seed in vain, because your enemies will eat it. ¹⁷I will set my face against you so that you

will be defeated by your enemies; those who hate you will rule over you, and you will flee even when no one is pursuing you.

¹⁸" 'If after all this you will not listen to me, I will punish you for your sins seven times over. ¹⁹I will break down your stubborn pride and make the sky above you like iron and the ground beneath you like bronze. ²⁰Your strength will be spent in vain, because your soil will not yield its crops, nor will the trees of the land yield their fruit.

²¹" 'If you remain hostile toward me and refuse to listen to me, I will multiply your afflictions seven times over, as your sins deserve. ²²I will send wild animals against you, and they will rob you of your children, destroy your cattle and make you so few in number that your roads will be deserted.

²³" 'If in spite of these things you do not accept my correction but continue to be hostile toward me, ²⁴I myself will be hostile toward you and will afflict you for your sins seven times over. ²⁵And I will bring the sword upon you to avenge the breaking of the covenant. When you withdraw into your cities, I will send a plague among you, and you will be given into enemy hands. ²⁶When I cut off your supply of bread, ten women will be able to bake your bread in one oven, and they will dole out the bread by weight. You will eat, but you will not be satisfied.

²⁷" 'If in spite of this you still do not listen to me but continue to be hostile toward me, ²⁸then in my anger I will be hostile toward you, and I myself will punish you for your sins seven times over. ²⁹You will eat the flesh of your sons and the flesh of your daughters. ³⁰I will destroy your high places, cut down your incense altars and pile your dead bodies on the lifeless forms of your idols, and I will abhor you. ³¹I will turn your cities into ruins and lay waste your sanctuaries, and I will take no delight in the pleasing aroma of your offerings. ³²I will lay waste the land, so that your enemies who live there will be appalled. ³³I will scatter you among the nations and will draw out my sword and pursue you. Your land will be laid waste, and your cities will lie in ruins. ³⁴Then the land will enjoy its sabbath

m 11 Or my tabernacle

years all the time that it lies desolate and you are in the country of your enemies; then the land will rest and enjoy its sabbaths. ³⁵All the time that it lies desolate, the land will have the rest it did not have during the sabbaths you lived in it.

³⁶" 'As for those of you who are left, I will make their hearts so fearful in the lands of their enemies that the sound of a windblown leaf will put them to flight. They will run as though fleeing from the sword, and they will fall, even though no one is pursuing them. ³⁷They will stumble over one another as though fleeing from the sword, even though no one is pursuing. So you will not be able to stand before your enemies. ³⁸You will perish among the nations; the land of your enemies will devour you. ³⁹Those of you who are left will waste away in the lands of their enemies because of their sins; also because of their fathers' sins they will waste away.

⁴⁰" 'But if they will confess their sins and the sins of their fathers—their treachery against me and their hostility toward me, ⁴¹which made me hostile toward them so that I sent them into the land of their enemies—then when their uncircumcised hearts are humbled and they pay for their sin, ⁴²I will remember my covenant with Jacob and my covenant with Isaac and my covenant with Abraham, and I will remember the land. ⁴³For the land will be deserted by them and will enjoy its sabbaths while it lies desolate without them. They will pay for their sins because they rejected my laws and abhorred my decrees. ⁴⁴Yet in spite of this, when they are in the land of their enemies, I will not reject them or abhor them so as to destroy them completely, breaking my covenant with them. I am the LORD their God. ⁴⁵But for their sake I will remember the covenant with their ancestors whom I brought out of Egypt in the sight of the nations to be their God. I am the LORD.' "

⁴⁶These are the decrees, the laws and the regulations that the LORD established on Mount Sinai between himself and the Israelites through Moses.

CHAPTER 27

The LORD said to Moses, ²"Speak to the Israelites and say to them: 'If anyone makes a special vow to dedicate persons to the LORD by giving equivalent values, ³set the value of a male between the ages of twenty and sixty at fifty shekels*ⁿ* of silver, according to the sanctuary shekel*ᵒ*; ⁴and if it is a female, set her value at thirty shekels.*ᵖ* ⁵If it is a person between the ages of five and twenty, set the value of a male at twenty shekels*�q* and of a female at ten shekels.*ʳ* ⁶If it is a person between one month and five years, set the value of a male at five shekels*ˢ* of silver and that of a female at three shekels*ᵗ* of silver. ⁷If it is a person sixty years old or more, set the value of a male at fifteen shekels*ᵘ* and of a female at ten shekels. ⁸If anyone making the vow is too poor to pay the specified amount, he is to present the person to the priest, who will set the value for him according to what the man making the vow can afford.

⁹" 'If what he vowed is an animal that is acceptable as an offering to the LORD, such an animal given to the LORD becomes holy. ¹⁰He must not exchange it or substitute a good one for a bad one, or a bad one for a good one; if he should substitute one animal for another, both it and the substitute become holy. ¹¹If what he vowed is a ceremonially unclean animal—one that is not acceptable as an offering to the LORD—the animal must be presented to the priest, ¹²who will judge its quality as good or bad. Whatever value the priest then sets, that is what it will be. ¹³If the owner wishes to redeem the animal, he must add a fifth to its value.

¹⁴" 'If a man dedicates his house as something holy to the LORD, the priest will judge its quality as good or bad. Whatever value the priest then sets, so it will remain. ¹⁵If the man who dedicates his house redeems it, he must add a fifth to its value, and the house will again become his.

¹⁶" 'If a man dedicates to the LORD part of his family land, its value is to be set according to the amount of seed required for it—fifty shekels of silver to a homer*ᵛ* of barley seed. ¹⁷If he dedicates his field

---

ⁿ3 That is, about 1 1/4 pounds (about 0.6 kilogram); also in verse 16   *ᵒ3* That is, about 2/5 ounce (about 11.5 grams); also in verse 25   *ᵖ4* That is, about 12 ounces (about 0.3 kilogram)   *q5* That is, about 8 ounces (about 0.2 kilogram)   *ʳ5* That is, about 4 ounces (about 110 grams); also in verse 7   *ˢ6* That is, about 2 ounces (about 55 grams)   *ᵗ6* That is, about 1 1/4 ounces (about 35 grams)   *ᵘ7* That is, about 6 ounces (about 170 grams)   *ᵛ16* That is, probably about 6 bushels (about 220 liters) during the Year of Jubilee, the value that has been set remains. [18]But if he dedicates his field after the Jubilee, the priest will determine the value according to the number of years that remain until the next Year of Jubilee, and its set value will be reduced. [19]If the man who dedicates the field wishes to redeem it, he must add a fifth to its value, and the field will again become his. [20]If, however, he does not redeem the field, or if he has sold it to someone else, it can never be redeemed. [21]When the field is released in the Jubilee, it will become holy, like a field devoted to the LORD; it will become the property of the priests.[w]

[22]" 'If a man dedicates to the LORD a field he has bought, which is not part of his family land, [23]the priest will determine its value up to the Year of Jubilee, and the man must pay its value on that day as something holy to the LORD. [24]In the Year of Jubilee the field will revert to the person from whom he bought it, the one whose land it was. [25]Every value is to be set according to the sanctuary shekel, twenty gerahs to the shekel.

[26]" 'No one, however, may dedicate the firstborn of an animal, since the firstborn already belongs to the LORD; whether an ox[x] or a sheep, it is the LORD's. [27]If it is one of the unclean animals, he may buy it back at its set value, adding a fifth of the value to it. If he does not redeem it, it is to be sold at its set value.

[28]" 'But nothing that a man owns and devotes[y] to the LORD—whether man or animal or family land—may be sold or redeemed; everything so devoted is most holy to the LORD.

[29]" 'No person devoted to destruction[z] may be ransomed; he must be put to death.

[30]" 'A tithe of everything from the land, whether grain from the soil or fruit from the trees, belongs to the LORD; it is holy to the LORD. [31]If a man redeems any of his tithe, he must add a fifth of the value to it. [32]The entire tithe of the herd and flock— every tenth animal that passes under the shepherd's rod—will be holy to the LORD. [33]He must not pick out the good from the bad or make any substitution. If he does make a substitution, both the animal and its substitute become holy and cannot be redeemed.' "

[34]These are the commands the LORD gave Moses on Mount Sinai for the Israelites.

---

[w]21 Or *priest*　[x]26 The Hebrew word can include both male and female.　[y]28 The Hebrew term refers to the irrevocable giving over of things or persons to the LORD.　[z]29 The Hebrew term refers to the irrevocable giving over of things or persons to the LORD, often by totally destroying them.

Numbers

BEGINNING with events about one year after the exodus from Egypt, Numbers is the book of divine discipline, showing the painful consequences of wrong choices by God's chosen people. Because of the nation's unbelief, Israel's eleven-day journey becomes a forty-year ordeal. Numbers contains the records of two generations, two censuses and two sets of instructions for enjoying the promised land. The lesson from history is clear: Obedience is the path to blessing in any generation.

Focus	Preparation			Punishment			Promise		
Divisions	The Nation Counted and Camped	The Nation Cleansed for Worship	The Nation Commences the Journey	Rebellion and Death in the Desert	The Staff, Red Heifer, and Rebellion	The Bronze Snake and Brash Seer	Recounting and Reviewing	The Last Days of a Great Leader	Laws of the Promised Land
	1 4	5 8	9 12	13 16	17 20	21 25	26 30	31 33	34 36
Topics	Old Generation			Degeneration			New Generation		
	A Bright Beginning			A Tragic Transition			The Grand Conclusion		
Place	On the Road to Kadesh			In the Desert			On the Road to Canaan		
Time	About 40 Years								

FEBRUARY 10 □ DAY 41
NUMBERS 1–4
The Nation Counted and Camped

OVERVIEW With the nation of Israel now poised, ready to begin its march toward Canaan, God commands Moses to number the fighting men and arrange the tribes around the camp with the tabernacle in the center. The census of the soldiers suggests a total population of 2 to 3 million people. The Levites are also counted and assigned specific tasks in connection with the care, erection and transportation of the tabernacle and its furnishings.

Chapter 1	Chapter 2	Chapter 3	Chapter 4
The Nation Counted	The Nation Camped	The Levites Arrayed	The Levites Assigned
God's People		God's Priests	

Life is a lot like tennis—the goal is to learn to serve best.

YOUR DAILY WALK *Question:* Which part of your physical body is more important? Your eye or ear? Your arm or Adam's apple?

Question: Which part of the spiritual body of Christ is more important? The teacher or administrator? The pastor or exhorter? (Now check Ephesians 4:16 for the answer.)

Because God accomplishes his purposes through people, he has given each of his children specific gifts, talents and skills to do his will. The sons of Merari, one family of the tribe of Levi, were told by God to carry parts of the tabernacle—an assignment so specific that everything they carried was itemized piece by piece (4:29–32). Every man in that family knew exactly what his job was. And the importance of their work was clear to all, for their employer was none other than the Lord.

What act of service has God given you to do? The task may seem small compared to what others are doing, but God never asks you to compare yourself with others. He simply desires your faithfulness.

Use a few of the more insignificant parts of your physical body to complete this sentence: "I'm so glad my [little finger, kneecap, eyelash, etc.] is a *faithful* part of my body, and that's what I want to be known as in the body of Christ—a faithful member."

INSIGHT Say, You Look Familiar!
God instructed Moses to arrange the twelve tribes in the camp of Israel by ancestry. The tribes were descended from four different mothers (the four wives of Jacob), and God placed those tribes that were the nearest of kin close to one another.

CHAPTER 1
The LORD spoke to Moses in the Tent of Meeting in the Desert of Sinai on the first day of the second month of the second year after the Israelites came out of Egypt. He said: ²"Take a census of the whole Israelite community by their clans and families, listing every man by name, one by one. ³You and Aaron are to number by their divisions all the men in Israel twenty years old or more who are able to serve in the army. ⁴One man from each tribe, each

the head of his family, is to help you.
⁵These are the names of the men who are
to assist you:

> from Reuben, Elizur son of Shedeur;
> ⁶from Simeon, Shelumiel son of Zuri-
> shaddai;
> ⁷from Judah, Nahshon son of Am-
> minadab;
> ⁸from Issachar, Nethanel son of Zuar;
> ⁹from Zebulun, Eliab son of Helon;
> ¹⁰from the sons of Joseph:
> from Ephraim, Elishama son of
> Ammihud;
> from Manasseh, Gamaliel son of
> Pedahzur;
> ¹¹from Benjamin, Abidan son of Gide-
> oni;
> ¹²from Dan, Ahiezer son of Ammi-
> shaddai;
> ¹³from Asher, Pagiel son of Ocran;
> ¹⁴from Gad, Eliasaph son of Deuel;
> ¹⁵from Naphtali, Ahira son of Enan."

¹⁶These were the men appointed from
the community, the leaders of their ancestral tribes. They were the heads of the
clans of Israel.

¹⁷Moses and Aaron took these men
whose names had been given, ¹⁸and they
called the whole community together on
the first day of the second month. The
people indicated their ancestry by their
clans and families, and the men twenty
years old or more were listed by name,
one by one, ¹⁹as the LORD commanded
Moses. And so he counted them in the
Desert of Sinai:

²⁰From the descendants of Reuben the
firstborn son of Israel:
All the men twenty years old or
more who were able to serve in
the army were listed by name, one
by one, according to the records
of their clans and families. ²¹The
number from the tribe of Reuben
was 46,500.

²²From the descendants of Simeon:
All the men twenty years old or
more who were able to serve in
the army were counted and listed
by name, one by one, according to
the records of their clans and families. ²³The number from the tribe
of Simeon was 59,300.

²⁴From the descendants of Gad:

All the men twenty years old or
more who were able to serve in
the army were listed by name, according to the records of their
clans and families. ²⁵The number
from the tribe of Gad was 45,650.

²⁶From the descendants of Judah:
All the men twenty years old or
more who were able to serve in
the army were listed by name, according to the records of their
clans and families. ²⁷The number
from the tribe of Judah was 74,600.

²⁸From the descendants of Issachar:
All the men twenty years old or
more who were able to serve in
the army were listed by name, according to the records of their
clans and families. ²⁹The number
from the tribe of Issachar was
54,400.

³⁰From the descendants of Zebulun:
All the men twenty years old or
more who were able to serve in
the army were listed by name, according to the records of their
clans and families. ³¹The number
from the tribe of Zebulun was
57,400.

³²From the sons of Joseph:
From the descendants of Ephraim:
All the men twenty years old or
more who were able to serve in
the army were listed by name, according to the records of their
clans and families. ³³The number
from the tribe of Ephraim was
40,500.

³⁴From the descendants of Manasseh:
All the men twenty years old or
more who were able to serve in
the army were listed by name, according to the records of their
clans and families. ³⁵The number
from the tribe of Manasseh was
32,200.

³⁶From the descendants of Benjamin:
All the men twenty years old or
more who were able to serve in
the army were listed by name, according to the records of their
clans and families. ³⁷The number
from the tribe of Benjamin was
35,400.

³⁸From the descendants of Dan:
All the men twenty years old or more who were able to serve in the army were listed by name, according to the records of their clans and families. ³⁹The number from the tribe of Dan was 62,700.

⁴⁰From the descendants of Asher:
All the men twenty years old or more who were able to serve in the army were listed by name, according to the records of their clans and families. ⁴¹The number from the tribe of Asher was 41,500.

⁴²From the descendants of Naphtali:
All the men twenty years old or more who were able to serve in the army were listed by name, according to the records of their clans and families. ⁴³The number from the tribe of Naphtali was 53,400.

⁴⁴These were the men counted by Moses and Aaron and the twelve leaders of Israel, each one representing his family. ⁴⁵All the Israelites twenty years old or more who were able to serve in Israel's army were counted according to their families. ⁴⁶The total number was 603,550.

⁴⁷The families of the tribe of Levi, however, were not counted along with the others. ⁴⁸The LORD had said to Moses: ⁴⁹"You must not count the tribe of Levi or include them in the census of the other Israelites. ⁵⁰Instead, appoint the Levites to be in charge of the tabernacle of the Testimony—over all its furnishings and everything belonging to it. They are to carry the tabernacle and all its furnishings; they are to take care of it and encamp around it. ⁵¹Whenever the tabernacle is to move, the Levites are to take it down, and whenever the tabernacle is to be set up, the Levites shall do it. Anyone else who goes near it shall be put to death. ⁵²The Israelites are to set up their tents by divisions, each man in his own camp under his own standard. ⁵³The Levites, however, are to set up their tents around the tabernacle of the Testimony so that wrath will not fall on the Israelite community. The Levites are to be responsible for the care of the tabernacle of the Testimony."

⁵⁴The Israelites did all this just as the LORD commanded Moses.

CHAPTER 2

The LORD said to Moses and Aaron: ²"The Israelites are to camp around the Tent of Meeting some distance from it, each man under his standard with the banners of his family."

³On the east, toward the sunrise, the divisions of the camp of Judah are to encamp under their standard. The leader of the people of Judah is Nahshon son of Amminadab. ⁴His division numbers 74,600.

⁵The tribe of Issachar will camp next to them. The leader of the people of Issachar is Nethanel son of Zuar. ⁶His division numbers 54,400.

⁷The tribe of Zebulun will be next. The leader of the people of Zebulun is Eliab son of Helon. ⁸His division numbers 57,400.

⁹All the men assigned to the camp of Judah, according to their divisions, number 186,400. They will set out first.

¹⁰On the south will be the divisions of the camp of Reuben under their standard. The leader of the people of Reuben is Elizur son of Shedeur. ¹¹His division numbers 46,500.

¹²The tribe of Simeon will camp next to them. The leader of the people of Simeon is Shelumiel son of Zurishaddai. ¹³His division numbers 59,300.

¹⁴The tribe of Gad will be next. The leader of the people of Gad is Eliasaph son of Deuel.^a ¹⁵His division numbers 45,650.

¹⁶All the men assigned to the camp of Reuben, according to their divisions, number 151,450. They will set out second.

¹⁷Then the Tent of Meeting and the camp of the Levites will set out in the middle of the camps. They will set out in the same order as they encamp, each in his own place under his standard.

¹⁸On the west will be the divisions of the camp of Ephraim under their

^a14 Many manuscripts of the Masoretic Text, Samaritan Pentateuch and Vulgate (see also Num. 1:14); most manuscripts of the Masoretic Text *Reuel*

standard. The leader of the people of Ephraim is Elishama son of Ammihud. ¹⁹His division numbers 40,500.

²⁰The tribe of Manasseh will be next to them. The leader of the people of Manasseh is Gamaliel son of Pedahzur. ²¹His division numbers 32,200.

²²The tribe of Benjamin will be next. The leader of the people of Benjamin is Abidan son of Gideoni. ²³His division numbers 35,400.

²⁴All the men assigned to the camp of Ephraim, according to their divisions, number 108,100. They will set out third.

²⁵On the north will be the divisions of the camp of Dan, under their standard. The leader of the people of Dan is Ahiezer son of Ammishaddai. ²⁶His division numbers 62,700.

²⁷The tribe of Asher will camp next to them. The leader of the people of Asher is Pagiel son of Ocran. ²⁸His division numbers 41,500.

²⁹The tribe of Naphtali will be next. The leader of the people of Naphtali is Ahira son of Enan. ³⁰His division numbers 53,400.

³¹All the men assigned to the camp of Dan number 157,600. They will set out last, under their standards.

³²These are the Israelites, counted according to their families. All those in the camps, by their divisions, number 603,550. ³³The Levites, however, were not counted along with the other Israelites, as the LORD commanded Moses.

³⁴So the Israelites did everything the LORD commanded Moses; that is the way they encamped under their standards, and that is the way they set out, each with his clan and family.

CHAPTER 3

This is the account of the family of Aaron and Moses at the time the LORD talked with Moses on Mount Sinai.

²The names of the sons of Aaron were Nadab the firstborn and Abihu, Eleazar and Ithamar. ³Those were the names of Aaron's sons, the anointed priests, who were ordained to serve as priests. ⁴Nadab and Abihu, however, fell dead before the LORD when they made an offering with unauthorized fire before him in the Desert of Sinai. They had no sons; so only Eleazar and Ithamar served as priests during the lifetime of their father Aaron.

⁵The LORD said to Moses, ⁶"Bring the tribe of Levi and present them to Aaron the priest to assist him. ⁷They are to perform duties for him and for the whole community at the Tent of Meeting by doing the work of the tabernacle. ⁸They are to take care of all the furnishings of the Tent of Meeting, fulfilling the obligations of the Israelites by doing the work of the tabernacle. ⁹Give the Levites to Aaron and his sons; they are the Israelites who are to be given wholly to him.^b ¹⁰Appoint Aaron and his sons to serve as priests; anyone else who approaches the sanctuary must be put to death."

¹¹The LORD also said to Moses, ¹²"I have taken the Levites from among the Israelites in place of the first male offspring of every Israelite woman. The Levites are mine, ¹³for all the firstborn are mine. When I struck down all the firstborn in Egypt, I set apart for myself every firstborn in Israel, whether man or animal. They are to be mine. I am the LORD."

¹⁴The LORD said to Moses in the Desert of Sinai, ¹⁵"Count the Levites by their families and clans. Count every male a month old or more." ¹⁶So Moses counted them, as he was commanded by the word of the LORD.

¹⁷These were the names of the sons of Levi:

Gershon, Kohath and Merari.

¹⁸These were the names of the Gershonite clans:

Libni and Shimei.

¹⁹The Kohathite clans:

Amram, Izhar, Hebron and Uzziel.

²⁰The Merarite clans:

Mahli and Mushi.

These were the Levite clans, according to their families.

²¹To Gershon belonged the clans of the Libnites and Shimeites; these were the Gershonite clans. ²²The number of all the males a month old or more who were

^b 9 Most manuscripts of the Masoretic Text; some manuscripts of the Masoretic Text, Samaritan Pentateuch and Septuagint (see also Num. 8:16) to me

counted was 7,500. ²³The Gershonite clans were to camp on the west, behind the tabernacle. ²⁴The leader of the families of the Gershonites was Eliasaph son of Lael. ²⁵At the Tent of Meeting the Gershonites were responsible for the care of the tabernacle and tent, its coverings, the curtain at the entrance to the Tent of Meeting, ²⁶the curtains of the courtyard, the curtain at the entrance to the courtyard surrounding the tabernacle and altar, and the ropes— and everything related to their use.

²⁷To Kohath belonged the clans of the Amramites, Izharites, Hebronites and Uzzielites; these were the Kohathite clans. ²⁸The number of all the males a month old or more was 8,600.ᶜ The Kohathites were responsible for the care of the sanctuary. ²⁹The Kohathite clans were to camp on the south side of the tabernacle. ³⁰The leader of the families of the Kohathite clans was Elizaphan son of Uzziel. ³¹They were responsible for the care of the ark, the table, the lampstand, the altars, the articles of the sanctuary used in ministering, the curtain, and everything related to their use. ³²The chief leader of the Levites was Eleazar son of Aaron, the priest. He was appointed over those who were responsible for the care of the sanctuary.

³³To Merari belonged the clans of the Mahlites and the Mushites; these were the Merarite clans. ³⁴The number of all the males a month old or more who were counted was 6,200. ³⁵The leader of the families of the Merarite clans was Zuriel son of Abihail; they were to camp on the north side of the tabernacle. ³⁶The Merarites were appointed to take care of the frames of the tabernacle, its crossbars, posts, bases, all its equipment, and everything related to their use, ³⁷as well as the posts of the surrounding courtyard with their bases, tent pegs and ropes.

³⁸Moses and Aaron and his sons were to camp to the east of the tabernacle, toward the sunrise, in front of the Tent of Meeting. They were responsible for the care of the sanctuary on behalf of the Israelites. Anyone else who approached the sanctuary was to be put to death.

³⁹The total number of Levites counted at the LORD's command by Moses and Aaron according to their clans, including every male a month old or more, was 22,000.

⁴⁰The LORD said to Moses, "Count all the firstborn Israelite males who are a month old or more and make a list of their names. ⁴¹Take the Levites for me in place of all the firstborn of the Israelites, and the livestock of the Levites in place of all the firstborn of the livestock of the Israelites. I am the LORD."

⁴²So Moses counted all the firstborn of the Israelites, as the LORD commanded him. ⁴³The total number of firstborn males a month old or more, listed by name, was 22,273.

⁴⁴The LORD also said to Moses, ⁴⁵"Take the Levites in place of all the firstborn of Israel, and the livestock of the Levites in place of their livestock. The Levites are to be mine. I am the LORD. ⁴⁶To redeem the 273 firstborn Israelites who exceed the number of the Levites, ⁴⁷collect five shekelsᵈ for each one, according to the sanctuary shekel, which weighs twenty gerahs. ⁴⁸Give the money for the redemption of the additional Israelites to Aaron and his sons."

⁴⁹So Moses collected the redemption money from those who exceeded the number redeemed by the Levites. ⁵⁰From the firstborn of the Israelites he collected silver weighing 1,365 shekels,ᵉ according to the sanctuary shekel. ⁵¹Moses gave the redemption money to Aaron and his sons, as he was commanded by the word of the LORD.

CHAPTER 4
The LORD said to Moses and Aaron: ²"Take a census of the Kohathite branch of the Levites by their clans and families. ³Count all the men from thirty to fifty years of age who come to serve in the work in the Tent of Meeting.

⁴"This is the work of the Kohathites in the Tent of Meeting: the care of the most holy things. ⁵When the camp is to move, Aaron and his sons are to go in and take down the shielding curtain and cover the ark of the Testimony with it. ⁶Then they are to cover this with hides of sea cows,ᶠ

ᶜ28 Hebrew; some Septuagint manuscripts 8,300   ᵈ47 That is, about 2 ounces (about 55 grams)   ᵉ50 That is, about 35 pounds (about 15.5 kilograms)   ᶠ6 That is, dugongs; also in verses 8, 10, 11, 12, 14 and 25 spread a cloth of solid blue over that and put the poles in place.

7"Over the table of the Presence they are to spread a blue cloth and put on it the plates, dishes and bowls, and the jars for drink offerings; the bread that is continually there is to remain on it. 8Over these they are to spread a scarlet cloth, cover that with hides of sea cows and put its poles in place.

9"They are to take a blue cloth and cover the lampstand that is for light, together with its lamps, its wick trimmers and trays, and all its jars for the oil used to supply it. 10Then they are to wrap it and all its accessories in a covering of hides of sea cows and put it on a carrying frame.

11"Over the gold altar they are to spread a blue cloth and cover that with hides of sea cows and put its poles in place.

12"They are to take all the articles used for ministering in the sanctuary, wrap them in a blue cloth, cover that with hides of sea cows and put them on a carrying frame.

13"They are to remove the ashes from the bronze altar and spread a purple cloth over it. 14Then they are to place on it all the utensils used for ministering at the altar, including the firepans, meat forks, shovels and sprinkling bowls. Over it they are to spread a covering of hides of sea cows and put its poles in place.

15"After Aaron and his sons have finished covering the holy furnishings and all the holy articles, and when the camp is ready to move, the Kohathites are to come to do the carrying. But they must not touch the holy things or they will die. The Kohathites are to carry those things that are in the Tent of Meeting.

16"Eleazar son of Aaron, the priest, is to have charge of the oil for the light, the fragrant incense, the regular grain offering and the anointing oil. He is to be in charge of the entire tabernacle and everything in it, including its holy furnishings and articles."

17The LORD said to Moses and Aaron, 18"See that the Kohathite tribal clans are not cut off from the Levites. 19So that they may live and not die when they come near the most holy things, do this for them: Aaron and his sons are to go into the sanctuary and assign to each man his work and what he is to carry. 20But the Kohathites must not go in to look at the holy things, even for a moment, or they will die."

21The LORD said to Moses, 22"Take a census also of the Gershonites by their families and clans. 23Count all the men from thirty to fifty years of age who come to serve in the work at the Tent of Meeting.

24"This is the service of the Gershonite clans as they work and carry burdens: 25They are to carry the curtains of the tabernacle, the Tent of Meeting, its covering and the outer covering of hides of sea cows, the curtains for the entrance to the Tent of Meeting, 26the curtains of the courtyard surrounding the tabernacle and altar, the curtain for the entrance, the ropes and all the equipment used in its service. The Gershonites are to do all that needs to be done with these things. 27All their service, whether carrying or doing other work, is to be done under the direction of Aaron and his sons. You shall assign to them as their responsibility all they are to carry. 28This is the service of the Gershonite clans at the Tent of Meeting. Their duties are to be under the direction of Ithamar son of Aaron, the priest.

29"Count the Merarites by their clans and families. 30Count all the men from thirty to fifty years of age who come to serve in the work at the Tent of Meeting. 31This is their duty as they perform service at the Tent of Meeting: to carry the frames of the tabernacle, its crossbars, posts and bases, 32as well as the posts of the surrounding courtyard with their bases, tent pegs, ropes, all their equipment and everything related to their use. Assign to each man the specific things he is to carry. 33This is the service of the Merarite clans as they work at the Tent of Meeting under the direction of Ithamar son of Aaron, the priest."

34Moses, Aaron and the leaders of the community counted the Kohathites by their clans and families. 35All the men from thirty to fifty years of age who came to serve in the work in the Tent of Meeting, 36counted by clans, were 2,750. 37This was the total of all those in the Kohathite clans who served in the Tent of Meeting. Moses and Aaron counted them according to the LORD's command through Moses.

38The Gershonites were counted by their clans and families. 39All the men from thirty to fifty years of age who came to serve in the work at the Tent of Meeting, ⁴⁰counted by their clans and families, were 2,630. ⁴¹This was the total of those in the Gershonite clans who served at the Tent of Meeting. Moses and Aaron counted them according to the LORD's command.

⁴²The Merarites were counted by their clans and families. ⁴³All the men from thirty to fifty years of age who came to serve in the work at the Tent of Meeting, ⁴⁴counted by their clans, were 3,200. ⁴⁵This was the total of those in the Mera-

rite clans. Moses and Aaron counted them according to the LORD's command through Moses.

⁴⁶So Moses, Aaron and the leaders of Israel counted all the Levites by their clans and families. ⁴⁷All the men from thirty to fifty years of age who came to do the work of serving and carrying the Tent of Meeting ⁴⁸numbered 8,580. ⁴⁹At the LORD's command through Moses, each was assigned his work and told what to carry.

Thus they were counted, as the LORD commanded Moses.

FEBRUARY 11 □ DAY 42
NUMBERS 5–8
The Nation Cleansed for Worship

 OVERVIEW God now further prepares the nation for the coming trip to Canaan by commanding Moses to deal with four specific problem areas: moral defilement, jealous suspicion, unmet needs in the tabernacle and uncleansed Levites in the service of the Lord. Israel's purity in moral conduct and interpersonal relationships is of utmost importance because the holy God of Israel dwells in her camp (5:3).

Chapter 5	Chapter 6	Chapter 7	Chapter 8
Defilement in Morals	Dedication to Service	Offerings of the Leaders	Offerings of the Levites
Cleansing	Dedication		

 YOUR DAILY WALK It is time for an easy, one-question quiz based on your reading of Leviticus and Numbers.

True or False: God demands holiness from his people.

A godly life is always the best advertisement for Christianity.

Absolutely true. But living a holy life is easier said than done because it involves maintaining personal purity while rubbing shoulders with a decidedly impure world.

As God prepared Israel to enter a land dominated by pagan influences, he knew his children would be exposed to all manner of idolatry and evil. So he required that they live a completely different way. His purpose was to *insulate* the Israelites from the influence of evil, but not to *isolate* them from the people to whom they could be a testimony. Israel was to witness about the true God in the midst of corruption, and the nation couldn't do that hidden away in the desert. Only as Israel's pagan neighbors saw the nation's godly lifestyle lived out before them would they be influenced toward righteousness.

Are the people around you influenced by your distinctive lifestyle, or do you blend inconspicuously into the world around you? Does your lifestyle *reflect* or *refute* your godly priorities and purity? Select one lifestyle goal for this coming week, and make it your "project in purity." Better yet, "team up" with another daily walker!

INSIGHT Twelve Offerings in One Service
Even though the offerings of the twelve leaders of the tribes of Israel
(given on the day the tabernacle worship was inaugurated) were
identical, each is recorded in great detail (7:10–83), showing God's
pleasure with their individual (and generous) gifts.

CHAPTER 5

The LORD said to Moses, 2"Command the Israelites to send away from the camp anyone who has an infectious skin disease*g* or a discharge of any kind, or who is ceremonially unclean because of a dead body. ³Send away male and female alike; send them outside the camp so they will not defile their camp, where I dwell among them." ⁴The Israelites did this; they sent them outside the camp. They did just as the LORD had instructed Moses.

⁵The LORD said to Moses, 6"Say to the Israelites: 'When a man or woman wrongs another in any way*h* and so is unfaithful to the LORD, that person is guilty ⁷and must confess the sin he has committed. He must make full restitution for his wrong, add one fifth to it and give it all to the person he has wronged. ⁸But if that person has no close relative to whom restitution can be made for the wrong, the restitution belongs to the LORD and must be given to the priest, along with the ram with which atonement is made for him. ⁹All the sacred contributions the Israelites bring to a priest will belong to him. ¹⁰Each man's sacred gifts are his own, but what he gives to the priest will belong to the priest.'"

¹¹Then the LORD said to Moses, 12"Speak to the Israelites and say to them: 'If a man's wife goes astray and is unfaithful to him ¹³by sleeping with another man, and this is hidden from her husband and her impurity is undetected (since there is no witness against her and she has not been caught in the act), ¹⁴and if feelings of jealousy come over her husband and he suspects his wife and she is impure—or if he is jealous and suspects her even though she is not impure— ¹⁵then he is to take his wife to the priest. He must also take an offering of a tenth of an ephah*i* of barley flour on her behalf. He must not pour oil on it or put incense on it, because it is a grain offering for jealousy, a reminder offering to draw attention to guilt.

16" 'The priest shall bring her and have her stand before the LORD. ¹⁷Then he shall take some holy water in a clay jar and put some dust from the tabernacle floor into the water. ¹⁸After the priest has had the woman stand before the LORD, he shall loosen her hair and place in her hands the reminder offering, the grain offering for jealousy, while he himself holds the bitter water that brings a curse. ¹⁹Then the priest shall put the woman under oath and say to her, "If no other man has slept with you and you have not gone astray and become impure while married to your husband, may this bitter water that brings a curse not harm you. ²⁰But if you have gone astray while married to your husband and you have defiled yourself by sleeping with a man other than your husband"— ²¹here the priest is to put the woman under this curse of the oath— "may the LORD cause your people to curse and denounce you when he causes your thigh to waste away and your abdomen to swell.*j* ²²May this water that brings a curse enter your body so that your abdomen swells and your thigh wastes away.*k*"

" 'Then the woman is to say, "Amen. So be it."

23" 'The priest is to write these curses on a scroll and then wash them off into the bitter water. ²⁴He shall have the woman drink the bitter water that brings a curse, and this water will enter her and cause bitter suffering. ²⁵The priest is to take from her hands the grain offering for jealousy, wave it before the LORD and bring it to the altar. ²⁶The priest is then to take a handful of the grain offering as a memorial offering and burn it on the altar; after that, he is to have the woman drink the water. ²⁷If she has defiled herself and been unfaithful to her husband, then when she is made to drink the water that brings a curse, it will go into her and cause bitter suffering; her abdomen will

---

*g*2 Traditionally *leprosy*; the Hebrew word was used for various diseases affecting the skin—not necessarily leprosy.
*h*6 Or *woman commits any wrong common to mankind*   *i*15 That is, probably about 2 quarts (about 2 liters)   *j*21 Or *causes you
to have a miscarrying womb and barrenness*   *k*22 Or *body and cause you to be barren and have a miscarrying womb*

swell and her thigh waste away,[1] and she will become accursed among her people. [28]If, however, the woman has not defiled herself and is free from impurity, she will be cleared of guilt and will be able to have children.

[29]" 'This, then, is the law of jealousy when a woman goes astray and defiles herself while married to her husband, [30]or when feelings of jealousy come over a man because he suspects his wife. The priest is to have her stand before the LORD and is to apply this entire law to her. [31]The husband will be innocent of any wrongdoing, but the woman will bear the consequences of her sin.' "

CHAPTER 6

The LORD said to Moses, [2]"Speak to the Israelites and say to them: 'If a man or woman wants to make a special vow, a vow of separation to the LORD as a Nazirite, [3]he must abstain from wine and other fermented drink and must not drink vinegar made from wine or from other fermented drink. He must not drink grape juice or eat grapes or raisins. [4]As long as he is a Nazirite, he must not eat anything that comes from the grapevine, not even the seeds or skins.

[5]" 'During the entire period of his vow of separation no razor may be used on his head. He must be holy until the period of his separation to the LORD is over; he must let the hair of his head grow long. [6]Throughout the period of his separation to the LORD he must not go near a dead body. [7]Even if his own father or mother or brother or sister dies, he must not make himself ceremonially unclean on account of them, because the symbol of his separation to God is on his head. [8]Throughout the period of his separation he is consecrated to the LORD.

[9]" 'If someone dies suddenly in his presence, thus defiling the hair he has dedicated, he must shave his head on the day of his cleansing—the seventh day. [10]Then on the eighth day he must bring two doves or two young pigeons to the priest at the entrance to the Tent of Meeting. [11]The priest is to offer one as a sin offering and the other as a burnt offering to make atonement for him because he sinned by being in the presence of the

dead body. That same day he is to consecrate his head. [12]He must dedicate himself to the LORD for the period of his separation and must bring a year-old male lamb as a guilt offering. The previous days do not count, because he became defiled during his separation.

[13]" 'Now this is the law for the Nazirite when the period of his separation is over. He is to be brought to the entrance to the Tent of Meeting. [14]There he is to present his offerings to the LORD: a year-old male lamb without defect for a burnt offering, a year-old ewe lamb without defect for a sin offering, a ram without defect for a fellowship offering,[m] [15]together with their grain offerings and drink offerings, and a basket of bread made without yeast—cakes made of fine flour mixed with oil, and wafers spread with oil.

[16]" 'The priest is to present them before the LORD and make the sin offering and the burnt offering. [17]He is to present the basket of unleavened bread and is to sacrifice the ram as a fellowship offering to the LORD, together with its grain offering and drink offering.

[18]" 'Then at the entrance to the Tent of Meeting, the Nazirite must shave off the hair that he dedicated. He is to take the hair and put it in the fire that is under the sacrifice of the fellowship offering.

[19]" 'After the Nazirite has shaved off the hair of his dedication, the priest is to place in his hands a boiled shoulder of the ram, and a cake and a wafer from the basket, both made without yeast. [20]The priest shall then wave them before the LORD as a wave offering; they are holy and belong to the priest, together with the breast that was waved and the thigh that was presented. After that, the Nazirite may drink wine.

[21]" 'This is the law of the Nazirite who vows his offering to the LORD in accordance with his separation, in addition to whatever else he can afford. He must fulfill the vow he has made, according to the law of the Nazirite.' "

[22]The LORD said to Moses, [23]"Tell Aaron and his sons, 'This is how you are to bless the Israelites. Say to them:

[24]" ' "The LORD bless you
　　and keep you;
[25]the LORD make his face shine upon you

---

[1]27 Or *suffering; she will have barrenness and a miscarrying womb*　　[m]14 Traditionally *peace offering*; also in verses 17 and 18

and be gracious to you;
²⁶the LORD turn his face toward you
    and give you peace." '

²⁷"So they will put my name on the Israelites, and I will bless them."

CHAPTER 7

When Moses finished setting up the tabernacle, he anointed it and consecrated it and all its furnishings. He also anointed and consecrated the altar and all its utensils. ²Then the leaders of Israel, the heads of families who were the tribal leaders in charge of those who were counted, made offerings. ³They brought as their gifts before the LORD six covered carts and twelve oxen—an ox from each leader and a cart from every two. These they presented before the tabernacle.

⁴The LORD said to Moses, ⁵"Accept these from them, that they may be used in the work at the Tent of Meeting. Give them to the Levites as each man's work requires."

⁶So Moses took the carts and oxen and gave them to the Levites. ⁷He gave two carts and four oxen to the Gershonites, as their work required, ⁸and he gave four carts and eight oxen to the Merarites, as their work required. They were all under the direction of Ithamar son of Aaron, the priest. ⁹But Moses did not give any to the Kohathites, because they were to carry on their shoulders the holy things, for which they were responsible.

¹⁰When the altar was anointed, the leaders brought their offerings for its dedication and presented them before the altar. ¹¹For the LORD had said to Moses, "Each day one leader is to bring his offering for the dedication of the altar."

¹²The one who brought his offering on the first day was Nahshon son of Amminadab of the tribe of Judah.

¹³His offering was one silver plate weighing a hundred and thirty shekels,ⁿ and one silver sprinkling bowl weighing seventy shekels,ᵒ both according to the sanctuary shekel, each filled with fine flour mixed with oil as a grain offering; ¹⁴one gold dish weighing ten shekels,ᵖ filled with incense; ¹⁵one young bull, one ram and one male lamb a year old, for a

burnt offering; ¹⁶one male goat for a sin offering; ¹⁷and two oxen, five rams, five male goats and five male lambs a year old, to be sacrificed as a fellowship offering.�q This was the offering of Nahshon son of Amminadab.

¹⁸On the second day Nethanel son of Zuar, the leader of Issachar, brought his offering.

¹⁹The offering he brought was one silver plate weighing a hundred and thirty shekels, and one silver sprinkling bowl weighing seventy shekels, both according to the sanctuary shekel, each filled with fine flour mixed with oil as a grain offering; ²⁰one gold dish weighing ten shekels, filled with incense; ²¹one young bull, one ram and one male lamb a year old, for a burnt offering; ²²one male goat for a sin offering; ²³and two oxen, five rams, five male goats and five male lambs a year old, to be sacrificed as a fellowship offering. This was the offering of Nethanel son of Zuar.

²⁴On the third day, Eliab son of Helon, the leader of the people of Zebulun, brought his offering.

²⁵His offering was one silver plate weighing a hundred and thirty shekels, and one silver sprinkling bowl weighing seventy shekels, both according to the sanctuary shekel, each filled with fine flour mixed with oil as a grain offering; ²⁶one gold dish weighing ten shekels, filled with incense; ²⁷one young bull, one ram and one male lamb a year old, for a burnt offering; ²⁸one male goat for a sin offering; ²⁹and two oxen, five rams, five male goats and five male lambs a year old, to be sacrificed as a fellowship offering. This was the offering of Eliab son of Helon.

³⁰On the fourth day Elizur son of Shedeur, the leader of the people of Reuben, brought his offering.

³¹His offering was one silver plate weighing a hundred and thirty shekels, and one silver sprinkling bowl

---

ⁿ13 That is, about 3 1/4 pounds (about 1.5 kilograms); also elsewhere in this chapter   ᵒ13 That is, about 1 3/4 pounds (about 0.8 kilogram); also elsewhere in this chapter   ᵖ14 That is, about 4 ounces (about 110 grams); also elsewhere in this chapter   q17 Traditionally *peace offering*; also elsewhere in this chapter weighing seventy shekels, both according to the sanctuary shekel, each filled with fine flour mixed with oil as a grain offering; ³²one gold dish weighing ten shekels, filled with incense; ³³one young bull, one ram and one male lamb a year old, for a burnt offering; ³⁴one male goat for a sin offering; ³⁵and two oxen, five rams, five male goats and five male lambs a year old, to be sacrificed as a fellowship offering. This was the offering of Elizur son of Shedeur.

³⁶On the fifth day Shelumiel son of Zurishaddai, the leader of the people of Simeon, brought his offering.

³⁷His offering was one silver plate weighing a hundred and thirty shekels, and one silver sprinkling bowl weighing seventy shekels, both according to the sanctuary shekel, each filled with fine flour mixed with oil as a grain offering; ³⁸one gold dish weighing ten shekels, filled with incense; ³⁹one young bull, one ram and one male lamb a year old, for a burnt offering; ⁴⁰one male goat for a sin offering; ⁴¹and two oxen, five rams, five male goats and five male lambs a year old, to be sacrificed as a fellowship offering. This was the offering of Shelumiel son of Zurishaddai.

⁴²On the sixth day Eliasaph son of Deuel, the leader of the people of Gad, brought his offering.

⁴³His offering was one silver plate weighing a hundred and thirty shekels, and one silver sprinkling bowl weighing seventy shekels, both according to the sanctuary shekel, each filled with fine flour mixed with oil as a grain offering; ⁴⁴one gold dish weighing ten shekels, filled with incense; ⁴⁵one young bull, one ram and one male lamb a year old, for a burnt offering; ⁴⁶one male goat for a sin offering; ⁴⁷and two oxen, five rams, five male goats and five male lambs a year old, to be sacrificed as a fellowship offering. This was the offering of Eliasaph son of Deuel.

⁴⁸On the seventh day Elishama son of Ammihud, the leader of the people of Ephraim, brought his offering.

⁴⁹His offering was one silver plate weighing a hundred and thirty shekels, and one silver sprinkling bowl weighing seventy shekels, both according to the sanctuary shekel, each filled with fine flour mixed with oil as a grain offering; ⁵⁰one gold dish weighing ten shekels, filled with incense; ⁵¹one young bull, one ram and one male lamb a year old, for a burnt offering; ⁵²one male goat for a sin offering; ⁵³and two oxen, five rams, five male goats and five male lambs a year old, to be sacrificed as a fellowship offering. This was the offering of Elishama son of Ammihud.

⁵⁴On the eighth day Gamaliel son of Pedahzur, the leader of the people of Manasseh, brought his offering.

⁵⁵His offering was one silver plate weighing a hundred and thirty shekels, and one silver sprinkling bowl weighing seventy shekels, both according to the sanctuary shekel, each filled with fine flour mixed with oil as a grain offering; ⁵⁶one gold dish weighing ten shekels, filled with incense; ⁵⁷one young bull, one ram and one male lamb a year old, for a burnt offering; ⁵⁸one male goat for a sin offering; ⁵⁹and two oxen, five rams, five male goats and five male lambs a year old, to be sacrificed as a fellowship offering. This was the offering of Gamaliel son of Pedahzur.

⁶⁰On the ninth day Abidan son of Gideoni, the leader of the people of Benjamin, brought his offering.

⁶¹His offering was one silver plate weighing a hundred and thirty shekels, and one silver sprinkling bowl weighing seventy shekels, both according to the sanctuary shekel, each filled with fine flour mixed with oil as a grain offering; ⁶²one gold dish weighing ten shekels, filled with incense; ⁶³one young bull, one ram and one male lamb a year old, for a burnt offering; ⁶⁴one male goat for a sin offering; ⁶⁵and two oxen, five rams, five male goats and five male lambs a year old, to be sacrificed as a fellowship offering. This was the offering of Abidan son of Gideoni.

⁶⁶On the tenth day Ahiezer son of

Ammishaddai, the leader of the people of Dan, brought his offering.

⁶⁷His offering was one silver plate weighing a hundred and thirty shekels, and one silver sprinkling bowl weighing seventy shekels, both according to the sanctuary shekel, each filled with fine flour mixed with oil as a grain offering; ⁶⁸one gold dish weighing ten shekels, filled with incense; ⁶⁹one young bull, one ram and one male lamb a year old, for a burnt offering; ⁷⁰one male goat for a sin offering; ⁷¹and two oxen, five rams, five male goats and five male lambs a year old, to be sacrificed as a fellowship offering. This was the offering of Ahiezer son of Ammishaddai.

⁷²On the eleventh day Pagiel son of Ocran, the leader of the people of Asher, brought his offering.

⁷³His offering was one silver plate weighing a hundred and thirty shekels, and one silver sprinkling bowl weighing seventy shekels, both according to the sanctuary shekel, each filled with fine flour mixed with oil as a grain offering; ⁷⁴one gold dish weighing ten shekels, filled with incense; ⁷⁵one young bull, one ram and one male lamb a year old, for a burnt offering; ⁷⁶one male goat for a sin offering; ⁷⁷and two oxen, five rams, five male goats and five male lambs a year old, to be sacrificed as a fellowship offering. This was the offering of Pagiel son of Ocran.

⁷⁸On the twelfth day Ahira son of Enan, the leader of the people of Naphtali, brought his offering.

⁷⁹His offering was one silver plate weighing a hundred and thirty shekels, and one silver sprinkling bowl weighing seventy shekels, both according to the sanctuary shekel, each filled with fine flour mixed with oil as a grain offering; ⁸⁰one gold dish weighing ten shekels, filled with incense; ⁸¹one young bull, one ram and one male lamb a year old, for a burnt offering; ⁸²one male goat for a sin offering; ⁸³and two oxen, five rams, five male goats and five male lambs a

year old, to be sacrificed as a fellowship offering. This was the offering of Ahira son of Enan.

⁸⁴These were the offerings of the Israelite leaders for the dedication of the altar when it was anointed: twelve silver plates, twelve silver sprinkling bowls and twelve gold dishes. ⁸⁵Each silver plate weighed a hundred and thirty shekels, and each sprinkling bowl seventy shekels. Altogether, the silver dishes weighed two thousand four hundred shekels,ʳ according to the sanctuary shekel. ⁸⁶The twelve gold dishes filled with incense weighed ten shekels each, according to the sanctuary shekel. Altogether, the gold dishes weighed a hundred and twenty shekels.ˢ ⁸⁷The total number of animals for the burnt offering came to twelve young bulls, twelve rams and twelve male lambs a year old, together with their grain offering. Twelve male goats were used for the sin offering. ⁸⁸The total number of animals for the sacrifice of the fellowship offering came to twenty-four oxen, sixty rams, sixty male goats and sixty male lambs a year old. These were the offerings for the dedication of the altar after it was anointed.

⁸⁹When Moses entered the Tent of Meeting to speak with the Lord, he heard the voice speaking to him from between the two cherubim above the atonement cover on the ark of the Testimony. And he spoke with him.

CHAPTER 8

The Lord said to Moses, ²"Speak to Aaron and say to him, 'When you set up the seven lamps, they are to light the area in front of the lampstand.' "

³Aaron did so; he set up the lamps so that they faced forward on the lampstand, just as the Lord commanded Moses. ⁴This is how the lampstand was made: It was made of hammered gold—from its base to its blossoms. The lampstand was made exactly like the pattern the Lord had shown Moses.

⁵The Lord said to Moses: ⁶"Take the Levites from among the other Israelites and make them ceremonially clean. ⁷To purify them, do this: Sprinkle the water of cleansing on them; then have them shave

---

ʳ 85 That is, about 60 pounds (about 28 kilograms)   ˢ 86 That is, about 3 pounds (about 1.4 kilograms) their whole bodies and wash their clothes, and so purify themselves. [8]Have them take a young bull with its grain offering of fine flour mixed with oil; then you are to take a second young bull for a sin offering. [9]Bring the Levites to the front of the Tent of Meeting and assemble the whole Israelite community. [10]You are to bring the Levites before the LORD, and the Israelites are to lay their hands on them. [11]Aaron is to present the Levites before the LORD as a wave offering from the Israelites, so that they may be ready to do the work of the LORD.

[12]"After the Levites lay their hands on the heads of the bulls, use the one for a sin offering to the LORD and the other for a burnt offering, to make atonement for the Levites. [13]Have the Levites stand in front of Aaron and his sons and then present them as a wave offering to the LORD. [14]In this way you are to set the Levites apart from the other Israelites, and the Levites will be mine.

[15]"After you have purified the Levites and presented them as a wave offering, they are to come to do their work at the Tent of Meeting. [16]They are the Israelites who are to be given wholly to me. I have taken them as my own in place of the firstborn, the first male offspring from every Israelite woman. [17]Every firstborn male in Israel, whether man or animal, is mine. When I struck down all the first-born in Egypt, I set them apart for myself. [18]And I have taken the Levites in place of all the firstborn sons in Israel. [19]Of all the Israelites, I have given the Levites as gifts to Aaron and his sons to do the work at the Tent of Meeting on behalf of the Israelites and to make atonement for them so that no plague will strike the Israelites when they go near the sanctuary."

[20]Moses, Aaron and the whole Israelite community did with the Levites just as the LORD commanded Moses. [21]The Levites purified themselves and washed their clothes. Then Aaron presented them as a wave offering before the LORD and made atonement for them to purify them. [22]After that, the Levites came to do their work at the Tent of Meeting under the supervision of Aaron and his sons. They did with the Levites just as the LORD commanded Moses.

[23]The LORD said to Moses, [24]"This applies to the Levites: Men twenty-five years old or more shall come to take part in the work at the Tent of Meeting, [25]but at the age of fifty, they must retire from their regular service and work no longer. [26]They may assist their brothers in performing their duties at the Tent of Meeting, but they themselves must not do the work. This, then, is how you are to assign the responsibilities of the Levites."

FEBRUARY 12 □ DAY 43
NUMBERS 9–12
The Nation Commences the Journey

 OVERVIEW After a special celebration of the Passover at Mount Sinai, the people watch as the cloud of his presence begins to move. Trumpets blare forth the exciting news: It is time to march! No sooner has Sinai faded from view than the congregation begins to grumble and complain. The manna is monotonous . . . water is scarce . . . the journey is hard. Egypt would have been far better than this! For every *problem* there is a corresponding *provision* from God until at last the people arrive at a desert oasis called Kadesh—the last scheduled stop before they enter the promised land. It is time for a crucial test of the people's commitment to walk by faith.

Chapter 9	Chapter 10	Chapter 11	Chapter 12
A Cloud to Guide	A Call to March	Complaining about Manna	Complaining about Moses
Getting Ready to March		Grumbling on the March	

YOUR DAILY WALK Have you ever spent the night in a desert? If so, you will have little trouble identifying with the complaints of the Israelites as they begin their march from Mount Sinai to the promised land.

The reason so many people know the solution is that they created the problem.

A desert is a hostile place. By day the sun beats down mercilessly, and the temperature soars. (God knew this and provided a traveling umbrella—the cloud.) Food is scarce and water is virtually nonexistent in a desert—unless, of course, you are eating manna from the dew and drinking water from rocks!

Do you see God's hand of provision in the life of his nation? More important, do you see God's hand of provision in your life? Repeatedly, the Israelites expressed *grumbling* instead of *gratitude.* Why not enjoy the blessing they missed by spending the next few minutes praising God for his daily provision!

INSIGHT Guided by a Cloud . . . and by Hobab

Though God provided divine guidance for the people in the form of the cloud of his presence, this did not preclude human agents. Moses persuaded his brother-in-law, Hobab, to act as a guide (10:31). God not only gives direction through his Word and through his Holy Spirit, he also uses people to guide our steps along life's journey.

CHAPTER 9

The LORD spoke to Moses in the Desert of Sinai in the first month of the second year after they came out of Egypt. He said, ²"Have the Israelites celebrate the Passover at the appointed time. ³Celebrate it at the appointed time, at twilight on the fourteenth day of this month, in accordance with all its rules and regulations."

⁴So Moses told the Israelites to celebrate the Passover, ⁵and they did so in the Desert of Sinai at twilight on the fourteenth day of the first month. The Israelites did everything just as the LORD commanded Moses.

⁶But some of them could not celebrate the Passover on that day because they were ceremonially unclean on account of a dead body. So they came to Moses and Aaron that same day ⁷and said to Moses, "We have become unclean because of a dead body, but why should we be kept from presenting the LORD's offering with the other Israelites at the appointed time?"

⁸Moses answered them, "Wait until I find out what the LORD commands concerning you."

⁹Then the LORD said to Moses, ¹⁰"Tell the Israelites: 'When any of you or your descendants are unclean because of a dead body or are away on a journey, they may still celebrate the LORD's Passover. ¹¹They are to celebrate it on the fourteenth day of the second month at twilight. They are to eat the lamb, together with unleavened bread and bitter herbs. ¹²They must not leave any of it till morning or break any of its bones. When they celebrate the Passover, they must follow all the regulations. ¹³But if a man who is ceremonially clean and not on a journey fails to celebrate the Passover, that person must be cut off from his people because he did not present the LORD's offering at the appointed time. That man will bear the consequences of his sin.

¹⁴"'An alien living among you who wants to celebrate the LORD's Passover must do so in accordance with its rules and regulations. You must have the same regulations for the alien and the native-born.'"

¹⁵On the day the tabernacle, the Tent of the Testimony, was set up, the cloud covered it. From evening till morning the cloud above the tabernacle looked like

fire. ¹⁶That is how it continued to be; the cloud covered it, and at night it looked like fire. ¹⁷Whenever the cloud lifted from above the Tent, the Israelites set out; wherever the cloud settled, the Israelites encamped. ¹⁸At the LORD's command the Israelites set out, and at his command they encamped. As long as the cloud stayed over the tabernacle, they remained in camp. ¹⁹When the cloud remained over the tabernacle a long time, the Israelites obeyed the LORD's order and did not set out. ²⁰Sometimes the cloud was over the tabernacle only a few days; at the LORD's command they would encamp, and then at his command they would set out. ²¹Sometimes the cloud stayed only from evening till morning, and when it lifted in the morning, they set out. Whether by day or by night, whenever the cloud lifted, they set out. ²²Whether the cloud stayed over the tabernacle for two days or a month or a year, the Israelites would remain in camp and not set out; but when it lifted, they would set out. ²³At the LORD's command they encamped, and at the LORD's command they set out. They obeyed the LORD's order, in accordance with his command through Moses.

CHAPTER 10

The LORD said to Moses: ²"Make two trumpets of hammered silver, and use them for calling the community together and for having the camps set out. ³When both are sounded, the whole community is to assemble before you at the entrance to the Tent of Meeting. ⁴If only one is sounded, the leaders—the heads of the clans of Israel—are to assemble before you. ⁵When a trumpet blast is sounded, the tribes camping on the east are to set out. ⁶At the sounding of a second blast, the camps on the south are to set out. The blast will be the signal for setting out. ⁷To gather the assembly, blow the trumpets, but not with the same signal.

⁸"The sons of Aaron, the priests, are to blow the trumpets. This is to be a lasting ordinance for you and the generations to come. ⁹When you go into battle in your own land against an enemy who is oppressing you, sound a blast on the trumpets. Then you will be remembered by the LORD your God and rescued from your enemies. ¹⁰Also at your times of rejoicing—your appointed feasts and New Moon festivals—you are to sound the trumpets over your burnt offerings and fellowship offerings,ᶦ and they will be a memorial for you before your God. I am the LORD your God."

¹¹On the twentieth day of the second month of the second year, the cloud lifted from above the tabernacle of the Testimony. ¹²Then the Israelites set out from the Desert of Sinai and traveled from place to place until the cloud came to rest in the Desert of Paran. ¹³They set out, this first time, at the LORD's command through Moses.

¹⁴The divisions of the camp of Judah went first, under their standard. Nahshon son of Amminadab was in command. ¹⁵Nethanel son of Zuar was over the division of the tribe of Issachar, ¹⁶and Eliab son of Helon was over the division of the tribe of Zebulun. ¹⁷Then the tabernacle was taken down, and the Gershonites and Merarites, who carried it, set out.

¹⁸The divisions of the camp of Reuben went next, under their standard. Elizur son of Shedeur was in command. ¹⁹Shelumiel son of Zurishaddai was over the division of the tribe of Simeon, ²⁰and Eliasaph son of Deuel was over the division of the tribe of Gad. ²¹Then the Kohathites set out, carrying the holy things. The tabernacle was to be set up before they arrived.

²²The divisions of the camp of Ephraim went next, under their standard. Elishama son of Ammihud was in command. ²³Gamaliel son of Pedahzur was over the division of the tribe of Manasseh, ²⁴and Abidan son of Gideoni was over the division of the tribe of Benjamin.

²⁵Finally, as the rear guard for all the units, the divisions of the camp of Dan set out, under their standard. Ahiezer son of Ammishaddai was in command. ²⁶Pagiel son of Ocran was over the division of the tribe of Asher, ²⁷and Ahira son of Enan was over the division of the tribe of Naphtali. ²⁸This was the order of march for the Israelite divisions as they set out.

²⁹Now Moses said to Hobab son of Reuel the Midianite, Moses' father-in-law, "We are setting out for the place about which the LORD said, 'I will give it

ᶦ10 Traditionally *peace offerings*

to you.' Come with us and we will treat you well, for the LORD has promised good things to Israel."

³⁰He answered, "No, I will not go; I am going back to my own land and my own people."

³¹But Moses said, "Please do not leave us. You know where we should camp in the desert, and you can be our eyes. ³²If you come with us, we will share with you whatever good things the LORD gives us."

³³So they set out from the mountain of the LORD and traveled for three days. The ark of the covenant of the LORD went before them during those three days to find them a place to rest. ³⁴The cloud of the LORD was over them by day when they set out from the camp.

³⁵Whenever the ark set out, Moses said,

"Rise up, O LORD!
    May your enemies be scattered;
    may your foes flee before you."

³⁶Whenever it came to rest, he said,

"Return, O LORD,
    to the countless thousands of Israel."

C H A P T E R   1 1
Now the people complained about their hardships in the hearing of the LORD, and when he heard them his anger was aroused. Then fire from the LORD burned among them and consumed some of the outskirts of the camp. ²When the people cried out to Moses, he prayed to the LORD and the fire died down. ³So that place was called Taberah,ᵘ because fire from the LORD had burned among them.

⁴The rabble with them began to crave other food, and again the Israelites started wailing and said, "If only we had meat to eat! ⁵We remember the fish we ate in Egypt at no cost—also the cucumbers, melons, leeks, onions and garlic. ⁶But now we have lost our appetite; we never see anything but this manna!"

⁷The manna was like coriander seed and looked like resin. ⁸The people went around gathering it, and then ground it in a handmill or crushed it in a mortar. They cooked it in a pot or made it into cakes. And it tasted like something made with olive oil. ⁹When the dew settled on the camp at night, the manna also came down.

¹⁰Moses heard the people of every family wailing, each at the entrance to his tent. The LORD became exceedingly angry, and Moses was troubled. ¹¹He asked the LORD, "Why have you brought this trouble on your servant? What have I done to displease you that you put the burden of all these people on me? ¹²Did I conceive all these people? Did I give them birth? Why do you tell me to carry them in my arms, as a nurse carries an infant, to the land you promised on oath to their forefathers? ¹³Where can I get meat for all these people? They keep wailing to me, 'Give us meat to eat!' ¹⁴I cannot carry all these people by myself; the burden is too heavy for me. ¹⁵If this is how you are going to treat me, put me to death right now—if I have found favor in your eyes—and do not let me face my own ruin."

¹⁶The LORD said to Moses: "Bring me seventy of Israel's elders who are known to you as leaders and officials among the people. Have them come to the Tent of Meeting, that they may stand there with you. ¹⁷I will come down and speak with you there, and I will take of the Spirit that is on you and put the Spirit on them. They will help you carry the burden of the people so that you will not have to carry it alone.

¹⁸"Tell the people: 'Consecrate yourselves in preparation for tomorrow, when you will eat meat. The LORD heard you when you wailed, "If only we had meat to eat! We were better off in Egypt!" Now the LORD will give you meat, and you will eat it. ¹⁹You will not eat it for just one day, or two days, or five, ten or twenty days, ²⁰but for a whole month—until it comes out of your nostrils and you loathe it—because you have rejected the LORD, who is among you, and have wailed before him, saying, "Why did we ever leave Egypt?" ' "

²¹But Moses said, "Here I am among six hundred thousand men on foot, and you say, 'I will give them meat to eat for a whole month!' ²²Would they have enough if flocks and herds were slaughtered for them? Would they have enough if all the fish in the sea were caught for them?"

²³The LORD answered Moses, "Is the LORD's arm too short? You will now see whether or not what I say will come true for you."

ᵘ3 *Taberah* means *burning.*

²⁴So Moses went out and told the people what the LORD had said. He brought together seventy of their elders and had them stand around the Tent. ²⁵Then the LORD came down in the cloud and spoke with him, and he took of the Spirit that was on him and put the Spirit on the seventy elders. When the Spirit rested on them, they prophesied, but they did not do so again.ᵛ

²⁶However, two men, whose names were Eldad and Medad, had remained in the camp. They were listed among the elders, but did not go out to the Tent. Yet the Spirit also rested on them, and they prophesied in the camp. ²⁷A young man ran and told Moses, "Eldad and Medad are prophesying in the camp."

²⁸Joshua son of Nun, who had been Moses' aide since youth, spoke up and said, "Moses, my lord, stop them!"

²⁹But Moses replied, "Are you jealous for my sake? I wish that all the LORD's people were prophets and that the LORD would put his Spirit on them!" ³⁰Then Moses and the elders of Israel returned to the camp.

³¹Now a wind went out from the LORD and drove quail in from the sea. It brought themʷ down all around the camp to about three feetˣ above the ground, as far as a day's walk in any direction. ³²All that day and night and all the next day the people went out and gathered quail. No one gathered less than ten homers.ʸ Then they spread them out all around the camp. ³³But while the meat was still between their teeth and before it could be consumed, the anger of the LORD burned against the people, and he struck them with a severe plague. ³⁴Therefore the place was named Kibroth Hattaavah,ᶻ because there they buried the people who had craved other food.

³⁵From Kibroth Hattaavah the people traveled to Hazeroth and stayed there.

CHAPTER 12
Miriam and Aaron began to talk against Moses because of his Cushite wife, for he had married a Cushite. ²"Has the LORD spoken only through Moses?" they asked.

"Hasn't he also spoken through us?" And the LORD heard this.

³(Now Moses was a very humble man, more humble than anyone else on the face of the earth.)

⁴At once the LORD said to Moses, Aaron and Miriam, "Come out to the Tent of Meeting, all three of you." So the three of them came out. ⁵Then the LORD came down in a pillar of cloud; he stood at the entrance to the Tent and summoned Aaron and Miriam. When both of them stepped forward, ⁶he said, "Listen to my words:

"When a prophet of the LORD is among you,
    I reveal myself to him in visions,
    I speak to him in dreams.
⁷But this is not true of my servant Moses;
    he is faithful in all my house.
⁸With him I speak face to face,
    clearly and not in riddles;
    he sees the form of the LORD.
Why then were you not afraid
    to speak against my servant Moses?"

⁹The anger of the LORD burned against them, and he left them.

¹⁰When the cloud lifted from above the Tent, there stood Miriam—leprous,ᵃ like snow. Aaron turned toward her and saw that she had leprosy; ¹¹and he said to Moses, "Please, my lord, do not hold against us the sin we have so foolishly committed. ¹²Do not let her be like a stillborn infant coming from its mother's womb with its flesh half eaten away."

¹³So Moses cried out to the LORD, "O God, please heal her!"

¹⁴The LORD replied to Moses, "If her father had spit in her face, would she not have been in disgrace for seven days? Confine her outside the camp for seven days; after that she can be brought back." ¹⁵So Miriam was confined outside the camp for seven days, and the people did not move on till she was brought back.

¹⁶After that, the people left Hazeroth and encamped in the Desert of Paran.

ᵛ25 Or prophesied and continued to do so   ʷ31 Or They flew   ˣ31 Hebrew two cubits (about 1 meter)   ʸ32 That is, probably about 60 bushels (about 2.2 kiloliters)   ᶻ34 Kibroth Hattaavah means graves of craving.   ᵃ10 The Hebrew word was used for various diseases affecting the skin—not necessarily leprosy.

FEBRUARY 13 □ DAY 44
NUMBERS 13–16
Rebellion and Death in the Desert

OVERVIEW As Israel camps at the edge of Canaan, the Lord commands Moses to select one man from each tribe to form a survey party to report on conditions in the land. The spies travel into Canaan and return with a report that stuns the people. The land is full of giants and fortified cities. By a vote of ten to two, the spies officially discourage the nation from claiming the land, and Caleb and Joshua's voices of faith are drowned out as the people cry, "Back to Egypt!" God punishes his children for their lack of faith by sentencing them to forty years of wandering in the desert—one year for each day the spies explored the land.

Chapter 13	Chapter 14	Chapter 15	Chapter 16
A Discouraging Word	A Disheartened People	A Divine Law	A Disobedient Korah
Rebellion against God		Judgment from God	

YOUR DAILY WALK *Action* and *reaction* have more in common than their spelling. They are inseparable halves of everything you do.

Because "no man is an island," your actions touch the lives of those close to you—family, friends and associates. Therefore, the decisions you make today spill over into the lives of others tomorrow—whether for good or evil.

Courage is the knowledge of how to fear what ought to be feared and how not to fear what ought not to be feared.

The Israelites who rejected God at Kadesh quickly realized the painful consequences of their willful disobedience. If they had remained faithful to God, not only they but their children as well would have enjoyed the blessings of the land immediately. Instead, parents and children alike suffered through forty years of desert wanderings until the unbelieving generation had all died.

Are you facing a seemingly insurmountable problem today—your own private "Canaan," full of giants and fortified cities? Remember, in times like this it's the size of your God—not the size of your giants—that counts. Take a few minutes today to share your "Canaan" with a prayer partner or family member. Then together ask God to help you make decisions that impact others for *good* and for *God*.

INSIGHT Warning! Warning! Warning!
Israel's revolt at Kadesh provides such a significant lesson on the price of unbelief that it is mentioned three times in the New Testament: 1 Corinthians 10:1–12; Hebrews 3:7–11; 4:1–11.

CHAPTER 13

The LORD said to Moses, 2 "Send some men to explore the land of Canaan, which I am giving to the Israelites. From each ancestral tribe send one of its leaders."

3 So at the LORD's command Moses sent them out from the Desert of Paran. All of them were leaders of the Israelites. 4 These are their names:

from the tribe of Reuben, Shammua son of Zaccur;

5 from the tribe of Simeon, Shaphat son of Hori;

6 from the tribe of Judah, Caleb son of Jephunneh;

7 from the tribe of Issachar, Igal son of Joseph;

8 from the tribe of Ephraim, Hoshea son of Nun;

9 from the tribe of Benjamin, Palti son of Raphu;

¹⁰from the tribe of Zebulun, Gaddiel son of Sodi;

¹¹from the tribe of Manasseh (a tribe of Joseph), Gaddi son of Susi;

¹²from the tribe of Dan, Ammiel son of Gemalli;

¹³from the tribe of Asher, Sethur son of Michael;

¹⁴from the tribe of Naphtali, Nahbi son of Vophsi;

¹⁵from the tribe of Gad, Geuel son of Maki.

¹⁶These are the names of the men Moses sent to explore the land. (Moses gave Hoshea son of Nun the name Joshua.)

¹⁷When Moses sent them to explore Canaan, he said, "Go up through the Negev and on into the hill country. ¹⁸See what the land is like and whether the people who live there are strong or weak, few or many. ¹⁹What kind of land do they live in? Is it good or bad? What kind of towns do they live in? Are they unwalled or fortified? ²⁰How is the soil? Is it fertile or poor? Are there trees on it or not? Do your best to bring back some of the fruit of the land." (It was the season for the first ripe grapes.)

²¹So they went up and explored the land from the Desert of Zin as far as Rehob, toward Lebo*ᵇ* Hamath. ²²They went up through the Negev and came to Hebron, where Ahiman, Sheshai and Talmai, the descendants of Anak, lived. (Hebron had been built seven years before Zoan in Egypt.) ²³When they reached the Valley of Eshcol,*ᶜ* they cut off a branch bearing a single cluster of grapes. Two of them carried it on a pole between them, along with some pomegranates and figs. ²⁴That place was called the Valley of Eshcol because of the cluster of grapes the Israelites cut off there. ²⁵At the end of forty days they returned from exploring the land.

²⁶They came back to Moses and Aaron and the whole Israelite community at Kadesh in the Desert of Paran. There they reported to them and to the whole assembly and showed them the fruit of the land. ²⁷They gave Moses this account: "We went into the land to which you sent us, and it does flow with milk and honey! Here is its fruit. ²⁸But the people who live there are powerful, and the cities are fortified

and very large. We even saw descendants of Anak there. ²⁹The Amalekites live in the Negev; the Hittites, Jebusites and Amorites live in the hill country; and the Canaanites live near the sea and along the Jordan."

³⁰Then Caleb silenced the people before Moses and said, "We should go up and take possession of the land, for we can certainly do it."

³¹But the men who had gone up with him said, "We can't attack those people; they are stronger than we are." ³²And they spread among the Israelites a bad report about the land they had explored. They said, "The land we explored devours those living in it. All the people we saw there are of great size. ³³We saw the Nephilim there (the descendants of Anak come from the Nephilim). We seemed like grasshoppers in our own eyes, and we looked the same to them."

CHAPTER 14

That night all the people of the community raised their voices and wept aloud. ²All the Israelites grumbled against Moses and Aaron, and the whole assembly said to them, "If only we had died in Egypt! Or in this desert! ³Why is the LORD bringing us to this land only to let us fall by the sword? Our wives and children will be taken as plunder. Wouldn't it be better for us to go back to Egypt?" ⁴And they said to each other, "We should choose a leader and go back to Egypt."

⁵Then Moses and Aaron fell facedown in front of the whole Israelite assembly gathered there. ⁶Joshua son of Nun and Caleb son of Jephunneh, who were among those who had explored the land, tore their clothes ⁷and said to the entire Israelite assembly, "The land we passed through and explored is exceedingly good. ⁸If the LORD is pleased with us, he will lead us into that land, a land flowing with milk and honey, and will give it to us. ⁹Only do not rebel against the LORD. And do not be afraid of the people of the land, because we will swallow them up. Their protection is gone, but the LORD is with us. Do not be afraid of them."

¹⁰But the whole assembly talked about stoning them. Then the glory of the LORD

appeared at the Tent of Meeting to all the Israelites. ¹¹The LORD said to Moses, "How long will these people treat me with contempt? How long will they refuse to believe in me, in spite of all the miraculous signs I have performed among them? ¹²I will strike them down with a plague and destroy them, but I will make you into a nation greater and stronger than they."

¹³Moses said to the LORD, "Then the Egyptians will hear about it! By your power you brought these people up from among them. ¹⁴And they will tell the inhabitants of this land about it. They have already heard that you, O LORD, are with these people and that you, O LORD, have been seen face to face, that your cloud stays over them, and that you go before them in a pillar of cloud by day and a pillar of fire by night. ¹⁵If you put these people to death all at one time, the nations who have heard this report about you will say, ¹⁶'The LORD was not able to bring these people into the land he promised them on oath; so he slaughtered them in the desert.'

¹⁷"Now may the Lord's strength be displayed, just as you have declared: ¹⁸'The LORD is slow to anger, abounding in love and forgiving sin and rebellion. Yet he does not leave the guilty unpunished; he punishes the children for the sin of the fathers to the third and fourth generation.' ¹⁹In accordance with your great love, forgive the sin of these people, just as you have pardoned them from the time they left Egypt until now."

²⁰The LORD replied, "I have forgiven them, as you asked. ²¹Nevertheless, as surely as I live and as surely as the glory of the LORD fills the whole earth, ²²not one of the men who saw my glory and the miraculous signs I performed in Egypt and in the desert but who disobeyed me and tested me ten times— ²³not one of them will ever see the land I promised on oath to their forefathers. No one who has treated me with contempt will ever see it. ²⁴But because my servant Caleb has a different spirit and follows me wholeheartedly, I will bring him into the land he went to, and his descendants will inherit it. ²⁵Since the Amalekites and Canaanites are living in the valleys, turn back tomor-

row and set out toward the desert along the route to the Red Sea.ᵈ"

²⁶The LORD said to Moses and Aaron: ²⁷"How long will this wicked community grumble against me? I have heard the complaints of these grumbling Israelites. ²⁸So tell them, 'As surely as I live, declares the LORD, I will do to you the very things I heard you say: ²⁹In this desert your bodies will fall—every one of you twenty years old or more who was counted in the census and who has grumbled against me. ³⁰Not one of you will enter the land I swore with uplifted hand to make your home, except Caleb son of Jephunneh and Joshua son of Nun. ³¹As for your children that you said would be taken as plunder, I will bring them in to enjoy the land you have rejected. ³²But you—your bodies will fall in this desert. ³³Your children will be shepherds here for forty years, suffering for your unfaithfulness, until the last of your bodies lies in the desert. ³⁴For forty years—one year for each of the forty days you explored the land—you will suffer for your sins and know what it is like to have me against you.' ³⁵I, the LORD, have spoken, and I will surely do these things to this whole wicked community, which has banded together against me. They will meet their end in this desert; here they will die."

³⁶So the men Moses had sent to explore the land, who returned and made the whole community grumble against him by spreading a bad report about it— ³⁷these men responsible for spreading the bad report about the land were struck down and died of a plague before the LORD. ³⁸Of the men who went to explore the land, only Joshua son of Nun and Caleb son of Jephunneh survived.

³⁹When Moses reported this to all the Israelites, they mourned bitterly. ⁴⁰Early the next morning they went up toward the high hill country. "We have sinned," they said. "We will go up to the place the LORD promised."

⁴¹But Moses said, "Why are you disobeying the LORD's command? This will not succeed! ⁴²Do not go up, because the LORD is not with you. You will be defeated by your enemies, ⁴³for the Amalekites and Canaanites will face you there. Because you have turned away from the LORD, he

ᵈ25 Hebrew *Yam Suph*; that is, Sea of Reeds

will not be with you and you will fall by the sword."

⁴⁴Nevertheless, in their presumption they went up toward the high hill country, though neither Moses nor the ark of the LORD's covenant moved from the camp. ⁴⁵Then the Amalekites and Canaanites who lived in that hill country came down and attacked them and beat them down all the way to Hormah.

CHAPTER 15
The LORD said to Moses, ²"Speak to the Israelites and say to them: 'After you enter the land I am giving you as a home ³and you present to the LORD offerings made by fire, from the herd or the flock, as an aroma pleasing to the LORD— whether burnt offerings or sacrifices, for special vows or freewill offerings or festival offerings— ⁴then the one who brings his offering shall present to the LORD a grain offering of a tenth of an ephah*ᵉ* of fine flour mixed with a quarter of a hin*ᶠ* of oil. ⁵With each lamb for the burnt offering or the sacrifice, prepare a quarter of a hin of wine as a drink offering.

⁶" 'With a ram prepare a grain offering of two-tenths of an ephah*ᵍ* of fine flour mixed with a third of a hin*ʰ* of oil, ⁷and a third of a hin of wine as a drink offering. Offer it as an aroma pleasing to the LORD.

⁸" 'When you prepare a young bull as a burnt offering or sacrifice, for a special vow or a fellowship offering*ⁱ* to the LORD, ⁹bring with the bull a grain offering of three-tenths of an ephah*ʲ* of fine flour mixed with half a hin*ᵏ* of oil. ¹⁰Also bring half a hin of wine as a drink offering. It will be an offering made by fire, an aroma pleasing to the LORD. ¹¹Each bull or ram, each lamb or young goat, is to be prepared in this manner. ¹²Do this for each one, for as many as you prepare.

¹³" 'Everyone who is native-born must do these things in this way when he brings an offering made by fire as an aroma pleasing to the LORD. ¹⁴For the generations to come, whenever an alien or anyone else living among you presents an offering made by fire as an aroma pleasing to the LORD, he must do exactly as you do. ¹⁵The community is to have the same

rules for you and for the alien living among you; this is a lasting ordinance for the generations to come. You and the alien shall be the same before the LORD: ¹⁶The same laws and regulations will apply both to you and to the alien living among you.' "

¹⁷The LORD said to Moses, ¹⁸"Speak to the Israelites and say to them: 'When you enter the land to which I am taking you ¹⁹and you eat the food of the land, present a portion as an offering to the LORD. ²⁰Present a cake from the first of your ground meal and present it as an offering from the threshing floor. ²¹Throughout the generations to come you are to give this offering to the LORD from the first of your ground meal.

²²" 'Now if you unintentionally fail to keep any of these commands the LORD gave Moses— ²³any of the LORD's commands to you through him, from the day the LORD gave them and continuing through the generations to come— ²⁴and if this is done unintentionally without the community being aware of it, then the whole community is to offer a young bull for a burnt offering as an aroma pleasing to the LORD, along with its prescribed grain offering and drink offering, and a male goat for a sin offering. ²⁵The priest is to make atonement for the whole Israelite community, and they will be forgiven, for it was not intentional and they have brought to the LORD for their wrong an offering made by fire and a sin offering. ²⁶The whole Israelite community and the aliens living among them will be forgiven, because all the people were involved in the unintentional wrong.

²⁷" 'But if just one person sins unintentionally, he must bring a year-old female goat for a sin offering. ²⁸The priest is to make atonement before the LORD for the one who erred by sinning unintentionally, and when atonement has been made for him, he will be forgiven. ²⁹One and the same law applies to everyone who sins unintentionally, whether he is a native-born Israelite or an alien.

³⁰" 'But anyone who sins defiantly, whether native-born or alien, blasphemes the LORD, and that person must be

---

ᵉ4 That is, probably about 2 quarts (about 2 liters)   *ᶠ4* That is, probably about 1 quart (about 1 liter); also in verse 5
ᵍ6 That is, probably about 4 quarts (about 4.5 liters)   *ʰ6* That is, probably about 1 1/4 quarts (about 1.2 liters); also in verse 7
ⁱ8 Traditionally *peace offering*   *ʲ9* That is, probably about 6 quarts (about 6.5 liters)   *ᵏ9* That is, probably about 2 quarts
(about 2 liters); also in verse 10

cut off from his people. ³¹Because he has despised the LORD's word and broken his commands, that person must surely be cut off; his guilt remains on him.' "

³²While the Israelites were in the desert, a man was found gathering wood on the Sabbath day. ³³Those who found him gathering wood brought him to Moses and Aaron and the whole assembly, ³⁴and they kept him in custody, because it was not clear what should be done to him. ³⁵Then the LORD said to Moses, "The man must die. The whole assembly must stone him outside the camp." ³⁶So the assembly took him outside the camp and stoned him to death, as the LORD commanded Moses.

³⁷The LORD said to Moses, ³⁸"Speak to the Israelites and say to them: 'Throughout the generations to come you are to make tassels on the corners of your garments, with a blue cord on each tassel. ³⁹You will have these tassels to look at and so you will remember all the commands of the LORD, that you may obey them and not prostitute yourselves by going after the lusts of your own hearts and eyes. ⁴⁰Then you will remember to obey all my commands and will be consecrated to your God. ⁴¹I am the LORD your God, who brought you out of Egypt to be your God. I am the LORD your God.' "

CHAPTER 16

Korah son of Izhar, the son of Kohath, the son of Levi, and certain Reubenites—Dathan and Abiram, sons of Eliab, and On son of Peleth—became insolent¹ ²and rose up against Moses. With them were 250 Israelite men, well-known community leaders who had been appointed members of the council. ³They came as a group to oppose Moses and Aaron and said to them, "You have gone too far! The whole community is holy, every one of them, and the LORD is with them. Why then do you set yourselves above the LORD's assembly?"

⁴When Moses heard this, he fell facedown. ⁵Then he said to Korah and all his followers: "In the morning the LORD will show who belongs to him and who is holy, and he will have that person come near him. The man he chooses he will

cause to come near him. ⁶You, Korah, and all your followers are to do this: Take censers ⁷and tomorrow put fire and incense in them before the LORD. The man the LORD chooses will be the one who is holy. You Levites have gone too far!"

⁸Moses also said to Korah, "Now listen, you Levites! ⁹Isn't it enough for you that the God of Israel has separated you from the rest of the Israelite community and brought you near himself to do the work at the LORD's tabernacle and to stand before the community and minister to them? ¹⁰He has brought you and all your fellow Levites near himself, but now you are trying to get the priesthood too. ¹¹It is against the LORD that you and all your followers have banded together. Who is Aaron that you should grumble against him?"

¹²Then Moses summoned Dathan and Abiram, the sons of Eliab. But they said, "We will not come! ¹³Isn't it enough that you have brought us up out of a land flowing with milk and honey to kill us in the desert? And now you also want to lord it over us? ¹⁴Moreover, you haven't brought us into a land flowing with milk and honey or given us an inheritance of fields and vineyards. Will you gouge out the eyes ofᵐ these men? No, we will not come!"

¹⁵Then Moses became very angry and said to the LORD, "Do not accept their offering. I have not taken so much as a donkey from them, nor have I wronged any of them."

¹⁶Moses said to Korah, "You and all your followers are to appear before the LORD tomorrow—you and they and Aaron. ¹⁷Each man is to take his censer and put incense in it—250 censers in all—and present it before the LORD. You and Aaron are to present your censers also." ¹⁸So each man took his censer, put fire and incense in it, and stood with Moses and Aaron at the entrance to the Tent of Meeting. ¹⁹When Korah had gathered all his followers in opposition to them at the entrance to the Tent of Meeting, the glory of the LORD appeared to the entire assembly. ²⁰The LORD said to Moses and Aaron, ²¹"Separate yourselves from this assembly so I can put an end to them at once." ²²But Moses and Aaron fell facedown

¹1 Or Peleth—took ⌐men⌐   ᵐ14 Or you make slaves of; or you deceive

and cried out, "O God, God of the spirits of all mankind, will you be angry with the entire assembly when only one man sins?"

23Then the LORD said to Moses, 24"Say to the assembly, 'Move away from the tents of Korah, Dathan and Abiram.' "

25Moses got up and went to Dathan and Abiram, and the elders of Israel followed him. 26He warned the assembly, "Move back from the tents of these wicked men! Do not touch anything belonging to them, or you will be swept away because of all their sins." 27So they moved away from the tents of Korah, Dathan and Abiram. Dathan and Abiram had come out and were standing with their wives, children and little ones at the entrances to their tents.

28Then Moses said, "This is how you will know that the LORD has sent me to do all these things and that it was not my idea: 29If these men die a natural death and experience only what usually happens to men, then the LORD has not sent me. 30But if the LORD brings about something totally new, and the earth opens its mouth and swallows them, with everything that belongs to them, and they go down alive into the grave,[n] then you will know that these men have treated the LORD with contempt."

31As soon as he finished saying all this, the ground under them split apart 32and the earth opened its mouth and swallowed them, with their households and all Korah's men and all their possessions. 33They went down alive into the grave, with everything they owned; the earth closed over them, and they perished and were gone from the community. 34At their cries, all the Israelites around them fled, shouting, "The earth is going to swallow us too!"

35And fire came out from the LORD and consumed the 250 men who were offering the incense.

36The LORD said to Moses, 37"Tell Eleazar son of Aaron, the priest, to take the censers out of the smoldering remains and

scatter the coals some distance away, for the censers are holy— 38the censers of the men who sinned at the cost of their lives. Hammer the censers into sheets to overlay the altar, for they were presented before the LORD and have become holy. Let them be a sign to the Israelites."

39So Eleazar the priest collected the bronze censers brought by those who had been burned up, and he had them hammered out to overlay the altar, 40as the LORD directed him through Moses. This was to remind the Israelites that no one except a descendant of Aaron should come to burn incense before the LORD, or he would become like Korah and his followers.

41The next day the whole Israelite community grumbled against Moses and Aaron. "You have killed the LORD's people," they said.

42But when the assembly gathered in opposition to Moses and Aaron and turned toward the Tent of Meeting, suddenly the cloud covered it and the glory of the LORD appeared. 43Then Moses and Aaron went to the front of the Tent of Meeting, 44and the LORD said to Moses, 45"Get away from this assembly so I can put an end to them at once." And they fell facedown.

46Then Moses said to Aaron, "Take your censer and put incense in it, along with fire from the altar, and hurry to the assembly to make atonement for them. Wrath has come out from the LORD; the plague has started." 47So Aaron did as Moses said, and ran into the midst of the assembly. The plague had already started among the people, but Aaron offered the incense and made atonement for them. 48He stood between the living and the dead, and the plague stopped. 49But 14,700 people died from the plague, in addition to those who had died because of Korah. 50Then Aaron returned to Moses at the entrance to the Tent of Meeting, for the plague had stopped.

n30 Hebrew *Sheol*; also in verse 33

FEBRUARY 14 ☐ DAY 45
Holy Habits for a Holy People

LOOK BACK Repetition is the key to retention. (Let me say that again.) Repetition is the key to retention. If you feel comfortable making notations in your Bible, the portions of Leviticus and Numbers you have read this past week have given you plenty of opportunity to mark words and phrases that are frequently repeated: "clean . . . unclean . . . atonement . . . I am the LORD your God . . . holy." They serve as a reminder that a holy God demanded nothing less than holy people in a holy camp. And when that holiness was interrupted by defilement or disobedience, God had already provided a way for the priest to make atonement (covering) for the sin. The sounds of animals being slaughtered, the smell of spilled blood and roasting flesh, the sight of smoke rising constantly from the altar—these were all too familiar to the nation. Without the shedding of blood there could be no forgiveness of sin or fellowship with God.

LOOK UP Take a handful of mud and coat your hands thoroughly. Now answer a series of questions.

Whitewashing the pump will not purify the water.

1. What would it take to get your hands clean enough to do work in the garage? (No problem. Just wipe them on your overalls, and that should do the trick.)
2. What would it take to get your hands clean enough to be allowed at the dinner table? (Soap and water might be needed there!)
3. What would it take to get your hands clean enough to put on your best white shirt or blouse without soiling it? (Lots of soap and hot water!)
4. What would it take to get your hands clean enough to do abdominal surgery? (Soap, water, a strong disinfectant and lots of scrubbing time.)

As one exasperated parent put it: "Cleanliness may be next to godliness, but around our house it's next to impossible."

But here's one more question to ponder.

5. What would it take to get your hands clean enough for God to allow you into heaven? (As one little boy was heard to exclaim: "You mean only people with clean hands get into heaven? Then I'm a goner!") Turn to Psalm 24:3–4, and see what God's Word says about clean hands!

LOOK AHEAD Heaven is a prepared place for a prepared people. Jesus prayed, "Father, hallowed be your name" (Luke 11:2). He knew that God, who is holy, cannot tolerate the presence of that which is unholy or defiled. So how is it possible for imperfect people to get into heaven? If no soap on earth can rid the stain of sin, what hope is there for any of us?

Answer: None at all . . . apart from the cleansing work of Jesus Christ, God's Son. "We have been made holy through the sacrifice of the body of Jesus Christ once for all" (Hebrews 10:10). What no soap, disinfectant or miracle detergent could do for our sinful condition, Jesus accomplished by his death, burial and resurrection. "The blood of Jesus, his Son, purifies us from all sin" (1 John 1:7).

"Have you washed your hands?" Mothers tend to ask questions like that a lot.

"Do you have clean hands and a pure heart?" The Father in heaven will one day ask you that question. If you're not sure what answer you would give, make Hebrews 10 your meditation today!

FEBRUARY 15 □ DAY 46
NUMBERS 17–20
The Staff, Red Heifer and Rebellion

OVERVIEW Two sounds accompany the people as they wander in the desert: the *rumbling* of a nation on the march and the *grumbling* of the people as they complain about the food, water and leadership. Mutiny against Moses and Aaron is avoided when God provides the miracle of Aaron's budding staff. In addition, the Levites are reaffirmed in their service in the tabernacle, and the sacrifice of the red heifer provides a constant source of cleansing from the ever present defilement of death. Yet, the grumbling continues. In a moment of anger, Moses does the right thing (bringing forth water) in the wrong way (striking the rock instead of speaking to it), thereby forfeiting his privilege to set foot in the promised land.

Chapter 17	Chapter 18	Chapter 19	Chapter 20
Staff of Aaron	Responsibilities of the Levites	Sacrifice of the Red Heifer	Sin of the People and Moses
Priesthood Established		Purity Enforced	

People always remember a kind deed— particularly if it was their own.

YOUR DAILY WALK Imagine for a moment that God has appeared to you to announce you will no longer be permitted to hold down a paying job or own property. Instead, you are to spend your full time in his service, and your compensation will be whatever your countrymen give to the Lord! Would that *comfort* you or *concern* you?

According to 18:20–21, those were basically God's instructions to Aaron and his descendants! Your local church today is in many ways a faith ministry like the priesthood of Aaron. You, like the Israelites, have been commanded to support the work of the Lord so God can be magnified in your community. Which word best describes your giving habits to your church: a *comfort* . . . or a *concern* to those ministering to you? Now read Acts 20:35, and enjoy a blessing this week!

INSIGHT A Family That Never Set Foot in Canaan
Neither Moses, his sister, Miriam, nor his brother, Aaron, ever enjoyed the blessings of the promised land. Numbers 20 details the fate of each of these three family members. Check out the details about
• Miriam (20:1)
• Moses (20:7–13)
• Aaron (20:22–29)

CHAPTER 17
The LORD said to Moses, ²"Speak to the Israelites and get twelve staffs from them, one from the leader of each of their ancestral tribes. Write the name of each man on his staff. ³On the staff of Levi write Aaron's name, for there must be one staff for the head of each ancestral tribe. ⁴Place them in the Tent of Meeting in front of the Testimony, where I meet with you. ⁵The staff belonging to the man I choose will sprout, and I will rid myself of this con-

stant grumbling against you by the Israelites."

⁶So Moses spoke to the Israelites, and their leaders gave him twelve staffs, one for the leader of each of their ancestral tribes, and Aaron's staff was among them. ⁷Moses placed the staffs before the LORD in the Tent of the Testimony.

⁸The next day Moses entered the Tent of the Testimony and saw that Aaron's staff, which represented the house of Levi, had not only sprouted but had

budded, blossomed and produced almonds. ⁹Then Moses brought out all the staffs from the LORD's presence to all the Israelites. They looked at them, and each man took his own staff.

¹⁰The LORD said to Moses, "Put back Aaron's staff in front of the Testimony, to be kept as a sign to the rebellious. This will put an end to their grumbling against me, so that they will not die." ¹¹Moses did just as the LORD commanded him.

¹²The Israelites said to Moses, "We will die! We are lost, we are all lost! ¹³Anyone who even comes near the tabernacle of the LORD will die. Are we all going to die?"

CHAPTER 18

The LORD said to Aaron, "You, your sons and your father's family are to bear the responsibility for offenses against the sanctuary, and you and your sons alone are to bear the responsibility for offenses against the priesthood. ²Bring your fellow Levites from your ancestral tribe to join you and assist you when you and your sons minister before the Tent of the Testimony. ³They are to be responsible to you and are to perform all the duties of the Tent, but they must not go near the furnishings of the sanctuary or the altar, or both they and you will die. ⁴They are to join you and be responsible for the care of the Tent of Meeting—all the work at the Tent—and no one else may come near where you are.

⁵"You are to be responsible for the care of the sanctuary and the altar, so that wrath will not fall on the Israelites again. ⁶I myself have selected your fellow Levites from among the Israelites as a gift to you, dedicated to the LORD to do the work at the Tent of Meeting. ⁷But only you and your sons may serve as priests in connection with everything at the altar and inside the curtain. I am giving you the service of the priesthood as a gift. Anyone else who comes near the sanctuary must be put to death."

⁸Then the LORD said to Aaron, "I myself have put you in charge of the offerings presented to me; all the holy offerings the Israelites give me I give to you and your sons as your portion and regular share. ⁹You are to have the part of the most holy offerings that is kept from the fire. From

all the gifts they bring me as most holy offerings, whether grain or sin or guilt offerings, that part belongs to you and your sons. ¹⁰Eat it as something most holy; every male shall eat it. You must regard it as holy.

¹¹"This also is yours: whatever is set aside from the gifts of all the wave offerings of the Israelites. I give this to you and your sons and daughters as your regular share. Everyone in your household who is ceremonially clean may eat it.

¹²"I give you all the finest olive oil and all the finest new wine and grain they give the LORD as the firstfruits of their harvest. ¹³All the land's firstfruits that they bring to the LORD will be yours. Everyone in your household who is ceremonially clean may eat it.

¹⁴"Everything in Israel that is devoted⁰ to the LORD is yours. ¹⁵The first offspring of every womb, both man and animal, that is offered to the LORD is yours. But you must redeem every firstborn son and every firstborn male of unclean animals. ¹⁶When they are a month old, you must redeem them at the redemption price set at five shekelsᵖ of silver, according to the sanctuary shekel, which weighs twenty gerahs.

¹⁷"But you must not redeem the firstborn of an ox, a sheep or a goat; they are holy. Sprinkle their blood on the altar and burn their fat as an offering made by fire, an aroma pleasing to the LORD. ¹⁸Their meat is to be yours, just as the breast of the wave offering and the right thigh are yours. ¹⁹Whatever is set aside from the holy offerings the Israelites present to the LORD I give to you and your sons and daughters as your regular share. It is an everlasting covenant of salt before the LORD for both you and your offspring."

²⁰The LORD said to Aaron, "You will have no inheritance in their land, nor will you have any share among them; I am your share and your inheritance among the Israelites.

²¹"I give to the Levites all the tithes in Israel as their inheritance in return for the work they do while serving at the Tent of Meeting. ²²From now on the Israelites must not go near the Tent of Meeting, or they will bear the consequences of their sin and will die. ²³It is the Levites who are

---

⁰14 The Hebrew term refers to the irrevocable giving over of things or persons to the LORD.   ᵖ16 That is, about 2 ounces (about 55 grams)

to do the work at the Tent of Meeting and bear the responsibility for offenses against it. This is a lasting ordinance for the generations to come. They will receive no inheritance among the Israelites. 24Instead, I give to the Levites as their inheritance the tithes that the Israelites present as an offering to the LORD. That is why I said concerning them: 'They will have no inheritance among the Israelites.' "

25The LORD said to Moses, 26"Speak to the Levites and say to them: 'When you receive from the Israelites the tithe I give you as your inheritance, you must present a tenth of that tithe as the LORD's offering. 27Your offering will be reckoned to you as grain from the threshing floor or juice from the winepress. 28In this way you also will present an offering to the LORD from all the tithes you receive from the Israelites. From these tithes you must give the LORD's portion to Aaron the priest. 29You must present as the LORD's portion the best and holiest part of everything given to you.'

30"Say to the Levites: 'When you present the best part, it will be reckoned to you as the product of the threshing floor or the winepress. 31You and your households may eat the rest of it anywhere, for it is your wages for your work at the Tent of Meeting. 32By presenting the best part of it you will not be guilty in this matter; then you will not defile the holy offerings of the Israelites, and you will not die.' "

CHAPTER 19
The LORD said to Moses and Aaron: 2"This is a requirement of the law that the LORD has commanded: Tell the Israelites to bring you a red heifer without defect or blemish and that has never been under a yoke. 3Give it to Eleazar the priest; it is to be taken outside the camp and slaughtered in his presence. 4Then Eleazar the priest is to take some of its blood on his finger and sprinkle it seven times toward the front of the Tent of Meeting. 5While he watches, the heifer is to be burned—its hide, flesh, blood and offal. 6The priest is to take some cedar wood, hyssop and scarlet wool and throw them onto the burning heifer. 7After that, the priest must wash his clothes and bathe himself with water. He may then come into the camp, but he will be ceremonially unclean till

evening. 8The man who burns it must also wash his clothes and bathe with water, and he too will be unclean till evening.

9"A man who is clean shall gather up the ashes of the heifer and put them in a ceremonially clean place outside the camp. They shall be kept by the Israelite community for use in the water of cleansing; it is for purification from sin. 10The man who gathers up the ashes of the heifer must also wash his clothes, and he too will be unclean till evening. This will be a lasting ordinance both for the Israelites and for the aliens living among them.

11"Whoever touches the dead body of anyone will be unclean for seven days. 12He must purify himself with the water on the third day and on the seventh day; then he will be clean. But if he does not purify himself on the third and seventh days, he will not be clean. 13Whoever touches the dead body of anyone and fails to purify himself defiles the LORD's tabernacle. That person must be cut off from Israel. Because the water of cleansing has not been sprinkled on him, he is unclean; his uncleanness remains on him.

14"This is the law that applies when a person dies in a tent: Anyone who enters the tent and anyone who is in it will be unclean for seven days, 15and every open container without a lid fastened on it will be unclean.

16"Anyone out in the open who touches someone who has been killed with a sword or someone who has died a natural death, or anyone who touches a human bone or a grave, will be unclean for seven days.

17"For the unclean person, put some ashes from the burned purification offering into a jar and pour fresh water over them. 18Then a man who is ceremonially clean is to take some hyssop, dip it in the water and sprinkle the tent and all the furnishings and the people who were there. He must also sprinkle anyone who has touched a human bone or a grave or someone who has been killed or someone who has died a natural death. 19The man who is clean is to sprinkle the unclean person on the third and seventh days, and on the seventh day he is to purify him. The person being cleansed must wash his clothes and bathe with water, and that evening he will be clean. 20But if a person who is unclean does not purify himself, he must be cut off from the community, because he has defiled the sanctuary of the LORD. The water of cleansing has not been sprinkled on him, and he is unclean. ²¹This is a lasting ordinance for them.

"The man who sprinkles the water of cleansing must also wash his clothes, and anyone who touches the water of cleansing will be unclean till evening. ²²Anything that an unclean person touches becomes unclean, and anyone who touches it becomes unclean till evening."

CHAPTER 20
In the first month the whole Israelite community arrived at the Desert of Zin, and they stayed at Kadesh. There Miriam died and was buried.

²Now there was no water for the community, and the people gathered in opposition to Moses and Aaron. ³They quarreled with Moses and said, "If only we had died when our brothers fell dead before the LORD! ⁴Why did you bring the LORD's community into this desert, that we and our livestock should die here? ⁵Why did you bring us up out of Egypt to this terrible place? It has no grain or figs, grapevines or pomegranates. And there is no water to drink!"

⁶Moses and Aaron went from the assembly to the entrance to the Tent of Meeting and fell facedown, and the glory of the LORD appeared to them. ⁷The LORD said to Moses, ⁸"Take the staff, and you and your brother Aaron gather the assembly together. Speak to that rock before their eyes and it will pour out its water. You will bring water out of the rock for the community so they and their livestock can drink."

⁹So Moses took the staff from the LORD's presence, just as he commanded him. ¹⁰He and Aaron gathered the assembly together in front of the rock and Moses said to them, "Listen, you rebels, must we bring you water out of this rock?" ¹¹Then Moses raised his arm and struck the rock twice with his staff. Water gushed out, and the community and their livestock drank.

¹²But the LORD said to Moses and Aaron, "Because you did not trust in me enough to honor me as holy in the sight of the Israelites, you will not bring this community into the land I give them."

¹³These were the waters of Meribah,�q where the Israelites quarreled with the LORD and where he showed himself holy among them.

¹⁴Moses sent messengers from Kadesh to the king of Edom, saying:

"This is what your brother Israel says: You know about all the hardships that have come upon us. ¹⁵Our forefathers went down into Egypt, and we lived there many years. The Egyptians mistreated us and our fathers, ¹⁶but when we cried out to the LORD, he heard our cry and sent an angel and brought us out of Egypt.

"Now we are here at Kadesh, a town on the edge of your territory. ¹⁷Please let us pass through your country. We will not go through any field or vineyard, or drink water from any well. We will travel along the king's highway and not turn to the right or to the left until we have passed through your territory."

¹⁸But Edom answered:

"You may not pass through here; if you try, we will march out and attack you with the sword."

¹⁹The Israelites replied:

"We will go along the main road, and if we or our livestock drink any of your water, we will pay for it. We only want to pass through on foot— nothing else."

²⁰Again they answered:

"You may not pass through."

Then Edom came out against them with a large and powerful army. ²¹Since Edom refused to let them go through their territory, Israel turned away from them.

²²The whole Israelite community set out from Kadesh and came to Mount Hor. ²³At Mount Hor, near the border of Edom, the LORD said to Moses and Aaron, ²⁴"Aaron will be gathered to his people. He will not enter the land I give the Israelites, because both of you rebelled

---

q13 *Meribah* means *quarreling.*

against my command at the waters of Meribah. ²⁵Get Aaron and his son Eleazar and take them up Mount Hor. ²⁶Remove Aaron's garments and put them on his son Eleazar, for Aaron will be gathered to his people; he will die there."

²⁷Moses did as the LORD commanded: They went up Mount Hor in the sight of the whole community. ²⁸Moses removed Aaron's garments and put them on his son Eleazar. And Aaron died there on top of the mountain. Then Moses and Eleazar came down from the mountain, ²⁹and when the whole community learned that Aaron had died, the entire house of Israel mourned for him thirty days.

FEBRUARY 16 □ DAY 47
NUMBERS 21–25
The Bronze Snake and Brash Seer

OVERVIEW There is warfare on the march to the promised land as the Israelites defeat the opposing Canaanites, Amorites and Bashanites—but the victories are soured by Israel's persistent complaining. Once again God's hand of discipline falls, this time in the form of venomous snakes. The reputation of Israel's God precedes the nation on its relentless march, causing the king of Moab to hire Balaam for the purpose of cursing Israel. The plot backfires when Balaam blesses Israel and predicts her future prosperity. But while Balaam could not bring misfortune upon Israel through a curse, the people of God bring it upon themselves through idolatry and mixed marriages.

Chapter 21	Chapters 22–24	Chapter 25
Conquest in the Midst of Complaining	Blessing in Spite of Balak	Defeat in the Midst of Disobedience
Bronze Snake	Balaam	Baal of Peor

YOUR DAILY WALK Look up the words *sovereignty* and *reign* in the dictionary, and read what it says about each. Chances are, the definitions will sound somewhat similar.

If God lights the candle, none can blow it out.

Balak, king of Moab, knew his days were numbered. In a desperate attempt to preserve his life and the life of his nation, he hired Balaam to bring down a curse upon Israel. Yet God so controlled the circumstances that Balaam uttered blessings instead of cursings. Rather than bring harm to Israel, Balaam became an agent of God's blessing upon his people. And all of this happened while the nation remained completely unaware of the threat to its safety! That is sovereignty: God reigning in the affairs of his people.

Sometimes it's difficult to see God's sovereignty in the present, but you can clearly observe it in the past. Looking back over the first few weeks of this year, how many times can you see God's sovereignty at work, protecting, guarding and keeping you from physical harm?

INSIGHT Immortalizing Balaam's Words
When Samuel Morse was looking for a suitable phrase to test out his new invention, the telegraph, his thoughts turned to the great statement of God's sovereignty in Numbers 23:23 (KJV): "What hath God wrought!"—an appropriate first "word by wire."

CHAPTER 21

When the Canaanite king of Arad, who lived in the Negev, heard that Israel was coming along the road to Atharim, he attacked the Israelites and captured some of them. ²Then Israel made this vow to the LORD: "If you will deliver these people into our hands, we will totally destroy^r their cities." ³The LORD listened to Israel's plea and gave the Canaanites over to them. They completely destroyed them and their towns; so the place was named Hormah.^s

⁴They traveled from Mount Hor along the route to the Red Sea,^t to go around Edom. But the people grew impatient on the way; ⁵they spoke against God and against Moses, and said, "Why have you brought us up out of Egypt to die in the desert? There is no bread! There is no water! And we detest this miserable food!"

⁶Then the LORD sent venomous snakes among them; they bit the people and many Israelites died. ⁷The people came to Moses and said, "We sinned when we spoke against the LORD and against you. Pray that the LORD will take the snakes away from us." So Moses prayed for the people.

⁸The LORD said to Moses, "Make a snake and put it up on a pole; anyone who is bitten can look at it and live." ⁹So Moses made a bronze snake and put it up on a pole. Then when anyone was bitten by a snake and looked at the bronze snake, he lived.

¹⁰The Israelites moved on and camped at Oboth. ¹¹Then they set out from Oboth and camped in Iye Abarim, in the desert that faces Moab toward the sunrise. ¹²From there they moved on and camped in the Zered Valley. ¹³They set out from there and camped alongside the Arnon, which is in the desert extending into Amorite territory. The Arnon is the border of Moab, between Moab and the Amorites. ¹⁴That is why the Book of the Wars of the LORD says:

"... Waheb in Suphah^u and the
          ravines,
    the Arnon ¹⁵and^v the slopes of the
          ravines

that lead to the site of Ar
    and lie along the border of Moab."

¹⁶From there they continued on to Beer, the well where the LORD said to Moses, "Gather the people together and I will give them water."

¹⁷Then Israel sang this song:

"Spring up, O well!
    Sing about it,
¹⁸about the well that the princes dug,
    that the nobles of the people sank—
    the nobles with scepters and staffs."

Then they went from the desert to Mattanah, ¹⁹from Mattanah to Nahaliel, from Nahaliel to Bamoth, ²⁰and from Bamoth to the valley in Moab where the top of Pisgah overlooks the wasteland.

²¹Israel sent messengers to say to Sihon king of the Amorites:

²²"Let us pass through your country. We will not turn aside into any field or vineyard, or drink water from any well. We will travel along the king's highway until we have passed through your territory."

²³But Sihon would not let Israel pass through his territory. He mustered his entire army and marched out into the desert against Israel. When he reached Jahaz, he fought with Israel. ²⁴Israel, however, put him to the sword and took over his land from the Arnon to the Jabbok, but only as far as the Ammonites, because their border was fortified. ²⁵Israel captured all the cities of the Amorites and occupied them, including Heshbon and all its surrounding settlements. ²⁶Heshbon was the city of Sihon king of the Amorites, who had fought against the former king of Moab and had taken from him all his land as far as the Arnon.

²⁷That is why the poets say:

"Come to Heshbon and let it be
          rebuilt;
    let Sihon's city be restored.

²⁸"Fire went out from Heshbon,
    a blaze from the city of Sihon.
It consumed Ar of Moab,
    the citizens of Arnon's heights.
²⁹Woe to you, O Moab!

---

^r2 The Hebrew term refers to the irrevocable giving over of things or persons to the LORD, often by totally destroying them; also in verse 3.   ^s3 *Hormah* means *destruction*.   ^t4 Hebrew *Yam Suph*; that is, Sea of Reeds   ^u14 The meaning of the Hebrew for this phrase is uncertain.   ^v14,15 Or *"I have been given from Suphah and the ravines / of the Arnon* ¹⁵*to*

You are destroyed, O people of
   Chemosh!
He has given up his sons as fugitives
   and his daughters as captives
   to Sihon king of the Amorites.

30"But we have overthrown them;
   Heshbon is destroyed all the way to
      Dibon.
We have demolished them as far as
   Nophah,
   which extends to Medeba."

31So Israel settled in the land of the
Amorites. 32After Moses had sent spies to Jazer,
the Israelites captured its surrounding
settlements and drove out the Amorites
who were there. 33Then they turned and
went up along the road toward Bashan,
and Og king of Bashan and his whole
army marched out to meet them in battle
at Edrei.

34The LORD said to Moses, "Do not be
afraid of him, for I have handed him over
to you, with his whole army and his land.
Do to him what you did to Sihon king of
the Amorites, who reigned in Heshbon."

35So they struck him down, together
with his sons and his whole army, leaving
them no survivors. And they took possession of his land.

CHAPTER 22
Then the Israelites traveled to the plains
of Moab and camped along the Jordan
across from Jericho.ʷ

2Now Balak son of Zippor saw all that
Israel had done to the Amorites, 3and
Moab was terrified because there were so
many people. Indeed, Moab was filled
with dread because of the Israelites.

4The Moabites said to the elders of
Midian, "This horde is going to lick up
everything around us, as an ox licks up
the grass of the field."

So Balak son of Zippor, who was king
of Moab at that time, 5sent messengers to
summon Balaam son of Beor, who was at
Pethor, near the River,ˣ in his native
land. Balak said:

   "A people has come out of Egypt;
   they cover the face of the land and
   have settled next to me. 6Now come
   and put a curse on these people, because they are too powerful for me.

Perhaps then I will be able to defeat
   them and drive them out of the
   country. For I know that those you
   bless are blessed, and those you curse
   are cursed."

7The elders of Moab and Midian left,
taking with them the fee for divination.
When they came to Balaam, they told him
what Balak had said.

8"Spend the night here," Balaam said to
them, "and I will bring you back the answer the LORD gives me." So the Moabite
princes stayed with him.

9God came to Balaam and asked, "Who
are these men with you?"

10Balaam said to God, "Balak son of
Zippor, king of Moab, sent me this message: 11'A people that has come out of
Egypt covers the face of the land. Now
come and put a curse on them for me.
Perhaps then I will be able to fight them
and drive them away.' "

12But God said to Balaam, "Do not go
with them. You must not put a curse on
those people, because they are blessed."

13The next morning Balaam got up and
said to Balak's princes, "Go back to your
own country, for the LORD has refused to
let me go with you."

14So the Moabite princes returned to
Balak and said, "Balaam refused to come
with us."

15Then Balak sent other princes, more
numerous and more distinguished than
the first. 16They came to Balaam and said:

   "This is what Balak son of Zippor
   says: Do not let anything keep you
   from coming to me, 17because I will
   reward you handsomely and do
   whatever you say. Come and put a
   curse on these people for me."

18But Balaam answered them, "Even if
Balak gave me his palace filled with silver
and gold, I could not do anything great or
small to go beyond the command of the
LORD my God. 19Now stay here tonight as
the others did, and I will find out what
else the LORD will tell me."

20That night God came to Balaam and
said, "Since these men have come to summon you, go with them, but do only what
I tell you."

21Balaam got up in the morning, saddled his donkey and went with the

ʷ1 Hebrew *Jordan of Jericho*; possibly an ancient name for the Jordan River   ˣ5 That is, the Euphrates princes of Moab. ²²But God was very angry when he went, and the angel of the LORD stood in the road to oppose him. Balaam was riding on his donkey, and his two servants were with him. ²³When the donkey saw the angel of the LORD standing in the road with a drawn sword in his hand, she turned off the road into a field. Balaam beat her to get her back on the road.

²⁴Then the angel of the LORD stood in a narrow path between two vineyards, with walls on both sides. ²⁵When the donkey saw the angel of the LORD, she pressed close to the wall, crushing Balaam's foot against it. So he beat her again.

²⁶Then the angel of the LORD moved on ahead and stood in a narrow place where there was no room to turn, either to the right or to the left. ²⁷When the donkey saw the angel of the LORD, she lay down under Balaam, and he was angry and beat her with his staff. ²⁸Then the LORD opened the donkey's mouth, and she said to Balaam, "What have I done to you to make you beat me these three times?"

²⁹Balaam answered the donkey, "You have made a fool of me! If I had a sword in my hand, I would kill you right now."

³⁰The donkey said to Balaam, "Am I not your own donkey, which you have always ridden, to this day? Have I been in the habit of doing this to you?"

"No," he said.

³¹Then the LORD opened Balaam's eyes, and he saw the angel of the LORD standing in the road with his sword drawn. So he bowed low and fell facedown.

³²The angel of the LORD asked him, "Why have you beaten your donkey these three times? I have come here to oppose you because your path is a reckless one before me.ʸ ³³The donkey saw me and turned away from me these three times. If she had not turned away, I would certainly have killed you by now, but I would have spared her."

³⁴Balaam said to the angel of the LORD, "I have sinned. I did not realize you were standing in the road to oppose me. Now if you are displeased, I will go back."

³⁵The angel of the LORD said to Balaam, "Go with the men, but speak only what I tell you." So Balaam went with the princes of Balak.

³⁶When Balak heard that Balaam was coming, he went out to meet him at the Moabite town on the Arnon border, at the edge of his territory. ³⁷Balak said to Balaam, "Did I not send you an urgent summons? Why didn't you come to me? Am I really not able to reward you?"

³⁸"Well, I have come to you now," Balaam replied. "But can I say just anything? I must speak only what God puts in my mouth."

³⁹Then Balaam went with Balak to Kiriath Huzoth. ⁴⁰Balak sacrificed cattle and sheep, and gave some to Balaam and the princes who were with him. ⁴¹The next morning Balak took Balaam up to Bamoth Baal, and from there he saw part of the people.

CHAPTER 23

Balaam said, "Build me seven altars here, and prepare seven bulls and seven rams for me." ²Balak did as Balaam said, and the two of them offered a bull and a ram on each altar.

³Then Balaam said to Balak, "Stay here beside your offering while I go aside. Perhaps the LORD will come to meet with me. Whatever he reveals to me I will tell you." Then he went off to a barren height.

⁴God met with him, and Balaam said, "I have prepared seven altars, and on each altar I have offered a bull and a ram."

⁵The LORD put a message in Balaam's mouth and said, "Go back to Balak and give him this message."

⁶So he went back to him and found him standing beside his offering, with all the princes of Moab. ⁷Then Balaam uttered his oracle:

"Balak brought me from Aram,
  the king of Moab from the eastern
    mountains.
'Come,' he said, 'curse Jacob for me;
  come, denounce Israel.'
⁸How can I curse
  those whom God has not cursed?
How can I denounce
  those whom the LORD has not
    denounced?
⁹From the rocky peaks I see them,
  from the heights I view them.
I see a people who live apart
  and do not consider themselves one
    of the nations.

ʸ32 The meaning of the Hebrew for this clause is uncertain.

¹⁰Who can count the dust of Jacob
  or number the fourth part of Israel?
Let me die the death of the righteous,
  and may my end be like theirs!"

¹¹Balak said to Balaam, "What have you
done to me? I brought you to curse my
enemies, but you have done nothing but
bless them!"

¹²He answered, "Must I not speak what
the LORD puts in my mouth?"

¹³Then Balak said to him, "Come with
me to another place where you can see
them; you will see only a part but not all
of them. And from there, curse them for
me." ¹⁴So he took him to the field of Zo-
phim on the top of Pisgah, and there he
built seven altars and offered a bull and a
ram on each altar.

¹⁵Balaam said to Balak, "Stay here beside your offering while I meet with him
over there."

¹⁶The LORD met with Balaam and put a
message in his mouth and said, "Go back
to Balak and give him this message."

¹⁷So he went to him and found him
standing beside his offering, with the
princes of Moab. Balak asked him, "What
did the LORD say?"

¹⁸Then he uttered his oracle:

"Arise, Balak, and listen;
  hear me, son of Zippor.
¹⁹God is not a man, that he should lie,
  nor a son of man, that he should
    change his mind.
Does he speak and then not act?
Does he promise and not fulfill?
²⁰I have received a command to bless;
  he has blessed, and I cannot change
    it.

²¹"No misfortune is seen in Jacob,
  no misery observed in Israel.ᶻ
The LORD their God is with them;
  the shout of the King is among
    them.
²²God brought them out of Egypt;
  they have the strength of a wild ox.
²³There is no sorcery against Jacob,
  no divination against Israel.
It will now be said of Jacob
  and of Israel, 'See what God has
    done!'
²⁴The people rise like a lioness;
  they rouse themselves like a lion

that does not rest till he devours his
    prey
  and drinks the blood of his victims."

²⁵Then Balak said to Balaam, "Neither
curse them at all nor bless them at all!"

²⁶Balaam answered, "Did I not tell you I
must do whatever the LORD says?"

²⁷Then Balak said to Balaam, "Come, let
me take you to another place. Perhaps it
will please God to let you curse them for
me from there." ²⁸And Balak took Balaam
to the top of Peor, overlooking the wasteland.

²⁹Balaam said, "Build me seven altars
here, and prepare seven bulls and seven
rams for me." ³⁰Balak did as Balaam had
said, and offered a bull and a ram on each
altar.

CHAPTER 24

Now when Balaam saw that it pleased the
LORD to bless Israel, he did not resort to
sorcery as at other times, but turned his
face toward the desert. ²When Balaam
looked out and saw Israel encamped tribe
by tribe, the Spirit of God came upon him
³and he uttered his oracle:

"The oracle of Balaam son of Beor,
  the oracle of one whose eye sees
    clearly,
⁴the oracle of one who hears the words
    of God,
  who sees a vision from the
    Almighty,ᵃ
  who falls prostrate, and whose eyes
    are opened:

⁵"How beautiful are your tents,
    O Jacob,
  your dwelling places, O Israel!

⁶"Like valleys they spread out,
  like gardens beside a river,
like aloes planted by the LORD,
  like cedars beside the waters.
⁷Water will flow from their buckets;
  their seed will have abundant water.

"Their king will be greater than Agag;
  their kingdom will be exalted.

⁸"God brought them out of Egypt;
  they have the strength of a wild ox.
They devour hostile nations
  and break their bones in pieces;
  with their arrows they pierce them.

ᶻ21 Or *He has not looked on Jacob's offenses / or on the wrongs found in Israel.*   ᵃ4 Hebrew *Shaddai;* also in verse 16

⁹Like a lion they crouch and lie down,
  like a lioness—who dares to rouse
    them?

"May those who bless you be blessed
  and those who curse you be cursed!"

¹⁰Then Balak's anger burned against Balaam. He struck his hands together and said to him, "I summoned you to curse my enemies, but you have blessed them these three times. ¹¹Now leave at once and go home! I said I would reward you handsomely, but the LORD has kept you from being rewarded."

¹²Balaam answered Balak, "Did I not tell the messengers you sent me, ¹³'Even if Balak gave me his palace filled with silver and gold, I could not do anything of my own accord, good or bad, to go beyond the command of the LORD—and I must say only what the LORD says'? ¹⁴Now I am going back to my people, but come, let me warn you of what this people will do to your people in days to come."

¹⁵Then he uttered his oracle:

"The oracle of Balaam son of Beor,
  the oracle of one whose eye sees
    clearly,
¹⁶the oracle of one who hears the words
    of God,
  who has knowledge from the Most
    High,
  who sees a vision from the Almighty,
    who falls prostrate, and whose eyes
    are opened:

¹⁷"I see him, but not now;
  I behold him, but not near.
A star will come out of Jacob;
  a scepter will rise out of Israel.
He will crush the foreheads of Moab,
  the skulls b ofᶜ all the sons of
    Sheth. d
¹⁸Edom will be conquered;
  Seir, his enemy, will be conquered,
  but Israel will grow strong.
¹⁹A ruler will come out of Jacob
  and destroy the survivors of the
    city."

²⁰Then Balaam saw Amalek and uttered his oracle:

"Amalek was first among the nations,
  but he will come to ruin at last."

²¹Then he saw the Kenites and uttered his oracle:

"Your dwelling place is secure,
  your nest is set in a rock;
²²yet you Kenites will be destroyed
  when Asshur takes you captive."

²³Then he uttered his oracle:

"Ah, who can live when God does
    this?ᵉ
²⁴ Ships will come from the shores of
    Kittim;
  they will subdue Asshur and Eber,
    but they too will come to ruin."

²⁵Then Balaam got up and returned home and Balak went his own way.

CHAPTER 25

While Israel was staying in Shittim, the men began to indulge in sexual immorality with Moabite women, ²who invited them to the sacrifices to their gods. The people ate and bowed down before these gods. ³So Israel joined in worshiping the Baal of Peor. And the LORD's anger burned against them.

⁴The LORD said to Moses, "Take all the leaders of these people, kill them and expose them in broad daylight before the LORD, so that the LORD's fierce anger may turn away from Israel."

⁵So Moses said to Israel's judges, "Each of you must put to death those of your men who have joined in worshiping the Baal of Peor."

⁶Then an Israelite man brought to his family a Midianite woman right before the eyes of Moses and the whole assembly of Israel while they were weeping at the entrance to the Tent of Meeting. ⁷When Phinehas son of Eleazar, the son of Aaron, the priest, saw this, he left the assembly, took a spear in his hand ⁸and followed the Israelite into the tent. He drove the spear through both of them—through the Israelite and into the woman's body. Then the plague against the Israelites was stopped; ⁹but those who died in the plague numbered 24,000.

¹⁰The LORD said to Moses, ¹¹"Phinehas son of Eleazar, the son of Aaron, the priest, has turned my anger away from

---

b 17 Samaritan Pentateuch (see also Jer. 48:45); the meaning of the word in the Masoretic Text is uncertain.   c 17 Or possibly
Moab, / batter   d 17 Or all the noisy boasters   e 23 Masoretic Text; with a different word division of the Hebrew A people will
gather from the north.

the Israelites; for he was as zealous as I am for my honor among them, so that in my zeal I did not put an end to them. ¹²Therefore tell him I am making my covenant of peace with him. ¹³He and his descendants will have a covenant of a lasting priesthood, because he was zealous for the honor of his God and made atonement for the Israelites."

¹⁴The name of the Israelite who was killed with the Midianite woman was Zimri son of Salu, the leader of a Simeon-ite family. ¹⁵And the name of the Midianite woman who was put to death was Cozbi daughter of Zur, a tribal chief of a Midianite family.

¹⁶The LORD said to Moses, ¹⁷"Treat the Midianites as enemies and kill them, ¹⁸because they treated you as enemies when they deceived you in the affair of Peor and their sister Cozbi, the daughter of a Midianite leader, the woman who was killed when the plague came as a result of Peor."

FEBRUARY 17 ☐ DAY 48
NUMBERS 26–30
Recounting and Reviewing

OVERVIEW Nearly forty years have passed; the unbelieving generation has vanished from the scene, and a new generation has grown to take its place. Once again it is time to number the people and assess Israel's military might. In spite of divine judgments that take the lives of more than thirty-eight thousand people (16:49; 25:9), the nation's fighting force still totals more than six hundred thousand. Moses, who has led the people from the beginning, will never live to see the conquest of Canaan. It remains for his successor, Joshua, to lead the people to victory.

Chapter 26	Chapter 27	Chapters 28–30
Repeating the Census	Replacing the Commander in Chief	Recounting the Code of Worship
A New Generation	A New General	A General Review

The object of teaching is to enable those taught to get along without a teacher.

YOUR DAILY WALK If you were suddenly incapacitated, who would be qualified to pick up your responsibilities and duties as they relate to . . . your job? . . . your family? . . . your church? As Moses approached his final days as Israel's leader, God instructed him not to leave "the LORD's people . . . like sheep without a shepherd" (27:17). Moses was commanded to take Joshua, lay his hands on him, deliver a charge to him before all the people and "give him some of [his] authority" (27:20). In this way the transition of leadership would be smooth so that when the man of God died, the work of God would not falter.

That's good advice for any generation. Are you letting others remain dependent upon you at home and church, or are you busy discipling them to one day take your place and carry on the work you've begun? Complete this sentence: "Knowing that no individual is indispensable in the program of God, today I will help prepare [whom?] to continue the work I am currently doing [where?] by [how?]."

INSIGHT Picking Your Lot by Lots (26:52–56)
There were two aspects to the partitioning of the land of Canaan. The size of each tribe's parcel was determined by the second census, each tribe receiving territory in proportion to the size of its population. The

location of each tribe's parcel was determined by lot so that no tribe could grumble about the quality of its land.

CHAPTER 26

After the plague the LORD said to Moses and Eleazar son of Aaron, the priest, 2"Take a census of the whole Israelite community by families—all those twenty years old or more who are able to serve in the army of Israel." 3So on the plains of Moab by the Jordan across from Jericho,*f* Moses and Eleazar the priest spoke with them and said, 4"Take a census of the men twenty years old or more, as the LORD commanded Moses."

These were the Israelites who came out of Egypt:

5The descendants of Reuben, the firstborn son of Israel, were:
through Hanoch, the Hanochite clan;
through Pallu, the Palluite clan;
6through Hezron, the Hezronite clan;
through Carmi, the Carmite clan.
7These were the clans of Reuben; those numbered were 43,730.

8The son of Pallu was Eliab, 9and the sons of Eliab were Nemuel, Dathan and Abiram. The same Dathan and Abiram were the community officials who rebelled against Moses and Aaron and were among Korah's followers when they rebelled against the LORD. 10The earth opened its mouth and swallowed them along with Korah, whose followers died when the fire devoured the 250 men. And they served as a warning sign. 11The line of Korah, however, did not die out.

12The descendants of Simeon by their clans were:
through Nemuel, the Nemuelite clan;
through Jamin, the Jaminite clan;
through Jakin, the Jakinite clan;
13through Zerah, the Zerahite clan;
through Shaul, the Shaulite clan.
14These were the clans of Simeon; there were 22,200 men.

15The descendants of Gad by their clans were:
through Zephon, the Zephonite clan;
through Haggi, the Haggite clan;
through Shuni, the Shunite clan;
16through Ozni, the Oznite clan;
through Eri, the Erite clan;
17through Arodi,*g* the Arodite clan;
through Areli, the Arelite clan.
18These were the clans of Gad; those numbered were 40,500.

19Er and Onan were sons of Judah, but they died in Canaan. 20The descendants of Judah by their clans were:
through Shelah, the Shelanite clan;
through Perez, the Perezite clan;
through Zerah, the Zerahite clan.
21The descendants of Perez were:
through Hezron, the Hezronite clan;
through Hamul, the Hamulite clan.
22These were the clans of Judah; those numbered were 76,500.

23The descendants of Issachar by their clans were:
through Tola, the Tolaite clan;
through Puah, the Puite*h* clan;
24through Jashub, the Jashubite clan;
through Shimron, the Shimronite clan.
25These were the clans of Issachar; those numbered were 64,300.

26The descendants of Zebulun by their clans were:
through Sered, the Seredite clan;
through Elon, the Elonite clan;
through Jahleel, the Jahleelite clan.
27These were the clans of Zebulun; those numbered were 60,500.

28The descendants of Joseph by their clans through Manasseh and Ephraim were:

29The descendants of Manasseh:
through Makir, the Makirite clan (Makir was the father of Gilead);
through Gilead, the Gileadite clan.
30These were the descendants of Gilead:
through Iezer, the Iezerite clan;
through Helek, the Helekite clan;
31through Asriel, the Asrielite clan;

f3 Hebrew *Jordan of Jericho*; possibly an ancient name for the Jordan River; also in verse 63   *g17* Samaritan Pentateuch and Syriac (see also Gen. 46:16); Masoretic Text *Arod*   *h23* Samaritan Pentateuch, Septuagint, Vulgate and Syriac (see also 1 Chron. 7:1); Masoretic Text *through Puvah, the Punite* through Shechem, the Shechemite clan;

³²through Shemida, the Shemidaite clan;

through Hepher, the Hepherite clan.

³³(Zelophehad son of Hepher had no sons; he had only daughters, whose names were Mahlah, Noah, Hoglah, Milcah and Tirzah.)

³⁴These were the clans of Manasseh; those numbered were 52,700.

³⁵These were the descendants of Ephraim by their clans:

through Shuthelah, the Shuthelahite clan;

through Beker, the Bekerite clan;

through Tahan, the Tahanite clan.

³⁶These were the descendants of Shuthelah:

through Eran, the Eranite clan.

³⁷These were the clans of Ephraim; those numbered were 32,500.

These were the descendants of Joseph by their clans.

³⁸The descendants of Benjamin by their clans were:

through Bela, the Belaite clan;

through Ashbel, the Ashbelite clan;

through Ahiram, the Ahiramite clan;

³⁹through Shupham,ⁱ the Shuphamite clan;

through Hupham, the Huphamite clan.

⁴⁰The descendants of Bela through Ard and Naaman were:

through Ard,^j the Ardite clan;

through Naaman, the Naamite clan.

⁴¹These were the clans of Benjamin; those numbered were 45,600.

⁴²These were the descendants of Dan by their clans:

through Shuham, the Shuhamite clan.

These were the clans of Dan: ⁴³All of them were Shuhamite clans; and those numbered were 64,400.

⁴⁴The descendants of Asher by their clans were:

through Imnah, the Imnite clan;

through Ishvi, the Ishvite clan;

through Beriah, the Beriite clan;

⁴⁵and through the descendants of Beriah:

through Heber, the Heberite clan;

through Malkiel, the Malkielite clan.

⁴⁶(Asher had a daughter named Serah.)

⁴⁷These were the clans of Asher; those numbered were 53,400.

⁴⁸The descendants of Naphtali by their clans were:

through Jahzeel, the Jahzeelite clan;

through Guni, the Gunite clan;

⁴⁹through Jezer, the Jezerite clan;

through Shillem, the Shillemite clan.

⁵⁰These were the clans of Naphtali; those numbered were 45,400.

⁵¹The total number of the men of Israel was 601,730.

⁵²The LORD said to Moses, ⁵³"The land is to be allotted to them as an inheritance based on the number of names. ⁵⁴To a larger group give a larger inheritance, and to a smaller group a smaller one; each is to receive its inheritance according to the number of those listed. ⁵⁵Be sure that the land is distributed by lot. What each group inherits will be according to the names for its ancestral tribe. ⁵⁶Each inheritance is to be distributed by lot among the larger and smaller groups."

⁵⁷These were the Levites who were counted by their clans:

through Gershon, the Gershonite clan;

through Kohath, the Kohathite clan;

through Merari, the Merarite clan.

⁵⁸These also were Levite clans:

the Libnite clan,

the Hebronite clan,

the Mahlite clan,

the Mushite clan,

the Korahite clan.

(Kohath was the forefather of Amram; ⁵⁹the name of Amram's wife was Jochebed, a descendant of Levi, who was born to the Levites^k in Egypt. To Amram she bore Aaron, Moses and their sister Miriam. ⁶⁰Aaron was the father of Nadab and

---

ⁱ39 A few manuscripts of the Masoretic Text, Samaritan Pentateuch, Vulgate and Syriac (see also Septuagint); most manuscripts of the Masoretic Text *Shephupham*   ^j40 Samaritan Pentateuch and Vulgate (see also Septuagint); Masoretic Text does not have *through Ard*.   ^k59 Or *Jochebed, a daughter of Levi, who was born to Levi*

Abihu, Eleazar and Ithamar. ⁶¹But Nadab and Abihu died when they made an offering before the LORD with unauthorized fire.)

⁶²All the male Levites a month old or more numbered 23,000. They were not counted along with the other Israelites because they received no inheritance among them.

⁶³These are the ones counted by Moses and Eleazar the priest when they counted the Israelites on the plains of Moab by the Jordan across from Jericho. ⁶⁴Not one of them was among those counted by Moses and Aaron the priest when they counted the Israelites in the Desert of Sinai. ⁶⁵For the LORD had told those Israelites they would surely die in the desert, and not one of them was left except Caleb son of Jephunneh and Joshua son of Nun.

CHAPTER 27
The daughters of Zelophehad son of Hepher, the son of Gilead, the son of Makir, the son of Manasseh, belonged to the clans of Manasseh son of Joseph. The names of the daughters were Mahlah, Noah, Hoglah, Milcah and Tirzah. They approached ²the entrance to the Tent of Meeting and stood before Moses, Eleazar the priest, the leaders and the whole assembly, and said, ³"Our father died in the desert. He was not among Korah's followers, who banded together against the LORD, but he died for his own sin and left no sons. ⁴Why should our father's name disappear from his clan because he had no son? Give us property among our father's relatives."

⁵So Moses brought their case before the LORD ⁶and the LORD said to him, ⁷"What Zelophehad's daughters are saying is right. You must certainly give them property as an inheritance among their father's relatives and turn their father's inheritance over to them.

⁸"Say to the Israelites, 'If a man dies and leaves no son, turn his inheritance over to his daughter. ⁹If he has no daughter, give his inheritance to his brothers. ¹⁰If he has no brothers, give his inheritance to his father's brothers. ¹¹If his father had no brothers, give his inheritance to the nearest relative in his clan, that he may pos-

sess it. This is to be a legal requirement for the Israelites, as the LORD commanded Moses.' "

¹²Then the LORD said to Moses, "Go up this mountain in the Abarim range and see the land I have given the Israelites. ¹³After you have seen it, you too will be gathered to your people, as your brother Aaron was, ¹⁴for when the community rebelled at the waters in the Desert of Zin, both of you disobeyed my command to honor me as holy before their eyes." (These were the waters of Meribah Kadesh, in the Desert of Zin.)

¹⁵Moses said to the LORD, ¹⁶"May the LORD, the God of the spirits of all mankind, appoint a man over this community ¹⁷to go out and come in before them, one who will lead them out and bring them in, so the LORD's people will not be like sheep without a shepherd."

¹⁸So the LORD said to Moses, "Take Joshua son of Nun, a man in whom is the spirit,ˡ and lay your hand on him. ¹⁹Have him stand before Eleazar the priest and the entire assembly and commission him in their presence. ²⁰Give him some of your authority so the whole Israelite community will obey him. ²¹He is to stand before Eleazar the priest, who will obtain decisions for him by inquiring of the Urim before the LORD. At his command he and the entire community of the Israelites will go out, and at his command they will come in."

²²Moses did as the LORD commanded him. He took Joshua and had him stand before Eleazar the priest and the whole assembly. ²³Then he laid his hands on him and commissioned him, as the LORD instructed through Moses.

CHAPTER 28
The LORD said to Moses, ²"Give this command to the Israelites and say to them: 'See that you present to me at the appointed time the food for my offerings made by fire, as an aroma pleasing to me.' ³Say to them: 'This is the offering made by fire that you are to present to the LORD: two lambs a year old without defect, as a regular burnt offering each day. ⁴Prepare one lamb in the morning and the other at twilight, ⁵together with a grain offering of a tenth of an ephahᵐ of fine flour mixed

ˡ18 Or Spirit   ᵐ5 That is, probably about 2 quarts (about 2 liters); also in verses 13, 21 and 29 with a quarter of a hin*ⁿ* of oil from pressed olives. ⁶This is the regular burnt offering instituted at Mount Sinai as a pleasing aroma, an offering made to the Lᴏʀᴅ by fire. ⁷The accompanying drink offering is to be a quarter of a hin of fermented drink with each lamb. Pour out the drink offering to the Lᴏʀᴅ at the sanctuary. ⁸Prepare the second lamb at twilight, along with the same kind of grain offering and drink offering that you prepare in the morning. This is an offering made by fire, an aroma pleasing to the Lᴏʀᴅ.

⁹" 'On the Sabbath day, make an offering of two lambs a year old without defect, together with its drink offering and a grain offering of two-tenths of an ephah*ᵒ* of fine flour mixed with oil. ¹⁰This is the burnt offering for every Sabbath, in addition to the regular burnt offering and its drink offering.

¹¹" 'On the first of every month, present to the Lᴏʀᴅ a burnt offering of two young bulls, one ram and seven male lambs a year old, all without defect. ¹²With each bull there is to be a grain offering of three-tenths of an ephah*ᵖ* of fine flour mixed with oil; with the ram, a grain offering of two-tenths of an ephah of fine flour mixed with oil; ¹³and with each lamb, a grain offering of a tenth of an ephah of fine flour mixed with oil. This is for a burnt offering, a pleasing aroma, an offering made to the Lᴏʀᴅ by fire. ¹⁴With each bull there is to be a drink offering of half a hin*�q* of wine; with the ram, a third of a hin*ʳ*; and with each lamb, a quarter of a hin. This is the monthly burnt offering to be made at each new moon during the year. ¹⁵Besides the regular burnt offering with its drink offering, one male goat is to be presented to the Lᴏʀᴅ as a sin offering.

¹⁶" 'On the fourteenth day of the first month the Lᴏʀᴅ's Passover is to be held. ¹⁷On the fifteenth day of this month there is to be a festival; for seven days eat bread made without yeast. ¹⁸On the first day hold a sacred assembly and do no regular work. ¹⁹Present to the Lᴏʀᴅ an offering made by fire, a burnt offering of two young bulls, one ram and seven male

lambs a year old, all without defect. ²⁰With each bull prepare a grain offering of three-tenths of an ephah of fine flour mixed with oil; with the ram, two-tenths; ²¹and with each of the seven lambs, one-tenth. ²²Include one male goat as a sin offering to make atonement for you. ²³Prepare these in addition to the regular morning burnt offering. ²⁴In this way prepare the food for the offering made by fire every day for seven days as an aroma pleasing to the Lᴏʀᴅ; it is to be prepared in addition to the regular burnt offering and its drink offering. ²⁵On the seventh day hold a sacred assembly and do no regular work.

²⁶" 'On the day of firstfruits, when you present to the Lᴏʀᴅ an offering of new grain during the Feast of Weeks, hold a sacred assembly and do no regular work. ²⁷Present a burnt offering of two young bulls, one ram and seven male lambs a year old as an aroma pleasing to the Lᴏʀᴅ. ²⁸With each bull there is to be a grain offering of three-tenths of an ephah of fine flour mixed with oil; with the ram, two-tenths; ²⁹and with each of the seven lambs, one-tenth. ³⁰Include one male goat to make atonement for you. ³¹Prepare these together with their drink offerings, in addition to the regular burnt offering and its grain offering. Be sure the animals are without defect.

CHAPTER 29

" 'On the first day of the seventh month hold a sacred assembly and do no regular work. It is a day for you to sound the trumpets. ²As an aroma pleasing to the Lᴏʀᴅ, prepare a burnt offering of one young bull, one ram and seven male lambs a year old, all without defect. ³With the bull prepare a grain offering of three-tenths of an ephah*ˢ* of fine flour mixed with oil; with the ram, two-tenths*ᵗ*; ⁴and with each of the seven lambs, one-tenth.*ᵘ* ⁵Include one male goat as a sin offering to make atonement for you. ⁶These are in addition to the monthly and daily burnt offerings with their grain offerings and drink offerings as specified. They are offerings made to the Lᴏʀᴅ by fire—a pleasing aroma.

ⁿ5 That is, probably about 1 quart (about 1 liter); also in verses 7 and 14　*ᵒ9* That is, probably about 4 quarts (about 4.5 liters); also in verses 12, 20 and 28　*ᵖ12* That is, probably about 6 quarts (about 6.5 liters); also in verses 20 and 28　*q14* That is, probably about 2 quarts (about 2 liters)　*ʳ14* That is, probably about 1 1/4 quarts (about 1.2 liters)　*ˢ3* That is, probably about 6 quarts (about 6.5 liters); also in verses 9 and 14　*ᵗ3* That is, probably about 4 quarts (about 4.5 liters); also in verses 9 and 14　*ᵘ4* That is, probably about 2 quarts (about 2 liters); also in verses 10 and 15

7" 'On the tenth day of this seventh month hold a sacred assembly. You must deny yourselves[v] and do no work. [8]Present as an aroma pleasing to the LORD a burnt offering of one young bull, one ram and seven male lambs a year old, all without defect. [9]With the bull prepare a grain offering of three-tenths of an ephah of fine flour mixed with oil; with the ram, two-tenths; [10]and with each of the seven lambs, one-tenth. [11]Include one male goat as a sin offering, in addition to the sin offering for atonement and the regular burnt offering with its grain offering, and their drink offerings.

12" 'On the fifteenth day of the seventh month, hold a sacred assembly and do no regular work. Celebrate a festival to the LORD for seven days. [13]Present an offering made by fire as an aroma pleasing to the LORD, a burnt offering of thirteen young bulls, two rams and fourteen male lambs a year old, all without defect. [14]With each of the thirteen bulls prepare a grain offering of three-tenths of an ephah of fine flour mixed with oil; with each of the two rams, two-tenths; [15]and with each of the fourteen lambs, one-tenth. [16]Include one male goat as a sin offering, in addition to the regular burnt offering with its grain offering and drink offering.

17" 'On the second day prepare twelve young bulls, two rams and fourteen male lambs a year old, all without defect. [18]With the bulls, rams and lambs, prepare their grain offerings and drink offerings according to the number specified. [19]Include one male goat as a sin offering, in addition to the regular burnt offering with its grain offering, and their drink offerings.

20" 'On the third day prepare eleven bulls, two rams and fourteen male lambs a year old, all without defect. [21]With the bulls, rams and lambs, prepare their grain offerings and drink offerings according to the number specified. [22]Include one male goat as a sin offering, in addition to the regular burnt offering with its grain offering and drink offering.

23" 'On the fourth day prepare ten bulls, two rams and fourteen male lambs a year old, all without defect. [24]With the bulls, rams and lambs, prepare their grain offerings and drink offerings according to

the number specified. [25]Include one male goat as a sin offering, in addition to the regular burnt offering with its grain offering and drink offering.

26" 'On the fifth day prepare nine bulls, two rams and fourteen male lambs a year old, all without defect. [27]With the bulls, rams and lambs, prepare their grain offerings and drink offerings according to the number specified. [28]Include one male goat as a sin offering, in addition to the regular burnt offering with its grain offering and drink offering.

29" 'On the sixth day prepare eight bulls, two rams and fourteen male lambs a year old, all without defect. [30]With the bulls, rams and lambs, prepare their grain offerings and drink offerings according to the number specified. [31]Include one male goat as a sin offering, in addition to the regular burnt offering with its grain offering and drink offering.

32" 'On the seventh day prepare seven bulls, two rams and fourteen male lambs a year old, all without defect. [33]With the bulls, rams and lambs, prepare their grain offerings and drink offerings according to the number specified. [34]Include one male goat as a sin offering, in addition to the regular burnt offering with its grain offering and drink offering.

35" 'On the eighth day hold an assembly and do no regular work. [36]Present an offering made by fire as an aroma pleasing to the LORD, a burnt offering of one bull, one ram and seven male lambs a year old, all without defect. [37]With the bull, the ram and the lambs, prepare their grain offerings and drink offerings according to the number specified. [38]Include one male goat as a sin offering, in addition to the regular burnt offering with its grain offering and drink offering.

39" 'In addition to what you vow and your freewill offerings, prepare these for the LORD at your appointed feasts: your burnt offerings, grain offerings, drink offerings and fellowship offerings.[w]' "

[40]Moses told the Israelites all that the LORD commanded him.

CHAPTER 30

Moses said to the heads of the tribes of Israel: "This is what the LORD commands:

[v]7 Or must fast   [w]39 Traditionally peace offerings

²When a man makes a vow to the LORD or takes an oath to obligate himself by a pledge, he must not break his word but must do everything he said.

³"When a young woman still living in her father's house makes a vow to the LORD or obligates herself by a pledge ⁴and her father hears about her vow or pledge but says nothing to her, then all her vows and every pledge by which she obligated herself will stand. ⁵But if her father forbids her when he hears about it, none of her vows or the pledges by which she obligated herself will stand; the LORD will release her because her father has forbidden her.

⁶"If she marries after she makes a vow or after her lips utter a rash promise by which she obligates herself ⁷and her husband hears about it but says nothing to her, then her vows or the pledges by which she obligated herself will stand. ⁸But if her husband forbids her when he hears about it, he nullifies the vow that obligates her or the rash promise by which she obligates herself, and the LORD will release her.

⁹"Any vow or obligation taken by a widow or divorced woman will be binding on her.

¹⁰"If a woman living with her husband makes a vow or obligates herself by a pledge under oath ¹¹and her husband hears about it but says nothing to her and does not forbid her, then all her vows or the pledges by which she obligated herself will stand. ¹²But if her husband nullifies them when he hears about them, then none of the vows or pledges that came from her lips will stand. Her husband has nullified them, and the LORD will release her. ¹³Her husband may confirm or nullify any vow she makes or any sworn pledge to deny herself. ¹⁴But if her husband says nothing to her about it from day to day, then he confirms all her vows or the pledges binding on her. He confirms them by saying nothing to her when he hears about them. ¹⁵If, however, he nullifies them some time after he hears about them, then he is responsible for her guilt."

¹⁶These are the regulations the LORD gave Moses concerning relationships between a man and his wife, and between a father and his young daughter still living in his house.

FEBRUARY 18 □ DAY 49
NUMBERS 31–33
The Last Days of a Great Leader

 OVERVIEW The final days of Moses' administration are just as productive as the first! As Israel's commander in chief, he leads a highly successful campaign against Midian; as administrator, he handles wisely the request of the tribes of Reuben and Gad that they be allowed to settle east of the Jordan River. He grants permission, provided the two tribes assist the other ten in conquering the promised land first. The remainder of the book of Numbers is a review of the Israelites' travels from Egypt to Moab.

Chapter 31	Chapter 32	Chapter 33
The Midianites Removed	A Problem Resolved	A Journey Recounted
Moses' Leadership	Moses' Wisdom	Moses' Travels

 YOUR DAILY WALK It could easily happen to you. You're doing some work around the house when suddenly your hand slips, and you come up with a finger full of splinters. After a half hour of "surgery,"

A little sin will add to your trouble, subtract from your energy and multiply your difficulties.

you figure you've pulled them all out, only to discover later that you (ouch) missed a few! At that point, the fact that you removed *most* of the splinters doesn't help much. It is the few remaining ones that really matter.

God clearly directed Israel to completely rid the land of its pagan inhabitants when the time came for conquest. He warned that any Canaanites left behind would become like painful splinters (thorns) to the Israelites (33:55–56). Disobeying God, Israel failed to rid the land of its pagan populace and was eventually corrupted by immorality and idolatry. The nation was *victimized* by forces it should have *controlled*.

Are there any "splinters" in your spiritual life—secret sins . . . nagging habits . . . little things you know displease God? Carry a pair of tweezers with you today as a reminder that what you fail to remove now will only fester and cause more pain in the future.

 INSIGHT Do Easy Paths Lead to Easy Living?
Moses handled the requests of the tribes of Reuben and Gad and the half-tribe of Manasseh in a prudent manner. However, their choice to remain outside the promised land in the rich grazing lands of Transjordan was comparable to Lot's selfish decision. And their choice manifested similar results of unbelief and conformity to the worldly standards of those about them (see 1 Chronicles 5:25–26).

CHAPTER 31

The LORD said to Moses, ²"Take vengeance on the Midianites for the Israelites. After that, you will be gathered to your people."

³So Moses said to the people, "Arm some of your men to go to war against the Midianites and to carry out the LORD's vengeance on them. ⁴Send into battle a thousand men from each of the tribes of Israel." ⁵So twelve thousand men armed for battle, a thousand from each tribe, were supplied from the clans of Israel. ⁶Moses sent them into battle, a thousand from each tribe, along with Phinehas son of Eleazar, the priest, who took with him articles from the sanctuary and the trumpets for signaling.

⁷They fought against Midian, as the LORD commanded Moses, and killed every man. ⁸Among their victims were Evi, Rekem, Zur, Hur and Reba—the five kings of Midian. They also killed Balaam son of Beor with the sword. ⁹The Israelites captured the Midianite women and children and took all the Midianite herds, flocks and goods as plunder. ¹⁰They burned all the towns where the Midianites had settled, as well as all their camps. ¹¹They took all the plunder and spoils, including the people and animals, ¹²and brought the captives, spoils and plunder to Moses and Eleazar the priest and the Israelite assembly at their camp on the plains of Moab, by the Jordan across from Jericho.ˣ

¹³Moses, Eleazar the priest and all the leaders of the community went to meet them outside the camp. ¹⁴Moses was angry with the officers of the army—the commanders of thousands and commanders of hundreds—who returned from the battle.

¹⁵"Have you allowed all the women to live?" he asked them. ¹⁶"They were the ones who followed Balaam's advice and were the means of turning the Israelites away from the LORD in what happened at Peor, so that a plague struck the LORD's people. ¹⁷Now kill all the boys. And kill every woman who has slept with a man, ¹⁸but save for yourselves every girl who has never slept with a man.

¹⁹"All of you who have killed anyone or touched anyone who was killed must stay outside the camp seven days. On the third and seventh days you must purify yourselves and your captives. ²⁰Purify every garment as well as everything made of leather, goat hair or wood."

²¹Then Eleazar the priest said to the soldiers who had gone into battle, "This is the requirement of the law that the LORD gave Moses: ²²Gold, silver, bronze, iron, tin, lead ²³and anything else that can withstand fire must be put through the fire, and then it will be clean. But it must also be purified with the water of cleans-

ˣ12 Hebrew *Jordan of Jericho*; possibly an ancient name for the Jordan River ing. And whatever cannot withstand fire must be put through that water. 24On the seventh day wash your clothes and you will be clean. Then you may come into the camp."

25The LORD said to Moses, 26"You and Eleazar the priest and the family heads of the community are to count all the people and animals that were captured. 27Divide the spoils between the soldiers who took part in the battle and the rest of the community. 28From the soldiers who fought in the battle, set apart as tribute for the LORD one out of every five hundred, whether persons, cattle, donkeys, sheep or goats. 29Take this tribute from their half share and give it to Eleazar the priest as the LORD's part. 30From the Israelites' half, select one out of every fifty, whether persons, cattle, donkeys, sheep, goats or other animals. Give them to the Levites, who are responsible for the care of the LORD's tabernacle." 31So Moses and Eleazar the priest did as the LORD commanded Moses.

32The plunder remaining from the spoils that the soldiers took was 675,000 sheep, 3372,000 cattle, 3461,000 donkeys 35and 32,000 women who had never slept with a man.

36The half share of those who fought in the battle was:

337,500 sheep, 37of which the tribute for the LORD was 675;
3836,000 cattle, of which the tribute for the LORD was 72;
3930,500 donkeys, of which the tribute for the LORD was 61;
4016,000 people, of which the tribute for the LORD was 32.

41Moses gave the tribute to Eleazar the priest as the LORD's part, as the LORD commanded Moses.

42The half belonging to the Israelites, which Moses set apart from that of the fighting men— 43the community's half— was 337,500 sheep, 4436,000 cattle, 4530,500 donkeys 46and 16,000 people. 47From the Israelites' half, Moses selected one out of every fifty persons and animals, as the LORD commanded him, and gave them to the Levites, who were responsible for the care of the LORD's tabernacle.

y52 That is, about 420 pounds (about 190 kilograms)

48Then the officers who were over the units of the army—the commanders of thousands and commanders of hundreds—went to Moses 49and said to him, "Your servants have counted the soldiers under our command, and not one is missing. 50So we have brought as an offering to the LORD the gold articles each of us acquired—armlets, bracelets, signet rings, earrings and necklaces—to make atonement for ourselves before the LORD."

51Moses and Eleazar the priest accepted from them the gold—all the crafted articles. 52All the gold from the commanders of thousands and commanders of hundreds that Moses and Eleazar presented as a gift to the LORD weighed 16,750 shekels.y 53Each soldier had taken plunder for himself. 54Moses and Eleazar the priest accepted the gold from the commanders of thousands and commanders of hundreds and brought it into the Tent of Meeting as a memorial for the Israelites before the LORD.

CHAPTER 32
The Reubenites and Gadites, who had very large herds and flocks, saw that the lands of Jazer and Gilead were suitable for livestock. 2So they came to Moses and Eleazar the priest and to the leaders of the community, and said, 3"Ataroth, Dibon, Jazer, Nimrah, Heshbon, Elealeh, Sebam, Nebo and Beon— 4the land the LORD subdued before the people of Israel—are suitable for livestock, and your servants have livestock. 5If we have found favor in your eyes," they said, "let this land be given to your servants as our possession. Do not make us cross the Jordan."

6Moses said to the Gadites and Reubenites, "Shall your countrymen go to war while you sit here? 7Why do you discourage the Israelites from going over into the land the LORD has given them? 8This is what your fathers did when I sent them from Kadesh Barnea to look over the land. 9After they went up to the Valley of Eshcol and viewed the land, they discouraged the Israelites from entering the land the LORD had given them. 10The LORD's anger was aroused that day and he swore this oath: 11'Because they have not followed me wholeheartedly, not one of the men twenty years old or more who came up out of Egypt will see the land I promised on oath to Abraham, Isaac and Jacob— [12]not one except Caleb son of Jephunneh the Kenizzite and Joshua son of Nun, for they followed the LORD wholeheartedly.' [13]The LORD's anger burned against Israel and he made them wander in the desert forty years, until the whole generation of those who had done evil in his sight was gone.

[14]"And here you are, a brood of sinners, standing in the place of your fathers and making the LORD even more angry with Israel. [15]If you turn away from following him, he will again leave all this people in the desert, and you will be the cause of their destruction."

[16]Then they came up to him and said, "We would like to build pens here for our livestock and cities for our women and children. [17]But we are ready to arm ourselves and go ahead of the Israelites until we have brought them to their place. Meanwhile our women and children will live in fortified cities, for protection from the inhabitants of the land. [18]We will not return to our homes until every Israelite has received his inheritance. [19]We will not receive any inheritance with them on the other side of the Jordan, because our inheritance has come to us on the east side of the Jordan."

[20]Then Moses said to them, "If you will do this—if you will arm yourselves before the LORD for battle, [21]and if all of you will go armed over the Jordan before the LORD until he has driven his enemies out before him— [22]then when the land is subdued before the LORD, you may return and be free from your obligation to the LORD and to Israel. And this land will be your possession before the LORD.

[23]"But if you fail to do this, you will be sinning against the LORD; and you may be sure that your sin will find you out. [24]Build cities for your women and children, and pens for your flocks, but do what you have promised."

[25]The Gadites and Reubenites said to Moses, "We your servants will do as our lord commands. [26]Our children and wives, our flocks and herds will remain here in the cities of Gilead. [27]But your servants, every man armed for battle, will cross over to fight before the LORD, just as our lord says."

[28]Then Moses gave orders about them to Eleazar the priest and Joshua son of Nun and to the family heads of the Israelite tribes. [29]He said to them, "If the Gadites and Reubenites, every man armed for battle, cross over the Jordan with you before the LORD, then when the land is subdued before you, give them the land of Gilead as their possession. [30]But if they do not cross over with you armed, they must accept their possession with you in Canaan."

[31]The Gadites and Reubenites answered, "Your servants will do what the LORD has said. [32]We will cross over before the LORD into Canaan armed, but the property we inherit will be on this side of the Jordan."

[33]Then Moses gave to the Gadites, the Reubenites and the half-tribe of Manasseh son of Joseph the kingdom of Sihon king of the Amorites and the kingdom of Og king of Bashan—the whole land with its cities and the territory around them.

[34]The Gadites built up Dibon, Ataroth, Aroer, [35]Atroth Shophan, Jazer, Jogbehah, [36]Beth Nimrah and Beth Haran as fortified cities, and built pens for their flocks. [37]And the Reubenites rebuilt Heshbon, Elealeh and Kiriathaim, [38]as well as Nebo and Baal Meon (these names were changed) and Sibmah. They gave names to the cities they rebuilt.

[39]The descendants of Makir son of Manasseh went to Gilead, captured it and drove out the Amorites who were there. [40]So Moses gave Gilead to the Makirites, the descendants of Manasseh, and they settled there. [41]Jair, a descendant of Manasseh, captured their settlements and called them Havvoth Jair.[z] [42]And Nobah captured Kenath and its surrounding settlements and called it Nobah after himself.

CHAPTER 33
Here are the stages in the journey of the Israelites when they came out of Egypt by divisions under the leadership of Moses and Aaron. [2]At the LORD's command Moses recorded the stages in their journey. This is their journey by stages:

[3]The Israelites set out from Rameses

[z]41 Or them the settlements of Jair

on the fifteenth day of the first month, the day after the Passover. They marched out boldly in full view of all the Egyptians, ⁴who were burying all their firstborn, whom the LORD had struck down among them; for the LORD had brought judgment on their gods.

⁵The Israelites left Rameses and camped at Succoth.

⁶They left Succoth and camped at Etham, on the edge of the desert.

⁷They left Etham, turned back to Pi Hahiroth, to the east of Baal Zephon, and camped near Migdol.

⁸They left Pi Hahiroth*a* and passed through the sea into the desert, and when they had traveled for three days in the Desert of Etham, they camped at Marah.

⁹They left Marah and went to Elim, where there were twelve springs and seventy palm trees, and they camped there.

¹⁰They left Elim and camped by the Red Sea.*b*

¹¹They left the Red Sea and camped in the Desert of Sin.

¹²They left the Desert of Sin and camped at Dophkah.

¹³They left Dophkah and camped at Alush.

¹⁴They left Alush and camped at Rephidim, where there was no water for the people to drink.

¹⁵They left Rephidim and camped in the Desert of Sinai.

¹⁶They left the Desert of Sinai and camped at Kibroth Hattaavah.

¹⁷They left Kibroth Hattaavah and camped at Hazeroth.

¹⁸They left Hazeroth and camped at Rithmah.

¹⁹They left Rithmah and camped at Rimmon Perez.

²⁰They left Rimmon Perez and camped at Libnah.

²¹They left Libnah and camped at Rissah.

²²They left Rissah and camped at Kehelathah.

²³They left Kehelathah and camped at Mount Shepher.

²⁴They left Mount Shepher and camped at Haradah.

²⁵They left Haradah and camped at Makheloth.

²⁶They left Makheloth and camped at Tahath.

²⁷They left Tahath and camped at Terah.

²⁸They left Terah and camped at Mithcah.

²⁹They left Mithcah and camped at Hashmonah.

³⁰They left Hashmonah and camped at Moseroth.

³¹They left Moseroth and camped at Bene Jaakan.

³²They left Bene Jaakan and camped at Hor Haggidgad.

³³They left Hor Haggidgad and camped at Jotbathah.

³⁴They left Jotbathah and camped at Abronah.

³⁵They left Abronah and camped at Ezion Geber.

³⁶They left Ezion Geber and camped at Kadesh, in the Desert of Zin.

³⁷They left Kadesh and camped at Mount Hor, on the border of Edom. ³⁸At the LORD's command Aaron the priest went up Mount Hor, where he died on the first day of the fifth month of the fortieth year after the Israelites came out of Egypt. ³⁹Aaron was a hundred and twenty-three years old when he died on Mount Hor.

⁴⁰The Canaanite king of Arad, who lived in the Negev of Canaan, heard that the Israelites were coming.

⁴¹They left Mount Hor and camped at Zalmonah.

⁴²They left Zalmonah and camped at Punon.

⁴³They left Punon and camped at Oboth.

⁴⁴They left Oboth and camped at Iye Abarim, on the border of Moab.

⁴⁵They left Iyim*c* and camped at Dibon Gad.

⁴⁶They left Dibon Gad and camped at Almon Diblathaim.

⁴⁷They left Almon Diblathaim and camped in the mountains of Abarim, near Nebo.

⁴⁸They left the mountains of Abarim and camped on the plains of

---

*a*8 Many manuscripts of the Masoretic Text, Samaritan Pentateuch and Vulgate; most manuscripts of the Masoretic Text *left from before Hahiroth*   *b*10 Hebrew *Yam Suph*; that is, Sea of Reeds; also in verse 11   *c*45 That is, Iye Abarim

Moab by the Jordan across from Jericho.[d] [49]There on the plains of Moab they camped along the Jordan from Beth Jeshimoth to Abel Shittim.

[50]On the plains of Moab by the Jordan across from Jericho the LORD said to Moses, [51]"Speak to the Israelites and say to them: 'When you cross the Jordan into Canaan, [52]drive out all the inhabitants of the land before you. Destroy all their carved images and their cast idols, and demolish all their high places. [53]Take possession of the land and settle in it, for I have given you the land to possess. [54]Distribute the land by lot, according to your clans. To a larger group give a larger inheritance, and to a smaller group a smaller one. Whatever falls to them by lot will be theirs. Distribute it according to your ancestral tribes.

[55]"'But if you do not drive out the inhabitants of the land, those you allow to remain will become barbs in your eyes and thorns in your sides. They will give you trouble in the land where you will live. [56]And then I will do to you what I plan to do to them.'"

[d]48 Hebrew *Jordan of Jericho*; possibly an ancient name for the Jordan River; also in verse 50

FEBRUARY 19 □ DAY 50
NUMBERS 34–36
Laws of the Promised Land

 OVERVIEW Perhaps no greater promises can be found in the pages of Scripture than those contained in Numbers 34–36, little-read chapters introduced with the phrase, "When you enter Canaan, . . ." (34:2). What follows is a detailed description of inheritances in the land of Canaan—the promise of thousands of square miles of real estate—when as yet the nation of Israel does not possess so much as a spadeful! Representatives from each of the twelve tribes cast lots for land they as yet do not own; the Levites are *given* forty-eight cities, not one of which has as yet been conquered. Fortified by faith, the people prepare to fight battles that have already been won!

Chapter 34	Chapter 35	Chapter 36
Borders around the Land	Refuge within the Land	Inheritance of the Land
Military Protection	Legal Protection	

 YOUR DAILY WALK With eyes riveted to the television screen, a group of hometown hockey fans howls its approval as the match progresses. When the home team falls behind 1–0 in the first period, the fans are delighted; when the score goes to 2–0 in the second period, the excitement grows; when in the third period the home team still trails 2–1, they go crazy with joy. Why? Because they're watching a videotape of the game, and they already know that the final score will be 3–2, in favor of the home team! The fans are confident their team will emerge victorious in the end.

Television has turned the family circle into a semicircle.

In the same way, the Israelites could face the walled cities and giant warriors of Canaan confident that their victory had already been won—in God's strength.

Tape the words of Luke 1:37 to the corner of your television screen to remind you that when the battle is the Lord's, the outcome is already certain.

INSIGHT Cities of Refuge, Savior of Refuge (35:32)
For the murderer of innocent blood, there was no refuge from death.
But for the accidental manslayer, six cities would later be designated
as places of protection (Joshua 20). Notice the parallels between these
cities of refuge in the Old Testament and the Savior of refuge in the
New Testament: Both were
- of divine origin,
- necessary to save from death,
- accessible to all and
- all-sufficient for salvation.

CHAPTER 34

The Lord said to Moses, [2]"Command the Israelites and say to them: 'When you enter Canaan, the land that will be allotted to you as an inheritance will have these boundaries:

[3]" 'Your southern side will include some of the Desert of Zin along the border of Edom. On the east, your southern boundary will start from the end of the Salt Sea,[e] [4]cross south of Scorpion[f] Pass, continue on to Zin and go south of Kadesh Barnea. Then it will go to Hazar Addar and over to Azmon, [5]where it will turn, join the Wadi of Egypt and end at the Sea.[g]

[6]" 'Your western boundary will be the coast of the Great Sea. This will be your boundary on the west.

[7]" 'For your northern boundary, run a line from the Great Sea to Mount Hor [8]and from Mount Hor to Lebo[h] Hamath. Then the boundary will go to Zedad, [9]continue to Ziphron and end at Hazar Enan. This will be your boundary on the north.

[10]" 'For your eastern boundary, run a line from Hazar Enan to Shepham. [11]The boundary will go down from Shepham to Riblah on the east side of Ain and continue along the slopes east of the Sea of Kinnereth.[i] [12]Then the boundary will go down along the Jordan and end at the Salt Sea.

" 'This will be your land, with its boundaries on every side.' "

[13]Moses commanded the Israelites: "Assign this land by lot as an inheritance. The Lord has ordered that it be given to the nine and a half tribes, [14]because the families of the tribe of Reuben, the tribe of Gad and the half-tribe of Manasseh have received their inheritance. [15]These two

and a half tribes have received their inheritance on the east side of the Jordan of Jericho,[j] toward the sunrise."

[16]The Lord said to Moses, [17]"These are the names of the men who are to assign the land for you as an inheritance: Eleazar the priest and Joshua son of Nun. [18]And appoint one leader from each tribe to help assign the land. [19]These are their names:

Caleb son of Jephunneh,
  from the tribe of Judah;
[20]Shemuel son of Ammihud,
  from the tribe of Simeon;
[21]Elidad son of Kislon,
  from the tribe of Benjamin;
[22]Bukki son of Jogli,
  the leader from the tribe of Dan;
[23]Hanniel son of Ephod,
  the leader from the tribe of Manasseh son of Joseph;
[24]Kemuel son of Shiphtan,
  the leader from the tribe of Ephraim son of Joseph;
[25]Elizaphan son of Parnach,
  the leader from the tribe of Zebulun;
[26]Paltiel son of Azzan,
  the leader from the tribe of Issachar;
[27]Ahihud son of Shelomi,
  the leader from the tribe of Asher;
[28]Pedahel son of Ammihud,
  the leader from the tribe of Naphtali."

[29]These are the men the Lord commanded to assign the inheritance to the Israelites in the land of Canaan.

CHAPTER 35

On the plains of Moab by the Jordan across from Jericho,[k] the Lord said to Moses, [2]"Command the Israelites to give the Levites towns to live in from the

---

[e]3 That is, the Dead Sea; also in verse 12   [f]4 Hebrew *Akrabbim*   [g]5 That is, the Mediterranean; also in verses 6 and 7
[h]8 Or *to the entrance to*   [i]11 That is, Galilee   [j]15 *Jordan of Jericho* was possibly an ancient name for the Jordan River.
[k]1 Hebrew *Jordan of Jericho*; possibly an ancient name for the Jordan River

inheritance the Israelites will possess. And give them pasturelands around the towns. [3]Then they will have towns to live in and pasturelands for their cattle, flocks and all their other livestock.

[4]"The pasturelands around the towns that you give the Levites will extend out fifteen hundred feet[l] from the town wall. [5]Outside the town, measure three thousand feet[m] on the east side, three thousand on the south side, three thousand on the west and three thousand on the north, with the town in the center. They will have this area as pastureland for the towns.

[6]"Six of the towns you give the Levites will be cities of refuge, to which a person who has killed someone may flee. In addition, give them forty-two other towns. [7]In all you must give the Levites forty-eight towns, together with their pasturelands. [8]The towns you give the Levites from the land the Israelites possess are to be given in proportion to the inheritance of each tribe: Take many towns from a tribe that has many, but few from one that has few."

[9]Then the LORD said to Moses: [10]"Speak to the Israelites and say to them: 'When you cross the Jordan into Canaan, [11]select some towns to be your cities of refuge, to which a person who has killed someone accidentally may flee. [12]They will be places of refuge from the avenger, so that a person accused of murder may not die before he stands trial before the assembly. [13]These six towns you give will be your cities of refuge. [14]Give three on this side of the Jordan and three in Canaan as cities of refuge. [15]These six towns will be a place of refuge for Israelites, aliens and any other people living among them, so that anyone who has killed another accidentally can flee there.

[16]"'If a man strikes someone with an iron object so that he dies, he is a murderer; the murderer shall be put to death. [17]Or if anyone has a stone in his hand that could kill, and he strikes someone so that he dies, he is a murderer; the murderer shall be put to death. [18]Or if anyone has a wooden object in his hand that could kill, and he hits someone so that he dies, he is a murderer; the murderer shall be put to death. [19]The avenger of blood shall put the murderer to death; when he meets him, he shall put him to death. [20]If anyone with malice aforethought shoves another or throws something at him intentionally so that he dies [21]or if in hostility he hits him with his fist so that he dies, that person shall be put to death; he is a murderer. The avenger of blood shall put the murderer to death when he meets him.

[22]"'But if without hostility someone suddenly shoves another or throws something at him unintentionally [23]or, without seeing him, drops a stone on him that could kill him, and he dies, then since he was not his enemy and he did not intend to harm him, [24]the assembly must judge between him and the avenger of blood according to these regulations. [25]The assembly must protect the one accused of murder from the avenger of blood and send him back to the city of refuge to which he fled. He must stay there until the death of the high priest, who was anointed with the holy oil.

[26]"'But if the accused ever goes outside the limits of the city of refuge to which he has fled [27]and the avenger of blood finds him outside the city, the avenger of blood may kill the accused without being guilty of murder. [28]The accused must stay in his city of refuge until the death of the high priest; only after the death of the high priest may he return to his own property.

[29]"'These are to be legal requirements for you throughout the generations to come, wherever you live.

[30]"'Anyone who kills a person is to be put to death as a murderer only on the testimony of witnesses. But no one is to be put to death on the testimony of only one witness.

[31]"'Do not accept a ransom for the life of a murderer, who deserves to die. He must surely be put to death.

[32]"'Do not accept a ransom for anyone who has fled to a city of refuge and so allow him to go back and live on his own land before the death of the high priest.

[33]"'Do not pollute the land where you are. Bloodshed pollutes the land, and atonement cannot be made for the land on which blood has been shed, except by the blood of the one who shed it. [34]Do not defile the land where you live and where

l4 Hebrew *a thousand cubits* (about 450 meters)   m5 Hebrew *two thousand cubits* (about 900 meters)

I dwell, for I, the LORD, dwell among the Israelites.' "

CHAPTER 36

The family heads of the clan of Gilead son of Makir, the son of Manasseh, who were from the clans of the descendants of Joseph, came and spoke before Moses and the leaders, the heads of the Israelite families. ²They said, "When the LORD commanded my lord to give the land as an inheritance to the Israelites by lot, he ordered you to give the inheritance of our brother Zelophehad to his daughters. ³Now suppose they marry men from other Israelite tribes; then their inheritance will be taken from our ancestral inheritance and added to that of the tribe they marry into. And so part of the inheritance allotted to us will be taken away. ⁴When the Year of Jubilee for the Israelites comes, their inheritance will be added to that of the tribe into which they marry, and their property will be taken from the tribal inheritance of our forefathers."

⁵Then at the LORD's command Moses gave this order to the Israelites: "What the tribe of the descendants of Joseph is saying is right. ⁶This is what the LORD commands for Zelophehad's daughters: They may marry anyone they please as long as they marry within the tribal clan of their father. ⁷No inheritance in Israel is to pass from tribe to tribe, for every Israelite shall keep the tribal land inherited from his forefathers. ⁸Every daughter who inherits land in any Israelite tribe must marry someone in her father's tribal clan, so that every Israelite will possess the inheritance of his fathers. ⁹No inheritance may pass from tribe to tribe, for each Israelite tribe is to keep the land it inherits."

¹⁰So Zelophehad's daughters did as the LORD commanded Moses. ¹¹Zelophehad's daughters—Mahlah, Tirzah, Hoglah, Milcah and Noah—married their cousins on their father's side. ¹²They married within the clans of the descendants of Manasseh son of Joseph, and their inheritance remained in their father's clan and tribe.

¹³These are the commands and regulations the LORD gave through Moses to the Israelites on the plains of Moab by the Jordan across from Jericho.ⁿ

ⁿ13 Hebrew *Jordan of Jericho*; possibly an ancient name for the Jordan River

Deuteronomy

THE LAST of the five books of Moses, Deuteronomy reviews the forty-year period of the nation's walk with God and previews the new relationship soon to begin in Canaan. Taking the form of a series of sermons, the book addresses the new generation emerging from the desert march. Moses reminds them of the central importance of obedience and stresses holiness as a way of life. Everything—possession of the land, victory over enemies, prosperity and enjoyment of life—depends on these valuable lessons.

Focus	Backward			Inward				Upward	
Divisions	Reviewing the Wanderings	Renewing God's Demands for Obedience	Remembering Lessons in Obedience	Religious Laws for Canaan	Civil Laws for Canaan	Societal Laws for Canaan	Commitment to the Covenant	Farewell and Death of Moses	
	1 4	5 7	8 11	12 16	17 20	21 26	27 30	31 34	
Topics	Lessons from the Past			Lessons for the Future				Lessons of a Leader	
	The Obedient Life			The Orderly Life				One Man's Life	
Place	Moab (North of the Dead Sea)								
Time	About 2 Months								

FEBRUARY 20 □ DAY 51
DEUTERONOMY 1–4
Reviewing the Wanderings

 OVERVIEW The first of Moses' three sermons in the book of Deuteronomy looks back over the history of the nation and traces God's dealings with his people. Because of unbelief the Israelites failed to possess the land God had promised them. But even their disobedience could not annul the promise of God. Israel would one day dwell in the land, though an entire generation had died in the desert for failing to believe God. True to his word, God overthrew nation after nation during Israel's relentless march to the Jordan River. The lesson from the past is painfully transparent: Blessing and victory follow obedience, but disobedience brings only defeat and heartache.

Chapter 1	Chapter 2	Chapter 3	Chapter 4
Postponement of the Land	Promise of the Land	Possession of the Land	Principle from the Land: Obey!
Looking to the Past			Learning from the Past

 YOUR DAILY WALK What have you learned during the months or years you've been walking with the Lord?

To overlook one's own faults is to miss a valuable free education.

The story is told of a high school teacher who spoke with excessive pride of her thirty-eight years of mediocre teaching experience. Her principal responded with a chuckle, "Well, that's not quite correct. Actually she's a first-year teacher—thirty-eight times over!" Do you see the difference? Each year that teacher was making the same mistakes she made during her first year—mistakes that should have been corrected long ago! She never profited from her past errors and so was destined to repeat them again and again.

Moses tried to shake the nation of Israel from its complacency by pointing out the deadly consequences of past disobedience. As you read today's section, you can almost hear him plead with the people to open their eyes and learn from their sordid history.

How about you? Are you wiser in the ways of God today for having seen him work in the past? Sometime this week, share with someone a "history lesson" from your life that is making a difference in your walk with God today!

 INSIGHT Words Worth Repeating

How much practical application do Moses' sermons to his people in the book of Deuteronomy carry? Just ask Jesus, who *three times* quoted this book to fend off Satan in the desert, one for each offer Satan made (Matthew 4:1–10). (By the way, it worked!)

CHAPTER 1

These are the words Moses spoke to all Israel in the desert east of the Jordan—that is, in the Arabah—opposite Suph, between Paran and Tophel, Laban, Haze- roth and Dizahab. ²(It takes eleven days to go from Horeb to Kadesh Barnea by the Mount Seir road.)

³In the fortieth year, on the first day of the eleventh month, Moses proclaimed to

the Israelites all that the LORD had commanded him concerning them. ⁴This was after he had defeated Sihon king of the Amorites, who reigned in Heshbon, and at Edrei had defeated Og king of Bashan, who reigned in Ashtaroth.

⁵East of the Jordan in the territory of Moab, Moses began to expound this law, saying:

⁶The LORD our God said to us at Horeb, "You have stayed long enough at this mountain. ⁷Break camp and advance into the hill country of the Amorites; go to all the neighboring peoples in the Arabah, in the mountains, in the western foothills, in the Negev and along the coast, to the land of the Canaanites and to Lebanon, as far as the great river, the Euphrates. ⁸See, I have given you this land. Go in and take possession of the land that the LORD swore he would give to your fathers—to Abraham, Isaac and Jacob—and to their descendants after them."

⁹At that time I said to you, "You are too heavy a burden for me to carry alone. ¹⁰The LORD your God has increased your numbers so that today you are as many as the stars in the sky. ¹¹May the LORD, the God of your fathers, increase you a thousand times and bless you as he has promised! ¹²But how can I bear your problems and your burdens and your disputes all by myself? ¹³Choose some wise, understanding and respected men from each of your tribes, and I will set them over you."

¹⁴You answered me, "What you propose to do is good."

¹⁵So I took the leading men of your tribes, wise and respected men, and appointed them to have authority over you—as commanders of thousands, of hundreds, of fifties and of tens and as tribal officials. ¹⁶And I charged your judges at that time: Hear the disputes between your brothers and judge fairly, whether the case is between brother Israelites or between one of them and an alien. ¹⁷Do not show partiality in judging; hear both small and great alike. Do not be afraid of any man, for judgment belongs to God. Bring me any case too hard for you, and I will hear it. ¹⁸And at that time I told you everything you were to do.

¹⁹Then, as the LORD our God commanded us, we set out from Horeb and went toward the hill country of the Amorites through all that vast and dreadful desert that you have seen, and so we reached Kadesh Barnea. ²⁰Then I said to you, "You have reached the hill country of the Amorites, which the LORD our God is giving us. ²¹See, the LORD your God has given you the land. Go up and take possession of it as the LORD, the God of your fathers, told you. Do not be afraid; do not be discouraged."

²²Then all of you came to me and said, "Let us send men ahead to spy out the land for us and bring back a report about the route we are to take and the towns we will come to."

²³The idea seemed good to me; so I selected twelve of you, one man from each tribe. ²⁴They left and went up into the hill country, and came to the Valley of Eshcol and explored it. ²⁵Taking with them some of the fruit of the land, they brought it down to us and reported, "It is a good land that the LORD our God is giving us."

²⁶But you were unwilling to go up; you rebelled against the command of the LORD your God. ²⁷You grumbled in your tents and said, "The LORD hates us; so he brought us out of Egypt to deliver us into the hands of the Amorites to destroy us. ²⁸Where can we go? Our brothers have made us lose heart. They say, 'The people are stronger and taller than we are; the cities are large, with walls up to the sky. We even saw the Anakites there.' "

²⁹Then I said to you, "Do not be terrified; do not be afraid of them. ³⁰The LORD your God, who is going before you, will fight for you, as he did for you in Egypt, before your very eyes, ³¹and in the desert. There you saw how the LORD your God carried you, as a father carries his son, all the way you went until you reached this place."

³²In spite of this, you did not trust in the LORD your God, ³³who went ahead of you on your journey, in fire by night and in a cloud by day, to search out places for you to camp and to show you the way you should go.

³⁴When the LORD heard what you said, he was angry and solemnly swore: ³⁵"Not a man of this evil generation shall see the good land I swore to give your forefathers, ³⁶except Caleb son of Jephunneh. He will see it, and I will give him and his descendants the land he set his feet on,

because he followed the LORD whole-heartedly."

37Because of you the LORD became angry with me also and said, "You shall not enter it, either. 38But your assistant, Joshua son of Nun, will enter it. Encourage him, because he will lead Israel to inherit it. 39And the little ones that you said would be taken captive, your children who do not yet know good from bad—they will enter the land. I will give it to them and they will take possession of it. 40But as for you, turn around and set out toward the desert along the route to the Red Sea.ᵃ"

41Then you replied, "We have sinned against the LORD. We will go up and fight, as the LORD our God commanded us." So every one of you put on his weapons, thinking it easy to go up into the hill country.

42But the LORD said to me, "Tell them, 'Do not go up and fight, because I will not be with you. You will be defeated by your enemies.'"

43So I told you, but you would not listen. You rebelled against the LORD's command and in your arrogance you marched up into the hill country. 44The Amorites who lived in those hills came out against you; they chased you like a swarm of bees and beat you down from Seir all the way to Hormah. 45You came back and wept before the LORD, but he paid no attention to your weeping and turned a deaf ear to you. 46And so you stayed in Kadesh many days—all the time you spent there.

CHAPTER 2

Then we turned back and set out toward the desert along the route to the Red Sea,ᵃ as the LORD had directed me. For a long time we made our way around the hill country of Seir.

2Then the LORD said to me, 3"You have made your way around this hill country long enough; now turn north. 4Give the people these orders: 'You are about to pass through the territory of your brothers the descendants of Esau, who live in Seir. They will be afraid of you, but be very careful. 5Do not provoke them to war, for I will not give you any of their land, not even enough to put your foot on. I have given Esau the hill country of

Seir as his own. 6You are to pay them in silver for the food you eat and the water you drink.'"

7The LORD your God has blessed you in all the work of your hands. He has watched over your journey through this vast desert. These forty years the LORD your God has been with you, and you have not lacked anything.

8So we went on past our brothers the descendants of Esau, who live in Seir. We turned from the Arabah road, which comes up from Elath and Ezion Geber, and traveled along the desert road of Moab.

9Then the LORD said to me, "Do not harass the Moabites or provoke them to war, for I will not give you any part of their land. I have given Ar to the descendants of Lot as a possession."

10(The Emites used to live there—a people strong and numerous, and as tall as the Anakites. 11Like the Anakites, they too were considered Rephaites, but the Moabites called them Emites. 12Horites used to live in Seir, but the descendants of Esau drove them out. They destroyed the Horites from before them and settled in their place, just as Israel did in the land the LORD gave them as their possession.)

13And the LORD said, "Now get up and cross the Zered Valley." So we crossed the valley.

14Thirty-eight years passed from the time we left Kadesh Barnea until we crossed the Zered Valley. By then, that entire generation of fighting men had perished from the camp, as the LORD had sworn to them. 15The LORD's hand was against them until he had completely eliminated them from the camp.

16Now when the last of these fighting men among the people had died, 17the LORD said to me, 18"Today you are to pass by the region of Moab at Ar. 19When you come to the Ammonites, do not harass them or provoke them to war, for I will not give you possession of any land belonging to the Ammonites. I have given it as a possession to the descendants of Lot."

20(That too was considered a land of the Rephaites, who used to live there; but the Ammonites called them Zamzummites. 21They were a people strong and numerous, and as tall as the Anakites. The LORD destroyed them from before the Ammonites, who drove them out and settled in their place. 22The LORD had done the same for the descendants of Esau, who lived in Seir, when he destroyed the Horites from before them. They drove them out and have lived in their place to this day. 23And as for the Avvites who lived in villages as far as Gaza, the Caphtorites coming out from Caphtor*b* destroyed them and settled in their place.)

24"Set out now and cross the Arnon Gorge. See, I have given into your hand Sihon the Amorite, king of Heshbon, and his country. Begin to take possession of it and engage him in battle. 25This very day I will begin to put the terror and fear of you on all the nations under heaven. They will hear reports of you and will tremble and be in anguish because of you."

26From the desert of Kedemoth I sent messengers to Sihon king of Heshbon offering peace and saying, 27"Let us pass through your country. We will stay on the main road; we will not turn aside to the right or to the left. 28Sell us food to eat and water to drink for their price in silver. Only let us pass through on foot— 29as the descendants of Esau, who live in Seir, and the Moabites, who live in Ar, did for us— until we cross the Jordan into the land the LORD our God is giving us." 30But Sihon king of Heshbon refused to let us pass through. For the LORD your God had made his spirit stubborn and his heart obstinate in order to give him into your hands, as he has now done.

31The LORD said to me, "See, I have begun to deliver Sihon and his country over to you. Now begin to conquer and possess his land."

32When Sihon and all his army came out to meet us in battle at Jahaz, 33the LORD our God delivered him over to us and we struck him down, together with his sons and his whole army. 34At that time we took all his towns and completely destroyed*c* them—men, women and children. We left no survivors. 35But the livestock and the plunder from the towns we had captured we carried off for ourselves. 36From Aroer on the rim of the Arnon Gorge, and from the town in the gorge, even as far as Gilead, not one town

was too strong for us. The LORD our God gave us all of them. 37But in accordance with the command of the LORD our God, you did not encroach on any of the land of the Ammonites, neither the land along the course of the Jabbok nor that around the towns in the hills.

CHAPTER 3
Next we turned and went up along the road toward Bashan, and Og king of Bashan with his whole army marched out to meet us in battle at Edrei. 2The LORD said to me, "Do not be afraid of him, for I have handed him over to you with his whole army and his land. Do to him what you did to Sihon king of the Amorites, who reigned in Heshbon."

3So the LORD our God also gave into our hands Og king of Bashan and all his army. We struck them down, leaving no survivors. 4At that time we took all his cities. There was not one of the sixty cities that we did not take from them—the whole region of Argob, Og's kingdom in Bashan. 5All these cities were fortified with high walls and with gates and bars, and there were also a great many unwalled villages. 6We completely destroyed*c* them, as we had done with Sihon king of Heshbon, destroying*c* every city—men, women and children. 7But all the livestock and the plunder from their cities we carried off for ourselves.

8So at that time we took from these two kings of the Amorites the territory east of the Jordan, from the Arnon Gorge as far as Mount Hermon. 9(Hermon is called Sirion by the Sidonians; the Amorites call it Senir.) 10We took all the towns on the plateau, and all Gilead, and all Bashan as far as Salecah and Edrei, towns of Og's kingdom in Bashan. 11(Only Og king of Bashan was left of the remnant of the Rephaites. His bed*d* was made of iron and was more than thirteen feet long and six feet wide.*e* It is still in Rabbah of the Ammonites.)

12Of the land that we took over at that time, I gave the Reubenites and the Gadites the territory north of Aroer by the Arnon Gorge, including half the hill country of Gilead, together with its towns. 13The rest of Gilead and also all of

*b*23 That is, Crete   *c*34,6 The Hebrew term refers to the irrevocable giving over of things or persons to the LORD, often by totally destroying them.   *d*11 Or *sarcophagus*   *e*11 Hebrew *nine cubits long and four cubits wide* (about 4 meters long and 1.8 meters wide)

Bashan, the kingdom of Og, I gave to the half tribe of Manasseh. (The whole region of Argob in Bashan used to be known as a land of the Rephaites. 14Jair, a descendant of Manasseh, took the whole region of Argob as far as the border of the Geshurites and the Maacathites; it was named after him, so that to this day Bashan is called Havvoth Jair.*f*) 15And I gave Gilead to Makir. 16But to the Reubenites and the Gadites I gave the territory extending from Gilead down to the Arnon Gorge (the middle of the gorge being the border) and out to the Jabbok River, which is the border of the Ammonites. 17Its western border was the Jordan in the Arabah, from Kinnereth to the Sea of the Arabah (the Salt Sea*g*), below the slopes of Pisgah.

18I commanded you at that time: "The LORD your God has given you this land to take possession of it. But all your able-bodied men, armed for battle, must cross over ahead of your brother Israelites. 19However, your wives, your children and your livestock (I know you have much livestock) may stay in the towns I have given you, 20until the LORD gives rest to your brothers as he has to you, and they too have taken over the land that the LORD your God is giving them, across the Jordan. After that, each of you may go back to the possession I have given you."

21At that time I commanded Joshua: "You have seen with your own eyes all that the LORD your God has done to these two kings. The LORD will do the same to all the kingdoms over there where you are going. 22Do not be afraid of them; the LORD your God himself will fight for you."

23At that time I pleaded with the LORD: 24"O Sovereign LORD, you have begun to show to your servant your greatness and your strong hand. For what god is there in heaven or on earth who can do the deeds and mighty works you do? 25Let me go over and see the good land beyond the Jordan—that fine hill country and Lebanon."

26But because of you the LORD was angry with me and would not listen to me. "That is enough," the LORD said. "Do not speak to me anymore about this matter. 27Go up to the top of Pisgah and look west and north and south and east. Look at the land with your own eyes, since you are not going to cross this Jordan. 28But commission Joshua, and encourage and strengthen him, for he will lead this people across and will cause them to inherit the land that you will see." 29So we stayed in the valley near Beth Peor.

CHAPTER 4

Hear now, O Israel, the decrees and laws I am about to teach you. Follow them so that you may live and may go in and take possession of the land that the LORD, the God of your fathers, is giving you. 2Do not add to what I command you and do not subtract from it, but keep the commands of the LORD your God that I give you.

3You saw with your own eyes what the LORD did at Baal Peor. The LORD your God destroyed from among you everyone who followed the Baal of Peor, 4but all of you who held fast to the LORD your God are still alive today.

5See, I have taught you decrees and laws as the LORD my God commanded me, so that you may follow them in the land you are entering to take possession of it. 6Observe them carefully, for this will show your wisdom and understanding to the nations, who will hear about all these decrees and say, "Surely this great nation is a wise and understanding people." 7What other nation is so great as to have their gods near them the way the LORD our God is near us whenever we pray to him? 8And what other nation is so great as to have such righteous decrees and laws as this body of laws I am setting before you today?

9Only be careful, and watch yourselves closely so that you do not forget the things your eyes have seen or let them slip from your heart as long as you live. Teach them to your children and to their children after them. 10Remember the day you stood before the LORD your God at Horeb, when he said to me, "Assemble the people before me to hear my words so that they may learn to revere me as long as they live in the land and may teach them to their children." 11You came near and stood at the foot of the mountain while it blazed with fire to the very heavens, with black clouds and deep darkness.

f14 Or called the settlements of Jair   g17 That is, the Dead Sea

¹²Then the LORD spoke to you out of the fire. You heard the sound of words but saw no form; there was only a voice. ¹³He declared to you his covenant, the Ten Commandments, which he commanded you to follow and then wrote them on two stone tablets. ¹⁴And the LORD directed me at that time to teach you the decrees and laws you are to follow in the land that you are crossing the Jordan to possess.

¹⁵You saw no form of any kind the day the LORD spoke to you at Horeb out of the fire. Therefore watch yourselves very carefully, ¹⁶so that you do not become corrupt and make for yourselves an idol, an image of any shape, whether formed like a man or a woman, ¹⁷or like any animal on earth or any bird that flies in the air, ¹⁸or like any creature that moves along the ground or any fish in the waters below. ¹⁹And when you look up to the sky and see the sun, the moon and the stars—all the heavenly array—do not be enticed into bowing down to them and worshiping things the LORD your God has apportioned to all the nations under heaven. ²⁰But as for you, the LORD took you and brought you out of the iron-smelting furnace, out of Egypt, to be the people of his inheritance, as you now are.

²¹The LORD was angry with me because of you, and he solemnly swore that I would not cross the Jordan and enter the good land the LORD your God is giving you as your inheritance. ²²I will die in this land; I will not cross the Jordan; but you are about to cross over and take possession of that good land. ²³Be careful not to forget the covenant of the LORD your God that he made with you; do not make for yourselves an idol in the form of anything the LORD your God has forbidden. ²⁴For the LORD your God is a consuming fire, a jealous God.

²⁵After you have had children and grandchildren and have lived in the land a long time—if you then become corrupt and make any kind of idol, doing evil in the eyes of the LORD your God and provoking him to anger, ²⁶I call heaven and earth as witnesses against you this day that you will quickly perish from the land that you are crossing the Jordan to possess. You will not live there long but will

certainly be destroyed. ²⁷The LORD will scatter you among the peoples, and only a few of you will survive among the nations to which the LORD will drive you. ²⁸There you will worship man-made gods of wood and stone, which cannot see or hear or eat or smell. ²⁹But if from there you seek the LORD your God, you will find him if you look for him with all your heart and with all your soul. ³⁰When you are in distress and all these things have happened to you, then in later days you will return to the LORD your God and obey him. ³¹For the LORD your God is a merciful God; he will not abandon or destroy you or forget the covenant with your forefathers, which he confirmed to them by oath.

³²Ask now about the former days, long before your time, from the day God created man on the earth; ask from one end of the heavens to the other. Has anything so great as this ever happened, or has anything like it ever been heard of? ³³Has any other people heard the voice of God^h speaking out of fire, as you have, and lived? ³⁴Has any god ever tried to take for himself one nation out of another nation, by testings, by miraculous signs and wonders, by war, by a mighty hand and an outstretched arm, or by great and awesome deeds, like all the things the LORD your God did for you in Egypt before your very eyes?

³⁵You were shown these things so that you might know that the LORD is God; besides him there is no other. ³⁶From heaven he made you hear his voice to discipline you. On earth he showed you his great fire, and you heard his words from out of the fire. ³⁷Because he loved your forefathers and chose their descendants after them, he brought you out of Egypt by his Presence and his great strength, ³⁸to drive out before you nations greater and stronger than you and to bring you into their land to give it to you for your inheritance, as it is today.

³⁹Acknowledge and take to heart this day that the LORD is God in heaven above and on the earth below. There is no other. ⁴⁰Keep his decrees and commands, which I am giving you today, so that it may go well with you and your children after you and that you may live long in the land the LORD your God gives you for all time.

h33 Or of a god

⁴¹Then Moses set aside three cities east of the Jordan, ⁴²to which anyone who had killed a person could flee if he had unintentionally killed his neighbor without malice aforethought. He could flee into one of these cities and save his life. ⁴³The cities were these: Bezer in the desert plateau, for the Reubenites; Ramoth in Gilead, for the Gadites; and Golan in Bashan, for the Manassites.

⁴⁴This is the law Moses set before the Israelites. ⁴⁵These are the stipulations, decrees and laws Moses gave them when they came out of Egypt ⁴⁶and were in the valley near Beth Peor east of the Jordan, in the land of Sihon king of the Amorites, who reigned in Heshbon and was defeated by Moses and the Israelites as they came out of Egypt. ⁴⁷They took possession of his land and the land of Og king of Bashan, the two Amorite kings east of the Jordan. ⁴⁸This land extended from Aroer on the rim of the Arnon Gorge to Mount Siyon*ⁱ* (that is, Hermon), ⁴⁹and included all the Arabah east of the Jordan, as far as the Sea of the Arabah,*ʲ* below the slopes of Pisgah.

i48 Hebrew; Syriac (see also Deut. 3:9) *Sirion*   *j49* That is, the Dead Sea

FEBRUARY 21 ☐ DAY 52
Lessons in the Desert

LOOK BACK In a book entitled *Numbers* you'd expect to find statistics and figures prominent, and this past week's reading has not disappointed! After an initial census to determine the strength of the fighting force, God instructed Moses to cleanse and consecrate the nation for worship and warfare. After a special celebration of the Passover at Mount Sinai, the people began the journey with great expectations. But rejoicing soon turned to rebellion, leading to a fateful decision at the Desert of Paran and forty years of fruitless wandering in the desert. Even in the midst of death and discouragement, God's grace was evident in the form of daily provisions of manna and water. The bronze snake was God's lifesaving antidote for venomous snakes, and a talking donkey showed Balaam the folly of trying to curse God's people. A second census (nearly forty years after the first) showed that the loss of a generation through unbelief had not decimated the nation. It would now remain for the new generation to learn from the errors of its elders.

Most people don't mind obstacles, as long as they don't get in their way.

LOOK UP You cannot get from Mount Sinai to the promised land without passing through the desert. The issue was not whether the children of Israel would pass through the desert (they would), but rather how long they would camp there. What should have been an eleven-day experience became a forty-year nightmare. What should have been a brief, uncomfortable inconvenience became instead a "terminal illness" for an entire generation. What should have produced a few blisters and first-degree burns ended up costing 1.2 million people their lives.

Deserts are never pleasant (unless they are on a picture postcard). Deserts tend to be dry, barren, lifeless and uncomfortable. You tend to get thirsty in a desert and find yourself yearning to be in a place of rest and refreshment.

But as you continue your daily walk through the Bible, you will discover something intriguing: Many of God's choicest servants spent time in a desertlike environment. Moses did (forty years, to be exact). David did. John the Baptist did. The apostle Paul did. And even our Lord was tempted for forty days in a barren wilderness region near the Dead Sea.

LOOK AHEAD A season in the desert does something interesting for a tree: It causes the roots to go down deeper in search of life-giving moisture. And the result is a stronger tree that is better able to weather the storms of life.

The same is true of the man or woman of God who faces the hot blast of desertlike conditions. What may at first glance appear to be barren, fruitless days on the "backside of God's blessing" may, in fact, be preparing you for days of great fruit bearing just ahead. Desert times will come—expect them! But don't allow the heat to make you bitter or disobedient toward God. "Perseverance must finish its work so that you may be mature and complete, not lacking anything" (James 1:4).

The tragedy of the book of Numbers is not that the nation went through the desert, but that through disobedience they camped there so long.

By the way, where are you camped these days?

FEBRUARY 22 □ DAY 53
DEUTERONOMY 5–7
Reviewing God's Demands

OVERVIEW The second (and longest) of Moses' three sermons begins in chapter 5 and ends in chapter 26. Moses begins by reviewing the Ten Commandments, the foundational expression of God's moral requirements for humanity. He then stresses the importance of loving God and passing on his law to succeeding generations. Moses realizes the need for the people of Israel to keep the law and teach future generations God's commands if they are to be what God desires of his children: an obedient people who conquer their foes in the strength God provides.

Chapter 5	Chapter 6	Chapter 7
Restating the Ten Commandments	Revealing a New Command	Repeating a Future Hope
Laws from Sinai	Law of Love	Certainty of Victory

YOUR DAILY WALK If a *god* is defined as anything that has the potential to replace God as the focus of your life, what will be the most dangerous god you encounter today at work? . . . at home? . . . on your campus? . . . in your leisure-time activities?

Idolatry is anything that cools your desire for Christ.

As Moses repeated God's law to the people, he emphasized one command: "You shall have no other gods before me" (5:7). Why that command? Because he had indelible memories of the golden calf incident at Mount Sinai. He knew the ever present danger of substituting *something* for the all-important *someone.* In addition, Moses had keen foresight. He knew the religious "climate" into which the people were about to move: a land filled with idolatry and unabashed immorality, which, if permitted, would turn the Israelites away from God.

Go back over your list of potential gods. Have you allowed one or more to take a controlling interest in your life? If so, make a note for yourself of the ones that need to be rooted out. Then invite the one true God to return to his desired (and proper) place in your life.

 INSIGHT Hear Ye, Hear Ye!
Deuteronomy 6:4 begins the celebrated Hebrew Shema ("hear"), which consists of 6:4–9, 11:13–21 and Numbers 15:37–41, and is recited twice daily by pious Jews. The command "Hear, O Israel" in some variation is repeated a total of seven times in this book (4:1; 5:1; 6:3–4; 9:1; 20:3; 27:9) to emphasize Moses' appeal for obedience on the part of the nation.

CHAPTER 5

Moses summoned all Israel and said:

Hear, O Israel, the decrees and laws I declare in your hearing today. Learn them and be sure to follow them. ²The LORD our God made a covenant with us at Horeb. ³It was not with our fathers that the LORD made this covenant, but with us, with all of us who are alive here today. ⁴The LORD spoke to you face to face out of the fire on the mountain. ⁵(At that time I stood between the LORD and you to declare to you the word of the LORD, because you were afraid of the fire and did not go up the mountain.) And he said:

⁶"I am the LORD your God, who brought you out of Egypt, out of the land of slavery.
⁷"You shall have no other gods before*k* me.
⁸"You shall not make for yourself an idol in the form of anything in heaven above or on the earth beneath or in the waters below. ⁹You shall not bow down to them or worship them; for I, the LORD your God, am a jealous God, punishing the children for the sin of the fathers to the third and fourth generation of those who hate me, ¹⁰but showing love to a thousand ⌊generations⌋ of those who love me and keep my commandments.
¹¹"You shall not misuse the name of the LORD your God, for the LORD will not hold anyone guiltless who misuses his name.
¹²"Observe the Sabbath day by keeping it holy, as the LORD your God has commanded you. ¹³Six days you shall labor and do all your work, ¹⁴but the seventh day is a Sabbath to the LORD

your God. On it you shall not do any work, neither you, nor your son or daughter, nor your manservant or maidservant, nor your ox, your donkey or any of your animals, nor the alien within your gates, so that your manservant and maidservant may rest, as you do. ¹⁵Remember that you were slaves in Egypt and that the LORD your God brought you out of there with a mighty hand and an outstretched arm. Therefore the LORD your God has commanded you to observe the Sabbath day.
¹⁶"Honor your father and your mother, as the LORD your God has commanded you, so that you may live long and that it may go well with you in the land the LORD your God is giving you.
¹⁷"You shall not murder.
¹⁸"You shall not commit adultery.
¹⁹"You shall not steal.
²⁰"You shall not give false testimony against your neighbor.
²¹"You shall not covet your neighbor's wife. You shall not set your desire on your neighbor's house or land, his manservant or maidservant, his ox or donkey, or anything that belongs to your neighbor."

²²These are the commandments the LORD proclaimed in a loud voice to your whole assembly there on the mountain from out of the fire, the cloud and the deep darkness; and he added nothing more. Then he wrote them on two stone tablets and gave them to me. ²³When you heard the voice out of the darkness, while the mountain was ablaze

k 7 Or besides

with fire, all the leading men of your tribes and your elders came to me. ²⁴And you said, "The LORD our God has shown us his glory and his majesty, and we have heard his voice from the fire. Today we have seen that a man can live even if God speaks with him. ²⁵But now, why should we die? This great fire will consume us, and we will die if we hear the voice of the LORD our God any longer. ²⁶For what mortal man has ever heard the voice of the living God speaking out of fire, as we have, and survived? ²⁷Go near and listen to all that the LORD our God says. Then tell us whatever the LORD our God tells you. We will listen and obey."

²⁸The LORD heard you when you spoke to me and the LORD said to me, "I have heard what this people said to you. Everything they said was good. ²⁹Oh, that their hearts would be inclined to fear me and keep all my commands always, so that it might go well with them and their children forever!

³⁰"Go, tell them to return to their tents. ³¹But you stay here with me so that I may give you all the commands, decrees and laws you are to teach them to follow in the land I am giving them to possess."

³²So be careful to do what the LORD your God has commanded you; do not turn aside to the right or to the left. ³³Walk in all the way that the LORD your God has commanded you, so that you may live and prosper and prolong your days in the land that you will possess.

CHAPTER 6

These are the commands, decrees and laws the LORD your God directed me to teach you to observe in the land that you are crossing the Jordan to possess, ²so that you, your children and their children after them may fear the LORD your God as long as you live by keeping all his decrees and commands that I give you, and so that you may enjoy long life. ³Hear, O Israel, and be careful to obey so that it may go well with you and that you may increase greatly in a land flowing with milk and honey, just as the LORD, the God of your fathers, promised you.

⁴Hear, O Israel: The LORD our God, the LORD is one.ˡ ⁵Love the LORD your God

with all your heart and with all your soul and with all your strength. ⁶These commandments that I give you today are to be upon your hearts. ⁷Impress them on your children. Talk about them when you sit at home and when you walk along the road, when you lie down and when you get up. ⁸Tie them as symbols on your hands and bind them on your foreheads. ⁹Write them on the doorframes of your houses and on your gates.

¹⁰When the LORD your God brings you into the land he swore to your fathers, to Abraham, Isaac and Jacob, to give you—a land with large, flourishing cities you did not build, ¹¹houses filled with all kinds of good things you did not provide, wells you did not dig, and vineyards and olive groves you did not plant—then when you eat and are satisfied, ¹²be careful that you do not forget the LORD, who brought you out of Egypt, out of the land of slavery.

¹³Fear the LORD your God, serve him only and take your oaths in his name. ¹⁴Do not follow other gods, the gods of the peoples around you; ¹⁵for the LORD your God, who is among you, is a jealous God and his anger will burn against you, and he will destroy you from the face of the land. ¹⁶Do not test the LORD your God as you did at Massah. ¹⁷Be sure to keep the commands of the LORD your God and the stipulations and decrees he has given you. ¹⁸Do what is right and good in the LORD's sight, so that it may go well with you and you may go in and take over the good land that the LORD promised on oath to your forefathers, ¹⁹thrusting out all your enemies before you, as the LORD said.

²⁰In the future, when your son asks you, "What is the meaning of the stipulations, decrees and laws the LORD our God has commanded you?" ²¹tell him: "We were slaves of Pharaoh in Egypt, but the LORD brought us out of Egypt with a mighty hand. ²²Before our eyes the LORD sent miraculous signs and wonders—great and terrible—upon Egypt and Pharaoh and his whole household. ²³But he brought us out from there to bring us in and give us the land that he promised on oath to our forefathers. ²⁴The LORD commanded us to

ˡ4 Or *The LORD our God is one LORD*; or *The LORD is our God, the LORD is one*; or *The LORD is our God, the LORD alone* obey all these decrees and to fear the LORD our God, so that we might always prosper and be kept alive, as is the case today. ²⁵And if we are careful to obey all this law before the LORD our God, as he has commanded us, that will be our righteousness."

CHAPTER 7

When the LORD your God brings you into the land you are entering to possess and drives out before you many nations—the Hittites, Girgashites, Amorites, Canaanites, Perizzites, Hivites and Jebusites, seven nations larger and stronger than you— ²and when the LORD your God has delivered them over to you and you have defeated them, then you must destroy them totally.ᵐ Make no treaty with them, and show them no mercy. ³Do not intermarry with them. Do not give your daughters to their sons or take their daughters for your sons, ⁴for they will turn your sons away from following me to serve other gods, and the LORD's anger will burn against you and will quickly destroy you. ⁵This is what you are to do to them: Break down their altars, smash their sacred stones, cut down their Asherah polesⁿ and burn their idols in the fire. ⁶For you are a people holy to the LORD your God. The LORD your God has chosen you out of all the peoples on the face of the earth to be his people, his treasured possession.

⁷The LORD did not set his affection on you and choose you because you were more numerous than other peoples, for you were the fewest of all peoples. ⁸But it was because the LORD loved you and kept the oath he swore to your forefathers that he brought you out with a mighty hand and redeemed you from the land of slavery, from the power of Pharaoh king of Egypt. ⁹Know therefore that the LORD your God is God; he is the faithful God, keeping his covenant of love to a thousand generations of those who love him and keep his commands. ¹⁰But

those who hate him he will repay to
their face by destruction;
he will not be slow to repay to their
face those who hate him.

¹¹Therefore, take care to follow the commands, decrees and laws I give you today. ¹²If you pay attention to these laws and are careful to follow them, then the LORD your God will keep his covenant of love with you, as he swore to your forefathers. ¹³He will love you and bless you and increase your numbers. He will bless the fruit of your womb, the crops of your land—your grain, new wine and oil—the calves of your herds and the lambs of your flocks in the land that he swore to your forefathers to give you. ¹⁴You will be blessed more than any other people; none of your men or women will be childless, nor any of your livestock without young. ¹⁵The LORD will keep you free from every disease. He will not inflict on you the horrible diseases you knew in Egypt, but he will inflict them on all who hate you. ¹⁶You must destroy all the peoples the LORD your God gives over to you. Do not look on them with pity and do not serve their gods, for that will be a snare to you.

¹⁷You may say to yourselves, "These nations are stronger than we are. How can we drive them out?" ¹⁸But do not be afraid of them; remember well what the LORD your God did to Pharaoh and to all Egypt. ¹⁹You saw with your own eyes the great trials, the miraculous signs and wonders, the mighty hand and outstretched arm, with which the LORD your God brought you out. The LORD your God will do the same to all the peoples you now fear. ²⁰Moreover, the LORD your God will send the hornet among them until even the survivors who hide from you have perished. ²¹Do not be terrified by them, for the LORD your God, who is among you, is a great and awesome God. ²²The LORD your God will drive out those nations before you, little by little. You will not be allowed to eliminate them all at once, or the wild animals will multiply around you. ²³But the LORD your God will deliver them over to you, throwing them into great confusion until they are destroyed. ²⁴He will give their kings into your hand, and you will wipe out their names from under heaven. No one will be able to stand up against you; you will destroy them. ²⁵The images of their gods you are to burn in the fire. Do not covet

---

ᵐ2 The Hebrew term refers to the irrevocable giving over of things or persons to the LORD, often by totally destroying them; also in verse 26.   ⁿ5 That is, symbols of the goddess Asherah; here and elsewhere in Deuteronomy the silver and gold on them, and do not take it for yourselves, or you will be ensnared by it, for it is detestable to the LORD your God. ²⁶Do not bring a detestable thing into your house or you, like it, will be set apart for destruction. Utterly abhor and detest it, for it is set apart for destruction.

FEBRUARY 23 □ DAY 54
DEUTERONOMY 8–11
Remembering Lessons in Obedience

OVERVIEW Moses continues his second sermon by calling upon Israel to remember God's miraculous care throughout the desert experience. As he provided abundantly in the past, so he will provide in the future. But Israel must not forget its sinful past—especially the golden calf incident and its tragic consequences. The choice is Israel's to make. If she will love and obey, God will shower her with blessings; if she rebels, God's judgment must surely follow.

Chapter 8	Chapter 9	Chapters 10–11
Remember the Lord's Provision	Remember Israel's Provocation	Respond with Obedience
God's Part	Moses' Part	The Nation's Part

YOUR DAILY WALK The descendants of Anak were a race of giants greatly feared by the Israelites. When the spies made their report about the promised land (Numbers 13:26–33), it included two specific references to the Anakites: first, an observation that was true ("We even saw descendants of Anak there," Numbers 13:28); second, an interpretation that was false ("We can't attack those people; they are stronger than we are," Numbers 13:31). For forty years these towering giants had stood as a taunting symbol of the nation's unbelief. So tall and formidable were they that the nation had coined a saying, "Who can stand up against the Anakites?" (Deuteronomy 9:2). But Moses assured the Israelites that God specializes in dealing with Anakites! God would go before his people to destroy the giants and give the Israelites the land as he had promised.

When your heart is filled with faith, there is no room left for fear.

Where are you facing "Anakites" in your life? What impossible situation seems to stand squarely in the way of your spiritual progress? God's word to Israel is also aimed at you: "The LORD your God is the one who goes across ahead of you like a devouring fire" (9:3). Stop by a grocery store today, and buy a giant-sized box of something you need, as a token of your faith in God to handle your "giant-sized" situation.

INSIGHT Phylacteries—A "Binding" Practice
The Pharisees of Jesus' day (and orthodox Jews of today) practiced Deuteronomy 11:18 by tying phylacteries, small receptacles containing verses of Scripture, to their foreheads and left arms during morning prayers.

CHAPTER 8

Be careful to follow every command I am giving you today, so that you may live and increase and may enter and possess the land that the LORD promised on oath to your forefathers. ²Remember how the LORD your God led you all the way in the desert these forty years, to humble you and to test you in order to know what was in your heart, whether or not you would keep his commands. ³He humbled you, causing you to hunger and then feeding you with manna, which neither you nor your fathers had known, to teach you that man does not live on bread alone but on every word that comes from the mouth of the LORD. ⁴Your clothes did not wear out and your feet did not swell during these forty years. ⁵Know then in your heart that as a man disciplines his son, so the LORD your God disciplines you.

⁶Observe the commands of the LORD your God, walking in his ways and revering him. ⁷For the LORD your God is bringing you into a good land—a land with streams and pools of water, with springs flowing in the valleys and hills; ⁸a land with wheat and barley, vines and fig trees, pomegranates, olive oil and honey; ⁹a land where bread will not be scarce and you will lack nothing; a land where the rocks are iron and you can dig copper out of the hills.

¹⁰When you have eaten and are satisfied, praise the LORD your God for the good land he has given you. ¹¹Be careful that you do not forget the LORD your God, failing to observe his commands, his laws and his decrees that I am giving you this day. ¹²Otherwise, when you eat and are satisfied, when you build fine houses and settle down, ¹³and when your herds and flocks grow large and your silver and gold increase and all you have is multiplied, ¹⁴then your heart will become proud and you will forget the LORD your God, who brought you out of Egypt, out of the land of slavery. ¹⁵He led you through the vast and dreadful desert, that thirsty and waterless land, with its venomous snakes and scorpions. He brought you water out of hard rock. ¹⁶He gave you manna to eat in the desert, something your fathers had never known, to humble and to test you so that in the end it might go well with you. ¹⁷You may say to yourself, "My power and the strength of my hands have produced this wealth for me." ¹⁸But remember the LORD your God, for it is he who gives you the ability to produce wealth, and so confirms his covenant, which he swore to your forefathers, as it is today.

¹⁹If you ever forget the LORD your God and follow other gods and worship and bow down to them, I testify against you today that you will surely be destroyed. ²⁰Like the nations the LORD destroyed before you, so you will be destroyed for not obeying the LORD your God.

CHAPTER 9

Hear, O Israel. You are now about to cross the Jordan to go in and dispossess nations greater and stronger than you, with large cities that have walls up to the sky. ²The people are strong and tall—Anakites! You know about them and have heard it said: "Who can stand up against the Anakites?" ³But be assured today that the LORD your God is the one who goes across ahead of you like a devouring fire. He will destroy them; he will subdue them before you. And you will drive them out and annihilate them quickly, as the LORD has promised you.

⁴After the LORD your God has driven them out before you, do not say to yourself, "The LORD has brought me here to take possession of this land because of my righteousness." No, it is on account of the wickedness of these nations that the LORD is going to drive them out before you. ⁵It is not because of your righteousness or your integrity that you are going in to take possession of their land; but on account of the wickedness of these nations, the LORD your God will drive them out before you, to accomplish what he swore to your fathers, to Abraham, Isaac and Jacob. ⁶Understand, then, that it is not because of your righteousness that the LORD your God is giving you this good land to possess, for you are a stiff-necked people.

⁷Remember this and never forget how you provoked the LORD your God to anger in the desert. From the day you left Egypt until you arrived here, you have been rebellious against the LORD. ⁸At Horeb you aroused the LORD's wrath so that he was angry enough to destroy you. ⁹When I went up on the mountain to receive the tablets of stone, the tablets of the covenant

that the LORD had made with you, I stayed on the mountain forty days and forty nights; I ate no bread and drank no water. [10]The LORD gave me two stone tablets inscribed by the finger of God. On them were all the commandments the LORD proclaimed to you on the mountain out of the fire, on the day of the assembly.

[11]At the end of the forty days and forty nights, the LORD gave me the two stone tablets, the tablets of the covenant. [12]Then the LORD told me, "Go down from here at once, because your people whom you brought out of Egypt have become corrupt. They have turned away quickly from what I commanded them and have made a cast idol for themselves."

[13]And the LORD said to me, "I have seen this people, and they are a stiff-necked people indeed! [14]Let me alone, so that I may destroy them and blot out their name from under heaven. And I will make you into a nation stronger and more numerous than they."

[15]So I turned and went down from the mountain while it was ablaze with fire. And the two tablets of the covenant were in my hands.[o] [16]When I looked, I saw that you had sinned against the LORD your God; you had made for yourselves an idol cast in the shape of a calf. You had turned aside quickly from the way that the LORD had commanded you. [17]So I took the two tablets and threw them out of my hands, breaking them to pieces before your eyes.

[18]Then once again I fell prostrate before the LORD for forty days and forty nights; I ate no bread and drank no water, because of all the sin you had committed, doing what was evil in the LORD's sight and so provoking him to anger. [19]I feared the anger and wrath of the LORD, for he was angry enough with you to destroy you. But again the LORD listened to me. [20]And the LORD was angry enough with Aaron to destroy him, but at that time I prayed for Aaron too. [21]Also I took that sinful thing of yours, the calf you had made, and burned it in the fire. Then I crushed it and ground it to powder as fine as dust and threw the dust into a stream that flowed down the mountain.

[22]You also made the LORD angry at Tab-

erah, at Massah and at Kibroth Hattaavah.

[23]And when the LORD sent you out from Kadesh Barnea, he said, "Go up and take possession of the land I have given you." But you rebelled against the command of the LORD your God. You did not trust him or obey him. [24]You have been rebellious against the LORD ever since I have known you.

[25]I lay prostrate before the LORD those forty days and forty nights because the LORD had said he would destroy you. [26]I prayed to the LORD and said, "O Sovereign LORD, do not destroy your people, your own inheritance that you redeemed by your great power and brought out of Egypt with a mighty hand. [27]Remember your servants Abraham, Isaac and Jacob. Overlook the stubbornness of this people, their wickedness and their sin. [28]Otherwise, the country from which you brought us will say, 'Because the LORD was not able to take them into the land he had promised them, and because he hated them, he brought them out to put them to death in the desert.' [29]But they are your people, your inheritance that you brought out by your great power and your outstretched arm."

CHAPTER 10

At that time the LORD said to me, "Chisel out two stone tablets like the first ones and come up to me on the mountain. Also make a wooden chest.[p] [2]I will write on the tablets the words that were on the first tablets, which you broke. Then you are to put them in the chest."

[3]So I made the ark out of acacia wood and chiseled out two stone tablets like the first ones, and I went up on the mountain with the two tablets in my hands. [4]The LORD wrote on these tablets what he had written before, the Ten Commandments he had proclaimed to you on the mountain, out of the fire, on the day of the assembly. And the LORD gave them to me. [5]Then I came back down the mountain and put the tablets in the ark I had made, as the LORD commanded me, and they are there now.

[6](The Israelites traveled from the wells of the Jaakanites to Moserah. There Aaron

died and was buried, and Eleazar his son succeeded him as priest. [7]From there they traveled to Gudgodah and on to Jotbathah, a land with streams of water. [8]At that time the LORD set apart the tribe of Levi to carry the ark of the covenant of the LORD, to stand before the LORD to minister and to pronounce blessings in his name, as they still do today. [9]That is why the Levites have no share or inheritance among their brothers; the LORD is their inheritance, as the LORD your God told them.)

[10]Now I had stayed on the mountain forty days and nights, as I did the first time, and the LORD listened to me at this time also. It was not his will to destroy you. [11]"Go," the LORD said to me, "and lead the people on their way, so that they may enter and possess the land that I swore to their fathers to give them."

[12]And now, O Israel, what does the LORD your God ask of you but to fear the LORD your God, to walk in all his ways, to love him, to serve the LORD your God with all your heart and with all your soul, [13]and to observe the LORD's commands and decrees that I am giving you today for your own good?

[14]To the LORD your God belong the heavens, even the highest heavens, the earth and everything in it. [15]Yet the LORD set his affection on your forefathers and loved them, and he chose you, their descendants, above all the nations, as it is today. [16]Circumcise your hearts, therefore, and do not be stiff-necked any longer. [17]For the LORD your God is God of gods and Lord of lords, the great God, mighty and awesome, who shows no partiality and accepts no bribes. [18]He defends the cause of the fatherless and the widow, and loves the alien, giving him food and clothing. [19]And you are to love those who are aliens, for you yourselves were aliens in Egypt. [20]Fear the LORD your God and serve him. Hold fast to him and take your oaths in his name. [21]He is your praise; he is your God, who performed for you those great and awesome wonders you saw with your own eyes. [22]Your forefathers who went down into Egypt were seventy in all, and now the LORD your God has made you as numerous as the stars in the sky.

CHAPTER 11

Love the LORD your God and keep his requirements, his decrees, his laws and his commands always. [2]Remember today that your children were not the ones who saw and experienced the discipline of the LORD your God: his majesty, his mighty hand, his outstretched arm; [3]the signs he performed and the things he did in the heart of Egypt, both to Pharaoh king of Egypt and to his whole country; [4]what he did to the Egyptian army, to its horses and chariots, how he overwhelmed them with the waters of the Red Sea[q] as they were pursuing you, and how the LORD brought lasting ruin on them. [5]It was not your children who saw what he did for you in the desert until you arrived at this place, [6]and what he did to Dathan and Abiram, sons of Eliab the Reubenite, when the earth opened its mouth right in the middle of all Israel and swallowed them up with their households, their tents and every living thing that belonged to them. [7]But it was your own eyes that saw all these great things the LORD has done.

[8]Observe therefore all the commands I am giving you today, so that you may have the strength to go in and take over the land that you are crossing the Jordan to possess, [9]and so that you may live long in the land that the LORD swore to your forefathers to give to them and their descendants, a land flowing with milk and honey. [10]The land you are entering to take over is not like the land of Egypt, from which you have come, where you planted your seed and irrigated it by foot as in a vegetable garden. [11]But the land you are crossing the Jordan to take possession of is a land of mountains and valleys that drinks rain from heaven. [12]It is a land the LORD your God cares for; the eyes of the LORD your God are continually on it from the beginning of the year to its end.

[13]So if you faithfully obey the commands I am giving you today—to love the LORD your God and to serve him with all your heart and with all your soul— [14]then I will send rain on your land in its season, both autumn and spring rains, so that you may gather in your grain, new wine and oil. [15]I will provide grass in the fields for your cattle, and you will eat and be satisfied.

---

[q]4 Hebrew *Yam Suph*; that is, Sea of Reeds

¹⁶Be careful, or you will be enticed to turn away and worship other gods and bow down to them. ¹⁷Then the LORD's anger will burn against you, and he will shut the heavens so that it will not rain and the ground will yield no produce, and you will soon perish from the good land the LORD is giving you. ¹⁸Fix these words of mine in your hearts and minds; tie them as symbols on your hands and bind them on your foreheads. ¹⁹Teach them to your children, talking about them when you sit at home and when you walk along the road, when you lie down and when you get up. ²⁰Write them on the doorframes of your houses and on your gates, ²¹so that your days and the days of your children may be many in the land that the LORD swore to give your forefathers, as many as the days that the heavens are above the earth.

²²If you carefully observe all these commands I am giving you to follow—to love the LORD your God, to walk in all his ways and to hold fast to him— ²³then the LORD will drive out all these nations before you, and you will dispossess nations larger and stronger than you. ²⁴Every place where you set your foot will be yours: Your territory will extend from the desert to Lebanon, and from the Euphrates River to the western sea.ʳ ²⁵No man will be able to stand against you. The LORD your God, as he promised you, will put the terror and fear of you on the whole land, wherever you go.

²⁶See, I am setting before you today a blessing and a curse— ²⁷the blessing if you obey the commands of the LORD your God that I am giving you today; ²⁸the curse if you disobey the commands of the LORD your God and turn from the way that I command you today by following other gods, which you have not known. ²⁹When the LORD your God has brought you into the land you are entering to possess, you are to proclaim on Mount Gerizim the blessings, and on Mount Ebal the curses. ³⁰As you know, these mountains are across the Jordan, west of the road,ˢ toward the setting sun, near the great trees of Moreh, in the territory of those Canaanites living in the Arabah in the vicinity of Gilgal. ³¹You are about to cross the Jordan to enter and take possession of the land the LORD your God is giving you. When you have taken it over and are living there, ³²be sure that you obey all the decrees and laws I am setting before you today.

ʳ24 That is, the Mediterranean   ˢ30 Or Jordan, westward

FEBRUARY 24 ☐ DAY 55
DEUTERONOMY 12–16
Religious Laws for Canaan

 OVERVIEW From the general principles of the law and exhortations to obedience, Moses now moves to more specific regulations governing life in the promised land. God himself would specify the place and manner of worship, and Israel must reject all idolatrous practices. Purity, tithing, release from debt and servanthood are all ways in which Israel can demonstrate her unique relationship with God. And the nation must be careful to observe all the feast days that mark important events in her miraculous history.

Chapter 12	Chapter 13	Chapter 14	Chapter 15	Chapter 16
Regulations for a Holy Land Involving				
Offerings	False Gods	Food	Finances	Feasts
"Obey . . . all these regulations . . . that it may always go well with you" (12:28).				

YOUR DAILY WALK Today pierced ears are considered by some to be highly fashionable. But in Israel ears were pierced for a vastly different reason!

Service is the overflow of superabounding devotion.

In today's reading Moses gives instructions concerning the release of servants after a six-year period. Once in a while there arose a situation in which a servant so loved his master that he did not wish to be set free. He would prefer to remain under his master's protection, devoted to his work, rather than to set out on his own. As a perpetual sign of this new relationship, the master would pierce the servant's ear, thereby proclaiming to the world: "This is my beloved servant; I am perpetually his beloved master."

In Psalm 40, David picks up this image: "Sacrifice and offering you did not desire, but my ears you have pierced; . . . I desire to do your will, O my God" (40:6, 8).

What about your ears? Have they been pierced yet for the Lord? Are you the property of the Father, ready to do his will as a loving servant? If not, give God your ears—and life—right now!

INSIGHT "You Are Not to Do as We Do Here Today" (12:8) The disruption of life caused by the conquest of the land east of the Jordan may have made orderly worship impossible. This verse may have been intended to prohibit the use of private altars for worship or sacrifice. Once in the land, only one place of worship would be sanctioned: the tabernacle in Jerusalem.

CHAPTER 12

These are the decrees and laws you must be careful to follow in the land that the LORD, the God of your fathers, has given you to possess—as long as you live in the land. ²Destroy completely all the places on the high mountains and on the hills and under every spreading tree where the nations you are dispossessing worship their gods. ³Break down their altars, smash their sacred stones and burn their Asherah poles in the fire; cut down the idols of their gods and wipe out their names from those places.

⁴You must not worship the LORD your God in their way. ⁵But you are to seek the place the LORD your God will choose from among all your tribes to put his Name there for his dwelling. To that place you must go; ⁶there bring your burnt offerings and sacrifices, your tithes and special gifts, what you have vowed to give and your freewill offerings, and the firstborn of your herds and flocks. ⁷There, in the presence of the LORD your God, you and your families shall eat and shall rejoice in everything you have put your hand to, because the LORD your God has blessed you.

⁸You are not to do as we do here today, everyone as he sees fit, ⁹since you have not yet reached the resting place and the inheritance the LORD your God is giving

you. ¹⁰But you will cross the Jordan and settle in the land the LORD your God is giving you as an inheritance, and he will give you rest from all your enemies around you so that you will live in safety. ¹¹Then to the place the LORD your God will choose as a dwelling for his Name— there you are to bring everything I command you: your burnt offerings and sacrifices, your tithes and special gifts, and all the choice possessions you have vowed to the LORD. ¹²And there rejoice before the LORD your God, you, your sons and daughters, your menservants and maidservants, and the Levites from your towns, who have no allotment or inheritance of their own. ¹³Be careful not to sacrifice your burnt offerings anywhere you please. ¹⁴Offer them only at the place the LORD will choose in one of your tribes, and there observe everything I command you.

¹⁵Nevertheless, you may slaughter your animals in any of your towns and eat as much of the meat as you want, as if it were gazelle or deer, according to the blessing the LORD your God gives you. Both the ceremonially unclean and the clean may eat it. ¹⁶But you must not eat the blood; pour it out on the ground like water. ¹⁷You must not eat in your own towns the tithe of your grain and new wine and oil, or the firstborn of your herds and flocks, or whatever you have

vowed to give, or your freewill offerings or special gifts. [18]Instead, you are to eat them in the presence of the LORD your God at the place the LORD your God will choose—you, your sons and daughters, your menservants and maidservants, and the Levites from your towns—and you are to rejoice before the LORD your God in everything you put your hand to. [19]Be careful not to neglect the Levites as long as you live in your land.

[20]When the LORD your God has enlarged your territory as he promised you, and you crave meat and say, "I would like some meat," then you may eat as much of it as you want. [21]If the place where the LORD your God chooses to put his Name is too far away from you, you may slaughter animals from the herds and flocks the LORD has given you, as I have commanded you, and in your own towns you may eat as much of them as you want. [22]Eat them as you would gazelle or deer. Both the ceremonially unclean and the clean may eat. [23]But be sure you do not eat the blood, because the blood is the life, and you must not eat the life with the meat. [24]You must not eat the blood; pour it out on the ground like water. [25]Do not eat it, so that it may go well with you and your children after you, because you will be doing what is right in the eyes of the LORD.

[26]But take your consecrated things and whatever you have vowed to give, and go to the place the LORD will choose. [27]Present your burnt offerings on the altar of the LORD your God, both the meat and the blood. The blood of your sacrifices must be poured beside the altar of the LORD your God, but you may eat the meat. [28]Be careful to obey all these regulations I am giving you, so that it may always go well with you and your children after you, because you will be doing what is good and right in the eyes of the LORD your God.

[29]The LORD your God will cut off before you the nations you are about to invade and dispossess. But when you have driven them out and settled in their land, [30]and after they have been destroyed before you, be careful not to be ensnared by inquiring about their gods, saying, "How do these nations serve their gods? We will do the same." [31]You must not worship the LORD your God in their way, because in worshiping their gods, they do all kinds of detestable things the LORD hates. They even burn their sons and daughters in the fire as sacrifices to their gods.

[32]See that you do all I command you; do not add to it or take away from it.

CHAPTER 13

If a prophet, or one who foretells by dreams, appears among you and announces to you a miraculous sign or wonder, [2]and if the sign or wonder of which he has spoken takes place, and he says, "Let us follow other gods" (gods you have not known) "and let us worship them," [3]you must not listen to the words of that prophet or dreamer. The LORD your God is testing you to find out whether you love him with all your heart and with all your soul. [4]It is the LORD your God you must follow, and him you must revere. Keep his commands and obey him; serve him and hold fast to him. [5]That prophet or dreamer must be put to death, because he preached rebellion against the LORD your God, who brought you out of Egypt and redeemed you from the land of slavery; he has tried to turn you from the way the LORD your God commanded you to follow. You must purge the evil from among you.

[6]If your very own brother, or your son or daughter, or the wife you love, or your closest friend secretly entices you, saying, "Let us go and worship other gods" (gods that neither you nor your fathers have known, [7]gods of the peoples around you, whether near or far, from one end of the land to the other), [8]do not yield to him or listen to him. Show him no pity. Do not spare him or shield him. [9]You must certainly put him to death. Your hand must be the first in putting him to death, and then the hands of all the people. [10]Stone him to death, because he tried to turn you away from the LORD your God, who brought you out of Egypt, out of the land of slavery. [11]Then all Israel will hear and be afraid, and no one among you will do such an evil thing again.

[12]If you hear it said about one of the towns the LORD your God is giving you to live in [13]that wicked men have arisen among you and have led the people of their town astray, saying, "Let us go and worship other gods" (gods you have not known), [14]then you must inquire, probe and investigate it thoroughly. And if it is

true and it has been proved that this detestable thing has been done among you, [15]you must certainly put to the sword all who live in that town. Destroy it completely,[t] both its people and its livestock. [16]Gather all the plunder of the town into the middle of the public square and completely burn the town and all its plunder as a whole burnt offering to the LORD your God. It is to remain a ruin forever, never to be rebuilt. [17]None of those condemned things[t] shall be found in your hands, so that the LORD will turn from his fierce anger; he will show you mercy, have compassion on you, and increase your numbers, as he promised on oath to your forefathers, [18]because you obey the LORD your God, keeping all his commands that I am giving you today and doing what is right in his eyes.

CHAPTER 14

You are the children of the LORD your God. Do not cut yourselves or shave the front of your heads for the dead, [2]for you are a people holy to the LORD your God. Out of all the peoples on the face of the earth, the LORD has chosen you to be his treasured possession.

[3]Do not eat any detestable thing. [4]These are the animals you may eat: the ox, the sheep, the goat, [5]the deer, the gazelle, the roe deer, the wild goat, the ibex, the antelope and the mountain sheep.[u] [6]You may eat any animal that has a split hoof divided in two and that chews the cud. [7]However, of those that chew the cud or that have a split hoof completely divided you may not eat the camel, the rabbit or the coney.[v] Although they chew the cud, they do not have a split hoof; they are ceremonially unclean for you. [8]The pig is also unclean; although it has a split hoof, it does not chew the cud. You are not to eat their meat or touch their carcasses.

[9]Of all the creatures living in the water, you may eat any that has fins and scales. [10]But anything that does not have fins and scales you may not eat; for you it is unclean.

[11]You may eat any clean bird. [12]But these you may not eat: the eagle, the vulture, the black vulture, [13]the red kite, the black kite, any kind of falcon, [14]any kind

of raven, [15]the horned owl, the screech owl, the gull, any kind of hawk, [16]the little owl, the great owl, the white owl, [17]the desert owl, the osprey, the cormorant, [18]the stork, any kind of heron, the hoopoe and the bat.

[19]All flying insects that swarm are unclean to you; do not eat them. [20]But any winged creature that is clean you may eat.

[21]Do not eat anything you find already dead. You may give it to an alien living in any of your towns, and he may eat it, or you may sell it to a foreigner. But you are a people holy to the LORD your God.

Do not cook a young goat in its mother's milk.

[22]Be sure to set aside a tenth of all that your fields produce each year. [23]Eat the tithe of your grain, new wine and oil, and the firstborn of your herds and flocks in the presence of the LORD your God at the place he will choose as a dwelling for his Name, so that you may learn to revere the LORD your God always. [24]But if that place is too distant and you have been blessed by the LORD your God and cannot carry your tithe (because the place where the LORD will choose to put his Name is so far away), [25]then exchange your tithe for silver, and take the silver with you and go to the place the LORD your God will choose. [26]Use the silver to buy whatever you like: cattle, sheep, wine or other fermented drink, or anything you wish. Then you and your household shall eat there in the presence of the LORD your God and rejoice. [27]And do not neglect the Levites living in your towns, for they have no allotment or inheritance of their own.

[28]At the end of every three years, bring all the tithes of that year's produce and store it in your towns, [29]so that the Levites (who have no allotment or inheritance of their own) and the aliens, the fatherless and the widows who live in your towns may come and eat and be satisfied, and so that the LORD your God may bless you in all the work of your hands.

CHAPTER 15

At the end of every seven years you must cancel debts. [2]This is how it is to be done: Every creditor shall cancel the loan he has made to his fellow Israelite. He shall not

---

[t]15,17 The Hebrew term refers to the irrevocable giving over of things or persons to the LORD, often by totally destroying them.   [u]5 The precise identification of some of the birds and animals in this chapter is uncertain.   [v]7 That is, the hyrax or rock badger

require payment from his fellow Israelite or brother, because the LORD's time for canceling debts has been proclaimed. ³You may require payment from a foreigner, but you must cancel any debt your brother owes you. ⁴However, there should be no poor among you, for in the land the LORD your God is giving you to possess as your inheritance, he will richly bless you, ⁵if only you fully obey the LORD your God and are careful to follow all these commands I am giving you today. ⁶For the LORD your God will bless you as he has promised, and you will lend to many nations but will borrow from none. You will rule over many nations but none will rule over you.

⁷If there is a poor man among your brothers in any of the towns of the land that the LORD your God is giving you, do not be hardhearted or tightfisted toward your poor brother. ⁸Rather be openhanded and freely lend him whatever he needs. ⁹Be careful not to harbor this wicked thought: "The seventh year, the year for canceling debts, is near," so that you do not show ill will toward your needy brother and give him nothing. He may then appeal to the LORD against you, and you will be found guilty of sin. ¹⁰Give generously to him and do so without a grudging heart; then because of this the LORD your God will bless you in all your work and in everything you put your hand to. ¹¹There will always be poor people in the land. Therefore I command you to be openhanded toward your brothers and toward the poor and needy in your land.

¹²If a fellow Hebrew, a man or a woman, sells himself to you and serves you six years, in the seventh year you must let him go free. ¹³And when you release him, do not send him away emptyhanded. ¹⁴Supply him liberally from your flock, your threshing floor and your winepress. Give to him as the LORD your God has blessed you. ¹⁵Remember that you were slaves in Egypt and the LORD your God redeemed you. That is why I give you this command today.

¹⁶But if your servant says to you, "I do not want to leave you," because he loves you and your family and is well off with you, ¹⁷then take an awl and push it through his ear lobe into the door, and he will become your servant for life. Do the same for your maidservant.

¹⁸Do not consider it a hardship to set your servant free, because his service to you these six years has been worth twice as much as that of a hired hand. And the LORD your God will bless you in everything you do.

¹⁹Set apart for the LORD your God every firstborn male of your herds and flocks. Do not put the firstborn of your oxen to work, and do not shear the firstborn of your sheep. ²⁰Each year you and your family are to eat them in the presence of the LORD your God at the place he will choose. ²¹If an animal has a defect, is lame or blind, or has any serious flaw, you must not sacrifice it to the LORD your God. ²²You are to eat it in your own towns. Both the ceremonially unclean and the clean may eat it, as if it were gazelle or deer. ²³But you must not eat the blood; pour it out on the ground like water.

CHAPTER 16

Observe the month of Abib and celebrate the Passover of the LORD your God, because in the month of Abib he brought you out of Egypt by night. ²Sacrifice as the Passover to the LORD your God an animal from your flock or herd at the place the LORD will choose as a dwelling for his Name. ³Do not eat it with bread made with yeast, but for seven days eat unleavened bread, the bread of affliction, because you left Egypt in haste—so that all the days of your life you may remember the time of your departure from Egypt. ⁴Let no yeast be found in your possession in all your land for seven days. Do not let any of the meat you sacrifice on the evening of the first day remain until morning.

⁵You must not sacrifice the Passover in any town the LORD your God gives you ⁶except in the place he will choose as a dwelling for his Name. There you must sacrifice the Passover in the evening, when the sun goes down, on the anniversaryʷ of your departure from Egypt. ⁷Roast it and eat it at the place the LORD your God will choose. Then in the morning return to your tents. ⁸For six days eat unleavened bread and on the seventh day

ʷ6 Or down, at the time of day

hold an assembly to the LORD your God and do no work.

⁹Count off seven weeks from the time you begin to put the sickle to the standing grain. ¹⁰Then celebrate the Feast of Weeks to the LORD your God by giving a freewill offering in proportion to the blessings the LORD your God has given you. ¹¹And rejoice before the LORD your God at the place he will choose as a dwelling for his Name—you, your sons and daughters, your menservants and maidservants, the Levites in your towns, and the aliens, the fatherless and the widows living among you. ¹²Remember that you were slaves in Egypt, and follow carefully these decrees.

¹³Celebrate the Feast of Tabernacles for seven days after you have gathered the produce of your threshing floor and your winepress. ¹⁴Be joyful at your Feast—you, your sons and daughters, your menservants and maidservants, and the Levites, the aliens, the fatherless and the widows who live in your towns. ¹⁵For seven days celebrate the Feast to the LORD your God at the place the LORD will choose. For the LORD your God will bless you in all your harvest and in all the work of your hands, and your joy will be complete.

¹⁶Three times a year all your men must appear before the LORD your God at the place he will choose: at the Feast of Unleavened Bread, the Feast of Weeks and the Feast of Tabernacles. No man should appear before the LORD empty-handed: ¹⁷Each of you must bring a gift in proportion to the way the LORD your God has blessed you.

¹⁸Appoint judges and officials for each of your tribes in every town the LORD your God is giving you, and they shall judge the people fairly. ¹⁹Do not pervert justice or show partiality. Do not accept a bribe, for a bribe blinds the eyes of the wise and twists the words of the righteous. ²⁰Follow justice and justice alone, so that you may live and possess the land the LORD your God is giving you.

²¹Do not set up any wooden Asherah pole˟ beside the altar you build to the LORD your God, ²²and do not erect a sacred stone, for these the LORD your God hates.

˟21 Or *Do not plant any tree dedicated to Asherah*

FEBRUARY 25 □ DAY 56
DEUTERONOMY 17–20
Civil Laws for Canaan

OVERVIEW Because Israel was a civil society as well as a religious community, laws governing national affairs were as vital as religious statutes. In today's reading Moses delivers a set of regulations providing for justice and impartiality in the settling of a wide variety of situations that might arise in the life of the nation. Included are laws governing kings, priests and prophets; peacetime and war; national and international affairs; the guilty and the innocent.

Chapter 17	Chapter 18	Chapter 19	Chapter 20
Choosing a King	Testing a Prophet	Providing a Refuge	Waging a War
National Affairs			International Affairs

YOUR DAILY WALK "Now, I don't know if this is true or not, but did you hear about so-and-so . . . ?"

　　If you've ever been the subject of such talk, you know the pain and destructiveness of hearsay. God hates rumor, hearsay and gossip. That's why he designated a system of justice in Israel whereby no

Envy is usually the mother of gossip. action could be taken against an accused person until two or three witnesses had testified to the truthfulness of the accusation (17:6–7). This law required a thorough investigation and gave the accused the right to be confronted by his accusers. The system was so effective that it became standard practice in the New Testament for handling church discipline (2 Corinthians 13:1). Jesus reaffirmed the Old Testament law when he said, "If your brother sins against you, go and show him his fault, just between the two of you. . . . But if he will not listen, take one or two others along, so that 'every matter may be established by the testimony of two or three witnesses' " (Matthew 18:15–16).

God's principle is clear: You are responsible to investigate a charge of wrongdoing against a fellow Christian before acting on it or telling someone else about it. Find an electrical fuse and carry it with you today as a reminder to "short-circuit" rumors and hearsay before they cause a "power failure" in your spiritual life!

INSIGHT The Motive behind the Monarch (17:14)
Although Israel's request for a king would seem harmless enough, 1 Samuel 8:4–9 reveals that this desire for a human king was indicative of Israel's refusal to retain God as her true King.

CHAPTER 17

Do not sacrifice to the LORD your God an ox or a sheep that has any defect or flaw in it, for that would be detestable to him.

²If a man or woman living among you in one of the towns the LORD gives you is found doing evil in the eyes of the LORD your God in violation of his covenant, ³and contrary to my command has worshiped other gods, bowing down to them or to the sun or the moon or the stars of the sky, ⁴and this has been brought to your attention, then you must investigate it thoroughly. If it is true and it has been proved that this detestable thing has been done in Israel, ⁵take the man or woman who has done this evil deed to your city gate and stone that person to death. ⁶On the testimony of two or three witnesses a man shall be put to death, but no one shall be put to death on the testimony of only one witness. ⁷The hands of the witnesses must be the first in putting him to death, and then the hands of all the people. You must purge the evil from among you.

⁸If cases come before your courts that are too difficult for you to judge—whether bloodshed, lawsuits or assaults—take them to the place the LORD your God will choose. ⁹Go to the priests, who are Levites, and to the judge who is in office at that time. Inquire of them and they will give you the verdict. ¹⁰You must act according to the decisions they give you at the place the LORD will choose. Be careful

to do everything they direct you to do. ¹¹Act according to the law they teach you and the decisions they give you. Do not turn aside from what they tell you, to the right or to the left. ¹²The man who shows contempt for the judge or for the priest who stands ministering there to the LORD your God must be put to death. You must purge the evil from Israel. ¹³All the people will hear and be afraid, and will not be contemptuous again.

¹⁴When you enter the land the LORD your God is giving you and have taken possession of it and settled in it, and you say, "Let us set a king over us like all the nations around us," ¹⁵be sure to appoint over you the king the LORD your God chooses. He must be from among your own brothers. Do not place a foreigner over you, one who is not a brother Israelite. ¹⁶The king, moreover, must not acquire great numbers of horses for himself or make the people return to Egypt to get more of them, for the LORD has told you, "You are not to go back that way again." ¹⁷He must not take many wives, or his heart will be led astray. He must not accumulate large amounts of silver and gold.

¹⁸When he takes the throne of his kingdom, he is to write for himself on a scroll a copy of this law, taken from that of the priests, who are Levites. ¹⁹It is to be with him, and he is to read it all the days of his life so that he may learn to revere the LORD his God and follow carefully all the words

of this law and these decrees [20]and not consider himself better than his brothers and turn from the law to the right or to the left. Then he and his descendants will reign a long time over his kingdom in Israel.

CHAPTER 18

The priests, who are Levites—indeed the whole tribe of Levi—are to have no allotment or inheritance with Israel. They shall live on the offerings made to the LORD by fire, for that is their inheritance. [2]They shall have no inheritance among their brothers; the LORD is their inheritance, as he promised them.

[3]This is the share due the priests from the people who sacrifice a bull or a sheep: the shoulder, the jowls and the inner parts. [4]You are to give them the firstfruits of your grain, new wine and oil, and the first wool from the shearing of your sheep, [5]for the LORD your God has chosen them and their descendants out of all your tribes to stand and minister in the LORD's name always.

[6]If a Levite moves from one of your towns anywhere in Israel where he is living, and comes in all earnestness to the place the LORD will choose, [7]he may minister in the name of the LORD his God like all his fellow Levites who serve there in the presence of the LORD. [8]He is to share equally in their benefits, even though he has received money from the sale of family possessions.

[9]When you enter the land the LORD your God is giving you, do not learn to imitate the detestable ways of the nations there. [10]Let no one be found among you who sacrifices his son or daughter in[y] the fire, who practices divination or sorcery, interprets omens, engages in witchcraft, [11]or casts spells, or who is a medium or spiritist or who consults the dead. [12]Anyone who does these things is detestable to the LORD, and because of these detestable practices the LORD your God will drive out those nations before you. [13]You must be blameless before the LORD your God.

[14]The nations you will dispossess listen to those who practice sorcery or divination. But as for you, the LORD your God has not permitted you to do so. [15]The LORD your God will raise up for you a prophet like me from among your own brothers. You must listen to him. [16]For this is what you asked of the LORD your God at Horeb on the day of the assembly when you said, "Let us not hear the voice of the LORD our God nor see this great fire anymore, or we will die."

[17]The LORD said to me: "What they say is good. [18]I will raise up for them a prophet like you from among their brothers; I will put my words in his mouth, and he will tell them everything I command him. [19]If anyone does not listen to my words that the prophet speaks in my name, I myself will call him to account. [20]But a prophet who presumes to speak in my name anything I have not commanded him to say, or a prophet who speaks in the name of other gods, must be put to death."

[21]You may say to yourselves, "How can we know when a message has not been spoken by the LORD?" [22]If what a prophet proclaims in the name of the LORD does not take place or come true, that is a message the LORD has not spoken. That prophet has spoken presumptuously. Do not be afraid of him.

CHAPTER 19

When the LORD your God has destroyed the nations whose land he is giving you, and when you have driven them out and settled in their towns and houses, [2]then set aside for yourselves three cities centrally located in the land the LORD your God is giving you to possess. [3]Build roads to them and divide into three parts the land the LORD your God is giving you as an inheritance, so that anyone who kills a man may flee there.

[4]This is the rule concerning the man who kills another and flees there to save his life—one who kills his neighbor unintentionally, without malice aforethought. [5]For instance, a man may go into the forest with his neighbor to cut wood, and as he swings his ax to fell a tree, the head may fly off and hit his neighbor and kill him. That man may flee to one of these cities and save his life. [6]Otherwise, the avenger of blood might pursue him in a rage, overtake him if the distance is too great, and kill him even though he is not deserving of death, since he did it to his neighbor without malice aforethought.

y10 Or who makes his son or daughter pass through

⁷This is why I command you to set aside for yourselves three cities.

⁸If the LORD your God enlarges your territory, as he promised on oath to your forefathers, and gives you the whole land he promised them, ⁹because you carefully follow all these laws I command you today—to love the LORD your God and to walk always in his ways—then you are to set aside three more cities. ¹⁰Do this so that innocent blood will not be shed in your land, which the LORD your God is giving you as your inheritance, and so that you will not be guilty of bloodshed.

¹¹But if a man hates his neighbor and lies in wait for him, assaults and kills him, and then flees to one of these cities, ¹²the elders of his town shall send for him, bring him back from the city, and hand him over to the avenger of blood to die. ¹³Show him no pity. You must purge from Israel the guilt of shedding innocent blood, so that it may go well with you.

¹⁴Do not move your neighbor's boundary stone set up by your predecessors in the inheritance you receive in the land the LORD your God is giving you to possess.

¹⁵One witness is not enough to convict a man accused of any crime or offense he may have committed. A matter must be established by the testimony of two or three witnesses.

¹⁶If a malicious witness takes the stand to accuse a man of a crime, ¹⁷the two men involved in the dispute must stand in the presence of the LORD before the priests and the judges who are in office at the time. ¹⁸The judges must make a thorough investigation, and if the witness proves to be a liar, giving false testimony against his brother, ¹⁹then do to him as he intended to do to his brother. You must purge the evil from among you. ²⁰The rest of the people will hear of this and be afraid, and never again will such an evil thing be done among you. ²¹Show no pity: life for life, eye for eye, tooth for tooth, hand for hand, foot for foot.

CHAPTER 20

When you go to war against your enemies and see horses and chariots and an army greater than yours, do not be afraid of them, because the LORD your God, who brought you up out of Egypt, will be with you. ²When you are about to go into battle, the priest shall come forward and address the army. ³He shall say: "Hear, O Israel, today you are going into battle against your enemies. Do not be faint-hearted or afraid; do not be terrified or give way to panic before them. ⁴For the LORD your God is the one who goes with you to fight for you against your enemies to give you victory."

⁵The officers shall say to the army: "Has anyone built a new house and not dedicated it? Let him go home, or he may die in battle and someone else may dedicate it. ⁶Has anyone planted a vineyard and not begun to enjoy it? Let him go home, or he may die in battle and someone else enjoy it. ⁷Has anyone become pledged to a woman and not married her? Let him go home, or he may die in battle and someone else marry her." ⁸Then the officers shall add, "Is any man afraid or faint-hearted? Let him go home so that his brothers will not become disheartened too." ⁹When the officers have finished speaking to the army, they shall appoint commanders over it.

¹⁰When you march up to attack a city, make its people an offer of peace. ¹¹If they accept and open their gates, all the people in it shall be subject to forced labor and shall work for you. ¹²If they refuse to make peace and they engage you in battle, lay siege to that city. ¹³When the LORD your God delivers it into your hand, put to the sword all the men in it. ¹⁴As for the women, the children, the livestock and everything else in the city, you may take these as plunder for yourselves. And you may use the plunder the LORD your God gives you from your enemies. ¹⁵This is how you are to treat all the cities that are at a distance from you and do not belong to the nations nearby.

¹⁶However, in the cities of the nations the LORD your God is giving you as an inheritance, do not leave alive anything that breathes. ¹⁷Completely destroyᶻ them—the Hittites, Amorites, Canaanites, Perizzites, Hivites and Jebusites—as the LORD your God has commanded you. ¹⁸Otherwise, they will teach you to follow all the detestable things they do in worshiping their gods, and you will sin against the LORD your God.

ᶻ17 The Hebrew term refers to the irrevocable giving over of things or persons to the LORD, often by totally destroying them.

¹⁹When you lay siege to a city for a long time, fighting against it to capture it, do not destroy its trees by putting an ax to them, because you can eat their fruit. Do not cut them down. Are the trees of the field people, that you should besiege them?ᵃ ²⁰However, you may cut down trees that you know are not fruit trees and use them to build siege works until the city at war with you falls.

ᵃ19 Or down to use in the siege, for the fruit trees are for the benefit of man.

FEBRUARY 26 □ DAY 57
DEUTERONOMY 21–26
Societal Laws for Canaan

OVERVIEW The concluding portion of Moses' second sermon contains a variety of wise guidelines for life in the promised land. Moses anticipates (and resolves) situations that could arise to disrupt the smooth functioning of Israel's society. In areas as diverse as marriage, capital punishment, purity and tithing, Moses provides God's view of what should and should not be done.

Chapters 21–22	Chapters 23–25	Chapter 26
Domestic Relationships	Defending the Weak	Donations to God
Family Matters	National Matters	Tabernacle Matters

YOUR DAILY WALK A man whose life was notoriously cluttered and confused asked that this epitaph be etched on his tombstone: "Organized at last!"

Many errors in life result from an inability to sit still long enough to read what God has written.

If you sometimes have trouble planning ahead for challenging situations, you may find Moses' example in today's reading very helpful. He greatly served Israel by giving the people clear directions in anticipation of a number of difficult situations. What can you learn from him?

Take the matter of potentially sinful situations. You have a child causing you disciplinary problems. You have a boss or fellow employee who irritates you. Why not plan right now the biblical, God-honoring response you will make the next time that situation arises? Make three columns on a sheet of paper, and write down (1) the anticipated situation; (2) your natural response; and (3) your prayerful, planned response. Keep that sheet handy and, with God's help, plan ahead to glorify him in the midst of a difficult situation!

INSIGHT High-Rise Living, Old Testament Style
God directed that all homes be built with a parapet or low wall around the roof (22:8). In a society where rooftops were used as recreation areas or extra bedrooms, this was wise to avoid accidental deaths!

CHAPTER 21

If a man is found slain, lying in a field in the land the LORD your God is giving you to possess, and it is not known who killed him, ²your elders and judges shall go out and measure the distance from the body to the neighboring towns. ³Then the elders of the town nearest the body shall take a heifer that has never been worked and has never worn a yoke ⁴and lead her down to a valley that has not been plowed or planted and where there is a flowing stream. There in the valley they are to break the heifer's neck. ⁵The priests, the sons of Levi, shall step forward, for the LORD your God has chosen them to minister and to pronounce blessings in the name of the LORD and to decide all cases of dispute and assault. ⁶Then all the elders of the town nearest the body shall wash their hands over the heifer whose neck was broken in the valley, ⁷and they shall declare: "Our hands did not shed this blood, nor did our eyes see it done. ⁸Accept this atonement for your people Israel, whom you have redeemed, O LORD, and do not hold your people guilty of the blood of an innocent man." And the bloodshed will be atoned for. ⁹So you will purge from yourselves the guilt of shedding innocent blood, since you have done what is right in the eyes of the LORD.

¹⁰When you go to war against your enemies and the LORD your God delivers them into your hands and you take captives, ¹¹if you notice among the captives a beautiful woman and are attracted to her, you may take her as your wife. ¹²Bring her into your home and have her shave her head, trim her nails ¹³and put aside the clothes she was wearing when captured. After she has lived in your house and mourned her father and mother for a full month, then you may go to her and be her husband and she shall be your wife. ¹⁴If you are not pleased with her, let her go wherever she wishes. You must not sell her or treat her as a slave, since you have dishonored her.

¹⁵If a man has two wives, and he loves one but not the other, and both bear him sons but the firstborn is the son of the wife he does not love, ¹⁶when he wills his property to his sons, he must not give the rights of the firstborn to the son of the wife he loves in preference to his actual firstborn, the son of the wife he does not love. ¹⁷He must acknowledge the son of his unloved wife as the firstborn by giving him a double share of all he has. That son is the first sign of his father's strength. The right of the firstborn belongs to him.

¹⁸If a man has a stubborn and rebellious son who does not obey his father and mother and will not listen to them when they discipline him, ¹⁹his father and mother shall take hold of him and bring him to the elders at the gate of his town. ²⁰They shall say to the elders, "This son of ours is stubborn and rebellious. He will not obey us. He is a profligate and a drunkard." ²¹Then all the men of his town shall stone him to death. You must purge the evil from among you. All Israel will hear of it and be afraid.

²²If a man guilty of a capital offense is put to death and his body is hung on a tree, ²³you must not leave his body on the tree overnight. Be sure to bury him that same day, because anyone who is hung on a tree is under God's curse. You must not desecrate the land the LORD your God is giving you as an inheritance.

CHAPTER 22

If you see your brother's ox or sheep straying, do not ignore it but be sure to take it back to him. ²If the brother does not live near you or if you do not know who he is, take it home with you and keep it until he comes looking for it. Then give it back to him. ³Do the same if you find your brother's donkey or his cloak or anything he loses. Do not ignore it.

⁴If you see your brother's donkey or his ox fallen on the road, do not ignore it. Help him get it to its feet.

⁵A woman must not wear men's clothing, nor a man wear women's clothing, for the LORD your God detests anyone who does this.

⁶If you come across a bird's nest beside the road, either in a tree or on the ground, and the mother is sitting on the young or on the eggs, do not take the mother with the young. ⁷You may take the young, but be sure to let the mother go, so that it may go well with you and you may have a long life.

⁸When you build a new house, make a parapet around your roof so that you may not bring the guilt of bloodshed on your house if someone falls from the roof.

⁹Do not plant two kinds of seed in your vineyard; if you do, not only the crops you plant but also the fruit of the vineyard will be defiled.ᵇ

¹⁰Do not plow with an ox and a donkey yoked together.

¹¹Do not wear clothes of wool and linen woven together.

¹²Make tassels on the four corners of the cloak you wear.

¹³If a man takes a wife and, after lying with her, dislikes her ¹⁴and slanders her and gives her a bad name, saying, "I married this woman, but when I approached her, I did not find proof of her virginity," ¹⁵then the girl's father and mother shall bring proof that she was a virgin to the town elders at the gate. ¹⁶The girl's father will say to the elders, "I gave my daughter in marriage to this man, but he dislikes her. ¹⁷Now he has slandered her and said, 'I did not find your daughter to be a virgin.' But here is the proof of my daughter's virginity." Then her parents shall display the cloth before the elders of the town, ¹⁸and the elders shall take the man and punish him. ¹⁹They shall fine him a hundred shekels of silverᶜ and give them to the girl's father, because this man has given an Israelite virgin a bad name. She shall continue to be his wife; he must not divorce her as long as he lives.

²⁰If, however, the charge is true and no proof of the girl's virginity can be found, ²¹she shall be brought to the door of her father's house and there the men of her town shall stone her to death. She has done a disgraceful thing in Israel by being promiscuous while still in her father's house. You must purge the evil from among you.

²²If a man is found sleeping with another man's wife, both the man who slept with her and the woman must die. You must purge the evil from Israel.

²³If a man happens to meet in a town a virgin pledged to be married and he sleeps with her, ²⁴you shall take both of them to the gate of that town and stone them to death—the girl because she was in a town and did not scream for help, and the man because he violated another man's wife. You must purge the evil from among you.

²⁵But if out in the country a man happens to meet a girl pledged to be married and rapes her, only the man who has done this shall die. ²⁶Do nothing to the girl; she has committed no sin deserving death. This case is like that of someone who attacks and murders his neighbor, ²⁷for the man found the girl out in the country, and though the betrothed girl screamed, there was no one to rescue her.

²⁸If a man happens to meet a virgin who is not pledged to be married and rapes her and they are discovered, ²⁹he shall pay the girl's father fifty shekels of silver.ᵈ He must marry the girl, for he has violated her. He can never divorce her as long as he lives.

³⁰A man is not to marry his father's wife; he must not dishonor his father's bed.

CHAPTER 23

No one who has been emasculated by crushing or cutting may enter the assembly of the LORD.

²No one born of a forbidden marriageᵉ nor any of his descendants may enter the assembly of the LORD, even down to the tenth generation.

³No Ammonite or Moabite or any of his descendants may enter the assembly of the LORD, even down to the tenth generation. ⁴For they did not come to meet you with bread and water on your way when you came out of Egypt, and they hired Balaam son of Beor from Pethor in Aram Naharaimᶠ to pronounce a curse on you. ⁵However, the LORD your God would not listen to Balaam but turned the curse into a blessing for you, because the LORD your God loves you. ⁶Do not seek a treaty of friendship with them as long as you live.

⁷Do not abhor an Edomite, for he is your brother. Do not abhor an Egyptian, because you lived as an alien in his country. ⁸The third generation of children born to them may enter the assembly of the LORD.

⁹When you are encamped against your enemies, keep away from everything impure. ¹⁰If one of your men is unclean because of a nocturnal emission, he is to go outside the camp and stay there. ¹¹But as evening approaches he is to wash himself, and at sunset he may return to the camp. ¹²Designate a place outside the camp

---

ᵇ9 Or be forfeited to the sanctuary   ᶜ19 That is, about 2 1/2 pounds (about 1 kilogram)   ᵈ29 That is, about 1 1/4 pounds (about 0.6 kilogram)   ᵉ2 Or one of illegitimate birth   ᶠ4 That is, Northwest Mesopotamia where you can go to relieve yourself. [13]As part of your equipment have something to dig with, and when you relieve yourself, dig a hole and cover up your excrement. [14]For the LORD your God moves about in your camp to protect you and to deliver your enemies to you. Your camp must be holy, so that he will not see among you anything indecent and turn away from you.

[15]If a slave has taken refuge with you, do not hand him over to his master. [16]Let him live among you wherever he likes and in whatever town he chooses. Do not oppress him.

[17]No Israelite man or woman is to become a shrine prostitute. [18]You must not bring the earnings of a female prostitute or of a male prostitute[g] into the house of the LORD your God to pay any vow, because the LORD your God detests them both.

[19]Do not charge your brother interest, whether on money or food or anything else that may earn interest. [20]You may charge a foreigner interest, but not a brother Israelite, so that the LORD your God may bless you in everything you put your hand to in the land you are entering to possess.

[21]If you make a vow to the LORD your God, do not be slow to pay it, for the LORD your God will certainly demand it of you and you will be guilty of sin. [22]But if you refrain from making a vow, you will not be guilty. [23]Whatever your lips utter you must be sure to do, because you made your vow freely to the LORD your God with your own mouth.

[24]If you enter your neighbor's vineyard, you may eat all the grapes you want, but do not put any in your basket. [25]If you enter your neighbor's grainfield, you may pick kernels with your hands, but you must not put a sickle to his standing grain.

CHAPTER 24

If a man marries a woman who becomes displeasing to him because he finds something indecent about her, and he writes her a certificate of divorce, gives it to her and sends her from his house, [2]and if after she leaves his house she becomes the wife of another man, [3]and her second husband dislikes her and writes her a certificate of divorce, gives it to her and sends her from his house, or if he dies, [4]then her first husband, who divorced her, is not allowed to marry her again after she has been defiled. That would be detestable in the eyes of the LORD. Do not bring sin upon the land the LORD your God is giving you as an inheritance.

[5]If a man has recently married, he must not be sent to war or have any other duty laid on him. For one year he is to be free to stay at home and bring happiness to the wife he has married.

[6]Do not take a pair of millstones—not even the upper one—as security for a debt, because that would be taking a man's livelihood as security.

[7]If a man is caught kidnapping one of his brother Israelites and treats him as a slave or sells him, the kidnapper must die. You must purge the evil from among you.

[8]In cases of leprous[h] diseases be very careful to do exactly as the priests, who are Levites, instruct you. You must follow carefully what I have commanded them. [9]Remember what the LORD your God did to Miriam along the way after you came out of Egypt.

[10]When you make a loan of any kind to your neighbor, do not go into his house to get what he is offering as a pledge. [11]Stay outside and let the man to whom you are making the loan bring the pledge out to you. [12]If the man is poor, do not go to sleep with his pledge in your possession. [13]Return his cloak to him by sunset so that he may sleep in it. Then he will thank you, and it will be regarded as a righteous act in the sight of the LORD your God.

[14]Do not take advantage of a hired man who is poor and needy, whether he is a brother Israelite or an alien living in one of your towns. [15]Pay him his wages each day before sunset, because he is poor and is counting on it. Otherwise he may cry to the LORD against you, and you will be guilty of sin.

[16]Fathers shall not be put to death for their children, nor children put to death for their fathers; each is to die for his own sin.

[17]Do not deprive the alien or the fatherless of justice, or take the cloak of the widow as a pledge. [18]Remember that you

[g]18 Hebrew of a dog   [h]8 The Hebrew word was used for various diseases affecting the skin—not necessarily leprosy.

were slaves in Egypt and the LORD your God redeemed you from there. That is why I command you to do this.

¹⁹When you are harvesting in your field and you overlook a sheaf, do not go back to get it. Leave it for the alien, the fatherless and the widow, so that the LORD your God may bless you in all the work of your hands. ²⁰When you beat the olives from your trees, do not go over the branches a second time. Leave what remains for the alien, the fatherless and the widow. ²¹When you harvest the grapes in your vineyard, do not go over the vines again. Leave what remains for the alien, the fatherless and the widow. ²²Remember that you were slaves in Egypt. That is why I command you to do this.

CHAPTER 25

When men have a dispute, they are to take it to court and the judges will decide the case, acquitting the innocent and condemning the guilty. ²If the guilty man deserves to be beaten, the judge shall make him lie down and have him flogged in his presence with the number of lashes his crime deserves, ³but he must not give him more than forty lashes. If he is flogged more than that, your brother will be degraded in your eyes.

⁴Do not muzzle an ox while it is treading out the grain.

⁵If brothers are living together and one of them dies without a son, his widow must not marry outside the family. Her husband's brother shall take her and marry her and fulfill the duty of a brother-in-law to her. ⁶The first son she bears shall carry on the name of the dead brother so that his name will not be blotted out from Israel.

⁷However, if a man does not want to marry his brother's wife, she shall go to the elders at the town gate and say, "My husband's brother refuses to carry on his brother's name in Israel. He will not fulfill the duty of a brother-in-law to me." ⁸Then the elders of his town shall summon him and talk to him. If he persists in saying, "I do not want to marry her," ⁹his brother's widow shall go up to him in the presence of the elders, take off one of his sandals, spit in his face and say, "This is what is done to the man who will not build up his brother's family line." ¹⁰That

man's line shall be known in Israel as The Family of the Unsandaled.

¹¹If two men are fighting and the wife of one of them comes to rescue her husband from his assailant, and she reaches out and seizes him by his private parts, ¹²you shall cut off her hand. Show her no pity.

¹³Do not have two differing weights in your bag—one heavy, one light. ¹⁴Do not have two differing measures in your house—one large, one small. ¹⁵You must have accurate and honest weights and measures, so that you may live long in the land the LORD your God is giving you. ¹⁶For the LORD your God detests anyone who does these things, anyone who deals dishonestly.

¹⁷Remember what the Amalekites did to you along the way when you came out of Egypt. ¹⁸When you were weary and worn out, they met you on your journey and cut off all who were lagging behind; they had no fear of God. ¹⁹When the LORD your God gives you rest from all the enemies around you in the land he is giving you to possess as an inheritance, you shall blot out the memory of Amalek from under heaven. Do not forget!

CHAPTER 26

When you have entered the land the LORD your God is giving you as an inheritance and have taken possession of it and settled in it, ²take some of the firstfruits of all that you produce from the soil of the land the LORD your God is giving you and put them in a basket. Then go to the place the LORD your God will choose as a dwelling for his Name ³and say to the priest in office at the time, "I declare today to the LORD your God that I have come to the land the LORD swore to our forefathers to give us." ⁴The priest shall take the basket from your hands and set it down in front of the altar of the LORD your God. ⁵Then you shall declare before the LORD your God: "My father was a wandering Aramean, and he went down into Egypt with a few people and lived there and became a great nation, powerful and numerous. ⁶But the Egyptians mistreated us and made us suffer, putting us to hard labor. ⁷Then we cried out to the LORD, the God of our fathers, and the LORD heard our voice and saw our misery, toil and oppression.

⁸So the LORD brought us out of Egypt with a mighty hand and an outstretched arm, with great terror and with miraculous signs and wonders. ⁹He brought us to this place and gave us this land, a land flowing with milk and honey; ¹⁰and now I bring the firstfruits of the soil that you, O LORD, have given me." Place the basket before the LORD your God and bow down before him. ¹¹And you and the Levites and the aliens among you shall rejoice in all the good things the LORD your God has given to you and your household.

¹²When you have finished setting aside a tenth of all your produce in the third year, the year of the tithe, you shall give it to the Levite, the alien, the fatherless and the widow, so that they may eat in your towns and be satisfied. ¹³Then say to the LORD your God: "I have removed from my house the sacred portion and have given it to the Levite, the alien, the fatherless and the widow, according to all you commanded. I have not turned aside from your commands nor have I forgotten any of them. ¹⁴I have not eaten any of the sa-

cred portion while I was in mourning, nor have I removed any of it while I was unclean, nor have I offered any of it to the dead. I have obeyed the LORD my God; I have done everything you commanded me. ¹⁵Look down from heaven, your holy dwelling place, and bless your people Israel and the land you have given us as you promised on oath to our forefathers, a land flowing with milk and honey."

¹⁶The LORD your God commands you this day to follow these decrees and laws; carefully observe them with all your heart and with all your soul. ¹⁷You have declared this day that the LORD is your God and that you will walk in his ways, that you will keep his decrees, commands and laws, and that you will obey him. ¹⁸And the LORD has declared this day that you are his people, his treasured possession as he promised, and that you are to keep all his commands. ¹⁹He has declared that he will set you in praise, fame and honor high above all the nations he has made and that you will be a people holy to the LORD your God, as he promised.

FEBRUARY 27 ☐ DAY 58
DEUTERONOMY 27–30
Commitment to the Covenant

OVERVIEW In today's reading Moses concludes his presentation of the new law for the new generation. First, he sets forth the blessings of obeying and the consequences of violating the covenant. Complete surrender to God's will as revealed in the laws will bring blessing upon the nation, the family and the individual. Crops will flourish, cattle will multiply and daily needs will be met. On the other hand, disobedience will result in disaster: pestilence, plagues and ultimately removal from the land. The responsibility is left squarely on the shoulders of the people. They are free to choose the path they will take, but they are not free to escape the consequences of their fateful choice.

Chapter 27	Chapter 28	Chapter 29	Chapter 30
Curses for Disobedience	Blessings for Obedience	The Covenant's Demands	A Life-or-Death Decision
The Covenant Concluded		The Covenant Ratified	

YOUR DAILY WALK Do you ever find the will of God elusive or unclear? You have an important decision to make, and you want to do the right thing. You want to honor God. But which direction should you turn? First, turn to the Word of God. God has something to say to

Perfect conformity to the will of God is the sole sovereign and perfect liberty. you, and it's written in the Bible. All that remains is for you to read and obey it!

God is not in the business of hiding his will or making it difficult to understand. To the Israelites Moses wrote, "Now what I am commanding you today is not too difficult for you or beyond your reach. It is not up in heaven, so that you have to ask, 'Who will ascend into heaven to get it and proclaim it to us so we may obey it?' " (30:11–12). God's will for you is not a heavenly fog; it is a down-to-earth reality you can understand.

Read Deuteronomy 30:11–20 twice. Then list three things that characterize God's will for you today. Don't worry about the things in the Bible you don't understand; worry about the things you do! And "do whatever he tells you" (John 2:5).

 INSIGHT The Day the Slave Markets Were Glutted
The horrible curse of 28:68 literally came true! After the fall of Jerusalem in A.D. 70, the slave markets of Egypt became so glutted with captive Israelites that there were not enough buyers for them all. God always keeps his promises—good and bad.

CHAPTER 27

Moses and the elders of Israel commanded the people: "Keep all these commands that I give you today. ²When you have crossed the Jordan into the land the LORD your God is giving you, set up some large stones and coat them with plaster. ³Write on them all the words of this law when you have crossed over to enter the land the LORD your God is giving you, a land flowing with milk and honey, just as the LORD, the God of your fathers, promised you. ⁴And when you have crossed the Jordan, set up these stones on Mount Ebal, as I command you today, and coat them with plaster. ⁵Build there an altar to the LORD your God, an altar of stones. Do not use any iron tool upon them. ⁶Build the altar of the LORD your God with fieldstones and offer burnt offerings on it to the LORD your God. ⁷Sacrifice fellowship offerings* there, eating them and rejoicing in the presence of the LORD your God. ⁸And you shall write very clearly all the words of this law on these stones you have set up."

⁹Then Moses and the priests, who are Levites, said to all Israel, "Be silent, O Israel, and listen! You have now become the people of the LORD your God. ¹⁰Obey the LORD your God and follow his commands and decrees that I give you today."

¹¹On the same day Moses commanded the people:

¹²When you have crossed the Jordan, these tribes shall stand on Mount Gerizim to bless the people: Simeon, Levi, Judah, Issachar, Joseph and Benjamin. ¹³And these tribes shall stand on Mount Ebal to pronounce curses: Reuben, Gad, Asher, Zebulun, Dan and Naphtali.

¹⁴The Levites shall recite to all the people of Israel in a loud voice:

¹⁵"Cursed is the man who carves an image or casts an idol—a thing detestable to the LORD, the work of the craftsman's hands—and sets it up in secret."

Then all the people shall say, "Amen!"

¹⁶"Cursed is the man who dishonors his father or his mother."

Then all the people shall say, "Amen!"

¹⁷"Cursed is the man who moves his neighbor's boundary stone."

Then all the people shall say, "Amen!"

¹⁸"Cursed is the man who leads the blind astray on the road."

Then all the people shall say, "Amen!"

¹⁹"Cursed is the man who withholds justice from the alien, the fatherless or the widow."

Then all the people shall say, "Amen!"

²⁰"Cursed is the man who sleeps with his father's wife, for he dishonors his father's bed."

7 Traditionally peace offerings

Then all the people shall say, "Amen!"

21"Cursed is the man who has sexual relations with any animal."

Then all the people shall say, "Amen!"

22"Cursed is the man who sleeps with his sister, the daughter of his father or the daughter of his mother."

Then all the people shall say, "Amen!"

23"Cursed is the man who sleeps with his mother-in-law."

Then all the people shall say, "Amen!"

24"Cursed is the man who kills his neighbor secretly."

Then all the people shall say, "Amen!"

25"Cursed is the man who accepts a bribe to kill an innocent person."

Then all the people shall say, "Amen!"

26"Cursed is the man who does not uphold the words of this law by carrying them out."

Then all the people shall say, "Amen!"

CHAPTER 28

If you fully obey the LORD your God and carefully follow all his commands I give you today, the LORD your God will set you high above all the nations on earth. 2All these blessings will come upon you and accompany you if you obey the LORD your God:

3You will be blessed in the city and blessed in the country.

4The fruit of your womb will be blessed, and the crops of your land and the young of your livestock—the calves of your herds and the lambs of your flocks.

5Your basket and your kneading trough will be blessed.

6You will be blessed when you come in and blessed when you go out.

7The LORD will grant that the enemies who rise up against you will be defeated before you. They will come at you from one direction but flee from you in seven.

8The LORD will send a blessing on your barns and on everything you put your hand to. The LORD your God will bless you in the land he is giving you.

9The LORD will establish you as his holy people, as he promised you on oath, if you keep the commands of the LORD your God and walk in his ways. 10Then all the peoples on earth will see that you are called by the name of the LORD, and they will fear you. 11The LORD will grant you abundant prosperity—in the fruit of your womb, the young of your livestock and the crops of your ground—in the land he swore to your forefathers to give you.

12The LORD will open the heavens, the storehouse of his bounty, to send rain on your land in season and to bless all the work of your hands. You will lend to many nations but will borrow from none. 13The LORD will make you the head, not the tail. If you pay attention to the commands of the LORD your God that I give you this day and carefully follow them, you will always be at the top, never at the bottom. 14Do not turn aside from any of the commands I give you today, to the right or to the left, following other gods and serving them.

15However, if you do not obey the LORD your God and do not carefully follow all his commands and decrees I am giving you today, all these curses will come upon you and overtake you:

16You will be cursed in the city and cursed in the country.

17Your basket and your kneading trough will be cursed.

18The fruit of your womb will be cursed, and the crops of your land, and the calves of your herds and the lambs of your flocks.

19You will be cursed when you come in and cursed when you go out.

20The LORD will send on you curses, confusion and rebuke in everything you put your hand to, until you are destroyed and come to sudden ruin because of the evil you have done in forsaking him.*j* 21The LORD will plague you with diseases until he has destroyed you from the land you are entering to possess. 22The LORD will strike you with wasting disease, with fever and inflammation, with scorching heat and drought, with blight and mil-

j20 Hebrew me

dew, which will plague you until you perish. ²³The sky over your head will be bronze, the ground beneath you iron. ²⁴The LORD will turn the rain of your country into dust and powder; it will come down from the skies until you are destroyed.

²⁵The LORD will cause you to be defeated before your enemies. You will come at them from one direction but flee from them in seven, and you will become a thing of horror to all the kingdoms on earth. ²⁶Your carcasses will be food for all the birds of the air and the beasts of the earth, and there will be no one to frighten them away. ²⁷The LORD will afflict you with the boils of Egypt and with tumors, festering sores and the itch, from which you cannot be cured. ²⁸The LORD will afflict you with madness, blindness and confusion of mind. ²⁹At midday you will grope about like a blind man in the dark. You will be unsuccessful in everything you do; day after day you will be oppressed and robbed, with no one to rescue you.

³⁰You will be pledged to be married to a woman, but another will take her and ravish her. You will build a house, but you will not live in it. You will plant a vineyard, but you will not even begin to enjoy its fruit. ³¹Your ox will be slaughtered before your eyes, but you will eat none of it. Your donkey will be forcibly taken from you and will not be returned. Your sheep will be given to your enemies, and no one will rescue them. ³²Your sons and daughters will be given to another nation, and you will wear out your eyes watching for them day after day, powerless to lift a hand. ³³A people that you do not know will eat what your land and labor produce, and you will have nothing but cruel oppression all your days. ³⁴The sights you see will drive you mad. ³⁵The LORD will afflict your knees and legs with painful boils that cannot be cured, spreading from the soles of your feet to the top of your head.

³⁶The LORD will drive you and the king you set over you to a nation unknown to you or your fathers. There you will worship other gods, gods of wood and stone. ³⁷You will become a thing of horror and an object of scorn and ridicule to all the nations where the LORD will drive you.

³⁸You will sow much seed in the field but you will harvest little, because locusts will devour it. ³⁹You will plant vineyards and cultivate them but you will not drink the wine or gather the grapes, because worms will eat them. ⁴⁰You will have olive trees throughout your country but you will not use the oil, because the olives will drop off. ⁴¹You will have sons and daughters but you will not keep them, because they will go into captivity. ⁴²Swarms of locusts will take over all your trees and the crops of your land.

⁴³The alien who lives among you will rise above you higher and higher, but you will sink lower and lower. ⁴⁴He will lend to you, but you will not lend to him. He will be the head, but you will be the tail.

⁴⁵All these curses will come upon you. They will pursue you and overtake you until you are destroyed, because you did not obey the LORD your God and observe the commands and decrees he gave you. ⁴⁶They will be a sign and a wonder to you and your descendants forever. ⁴⁷Because you did not serve the LORD your God joyfully and gladly in the time of prosperity, ⁴⁸therefore in hunger and thirst, in nakedness and dire poverty, you will serve the enemies the LORD sends against you. He will put an iron yoke on your neck until he has destroyed you.

⁴⁹The LORD will bring a nation against you from far away, from the ends of the earth, like an eagle swooping down, a nation whose language you will not understand, ⁵⁰a fierce-looking nation without respect for the old or pity for the young. ⁵¹They will devour the young of your livestock and the crops of your land until you are destroyed. They will leave you no grain, new wine or oil, nor any calves of your herds or lambs of your flocks until you are ruined. ⁵²They will lay siege to all the cities throughout your land until the high fortified walls in which you trust fall down. They will besiege all the cities throughout the land the LORD your God is giving you.

⁵³Because of the suffering that your enemy will inflict on you during the siege, you will eat the fruit of the womb, the flesh of the sons and daughters the LORD your God has given you. ⁵⁴Even the most gentle and sensitive man among you will have no compassion on his own brother or the wife he loves or his surviving children, ⁵⁵and he will not give to one of them

any of the flesh of his children that he is eating. It will be all he has left because of the suffering your enemy will inflict on you during the siege of all your cities. 56The most gentle and sensitive woman among you—so sensitive and gentle that she would not venture to touch the ground with the sole of her foot—will begrudge the husband she loves and her own son or daughter 57the afterbirth from her womb and the children she bears. For she intends to eat them secretly during the siege and in the distress that your enemy will inflict on you in your cities.

58If you do not carefully follow all the words of this law, which are written in this book, and do not revere this glorious and awesome name—the LORD your God— 59the LORD will send fearful plagues on you and your descendants, harsh and prolonged disasters, and severe and lingering illnesses. 60He will bring upon you all the diseases of Egypt that you dreaded, and they will cling to you. 61The LORD will also bring on you every kind of sickness and disaster not recorded in this Book of the Law, until you are destroyed. 62You who were as numerous as the stars in the sky will be left but few in number, because you did not obey the LORD your God. 63Just as it pleased the LORD to make you prosper and increase in number, so it will please him to ruin and destroy you. You will be uprooted from the land you are entering to possess.

64Then the LORD will scatter you among all nations, from one end of the earth to the other. There you will worship other gods—gods of wood and stone, which neither you nor your fathers have known. 65Among those nations you will find no repose, no resting place for the sole of your foot. There the LORD will give you an anxious mind, eyes weary with longing, and a despairing heart. 66You will live in constant suspense, filled with dread both night and day, never sure of your life. 67In the morning you will say, "If only it were evening!" and in the evening, "If only it were morning!"—because of the terror that will fill your hearts and the sights that your eyes will see. 68The LORD will send you back in ships to Egypt on a journey I said you should never make again. There you will offer yourselves for sale to your enemies as male and female slaves, but no one will buy you.

CHAPTER 29

These are the terms of the covenant the LORD commanded Moses to make with the Israelites in Moab, in addition to the covenant he had made with them at Horeb.

2Moses summoned all the Israelites and said to them:

Your eyes have seen all that the LORD did in Egypt to Pharaoh, to all his officials and to all his land. 3With your own eyes you saw those great trials, those miraculous signs and great wonders. 4But to this day the LORD has not given you a mind that understands or eyes that see or ears that hear. 5During the forty years that I led you through the desert, your clothes did not wear out, nor did the sandals on your feet. 6You ate no bread and drank no wine or other fermented drink. I did this so that you might know that I am the LORD your God.

7When you reached this place, Sihon king of Heshbon and Og king of Bashan came out to fight against us, but we defeated them. 8We took their land and gave it as an inheritance to the Reubenites, the Gadites and the half-tribe of Manasseh.

9Carefully follow the terms of this covenant, so that you may prosper in everything you do. 10All of you are standing today in the presence of the LORD your God—your leaders and chief men, your elders and officials, and all the other men of Israel, 11together with your children and your wives, and the aliens living in your camps who chop your wood and carry your water. 12You are standing here in order to enter into a covenant with the LORD your God, a covenant the LORD is making with you this day and sealing with an oath, 13to confirm you this day as his people, that he may be your God as he promised you and as he swore to your fathers, Abraham, Isaac and Jacob. 14I am making this covenant, with its oath, not only with you 15who are standing here with us today in the presence of the LORD our God but also with those who are not here today.

16You yourselves know how we lived in Egypt and how we passed through the countries on the way here. 17You saw among them their detestable images and idols of wood and stone, of silver and gold. [18]Make sure there is no man or woman, clan or tribe among you today whose heart turns away from the LORD our God to go and worship the gods of those nations; make sure there is no root among you that produces such bitter poison.

[19]When such a person hears the words of this oath, he invokes a blessing on himself and therefore thinks, "I will be safe, even though I persist in going my own way." This will bring disaster on the watered land as well as the dry.[k] [20]The LORD will never be willing to forgive him; his wrath and zeal will burn against that man. All the curses written in this book will fall upon him, and the LORD will blot out his name from under heaven. [21]The LORD will single him out from all the tribes of Israel for disaster, according to all the curses of the covenant written in this Book of the Law.

[22]Your children who follow you in later generations and foreigners who come from distant lands will see the calamities that have fallen on the land and the diseases with which the LORD has afflicted it. [23]The whole land will be a burning waste of salt and sulfur—nothing planted, nothing sprouting, no vegetation growing on it. It will be like the destruction of Sodom and Gomorrah, Admah and Zeboiim, which the LORD overthrew in fierce anger. [24]All the nations will ask: "Why has the LORD done this to this land? Why this fierce, burning anger?"

[25]And the answer will be: "It is because this people abandoned the covenant of the LORD, the God of their fathers, the covenant he made with them when he brought them out of Egypt. [26]They went off and worshiped other gods and bowed down to them, gods they did not know, gods he had not given them. [27]Therefore the LORD's anger burned against this land, so that he brought on it all the curses written in this book. [28]In furious anger and in great wrath the LORD uprooted them from their land and thrust them into another land, as it is now."

[29]The secret things belong to the LORD our God, but the things revealed belong to us and to our children forever, that we may follow all the words of this law.

CHAPTER 30

When all these blessings and curses I have set before you come upon you and you take them to heart wherever the LORD your God disperses you among the nations, [2]and when you and your children return to the LORD your God and obey him with all your heart and with all your soul according to everything I command you today, [3]then the LORD your God will restore your fortunes[l] and have compassion on you and gather you again from all the nations where he scattered you. [4]Even if you have been banished to the most distant land under the heavens, from there the LORD your God will gather you and bring you back. [5]He will bring you to the land that belonged to your fathers, and you will take possession of it. He will make you more prosperous and numerous than your fathers. [6]The LORD your God will circumcise your hearts and the hearts of your descendants, so that you may love him with all your heart and with all your soul, and live. [7]The LORD your God will put all these curses on your enemies who hate and persecute you. [8]You will again obey the LORD and follow all his commands I am giving you today. [9]Then the LORD your God will make you most prosperous in all the work of your hands and in the fruit of your womb, the young of your livestock and the crops of your land. The LORD will again delight in you and make you prosperous, just as he delighted in your fathers, [10]if you obey the LORD your God and keep his commands and decrees that are written in this Book of the Law and turn to the LORD your God with all your heart and with all your soul.

[11]Now what I am commanding you today is not too difficult for you or beyond your reach. [12]It is not up in heaven, so that you have to ask, "Who will ascend into heaven to get it and proclaim it to us so we may obey it?" [13]Nor is it beyond the sea, so that you have to ask, "Who will cross the sea to get it and proclaim it to us so we may obey it?" [14]No, the word is very near you; it is in your mouth and in your heart so you may obey it.

[15]See, I set before you today life and prosperity, death and destruction. [16]For I command you today to love the LORD

---

k 19 Or way, in order to add drunkenness to thirst."   *l 3 Or will bring you back from captivity* your God, to walk in his ways, and to keep his commands, decrees and laws; then you will live and increase, and the LORD your God will bless you in the land you are entering to possess.

¹⁷But if your heart turns away and you are not obedient, and if you are drawn away to bow down to other gods and worship them, ¹⁸I declare to you this day that you will certainly be destroyed. You will not live long in the land you are crossing the Jordan to enter and possess.

¹⁹This day I call heaven and earth as witnesses against you that I have set before you life and death, blessings and curses. Now choose life, so that you and your children may live ²⁰and that you may love the LORD your God, listen to his voice, and hold fast to him. For the LORD is your life, and he will give you many years in the land he swore to give to your fathers, Abraham, Isaac and Jacob.

FEBRUARY 28 ☐ DAY 59
DEUTERONOMY 31–34
Farewell and Death of Moses

 OVERVIEW Moses' long and illustrious life is drawing to a close. During his final days as Israel's leader, he delivers some significant words of counsel to the priests, Levites, his successor, Joshua, and the entire nation. He has learned much during his 120-year walk with God, and his final words of warning and encouragement deserve careful attention. To make his last utterances easily remembered, Moses writes them down in the form of a song, which he teaches to the people. After blessing each of the twelve tribes, Moses climbs Mount Nebo for a final look at the promised land, and there he dies—still in the prime of life!

Chapter 31	Chapter 32	Chapter 33	Chapter 34
Moses' Successor	Moses' Song	Moses' Farewell	Moses' Funeral
The Final Days of Moses			

 YOUR DAILY WALK Do you have trouble identifying with a great Old Testament saint such as Moses? After all, in many ways Moses was unique in history. He stood in the very presence of God, performed miracles before Pharaoh, parted the Red Sea, turned rocks into drinking fountains and died at the age of 120, still full of youthful vigor.

No one is so old as the one who has outlived enthusiasm.

And yet the Bible paints Moses in very human tones. He spent the first two-thirds of his life wrestling with his calling before he finally yielded to God's will. Being a man of action, he found it frustrating to administer the affairs of a large, rebellious nation. Finally, in a moment of impatience and anger, he disobeyed God's direct instructions, thus denying himself the opportunity to set foot in the promised land. And yet, God's commentary on Moses is this: "Since then, no prophet has risen in Israel like Moses, whom the LORD knew face to face" (34:10).

Let the words of Deuteronomy 29:29 provide a fresh motivation for you to *know* and *do* God's will next month as you follow in the footsteps of Moses!

 INSIGHT The Promised Land at Last
Sadly, Moses, deliverer of his people, never set foot in the promised land. Or did he? Though he climbs Mount Nebo for one last faraway

look at Canaan before his death, he is seen *inside* the promised land years later on the mountain in which Jesus was transfigured (Matthew 17:3; Luke 9:30–31).

CHAPTER 31

Then Moses went out and spoke these words to all Israel: ²"I am now a hundred and twenty years old and I am no longer able to lead you. The LORD has said to me, 'You shall not cross the Jordan.' ³The LORD your God himself will cross over ahead of you. He will destroy these nations before you, and you will take possession of their land. Joshua also will cross over ahead of you, as the LORD said. ⁴And the LORD will do to them what he did to Sihon and Og, the kings of the Amorites, whom he destroyed along with their land. ⁵The LORD will deliver them to you, and you must do to them all that I have commanded you. ⁶Be strong and courageous. Do not be afraid or terrified because of them, for the LORD your God goes with you; he will never leave you nor forsake you."

⁷Then Moses summoned Joshua and said to him in the presence of all Israel, "Be strong and courageous, for you must go with this people into the land that the LORD swore to their forefathers to give them, and you must divide it among them as their inheritance. ⁸The LORD himself goes before you and will be with you; he will never leave you nor forsake you. Do not be afraid; do not be discouraged."

⁹So Moses wrote down this law and gave it to the priests, the sons of Levi, who carried the ark of the covenant of the LORD, and to all the elders of Israel. ¹⁰Then Moses commanded them: "At the end of every seven years, in the year for canceling debts, during the Feast of Tabernacles, ¹¹when all Israel comes to appear before the LORD your God at the place he will choose, you shall read this law before them in their hearing. ¹²Assemble the people—men, women and children, and the aliens living in your towns—so they can listen and learn to fear the LORD your God and follow carefully all the words of this law. ¹³Their children, who do not know this law, must hear it and learn to fear the LORD your God as long as you live in the land you are crossing the Jordan to possess."

¹⁴The LORD said to Moses, "Now the day of your death is near. Call Joshua and present yourselves at the Tent of Meeting, where I will commission him." So Moses and Joshua came and presented themselves at the Tent of Meeting.

¹⁵Then the LORD appeared at the Tent in a pillar of cloud, and the cloud stood over the entrance to the Tent. ¹⁶And the LORD said to Moses: "You are going to rest with your fathers, and these people will soon prostitute themselves to the foreign gods of the land they are entering. They will forsake me and break the covenant I made with them. ¹⁷On that day I will become angry with them and forsake them; I will hide my face from them, and they will be destroyed. Many disasters and difficulties will come upon them, and on that day they will ask, 'Have not these disasters come upon us because our God is not with us?' ¹⁸And I will certainly hide my face on that day because of all their wickedness in turning to other gods.

¹⁹"Now write down for yourselves this song and teach it to the Israelites and have them sing it, so that it may be a witness for me against them. ²⁰When I have brought them into the land flowing with milk and honey, the land I promised on oath to their forefathers, and when they eat their fill and thrive, they will turn to other gods and worship them, rejecting me and breaking my covenant. ²¹And when many disasters and difficulties come upon them, this song will testify against them, because it will not be forgotten by their descendants. I know what they are disposed to do, even before I bring them into the land I promised them on oath." ²²So Moses wrote down this song that day and taught it to the Israelites.

²³The LORD gave this command to Joshua son of Nun: "Be strong and courageous, for you will bring the Israelites into the land I promised them on oath, and I myself will be with you."

²⁴After Moses finished writing in a book the words of this law from beginning to end, ²⁵he gave this command to the Levites who carried the ark of the covenant of the LORD: ²⁶"Take this Book of the Law and place it beside the ark of the

covenant of the LORD your God. There it will remain as a witness against you. ²⁷For I know how rebellious and stiff-necked you are. If you have been rebellious against the LORD while I am still alive and with you, how much more will you rebel after I die! ²⁸Assemble before me all the elders of your tribes and all your officials, so that I can speak these words in their hearing and call heaven and earth to testify against them. ²⁹For I know that after my death you are sure to become utterly corrupt and to turn from the way I have commanded you. In days to come, disaster will fall upon you because you will do evil in the sight of the LORD and provoke him to anger by what your hands have made."

³⁰And Moses recited the words of this song from beginning to end in the hearing of the whole assembly of Israel:

CHAPTER 32

Listen, O heavens, and I will speak;
  hear, O earth, the words of my
    mouth.
²Let my teaching fall like rain
  and my words descend like dew,
like showers on new grass,
  like abundant rain on tender plants.

³I will proclaim the name of the LORD.
  Oh, praise the greatness of our God!
⁴He is the Rock, his works are perfect,
  and all his ways are just.
A faithful God who does no wrong,
  upright and just is he.

⁵They have acted corruptly toward him;
  to their shame they are no longer his
    children,
  but a warped and crooked
    generation.ᵐ
⁶Is this the way you repay the LORD,
  O foolish and unwise people?
Is he not your Father, your Creator,ⁿ
  who made you and formed you?

⁷Remember the days of old;
  consider the generations long past.
Ask your father and he will tell you,
  your elders, and they will explain to
    you.
⁸When the Most High gave the nations
    their inheritance,
  when he divided all mankind,

he set up boundaries for the peoples
  according to the number of the sons
    of Israel.ᵒ
⁹For the LORD's portion is his people,
  Jacob his allotted inheritance.

¹⁰In a desert land he found him,
  in a barren and howling waste.
He shielded him and cared for him;
  he guarded him as the apple of his
    eye,
¹¹like an eagle that stirs up its nest
  and hovers over its young,
that spreads its wings to catch them
  and carries them on its pinions.
¹²The LORD alone led him;
  no foreign god was with him.

¹³He made him ride on the heights of
    the land
  and fed him with the fruit of the
    fields.
He nourished him with honey from
    the rock,
  and with oil from the flinty crag,
¹⁴with curds and milk from herd and
    flock
  and with fattened lambs and goats,
with choice rams of Bashan
  and the finest kernels of wheat.
You drank the foaming blood of the
    grape.

¹⁵Jeshurunᵖ grew fat and kicked;
  filled with food, he became heavy
    and sleek.
He abandoned the God who made him
  and rejected the Rock his Savior.
¹⁶They made him jealous with their
    foreign gods
  and angered him with their
    detestable idols.
¹⁷They sacrificed to demons, which are
    not God—
  gods they had not known,
  gods that recently appeared,
  gods your fathers did not fear.
¹⁸You deserted the Rock, who fathered
    you;
  you forgot the God who gave you
    birth.

¹⁹The LORD saw this and rejected them
  because he was angered by his sons
    and daughters.
²⁰"I will hide my face from them," he
    said,

ᵐ5 Or *Corrupt are they and not his children,* / *a generation warped and twisted to their shame*   ⁿ6 Or *Father, who bought you*
ᵒ8 Masoretic Text; Dead Sea Scrolls (see also Septuagint) *sons of God*   ᵖ15 *Jeshurun* means *the upright one,* that is, Israel.

"and see what their end will be;
for they are a perverse generation,
    children who are unfaithful.
²¹They made me jealous by what is no
        god
    and angered me with their worthless
        idols.
I will make them envious by those
        who are not a people;
    I will make them angry by a nation
        that has no understanding.
²²For a fire has been kindled by my
        wrath,
    one that burns to the realm of
        death^q below.
It will devour the earth and its
        harvests
    and set afire the foundations of the
        mountains.

²³"I will heap calamities upon them
    and spend my arrows against them.
²⁴I will send wasting famine against
        them,
    consuming pestilence and deadly
        plague;
I will send against them the fangs of
        wild beasts,
    the venom of vipers that glide in the
        dust.
²⁵In the street the sword will make them
        childless;
    in their homes terror will reign.
Young men and young women will
        perish,
    infants and gray-haired men.
²⁶I said I would scatter them
    and blot out their memory from
        mankind,
²⁷but I dreaded the taunt of the enemy,
    lest the adversary misunderstand
and say, 'Our hand has triumphed;
    the LORD has not done all this.' "

²⁸They are a nation without sense,
    there is no discernment in them.
²⁹If only they were wise and would
        understand this
    and discern what their end will be!
³⁰How could one man chase a thousand,
    or two put ten thousand to flight,
unless their Rock had sold them,
    unless the LORD had given them up?
³¹For their rock is not like our Rock,
    as even our enemies concede.

³²Their vine comes from the vine of
        Sodom
    and from the fields of Gomorrah.
Their grapes are filled with poison,
    and their clusters with bitterness.
³³Their wine is the venom of serpents,
    the deadly poison of cobras.

³⁴"Have I not kept this in reserve
    and sealed it in my vaults?
³⁵It is mine to avenge; I will repay.
    In due time their foot will slip;
their day of disaster is near
    and their doom rushes upon them."

³⁶The LORD will judge his people
    and have compassion on his
        servants
when he sees their strength is gone
    and no one is left, slave or free.
³⁷He will say: "Now where are their
        gods,
    the rock they took refuge in,
³⁸the gods who ate the fat of their
        sacrifices
    and drank the wine of their drink
        offerings?
Let them rise up to help you!
    Let them give you shelter!

³⁹"See now that I myself am He!
    There is no god besides me.
I put to death and I bring to life,
    I have wounded and I will heal,
    and no one can deliver out of my
        hand.
⁴⁰I lift my hand to heaven and declare:
    As surely as I live forever,
⁴¹when I sharpen my flashing sword
    and my hand grasps it in judgment,
I will take vengeance on my
        adversaries
    and repay those who hate me.
⁴²I will make my arrows drunk with
        blood,
    while my sword devours flesh:
the blood of the slain and the captives,
    the heads of the enemy leaders."

⁴³Rejoice, O nations, with his people,^r,s
    for he will avenge the blood of his
        servants;
he will take vengeance on his enemies
    and make atonement for his land
        and people.

⁴⁴Moses came with Joshua^t son of Nun

---

^q22 Hebrew *to Sheol*   ^r43 Or *Make his people rejoice, O nations people, / and let all the angels worship him /*   ^s43 Masoretic Text; Dead Sea Scrolls (see also Septuagint)   ^t44 Hebrew *Hoshea,* a variant of *Joshua* and spoke all the words of this song in the hearing of the people. ⁴⁵When Moses finished reciting all these words to all Israel, ⁴⁶he said to them, "Take to heart all the words I have solemnly declared to you this day, so that you may command your children to obey carefully all the words of this law. ⁴⁷They are not just idle words for you—they are your life. By them you will live long in the land you are crossing the Jordan to possess."

⁴⁸On that same day the LORD told Moses, ⁴⁹"Go up into the Abarim Range to Mount Nebo in Moab, across from Jericho, and view Canaan, the land I am giving the Israelites as their own possession. ⁵⁰There on the mountain that you have climbed you will die and be gathered to your people, just as your brother Aaron died on Mount Hor and was gathered to his people. ⁵¹This is because both of you broke faith with me in the presence of the Israelites at the waters of Meribah Kadesh in the Desert of Zin and because you did not uphold my holiness among the Israelites. ⁵²Therefore, you will see the land only from a distance; you will not enter the land I am giving to the people of Israel."

C H A P T E R   3 3

This is the blessing that Moses the man of God pronounced on the Israelites before his death. ²He said:

"The LORD came from Sinai
    and dawned over them from Seir;
    he shone forth from Mount Paran.
He came with ᵘ myriads of holy ones
    from the south, from his mountain
        slopes. ᵛ
³Surely it is you who love the people;
    all the holy ones are in your hand.
At your feet they all bow down,
    and from you receive instruction,
⁴the law that Moses gave us,
    the possession of the assembly of
        Jacob.
⁵He was king over Jeshurun ʷ
    when the leaders of the people
        assembled,
    along with the tribes of Israel.

⁶"Let Reuben live and not die,
    nor ˣ his men be few."

⁷And this he said about Judah:

"Hear, O LORD, the cry of Judah;
    bring him to his people.
With his own hands he defends his
        cause.
    Oh, be his help against his foes!"

⁸About Levi he said:

"Your Thummim and Urim belong
    to the man you favored.
You tested him at Massah;
    you contended with him at the
        waters of Meribah.
⁹He said of his father and mother,
    'I have no regard for them.'
He did not recognize his brothers
    or acknowledge his own children,
but he watched over your word
    and guarded your covenant.
¹⁰He teaches your precepts to Jacob
    and your law to Israel.
He offers incense before you
    and whole burnt offerings on your
        altar.
¹¹Bless all his skills, O LORD,
    and be pleased with the work of his
        hands.
Smite the loins of those who rise up
        against him;
    strike his foes till they rise no more."

¹²About Benjamin he said:

"Let the beloved of the LORD rest
        secure in him,
    for he shields him all day long,
    and the one the LORD loves rests
        between his shoulders."

¹³About Joseph he said:

"May the LORD bless his land
    with the precious dew from heaven
        above
    and with the deep waters that lie
        below;
¹⁴with the best the sun brings forth
    and the finest the moon can yield;
¹⁵with the choicest gifts of the ancient
        mountains
    and the fruitfulness of the
        everlasting hills;
¹⁶with the best gifts of the earth and its
        fullness
    and the favor of him who dwelt in
        the burning bush.

ᵘ2 Or *from*   ᵛ2 The meaning of the Hebrew for this phrase is uncertain.   ʷ5 *Jeshurun* means *the upright one,* that is, Israel; also in verse 26.   ˣ6 Or *but let*

Let all these rest on the head of
  Joseph,
  on the brow of the prince among[y]
  his brothers.
¹⁷In majesty he is like a firstborn bull;
  his horns are the horns of a wild ox.
With them he will gore the nations,
  even those at the ends of the earth.
Such are the ten thousands of
  Ephraim;
  such are the thousands of
  Manasseh."

¹⁸About Zebulun he said:

"Rejoice, Zebulun, in your going out,
  and you, Issachar, in your tents.
¹⁹They will summon peoples to the
  mountain
  and there offer sacrifices of
  righteousness;
they will feast on the abundance of the
  seas,
  on the treasures hidden in the sand."

²⁰About Gad he said:

"Blessed is he who enlarges Gad's
  domain!
  Gad lives there like a lion,
  tearing at arm or head.
²¹He chose the best land for himself;
  the leader's portion was kept for
  him.
When the heads of the people
  assembled,
he carried out the LORD's righteous
  will,
  and his judgments concerning
  Israel."

²²About Dan he said:

"Dan is a lion's cub,
  springing out of Bashan."

²³About Naphtali he said:

"Naphtali is abounding with the favor
  of the LORD
  and is full of his blessing;
he will inherit southward to the
  lake."

²⁴About Asher he said:

"Most blessed of sons is Asher;
  let him be favored by his brothers,
  and let him bathe his feet in oil.

²⁵The bolts of your gates will be iron
  and bronze,
  and your strength will equal your
  days.

²⁶"There is no one like the God of
  Jeshurun,
  who rides on the heavens to help
  you
  and on the clouds in his majesty.
²⁷The eternal God is your refuge,
  and underneath are the everlasting
  arms.
He will drive out your enemy before
  you,
  saying, 'Destroy him!'
²⁸So Israel will live in safety alone;
  Jacob's spring is secure
in a land of grain and new wine,
  where the heavens drop dew.
²⁹Blessed are you, O Israel!
  Who is like you,
  a people saved by the LORD?
He is your shield and helper
  and your glorious sword.
Your enemies will cower before you,
  and you will trample down their
  high places.[z]"

CHAPTER 34

Then Moses climbed Mount Nebo from
the plains of Moab to the top of Pisgah,
across from Jericho. There the LORD
showed him the whole land—from Gilead
to Dan, ²all of Naphtali, the territory of
Ephraim and Manasseh, all the land of
Judah as far as the western sea,[a] ³the
Negev and the whole region from the
Valley of Jericho, the City of Palms, as far
as Zoar. ⁴Then the LORD said to him, "This
is the land I promised on oath to Abraham, Isaac and Jacob when I said, 'I will
give it to your descendants.' I have let you
see it with your eyes, but you will not
cross over into it."

⁵And Moses the servant of the LORD
died there in Moab, as the LORD had said.
⁶He buried him[b] in Moab, in the valley
opposite Beth Peor, but to this day no one
knows where his grave is. ⁷Moses was a
hundred and twenty years old when he
died, yet his eyes were not weak nor his
strength gone. ⁸The Israelites grieved for
Moses in the plains of Moab thirty days,
until the time of weeping and mourning
was over.

---

y16 Or *of the one separated from*   z29 Or *will tread upon their bodies*   a2 That is, the Mediterranean   b6 Or *He was buried*

⁹Now Joshua son of Nun was filled with the spirit*c* of wisdom because Moses had laid his hands on him. So the Israelites listened to him and did what the LORD had commanded Moses.

¹⁰Since then, no prophet has risen in Israel like Moses, whom the LORD knew face to face, ¹¹who did all those miraculous signs and wonders the LORD sent him to do in Egypt—to Pharaoh and to all his officials and to his whole land. ¹²For no one has ever shown the mighty power or performed the awesome deeds that Moses did in the sight of all Israel.

c9 Or *Spirit*

FEBRUARY 29 □ DAY 60
All God Requires

LOOK BACK "Take two," says your doctor, instructing you to take two tablets of medication every day until you feel better.

"Take two," says the director, instructing the actors to repeat a part of the drama that didn't come off right the first time.

Both would be accurate summaries of the chapters you have read this past week. "Take two tablets of the law," says Moses, and make them, not your daily *medication,* but your daily *meditation.* In so doing, the new generation would avoid the folly and heartache of their parents, who died in the desert rather than in the land of milk and honey. The nation is given a second chance to discover that the law is designed, not to restrict and shackle, but to align the nation with God's holy purposes, resulting in provision, protection and prolonged life (5:32–33).

It's a lesson God wants parents to teach their children, and Israel to teach the nations around them: "And now, O Israel, what does the LORD your God ask of you but to fear the LORD your God, to walk in all his ways, to love him, to serve the LORD your God with all your heart and with all your soul, and to observe the LORD's commands and decrees that I am giving you today *for your own good?*" (10:12–13, emphasis added).

LOOK UP What does the highway patrol in your state require of motorists if they are going to use the highways? (Stay within the speed limit; don't endanger others; keep your car under control; don't drive without a license—simple things designed for the well-being of all.) Would you say that the highway patrol is heavy-handed and unfair to make such demands of motorists who want to drive on the highways, or that it is their intent to ensure that everyone is able to use and enjoy the highways to the fullest? The latter, of course.

A person who "knows everything" has a lot to learn.

In the same way, the author of life, who ought to know how life was meant to be lived, desires you to discover how to live life to the fullest. After all, it was Jesus who said, "I have come that they may have life, and have it to the full" (John 10:10). God is no cosmic killjoy, out to make you miserable with needless rules and regulations. His commands and warnings are for our ultimate good, and those who ignore them are an accident waiting to happen.

You can be sure if God says something more than once (such as the Ten Commandments in Exodus 20 and Deuteronomy 5), it's no accident!

LOOK AHEAD Perhaps the prophet Micah said it best. Read his words out loud twice, looking for the answer to the question, What is God expecting me to do?

> "He has showed you, O man, what is good.
>   And what does the LORD require of you?
> To act justly and to love mercy
>   And to walk humbly with your God." (Micah 6:8)

Now close your eyes, tell God what you read, and what you intend to do about it.

Joshua

THE BOOK of Joshua is a tale of war and peace. In the first twelve chapters, the people of Israel conquer the land of Canaan. Through three military campaigns involving more than thirty enemy armies, they learn a valuable lesson under Joshua's capable leadership: Victory comes through faith in God and obedience to his word rather than by military might or numerical superiority. In the final twelve chapters, peace reigns as the people of God divide up their new homeland.

Focus	Divide and Conquer			Divide and Settle		
Divisions	Preparation	Central Campaign	Moving South & North	Portions for 5 Tribes	Portions for 7 Tribes	Joshua's Last Words
	1　　5	6　　8	9　　12	13　　17	18　　21	22　　24
Topics	Possessing Canaan			Partitioning Canaan		
	Subduing the Land			Settling the Land		
Place	9½ Tribes West of the Jordan (Canaan) 2½ Tribes East of the Jordan (Transjordan)					
Time	About 7 Years			About 18 Years		

MARCH 1 □ DAY 61
JOSHUA 1–5
Preparation of the People for War

OVERVIEW Moses, "the servant of the LORD," is dead. In his place stands General Joshua, one of only two adults surviving the forty years of desert wandering. Joshua must guide the nation across the flood-swollen Jordan River and into battle against the fortified cities of Canaan—certainly not an assignment for the fainthearted! Spying out the city of Jericho . . . crossing the Jordan . . . circumcising the new generation—each step brings comforting reminders of God's promise to fight on behalf of his people.

Chapter 1	Chapter 2	Chapters 3–4	Chapter 5
Commands for Joshua	Close Call at Jericho	Crossing the Jordan	Commemorating the Passover
"Be strong"	"Go look"	"Go over"	"Circumcise"

YOUR DAILY WALK The coach is giving his pregame pep talk to the local football team. To the players, the opposing team looks enormous, obviously outweighing (and no doubt outplaying) them at every position. Somehow the coach's encouragement rings hollow: "OK, men, now I want you to go out there and be strong . . . be courageous . . . don't let their size terrify you." But then an amazing thing happens. The coach, a man of unequaled strength and skill, lays aside his whistle and playbook, dons a jersey, and announces to the team: "I will be your quarterback, and in my strength we cannot fail. So be strong!"

Confidence is the feeling you have just before you fully understand the situation.

The opening chapter of Joshua was no mere divine pep talk. Rather, God was providing Joshua with the bedrock assurance he needed to face the towering giants and fortified strongholds of Canaan. Humanly speaking, the battle seemed already lost; but from God's perspective, the battle was already won—because it would be fought in his strength! What is one situation in your life today in which you too can draw courage from the promise of Joshua 1:5?

INSIGHT Joshua, the Renamed General
Joshua's original name was *Hoshea* (Numbers 13:8), which means "salvation." But during the desert wanderings Moses changed his name to *Jehoshua*, "the LORD is salvation" (Numbers 13:16). *Joshua* is a contracted form of *Jehoshua* and the Hebrew form of the New Testament Greek name *Jesus*.

CHAPTER 1
After the death of Moses the servant of the LORD, the LORD said to Joshua son of Nun, Moses' aide: ²"Moses my servant is dead. Now then, you and all these people, get ready to cross the Jordan River into the land I am about to give to them—to the Israelites. ³I will give you every place where you set your foot, as I promised Moses. ⁴Your territory will extend from the desert to Lebanon, and from the great river, the Euphrates—all the Hittite

country—to the Great Sea[a] on the west. [5]No one will be able to stand up against you all the days of your life. As I was with Moses, so I will be with you; I will never leave you nor forsake you.

[6]"Be strong and courageous, because you will lead these people to inherit the land I swore to their forefathers to give them. [7]Be strong and very courageous. Be careful to obey all the law my servant Moses gave you; do not turn from it to the right or to the left, that you may be successful wherever you go. [8]Do not let this Book of the Law depart from your mouth; meditate on it day and night, so that you may be careful to do everything written in it. Then you will be prosperous and successful. [9]Have I not commanded you? Be strong and courageous. Do not be terrified; do not be discouraged, for the LORD your God will be with you wherever you go."

[10]So Joshua ordered the officers of the people: [11]"Go through the camp and tell the people, 'Get your supplies ready. Three days from now you will cross the Jordan here to go in and take possession of the land the LORD your God is giving you for your own.'"

[12]But to the Reubenites, the Gadites and the half-tribe of Manasseh, Joshua said, [13]"Remember the command that Moses the servant of the LORD gave you: 'The LORD your God is giving you rest and has granted you this land.' [14]Your wives, your children and your livestock may stay in the land that Moses gave you east of the Jordan, but all your fighting men, fully armed, must cross over ahead of your brothers. You are to help your brothers [15]until the LORD gives them rest, as he has done for you, and until they too have taken possession of the land that the LORD your God is giving them. After that, you may go back and occupy your own land, which Moses the servant of the LORD gave you east of the Jordan toward the sunrise."

[16]Then they answered Joshua, "Whatever you have commanded us we will do, and wherever you send us we will go. [17]Just as we fully obeyed Moses, so we will obey you. Only may the LORD your God be with you as he was with Moses. [18]Whoever rebels against your word and does not obey your words, whatever you may command them, will be put to death. Only be strong and courageous!"

CHAPTER 2

Then Joshua son of Nun secretly sent two spies from Shittim. "Go, look over the land," he said, "especially Jericho." So they went and entered the house of a prostitute[b] named Rahab and stayed there.

[2]The king of Jericho was told, "Look! Some of the Israelites have come here tonight to spy out the land." [3]So the king of Jericho sent this message to Rahab: "Bring out the men who came to you and entered your house, because they have come to spy out the whole land."

[4]But the woman had taken the two men and hidden them. She said, "Yes, the men came to me, but I did not know where they had come from. [5]At dusk, when it was time to close the city gate, the men left. I don't know which way they went. Go after them quickly. You may catch up with them." [6](But she had taken them up to the roof and hidden them under the stalks of flax she had laid out on the roof.) [7]So the men set out in pursuit of the spies on the road that leads to the fords of the Jordan, and as soon as the pursuers had gone out, the gate was shut.

[8]Before the spies lay down for the night, she went up on the roof [9]and said to them, "I know that the LORD has given this land to you and that a great fear of you has fallen on us, so that all who live in this country are melting in fear because of you. [10]We have heard how the LORD dried up the water of the Red Sea[c] for you when you came out of Egypt, and what you did to Sihon and Og, the two kings of the Amorites east of the Jordan, whom you completely destroyed.[d] [11]When we heard of it, our hearts melted and everyone's courage failed because of you, for the LORD your God is God in heaven above and on the earth below. [12]Now then, please swear to me by the LORD that you will show kindness to my family, because I have shown kindness to you. Give me a sure sign [13]that you will spare the lives of my father and mother, my brothers and sisters, and all who belong to them, and that you will save us from death."

¹⁴"Our lives for your lives!" the men assured her. "If you don't tell what we are doing, we will treat you kindly and faithfully when the LORD gives us the land."

¹⁵So she let them down by a rope through the window, for the house she lived in was part of the city wall. ¹⁶Now she had said to them, "Go to the hills so the pursuers will not find you. Hide yourselves there three days until they return, and then go on your way."

¹⁷The men said to her, "This oath you made us swear will not be binding on us ¹⁸unless, when we enter the land, you have tied this scarlet cord in the window through which you let us down, and unless you have brought your father and mother, your brothers and all your family into your house. ¹⁹If anyone goes outside your house into the street, his blood will be on his own head; we will not be responsible. As for anyone who is in the house with you, his blood will be on our head if a hand is laid on him. ²⁰But if you tell what we are doing, we will be released from the oath you made us swear."

²¹"Agreed," she replied. "Let it be as you say." So she sent them away and they departed. And she tied the scarlet cord in the window.

²²When they left, they went into the hills and stayed there three days, until the pursuers had searched all along the road and returned without finding them. ²³Then the two men started back. They went down out of the hills, forded the river and came to Joshua son of Nun and told him everything that had happened to them. ²⁴They said to Joshua, "The LORD has surely given the whole land into our hands; all the people are melting in fear because of us."

CHAPTER 3

Early in the morning Joshua and all the Israelites set out from Shittim and went to the Jordan, where they camped before crossing over. ²After three days the officers went throughout the camp, ³giving orders to the people: "When you see the ark of the covenant of the LORD your God, and the priests, who are Levites, carrying it, you are to move out from your positions and follow it. ⁴Then you will know

which way to go, since you have never been this way before. But keep a distance of about a thousand yardsᵉ between you and the ark; do not go near it."

⁵Joshua told the people, "Consecrate yourselves, for tomorrow the LORD will do amazing things among you."

⁶Joshua said to the priests, "Take up the ark of the covenant and pass on ahead of the people." So they took it up and went ahead of them.

⁷And the LORD said to Joshua, "Today I will begin to exalt you in the eyes of all Israel, so they may know that I am with you as I was with Moses. ⁸Tell the priests who carry the ark of the covenant: 'When you reach the edge of the Jordan's waters, go and stand in the river.' "

⁹Joshua said to the Israelites, "Come here and listen to the words of the LORD your God. ¹⁰This is how you will know that the living God is among you and that he will certainly drive out before you the Canaanites, Hittites, Hivites, Perizzites, Girgashites, Amorites and Jebusites. ¹¹See, the ark of the covenant of the Lord of all the earth will go into the Jordan ahead of you. ¹²Now then, choose twelve men from the tribes of Israel, one from each tribe. ¹³And as soon as the priests who carry the ark of the LORD—the Lord of all the earth—set foot in the Jordan, its waters flowing downstream will be cut off and stand up in a heap."

¹⁴So when the people broke camp to cross the Jordan, the priests carrying the ark of the covenant went ahead of them. ¹⁵Now the Jordan is at flood stage all during harvest. Yet as soon as the priests who carried the ark reached the Jordan and their feet touched the water's edge, ¹⁶the water from upstream stopped flowing. It piled up in a heap a great distance away, at a town called Adam in the vicinity of Zarethan, while the water flowing down to the Sea of the Arabah (the Salt Sea ᶠ) was completely cut off. So the people crossed over opposite Jericho. ¹⁷The priests who carried the ark of the covenant of the LORD stood firm on dry ground in the middle of the Jordan, while all Israel passed by until the whole nation had completed the crossing on dry ground.

ᵉ4 Hebrew *about two thousand cubits* (about 900 meters)   ᶠ16 That is, the Dead Sea

CHAPTER 4

When the whole nation had finished crossing the Jordan, the LORD said to Joshua, ²"Choose twelve men from among the people, one from each tribe, ³and tell them to take up twelve stones from the middle of the Jordan from right where the priests stood and to carry them over with you and put them down at the place where you stay tonight."

⁴So Joshua called together the twelve men he had appointed from the Israelites, one from each tribe, ⁵and said to them, "Go over before the ark of the LORD your God into the middle of the Jordan. Each of you is to take up a stone on his shoulder, according to the number of the tribes of the Israelites, ⁶to serve as a sign among you. In the future, when your children ask you, 'What do these stones mean?' ⁷tell them that the flow of the Jordan was cut off before the ark of the covenant of the LORD. When it crossed the Jordan, the waters of the Jordan were cut off. These stones are to be a memorial to the people of Israel forever."

⁸So the Israelites did as Joshua commanded them. They took twelve stones from the middle of the Jordan, according to the number of the tribes of the Israelites, as the LORD had told Joshua; and they carried them over with them to their camp, where they put them down. ⁹Joshua set up the twelve stones that had beenᵍ in the middle of the Jordan at the spot where the priests who carried the ark of the covenant had stood. And they are there to this day.

¹⁰Now the priests who carried the ark remained standing in the middle of the Jordan until everything the LORD had commanded Joshua was done by the people, just as Moses had directed Joshua. The people hurried over, ¹¹and as soon as all of them had crossed, the ark of the LORD and the priests came to the other side while the people watched. ¹²The men of Reuben, Gad and the half-tribe of Manasseh crossed over, armed, in front of the Israelites, as Moses had directed them. ¹³About forty thousand armed for battle crossed over before the LORD to the plains of Jericho for war.

¹⁴That day the LORD exalted Joshua in the sight of all Israel; and they revered him all the days of his life, just as they had revered Moses.

¹⁵Then the LORD said to Joshua, ¹⁶"Command the priests carrying the ark of the Testimony to come up out of the Jordan."

¹⁷So Joshua commanded the priests, "Come up out of the Jordan."

¹⁸And the priests came up out of the river carrying the ark of the covenant of the LORD. No sooner had they set their feet on the dry ground than the waters of the Jordan returned to their place and ran at flood stage as before.

¹⁹On the tenth day of the first month the people went up from the Jordan and camped at Gilgal on the eastern border of Jericho. ²⁰And Joshua set up at Gilgal the twelve stones they had taken out of the Jordan. ²¹He said to the Israelites, "In the future when your descendants ask their fathers, 'What do these stones mean?' ²²tell them, 'Israel crossed the Jordan on dry ground.' ²³For the LORD your God dried up the Jordan before you until you had crossed over. The LORD your God did to the Jordan just what he had done to the Red Seaʰ when he dried it up before us until we had crossed over. ²⁴He did this so that all the peoples of the earth might know that the hand of the LORD is powerful and so that you might always fear the LORD your God."

CHAPTER 5

Now when all the Amorite kings west of the Jordan and all the Canaanite kings along the coast heard how the LORD had dried up the Jordan before the Israelites until we had crossed over, their hearts melted and they no longer had the courage to face the Israelites.

²At that time the LORD said to Joshua, "Make flint knives and circumcise the Israelites again." ³So Joshua made flint knives and circumcised the Israelites at Gibeath Haaraloth.ⁱ

⁴Now this is why he did so: All those who came out of Egypt—all the men of military age—died in the desert on the way after leaving Egypt. ⁵All the people that came out had been circumcised, but all the people born in the desert during the journey from Egypt had not. ⁶The Israelites had moved about in the desert forty years until all the men who were of

ᵍ9 Or *Joshua also set up twelve stones*   ʰ23 Hebrew *Yam Suph*; that is, Sea of Reeds   ⁱ3 *Gibeath Haaraloth* means *hill of foreskins*.

military age when they left Egypt had died, since they had not obeyed the LORD. For the LORD had sworn to them that they would not see the land that he had solemnly promised their fathers to give us, a land flowing with milk and honey. ⁷So he raised up their sons in their place, and these were the ones Joshua circumcised. They were still uncircumcised because they had not been circumcised on the way. ⁸And after the whole nation had been circumcised, they remained where they were in camp until they were healed.

⁹Then the LORD said to Joshua, "Today I have rolled away the reproach of Egypt from you." So the place has been called Gilgalʲ to this day.

¹⁰On the evening of the fourteenth day of the month, while camped at Gilgal on the plains of Jericho, the Israelites celebrated the Passover. ¹¹The day after the Passover, that very day, they ate some of the produce of the land: unleavened bread and roasted grain. ¹²The manna stopped the day afterᵏ they ate this food from the land; there was no longer any manna for the Israelites, but that year they ate of the produce of Canaan.

¹³Now when Joshua was near Jericho, he looked up and saw a man standing in front of him with a drawn sword in his hand. Joshua went up to him and asked, "Are you for us or for our enemies?"

¹⁴"Neither," he replied, "but as commander of the army of the LORD I have now come." Then Joshua fell facedown to the ground in reverence, and asked him, "What message does my Lordˡ have for his servant?"

¹⁵The commander of the LORD's army replied, "Take off your sandals, for the place where you are standing is holy." And Joshua did so.

ʲ9 *Gilgal* sounds like the Hebrew for *roll.*   ᵏ12 Or *the day*   ˡ14 Or *lord*

MARCH 2 ☐ DAY 62
JOSHUA 6–8
Central Campaign

 OVERVIEW Standing like a taunting giant in the path of the approaching Israelites is the walled fortress of Jericho. There can be no skirting the issue: Jericho must be conquered. But how? The strategy God delivers to Joshua is truly unique and is designed to ensure that if the walls fall down, there can be only one explanation—God did it! Joshua leads the people on a daily lap around the city walls, culminating in a seven-lap marathon on the seventh day. At last comes the moment to shout . . . and Jericho's walls turn to rubble. But even in victory the people of God disobey. Achan steals some of the forbidden booty, resulting in death and defeat for the Israelite army.

Chapter 6	Chapter 7	Chapter 8
Obedient Victory at Jericho	Disobedient Defeat at Ai	Obedient Rematch at Ai
The Thrill of Victory	The Agony of Defeat	

 YOUR DAILY WALK *Hate* is a strong word. And to say that God hates is even stronger!

Yet the Bible lists many things that God hates: idolatry (Deuteronomy 16:22), wickedness (Psalm 45:7), pride, lying, murder, discord, wicked scheming (Proverbs 6:16–19)—in a word, SIN!

Today's reading explains one reason why God finds sin so abhorrent: It leaves scars on the innocent as well as the guilty. Achan's

There is no biblical authority for believing there is any such thing as a little sin. sin—seemingly so private and harmless—resulted in thirty-six lives needlessly lost in battle and an entire nation left in disarray.

Are you tempted to disobey God today, concluding, "It's my life and I can do with it as I please"? Then stop and consider. What will disobedience cost you personally? How will it affect others around you? God has strength for you to be a conqueror instead (Romans 8:37). Will you turn to him right now and use that strength?

 INSIGHT Long Odds at Ai
Overconfident from their smashing victory at Jericho, the people urge Joshua to send only a token force against Ai (7:3). Joshua agrees, sending only three thousand soldiers (7:4). In their own strength—and facing an enemy that outnumbers them four-to-one (8:25)—the Israelite troops suffer a staggering defeat. The lesson is clear: With God on your side, you cannot lose; without him, you cannot win!

CHAPTER 6

Now Jericho was tightly shut up because of the Israelites. No one went out and no one came in.

²Then the LORD said to Joshua, "See, I have delivered Jericho into your hands, along with its king and its fighting men. ³March around the city once with all the armed men. Do this for six days. ⁴Have seven priests carry trumpets of rams' horns in front of the ark. On the seventh day, march around the city seven times, with the priests blowing the trumpets. ⁵When you hear them sound a long blast on the trumpets, have all the people give a loud shout; then the wall of the city will collapse and the people will go up, every man straight in."

⁶So Joshua son of Nun called the priests and said to them, "Take up the ark of the covenant of the LORD and have seven priests carry trumpets in front of it." ⁷And he ordered the people, "Advance! March around the city, with the armed guard going ahead of the ark of the LORD."

⁸When Joshua had spoken to the people, the seven priests carrying the seven trumpets before the LORD went forward, blowing their trumpets, and the ark of the LORD's covenant followed them. ⁹The armed guard marched ahead of the priests who blew the trumpets, and the rear guard followed the ark. All this time the trumpets were sounding. ¹⁰But Joshua had commanded the people, "Do not give a war cry, do not raise your voices, do not say a word until the day I tell you to shout. Then shout!" ¹¹So he had the ark of the LORD carried around the city, circling it once. Then the people returned to camp and spent the night there.

¹²Joshua got up early the next morning and the priests took up the ark of the LORD. ¹³The seven priests carrying the seven trumpets went forward, marching before the ark of the LORD and blowing the trumpets. The armed men went ahead of them and the rear guard followed the ark of the LORD, while the trumpets kept sounding. ¹⁴So on the second day they marched around the city once and returned to the camp. They did this for six days.

¹⁵On the seventh day, they got up at daybreak and marched around the city seven times in the same manner, except that on that day they circled the city seven times. ¹⁶The seventh time around, when the priests sounded the trumpet blast, Joshua commanded the people, "Shout! For the LORD has given you the city! ¹⁷The city and all that is in it are to be devoted ᵐ to the LORD. Only Rahab the prostitute ⁿ and all who are with her in her house shall be spared, because she hid the spies we sent. ¹⁸But keep away from the devoted things, so that you will not bring about your own destruction by taking any of them. Otherwise you will make the camp of Israel liable to destruction and bring trouble on it. ¹⁹All the silver and gold and the articles of bronze and iron are sacred to the LORD and must go into his treasury."

²⁰When the trumpets sounded, the people shouted, and at the sound of the trumpet, when the people gave a loud shout, the wall collapsed; so every man

---

ᵐ17 The Hebrew term refers to the irrevocable giving over of things or persons to the LORD, often by totally destroying them; also in verses 18 and 21.   ⁿ17 Or possibly *innkeeper*; also in verses 22 and 25 charged straight in, and they took the city. [21]They devoted the city to the LORD and destroyed with the sword every living thing in it—men and women, young and old, cattle, sheep and donkeys.

[22]Joshua said to the two men who had spied out the land, "Go into the prostitute's house and bring her out and all who belong to her, in accordance with your oath to her." [23]So the young men who had done the spying went in and brought out Rahab, her father and mother and brothers and all who belonged to her. They brought out her entire family and put them in a place outside the camp of Israel.

[24]Then they burned the whole city and everything in it, but they put the silver and gold and the articles of bronze and iron into the treasury of the LORD's house. [25]But Joshua spared Rahab the prostitute, with her family and all who belonged to her, because she hid the men Joshua had sent as spies to Jericho—and she lives among the Israelites to this day.

[26]At that time Joshua pronounced this solemn oath: "Cursed before the LORD is the man who undertakes to rebuild this city, Jericho:

"At the cost of his firstborn son
    will he lay its foundations;
at the cost of his youngest
    will he set up its gates."

[27]So the LORD was with Joshua, and his fame spread throughout the land.

CHAPTER 7

But the Israelites acted unfaithfully in regard to the devoted things[o]; Achan son of Carmi, the son of Zimri,[p] the son of Zerah, of the tribe of Judah, took some of them. So the LORD's anger burned against Israel.

[2]Now Joshua sent men from Jericho to Ai, which is near Beth Aven to the east of Bethel, and told them, "Go up and spy out the region." So the men went up and spied out Ai.

[3]When they returned to Joshua, they said, "Not all the people will have to go up against Ai. Send two or three thousand men to take it and do not weary all the people, for only a few men are there." [4]So

about three thousand men went up; but they were routed by the men of Ai, [5]who killed about thirty-six of them. They chased the Israelites from the city gate as far as the stone quarries[q] and struck them down on the slopes. At this the hearts of the people melted and became like water.

[6]Then Joshua tore his clothes and fell facedown to the ground before the ark of the LORD, remaining there till evening. The elders of Israel did the same, and sprinkled dust on their heads. [7]And Joshua said, "Ah, Sovereign LORD, why did you ever bring this people across the Jordan to deliver us into the hands of the Amorites to destroy us? If only we had been content to stay on the other side of the Jordan! [8]O Lord, what can I say, now that Israel has been routed by its enemies? [9]The Canaanites and the other people of the country will hear about this and they will surround us and wipe out our name from the earth. What then will you do for your own great name?"

[10]The LORD said to Joshua, "Stand up! What are you doing down on your face? [11]Israel has sinned; they have violated my covenant, which I commanded them to keep. They have taken some of the devoted things; they have stolen, they have lied, they have put them with their own possessions. [12]That is why the Israelites cannot stand against their enemies; they turn their backs and run because they have been made liable to destruction. I will not be with you anymore unless you destroy whatever among you is devoted to destruction.

[13]"Go, consecrate the people. Tell them, 'Consecrate yourselves in preparation for tomorrow; for this is what the LORD, the God of Israel, says: That which is devoted is among you, O Israel. You cannot stand against your enemies until you remove it.

[14]" 'In the morning, present yourselves tribe by tribe. The tribe that the LORD takes shall come forward clan by clan; the clan that the LORD takes shall come forward family by family; and the family that the LORD takes shall come forward man by man. [15]He who is caught with the devoted things shall be destroyed by fire, along with all that belongs to him. He has

violated the covenant of the LORD and has done a disgraceful thing in Israel!' "

¹⁶Early the next morning Joshua had Israel come forward by tribes, and Judah was taken. ¹⁷The clans of Judah came forward, and he took the Zerahites. He had the clan of the Zerahites come forward by families, and Zimri was taken. ¹⁸Joshua had his family come forward man by man, and Achan son of Carmi, the son of Zimri, the son of Zerah, of the tribe of Judah, was taken.

¹⁹Then Joshua said to Achan, "My son, give glory to the LORD,ʳ the God of Israel, and give him the praise.ˢ Tell me what you have done; do not hide it from me."

²⁰Achan replied, "It is true! I have sinned against the LORD, the God of Israel. This is what I have done: ²¹When I saw in the plunder a beautiful robe from Babylonia,ᵗ two hundred shekelsᵘ of silver and a wedge of gold weighing fifty shekels,ᵛ I coveted them and took them. They are hidden in the ground inside my tent, with the silver underneath."

²²So Joshua sent messengers, and they ran to the tent, and there it was, hidden in his tent, with the silver underneath. ²³They took the things from the tent, brought them to Joshua and all the Israelites and spread them out before the LORD.

²⁴Then Joshua, together with all Israel, took Achan son of Zerah, the silver, the robe, the gold wedge, his sons and daughters, his cattle, donkeys and sheep, his tent and all that he had, to the Valley of Achor. ²⁵Joshua said, "Why have you brought this trouble on us? The LORD will bring trouble on you today."

Then all Israel stoned him, and after they had stoned the rest, they burned them. ²⁶Over Achan they heaped up a large pile of rocks, which remains to this day. Then the LORD turned from his fierce anger. Therefore that place has been called the Valley of Achorʷ ever since.

CHAPTER 8

Then the LORD said to Joshua, "Do not be afraid; do not be discouraged. Take the whole army with you, and go up and attack Ai. For I have delivered into your hands the king of Ai, his people, his city and his land. ²You shall do to Ai and its king as you did to Jericho and its king,

except that you may carry off their plunder and livestock for yourselves. Set an ambush behind the city."

³So Joshua and the whole army moved out to attack Ai. He chose thirty thousand of his best fighting men and sent them out at night ⁴with these orders: "Listen carefully. You are to set an ambush behind the city. Don't go very far from it. All of you be on the alert. ⁵I and all those with me will advance on the city, and when the men come out against us, as they did before, we will flee from them. ⁶They will pursue us until we have lured them away from the city, for they will say, 'They are running away from us as they did before.' So when we flee from them, ⁷you are to rise up from ambush and take the city. The LORD your God will give it into your hand. ⁸When you have taken the city, set it on fire. Do what the LORD has commanded. See to it; you have my orders."

⁹Then Joshua sent them off, and they went to the place of ambush and lay in wait between Bethel and Ai, to the west of Ai—but Joshua spent that night with the people.

¹⁰Early the next morning Joshua mustered his men, and he and the leaders of Israel marched before them to Ai. ¹¹The entire force that was with him marched up and approached the city and arrived in front of it. They set up camp north of Ai, with the valley between them and the city. ¹²Joshua had taken about five thousand men and set them in ambush between Bethel and Ai, to the west of the city. ¹³They had the soldiers take up their positions—all those in the camp to the north of the city and the ambush to the west of it. That night Joshua went into the valley.

¹⁴When the king of Ai saw this, he and all the men of the city hurried out early in the morning to meet Israel in battle at a certain place overlooking the Arabah. But he did not know that an ambush had been set against him behind the city. ¹⁵Joshua and all Israel let themselves be driven back before them, and they fled toward the desert. ¹⁶All the men of Ai were called to pursue them, and they pursued Joshua and were lured away from the city. ¹⁷Not a man remained in Ai or Bethel who did

---

ʳ19 A solemn charge to tell the truth   ˢ19 Or and confess to him   ᵗ21 Hebrew Shinar   ᵘ21 That is, about 5 pounds (about 2.3 kilograms)   ᵛ21 That is, about 1 1/4 pounds (about 0.6 kilogram)   ʷ26 Achor means trouble.

not go after Israel. They left the city open and went in pursuit of Israel.

[18]Then the LORD said to Joshua, "Hold out toward Ai the javelin that is in your hand, for into your hand I will deliver the city." So Joshua held out his javelin toward Ai. [19]As soon as he did this, the men in the ambush rose quickly from their position and rushed forward. They entered the city and captured it and quickly set it on fire.

[20]The men of Ai looked back and saw the smoke of the city rising against the sky, but they had no chance to escape in any direction, for the Israelites who had been fleeing toward the desert had turned back against their pursuers. [21]For when Joshua and all Israel saw that the ambush had taken the city and that smoke was going up from the city, they turned around and attacked the men of Ai. [22]The men of the ambush also came out of the city against them, so that they were caught in the middle, with Israelites on both sides. Israel cut them down, leaving them neither survivors nor fugitives. [23]But they took the king of Ai alive and brought him to Joshua.

[24]When Israel had finished killing all the men of Ai in the fields and in the desert where they had chased them, and when every one of them had been put to the sword, all the Israelites returned to Ai and killed those who were in it. [25]Twelve thousand men and women fell that day— all the people of Ai. [26]For Joshua did not draw back the hand that held out his javelin until he had destroyed[x] all who lived in Ai. [27]But Israel did carry off for themselves the livestock and plunder of this city, as the LORD had instructed Joshua.

[28]So Joshua burned Ai and made it a permanent heap of ruins, a desolate place to this day. [29]He hung the king of Ai on a tree and left him there until evening. At sunset, Joshua ordered them to take his body from the tree and throw it down at the entrance of the city gate. And they raised a large pile of rocks over it, which remains to this day.

[30]Then Joshua built on Mount Ebal an altar to the LORD, the God of Israel, [31]as Moses the servant of the LORD had commanded the Israelites. He built it according to what is written in the Book of the Law of Moses—an altar of uncut stones, on which no iron tool had been used. On it they offered to the LORD burnt offerings and sacrificed fellowship offerings.[y] [32]There, in the presence of the Israelites, Joshua copied on stones the law of Moses, which he had written. [33]All Israel, aliens and citizens alike, with their elders, officials and judges, were standing on both sides of the ark of the covenant of the LORD, facing those who carried it—the priests, who were Levites. Half of the people stood in front of Mount Gerizim and half of them in front of Mount Ebal, as Moses the servant of the LORD had formerly commanded when he gave instructions to bless the people of Israel.

[34]Afterward, Joshua read all the words of the law—the blessings and the curses— just as it is written in the Book of the Law. [35]There was not a word of all that Moses had commanded that Joshua did not read to the whole assembly of Israel, including the women and children, and the aliens who lived among them.

[x]26 The Hebrew term refers to the irrevocable giving over of things or persons to the LORD, often by totally destroying them.
[y]31 Traditionally *peace offerings*

MARCH 3 ☐ DAY 63
JOSHUA 9–12
Moving South and North

 OVERVIEW "Divide and conquer" is a classic strategy for military conquest, and Joshua uses it to perfection. With Jericho and Ai secured, he has accomplished phase one—dividing the land in half, thereby isolating the northern and southern confederacies. Next he begins a "mopping up" operation in the south and north. But the thrill of victory is tempered by the knowledge of what should have been. The Gibeonites, hearing the sad fate of Jericho and Ai, trick Joshua into signing a pact of protection, causing the Israelites to defend rather than defeat one of their enemies.

Chapter 9	Chapter 10	Chapter 11	Chapter 12
Craftiness of Gibeon	Conquest of Five Kings	Conquest of the North	Counting Up the Score
Southern Campaign		Northern Campaign	

YOUR DAILY WALK "Dr. Livingstone, I presume?" Fortunately for Sir Henry Stanley on that fateful day in 1871 deep in the heart of central Africa, he "presumed" correctly. But more often than not, presumption can get you into trouble—particularly if it is presumption about God's Word.

Understanding can wait; obedience can't.

Yesterday you read about Achan, a man who presumed that God wouldn't mind if he stole a few trinkets from the crumbling ruins of Jericho—and paid for it with his life. Today you read about godly Joshua falling into a presumptuous sin by failing to consult the Lord. The Scriptures make it very clear that presumption can bring pretty serious consequences!

What important decision are you facing today? Don't presume you can make a wise choice without God's help. With his Spirit indwelling you and his Word available to you, he can guide you into a wise course of action—if you'll let him.

INSIGHT A Hungry Homeland

Earlier the spies described Canaan as a "land . . . [that] devours those living in it" (Numbers 13:32). During the seven-year conquest, Joshua's army destroyed thirty-one kings and most of the Canaanites, making the spies' statement ironically prophetic!

CHAPTER 9

Now when all the kings west of the Jordan heard about these things—those in the hill country, in the western foothills, and along the entire coast of the Great Sea[z] as far as Lebanon (the kings of the Hittites, Amorites, Canaanites, Perizzites, Hivites and Jebusites)— [2]they came together to make war against Joshua and Israel.

[3]However, when the people of Gibeon heard what Joshua had done to Jericho and Ai, [4]they resorted to a ruse: They went as a delegation whose donkeys were loaded[a] with worn-out sacks and old wineskins, cracked and mended. [5]The men put worn and patched sandals on their feet and wore old clothes. All the bread of their food supply was dry and moldy. [6]Then they went to Joshua in the camp at Gilgal and said to him and the men of Israel, "We have come from a distant country; make a treaty with us."

[7]The men of Israel said to the Hivites, "But perhaps you live near us. How then can we make a treaty with you?"

[8]"We are your servants," they said to Joshua.

But Joshua asked, "Who are you and where do you come from?"

[9]They answered: "Your servants have come from a very distant country because of the fame of the LORD your God. For we have heard reports of him: all that he did in Egypt, [10]and all that he did to the two kings of the Amorites east of the Jordan— Sihon king of Heshbon, and Og king of Bashan, who reigned in Ashtaroth. [11]And our elders and all those living in our country said to us, 'Take provisions for your journey; go and meet them and say to them, "We are your servants; make a treaty with us." ' [12]This bread of ours was

[z]1 That is, the Mediterranean   [a]4 Most Hebrew manuscripts; some Hebrew manuscripts, Vulgate and Syriac (see also Septuagint) *They prepared provisions and loaded their donkeys*

warm when we packed it at home on the day we left to come to you. But now see how dry and moldy it is. [13]And these wineskins that we filled were new, but see how cracked they are. And our clothes and sandals are worn out by the very long journey."

[14]The men of Israel sampled their provisions but did not inquire of the LORD. [15]Then Joshua made a treaty of peace with them to let them live, and the leaders of the assembly ratified it by oath.

[16]Three days after they made the treaty with the Gibeonites, the Israelites heard that they were neighbors, living near them. [17]So the Israelites set out and on the third day came to their cities: Gibeon, Kephirah, Beeroth and Kiriath Jearim. [18]But the Israelites did not attack them, because the leaders of the assembly had sworn an oath to them by the LORD, the God of Israel.

The whole assembly grumbled against the leaders, [19]but all the leaders answered, "We have given them our oath by the LORD, the God of Israel, and we cannot touch them now. [20]This is what we will do to them: We will let them live, so that wrath will not fall on us for breaking the oath we swore to them." [21]They continued, "Let them live, but let them be woodcutters and water carriers for the entire community." So the leaders' promise to them was kept.

[22]Then Joshua summoned the Gibeonites and said, "Why did you deceive us by saying, 'We live a long way from you,' while actually you live near us? [23]You are now under a curse: You will never cease to serve as woodcutters and water carriers for the house of my God."

[24]They answered Joshua, "Your servants were clearly told how the LORD your God had commanded his servant Moses to give you the whole land and to wipe out all its inhabitants from before you. So we feared for our lives because of you, and that is why we did this. [25]We are now in your hands. Do to us whatever seems good and right to you."

[26]So Joshua saved them from the Israelites, and they did not kill them. [27]That day he made the Gibeonites woodcutters and water carriers for the community and for the altar of the LORD at the place the LORD

would choose. And that is what they are to this day.

CHAPTER 10

Now Adoni-Zedek king of Jerusalem heard that Joshua had taken Ai and totally destroyed[b] it, doing to Ai and its king as he had done to Jericho and its king, and that the people of Gibeon had made a treaty of peace with Israel and were living near them. [2]He and his people were very much alarmed at this, because Gibeon was an important city, like one of the royal cities; it was larger than Ai, and all its men were good fighters. [3]So Adoni-Zedek king of Jerusalem appealed to Hoham king of Hebron, Piram king of Jarmuth, Japhia king of Lachish and Debir king of Eglon. [4]"Come up and help me attack Gibeon," he said, "because it has made peace with Joshua and the Israelites."

[5]Then the five kings of the Amorites—the kings of Jerusalem, Hebron, Jarmuth, Lachish and Eglon—joined forces. They moved up with all their troops and took up positions against Gibeon and attacked it.

[6]The Gibeonites then sent word to Joshua in the camp at Gilgal: "Do not abandon your servants. Come up to us quickly and save us! Help us, because all the Amorite kings from the hill country have joined forces against us."

[7]So Joshua marched up from Gilgal with his entire army, including all the best fighting men. [8]The LORD said to Joshua, "Do not be afraid of them; I have given them into your hand. Not one of them will be able to withstand you."

[9]After an all-night march from Gilgal, Joshua took them by surprise. [10]The LORD threw them into confusion before Israel, who defeated them in a great victory at Gibeon. Israel pursued them along the road going up to Beth Horon and cut them down all the way to Azekah and Makkedah. [11]As they fled before Israel on the road down from Beth Horon to Azekah, the LORD hurled large hailstones down on them from the sky, and more of them died from the hailstones than were killed by the swords of the Israelites.

[12]On the day the LORD gave the

---

[b]1 The Hebrew term refers to the irrevocable giving over of things or persons to the LORD, often by totally destroying them; also in verses 28, 35, 37, 39 and 40.

Amorites over to Israel, Joshua said to the LORD in the presence of Israel:

"O sun, stand still over Gibeon,
O moon, over the Valley of Aijalon."
[13]So the sun stood still,
and the moon stopped,
till the nation avenged itself on[c] its
enemies,

as it is written in the Book of Jashar.

The sun stopped in the middle of the sky and delayed going down about a full day. [14]There has never been a day like it before or since, a day when the LORD listened to a man. Surely the LORD was fighting for Israel!

[15]Then Joshua returned with all Israel to the camp at Gilgal.

[16]Now the five kings had fled and hidden in the cave at Makkedah. [17]When Joshua was told that the five kings had been found hiding in the cave at Makkedah, [18]he said, "Roll large rocks up to the mouth of the cave, and post some men there to guard it. [19]But don't stop! Pursue your enemies, attack them from the rear and don't let them reach their cities, for the LORD your God has given them into your hand."

[20]So Joshua and the Israelites destroyed them completely—almost to a man—but the few who were left reached their fortified cities. [21]The whole army then returned safely to Joshua in the camp at Makkedah, and no one uttered a word against the Israelites.

[22]Joshua said, "Open the mouth of the cave and bring those five kings out to me." [23]So they brought the five kings out of the cave—the kings of Jerusalem, Hebron, Jarmuth, Lachish and Eglon. [24]When they had brought these kings to Joshua, he summoned all the men of Israel and said to the army commanders who had come with him, "Come here and put your feet on the necks of these kings." So they came forward and placed their feet on their necks.

[25]Joshua said to them, "Do not be afraid; do not be discouraged. Be strong and courageous. This is what the LORD will do to all the enemies you are going to fight." [26]Then Joshua struck and killed the kings and hung them on five trees, and they were left hanging on the trees until evening.

[27]At sunset Joshua gave the order and they took them down from the trees and threw them into the cave where they had been hiding. At the mouth of the cave they placed large rocks, which are there to this day.

[28]That day Joshua took Makkedah. He put the city and its king to the sword and totally destroyed everyone in it. He left no survivors. And he did to the king of Makkedah as he had done to the king of Jericho.

[29]Then Joshua and all Israel with him moved on from Makkedah to Libnah and attacked it. [30]The LORD also gave that city and its king into Israel's hand. The city and everyone in it Joshua put to the sword. He left no survivors there. And he did to its king as he had done to the king of Jericho.

[31]Then Joshua and all Israel with him moved on from Libnah to Lachish; he took up positions against it and attacked it. [32]The LORD handed Lachish over to Israel, and Joshua took it on the second day. The city and everyone in it he put to the sword, just as he had done to Libnah. [33]Meanwhile, Horam king of Gezer had come up to help Lachish, but Joshua defeated him and his army—until no survivors were left.

[34]Then Joshua and all Israel with him moved on from Lachish to Eglon; they took up positions against it and attacked it. [35]They captured it that same day and put it to the sword and totally destroyed everyone in it, just as they had done to Lachish.

[36]Then Joshua and all Israel with him went up from Eglon to Hebron and attacked it. [37]They took the city and put it to the sword, together with its king, its villages and everyone in it. They left no survivors. Just as at Eglon, they totally destroyed it and everyone in it.

[38]Then Joshua and all Israel with him turned around and attacked Debir. [39]They took the city, its king and its villages, and put them to the sword. Everyone in it they totally destroyed. They left no survivors. They did to Debir and its king as they had done to Libnah and its king and to Hebron.

[c]13 Or *nation triumphed over*

⁴⁰So Joshua subdued the whole region, including the hill country, the Negev, the western foothills and the mountain slopes, together with all their kings. He left no survivors. He totally destroyed all who breathed, just as the LORD, the God of Israel, had commanded. ⁴¹Joshua subdued them from Kadesh Barnea to Gaza and from the whole region of Goshen to Gibeon. ⁴²All these kings and their lands Joshua conquered in one campaign, because the LORD, the God of Israel, fought for Israel.

⁴³Then Joshua returned with all Israel to the camp at Gilgal.

CHAPTER 11

When Jabin king of Hazor heard of this, he sent word to Jobab king of Madon, to the kings of Shimron and Acshaph, ²and to the northern kings who were in the mountains, in the Arabah south of Kinnereth, in the western foothills and in Naphoth Dorᵈ on the west; ³to the Canaanites in the east and west; to the Amorites, Hittites, Perizzites and Jebusites in the hill country; and to the Hivites below Hermon in the region of Mizpah. ⁴They came out with all their troops and a large number of horses and chariots—a huge army, as numerous as the sand on the seashore. ⁵All these kings joined forces and made camp together at the Waters of Merom, to fight against Israel.

⁶The LORD said to Joshua, "Do not be afraid of them, because by this time tomorrow I will hand all of them over to Israel, slain. You are to hamstring their horses and burn their chariots."

⁷So Joshua and his whole army came against them suddenly at the Waters of Merom and attacked them, ⁸and the LORD gave them into the hand of Israel. They defeated them and pursued them all the way to Greater Sidon, to Misrephoth Maim, and to the Valley of Mizpah on the east, until no survivors were left. ⁹Joshua did to them as the LORD had directed: He hamstrung their horses and burned their chariots.

¹⁰At that time Joshua turned back and captured Hazor and put its king to the sword. (Hazor had been the head of all these kingdoms.) ¹¹Everyone in it they put to the sword. They totally destroyedᵉ them, not sparing anything that breathed, and he burned up Hazor itself.

¹²Joshua took all these royal cities and their kings and put them to the sword. He totally destroyed them, as Moses the servant of the LORD had commanded. ¹³Yet Israel did not burn any of the cities built on their mounds—except Hazor, which Joshua burned. ¹⁴The Israelites carried off for themselves all the plunder and livestock of these cities, but all the people they put to the sword until they completely destroyed them, not sparing anyone that breathed. ¹⁵As the LORD commanded his servant Moses, so Moses commanded Joshua, and Joshua did it; he left nothing undone of all that the LORD commanded Moses.

¹⁶So Joshua took this entire land: the hill country, all the Negev, the whole region of Goshen, the western foothills, the Arabah and the mountains of Israel with their foothills, ¹⁷from Mount Halak, which rises toward Seir, to Baal Gad in the Valley of Lebanon below Mount Hermon. He captured all their kings and struck them down, putting them to death. ¹⁸Joshua waged war against all these kings for a long time. ¹⁹Except for the Hivites living in Gibeon, not one city made a treaty of peace with the Israelites, who took them all in battle. ²⁰For it was the LORD himself who hardened their hearts to wage war against Israel, so that he might destroy them totally, exterminating them without mercy, as the LORD had commanded Moses.

²¹At that time Joshua went and destroyed the Anakites from the hill country: from Hebron, Debir and Anab, from all the hill country of Judah, and from all the hill country of Israel. Joshua totally destroyed them and their towns. ²²No Anakites were left in Israelite territory; only in Gaza, Gath and Ashdod did any survive. ²³So Joshua took the entire land, just as the LORD had directed Moses, and he gave it as an inheritance to Israel according to their tribal divisions.

Then the land had rest from war.

CHAPTER 12

These are the kings of the land whom the Israelites had defeated and whose territory they took over east of the Jordan,

ᵈ2 Or *in the heights of Dor*   ᵉ11 The Hebrew term refers to the irrevocable giving over of things or persons to the LORD, often by totally destroying them; also in verses 12, 20 and 21.

from the Arnon Gorge to Mount Hermon, including all the eastern side of the Arabah:

2Sihon king of the Amorites,
who reigned in Heshbon. He ruled from Aroer on the rim of the Arnon Gorge—from the middle of the gorge—to the Jabbok River, which is the border of the Ammonites. This included half of Gilead. 3He also ruled over the eastern Arabah from the Sea of Kinnereth[f] to the Sea of the Arabah (the Salt Sea[g]), to Beth Jeshimoth, and then southward below the slopes of Pisgah.

4And the territory of Og king of Bashan, one of the last of the Rephaites, who reigned in Ashtaroth and Edrei. 5He ruled over Mount Hermon, Salecah, all of Bashan to the border of the people of Geshur and Maacah, and half of Gilead to the border of Sihon king of Heshbon.

6Moses, the servant of the LORD, and the Israelites conquered them. And Moses the servant of the LORD gave their land to the Reubenites, the Gadites and the half-tribe of Manasseh to be their possession.

7These are the kings of the land that Joshua and the Israelites conquered on the west side of the Jordan, from Baal Gad in the Valley of Lebanon to Mount Halak, which rises toward Seir (their lands Joshua gave as an inheritance to the tribes of Israel according to their tribal divisions— 8the hill country, the western foothills, the Arabah, the mountain slopes, the desert and the Negev—the lands of the Hittites, Amorites, Canaanites, Perizzites, Hivites and Jebusites):

9the king of Jericho	one
the king of Ai (near Bethel)	one
10the king of Jerusalem	one
the king of Hebron	one
11the king of Jarmuth	one
the king of Lachish	one
12the king of Eglon	one
the king of Gezer	one
13the king of Debir	one
the king of Geder	one
14the king of Hormah	one
the king of Arad	one
15the king of Libnah	one
the king of Adullam	one
16the king of Makkedah	one
the king of Bethel	one
17the king of Tappuah	one
the king of Hepher	one
18the king of Aphek	one
the king of Lasharon	one
19the king of Madon	one
the king of Hazor	one
20the king of Shimron Meron	one
the king of Acshaph	one
21the king of Taanach	one
the king of Megiddo	one
22the king of Kedesh	one
the king of Jokneam in Carmel	one
23the king of Dor (in Naphoth Dor[h])	one
the king of Goyim in Gilgal	one
24the king of Tirzah	one
thirty-one kings in all.	

f3 That is, Galilee   *g3* That is, the Dead Sea   *h23* Or *in the heights of Dor*

MARCH 4 □ DAY 64
JOSHUA 13–17
Portions for Five Tribes

 OVERVIEW The conquest is complete, and now it is time to assign portions of the land to the tribes that have fought so valiantly in the strength of the Lord. Reuben, Gad and half the tribe of Manasseh have previously requested land east of the Jordan, and now they receive their new homesteads. Caleb, still full of vigor at the age of eighty-five, requests and receives Hebron in Judah's area as his inheritance—even though it contains giants and fortified cities!

Chapter 13	Chapter 14	Chapter 15	Chapters 16–17
Portions for			
2½ Tribes	Caleb	Judah	Joseph's Sons
East of Jordan	West of Jordan		

YOUR DAILY WALK Joshua 14 features Caleb, and at first glance he may appear to be a proud, self-reliant soldier. After all, how often do you hear an eighty-five-year-old claim to have the energy of someone half his age? But Caleb wasn't blowing his own horn. Rather, he was boasting in the Lord: "I, however, followed the LORD my God wholeheartedly. . . . Now then, just as the LORD promised, he has kept me alive . . . " (14:8, 10). He was merely giving credit where credit was due!

When we are truly witnessing, we are not talking about ourselves but about Christ.

Stop right now and brag a little on the Lord. Think of one way God has shown himself strong on your behalf over the past week, and tell a friend or loved one about it sometime today. Then you'll be doing what Caleb, the soldier, (and David, the psalmist) loved to do so much: "My soul will boast in the LORD" (Psalm 34:2).

INSIGHT Locating the Allocator of the Land
Who, in fact, made the final decision regarding *which* tribe received *which* part of the land? According to 13:1–6, it was Joshua; 14:1 suggests Eleazar and the heads of the tribal clans of Israel; 14:5 implies the people as a whole. One commentator has suggested that Eleazar cast the lots, assisted by the heads of the tribal clans of Israel; the people accepted the allocations; and Joshua took the ultimate responsibility.

CHAPTER 13

When Joshua was old and well advanced in years, the LORD said to him, "You are very old, and there are still very large areas of land to be taken over.

2"This is the land that remains: all the regions of the Philistines and Geshurites: 3from the Shihor River on the east of Egypt to the territory of Ekron on the north, all of it counted as Canaanite (the territory of the five Philistine rulers in Gaza, Ashdod, Ashkelon, Gath and Ekron—that of the Avvites); 4from the south, all the land of the Canaanites, from Arah of the Sidonians as far as Aphek, the region of the Amorites, 5the area of the Gebalites[i]; and all Lebanon to the east, from Baal Gad below Mount Hermon to Lebo[j] Hamath.

6"As for all the inhabitants of the mountain regions from Lebanon to Misrephoth Maim, that is, all the Sidonians, I myself will drive them out before the Israelites. Be sure to allocate this land to Israel for an inheritance, as I have instructed you, 7and divide it as an inheritance among the nine tribes and half of the tribe of Manasseh."

8The other half of Manasseh,[k] the Reubenites and the Gadites had received the inheritance that Moses had given them east of the Jordan, as he, the servant of the LORD, had assigned it to them.

9It extended from Aroer on the rim of the Arnon Gorge, and from the town in the middle of the gorge, and included the whole plateau of Medeba as far as Dibon, 10and all the towns of Sihon king of the Amorites, who ruled in Heshbon, out to the border of the Ammonites. 11It also included Gilead, the territory of the people of Geshur and Maacah, all of Mount Hermon and all Bashan as far as Salecah— 12that is, the whole kingdom of Og in Bashan, who had reigned in Ashtaroth and Edrei and had survived as one of the last of the Rephaites. Moses had defeated them and

i5 That is, the area of Byblos   j5 Or to the entrance to   k8 Hebrew With it (that is, with the other half of Manasseh) taken over their land. [13]But the Israelites did not drive out the people of Geshur and Maacah, so they continue to live among the Israelites to this day.

[14]But to the tribe of Levi he gave no inheritance, since the offerings made by fire to the LORD, the God of Israel, are their inheritance, as he promised them.

[15]This is what Moses had given to the tribe of Reuben, clan by clan:

[16]The territory from Aroer on the rim of the Arnon Gorge, and from the town in the middle of the gorge, and the whole plateau past Medeba [17]to Heshbon and all its towns on the plateau, including Dibon, Bamoth Baal, Beth Baal Meon, [18]Jahaz, Kedemoth, Mephaath, [19]Kiriathaim, Sibmah, Zereth Shahar on the hill in the valley, [20]Beth Peor, the slopes of Pisgah, and Beth Jeshimoth [21]—all the towns on the plateau and the entire realm of Sihon king of the Amorites, who ruled at Heshbon. Moses had defeated him and the Midianite chiefs, Evi, Rekem, Zur, Hur and Reba—princes allied with Sihon—who lived in that country. [22]In addition to those slain in battle, the Israelites had put to the sword Balaam son of Beor, who practiced divination. [23]The boundary of the Reubenites was the bank of the Jordan. These towns and their villages were the inheritance of the Reubenites, clan by clan.

[24]This is what Moses had given to the tribe of Gad, clan by clan:

[25]The territory of Jazer, all the towns of Gilead and half the Ammonite country as far as Aroer, near Rabbah; [26]and from Heshbon to Ramath Mizpah and Betonim, and from Mahanaim to the territory of Debir; [27]and in the valley, Beth Haram, Beth Nimrah, Succoth and Zaphon with the rest of the realm of Sihon king of Heshbon (the east side of the Jordan, the territory up to the end of the Sea of Kinnereth[l]). [28]These towns and their villages were the inheritance of the Gadites, clan by clan.

[29]This is what Moses had given to the half-tribe of Manasseh, that is, to half the family of the descendants of Manasseh, clan by clan:

[30]The territory extending from Mahanaim and including all of Bashan, the entire realm of Og king of Bashan—all the settlements of Jair in Bashan, sixty towns, [31]half of Gilead, and Ashtaroth and Edrei (the royal cities of Og in Bashan). This was for the descendants of Makir son of Manasseh—for half of the sons of Makir, clan by clan.

[32]This is the inheritance Moses had given when he was in the plains of Moab across the Jordan east of Jericho. [33]But to the tribe of Levi, Moses had given no inheritance; the LORD, the God of Israel, is their inheritance, as he promised them.

C H A P T E R   14

Now these are the areas the Israelites received as an inheritance in the land of Canaan, which Eleazar the priest, Joshua son of Nun and the heads of the tribal clans of Israel allotted to them. [2]Their inheritances were assigned by lot to the nine-and-a-half tribes, as the LORD had commanded through Moses. [3]Moses had granted the two-and-a-half tribes their inheritance east of the Jordan but had not granted the Levites an inheritance among the rest, [4]for the sons of Joseph had become two tribes—Manasseh and Ephraim. The Levites received no share of the land but only towns to live in, with pasturelands for their flocks and herds. [5]So the Israelites divided the land, just as the LORD had commanded them.

[6]Now the men of Judah approached Joshua at Gilgal, and Caleb son of Jephunneh the Kenizzite said to him, "You know what the LORD said to Moses the man of God at Kadesh Barnea about you and me. [7]I was forty years old when Moses the servant of the LORD sent me from Kadesh Barnea to explore the land. And I brought him back a report according to my convictions, [8]but my brothers who went up with me made the hearts of the people melt with fear. I, however, followed the LORD my God wholeheartedly. [9]So on that day Moses swore to me, 'The

[l]27 That is, Galilee

land on which your feet have walked will be your inheritance and that of your children forever, because you have followed the LORD my God wholeheartedly.'[m]

[10]"Now then, just as the LORD promised, he has kept me alive for forty-five years since the time he said this to Moses, while Israel moved about in the desert. So here I am today, eighty-five years old! [11]I am still as strong today as the day Moses sent me out; I'm just as vigorous to go out to battle now as I was then. [12]Now give me this hill country that the LORD promised me that day. You yourself heard then that the Anakites were there and their cities were large and fortified, but, the LORD helping me, I will drive them out just as he said."

[13]Then Joshua blessed Caleb son of Jephunneh and gave him Hebron as his inheritance. [14]So Hebron has belonged to Caleb son of Jephunneh the Kenizzite ever since, because he followed the LORD, the God of Israel, wholeheartedly. [15](Hebron used to be called Kiriath Arba after Arba, who was the greatest man among the Anakites.)

Then the land had rest from war.

CHAPTER 15

The allotment for the tribe of Judah, clan by clan, extended down to the territory of Edom, to the Desert of Zin in the extreme south.

[2]Their southern boundary started from the bay at the southern end of the Salt Sea,[n] [3]crossed south of Scorpion[o] Pass, continued on to Zin and went over to the south of Kadesh Barnea. Then it ran past Hezron up to Addar and curved around to Karka. [4]It then passed along to Azmon and joined the Wadi of Egypt, ending at the sea. This is their[p] southern boundary.

[5]The eastern boundary is the Salt Sea as far as the mouth of the Jordan.

The northern boundary started from the bay of the sea at the mouth of the Jordan, [6]went up to Beth Hoglah and continued north of Beth Arabah to the Stone of Bohan son of Reuben. [7]The boundary then went up to Debir from the Valley of Achor

and turned north to Gilgal, which faces the Pass of Adummim south of the gorge. It continued along to the waters of En Shemesh and came out at En Rogel. [8]Then it ran up the Valley of Ben Hinnom along the southern slope of the Jebusite city (that is, Jerusalem). From there it climbed to the top of the hill west of the Hinnom Valley at the northern end of the Valley of Rephaim. [9]From the hilltop the boundary headed toward the spring of the waters of Nephtoah, came out at the towns of Mount Ephron and went down toward Baalah (that is, Kiriath Jearim). [10]Then it curved westward from Baalah to Mount Seir, ran along the northern slope of Mount Jearim (that is, Kesalon), continued down to Beth Shemesh and crossed to Timnah. [11]It went to the northern slope of Ekron, turned toward Shikkeron, passed along to Mount Baalah and reached Jabneel. The boundary ended at the sea.

[12]The western boundary is the coastline of the Great Sea.[q]

These are the boundaries around the people of Judah by their clans.

[13]In accordance with the LORD's command to him, Joshua gave to Caleb son of Jephunneh a portion in Judah—Kiriath Arba, that is, Hebron. (Arba was the forefather of Anak.) [14]From Hebron Caleb drove out the three Anakites—Sheshai, Ahiman and Talmai—descendants of Anak. [15]From there he marched against the people living in Debir (formerly called Kiriath Sepher). [16]And Caleb said, "I will give my daughter Acsah in marriage to the man who attacks and captures Kiriath Sepher." [17]Othniel son of Kenaz, Caleb's brother, took it; so Caleb gave his daughter Acsah to him in marriage.

[18]One day when she came to Othniel, she urged him[r] to ask her father for a field. When she got off her donkey, Caleb asked her, "What can I do for you?"

[19]She replied, "Do me a special favor. Since you have given me land in the Negev, give me also springs of water." So

m 9 Deut. 1:36   *n* 2 That is, the Dead Sea; also in verse 5   *o* 3 Hebrew *Akrabbim*   *p* 4 Hebrew *your*   *q* 12 That is, the Mediterranean; also in verse 47   *r* 18 Hebrew and some Septuagint manuscripts; other Septuagint manuscripts (see also note at Judges 1:14) *Othniel, he urged her*

Caleb gave her the upper and lower springs.

²⁰This is the inheritance of the tribe of Judah, clan by clan:

²¹The southernmost towns of the tribe of Judah in the Negev toward the boundary of Edom were:

Kabzeel, Eder, Jagur, ²²Kinah, Dimonah, Adadah, ²³Kedesh, Hazor, Ithnan, ²⁴Ziph, Telem, Bealoth, ²⁵Hazor Hadattah, Kerioth Hezron (that is, Hazor), ²⁶Amam, Shema, Moladah, ²⁷Hazar Gaddah, Heshmon, Beth Pelet, ²⁸Hazar Shual, Beersheba, Biziothiah, ²⁹Baalah, Iim, Ezem, ³⁰Eltolad, Kesil, Hormah, ³¹Ziklag, Madmannah, Sansannah, ³²Lebaoth, Shilhim, Ain and Rimmon—a total of twenty-nine towns and their villages.

³³In the western foothills:

Eshtaol, Zorah, Ashnah, ³⁴Zanoah, En Gannim, Tappuah, Enam, ³⁵Jarmuth, Adullam, Socoh, Azekah, ³⁶Shaaraim, Adithaim and Gederah (or Gederothaim)ˢ—fourteen towns and their villages.

³⁷Zenan, Hadashah, Migdal Gad, ³⁸Dilean, Mizpah, Joktheel, ³⁹Lachish, Bozkath, Eglon, ⁴⁰Cabbon, Lahmas, Kitlish, ⁴¹Gederoth, Beth Dagon, Naamah and Makkedah—sixteen towns and their villages.

⁴²Libnah, Ether, Ashan, ⁴³Iphtah, Ashnah, Nezib, ⁴⁴Keilah, Aczib and Mareshah—nine towns and their villages.

⁴⁵Ekron, with its surrounding settlements and villages; ⁴⁶west of Ekron, all that were in the vicinity of Ashdod, together with their villages; ⁴⁷Ashdod, its surrounding settlements and villages; and Gaza, its settlements and villages, as far as the Wadi of Egypt and the coastline of the Great Sea.

⁴⁸In the hill country:

Shamir, Jattir, Socoh, ⁴⁹Dannah, Kiriath Sannah (that is, Debir), ⁵⁰Anab, Eshtemoh, Anim, ⁵¹Goshen, Holon and Giloh—eleven towns and their villages.

⁵²Arab, Dumah, Eshan, ⁵³Janim,

Beth Tappuah, Aphekah, ⁵⁴Humtah, Kiriath Arba (that is, Hebron) and Zior—nine towns and their villages.

⁵⁵Maon, Carmel, Ziph, Juttah, ⁵⁶Jezreel, Jokdeam, Zanoah, ⁵⁷Kain, Gibeah and Timnah—ten towns and their villages.

⁵⁸Halhul, Beth Zur, Gedor, ⁵⁹Maarath, Beth Anoth and Eltekon—six towns and their villages.

⁶⁰Kiriath Baal (that is, Kiriath Jearim) and Rabbah—two towns and their villages.

⁶¹In the desert:

Beth Arabah, Middin, Secacah, ⁶²Nibshan, the City of Salt and En Gedi—six towns and their villages.

⁶³Judah could not dislodge the Jebusites, who were living in Jerusalem; to this day the Jebusites live there with the people of Judah.

CHAPTER 16

The allotment for Joseph began at the Jordan of Jericho,ᵗ east of the waters of Jericho, and went up from there through the desert into the hill country of Bethel. ²It went on from Bethel (that is, Luz),ᵘ crossed over to the territory of the Arkites in Ataroth, ³descended westward to the territory of the Japhletites as far as the region of Lower Beth Horon and on to Gezer, ending at the sea.

⁴So Manasseh and Ephraim, the descendants of Joseph, received their inheritance.

⁵This was the territory of Ephraim, clan by clan:

The boundary of their inheritance went from Ataroth Addar in the east to Upper Beth Horon ⁶and continued to the sea. From Micmethath on the north it curved eastward to Taanath Shiloh, passing by it to Janoah on the east. ⁷Then it went down from Janoah to Ataroth and Naarah, touched Jericho and came out at the Jordan. ⁸From Tappuah the border went west to the Kanah Ravine and ended at the sea. This was the inheritance of the tribe of the Ephraimites, clan by clan. ⁹It also included all the towns and their villages that were set aside for

ˢ36 Or Gederah and Gederothaim   ᵗ1 Jordan of Jericho was possibly an ancient name for the Jordan River.   ᵘ2 Septuagint; Hebrew Bethel to Luz the Ephraimites within the inheritance of the Manassites. ¹⁰They did not dislodge the Canaanites living in Gezer; to this day the Canaanites live among the people of Ephraim but are required to do forced labor.

CHAPTER 17

This was the allotment for the tribe of Manasseh as Joseph's firstborn, that is, for Makir, Manasseh's firstborn. Makir was the ancestor of the Gileadites, who had received Gilead and Bashan because the Makirites were great soldiers. ²So this allotment was for the rest of the people of Manasseh—the clans of Abiezer, Helek, Asriel, Shechem, Hepher and Shemida. These are the other male descendants of Manasseh son of Joseph by their clans.

³Now Zelophehad son of Hepher, the son of Gilead, the son of Makir, the son of Manasseh, had no sons but only daughters, whose names were Mahlah, Noah, Hoglah, Milcah and Tirzah. ⁴They went to Eleazar the priest, Joshua son of Nun, and the leaders and said, "The LORD commanded Moses to give us an inheritance among our brothers." So Joshua gave them an inheritance along with the brothers of their father, according to the LORD's command. ⁵Manasseh's share consisted of ten tracts of land besides Gilead and Bashan east of the Jordan, ⁶because the daughters of the tribe of Manasseh received an inheritance among the sons. The land of Gilead belonged to the rest of the descendants of Manasseh.

⁷The territory of Manasseh extended from Asher to Micmethath east of Shechem. The boundary ran southward from there to include the people living at En Tappuah. ⁸(Manasseh had the land of Tappuah, but Tappuah itself, on the boundary of Manasseh, belonged to the Ephraimites.) ⁹Then the boundary continued south to the Kanah Ravine. There were towns belonging to Ephraim

lying among the towns of Manasseh, but the boundary of Manasseh was the northern side of the ravine and ended at the sea. ¹⁰On the south the land belonged to Ephraim, on the north to Manasseh. The territory of Manasseh reached the sea and bordered Asher on the north and Issachar on the east.

¹¹Within Issachar and Asher, Manasseh also had Beth Shan, Ibleam and the people of Dor, Endor, Taanach and Megiddo, together with their surrounding settlements (the third in the list is Naphoth ᵛ).

¹²Yet the Manassites were not able to occupy these towns, for the Canaanites were determined to live in that region. ¹³However, when the Israelites grew stronger, they subjected the Canaanites to forced labor but did not drive them out completely.

¹⁴The people of Joseph said to Joshua, "Why have you given us only one allotment and one portion for an inheritance? We are a numerous people and the LORD has blessed us abundantly."

¹⁵"If you are so numerous," Joshua answered, "and if the hill country of Ephraim is too small for you, go up into the forest and clear land for yourselves there in the land of the Perizzites and Rephaites."

¹⁶The people of Joseph replied, "The hill country is not enough for us, and all the Canaanites who live in the plain have iron chariots, both those in Beth Shan and its settlements and those in the Valley of Jezreel."

¹⁷But Joshua said to the house of Joseph—to Ephraim and Manasseh—"You are numerous and very powerful. You will have not only one allotment ¹⁸but the forested hill country as well. Clear it, and its farthest limits will be yours; though the Canaanites have iron chariots and though they are strong, you can drive them out."

ᵛ11 That is, Naphoth Dor

MARCH 5 □ DAY 65
JOSHUA 18–21
Portions for Seven Tribes

OVERVIEW Seven tribes remain to receive their hard-earned "property inheritance." After ordering a survey of the land, Joshua divides it into seven parts and distributes it by lot. In addition, six cities of refuge are designated to protect innocent manslayers. The Levites, whose inheritance is the priesthood rather than property, are given forty-eight cities in which to live. With the tabernacle in place in Shiloh, the task of dividing up the land is complete.

Chapter 18	Chapter 19	Chapter 20	Chapter 21
Portions for		Protection for	Provision for
Benjamin	6 Tribes	Slayers	Levites
A Hard-Earned Reward		A Gracious Refuge	

YOUR DAILY WALK Today's passage will either excite you or exasperate you!

On the surface it appears to be little more than a long list of unknown towns, obscure families and meaningless details. You'll be tempted to skim the material—and skip the blessing God has for you.

God will keep all his promises whether you believe them or not!

Put yourself in Joshua's sandals for a moment. Imagine that your home state is the promised land. For seven long years you have been taking stronghold after stronghold in the quest to rid the land of its pagan occupants. Then one morning trumpets blare forth the news: The war is over! The land is yours. Victory is complete. It is time to celebrate and to learn which part of the new territory will be your home.

You listen breathlessly as Joshua describes its borders: "Norman and Norma Christian, your family now owns all of Jefferson County, from Route 16 to the state line." You pinch yourself. After all the years of waiting, it's finally happened. God has kept his word!

Does that do anything for your faith in God and your confidence in his promises to care for you? If so, write the words of Philippians 4:19 on a card, sign it and date it. Let it be a reminder today—and every day—that you are taking God at his word!

INSIGHT Growing Room for the Tribe of Dan

Dan's allotment was a small territory compressed between the northwestern hills of Judah and the Mediterranean Sea—a portion that proved too small for Dan's 64,400 families (Numbers 26:42–43). The majority of the tribe migrated farther north and settled in Laish—with disastrous consequences (Judges 18).

CHAPTER 18

The whole assembly of the Israelites gathered at Shiloh and set up the Tent of Meeting there. The country was brought under their control, ²but there were still seven Israelite tribes who had not yet received their inheritance.

³So Joshua said to the Israelites: "How long will you wait before you begin to take possession of the land that the LORD, the God of your fathers, has given you? ⁴Appoint three men from each tribe. I will send them out to make a survey of the land and to write a description of it, according to the inheritance of each. Then they will return to me. ⁵You are to divide the land into seven parts. Judah is to remain in its territory on the south and the house of Joseph in its territory on the north. ⁶After you have written descrip-

tions of the seven parts of the land, bring them here to me and I will cast lots for you in the presence of the LORD our God. [7]The Levites, however, do not get a portion among you, because the priestly service of the LORD is their inheritance. And Gad, Reuben and the half-tribe of Manasseh have already received their inheritance on the east side of the Jordan. Moses the servant of the LORD gave it to them."

[8]As the men started on their way to map out the land, Joshua instructed them, "Go and make a survey of the land and write a description of it. Then return to me, and I will cast lots for you here at Shiloh in the presence of the LORD." [9]So the men left and went through the land. They wrote its description on a scroll, town by town, in seven parts, and returned to Joshua in the camp at Shiloh. [10]Joshua then cast lots for them in Shiloh in the presence of the LORD, and there he distributed the land to the Israelites according to their tribal divisions.

[11]The lot came up for the tribe of Benjamin, clan by clan. Their allotted territory lay between the tribes of Judah and Joseph:

[12]On the north side their boundary began at the Jordan, passed the northern slope of Jericho and headed west into the hill country, coming out at the desert of Beth Aven. [13]From there it crossed to the south slope of Luz (that is, Bethel) and went down to Ataroth Addar on the hill south of Lower Beth Horon.

[14]From the hill facing Beth Horon on the south the boundary turned south along the western side and came out at Kiriath Baal (that is, Kiriath Jearim), a town of the people of Judah. This was the western side.

[15]The southern side began at the outskirts of Kiriath Jearim on the west, and the boundary came out at the spring of the waters of Nephtoah. [16]The boundary went down to the foot of the hill facing the Valley of Ben Hinnom, north of the Valley of Rephaim. It continued down the Hinnom Valley along the southern slope of the Jebusite city and so to En

Rogel. [17]It then curved north, went to En Shemesh, continued to Geliloth, which faces the Pass of Adummim, and ran down to the Stone of Bohan son of Reuben. [18]It continued to the northern slope of Beth Arabah[w] and on down into the Arabah. [19]It then went to the northern slope of Beth Hoglah and came out at the northern bay of the Salt Sea,[x] at the mouth of the Jordan in the south. This was the southern boundary.

[20]The Jordan formed the boundary on the eastern side.

These were the boundaries that marked out the inheritance of the clans of Benjamin on all sides.

[21]The tribe of Benjamin, clan by clan, had the following cities:

Jericho, Beth Hoglah, Emek Keziz, [22]Beth Arabah, Zemaraim, Bethel, [23]Avvim, Parah, Ophrah, [24]Kephar Ammoni, Ophni and Geba—twelve towns and their villages.

[25]Gibeon, Ramah, Beeroth, [26]Mizpah, Kephirah, Mozah, [27]Rekem, Irpeel, Taralah, [28]Zelah, Haeleph, the Jebusite city (that is, Jerusalem), Gibeah and Kiriath—fourteen towns and their villages.

This was the inheritance of Benjamin for its clans.

CHAPTER 19

The second lot came out for the tribe of Simeon, clan by clan. Their inheritance lay within the territory of Judah. [2]It included:

Beersheba (or Sheba),[y] Moladah, [3]Hazar Shual, Balah, Ezem, [4]Eltolad, Bethul, Hormah, [5]Ziklag, Beth Marcaboth, Hazar Susah, [6]Beth Lebaoth and Sharuhen—thirteen towns and their villages;

[7]Ain, Rimmon, Ether and Ashan—four towns and their villages— [8]and all the villages around these towns as far as Baalath Beer (Ramah in the Negev).

This was the inheritance of the tribe of the Simeonites, clan by clan. [9]The inheritance of the Simeonites was taken from the share of Judah, because Judah's portion was more than they needed. So the

---

[w]18 Septuagint; Hebrew *slope facing the Arabah*   [x]19 That is, the Dead Sea   [y]2 Or *Beersheba, Sheba;* 1 Chron. 4:28 does not have *Sheba.*

Simeonites received their inheritance within the territory of Judah.

[10]The third lot came up for Zebulun, clan by clan:

The boundary of their inheritance went as far as Sarid. [11]Going west it ran to Maralah, touched Dabbesheth, and extended to the ravine near Jokneam. [12]It turned east from Sarid toward the sunrise to the territory of Kisloth Tabor and went on to Daberath and up to Japhia. [13]Then it continued eastward to Gath Hepher and Eth Kazin; it came out at Rimmon and turned toward Neah. [14]There the boundary went around on the north to Hannathon and ended at the Valley of Iphtah El. [15]Included were Kattath, Nahalal, Shimron, Idalah and Bethlehem. There were twelve towns and their villages.

[16]These towns and their villages were the inheritance of Zebulun, clan by clan.

[17]The fourth lot came out for Issachar, clan by clan. [18]Their territory included:

Jezreel, Kesulloth, Shunem, [19]Hapharaim, Shion, Anaharath, [20]Rabbith, Kishion, Ebez, [21]Remeth, En Gannim, En Haddah and Beth Pazzez. [22]The boundary touched Tabor, Shahazumah and Beth Shemesh, and ended at the Jordan. There were sixteen towns and their villages.

[23]These towns and their villages were the inheritance of the tribe of Issachar, clan by clan.

[24]The fifth lot came out for the tribe of Asher, clan by clan. [25]Their territory included:

Helkath, Hali, Beten, Acshaph, [26]Allammelech, Amad and Mishal. On the west the boundary touched Carmel and Shihor Libnath. [27]It then turned east toward Beth Dagon, touched Zebulun and the Valley of Iphtah El, and went north to Beth Emek and Neiel, passing Cabul on the left. [28]It went to Abdon,[z] Rehob, Hammon and Kanah, as far as Greater Sidon. [29]The boundary then turned back toward Ramah and went to the fortified city of Tyre, turned toward Hosah and came out at the sea in the region of Aczib, [30]Ummah, Aphek and Rehob. There were twenty-two towns and their villages.

[31]These towns and their villages were the inheritance of the tribe of Asher, clan by clan.

[32]The sixth lot came out for Naphtali, clan by clan:

[33]Their boundary went from Heleph and the large tree in Zaanannim, passing Adami Nekeb and Jabneel to Lakkum and ending at the Jordan. [34]The boundary ran west through Aznoth Tabor and came out at Hukkok. It touched Zebulun on the south, Asher on the west and the Jordan[a] on the east. [35]The fortified cities were Ziddim, Zer, Hammath, Rakkath, Kinnereth, [36]Adamah, Ramah, Hazor, [37]Kedesh, Edrei, En Hazor, [38]Iron, Migdal El, Horem, Beth Anath and Beth Shemesh. There were nineteen towns and their villages.

[39]These towns and their villages were the inheritance of the tribe of Naphtali, clan by clan.

[40]The seventh lot came out for the tribe of Dan, clan by clan. [41]The territory of their inheritance included:

Zorah, Eshtaol, Ir Shemesh, [42]Shaalabbin, Aijalon, Ithlah, [43]Elon, Timnah, Ekron, [44]Eltekeh, Gibbethon, Baalath, [45]Jehud, Bene Berak, Gath Rimmon, [46]Me Jarkon and Rakkon, with the area facing Joppa.

[47](But the Danites had difficulty taking possession of their territory, so they went up and attacked Leshem, took it, put it to the sword and occupied it. They settled in Leshem and named it Dan after their forefather.)

[48]These towns and their villages were the inheritance of the tribe of Dan, clan by clan.

[49]When they had finished dividing the land into its allotted portions, the Israelites gave Joshua son of Nun an inheritance among them, [50]as the LORD had commanded. They gave him the town he asked for—Timnath Serah[b] in the hill country of Ephraim. And he built up the town and settled there.

[51]These are the territories that Eleazar

---

[z]28 Some Hebrew manuscripts (see also Joshua 21:30); most Hebrew manuscripts *Ebron*   [a]34 Septuagint; Hebrew *west, and Judah, the Jordan,*   [b]50 Also known as *Timnath Heres* (see Judges 2:9)

the priest, Joshua son of Nun and the heads of the tribal clans of Israel assigned by lot at Shiloh in the presence of the LORD at the entrance to the Tent of Meeting. And so they finished dividing the land.

CHAPTER 20

Then the LORD said to Joshua: 2"Tell the Israelites to designate the cities of refuge, as I instructed you through Moses, 3so that anyone who kills a person accidentally and unintentionally may flee there and find protection from the avenger of blood.

4"When he flees to one of these cities, he is to stand in the entrance of the city gate and state his case before the elders of that city. Then they are to admit him into their city and give him a place to live with them. 5If the avenger of blood pursues him, they must not surrender the one accused, because he killed his neighbor unintentionally and without malice aforethought. 6He is to stay in that city until he has stood trial before the assembly and until the death of the high priest who is serving at that time. Then he may go back to his own home in the town from which he fled."

7So they set apart Kedesh in Galilee in the hill country of Naphtali, Shechem in the hill country of Ephraim, and Kiriath Arba (that is, Hebron) in the hill country of Judah. 8On the east side of the Jordan of Jericho[c] they designated Bezer in the desert on the plateau in the tribe of Reuben, Ramoth in Gilead in the tribe of Gad, and Golan in Bashan in the tribe of Manasseh. 9Any of the Israelites or any alien living among them who killed someone accidentally could flee to these designated cities and not be killed by the avenger of blood prior to standing trial before the assembly.

CHAPTER 21

Now the family heads of the Levites approached Eleazar the priest, Joshua son of Nun, and the heads of the other tribal families of Israel 2at Shiloh in Canaan and said to them, "The LORD commanded through Moses that you give us towns to live in, with pasturelands for our livestock." 3So, as the LORD had commanded, the Israelites gave the Levites the follow-

ing towns and pasturelands out of their own inheritance:

4The first lot came out for the Kohathites, clan by clan. The Levites who were descendants of Aaron the priest were allotted thirteen towns from the tribes of Judah, Simeon and Benjamin. 5The rest of Kohath's descendants were allotted ten towns from the clans of the tribes of Ephraim, Dan and half of Manasseh.

6The descendants of Gershon were allotted thirteen towns from the clans of the tribes of Issachar, Asher, Naphtali and the half-tribe of Manasseh in Bashan.

7The descendants of Merari, clan by clan, received twelve towns from the tribes of Reuben, Gad and Zebulun.

8So the Israelites allotted to the Levites these towns and their pasturelands, as the LORD had commanded through Moses.

9From the tribes of Judah and Simeon they allotted the following towns by name 10(these towns were assigned to the descendants of Aaron who were from the Kohathite clans of the Levites, because the first lot fell to them):

11They gave them Kiriath Arba (that is, Hebron), with its surrounding pastureland, in the hill country of Judah. (Arba was the forefather of Anak.) 12But the fields and villages around the city they had given to Caleb son of Jephunneh as his possession.

13So to the descendants of Aaron the priest they gave Hebron (a city of refuge for one accused of murder), Libnah, 14Jattir, Eshtemoa, 15Holon, Debir, 16Ain, Juttah and Beth Shemesh, together with their pasturelands—nine towns from these two tribes.

17And from the tribe of Benjamin they gave them Gibeon, Geba, 18Anathoth and Almon, together with their pasturelands—four towns.

19All the towns for the priests, the descendants of Aaron, were thirteen, together with their pasturelands.

20The rest of the Kohathite clans of the Levites were allotted towns from the tribe of Ephraim:

21In the hill country of Ephraim they were given Shechem (a city of

---

[c]8 Jordan of Jericho was possibly an ancient name for the Jordan River.

refuge for one accused of murder) and Gezer, ²²Kibzaim and Beth Horon, together with their pasturelands—four towns.

²³Also from the tribe of Dan they received Eltekeh, Gibbethon, ²⁴Aijalon and Gath Rimmon, together with their pasturelands—four towns.

²⁵From half the tribe of Manasseh they received Taanach and Gath Rimmon, together with their pasturelands—two towns.

²⁶All these ten towns and their pasturelands were given to the rest of the Kohathite clans.

²⁷The Levite clans of the Gershonites were given:

from the half-tribe of Manasseh,
Golan in Bashan (a city of refuge for one accused of murder) and Be Eshtarah, together with their pasturelands—two towns;

²⁸from the tribe of Issachar,
Kishion, Daberath, ²⁹Jarmuth and En Gannim, together with their pasturelands—four towns;

³⁰from the tribe of Asher,
Mishal, Abdon, ³¹Helkath and Rehob, together with their pasturelands—four towns;

³²from the tribe of Naphtali,
Kedesh in Galilee (a city of refuge for one accused of murder), Hammoth Dor and Kartan, together with their pasturelands—three towns.

³³All the towns of the Gershonite clans were thirteen, together with their pasturelands.

³⁴The Merarite clans (the rest of the Levites) were given:

from the tribe of Zebulun,
Jokneam, Kartah, ³⁵Dimnah and Nahalal, together with their pasturelands—four towns;

³⁶from the tribe of Reuben,
Bezer, Jahaz, ³⁷Kedemoth and Mephaath, together with their pasturelands—four towns;

³⁸from the tribe of Gad,
Ramoth in Gilead (a city of refuge for one accused of murder), Mahanaim, ³⁹Heshbon and Jazer, together with their pasturelands—four towns in all.

⁴⁰All the towns allotted to the Merarite clans, who were the rest of the Levites, were twelve.

⁴¹The towns of the Levites in the territory held by the Israelites were forty-eight in all, together with their pasturelands. ⁴²Each of these towns had pasturelands surrounding it; this was true for all these towns.

⁴³So the LORD gave Israel all the land he had sworn to give their forefathers, and they took possession of it and settled there. ⁴⁴The LORD gave them rest on every side, just as he had sworn to their forefathers. Not one of their enemies withstood them; the LORD handed all their enemies over to them. ⁴⁵Not one of all the LORD's good promises to the house of Israel failed; every one was fulfilled.

MARCH 6 □ DAY 66
JOSHUA 22–24
Joshua's Last Words

 OVERVIEW In his one-hundred-plus years, Joshua has seldom seen an uneventful day—and the closing chapters of his life are no exception! Scarcely have the tribes unpacked in their new homeland when civil war threatens to break out. A memorial built by the eastern tribes is misinterpreted as an idol by their western neighbors, and only quick action by Joshua prevents bloodshed. Years later, in the final hours of Joshua's life, he gathers the nation together and delivers an emotional charge, pleading with them to remain true to the Lord—yet knowing full well they would depart from him. He concludes with a ringing challenge: ". . . choose for yourselves this day whom you will serve . . . . But as for me and my household, we will serve the LORD" (24:15).

Chapter 22	Chapter 23	Chapter 24
An Altar Misinterpreted	A Charge Given: "Hold Fast to the Lord"	A Covenant Renewed "We Will Serve the Lord"
National Conflict	National Challenge	National Commitment

YOUR DAILY WALK When a person lies on his or her deathbed facing the final hours of earthly life, you can be sure he or she won't fritter away those precious moments in small talk. That person's every word will be fraught with importance. Listen carefully, for that person

A man can't go anywhere while he's straddling a fence.

is sharing his or her innermost thoughts.

Joshua gathered his dwindling strength and made one last appeal to Israel for a fresh resolve to put away idolatry and serve God alone. After all, it was God who brought their fathers out of Egypt. It was God who parted the Red Sea and decimated the Egyptian army. It was God who stopped the Jordan, flattened Jericho and put the Canaanite armies to flight. It was God who gave them a land they did not deserve, cities they had not built and vineyards they did not plant. Is it any wonder Joshua drew an imaginary line in the dust and declared, "Choose for yourselves this day whom you will serve"?

What is keeping you from making a clear-cut commitment to serve God? Has something or someone replaced God as the object of your affection? Choose this day whom you will serve.

INSIGHT Joshua's One Glaring Failure
When Moses died, his right-hand man, Joshua, stepped in to fill the void. When Joshua died, he did not have a right-hand man to take over. The resulting lack of trained leadership set the stage for the chaotic period of the judges when "everyone did as he saw fit."

CHAPTER 22
Then Joshua summoned the Reubenites, the Gadites and the half-tribe of Manasseh ²and said to them, "You have done all that Moses the servant of the LORD commanded, and you have obeyed me in everything I commanded. ³For a long time now—to this very day—you have not deserted your brothers but have carried out the mission the LORD your God gave you. ⁴Now that the LORD your God has given your brothers rest as he promised, return to your homes in the land that Moses the servant of the LORD gave you on the other side of the Jordan. ⁵But be very careful to keep the commandment and the law that Moses the servant of the LORD gave you: to love the LORD your God, to walk in all his ways, to obey his commands, to hold fast to him and to serve him with all your heart and all your soul."

⁶Then Joshua blessed them and sent them away, and they went to their homes. ⁷(To the half-tribe of Manasseh Moses had given land in Bashan, and to the other half of the tribe Joshua gave land on the west side of the Jordan with their brothers.) When Joshua sent them home, he blessed them, ⁸saying, "Return to your homes with your great wealth—with large herds of livestock, with silver, gold, bronze and iron, and a great quantity of clothing—and divide with your brothers the plunder from your enemies."

⁹So the Reubenites, the Gadites and the half-tribe of Manasseh left the Israelites at Shiloh in Canaan to return to Gilead, their own land, which they had acquired in accordance with the command of the LORD through Moses.

¹⁰When they came to Geliloth near the Jordan in the land of Canaan, the Reubenites, the Gadites and the half-tribe of Manasseh built an imposing altar there by the Jordan. ¹¹And when the Israelites heard that they had built the altar on the border of Canaan at Geliloth near the Jordan on the Israelite side, ¹²the whole assembly of Israel gathered at Shiloh to go to war against them.

¹³So the Israelites sent Phinehas son of Eleazar, the priest, to the land of Gilead—to Reuben, Gad and the half-tribe of Manasseh. ¹⁴With him they sent ten of the

chief men, one for each of the tribes of Israel, each the head of a family division among the Israelite clans.

[15]When they went to Gilead—to Reuben, Gad and the half-tribe of Manasseh—they said to them: [16]"The whole assembly of the LORD says: 'How could you break faith with the God of Israel like this? How could you turn away from the LORD and build yourselves an altar in rebellion against him now? [17]Was not the sin of Peor enough for us? Up to this very day we have not cleansed ourselves from that sin, even though a plague fell on the community of the LORD! [18]And are you now turning away from the LORD?

" 'If you rebel against the LORD today, tomorrow he will be angry with the whole community of Israel. [19]If the land you possess is defiled, come over to the LORD's land, where the LORD's tabernacle stands, and share the land with us. But do not rebel against the LORD or against us by building an altar for yourselves, other than the altar of the LORD our God. [20]When Achan son of Zerah acted unfaithfully regarding the devoted things,[d] did not wrath come upon the whole community of Israel? He was not the only one who died for his sin.' "

[21]Then Reuben, Gad and the half-tribe of Manasseh replied to the heads of the clans of Israel: [22]"The Mighty One, God, the LORD! The Mighty One, God, the LORD! He knows! And let Israel know! If this has been in rebellion or disobedience to the LORD, do not spare us this day. [23]If we have built our own altar to turn away from the LORD and to offer burnt offerings and grain offerings, or to sacrifice fellowship offerings[e] on it, may the LORD himself call us to account.

[24]"No! We did it for fear that some day your descendants might say to ours, 'What do you have to do with the LORD, the God of Israel? [25]The LORD has made the Jordan a boundary between us and you—you Reubenites and Gadites! You have no share in the LORD.' So your descendants might cause ours to stop fearing the LORD.

[26]"That is why we said, 'Let us get ready and build an altar—but not for burnt offerings or sacrifices.' [27]On the contrary, it is to be a witness between us and you and the generations that follow, that we will worship the LORD at his sanctuary with our burnt offerings, sacrifices and fellowship offerings. Then in the future your descendants will not be able to say to ours, 'You have no share in the LORD.'

[28]"And we said, 'If they ever say this to us, or to our descendants, we will answer: Look at the replica of the LORD's altar, which our fathers built, not for burnt offerings and sacrifices, but as a witness between us and you.'

[29]"Far be it from us to rebel against the LORD and turn away from him today by building an altar for burnt offerings, grain offerings and sacrifices, other than the altar of the LORD our God that stands before his tabernacle."

[30]When Phinehas the priest and the leaders of the community—the heads of the clans of the Israelites—heard what Reuben, Gad and Manasseh had to say, they were pleased. [31]And Phinehas son of Eleazar, the priest, said to Reuben, Gad and Manasseh, "Today we know that the LORD is with us, because you have not acted unfaithfully toward the LORD in this matter. Now you have rescued the Israelites from the LORD's hand."

[32]Then Phinehas son of Eleazar, the priest, and the leaders returned to Canaan from their meeting with the Reubenites and Gadites in Gilead and reported to the Israelites. [33]They were glad to hear the report and praised God. And they talked no more about going to war against them to devastate the country where the Reubenites and the Gadites lived.

[34]And the Reubenites and the Gadites gave the altar this name: A Witness Between Us that the LORD is God.

CHAPTER 23

After a long time had passed and the LORD had given Israel rest from all their enemies around them, Joshua, by then old and well advanced in years, [2]summoned all Israel—their elders, leaders, judges and officials—and said to them: "I am old and well advanced in years. [3]You yourselves have seen everything the LORD your God has done to all these nations for your sake; it was the LORD your God who fought for you. [4]Remember how I have allotted as an inheritance for your tribes

[d]20 The Hebrew term refers to the irrevocable giving over of things or persons to the LORD, often by totally destroying them.
[e]23 Traditionally *peace offerings*; also in verse 27

all the land of the nations that remain—the nations I conquered—between the Jordan and the Great Sea[f] in the west. [5]The LORD your God himself will drive them out of your way. He will push them out before you, and you will take possession of their land, as the LORD your God promised you.

[6]"Be very strong; be careful to obey all that is written in the Book of the Law of Moses, without turning aside to the right or to the left. [7]Do not associate with these nations that remain among you; do not invoke the names of their gods or swear by them. You must not serve them or bow down to them. [8]But you are to hold fast to the LORD your God, as you have until now.

[9]"The LORD has driven out before you great and powerful nations; to this day no one has been able to withstand you. [10]One of you routs a thousand, because the LORD your God fights for you, just as he promised. [11]So be very careful to love the LORD your God.

[12]"But if you turn away and ally yourselves with the survivors of these nations that remain among you and if you intermarry with them and associate with them, [13]then you may be sure that the LORD your God will no longer drive out these nations before you. Instead, they will become snares and traps for you, whips on your backs and thorns in your eyes, until you perish from this good land, which the LORD your God has given you.

[14]"Now I am about to go the way of all the earth. You know with all your heart and soul that not one of all the good promises the LORD your God gave you has failed. Every promise has been fulfilled; not one has failed. [15]But just as every good promise of the LORD your God has come true, so the LORD will bring on you all the evil he has threatened, until he has destroyed you from this good land he has given you. [16]If you violate the covenant of the LORD your God, which he commanded you, and go and serve other gods and bow down to them, the LORD's anger will burn against you, and you will quickly perish from the good land he has given you."

CHAPTER 24

Then Joshua assembled all the tribes of Israel at Shechem. He summoned the elders, leaders, judges and officials of Israel, and they presented themselves before God.

[2]Joshua said to all the people, "This is what the LORD, the God of Israel, says: 'Long ago your forefathers, including Terah the father of Abraham and Nahor, lived beyond the River[g] and worshiped other gods. [3]But I took your father Abraham from the land beyond the River and led him throughout Canaan and gave him many descendants. I gave him Isaac, [4]and to Isaac I gave Jacob and Esau. I assigned the hill country of Seir to Esau, but Jacob and his sons went down to Egypt.

[5]"'Then I sent Moses and Aaron, and I afflicted the Egyptians by what I did there, and I brought you out. [6]When I brought your fathers out of Egypt, you came to the sea, and the Egyptians pursued them with chariots and horsemen[h] as far as the Red Sea.[i] [7]But they cried to the LORD for help, and he put darkness between you and the Egyptians; he brought the sea over them and covered them. You saw with your own eyes what I did to the Egyptians. Then you lived in the desert for a long time.

[8]"'I brought you to the land of the Amorites who lived east of the Jordan. They fought against you, but I gave them into your hands. I destroyed them from before you, and you took possession of their land. [9]When Balak son of Zippor, the king of Moab, prepared to fight against Israel, he sent for Balaam son of Beor to put a curse on you. [10]But I would not listen to Balaam, so he blessed you again and again, and I delivered you out of his hand.

[11]"'Then you crossed the Jordan and came to Jericho. The citizens of Jericho fought against you, as did also the Amorites, Perizzites, Canaanites, Hittites, Girgashites, Hivites and Jebusites, but I gave them into your hands. [12]I sent the hornet ahead of you, which drove them out before you—also the two Amorite kings. You did not do it with your own sword and bow. [13]So I gave you a land on which you did not toil and cities you did not build; and you live in them and eat from

---

[f]4 That is, the Mediterranean   [g]2 That is, the Euphrates; also in verses 3, 14 and 15   [h]6 Or *charioteers*   [i]6 Hebrew *Yam Suph*; that is, Sea of Reeds

vineyards and olive groves that you did not plant.'

¹⁴"Now fear the LORD and serve him with all faithfulness. Throw away the gods your forefathers worshiped beyond the River and in Egypt, and serve the LORD. ¹⁵But if serving the LORD seems undesirable to you, then choose for yourselves this day whom you will serve, whether the gods your forefathers served beyond the River, or the gods of the Amorites, in whose land you are living. But as for me and my household, we will serve the LORD."

¹⁶Then the people answered, "Far be it from us to forsake the LORD to serve other gods! ¹⁷It was the LORD our God himself who brought us and our fathers up out of Egypt, from that land of slavery, and performed those great signs before our eyes. He protected us on our entire journey and among all the nations through which we traveled. ¹⁸And the LORD drove out before us all the nations, including the Amorites, who lived in the land. We too will serve the LORD, because he is our God."

¹⁹Joshua said to the people, "You are not able to serve the LORD. He is a holy God; he is a jealous God. He will not forgive your rebellion and your sins. ²⁰If you forsake the LORD and serve foreign gods, he will turn and bring disaster on you and make an end of you, after he has been good to you."

²¹But the people said to Joshua, "No! We will serve the LORD."

²²Then Joshua said, "You are witnesses against yourselves that you have chosen to serve the LORD."

"Yes, we are witnesses," they replied.

²³"Now then," said Joshua, "throw away the foreign gods that are among you and yield your hearts to the LORD, the God of Israel."

²⁴And the people said to Joshua, "We will serve the LORD our God and obey him."

²⁵On that day Joshua made a covenant for the people, and there at Shechem he drew up for them decrees and laws. ²⁶And Joshua recorded these things in the Book of the Law of God. Then he took a large stone and set it up there under the oak near the holy place of the LORD.

²⁷"See!" he said to all the people. "This stone will be a witness against us. It has heard all the words the LORD has said to us. It will be a witness against you if you are untrue to your God."

²⁸Then Joshua sent the people away, each to his own inheritance.

²⁹After these things, Joshua son of Nun, the servant of the LORD, died at the age of a hundred and ten. ³⁰And they buried him in the land of his inheritance, at Timnath Serahʲ in the hill country of Ephraim, north of Mount Gaash.

³¹Israel served the LORD throughout the lifetime of Joshua and of the elders who outlived him and who had experienced everything the LORD had done for Israel.

³²And Joseph's bones, which the Israelites had brought up from Egypt, were buried at Shechem in the tract of land that Jacob bought for a hundred pieces of silverᵏ from the sons of Hamor, the father of Shechem. This became the inheritance of Joseph's descendants.

³³And Eleazar son of Aaron died and was buried at Gibeah, which had been allotted to his son Phinehas in the hill country of Ephraim.

ʲ30 Also known as *Timnath Heres* (see Judges 2:9)   ᵏ32 Hebrew *hundred kesitahs*; a kesitah was a unit of money of unknown weight and value.

MARCH 7 ☐ DAY 67
Leading the Way

 LOOK BACK Last month we read about Moses' leadership of God's people. Now we've just finished the book of Joshua, in which the general by that name filled Moses' sandals. Leadership transitions are never easy. Any time a leader of the stature and longevity of a Moses passes from the scene, there is good reason for the followers to be nervous: How will our new leader compare with his predecessor? Will he be kind or cruel? Will he walk in the footsteps of his predecessor? Will he have his own agenda or follow God faithfully?

What allowed the transition to move smoothly from Moses to Joshua, in the final analysis, was the realization that the nation's true leader had never changed—only the human instrument through whom that leader worked. Joshua the servant of Moses became Joshua the servant of the LORD and continued the pattern of servant leadership the nation had known for forty years. After a fitting farewell for Moses, Joshua led the nation on a memorable crossing of the flood-swollen Jordan River and began a seven-year campaign to conquer and cleanse the promised land. Out of a total of thirty-one battles, Joshua would lose only one (can you name it?)—a temporary setback quickly corrected.

LOOK UP With small children, leadership is seldom a problem. When playing "Follow the Leader," everyone takes a turn.

Be careful if you think you are leading people—they may be chasing you.

But what about leadership in the household of faith? Are leaders made or born? And how do you know when you have the qualifications for leadership?

Regardless of your present role of leadership or "followership" in the family of God, it is a worthy ambition to aspire to become a leader (1 Timothy 3:1). But leadership is not for everyone. In fact, the qualifications set forth in 1 Timothy 3 and Titus 1 may surprise you. They have nothing to do with your net worth, your degrees or the number of civic clubs you belong to. Leadership isn't something to be earned. It is a recognition of spiritual maturity, proven character and the reputation you have developed both inside and outside the church.

If you aspire to help "manage the ministry" within the family of God, then ask yourself, How well have I managed the other responsibilities I have been entrusted with? Have I managed well my physical body? . . . my mind? . . . my money? . . . my family? . . . my tongue? . . . my reputation? Am I worthy of respect? Am I self-controlled? . . . hospitable? . . . teachable? . . . above reproach? . . . mature? . . . honest in all my dealings? If the answer to these questions is yes, then an expanded leadership role may be appropriate for you.

LOOK AHEAD Regardless of whether an enlarged leadership responsibility may be in your future, the attitude of a servant-leader ought to be your ambition. Listen to this exhortation from the apostle Peter: "Be shepherds of God's flock that is under your care, *serving* as overseers—not because you must, but because you are *willing,* as God wants you to be; not greedy for money, but *eager* to serve; not lording it over those entrusted to you, but being *examples* to the flock. . . . Young men, in the same way be *submissive* to those who are older. All of you, clothe yourselves with *humility* toward one another" (1 Peter 5:2–5, emphasis added).

Leaders like that are always in short supply—perhaps because they are too humble to admit they have what it takes.

Judges

FOLLOWING the conquest of Canaan, Israel plunges into a 350-year period of national deterioration. A monotonous and deadly pattern develops: The people fall into sin, God disciplines them with foreign oppression, the people cry out in repentance, God raises up a deliverer, peace is restored. The cycle of sin repeats itself a total of seven times in the book. But God, ever faithful to his covenant people, extends his grace again and again by sending such leaders as Deborah, Gideon and Samson.

Focus	Deterioration	Deliverance				Depravity
Divisions	Introduction to the Judges	First 5 Judges	Gideon, the Hesitant Hero	Gideon's Son and 6 Judges	Samson, the Carnal Champion	2 Examples of National Degradation
	1 2	3 5	6 8	9 12	13 16	17 21
Topics	Situation	Sin, Servitude and Salvation				Shocking Decline
	Religious Laxity	Political Uncertainty				Moral Anarchy
Place	Canaan and Transjordan					
Time	About 350 Years					

MARCH 8 ☐ DAY 68
JUDGES 1–5
First Five Judges

OVERVIEW Efforts by Judah, Simeon and the other tribes to purge the land of its pagan inhabitants are not completely successful. Pockets of godless influence remain, always a source of spiritual stumbling to Israel. Over and over the cycle repeats itself. Israel falls into national immorality and idolatry, causing God to allow powerful neighboring countries to oppress and enslave her. When the people cry out in repentance, God responds to their renewed commitment by raising up yet another judge to deliver them. But the cycle soon begins again as the nation's spiritual temperature grows steadily colder.

Chapters 1–2	Chapter 3			Chapters 4–5
Background of the Judges	Three Early Judges			Deborah and Barak
	Othniel	Ehud	Shamgar	
	1 11	12 30	31	
God's Message	God's Messengers			God's Miracles

YOUR DAILY WALK Look up Romans 12:1–2, and read it several times. Now write your own paraphrase of what it means to be conformed "to the pattern of this world."

When a sin is fashionable, Christians should be out of fashion.

You will spend nearly every day of your earthly life surrounded by unbelievers. And when you stop to think about it, you really have no choice in the matter. To eliminate all contact with non-Christians, as Paul writes, would require leaving the world (1 Corinthians 5:9–10). Besides, how can you witness to unbelievers and lead them to the Savior if you spend no time with them?

But while you must have contact with the world, you are commanded not to be conformed to the world. That was Israel's problem. Her people not only had contact with sinners (as a result of their failure to obey God and clear them out), but they also embraced the sinner's sin. They became indistinguishable from the heathen.

Here is a sentence to ponder and complete: One way in which my lifestyle differs from the world around me because of my commitment to Christ is _____. If you have trouble supplying an answer, consult 1 Peter 2:9–17 for suggestions!

INSIGHT Reconstructing the Colorful Period of the Judges
An excellent way to trace the cyclical period of the judges is by color-coding your Bible. Select five colored pens, and use one color to highlight each part of the "sin cycle": *sin, servitude, supplication, salvation, silence* (you'll use each pen seven times).

CHAPTER 1

After the death of Joshua, the Israelites asked the LORD, "Who will be the first to go up and fight for us against the Canaanites?"

²The LORD answered, "Judah is to go; I have given the land into their hands."

³Then the men of Judah said to the Simeonites their brothers, "Come up with us into the territory allotted to us, to fight against the Canaanites. We in turn will go

with you into yours." So the Simeonites went with them.

[4]When Judah attacked, the LORD gave the Canaanites and Perizzites into their hands and they struck down ten thousand men at Bezek. [5]It was there that they found Adoni-Bezek and fought against him, putting to rout the Canaanites and Perizzites. [6]Adoni-Bezek fled, but they chased him and caught him, and cut off his thumbs and big toes.

[7]Then Adoni-Bezek said, "Seventy kings with their thumbs and big toes cut off have picked up scraps under my table. Now God has paid me back for what I did to them." They brought him to Jerusalem, and he died there.

[8]The men of Judah attacked Jerusalem also and took it. They put the city to the sword and set it on fire.

[9]After that, the men of Judah went down to fight against the Canaanites living in the hill country, the Negev and the western foothills. [10]They advanced against the Canaanites living in Hebron (formerly called Kiriath Arba) and defeated Sheshai, Ahiman and Talmai.

[11]From there they advanced against the people living in Debir (formerly called Kiriath Sepher). [12]And Caleb said, "I will give my daughter Acsah in marriage to the man who attacks and captures Kiriath Sepher." [13]Othniel son of Kenaz, Caleb's younger brother, took it; so Caleb gave his daughter Acsah to him in marriage.

[14]One day when she came to Othniel, she urged him[a] to ask her father for a field. When she got off her donkey, Caleb asked her, "What can I do for you?"

[15]She replied, "Do me a special favor. Since you have given me land in the Negev, give me also springs of water." Then Caleb gave her the upper and lower springs.

[16]The descendants of Moses' father-in-law, the Kenite, went up from the City of Palms[b] with the men of Judah to live among the people of the Desert of Judah in the Negev near Arad.

[17]Then the men of Judah went with the Simeonites their brothers and attacked the Canaanites living in Zephath, and they totally destroyed[c] the city. Therefore it was called Hormah.[d] [18]The men of Judah

also took[e] Gaza, Ashkelon and Ekron—each city with its territory.

[19]The LORD was with the men of Judah. They took possession of the hill country, but they were unable to drive the people from the plains, because they had iron chariots. [20]As Moses had promised, Hebron was given to Caleb, who drove from it the three sons of Anak. [21]The Benjamites, however, failed to dislodge the Jebusites, who were living in Jerusalem; to this day the Jebusites live there with the Benjamites.

[22]Now the house of Joseph attacked Bethel, and the LORD was with them. [23]When they sent men to spy out Bethel (formerly called Luz), [24]the spies saw a man coming out of the city and they said to him, "Show us how to get into the city and we will see that you are treated well." [25]So he showed them, and they put the city to the sword but spared the man and his whole family. [26]He then went to the land of the Hittites, where he built a city and called it Luz, which is its name to this day.

[27]But Manasseh did not drive out the people of Beth Shan or Taanach or Dor or Ibleam or Megiddo and their surrounding settlements, for the Canaanites were determined to live in that land. [28]When Israel became strong, they pressed the Canaanites into forced labor but never drove them out completely. [29]Nor did Ephraim drive out the Canaanites living in Gezer, but the Canaanites continued to live there among them. [30]Neither did Zebulun drive out the Canaanites living in Kitron or Nahalol, who remained among them; but they did subject them to forced labor. [31]Nor did Asher drive out those living in Acco or Sidon or Ahlab or Aczib or Helbah or Aphek or Rehob, [32]and because of this the people of Asher lived among the Canaanite inhabitants of the land. [33]Neither did Naphtali drive out those living in Beth Shemesh or Beth Anath; but the Naphtalites too lived among the Canaanite inhabitants of the land, and those living in Beth Shemesh and Beth Anath became forced laborers for them. [34]The Amorites confined the Danites to the hill country, not allowing them to come down into the plain. [35]And the Amorites were

---

[a]14 Hebrew; Septuagint and Vulgate *Othniel, he urged her*   [b]16 That is, Jericho   [c]17 The Hebrew term refers to the irrevocable giving over of things or persons to the LORD, often by totally destroying them.   [d]17 *Hormah* means *destruction*.   [e]18 Hebrew; Septuagint *Judah did not take*

determined also to hold out in Mount Heres, Aijalon and Shaalbim, but when the power of the house of Joseph increased, they too were pressed into forced labor. 36The boundary of the Amorites was from Scorpion*f* Pass to Sela and beyond.

CHAPTER 2

The angel of the LORD went up from Gilgal to Bokim and said, "I brought you up out of Egypt and led you into the land that I swore to give to your forefathers. I said, 'I will never break my covenant with you, 2and you shall not make a covenant with the people of this land, but you shall break down their altars.' Yet you have disobeyed me. Why have you done this? 3Now therefore I tell you that I will not drive them out before you; they will be ,thorns, in your sides and their gods will be a snare to you."

4When the angel of the LORD had spoken these things to all the Israelites, the people wept aloud, 5and they called that place Bokim.*g* There they offered sacrifices to the LORD.

6After Joshua had dismissed the Israelites, they went to take possession of the land, each to his own inheritance. 7The people served the LORD throughout the lifetime of Joshua and of the elders who outlived him and who had seen all the great things the LORD had done for Israel.

8Joshua son of Nun, the servant of the LORD, died at the age of a hundred and ten. 9And they buried him in the land of his inheritance, at Timnath Heres*h* in the hill country of Ephraim, north of Mount Gaash.

10After that whole generation had been gathered to their fathers, another generation grew up, who knew neither the LORD nor what he had done for Israel. 11Then the Israelites did evil in the eyes of the LORD and served the Baals. 12They forsook the LORD, the God of their fathers, who had brought them out of Egypt. They followed and worshiped various gods of the peoples around them. They provoked the LORD to anger 13because they forsook him and served Baal and the Ashtoreths. 14In his anger against Israel the LORD handed them over to raiders who plundered them. He sold them to their enemies all

around, whom they were no longer able to resist. 15Whenever Israel went out to fight, the hand of the LORD was against them to defeat them, just as he had sworn to them. They were in great distress.

16Then the LORD raised up judges,*i* who saved them out of the hands of these raiders. 17Yet they would not listen to their judges but prostituted themselves to other gods and worshiped them. Unlike their fathers, they quickly turned from the way in which their fathers had walked, the way of obedience to the LORD's commands. 18Whenever the LORD raised up a judge for them, he was with the judge and saved them out of the hands of their enemies as long as the judge lived; for the LORD had compassion on them as they groaned under those who oppressed and afflicted them. 19But when the judge died, the people returned to ways even more corrupt than those of their fathers, following other gods and serving and worshiping them. They refused to give up their evil practices and stubborn ways.

20Therefore the LORD was very angry with Israel and said, "Because this nation has violated the covenant that I laid down for their forefathers and has not listened to me, 21I will no longer drive out before them any of the nations Joshua left when he died. 22I will use them to test Israel and see whether they will keep the way of the LORD and walk in it as their forefathers did." 23The LORD had allowed those nations to remain; he did not drive them out at once by giving them into the hands of Joshua.

CHAPTER 3

These are the nations the LORD left to test all those Israelites who had not experienced any of the wars in Canaan 2(he did this only to teach warfare to the descendants of the Israelites who had not had previous battle experience): 3the five rulers of the Philistines, all the Canaanites, the Sidonians, and the Hivites living in the Lebanon mountains from Mount Baal Hermon to Lebo*j* Hamath. 4They were left to test the Israelites to see whether they would obey the LORD's commands, which he had given their forefathers through Moses.

5The Israelites lived among the

---

*f*36 Hebrew *Akrabbim*   *g*5 *Bokim* means *weepers.*   *h*9 Also known as *Timnath Serah* (see Joshua 19:50 and 24:30)
*i*16 Or *leaders;* similarly in verses 17-19   *j*3 Or *to the entrance to*

Canaanites, Hittites, Amorites, Perizzites, Hivites and Jebusites. [6]They took their daughters in marriage and gave their own daughters to their sons, and served their gods.

[7]The Israelites did evil in the eyes of the LORD; they forgot the LORD their God and served the Baals and the Asherahs. [8]The anger of the LORD burned against Israel so that he sold them into the hands of Cushan-Rishathaim king of Aram Naharaim,[k] to whom the Israelites were subject for eight years. [9]But when they cried out to the LORD, he raised up for them a deliverer, Othniel son of Kenaz, Caleb's younger brother, who saved them. [10]The Spirit of the LORD came upon him, so that he became Israel's judge[l] and went to war. The LORD gave Cushan-Rishathaim king of Aram into the hands of Othniel, who overpowered him. [11]So the land had peace for forty years, until Othniel son of Kenaz died.

[12]Once again the Israelites did evil in the eyes of the LORD, and because they did this evil the LORD gave Eglon king of Moab power over Israel. [13]Getting the Ammonites and Amalekites to join him, Eglon came and attacked Israel, and they took possession of the City of Palms.[m] [14]The Israelites were subject to Eglon king of Moab for eighteen years.

[15]Again the Israelites cried out to the LORD, and he gave them a deliverer— Ehud, a left-handed man, the son of Gera the Benjamite. The Israelites sent him with tribute to Eglon king of Moab. [16]Now Ehud had made a double-edged sword about a foot and a half[n] long, which he strapped to his right thigh under his clothing. [17]He presented the tribute to Eglon king of Moab, who was a very fat man. [18]After Ehud had presented the tribute, he sent on their way the men who had carried it. [19]At the idols[o] near Gilgal he himself turned back and said, "I have a secret message for you, O king."

The king said, "Quiet!" And all his attendants left him.

[20]Ehud then approached him while he was sitting alone in the upper room of his summer palace[p] and said, "I have a message from God for you." As the king rose from his seat, [21]Ehud reached with his left hand, drew the sword from his right thigh and plunged it into the king's belly. [22]Even the handle sank in after the blade, which came out his back. Ehud did not pull the sword out, and the fat closed in over it. [23]Then Ehud went out to the porch[q]; he shut the doors of the upper room behind him and locked them.

[24]After he had gone, the servants came and found the doors of the upper room locked. They said, "He must be relieving himself in the inner room of the house." [25]They waited to the point of embarrassment, but when he did not open the doors of the room, they took a key and unlocked them. There they saw their lord fallen to the floor, dead.

[26]While they waited, Ehud got away. He passed by the idols and escaped to Seirah. [27]When he arrived there, he blew a trumpet in the hill country of Ephraim, and the Israelites went down with him from the hills, with him leading them.

[28]"Follow me," he ordered, "for the LORD has given Moab, your enemy, into your hands." So they followed him down and, taking possession of the fords of the Jordan that led to Moab, they allowed no one to cross over. [29]At that time they struck down about ten thousand Moabites, all vigorous and strong; not a man escaped. [30]That day Moab was made subject to Israel, and the land had peace for eighty years.

[31]After Ehud came Shamgar son of Anath, who struck down six hundred Philistines with an oxgoad. He too saved Israel.

CHAPTER 4

After Ehud died, the Israelites once again did evil in the eyes of the LORD. [2]So the LORD sold them into the hands of Jabin, a king of Canaan, who reigned in Hazor. The commander of his army was Sisera, who lived in Harosheth Haggoyim. [3]Because he had nine hundred iron chariots and had cruelly oppressed the Israelites for twenty years, they cried to the LORD for help.

[4]Deborah, a prophetess, the wife of Lappidoth, was leading[r] Israel at that time. [5]She held court under the Palm of Deborah between Ramah and Bethel in

[k]8 That is, Northwest Mesopotamia   [l]10 Or leader   [m]13 That is, Jericho   [n]16 Hebrew a cubit (about 0.5 meter)
[o]19 Or the stone quarries; also in verse 26   [p]20 The meaning of the Hebrew for this phrase is uncertain.   [q]23 The meaning of the Hebrew for this word is uncertain.   [r]4 Traditionally judging

the hill country of Ephraim, and the Isra-elites came to her to have their disputes decided. ⁶She sent for Barak son of Abin-oam from Kedesh in Naphtali and said to him, "The LORD, the God of Israel, com-mands you: 'Go, take with you ten thou-sand men of Naphtali and Zebulun and lead the way to Mount Tabor. ⁷I will lure Sisera, the commander of Jabin's army, with his chariots and his troops to the Ki-shon River and give him into your hands.' "

⁸Barak said to her, "If you go with me, I will go; but if you don't go with me, I won't go."

⁹"Very well," Deborah said, "I will go with you. But because of the way you are going about this,ˢ the honor will not be yours, for the LORD will hand Sisera over to a woman." So Deborah went with Barak to Kedesh, ¹⁰where he summoned Zebulun and Naphtali. Ten thousand men followed him, and Deborah also went with him.

¹¹Now Heber the Kenite had left the other Kenites, the descendants of Hobab, Moses' brother-in-law,ᵗ and pitched his tent by the great tree in Zaanannim near Kedesh.

¹²When they told Sisera that Barak son of Abinoam had gone up to Mount Tabor, ¹³Sisera gathered together his nine hun-dred iron chariots and all the men with him, from Harosheth Haggoyim to the Kishon River.

¹⁴Then Deborah said to Barak, "Go! This is the day the LORD has given Sisera into your hands. Has not the LORD gone ahead of you?" So Barak went down Mount Ta-bor, followed by ten thousand men. ¹⁵At Barak's advance, the LORD routed Sisera and all his chariots and army by the sword, and Sisera abandoned his chariot and fled on foot. ¹⁶But Barak pursued the chariots and army as far as Harosheth Haggoyim. All the troops of Sisera fell by the sword; not a man was left.

¹⁷Sisera, however, fled on foot to the tent of Jael, the wife of Heber the Kenite, because there were friendly relations be-tween Jabin king of Hazor and the clan of Heber the Kenite.

¹⁸Jael went out to meet Sisera and said to him, "Come, my lord, come right in.

Don't be afraid." So he entered her tent, and she put a covering over him.

¹⁹"I'm thirsty," he said. "Please give me some water." She opened a skin of milk, gave him a drink, and covered him up.

²⁰"Stand in the doorway of the tent," he told her. "If someone comes by and asks you, 'Is anyone here?' say 'No.' "

²¹But Jael, Heber's wife, picked up a tent peg and a hammer and went quietly to him while he lay fast asleep, exhausted. She drove the peg through his temple into the ground, and he died.

²²Barak came by in pursuit of Sisera, and Jael went out to meet him. "Come," she said, "I will show you the man you're looking for." So he went in with her, and there lay Sisera with the tent peg through his temple—dead.

²³On that day God subdued Jabin, the Canaanite king, before the Israelites. ²⁴And the hand of the Israelites grew stronger and stronger against Jabin, the Canaanite king, until they destroyed him.

CHAPTER 5

On that day Deborah and Barak son of Abinoam sang this song:

²"When the princes in Israel take the
        lead,
    when the people willingly offer
        themselves—
    praise the LORD!

³"Hear this, you kings! Listen, you
        rulers!
    I will sing toᵘ the LORD, I will sing;
    I will make music toᵛ the LORD, the
        God of Israel.

⁴"O LORD, when you went out from
        Seir,
    when you marched from the land of
        Edom,
    the earth shook, the heavens poured,
        the clouds poured down water.
⁵The mountains quaked before the
        LORD, the One of Sinai,
    before the LORD, the God of Israel.

⁶"In the days of Shamgar son of Anath,
    in the days of Jael, the roads were
        abandoned;
    travelers took to winding paths.
⁷Village lifeʷ in Israel ceased,
    ceased until I,ˣ Deborah, arose,

ˢ9 Or But on the expedition you are undertaking   ᵗ11 Or father-in-law   ᵘ3 Or of   ᵛ3 Or / with song I will praise
ʷ7 Or Warriors   ˣ7 Or you

arose a mother in Israel.
[8]When they chose new gods,
　　war came to the city gates,
and not a shield or spear was seen
　　among forty thousand in Israel.
[9]My heart is with Israel's princes,
　　with the willing volunteers among
　　　　the people.
　　Praise the LORD!'

[10]"You who ride on white donkeys,
　　sitting on your saddle blankets,
　　and you who walk along the road,
consider [11]the voice of the singers[y] at
　　　　the watering places.
　　They recite the righteous acts of the
　　　　LORD,
　　the righteous acts of his warriors[z]
　　　　in Israel.

"Then the people of the LORD
　　went down to the city gates.
[12]'Wake up, wake up, Deborah!
　　Wake up, wake up, break out in
　　　　song!
Arise, O Barak!
　　Take captive your captives, O son of
　　　　Abinoam.'

[13]"Then the men who were left
　　came down to the nobles;
the people of the LORD
　　came to me with the mighty.
[14]Some came from Ephraim, whose roots
　　　　were in Amalek;
　　Benjamin was with the people who
　　　　followed you.
From Makir captains came down,
　　from Zebulun those who bear a
　　　　commander's staff.
[15]The princes of Issachar were with
　　　　Deborah;
　　yes, Issachar was with Barak,
　　rushing after him into the valley.
In the districts of Reuben
　　there was much searching of heart.
[16]Why did you stay among the
　　　　campfires[a]
　　to hear the whistling for the flocks?
In the districts of Reuben
　　there was much searching of heart.
[17]Gilead stayed beyond the Jordan.
　　And Dan, why did he linger by the
　　　　ships?
Asher remained on the coast
　　and stayed in his coves.

[18]The people of Zebulun risked their
　　　　very lives;
　　so did Naphtali on the heights of the
　　　　field.

[19]"Kings came, they fought;
　　the kings of Canaan fought
at Taanach by the waters of Megiddo,
　　but they carried off no silver, no
　　　　plunder.
[20]From the heavens the stars fought,
　　from their courses they fought
　　　　against Sisera.
[21]The river Kishon swept them away,
　　the age-old river, the river Kishon.
　　March on, my soul; be strong!
[22]Then thundered the horses' hoofs—
　　galloping, galloping go his mighty
　　　　steeds.
[23]'Curse Meroz,' said the angel of the
　　　　LORD.
　　'Curse its people bitterly,
because they did not come to help the
　　　　LORD,
　　to help the LORD against the mighty.'

[24]"Most blessed of women be Jael,
　　the wife of Heber the Kenite,
　　most blessed of tent-dwelling
　　　　women.
[25]He asked for water, and she gave him
　　　　milk;
　　in a bowl fit for nobles she brought
　　　　him curdled milk.
[26]Her hand reached for the tent peg,
　　her right hand for the workman's
　　　　hammer.
She struck Sisera, she crushed his
　　　　head,
　　she shattered and pierced his
　　　　temple.
[27]At her feet he sank,
　　he fell; there he lay.
At her feet he sank, he fell;
　　where he sank, there he fell—dead.

[28]"Through the window peered Sisera's
　　　　mother;
　　behind the lattice she cried out,
　　'Why is his chariot so long in coming?
　　Why is the clatter of his chariots
　　　　delayed?'
[29]The wisest of her ladies answer her;
　　indeed, she keeps saying to herself,
[30]'Are they not finding and dividing the
　　　　spoils:

[y]11 Or *archers*; the meaning of the Hebrew for this word is uncertain.　[z]11 Or *villagers*　[a]16 Or *saddlebags*

a girl or two for each man,
  colorful garments as plunder for
    Sisera,
  colorful garments embroidered,
  highly embroidered garments for my
    neck—
all this as plunder?'

³¹"So may all your enemies perish,
    O Lᴏʀᴅ!
But may they who love you be like
    the sun
  when it rises in its strength."

Then the land had peace forty years.

MARCH 9 □ DAY 69
JUDGES 6–8
Gideon, the Hesitant Hero

 OVERVIEW Israel's oppression under Midian is brief but severe, as Midian forcibly takes Israel's harvest. Gideon, called by a divine messenger to deliver God's people, is a reluctant savior and doubtful candidate for greatness. It takes a pair of confirming signs (first a soggy fleece, then a dry one) to convince Gideon that God can use him. But once his faith is sparked, Gideon watches as God removes all the props upon which he might have trusted: his army (reduced 99 percent); his weapons (reduced to pitchers, torches and trumpets); and his military strategy (reduced to a single command: "Stand still!"). When a miracle of deliverance occurs, there can be only one explanation—God did it!

Chapter 6	Chapter 7	Chapter 8
Call of Gideon	Defeat of Midian	Rest for Israel
God's Man	God's Plan	God's Glory

 YOUR DAILY WALK Are you a skeptic—the kind of person who never takes anything at face value, asks a lot of questions and always requires confirmation of the facts? Then you will appreciate the life of Gideon!

If seeing is believing, the true skeptic will refuse to look.

In 1 Corinthians 1:22, Paul comments that the "Jews demand miraculous signs," and such was the case with Gideon. Faced with an overwhelming assignment and equipped with rather dubious human qualifications for the task, Gideon needed a bolstered faith before he was ready to answer God's call. Nowhere in the passage did God chide Gideon for his request for a confirming sign. Rather, he gladly and patiently provided what Gideon needed to overcome his inferiority complex.

When the will of God is clear, to demand a sign is evidence of unwillingness to obey. When God's will is uncertain, but you are earnestly seeking to find it (like Gideon), God will make it clear to you. Take a decision you are wrestling with today, and ask God to confirm his will through the Bible, Christian counsel, circumstances or inner assurance. But, remember, once you know what he wants you to do, delayed obedience is really disobedience.

 INSIGHT God Plus One: An Unbeatable Team (7:14)
In Leviticus 26:8, God had promised Israel that "five of you will chase a hundred [a ratio of one to twenty], and a hundred of you will chase ten thousand [one to one hundred]. . . ." With Gideon's band of 300

men, God fulfilled that promise and proved he doesn't worry about the odds!

CHAPTER 6

Again the Israelites did evil in the eyes of the Lord, and for seven years he gave them into the hands of the Midianites. ²Because the power of Midian was so oppressive, the Israelites prepared shelters for themselves in mountain clefts, caves and strongholds. ³Whenever the Israelites planted their crops, the Midianites, Amalekites and other eastern peoples invaded the country. ⁴They camped on the land and ruined the crops all the way to Gaza and did not spare a living thing for Israel, neither sheep nor cattle nor donkeys. ⁵They came up with their livestock and their tents like swarms of locusts. It was impossible to count the men and their camels; they invaded the land to ravage it. ⁶Midian so impoverished the Israelites that they cried out to the Lord for help.

⁷When the Israelites cried to the Lord because of Midian, ⁸he sent them a prophet, who said, "This is what the Lord, the God of Israel, says: I brought you up out of Egypt, out of the land of slavery. ⁹I snatched you from the power of Egypt and from the hand of all your oppressors. I drove them from before you and gave you their land. ¹⁰I said to you, 'I am the Lord your God; do not worship the gods of the Amorites, in whose land you live.' But you have not listened to me."

¹¹The angel of the Lord came and sat down under the oak in Ophrah that belonged to Joash the Abiezrite, where his son Gideon was threshing wheat in a winepress to keep it from the Midianites. ¹²When the angel of the Lord appeared to Gideon, he said, "The Lord is with you, mighty warrior."

¹³"But sir," Gideon replied, "if the Lord is with us, why has all this happened to us? Where are all his wonders that our fathers told us about when they said, 'Did not the Lord bring us up out of Egypt?' But now the Lord has abandoned us and put us into the hand of Midian."

¹⁴The Lord turned to him and said, "Go in the strength you have and save Israel out of Midian's hand. Am I not sending you?"

¹⁵"But Lord,ᵇ" Gideon asked, "how can I save Israel? My clan is the weakest in Manasseh, and I am the least in my family."

¹⁶The Lord answered, "I will be with you, and you will strike down all the Midianites together."

¹⁷Gideon replied, "If now I have found favor in your eyes, give me a sign that it is really you talking to me. ¹⁸Please do not go away until I come back and bring my offering and set it before you."

And the Lord said, "I will wait until you return."

¹⁹Gideon went in, prepared a young goat, and from an ephahᶜ of flour he made bread without yeast. Putting the meat in a basket and its broth in a pot, he brought them out and offered them to him under the oak.

²⁰The angel of God said to him, "Take the meat and the unleavened bread, place them on this rock, and pour out the broth." And Gideon did so. ²¹With the tip of the staff that was in his hand, the angel of the Lord touched the meat and the unleavened bread. Fire flared from the rock, consuming the meat and the bread. And the angel of the Lord disappeared. ²²When Gideon realized that it was the angel of the Lord, he exclaimed, "Ah, Sovereign Lord! I have seen the angel of the Lord face to face!"

²³But the Lord said to him, "Peace! Do not be afraid. You are not going to die."

²⁴So Gideon built an altar to the Lord there and called it The Lord is Peace. To this day it stands in Ophrah of the Abiezrites.

²⁵That same night the Lord said to him, "Take the second bull from your father's herd, the one seven years old.ᵈ Tear down your father's altar to Baal and cut down the Asherah poleᵉ beside it. ²⁶Then build a proper kind ofᶠ altar to the Lord your God on the top of this height. Using the wood of the Asherah pole that you cut down, offer the secondᵍ bull as a burnt offering."

²⁷So Gideon took ten of his servants and did as the Lord told him. But because he

---

ᵇ15 Or sir   ᶜ19 That is, probably about 3/5 bushel (about 22 liters)   ᵈ25 Or Take a full-grown, mature bull from your father's herd   ᵉ25 That is, a symbol of the goddess Asherah; here and elsewhere in Judges   ᶠ26 Or build with layers of stone an
ᵍ26 Or full-grown; also in verse 28

was afraid of his family and the men of the town, he did it at night rather than in the daytime.

²⁸In the morning when the men of the town got up, there was Baal's altar, demolished, with the Asherah pole beside it cut down and the second bull sacrificed on the newly built altar!

²⁹They asked each other, "Who did this?"

When they carefully investigated, they were told, "Gideon son of Joash did it."

³⁰The men of the town demanded of Joash, "Bring out your son. He must die, because he has broken down Baal's altar and cut down the Asherah pole beside it."

³¹But Joash replied to the hostile crowd around him, "Are you going to plead Baal's cause? Are you trying to save him? Whoever fights for him shall be put to death by morning! If Baal really is a god, he can defend himself when someone breaks down his altar." ³²So that day they called Gideon "Jerub-Baal,^h" saying, "Let Baal contend with him," because he broke down Baal's altar.

³³Now all the Midianites, Amalekites and other eastern peoples joined forces and crossed over the Jordan and camped in the Valley of Jezreel. ³⁴Then the Spirit of the LORD came upon Gideon, and he blew a trumpet, summoning the Abiezrites to follow him. ³⁵He sent messengers throughout Manasseh, calling them to arms, and also into Asher, Zebulun and Naphtali, so that they too went up to meet them.

³⁶Gideon said to God, "If you will save Israel by my hand as you have promised— ³⁷look, I will place a wool fleece on the threshing floor. If there is dew only on the fleece and all the ground is dry, then I will know that you will save Israel by my hand, as you said." ³⁸And that is what happened. Gideon rose early the next day; he squeezed the fleece and wrung out the dew—a bowlful of water.

³⁹Then Gideon said to God, "Do not be angry with me. Let me make just one more request. Allow me one more test with the fleece. This time make the fleece dry and the ground covered with dew." ⁴⁰That night God did so. Only the fleece was dry; all the ground was covered with dew.

CHAPTER 7

Early in the morning, Jerub-Baal (that is, Gideon) and all his men camped at the spring of Harod. The camp of Midian was north of them in the valley near the hill of Moreh. ²The LORD said to Gideon, "You have too many men for me to deliver Midian into their hands. In order that Israel may not boast against me that her own strength has saved her, ³announce now to the people, 'Anyone who trembles with fear may turn back and leave Mount Gilead.'" So twenty-two thousand men left, while ten thousand remained.

⁴But the LORD said to Gideon, "There are still too many men. Take them down to the water, and I will sift them for you there. If I say, 'This one shall go with you,' he shall go; but if I say, 'This one shall not go with you,' he shall not go."

⁵So Gideon took the men down to the water. There the LORD told him, "Separate those who lap the water with their tongues like a dog from those who kneel down to drink." ⁶Three hundred men lapped with their hands to their mouths. All the rest got down on their knees to drink.

⁷The LORD said to Gideon, "With the three hundred men that lapped I will save you and give the Midianites into your hands. Let all the other men go, each to his own place." ⁸So Gideon sent the rest of the Israelites to their tents but kept the three hundred, who took over the provisions and trumpets of the others.

Now the camp of Midian lay below him in the valley. ⁹During that night the LORD said to Gideon, "Get up, go down against the camp, because I am going to give it into your hands. ¹⁰If you are afraid to attack, go down to the camp with your servant Purah ¹¹and listen to what they are saying. Afterward, you will be encouraged to attack the camp." So he and Purah his servant went down to the outposts of the camp. ¹²The Midianites, the Amalekites and all the other eastern peoples had settled in the valley, thick as locusts. Their camels could no more be counted than the sand on the seashore.

¹³Gideon arrived just as a man was telling a friend his dream. "I had a dream," he was saying. "A round loaf of barley bread came tumbling into the Midianite camp. It

h 32 Jerub-Baal means let Baal contend.

struck the tent with such force that the tent overturned and collapsed."

[14]His friend responded, "This can be nothing other than the sword of Gideon son of Joash, the Israelite. God has given the Midianites and the whole camp into his hands."

[15]When Gideon heard the dream and its interpretation, he worshiped God. He returned to the camp of Israel and called out, "Get up! The LORD has given the Midianite camp into your hands." [16]Dividing the three hundred men into three companies, he placed trumpets and empty jars in the hands of all of them, with torches inside.

[17]"Watch me," he told them. "Follow my lead. When I get to the edge of the camp, do exactly as I do. [18]When I and all who are with me blow our trumpets, then from all around the camp blow yours and shout, 'For the LORD and for Gideon.' "

[19]Gideon and the hundred men with him reached the edge of the camp at the beginning of the middle watch, just after they had changed the guard. They blew their trumpets and broke the jars that were in their hands. [20]The three companies blew the trumpets and smashed the jars. Grasping the torches in their left hands and holding in their right hands the trumpets they were to blow, they shouted, "A sword for the LORD and for Gideon!" [21]While each man held his position around the camp, all the Midianites ran, crying out as they fled.

[22]When the three hundred trumpets sounded, the LORD caused the men throughout the camp to turn on each other with their swords. The army fled to Beth Shittah toward Zererah as far as the border of Abel Meholah near Tabbath. [23]Israelites from Naphtali, Asher and all Manasseh were called out, and they pursued the Midianites. [24]Gideon sent messengers throughout the hill country of Ephraim, saying, "Come down against the Midianites and seize the waters of the Jordan ahead of them as far as Beth Barah."

So all the men of Ephraim were called out and they took the waters of the Jordan as far as Beth Barah. [25]They also captured two of the Midianite leaders, Oreb and Zeeb. They killed Oreb at the rock of Oreb, and Zeeb at the winepress of Zeeb. They pursued the Midianites and brought the heads of Oreb and Zeeb to Gideon, who was by the Jordan.

CHAPTER 8

Now the Ephraimites asked Gideon, "Why have you treated us like this? Why didn't you call us when you went to fight Midian?" And they criticized him sharply. [2]But he answered them, "What have I accomplished compared to you? Aren't the gleanings of Ephraim's grapes better than the full grape harvest of Abiezer? [3]God gave Oreb and Zeeb, the Midianite leaders, into your hands. What was I able to do compared to you?" At this, their resentment against him subsided.

[4]Gideon and his three hundred men, exhausted yet keeping up the pursuit, came to the Jordan and crossed it. [5]He said to the men of Succoth, "Give my troops some bread; they are worn out, and I am still pursuing Zebah and Zalmunna, the kings of Midian."

[6]But the officials of Succoth said, "Do you already have the hands of Zebah and Zalmunna in your possession? Why should we give bread to your troops?"

[7]Then Gideon replied, "Just for that, when the LORD has given Zebah and Zalmunna into my hand, I will tear your flesh with desert thorns and briers."

[8]From there he went up to Peniel[i] and made the same request of them, but they answered as the men of Succoth had. [9]So he said to the men of Peniel, "When I return in triumph, I will tear down this tower."

[10]Now Zebah and Zalmunna were in Karkor with a force of about fifteen thousand men, all that were left of the armies of the eastern peoples; a hundred and twenty thousand swordsmen had fallen. [11]Gideon went up by the route of the nomads east of Nobah and Jogbehah and fell upon the unsuspecting army. [12]Zebah and Zalmunna, the two kings of Midian, fled, but he pursued them and captured them, routing their entire army.

[13]Gideon son of Joash then returned from the battle by the Pass of Heres. [14]He caught a young man of Succoth and questioned him, and the young man wrote down for him the names of the

[i]8 Hebrew *Penuel*, a variant of *Peniel*; also in verses 9 and 17

seventy-seven officials of Succoth, the elders of the town. ¹⁵Then Gideon came and said to the men of Succoth, "Here are Zebah and Zalmunna, about whom you taunted me by saying, 'Do you already have the hands of Zebah and Zalmunna in your possession? Why should we give bread to your exhausted men?' " ¹⁶He took the elders of the town and taught the men of Succoth a lesson by punishing them with desert thorns and briers. ¹⁷He also pulled down the tower of Peniel and killed the men of the town.

¹⁸Then he asked Zebah and Zalmunna, "What kind of men did you kill at Tabor?"

"Men like you," they answered, "each one with the bearing of a prince."

¹⁹Gideon replied, "Those were my brothers, the sons of my own mother. As surely as the LORD lives, if you had spared their lives, I would not kill you." ²⁰Turning to Jether, his oldest son, he said, "Kill them!" But Jether did not draw his sword, because he was only a boy and was afraid.

²¹Zebah and Zalmunna said, "Come, do it yourself. 'As is the man, so is his strength.' " So Gideon stepped forward and killed them, and took the ornaments off their camels' necks.

²²The Israelites said to Gideon, "Rule over us—you, your son and your grandson—because you have saved us out of the hand of Midian."

²³But Gideon told them, "I will not rule over you, nor will my son rule over you. The LORD will rule over you." ²⁴And he said, "I do have one request, that each of you give me an earring from your share

j26 That is, about 43 pounds (about 19.5 kilograms)

of the plunder." (It was the custom of the Ishmaelites to wear gold earrings.)

²⁵They answered, "We'll be glad to give them." So they spread out a garment, and each man threw a ring from his plunder onto it. ²⁶The weight of the gold rings he asked for came to seventeen hundred shekels,ʲ not counting the ornaments, the pendants and the purple garments worn by the kings of Midian or the chains that were on their camels' necks. ²⁷Gideon made the gold into an ephod, which he placed in Ophrah, his town. All Israel prostituted themselves by worshiping it there, and it became a snare to Gideon and his family.

²⁸Thus Midian was subdued before the Israelites and did not raise its head again. During Gideon's lifetime, the land enjoyed peace forty years.

²⁹Jerub-Baal son of Joash went back home to live. ³⁰He had seventy sons of his own, for he had many wives. ³¹His concubine, who lived in Shechem, also bore him a son, whom he named Abimelech. ³²Gideon son of Joash died at a good old age and was buried in the tomb of his father Joash in Ophrah of the Abiezrites.

³³No sooner had Gideon died than the Israelites again prostituted themselves to the Baals. They set up Baal-Berith as their god and ³⁴did not remember the LORD their God, who had rescued them from the hands of all their enemies on every side. ³⁵They also failed to show kindness to the family of Jerub-Baal (that is, Gideon) for all the good things he had done for them.

MARCH 10 □ DAY 70
JUDGES 9–12
Gideon's Son and Six Judges

 OVERVIEW Abimelech, Gideon's son by a concubine, is never called a judge in Israel, though he sets himself up as king and murders his seventy brothers. As Jotham (the only surviving brother) predicts, Abimelech dies as violently as he lived. The brief records of two minor judges, Tola and Jair, are followed by a lengthy treatment of Jephthah in the days of oppression by the Philistines and Ammonites. In contrast to Gideon, who sought to appease the tribe of Ephraim, Jephthah ends up going to war against Ephraim. His action-filled reign as

judge is best remembered for his presumptuous vow, which seals forever the fate of his virgin daughter. The section closes with a brief
look at three other minor judges who are most noteworthy for their
enormous families!

Chapter 9	Chapter 10	Chapter 11	Chapter 12
God's Retribution	God's Rebuke	Jephthah's Vow	Jephthah's Vengeance
Abimelech	Tola/Jair	Jephthah and 3 Other Judges	

YOUR DAILY WALK Should Christians take oaths or make vows today? Those who respond no will find ample support for their view in
the tragic consequences of Jephthah's presumptuous vow (11:30–31,
34–40).

*No one can be
called mature
who does not
learn from his
or her own
mistakes.*

Vows are not to be taken lightly. But the real tragedy of Jephthah
was his unwillingness to admit he had acted foolishly and had made a
mistake. A willingness to admit errors and seek help is evidence of
maturity and strength, not weakness.

Is there a family member or friend you have wronged through a
mistake? Going to that person, admitting you were wrong, asking for
forgiveness and making restitution for any damage can open new opportunities for fellowship and service with him or her. God wants you
to be an open, honest person with a realistic view of yourself—one
who (unlike Jephthah) is quick to admit mistakes and knows when to
seek wise counsel.

INSIGHT A Deadly Slip of the Tongue
The forty-two thousand Ephraimites Jephthah slew were identified by
the fact that they said, *Sibboleth* instead of *Shibboleth* (12:6). But they
aren't the only ones in Scripture who were betrayed by an accent.
When Peter was in the high priest's courtyard the night Jesus was arrested, he was accused of being a follower of Jesus because of his Galilean accent (Matthew 26:73)!

CHAPTER 9
Abimelech son of Jerub-Baal went to his
mother's brothers in Shechem and said to
them and to all his mother's clan, ²"Ask
all the citizens of Shechem, 'Which is better for you: to have all seventy of Jerub-
Baal's sons rule over you, or just one
man?' Remember, I am your flesh and
blood."

³When the brothers repeated all this to
the citizens of Shechem, they were inclined to follow Abimelech, for they said,
"He is our brother." ⁴They gave him seventy shekelsᵏ of silver from the temple
of Baal-Berith, and Abimelech used it to
hire reckless adventurers, who became his
followers. ⁵He went to his father's home
in Ophrah and on one stone murdered his
seventy brothers, the sons of Jerub-Baal.
But Jotham, the youngest son of Jerub-
Baal, escaped by hiding. ⁶Then all the cit-

izens of Shechem and Beth Millo gathered
beside the great tree at the pillar in Shechem to crown Abimelech king.

⁷When Jotham was told about this, he
climbed up on the top of Mount Gerizim
and shouted to them, "Listen to me, citizens of Shechem, so that God may listen
to you. ⁸One day the trees went out to
anoint a king for themselves. They said to
the olive tree, 'Be our king.'

⁹"But the olive tree answered, 'Should I
give up my oil, by which both gods and
men are honored, to hold sway over the
trees?'

¹⁰"Next, the trees said to the fig tree,
'Come and be our king.'

¹¹"But the fig tree replied, 'Should I give
up my fruit, so good and sweet, to hold
sway over the trees?'

¹²"Then the trees said to the vine, 'Come
and be our king.'

ᵏ4 That is, about 1 3/4 pounds (about 0.8 kilogram)

¹³"But the vine answered, 'Should I give up my wine, which cheers both gods and men, to hold sway over the trees?'

¹⁴"Finally all the trees said to the thornbush, 'Come and be our king.'

¹⁵"The thornbush said to the trees, 'If you really want to anoint me king over you, come and take refuge in my shade; but if not, then let fire come out of the thornbush and consume the cedars of Lebanon!'

¹⁶"Now if you have acted honorably and in good faith when you made Abimelech king, and if you have been fair to Jerub-Baal and his family, and if you have treated him as he deserves— ¹⁷and to think that my father fought for you, risked his life to rescue you from the hand of Midian ¹⁸(but today you have revolted against my father's family, murdered his seventy sons on a single stone, and made Abimelech, the son of his slave girl, king over the citizens of Shechem because he is your brother)— ¹⁹if then you have acted honorably and in good faith toward Jerub-Baal and his family today, may Abimelech be your joy, and may you be his, too! ²⁰But if you have not, let fire come out from Abimelech and consume you, citizens of Shechem and Beth Millo, and let fire come out from you, citizens of Shechem and Beth Millo, and consume Abimelech!"

²¹Then Jotham fled, escaping to Beer, and he lived there because he was afraid of his brother Abimelech.

²²After Abimelech had governed Israel three years, ²³God sent an evil spirit between Abimelech and the citizens of Shechem, who acted treacherously against Abimelech. ²⁴God did this in order that the crime against Jerub-Baal's seventy sons, the shedding of their blood, might be avenged on their brother Abimelech and on the citizens of Shechem, who had helped him murder his brothers. ²⁵In opposition to him these citizens of Shechem set men on the hilltops to ambush and rob everyone who passed by, and this was reported to Abimelech.

²⁶Now Gaal son of Ebed moved with his brothers into Shechem, and its citizens put their confidence in him. ²⁷After they had gone out into the fields and gathered the grapes and trodden them, they held a festival in the temple of their god. While they were eating and drinking, they cursed Abimelech. ²⁸Then Gaal son of Ebed said, "Who is Abimelech, and who is Shechem, that we should be subject to him? Isn't he Jerub-Baal's son, and isn't Zebul his deputy? Serve the men of Hamor, Shechem's father! Why should we serve Abimelech? ²⁹If only this people were under my command! Then I would get rid of him. I would say to Abimelech, 'Call out your whole army!' "[l]

³⁰When Zebul the governor of the city heard what Gaal son of Ebed said, he was very angry. ³¹Under cover he sent messengers to Abimelech, saying, "Gaal son of Ebed and his brothers have come to Shechem and are stirring up the city against you. ³²Now then, during the night you and your men should come and lie in wait in the fields. ³³In the morning at sunrise, advance against the city. When Gaal and his men come out against you, do whatever your hand finds to do."

³⁴So Abimelech and all his troops set out by night and took up concealed positions near Shechem in four companies. ³⁵Now Gaal son of Ebed had gone out and was standing at the entrance to the city gate just as Abimelech and his soldiers came out from their hiding place.

³⁶When Gaal saw them, he said to Zebul, "Look, people are coming down from the tops of the mountains!"

Zebul replied, "You mistake the shadows of the mountains for men."

³⁷But Gaal spoke up again: "Look, people are coming down from the center of the land, and a company is coming from the direction of the soothsayers' tree."

³⁸Then Zebul said to him, "Where is your big talk now, you who said, 'Who is Abimelech that we should be subject to him?' Aren't these the men you ridiculed? Go out and fight them!"

³⁹So Gaal led out[m] the citizens of Shechem and fought Abimelech. ⁴⁰Abimelech chased him, and many fell wounded in the flight—all the way to the entrance to the gate. ⁴¹Abimelech stayed in Arumah, and Zebul drove Gaal and his brothers out of Shechem.

⁴²The next day the people of Shechem went out to the fields, and this was reported to Abimelech. ⁴³So he took his

men, divided them into three companies and set an ambush in the fields. When he saw the people coming out of the city, he rose to attack them. ⁴⁴Abimelech and the companies with him rushed forward to a position at the entrance to the city gate. Then two companies rushed upon those in the fields and struck them down. ⁴⁵All that day Abimelech pressed his attack against the city until he had captured it and killed its people. Then he destroyed the city and scattered salt over it.

⁴⁶On hearing this, the citizens in the tower of Shechem went into the stronghold of the temple of El-Berith. ⁴⁷When Abimelech heard that they had assembled there, ⁴⁸he and all his men went up Mount Zalmon. He took an ax and cut off some branches, which he lifted to his shoulders. He ordered the men with him, "Quick! Do what you have seen me do!" ⁴⁹So all the men cut branches and followed Abimelech. They piled them against the stronghold and set it on fire over the people inside. So all the people in the tower of Shechem, about a thousand men and women, also died.

⁵⁰Next Abimelech went to Thebez and besieged it and captured it. ⁵¹Inside the city, however, was a strong tower, to which all the men and women—all the people of the city—fled. They locked themselves in and climbed up on the tower roof. ⁵²Abimelech went to the tower and stormed it. But as he approached the entrance to the tower to set it on fire, ⁵³a woman dropped an upper millstone on his head and cracked his skull.

⁵⁴Hurriedly he called to his armor-bearer, "Draw your sword and kill me, so that they can't say, 'A woman killed him.' " So his servant ran him through, and he died. ⁵⁵When the Israelites saw that Abimelech was dead, they went home.

⁵⁶Thus God repaid the wickedness that Abimelech had done to his father by murdering his seventy brothers. ⁵⁷God also made the men of Shechem pay for all their wickedness. The curse of Jotham son of Jerub-Baal came on them.

CHAPTER 10

After the time of Abimelech a man of Issachar, Tola son of Puah, the son of Dodo,

rose to save Israel. He lived in Shamir, in the hill country of Ephraim. ²He led[n] Israel twenty-three years; then he died, and was buried in Shamir.

³He was followed by Jair of Gilead, who led Israel twenty-two years. ⁴He had thirty sons, who rode thirty donkeys. They controlled thirty towns in Gilead, which to this day are called Havvoth Jair.[o] ⁵When Jair died, he was buried in Kamon.

⁶Again the Israelites did evil in the eyes of the LORD. They served the Baals and the Ashtoreths, and the gods of Aram, the gods of Sidon, the gods of Moab, the gods of the Ammonites and the gods of the Philistines. And because the Israelites forsook the LORD and no longer served him, ⁷he became angry with them. He sold them into the hands of the Philistines and the Ammonites, ⁸who that year shattered and crushed them. For eighteen years they oppressed all the Israelites on the east side of the Jordan in Gilead, the land of the Amorites. ⁹The Ammonites also crossed the Jordan to fight against Judah, Benjamin and the house of Ephraim; and Israel was in great distress. ¹⁰Then the Israelites cried out to the LORD, "We have sinned against you, forsaking our God and serving the Baals."

¹¹The LORD replied, "When the Egyptians, the Amorites, the Ammonites, the Philistines, ¹²the Sidonians, the Amalekites and the Maonites[p] oppressed you and you cried to me for help, did I not save you from their hands? ¹³But you have forsaken me and served other gods, so I will no longer save you. ¹⁴Go and cry out to the gods you have chosen. Let them save you when you are in trouble!"

¹⁵But the Israelites said to the LORD, "We have sinned. Do with us whatever you think best, but please rescue us now." ¹⁶Then they got rid of the foreign gods among them and served the LORD. And he could bear Israel's misery no longer.

¹⁷When the Ammonites were called to arms and camped in Gilead, the Israelites assembled and camped at Mizpah. ¹⁸The leaders of the people of Gilead said to each other, "Whoever will launch the attack against the Ammonites will be the head of all those living in Gilead."

ⁿ2 Traditionally *judged*; also in verse 3   ^o4 Or *called the settlements of Jair*   ^p12 Hebrew; some Septuagint manuscripts *Midianites*

CHAPTER 11

Jephthah the Gileadite was a mighty warrior. His father was Gilead; his mother was a prostitute. ²Gilead's wife also bore him sons, and when they were grown up, they drove Jephthah away. "You are not going to get any inheritance in our family," they said, "because you are the son of another woman." ³So Jephthah fled from his brothers and settled in the land of Tob, where a group of adventurers gathered around him and followed him.

⁴Some time later, when the Ammonites made war on Israel, ⁵the elders of Gilead went to get Jephthah from the land of Tob. ⁶"Come," they said, "be our commander, so we can fight the Ammonites."

⁷Jephthah said to them, "Didn't you hate me and drive me from my father's house? Why do you come to me now, when you're in trouble?"

⁸The elders of Gilead said to him, "Nevertheless, we are turning to you now; come with us to fight the Ammonites, and you will be our head over all who live in Gilead."

⁹Jephthah answered, "Suppose you take me back to fight the Ammonites and the LORD gives them to me—will I really be your head?"

¹⁰The elders of Gilead replied, "The LORD is our witness; we will certainly do as you say." ¹¹So Jephthah went with the elders of Gilead, and the people made him head and commander over them. And he repeated all his words before the LORD in Mizpah.

¹²Then Jephthah sent messengers to the Ammonite king with the question: "What do you have against us that you have attacked our country?"

¹³The king of the Ammonites answered Jephthah's messengers, "When Israel came up out of Egypt, they took away my land from the Arnon to the Jabbok, all the way to the Jordan. Now give it back peaceably."

¹⁴Jephthah sent back messengers to the Ammonite king, ¹⁵saying:

"This is what Jephthah says: Israel did not take the land of Moab or the land of the Ammonites. ¹⁶But when they came up out of Egypt, Israel went through the desert to the Red Sea*q* and on to Kadesh. ¹⁷Then Israel sent messengers to the king of Edom, saying, 'Give us permission to go through your country,' but the king of Edom would not listen. They sent also to the king of Moab, and he refused. So Israel stayed at Kadesh.

¹⁸"Next they traveled through the desert, skirted the lands of Edom and Moab, passed along the eastern side of the country of Moab, and camped on the other side of the Arnon. They did not enter the territory of Moab, for the Arnon was its border.

¹⁹"Then Israel sent messengers to Sihon king of the Amorites, who ruled in Heshbon, and said to him, 'Let us pass through your country to our own place.' ²⁰Sihon, however, did not trust Israel*r* to pass through his territory. He mustered all his men and encamped at Jahaz and fought with Israel.

²¹"Then the LORD, the God of Israel, gave Sihon and all his men into Israel's hands, and they defeated them. Israel took over all the land of the Amorites who lived in that country, ²²capturing all of it from the Arnon to the Jabbok and from the desert to the Jordan.

²³"Now since the LORD, the God of Israel, has driven the Amorites out before his people Israel, what right have you to take it over? ²⁴Will you not take what your god Chemosh gives you? Likewise, whatever the LORD our God has given us, we will possess. ²⁵Are you better than Balak son of Zippor, king of Moab? Did he ever quarrel with Israel or fight with them? ²⁶For three hundred years Israel occupied Heshbon, Aroer, the surrounding settlements and all the towns along the Arnon. Why didn't you retake them during that time? ²⁷I have not wronged you, but you are doing me wrong by waging war against me. Let the LORD, the Judge,*s* decide the dispute this day between the Israelites and the Ammonites."

²⁸The king of Ammon, however, paid no attention to the message Jephthah sent him.

²⁹Then the Spirit of the LORD came upon Jephthah. He crossed Gilead and

---

q16 Hebrew *Yam Suph*; that is, Sea of Reeds   *r20* Or *however, would not make an agreement for Israel*   *s27* Or Ruler

Manasseh, passed through Mizpah of Gilead, and from there he advanced against the Ammonites. [30]And Jephthah made a vow to the LORD: "If you give the Ammonites into my hands, [31]whatever comes out of the door of my house to meet me when I return in triumph from the Ammonites will be the LORD's, and I will sacrifice it as a burnt offering."

[32]Then Jephthah went over to fight the Ammonites, and the LORD gave them into his hands. [33]He devastated twenty towns from Aroer to the vicinity of Minnith, as far as Abel Keramim. Thus Israel subdued Ammon.

[34]When Jephthah returned to his home in Mizpah, who should come out to meet him but his daughter, dancing to the sound of tambourines! She was an only child. Except for her he had neither son nor daughter. [35]When he saw her, he tore his clothes and cried, "Oh! My daughter! You have made me miserable and wretched, because I have made a vow to the LORD that I cannot break."

[36]"My father," she replied, "you have given your word to the LORD. Do to me just as you promised, now that the LORD has avenged you of your enemies, the Ammonites. [37]But grant me this one request," she said. "Give me two months to roam the hills and weep with my friends, because I will never marry."

[38]"You may go," he said. And he let her go for two months. She and the girls went into the hills and wept because she would never marry. [39]After the two months, she returned to her father and he did to her as he had vowed. And she was a virgin.

From this comes the Israelite custom [40]that each year the young women of Israel go out for four days to commemorate the daughter of Jephthah the Gileadite.

CHAPTER 12
The men of Ephraim called out their forces, crossed over to Zaphon and said to Jephthah, "Why did you go to fight the Ammonites without calling us to go with you? We're going to burn down your house over your head."

[2]Jephthah answered, "I and my people were engaged in a great struggle with the Ammonites, and although I called, you didn't save me out of their hands. [3]When I saw that you wouldn't help, I took my life in my hands and crossed over to fight the Ammonites, and the LORD gave me the victory over them. Now why have you come up today to fight me?"

[4]Jephthah then called together the men of Gilead and fought against Ephraim. The Gileadites struck them down because the Ephraimites had said, "You Gileadites are renegades from Ephraim and Manasseh." [5]The Gileadites captured the fords of the Jordan leading to Ephraim, and whenever a survivor of Ephraim said, "Let me cross over," the men of Gilead asked him, "Are you an Ephraimite?" If he replied, "No," [6]they said, "All right, say 'Shibboleth.' " If he said, "Sibboleth," because he could not pronounce the word correctly, they seized him and killed him at the fords of the Jordan. Forty-two thousand Ephraimites were killed at that time.

[7]Jephthah led[f] Israel six years. Then Jephthah the Gileadite died, and was buried in a town in Gilead.

[8]After him, Ibzan of Bethlehem led Israel. [9]He had thirty sons and thirty daughters. He gave his daughters away in marriage to those outside his clan, and for his sons he brought in thirty young women as wives from outside his clan. Ibzan led Israel seven years. [10]Then Ibzan died, and was buried in Bethlehem.

[11]After him, Elon the Zebulunite led Israel ten years. [12]Then Elon died, and was buried in Aijalon in the land of Zebulun.

[13]After him, Abdon son of Hillel, from Pirathon, led Israel. [14]He had forty sons and thirty grandsons, who rode on seventy donkeys. He led Israel eight years. [15]Then Abdon son of Hillel died, and was buried at Pirathon in Ephraim, in the hill country of the Amalekites.

[f]7 Traditionally *judged*; also in verses 8-14

MARCH 11 □ DAY 71
JUDGES 13–16
Samson, the Carnal Champion

OVERVIEW The life of Samson is a study in unfulfilled potential. The only child of an elderly couple, designated by God a Nazirite from birth, blessed with superhuman strength and commissioned to "begin the deliverance Israel from the hands of the Philistines" (13:5), Samson instead spends most of his life fulfilling his own passions and desires. His lack of self-control eventually results in blindness and bondage. But God gives him one last portion of power, and in his death Samson destroys more Philistines than during his entire life of compromise.

Chapter 13	Chapter 14	Chapter 15	Chapter 16
Manoah's Prayer	Samson's Power	Samson's Passion	Samson's Passing
Calling		Compromise	

YOUR DAILY WALK Here are some of the wisest words ever penned by Benjamin Franklin: "Doing an injury puts you below your enemy; revenging one makes you but even with him; forgiving one sets you above him." You may want to create a plaque or stitchery featuring them!

Forgiveness warms the heart and cools the sting.

Revenge is one of the most natural—and destructive—of all human responses. Rather than reacting to a wrong with forgiveness, the most common reaction is to commit another wrong—namely, lashing out at the other person. Such was the problem with Samson. He spent much of his time burning with anger (14:19) and doing harm to those who had wronged him (15:3). But his temper only complicated the problem, never corrected it.

What is your response when someone has wronged you? Do you count to ten before blasting off, or do you go into orbit immediately? To help you cultivate a proper response to others, put this verse to work today: "A gentle answer turns away wrath, but a harsh word stirs up anger" (Proverbs 15:1). Be the one to break anger's destructive cycle in your interactions with others today.

INSIGHT Nazirite or Nazarene: What's the Difference?
Many confuse the two terms *Nazirite* and *Nazarene.* Jesus, a Nazarene, was so called because he lived in Nazareth. Samson, a Nazirite, was so called because he did not drink wine or touch dead bodies or cut his hair—all prohibitions of a Nazirite vow. (For added details concerning this vow, see Numbers 6:1–21.)

CHAPTER 13
Again the Israelites did evil in the eyes of the LORD, so the LORD delivered them into the hands of the Philistines for forty years.

²A certain man of Zorah, named Manoah, from the clan of the Danites, had a wife who was sterile and remained childless. ³The angel of the LORD appeared to her and said, "You are sterile and childless, but you are going to conceive and have a son. ⁴Now see to it that you drink no wine or other fermented drink and that you do not eat anything unclean, ⁵because you will conceive and give birth to a son. No razor may be used on his head, because the boy is to be a Nazirite, set apart to God from birth, and he will begin the deliverance of Israel from the hands of the Philistines."

⁶Then the woman went to her husband and told him, "A man of God came to me. He looked like an angel of God, very

awesome. I didn't ask him where he came from, and he didn't tell me his name. [7]But he said to me, 'You will conceive and give birth to a son. Now then, drink no wine or other fermented drink and do not eat anything unclean, because the boy will be a Nazirite of God from birth until the day of his death.' "

[8]Then Manoah prayed to the LORD: "O Lord, I beg you, let the man of God you sent to us come again to teach us how to bring up the boy who is to be born."

[9]God heard Manoah, and the angel of God came again to the woman while she was out in the field; but her husband Manoah was not with her. [10]The woman hurried to tell her husband, "He's here! The man who appeared to me the other day!"

[11]Manoah got up and followed his wife. When he came to the man, he said, "Are you the one who talked to my wife?"

"I am," he said.

[12]So Manoah asked him, "When your words are fulfilled, what is to be the rule for the boy's life and work?"

[13]The angel of the LORD answered, "Your wife must do all that I have told her. [14]She must not eat anything that comes from the grapevine, nor drink any wine or other fermented drink nor eat anything unclean. She must do everything I have commanded her."

[15]Manoah said to the angel of the LORD, "We would like you to stay until we prepare a young goat for you."

[16]The angel of the LORD replied, "Even though you detain me, I will not eat any of your food. But if you prepare a burnt offering, offer it to the LORD." (Manoah did not realize that it was the angel of the LORD.)

[17]Then Manoah inquired of the angel of the LORD, "What is your name, so that we may honor you when your word comes true?"

[18]He replied, "Why do you ask my name? It is beyond understanding.[u]"

[19]Then Manoah took a young goat, together with the grain offering, and sacrificed it on a rock to the LORD. And the LORD did an amazing thing while Manoah and his wife watched: [20]As the flame blazed up from the altar toward heaven, the angel of the LORD ascended in the flame. Seeing this, Manoah and his wife fell with their faces to the ground. [21]When the angel of the LORD did not show himself again to Manoah and his wife, Manoah realized that it was the angel of the LORD.

[22]"We are doomed to die!" he said to his wife. "We have seen God!"

[23]But his wife answered, "If the LORD had meant to kill us, he would not have accepted a burnt offering and grain offering from our hands, nor shown us all these things or now told us this."

[24]The woman gave birth to a boy and named him Samson. He grew and the LORD blessed him, [25]and the Spirit of the LORD began to stir him while he was in Mahaneh Dan, between Zorah and Eshtaol.

CHAPTER 14

Samson went down to Timnah and saw there a young Philistine woman. [2]When he returned, he said to his father and mother, "I have seen a Philistine woman in Timnah; now get her for me as my wife."

[3]His father and mother replied, "Isn't there an acceptable woman among your relatives or among all our people? Must you go to the uncircumcised Philistines to get a wife?"

But Samson said to his father, "Get her for me. She's the right one for me." [4](His parents did not know that this was from the LORD, who was seeking an occasion to confront the Philistines; for at that time they were ruling over Israel.) [5]Samson went down to Timnah together with his father and mother. As they approached the vineyards of Timnah, suddenly a young lion came roaring toward him. [6]The Spirit of the LORD came upon him in power so that he tore the lion apart with his bare hands as he might have torn a young goat. But he told neither his father nor his mother what he had done. [7]Then he went down and talked with the woman, and he liked her.

[8]Some time later, when he went back to marry her, he turned aside to look at the lion's carcass. In it was a swarm of bees and some honey, [9]which he scooped out with his hands and ate as he went along. When he rejoined his parents, he gave

[u]18 Or is wonderful

them some, and they too ate it. But he did not tell them that he had taken the honey from the lion's carcass.

[10]Now his father went down to see the woman. And Samson made a feast there, as was customary for bridegrooms. [11]When he appeared, he was given thirty companions.

[12]"Let me tell you a riddle," Samson said to them. "If you can give me the answer within the seven days of the feast, I will give you thirty linen garments and thirty sets of clothes. [13]If you can't tell me the answer, you must give me thirty linen garments and thirty sets of clothes."

"Tell us your riddle," they said. "Let's hear it."

[14]He replied,

"Out of the eater, something to eat;
    out of the strong, something sweet."

For three days they could not give the answer.

[15]On the fourth[v] day, they said to Samson's wife, "Coax your husband into explaining the riddle for us, or we will burn you and your father's household to death. Did you invite us here to rob us?"

[16]Then Samson's wife threw herself on him, sobbing, "You hate me! You don't really love me. You've given my people a riddle, but you haven't told me the answer."

"I haven't even explained it to my father or mother," he replied, "so why should I explain it to you?" [17]She cried the whole seven days of the feast. So on the seventh day he finally told her, because she continued to press him. She in turn explained the riddle to her people.

[18]Before sunset on the seventh day the men of the town said to him,

"What is sweeter than honey?
    What is stronger than a lion?"

Samson said to them,

"If you had not plowed with my
    heifer,
  you would not have solved my
    riddle."

[19]Then the Spirit of the LORD came upon him in power. He went down to Ashkelon, struck down thirty of their men, stripped them of their belongings and gave their clothes to those who had explained the riddle. Burning with anger, he went up to his father's house. [20]And Samson's wife was given to the friend who had attended him at his wedding.

CHAPTER 15

Later on, at the time of wheat harvest, Samson took a young goat and went to visit his wife. He said, "I'm going to my wife's room." But her father would not let him go in.

[2]"I was so sure you thoroughly hated her," he said, "that I gave her to your friend. Isn't her younger sister more attractive? Take her instead."

[3]Samson said to them, "This time I have a right to get even with the Philistines; I will really harm them." [4]So he went out and caught three hundred foxes and tied them tail to tail in pairs. He then fastened a torch to every pair of tails, [5]lit the torches and let the foxes loose in the standing grain of the Philistines. He burned up the shocks and standing grain, together with the vineyards and olive groves.

[6]When the Philistines asked, "Who did this?" they were told, "Samson, the Timnite's son-in-law, because his wife was given to his friend."

So the Philistines went up and burned her and her father to death. [7]Samson said to them, "Since you've acted like this, I won't stop until I get my revenge on you." [8]He attacked them viciously and slaughtered many of them. Then he went down and stayed in a cave in the rock of Etam.

[9]The Philistines went up and camped in Judah, spreading out near Lehi. [10]The men of Judah asked, "Why have you come to fight us?"

"We have come to take Samson prisoner," they answered, "to do to him as he did to us."

[11]Then three thousand men from Judah went down to the cave in the rock of Etam and said to Samson, "Don't you realize that the Philistines are rulers over us? What have you done to us?"

He answered, "I merely did to them what they did to me."

[12]They said to him, "We've come to tie you up and hand you over to the Philistines."

v[15] Some Septuagint manuscripts and Syriac; Hebrew *seventh*

Samson said, "Swear to me that you won't kill me yourselves."

¹³"Agreed," they answered. "We will only tie you up and hand you over to them. We will not kill you." So they bound him with two new ropes and led him up from the rock. ¹⁴As he approached Lehi, the Philistines came toward him shouting. The Spirit of the LORD came upon him in power. The ropes on his arms became like charred flax, and the bindings dropped from his hands. ¹⁵Finding a fresh jawbone of a donkey, he grabbed it and struck down a thousand men.

¹⁶Then Samson said,

"With a donkey's jawbone
　I have made donkeys of them.ʷ
With a donkey's jawbone
　I have killed a thousand men."

¹⁷When he finished speaking, he threw away the jawbone; and the place was called Ramath Lehi.ˣ

¹⁸Because he was very thirsty, he cried out to the LORD, "You have given your servant this great victory. Must I now die of thirst and fall into the hands of the uncircumcised?" ¹⁹Then God opened up the hollow place in Lehi, and water came out of it. When Samson drank, his strength returned and he revived. So the spring was called En Hakkore,ʸ and it is still there in Lehi.

²⁰Samson ledᶻ Israel for twenty years in the days of the Philistines.

CHAPTER 16
One day Samson went to Gaza, where he saw a prostitute. He went in to spend the night with her. ²The people of Gaza were told, "Samson is here!" So they surrounded the place and lay in wait for him all night at the city gate. They made no move during the night, saying, "At dawn we'll kill him."

³But Samson lay there only until the middle of the night. Then he got up and took hold of the doors of the city gate, together with the two posts, and tore them loose, bar and all. He lifted them to his shoulders and carried them to the top of the hill that faces Hebron.

⁴Some time later, he fell in love with a woman in the Valley of Sorek whose name was Delilah. ⁵The rulers of the Philistines went to her and said, "See if you can lure him into showing you the secret of his great strength and how we can overpower him so we may tie him up and subdue him. Each one of us will give you eleven hundred shekelsᵃ of silver."

⁶So Delilah said to Samson, "Tell me the secret of your great strength and how you can be tied up and subdued."

⁷Samson answered her, "If anyone ties me with seven fresh thongsᵇ that have not been dried, I'll become as weak as any other man."

⁸Then the rulers of the Philistines brought her seven fresh thongs that had not been dried, and she tied him with them. ⁹With men hidden in the room, she called to him, "Samson, the Philistines are upon you!" But he snapped the thongs as easily as a piece of string snaps when it comes close to a flame. So the secret of his strength was not discovered.

¹⁰Then Delilah said to Samson, "You have made a fool of me; you lied to me. Come now, tell me how you can be tied."

¹¹He said, "If anyone ties me securely with new ropes that have never been used, I'll become as weak as any other man."

¹²So Delilah took new ropes and tied him with them. Then, with men hidden in the room, she called to him, "Samson, the Philistines are upon you!" But he snapped the ropes off his arms as if they were threads.

¹³Delilah then said to Samson, "Until now, you have been making a fool of me and lying to me. Tell me how you can be tied."

He replied, "If you weave the seven braids of my head into the fabric ⌊on the loom⌋ and tighten it with the pin, I'll become as weak as any other man." So while he was sleeping, Delilah took the seven braids of his head, wove them into the fabric ¹⁴andᶜ tightened it with the pin.

Again she called to him, "Samson, the Philistines are upon you!" He awoke from his sleep and pulled up the pin and the loom, with the fabric.

ʷ16 Or *made a heap or two*; the Hebrew for *donkey* sounds like the Hebrew for *heap*.　　ˣ17 *Ramath Lehi* means *jawbone hill.*
ʸ19 *En Hakkore* means *caller's spring.*　　ᶻ20 Traditionally *judged*　　ᵃ5 That is, about 28 pounds (about 13 kilograms)
ᵇ7 Or *bowstrings*; also in verses 8 and 9　　ᶜ13,14 Some Septuagint manuscripts; Hebrew "⌊*I can⌋, if you weave the seven braids of my head into the fabric ⌊on the loom⌋.*" ¹⁴*So she*

¹⁵Then she said to him, "How can you say, 'I love you,' when you won't confide in me? This is the third time you have made a fool of me and haven't told me the secret of your great strength." ¹⁶With such nagging she prodded him day after day until he was tired to death.

¹⁷So he told her everything. "No razor has ever been used on my head," he said, "because I have been a Nazirite set apart to God since birth. If my head were shaved, my strength would leave me, and I would become as weak as any other man."

¹⁸When Delilah saw that he had told her everything, she sent word to the rulers of the Philistines, "Come back once more; he has told me everything." So the rulers of the Philistines returned with the silver in their hands. ¹⁹Having put him to sleep on her lap, she called a man to shave off the seven braids of his hair, and so began to subdue him.ᵈ And his strength left him.

²⁰Then she called, "Samson, the Philistines are upon you!"

He awoke from his sleep and thought, "I'll go out as before and shake myself free." But he did not know that the LORD had left him.

²¹Then the Philistines seized him, gouged out his eyes and took him down to Gaza. Binding him with bronze shackles, they set him to grinding in the prison. ²²But the hair on his head began to grow again after it had been shaved.

²³Now the rulers of the Philistines assembled to offer a great sacrifice to Dagon their god and to celebrate, saying, "Our god has delivered Samson, our enemy, into our hands."

²⁴When the people saw him, they praised their god, saying,

"Our god has delivered our enemy
  into our hands,
the one who laid waste our land
  and multiplied our slain."

²⁵While they were in high spirits, they shouted, "Bring out Samson to entertain us." So they called Samson out of the prison, and he performed for them.

When they stood him among the pillars, ²⁶Samson said to the servant who held his hand, "Put me where I can feel the pillars that support the temple, so that I may lean against them." ²⁷Now the temple was crowded with men and women; all the rulers of the Philistines were there, and on the roof were about three thousand men and women watching Samson perform. ²⁸Then Samson prayed to the LORD, "O Sovereign LORD, remember me. O God, please strengthen me just once more, and let me with one blow get revenge on the Philistines for my two eyes." ²⁹Then Samson reached toward the two central pillars on which the temple stood. Bracing himself against them, his right hand on the one and his left hand on the other, ³⁰Samson said, "Let me die with the Philistines!" Then he pushed with all his might, and down came the temple on the rulers and all the people in it. Thus he killed many more when he died than while he lived.

³¹Then his brothers and his father's whole family went down to get him. They brought him back and buried him between Zorah and Eshtaol in the tomb of Manoah his father. He had ledᵉ Israel twenty years.

ᵈ19 Hebrew; some Septuagint manuscripts *and he began to weaken*   ᵉ31 Traditionally *judged*

MARCH 12 □ DAY 72
JUDGES 17–21
Two Examples of National Degradation

 OVERVIEW The closing chapters of Judges provide graphic snapshots of the spiritual and moral degeneration of a nation in which "everyone did as he saw fit" (17:6; 21:25). Chronologically, these events belong with chapter 3, but thematically they form a fitting conclusion to the book. The spiritual decline is illustrated by Micah, who carves his own idol, consecrates his own son as priest and hires a traveling Levite to minister on his behalf! The tribe of Dan confiscates both the idol and the priest to serve their own interests instead. The story of the Levite and his concubine is a grisly flashback to the days of Sodom and Gomorrah. In the ensuing civil war, the tribe of Benjamin is decimated, and efforts to repopulate it result in little more than anarchy.

Chapter 17	Chapter 18	Chapter 19	Chapters 20–21
Man-made Religion	Idolatrous Religion	Violent Immorality	Violent Vengeance
Religious Confusion		Moral and Civil Confusion	

YOUR DAILY WALK Is it possible that one of the reasons the forces of evil and wickedness are so successful is that the children of God are simply naive?

Those who believe that people aren't so bad must never have been parents.

When you read chapters in the Bible like Judges 17–21, your immediate reaction may be, "It can't happen here." No one wants to believe the veneer of civilization is really that thin and fragile. But until you recognize the problem, there is little hope of finding a solution.

Check up on your own IQ (Information Quotient). Do you know what the crime rate is in your area? What percent of your community is unchurched? How many babies were aborted last year? How many incidents of divorce, child abuse, homosexuality and substance abuse were recorded? If you don't know, a local social service agency can tell you. Knowing some of those statistics can help you pray more intelligently (and perhaps enable you to make a difference for Christ by helping some of the hurting people who are responsible for those statistics).

INSIGHT My, How Times Have Changed!

The book of Joshua records the history of the nation of Israel in days of victory with faith in God, spiritual vision, strength and unity. But as you read in Judges of Israel's defeats, unbelief, apostasy, worldliness, weakness and anarchy, you may have thought you were reading about an entirely different nation!

CHAPTER 17

Now a man named Micah from the hill country of Ephraim ²said to his mother, "The eleven hundred shekels*f* of silver that were taken from you and about which I heard you utter a curse—I have that silver with me; I took it."

Then his mother said, "The LORD bless you, my son!"

³When he returned the eleven hundred shekels of silver to his mother, she said, "I solemnly consecrate my silver to the LORD for my son to make a carved image and a cast idol. I will give it back to you."

⁴So he returned the silver to his mother, and she took two hundred shekels*g* of silver and gave them to a silversmith, who made them into the image and the idol. And they were put in Micah's house.

⁵Now this man Micah had a shrine, and he made an ephod and some idols and installed one of his sons as his priest. ⁶In those days Israel had no king; everyone did as he saw fit.

⁷A young Levite from Bethlehem in Judah, who had been living within the clan of Judah, ⁸left that town in search of some other place to stay. On his way*h* he came to Micah's house in the hill country of Ephraim.

⁹Micah asked him, "Where are you from?"

"I'm a Levite from Bethlehem in Judah," he said, "and I'm looking for a place to stay."

¹⁰Then Micah said to him, "Live with me and be my father and priest, and I'll give you ten shekels*i* of silver a year,

f2 That is, about 28 pounds (about 13 kilograms)   *g4* That is, about 5 pounds (about 2.3 kilograms)   *h8* Or *To carry on his profession*   *i10* That is, about 4 ounces (about 110 grams) your clothes and your food." [11]So the Levite agreed to live with him, and the young man was to him like one of his sons. [12]Then Micah installed the Levite, and the young man became his priest and lived in his house. [13]And Micah said, "Now I know that the LORD will be good to me, since this Levite has become my priest."

CHAPTER 18

In those days Israel had no king.

And in those days the tribe of the Danites was seeking a place of their own where they might settle, because they had not yet come into an inheritance among the tribes of Israel. [2]So the Danites sent five warriors from Zorah and Eshtaol to spy out the land and explore it. These men represented all their clans. They told them, "Go, explore the land."

The men entered the hill country of Ephraim and came to the house of Micah, where they spent the night. [3]When they were near Micah's house, they recognized the voice of the young Levite; so they turned in there and asked him, "Who brought you here? What are you doing in this place? Why are you here?"

[4]He told them what Micah had done for him, and said, "He has hired me and I am his priest."

[5]Then they said to him, "Please inquire of God to learn whether our journey will be successful."

[6]The priest answered them, "Go in peace. Your journey has the LORD's approval."

[7]So the five men left and came to Laish, where they saw that the people were living in safety, like the Sidonians, unsuspecting and secure. And since their land lacked nothing, they were prosperous.[j] Also, they lived a long way from the Sidonians and had no relationship with anyone else.[k]

[8]When they returned to Zorah and Eshtaol, their brothers asked them, "How did you find things?"

[9]They answered, "Come on, let's attack them! We have seen that the land is very good. Aren't you going to do something? Don't hesitate to go there and take it over. [10]When you get there, you will find an unsuspecting people and a spacious land

that God has put into your hands, a land that lacks nothing whatever."

[11]Then six hundred men from the clan of the Danites, armed for battle, set out from Zorah and Eshtaol. [12]On their way they set up camp near Kiriath Jearim in Judah. This is why the place west of Kiriath Jearim is called Mahaneh Dan[l] to this day. [13]From there they went on to the hill country of Ephraim and came to Micah's house.

[14]Then the five men who had spied out the land of Laish said to their brothers, "Do you know that one of these houses has an ephod, other household gods, a carved image and a cast idol? Now you know what to do." [15]So they turned in there and went to the house of the young Levite at Micah's place and greeted him. [16]The six hundred Danites, armed for battle, stood at the entrance to the gate. [17]The five men who had spied out the land went inside and took the carved image, the ephod, the other household gods and the cast idol while the priest and the six hundred armed men stood at the entrance to the gate.

[18]When these men went into Micah's house and took the carved image, the ephod, the other household gods and the cast idol, the priest said to them, "What are you doing?"

[19]They answered him, "Be quiet! Don't say a word. Come with us, and be our father and priest. Isn't it better that you serve a tribe and clan in Israel as priest rather than just one man's household?" [20]Then the priest was glad. He took the ephod, the other household gods and the carved image and went along with the people. [21]Putting their little children, their livestock and their possessions in front of them, they turned away and left.

[22]When they had gone some distance from Micah's house, the men who lived near Micah were called together and overtook the Danites. [23]As they shouted after them, the Danites turned and said to Micah, "What's the matter with you that you called out your men to fight?"

[24]He replied, "You took the gods I made, and my priest, and went away. What else do I have? How can you ask, 'What's the matter with you?'"

[25]The Danites answered, "Don't argue

---

[j]7 The meaning of the Hebrew for this clause is uncertain.   [k]7 Hebrew; some Septuagint manuscripts *with the Arameans*
[l]12 *Mahaneh Dan* means *Dan's camp.*

with us, or some hot-tempered men will attack you, and you and your family will lose your lives." 26So the Danites went their way, and Micah, seeing that they were too strong for him, turned around and went back home.

27Then they took what Micah had made, and his priest, and went on to Laish, against a peaceful and unsuspecting people. They attacked them with the sword and burned down their city. 28There was no one to rescue them because they lived a long way from Sidon and had no relationship with anyone else. The city was in a valley near Beth Rehob.

The Danites rebuilt the city and settled there. 29They named it Dan after their forefather Dan, who was born to Israel—though the city used to be called Laish. 30There the Danites set up for themselves the idols, and Jonathan son of Gershom, the son of Moses,m and his sons were priests for the tribe of Dan until the time of the captivity of the land. 31They continued to use the idols Micah had made, all the time the house of God was in Shiloh.

CHAPTER 19

In those days Israel had no king.

Now a Levite who lived in a remote area in the hill country of Ephraim took a concubine from Bethlehem in Judah. 2But she was unfaithful to him. She left him and went back to her father's house in Bethlehem, Judah. After she had been there four months, 3her husband went to her to persuade her to return. He had with him his servant and two donkeys. She took him into her father's house, and when her father saw him, he gladly welcomed him. 4His father-in-law, the girl's father, prevailed upon him to stay; so he remained with him three days, eating and drinking, and sleeping there.

5On the fourth day they got up early and he prepared to leave, but the girl's father said to his son-in-law, "Refresh yourself with something to eat; then you can go." 6So the two of them sat down to eat and drink together. Afterward the girl's father said, "Please stay tonight and enjoy yourself." 7And when the man got up to go, his father-in-law persuaded him, so he stayed there that night. 8On the

morning of the fifth day, when he rose to go, the girl's father said, "Refresh yourself. Wait till afternoon!" So the two of them ate together.

9Then when the man, with his concubine and his servant, got up to leave, his father-in-law, the girl's father, said, "Now look, it's almost evening. Spend the night here; the day is nearly over. Stay and enjoy yourself. Early tomorrow morning you can get up and be on your way home." 10But, unwilling to stay another night, the man left and went toward Jebus (that is, Jerusalem), with his two saddled donkeys and his concubine.

11When they were near Jebus and the day was almost gone, the servant said to his master, "Come, let's stop at this city of the Jebusites and spend the night."

12His master replied, "No. We won't go into an alien city, whose people are not Israelites. We will go on to Gibeah." 13He added, "Come, let's try to reach Gibeah or Ramah and spend the night in one of those places." 14So they went on, and the sun set as they neared Gibeah in Benjamin. 15There they stopped to spend the night. They went and sat in the city square, but no one took them into his home for the night.

16That evening an old man from the hill country of Ephraim, who was living in Gibeah (the men of the place were Benjamites), came in from his work in the fields. 17When he looked and saw the traveler in the city square, the old man asked, "Where are you going? Where did you come from?"

18He answered, "We are on our way from Bethlehem in Judah to a remote area in the hill country of Ephraim where I live. I have been to Bethlehem in Judah and now I am going to the house of the LORD. No one has taken me into his house. 19We have both straw and fodder for our donkeys and bread and wine for ourselves your servants—me, your maidservant, and the young man with us. We don't need anything."

20"You are welcome at my house," the old man said. "Let me supply whatever you need. Only don't spend the night in the square." 21So he took him into his house and fed his donkeys. After they

m 30 An ancient Hebrew scribal tradition, some Septuagint manuscripts and Vulgate; Masoretic Text Manasseh had washed their feet, they had something to eat and drink.

22While they were enjoying themselves, some of the wicked men of the city surrounded the house. Pounding on the door, they shouted to the old man who owned the house, "Bring out the man who came to your house so we can have sex with him."

23The owner of the house went outside and said to them, "No, my friends, don't be so vile. Since this man is my guest, don't do this disgraceful thing. 24Look, here is my virgin daughter, and his concubine. I will bring them out to you now, and you can use them and do to them whatever you wish. But to this man, don't do such a disgraceful thing."

25But the men would not listen to him. So the man took his concubine and sent her outside to them, and they raped her and abused her throughout the night, and at dawn they let her go. 26At daybreak the woman went back to the house where her master was staying, fell down at the door and lay there until daylight.

27When her master got up in the morning and opened the door of the house and stepped out to continue on his way, there lay his concubine, fallen in the doorway of the house, with her hands on the threshold. 28He said to her, "Get up; let's go." But there was no answer. Then the man put her on his donkey and set out for home.

29When he reached home, he took a knife and cut up his concubine, limb by limb, into twelve parts and sent them into all the areas of Israel. 30Everyone who saw it said, "Such a thing has never been seen or done, not since the day the Israelites came up out of Egypt. Think about it! Consider it! Tell us what to do!"

CHAPTER 20
Then all the Israelites from Dan to Beersheba and from the land of Gilead came out as one man and assembled before the LORD in Mizpah. 2The leaders of all the people of the tribes of Israel took their places in the assembly of the people of God, four hundred thousand soldiers armed with swords. 3(The Benjamites heard that the Israelites had gone up to Mizpah.) Then the Israelites said, "Tell us how this awful thing happened."

4So the Levite, the husband of the murdered woman, said, "I and my concubine came to Gibeah in Benjamin to spend the night. 5During the night the men of Gibeah came after me and surrounded the house, intending to kill me. They raped my concubine, and she died. 6I took my concubine, cut her into pieces and sent one piece to each region of Israel's inheritance, because they committed this lewd and disgraceful act in Israel. 7Now, all you Israelites, speak up and give your verdict."

8All the people rose as one man, saying, "None of us will go home. No, not one of us will return to his house. 9But now this is what we'll do to Gibeah: We'll go up against it as the lot directs. 10We'll take ten men out of every hundred from all the tribes of Israel, and a hundred from a thousand, and a thousand from ten thousand, to get provisions for the army. Then, when the army arrives at Gibeah[n] in Benjamin, it can give them what they deserve for all this vileness done in Israel." 11So all the men of Israel got together and united as one man against the city.

12The tribes of Israel sent men throughout the tribe of Benjamin, saying, "What about this awful crime that was committed among you? 13Now surrender those wicked men of Gibeah so that we may put them to death and purge the evil from Israel."

But the Benjamites would not listen to their fellow Israelites. 14From their towns they came together at Gibeah to fight against the Israelites. 15At once the Benjamites mobilized twenty-six thousand swordsmen from their towns, in addition to seven hundred chosen men from those living in Gibeah. 16Among all these soldiers there were seven hundred chosen men who were left-handed, each of whom could sling a stone at a hair and not miss.

17Israel, apart from Benjamin, mustered four hundred thousand swordsmen, all of them fighting men.

18The Israelites went up to Bethel[o] and inquired of God. They said, "Who of us

n10 One Hebrew manuscript; most Hebrew manuscripts Geba, a variant of Gibeah   o18 Or to the house of God; also in verse 26 shall go first to fight against the Benjamites?"

The LORD replied, "Judah shall go first." [19]The next morning the Israelites got up and pitched camp near Gibeah. [20]The men of Israel went out to fight the Benjamites and took up battle positions against them at Gibeah. [21]The Benjamites came out of Gibeah and cut down twenty-two thousand Israelites on the battlefield that day. [22]But the men of Israel encouraged one another and again took up their positions where they had stationed themselves the first day. [23]The Israelites went up and wept before the LORD until evening, and they inquired of the LORD. They said, "Shall we go up again to battle against the Benjamites, our brothers?"

The LORD answered, "Go up against them."

[24]Then the Israelites drew near to Benjamin the second day. [25]This time, when the Benjamites came out from Gibeah to oppose them, they cut down another eighteen thousand Israelites, all of them armed with swords.

[26]Then the Israelites, all the people, went up to Bethel, and there they sat weeping before the LORD. They fasted that day until evening and presented burnt offerings and fellowship offerings[p] to the LORD. [27]And the Israelites inquired of the LORD. (In those days the ark of the covenant of God was there, [28]with Phinehas son of Eleazar, the son of Aaron, ministering before it.) They asked, "Shall we go up again to battle with Benjamin our brother, or not?"

The LORD responded, "Go, for tomorrow I will give them into your hands."

[29]Then Israel set an ambush around Gibeah. [30]They went up against the Benjamites on the third day and took up positions against Gibeah as they had done before. [31]The Benjamites came out to meet them and were drawn away from the city. They began to inflict casualties on the Israelites as before, so that about thirty men fell in the open field and on the roads—the one leading to Bethel and the other to Gibeah.

[32]While the Benjamites were saying, "We are defeating them as before," the Israelites were saying, "Let's retreat and draw them away from the city to the roads."

[33]All the men of Israel moved from their places and took up positions at Baal Tamar, and the Israelite ambush charged out of its place on the west[q] of Gibeah.[r] [34]Then ten thousand of Israel's finest men made a frontal attack on Gibeah. The fighting was so heavy that the Benjamites did not realize how near disaster was. [35]The LORD defeated Benjamin before Israel, and on that day the Israelites struck down 25,100 Benjamites, all armed with swords. [36]Then the Benjamites saw that they were beaten.

Now the men of Israel had given way before Benjamin, because they relied on the ambush they had set near Gibeah. [37]The men who had been in ambush made a sudden dash into Gibeah, spread out and put the whole city to the sword. [38]The men of Israel had arranged with the ambush that they should send up a great cloud of smoke from the city, [39]and then the men of Israel would turn in the battle.

The Benjamites had begun to inflict casualties on the men of Israel (about thirty), and they said, "We are defeating them as in the first battle." [40]But when the column of smoke began to rise from the city, the Benjamites turned and saw the smoke of the whole city going up into the sky. [41]Then the men of Israel turned on them, and the men of Benjamin were terrified, because they realized that disaster had come upon them. [42]So they fled before the Israelites in the direction of the desert, but they could not escape the battle. And the men of Israel who came out of the towns cut them down there. [43]They surrounded the Benjamites, chased them and easily[s] overran them in the vicinity of Gibeah on the east. [44]Eighteen thousand Benjamites fell, all of them valiant fighters. [45]As they turned and fled toward the desert to the rock of Rimmon, the Israelites cut down five thousand men along the roads. They kept pressing after the Benjamites as far as Gidom and struck down two thousand more.

[46]On that day twenty-five thousand Benjamite swordsmen fell, all of them valiant fighters. [47]But six hundred men turned and fled into the desert to the rock of Rimmon, where they stayed four

---

[p]26 Traditionally *peace offerings*   [q]33 Some Septuagint manuscripts and Vulgate; the meaning of the Hebrew for this word is uncertain.   [r]33 Hebrew *Geba*, a variant of *Gibeah*   [s]43 The meaning of the Hebrew for this word is uncertain.

months. [48]The men of Israel went back to Benjamin and put all the towns to the sword, including the animals and everything else they found. All the towns they came across they set on fire.

CHAPTER 21

The men of Israel had taken an oath at Mizpah: "Not one of us will give his daughter in marriage to a Benjamite."

[2]The people went to Bethel,[t] where they sat before God until evening, raising their voices and weeping bitterly. [3]"O LORD, the God of Israel," they cried, "why has this happened to Israel? Why should one tribe be missing from Israel today?"

[4]Early the next day the people built an altar and presented burnt offerings and fellowship offerings.[u]

[5]Then the Israelites asked, "Who from all the tribes of Israel has failed to assemble before the LORD?" For they had taken a solemn oath that anyone who failed to assemble before the LORD at Mizpah should certainly be put to death.

[6]Now the Israelites grieved for their brothers, the Benjamites. "Today one tribe is cut off from Israel," they said. [7]"How can we provide wives for those who are left, since we have taken an oath by the LORD not to give them any of our daughters in marriage?" [8]Then they asked, "Which one of the tribes of Israel failed to assemble before the LORD at Mizpah?" They discovered that no one from Jabesh Gilead had come to the camp for the assembly. [9]For when they counted the people, they found that none of the people of Jabesh Gilead were there.

[10]So the assembly sent twelve thousand fighting men with instructions to go to Jabesh Gilead and put to the sword those living there, including the women and children. [11]"This is what you are to do," they said. "Kill every male and every woman who is not a virgin." [12]They found among the people living in Jabesh Gilead four hundred young women who had

never slept with a man, and they took them to the camp at Shiloh in Canaan.

[13]Then the whole assembly sent an offer of peace to the Benjamites at the rock of Rimmon. [14]So the Benjamites returned at that time and were given the women of Jabesh Gilead who had been spared. But there were not enough for all of them.

[15]The people grieved for Benjamin, because the LORD had made a gap in the tribes of Israel. [16]And the elders of the assembly said, "With the women of Benjamin destroyed, how shall we provide wives for the men who are left? [17]The Benjamite survivors must have heirs," they said, "so that a tribe of Israel will not be wiped out. [18]We can't give them our daughters as wives, since we Israelites have taken this oath: 'Cursed be anyone who gives a wife to a Benjamite.' [19]But look, there is the annual festival of the LORD in Shiloh, to the north of Bethel, and east of the road that goes from Bethel to Shechem, and to the south of Lebonah."

[20]So they instructed the Benjamites, saying, "Go and hide in the vineyards [21]and watch. When the girls of Shiloh come out to join in the dancing, then rush from the vineyards and each of you seize a wife from the girls of Shiloh and go to the land of Benjamin. [22]When their fathers or brothers complain to us, we will say to them, 'Do us a kindness by helping them, because we did not get wives for them during the war, and you are innocent, since you did not give your daughters to them.'"

[23]So that is what the Benjamites did. While the girls were dancing, each man caught one and carried her off to be his wife. Then they returned to their inheritance and rebuilt the towns and settled in them.

[24]At that time the Israelites left that place and went home to their tribes and clans, each to his own inheritance.

[25]In those days Israel had no king; everyone did as he saw fit.

---

[t]2 Or *to the house of God*   [u]4 Traditionally *peace offerings*

Ruth

AGAINST the dark backdrop of the time of the judges in Israel—filled with apostasy and judgment—the story of Ruth is a cameo of love and redemption. Ruth, a young widow, leaves her native Moab to help her mother-in-law and gleans in the fields belonging to a relative, Boaz, who grows to love this faithful woman. The two marry and become the great-grandparents of King David, ancestor of Jesus Christ. By marrying the widow and redeeming the family's property, Boaz is a picture of Christ as the "kinsman-redeemer."

Focus	Ruth's Faithfulness Revealed		Ruth's Faithfulness Rewarded	
Divisions	Ruth's Decision	Ruth's Devotion	Ruth's Deliverer	Ruth's Delight
	1:1　　　　1:22	2:1　　　　2:23	3:1　　　　3:18	4:1　　　　4:22
Topics	Ruth and Naomi		Ruth and Boaz	
	Going with Naomi	Gleaning for Naomi	Loved by Boaz	Married to Boaz
Place	Moab	Fields in Bethlehem	Threshing Floor in Bethlehem	Home in Bethlehem
Time	About 30 Years			

MARCH 13 ☐ DAY 73
RUTH 1–4
Ruth: An Old Testament Love Story

OVERVIEW Yesterday you read five of the darkest chapters in all of Scripture; today you're reading four of the brightest. The remarkable thing to keep in mind is this: The events described in both portions take place at approximately the same time! The book of Ruth is a cameo story of love, devotion and redemption set in the black context of the era of the judges. It is the story of a Moabite woman who was willing to forsake her pagan heritage in order to cling to the people of Israel and the God of Israel. Because of her *faithfulness* in a time of national *faithlessness*, God rewards her by giving her a new husband (Boaz), a baby son (Obed) and a privileged position in the lineage of Christ (she is the great-grandmother of King David).

Chapter 1	Chapter 2	Chapter 3	Chapter 4
Ruth's Decision	Ruth's Devotion	Ruth's Deliverer	Ruth's Delight
Love Revealed		Love Rewarded	

YOUR DAILY WALK After reading Ruth's four-chapter love story, turn to Hebrews 11:6. The words will have a familiar ring, but don't slide over them casually. Then ask yourself this question: Do I truly believe that God rewards those who diligently seek him?

The world crowns success, but God crowns faithfulness.

Think back over the difficult decisions that confronted Ruth: staying in her homeland of Moab, where she was known and loved, or moving to Israel, where she was largely unknown and unloved; starting a new home of her own, or living with her bereaved mother-in-law; worshiping the familiar gods of Moab, or worshiping the true God of Israel. As she diligently sought to walk with God in the midst of a godless nation, Ruth learned firsthand that God rewards God-seekers!

Are you struggling with misfortune, bereavement or strange new surroundings today? Take heart from Ruth's example. Why not share with your in-laws (if you have some) a difficult decision you are facing today, and ask them to join you in prayer!

INSIGHT Typecasting in the Book of Ruth
Notice how the characters' names foreshadow the action in the book of Ruth: *Naomi,* "pleasant"; *Elimelech,* "my God is King"; *Mahlon,* "sick"; *Chilion,* "pining"; *Orpah,* "stubbornness"; *Ruth,* "friendship"; *Boaz,* "in him is strength."

CHAPTER 1
In the days when the judges ruled,[a] there was a famine in the land, and a man from Bethlehem in Judah, together with his wife and two sons, went to live for a while in the country of Moab. ²The man's name was Elimelech, his wife's name Naomi, and the names of his two sons were Mahlon and Kilion. They were Ephrathites from Bethlehem, Judah. And they went to Moab and lived there.

³Now Elimelech, Naomi's husband,

[a] 1 Traditionally *judged*

died, and she was left with her two sons. ⁴They married Moabite women, one named Orpah and the other Ruth. After they had lived there about ten years, ⁵both Mahlon and Kilion also died, and Naomi was left without her two sons and her husband.

⁶When she heard in Moab that the LORD had come to the aid of his people by providing food for them, Naomi and her daughters-in-law prepared to return home from there. ⁷With her two daughters-in-law she left the place where she had been living and set out on the road that would take them back to the land of Judah.

⁸Then Naomi said to her two daughters-in-law, "Go back, each of you, to your mother's home. May the LORD show kindness to you, as you have shown to your dead and to me. ⁹May the LORD grant that each of you will find rest in the home of another husband."

Then she kissed them and they wept aloud ¹⁰and said to her, "We will go back with you to your people."

¹¹But Naomi said, "Return home, my daughters. Why would you come with me? Am I going to have any more sons, who could become your husbands? ¹²Return home, my daughters; I am too old to have another husband. Even if I thought there was still hope for me—even if I had a husband tonight and then gave birth to sons— ¹³would you wait until they grew up? Would you remain unmarried for them? No, my daughters. It is more bitter for me than for you, because the LORD's hand has gone out against me!"

¹⁴At this they wept again. Then Orpah kissed her mother-in-law good-by, but Ruth clung to her.

¹⁵"Look," said Naomi, "your sister-in-law is going back to her people and her gods. Go back with her."

¹⁶But Ruth replied, "Don't urge me to leave you or to turn back from you. Where you go I will go, and where you stay I will stay. Your people will be my people and your God my God. ¹⁷Where you die I will die, and there I will be buried. May the LORD deal with me, be it ever so severely, if anything but death separates you and me." ¹⁸When Naomi real-

ized that Ruth was determined to go with her, she stopped urging her.

¹⁹So the two women went on until they came to Bethlehem. When they arrived in Bethlehem, the whole town was stirred because of them, and the women exclaimed, "Can this be Naomi?"

²⁰"Don't call me Naomi,ᵇ" she told them. "Call me Mara,ᶜ because the Almightyᵈ has made my life very bitter. ²¹I went away full, but the LORD has brought me back empty. Why call me Naomi? The LORD has afflictedᵉ me; the Almighty has brought misfortune upon me."

²²So Naomi returned from Moab accompanied by Ruth the Moabitess, her daughter-in-law, arriving in Bethlehem as the barley harvest was beginning.

CHAPTER 2

Now Naomi had a relative on her husband's side, from the clan of Elimelech, a man of standing, whose name was Boaz.

²And Ruth the Moabitess said to Naomi, "Let me go to the fields and pick up the leftover grain behind anyone in whose eyes I find favor."

Naomi said to her, "Go ahead, my daughter." ³So she went out and began to glean in the fields behind the harvesters. As it turned out, she found herself working in a field belonging to Boaz, who was from the clan of Elimelech.

⁴Just then Boaz arrived from Bethlehem and greeted the harvesters, "The LORD be with you!"

"The LORD bless you!" they called back. ⁵Boaz asked the foreman of his harvesters, "Whose young woman is that?"

⁶The foreman replied, "She is the Moabitess who came back from Moab with Naomi. ⁷She said, 'Please let me glean and gather among the sheaves behind the harvesters.' She went into the field and has worked steadily from morning till now, except for a short rest in the shelter."

⁸So Boaz said to Ruth, "My daughter, listen to me. Don't go and glean in another field and don't go away from here. Stay here with my servant girls. ⁹Watch the field where the men are harvesting, and follow along after the girls. I have told the men not to touch you. And whenever you are thirsty, go and get a

---

ᵇ20 Naomi means *pleasant*; also in verse 21.   ᶜ20 Mara means *bitter*.   ᵈ20 Hebrew *Shaddai*; also in verse 21   ᵉ21 Or *has testified against* drink from the water jars the men have filled."

[10]At this, she bowed down with her face to the ground. She exclaimed, "Why have I found such favor in your eyes that you notice me—a foreigner?"

[11]Boaz replied, "I've been told all about what you have done for your mother-in-law since the death of your husband—how you left your father and mother and your homeland and came to live with a people you did not know before. [12]May the LORD repay you for what you have done. May you be richly rewarded by the LORD, the God of Israel, under whose wings you have come to take refuge."

[13]"May I continue to find favor in your eyes, my lord," she said. "You have given me comfort and have spoken kindly to your servant—though I do not have the standing of one of your servant girls."

[14]At mealtime Boaz said to her, "Come over here. Have some bread and dip it in the wine vinegar."

When she sat down with the harvesters, he offered her some roasted grain. She ate all she wanted and had some left over. [15]As she got up to glean, Boaz gave orders to his men, "Even if she gathers among the sheaves, don't embarrass her. [16]Rather, pull out some stalks for her from the bundles and leave them for her to pick up, and don't rebuke her."

[17]So Ruth gleaned in the field until evening. Then she threshed the barley she had gathered, and it amounted to about an ephah.[f] [18]She carried it back to town, and her mother-in-law saw how much she had gathered. Ruth also brought out and gave her what she had left over after she had eaten enough.

[19]Her mother-in-law asked her, "Where did you glean today? Where did you work? Blessed be the man who took notice of you!"

Then Ruth told her mother-in-law about the one at whose place she had been working. "The name of the man I worked with today is Boaz," she said.

[20]"The LORD bless him!" Naomi said to her daughter-in-law. "He has not stopped showing his kindness to the living and the dead." She added, "That man is our close relative; he is one of our kinsman-redeemers."

[21]Then Ruth the Moabitess said, "He even said to me, 'Stay with my workers until they finish harvesting all my grain.' "

[22]Naomi said to Ruth her daughter-in-law, "It will be good for you, my daughter, to go with his girls, because in someone else's field you might be harmed."

[23]So Ruth stayed close to the servant girls of Boaz to glean until the barley and wheat harvests were finished. And she lived with her mother-in-law.

CHAPTER 3

One day Naomi her mother-in-law said to her, "My daughter, should I not try to find a home[g] for you, where you will be well provided for? [2]Is not Boaz, with whose servant girls you have been, a kinsman of ours? Tonight he will be winnowing barley on the threshing floor. [3]Wash and perfume yourself, and put on your best clothes. Then go down to the threshing floor, but don't let him know you are there until he has finished eating and drinking. [4]When he lies down, note the place where he is lying. Then go and uncover his feet and lie down. He will tell you what to do."

[5]"I will do whatever you say," Ruth answered. [6]So she went down to the threshing floor and did everything her mother-in-law told her to do.

[7]When Boaz had finished eating and drinking and was in good spirits, he went over to lie down at the far end of the grain pile. Ruth approached quietly, uncovered his feet and lay down. [8]In the middle of the night something startled the man, and he turned and discovered a woman lying at his feet.

[9]"Who are you?" he asked.

"I am your servant Ruth," she said. "Spread the corner of your garment over me, since you are a kinsman-redeemer."

[10]"The LORD bless you, my daughter," he replied. "This kindness is greater than that which you showed earlier: You have not run after the younger men, whether rich or poor. [11]And now, my daughter, don't be afraid. I will do for you all you ask. All my fellow townsmen know that you are a woman of noble character. [12]Although it is true that I am near of kin, there is a kinsman-redeemer nearer than I. [13]Stay here for the night, and in the morning if

f17 That is, probably about 3/5 bushel (about 22 liters)   g1 Hebrew find rest (see Ruth 1:9) he wants to redeem, good; let him redeem. But if he is not willing, as surely as the LORD lives I will do it. Lie here until morning."

¹⁴So she lay at his feet until morning, but got up before anyone could be recognized; and he said, "Don't let it be known that a woman came to the threshing floor."

¹⁵He also said, "Bring me the shawl you are wearing and hold it out." When she did so, he poured into it six measures of barley and put it on her. Then he*ʰ* went back to town.

¹⁶When Ruth came to her mother-in-law, Naomi asked, "How did it go, my daughter?"

Then she told her everything Boaz had done for her ¹⁷and added, "He gave me these six measures of barley, saying, 'Don't go back to your mother-in-law empty-handed.' "

¹⁸Then Naomi said, "Wait, my daughter, until you find out what happens. For the man will not rest until the matter is settled today."

CHAPTER 4

Meanwhile Boaz went up to the town gate and sat there. When the kinsman-redeemer he had mentioned came along, Boaz said, "Come over here, my friend, and sit down." So he went over and sat down.

²Boaz took ten of the elders of the town and said, "Sit here," and they did so. ³Then he said to the kinsman-redeemer, "Naomi, who has come back from Moab, is selling the piece of land that belonged to our brother Elimelech. ⁴I thought I should bring the matter to your attention and suggest that you buy it in the presence of these seated here and in the presence of the elders of my people. If you will redeem it, do so. But if you*ⁱ* will not, tell me, so I will know. For no one has the right to do it except you, and I am next in line."

"I will redeem it," he said.

⁵Then Boaz said, "On the day you buy the land from Naomi and from Ruth the Moabitess, you acquire*ʲ* the dead man's widow, in order to maintain the name of the dead with his property."

⁶At this, the kinsman-redeemer said, "Then I cannot redeem it because I might endanger my own estate. You redeem it yourself. I cannot do it."

⁷(Now in earlier times in Israel, for the redemption and transfer of property to become final, one party took off his sandal and gave it to the other. This was the method of legalizing transactions in Israel.)

⁸So the kinsman-redeemer said to Boaz, "Buy it yourself." And he removed his sandal.

⁹Then Boaz announced to the elders and all the people, "Today you are witnesses that I have bought from Naomi all the property of Elimelech, Kilion and Mahlon. ¹⁰I have also acquired Ruth the Moabitess, Mahlon's widow, as my wife, in order to maintain the name of the dead with his property, so that his name will not disappear from among his family or from the town records. Today you are witnesses!"

¹¹Then the elders and all those at the gate said, "We are witnesses. May the LORD make the woman who is coming into your home like Rachel and Leah, who together built up the house of Israel. May you have standing in Ephrathah and be famous in Bethlehem. ¹²Through the offspring the LORD gives you by this young woman, may your family be like that of Perez, whom Tamar bore to Judah."

¹³So Boaz took Ruth and she became his wife. Then he went to her, and the LORD enabled her to conceive, and she gave birth to a son. ¹⁴The women said to Naomi: "Praise be to the LORD, who this day has not left you without a kinsman-redeemer. May he become famous throughout Israel! ¹⁵He will renew your life and sustain you in your old age. For your daughter-in-law, who loves you and who is better to you than seven sons, has given him birth."

¹⁶Then Naomi took the child, laid him in her lap and cared for him. ¹⁷The women living there said, "Naomi has a son." And they named him Obed. He was the father of Jesse, the father of David.

¹⁸This, then, is the family line of Perez:

Perez was the father of Hezron,

---

*ʰ*15 Most Hebrew manuscripts; many Hebrew manuscripts, Vulgate and Syriac *she*   *ⁱ*4 Many Hebrew manuscripts, Septuagint, Vulgate and Syriac; most Hebrew manuscripts *he*   *ʲ*5 Hebrew; Vulgate and Syriac *Naomi, you acquire Ruth the Moabitess,*

¹⁹Hezron the father of Ram,
  Ram the father of Amminadab,
²⁰Amminadab the father of Nahshon,
  Nahshon the father of Salmon,ᵏ

²¹Salmon the father of Boaz,
  Boaz the father of Obed,
²²Obed the father of Jesse,
  and Jesse the father of David.

ᵏ20 A few Hebrew manuscripts, some Septuagint manuscripts and Vulgate (see also verse 21 and Septuagint of 1 Chron. 2:11); most Hebrew manuscripts *Salma*

MARCH 14 □ DAY 74
Against the Odds

 LOOK BACK This week you have read about the judges of Israel, military leaders who fought to deliver the nation from the effects of its persistent sin. More than a dozen are described in the book of Judges, but Deborah and Gideon are two of the best. Deborah, a prophetess and songwriter, is instrumental in delivering the nation from Canaanite oppression. Gideon, a timid man with dubious credentials, leads the world's most unusual military band in the destruction of Midian's army—without a shot being fired!

Casting a shadow bigger than life across the last half of the book of Judges is Samson, a man with incredible physical strength and equally remarkable moral weakness. Set apart by his parents from birth for special service to God, Samson ends his life in failure and dishonor. His great potential and equally great moral collapse mirror the condition of the nation, which becomes so corrupt and degraded by the end of the book that even shocking brutality and immorality no longer cause the people to blush. Against this dark backdrop, the story of Ruth shines as a bright exception. Ruth the Moabitess forfeits the security of her homeland for the privilege of knowing the one true God.

 LOOK UP The plans may be man's, but the odds are God's. And chances are good you wouldn't want to face the odds Gideon faced as God whittled down his fighting force to something that would bring great glory to the Lord of hosts. Get your pen or pencil, and let's do a little arithmetic:

When we put our cares in God's hands, he puts his peace in our hearts.

(1) How large was the Midianite army before the battle began? (According to Judges 8:10, there were only 15,000 soldiers left after 120,000 had fallen in battle. That would make a total of _____,000 enemy soldiers to begin with.)

(2) According to Judges 7:3, Gideon had 10,000 soldiers left after 22,000 had gone home fearful. Add those two numbers together, and he had started with _____,000 men.

(3) That means initially Gideon faced "odds" of 135,000:32,000 or roughly 4:1. What did God say about those odds (Judges 7:2)?

_____

(4) After the fearful ones left, Gideon's army was reduced to just _____,000. The Midianite army was still the same size: _____,000. Now Gideon faced odds of 135,000:10,000 or roughly 13:1. What did God say about those odds (Judges 7:4)?

_____

(5) After the water-drinking experience, Gideon's army was further reduced to just _____ men (Judges 7:7). Meanwhile the Midianite army was still the same size: _____,000. That means Gideon now faced odds of 135,000:300 or roughly 450:1. And what did God say about those odds (Judges 7:7)? _____

LOOK AHEAD God delights to bring great victory out of certain defeat. At times he seems to go out of his way to ensure that the odds are overwhelmingly against his people so that when victory is achieved, there can be only one explanation: God did it!

Would you have had the courage to do what Gideon did? Before you conclude that Gideon was some sort of Old Testament "super saint," recall that when the story began he was cowering in a winepress trying to escape the all-seeing eye of the Midianites (Judges 6:11–12). This was just a humble servant willing to obey God in spite of the odds.

Perhaps the odds look no better from where you are standing as you look at your own prospects for victory over a physical disability, an uncertain future, a family situation that defies solution. Give God a chance to show himself strong, and you may see the odds swing decidedly in your favor!

1 Samuel

AS Israel's last judge, Samuel is raised up by God to bring to a close this chaotic period in the nation's history. To restore order, God instructs Samuel to anoint an impressive soldier named Saul. Though qualified outwardly, Saul is soon disqualified inwardly. Once again Samuel takes his anointing flask in search of a king—one with a heart like God's. Thus, 1 Samuel recounts the rise and decline of Saul and sets the stage for Israel's greatest king, David.

Focus	Final Judge		First King		King-Elect			
Divisions	The Dedicated Servant	The Faithful Servant	The Chosen King	The Rejected King	The Secret King-Elect	The Pursued King-Elect	The Recognized King-Elect	The Exiled King-Elect
	1　　3	4　　8	9　　12	13　　15	16　　19	20　　23	24　　26	27　　31
Topics	Samuel		Saul		David			
	Rebuilding		Rebelling		Running			
Place	Israel in Canaan							
Time	About 94 Years							

MARCH 15 □ DAY 75
1 SAMUEL 1–3
Samuel, the Dedicated Servant

OVERVIEW As the period of the judges draws to a close, God blesses a man named Elkanah and his barren wife, Hannah, with a son. The child Samuel, destined to be the last judge and first great prophet in Israel, is dedicated to the Lord's service and grows up in the household of Eli the priest. Through Samuel God delivers an ear-tingling message of judgment upon Eli's house for his failure to discipline his wayward sons. Samuel's obedience from earliest childhood demonstrates to "all Israel from Dan to Beersheba . . . that Samuel [is] attested as a prophet of the Lord" (3:20).

Chapter 1		Chapter 2		Chapter 3
Hannah's Request	God's Reward	Hannah's Rejoicing	Eli's Rejection	Samuel's Response
1 18	19 28	1 11	12 36	
Birth of Samuel		Boyhood of Samuel		

Keep your heart right, even when it is sorely wounded.

YOUR DAILY WALK Your best friend comes to you and says, "I've been praying about something for weeks, and God still hasn't answered my prayer. Can you tell me why?" What would you tell that person? How many reasons can you think of why God might not answer a certain prayer?

According to the Bible, unanswered prayer may result from
• sin in the life of the person praying (Psalm 66:18)
• lack of faith (James 1:6–7)
• not praying according to God's will (1 John 5:14)
• praying from impure motives (James 4:3)

But what if you pray, meet all the requirements and still don't receive an answer (like Hannah)? The answer is simple, yet complex: God is sovereign. He answers prayer in his time and for his purposes. Hannah prayed and wept and longed for a child. At the right time God gave her a son who would be a blessing to the entire nation.

Today, compile an "unanswered prayer list" of those requests you've been praying about for some time. Across the top, write "Remember Hannah" as a reminder that God never leaves a prayer unanswered too long.

INSIGHT A Prayer God Loves to Answer
Hannah is one of several Bible women who, in answer to specific prayer, was blessed with a son. How many others can you name? (Hint: Genesis 17:15–16; 25:21; 30:22; Luke 1:13).

CHAPTER 1

There was a certain man from Ramathaim, a Zuphite*a* from the hill country of Ephraim, whose name was Elkanah son of Jeroham, the son of Elihu, the son of Tohu, the son of Zuph, an Ephraimite. ²He had two wives; one was called Hannah and the other Peninnah. Peninnah had children, but Hannah had none.

³Year after year this man went up from

*a*1 Or *from Ramathaim Zuphim*

his town to worship and sacrifice to the LORD Almighty at Shiloh, where Hophni and Phinehas, the two sons of Eli, were priests of the LORD. [4]Whenever the day came for Elkanah to sacrifice, he would give portions of the meat to his wife Peninnah and to all her sons and daughters. [5]But to Hannah he gave a double portion because he loved her, and the LORD had closed her womb. [6]And because the LORD had closed her womb, her rival kept provoking her in order to irritate her. [7]This went on year after year. Whenever Hannah went up to the house of the LORD, her rival provoked her till she wept and would not eat. [8]Elkanah her husband would say to her, "Hannah, why are you weeping? Why don't you eat? Why are you downhearted? Don't I mean more to you than ten sons?"

[9]Once when they had finished eating and drinking in Shiloh, Hannah stood up. Now Eli the priest was sitting on a chair by the doorpost of the LORD's temple.[b] [10]In bitterness of soul Hannah wept much and prayed to the LORD. [11]And she made a vow, saying, "O LORD Almighty, if you will only look upon your servant's misery and remember me, and not forget your servant but give her a son, then I will give him to the LORD for all the days of his life, and no razor will ever be used on his head."

[12]As she kept on praying to the LORD, Eli observed her mouth. [13]Hannah was praying in her heart, and her lips were moving but her voice was not heard. Eli thought she was drunk [14]and said to her, "How long will you keep on getting drunk? Get rid of your wine."

[15]"Not so, my lord," Hannah replied, "I am a woman who is deeply troubled. I have not been drinking wine or beer; I was pouring out my soul to the LORD. [16]Do not take your servant for a wicked woman; I have been praying here out of my great anguish and grief."

[17]Eli answered, "Go in peace, and may the God of Israel grant you what you have asked of him."

[18]She said, "May your servant find favor in your eyes." Then she went her way and ate something, and her face was no longer downcast.

[19]Early the next morning they arose and worshiped before the LORD and then went back to their home at Ramah. Elkanah lay with Hannah his wife, and the LORD remembered her. [20]So in the course of time Hannah conceived and gave birth to a son. She named him Samuel,[c] saying, "Because I asked the LORD for him."

[21]When the man Elkanah went up with all his family to offer the annual sacrifice to the LORD and to fulfill his vow, [22]Hannah did not go. She said to her husband, "After the boy is weaned, I will take him and present him before the LORD, and he will live there always."

[23]"Do what seems best to you," Elkanah her husband told her. "Stay here until you have weaned him; only may the LORD make good his[d] word." So the woman stayed at home and nursed her son until she had weaned him.

[24]After he was weaned, she took the boy with her, young as he was, along with a three-year-old bull,[e] an ephah[f] of flour and a skin of wine, and brought him to the house of the LORD at Shiloh. [25]When they had slaughtered the bull, they brought the boy to Eli, [26]and she said to him, "As surely as you live, my lord, I am the woman who stood here beside you praying to the LORD. [27]I prayed for this child, and the LORD has granted me what I asked of him. [28]So now I give him to the LORD. For his whole life he will be given over to the LORD." And he worshiped the LORD there.

CHAPTER 2

Then Hannah prayed and said:

"My heart rejoices in the LORD;
    in the LORD my horn[g] is lifted high.
My mouth boasts over my enemies,
    for I delight in your deliverance.

[2]"There is no one holy[h] like the LORD;
    there is no one besides you;
    there is no Rock like our God.

[3]"Do not keep talking so proudly
    or let your mouth speak such arrogance,
for the LORD is a God who knows,
    and by him deeds are weighed.

[4]"The bows of the warriors are broken,

---

[b]9 That is, tabernacle   [c]20 *Samuel* sounds like the Hebrew for *heard of God.*   [d]23 Masoretic Text; Dead Sea Scrolls, Septuagint and Syriac *your*   [e]24 Dead Sea Scrolls, Septuagint and Syriac; Masoretic Text *with three bulls*   [f]24 That is, probably about 3/5 bushel (about 22 liters)   [g]1 *Horn* here symbolizes strength; also in verse 10.   [h]2 Or *no Holy One*

but those who stumbled are armed
  with strength.
⁵Those who were full hire themselves
    out for food,
  but those who were hungry hunger
    no more.
She who was barren has borne seven
  children,
  but she who has had many sons
    pines away.

⁶"The LORD brings death and makes
    alive;
  he brings down to the grave*i* and
    raises up.
⁷The LORD sends poverty and wealth;
  he humbles and he exalts.
⁸He raises the poor from the dust
  and lifts the needy from the ash
    heap;
  he seats them with princes
    and has them inherit a throne of
      honor.

"For the foundations of the earth are
    the LORD's;
  upon them he has set the world.
⁹He will guard the feet of his saints,
  but the wicked will be silenced in
    darkness.

"It is not by strength that one prevails;
10   those who oppose the LORD will be
    shattered.
He will thunder against them from
    heaven;
  the LORD will judge the ends of the
    earth.

"He will give strength to his king
  and exalt the horn of his anointed."

¹¹Then Elkanah went home to Ramah,
but the boy ministered before the LORD
under Eli the priest.

¹²Eli's sons were wicked men; they had
no regard for the LORD. ¹³Now it was the
practice of the priests with the people that
whenever anyone offered a sacrifice, and
while the meat was being boiled, the servant of the priest would come with a
three-pronged fork in his hand. ¹⁴He
would plunge it into the pan or kettle or
caldron or pot, and the priest would take
for himself whatever the fork brought up.
This is how they treated all the Israelites
who came to Shiloh. ¹⁵But even before the
fat was burned, the servant of the priest

would come and say to the man who was
sacrificing, "Give the priest some meat to
roast; he won't accept boiled meat from
you, but only raw."

¹⁶If the man said to him, "Let the fat be
burned up first, and then take whatever
you want," the servant would then answer, "No, hand it over now; if you don't,
I'll take it by force."

¹⁷This sin of the young men was very
great in the LORD's sight, for they*j* were
treating the LORD's offering with contempt.

¹⁸But Samuel was ministering before
the LORD—a boy wearing a linen ephod.
¹⁹Each year his mother made him a little
robe and took it to him when she went up
with her husband to offer the annual sacrifice. ²⁰Eli would bless Elkanah and his
wife, saying, "May the LORD give you children by this woman to take the place of
the one she prayed for and gave to the
LORD." Then they would go home. ²¹And
the LORD was gracious to Hannah; she
conceived and gave birth to three sons
and two daughters. Meanwhile, the boy
Samuel grew up in the presence of the
LORD.

²²Now Eli, who was very old, heard
about everything his sons were doing to
all Israel and how they slept with the
women who served at the entrance to the
Tent of Meeting. ²³So he said to them,
"Why do you do such things? I hear from
all the people about these wicked deeds of
yours. ²⁴No, my sons; it is not a good report that I hear spreading among the
LORD's people. ²⁵If a man sins against another man, God*k* may mediate for him;
but if a man sins against the LORD, who
will intercede for him?" His sons, however, did not listen to their father's rebuke, for it was the LORD's will to put
them to death.

²⁶And the boy Samuel continued to
grow in stature and in favor with the LORD
and with men.

²⁷Now a man of God came to Eli and
said to him, "This is what the LORD says:
'Did I not clearly reveal myself to your
father's house when they were in Egypt
under Pharaoh? ²⁸I chose your father out
of all the tribes of Israel to be my priest, to
go up to my altar, to burn incense, and
to wear an ephod in my presence. I also

*i*6 Hebrew *Sheol*   *j*17 Or *men*   *k*25 Or *the judges* gave your father's house all the offerings made with fire by the Israelites. [29]Why do you[j] scorn my sacrifice and offering that I prescribed for my dwelling? Why do you honor your sons more than me by fattening yourselves on the choice parts of every offering made by my people Israel?'

[30]"Therefore the LORD, the God of Israel, declares: 'I promised that your house and your father's house would minister before me forever.' But now the LORD declares: 'Far be it from me! Those who honor me I will honor, but those who despise me will be disdained. [31]The time is coming when I will cut short your strength and the strength of your father's house, so that there will not be an old man in your family line [32]and you will see distress in my dwelling. Although good will be done to Israel, in your family line there will never be an old man. [33]Every one of you that I do not cut off from my altar will be spared only to blind your eyes with tears and to grieve your heart, and all your descendants will die in the prime of life.

[34]" 'And what happens to your two sons, Hophni and Phinehas, will be a sign to you—they will both die on the same day. [35]I will raise up for myself a faithful priest, who will do according to what is in my heart and mind. I will firmly establish his house, and he will minister before my anointed one always. [36]Then everyone left in your family line will come and bow down before him for a piece of silver and a crust of bread and plead, "Appoint me to some priestly office so I can have food to eat." ' "

CHAPTER 3

The boy Samuel ministered before the LORD under Eli. In those days the word of the LORD was rare; there were not many visions.

[2]One night Eli, whose eyes were becoming so weak that he could barely see, was lying down in his usual place. [3]The lamp of God had not yet gone out, and Samuel was lying down in the temple[m] of the LORD, where the ark of God was. [4]Then the LORD called Samuel.

Samuel answered, "Here I am." [5]And he ran to Eli and said, "Here I am; you called me."

But Eli said, "I did not call; go back and lie down." So he went and lay down.

[6]Again the LORD called, "Samuel!" And Samuel got up and went to Eli and said, "Here I am; you called me."

"My son," Eli said, "I did not call; go back and lie down."

[7]Now Samuel did not yet know the LORD: The word of the LORD had not yet been revealed to him.

[8]The LORD called Samuel a third time, and Samuel got up and went to Eli and said, "Here I am; you called me."

Then Eli realized that the LORD was calling the boy. [9]So Eli told Samuel, "Go and lie down, and if he calls you, say, 'Speak, LORD, for your servant is listening.' " So Samuel went and lay down in his place.

[10]The LORD came and stood there, calling as at the other times, "Samuel! Samuel!"

Then Samuel said, "Speak, for your servant is listening."

[11]And the LORD said to Samuel: "See, I am about to do something in Israel that will make the ears of everyone who hears of it tingle. [12]At that time I will carry out against Eli everything I spoke against his family—from beginning to end. [13]For I told him that I would judge his family forever because of the sin he knew about; his sons made themselves contemptible,[n] and he failed to restrain them. [14]Therefore, I swore to the house of Eli, 'The guilt of Eli's house will never be atoned for by sacrifice or offering.' "

[15]Samuel lay down until morning and then opened the doors of the house of the LORD. He was afraid to tell Eli the vision, [16]but Eli called him and said, "Samuel, my son."

Samuel answered, "Here I am."

[17]"What was it he said to you?" Eli asked. "Do not hide it from me. May God deal with you, be it ever so severely, if you hide from me anything he told you." [18]So Samuel told him everything, hiding nothing from him. Then Eli said, "He is the LORD; let him do what is good in his eyes."

---

j 29 The Hebrew is plural.   m 3 That is, tabernacle   n 13 Masoretic Text; an ancient Hebrew scribal tradition and Septuagint sons blasphemed God

¹⁹The LORD was with Samuel as he grew up, and he let none of his words fall to the ground. ²⁰And all Israel from Dan to Beersheba recognized that Samuel was attested as a prophet of the LORD. ²¹The LORD continued to appear at Shiloh, and there he revealed himself to Samuel through his word.

MARCH 16 ☐ DAY 76
1 SAMUEL 4–8
Samuel, the Faithful Servant

 OVERVIEW The Philistines, enemies and oppressors of Israel since the days of Samson, are God's instrument of judgment upon Eli and his wicked sons. Using the ark of God as a good-luck charm, Israel carries it into battle and is soundly defeated. The ark is captured, and Hophni and Phinehas (who carried it into battle) are slain—events that serve as a deathblow for Eli. Truly *Ichabod* ("The glory has departed from Israel") can be written over Israel. But though the symbol of God's presence is gone, God himself is still very much alive! He afflicts the Philistines with grievous plagues, even causing the Philistine objects of worship to fall down before the ark. When at last the ark is returned, Samuel leads the nation in repentance before God and victory over the enemy. But the days of the judges are numbered, for the people demand a king "like all the other nations" (8:20)—a request with painful repercussions.

Chapter 4	Chapters 5–6	Chapter 7	Chapter 8
The Ark Removed	The Ark Returned	The Nation Repentant	A King Requested
Defeat in the Nation		Revival in the Nation	

 YOUR DAILY WALK There are really only two things you can do with someone else's mistakes: (1) You can learn from them, or (2) you can duplicate them.

Samuel should have learned the necessity of proper parental discipline from his observance of Eli's failure with his sons. But apparently he did not because his own sons were equally undisciplined. They were covetous, took bribes and perverted justice—just like Hophni and Phinehas! How could such a tragic turn of events repeat itself? How could Samuel duplicate Eli's folly? How could any generation not learn from its predecessors?

What a father says to his children is not heard by the world, but it will be heard by posterity.

Answer: Neglect. Samuel's circuit-riding schedule (7:15–17) left scant time to spend with his children during their formative years. How about you? Does your schedule reflect that your children are a priority in your life? Make an appointment to take each one to breakfast sometime next week. It will be time well spent—for both of you!

 INSIGHT The Heartbreak of Having a King
In the space of eight verses, Samuel warns the people of at least ten painful consequences of having a king (8:11–18). How many can you find? (Hint: Watch for the telltale words *he will.*)

CHAPTER 4

And Samuel's word came to all Israel.

Now the Israelites went out to fight against the Philistines. The Israelites camped at Ebenezer, and the Philistines at Aphek. ²The Philistines deployed their forces to meet Israel, and as the battle spread, Israel was defeated by the Philistines, who killed about four thousand of them on the battlefield. ³When the soldiers returned to camp, the elders of Israel asked, "Why did the LORD bring defeat upon us today before the Philistines? Let us bring the ark of the LORD's covenant from Shiloh, so that itᵒ may go with us and save us from the hand of our enemies."

⁴So the people sent men to Shiloh, and they brought back the ark of the covenant of the LORD Almighty, who is enthroned between the cherubim. And Eli's two sons, Hophni and Phinehas, were there with the ark of the covenant of God.

⁵When the ark of the LORD's covenant came into the camp, all Israel raised such a great shout that the ground shook. ⁶Hearing the uproar, the Philistines asked, "What's all this shouting in the Hebrew camp?"

When they learned that the ark of the LORD had come into the camp, ⁷the Philistines were afraid. "A god has come into the camp," they said. "We're in trouble! Nothing like this has happened before. ⁸Woe to us! Who will deliver us from the hand of these mighty gods? They are the gods who struck the Egyptians with all kinds of plagues in the desert. ⁹Be strong, Philistines! Be men, or you will be subject to the Hebrews, as they have been to you. Be men, and fight!"

¹⁰So the Philistines fought, and the Israelites were defeated and every man fled to his tent. The slaughter was very great; Israel lost thirty thousand foot soldiers. ¹¹The ark of God was captured, and Eli's two sons, Hophni and Phinehas, died.

¹²That same day a Benjamite ran from the battle line and went to Shiloh, his clothes torn and dust on his head. ¹³When he arrived, there was Eli sitting on his chair by the side of the road, watching, because his heart feared for the ark of God. When the man entered the town and told what had happened, the whole town sent up a cry.

¹⁴Eli heard the outcry and asked, "What is the meaning of this uproar?"

The man hurried over to Eli, ¹⁵who was ninety-eight years old and whose eyes were set so that he could not see. ¹⁶He told Eli, "I have just come from the battle line; I fled from it this very day."

Eli asked, "What happened, my son?"

¹⁷The man who brought the news replied, "Israel fled before the Philistines, and the army has suffered heavy losses. Also your two sons, Hophni and Phinehas, are dead, and the ark of God has been captured."

¹⁸When he mentioned the ark of God, Eli fell backward off his chair by the side of the gate. His neck was broken and he died, for he was an old man and heavy. He had ledᵖ Israel forty years.

¹⁹His daughter-in-law, the wife of Phinehas, was pregnant and near the time of delivery. When she heard the news that the ark of God had been captured and that her father-in-law and her husband were dead, she went into labor and gave birth, but was overcome by her labor pains. ²⁰As she was dying, the women attending her said, "Don't despair; you have given birth to a son." But she did not respond or pay any attention.

²¹She named the boy Ichabod,�q saying, "The glory has departed from Israel"—because of the capture of the ark of God and the deaths of her father-in-law and her husband. ²²She said, "The glory has departed from Israel, for the ark of God has been captured."

CHAPTER 5

After the Philistines had captured the ark of God, they took it from Ebenezer to Ashdod. ²Then they carried the ark into Dagon's temple and set it beside Dagon. ³When the people of Ashdod rose early the next day, there was Dagon, fallen on his face on the ground before the ark of the LORD! They took Dagon and put him back in his place. ⁴But the following morning when they rose, there was Dagon, fallen on his face on the ground before the ark of the LORD! His head and hands had been broken off and were lying on the threshold; only his body remained.

ᵒ3 Or *he*   ᵖ18 Traditionally *judged*   q21 *Ichabod* means *no glory.*

⁵That is why to this day neither the priests of Dagon nor any others who enter Dagon's temple at Ashdod step on the threshold.

⁶The LORD's hand was heavy upon the people of Ashdod and its vicinity; he brought devastation upon them and afflicted them with tumors.ʳ ⁷When the men of Ashdod saw what was happening, they said, "The ark of the god of Israel must not stay here with us, because his hand is heavy upon us and upon Dagon our god." ⁸So they called together all the rulers of the Philistines and asked them, "What shall we do with the ark of the god of Israel?"

They answered, "Have the ark of the god of Israel moved to Gath." So they moved the ark of the God of Israel.

⁹But after they had moved it, the LORD's hand was against that city, throwing it into a great panic. He afflicted the people of the city, both young and old, with an outbreak of tumors.ˢ ¹⁰So they sent the ark of God to Ekron.

As the ark of God was entering Ekron, the people of Ekron cried out, "They have brought the ark of the god of Israel around to us to kill us and our people." ¹¹So they called together all the rulers of the Philistines and said, "Send the ark of the god of Israel away; let it go back to its own place, or itᵗ will kill us and our people." For death had filled the city with panic; God's hand was very heavy upon it. ¹²Those who did not die were afflicted with tumors, and the outcry of the city went up to heaven.

CHAPTER 6

When the ark of the LORD had been in Philistine territory seven months, ²the Philistines called for the priests and the diviners and said, "What shall we do with the ark of the LORD? Tell us how we should send it back to its place."

³They answered, "If you return the ark of the god of Israel, do not send it away empty, but by all means send a guilt offering to him. Then you will be healed, and you will know why his hand has not been lifted from you."

⁴The Philistines asked, "What guilt offering should we send to him?"

They replied, "Five gold tumors and five gold rats, according to the number of the Philistine rulers, because the same plague has struck both you and your rulers. ⁵Make models of the tumors and of the rats that are destroying the country, and pay honor to Israel's god. Perhaps he will lift his hand from you and your gods and your land. ⁶Why do you harden your hearts as the Egyptians and Pharaoh did? When heᵘ treated them harshly, did they not send the Israelites out so they could go on their way?

⁷"Now then, get a new cart ready, with two cows that have calved and have never been yoked. Hitch the cows to the cart, but take their calves away and pen them up. ⁸Take the ark of the LORD and put it on the cart, and in a chest beside it put the gold objects you are sending back to him as a guilt offering. Send it on its way, ⁹but keep watching it. If it goes up to its own territory, toward Beth Shemesh, then the LORD has brought this great disaster on us. But if it does not, then we will know that it was not his hand that struck us and that it happened to us by chance."

¹⁰So they did this. They took two such cows and hitched them to the cart and penned up their calves. ¹¹They placed the ark of the LORD on the cart and along with it the chest containing the gold rats and the models of the tumors. ¹²Then the cows went straight up toward Beth Shemesh, keeping on the road and lowing all the way; they did not turn to the right or to the left. The rulers of the Philistines followed them as far as the border of Beth Shemesh.

¹³Now the people of Beth Shemesh were harvesting their wheat in the valley, and when they looked up and saw the ark, they rejoiced at the sight. ¹⁴The cart came to the field of Joshua of Beth Shemesh, and there it stopped beside a large rock. The people chopped up the wood of the cart and sacrificed the cows as a burnt offering to the LORD. ¹⁵The Levites took down the ark of the LORD, together with the chest containing the gold objects, and placed them on the large rock. On that day the people of Beth Shemesh offered burnt offerings and made sacrifices to the LORD. ¹⁶The five rulers of the Philistines

---

ʳ6 Hebrew; Septuagint and Vulgate *tumors. And rats appeared in their land, and death and destruction were throughout the city*
ˢ9 Or *with tumors in the groin* (see Septuagint) ᵗ11 Or *he* ᵘ6 That is, God

saw all this and then returned that same day to Ekron.

¹⁷These are the gold tumors the Philistines sent as a guilt offering to the Lord— one each for Ashdod, Gaza, Ashkelon, Gath and Ekron. ¹⁸And the number of the gold rats was according to the number of Philistine towns belonging to the five rulers—the fortified towns with their country villages. The large rock, on whichᵛ they set the ark of the Lord, is a witness to this day in the field of Joshua of Beth Shemesh.

¹⁹But God struck down some of the men of Beth Shemesh, putting seventyʷ of them to death because they had looked into the ark of the Lord. The people mourned because of the heavy blow the Lord had dealt them, ²⁰and the men of Beth Shemesh asked, "Who can stand in the presence of the Lord, this holy God? To whom will the ark go up from here?" ²¹Then they sent messengers to the people of Kiriath Jearim, saying, "The Philistines have returned the ark of the Lord. Come down and take it up to your C H A P T E R 7 place." ¹So the men of Kiriath Jearim came and took up the ark of the Lord. They took it to Abinadab's house on the hill and consecrated Eleazar his son to guard the ark of the Lord.

²It was a long time, twenty years in all, that the ark remained at Kiriath Jearim, and all the people of Israel mourned and sought after the Lord. ³And Samuel said to the whole house of Israel, "If you are returning to the Lord with all your hearts, then rid yourselves of the foreign gods and the Ashtoreths and commit yourselves to the Lord and serve him only, and he will deliver you out of the hand of the Philistines." ⁴So the Israelites put away their Baals and Ashtoreths, and served the Lord only.

⁵Then Samuel said, "Assemble all Israel at Mizpah and I will intercede with the Lord for you." ⁶When they had assembled at Mizpah, they drew water and poured it out before the Lord. On that day they fasted and there they confessed, "We have sinned against the Lord." And Samuel was leaderˣ of Israel at Mizpah.

⁷When the Philistines heard that Israel had assembled at Mizpah, the rulers of the Philistines came up to attack them. And when the Israelites heard of it, they were afraid because of the Philistines. ⁸They said to Samuel, "Do not stop crying out to the Lord our God for us, that he may rescue us from the hand of the Philistines." ⁹Then Samuel took a suckling lamb and offered it up as a whole burnt offering to the Lord. He cried out to the Lord on Israel's behalf, and the Lord answered him.

¹⁰While Samuel was sacrificing the burnt offering, the Philistines drew near to engage Israel in battle. But that day the Lord thundered with loud thunder against the Philistines and threw them into such a panic that they were routed before the Israelites. ¹¹The men of Israel rushed out of Mizpah and pursued the Philistines, slaughtering them along the way to a point below Beth Car.

¹²Then Samuel took a stone and set it up between Mizpah and Shen. He named it Ebenezer,ʸ saying, "Thus far has the Lord helped us." ¹³So the Philistines were subdued and did not invade Israelite territory again.

Throughout Samuel's lifetime, the hand of the Lord was against the Philistines. ¹⁴The towns from Ekron to Gath that the Philistines had captured from Israel were restored to her, and Israel delivered the neighboring territory from the power of the Philistines. And there was peace between Israel and the Amorites.

¹⁵Samuel continued as judge over Israel all the days of his life. ¹⁶From year to year he went on a circuit from Bethel to Gilgal to Mizpah, judging Israel in all those places. ¹⁷But he always went back to Ramah, where his home was, and there he also judged Israel. And he built an altar there to the Lord.

C H A P T E R 8
When Samuel grew old, he appointed his sons as judges for Israel. ²The name of his firstborn was Joel and the name of his second was Abijah, and they served at Beersheba. ³But his sons did not walk in his ways. They turned aside after dishonest gain and accepted bribes and perverted justice.

⁴So all the elders of Israel gathered

ᵛ18 A few Hebrew manuscripts (see also Septuagint); most Hebrew manuscripts *villages as far as Greater Abel, where*
ʷ19 A few Hebrew manuscripts; most Hebrew manuscripts and Septuagint *50,070*   ˣ6 Traditionally *judge*   ʸ12 *Ebenezer* means *stone of help.*

together and came to Samuel at Ramah. [5]They said to him, "You are old, and your sons do not walk in your ways; now appoint a king to lead[z] us, such as all the other nations have."

[6]But when they said, "Give us a king to lead us," this displeased Samuel; so he prayed to the LORD. [7]And the LORD told him: "Listen to all that the people are saying to you; it is not you they have rejected, but they have rejected me as their king. [8]As they have done from the day I brought them up out of Egypt until this day, forsaking me and serving other gods, so they are doing to you. [9]Now listen to them; but warn them solemnly and let them know what the king who will reign over them will do."

[10]Samuel told all the words of the LORD to the people who were asking him for a king. [11]He said, "This is what the king who will reign over you will do: He will take your sons and make them serve with his chariots and horses, and they will run in front of his chariots. [12]Some he will assign to be commanders of thousands and commanders of fifties, and others to plow his ground and reap his harvest, and still others to make weapons of war and equipment for his chariots. [13]He will take your daughters to be perfumers and cooks and bakers. [14]He will take the best of your fields and vineyards and olive groves and give them to his attendants. [15]He will take a tenth of your grain and of your vintage and give it to his officials and attendants. [16]Your menservants and maidservants and the best of your cattle[a] and donkeys he will take for his own use. [17]He will take a tenth of your flocks, and you yourselves will become his slaves. [18]When that day comes, you will cry out for relief from the king you have chosen, and the LORD will not answer you in that day."

[19]But the people refused to listen to Samuel. "No!" they said. "We want a king over us. [20]Then we will be like all the other nations, with a king to lead us and to go out before us and fight our battles."

[21]When Samuel heard all that the people said, he repeated it before the LORD. [22]The LORD answered, "Listen to them and give them a king."

Then Samuel said to the men of Israel, "Everyone go back to his town."

[z]5 Traditionally *judge*; also in verses 6 and 20   [a]16 Septuagint; Hebrew *young men*

MARCH 17 □ DAY 77
1 SAMUEL 9–12
Saul, the Chosen King

OVERVIEW Part of Samuel's "rebuilding program" for the nation involves anointing the first king, a giant of a man named Saul. Installed as king at Mizpah, proven in battle against the Ammonites and confirmed as king at Gilgal, Saul shows promising potential as the leader of God's people. But as Samuel points out in his farewell address, the very presence of a human king shows the rebellious attitude of the nation toward their divine king (12:19–20) and foreshadows disaster to come.

Chapter 9	Chapter 10	Chapter 11	Chapter 12
Finding a King	Anointing a King	Confirming a King	Counseling a King
Saul's Coronation			Samuel's Caution

YOUR DAILY WALK Try as you may, you will not find listed among the spiritual gifts in the New Testament the gift of criticism. But criticizing the actions and motives of others continues to be a popular

No one so Christian sport. After all, it's a game everyone can play, with no age
thoroughly limit or experience required. And it's especially gratifying when the
appreciates criticism is justified—when the other person is truly out of line.
the value of
constructive   Samuel had every right to judge the people for demanding a king.
criticism as the Their motives were wrong, and Samuel knew it; their end would be
one who is destruction, and Samuel knew it. But after delivering his blistering re-
giving it. buke to the people, Samuel tempered it with love. Like a tender father
disciplining an erring son, Samuel allowed his true affections to show
through. "You have done all this evil; . . . [but] far be it from me that I
should sin against the LORD by failing to pray for you" (12:20, 23).
Though the failure of others gave him reason to criticize, it instead
drove him to his knees.

How do you react when others stumble and fall? Are you quick to
criticize or quick to intercede? Samuel turned his criticisms into a
cause for prayer; think of one person for whom you'll practice doing
the same today.

 INSIGHT Lend Me Your Ear
The phrase "the LORD had revealed this to Samuel" (9:15) literally
means "the LORD had uncovered Samuel's ear," an expression derived
from the Middle East practice of pushing aside another man's hair or
the corner of his turban in order to whisper a secret into his ear.

CHAPTER 9
There was a Benjamite, a man of standing,
whose name was Kish son of Abiel, the
son of Zeror, the son of Becorath, the son
of Aphiah of Benjamin. ²He had a son
named Saul, an impressive young man
without equal among the Israelites—a
head taller than any of the others.

³Now the donkeys belonging to Saul's
father Kish were lost, and Kish said to his
son Saul, "Take one of the servants with
you and go and look for the donkeys." ⁴So
he passed through the hill country of
Ephraim and through the area around
Shalisha, but they did not find them. They
went on into the district of Shaalim, but
the donkeys were not there. Then he
passed through the territory of Benjamin,
but they did not find them.

⁵When they reached the district of
Zuph, Saul said to the servant who was
with him, "Come, let's go back, or my father will stop thinking about the donkeys
and start worrying about us."

⁶But the servant replied, "Look, in this
town there is a man of God; he is highly
respected, and everything he says comes
true. Let's go there now. Perhaps he will
tell us what way to take."

⁷Saul said to his servant, "If we go, what
can we give the man? The food in our
sacks is gone. We have no gift to take to
the man of God. What do we have?"

⁸The servant answered him again.
"Look," he said, "I have a quarter of a
shekel*ᵇ* of silver. I will give it to the man
of God so that he will tell us what way to
take." ⁹(Formerly in Israel, if a man went
to inquire of God, he would say, "Come,
let us go to the seer," because the prophet
of today used to be called a seer.)

¹⁰"Good," Saul said to his servant.
"Come, let's go." So they set out for the
town where the man of God was.

¹¹As they were going up the hill to the
town, they met some girls coming out to
draw water, and they asked them, "Is the
seer here?"

¹²"He is," they answered. "He's ahead of
you. Hurry now; he has just come to our
town today, for the people have a sacrifice
at the high place. ¹³As soon as you enter
the town, you will find him before he
goes up to the high place to eat. The people will not begin eating until he comes,
because he must bless the sacrifice; afterward, those who are invited will eat. Go
up now; you should find him about this
time."

¹⁴They went up to the town, and as they
were entering it, there was Samuel, coming toward them on his way up to the
high place.

¹⁵Now the day before Saul came, the
LORD had revealed this to Samuel:
¹⁶"About this time tomorrow I will send

ᵇ8 That is, about 1/10 ounce (about 3 grams)

you a man from the land of Benjamin. Anoint him leader over my people Israel; he will deliver my people from the hand of the Philistines. I have looked upon my people, for their cry has reached me."

¹⁷When Samuel caught sight of Saul, the LORD said to him, "This is the man I spoke to you about; he will govern my people."

¹⁸Saul approached Samuel in the gateway and asked, "Would you please tell me where the seer's house is?"

¹⁹"I am the seer," Samuel replied. "Go up ahead of me to the high place, for today you are to eat with me, and in the morning I will let you go and will tell you all that is in your heart. ²⁰As for the donkeys you lost three days ago, do not worry about them; they have been found. And to whom is all the desire of Israel turned, if not to you and all your father's family?"

²¹Saul answered, "But am I not a Benjamite, from the smallest tribe of Israel, and is not my clan the least of all the clans of the tribe of Benjamin? Why do you say such a thing to me?"

²²Then Samuel brought Saul and his servant into the hall and seated them at the head of those who were invited—about thirty in number. ²³Samuel said to the cook, "Bring the piece of meat I gave you, the one I told you to lay aside."

²⁴So the cook took up the leg with what was on it and set it in front of Saul. Samuel said, "Here is what has been kept for you. Eat, because it was set aside for you for this occasion, from the time I said, 'I have invited guests.'" And Saul dined with Samuel that day.

²⁵After they came down from the high place to the town, Samuel talked with Saul on the roof of his house. ²⁶They rose about daybreak and Samuel called to Saul on the roof, "Get ready, and I will send you on your way." When Saul got ready, he and Samuel went outside together. ²⁷As they were going down to the edge of the town, Samuel said to Saul, "Tell the servant to go on ahead of us"—and the servant did so—"but you stay here awhile, so that I may give you a message from God."

CHAPTER 10

Then Samuel took a flask of oil and poured it on Saul's head and kissed him, saying, "Has not the LORD anointed you leader over his inheritance?ᶜ ²When you leave me today, you will meet two men near Rachel's tomb, at Zelzah on the border of Benjamin. They will say to you, 'The donkeys you set out to look for have been found. And now your father has stopped thinking about them and is worried about you. He is asking, "What shall I do about my son?"'

³"Then you will go on from there until you reach the great tree of Tabor. Three men going up to God at Bethel will meet you there. One will be carrying three young goats, another three loaves of bread, and another a skin of wine. ⁴They will greet you and offer you two loaves of bread, which you will accept from them.

⁵"After that you will go to Gibeah of God, where there is a Philistine outpost. As you approach the town, you will meet a procession of prophets coming down from the high place with lyres, tambourines, flutes and harps being played before them, and they will be prophesying. ⁶The Spirit of the LORD will come upon you in power, and you will prophesy with them; and you will be changed into a different person. ⁷Once these signs are fulfilled, do whatever your hand finds to do, for God is with you.

⁸"Go down ahead of me to Gilgal. I will surely come down to you to sacrifice burnt offerings and fellowship offerings,ᵈ but you must wait seven days until I come to you and tell you what you are to do."

⁹As Saul turned to leave Samuel, God changed Saul's heart, and all these signs were fulfilled that day. ¹⁰When they arrived at Gibeah, a procession of prophets met him; the Spirit of God came upon him in power, and he joined in their prophesying. ¹¹When all those who had formerly known him saw him prophesying with the prophets, they asked each other, "What is this that has happened to the son of Kish? Is Saul also among the prophets?"

¹²A man who lived there answered, "And who is their father?" So it became a saying: "Is Saul also among the prophets?"

ᶜ**1** Hebrew; Septuagint and Vulgate *over his people Israel? You will reign over the LORD's people and save them from the power of their enemies round about. And this will be a sign to you that the LORD has anointed you leader over his inheritance:*   ᵈ**8** Traditionally *peace offerings*

¹³After Saul stopped prophesying, he went to the high place.

¹⁴Now Saul's uncle asked him and his servant, "Where have you been?"

"Looking for the donkeys," he said. "But when we saw they were not to be found, we went to Samuel."

¹⁵Saul's uncle said, "Tell me what Samuel said to you."

¹⁶Saul replied, "He assured us that the donkeys had been found." But he did not tell his uncle what Samuel had said about the kingship.

¹⁷Samuel summoned the people of Israel to the LORD at Mizpah ¹⁸and said to them, "This is what the LORD, the God of Israel, says: 'I brought Israel up out of Egypt, and I delivered you from the power of Egypt and all the kingdoms that oppressed you.' ¹⁹But you have now rejected your God, who saves you out of all your calamities and distresses. And you have said, 'No, set a king over us.' So now present yourselves before the LORD by your tribes and clans."

²⁰When Samuel brought all the tribes of Israel near, the tribe of Benjamin was chosen. ²¹Then he brought forward the tribe of Benjamin, clan by clan, and Matri's clan was chosen. Finally Saul son of Kish was chosen. But when they looked for him, he was not to be found. ²²So they inquired further of the LORD, "Has the man come here yet?"

And the LORD said, "Yes, he has hidden himself among the baggage."

²³They ran and brought him out, and as he stood among the people he was a head taller than any of the others. ²⁴Samuel said to all the people, "Do you see the man the LORD has chosen? There is no one like him among all the people."

Then the people shouted, "Long live the king!"

²⁵Samuel explained to the people the regulations of the kingship. He wrote them down on a scroll and deposited it before the LORD. Then Samuel dismissed the people, each to his own home.

²⁶Saul also went to his home in Gibeah, accompanied by valiant men whose hearts God had touched. ²⁷But some troublemakers said, "How can this fellow save us?" They despised him and brought him no gifts. But Saul kept silent.

CHAPTER 11

Nahash the Ammonite went up and besieged Jabesh Gilead. And all the men of Jabesh said to him, "Make a treaty with us, and we will be subject to you."

²But Nahash the Ammonite replied, "I will make a treaty with you only on the condition that I gouge out the right eye of every one of you and so bring disgrace on all Israel."

³The elders of Jabesh said to him, "Give us seven days so we can send messengers throughout Israel; if no one comes to rescue us, we will surrender to you."

⁴When the messengers came to Gibeah of Saul and reported these terms to the people, they all wept aloud. ⁵Just then Saul was returning from the fields, behind his oxen, and he asked, "What is wrong with the people? Why are they weeping?" Then they repeated to him what the men of Jabesh had said.

⁶When Saul heard their words, the Spirit of God came upon him in power, and he burned with anger. ⁷He took a pair of oxen, cut them into pieces, and sent the pieces by messengers throughout Israel, proclaiming, "This is what will be done to the oxen of anyone who does not follow Saul and Samuel." Then the terror of the LORD fell on the people, and they turned out as one man. ⁸When Saul mustered them at Bezek, the men of Israel numbered three hundred thousand and the men of Judah thirty thousand.

⁹They told the messengers who had come, "Say to the men of Jabesh Gilead, 'By the time the sun is hot tomorrow, you will be delivered.' " When the messengers went and reported this to the men of Jabesh, they were elated. ¹⁰They said to the Ammonites, "Tomorrow we will surrender to you, and you can do to us whatever seems good to you."

¹¹The next day Saul separated his men into three divisions; during the last watch of the night they broke into the camp of the Ammonites and slaughtered them until the heat of the day. Those who survived were scattered, so that no two of them were left together.

¹²The people then said to Samuel, "Who was it that asked, 'Shall Saul reign over us?' Bring these men to us and we will put them to death."

¹³But Saul said, "No one shall be put to

death today, for this day the LORD has rescued Israel."

¹⁴Then Samuel said to the people, "Come, let us go to Gilgal and there reaffirm the kingship." ¹⁵So all the people went to Gilgal and confirmed Saul as king in the presence of the LORD. There they sacrificed fellowship offerings^e before the LORD, and Saul and all the Israelites held a great celebration.

CHAPTER 12

Samuel said to all Israel, "I have listened to everything you said to me and have set a king over you. ²Now you have a king as your leader. As for me, I am old and gray, and my sons are here with you. I have been your leader from my youth until this day. ³Here I stand. Testify against me in the presence of the LORD and his anointed. Whose ox have I taken? Whose donkey have I taken? Whom have I cheated? Whom have I oppressed? From whose hand have I accepted a bribe to make me shut my eyes? If I have done any of these, I will make it right."

⁴"You have not cheated or oppressed us," they replied. "You have not taken anything from anyone's hand."

⁵Samuel said to them, "The LORD is witness against you, and also his anointed is witness this day, that you have not found anything in my hand."

"He is witness," they said.

⁶Then Samuel said to the people, "It is the LORD who appointed Moses and Aaron and brought your forefathers up out of Egypt. ⁷Now then, stand here, because I am going to confront you with evidence before the LORD as to all the righteous acts performed by the LORD for you and your fathers.

⁸"After Jacob entered Egypt, they cried to the LORD for help, and the LORD sent Moses and Aaron, who brought your forefathers out of Egypt and settled them in this place.

⁹"But they forgot the LORD their God; so he sold them into the hand of Sisera, the commander of the army of Hazor, and into the hands of the Philistines and the king of Moab, who fought against them. ¹⁰They cried out to the LORD and said, 'We have sinned; we have forsaken the LORD and served the Baals and the Ashtoreths.

But now deliver us from the hands of our enemies, and we will serve you.' ¹¹Then the LORD sent Jerub-Baal,^f Barak,^g Jephthah and Samuel,^h and he delivered you from the hands of your enemies on every side, so that you lived securely.

¹²"But when you saw that Nahash king of the Ammonites was moving against you, you said to me, 'No, we want a king to rule over us'—even though the LORD your God was your king. ¹³Now here is the king you have chosen, the one you asked for; see, the LORD has set a king over you. ¹⁴If you fear the LORD and serve and obey him and do not rebel against his commands, and if both you and the king who reigns over you follow the LORD your God—good! ¹⁵But if you do not obey the LORD, and if you rebel against his commands, his hand will be against you, as it was against your fathers.

¹⁶"Now then, stand still and see this great thing the LORD is about to do before your eyes! ¹⁷Is it not wheat harvest now? I will call upon the LORD to send thunder and rain. And you will realize what an evil thing you did in the eyes of the LORD when you asked for a king."

¹⁸Then Samuel called upon the LORD, and that same day the LORD sent thunder and rain. So all the people stood in awe of the LORD and of Samuel.

¹⁹The people all said to Samuel, "Pray to the LORD your God for your servants so that we will not die, for we have added to all our other sins the evil of asking for a king."

²⁰"Do not be afraid," Samuel replied. "You have done all this evil; yet do not turn away from the LORD, but serve the LORD with all your heart. ²¹Do not turn away after useless idols. They can do you no good, nor can they rescue you, because they are useless. ²²For the sake of his great name the LORD will not reject his people, because the LORD was pleased to make you his own. ²³As for me, far be it from me that I should sin against the LORD by failing to pray for you. And I will teach you the way that is good and right. ²⁴But be sure to fear the LORD and serve him faithfully with all your heart; consider what great things he has done for you. ²⁵Yet if you persist in doing evil, both you and your king will be swept away."

^e15 Traditionally *peace offerings*   ^f11 Also called *Gideon*   ^g11 Some Septuagint manuscripts and Syriac; Hebrew *Bedan*
^h11 Hebrew; some Septuagint manuscripts and Syriac *Samson*

MARCH 18 ☐ DAY 78
1 SAMUEL 13–15
Saul, the Rejected King

OVERVIEW After his promising beginning, Saul soon begins to show his true colors. When a Philistine invasion threatens, Saul takes over the role of the priest and offers sacrifices himself in defiance of God's clear command. Later, an impulsive oath nearly costs Saul the life of his devoted son Jonathan. Finally, Saul is given a make-or-break assignment: Destroy the Amalekites and all they possess. However, Saul chooses to spare the choicest livestock and the king of the land. Confronted with his disobedience, Saul passes the blame to the people, prompting the prophet to declare, "The LORD has rejected you" (15:26).

Chapter 13	Chapter 14	Chapter 15
Saul's Impatience	Saul's Impulsiveness	Saul's Incomplete Obedience
Tested and Rebuked		Tested and Rejected

YOUR DAILY WALK Have you discovered that God's heavenly timetable doesn't always make good earthly sense?

You know God has the perfect marriage partner for you, but as the years slip by you grow more and more impatient. . . .

Patience is accepting a difficult situation without giving God a deadline for removing it.

You know God wants you to succeed in your work, but year after year you labor at the same task with no promotion in sight. . . .

You know God wants you to help win the world for him, but after twelve years of teaching fifth-grade Sunday school. . . .

When Saul offered the sacrifices that only priests were permitted to offer, it cost him more than God's approval; it also cost him the kingdom. Because God's timetable didn't coincide with Saul's, Israel's first king responded impatiently. In the process he discovered there is something worse than having to wait for God—and that is wishing you had!

Are you becoming impatient with God's timetable for your life? Then do some "wait" watching today. Look up these verses and meditate upon their truth: Isaiah 25:9; 30:18; 40:31.

INSIGHT A Sword in the Hand, But None in the Land
The Philistines had the military advantage over Israel because they held the monopoly on iron and strictly controlled its use among subject peoples (13:19–22). Swords and spears were very rare. The monopoly was broken when Saul and David overthrew the Philistines and armed the Israelites.

CHAPTER 13

Saul was ⸢thirty⸣[i] years old when he became king, and he reigned over Israel ⸢forty-⸣[j] two years. ²Saul[k] chose three thousand men from Israel; two thousand were with him at Micmash and in the hill country of Bethel, and a thousand were with Jonathan at

Gibeah in Benjamin. The rest of the men he sent back to their homes.

³Jonathan attacked the Philistine outpost at Geba, and the Philistines heard about it. Then Saul had the trumpet blown throughout the land and said, "Let the Hebrews hear!" ⁴So all Israel heard the news: "Saul has attacked the Philistine

---

[i]1 A few late manuscripts of the Septuagint; Hebrew does not have *thirty*. [j]1 See the round number in Acts 13:21; Hebrew does not have *forty-*. [k]1,2 Or *and when he had reigned over Israel two years*, ²*he*

outpost, and now Israel has become a stench to the Philistines." And the people were summoned to join Saul at Gilgal.

[5]The Philistines assembled to fight Israel, with three thousand[l] chariots, six thousand charioteers, and soldiers as numerous as the sand on the seashore. They went up and camped at Micmash, east of Beth Aven. [6]When the men of Israel saw that their situation was critical and that their army was hard pressed, they hid in caves and thickets, among the rocks, and in pits and cisterns. [7]Some Hebrews even crossed the Jordan to the land of Gad and Gilead.

Saul remained at Gilgal, and all the troops with him were quaking with fear. [8]He waited seven days, the time set by Samuel; but Samuel did not come to Gilgal, and Saul's men began to scatter. [9]So he said, "Bring me the burnt offering and the fellowship offerings.[m]" And Saul offered up the burnt offering. [10]Just as he finished making the offering, Samuel arrived, and Saul went out to greet him.

[11]"What have you done?" asked Samuel.

Saul replied, "When I saw that the men were scattering, and that you did not come at the set time, and that the Philistines were assembling at Micmash, [12]I thought, 'Now the Philistines will come down against me at Gilgal, and I have not sought the LORD's favor.' So I felt compelled to offer the burnt offering."

[13]"You acted foolishly," Samuel said. "You have not kept the command the LORD your God gave you; if you had, he would have established your kingdom over Israel for all time. [14]But now your kingdom will not endure; the LORD has sought out a man after his own heart and appointed him leader of his people, because you have not kept the LORD's command."

[15]Then Samuel left Gilgal[n] and went up to Gibeah in Benjamin, and Saul counted the men who were with him. They numbered about six hundred.

[16]Saul and his son Jonathan and the men with them were staying in Gibeah[o] in Benjamin, while the Philistines camped at Micmash. [17]Raiding parties went out from the Philistine camp in three detachments. One turned toward Ophrah in the vicinity of Shual, [18]another toward Beth Horon, and the third toward the borderland overlooking the Valley of Zeboim facing the desert.

[19]Not a blacksmith could be found in the whole land of Israel, because the Philistines had said, "Otherwise the Hebrews will make swords or spears!" [20]So all Israel went down to the Philistines to have their plowshares, mattocks, axes and sickles[p] sharpened. [21]The price was two thirds of a shekel[q] for sharpening plowshares and mattocks, and a third of a shekel[r] for sharpening forks and axes and for repointing goads.

[22]So on the day of the battle not a soldier with Saul and Jonathan had a sword or spear in his hand; only Saul and his son Jonathan had them.

[23]Now a detachment of Philistines had gone out to the pass at Micmash.

CHAPTER 14 [1]One day Jonathan son of Saul said to the young man bearing his armor, "Come, let's go over to the Philistine outpost on the other side." But he did not tell his father.

[2]Saul was staying on the outskirts of Gibeah under a pomegranate tree in Migron. With him were about six hundred men, [3]among whom was Ahijah, who was wearing an ephod. He was a son of Ichabod's brother Ahitub son of Phinehas, the son of Eli, the LORD's priest in Shiloh. No one was aware that Jonathan had left.

[4]On each side of the pass that Jonathan intended to cross to reach the Philistine outpost was a cliff; one was called Bozez, and the other Seneh. [5]One cliff stood to the north toward Micmash, the other to the south toward Geba.

[6]Jonathan said to his young armorbearer, "Come, let's go over to the outpost of those uncircumcised fellows. Perhaps the LORD will act in our behalf. Nothing can hinder the LORD from saving, whether by many or by few."

[7]"Do all that you have in mind," his armor-bearer said. "Go ahead; I am with you heart and soul."

[8]Jonathan said, "Come, then; we will cross over toward the men and let them see us. [9]If they say to us, 'Wait there until

we come to you,' we will stay where we are and not go up to them. [10]But if they say, 'Come up to us,' we will climb up, because that will be our sign that the LORD has given them into our hands."

[11]So both of them showed themselves to the Philistine outpost. "Look!" said the Philistines. "The Hebrews are crawling out of the holes they were hiding in." [12]The men of the outpost shouted to Jonathan and his armor-bearer, "Come up to us and we'll teach you a lesson."

So Jonathan said to his armor-bearer, "Climb up after me; the LORD has given them into the hand of Israel."

[13]Jonathan climbed up, using his hands and feet, with his armor-bearer right behind him. The Philistines fell before Jonathan, and his armor-bearer followed and killed behind him. [14]In that first attack Jonathan and his armor-bearer killed some twenty men in an area of about half an acre.[s]

[15]Then panic struck the whole army—those in the camp and field, and those in the outposts and raiding parties—and the ground shook. It was a panic sent by God.[t]

[16]Saul's lookouts at Gibeah in Benjamin saw the army melting away in all directions. [17]Then Saul said to the men who were with him, "Muster the forces and see who has left us." When they did, it was Jonathan and his armor-bearer who were not there.

[18]Saul said to Ahijah, "Bring the ark of God." (At that time it was with the Israelites.)[u] [19]While Saul was talking to the priest, the tumult in the Philistine camp increased more and more. So Saul said to the priest, "Withdraw your hand."

[20]Then Saul and all his men assembled and went to the battle. They found the Philistines in total confusion, striking each other with their swords. [21]Those Hebrews who had previously been with the Philistines and had gone up with them to their camp went over to the Israelites who were with Saul and Jonathan. [22]When all the Israelites who had hidden in the hill country of Ephraim heard that the Philistines were on the run, they joined the battle in hot pursuit. [23]So the LORD rescued

Israel that day, and the battle moved on beyond Beth Aven.

[24]Now the men of Israel were in distress that day, because Saul had bound the people under an oath, saying, "Cursed be any man who eats food before evening comes, before I have avenged myself on my enemies!" So none of the troops tasted food.

[25]The entire army[v] entered the woods, and there was honey on the ground. [26]When they went into the woods, they saw the honey oozing out, yet no one put his hand to his mouth, because they feared the oath. [27]But Jonathan had not heard that his father had bound the people with the oath, so he reached out the end of the staff that was in his hand and dipped it into the honeycomb. He raised his hand to his mouth, and his eyes brightened.[w] [28]Then one of the soldiers told him, "Your father bound the army under a strict oath, saying, 'Cursed be any man who eats food today!' That is why the men are faint."

[29]Jonathan said, "My father has made trouble for the country. See how my eyes brightened[x] when I tasted a little of this honey. [30]How much better it would have been if the men had eaten today some of the plunder they took from their enemies. Would not the slaughter of the Philistines have been even greater?"

[31]That day, after the Israelites had struck down the Philistines from Micmash to Aijalon, they were exhausted. [32]They pounced on the plunder and, taking sheep, cattle and calves, they butchered them on the ground and ate them, together with the blood. [33]Then someone said to Saul, "Look, the men are sinning against the LORD by eating meat that has blood in it."

"You have broken faith," he said. "Roll a large stone over here at once." [34]Then he said, "Go out among the men and tell them, 'Each of you bring me your cattle and sheep, and slaughter them here and eat them. Do not sin against the LORD by eating meat with blood still in it.' "

So everyone brought his ox that night and slaughtered it there. [35]Then Saul built an altar to the LORD; it was the first time he had done this.

[s]**14** Hebrew *half a yoke;* a "yoke" was the land plowed by a yoke of oxen in one day.   [t]**15** Or *a terrible panic*   [u]**18** Hebrew; Septuagint *"Bring the ephod." (At that time he wore the ephod before the Israelites.)*   [v]**25** Or *Now all the people of the land*   [w]**27** Or *his strength was renewed*   [x]**29** Or *my strength was renewed*

³⁶Saul said, "Let us go down after the Philistines by night and plunder them till dawn, and let us not leave one of them alive."

"Do whatever seems best to you," they replied.

But the priest said, "Let us inquire of God here."

³⁷So Saul asked God, "Shall I go down after the Philistines? Will you give them into Israel's hand?" But God did not answer him that day.

³⁸Saul therefore said, "Come here, all you who are leaders of the army, and let us find out what sin has been committed today. ³⁹As surely as the LORD who rescues Israel lives, even if it lies with my son Jonathan, he must die." But not one of the men said a word.

⁴⁰Saul then said to all the Israelites, "You stand over there; I and Jonathan my son will stand over here."

"Do what seems best to you," the men replied.

⁴¹Then Saul prayed to the LORD, the God of Israel, "Give me the right answer."ʸ And Jonathan and Saul were taken by lot, and the men were cleared. ⁴²Saul said, "Cast the lot between me and Jonathan my son." And Jonathan was taken.

⁴³Then Saul said to Jonathan, "Tell me what you have done."

So Jonathan told him, "I merely tasted a little honey with the end of my staff. And now must I die?"

⁴⁴Saul said, "May God deal with me, be it ever so severely, if you do not die, Jonathan."

⁴⁵But the men said to Saul, "Should Jonathan die—he who has brought about this great deliverance in Israel? Never! As surely as the LORD lives, not a hair of his head will fall to the ground, for he did this today with God's help." So the men rescued Jonathan, and he was not put to death.

⁴⁶Then Saul stopped pursuing the Philistines, and they withdrew to their own land.

⁴⁷After Saul had assumed rule over Israel, he fought against their enemies on every side: Moab, the Ammonites, Edom, the kingsᶻ of Zobah, and the Philistines.

Wherever he turned, he inflicted punishment on them.ᵃ ⁴⁸He fought valiantly and defeated the Amalekites, delivering Israel from the hands of those who had plundered them.

⁴⁹Saul's sons were Jonathan, Ishvi and Malki-Shua. The name of his older daughter was Merab, and that of the younger was Michal. ⁵⁰His wife's name was Ahinoam daughter of Ahimaaz. The name of the commander of Saul's army was Abner son of Ner, and Ner was Saul's uncle. ⁵¹Saul's father Kish and Abner's father Ner were sons of Abiel.

⁵²All the days of Saul there was bitter war with the Philistines, and whenever Saul saw a mighty or brave man, he took him into his service.

C H A P T E R   1 5

Samuel said to Saul, "I am the one the LORD sent to anoint you king over his people Israel; so listen now to the message from the LORD. ²This is what the LORD Almighty says: 'I will punish the Amalekites for what they did to Israel when they waylaid them as they came up from Egypt. ³Now go, attack the Amalekites and totally destroyᵇ everything that belongs to them. Do not spare them; put to death men and women, children and infants, cattle and sheep, camels and donkeys.' "

⁴So Saul summoned the men and mustered them at Telaim—two hundred thousand foot soldiers and ten thousand men from Judah. ⁵Saul went to the city of Amalek and set an ambush in the ravine. ⁶Then he said to the Kenites, "Go away, leave the Amalekites so that I do not destroy you along with them; for you showed kindness to all the Israelites when they came up out of Egypt." So the Kenites moved away from the Amalekites.

⁷Then Saul attacked the Amalekites all the way from Havilah to Shur, to the east of Egypt. ⁸He took Agag king of the Amalekites alive, and all his people he totally destroyed with the sword. ⁹But Saul and the army spared Agag and the best of the sheep and cattle, the fat calvesᶜ and lambs—everything that was good. These they were unwilling to destroy com-

---

ʸ41 Hebrew; Septuagint "Why have you not answered your servant today? If the fault is in me or my son Jonathan, respond with Urim, but if the men of Israel are at fault, respond with Thummim."   ᶻ47 Masoretic Text; Dead Sea Scrolls and Septuagint king
ᵃ47 Hebrew; Septuagint he was victorious   ᵇ3 The Hebrew term refers to the irrevocable giving over of things or persons to the LORD, often by totally destroying them; also in verses 8, 9, 15, 18, 20 and 21.   ᶜ9 Or the grown bulls; the meaning of the Hebrew for this phrase is uncertain.

pletely, but everything that was despised and weak they totally destroyed.

[10]Then the word of the LORD came to Samuel: [11]"I am grieved that I have made Saul king, because he has turned away from me and has not carried out my instructions." Samuel was troubled, and he cried out to the LORD all that night.

[12]Early in the morning Samuel got up and went to meet Saul, but he was told, "Saul has gone to Carmel. There he has set up a monument in his own honor and has turned and gone on down to Gilgal."

[13]When Samuel reached him, Saul said, "The LORD bless you! I have carried out the LORD's instructions."

[14]But Samuel said, "What then is this bleating of sheep in my ears? What is this lowing of cattle that I hear?"

[15]Saul answered, "The soldiers brought them from the Amalekites; they spared the best of the sheep and cattle to sacrifice to the LORD your God, but we totally destroyed the rest."

[16]"Stop!" Samuel said to Saul. "Let me tell you what the LORD said to me last night."

"Tell me," Saul replied.

[17]Samuel said, "Although you were once small in your own eyes, did you not become the head of the tribes of Israel? The LORD anointed you king over Israel. [18]And he sent you on a mission, saying, 'Go and completely destroy those wicked people, the Amalekites; make war on them until you have wiped them out.' [19]Why did you not obey the LORD? Why did you pounce on the plunder and do evil in the eyes of the LORD?"

[20]"But I did obey the LORD," Saul said. "I went on the mission the LORD assigned me. I completely destroyed the Amalekites and brought back Agag their king. [21]The soldiers took sheep and cattle from the plunder, the best of what was devoted to God, in order to sacrifice them to the LORD your God at Gilgal."

[22]But Samuel replied:

"Does the LORD delight in burnt
    offerings and sacrifices
  as much as in obeying the voice of
    the LORD?
To obey is better than sacrifice,

[footnote d32 Or him trembling, yet]

and to heed is better than the fat of
    rams.
[23]For rebellion is like the sin of
    divination,
  and arrogance like the evil of
    idolatry.
Because you have rejected the word of
    the LORD,
  he has rejected you as king."

[24]Then Saul said to Samuel, "I have sinned. I violated the LORD's command and your instructions. I was afraid of the people and so I gave in to them. [25]Now I beg you, forgive my sin and come back with me, so that I may worship the LORD."

[26]But Samuel said to him, "I will not go back with you. You have rejected the word of the LORD, and the LORD has rejected you as king over Israel!"

[27]As Samuel turned to leave, Saul caught hold of the hem of his robe, and it tore. [28]Samuel said to him, "The LORD has torn the kingdom of Israel from you today and has given it to one of your neighbors—to one better than you. [29]He who is the Glory of Israel does not lie or change his mind; for he is not a man, that he should change his mind."

[30]Saul replied, "I have sinned. But please honor me before the elders of my people and before Israel; come back with me, so that I may worship the LORD your God." [31]So Samuel went back with Saul, and Saul worshiped the LORD.

[32]Then Samuel said, "Bring me Agag king of the Amalekites."

Agag came to him confidently,[d] thinking, "Surely the bitterness of death is past."

[33]But Samuel said,

"As your sword has made women
    childless,
  so will your mother be childless
    among women."

And Samuel put Agag to death before the LORD at Gilgal.

[34]Then Samuel left for Ramah, but Saul went up to his home in Gibeah of Saul. [35]Until the day Samuel died, he did not go to see Saul again, though Samuel mourned for him. And the LORD was grieved that he had made Saul king over Israel.

MARCH 19 □ DAY 79
1 SAMUEL 16–19
David, the Secret King-Elect

OVERVIEW While Saul is losing favor with God, the shepherd boy David is being secretly anointed by Samuel as Saul's replacement. From that moment on, the lives of Saul and David will be intricately intertwined. Because of his skill as a musician, David is selected to play for King Saul and soothe his troubled mind. Next, David becomes a national hero by challenging and killing Goliath, the Philistine giant whom Saul himself actually should have fought. Clearly, God is with David—an observation that drives Saul into a jealous frenzy and puts David's life in jeopardy.

Chapter 16		Chapter 17	Chapters 18–19
David the King-Elect	David the Musician	David the Fighter	David the Fugitive
In the Field	In the Court	In the Valley	On the Run

YOUR DAILY WALK It is one thing to keep a level head when things are running smoothly. It is quite another to behave wisely when you are on the run, pressure is on, the future seems uncertain and every breath you take may be your last!

Most of us don't put our best foot forward until we get the other one in hot water.

David faced a peculiar set of pressures. God was with him, causing his every endeavor to prosper. And because of his constant success and growing acclaim, David's life became more and more uncertain! "Because the LORD was with David" (18:12), Saul sought to snuff out David's life. Yet, in spite of the temptation to retaliate and grow bitter, David did what was right, and "in everything he did he had great success" (18:14).

Are you in a similar situation at your job? . . . in your home? . . . or on your campus? Because of God's blessing upon your life or ministry, are you faced with jealous opposition and undeserved suffering? God wants you, like David, to maintain an honorable attitude and blameless behavior in the face of persecution. Turn to Matthew 10:16, and notice what it says: *Shrewd* and *innocent* should be your watchwords!

INSIGHT David, First-Rate Candidate for King
David's qualifications, as stated by one of Saul's own servants (16:18), were impeccable: He was good-looking, a fine musician, a skilled warrior and a quick learner, and the Lord was with him. Everything that a king needed for success, David had. Little wonder that Saul was jealous.

CHAPTER 16

The LORD said to Samuel, "How long will you mourn for Saul, since I have rejected him as king over Israel? Fill your horn with oil and be on your way; I am sending you to Jesse of Bethlehem. I have chosen one of his sons to be king."

²But Samuel said, "How can I go? Saul will hear about it and kill me."

The LORD said, "Take a heifer with you and say, 'I have come to sacrifice to the LORD.' ³Invite Jesse to the sacrifice, and I will show you what to do. You are to anoint for me the one I indicate."

⁴Samuel did what the LORD said. When he arrived at Bethlehem, the elders of the town trembled when they met him. They asked, "Do you come in peace?"

⁵Samuel replied, "Yes, in peace; I have come to sacrifice to the LORD. Consecrate yourselves and come to the sacrifice with

me." Then he consecrated Jesse and his sons and invited them to the sacrifice.

⁶When they arrived, Samuel saw Eliab and thought, "Surely the Lord's anointed stands here before the Lord."

⁷But the Lord said to Samuel, "Do not consider his appearance or his height, for I have rejected him. The Lord does not look at the things man looks at. Man looks at the outward appearance, but the Lord looks at the heart."

⁸Then Jesse called Abinadab and had him pass in front of Samuel. But Samuel said, "The Lord has not chosen this one either." ⁹Jesse then had Shammah pass by, but Samuel said, "Nor has the Lord chosen this one." ¹⁰Jesse had seven of his sons pass before Samuel, but Samuel said to him, "The Lord has not chosen these." ¹¹So he asked Jesse, "Are these all the sons you have?"

"There is still the youngest," Jesse answered, "but he is tending the sheep."

Samuel said, "Send for him; we will not sit down*ᵉ* until he arrives."

¹²So he sent and had him brought in. He was ruddy, with a fine appearance and handsome features.

Then the Lord said, "Rise and anoint him; he is the one."

¹³So Samuel took the horn of oil and anointed him in the presence of his brothers, and from that day on the Spirit of the Lord came upon David in power. Samuel then went to Ramah.

¹⁴Now the Spirit of the Lord had departed from Saul, and an evil*ᶠ* spirit from the Lord tormented him.

¹⁵Saul's attendants said to him, "See, an evil spirit from God is tormenting you. ¹⁶Let our lord command his servants here to search for someone who can play the harp. He will play when the evil spirit from God comes upon you, and you will feel better."

¹⁷So Saul said to his attendants, "Find someone who plays well and bring him to me."

¹⁸One of the servants answered, "I have seen a son of Jesse of Bethlehem who knows how to play the harp. He is a brave man and a warrior. He speaks well and is a fine-looking man. And the Lord is with him."

¹⁹Then Saul sent messengers to Jesse and said, "Send me your son David, who is with the sheep." ²⁰So Jesse took a donkey loaded with bread, a skin of wine and a young goat and sent them with his son David to Saul.

²¹David came to Saul and entered his service. Saul liked him very much, and David became one of his armor-bearers. ²²Then Saul sent word to Jesse, saying, "Allow David to remain in my service, for I am pleased with him."

²³Whenever the spirit from God came upon Saul, David would take his harp and play. Then relief would come to Saul; he would feel better, and the evil spirit would leave him.

CHAPTER 17

Now the Philistines gathered their forces for war and assembled at Socoh in Judah. They pitched camp at Ephes Dammim, between Socoh and Azekah. ²Saul and the Israelites assembled and camped in the Valley of Elah and drew up their battle line to meet the Philistines. ³The Philistines occupied one hill and the Israelites another, with the valley between them.

⁴A champion named Goliath, who was from Gath, came out of the Philistine camp. He was over nine feet*ᵍ* tall. ⁵He had a bronze helmet on his head and wore a coat of scale armor of bronze weighing five thousand shekels*ʰ*; ⁶on his legs he wore bronze greaves, and a bronze javelin was slung on his back. ⁷His spear shaft was like a weaver's rod, and its iron point weighed six hundred shekels.*ⁱ* His shield bearer went ahead of him.

⁸Goliath stood and shouted to the ranks of Israel, "Why do you come out and line up for battle? Am I not a Philistine, and are you not the servants of Saul? Choose a man and have him come down to me. ⁹If he is able to fight and kill me, we will become your subjects; but if I overcome him and kill him, you will become our subjects and serve us." ¹⁰Then the Philistine said, "This day I defy the ranks of Israel! Give me a man and let us fight each other." ¹¹On hearing the Philistine's words, Saul and all the Israelites were dismayed and terrified.

ᵉ11 Some Septuagint manuscripts; Hebrew *not gather around six cubits and a span* (about 3 meters)   ʰ5 That is, about 125 pounds (about 57 kilograms)   ᶠ14 Or *injurious*; also in verses 15, 16 and 23   ᵍ4 Hebrew *was*   ⁱ7 That is, about 15 pounds (about 7 kilograms)

¹²Now David was the son of an Ephrathite named Jesse, who was from Bethlehem in Judah. Jesse had eight sons, and in Saul's time he was old and well advanced in years. ¹³Jesse's three oldest sons had followed Saul to the war: The firstborn was Eliab; the second, Abinadab; and the third, Shammah. ¹⁴David was the youngest. The three oldest followed Saul, ¹⁵but David went back and forth from Saul to tend his father's sheep at Bethlehem.

¹⁶For forty days the Philistine came forward every morning and evening and took his stand.

¹⁷Now Jesse said to his son David, "Take this ephah*ʲ* of roasted grain and these ten loaves of bread for your brothers and hurry to their camp. ¹⁸Take along these ten cheeses to the commander of their unit.*ᵏ* See how your brothers are and bring back some assurance*ˡ* from them. ¹⁹They are with Saul and all the men of Israel in the Valley of Elah, fighting against the Philistines."

²⁰Early in the morning David left the flock with a shepherd, loaded up and set out, as Jesse had directed. He reached the camp as the army was going out to its battle positions, shouting the war cry. ²¹Israel and the Philistines were drawing up their lines facing each other. ²²David left his things with the keeper of supplies, ran to the battle lines and greeted his brothers. ²³As he was talking with them, Goliath, the Philistine champion from Gath, stepped out from his lines and shouted his usual defiance, and David heard it. ²⁴When the Israelites saw the man, they all ran from him in great fear.

²⁵Now the Israelites had been saying, "Do you see how this man keeps coming out? He comes out to defy Israel. The king will give great wealth to the man who kills him. He will also give him his daughter in marriage and will exempt his father's family from taxes in Israel."

²⁶David asked the men standing near him, "What will be done for the man who kills this Philistine and removes this disgrace from Israel? Who is this uncircumcised Philistine that he should defy the armies of the living God?"

²⁷They repeated to him what they had been saying and told him, "This is what will be done for the man who kills him."

²⁸When Eliab, David's oldest brother, heard him speaking with the men, he burned with anger at him and asked, "Why have you come down here? And with whom did you leave those few sheep in the desert? I know how conceited you are and how wicked your heart is; you came down only to watch the battle."

²⁹"Now what have I done?" said David. "Can't I even speak?" ³⁰He then turned away to someone else and brought up the same matter, and the men answered him as before. ³¹What David said was overheard and reported to Saul, and Saul sent for him.

³²David said to Saul, "Let no one lose heart on account of this Philistine; your servant will go and fight him."

³³Saul replied, "You are not able to go out against this Philistine and fight him; you are only a boy, and he has been a fighting man from his youth."

³⁴But David said to Saul, "Your servant has been keeping his father's sheep. When a lion or a bear came and carried off a sheep from the flock, ³⁵I went after it, struck it and rescued the sheep from its mouth. When it turned on me, I seized it by its hair, struck it and killed it. ³⁶Your servant has killed both the lion and the bear; this uncircumcised Philistine will be like one of them, because he has defied the armies of the living God. ³⁷The LORD who delivered me from the paw of the lion and the paw of the bear will deliver me from the hand of this Philistine."

Saul said to David, "Go, and the LORD be with you."

³⁸Then Saul dressed David in his own tunic. He put a coat of armor on him and a bronze helmet on his head. ³⁹David fastened on his sword over the tunic and tried walking around, because he was not used to them.

"I cannot go in these," he said to Saul, "because I am not used to them." So he took them off. ⁴⁰Then he took his staff in his hand, chose five smooth stones from the stream, put them in the pouch of his shepherd's bag and, with his sling in his hand, approached the Philistine.

⁴¹Meanwhile, the Philistine, with his shield bearer in front of him, kept coming

closer to David. [42]He looked David over and saw that he was only a boy, ruddy and handsome, and he despised him. [43]He said to David, "Am I a dog, that you come at me with sticks?" And the Philistine cursed David by his gods. [44]"Come here," he said, "and I'll give your flesh to the birds of the air and the beasts of the field!"

[45]David said to the Philistine, "You come against me with sword and spear and javelin, but I come against you in the name of the LORD Almighty, the God of the armies of Israel, whom you have defied. [46]This day the LORD will hand you over to me, and I'll strike you down and cut off your head. Today I will give the carcasses of the Philistine army to the birds of the air and the beasts of the earth, and the whole world will know that there is a God in Israel. [47]All those gathered here will know that it is not by sword or spear that the LORD saves; for the battle is the LORD's, and he will give all of you into our hands."

[48]As the Philistine moved closer to attack him, David ran quickly toward the battle line to meet him. [49]Reaching into his bag and taking out a stone, he slung it and struck the Philistine on the forehead. The stone sank into his forehead, and he fell facedown on the ground.

[50]So David triumphed over the Philistine with a sling and a stone; without a sword in his hand he struck down the Philistine and killed him.

[51]David ran and stood over him. He took hold of the Philistine's sword and drew it from the scabbard. After he killed him, he cut off his head with the sword.

When the Philistines saw that their hero was dead, they turned and ran. [52]Then the men of Israel and Judah surged forward with a shout and pursued the Philistines to the entrance of Gath[m] and to the gates of Ekron. Their dead were strewn along the Shaaraim road to Gath and Ekron. [53]When the Israelites returned from chasing the Philistines, they plundered their camp. [54]David took the Philistine's head and brought it to Jerusalem, and he put the Philistine's weapons in his own tent.

[55]As Saul watched David going out to meet the Philistine, he said to Abner, commander of the army, "Abner, whose son is that young man?"

Abner replied, "As surely as you live, O king, I don't know."

[56]The king said, "Find out whose son this young man is."

[57]As soon as David returned from killing the Philistine, Abner took him and brought him before Saul, with David still holding the Philistine's head.

[58]"Whose son are you, young man?" Saul asked him.

David said, "I am the son of your servant Jesse of Bethlehem."

CHAPTER 18

After David had finished talking with Saul, Jonathan became one in spirit with David, and he loved him as himself. [2]From that day Saul kept David with him and did not let him return to his father's house. [3]And Jonathan made a covenant with David because he loved him as himself. [4]Jonathan took off the robe he was wearing and gave it to David, along with his tunic, and even his sword, his bow and his belt.

[5]Whatever Saul sent him to do, David did it so successfully[n] that Saul gave him a high rank in the army. This pleased all the people, and Saul's officers as well.

[6]When the men were returning home after David had killed the Philistine, the women came out from all the towns of Israel to meet King Saul with singing and dancing, with joyful songs and with tambourines and lutes. [7]As they danced, they sang:

"Saul has slain his thousands,
    and David his tens of thousands."

[8]Saul was very angry; this refrain galled him. "They have credited David with tens of thousands," he thought, "but me with only thousands. What more can he get but the kingdom?" [9]And from that time on Saul kept a jealous eye on David.

[10]The next day an evil[o] spirit from God came forcefully upon Saul. He was prophesying in his house, while David was playing the harp, as he usually did. Saul had a spear in his hand [11]and he hurled it, saying to himself, "I'll pin David to the wall." But David eluded him twice.

[12]Saul was afraid of David, because the

[m]52 Some Septuagint manuscripts; Hebrew *a valley*   [n]5 Or *wisely*   [o]10 Or *injurious*

LORD was with David but had left Saul. ¹³So he sent David away from him and gave him command over a thousand men, and David led the troops in their campaigns. ¹⁴In everything he did he had great success,ᵖ because the LORD was with him. ¹⁵When Saul saw how successfulᵠ he was, he was afraid of him. ¹⁶But all Israel and Judah loved David, because he led them in their campaigns.

¹⁷Saul said to David, "Here is my older daughter Merab. I will give her to you in marriage; only serve me bravely and fight the battles of the LORD." For Saul said to himself, "I will not raise a hand against him. Let the Philistines do that!"

¹⁸But David said to Saul, "Who am I, and what is my family or my father's clan in Israel, that I should become the king's son-in-law?" ¹⁹Soʳ when the time came for Merab, Saul's daughter, to be given to David, she was given in marriage to Adriel of Meholah.

²⁰Now Saul's daughter Michal was in love with David, and when they told Saul about it, he was pleased. ²¹"I will give her to him," he thought, "so that she may be a snare to him and so that the hand of the Philistines may be against him." So Saul said to David, "Now you have a second opportunity to become my son-in-law."

²²Then Saul ordered his attendants: "Speak to David privately and say, 'Look, the king is pleased with you, and his attendants all like you; now become his son-in-law.' "

²³They repeated these words to David. But David said, "Do you think it is a small matter to become the king's son-in-law? I'm only a poor man and little known."

²⁴When Saul's servants told him what David had said, ²⁵Saul replied, "Say to David, 'The king wants no other price for the bride than a hundred Philistine foreskins, to take revenge on his enemies.' " Saul's plan was to have David fall by the hands of the Philistines.

²⁶When the attendants told David these things, he was pleased to become the king's son-in-law. So before the allotted time elapsed, ²⁷David and his men went out and killed two hundred Philistines. He brought their foreskins and presented the full number to the king so that he might become the king's son-in-law. Then Saul gave him his daughter Michal in marriage.

²⁸When Saul realized that the LORD was with David and that his daughter Michal loved David, ²⁹Saul became still more afraid of him, and he remained his enemy the rest of his days.

³⁰The Philistine commanders continued to go out to battle, and as often as they did, David met with more successˢ than the rest of Saul's officers, and his name became well known.

C H A P T E R   1 9

Saul told his son Jonathan and all the attendants to kill David. But Jonathan was very fond of David ²and warned him, "My father Saul is looking for a chance to kill you. Be on your guard tomorrow morning; go into hiding and stay there. ³I will go out and stand with my father in the field where you are. I'll speak to him about you and will tell you what I find out."

⁴Jonathan spoke well of David to Saul his father and said to him, "Let not the king do wrong to his servant David; he has not wronged you, and what he has done has benefited you greatly. ⁵He took his life in his hands when he killed the Philistine. The LORD won a great victory for all Israel, and you saw it and were glad. Why then would you do wrong to an innocent man like David by killing him for no reason?"

⁶Saul listened to Jonathan and took this oath: "As surely as the LORD lives, David will not be put to death."

⁷So Jonathan called David and told him the whole conversation. He brought him to Saul, and David was with Saul as before.

⁸Once more war broke out, and David went out and fought the Philistines. He struck them with such force that they fled before him.

⁹But an evilᵗ spirit from the LORD came upon Saul as he was sitting in his house with his spear in his hand. While David was playing the harp, ¹⁰Saul tried to pin him to the wall with his spear, but David eluded him as Saul drove the spear into the wall. That night David made good his escape.

¹¹Saul sent men to David's house to

ᵖ14 Or he was very wise   ᵠ15 Or wise   ʳ19 Or However,   ˢ30 Or David acted more wisely   ᵗ9 Or injurious watch it and to kill him in the morning. But Michal, David's wife, warned him, "If you don't run for your life tonight, tomorrow you'll be killed." ¹²So Michal let David down through a window, and he fled and escaped. ¹³Then Michal took an idol^u and laid it on the bed, covering it with a garment and putting some goats' hair at the head.

¹⁴When Saul sent the men to capture David, Michal said, "He is ill."

¹⁵Then Saul sent the men back to see David and told them, "Bring him up to me in his bed so that I may kill him." ¹⁶But when the men entered, there was the idol in the bed, and at the head was some goats' hair.

¹⁷Saul said to Michal, "Why did you deceive me like this and send my enemy away so that he escaped?"

Michal told him, "He said to me, 'Let me get away. Why should I kill you?' "

¹⁸When David had fled and made his escape, he went to Samuel at Ramah and told him all that Saul had done to him. Then he and Samuel went to Naioth and stayed there. ¹⁹Word came to Saul: "David is in Naioth at Ramah"; ²⁰so he sent men to capture him. But when they saw a group of prophets prophesying, with Samuel standing there as their leader, the Spirit of God came upon Saul's men and they also prophesied. ²¹Saul was told about it, and he sent more men, and they prophesied too. Saul sent men a third time, and they also prophesied. ²²Finally, he himself left for Ramah and went to the great cistern at Secu. And he asked, "Where are Samuel and David?"

"Over in Naioth at Ramah," they said.

²³So Saul went to Naioth at Ramah. But the Spirit of God came even upon him, and he walked along prophesying until he came to Naioth. ²⁴He stripped off his robes and also prophesied in Samuel's presence. He lay that way all that day and night. This is why people say, "Is Saul also among the prophets?"

^u13 Hebrew *teraphim*; also in verse 16

MARCH 20 □ DAY 80
1 SAMUEL 20–23
David, the Pursued King-Elect

OVERVIEW Ironically, as the rift grows between David and Saul, the relationship deepens between David and Saul's son Jonathan. Knowing he himself will never sit upon the throne of Israel, Jonathan seeks to assist and protect the pursued king-elect. He alerts David to his father's murderous intent and sends David on the first leg of a journey that will cover hundreds of miles and span nearly a decade. From Nob . . . to Gath . . . to Adullam . . . to the Desert of Ziph, the king-elect is hunted by the king-rejected in a desperate and deadly game of hide-and-seek, from which only one will emerge victorious.

Chapter 20	Chapter 21	Chapter 22	Chapter 23
David's Faithful Friend Jonathan	Nob	David's Frantic Flight to Adullam	Ziph
A Friend Indeed	A Fugitive in Need		

YOUR DAILY WALK Have you found a Jonathan in your Christian life:
- someone who knows you fully and accepts you completely?
- someone with whom you can share your deepest hurts?
- someone who will listen without lecturing . . . comfort without condemning . . . encourage without criticizing?
- someone who will defend you when you're not around?

The more hot arguments you win, the fewer warm friends you'll have.

- someone whose greatest joy comes from your happiness?
- someone who watches out for your well-being, even at the potential risk of his own?
- someone who grieves when you are grieved, rejoices when you are promoted, bleeds when you are wounded?

Jonathans are rare, perhaps because the key to finding a Jonathan is becoming a David. Friendship is costly, demanding sacrifice and sensitivity; but that's what makes it so precious. Have you discovered the priceless treasure of finding—or becoming—a Jonathan?

 INSIGHT The Nob of a Hill Called Nob
Nob, also known as "the town of the priests" (22:19), was located about one mile north of Jerusalem on a ridge overlooking what later became the site of Solomon's temple. During the time of David, the tabernacle was located in Nob, and national worship was conducted from there.

CHAPTER 20

Then David fled from Naioth at Ramah and went to Jonathan and asked, "What have I done? What is my crime? How have I wronged your father, that he is trying to take my life?"

²"Never!" Jonathan replied. "You are not going to die! Look, my father doesn't do anything, great or small, without confiding in me. Why would he hide this from me? It's not so!"

³But David took an oath and said, "Your father knows very well that I have found favor in your eyes, and he has said to himself, 'Jonathan must not know this or he will be grieved.' Yet as surely as the LORD lives and as you live, there is only a step between me and death."

⁴Jonathan said to David, "Whatever you want me to do, I'll do for you."

⁵So David said, "Look, tomorrow is the New Moon festival, and I am supposed to dine with the king; but let me go and hide in the field until the evening of the day after tomorrow. ⁶If your father misses me at all, tell him, 'David earnestly asked my permission to hurry to Bethlehem, his hometown, because an annual sacrifice is being made there for his whole clan.' ⁷If he says, 'Very well,' then your servant is safe. But if he loses his temper, you can be sure that he is determined to harm me. ⁸As for you, show kindness to your servant, for you have brought him into a covenant with you before the LORD. If I am guilty, then kill me yourself! Why hand me over to your father?"

⁹"Never!" Jonathan said. "If I had the least inkling that my father was determined to harm you, wouldn't I tell you?"

¹⁰David asked, "Who will tell me if your father answers you harshly?"

¹¹"Come," Jonathan said, "let's go out into the field." So they went there together.

¹²Then Jonathan said to David: "By the LORD, the God of Israel, I will surely sound out my father by this time the day after tomorrow! If he is favorably disposed toward you, will I not send you word and let you know? ¹³But if my father is inclined to harm you, may the LORD deal with me, be it ever so severely, if I do not let you know and send you away safely. May the LORD be with you as he has been with my father. ¹⁴But show me unfailing kindness like that of the LORD as long as I live, so that I may not be killed, ¹⁵and do not ever cut off your kindness from my family—not even when the LORD has cut off every one of David's enemies from the face of the earth."

¹⁶So Jonathan made a covenant with the house of David, saying, "May the LORD call David's enemies to account." ¹⁷And Jonathan had David reaffirm his oath out of love for him, because he loved him as he loved himself.

¹⁸Then Jonathan said to David: "Tomorrow is the New Moon festival. You will be missed, because your seat will be empty. ¹⁹The day after tomorrow, toward evening, go to the place where you hid when this trouble began, and wait by the stone Ezel. ²⁰I will shoot three arrows to the side of it, as though I were shooting at a target. ²¹Then I will send a boy and say, 'Go, find the arrows.' If I say to him, 'Look, the arrows are on this side of you; bring them here,' then come, because, as

surely as the LORD lives, you are safe; there is no danger. ²²But if I say to the boy, 'Look, the arrows are beyond you,' then you must go, because the LORD has sent you away. ²³And about the matter you and I discussed—remember, the LORD is witness between you and me forever."

²⁴So David hid in the field, and when the New Moon festival came, the king sat down to eat. ²⁵He sat in his customary place by the wall, opposite Jonathan,ᵛ and Abner sat next to Saul, but David's place was empty. ²⁶Saul said nothing that day, for he thought, "Something must have happened to David to make him ceremonially unclean—surely he is unclean." ²⁷But the next day, the second day of the month, David's place was empty again. Then Saul said to his son Jonathan, "Why hasn't the son of Jesse come to the meal, either yesterday or today?"

²⁸Jonathan answered, "David earnestly asked me for permission to go to Bethlehem. ²⁹He said, 'Let me go, because our family is observing a sacrifice in the town and my brother has ordered me to be there. If I have found favor in your eyes, let me get away to see my brothers.' That is why he has not come to the king's table."

³⁰Saul's anger flared up at Jonathan and he said to him, "You son of a perverse and rebellious woman! Don't I know that you have sided with the son of Jesse to your own shame and to the shame of the mother who bore you? ³¹As long as the son of Jesse lives on this earth, neither you nor your kingdom will be established. Now send and bring him to me, for he must die!"

³²"Why should he be put to death? What has he done?" Jonathan asked his father. ³³But Saul hurled his spear at him to kill him. Then Jonathan knew that his father intended to kill David.

³⁴Jonathan got up from the table in fierce anger; on that second day of the month he did not eat, because he was grieved at his father's shameful treatment of David.

³⁵In the morning Jonathan went out to the field for his meeting with David. He had a small boy with him, ³⁶and he said to the boy, "Run and find the arrows I shoot." As the boy ran, he shot an arrow beyond him. ³⁷When the boy came to the place where Jonathan's arrow had fallen, Jonathan called out after him, "Isn't the arrow beyond you?" ³⁸Then he shouted, "Hurry! Go quickly! Don't stop!" The boy picked up the arrow and returned to his master. ³⁹(The boy knew nothing of all this; only Jonathan and David knew.) ⁴⁰Then Jonathan gave his weapons to the boy and said, "Go, carry them back to town."

⁴¹After the boy had gone, David got up from the south side ⸢of the stone⸣ and bowed down before Jonathan three times, with his face to the ground. Then they kissed each other and wept together—but David wept the most.

⁴²Jonathan said to David, "Go in peace, for we have sworn friendship with each other in the name of the LORD, saying, 'The LORD is witness between you and me, and between your descendants and my descendants forever.'" Then David left, and Jonathan went back to the town.

CHAPTER 21

David went to Nob, to Ahimelech the priest. Ahimelech trembled when he met him, and asked, "Why are you alone? Why is no one with you?"

²David answered Ahimelech the priest, "The king charged me with a certain matter and said to me, 'No one is to know anything about your mission and your instructions.' As for my men, I have told them to meet me at a certain place. ³Now then, what do you have on hand? Give me five loaves of bread, or whatever you can find."

⁴But the priest answered David, "I don't have any ordinary bread on hand; however, there is some consecrated bread here—provided the men have kept themselves from women."

⁵David replied, "Indeed women have been kept from us, as usual wheneverʷ I set out. The men's thingsˣ are holy even on missions that are not holy. How much more so today!" ⁶So the priest gave him the consecrated bread, since there was no bread there except the bread of the Presence that had been removed from before the LORD and replaced by hot bread on the day it was taken away.

⁷Now one of Saul's servants was there

that day, detained before the LORD; he was Doeg the Edomite, Saul's head shepherd.

⁸David asked Ahimelech, "Don't you have a spear or a sword here? I haven't brought my sword or any other weapon, because the king's business was urgent."

⁹The priest replied, "The sword of Goliath the Philistine, whom you killed in the Valley of Elah, is here; it is wrapped in a cloth behind the ephod. If you want it, take it; there is no sword here but that one."

David said, "There is none like it; give it to me."

¹⁰That day David fled from Saul and went to Achish king of Gath. ¹¹But the servants of Achish said to him, "Isn't this David, the king of the land? Isn't he the one they sing about in their dances:

" 'Saul has slain his thousands,
    and David his tens of thousands'?"

¹²David took these words to heart and was very much afraid of Achish king of Gath. ¹³So he pretended to be insane in their presence; and while he was in their hands he acted like a madman, making marks on the doors of the gate and letting saliva run down his beard.

¹⁴Achish said to his servants, "Look at the man! He is insane! Why bring him to me? ¹⁵Am I so short of madmen that you have to bring this fellow here to carry on like this in front of me? Must this man come into my house?"

CHAPTER 22

David left Gath and escaped to the cave of Adullam. When his brothers and his father's household heard about it, they went down to him there. ²All those who were in distress or in debt or discontented gathered around him, and he became their leader. About four hundred men were with him.

³From there David went to Mizpah in Moab and said to the king of Moab, "Would you let my father and mother come and stay with you until I learn what God will do for me?" ⁴So he left them with the king of Moab, and they stayed with him as long as David was in the stronghold.

⁵But the prophet Gad said to David, "Do not stay in the stronghold. Go into the land of Judah." So David left and went to the forest of Hereth.

⁶Now Saul heard that David and his men had been discovered. And Saul, spear in hand, was seated under the tamarisk tree on the hill at Gibeah, with all his officials standing around him. ⁷Saul said to them, "Listen, men of Benjamin! Will the son of Jesse give all of you fields and vineyards? Will he make all of you commanders of thousands and commanders of hundreds? ⁸Is that why you have all conspired against me? No one tells me when my son makes a covenant with the son of Jesse. None of you is concerned about me or tells me that my son has incited my servant to lie in wait for me, as he does today."

⁹But Doeg the Edomite, who was standing with Saul's officials, said, "I saw the son of Jesse come to Ahimelech son of Ahitub at Nob. ¹⁰Ahimelech inquired of the LORD for him; he also gave him provisions and the sword of Goliath the Philistine."

¹¹Then the king sent for the priest Ahimelech son of Ahitub and his father's whole family, who were the priests at Nob, and they all came to the king. ¹²Saul said, "Listen now, son of Ahitub."

"Yes, my lord," he answered.

¹³Saul said to him, "Why have you conspired against me, you and the son of Jesse, giving him bread and a sword and inquiring of God for him, so that he has rebelled against me and lies in wait for me, as he does today?"

¹⁴Ahimelech answered the king, "Who of all your servants is as loyal as David, the king's son-in-law, captain of your bodyguard and highly respected in your household? ¹⁵Was that day the first time I inquired of God for him? Of course not! Let not the king accuse your servant or any of his father's family, for your servant knows nothing at all about this whole affair."

¹⁶But the king said, "You will surely die, Ahimelech, you and your father's whole family."

¹⁷Then the king ordered the guards at his side: "Turn and kill the priests of the LORD, because they too have sided with David. They knew he was fleeing, yet they did not tell me."

But the king's officials were not willing to raise a hand to strike the priests of the LORD.

¹⁸The king then ordered Doeg, "You

turn and strike down the priests." So Doeg the Edomite turned and struck them down. That day he killed eighty-five men who wore the linen ephod. ¹⁹He also put to the sword Nob, the town of the priests, with its men and women, its children and infants, and its cattle, donkeys and sheep.

²⁰But Abiathar, a son of Ahimelech son of Ahitub, escaped and fled to join David. ²¹He told David that Saul had killed the priests of the LORD. ²²Then David said to Abiathar: "That day, when Doeg the Edomite was there, I knew he would be sure to tell Saul. I am responsible for the death of your father's whole family. ²³Stay with me; don't be afraid; the man who is seeking your life is seeking mine also. You will be safe with me."

CHAPTER 23

When David was told, "Look, the Philistines are fighting against Keilah and are looting the threshing floors," ²he inquired of the LORD, saying, "Shall I go and attack these Philistines?"

The LORD answered him, "Go, attack the Philistines and save Keilah."

³But David's men said to him, "Here in Judah we are afraid. How much more, then, if we go to Keilah against the Philistine forces!"

⁴Once again David inquired of the LORD, and the LORD answered him, "Go down to Keilah, for I am going to give the Philistines into your hand." ⁵So David and his men went to Keilah, fought the Philistines and carried off their livestock. He inflicted heavy losses on the Philistines and saved the people of Keilah. ⁶(Now Abiathar son of Ahimelech had brought the ephod down with him when he fled to David at Keilah.)

⁷Saul was told that David had gone to Keilah, and he said, "God has handed him over to me, for David has imprisoned himself by entering a town with gates and bars." ⁸And Saul called up all his forces for battle, to go down to Keilah to besiege David and his men.

⁹When David learned that Saul was plotting against him, he said to Abiathar the priest, "Bring the ephod." ¹⁰David said, "O LORD, God of Israel, your servant has heard definitely that Saul plans to come to Keilah and destroy the town on account of me. ¹¹Will the citizens of Keilah surrender me to him? Will Saul come down, as your servant has heard? O LORD, God of Israel, tell your servant."

And the LORD said, "He will."

¹²Again David asked, "Will the citizens of Keilah surrender me and my men to Saul?"

And the LORD said, "They will."

¹³So David and his men, about six hundred in number, left Keilah and kept moving from place to place. When Saul was told that David had escaped from Keilah, he did not go there.

¹⁴David stayed in the desert strongholds and in the hills of the Desert of Ziph. Day after day Saul searched for him, but God did not give David into his hands.

¹⁵While David was at Horesh in the Desert of Ziph, he learned that Saul had come out to take his life. ¹⁶And Saul's son Jonathan went to David at Horesh and helped him find strength in God. ¹⁷"Don't be afraid," he said. "My father Saul will not lay a hand on you. You will be king over Israel, and I will be second to you. Even my father Saul knows this." ¹⁸The two of them made a covenant before the LORD. Then Jonathan went home, but David remained at Horesh.

¹⁹The Ziphites went up to Saul at Gibeah and said, "Is not David hiding among us in the strongholds at Horesh, on the hill of Hakilah, south of Jeshimon? ²⁰Now, O king, come down whenever it pleases you to do so, and we will be responsible for handing him over to the king."

²¹Saul replied, "The LORD bless you for your concern for me. ²²Go and make further preparation. Find out where David usually goes and who has seen him there. They tell me he is very crafty. ²³Find out about all the hiding places he uses and come back to me with definite information.ʸ Then I will go with you; if he is in the area, I will track him down among all the clans of Judah."

²⁴So they set out and went to Ziph ahead of Saul. Now David and his men were in the Desert of Maon, in the Arabah south of Jeshimon. ²⁵Saul and his men began the search, and when David was told about it, he went down to the rock and

ʸ23 Or me at Nacon

stayed in the Desert of Maon. When Saul heard this, he went into the Desert of Maon in pursuit of David.

²⁶Saul was going along one side of the mountain, and David and his men were on the other side, hurrying to get away from Saul. As Saul and his forces were closing in on David and his men to capture them, ²⁷a messenger came to Saul, saying, "Come quickly! The Philistines are raiding the land." ²⁸Then Saul broke off his pursuit of David and went to meet the Philistines. That is why they call this place Sela Hammahlekoth.ᶻ ²⁹And David went up from there and lived in the strongholds of En Gedi.

ᶻ 28 *Sela Hammahlekoth* means *rock of parting.*

MARCH 21 ☐ DAY 81
True Strength

 LOOK BACK The young boy Samuel shows that you don't have to be old—just attentive—to hear and obey the voice of God.

Though "tuned in" to God in many ways, Samuel neglects the proper discipline of his sons, resulting in a national call for a king. In spite of dire predictions of what a king would do, God instructs Samuel to anoint Saul, a man of great physical stature but scant spiritual character. Saul's early *successes* soon give way to disobedient *excesses,* resulting in God's verdict of "rejected" and the anointing of Saul's successor. David, the young shepherd boy plucked from the pasture, would soon sing and "sling" his way into the hearts of his countrymen. But the path to the palace would be fraught with danger, discouragement and deadly intrigue as David runs for his life before a crazed King Saul.

 LOOK UP Q: Who had more strength—Samuel or Samson?
A: It all depends upon your definition of *strength.*

If by *strength* you mean "the physical ability to bring down the house," then it's no contest. He-man Samson beats little boy Samuel every time.

Good character is like good soup—it is usually homemade.

But if by *strength* you mean inner moral character, the ability to do what is right even when no one is watching, godliness, self-control and ethical integrity, then little boy Samuel beats Samson hands down.

Samson spent his entire life seeing how close to the edge of moral collapse he could get without falling over. In the end he lost his sight, his influence and eventually his life. To be sure, God won a great victory over the Philistines at Samson's death, but imagine how many other victories were never achieved because of Samson's compromising stance toward right and wrong.

By contrast, even in his early years Samuel was intent on hearing and obeying God's voice. "The LORD was with Samuel as he grew up, and he let none of his words fall to the ground" (3:19). Samuel never seemed to tire of "tuning in" to what God was trying to say. He wanted to get as close to God as possible, lest he miss a single word. It's true that Samuel's later years were marked by the failure of over-commitment as he reaped the tearful harvest of having neglected the discipline of his sons. But over his life could be written the epitaph "He yearned to hear God's voice."

 LOOK AHEAD What a strange, upside-down world we live in when those receiving the greatest public applause and financial reward are those who can dunk a basketball, act in front of a camera or sell a million albums—with no regard to their moral character or ethical conduct.

By contrast, those in line for God's recognition and reward are those who are "poor in spirit . . . meek . . . merciful . . . pure in heart . . . peacemakers . . . persecuted because of righteousness" (Matthew 5:3–10). No, you're not likely to see them in the spotlight this side of heaven. But when God hands out his "Well done, good and faithful servant" awards (Matthew 25:21, 23), you can be sure there will be some surprises!

Incidentally, which type of recognition are you striving to receive?

MARCH 22 □ DAY 82
1 SAMUEL 24–26
David, the Recognized King-Elect

OVERVIEW In today's reading you will encounter four different people and will view each from God's perspective. The focus is not on their external appearance but on their internal motivation, for "man looks at the outward appearance, but the LORD looks at the heart" (16:7). David demonstrates a heart of true compassion and righteousness when he twice refuses to kill the helpless king. Saul portrays a heart of repentance when he humbly acknowledges his sin of pursuing David. Nabal reveals his foolish heart by refusing to assist the king-elect. Nabal's wife, Abigail, shows her discerning heart by offering to David and his weary men the hospitality that her reckless husband withheld.

Chapter 24	Chapter 25	Chapter 26
A Demonstration of Righteousness	A Demonstration of Foolishness	A Demonstration of Faithfulness
David Spares Saul	Abigail Spares Nabal	David Spares Saul Again

YOUR DAILY WALK "If I ran the show, I would . . ."

Have you ever been convinced you could do a better job than the leader in charge? If so, how did you handle the situation? Were you openly supportive . . . or openly critical?

The best thing to do behind a person's back is pat it.

David showed unique strength of character when faced with an inept, jealous leader. Though David fled for his life, he never fought for his rights, even when twice given the opportunity to rid himself of his pursuer. David's conduct demonstrates that a righteous person recognizes God's chosen leader even when the leader fails.

How do you respond to the leaders God has placed over you? Do you honor them with the respect due their position? Do you permit them the luxury of an occasional mistake? (After all, what if you hadn't been given a second, third or even fourth chance?) Take the time today to write an encouraging note to one of your civic, national or spiritual leaders, pledging your continued support as that individual exercises God-given authority.

INSIGHT A Fragile Peace with a Fickle King

Although chapter 26 ends on a note of reconciliation (vv. 21–25), David is wise enough not to return with King Saul. As the opening verse of tomorrow's reading will show, from that time on, no trust remained between the two rivals.

CHAPTER 24

After Saul returned from pursuing the Philistines, he was told, "David is in the Desert of En Gedi." ²So Saul took three thousand chosen men from all Israel and set out to look for David and his men near the Crags of the Wild Goats.

³He came to the sheep pens along the way; a cave was there, and Saul went in to relieve himself. David and his men were far back in the cave. ⁴The men said, "This is the day the LORD spoke of when he said*ᵃ* to you, 'I will give your enemy into your hands for you to deal with as you wish.' " Then David crept up unnoticed and cut off a corner of Saul's robe.

⁵Afterward, David was conscience-stricken for having cut off a corner of his robe. ⁶He said to his men, "The LORD forbid that I should do such a thing to my master, the LORD's anointed, or lift my hand against him; for he is the anointed of the LORD." ⁷With these words David rebuked his men and did not allow them to attack Saul. And Saul left the cave and went his way.

⁸Then David went out of the cave and called out to Saul, "My lord the king!" When Saul looked behind him, David bowed down and prostrated himself with his face to the ground. ⁹He said to Saul, "Why do you listen when men say, 'David is bent on harming you'? ¹⁰This day you have seen with your own eyes how the LORD delivered you into my hands in the cave. Some urged me to kill you, but I spared you; I said, 'I will not lift my hand against my master, because he is the LORD's anointed.' ¹¹See, my father, look at this piece of your robe in my hand! I cut off the corner of your robe but did not kill you. Now understand and recognize that I am not guilty of wrongdoing or rebellion. I have not wronged you, but you are hunting me down to take my life. ¹²May the LORD judge between you and me. And may the LORD avenge the wrongs you have done to me, but my hand will not touch you. ¹³As the old saying goes, 'From evildoers come evil deeds,' so my hand will not touch you.

¹⁴"Against whom has the king of Israel come out? Whom are you pursuing? A dead dog? A flea? ¹⁵May the LORD be our judge and decide between us. May he consider my cause and uphold it; may he vindicate me by delivering me from your hand."

¹⁶When David finished saying this, Saul asked, "Is that your voice, David my son?" And he wept aloud. ¹⁷"You are more righteous than I," he said. "You have treated me well, but I have treated you badly. ¹⁸You have just now told me of the good you did to me; the LORD delivered me into your hands, but you did not kill me. ¹⁹When a man finds his enemy, does he let him get away unharmed? May the LORD reward you well for the way you treated me today. ²⁰I know that you will surely be king and that the kingdom of Israel will be established in your hands. ²¹Now swear to me by the LORD that you will not cut off my descendants or wipe out my name from my father's family."

²²So David gave his oath to Saul. Then Saul returned home, but David and his men went up to the stronghold.

CHAPTER 25

Now Samuel died, and all Israel assembled and mourned for him; and they buried him at his home in Ramah.

Then David moved down into the Desert of Maon.*ᵇ* ²A certain man in Maon, who had property there at Carmel, was very wealthy. He had a thousand goats and three thousand sheep, which he was shearing in Carmel. ³His name was Nabal and his wife's name was Abigail. She was an intelligent and beautiful woman, but her husband, a Calebite, was surly and mean in his dealings.

⁴While David was in the desert, he heard that Nabal was shearing sheep. ⁵So he sent ten young men and said to them, "Go up to Nabal at Carmel and greet him in my name. ⁶Say to him: 'Long life to you! Good health to you and your household! And good health to all that is yours!

⁷" 'Now I hear that it is sheep-shearing time. When your shepherds were with us, we did not mistreat them, and the whole time they were at Carmel nothing of

---

*ᵃ*4 Or *"Today the LORD is saying*   *ᵇ*1 Some Septuagint manuscripts; Hebrew *Paran* theirs was missing. [8]Ask your own servants and they will tell you. Therefore be favorable toward my young men, since we come at a festive time. Please give your servants and your son David whatever you can find for them.' "

[9]When David's men arrived, they gave Nabal this message in David's name. Then they waited.

[10]Nabal answered David's servants, "Who is this David? Who is this son of Jesse? Many servants are breaking away from their masters these days. [11]Why should I take my bread and water, and the meat I have slaughtered for my shearers, and give it to men coming from who knows where?"

[12]David's men turned around and went back. When they arrived, they reported every word. [13]David said to his men, "Put on your swords!" So they put on their swords, and David put on his. About four hundred men went up with David, while two hundred stayed with the supplies.

[14]One of the servants told Nabal's wife Abigail: "David sent messengers from the desert to give our master his greetings, but he hurled insults at them. [15]Yet these men were very good to us. They did not mistreat us, and the whole time we were out in the fields near them nothing was missing. [16]Night and day they were a wall around us all the time we were herding our sheep near them. [17]Now think it over and see what you can do, because disaster is hanging over our master and his whole household. He is such a wicked man that no one can talk to him."

[18]Abigail lost no time. She took two hundred loaves of bread, two skins of wine, five dressed sheep, five seahs[c] of roasted grain, a hundred cakes of raisins and two hundred cakes of pressed figs, and loaded them on donkeys. [19]Then she told her servants, "Go on ahead; I'll follow you." But she did not tell her husband Nabal.

[20]As she came riding her donkey into a mountain ravine, there were David and his men descending toward her, and she met them. [21]David had just said, "It's been useless—all my watching over this fellow's property in the desert so that nothing of his was missing. He has paid me back evil for good. [22]May God deal with David,[d] be it ever so severely, if by morning I leave alive one male of all who belong to him!"

[23]When Abigail saw David, she quickly got off her donkey and bowed down before David with her face to the ground. [24]She fell at his feet and said: "My lord, let the blame be on me alone. Please let your servant speak to you; hear what your servant has to say. [25]May my lord pay no attention to that wicked man Nabal. He is just like his name—his name is Fool, and folly goes with him. But as for me, your servant, I did not see the men my master sent.

[26]"Now since the LORD has kept you, my master, from bloodshed and from avenging yourself with your own hands, as surely as the LORD lives and as you live, may your enemies and all who intend to harm my master be like Nabal. [27]And let this gift, which your servant has brought to my master, be given to the men who follow you. [28]Please forgive your servant's offense, for the LORD will certainly make a lasting dynasty for my master, because he fights the LORD's battles. Let no wrongdoing be found in you as long as you live. [29]Even though someone is pursuing you to take your life, the life of my master will be bound securely in the bundle of the living by the LORD your God. But the lives of your enemies he will hurl away as from the pocket of a sling. [30]When the LORD has done for my master every good thing he promised concerning him and has appointed him leader over Israel, [31]my master will not have on his conscience the staggering burden of needless bloodshed or of having avenged himself. And when the LORD has brought my master success, remember your servant."

[32]David said to Abigail, "Praise be to the LORD, the God of Israel, who has sent you today to meet me. [33]May you be blessed for your good judgment and for keeping me from bloodshed this day and from avenging myself with my own hands. [34]Otherwise, as surely as the LORD, the God of Israel, lives, who has kept me from harming you, if you had not come quickly to meet me, not one male belonging to Nabal would have been left alive by daybreak."

---

[c]18 That is, probably about a bushel (about 37 liters)   [d]22 Some Septuagint manuscripts; Hebrew *with David's enemies*

³⁵Then David accepted from her hand what she had brought him and said, "Go home in peace. I have heard your words and granted your request."

³⁶When Abigail went to Nabal, he was in the house holding a banquet like that of a king. He was in high spirits and very drunk. So she told him nothing until daybreak. ³⁷Then in the morning, when Nabal was sober, his wife told him all these things, and his heart failed him and he became like a stone. ³⁸About ten days later, the LORD struck Nabal and he died.

³⁹When David heard that Nabal was dead, he said, "Praise be to the LORD, who has upheld my cause against Nabal for treating me with contempt. He has kept his servant from doing wrong and has brought Nabal's wrongdoing down on his own head."

Then David sent word to Abigail, asking her to become his wife. ⁴⁰His servants went to Carmel and said to Abigail, "David has sent us to you to take you to become his wife."

⁴¹She bowed down with her face to the ground and said, "Here is your maidservant, ready to serve you and wash the feet of my master's servants." ⁴²Abigail quickly got on a donkey and, attended by her five maids, went with David's messengers and became his wife. ⁴³David had also married Ahinoam of Jezreel, and they both were his wives. ⁴⁴But Saul had given his daughter Michal, David's wife, to Paltiel*e* son of Laish, who was from Gallim.

CHAPTER 26

The Ziphites went to Saul at Gibeah and said, "Is not David hiding on the hill of Hakilah, which faces Jeshimon?"

²So Saul went down to the Desert of Ziph, with his three thousand chosen men of Israel, to search there for David. ³Saul made his camp beside the road on the hill of Hakilah facing Jeshimon, but David stayed in the desert. When he saw that Saul had followed him there, ⁴he sent out scouts and learned that Saul had definitely arrived.*f*

⁵Then David set out and went to the place where Saul had camped. He saw where Saul and Abner son of Ner, the commander of the army, had lain down.

Saul was lying inside the camp, with the army encamped around him.

⁶David then asked Ahimelech the Hittite and Abishai son of Zeruiah, Joab's brother, "Who will go down into the camp with me to Saul?"

"I'll go with you," said Abishai.

⁷So David and Abishai went to the army by night, and there was Saul, lying asleep inside the camp with his spear stuck in the ground near his head. Abner and the soldiers were lying around him.

⁸Abishai said to David, "Today God has delivered your enemy into your hands. Now let me pin him to the ground with one thrust of my spear; I won't strike him twice."

⁹But David said to Abishai, "Don't destroy him! Who can lay a hand on the LORD's anointed and be guiltless? ¹⁰As surely as the LORD lives," he said, "the LORD himself will strike him; either his time will come and he will die, or he will go into battle and perish. ¹¹But the LORD forbid that I should lay a hand on the LORD's anointed. Now get the spear and water jug that are near his head, and let's go."

¹²So David took the spear and water jug near Saul's head, and they left. No one saw or knew about it, nor did anyone wake up. They were all sleeping, because the LORD had put them into a deep sleep.

¹³Then David crossed over to the other side and stood on top of the hill some distance away; there was a wide space between them. ¹⁴He called out to the army and to Abner son of Ner, "Aren't you going to answer me, Abner?"

Abner replied, "Who are you who calls to the king?"

¹⁵David said, "You're a man, aren't you? And who is like you in Israel? Why didn't you guard your lord the king? Someone came to destroy your lord the king. ¹⁶What you have done is not good. As surely as the LORD lives, you and your men deserve to die, because you did not guard your master, the LORD's anointed. Look around you. Where are the king's spear and water jug that were near his head?"

¹⁷Saul recognized David's voice and said, "Is that your voice, David my son?"

David replied, "Yes it is, my lord the king." ¹⁸And he added, "Why is my lord pursuing his servant? What have I done, and what wrong am I guilty of? ¹⁹Now let my lord the king listen to his servant's words. If the LORD has incited you against me, then may he accept an offering. If, however, men have done it, may they be cursed before the LORD! They have now driven me from my share in the LORD's inheritance and have said, 'Go, serve other gods.' ²⁰Now do not let my blood fall to the ground far from the presence of the LORD. The king of Israel has come out to look for a flea—as one hunts a partridge in the mountains."

²¹Then Saul said, "I have sinned. Come back, David my son. Because you considered my life precious today, I will not try to harm you again. Surely I have acted like a fool and have erred greatly."

²²"Here is the king's spear," David answered. "Let one of your young men come over and get it. ²³The LORD rewards every man for his righteousness and faithfulness. The LORD delivered you into my hands today, but I would not lay a hand on the LORD's anointed. ²⁴As surely as I valued your life today, so may the LORD value my life and deliver me from all trouble."

²⁵Then Saul said to David, "May you be blessed, my son David; you will do great things and surely triumph."

So David went on his way, and Saul returned home.

MARCH 23 □ DAY 83
1 SAMUEL 27–31
David, the Exiled King-Elect

 OVERVIEW After Saul's second brush with death in the Desert of Ziph, he discontinues the hunt for David. But the reprieve is only temporary, as David expects from past experience. Fleeing again to Gath of Philistines (the hometown of Goliath!), David pretends that he has defected to the enemy. In fact, he is busy destroying Philistine strongholds without leaving a single survivor to disclose his ingenious plan. When the Philistine kings mount a united war against Israel, David narrowly escapes fighting against his own nation. He returns instead to Ziklag to find it destroyed by the Amalekites, whom he pursues and defeats. Meanwhile, Saul is confronted with a Philistine invasion. Since the Spirit of God has left him, he seeks direction by divination—and receives instead a prediction of death and defeat.

Chapter 27	Chapter 28	Chapter 29	Chapter 30	Chapter 31
David's Defection	Saul's Distress	David's Dismissal	Amalekites' Defeat	Saul's Death
End of a Deadly Chase			End of a Dynasty	

 YOUR DAILY WALK In contemporary English, the word *tragedy* is used to describe any severe adversity, regardless of its cause. But more specifically, a tragedy is a calamity that results from a wrong decision arising from a flawed character. Using this definition, Saul's life was a true tragedy. It held much promise of success for himself and the nation, yet it ended in defeat and disgrace—all because pride and self-will led him to rebel against God's commands.

The number of times the average person says no to temptation is once weakly.

Becoming a Christian doesn't mark the end of your battle with sin and temptation; in many ways it marks the beginning! As a Christian you still have a fallen nature that seeks to express itself in your daily actions. You also have a personal will that desires to direct your life. Both need to come under the lordship of Jesus Christ. Take the four major areas of your life (spiritual, social, physical, emotional) and give each back to God right now, asking for his help to make your attitudes, decisions and actions pleasing to him.

INSIGHT A King's Life Comes Full Circle
First Samuel ends on a fitting note. Saul's first official act had been to rescue Jabesh Gilead (1 Samuel 11). Now its citizens have an opportunity to repay his kindness . . . posthumously (31:8–13).

CHAPTER 27

But David thought to himself, "One of these days I will be destroyed by the hand of Saul. The best thing I can do is to escape to the land of the Philistines. Then Saul will give up searching for me anywhere in Israel, and I will slip out of his hand."

²So David and the six hundred men with him left and went over to Achish son of Maoch king of Gath. ³David and his men settled in Gath with Achish. Each man had his family with him, and David had his two wives: Ahinoam of Jezreel and Abigail of Carmel, the widow of Nabal. ⁴When Saul was told that David had fled to Gath, he no longer searched for him.

⁵Then David said to Achish, "If I have found favor in your eyes, let a place be assigned to me in one of the country towns, that I may live there. Why should your servant live in the royal city with you?"

⁶So on that day Achish gave him Ziklag, and it has belonged to the kings of Judah ever since. ⁷David lived in Philistine territory a year and four months.

⁸Now David and his men went up and raided the Geshurites, the Girzites and the Amalekites. (From ancient times these peoples had lived in the land extending to Shur and Egypt.) ⁹Whenever David attacked an area, he did not leave a man or woman alive, but took sheep and cattle, donkeys and camels, and clothes. Then he returned to Achish.

¹⁰When Achish asked, "Where did you go raiding today?" David would say, "Against the Negev of Judah" or "Against the Negev of Jerahmeel" or "Against the Negev of the Kenites." ¹¹He did not leave a man or woman alive to be brought to Gath, for he thought, "They might inform on us and say, 'This is what David did.'" And such was his practice as long as he lived in Philistine territory. ¹²Achish trusted David and said to himself, "He has become so odious to his people, the Israelites, that he will be my servant forever."

CHAPTER 28

In those days the Philistines gathered their forces to fight against Israel. Achish said to David, "You must understand that you and your men will accompany me in the army."

²David said, "Then you will see for yourself what your servant can do."

Achish replied, "Very well, I will make you my bodyguard for life."

³Now Samuel was dead, and all Israel had mourned for him and buried him in his own town of Ramah. Saul had expelled the mediums and spiritists from the land.

⁴The Philistines assembled and came and set up camp at Shunem, while Saul gathered all the Israelites and set up camp at Gilboa. ⁵When Saul saw the Philistine army, he was afraid; terror filled his heart. ⁶He inquired of the LORD, but the LORD did not answer him by dreams or Urim or prophets. ⁷Saul then said to his attendants, "Find me a woman who is a medium, so I may go and inquire of her."

"There is one in Endor," they said.

⁸So Saul disguised himself, putting on other clothes, and at night he and two men went to the woman. "Consult a spirit for me," he said, "and bring up for me the one I name."

⁹But the woman said to him, "Surely you know what Saul has done. He has cut off the mediums and spiritists from the land. Why have you set a trap for my life to bring about my death?"

¹⁰Saul swore to her by the LORD, "As surely as the LORD lives, you will not be punished for this."

¹¹Then the woman asked, "Whom shall I bring up for you?"

"Bring up Samuel," he said.

¹²When the woman saw Samuel, she cried out at the top of her voice and said

to Saul, "Why have you deceived me? You are Saul!"

[13]The king said to her, "Don't be afraid. What do you see?"

The woman said, "I see a spirit[g] coming up out of the ground."

[14]"What does he look like?" he asked.

"An old man wearing a robe is coming up," she said.

Then Saul knew it was Samuel, and he bowed down and prostrated himself with his face to the ground.

[15]Samuel said to Saul, "Why have you disturbed me by bringing me up?"

"I am in great distress," Saul said. "The Philistines are fighting against me, and God has turned away from me. He no longer answers me, either by prophets or by dreams. So I have called on you to tell me what to do."

[16]Samuel said, "Why do you consult me, now that the LORD has turned away from you and become your enemy? [17]The LORD has done what he predicted through me. The LORD has torn the kingdom out of your hands and given it to one of your neighbors—to David. [18]Because you did not obey the LORD or carry out his fierce wrath against the Amalekites, the LORD has done this to you today. [19]The LORD will hand over both Israel and you to the Philistines, and tomorrow you and your sons will be with me. The LORD will also hand over the army of Israel to the Philistines."

[20]Immediately Saul fell full length on the ground, filled with fear because of Samuel's words. His strength was gone, for he had eaten nothing all that day and night.

[21]When the woman came to Saul and saw that he was greatly shaken, she said, "Look, your maidservant has obeyed you. I took my life in my hands and did what you told me to do. [22]Now please listen to your servant and let me give you some food so you may eat and have the strength to go on your way."

[23]He refused and said, "I will not eat."

But his men joined the woman in urging him, and he listened to them. He got up from the ground and sat on the couch.

[24]The woman had a fattened calf at the house, which she butchered at once. She took some flour, kneaded it and baked bread without yeast. [25]Then she set it before Saul and his men, and they ate. That same night they got up and left.

CHAPTER 29

The Philistines gathered all their forces at Aphek, and Israel camped by the spring in Jezreel. [2]As the Philistine rulers marched with their units of hundreds and thousands, David and his men were marching at the rear with Achish. [3]The commanders of the Philistines asked, "What about these Hebrews?"

Achish replied, "Is this not David, who was an officer of Saul king of Israel? He has already been with me for over a year, and from the day he left Saul until now, I have found no fault in him."

[4]But the Philistine commanders were angry with him and said, "Send the man back, that he may return to the place you assigned him. He must not go with us into battle, or he will turn against us during the fighting. How better could he regain his master's favor than by taking the heads of our own men? [5]Isn't this the David they sang about in their dances:

" 'Saul has slain his thousands,
    and David his tens of thousands'?"

[6]So Achish called David and said to him, "As surely as the LORD lives, you have been reliable, and I would be pleased to have you serve with me in the army. From the day you came to me until now, I have found no fault in you, but the rulers don't approve of you. [7]Turn back and go in peace; do nothing to displease the Philistine rulers."

[8]"But what have I done?" asked David. "What have you found against your servant from the day I came to you until now? Why can't I go and fight against the enemies of my lord the king?"

[9]Achish answered, "I know that you have been as pleasing in my eyes as an angel of God; nevertheless, the Philistine commanders have said, 'He must not go up with us into battle.' [10]Now get up early, along with your master's servants who have come with you, and leave in the morning as soon as it is light."

[11]So David and his men got up early in the morning to go back to the land of the

g 13 Or see spirits; or see gods

Philistines, and the Philistines went up to Jezreel.

CHAPTER 30

David and his men reached Ziklag on the third day. Now the Amalekites had raided the Negev and Ziklag. They had attacked Ziklag and burned it, 2and had taken captive the women and all who were in it, both young and old. They killed none of them, but carried them off as they went on their way.

3When David and his men came to Ziklag, they found it destroyed by fire and their wives and sons and daughters taken captive. 4So David and his men wept aloud until they had no strength left to weep. 5David's two wives had been captured—Ahinoam of Jezreel and Abigail, the widow of Nabal of Carmel. 6David was greatly distressed because the men were talking of stoning him; each one was bitter in spirit because of his sons and daughters. But David found strength in the LORD his God.

7Then David said to Abiathar the priest, the son of Ahimelech, "Bring me the ephod." Abiathar brought it to him, 8and David inquired of the LORD, "Shall I pursue this raiding party? Will I overtake them?"

"Pursue them," he answered. "You will certainly overtake them and succeed in the rescue."

9David and the six hundred men with him came to the Besor Ravine, where some stayed behind, 10for two hundred men were too exhausted to cross the ravine. But David and four hundred men continued the pursuit.

11They found an Egyptian in a field and brought him to David. They gave him water to drink and food to eat— 12part of a cake of pressed figs and two cakes of raisins. He ate and was revived, for he had not eaten any food or drunk any water for three days and three nights.

13David asked him, "To whom do you belong, and where do you come from?"

He said, "I am an Egyptian, the slave of an Amalekite. My master abandoned me when I became ill three days ago. 14We raided the Negev of the Kerethites and the territory belonging to Judah and the Negev of Caleb. And we burned Ziklag." 15David asked him, "Can you lead me down to this raiding party?"

He answered, "Swear to me before God that you will not kill me or hand me over to my master, and I will take you down to them."

16He led David down, and there they were, scattered over the countryside, eating, drinking and reveling because of the great amount of plunder they had taken from the land of the Philistines and from Judah. 17David fought them from dusk until the evening of the next day, and none of them got away, except four hundred young men who rode off on camels and fled. 18David recovered everything the Amalekites had taken, including his two wives. 19Nothing was missing: young or old, boy or girl, plunder or anything else they had taken. David brought everything back. 20He took all the flocks and herds, and his men drove them ahead of the other livestock, saying, "This is David's plunder."

21Then David came to the two hundred men who had been too exhausted to follow him and who were left behind at the Besor Ravine. They came out to meet David and the people with him. As David and his men approached, he greeted them. 22But all the evil men and troublemakers among David's followers said, "Because they did not go out with us, we will not share with them the plunder we recovered. However, each man may take his wife and children and go."

23David replied, "No, my brothers, you must not do that with what the LORD has given us. He has protected us and handed over to us the forces that came against us. 24Who will listen to what you say? The share of the man who stayed with the supplies is to be the same as that of him who went down to the battle. All will share alike." 25David made this a statute and ordinance for Israel from that day to this.

26When David arrived in Ziklag, he sent some of the plunder to the elders of Judah, who were his friends, saying, "Here is a present for you from the plunder of the LORD's enemies."

27He sent it to those who were in Bethel, Ramoth Negev and Jattir; 28to those in Aroer, Siphmoth, Eshtemoa 29and Racal; to those in the towns of the Jerahmeelites and the Kenites; 30to those in Hormah, Bor Ashan, Athach 31and Hebron; and to those in all the other places where David and his men had roamed.

CHAPTER 31

Now the Philistines fought against Israel; the Israelites fled before them, and many fell slain on Mount Gilboa. ²The Philistines pressed hard after Saul and his sons, and they killed his sons Jonathan, Abinadab and Malki-Shua. ³The fighting grew fierce around Saul, and when the archers overtook him, they wounded him critically.

⁴Saul said to his armor-bearer, "Draw your sword and run me through, or these uncircumcised fellows will come and run me through and abuse me."

But his armor-bearer was terrified and would not do it; so Saul took his own sword and fell on it. ⁵When the armor-bearer saw that Saul was dead, he too fell on his sword and died with him. ⁶So Saul and his three sons and his armor-bearer and all his men died together that same day.

⁷When the Israelites along the valley and those across the Jordan saw that the Israelite army had fled and that Saul and his sons had died, they abandoned their towns and fled. And the Philistines came and occupied them.

⁸The next day, when the Philistines came to strip the dead, they found Saul and his three sons fallen on Mount Gilboa. ⁹They cut off his head and stripped off his armor, and they sent messengers throughout the land of the Philistines to proclaim the news in the temple of their idols and among their people. ¹⁰They put his armor in the temple of the Ashtoreths and fastened his body to the wall of Beth Shan.

¹¹When the people of Jabesh Gilead heard of what the Philistines had done to Saul, ¹²all their valiant men journeyed through the night to Beth Shan. They took down the bodies of Saul and his sons from the wall of Beth Shan and went to Jabesh, where they burned them. ¹³Then they took their bones and buried them under a tamarisk tree at Jabesh, and they fasted seven days.

2 Samuel

THE BOOK of 2 Samuel chronicles the remarkable forty-year reign of King David, a man who lives at the halfway point between Moses and Christ (about 1000 B.C.). David's triumphs and successes bring Israel to the very zenith of her power. But his all-too-human weaknesses become a national scandal, leading to rebellion within his own family and temporary exile for himself and his court. Through it all, David seeks God zealously and confesses his sins promptly.

Focus	Success			Sin	Suffering		
Divisions	David, King of Judah	David, King of Israel	David's Growing Kingdom	David's Tragic Downfall	Absalom's Quest to Rule	David's Return to the Throne	David's Final Days
	1 4	5 7	8 10	11 14	15 18	19 20	21 24
Topics	David's Rise			David's Demise			
	Victory and Expansion			Violence and Struggle			
Place	Hebron			Jerusalem			
Time	7½ Years			33 Years			

MARCH 24 ☐ DAY 84
2 SAMUEL 1–4
David, King of Judah

OVERVIEW Second Samuel continues the narrative of 1 Samuel and chronicles David's rise to prominence as Israel's leader. After mourning the deaths of Saul and Jonathan, David assumes the throne as king over Judah. But Saul's dynasty is not to be replaced without a fight! Ish-bosheth, Saul's son, claims the throne of Israel, initiating seven years of bloody civil war, intrigue, defections, assassinations, suspense, rival factions and rebellions. But when at last the opposition has been quelled, David rules as king over a united kingdom.

Chapter 1	Chapters 2–3	Chapter 4
David Weeps	David Wars	David Wins
Mourning Saul's Death	Fighting Saul's House	

YOUR DAILY WALK Look up Matthew 12:25, and thoughtfully read it twice. Now ask yourself these two questions:
  1. How was this verse proved true in David's kingdom?
  2. What does this verse mean in my home?

The family altar would alter many a family.

In David's day many individuals were striving for positions of leadership and power. Some would even scheme, kill or change sides to gain their personal ends. The result was chaos, frustration and death until the nation was united under one head.

Many activities compete for your attention. Television, clubs, school activities, civic functions, church meetings—all demand your time and energy. In many homes the result is confusion, frustration and lack of family unity.

Families, like nations, function best when they operate under one head. Hold a family council to talk about leadership in your home. Spend some time looking at Bible passages dealing with headship in the home (Ephesians 5:22–6:4; Colossians 3:18–21). Then select a family goal for the coming week—something that will honor the Lord and benefit each family member!

INSIGHT Did You Ever Read the One by . . .
Lost in ancient times, the book of Jasher was apparently a collection of verse describing great events in Israel's history. It contained an account of Joshua's triumph at the battle of Gibeon (Joshua 10:12–13) as well as David's lament over Saul and Jonathan. Second Chronicles 9:29 mentions other writings that have been lost.

CHAPTER 1
After the death of Saul, David returned from defeating the Amalekites and stayed in Ziklag two days. ²On the third day a man arrived from Saul's camp, with his clothes torn and with dust on his head. When he came to David, he fell to the ground to pay him honor.

³"Where have you come from?" David asked him.

He answered, "I have escaped from the Israelite camp."

4"What happened?" David asked. "Tell me."

He said, "The men fled from the battle. Many of them fell and died. And Saul and his son Jonathan are dead."

5Then David said to the young man who brought him the report, "How do you know that Saul and his son Jonathan are dead?"

6"I happened to be on Mount Gilboa," the young man said, "and there was Saul, leaning on his spear, with the chariots and riders almost upon him. 7When he turned around and saw me, he called out to me, and I said, 'What can I do?'

8"He asked me, 'Who are you?'

" 'An Amalekite,' I answered.

9"Then he said to me, 'Stand over me and kill me! I am in the throes of death, but I'm still alive.'

10"So I stood over him and killed him, because I knew that after he had fallen he could not survive. And I took the crown that was on his head and the band on his arm and have brought them here to my lord."

11Then David and all the men with him took hold of their clothes and tore them. 12They mourned and wept and fasted till evening for Saul and his son Jonathan, and for the army of the LORD and the house of Israel, because they had fallen by the sword.

13David said to the young man who brought him the report, "Where are you from?"

"I am the son of an alien, an Amalekite," he answered.

14David asked him, "Why were you not afraid to lift your hand to destroy the LORD's anointed?"

15Then David called one of his men and said, "Go, strike him down!" So he struck him down, and he died. 16For David had said to him, "Your blood be on your own head. Your own mouth testified against you when you said, 'I killed the LORD's anointed.' "

17David took up this lament concerning Saul and his son Jonathan, 18and ordered that the men of Judah be taught this lament of the bow (it is written in the Book of Jashar):

19"Your glory, O Israel, lies slain on your heights.
How the mighty have fallen!

20"Tell it not in Gath,
proclaim it not in the streets of Ashkelon,
lest the daughters of the Philistines be glad,
lest the daughters of the uncircumcised rejoice.

21"O mountains of Gilboa,
may you have neither dew nor rain,
nor fields that yield offerings ⌐of grain⌐.
For there the shield of the mighty was defiled,
the shield of Saul—no longer rubbed with oil.

22From the blood of the slain,
from the flesh of the mighty,
the bow of Jonathan did not turn back,
the sword of Saul did not return unsatisfied.

23"Saul and Jonathan—
in life they were loved and gracious,
and in death they were not parted.
They were swifter than eagles,
they were stronger than lions.

24"O daughters of Israel,
weep for Saul,
who clothed you in scarlet and finery,
who adorned your garments with ornaments of gold.

25"How the mighty have fallen in battle!
Jonathan lies slain on your heights.
26I grieve for you, Jonathan my brother;
you were very dear to me.
Your love for me was wonderful,
more wonderful than that of women.

27"How the mighty have fallen!
The weapons of war have perished!"

CHAPTER 2

In the course of time, David inquired of the LORD. "Shall I go up to one of the towns of Judah?" he asked.

The LORD said, "Go up."

David asked, "Where shall I go?"

"To Hebron," the LORD answered.

2So David went up there with his two wives, Ahinoam of Jezreel and Abigail, the widow of Nabal of Carmel. 3David also took the men who were with him, each with his family, and they settled in Hebron and its towns. 4Then the men of Judah came to Hebron and there they anointed David king over the house of Judah.

When David was told that it was the men of Jabesh Gilead who had buried Saul, [5]he sent messengers to the men of Jabesh Gilead to say to them, "The LORD bless you for showing this kindness to Saul your master by burying him. [6]May the LORD now show you kindness and faithfulness, and I too will show you the same favor because you have done this. [7]Now then, be strong and brave, for Saul your master is dead, and the house of Judah has anointed me king over them."

[8]Meanwhile, Abner son of Ner, the commander of Saul's army, had taken Ish-Bosheth son of Saul and brought him over to Mahanaim. [9]He made him king over Gilead, Ashuri[a] and Jezreel, and also over Ephraim, Benjamin and all Israel.

[10]Ish-Bosheth son of Saul was forty years old when he became king over Israel, and he reigned two years. The house of Judah, however, followed David. [11]The length of time David was king in Hebron over the house of Judah was seven years and six months.

[12]Abner son of Ner, together with the men of Ish-Bosheth son of Saul, left Mahanaim and went to Gibeon. [13]Joab son of Zeruiah and David's men went out and met them at the pool of Gibeon. One group sat down on one side of the pool and one group on the other side.

[14]Then Abner said to Joab, "Let's have some of the young men get up and fight hand to hand in front of us."

"All right, let them do it," Joab said.

[15]So they stood up and were counted off—twelve men for Benjamin and Ish-Bosheth son of Saul, and twelve for David. [16]Then each man grabbed his opponent by the head and thrust his dagger into his opponent's side, and they fell down together. So that place in Gibeon was called Helkath Hazzurim.[b]

[17]The battle that day was very fierce, and Abner and the men of Israel were defeated by David's men.

[18]The three sons of Zeruiah were there: Joab, Abishai and Asahel. Now Asahel was as fleet-footed as a wild gazelle. [19]He chased Abner, turning neither to the right

nor to the left as he pursued him. [20]Abner looked behind him and asked, "Is that you, Asahel?"

"It is," he answered.

[21]Then Abner said to him, "Turn aside to the right or to the left; take on one of the young men and strip him of his weapons." But Asahel would not stop chasing him.

[22]Again Abner warned Asahel, "Stop chasing me! Why should I strike you down? How could I look your brother Joab in the face?"

[23]But Asahel refused to give up the pursuit; so Abner thrust the butt of his spear into Asahel's stomach, and the spear came out through his back. He fell there and died on the spot. And every man stopped when he came to the place where Asahel had fallen and died.

[24]But Joab and Abishai pursued Abner, and as the sun was setting, they came to the hill of Ammah, near Giah on the way to the wasteland of Gibeon. [25]Then the men of Benjamin rallied behind Abner. They formed themselves into a group and took their stand on top of a hill.

[26]Abner called out to Joab, "Must the sword devour forever? Don't you realize that this will end in bitterness? How long before you order your men to stop pursuing their brothers?"

[27]Joab answered, "As surely as God lives, if you had not spoken, the men would have continued the pursuit of their brothers until morning.[c]"

[28]So Joab blew the trumpet, and all the men came to a halt; they no longer pursued Israel, nor did they fight anymore.

[29]All that night Abner and his men marched through the Arabah. They crossed the Jordan, continued through the whole Bithron[d] and came to Mahanaim.

[30]Then Joab returned from pursuing Abner and assembled all his men. Besides Asahel, nineteen of David's men were found missing. [31]But David's men had killed three hundred and sixty Benjamites who were with Abner. [32]They took Asahel and buried him in his father's tomb at Bethlehem. Then Joab and his men marched all night and arrived at Hebron by daybreak.

CHAPTER 3

The war between the house of Saul and the house of David lasted a long time. David grew stronger and stronger, while the house of Saul grew weaker and weaker.

²Sons were born to David in Hebron:

His firstborn was Amnon the son of Ahinoam of Jezreel;

³his second, Kileab the son of Abigail the widow of Nabal of Carmel;

the third, Absalom the son of Maacah daughter of Talmai king of Geshur;

⁴the fourth, Adonijah the son of Haggith;

the fifth, Shephatiah the son of Abital;

⁵and the sixth, Ithream the son of David's wife Eglah.

These were born to David in Hebron.

⁶During the war between the house of Saul and the house of David, Abner had been strengthening his own position in the house of Saul. ⁷Now Saul had had a concubine named Rizpah daughter of Aiah. And Ish-Bosheth said to Abner, "Why did you sleep with my father's concubine?"

⁸Abner was very angry because of what Ish-Bosheth said and he answered, "Am I a dog's head—on Judah's side? This very day I am loyal to the house of your father Saul and to his family and friends. I haven't handed you over to David. Yet now you accuse me of an offense involving this woman! ⁹May God deal with Abner, be it ever so severely, if I do not do for David what the LORD promised him on oath ¹⁰and transfer the kingdom from the house of Saul and establish David's throne over Israel and Judah from Dan to Beersheba." ¹¹Ish-Bosheth did not dare to say another word to Abner, because he was afraid of him.

¹²Then Abner sent messengers on his behalf to say to David, "Whose land is it? Make an agreement with me, and I will help you bring all Israel over to you."

¹³"Good," said David. "I will make an agreement with you. But I demand one thing of you: Do not come into my presence unless you bring Michal daughter of Saul when you come to see me." ¹⁴Then David sent messengers to Ish-Bosheth son of Saul, demanding, "Give me my wife Michal, whom I betrothed to myself for the price of a hundred Philistine foreskins."

¹⁵So Ish-Bosheth gave orders and had her taken away from her husband Paltiel son of Laish. ¹⁶Her husband, however, went with her, weeping behind her all the way to Bahurim. Then Abner said to him, "Go back home!" So he went back.

¹⁷Abner conferred with the elders of Israel and said, "For some time you have wanted to make David your king. ¹⁸Now do it! For the LORD promised David, 'By my servant David I will rescue my people Israel from the hand of the Philistines and from the hand of all their enemies.' "

¹⁹Abner also spoke to the Benjamites in person. Then he went to Hebron to tell David everything that Israel and the whole house of Benjamin wanted to do. ²⁰When Abner, who had twenty men with him, came to David at Hebron, David prepared a feast for him and his men. ²¹Then Abner said to David, "Let me go at once and assemble all Israel for my lord the king, so that they may make a compact with you, and that you may rule over all that your heart desires." So David sent Abner away, and he went in peace.

²²Just then David's men and Joab returned from a raid and brought with them a great deal of plunder. But Abner was no longer with David in Hebron, because David had sent him away, and he had gone in peace. ²³When Joab and all the soldiers with him arrived, he was told that Abner son of Ner had come to the king and that the king had sent him away and that he had gone in peace.

²⁴So Joab went to the king and said, "What have you done? Look, Abner came to you. Why did you let him go? Now he is gone! ²⁵You know Abner son of Ner; he came to deceive you and observe your movements and find out everything you are doing."

²⁶Joab then left David and sent messengers after Abner, and they brought him back from the well of Sirah. But David did not know it. ²⁷Now when Abner returned to Hebron, Joab took him aside into the gateway, as though to speak with him privately. And there, to avenge the blood of his brother Asahel, Joab stabbed him in the stomach, and he died.

²⁸Later, when David heard about this, he said, "I and my kingdom are forever innocent before the LORD concerning the blood of Abner son of Ner. ²⁹May his blood fall upon the head of Joab and upon all his father's house! May Joab's house never be without someone who has a running sore or leprosy* or who leans on a crutch or who falls by the sword or who lacks food."

³⁰(Joab and his brother Abishai murdered Abner because he had killed their brother Asahel in the battle at Gibeon.)

³¹Then David said to Joab and all the people with him, "Tear your clothes and put on sackcloth and walk in mourning in front of Abner." King David himself walked behind the bier. ³²They buried Abner in Hebron, and the king wept aloud at Abner's tomb. All the people wept also.

³³The king sang this lament for Abner:

"Should Abner have died as the
        lawless die?
³⁴   Your hands were not bound,
     your feet were not fettered.
You fell as one falls before wicked
        men."

And all the people wept over him again.

³⁵Then they all came and urged David to eat something while it was still day; but David took an oath, saying, "May God deal with me, be it ever so severely, if I taste bread or anything else before the sun sets!"

³⁶All the people took note and were pleased; indeed, everything the king did pleased them. ³⁷So on that day all the people and all Israel knew that the king had no part in the murder of Abner son of Ner.

³⁸Then the king said to his men, "Do you not realize that a prince and a great man has fallen in Israel this day? ³⁹And today, though I am the anointed king, I am weak, and these sons of Zeruiah are too strong for me. May the LORD repay the evildoer according to his evil deeds!"

CHAPTER 4
When Ish-Bosheth son of Saul heard that Abner had died in Hebron, he lost courage, and all Israel became alarmed. ²Now

Saul's son had two men who were leaders of raiding bands. One was named Baanah and the other Recab; they were sons of Rimmon the Beerothite from the tribe of Benjamin—Beeroth is considered part of Benjamin, ³because the people of Beeroth fled to Gittaim and have lived there as aliens to this day.

⁴(Jonathan son of Saul had a son who was lame in both feet. He was five years old when the news about Saul and Jonathan came from Jezreel. His nurse picked him up and fled, but as she hurried to leave, he fell and became crippled. His name was Mephibosheth.)

⁵Now Recab and Baanah, the sons of Rimmon the Beerothite, set out for the house of Ish-Bosheth, and they arrived there in the heat of the day while he was taking his noonday rest. ⁶They went into the inner part of the house as if to get some wheat, and they stabbed him in the stomach. Then Recab and his brother Baanah slipped away.

⁷They had gone into the house while he was lying on the bed in his bedroom. After they stabbed and killed him, they cut off his head. Taking it with them, they traveled all night by way of the Arabah. ⁸They brought the head of Ish-Bosheth to David at Hebron and said to the king, "Here is the head of Ish-Bosheth son of Saul, your enemy, who tried to take your life. This day the LORD has avenged my lord the king against Saul and his offspring."

⁹David answered Recab and his brother Baanah, the sons of Rimmon the Beerothite, "As surely as the LORD lives, who has delivered me out of all trouble, ¹⁰when a man told me, 'Saul is dead,' and thought he was bringing good news, I seized him and put him to death in Ziklag. That was the reward I gave him for his news! ¹¹How much more—when wicked men have killed an innocent man in his own house and on his own bed—should I not now demand his blood from your hand and rid the earth of you!"

¹²So David gave an order to his men, and they killed them. They cut off their hands and feet and hung the bodies by the pool in Hebron. But they took the head of Ish-Bosheth and buried it in Abner's tomb at Hebron.

*29 The Hebrew word was used for various diseases affecting the skin—not necessarily leprosy.

MARCH 25 ☐ DAY 85
2 SAMUEL 5–7
David's Reign over a United Nation

 OVERVIEW Initially, David's rule extends only over the tribe of Judah. But with the death of Ish-bosheth, all Israel transfers her allegiance to David as the rightful ruler. After making Jerusalem his new capital, David wastes no time in bringing the ark of God back from Baalah of Judah where it had sat for years. Intent on building a beautiful house for God, David learns that God will build an eternal house for him instead: His throne, family and kingdom will be established forever, and he will take his place among the great men of history.

Chapter 5	Chapter 6	Chapter 7	
Reuniting the Nation	Returning the Ark	A House for God Planned	A House for David Promised
David's Power	David's Passion	David's Plan	David's Praise

 YOUR DAILY WALK The motto "Attempt great things for God, expect great things from God" would provide an apt summary of David's early years in office as king over the twelve tribes of Israel. He moved speedily to implement his godly convictions both politically and religiously, reversing the godless influences of his predecessor, Saul. And though God would not permit him to fulfill certain dreams (such as building the temple), he never rebuked David for his motives or discouraged him from attempting other great enterprises for him.

One person with a dream is equal to ninety-nine who only have interests.

Building projects for God are costly. They demand vision . . . time . . . sacrifice . . . perseverance. The great Christian schools we enjoy today, the majestic churches whose pulpits are aflame with righteousness, the missionary organizations that touch millions of lives spiritually and physically—each began with a dream in the heart of a committed child of God.

Do you have a dream of how God might want to use you? . . . your family? . . . your church? . . . your skills? . . . your resources to impact your world for him? If not, allow God to implant a dream for his glory; then dream it, plan it, pursue it—and as God enables—achieve it!

 INSIGHT Chronicling a Coronation
The account of David's coronation in 2 Samuel covers just three verses (5:1–3). For a fuller treatment of this very impressive ceremony, read 1 Chronicles 12:23–40, which describes the massive assembly of more than 340,000 troops for the gala event.

CHAPTER 5
All the tribes of Israel came to David at Hebron and said, "We are your own flesh and blood. ²In the past, while Saul was king over us, you were the one who led Israel on their military campaigns. And the LORD said to you, 'You will shepherd my people Israel, and you will become their ruler.' "

³When all the elders of Israel had come to King David at Hebron, the king made a compact with them at Hebron before the LORD, and they anointed David king over Israel.

⁴David was thirty years old when he became king, and he reigned forty years. ⁵In Hebron he reigned over Judah seven years and six months, and in Jerusalem he reigned over all Israel and Judah thirty-three years.

⁶The king and his men marched to Jerusalem to attack the Jebusites, who lived

there. The Jebusites said to David, "You will not get in here; even the blind and the lame can ward you off." They thought, "David cannot get in here." [7]Nevertheless, David captured the fortress of Zion, the City of David.

[8]On that day, David said, "Anyone who conquers the Jebusites will have to use the water shaft[f] to reach those 'lame and blind' who are David's enemies.[g]" That is why they say, "The 'blind and lame' will not enter the palace."

[9]David then took up residence in the fortress and called it the City of David. He built up the area around it, from the supporting terraces[h] inward. [10]And he became more and more powerful, because the LORD God Almighty was with him.

[11]Now Hiram king of Tyre sent messengers to David, along with cedar logs and carpenters and stonemasons, and they built a palace for David. [12]And David knew that the LORD had established him as king over Israel and had exalted his kingdom for the sake of his people Israel.

[13]After he left Hebron, David took more concubines and wives in Jerusalem, and more sons and daughters were born to him. [14]These are the names of the children born to him there: Shammua, Shobab, Nathan, Solomon, [15]Ibhar, Elishua, Nepheg, Japhia, [16]Elishama, Eliada and Eliphelet.

[17]When the Philistines heard that David had been anointed king over Israel, they went up in full force to search for him, but David heard about it and went down to the stronghold. [18]Now the Philistines had come and spread out in the Valley of Rephaim; [19]so David inquired of the LORD, "Shall I go and attack the Philistines? Will you hand them over to me?"

The LORD answered him, "Go, for I will surely hand the Philistines over to you."

[20]So David went to Baal Perazim, and there he defeated them. He said, "As waters break out, the LORD has broken out against my enemies before me." So that place was called Baal Perazim.[i] [21]The Philistines abandoned their idols there,

and David and his men carried them off.

[22]Once more the Philistines came up and spread out in the Valley of Rephaim; [23]so David inquired of the LORD, and he answered, "Do not go straight up, but circle around behind them and attack them in front of the balsam trees. [24]As soon as you hear the sound of marching in the tops of the balsam trees, move quickly, because that will mean the LORD has gone out in front of you to strike the Philistine army." [25]So David did as the LORD commanded him, and he struck down the Philistines all the way from Gibeon[j] to Gezer.

CHAPTER 6

David again brought together out of Israel chosen men, thirty thousand in all. [2]He and all his men set out from Baalah of Judah[k] to bring up from there the ark of God, which is called by the Name,[l] the name of the LORD Almighty, who is enthroned between the cherubim that are on the ark. [3]They set the ark of God on a new cart and brought it from the house of Abinadab, which was on the hill. Uzzah and Ahio, sons of Abinadab, were guiding the new cart [4]with the ark of God on it,[m] and Ahio was walking in front of it. [5]David and the whole house of Israel were celebrating with all their might before the LORD, with songs[n] and with harps, lyres, tambourines, sistrums and cymbals.

[6]When they came to the threshing floor of Nacon, Uzzah reached out and took hold of the ark of God, because the oxen stumbled. [7]The LORD's anger burned against Uzzah because of his irreverent act; therefore God struck him down and he died there beside the ark of God.

[8]Then David was angry because the LORD's wrath had broken out against Uzzah, and to this day that place is called Perez Uzzah.[o]

[9]David was afraid of the LORD that day and said, "How can the ark of the LORD ever come to me?" [10]He was not willing to take the ark of the LORD to be with him in the City of David. Instead, he took it aside

---

[f]8 Or use scaling hooks   [g]8 Or are hated by David   [h]9 Or the Millo   [i]20 Baal Perazim means the lord who breaks out.
[j]25 Septuagint (see also 1 Chron. 14:16); Hebrew Geba   [k]2 That is, Kiriath Jearim; Hebrew Baale Judah, a variant of Baalah of Judah   [l]2 Hebrew; Septuagint and Vulgate do not have the Name.   [m]3,4 Dead Sea Scrolls and some Septuagint manuscripts; Masoretic Text cart [4]and they brought it with the ark of God from the house of Abinadab, which was on the hill   [n]5 See Dead Sea Scrolls, Septuagint and 1 Chronicles 13:8; Masoretic Text celebrating before the LORD with all kinds of instruments made of pine.
[o]8 Perez Uzzah means outbreak against Uzzah.

to the house of Obed-Edom the Gittite. ¹¹The ark of the LORD remained in the house of Obed-Edom the Gittite for three months, and the LORD blessed him and his entire household.

¹²Now King David was told, "The LORD has blessed the household of Obed-Edom and everything he has, because of the ark of God." So David went down and brought up the ark of God from the house of Obed-Edom to the City of David with rejoicing. ¹³When those who were carrying the ark of the LORD had taken six steps, he sacrificed a bull and a fattened calf. ¹⁴David, wearing a linen ephod, danced before the LORD with all his might, ¹⁵while he and the entire house of Israel brought up the ark of the LORD with shouts and the sound of trumpets.

¹⁶As the ark of the LORD was entering the City of David, Michal daughter of Saul watched from a window. And when she saw King David leaping and dancing before the LORD, she despised him in her heart.

¹⁷They brought the ark of the LORD and set it in its place inside the tent that David had pitched for it, and David sacrificed burnt offerings and fellowship offerings*ᵖ* before the LORD. ¹⁸After he had finished sacrificing the burnt offerings and fellowship offerings, he blessed the people in the name of the LORD Almighty. ¹⁹Then he gave a loaf of bread, a cake of dates and a cake of raisins to each person in the whole crowd of Israelites, both men and women. And all the people went to their homes.

²⁰When David returned home to bless his household, Michal daughter of Saul came out to meet him and said, "How the king of Israel has distinguished himself today, disrobing in the sight of the slave girls of his servants as any vulgar fellow would!"

²¹David said to Michal, "It was before the LORD, who chose me rather than your father or anyone from his house when he appointed me ruler over the LORD's people Israel—I will celebrate before the LORD. ²²I will become even more undignified than this, and I will be humiliated in my own eyes. But by these slave girls you spoke of, I will be held in honor."

²³And Michal daughter of Saul had no children to the day of her death.

CHAPTER 7

After the king was settled in his palace and the LORD had given him rest from all his enemies around him, ²he said to Nathan the prophet, "Here I am, living in a palace of cedar, while the ark of God remains in a tent."

³Nathan replied to the king, "Whatever you have in mind, go ahead and do it, for the LORD is with you."

⁴That night the word of the LORD came to Nathan, saying:

⁵"Go and tell my servant David, 'This is what the LORD says: Are you the one to build me a house to dwell in? ⁶I have not dwelt in a house from the day I brought the Israelites up out of Egypt to this day. I have been moving from place to place with a tent as my dwelling. ⁷Wherever I have moved with all the Israelites, did I ever say to any of their rulers whom I commanded to shepherd my people Israel, "Why have you not built me a house of cedar?" '

⁸"Now then, tell my servant David, 'This is what the LORD Almighty says: I took you from the pasture and from following the flock to be ruler over my people Israel. ⁹I have been with you wherever you have gone, and I have cut off all your enemies from before you. Now I will make your name great, like the names of the greatest men of the earth. ¹⁰And I will provide a place for my people Israel and will plant them so that they can have a home of their own and no longer be disturbed. Wicked people will not oppress them anymore, as they did at the beginning ¹¹and have done ever since the time I appointed leaders*�q* over my people Israel. I will also give you rest from all your enemies.

" 'The LORD declares to you that the LORD himself will establish a house for you: ¹²When your days are over and you rest with your fathers, I will raise up your offspring to succeed you, who will come from your own body, and I will establish his kingdom. ¹³He is the one who will build a house for my Name, and I will establish the throne of his kingdom for-

---

ᵖ17 Traditionally *peace offerings*; also in verse 18   *�q11* Traditionally *judges* ever. ¹⁴I will be his father, and he will be my son. When he does wrong, I will punish him with the rod of men, with floggings inflicted by men. ¹⁵But my love will never be taken away from him, as I took it away from Saul, whom I removed from before you. ¹⁶Your house and your kingdom will endure forever before me*ʳ*; your throne will be established forever.' "

¹⁷Nathan reported to David all the words of this entire revelation.

¹⁸Then King David went in and sat before the LORD, and he said:

"Who am I, O Sovereign LORD, and what is my family, that you have brought me this far? ¹⁹And as if this were not enough in your sight, O Sovereign LORD, you have also spoken about the future of the house of your servant. Is this your usual way of dealing with man, O Sovereign LORD?

²⁰"What more can David say to you? For you know your servant, O Sovereign LORD. ²¹For the sake of your word and according to your will, you have done this great thing and made it known to your servant.

²²"How great you are, O Sovereign LORD! There is no one like you, and there is no God but you, as we have heard with our own ears. ²³And who

is like your people Israel—the one nation on earth that God went out to redeem as a people for himself, and to make a name for himself, and to perform great and awesome wonders by driving out nations and their gods from before your people, whom you redeemed from Egypt?*ˢ* ²⁴You have established your people Israel as your very own forever, and you, O LORD, have become their God.

²⁵"And now, LORD God, keep forever the promise you have made concerning your servant and his house. Do as you promised, ²⁶so that your name will be great forever. Then men will say, 'The LORD Almighty is God over Israel!' And the house of your servant David will be established before you.

²⁷"O LORD Almighty, God of Israel, you have revealed this to your servant, saying, 'I will build a house for you.' So your servant has found courage to offer you this prayer. ²⁸O Sovereign LORD, you are God! Your words are trustworthy, and you have promised these good things to your servant. ²⁹Now be pleased to bless the house of your servant, that it may continue forever in your sight; for you, O Sovereign LORD, have spoken, and with your blessing the house of your servant will be blessed forever."

ʳ16 Some Hebrew manuscripts and Septuagint; most Hebrew manuscripts *you*   *ˢ23* See Septuagint and 1 Chron. 17:21; Hebrew *wonders for your land and before your people, whom you redeemed from Egypt, from the nations and their gods.*

MARCH 26 ☐ DAY 86
2 SAMUEL 8–10
David's Growing Kingdom

 OVERVIEW Once the internal security of the nation has been restored, David begins the task of securing and enlarging its borders. The Philistines, Moabites and Arameans fall in quick succession before Israel's mighty army. But in spite of David's many military conquests, his tenderness and compassion are evident in his invitation to Mephibosheth, the crippled son of Jonathan, to live in the king's palace. When the Ammonites question another of David's acts of kindness, he teaches them a stern lesson in respect.

Chapter 8	Chapter 9	Chapter 10
David Expands the Kingdom	David Expresses His Kindness	David Extends His Justice
Moab	Mephibosheth	Ammon

YOUR DAILY WALK When was the last time you
- visited a shut-in?
- cooked a meal for someone outside your family?
- offered to take an elderly person shopping?
- did something for someone who couldn't repay you?

To feel sorry for the needy is not the mark of a Christian—to help them is.

King David demonstrated great depth of character when he showed mercy to Jonathan's crippled son. Kings seldom concerned themselves with the welfare of the disadvantaged, and the heirs of former kings were usually killed, not comforted. But out of a heart of compassion and because he had made a covenant with Jonathan, David took the unprecedented step of making Mephibosheth an adopted member of his family. With no thought of repayment or publicity, David acted in faithfulness to his friend by caring for Mephibosheth.

Where has God brought a Mephibosheth across your path? You may not find it very convenient . . . or glamorous . . . or financially rewarding to help that person. But remember, "Whatever you did for one of the least of these brothers of mine," Jesus said, "you did for me" (Matthew 25:40).

INSIGHT Flaunting the Kindness of the King
Compare the response of Mephibosheth (9:8) with that of the Ammonites (10:1–4) when each was extended King David's kindness. Mephibosheth was humbly grateful and lived in the palace, but the Ammonites remained arrogant and died on the battlefield.

CHAPTER 8
In the course of time, David defeated the Philistines and subdued them, and he took Metheg Ammah from the control of the Philistines.

²David also defeated the Moabites. He made them lie down on the ground and measured them off with a length of cord. Every two lengths of them were put to death, and the third length was allowed to live. So the Moabites became subject to David and brought tribute.

³Moreover, David fought Hadadezer son of Rehob, king of Zobah, when he went to restore his control along the Euphrates River. ⁴David captured a thousand of his chariots, seven thousand charioteers*ᵗ* and twenty thousand foot soldiers. He hamstrung all but a hundred of the chariot horses.

⁵When the Arameans of Damascus came to help Hadadezer king of Zobah, David struck down twenty-two thousand of them. ⁶He put garrisons in the Aramean kingdom of Damascus, and the Arameans became subject to him and brought tribute. The LORD gave David victory wherever he went.

⁷David took the gold shields that belonged to the officers of Hadadezer and brought them to Jerusalem. ⁸From Tebah*ᵘ* and Berothai, towns that belonged to Hadadezer, King David took a great quantity of bronze.

⁹When Tou*ᵛ* king of Hamath heard that David had defeated the entire army of Hadadezer, ¹⁰he sent his son Joram*ʷ* to King David to greet him and congratulate him on his victory in battle over Hadadezer, who had been at war with Tou. Joram brought with him articles of silver and gold and bronze.

¹¹King David dedicated these articles to the LORD, as he had done with the silver and gold from all the nations he had subdued: ¹²Edom*ˣ* and Moab, the Ammon-

---
ᵗ4 Septuagint (see also Dead Sea Scrolls and 1 Chron. 18:4); Masoretic Text *captured seventeen hundred of his charioteers*
ᵘ8 See some Septuagint manuscripts (see also 1 Chron. 18:8); Hebrew *Betah.*   *ᵛ9* Hebrew *Toi,* a variant of *Tou;* also in verse 10   *ʷ10* A variant of *Hadoram*   *ˣ12* Some Hebrew manuscripts, Septuagint and Syriac (see also 1 Chron. 18:11); most Hebrew manuscripts *Aram*

ites and the Philistines, and Amalek. He also dedicated the plunder taken from Hadadezer son of Rehob, king of Zobah.

¹³And David became famous after he returned from striking down eighteen thousand Edomites⁹ in the Valley of Salt.

¹⁴He put garrisons throughout Edom, and all the Edomites became subject to David. The LORD gave David victory wherever he went.

¹⁵David reigned over all Israel, doing what was just and right for all his people. ¹⁶Joab son of Zeruiah was over the army; Jehoshaphat son of Ahilud was recorder; ¹⁷Zadok son of Ahitub and Ahimelech son of Abiathar were priests; Seraiah was secretary; ¹⁸Benaiah son of Jehoiada was over the Kerethites and Pelethites; and David's sons were royal advisers.ᶻ

CHAPTER 9

David asked, "Is there anyone still left of the house of Saul to whom I can show kindness for Jonathan's sake?"

²Now there was a servant of Saul's household named Ziba. They called him to appear before David, and the king said to him, "Are you Ziba?"

"Your servant," he replied.

³The king asked, "Is there no one still left of the house of Saul to whom I can show God's kindness?"

Ziba answered the king, "There is still a son of Jonathan; he is crippled in both feet."

⁴"Where is he?" the king asked.

Ziba answered, "He is at the house of Makir son of Ammiel in Lo Debar."

⁵So King David had him brought from Lo Debar, from the house of Makir son of Ammiel.

⁶When Mephibosheth son of Jonathan, the son of Saul, came to David, he bowed down to pay him honor.

David said, "Mephibosheth!"

"Your servant," he replied.

⁷"Don't be afraid," David said to him, "for I will surely show you kindness for the sake of your father Jonathan. I will restore to you all the land that belonged to your grandfather Saul, and you will always eat at my table."

⁸Mephibosheth bowed down and said, "What is your servant, that you should notice a dead dog like me?"

⁹Then the king summoned Ziba, Saul's servant, and said to him, "I have given your master's grandson everything that belonged to Saul and his family. ¹⁰You and your sons and your servants are to farm the land for him and bring in the crops, so that your master's grandson may be provided for. And Mephibosheth, grandson of your master, will always eat at my table." (Now Ziba had fifteen sons and twenty servants.)

¹¹Then Ziba said to the king, "Your servant will do whatever my lord the king commands his servant to do." So Mephibosheth ate at David'sᵃ table like one of the king's sons.

¹²Mephibosheth had a young son named Mica, and all the members of Ziba's household were servants of Mephibosheth. ¹³And Mephibosheth lived in Jerusalem, because he always ate at the king's table, and he was crippled in both feet.

CHAPTER 10

In the course of time, the king of the Ammonites died, and his son Hanun succeeded him as king. ²David thought, "I will show kindness to Hanun son of Nahash, just as his father showed kindness to me." So David sent a delegation to express his sympathy to Hanun concerning his father.

When David's men came to the land of the Ammonites, ³the Ammonite nobles said to Hanun their lord, "Do you think David is honoring your father by sending men to you to express sympathy? Hasn't David sent them to you to explore the city and spy it out and overthrow it?" ⁴So Hanun seized David's men, shaved off half of each man's beard, cut off their garments in the middle at the buttocks, and sent them away.

⁵When David was told about this, he sent messengers to meet the men, for they were greatly humiliated. The king said, "Stay at Jericho till your beards have grown, and then come back."

⁶When the Ammonites realized that they had become a stench in David's nostrils, they hired twenty thousand Aramean foot soldiers from Beth Rehob and Zobah, as well as the king of Maacah with

ʸ13 A few Hebrew manuscripts, Septuagint and Syriac (see also 1 Chron. 18:12); most Hebrew manuscripts Aram (that is, Arameans)   ᶻ18 Or were priests   ᵃ11 Septuagint; Hebrew my a thousand men, and also twelve thousand men from Tob.

⁷On hearing this, David sent Joab out with the entire army of fighting men. ⁸The Ammonites came out and drew up in battle formation at the entrance to their city gate, while the Arameans of Zobah and Rehob and the men of Tob and Maacah were by themselves in the open country.

⁹Joab saw that there were battle lines in front of him and behind him; so he selected some of the best troops in Israel and deployed them against the Arameans. ¹⁰He put the rest of the men under the command of Abishai his brother and deployed them against the Ammonites. ¹¹Joab said, "If the Arameans are too strong for me, then you are to come to my rescue; but if the Ammonites are too strong for you, then I will come to rescue you. ¹²Be strong and let us fight bravely for our people and the cities of our God. The LORD will do what is good in his sight."

¹³Then Joab and the troops with him advanced to fight the Arameans, and they fled before him. ¹⁴When the Ammonites saw that the Arameans were fleeing, they fled before Abishai and went inside the city. So Joab returned from fighting the Ammonites and came to Jerusalem.

¹⁵After the Arameans saw that they had been routed by Israel, they regrouped. ¹⁶Hadadezer had Arameans brought from beyond the River[b]; they went to Helam, with Shobach the commander of Hadadezer's army leading them.

¹⁷When David was told of this, he gathered all Israel, crossed the Jordan and went to Helam. The Arameans formed their battle lines to meet David and fought against him. ¹⁸But they fled before Israel, and David killed seven hundred of their charioteers and forty thousand of their foot soldiers.[c] He also struck down Shobach the commander of their army, and he died there. ¹⁹When all the kings who were vassals of Hadadezer saw that they had been defeated by Israel, they made peace with the Israelites and became subject to them.

So the Arameans were afraid to help the Ammonites anymore.

[b]16 That is, the Euphrates   [c]18 Some Septuagint manuscripts (see also 1 Chron. 19:18); Hebrew *horsemen*

MARCH 27 □ DAY 87
2 SAMUEL 11–14
David's Tragic Downfall

 OVERVIEW Today's section marks a tragic turning point in David's life. While idling in the palace instead of fighting on the battlefield, David yields to temptation and commits adultery with Bathsheba—an act the king then attempts to hide with lies, deceit and eventually murder. Though David's sin is grave, his response to the uncovering of that sin is exemplary: "I have sinned against the LORD" (12:13). Forgiveness and restoration follow, but there can be no reversing the ugly consequences of David's act: death for the unnamed infant and open revolt in David's household and nation.

Chapter 11	Chapter 12	Chapters 13–14
David's Sin	Nathan's Rebuke	David's Regret
A Palace Corrupted		A Family Divided

 YOUR DAILY WALK Take a sheet of paper and write on it: "Things That Could Never Happen to Me." Then make a list of at least five moral, spiritual and financial disasters that you feel certain could never

One test of
a person's
strength is that
person's
knowledge of
his or her
weakness.

happen to you: bankruptcy, divorce, prodigal children, nervous break-down, etc.

David's reign was marked by material wealth, military success, social prestige and the promise of future prosperity. From all outward appearances, things couldn't have been better for the king and his magnificent kingdom.

But in David's heart, a steady erosion was taking place in his ability to withstand temptation—a spiritual slide away from God prompted by an undisciplined life of passion, polygamy and idle pleasure. When the moment of temptation came, David had no power to resist, and the rest is history.

Where is erosion taking place in your spiritual life? Where are you setting yourself up for future heartache by ignoring danger signs in the present? Look again at your list of "impossible disasters," and scratch out the word *never* in the title. Tragedy could happen to you, just as it did to David, if you take your eyes off the Lord.

 INSIGHT Heavy, Heavy Hangs over Your Head
A "hand on the head" (13:19; compare Jeremiah 2:37) was the sign that terrible calamity had befallen the victim and that the hand of God was against him—a heavy burden indeed!

CHAPTER 11

In the spring, at the time when kings go off to war, David sent Joab out with the king's men and the whole Israelite army. They destroyed the Ammonites and besieged Rabbah. But David remained in Jerusalem.

²One evening David got up from his bed and walked around on the roof of the palace. From the roof he saw a woman bathing. The woman was very beautiful, ³and David sent someone to find out about her. The man said, "Isn't this Bathsheba, the daughter of Eliam and the wife of Uriah the Hittite?" ⁴Then David sent messengers to get her. She came to him, and he slept with her. (She had purified herself from her uncleanness.) Then*d* she went back home. ⁵The woman conceived and sent word to David, saying, "I am pregnant."

⁶So David sent this word to Joab: "Send me Uriah the Hittite." And Joab sent him to David. ⁷When Uriah came to him, David asked him how Joab was, how the soldiers were and how the war was going. ⁸Then David said to Uriah, "Go down to your house and wash your feet." So Uriah left the palace, and a gift from the king was sent after him. ⁹But Uriah slept at the entrance to the palace with all his master's servants and did not go down to his house.

¹⁰When David was told, "Uriah did not go home," he asked him, "Haven't you just come from a distance? Why didn't you go home?"

¹¹Uriah said to David, "The ark and Israel and Judah are staying in tents, and my master Joab and my lord's men are camped in the open fields. How could I go to my house to eat and drink and lie with my wife? As surely as you live, I will not do such a thing!"

¹²Then David said to him, "Stay here one more day, and tomorrow I will send you back." So Uriah remained in Jerusalem that day and the next. ¹³At David's invitation, he ate and drank with him, and David made him drunk. But in the evening Uriah went out to sleep on his mat among his master's servants; he did not go home.

¹⁴In the morning David wrote a letter to Joab and sent it with Uriah. ¹⁵In it he wrote, "Put Uriah in the front line where the fighting is fiercest. Then withdraw from him so he will be struck down and die."

¹⁶So while Joab had the city under siege, he put Uriah at a place where he knew the strongest defenders were. ¹⁷When the men of the city came out and fought against Joab, some of the men in David's army fell; moreover, Uriah the Hittite died.

¹⁸Joab sent David a full account of the battle. ¹⁹He instructed the messenger:

*d*4 Or *with her. When she purified herself from her uncleanness,*

"When you have finished giving the king this account of the battle, ²⁰the king's anger may flare up, and he may ask you, 'Why did you get so close to the city to fight? Didn't you know they would shoot arrows from the wall? ²¹Who killed Abimelech son of Jerub-Besheth*? Didn't a woman throw an upper millstone on him from the wall, so that he died in Thebez? Why did you get so close to the wall?' If he asks you this, then say to him, 'Also, your servant Uriah the Hittite is dead.' "

²²The messenger set out, and when he arrived he told David everything Joab had sent him to say. ²³The messenger said to David, "The men overpowered us and came out against us in the open, but we drove them back to the entrance to the city gate. ²⁴Then the archers shot arrows at your servants from the wall, and some of the king's men died. Moreover, your servant Uriah the Hittite is dead."

²⁵David told the messenger, "Say this to Joab: 'Don't let this upset you; the sword devours one as well as another. Press the attack against the city and destroy it.' Say this to encourage Joab."

²⁶When Uriah's wife heard that her husband was dead, she mourned for him. ²⁷After the time of mourning was over, David had her brought to his house, and she became his wife and bore him a son. But the thing David had done displeased the LORD.

CHAPTER 12

The LORD sent Nathan to David. When he came to him, he said, "There were two men in a certain town, one rich and the other poor. ²The rich man had a very large number of sheep and cattle, ³but the poor man had nothing except one little ewe lamb he had bought. He raised it, and it grew up with him and his children. It shared his food, drank from his cup and even slept in his arms. It was like a daughter to him.

⁴"Now a traveler came to the rich man, but the rich man refrained from taking one of his own sheep or cattle to prepare a meal for the traveler who had come to him. Instead, he took the ewe lamb that belonged to the poor man and prepared it for the one who had come to him."

⁵David burned with anger against the man and said to Nathan, "As surely as the LORD lives, the man who did this deserves to die! ⁶He must pay for that lamb four times over, because he did such a thing and had no pity."

⁷Then Nathan said to David, "You are the man! This is what the LORD, the God of Israel, says: 'I anointed you king over Israel, and I delivered you from the hand of Saul. ⁸I gave your master's house to you, and your master's wives into your arms. I gave you the house of Israel and Judah. And if all this had been too little, I would have given you even more. ⁹Why did you despise the word of the LORD by doing what is evil in his eyes? You struck down Uriah the Hittite with the sword and took his wife to be your own. You killed him with the sword of the Ammonites. ¹⁰Now, therefore, the sword will never depart from your house, because you despised me and took the wife of Uriah the Hittite to be your own.'

¹¹"This is what the LORD says: 'Out of your own household I am going to bring calamity upon you. Before your very eyes I will take your wives and give them to one who is close to you, and he will lie with your wives in broad daylight. ¹²You did it in secret, but I will do this thing in broad daylight before all Israel.' "

¹³Then David said to Nathan, "I have sinned against the LORD."

Nathan replied, "The LORD has taken away your sin. You are not going to die. ¹⁴But because by doing this you have made the enemies of the LORD show utter contempt,^f the son born to you will die."

¹⁵After Nathan had gone home, the LORD struck the child that Uriah's wife had borne to David, and he became ill. ¹⁶David pleaded with God for the child. He fasted and went into his house and spent the nights lying on the ground. ¹⁷The elders of his household stood beside him to get him up from the ground, but he refused, and he would not eat any food with them.

¹⁸On the seventh day the child died. David's servants were afraid to tell him that the child was dead, for they thought, "While the child was still living, we spoke to David but he would not listen to us.

---

*21 Also known as *Jerub-Baal* (that is, Gideon)   *14 Masoretic Text; an ancient Hebrew scribal tradition *this you have shown utter contempt for the* LORD

How can we tell him the child is dead? He may do something desperate."

¹⁹David noticed that his servants were whispering among themselves and he realized the child was dead. "Is the child dead?" he asked.

"Yes," they replied, "he is dead."

²⁰Then David got up from the ground. After he had washed, put on lotions and changed his clothes, he went into the house of the LORD and worshiped. Then he went to his own house, and at his request they served him food, and he ate.

²¹His servants asked him, "Why are you acting this way? While the child was alive, you fasted and wept, but now that the child is dead, you get up and eat!"

²²He answered, "While the child was still alive, I fasted and wept. I thought, 'Who knows? The LORD may be gracious to me and let the child live.' ²³But now that he is dead, why should I fast? Can I bring him back again? I will go to him, but he will not return to me."

²⁴Then David comforted his wife Bathsheba, and he went to her and lay with her. She gave birth to a son, and they named him Solomon. The LORD loved him; ²⁵and because the LORD loved him, he sent word through Nathan the prophet to name him Jedidiah.⁸

²⁶Meanwhile Joab fought against Rabbah of the Ammonites and captured the royal citadel. ²⁷Joab then sent messengers to David, saying, "I have fought against Rabbah and taken its water supply. ²⁸Now muster the rest of the troops and besiege the city and capture it. Otherwise I will take the city, and it will be named after me."

²⁹So David mustered the entire army and went to Rabbah, and attacked and captured it. ³⁰He took the crown from the head of their king*ʰ*—its weight was a talent*ⁱ* of gold, and it was set with precious stones—and it was placed on David's head. He took a great quantity of plunder from the city ³¹and brought out the people who were there, consigning them to labor with saws and with iron picks and axes, and he made them work at brickmaking.ʲ He did this to all the Ammonite towns. Then David and his entire army returned to Jerusalem.

CHAPTER 13

In the course of time, Amnon son of David fell in love with Tamar, the beautiful sister of Absalom son of David.

²Amnon became frustrated to the point of illness on account of his sister Tamar, for she was a virgin, and it seemed impossible for him to do anything to her.

³Now Amnon had a friend named Jonadab son of Shimeah, David's brother. Jonadab was a very shrewd man. ⁴He asked Amnon, "Why do you, the king's son, look so haggard morning after morning? Won't you tell me?"

Amnon said to him, "I'm in love with Tamar, my brother Absalom's sister."

⁵"Go to bed and pretend to be ill," Jonadab said. "When your father comes to see you, say to him, 'I would like my sister Tamar to come and give me something to eat. Let her prepare the food in my sight so I may watch her and then eat it from her hand.'"

⁶So Amnon lay down and pretended to be ill. When the king came to see him, Amnon said to him, "I would like my sister Tamar to come and make some special bread in my sight, so I may eat from her hand."

⁷David sent word to Tamar at the palace: "Go to the house of your brother Amnon and prepare some food for him." ⁸So Tamar went to the house of her brother Amnon, who was lying down. She took some dough, kneaded it, made the bread in his sight and baked it. ⁹Then she took the pan and served him the bread, but he refused to eat.

"Send everyone out of here," Amnon said. So everyone left him. ¹⁰Then Amnon said to Tamar, "Bring the food here into my bedroom so I may eat from your hand." And Tamar took the bread she had prepared and brought it to her brother Amnon in his bedroom. ¹¹But when she took it to him to eat, he grabbed her and said, "Come to bed with me, my sister."

¹²"Don't, my brother!" she said to him. "Don't force me. Such a thing should not be done in Israel! Don't do this wicked thing. ¹³What about me? Where could I get rid of my disgrace? And what about you? You would be like one of the wicked fools in Israel. Please speak to the king; he will not keep me from being married to

---

ᵍ25 *Jedidiah* means *loved by the* LORD.   *ʰ30* Or *of Milcom* (that is, Molech)   *ⁱ30* That is, about 75 pounds (about 34 kilograms)
ʲ31 The meaning of the Hebrew for this clause is uncertain.

you." ¹⁴But he refused to listen to her, and since he was stronger than she, he raped her.

¹⁵Then Amnon hated her with intense hatred. In fact, he hated her more than he had loved her. Amnon said to her, "Get up and get out!"

¹⁶"No!" she said to him. "Sending me away would be a greater wrong than what you have already done to me."

But he refused to listen to her. ¹⁷He called his personal servant and said, "Get this woman out of here and bolt the door after her." ¹⁸So his servant put her out and bolted the door after her. She was wearing a richly ornamented ^{k} robe, for this was the kind of garment the virgin daughters of the king wore. ¹⁹Tamar put ashes on her head and tore the ornamented ^{l} robe she was wearing. She put her hand on her head and went away, weeping aloud as she went.

²⁰Her brother Absalom said to her, "Has that Amnon, your brother, been with you? Be quiet now, my sister; he is your brother. Don't take this thing to heart." And Tamar lived in her brother Absalom's house, a desolate woman.

²¹When King David heard all this, he was furious. ²²Absalom never said a word to Amnon, either good or bad; he hated Amnon because he had disgraced his sister Tamar.

²³Two years later, when Absalom's sheepshearers were at Baal Hazor near the border of Ephraim, he invited all the king's sons to come there. ²⁴Absalom went to the king and said, "Your servant has had shearers come. Will the king and his officials please join me?"

²⁵"No, my son," the king replied. "All of us should not go; we would only be a burden to you." Although Absalom urged him, he still refused to go, but gave him his blessing.

²⁶Then Absalom said, "If not, please let my brother Amnon come with us."

The king asked him, "Why should he go with you?" ²⁷But Absalom urged him, so he sent with him Amnon and the rest of the king's sons.

²⁸Absalom ordered his men, "Listen! When Amnon is in high spirits from drinking wine and I say to you, 'Strike Amnon down,' then kill him. Don't be afraid. Have not I given you this order? Be strong and brave." ²⁹So Absalom's men did to Amnon what Absalom had ordered. Then all the king's sons got up, mounted their mules and fled.

³⁰While they were on their way, the report came to David: "Absalom has struck down all the king's sons; not one of them is left." ³¹The king stood up, tore his clothes and lay down on the ground; and all his servants stood by with their clothes torn.

³²But Jonadab son of Shimeah, David's brother, said, "My lord should not think that they killed all the princes; only Amnon is dead. This has been Absalom's expressed intention ever since the day Amnon raped his sister Tamar. ³³My lord the king should not be concerned about the report that all the king's sons are dead. Only Amnon is dead."

³⁴Meanwhile, Absalom had fled.

Now the man standing watch looked up and saw many people on the road west of him, coming down the side of the hill. The watchman went and told the king, "I see men in the direction of Horonaim, on the side of the hill." ^{m}

³⁵Jonadab said to the king, "See, the king's sons are here; it has happened just as your servant said."

³⁶As he finished speaking, the king's sons came in, wailing loudly. The king, too, and all his servants wept very bitterly.

³⁷Absalom fled and went to Talmai son of Ammihud, the king of Geshur. But King David mourned for his son every day.

³⁸After Absalom fled and went to Geshur, he stayed there three years. ³⁹And the spirit of the king ^{n} longed to go to Absalom, for he was consoled concerning Amnon's death.

CHAPTER 14

Joab son of Zeruiah knew that the king's heart longed for Absalom. ²So Joab sent someone to Tekoa and had a wise woman brought from there. He said to her, "Pretend you are in mourning. Dress in mourning clothes, and don't use any cosmetic lotions. Act like a woman who has

$^k18$ The meaning of the Hebrew for this phrase is uncertain. $^l19$ The meaning of the Hebrew for this word is uncertain.
$^m34$ Septuagint; Hebrew does not have this sentence. $^n39$ Dead Sea Scrolls and some Septuagint manuscripts; Masoretic Text But ⌊the spirit of⌋ David the king

spent many days grieving for the dead. ³Then go to the king and speak these words to him." And Joab put the words in her mouth.

⁴When the woman from Tekoa went⁰ to the king, she fell with her face to the ground to pay him honor, and she said, "Help me, O king!"

⁵The king asked her, "What is troubling you?"

She said, "I am indeed a widow; my husband is dead. ⁶I your servant had two sons. They got into a fight with each other in the field, and no one was there to separate them. One struck the other and killed him. ⁷Now the whole clan has risen up against your servant; they say, 'Hand over the one who struck his brother down, so that we may put him to death for the life of his brother whom he killed; then we will get rid of the heir as well.' They would put out the only burning coal I have left, leaving my husband neither name nor descendant on the face of the earth."

⁸The king said to the woman, "Go home, and I will issue an order in your behalf."

⁹But the woman from Tekoa said to him, "My lord the king, let the blame rest on me and on my father's family, and let the king and his throne be without guilt."

¹⁰The king replied, "If anyone says anything to you, bring him to me, and he will not bother you again."

¹¹She said, "Then let the king invoke the LORD his God to prevent the avenger of blood from adding to the destruction, so that my son will not be destroyed."

"As surely as the LORD lives," he said, "not one hair of your son's head will fall to the ground."

¹²Then the woman said, "Let your servant speak a word to my lord the king."

"Speak," he replied.

¹³The woman said, "Why then have you devised a thing like this against the people of God? When the king says this, does he not convict himself, for the king has not brought back his banished son? ¹⁴Like water spilled on the ground, which cannot be recovered, so we must die. But God does not take away life; instead, he devises ways so that a banished person may not remain estranged from him.

¹⁵"And now I have come to say this to my lord the king because the people have made me afraid. Your servant thought, 'I will speak to the king; perhaps he will do what his servant asks. ¹⁶Perhaps the king will agree to deliver his servant from the hand of the man who is trying to cut off both me and my son from the inheritance God gave us.'

¹⁷"And now your servant says, 'May the word of my lord the king bring me rest, for my lord the king is like an angel of God in discerning good and evil. May the LORD your God be with you.' "

¹⁸Then the king said to the woman, "Do not keep from me the answer to what I am going to ask you."

"Let my lord the king speak," the woman said.

¹⁹The king asked, "Isn't the hand of Joab with you in all this?"

The woman answered, "As surely as you live, my lord the king, no one can turn to the right or to the left from anything my lord the king says. Yes, it was your servant Joab who instructed me to do this and who put all these words into the mouth of your servant. ²⁰Your servant Joab did this to change the present situation. My lord has wisdom like that of an angel of God—he knows everything that happens in the land."

²¹The king said to Joab, "Very well, I will do it. Go, bring back the young man Absalom."

²²Joab fell with his face to the ground to pay him honor, and he blessed the king. Joab said, "Today your servant knows that he has found favor in your eyes, my lord the king, because the king has granted his servant's request."

²³Then Joab went to Geshur and brought Absalom back to Jerusalem. ²⁴But the king said, "He must go to his own house; he must not see my face." So Absalom went to his own house and did not see the face of the king.

²⁵In all Israel there was not a man so highly praised for his handsome appearance as Absalom. From the top of his head to the sole of his foot there was no blemish in him. ²⁶Whenever he cut the hair of his head—he used to cut his hair from time to time when it became too heavy for him—he would weigh it, and its weight

---

⁰4 Many Hebrew manuscripts, Septuagint, Vulgate and Syriac; most Hebrew manuscripts *spoke*

was two hundred shekels[p] by the royal standard.

[27] Three sons and a daughter were born to Absalom. The daughter's name was Tamar, and she became a beautiful woman.

[28] Absalom lived two years in Jerusalem without seeing the king's face. [29] Then Absalom sent for Joab in order to send him to the king, but Joab refused to come to him. So he sent a second time, but he refused to come. [30] Then he said to his servants, "Look, Joab's field is next to mine, and he has barley there. Go and set it on fire." So Absalom's servants set the field on fire.

[31] Then Joab did go to Absalom's house and he said to him, "Why have your servants set my field on fire?"

[32] Absalom said to Joab, "Look, I sent word to you and said, 'Come here so I can send you to the king to ask, "Why have I come from Geshur? It would be better for me if I were still there!"' Now then, I want to see the king's face, and if I am guilty of anything, let him put me to death."

[33] So Joab went to the king and told him this. Then the king summoned Absalom, and he came in and bowed down with his face to the ground before the king. And the king kissed Absalom.

p26 That is, about 5 pounds (about 2.3 kilograms)

MARCH 28 □ DAY 88
Learning to WOTL

LOOK BACK Here is a hint to help you keep track of 1 and 2 Samuel and 1 and 2 Kings:
- 1 Samuel describes the life of Samuel and the first king he anointed (Saul).
- 2 Samuel describes the life of the second king Samuel anointed (David).
- 1 Kings describes the life of the last king to rule over one kingdom (Solomon).
- 2 Kings describes the demise of two kingdoms (Israel and Judah).

LOOK UP Have you learned how to WOTL yet?

No, we're not talking about how to waddle like a duck but rather how to **W**ait **O**n **T**he **L**ord, like the young shepherd boy David did. The youngest of eight brothers, entrusted with the unenviable "chore" of tending the family's flocks, David could have viewed his job as monotonous and his future as bleak. Instead, he looked for and found constructive ways to pass the time while tending the sheep.

There are times when God asks nothing of his children except silence, patience and tears.

Notice the way this young shepherd is described in 1 Samuel 16:18. He had earned a remarkable reputation in the obscurity of the sheepfold:
- "knows how to play the harp"; he was an accomplished musician who practiced long hours, though his only audience consisted of sheep and stars.
- "a brave man"; he taught bears and lions not to fool with his flock.
- "a warrior"; he had a slingshot that seldom missed its mark.
- "he speaks well"; he didn't butcher the king's Hebrew.
- "a fine-looking man"; he lived in the bush but didn't look like one.
- "the LORD is with him"; God's blessing upon his life was evident to all.

LOOK AHEAD It's not much fun tending sheep. The hours are long, the task demanding, the pay disappointing—and the sheep almost never say *thaaaaaaanks.*

But it's remarkable how many people take on the challenge nonetheless: teachers, their students; parents, their infant children; ministers, their congregations. They understand the importance of a long-term perspective, the need for patience and determination if a harvest is ever to be realized in the next generation.

David saw each day as an opportunity to develop his walk with God. He composed songs, practiced his harp and sling, defended his flock against all predators and sought to develop himself in body, soul and spirit. Twice presented with a tempting opportunity to cut short the wait, David chose to WOTL rather than lift his hand against King Saul.

Write *WOTL* on a three-by-five-inch card, and place it where you're likely to see it often today (such as next to the telephone or on the refrigerator). Let it remind you that you're never *late* when you *wait* on the Lord!

MARCH 29 ☐ DAY 89
2 SAMUEL 15–18
Absalom's Quest to Rule

 OVERVIEW Absalom, David's handsome but undisciplined son, initiates a plot to take away the reins of leadership from his father. True to Nathan's prophecy (12:11–12), Absalom first sows seeds of discontent in Israel, then leads an invasion against Jerusalem that forces David to flee for his life. The nation temporarily sides with Absalom until his humiliating death, while hanging from an oak tree, cuts short his brief revolt. Though David wins the battle, he loses a son, leaving him a broken parent who has paid a staggering price for lax discipline.

Chapter 15	Chapter 16	Chapter 17	Chapter 18
Absalom's Conspiracy	Shimei's Curse	Ahithophel's Counsel	Joab's Cruelty
Starting a Rebellion		Stopping a Rebellion	

 YOUR DAILY WALK "This is going to hurt me more than it hurts you" is probably one of the most "unbelievable" things a parent can say to a child—at least from the child's perspective! Though the parent's words are sincere, the child finds them hard to believe since it isn't
The alternative Mom or Dad who feels the sting of the paddle.
to discipline 　Discipline, regardless of the form it takes, is never pleasant for the
is disaster. moment (Hebrews 12:11). But it is necessary in order to ensure that both parent and child aren't hurt even more in the future when they begin to reap the consequences of a lack of discipline.

King David, preoccupied with his royal duties, allowed his wayward son to continue in disobedience. Had David attempted to curb Absalom's rebellion, it would have been painful to be sure—but not nearly as painful as the grief David experienced when his son died a rebel. Do you see discipline as a pain to be avoided or as a means of avoiding pain? In the margin, write down three reasons why children need to be disciplined in love. If you're a parent, learn from David's sad example. If you're not a parent, pass along your insights to someone who can use them!

INSIGHT The High Cost of High-Mindedness
Absalom was noted for being a fine physical specimen who gloried in his phenomenal head of hair, from which seven pounds were trimmed annually. Ironically, it was his ego that led him astray (14:25–26) and his hair that trapped him and led to his death.

CHAPTER 15
In the course of time, Absalom provided himself with a chariot and horses and with fifty men to run ahead of him. ²He would get up early and stand by the side of the road leading to the city gate. Whenever anyone came with a complaint to be placed before the king for a decision, Absalom would call out to him, "What town are you from?" He would answer, "Your servant is from one of the tribes of Israel." ³Then Absalom would say to him, "Look, your claims are valid and proper, but there is no representative of the king to hear you." ⁴And Absalom would add, "If only I were appointed judge in the land! Then everyone who has a complaint or case could come to me and I would see that he gets justice."

⁵Also, whenever anyone approached him to bow down before him, Absalom would reach out his hand, take hold of him and kiss him. ⁶Absalom behaved in this way toward all the Israelites who came to the king asking for justice, and so he stole the hearts of the men of Israel.

⁷At the end of four*q* years, Absalom said to the king, "Let me go to Hebron and fulfill a vow I made to the LORD. ⁸While your servant was living at Geshur in Aram, I made this vow: 'If the LORD takes me back to Jerusalem, I will worship the LORD in Hebron.'*r*'"

⁹The king said to him, "Go in peace." So he went to Hebron.

¹⁰Then Absalom sent secret messengers throughout the tribes of Israel to say, "As soon as you hear the sound of the trumpets, then say, 'Absalom is king in Hebron.'" ¹¹Two hundred men from Jerusalem had accompanied Absalom. They had been invited as guests and went quite innocently, knowing nothing about the matter. ¹²While Absalom was offering sacrifices, he also sent for Ahithophel the Gilonite, David's counselor, to come from

Giloh, his hometown. And so the conspiracy gained strength, and Absalom's following kept on increasing.

¹³A messenger came and told David, "The hearts of the men of Israel are with Absalom."

¹⁴Then David said to all his officials who were with him in Jerusalem, "Come! We must flee, or none of us will escape from Absalom. We must leave immediately, or he will move quickly to overtake us and bring ruin upon us and put the city to the sword."

¹⁵The king's officials answered him, "Your servants are ready to do whatever our lord the king chooses."

¹⁶The king set out, with his entire household following him; but he left ten concubines to take care of the palace. ¹⁷So the king set out, with all the people following him, and they halted at a place some distance away. ¹⁸All his men marched past him, along with all the Kerethites and Pelethites; and all the six hundred Gittites who had accompanied him from Gath marched before the king.

¹⁹The king said to Ittai the Gittite, "Why should you come along with us? Go back and stay with King Absalom. You are a foreigner, an exile from your homeland. ²⁰You came only yesterday. And today shall I make you wander about with us, when I do not know where I am going? Go back, and take your countrymen. May kindness and faithfulness be with you."

²¹But Ittai replied to the king, "As surely as the LORD lives, and as my lord the king lives, wherever my lord the king may be, whether it means life or death, there will your servant be."

²²David said to Ittai, "Go ahead, march on." So Ittai the Gittite marched on with all his men and the families that were with him.

²³The whole countryside wept aloud as all the people passed by. The king also

q7 Some Septuagint manuscripts, Syriac and Josephus; Hebrew forty   r8 Some Septuagint manuscripts; Hebrew does not have in Hebron.

crossed the Kidron Valley, and all the people moved on toward the desert.

²⁴Zadok was there, too, and all the Levites who were with him were carrying the ark of the covenant of God. They set down the ark of God, and Abiathar offered sacrificesˢ until all the people had finished leaving the city.

²⁵Then the king said to Zadok, "Take the ark of God back into the city. If I find favor in the LORD's eyes, he will bring me back and let me see it and his dwelling place again. ²⁶But if he says, 'I am not pleased with you,' then I am ready; let him do to me whatever seems good to him."

²⁷The king also said to Zadok the priest, "Aren't you a seer? Go back to the city in peace, with your son Ahimaaz and Jonathan son of Abiathar. You and Abiathar take your two sons with you. ²⁸I will wait at the fords in the desert until word comes from you to inform me." ²⁹So Zadok and Abiathar took the ark of God back to Jerusalem and stayed there.

³⁰But David continued up the Mount of Olives, weeping as he went; his head was covered and he was barefoot. All the people with him covered their heads too and were weeping as they went up. ³¹Now David had been told, "Ahithophel is among the conspirators with Absalom." So David prayed, "O LORD, turn Ahithophel's counsel into foolishness."

³²When David arrived at the summit, where people used to worship God, Hushai the Arkite was there to meet him, his robe torn and dust on his head. ³³David said to him, "If you go with me, you will be a burden to me. ³⁴But if you return to the city and say to Absalom, 'I will be your servant, O king; I was your father's servant in the past, but now I will be your servant,' then you can help me by frustrating Ahithophel's advice. ³⁵Won't the priests Zadok and Abiathar be there with you? Tell them anything you hear in the king's palace. ³⁶Their two sons, Ahimaaz son of Zadok and Jonathan son of Abiathar, are there with them. Send them to me with anything you hear."

³⁷So David's friend Hushai arrived at Jerusalem as Absalom was entering the city.

ˢ24 Or *Abiathar went up*

CHAPTER 16

When David had gone a short distance beyond the summit, there was Ziba, the steward of Mephibosheth, waiting to meet him. He had a string of donkeys saddled and loaded with two hundred loaves of bread, a hundred cakes of raisins, a hundred cakes of figs and a skin of wine.

²The king asked Ziba, "Why have you brought these?"

Ziba answered, "The donkeys are for the king's household to ride on, the bread and fruit are for the men to eat, and the wine is to refresh those who become exhausted in the desert."

³The king then asked, "Where is your master's grandson?"

Ziba said to him, "He is staying in Jerusalem, because he thinks, 'Today the house of Israel will give me back my grandfather's kingdom.' "

⁴Then the king said to Ziba, "All that belonged to Mephibosheth is now yours."

"I humbly bow," Ziba said. "May I find favor in your eyes, my lord the king."

⁵As King David approached Bahurim, a man from the same clan as Saul's family came out from there. His name was Shimei son of Gera, and he cursed as he came out. ⁶He pelted David and all the king's officials with stones, though all the troops and the special guard were on David's right and left. ⁷As he cursed, Shimei said, "Get out, get out, you man of blood, you scoundrel! ⁸The LORD has repaid you for all the blood you shed in the household of Saul, in whose place you have reigned. The LORD has handed the kingdom over to your son Absalom. You have come to ruin because you are a man of blood!"

⁹Then Abishai son of Zeruiah said to the king, "Why should this dead dog curse my lord the king? Let me go over and cut off his head."

¹⁰But the king said, "What do you and I have in common, you sons of Zeruiah? If he is cursing because the LORD said to him, 'Curse David,' who can ask, 'Why do you do this?' "

¹¹David then said to Abishai and all his officials, "My son, who is of my own flesh, is trying to take my life. How much more, then, this Benjamite! Leave him alone; let

him curse, for the LORD has told him to. ¹²It may be that the LORD will see my distress and repay me with good for the cursing I am receiving today."

¹³So David and his men continued along the road while Shimei was going along the hillside opposite him, cursing as he went and throwing stones at him and showering him with dirt. ¹⁴The king and all the people with him arrived at their destination exhausted. And there he refreshed himself.

¹⁵Meanwhile, Absalom and all the men of Israel came to Jerusalem, and Ahithophel was with him. ¹⁶Then Hushai the Arkite, David's friend, went to Absalom and said to him, "Long live the king! Long live the king!"

¹⁷Absalom asked Hushai, "Is this the love you show your friend? Why didn't you go with your friend?"

¹⁸Hushai said to Absalom, "No, the one chosen by the LORD, by these people, and by all the men of Israel—his I will be, and I will remain with him. ¹⁹Furthermore, whom should I serve? Should I not serve the son? Just as I served your father, so I will serve you."

²⁰Absalom said to Ahithophel, "Give us your advice. What should we do?"

²¹Ahithophel answered, "Lie with your father's concubines whom he left to take care of the palace. Then all Israel will hear that you have made yourself a stench in your father's nostrils, and the hands of everyone with you will be strengthened." ²²So they pitched a tent for Absalom on the roof, and he lay with his father's concubines in the sight of all Israel.

²³Now in those days the advice Ahithophel gave was like that of one who inquires of God. That was how both David and Absalom regarded all of Ahithophel's advice.

CHAPTER 17
Ahithophel said to Absalom, "I would ᵗ choose twelve thousand men and set out tonight in pursuit of David. ²I would ᵘ attack him while he is weary and weak. I would ᵘ strike him with terror, and then all the people with him will flee. I would ᵘ strike down only the king ³and bring all the people back to you. The death of the man you seek will mean the

return of all; all the people will be unharmed." ⁴This plan seemed good to Absalom and to all the elders of Israel.

⁵But Absalom said, "Summon also Hushai the Arkite, so we can hear what he has to say." ⁶When Hushai came to him, Absalom said, "Ahithophel has given this advice. Should we do what he says? If not, give us your opinion."

⁷Hushai replied to Absalom, "The advice Ahithophel has given is not good this time. ⁸You know your father and his men; they are fighters, and as fierce as a wild bear robbed of her cubs. Besides, your father is an experienced fighter; he will not spend the night with the troops. ⁹Even now, he is hidden in a cave or some other place. If he should attack your troops first,ᵛ whoever hears about it will say, 'There has been a slaughter among the troops who follow Absalom.' ¹⁰Then even the bravest soldier, whose heart is like the heart of a lion, will melt with fear, for all Israel knows that your father is a fighter and that those with him are brave.

¹¹"So I advise you: Let all Israel, from Dan to Beersheba—as numerous as the sand on the seashore—be gathered to you, with you yourself leading them into battle. ¹²Then we will attack him wherever he may be found, and we will fall on him as dew settles on the ground. Neither he nor any of his men will be left alive. ¹³If he withdraws into a city, then all Israel will bring ropes to that city, and we will drag it down to the valley until not even a piece of it can be found."

¹⁴Absalom and all the men of Israel said, "The advice of Hushai the Arkite is better than that of Ahithophel." For the LORD had determined to frustrate the good advice of Ahithophel in order to bring disaster on Absalom.

¹⁵Hushai told Zadok and Abiathar, the priests, "Ahithophel has advised Absalom and the elders of Israel to do such and such, but I have advised them to do so and so. ¹⁶Now send a message immediately and tell David, 'Do not spend the night at the fords in the desert; cross over without fail, or the king and all the people with him will be swallowed up.' "

¹⁷Jonathan and Ahimaaz were staying at En Rogel. A servant girl was to go and inform them, and they were to go and tell

King David, for they could not risk being seen entering the city. [18]But a young man saw them and told Absalom. So the two of them left quickly and went to the house of a man in Bahurim. He had a well in his courtyard, and they climbed down into it. [19]His wife took a covering and spread it out over the opening of the well and scattered grain over it. No one knew anything about it.

[20]When Absalom's men came to the woman at the house, they asked, "Where are Ahimaaz and Jonathan?"

The woman answered them, "They crossed over the brook."[w] The men searched but found no one, so they returned to Jerusalem.

[21]After the men had gone, the two climbed out of the well and went to inform King David. They said to him, "Set out and cross the river at once; Ahithophel has advised such and such against you." [22]So David and all the people with him set out and crossed the Jordan. By daybreak, no one was left who had not crossed the Jordan.

[23]When Ahithophel saw that his advice had not been followed, he saddled his donkey and set out for his house in his hometown. He put his house in order and then hanged himself. So he died and was buried in his father's tomb.

[24]David went to Mahanaim, and Absalom crossed the Jordan with all the men of Israel. [25]Absalom had appointed Amasa over the army in place of Joab. Amasa was the son of a man named Jether,[x] an Israelite[y] who had married Abigail,[z] the daughter of Nahash and sister of Zeruiah the mother of Joab. [26]The Israelites and Absalom camped in the land of Gilead.

[27]When David came to Mahanaim, Shobi son of Nahash from Rabbah of the Ammonites, and Makir son of Ammiel from Lo Debar, and Barzillai the Gileadite from Rogelim [28]brought bedding and bowls and articles of pottery. They also brought wheat and barley, flour and roasted grain, beans and lentils,[a] [29]honey and curds, sheep, and cheese from cows' milk for David and his people to eat. For they said, "The people have become hungry and tired and thirsty in the desert."

CHAPTER 18

David mustered the men who were with him and appointed over them commanders of thousands and commanders of hundreds. [2]David sent the troops out—a third under the command of Joab, a third under Joab's brother Abishai son of Zeruiah, and a third under Ittai the Gittite. The king told the troops, "I myself will surely march out with you."

[3]But the men said, "You must not go out; if we are forced to flee, they won't care about us. Even if half of us die, they won't care; but you are worth ten thousand of us.[b] It would be better now for you to give us support from the city."

[4]The king answered, "I will do whatever seems best to you."

So the king stood beside the gate while all the men marched out in units of hundreds and of thousands. [5]The king commanded Joab, Abishai and Ittai, "Be gentle with the young man Absalom for my sake." And all the troops heard the king giving orders concerning Absalom to each of the commanders.

[6]The army marched into the field to fight Israel, and the battle took place in the forest of Ephraim. [7]There the army of Israel was defeated by David's men, and the casualties that day were great—twenty thousand men. [8]The battle spread out over the whole countryside, and the forest claimed more lives that day than the sword.

[9]Now Absalom happened to meet David's men. He was riding his mule, and as the mule went under the thick branches of a large oak, Absalom's head got caught in the tree. He was left hanging in midair, while the mule he was riding kept on going.

[10]When one of the men saw this, he told Joab, "I just saw Absalom hanging in an oak tree."

[11]Joab said to the man who had told him this, "What! You saw him? Why didn't you strike him to the ground right there? Then I would have had to give you ten shekels[c] of silver and a warrior's belt."

[12]But the man replied, "Even if a thousand shekels[d] were weighed out into my

hands, I would not lift my hand against the king's son. In our hearing the king commanded you and Abishai and Ittai, 'Protect the young man Absalom for my sake.'*ᵉ* ¹³And if I had put my life in jeopardy*ᶠ*—and nothing is hidden from the king—you would have kept your distance from me."

¹⁴Joab said, "I'm not going to wait like this for you." So he took three javelins in his hand and plunged them into Absalom's heart while Absalom was still alive in the oak tree. ¹⁵And ten of Joab's armor-bearers surrounded Absalom, struck him and killed him.

¹⁶Then Joab sounded the trumpet, and the troops stopped pursuing Israel, for Joab halted them. ¹⁷They took Absalom, threw him into a big pit in the forest and piled up a large heap of rocks over him. Meanwhile, all the Israelites fled to their homes.

¹⁸During his lifetime Absalom had taken a pillar and erected it in the King's Valley as a monument to himself, for he thought, "I have no son to carry on the memory of my name." He named the pillar after himself, and it is called Absalom's Monument to this day.

¹⁹Now Ahimaaz son of Zadok said, "Let me run and take the news to the king that the LORD has delivered him from the hand of his enemies."

²⁰"You are not the one to take the news today," Joab told him. "You may take the news another time, but you must not do so today, because the king's son is dead."

²¹Then Joab said to a Cushite, "Go, tell the king what you have seen." The Cushite bowed down before Joab and ran off.

²²Ahimaaz son of Zadok again said to Joab, "Come what may, please let me run behind the Cushite."

But Joab replied, "My son, why do you want to go? You don't have any news that will bring you a reward."

²³He said, "Come what may, I want to run."

So Joab said, "Run!" Then Ahimaaz ran by way of the plain*ᵍ* and outran the Cushite.

²⁴While David was sitting between the inner and outer gates, the watchman went up to the roof of the gateway by the wall. As he looked out, he saw a man running alone. ²⁵The watchman called out to the king and reported it.

The king said, "If he is alone, he must have good news." And the man came closer and closer.

²⁶Then the watchman saw another man running, and he called down to the gatekeeper, "Look, another man running alone!"

The king said, "He must be bringing good news, too."

²⁷The watchman said, "It seems to me that the first one runs like Ahimaaz son of Zadok."

"He's a good man," the king said. "He comes with good news."

²⁸Then Ahimaaz called out to the king, "All is well!" He bowed down before the king with his face to the ground and said, "Praise be to the LORD your God! He has delivered up the men who lifted their hands against my lord the king."

²⁹The king asked, "Is the young man Absalom safe?"

Ahimaaz answered, "I saw great confusion just as Joab was about to send the king's servant and me, your servant, but I don't know what it was."

³⁰The king said, "Stand aside and wait here." So he stepped aside and stood there.

³¹Then the Cushite arrived and said, "My lord the king, hear the good news! The LORD has delivered you today from all who rose up against you."

³²The king asked the Cushite, "Is the young man Absalom safe?"

The Cushite replied, "May the enemies of my lord the king and all who rise up to harm you be like that young man."

³³The king was shaken. He went up to the room over the gateway and wept. As he went, he said: "O my son Absalom! My son, my son Absalom! If only I had died instead of you—O Absalom, my son, my son!"

ᵉ12 A few Hebrew manuscripts, Septuagint, Vulgate and Syriac; most Hebrew manuscripts may be translated *Absalom, whoever you may be.*   *ᶠ13* Or *Otherwise, if I had acted treacherously toward him*   *ᵍ23* That is, the plain of the Jordan

MARCH 30 □ DAY 90
2 SAMUEL 19–20
David's Return to the Throne

OVERVIEW David's grief over the death of Absalom causes him to overlook the people who risked their lives to help restore his rule over Israel. Alerted to the danger of this situation by General Joab, David responds by accompanying his faithful followers in a triumphal return to Jerusalem. But though David has been successful in putting down one rebellion, he must soon confront another in the person of Sheba. Only when it has been crushed can David reign over a reunited kingdom.

Chapter 19			Chapter 20
Joab's Rebuke		David's Return	Sheba's Revolt
1	14	15	43
David's Throne Restored			David's Throne Threatened

There is a vast difference between putting your nose in other people's business and putting your heart in other people's problems.

YOUR DAILY WALK In a humorous television commercial, a man nervously rehearses the words he will use to tell his boss he has bad breath (which, of course, can only be eliminated by using a particular brand of mouthwash). Fortunately for the employee, the boss discovers the "cure" on his own, thus avoiding the confrontation.

Two men in David's life faced situations far more serious than that of telling the king he needed to freshen his breath. Both were used by God to "freshen up" David's spiritual life and jar him back to reality. When David was seeking to cover up his sin with Bathsheba, Nathan boldly announced to the king, "You are the man!" (12:7)—words that helped David come to grips with his sin. Later, as David mourned the death of Absalom, Joab prevented mutiny in the army by exhorting his commander in chief, "Now go out and encourage your men" (19:7)—strong words that could have cost Joab his job and his life. Yet he had the courage to exhort his king and friend.

Do you have the holy boldness of a Nathan or a Joab? When those you love need to hear the truth about themselves, can you speak the truth in love? To help you recognize the importance of sensitive confrontation, meditate on Proverbs 27:6: "Wounds from a friend can be trusted, but an enemy multiplies kisses."

INSIGHT Politics in David's Day
Compare the list of David's "cabinet members" in 20:23–26 with an earlier list in 8:15–18 and watch for the differences. Can you spot who has been replaced and who is still "in office"?

CHAPTER 19
Joab was told, "The king is weeping and mourning for Absalom." ²And for the whole army the victory that day was turned into mourning, because on that day the troops heard it said, "The king is grieving for his son." ³The men stole into the city that day as men steal in who are ashamed when they flee from battle. ⁴The king covered his face and cried aloud,

"O my son Absalom! O Absalom, my son, my son!"

⁵Then Joab went into the house to the king and said, "Today you have humiliated all your men, who have just saved your life and the lives of your sons and daughters and the lives of your wives and concubines. ⁶You love those who hate you and hate those who love you. You have made it clear today that the commanders

and their men mean nothing to you. I see that you would be pleased if Absalom were alive today and all of us were dead. [7]Now go out and encourage your men. I swear by the LORD that if you don't go out, not a man will be left with you by nightfall. This will be worse for you than all the calamities that have come upon you from your youth till now."

[8]So the king got up and took his seat in the gateway. When the men were told, "The king is sitting in the gateway," they all came before him.

Meanwhile, the Israelites had fled to their homes. [9]Throughout the tribes of Israel, the people were all arguing with each other, saying, "The king delivered us from the hand of our enemies; he is the one who rescued us from the hand of the Philistines. But now he has fled the country because of Absalom; [10]and Absalom, whom we anointed to rule over us, has died in battle. So why do you say nothing about bringing the king back?"

[11]King David sent this message to Zadok and Abiathar, the priests: "Ask the elders of Judah, 'Why should you be the last to bring the king back to his palace, since what is being said throughout Israel has reached the king at his quarters? [12]You are my brothers, my own flesh and blood. So why should you be the last to bring back the king?' [13]And say to Amasa, 'Are you not my own flesh and blood? May God deal with me, be it ever so severely, if from now on you are not the commander of my army in place of Joab.'"

[14]He won over the hearts of all the men of Judah as though they were one man. They sent word to the king, "Return, you and all your men." [15]Then the king returned and went as far as the Jordan.

Now the men of Judah had come to Gilgal to go out and meet the king and bring him across the Jordan. [16]Shimei son of Gera, the Benjamite from Bahurim, hurried down with the men of Judah to meet King David. [17]With him were a thousand Benjamites, along with Ziba, the steward of Saul's household, and his fifteen sons and twenty servants. They rushed to the Jordan, where the king was. [18]They crossed at the ford to take the king's household over and to do whatever he wished.

When Shimei son of Gera crossed the Jordan, he fell prostrate before the king [19]and said to him, "May my lord not hold me guilty. Do not remember how your servant did wrong on the day my lord the king left Jerusalem. May the king put it out of his mind. [20]For I your servant know that I have sinned, but today I have come here as the first of the whole house of Joseph to come down and meet my lord the king."

[21]Then Abishai son of Zeruiah said, "Shouldn't Shimei be put to death for this? He cursed the LORD's anointed."

[22]David replied, "What do you and I have in common, you sons of Zeruiah? This day you have become my adversaries! Should anyone be put to death in Israel today? Do I not know that today I am king over Israel?" [23]So the king said to Shimei, "You shall not die." And the king promised him on oath.

[24]Mephibosheth, Saul's grandson, also went down to meet the king. He had not taken care of his feet or trimmed his mustache or washed his clothes from the day the king left until the day he returned safely. [25]When he came from Jerusalem to meet the king, the king asked him, "Why didn't you go with me, Mephibosheth?"

[26]He said, "My lord the king, since I your servant am lame, I said, 'I will have my donkey saddled and will ride on it, so I can go with the king.' But Ziba my servant betrayed me. [27]And he has slandered your servant to my lord the king. My lord the king is like an angel of God; so do whatever pleases you. [28]All my grandfather's descendants deserved nothing but death from my lord the king, but you gave your servant a place among those who eat at your table. So what right do I have to make any more appeals to the king?"

[29]The king said to him, "Why say more? I order you and Ziba to divide the fields."

[30]Mephibosheth said to the king, "Let him take everything, now that my lord the king has arrived home safely."

[31]Barzillai the Gileadite also came down from Rogelim to cross the Jordan with the king and to send him on his way from there. [32]Now Barzillai was a very old man, eighty years of age. He had provided for the king during his stay in Mahanaim, for he was a very wealthy man. [33]The king said to Barzillai, "Cross over

with me and stay with me in Jerusalem, and I will provide for you."

³⁴But Barzillai answered the king, "How many more years will I live, that I should go up to Jerusalem with the king? ³⁵I am now eighty years old. Can I tell the difference between what is good and what is not? Can your servant taste what he eats and drinks? Can I still hear the voices of men and women singers? Why should your servant be an added burden to my lord the king? ³⁶Your servant will cross over the Jordan with the king for a short distance, but why should the king reward me in this way? ³⁷Let your servant return, that I may die in my own town near the tomb of my father and mother. But here is your servant Kimham. Let him cross over with my lord the king. Do for him whatever pleases you."

³⁸The king said, "Kimham shall cross over with me, and I will do for him whatever pleases you. And anything you desire from me I will do for you."

³⁹So all the people crossed the Jordan, and then the king crossed over. The king kissed Barzillai and gave him his blessing, and Barzillai returned to his home.

⁴⁰When the king crossed over to Gilgal, Kimham crossed with him. All the troops of Judah and half the troops of Israel had taken the king over.

⁴¹Soon all the men of Israel were coming to the king and saying to him, "Why did our brothers, the men of Judah, steal the king away and bring him and his household across the Jordan, together with all his men?"

⁴²All the men of Judah answered the men of Israel, "We did this because the king is closely related to us. Why are you angry about it? Have we eaten any of the king's provisions? Have we taken anything for ourselves?"

⁴³Then the men of Israel answered the men of Judah, "We have ten shares in the king; and besides, we have a greater claim on David than you have. So why do you treat us with contempt? Were we not the first to speak of bringing back our king?"

But the men of Judah responded even more harshly than the men of Israel.

CHAPTER 20

Now a troublemaker named Sheba son of Bicri, a Benjamite, happened to be there.

He sounded the trumpet and shouted,

"We have no share in David,
  no part in Jesse's son!
Every man to his tent, O Israel!"

²So all the men of Israel deserted David to follow Sheba son of Bicri. But the men of Judah stayed by their king all the way from the Jordan to Jerusalem.

³When David returned to his palace in Jerusalem, he took the ten concubines he had left to take care of the palace and put them in a house under guard. He provided for them, but did not lie with them. They were kept in confinement till the day of their death, living as widows.

⁴Then the king said to Amasa, "Summon the men of Judah to come to me within three days, and be here yourself." ⁵But when Amasa went to summon Judah, he took longer than the time the king had set for him.

⁶David said to Abishai, "Now Sheba son of Bicri will do us more harm than Absalom did. Take your master's men and pursue him, or he will find fortified cities and escape from us." ⁷So Joab's men and the Kerethites and Pelethites and all the mighty warriors went out under the command of Abishai. They marched out from Jerusalem to pursue Sheba son of Bicri.

⁸While they were at the great rock in Gibeon, Amasa came to meet them. Joab was wearing his military tunic, and strapped over it at his waist was a belt with a dagger in its sheath. As he stepped forward, it dropped out of its sheath.

⁹Joab said to Amasa, "How are you, my brother?" Then Joab took Amasa by the beard with his right hand to kiss him. ¹⁰Amasa was not on his guard against the dagger in Joab's hand, and Joab plunged it into his belly, and his intestines spilled out on the ground. Without being stabbed again, Amasa died. Then Joab and his brother Abishai pursued Sheba son of Bicri.

¹¹One of Joab's men stood beside Amasa and said, "Whoever favors Joab, and whoever is for David, let him follow Joab!" ¹²Amasa lay wallowing in his blood in the middle of the road, and the man saw that all the troops came to a halt there. When he realized that everyone who came up to Amasa stopped, he

dragged him from the road into a field and threw a garment over him. [13]After Amasa had been removed from the road, all the men went on with Joab to pursue Sheba son of Bicri.

[14]Sheba passed through all the tribes of Israel to Abel Beth Maacah[h] and through the entire region of the Berites, who gathered together and followed him. [15]All the troops with Joab came and besieged Sheba in Abel Beth Maacah. They built a siege ramp up to the city, and it stood against the outer fortifications. While they were battering the wall to bring it down, [16]a wise woman called from the city, "Listen! Listen! Tell Joab to come here so I can speak to him." [17]He went toward her, and she asked, "Are you Joab?"

"I am," he answered.

She said, "Listen to what your servant has to say."

"I'm listening," he said.

[18]She continued, "Long ago they used to say, 'Get your answer at Abel,' and that settled it. [19]We are the peaceful and faithful in Israel. You are trying to destroy a city that is a mother in Israel. Why do you want to swallow up the LORD's inheritance?"

[20]"Far be it from me!" Joab replied, "Far be it from me to swallow up or destroy! [21]That is not the case. A man named Sheba son of Bicri, from the hill country of Ephraim, has lifted up his hand against the king, against David. Hand over this one man, and I'll withdraw from the city."

The woman said to Joab, "His head will be thrown to you from the wall."

[22]Then the woman went to all the people with her wise advice, and they cut off the head of Sheba son of Bicri and threw it to Joab. So he sounded the trumpet, and his men dispersed from the city, each returning to his home. And Joab went back to the king in Jerusalem.

[23]Joab was over Israel's entire army; Benaiah son of Jehoiada was over the Kerethites and Pelethites; [24]Adoniram[i] was in charge of forced labor; Jehoshaphat son of Ahilud was recorder; [25]Sheva was secretary; Zadok and Abiathar were priests; [26]and Ira the Jairite was David's priest.

[h]14 Or *Abel, even Beth Maacah*; also in verse 15   [i]24 Some Septuagint manuscripts (see also 1 Kings 4:6 and 5:14); Hebrew *Adoram*

MARCH 31 □ DAY 91
2 SAMUEL 21–24
David's Final Words and Acts

 OVERVIEW Today's section covers six topics that, although out of strict chronological order, form an appendix supplementing the main body of 2 Samuel and, as such, provide a fitting conclusion to the book. The topics include a severe famine sent in judgment for Saul's treatment of the Gibeonites (whom he was committed by oath to protect—21:1); a series of wars with Philistines (apparently toward the very end of David's life—21:15–22); a beautiful psalm of deliverance and praise (including David's last words—23:1–7); a list of David's mighty men of valor (with one startling addition—Uriah!); a sinful census (apparently motivated by pride); and the severe punishment by pestilence that followed it. The closing paragraph of the book portrays David in his most natural pose: worshiping the Lord in humility.

Chapter 21	Chapters 22–23	Chapter 24
Famine and Philistines	Music and Mighty Men	A Proud Census and Painful Punishment
David's Final Words and Acts		

YOUR DAILY WALK Are you on God's list of "mighty men and women"? Don't answer too quickly. God's choices may surprise you!

David composed a list of thirty-seven soldiers from his vast armies, thirty-seven men who, in his estimation, deserved the title "mighty."

A man can be no bigger than the number of people for whom he genuinely cares.

Most of his selections make good sense. After all, who could possibly forget Adino the Eznite, who killed eight hundred men single-handedly? Or Eleazar, the son of Dodai, who one day fought Philistines until his hand "grew tired and froze to the sword"! But there are some curious additions as well. Three men broke through the Philistine lines to bring thirsty King David a cup of cold water from the well near the gate of Bethlehem—and for that they received the same praise as a warrior who killed hundreds.

Stop and think of one specific act you can do today that would be mighty in God's eyes. (Remember, even a cup of cold water given in his name will not go unrewarded.) Now include it in your schedule, and do it! You'll be "mighty" glad you did.

INSIGHT Real Estate Rich with Significance
The book closes with David purchasing the threshing floor on Mount Moriah—the place where Abraham offered Isaac centuries before and where Solomon's temple would soon stand.

CHAPTER 21

During the reign of David, there was a famine for three successive years; so David sought the face of the LORD. The LORD said, "It is on account of Saul and his blood-stained house; it is because he put the Gibeonites to death."

²The king summoned the Gibeonites and spoke to them. (Now the Gibeonites were not a part of Israel but were survivors of the Amorites; the Israelites had sworn to ⌊spare⌋ them, but Saul in his zeal for Israel and Judah had tried to annihilate them.) ³David asked the Gibeonites, "What shall I do for you? How shall I make amends so that you will bless the LORD's inheritance?"

⁴The Gibeonites answered him, "We have no right to demand silver or gold from Saul or his family, nor do we have the right to put anyone in Israel to death."

"What do you want me to do for you?" David asked.

⁵They answered the king, "As for the man who destroyed us and plotted against us so that we have been decimated and have no place anywhere in Israel, ⁶let seven of his male descendants be given to us to be killed and exposed before the LORD at Gibeah of Saul—the LORD's chosen one."

So the king said, "I will give them to you."

⁷The king spared Mephibosheth son of Jonathan, the son of Saul, because of the oath before the LORD between David and Jonathan son of Saul. ⁸But the king took Armoni and Mephibosheth, the two sons of Aiah's daughter Rizpah, whom she had borne to Saul, together with the five sons of Saul's daughter Merab,ʲ whom she had borne to Adriel son of Barzillai the Meholathite. ⁹He handed them over to the Gibeonites, who killed and exposed them on a hill before the LORD. All seven of them fell together; they were put to death during the first days of the harvest, just as the barley harvest was beginning.

¹⁰Rizpah daughter of Aiah took sackcloth and spread it out for herself on a rock. From the beginning of the harvest till the rain poured down from the heavens on the bodies, she did not let the birds of the air touch them by day or the wild animals by night. ¹¹When David was told what Aiah's daughter Rizpah, Saul's concubine, had done, ¹²he went and took the bones of Saul and his son Jonathan from the citizens of Jabesh Gilead. (They had taken them secretly from the public square at Beth Shan, where the Philistines had hung them after they struck Saul down on Gilboa.) ¹³David brought the bones of Saul and his son Jonathan from there, and the bones of those who had been killed and exposed were gathered up.

¹⁴They buried the bones of Saul and his

ʲ8 Two Hebrew manuscripts, some Septuagint manuscripts and Syriac (see also 1 Samuel 18:19); most Hebrew and Septuagint manuscripts *Michal* son Jonathan in the tomb of Saul's father Kish, at Zela in Benjamin, and did everything the king commanded. After that, God answered prayer in behalf of the land.

¹⁵Once again there was a battle between the Philistines and Israel. David went down with his men to fight against the Philistines, and he became exhausted. ¹⁶And Ishbi-Benob, one of the descendants of Rapha, whose bronze spearhead weighed three hundred shekels*ᵏ* and who was armed with a new ₍sword₎, said he would kill David. ¹⁷But Abishai son of Zeruiah came to David's rescue; he struck the Philistine down and killed him. Then David's men swore to him, saying, "Never again will you go out with us to battle, so that the lamp of Israel will not be extinguished."

¹⁸In the course of time, there was another battle with the Philistines, at Gob. At that time Sibbecai the Hushathite killed Saph, one of the descendants of Rapha.

¹⁹In another battle with the Philistines at Gob, Elhanan son of Jaare-Oregim*ˡ* the Bethlehemite killed Goliath*ᵐ* the Gittite, who had a spear with a shaft like a weaver's rod.

²⁰In still another battle, which took place at Gath, there was a huge man with six fingers on each hand and six toes on each foot—twenty-four in all. He also was descended from Rapha. ²¹When he taunted Israel, Jonathan son of Shimeah, David's brother, killed him.

²²These four were descendants of Rapha in Gath, and they fell at the hands of David and his men.

CHAPTER 22

David sang to the LORD the words of this song when the LORD delivered him from the hand of all his enemies and from the hand of Saul. ²He said:

"The LORD is my rock, my fortress and my deliverer;
³   my God is my rock, in whom I take refuge,
   my shield and the horn*ⁿ* of my salvation.

He is my stronghold, my refuge and my savior—
   from violent men you save me.
⁴I call to the LORD, who is worthy of praise,
   and I am saved from my enemies.

⁵"The waves of death swirled about me;
   the torrents of destruction overwhelmed me.
⁶The cords of the grave*ᵒ* coiled around me;
   the snares of death confronted me.
⁷In my distress I called to the LORD;
   I called out to my God.
From his temple he heard my voice;
   my cry came to his ears.

⁸"The earth trembled and quaked,
   the foundations of the heavens*ᵖ* shook;
   they trembled because he was angry.
⁹Smoke rose from his nostrils;
   consuming fire came from his mouth,
   burning coals blazed out of it.
¹⁰He parted the heavens and came down;
   dark clouds were under his feet.
¹¹He mounted the cherubim and flew;
   he soared*�q* on the wings of the wind.
¹²He made darkness his canopy around him—
   the dark*ʳ* rain clouds of the sky.
¹³Out of the brightness of his presence
   bolts of lightning blazed forth.
¹⁴The LORD thundered from heaven;
   the voice of the Most High resounded.
¹⁵He shot arrows and scattered ₍the enemies₎,
   bolts of lightning and routed them.
¹⁶The valleys of the sea were exposed
   and the foundations of the earth laid bare
at the rebuke of the LORD,
   at the blast of breath from his nostrils.

¹⁷"He reached down from on high and took hold of me;
   he drew me out of deep waters.
¹⁸He rescued me from my powerful enemy,

ᵏ16 That is, about 7 1/2 pounds (about 3.5 kilograms)   *ˡ19* Or *son of Jair the weaver*   *ᵐ19* Hebrew and Septuagint; 1 Chron. 20:5 *son of Jair killed Lahmi the brother of Goliath*   *ⁿ3* Horn *here symbolizes strength.*   *ᵒ6* Hebrew *Sheol*   *ᵖ8* Hebrew; Vulgate and Syriac (see also Psalm 18:7) *mountains*   *q11* Many Hebrew manuscripts (see also Psalm 18:10); most Hebrew manuscripts *appeared*   *ʳ12* Septuagint and Vulgate (see also Psalm 18:11); Hebrew *massed*

from my foes, who were too strong
    for me.
¹⁹They confronted me in the day of my
    disaster,
    but the LORD was my support.
²⁰He brought me out into a spacious
    place;
    he rescued me because he delighted
    in me.

²¹"The LORD has dealt with me according
    to my righteousness;
    according to the cleanness of my
    hands he has rewarded me.
²²For I have kept the ways of the LORD;
    I have not done evil by turning from
    my God.
²³All his laws are before me;
    I have not turned away from his
    decrees.
²⁴I have been blameless before him
    and have kept myself from sin.
²⁵The LORD has rewarded me according
    to my righteousness,
    according to my cleanness⁵ in his
    sight.

²⁶"To the faithful you show yourself
    faithful,
    to the blameless you show yourself
    blameless,
²⁷to the pure you show yourself pure,
    but to the crooked you show
    yourself shrewd.
²⁸You save the humble,
    but your eyes are on the haughty to
    bring them low.
²⁹You are my lamp, O LORD;
    the LORD turns my darkness into
    light.
³⁰With your help I can advance against
    a troop ᵗ;
    with my God I can scale a wall.

³¹"As for God, his way is perfect;
    the word of the LORD is flawless.
    He is a shield
    for all who take refuge in him.
³²For who is God besides the LORD?
    And who is the Rock except our
    God?
³³It is God who arms me with strength ᵘ
    and makes my way perfect.
³⁴He makes my feet like the feet of a
    deer;

he enables me to stand on the
    heights.
³⁵He trains my hands for battle;
    my arms can bend a bow of bronze.
³⁶You give me your shield of victory;
    you stoop down to make me great.
³⁷You broaden the path beneath me,
    so that my ankles do not turn.

³⁸"I pursued my enemies and crushed
    them;
    I did not turn back till they were
    destroyed.
³⁹I crushed them completely, and they
    could not rise;
    they fell beneath my feet.
⁴⁰You armed me with strength for battle;
    you made my adversaries bow at
    my feet.
⁴¹You made my enemies turn their
    backs in flight,
    and I destroyed my foes.
⁴²They cried for help, but there was no
    one to save them—
    to the LORD, but he did not answer.
⁴³I beat them as fine as the dust of the
    earth;
    I pounded and trampled them like
    mud in the streets.

⁴⁴"You have delivered me from the
    attacks of my people;
    you have preserved me as the head
    of nations.
People I did not know are subject to
    me,
⁴⁵   and foreigners come cringing to me;
    as soon as they hear me, they obey
    me.
⁴⁶They all lose heart;
    they come trembling ᵛ from their
    strongholds.

⁴⁷"The LORD lives! Praise be to my Rock!
    Exalted be God, the Rock, my
    Savior!
⁴⁸He is the God who avenges me,
    who puts the nations under me,
⁴⁹   who sets me free from my enemies.
You exalted me above my foes;
    from violent men you rescued me.
⁵⁰Therefore I will praise you, O LORD,
    among the nations;
    I will sing praises to your name.
⁵¹He gives his king great victories;

ˢ25 Hebrew; Septuagint and Vulgate (see also Psalm 18:24) *to the cleanness of my hands*   ᵗ30 Or *can run through a barricade*
ᵘ33 Dead Sea Scrolls, some Septuagint manuscripts, Vulgate and Syriac (see also Psalm 18:32); Masoretic Text *who is my strong refuge*   ᵛ46 Some Septuagint manuscripts and Vulgate (see also Psalm 18:45); Masoretic Text *they arm themselves.*

he shows unfailing kindness to his
anointed,
to David and his descendants
forever."

CHAPTER 23
These are the last words of David:

"The oracle of David son of Jesse,
the oracle of the man exalted by the
Most High,
the man anointed by the God of Jacob,
Israel's singer of songs[w]:

[2]"The Spirit of the LORD spoke through
me;
his word was on my tongue.
[3]The God of Israel spoke,
the Rock of Israel said to me:
'When one rules over men in
righteousness,
when he rules in the fear of God,
[4]he is like the light of morning at
sunrise
on a cloudless morning,
like the brightness after rain
that brings the grass from the earth.'

[5]"Is not my house right with God?
Has he not made with me an
everlasting covenant,
arranged and secured in every part?
Will he not bring to fruition my
salvation
and grant me my every desire?
[6]But evil men are all to be cast aside
like thorns,
which are not gathered with the
hand.
[7]Whoever touches thorns
uses a tool of iron or the shaft of a
spear;
they are burned up where they lie."

[8]These are the names of David's mighty
men:
Josheb-Basshebeth,[x] a Tahkemonite,[y]
was chief of the Three; he raised his spear
against eight hundred men, whom he
killed[z] in one encounter.
[9]Next to him was Eleazar son of Dodai
the Ahohite. As one of the three mighty
men, he was with David when they
taunted the Philistines gathered ᴊat Pas
Dammim,[a] for battle. Then the men of

Israel retreated, [10]but he stood his ground
and struck down the Philistines till his
hand grew tired and froze to the sword.
The LORD brought about a great victory
that day. The troops returned to Eleazar,
but only to strip the dead.
[11]Next to him was Shammah son of
Agee the Hararite. When the Philistines
banded together at a place where there
was a field full of lentils, Israel's troops
fled from them. [12]But Shammah took his
stand in the middle of the field. He defended it and struck the Philistines down,
and the LORD brought about a great victory.
[13]During harvest time, three of the
thirty chief men came down to David at
the cave of Adullam, while a band of Philistines was encamped in the Valley of
Rephaim. [14]At that time David was in the
stronghold, and the Philistine garrison
was at Bethlehem. [15]David longed for
water and said, "Oh, that someone would
get me a drink of water from the well near
the gate of Bethlehem!" [16]So the three
mighty men broke through the Philistine
lines, drew water from the well near the
gate of Bethlehem and carried it back to
David. But he refused to drink it; instead,
he poured it out before the LORD. [17]"Far be
it from me, O LORD, to do this!" he said. "Is
it not the blood of men who went at the
risk of their lives?" And David would not
drink it.
Such were the exploits of the three
mighty men.
[18]Abishai the brother of Joab son of
Zeruiah was chief of the Three.[b] He
raised his spear against three hundred
men, whom he killed, and so he became
as famous as the Three. [19]Was he not held
in greater honor than the Three? He became their commander, even though he
was not included among them.
[20]Benaiah son of Jehoiada was a valiant
fighter from Kabzeel, who performed
great exploits. He struck down two of
Moab's best men. He also went down into
a pit on a snowy day and killed a lion.
[21]And he struck down a huge Egyptian.
Although the Egyptian had a spear in his
hand, Benaiah went against him with a
club. He snatched the spear from the

[w]1 Or Israel's beloved singer   [x]8 Hebrew; some Septuagint manuscripts suggest Ish-Bosheth, that is, Esh-Baal (see also
1 Chron. 11:11 Jashobeam).   [y]8 Probably a variant of Hacmonite (see 1 Chron. 11:11)   [z]8 Some Septuagint manuscripts (see
also 1 Chron. 11:11); Hebrew and other Septuagint manuscripts Three; it was Adino the Eznite who killed eight hundred men
[a]9 See 1 Chron. 11:13; Hebrew gathered there.   [b]18 Most Hebrew manuscripts (see also 1 Chron. 11:20); two Hebrew
manuscripts and Syriac Thirty

Egyptian's hand and killed him with his own spear. ²²Such were the exploits of Benaiah son of Jehoiada; he too was as famous as the three mighty men. ²³He was held in greater honor than any of the Thirty, but he was not included among the Three. And David put him in charge of his bodyguard.

²⁴Among the Thirty were:
Asahel the brother of Joab,
Elhanan son of Dodo from Bethle-
    hem,
²⁵Shammah the Harodite,
Elika the Harodite,
²⁶Helez the Paltite,
Ira son of Ikkesh from Tekoa,
²⁷Abiezer from Anathoth,
Mebunnai^c the Hushathite,
²⁸Zalmon the Ahohite,
Maharai the Netophathite,
²⁹Heled^d son of Baanah the Ne-
    tophathite,
Ithai son of Ribai from Gibeah in
    Benjamin,
³⁰Benaiah the Pirathonite,
Hiddai^e from the ravines of Ga-
    ash,
³¹Abi-Albon the Arbathite,
Azmaveth the Barhumite,
³²Eliahba the Shaalbonite,
the sons of Jashen,
Jonathan ³³son of^f Shammah the
    Hararite,
Ahiam son of Sharar^g the Hara-
    rite,
³⁴Eliphelet son of Ahasbai the Maac-
    athite,
Eliam son of Ahithophel the Gilo-
    nite,
³⁵Hezro the Carmelite,
Paarai the Arbite,
³⁶Igal son of Nathan from Zobah,
the son of Hagri,^{h}
³⁷Zelek the Ammonite,
Naharai the Beerothite, the armor-
    bearer of Joab son of Zeruiah,
³⁸Ira the Ithrite,
Gareb the Ithrite,
³⁹and Uriah the Hittite.
There were thirty-seven in all.

CHAPTER 24

Again the anger of the LORD burned against Israel, and he incited David against them, saying, "Go and take a census of Israel and Judah."

²So the king said to Joab and the army commanders^i with him, "Go throughout the tribes of Israel from Dan to Beersheba and enroll the fighting men, so that I may know how many there are."

³But Joab replied to the king, "May the LORD your God multiply the troops a hundred times over, and may the eyes of my lord the king see it. But why does my lord the king want to do such a thing?"

⁴The king's word, however, overruled Joab and the army commanders; so they left the presence of the king to enroll the fighting men of Israel.

⁵After crossing the Jordan, they camped near Aroer, south of the town in the gorge, and then went through Gad and on to Jazer. ⁶They went to Gilead and the region of Tahtim Hodshi, and on to Dan Jaan and around toward Sidon. ⁷Then they went toward the fortress of Tyre and all the towns of the Hivites and Canaanites. Finally, they went on to Beersheba in the Negev of Judah.

⁸After they had gone through the entire land, they came back to Jerusalem at the end of nine months and twenty days.

⁹Joab reported the number of the fighting men to the king: In Israel there were eight hundred thousand able-bodied men who could handle a sword, and in Judah five hundred thousand.

¹⁰David was conscience-stricken after he had counted the fighting men, and he said to the LORD, "I have sinned greatly in what I have done. Now, O LORD, I beg you, take away the guilt of your servant. I have done a very foolish thing."

¹¹Before David got up the next morning, the word of the LORD had come to Gad the prophet, David's seer: ¹²"Go and tell David, 'This is what the LORD says: I am giving you three options. Choose one of them for me to carry out against you.' "

¹³So Gad went to David and said to him, "Shall there come upon you three^j years of famine in your land? Or three

^{c}27 Hebrew; some Septuagint manuscripts (see also 1 Chron. 11:29) *Sibbecai* ^{d}29 Some Hebrew manuscripts and Vulgate (see also 1 Chron. 11:30); most Hebrew manuscripts *Heleb* ^{e}30 Hebrew; some Septuagint manuscripts (see also 1 Chron. 11:32) *Hurai* ^{f}33 Some Septuagint manuscripts (see also 1 Chron. 11:34); Hebrew does not have *son of*. ^{g}33 Hebrew; some Septuagint manuscripts (see also 1 Chron. 11:35) *Sacar* ^{h}36 Some Septuagint manuscripts (see also 1 Chron. 11:38); Hebrew *Haggadi* ^{i}2 Septuagint (see also verse 4 and 1 Chron. 21:2); Hebrew *Joab the army commander* ^{j}13 Septuagint (see also 1 Chron. 21:12); Hebrew *seven* months of fleeing from your enemies while they pursue you? Or three days of plague in your land? Now then, think it over and decide how I should answer the one who sent me."

¹⁴David said to Gad, "I am in deep distress. Let us fall into the hands of the LORD, for his mercy is great; but do not let me fall into the hands of men."

¹⁵So the LORD sent a plague on Israel from that morning until the end of the time designated, and seventy thousand of the people from Dan to Beersheba died. ¹⁶When the angel stretched out his hand to destroy Jerusalem, the LORD was grieved because of the calamity and said to the angel who was afflicting the people, "Enough! Withdraw your hand." The angel of the LORD was then at the threshing floor of Araunah the Jebusite.

¹⁷When David saw the angel who was striking down the people, he said to the LORD, "I am the one who has sinned and done wrong. These are but sheep. What have they done? Let your hand fall upon me and my family."

¹⁸On that day Gad went to David and said to him, "Go up and build an altar to the LORD on the threshing floor of Araunah the Jebusite." ¹⁹So David went up, as the LORD had commanded through Gad.

²⁰When Araunah looked and saw the king and his men coming toward him, he went out and bowed down before the king with his face to the ground.

²¹Araunah said, "Why has my lord the king come to his servant?"

"To buy your threshing floor," David answered, "so I can build an altar to the LORD, that the plague on the people may be stopped."

²²Araunah said to David, "Let my lord the king take whatever pleases him and offer it up. Here are oxen for the burnt offering, and here are threshing sledges and ox yokes for the wood. ²³O king, Araunah gives all this to the king." Araunah also said to him, "May the LORD your God accept you."

²⁴But the king replied to Araunah, "No, I insist on paying you for it. I will not sacrifice to the LORD my God burnt offerings that cost me nothing."

So David bought the threshing floor and the oxen and paid fifty shekels[k] of silver for them. ²⁵David built an altar to the LORD there and sacrificed burnt offerings and fellowship offerings.[l] Then the LORD answered prayer in behalf of the land, and the plague on Israel was stopped.

---

[k]24 That is, about 1 1/4 pounds (about 0.6 kilogram)   [l]25 Traditionally *peace offerings*

1 Kings

AS 1 Kings opens, the golden era of David's reign is drawing to a close, and David's son Solomon prepares to take the throne. While Solomon is able to fulfill his father's dream by building the temple in Jerusalem, he fails to center his life on the faith it signified (1 Kings 1–11). Solomon's death marks the end of a unified nation of twelve tribes and introduces the chaotic period of the divided kingdom, with Israel in the north and Judah in the south (1 Kings 12–22).

Focus	A King's Divided Heart			A Divided Kingdom		
Divisions	Solomon's Commission: A Throne from God	Solomon's Construction: A Temple for God	Solomon's Compromise: Turning from God	Israel's Civil War	Ahab's Battle with Elijah	Ahab's Battle with Aram
	1　　　　　4	5　　　　　8	9　　　　11	12　　　16	17　　　19	20　　　22
Topics	The Glory Years			The Declining Years		
	One King (Solomon)			Many Kings	One Prophet (Elijah)	
Place	Jerusalem			Northern Kingdom: Israel Southern Kingdom: Judah		
Time	About 40 Years			About 90 Years		

APRIL 1 □ DAY 92
1 KINGS 1–4
Solomon's Commission: A Throne from God

OVERVIEW The final days of David's forty-year reign provide bitter-sweet reminders of his conduct as king: bitter memories of past family failures as seen in Adonijah's attempt to usurp the throne and sweet recollections of a promised dynasty as personified in Solomon, the king-elect. After David's death, Solomon steps into the enormous responsibilities as God's anointed. When confronted by God with the invitation "Ask for whatever you want me to give you?" (3:5), Solomon responds, "Give your servant a discerning heart to govern your people" (3:9)—a request God is only too willing to grant. In addition, God provides the things Solomon could have asked for but didn't: wealth, victory, fame and long life.

Chapter 1		Chapter 2	Chapters 3–4
A False "King" Overthrown	A New King Anointed	Justice in the Palace	Wisdom in the Palace
1 27	28 53		
Solomon's Rise		Solomon's Rule	

YOUR DAILY WALK Think back over the great personalities of the past century. Would you like to have been
  • the son or daughter of Albert Einstein?
  • the center fielder who succeeded Mickey Mantle?
  • the conductor who picked up the baton of Arthur Fiedler?

Wise men talk because they have something to say; fools, because they have to say something.

Following in the footsteps of greatness is never easy. Imagine the burden that Solomon carried as he assumed the reins of power formerly held by his father David. And yet, in God's strength and wisdom, he did it, taking the nation of Israel to even greater heights spiritually and economically. Instead of falling over his father's reputation, Solomon followed in his father's footsteps . . . and then some.

Write the words of 1 Kings 3:9 on a piece of paper and place it by the shoes you will wear tomorrow. Let this verse remind you that God has new paths of service for you to blaze, regardless of who has preceded you.

INSIGHT I'd Like the Chef to Prepare . . .
Solomon's court, which included his enormous harem, his ministers, officials, family members and servants, required two or three meals a day, just like everyone else. Solomon appointed twelve governors over various regions of Israel to supply the necessary provisions—a job worthy of a military quartermaster corps.

CHAPTER 1
When King David was old and well advanced in years, he could not keep warm even when they put covers over him. ²So his servants said to him, "Let us look for a young virgin to attend the king and take care of him. She can lie beside him so that our lord the king may keep warm."

³Then they searched throughout Israel for a beautiful girl and found Abishag, a

Shunammite, and brought her to the king. ⁴The girl was very beautiful; she took care of the king and waited on him, but the king had no intimate relations with her.

⁵Now Adonijah, whose mother was Haggith, put himself forward and said, "I will be king." So he got chariots and horses*a* ready, with fifty men to run ahead of him. ⁶(His father had never interfered with him by asking, "Why do you behave as you do?" He was also very handsome and was born next after Absalom.)

⁷Adonijah conferred with Joab son of Zeruiah and with Abiathar the priest, and they gave him their support. ⁸But Zadok the priest, Benaiah son of Jehoiada, Nathan the prophet, Shimei and Rei*b* and David's special guard did not join Adonijah.

⁹Adonijah then sacrificed sheep, cattle and fattened calves at the Stone of Zoheleth near En Rogel. He invited all his brothers, the king's sons, and all the men of Judah who were royal officials, ¹⁰but he did not invite Nathan the prophet or Benaiah or the special guard or his brother Solomon.

¹¹Then Nathan asked Bathsheba, Solomon's mother, "Have you not heard that Adonijah, the son of Haggith, has become king without our lord David's knowing it? ¹²Now then, let me advise you how you can save your own life and the life of your son Solomon. ¹³Go in to King David and say to him, 'My lord the king, did you not swear to me your servant: "Surely Solomon your son shall be king after me, and he will sit on my throne"? Why then has Adonijah become king?' ¹⁴While you are still there talking to the king, I will come in and confirm what you have said."

¹⁵So Bathsheba went to see the aged king in his room, where Abishag the Shunammite was attending him. ¹⁶Bathsheba bowed low and knelt before the king.

"What is it you want?" the king asked.

¹⁷She said to him, "My lord, you yourself swore to me your servant by the LORD your God: 'Solomon your son shall be king after me, and he will sit on my throne.' ¹⁸But now Adonijah has become king, and you, my lord the king, do not know about it. ¹⁹He has sacrificed great numbers of cattle, fattened calves, and

sheep, and has invited all the king's sons, Abiathar the priest and Joab the commander of the army, but he has not invited Solomon your servant. ²⁰My lord the king, the eyes of all Israel are on you, to learn from you who will sit on the throne of my lord the king after him. ²¹Otherwise, as soon as my lord the king is laid to rest with his fathers, I and my son Solomon will be treated as criminals."

²²While she was still speaking with the king, Nathan the prophet arrived. ²³And they told the king, "Nathan the prophet is here." So he went before the king and bowed with his face to the ground.

²⁴Nathan said, "Have you, my lord the king, declared that Adonijah shall be king after you, and that he will sit on your throne? ²⁵Today he has gone down and sacrificed great numbers of cattle, fattened calves, and sheep. He has invited all the king's sons, the commanders of the army and Abiathar the priest. Right now they are eating and drinking with him and saying, 'Long live King Adonijah!' ²⁶But me your servant, and Zadok the priest, and Benaiah son of Jehoiada, and your servant Solomon he did not invite. ²⁷Is this something my lord the king has done without letting his servants know who should sit on the throne of my lord the king after him?"

²⁸Then King David said, "Call in Bathsheba." So she came into the king's presence and stood before him.

²⁹The king then took an oath: "As surely as the LORD lives, who has delivered me out of every trouble, ³⁰I will surely carry out today what I swore to you by the LORD, the God of Israel: Solomon your son shall be king after me, and he will sit on my throne in my place."

³¹Then Bathsheba bowed low with her face to the ground and, kneeling before the king, said, "May my lord King David live forever!"

³²King David said, "Call in Zadok the priest, Nathan the prophet and Benaiah son of Jehoiada." When they came before the king, ³³he said to them: "Take your lord's servants with you and set Solomon my son on my own mule and take him down to Gihon. ³⁴There have Zadok the priest and Nathan the prophet anoint him king over Israel. Blow the trumpet and

---

*a*5 Or *charioteers*   *b*8 Or *and his friends*

shout, 'Long live King Solomon!' ³⁵Then you are to go up with him, and he is to come and sit on my throne and reign in my place. I have appointed him ruler over Israel and Judah."

³⁶Benaiah son of Jehoiada answered the king, "Amen! May the LORD, the God of my lord the king, so declare it. ³⁷As the LORD was with my lord the king, so may he be with Solomon to make his throne even greater than the throne of my lord King David!"

³⁸So Zadok the priest, Nathan the prophet, Benaiah son of Jehoiada, the Kerethites and the Pelethites went down and put Solomon on King David's mule and escorted him to Gihon. ³⁹Zadok the priest took the horn of oil from the sacred tent and anointed Solomon. Then they sounded the trumpet and all the people shouted, "Long live King Solomon!" ⁴⁰And all the people went up after him, playing flutes and rejoicing greatly, so that the ground shook with the sound.

⁴¹Adonijah and all the guests who were with him heard it as they were finishing their feast. On hearing the sound of the trumpet, Joab asked, "What's the meaning of all the noise in the city?"

⁴²Even as he was speaking, Jonathan son of Abiathar the priest arrived. Adonijah said, "Come in. A worthy man like you must be bringing good news."

⁴³"Not at all!" Jonathan answered. "Our lord King David has made Solomon king. ⁴⁴The king has sent with him Zadok the priest, Nathan the prophet, Benaiah son of Jehoiada, the Kerethites and the Pelethites, and they have put him on the king's mule, ⁴⁵and Zadok the priest and Nathan the prophet have anointed him king at Gihon. From there they have gone up cheering, and the city resounds with it. That's the noise you hear. ⁴⁶Moreover, Solomon has taken his seat on the royal throne. ⁴⁷Also, the royal officials have come to congratulate our lord King David, saying, 'May your God make Solomon's name more famous than yours and his throne greater than yours!' And the king bowed in worship on his bed ⁴⁸and said, 'Praise be to the LORD, the God of Israel, who has allowed my eyes to see a successor on my throne today.' "

⁴⁹At this, all Adonijah's guests rose in alarm and dispersed. ⁵⁰But Adonijah, in fear of Solomon, went and took hold of the horns of the altar. ⁵¹Then Solomon was told, "Adonijah is afraid of King Solomon and is clinging to the horns of the altar. He says, 'Let King Solomon swear to me today that he will not put his servant to death with the sword.' "

⁵²Solomon replied, "If he shows himself to be a worthy man, not a hair of his head will fall to the ground; but if evil is found in him, he will die." ⁵³Then King Solomon sent men, and they brought him down from the altar. And Adonijah came and bowed down to King Solomon, and Solomon said, "Go to your home."

C H A P T E R   2
When the time drew near for David to die, he gave a charge to Solomon his son.

²"I am about to go the way of all the earth," he said. "So be strong, show yourself a man, ³and observe what the LORD your God requires: Walk in his ways, and keep his decrees and commands, his laws and requirements, as written in the Law of Moses, so that you may prosper in all you do and wherever you go, ⁴and that the LORD may keep his promise to me: 'If your descendants watch how they live, and if they walk faithfully before me with all their heart and soul, you will never fail to have a man on the throne of Israel.'

⁵"Now you yourself know what Joab son of Zeruiah did to me—what he did to the two commanders of Israel's armies, Abner son of Ner and Amasa son of Jether. He killed them, shedding their blood in peacetime as if in battle, and with that blood stained the belt around his waist and the sandals on his feet. ⁶Deal with him according to your wisdom, but do not let his gray head go down to the grave^c in peace.

⁷"But show kindness to the sons of Barzillai of Gilead and let them be among those who eat at your table. They stood by me when I fled from your brother Absalom.

⁸"And remember, you have with you Shimei son of Gera, the Benjamite from Bahurim, who called down bitter curses on me the day I went to Mahanaim. When he came down to meet me at the Jordan, I swore to him by the LORD: 'I will not put

^c6 Hebrew *Sheol*; also in verse 9

you to death by the sword.' ⁹But now, do not consider him innocent. You are a man of wisdom; you will know what to do to him. Bring his gray head down to the grave in blood."

¹⁰Then David rested with his fathers and was buried in the City of David. ¹¹He had reigned forty years over Israel—seven years in Hebron and thirty-three in Jerusalem. ¹²So Solomon sat on the throne of his father David, and his rule was firmly established.

¹³Now Adonijah, the son of Haggith, went to Bathsheba, Solomon's mother. Bathsheba asked him, "Do you come peacefully?"

He answered, "Yes, peacefully." ¹⁴Then he added, "I have something to say to you."

"You may say it," she replied.

¹⁵"As you know," he said, "the kingdom was mine. All Israel looked to me as their king. But things changed, and the kingdom has gone to my brother; for it has come to him from the LORD. ¹⁶Now I have one request to make of you. Do not refuse me."

"You may make it," she said.

¹⁷So he continued, "Please ask King Solomon—he will not refuse you—to give me Abishag the Shunammite as my wife."

¹⁸"Very well," Bathsheba replied, "I will speak to the king for you."

¹⁹When Bathsheba went to King Solomon to speak to him for Adonijah, the king stood up to meet her, bowed down to her and sat down on his throne. He had a throne brought for the king's mother, and she sat down at his right hand.

²⁰"I have one small request to make of you," she said. "Do not refuse me."

The king replied, "Make it, my mother; I will not refuse you."

²¹So she said, "Let Abishag the Shunammite be given in marriage to your brother Adonijah."

²²King Solomon answered his mother, "Why do you request Abishag the Shunammite for Adonijah? You might as well request the kingdom for him—after all, he is my older brother—yes, for him and for Abiathar the priest and Joab son of Zeruiah!"

²³Then King Solomon swore by the LORD: "May God deal with me, be it ever

so severely, if Adonijah does not pay with his life for this request! ²⁴And now, as surely as the LORD lives—he who has established me securely on the throne of my father David and has founded a dynasty for me as he promised—Adonijah shall be put to death today!" ²⁵So King Solomon gave orders to Benaiah son of Jehoiada, and he struck down Adonijah and he died.

²⁶To Abiathar the priest the king said, "Go back to your fields in Anathoth. You deserve to die, but I will not put you to death now, because you carried the ark of the Sovereign LORD before my father David and shared all my father's hardships." ²⁷So Solomon removed Abiathar from the priesthood of the LORD, fulfilling the word the LORD had spoken at Shiloh about the house of Eli.

²⁸When the news reached Joab, who had conspired with Adonijah though not with Absalom, he fled to the tent of the LORD and took hold of the horns of the altar. ²⁹King Solomon was told that Joab had fled to the tent of the LORD and was beside the altar. Then Solomon ordered Benaiah son of Jehoiada, "Go, strike him down!"

³⁰So Benaiah entered the tent of the LORD and said to Joab, "The king says, 'Come out!'"

But he answered, "No, I will die here."

Benaiah reported to the king, "This is how Joab answered me."

³¹Then the king commanded Benaiah, "Do as he says. Strike him down and bury him, and so clear me and my father's house of the guilt of the innocent blood that Joab shed. ³²The LORD will repay him for the blood he shed, because without the knowledge of my father David he attacked two men and killed them with the sword. Both of them—Abner son of Ner, commander of Israel's army, and Amasa son of Jether, commander of Judah's army—were better men and more upright than he. ³³May the guilt of their blood rest on the head of Joab and his descendants forever. But on David and his descendants, his house and his throne, may there be the LORD's peace forever."

³⁴So Benaiah son of Jehoiada went up and struck down Joab and killed him, and he was buried on his own land*ᵈ* in the

*ᵈ*34 Or *buried in his tomb*

desert. ³⁵The king put Benaiah son of Jehoiada over the army in Joab's position
and replaced Abiathar with Zadok the
priest.

³⁶Then the king sent for Shimei and said
to him, "Build yourself a house in Jerusalem and live there, but do not go anywhere else. ³⁷The day you leave and cross
the Kidron Valley, you can be sure you
will die; your blood will be on your own
head."

³⁸Shimei answered the king, "What you
say is good. Your servant will do as my
lord the king has said." And Shimei
stayed in Jerusalem for a long time.

³⁹But three years later, two of Shimei's
slaves ran off to Achish son of Maacah,
king of Gath, and Shimei was told, "Your
slaves are in Gath." ⁴⁰At this, he saddled
his donkey and went to Achish at Gath in
search of his slaves. So Shimei went away
and brought the slaves back from Gath.

⁴¹When Solomon was told that Shimei
had gone from Jerusalem to Gath and had
returned, ⁴²the king summoned Shimei
and said to him, "Did I not make you
swear by the LORD and warn you, 'On the
day you leave to go anywhere else, you
can be sure you will die'? At that time you
said to me, 'What you say is good. I will
obey.' ⁴³Why then did you not keep your
oath to the LORD and obey the command I
gave you?"

⁴⁴The king also said to Shimei, "You
know in your heart all the wrong you did
to my father David. Now the LORD will
repay you for your wrongdoing. ⁴⁵But
King Solomon will be blessed, and David's throne will remain secure before the
LORD forever."

⁴⁶Then the king gave the order to Benaiah son of Jehoiada, and he went out and
struck Shimei down and killed him.

The kingdom was now firmly established in Solomon's hands.

CHAPTER 3
Solomon made an alliance with Pharaoh
king of Egypt and married his daughter.
He brought her to the City of David until
he finished building his palace and the
temple of the LORD, and the wall around
Jerusalem. ²The people, however, were
still sacrificing at the high places, because
a temple had not yet been built for the

Name of the LORD. ³Solomon showed his
love for the LORD by walking according to
the statutes of his father David, except
that he offered sacrifices and burned incense on the high places.

⁴The king went to Gibeon to offer sacrifices, for that was the most important
high place, and Solomon offered a thousand burnt offerings on that altar. ⁵At
Gibeon the LORD appeared to Solomon
during the night in a dream, and God
said, "Ask for whatever you want me to
give you."

⁶Solomon answered, "You have shown
great kindness to your servant, my father
David, because he was faithful to you and
righteous and upright in heart. You have
continued this great kindness to him and
have given him a son to sit on his throne
this very day.

⁷"Now, O LORD my God, you have
made your servant king in place of my
father David. But I am only a little child
and do not know how to carry out my
duties. ⁸Your servant is here among the
people you have chosen, a great people,
too numerous to count or number. ⁹So
give your servant a discerning heart to
govern your people and to distinguish
between right and wrong. For who is able
to govern this great people of yours?"

¹⁰The Lord was pleased that Solomon
had asked for this. ¹¹So God said to him,
"Since you have asked for this and not for
long life or wealth for yourself, nor have
asked for the death of your enemies but
for discernment in administering justice,
¹²I will do what you have asked. I will
give you a wise and discerning heart, so
that there will never have been anyone
like you, nor will there ever be. ¹³More-
over, I will give you what you have not
asked for—both riches and honor—so that
in your lifetime you will have no equal
among kings. ¹⁴And if you walk in my
ways and obey my statutes and commands as David your father did, I will
give you a long life." ¹⁵Then Solomon
awoke—and he realized it had been a
dream.

He returned to Jerusalem, stood before
the ark of the Lord's covenant and sacrificed burnt offerings and fellowship of-
ferings.ᵉ Then he gave a feast for all his
court.

ᵉ15 Traditionally *peace offerings*

¹⁶Now two prostitutes came to the king and stood before him. ¹⁷One of them said, "My lord, this woman and I live in the same house. I had a baby while she was there with me. ¹⁸The third day after my child was born, this woman also had a baby. We were alone; there was no one in the house but the two of us.

¹⁹"During the night this woman's son died because she lay on him. ²⁰So she got up in the middle of the night and took my son from my side while I your servant was asleep. She put him by her breast and put her dead son by my breast. ²¹The next morning, I got up to nurse my son—and he was dead! But when I looked at him closely in the morning light, I saw that it wasn't the son I had borne."

²²The other woman said, "No! The living one is my son; the dead one is yours."

But the first one insisted, "No! The dead one is yours; the living one is mine." And so they argued before the king.

²³The king said, "This one says, 'My son is alive and your son is dead,' while that one says, 'No! Your son is dead and mine is alive.'"

²⁴Then the king said, "Bring me a sword." So they brought a sword for the king. ²⁵He then gave an order: "Cut the living child in two and give half to one and half to the other."

²⁶The woman whose son was alive was filled with compassion for her son and said to the king, "Please, my lord, give her the living baby! Don't kill him!"

But the other said, "Neither I nor you shall have him. Cut him in two!"

²⁷Then the king gave his ruling: "Give the living baby to the first woman. Do not kill him; she is his mother."

²⁸When all Israel heard the verdict the king had given, they held the king in awe, because they saw that he had wisdom from God to administer justice.

CHAPTER 4

So King Solomon ruled over all Israel. ²And these were his chief officials:

Azariah son of Zadok—the priest;
³Elihoreph and Ahijah, sons of Shisha—secretaries;
Jehoshaphat son of Ahilud—recorder;
⁴Benaiah son of Jehoiada—commander in chief;
Zadok and Abiathar—priests;
⁵Azariah son of Nathan—in charge of the district officers;
Zabud son of Nathan—a priest and personal adviser to the king;
⁶Ahishar—in charge of the palace;
Adoniram son of Abda—in charge of forced labor.

⁷Solomon also had twelve district governors over all Israel, who supplied provisions for the king and the royal household. Each one had to provide supplies for one month in the year. ⁸These are their names:

Ben-Hur—in the hill country of Ephraim;
⁹Ben-Deker—in Makaz, Shaalbim, Beth Shemesh and Elon Bethhanan;
¹⁰Ben-Hesed—in Arubboth (Socoh and all the land of Hepher were his);
¹¹Ben-Abinadab—in Naphoth Dorᶠ (he was married to Taphath daughter of Solomon);
¹²Baana son of Ahilud—in Taanach and Megiddo, and in all of Beth Shan next to Zarethan below Jezreel, from Beth Shan to Abel Meholah across to Jokmeam;
¹³Ben-Geber—in Ramoth Gilead (the settlements of Jair son of Manasseh in Gilead were his, as well as the district of Argob in Bashan and its sixty large walled cities with bronze gate bars);
¹⁴Ahinadab son of Iddo—in Mahanaim;
¹⁵Ahimaaz—in Naphtali (he had married Basemath daughter of Solomon);
¹⁶Baana son of Hushai—in Asher and in Aloth;
¹⁷Jehoshaphat son of Paruah—in Issachar;
¹⁸Shimei son of Ela—in Benjamin;
¹⁹Geber son of Uri—in Gilead (the country of Sihon king of the Amorites and the country of Og king of Bashan). He was the only governor over the district.

²⁰The people of Judah and Israel were

f11 Or in the heights of Dor

as numerous as the sand on the seashore; they ate, they drank and they were happy. [21]And Solomon ruled over all the kingdoms from the River[g] to the land of the Philistines, as far as the border of Egypt. These countries brought tribute and were Solomon's subjects all his life.

[22]Solomon's daily provisions were thirty cors[h] of fine flour and sixty cors[i] of meal, [23]ten head of stall-fed cattle, twenty of pasture-fed cattle and a hundred sheep and goats, as well as deer, gazelles, roebucks and choice fowl. [24]For he ruled over all the kingdoms west of the River, from Tiphsah to Gaza, and had peace on all sides. [25]During Solomon's lifetime Judah and Israel, from Dan to Beersheba, lived in safety, each man under his own vine and fig tree.

[26]Solomon had four[j] thousand stalls for chariot horses, and twelve thousand horses.[k]

[27]The district officers, each in his month, supplied provisions for King Solomon and all who came to the king's table. They saw to it that nothing was lacking. [28]They also brought to the proper place their quotas of barley and straw for the chariot horses and the other horses.

[29]God gave Solomon wisdom and very great insight, and a breadth of understanding as measureless as the sand on the seashore. [30]Solomon's wisdom was greater than the wisdom of all the men of the East, and greater than all the wisdom of Egypt. [31]He was wiser than any other man, including Ethan the Ezrahite—wiser than Heman, Calcol and Darda, the sons of Mahol. And his fame spread to all the surrounding nations. [32]He spoke three thousand proverbs and his songs numbered a thousand and five. [33]He described plant life, from the cedar of Lebanon to the hyssop that grows out of walls. He also taught about animals and birds, reptiles and fish. [34]Men of all nations came to listen to Solomon's wisdom, sent by all the kings of the world, who had heard of his wisdom.

g21 That is, the Euphrates; also in verse 24   h22 That is, probably about 185 bushels (about 6.6 kiloliters)   i22 That is, probably about 375 bushels (about 13.2 kiloliters)   j26 Some Septuagint manuscripts (see also 2 Chron. 9:25); Hebrew forty   k26 Or charioteers

APRIL 2 □ DAY 93
1 KINGS 5–8
Solomon's Construction: A Temple for God

OVERVIEW David's lifelong dream to build a house for God now becomes Solomon's consuming passion. Building upon the ample preparations of his father, Solomon secures the remaining supplies and manpower to accomplish the task: cedar from Lebanon, huge stones from mountain quarries, conscripted laborers from all over the country. Seven long years pass before the work is finished and worship can begin. Elders, Levites, priests and the people congregate to exalt the God whom no earthly house can contain. When at last the glory of the Lord fills the temple, Solomon lifts his hands toward heaven and leads the nation in a stirring prayer of praise and petition.

Chapter 5	Chapter 6	Chapter 7	Chapter 8
Temple Builders	Temple Blueprint	Temple Construction	Temple Consecration
"I intend . . . to build a temple for . . . the LORD my God" (5:5).			

YOUR DAILY WALK If your prayer life has been a little anemic lately, spend some extra moments savoring chapter 8.
     In the space of thirty-one verses (8:23–53), Solomon pours out his

Prayer at its best employs four statements: Thank you; I'm sorry; teach me; go with me.

heart to God in a prayer of unparalleled worship and adoration. With hands held high to heaven (v. 22) and kneeling in humility before the Lord (v. 54), Solomon recalls God's covenant promises to his people. Knowing full well that God cannot be contained by the temple he has built (v. 27), Solomon is equally confident that God answers prayers in keeping with his covenant (v. 23). Then Solomon makes seven specific petitions covering different cases in which future prayers would be offered to God in the temple. (Can you find all seven, each containing the phrase "hear from heaven"?)

How confident are you that God hears and answers your prayers when they are consistent with his promises? Make 1 John 5:14 your meditation for the day: "If we ask anything according to his will, he hears us." Then pray with the same confidence that Solomon prayed!

 INSIGHT Unholey Walls for a Holy Temple (7:9)
Walls in Solomon's time were commonly made of sun-dried mud or sandstone blocks, often with gaps between. The wealthy would avoid this problem by substituting expensive, close-fitting hewn stones. This was the building method used for the temple.

CHAPTER 5

When Hiram king of Tyre heard that Solomon had been anointed king to succeed his father David, he sent his envoys to Solomon, because he had always been on friendly terms with David. ²Solomon sent back this message to Hiram:

³"You know that because of the wars waged against my father David from all sides, he could not build a temple for the Name of the LORD his God until the LORD put his enemies under his feet. ⁴But now the LORD my God has given me rest on every side, and there is no adversary or disaster. ⁵I intend, therefore, to build a temple for the Name of the LORD my God, as the LORD told my father David, when he said, 'Your son whom I will put on the throne in your place will build the temple for my Name.'

⁶"So give orders that cedars of Lebanon be cut for me. My men will work with yours, and I will pay you for your men whatever wages you set. You know that we have no one so skilled in felling timber as the Sidonians."

⁷When Hiram heard Solomon's message, he was greatly pleased and said, "Praise be to the LORD today, for he has given David a wise son to rule over this great nation."

⁸So Hiram sent word to Solomon:

"I have received the message you sent me and will do all you want in providing the cedar and pine logs. ⁹My men will haul them down from Lebanon to the sea, and I will float them in rafts by sea to the place you specify. There I will separate them and you can take them away. And you are to grant my wish by providing food for my royal household."

¹⁰In this way Hiram kept Solomon supplied with all the cedar and pine logs he wanted, ¹¹and Solomon gave Hiram twenty thousand cors*ˡ* of wheat as food for his household, in addition to twenty thousand baths*ᵐ,ⁿ* of pressed olive oil. Solomon continued to do this for Hiram year after year. ¹²The LORD gave Solomon wisdom, just as he had promised him. There were peaceful relations between Hiram and Solomon, and the two of them made a treaty.

¹³King Solomon conscripted laborers from all Israel—thirty thousand men. ¹⁴He sent them off to Lebanon in shifts of ten thousand a month, so that they spent one month in Lebanon and two months at home. Adoniram was in charge of the forced labor. ¹⁵Solomon had seventy thousand carriers and eighty thousand stonecutters in the hills, ¹⁶as well as thirty-three hundred*ᵒ* foremen who

---

ˡ11 That is, probably about 125,000 bushels (about 4,400 kiloliters)
cors   ⁿ11 That is, about 115,000 gallons (about 440 kiloliters)
2:2, 18) *thirty-six hundred*   *ᵐ11* Septuagint (see also 2 Chron. 2:10); Hebrew *twenty*   *ᵒ16* Hebrew; some Septuagint manuscripts (see also 2 Chron.

supervised the project and directed the workmen. [17]At the king's command they removed from the quarry large blocks of quality stone to provide a foundation of dressed stone for the temple. [18]The craftsmen of Solomon and Hiram and the men of Gebal[p] cut and prepared the timber and stone for the building of the temple.

CHAPTER 6

In the four hundred and eightieth[q] year after the Israelites had come out of Egypt, in the fourth year of Solomon's reign over Israel, in the month of Ziv, the second month, he began to build the temple of the LORD.

[2]The temple that King Solomon built for the LORD was sixty cubits long, twenty wide and thirty high.[r] [3]The portico at the front of the main hall of the temple extended the width of the temple, that is twenty cubits,[s] and projected ten cubits[t] from the front of the temple. [4]He made narrow clerestory windows in the temple. [5]Against the walls of the main hall and inner sanctuary he built a structure around the building, in which there were side rooms. [6]The lowest floor was five cubits[u] wide, the middle floor six cubits[v] and the third floor seven.[w] He made offset ledges around the outside of the temple so that nothing would be inserted into the temple walls.

[7]In building the temple, only blocks dressed at the quarry were used, and no hammer, chisel or any other iron tool was heard at the temple site while it was being built.

[8]The entrance to the lowest[x] floor was on the south side of the temple; a stairway led up to the middle level and from there to the third. [9]So he built the temple and completed it, roofing it with beams and cedar planks. [10]And he built the side rooms all along the temple. The height of each was five cubits, and they were attached to the temple by beams of cedar.

[11]The word of the LORD came to Solomon: [12]"As for this temple you are building, if you follow my decrees, carry out my regulations and keep all my commands and obey them, I will fulfill through you the promise I gave to David

your father. [13]And I will live among the Israelites and will not abandon my people Israel."

[14]So Solomon built the temple and completed it. [15]He lined its interior walls with cedar boards, paneling them from the floor of the temple to the ceiling, and covered the floor of the temple with planks of pine. [16]He partitioned off twenty cubits[s] at the rear of the temple with cedar boards from floor to ceiling to form within the temple an inner sanctuary, the Most Holy Place. [17]The main hall in front of this room was forty cubits[y] long. [18]The inside of the temple was cedar, carved with gourds and open flowers. Everything was cedar; no stone was to be seen.

[19]He prepared the inner sanctuary within the temple to set the ark of the covenant of the LORD there. [20]The inner sanctuary was twenty cubits long, twenty wide and twenty high.[z] He overlaid the inside with pure gold, and he also overlaid the altar of cedar. [21]Solomon covered the inside of the temple with pure gold, and he extended gold chains across the front of the inner sanctuary, which was overlaid with gold. [22]So he overlaid the whole interior with gold. He also overlaid with gold the altar that belonged to the inner sanctuary.

[23]In the inner sanctuary he made a pair of cherubim of olive wood, each ten cubits[t] high. [24]One wing of the first cherub was five cubits long, and the other wing five cubits—ten cubits from wing tip to wing tip. [25]The second cherub also measured ten cubits, for the two cherubim were identical in size and shape. [26]The height of each cherub was ten cubits. [27]He placed the cherubim inside the innermost room of the temple, with their wings spread out. The wing of one cherub touched one wall, while the wing of the other touched the other wall, and their wings touched each other in the middle of the room. [28]He overlaid the cherubim with gold.

[29]On the walls all around the temple, in both the inner and outer rooms, he carved cherubim, palm trees and open flowers. [30]He also covered the floors of both the

inner and outer rooms of the temple with gold. ³¹For the entrance of the inner sanctuary he made doors of olive wood with five-sided jambs. ³²And on the two olive wood doors he carved cherubim, palm trees and open flowers, and overlaid the cherubim and palm trees with beaten gold. ³³In the same way he made four-sided jambs of olive wood for the entrance to the main hall. ³⁴He also made two pine doors, each having two leaves that turned in sockets. ³⁵He carved cherubim, palm trees and open flowers on them and overlaid them with gold hammered evenly over the carvings.

³⁶And he built the inner courtyard of three courses of dressed stone and one course of trimmed cedar beams.

³⁷The foundation of the temple of the LORD was laid in the fourth year, in the month of Ziv. ³⁸In the eleventh year in the month of Bul, the eighth month, the temple was finished in all its details according to its specifications. He had spent seven years building it.

CHAPTER 7

It took Solomon thirteen years, however, to complete the construction of his palace. ²He built the Palace of the Forest of Lebanon a hundred cubits long, fifty wide and thirty high,^a with four rows of cedar columns supporting trimmed cedar beams. ³It was roofed with cedar above the beams that rested on the columns—forty-five beams, fifteen to a row. ⁴Its windows were placed high in sets of three, facing each other. ⁵All the doorways had rectangular frames; they were in the front part in sets of three, facing each other.^b

⁶He made a colonnade fifty cubits long and thirty wide.^c In front of it was a portico, and in front of that were pillars and an overhanging roof.

⁷He built the throne hall, the Hall of Justice, where he was to judge, and he covered it with cedar from floor to ceiling.^d ⁸And the palace in which he was to live, set farther back, was similar in design. Solomon also made a palace like this

hall for Pharaoh's daughter, whom he had married.

⁹All these structures, from the outside to the great courtyard and from foundation to eaves, were made of blocks of high-grade stone cut to size and trimmed with a saw on their inner and outer faces. ¹⁰The foundations were laid with large stones of good quality, some measuring ten cubits^e and some eight.^f ¹¹Above were high-grade stones, cut to size, and cedar beams. ¹²The great courtyard was surrounded by a wall of three courses of dressed stone and one course of trimmed cedar beams, as was the inner courtyard of the temple of the LORD with its portico.

¹³King Solomon sent to Tyre and brought Huram,^g ¹⁴whose mother was a widow from the tribe of Naphtali and whose father was a man of Tyre and a craftsman in bronze. Huram was highly skilled and experienced in all kinds of bronze work. He came to King Solomon and did all the work assigned to him.

¹⁵He cast two bronze pillars, each eighteen cubits high and twelve cubits around,^h by line. ¹⁶He also made two capitals of cast bronze to set on the tops of the pillars; each capital was five cubitsⁱ high. ¹⁷A network of interwoven chains festooned the capitals on top of the pillars, seven for each capital. ¹⁸He made pomegranates in two rows^j encircling each network to decorate the capitals on top of the pillars.^k He did the same for each capital. ¹⁹The capitals on top of the pillars in the portico were in the shape of lilies, four cubits^l high. ²⁰On the capitals of both pillars, above the bowl-shaped part next to the network, were the two hundred pomegranates in rows all around. ²¹He erected the pillars at the portico of the temple. The pillar to the south he named Jakin^m and the one to the north Boaz.ⁿ ²²The capitals on top were in the shape of lilies. And so the work on the pillars was completed.

²³He made the Sea of cast metal, circular in shape, measuring ten cubits^e from rim to rim and five cubits high. It took a

---

^a2 That is, about 150 feet (about 46 meters) long, 75 feet (about 23 meters) wide and 45 feet (about 13.5 meters) high
^b5 The meaning of the Hebrew for this verse is uncertain.   ^c6 That is, about 75 feet (about 23 meters) long and 45 feet (about 13.5 meters) wide   ^d7 Vulgate and Syriac; Hebrew *floor*   ^e10,23 That is, about 15 feet (about 4.5 meters)   ^f10 That is, about 12 feet (about 3.6 meters)   ^g13 Hebrew *Hiram*, a variant of *Huram*; also in verses 40 and 45   ^h15 That is, about 27 feet (about 8.1 meters) high and 18 feet (about 5.4 meters) around   ⁱ16 That is, about 7 1/2 feet (about 2.3 meters); also in verse 23   ^j18 Two Hebrew manuscripts and Septuagint; most Hebrew manuscripts *made the pillars, and there were two rows* ^k18 Many Hebrew manuscripts and Syriac; most Hebrew manuscripts *pomegranates*   ^l19 That is, about 6 feet (about 1.8 meters); also in verse 38   ^m21 *Jakin* probably means *he establishes.*   ⁿ21 *Boaz* probably means *in him is strength.*

line of thirty cubits⁰ to measure around it. ²⁴Below the rim, gourds encircled it— ten to a cubit. The gourds were cast in two rows in one piece with the Sea.

²⁵The Sea stood on twelve bulls, three facing north, three facing west, three facing south and three facing east. The Sea rested on top of them, and their hindquarters were toward the center. ²⁶It was a handbreadthᵖ in thickness, and its rim was like the rim of a cup, like a lily blossom. It held two thousand baths.�q

²⁷He also made ten movable stands of bronze; each was four cubits long, four wide and three high.ʳ ²⁸This is how the stands were made: They had side panels attached to uprights. ²⁹On the panels between the uprights were lions, bulls and cherubim—and on the uprights as well. Above and below the lions and bulls were wreaths of hammered work. ³⁰Each stand had four bronze wheels with bronze axles, and each had a basin resting on four supports, cast with wreaths on each side. ³¹On the inside of the stand there was an opening that had a circular frame one cubitˢ deep. This opening was round, and with its basework it measured a cubit and a half.ᵗ Around its opening there was engraving. The panels of the stands were square, not round. ³²The four wheels were under the panels, and the axles of the wheels were attached to the stand. The diameter of each wheel was a cubit and a half. ³³The wheels were made like chariot wheels; the axles, rims, spokes and hubs were all of cast metal.

³⁴Each stand had four handles, one on each corner, projecting from the stand. ³⁵At the top of the stand there was a circular band half a cubitᵘ deep. The supports and panels were attached to the top of the stand. ³⁶He engraved cherubim, lions and palm trees on the surfaces of the supports and on the panels, in every available space, with wreaths all around. ³⁷This is the way he made the ten stands. They were all cast in the same molds and were identical in size and shape.

³⁸He then made ten bronze basins, each holding forty bathsᵛ and measuring four cubits across, one basin to go on each of the ten stands. ³⁹He placed five of the

stands on the south side of the temple and five on the north. He placed the Sea on the south side, at the southeast corner of the temple. ⁴⁰He also made the basins and shovels and sprinkling bowls.

So Huram finished all the work he had undertaken for King Solomon in the temple of the LORD:

⁴¹the two pillars;
the two bowl-shaped capitals on top of the pillars;
the two sets of network decorating the two bowl-shaped capitals on top of the pillars;
⁴²the four hundred pomegranates for the two sets of network (two rows of pomegranates for each network, decorating the bowl-shaped capitals on top of the pillars);
⁴³the ten stands with their ten basins;
⁴⁴the Sea and the twelve bulls under it;
⁴⁵the pots, shovels and sprinkling bowls.

All these objects that Huram made for King Solomon for the temple of the LORD were of burnished bronze. ⁴⁶The king had them cast in clay molds in the plain of the Jordan between Succoth and Zarethan. ⁴⁷Solomon left all these things unweighed, because there were so many; the weight of the bronze was not determined.

⁴⁸Solomon also made all the furnishings that were in the LORD's temple:

the golden altar;
the golden table on which was the bread of the Presence;
⁴⁹the lampstands of pure gold (five on the right and five on the left, in front of the inner sanctuary);
the gold floral work and lamps and tongs;
⁵⁰the pure gold basins, wick trimmers, sprinkling bowls, dishes and censers;
and the gold sockets for the doors of the innermost room, the Most Holy Place, and also for the doors of the main hall of the temple.

⁵¹When all the work King Solomon had

⁰23 That is, about 45 feet (about 13.5 meters)   ᵖ26 That is, about 3 inches (about 8 centimeters)   q26 That is, probably about 11,500 gallons (about 44 kiloliters); the Septuagint does not have this sentence.   ʳ27 That is, about 6 feet (about 1.8 meters) long and wide and about 4 1/2 feet (about 1.3 meters) high   ˢ31 That is, about 1 1/2 feet (about 0.5 meter)   ᵗ31 That is, about 2 1/4 feet (about 0.7 meter); also in verse 32   ᵘ35 That is, about 3/4 foot (about 0.2 meter)   ᵛ38 That is, about 230 gallons (about 880 liters)

done for the temple of the LORD was finished, he brought in the things his father David had dedicated—the silver and gold and the furnishings—and he placed them in the treasuries of the LORD's temple.

CHAPTER 8

Then King Solomon summoned into his presence at Jerusalem the elders of Israel, all the heads of the tribes and the chiefs of the Israelite families, to bring up the ark of the LORD's covenant from Zion, the City of David. ²All the men of Israel came together to King Solomon at the time of the festival in the month of Ethanim, the seventh month.

³When all the elders of Israel had arrived, the priests took up the ark, ⁴and they brought up the ark of the LORD and the Tent of Meeting and all the sacred furnishings in it. The priests and Levites carried them up, ⁵and King Solomon and the entire assembly of Israel that had gathered about him were before the ark, sacrificing so many sheep and cattle that they could not be recorded or counted.

⁶The priests then brought the ark of the LORD's covenant to its place in the inner sanctuary of the temple, the Most Holy Place, and put it beneath the wings of the cherubim. ⁷The cherubim spread their wings over the place of the ark and overshadowed the ark and its carrying poles. ⁸These poles were so long that their ends could be seen from the Holy Place in front of the inner sanctuary, but not from outside the Holy Place; and they are still there today. ⁹There was nothing in the ark except the two stone tablets that Moses had placed in it at Horeb, where the LORD made a covenant with the Israelites after they came out of Egypt.

¹⁰When the priests withdrew from the Holy Place, the cloud filled the temple of the LORD. ¹¹And the priests could not perform their service because of the cloud, for the glory of the LORD filled his temple. ¹²Then Solomon said, "The LORD has said that he would dwell in a dark cloud; ¹³I have indeed built a magnificent temple for you, a place for you to dwell forever."

¹⁴While the whole assembly of Israel was standing there, the king turned around and blessed them. ¹⁵Then he said:

"Praise be to the LORD, the God of Israel, who with his own hand has fulfilled what he promised with his own mouth to my father David. For he said, ¹⁶'Since the day I brought my people Israel out of Egypt, I have not chosen a city in any tribe of Israel to have a temple built for my Name to be there, but I have chosen David to rule my people Israel.'

¹⁷"My father David had it in his heart to build a temple for the Name of the LORD, the God of Israel. ¹⁸But the LORD said to my father David, 'Because it was in your heart to build a temple for my Name, you did well to have this in your heart. ¹⁹Nevertheless, you are not the one to build the temple, but your son, who is your own flesh and blood—he is the one who will build the temple for my Name.'

²⁰"The LORD has kept the promise he made: I have succeeded David my father and now I sit on the throne of Israel, just as the LORD promised, and I have built the temple for the Name of the LORD, the God of Israel. ²¹I have provided a place there for the ark, in which is the covenant of the LORD that he made with our fathers when he brought them out of Egypt."

²²Then Solomon stood before the altar of the LORD in front of the whole assembly of Israel, spread out his hands toward heaven ²³and said:

"O LORD, God of Israel, there is no God like you in heaven above or on earth below—you who keep your covenant of love with your servants who continue wholeheartedly in your way. ²⁴You have kept your promise to your servant David my father; with your mouth you have promised and with your hand you have fulfilled it—as it is today.

²⁵"Now LORD, God of Israel, keep for your servant David my father the promises you made to him when you said, 'You shall never fail to have a man to sit before me on the throne of Israel, if only your sons are careful in all they do to walk before me as you have done.' ²⁶And now, O God of Israel, let your word that you promised your servant David my father come true.

²⁷"But will God really dwell on

earth? The heavens, even the highest heaven, cannot contain you. How much less this temple I have built! [28]Yet give attention to your servant's prayer and his plea for mercy, O LORD my God. Hear the cry and the prayer that your servant is praying in your presence this day. [29]May your eyes be open toward this temple night and day, this place of which you said, 'My Name shall be there,' so that you will hear the prayer your servant prays toward this place. [30]Hear the supplication of your servant and of your people Israel when they pray toward this place. Hear from heaven, your dwelling place, and when you hear, forgive.

[31]"When a man wrongs his neighbor and is required to take an oath and he comes and swears the oath before your altar in this temple, [32]then hear from heaven and act. Judge between your servants, condemning the guilty and bringing down on his own head what he has done. Declare the innocent not guilty, and so establish his innocence.

[33]"When your people Israel have been defeated by an enemy because they have sinned against you, and when they turn back to you and confess your name, praying and making supplication to you in this temple, [34]then hear from heaven and forgive the sin of your people Israel and bring them back to the land you gave to their fathers.

[35]"When the heavens are shut up and there is no rain because your people have sinned against you, and when they pray toward this place and confess your name and turn from their sin because you have afflicted them, [36]then hear from heaven and forgive the sin of your servants, your people Israel. Teach them the right way to live, and send rain on the land you gave your people for an inheritance.

[37]"When famine or plague comes to the land, or blight or mildew, locusts or grasshoppers, or when an enemy besieges them in any of their cities, whatever disaster or disease may come, [38]and when a prayer or plea is made by any of your people Israel—

each one aware of the afflictions of his own heart, and spreading out his hands toward this temple— [39]then hear from heaven, your dwelling place. Forgive and act; deal with each man according to all he does, since you know his heart (for you alone know the hearts of all men), [40]so that they will fear you all the time they live in the land you gave our fathers.

[41]"As for the foreigner who does not belong to your people Israel but has come from a distant land because of your name— [42]for men will hear of your great name and your mighty hand and your outstretched arm—when he comes and prays toward this temple, [43]then hear from heaven, your dwelling place, and do whatever the foreigner asks of you, so that all the peoples of the earth may know your name and fear you, as do your own people Israel, and may know that this house I have built bears your Name.

[44]"When your people go to war against their enemies, wherever you send them, and when they pray to the LORD toward the city you have chosen and the temple I have built for your Name, [45]then hear from heaven their prayer and their plea, and uphold their cause.

[46]"When they sin against you—for there is no one who does not sin—and you become angry with them and give them over to the enemy, who takes them captive to his own land, far away or near; [47]and if they have a change of heart in the land where they are held captive, and repent and plead with you in the land of their conquerors and say, 'We have sinned, we have done wrong, we have acted wickedly'; [48]and if they turn back to you with all their heart and soul in the land of their enemies who took them captive, and pray to you toward the land you gave their fathers, toward the city you have chosen and the temple I have built for your Name; [49]then from heaven, your dwelling place, hear their prayer and their plea, and uphold their cause. [50]And forgive your people, who have sinned against you; forgive all the offenses

they have committed against you, and cause their conquerors to show them mercy; [51]for they are your people and your inheritance, whom you brought out of Egypt, out of that iron-smelting furnace.

[52]"May your eyes be open to your servant's plea and to the plea of your people Israel, and may you listen to them whenever they cry out to you. [53]For you singled them out from all the nations of the world to be your own inheritance, just as you declared through your servant Moses when you, O Sovereign LORD, brought our fathers out of Egypt."

[54]When Solomon had finished all these prayers and supplications to the LORD, he rose from before the altar of the LORD, where he had been kneeling with his hands spread out toward heaven. [55]He stood and blessed the whole assembly of Israel in a loud voice, saying:

[56]"Praise be to the LORD, who has given rest to his people Israel just as he promised. Not one word has failed of all the good promises he gave through his servant Moses. [57]May the LORD our God be with us as he was with our fathers; may he never leave us nor forsake us. [58]May he turn our hearts to him, to walk in all his ways and to keep the commands, decrees and regulations he gave our fathers. [59]And may these words of mine, which I have prayed before the LORD, be near to the LORD our God day and night, that he may uphold the cause of his servant and the cause of his people Israel according to each day's need, [60]so that all the peoples of the earth may know that the LORD is God and that there is no other. [61]But your hearts must be fully committed to the LORD our God, to live by his decrees and obey his commands, as at this time."

[62]Then the king and all Israel with him offered sacrifices before the LORD. [63]Solomon offered a sacrifice of fellowship offerings[w] to the LORD: twenty-two thousand cattle and a hundred and twenty thousand sheep and goats. So the king and all the Israelites dedicated the temple of the LORD.

[64]On that same day the king consecrated the middle part of the courtyard in front of the temple of the LORD, and there he offered burnt offerings, grain offerings and the fat of the fellowship offerings, because the bronze altar before the LORD was too small to hold the burnt offerings, the grain offerings and the fat of the fellowship offerings.

[65]So Solomon observed the festival at that time, and all Israel with him—a vast assembly, people from Lebo[x] Hamath to the Wadi of Egypt. They celebrated it before the LORD our God for seven days and seven days more, fourteen days in all. [66]On the following day he sent the people away. They blessed the king and then went home, joyful and glad in heart for all the good things the LORD had done for his servant David and his people Israel.

[w]63 Traditionally *peace offerings*; also in verse 64   [x]65 Or *from the entrance to*

APRIL 3 □ DAY 94
1 KINGS 9–11
Solomon's Compromise: Turning from God

 OVERVIEW With the completion of the temple in Jerusalem, Solomon reaches the zenith of his reign. At this crucial moment, God brings both a promise and a warning to his kingly representative. If Solomon will continue to walk in the footsteps of his father, David, God promises to bless and prosper him. But if Solomon strays into paths of idolatry and immorality, God warns that he will severely discipline both the king and his people. Hardly has the ring of God's words left Solomon's ears when he begins to amass wealth and wives—the very things that will lead to his undoing. Earthly pursuits and pagan women soon turn his heart away from God, leading to yet another declaration from God: "I will most certainly tear the kingdom away from you and give it to one of your subordinates" (11:11).

Chapter 9	Chapter 10	Chapter 11
Warning to Solomon	Wealth of Solomon	Wives of Solomon
Solomon's Fame		Solomon's Failure

YOUR DAILY WALK In the margin make a list of three or more issues about which you are currently straddling the fence (that is, you are considering the different sides of the issue but as yet haven't come to a firm conviction regarding which side you want to take).

The highest reward for a person's toil is not what he or she gets for it but rather what he or she becomes by it.

Straddling the proverbial fence may be desirable when an issue is still in question. But once the proper course of action is clear, fence-straddling can be dangerous—even deadly. Solomon straddled the fence in his relationship with God. He worshiped God one day and pagan gods the next; he built his life upon God's promises one day, then disregarded them the next; he sought God's wisdom one day but ignored God's warnings the next. And in the end his divided heart resulted in a divided kingdom.

Take an issue on which you are straddling the fence, and search the Scriptures until God's mind on the matter is clear to you. Then decide what—with God's help—you can do in the next week to declare which side you're on!

INSIGHT Three Strikes and You're Out
Deuteronomy 17:14–20 sets forth God's three commands specifically aimed at Israel's kings in the promised land (vv. 16–17, 19). What was Solomon's "batting average" on these three important prohibitions (10:28; 11:3, 6–8)?

CHAPTER 9

When Solomon had finished building the temple of the LORD and the royal palace, and had achieved all he had desired to do, [2]the LORD appeared to him a second time, as he had appeared to him at Gibeon. [3]The LORD said to him:

"I have heard the prayer and plea you have made before me; I have consecrated this temple, which you have built, by putting my Name there forever. My eyes and my heart will always be there.

[4]"As for you, if you walk before me in integrity of heart and uprightness, as David your father did, and do all I command and observe my decrees and laws, [5]I will establish your royal throne over Israel forever, as I promised David your father when I said,

'You shall never fail to have a man on the throne of Israel.'

[6]"But if you[y] or your sons turn away from me and do not observe the commands and decrees I have given you[y] and go off to serve other gods and worship them, [7]then I will cut off Israel from the land I have given them and will reject this temple I have consecrated for my Name. Israel will then become a byword and an object of ridicule among all peoples. [8]And though this temple is now imposing, all who pass by will be appalled and will scoff and say, 'Why has the LORD done such a thing to this land and to this temple?' [9]People will answer, 'Because they have forsaken the LORD their God, who brought their fathers out of Egypt, and have embraced other gods, worshiping

[y]6 The Hebrew is plural.

and serving them—that is why the LORD brought all this disaster on them.' "

¹⁰At the end of twenty years, during which Solomon built these two buildings—the temple of the LORD and the royal palace— ¹¹King Solomon gave twenty towns in Galilee to Hiram king of Tyre, because Hiram had supplied him with all the cedar and pine and gold he wanted. ¹²But when Hiram went from Tyre to see the towns that Solomon had given him, he was not pleased with them. ¹³"What kind of towns are these you have given me, my brother?" he asked. And he called them the Land of Cabul,ᶻ a name they have to this day. ¹⁴Now Hiram had sent to the king 120 talentsᵃ of gold.

¹⁵Here is the account of the forced labor King Solomon conscripted to build the LORD's temple, his own palace, the supporting terraces,ᵇ the wall of Jerusalem, and Hazor, Megiddo and Gezer. ¹⁶(Pharaoh king of Egypt had attacked and captured Gezer. He had set it on fire. He killed its Canaanite inhabitants and then gave it as a wedding gift to his daughter, Solomon's wife. ¹⁷And Solomon rebuilt Gezer.) He built up Lower Beth Horon, ¹⁸Baalath, and Tadmorᶜ in the desert, within his land, ¹⁹as well as all his store cities and the towns for his chariots and for his horsesᵈ—whatever he desired to build in Jerusalem, in Lebanon and throughout all the territory he ruled.

²⁰All the people left from the Amorites, Hittites, Perizzites, Hivites and Jebusites (these peoples were not Israelites), ²¹that is, their descendants remaining in the land, whom the Israelites could not exterminateᵉ—these Solomon conscripted for his slave labor force, as it is to this day. ²²But Solomon did not make slaves of any of the Israelites; they were his fighting men, his government officials, his officers, his captains, and the commanders of his chariots and charioteers. ²³They were also the chief officials in charge of Solomon's projects—550 officials supervising the men who did the work.

²⁴After Pharaoh's daughter had come up from the City of David to the palace Solomon had built for her, he constructed the supporting terraces.

²⁵Three times a year Solomon sacrificed burnt offerings and fellowship offeringsᶠ on the altar he had built for the LORD, burning incense before the LORD along with them, and so fulfilled the temple obligations.

²⁶King Solomon also built ships at Ezion Geber, which is near Elath in Edom, on the shore of the Red Sea.ᵍ ²⁷And Hiram sent his men—sailors who knew the sea—to serve in the fleet with Solomon's men. ²⁸They sailed to Ophir and brought back 420 talentsʰ of gold, which they delivered to King Solomon.

CHAPTER 10

When the queen of Sheba heard about the fame of Solomon and his relation to the name of the LORD, she came to test him with hard questions. ²Arriving at Jerusalem with a very great caravan—with camels carrying spices, large quantities of gold, and precious stones—she came to Solomon and talked with him about all that she had on her mind. ³Solomon answered all her questions; nothing was too hard for the king to explain to her. ⁴When the queen of Sheba saw all the wisdom of Solomon and the palace he had built, ⁵the food on his table, the seating of his officials, the attending servants in their robes, his cupbearers, and the burnt offerings he made atⁱ the temple of the LORD, she was overwhelmed.

⁶She said to the king, "The report I heard in my own country about your achievements and your wisdom is true. ⁷But I did not believe these things until I came and saw with my own eyes. Indeed, not even half was told me; in wisdom and wealth you have far exceeded the report I heard. ⁸How happy your men must be! How happy your officials, who continually stand before you and hear your wisdom! ⁹Praise be to the LORD your God, who has delighted in you and placed you on the throne of Israel. Because of the LORD's eternal love for Israel, he has made you king, to maintain justice and righteousness."

¹⁰And she gave the king 120 talentsᵃ of

ᶻ13 Cabul sounds like the Hebrew for good-for-nothing.   ᵃ14,10 That is, about 4 1/2 tons (about 4 metric tons)   ᵇ15 Or the Millo; also in verse 24   ᶜ18 The Hebrew may also be read Tamar.   ᵈ19 Or charioteers   ᵉ21 The Hebrew term refers to the irrevocable giving over of things or persons to the LORD, often by totally destroying them.   ᶠ25 Traditionally peace offerings   ᵍ26 Hebrew Yam Suph; that is, Sea of Reeds   ʰ28 That is, about 16 tons (about 14.5 metric tons)   ⁱ5 Or the ascent by which he went up to gold, large quantities of spices, and precious stones. Never again were so many spices brought in as those the queen of Sheba gave to King Solomon.

[11](Hiram's ships brought gold from Ophir; and from there they brought great cargoes of almugwood[j] and precious stones. [12]The king used the almugwood to make supports for the temple of the Lord and for the royal palace, and to make harps and lyres for the musicians. So much almugwood has never been imported or seen since that day.)

[13]King Solomon gave the queen of Sheba all she desired and asked for, besides what he had given her out of his royal bounty. Then she left and returned with her retinue to her own country.

[14]The weight of the gold that Solomon received yearly was 666 talents,[k] [15]not including the revenues from merchants and traders and from all the Arabian kings and the governors of the land.

[16]King Solomon made two hundred large shields of hammered gold; six hundred bekas[l] of gold went into each shield. [17]He also made three hundred small shields of hammered gold, with three minas[m] of gold in each shield. The king put them in the Palace of the Forest of Lebanon.

[18]Then the king made a great throne inlaid with ivory and overlaid with fine gold. [19]The throne had six steps, and its back had a rounded top. On both sides of the seat were armrests, with a lion standing beside each of them. [20]Twelve lions stood on the six steps, one at either end of each step. Nothing like it had ever been made for any other kingdom. [21]All King Solomon's goblets were gold, and all the household articles in the Palace of the Forest of Lebanon were pure gold. Nothing was made of silver, because silver was considered of little value in Solomon's days. [22]The king had a fleet of trading ships[n] at sea along with the ships of Hiram. Once every three years it returned, carrying gold, silver and ivory, and apes and baboons.

[23]King Solomon was greater in riches and wisdom than all the other kings of the earth. [24]The whole world sought audience

with Solomon to hear the wisdom God had put in his heart. [25]Year after year, everyone who came brought a gift—articles of silver and gold, robes, weapons and spices, and horses and mules.

[26]Solomon accumulated chariots and horses; he had fourteen hundred chariots and twelve thousand horses,[o] which he kept in the chariot cities and also with him in Jerusalem. [27]The king made silver as common in Jerusalem as stones, and cedar as plentiful as sycamore-fig trees in the foothills. [28]Solomon's horses were imported from Egypt[p] and from Kue[q]—the royal merchants purchased them from Kue. [29]They imported a chariot from Egypt for six hundred shekels[r] of silver, and a horse for a hundred and fifty.[m] They also exported them to all the kings of the Hittites and of the Arameans.

CHAPTER 11

King Solomon, however, loved many foreign women besides Pharaoh's daughter—Moabites, Ammonites, Edomites, Sidonians and Hittites. [2]They were from nations about which the Lord had told the Israelites, "You must not intermarry with them, because they will surely turn your hearts after their gods." Nevertheless, Solomon held fast to them in love. [3]He had seven hundred wives of royal birth and three hundred concubines, and his wives led him astray. [4]As Solomon grew old, his wives turned his heart after other gods, and his heart was not fully devoted to the Lord his God, as the heart of David his father had been. [5]He followed Ashtoreth the goddess of the Sidonians, and Molech[s] the detestable god of the Ammonites. [6]So Solomon did evil in the eyes of the Lord; he did not follow the Lord completely, as David his father had done.

[7]On a hill east of Jerusalem, Solomon built a high place for Chemosh the detestable god of Moab, and for Molech the detestable god of the Ammonites. [8]He did the same for all his foreign wives, who burned incense and offered sacrifices to their gods.

[9]The Lord became angry with Solomon because his heart had turned away from the Lord, the God of Israel, who had ap-

---

j 11 Probably a variant of *algumwood*; also in verse 12   *k 14* That is, about 25 tons (about 23 metric tons)   *l 16* That is, about 7 1/2 pounds (about 3.5 kilograms)   *m 17,29* That is, about 3 3/4 pounds (about 1.7 kilograms)   *n 22* Hebrew *of ships of Tarshish*   *o 26* Or *charioteers*   *p 28* Or possibly *Muzur*, a region in Cilicia; also in verse 29   *q 28* Probably *Cilicia*   *r 29* That is, about 15 pounds (about 7 kilograms)   *s 5* Hebrew *Milcom*; also in verse 33 peared to him twice. [10]Although he had forbidden Solomon to follow other gods, Solomon did not keep the LORD's command. [11]So the LORD said to Solomon, "Since this is your attitude and you have not kept my covenant and my decrees, which I commanded you, I will most certainly tear the kingdom away from you and give it to one of your subordinates. [12]Nevertheless, for the sake of David your father, I will not do it during your lifetime. I will tear it out of the hand of your son. [13]Yet I will not tear the whole kingdom from him, but will give him one tribe for the sake of David my servant and for the sake of Jerusalem, which I have chosen."

[14]Then the LORD raised up against Solomon an adversary, Hadad the Edomite, from the royal line of Edom. [15]Earlier when David was fighting with Edom, Joab the commander of the army, who had gone up to bury the dead, had struck down all the men in Edom. [16]Joab and all the Israelites stayed there for six months, until they had destroyed all the men in Edom. [17]But Hadad, still only a boy, fled to Egypt with some Edomite officials who had served his father. [18]They set out from Midian and went to Paran. Then taking men from Paran with them, they went to Egypt, to Pharaoh king of Egypt, who gave Hadad a house and land and provided him with food.

[19]Pharaoh was so pleased with Hadad that he gave him a sister of his own wife, Queen Tahpenes, in marriage. [20]The sister of Tahpenes bore him a son named Genubath, whom Tahpenes brought up in the royal palace. There Genubath lived with Pharaoh's own children.

[21]While he was in Egypt, Hadad heard that David rested with his fathers and that Joab the commander of the army was also dead. Then Hadad said to Pharaoh, "Let me go, that I may return to my own country."

[22]"What have you lacked here that you want to go back to your own country?" Pharaoh asked.

"Nothing," Hadad replied, "but do let me go!"

[23]And God raised up against Solomon another adversary, Rezon son of Eliada, who had fled from his master, Hadadezer king of Zobah. [24]He gathered men around him and became the leader of a band of rebels when David destroyed the forces[t] ⌊of Zobah⌋; the rebels went to Damascus, where they settled and took control. [25]Rezon was Israel's adversary as long as Solomon lived, adding to the trouble caused by Hadad. So Rezon ruled in Aram and was hostile toward Israel.

[26]Also, Jeroboam son of Nebat rebelled against the king. He was one of Solomon's officials, an Ephraimite from Zeredah, and his mother was a widow named Zeruah.

[27]Here is the account of how he rebelled against the king: Solomon had built the supporting terraces[u] and had filled in the gap in the wall of the city of David his father. [28]Now Jeroboam was a man of standing, and when Solomon saw how well the young man did his work, he put him in charge of the whole labor force of the house of Joseph.

[29]About that time Jeroboam was going out of Jerusalem, and Ahijah the prophet of Shiloh met him on the way, wearing a new cloak. The two of them were alone out in the country, [30]and Ahijah took hold of the new cloak he was wearing and tore it into twelve pieces. [31]Then he said to Jeroboam, "Take ten pieces for yourself, for this is what the LORD, the God of Israel, says: 'See, I am going to tear the kingdom out of Solomon's hand and give you ten tribes. [32]But for the sake of my servant David and the city of Jerusalem, which I have chosen out of all the tribes of Israel, he will have one tribe. [33]I will do this because they have[v] forsaken me and worshiped Ashtoreth the goddess of the Sidonians, Chemosh the god of the Moabites, and Molech the god of the Ammonites, and have not walked in my ways, nor done what is right in my eyes, nor kept my statutes and laws as David, Solomon's father, did.

[34]" 'But I will not take the whole kingdom out of Solomon's hand; I have made him ruler all the days of his life for the sake of David my servant, whom I chose and who observed my commands and statutes. [35]I will take the kingdom from his son's hands and give you ten tribes. [36]I will give one tribe to his son so that David my servant may always have a lamp

before me in Jerusalem, the city where I chose to put my Name. ³⁷However, as for you, I will take you, and you will rule over all that your heart desires; you will be king over Israel. ³⁸If you do whatever I command you and walk in my ways and do what is right in my eyes by keeping my statutes and commands, as David my servant did, I will be with you. I will build you a dynasty as enduring as the one I built for David and will give Israel to you. ³⁹I will humble David's descendants because of this, but not forever.' "

⁴⁰Solomon tried to kill Jeroboam, but Jeroboam fled to Egypt, to Shishak the king, and stayed there until Solomon's death.

⁴¹As for the other events of Solomon's reign—all he did and the wisdom he displayed—are they not written in the book of the annals of Solomon? ⁴²Solomon reigned in Jerusalem over all Israel forty years. ⁴³Then he rested with his fathers and was buried in the city of David his father. And Rehoboam his son succeeded him as king.

APRIL 4 ☐ DAY 95
1 KINGS 12–16
Israel's Civil War

 OVERVIEW What was sown by Solomon is now reaped by Rehoboam. Solomon's great wealth was accumulated partially through excessive taxation of the people. Rehoboam, his son, faced with the choice of decreasing or increasing taxes, foolishly follows the counsel of his young advisors. He increases the tax burden on the people, prompting open revolt and the fracturing of the kingdom. One nation becomes two, with Jeroboam ruling the ten tribes in the north (Israel) and Rehoboam ruling only two tribes in the south (Judah). Jeroboam charts a godless course of idol worship in Israel that every one of his successors will imitate. In Judah the picture is somewhat brighter as godly kings (such as Asa) introduce periodic revivals that, although short-lived, profoundly influence their nation for God.

Chapters 12–13	Chapter 14	Chapters 15–16
Reign by Jeroboam	Reign by Rehoboam	Reigns of Eight Kings
Israel	Judah	Israel and Judah

 YOUR DAILY WALK Rate the following six influences in the order that you feel they have affected the lives of your children (or your own life if you are not a parent). Use 1 for "most influential," 2 for "next most influential," etc.

Others will follow your footsteps more easily than they will follow your advice.

_____ Television   _____ Church
_____ Parents   _____ Friends
_____ School   _____ Brothers/Sisters

The epitaph "He walked in the ways of his father" could be penned over almost every king you will read about in today's section. With surprising regularity the son became a carbon copy of his father, patterning his spiritual and moral actions after those of his parent.

Parent, if your children walk in your ways, will you be happy or horrified? Tonight before putting them to bed, give them the above quiz. Then discuss ways that as a family you can walk in the way of the Lord.

INSIGHT Six Decades of Kingly Calamity
Of the six kings of Israel in today's reading, only two died of natural causes. Two others were murdered, one was stricken by God and one committed suicide—all in the space of fifty-seven years!

CHAPTER 12

Rehoboam went to Shechem, for all the Israelites had gone there to make him king. [2]When Jeroboam son of Nebat heard this (he was still in Egypt, where he had fled from King Solomon), he returned from[w] Egypt. [3]So they sent for Jeroboam, and he and the whole assembly of Israel went to Rehoboam and said to him: [4]"Your father put a heavy yoke on us, but now lighten the harsh labor and the heavy yoke he put on us, and we will serve you."

[5]Rehoboam answered, "Go away for three days and then come back to me." So the people went away.

[6]Then King Rehoboam consulted the elders who had served his father Solomon during his lifetime. "How would you advise me to answer these people?" he asked.

[7]They replied, "If today you will be a servant to these people and serve them and give them a favorable answer, they will always be your servants."

[8]But Rehoboam rejected the advice the elders gave him and consulted the young men who had grown up with him and were serving him. [9]He asked them, "What is your advice? How should we answer these people who say to me, 'Lighten the yoke your father put on us'?"

[10]The young men who had grown up with him replied, "Tell these people who have said to you, 'Your father put a heavy yoke on us, but make our yoke lighter'— tell them, 'My little finger is thicker than my father's waist. [11]My father laid on you a heavy yoke; I will make it even heavier. My father scourged you with whips; I will scourge you with scorpions.'"

[12]Three days later Jeroboam and all the people returned to Rehoboam, as the king had said, "Come back to me in three days." [13]The king answered the people harshly. Rejecting the advice given him by the elders, [14]he followed the advice of the young men and said, "My father made your yoke heavy; I will make it even heavier. My father scourged you with whips; I will scourge you with scorpions."

[15]So the king did not listen to the people, for this turn of events was from the LORD, to fulfill the word the LORD had spoken to Jeroboam son of Nebat through Ahijah the Shilonite.

[16]When all Israel saw that the king refused to listen to them, they answered the king:

> "What share do we have in David,
>   what part in Jesse's son?
> To your tents, O Israel!
>   Look after your own house,
>   O David!"

So the Israelites went home. [17]But as for the Israelites who were living in the towns of Judah, Rehoboam still ruled over them.

[18]King Rehoboam sent out Adoniram,[x] who was in charge of forced labor, but all Israel stoned him to death. King Rehoboam, however, managed to get into his chariot and escape to Jerusalem. [19]So Israel has been in rebellion against the house of David to this day.

[20]When all the Israelites heard that Jeroboam had returned, they sent and called him to the assembly and made him king over all Israel. Only the tribe of Judah remained loyal to the house of David.

[21]When Rehoboam arrived in Jerusalem, he mustered the whole house of Judah and the tribe of Benjamin—a hundred and eighty thousand fighting men—to make war against the house of Israel and to regain the kingdom for Rehoboam son of Solomon.

[22]But this word of God came to Shemaiah the man of God: [23]"Say to Rehoboam son of Solomon king of Judah, to the whole house of Judah and Benjamin, and to the rest of the people, [24]'This is what the LORD says: Do not go up to fight against your brothers, the Israelites. Go home, every one of you, for this is my doing.'" So they obeyed the word of the LORD and went home again, as the LORD had ordered.

[25]Then Jeroboam fortified Shechem in the hill country of Ephraim and lived

---

[w]*2* Or *he remained in*   [x]*18* Some Septuagint manuscripts and Syriac (see also 1 Kings 4:6 and 5:14); Hebrew *Adoram*

there. From there he went out and built up Peniel.ʸ

²⁶Jeroboam thought to himself, "The kingdom will now likely revert to the house of David. ²⁷If these people go up to offer sacrifices at the temple of the LORD in Jerusalem, they will again give their allegiance to their lord, Rehoboam king of Judah. They will kill me and return to King Rehoboam."

²⁸After seeking advice, the king made two golden calves. He said to the people, "It is too much for you to go up to Jerusalem. Here are your gods, O Israel, who brought you up out of Egypt." ²⁹One he set up in Bethel, and the other in Dan. ³⁰And this thing became a sin; the people went even as far as Dan to worship the one there.

³¹Jeroboam built shrines on high places and appointed priests from all sorts of people, even though they were not Levites. ³²He instituted a festival on the fifteenth day of the eighth month, like the festival held in Judah, and offered sacrifices on the altar. This he did in Bethel, sacrificing to the calves he had made. And at Bethel he also installed priests at the high places he had made. ³³On the fifteenth day of the eighth month, a month of his own choosing, he offered sacrifices on the altar he had built at Bethel. So he instituted the festival for the Israelites and went up to the altar to make offerings.

CHAPTER 13
By the word of the LORD a man of God came from Judah to Bethel, as Jeroboam was standing by the altar to make an offering. ²He cried out against the altar by the word of the LORD: "O altar, altar! This is what the LORD says: 'A son named Josiah will be born to the house of David. On you he will sacrifice the priests of the high places who now make offerings here, and human bones will be burned on you.' " ³That same day the man of God gave a sign: "This is the sign the LORD has declared: The altar will be split apart and the ashes on it will be poured out."

⁴When King Jeroboam heard what the man of God cried out against the altar at Bethel, he stretched out his hand from the altar and said, "Seize him!" But the hand he stretched out toward the man shriv-

eled up, so that he could not pull it back. ⁵Also, the altar was split apart and its ashes poured out according to the sign given by the man of God by the word of the LORD.

⁶Then the king said to the man of God, "Intercede with the LORD your God and pray for me that my hand may be restored." So the man of God interceded with the LORD, and the king's hand was restored and became as it was before.

⁷The king said to the man of God, "Come home with me and have something to eat, and I will give you a gift."

⁸But the man of God answered the king, "Even if you were to give me half your possessions, I would not go with you, nor would I eat bread or drink water here. ⁹For I was commanded by the word of the LORD: 'You must not eat bread or drink water or return by the way you came.' " ¹⁰So he took another road and did not return by the way he had come to Bethel.

¹¹Now there was a certain old prophet living in Bethel, whose sons came and told him all that the man of God had done there that day. They also told their father what he had said to the king. ¹²Their father asked them, "Which way did he go?" And his sons showed him which road the man of God from Judah had taken. ¹³So he said to his sons, "Saddle the donkey for me." And when they had saddled the donkey for him, he mounted it ¹⁴and rode after the man of God. He found him sitting under an oak tree and asked, "Are you the man of God who came from Judah?"

"I am," he replied.

¹⁵So the prophet said to him, "Come home with me and eat."

¹⁶The man of God said, "I cannot turn back and go with you, nor can I eat bread or drink water with you in this place. ¹⁷I have been told by the word of the LORD: 'You must not eat bread or drink water there or return by the way you came.' "

¹⁸The old prophet answered, "I too am a prophet, as you are. And an angel said to me by the word of the LORD: 'Bring him back with you to your house so that he may eat bread and drink water.' " (But he was lying to him.) ¹⁹So the man of God returned with him and ate and drank in his house.

ʸ25 Hebrew *Penuel*, a variant of *Peniel*

²⁰While they were sitting at the table, the word of the LORD came to the old prophet who had brought him back. ²¹He cried out to the man of God who had come from Judah, "This is what the LORD says: 'You have defied the word of the LORD and have not kept the command the LORD your God gave you. ²²You came back and ate bread and drank water in the place where he told you not to eat or drink. Therefore your body will not be buried in the tomb of your fathers.' "

²³When the man of God had finished eating and drinking, the prophet who had brought him back saddled his donkey for him. ²⁴As he went on his way, a lion met him on the road and killed him, and his body was thrown down on the road, with both the donkey and the lion standing beside it. ²⁵Some people who passed by saw the body thrown down there, with the lion standing beside the body, and they went and reported it in the city where the old prophet lived.

²⁶When the prophet who had brought him back from his journey heard of it, he said, "It is the man of God who defied the word of the LORD. The LORD has given him over to the lion, which has mauled him and killed him, as the word of the LORD had warned him."

²⁷The prophet said to his sons, "Saddle the donkey for me," and they did so. ²⁸Then he went out and found the body thrown down on the road, with the donkey and the lion standing beside it. The lion had neither eaten the body nor mauled the donkey. ²⁹So the prophet picked up the body of the man of God, laid it on the donkey, and brought it back to his own city to mourn for him and bury him. ³⁰Then he laid the body in his own tomb, and they mourned over him and said, "Oh, my brother!"

³¹After burying him, he said to his sons, "When I die, bury me in the grave where the man of God is buried; lay my bones beside his bones. ³²For the message he declared by the word of the LORD against the altar in Bethel and against all the shrines on the high places in the towns of Samaria will certainly come true."

³³Even after this, Jeroboam did not change his evil ways, but once more appointed priests for the high places from all sorts of people. Anyone who wanted to become a priest he consecrated for the high places. ³⁴This was the sin of the house of Jeroboam that led to its downfall and to its destruction from the face of the earth.

CHAPTER 14

At that time Abijah son of Jeroboam became ill, ²and Jeroboam said to his wife, "Go, disguise yourself, so you won't be recognized as the wife of Jeroboam. Then go to Shiloh. Ahijah the prophet is there—the one who told me I would be king over this people. ³Take ten loaves of bread with you, some cakes and a jar of honey, and go to him. He will tell you what will happen to the boy." ⁴So Jeroboam's wife did what he said and went to Ahijah's house in Shiloh.

Now Ahijah could not see; his sight was gone because of his age. ⁵But the LORD had told Ahijah, "Jeroboam's wife is coming to ask you about her son, for he is ill, and you are to give her such and such an answer. When she arrives, she will pretend to be someone else."

⁶So when Ahijah heard the sound of her footsteps at the door, he said, "Come in, wife of Jeroboam. Why this pretense? I have been sent to you with bad news. ⁷Go, tell Jeroboam that this is what the LORD, the God of Israel, says: 'I raised you up from among the people and made you a leader over my people Israel. ⁸I tore the kingdom away from the house of David and gave it to you, but you have not been like my servant David, who kept my commands and followed me with all his heart, doing only what was right in my eyes. ⁹You have done more evil than all who lived before you. You have made for yourself other gods, idols made of metal; you have provoked me to anger and thrust me behind your back.

¹⁰" 'Because of this, I am going to bring disaster on the house of Jeroboam. I will cut off from Jeroboam every last male in Israel—slave or free. I will burn up the house of Jeroboam as one burns dung, until it is all gone. ¹¹Dogs will eat those belonging to Jeroboam who die in the city, and the birds of the air will feed on those who die in the country. The LORD has spoken!'

¹²"As for you, go back home. When you set foot in your city, the boy will die. ¹³All Israel will mourn for him and bury him. He is the only one belonging to Jeroboam

who will be buried, because he is the only one in the house of Jeroboam in whom the LORD, the God of Israel, has found anything good.

[14]"The LORD will raise up for himself a king over Israel who will cut off the family of Jeroboam. This is the day! What? Yes, even now.[z] [15]And the LORD will strike Israel, so that it will be like a reed swaying in the water. He will uproot Israel from this good land that he gave to their forefathers and scatter them beyond the River,[a] because they provoked the LORD to anger by making Asherah poles.[b] [16]And he will give Israel up because of the sins Jeroboam has committed and has caused Israel to commit."

[17]Then Jeroboam's wife got up and left and went to Tirzah. As soon as she stepped over the threshold of the house, the boy died. [18]They buried him, and all Israel mourned for him, as the LORD had said through his servant the prophet Ahijah.

[19]The other events of Jeroboam's reign, his wars and how he ruled, are written in the book of the annals of the kings of Israel. [20]He reigned for twenty-two years and then rested with his fathers. And Nadab his son succeeded him as king.

[21]Rehoboam son of Solomon was king in Judah. He was forty-one years old when he became king, and he reigned seventeen years in Jerusalem, the city the LORD had chosen out of all the tribes of Israel in which to put his Name. His mother's name was Naamah; she was an Ammonite.

[22]Judah did evil in the eyes of the LORD. By the sins they committed they stirred up his jealous anger more than their fathers had done. [23]They also set up for themselves high places, sacred stones and Asherah poles on every high hill and under every spreading tree. [24]There were even male shrine prostitutes in the land; the people engaged in all the detestable practices of the nations the LORD had driven out before the Israelites.

[25]In the fifth year of King Rehoboam, Shishak king of Egypt attacked Jerusalem. [26]He carried off the treasures of the temple of the LORD and the treasures of the royal palace. He took everything, including all the gold shields Solomon had made. [27]So King Rehoboam made bronze shields to replace them and assigned these to the commanders of the guard on duty at the entrance to the royal palace. [28]Whenever the king went to the LORD's temple, the guards bore the shields, and afterward they returned them to the guardroom.

[29]As for the other events of Rehoboam's reign, and all he did, are they not written in the book of the annals of the kings of Judah? [30]There was continual warfare between Rehoboam and Jeroboam. [31]And Rehoboam rested with his fathers and was buried with them in the City of David. His mother's name was Naamah; she was an Ammonite. And Abijah[c] his son succeeded him as king.

CHAPTER 15

In the eighteenth year of the reign of Jeroboam son of Nebat, Abijah[d] became king of Judah, [2]and he reigned in Jerusalem three years. His mother's name was Maacah daughter of Abishalom.[e]

[3]He committed all the sins his father had done before him; his heart was not fully devoted to the LORD his God, as the heart of David his forefather had been. [4]Nevertheless, for David's sake the LORD his God gave him a lamp in Jerusalem by raising up a son to succeed him and by making Jerusalem strong. [5]For David had done what was right in the eyes of the LORD and had not failed to keep any of the LORD's commands all the days of his life—except in the case of Uriah the Hittite.

[6]There was war between Rehoboam[f] and Jeroboam throughout ⌊Abijah's⌋ lifetime. [7]As for the other events of Abijah's reign, and all he did, are they not written in the book of the annals of the kings of Judah? There was war between Abijah and Jeroboam. [8]And Abijah rested with his fathers and was buried in the City of David. And Asa his son succeeded him as king.

[9]In the twentieth year of Jeroboam king of Israel, Asa became king of Judah, [10]and he reigned in Jerusalem forty-one years.

[z]14 The meaning of the Hebrew for this sentence is uncertain.   [a]15 That is, the Euphrates   [b]15 That is, symbols of the goddess Asherah; here and elsewhere in 1 Kings   [c]31 Some Hebrew manuscripts and Septuagint (see also 2 Chron. 12:16); most Hebrew manuscripts Abijam   [d]1 Some Hebrew manuscripts and Septuagint (see also 2 Chron. 12:16); most Hebrew manuscripts Abijam; also in verses 7 and 8   [e]2 A variant of Absalom; also in verse 10   [f]6 Most Hebrew manuscripts; some Hebrew manuscripts and Syriac Abijam (that is, Abijah)

His grandmother's name was Maacah daughter of Abishalom.

[11] Asa did what was right in the eyes of the LORD, as his father David had done. [12] He expelled the male shrine prostitutes from the land and got rid of all the idols his fathers had made. [13] He even deposed his grandmother Maacah from her position as queen mother, because she had made a repulsive Asherah pole. Asa cut the pole down and burned it in the Kidron Valley. [14] Although he did not remove the high places, Asa's heart was fully committed to the LORD all his life. [15] He brought into the temple of the LORD the silver and gold and the articles that he and his father had dedicated.

[16] There was war between Asa and Baasha king of Israel throughout their reigns. [17] Baasha king of Israel went up against Judah and fortified Ramah to prevent anyone from leaving or entering the territory of Asa king of Judah.

[18] Asa then took all the silver and gold that was left in the treasuries of the LORD's temple and of his own palace. He entrusted it to his officials and sent them to Ben-Hadad son of Tabrimmon, the son of Hezion, the king of Aram, who was ruling in Damascus. [19] "Let there be a treaty between me and you," he said, "as there was between my father and your father. See, I am sending you a gift of silver and gold. Now break your treaty with Baasha king of Israel so he will withdraw from me."

[20] Ben-Hadad agreed with King Asa and sent the commanders of his forces against the towns of Israel. He conquered Ijon, Dan, Abel Beth Maacah and all Kinnereth in addition to Naphtali. [21] When Baasha heard this, he stopped building Ramah and withdrew to Tirzah. [22] Then King Asa issued an order to all Judah—no one was exempt—and they carried away from Ramah the stones and timber Baasha had been using there. With them King Asa built up Geba in Benjamin, and also Mizpah.

[23] As for all the other events of Asa's reign, all his achievements, all he did and the cities he built, are they not written in the book of the annals of the kings of Judah? In his old age, however, his feet became diseased. [24] Then Asa rested with his fathers and was buried with them in the city of his father David. And Jehoshaphat his son succeeded him as king.

[25] Nadab son of Jeroboam became king of Israel in the second year of Asa king of Judah, and he reigned over Israel two years. [26] He did evil in the eyes of the LORD, walking in the ways of his father and in his sin, which he had caused Israel to commit.

[27] Baasha son of Ahijah of the house of Issachar plotted against him, and he struck him down at Gibbethon, a Philistine town, while Nadab and all Israel were besieging it. [28] Baasha killed Nadab in the third year of Asa king of Judah and succeeded him as king.

[29] As soon as he began to reign, he killed Jeroboam's whole family. He did not leave Jeroboam anyone that breathed, but destroyed them all, according to the word of the LORD given through his servant Ahijah the Shilonite— [30] because of the sins Jeroboam had committed and had caused Israel to commit, and because he provoked the LORD, the God of Israel, to anger.

[31] As for the other events of Nadab's reign, and all he did, are they not written in the book of the annals of the kings of Israel? [32] There was war between Asa and Baasha king of Israel throughout their reigns.

[33] In the third year of Asa king of Judah, Baasha son of Ahijah became king of all Israel in Tirzah, and he reigned twenty-four years. [34] He did evil in the eyes of the LORD, walking in the ways of Jeroboam and in his sin, which he had caused Israel to commit.

CHAPTER 16
Then the word of the LORD came to Jehu son of Hanani against Baasha: [2] "I lifted you up from the dust and made you leader of my people Israel, but you walked in the ways of Jeroboam and caused my people Israel to sin and to provoke me to anger by their sins. [3] So I am about to consume Baasha and his house, and I will make your house like that of Jeroboam son of Nebat. [4] Dogs will eat those belonging to Baasha who die in the city, and the birds of the air will feed on those who die in the country."

[5] As for the other events of Baasha's reign, what he did and his achievements, are they not written in the book of the annals of the kings of Israel? [6] Baasha rested with his fathers and was buried in

Tirzah. And Elah his son succeeded him as king.

[7]Moreover, the word of the LORD came through the prophet Jehu son of Hanani to Baasha and his house, because of all the evil he had done in the eyes of the LORD, provoking him to anger by the things he did, and becoming like the house of Jeroboam—and also because he destroyed it.

[8]In the twenty-sixth year of Asa king of Judah, Elah son of Baasha became king of Israel, and he reigned in Tirzah two years.

[9]Zimri, one of his officials, who had command of half his chariots, plotted against him. Elah was in Tirzah at the time, getting drunk in the home of Arza, the man in charge of the palace at Tirzah. [10]Zimri came in, struck him down and killed him in the twenty-seventh year of Asa king of Judah. Then he succeeded him as king.

[11]As soon as he began to reign and was seated on the throne, he killed off Baasha's whole family. He did not spare a single male, whether relative or friend. [12]So Zimri destroyed the whole family of Baasha, in accordance with the word of the LORD spoken against Baasha through the prophet Jehu— [13]because of all the sins Baasha and his son Elah had committed and had caused Israel to commit, so that they provoked the LORD, the God of Israel, to anger by their worthless idols.

[14]As for the other events of Elah's reign, and all he did, are they not written in the book of the annals of the kings of Israel?

[15]In the twenty-seventh year of Asa king of Judah, Zimri reigned in Tirzah seven days. The army was encamped near Gibbethon, a Philistine town. [16]When the Israelites in the camp heard that Zimri had plotted against the king and murdered him, they proclaimed Omri, the commander of the army, king over Israel that very day there in the camp. [17]Then Omri and all the Israelites with him withdrew from Gibbethon and laid siege to Tirzah. [18]When Zimri saw that the city was taken, he went into the citadel of the royal palace and set the palace on fire around him. So he died, [19]because of the sins he had committed, doing evil in the eyes of the LORD and walking in the ways of Jeroboam and in the sin he had committed and had caused Israel to commit.

[20]As for the other events of Zimri's reign, and the rebellion he carried out, are they not written in the book of the annals of the kings of Israel?

[21]Then the people of Israel were split into two factions; half supported Tibni son of Ginath for king, and the other half supported Omri. [22]But Omri's followers proved stronger than those of Tibni son of Ginath. So Tibni died and Omri became king.

[23]In the thirty-first year of Asa king of Judah, Omri became king of Israel, and he reigned twelve years, six of them in Tirzah. [24]He bought the hill of Samaria from Shemer for two talents[g] of silver and built a city on the hill, calling it Samaria, after Shemer, the name of the former owner of the hill.

[25]But Omri did evil in the eyes of the LORD and sinned more than all those before him. [26]He walked in all the ways of Jeroboam son of Nebat and in his sin, which he had caused Israel to commit, so that they provoked the LORD, the God of Israel, to anger by their worthless idols.

[27]As for the other events of Omri's reign, what he did and the things he achieved, are they not written in the book of the annals of the kings of Israel? [28]Omri rested with his fathers and was buried in Samaria. And Ahab his son succeeded him as king.

[29]In the thirty-eighth year of Asa king of Judah, Ahab son of Omri became king of Israel, and he reigned in Samaria over Israel twenty-two years. [30]Ahab son of Omri did more evil in the eyes of the LORD than any of those before him. [31]He not only considered it trivial to commit the sins of Jeroboam son of Nebat, but he also married Jezebel daughter of Ethbaal king of the Sidonians, and began to serve Baal and worship him. [32]He set up an altar for Baal in the temple of Baal that he built in Samaria. [33]Ahab also made an Asherah pole and did more to provoke the LORD, the God of Israel, to anger than did all the kings of Israel before him.

[34]In Ahab's time, Hiel of Bethel rebuilt Jericho. He laid its foundations at the cost of his firstborn son Abiram, and he set up its gates at the cost of his youngest son Segub, in accordance with the word of the LORD spoken by Joshua son of Nun.

g24 That is, about 150 pounds (about 70 kilograms)

APRIL 5 □ DAY 96
1 KINGS 17–19
Ahab's Battle with Elijah

OVERVIEW Without fanfare or announcement, the prophet Elijah bursts upon the scene of Israel's history to predict a severe drought during the reign of King Ahab. At the peak of the drought, the prophet returns to challenge Ahab and the prophets of Baal to a "battle of the gods" on Mount Carmel. In a fiery display of power and majesty, God consumes the offering, wood, stones, dirt and water of Elijah's sacrifice, proving to the onlooking nation that he alone is the Lord God. When the news of Elijah's victory reaches Queen Jezebel, she vows to end his life. Once again the prophet returns to seclusion where God ministers to his exhausted and discouraged servant.

Chapter 17	Chapter 18	Chapter 19
Elijah and the Widow at Zarephath	Elijah and the Prophets of Baal	Elijah and the Fear of Jezebel
God's Provision	God's Power	God's Persistence

YOUR DAILY WALK When was the last time you suffered a bout of depression or self-pity? Do you remember what caused it? How long did it last? What finally helped you to overcome it?

To hatch despair, just brood over your troubles.

In 1 Kings 19 you will see Elijah in one of those blue moods of depression, his thoughts filled with self-pity: "I have been very zealous for the LORD God Almighty. . . . I am the only one left, and now they are trying to kill me too" (19:10). Did you notice when the prophet of God fell into the doldrums of depression? It was immediately after one of the greatest spiritual victories of his life! He had just confronted wicked Ahab and 450 of his pagan prophets and won by a score of 450 to nothing! Then . . . depression set in.

Think back to the last low time in your walk with God. What happened immediately before it? Were you perhaps physically or emotionally drained from ministering to the needs of others? Elijah found strength to continue by hearing the gentle whisper of God (19:12). Spend some extra moments in prayer and meditation today. It's one sure cure for a run-down spiritual battery!

INSIGHT Before All Else Fails, Read the Directions!
Sometimes the greatest challenge is sitting long enough to learn God's will, rather than acting first and praying later. Read 17:2, 5, 8, 10 and 18:1–2 to discover Elijah's pattern for godly service.

CHAPTER 17

Now Elijah the Tishbite, from Tishbe[h] in Gilead, said to Ahab, "As the LORD, the God of Israel, lives, whom I serve, there will be neither dew nor rain in the next few years except at my word."

²Then the word of the LORD came to Elijah: ³"Leave here, turn eastward and hide in the Kerith Ravine, east of the Jordan. ⁴You will drink from the brook, and I have ordered the ravens to feed you there."

⁵So he did what the LORD had told him. He went to the Kerith Ravine, east of the Jordan, and stayed there. ⁶The ravens brought him bread and meat in the morning and bread and meat in the evening, and he drank from the brook.

⁷Some time later the brook dried up because there had been no rain in the land.

[h]1 Or *Tishbite, of the settlers*

⁸Then the word of the LORD came to him: ⁹"Go at once to Zarephath of Sidon and stay there. I have commanded a widow in that place to supply you with food." ¹⁰So he went to Zarephath. When he came to the town gate, a widow was there gathering sticks. He called to her and asked, "Would you bring me a little water in a jar so I may have a drink?" ¹¹As she was going to get it, he called, "And bring me, please, a piece of bread."

¹²"As surely as the LORD your God lives," she replied, "I don't have any bread—only a handful of flour in a jar and a little oil in a jug. I am gathering a few sticks to take home and make a meal for myself and my son, that we may eat it—and die."

¹³Elijah said to her, "Don't be afraid. Go home and do as you have said. But first make a small cake of bread for me from what you have and bring it to me, and then make something for yourself and your son. ¹⁴For this is what the LORD, the God of Israel, says: 'The jar of flour will not be used up and the jug of oil will not run dry until the day the LORD gives rain on the land.'"

¹⁵She went away and did as Elijah had told her. So there was food every day for Elijah and for the woman and her family. ¹⁶For the jar of flour was not used up and the jug of oil did not run dry, in keeping with the word of the LORD spoken by Elijah.

¹⁷Some time later the son of the woman who owned the house became ill. He grew worse and worse, and finally stopped breathing. ¹⁸She said to Elijah, "What do you have against me, man of God? Did you come to remind me of my sin and kill my son?"

¹⁹"Give me your son," Elijah replied. He took him from her arms, carried him to the upper room where he was staying, and laid him on his bed. ²⁰Then he cried out to the LORD, "O LORD my God, have you brought tragedy also upon this widow I am staying with, by causing her son to die?" ²¹Then he stretched himself out on the boy three times and cried to the LORD, "O LORD my God, let this boy's life return to him!"

²²The LORD heard Elijah's cry, and the boy's life returned to him, and he lived. ²³Elijah picked up the child and carried him down from the room into the house. He gave him to his mother and said, "Look, your son is alive!"

²⁴Then the woman said to Elijah, "Now I know that you are a man of God and that the word of the LORD from your mouth is the truth."

CHAPTER 18
After a long time, in the third year, the word of the LORD came to Elijah: "Go and present yourself to Ahab, and I will send rain on the land." ²So Elijah went to present himself to Ahab.

Now the famine was severe in Samaria, ³and Ahab had summoned Obadiah, who was in charge of his palace. (Obadiah was a devout believer in the LORD. ⁴While Jezebel was killing off the LORD's prophets, Obadiah had taken a hundred prophets and hidden them in two caves, fifty in each, and had supplied them with food and water.) ⁵Ahab had said to Obadiah, "Go through the land to all the springs and valleys. Maybe we can find some grass to keep the horses and mules alive so we will not have to kill any of our animals." ⁶So they divided the land they were to cover, Ahab going in one direction and Obadiah in another.

⁷As Obadiah was walking along, Elijah met him. Obadiah recognized him, bowed down to the ground, and said, "Is it really you, my lord Elijah?"

⁸"Yes," he replied. "Go tell your master, 'Elijah is here.'"

⁹"What have I done wrong," asked Obadiah, "that you are handing your servant over to Ahab to be put to death? ¹⁰As surely as the LORD your God lives, there is not a nation or kingdom where my master has not sent someone to look for you. And whenever a nation or kingdom claimed you were not there, he made them swear they could not find you. ¹¹But now you tell me to go to my master and say, 'Elijah is here.' ¹²I don't know where the Spirit of the LORD may carry you when I leave you. If I go and tell Ahab and he doesn't find you, he will kill me. Yet I your servant have worshiped the LORD since my youth. ¹³Haven't you heard, my lord, what I did while Jezebel was killing the prophets of the LORD? I hid a hundred of the LORD's prophets in two caves, fifty in each, and supplied them with food and water. ¹⁴And now you tell me to go to my mas-

ter and say, 'Elijah is here.' He will kill me!"

¹⁵Elijah said, "As the LORD Almighty lives, whom I serve, I will surely present myself to Ahab today."

¹⁶So Obadiah went to meet Ahab and told him, and Ahab went to meet Elijah. ¹⁷When he saw Elijah, he said to him, "Is that you, you troubler of Israel?"

¹⁸"I have not made trouble for Israel," Elijah replied. "But you and your father's family have. You have abandoned the LORD's commands and have followed the Baals. ¹⁹Now summon the people from all over Israel to meet me on Mount Carmel. And bring the four hundred and fifty prophets of Baal and the four hundred prophets of Asherah, who eat at Jezebel's table."

²⁰So Ahab sent word throughout all Israel and assembled the prophets on Mount Carmel. ²¹Elijah went before the people and said, "How long will you waver between two opinions? If the LORD is God, follow him; but if Baal is God, follow him."

But the people said nothing.

²²Then Elijah said to them, "I am the only one of the LORD's prophets left, but Baal has four hundred and fifty prophets. ²³Get two bulls for us. Let them choose one for themselves, and let them cut it into pieces and put it on the wood but not set fire to it. I will prepare the other bull and put it on the wood but not set fire to it. ²⁴Then you call on the name of your god, and I will call on the name of the LORD. The god who answers by fire—he is God."

Then all the people said, "What you say is good."

²⁵Elijah said to the prophets of Baal, "Choose one of the bulls and prepare it first, since there are so many of you. Call on the name of your god, but do not light the fire." ²⁶So they took the bull given them and prepared it.

Then they called on the name of Baal from morning till noon. "O Baal, answer us!" they shouted. But there was no response; no one answered. And they danced around the altar they had made.

²⁷At noon Elijah began to taunt them. "Shout louder!" he said. "Surely he is a god! Perhaps he is deep in thought, or busy, or traveling. Maybe he is sleeping and must be awakened." ²⁸So they shouted louder and slashed themselves with swords and spears, as was their custom, until their blood flowed. ²⁹Midday passed, and they continued their frantic prophesying until the time for the evening sacrifice. But there was no response, no one answered, no one paid attention.

³⁰Then Elijah said to all the people, "Come here to me." They came to him, and he repaired the altar of the LORD, which was in ruins. ³¹Elijah took twelve stones, one for each of the tribes descended from Jacob, to whom the word of the LORD had come, saying, "Your name shall be Israel." ³²With the stones he built an altar in the name of the LORD, and he dug a trench around it large enough to hold two seahs[i] of seed. ³³He arranged the wood, cut the bull into pieces and laid it on the wood. Then he said to them, "Fill four large jars with water and pour it on the offering and on the wood."

³⁴"Do it again," he said, and they did it again.

"Do it a third time," he ordered, and they did it the third time. ³⁵The water ran down around the altar and even filled the trench.

³⁶At the time of sacrifice, the prophet Elijah stepped forward and prayed: "O LORD, God of Abraham, Isaac and Israel, let it be known today that you are God in Israel and that I am your servant and have done all these things at your command. ³⁷Answer me, O LORD, answer me, so these people will know that you, O LORD, are God, and that you are turning their hearts back again."

³⁸Then the fire of the LORD fell and burned up the sacrifice, the wood, the stones and the soil, and also licked up the water in the trench.

³⁹When all the people saw this, they fell prostrate and cried, "The LORD—he is God! The LORD—he is God!"

⁴⁰Then Elijah commanded them, "Seize the prophets of Baal. Don't let anyone get away!" They seized them, and Elijah had them brought down to the Kishon Valley and slaughtered there.

i32 That is, probably about 13 quarts (about 15 liters)

⁴¹And Elijah said to Ahab, "Go, eat and drink, for there is the sound of a heavy rain." ⁴²So Ahab went off to eat and drink, but Elijah climbed to the top of Carmel, bent down to the ground and put his face between his knees.

⁴³"Go and look toward the sea," he told his servant. And he went up and looked. "There is nothing there," he said.

Seven times Elijah said, "Go back."

⁴⁴The seventh time the servant reported, "A cloud as small as a man's hand is rising from the sea."

So Elijah said, "Go and tell Ahab, 'Hitch up your chariot and go down before the rain stops you.' "

⁴⁵Meanwhile, the sky grew black with clouds, the wind rose, a heavy rain came on and Ahab rode off to Jezreel. ⁴⁶The power of the LORD came upon Elijah and, tucking his cloak into his belt, he ran ahead of Ahab all the way to Jezreel.

CHAPTER 19
Now Ahab told Jezebel everything Elijah had done and how he had killed all the prophets with the sword. ²So Jezebel sent a messenger to Elijah to say, "May the gods deal with me, be it ever so severely, if by this time tomorrow I do not make your life like that of one of them."

³Elijah was afraidʲ and ran for his life. When he came to Beersheba in Judah, he left his servant there, ⁴while he himself went a day's journey into the desert. He came to a broom tree, sat down under it and prayed that he might die. "I have had enough, LORD," he said. "Take my life; I am no better than my ancestors." ⁵Then he lay down under the tree and fell asleep.

All at once an angel touched him and said, "Get up and eat." ⁶He looked around, and there by his head was a cake of bread baked over hot coals, and a jar of water. He ate and drank and then lay down again.

⁷The angel of the LORD came back a second time and touched him and said, "Get up and eat, for the journey is too much for you." ⁸So he got up and ate and drank. Strengthened by that food, he traveled forty days and forty nights until he reached Horeb, the mountain of God. ⁹There he went into a cave and spent the night.

And the word of the LORD came to him: "What are you doing here, Elijah?"

¹⁰He replied, "I have been very zealous for the LORD God Almighty. The Israelites have rejected your covenant, broken down your altars, and put your prophets to death with the sword. I am the only one left, and now they are trying to kill me too."

¹¹The LORD said, "Go out and stand on the mountain in the presence of the LORD, for the LORD is about to pass by."

Then a great and powerful wind tore the mountains apart and shattered the rocks before the LORD, but the LORD was not in the wind. After the wind there was an earthquake, but the LORD was not in the earthquake. ¹²After the earthquake came a fire, but the LORD was not in the fire. And after the fire came a gentle whisper. ¹³When Elijah heard it, he pulled his cloak over his face and went out and stood at the mouth of the cave.

Then a voice said to him, "What are you doing here, Elijah?"

¹⁴He replied, "I have been very zealous for the LORD God Almighty. The Israelites have rejected your covenant, broken down your altars, and put your prophets to death with the sword. I am the only one left, and now they are trying to kill me too."

¹⁵The LORD said to him, "Go back the way you came, and go to the Desert of Damascus. When you get there, anoint Hazael king over Aram. ¹⁶Also, anoint Jehu son of Nimshi king over Israel, and anoint Elisha son of Shaphat from Abel Meholah to succeed you as prophet. ¹⁷Jehu will put to death any who escape the sword of Hazael, and Elisha will put to death any who escape the sword of Jehu. ¹⁸Yet I reserve seven thousand in Israel—all whose knees have not bowed down to Baal and all whose mouths have not kissed him."

¹⁹So Elijah went from there and found Elisha son of Shaphat. He was plowing with twelve yoke of oxen, and he himself was driving the twelfth pair. Elijah went up to him and threw his cloak around him. ²⁰Elisha then left his oxen and ran after Elijah. "Let me kiss my father and mother good-by," he said, "and then I will come with you."

ʲ3 Or Elijah saw

"Go back," Elijah replied. "What have I done to you?"

²¹So Elisha left him and went back. He took his yoke of oxen and slaughtered them. He burned the plowing equipment to cook the meat and gave it to the people, and they ate. Then he set out to follow Elijah and became his attendant.

APRIL 6 ☐ DAY 97
1 KINGS 20–22
Ahab's Battle with Aram

OVERVIEW Ahab's life illustrates the disastrous consequences of persistent disobedience. Even after seeing God's power exhibited on Mount Carmel, Ahab refuses to seek God's assistance against the Aramean army. Twice God gives Ahab victory over the Arameans, yet the king responds by sparing Ben-Hadad rather than killing him as the Lord had commanded. For Ahab's refusal to obey, a prophet declares that the king of Israel will forfeit his life for the life of the king of Aram. True to the prophet's word, Ahab suffers a mortal (and divinely guided) wound in the third campaign that was waged against Aram.

Chapter 20	Chapter 21	Chapter 22
Samaria under Siege	Vying for Naboth's Vineyard	Dying on the Field of Battle
Ahab's Life		Ahab's Death

YOUR DAILY WALK There are many ways you can discover that it is dangerous to jump off a ten-story building: You can read about the law of gravity in a book. You can learn from the sad experience of someone who tried it. You can listen to the wise counsel of a fireman or physician who claims it would be "hazardous to your health." Or you can jump. Each provides the information you are seeking; the only difference is the amount of pain involved in gaining that information.

A person becomes wise by observing what happens when he or she isn't.

God wanted Ahab to learn that he alone is Lord of the nations. Fire at Mount Carmel . . . victory over vast armies . . . drought and rain—each was for Ahab's benefit: "And then you will know that I am the LORD" (20:13, 28). Only after being mortally wounded did Ahab learn the lesson, but then it was too late.

What about you? Jot down in the margin a few of the signs of God's sovereignty that you have observed in recent days. How should you respond? How will you respond . . . today?

INSIGHT 1 Kings in Capsule Form

The book of 1 Kings ("one kings") traces the rise and fall of "one kingdom." Solomon, the king who built the temple for God, was not careful to guard the temple of his own heart. After his death the kingdom splits, as does the spiritual loyalty of the people. The book of 2 Kings ("two kings") traces the decline of these "two kingdoms" at the hands of Assyria and Babylonia.

CHAPTER 20

Now Ben-Hadad king of Aram mustered his entire army. Accompanied by thirty-two kings with their horses and chariots, he went up and besieged Samaria and attacked it. ²He sent messengers into the city to Ahab king of Israel, saying, "This is what Ben-Hadad says: ³'Your silver and gold are mine, and the best of your wives and children are mine.' "

⁴The king of Israel answered, "Just as you say, my lord the king. I and all I have are yours."

⁵The messengers came again and said, "This is what Ben-Hadad says: 'I sent to demand your silver and gold, your wives and your children. ⁶But about this time tomorrow I am going to send my officials to search your palace and the houses of your officials. They will seize everything you value and carry it away.' "

⁷The king of Israel summoned all the elders of the land and said to them, "See how this man is looking for trouble! When he sent for my wives and my children, my silver and my gold, I did not refuse him."

⁸The elders and the people all answered, "Don't listen to him or agree to his demands."

⁹So he replied to Ben-Hadad's messengers, "Tell my lord the king, 'Your servant will do all you demanded the first time, but this demand I cannot meet.' " They left and took the answer back to Ben-Hadad.

¹⁰Then Ben-Hadad sent another message to Ahab: "May the gods deal with me, be it ever so severely, if enough dust remains in Samaria to give each of my men a handful."

¹¹The king of Israel answered, "Tell him: 'One who puts on his armor should not boast like one who takes it off.' "

¹²Ben-Hadad heard this message while he and the kings were drinking in their tents,ᵏ and he ordered his men: "Prepare to attack." So they prepared to attack the city.

¹³Meanwhile a prophet came to Ahab king of Israel and announced, "This is what the LORD says: 'Do you see this vast army? I will give it into your hand today, and then you will know that I am the LORD.' "

¹⁴"But who will do this?" asked Ahab.

The prophet replied, "This is what the LORD says: 'The young officers of the provincial commanders will do it.' "

"And who will start the battle?" he asked.

The prophet answered, "You will."

¹⁵So Ahab summoned the young officers of the provincial commanders, 232 men. Then he assembled the rest of the Israelites, 7,000 in all. ¹⁶They set out at noon while Ben-Hadad and the 32 kings allied with him were in their tents getting drunk. ¹⁷The young officers of the provincial commanders went out first.

Now Ben-Hadad had dispatched scouts, who reported, "Men are advancing from Samaria."

¹⁸He said, "If they have come out for peace, take them alive; if they have come out for war, take them alive."

¹⁹The young officers of the provincial commanders marched out of the city with the army behind them ²⁰and each one struck down his opponent. At that, the Arameans fled, with the Israelites in pursuit. But Ben-Hadad king of Aram escaped on horseback with some of his horsemen. ²¹The king of Israel advanced and overpowered the horses and chariots and inflicted heavy losses on the Arameans.

²²Afterward, the prophet came to the king of Israel and said, "Strengthen your position and see what must be done, because next spring the king of Aram will attack you again."

²³Meanwhile, the officials of the king of Aram advised him, "Their gods are gods of the hills. That is why they were too strong for us. But if we fight them on the plains, surely we will be stronger than they. ²⁴Do this: Remove all the kings from their commands and replace them with other officers. ²⁵You must also raise an army like the one you lost—horse for horse and chariot for chariot—so we can fight Israel on the plains. Then surely we will be stronger than they." He agreed with them and acted accordingly.

²⁶The next spring Ben-Hadad mustered the Arameans and went up to Aphek to fight against Israel. ²⁷When the Israelites were also mustered and given provisions, they marched out to meet

ᵏ12 Or in Succoth; also in verse 16

them. The Israelites camped opposite them like two small flocks of goats, while the Arameans covered the countryside.

²⁸The man of God came up and told the king of Israel, "This is what the LORD says: 'Because the Arameans think the LORD is a god of the hills and not a god of the valleys, I will deliver this vast army into your hands, and you will know that I am the LORD.' "

²⁹For seven days they camped opposite each other, and on the seventh day the battle was joined. The Israelites inflicted a hundred thousand casualties on the Aramean foot soldiers in one day. ³⁰The rest of them escaped to the city of Aphek, where the wall collapsed on twenty-seven thousand of them. And Ben-Hadad fled to the city and hid in an inner room.

³¹His officials said to him, "Look, we have heard that the kings of the house of Israel are merciful. Let us go to the king of Israel with sackcloth around our waists and ropes around our heads. Perhaps he will spare your life."

³²Wearing sackcloth around their waists and ropes around their heads, they went to the king of Israel and said, "Your servant Ben-Hadad says: 'Please let me live.' "

The king answered, "Is he still alive? He is my brother."

³³The men took this as a good sign and were quick to pick up his word. "Yes, your brother Ben-Hadad!" they said.

"Go and get him," the king said. When Ben-Hadad came out, Ahab had him come up into his chariot.

³⁴"I will return the cities my father took from your father," Ben-Hadad offered. "You may set up your own market areas in Damascus, as my father did in Samaria."

⌊Ahab said,⌋ "On the basis of a treaty I will set you free." So he made a treaty with him, and let him go.

³⁵By the word of the LORD one of the sons of the prophets said to his companion, "Strike me with your weapon," but the man refused.

³⁶So the prophet said, "Because you have not obeyed the LORD, as soon as you leave me a lion will kill you." And after

the man went away, a lion found him and killed him.

³⁷The prophet found another man and said, "Strike me, please." So the man struck him and wounded him. ³⁸Then the prophet went and stood by the road waiting for the king. He disguised himself with his headband down over his eyes. ³⁹As the king passed by, the prophet called out to him, "Your servant went into the thick of the battle, and someone came to me with a captive and said, 'Guard this man. If he is missing, it will be your life for his life, or you must pay a talent¹ of silver.' ⁴⁰While your servant was busy here and there, the man disappeared."

"That is your sentence," the king of Israel said. "You have pronounced it yourself."

⁴¹Then the prophet quickly removed the headband from his eyes, and the king of Israel recognized him as one of the prophets. ⁴²He said to the king, "This is what the LORD says: 'You have set free a man I had determined should die.ᵐ Therefore it is your life for his life, your people for his people.' " ⁴³Sullen and angry, the king of Israel went to his palace in Samaria.

CHAPTER 21
Some time later there was an incident involving a vineyard belonging to Naboth the Jezreelite. The vineyard was in Jezreel, close to the palace of Ahab king of Samaria. ²Ahab said to Naboth, "Let me have your vineyard to use for a vegetable garden, since it is close to my palace. In exchange I will give you a better vineyard or, if you prefer, I will pay you whatever it is worth."

³But Naboth replied, "The LORD forbid that I should give you the inheritance of my fathers."

⁴So Ahab went home, sullen and angry because Naboth the Jezreelite had said, "I will not give you the inheritance of my fathers." He lay on his bed sulking and refused to eat.

⁵His wife Jezebel came in and asked him, "Why are you so sullen? Why won't you eat?"

⁶He answered her, "Because I said to Naboth the Jezreelite, 'Sell me your vineyard; or if you prefer, I will give you

---

¹39 That is, about 75 pounds (about 34 kilograms)   ᵐ42 The Hebrew term refers to the irrevocable giving over of things or persons to the LORD, often by totally destroying them.

another vineyard in its place.' But he said, 'I will not give you my vineyard.' "

⁷Jezebel his wife said, "Is this how you act as king over Israel? Get up and eat! Cheer up. I'll get you the vineyard of Naboth the Jezreelite."

⁸So she wrote letters in Ahab's name, placed his seal on them, and sent them to the elders and nobles who lived in Naboth's city with him. ⁹In those letters she wrote:

> "Proclaim a day of fasting and seat Naboth in a prominent place among the people. ¹⁰But seat two scoundrels opposite him and have them testify that he has cursed both God and the king. Then take him out and stone him to death."

¹¹So the elders and nobles who lived in Naboth's city did as Jezebel directed in the letters she had written to them. ¹²They proclaimed a fast and seated Naboth in a prominent place among the people. ¹³Then two scoundrels came and sat opposite him and brought charges against Naboth before the people, saying, "Naboth has cursed both God and the king." So they took him outside the city and stoned him to death. ¹⁴Then they sent word to Jezebel: "Naboth has been stoned and is dead."

¹⁵As soon as Jezebel heard that Naboth had been stoned to death, she said to Ahab, "Get up and take possession of the vineyard of Naboth the Jezreelite that he refused to sell you. He is no longer alive, but dead." ¹⁶When Ahab heard that Naboth was dead, he got up and went down to take possession of Naboth's vineyard.

¹⁷Then the word of the LORD came to Elijah the Tishbite: ¹⁸"Go down to meet Ahab king of Israel, who rules in Samaria. He is now in Naboth's vineyard, where he has gone to take possession of it. ¹⁹Say to him, 'This is what the LORD says: Have you not murdered a man and seized his property?' Then say to him, 'This is what the LORD says: In the place where dogs licked up Naboth's blood, dogs will lick up your blood—yes, yours!' "

²⁰Ahab said to Elijah, "So you have found me, my enemy!"

"I have found you," he answered, "because you have sold yourself to do evil in the eyes of the LORD. ²¹'I am going to bring disaster on you. I will consume your descendants and cut off from Ahab every last male in Israel—slave or free. ²²I will make your house like that of Jeroboam son of Nebat and that of Baasha son of Ahijah, because you have provoked me to anger and have caused Israel to sin.'

²³"And also concerning Jezebel the LORD says: 'Dogs will devour Jezebel by the wall of^n Jezreel.'

²⁴"Dogs will eat those belonging to Ahab who die in the city, and the birds of the air will feed on those who die in the country."

²⁵(There was never a man like Ahab, who sold himself to do evil in the eyes of the LORD, urged on by Jezebel his wife. ²⁶He behaved in the vilest manner by going after idols, like the Amorites the LORD drove out before Israel.)

²⁷When Ahab heard these words, he tore his clothes, put on sackcloth and fasted. He lay in sackcloth and went around meekly.

²⁸Then the word of the LORD came to Elijah the Tishbite: ²⁹"Have you noticed how Ahab has humbled himself before me? Because he has humbled himself, I will not bring this disaster in his day, but I will bring it on his house in the days of his son."

CHAPTER 22

For three years there was no war between Aram and Israel. ²But in the third year Jehoshaphat king of Judah went down to see the king of Israel. ³The king of Israel had said to his officials, "Don't you know that Ramoth Gilead belongs to us and yet we are doing nothing to retake it from the king of Aram?"

⁴So he asked Jehoshaphat, "Will you go with me to fight against Ramoth Gilead?"

Jehoshaphat replied to the king of Israel, "I am as you are, my people as your people, my horses as your horses." ⁵But Jehoshaphat also said to the king of Israel, "First seek the counsel of the LORD."

⁶So the king of Israel brought together the prophets—about four hundred men—and asked them, "Shall I go to war against Ramoth Gilead, or shall I refrain?"

"Go," they answered, "for the Lord will give it into the king's hand."

^{n}23 Most Hebrew manuscripts; a few Hebrew manuscripts, Vulgate and Syriac (see also 2 Kings 9:26) *the plot of ground at*

⁷But Jehoshaphat asked, "Is there not a prophet of the LORD here whom we can inquire of?"

⁸The king of Israel answered Jehoshaphat, "There is still one man through whom we can inquire of the LORD, but I hate him because he never prophesies anything good about me, but always bad. He is Micaiah son of Imlah."

"The king should not say that," Jehoshaphat replied.

⁹So the king of Israel called one of his officials and said, "Bring Micaiah son of Imlah at once."

¹⁰Dressed in their royal robes, the king of Israel and Jehoshaphat king of Judah were sitting on their thrones at the threshing floor by the entrance of the gate of Samaria, with all the prophets prophesying before them. ¹¹Now Zedekiah son of Kenaanah had made iron horns and he declared, "This is what the LORD says: 'With these you will gore the Arameans until they are destroyed.' "

¹²All the other prophets were prophesying the same thing. "Attack Ramoth Gilead and be victorious," they said, "for the LORD will give it into the king's hand."

¹³The messenger who had gone to summon Micaiah said to him, "Look, as one man the other prophets are predicting success for the king. Let your word agree with theirs, and speak favorably."

¹⁴But Micaiah said, "As surely as the LORD lives, I can tell him only what the LORD tells me."

¹⁵When he arrived, the king asked him, "Micaiah, shall we go to war against Ramoth Gilead, or shall I refrain?"

"Attack and be victorious," he answered, "for the LORD will give it into the king's hand."

¹⁶The king said to him, "How many times must I make you swear to tell me nothing but the truth in the name of the LORD?"

¹⁷Then Micaiah answered, "I saw all Israel scattered on the hills like sheep without a shepherd, and the LORD said, 'These people have no master. Let each one go home in peace.' "

¹⁸The king of Israel said to Jehoshaphat, "Didn't I tell you that he never prophesies anything good about me, but only bad?"

¹⁹Micaiah continued, "Therefore hear the word of the LORD: I saw the LORD sitting on his throne with all the host of heaven standing around him on his right and on his left. ²⁰And the LORD said, 'Who will entice Ahab into attacking Ramoth Gilead and going to his death there?'

"One suggested this, and another that. ²¹Finally, a spirit came forward, stood before the LORD and said, 'I will entice him.'

²²" 'By what means?' the LORD asked.

" 'I will go out and be a lying spirit in the mouths of all his prophets,' he said.

" 'You will succeed in enticing him,' said the LORD. 'Go and do it.'

²³"So now the LORD has put a lying spirit in the mouths of all these prophets of yours. The LORD has decreed disaster for you."

²⁴Then Zedekiah son of Kenaanah went up and slapped Micaiah in the face. "Which way did the spirit from° the LORD go when he went from me to speak to you?" he asked.

²⁵Micaiah replied, "You will find out on the day you go to hide in an inner room."

²⁶The king of Israel then ordered, "Take Micaiah and send him back to Amon the ruler of the city and to Joash the king's son ²⁷and say, 'This is what the king says: Put this fellow in prison and give him nothing but bread and water until I return safely.' "

²⁸Micaiah declared, "If you ever return safely, the LORD has not spoken through me." Then he added, "Mark my words, all you people!"

²⁹So the king of Israel and Jehoshaphat king of Judah went up to Ramoth Gilead. ³⁰The king of Israel said to Jehoshaphat, "I will enter the battle in disguise, but you wear your royal robes." So the king of Israel disguised himself and went into battle.

³¹Now the king of Aram had ordered his thirty-two chariot commanders, "Do not fight with anyone, small or great, except the king of Israel." ³²When the chariot commanders saw Jehoshaphat, they thought, "Surely this is the king of Israel." So they turned to attack him, but when Jehoshaphat cried out, ³³the chariot commanders saw that he was not the king of Israel and stopped pursuing him.

³⁴But someone drew his bow at random and hit the king of Israel between the

°24 Or *Spirit of*

sections of his armor. The king told his chariot driver, "Wheel around and get me out of the fighting. I've been wounded." [35]All day long the battle raged, and the king was propped up in his chariot facing the Arameans. The blood from his wound ran onto the floor of the chariot, and that evening he died. [36]As the sun was setting, a cry spread through the army: "Every man to his town; everyone to his land!"

[37]So the king died and was brought to Samaria, and they buried him there. [38]They washed the chariot at a pool in Samaria (where the prostitutes bathed),[p] and the dogs licked up his blood, as the word of the LORD had declared.

[39]As for the other events of Ahab's reign, including all he did, the palace he built and inlaid with ivory, and the cities he fortified, are they not written in the book of the annals of the kings of Israel? [40]Ahab rested with his fathers. And Ahaziah his son succeeded him as king.

[41]Jehoshaphat son of Asa became king of Judah in the fourth year of Ahab king of Israel. [42]Jehoshaphat was thirty-five years old when he became king, and he reigned in Jerusalem twenty-five years. His mother's name was Azubah daughter of Shilhi. [43]In everything he walked in the ways of his father Asa and did not stray from them; he did what was right in the eyes of the LORD. The high places, however, were not removed, and the people continued to offer sacrifices and burn incense there. [44]Jehoshaphat was also at peace with the king of Israel.

[45]As for the other events of Jehoshaphat's reign, the things he achieved and his military exploits, are they not written in the book of the annals of the kings of Judah? [46]He rid the land of the rest of the male shrine prostitutes who remained there even after the reign of his father Asa. [47]There was then no king in Edom; a deputy ruled.

[48]Now Jehoshaphat built a fleet of trading ships[q] to go to Ophir for gold, but they never set sail—they were wrecked at Ezion Geber. [49]At that time Ahaziah son of Ahab said to Jehoshaphat, "Let my men sail with your men," but Jehoshaphat refused.

[50]Then Jehoshaphat rested with his fathers and was buried with them in the city of David his father. And Jehoram his son succeeded him.

[51]Ahaziah son of Ahab became king of Israel in Samaria in the seventeenth year of Jehoshaphat king of Judah, and he reigned over Israel two years. [52]He did evil in the eyes of the LORD, because he walked in the ways of his father and mother and in the ways of Jeroboam son of Nebat, who caused Israel to sin. [53]He served and worshiped Baal and provoked the LORD, the God of Israel, to anger, just as his father had done.

p38 Or Samaria and cleaned the weapons   q48 Hebrew of ships of Tarshish

APRIL 7 □ DAY 98
The Danger of a Divided Heart

 LOOK BACK Solomon's request for wisdom from God, combined with his commitment to walk in the footsteps of his father (3:3), ensure that Solomon's reign will mark the Golden Age of Israel's kings. People come from as far away as Africa to see for themselves the splendor and wisdom of Solomon's administration—and they are not disappointed.

Blessed with an international reputation and indescribable wealth, Solomon sets out to fulfill the dream of his father, David: a suitable temple in which to worship the God of heaven. Curiously, God's house takes only half as long to build as Solomon's own house.

Soon there are other warning signs that all is not well in Solomon's palace. Wealth, women, weapons of war and worship of idols soon crowd God out of Solomon's heart. Under the selfish leadership of his son Rehoboam, Solomon's kingdom fractures. Under the godless leadership of such kings as Jeroboam and Ahab, the twin kingdoms disintegrate. The call goes out for a striking figure with a penetrating message: Elijah the Tishbite.

LOOK UP What would you think of an athlete who ran as fast as the wind . . . for the first half of the race, then walked the rest of the way and came in dead last?

The inconsistent Christian is one of the devil's best workers.

What would you think of a builder whose high-rise buildings were strong and safe . . . for the first ten stories but were marked by shoddy workmanship and half-finished rooms on the rest of the floors?

What would you think of a baker whose bread and pastries had a marvelous aroma . . . but upon taking a bite you discovered they were half-baked?

Chances are you would look for someone who gave as much attention to the *finish* as to the *start*. In every pursuit of life—whether running, building, baking or serving God—a job half done is little better than a job that was never begun.

Solomon's reign started with great promise and potential. The king who "was greater in riches and wisdom than all the other kings of the earth" (10:23) seemed to have everything going for him. But in his final years, the wisest man who ever lived began to play the fool. Once his heart had focused on God alone, but now Solomon's heart was turned to other loves: foreign women, fast chariots, glittering wealth. And when the last (and saddest) chapter of his life was written, the king with a divided heart had left behind a divided kingdom.

LOOK AHEAD The Bible has many sobering things to say about the danger of halfheartedness. The church at Laodicea was neither hot nor cold. It was merely lukewarm in its zeal for God. And notice God's surprising reaction to a church like that (Revelation 3:15–16).

Neglect and preoccupation can be lethal, as Solomon observed when he wrote about the field of a sluggard in Proverbs 24:30–34. Without knowing it, Solomon was writing a parable about his own life. Don't let his words become a parable about your life. If you have made a halfhearted commitment to God or a family member, what better time than today to put your whole heart into it?

2 Kings

IN 1 Kings one nation becomes two; in 2 Kings two nations become one. Nineteen consecutive evil kings consistently lead Israel downhill. Even the miracle-working ministry of Elisha cannot stop the nation's slide. Meanwhile, to the south, the occasional good king in Judah is powerless to reform the evils of his many bad predecessors. The "tale of two nations" ends disastrously: Israel is dispersed by Assyria (2 Kings 1–17); and Judah is marched off to exile by Babylon (2 Kings 18–25).

Focus	Two Nations Become One					
Divisions	Reign of Joram	Record of Elisha	Jehu's Revenge / Joash's Reforms	Ruin of Israel	Reforms of Hezekiah	Ruin of Judah
	1 3	4 8	9 12	13 17	18 21	22 25
Topics	Elisha		Kings and Queens of Israel and Judah			
	Downfall of Israel				Downfall of Judah	
Place	Israel and Judah				Judah	
Time	About 130 Years				About 155 Years	

APRIL 8 ☐ DAY 99
2 KINGS 1–3
Reign of Joram

OVERVIEW While 1 Kings centers around the ministry of Elijah, 2 Kings focuses on the ministry of Elisha. After Elijah makes his last prophetic utterance—the prediction of Ahaziah's death for turning to lifeless idols rather than to the living God—he is taken up to heaven in a whirlwind, leaving his understudy, Elisha, to continue the prophetic work of calling the nation back to God. With the cloak of Elijah on his shoulders and a double portion of Elijah's spirit to fortify him, Elisha wastes no time in beginning his prophetic and miraculous ministry. He predicts that God will fill the valleys of Edom with water, enabling King Joram to defeat the forces of Moab and turn back the enemy threat.

Chapter 1	Chapter 2	Chapter 3
Fire from Heaven	Whirlwind from Heaven	Water from Heaven
Elijah's Ministry Ends and Elisha's Ministry Begins		

YOUR DAILY WALK If a miracle is defined as "something so difficult that only God can do it," what area of your life is most in need of a miracle? And how does it compare with these "miracle stories"?

Though you may ask God to do something for you, he generally wants to do something in you.

The Lord said to Abraham, "Is anything too hard for the LORD?" (Genesis 18:14). And Abraham fathered Isaac at age one hundred.

When Elisha instructed Joram to dig ditches in the valley because God was going to fill them with water in spite of a drought, Elisha assured the king, "This is an easy thing in the eyes of the LORD" (2 Kings 3:18). The next morning the waters came.

Jeremiah affirmed, "Nothing is too hard for you" (Jeremiah 32:17). And God delivered his people from exile.

The angel told Mary, "For nothing is impossible with God" (Luke 1:37). And a virgin gave birth to the Savior.

What challenge in your life seems too big for anyone but God? Write your name by one of the stories above as your testimony of confidence in God's ability to do the impossible in your life as well.

INSIGHT Going to School with the Prophets
The "company of the prophets" (1 Kings 20:35; 2 Kings 2:3, 5, 7, 15; 4:1, 38; 5:22; 6:1) were probably young men studying the law and the history of Israel in order to teach the people. Samuel may have set up these schools as part of his circuit-riding ministry (1 Samuel 7:15–17).

CHAPTER 1
After Ahab's death, Moab rebelled against Israel. ²Now Ahaziah had fallen through the lattice of his upper room in Samaria and injured himself. So he sent messengers, saying to them, "Go and consult Baal-Zebub, the god of Ekron, to see if I will recover from this injury."

³But the angel of the LORD said to Elijah the Tishbite, "Go up and meet the messengers of the king of Samaria and ask them, 'Is it because there is no God in

Israel that you are going off to consult Baal-Zebub, the god of Ekron?' [4]Therefore this is what the LORD says: 'You will not leave the bed you are lying on. You will certainly die!' " So Elijah went.

[5]When the messengers returned to the king, he asked them, "Why have you come back?"

[6]"A man came to meet us," they replied. "And he said to us, 'Go back to the king who sent you and tell him, "This is what the LORD says: Is it because there is no God in Israel that you are sending men to consult Baal-Zebub, the god of Ekron? Therefore you will not leave the bed you are lying on. You will certainly die!" ' "

[7]The king asked them, "What kind of man was it who came to meet you and told you this?"

[8]They replied, "He was a man with a garment of hair and with a leather belt around his waist."

The king said, "That was Elijah the Tishbite."

[9]Then he sent to Elijah a captain with his company of fifty men. The captain went up to Elijah, who was sitting on the top of a hill, and said to him, "Man of God, the king says, 'Come down!' "

[10]Elijah answered the captain, "If I am a man of God, may fire come down from heaven and consume you and your fifty men!" Then fire fell from heaven and consumed the captain and his men.

[11]At this the king sent to Elijah another captain with his fifty men. The captain said to him, "Man of God, this is what the king says, 'Come down at once!' "

[12]"If I am a man of God," Elijah replied, "may fire come down from heaven and consume you and your fifty men!" Then the fire of God fell from heaven and consumed him and his fifty men.

[13]So the king sent a third captain with his fifty men. This third captain went up and fell on his knees before Elijah. "Man of God," he begged, "please have respect for my life and the lives of these fifty men, your servants! [14]See, fire has fallen from heaven and consumed the first two captains and all their men. But now have respect for my life!"

[15]The angel of the LORD said to Elijah, "Go down with him; do not be afraid of

him." So Elijah got up and went down with him to the king.

[16]He told the king, "This is what the LORD says: Is it because there is no God in Israel for you to consult that you have sent messengers to consult Baal-Zebub, the god of Ekron? Because you have done this, you will never leave the bed you are lying on. You will certainly die!" [17]So he died, according to the word of the LORD that Elijah had spoken.

Because Ahaziah had no son, Joram[a] succeeded him as king in the second year of Jehoram son of Jehoshaphat king of Judah. [18]As for all the other events of Ahaziah's reign, and what he did, are they not written in the book of the annals of the kings of Israel?

CHAPTER 2

When the LORD was about to take Elijah up to heaven in a whirlwind, Elijah and Elisha were on their way from Gilgal. [2]Elijah said to Elisha, "Stay here; the LORD has sent me to Bethel."

But Elisha said, "As surely as the LORD lives and as you live, I will not leave you." So they went down to Bethel.

[3]The company of the prophets at Bethel came out to Elisha and asked, "Do you know that the LORD is going to take your master from you today?"

"Yes, I know," Elisha replied, "but do not speak of it."

[4]Then Elijah said to him, "Stay here, Elisha; the LORD has sent me to Jericho."

And he replied, "As surely as the LORD lives and as you live, I will not leave you." So they went to Jericho.

[5]The company of the prophets at Jericho went up to Elisha and asked him, "Do you know that the LORD is going to take your master from you today?"

"Yes, I know," he replied, "but do not speak of it."

[6]Then Elijah said to him, "Stay here; the LORD has sent me to the Jordan."

And he replied, "As surely as the LORD lives and as you live, I will not leave you." So the two of them walked on.

[7]Fifty men of the company of the prophets went and stood at a distance, facing the place where Elijah and Elisha had stopped at the Jordan. [8]Elijah took his cloak, rolled it up and struck the water

[a]17 Hebrew *Jehoram*, a variant of *Joram*

with it. The water divided to the right and to the left, and the two of them crossed over on dry ground.

⁹When they had crossed, Elijah said to Elisha, "Tell me, what can I do for you before I am taken from you?"

"Let me inherit a double portion of your spirit," Elisha replied.

¹⁰"You have asked a difficult thing," Elijah said, "yet if you see me when I am taken from you, it will be yours—otherwise not."

¹¹As they were walking along and talking together, suddenly a chariot of fire and horses of fire appeared and separated the two of them, and Elijah went up to heaven in a whirlwind. ¹²Elisha saw this and cried out, "My father! My father! The chariots and horsemen of Israel!" And Elisha saw him no more. Then he took hold of his own clothes and tore them apart.

¹³He picked up the cloak that had fallen from Elijah and went back and stood on the bank of the Jordan. ¹⁴Then he took the cloak that had fallen from him and struck the water with it. "Where now is the LORD, the God of Elijah?" he asked. When he struck the water, it divided to the right and to the left, and he crossed over.

¹⁵The company of the prophets from Jericho, who were watching, said, "The spirit of Elijah is resting on Elisha." And they went to meet him and bowed to the ground before him. ¹⁶"Look," they said, "we your servants have fifty able men. Let them go and look for your master. Perhaps the Spirit of the LORD has picked him up and set him down on some mountain or in some valley."

"No," Elisha replied, "do not send them."

¹⁷But they persisted until he was too ashamed to refuse. So he said, "Send them." And they sent fifty men, who searched for three days but did not find him. ¹⁸When they returned to Elisha, who was staying in Jericho, he said to them, "Didn't I tell you not to go?"

¹⁹The men of the city said to Elisha, "Look, our lord, this town is well situated, as you can see, but the water is bad and the land is unproductive."

²⁰"Bring me a new bowl," he said, "and put salt in it." So they brought it to him.

²¹Then he went out to the spring and threw the salt into it, saying, "This is what the LORD says: 'I have healed this water. Never again will it cause death or make the land unproductive.' " ²²And the water has remained wholesome to this day, according to the word Elisha had spoken.

²³From there Elisha went up to Bethel. As he was walking along the road, some youths came out of the town and jeered at him. "Go on up, you baldhead!" they said. "Go on up, you baldhead!" ²⁴He turned around, looked at them and called down a curse on them in the name of the LORD. Then two bears came out of the woods and mauled forty-two of the youths. ²⁵And he went on to Mount Carmel and from there returned to Samaria.

CHAPTER 3

Joram*b* son of Ahab became king of Israel in Samaria in the eighteenth year of Jehoshaphat king of Judah, and he reigned twelve years. ²He did evil in the eyes of the LORD, but not as his father and mother had done. He got rid of the sacred stone of Baal that his father had made. ³Nevertheless he clung to the sins of Jeroboam son of Nebat, which he had caused Israel to commit; he did not turn away from them.

⁴Now Mesha king of Moab raised sheep, and he had to supply the king of Israel with a hundred thousand lambs and with the wool of a hundred thousand rams. ⁵But after Ahab died, the king of Moab rebelled against the king of Israel. ⁶So at that time King Joram set out from Samaria and mobilized all Israel. ⁷He also sent this message to Jehoshaphat king of Judah: "The king of Moab has rebelled against me. Will you go with me to fight against Moab?"

"I will go with you," he replied. "I am as you are, my people as your people, my horses as your horses."

⁸"By what route shall we attack?" he asked.

"Through the Desert of Edom," he answered.

⁹So the king of Israel set out with the king of Judah and the king of Edom. After a roundabout march of seven days, the army had no more water for themselves or for the animals with them.

b1 Hebrew Jehoram, a variant of Joram; also in verse 6

10"What!" exclaimed the king of Israel. "Has the LORD called us three kings together only to hand us over to Moab?"

11But Jehoshaphat asked, "Is there no prophet of the LORD here, that we may inquire of the LORD through him?"

An officer of the king of Israel answered, "Elisha son of Shaphat is here. He used to pour water on the hands of Elijah.c"

12Jehoshaphat said, "The word of the LORD is with him." So the king of Israel and Jehoshaphat and the king of Edom went down to him.

13Elisha said to the king of Israel, "What do we have to do with each other? Go to the prophets of your father and the prophets of your mother."

"No," the king of Israel answered, "because it was the LORD who called us three kings together to hand us over to Moab."

14Elisha said, "As surely as the LORD Almighty lives, whom I serve, if I did not have respect for the presence of Jehoshaphat king of Judah, I would not look at you or even notice you. 15But now bring me a harpist."

While the harpist was playing, the hand of the LORD came upon Elisha 16and he said, "This is what the LORD says: Make this valley full of ditches. 17For this is what the LORD says: You will see neither wind nor rain, yet this valley will be filled with water, and you, your cattle and your other animals will drink. 18This is an easy thing in the eyes of the LORD; he will also hand Moab over to you. 19You will overthrow every fortified city and every major town. You will cut down every good tree,

stop up all the springs, and ruin every good field with stones."

20The next morning, about the time for offering the sacrifice, there it was—water flowing from the direction of Edom! And the land was filled with water.

21Now all the Moabites had heard that the kings had come to fight against them; so every man, young and old, who could bear arms was called up and stationed on the border. 22When they got up early in the morning, the sun was shining on the water. To the Moabites across the way, the water looked red—like blood. 23"That's blood!" they said. "Those kings must have fought and slaughtered each other. Now to the plunder, Moab!"

24But when the Moabites came to the camp of Israel, the Israelites rose up and fought them until they fled. And the Israelites invaded the land and slaughtered the Moabites. 25They destroyed the towns, and each man threw a stone on every good field until it was covered. They stopped up all the springs and cut down every good tree. Only Kir Hareseth was left with its stones in place, but men armed with slings surrounded it and attacked it as well.

26When the king of Moab saw that the battle had gone against him, he took with him seven hundred swordsmen to break through to the king of Edom, but they failed. 27Then he took his firstborn son, who was to succeed him as king, and offered him as a sacrifice on the city wall. The fury against Israel was great; they withdrew and returned to their own land.

c11 That is, he was Elijah's personal servant.

APRIL 9 □ DAY 100
2 KINGS 4–8
Record of Elisha

 OVERVIEW Elisha, the great miracle worker of God, performs no fewer than nine miracles in the space of today's section: providing an "oil well" for a destitute widow, giving new life to a dead boy, making poisoned stew harmless, multiplying bread for a hungry crowd, curing a leprous army commander, making an ax head defy the law of gravity, reading the mind of an enemy king, opening the eyes of a servant to see the angels of God and closing the eyes of the enemy to the same spectacle. In each case, God's power at work in the *individ-*

ual shows his readiness to do the same in the *nation* he has called his own.

Chapter 4	Chapter 5	Chapters 6–8
Elisha and the Shunammite Woman	Elisha and the Aramean Commander	Elisha and the Aramean King
Provision	Purification	Protection

It is not the darkness that blocks your vision so much as what is between you and God.

YOUR DAILY WALK If you wear glasses, then you're probably familiar with the term *myopia*. Myopia, simply defined, is improper focus. Images appear fuzzy or blurred because the eye is incapable of bringing the light to a sharp focus. Physical myopia can be detected and compensated for quite easily.

But there is a similar visual problem in the spiritual realm. Let's call it "spiritual myopia." The symptoms: clear focus when it comes to identifying problems, obstacles and difficulties in everyday life, but great difficulty in focusing on the reservoir of power and protection God has provided to meet those problems head-on. Spiritual myopia is the condition from which Elisha's servant suffered when he focused on the *problem* (6:15) but not the *provision* (6:17). He saw only an army of Arameans, while Elisha saw the host of angels.

On a three-by-five-inch card, draw a small eye chart (similar to what you would find in an optometrist's office) using the words of 2 Kings 6:16 and place it on your mirror or mantel. Let it remind you often of the importance of proper spiritual focus in your walk with God.

INSIGHT How to Fly off the Handle

In biblical times the iron head of an ax was attached to the handle by thongs. Thus, it was common for the head to fly off the handle whenever the thongs broke or slipped. Accidents with axes were so common that a special provision was included in the law of Moses to handle such cases (Deuteronomy 19:1–6).

CHAPTER 4

The wife of a man from the company of the prophets cried out to Elisha, "Your servant my husband is dead, and you know that he revered the LORD. But now his creditor is coming to take my two boys as his slaves."

²Elisha replied to her, "How can I help you? Tell me, what do you have in your house?"

"Your servant has nothing there at all," she said, "except a little oil."

³Elisha said, "Go around and ask all your neighbors for empty jars. Don't ask for just a few. ⁴Then go inside and shut the door behind you and your sons. Pour oil into all the jars, and as each is filled, put it to one side."

⁵She left him and afterward shut the door behind her and her sons. They brought the jars to her and she kept pouring. ⁶When all the jars were full, she said to her son, "Bring me another one."

But he replied, "There is not a jar left." Then the oil stopped flowing.

⁷She went and told the man of God, and he said, "Go, sell the oil and pay your debts. You and your sons can live on what is left."

⁸One day Elisha went to Shunem. And a well-to-do woman was there, who urged him to stay for a meal. So whenever he came by, he stopped there to eat. ⁹She said to her husband, "I know that this man who often comes our way is a holy man of God. ¹⁰Let's make a small room on the roof and put in it a bed and a table, a chair and a lamp for him. Then he can stay there whenever he comes to us."

¹¹One day when Elisha came, he went up to his room and lay down there. ¹²He said to his servant Gehazi, "Call the Shunammite." So he called her, and she stood before him. ¹³Elisha said to him, "Tell her, 'You have gone to all this trouble for us. Now what can be done for you? Can we

speak on your behalf to the king or the commander of the army?' "

She replied, "I have a home among my own people."

¹⁴"What can be done for her?" Elisha asked.

Gehazi said, "Well, she has no son and her husband is old."

¹⁵Then Elisha said, "Call her." So he called her, and she stood in the doorway. ¹⁶"About this time next year," Elisha said, "you will hold a son in your arms."

"No, my lord," she objected. "Don't mislead your servant, O man of God!"

¹⁷But the woman became pregnant, and the next year about that same time she gave birth to a son, just as Elisha had told her.

¹⁸The child grew, and one day he went out to his father, who was with the reapers. ¹⁹"My head! My head!" he said to his father.

His father told a servant, "Carry him to his mother." ²⁰After the servant had lifted him up and carried him to his mother, the boy sat on her lap until noon, and then he died. ²¹She went up and laid him on the bed of the man of God, then shut the door and went out.

²²She called her husband and said, "Please send me one of the servants and a donkey so I can go to the man of God quickly and return."

²³"Why go to him today?" he asked. "It's not the New Moon or the Sabbath."

"It's all right," she said.

²⁴She saddled the donkey and said to her servant, "Lead on; don't slow down for me unless I tell you." ²⁵So she set out and came to the man of God at Mount Carmel.

When he saw her in the distance, the man of God said to his servant Gehazi, "Look! There's the Shunammite! ²⁶Run to meet her and ask her, 'Are you all right? Is your husband all right? Is your child all right?' "

"Everything is all right," she said.

²⁷When she reached the man of God at the mountain, she took hold of his feet. Gehazi came over to push her away, but the man of God said, "Leave her alone! She is in bitter distress, but the LORD has hidden it from me and has not told me why."

²⁸"Did I ask you for a son, my lord?" she said. "Didn't I tell you, 'Don't raise my hopes'?"

²⁹Elisha said to Gehazi, "Tuck your cloak into your belt, take my staff in your hand and run. If you meet anyone, do not greet him, and if anyone greets you, do not answer. Lay my staff on the boy's face."

³⁰But the child's mother said, "As surely as the LORD lives and as you live, I will not leave you." So he got up and followed her.

³¹Gehazi went on ahead and laid the staff on the boy's face, but there was no sound or response. So Gehazi went back to meet Elisha and told him, "The boy has not awakened."

³²When Elisha reached the house, there was the boy lying dead on his couch. ³³He went in, shut the door on the two of them and prayed to the LORD. ³⁴Then he got on the bed and lay upon the boy, mouth to mouth, eyes to eyes, hands to hands. As he stretched himself out upon him, the boy's body grew warm. ³⁵Elisha turned away and walked back and forth in the room and then got on the bed and stretched out upon him once more. The boy sneezed seven times and opened his eyes.

³⁶Elisha summoned Gehazi and said, "Call the Shunammite." And he did. When she came, he said, "Take your son." ³⁷She came in, fell at his feet and bowed to the ground. Then she took her son and went out.

³⁸Elisha returned to Gilgal and there was a famine in that region. While the company of the prophets was meeting with him, he said to his servant, "Put on the large pot and cook some stew for these men."

³⁹One of them went out into the fields to gather herbs and found a wild vine. He gathered some of its gourds and filled the fold of his cloak. When he returned, he cut them up into the pot of stew, though no one knew what they were. ⁴⁰The stew was poured out for the men, but as they began to eat it, they cried out, "O man of God, there is death in the pot!" And they could not eat it.

⁴¹Elisha said, "Get some flour." He put it into the pot and said, "Serve it to the people to eat." And there was nothing harmful in the pot.

⁴²A man came from Baal Shalishah, bringing the man of God twenty loaves

of barley bread baked from the first ripe grain, along with some heads of new grain. "Give it to the people to eat," Elisha said.

⁴³"How can I set this before a hundred men?" his servant asked.

But Elisha answered, "Give it to the people to eat. For this is what the LORD says: 'They will eat and have some left over.' " ⁴⁴Then he set it before them, and they ate and had some left over, according to the word of the LORD.

CHAPTER 5

Now Naaman was commander of the army of the king of Aram. He was a great man in the sight of his master and highly regarded, because through him the LORD had given victory to Aram. He was a valiant soldier, but he had leprosy.ᵈ

²Now bands from Aram had gone out and had taken captive a young girl from Israel, and she served Naaman's wife. ³She said to her mistress, "If only my master would see the prophet who is in Samaria! He would cure him of his leprosy."

⁴Naaman went to his master and told him what the girl from Israel had said. ⁵"By all means, go," the king of Aram replied. "I will send a letter to the king of Israel." So Naaman left, taking with him ten talentsᵉ of silver, six thousand shekelsᶠ of gold and ten sets of clothing. ⁶The letter that he took to the king of Israel read: "With this letter I am sending my servant Naaman to you so that you may cure him of his leprosy."

⁷As soon as the king of Israel read the letter, he tore his robes and said, "Am I God? Can I kill and bring back to life? Why does this fellow send someone to me to be cured of his leprosy? See how he is trying to pick a quarrel with me!"

⁸When Elisha the man of God heard that the king of Israel had torn his robes, he sent him this message: "Why have you torn your robes? Have the man come to me and he will know that there is a prophet in Israel." ⁹So Naaman went with his horses and chariots and stopped at the door of Elisha's house. ¹⁰Elisha sent a messenger to say to him, "Go, wash yourself seven times in the Jordan, and your

flesh will be restored and you will be cleansed."

¹¹But Naaman went away angry and said, "I thought that he would surely come out to me and stand and call on the name of the LORD his God, wave his hand over the spot and cure me of my leprosy. ¹²Are not Abana and Pharpar, the rivers of Damascus, better than any of the waters of Israel? Couldn't I wash in them and be cleansed?" So he turned and went off in a rage.

¹³Naaman's servants went to him and said, "My father, if the prophet had told you to do some great thing, would you not have done it? How much more, then, when he tells you, 'Wash and be cleansed'!" ¹⁴So he went down and dipped himself in the Jordan seven times, as the man of God had told him, and his flesh was restored and became clean like that of a young boy.

¹⁵Then Naaman and all his attendants went back to the man of God. He stood before him and said, "Now I know that there is no God in all the world except in Israel. Please accept now a gift from your servant."

¹⁶The prophet answered, "As surely as the LORD lives, whom I serve, I will not accept a thing." And even though Naaman urged him, he refused.

¹⁷"If you will not," said Naaman, "please let me, your servant, be given as much earth as a pair of mules can carry, for your servant will never again make burnt offerings and sacrifices to any other god but the LORD. ¹⁸But may the LORD forgive your servant for this one thing: When my master enters the temple of Rimmon to bow down and he is leaning on my arm and I bow there also—when I bow down in the temple of Rimmon, may the LORD forgive your servant for this."

¹⁹"Go in peace," Elisha said.

After Naaman had traveled some distance, ²⁰Gehazi, the servant of Elisha the man of God, said to himself, "My master was too easy on Naaman, this Aramean, by not accepting from him what he brought. As surely as the LORD lives, I will run after him and get something from him."

²¹So Gehazi hurried after Naaman. When Naaman saw him running toward

ᵈ1 The Hebrew word was used for various diseases affecting the skin—not necessarily leprosy; also in verses 3, 6, 7, 11 and 27.   ᵉ5 That is, about 750 pounds (about 340 kilograms)   ᶠ5 That is, about 150 pounds (about 70 kilograms) him, he got down from the chariot to meet him. "Is everything all right?" he asked.

²²"Everything is all right," Gehazi answered. "My master sent me to say, 'Two young men from the company of the prophets have just come to me from the hill country of Ephraim. Please give them a talent⁸ of silver and two sets of clothing.' "

²³"By all means, take two talents," said Naaman. He urged Gehazi to accept them, and then tied up the two talents of silver in two bags, with two sets of clothing. He gave them to two of his servants, and they carried them ahead of Gehazi. ²⁴When Gehazi came to the hill, he took the things from the servants and put them away in the house. He sent the men away and they left. ²⁵Then he went in and stood before his master Elisha.

"Where have you been, Gehazi?" Elisha asked.

"Your servant didn't go anywhere," Gehazi answered.

²⁶But Elisha said to him, "Was not my spirit with you when the man got down from his chariot to meet you? Is this the time to take money, or to accept clothes, olive groves, vineyards, flocks, herds, or menservants and maidservants? ²⁷Naaman's leprosy will cling to you and to your descendants forever." Then Gehazi went from Elisha's presence and he was leprous, as white as snow.

CHAPTER 6

The company of the prophets said to Elisha, "Look, the place where we meet with you is too small for us. ²Let us go to the Jordan, where each of us can get a pole; and let us build a place there for us to live."

And he said, "Go."

³Then one of them said, "Won't you please come with your servants?"

"I will," Elisha replied. ⁴And he went with them.

They went to the Jordan and began to cut down trees. ⁵As one of them was cutting down a tree, the iron axhead fell into the water. "Oh, my lord," he cried out, "it was borrowed!"

⁶The man of God asked, "Where did it fall?" When he showed him the place, Elisha cut a stick and threw it there, and

made the iron float. ⁷"Lift it out," he said. Then the man reached out his hand and took it.

⁸Now the king of Aram was at war with Israel. After conferring with his officers, he said, "I will set up my camp in such and such a place."

⁹The man of God sent word to the king of Israel: "Beware of passing that place, because the Arameans are going down there." ¹⁰So the king of Israel checked on the place indicated by the man of God. Time and again Elisha warned the king, so that he was on his guard in such places.

¹¹This enraged the king of Aram. He summoned his officers and demanded of them, "Will you not tell me which of us is on the side of the king of Israel?"

¹²"None of us, my lord the king," said one of his officers, "but Elisha, the prophet who is in Israel, tells the king of Israel the very words you speak in your bedroom."

¹³"Go, find out where he is," the king ordered, "so I can send men and capture him." The report came back: "He is in Dothan." ¹⁴Then he sent horses and chariots and a strong force there. They went by night and surrounded the city.

¹⁵When the servant of the man of God got up and went out early the next morning, an army with horses and chariots had surrounded the city. "Oh, my lord, what shall we do?" the servant asked.

¹⁶"Don't be afraid," the prophet answered. "Those who are with us are more than those who are with them."

¹⁷And Elisha prayed, "O LORD, open his eyes so he may see." Then the LORD opened the servant's eyes, and he looked and saw the hills full of horses and chariots of fire all around Elisha.

¹⁸As the enemy came down toward him, Elisha prayed to the LORD, "Strike these people with blindness." So he struck them with blindness, as Elisha had asked.

¹⁹Elisha told them, "This is not the road and this is not the city. Follow me, and I will lead you to the man you are looking for." And he led them to Samaria.

²⁰After they entered the city, Elisha said, "LORD, open the eyes of these men so they can see." Then the LORD opened their eyes and they looked, and there they were, inside Samaria.

⁸22 That is, about 75 pounds (about 34 kilograms)

²¹When the king of Israel saw them, he asked Elisha, "Shall I kill them, my father? Shall I kill them?"

²²"Do not kill them," he answered. "Would you kill men you have captured with your own sword or bow? Set food and water before them so that they may eat and drink and then go back to their master." ²³So he prepared a great feast for them, and after they had finished eating and drinking, he sent them away, and they returned to their master. So the bands from Aram stopped raiding Israel's territory.

²⁴Some time later, Ben-Hadad king of Aram mobilized his entire army and marched up and laid siege to Samaria. ²⁵There was a great famine in the city; the siege lasted so long that a donkey's head sold for eighty shekels[h] of silver, and a quarter of a cab[i] of seed pods[j] for five shekels.[k]

²⁶As the king of Israel was passing by on the wall, a woman cried to him, "Help me, my lord the king!"

²⁷The king replied, "If the LORD does not help you, where can I get help for you? From the threshing floor? From the winepress?" ²⁸Then he asked her, "What's the matter?"

She answered, "This woman said to me, 'Give up your son so we may eat him today, and tomorrow we'll eat my son.' ²⁹So we cooked my son and ate him. The next day I said to her, 'Give up your son so we may eat him,' but she had hidden him."

³⁰When the king heard the woman's words, he tore his robes. As he went along the wall, the people looked, and there, underneath, he had sackcloth on his body. ³¹He said, "May God deal with me, be it ever so severely, if the head of Elisha son of Shaphat remains on his shoulders today!"

³²Now Elisha was sitting in his house, and the elders were sitting with him. The king sent a messenger ahead, but before he arrived, Elisha said to the elders, "Don't you see how this murderer is sending someone to cut off my head? Look, when the messenger comes, shut the door and hold it shut against him. Is not the sound of his master's footsteps behind him?"

³³While he was still talking to them, the messenger came down to him. And ⌞the king⌟ said, "This disaster is from the LORD. Why should I wait for the LORD any longer?"

CHAPTER 7

Elisha said, "Hear the word of the LORD. This is what the LORD says: About this time tomorrow, a seah[l] of flour will sell for a shekel[m] and two seahs[n] of barley for a shekel at the gate of Samaria."

²The officer on whose arm the king was leaning said to the man of God, "Look, even if the LORD should open the floodgates of the heavens, could this happen?"

"You will see it with your own eyes," answered Elisha, "but you will not eat any of it!"

³Now there were four men with leprosy[o] at the entrance of the city gate. They said to each other, "Why stay here until we die? ⁴If we say, 'We'll go into the city'—the famine is there, and we will die. And if we stay here, we will die. So let's go over to the camp of the Arameans and surrender. If they spare us, we live; if they kill us, then we die."

⁵At dusk they got up and went to the camp of the Arameans. When they reached the edge of the camp, not a man was there, ⁶for the Lord had caused the Arameans to hear the sound of chariots and horses and a great army, so that they said to one another, "Look, the king of Israel has hired the Hittite and Egyptian kings to attack us!" ⁷So they got up and fled in the dusk and abandoned their tents and their horses and donkeys. They left the camp as it was and ran for their lives.

⁸The men who had leprosy reached the edge of the camp and entered one of the tents. They ate and drank, and carried away silver, gold and clothes, and went off and hid them. They returned and entered another tent and took some things from it and hid them also.

⁹Then they said to each other, "We're not doing right. This is a day of good news and we are keeping it to ourselves.

h25 That is, about 2 pounds (about 1 kilogram)   i25 That is, probably about 1/2 pint (about 0.3 liter)   j25 Or of dove's dung   k25 That is, about 2 ounces (about 55 grams)   l1 That is, probably about 7 quarts (about 7.3 liters); also in verses 16 and 18   m1 That is, about 2/5 ounce (about 11 grams); also in verses 16 and 18   n1 That is, probably about 13 quarts (about 15 liters); also in verses 16 and 18   o3 The Hebrew word is used for various diseases affecting the skin—not necessarily leprosy; also in verse 8.

If we wait until daylight, punishment will overtake us. Let's go at once and report this to the royal palace."

¹⁰So they went and called out to the city gatekeepers and told them, "We went into the Aramean camp and not a man was there—not a sound of anyone—only tethered horses and donkeys, and the tents left just as they were." ¹¹The gatekeepers shouted the news, and it was reported within the palace.

¹²The king got up in the night and said to his officers, "I will tell you what the Arameans have done to us. They know we are starving; so they have left the camp to hide in the countryside, thinking, 'They will surely come out, and then we will take them alive and get into the city.' "

¹³One of his officers answered, "Have some men take five of the horses that are left in the city. Their plight will be like that of all the Israelites left here—yes, they will only be like all these Israelites who are doomed. So let us send them to find out what happened."

¹⁴So they selected two chariots with their horses, and the king sent them after the Aramean army. He commanded the drivers, "Go and find out what has happened." ¹⁵They followed them as far as the Jordan, and they found the whole road strewn with the clothing and equipment the Arameans had thrown away in their headlong flight. So the messengers returned and reported to the king. ¹⁶Then the people went out and plundered the camp of the Arameans. So a seah of flour sold for a shekel, and two seahs of barley sold for a shekel, as the LORD had said.

¹⁷Now the king had put the officer on whose arm he leaned in charge of the gate, and the people trampled him in the gateway, and he died, just as the man of God had foretold when the king came down to his house. ¹⁸It happened as the man of God had said to the king: "About this time tomorrow, a seah of flour will sell for a shekel and two seahs of barley for a shekel at the gate of Samaria."

¹⁹The officer had said to the man of God, "Look, even if the LORD should open the floodgates of the heavens, could this happen?" The man of God had replied, "You will see it with your own eyes, but

you will not eat any of it!" ²⁰And that is exactly what happened to him, for the people trampled him in the gateway, and he died.

CHAPTER 8

Now Elisha had said to the woman whose son he had restored to life, "Go away with your family and stay for a while wherever you can, because the LORD has decreed a famine in the land that will last seven years." ²The woman proceeded to do as the man of God said. She and her family went away and stayed in the land of the Philistines seven years.

³At the end of the seven years she came back from the land of the Philistines and went to the king to beg for her house and land. ⁴The king was talking to Gehazi, the servant of the man of God, and had said, "Tell me about all the great things Elisha has done." ⁵Just as Gehazi was telling the king how Elisha had restored the dead to life, the woman whose son Elisha had brought back to life came to beg the king for her house and land.

Gehazi said, "This is the woman, my lord the king, and this is her son whom Elisha restored to life." ⁶The king asked the woman about it, and she told him.

Then he assigned an official to her case and said to him, "Give back everything that belonged to her, including all the income from her land from the day she left the country until now."

⁷Elisha went to Damascus, and Ben-Hadad king of Aram was ill. When the king was told, "The man of God has come all the way up here," ⁸he said to Hazael, "Take a gift with you and go to meet the man of God. Consult the LORD through him; ask him, 'Will I recover from this illness?' "

⁹Hazael went to meet Elisha, taking with him as a gift forty camel-loads of all the finest wares of Damascus. He went in and stood before him, and said, "Your son Ben-Hadad king of Aram has sent me to ask, 'Will I recover from this illness?' "

¹⁰Elisha answered, "Go and say to him, 'You will certainly recover'; but[p] the LORD has revealed to me that he will in fact die." ¹¹He stared at him with a fixed gaze until Hazael felt ashamed. Then the man of God began to weep.

p10 The Hebrew may also be read *Go and say, 'You will certainly not recover,' for.*

¹²"Why is my lord weeping?" asked Hazael.

"Because I know the harm you will do to the Israelites," he answered. "You will set fire to their fortified places, kill their young men with the sword, dash their little children to the ground, and rip open their pregnant women."

¹³Hazael said, "How could your servant, a mere dog, accomplish such a feat?"

"The LORD has shown me that you will become king of Aram," answered Elisha.

¹⁴Then Hazael left Elisha and returned to his master. When Ben-Hadad asked, "What did Elisha say to you?" Hazael replied, "He told me that you would certainly recover." ¹⁵But the next day he took a thick cloth, soaked it in water and spread it over the king's face, so that he died. Then Hazael succeeded him as king.

¹⁶In the fifth year of Joram son of Ahab king of Israel, when Jehoshaphat was king of Judah, Jehoram son of Jehoshaphat began his reign as king of Judah. ¹⁷He was thirty-two years old when he became king, and he reigned in Jerusalem eight years. ¹⁸He walked in the ways of the kings of Israel, as the house of Ahab had done, for he married a daughter of Ahab. He did evil in the eyes of the LORD. ¹⁹Nevertheless, for the sake of his servant David, the LORD was not willing to destroy Judah. He had promised to maintain a lamp for David and his descendants forever.

²⁰In the time of Jehoram, Edom rebelled against Judah and set up its own king.

²¹So Jehoram⁹ went to Zair with all his chariots. The Edomites surrounded him and his chariot commanders, but he rose up and broke through by night; his army, however, fled back home. ²²To this day Edom has been in rebellion against Judah. Libnah revolted at the same time.

²³As for the other events of Jehoram's reign, and all he did, are they not written in the book of the annals of the kings of Judah? ²⁴Jehoram rested with his fathers and was buried with them in the City of David. And Ahaziah his son succeeded him as king.

²⁵In the twelfth year of Joram son of Ahab king of Israel, Ahaziah son of Jehoram king of Judah began to reign. ²⁶Ahaziah was twenty-two years old when he became king, and he reigned in Jerusalem one year. His mother's name was Athaliah, a granddaughter of Omri king of Israel. ²⁷He walked in the ways of the house of Ahab and did evil in the eyes of the LORD, as the house of Ahab had done, for he was related by marriage to Ahab's family.

²⁸Ahaziah went with Joram son of Ahab to war against Hazael king of Aram at Ramoth Gilead. The Arameans wounded Joram; ²⁹so King Joram returned to Jezreel to recover from the wounds the Arameans had inflicted on him at Ramothʳ in his battle with Hazael king of Aram.

Then Ahaziah son of Jehoram king of Judah went down to Jezreel to see Joram son of Ahab, because he had been wounded.

ᑫ21 Hebrew *Joram*, a variant of *Jehoram*; also in verses 23 and 24   ʳ29 Hebrew *Ramah*, a variant of *Ramoth*

APRIL 10 □ DAY 101
2 KINGS 9–12
Jehu's Revenge, Joash's Reforms

OVERVIEW Anointed king over Israel at Elisha's direction, Jehu wastes no time in carrying out his mission. He heads straight for the city of Jezreel, where Joram is recuperating from his battle wounds. There he slays the ruling heir of Ahab's house in the vineyard of Naboth for which Ahab had committed murder a generation before! But Jehu is far from finished. In addition, he kills Ahaziah, king of Judah (who was making an untimely visit to Joram), Jezebel (Joram's wicked mother-in-law) and finally the entire surviving family of Ahab, thus fulfilling God's sentence of death. But while Jehu is executing judgment in Israel, a different and potentially more dangerous execution is taking place in Judah. Athaliah, Ahab's daughter and the mother of Ahaziah, seizes the throne and seeks to liquidate the rest of the royal line. The sole surviving heir, Joash, grows up to be Judah's youngest king and one of its greatest reformers.

Chapter 9	Chapter 10	Chapter 11	Chapter 12
Jehu Kills Two Kings	Jehu Kills Ahab's Family	Athaliah Kills Her Own Family	Joash Repairs the Temple
Jehu's Ministry of Judgment		Joash's Ministry of Reform	

Get on fire for God, and people will watch you burn.

YOUR DAILY WALK Whatever else you can say about Jehu (and you can say plenty!), his single-minded attention to the task God had given him is exemplary. Jehu was a man with a divine calling, a man with a mission, who lost no time in carrying it out. He brought to fulfillment the prophecy of Elijah against the house of Ahab (1 Kings 21:19–24) and completely rid Israel of the heathen worship of Baal for a time. God approved of Jehu's ministry and rewarded him for it.

How do you tackle the assignment God has set before you? carelessly? halfheartedly? or with the zeal of a Jehu? Whether you are a student or a parent, a minister or an office worker, you can put your heart into your work—if the God of Jehu is in your heart.

INSIGHT Judgment Can Be Murder
Jehu was anointed as God's instrument for the task of exterminating the house of Ahab and, along with it, the worship of Baal. Baalism was so viciously cruel that only a person of Jehu's relentlessness could have done the job. By the end, Jehu had indeed wiped out the entire house of Ahab and had thoroughly purged the nation of Baal worshipers.

CHAPTER 9

The prophet Elisha summoned a man from the company of the prophets and said to him, "Tuck your cloak into your belt, take this flask of oil with you and go to Ramoth Gilead. ²When you get there, look for Jehu son of Jehoshaphat, the son of Nimshi. Go to him, get him away from his companions and take him into an inner room. ³Then take the flask and pour the oil on his head and declare, 'This is what the LORD says: I anoint you king over Israel.' Then open the door and run; don't delay!"

⁴So the young man, the prophet, went to Ramoth Gilead. ⁵When he arrived, he found the army officers sitting together. "I have a message for you, commander," he said.

"For which of us?" asked Jehu.

"For you, commander," he replied.

⁶Jehu got up and went into the house. Then the prophet poured the oil on Jehu's head and declared, "This is what the LORD, the God of Israel, says: 'I anoint you king over the LORD's people Israel. ⁷You are to destroy the house of Ahab your master,

and I will avenge the blood of my servants the prophets and the blood of all the LORD's servants shed by Jezebel. ⁸The whole house of Ahab will perish. I will cut off from Ahab every last male in Israel—slave or free. ⁹I will make the house of Ahab like the house of Jeroboam son of Nebat and like the house of Baasha son of Ahijah. ¹⁰As for Jezebel, dogs will devour her on the plot of ground at Jezreel, and no one will bury her.' " Then he opened the door and ran.

¹¹When Jehu went out to his fellow officers, one of them asked him, "Is everything all right? Why did this madman come to you?"

"You know the man and the sort of things he says," Jehu replied.

¹²"That's not true!" they said. "Tell us." Jehu said, "Here is what he told me: 'This is what the LORD says: I anoint you king over Israel.' "

¹³They hurried and took their cloaks and spread them under him on the bare steps. Then they blew the trumpet and shouted, "Jehu is king!"

¹⁴So Jehu son of Jehoshaphat, the son of

Nimshi, conspired against Joram. (Now Joram and all Israel had been defending Ramoth Gilead against Hazael king of Aram, [15]but King Joram[s] had returned to Jezreel to recover from the wounds the Arameans had inflicted on him in the battle with Hazael king of Aram.) Jehu said, "If this is the way you feel, don't let anyone slip out of the city to go and tell the news in Jezreel." [16]Then he got into his chariot and rode to Jezreel, because Joram was resting there and Ahaziah king of Judah had gone down to see him.

[17]When the lookout standing on the tower in Jezreel saw Jehu's troops approaching, he called out, "I see some troops coming."

"Get a horseman," Joram ordered. "Send him to meet them and ask, 'Do you come in peace?' "

[18]The horseman rode off to meet Jehu and said, "This is what the king says: 'Do you come in peace?' "

"What do you have to do with peace?" Jehu replied. "Fall in behind me."

The lookout reported, "The messenger has reached them, but he isn't coming back."

[19]So the king sent out a second horseman. When he came to them he said, "This is what the king says: 'Do you come in peace?' "

Jehu replied, "What do you have to do with peace? Fall in behind me."

[20]The lookout reported, "He has reached them, but he isn't coming back either. The driving is like that of Jehu son of Nimshi—he drives like a madman."

[21]"Hitch up my chariot," Joram ordered. And when it was hitched up, Joram king of Israel and Ahaziah king of Judah rode out, each in his own chariot, to meet Jehu. They met him at the plot of ground that had belonged to Naboth the Jezreelite. [22]When Joram saw Jehu he asked, "Have you come in peace, Jehu?"

"How can there be peace," Jehu replied, "as long as all the idolatry and witchcraft of your mother Jezebel abound?"

[23]Joram turned about and fled, calling out to Ahaziah, "Treachery, Ahaziah!"

[24]Then Jehu drew his bow and shot Joram between the shoulders. The arrow pierced his heart and he slumped down in his chariot. [25]Jehu said to Bidkar, his chariot officer, "Pick him up and throw him on the field that belonged to Naboth the Jezreelite. Remember how you and I were riding together in chariots behind Ahab his father when the LORD made this prophecy about him: [26]'Yesterday I saw the blood of Naboth and the blood of his sons, declares the LORD, and I will surely make you pay for it on this plot of ground, declares the LORD.'[t] Now then, pick him up and throw him on that plot, in accordance with the word of the LORD."

[27]When Ahaziah king of Judah saw what had happened, he fled up the road to Beth Haggan.[u] Jehu chased him, shouting, "Kill him too!" They wounded him in his chariot on the way up to Gur near Ibleam, but he escaped to Megiddo and died there. [28]His servants took him by chariot to Jerusalem and buried him with his fathers in his tomb in the City of David. [29](In the eleventh year of Joram son of Ahab, Ahaziah had become king of Judah.)

[30]Then Jehu went to Jezreel. When Jezebel heard about it, she painted her eyes, arranged her hair and looked out of a window. [31]As Jehu entered the gate, she asked, "Have you come in peace, Zimri, you murderer of your master?"[v]

[32]He looked up at the window and called out, "Who is on my side? Who?" Two or three eunuchs looked down at him. [33]"Throw her down!" Jehu said. So they threw her down, and some of her blood spattered the wall and the horses as they trampled her underfoot.

[34]Jehu went in and ate and drank. "Take care of that cursed woman," he said, "and bury her, for she was a king's daughter." [35]But when they went out to bury her, they found nothing except her skull, her feet and her hands. [36]They went back and told Jehu, who said, "This is the word of the LORD that he spoke through his servant Elijah the Tishbite: On the plot of ground at Jezreel dogs will devour Jezebel's flesh.[w] [37]Jezebel's body will be like refuse on the ground in the plot at Jezreel, so that no one will be able to say, 'This is Jezebel.' "

CHAPTER 10

Now there were in Samaria seventy sons of the house of Ahab. So Jehu wrote

[s]15 Hebrew *Jehoram,* a variant of *Joram;* also in verses 17 and 21-24 house   [v]31 Or *"Did Zimri have peace, who murdered his master?"*   [t]26 See 1 Kings 21:19.   [u]27 Or *fled by way of the garden*   [w]36 See 1 Kings 21:23.

letters and sent them to Samaria: to the officials of Jezreel,[x] to the elders and to the guardians of Ahab's children. He said, [2]"As soon as this letter reaches you, since your master's sons are with you and you have chariots and horses, a fortified city and weapons, [3]choose the best and most worthy of your master's sons and set him on his father's throne. Then fight for your master's house."

[4]But they were terrified and said, "If two kings could not resist him, how can we?"

[5]So the palace administrator, the city governor, the elders and the guardians sent this message to Jehu: "We are your servants and we will do anything you say. We will not appoint anyone as king; you do whatever you think best."

[6]Then Jehu wrote them a second letter, saying, "If you are on my side and will obey me, take the heads of your master's sons and come to me in Jezreel by this time tomorrow."

Now the royal princes, seventy of them, were with the leading men of the city, who were rearing them. [7]When the letter arrived, these men took the princes and slaughtered all seventy of them. They put their heads in baskets and sent them to Jehu in Jezreel. [8]When the messenger arrived, he told Jehu, "They have brought the heads of the princes."

Then Jehu ordered, "Put them in two piles at the entrance of the city gate until morning."

[9]The next morning Jehu went out. He stood before all the people and said, "You are innocent. It was I who conspired against my master and killed him, but who killed all these? [10]Know then, that not a word the LORD has spoken against the house of Ahab will fail. The LORD has done what he promised through his servant Elijah." [11]So Jehu killed everyone in Jezreel who remained of the house of Ahab, as well as all his chief men, his close friends and his priests, leaving him no survivor.

[12]Jehu then set out and went toward Samaria. At Beth Eked of the Shepherds, [13]he met some relatives of Ahaziah king of Judah and asked, "Who are you?"

They said, "We are relatives of Ahaziah, and we have come down to greet the families of the king and of the queen mother."

[14]"Take them alive!" he ordered. So they took them alive and slaughtered them by the well of Beth Eked—forty-two men. He left no survivor.

[15]After he left there, he came upon Jehonadab son of Recab, who was on his way to meet him. Jehu greeted him and said, "Are you in accord with me, as I am with you?"

"I am," Jehonadab answered.

"If so," said Jehu, "give me your hand." So he did, and Jehu helped him up into the chariot. [16]Jehu said, "Come with me and see my zeal for the LORD." Then he had him ride along in his chariot.

[17]When Jehu came to Samaria, he killed all who were left there of Ahab's family; he destroyed them, according to the word of the LORD spoken to Elijah.

[18]Then Jehu brought all the people together and said to them, "Ahab served Baal a little; Jehu will serve him much. [19]Now summon all the prophets of Baal, all his ministers and all his priests. See that no one is missing, because I am going to hold a great sacrifice for Baal. Anyone who fails to come will no longer live." But Jehu was acting deceptively in order to destroy the ministers of Baal.

[20]Jehu said, "Call an assembly in honor of Baal." So they proclaimed it. [21]Then he sent word throughout Israel, and all the ministers of Baal came; not one stayed away. They crowded into the temple of Baal until it was full from one end to the other. [22]And Jehu said to the keeper of the wardrobe, "Bring robes for all the ministers of Baal." So he brought out robes for them.

[23]Then Jehu and Jehonadab son of Recab went into the temple of Baal. Jehu said to the ministers of Baal, "Look around and see that no servants of the LORD are here with you—only ministers of Baal." [24]So they went in to make sacrifices and burnt offerings. Now Jehu had posted eighty men outside with this warning: "If one of you lets any of the men I am placing in your hands escape, it will be your life for his life."

[25]As soon as Jehu had finished making the burnt offering, he ordered the guards and officers: "Go in and kill them; let no

[x]1 Hebrew; some Septuagint manuscripts and Vulgate *of the city*

one escape." So they cut them down with the sword. The guards and officers threw the bodies out and then entered the inner shrine of the temple of Baal. ²⁶They brought the sacred stone out of the temple of Baal and burned it. ²⁷They demolished the sacred stone of Baal and tore down the temple of Baal, and people have used it for a latrine to this day.

²⁸So Jehu destroyed Baal worship in Israel. ²⁹However, he did not turn away from the sins of Jeroboam son of Nebat, which he had caused Israel to commit—the worship of the golden calves at Bethel and Dan.

³⁰The LORD said to Jehu, "Because you have done well in accomplishing what is right in my eyes and have done to the house of Ahab all I had in mind to do, your descendants will sit on the throne of Israel to the fourth generation." ³¹Yet Jehu was not careful to keep the law of the LORD, the God of Israel, with all his heart. He did not turn away from the sins of Jeroboam, which he had caused Israel to commit.

³²In those days the LORD began to reduce the size of Israel. Hazael overpowered the Israelites throughout their territory ³³east of the Jordan in all the land of Gilead (the region of Gad, Reuben and Manasseh), from Aroer by the Arnon Gorge through Gilead to Bashan.

³⁴As for the other events of Jehu's reign, all he did, and all his achievements, are they not written in the book of the annals of the kings of Israel?

³⁵Jehu rested with his fathers and was buried in Samaria. And Jehoahaz his son succeeded him as king. ³⁶The time that Jehu reigned over Israel in Samaria was twenty-eight years.

CHAPTER 11

When Athaliah the mother of Ahaziah saw that her son was dead, she proceeded to destroy the whole royal family. ²But Jehosheba, the daughter of King Jehoram*ʸ* and sister of Ahaziah, took Joash son of Ahaziah and stole him away from among the royal princes, who were about to be murdered. She put him and his nurse in a bedroom to hide him from Athaliah; so he was not killed. ³He remained hidden with his nurse at the tem-

ple of the LORD for six years while Athaliah ruled the land.

⁴In the seventh year Jehoiada sent for the commanders of units of a hundred, the Carites and the guards and had them brought to him at the temple of the LORD. He made a covenant with them and put them under oath at the temple of the LORD. Then he showed them the king's son. ⁵He commanded them, saying, "This is what you are to do: You who are in the three companies that are going on duty on the Sabbath—a third of you guarding the royal palace, ⁶a third at the Sur Gate, and a third at the gate behind the guard, who take turns guarding the temple— ⁷and you who are in the other two companies that normally go off Sabbath duty are all to guard the temple for the king. ⁸Station yourselves around the king, each man with his weapon in his hand. Anyone who approaches your ranks*ᶻ* must be put to death. Stay close to the king wherever he goes."

⁹The commanders of units of a hundred did just as Jehoiada the priest ordered. Each one took his men—those who were going on duty on the Sabbath and those who were going off duty—and came to Jehoiada the priest. ¹⁰Then he gave the commanders the spears and shields that had belonged to King David and that were in the temple of the LORD. ¹¹The guards, each with his weapon in his hand, stationed themselves around the king—near the altar and the temple, from the south side to the north side of the temple.

¹²Jehoiada brought out the king's son and put the crown on him; he presented him with a copy of the covenant and proclaimed him king. They anointed him, and the people clapped their hands and shouted, "Long live the king!"

¹³When Athaliah heard the noise made by the guards and the people, she went to the people at the temple of the LORD. ¹⁴She looked and there was the king, standing by the pillar, as the custom was. The officers and the trumpeters were beside the king, and all the people of the land were rejoicing and blowing trumpets. Then Athaliah tore her robes and called out, "Treason! Treason!"

¹⁵Jehoiada the priest ordered the commanders of units of a hundred, who were

ʸ2 Hebrew Joram, a variant of Jehoram   ᶻ8 Or approaches the precincts in charge of the troops: "Bring her out between the ranks[a] and put to the sword anyone who follows her." For the priest had said, "She must not be put to death in the temple of the LORD." [16]So they seized her as she reached the place where the horses enter the palace grounds, and there she was put to death.

[17]Jehoiada then made a covenant between the LORD and the king and people that they would be the LORD's people. He also made a covenant between the king and the people. [18]All the people of the land went to the temple of Baal and tore it down. They smashed the altars and idols to pieces and killed Mattan the priest of Baal in front of the altars.

Then Jehoiada the priest posted guards at the temple of the LORD. [19]He took with him the commanders of hundreds, the Carites, the guards and all the people of the land, and together they brought the king down from the temple of the LORD and went into the palace, entering by way of the gate of the guards. The king then took his place on the royal throne, [20]and all the people of the land rejoiced. And the city was quiet, because Athaliah had been slain with the sword at the palace.

[21]Joash[b] was seven years old when he began to reign.

CHAPTER 12

In the seventh year of Jehu, Joash[c] became king, and he reigned in Jerusalem forty years. His mother's name was Zibiah; she was from Beersheba. [2]Joash did what was right in the eyes of the LORD all the years Jehoiada the priest instructed him. [3]The high places, however, were not removed; the people continued to offer sacrifices and burn incense there.

[4]Joash said to the priests, "Collect all the money that is brought as sacred offerings to the temple of the LORD—the money collected in the census, the money received from personal vows and the money brought voluntarily to the temple. [5]Let every priest receive the money from one of the treasurers, and let it be used to repair whatever damage is found in the temple."

[6]But by the twenty-third year of King Joash the priests still had not repaired the temple. [7]Therefore King Joash summoned Jehoiada the priest and the other priests and asked them, "Why aren't you repairing the damage done to the temple? Take no more money from your treasurers, but hand it over for repairing the temple." [8]The priests agreed that they would not collect any more money from the people and that they would not repair the temple themselves.

[9]Jehoiada the priest took a chest and bored a hole in its lid. He placed it beside the altar, on the right side as one enters the temple of the LORD. The priests who guarded the entrance put into the chest all the money that was brought to the temple of the LORD. [10]Whenever they saw that there was a large amount of money in the chest, the royal secretary and the high priest came, counted the money that had been brought into the temple of the LORD and put it into bags. [11]When the amount had been determined, they gave the money to the men appointed to supervise the work on the temple. With it they paid those who worked on the temple of the LORD—the carpenters and builders, [12]the masons and stonecutters. They purchased timber and dressed stone for the repair of the temple of the LORD, and met all the other expenses of restoring the temple.

[13]The money brought into the temple was not spent for making silver basins, wick trimmers, sprinkling bowls, trumpets or any other articles of gold or silver for the temple of the LORD; [14]it was paid to the workmen, who used it to repair the temple. [15]They did not require an accounting from those to whom they gave the money to pay the workers, because they acted with complete honesty. [16]The money from the guilt offerings and sin offerings was not brought into the temple of the LORD; it belonged to the priests.

[17]About this time Hazael king of Aram went up and attacked Gath and captured it. Then he turned to attack Jerusalem. [18]But Joash king of Judah took all the sacred objects dedicated by his fathers—Jehoshaphat, Jehoram and Ahaziah, the kings of Judah—and the gifts he himself had dedicated and all the gold found in the treasuries of the temple of the LORD

[a]15 Or out from the precincts   [b]21 Hebrew Jehoash, a variant of Joash   [c]1 Hebrew Jehoash, a variant of Joash; also in verses 2, 4, 6, 7 and 18

and of the royal palace, and he sent them to Hazael king of Aram, who then withdrew from Jerusalem.

¹⁹As for the other events of the reign of Joash, and all he did, are they not written in the book of the annals of the kings of Judah? ²⁰His officials conspired against him and assassinated him at Beth Millo, on the road down to Silla. ²¹The officials who murdered him were Jozabad son of Shimeath and Jehozabad son of Shomer. He died and was buried with his fathers in the City of David. And Amaziah his son succeeded him as king.

APRIL 11 ☐ DAY 102
2 KINGS 13–17
Ruin of Israel

OVERVIEW On his deathbed, Elisha offers King Jehoash of Israel the opportunity to utterly rout his Aramean enemy. But the king's lack of faith results in something far short of complete victory and presents a picture of the problem that has plagued Israel's kings for centuries. The alliance between Israel and Judah, secured under Jehoshaphat, now gives way to constant warfare. Anarchy and apostasy rip the land of Israel as first one king and then another is assassinated. When Israel and Aram form an alliance against Judah, Ahaz (king of Judah) buys the help of Assyria. But the downward spiral continues, and soon the ten tribes in the north are deported to the remotest corners of the Assyrian Empire, while other conquered peoples are imported to fill the vacuum.

Chapter 13	Chapter 14	Chapter 15	Chapters 16–17
Elisha Dies	Jeroboam II Reigns	Anarchy Reigns	Assyria Prevails
Decline in Israel		Dispersion of Israel	

The power of humans can never reverse the sentence of God.

YOUR DAILY WALK Historians and political scientists have developed elaborate explanations for the conquest of Israel and, later, Judah. "These were small countries," they say, "in the buffer zone between large, powerful neighbors to the south [Egypt] and north [Assyria and Babylonia]." But the Bible states that the conquest and exile were God's judgment because of the sin of his people. Israel abandoned the Lord, turned to idols and ignored the repeated message of God's prophets to "shape up or ship out." They had no one to blame but themselves.

That biblical principle remains in force today for nations as well as individuals, Christians as well as unbelievers. God will deal with an individual, with a family or with a nation according to the unchanging principle that "a man reaps what he sows" (Galatians 6:7). By the way, when was the last time you "sowed" a word for God by means of a brief phone call or letter to one of your elected officials? If an issue is crucial and God has spoken in his Word concerning it, can you afford to remain silent?

INSIGHT It's a Long Way to Captivity
In the Assyrian dispersion many Israelites were resettled in northern Mesopotamia (more than four hundred miles away) and others in the area of the Medes (a full thousand miles from Samaria).

CHAPTER 13

In the twenty-third year of Joash son of Ahaziah king of Judah, Jehoahaz son of Jehu became king of Israel in Samaria, and he reigned seventeen years. ²He did evil in the eyes of the LORD by following the sins of Jeroboam son of Nebat, which he had caused Israel to commit, and he did not turn away from them. ³So the LORD's anger burned against Israel, and for a long time he kept them under the power of Hazael king of Aram and Ben-Hadad his son.

⁴Then Jehoahaz sought the LORD's favor, and the LORD listened to him, for he saw how severely the king of Aram was oppressing Israel. ⁵The LORD provided a deliverer for Israel, and they escaped from the power of Aram. So the Israelites lived in their own homes as they had before. ⁶But they did not turn away from the sins of the house of Jeroboam, which he had caused Israel to commit; they continued in them. Also, the Asherah pole^d remained standing in Samaria.

⁷Nothing had been left of the army of Jehoahaz except fifty horsemen, ten chariots and ten thousand foot soldiers, for the king of Aram had destroyed the rest and made them like the dust at threshing time.

⁸As for the other events of the reign of Jehoahaz, all he did and his achievements, are they not written in the book of the annals of the kings of Israel? ⁹Jehoahaz rested with his fathers and was buried in Samaria. And Jehoash^e his son succeeded him as king.

¹⁰In the thirty-seventh year of Joash king of Judah, Jehoash son of Jehoahaz became king of Israel in Samaria, and he reigned sixteen years. ¹¹He did evil in the eyes of the LORD and did not turn away from any of the sins of Jeroboam son of Nebat, which he had caused Israel to commit; he continued in them.

¹²As for the other events of the reign of Jehoash, all he did and his achievements, including his war against Amaziah king of Judah, are they not written in the book of the annals of the kings of Israel? ¹³Jehoash rested with his fathers, and Jeroboam succeeded him on the throne. Jehoash was buried in Samaria with the kings of Israel.

¹⁴Now Elisha was suffering from the illness from which he died. Jehoash king of Israel went down to see him and wept over him. "My father! My father!" he cried. "The chariots and horsemen of Israel!"

¹⁵Elisha said, "Get a bow and some arrows," and he did so. ¹⁶"Take the bow in your hands," he said to the king of Israel. When he had taken it, Elisha put his hands on the king's hands.

¹⁷"Open the east window," he said, and he opened it. "Shoot!" Elisha said, and he shot. "The LORD's arrow of victory, the arrow of victory over Aram!" Elisha declared. "You will completely destroy the Arameans at Aphek."

¹⁸Then he said, "Take the arrows," and the king took them. Elisha told him, "Strike the ground." He struck it three times and stopped. ¹⁹The man of God was angry with him and said, "You should have struck the ground five or six times; then you would have defeated Aram and completely destroyed it. But now you will defeat it only three times."

²⁰Elisha died and was buried.

Now Moabite raiders used to enter the country every spring. ²¹Once while some Israelites were burying a man, suddenly they saw a band of raiders; so they threw the man's body into Elisha's tomb. When the body touched Elisha's bones, the man came to life and stood up on his feet.

²²Hazael king of Aram oppressed Israel throughout the reign of Jehoahaz. ²³But the LORD was gracious to them and had compassion and showed concern for them because of his covenant with Abraham, Isaac and Jacob. To this day he has been unwilling to destroy them or banish them from his presence.

²⁴Hazael king of Aram died, and Ben-Hadad his son succeeded him as king. ²⁵Then Jehoash son of Jehoahaz recaptured from Ben-Hadad son of Hazael the towns he had taken in battle from his father Jehoahaz. Three times Jehoash defeated him, and so he recovered the Israelite towns.

CHAPTER 14

In the second year of Jehoash^f son of Jehoahaz king of Israel, Amaziah son of Joash king of Judah began to reign. ²He was twenty-five years old when he became king, and he reigned in Jerusalem

---

^{d}6 That is, a symbol of the goddess Asherah; here and elsewhere in 2 Kings ^{e}9 Hebrew *Joash*, a variant of *Jehoash*; also in verses 12-14 and 25 ^{f}1 Hebrew *Joash*, a variant of *Jehoash*; also in verses 13, 23 and 27 twenty-nine years. His mother's name was Jehoaddin; she was from Jerusalem. ³He did what was right in the eyes of the LORD, but not as his father David had done. In everything he followed the example of his father Joash. ⁴The high places, however, were not removed; the people continued to offer sacrifices and burn incense there.

⁵After the kingdom was firmly in his grasp, he executed the officials who had murdered his father the king. ⁶Yet he did not put the sons of the assassins to death, in accordance with what is written in the Book of the Law of Moses where the LORD commanded: "Fathers shall not be put to death for their children, nor children put to death for their fathers; each is to die for his own sins."ᵍ

⁷He was the one who defeated ten thousand Edomites in the Valley of Salt and captured Sela in battle, calling it Joktheel, the name it has to this day.

⁸Then Amaziah sent messengers to Jehoash son of Jehoahaz, the son of Jehu, king of Israel, with the challenge: "Come, meet me face to face."

⁹But Jehoash king of Israel replied to Amaziah king of Judah: "A thistle in Lebanon sent a message to a cedar in Lebanon, 'Give your daughter to my son in marriage.' Then a wild beast in Lebanon came along and trampled the thistle underfoot. ¹⁰You have indeed defeated Edom and now you are arrogant. Glory in your victory, but stay at home! Why ask for trouble and cause your own downfall and that of Judah also?"

¹¹Amaziah, however, would not listen, so Jehoash king of Israel attacked. He and Amaziah king of Judah faced each other at Beth Shemesh in Judah. ¹²Judah was routed by Israel, and every man fled to his home. ¹³Jehoash king of Israel captured Amaziah king of Judah, the son of Joash, the son of Ahaziah, at Beth Shemesh. Then Jehoash went to Jerusalem and broke down the wall of Jerusalem from the Ephraim Gate to the Corner Gate—a section about six hundred feet long.ʰ ¹⁴He took all the gold and silver and all the articles found in the temple of the LORD and in the treasuries of the royal palace. He also took hostages and returned to Samaria.

¹⁵As for the other events of the reign of Jehoash, what he did and his achievements, including his war against Amaziah king of Judah, are they not written in the book of the annals of the kings of Israel? ¹⁶Jehoash rested with his fathers and was buried in Samaria with the kings of Israel. And Jeroboam his son succeeded him as king.

¹⁷Amaziah son of Joash king of Judah lived for fifteen years after the death of Jehoash son of Jehoahaz king of Israel. ¹⁸As for the other events of Amaziah's reign, are they not written in the book of the annals of the kings of Judah?

¹⁹They conspired against him in Jerusalem, and he fled to Lachish, but they sent men after him to Lachish and killed him there. ²⁰He was brought back by horse and was buried in Jerusalem with his fathers, in the City of David.

²¹Then all the people of Judah took Azariah,ⁱ who was sixteen years old, and made him king in place of his father Amaziah. ²²He was the one who rebuilt Elath and restored it to Judah after Amaziah rested with his fathers.

²³In the fifteenth year of Amaziah son of Joash king of Judah, Jeroboam son of Jehoash king of Israel became king in Samaria, and he reigned forty-one years. ²⁴He did evil in the eyes of the LORD and did not turn away from any of the sins of Jeroboam son of Nebat, which he had caused Israel to commit. ²⁵He was the one who restored the boundaries of Israel from Leboʲ Hamath to the Sea of the Arabah,ᵏ in accordance with the word of the LORD, the God of Israel, spoken through his servant Jonah son of Amittai, the prophet from Gath Hepher.

²⁶The LORD had seen how bitterly everyone in Israel, whether slave or free, was suffering; there was no one to help them. ²⁷And since the LORD had not said he would blot out the name of Israel from under heaven, he saved them by the hand of Jeroboam son of Jehoash.

²⁸As for the other events of Jeroboam's reign, all he did, and his military achievements, including how he recovered for Israel both Damascus and Hamath, which had belonged to Yaudi,ˡ are they not written in the book of the annals of the kings of Israel? ²⁹Jeroboam rested with his

ᵍ6 Deut. 24:16   ʰ13 Hebrew *four hundred cubits* (about 180 meters)   ⁱ21 Also called *Uzziah*   ʲ25 Or *from the entrance to*
ᵏ25 That is, the Dead Sea   ˡ28 Or *Judah*

fathers, the kings of Israel. And Zechariah his son succeeded him as king.

CHAPTER 15

In the twenty-seventh year of Jeroboam king of Israel, Azariah son of Amaziah king of Judah began to reign. ²He was sixteen years old when he became king, and he reigned in Jerusalem fifty-two years. His mother's name was Jecoliah; she was from Jerusalem. ³He did what was right in the eyes of the LORD, just as his father Amaziah had done. ⁴The high places, however, were not removed; the people continued to offer sacrifices and burn incense there.

⁵The LORD afflicted the king with leprosy*ᵐ* until the day he died, and he lived in a separate house.*ⁿ* Jotham the king's son had charge of the palace and governed the people of the land.

⁶As for the other events of Azariah's reign, and all he did, are they not written in the book of the annals of the kings of Judah? ⁷Azariah rested with his fathers and was buried near them in the City of David. And Jotham his son succeeded him as king.

⁸In the thirty-eighth year of Azariah king of Judah, Zechariah son of Jeroboam became king of Israel in Samaria, and he reigned six months. ⁹He did evil in the eyes of the LORD, as his fathers had done. He did not turn away from the sins of Jeroboam son of Nebat, which he had caused Israel to commit.

¹⁰Shallum son of Jabesh conspired against Zechariah. He attacked him in front of the people,*ᵒ* assassinated him and succeeded him as king. ¹¹The other events of Zechariah's reign are written in the book of the annals of the kings of Israel. ¹²So the word of the LORD spoken to Jehu was fulfilled: "Your descendants will sit on the throne of Israel to the fourth generation."*ᵖ*

¹³Shallum son of Jabesh became king in the thirty-ninth year of Uzziah king of Judah, and he reigned in Samaria one month. ¹⁴Then Menahem son of Gadi went from Tirzah up to Samaria. He attacked Shallum son of Jabesh in Samaria, assassinated him and succeeded him as king.

¹⁵The other events of Shallum's reign, and the conspiracy he led, are written in the book of the annals of the kings of Israel.

¹⁶At that time Menahem, starting out from Tirzah, attacked Tiphsah and everyone in the city and its vicinity, because they refused to open their gates. He sacked Tiphsah and ripped open all the pregnant women.

¹⁷In the thirty-ninth year of Azariah king of Judah, Menahem son of Gadi became king of Israel, and he reigned in Samaria ten years. ¹⁸He did evil in the eyes of the LORD. During his entire reign he did not turn away from the sins of Jeroboam son of Nebat, which he had caused Israel to commit.

¹⁹Then Pul*�q* king of Assyria invaded the land, and Menahem gave him a thousand talents*ʳ* of silver to gain his support and strengthen his own hold on the kingdom. ²⁰Menahem exacted this money from Israel. Every wealthy man had to contribute fifty shekels*ˢ* of silver to be given to the king of Assyria. So the king of Assyria withdrew and stayed in the land no longer.

²¹As for the other events of Menahem's reign, and all he did, are they not written in the book of the annals of the kings of Israel? ²²Menahem rested with his fathers. And Pekahiah his son succeeded him as king.

²³In the fiftieth year of Azariah king of Judah, Pekahiah son of Menahem became king of Israel in Samaria, and he reigned two years. ²⁴Pekahiah did evil in the eyes of the LORD. He did not turn away from the sins of Jeroboam son of Nebat, which he had caused Israel to commit. ²⁵One of his chief officers, Pekah son of Remaliah, conspired against him. Taking fifty men of Gilead with him, he assassinated Pekahiah, along with Argob and Arieh, in the citadel of the royal palace at Samaria. So Pekah killed Pekahiah and succeeded him as king.

²⁶The other events of Pekahiah's reign, and all he did, are written in the book of the annals of the kings of Israel.

²⁷In the fifty-second year of Azariah king of Judah, Pekah son of Remaliah became king of Israel in Samaria, and he

---

ᵐ5 The Hebrew word was used for various diseases affecting the skin—not necessarily leprosy.   *ⁿ5* Or *in a house where he was relieved of responsibility*   *ᵒ10* Hebrew; some Septuagint manuscripts *in Ibleam*   *ᵖ12* 2 Kings 10:30   *�q19* Also called Tiglath-Pileser   *ʳ19* That is, about 37 tons (about 34 metric tons)   *ˢ20* That is, about 1 1/4 pounds (about 0.6 kilogram) reigned twenty years. 28He did evil in the eyes of the LORD. He did not turn away from the sins of Jeroboam son of Nebat, which he had caused Israel to commit.

29In the time of Pekah king of Israel, Tiglath-Pileser king of Assyria came and took Ijon, Abel Beth Maacah, Janoah, Kedesh and Hazor. He took Gilead and Galilee, including all the land of Naphtali, and deported the people to Assyria. 30Then Hoshea son of Elah conspired against Pekah son of Remaliah. He attacked and assassinated him, and then succeeded him as king in the twentieth year of Jotham son of Uzziah.

31As for the other events of Pekah's reign, and all he did, are they not written in the book of the annals of the kings of Israel?

32In the second year of Pekah son of Remaliah king of Israel, Jotham son of Uzziah king of Judah began to reign. 33He was twenty-five years old when he became king, and he reigned in Jerusalem sixteen years. His mother's name was Jerusha daughter of Zadok. 34He did what was right in the eyes of the LORD, just as his father Uzziah had done. 35The high places, however, were not removed; the people continued to offer sacrifices and burn incense there. Jotham rebuilt the Upper Gate of the temple of the LORD.

36As for the other events of Jotham's reign, and what he did, are they not written in the book of the annals of the kings of Judah? 37(In those days the LORD began to send Rezin king of Aram and Pekah son of Remaliah against Judah.) 38Jotham rested with his fathers and was buried with them in the City of David, the city of his father. And Ahaz his son succeeded him as king.

CHAPTER 16
In the seventeenth year of Pekah son of Remaliah, Ahaz son of Jotham king of Judah began to reign. 2Ahaz was twenty years old when he became king, and he reigned in Jerusalem sixteen years. Unlike David his father, he did not do what was right in the eyes of the LORD his God. 3He walked in the ways of the kings of Israel and even sacrificed his son in*t* the fire, following the detestable ways of the nations the LORD had driven out before the

Israelites. 4He offered sacrifices and burned incense at the high places, on the hilltops and under every spreading tree.

5Then Rezin king of Aram and Pekah son of Remaliah king of Israel marched up to fight against Jerusalem and besieged Ahaz, but they could not overpower him. 6At that time, Rezin king of Aram recovered Elath for Aram by driving out the men of Judah. Edomites then moved into Elath and have lived there to this day.

7Ahaz sent messengers to say to Tiglath-Pileser king of Assyria, "I am your servant and vassal. Come up and save me out of the hand of the king of Aram and of the king of Israel, who are attacking me." 8And Ahaz took the silver and gold found in the temple of the LORD and in the treasuries of the royal palace and sent it as a gift to the king of Assyria. 9The king of Assyria complied by attacking Damascus and capturing it. He deported its inhabitants to Kir and put Rezin to death.

10Then King Ahaz went to Damascus to meet Tiglath-Pileser king of Assyria. He saw an altar in Damascus and sent to Uriah the priest a sketch of the altar, with detailed plans for its construction. 11So Uriah the priest built an altar in accordance with all the plans that King Ahaz had sent from Damascus and finished it before King Ahaz returned. 12When the king came back from Damascus and saw the altar, he approached it and presented offerings*u* on it. 13He offered up his burnt offering and grain offering, poured out his drink offering, and sprinkled the blood of his fellowship offerings*v* on the altar. 14The bronze altar that stood before the LORD he brought from the front of the temple—from between the new altar and the temple of the LORD—and put it on the north side of the new altar.

15King Ahaz then gave these orders to Uriah the priest: "On the large new altar, offer the morning burnt offering and the evening grain offering, the king's burnt offering and his grain offering, and the burnt offering of all the people of the land, and their grain offering and their drink offering. Sprinkle on the altar all the blood of the burnt offerings and sacrifices. But I will use the bronze altar for seeking

*t*3 Or *even made his son pass through*   *u*12 Or *and went up*   *v*13 Traditionally *peace offerings* guidance." [16]And Uriah the priest did just as King Ahaz had ordered.

[17]King Ahaz took away the side panels and removed the basins from the movable stands. He removed the Sea from the bronze bulls that supported it and set it on a stone base. [18]He took away the Sabbath canopy[w] that had been built at the temple and removed the royal entryway outside the temple of the LORD, in deference to the king of Assyria.

[19]As for the other events of the reign of Ahaz, and what he did, are they not written in the book of the annals of the kings of Judah? [20]Ahaz rested with his fathers and was buried with them in the City of David. And Hezekiah his son succeeded him as king.

CHAPTER 17

In the twelfth year of Ahaz king of Judah, Hoshea son of Elah became king of Israel in Samaria, and he reigned nine years. [2]He did evil in the eyes of the LORD, but not like the kings of Israel who preceded him.

[3]Shalmaneser king of Assyria came up to attack Hoshea, who had been Shalmaneser's vassal and had paid him tribute. [4]But the king of Assyria discovered that Hoshea was a traitor, for he had sent envoys to So[x] king of Egypt, and he no longer paid tribute to the king of Assyria, as he had done year by year. Therefore Shalmaneser seized him and put him in prison. [5]The king of Assyria invaded the entire land, marched against Samaria and laid siege to it for three years. [6]In the ninth year of Hoshea, the king of Assyria captured Samaria and deported the Israelites to Assyria. He settled them in Halah, in Gozan on the Habor River and in the towns of the Medes.

[7]All this took place because the Israelites had sinned against the LORD their God, who had brought them up out of Egypt from under the power of Pharaoh king of Egypt. They worshiped other gods [8]and followed the practices of the nations the LORD had driven out before them, as well as the practices that the kings of Israel had introduced. [9]The Israelites secretly did things against the LORD their God that were not right. From watchtower to fortified city they built themselves high places in all their towns. [10]They set up sacred stones and Asherah poles on every high hill and under every spreading tree. [11]At every high place they burned incense, as the nations whom the LORD had driven out before them had done. They did wicked things that provoked the LORD to anger. [12]They worshiped idols, though the LORD had said, "You shall not do this."[y] [13]The LORD warned Israel and Judah through all his prophets and seers: "Turn from your evil ways. Observe my commands and decrees, in accordance with the entire Law that I commanded your fathers to obey and that I delivered to you through my servants the prophets."

[14]But they would not listen and were as stiff-necked as their fathers, who did not trust in the LORD their God. [15]They rejected his decrees and the covenant he had made with their fathers and the warnings he had given them. They followed worthless idols and themselves became worthless. They imitated the nations around them although the LORD had ordered them, "Do not do as they do," and they did the things the LORD had forbidden them to do.

[16]They forsook all the commands of the LORD their God and made for themselves two idols cast in the shape of calves, and an Asherah pole. They bowed down to all the starry hosts, and they worshiped Baal. [17]They sacrificed their sons and daughters in[z] the fire. They practiced divination and sorcery and sold themselves to do evil in the eyes of the LORD, provoking him to anger.

[18]So the LORD was very angry with Israel and removed them from his presence. Only the tribe of Judah was left, [19]and even Judah did not keep the commands of the LORD their God. They followed the practices Israel had introduced. [20]Therefore the LORD rejected all the people of Israel; he afflicted them and gave them into the hands of plunderers, until he thrust them from his presence.

[21]When he tore Israel away from the house of David, they made Jeroboam son of Nebat their king. Jeroboam enticed Israel away from following the LORD and caused them to commit a great sin. [22]The Israelites persisted in all the sins of Jero-

[w]18 Or the dais of his throne (see Septuagint)   [x]4 Or to Sais, to the; So is possibly an abbreviation for Osorkon.
[y]12 Exodus 20:4, 5   [z]17 Or They made their sons and daughters pass through

boam and did not turn away from them ²³until the LORD removed them from his presence, as he had warned through all his servants the prophets. So the people of Israel were taken from their homeland into exile in Assyria, and they are still there.

²⁴The king of Assyria brought people from Babylon, Cuthah, Avva, Hamath and Sepharvaim and settled them in the towns of Samaria to replace the Israelites. They took over Samaria and lived in its towns. ²⁵When they first lived there, they did not worship the LORD; so he sent lions among them and they killed some of the people. ²⁶It was reported to the king of Assyria: "The people you deported and resettled in the towns of Samaria do not know what the god of that country requires. He has sent lions among them, which are killing them off, because the people do not know what he requires."

²⁷Then the king of Assyria gave this order: "Have one of the priests you took captive from Samaria go back to live there and teach the people what the god of the land requires." ²⁸So one of the priests who had been exiled from Samaria came to live in Bethel and taught them how to worship the LORD.

²⁹Nevertheless, each national group made its own gods in the several towns where they settled, and set them up in the shrines the people of Samaria had made at the high places. ³⁰The men from Babylon made Succoth Benoth, the men from Cuthah made Nergal, and the men from Hamath made Ashima; ³¹the Avvites made Nibhaz and Tartak, and the Se-

pharvites burned their children in the fire as sacrifices to Adrammelech and Anammelech, the gods of Sepharvaim. ³²They worshiped the LORD, but they also appointed all sorts of their own people to officiate for them as priests in the shrines at the high places. ³³They worshiped the LORD, but they also served their own gods in accordance with the customs of the nations from which they had been brought.

³⁴To this day they persist in their former practices. They neither worship the LORD nor adhere to the decrees and ordinances, the laws and commands that the LORD gave the descendants of Jacob, whom he named Israel. ³⁵When the LORD made a covenant with the Israelites, he commanded them: "Do not worship any other gods or bow down to them, serve them or sacrifice to them. ³⁶But the LORD, who brought you up out of Egypt with mighty power and outstretched arm, is the one you must worship. To him you shall bow down and to him offer sacrifices. ³⁷You must always be careful to keep the decrees and ordinances, the laws and commands he wrote for you. Do not worship other gods. ³⁸Do not forget the covenant I have made with you, and do not worship other gods. ³⁹Rather, worship the LORD your God; it is he who will deliver you from the hand of all your enemies."

⁴⁰They would not listen, however, but persisted in their former practices. ⁴¹Even while these people were worshiping the LORD, they were serving their idols. To this day their children and grandchildren continue to do as their fathers did.

APRIL 12 ☐ DAY 103
2 KINGS 18–21
Reforms of Hezekiah

 OVERVIEW With the captivity and deportation of Israel, the curtain drops on the northern ten tribes. But what of their countrymen in the south? Will they learn from Israel's calamity and turn back to God? At this crucial juncture, God raises up Hezekiah, who does "what [is] right in the eyes of the LORD, just as his father David had done" (18:3). Spiritually, Hezekiah institutes sweeping reforms to bring the nation back to a wholehearted worship of God. Politically, he refuses to pay tribute any longer to Assyria, choosing instead to trust God for protection from reprisal. In answer to his prayer, God decimates the Assyrian army, breaking the back of that once mighty nation. However, by the time of his death, Hezekiah's pride and family negligence ensure that Judah's days are numbered.

Chapter 18	Chapter 19	Chapter 20	Chapter 21
Assyria at the Door	Assyria on the Run	Hezekiah on His Deathbed	Manasseh on the Rampage
Hezekiah's National Problems		Hezekiah's Personal Problems	

YOUR DAILY WALK If you're looking for some help in your prayer life, why not spend some time studying an Old Testament character whose every recorded prayer was answered!

People may spurn your appeals, reject your messages and oppose your arguments, but they are helpless against your prayers.

Hezekiah was a man of faith (18:5) and a man of prayer. His first reaction when confronted with a problem was to bring it before the Lord. Whether the problem was 185,000 uninvited Assyrians (19:35) or a painful illness (20:1, 7), Hezekiah took it to the Lord in prayer. And when he prayed, things happened!

Prayer is not a magic formula, but verbal communication with the sovereign God of creation. Examine your own prayer habits. Are they built on a personal relationship with God? Are you strengthening your prayer life with daily exercise? Are you more comfortable talking to God today than you were a year ago? Try this: Every time you get into or out of your car today, spend a few seconds in prayer. You'll find it habit-forming!

INSIGHT Smashing a Pagan Python
Hezekiah's zealous reforms included even the destruction of the bronze snake Moses had made in the desert (Numbers 21:8–9), to which the people were burning incense.

CHAPTER 18

In the third year of Hoshea son of Elah king of Israel, Hezekiah son of Ahaz king of Judah began to reign. ²He was twenty-five years old when he became king, and he reigned in Jerusalem twenty-nine years. His mother's name was Abijah*a* daughter of Zechariah. ³He did what was right in the eyes of the LORD, just as his father David had done. ⁴He removed the high places, smashed the sacred stones and cut down the Asherah poles. He broke into pieces the bronze snake Moses had made, for up to that time the Israelites had been burning incense to it. (It was called*b* Nehushtan.*c*)

⁵Hezekiah trusted in the LORD, the God of Israel. There was no one like him among all the kings of Judah, either before him or after him. ⁶He held fast to the LORD and did not cease to follow him; he kept the commands the LORD had given Moses. ⁷And the LORD was with him; he was successful in whatever he undertook.

He rebelled against the king of Assyria and did not serve him. ⁸From watchtower to fortified city, he defeated the Philistines, as far as Gaza and its territory.

⁹In King Hezekiah's fourth year, which was the seventh year of Hoshea son of Elah king of Israel, Shalmaneser king of Assyria marched against Samaria and laid siege to it. ¹⁰At the end of three years the Assyrians took it. So Samaria was captured in Hezekiah's sixth year, which was the ninth year of Hoshea king of Israel. ¹¹The king of Assyria deported Israel to Assyria and settled them in Halah, in Gozan on the Habor River and in towns of the Medes. ¹²This happened because they had not obeyed the LORD their God, but had violated his covenant—all that Moses the servant of the LORD commanded. They neither listened to the commands nor carried them out.

¹³In the fourteenth year of King Hezekiah's reign, Sennacherib king of Assyria attacked all the fortified cities of Judah

a2 Hebrew Abi, a variant of Abijah b4 Or He called it c4 Nehushtan sounds like the Hebrew for bronze and snake and unclean thing.

and captured them. ¹⁴So Hezekiah king of Judah sent this message to the king of Assyria at Lachish: "I have done wrong. Withdraw from me, and I will pay whatever you demand of me." The king of Assyria exacted from Hezekiah king of Judah three hundred talents*ᵈ* of silver and thirty talents*ᵉ* of gold. ¹⁵So Hezekiah gave him all the silver that was found in the temple of the LORD and in the treasuries of the royal palace.

¹⁶At this time Hezekiah king of Judah stripped off the gold with which he had covered the doors and doorposts of the temple of the LORD, and gave it to the king of Assyria.

¹⁷The king of Assyria sent his supreme commander, his chief officer and his field commander with a large army, from Lachish to King Hezekiah at Jerusalem. They came up to Jerusalem and stopped at the aqueduct of the Upper Pool, on the road to the Washerman's Field. ¹⁸They called for the king; and Eliakim son of Hilkiah the palace administrator, Shebna the secretary, and Joah son of Asaph the recorder went out to them.

¹⁹The field commander said to them, "Tell Hezekiah:

" 'This is what the great king, the king of Assyria, says: On what are you basing this confidence of yours? ²⁰You say you have strategy and military strength—but you speak only empty words. On whom are you depending, that you rebel against me? ²¹Look now, you are depending on Egypt, that splintered reed of a staff, which pierces a man's hand and wounds him if he leans on it! Such is Pharaoh king of Egypt to all who depend on him. ²²And if you say to me, "We are depending on the LORD our God"—isn't he the one whose high places and altars Hezekiah removed, saying to Judah and Jerusalem, "You must worship before this altar in Jerusalem"?

²³" 'Come now, make a bargain with my master, the king of Assyria: I will give you two thousand horses—if you can put riders on them! ²⁴How can you repulse one officer of the least of my master's officials, even though you are depending on Egypt

for chariots and horsemen*ᶠ*? ²⁵Furthermore, have I come to attack and destroy this place without word from the LORD? The LORD himself told me to march against this country and destroy it.' "

²⁶Then Eliakim son of Hilkiah, and Shebna and Joah said to the field commander, "Please speak to your servants in Aramaic, since we understand it. Don't speak to us in Hebrew in the hearing of the people on the wall."

²⁷But the commander replied, "Was it only to your master and you that my master sent me to say these things, and not to the men sitting on the wall—who, like you, will have to eat their own filth and drink their own urine?"

²⁸Then the commander stood and called out in Hebrew: "Hear the word of the great king, the king of Assyria! ²⁹This is what the king says: Do not let Hezekiah deceive you. He cannot deliver you from my hand. ³⁰Do not let Hezekiah persuade you to trust in the LORD when he says, 'The LORD will surely deliver us; this city will not be given into the hand of the king of Assyria.'

³¹"Do not listen to Hezekiah. This is what the king of Assyria says: Make peace with me and come out to me. Then every one of you will eat from his own vine and fig tree and drink water from his own cistern, ³²until I come and take you to a land like your own, a land of grain and new wine, a land of bread and vineyards, a land of olive trees and honey. Choose life and not death!

"Do not listen to Hezekiah, for he is misleading you when he says, 'The LORD will deliver us.' ³³Has the god of any nation ever delivered his land from the hand of the king of Assyria? ³⁴Where are the gods of Hamath and Arpad? Where are the gods of Sepharvaim, Hena and Ivvah? Have they rescued Samaria from my hand? ³⁵Who of all the gods of these countries has been able to save his land from me? How then can the LORD deliver Jerusalem from my hand?"

³⁶But the people remained silent and said nothing in reply, because the king had commanded, "Do not answer him."

³⁷Then Eliakim son of Hilkiah the palace administrator, Shebna the secretary

and Joah son of Asaph the recorder went to Hezekiah, with their clothes torn, and told him what the field commander had said.

CHAPTER 19

When King Hezekiah heard this, he tore his clothes and put on sackcloth and went into the temple of the LORD. ²He sent Eliakim the palace administrator, Shebna the secretary and the leading priests, all wearing sackcloth, to the prophet Isaiah son of Amoz. ³They told him, "This is what Hezekiah says: This day is a day of distress and rebuke and disgrace, as when children come to the point of birth and there is no strength to deliver them. ⁴It may be that the LORD your God will hear all the words of the field commander, whom his master, the king of Assyria, has sent to ridicule the living God, and that he will rebuke him for the words the LORD your God has heard. Therefore pray for the remnant that still survives."

⁵When King Hezekiah's officials came to Isaiah, ⁶Isaiah said to them, "Tell your master, 'This is what the LORD says: Do not be afraid of what you have heard—those words with which the underlings of the king of Assyria have blasphemed me. ⁷Listen! I am going to put such a spirit in him that when he hears a certain report, he will return to his own country, and there I will have him cut down with the sword.' "

⁸When the field commander heard that the king of Assyria had left Lachish, he withdrew and found the king fighting against Libnah.

⁹Now Sennacherib received a report that Tirhakah, the Cushite⁸ king ₗof Egypt₎, was marching out to fight against him. So he again sent messengers to Hezekiah with this word: ¹⁰"Say to Hezekiah king of Judah: Do not let the god you depend on deceive you when he says, 'Jerusalem will not be handed over to the king of Assyria.' ¹¹Surely you have heard what the kings of Assyria have done to all the countries, destroying them completely. And will you be delivered? ¹²Did the gods of the nations that were destroyed by my forefathers deliver them: the gods of Gozan, Haran, Rezeph and the people of Eden who were in Tel Assar? ¹³Where is

the king of Hamath, the king of Arpad, the king of the city of Sepharvaim, or of Hena or Ivvah?"

¹⁴Hezekiah received the letter from the messengers and read it. Then he went up to the temple of the LORD and spread it out before the LORD. ¹⁵And Hezekiah prayed to the LORD: "O LORD, God of Israel, enthroned between the cherubim, you alone are God over all the kingdoms of the earth. You have made heaven and earth. ¹⁶Give ear, O LORD, and hear; open your eyes, O LORD, and see; listen to the words Sennacherib has sent to insult the living God.

¹⁷"It is true, O LORD, that the Assyrian kings have laid waste these nations and their lands. ¹⁸They have thrown their gods into the fire and destroyed them, for they were not gods but only wood and stone, fashioned by men's hands. ¹⁹Now, O LORD our God, deliver us from his hand, so that all kingdoms on earth may know that you alone, O LORD, are God."

²⁰Then Isaiah son of Amoz sent a message to Hezekiah: "This is what the LORD, the God of Israel, says: I have heard your prayer concerning Sennacherib king of Assyria. ²¹This is the word that the LORD has spoken against him:

" 'The Virgin Daughter of Zion
    despises you and mocks you.
The Daughter of Jerusalem
    tosses her head as you flee.
²²Who is it you have insulted and
        blasphemed?
    Against whom have you raised your
        voice
and lifted your eyes in pride?
    Against the Holy One of Israel!
²³By your messengers
    you have heaped insults on the
        Lord.
And you have said,
    "With my many chariots
I have ascended the heights of the
        mountains,
    the utmost heights of Lebanon.
I have cut down its tallest cedars,
    the choicest of its pines.
I have reached its remotest parts,
    the finest of its forests.
²⁴I have dug wells in foreign lands
    and drunk the water there.
With the soles of my feet

⁸⁹ That is, from the upper Nile region

I have dried up all the streams of
    Egypt."

25" 'Have you not heard?
    Long ago I ordained it.
In days of old I planned it;
    now I have brought it to pass,
that you have turned fortified cities
    into piles of stone.
26Their people, drained of power,
    are dismayed and put to shame.
They are like plants in the field,
    like tender green shoots,
like grass sprouting on the roof,
    scorched before it grows up.

27" 'But I know where you stay
    and when you come and go
    and how you rage against me.
28Because you rage against me
    and your insolence has reached my
        ears,
I will put my hook in your nose
    and my bit in your mouth,
and I will make you return
    by the way you came.'

29"This will be the sign for you,
O Hezekiah:

"This year you will eat what grows by
    itself,
    and the second year what springs
        from that.
But in the third year sow and reap,
    plant vineyards and eat their fruit.
30Once more a remnant of the house of
    Judah
    will take root below and bear fruit
        above.
31For out of Jerusalem will come a
    remnant,
    and out of Mount Zion a band of
        survivors.
The zeal of the LORD Almighty will accomplish this.

32"Therefore this is what the LORD says
concerning the king of Assyria:

"He will not enter this city
    or shoot an arrow here.
He will not come before it with shield
    or build a siege ramp against it.
33By the way that he came he will
    return;
    he will not enter this city,
            declares the LORD.
34I will defend this city and save it,

for my sake and for the sake of
    David my servant."

35That night the angel of the LORD went
out and put to death a hundred and
eighty-five thousand men in the Assyrian camp. When the people got up the
next morning—there were all the dead
bodies! 36So Sennacherib king of Assyria
broke camp and withdrew. He returned
to Nineveh and stayed there.

37One day, while he was worshiping in
the temple of his god Nisroch, his sons
Adrammelech and Sharezer cut him
down with the sword, and they escaped
to the land of Ararat. And Esarhaddon his
son succeeded him as king.

CHAPTER 20

In those days Hezekiah became ill and
was at the point of death. The prophet
Isaiah son of Amoz went to him and said,
"This is what the LORD says: Put your
house in order, because you are going to
die; you will not recover."

2Hezekiah turned his face to the wall
and prayed to the LORD, 3 "Remember,
O LORD, how I have walked before you
faithfully and with wholehearted devotion and have done what is good in your
eyes." And Hezekiah wept bitterly.

4Before Isaiah had left the middle court,
the word of the LORD came to him: 5 "Go
back and tell Hezekiah, the leader of my
people, 'This is what the LORD, the God
of your father David, says: I have heard
your prayer and seen your tears; I will
heal you. On the third day from now you
will go up to the temple of the LORD. 6I
will add fifteen years to your life. And
I will deliver you and this city from
the hand of the king of Assyria. I will defend this city for my sake and for the
sake of my servant David.' "

7Then Isaiah said, "Prepare a poultice of
figs." They did so and applied it to the
boil, and he recovered.

8Hezekiah had asked Isaiah, "What will
be the sign that the LORD will heal me and
that I will go up to the temple of the LORD
on the third day from now?"

9Isaiah answered, "This is the LORD's
sign to you that the LORD will do what he
has promised: Shall the shadow go forward ten steps, or shall it go back ten
steps?"

10"It is a simple matter for the shadow

to go forward ten steps," said Hezekiah. "Rather, have it go back ten steps."

[11]Then the prophet Isaiah called upon the LORD, and the LORD made the shadow go back the ten steps it had gone down on the stairway of Ahaz.

[12]At that time Merodach-Baladan son of Baladan king of Babylon sent Hezekiah letters and a gift, because he had heard of Hezekiah's illness. [13]Hezekiah received the messengers and showed them all that was in his storehouses—the silver, the gold, the spices and the fine oil—his armory and everything found among his treasures. There was nothing in his palace or in all his kingdom that Hezekiah did not show them.

[14]Then Isaiah the prophet went to King Hezekiah and asked, "What did those men say, and where did they come from?"

"From a distant land," Hezekiah replied. "They came from Babylon."

[15]The prophet asked, "What did they see in your palace?"

"They saw everything in my palace," Hezekiah said. "There is nothing among my treasures that I did not show them."

[16]Then Isaiah said to Hezekiah, "Hear the word of the LORD: [17]The time will surely come when everything in your palace, and all that your fathers have stored up until this day, will be carried off to Babylon. Nothing will be left, says the LORD. [18]And some of your descendants, your own flesh and blood, that will be born to you, will be taken away, and they will become eunuchs in the palace of the king of Babylon."

[19]"The word of the LORD you have spoken is good," Hezekiah replied. For he thought, "Will there not be peace and security in my lifetime?"

[20]As for the other events of Hezekiah's reign, all his achievements and how he made the pool and the tunnel by which he brought water into the city, are they not written in the book of the annals of the kings of Judah? [21]Hezekiah rested with his fathers. And Manasseh his son succeeded him as king.

CHAPTER 21

Manasseh was twelve years old when he became king, and he reigned in Jerusalem fifty-five years. His mother's name was Hephzibah. [2]He did evil in the eyes of the LORD, following the detestable practices of the nations the LORD had driven out before the Israelites. [3]He rebuilt the high places his father Hezekiah had destroyed; he also erected altars to Baal and made an Asherah pole, as Ahab king of Israel had done. He bowed down to all the starry hosts and worshiped them. [4]He built altars in the temple of the LORD, of which the LORD had said, "In Jerusalem I will put my Name." [5]In both courts of the temple of the LORD, he built altars to all the starry hosts. [6]He sacrificed his own son in[h] the fire, practiced sorcery and divination, and consulted mediums and spiritists. He did much evil in the eyes of the LORD, provoking him to anger.

[7]He took the carved Asherah pole he had made and put it in the temple, of which the LORD had said to David and to his son Solomon, "In this temple and in Jerusalem, which I have chosen out of all the tribes of Israel, I will put my Name forever. [8]I will not again make the feet of the Israelites wander from the land I gave their forefathers, if only they will be careful to do everything I commanded them and will keep the whole Law that my servant Moses gave them." [9]But the people did not listen. Manasseh led them astray, so that they did more evil than the nations the LORD had destroyed before the Israelites.

[10]The LORD said through his servants the prophets: [11]"Manasseh king of Judah has committed these detestable sins. He has done more evil than the Amorites who preceded him and has led Judah into sin with his idols. [12]Therefore this is what the LORD, the God of Israel, says: I am going to bring such disaster on Jerusalem and Judah that the ears of everyone who hears of it will tingle. [13]I will stretch out over Jerusalem the measuring line used against Samaria and the plumb line used against the house of Ahab. I will wipe out Jerusalem as one wipes a dish, wiping it and turning it upside down. [14]I will forsake the remnant of my inheritance and hand them over to their enemies. They will be looted and plundered by all their foes, [15]because they have done evil in my eyes and have provoked me to anger from

[h]6 Or He made his own son pass through

the day their forefathers came out of Egypt until this day."

¹⁶Moreover, Manasseh also shed so much innocent blood that he filled Jerusalem from end to end—besides the sin that he had caused Judah to commit, so that they did evil in the eyes of the LORD.

¹⁷As for the other events of Manasseh's reign, and all he did, including the sin he committed, are they not written in the book of the annals of the kings of Judah? ¹⁸Manasseh rested with his fathers and was buried in his palace garden, the garden of Uzza. And Amon his son succeeded him as king.

¹⁹Amon was twenty-two years old when he became king, and he reigned in Jerusalem two years. His mother's name was Meshullemeth daughter of Haruz; she was from Jotbah. ²⁰He did evil in the eyes of the LORD, as his father Manasseh had done. ²¹He walked in all the ways of his father; he worshiped the idols his father had worshiped, and bowed down to them. ²²He forsook the LORD, the God of his fathers, and did not walk in the way of the LORD.

²³Amon's officials conspired against him and assassinated the king in his palace. ²⁴Then the people of the land killed all who had plotted against King Amon, and they made Josiah his son king in his place.

²⁵As for the other events of Amon's reign, and what he did, are they not written in the book of the annals of the kings of Judah? ²⁶He was buried in his grave in the garden of Uzza. And Josiah his son succeeded him as king.

APRIL 13 □ DAY 104
2 KINGS 22–25
Ruin of Judah

OVERVIEW Those who do not learn from history are destined to repeat it, and Judah is no exception. Though Israel has been swept away in judgment, the southern kingdom continues its pagan "business as usual." Good king Josiah makes a last desperate attempt to turn the nation back to God. He locates the long-lost Book of the Law and institutes sweeping reforms. But though he can impose a change of *actions* on the people, only wholehearted repentance can change the *attitudes* of godlessness and self-indulgence that are the root of the problem. When Josiah dies, his successors revert to their pagan patterns and practices. At last, God brings down the curtain on the southern kingdom as Babylonian soldiers topple the walls, homes and temple of once-mighty Jerusalem.

Chapter 22	Chapter 23	Chapter 24	Chapter 25
Recovery of the Law	Reform of the Nation	Siege of Jerusalem	Fall of Jerusalem
Reform by Josiah		Removal by Nebuchadnezzar	

YOUR DAILY WALK What is the most important book in the world to you? Assuming your answer is "the Bible" . . .

How many days this month have you spent time in the Bible? Assuming your answer is at least one . . .

How did you respond to the truth you encountered there? Assuming your answer is an honest one . . .

Are you satisfied with how you responded to that truth? Assuming your answer is anything less than a resounding yes . . .

The degree of our spiritual vigor is in direct proportion to the time we spend in God's Word.

Reread 2 Kings 23:2–3. The power of God's Word to change lives is perhaps nowhere more evident than in those two verses. The Word pierced where no man-made sword could reach: to the very heart of the king, priests, prophets and people, turning their hearts collectively back to God. The result: a national spiritual awakening.

God's Word convicts, but only you can commit yourself to doing God's will. Is there an area of your life where a response is overdue? THINK.

INSIGHT The Short and Long and Short and Long of It
The length of time each of the last four kings in Judah reigned is easy to remember once you see the pattern. The sequence is 3 months—11 years—3 months—11 years.

CHAPTER 22

Josiah was eight years old when he became king, and he reigned in Jerusalem thirty-one years. His mother's name was Jedidah daughter of Adaiah; she was from Bozkath. ²He did what was right in the eyes of the LORD and walked in all the ways of his father David, not turning aside to the right or to the left.

³In the eighteenth year of his reign, King Josiah sent the secretary, Shaphan son of Azaliah, the son of Meshullam, to the temple of the LORD. He said: ⁴"Go up to Hilkiah the high priest and have him get ready the money that has been brought into the temple of the LORD, which the doorkeepers have collected from the people. ⁵Have them entrust it to the men appointed to supervise the work on the temple. And have these men pay the workers who repair the temple of the LORD— ⁶the carpenters, the builders and the masons. Also have them purchase timber and dressed stone to repair the temple. ⁷But they need not account for the money entrusted to them, because they are acting faithfully."

⁸Hilkiah the high priest said to Shaphan the secretary, "I have found the Book of the Law in the temple of the LORD." He gave it to Shaphan, who read it. ⁹Then Shaphan the secretary went to the king and reported to him: "Your officials have paid out the money that was in the temple of the LORD and have entrusted it to the workers and supervisors at the temple." ¹⁰Then Shaphan the secretary informed the king, "Hilkiah the priest has given me a book." And Shaphan read from it in the presence of the king.

¹¹When the king heard the words of the Book of the Law, he tore his robes. ¹²He gave these orders to Hilkiah the priest, Ahikam son of Shaphan, Acbor son of Micaiah, Shaphan the secretary and Asaiah the king's attendant: ¹³"Go and inquire of the LORD for me and for the people and for all Judah about what is written in this book that has been found. Great is the LORD's anger that burns against us because our fathers have not obeyed the words of this book; they have not acted in accordance with all that is written there concerning us."

¹⁴Hilkiah the priest, Ahikam, Acbor, Shaphan and Asaiah went to speak to the prophetess Huldah, who was the wife of Shallum son of Tikvah, the son of Harhas, keeper of the wardrobe. She lived in Jerusalem, in the Second District.

¹⁵She said to them, "This is what the LORD, the God of Israel, says: Tell the man who sent you to me, ¹⁶'This is what the LORD says: I am going to bring disaster on this place and its people, according to everything written in the book the king of Judah has read. ¹⁷Because they have forsaken me and burned incense to other gods and provoked me to anger by all the idols their hands have made,ⁱ my anger will burn against this place and will not be quenched.' ¹⁸Tell the king of Judah, who sent you to inquire of the LORD, 'This is what the LORD, the God of Israel, says concerning the words you heard: ¹⁹Because your heart was responsive and you humbled yourself before the LORD when you heard what I have spoken against this place and its people, that they would become accursed and laid waste, and because you tore your robes and wept in my presence, I have heard you, declares the LORD. ²⁰Therefore I will gather you to your fathers, and you will be buried in peace.

ⁱ17 Or *by everything they have done*

Your eyes will not see all the disaster I am going to bring on this place.' "

So they took her answer back to the king.

CHAPTER 23
Then the king called together all the elders of Judah and Jerusalem. ²He went up to the temple of the LORD with the men of Judah, the people of Jerusalem, the priests and the prophets—all the people from the least to the greatest. He read in their hearing all the words of the Book of the Covenant, which had been found in the temple of the LORD. ³The king stood by the pillar and renewed the covenant in the presence of the LORD—to follow the LORD and keep his commands, regulations and decrees with all his heart and all his soul, thus confirming the words of the covenant written in this book. Then all the people pledged themselves to the covenant.

⁴The king ordered Hilkiah the high priest, the priests next in rank and the doorkeepers to remove from the temple of the LORD all the articles made for Baal and Asherah and all the starry hosts. He burned them outside Jerusalem in the fields of the Kidron Valley and took the ashes to Bethel. ⁵He did away with the pagan priests appointed by the kings of Judah to burn incense on the high places of the towns of Judah and on those around Jerusalem—those who burned incense to Baal, to the sun and moon, to the constellations and to all the starry hosts. ⁶He took the Asherah pole from the temple of the LORD to the Kidron Valley outside Jerusalem and burned it there. He ground it to powder and scattered the dust over the graves of the common people. ⁷He also tore down the quarters of the male shrine prostitutes, which were in the temple of the LORD and where women did weaving for Asherah.

⁸Josiah brought all the priests from the towns of Judah and desecrated the high places, from Geba to Beersheba, where the priests had burned incense. He broke down the shrinesʲ at the gates—at the entrance to the Gate of Joshua, the city governor, which is on the left of the city gate. ⁹Although the priests of the high places did not serve at the altar of the

LORD in Jerusalem, they ate unleavened bread with their fellow priests.

¹⁰He desecrated Topheth, which was in the Valley of Ben Hinnom, so no one could use it to sacrifice his son or daughter inᵏ the fire to Molech. ¹¹He removed from the entrance to the temple of the LORD the horses that the kings of Judah had dedicated to the sun. They were in the court near the room of an official named Nathan-Melech. Josiah then burned the chariots dedicated to the sun.

¹²He pulled down the altars the kings of Judah had erected on the roof near the upper room of Ahaz, and the altars Manasseh had built in the two courts of the temple of the LORD. He removed them from there, smashed them to pieces and threw the rubble into the Kidron Valley. ¹³The king also desecrated the high places that were east of Jerusalem on the south of the Hill of Corruption—the ones Solomon king of Israel had built for Ashtoreth the vile goddess of the Sidonians, for Chemosh the vile god of Moab, and for Molechˡ the detestable god of the people of Ammon. ¹⁴Josiah smashed the sacred stones and cut down the Asherah poles and covered the sites with human bones.

¹⁵Even the altar at Bethel, the high place made by Jeroboam son of Nebat, who had caused Israel to sin—even that altar and high place he demolished. He burned the high place and ground it to powder, and burned the Asherah pole also. ¹⁶Then Josiah looked around, and when he saw the tombs that were there on the hillside, he had the bones removed from them and burned on the altar to defile it, in accordance with the word of the LORD proclaimed by the man of God who foretold these things.

¹⁷The king asked, "What is that tombstone I see?"

The men of the city said, "It marks the tomb of the man of God who came from Judah and pronounced against the altar of Bethel the very things you have done to it."

¹⁸"Leave it alone," he said. "Don't let anyone disturb his bones." So they spared his bones and those of the prophet who had come from Samaria.

¹⁹Just as he had done at Bethel, Josiah removed and defiled all the shrines at the

ʲ8 Or high places   ᵏ10 Or to make his son or daughter pass through   ˡ13 Hebrew Milcom high places that the kings of Israel had built in the towns of Samaria that had provoked the LORD to anger. ²⁰Josiah slaughtered all the priests of those high places on the altars and burned human bones on them. Then he went back to Jerusalem.

²¹The king gave this order to all the people: "Celebrate the Passover to the LORD your God, as it is written in this Book of the Covenant." ²²Not since the days of the judges who led Israel, nor throughout the days of the kings of Israel and the kings of Judah, had any such Passover been observed. ²³But in the eighteenth year of King Josiah, this Passover was celebrated to the LORD in Jerusalem.

²⁴Furthermore, Josiah got rid of the mediums and spiritists, the household gods, the idols and all the other detestable things seen in Judah and Jerusalem. This he did to fulfill the requirements of the law written in the book that Hilkiah the priest had discovered in the temple of the LORD. ²⁵Neither before nor after Josiah was there a king like him who turned to the LORD as he did—with all his heart and with all his soul and with all his strength, in accordance with all the Law of Moses.

²⁶Nevertheless, the LORD did not turn away from the heat of his fierce anger, which burned against Judah because of all that Manasseh had done to provoke him to anger. ²⁷So the LORD said, "I will remove Judah also from my presence as I removed Israel, and I will reject Jerusalem, the city I chose, and this temple, about which I said, 'There shall my Name be.'ᵐ"

²⁸As for the other events of Josiah's reign, and all he did, are they not written in the book of the annals of the kings of Judah?

²⁹While Josiah was king, Pharaoh Neco king of Egypt went up to the Euphrates River to help the king of Assyria. King Josiah marched out to meet him in battle, but Neco faced him and killed him at Megiddo. ³⁰Josiah's servants brought his body in a chariot from Megiddo to Jerusalem and buried him in his own tomb. And the people of the land took Jehoahaz son of Josiah and anointed him and made him king in place of his father.

³¹Jehoahaz was twenty-three years old when he became king, and he reigned in Jerusalem three months. His mother's name was Hamutal daughter of Jeremiah; she was from Libnah. ³²He did evil in the eyes of the LORD, just as his fathers had done. ³³Pharaoh Neco put him in chains at Riblah in the land of Hamathⁿ so that he might not reign in Jerusalem, and he imposed on Judah a levy of a hundred talentsᵒ of silver and a talentᵖ of gold. ³⁴Pharaoh Neco made Eliakim son of Josiah king in place of his father Josiah and changed Eliakim's name to Jehoiakim. But he took Jehoahaz and carried him off to Egypt, and there he died. ³⁵Jehoiakim paid Pharaoh Neco the silver and gold he demanded. In order to do so, he taxed the land and exacted the silver and gold from the people of the land according to their assessments.

³⁶Jehoiakim was twenty-five years old when he became king, and he reigned in Jerusalem eleven years. His mother's name was Zebidah daughter of Pedaiah; she was from Rumah. ³⁷And he did evil in the eyes of the LORD, just as his fathers had done.

CHAPTER 24

During Jehoiakim's reign, Nebuchadnezzar king of Babylon invaded the land, and Jehoiakim became his vassal for three years. But then he changed his mind and rebelled against Nebuchadnezzar. ²The LORD sent Babylonian,�q Aramean, Moabite and Ammonite raiders against him. He sent them to destroy Judah, in accordance with the word of the LORD proclaimed by his servants the prophets. ³Surely these things happened to Judah according to the LORD's command, in order to remove them from his presence because of the sins of Manasseh and all he had done, ⁴including the shedding of innocent blood. For he had filled Jerusalem with innocent blood, and the LORD was not willing to forgive.

⁵As for the other events of Jehoiakim's reign, and all he did, are they not written in the book of the annals of the kings of Judah? ⁶Jehoiakim rested with his fathers. And Jehoiachin his son succeeded him as king.

⁷The king of Egypt did not march out

ᵐ27 1 Kings 8:29   ⁿ33 Hebrew; Septuagint (see also 2 Chron. 36:3) *Neco at Riblah in Hamath removed him*   ᵒ33 That is, about 3 3/4 tons (about 3.4 metric tons)   ᵖ33 That is, about 75 pounds (about 34 kilograms)   q2 Or *Chaldean* from his own country again, because the king of Babylon had taken all his territory, from the Wadi of Egypt to the Euphrates River.

⁸Jehoiachin was eighteen years old when he became king, and he reigned in Jerusalem three months. His mother's name was Nehushta daughter of Elnathan; she was from Jerusalem. ⁹He did evil in the eyes of the LORD, just as his father had done.

¹⁰At that time the officers of Nebuchadnezzar king of Babylon advanced on Jerusalem and laid siege to it, ¹¹and Nebuchadnezzar himself came up to the city while his officers were besieging it. ¹²Jehoiachin king of Judah, his mother, his attendants, his nobles and his officials all surrendered to him.

In the eighth year of the reign of the king of Babylon, he took Jehoiachin prisoner. ¹³As the LORD had declared, Nebuchadnezzar removed all the treasures from the temple of the LORD and from the royal palace, and took away all the gold articles that Solomon king of Israel had made for the temple of the LORD. ¹⁴He carried into exile all Jerusalem: all the officers and fighting men, and all the craftsmen and artisans—a total of ten thousand. Only the poorest people of the land were left.

¹⁵Nebuchadnezzar took Jehoiachin captive to Babylon. He also took from Jerusalem to Babylon the king's mother, his wives, his officials and the leading men of the land. ¹⁶The king of Babylon also deported to Babylon the entire force of seven thousand fighting men, strong and fit for war, and a thousand craftsmen and artisans. ¹⁷He made Mattaniah, Jehoiachin's uncle, king in his place and changed his name to Zedekiah.

¹⁸Zedekiah was twenty-one years old when he became king, and he reigned in Jerusalem eleven years. His mother's name was Hamutal daughter of Jeremiah; she was from Libnah. ¹⁹He did evil in the eyes of the LORD, just as Jehoiakim had done. ²⁰It was because of the LORD's anger that all this happened to Jerusalem and Judah, and in the end he thrust them from his presence.

Now Zedekiah rebelled against the king of Babylon.

CHAPTER 25

So in the ninth year of Zedekiah's reign, on the tenth day of the tenth month, Nebuchadnezzar king of Babylon marched against Jerusalem with his whole army. He encamped outside the city and built siege works all around it. ²The city was kept under siege until the eleventh year of King Zedekiah. ³By the ninth day of the ⌊fourth⌋ʳ month the famine in the city had become so severe that there was no food for the people to eat. ⁴Then the city wall was broken through, and the whole army fled at night through the gate between the two walls near the king's garden, though the Babyloniansˢ were surrounding the city. They fled toward the Arabah,ᵗ ⁵but the Babylonianᵘ army pursued the king and overtook him in the plains of Jericho. All his soldiers were separated from him and scattered, ⁶and he was captured. He was taken to the king of Babylon at Riblah, where sentence was pronounced on him. ⁷They killed the sons of Zedekiah before his eyes. Then they put out his eyes, bound him with bronze shackles and took him to Babylon.

⁸On the seventh day of the fifth month, in the nineteenth year of Nebuchadnezzar king of Babylon, Nebuzaradan commander of the imperial guard, an official of the king of Babylon, came to Jerusalem. ⁹He set fire to the temple of the LORD, the royal palace and all the houses of Jerusalem. Every important building he burned down. ¹⁰The whole Babylonian army, under the commander of the imperial guard, broke down the walls around Jerusalem. ¹¹Nebuzaradan the commander of the guard carried into exile the people who remained in the city, along with the rest of the populace and those who had gone over to the king of Babylon. ¹²But the commander left behind some of the poorest people of the land to work the vineyards and fields.

¹³The Babylonians broke up the bronze pillars, the movable stands and the bronze Sea that were at the temple of the LORD and they carried the bronze to Babylon. ¹⁴They also took away the pots, shovels, wick trimmers, dishes and all the bronze articles used in the temple service. ¹⁵The commander of the imperial guard took away the censers and sprinkling

ʳ3 See Jer. 52:6.   ˢ4 Or Chaldeans; also in verses 13, 25 and 26   ᵗ4 Or the Jordan Valley   ᵘ5 Or Chaldean; also in verses 10 and 24 bowls—all that were made of pure gold or silver.

¹⁶The bronze from the two pillars, the Sea and the movable stands, which Solomon had made for the temple of the LORD, was more than could be weighed. ¹⁷Each pillar was twenty-seven feet^v high. The bronze capital on top of one pillar was four and a half feet^w high and was decorated with a network and pomegranates of bronze all around. The other pillar, with its network, was similar.

¹⁸The commander of the guard took as prisoners Seraiah the chief priest, Zephaniah the priest next in rank and the three doorkeepers. ¹⁹Of those still in the city, he took the officer in charge of the fighting men and five royal advisers. He also took the secretary who was chief officer in charge of conscripting the people of the land and sixty of his men who were found in the city. ²⁰Nebuzaradan the commander took them all and brought them to the king of Babylon at Riblah. ²¹There at Riblah, in the land of Hamath, the king had them executed.

So Judah went into captivity, away from her land.

²²Nebuchadnezzar king of Babylon appointed Gedaliah son of Ahikam, the son of Shaphan, to be over the people he had left behind in Judah. ²³When all the army officers and their men heard that the king

of Babylon had appointed Gedaliah as governor, they came to Gedaliah at Mizpah—Ishmael son of Nethaniah, Johanan son of Kareah, Seraiah son of Tanhumeth the Netophathite, Jaazaniah the son of the Maacathite, and their men. ²⁴Gedaliah took an oath to reassure them and their men. "Do not be afraid of the Babylonian officials," he said. "Settle down in the land and serve the king of Babylon, and it will go well with you."

²⁵In the seventh month, however, Ishmael son of Nethaniah, the son of Elishama, who was of royal blood, came with ten men and assassinated Gedaliah and also the men of Judah and the Babylonians who were with him at Mizpah. ²⁶At this, all the people from the least to the greatest, together with the army officers, fled to Egypt for fear of the Babylonians.

²⁷In the thirty-seventh year of the exile of Jehoiachin king of Judah, in the year Evil-Merodach^x became king of Babylon, he released Jehoiachin from prison on the twenty-seventh day of the twelfth month. ²⁸He spoke kindly to him and gave him a seat of honor higher than those of the other kings who were with him in Babylon. ²⁹So Jehoiachin put aside his prison clothes and for the rest of his life ate regularly at the king's table. ³⁰Day by day the king gave Jehoiachin a regular allowance as long as he lived.

^{v}17 Hebrew *eighteen cubits* (about 8.1 meters) ^{w}17 Hebrew *three cubits* (about 1.3 meters) ^{x}27 Also called *Amel-Marduk*

APRIL 14 □ DAY 105
Prayers God Delights to Answer

 LOOK BACK One nation under Solomon (Israel) becomes two nations fractured by civil war (Israel and Judah). Beginning with 1 Kings 12, you have been reading the parallel histories of these two kingdoms.

Elijah's prophetic ministry (1 Kings) is mostly public and national in scope. His encounter with the prophets of Baal on Mount Carmel is a classic "battle of the gods," and his prayer life an example to all believers (James 5:17–18). By contrast, his successor, Elisha (2 Kings), ministers with equal power and a double portion of Elijah's spirit, but mostly in private, one-on-one encounters.

The northern kingdom of Israel, clearly on a collision course with disaster since the days of Ahab, finally meets its fate at the hands of the cruel Assyrians. The surviving kingdom of Judah narrowly averts a similar end and is revived during the reign of good king Hezekiah. His zealous reforms and heartfelt prayers temporarily turn the tide of national apostasy and halfhearted religion.

True prayer is a way of life, not just an emergency detour.

LOOK UP When you pray, does God *(a)* always answer your prayers? *(b)* sometimes answer your prayers? *(c)* seldom answer your prayers?

If the frequency of God's answers makes you suspect you still have much to learn about prayer, you are in good company. Even Jesus' closest traveling companions came to him one day and said, "Lord, teach us to pray" (Luke 11:1). It was a request Jesus was only too happy to grant!

In your reading of 1 and 2 Kings you have encountered two remarkable examples of people who prayed the kinds of prayers God delights to answer.

Elijah prayed a prayer of *self-sacrifice*. In order to bring his countrymen to a spiritual crossroads, Elijah prayed that it wouldn't rain—knowing that if God answered his prayer, Elijah's own brook would dry up, and his life would be in jeopardy.

Hezekiah prayed a prayer of *total dependence*. Spreading before the Lord the threatening letter he had received from the Assyrian commander, Hezekiah affirmed that God and God alone had the power to deliver his people. Hezekiah's confidence was not in his wealth, his wisdom, the size of his army or the eloquence of his words—but in God's omnipotent greatness.

LOOK AHEAD Close your time in the Word today by following the exhortation of Peter (one of the disciples who asked Jesus to teach him to pray) in 1 Peter 5:5–7: "All of you, clothe yourselves with humility toward one another, because 'God opposes the proud, but gives grace to the humble.' Humble yourselves, therefore, under God's mighty hand, that he may lift you up in due time. Cast all your anxiety on him because he cares for you."

Think of a problem or decision you are facing right now, and pray it through like Elijah or Hezekiah. Lay your request before the Lord; be honest and transparent before him. Are you willing to obey God totally, even if it means personal inconvenience or risk? Are you willing to lean on God alone, even if others criticize or ostracize you? Tell him so right now!

It's a humbling thing to acknowledge that you cannot solve your own problems—but when you let God be your problem solver, don't be surprised if you see enemies flee and fireworks begin!

1 Chronicles

THE TWO books of Chronicles are priestly recollections and interpretations of the historical facts surrounding God's people from the reign of David to the Babylonian exile. First Chronicles recounts the righteous reign of David. Chapters 1–9 date David's ancestry back to Adam, and chapters 10–29 focus on the details of David's administration. The book's emphasis is on proper worship of the one true God—a worship David's life consistently exemplifies.

Focus	David's Line	David's Reign			
Divisions	David's Ancestors	David's Early Years as King	David's Kingdom and Covenant	David's Preparations for Temple Worship	David's Final Words and Deeds
	1 9	10 16	17 21	22 27	28 29
Topics	Genealogy	Biography			
	Ancestry	Anointing	Administration		Advice
Place	United Kingdom of Israel				
Time	Many Years	About 40 Years			

APRIL 15 ☐ DAY 106
1 CHRONICLES 1–9
David's Ancestors

OVERVIEW Chronicles gives a priestly perspective on the history of God's people. The anonymous chronicler (possibly Ezra) carefully weds the nation's history with the sovereign hand of God to show God's purposes at work in the affairs of his people. For generations God has been preparing a people (the Jews), a king (David) and a kingdom (Judah) through whom he would bless the world. In spite of the nation's unbelief, disobedience and even displacement from the land, God's plan for them is still at work—a warming comfort for those about to return to rubble-strewn Jerusalem after a seventy-year absence.

Chapters 1–3	Chapters 4–8	Chapter 9
Genealogy from Adam to the Exile	Genealogy of the Twelve Tribes	Genealogy after the Exile
Family Tree of David and Israel		

YOUR DAILY WALK One wag has commented, "Always treat your mother and father with respect, for without them you might be somebody else!"

Never try to make your son or daughter another you; one is enough.

The chronicler spends nine chapters showing how important it was for God's people to trace their roots and cling to their ancestral ties. Why? Because many of God's promises were made to an individual and his descendants, such as Abraham (Genesis 15) and David (2 Samuel 7). Take away the roots, and you take away the promises. For a people languishing in exile and wondering if God had forgotten them, their heritage became their hope.

Do a little New Testament research to discover what your rich heritage is because of your position in the family of God. Start with Galatians 3:29; 4:7; Titus 3:7; James 2:5; 1 Peter 1:3–4.

INSIGHT Shame on a Name

Baal is not a proper name but a title: "master." It is used to describe the owner of a house, land or cattle. During the period of the judges, it was applied by many to the Lord and appeared in many individuals' names. (For example, see Judges 7:1.) But *Baal* was also the name of the chief male god of Canaan. Later, scribes found the custom of using *Baal* in personal names so abhorrent that they put the word *bosheth* (which means "shame") in place of *Baal.* Hence the name *Ishbosheth* in place of *Esh-Baal* (8:33; see 2 Samuel 2:8) and *Mephibosheth* in place of *Merib-Baal* (8:34; see 2 Samuel 9:6).

CHAPTER 1
Adam, Seth, Enosh, ²Kenan, Mahalalel, Jared, ³Enoch, Methuselah, Lamech, Noah.

⁴The sons of Noah:ᵃ
  Shem, Ham and Japheth.

⁵The sonsᵇ of Japheth:

ᵃ4 Septuagint; Hebrew does not have *The sons of Noah:*   ᵇ5 *Sons* may mean *descendants* or *successors* or *nations*; also in verses 6-10, 17 and 20.

Gomer, Magog, Madai, Javan, Tubal, Meshech and Tiras.
⁶The sons of Gomer:
Ashkenaz, Riphath*c* and Togarmah.
⁷The sons of Javan:
Elishah, Tarshish, the Kittim and the Rodanim.
⁸The sons of Ham:
Cush, Mizraim,*d* Put and Canaan.
⁹The sons of Cush:
Seba, Havilah, Sabta, Raamah and Sabteca.
The sons of Raamah:
Sheba and Dedan.
¹⁰Cush was the father*e* of
Nimrod, who grew to be a mighty warrior on earth.
¹¹Mizraim was the father of
the Ludites, Anamites, Lehabites, Naphtuhites, ¹²Pathrusites, Casluhites (from whom the Philistines came) and Caphtorites.
¹³Canaan was the father of
Sidon his firstborn,*f* and of the Hittites, ¹⁴Jebusites, Amorites, Girgashites, ¹⁵Hivites, Arkites, Sinites, ¹⁶Arvadites, Zemarites and Hamathites.

¹⁷The sons of Shem:
Elam, Asshur, Arphaxad, Lud and Aram.
The sons of Aram*g*:
Uz, Hul, Gether and Meshech.
¹⁸Arphaxad was the father of Shelah,
and Shelah the father of Eber.
¹⁹Two sons were born to Eber:
One was named Peleg,*h* because in his time the earth was divided; his brother was named Joktan.
²⁰Joktan was the father of
Almodad, Sheleph, Hazarmaveth, Jerah, ²¹Hadoram, Uzal, Diklah, ²²Obal,*i* Abimael, Sheba, ²³Ophir, Havilah and Jobab. All these were sons of Joktan.

²⁴Shem, Arphaxad,*j* Shelah,
²⁵Eber, Peleg, Reu,
²⁶Serug, Nahor, Terah

²⁷and Abram (that is, Abraham).

²⁸The sons of Abraham:
Isaac and Ishmael.
²⁹These were their descendants:
Nebaioth the firstborn of Ishmael, Kedar, Adbeel, Mibsam, ³⁰Mishma, Dumah, Massa, Hadad, Tema, ³¹Jetur, Naphish and Kedemah. These were the sons of Ishmael.

³²The sons born to Keturah, Abraham's concubine:
Zimran, Jokshan, Medan, Midian, Ishbak and Shuah.
The sons of Jokshan:
Sheba and Dedan.
³³The sons of Midian:
Ephah, Epher, Hanoch, Abida and Eldaah.
All these were descendants of Keturah.

³⁴Abraham was the father of Isaac.
The sons of Isaac:
Esau and Israel.
³⁵The sons of Esau:
Eliphaz, Reuel, Jeush, Jalam and Korah.
³⁶The sons of Eliphaz:
Teman, Omar, Zepho,*k* Gatam and Kenaz;
by Timna: Amalek.*l*
³⁷The sons of Reuel:
Nahath, Zerah, Shammah and Mizzah.

³⁸The sons of Seir:
Lotan, Shobal, Zibeon, Anah, Dishon, Ezer and Dishan.
³⁹The sons of Lotan:
Hori and Homam. Timna was Lotan's sister.
⁴⁰The sons of Shobal:
Alvan,*m* Manahath, Ebal, Shepho and Onam.
The sons of Zibeon:
Aiah and Anah.
⁴¹The son of Anah:
Dishon.
The sons of Dishon:

---

*c*6 Many Hebrew manuscripts and Vulgate (see also Septuagint and Gen. 10:3); most Hebrew manuscripts *Diphath*   *d*8 That is, Egypt; also in verse 11   *e*10 *Father* may mean *ancestor* or *predecessor* or *founder*; also in verses 11, 13, 18 and 20.   *f*13 Or *of the Sidonians, the foremost*   *g*17 One Hebrew manuscript and some Septuagint manuscripts (see also Gen. 10:23); most Hebrew manuscripts do not have this line.   *h*19 *Peleg* means *division*.   *i*22 Some Hebrew manuscripts and Syriac (see also Gen. 10:28); most Hebrew manuscripts *Ebal*   *j*24 Hebrew; some Septuagint manuscripts *Arphaxad, Cainan* (see also note at Gen. 11:10)   *k*36 Many Hebrew manuscripts, some Septuagint manuscripts and Syriac (see also Gen. 36:11); most Hebrew manuscripts *Zephi*   *l*36 Some Septuagint manuscripts (see also Gen. 36:12); Hebrew *Gatam, Kenaz, Timna and Amalek*   *m*40 Many Hebrew manuscripts and some Septuagint manuscripts (see also Gen. 36:23); most Hebrew manuscripts *Alian*

Hemdan,ⁿ Eshban, Ithran and Keran.

⁴²The sons of Ezer:
Bilhan, Zaavan and Akan.^o
The sons of Dishan^p:
Uz and Aran.

⁴³These were the kings who reigned in Edom before any Israelite king reigned^q:
Bela son of Beor, whose city was named Dinhabah.

⁴⁴When Bela died, Jobab son of Zerah from Bozrah succeeded him as king.

⁴⁵When Jobab died, Husham from the land of the Temanites succeeded him as king.

⁴⁶When Husham died, Hadad son of Bedad, who defeated Midian in the country of Moab, succeeded him as king. His city was named Avith.

⁴⁷When Hadad died, Samlah from Masrekah succeeded him as king.

⁴⁸When Samlah died, Shaul from Rehoboth on the river^r succeeded him as king.

⁴⁹When Shaul died, Baal-Hanan son of Acbor succeeded him as king.

⁵⁰When Baal-Hanan died, Hadad succeeded him as king. His city was named Pau,^s and his wife's name was Mehetabel daughter of Matred, the daughter of Me-Zahab. ⁵¹Hadad also died.

The chiefs of Edom were:
Timna, Alvah, Jetheth, ⁵²Oholibamah, Elah, Pinon, ⁵³Kenaz, Teman, Mibzar, ⁵⁴Magdiel and Iram. These were the chiefs of Edom.

CHAPTER 2

These were the sons of Israel:
Reuben, Simeon, Levi, Judah, Issachar, Zebulun, ²Dan, Joseph, Benjamin, Naphtali, Gad and Asher.

³The sons of Judah:
Er, Onan and Shelah. These three

were born to him by a Canaanite woman, the daughter of Shua. Er, Judah's firstborn, was wicked in the LORD's sight; so the LORD put him to death. ⁴Tamar, Judah's daughter-in-law, bore him Perez and Zerah. Judah had five sons in all.

⁵The sons of Perez:
Hezron and Hamul.

⁶The sons of Zerah:
Zimri, Ethan, Heman, Calcol and Darda^t—five in all.

⁷The son of Carmi:
Achar,^u who brought trouble on Israel by violating the ban on taking devoted things.^v

⁸The son of Ethan:
Azariah.

⁹The sons born to Hezron were:
Jerahmeel, Ram and Caleb.^w

¹⁰Ram was the father of
Amminadab, and Amminadab the father of Nahshon, the leader of the people of Judah. ¹¹Nahshon was the father of Salmon,^x Salmon the father of Boaz, ¹²Boaz the father of Obed and Obed the father of Jesse.

¹³Jesse was the father of
Eliab his firstborn; the second son was Abinadab, the third Shimea, ¹⁴the fourth Nethanel, the fifth Raddai, ¹⁵the sixth Ozem and the seventh David. ¹⁶Their sisters were Zeruiah and Abigail. Zeruiah's three sons were Abishai, Joab and Asahel. ¹⁷Abigail was the mother of Amasa, whose father was Jether the Ishmaelite.

¹⁸Caleb son of Hezron had children by his wife Azubah (and by Jerioth). These were her sons: Jesher, Shobab and Ardon. ¹⁹When Azubah died, Caleb married Ephrath, who bore him Hur. ²⁰Hur was the father of Uri, and Uri the father of Bezalel.

²¹Later, Hezron lay with the daughter

ⁿ41 Many Hebrew manuscripts and some Septuagint manuscripts (see also Gen. 36:26); most Hebrew manuscripts *Hamran*
^o42 Many Hebrew and Septuagint manuscripts (see also Gen. 36:27); most Hebrew manuscripts *Zaavan, Jaakan*   ^p42 Hebrew *Dishon*, a variant of *Dishan*   ^q43 Or *before an Israelite king reigned over them*   ^r48 Possibly the Euphrates   ^s50 Many Hebrew manuscripts, some Septuagint manuscripts, Vulgate and Syriac (see also Gen. 36:39); most Hebrew manuscripts *Pai*
^t6 Many Hebrew manuscripts, some Septuagint manuscripts and Syriac (see also 1 Kings 4:31); most Hebrew manuscripts *Dara*   ^u7 *Achar* means *trouble*; *Achar* is called *Achan* in Joshua.   ^v7 The Hebrew term refers to the irrevocable giving over of things or persons to the LORD, often by totally destroying them.   ^w9 Hebrew *Kelubai*, a variant of *Caleb*   ^x11 Septuagint (see also Ruth 4:21); Hebrew *Salma*

of Makir the father of Gilead (he had married her when he was sixty years old), and she bore him Segub. ²²Segub was the father of Jair, who controlled twenty-three towns in Gilead. ²³(But Geshur and Aram captured Havvoth Jair,^y as well as Kenath with its surrounding settlements—sixty towns.) All these were descendants of Makir the father of Gilead.

²⁴After Hezron died in Caleb Ephrathah, Abijah the wife of Hezron bore him Ashhur the father^z of Tekoa.

²⁵The sons of Jerahmeel the firstborn of Hezron:
Ram his firstborn, Bunah, Oren, Ozem and^a Ahijah. ²⁶Jerahmeel had another wife, whose name was Atarah; she was the mother of Onam.

²⁷The sons of Ram the firstborn of Jerahmeel:
Maaz, Jamin and Eker.

²⁸The sons of Onam:
Shammai and Jada.
The sons of Shammai:
Nadab and Abishur.

²⁹Abishur's wife was named Abihail, who bore him Ahban and Molid.

³⁰The sons of Nadab:
Seled and Appaim. Seled died without children.

³¹The son of Appaim:
Ishi, who was the father of Sheshan.
Sheshan was the father of Ahlai.

³²The sons of Jada, Shammai's brother:
Jether and Jonathan. Jether died without children.

³³The sons of Jonathan:
Peleth and Zaza.
These were the descendants of Jerahmeel.

³⁴Sheshan had no sons—only daughters.
He had an Egyptian servant named Jarha. ³⁵Sheshan gave his daughter in marriage to his servant Jarha, and she bore him Attai.

³⁶Attai was the father of Nathan,

Nathan the father of Zabad,
³⁷Zabad the father of Ephlal,
Ephlal the father of Obed,
³⁸Obed the father of Jehu,
Jehu the father of Azariah,
³⁹Azariah the father of Helez,
Helez the father of Eleasah,
⁴⁰Eleasah the father of Sismai,
Sismai the father of Shallum,
⁴¹Shallum the father of Jekamiah,
and Jekamiah the father of Elishama.

⁴²The sons of Caleb the brother of Jerahmeel:
Mesha his firstborn, who was the father of Ziph, and his son Mareshah,^b who was the father of Hebron.

⁴³The sons of Hebron:
Korah, Tappuah, Rekem and Shema. ⁴⁴Shema was the father of Raham, and Raham the father of Jorkeam. Rekem was the father of Shammai. ⁴⁵The son of Shammai was Maon, and Maon was the father of Beth Zur.

⁴⁶Caleb's concubine Ephah was the mother of Haran, Moza and Gazez. Haran was the father of Gazez.

⁴⁷The sons of Jahdai:
Regem, Jotham, Geshan, Pelet, Ephah and Shaaph.

⁴⁸Caleb's concubine Maacah was the mother of Sheber and Tirhanah. ⁴⁹She also gave birth to Shaaph the father of Madmannah and to Sheva the father of Macbenah and Gibea. Caleb's daughter was Acsah. ⁵⁰These were the descendants of Caleb.

The sons of Hur the firstborn of Ephrathah:
Shobal the father of Kiriath Jearim, ⁵¹Salma the father of Bethlehem, and Hareph the father of Beth Gader.

⁵²The descendants of Shobal the father of Kiriath Jearim were:
Haroeh, half the Manahathites, ⁵³and the clans of Kiriath Jearim: the Ithrites, Puthites, Shumathites and Mishraites. From these de-

---

^y23 Or *captured the settlements of Jair*   ^z24 *Father* may mean *civic leader* or *military leader*; also in verses 42, 45, 49-52 and possibly elsewhere.   ^a25 Or *Oren and Ozem, by*   ^b42 The meaning of the Hebrew for this phrase is uncertain.

scended the Zorathites and Eshta-
olites.
⁵⁴The descendants of Salma:
Bethlehem, the Netophathites, At-
roth Beth Joab, half the Manahathites, the Zorites, ⁵⁵and the
clans of scribes*c* who lived at Jabez: the Tirathites, Shimeathites
and Sucathites. These are the Kenites who came from Hammath,
the father of the house of Recab.*d*

CHAPTER 3

These were the sons of David born to him
in Hebron:
The firstborn was Amnon the son
of Ahinoam of Jezreel;
the second, Daniel the son of Abigail of Carmel;
²the third, Absalom the son of Maacah daughter of Talmai king of
Geshur;
the fourth, Adonijah the son of
Haggith;
³the fifth, Shephatiah the son of
Abital;
and the sixth, Ithream, by his wife
Eglah.
⁴These six were born to David in
Hebron, where he reigned seven
years and six months.
David reigned in Jerusalem thirty-three
years, ⁵and these were the children born
to him there:
Shammua,*e* Shobab, Nathan and
Solomon. These four were by
Bathsheba*f* daughter of Ammiel.
⁶There were also Ibhar, Elishua,*g*
Eliphelet, ⁷Nogah, Nepheg, Ja-
phia, ⁸Elishama, Eliada and
Eliphelet—nine in all. ⁹All these
were the sons of David, besides
his sons by his concubines. And
Tamar was their sister.

¹⁰Solomon's son was Rehoboam,
Abijah his son,
Asa his son,
Jehoshaphat his son,
¹¹Jehoram*h* his son,
Ahaziah his son,
Joash his son,
¹²Amaziah his son,
Azariah his son,

Jotham his son,
¹³Ahaz his son,
Hezekiah his son,
Manasseh his son,
¹⁴Amon his son,
Josiah his son.
¹⁵The sons of Josiah:
Johanan the firstborn,
Jehoiakim the second son,
Zedekiah the third,
Shallum the fourth.
¹⁶The successors of Jehoiakim:
Jehoiachin*i* his son,
and Zedekiah.

¹⁷The descendants of Jehoiachin the
captive:
Shealtiel his son, ¹⁸Malkiram,
Pedaiah, Shenazzar, Jekamiah,
Hoshama and Nedabiah.
¹⁹The sons of Pedaiah:
Zerubbabel and Shimei.
The sons of Zerubbabel:
Meshullam and Hananiah.
Shelomith was their sister.
²⁰There were also five others:
Hashubah, Ohel, Berekiah, Hasa-
diah and Jushab-Hesed.
²¹The descendants of Hananiah:
Pelatiah and Jeshaiah, and the
sons of Rephaiah, of Arnan, of
Obadiah and of Shecaniah.
²²The descendants of Shecaniah:
Shemaiah and his sons:
Hattush, Igal, Bariah, Neariah and
Shaphat—six in all.
²³The sons of Neariah:
Elioenai, Hizkiah and Azrikam—
three in all.
²⁴The sons of Elioenai:
Hodaviah, Eliashib, Pelaiah, Ak-
kub, Johanan, Delaiah and
Anani—seven in all.

CHAPTER 4

The descendants of Judah:
Perez, Hezron, Carmi, Hur and
Shobal.
²Reaiah son of Shobal was the father
of Jahath, and Jahath the father of
Ahumai and Lahad. These were
the clans of the Zorathites.

---

*c*55 Or of the Sopherites   *d*55 Or father of Beth Recab   *e*5 Hebrew Shimea, a variant of Shammua   *f*5 One Hebrew manuscript
and Vulgate (see also Septuagint and 2 Samuel 11:3); most Hebrew manuscripts Bathshua   *g*6 Two Hebrew manuscripts (see
also 2 Samuel 5:15 and 1 Chron. 14:5); most Hebrew manuscripts Elishama   *h*11 Hebrew Joram, a variant of Jehoram
*i*16 Hebrew Jeconiah, a variant of Jehoiachin; also in verse 17

³These were the sons^j of Etam:
Jezreel, Ishma and Idbash. Their sister was named Hazzelelponi. ⁴Penuel was the father of Gedor, and Ezer the father of Hushah.

These were the descendants of Hur, the firstborn of Ephrathah and father^k of Bethlehem.

⁵Ashhur the father of Tekoa had two wives, Helah and Naarah.

⁶Naarah bore him Ahuzzam, Hepher, Temeni and Haahashtari. These were the descendants of Naarah.

⁷The sons of Helah:
Zereth, Zohar, Ethnan, ⁸and Koz, who was the father of Anub and Hazzobebah and of the clans of Aharhel son of Harum.

⁹Jabez was more honorable than his brothers. His mother had named him Jabez,^{l} saying, "I gave birth to him in pain." ¹⁰Jabez cried out to the God of Israel, "Oh, that you would bless me and enlarge my territory! Let your hand be with me, and keep me from harm so that I will be free from pain." And God granted his request.

¹¹Kelub, Shuhah's brother, was the father of Mehir, who was the father of Eshton. ¹²Eshton was the father of Beth Rapha, Paseah and Tehinnah the father of Ir Nahash.^{m} These were the men of Recah.

¹³The sons of Kenaz:
Othniel and Seraiah.

The sons of Othniel:
Hathath and Meonothai.^{n} ¹⁴Meonothai was the father of Ophrah.

Seraiah was the father of Joab, the father of Ge Harashim.^{o} It was called this because its people were craftsmen.

¹⁵The sons of Caleb son of Jephunneh:
Iru, Elah and Naam.

The son of Elah:
Kenaz.

¹⁶The sons of Jehallelel:
Ziph, Ziphah, Tiria and Asarel.

¹⁷The sons of Ezrah:
Jether, Mered, Epher and Jalon. One of Mered's wives gave birth to Miriam, Shammai and Ishbah

the father of Eshtemoa. ¹⁸(His Judean wife gave birth to Jered the father of Gedor, Heber the father of Soco, and Jekuthiel the father of Zanoah.) These were the children of Pharaoh's daughter Bithiah, whom Mered had married.

¹⁹The sons of Hodiah's wife, the sister of Naham:
the father of Keilah the Garmite, and Eshtemoa the Maacathite.

²⁰The sons of Shimon:
Amnon, Rinnah, Ben-Hanan and Tilon.

The descendants of Ishi:
Zoheth and Ben-Zoheth.

²¹The sons of Shelah son of Judah:
Er the father of Lecah, Laadah the father of Mareshah and the clans of the linen workers at Beth Ashbea, ²²Jokim, the men of Cozeba, and Joash and Saraph, who ruled in Moab and Jashubi Lehem. (These records are from ancient times.) ²³They were the potters who lived at Netaim and Gederah; they stayed there and worked for the king.

²⁴The descendants of Simeon:
Nemuel, Jamin, Jarib, Zerah and Shaul;
²⁵Shallum was Shaul's son, Mibsam his son and Mishma his son.

²⁶The descendants of Mishma:
Hammuel his son, Zaccur his son and Shimei his son.

²⁷Shimei had sixteen sons and six daughters, but his brothers did not have many children; so their entire clan did not become as numerous as the people of Judah. ²⁸They lived in Beersheba, Moladah, Hazar Shual, ²⁹Bilhah, Ezem, Tolad, ³⁰Bethuel, Hormah, Ziklag, ³¹Beth Marcaboth, Hazar Susim, Beth Biri and Shaaraim. These were their towns until the reign of David. ³²Their surrounding villages were Etam, Ain, Rimmon, Token and Ashan—five towns— ³³and all the villages around these towns as far as Baalath.^{p} These were their settlements. And they kept a genealogical record.

³⁴Meshobab, Jamlech, Joshah son of

---

^{j}3 Some Septuagint manuscripts (see also Vulgate); Hebrew *father* ^{k}4 *Father* may mean *civic leader* or *military leader*; also in verses 12, 14, 17, 18 and possibly elsewhere. ^{l}9 *Jabez* sounds like the Hebrew for *pain*. ^{m}12 Or *of the city of Nahash*
^{n}13 Some Septuagint manuscripts and Vulgate; Hebrew does not have *and Meonothai*. ^{o}14 *Ge Harashim* means *valley of craftsmen*. ^{p}33 Some Septuagint manuscripts (see also Joshua 19:8); Hebrew *Baal*

Amaziah, ³⁵Joel, Jehu son of Joshibiah, the son of Seraiah, the son of Asiel, ³⁶also Elioenai, Jaakobah, Jeshohaiah, Asaiah, Adiel, Jesimiel, Benaiah, ³⁷and Ziza son of Shiphi, the son of Allon, the son of Jedaiah, the son of Shimri, the son of Shemaiah.

³⁸The men listed above by name were leaders of their clans. Their families increased greatly, ³⁹and they went to the outskirts of Gedor to the east of the valley in search of pasture for their flocks. ⁴⁰They found rich, good pasture, and the land was spacious, peaceful and quiet. Some Hamites had lived there formerly. ⁴¹The men whose names were listed came in the days of Hezekiah king of Judah. They attacked the Hamites in their dwellings and also the Meunites who were there and completely destroyed⁹ them, as is evident to this day. Then they settled in their place, because there was pasture for their flocks. ⁴²And five hundred of these Simeonites, led by Pelatiah, Neariah, Rephaiah and Uzziel, the sons of Ishi, invaded the hill country of Seir. ⁴³They killed the remaining Amalekites who had escaped, and they have lived there to this day.

CHAPTER 5

The sons of Reuben the firstborn of Israel (he was the firstborn, but when he defiled his father's marriage bed, his rights as firstborn were given to the sons of Joseph son of Israel; so he could not be listed in the genealogical record in accordance with his birthright, ²and though Judah was the strongest of his brothers and a ruler came from him, the rights of the firstborn belonged to Joseph)— ³the sons of Reuben the firstborn of Israel:

Hanoch, Pallu, Hezron and Carmi.
⁴The descendants of Joel:
Shemaiah his son, Gog his son, Shimei his son, ⁵Micah his son, Reaiah his son, Baal his son,
⁶and Beerah his son, whom Tiglath-Pileserʳ king of Assyria took into exile. Beerah was a leader of the Reubenites.
⁷Their relatives by clans, listed according to their genealogical records:

Jeiel the chief, Zechariah, ⁸and Bela son of Azaz, the son of Shema, the son of Joel. They settled in the area from Aroer to Nebo and Baal Meon. ⁹To the east they occupied the land up to the edge of the desert that extends to the Euphrates River, because their livestock had increased in Gilead. ¹⁰During Saul's reign they waged war against the Hagrites, who were defeated at their hands; they occupied the dwellings of the Hagrites throughout the entire region east of Gilead.

¹¹The Gadites lived next to them in Bashan, as far as Salecah:
¹²Joel was the chief, Shapham the second, then Janai and Shaphat, in Bashan.
¹³Their relatives, by families, were:
Michael, Meshullam, Sheba, Jorai, Jacan, Zia and Eber—seven in all.
¹⁴These were the sons of Abihail son of Huri, the son of Jaroah, the son of Gilead, the son of Michael, the son of Jeshishai, the son of Jahdo, the son of Buz.
¹⁵Ahi son of Abdiel, the son of Guni, was head of their family.
¹⁶The Gadites lived in Gilead, in Bashan and its outlying villages, and on all the pasturelands of Sharon as far as they extended.

¹⁷All these were entered in the genealogical records during the reigns of Jotham king of Judah and Jeroboam king of Israel.

¹⁸The Reubenites, the Gadites and the half-tribe of Manasseh had 44,760 men ready for military service—able-bodied men who could handle shield and sword, who could use a bow, and who were trained for battle. ¹⁹They waged war against the Hagrites, Jetur, Naphish and Nodab. ²⁰They were helped in fighting them, and God handed the Hagrites and all their allies over to them, because they cried out to him during the battle. He answered their prayers, because they trusted in him. ²¹They seized the livestock of the Hagrites—fifty thousand camels, two hundred fifty thousand sheep and two thousand donkeys. They also took

---

q41 The Hebrew term refers to the irrevocable giving over of things or persons to the LORD, often by totally destroying them.
r6 Hebrew Tilgath-Pilneser, a variant of Tiglath-Pileser; also in verse 26

one hundred thousand people captive, [22]and many others fell slain, because the battle was God's. And they occupied the land until the exile.

[23]The people of the half-tribe of Manasseh were numerous; they settled in the land from Bashan to Baal Hermon, that is, to Senir (Mount Hermon).

[24]These were the heads of their families: Epher, Ishi, Eliel, Azriel, Jeremiah, Hodaviah and Jahdiel. They were brave warriors, famous men, and heads of their families. [25]But they were unfaithful to the God of their fathers and prostituted themselves to the gods of the peoples of the land, whom God had destroyed before them. [26]So the God of Israel stirred up the spirit of Pul king of Assyria (that is, Tiglath-Pileser king of Assyria), who took the Reubenites, the Gadites and the half-tribe of Manasseh into exile. He took them to Halah, Habor, Hara and the river of Gozan, where they are to this day.

CHAPTER 6

The sons of Levi:
   Gershon, Kohath and Merari.
[2]The sons of Kohath:
   Amram, Izhar, Hebron and Uzziel.
[3]The children of Amram:
   Aaron, Moses and Miriam.
   The sons of Aaron:
   Nadab, Abihu, Eleazar and Ithamar.
[4]Eleazar was the father of Phinehas,
   Phinehas the father of Abishua,
[5]Abishua the father of Bukki,
   Bukki the father of Uzzi,
[6]Uzzi the father of Zerahiah,
   Zerahiah the father of Meraioth,
[7]Meraioth the father of Amariah,
   Amariah the father of Ahitub,
[8]Ahitub the father of Zadok,
   Zadok the father of Ahimaaz,
[9]Ahimaaz the father of Azariah,
   Azariah the father of Johanan,
[10]Johanan the father of Azariah (it was he who served as priest in the temple Solomon built in Jerusalem),
[11]Azariah the father of Amariah,

   Amariah the father of Ahitub,
[12]Ahitub the father of Zadok,
   Zadok the father of Shallum,
[13]Shallum the father of Hilkiah,
   Hilkiah the father of Azariah,
[14]Azariah the father of Seraiah,
   and Seraiah the father of Jehozadak.

[15]Jehozadak was deported when the LORD sent Judah and Jerusalem into exile by the hand of Nebuchadnezzar.

[16]The sons of Levi:
   Gershon,[s] Kohath and Merari.
[17]These are the names of the sons of Gershon:
   Libni and Shimei.
[18]The sons of Kohath:
   Amram, Izhar, Hebron and Uzziel.
[19]The sons of Merari:
   Mahli and Mushi.
These are the clans of the Levites listed according to their fathers:
[20]Of Gershon:
   Libni his son, Jehath his son,
   Zimmah his son, [21]Joah his son,
   Iddo his son, Zerah his son
   and Jeatherai his son.
[22]The descendants of Kohath:
   Amminadab his son, Korah his son,
   Assir his son, [23]Elkanah his son,
   Ebiasaph his son, Assir his son,
[24]Tahath his son, Uriel his son,
   Uzziah his son and Shaul his son.
[25]The descendants of Elkanah:
   Amasai, Ahimoth,
[26]Elkanah his son,[t] Zophai his son,
   Nahath his son, [27]Eliab his son,
   Jeroham his son, Elkanah his son
   and Samuel his son.[u]
[28]The sons of Samuel:
   Joel[v] the firstborn
   and Abijah the second son.
[29]The descendants of Merari:
   Mahli, Libni his son,
   Shimei his son, Uzzah his son,
[30]Shimea his son, Haggiah his son
   and Asaiah his son.

[31]These are the men David put in charge of the music in the house of the

[s]16 Hebrew Gershom, a variant of Gershon; also in verses 17, 20, 43, 62 and 71   [t]26 Some Hebrew manuscripts, Septuagint and Syriac; most Hebrew manuscripts Ahimoth 26and Elkanah. The sons of Elkanah: [u]27 Some Septuagint manuscripts (see also 1 Samuel 1:19,20 and 1 Chron. 6:33,34); Hebrew does not have and Samuel his son.   [v]28 Some Septuagint manuscripts and Syriac (see also 1 Samuel 8:2 and 1 Chron. 6:33); Hebrew does not have Joel.

LORD after the ark came to rest there. ³²They ministered with music before the tabernacle, the Tent of Meeting, until Solomon built the temple of the LORD in Jerusalem. They performed their duties according to the regulations laid down for them.

³³Here are the men who served, together with their sons:

From the Kohathites:
Heman, the musician,
the son of Joel, the son of Samuel,
³⁴the son of Elkanah, the son of Jeroham,
the son of Eliel, the son of Toah,
³⁵the son of Zuph, the son of Elkanah,
the son of Mahath, the son of Amasai,
³⁶the son of Elkanah, the son of Joel,
the son of Azariah, the son of Zephaniah,
³⁷the son of Tahath, the son of Assir,
the son of Ebiasaph, the son of Korah,
³⁸the son of Izhar, the son of Kohath,
the son of Levi, the son of Israel;
³⁹and Heman's associate Asaph, who served at his right hand:
Asaph son of Berekiah, the son of Shimea,
⁴⁰the son of Michael, the son of Baaseiah,ʷ
the son of Malkijah, ⁴¹the son of Ethni,
the son of Zerah, the son of Adaiah,
⁴²the son of Ethan, the son of Zimmah,
the son of Shimei, ⁴³the son of Jahath,
the son of Gershon, the son of Levi;
⁴⁴and from their associates, the Merarites, at his left hand:
Ethan son of Kishi, the son of Abdi,
the son of Malluch, ⁴⁵the son of Hashabiah,
the son of Amaziah, the son of Hilkiah,
⁴⁶the son of Amzi, the son of Bani,

the son of Shemer, ⁴⁷the son of Mahli,
the son of Mushi, the son of Merari,
the son of Levi.

⁴⁸Their fellow Levites were assigned to all the other duties of the tabernacle, the house of God. ⁴⁹But Aaron and his descendants were the ones who presented offerings on the altar of burnt offering and on the altar of incense in connection with all that was done in the Most Holy Place, making atonement for Israel, in accordance with all that Moses the servant of God had commanded.

⁵⁰These were the descendants of Aaron:
Eleazar his son, Phinehas his son, Abishua his son, ⁵¹Bukki his son, Uzzi his son, Zerahiah his son, ⁵²Meraioth his son, Amariah his son,
Ahitub his son, ⁵³Zadok his son and Ahimaaz his son.

⁵⁴These were the locations of their settlements allotted as their territory (they were assigned to the descendants of Aaron who were from the Kohathite clan, because the first lot was for them):
⁵⁵They were given Hebron in Judah with its surrounding pasturelands. ⁵⁶But the fields and villages around the city were given to Caleb son of Jephunneh. ⁵⁷So the descendants of Aaron were given Hebron (a city of refuge), and Libnah,ˣ Jattir, Eshtemoa, ⁵⁸Hilen, Debir, ⁵⁹Ashan, Juttahʸ and Beth Shemesh, together with their pasturelands. ⁶⁰And from the tribe of Benjamin they were given Gibeon,ᶻ Geba, Alemeth and Anathoth, together with their pasturelands.

These towns, which were distributed among the Kohathite clans, were thirteen in all.
⁶¹The rest of Kohath's descendants were allotted ten towns from the clans of half the tribe of Manasseh.
⁶²The descendants of Gershon, clan by clan, were allotted thirteen towns from the tribes of Issachar, Asher and Naphtali,

ʷ40 Most Hebrew manuscripts; some Hebrew manuscripts, one Septuagint manuscript and Syriac *Maaseiah*   ˣ57 See Joshua 21:13; Hebrew *given the cities of refuge: Hebron, Libnah.*   ʸ59 Syriac (see also Septuagint and Joshua 21:16); Hebrew does not have *Juttah.*   ᶻ60 See Joshua 21:17; Hebrew does not have *Gibeon.*

and from the part of the tribe of Manasseh that is in Bashan.

⁶³The descendants of Merari, clan by clan, were allotted twelve towns from the tribes of Reuben, Gad and Zebulun.

⁶⁴So the Israelites gave the Levites these towns and their pasturelands. ⁶⁵From the tribes of Judah, Simeon and Benjamin they allotted the previously named towns.

⁶⁶Some of the Kohathite clans were given as their territory towns from the tribe of Ephraim.

⁶⁷In the hill country of Ephraim they were given Shechem (a city of refuge), and Gezer,ᵃ ⁶⁸Jokmeam, Beth Horon, ⁶⁹Aijalon and Gath Rimmon, together with their pasturelands.

⁷⁰And from half the tribe of Manasseh the Israelites gave Aner and Bileam, together with their pasturelands, to the rest of the Kohathite clans.

⁷¹The Gershonites received the following:

From the clan of the half-tribe of Manasseh
they received Golan in Bashan and also Ashtaroth, together with their pasturelands;
⁷²from the tribe of Issachar
they received Kedesh, Daberath, ⁷³Ramoth and Anem, together with their pasturelands;
⁷⁴from the tribe of Asher
they received Mashal, Abdon, ⁷⁵Hukok and Rehob, together with their pasturelands;
⁷⁶and from the tribe of Naphtali
they received Kedesh in Galilee, Hammon and Kiriathaim, together with their pasturelands.

⁷⁷The Merarites (the rest of the Levites) received the following:

From the tribe of Zebulun
they received Jokneam, Kartah,ᵇ Rimmono and Tabor, together with their pasturelands;
⁷⁸from the tribe of Reuben across the Jordan east of Jericho
they received Bezer in the desert, Jahzah, ⁷⁹Kedemoth and Mepha-

ath, together with their pasturelands;
⁸⁰and from the tribe of Gad
they received Ramoth in Gilead, Mahanaim, ⁸¹Heshbon and Jazer, together with their pasturelands.

CHAPTER 7

The sons of Issachar:
Tola, Puah, Jashub and Shimron—four in all.
²The sons of Tola:
Uzzi, Rephaiah, Jeriel, Jahmai, Ibsam and Samuel—heads of their families. During the reign of David, the descendants of Tola listed as fighting men in their genealogy numbered 22,600.
³The son of Uzzi:
Izrahiah.
The sons of Izrahiah:
Michael, Obadiah, Joel and Isshiah. All five of them were chiefs. ⁴According to their family genealogy, they had 36,000 men ready for battle, for they had many wives and children.
⁵The relatives who were fighting men belonging to all the clans of Issachar, as listed in their genealogy, were 87,000 in all.

⁶Three sons of Benjamin:
Bela, Beker and Jediael.
⁷The sons of Bela:
Ezbon, Uzzi, Uzziel, Jerimoth and Iri, heads of families—five in all. Their genealogical record listed 22,034 fighting men.
⁸The sons of Beker:
Zemirah, Joash, Eliezer, Elioenai, Omri, Jeremoth, Abijah, Anathoth and Alemeth. All these were the sons of Beker. ⁹Their genealogical record listed the heads of families and 20,200 fighting men.
¹⁰The son of Jediael:
Bilhan.
The sons of Bilhan:
Jeush, Benjamin, Ehud, Kenaanah, Zethan, Tarshish and Ahishahar. ¹¹All these sons of Jediael were heads of families. There were 17,200 fighting men ready to go out to war.

ᵃ67 See Joshua 21:21; Hebrew *given the cities of refuge: Shechem, Gezer.*   ᵇ77 See Septuagint and Joshua 21:34; Hebrew does not have *Jokneam, Kartah.*

[12]The Shuppites and Huppites were the descendants of Ir, and the Hushites the descendants of Aher.

[13]The sons of Naphtali:
Jahziel, Guni, Jezer and Shillem[c]—the descendants of Bilhah.

[14]The descendants of Manasseh:
Asriel was his descendant through his Aramean concubine. She gave birth to Makir the father of Gilead. [15]Makir took a wife from among the Huppites and Shuppites. His sister's name was Maacah.

Another descendant was named Zelophehad, who had only daughters.

[16]Makir's wife Maacah gave birth to a son and named him Peresh. His brother was named Sheresh, and his sons were Ulam and Rakem.
[17]The son of Ulam:
Bedan.

These were the sons of Gilead son of Makir, the son of Manasseh. [18]His sister Hammoleketh gave birth to Ishhod, Abiezer and Mahlah.

[19]The sons of Shemida were:
Ahian, Shechem, Likhi and Aniam.

[20]The descendants of Ephraim:
Shuthelah, Bered his son,
Tahath his son, Eleadah his son,
Tahath his son, [21]Zabad his son
and Shuthelah his son.

Ezer and Elead were killed by the native-born men of Gath, when they went down to seize their livestock. [22]Their father Ephraim mourned for them many days, and his relatives came to comfort him. [23]Then he lay with his wife again, and she became pregnant and gave birth to a son. He named him Beriah,[d] because there had been misfortune in his family. [24]His daughter was Sheerah, who built Lower and Upper Beth Horon as well as Uzzen Sheerah.
[25]Rephah was his son, Resheph his son,[e]
Telah his son, Tahan his son,
[26]Ladan his son, Ammihud his son,

Elishama his son, [27]Nun his son
and Joshua his son.

[28]Their lands and settlements included Bethel and its surrounding villages, Naaran to the east, Gezer and its villages to the west, and Shechem and its villages all the way to Ayyah and its villages. [29]Along the borders of Manasseh were Beth Shan, Taanach, Megiddo and Dor, together with their villages. The descendants of Joseph son of Israel lived in these towns.

[30]The sons of Asher:
Imnah, Ishvah, Ishvi and Beriah.
Their sister was Serah.
[31]The sons of Beriah:
Heber and Malkiel, who was the father of Birzaith.
[32]Heber was the father of Japhlet, Shomer and Hotham and of their sister Shua.
[33]The sons of Japhlet:
Pasach, Bimhal and Ashvath.
These were Japhlet's sons.
[34]The sons of Shomer:
Ahi, Rohgah,[f] Hubbah and Aram.
[35]The sons of his brother Helem:
Zophah, Imna, Shelesh and Amal.
[36]The sons of Zophah:
Suah, Harnepher, Shual, Beri, Imrah, [37]Bezer, Hod, Shamma, Shilshah, Ithran[g] and Beera.
[38]The sons of Jether:
Jephunneh, Pispah and Ara.
[39]The sons of Ulla:
Arah, Hanniel and Rizia.
[40]All these were descendants of Asher—heads of families, choice men, brave warriors and outstanding leaders. The number of men ready for battle, as listed in their genealogy, was 26,000.

C H A P T E R 8
Benjamin was the father of Bela his firstborn,
Ashbel the second son, Aharah the third,
[2]Nohah the fourth and Rapha the fifth.
[3]The sons of Bela were:
Addar, Gera, Abihud,[h] [4]Abishua, Naaman, Ahoah, [5]Gera, Shephuphan and Huram.
[6]These were the descendants of

---

[c]13 Some Hebrew and Septuagint manuscripts (see also Gen. 46:24 and Num. 26:49); most Hebrew manuscripts *Shallum*
[d]23 *Beriah* sounds like the Hebrew for *misfortune.*   [e]25 Some Septuagint manuscripts; Hebrew does not have *his son.*
[f]34 Or *of his brother Shomer: Rohgah*   [g]37 Possibly a variant of *Jether*   [h]3 Or *Gera the father of Ehud*

Ehud, who were heads of families of those living in Geba and were deported to Manahath:

[7]Naaman, Ahijah, and Gera, who deported them and who was the father of Uzza and Ahihud.

[8]Sons were born to Shaharaim in Moab after he had divorced his wives Hushim and Baara. [9]By his wife Hodesh he had Jobab, Zibia, Mesha, Malcam, [10]Jeuz, Sakia and Mirmah. These were his sons, heads of families. [11]By Hushim he had Abitub and Elpaal.

[12]The sons of Elpaal:

Eber, Misham, Shemed (who built Ono and Lod with its surrounding villages), [13]and Beriah and Shema, who were heads of families of those living in Aijalon and who drove out the inhabitants of Gath.

[14]Ahio, Shashak, Jeremoth, [15]Zebadiah, Arad, Eder, [16]Michael, Ishpah and Joha were the sons of Beriah.

[17]Zebadiah, Meshullam, Hizki, Heber, [18]Ishmerai, Izliah and Jobab were the sons of Elpaal.

[19]Jakim, Zicri, Zabdi, [20]Elienai, Zillethai, Eliel, [21]Adaiah, Beraiah and Shimrath were the sons of Shimei.

[22]Ishpan, Eber, Eliel, [23]Abdon, Zicri, Hanan, [24]Hananiah, Elam, Anthothijah, [25]Iphdeiah and Penuel were the sons of Shashak.

[26]Shamsherai, Shehariah, Athaliah, [27]Jaareshiah, Elijah and Zicri were the sons of Jeroham.

[28]All these were heads of families, chiefs as listed in their genealogy, and they lived in Jerusalem.

[29]Jeiel[i] the father[j] of Gibeon lived in Gibeon.

His wife's name was Maacah, [30]and his firstborn son was Abdon, followed by Zur, Kish, Baal, Ner,[k] Nadab, [31]Gedor, Ahio, Zeker [32]and Mikloth, who was the father of Shimeah. They too lived near their relatives in Jerusalem.

[33]Ner was the father of Kish, Kish the father of Saul, and Saul the father of Jonathan, Malki-Shua, Abinadab and Esh-Baal.[l]

[34]The son of Jonathan:

Merib-Baal,[m] who was the father of Micah.

[35]The sons of Micah:

Pithon, Melech, Tarea and Ahaz.

[36]Ahaz was the father of Jehoaddah, Jehoaddah was the father of Alemeth, Azmaveth and Zimri, and Zimri was the father of Moza. [37]Moza was the father of Binea; Raphah was his son, Eleasah his son and Azel his son.

[38]Azel had six sons, and these were their names:

Azrikam, Bokeru, Ishmael, Sheariah, Obadiah and Hanan. All these were the sons of Azel.

[39]The sons of his brother Eshek:

Ulam his firstborn, Jeush the second son and Eliphelet the third. [40]The sons of Ulam were brave warriors who could handle the bow. They had many sons and grandsons—150 in all.

All these were the descendants of Benjamin.

CHAPTER 9

All Israel was listed in the genealogies recorded in the book of the kings of Israel.

The people of Judah were taken captive to Babylon because of their unfaithfulness. [2]Now the first to resettle on their own property in their own towns were some Israelites, priests, Levites and temple servants.

[3]Those from Judah, from Benjamin, and from Ephraim and Manasseh who lived in Jerusalem were:

[4]Uthai son of Ammihud, the son of Omri, the son of Imri, the son of Bani, a descendant of Perez son of Judah.

[5]Of the Shilonites:

Asaiah the firstborn and his sons.

[6]Of the Zerahites:

Jeuel.

The people from Judah numbered 690.

[7]Of the Benjamites:

Sallu son of Meshullam, the son of Hodaviah, the son of Hassenuah;

i29 Some Septuagint manuscripts (see also 1 Chron. 9:35); Hebrew does not have Jeiel.   j29 Father may mean civic leader or military leader.   k30 Some Septuagint manuscripts (see also 1 Chron. 9:36); Hebrew does not have Ner.   l33 Also known as Ish-Bosheth   m34 Also known as Mephibosheth

⁸Ibneiah son of Jeroham; Elah son of Uzzi, the son of Micri; and Meshullam son of Shephatiah, the son of Reuel, the son of Ibnijah.

⁹The people from Benjamin, as listed in their genealogy, numbered 956. All these men were heads of their families.

¹⁰Of the priests:

Jedaiah; Jehoiarib; Jakin;

¹¹Azariah son of Hilkiah, the son of Meshullam, the son of Zadok, the son of Meraioth, the son of Ahitub, the official in charge of the house of God;

¹²Adaiah son of Jeroham, the son of Pashhur, the son of Malkijah; and Maasai son of Adiel, the son of Jahzerah, the son of Meshullam, the son of Meshillemith, the son of Immer.

¹³The priests, who were heads of families, numbered 1,760. They were able men, responsible for ministering in the house of God.

¹⁴Of the Levites:

Shemaiah son of Hasshub, the son of Azrikam, the son of Hashabiah, a Merarite; ¹⁵Bakbakkar, Heresh, Galal and Mattaniah son of Mica, the son of Zicri, the son of Asaph; ¹⁶Obadiah son of Shemaiah, the son of Galal, the son of Jeduthun; and Berekiah son of Asa, the son of Elkanah, who lived in the villages of the Netophathites.

¹⁷The gatekeepers:

Shallum, Akkub, Talmon, Ahiman and their brothers, Shallum their chief ¹⁸being stationed at the King's Gate on the east, up to the present time. These were the gatekeepers belonging to the camp of the Levites. ¹⁹Shallum son of Kore, the son of Ebiasaph, the son of Korah, and his fellow gatekeepers from his family (the Korahites) were responsible for guarding the thresholds of the Tent^n just as their fathers had been responsible for guarding the entrance to the dwelling of the LORD. ²⁰In earlier times Phinehas son of Eleazar was in charge of the gatekeepers, and the LORD was with him. ²¹Zecha-

riah son of Meshelemiah was the gatekeeper at the entrance to the Tent of Meeting.

²²Altogether, those chosen to be gatekeepers at the thresholds numbered 212. They were registered by genealogy in their villages. The gatekeepers had been assigned to their positions of trust by David and Samuel the seer. ²³They and their descendants were in charge of guarding the gates of the house of the LORD—the house called the Tent. ²⁴The gatekeepers were on the four sides: east, west, north and south. ²⁵Their brothers in their villages had to come from time to time and share their duties for seven-day periods. ²⁶But the four principal gatekeepers, who were Levites, were entrusted with the responsibility for the rooms and treasuries in the house of God. ²⁷They would spend the night stationed around the house of God, because they had to guard it; and they had charge of the key for opening it each morning.

²⁸Some of them were in charge of the articles used in the temple service; they counted them when they were brought in and when they were taken out. ²⁹Others were assigned to take care of the furnishings and all the other articles of the sanctuary, as well as the flour and wine, and the oil, incense and spices. ³⁰But some of the priests took care of mixing the spices. ³¹A Levite named Mattithiah, the firstborn son of Shallum the Korahite, was entrusted with the responsibility for baking the offering bread. ³²Some of their Kohathite brothers were in charge of preparing for every Sabbath the bread set out on the table.

³³Those who were musicians, heads of Levite families, stayed in the rooms of the temple and were exempt from other duties because they were responsible for the work day and night.

³⁴All these were heads of Levite families, chiefs as listed in their genealogy, and they lived in Jerusalem.

³⁵Jeiel the father^o of Gibeon lived in Gibeon.

His wife's name was Maacah, ³⁶and his firstborn son was Abdon, followed by Zur, Kish, Baal, Ner, Nadab, ³⁷Gedor, Ahio, Zechariah and Mikloth. ³⁸Mikloth was

---

^{n}19 That is, the temple; also in verses 21 and 23 ^{o}35 Father may mean civic leader or military leader.

the father of Shimeam. They too lived near their relatives in Jerusalem.

³⁹Ner was the father of Kish, Kish the father of Saul, and Saul the father of Jonathan, Malki-Shua, Abinadab and Esh-Baal.ᵖ

⁴⁰The son of Jonathan:

Merib-Baal,�q who was the father of Micah.

⁴¹The sons of Micah:

Pithon, Melech, Tahrea and Ahaz.ʳ

⁴²Ahaz was the father of Jadah, Jadahˢ was the father of Alemeth, Azmaveth and Zimri, and Zimri was the father of Moza. ⁴³Moza was the father of Binea; Rephaiah was his son, Eleasah his son and Azel his son.

⁴⁴Azel had six sons, and these were their names:

Azrikam, Bokeru, Ishmael, Sheariah, Obadiah and Hanan. These were the sons of Azel.

ᵖ39 Also known as *Ish-Bosheth*   �q40 Also known as *Mephibosheth*   ʳ41 Vulgate and Syriac (see also Septuagint and 1 Chron. 8:35); Hebrew does not have *and Ahaz*.   ˢ42 Some Hebrew manuscripts and Septuagint (see also 1 Chron. 8:36); most Hebrew manuscripts *Jarah, Jarah*

APRIL 16 ☐ DAY 107
1 CHRONICLES 10–16
David's Early Years as King

OVERVIEW Because Chronicles is written from the perspective of a priest, not a palace dweller, the temple and temple worship are central themes in the chronicler's work. Thus, David's efforts to return the ark of the covenant to its rightful place—an event that is scarcely mentioned in 2 Samuel—consumes three entire chapters in today's reading! With right motives but wrong methods, David learns that God's will done in something other than God's way is not God's will. When at last the ark is installed in Jerusalem, there is cause for national rejoicing, for God's presence is in the midst of his people.

Chapter 10	Chapters 11–12	Chapters 13–15	Chapter 16
David's Accession	David's Army	David's Ark Adventures	David's Anthem of Praise
David on the Throne		David on His Knees	

YOUR DAILY WALK "It must be OK. After all, I'm doing it for God." That statement reflects a common misconception about what it means to serve God. But does the end justify the means in serving God?

David had a godly ambition. He wanted to return the ark to its rightful place in Jerusalem. But in his zeal, he paid no attention to God's law regarding how the ark should be carried (Numbers 4:15). Instead, he substituted a *convenient* way for the *obedient* way, and the result was that Uzzah lost his life.

Motivation is what gets you started; habit is what keeps you going.

Sincerity in serving God is important, but it is possible to be sincerely wrong. Select an area of service that you participate in weekly. Then answer this question: What does the Bible say about *how* I should do this? Motives and methods—both are important in God's service.

INSIGHT Valiant Warriors, Loyal Friends

David's mighty men were an elite group of warriors, famous for their courage in battle, their personal valor and their leadership. For instance,

Benaiah earned his reputation by three acts: killing two Moabite warriors, killing a lion in a pit and killing an Egyptian giant with the giant's
own weapon. Above all, the mighty men showed loyalty to David—a
character quality of great worth in the turbulent political intrigues of
the day.

CHAPTER 10

Now the Philistines fought against Israel;
the Israelites fled before them, and many
fell slain on Mount Gilboa. ²The Philistines pressed hard after Saul and his sons,
and they killed his sons Jonathan, Abinadab and Malki-Shua. ³The fighting grew
fierce around Saul, and when the archers
overtook him, they wounded him.

⁴Saul said to his armor-bearer, "Draw
your sword and run me through, or these
uncircumcised fellows will come and
abuse me."

But his armor-bearer was terrified and
would not do it; so Saul took his own
sword and fell on it. ⁵When the armor-
bearer saw that Saul was dead, he too fell
on his sword and died. ⁶So Saul and his
three sons died, and all his house died
together.

⁷When all the Israelites in the valley
saw that the army had fled and that Saul
and his sons had died, they abandoned
their towns and fled. And the Philistines
came and occupied them.

⁸The next day, when the Philistines
came to strip the dead, they found Saul
and his sons fallen on Mount Gilboa.
⁹They stripped him and took his head and
his armor, and sent messengers throughout the land of the Philistines to proclaim
the news among their idols and their
people. ¹⁰They put his armor in the temple of their gods and hung up his head in
the temple of Dagon.

¹¹When all the inhabitants of Jabesh
Gilead heard of everything the Philistines
had done to Saul, ¹²all their valiant men
went and took the bodies of Saul and his
sons and brought them to Jabesh. Then
they buried their bones under the great
tree in Jabesh, and they fasted seven days.

¹³Saul died because he was unfaithful to
the LORD; he did not keep the word of the
LORD and even consulted a medium for
guidance, ¹⁴and did not inquire of the
LORD. So the LORD put him to death and
turned the kingdom over to David son of
Jesse.

CHAPTER 11

All Israel came together to David at Hebron and said, "We are your own flesh
and blood. ²In the past, even while Saul
was king, you were the one who led Israel
on their military campaigns. And the LORD
your God said to you, 'You will shepherd
my people Israel, and you will become
their ruler.' "

³When all the elders of Israel had come
to King David at Hebron, he made a compact with them at Hebron before the LORD,
and they anointed David king over Israel,
as the LORD had promised through Samuel.

⁴David and all the Israelites marched to
Jerusalem (that is, Jebus). The Jebusites
who lived there ⁵said to David, "You will
not get in here." Nevertheless, David captured the fortress of Zion, the City of David.

⁶David had said, "Whoever leads the
attack on the Jebusites will become
commander-in-chief." Joab son of Zeruiah went up first, and so he received the
command.

⁷David then took up residence in the
fortress, and so it was called the City of
David. ⁸He built up the city around it,
from the supporting terraces ᶠ to the surrounding wall, while Joab restored the
rest of the city. ⁹And David became more
and more powerful, because the LORD Almighty was with him.

¹⁰These were the chiefs of David's
mighty men—they, together with all Israel, gave his kingship strong support to
extend it over the whole land, as the LORD
had promised— ¹¹this is the list of David's
mighty men:

Jashobeam,ᵘ a Hacmonite, was chief of
the officersᵛ; he raised his spear against
three hundred men, whom he killed in
one encounter.

¹²Next to him was Eleazar son of Dodai
the Ahohite, one of the three mighty men.
¹³He was with David at Pas Dammim
when the Philistines gathered there for
battle. At a place where there was a field

ᶠ8 Or the Millo   ᵘ11 Possibly a variant of Jashob-Baal   ᵛ11 Or Thirty; some Septuagint manuscripts Three (see also 2 Samuel
23:8)

full of barley, the troops fled from the Philistines. [14]But they took their stand in the middle of the field. They defended it and struck the Philistines down, and the LORD brought about a great victory.

[15]Three of the thirty chiefs came down to David to the rock at the cave of Adullam, while a band of Philistines was encamped in the Valley of Rephaim. [16]At that time David was in the stronghold, and the Philistine garrison was at Bethlehem. [17]David longed for water and said, "Oh, that someone would get me a drink of water from the well near the gate of Bethlehem!" [18]So the Three broke through the Philistine lines, drew water from the well near the gate of Bethlehem and carried it back to David. But he refused to drink it; instead, he poured it out before the LORD. [19]"God forbid that I should do this!" he said. "Should I drink the blood of these men who went at the risk of their lives?" Because they risked their lives to bring it back, David would not drink it.

Such were the exploits of the three mighty men.

[20]Abishai the brother of Joab was chief of the Three. He raised his spear against three hundred men, whom he killed, and so he became as famous as the Three. [21]He was doubly honored above the Three and became their commander, even though he was not included among them.

[22]Benaiah son of Jehoiada was a valiant fighter from Kabzeel, who performed great exploits. He struck down two of Moab's best men. He also went down into a pit on a snowy day and killed a lion. [23]And he struck down an Egyptian who was seven and a half feet[w] tall. Although the Egyptian had a spear like a weaver's rod in his hand, Benaiah went against him with a club. He snatched the spear from the Egyptian's hand and killed him with his own spear. [24]Such were the exploits of Benaiah son of Jehoiada; he too was as famous as the three mighty men. [25]He was held in greater honor than any of the Thirty, but he was not included among the Three. And David put him in charge of his bodyguard.

[26]The mighty men were:
    Asahel the brother of Joab,
    Elhanan son of Dodo from Bethlehem,

[27]Shammoth the Harorite,
    Helez the Pelonite,
[28]Ira son of Ikkesh from Tekoa,
    Abiezer from Anathoth,
[29]Sibbecai the Hushathite,
    Ilai the Ahohite,
[30]Maharai the Netophathite,
    Heled son of Baanah the Netophathite,
[31]Ithai son of Ribai from Gibeah in Benjamin,
    Benaiah the Pirathonite,
[32]Hurai from the ravines of Gaash,
    Abiel the Arbathite,
[33]Azmaveth the Baharumite,
    Eliahba the Shaalbonite,
[34]the sons of Hashem the Gizonite,
    Jonathan son of Shagee the Hararite,
[35]Ahiam son of Sacar the Hararite,
    Eliphal son of Ur,
[36]Hepher the Mekerathite,
    Ahijah the Pelonite,
[37]Hezro the Carmelite,
    Naarai son of Ezbai,
[38]Joel the brother of Nathan,
    Mibhar son of Hagri,
[39]Zelek the Ammonite,
    Naharai the Berothite, the armorbearer of Joab son of Zeruiah,
[40]Ira the Ithrite,
    Gareb the Ithrite,
[41]Uriah the Hittite,
    Zabad son of Ahlai,
[42]Adina son of Shiza the Reubenite, who was chief of the Reubenites, and the thirty with him,
[43]Hanan son of Maacah,
    Joshaphat the Mithnite,
[44]Uzzia the Ashterathite,
    Shama and Jeiel the sons of Hotham the Aroerite,
[45]Jediael son of Shimri,
    his brother Joha the Tizite,
[46]Eliel the Mahavite,
    Jeribai and Joshaviah the sons of Elnaam,
    Ithmah the Moabite,
[47]Eliel, Obed and Jaasiel the Mezobaite,

CHAPTER 12
These were the men who came to David at Ziklag, while he was banished from the presence of Saul son of Kish (they were

[w]23 Hebrew *five cubits* (about 2.3 meters)

among the warriors who helped him in battle; ²they were armed with bows and were able to shoot arrows or to sling stones right-handed or left-handed; they were kinsmen of Saul from the tribe of Benjamin):

³Ahiezer their chief and Joash the sons of Shemaah the Gibeathite; Jeziel and Pelet the sons of Azmaveth; Beracah, Jehu the Anathothite, ⁴and Ishmaiah the Gibeonite, a mighty man among the Thirty, who was a leader of the Thirty; Jeremiah, Jahaziel, Johanan, Jozabad the Gederathite, ⁵Eluzai, Jerimoth, Bealiah, Shemariah and Shephatiah the Haruphite; ⁶Elkanah, Isshiah, Azarel, Joezer and Jashobeam the Korahites; ⁷and Joelah and Zebadiah the sons of Jeroham from Gedor.

⁸Some Gadites defected to David at his stronghold in the desert. They were brave warriors, ready for battle and able to handle the shield and spear. Their faces were the faces of lions, and they were as swift as gazelles in the mountains.

⁹Ezer was the chief,
  Obadiah the second in command,
    Eliab the third,
¹⁰Mishmannah the fourth, Jeremiah the fifth,
¹¹Attai the sixth, Eliel the seventh,
¹²Johanan the eighth, Elzabad the ninth,
¹³Jeremiah the tenth and Macbannai the eleventh.

¹⁴These Gadites were army commanders; the least was a match for a hundred, and the greatest for a thousand. ¹⁵It was they who crossed the Jordan in the first month when it was overflowing all its banks, and they put to flight everyone living in the valleys, to the east and to the west.

¹⁶Other Benjamites and some men from Judah also came to David in his stronghold. ¹⁷David went out to meet them and said to them, "If you have come to me in peace, to help me, I am ready to have you unite with me. But if you have come to betray me to my enemies when my hands are free from violence, may the God of our fathers see it and judge you."

¹⁸Then the Spirit came upon Amasai, chief of the Thirty, and he said:

"We are yours, O David!
  We are with you, O son of Jesse!
Success, success to you,
  and success to those who help you,
    for your God will help you."

So David received them and made them leaders of his raiding bands.

¹⁹Some of the men of Manasseh defected to David when he went with the Philistines to fight against Saul. (He and his men did not help the Philistines because, after consultation, their rulers sent him away. They said, "It will cost us our heads if he deserts to his master Saul.") ²⁰When David went to Ziklag, these were the men of Manasseh who defected to him: Adnah, Jozabad, Jediael, Michael, Jozabad, Elihu and Zillethai, leaders of units of a thousand in Manasseh. ²¹They helped David against raiding bands, for all of them were brave warriors, and they were commanders in his army. ²²Day after day men came to help David, until he had a great army, like the army of God.ˣ

²³These are the numbers of the men armed for battle who came to David at Hebron to turn Saul's kingdom over to him, as the LORD had said:
²⁴men of Judah, carrying shield and spear—6,800 armed for battle;
²⁵men of Simeon, warriors ready for battle—7,100;
²⁶men of Levi—4,600, ²⁷including Jehoiada, leader of the family of Aaron, with 3,700 men, ²⁸and Zadok, a brave young warrior, with 22 officers from his family;
²⁹men of Benjamin, Saul's kinsmen—3,000, most of whom had remained loyal to Saul's house until then;
³⁰men of Ephraim, brave warriors, famous in their own clans—20,800;
³¹men of half the tribe of Manasseh, designated by name to come and make David king—18,000;
³²men of Issachar, who understood the times and knew what Israel should do—200 chiefs, with all their relatives under their command;
³³men of Zebulun, experienced

soldiers prepared for battle with every type of weapon, to help David with undivided loyalty—50,000;

[34] men of Naphtali—1,000 officers, together with 37,000 men carrying shields and spears;

[35] men of Dan, ready for battle—28,600;

[36] men of Asher, experienced soldiers prepared for battle—40,000;

[37] and from east of the Jordan, men of Reuben, Gad and the half-tribe of Manasseh, armed with every type of weapon—120,000.

[38] All these were fighting men who volunteered to serve in the ranks. They came to Hebron fully determined to make David king over all Israel. All the rest of the Israelites were also of one mind to make David king. [39] The men spent three days there with David, eating and drinking, for their families had supplied provisions for them. [40] Also, their neighbors from as far away as Issachar, Zebulun and Naphtali came bringing food on donkeys, camels, mules and oxen. There were plentiful supplies of flour, fig cakes, raisin cakes, wine, oil, cattle and sheep, for there was joy in Israel.

CHAPTER 13

David conferred with each of his officers, the commanders of thousands and commanders of hundreds. [2] He then said to the whole assembly of Israel, "If it seems good to you and if it is the will of the LORD our God, let us send word far and wide to the rest of our brothers throughout the territories of Israel, and also to the priests and Levites who are with them in their towns and pasturelands, to come and join us. [3] Let us bring the ark of our God back to us, for we did not inquire of[y] it[z] during the reign of Saul." [4] The whole assembly agreed to do this, because it seemed right to all the people.

[5] So David assembled all the Israelites, from the Shihor River in Egypt to Lebo[a] Hamath, to bring the ark of God from Kiriath Jearim. [6] David and all the Israelites with him went to Baalah of Judah (Kiriath Jearim) to bring up from there the ark of God the LORD, who is enthroned between the cherubim—the ark that is called by the Name.

[7] They moved the ark of God from Abinadab's house on a new cart, with Uzzah and Ahio guiding it. [8] David and all the Israelites were celebrating with all their might before God, with songs and with harps, lyres, tambourines, cymbals and trumpets.

[9] When they came to the threshing floor of Kidon, Uzzah reached out his hand to steady the ark, because the oxen stumbled. [10] The LORD's anger burned against Uzzah, and he struck him down because he had put his hand on the ark. So he died there before God.

[11] Then David was angry because the LORD's wrath had broken out against Uzzah, and to this day that place is called Perez Uzzah.[b]

[12] David was afraid of God that day and asked, "How can I ever bring the ark of God to me?" [13] He did not take the ark to be with him in the City of David. Instead, he took it aside to the house of Obed-Edom the Gittite. [14] The ark of God remained with the family of Obed-Edom in his house for three months, and the LORD blessed his household and everything he had.

CHAPTER 14

Now Hiram king of Tyre sent messengers to David, along with cedar logs, stonemasons and carpenters to build a palace for him. [2] And David knew that the LORD had established him as king over Israel and that his kingdom had been highly exalted for the sake of his people Israel.

[3] In Jerusalem David took more wives and became the father of more sons and daughters. [4] These are the names of the children born to him there: Shammua, Shobab, Nathan, Solomon, [5] Ibhar, Elishua, Elpelet, [6] Nogah, Nepheg, Japhia, [7] Elishama, Beeliada[c] and Eliphelet.

[8] When the Philistines heard that David had been anointed king over all Israel, they went up in full force to search for him, but David heard about it and went out to meet them. [9] Now the Philistines had come and raided the Valley of Rephaim; [10] so David inquired of God: "Shall I go and attack the Philistines? Will you hand them over to me?"

The LORD answered him, "Go, I will hand them over to you."

[11] So David and his men went up to Baal

---

[y]3 Or *we neglected*   [z]3 Or *him*   [a]5 Or *to the entrance to*   [b]11 *Perez Uzzah* means *outbreak against Uzzah.*   [c]7 A variant of *Eliada*

Perazim, and there he defeated them. He said, "As waters break out, God has broken out against my enemies by my hand." So that place was called Baal Perazim.[d] [12]The Philistines had abandoned their gods there, and David gave orders to burn them in the fire.

[13]Once more the Philistines raided the valley; [14]so David inquired of God again, and God answered him, "Do not go straight up, but circle around them and attack them in front of the balsam trees. [15]As soon as you hear the sound of marching in the tops of the balsam trees, move out to battle, because that will mean God has gone out in front of you to strike the Philistine army." [16]So David did as God commanded him, and they struck down the Philistine army, all the way from Gibeon to Gezer.

[17]So David's fame spread throughout every land, and the LORD made all the nations fear him.

CHAPTER 15

After David had constructed buildings for himself in the City of David, he prepared a place for the ark of God and pitched a tent for it. [2]Then David said, "No one but the Levites may carry the ark of God, because the LORD chose them to carry the ark of the LORD and to minister before him forever."

[3]David assembled all Israel in Jerusalem to bring up the ark of the LORD to the place he had prepared for it. [4]He called together the descendants of Aaron and the Levites:

[5]From the descendants of Kohath,
　　Uriel the leader and 120 relatives;
[6]from the descendants of Merari,
　　Asaiah the leader and 220 relatives;
[7]from the descendants of Gershon,[e]
　　Joel the leader and 130 relatives;
[8]from the descendants of Elizaphan,
　　Shemaiah the leader and 200 relatives;
[9]from the descendants of Hebron,
　　Eliel the leader and 80 relatives;
[10]from the descendants of Uzziel,
　　Amminadab the leader and 112 relatives.
[11]Then David summoned Zadok and Abiathar the priests, and Uriel, Asaiah, Joel, Shemaiah, Eliel and Amminadab the Levites. [12]He said to them, "You are the heads of the Levitical families; you and your fellow Levites are to consecrate yourselves and bring up the ark of the LORD, the God of Israel, to the place I have prepared for it. [13]It was because you, the Levites, did not bring it up the first time that the LORD our God broke out in anger against us. We did not inquire of him about how to do it in the prescribed way." [14]So the priests and Levites consecrated themselves in order to bring up the ark of the LORD, the God of Israel. [15]And the Levites carried the ark of God with the poles on their shoulders, as Moses had commanded in accordance with the word of the LORD.

[16]David told the leaders of the Levites to appoint their brothers as singers to sing joyful songs, accompanied by musical instruments: lyres, harps and cymbals.

[17]So the Levites appointed Heman son of Joel; from his brothers, Asaph son of Berekiah; and from their brothers the Merarites, Ethan son of Kushaiah; [18]and with them their brothers next in rank: Zechariah,[f] Jaaziel, Shemiramoth, Jehiel, Unni, Eliab, Benaiah, Maaseiah, Mattithiah, Eliphelehu, Mikneiah, Obed-Edom and Jeiel,[g] the gatekeepers. [19]The musicians Heman, Asaph and Ethan were to sound the bronze cymbals; [20]Zechariah, Aziel, Shemiramoth, Jehiel, Unni, Eliab, Maaseiah and Benaiah were to play the lyres according to alamoth,[h] [21]and Mattithiah, Eliphelehu, Mikneiah, Obed-Edom, Jeiel and Azaziah were to play the harps, directing according to sheminith.[h] [22]Kenaniah the head Levite was in charge of the singing; that was his responsibility because he was skillful at it.

[23]Berekiah and Elkanah were to be doorkeepers for the ark. [24]Shebaniah, Joshaphat, Nethanel, Amasai, Zechariah, Benaiah and Eliezer the priests were to blow trumpets before the ark of God. Obed-Edom and Jehiah were also to be doorkeepers for the ark.

[25]So David and the elders of Israel and the commanders of units of a thousand went to bring up the ark of the covenant

d11 Baal Perazim means the lord who breaks out.　_e7 Hebrew Gershom, a variant of Gershon_　_f18 Three Hebrew manuscripts and most Septuagint manuscripts (see also verse 20 and 1 Chron. 16:5); most Hebrew manuscripts Zechariah son and or Zechariah, Ben and_　_g18 Hebrew; Septuagint (see also verse 21) Jeiel and Azaziah_　_h20,21 Probably a musical term_ of the LORD from the house of Obed-Edom, with rejoicing. 26Because God had helped the Levites who were carrying the ark of the covenant of the LORD, seven bulls and seven rams were sacrificed. 27Now David was clothed in a robe of fine linen, as were all the Levites who were carrying the ark, and as were the singers, and Kenaniah, who was in charge of the singing of the choirs. David also wore a linen ephod. 28So all Israel brought up the ark of the covenant of the LORD with shouts, with the sounding of rams' horns and trumpets, and of cymbals, and the playing of lyres and harps.

29As the ark of the covenant of the LORD was entering the City of David, Michal daughter of Saul watched from a window. And when she saw King David dancing and celebrating, she despised him in her heart.

C H A P T E R   1 6
They brought the ark of God and set it inside the tent that David had pitched for it, and they presented burnt offerings and fellowship offerings[i] before God. 2After David had finished sacrificing the burnt offerings and fellowship offerings, he blessed the people in the name of the LORD. 3Then he gave a loaf of bread, a cake of dates and a cake of raisins to each Israelite man and woman.

4He appointed some of the Levites to minister before the ark of the LORD, to make petition, to give thanks, and to praise the LORD, the God of Israel: 5Asaph was the chief, Zechariah second, then Jeiel, Shemiramoth, Jehiel, Mattithiah, Eliab, Benaiah, Obed-Edom and Jeiel. They were to play the lyres and harps, Asaph was to sound the cymbals, 6and Benaiah and Jahaziel the priests were to blow the trumpets regularly before the ark of the covenant of God.

7That day David first committed to Asaph and his associates this psalm of thanks to the LORD:

8Give thanks to the LORD, call on his
        name;
    make known among the nations
        what he has done.
9Sing to him, sing praise to him;

    tell of all his wonderful acts.
10Glory in his holy name;
    let the hearts of those who seek the
        LORD rejoice.
11Look to the LORD and his strength;
    seek his face always.
12Remember the wonders he has done,
    his miracles, and the judgments he
        pronounced,
13O descendants of Israel his servant,
    O sons of Jacob, his chosen ones.

14He is the LORD our God;
    his judgments are in all the earth.
15He remembers[j] his covenant forever,
    the word he commanded, for a
        thousand generations,
16the covenant he made with Abraham,
    the oath he swore to Isaac.
17He confirmed it to Jacob as a decree,
    to Israel as an everlasting covenant:
18"To you I will give the land of Canaan
    as the portion you will inherit."

19When they were but few in number,
    few indeed, and strangers in it,
20they[k] wandered from nation to
        nation,
    from one kingdom to another.
21He allowed no man to oppress them;
    for their sake he rebuked kings:
22"Do not touch my anointed ones;
    do my prophets no harm."

23Sing to the LORD, all the earth;
    proclaim his salvation day after day.
24Declare his glory among the nations,
    his marvelous deeds among all
        peoples.
25For great is the LORD and most worthy
        of praise;
    he is to be feared above all gods.
26For all the gods of the nations are
        idols,
    but the LORD made the heavens.
27Splendor and majesty are before him;
    strength and joy in his dwelling
        place.
28Ascribe to the LORD, O families of
        nations,
    ascribe to the LORD glory and
        strength,
29   ascribe to the LORD the glory due his
        name.

i1 Traditionally peace offerings; also in verse 2   j15 Some Septuagint manuscripts (see also Psalm 105:8); Hebrew Remember   k18-20 One Hebrew manuscript, Septuagint and Vulgate (see also Psalm 105:12); most Hebrew manuscripts inherit, / 19though you are but few in number, / few indeed, and strangers in it." / 20They

Bring an offering and come before
   him;
   worship the Lord in the splendor of
   his^l holiness.
30Tremble before him, all the earth!
   The world is firmly established; it
      cannot be moved.
31Let the heavens rejoice, let the earth be
   glad;
   let them say among the nations,
      "The Lord reigns!"
32Let the sea resound, and all that is in
   it;
   let the fields be jubilant, and
      everything in them!
33Then the trees of the forest will sing,
   they will sing for joy before the
      Lord,
   for he comes to judge the earth.

34Give thanks to the Lord, for he is
   good;
   his love endures forever.
35Cry out, "Save us, O God our Savior;
   gather us and deliver us from the
      nations,
   that we may give thanks to your holy
      name,
   that we may glory in your praise."
36Praise be to the Lord, the God of
   Israel,
   from everlasting to everlasting.

^{l}29 Or Lord with the splendor of

Then all the people said "Amen" and
"Praise the Lord."

37David left Asaph and his associates
before the ark of the covenant of the Lord
to minister there regularly, according to
each day's requirements. 38He also left
Obed-Edom and his sixty-eight associates to minister with them. Obed-Edom
son of Jeduthun, and also Hosah, were
gatekeepers.
   39David left Zadok the priest and his
fellow priests before the tabernacle of the
Lord at the high place in Gibeon 40to
present burnt offerings to the Lord on the
altar of burnt offering regularly, morning
and evening, in accordance with everything written in the Law of the Lord,
which he had given Israel. 41With them
were Heman and Jeduthun and the rest of
those chosen and designated by name to
give thanks to the Lord, "for his love endures forever." 42Heman and Jeduthun
were responsible for the sounding of the
trumpets and cymbals and for the playing
of the other instruments for sacred song.
The sons of Jeduthun were stationed at
the gate.
   43Then all the people left, each for his
own home, and David returned home to
bless his family.

APRIL 17 ☐ DAY 108
1 CHRONICLES 17–21
David's Kingdom and Covenant

 OVERVIEW David's dream of building a fitting place for God to dwell
and be worshiped meets with the prophet's approval . . . and God's
disapproval. Solomon, not David, is God's choice to build the temple.
But while David's house for God must be postponed, God has a house
for David that begins immediately and never ends: an eternal kingdom
and perpetual dynasty. In peacetime and war, through times of faithfulness and faltering, God keeps his promise by preserving David's
line.

Chapter 17	Chapter 18	Chapters 19–20	Chapter 21
An Eternal House	An Extended Kingdom	An Exterminated Enemy	An Evil Idea
Covenant	Conquest		Census

YOUR DAILY WALK If a chronicler were to write the priestly view of your life, what would he include? And what would he exclude from his account?

There are some Christians who can't be called pilgrims because they never make any progress.

There are some notable omissions in the book of 1 Chronicles. Try as you might, you will find nothing about Saul's reign or David's great sin with Bathsheba, Absalom's rebellion or Adonijah's attempted coup. Why are these bleak events in Israel's history deleted? Not to white-wash the story of the nation, but to put the emphasis on God's positive purpose for the nation's existence. In spite of repeated human failings, God's program for his people will be accomplished!

If you were to diagram your own spiritual pilgrimage, chances are it wouldn't have any more ups and downs than Israel's. And God is just as committed to *your* spiritual maturity and the fulfilling of his purpose for your life. ". . . he who began a good work in you will carry it on to completion until the day of Christ Jesus" (Philippians 1:6). Pretend that you are the chronicler writing the autobiography of your own walk with God. What spiritual milestones would you highlight? Jot them down in your journal or inside the cover of this Bible. But leave room—God isn't finished yet!

INSIGHT How's That Name Again?
David's secretary, Shavsha, of 18:16 is also called Shisha (1 Kings 4:3) and Sheva (2 Samuel 20:25). The variations in spelling are perhaps due to a non-Hebrew origin for his name, giving rise to different transliterations.

CHAPTER 17

After David was settled in his palace, he said to Nathan the prophet, "Here I am, living in a palace of cedar, while the ark of the covenant of the LORD is under a tent."

²Nathan replied to David, "Whatever you have in mind, do it, for God is with you."

³That night the word of God came to Nathan, saying:

⁴"Go and tell my servant David, 'This is what the LORD says: You are not the one to build me a house to dwell in. ⁵I have not dwelt in a house from the day I brought Israel up out of Egypt to this day. I have moved from one tent site to another, from one dwelling place to another. ⁶Wherever I have moved with all the Israelites, did I ever say to any of their leaders*m* whom I commanded to shepherd my people, "Why have you not built me a house of cedar?" '

⁷"Now then, tell my servant David, 'This is what the LORD Almighty says: I took you from the pasture and from following the flock, to be ruler over my people Israel. ⁸I have been with you wherever you have gone, and I

have cut off all your enemies from before you. Now I will make your name like the names of the greatest men of the earth. ⁹And I will provide a place for my people Israel and will plant them so that they can have a home of their own and no longer be disturbed. Wicked people will not oppress them anymore, as they did at the beginning ¹⁰and have done ever since the time I appointed leaders over my people Israel. I will also subdue all your enemies.

" 'I declare to you that the LORD will build a house for you: ¹¹When your days are over and you go to be with your fathers, I will raise up your off-spring to succeed you, one of your own sons, and I will establish his kingdom. ¹²He is the one who will build a house for me, and I will establish his throne forever. ¹³I will be his father, and he will be my son. I will never take my love away from him, as I took it away from your predecessor. ¹⁴I will set him over my house and my kingdom forever; his throne will be established forever.' "

¹⁵Nathan reported to David all the words of this entire revelation.

m 6 Traditionally judges; also in verse 10

¹⁶Then King David went in and sat before the LORD, and he said:

"Who am I, O LORD God, and what is my family, that you have brought me this far? ¹⁷And as if this were not enough in your sight, O God, you have spoken about the future of the house of your servant. You have looked on me as though I were the most exalted of men, O LORD God.

¹⁸"What more can David say to you for honoring your servant? For you know your servant, ¹⁹O LORD. For the sake of your servant and according to your will, you have done this great thing and made known all these great promises.

²⁰"There is no one like you, O LORD, and there is no God but you, as we have heard with our own ears. ²¹And who is like your people Israel—the one nation on earth whose God went out to redeem a people for himself, and to make a name for yourself, and to perform great and awesome wonders by driving out nations from before your people, whom you redeemed from Egypt? ²²You made your people Israel your very own forever, and you, O LORD, have become their God.

²³"And now, LORD, let the promise you have made concerning your servant and his house be established forever. Do as you promised, ²⁴so that it will be established and that your name will be great forever. Then men will say, 'The LORD Almighty, the God over Israel, is Israel's God!' And the house of your servant David will be established before you.

²⁵"You, my God, have revealed to your servant that you will build a house for him. So your servant has found courage to pray to you. ²⁶O LORD, you are God! You have promised these good things to your servant. ²⁷Now you have been pleased to bless the house of your servant, that it may continue forever in your sight; for you, O LORD, have blessed it, and it will be blessed forever."

CHAPTER 18

In the course of time, David defeated the Philistines and subdued them, and he took Gath and its surrounding villages from the control of the Philistines.

²David also defeated the Moabites, and they became subject to him and brought tribute.

³Moreover, David fought Hadadezer king of Zobah, as far as Hamath, when he went to establish his control along the Euphrates River. ⁴David captured a thousand of his chariots, seven thousand charioteers and twenty thousand foot soldiers. He hamstrung all but a hundred of the chariot horses.

⁵When the Arameans of Damascus came to help Hadadezer king of Zobah, David struck down twenty-two thousand of them. ⁶He put garrisons in the Aramean kingdom of Damascus, and the Arameans became subject to him and brought tribute. The LORD gave David victory everywhere he went.

⁷David took the gold shields carried by the officers of Hadadezer and brought them to Jerusalem. ⁸From Tebah[n] and Cun, towns that belonged to Hadadezer, David took a great quantity of bronze, which Solomon used to make the bronze Sea, the pillars and various bronze articles.

⁹When Tou king of Hamath heard that David had defeated the entire army of Hadadezer king of Zobah, ¹⁰he sent his son Hadoram to King David to greet him and congratulate him on his victory in battle over Hadadezer, who had been at war with Tou. Hadoram brought all kinds of articles of gold and silver and bronze.

¹¹King David dedicated these articles to the LORD, as he had done with the silver and gold he had taken from all these nations: Edom and Moab, the Ammonites and the Philistines, and Amalek.

¹²Abishai son of Zeruiah struck down eighteen thousand Edomites in the Valley of Salt. ¹³He put garrisons in Edom, and all the Edomites became subject to David. The LORD gave David victory everywhere he went.

¹⁴David reigned over all Israel, doing what was just and right for all his people. ¹⁵Joab son of Zeruiah was over the army; Jehoshaphat son of Ahilud was recorder;

<hr>

n 8 Hebrew *Tibhath*, a variant of *Tebah*

¹⁶Zadok son of Ahitub and Ahimelech⁰ son of Abiathar were priests; Shavsha was secretary; ¹⁷Benaiah son of Jehoiada was over the Kerethites and Pelethites; and David's sons were chief officials at the king's side.

CHAPTER 19

In the course of time, Nahash king of the Ammonites died, and his son succeeded him as king. ²David thought, "I will show kindness to Hanun son of Nahash, because his father showed kindness to me." So David sent a delegation to express his sympathy to Hanun concerning his father.

When David's men came to Hanun in the land of the Ammonites to express sympathy to him, ³the Ammonite nobles said to Hanun, "Do you think David is honoring your father by sending men to you to express sympathy? Haven't his men come to you to explore and spy out the country and overthrow it?" ⁴So Hanun seized David's men, shaved them, cut off their garments in the middle at the buttocks, and sent them away.

⁵When someone came and told David about the men, he sent messengers to meet them, for they were greatly humiliated. The king said, "Stay at Jericho till your beards have grown, and then come back."

⁶When the Ammonites realized that they had become a stench in David's nostrils, Hanun and the Ammonites sent a thousand talentsᴾ of silver to hire chariots and charioteers from Aram Naharaim,�q Aram Maacah and Zobah. ⁷They hired thirty-two thousand chariots and charioteers, as well as the king of Maacah with his troops, who came and camped near Medeba, while the Ammonites were mustered from their towns and moved out for battle.

⁸On hearing this, David sent Joab out with the entire army of fighting men. ⁹The Ammonites came out and drew up in battle formation at the entrance to their city, while the kings who had come were by themselves in the open country.

¹⁰Joab saw that there were battle lines in front of him and behind him; so he selected some of the best troops in Israel and deployed them against the Arameans. ¹¹He put the rest of the men under the command of Abishai his brother, and they were deployed against the Ammonites. ¹²Joab said, "If the Arameans are too strong for me, then you are to rescue me; but if the Ammonites are too strong for you, then I will rescue you. ¹³Be strong and let us fight bravely for our people and the cities of our God. The LORD will do what is good in his sight."

¹⁴Then Joab and the troops with him advanced to fight the Arameans, and they fled before him. ¹⁵When the Ammonites saw that the Arameans were fleeing, they too fled before his brother Abishai and went inside the city. So Joab went back to Jerusalem.

¹⁶After the Arameans saw that they had been routed by Israel, they sent messengers and had Arameans brought from beyond the River,ʳ with Shophach the commander of Hadadezer's army leading them.

¹⁷When David was told of this, he gathered all Israel and crossed the Jordan; he advanced against them and formed his battle lines opposite them. David formed his lines to meet the Arameans in battle, and they fought against him. ¹⁸But they fled before Israel, and David killed seven thousand of their charioteers and forty thousand of their foot soldiers. He also killed Shophach the commander of their army.

¹⁹When the vassals of Hadadezer saw that they had been defeated by Israel, they made peace with David and became subject to him.

So the Arameans were not willing to help the Ammonites anymore.

CHAPTER 20

In the spring, at the time when kings go off to war, Joab led out the armed forces. He laid waste the land of the Ammonites and went to Rabbah and besieged it, but David remained in Jerusalem. Joab attacked Rabbah and left it in ruins. ²David took the crown from the head of their kingˢ—its weight was found to be a talentᵗ of gold, and it was set with precious stones—and it was placed on David's head. He took a great quantity of plunder from the city ³and brought out the people

⁰16 Some Hebrew manuscripts, Vulgate and Syriac (see also 2 Samuel 8:17); most Hebrew manuscripts *Abimelech*   ᴾ6 That is, about 37 tons (about 34 metric tons)   q6 That is, Northwest Mesopotamia   ʳ16 That is, the Euphrates   ˢ2 Or *of Milcom*, that is, Molech   ᵗ2 That is, about 75 pounds (about 34 kilograms)

who were there, consigning them to labor with saws and with iron picks and axes. David did this to all the Ammonite towns. Then David and his entire army returned to Jerusalem.

⁴In the course of time, war broke out with the Philistines, at Gezer. At that time Sibbecai the Hushathite killed Sippai, one of the descendants of the Rephaites, and the Philistines were subjugated.

⁵In another battle with the Philistines, Elhanan son of Jair killed Lahmi the brother of Goliath the Gittite, who had a spear with a shaft like a weaver's rod.

⁶In still another battle, which took place at Gath, there was a huge man with six fingers on each hand and six toes on each foot—twenty-four in all. He also was descended from Rapha. ⁷When he taunted Israel, Jonathan son of Shimea, David's brother, killed him.

⁸These were descendants of Rapha in Gath, and they fell at the hands of David and his men.

CHAPTER 21

Satan rose up against Israel and incited David to take a census of Israel. ²So David said to Joab and the commanders of the troops, "Go and count the Israelites from Beersheba to Dan. Then report back to me so that I may know how many there are."

³But Joab replied, "May the LORD multiply his troops a hundred times over. My lord the king, are they not all my lord's subjects? Why does my lord want to do this? Why should he bring guilt on Israel?"

⁴The king's word, however, overruled Joab; so Joab left and went throughout Israel and then came back to Jerusalem. ⁵Joab reported the number of the fighting men to David: In all Israel there were one million one hundred thousand men who could handle a sword, including four hundred and seventy thousand in Judah.

⁶But Joab did not include Levi and Benjamin in the numbering, because the king's command was repulsive to him. ⁷This command was also evil in the sight of God; so he punished Israel.

⁸Then David said to God, "I have sinned greatly by doing this. Now, I beg you, take away the guilt of your servant. I have done a very foolish thing."

⁹The LORD said to Gad, David's seer, ¹⁰"Go and tell David, 'This is what the LORD says: I am giving you three options. Choose one of them for me to carry out against you.' "

¹¹So Gad went to David and said to him, "This is what the LORD says: 'Take your choice: ¹²three years of famine, three months of being swept awayᵘ before your enemies, with their swords overtaking you, or three days of the sword of the LORD—days of plague in the land, with the angel of the LORD ravaging every part of Israel.' Now then, decide how I should answer the one who sent me."

¹³David said to Gad, "I am in deep distress. Let me fall into the hands of the LORD, for his mercy is very great; but do not let me fall into the hands of men."

¹⁴So the LORD sent a plague on Israel, and seventy thousand men of Israel fell dead. ¹⁵And God sent an angel to destroy Jerusalem. But as the angel was doing so, the LORD saw it and was grieved because of the calamity and said to the angel who was destroying the people, "Enough! Withdraw your hand." The angel of the LORD was then standing at the threshing floor of Araunahᵛ the Jebusite.

¹⁶David looked up and saw the angel of the LORD standing between heaven and earth, with a drawn sword in his hand extended over Jerusalem. Then David and the elders, clothed in sackcloth, fell facedown.

¹⁷David said to God, "Was it not I who ordered the fighting men to be counted? I am the one who has sinned and done wrong. These are but sheep. What have they done? O LORD my God, let your hand fall upon me and my family, but do not let this plague remain on your people."

¹⁸Then the angel of the LORD ordered Gad to tell David to go up and build an altar to the LORD on the threshing floor of Araunah the Jebusite. ¹⁹So David went up in obedience to the word that Gad had spoken in the name of the LORD.

²⁰While Araunah was threshing wheat, he turned and saw the angel; his four sons who were with him hid themselves. ²¹Then David approached, and when Araunah looked and saw him, he left the threshing floor and bowed down before David with his face to the ground.

ᵘ12 Hebrew; Septuagint and Vulgate (see also 2 Samuel 24:13) of fleeing   ᵛ15 Hebrew Ornan, a variant of Araunah; also in verses 18-28

²²David said to him, "Let me have the site of your threshing floor so I can build an altar to the LORD, that the plague on the people may be stopped. Sell it to me at the full price."

²³Araunah said to David, "Take it! Let my lord the king do whatever pleases him. Look, I will give the oxen for the burnt offerings, the threshing sledges for the wood, and the wheat for the grain offering. I will give all this."

²⁴But King David replied to Araunah, "No, I insist on paying the full price. I will not take for the LORD what is yours, or sacrifice a burnt offering that costs me nothing."

²⁵So David paid Araunah six hundred shekels*ʷ* of gold for the site. ²⁶David built an altar to the LORD there and sacrificed burnt offerings and fellowship offerings.*ˣ* He called on the LORD, and the LORD answered him with fire from heaven on the altar of burnt offering.

²⁷Then the LORD spoke to the angel, and he put his sword back into its sheath. ²⁸At that time, when David saw that the LORD had answered him on the threshing floor of Araunah the Jebusite, he offered sacrifices there. ²⁹The tabernacle of the LORD, which Moses had made in the desert, and the altar of burnt offering were at that time on the high place at Gibeon. ³⁰But David could not go before it to inquire of God, because he was afraid of the sword of the angel of the LORD.

*ʷ*25 That is, about 15 pounds (about 7 kilograms)   *ˣ*26 Traditionally *peace offerings*

APRIL 18 ☐ DAY 109
1 CHRONICLES 22–27
David's Preparations for the Temple

OVERVIEW Though David is denied the privilege of building the temple in Jerusalem, he nevertheless can begin preparations for that mammoth project. Every detail—from selecting a site to securing materials—must be carefully planned and coordinated. Most important, David spends his time training the foreman who will oversee the entire project: Solomon, his son. David informs Solomon of God's decision to have his temple built by a man of peace and tells his son of the detailed preparations that have already been made. Finally, David sends Solomon off to the task with a command and a promise: "Now begin the work, and the LORD be with you" (22:16).

Chapter 22	Chapters 23–24	Chapter 25	Chapters 26–27
David's Charge to Solomon	Levites	David's Commissioning of the Musicians	Officers
Father to Son	Leader to Followers		

YOUR DAILY WALK How successful are you at making other people successful?

Divide a sheet of paper in half, and label the left side "Things I am doing to make myself successful." Fill in that column with all the activities you do to make yourself successful spiritually (e.g., praying), physically (jogging), vocationally (reading), etc.

Now title the right column "Things I am doing to make _____ successful." Add the name of a spouse, child, employee or someone else in whose life you have an influence. Then complete as before.

Which was easier to fill out: the right side or the left? Now stop and think: Even though God would not allow David to be successful in his

Length of service for God is not nearly as important as breadth and depth of service.

desire to build the temple (left column), he did allow David to make preparations for his son Solomon to successfully complete the task (right column). What specific action can you begin today to help the person you named become successful in his or her God-given roles?

 INSIGHT Priestly Lots for Lots of Priests
With the growing population came a growing number of priests, seemingly far more than were needed in the temple of Jerusalem. So they were divided into twenty-four "lots," with each group serving for a two-week period each year and being on call during the feast days (24:1–19).

CHAPTER 22

Then David said, "The house of the LORD God is to be here, and also the altar of burnt offering for Israel."

2So David gave orders to assemble the aliens living in Israel, and from among them he appointed stonecutters to prepare dressed stone for building the house of God. 3He provided a large amount of iron to make nails for the doors of the gateways and for the fittings, and more bronze than could be weighed. 4He also provided more cedar logs than could be counted, for the Sidonians and Tyrians had brought large numbers of them to David.

5David said, "My son Solomon is young and inexperienced, and the house to be built for the LORD should be of great magnificence and fame and splendor in the sight of all the nations. Therefore I will make preparations for it." So David made extensive preparations before his death.

6Then he called for his son Solomon and charged him to build a house for the LORD, the God of Israel. 7David said to Solomon: "My son, I had it in my heart to build a house for the Name of the LORD my God. 8But this word of the LORD came to me: 'You have shed much blood and have fought many wars. You are not to build a house for my Name, because you have shed much blood on the earth in my sight. 9But you will have a son who will be a man of peace and rest, and I will give him rest from all his enemies on every side. His name will be Solomon,ʸ and I will grant Israel peace and quiet during his reign. 10He is the one who will build a house for my Name. He will be my son, and I will be his father. And I will establish the throne of his kingdom over Israel forever.'

11"Now, my son, the LORD be with you, and may you have success and build the house of the LORD your God, as he said you would. 12May the LORD give you discretion and understanding when he puts you in command over Israel, so that you may keep the law of the LORD your God. 13Then you will have success if you are careful to observe the decrees and laws that the LORD gave Moses for Israel. Be strong and courageous. Do not be afraid or discouraged.

14"I have taken great pains to provide for the temple of the LORD a hundred thousand talentsᶻ of gold, a million talentsᵃ of silver, quantities of bronze and iron too great to be weighed, and wood and stone. And you may add to them. 15You have many workmen: stonecutters, masons and carpenters, as well as men skilled in every kind of work 16in gold and silver, bronze and iron—craftsmen beyond number. Now begin the work, and the LORD be with you."

17Then David ordered all the leaders of Israel to help his son Solomon. 18He said to them, "Is not the LORD your God with you? And has he not granted you rest on every side? For he has handed the inhabitants of the land over to me, and the land is subject to the LORD and to his people. 19Now devote your heart and soul to seeking the LORD your God. Begin to build the sanctuary of the LORD God, so that you may bring the ark of the covenant of the LORD and the sacred articles belonging to God into the temple that will be built for the Name of the LORD."

CHAPTER 23

When David was old and full of years, he made his son Solomon king over Israel.

2He also gathered together all the

ʸ9 *Solomon* sounds like and may be derived from the Hebrew for *peace*.   ᶻ14 That is, about 3,750 tons (about 3,450 metric tons)   ᵃ14 That is, about 37,500 tons (about 34,500 metric tons) leaders of Israel, as well as the priests and Levites. ³The Levites thirty years old or more were counted, and the total number of men was thirty-eight thousand. ⁴David said, "Of these, twenty-four thousand are to supervise the work of the temple of the LORD and six thousand are to be officials and judges. ⁵Four thousand are to be gatekeepers and four thousand are to praise the LORD with the musical instruments I have provided for that purpose."

⁶David divided the Levites into groups corresponding to the sons of Levi: Gershon, Kohath and Merari.

⁷Belonging to the Gershonites:
  Ladan and Shimei.
⁸The sons of Ladan:
  Jehiel the first, Zetham and Joel—three in all.
⁹The sons of Shimei:
  Shelomoth, Haziel and Haran—three in all.
  These were the heads of the families of Ladan.
¹⁰And the sons of Shimei:
  Jahath, Ziza,ᵇ Jeush and Beriah.
  These were the sons of Shimei—four in all.
¹¹Jahath was the first and Ziza the second, but Jeush and Beriah did not have many sons; so they were counted as one family with one assignment.

¹²The sons of Kohath:
  Amram, Izhar, Hebron and Uzziel—four in all.
¹³The sons of Amram:
  Aaron and Moses.
  Aaron was set apart, he and his descendants forever, to consecrate the most holy things, to offer sacrifices before the LORD, to minister before him and to pronounce blessings in his name forever.
¹⁴The sons of Moses the man of God were counted as part of the tribe of Levi.
¹⁵The sons of Moses:
  Gershom and Eliezer.
¹⁶The descendants of Gershom:
  Shubael was the first.
¹⁷The descendants of Eliezer:
  Rehabiah was the first.
  Eliezer had no other sons, but the sons of Rehabiah were very numerous.
¹⁸The sons of Izhar:
  Shelomith was the first.
¹⁹The sons of Hebron:
  Jeriah the first, Amariah the second, Jahaziel the third and Jekameam the fourth.
²⁰The sons of Uzziel:
  Micah the first and Isshiah the second.

²¹The sons of Merari:
  Mahli and Mushi.
  The sons of Mahli:
  Eleazar and Kish.
²²Eleazar died without having sons: he had only daughters. Their cousins, the sons of Kish, married them.
²³The sons of Mushi:
  Mahli, Eder and Jerimoth—three in all.

²⁴These were the descendants of Levi by their families—the heads of families as they were registered under their names and counted individually, that is, the workers twenty years old or more who served in the temple of the LORD. ²⁵For David had said, "Since the LORD, the God of Israel, has granted rest to his people and has come to dwell in Jerusalem forever, ²⁶the Levites no longer need to carry the tabernacle or any of the articles used in its service." ²⁷According to the last instructions of David, the Levites were counted from those twenty years old or more.

²⁸The duty of the Levites was to help Aaron's descendants in the service of the temple of the LORD: to be in charge of the courtyards, the side rooms, the purification of all sacred things and the performance of other duties at the house of God. ²⁹They were in charge of the bread set out on the table, the flour for the grain offerings, the unleavened wafers, the baking and the mixing, and all measurements of quantity and size. ³⁰They were also to stand every morning to thank and praise the LORD. They were to do the same in the evening ³¹and whenever burnt offerings were presented to the LORD on Sabbaths and at New Moon festivals and at appointed feasts. They were to serve before

ᵇ10 One Hebrew manuscript, Septuagint and Vulgate (see also verse 11); most Hebrew manuscripts *Zina* the LORD regularly in the proper number and in the way prescribed for them.

³²And so the Levites carried out their responsibilities for the Tent of Meeting, for the Holy Place and, under their brothers the descendants of Aaron, for the service of the temple of the LORD.

CHAPTER 24

These were the divisions of the sons of Aaron:

The sons of Aaron were Nadab, Abihu, Eleazar and Ithamar. ²But Nadab and Abihu died before their father did, and they had no sons; so Eleazar and Ithamar served as the priests. ³With the help of Zadok a descendant of Eleazar and Ahimelech a descendant of Ithamar, David separated them into divisions for their appointed order of ministering. ⁴A larger number of leaders were found among Eleazar's descendants than among Ithamar's, and they were divided accordingly: sixteen heads of families from Eleazar's descendants and eight heads of families from Ithamar's descendants. ⁵They divided them impartially by drawing lots, for there were officials of the sanctuary and officials of God among the descendants of both Eleazar and Ithamar.

⁶The scribe Shemaiah son of Nethanel, a Levite, recorded their names in the presence of the king and of the officials: Zadok the priest, Ahimelech son of Abiathar and the heads of families of the priests and of the Levites—one family being taken from Eleazar and then one from Ithamar.

⁷The first lot fell to Jehoiarib,
  the second to Jedaiah,
⁸the third to Harim,
  the fourth to Seorim,
⁹the fifth to Malkijah,
  the sixth to Mijamin,
¹⁰the seventh to Hakkoz,
  the eighth to Abijah,
¹¹the ninth to Jeshua,
  the tenth to Shecaniah,
¹²the eleventh to Eliashib,
  the twelfth to Jakim,
¹³the thirteenth to Huppah,
  the fourteenth to Jeshebeab,
¹⁴the fifteenth to Bilgah,
  the sixteenth to Immer,

¹⁵the seventeenth to Hezir,
  the eighteenth to Happizzez,
¹⁶the nineteenth to Pethahiah,
  the twentieth to Jehezkel,
¹⁷the twenty-first to Jakin,
  the twenty-second to Gamul,
¹⁸the twenty-third to Delaiah
  and the twenty-fourth to Maaziah.

¹⁹This was their appointed order of ministering when they entered the temple of the LORD, according to the regulations prescribed for them by their forefather Aaron, as the LORD, the God of Israel, had commanded him.

²⁰As for the rest of the descendants of Levi:
  from the sons of Amram: Shubael;
    from the sons of Shubael: Jehdeiah.
  ²¹As for Rehabiah, from his sons:
    Isshiah was the first.
²²From the Izharites: Shelomoth;
  from the sons of Shelomoth: Jahath.
²³The sons of Hebron: Jeriah the first,ᶜ Amariah the second, Jahaziel the third and Jekameam the fourth.
²⁴The son of Uzziel: Micah;
  from the sons of Micah: Shamir.
  ²⁵The brother of Micah: Isshiah;
    from the sons of Isshiah: Zechariah.
²⁶The sons of Merari: Mahli and Mushi.
  The son of Jaaziah: Beno.
²⁷The sons of Merari:
  from Jaaziah: Beno, Shoham, Zaccur and Ibri.
²⁸From Mahli: Eleazar, who had no sons.
²⁹From Kish: the son of Kish: Jerahmeel.
³⁰And the sons of Mushi: Mahli, Eder and Jerimoth.

These were the Levites, according to their families. ³¹They also cast lots, just as their brothers the descendants of Aaron did, in the presence of King David and of Zadok, Ahimelech, and the heads of families of the priests and of the Levites. The families of the oldest brother were treated the same as those of the youngest.

ᶜ23 Two Hebrew manuscripts and some Septuagint manuscripts (see also 1 Chron. 23:19); most Hebrew manuscripts *The sons of Jeriah:*

CHAPTER 25

David, together with the commanders of the army, set apart some of the sons of Asaph, Heman and Jeduthun for the ministry of prophesying, accompanied by harps, lyres and cymbals. Here is the list of the men who performed this service:

²From the sons of Asaph:
Zaccur, Joseph, Nethaniah and Asa-relah. The sons of Asaph were under the supervision of Asaph, who prophesied under the king's supervision.

³As for Jeduthun, from his sons:
Gedaliah, Zeri, Jeshaiah, Shimei,ᵈ Hashabiah and Mattithiah, six in all, under the supervision of their father Jeduthun, who prophesied, using the harp in thanking and praising the LORD.

⁴As for Heman, from his sons:
Bukkiah, Mattaniah, Uzziel, Shubael and Jerimoth; Hananiah, Hanani, Eliathah, Giddalti and Romamti-Ezer; Joshbekashah, Mallothi, Hothir and Mahazioth. ⁵All these were sons of Heman the king's seer. They were given him through the promises of God to exalt him.ᵉ God gave Heman fourteen sons and three daughters.

⁶All these men were under the supervision of their fathers for the music of the temple of the LORD, with cymbals, lyres and harps, for the ministry at the house of God. Asaph, Jeduthun and Heman were under the supervision of the king. ⁷Along with their relatives—all of them trained and skilled in music for the LORD—they numbered 288. ⁸Young and old alike, teacher as well as student, cast lots for their duties.

⁹The first lot, which was for Asaph, fell to Joseph,
his sons and relatives,ᶠ   12ᵍ
the second to Gedaliah,
he and his relatives and sons,   12
¹⁰the third to Zaccur,
his sons and relatives,   12
¹¹the fourth to Izri,ʰ
his sons and relatives,   12
¹²the fifth to Nethaniah,
his sons and relatives,   12

¹³the sixth to Bukkiah,
his sons and relatives,   12
¹⁴the seventh to Jesarelah,ⁱ
his sons and relatives,   12
¹⁵the eighth to Jeshaiah,
his sons and relatives,   12
¹⁶the ninth to Mattaniah,
his sons and relatives,   12
¹⁷the tenth to Shimei,
his sons and relatives,   12
¹⁸the eleventh to Azarel,ʲ
his sons and relatives,   12
¹⁹the twelfth to Hashabiah,
his sons and relatives,   12
²⁰the thirteenth to Shubael,
his sons and relatives,   12
²¹the fourteenth to Mattithiah,
his sons and relatives,   12
²²the fifteenth to Jerimoth,
his sons and relatives,   12
²³the sixteenth to Hananiah,
his sons and relatives,   12
²⁴the seventeenth to Joshbekashah,
his sons and relatives,   12
²⁵the eighteenth to Hanani,
his sons and relatives,   12
²⁶the nineteenth to Mallothi,
his sons and relatives,   12
²⁷the twentieth to Eliathah,
his sons and relatives,   12
²⁸the twenty-first to Hothir,
his sons and relatives,   12
²⁹the twenty-second to Giddalti,
his sons and relatives,   12
³⁰the twenty-third to Mahazioth,
his sons and relatives,   12
³¹the twenty-fourth to Romamti-Ezer,
his sons and relatives,   12

CHAPTER 26

The divisions of the gatekeepers:

From the Korahites: Meshelemiah son of Kore, one of the sons of Asaph.
²Meshelemiah had sons:
Zechariah the firstborn,
Jediael the second,
Zebadiah the third,
Jathniel the fourth,
³Elam the fifth,

ᵈ3 One Hebrew manuscript and some Septuagint manuscripts (see also verse 17); most Hebrew manuscripts do not have Shimei.   ᵉ5 Hebrew exalt the horn   ᶠ9 See Septuagint; Hebrew does not have his sons and relatives.   ᵍ9 See the total in verse 7; Hebrew does not have twelve.   ʰ11 A variant of Zeri   ⁱ14 A variant of Asarelah   ʲ18 A variant of Uzziel

Jehohanan the sixth
and Eliehoenai the seventh.
[4]Obed-Edom also had sons:
Shemaiah the firstborn,
Jehozabad the second,
Joah the third,
Sacar the fourth,
Nethanel the fifth,
[5]Ammiel the sixth,
Issachar the seventh
and Peullethai the eighth.
(For God had blessed Obed-
Edom.)

[6]His son Shemaiah also had sons,
who were leaders in their father's
family because they were very capable men. [7]The sons of Shemaiah:
Othni, Rephael, Obed and Elzabad; his relatives Elihu and Sema-
kiah were also able men. [8]All
these were descendants of Obed-
Edom; they and their sons and
their relatives were capable men
with the strength to do the work—
descendants of Obed-Edom, 62 in
all.
[9]Meshelemiah had sons and relatives,
who were able men—18 in all.

[10]Hosah the Merarite had sons: Shimri
the first (although he was not the
firstborn, his father had appointed
him the first), [11]Hilkiah the second, Tabaliah the third and Zechariah the fourth. The sons and
relatives of Hosah were 13 in all.
[12]These divisions of the gatekeepers,
through their chief men, had duties for
ministering in the temple of the LORD, just
as their relatives had. [13]Lots were cast for
each gate, according to their families,
young and old alike.
[14]The lot for the East Gate fell to Shelemiah.[k] Then lots were cast for his son
Zechariah, a wise counselor, and the lot
for the North Gate fell to him. [15]The lot
for the South Gate fell to Obed-Edom,
and the lot for the storehouse fell to his
sons. [16]The lots for the West Gate and the
Shalleketh Gate on the upper road fell to
Shuppim and Hosah.
Guard was alongside of guard: [17]There
were six Levites a day on the east, four a
day on the north, four a day on the south
and two at a time at the storehouse. [18]As

for the court to the west, there were four
at the road and two at the court itself.
[19]These were the divisions of the gatekeepers who were descendants of Korah
and Merari.

[20]Their fellow Levites were[l] in charge
of the treasuries of the house of God and
the treasuries for the dedicated things.
[21]The descendants of Ladan, who were
Gershonites through Ladan and who
were heads of families belonging to Ladan the Gershonite, were Jehieli, [22]the
sons of Jehieli, Zetham and his brother
Joel. They were in charge of the treasuries
of the temple of the LORD.
[23]From the Amramites, the Izharites,
the Hebronites and the Uzzielites:

[24]Shubael, a descendant of Gershom
son of Moses, was the officer in
charge of the treasuries. [25]His relatives through Eliezer: Rehabiah
his son, Jeshaiah his son, Joram his
son, Zicri his son and Shelomith
his son. [26]Shelomith and his relatives were in charge of all the
treasuries for the things dedicated
by King David, by the heads of
families who were the commanders of thousands and commanders
of hundreds, and by the other
army commanders. [27]Some of the
plunder taken in battle they dedicated for the repair of the temple
of the LORD. [28]And everything
dedicated by Samuel the seer and
by Saul son of Kish, Abner son of
Ner and Joab son of Zeruiah, and
all the other dedicated things were
in the care of Shelomith and his
relatives.
[29]From the Izharites: Kenaniah and his
sons were assigned duties away
from the temple, as officials and
judges over Israel.
[30]From the Hebronites: Hashabiah
and his relatives—seventeen hundred able men—were responsible
in Israel west of the Jordan for all
the work of the LORD and for the
king's service. [31]As for the Hebronites, Jeriah was their chief
according to the genealogical
records of their families. In the
fortieth year of David's reign a

search was made in the records, and capable men among the Hebronites were found at Jazer in Gilead. ³²Jeriah had twenty-seven hundred relatives, who were able men and heads of families, and King David put them in charge of the Reubenites, the Gadites and the half-tribe of Manasseh for every matter pertaining to God and for the affairs of the king.

CHAPTER 27

This is the list of the Israelites—heads of families, commanders of thousands and commanders of hundreds, and their officers, who served the king in all that concerned the army divisions that were on duty month by month throughout the year. Each division consisted of 24,000 men.

²In charge of the first division, for the first month, was Jashobeam son of Zabdiel. There were 24,000 men in his division. ³He was a descendant of Perez and chief of all the army officers for the first month.

⁴In charge of the division for the second month was Dodai the Ahohite; Mikloth was the leader of his division. There were 24,000 men in his division.

⁵The third army commander, for the third month, was Benaiah son of Jehoiada the priest. He was chief and there were 24,000 men in his division. ⁶This was the Benaiah who was a mighty man among the Thirty and was over the Thirty. His son Ammizabad was in charge of his division.

⁷The fourth, for the fourth month, was Asahel the brother of Joab; his son Zebadiah was his successor. There were 24,000 men in his division.

⁸The fifth, for the fifth month, was the commander Shamhuth the Izrahite. There were 24,000 men in his division.

⁹The sixth, for the sixth month, was Ira the son of Ikkesh the Tekoite. There were 24,000 men in his division.

¹⁰The seventh, for the seventh month, was Helez the Pelonite, an Ephraimite. There were 24,000 men in his division.

¹¹The eighth, for the eighth month, was Sibbecai the Hushathite, a Zerahite. There were 24,000 men in his division.

¹²The ninth, for the ninth month, was Abiezer the Anathothite, a Benjamite. There were 24,000 men in his division.

¹³The tenth, for the tenth month, was Maharai the Netophathite, a Zerahite. There were 24,000 men in his division.

¹⁴The eleventh, for the eleventh month, was Benaiah the Pirathonite, an Ephraimite. There were 24,000 men in his division.

¹⁵The twelfth, for the twelfth month, was Heldai the Netophathite, from the family of Othniel. There were 24,000 men in his division.

¹⁶The officers over the tribes of Israel:

over the Reubenites: Eliezer son of Zicri;

over the Simeonites: Shephatiah son of Maacah;

¹⁷over Levi: Hashabiah son of Kemuel;

over Aaron: Zadok;

¹⁸over Judah: Elihu, a brother of David;

over Issachar: Omri son of Michael;

¹⁹over Zebulun: Ishmaiah son of Obadiah;

over Naphtali: Jerimoth son of Azriel;

²⁰over the Ephraimites: Hoshea son of Azaziah;

over half the tribe of Manasseh: Joel son of Pedaiah;

²¹over the half-tribe of Manasseh in Gilead: Iddo son of Zechariah;

over Benjamin: Jaasiel son of Abner;

²²over Dan: Azarel son of Jeroham.

These were the officers over the tribes of Israel.

²³David did not take the number of the men twenty years old or less, because the LORD had promised to make Israel as numerous as the stars in the sky. ²⁴Joab son of Zeruiah began to count the men but did not finish. Wrath came on Israel on account of this numbering, and the number was not entered in the book^m of the annals of King David.

²⁵Azmaveth son of Adiel was in charge of the royal storehouses.

Jonathan son of Uzziah was in charge of the storehouses in the outlying districts, in the towns, the villages and the watchtowers.

---

^m 24 Septuagint; Hebrew *number*

²⁶Ezri son of Kelub was in charge of the field workers who farmed the land.

²⁷Shimei the Ramathite was in charge of the vineyards.

Zabdi the Shiphmite was in charge of the produce of the vineyards for the wine vats.

²⁸Baal-Hanan the Gederite was in charge of the olive and sycamore-fig trees in the western foothills.

Joash was in charge of the supplies of olive oil.

²⁹Shitrai the Sharonite was in charge of the herds grazing in Sharon.

Shaphat son of Adlai was in charge of the herds in the valleys.

³⁰Obil the Ishmaelite was in charge of the camels.

Jehdeiah the Meronothite was in charge of the donkeys.

³¹Jaziz the Hagrite was in charge of the flocks.

All these were the officials in charge of King David's property.

³²Jonathan, David's uncle, was a counselor, a man of insight and a scribe. Jehiel son of Hacmoni took care of the king's sons.

³³Ahithophel was the king's counselor.

Hushai the Arkite was the king's friend. ³⁴Ahithophel was succeeded by Jehoiada son of Benaiah and by Abiathar.

Joab was the commander of the royal army.

APRIL 19 ☐ DAY 110
1 CHRONICLES 28–29
David's Final Words and Deeds

OVERVIEW Compare the opening chapters of David's life with the closing ones, and you will come to a startling conclusion: David ended his life the same way he began it—with humble confidence in God. In spite of his great and numerous accomplishments, he never let greatness go to his head. David's final words to Solomon and the nation reflect the same wholehearted devotion to God that he first expressed as a youthful shepherd in the pasturelands of Judea. With the dream of his heart (building a temple) entrusted to his son and the tokens of God's blessing all around him, David dies "a good old age, having enjoyed long life, wealth and honor. His son Solomon succeeded him as king" (29:28).

Chapter 28		Chapter 29	
David's Final Words		David's Final	David's Fitting
to Israel	to Solomon	Act of Worship	Epitaph
1	8 9	21 1	21 22	30
Advice		Adoration	Acclaim

YOUR DAILY WALK Close your study of David's life in 1 Chronicles by reading his prayer slowly and prayerfully. Is his expression of thanksgiving to God the prayer of your heart?

The person who forgets the language of gratitude can never be on speaking terms with happiness.

"Yours, O LORD, is the greatness and the power and the glory and the majesty and the splendor, for everything in heaven and earth is yours. Yours, O LORD, is the kingdom; you are exalted as head over all. Wealth and honor come from you; you are the ruler of all things. In your hands are strength and power to exalt and give strength to all. Now, our God, we give you thanks, and praise your glorious name" (29:11–13).

David offered this prayer in gratitude for the generous, voluntary contributions of the congregation for the service of God's house. Why not prepare a special offering for your church this weekend?

 INSIGHT All That Glitters Is Not Gold (It May Be Silver!) Don't miss the incredible statistics (29:4–7) that describe the materials David set aside for building the temple: 300 tons of gold, 635 tons of silver, and nearly 4,000 tons of iron! Find the current price of gold and silver, and calculate what those tons of precious metals would be worth today!

CHAPTER 28

David summoned all the officials of Israel to assemble at Jerusalem: the officers over the tribes, the commanders of the divisions in the service of the king, the commanders of thousands and commanders of hundreds, and the officials in charge of all the property and livestock belonging to the king and his sons, together with the palace officials, the mighty men and all the brave warriors.

²King David rose to his feet and said: "Listen to me, my brothers and my people. I had it in my heart to build a house as a place of rest for the ark of the covenant of the LORD, for the footstool of our God, and I made plans to build it. ³But God said to me, 'You are not to build a house for my Name, because you are a warrior and have shed blood.'

⁴"Yet the LORD, the God of Israel, chose me from my whole family to be king over Israel forever. He chose Judah as leader, and from the house of Judah he chose my family, and from my father's sons he was pleased to make me king over all Israel. ⁵Of all my sons—and the LORD has given me many—he has chosen my son Solomon to sit on the throne of the kingdom of the LORD over Israel. ⁶He said to me: 'Solomon your son is the one who will build my house and my courts, for I have chosen him to be my son, and I will be his father. ⁷I will establish his kingdom forever if he is unswerving in carrying out my commands and laws, as is being done at this time.'

⁸"So now I charge you in the sight of all Israel and of the assembly of the LORD, and in the hearing of our God: Be careful to follow all the commands of the LORD your God, that you may possess this good land and pass it on as an inheritance to your descendants forever.

⁹"And you, my son Solomon, acknowledge the God of your father, and serve him with wholehearted devotion and with a willing mind, for the LORD searches every heart and understands every motive behind the thoughts. If you seek him, he will be found by you; but if you forsake him, he will reject you forever. ¹⁰Consider now, for the LORD has chosen you to build a temple as a sanctuary. Be strong and do the work."

¹¹Then David gave his son Solomon the plans for the portico of the temple, its buildings, its storerooms, its upper parts, its inner rooms and the place of atonement. ¹²He gave him the plans of all that the Spirit had put in his mind for the courts of the temple of the LORD and all the surrounding rooms, for the treasuries of the temple of God and for the treasuries for the dedicated things. ¹³He gave him instructions for the divisions of the priests and Levites, and for all the work of serving in the temple of the LORD, as well as for all the articles to be used in its service. ¹⁴He designated the weight of gold for all the gold articles to be used in various kinds of service, and the weight of silver for all the silver articles to be used in various kinds of service: ¹⁵the weight of gold for the gold lampstands and their lamps, with the weight for each lampstand and its lamps; and the weight of silver for each silver lampstand and its lamps, according to the use of each lampstand; ¹⁶the weight of gold for each table for consecrated bread; the weight of silver for the silver tables; ¹⁷the weight of pure gold for the forks, sprinkling bowls and pitchers; the weight of gold for each gold dish; the weight of silver for each silver dish; ¹⁸and the weight of the refined gold for the altar of incense. He also gave him the plan for the chariot, that is, the cherubim of gold that spread their wings and shelter the ark of the covenant of the LORD.

¹⁹"All this," David said, "I have in writing from the hand of the LORD upon me,

and he gave me understanding in all the details of the plan."

²⁰David also said to Solomon his son, "Be strong and courageous, and do the work. Do not be afraid or discouraged, for the LORD God, my God, is with you. He will not fail you or forsake you until all the work for the service of the temple of the LORD is finished. ²¹The divisions of the priests and Levites are ready for all the work on the temple of God, and every willing man skilled in any craft will help you in all the work. The officials and all the people will obey your every command."

CHAPTER 29

Then King David said to the whole assembly: "My son Solomon, the one whom God has chosen, is young and inexperienced. The task is great, because this palatial structure is not for man but for the LORD God. ²With all my resources I have provided for the temple of my God—gold for the gold work, silver for the silver, bronze for the bronze, iron for the iron and wood for the wood, as well as onyx for the settings, turquoise,ⁿ stones of various colors, and all kinds of fine stone and marble—all of these in large quantities. ³Besides, in my devotion to the temple of my God I now give my personal treasures of gold and silver for the temple of my God, over and above everything I have provided for this holy temple: ⁴three thousand talents^o of gold (gold of Ophir) and seven thousand talents^p of refined silver, for the overlaying of the walls of the buildings, ⁵for the gold work and the silver work, and for all the work to be done by the craftsmen. Now, who is willing to consecrate himself today to the LORD?"

⁶Then the leaders of families, the officers of the tribes of Israel, the commanders of thousands and commanders of hundreds, and the officials in charge of the king's work gave willingly. ⁷They gave toward the work on the temple of God five thousand talents^q and ten thousand darics^r of gold, ten thousand talents^s of silver, eighteen thousand talents^t of bronze and a hundred thousand

talents^u of iron. ⁸Any who had precious stones gave them to the treasury of the temple of the LORD in the custody of Jehiel the Gershonite. ⁹The people rejoiced at the willing response of their leaders, for they had given freely and wholeheartedly to the LORD. David the king also rejoiced greatly.

¹⁰David praised the LORD in the presence of the whole assembly, saying,

"Praise be to you, O LORD,
   God of our father Israel,
   from everlasting to everlasting.
¹¹Yours, O LORD, is the greatness and the
     power
   and the glory and the majesty and
     the splendor,
   for everything in heaven and earth
     is yours.
Yours, O LORD, is the kingdom;
   you are exalted as head over all.
¹²Wealth and honor come from you;
   you are the ruler of all things.
In your hands are strength and power
   to exalt and give strength to all.
¹³Now, our God, we give you thanks,
   and praise your glorious name.

¹⁴"But who am I, and who are my people, that we should be able to give as generously as this? Everything comes from you, and we have given you only what comes from your hand. ¹⁵We are aliens and strangers in your sight, as were all our forefathers. Our days on earth are like a shadow, without hope. ¹⁶O LORD our God, as for all this abundance that we have provided for building you a temple for your Holy Name, it comes from your hand, and all of it belongs to you. ¹⁷I know, my God, that you test the heart and are pleased with integrity. All these things have I given willingly and with honest intent. And now I have seen with joy how willingly your people who are here have given to you. ¹⁸O LORD, God of our fathers Abraham, Isaac and Israel, keep this desire in the hearts of your people forever, and keep their hearts loyal to you. ¹⁹And give my son Solomon the wholehearted devotion to keep your commands, requirements and decrees

ⁿ2 The meaning of the Hebrew for this word is uncertain.   ^o4 That is, about 110 tons (about 100 metric tons)   ^p4 That is, about 260 tons (about 240 metric tons)   ^q7 That is, about 190 tons (about 170 metric tons)   ^r7 That is, about 185 pounds (about 84 kilograms)   ^s7 That is, about 375 tons (about 345 metric tons)   ^t7 That is, about 675 tons (about 610 metric tons)   ^u7 That is, about 3,750 tons (about 3,450 metric tons)

and to do everything to build the palatial structure for which I have provided."

²⁰Then David said to the whole assembly, "Praise the LORD your God." So they all praised the LORD, the God of their fathers; they bowed low and fell prostrate before the LORD and the king.

²¹The next day they made sacrifices to the LORD and presented burnt offerings to him: a thousand bulls, a thousand rams and a thousand male lambs, together with their drink offerings, and other sacrifices in abundance for all Israel. ²²They ate and drank with great joy in the presence of the LORD that day.

Then they acknowledged Solomon son of David as king a second time, anointing him before the LORD to be ruler and Zadok to be priest. ²³So Solomon sat on the throne of the LORD as king in place of his father David. He prospered and all Israel obeyed him. ²⁴All the officers and mighty men, as well as all of King David's sons, pledged their submission to King Solomon.

²⁵The LORD highly exalted Solomon in the sight of all Israel and bestowed on him royal splendor such as no king over Israel ever had before.

²⁶David son of Jesse was king over all Israel. ²⁷He ruled over Israel forty years—seven in Hebron and thirty-three in Jerusalem. ²⁸He died at a good old age, having enjoyed long life, wealth and honor. His son Solomon succeeded him as king.

²⁹As for the events of King David's reign, from beginning to end, they are written in the records of Samuel the seer, the records of Nathan the prophet and the records of Gad the seer, ³⁰together with the details of his reign and power, and the circumstances that surrounded him and Israel and the kingdoms of all the other lands.

2 Chronicles

THE BOOK of 2 Chronicles begins with the construction of Solomon's temple and concludes with Cyrus's edict to rebuild the temple more than four hundred years later! In between, 2 Chronicles is the story of fading glory—the downward spiral of the kingdom of Judah in spite of the energetic efforts of a handful of reformers. The temple and temple worship remain central throughout the book, although the people stray far from it and ultimately pay the price for their waywardness.

Focus	Descendants of King David								
Divisions	Solomon's Magnificent Temple	Solomon's Worship and Works	Rebellion against Rehoboam	Reigns of Abijah and Asa	Reform under Jehoshaphat	Reigns of Jehoram to Amaziah	Reigns of Uzziah to Ahaz	Reform under Hezekiah	Reigns of Judah's Last Kings
	1 5	6 9	10 12	13 16	17 20	21 25	26 28	29 32	33 36
Topics	Solomon's Glory				Judah's Decline				
	Construction of the Temple				Desecration of the Temple				
Place	Southern Kingdom of Judah								
Time	About 40 Years				About 400 Years				

APRIL 20 ☐ DAY 111
2 CHRONICLES 1–5
Solomon's Magnificent Temple

OVERVIEW Solomon's wealth and wisdom are legendary. But they pale by comparison to the one project with which history would later connect his name: Solomon's temple. In only seven years, Solomon uses the efforts of 153,000 workers to fashion tons of gold and silver, bronze and cedar, into a breathtaking abode for the God who is "greater than all other gods" (2:5). When at last the task is complete, the glory of God fills the temple with such radiance that even the people who work there must temporarily evacuate—a token of God's pleasure with the finished project.

Chapter 1	Chapters 2–3	Chapter 4	Chapter 5
Solomon's Wealth and Wisdom	Solomon's Wondrous Temple		
	Fashioned	Furnished	Filled
Promise from God	Place to Worship God		

YOUR DAILY WALK What is your reaction when you encounter a wealthy businessman? . . . a wealthy politician? . . . a wealthy Christian? . . . a wealthy minister? Do the terms *rich* and *Christian* seem contradictory?

Don't knock the rich. When was the last time you were hired by somebody poor?

The real issue for a Christian living in an age of plenty is not how much money he or she has. Christians can be rich or poor, in or out of the will of God. The rich man in James 5 is not so much a man who possesses much as he is a man who is preoccupied with what he possesses. King Solomon had much, but he recognized it all as a gift from God (1:11–12), which, if used wisely, would become a constant source of blessing to himself and others.

How can you use a part of your material blessings from God to become in turn a blessing in someone else's life today? To be truly rich, reach out!

INSIGHT Temples Old and New
When you come across the word *temple* in your Bible, be sure to check the context. Is the author speaking of
- Solomon's temple?
- Zerubbabel's temple? (Ezra 3:8—the one built to replace Solomon's temple after Nebuchadnezzar destroyed it in 586 B.C.)
- Herod's temple? (Matthew 24:1; John 2:20—Zerubbabel's temple expanded and elaborated that stood in Jesus' day)
- Ezekiel's temple? (Ezekiel 40–48—a temple as yet unbuilt whose details were given to Ezekiel in a vision)
- Artemis's temple? (Acts 19:27—a pagan shrine in Ephesus and one of the seven wonders of the ancient world)

CHAPTER 1

Solomon son of David established himself firmly over his kingdom, for the LORD his God was with him and made him exceedingly great.

²Then Solomon spoke to all Israel—to

the commanders of thousands and commanders of hundreds, to the judges and to all the leaders in Israel, the heads of families— ³and Solomon and the whole assembly went to the high place at Gibeon, for God's Tent of Meeting was there, which Moses the LORD's servant had made in the desert. ⁴Now David had brought up the ark of God from Kiriath Jearim to the place he had prepared for it, because he had pitched a tent for it in Jerusalem. ⁵But the bronze altar that Bezalel son of Uri, the son of Hur, had made was in Gibeon in front of the tabernacle of the LORD; so Solomon and the assembly inquired of him there. ⁶Solomon went up to the bronze altar before the LORD in the Tent of Meeting and offered a thousand burnt offerings on it.

⁷That night God appeared to Solomon and said to him, "Ask for whatever you want me to give you."

⁸Solomon answered God, "You have shown great kindness to David my father and have made me king in his place. ⁹Now, LORD God, let your promise to my father David be confirmed, for you have made me king over a people who are as numerous as the dust of the earth. ¹⁰Give me wisdom and knowledge, that I may lead this people, for who is able to govern this great people of yours?"

¹¹God said to Solomon, "Since this is your heart's desire and you have not asked for wealth, riches or honor, nor for the death of your enemies, and since you have not asked for a long life but for wisdom and knowledge to govern my people over whom I have made you king, ¹²therefore wisdom and knowledge will be given you. And I will also give you wealth, riches and honor, such as no king who was before you ever had and none after you will have."

¹³Then Solomon went to Jerusalem from the high place at Gibeon, from before the Tent of Meeting. And he reigned over Israel.

¹⁴Solomon accumulated chariots and horses; he had fourteen hundred chariots and twelve thousand horses,ᵃ which he kept in the chariot cities and also with him in Jerusalem. ¹⁵The king made silver and gold as common in Jerusalem as

stones, and cedar as plentiful as sycamore-fig trees in the foothills. ¹⁶Solomon's horses were imported from Egyptᵇ and from Kueᶜ—the royal merchants purchased them from Kue. ¹⁷They imported a chariot from Egypt for six hundred shekelsᵈ of silver, and a horse for a hundred and fifty.ᵉ They also exported them to all the kings of the Hittites and of the Arameans.

CHAPTER 2

Solomon gave orders to build a temple for the Name of the LORD and a royal palace for himself. ²He conscripted seventy thousand men as carriers and eighty thousand as stonecutters in the hills and thirty-six hundred as foremen over them.

³Solomon sent this message to Hiramᶠ king of Tyre:

"Send me cedar logs as you did for my father David when you sent him cedar to build a palace to live in. ⁴Now I am about to build a temple for the Name of the LORD my God and to dedicate it to him for burning fragrant incense before him, for setting out the consecrated bread regularly, and for making burnt offerings every morning and evening and on Sabbaths and New Moons and at the appointed feasts of the LORD our God. This is a lasting ordinance for Israel.

⁵"The temple I am going to build will be great, because our God is greater than all other gods. ⁶But who is able to build a temple for him, since the heavens, even the highest heavens, cannot contain him? Who then am I to build a temple for him, except as a place to burn sacrifices before him?

⁷"Send me, therefore, a man skilled to work in gold and silver, bronze and iron, and in purple, crimson and blue yarn, and experienced in the art of engraving, to work in Judah and Jerusalem with my skilled craftsmen, whom my father David provided.

⁸"Send me also cedar, pine and algumᵍ logs from Lebanon, for I know that your men are skilled in cutting timber there. My men will work with yours ⁹to provide me with plenty of

---

ᵃ14 Or charioteers   ᵇ16 Or possibly Muzur, a region in Cilicia; also in verse 17   ᶜ16 Probably Cilicia   ᵈ17 That is, about 15 pounds (about 7 kilograms)   ᵉ17 That is, about 3 3/4 pounds (about 1.7 kilograms)   ᶠ3 Hebrew Huram, a variant of Hiram; also in verses 11 and 12   ᵍ8 Probably a variant of almug; possibly juniper lumber, because the temple I build must be large and magnificent. ¹⁰I will give your servants, the woodsmen who cut the timber, twenty thousand cors^h of ground wheat, twenty thousand cors of barley, twenty thousand bathsⁱ of wine and twenty thousand baths of olive oil."

¹¹Hiram king of Tyre replied by letter to Solomon:

"Because the Lord loves his people, he has made you their king."

¹²And Hiram added:

"Praise be to the Lord, the God of Israel, who made heaven and earth! He has given King David a wise son, endowed with intelligence and discernment, who will build a temple for the Lord and a palace for himself. ¹³"I am sending you Huram-Abi, a man of great skill, ¹⁴whose mother was from Dan and whose father was from Tyre. He is trained to work in gold and silver, bronze and iron, stone and wood, and with purple and blue and crimson yarn and fine linen. He is experienced in all kinds of engraving and can execute any design given to him. He will work with your craftsmen and with those of my lord, David your father.

¹⁵"Now let my lord send his servants the wheat and barley and the olive oil and wine he promised, ¹⁶and we will cut all the logs from Lebanon that you need and will float them in rafts by sea down to Joppa. You can then take them up to Jerusalem."

¹⁷Solomon took a census of all the aliens who were in Israel, after the census his father David had taken; and they were found to be 153,600. ¹⁸He assigned 70,000 of them to be carriers and 80,000 to be stonecutters in the hills, with 3,600 foremen over them to keep the people working.

CHAPTER 3
Then Solomon began to build the temple of the Lord in Jerusalem on Mount Moriah, where the Lord had appeared to his father David. It was on the threshing floor of Araunah^j the Jebusite, the place provided by David. ²He began building on the second day of the second month in the fourth year of his reign.

³The foundation Solomon laid for building the temple of God was sixty cubits long and twenty cubits wide^k (using the cubit of the old standard). ⁴The portico at the front of the temple was twenty cubits^l long across the width of the building and twenty cubits^m high. He overlaid the inside with pure gold. ⁵He paneled the main hall with pine and covered it with fine gold and decorated it with palm tree and chain designs. ⁶He adorned the temple with precious stones. And the gold he used was gold of Parvaim. ⁷He overlaid the ceiling beams, doorframes, walls and doors of the temple with gold, and he carved cherubim on the walls.

⁸He built the Most Holy Place, its length corresponding to the width of the temple—twenty cubits long and twenty cubits wide. He overlaid the inside with six hundred talentsⁿ of fine gold. ⁹The gold nails weighed fifty shekels.^o He also overlaid the upper parts with gold.

¹⁰In the Most Holy Place he made a pair of sculptured cherubim and overlaid them with gold. ¹¹The total wingspan of the cherubim was twenty cubits. One wing of the first cherub was five cubits^p long and touched the temple wall, while its other wing, also five cubits long, touched the wing of the other cherub. ¹²Similarly one wing of the second cherub was five cubits long and touched the other temple wall, and its other wing, also five cubits long, touched the wing of the first cherub. ¹³The wings of these cherubim extended twenty cubits. They stood on their feet, facing the main hall.^q

¹⁴He made the curtain of blue, purple and crimson yarn and fine linen, with cherubim worked into it.

¹⁵In the front of the temple he made two pillars, which ₗtogetherₗ were thirty-five

ʰ10 That is, probably about 125,000 bushels (about 4,400 kiloliters)   ⁱ10 That is, probably about 115,000 gallons (about 440 kiloliters)   ʲ1 Hebrew Ornan, a variant of Araunah   ᵏ3 That is, about 90 feet (about 27 meters) long and 30 feet (about 9 meters) wide   ˡ4 That is, about 30 feet (about 9 meters); also in verses 8, 11 and 13   ᵐ4 Some Septuagint and Syriac manuscripts; Hebrew and a hundred and twenty   ⁿ8 That is, about 23 tons (about 21 metric tons)   ᵒ9 That is, about 1 1/4 pounds (about 0.6 kilogram)   ᵖ11 That is, about 7 1/2 feet (about 2.3 meters); also in verse 15   ۹13 Or facing inward cubits[r] long, each with a capital on top measuring five cubits. [16]He made interwoven chains[s] and put them on top of the pillars. He also made a hundred pomegranates and attached them to the chains. [17]He erected the pillars in the front of the temple, one to the south and one to the north. The one to the south he named Jakin[t] and the one to the north Boaz.[u]

CHAPTER 4
He made a bronze altar twenty cubits long, twenty cubits wide and ten cubits high.[v] [2]He made the Sea of cast metal, circular in shape, measuring ten cubits from rim to rim and five cubits[w] high. It took a line of thirty cubits[x] to measure around it. [3]Below the rim, figures of bulls encircled it—ten to a cubit.[y] The bulls were cast in two rows in one piece with the Sea.

[4]The Sea stood on twelve bulls, three facing north, three facing west, three facing south and three facing east. The Sea rested on top of them, and their hindquarters were toward the center. [5]It was a handbreadth[z] in thickness, and its rim was like the rim of a cup, like a lily blossom. It held three thousand baths.[a]

[6]He then made ten basins for washing and placed five on the south side and five on the north. In them the things to be used for the burnt offerings were rinsed, but the Sea was to be used by the priests for washing.

[7]He made ten gold lampstands according to the specifications for them and placed them in the temple, five on the south side and five on the north.

[8]He made ten tables and placed them in the temple, five on the south side and five on the north. He also made a hundred gold sprinkling bowls.

[9]He made the courtyard of the priests, and the large court and the doors for the court, and overlaid the doors with bronze. [10]He placed the Sea on the south side, at the southeast corner.

[11]He also made the pots and shovels and sprinkling bowls.

So Huram finished the work he had undertaken for King Solomon in the temple of God:

[12]the two pillars;
the two bowl-shaped capitals on top of the pillars;
the two sets of network decorating the two bowl-shaped capitals on top of the pillars;
[13]the four hundred pomegranates for the two sets of network (two rows of pomegranates for each network, decorating the bowl-shaped capitals on top of the pillars);
[14]the stands with their basins;
[15]the Sea and the twelve bulls under it;
[16]the pots, shovels, meat forks and all related articles.

All the objects that Huram-Abi made for King Solomon for the temple of the LORD were of polished bronze. [17]The king had them cast in clay molds in the plain of the Jordan between Succoth and Zarethan.[b] [18]All these things that Solomon made amounted to so much that the weight of the bronze was not determined.

[19]Solomon also made all the furnishings that were in God's temple:

the golden altar;
the tables on which was the bread of the Presence;
[20]the lampstands of pure gold with their lamps, to burn in front of the inner sanctuary as prescribed;
[21]the gold floral work and lamps and tongs (they were solid gold);
[22]the pure gold wick trimmers, sprinkling bowls, dishes and censers; and the gold doors of the temple: the inner doors to the Most Holy Place and the doors of the main hall.

CHAPTER 5
When all the work Solomon had done for the temple of the LORD was finished, he brought in the things his father David had dedicated—the silver and gold and all the

---

[r]15 That is, about 52 feet (about 16 meters)   [s]16 Or possibly *made chains in the inner sanctuary*; the meaning of the Hebrew for this phrase is uncertain.   [t]17 *Jakin* probably means *he establishes.*   [u]17 *Boaz* probably means *in him is strength.*   [v]1 That is, about 30 feet (about 9 meters) long and wide, and about 15 feet (about 4.5 meters) high   [w]2 That is, about 7 1/2 feet (about 2.3 meters)   [x]2 That is, about 45 feet (about 13.5 meters)   [y]3 That is, about 1 1/2 feet (about 0.5 meter)   [z]5 That is, about 3 inches (about 8 centimeters)   [a]5 That is, about 17,500 gallons (about 66 kiloliters)   [b]17 Hebrew *Zeredatha*, a variant of *Zarethan*

furnishings—and he placed them in the treasuries of God's temple.

²Then Solomon summoned to Jerusalem the elders of Israel, all the heads of the tribes and the chiefs of the Israelite families, to bring up the ark of the LORD's covenant from Zion, the City of David. ³And all the men of Israel came together to the king at the time of the festival in the seventh month.

⁴When all the elders of Israel had arrived, the Levites took up the ark, ⁵and they brought up the ark and the Tent of Meeting and all the sacred furnishings in it. The priests, who were Levites, carried them up; ⁶and King Solomon and the entire assembly of Israel that had gathered about him were before the ark, sacrificing so many sheep and cattle that they could not be recorded or counted.

⁷The priests then brought the ark of the LORD's covenant to its place in the inner sanctuary of the temple, the Most Holy Place, and put it beneath the wings of the cherubim. ⁸The cherubim spread their wings over the place of the ark and covered the ark and its carrying poles. ⁹These poles were so long that their ends, extending from the ark, could be seen from in front of the inner sanctuary, but not from outside the Holy Place; and they are still there today. ¹⁰There was nothing in the ark except the two tablets that Moses had placed in it at Horeb, where the LORD made a covenant with the Israelites after they came out of Egypt.

¹¹The priests then withdrew from the Holy Place. All the priests who were there had consecrated themselves, regardless of their divisions. ¹²All the Levites who were musicians—Asaph, Heman, Jeduthun and their sons and relatives—stood on the east side of the altar, dressed in fine linen and playing cymbals, harps and lyres. They were accompanied by 120 priests sounding trumpets. ¹³The trumpeters and singers joined in unison, as with one voice, to give praise and thanks to the LORD. Accompanied by trumpets, cymbals and other instruments, they raised their voices in praise to the LORD and sang:

"He is good;
   his love endures forever."

Then the temple of the LORD was filled with a cloud, ¹⁴and the priests could not perform their service because of the cloud, for the glory of the LORD filled the temple of God.

APRIL 21 □ DAY 112
Sounds of Celebration

LOOK BACK The end of 2 Kings marks the end of two kingdoms. Assyria ransacks Israel, dispersing its population in the process (2 Kings 17). Babylonia descends upon defenseless Jerusalem, destroying its walls, burning its temple and dislocating many of its inhabitants (2 Kings 25).

Beginning with 1 Chronicles, the story takes a leap back in time, returning again to the days of King David. Don't worry, there's nothing wrong with your Bible. The books of 1 and 2 Chronicles retrace the same portion of the story you have already read in 2 Samuel through 2 Kings. Only this time you will see it through the eyes of a priest (perhaps Ezra, though we don't know for sure).

Parts of the story that were covered briefly in 2 Samuel through 2 Kings now unfold with exciting new detail in 1 and 2 Chronicles. Other accounts you've read in the books of Kings are omitted completely in the books of Chronicles in order to focus on the events that have the most profound spiritual impact upon David and his descendants. You'll enjoy this "second look" at the man after God's own heart (David), the son who followed in his footsteps (Solomon) and the descendants who perpetuated his dynasty (Judah).

LOOK UP In a few short weeks we'll reach the book of Psalms—the longest book in the Bible and the halfway point in your journey through the Bible. But you needn't wait till then to begin to read and enjoy these majestic anthems of praise and adoration penned by King David, for in 1 Chronicles 16 you'll discover portions of three psalms blended into one:

Since we fight for the liberty to worship, should we not make more use of that liberty?

Verses 8–22 are drawn from Psalm 105:1–15.
Verses 23–33 come from Psalm 96:1–13.
Verses 34–36 echo Psalm 106:1, 47–48.

As David and his appointed assistants ministered before the Lord, they found their hearts tugging in three directions: *upward* (in spontaneous praise to God), *outward* (in public testimony and thanksgiving for God's greatness) and *inward* (in humble dependence upon God). As you read the words of 1 Chronicles 16, you can almost hear the music ascending to heaven as the king and his people sing for joy before the Lord.

LOOK AHEAD Whether you are vocally gifted, instrumentally talented or "musically challenged," you will find ample motivation this week to sing to the Lord . . . praise the Lord . . . and give thanks to the Lord in musical worship. Set aside a few minutes to lift your voice or play your instrument to the glory of God. (No audience necessary but the Lord!) Here are the titles of several hymns and gospel songs you may want to use to focus your thoughts (along with the Scripture from which they are drawn):

• "How Great Thou Art" (Psalm 86:10)
• "Great Is the Lord" (Psalm 145:3)
• "Be Exalted, O God" (Psalm 57:10–11)
• "O Worship the King" (Psalm 104:1)
• "A Mighty Fortress Is Our God" (Psalm 46:1–7)
• "Holy, Holy, Holy" (Revelation 4:8)

Have you ever thought of composing your own poem of praise or song of celebration? Remember, God delights to hear our "joyful noise" made in adoration of him.

APRIL 22 ☐ DAY 113
2 CHRONICLES 6–9
Solomon's Worship and Works

OVERVIEW Humbly on his knees with hands outstretched to heaven, Solomon dedicates the temple worship with a moving prayer of consecration. This is more than the dedication of a building, however. It is also the dedication of a nation to make the temple of God and the God of the temple the center of everyday life. God appears to Solomon by night to make this promise: If Solomon will walk in the steps of his father, David, God will establish his dynasty forever. True to his word, God blesses Solomon's early years with immense wealth, national allegiance and international fame.

Chapter 6	Chapter 7	Chapter 8	Chapter 9	
Solomon's Prayer	God's Promise	Solomon's Fame	Solomon's Fortune	Solomon's Funeral
			1 28	29 31
Solomon's Worship		Solomon's Wealth		

YOUR DAILY WALK If your prayer life is normal, you have probably prayed often for God to bless you. But when was the last time you blessed God?

Bless the Lord today; he blesses you every day.

There is something God desires from you, something he is incapable of providing for himself. Naturally it's not money or power or possessions. God owns the cattle on a thousand hills (Psalm 50:10). He is high above all people (Psalm 99:2). So what could he possibly want that he does not already possess?

He wants your *praise.* Praise is a response of gratitude and worship to the goodness and blessing of God, a heartfelt thank-you from one of God's creatures for the benefits provided by the loving Creator. At the dedication of the temple, Solomon "turned around and blessed [the entire community of Israel]" (6:3). And then he did what his father, David, had urged in Psalm 103:2. "Praise the LORD, O my soul, and forget not all his benefits." Count how many blessings Solomon mentions in 6:4–11. (Can you find a dozen?) Then turn each benefit into an occasion to bless the Lord in a prayer of praise.

INSIGHT The Offering That Lasted Two Weeks
At the dedication of the temple, Solomon offered 22,000 bulls and 120,000 sheep in a peace offering to God (1 Kings 8:63). According to Leviticus, the peace offering was to be eaten by the offerer, which helps explain the fifteen days of feasting and the fact that the people returned home "joyful and glad" (7:5–10).

CHAPTER 6

Then Solomon said, "The LORD has said that he would dwell in a dark cloud; ²I have built a magnificent temple for you, a place for you to dwell forever."

³While the whole assembly of Israel was standing there, the king turned around and blessed them. ⁴Then he said:

"Praise be to the LORD, the God of Israel, who with his hands has fulfilled what he promised with his mouth to my father David. For he said, ⁵'Since the day I brought my people out of Egypt, I have not chosen a city in any tribe of Israel to have a temple built for my Name to be there, nor have I chosen anyone to be the leader over my people Israel. ⁶But now I have chosen Jerusalem for my Name to be there, and I have chosen David to rule my people Israel.'

⁷"My father David had it in his heart to build a temple for the Name of the LORD, the God of Israel. ⁸But the LORD said to my father David, 'Because it was in your heart to build a temple for my Name, you did well to have this in your heart. ⁹Nevertheless, you are not the one to build the temple, but your son, who is your own flesh and blood—he is the one who will build the temple for my Name.'

¹⁰"The LORD has kept the promise he made. I have succeeded David my father and now I sit on the throne of Israel, just as the LORD promised, and I have built the temple for the Name of the LORD, the God of Israel. ¹¹There I have placed the ark, in which is the covenant of the LORD that he made with the people of Israel."

¹²Then Solomon stood before the altar of the LORD in front of the whole assembly of Israel and spread out his hands. ¹³Now he had made a bronze platform, five cubits*c* long, five cubits wide and three cubits*d* high, and had placed it in the center

c13 That is, about 7 1/2 feet (about 2.3 meters)   *d13* That is, about 4 1/2 feet (about 1.3 meters) of the outer court. He stood on the platform and then knelt down before the whole assembly of Israel and spread out his hands toward heaven. [14]He said:

"O LORD, God of Israel, there is no God like you in heaven or on earth—you who keep your covenant of love with your servants who continue wholeheartedly in your way. [15]You have kept your promise to your servant David my father; with your mouth you have promised and with your hand you have fulfilled it—as it is today.

[16]"Now LORD, God of Israel, keep for your servant David my father the promises you made to him when you said, 'You shall never fail to have a man to sit before me on the throne of Israel, if only your sons are careful in all they do to walk before me according to my law, as you have done.' [17]And now, O LORD, God of Israel, let your word that you promised your servant David come true.

[18]"But will God really dwell on earth with men? The heavens, even the highest heavens, cannot contain you. How much less this temple I have built! [19]Yet give attention to your servant's prayer and his plea for mercy, O LORD my God. Hear the cry and the prayer that your servant is praying in your presence. [20]May your eyes be open toward this temple day and night, this place of which you said you would put your Name there. May you hear the prayer your servant prays toward this place. [21]Hear the supplications of your servant and of your people Israel when they pray toward this place. Hear from heaven, your dwelling place; and when you hear, forgive.

[22]"When a man wrongs his neighbor and is required to take an oath and he comes and swears the oath before your altar in this temple, [23]then hear from heaven and act. Judge between your servants, repaying the guilty by bringing down on his own head what he has done. Declare the innocent not guilty and so establish his innocence.

[24]"When your people Israel have been defeated by an enemy because they have sinned against you and when they turn back and confess your name, praying and making supplication before you in this temple, [25]then hear from heaven and forgive the sin of your people Israel and bring them back to the land you gave to them and their fathers.

[26]"When the heavens are shut up and there is no rain because your people have sinned against you, and when they pray toward this place and confess your name and turn from their sin because you have afflicted them, [27]then hear from heaven and forgive the sin of your servants, your people Israel. Teach them the right way to live, and send rain on the land you gave your people for an inheritance.

[28]"When famine or plague comes to the land, or blight or mildew, locusts or grasshoppers, or when enemies besiege them in any of their cities, whatever disaster or disease may come, [29]and when a prayer or plea is made by any of your people Israel—each one aware of his afflictions and pains, and spreading out his hands toward this temple— [30]then hear from heaven, your dwelling place. Forgive, and deal with each man according to all he does, since you know his heart (for you alone know the hearts of men), [31]so that they will fear you and walk in your ways all the time they live in the land you gave our fathers.

[32]"As for the foreigner who does not belong to your people Israel but has come from a distant land because of your great name and your mighty hand and your outstretched arm—when he comes and prays toward this temple, [33]then hear from heaven, your dwelling place, and do whatever the foreigner asks of you, so that all the peoples of the earth may know your name and fear you, as do your own people Israel, and may know that this house I have built bears your Name.

[34]"When your people go to war against their enemies, wherever you send them, and when they pray to you toward this city you have chosen and the temple I have built for your

Name, [35]then hear from heaven their prayer and their plea, and uphold their cause.

[36]"When they sin against you—for there is no one who does not sin—and you become angry with them and give them over to the enemy, who takes them captive to a land far away or near; [37]and if they have a change of heart in the land where they are held captive, and repent and plead with you in the land of their captivity and say, 'We have sinned, we have done wrong and acted wickedly'; [38]and if they turn back to you with all their heart and soul in the land of their captivity where they were taken, and pray toward the land you gave their fathers, toward the city you have chosen and toward the temple I have built for your Name; [39]then from heaven, your dwelling place, hear their prayer and their pleas, and uphold their cause. And forgive your people, who have sinned against you.

[40]"Now, my God, may your eyes be open and your ears attentive to the prayers offered in this place.

[41]"Now arise, O Lord God, and
　　come to your resting place,
　　you and the ark of your might.
May your priests, O Lord God, be
　　clothed with salvation,
　　may your saints rejoice in your
　　　goodness.
[42]O Lord God, do not reject your
　　anointed one.
　Remember the great love
　　promised to David your
　　servant."

CHAPTER 7

When Solomon finished praying, fire came down from heaven and consumed the burnt offering and the sacrifices, and the glory of the Lord filled the temple. [2]The priests could not enter the temple of the Lord because the glory of the Lord filled it. [3]When all the Israelites saw the fire coming down and the glory of the Lord above the temple, they knelt on the pavement with their faces to the ground, and they worshiped and gave thanks to the Lord, saying,

"He is good;
　his love endures forever."

[4]Then the king and all the people offered sacrifices before the Lord. [5]And King Solomon offered a sacrifice of twenty-two thousand head of cattle and a hundred and twenty thousand sheep and goats. So the king and all the people dedicated the temple of God. [6]The priests took their positions, as did the Levites with the Lord's musical instruments, which King David had made for praising the Lord and which were used when he gave thanks, saying, "His love endures forever." Opposite the Levites, the priests blew their trumpets, and all the Israelites were standing.

[7]Solomon consecrated the middle part of the courtyard in front of the temple of the Lord, and there he offered burnt offerings and the fat of the fellowship offerings,[e] because the bronze altar he had made could not hold the burnt offerings, the grain offerings and the fat portions.

[8]So Solomon observed the festival at that time for seven days, and all Israel with him—a vast assembly, people from Lebo[f] Hamath to the Wadi of Egypt. [9]On the eighth day they held an assembly, for they had celebrated the dedication of the altar for seven days and the festival for seven days more. [10]On the twenty-third day of the seventh month he sent the people to their homes, joyful and glad in heart for the good things the Lord had done for David and Solomon and for his people Israel.

[11]When Solomon had finished the temple of the Lord and the royal palace, and had succeeded in carrying out all he had in mind to do in the temple of the Lord and in his own palace, [12]the Lord appeared to him at night and said:

"I have heard your prayer and have chosen this place for myself as a temple for sacrifices.

[13]"When I shut up the heavens so that there is no rain, or command locusts to devour the land or send a plague among my people, [14]if my people, who are called by my name, will humble themselves and pray and seek my face and turn from their wicked ways, then will I hear from

---

[e]7 Traditionally *peace offerings*　　[f]8 Or *from the entrance to*

heaven and will forgive their sin and will heal their land. [15]Now my eyes will be open and my ears attentive to the prayers offered in this place. [16]I have chosen and consecrated this temple so that my Name may be there forever. My eyes and my heart will always be there.

[17]"As for you, if you walk before me as David your father did, and do all I command, and observe my decrees and laws, [18]I will establish your royal throne, as I covenanted with David your father when I said, 'You shall never fail to have a man to rule over Israel.'

[19]"But if you[g] turn away and forsake the decrees and commands I have given you[g] and go off to serve other gods and worship them, [20]then I will uproot Israel from my land, which I have given them, and will reject this temple I have consecrated for my Name. I will make it a byword and an object of ridicule among all peoples. [21]And though this temple is now so imposing, all who pass by will be appalled and say, 'Why has the LORD done such a thing to this land and to this temple?' [22]People will answer, 'Because they have forsaken the LORD, the God of their fathers, who brought them out of Egypt, and have embraced other gods, worshiping and serving them— that is why he brought all this disaster on them.' "

CHAPTER 8

At the end of twenty years, during which Solomon built the temple of the LORD and his own palace, [2]Solomon rebuilt the villages that Hiram[h] had given him, and settled Israelites in them. [3]Solomon then went to Hamath Zobah and captured it. [4]He also built up Tadmor in the desert and all the store cities he had built in Hamath. [5]He rebuilt Upper Beth Horon and Lower Beth Horon as fortified cities, with walls and with gates and bars, [6]as well as Baalath and all his store cities, and all the cities for his chariots and for his horses[i]—whatever he desired to build in

Jerusalem, in Lebanon and throughout all the territory he ruled.

[7]All the people left from the Hittites, Amorites, Perizzites, Hivites and Jebusites (these peoples were not Israelites), [8]that is, their descendants remaining in the land, whom the Israelites had not destroyed—these Solomon conscripted for his slave labor force, as it is to this day. [9]But Solomon did not make slaves of the Israelites for his work; they were his fighting men, commanders of his captains, and commanders of his chariots and charioteers. [10]They were also King Solomon's chief officials—two hundred and fifty officials supervising the men.

[11]Solomon brought Pharaoh's daughter up from the City of David to the palace he had built for her, for he said, "My wife must not live in the palace of David king of Israel, because the places the ark of the LORD has entered are holy."

[12]On the altar of the LORD that he had built in front of the portico, Solomon sacrificed burnt offerings to the LORD, [13]according to the daily requirement for offerings commanded by Moses for Sabbaths, New Moons and the three annual feasts—the Feast of Unleavened Bread, the Feast of Weeks and the Feast of Tabernacles. [14]In keeping with the ordinance of his father David, he appointed the divisions of the priests for their duties, and the Levites to lead the praise and to assist the priests according to each day's requirement. He also appointed the gatekeepers by divisions for the various gates, because this was what David the man of God had ordered. [15]They did not deviate from the king's commands to the priests or to the Levites in any matter, including that of the treasuries.

[16]All Solomon's work was carried out, from the day the foundation of the temple of the LORD was laid until its completion. So the temple of the LORD was finished.

[17]Then Solomon went to Ezion Geber and Elath on the coast of Edom. [18]And Hiram sent him ships commanded by his own officers, men who knew the sea. These, with Solomon's men, sailed to Ophir and brought back four hundred and fifty talents[j] of gold, which they delivered to King Solomon.

---

[g]19 The Hebrew is plural.　[h]2 Hebrew *Huram*, a variant of *Hiram*; also in verse 18　[i]6 Or *charioteers*　[j]18 That is, about 17 tons (about 16 metric tons)

CHAPTER 9

When the queen of Sheba heard of Solomon's fame, she came to Jerusalem to test him with hard questions. Arriving with a very great caravan—with camels carrying spices, large quantities of gold, and precious stones—she came to Solomon and talked with him about all she had on her mind. [2]Solomon answered all her questions; nothing was too hard for him to explain to her. [3]When the queen of Sheba saw the wisdom of Solomon, as well as the palace he had built, [4]the food on his table, the seating of his officials, the attending servants in their robes, the cupbearers in their robes and the burnt offerings he made at[k] the temple of the LORD, she was overwhelmed.

[5]She said to the king, "The report I heard in my own country about your achievements and your wisdom is true. [6]But I did not believe what they said until I came and saw with my own eyes. Indeed, not even half the greatness of your wisdom was told me; you have far exceeded the report I heard. [7]How happy your men must be! How happy your officials, who continually stand before you and hear your wisdom! [8]Praise be to the LORD your God, who has delighted in you and placed you on his throne as king to rule for the LORD your God. Because of the love of your God for Israel and his desire to uphold them forever, he has made you king over them, to maintain justice and righteousness."

[9]Then she gave the king 120 talents[l] of gold, large quantities of spices, and precious stones. There had never been such spices as those the queen of Sheba gave to King Solomon.

[10](The men of Hiram and the men of Solomon brought gold from Ophir; they also brought algumwood[m] and precious stones. [11]The king used the algumwood to make steps for the temple of the LORD and for the royal palace, and to make harps and lyres for the musicians. Nothing like them had ever been seen in Judah.)

[12]King Solomon gave the queen of Sheba all she desired and asked for; he gave her more than she had brought to him. Then she left and returned with her retinue to her own country.

[13]The weight of the gold that Solomon received yearly was 666 talents,[n] [14]not including the revenues brought in by merchants and traders. Also all the kings of Arabia and the governors of the land brought gold and silver to Solomon.

[15]King Solomon made two hundred large shields of hammered gold; six hundred bekas[o] of hammered gold went into each shield. [16]He also made three hundred small shields of hammered gold, with three hundred bekas[p] of gold in each shield. The king put them in the Palace of the Forest of Lebanon.

[17]Then the king made a great throne inlaid with ivory and overlaid with pure gold. [18]The throne had six steps, and a footstool of gold was attached to it. On both sides of the seat were armrests, with a lion standing beside each of them. [19]Twelve lions stood on the six steps, one at either end of each step. Nothing like it had ever been made for any other kingdom. [20]All King Solomon's goblets were gold, and all the household articles in the Palace of the Forest of Lebanon were pure gold. Nothing was made of silver, because silver was considered of little value in Solomon's day. [21]The king had a fleet of trading ships[q] manned by Hiram's[r] men. Once every three years it returned, carrying gold, silver and ivory, and apes and baboons.

[22]King Solomon was greater in riches and wisdom than all the other kings of the earth. [23]All the kings of the earth sought audience with Solomon to hear the wisdom God had put in his heart. [24]Year after year, everyone who came brought a gift—articles of silver and gold, and robes, weapons and spices, and horses and mules.

[25]Solomon had four thousand stalls for horses and chariots, and twelve thousand horses,[s] which he kept in the chariot cities and also with him in Jerusalem. [26]He ruled over all the kings from the River[t] to the land of the Philistines, as far as the border of Egypt. [27]The king made silver as common in Jerusalem as stones, and cedar as plentiful as sycamore-fig trees in the

---

[k]4 Or the ascent by which he went up to   [l]9 That is, about 4 1/2 tons (about 4 metric tons)   [m]10 Probably a variant of almugwood   [n]13 That is, about 25 tons (about 23 metric tons)   [o]15 That is, about 7 1/2 pounds (about 3.5 kilograms)   [p]16 That is, about 3 3/4 pounds (about 1.7 kilograms)   [q]21 Hebrew of ships that could go to Tarshish   [r]21 Hebrew Huram, a variant of Hiram   [s]25 Or charioteers   [t]26 That is, the Euphrates

foothills. ²⁸Solomon's horses were imported from Egypt^u and from all other countries.

²⁹As for the other events of Solomon's reign, from beginning to end, are they not written in the records of Nathan the prophet, in the prophecy of Ahijah the Shilonite and in the visions of Iddo the seer concerning Jeroboam son of Nebat? ³⁰Solomon reigned in Jerusalem over all Israel forty years. ³¹Then he rested with his fathers and was buried in the city of David his father. And Rehoboam his son succeeded him as king.

^u28 Or possibly *Muzur*, a region in Cilicia

APRIL 23 ☐ DAY 114
2 CHRONICLES 10–12
Rebellion against Rehoboam

 OVERVIEW Everything about Rehoboam is divided: from his counselors to his kingdom to his heart attitude toward God. While 1 Kings recounted the predicament in which Rehoboam found himself, Chronicles centers around the divine purpose behind it all: "So the king did not listen to the people, for this turn of events was from God, to fulfill the word the LORD had spoken . . . " (10:15). The result is open hostility between the north and south and the formation of two distinct national entities: Israel and Judah. After three years of outward compliance with God's law, Rehoboam once again shows his true colors by forsaking God and drawing away most of the people. At his death these words provide the divine commentary on his life: "He did evil because he had not set his heart on seeking the LORD" (12:14).

Chapter 10		Chapter 11	Chapter 12
A Divided Opinion	A Divided Nation	A Divided Heart	A Defaced Temple
1 15	16 19		
Rehoboam's Political Life		Rehoboam's Spiritual Life	

 YOUR DAILY WALK Here are some symptoms of a halfhearted love for God taken from the life of Rehoboam:
- Your words and actions promote division, not peace.
- You rely on your own strength, rather than God's.
- You worship God only when it is expedient for you.
- You distort God's plan and purpose for the family.
- You acknowledge God only when you feel helpless.

The more a person takes the needs of others to heart, the more he or she will take his or her own heart to God.

Rehoboam's self-serving indifference came to a sudden halt when God brought him face-to-face with death in the person of Shishak, king of Egypt. In humble helplessness, Rehoboam acknowledged his own wickedness and God's righteousness.

Are you halfhearted in your love for God? Then clear the channels of communication with him. Admit your waywardness, acknowledge his righteousness and get back in step with him. Don't wait until you're staring death in the face to set things right.

INSIGHT Double Coverage for Good News
The chronicler does not recognize the kings of the northern kingdom, Israel. From his viewpoint, only the descendants of David are legitimate rulers of the nation, even though it is sadly divided. Furthermore, the reigns of the eight good kings of Judah are given twice as much coverage as the twelve evil rulers.

CHAPTER 10

Rehoboam went to Shechem, for all the Israelites had gone there to make him king. [2]When Jeroboam son of Nebat heard this (he was in Egypt, where he had fled from King Solomon), he returned from Egypt. [3]So they sent for Jeroboam, and he and all Israel went to Rehoboam and said to him: [4]"Your father put a heavy yoke on us, but now lighten the harsh labor and the heavy yoke he put on us, and we will serve you."

[5]Rehoboam answered, "Come back to me in three days." So the people went away.

[6]Then King Rehoboam consulted the elders who had served his father Solomon during his lifetime. "How would you advise me to answer these people?" he asked.

[7]They replied, "If you will be kind to these people and please them and give them a favorable answer, they will always be your servants."

[8]But Rehoboam rejected the advice the elders gave him and consulted the young men who had grown up with him and were serving him. [9]He asked them, "What is your advice? How should we answer these people who say to me, 'Lighten the yoke your father put on us'?"

[10]The young men who had grown up with him replied, "Tell the people who have said to you, 'Your father put a heavy yoke on us, but make our yoke lighter'—tell them, 'My little finger is thicker than my father's waist. [11]My father laid on you a heavy yoke; I will make it even heavier. My father scourged you with whips; I will scourge you with scorpions.' "

[12]Three days later Jeroboam and all the people returned to Rehoboam, as the king had said, "Come back to me in three days." [13]The king answered them harshly. Rejecting the advice of the elders, [14]he followed the advice of the young men and said, "My father made your yoke heavy; I will make it even heavier. My father scourged you with whips; I will scourge you with scorpions." [15]So the king did not listen to the people, for this turn of events was from God, to fulfill the word the LORD had spoken to Jeroboam son of Nebat through Ahijah the Shilonite.

[16]When all Israel saw that the king refused to listen to them, they answered the king:

"What share do we have in David,
  what part in Jesse's son?
To your tents, O Israel!
  Look after your own house,
    O David!"

So all the Israelites went home. [17]But as for the Israelites who were living in the towns of Judah, Rehoboam still ruled over them.

[18]King Rehoboam sent out Adoniram,[v] who was in charge of forced labor, but the Israelites stoned him to death. King Rehoboam, however, managed to get into his chariot and escape to Jerusalem. [19]So Israel has been in rebellion against the house of David to this day.

CHAPTER 11

When Rehoboam arrived in Jerusalem, he mustered the house of Judah and Benjamin—a hundred and eighty thousand fighting men—to make war against Israel and to regain the kingdom for Rehoboam.

[2]But this word of the LORD came to Shemaiah the man of God: [3]"Say to Rehoboam son of Solomon king of Judah and to all the Israelites in Judah and Benjamin, [4]'This is what the LORD says: Do not go up to fight against your brothers. Go home, every one of you, for this is my doing.' " So they obeyed the words of the LORD and turned back from marching against Jeroboam.

[5]Rehoboam lived in Jerusalem and built up towns for defense in Judah: [6]Bethlehem, Etam, Tekoa, [7]Beth Zur, Soco, Adullam, [8]Gath, Mareshah, Ziph, [9]Adoraim, Lachish, Azekah, [10]Zorah, Aijalon and Hebron. These were fortified cities in Judah and Benjamin. [11]He strengthened their defenses and put commanders in them, with supplies of food, olive oil and wine. [12]He put shields and spears in all the cities, and made them very strong. So Judah and Benjamin were his.

[13]The priests and Levites from all their districts throughout Israel sided with him. [14]The Levites even abandoned their pasturelands and property, and came to Judah and Jerusalem because Jeroboam and his sons had rejected them as priests of the LORD. [15]And he appointed his own

[v]18 Hebrew Hadoram, a variant of Adoniram

priests for the high places and for the goat and calf idols he had made. [16]Those from every tribe of Israel who set their hearts on seeking the LORD, the God of Israel, followed the Levites to Jerusalem to offer sacrifices to the LORD, the God of their fathers. [17]They strengthened the kingdom of Judah and supported Rehoboam son of Solomon three years, walking in the ways of David and Solomon during this time.

[18]Rehoboam married Mahalath, who was the daughter of David's son Jerimoth and of Abihail, the daughter of Jesse's son Eliab. [19]She bore him sons: Jeush, Shemariah and Zaham. [20]Then he married Maacah daughter of Absalom, who bore him Abijah, Attai, Ziza and Shelomith. [21]Rehoboam loved Maacah daughter of Absalom more than any of his other wives and concubines. In all, he had eighteen wives and sixty concubines, twenty-eight sons and sixty daughters.

[22]Rehoboam appointed Abijah son of Maacah to be the chief prince among his brothers, in order to make him king. [23]He acted wisely, dispersing some of his sons throughout the districts of Judah and Benjamin, and to all the fortified cities. He gave them abundant provisions and took many wives for them.

CHAPTER 12

After Rehoboam's position as king was established and he had become strong, he and all Israel[w] with him abandoned the law of the LORD. [2]Because they had been unfaithful to the LORD, Shishak king of Egypt attacked Jerusalem in the fifth year of King Rehoboam. [3]With twelve hundred chariots and sixty thousand horsemen and the innumerable troops of Libyans, Sukkites and Cushites[x] that came with him from Egypt, [4]he captured the fortified cities of Judah and came as far as Jerusalem.

[5]Then the prophet Shemaiah came to Rehoboam and to the leaders of Judah who had assembled in Jerusalem for fear of Shishak, and he said to them, "This is what the LORD says, 'You have abandoned

me; therefore, I now abandon you to Shishak.' "

[6]The leaders of Israel and the king humbled themselves and said, "The LORD is just."

[7]When the LORD saw that they humbled themselves, this word of the LORD came to Shemaiah: "Since they have humbled themselves, I will not destroy them but will soon give them deliverance. My wrath will not be poured out on Jerusalem through Shishak. [8]They will, however, become subject to him, so that they may learn the difference between serving me and serving the kings of other lands."

[9]When Shishak king of Egypt attacked Jerusalem, he carried off the treasures of the temple of the LORD and the treasures of the royal palace. He took everything, including the gold shields Solomon had made. [10]So King Rehoboam made bronze shields to replace them and assigned these to the commanders of the guard on duty at the entrance to the royal palace. [11]Whenever the king went to the LORD's temple, the guards went with him, bearing the shields, and afterward they returned them to the guardroom.

[12]Because Rehoboam humbled himself, the LORD's anger turned from him, and he was not totally destroyed. Indeed, there was some good in Judah.

[13]King Rehoboam established himself firmly in Jerusalem and continued as king. He was forty-one years old when he became king, and he reigned seventeen years in Jerusalem, the city the LORD had chosen out of all the tribes of Israel in which to put his Name. His mother's name was Naamah; she was an Ammonite. [14]He did evil because he had not set his heart on seeking the LORD.

[15]As for the events of Rehoboam's reign, from beginning to end, are they not written in the records of Shemaiah the prophet and of Iddo the seer that deal with genealogies? There was continual warfare between Rehoboam and Jeroboam. [16]Rehoboam rested with his fathers and was buried in the City of David. And Abijah his son succeeded him as king.

[w]1 That is, Judah, as frequently in 2 Chronicles   [x]3 That is, people from the upper Nile region

APRIL 24 ☐ DAY 115
2 CHRONICLES 13–16
Reigns of Abijah and Asa

OVERVIEW Abijah, who "committed all the sins his father had done before him" (1 Kings 15:3), nevertheless is used by God to judge an even more corrupt king, Jeroboam in the north. Through Abijah God vindicates the temple in Jerusalem as the true place of worship. By contrast, Abijah's son Asa demonstrates a faith in God unparalleled since the days of Solomon and David! He removes idols, restores pure worship and reminds God often of his promise to fight on behalf of his people: "Lord, there is no one like you to help the powerless against the mighty. Help us, O Lord our God, for we rely on you, and in your name we have come against this vast army" (14:11).

Chapter 13	Chapters 14–15	Chapter 16
Abijah's Civil Struggle	Asa's Reliance on God	Asa's Alliance with Aram
Divine Deliverance		Divine Discipline

YOUR DAILY WALK Today's section contains a divine "classified ad." God is looking for a certain kind of person—someone to do an important job for him. Do you have the qualifications for the position?

The capital of heaven is the heart in which God is enthroned as king.

"Wanted: People with a heart loyal to God. No age limit. Experience not necessary. Educational background immaterial. Physical limitations no problem. Open to anyone, regardless of race, color, gender or national origin. Equal opportunity employer. No mandatory retirement age."

That's the gist of 16:9. God is searching diligently for men and women, boys and girls, whose heart attitude is right toward him. No matter if you're weak; God has strength in abundance! He's looking for those who are willing to make their lives a showcase for his power. Are you interested in the position? Then give heaven a call right now. (It's toll-free.) God is standing by to talk to you personally.

Just tell him Asa sent you!

INSIGHT Calling Out the Troops, One and All
In the war between Abijah and Jeroboam, 1.2 million troops were committed to the battle—800,000 for Israel and 400,000 for Judah (13:3). Compare these numbers with the census figures recorded in 2 Samuel 24:9 and 1 Chronicles 21:5. This was all-out war!

CHAPTER 13
In the eighteenth year of the reign of Jeroboam, Abijah became king of Judah, ²and he reigned in Jerusalem three years. His mother's name was Maacah,ʸ a daughterᶻ of Uriel of Gibeah.

There was war between Abijah and Jeroboam. ³Abijah went into battle with a force of four hundred thousand able fighting men, and Jeroboam drew up a battle line against him with eight hundred thousand able troops.

⁴Abijah stood on Mount Zemaraim, in the hill country of Ephraim, and said, "Jeroboam and all Israel, listen to me! ⁵Don't you know that the Lord, the God of Israel, has given the kingship of Israel to David and his descendants forever by a covenant of salt? ⁶Yet Jeroboam son of Nebat, an official of Solomon son of David, rebelled against his master. ⁷Some worthless scoundrels gathered around him and opposed Rehoboam son of Solomon when he was young and inde-

ʸ2 Most Septuagint manuscripts and Syriac (see also 2 Chron. 11:20 and 1 Kings 15:2); Hebrew *Micaiah*   ᶻ2 Or *granddaughter* cisive and not strong enough to resist them.

8"And now you plan to resist the kingdom of the LORD, which is in the hands of David's descendants. You are indeed a vast army and have with you the golden calves that Jeroboam made to be your gods. 9But didn't you drive out the priests of the LORD, the sons of Aaron, and the Levites, and make priests of your own as the peoples of other lands do? Whoever comes to consecrate himself with a young bull and seven rams may become a priest of what are not gods.

10"As for us, the LORD is our God, and we have not forsaken him. The priests who serve the LORD are sons of Aaron, and the Levites assist them. 11Every morning and evening they present burnt offerings and fragrant incense to the LORD. They set out the bread on the ceremonially clean table and light the lamps on the gold lampstand every evening. We are observing the requirements of the LORD our God. But you have forsaken him. 12God is with us; he is our leader. His priests with their trumpets will sound the battle cry against you. Men of Israel, do not fight against the LORD, the God of your fathers, for you will not succeed."

13Now Jeroboam had sent troops around to the rear, so that while he was in front of Judah the ambush was behind them. 14Judah turned and saw that they were being attacked at both front and rear. Then they cried out to the LORD. The priests blew their trumpets 15and the men of Judah raised the battle cry. At the sound of their battle cry, God routed Jeroboam and all Israel before Abijah and Judah. 16The Israelites fled before Judah, and God delivered them into their hands. 17Abijah and his men inflicted heavy losses on them, so that there were five hundred thousand casualties among Israel's able men. 18The men of Israel were subdued on that occasion, and the men of Judah were victorious because they relied on the LORD, the God of their fathers.

19Abijah pursued Jeroboam and took from him the towns of Bethel, Jeshanah and Ephron, with their surrounding villages. 20Jeroboam did not regain power during the time of Abijah. And the LORD struck him down and he died.

21But Abijah grew in strength. He married fourteen wives and had twenty-two sons and sixteen daughters. 22The other events of Abijah's reign, what he did and what he said, are written in the annotations of the prophet Iddo.

CHAPTER 14

And Abijah rested with his fathers and was buried in the City of David. Asa his son succeeded him as king, and in his days the country was at peace for ten years.

2Asa did what was good and right in the eyes of the LORD his God. 3He removed the foreign altars and the high places, smashed the sacred stones and cut down the Asherah poles.a 4He commanded Judah to seek the LORD, the God of their fathers, and to obey his laws and commands. 5He removed the high places and incense altars in every town in Judah, and the kingdom was at peace under him. 6He built up the fortified cities of Judah, since the land was at peace. No one was at war with him during those years, for the LORD gave him rest.

7"Let us build up these towns," he said to Judah, "and put walls around them, with towers, gates and bars. The land is still ours, because we have sought the LORD our God; we sought him and he has given us rest on every side." So they built and prospered.

8Asa had an army of three hundred thousand men from Judah, equipped with large shields and with spears, and two hundred and eighty thousand from Benjamin, armed with small shields and with bows. All these were brave fighting men.

9Zerah the Cushite marched out against them with a vast armyb and three hundred chariots, and came as far as Mareshah. 10Asa went out to meet him, and they took up battle positions in the Valley of Zephathah near Mareshah.

11Then Asa called to the LORD his God and said, "LORD, there is no one like you to help the powerless against the mighty. Help us, O LORD our God, for we rely on you, and in your name we have come against this vast army. O LORD, you are our God; do not let man prevail against you."

12The LORD struck down the Cushites

---

a3 That is, symbols of the goddess Asherah; here and elsewhere in 2 Chronicles   b9 Hebrew with an army of a thousand thousands or with an army of thousands upon thousands before Asa and Judah. The Cushites fled, [13]and Asa and his army pursued them as far as Gerar. Such a great number of Cushites fell that they could not recover; they were crushed before the LORD and his forces. The men of Judah carried off a large amount of plunder. [14]They destroyed all the villages around Gerar, for the terror of the LORD had fallen upon them. They plundered all these villages, since there was much booty there. [15]They also attacked the camps of the herdsmen and carried off droves of sheep and goats and camels. Then they returned to Jerusalem.

CHAPTER 15

The Spirit of God came upon Azariah son of Oded. [2]He went out to meet Asa and said to him, "Listen to me, Asa and all Judah and Benjamin. The LORD is with you when you are with him. If you seek him, he will be found by you, but if you forsake him, he will forsake you. [3]For a long time Israel was without the true God, without a priest to teach and without the law. [4]But in their distress they turned to the LORD, the God of Israel, and sought him, and he was found by them. [5]In those days it was not safe to travel about, for all the inhabitants of the lands were in great turmoil. [6]One nation was being crushed by another and one city by another, because God was troubling them with every kind of distress. [7]But as for you, be strong and do not give up, for your work will be rewarded."

[8]When Asa heard these words and the prophecy of Azariah son of[c] Oded the prophet, he took courage. He removed the detestable idols from the whole land of Judah and Benjamin and from the towns he had captured in the hills of Ephraim. He repaired the altar of the LORD that was in front of the portico of the LORD's temple.

[9]Then he assembled all Judah and Benjamin and the people from Ephraim, Manasseh and Simeon who had settled among them, for large numbers had come over to him from Israel when they saw that the LORD his God was with him.

[10]They assembled at Jerusalem in the third month of the fifteenth year of Asa's reign. [11]At that time they sacrificed to the LORD seven hundred head of cattle and seven thousand sheep and goats from the plunder they had brought back. [12]They entered into a covenant to seek the LORD, the God of their fathers, with all their heart and soul. [13]All who would not seek the LORD, the God of Israel, were to be put to death, whether small or great, man or woman. [14]They took an oath to the LORD with loud acclamation, with shouting and with trumpets and horns. [15]All Judah rejoiced about the oath because they had sworn it wholeheartedly. They sought God eagerly, and he was found by them. So the LORD gave them rest on every side.

[16]King Asa also deposed his grandmother Maacah from her position as queen mother, because she had made a repulsive Asherah pole. Asa cut the pole down, broke it up and burned it in the Kidron Valley. [17]Although he did not remove the high places from Israel, Asa's heart was fully committed ⌊to the LORD⌋ all his life. [18]He brought into the temple of God the silver and gold and the articles that he and his father had dedicated.

[19]There was no more war until the thirty-fifth year of Asa's reign.

CHAPTER 16

In the thirty-sixth year of Asa's reign Baasha king of Israel went up against Judah and fortified Ramah to prevent anyone from leaving or entering the territory of Asa king of Judah.

[2]Asa then took the silver and gold out of the treasuries of the LORD's temple and of his own palace and sent it to Ben-Hadad king of Aram, who was ruling in Damascus. [3]"Let there be a treaty between me and you," he said, "as there was between my father and your father. See, I am sending you silver and gold. Now break your treaty with Baasha king of Israel so he will withdraw from me."

[4]Ben-Hadad agreed with King Asa and sent the commanders of his forces against the towns of Israel. They conquered Ijon, Dan, Abel Maim[d] and all the store cities of Naphtali. [5]When Baasha heard this, he stopped building Ramah and abandoned his work. [6]Then King Asa brought all the men of Judah, and they carried away from Ramah the stones and timber Baasha

had been using. With them he built up Geba and Mizpah.

⁷At that time Hanani the seer came to Asa king of Judah and said to him: "Because you relied on the king of Aram and not on the LORD your God, the army of the king of Aram has escaped from your hand. ⁸Were not the Cushites*e* and Libyans a mighty army with great numbers of chariots and horsemen*f*? Yet when you relied on the LORD, he delivered them into your hand. ⁹For the eyes of the LORD range throughout the earth to strengthen those whose hearts are fully committed to him. You have done a foolish thing, and from now on you will be at war."

¹⁰Asa was angry with the seer because

of this; he was so enraged that he put him in prison. At the same time Asa brutally oppressed some of the people.

¹¹The events of Asa's reign, from beginning to end, are written in the book of the kings of Judah and Israel. ¹²In the thirty-ninth year of his reign Asa was afflicted with a disease in his feet. Though his disease was severe, even in his illness he did not seek help from the LORD, but only from the physicians. ¹³Then in the forty-first year of his reign Asa died and rested with his fathers. ¹⁴They buried him in the tomb that he had cut out for himself in the City of David. They laid him on a bier covered with spices and various blended perfumes, and they made a huge fire in his honor.

*e*8 That is, people from the upper Nile region   *f*8 Or *charioteers*

APRIL 25 ☐ DAY 116
2 CHRONICLES 17–20
Reform under Jehoshaphat

 OVERVIEW Building upon the foundation of his reformer father, Asa, Jehoshaphat appoints Levites to travel around the country carrying the law of the Lord and teaching the people the ways of the Lord. A quarter-century of godly leadership is nearly cut short by a foolish alliance between Jehoshaphat and Ahab, king of Israel. After being rebuked for his momentary lapse of faith, Jehoshaphat continues his reforming ways by destroying idols in the land and appointing judges to render righteous and impartial decisions in the courts.

Chapter 17	Chapter 18	Chapter 19	Chapter 20
Jehoshaphat's Teachers	Ahab's Death	Jehoshaphat's Judges	Moab's Defeat
Revival in the Cities		Reform in the Courts	

 YOUR DAILY WALK When times of crisis come to your family, how do you respond? Does the pressure pull you apart or weld you closer together? Do you find yourself praying less as a family or more?

Pessimism is pulling tomorrow's cloud over today's sunshine.

Jehoshaphat faced a crisis. The Moabites and Ammonites were massing their troops in preparation for an all-out assault on Judah. Jehoshaphat had every right to be afraid . . . withdrawn . . . worried . . . and indecisive. But instead, his response was exemplary. He gathered all Judah together to seek help from the Lord. In an unprecedented national call to prayer, "all the men of Judah, with their wives and children and little ones, stood there before the LORD" (20:13)—a prayer meeting involving every member of the family!

Is that what happens in your home? If not, gather your family together to discuss a crisis you are facing as a family or as a nation. Allow each person to pray for God's strength and wisdom in the midst of the crisis. You'll find your love deepening for the God to whom you pray, as well as for the people you pray with and those you pray for.

 INSIGHT Beating Yourself at Your Own Game
As part of God's divine strategy for giving Jehoshaphat the victory over Moab and Ammon, "they helped to destroy one another" (20:23, i.e., the enemy forces fought and killed each other). Can you think of another Old Testament battle where the same thing happened? (Hint: See Judges 7:22.)

CHAPTER 17

Jehoshaphat his son succeeded him as king and strengthened himself against Israel. ²He stationed troops in all the fortified cities of Judah and put garrisons in Judah and in the towns of Ephraim that his father Asa had captured.

³The LORD was with Jehoshaphat because in his early years he walked in the ways his father David had followed. He did not consult the Baals ⁴but sought the God of his father and followed his commands rather than the practices of Israel. ⁵The LORD established the kingdom under his control; and all Judah brought gifts to Jehoshaphat, so that he had great wealth and honor. ⁶His heart was devoted to the ways of the LORD; furthermore, he removed the high places and the Asherah poles from Judah.

⁷In the third year of his reign he sent his officials Ben-Hail, Obadiah, Zechariah, Nethanel and Micaiah to teach in the towns of Judah. ⁸With them were certain Levites—Shemaiah, Nethaniah, Zebadiah, Asahel, Shemiramoth, Jehonathan, Adonijah, Tobijah and Tob-Adonijah—and the priests Elishama and Jehoram. ⁹They taught throughout Judah, taking with them the Book of the Law of the LORD; they went around to all the towns of Judah and taught the people.

¹⁰The fear of the LORD fell on all the kingdoms of the lands surrounding Judah, so that they did not make war with Jehoshaphat. ¹¹Some Philistines brought Jehoshaphat gifts and silver as tribute, and the Arabs brought him flocks: seven thousand seven hundred rams and seven thousand seven hundred goats.

¹²Jehoshaphat became more and more powerful; he built forts and store cities in Judah ¹³and had large supplies in the towns of Judah. He also kept experienced fighting men in Jerusalem. ¹⁴Their enrollment by families was as follows:

From Judah, commanders of units of 1,000:
Adnah the commander, with 300,000 fighting men;
¹⁵next, Jehohanan the commander, with 280,000;
¹⁶next, Amasiah son of Zicri, who volunteered himself for the service of the LORD, with 200,000.
¹⁷From Benjamin:
Eliada, a valiant soldier, with 200,000 men armed with bows and shields;
¹⁸next, Jehozabad, with 180,000 men armed for battle.

¹⁹These were the men who served the king, besides those he stationed in the fortified cities throughout Judah.

CHAPTER 18

Now Jehoshaphat had great wealth and honor, and he allied himself with Ahab by marriage. ²Some years later he went down to visit Ahab in Samaria. Ahab slaughtered many sheep and cattle for him and the people with him and urged him to attack Ramoth Gilead. ³Ahab king of Israel asked Jehoshaphat king of Judah, "Will you go with me against Ramoth Gilead?"

Jehoshaphat replied, "I am as you are, and my people as your people; we will join you in the war." ⁴But Jehoshaphat also said to the king of Israel, "First seek the counsel of the LORD."

⁵So the king of Israel brought together the prophets—four hundred men—and asked them, "Shall we go to war against Ramoth Gilead, or shall I refrain?"

"Go," they answered, "for God will give it into the king's hand."

⁶But Jehoshaphat asked, "Is there not a prophet of the LORD here whom we can inquire of?"

⁷The king of Israel answered Jehoshaphat, "There is still one man through

whom we can inquire of the LORD, but I hate him because he never prophesies anything good about me, but always bad. He is Micaiah son of Imlah."

"The king should not say that," Jehoshaphat replied.

⁸So the king of Israel called one of his officials and said, "Bring Micaiah son of Imlah at once."

⁹Dressed in their royal robes, the king of Israel and Jehoshaphat king of Judah were sitting on their thrones at the threshing floor by the entrance to the gate of Samaria, with all the prophets prophesying before them. ¹⁰Now Zedekiah son of Kenaanah had made iron horns, and he declared, "This is what the LORD says: 'With these you will gore the Arameans until they are destroyed.' "

¹¹All the other prophets were prophesying the same thing. "Attack Ramoth Gilead and be victorious," they said, "for the LORD will give it into the king's hand."

¹²The messenger who had gone to summon Micaiah said to him, "Look, as one man the other prophets are predicting success for the king. Let your word agree with theirs, and speak favorably."

¹³But Micaiah said, "As surely as the LORD lives, I can tell him only what my God says."

¹⁴When he arrived, the king asked him, "Micaiah, shall we go to war against Ramoth Gilead, or shall I refrain?"

"Attack and be victorious," he answered, "for they will be given into your hand."

¹⁵The king said to him, "How many times must I make you swear to tell me nothing but the truth in the name of the LORD?"

¹⁶Then Micaiah answered, "I saw all Israel scattered on the hills like sheep without a shepherd, and the LORD said, 'These people have no master. Let each one go home in peace.' "

¹⁷The king of Israel said to Jehoshaphat, "Didn't I tell you that he never prophesies anything good about me, but only bad?"

¹⁸Micaiah continued, "Therefore hear the word of the LORD: I saw the LORD sitting on his throne with all the host of heaven standing on his right and on his left. ¹⁹And the LORD said, 'Who will entice Ahab king of Israel into attacking Ramoth Gilead and going to his death there?'

"One suggested this, and another that. ²⁰Finally, a spirit came forward, stood before the LORD and said, 'I will entice him.'

" 'By what means?' the LORD asked.

²¹" 'I will go and be a lying spirit in the mouths of all his prophets,' he said.

" 'You will succeed in enticing him,' said the LORD. 'Go and do it.'

²²"So now the LORD has put a lying spirit in the mouths of these prophets of yours. The LORD has decreed disaster for you."

²³Then Zedekiah son of Kenaanah went up and slapped Micaiah in the face. "Which way did the spirit from⁸ the LORD go when he went from me to speak to you?" he asked.

²⁴Micaiah replied, "You will find out on the day you go to hide in an inner room."

²⁵The king of Israel then ordered, "Take Micaiah and send him back to Amon the ruler of the city and to Joash the king's son, ²⁶and say, 'This is what the king says: Put this fellow in prison and give him nothing but bread and water until I return safely.' "

²⁷Micaiah declared, "If you ever return safely, the LORD has not spoken through me." Then he added, "Mark my words, all you people!"

²⁸So the king of Israel and Jehoshaphat king of Judah went up to Ramoth Gilead. ²⁹The king of Israel said to Jehoshaphat, "I will enter the battle in disguise, but you wear your royal robes." So the king of Israel disguised himself and went into battle.

³⁰Now the king of Aram had ordered his chariot commanders, "Do not fight with anyone, small or great, except the king of Israel." ³¹When the chariot commanders saw Jehoshaphat, they thought, "This is the king of Israel." So they turned to attack him, but Jehoshaphat cried out, and the LORD helped him. God drew them away from him, ³²for when the chariot commanders saw that he was not the king of Israel, they stopped pursuing him.

³³But someone drew his bow at random and hit the king of Israel between the sections of his armor. The king told the chariot driver, "Wheel around and get me out

⁸23 Or Spirit of

of the fighting. I've been wounded." ³⁴All day long the battle raged, and the king of Israel propped himself up in his chariot facing the Arameans until evening. Then at sunset he died.

CHAPTER 19

When Jehoshaphat king of Judah returned safely to his palace in Jerusalem, ²Jehu the seer, the son of Hanani, went out to meet him and said to the king, "Should you help the wicked and love*ʰ* those who hate the Lord? Because of this, the wrath of the Lord is upon you. ³There is, however, some good in you, for you have rid the land of the Asherah poles and have set your heart on seeking God."

⁴Jehoshaphat lived in Jerusalem, and he went out again among the people from Beersheba to the hill country of Ephraim and turned them back to the Lord, the God of their fathers. ⁵He appointed judges in the land, in each of the fortified cities of Judah. ⁶He told them, "Consider carefully what you do, because you are not judging for man but for the Lord, who is with you whenever you give a verdict. ⁷Now let the fear of the Lord be upon you. Judge carefully, for with the Lord our God there is no injustice or partiality or bribery."

⁸In Jerusalem also, Jehoshaphat appointed some of the Levites, priests and heads of Israelite families to administer the law of the Lord and to settle disputes. And they lived in Jerusalem. ⁹He gave them these orders: "You must serve faithfully and wholeheartedly in the fear of the Lord. ¹⁰In every case that comes before you from your fellow countrymen who live in the cities—whether bloodshed or other concerns of the law, commands, decrees or ordinances—you are to warn them not to sin against the Lord; otherwise his wrath will come on you and your brothers. Do this, and you will not sin.

¹¹"Amariah the chief priest will be over you in any matter concerning the Lord, and Zebadiah son of Ishmael, the leader of the tribe of Judah, will be over you in any matter concerning the king, and the Levites will serve as officials before you. Act with courage, and may the Lord be with those who do well."

CHAPTER 20

After this, the Moabites and Ammonites with some of the Meunites*ⁱ* came to make war on Jehoshaphat.

²Some men came and told Jehoshaphat, "A vast army is coming against you from Edom,*ʲ* from the other side of the Sea.*ᵏ* It is already in Hazazon Tamar" (that is, En Gedi). ³Alarmed, Jehoshaphat resolved to inquire of the Lord, and he proclaimed a fast for all Judah. ⁴The people of Judah came together to seek help from the Lord; indeed, they came from every town in Judah to seek him.

⁵Then Jehoshaphat stood up in the assembly of Judah and Jerusalem at the temple of the Lord in the front of the new courtyard ⁶and said:

"O Lord, God of our fathers, are you not the God who is in heaven? You rule over all the kingdoms of the nations. Power and might are in your hand, and no one can withstand you. ⁷O our God, did you not drive out the inhabitants of this land before your people Israel and give it forever to the descendants of Abraham your friend? ⁸They have lived in it and have built in it a sanctuary for your Name, saying, ⁹'If calamity comes upon us, whether the sword of judgment, or plague or famine, we will stand in your presence before this temple that bears your Name and will cry out to you in our distress, and you will hear us and save us.'

¹⁰"But now here are men from Ammon, Moab and Mount Seir, whose territory you would not allow Israel to invade when they came from Egypt; so they turned away from them and did not destroy them. ¹¹See how they are repaying us by coming to drive us out of the possession you gave us as an inheritance. ¹²O our God, will you not judge them? For we have no power to face this vast army that is attacking us. We do not know what to do, but our eyes are upon you."

¹³All the men of Judah, with their wives and children and little ones, stood there before the Lord. ¹⁴Then the Spirit of the Lord came upon

---

*ʰ*2 Or *and make alliances with*   *ⁱ*1 Some Septuagint manuscripts; Hebrew *Ammonites*   *ʲ*2 One Hebrew manuscript; most Hebrew manuscripts, Septuagint and Vulgate *Aram*   *ᵏ*2 That is, the Dead Sea

Jahaziel son of Zechariah, the son of Benaiah, the son of Jeiel, the son of Mattaniah, a Levite and descendant of Asaph, as he stood in the assembly.

¹⁵He said: "Listen, King Jehoshaphat and all who live in Judah and Jerusalem! This is what the LORD says to you: 'Do not be afraid or discouraged because of this vast army. For the battle is not yours, but God's. ¹⁶Tomorrow march down against them. They will be climbing up by the Pass of Ziz, and you will find them at the end of the gorge in the Desert of Jeruel. ¹⁷You will not have to fight this battle. Take up your positions; stand firm and see the deliverance the LORD will give you, O Judah and Jerusalem. Do not be afraid; do not be discouraged. Go out to face them tomorrow, and the LORD will be with you.' "

¹⁸Jehoshaphat bowed with his face to the ground, and all the people of Judah and Jerusalem fell down in worship before the LORD. ¹⁹Then some Levites from the Kohathites and Korahites stood up and praised the LORD, the God of Israel, with very loud voice.

²⁰Early in the morning they left for the Desert of Tekoa. As they set out, Jehoshaphat stood and said, "Listen to me, Judah and people of Jerusalem! Have faith in the LORD your God and you will be upheld; have faith in his prophets and you will be successful." ²¹After consulting the people, Jehoshaphat appointed men to sing to the LORD and to praise him for the splendor of his[l] holiness as they went out at the head of the army, saying:

"Give thanks to the LORD,
    for his love endures forever."

²²As they began to sing and praise, the LORD set ambushes against the men of Ammon and Moab and Mount Seir who were invading Judah, and they were defeated. ²³The men of Ammon and Moab rose up against the men from Mount Seir to destroy and annihilate them. After they finished slaughtering the men from Seir, they helped to destroy one another.

²⁴When the men of Judah came to the place that overlooks the desert and looked toward the vast army, they saw only dead bodies lying on the ground; no one had escaped. ²⁵So Jehoshaphat and his men went to carry off their plunder, and they found among them a great amount of equipment and clothing[m] and also articles of value—more than they could take away. There was so much plunder that it took three days to collect it. ²⁶On the fourth day they assembled in the Valley of Beracah, where they praised the LORD. This is why it is called the Valley of Beracah[n] to this day.

²⁷Then, led by Jehoshaphat, all the men of Judah and Jerusalem returned joyfully to Jerusalem, for the LORD had given them cause to rejoice over their enemies. ²⁸They entered Jerusalem and went to the temple of the LORD with harps and lutes and trumpets.

²⁹The fear of God came upon all the kingdoms of the countries when they heard how the LORD had fought against the enemies of Israel. ³⁰And the kingdom of Jehoshaphat was at peace, for his God had given him rest on every side.

³¹So Jehoshaphat reigned over Judah. He was thirty-five years old when he became king of Judah, and he reigned in Jerusalem twenty-five years. His mother's name was Azubah daughter of Shilhi. ³²He walked in the ways of his father Asa and did not stray from them; he did what was right in the eyes of the LORD. ³³The high places, however, were not removed, and the people still had not set their hearts on the God of their fathers.

³⁴The other events of Jehoshaphat's reign, from beginning to end, are written in the annals of Jehu son of Hanani, which are recorded in the book of the kings of Israel.

³⁵Later, Jehoshaphat king of Judah made an alliance with Ahaziah king of Israel, who was guilty of wickedness. ³⁶He agreed with him to construct a fleet of trading ships.[o] After these were built at Ezion Geber, ³⁷Eliezer son of Dodavahu of Mareshah prophesied against Jehoshaphat, saying, "Because you have made an alliance with Ahaziah, the LORD will destroy what you have made." The ships were wrecked and were not able to set sail to trade.[p]

---

[l]21 Or *him with the splendor of*   [m]25 Some Hebrew manuscripts and Vulgate; most Hebrew manuscripts *corpses*   [n]26 *Beracah* means *praise*.   [o]36 Hebrew *of ships that could go to Tarshish*   [p]37 Hebrew *sail for Tarshish*

APRIL 26 ☐ DAY 117
2 CHRONICLES 21–25
Reigns of Jehoram to Amaziah

 OVERVIEW Jehoshaphat's spiritual gains in the nation are all too soon wiped out by the wicked reigns of Jehoram, Ahaziah and Athaliah. Before reading the tale of intrigue and bloodshed, be sure you understand the family relationships between the main characters and the significance of little Joash's survival as the sole remaining heir of David's dynasty.

North (Israel)		South (Judah)
Ahab ──┬── Jezebel		Jehoshaphat
(husband) │ (wife)		│
Athaliah ──────── (wife/husband) ──────── Jehoram (son)		│
(daughter)	└──── Ahaziah (son)
	│
	Joash (son)

Chapter 21	Chapter 22		Chapters 23–24	Chapter 25
Idolatry in the Palace			Inconsistency in the Palace	
Jehoram	Ahaziah	Athaliah	Joash	Amaziah
	9	10 12		
"Evil in the eyes of the LORD"			"Right in the eyes of the LORD"	

 YOUR DAILY WALK There are two parts to any military conquest: (1) the initial assault, and (2) the "mopping up" operation that deals with any lingering resistance. Keeping that in mind, consider this principle that holds true both in military and spiritual realms: Pockets of resistance, if left unchallenged, can lead to rebellion. Dealing with those pockets is not optional; it is essential if complete victory is to be achieved.

When evil thoughts come into your heart, dash them at once on the rock of Christ.

Study the life of good king Joash, and you will quickly detect some pockets of resistance in his spiritual life: idolatry (24:18), insensitivity to the message of God's prophet (24:19–21) and cruelty in the face of kindness (24:22). How about you? Are there any areas of your life that have become pockets of resistance, such as

- Finances?
- Pride?
- Time with God?
- Gossip?
- Thought life?
- Time with family?

Pick an area of resistance and deal with it today!

 INSIGHT The Reign of Joash—Judah's History in Miniature
The life of Joash reads like a condensed history of Judah. He began his reign by living righteously, yet in later years abandoned the Lord, killed the prophet who rebuked him, was defeated by a foreign power and died a humiliating death for his many crimes.

CHAPTER 21

Then Jehoshaphat rested with his fathers and was buried with them in the City of David. And Jehoram his son succeeded him as king. ²Jehoram's brothers, the sons of Jehoshaphat, were Azariah, Jehiel, Zechariah, Azariahu, Michael and Shephatiah. All these were sons of Jehoshaphat king of Israel.*ᑫ* ³Their father had given them many gifts of silver and gold and articles of value, as well as fortified cities in Judah, but he had given the kingdom to

ᑫ2 That is, Judah, as frequently in 2 Chronicles

Jehoram because he was his firstborn son.

⁴When Jehoram established himself firmly over his father's kingdom, he put all his brothers to the sword along with some of the princes of Israel. ⁵Jehoram was thirty-two years old when he became king, and he reigned in Jerusalem eight years. ⁶He walked in the ways of the kings of Israel, as the house of Ahab had done, for he married a daughter of Ahab. He did evil in the eyes of the LORD. ⁷Nevertheless, because of the covenant the LORD had made with David, the LORD was not willing to destroy the house of David. He had promised to maintain a lamp for him and his descendants forever.

⁸In the time of Jehoram, Edom rebelled against Judah and set up its own king. ⁹So Jehoram went there with his officers and all his chariots. The Edomites surrounded him and his chariot commanders, but he rose up and broke through by night. ¹⁰To this day Edom has been in rebellion against Judah.

Libnah revolted at the same time, because Jehoram had forsaken the LORD, the God of his fathers. ¹¹He had also built high places on the hills of Judah and had caused the people of Jerusalem to prostitute themselves and had led Judah astray.

¹²Jehoram received a letter from Elijah the prophet, which said:

"This is what the LORD, the God of your father David, says: 'You have not walked in the ways of your father Jehoshaphat or of Asa king of Judah. ¹³But you have walked in the ways of the kings of Israel, and you have led Judah and the people of Jerusalem to prostitute themselves, just as the house of Ahab did. You have also murdered your own brothers, members of your father's house, men who were better than you. ¹⁴So now the LORD is about to strike your people, your sons, your wives and everything that is yours, with a heavy blow. ¹⁵You yourself will be very ill with a lingering disease of the bowels, until the disease causes your bowels to come out.' "

¹⁶The LORD aroused against Jehoram the hostility of the Philistines and of the Arabs who lived near the Cushites. ¹⁷They attacked Judah, invaded it and carried off all the goods found in the king's palace, together with his sons and wives. Not a son was left to him except Ahaziah,ʳ the youngest.

¹⁸After all this, the LORD afflicted Jehoram with an incurable disease of the bowels. ¹⁹In the course of time, at the end of the second year, his bowels came out because of the disease, and he died in great pain. His people made no fire in his honor, as they had for his fathers.

²⁰Jehoram was thirty-two years old when he became king, and he reigned in Jerusalem eight years. He passed away, to no one's regret, and was buried in the City of David, but not in the tombs of the kings.

CHAPTER 22

The people of Jerusalem made Ahaziah, Jehoram's youngest son, king in his place, since the raiders, who came with the Arabs into the camp, had killed all the older sons. So Ahaziah son of Jehoram king of Judah began to reign.

²Ahaziah was twenty-twoˢ years old when he became king, and he reigned in Jerusalem one year. His mother's name was Athaliah, a granddaughter of Omri.

³He too walked in the ways of the house of Ahab, for his mother encouraged him in doing wrong. ⁴He did evil in the eyes of the LORD, as the house of Ahab had done, for after his father's death they became his advisers, to his undoing. ⁵He also followed their counsel when he went with Joramᵗ son of Ahab king of Israel to war against Hazael king of Aram at Ramoth Gilead. The Arameans wounded Joram; ⁶so he returned to Jezreel to recover from the wounds they had inflicted on him at Ramothᵘ in his battle with Hazael king of Aram.

Then Ahaziahᵛ son of Jehoram king of Judah went down to Jezreel to see Joram son of Ahab because he had been wounded.

⁷Through Ahaziah's visit to Joram, God brought about Ahaziah's downfall. When Ahaziah arrived, he went out with Joram to meet Jehu son of Nimshi, whom the LORD had anointed to destroy the house of

ʳ17 Hebrew Jehoahaz, a variant of Ahaziah   ˢ2 Some Septuagint manuscripts and Syriac (see also 2 Kings 8:26); Hebrew forty-two   ᵗ5 Hebrew Jehoram, a variant of Joram; also in verses 6 and 7   ᵘ6 Hebrew Ramah, a variant of Ramoth   ᵛ6 Some Hebrew manuscripts, Septuagint, Vulgate and Syriac (see also 2 Kings 8:29); most Hebrew manuscripts Azariah

Ahab. ⁸While Jehu was executing judgment on the house of Ahab, he found the princes of Judah and the sons of Ahaziah's relatives, who had been attending Ahaziah, and he killed them. ⁹He then went in search of Ahaziah, and his men captured him while he was hiding in Samaria. He was brought to Jehu and put to death. They buried him, for they said, "He was a son of Jehoshaphat, who sought the LORD with all his heart." So there was no one in the house of Ahaziah powerful enough to retain the kingdom.

¹⁰When Athaliah the mother of Ahaziah saw that her son was dead, she proceeded to destroy the whole royal family of the house of Judah. ¹¹But Jehosheba,ʷ the daughter of King Jehoram, took Joash son of Ahaziah and stole him away from among the royal princes who were about to be murdered and put him and his nurse in a bedroom. Because Jehosheba,ʷ the daughter of King Jehoram and wife of the priest Jehoiada, was Ahaziah's sister, she hid the child from Athaliah so she could not kill him. ¹²He remained hidden with them at the temple of God for six years while Athaliah ruled the land.

CHAPTER 23

In the seventh year Jehoiada showed his strength. He made a covenant with the commanders of units of a hundred: Azariah son of Jeroham, Ishmael son of Jehohanan, Azariah son of Obed, Maaseiah son of Adaiah, and Elishaphat son of Zicri. ²They went throughout Judah and gathered the Levites and the heads of Israelite families from all the towns. When they came to Jerusalem, ³the whole assembly made a covenant with the king at the temple of God.

Jehoiada said to them, "The king's son shall reign, as the LORD promised concerning the descendants of David. ⁴Now this is what you are to do: A third of you priests and Levites who are going on duty on the Sabbath are to keep watch at the doors, ⁵a third of you at the royal palace and a third at the Foundation Gate, and all the other men are to be in the courtyards of the temple of the LORD. ⁶No one is to enter the temple of the LORD except the priests and Levites on duty; they may enter because they are consecrated, but all

the other men are to guard what the LORD has assigned to them.ˣ ⁷The Levites are to station themselves around the king, each man with his weapons in his hand. Anyone who enters the temple must be put to death. Stay close to the king wherever he goes."

⁸The Levites and all the men of Judah did just as Jehoiada the priest ordered. Each one took his men—those who were going on duty on the Sabbath and those who were going off duty—for Jehoiada the priest had not released any of the divisions. ⁹Then he gave the commanders of units of a hundred the spears and the large and small shields that had belonged to King David and that were in the temple of God. ¹⁰He stationed all the men, each with his weapon in his hand, around the king—near the altar and the temple, from the south side to the north side of the temple.

¹¹Jehoiada and his sons brought out the king's son and put the crown on him; they presented him with a copy of the covenant and proclaimed him king. They anointed him and shouted, "Long live the king!"

¹²When Athaliah heard the noise of the people running and cheering the king, she went to them at the temple of the LORD. ¹³She looked, and there was the king, standing by his pillar at the entrance. The officers and the trumpeters were beside the king, and all the people of the land were rejoicing and blowing trumpets, and singers with musical instruments were leading the praises. Then Athaliah tore her robes and shouted, "Treason! Treason!"

¹⁴Jehoiada the priest sent out the commanders of units of a hundred, who were in charge of the troops, and said to them: "Bring her out between the ranksʸ and put to the sword anyone who follows her." For the priest had said, "Do not put her to death at the temple of the LORD." ¹⁵So they seized her as she reached the entrance of the Horse Gate on the palace grounds, and there they put her to death.

¹⁶Jehoiada then made a covenant that he and the people and the kingᶻ would be the LORD's people. ¹⁷All the people went to the temple of Baal and tore it down. They smashed the altars and idols

---

ʷ11 Hebrew *Jehoshabeath*, a variant of *Jehosheba*   ˣ6 Or *to observe the LORD's command*ᵧ*not to enter*ᵧ   ʸ14 Or *out from the precincts*   ᶻ16 Or *covenant between*ᵧ*the LORD*ᵧ*and the people and the king that they* (see 2 Kings 11:17) and killed Mattan the priest of Baal in front of the altars.

¹⁸Then Jehoiada placed the oversight of the temple of the LORD in the hands of the priests, who were Levites, to whom David had made assignments in the temple, to present the burnt offerings of the LORD as written in the Law of Moses, with rejoicing and singing, as David had ordered. ¹⁹He also stationed doorkeepers at the gates of the LORD's temple so that no one who was in any way unclean might enter.

²⁰He took with him the commanders of hundreds, the nobles, the rulers of the people and all the people of the land and brought the king down from the temple of the LORD. They went into the palace through the Upper Gate and seated the king on the royal throne, ²¹and all the people of the land rejoiced. And the city was quiet, because Athaliah had been slain with the sword.

CHAPTER 24
Joash was seven years old when he became king, and he reigned in Jerusalem forty years. His mother's name was Zibiah; she was from Beersheba. ²Joash did what was right in the eyes of the LORD all the years of Jehoiada the priest. ³Jehoiada chose two wives for him, and he had sons and daughters.

⁴Some time later Joash decided to restore the temple of the LORD. ⁵He called together the priests and Levites and said to them, "Go to the towns of Judah and collect the money due annually from all Israel, to repair the temple of your God. Do it now." But the Levites did not act at once.

⁶Therefore the king summoned Jehoiada the chief priest and said to him, "Why haven't you required the Levites to bring in from Judah and Jerusalem the tax imposed by Moses the servant of the LORD and by the assembly of Israel for the Tent of the Testimony?"

⁷Now the sons of that wicked woman Athaliah had broken into the temple of God and had used even its sacred objects for the Baals.

⁸At the king's command, a chest was made and placed outside, at the gate of the temple of the LORD. ⁹A proclamation was then issued in Judah and Jerusalem that they should bring to the LORD the tax that Moses the servant of God had required of Israel in the desert. ¹⁰All the officials and all the people brought their contributions gladly, dropping them into the chest until it was full. ¹¹Whenever the chest was brought in by the Levites to the king's officials and they saw that there was a large amount of money, the royal secretary and the officer of the chief priest would come and empty the chest and carry it back to its place. They did this regularly and collected a great amount of money. ¹²The king and Jehoiada gave it to the men who carried out the work required for the temple of the LORD. They hired masons and carpenters to restore the LORD's temple, and also workers in iron and bronze to repair the temple.

¹³The men in charge of the work were diligent, and the repairs progressed under them. They rebuilt the temple of God according to its original design and reinforced it. ¹⁴When they had finished, they brought the rest of the money to the king and Jehoiada, and with it were made articles for the LORD's temple: articles for the service and for the burnt offerings, and also dishes and other objects of gold and silver. As long as Jehoiada lived, burnt offerings were presented continually in the temple of the LORD.

¹⁵Now Jehoiada was old and full of years, and he died at the age of a hundred and thirty. ¹⁶He was buried with the kings in the City of David, because of the good he had done in Israel for God and his temple.

¹⁷After the death of Jehoiada, the officials of Judah came and paid homage to the king, and he listened to them. ¹⁸They abandoned the temple of the LORD, the God of their fathers, and worshiped Asherah poles and idols. Because of their guilt, God's anger came upon Judah and Jerusalem. ¹⁹Although the LORD sent prophets to the people to bring them back to him, and though they testified against them, they would not listen.

²⁰Then the Spirit of God came upon Zechariah son of Jehoiada the priest. He stood before the people and said, "This is what God says: 'Why do you disobey the LORD's commands? You will not prosper. Because you have forsaken the LORD, he has forsaken you.'"

²¹But they plotted against him, and by order of the king they stoned him to death in the courtyard of the LORD's temple.

²²King Joash did not remember the kindness Zechariah's father Jehoiada had shown him but killed his son, who said as he lay dying, "May the LORD see this and call you to account."

²³At the turn of the year,ᵃ the army of Aram marched against Joash; it invaded Judah and Jerusalem and killed all the leaders of the people. They sent all the plunder to their king in Damascus. ²⁴Although the Aramean army had come with only a few men, the LORD delivered into their hands a much larger army. Because Judah had forsaken the LORD, the God of their fathers, judgment was executed on Joash. ²⁵When the Arameans withdrew, they left Joash severely wounded. His officials conspired against him for murdering the son of Jehoiada the priest, and they killed him in his bed. So he died and was buried in the City of David, but not in the tombs of the kings.

²⁶Those who conspired against him were Zabad,ᵇ son of Shimeath an Ammonite woman, and Jehozabad, son of Shimrithᶜ a Moabite woman. ²⁷The account of his sons, the many prophecies about him, and the record of the restoration of the temple of God are written in the annotations on the book of the kings. And Amaziah his son succeeded him as king.

CHAPTER 25

Amaziah was twenty-five years old when he became king, and he reigned in Jerusalem twenty-nine years. His mother's name was Jehoaddinᵈ; she was from Jerusalem. ²He did what was right in the eyes of the LORD, but not wholeheartedly. ³After the kingdom was firmly in his control, he executed the officials who had murdered his father the king. ⁴Yet he did not put their sons to death, but acted in accordance with what is written in the Law, in the Book of Moses, where the LORD commanded: "Fathers shall not be put to death for their children, nor children put to death for their fathers; each is to die for his own sins."ᵉ

⁵Amaziah called the people of Judah together and assigned them according to their families to commanders of thousands and commanders of hundreds for all Judah and Benjamin. He then mustered those twenty years old or more and found that there were three hundred thousand men ready for military service, able to handle the spear and shield. ⁶He also hired a hundred thousand fighting men from Israel for a hundred talentsᶠ of silver.

⁷But a man of God came to him and said, "O king, these troops from Israel must not march with you, for the LORD is not with Israel—not with any of the people of Ephraim. ⁸Even if you go and fight courageously in battle, God will overthrow you before the enemy, for God has the power to help or to overthrow."

⁹Amaziah asked the man of God, "But what about the hundred talents I paid for these Israelite troops?"

The man of God replied, "The LORD can give you much more than that."

¹⁰So Amaziah dismissed the troops who had come to him from Ephraim and sent them home. They were furious with Judah and left for home in a great rage.

¹¹Amaziah then marshaled his strength and led his army to the Valley of Salt, where he killed ten thousand men of Seir. ¹²The army of Judah also captured ten thousand men alive, took them to the top of a cliff and threw them down so that all were dashed to pieces.

¹³Meanwhile the troops that Amaziah had sent back and had not allowed to take part in the war raided Judean towns from Samaria to Beth Horon. They killed three thousand people and carried off great quantities of plunder.

¹⁴When Amaziah returned from slaughtering the Edomites, he brought back the gods of the people of Seir. He set them up as his own gods, bowed down to them and burned sacrifices to them. ¹⁵The anger of the LORD burned against Amaziah, and he sent a prophet to him, who said, "Why do you consult this people's gods, which could not save their own people from your hand?"

¹⁶While he was still speaking, the king said to him, "Have we appointed you an adviser to the king? Stop! Why be struck down?"

So the prophet stopped but said, "I know that God has determined to destroy you, because you have done this and have not listened to my counsel."

ᵃ23 Probably in the spring   ᵇ26 A variant of *Jozabad*   ᶜ26 A variant of *Shomer*   ᵈ1 Hebrew *Jehoaddan*, a variant of *Jehoaddin*   ᵉ4 Deut. 24:16   ᶠ6 That is, about 3 3/4 tons (about 3.4 metric tons); also in verse 9

¹⁷After Amaziah king of Judah consulted his advisers, he sent this challenge to Jehoash⁸ son of Jehoahaz, the son of Jehu, king of Israel: "Come, meet me face to face."

¹⁸But Jehoash king of Israel replied to Amaziah king of Judah: "A thistle in Lebanon sent a message to a cedar in Lebanon, 'Give your daughter to my son in marriage.' Then a wild beast in Lebanon came along and trampled the thistle underfoot. ¹⁹You say to yourself that you have defeated Edom, and now you are arrogant and proud. But stay at home! Why ask for trouble and cause your own downfall and that of Judah also?"

²⁰Amaziah, however, would not listen, for God so worked that he might hand them over to ₗJehoashₗ, because they sought the gods of Edom. ²¹So Jehoash king of Israel attacked. He and Amaziah king of Judah faced each other at Beth Shemesh in Judah. ²²Judah was routed by Israel, and every man fled to his home. ²³Jehoash king of Israel captured Amaziah

king of Judah, the son of Joash, the son of Ahaziah,ʰ at Beth Shemesh. Then Jehoash brought him to Jerusalem and broke down the wall of Jerusalem from the Ephraim Gate to the Corner Gate—a section about six hundred feetⁱ long. ²⁴He took all the gold and silver and all the articles found in the temple of God that had been in the care of Obed-Edom, together with the palace treasures and the hostages, and returned to Samaria.

²⁵Amaziah son of Joash king of Judah lived for fifteen years after the death of Jehoash son of Jehoahaz king of Israel. ²⁶As for the other events of Amaziah's reign, from beginning to end, are they not written in the book of the kings of Judah and Israel? ²⁷From the time that Amaziah turned away from following the LORD, they conspired against him in Jerusalem and he fled to Lachish, but they sent men after him to Lachish and killed him there. ²⁸He was brought back by horse and was buried with his fathers in the City of Judah.

⁸17 Hebrew *Joash*, a variant of *Jehoash*; also in verses 18, 21, 23 and 25   ʰ23 Hebrew *Jehoahaz*, a variant of *Ahaziah*
ⁱ23 Hebrew *four hundred cubits* (about 180 meters)

APRIL 27 □ DAY 118
2 CHRONICLES 26–28
Reigns of Uzziah to Ahaz

 OVERVIEW Uzziah's fifty-two-year reign can be summarized in a dozen words: "As long as he sought the LORD, God gave him success" (26:5). His administration sparkles with military, architectural and agricultural achievements. But the luster is dimmed in his final years when he intrudes into the priests' functions and dies of leprosy. His son Jotham picks up where his father left off by becoming "powerful because he walked steadfastly before the LORD his God" (27:6). But after nearly seven decades of godly national leadership, Ahaz emerges to undo much of what his father and grandfather had accomplished. Forbidden alliances, infant sacrifices and rank idolatry bring the nation of Judah to its knees "because of Ahaz . . . for he had promoted wickedness in Judah and had been most unfaithful to the LORD" (28:19).

Chapter 26	Chapter 27	Chapter 28
Uzziah, Usurper in the Temple	Jotham, Giant on the Battlefield	Ahaz, Heathen in the Palace
Pride	Prosperity	Pollution

YOUR DAILY WALK Take a few minutes to complete the following statements:

"You will stay stronger and healthier *physically* if you . . ."

"You will stay stronger and healthier *financially* if you . . ."

When you see a worthy person, emulate him or her; when you see an unworthy person, examine yourself.

"You will stay stronger and healthier *emotionally* if you . . ."

Now that you have the hang of it, try the really hard one!

"You will stay stronger and healthier *spiritually* if you . . ."

Just as there are God-given principles for physical, financial and emotional health, so, too, there are God-given principles for spiritual health. Keep them and you will enjoy the benefits; violate them and you will pay the penalty. Uzziah and Jotham learned that painful lesson. Have you? Take your own counsel (as revealed in the way you completed the last sentence), compare it with Scripture and look for a way to put it to work today.

INSIGHT A Century of Unemployed Prophets

As long as Judah's kings were obeying God's commands, there was no need for the prophet's ultimatum: Shape up or judgment will fall! That message was reserved for wicked kings and wicked times in the nation. Thus, during the century of godly leadership under Joash, Amaziah, Uzziah and Jotham (835–732 B.C.), prophets were largely out of work!

CHAPTER 26

Then all the people of Judah took Uzziah,[j] who was sixteen years old, and made him king in place of his father Amaziah. [2]He was the one who rebuilt Elath and restored it to Judah after Amaziah rested with his fathers.

[3]Uzziah was sixteen years old when he became king, and he reigned in Jerusalem fifty-two years. His mother's name was Jecoliah; she was from Jerusalem. [4]He did what was right in the eyes of the LORD, just as his father Amaziah had done. [5]He sought God during the days of Zechariah, who instructed him in the fear[k] of God. As long as he sought the LORD, God gave him success.

[6]He went to war against the Philistines and broke down the walls of Gath, Jabneh and Ashdod. He then rebuilt towns near Ashdod and elsewhere among the Philistines. [7]God helped him against the Philistines and against the Arabs who lived in Gur Baal and against the Meunites. [8]The Ammonites brought tribute to Uzziah, and his fame spread as far as the border of Egypt, because he had become very powerful.

[9]Uzziah built towers in Jerusalem at the Corner Gate, at the Valley Gate and at the angle of the wall, and he fortified them. [10]He also built towers in the desert and dug many cisterns, because he had much livestock in the foothills and in the plain. He had people working his fields and vineyards in the hills and in the fertile lands, for he loved the soil.

[11]Uzziah had a well-trained army, ready to go out by divisions according to their numbers as mustered by Jeiel the secretary and Maaseiah the officer under the direction of Hananiah, one of the royal officials. [12]The total number of family leaders over the fighting men was 2,600. [13]Under their command was an army of 307,500 men trained for war, a powerful force to support the king against his enemies. [14]Uzziah provided shields, spears, helmets, coats of armor, bows and slingstones for the entire army. [15]In Jerusalem he made machines designed by skillful men for use on the towers and on the corner defenses to shoot arrows and hurl large stones. His fame spread far and wide, for he was greatly helped until he became powerful.

[16]But after Uzziah became powerful, his pride led to his downfall. He was unfaithful to the LORD his God, and entered the temple of the LORD to burn incense on the altar of incense. [17]Azariah the priest with eighty other courageous priests of the LORD followed him in. [18]They confronted him and said, "It is not right for you, Uzziah, to burn incense to the LORD. That is for the priests, the descendants of

j1 Also called Azariah   k5 Many Hebrew manuscripts, Septuagint and Syriac; other Hebrew manuscripts vision

Aaron, who have been consecrated to burn incense. Leave the sanctuary, for you have been unfaithful; and you will not be honored by the LORD God."

[19]Uzziah, who had a censer in his hand ready to burn incense, became angry. While he was raging at the priests in their presence before the incense altar in the LORD's temple, leprosy[l] broke out on his forehead. [20]When Azariah the chief priest and all the other priests looked at him, they saw that he had leprosy on his forehead, so they hurried him out. Indeed, he himself was eager to leave, because the LORD had afflicted him.

[21]King Uzziah had leprosy until the day he died. He lived in a separate house[m]— leprous, and excluded from the temple of the LORD. Jotham his son had charge of the palace and governed the people of the land.

[22]The other events of Uzziah's reign, from beginning to end, are recorded by the prophet Isaiah son of Amoz. [23]Uzziah rested with his fathers and was buried near them in a field for burial that belonged to the kings, for people said, "He had leprosy." And Jotham his son succeeded him as king.

CHAPTER 27

Jotham was twenty-five years old when he became king, and he reigned in Jerusalem sixteen years. His mother's name was Jerusha daughter of Zadok. [2]He did what was right in the eyes of the LORD, just as his father Uzziah had done, but unlike him he did not enter the temple of the LORD. The people, however, continued their corrupt practices. [3]Jotham rebuilt the Upper Gate of the temple of the LORD and did extensive work on the wall at the hill of Ophel. [4]He built towns in the Judean hills and forts and towers in the wooded areas.

[5]Jotham made war on the king of the Ammonites and conquered them. That year the Ammonites paid him a hundred talents[n] of silver, ten thousand cors[o] of wheat and ten thousand cors of barley. The Ammonites brought him the same amount also in the second and third years.

[6]Jotham grew powerful because he

walked steadfastly before the LORD his God.

[7]The other events in Jotham's reign, including all his wars and the other things he did, are written in the book of the kings of Israel and Judah. [8]He was twenty-five years old when he became king, and he reigned in Jerusalem sixteen years. [9]Jotham rested with his fathers and was buried in the City of David. And Ahaz his son succeeded him as king.

CHAPTER 28

Ahaz was twenty years old when he became king, and he reigned in Jerusalem sixteen years. Unlike David his father, he did not do what was right in the eyes of the LORD. [2]He walked in the ways of the kings of Israel and also made cast idols for worshiping the Baals. [3]He burned sacrifices in the Valley of Ben Hinnom and sacrificed his sons in the fire, following the detestable ways of the nations the LORD had driven out before the Israelites. [4]He offered sacrifices and burned incense at the high places, on the hilltops and under every spreading tree.

[5]Therefore the LORD his God handed him over to the king of Aram. The Arameans defeated him and took many of his people as prisoners and brought them to Damascus.

He was also given into the hands of the king of Israel, who inflicted heavy casualties on him. [6]In one day Pekah son of Remaliah killed a hundred and twenty thousand soldiers in Judah—because Judah had forsaken the LORD, the God of their fathers. [7]Zicri, an Ephraimite warrior, killed Maaseiah the king's son, Azrikam the officer in charge of the palace, and Elkanah, second to the king. [8]The Israelites took captive from their kinsmen two hundred thousand wives, sons and daughters. They also took a great deal of plunder, which they carried back to Samaria.

[9]But a prophet of the LORD named Oded was there, and he went out to meet the army when it returned to Samaria. He said to them, "Because the LORD, the God of your fathers, was angry with Judah, he gave them into your hand. But you have slaughtered them in a rage that reaches to

[l]19 The Hebrew word was used for various diseases affecting the skin—not necessarily leprosy; also in verses 20, 21 and 23.
[m]21 Or *in a house where he was relieved of responsibilities*   [n]5 That is, about 3 3/4 tons (about 3.4 metric tons)   [o]5 That is, probably about 62,000 bushels (about 2,200 kiloliters)

heaven. ¹⁰And now you intend to make the men and women of Judah and Jerusalem your slaves. But aren't you also guilty of sins against the LORD your God? ¹¹Now listen to me! Send back your fellow countrymen you have taken as prisoners, for the LORD's fierce anger rests on you."

¹²Then some of the leaders in Ephraim—Azariah son of Jehohanan, Berekiah son of Meshillemoth, Jehizkiah son of Shallum, and Amasa son of Hadlai—confronted those who were arriving from the war. ¹³"You must not bring those prisoners here," they said, "or we will be guilty before the LORD. Do you intend to add to our sin and guilt? For our guilt is already great, and his fierce anger rests on Israel."

¹⁴So the soldiers gave up the prisoners and plunder in the presence of the officials and all the assembly. ¹⁵The men designated by name took the prisoners, and from the plunder they clothed all who were naked. They provided them with clothes and sandals, food and drink, and healing balm. All those who were weak they put on donkeys. So they took them back to their fellow countrymen at Jericho, the City of Palms, and returned to Samaria.

¹⁶At that time King Ahaz sent to the king[p] of Assyria for help. ¹⁷The Edomites had again come and attacked Judah and carried away prisoners, ¹⁸while the Philistines had raided towns in the foothills and in the Negev of Judah. They captured and occupied Beth Shemesh, Aijalon and Gederoth, as well as Soco, Timnah and Gimzo, with their surrounding villages. ¹⁹The LORD had humbled Judah because of Ahaz king of Israel,[q] for he had promoted wickedness in Judah and had been most unfaithful to the LORD. ²⁰Tiglath-Pileser[r] king of Assyria came to him, but he gave him trouble instead of help. ²¹Ahaz took some of the things from the temple of the LORD and from the royal palace and from the princes and presented them to the king of Assyria, but that did not help him.

²²In his time of trouble King Ahaz became even more unfaithful to the LORD. ²³He offered sacrifices to the gods of Damascus, who had defeated him; for he thought, "Since the gods of the kings of Aram have helped them, I will sacrifice to them so they will help me." But they were his downfall and the downfall of all Israel.

²⁴Ahaz gathered together the furnishings from the temple of God and took them away.[s] He shut the doors of the LORD's temple and set up altars at every street corner in Jerusalem. ²⁵In every town in Judah he built high places to burn sacrifices to other gods and provoked the LORD, the God of his fathers, to anger.

²⁶The other events of his reign and all his ways, from beginning to end, are written in the book of the kings of Judah and Israel. ²⁷Ahaz rested with his fathers and was buried in the city of Jerusalem, but he was not placed in the tombs of the kings of Israel. And Hezekiah his son succeeded him as king.

[p]16 One Hebrew manuscript, Septuagint and Vulgate (see also 2 Kings 16:7); most Hebrew manuscripts *kings*   [q]19 That is, Judah, as frequently in 2 Chronicles   [r]20 Hebrew *Tilgath-Pilneser*, a variant of *Tiglath-Pileser*   [s]24 Or *and cut them up*

APRIL 28 □ DAY 119
Ageless Obedience

 LOOK BACK First Chronicles provides a priestly view of David's reign. Second Chronicles continues this "divine editorial" by focusing on David's descendants, the kings who ruled over the southern kingdom of Judah. Kings whose names were barely mentioned in 2 Kings receive extensive space in 2 Chronicles, and for good reason. Asa, Jehoshaphat, Joash, Uzziah and Jotham led reforms that helped to restore righteousness and postpone judgment for decades. They made a difference in their generation because they walked with God and used their God-given influence for good.

Notice how the chronicler highlights both the *what* of their reign and the *why* behind their success (emphasis added):

"The LORD was with Jehoshaphat *because* in his early years he walked in the ways his father David had followed" (2 Chronicles 17:3).

"*As long as* [Uzziah] sought the LORD, God gave him success" (2 Chronicles 26:5).

"Jotham grew powerful *because* he walked steadfastly before the LORD his God" (2 Chronicles 27:6).

Sadly, the influence of these godly kings is largely blunted by the cumulative effect of many more ungodly kings. The spiral is clearly downward, and time is running out for Judah.

LOOK UP There were no headlines in Uzziah's day, but if there had been, they might have read: "Teenager Takes Over Reins of Government."

Obedience sheds light on the hidden things of God.

At the tender age of sixteen, the boy-king Uzziah began a reign that would eventually stretch more than half a century. Barely old enough to drive a chariot, Uzziah suddenly found himself steering an entire nation! Armed with a healthy fear of God, a robust commitment to do what was right and a circle of godly advisers, Uzziah wasted no time "going to school" on his nation. Here's how his report card might have looked, according to 2 Chronicles 26:

Achievements: "He went to war . . . and broke down the walls of Gath, Jabneh and Ashdod."

Architecture: "He also built towers . . . and dug many cisterns . . ."

Agriculture: "He had much livestock . . . He had people working his fields and vineyards . . ."

Armed forces: "[He] had a well-trained army . . . of 307,500 men trained for war."

Accolades: "His fame spread far and wide, for . . . he became powerful."

Straight A's in his kingly curriculum, to be sure. And yet, when the final report card was in, Uzziah had failed in the role of king because "after [he] became powerful, his pride led to his downfall" (26:16). Arrogance and presumption later in life resulted in his being stricken with leprosy and dying a tragic death.

LOOK AHEAD Believe it or not, an even younger king than Uzziah once sat upon the throne of Judah—a seven-year-old named Joash (2 Chronicles 24:1)! Faithfulness to God knows no age limit. Whether young or old, you are the right age to seek God and obey him with a whole heart.

The apostle Paul underscored this point when he told his youthful understudy Timothy, "Don't let anyone look down on you because you are young, but set an example for the believers in speech, in life, in love, in faith and in purity" (1 Timothy 4:12).

Now there's a homework assignment you can spend a lifetime completing!

APRIL 29 ☐ DAY 120
2 CHRONICLES 29–32
Reform under Hezekiah

OVERVIEW Ahaz's son Hezekiah inherits a nation that is spiritually cold, militarily weak and politically disorganized. And brutal Assyrian forces threaten Judah's very existence. What should Hezekiah do first: reorganize the palace or rearm his troops? Wisely he chooses to reestablish the worship of God as the nation's top priority. In the first month of his administration, Hezekiah reopens and repairs the house of the Lord, restores observance of the Passover and declares war on idol worship and pagan practices. When the Assyrians come, Hezekiah handles the danger as he has handled so many decisions before: on his knees. God answers Hezekiah's prayer and honors his faith by bringing Assyria to defeat without a single Israelite soldier being lost in battle!

Chapter 29	Chapters 30–31	Chapter 32
Hezekiah's Rapid Reforms	Hezekiah's Passover Preparations	Hezekiah's Divine Deliverance
Correction	Celebration	Confrontation

YOUR DAILY WALK Some of the kings in 2 Chronicles are described in as few as nine verses (e.g., Jotham, 27:1–9); others command as much as four chapters (e.g., Jehoshaphat and Hezekiah). Can you suggest a reason for this uneven treatment and selective emphasis on Judah's kings?

Faith is the tendril by which the soul clings to God.

God's Word is not blind to the failures of his children, but neither is it stingy in its praise of those who lived out their faith day by day. Do you need a godly model to encourage you in your walk with God? Then look no further than such heroes of the faith as Solomon, Asa, Jehoshaphat, Joash or Hezekiah.

Walking by faith is not an impossible assignment. In God's strength it can be done. They did it . . . and so can you! Complete this sentence: "The hero of the faith from 2 Chronicles I most admire is _____ because _____."

INSIGHT The Day the People Led the Priests in Worship
In the days of Ahaz, the priests had done nothing to oppose the godless activities of the king (2 Kings 16:10–16). Now the zeal of the people in returning to the worship of the Lord and observance of the Passover shamed the priests into action. They, too, sanctified themselves and brought burnt offerings to the temple (30:15).

CHAPTER 29

Hezekiah was twenty-five years old when he became king, and he reigned in Jerusalem twenty-nine years. His mother's name was Abijah daughter of Zechariah. ²He did what was right in the eyes of the LORD, just as his father David had done.

³In the first month of the first year of his reign, he opened the doors of the temple of the LORD and repaired them. ⁴He brought in the priests and the Levites, assembled them in the square on the east side ⁵and said: "Listen to me, Levites! Consecrate yourselves now and consecrate the temple of the LORD, the God of your fathers. Remove all defilement from the sanctuary. ⁶Our fathers were unfaithful; they did evil in the eyes of the LORD our God and forsook him. They turned their faces away from the LORD's dwelling place and turned their backs on him.

[7]They also shut the doors of the portico and put out the lamps. They did not burn incense or present any burnt offerings at the sanctuary to the God of Israel. [8]Therefore, the anger of the LORD has fallen on Judah and Jerusalem; he has made them an object of dread and horror and scorn, as you can see with your own eyes. [9]This is why our fathers have fallen by the sword and why our sons and daughters and our wives are in captivity. [10]Now I intend to make a covenant with the LORD, the God of Israel, so that his fierce anger will turn away from us. [11]My sons, do not be negligent now, for the LORD has chosen you to stand before him and serve him, to minister before him and to burn incense."

[12]Then these Levites set to work:

from the Kohathites,
> Mahath son of Amasai and Joel son of Azariah;

from the Merarites,
> Kish son of Abdi and Azariah son of Jehallelel;

from the Gershonites,
> Joah son of Zimmah and Eden son of Joah;

[13]from the descendants of Elizaphan,
> Shimri and Jeiel;

from the descendants of Asaph,
> Zechariah and Mattaniah;

[14]from the descendants of Heman,
> Jehiel and Shimei;

from the descendants of Jeduthun,
> Shemaiah and Uzziel.

[15]When they had assembled their brothers and consecrated themselves, they went in to purify the temple of the LORD, as the king had ordered, following the word of the LORD. [16]The priests went into the sanctuary of the LORD to purify it. They brought out to the courtyard of the LORD's temple everything unclean that they found in the temple of the LORD. The Levites took it and carried it out to the Kidron Valley. [17]They began the consecration on the first day of the first month, and by the eighth day of the month they reached the portico of the LORD. For eight more days they consecrated the temple of the LORD itself, finishing on the sixteenth day of the first month.

[18]Then they went in to King Hezekiah and reported: "We have purified the entire temple of the LORD, the altar of burnt offering with all its utensils, and the table for setting out the consecrated bread, with all its articles. [19]We have prepared and consecrated all the articles that King Ahaz removed in his unfaithfulness while he was king. They are now in front of the LORD's altar."

[20]Early the next morning King Hezekiah gathered the city officials together and went up to the temple of the LORD. [21]They brought seven bulls, seven rams, seven male lambs and seven male goats as a sin offering for the kingdom, for the sanctuary and for Judah. The king commanded the priests, the descendants of Aaron, to offer these on the altar of the LORD. [22]So they slaughtered the bulls, and the priests took the blood and sprinkled it on the altar; next they slaughtered the rams and sprinkled their blood on the altar; then they slaughtered the lambs and sprinkled their blood on the altar. [23]The goats for the sin offering were brought before the king and the assembly, and they laid their hands on them. [24]The priests then slaughtered the goats and presented their blood on the altar for a sin offering to atone for all Israel, because the king had ordered the burnt offering and the sin offering for all Israel.

[25]He stationed the Levites in the temple of the LORD with cymbals, harps and lyres in the way prescribed by David and Gad the king's seer and Nathan the prophet; this was commanded by the LORD through his prophets. [26]So the Levites stood ready with David's instruments, and the priests with their trumpets.

[27]Hezekiah gave the order to sacrifice the burnt offering on the altar. As the offering began, singing to the LORD began also, accompanied by trumpets and the instruments of David king of Israel. [28]The whole assembly bowed in worship, while the singers sang and the trumpeters played. All this continued until the sacrifice of the burnt offering was completed.

[29]When the offerings were finished, the king and everyone present with him knelt down and worshiped. [30]King Hezekiah and his officials ordered the Levites to praise the LORD with the words of David and of Asaph the seer. So they sang praises with gladness and bowed their heads and worshiped.

[31]Then Hezekiah said, "You have now dedicated yourselves to the LORD. Come and bring sacrifices and thank offerings to

the temple of the LORD." So the assembly brought sacrifices and thank offerings, and all whose hearts were willing brought burnt offerings.

³²The number of burnt offerings the assembly brought was seventy bulls, a hundred rams and two hundred male lambs—all of them for burnt offerings to the LORD. ³³The animals consecrated as sacrifices amounted to six hundred bulls and three thousand sheep and goats. ³⁴The priests, however, were too few to skin all the burnt offerings; so their kinsmen the Levites helped them until the task was finished and until other priests had been consecrated, for the Levites had been more conscientious in consecrating themselves than the priests had been. ³⁵There were burnt offerings in abundance, together with the fat of the fellowship offerings^l and the drink offerings that accompanied the burnt offerings.

So the service of the temple of the LORD was reestablished. ³⁶Hezekiah and all the people rejoiced at what God had brought about for his people, because it was done so quickly.

CHAPTER 30

Hezekiah sent word to all Israel and Judah and also wrote letters to Ephraim and Manasseh, inviting them to come to the temple of the LORD in Jerusalem and celebrate the Passover to the LORD, the God of Israel. ²The king and his officials and the whole assembly in Jerusalem decided to celebrate the Passover in the second month. ³They had not been able to celebrate it at the regular time because not enough priests had consecrated themselves and the people had not assembled in Jerusalem. ⁴The plan seemed right both to the king and to the whole assembly. ⁵They decided to send a proclamation throughout Israel, from Beersheba to Dan, calling the people to come to Jerusalem and celebrate the Passover to the LORD, the God of Israel. It had not been celebrated in large numbers according to what was written.

⁶At the king's command, couriers went throughout Israel and Judah with letters from the king and from his officials, which read:

"People of Israel, return to the

LORD, the God of Abraham, Isaac and Israel, that he may return to you who are left, who have escaped from the hand of the kings of Assyria. ⁷Do not be like your fathers and brothers, who were unfaithful to the LORD, the God of their fathers, so that he made them an object of horror, as you see. ⁸Do not be stiff-necked, as your fathers were; submit to the LORD. Come to the sanctuary, which he has consecrated forever. Serve the LORD your God, so that his fierce anger will turn away from you. ⁹If you return to the LORD, then your brothers and your children will be shown compassion by their captors and will come back to this land, for the LORD your God is gracious and compassionate. He will not turn his face from you if you return to him."

¹⁰The couriers went from town to town in Ephraim and Manasseh, as far as Zebulun, but the people scorned and ridiculed them. ¹¹Nevertheless, some men of Asher, Manasseh and Zebulun humbled themselves and went to Jerusalem. ¹²Also in Judah the hand of God was on the people to give them unity of mind to carry out what the king and his officials had ordered, following the word of the LORD.

¹³A very large crowd of people assembled in Jerusalem to celebrate the Feast of Unleavened Bread in the second month. ¹⁴They removed the altars in Jerusalem and cleared away the incense altars and threw them into the Kidron Valley.

¹⁵They slaughtered the Passover lamb on the fourteenth day of the second month. The priests and the Levites were ashamed and consecrated themselves and brought burnt offerings to the temple of the LORD. ¹⁶Then they took up their regular positions as prescribed in the Law of Moses the man of God. The priests sprinkled the blood handed to them by the Levites. ¹⁷Since many in the crowd had not consecrated themselves, the Levites had to kill the Passover lambs for all those who were not ceremonially clean and could not consecrate ₜtheir lambs₎ to the LORD. ¹⁸Although most of the many people who came from Ephraim, Manasseh, Issachar and Zebulun had not purified themselves, yet they ate the Passover,

^{l}35 Traditionally *peace offerings*

contrary to what was written. But Hezekiah prayed for them, saying, "May the LORD, who is good, pardon everyone [19]who sets his heart on seeking God—the LORD, the God of his fathers—even if he is not clean according to the rules of the sanctuary." [20]And the LORD heard Hezekiah and healed the people.

[21]The Israelites who were present in Jerusalem celebrated the Feast of Unleavened Bread for seven days with great rejoicing, while the Levites and priests sang to the LORD every day, accompanied by the LORD's instruments of praise.[u]

[22]Hezekiah spoke encouragingly to all the Levites, who showed good understanding of the service of the LORD. For the seven days they ate their assigned portion and offered fellowship offerings[v] and praised the LORD, the God of their fathers.

[23]The whole assembly then agreed to celebrate the festival seven more days; so for another seven days they celebrated joyfully. [24]Hezekiah king of Judah provided a thousand bulls and seven thousand sheep and goats for the assembly, and the officials provided them with a thousand bulls and ten thousand sheep and goats. A great number of priests consecrated themselves. [25]The entire assembly of Judah rejoiced, along with the priests and Levites and all who had assembled from Israel, including the aliens who had come from Israel and those who lived in Judah. [26]There was great joy in Jerusalem, for since the days of Solomon son of David king of Israel there had been nothing like this in Jerusalem. [27]The priests and the Levites stood to bless the people, and God heard them, for their prayer reached heaven, his holy dwelling place.

CHAPTER 31
When all this had ended, the Israelites who were there went out to the towns of Judah, smashed the sacred stones and cut down the Asherah poles. They destroyed the high places and the altars throughout Judah and Benjamin and in Ephraim and Manasseh. After they had destroyed all of them, the Israelites returned to their own towns and to their own property.

[2]Hezekiah assigned the priests and Levites to divisions—each of them according to their duties as priests or Levites—to offer burnt offerings and fellowship offerings,[v] to minister, to give thanks and to sing praises at the gates of the LORD's dwelling. [3]The king contributed from his own possessions for the morning and evening burnt offerings and for the burnt offerings on the Sabbaths, New Moons and appointed feasts as written in the Law of the LORD. [4]He ordered the people living in Jerusalem to give the portion due the priests and Levites so they could devote themselves to the Law of the LORD. [5]As soon as the order went out, the Israelites generously gave the firstfruits of their grain, new wine, oil and honey and all that the fields produced. They brought a great amount, a tithe of everything. [6]The men of Israel and Judah who lived in the towns of Judah also brought a tithe of their herds and flocks and a tithe of the holy things dedicated to the LORD their God, and they piled them in heaps. [7]They began doing this in the third month and finished in the seventh month. [8]When Hezekiah and his officials came and saw the heaps, they praised the LORD and blessed his people Israel.

[9]Hezekiah asked the priests and Levites about the heaps; [10]and Azariah the chief priest, from the family of Zadok, answered, "Since the people began to bring their contributions to the temple of the LORD, we have had enough to eat and plenty to spare, because the LORD has blessed his people, and this great amount is left over."

[11]Hezekiah gave orders to prepare storerooms in the temple of the LORD, and this was done. [12]Then they faithfully brought in the contributions, tithes and dedicated gifts. Conaniah, a Levite, was in charge of these things, and his brother Shimei was next in rank. [13]Jehiel, Azaziah, Nahath, Asahel, Jerimoth, Jozabad, Eliel, Ismakiah, Mahath and Benaiah were supervisors under Conaniah and Shimei his brother, by appointment of King Hezekiah and Azariah the official in charge of the temple of God.

[14]Kore son of Imnah the Levite, keeper of the East Gate, was in charge of the freewill offerings given to God, distributing the contributions made to the LORD and also the consecrated gifts. [15]Eden,

[u]21 Or priests praised the LORD every day with resounding instruments belonging to the LORD   [v]22,2 Traditionally peace offerings

Miniamin, Jeshua, Shemaiah, Amariah and Shecaniah assisted him faithfully in the towns of the priests, distributing to their fellow priests according to their divisions, old and young alike. ¹⁶In addition, they distributed to the males three years old or more whose names were in the genealogical records—all who would enter the temple of the Lord to perform the daily duties of their various tasks, according to their responsibilities and their divisions. ¹⁷And they distributed to the priests enrolled by their families in the genealogical records and likewise to the Levites twenty years old or more, according to their responsibilities and their divisions. ¹⁸They included all the little ones, the wives, and the sons and daughters of the whole community listed in these genealogical records. For they were faithful in consecrating themselves.

¹⁹As for the priests, the descendants of Aaron, who lived on the farm lands around their towns or in any other towns, men were designated by name to distribute portions to every male among them and to all who were recorded in the genealogies of the Levites.

²⁰This is what Hezekiah did throughout Judah, doing what was good and right and faithful before the Lord his God. ²¹In everything that he undertook in the service of God's temple and in obedience to the law and the commands, he sought his God and worked wholeheartedly. And so he prospered.

CHAPTER 32
After all that Hezekiah had so faithfully done, Sennacherib king of Assyria came and invaded Judah. He laid siege to the fortified cities, thinking to conquer them for himself. ²When Hezekiah saw that Sennacherib had come and that he intended to make war on Jerusalem, ³he consulted with his officials and military staff about blocking off the water from the springs outside the city, and they helped him. ⁴A large force of men assembled, and they blocked all the springs and the stream that flowed through the land. "Why should the kings*ʷ* of Assyria come and find plenty of water?" they said. ⁵Then he worked hard repairing all the broken sections of the wall and building

towers on it. He built another wall outside that one and reinforced the supporting terraces*ˣ* of the City of David. He also made large numbers of weapons and shields.

⁶He appointed military officers over the people and assembled them before him in the square at the city gate and encouraged them with these words: ⁷"Be strong and courageous. Do not be afraid or discouraged because of the king of Assyria and the vast army with him, for there is a greater power with us than with him. ⁸With him is only the arm of flesh, but with us is the Lord our God to help us and to fight our battles." And the people gained confidence from what Hezekiah the king of Judah said.

⁹Later, when Sennacherib king of Assyria and all his forces were laying siege to Lachish, he sent his officers to Jerusalem with this message for Hezekiah king of Judah and for all the people of Judah who were there:

¹⁰"This is what Sennacherib king of Assyria says: On what are you basing your confidence, that you remain in Jerusalem under siege? ¹¹When Hezekiah says, 'The Lord our God will save us from the hand of the king of Assyria,' he is misleading you, to let you die of hunger and thirst. ¹²Did not Hezekiah himself remove this god's high places and altars, saying to Judah and Jerusalem, 'You must worship before one altar and burn sacrifices on it'?

¹³"Do you not know what I and my fathers have done to all the peoples of the other lands? Were the gods of those nations ever able to deliver their land from my hand? ¹⁴Who of all the gods of these nations that my fathers destroyed has been able to save his people from me? How then can your god deliver you from my hand? ¹⁵Now do not let Hezekiah deceive you and mislead you like this. Do not believe him, for no god of any nation or kingdom has been able to deliver his people from my hand or the hand of my fathers. How much less will your god deliver you from my hand!"

*ʷ*4 Hebrew; Septuagint and Syriac *king*   *ˣ*5 Or *the Millo*

¹⁶Sennacherib's officers spoke further against the LORD God and against his servant Hezekiah. ¹⁷The king also wrote letters insulting the LORD, the God of Israel, and saying this against him: "Just as the gods of the peoples of the other lands did not rescue their people from my hand, so the god of Hezekiah will not rescue his people from my hand." ¹⁸Then they called out in Hebrew to the people of Jerusalem who were on the wall, to terrify them and make them afraid in order to capture the city. ¹⁹They spoke about the God of Jerusalem as they did about the gods of the other peoples of the world—the work of men's hands.

²⁰King Hezekiah and the prophet Isaiah son of Amoz cried out in prayer to heaven about this. ²¹And the LORD sent an angel, who annihilated all the fighting men and the leaders and officers in the camp of the Assyrian king. So he withdrew to his own land in disgrace. And when he went into the temple of his god, some of his sons cut him down with the sword.

²²So the LORD saved Hezekiah and the people of Jerusalem from the hand of Sennacherib king of Assyria and from the hand of all others. He took care of them ʸ on every side. ²³Many brought offerings to Jerusalem for the LORD and valuable gifts for Hezekiah king of Judah. From then on he was highly regarded by all the nations.

²⁴In those days Hezekiah became ill and was at the point of death. He prayed to the LORD, who answered him and gave him a miraculous sign. ²⁵But Hezekiah's heart was proud and he did not respond to the kindness shown him; therefore the LORD's wrath was on him and on Judah and Jerusalem. ²⁶Then Hezekiah repented of the pride of his heart, as did the people of Jerusalem; therefore the LORD's wrath did not come upon them during the days of Hezekiah.

²⁷Hezekiah had very great riches and honor, and he made treasuries for his silver and gold and for his precious stones, spices, shields and all kinds of valuables. ²⁸He also made buildings to store the harvest of grain, new wine and oil; and he made stalls for various kinds of cattle, and pens for the flocks. ²⁹He built villages and acquired great numbers of flocks and herds, for God had given him very great riches.

³⁰It was Hezekiah who blocked the upper outlet of the Gihon spring and channeled the water down to the west side of the City of David. He succeeded in everything he undertook. ³¹But when envoys were sent by the rulers of Babylon to ask him about the miraculous sign that had occurred in the land, God left him to test him and to know everything that was in his heart.

³²The other events of Hezekiah's reign and his acts of devotion are written in the vision of the prophet Isaiah son of Amoz in the book of the kings of Judah and Israel. ³³Hezekiah rested with his fathers and was buried on the hill where the tombs of David's descendants are. All Judah and the people of Jerusalem honored him when he died. And Manasseh his son succeeded him as king.

ʸ22 Hebrew; Septuagint and Vulgate *He gave them rest*

APRIL 30 ☐ DAY 121
2 CHRONICLES 33–36
Reigns of Judah's Last Kings

 OVERVIEW The book of 2 Chronicles closes with bad news and good news. The bad news begins with the fifty-five-year reign of Manasseh, the longest ruling and most corrupt king in Judah. His reign of horror creates such a sinful situation in the nation that even the reforms of his successor, Josiah, cannot divert the coming judgment. Ultimately, the Babylonians sweep down upon Jerusalem, destroying the temple, breaking down the walls and carrying the inhabitants into exile in Babylon, where they will remain for seventy long years. But the book ends on a note of hope and good news! God has not forgotten his exiled nation. Seventy years later he raises up the Persian king Cyrus to give a proclamation: The people of Jerusalem are free to return home and rebuild the temple of their God in Jerusalem.

Chapter 33	Chapters 34–35	Chapter 36
Manasseh's Evil	Josiah's Excellence	Judah's Exile
Law Ignored	Law Restored	People Removed

YOUR DAILY WALK Congratulations, you made it! You have finished another month of reading through the Bible. Your mind is probably buzzing with names and places you have encountered this month. But before you tackle next month's reading, spend a few minutes reviewing the books of Kings and Chronicles. Flip back through the pages, and then answer these questions:

Better to master one mountain than a thousand foothills.

- Who was your favorite character?
- Who was your least favorite character?
- Which day's reading did you enjoy the most?
- Which "Insight" did you enjoy the most?
- Which "Daily Walk" was most meaningful?
- How have you grown in your spiritual life this month?

INSIGHT Don't Throw Away God's Gifts to the Family
The ritual murder of children in the name of religion was common in heathen nations. Archaeologists have uncovered piles of ashes and infant skeletons around heathen altars. For God's people to engage in such demonic practices was against God's law; for their king to be the foremost practitioner of the occult—as was Manasseh—was complete apostasy, deserving of God's judgment.

CHAPTER 33

Manasseh was twelve years old when he became king, and he reigned in Jerusalem fifty-five years. ²He did evil in the eyes of the LORD, following the detestable practices of the nations the LORD had driven out before the Israelites. ³He rebuilt the high places his father Hezekiah had demolished; he also erected altars to the Baals and made Asherah poles. He bowed down to all the starry hosts and worshiped them. ⁴He built altars in the temple of the LORD, of which the LORD had said, "My Name will remain in Jerusalem forever." ⁵In both courts of the temple of the LORD, he built altars to all the starry hosts. ⁶He sacrificed his sons in^z the fire in the Valley of Ben Hinnom, practiced sorcery, divination and witchcraft, and consulted mediums and spiritists. He did much evil in the eyes of the LORD, provoking him to anger.

⁷He took the carved image he had made

and put it in God's temple, of which God had said to David and to his son Solomon, "In this temple and in Jerusalem, which I have chosen out of all the tribes of Israel, I will put my Name forever. ⁸I will not again make the feet of the Israelites leave the land I assigned to your forefathers, if only they will be careful to do everything I commanded them concerning all the laws, decrees and ordinances given through Moses." ⁹But Manasseh led Judah and the people of Jerusalem astray, so that they did more evil than the nations the LORD had destroyed before the Israelites.

¹⁰The LORD spoke to Manasseh and his people, but they paid no attention. ¹¹So the LORD brought against them the army commanders of the king of Assyria, who took Manasseh prisoner, put a hook in his nose, bound him with bronze shackles and took him to Babylon. ¹²In his distress he sought the favor of the LORD his God

^{z}6 Or *He made his sons pass through*

and humbled himself greatly before the God of his fathers. ¹³And when he prayed to him, the LORD was moved by his entreaty and listened to his plea; so he brought him back to Jerusalem and to his kingdom. Then Manasseh knew that the LORD is God.

¹⁴Afterward he rebuilt the outer wall of the City of David, west of the Gihon spring in the valley, as far as the entrance of the Fish Gate and encircling the hill of Ophel; he also made it much higher. He stationed military commanders in all the fortified cities in Judah.

¹⁵He got rid of the foreign gods and removed the image from the temple of the LORD, as well as all the altars he had built on the temple hill and in Jerusalem; and he threw them out of the city. ¹⁶Then he restored the altar of the LORD and sacrificed fellowship offeringsª and thank offerings on it, and told Judah to serve the LORD, the God of Israel. ¹⁷The people, however, continued to sacrifice at the high places, but only to the LORD their God.

¹⁸The other events of Manasseh's reign, including his prayer to his God and the words the seers spoke to him in the name of the LORD, the God of Israel, are written in the annals of the kings of Israel.ᵇ ¹⁹His prayer and how God was moved by his entreaty, as well as all his sins and unfaithfulness, and the sites where he built high places and set up Asherah poles and idols before he humbled himself—all are written in the records of the seers.ᶜ ²⁰Manasseh rested with his fathers and was buried in his palace. And Amon his son succeeded him as king.

²¹Amon was twenty-two years old when he became king, and he reigned in Jerusalem two years. ²²He did evil in the eyes of the LORD, as his father Manasseh had done. Amon worshiped and offered sacrifices to all the idols Manasseh had made. ²³But unlike his father Manasseh, he did not humble himself before the LORD; Amon increased his guilt.

²⁴Amon's officials conspired against him and assassinated him in his palace. ²⁵Then the people of the land killed all who had plotted against King Amon, and they made Josiah his son king in his place.

CHAPTER 34

Josiah was eight years old when he became king, and he reigned in Jerusalem thirty-one years. ²He did what was right in the eyes of the LORD and walked in the ways of his father David, not turning aside to the right or to the left.

³In the eighth year of his reign, while he was still young, he began to seek the God of his father David. In his twelfth year he began to purge Judah and Jerusalem of high places, Asherah poles, carved idols and cast images. ⁴Under his direction the altars of the Baals were torn down; he cut to pieces the incense altars that were above them, and smashed the Asherah poles, the idols and the images. These he broke to pieces and scattered over the graves of those who had sacrificed to them. ⁵He burned the bones of the priests on their altars, and so he purged Judah and Jerusalem. ⁶In the towns of Manasseh, Ephraim and Simeon, as far as Naphtali, and in the ruins around them, ⁷he tore down the altars and the Asherah poles and crushed the idols to powder and cut to pieces all the incense altars throughout Israel. Then he went back to Jerusalem.

⁸In the eighteenth year of Josiah's reign, to purify the land and the temple, he sent Shaphan son of Azaliah and Maaseiah the ruler of the city, with Joah son of Joahaz, the recorder, to repair the temple of the LORD his God.

⁹They went to Hilkiah the high priest and gave him the money that had been brought into the temple of God, which the Levites who were the doorkeepers had collected from the people of Manasseh, Ephraim and the entire remnant of Israel and from all the people of Judah and Benjamin and the inhabitants of Jerusalem. ¹⁰Then they entrusted it to the men appointed to supervise the work on the LORD's temple. These men paid the workers who repaired and restored the temple. ¹¹They also gave money to the carpenters and builders to purchase dressed stone, and timber for joists and beams for the buildings that the kings of Judah had allowed to fall into ruin.

¹²The men did the work faithfully. Over them to direct them were Jahath and Obadiah, Levites descended from Merari,

and Zechariah and Meshullam, descended from Kohath. The Levites—all who were skilled in playing musical instruments— [13]had charge of the laborers and supervised all the workers from job to job. Some of the Levites were secretaries, scribes and doorkeepers.

[14]While they were bringing out the money that had been taken into the temple of the LORD, Hilkiah the priest found the Book of the Law of the LORD that had been given through Moses. [15]Hilkiah said to Shaphan the secretary, "I have found the Book of the Law in the temple of the LORD." He gave it to Shaphan.

[16]Then Shaphan took the book to the king and reported to him: "Your officials are doing everything that has been committed to them. [17]They have paid out the money that was in the temple of the LORD and have entrusted it to the supervisors and workers." [18]Then Shaphan the secretary informed the king, "Hilkiah the priest has given me a book." And Shaphan read from it in the presence of the king.

[19]When the king heard the words of the Law, he tore his robes. [20]He gave these orders to Hilkiah, Ahikam son of Shaphan, Abdon son of Micah,[d] Shaphan the secretary and Asaiah the king's attendant: [21]"Go and inquire of the LORD for me and for the remnant in Israel and Judah about what is written in this book that has been found. Great is the LORD's anger that is poured out on us because our fathers have not kept the word of the LORD; they have not acted in accordance with all that is written in this book."

[22]Hilkiah and those the king had sent with him[e] went to speak to the prophetess Huldah, who was the wife of Shallum son of Tokhath,[f] the son of Hasrah,[g] keeper of the wardrobe. She lived in Jerusalem, in the Second District.

[23]She said to them, "This is what the LORD, the God of Israel, says: Tell the man who sent you to me, [24]'This is what the LORD says: I am going to bring disaster on this place and its people—all the curses written in the book that has been read in the presence of the king of Judah. [25]Because they have forsaken me and burned incense to other gods and provoked me to anger by all that their hands have made,[h] my anger will be poured out on this place

and will not be quenched.' [26]Tell the king of Judah, who sent you to inquire of the LORD, 'This is what the LORD, the God of Israel, says concerning the words you heard: [27]Because your heart was responsive and you humbled yourself before God when you heard what he spoke against this place and its people, and because you humbled yourself before me and tore your robes and wept in my presence, I have heard you, declares the LORD. [28]Now I will gather you to your fathers, and you will be buried in peace. Your eyes will not see all the disaster I am going to bring on this place and on those who live here.' "

So they took her answer back to the king.

[29]Then the king called together all the elders of Judah and Jerusalem. [30]He went up to the temple of the LORD with the men of Judah, the people of Jerusalem, the priests and the Levites—all the people from the least to the greatest. He read in their hearing all the words of the Book of the Covenant, which had been found in the temple of the LORD. [31]The king stood by his pillar and renewed the covenant in the presence of the LORD—to follow the LORD and keep his commands, regulations and decrees with all his heart and all his soul, and to obey the words of the covenant written in this book.

[32]Then he had everyone in Jerusalem and Benjamin pledge themselves to it; the people of Jerusalem did this in accordance with the covenant of God, the God of their fathers.

[33]Josiah removed all the detestable idols from all the territory belonging to the Israelites, and he had all who were present in Israel serve the LORD their God. As long as he lived, they did not fail to follow the LORD, the God of their fathers.

CHAPTER 35

Josiah celebrated the Passover to the LORD in Jerusalem, and the Passover lamb was slaughtered on the fourteenth day of the first month. [2]He appointed the priests to their duties and encouraged them in the service of the LORD's temple. [3]He said to the Levites, who instructed all Israel and who had been consecrated to the LORD: "Put the sacred ark in the temple that Solomon son of David king of Israel built. It is not to be carried about on your shoulders. Now serve the LORD your God and his people Israel. ⁴Prepare yourselves by families in your divisions, according to the directions written by David king of Israel and by his son Solomon.

⁵"Stand in the holy place with a group of Levites for each subdivision of the families of your fellow countrymen, the lay people. ⁶Slaughter the Passover lambs, consecrate yourselves and prepare ˌthe lambsˌ for your fellow countrymen, doing what the LORD commanded through Moses."

⁷Josiah provided for all the lay people who were there a total of thirty thousand sheep and goats for the Passover offerings, and also three thousand cattle—all from the king's own possessions.

⁸His officials also contributed voluntarily to the people and the priests and Levites. Hilkiah, Zechariah and Jehiel, the administrators of God's temple, gave the priests twenty-six hundred Passover offerings and three hundred cattle. ⁹Also Conaniah along with Shemaiah and Nethanel, his brothers, and Hashabiah, Jeiel and Jozabad, the leaders of the Levites, provided five thousand Passover offerings and five hundred head of cattle for the Levites.

¹⁰The service was arranged and the priests stood in their places with the Levites in their divisions as the king had ordered. ¹¹The Passover lambs were slaughtered, and the priests sprinkled the blood handed to them, while the Levites skinned the animals. ¹²They set aside the burnt offerings to give them to the subdivisions of the families of the people to offer to the LORD, as is written in the Book of Moses. They did the same with the cattle. ¹³They roasted the Passover animals over the fire as prescribed, and boiled the holy offerings in pots, caldrons and pans and served them quickly to all the people. ¹⁴After this, they made preparations for themselves and for the priests, because the priests, the descendants of Aaron, were sacrificing the burnt offerings and the fat portions until nightfall. So the Levites made preparations for themselves and for the Aaronic priests.

¹⁵The musicians, the descendants of Asaph, were in the places prescribed by David, Asaph, Heman and Jeduthun the king's seer. The gatekeepers at each gate did not need to leave their posts, because their fellow Levites made the preparations for them.

¹⁶So at that time the entire service of the LORD was carried out for the celebration of the Passover and the offering of burnt offerings on the altar of the LORD, as King Josiah had ordered. ¹⁷The Israelites who were present celebrated the Passover at that time and observed the Feast of Unleavened Bread for seven days. ¹⁸The Passover had not been observed like this in Israel since the days of the prophet Samuel; and none of the kings of Israel had ever celebrated such a Passover as did Josiah, with the priests, the Levites and all Judah and Israel who were there with the people of Jerusalem. ¹⁹This Passover was celebrated in the eighteenth year of Josiah's reign.

²⁰After all this, when Josiah had set the temple in order, Neco king of Egypt went up to fight at Carchemish on the Euphrates, and Josiah marched out to meet him in battle. ²¹But Neco sent messengers to him, saying, "What quarrel is there between you and me, O king of Judah? It is not you I am attacking at this time, but the house with which I am at war. God has told me to hurry; so stop opposing God, who is with me, or he will destroy you."

²²Josiah, however, would not turn away from him, but disguised himself to engage him in battle. He would not listen to what Neco had said at God's command but went to fight him on the plain of Megiddo.

²³Archers shot King Josiah, and he told his officers, "Take me away; I am badly wounded." ²⁴So they took him out of his chariot, put him in the other chariot he had and brought him to Jerusalem, where he died. He was buried in the tombs of his fathers, and all Judah and Jerusalem mourned for him.

²⁵Jeremiah composed laments for Josiah, and to this day all the men and women singers commemorate Josiah in the laments. These became a tradition in Israel and are written in the Laments.

²⁶The other events of Josiah's reign and his acts of devotion, according to what is written in the Law of the LORD— ²⁷all the events, from beginning to end, are written in the book of the kings of Israel and

CHAPTER 36 Judah. [1]And the people of the land took Jehoahaz son of Josiah and made him king in Jerusalem in place of his father.

[2]Jehoahaz[i] was twenty-three years old when he became king, and he reigned in Jerusalem three months. [3]The king of Egypt dethroned him in Jerusalem and imposed on Judah a levy of a hundred talents[j] of silver and a talent[k] of gold. [4]The king of Egypt made Eliakim, a brother of Jehoahaz, king over Judah and Jerusalem and changed Eliakim's name to Jehoiakim. But Neco took Eliakim's brother Jehoahaz and carried him off to Egypt.

[5]Jehoiakim was twenty-five years old when he became king, and he reigned in Jerusalem eleven years. He did evil in the eyes of the LORD his God. [6]Nebuchadnezzar king of Babylon attacked him and bound him with bronze shackles to take him to Babylon. [7]Nebuchadnezzar also took to Babylon articles from the temple of the LORD and put them in his temple[l] there.

[8]The other events of Jehoiakim's reign, the detestable things he did and all that was found against him, are written in the book of the kings of Israel and Judah. And Jehoiachin his son succeeded him as king.

[9]Jehoiachin was eighteen[m] years old when he became king, and he reigned in Jerusalem three months and ten days. He did evil in the eyes of the LORD. [10]In the spring, King Nebuchadnezzar sent for him and brought him to Babylon, together with articles of value from the temple of the LORD, and he made Jehoiachin's uncle,[n] Zedekiah, king over Judah and Jerusalem.

[11]Zedekiah was twenty-one years old when he became king, and he reigned in Jerusalem eleven years. [12]He did evil in the eyes of the LORD his God and did not humble himself before Jeremiah the prophet, who spoke the word of the LORD. [13]He also rebelled against King Nebuchadnezzar, who had made him take an oath in God's name. He became stiff-necked and hardened his heart and would not turn to the LORD, the God of Israel. [14]Furthermore, all the leaders of the priests and the people became more and more unfaithful, following all the detestable practices of the nations and defiling the temple of the LORD, which he had consecrated in Jerusalem.

[15]The LORD, the God of their fathers, sent word to them through his messengers again and again, because he had pity on his people and on his dwelling place. [16]But they mocked God's messengers, despised his words and scoffed at his prophets until the wrath of the LORD was aroused against his people and there was no remedy. [17]He brought up against them the king of the Babylonians,[o] who killed their young men with the sword in the sanctuary, and spared neither young man nor young woman, old man or aged. God handed all of them over to Nebuchadnezzar. [18]He carried to Babylon all the articles from the temple of God, both large and small, and the treasures of the LORD's temple and the treasures of the king and his officials. [19]They set fire to God's temple and broke down the wall of Jerusalem; they burned all the palaces and destroyed everything of value there.

[20]He carried into exile to Babylon the remnant, who escaped from the sword, and they became servants to him and his sons until the kingdom of Persia came to power. [21]The land enjoyed its sabbath rests; all the time of its desolation it rested, until the seventy years were completed in fulfillment of the word of the LORD spoken by Jeremiah.

[22]In the first year of Cyrus king of Persia, in order to fulfill the word of the LORD spoken by Jeremiah, the LORD moved the heart of Cyrus king of Persia to make a proclamation throughout his realm and to put it in writing:

[23]"This is what Cyrus king of Persia says:

" 'The LORD, the God of heaven, has given me all the kingdoms of the earth and he has appointed me to build a temple for him at Jerusalem in Judah. Anyone of his people among you—may the LORD his God be with him, and let him go up.' "

---

[i]2 Hebrew *Joahaz*, a variant of *Jehoahaz*; also in verse 4   [j]3 That is, about 3 3/4 tons (about 3.4 metric tons)   [k]3 That is, about 75 pounds (about 34 kilograms)   [l]7 Or *palace*   [m]9 One Hebrew manuscript, some Septuagint manuscripts and Syriac (see also 2 Kings 24:8); most Hebrew manuscripts *eight*   [n]10 Hebrew *brother*, that is, relative (see 2 Kings 24:17)   [o]17 Or *Chaldeans*

Ezra

THE JEWS held captive in Babylonia for seventy years are allowed at last to return to their homeland. The book of Ezra begins with the proclamation of King Cyrus of Persia and the homeward journey of the first returnees under Zerubbabel (Ezra 1–6). With the temple rebuilt, a second group returns under Ezra, the priest, this time to rebuild the spiritual vitality of the nation (Ezra 7–10). Between those two homecomings you'll find a fifty-eight-year interlude during which the book of Esther takes place.

Focus	Restoration of the Temple		58-Year Gap—The Book of Esther	Reformation of the People	
Divisions	Commission of the Temple Builders	Completion of the Temple Project		Commission of the Spiritual Leaders	Completion of the Spiritual Reforms
	1　　　　　3	4　　　　　6		7　　　　　8	9　　　　　10
Topics	Return under Zerubbabel			Return under Ezra	
	Building Construction			Rebuilding Commitment	
Place	Persia to Jerusalem			Persia to Jerusalem	
Time	23 Years (538–515 B.C.)			1 Year (457 B.C.)	

MAY 1 □ DAY 122
EZRA 1–3
Commission of the Temple Builders

OVERVIEW At last the wearisome Babylonian captivity is at an end. With the proclamation of King Cyrus, permitting the people to leave Persia and return to their homeland, the hard work of rebuilding the nation can begin. Nearly fifty thousand pilgrims journey with Zerubbabel back to Jerusalem to rebuild the temple. But laying the temple foundation brings tears of remembrance as the builders recall the splendor that was once Solomon's temple—a splendor never to be regained.

Chapter 1	Chapter 2	Chapter 3
A Call for Temple Builders	A Catalog of Temple Builders	Commencing to Build the Temple
Proclamation	Presentation	Progress

YOUR DAILY WALK How long have you lived at your present location? Based on the national average, one family in three will move this year. And that means if you have lived in the place you call home for five years or longer, you are a vanishing breed!

Little people with little minds jog through life in little ruts, smugly resisting all changes that would jar their little worlds.

Pulling up stakes is never easy. Anticipation and anxiety can make the ordeal as difficult emotionally as it is physically. Consider the caravan of pioneers listed in Ezra 2. The trail ahead of them was long—a hike of nearly a thousand miles. There was the constant danger of ambush from robbers, especially since the people were transporting a wealth of temple treasures (1:9–11). Notwithstanding, God had stirred up the hearts of the people to respond to the invitation of a pagan king. With such internal compulsion and external confirmation, how could they help but move out for God!

Is God calling you to pull up stakes—to move to a new home, a new school, a new church, a new job, a new level of commitment to him? Then here is a motto you may want to copy and display in your home or office: "Even a long, dangerous journey can be faced confidently when God is leading the expedition."

INSIGHT Cyrus, God's Pagan Messiah
About 150 years before the dramatic proclamation of Ezra 1:1–4, Isaiah delivered a detailed prophecy concerning King Cyrus (Isaiah 44:28–45:7). Because the Lord would prompt Cyrus to do all these things for the Jews, he is called "my shepherd" (44:28) and "his anointed" (literally, *messiah;* 45:1).

CHAPTER 1

In the first year of Cyrus king of Persia, in order to fulfill the word of the LORD spoken by Jeremiah, the LORD moved the heart of Cyrus king of Persia to make a proclamation throughout his realm and to put it in writing:

2"This is what Cyrus king of Persia says:

" 'The LORD, the God of heaven, has given me all the kingdoms of the earth and he has appointed me to build a temple for him at Jerusalem in Judah. 3Anyone of his people among you—may his God be with him, and let him go up to Jerusalem in Judah and build the temple of the LORD, the God of Israel, the God who is in Jerusalem. [4]And the people of any place where survivors may now be living are to provide him with silver and gold, with goods and livestock, and with freewill offerings for the temple of God in Jerusalem.' "

[5]Then the family heads of Judah and Benjamin, and the priests and Levites—everyone whose heart God had moved—prepared to go up and build the house of the LORD in Jerusalem. [6]All their neighbors assisted them with articles of silver and gold, with goods and livestock, and with valuable gifts, in addition to all the freewill offerings. [7]Moreover, King Cyrus brought out the articles belonging to the temple of the LORD, which Nebuchadnezzar had carried away from Jerusalem and had placed in the temple of his god.[a] [8]Cyrus king of Persia had them brought by Mithredath the treasurer, who counted them out to Sheshbazzar the prince of Judah.

[9]This was the inventory:

gold dishes	30
silver dishes	1,000
silver pans[b]	29
[10]gold bowls	30
matching silver bowls	410
other articles	1,000

[11]In all, there were 5,400 articles of gold and of silver. Sheshbazzar brought all these along when the exiles came up from Babylon to Jerusalem.

CHAPTER 2
Now these are the people of the province who came up from the captivity of the exiles, whom Nebuchadnezzar king of Babylon had taken captive to Babylon (they returned to Jerusalem and Judah, each to his own town, [2]in company with Zerubbabel, Jeshua, Nehemiah, Seraiah, Reelaiah, Mordecai, Bilshan, Mispar, Bigvai, Rehum and Baanah):

The list of the men of the people of Israel:

[3]the descendants of Parosh   2,172

[4]of Shephatiah	372
[5]of Arah	775
[6]of Pahath-Moab (through the line of Jeshua and Joab)	2,812
[7]of Elam	1,254
[8]of Zattu	945
[9]of Zaccai	760
[10]of Bani	642
[11]of Bebai	623
[12]of Azgad	1,222
[13]of Adonikam	666
[14]of Bigvai	2,056
[15]of Adin	454
[16]of Ater (through Hezekiah)	98
[17]of Bezai	323
[18]of Jorah	112
[19]of Hashum	223
[20]of Gibbar	95
[21]the men of Bethlehem	123
[22]of Netophah	56
[23]of Anathoth	128
[24]of Azmaveth	42
[25]of Kiriath Jearim,[c] Kephirah and Beeroth	743
[26]of Ramah and Geba	621
[27]of Micmash	122
[28]of Bethel and Ai	223
[29]of Nebo	52
[30]of Magbish	156
[31]of the other Elam	1,254
[32]of Harim	320
[33]of Lod, Hadid and Ono	725
[34]of Jericho	345
[35]of Senaah	3,630

[36]The priests:

the descendants of Jedaiah (through the family of Jeshua)	973
[37]of Immer	1,052
[38]of Pashhur	1,247
[39]of Harim	1,017

[40]The Levites:

the descendants of Jeshua and Kadmiel (through the line of Hodaviah)	74

[41]The singers:

the descendants of Asaph	128

[42]The gatekeepers of the temple:

the descendants of

[a]7 Or gods   [b]9 The meaning of the Hebrew for this word is uncertain.   [c]25 See Septuagint (see also Neh. 7:29); Hebrew Kiriath Arim.

Shallum, Ater, Talmon,
Akkub, Hatita and Shobai   139

⁴³The temple servants:

the descendants of
Ziha, Hasupha, Tabbaoth,
⁴⁴Keros, Siaha, Padon,
⁴⁵Lebanah, Hagabah, Akkub,
⁴⁶Hagab, Shalmai, Hanan,
⁴⁷Giddel, Gahar, Reaiah,
⁴⁸Rezin, Nekoda, Gazzam,
⁴⁹Uzza, Paseah, Besai,
⁵⁰Asnah, Meunim, Nephussim,
⁵¹Bakbuk, Hakupha, Harhur,
⁵²Bazluth, Mehida, Harsha,
⁵³Barkos, Sisera, Temah,
⁵⁴Neziah and Hatipha

⁵⁵The descendants of the servants of
Solomon:

the descendants of
Sotai, Hassophereth, Peruda,
⁵⁶Jaala, Darkon, Giddel,
⁵⁷Shephatiah, Hattil,
Pokereth-Hazzebaim and Ami

⁵⁸The temple servants and the
descendants of the servants
of Solomon   392

⁵⁹The following came up from the
towns of Tel Melah, Tel Harsha, Kerub, Addon and Immer, but they
could not show that their families
were descended from Israel:

⁶⁰The descendants of
Delaiah, Tobiah and Nekoda   652

⁶¹And from among the priests:

The descendants of
Hobaiah, Hakkoz and Barzillai
(a man who had married a
daughter of Barzillai the
Gileadite and was called by that
name).
⁶²These searched for their family
records, but they could not find them
and so were excluded from the
priesthood as unclean. ⁶³The governor ordered them not to eat any of
the most sacred food until there was
a priest ministering with the Urim
and Thummim.

⁶⁴The whole company numbered
42,360, ⁶⁵besides their 7,337 menservants and maidservants; and they
also had 200 men and women singers. ⁶⁶They had 736 horses, 245 mules,
⁶⁷435 camels and 6,720 donkeys.

⁶⁸When they arrived at the house of the
LORD in Jerusalem, some of the heads of
the families gave freewill offerings toward the rebuilding of the house of God
on its site. ⁶⁹According to their ability
they gave to the treasury for this work
61,000 drachmas*d* of gold, 5,000 minas*e*
of silver and 100 priestly garments.
⁷⁰The priests, the Levites, the singers,
the gatekeepers and the temple servants
settled in their own towns, along with
some of the other people, and the rest of
the Israelites settled in their towns.

CHAPTER 3

When the seventh month came and the
Israelites had settled in their towns, the
people assembled as one man in Jerusalem. ²Then Jeshua son of Jozadak and his
fellow priests and Zerubbabel son of Shealtiel and his associates began to build the
altar of the God of Israel to sacrifice burnt
offerings on it, in accordance with what is
written in the Law of Moses the man of
God. ³Despite their fear of the peoples
around them, they built the altar on its
foundation and sacrificed burnt offerings
on it to the LORD, both the morning and
evening sacrifices. ⁴Then in accordance
with what is written, they celebrated the
Feast of Tabernacles with the required
number of burnt offerings prescribed for
each day. ⁵After that, they presented the
regular burnt offerings, the New Moon
sacrifices and the sacrifices for all the appointed sacred feasts of the LORD, as well
as those brought as freewill offerings to
the LORD. ⁶On the first day of the seventh
month they began to offer burnt offerings
to the LORD, though the foundation of the
LORD's temple had not yet been laid.
⁷Then they gave money to the masons
and carpenters, and gave food and drink
and oil to the people of Sidon and Tyre, so
that they would bring cedar logs by sea
from Lebanon to Joppa, as authorized by
Cyrus king of Persia.
⁸In the second month of the second year
after their arrival at the house of God in
Jerusalem, Zerubbabel son of Shealtiel,
Jeshua son of Jozadak and the rest of their

d69 That is, about 1,100 pounds (about 500 kilograms)   *e69* That is, about 3 tons (about 2.9 metric tons) brothers (the priests and the Levites and all who had returned from the captivity to Jerusalem) began the work, appointing Levites twenty years of age and older to supervise the building of the house of the LORD. ⁹Jeshua and his sons and brothers and Kadmiel and his sons (descendants of Hodaviah*f*) and the sons of Henadad and their sons and brothers—all Levites— joined together in supervising those working on the house of God.

¹⁰When the builders laid the foundation of the temple of the LORD, the priests in their vestments and with trumpets, and the Levites (the sons of Asaph) with cymbals, took their places to praise the LORD, as prescribed by David king of Israel.

f9 Hebrew *Yehudah*, probably a variant of *Hodaviah*

¹¹With praise and thanksgiving they sang to the LORD:

"He is good;
      his love to Israel endures forever."

And all the people gave a great shout of praise to the LORD, because the foundation of the house of the LORD was laid. ¹²But many of the older priests and Levites and family heads, who had seen the former temple, wept aloud when they saw the foundation of this temple being laid, while many others shouted for joy. ¹³No one could distinguish the sound of the shouts of joy from the sound of weeping, because the people made so much noise. And the sound was heard far away.

MAY 2 □ DAY 123
EZRA 4–6
Completion of the Temple Project

OVERVIEW The task of rebuilding the temple involves more than simply organizing men and materials. Antagonism from local citizens soon arises to threaten the project. Deceitful offers of help, open attack, false accusations—each must be handled by Zerubbabel with conviction and courage. Although the builders are temporarily stopped, the prophets Haggai and Zechariah emerge to exhort the people not to throw in the trowel, so to speak. Darius, a sympathetic new Persian king, at last ends the fifteen-year construction delay by reconfirming the proclamation of Cyrus: God's temple must be completed!

Chapter 4	Chapter 5	Chapter 6
Restraining the Builders	Reinstating the Builders	Reaching the Goal
Opposition	Resolution	Completion

YOUR DAILY WALK In the margin see if you can list at least ten instant products that are popular today: instant coffee, instant cameras, etc.

When you cannot remove an obstacle, plow around it. But in God's strength, keep plowing.

Ours is an "instant" society in which immediate results have become our expectation. And yet there are many endeavors for God that will only be accomplished if the long-range perspective is maintained. Parenting a child . . . developing a spiritual gift . . . discipling a new Christian . . . gaining an education—all these take time, the investment of years of practice and patience and perseverance, if the goal is to be achieved.

If Zerubbabel had allowed the short-term discouragements to deter him from his long-range determination to rebuild the temple, he never would have finished the task. But with his goal clearly in view and his faith firmly fixed in God, Zerubbabel was able to stay on target . . . for more than twenty years!

Use one of your long-range roles or goals to complete this sentence: "Though I may not experience instant success in my goal of _____, with God's help I will commit myself to be faithful a day at a time, beginning today."

INSIGHT Ezra the Priest—Which Way Did He Go?
In a book entitled *Ezra,* you would expect the title character to play a prominent role. With the help of a Bible concordance (or just by retracing your steps), see how many times Ezra's name appears in the first six chapters. The answer may surprise you!

CHAPTER 4

When the enemies of Judah and Benjamin heard that the exiles were building a temple for the LORD, the God of Israel, ²they came to Zerubbabel and to the heads of the families and said, "Let us help you build because, like you, we seek your God and have been sacrificing to him since the time of Esarhaddon king of Assyria, who brought us here."

³But Zerubbabel, Jeshua and the rest of the heads of the families of Israel answered, "You have no part with us in building a temple to our God. We alone will build it for the LORD, the God of Israel, as King Cyrus, the king of Persia, commanded us."

⁴Then the peoples around them set out to discourage the people of Judah and make them afraid to go on building.*ᵍ* ⁵They hired counselors to work against them and frustrate their plans during the entire reign of Cyrus king of Persia and down to the reign of Darius king of Persia.

⁶At the beginning of the reign of Xerxes,*ʰ* they lodged an accusation against the people of Judah and Jerusalem.

⁷And in the days of Artaxerxes king of Persia, Bishlam, Mithredath, Tabeel and the rest of his associates wrote a letter to Artaxerxes. The letter was written in Aramaic script and in the Aramaic language.*ⁱ,ʲ*

⁸Rehum the commanding officer and Shimshai the secretary wrote a letter against Jerusalem to Artaxerxes the king as follows:

⁹Rehum the commanding officer and Shimshai the secretary, together with the rest of their associates—the judges and officials over the men from Tripolis, Persia,*ᵏ* Erech and Babylon, the Elamites of Susa, ¹⁰and the other people whom the great and honorable Ashurbanipal*ˡ* deported and settled in the city of Samaria and elsewhere in Trans-Euphrates.

¹¹(This is a copy of the letter they sent him.)

To King Artaxerxes,

From your servants, the men of Trans-Euphrates:

¹²The king should know that the Jews who came up to us from you have gone to Jerusalem and are rebuilding that rebellious and wicked city. They are restoring the walls and repairing the foundations.

¹³Furthermore, the king should know that if this city is built and its walls are restored, no more taxes, tribute or duty will be paid, and the royal revenues will suffer. ¹⁴Now since we are under obligation to the palace and it is not proper for us to see the king dishonored, we are sending this message to inform the king, ¹⁵so that a search may be made in the archives of your predecessors. In these records you will find that this city is a rebellious city, troublesome to kings and provinces, a place of rebellion from ancient times. That is why this city was destroyed. ¹⁶We inform the king that if this city is built and its walls are restored, you will be left with nothing in Trans-Euphrates.

¹⁷The king sent this reply:

ᵍ4 Or *and troubled them as they built*   *ʰ6* Hebrew *Ahasuerus,* a variant of Xerxes' Persian name   *ⁱ7* Or *written in Aramaic and translated*   *ʲ7* The text of Ezra 4:8—6:18 is in Aramaic.   *ᵏ9* Or *officials, magistrates and governors over the men from*
ˡ10 Aramaic *Osnappar,* a variant of *Ashurbanipal*

To Rehum the commanding officer, Shimshai the secretary and the rest of their associates living in Samaria and elsewhere in Trans-Euphrates:

Greetings.

¹⁸The letter you sent us has been read and translated in my presence. ¹⁹I issued an order and a search was made, and it was found that this city has a long history of revolt against kings and has been a place of rebellion and sedition. ²⁰Jerusalem has had powerful kings ruling over the whole of Trans-Euphrates, and taxes, tribute and duty were paid to them. ²¹Now issue an order to these men to stop work, so that this city will not be rebuilt until I so order. ²²Be careful not to neglect this matter. Why let this threat grow, to the detriment of the royal interests?

²³As soon as the copy of the letter of King Artaxerxes was read to Rehum and Shimshai the secretary and their associates, they went immediately to the Jews in Jerusalem and compelled them by force to stop.

²⁴Thus the work on the house of God in Jerusalem came to a standstill until the second year of the reign of Darius king of Persia.

CHAPTER 5

Now Haggai the prophet and Zechariah the prophet, a descendant of Iddo, prophesied to the Jews in Judah and Jerusalem in the name of the God of Israel, who was over them. ²Then Zerubbabel son of Shealtiel and Jeshua son of Jozadak set to work to rebuild the house of God in Jerusalem. And the prophets of God were with them, helping them.

³At that time Tattenai, governor of Trans-Euphrates, and Shethar-Bozenai and their associates went to them and asked, "Who authorized you to rebuild this temple and restore this structure?" ⁴They also asked, "What are the names of the men constructing this building?" *m* ⁵But the eye of their God was watching over the elders of the Jews, and they were not stopped until a report could go to Darius and his written reply be received.

⁶This is a copy of the letter that Tattenai, governor of Trans-Euphrates, and Shethar-Bozenai and their associates, the officials of Trans-Euphrates, sent to King Darius. ⁷The report they sent him read as follows:

To King Darius:

Cordial greetings.

⁸The king should know that we went to the district of Judah, to the temple of the great God. The people are building it with large stones and placing the timbers in the walls. The work is being carried on with diligence and is making rapid progress under their direction.

⁹We questioned the elders and asked them, "Who authorized you to rebuild this temple and restore this structure?" ¹⁰We also asked them their names, so that we could write down the names of their leaders for your information.

¹¹This is the answer they gave us:

"We are the servants of the God of heaven and earth, and we are rebuilding the temple that was built many years ago, one that a great king of Israel built and finished. ¹²But because our fathers angered the God of heaven, he handed them over to Nebuchadnezzar the Chaldean, king of Babylon, who destroyed this temple and deported the people to Babylon.

¹³"However, in the first year of Cyrus king of Babylon, King Cyrus issued a decree to rebuild this house of God. ¹⁴He even removed from the temple *n* of Babylon the gold and silver articles of the house of God, which Nebuchadnezzar had taken from the temple in Jerusalem and brought to the temple *n* in Babylon.

"Then King Cyrus gave them to a man named Sheshbazzar, whom he had appointed governor, ¹⁵and he told him, 'Take these articles and go and deposit them in the temple in Jerusalem. And rebuild the house of God on its site.' ¹⁶So this Sheshbazzar came and laid the foundations of the house of God in Jerusalem. From that

m 4 See Septuagint; Aramaic *4 We told them the names of the men constructing this building.*   *n 14* Or *palace* day to the present it has been under construction but is not yet finished."

17Now if it pleases the king, let a search be made in the royal archives of Babylon to see if King Cyrus did in fact issue a decree to rebuild this house of God in Jerusalem. Then let the king send us his decision in this matter.

CHAPTER 6

King Darius then issued an order, and they searched in the archives stored in the treasury at Babylon. 2A scroll was found in the citadel of Ecbatana in the province of Media, and this was written on it:

Memorandum:

3In the first year of King Cyrus, the king issued a decree concerning the temple of God in Jerusalem:

Let the temple be rebuilt as a place to present sacrifices, and let its foundations be laid. It is to be ninety feet° high and ninety feet wide, 4with three courses of large stones and one of timbers. The costs are to be paid by the royal treasury. 5Also, the gold and silver articles of the house of God, which Nebuchadnezzar took from the temple in Jerusalem and brought to Babylon, are to be returned to their places in the temple in Jerusalem; they are to be deposited in the house of God.

6Now then, Tattenai, governor of Trans-Euphrates, and Shethar-Bozenai and you, their fellow officials of that province, stay away from there. 7Do not interfere with the work on this temple of God. Let the governor of the Jews and the Jewish elders rebuild this house of God on its site.

8Moreover, I hereby decree what you are to do for these elders of the Jews in the construction of this house of God:

The expenses of these men are to be fully paid out of the royal treasury, from the revenues of Trans-Euphrates, so that the work will not stop. 9Whatever is needed—young bulls, rams, male lambs for burnt of-

ferings to the God of heaven, and wheat, salt, wine and oil, as requested by the priests in Jerusalem—must be given them daily without fail, 10so that they may offer sacrifices pleasing to the God of heaven and pray for the well-being of the king and his sons.

11Furthermore, I decree that if anyone changes this edict, a beam is to be pulled from his house and he is to be lifted up and impaled on it. And for this crime his house is to be made a pile of rubble. 12May God, who has caused his Name to dwell there, overthrow any king or people who lifts a hand to change this decree or to destroy this temple in Jerusalem.

I Darius have decreed it. Let it be carried out with diligence.

13Then, because of the decree King Darius had sent, Tattenai, governor of Trans-Euphrates, and Shethar-Bozenai and his associates carried it out with diligence. 14So the elders of the Jews continued to build and prosper under the preaching of Haggai the prophet and Zechariah, a descendant of Iddo. They finished building the temple according to the command of the God of Israel and the decrees of Cyrus, Darius and Artaxerxes, kings of Persia. 15The temple was completed on the third day of the month Adar, in the sixth year of the reign of King Darius.

16Then the people of Israel—the priests, the Levites and the rest of the exiles—celebrated the dedication of the house of God with joy. 17For the dedication of this house of God they offered a hundred bulls, two hundred rams, four hundred male lambs and, as a sin offering for all Israel, twelve male goats, one for each of the tribes of Israel. 18And they installed the priests in their divisions and the Levites in their groups for the service of God at Jerusalem, according to what is written in the Book of Moses.

19On the fourteenth day of the first month, the exiles celebrated the Passover. 20The priests and Levites had purified themselves and were all ceremonially clean. The Levites slaughtered the Passover lamb for all the exiles, for their

°3 Aramaic *sixty cubits* (about 27 meters)

brothers the priests and for themselves. ²¹So the Israelites who had returned from the exile ate it, together with all who had separated themselves from the unclean practices of their Gentile neighbors in order to seek the LORD, the God of Israel.

²²For seven days they celebrated with joy the Feast of Unleavened Bread, because the LORD had filled them with joy by changing the attitude of the king of Assyria, so that he assisted them in the work on the house of God, the God of Israel.

MAY 3 □ DAY 124
EZRA 7–8
Commission of the Spiritual Leaders

OVERVIEW Chapter 7 breaks a fifty-eight-year silence with the introduction of a priest and teacher named Ezra. Another kingly proclamation, this time by Artaxerxes, sets the stage for Ezra to return to Jerusalem, accompanied by 1,753 priests, Levites and laymen. After praying and fasting, Ezra and his caravan begin the four-month journey, weighted down with treasures for the temple and buoyed up by their confidence in God.

Chapter 7	Chapter 8
Preparations for the Return	Protection during the Return
Ezra's Commission	Ezra's Companions

YOUR DAILY WALK Have you ever tried to help God out by doing for him what he has already promised to do for himself?

Abraham tried it (Genesis 16) by fathering Ishmael, even though God had promised to give him a son by Sarah. Saul tried it (1 Samuel 17:38–39) by covering David with the king's bulky armor, but the young shepherd boy knew God wanted him to use a proven, less cumbersome method to fell the giant Goliath.

We would worry less about what others think of us if we realized how seldom they do.

Ezra was tempted to try it, too. When presented with the chance to enlist pagan soldiers and horsemen as a protection against enemies along the way, Ezra went to his knees and received the assurance of something he had previously told pagan king Artaxerxes: "The gracious hand of our God is on everyone who looks to him, but his great anger is against all who forsake him" (8:22). Armed with that confidence, Ezra and the people set out on a four-month adventure in trusting God. And God proved his faithfulness once more!

How are you tempted to substitute human crutches for wholehearted trust in the Lord? Where do you turn when things get tough? To your checkbook? . . . investments? . . . friends? . . . job security? . . . spouse? . . . or to the Lord? Turn to him right now in confident prayer, and watch him guide your pilgrimage!

INSIGHT Three Leaders, Three Backgrounds
God chose three very different men to lead the three Jerusalem "homecomings." Zerubbabel was a prince of Judah; Ezra was a priest and Levite; and Nehemiah was a politician from an unspecified tribe.

CHAPTER 7

After these things, during the reign of Artaxerxes king of Persia, Ezra son of Seraiah, the son of Azariah, the son of Hilkiah, ²the son of Shallum, the son of Zadok, the son of Ahitub, ³the son of Amariah, the son of Azariah, the son of Meraioth, ⁴the son of Zerahiah, the son of Uzzi, the son of Bukki, ⁵the son of Abishua, the son of Phinehas, the son of Eleazar, the son of Aaron the chief priest— ⁶this Ezra came up from Babylon. He was a teacher well versed in the Law of Moses, which the LORD, the God of Israel, had given. The king had granted him everything he asked, for the hand of the LORD his God was on him. ⁷Some of the Israelites, including priests, Levites, singers, gatekeepers and temple servants, also came up to Jerusalem in the seventh year of King Artaxerxes.

⁸Ezra arrived in Jerusalem in the fifth month of the seventh year of the king. ⁹He had begun his journey from Babylon on the first day of the first month, and he arrived in Jerusalem on the first day of the fifth month, for the gracious hand of his God was on him. ¹⁰For Ezra had devoted himself to the study and observance of the Law of the LORD, and to teaching its decrees and laws in Israel.

¹¹This is a copy of the letter King Artaxerxes had given to Ezra the priest and teacher, a man learned in matters concerning the commands and decrees of the LORD for Israel:

¹²ᵖArtaxerxes, king of kings,

To Ezra the priest, a teacher of the Law of the God of heaven:

Greetings.

¹³Now I decree that any of the Israelites in my kingdom, including priests and Levites, who wish to go to Jerusalem with you, may go. ¹⁴You are sent by the king and his seven advisers to inquire about Judah and Jerusalem with regard to the Law of your God, which is in your hand. ¹⁵Moreover, you are to take with you the silver and gold that the king and his advisers have freely given to the God of Israel, whose dwelling is in Jerusalem, ¹⁶together with all the silver and gold you may obtain from the province of Babylon, as well as the freewill offerings of the people and priests for the temple of their God in Jerusalem. ¹⁷With this money be sure to buy bulls, rams and male lambs, together with their grain offerings and drink offerings, and sacrifice them on the altar of the temple of your God in Jerusalem.

¹⁸You and your brother Jews may then do whatever seems best with the rest of the silver and gold, in accordance with the will of your God. ¹⁹Deliver to the God of Jerusalem all the articles entrusted to you for worship in the temple of your God. ²⁰And anything else needed for the temple of your God that you may have occasion to supply, you may provide from the royal treasury.

²¹Now I, King Artaxerxes, order all the treasurers of Trans-Euphrates to provide with diligence whatever Ezra the priest, a teacher of the Law of the God of heaven, may ask of you— ²²up to a hundred talents�q of silver, a hundred corsʳ of wheat, a hundred bathsˢ of wine, a hundred bathsˢ of olive oil, and salt without limit. ²³Whatever the God of heaven has prescribed, let it be done with diligence for the temple of the God of heaven. Why should there be wrath against the realm of the king and of his sons? ²⁴You are also to know that you have no authority to impose taxes, tribute or duty on any of the priests, Levites, singers, gatekeepers, temple servants or other workers at this house of God.

²⁵And you, Ezra, in accordance with the wisdom of your God, which you possess, appoint magistrates and judges to administer justice to all the people of Trans-Euphrates—all who know the laws of your God. And you are to teach any who do not know them. ²⁶Whoever does not obey the law of your God and the law of the king must surely be punished by death, banishment, confiscation of property, or imprisonment.

²⁷Praise be to the LORD, the God of our

ᵖ12 The text of Ezra 7:12-26 is in Aramaic.   q22 That is, about 3 3/4 tons (about 3.4 metric tons)   ʳ22 That is, probably about 600 bushels (about 22 kiloliters)   ˢ22 That is, probably about 600 gallons (about 2.2 kiloliters) fathers, who has put it into the king's heart to bring honor to the house of the LORD in Jerusalem in this way ²⁸and who has extended his good favor to me before the king and his advisers and all the king's powerful officials. Because the hand of the LORD my God was on me, I took courage and gathered leading men from Israel to go up with me.

CHAPTER 8

These are the family heads and those registered with them who came up with me from Babylon during the reign of King Artaxerxes:

²of the descendants of Phinehas, Gershom;

of the descendants of Ithamar, Daniel;

of the descendants of David, Hattush ³of the descendants of Shecaniah;

of the descendants of Parosh, Zechariah, and with him were registered 150 men;

⁴of the descendants of Pahath-Moab, Eliehoenai son of Zerahiah, and with him 200 men;

⁵of the descendants of Zattu,ᵗ Shecaniah son of Jahaziel, and with him 300 men;

⁶of the descendants of Adin, Ebed son of Jonathan, and with him 50 men;

⁷of the descendants of Elam, Jeshaiah son of Athaliah, and with him 70 men;

⁸of the descendants of Shephatiah, Zebadiah son of Michael, and with him 80 men;

⁹of the descendants of Joab, Obadiah son of Jehiel, and with him 218 men;

¹⁰of the descendants of Bani,ᵘ Shelomith son of Josiphiah, and with him 160 men;

¹¹of the descendants of Bebai, Zechariah son of Bebai, and with him 28 men;

¹²of the descendants of Azgad, Johanan son of Hakkatan, and with him 110 men;

¹³of the descendants of Adonikam, the last ones, whose names were

Eliphelet, Jeuel and Shemaiah, and with them 60 men;

¹⁴of the descendants of Bigvai, Uthai and Zaccur, and with them 70 men.

¹⁵I assembled them at the canal that flows toward Ahava, and we camped there three days. When I checked among the people and the priests, I found no Levites there. ¹⁶So I summoned Eliezer, Ariel, Shemaiah, Elnathan, Jarib, Elnathan, Nathan, Zechariah and Meshullam, who were leaders, and Joiarib and Elnathan, who were men of learning, ¹⁷and I sent them to Iddo, the leader in Casiphia. I told them what to say to Iddo and his kinsmen, the temple servants in Casiphia, so that they might bring attendants to us for the house of our God. ¹⁸Because the gracious hand of our God was on us, they brought us Sherebiah, a capable man, from the descendants of Mahli son of Levi, the son of Israel, and Sherebiah's sons and brothers, 18 men; ¹⁹and Hashabiah, together with Jeshaiah from the descendants of Merari, and his brothers and nephews, 20 men. ²⁰They also brought 220 of the temple servants—a body that David and the officials had established to assist the Levites. All were registered by name.

²¹There, by the Ahava Canal, I proclaimed a fast, so that we might humble ourselves before our God and ask him for a safe journey for us and our children, with all our possessions. ²²I was ashamed to ask the king for soldiers and horsemen to protect us from enemies on the road, because we had told the king, "The gracious hand of our God is on everyone who looks to him, but his great anger is against all who forsake him." ²³So we fasted and petitioned our God about this, and he answered our prayer.

²⁴Then I set apart twelve of the leading priests, together with Sherebiah, Hashabiah and ten of their brothers, ²⁵and I weighed out to them the offering of silver and gold and the articles that the king, his advisers, his officials and all Israel present there had donated for the house of our God. ²⁶I weighed out to them 650 talentsᵛ

ᵗ5 Some Septuagint manuscripts (also 1 Esdras 8:32); Hebrew does not have *Zattu.*   ᵘ10 Some Septuagint manuscripts (also 1 Esdras 8:36); Hebrew does not have *Bani.*   ᵛ26 That is, about 25 tons (about 22 metric tons) of silver, silver articles weighing 100 talents,[w] 100 talents[w] of gold, ²⁷20 bowls of gold valued at 1,000 darics,[x] and two fine articles of polished bronze, as precious as gold.

²⁸I said to them, "You as well as these articles are consecrated to the LORD. The silver and gold are a freewill offering to the LORD, the God of your fathers. ²⁹Guard them carefully until you weigh them out in the chambers of the house of the LORD in Jerusalem before the leading priests and the Levites and the family heads of Israel." ³⁰Then the priests and Levites received the silver and gold and sacred articles that had been weighed out to be taken to the house of our God in Jerusalem.

³¹On the twelfth day of the first month we set out from the Ahava Canal to go to Jerusalem. The hand of our God was on us, and he protected us from enemies and bandits along the way. ³²So we ar-

rived in Jerusalem, where we rested three days.

³³On the fourth day, in the house of our God, we weighed out the silver and gold and the sacred articles into the hands of Meremoth son of Uriah, the priest. Eleazar son of Phinehas was with him, and so were the Levites Jozabad son of Jeshua and Noadiah son of Binnui. ³⁴Everything was accounted for by number and weight, and the entire weight was recorded at that time.

³⁵Then the exiles who had returned from captivity sacrificed burnt offerings to the God of Israel: twelve bulls for all Israel, ninety-six rams, seventy-seven male lambs and, as a sin offering, twelve male goats. All this was a burnt offering to the LORD. ³⁶They also delivered the king's orders to the royal satraps and to the governors of Trans-Euphrates, who then gave assistance to the people and to the house of God.

---

[w]26 That is, about 3 3/4 tons (about 3.4 metric tons)   [x]27 That is, about 19 pounds (about 8.5 kilograms)

MAY 4 □ DAY 125
EZRA 9–10
Completion of the Spiritual Reforms

OVERVIEW Upon his arrival in Jerusalem, Ezra is greeted by reports of pollution in the city. Spiritually mixed marriages—expressly forbidden in the law of God—are taking place among people and priesthood alike. The news brings instant anguish to the "well versed in the Law of Moses" (7:6). Identifying himself with his disobedient countrymen, Ezra intercedes with an emotional prayer of confession. The guilty parties, moved by Ezra's example, assemble to bring forth fruits befitting repentance. In spite of poor weather, the difficult and time-consuming job of restoring purity in Israel's family life begins.

	Chapter 9		Chapter 10
Ezra's Anguish		Ezra's Acknowledgment	Ezra's Action
1	4	5 15	
Pollution Discovered			Purging Demanded

YOUR DAILY WALK The statement "Confession is good for the soul" is not a biblical quote, but it is a biblical concept. Look up the following verses to see what each says about the importance of confession:
- Acts 19:18–20
- James 5:16
- 1 John 1:9

Confession without change is just a game. Real confession involves two elements: (1) an acknowledgment of wrong committed and (2) a forsaking of wrong conduct. Ezra 9–10 describes a grievous condition in Jerusalem, a situation that demanded both acknowledging ("we have been unfaithful," 10:2) and forsaking ("separate yourselves," 10:11). Though the cure was perhaps as painful as the disease, God was pleased with the nation's prompt and whole-hearted confession.

Is confession overdue in your life today? There's no better time to complete this prayer: "God, I acknowledge that I have sinned against you, and beginning today with your help I will forsake _____."

INSIGHT Putting Yourself into Your Prayers
More than thirty occurrences of the plural pronouns *us, we* and *our* in Ezra's prayer of intercession (9:5–15) show that Ezra—though innocent of the charges—identified himself with the condition of his country-men. Do you pray that way for your family, church and nation?

CHAPTER 9
After these things had been done, the leaders came to me and said, "The people of Israel, including the priests and the Le-vites, have not kept themselves separate from the neighboring peoples with their detestable practices, like those of the Ca-naanites, Hittites, Perizzites, Jebusites, Ammonites, Moabites, Egyptians and Amorites. ²They have taken some of their daughters as wives for themselves and their sons, and have mingled the holy race with the peoples around them. And the leaders and officials have led the way in this unfaithfulness."

³When I heard this, I tore my tunic and cloak, pulled hair from my head and beard and sat down appalled. ⁴Then ev-eryone who trembled at the words of the God of Israel gathered around me be-cause of this unfaithfulness of the exiles. And I sat there appalled until the evening sacrifice.

⁵Then, at the evening sacrifice, I rose from my self-abasement, with my tunic and cloak torn, and fell on my knees with my hands spread out to the LORD my God ⁶and prayed:

"O my God, I am too ashamed and disgraced to lift up my face to you, my God, because our sins are higher than our heads and our guilt has reached to the heavens. ⁷From the days of our forefathers until now, our guilt has been great. Because of our sins, we and our kings and our priests have been subjected to the sword and captivity, to pillage and

humiliation at the hand of foreign kings, as it is today.

⁸"But now, for a brief moment, the LORD our God has been gracious in leaving us a remnant and giving us a firm place in his sanctuary, and so our God gives light to our eyes and a little relief in our bondage. ⁹Though we are slaves, our God has not de-serted us in our bondage. He has shown us kindness in the sight of the kings of Persia: He has granted us new life to rebuild the house of our God and repair its ruins, and he has given us a wall of protection in Judah and Jerusalem.

¹⁰"But now, O our God, what can we say after this? For we have disre-garded the commands ¹¹you gave through your servants the prophets when you said: 'The land you are en-tering to possess is a land polluted by the corruption of its peoples. By their detestable practices they have filled it with their impurity from one end to the other. ¹²Therefore, do not give your daughters in marriage to their sons or take their daughters for your sons. Do not seek a treaty of friend-ship with them at any time, that you may be strong and eat the good things of the land and leave it to your children as an everlasting inheri-tance.'

¹³"What has happened to us is a result of our evil deeds and our great guilt, and yet, our God, you have punished us less than our sins have deserved and have given us a

remnant like this. [14]Shall we again break your commands and intermarry with the peoples who commit such detestable practices? Would you not be angry enough with us to destroy us, leaving us no remnant or survivor? [15]O LORD, God of Israel, you are righteous! We are left this day as a remnant. Here we are before you in our guilt, though because of it not one of us can stand in your presence."

CHAPTER 10

While Ezra was praying and confessing, weeping and throwing himself down before the house of God, a large crowd of Israelites—men, women and children—gathered around him. They too wept bitterly. [2]Then Shecaniah son of Jehiel, one of the descendants of Elam, said to Ezra, "We have been unfaithful to our God by marrying foreign women from the peoples around us. But in spite of this, there is still hope for Israel. [3]Now let us make a covenant before our God to send away all these women and their children, in accordance with the counsel of my lord and of those who fear the commands of our God. Let it be done according to the Law. [4]Rise up; this matter is in your hands. We will support you, so take courage and do it."

[5]So Ezra rose up and put the leading priests and Levites and all Israel under oath to do what had been suggested. And they took the oath. [6]Then Ezra withdrew from before the house of God and went to the room of Jehohanan son of Eliashib. While he was there, he ate no food and drank no water, because he continued to mourn over the unfaithfulness of the exiles.

[7]A proclamation was then issued throughout Judah and Jerusalem for all the exiles to assemble in Jerusalem. [8]Anyone who failed to appear within three days would forfeit all his property, in accordance with the decision of the officials and elders, and would himself be expelled from the assembly of the exiles.

[9]Within the three days, all the men of Judah and Benjamin had gathered in Jerusalem. And on the twentieth day of the ninth month, all the people were sitting in the square before the house of God, greatly distressed by the occasion and because of the rain. [10]Then Ezra the priest

stood up and said to them, "You have been unfaithful; you have married foreign women, adding to Israel's guilt. [11]Now make confession to the LORD, the God of your fathers, and do his will. Separate yourselves from the peoples around you and from your foreign wives."

[12]The whole assembly responded with a loud voice: "You are right! We must do as you say. [13]But there are many people here and it is the rainy season; so we cannot stand outside. Besides, this matter cannot be taken care of in a day or two, because we have sinned greatly in this thing. [14]Let our officials act for the whole assembly. Then let everyone in our towns who has married a foreign woman come at a set time, along with the elders and judges of each town, until the fierce anger of our God in this matter is turned away from us." [15]Only Jonathan son of Asahel and Jahzeiah son of Tikvah, supported by Meshullam and Shabbethai the Levite, opposed this.

[16]So the exiles did as was proposed. Ezra the priest selected men who were family heads, one from each family division, and all of them designated by name. On the first day of the tenth month they sat down to investigate the cases, [17]and by the first day of the first month they finished dealing with all the men who had married foreign women.

[18]Among the descendants of the priests, the following had married foreign women:

From the descendants of Jeshua son of Jozadak, and his brothers: Maaseiah, Eliezer, Jarib and Gedaliah. [19](They all gave their hands in pledge to put away their wives, and for their guilt they each presented a ram from the flock as a guilt offering.)

[20]From the descendants of Immer: Hanani and Zebadiah.

[21]From the descendants of Harim: Maaseiah, Elijah, Shemaiah, Jehiel and Uzziah.

[22]From the descendants of Pashhur: Elioenai, Maaseiah, Ishmael, Nethanel, Jozabad and Elasah.

[23]Among the Levites:

Jozabad, Shimei, Kelaiah (that is,

Kelita), Pethahiah, Judah and Eli-
ezer.
24From the singers:
Eliashib.
From the gatekeepers:
Shallum, Telem and Uri.

25And among the other Israelites:

From the descendants of Parosh:
Ramiah, Izziah, Malkijah, Mijamin, Eleazar, Malkijah and Benaiah.
26From the descendants of Elam:
Mattaniah, Zechariah, Jehiel,
Abdi, Jeremoth and Elijah.
27From the descendants of Zattu:
Elioenai, Eliashib, Mattaniah, Jeremoth, Zabad and Aziza.
28From the descendants of Bebai:
Jehohanan, Hananiah, Zabbai and
Athlai.
29From the descendants of Bani:
Meshullam, Malluch, Adaiah, Jashub, Sheal and Jeremoth.
30From the descendants of Pahath-
Moab:
Adna, Kelal, Benaiah, Maaseiah,

Mattaniah, Bezalel, Binnui and
Manasseh.
31From the descendants of Harim:
Eliezer, Ishijah, Malkijah, Shema-
iah, Shimeon, 32Benjamin, Malluch
and Shemariah.
33From the descendants of Hashum:
Mattenai, Mattattah, Zabad,
Eliphelet, Jeremai, Manasseh and
Shimei.
34From the descendants of Bani:
Maadai, Amram, Uel, 35Benaiah,
Bedeiah, Keluhi, 36Vaniah, Mere-
moth, Eliashib, 37Mattaniah, Mat-
tenai and Jaasu.
38From the descendants of Binnui:y
Shimei, 39Shelemiah, Nathan,
Adaiah, 40Macnadebai, Shashai,
Sharai, 41Azarel, Shelemiah,
Shemariah, 42Shallum, Amariah
and Joseph.
43From the descendants of Nebo:
Jeiel, Mattithiah, Zabad, Zebina,
Jaddai, Joel and Benaiah.

44All these had married foreign women,
and some of them had children by these
wives.z

y37,38 See Septuagint (also 1 Esdras 9:34); Hebrew *Jaasu* 38*and Bani and Binnui,*   z44 Or *and they sent them away with their children*

Nehemiah

A CONTEMPORARY of Ezra and cupbearer to the king of Persia, Nehemiah leads the third and final return of the Jews to Jerusalem after the Babylonian exile. Under his leadership the people undertake the enormous task of rebuilding the holy city's battered walls, destroyed almost a century earlier. Despite opposition from without and abuse from within, the task is completed in only fifty-two days—a feat that even Israel's enemies must attribute to God's power.

Focus	New Walls			New Worship	Renewed Nation
Divisions	Wall Plans Conceived	Wall Plans Commenced	Wall Plans Concluded	Renewed Worship Commenced	Renewed Nation Cleansed
	1　2	3　4	5　7	8　10	11　13
Topics	Reconstructing the City			Reforming the Citizens	
	Security			Purity	
Place	Jerusalem				
Time	About 25 Years (445–420 B.C.)				

MAY 5 ☐ DAY 126
NEHEMIAH 1–2
Wall Plans Conceived

OVERVIEW Nearly a century has passed since Zerubbabel led the first group of Jewish exiles from Babylon back to their homeland. But though the temple stands complete, inviting worshipers from near and far, the walls lie in rubble, inviting enemy attacks. Nehemiah, cup-bearer to King Artaxerxes of Persia, hears this heartbreaking news. With a carefully and prayerfully conceived plan, he is ready when the king inquires, "What is it you want?" (2:4). Accompanied by army officers and cavalry, Nehemiah returns to Jerusalem to inspect the damage and infuse his countrymen with the will to raise the walls.

Chapter 1		Chapter 2
Jerusalem's Broken Walls	Nehemiah's Broken Heart	Nehemiah's Building Plans
1 3	4 11	
Problem	Prayer	Preparation

YOUR DAILY WALK Find a small electric appliance (an iron will do nicely), plug it in and turn it on. Does it work? Were you surprised that it worked? If not, why not?

Prayer can do anything God can do.

What would you think of a person who, upon plugging in an iron and finding that it didn't work, responded, "Well, I guess it just wasn't God's will for it to get hot"? Irons are supposed to get hot! And when they don't, you need to check the connections because something is obviously wrong. You expect a hot iron . . . and rightly so!

Now consider your prayer life. Does it "get hot"? That is, does God answer your prayers in regular, discernible ways? Or are you surprised when an answer to prayer comes? Your expectation should be an-swered prayer, for God has staked his reputation on it. Nehemiah learned that exciting truth, and you can, too! Spend a few extra min-utes basking in these biblical prayer promises: Jeremiah 33:3; Matthew 7:7–11; John 16:24; 1 John 5:14–15. Pick one and "plug it in" to your prayer life today. Watch for God's answer . . . and be thankful when it comes! That's what prayer is all about.

INSIGHT Persian Cupbearer: Servant or Something Else?
Nehemiah was more than a royal waiter. His duties included confi-dant, adviser, administrator, bodyguard and food taster (to protect the king from poisoning)—a position of high trust and authority. Today we would call him a prime minister.

CHAPTER 1
The words of Nehemiah son of Hacaliah:

In the month of Kislev in the twentieth year, while I was in the citadel of Susa, [2]Hanani, one of my brothers, came from Judah with some other men, and I ques-tioned them about the Jewish remnant that survived the exile, and also about Je-rusalem.

[3]They said to me, "Those who survived the exile and are back in the province are in great trouble and disgrace. The wall of Jerusalem is broken down, and its gates have been burned with fire."

[4]When I heard these things, I sat down

and wept. For some days I mourned and fasted and prayed before the God of heaven. [5]Then I said:

"O LORD, God of heaven, the great and awesome God, who keeps his covenant of love with those who love him and obey his commands, [6]let your ear be attentive and your eyes open to hear the prayer your servant is praying before you day and night for your servants, the people of Israel. I confess the sins we Israelites, including myself and my father's house, have committed against you. [7]We have acted very wickedly toward you. We have not obeyed the commands, decrees and laws you gave your servant Moses.

[8]"Remember the instruction you gave your servant Moses, saying, 'If you are unfaithful, I will scatter you among the nations, [9]but if you return to me and obey my commands, then even if your exiled people are at the farthest horizon, I will gather them from there and bring them to the place I have chosen as a dwelling for my Name.'

[10]"They are your servants and your people, whom you redeemed by your great strength and your mighty hand. [11]O Lord, let your ear be attentive to the prayer of this your servant and to the prayer of your servants who delight in revering your name. Give your servant success today by granting him favor in the presence of this man."

I was cupbearer to the king.

CHAPTER 2

In the month of Nisan in the twentieth year of King Artaxerxes, when wine was brought for him, I took the wine and gave it to the king. I had not been sad in his presence before; [2]so the king asked me, "Why does your face look so sad when you are not ill? This can be nothing but sadness of heart."

I was very much afraid, [3]but I said to the king, "May the king live forever! Why should my face not look sad when the city where my fathers are buried lies in ruins,

and its gates have been destroyed by fire?"

[4]The king said to me, "What is it you want?"

Then I prayed to the God of heaven, [5]and I answered the king, "If it pleases the king and if your servant has found favor in his sight, let him send me to the city in Judah where my fathers are buried so that I can rebuild it."

[6]Then the king, with the queen sitting beside him, asked me, "How long will your journey take, and when will you get back?" It pleased the king to send me; so I set a time.

[7]I also said to him, "If it pleases the king, may I have letters to the governors of Trans-Euphrates, so that they will provide me safe-conduct until I arrive in Judah? [8]And may I have a letter to Asaph, keeper of the king's forest, so he will give me timber to make beams for the gates of the citadel by the temple and for the city wall and for the residence I will occupy?" And because the gracious hand of my God was upon me, the king granted my requests. [9]So I went to the governors of Trans-Euphrates and gave them the king's letters. The king had also sent army officers and cavalry with me.

[10]When Sanballat the Horonite and Tobiah the Ammonite official heard about this, they were very much disturbed that someone had come to promote the welfare of the Israelites.

[11]I went to Jerusalem, and after staying there three days [12]I set out during the night with a few men. I had not told anyone what my God had put in my heart to do for Jerusalem. There were no mounts with me except the one I was riding on. [13]By night I went out through the Valley Gate toward the Jackal[a] Well and the Dung Gate, examining the walls of Jerusalem, which had been broken down, and its gates, which had been destroyed by fire. [14]Then I moved on toward the Fountain Gate and the King's Pool, but there was not enough room for my mount to get through; [15]so I went up the valley by night, examining the wall. Finally, I turned back and reentered through the Valley Gate. [16]The officials did not know where I had gone or what I was doing, because as yet I had said nothing to the

[a]13 Or Serpent or Fig

Jews or the priests or nobles or officials or any others who would be doing the work.

¹⁷Then I said to them, "You see the trouble we are in: Jerusalem lies in ruins, and its gates have been burned with fire. Come, let us rebuild the wall of Jerusalem, and we will no longer be in disgrace." ¹⁸I also told them about the gracious hand of my God upon me and what the king had said to me.

They replied, "Let us start rebuilding." So they began this good work.

¹⁹But when Sanballat the Horonite, Tobiah the Ammonite official and Geshem the Arab heard about it, they mocked and ridiculed us. "What is this you are doing?" they asked. "Are you rebelling against the king?"

²⁰I answered them by saying, "The God of heaven will give us success. We his servants will start rebuilding, but as for you, you have no share in Jerusalem or any claim or historic right to it."

MAY 6 □ DAY 127
NEHEMIAH 3–4
Wall Plans Commenced

OVERVIEW Nehemiah's dream of rebuilding the walls now becomes contagious! The people rise up in unison, trowels in hand, to begin repairing the eight gates and more than two miles of wall surrounding the city. Nehemiah's strategy is simple: Give each person a vested interest in the work. To ensure both speed and quality of workmanship, he assigns each worker the portion of the wall nearest the worker's own house! There's a lot of incentive to do a good job when you know that if enemies break through a defective portion of the wall, the first people jeopardized will be your own family. But soon the entire project is threatened by outside opposition. Harmless ridicule gives way to threats of violence, and Nehemiah responds with a combination of prayer and preparation.

Chapter 3		Chapter 4	
Repairing the Walls	Ridiculing the Workers	Rallying the Workers	
		Prayerfully	Militarily
1	3	4 12	13 23
The Work Initiated		The Work Interrupted	

Too many people pray like little children who knock on doors, then run away.

YOUR DAILY WALK "Pray like it's up to God; then act like it's up to you." Those words are found nowhere in Scripture, but they contain more than a little truth. Over and over, God has told you to take your problems and anxieties to him. "Do not be anxious about anything, but in everything, by prayer and petition, with thanksgiving, present your requests to God" (Philippians 4:6). Take a lesson from Nehemiah. When troubles come, turn your problems into prayers . . . pronto!

But once you have prayed through your problems, don't expect angels to finish building your walls! Pick up your trowel and finish the job God has given you. "Continue to work . . . for it is God who works in you" (Philippians 2:12–13) is a great balance to achieve.

Pick a situation in your life that needs *prayer* coupled with *preparation*. Pray it through, work it out and share it with a friend or family member!

INSIGHT The Special Gate for God
Among the list of gates is the East Gate (3:29), through which the shekinah glory (a visible manifestation of the presence of God) left and

by which it will return. Ezekiel sees the return of God's glory through the East Gate (Ezekiel 43:1–17) to reside in the temple's Most Holy Place during the kingdom age, as he had seen its departure during the fall of Jerusalem.

CHAPTER 3

Eliashib the high priest and his fellow priests went to work and rebuilt the Sheep Gate. They dedicated it and set its doors in place, building as far as the Tower of the Hundred, which they dedicated, and as far as the Tower of Hananel. ²The men of Jericho built the adjoining section, and Zaccur son of Imri built next to them.

³The Fish Gate was rebuilt by the sons of Hassenaah. They laid its beams and put its doors and bolts and bars in place. ⁴Meremoth son of Uriah, the son of Hakkoz, repaired the next section. Next to him Meshullam son of Berekiah, the son of Meshezabel, made repairs, and next to him Zadok son of Baana also made repairs. ⁵The next section was repaired by the men of Tekoa, but their nobles would not put their shoulders to the work under their supervisors.ᵇ

⁶The Jeshanahᶜ Gate was repaired by Joiada son of Paseah and Meshullam son of Besodeiah. They laid its beams and put its doors and bolts and bars in place. ⁷Next to them, repairs were made by men from Gibeon and Mizpah—Melatiah of Gibeon and Jadon of Meronoth—places under the authority of the governor of Trans-Euphrates. ⁸Uzziel son of Harhaiah, one of the goldsmiths, repaired the next section; and Hananiah, one of the perfume-makers, made repairs next to that. They restoredᵈ Jerusalem as far as the Broad Wall. ⁹Rephaiah son of Hur, ruler of a half-district of Jerusalem, repaired the next section. ¹⁰Adjoining this, Jedaiah son of Harumaph made repairs opposite his house, and Hattush son of Hashabneiah made repairs next to him. ¹¹Malkijah son of Harim and Hasshub son of Pahath-Moab repaired another section and the Tower of the Ovens. ¹²Shallum son of Hallohesh, ruler of a half-district of Jerusalem, repaired the next section with the help of his daughters.

¹³The Valley Gate was repaired by Hanun and the residents of Zanoah. They rebuilt it and put its doors and bolts and bars in place. They also repaired five hundred yardsᵉ of the wall as far as the Dung Gate.

¹⁴The Dung Gate was repaired by Malkijah son of Recab, ruler of the district of Beth Hakkerem. He rebuilt it and put its doors and bolts and bars in place.

¹⁵The Fountain Gate was repaired by Shallun son of Col-Hozeh, ruler of the district of Mizpah. He rebuilt it, roofing it over and putting its doors and bolts and bars in place. He also repaired the wall of the Pool of Siloam,ᶠ by the King's Garden, as far as the steps going down from the City of David. ¹⁶Beyond him, Nehemiah son of Azbuk, ruler of a half-district of Beth Zur, made repairs up to a point opposite the tombsᵍ of David, as far as the artificial pool and the House of the Heroes.

¹⁷Next to him, the repairs were made by the Levites under Rehum son of Bani. Beside him, Hashabiah, ruler of half the district of Keilah, carried out repairs for his district. ¹⁸Next to him, the repairs were made by their countrymen under Binnuiʰ son of Henadad, ruler of the other half-district of Keilah. ¹⁹Next to him, Ezer son of Jeshua, ruler of Mizpah, repaired another section, from a point facing the ascent to the armory as far as the angle. ²⁰Next to him, Baruch son of Zabbai zealously repaired another section, from the angle to the entrance of the house of Eliashib the high priest. ²¹Next to him, Meremoth son of Uriah, the son of Hakkoz, repaired another section, from the entrance of Eliashib's house to the end of it.

²²The repairs next to him were made by the priests from the surrounding region. ²³Beyond them, Benjamin and Hasshub made repairs in front of their house; and next to them, Azariah son of Maaseiah, the son of Ananiah, made repairs beside

---

ᵇ5 Or their Lord or the governor   ᶜ6 Or Old   ᵈ8 Or They left out part of   ᵉ13 Hebrew a thousand cubits (about 450 meters)
ᶠ15 Hebrew Shelah, a variant of Shiloah, that is, Siloam   ᵍ16 Hebrew; Septuagint, some Vulgate manuscripts and Syriac tomb
ʰ18 Two Hebrew manuscripts and Syriac (see also Septuagint and verse 24); most Hebrew manuscripts Bavvai

his house. ²⁴Next to him, Binnui son of Henadad repaired another section, from Azariah's house to the angle and the corner, ²⁵and Palal son of Uzai worked opposite the angle and the tower projecting from the upper palace near the court of the guard. Next to him, Pedaiah son of Parosh ²⁶and the temple servants living on the hill of Ophel made repairs up to a point opposite the Water Gate toward the east and the projecting tower. ²⁷Next to them, the men of Tekoa repaired another section, from the great projecting tower to the wall of Ophel.

²⁸Above the Horse Gate, the priests made repairs, each in front of his own house. ²⁹Next to them, Zadok son of Immer made repairs opposite his house. Next to him, Shemaiah son of Shecaniah, the guard at the East Gate, made repairs. ³⁰Next to him, Hananiah son of Shelemiah, and Hanun, the sixth son of Zalaph, repaired another section. Next to them, Meshullam son of Berekiah made repairs opposite his living quarters. ³¹Next to him, Malkijah, one of the goldsmiths, made repairs as far as the house of the temple servants and the merchants, opposite the Inspection Gate, and as far as the room above the corner; ³²and between the room above the corner and the Sheep Gate the goldsmiths and merchants made repairs.

CHAPTER 4

When Sanballat heard that we were rebuilding the wall, he became angry and was greatly incensed. He ridiculed the Jews, ²and in the presence of his associates and the army of Samaria, he said, "What are those feeble Jews doing? Will they restore their wall? Will they offer sacrifices? Will they finish in a day? Can they bring the stones back to life from those heaps of rubble—burned as they are?"

³Tobiah the Ammonite, who was at his side, said, "What they are building—if even a fox climbed up on it, he would break down their wall of stones!"

⁴Hear us, O our God, for we are despised. Turn their insults back on their own heads. Give them over as plunder in a land of captivity. ⁵Do not cover up their

guilt or blot out their sins from your sight, for they have thrown insults in the face of[i] the builders.

⁶So we rebuilt the wall till all of it reached half its height, for the people worked with all their heart.

⁷But when Sanballat, Tobiah, the Arabs, the Ammonites and the men of Ashdod heard that the repairs to Jerusalem's walls had gone ahead and that the gaps were being closed, they were very angry. ⁸They all plotted together to come and fight against Jerusalem and stir up trouble against it. ⁹But we prayed to our God and posted a guard day and night to meet this threat.

¹⁰Meanwhile, the people in Judah said, "The strength of the laborers is giving out, and there is so much rubble that we cannot rebuild the wall."

¹¹Also our enemies said, "Before they know it or see us, we will be right there among them and will kill them and put an end to the work."

¹²Then the Jews who lived near them came and told us ten times over, "Wherever you turn, they will attack us."

¹³Therefore I stationed some of the people behind the lowest points of the wall at the exposed places, posting them by families, with their swords, spears and bows. ¹⁴After I looked things over, I stood up and said to the nobles, the officials and the rest of the people, "Don't be afraid of them. Remember the Lord, who is great and awesome, and fight for your brothers, your sons and your daughters, your wives and your homes."

¹⁵When our enemies heard that we were aware of their plot and that God had frustrated it, we all returned to the wall, each to his own work.

¹⁶From that day on, half of my men did the work, while the other half were equipped with spears, shields, bows and armor. The officers posted themselves behind all the people of Judah ¹⁷who were building the wall. Those who carried materials did their work with one hand and held a weapon in the other, ¹⁸and each of the builders wore his sword at his side as he worked. But the man who sounded the trumpet stayed with me.

¹⁹Then I said to the nobles, the officials and the rest of the people, "The work is

extensive and spread out, and we are widely separated from each other along the wall. ²⁰Wherever you hear the sound of the trumpet, join us there. Our God will fight for us!"

²¹So we continued the work with half the men holding spears, from the first light of dawn till the stars came out. ²²At that time I also said to the people, "Have every man and his helper stay inside Jerusalem at night, so they can serve us as guards by night and workmen by day." ²³Neither I nor my brothers nor my men nor the guards with me took off our clothes; each had his weapon, even when he went for water.ʲ

ʲ23 The meaning of the Hebrew for this clause is uncertain.

MAY 7 □ DAY 128
Strength of the Lord

 LOOK BACK Hezekiah and Ezra. Their names sound alike and have similar meanings. *Ezra* means "help"; *Hezekiah* means "God strengthens." But there the similarity ends. Hezekiah was a king; Ezra was a priest. They never met since they lived hundreds of years apart in different parts of the world: Hezekiah in Jerusalem; Ezra in Persia. Hezekiah was trying to protect his nation from enemy attack; Ezra was intent on rebuilding his nation after seventy years of exile.

And yet these two heroes of the Old Testament accomplished great things for God because they shared a common passion to read, study and obey the law of God. They were able to provide help and strength in the lives of others because their own lives were anchored to the unchanging foundation of God's Word.

Hezekiah and Ezra, Ruth and Esther—what a rich heritage of heroes and heroines you'll find in the pages of the Old Testament. Men and women who walked with God in uncertain days, made tough decisions, faced giant-sized enemies, prayed powerful prayers and accomplished mighty feats in the strength of the Lord.

 LOOK UP Ezra learned firsthand about the hand of the Lord his God (Ezra 7:6, 9; 8:18, 22). When an attribute of God is described in human terms, it's called an anthropomorphism. Here are just a few of the many ways in which God is described in human terms. Can you explain the significance of each analogy?

The finger that points the way is part of the hand that provides the need.

The "hand" of the Lord (Joshua 4:24) helps us come to grips with his _____.

The "voice" of the Lord (1 Samuel 15:22) speaks of his _____.

The "eyes" of the Lord (2 Chronicles 16:9) causes us to view his _____.

The "arm" of the Lord (Isaiah 51:9) refers to his _____.

When a boxer throws a jab, his intent is to cause his opponent to feel the power of his hand. All the strength of the boxer is channeled and directed through his hand. In the same way, God desires to channel his power through the life of the believer. Ezra's life was full of God's power because Ezra's heart and mind were full of God's Word.

 LOOK AHEAD If you're experiencing a season of weakness or fruitlessness in your spiritual life in recent days, perhaps you need to check your "power supply." A branch that is wilted and fruitless has obviously become severed from the vine, its source of strength and life (John 15:1–8).

Happiness, fruitfulness, prosperity—each is the heritage of anyone who makes the law of the Lord his or her daily meditation (Psalm 1:1–3). It's a truth Ezra learned, and so can you.

To meditate is to chew the cud, drawing nourishment from the life-giving truths of the Bible just like a cow draws nourishment from the life-giving grass. And typically one "chew" isn't enough! There is ample reason to meditate upon the same passage over and over again, for God delights to give fresh insight from previously digested passages!

Thumb back through the readings you've covered so far this year, and find a favorite passage or devotional. Read it again thoughtfully, reflecting on how the intervening months have helped to sharpen your insight into its meaning and application.

MAY 8 □ DAY 129
NEHEMIAH 5–7
Wall Plans Concluded

OVERVIEW Internal strife in the Israelite camp causes as much unrest as the attacks from outside the camp. The people are suffering under financial stress imposed by their Persian masters. Worse yet, the Hebrews are exacting interest from their own brothers who have borrowed to pay their debts. After correcting this abuse, Nehemiah again turns his attention toward the threats from without. He refuses to be lured into an assassination plot on his life, nor will he be intimidated by the threats of a slanderous letter. After fifty-two days of building and battling, the walls stand completed. At last the order can go forth to repopulate the holy city of Jerusalem!

Chapter 5		Chapter 6		Chapter 7
Usury Abolished	Murder Averted	Deceit Avoided	Mission Accomplished	Population Assigned
1	4	5 14	15 19	1 73a
Opposition		Outcome		

YOUR DAILY WALK How do you react when you see the poor exploited? Does your heart beat a little faster . . . your temperature go up a degree or two? Now imagine it is a member of your family being exploited. How would you respond to that?

Injustice anywhere is a threat to justice everywhere.

Lack of grain and oppressive Persian rule had forced some of the Hebrews in Jerusalem to mortgage their homes and sell themselves into slavery in order to pay their debts. When Nehemiah heard that the rich were extorting money from their own countrymen, his reaction was immediate . . . and unmistakable!

You may never have exacted interest from someone suffering hardships, but have you been guilty of taking advantage of another Christian by ignoring his or her difficult circumstances? Carry your money somewhere other than in your wallet or purse today, and let the empty wallet (or purse) remind you of the usury tactics of Nehemiah's day. Then look for a way to assist, rather than simply avoid, a Christian brother or sister who is in difficult financial straits.

INSIGHT Doing Wrong to Do Right Is Wrong, Right?
Shemaiah's offer of safety in the temple for Nehemiah (6:10–14) was a direct violation of God's law that forbade laymen from entering the sanctuary. Even if Shemaiah had been telling the truth (which he wasn't), to enter the temple would have been a fatal mistake.

CHAPTER 5

Now the men and their wives raised a great outcry against their Jewish brothers. ²Some were saying, "We and our sons and daughters are numerous; in order for us to eat and stay alive, we must get grain."

³Others were saying, "We are mortgaging our fields, our vineyards and our homes to get grain during the famine."

⁴Still others were saying, "We have had to borrow money to pay the king's tax on our fields and vineyards. ⁵Although we are of the same flesh and blood as our countrymen and though our sons are as good as theirs, yet we have to subject our sons and daughters to slavery. Some of our daughters have already been enslaved, but we are powerless, because our fields and our vineyards belong to others."

⁶When I heard their outcry and these charges, I was very angry. ⁷I pondered them in my mind and then accused the nobles and officials. I told them, "You are exacting usury from your own countrymen!" So I called together a large meeting to deal with them ⁸and said: "As far as possible, we have bought back our Jewish brothers who were sold to the Gentiles. Now you are selling your brothers, only for them to be sold back to us!" They kept quiet, because they could find nothing to say.

⁹So I continued, "What you are doing is not right. Shouldn't you walk in the fear of our God to avoid the reproach of our Gentile enemies? ¹⁰I and my brothers and my men are also lending the people money and grain. But let the exacting of usury stop! ¹¹Give back to them immediately their fields, vineyards, olive groves and houses, and also the usury you are charging them—the hundredth part of the money, grain, new wine and oil."

¹²"We will give it back," they said. "And we will not demand anything more from them. We will do as you say."

Then I summoned the priests and made the nobles and officials take an oath to do what they had promised. ¹³I also shook out the folds of my robe and said, "In this way may God shake out of his house and possessions every man who does not keep this promise. So may such a man be shaken out and emptied!"

At this the whole assembly said, "Amen," and praised the LORD. And the people did as they had promised.

¹⁴Moreover, from the twentieth year of King Artaxerxes, when I was appointed to be their governor in the land of Judah, until his thirty-second year—twelve years—neither I nor my brothers ate the food allotted to the governor. ¹⁵But the earlier governors—those preceding me—placed a heavy burden on the people and took forty shekels*ᵏ* of silver from them in addition to food and wine. Their assistants also lorded it over the people. But out of reverence for God I did not act like that. ¹⁶Instead, I devoted myself to the work on this wall. All my men were assembled there for the work; we*ˡ* did not acquire any land.

¹⁷Furthermore, a hundred and fifty Jews and officials ate at my table, as well as those who came to us from the surrounding nations. ¹⁸Each day one ox, six choice sheep and some poultry were prepared for me, and every ten days an abundant supply of wine of all kinds. In spite of all this, I never demanded the food allotted to the governor, because the demands were heavy on these people.

¹⁹Remember me with favor, O my God, for all I have done for these people.

CHAPTER 6

When word came to Sanballat, Tobiah, Geshem the Arab and the rest of our enemies that I had rebuilt the wall and not a gap was left in it—though up to that time I had not set the doors in the gates—²Sanballat and Geshem sent me this message: "Come, let us meet together in one of the villages*ᵐ* on the plain of Ono."

But they were scheming to harm me;

ᵏ15 That is, about 1 pound (about 0.5 kilogram)   *ˡ16* Most Hebrew manuscripts; some Hebrew manuscripts, Septuagint, Vulgate and Syriac *I*   *ᵐ2* Or *in Kephirim*

³so I sent messengers to them with this reply: "I am carrying on a great project and cannot go down. Why should the work stop while I leave it and go down to you?" ⁴Four times they sent me the same message, and each time I gave them the same answer.

⁵Then, the fifth time, Sanballat sent his aide to me with the same message, and in his hand was an unsealed letter ⁶in which was written:

"It is reported among the nations— and Geshem" says it is true—that you and the Jews are plotting to revolt, and therefore you are building the wall. Moreover, according to these reports you are about to become their king ⁷and have even appointed prophets to make this proclamation about you in Jerusalem: 'There is a king in Judah!' Now this report will get back to the king; so come, let us confer together."

⁸I sent him this reply: "Nothing like what you are saying is happening; you are just making it up out of your head."

⁹They were all trying to frighten us, thinking, "Their hands will get too weak for the work, and it will not be completed."

But I prayed, "Now strengthen my hands."

¹⁰One day I went to the house of Shemaiah son of Delaiah, the son of Mehetabel, who was shut in at his home. He said, "Let us meet in the house of God, inside the temple, and let us close the temple doors, because men are coming to kill you—by night they are coming to kill you."

¹¹But I said, "Should a man like me run away? Or should one like me go into the temple to save his life? I will not go!" ¹²I realized that God had not sent him, but that he had prophesied against me because Tobiah and Sanballat had hired him. ¹³He had been hired to intimidate me so that I would commit a sin by doing this, and then they would give me a bad name to discredit me.

¹⁴Remember Tobiah and Sanballat, O my God, because of what they have done; remember also the prophetess No-

adiah and the rest of the prophets who have been trying to intimidate me.

¹⁵So the wall was completed on the twenty-fifth of Elul, in fifty-two days. ¹⁶When all our enemies heard about this, all the surrounding nations were afraid and lost their self-confidence, because they realized that this work had been done with the help of our God.

¹⁷Also, in those days the nobles of Judah were sending many letters to Tobiah, and replies from Tobiah kept coming to them. ¹⁸For many in Judah were under oath to him, since he was son-in-law to Shecaniah son of Arah, and his son Jehohanan had married the daughter of Meshullam son of Berekiah. ¹⁹Moreover, they kept reporting to me his good deeds and then telling him what I said. And Tobiah sent letters to intimidate me.

CHAPTER 7

After the wall had been rebuilt and I had set the doors in place, the gatekeepers and the singers and the Levites were appointed. ²I put in charge of Jerusalem my brother Hanani, along withᵒ Hananiah the commander of the citadel, because he was a man of integrity and feared God more than most men do. ³I said to them, "The gates of Jerusalem are not to be opened until the sun is hot. While the gatekeepers are still on duty, have them shut the doors and bar them. Also appoint residents of Jerusalem as guards, some at their posts and some near their own houses."

⁴Now the city was large and spacious, but there were few people in it, and the houses had not yet been rebuilt. ⁵So my God put it into my heart to assemble the nobles, the officials and the common people for registration by families. I found the genealogical record of those who had been the first to return. This is what I found written there:

⁶These are the people of the province who came up from the captivity of the exiles whom Nebuchadnezzar king of Babylon had taken captive (they returned to Jerusalem and Judah, each to his own town, ⁷in company with Zerubbabel, Jeshua, Nehemiah, Azariah, Raamiah,

---

ⁿ6 Hebrew *Gashmu*, a variant of *Geshem*   ᵒ2 Or *Hanani, that is,*

Nahamani, Mordecai, Bilshan, Mispereth, Bigvai, Nehum and Baanah):

The list of the men of Israel:

8the descendants of Parosh   2,172
9of Shephatiah   372
10of Arah   652
11of Pahath-Moab (through
   the line of Jeshua and
   Joab)   2,818
12of Elam   1,254
13of Zattu   845
14of Zaccai   760
15of Binnui   648
16of Bebai   628
17of Azgad   2,322
18of Adonikam   667
19of Bigvai   2,067
20of Adin   655
21of Ater (through Hezekiah)   98
22of Hashum   328
23of Bezai   324
24of Hariph   112
25of Gibeon   95

26the men of Bethlehem and
   Netophah   188
27of Anathoth   128
28of Beth Azmaveth   42
29of Kiriath Jearim, Kephirah
   and Beeroth   743
30of Ramah and Geba   621
31of Micmash   122
32of Bethel and Ai   123
33of the other Nebo   52
34of the other Elam   1,254
35of Harim   320
36of Jericho   345
37of Lod, Hadid and Ono   721
38of Senaah   3,930

39The priests:

the descendants of Jedaiah
   (through the family of
   Jeshua)   973
40of Immer   1,052
41of Pashhur   1,247
42of Harim   1,017

43The Levites:

the descendants of Jeshua
   (through Kadmiel through
   the line of Hodaviah)   74

44The singers:

the descendants of Asaph   148

45The gatekeepers:

the descendants of
   Shallum, Ater, Talmon,
   Akkub, Hatita and Shobai   138

46The temple servants:

the descendants of
   Ziha, Hasupha, Tabbaoth,
47Keros, Sia, Padon,
48Lebana, Hagaba, Shalmai,
49Hanan, Giddel, Gahar,
50Reaiah, Rezin, Nekoda,
51Gazzam, Uzza, Paseah,
52Besai, Meunim, Nephussim,
53Bakbuk, Hakupha, Harhur,
54Bazluth, Mehida, Harsha,
55Barkos, Sisera, Temah,
56Neziah and Hatipha

57The descendants of the servants of
Solomon:

the descendants of
   Sotai, Sophereth, Perida,
58Jaala, Darkon, Giddel,
59Shephatiah, Hattil,
   Pokereth-Hazzebaim and Amon

60The temple servants and the
   descendants of the servants
   of Solomon   392

61The following came up from the
towns of Tel Melah, Tel Harsha, Kerub, Addon and Immer, but they
could not show that their families
were descended from Israel:

62the descendants of
   Delaiah, Tobiah and Nekoda   642

63And from among the priests:

the descendants of
   Hobaiah, Hakkoz and Barzillai
   (a man who had married a
   daughter of Barzillai the
   Gileadite and was called by that
   name).

64These searched for their family
records, but they could not find them
and so were excluded from the
priesthood as unclean. 65The governor, therefore, ordered them not to
eat any of the most sacred food until
there should be a priest ministering
with the Urim and Thummim.

66The whole company numbered
42,360, 67besides their 7,337 menservants and maidservants; and they

also had 245 men and women singers. ⁶⁸There were 736 horses, 245
mules,ᵖ ⁶⁹435 camels and 6,720 donkeys.

⁷⁰Some of the heads of the families
contributed to the work. The governor gave to the treasury 1,000 drach-
mas�q of gold, 50 bowls and 530 garments for priests. ⁷¹Some of the heads
of the families gave to the treasury

for the work 20,000 drachmasʳ of
gold and 2,200 minasˢ of silver.
⁷²The total given by the rest of the
people was 20,000 drachmas of gold,
2,000 minasᵗ of silver and 67 garments for priests.

⁷³The priests, the Levites, the gatekeepers, the singers and the temple
servants, along with certain of the
people and the rest of the Israelites,
settled in their own towns.

ᵖ68 Some Hebrew manuscripts (see also Ezra 2:66); most Hebrew manuscripts do not have this verse.   �q70 That is, about 19
pounds (about 8.5 kilograms)   ʳ71 That is, about 375 pounds (about 170 kilograms); also in verse 72   ˢ71 That is, about
1 1/3 tons (about 1.2 metric tons)   ᵗ72 That is, about 1 1/4 tons (about 1.1 metric tons)

MAY 9 ☐ DAY 130
NEHEMIAH 8–10
Renewed Worship Commenced

OVERVIEW The first half of Nehemiah's account describes the construction of the city walls; the second half contains instruction for the
city worshipers. Beginning with chapter 8 the account becomes bio-
graphical rather than autobiographical as Nehemiah deals with the
spiritual rather than the physical well-being of the inhabitants of Jerusalem. Revival breaks out when the Word of God is translated, "broadcast" and explained for the common people. The preaching of Ezra
the priest produces heartfelt confession, wholehearted worship and refreshing resolve to bring the nation's wayward conduct in line with
the nation's covenant relationship with God.

Chapters 7–8		Chapter 9	Chapter 10
Reading the Law 7:73b 8:12	Restoring the Law 13 18	Responding to the Law	Resolving to Keep the Law
Conviction	Commemoration	Confession	Commitment

Freedom decays as material society expands.

YOUR DAILY WALK This evening go through your house and gather
up every trace of Scripture you can find: every copy of the Bible . . .
every Bible motto or poster hanging on your walls . . . every hymnbook or gospel recording . . . every gospel tract or Christian biography. Pile them all together on a table in the living room. Then find a
book of matches and strike one as you ponder this sobering thought:
Someday you may lose the priceless freedom you enjoy today of surrounding yourself with God's Word.

If that ever happened, how much of God's Word would you have
hidden away in your heart, where no tyrant can invade (Psalm
119:11)? Ezra's reading of the long-neglected Book of the Law produced tears of gladness and grief—gladness over the return of God's
Word to a place of primacy in the nation, and grief that the nation
had drifted so far from God's will and way. It could never happen in
our country . . . or could it? And isn't it worth five minutes of prayer
daily to help see that it won't?

INSIGHT Ezra, the Elusive Priest

Ezra did not appear until chapter 7 of the book that bears his own name, and he does not appear until chapter 8 of the book of Nehemiah—a natural dividing point for the book. Chapters 1–7 center around the *work* of God in building the wall; chapters 8–13 focus on the *worship* of God in obedience to the law.

When the seventh month came and the Israelites had settled in their CHAPTER 8 towns, ¹all the people assembled as one man in the square before the Water Gate. They told Ezra the scribe to bring out the Book of the Law of Moses, which the LORD had commanded for Israel.

²So on the first day of the seventh month Ezra the priest brought the Law before the assembly, which was made up of men and women and all who were able to understand. ³He read it aloud from daybreak till noon as he faced the square before the Water Gate in the presence of the men, women and others who could understand. And all the people listened attentively to the Book of the Law.

⁴Ezra the scribe stood on a high wooden platform built for the occasion. Beside him on his right stood Mattithiah, Shema, Anaiah, Uriah, Hilkiah and Maaseiah; and on his left were Pedaiah, Mishael, Malkijah, Hashum, Hashbaddanah, Zechariah and Meshullam.

⁵Ezra opened the book. All the people could see him because he was standing above them; and as he opened it, the people all stood up. ⁶Ezra praised the LORD, the great God; and all the people lifted their hands and responded, "Amen! Amen!" Then they bowed down and worshiped the LORD with their faces to the ground.

⁷The Levites—Jeshua, Bani, Sherebiah, Jamin, Akkub, Shabbethai, Hodiah, Maaseiah, Kelita, Azariah, Jozabad, Hanan and Pelaiah—instructed the people in the Law while the people were standing there. ⁸They read from the Book of the Law of God, making it clear[u] and giving the meaning so that the people could understand what was being read.

⁹Then Nehemiah the governor, Ezra the priest and scribe, and the Levites who were instructing the people said to them all, "This day is sacred to the LORD your God. Do not mourn or weep." For all the people had been weeping as they listened to the words of the Law.

¹⁰Nehemiah said, "Go and enjoy choice food and sweet drinks, and send some to those who have nothing prepared. This day is sacred to our Lord. Do not grieve, for the joy of the LORD is your strength."

¹¹The Levites calmed all the people, saying, "Be still, for this is a sacred day. Do not grieve."

¹²Then all the people went away to eat and drink, to send portions of food and to celebrate with great joy, because they now understood the words that had been made known to them.

¹³On the second day of the month, the heads of all the families, along with the priests and the Levites, gathered around Ezra the scribe to give attention to the words of the Law. ¹⁴They found written in the Law, which the LORD had commanded through Moses, that the Israelites were to live in booths during the feast of the seventh month ¹⁵and that they should proclaim this word and spread it throughout their towns and in Jerusalem: "Go out into the hill country and bring back branches from olive and wild olive trees, and from myrtles, palms and shade trees, to make booths"—as it is written.[v]

¹⁶So the people went out and brought back branches and built themselves booths on their own roofs, in their courtyards, in the courts of the house of God and in the square by the Water Gate and the one by the Gate of Ephraim. ¹⁷The whole company that had returned from exile built booths and lived in them. From the days of Joshua son of Nun until that day, the Israelites had not celebrated it like this. And their joy was very great.

¹⁸Day after day, from the first day to the last, Ezra read from the Book of the Law of God. They celebrated the feast for seven days, and on the eighth day, in accordance with the regulation, there was an assembly.

u 8 Or *God, translating it   v 15* See Lev. 23:37-40.

CHAPTER 9

On the twenty-fourth day of the same month, the Israelites gathered together, fasting and wearing sackcloth and having dust on their heads. ²Those of Israelite descent had separated themselves from all foreigners. They stood in their places and confessed their sins and the wickedness of their fathers. ³They stood where they were and read from the Book of the Law of the LORD their God for a quarter of the day, and spent another quarter in confession and in worshiping the LORD their God. ⁴Standing on the stairs were the Levites—Jeshua, Bani, Kadmiel, Shebaniah, Bunni, Sherebiah, Bani and Kenani—who called with loud voices to the LORD their God. ⁵And the Levites—Jeshua, Kadmiel, Bani, Hashabneiah, Sherebiah, Hodiah, Shebaniah and Pethahiah—said: "Stand up and praise the LORD your God, who is from everlasting to everlasting.ʷ"

"Blessed be your glorious name, and may it be exalted above all blessing and praise. ⁶You alone are the LORD. You made the heavens, even the highest heavens, and all their starry host, the earth and all that is on it, the seas and all that is in them. You give life to everything, and the multitudes of heaven worship you.

⁷"You are the LORD God, who chose Abram and brought him out of Ur of the Chaldeans and named him Abraham. ⁸You found his heart faithful to you, and you made a covenant with him to give to his descendants the land of the Canaanites, Hittites, Amorites, Perizzites, Jebusites and Girgashites. You have kept your promise because you are righteous.

⁹"You saw the suffering of our forefathers in Egypt; you heard their cry at the Red Sea.ˣ ¹⁰You sent miraculous signs and wonders against Pharaoh, against all his officials and all the people of his land, for you knew how arrogantly the Egyptians treated them. You made a name for yourself, which remains to this day. ¹¹You divided the sea before them, so that they passed through it on dry ground, but you hurled their pursuers into the depths, like a stone into mighty waters. ¹²By day you led them with a pillar of cloud, and by night with a pillar of fire to give them light on the way they were to take.

¹³"You came down on Mount Sinai; you spoke to them from heaven. You gave them regulations and laws that are just and right, and decrees and commands that are good. ¹⁴You made known to them your holy Sabbath and gave them commands, decrees and laws through your servant Moses. ¹⁵In their hunger you gave them bread from heaven and in their thirst you brought them water from the rock; you told them to go in and take possession of the land you had sworn with uplifted hand to give them.

¹⁶"But they, our forefathers, became arrogant and stiff-necked, and did not obey your commands. ¹⁷They refused to listen and failed to remember the miracles you performed among them. They became stiff-necked and in their rebellion appointed a leader in order to return to their slavery. But you are a forgiving God, gracious and compassionate, slow to anger and abounding in love. Therefore you did not desert them, ¹⁸even when they cast for themselves an image of a calf and said, 'This is your god, who brought you up out of Egypt,' or when they committed awful blasphemies.

¹⁹"Because of your great compassion you did not abandon them in the desert. By day the pillar of cloud did not cease to guide them on their path, nor the pillar of fire by night to shine on the way they were to take. ²⁰You gave your good Spirit to instruct them. You did not withhold your manna from their mouths, and you gave them water for their thirst. ²¹For forty years you sustained them in the desert; they lacked nothing, their clothes did not wear out nor did their feet become swollen.

²²"You gave them kingdoms and nations, allotting to them even the remotest frontiers. They took over the country of Sihonʸ king of Heshbon and the country of Og king of

---

ʷ5 Or *God for ever and ever*   ˣ9 Hebrew *Yam Suph*; that is, Sea of Reeds   ʸ22 One Hebrew manuscript and Septuagint; most Hebrew manuscripts *Sihon, that is, the country of the*

Bashan. [23]You made their sons as numerous as the stars in the sky, and you brought them into the land that you told their fathers to enter and possess. [24]Their sons went in and took possession of the land. You subdued before them the Canaanites, who lived in the land; you handed the Canaanites over to them, along with their kings and the peoples of the land, to deal with them as they pleased. [25]They captured fortified cities and fertile land; they took possession of houses filled with all kinds of good things, wells already dug, vineyards, olive groves and fruit trees in abundance. They ate to the full and were well-nourished; they reveled in your great goodness.

[26]"But they were disobedient and rebelled against you; they put your law behind their backs. They killed your prophets, who had admonished them in order to turn them back to you; they committed awful blasphemies. [27]So you handed them over to their enemies, who oppressed them. But when they were oppressed they cried out to you. From heaven you heard them, and in your great compassion you gave them deliverers, who rescued them from the hand of their enemies.

[28]"But as soon as they were at rest, they again did what was evil in your sight. Then you abandoned them to the hand of their enemies so that they ruled over them. And when they cried out to you again, you heard from heaven, and in your compassion you delivered them time after time.

[29]"You warned them to return to your law, but they became arrogant and disobeyed your commands. They sinned against your ordinances, by which a man will live if he obeys them. Stubbornly they turned their backs on you, became stiff-necked and refused to listen. [30]For many years you were patient with them. By your Spirit you admonished them through your prophets. Yet they paid no attention, so you handed them over to the neighboring peoples. [31]But in your great mercy you did not put an end to them or abandon them,

for you are a gracious and merciful God.

[32]"Now therefore, O our God, the great, mighty and awesome God, who keeps his covenant of love, do not let all this hardship seem trifling in your eyes—the hardship that has come upon us, upon our kings and leaders, upon our priests and prophets, upon our fathers and all your people, from the days of the kings of Assyria until today. [33]In all that has happened to us, you have been just; you have acted faithfully, while we did wrong. [34]Our kings, our leaders, our priests and our fathers did not follow your law; they did not pay attention to your commands or the warnings you gave them. [35]Even while they were in their kingdom, enjoying your great goodness to them in the spacious and fertile land you gave them, they did not serve you or turn from their evil ways.

[36]"But see, we are slaves today, slaves in the land you gave our forefathers so they could eat its fruit and the other good things it produces. [37]Because of our sins, its abundant harvest goes to the kings you have placed over us. They rule over our bodies and our cattle as they please. We are in great distress.

[38]"In view of all this, we are making a binding agreement, putting it in writing, and our leaders, our Levites and our priests are affixing their seals to it."

CHAPTER 10

Those who sealed it were:

> Nehemiah the governor, the son of Hacaliah.
>
> Zedekiah, [2]Seraiah, Azariah, Jeremiah,
> [3]Pashhur, Amariah, Malkijah,
> [4]Hattush, Shebaniah, Malluch,
> [5]Harim, Meremoth, Obadiah,
> [6]Daniel, Ginnethon, Baruch,
> [7]Meshullam, Abijah, Mijamin,
> [8]Maaziah, Bilgai and Shemaiah.
> These were the priests.

[9]The Levites:

> Jeshua son of Azaniah, Binnui of the sons of Henadad, Kadmiel,

¹⁰and their associates: Shebaniah, Hodiah, Kelita, Pelaiah, Hanan, ¹¹Mica, Rehob, Hashabiah, ¹²Zaccur, Sherebiah, Shebaniah, ¹³Hodiah, Bani and Beninu.

¹⁴The leaders of the people:

Parosh, Pahath-Moab, Elam, Zattu, Bani,
¹⁵Bunni, Azgad, Bebai,
¹⁶Adonijah, Bigvai, Adin,
¹⁷Ater, Hezekiah, Azzur,
¹⁸Hodiah, Hashum, Bezai,
¹⁹Hariph, Anathoth, Nebai,
²⁰Magpiash, Meshullam, Hezir,
²¹Meshezabel, Zadok, Jaddua,
²²Pelatiah, Hanan, Anaiah,
²³Hoshea, Hananiah, Hasshub,
²⁴Hallohesh, Pilha, Shobek,
²⁵Rehum, Hashabnah, Maaseiah,
²⁶Ahiah, Hanan, Anan,
²⁷Malluch, Harim and Baanah.

²⁸"The rest of the people—priests, Levites, gatekeepers, singers, temple servants and all who separated themselves from the neighboring peoples for the sake of the Law of God, together with their wives and all their sons and daughters who are able to understand— ²⁹all these now join their brothers the nobles, and bind themselves with a curse and an oath to follow the Law of God given through Moses the servant of God and to obey carefully all the commands, regulations and decrees of the LORD our Lord.

³⁰"We promise not to give our daughters in marriage to the peoples around us or take their daughters for our sons.

³¹"When the neighboring peoples bring merchandise or grain to sell on the Sabbath, we will not buy from them on the Sabbath or on any holy day. Every seventh year we will forgo working the land and will cancel all debts.

³²"We assume the responsibility for carrying out the commands to give a

ᶻ32 That is, about 1/8 ounce (about 4 grams)

third of a shekelᶻ each year for the service of the house of our God: ³³for the bread set out on the table; for the regular grain offerings and burnt offerings; for the offerings on the Sabbaths, New Moon festivals and appointed feasts; for the holy offerings; for sin offerings to make atonement for Israel; and for all the duties of the house of our God.

³⁴"We—the priests, the Levites and the people—have cast lots to determine when each of our families is to bring to the house of our God at set times each year a contribution of wood to burn on the altar of the LORD our God, as it is written in the Law.

³⁵"We also assume responsibility for bringing to the house of the LORD each year the firstfruits of our crops and of every fruit tree.

³⁶"As it is also written in the Law, we will bring the firstborn of our sons and of our cattle, of our herds and of our flocks to the house of our God, to the priests ministering there.

³⁷"Moreover, we will bring to the storerooms of the house of our God, to the priests, the first of our ground meal, of our ˻grain˼ offerings, of the fruit of all our trees and of our new wine and oil. And we will bring a tithe of our crops to the Levites, for it is the Levites who collect the tithes in all the towns where we work. ³⁸A priest descended from Aaron is to accompany the Levites when they receive the tithes, and the Levites are to bring a tenth of the tithes up to the house of our God, to the storerooms of the treasury. ³⁹The people of Israel, including the Levites, are to bring their contributions of grain, new wine and oil to the storerooms where the articles for the sanctuary are kept and where the ministering priests, the gatekeepers and the singers stay.

"We will not neglect the house of our God."

MAY 10 □ DAY 131
NEHEMIAH 11–13
Renewed Nation Cleansed

OVERVIEW With his time in Jerusalem nearly at an end, Nehemiah busies himself with the final duties of his mission. He oversees the redistribution of the people in the cities—one tenth of the population in Jerusalem and the rest in surrounding suburbs. A massive ceremony is held in which two processions of praising people march along the walls to dedicate them to God. Nine years after returning to Persia, Nehemiah again hears disturbing news from his homeland. He returns to correct abuses in the temple and deal again with the stubborn problem of mixed marriages.

Chapter 11	Chapter 12	Chapter 13
Resettling the People	Recognizing the People	Reforming the People
New Homes	Old Names	Old Problems

Prayer becomes a flat and arduous business when we refuse to follow the lights and leads God has given us.

YOUR DAILY WALK It is sad but true that those who do not learn from history are destined to repeat it. The closing chapters of Nehemiah provide a sobering warning . . . and an opportunity to learn from the past.

The people under Nehemiah had made several vows in chapter 10: They agreed to obey God's Word, abstain from intermarriage with pagans, keep the Sabbath and support temple worship. Less than a decade later, they had broken every promise!

Today would be a great time to renew old promises and vows before the Lord. If you are married, spend some quiet moments with your spouse, reminding one another of the vows you made on your wedding day. Confess your areas of failure, and praise your partner for the vow he or she has faithfully kept. If you are single, reflect on your extra privilege (and responsibility) to serve God with undivided attention (1 Corinthians 7:32–33).

If you have made a promise to serve God faithfully, take some time to renew that promise today. If you've never done so, this would be a great time to start!

INSIGHT Nehemiah's Prophetic Partner

Malachi, who lived and ministered during the same time as Nehemiah, spoke to the moral condition of the Jews who returned to Jerusalem. You might want to read his short, four-chapter book in connection with Nehemiah. Malachi paints a bleak picture of coldhearted indifference toward God—a condition that persisted for four hundred years until the appearance of the Messiah (John 1:29).

C H A P T E R 11

Now the leaders of the people settled in Jerusalem, and the rest of the people cast lots to bring one out of every ten to live in Jerusalem, the holy city, while the remaining nine were to stay in their own towns. ²The people commended all the men who volunteered to live in Jerusalem.

³These are the provincial leaders who settled in Jerusalem (now some Israelites, priests, Levites, temple servants and descendants of Solomon's servants lived in the towns of Judah, each on his own property in the various towns, ⁴while other people from both Judah and Benjamin lived in Jerusalem):

From the descendants of Judah:

Athaiah son of Uzziah, the son of Zechariah, the son of Amariah, the son of Shephatiah, the son of Mahalalel, a descendant of Perez; [5]and Maaseiah son of Baruch, the son of Col-Hozeh, the son of Hazaiah, the son of Adaiah, the son of Joiarib, the son of Zechariah, a descendant of Shelah. [6]The descendants of Perez who lived in Jerusalem totaled 468 able men.

[7]From the descendants of Benjamin:

Sallu son of Meshullam, the son of Joed, the son of Pedaiah, the son of Kolaiah, the son of Maaseiah, the son of Ithiel, the son of Jeshaiah, [8]and his followers, Gabbai and Sallai—928 men. [9]Joel son of Zicri was their chief officer, and Judah son of Hassenuah was over the Second District of the city.

[10]From the priests:

Jedaiah; the son of Joiarib; Jakin; [11]Seraiah son of Hilkiah, the son of Meshullam, the son of Zadok, the son of Meraioth, the son of Ahitub, supervisor in the house of God, [12]and their associates, who carried on work for the temple—822 men; Adaiah son of Jeroham, the son of Pelaliah, the son of Amzi, the son of Zechariah, the son of Pashhur, the son of Malkijah, [13]and his associates, who were heads of families—242 men; Amashsai son of Azarel, the son of Ahzai, the son of Meshillemoth, the son of Immer, [14]and his[a] associates, who were able men—128. Their chief officer was Zabdiel son of Haggedolim.

[15]From the Levites:

Shemaiah son of Hasshub, the son of Azrikam, the son of Hashabiah, the son of Bunni; [16]Shabbethai and Jozabad, two of the heads of the Levites, who had charge of the outside work of the house of God; [17]Mattaniah son of Mica, the son of Zabdi, the son of Asaph, the director who led in thanksgiving and prayer; Bakbukiah, second among his associates; and Abda son of Shammua, the son of Galal, the son of Jeduthun. [18]The Levites in the holy city totaled 284.

[19]The gatekeepers:

Akkub, Talmon and their associates, who kept watch at the gates—172 men.

[20]The rest of the Israelites, with the priests and Levites, were in all the towns of Judah, each on his ancestral property. [21]The temple servants lived on the hill of Ophel, and Ziha and Gishpa were in charge of them. [22]The chief officer of the Levites in Jerusalem was Uzzi son of Bani, the son of Hashabiah, the son of Mattaniah, the son of Mica. Uzzi was one of Asaph's descendants, who were the singers responsible for the service of the house of God. [23]The singers were under the king's orders, which regulated their daily activity.

[24]Pethahiah son of Meshezabel, one of the descendants of Zerah son of Judah, was the king's agent in all affairs relating to the people.

[25]As for the villages with their fields, some of the people of Judah lived in Kiriath Arba and its surrounding settlements, in Dibon and its settlements, in Jekabzeel and its villages, [26]in Jeshua, in Moladah, in Beth Pelet, [27]in Hazar Shual, in Beersheba and its settlements, [28]in Ziklag, in Meconah and its settlements, [29]in En Rimmon, in Zorah, in Jarmuth, [30]Zanoah, Adullam and their villages, in Lachish and its fields, and in Azekah and its settlements. So they were living all the way from Beersheba to the Valley of Hinnom.

[31]The descendants of the Benjamites from Geba lived in Micmash, Aija, Bethel and its settlements, [32]in Anathoth, Nob and Ananiah, [33]in Hazor, Ramah and Gittaim, [34]in Hadid, Zeboim and Neballat, [35]in Lod and Ono, and in the Valley of the Craftsmen.

[36]Some of the divisions of the Levites of Judah settled in Benjamin.

CHAPTER 12

These were the priests and Levites who returned with Zerubbabel son of Shealtiel and with Jeshua:

Seraiah, Jeremiah, Ezra,
[2]Amariah, Malluch, Hattush,
[3]Shecaniah, Rehum, Meremoth,

[a]14 Most Septuagint manuscripts; Hebrew *their*

⁴Iddo, Ginnethon,ᵇ Abijah, ⁵Mijamin,ᶜ Moadiah, Bilgah, ⁶Shemaiah, Joiarib, Jedaiah, ⁷Sallu, Amok, Hilkiah and Jedaiah.

These were the leaders of the priests and their associates in the days of Jeshua.

⁸The Levites were Jeshua, Binnui, Kadmiel, Sherebiah, Judah, and also Mattaniah, who, together with his associates, was in charge of the songs of thanksgiving. ⁹Bakbukiah and Unni, their associates, stood opposite them in the services.

¹⁰Jeshua was the father of Joiakim, Joiakim the father of Eliashib, Eliashib the father of Joiada, ¹¹Joiada the father of Jonathan, and Jonathan the father of Jaddua.

¹²In the days of Joiakim, these were the heads of the priestly families:

of Seraiah's family, Meraiah;
of Jeremiah's, Hananiah;
¹³of Ezra's, Meshullam;
of Amariah's, Jehohanan;
¹⁴of Malluch's, Jonathan;
of Shecaniah's,ᵈ Joseph;
¹⁵of Harim's, Adna;
of Meremoth's,ᵉ Helkai;
¹⁶of Iddo's, Zechariah;
of Ginnethon's, Meshullam;
¹⁷of Abijah's, Zicri;
of Miniamin's and of Moadiah's, Piltai;
¹⁸of Bilgah's, Shammua;
of Shemaiah's, Jehonathan;
¹⁹of Joiarib's, Mattenai;
of Jedaiah's, Uzzi;
²⁰of Sallu's, Kallai;
of Amok's, Eber;
²¹of Hilkiah's, Hashabiah;
of Jedaiah's, Nethanel.

²²The family heads of the Levites in the days of Eliashib, Joiada, Johanan and Jaddua, as well as those of the priests, were recorded in the reign of Darius the Persian. ²³The family heads among the descendants of Levi up to the time of Johanan son of Eliashib were recorded in the book of the annals. ²⁴And the leaders of the Levites were Hashabiah, Sherebiah, Jeshua son of Kadmiel, and their associates, who stood opposite them to give praise and thanksgiving, one section responding to the other, as prescribed by David the man of God.

²⁵Mattaniah, Bakbukiah, Obadiah, Meshullam, Talmon and Akkub were gatekeepers who guarded the storerooms at the gates. ²⁶They served in the days of Joiakim son of Jeshua, the son of Jozadak, and in the days of Nehemiah the governor and of Ezra the priest and scribe.

²⁷At the dedication of the wall of Jerusalem, the Levites were sought out from where they lived and were brought to Jerusalem to celebrate joyfully the dedication with songs of thanksgiving and with the music of cymbals, harps and lyres. ²⁸The singers also were brought together from the region around Jerusalem—from the villages of the Netophathites, ²⁹from Beth Gilgal, and from the area of Geba and Azmaveth, for the singers had built villages for themselves around Jerusalem. ³⁰When the priests and Levites had purified themselves ceremonially, they purified the people, the gates and the wall.

³¹I had the leaders of Judah go up on topᶠ of the wall. I also assigned two large choirs to give thanks. One was to proceed on topᵍ of the wall to the right, toward the Dung Gate. ³²Hoshaiah and half the leaders of Judah followed them, ³³along with Azariah, Ezra, Meshullam, ³⁴Judah, Benjamin, Shemaiah, Jeremiah, ³⁵as well as some priests with trumpets, and also Zechariah son of Jonathan, the son of Shemaiah, the son of Mattaniah, the son of Micaiah, the son of Zaccur, the son of Asaph, ³⁶and his associates—Shemaiah, Azarel, Milalai, Gilalai, Maai, Nethanel, Judah and Hanani—with musical instruments ∟prescribed by⌐ David the man of God. Ezra the scribe led the procession. ³⁷At the Fountain Gate they continued directly up the steps of the City of David on the ascent to the wall and passed above the house of David to the Water Gate on the east.

³⁸The second choir proceeded in the opposite direction. I followed them on topʰ of the wall, together with half the people—past the Tower of the Ovens to the Broad Wall, ³⁹over the Gate of Ephraim, the Jeshanahⁱ Gate, the Fish Gate, the Tower of Hananel and the Tower of the Hundred, as far as the Sheep

ᵇ4 Many Hebrew manuscripts and Vulgate (see also Neh. 12:16); most Hebrew manuscripts Ginnethoi   ᶜ5 A variant of Miniamin   ᵈ14 Very many Hebrew manuscripts, some Septuagint manuscripts and Syriac (see also Neh. 12:3); most Hebrew manuscripts Shebaniah's   ᵉ15 Some Septuagint manuscripts (see also Neh. 12:3); Hebrew Meraioth's   ᶠ31 Or go alongside   ᵍ31 Or proceed alongside   ʰ38 Or them alongside   ⁱ39 Or Old

Gate. At the Gate of the Guard they stopped.

⁴⁰The two choirs that gave thanks then took their places in the house of God; so did I, together with half the officials, ⁴¹as well as the priests—Eliakim, Maaseiah, Miniamin, Micaiah, Elioenai, Zechariah and Hananiah with their trumpets— ⁴²and also Maaseiah, Shemaiah, Eleazar, Uzzi, Jehohanan, Malkijah, Elam and Ezer. The choirs sang under the direction of Jezrahiah. ⁴³And on that day they offered great sacrifices, rejoicing because God had given them great joy. The women and children also rejoiced. The sound of rejoicing in Jerusalem could be heard far away.

⁴⁴At that time men were appointed to be in charge of the storerooms for the contributions, firstfruits and tithes. From the fields around the towns they were to bring into the storerooms the portions required by the Law for the priests and the Levites, for Judah was pleased with the ministering priests and Levites. ⁴⁵They performed the service of their God and the service of purification, as did also the singers and gatekeepers, according to the commands of David and his son Solomon. ⁴⁶For long ago, in the days of David and Asaph, there had been directors for the singers and for the songs of praise and thanksgiving to God. ⁴⁷So in the days of Zerubbabel and of Nehemiah, all Israel contributed the daily portions for the singers and gatekeepers. They also set aside the portion for the other Levites, and the Levites set aside the portion for the descendants of Aaron.

CHAPTER 13

On that day the Book of Moses was read aloud in the hearing of the people and there it was found written that no Ammonite or Moabite should ever be admitted into the assembly of God, ²because they had not met the Israelites with food and water but had hired Balaam to call a curse down on them. (Our God, however, turned the curse into a blessing.) ³When the people heard this law, they excluded from Israel all who were of foreign descent.

⁴Before this, Eliashib the priest had been put in charge of the storerooms of the house of our God. He was closely associated with Tobiah, ⁵and he had pro-

vided him with a large room formerly used to store the grain offerings and incense and temple articles, and also the tithes of grain, new wine and oil prescribed for the Levites, singers and gatekeepers, as well as the contributions for the priests.

⁶But while all this was going on, I was not in Jerusalem, for in the thirty-second year of Artaxerxes king of Babylon I had returned to the king. Some time later I asked his permission ⁷and came back to Jerusalem. Here I learned about the evil thing Eliashib had done in providing Tobiah a room in the courts of the house of God. ⁸I was greatly displeased and threw all Tobiah's household goods out of the room. ⁹I gave orders to purify the rooms, and then I put back into them the equipment of the house of God, with the grain offerings and the incense.

¹⁰I also learned that the portions assigned to the Levites had not been given to them, and that all the Levites and singers responsible for the service had gone back to their own fields. ¹¹So I rebuked the officials and asked them, "Why is the house of God neglected?" Then I called them together and stationed them at their posts.

¹²All Judah brought the tithes of grain, new wine and oil into the storerooms. ¹³I put Shelemiah the priest, Zadok the scribe, and a Levite named Pedaiah in charge of the storerooms and made Hanan son of Zaccur, the son of Mattaniah, their assistant, because these men were considered trustworthy. They were made responsible for distributing the supplies to their brothers.

¹⁴Remember me for this, O my God, and do not blot out what I have so faithfully done for the house of my God and its services.

¹⁵In those days I saw men in Judah treading winepresses on the Sabbath and bringing in grain and loading it on donkeys, together with wine, grapes, figs and all other kinds of loads. And they were bringing all this into Jerusalem on the Sabbath. Therefore I warned them against selling food on that day. ¹⁶Men from Tyre who lived in Jerusalem were bringing in fish and all kinds of merchandise and selling them in Jerusalem on the Sabbath to the people of Judah. ¹⁷I rebuked the

nobles of Judah and said to them, "What is this wicked thing you are doing—desecrating the Sabbath day? [18]Didn't your forefathers do the same things, so that our God brought all this calamity upon us and upon this city? Now you are stirring up more wrath against Israel by desecrating the Sabbath."

[19]When evening shadows fell on the gates of Jerusalem before the Sabbath, I ordered the doors to be shut and not opened until the Sabbath was over. I stationed some of my own men at the gates so that no load could be brought in on the Sabbath day. [20]Once or twice the merchants and sellers of all kinds of goods spent the night outside Jerusalem. [21]But I warned them and said, "Why do you spend the night by the wall? If you do this again, I will lay hands on you." From that time on they no longer came on the Sabbath. [22]Then I commanded the Levites to purify themselves and go and guard the gates in order to keep the Sabbath day holy.

Remember me for this also, O my God, and show mercy to me according to your great love.

[23]Moreover, in those days I saw men of Judah who had married women from Ashdod, Ammon and Moab. [24]Half of their children spoke the language of Ashdod or the language of one of the other peoples, and did not know how to speak the language of Judah. [25]I rebuked them and called curses down on them. I beat some of the men and pulled out their hair. I made them take an oath in God's name and said: "You are not to give your daughters in marriage to their sons, nor are you to take their daughters in marriage for your sons or for yourselves. [26]Was it not because of marriages like these that Solomon king of Israel sinned? Among the many nations there was no king like him. He was loved by his God, and God made him king over all Israel, but even he was led into sin by foreign women. [27]Must we hear now that you too are doing all this terrible wickedness and are being unfaithful to our God by marrying foreign women?"

[28]One of the sons of Joiada son of Eliashib the high priest was son-in-law to Sanballat the Horonite. And I drove him away from me.

[29]Remember them, O my God, because they defiled the priestly office and the covenant of the priesthood and of the Levites.

[30]So I purified the priests and the Levites of everything foreign, and assigned them duties, each to his own task. [31]I also made provision for contributions of wood at designated times, and for the firstfruits.

Remember me with favor, O my God.

Esther

WHILE Zerubbabel, Ezra and Nehemiah led some fifty thousand people to their homeland, many more were reluctant to leave their adopted home of Persia. Esther's story takes place against this Persian background. Chosen to replace the banished queen, Esther soon finds herself—and her countrymen—threatened by a bizarre plot. Her faithful and courageous action saves God's people from destruction and provides the occasion for an annual celebration still observed by Jews today: the Feast of Purim.

Focus	Grave Danger		Great Deliverance	
Divisions	Esther's Exaltation	Haman's Cunning Plot	Haman's Humiliation	Mordecai's Exaltation
	1 2	3 4	5 7	8 10
Topics	Feast of Xerxes	Fast of Mordecai	Feasts of Esther	Feast of Purim
	Exaltation	Persecution	Preservation	Commemoration
Place	Persia			
Time	About 10 Years (483–473 B.C.)			

MAY 11 ☐ DAY 132
ESTHER 1–2
Esther's Exaltation

OVERVIEW The book of Esther is the story of a beautiful Jewish girl who rises from obscurity to prominence when she becomes the new queen of Persia. Although God's name is not mentioned anywhere in the account, his hand is visible everywhere as he places Esther in the Persian palace and her cousin Mordecai's name in the book of the annals "for such a time as this" (4:14).

Chapter 1		Chapter 2	
Xerxes' Dinner	Vashti's Divorce	Esther's Coronation	Mordecai's Loyalty
1　　　　9	10　　　　22	1　　　　18	19　　　　23
Banishment		Bravery	

YOUR DAILY WALK "Of all the bad luck! Why did that have to happen to me?"

It's truly amazing how quickly we credit our setbacks in life to "bad luck" and our successes to "hard work"!

Man proposes, God disposes.

As you read the book of Esther, you'll find a remarkable assortment of setbacks and successes. (Divide a sheet of paper in half, and see how many of each you can record over the next four days!) But one common thread runs through them all: God was at work behind the scenes. Esther's unexpected promotion, Mordecai's forgotten act of heroism—neither was an accident! Rather, God was weaving a beautiful lesson on sovereignty from the threads in their lives, showing that in their day—as in yours—God is in control.

It's a truth found not only in the book of Esther. Read about it as well in Exodus 4:11; Psalm 115:3; Daniel 4:17, 25, 32; Romans 8:28.

INSIGHT A Fatal Plot at a Fateful Moment

At a strategic moment, Mordecai became aware of a plot devised by two of the king's officers to assassinate King Xerxes (2:21–23). On this occasion, Mordecai secretly passed the news to Esther, Esther reported it in Mordecai's name, the conspirators were hanged and the incident was written up in the book of the annals. Ironically, about fifteen years later Xerxes would finally lose his life as a result of a similar plot.

CHAPTER 1

This is what happened during the time of Xerxes,*a* the Xerxes who ruled over 127 provinces stretching from India to Cush*b*: ²At that time King Xerxes reigned from his royal throne in the citadel of Susa, ³and in the third year of his reign he gave a banquet for all his nobles and officials. The military leaders of Persia and Media, the princes,

and the nobles of the provinces were present.

⁴For a full 180 days he displayed the vast wealth of his kingdom and the splendor and glory of his majesty. ⁵When these days were over, the king gave a banquet, lasting seven days, in the enclosed garden of the king's palace, for all the people from the least to the greatest, who were in the citadel of Susa. ⁶The gar-

---

*a*1 Hebrew *Ahasuerus*, a variant of Xerxes' Persian name; here and throughout Esther　　*b*1 That is, the upper Nile region den had hangings of white and blue linen, fastened with cords of white linen and purple material to silver rings on marble pillars. There were couches of gold and silver on a mosaic pavement of porphyry, marble, mother-of-pearl and other costly stones. [7]Wine was served in goblets of gold, each one different from the other, and the royal wine was abundant, in keeping with the king's liberality. [8]By the king's command each guest was allowed to drink in his own way, for the king instructed all the wine stewards to serve each man what he wished.

[9]Queen Vashti also gave a banquet for the women in the royal palace of King Xerxes.

[10]On the seventh day, when King Xerxes was in high spirits from wine, he commanded the seven eunuchs who served him—Mehuman, Biztha, Harbona, Bigtha, Abagtha, Zethar and Carcas— [11]to bring before him Queen Vashti, wearing her royal crown, in order to display her beauty to the people and nobles, for she was lovely to look at. [12]But when the attendants delivered the king's command, Queen Vashti refused to come. Then the king became furious and burned with anger.

[13]Since it was customary for the king to consult experts in matters of law and justice, he spoke with the wise men who understood the times [14]and were closest to the king—Carshena, Shethar, Admatha, Tarshish, Meres, Marsena and Memucan, the seven nobles of Persia and Media who had special access to the king and were highest in the kingdom.

[15]"According to law, what must be done to Queen Vashti?" he asked. "She has not obeyed the command of King Xerxes that the eunuchs have taken to her."

[16]Then Memucan replied in the presence of the king and the nobles, "Queen Vashti has done wrong, not only against the king but also against all the nobles and the peoples of all the provinces of King Xerxes. [17]For the queen's conduct will become known to all the women, and so they will despise their husbands and say, 'King Xerxes commanded Queen Vashti to be brought before him, but she would not come.' [18]This very day the Persian and Median women of the nobility

who have heard about the queen's conduct will respond to all the king's nobles in the same way. There will be no end of disrespect and discord.

[19]"Therefore, if it pleases the king, let him issue a royal decree and let it be written in the laws of Persia and Media, which cannot be repealed, that Vashti is never again to enter the presence of King Xerxes. Also let the king give her royal position to someone else who is better than she. [20]Then when the king's edict is proclaimed throughout all his vast realm, all the women will respect their husbands, from the least to the greatest."

[21]The king and his nobles were pleased with this advice, so the king did as Memucan proposed. [22]He sent dispatches to all parts of the kingdom, to each province in its own script and to each people in its own language, proclaiming in each people's tongue that every man should be ruler over his own household.

CHAPTER 2

Later when the anger of King Xerxes had subsided, he remembered Vashti and what she had done and what he had decreed about her. [2]Then the king's personal attendants proposed, "Let a search be made for beautiful young virgins for the king. [3]Let the king appoint commissioners in every province of his realm to bring all these beautiful girls to the harem at the citadel of Susa. Let them be placed under the care of Hegai, the king's eunuch, who is in charge of the women; and let beauty treatments be given to them. [4]Then let the girl who pleases the king be queen instead of Vashti." This advice appealed to the king, and he followed it.

[5]Now there was in the citadel of Susa a Jew of the tribe of Benjamin, named Mordecai son of Jair, the son of Shimei, the son of Kish, [6]who had been carried into exile from Jerusalem by Nebuchadnezzar king of Babylon, among those taken captive with Jehoiachin[c] king of Judah. [7]Mordecai had a cousin named Hadassah, whom he had brought up because she had neither father nor mother. This girl, who was also known as Esther, was lovely in form and features, and Mordecai had taken her as his own daughter when her father and mother died.

[c]6 Hebrew *Jeconiah*, a variant of *Jehoiachin*

⁸When the king's order and edict had been proclaimed, many girls were brought to the citadel of Susa and put under the care of Hegai. Esther also was taken to the king's palace and entrusted to Hegai, who had charge of the harem. ⁹The girl pleased him and won his favor. Immediately he provided her with her beauty treatments and special food. He assigned to her seven maids selected from the king's palace and moved her and her maids into the best place in the harem.

¹⁰Esther had not revealed her nationality and family background, because Mordecai had forbidden her to do so. ¹¹Every day he walked back and forth near the courtyard of the harem to find out how Esther was and what was happening to her.

¹²Before a girl's turn came to go in to King Xerxes, she had to complete twelve months of beauty treatments prescribed for the women, six months with oil of myrrh and six with perfumes and cosmetics. ¹³And this is how she would go to the king: Anything she wanted was given her to take with her from the harem to the king's palace. ¹⁴In the evening she would go there and in the morning return to another part of the harem to the care of Shaashgaz, the king's eunuch who was in charge of the concubines. She would not return to the king unless he was pleased with her and summoned her by name.

¹⁵When the turn came for Esther (the girl Mordecai had adopted, the daughter of his uncle Abihail) to go to the king, she asked for nothing other than what Hegai, the king's eunuch who was in charge of the harem, suggested. And Esther won the favor of everyone who saw her. ¹⁶She was taken to King Xerxes in the royal residence in the tenth month, the month of Tebeth, in the seventh year of his reign.

¹⁷Now the king was attracted to Esther more than to any of the other women, and she won his favor and approval more than any of the other virgins. So he set a royal crown on her head and made her queen instead of Vashti. ¹⁸And the king gave a great banquet, Esther's banquet, for all his nobles and officials. He proclaimed a holiday throughout the provinces and distributed gifts with royal liberality.

¹⁹When the virgins were assembled a second time, Mordecai was sitting at the king's gate. ²⁰But Esther had kept secret her family background and nationality just as Mordecai had told her to do, for she continued to follow Mordecai's instructions as she had done when he was bringing her up.

²¹During the time Mordecai was sitting at the king's gate, Bigthana*d* and Teresh, two of the king's officers who guarded the doorway, became angry and conspired to assassinate King Xerxes. ²²But Mordecai found out about the plot and told Queen Esther, who in turn reported it to the king, giving credit to Mordecai. ²³And when the report was investigated and found to be true, the two officials were hanged on a gallows.*e* All this was recorded in the book of the annals in the presence of the king.

---

*d*21 Hebrew *Bigthan,* a variant of *Bigthana*   *e*23 Or *were hung* (or *impaled*) *on poles;* similarly elsewhere in Esther

MAY 12 □ DAY 133
ESTHER 3–4
Haman's Cunning Plot

OVERVIEW Esther has been made queen without her nationality being known. But now a new danger arises in the person of Haman, another recipient of a kingly promotion. Mordecai, who has already proven his loyalty to the king, refuses to kneel down before Haman as the king has decreed, prompting Haman to respond with insane anger. Both Mordecai and his countrymen must die. False charges and a sizable bribe secure what Haman desires: the king's permission to liquidate the Jewish population. Now Queen Esther is faced with a life-and-death decision. Should she risk revealing her nationality in order to dissuade the king? Or should she protect her life and watch her countrymen be exterminated?

Chapter 3		Chapter 4	
Haman's Promotion	Haman's Plot	Mordecai's Fast	Esther's Faith
1 5	6 15	1 12	13 17
A Deadly Plan		A Desperate Decision	

YOUR DAILY WALK "If I must die, I am willing to die." Is this the fatalistic cry of a queen resigned to her death, or the faith-inspired statement of a woman who serves a sovereign God?

Don't miss the context: Mordecai has just warned Esther that she will not escape Haman's plot just because she is the queen. And he challenges her with this thought: "And who knows but that you have come to royal position for such a time as this?" Paraphrased, he was saying: "Esther, God has placed you in a strategic place at a critical moment to be the instrument of deliverance for his people. Your presence in the palace is not by accident, but by divine appointment."

Only when we place ourselves in God's hands can we bring glory to him and growth to ourselves.

Do you find yourself in a situation similar to Esther's where you wish you could hide in the palace, so to speak? Then get ready! God has put you where you are for a purpose.

INSIGHT The High Price of Cold Blood
One commentator has valued the Hebrew talent of silver at $12,000. That means Haman was willing to pay $120 million to exterminate the Jews—a fabulous sum for a Persian hit man!

CHAPTER 3
After these events, King Xerxes honored Haman son of Hammedatha, the Agagite, elevating him and giving him a seat of honor higher than that of all the other nobles. ²All the royal officials at the king's gate knelt down and paid honor to Haman, for the king had commanded this concerning him. But Mordecai would not kneel down or pay him honor.

³Then the royal officials at the king's gate asked Mordecai, "Why do you disobey the king's command?" ⁴Day after day they spoke to him but he refused to comply. Therefore they told Haman about it to see whether Mordecai's behavior would be tolerated, for he had told them he was a Jew.

⁵When Haman saw that Mordecai would not kneel down or pay him honor, he was enraged. ⁶Yet having learned who Mordecai's people were, he scorned the idea of killing only Mordecai. Instead Haman looked for a way to destroy all Mordecai's people, the Jews, throughout the whole kingdom of Xerxes.

⁷In the twelfth year of King Xerxes, in the first month, the month of Nisan, they cast the *pur* (that is, the lot) in the presence of Haman to select a day and month. And the lot fell on^f the twelfth month, the month of Adar.

⁸Then Haman said to King Xerxes, "There is a certain people dispersed and scattered among the peoples in all the provinces of your kingdom whose customs are different from those of all other people and who do not obey the king's laws; it is not in the king's best interest to tolerate them. ⁹If it pleases the king, let a decree be issued to destroy them, and I will put ten thousand talents^g of silver into the royal treasury for the men who carry out this business."

¹⁰So the king took his signet ring from his finger and gave it to Haman son of Hammedatha, the Agagite, the enemy of the Jews. ¹¹"Keep the money," the king said to Haman, "and do with the people as you please."

¹²Then on the thirteenth day of the first month the royal secretaries were summoned. They wrote out in the script of each province and in the language of each people all Haman's orders to the king's satraps, the governors of the various

f7 Septuagint; Hebrew does not have *And the lot fell on.*   g9 That is, about 375 tons (about 345 metric tons) provinces and the nobles of the various peoples. These were written in the name of King Xerxes himself and sealed with his own ring. [13]Dispatches were sent by couriers to all the king's provinces with the order to destroy, kill and annihilate all the Jews—young and old, women and little children—on a single day, the thirteenth day of the twelfth month, the month of Adar, and to plunder their goods. [14]A copy of the text of the edict was to be issued as law in every province and made known to the people of every nationality so they would be ready for that day.

[15]Spurred on by the king's command, the couriers went out, and the edict was issued in the citadel of Susa. The king and Haman sat down to drink, but the city of Susa was bewildered.

CHAPTER 4

When Mordecai learned of all that had been done, he tore his clothes, put on sackcloth and ashes, and went out into the city, wailing loudly and bitterly. [2]But he went only as far as the king's gate, because no one clothed in sackcloth was allowed to enter it. [3]In every province to which the edict and order of the king came, there was great mourning among the Jews, with fasting, weeping and wailing. Many lay in sackcloth and ashes.

[4]When Esther's maids and eunuchs came and told her about Mordecai, she was in great distress. She sent clothes for him to put on instead of his sackcloth, but he would not accept them. [5]Then Esther summoned Hathach, one of the king's eunuchs assigned to attend her, and ordered him to find out what was troubling Mordecai and why.

[6]So Hathach went out to Mordecai in the open square of the city in front of the king's gate. [7]Mordecai told him everything that had happened to him, including the exact amount of money Haman had promised to pay into the royal treasury for the destruction of the Jews. [8]He also gave him a copy of the text of the edict for their annihilation, which had been published in Susa, to show to Esther and explain it to her, and he told him to urge her to go into the king's presence to beg for mercy and plead with him for her people.

[9]Hathach went back and reported to Esther what Mordecai had said. [10]Then she instructed him to say to Mordecai, [11]"All the king's officials and the people of the royal provinces know that for any man or woman who approaches the king in the inner court without being summoned the king has but one law: that he be put to death. The only exception to this is for the king to extend the gold scepter to him and spare his life. But thirty days have passed since I was called to go to the king."

[12]When Esther's words were reported to Mordecai, [13]he sent back this answer: "Do not think that because you are in the king's house you alone of all the Jews will escape. [14]For if you remain silent at this time, relief and deliverance for the Jews will arise from another place, but you and your father's family will perish. And who knows but that you have come to royal position for such a time as this?"

[15]Then Esther sent this reply to Mordecai: [16]"Go, gather together all the Jews who are in Susa, and fast for me. Do not eat or drink for three days, night or day. I and my maids will fast as you do. When this is done, I will go to the king, even though it is against the law. And if I perish, I perish."

[17]So Mordecai went away and carried out all of Esther's instructions.

MAY 13 □ DAY 134
ESTHER 5–7
Haman's Humiliation

OVERVIEW Esther knows full well that entering the king's throne room uninvited could prove hazardous to her health. But Esther courageously discovers that God has once again prepared the way. She invites Xerxes and Haman to a special banquet in their honor and there repeats the invitation for the next day as well. But before that fateful second banquet, Haman builds a gallows seventy-five feet high on which to hang Mordecai; Xerxes discovers Mordecai's unrewarded heroism; and Haman watches the honor he had craved go to Mordecai. At the second banquet Haman is unmasked and dies the very death he had planned for Mordecai.

Chapter 5	Chapter 6	Chapter 7
Haman's Haughtiness	Haman's Humiliation	Haman's Hanging
First Banquet	Forgotten Bravery	Fateful Banquet

YOUR DAILY WALK Do you believe in prayer? Do you really? Esther believed in prayer enough to go before the king at an unappointed time with an unlikely request, though it could have meant swift death (4:11, 16; 5:2). Would you have done that?

Believing supplications are forecasts of the future.

The story is told of a midwestern town suffering under a searing drought. All the townspeople finally decided it was time to gather the clergy and assemble for prayer. The whole town turned out to pray for rain, but only one person, a small girl, brought her umbrella.

When you pray, are you like the townspeople or the little girl? Do you, like Esther, pray first and then live in the confidence of God's answer? Are your prayers specific enough that, when God answers, you notice a difference? In the margin write down a specific request for provision, protection or guidance. For the next week focus your prayers on that item. You might even want to put your umbrella in an unusual place to remind you throughout the week to watch for God's answer!

INSIGHT The Hanging All Susa Would See
The excessive height of Haman's gallows (seventy-five feet, or at least as high as the city walls) was designed to ensure that Mordecai's downfall would be a citywide spectacle, visible both inside and outside the walls. Instead, Haman himself received the notoriety!

CHAPTER 5
On the third day Esther put on her royal robes and stood in the inner court of the palace, in front of the king's hall. The king was sitting on his royal throne in the hall, facing the entrance. ²When he saw Queen Esther standing in the court, he was pleased with her and held out to her the gold scepter that was in his hand. So Esther approached and touched the tip of the scepter.

³Then the king asked, "What is it, Queen Esther? What is your request? Even up to half the kingdom, it will be given you."

⁴"If it pleases the king," replied Esther, "let the king, together with Haman, come today to a banquet I have prepared for him."

⁵"Bring Haman at once," the king said, "so that we may do what Esther asks."

So the king and Haman went to the banquet Esther had prepared. ⁶As they were drinking wine, the king again asked

Esther, "Now what is your petition? It will be given you. And what is your request? Even up to half the kingdom, it will be granted."

[7]Esther replied, "My petition and my request is this: [8]If the king regards me with favor and if it pleases the king to grant my petition and fulfill my request, let the king and Haman come tomorrow to the banquet I will prepare for them. Then I will answer the king's question."

[9]Haman went out that day happy and in high spirits. But when he saw Mordecai at the king's gate and observed that he neither rose nor showed fear in his presence, he was filled with rage against Mordecai. [10]Nevertheless, Haman restrained himself and went home.

Calling together his friends and Zeresh, his wife, [11]Haman boasted to them about his vast wealth, his many sons, and all the ways the king had honored him and how he had elevated him above the other nobles and officials. [12]"And that's not all," Haman added. "I'm the only person Queen Esther invited to accompany the king to the banquet she gave. And she has invited me along with the king tomorrow. [13]But all this gives me no satisfaction as long as I see that Jew Mordecai sitting at the king's gate."

[14]His wife Zeresh and all his friends said to him, "Have a gallows built, seventy-five feet[h] high, and ask the king in the morning to have Mordecai hanged on it. Then go with the king to the dinner and be happy." This suggestion delighted Haman, and he had the gallows built.

CHAPTER 6

That night the king could not sleep; so he ordered the book of the chronicles, the record of his reign, to be brought in and read to him. [2]It was found recorded there that Mordecai had exposed Bigthana and Teresh, two of the king's officers who guarded the doorway, who had conspired to assassinate King Xerxes.

[3]"What honor and recognition has Mordecai received for this?" the king asked.

"Nothing has been done for him," his attendants answered.

[4]The king said, "Who is in the court?" Now Haman had just entered the outer court of the palace to speak to the king

about hanging Mordecai on the gallows he had erected for him.

[5]His attendants answered, "Haman is standing in the court."

"Bring him in," the king ordered.

[6]When Haman entered, the king asked him, "What should be done for the man the king delights to honor?"

Now Haman thought to himself, "Who is there that the king would rather honor than me?" [7]So he answered the king, "For the man the king delights to honor, [8]have them bring a royal robe the king has worn and a horse the king has ridden, one with a royal crest placed on its head. [9]Then let the robe and horse be entrusted to one of the king's most noble princes. Let them robe the man the king delights to honor, and lead him on the horse through the city streets, proclaiming before him, 'This is what is done for the man the king delights to honor!' "

[10]"Go at once," the king commanded Haman. "Get the robe and the horse and do just as you have suggested for Mordecai the Jew, who sits at the king's gate. Do not neglect anything you have recommended."

[11]So Haman got the robe and the horse. He robed Mordecai, and led him on horseback through the city streets, proclaiming before him, "This is what is done for the man the king delights to honor!"

[12]Afterward Mordecai returned to the king's gate. But Haman rushed home, with his head covered in grief, [13]and told Zeresh his wife and all his friends everything that had happened to him.

His advisers and his wife Zeresh said to him, "Since Mordecai, before whom your downfall has started, is of Jewish origin, you cannot stand against him—you will surely come to ruin!" [14]While they were still talking with him, the king's eunuchs arrived and hurried Haman away to the banquet Esther had prepared.

CHAPTER 7

So the king and Haman went to dine with Queen Esther, [2]and as they were drinking wine on that second day, the king again asked, "Queen Esther, what is your petition? It will be given you. What is your request? Even up to half the kingdom, it will be granted."

[h]14 Hebrew *fifty cubits* (about 23 meters)

³Then Queen Esther answered, "If I have found favor with you, O king, and if it pleases your majesty, grant me my life—this is my petition. And spare my people—this is my request. ⁴For I and my people have been sold for destruction and slaughter and annihilation. If we had merely been sold as male and female slaves, I would have kept quiet, because no such distress would justify disturbing the king.ⁱ"

⁵King Xerxes asked Queen Esther, "Who is he? Where is the man who has dared to do such a thing?"

⁶Esther said, "The adversary and enemy is this vile Haman."

Then Haman was terrified before the king and queen. ⁷The king got up in a rage, left his wine and went out into the palace garden. But Haman, realizing that the king had already decided his fate, stayed behind to beg Queen Esther for his life.

⁸Just as the king returned from the palace garden to the banquet hall, Haman was falling on the couch where Esther was reclining.

The king exclaimed, "Will he even molest the queen while she is with me in the house?"

As soon as the word left the king's mouth, they covered Haman's face. ⁹Then Harbona, one of the eunuchs attending the king, said, "A gallows seventy-five feetʲ high stands by Haman's house. He had it made for Mordecai, who spoke up to help the king."

The king said, "Hang him on it!" ¹⁰So they hanged Haman on the gallows he had prepared for Mordecai. Then the king's fury subsided.

ⁱ4 Or quiet, but the compensation our adversary offers cannot be compared with the loss the king would suffer   ʲ9 Hebrew fifty cubits (about 23 meters)

MAY 14 ☐ DAY 135
Going and Coming with God

LOOK BACK "Go home!" (That's what Artaxerxes told Nehemiah to do.)

"Stay put!" (That, in essence, is what Mordecai told Esther to do.)

Sounds a bit confusing until you realize that both commands were God's will for his choice servants. When Nehemiah saw there was a rebuilding job to do hundreds of miles away in his beloved Jerusalem, he prayerfully began to form a plan to tackle the job. When the king inquired, Nehemiah was ready.

By contrast, Esther saw a need right where she lived in Persia. Her Jewish countrymen were threatened with annihilation at the hands of wicked Haman. With the help of her cousin Mordecai, Esther fasted, prayed and formed a plan. And when the king inquired, Esther was ready.

Each faced withering opposition and seemingly insurmountable odds. They both had plenty of reason never to attempt what they did! And each saw God work a miracle through his available servant. What exciting walks of faith to study and model your life after as you seek to obey God in the daily decisions of life.

LOOK UP Rome wasn't built in a day. Neither are most other things that have the potential to touch many lives or accomplish great good. But careful planning, combined with fervent prayer and plenty of hard work, can accomplish things for God that would never be possible on the spur of the moment.

We must ask ourselves, How much of eternity is in what we are doing?

Here is a partial list of long-range projects you might want to consider. If one person can't accomplish them alone, why not share your vision and burden with a circle of close praying friends, and see if God might want you to tackle something together:

- Get completely out of debt (including any mortgages on your own house).
- Start a backyard Bible class or weekly evangelistic Bible study in your neighborhood.
- Begin a recreation program with inner-city youth.
- Write a book.
- Take a short-term mission trip to another country.
- Call your former classmates from high school or college, and tell them the difference Jesus has made in your life.
- Build a low-cost house for a family who is dependent on government aid.
- Run for public office.
- Go back to school and finish that bachelor's, master's or doctoral degree.

 LOOK AHEAD No one believed Nehemiah could rebuild the walls of Jerusalem that lay in rubble and ruin. Fortified by long hours of prayer and tears, and joined by fifty thousand of his motivated countrymen, they completed the task miraculously in fifty-two days despite intense opposition!

No one believed Esther could stay the death sentence hanging over her countrymen. But with her heart prepared through prayer and fasting, and counseled by her godly cousin, Mordecai, Esther ventured into the very presence of the king to make her bold request. As a result, thousands of Jews were spared.

No one may believe that you can accomplish what God has laid upon your heart either . . . until you attempt it in the strength of the Lord.

MAY 15 ☐ DAY 136
ESTHER 8–10
Mordecai's Exaltation

 OVERVIEW A Persian law sealed with the king's ring could never be revoked. And although Haman is dead, the king's edict calling for the extermination of the Jewish race lives on. Mordecai, who now occupies Haman's former position of power, issues a counter-edict allowing the Jews to defend themselves on the same day as Haman's edict. When the day of destruction arrives, the enemies of the Jews—not the Jews themselves—are annihilated. Future generations will henceforth celebrate the Feast of Purim (so named for the lots Haman cast and God directed), recalling the days of earnest appeal to God and the stunning deliverance he provided.

Chapter 8	Chapter 9	Chapter 10
Mordecai's Vindication	The Jews' Vengeance	Mordecai's Veneration
Promotion	Protection	Praise

 YOUR DAILY WALK Think back over the troubles of the Jews as recorded in the historical books of the Bible. During the years of the judges and kings they experienced wars, famines, political upheavals,

To know God's will is life's greatest treasure; to do God's will is life's greatest pleasure. shattered families and premature death. Later came captivity, dispersion and exile at the hands of the Assyrians and Babylonians. During the four hundred years between the close of the Old Testament and the opening of the New, they would be characterized by coldhearted indifference, culminating in the outright rejection of the Messiah. They would be dispersed worldwide once again; attempts would be made to liquidate them once and for all. And yet, as you look at your map of the Middle East today, there boldly stands the tiny nation of Israel— still very much a part of God's continuing plan.

If God can bring his chosen people through centuries of chaotic history and preserve them from extinction in spite of unbelief, disobedience and indifference, what do you suppose he is capable of doing in your life . . . especially if he has your cooperation? God wants to make Esther's story your story; will you let him?

 INSIGHT The Verse That Says It All—or Nearly So! There is something striking about Esther 8:9. Can you discover what it is? (Hint: John 11:35 is just the opposite!) Give up? The seventy-two words contained in that verse make it the longest in the Bible.

CHAPTER 8

That same day King Xerxes gave Queen Esther the estate of Haman, the enemy of the Jews. And Mordecai came into the presence of the king, for Esther had told how he was related to her. ²The king took off his signet ring, which he had reclaimed from Haman, and presented it to Mordecai. And Esther appointed him over Haman's estate.

³Esther again pleaded with the king, falling at his feet and weeping. She begged him to put an end to the evil plan of Haman the Agagite, which he had devised against the Jews. ⁴Then the king extended the gold scepter to Esther and she arose and stood before him.

⁵"If it pleases the king," she said, "and if he regards me with favor and thinks it the right thing to do, and if he is pleased with me, let an order be written overruling the dispatches that Haman son of Hammedatha, the Agagite, devised and wrote to destroy the Jews in all the king's provinces. ⁶For how can I bear to see disaster fall on my people? How can I bear to see the destruction of my family?"

⁷King Xerxes replied to Queen Esther and to Mordecai the Jew, "Because Haman attacked the Jews, I have given his estate to Esther, and they have hanged him on the gallows. ⁸Now write another decree in the king's name in behalf of the Jews as seems best to you, and seal it with the king's signet ring—for no document

written in the king's name and sealed with his ring can be revoked."

⁹At once the royal secretaries were summoned—on the twenty-third day of the third month, the month of Sivan. They wrote out all Mordecai's orders to the Jews, and to the satraps, governors and nobles of the 127 provinces stretching from India to Cush.ᵏ These orders were written in the script of each province and the language of each people and also to the Jews in their own script and language. ¹⁰Mordecai wrote in the name of King Xerxes, sealed the dispatches with the king's signet ring, and sent them by mounted couriers, who rode fast horses especially bred for the king.

¹¹The king's edict granted the Jews in every city the right to assemble and protect themselves; to destroy, kill and annihilate any armed force of any nationality or province that might attack them and their women and children; and to plunder the property of their enemies. ¹²The day appointed for the Jews to do this in all the provinces of King Xerxes was the thirteenth day of the twelfth month, the month of Adar. ¹³A copy of the text of the edict was to be issued as law in every province and made known to the people of every nationality so that the Jews would be ready on that day to avenge themselves on their enemies.

¹⁴The couriers, riding the royal horses, raced out, spurred on by the king's

ᵏ**9** That is, the upper Nile region

command. And the edict was also issued in the citadel of Susa.

¹⁵Mordecai left the king's presence wearing royal garments of blue and white, a large crown of gold and a purple robe of fine linen. And the city of Susa held a joyous celebration. ¹⁶For the Jews it was a time of happiness and joy, gladness and honor. ¹⁷In every province and in every city, wherever the edict of the king went, there was joy and gladness among the Jews, with feasting and celebrating. And many people of other nationalities became Jews because fear of the Jews had seized them.

CHAPTER 9

On the thirteenth day of the twelfth month, the month of Adar, the edict commanded by the king was to be carried out. On this day the enemies of the Jews had hoped to overpower them, but now the tables were turned and the Jews got the upper hand over those who hated them. ²The Jews assembled in their cities in all the provinces of King Xerxes to attack those seeking their destruction. No one could stand against them, because the people of all the other nationalities were afraid of them. ³And all the nobles of the provinces, the satraps, the governors and the king's administrators helped the Jews, because fear of Mordecai had seized them. ⁴Mordecai was prominent in the palace; his reputation spread throughout the provinces, and he became more and more powerful.

⁵The Jews struck down all their enemies with the sword, killing and destroying them, and they did what they pleased to those who hated them. ⁶In the citadel of Susa, the Jews killed and destroyed five hundred men. ⁷They also killed Parshandatha, Dalphon, Aspatha, ⁸Poratha, Adalia, Aridatha, ⁹Parmashta, Arisai, Aridai and Vaizatha, ¹⁰the ten sons of Haman son of Hammedatha, the enemy of the Jews. But they did not lay their hands on the plunder.

¹¹The number of those slain in the citadel of Susa was reported to the king that same day. ¹²The king said to Queen Esther, "The Jews have killed and destroyed five hundred men and the ten sons of Haman in the citadel of Susa. What have they done in the rest of the king's provinces? Now what is your petition? It will

be given you. What is your request? It will also be granted."

¹³"If it pleases the king," Esther answered, "give the Jews in Susa permission to carry out this day's edict tomorrow also, and let Haman's ten sons be hanged on gallows."

¹⁴So the king commanded that this be done. An edict was issued in Susa, and they hanged the ten sons of Haman. ¹⁵The Jews in Susa came together on the fourteenth day of the month of Adar, and they put to death in Susa three hundred men, but they did not lay their hands on the plunder.

¹⁶Meanwhile, the remainder of the Jews who were in the king's provinces also assembled to protect themselves and get relief from their enemies. They killed seventy-five thousand of them but did not lay their hands on the plunder. ¹⁷This happened on the thirteenth day of the month of Adar, and on the fourteenth they rested and made it a day of feasting and joy.

¹⁸The Jews in Susa, however, had assembled on the thirteenth and fourteenth, and then on the fifteenth they rested and made it a day of feasting and joy.

¹⁹That is why rural Jews—those living in villages—observe the fourteenth of the month of Adar as a day of joy and feasting, a day for giving presents to each other.

²⁰Mordecai recorded these events, and he sent letters to all the Jews throughout the provinces of King Xerxes, near and far, ²¹to have them celebrate annually the fourteenth and fifteenth days of the month of Adar ²²as the time when the Jews got relief from their enemies, and as the month when their sorrow was turned into joy and their mourning into a day of celebration. He wrote them to observe the days as days of feasting and joy and giving presents of food to one another and gifts to the poor.

²³So the Jews agreed to continue the celebration they had begun, doing what Mordecai had written to them. ²⁴For Haman son of Hammedatha, the Agagite, the enemy of all the Jews, had plotted against the Jews to destroy them and had cast the *pur* (that is, the lot) for their ruin and destruction. ²⁵But when the plot came

to the king's attention,[1] he issued written orders that the evil scheme Haman had devised against the Jews should come back onto his own head, and that he and his sons should be hanged on the gallows. [26](Therefore these days were called Purim, from the word *pur*.) Because of everything written in this letter and because of what they had seen and what had happened to them, [27]the Jews took it upon themselves to establish the custom that they and their descendants and all who join them should without fail observe these two days every year, in the way prescribed and at the time appointed. [28]These days should be remembered and observed in every generation by every family, and in every province and in every city. And these days of Purim should never cease to be celebrated by the Jews, nor should the memory of them die out among their descendants.

[29]So Queen Esther, daughter of Abihail, along with Mordecai the Jew, wrote with full authority to confirm this second letter concerning Purim. [30]And Mordecai sent

[1]25 Or *when Esther came before the king*

letters to all the Jews in the 127 provinces of the kingdom of Xerxes—words of goodwill and assurance— [31]to establish these days of Purim at their designated times, as Mordecai the Jew and Queen Esther had decreed for them, and as they had established for themselves and their descendants in regard to their times of fasting and lamentation. [32]Esther's decree confirmed these regulations about Purim, and it was written down in the records.

C H A P T E R   1 0

King Xerxes imposed tribute throughout the empire, to its distant shores. [2]And all his acts of power and might, together with a full account of the greatness of Mordecai to which the king had raised him, are they not written in the book of the annals of the kings of Media and Persia? [3]Mordecai the Jew was second in rank to King Xerxes, preeminent among the Jews, and held in high esteem by his many fellow Jews, because he worked for the good of his people and spoke up for the welfare of all the Jews.

Job

THE BOOK of Job examines one of life's most perplexing questions. It introduces a pious man of God named Job, who lived perhaps four thousand years ago. In a sudden series of catastrophes, Job loses his family, fame, fortune and fitness. For more than thirty chapters he searches his soul and debates his best friends to find a reason for his misfortune. After exhausting the conventional wisdom of his counselors, Job is confronted by God himself, and his demanding *why* melts into humble worship.

Focus	Situation	Search			Solution
Divisions	Controversy between the Lord and Satan	Controversy with Job's Four Friends:	Cycle 1 { Eliphaz and Job (4–7) Bildad and Job (8–10) Zophar and Job (11–14)	Cycle 2 { Eliphaz and Job (15–17) Bildad and Job (18–19) Zophar and Job (20–21) — Cycle 3 { Eliphaz and Job (22–24) Bildad and Job (25–31) Elihu (32–37)	Controversy between the Lord and Job
	1 3	4		37	38 42
Topics	Dialogue in Heaven	Dialogue on Earth			Dialogue between Heaven & Earth
	The Onset of Suffering	The Failure of Human Wisdom			The Final Word from God
Place	Land of Uz (North Arabia)				
Time	Patriarchal Period (about 2000 B.C.)				

MAY 16 □ DAY 137
JOB 1–3
Controversy between the Lord and Satan

OVERVIEW Southeast of the Dead Sea lies the land of Uz, a sheep and cattle ranching region and home of the wealthy herdsman Job. Job's exemplary life of service for God is placed in the furnace of testing. In a heavenly drama (unknown to Job but revealed to the reader), Satan accuses Job of serving God for material reward. By divine permission, Satan tests Job by removing all that he holds dear: his family, wealth, health and prestige. Yet through it all Job maintains his steadfast worship of God, though nagging questions remain.

Chapter 1		Chapter 2		Chapter 3
Satan's First Attack		Satan's Second Attack		Job's Agony
Planned	Performed	Planned	Performed	
1 11	12 22	1 6	7 13	
Disaster				Doubt

YOUR DAILY WALK What is your first response when someone points a finger at you? Do you find it a painful or a pleasant experience?

There is someone who takes great delight in pointing an accusing finger at your life. One of his names is *devil* (1 Peter 5:8), which literally means "slanderer." (Some of his other names are equally revealing—see Matthew 12:24; 13:19; Luke 10:18; John 8:44; Ephesians 6:12; Revelation 9:11; 12:10; 20:2).

Of all the devil's tools for making us miserable, discouragement is his finest and most frequently used.

Now that you know something about your enemy, you'll want to know how you—like Job—can stand firm against his fiery attacks. Job, who experienced the worst Satan could hurl against him, maintained an attitude of confident trust in his sovereign God.

Did that mean . . .
• Job deserved the treatment he received? (2:3)
• all of Job's questions were answered? (3:11–12, 23)

The answer in both cases is no! But even though Job's misery came unexplained and undeserved, Job demonstrated in the midst of it an unshakable confidence in the one who held his life in his very hands. It wasn't *what* he knew but *whom* he knew that gave him strength to stand against any trial.

INSIGHT A Name from Ancient Time
The name of both the book and its hero, Job (Hebrew, *iyyob*), appears in extrabiblical texts as early as 2000 B.C., indicating that Job is perhaps the oldest book of the Bible.

CHAPTER 1
In the land of Uz there lived a man whose name was Job. This man was blameless and upright; he feared God and shunned evil. ²He had seven sons and three daughters, ³and he owned seven thousand sheep, three thousand camels, five

hundred yoke of oxen and five hundred donkeys, and had a large number of servants. He was the greatest man among all the people of the East.

⁴His sons used to take turns holding feasts in their homes, and they would invite their three sisters to eat and drink

with them. ⁵When a period of feasting had run its course, Job would send and have them purified. Early in the morning he would sacrifice a burnt offering for each of them, thinking, "Perhaps my children have sinned and cursed God in their hearts." This was Job's regular custom.

⁶One day the angels*ᵃ* came to present themselves before the LORD, and Satan*ᵇ* also came with them. ⁷The LORD said to Satan, "Where have you come from?"

Satan answered the LORD, "From roaming through the earth and going back and forth in it."

⁸Then the LORD said to Satan, "Have you considered my servant Job? There is no one on earth like him; he is blameless and upright, a man who fears God and shuns evil."

⁹"Does Job fear God for nothing?" Satan replied. ¹⁰"Have you not put a hedge around him and his household and everything he has? You have blessed the work of his hands, so that his flocks and herds are spread throughout the land. ¹¹But stretch out your hand and strike everything he has, and he will surely curse you to your face."

¹²The LORD said to Satan, "Very well, then, everything he has is in your hands, but on the man himself do not lay a finger."

Then Satan went out from the presence of the LORD.

¹³One day when Job's sons and daughters were feasting and drinking wine at the oldest brother's house, ¹⁴a messenger came to Job and said, "The oxen were plowing and the donkeys were grazing nearby, ¹⁵and the Sabeans attacked and carried them off. They put the servants to the sword, and I am the only one who has escaped to tell you!"

¹⁶While he was still speaking, another messenger came and said, "The fire of God fell from the sky and burned up the sheep and the servants, and I am the only one who has escaped to tell you!"

¹⁷While he was still speaking, another messenger came and said, "The Chaldeans formed three raiding parties and swept down on your camels and carried them off. They put the servants to the sword, and I am the only one who has escaped to tell you!"

¹⁸While he was still speaking, yet another messenger came and said, "Your sons and daughters were feasting and drinking wine at the oldest brother's house, ¹⁹when suddenly a mighty wind swept in from the desert and struck the four corners of the house. It collapsed on them and they are dead, and I am the only one who has escaped to tell you!"

²⁰At this, Job got up and tore his robe and shaved his head. Then he fell to the ground in worship ²¹and said:

> "Naked I came from my mother's
>   womb,
>   and naked I will depart.*ᶜ*
> The LORD gave and the LORD has taken
>   away;
>   may the name of the LORD be
>   praised."

²²In all this, Job did not sin by charging God with wrongdoing.

CHAPTER 2

On another day the angels*ᵃ* came to present themselves before the LORD, and Satan also came with them to present himself before him. ²And the LORD said to Satan, "Where have you come from?"

Satan answered the LORD, "From roaming through the earth and going back and forth in it."

³Then the LORD said to Satan, "Have you considered my servant Job? There is no one on earth like him; he is blameless and upright, a man who fears God and shuns evil. And he still maintains his integrity, though you incited me against him to ruin him without any reason."

⁴"Skin for skin!" Satan replied. "A man will give all he has for his own life. ⁵But stretch out your hand and strike his flesh and bones, and he will surely curse you to your face."

⁶The LORD said to Satan, "Very well, then, he is in your hands; but you must spare his life."

⁷So Satan went out from the presence of the LORD and afflicted Job with painful sores from the soles of his feet to the top of his head. ⁸Then Job took a piece of broken pottery and scraped himself with it as he sat among the ashes.

⁹His wife said to him, "Are you still

holding on to your integrity? Curse God and die!"

[10]He replied, "You are talking like a foolish[d] woman. Shall we accept good from God, and not trouble?"

In all this, Job did not sin in what he said.

[11]When Job's three friends, Eliphaz the Temanite, Bildad the Shuhite and Zophar the Naamathite, heard about all the troubles that had come upon him, they set out from their homes and met together by agreement to go and sympathize with him and comfort him. [12]When they saw him from a distance, they could hardly recognize him; they began to weep aloud, and they tore their robes and sprinkled dust on their heads. [13]Then they sat on the ground with him for seven days and seven nights. No one said a word to him, because they saw how great his suffering was.

CHAPTER 3
After this, Job opened his mouth and cursed the day of his birth. [2]He said:

[3]"May the day of my birth perish,
    and the night it was said, 'A boy is
        born!'
[4]That day—may it turn to darkness;
    may God above not care about it;
    may no light shine upon it.
[5]May darkness and deep shadow[e]
        claim it once more;
    may a cloud settle over it;
    may blackness overwhelm its light.
[6]That night—may thick darkness seize
        it;
    may it not be included among the
        days of the year
    nor be entered in any of the months.
[7]May that night be barren;
    may no shout of joy be heard in it.
[8]May those who curse days[f] curse that
        day,
    those who are ready to rouse
        Leviathan.
[9]May its morning stars become dark;
    may it wait for daylight in vain

and not see the first rays of dawn,
[10]for it did not shut the doors of the
        womb on me
    to hide trouble from my eyes.

[11]"Why did I not perish at birth,
    and die as I came from the womb?
[12]Why were there knees to receive me
    and breasts that I might be nursed?
[13]For now I would be lying down in
        peace;
    I would be asleep and at rest
[14]with kings and counselors of the earth,
    who built for themselves places now
        lying in ruins,
[15]with rulers who had gold,
    who filled their houses with silver.
[16]Or why was I not hidden in the
        ground like a stillborn child,
    like an infant who never saw the
        light of day?
[17]There the wicked cease from turmoil,
    and there the weary are at rest.
[18]Captives also enjoy their ease;
    they no longer hear the slave
        driver's shout.
[19]The small and the great are there,
    and the slave is freed from his
        master.

[20]"Why is light given to those in misery,
    and life to the bitter of soul,
[21]to those who long for death that does
        not come,
    who search for it more than for
        hidden treasure,
[22]who are filled with gladness
    and rejoice when they reach the
        grave?
[23]Why is life given to a man
    whose way is hidden,
    whom God has hedged in?
[24]For sighing comes to me instead of
        food;
    my groans pour out like water.
[25]What I feared has come upon me;
    what I dreaded has happened to me.
[26]I have no peace, no quietness;
    I have no rest, but only turmoil."

[d]10 The Hebrew word rendered *foolish* denotes moral deficiency.   [e]5 Or *and the shadow of death*   [f]8 Or *the sea*

MAY 17 ☐ DAY 138
JOB 4–7
Eliphaz and Job (First Debate)

OVERVIEW Onto the stage now step three counselors to begin a series of poetic debates with Job, which will stretch from chapter 4 through chapter 31. These three personal friends, previously introduced in 2:11, represent three differing points of view as they analyze Job's sorry plight. Eliphaz, the senior spokesman, bases much of his insight on personal experience. Courteously, Eliphaz reasons from the general assumption that all people stand guilty before a perfect God. All suffering results from sin—a diagnosis that proves inadequate in Job's case. Job expresses disappointment with Eliphaz's counsel and challenges him to identify anything standing between Job and his God.

Chapter 4	Chapter 5	Chapter 6	Chapter 7
Sin's Suffering	Sin's Solution	The Sufferer's Sorrow	The Sufferer's Self-Analysis
Counsel by Eliphaz		Evaluation by Job	

YOUR DAILY WALK Put yourself in this fatherly role for a moment. You have just come home from work to find a baseball and bat lying in front of the shattered remains of what used to be your patio window. Without investigating further (an open-and-shut case, you conclude), you storm into the house, corral the guilty party and administer a sound spanking. Satisfied that justice has been served, you sit down with the evening paper . . . just as your wife returns with the boy next door who has confessed to the whole thing!

No one gives advice with more enthusiasm than an ignorant person.

Jumping to conclusions is not nearly as good an exercise as digging for the facts. The Bible tells us to be "quick to listen, slow to speak and slow to become angry" (James 1:19). Take a counseling lesson from the book of Job. What situation today requires you to act as referee? Spend adequate time looking at all the issues first. Give your counsel only after thoughtful, prayerful consideration of all the facts.

INSIGHT What's Ailing You?

Job's disease included all of these symptoms: painful sores (2:7), itching (2:8), disfigurement (2:12), loss of appetite (3:24), severe depression (3:24–25), broken skin (7:5), red eyes (16:16), bad breath (19:17), constant pain (30:17), discoloration and fever (30:30) and an emaciated appearance (33:21).

CHAPTER 4

Then Eliphaz the Temanite replied:

2"If someone ventures a word with you,
    will you be impatient?
But who can keep from speaking?
3Think how you have instructed many,
    how you have strengthened feeble
        hands.
4Your words have supported those who
        stumbled;

you have strengthened faltering knees.
5But now trouble comes to you, and
    you are discouraged;
it strikes you, and you are
    dismayed.
6Should not your piety be your
        confidence
and your blameless ways your hope?

7"Consider now: Who, being innocent,
    has ever perished?

Where were the upright ever
destroyed?
⁸As I have observed, those who plow
evil
and those who sow trouble reap it.
⁹At the breath of God they are
destroyed;
at the blast of his anger they perish.
¹⁰The lions may roar and growl,
yet the teeth of the great lions are
broken.
¹¹The lion perishes for lack of prey,
and the cubs of the lioness are
scattered.

¹²"A word was secretly brought to me,
my ears caught a whisper of it.
¹³Amid disquieting dreams in the
night,
when deep sleep falls on men,
¹⁴fear and trembling seized me
and made all my bones shake.
¹⁵A spirit glided past my face,
and the hair on my body stood on
end.
¹⁶It stopped,
but I could not tell what it was.
A form stood before my eyes,
and I heard a hushed voice:
¹⁷'Can a mortal be more righteous than
God?
Can a man be more pure than his
Maker?
¹⁸If God places no trust in his servants,
if he charges his angels with
error,
¹⁹how much more those who live in
houses of clay,
whose foundations are in the dust,
who are crushed more readily than
a moth!
²⁰Between dawn and dusk they are
broken to pieces;
unnoticed, they perish forever.
²¹Are not the cords of their tent pulled
up,
so that they die without wisdom?'ᵍ

CHAPTER 5
"Call if you will, but who will answer
you?
To which of the holy ones will you
turn?
²Resentment kills a fool,
and envy slays the simple.
³I myself have seen a fool taking root,

but suddenly his house was cursed.
⁴His children are far from safety,
crushed in court without a defender.
⁵The hungry consume his harvest,
taking it even from among thorns,
and the thirsty pant after his wealth.
⁶For hardship does not spring from the
soil,
nor does trouble sprout from the
ground.
⁷Yet man is born to trouble
as surely as sparks fly upward.

⁸"But if it were I, I would appeal to
God;
I would lay my cause before him.
⁹He performs wonders that cannot be
fathomed,
miracles that cannot be counted.
¹⁰He bestows rain on the earth;
he sends water upon the
countryside.
¹¹The lowly he sets on high,
and those who mourn are lifted to
safety.
¹²He thwarts the plans of the crafty,
so that their hands achieve no
success.
¹³He catches the wise in their craftiness,
and the schemes of the wily are
swept away.
¹⁴Darkness comes upon them in the
daytime;
at noon they grope as in the night.
¹⁵He saves the needy from the sword in
their mouth;
he saves them from the clutches of
the powerful.
¹⁶So the poor have hope,
and injustice shuts its mouth.

¹⁷"Blessed is the man whom God
corrects;
so do not despise the discipline of
the Almighty.ʰ
¹⁸For he wounds, but he also binds up;
he injures, but his hands also heal.
¹⁹From six calamities he will rescue you;
in seven no harm will befall you.
²⁰In famine he will ransom you from
death,
and in battle from the stroke of the
sword.
²¹You will be protected from the lash of
the tongue,

ᵍ21 Some interpreters end the quotation after verse 17.   ʰ17 Hebrew *Shaddai*; here and throughout Job

and need not fear when destruction
    comes.
²²You will laugh at destruction and
    famine,
    and need not fear the beasts of the
    earth.
²³For you will have a covenant with the
    stones of the field,
    and the wild animals will be at
    peace with you.
²⁴You will know that your tent is secure;
    you will take stock of your property
    and find nothing missing.
²⁵You will know that your children will
    be many,
    and your descendants like the grass
    of the earth.
²⁶You will come to the grave in full
    vigor,
    like sheaves gathered in season.

²⁷"We have examined this, and it is true.
    So hear it and apply it to yourself."

CHAPTER 6
Then Job replied:

²"If only my anguish could be weighed
    and all my misery be placed on the
    scales!
³It would surely outweigh the sand of
    the seas—
    no wonder my words have been
    impetuous.
⁴The arrows of the Almighty are in me,
    my spirit drinks in their poison;
    God's terrors are marshaled against
    me.
⁵Does a wild donkey bray when it has
    grass,
    or an ox bellow when it has fodder?
⁶Is tasteless food eaten without salt,
    or is there flavor in the white of an
    egg^i?
⁷I refuse to touch it;
    such food makes me ill.

⁸"Oh, that I might have my request,
    that God would grant what I hope
    for,
⁹that God would be willing to crush
    me,
    to let loose his hand and cut me off!
¹⁰Then I would still have this
    consolation—
    my joy in unrelenting pain—

that I had not denied the words of
    the Holy One.

¹¹"What strength do I have, that I should
    still hope?
    What prospects, that I should be
    patient?
¹²Do I have the strength of stone?
    Is my flesh bronze?
¹³Do I have any power to help myself,
    now that success has been driven
    from me?

¹⁴"A despairing man should have the
    devotion of his friends,
    even though he forsakes the fear of
    the Almighty.
¹⁵But my brothers are as undependable
    as intermittent streams,
    as the streams that overflow
¹⁶when darkened by thawing ice
    and swollen with melting snow,
¹⁷but that cease to flow in the dry
    season,
    and in the heat vanish from their
    channels.
¹⁸Caravans turn aside from their routes;
    they go up into the wasteland and
    perish.
¹⁹The caravans of Tema look for water,
    the traveling merchants of Sheba
    look in hope.
²⁰They are distressed, because they had
    been confident;
    they arrive there, only to be
    disappointed.
²¹Now you too have proved to be of no
    help;
    you see something dreadful and are
    afraid.
²²Have I ever said, 'Give something on
    my behalf,
    pay a ransom for me from your
    wealth,
²³deliver me from the hand of the
    enemy,
    ransom me from the clutches of the
    ruthless'?

²⁴"Teach me, and I will be quiet;
    show me where I have been wrong.
²⁵How painful are honest words!
    But what do your arguments prove?
²⁶Do you mean to correct what I say,
    and treat the words of a despairing
    man as wind?

ⁱ6 The meaning of the Hebrew for this phrase is uncertain.

²⁷You would even cast lots for the
　　fatherless
　　and barter away your friend.

²⁸"But now be so kind as to look at me.
　　Would I lie to your face?
²⁹Relent, do not be unjust;
　　reconsider, for my integrity is at
　　stake.ʲ
³⁰Is there any wickedness on my lips?
　　Can my mouth not discern malice?

CHAPTER 7

"Does not man have hard service on
　　earth?
　　Are not his days like those of a
　　hired man?
²Like a slave longing for the evening
　　shadows,
　　or a hired man waiting eagerly for
　　his wages,
³so I have been allotted months of
　　futility,
　　and nights of misery have been
　　assigned to me.
⁴When I lie down I think, 'How long
　　before I get up?'
　　The night drags on, and I toss till
　　dawn.
⁵My body is clothed with worms and
　　scabs,
　　my skin is broken and festering.

⁶"My days are swifter than a weaver's
　　shuttle,
　　and they come to an end without
　　hope.
⁷Remember, O God, that my life is but
　　a breath;
　　my eyes will never see happiness
　　again.
⁸The eye that now sees me will see me
　　no longer;
　　you will look for me, but I will be
　　no more.

⁹As a cloud vanishes and is gone,
　　so he who goes down to the graveᵏ
　　does not return.
¹⁰He will never come to his house again;
　　his place will know him no more.

¹¹"Therefore I will not keep silent;
　　I will speak out in the anguish of
　　my spirit,
　　I will complain in the bitterness of
　　my soul.
¹²Am I the sea, or the monster of the
　　deep,
　　that you put me under guard?
¹³When I think my bed will comfort me
　　and my couch will ease my
　　complaint,
¹⁴even then you frighten me with
　　dreams
　　and terrify me with visions,
¹⁵so that I prefer strangling and death,
　　rather than this body of mine.
¹⁶I despise my life; I would not live
　　forever.
　　Let me alone; my days have no
　　meaning.

¹⁷"What is man that you make so much
　　of him,
　　that you give him so much attention,
¹⁸that you examine him every morning
　　and test him every moment?
¹⁹Will you never look away from me,
　　or let me alone even for an instant?
²⁰If I have sinned, what have I done to
　　you,
　　O watcher of men?
　　Why have you made me your target?
　　Have I become a burden to you?ˡ
²¹Why do you not pardon my offenses
　　and forgive my sins?
　　For I will soon lie down in the dust;
　　you will search for me, but I will be
　　no more."

ʲ29 Or my righteousness still stands   ᵏ9 Hebrew Sheol   ˡ20 A few manuscripts of the Masoretic Text, an ancient Hebrew
scribal tradition and Septuagint; most manuscripts of the Masoretic Text I have become a burden to myself.

MAY 18 □ DAY 139
JOB 8–10
Bildad and Job (First Debate)

OVERVIEW Eliphaz has based his arguments on a cause-and-effect view of sin and suffering. Now Bildad the Shuhite arises to argue the same case, but from the perspective of tradition rather than experience. He calls on Job to meditate upon the attribute of God's justice as seen repeatedly in history. God shows his salvation and mercy to the upright, but brings down the wicked. Therefore, there can be only one conclusion regarding Job's plight: He is guilty of some secret sin. Again the suffering patriarch concedes that God is perfect and just, but he also maintains his own innocence—and expresses his bewilderment as he struggles to understand his suffering.

Chapter 8	Chapter 9	Chapter 10
"God Is Just"	"I Know God Is Just!"	"Why Then Do I Suffer?"
Bildad's Comments	Job's Concession	Job's Confusion

The best of saints have borne the worst of sufferings.

YOUR DAILY WALK The need for someone who can reconcile holy God and sinful humanity is as old as the early chapters of Genesis. The sin of Adam and Eve in the Garden of Eden (Genesis 3:6) interrupted their fellowship with God, brought forth God's anger and judgment and placed a barrier between God and humanity. Later, prophets would represent God to the people, and priests would establish God's order on earth for humanity. Yet throughout the Old Testament there was never one who could fully heal the breach. To do that would require a man to be God and God to become a man.

Job lived during a period of history when a perfect and sinless mediator was unknown. The one who alone can bring God and humanity together and restore that lost fellowship is Jesus Christ (1 Timothy 2:5). Do you know Jesus as your personal Savior and Mediator before God? He is waiting to bring you to God, to settle the sin problem that has estranged you from him, to lay his loving hand upon you right now (Psalm 139:5–6). Will you let him?

INSIGHT Here Comes the Judge
The phrase translated *someone to arbitrate* in 9:33 does not merely mean a judge who decides what is right. Rather, it means one who mediates between or reconciles two parties by bringing them together and then lays his hands on them both as a mutual friend.

CHAPTER 8
Then Bildad the Shuhite replied:

2"How long will you say such things?
Your words are a blustering wind.
3Does God pervert justice?
Does the Almighty pervert what is
right?
4When your children sinned against
him,
he gave them over to the penalty of
their sin.
5But if you will look to God

and plead with the Almighty,
6if you are pure and upright,
even now he will rouse himself on
your behalf
and restore you to your rightful
place.
7Your beginnings will seem humble,
so prosperous will your future be.

8"Ask the former generations
and find out what their fathers
learned,

[9]for we were born only yesterday and
know nothing,
and our days on earth are but a
shadow.
[10]Will they not instruct you and tell
you?
Will they not bring forth words
from their understanding?
[11]Can papyrus grow tall where there is
no marsh?
Can reeds thrive without water?
[12]While still growing and uncut,
they wither more quickly than grass.
[13]Such is the destiny of all who forget
God;
so perishes the hope of the godless.
[14]What he trusts in is fragile[m];
what he relies on is a spider's web.
[15]He leans on his web, but it gives way;
he clings to it, but it does not hold.
[16]He is like a well-watered plant in the
sunshine,
spreading its shoots over the garden;
[17]it entwines its roots around a pile of
rocks
and looks for a place among the
stones.
[18]But when it is torn from its spot,
that place disowns it and says, 'I
never saw you.'
[19]Surely its life withers away,
and[n] from the soil other plants
grow.

[20]"Surely God does not reject a
blameless man
or strengthen the hands of evildoers.
[21]He will yet fill your mouth with
laughter
and your lips with shouts of joy.
[22]Your enemies will be clothed in
shame,
and the tents of the wicked will be
no more."

CHAPTER 9
Then Job replied:

[2]"Indeed, I know that this is true.
But how can a mortal be righteous
before God?
[3]Though one wished to dispute with
him,
he could not answer him one time
out of a thousand.

[4]His wisdom is profound, his power is
vast.
Who has resisted him and come out
unscathed?
[5]He moves mountains without their
knowing it
and overturns them in his anger.
[6]He shakes the earth from its place
and makes its pillars tremble.
[7]He speaks to the sun and it does not
shine;
he seals off the light of the stars.
[8]He alone stretches out the heavens
and treads on the waves of the sea.
[9]He is the Maker of the Bear and
Orion,
the Pleiades and the constellations of
the south.
[10]He performs wonders that cannot be
fathomed,
miracles that cannot be counted.
[11]When he passes me, I cannot see him;
when he goes by, I cannot perceive
him.
[12]If he snatches away, who can stop
him?
Who can say to him, 'What are you
doing?'
[13]God does not restrain his anger;
even the cohorts of Rahab cowered
at his feet.

[14]"How then can I dispute with him?
How can I find words to argue with
him?
[15]Though I were innocent, I could not
answer him;
I could only plead with my Judge
for mercy.
[16]Even if I summoned him and he
responded,
I do not believe he would give me a
hearing.
[17]He would crush me with a storm
and multiply my wounds for no
reason.
[18]He would not let me regain my breath
but would overwhelm me with
misery.
[19]If it is a matter of strength, he is
mighty!
And if it is a matter of justice, who
will summon him[o]?
[20]Even if I were innocent, my mouth
would condemn me;

[m]14 The meaning of the Hebrew for this word is uncertain.   _[n]19 Or Surely all the joy it has / is that_   _[o]19 See Septuagint;_
Hebrew me.

if I were blameless, it would
  pronounce me guilty.

21"Although I am blameless,
  I have no concern for myself;
  I despise my own life.
22It is all the same; that is why I say,
  'He destroys both the blameless and
    the wicked.'
23When a scourge brings sudden death,
  he mocks the despair of the
    innocent.
24When a land falls into the hands of the
    wicked,
  he blindfolds its judges.
  If it is not he, then who is it?

25"My days are swifter than a runner;
  they fly away without a glimpse of
    joy.
26They skim past like boats of papyrus,
  like eagles swooping down on their
    prey.
27If I say, 'I will forget my complaint,
  I will change my expression, and
    smile,'
28I still dread all my sufferings,
  for I know you will not hold me
    innocent.
29Since I am already found guilty,
  why should I struggle in vain?
30Even if I washed myself with soap*p*
  and my hands with washing soda,
31you would plunge me into a slime pit
  so that even my clothes would
    detest me.

32"He is not a man like me that I might
    answer him,
  that we might confront each other in
    court.
33If only there were someone to arbitrate
    between us,
  to lay his hand upon us both,
34someone to remove God's rod from
    me,
  so that his terror would frighten me
    no more.
35Then I would speak up without fear of
    him,
  but as it now stands with me, I
    cannot.

CHAPTER 10
  "I loathe my very life;
  therefore I will give free rein to my
    complaint

and speak out in the bitterness of
  my soul.
2I will say to God: Do not condemn me,
  but tell me what charges you have
    against me.
3Does it please you to oppress me,
  to spurn the work of your hands,
  while you smile on the schemes of
    the wicked?
4Do you have eyes of flesh?
  Do you see as a mortal sees?
5Are your days like those of a mortal
  or your years like those of a man,
6that you must search out my faults
  and probe after my sin—
7though you know that I am not guilty
  and that no one can rescue me from
    your hand?

8"Your hands shaped me and made me.
  Will you now turn and destroy me?
9Remember that you molded me like
    clay.
  Will you now turn me to dust
    again?
10Did you not pour me out like milk
  and curdle me like cheese,
11clothe me with skin and flesh
  and knit me together with bones
    and sinews?
12You gave me life and showed me
    kindness,
  and in your providence watched
    over my spirit.

13"But this is what you concealed in
    your heart,
  and I know that this was in your
    mind:
14If I sinned, you would be watching me
  and would not let my offense go
    unpunished.
15If I am guilty—woe to me!
  Even if I am innocent, I cannot lift
    my head,
  for I am full of shame
  and drowned in*q* my affliction.
16If I hold my head high, you stalk me
    like a lion
  and again display your awesome
    power against me.
17You bring new witnesses against me
  and increase your anger toward me;
  your forces come against me wave
    upon wave.

p 30 Or snow   q 15 Or and aware of

¹⁸"Why then did you bring me out of
the womb?
I wish I had died before any eye
saw me.
¹⁹If only I had never come into
being,
or had been carried straight from
the womb to the grave!
²⁰Are not my few days almost over?

Turn away from me so I can have a
moment's joy
²¹before I go to the place of no return,
to the land of gloom and deep
shadow,^r
²²to the land of deepest night,
of deep shadow and disorder,
where even the light is like
darkness."

^r21 Or *and the shadow of death*; also in verse 22

MAY 19 ☐ DAY 140
JOB 11–14
Zophar and Job (First Debate)

OVERVIEW Zophar wastes little time boring straight to the heart of
the matter (as he interprets it). By comparison with Eliphaz and Bildad, he is almost brutal in his bluntness. "Will your idle talk reduce
men to silence? . . . Oh, how I wish that God would speak, that he
would open his lips against you . . . Know this: God has even forgotten some of your sin" (11:3, 5–6). He appeals to God's great wisdom
and control, which dwarf those of vain and ignorant men, and urges
Job to return to God, where he will find both security and hope. Job
responds with a lengthy defense in which he acknowledges God's
power, defends his own integrity and reaffirms his steadfast confidence
in God.

Chapter 11		Chapter 12	Chapter 13	Chapter 14
"God Is in Control"	"Turn Back to Him"	"I Never Left Him"	"You're No Help"	"Help Me, God"
1 12	13 20			
Zophar's Plea for Piety		Job's Persistent Denial		

YOUR DAILY WALK Few passages in Scripture paint as dark a picture
of depression as that found in Job 14. What makes it more remarkable
is that the author is describing a believer. Believers are not immune to
the despair and despondency that accompany painful circumstances.

If we could avoid that portion of suffering we bring upon ourselves, we might be surprised at how little would be left.

But believers do have a reservoir for coping with depression that the
world knows nothing about!
• They know God is on their side (Romans 8:31).
• They know God is in control of both the oppressed and the oppressor (Job 12:16).
• They know justice will ultimately triumph (Job 13:18).
Are you given to times of depression about a particular circumstance
in your life? The answer is not to dwell on your circumstance but on
the greatness of your Creator. He is your salvation (13:16); he numbers your every step (14:16); and he cares about you. Spend some
quiet moments pondering his greatness until you can respond as Job
did: "May the name of the LORD be praised" (1:21).

INSIGHT Zophar, the Friend Job Could Do Without
Zophar (whose name means "hairy" or "rough") appears as a mean,
self-made authority who thought he understood Job's problem (and

didn't), making life all the more miserable for Job, who wanted to understand his problem (and couldn't)!

CHAPTER 11
Then Zophar the Naamathite replied:

2"Are all these words to go
    unanswered?
Is this talker to be vindicated?
3Will your idle talk reduce men to
    silence?
Will no one rebuke you when you
    mock?
4You say to God, 'My beliefs are
    flawless
and I am pure in your sight.'
5Oh, how I wish that God would speak,
    that he would open his lips against
    you
6and disclose to you the secrets of
    wisdom,
for true wisdom has two sides.
Know this: God has even forgotten
    some of your sin.

7"Can you fathom the mysteries of
    God?
Can you probe the limits of the
    Almighty?
8They are higher than the heavens—
    what can you do?
They are deeper than the depths of
    the grave^s—what can you
    know?
9Their measure is longer than the earth
    and wider than the sea.

10"If he comes along and confines you in
    prison
and convenes a court, who can
    oppose him?
11Surely he recognizes deceitful men;
    and when he sees evil, does he not
    take note?
12But a witless man can no more become
    wise
than a wild donkey's colt can be
    born a man.^t

13"Yet if you devote your heart to him
    and stretch out your hands to him,
14if you put away the sin that is in your
    hand
and allow no evil to dwell in your
    tent,
15then you will lift up your face without
    shame;

you will stand firm and without
    fear.
16You will surely forget your trouble,
    recalling it only as waters gone by.
17Life will be brighter than noonday,
    and darkness will become like
    morning.
18You will be secure, because there is
    hope;
you will look about you and take
    your rest in safety.
19You will lie down, with no one to
    make you afraid,
and many will court your favor.
20But the eyes of the wicked will fail,
    and escape will elude them;
their hope will become a dying
    gasp."

CHAPTER 12
Then Job replied:

2"Doubtless you are the people,
    and wisdom will die with you!
3But I have a mind as well as you;
    I am not inferior to you.
Who does not know all these things?

4"I have become a laughingstock to my
    friends,
though I called upon God and he
    answered—
a mere laughingstock, though
    righteous and blameless!
5Men at ease have contempt for
    misfortune
as the fate of those whose feet are
    slipping.
6The tents of marauders are
    undisturbed,
and those who provoke God are
    secure—
those who carry their god in their
    hands.^u

7"But ask the animals, and they will
    teach you,
or the birds of the air, and they will
    tell you;
8or speak to the earth, and it will teach
    you,
or let the fish of the sea inform you.
9Which of all these does not know

^s8 Hebrew than Sheol   ^t12 Or wild donkey can be born tame   ^u6 Or secure / in what God's hand brings them

that the hand of the LORD has done
  this?
¹⁰In his hand is the life of every creature
  and the breath of all mankind.
¹¹Does not the ear test words
  as the tongue tastes food?
¹²Is not wisdom found among the aged?
  Does not long life bring
    understanding?

¹³"To God belong wisdom and power;
  counsel and understanding are his.
¹⁴What he tears down cannot be rebuilt;
  the man he imprisons cannot be
    released.
¹⁵If he holds back the waters, there is
    drought;
  if he lets them loose, they devastate
    the land.
¹⁶To him belong strength and victory;
  both deceived and deceiver are his.
¹⁷He leads counselors away stripped
  and makes fools of judges.
¹⁸He takes off the shackles put on by
    kings
  and ties a loincloth^v around their
    waist.
¹⁹He leads priests away stripped
  and overthrows men long
    established.
²⁰He silences the lips of trusted advisers
  and takes away the discernment of
    elders.
²¹He pours contempt on nobles
  and disarms the mighty.
²²He reveals the deep things of darkness
  and brings deep shadows into the
    light.
²³He makes nations great, and destroys
    them;
  he enlarges nations, and disperses
    them.
²⁴He deprives the leaders of the earth of
    their reason;
  he sends them wandering through a
    trackless waste.
²⁵They grope in darkness with no light;
  he makes them stagger like
    drunkards.

CHAPTER 13
  "My eyes have seen all this,
    my ears have heard and understood
      it.
  ²What you know, I also know;
    I am not inferior to you.

³But I desire to speak to the Almighty
  and to argue my case with God.
⁴You, however, smear me with lies;
  you are worthless physicians, all of
    you!
⁵If only you would be altogether silent!
  For you, that would be wisdom.
⁶Hear now my argument;
  listen to the plea of my lips.
⁷Will you speak wickedly on God's
    behalf?
  Will you speak deceitfully for him?
⁸Will you show him partiality?
  Will you argue the case for God?
⁹Would it turn out well if he examined
    you?
  Could you deceive him as you
    might deceive men?
¹⁰He would surely rebuke you
  if you secretly showed partiality.
¹¹Would not his splendor terrify you?
  Would not the dread of him fall on
    you?
¹²Your maxims are proverbs of ashes;
  your defenses are defenses of clay.

¹³"Keep silent and let me speak;
  then let come to me what may.
¹⁴Why do I put myself in jeopardy
  and take my life in my hands?
¹⁵Though he slay me, yet will I hope in
    him;
  I will surely^w defend my ways to
    his face.
¹⁶Indeed, this will turn out for my
    deliverance,
  for no godless man would dare
    come before him!
¹⁷Listen carefully to my words;
  let your ears take in what I say.
¹⁸Now that I have prepared my case,
  I know I will be vindicated.
¹⁹Can anyone bring charges against me?
  If so, I will be silent and die.

²⁰"Only grant me these two things,
    O God,
  and then I will not hide from you:
²¹Withdraw your hand far from me,
  and stop frightening me with your
    terrors.
²²Then summon me and I will answer,
  or let me speak, and you reply.
²³How many wrongs and sins have I
    committed?
  Show me my offense and my sin.

^{v}18 Or shackles of kings / and ties a belt ^{w}15 Or He will surely slay me; I have no hope — / yet I will

²⁴Why do you hide your face
and consider me your enemy?
²⁵Will you torment a windblown leaf?
Will you chase after dry chaff?
²⁶For you write down bitter things
against me
and make me inherit the sins of my
youth.
²⁷You fasten my feet in shackles;
you keep close watch on all my
paths
by putting marks on the soles of my
feet.

²⁸"So man wastes away like something
rotten,
like a garment eaten by moths.

CHAPTER 14

"Man born of woman
is of few days and full of trouble.
²He springs up like a flower and
withers away;
like a fleeting shadow, he does not
endure.
³Do you fix your eye on such a one?
Will you bring him˟ before you for
judgment?
⁴Who can bring what is pure from the
impure?
No one!
⁵Man's days are determined;
you have decreed the number of his
months
and have set limits he cannot
exceed.
⁶So look away from him and let him
alone,
till he has put in his time like a
hired man.

⁷"At least there is hope for a tree:
If it is cut down, it will sprout
again,
and its new shoots will not fail.
⁸Its roots may grow old in the ground
and its stump die in the soil,
⁹yet at the scent of water it will bud

and put forth shoots like a plant.
¹⁰But man dies and is laid low;
he breathes his last and is no more.
¹¹As water disappears from the sea
or a riverbed becomes parched and
dry,
¹²so man lies down and does not rise;
till the heavens are no more, men
will not awake
or be roused from their sleep.

¹³"If only you would hide me in the
graveʸ
and conceal me till your anger has
passed!
If only you would set me a time
and then remember me!
¹⁴If a man dies, will he live again?
All the days of my hard service
I will wait for my renewalᶻ to
come.
¹⁵You will call and I will answer you;
you will long for the creature your
hands have made.
¹⁶Surely then you will count my steps
but not keep track of my sin.
¹⁷My offenses will be sealed up in a bag;
you will cover over my sin.

¹⁸"But as a mountain erodes and
crumbles
and as a rock is moved from its
place,
¹⁹as water wears away stones
and torrents wash away the soil,
so you destroy man's hope.
²⁰You overpower him once for all, and
he is gone;
you change his countenance and
send him away.
²¹If his sons are honored, he does not
know it;
if they are brought low, he does not
see it.
²²He feels but the pain of his own body
and mourns only for himself."

˟3 Septuagint, Vulgate and Syriac; Hebrew *me*   ʸ13 Hebrew *Sheol*   ᶻ14 Or *release*

MAY 20 □ DAY 141
JOB 15–17
Eliphaz and Job (Second Debate)

OVERVIEW Like a second wave of attacking soldiers, the three counselors launch their second cycle of debates without giving Job so much as a moment's rest! Eliphaz again leads the assault, this time increasing the intensity of his verbal attack. He describes Job's words as worthless talk; he denies that Job understands anything new or true about God; and he broadly condemns all wickedness in man—a thinly disguised slander of Job's character. Job rejects these bitter accusations. Then, speaking to himself, he agonizes over God's apparent plot to destroy him. Depression once again overwhelms him.

Chapter 15	Chapter 16	Chapter 17
Eliphaz's Broken Record	Job's Broken Heart	Job's Broken Hope
Wicked People Die	God Shatters Me	God, Deliver Me

YOUR DAILY WALK "Anything true is not new; anything new is not true."

This closed-minded attitude that excludes any possibility of learning is a perfect description of the elder counselor, Eliphaz (15:9–10, 17–19). Such is the fate of all who claim to know it all by reason of their years of experience. Age alone, whether chronological or spiritual, is no sure measure of a person's wisdom.

Your ability to learn depends in part on your ability to relinquish what you have held.

Maintain a teachable spirit today. Take an index card with you everywhere you go, and write down at least four new thoughts that other people express today. Be a ready learner. Don't attempt to convince the other person of your point of view until first you are sure you understand his or hers. Then at the end of the day, evaluate the things you have written down. Are they biblical? Are they practical? Are they appropriate? See if you can learn something new and useful today.

And remember this little slogan: If you think you're green, you'll grow; if you think you're ripe, you'll rot.

INSIGHT The Agony of Defeat

When a wounded bull has spent his last energy, he will often scrape at the ground with his horns. Job sensed that he was doomed. In 16:15 he likens himself to a defeated animal who has laid his head in the dust—a pathetic picture of a discouraged saint.

CHAPTER 15
Then Eliphaz the Temanite replied:

2"Would a wise man answer with
    empty notions
  or fill his belly with the hot east
    wind?
3Would he argue with useless words,
  with speeches that have no value?
4But you even undermine piety
  and hinder devotion to God.
5Your sin prompts your mouth;
  you adopt the tongue of the crafty.

6Your own mouth condemns you, not
    mine;
  your own lips testify against you.
7"Are you the first man ever born?
  Were you brought forth before the
    hills?
8Do you listen in on God's council?
  Do you limit wisdom to yourself?
9What do you know that we do not
    know?
  What insights do you have that we
    do not have?

¹⁰The gray-haired and the aged are on
    our side,
  men even older than your father.
¹¹Are God's consolations not enough for
    you,
  words spoken gently to you?
¹²Why has your heart carried you away,
  and why do your eyes flash,
¹³so that you vent your rage against
    God
  and pour out such words from your
    mouth?

¹⁴"What is man, that he could be pure,
  or one born of woman, that he could
    be righteous?
¹⁵If God places no trust in his holy ones,
  if even the heavens are not pure in
    his eyes,
¹⁶how much less man, who is vile and
    corrupt,
  who drinks up evil like water!

¹⁷"Listen to me and I will explain to
    you;
  let me tell you what I have seen,
¹⁸what wise men have declared,
  hiding nothing received from their
    fathers
¹⁹(to whom alone the land was given
  when no alien passed among them):
²⁰All his days the wicked man suffers
    torment,
  the ruthless through all the years
    stored up for him.
²¹Terrifying sounds fill his ears;
  when all seems well, marauders
    attack him.
²²He despairs of escaping the darkness;
  he is marked for the sword.
²³He wanders about—food for
    vultures*;
  he knows the day of darkness is at
    hand.
²⁴Distress and anguish fill him with
    terror;
  they overwhelm him, like a king
    poised to attack,
²⁵because he shakes his fist at God
  and vaunts himself against the
    Almighty,
²⁶defiantly charging against him
  with a thick, strong shield.

²⁷"Though his face is covered with fat
  and his waist bulges with flesh,
²⁸he will inhabit ruined towns

*23 Or about, looking for food

and houses where no one lives,
  houses crumbling to rubble.
²⁹He will no longer be rich and his
    wealth will not endure,
  nor will his possessions spread over
    the land.
³⁰He will not escape the darkness;
  a flame will wither his shoots,
  and the breath of God's mouth will
    carry him away.
³¹Let him not deceive himself by
    trusting what is worthless,
  for he will get nothing in return.
³²Before his time he will be paid in full,
  and his branches will not flourish.
³³He will be like a vine stripped of its
    unripe grapes,
  like an olive tree shedding its
    blossoms.
³⁴For the company of the godless will be
    barren,
  and fire will consume the tents of
    those who love bribes.
³⁵They conceive trouble and give birth
    to evil;
  their womb fashions deceit."

CHAPTER 16

Then Job replied:

²"I have heard many things like these;
  miserable comforters are you all!
³Will your long-winded speeches
    never end?
  What ails you that you keep on
    arguing?
⁴I also could speak like you,
  if you were in my place;
  I could make fine speeches against you
  and shake my head at you.
⁵But my mouth would encourage you;
  comfort from my lips would bring
    you relief.

⁶"Yet if I speak, my pain is not relieved;
  and if I refrain, it does not go away.
⁷Surely, O God, you have worn me out;
  you have devastated my entire
    household.
⁸You have bound me—and it has
    become a witness;
  my gauntness rises up and testifies
    against me.
⁹God assails me and tears me in his
    anger
  and gnashes his teeth at me;

my opponent fastens on me his
    piercing eyes.
¹⁰Men open their mouths to jeer at me;
    they strike my cheek in scorn
    and unite together against me.
¹¹God has turned me over to evil men
    and thrown me into the clutches of
        the wicked.
¹²All was well with me, but he shattered
    me;
    he seized me by the neck and
        crushed me.
    He has made me his target;
¹³ his archers surround me.
    Without pity, he pierces my kidneys
    and spills my gall on the ground.
¹⁴Again and again he bursts upon me;
    he rushes at me like a warrior.

¹⁵"I have sewed sackcloth over my skin
    and buried my brow in the dust.
¹⁶My face is red with weeping,
    deep shadows ring my eyes;
¹⁷yet my hands have been free of
        violence
    and my prayer is pure.

¹⁸"O earth, do not cover my blood;
    may my cry never be laid to rest!
¹⁹Even now my witness is in heaven;
    my advocate is on high.
²⁰My intercessor is my friend[b]
    as my eyes pour out tears to God;
²¹on behalf of a man he pleads with
        God
    as a man pleads for his friend.

²²"Only a few years will pass
    before I go on the journey of no
        return.
C H A P T E R   1 7
¹My spirit is broken,
    my days are cut short,
    the grave awaits me.
²Surely mockers surround me;
    my eyes must dwell on their
        hostility.

³"Give me, O God, the pledge you
        demand.
    Who else will put up security for
        me?
⁴You have closed their minds to
        understanding;
    therefore you will not let them
        triumph.
⁵If a man denounces his friends for
        reward,
    the eyes of his children will fail.

⁶"God has made me a byword to
        everyone,
    a man in whose face people spit.
⁷My eyes have grown dim with grief;
    my whole frame is but a shadow.
⁸Upright men are appalled at this;
    the innocent are aroused against the
        ungodly.
⁹Nevertheless, the righteous will hold
    to their ways,
    and those with clean hands will
        grow stronger.

¹⁰"But come on, all of you, try again!
    I will not find a wise man among
        you.
¹¹My days have passed, my plans are
        shattered,
    and so are the desires of my heart.
¹²These men turn night into day;
    in the face of darkness they say,
        'Light is near.'
¹³If the only home I hope for is the
        grave,[c]
    if I spread out my bed in darkness,
¹⁴if I say to corruption, 'You are my
        father,'
    and to the worm, 'My mother' or
        'My sister,'
¹⁵where then is my hope?
    Who can see any hope for me?
¹⁶Will it go down to the gates of
        death[c]?
    Will we descend together into the
        dust?"

[b]20 Or *My friends treat me with scorn*   [c]13,16 Hebrew *Sheol*

MAY 21 ☐ DAY 142
Our God Reigns

LOOK BACK Your reading this week has carried you from the palace of Queen Esther to the pit of Job's suffering. You've seen God deliver his people from certain death and allow his servant Job to experience suffering to the point of death. You've seen God's mighty arm at work in the days of Esther, and you've seen God strangely quiet and inactive in the midst of Job's sufferings. You've read about Mordecai's promotion for looking out for the welfare of his people and Job's agonizing calamities even though he was "blameless and upright" (2:3).

Perhaps you've wondered, *What's going on here, anyway? Is this really the same God at work? How can he be so benevolent to one of his children and seemingly so cruel and passive toward another?*

If so, you are not alone! Job asked himself many of those same questions. He struggled with the why of his predicament: God, where are you when it hurts? Why have you allowed such sadness and pain to come into my life? What have I done to deserve all this? The answers Job found—and which you will find, too, as you continue to read—changed forever the way he looked at the God of creation.

LOOK UP Reputation is what others think you are; character is what God knows you are. And when your reputation and character are both blameless, you have integrity—the ring of authenticity in the life of the child of God.

The longer you dwell on your misfortunes, the greater is their power to harm you.

Integrity is behaving in the dark just as you would in the light. It is being what you say you are and doing what you said you would even when no one is watching. It is consistency of character, with no hidden agenda or twisted motive.

Integrity is what causes you to tell the truth, regardless of how tempting it might be to shade the truth. It's what prompts you to tell the cashier you've received too much change, to give back the wallet someone lost without first counting its contents, to drive one mile under (rather than over) the speed limit, to be one minute early (rather than late) for an appointment, to stand up for what is right even if you stand alone.

When Job's world came crashing down around him, he no doubt faced an avalanche of emotional responses: fear, frustration, anger, bitterness, confusion, bewilderment. Unknown to Job, a celestial drama was unfolding between God and Satan—with Job as the center of attention! God was inviting Satan to observe one of his choicest servants and to discover what a blameless and upright man looks like—one who holds fast to his integrity. Job's character in the crucible of adversity was so remarkable, even his wife found it unbelievable (2:9)!

LOOK AHEAD Do you hold to your integrity in the midst of trying circumstances? Here's a little quiz to help you measure your "Integrity Quotient": *If you knew no one was watching or would ever know . . .*

- How much would someone have to pay you to get you to lie or shade the truth?
- How long would you watch a sexually suggestive TV program before you changed the channel?
- How much "too much" would a cashier have to pay you before you went to the trouble of pointing out the error and returning the money?
- How bad would things have to get before you were tempted to curse God?

MAY 22 ☐ DAY 143
JOB 18–19
Bildad and Job (Second Debate)

 OVERVIEW Bildad continues the seemingly endless debate by painting a horrifying picture of the terror and destruction awaiting the wicked. Job is pained, but he refuses to collapse under the pressure of his counselors-turned-accusers. Once again placing the responsibility for his plight on the Lord, Job dwells on the history of his disaster. He has been abandoned by family and friends, servants and spouse. Yet in spite of his despair, there is reason to hope. For Job knows that the future holds the promise both of resurrection and his ultimate vindication from wrong.

Chapter 18		Chapter 19		
Bildad's Hostility	Bildad's Harassment	Job's Hurt	Job's History	Job's Hope
1 4	5 21	1 12	13 22	23 29
Bildad's Taunts		Job's Thoughts		

 YOUR DAILY WALK "There is no medicine like hope, no incentive so great, no tonic so powerful as expectation of something better tomorrow."

There is no medicine like hope. It is one thing to speak of hope when things look doubtful . . . when the future is uncertain . . . when circumstances are crowding in. It is something else to speak of hope when there is no doubt about the present (it is a disaster), when the future is certain (and definitely uninviting), when circumstances have crushed you to the floor. Hope in the midst of utter turmoil cannot simply be starry-eyed optimism; it must be built upon bedrock reality.

Job's testimony in 19:25–26 was no mere poetic sentiment. (Remember his plight; it was hopeless!) Rather, Job was drawing strength from the person to whom he had entrusted his life and from the promises that person had made on his behalf.

Imagine that you have been deprived of possessions, health and loved ones. Could you proclaim with Job that your hope was still in the Lord? Pick one of God's many promises (1 Corinthians 10:13 would do nicely), and make it your "Project Hope" today!

 INSIGHT Count to Ten . . . Slowly
Ten is a prominent number in the Bible indicating patient endurance. Jacob endured ten changes in his wages (Genesis 31:7); the Israelites tempted God ten times with their rebellion (Numbers 14:22); and Job put up with ten insults from his companions (Job 19:3).

CHAPTER 18
Then Bildad the Shuhite replied:

²"When will you end these speeches?
    Be sensible, and then we can talk.
³Why are we regarded as cattle
    and considered stupid in your sight?
⁴You who tear yourself to pieces in
        your anger,
    is the earth to be abandoned for
        your sake?

Or must the rocks be moved from
    their place?

⁵"The lamp of the wicked is snuffed
        out;
    the flame of his fire stops burning.
⁶The light in his tent becomes dark;
    the lamp beside him goes out.
⁷The vigor of his step is weakened;
    his own schemes throw him down.
⁸His feet thrust him into a net

and he wanders into its mesh.
⁹A trap seizes him by the heel;
    a snare holds him fast.
¹⁰A noose is hidden for him on the
        ground;
    a trap lies in his path.
¹¹Terrors startle him on every side
    and dog his every step.
¹²Calamity is hungry for him;
    disaster is ready for him when he
        falls.
¹³It eats away parts of his skin;
    death's firstborn devours his limbs.
¹⁴He is torn from the security of his tent
    and marched off to the king of
        terrors.
¹⁵Fire resides*d* in his tent;
    burning sulfur is scattered over his
        dwelling.
¹⁶His roots dry up below
    and his branches wither above.
¹⁷The memory of him perishes from the
        earth;
    he has no name in the land.
¹⁸He is driven from light into darkness
    and is banished from the world.
¹⁹He has no offspring or descendants
        among his people,
    no survivor where once he lived.
²⁰Men of the west are appalled at his
        fate;
    men of the east are seized with
        horror.
²¹Surely such is the dwelling of an evil
        man;
    such is the place of one who knows
        not God."

CHAPTER 19
Then Job replied:

²"How long will you torment me
    and crush me with words?
³Ten times now you have reproached
        me;
    shamelessly you attack me.
⁴If it is true that I have gone astray,
    my error remains my concern alone.
⁵If indeed you would exalt yourselves
        above me
    and use my humiliation against me,
⁶then know that God has wronged me
    and drawn his net around me.

⁷"Though I cry, 'I've been wronged!' I
        get no response;

though I call for help, there is no
        justice.
⁸He has blocked my way so I cannot
        pass;
    he has shrouded my paths in
        darkness.
⁹He has stripped me of my honor
    and removed the crown from my
        head.
¹⁰He tears me down on every side till I
        am gone;
    he uproots my hope like a tree.
¹¹His anger burns against me;
    he counts me among his enemies.
¹²His troops advance in force;
    they build a siege ramp against me
    and encamp around my tent.

¹³"He has alienated my brothers from
        me;
    my acquaintances are completely
        estranged from me.
¹⁴My kinsmen have gone away;
    my friends have forgotten me.
¹⁵My guests and my maidservants count
        me a stranger;
    they look upon me as an alien.
¹⁶I summon my servant, but he does not
        answer,
    though I beg him with my own
        mouth.
¹⁷My breath is offensive to my wife;
    I am loathsome to my own brothers.
¹⁸Even the little boys scorn me;
    when I appear, they ridicule me.
¹⁹All my intimate friends detest me;
    those I love have turned against me.
²⁰I am nothing but skin and bones;
    I have escaped with only the skin of
        my teeth.*e*

²¹"Have pity on me, my friends, have
        pity,
    for the hand of God has struck me.
²²Why do you pursue me as God does?
    Will you never get enough of my
        flesh?

²³"Oh, that my words were recorded,
    that they were written on a scroll,
²⁴that they were inscribed with an iron
        tool on*f* lead,
    or engraved in rock forever!
²⁵I know that my Redeemer*g* lives,
    and that in the end he will stand
        upon the earth.*h*
²⁶And after my skin has been destroyed,

*d*15 Or *Nothing he had remains*   *e*20 Or *only my gums*   *f*24 Or *and*   *g*25 Or *defender*   *h*25 Or *upon my grave*

yet[i] in[j] my flesh I will see God;
[27]I myself will see him
    with my own eyes—I, and not
        another.
    How my heart yearns within me!

[28]"If you say, 'How we will hound him,

since the root of the trouble lies in
    him,[k']
[29]you should fear the sword yourselves;
    for wrath will bring punishment by
        the sword,
    and then you will know that there is
        judgment.[l']"

[i]26 Or And after I awake, / though this body, has been destroyed, / then   [j]26 Or / apart from   [k]28 Many Hebrew manuscripts, Septuagint and Vulgate; most Hebrew manuscripts me   [l]29 Or / that you may come to know the Almighty

MAY 23 □ DAY 144
JOB 20–21
Zophar and Job (Second Debate)

OVERVIEW Zophar—who specializes in easy answers to difficult questions—now makes his last public appearance. His comments are addressed to "the wicked" (20:5) but are aimed straight at Job. The wicked will be cut off; sin and riches will devour him; those he oppressed shall see his defeat; and the fury of God's wrath shall strike him down. Then Job interrupts. The wicked do sometimes prosper and enjoy the luxury of their wealth, but they ultimately die just like everyone else. The wicked are mighty in power while they live, but then comes their destruction by God. Job concludes, "So how can you console me with your nonsense? Nothing is left of your answers but falsehood" (21:34).

Chapter 20		Chapter 21	
Righteous Indignation	Repeated Insight	Understandable Impatience	Undeniable Injustice
1 3	4 29	1 6	7 34
Zophar's Insistence		Job's Innocence	

YOUR DAILY WALK How can you explain the seeming inequities in the world today? The wicked generally go unpunished, the rich get richer, the poor get poorer, the swindler prospers, while the honest man goes bankrupt. Isn't God concerned about such things?

Do not pray that the poor be fed unless you are willing to provide the bread.

If you have pondered thoughts like those, you're not alone. Centuries ago, Job asked the same penetrating questions about the prosperity of the wicked. He looked around him and saw distorted business ethics, perverted justice, unpunished criminals and unjust suffering. Everywhere he looked there was cause for pessimism—until he looked up!

And suddenly everything snapped into sharp focus. The God of eternity works out his plan from the perspective of eternity. In the end, all accounts will be settled justly. But for now, God calls upon the righteous to trust him, leave vengeance in his hands and walk by faith.

Pick an unfair situation from daily life, and look at it from God's perspective. What do you see? How will you respond?

INSIGHT Words with a Hollow (and Familiar) Ring
In his rebuttal, Job skillfully employs the words of his opponents. For example, in the space of a single verse (21:28), Job paraphrases (and parodies) the words of all three counselors: Bildad (8:22), Eliphaz (15:34) and Zophar (20:26).

CHAPTER 20

Then Zophar the Naamathite replied:

²"My troubled thoughts prompt me to answer
because I am greatly disturbed.
³I hear a rebuke that dishonors me,
and my understanding inspires me to reply.

⁴"Surely you know how it has been from of old,
ever since man*m* was placed on the earth,
⁵that the mirth of the wicked is brief,
the joy of the godless lasts but a moment.
⁶Though his pride reaches to the heavens
and his head touches the clouds,
⁷he will perish forever, like his own dung;
those who have seen him will say, 'Where is he?'
⁸Like a dream he flies away, no more to be found,
banished like a vision of the night.
⁹The eye that saw him will not see him again;
his place will look on him no more.
¹⁰His children must make amends to the poor;
his own hands must give back his wealth.
¹¹The youthful vigor that fills his bones
will lie with him in the dust.

¹²"Though evil is sweet in his mouth
and he hides it under his tongue,
¹³though he cannot bear to let it go
and keeps it in his mouth,
¹⁴yet his food will turn sour in his stomach;
it will become the venom of serpents within him.
¹⁵He will spit out the riches he swallowed;
God will make his stomach vomit them up.
¹⁶He will suck the poison of serpents;
the fangs of an adder will kill him.
¹⁷He will not enjoy the streams,
the rivers flowing with honey and cream.
¹⁸What he toiled for he must give back uneaten;

he will not enjoy the profit from his trading.
¹⁹For he has oppressed the poor and left them destitute;
he has seized houses he did not build.

²⁰"Surely he will have no respite from his craving;
he cannot save himself by his treasure.
²¹Nothing is left for him to devour;
his prosperity will not endure.
²²In the midst of his plenty, distress will overtake him;
the full force of misery will come upon him.
²³When he has filled his belly,
God will vent his burning anger against him
and rain down his blows upon him.
²⁴Though he flees from an iron weapon,
a bronze-tipped arrow pierces him.
²⁵He pulls it out of his back,
the gleaming point out of his liver.
Terrors will come over him;
²⁶   total darkness lies in wait for his treasures.
A fire unfanned will consume him
and devour what is left in his tent.
²⁷The heavens will expose his guilt;
the earth will rise up against him.
²⁸A flood will carry off his house,
rushing waters*n* on the day of God's wrath.
²⁹Such is the fate God allots the wicked,
the heritage appointed for them by God."

CHAPTER 21

Then Job replied:

²"Listen carefully to my words;
let this be the consolation you give me.
³Bear with me while I speak,
and after I have spoken, mock on.

⁴"Is my complaint directed to man?
Why should I not be impatient?
⁵Look at me and be astonished;
clap your hand over your mouth.
⁶When I think about this, I am terrified;
trembling seizes my body.
⁷Why do the wicked live on,
growing old and increasing in power?

*m*4 Or *Adam*   *n*28 Or *The possessions in his house will be carried off, / washed away*

⁸They see their children established
around them,
their offspring before their eyes.
⁹Their homes are safe and free from
fear;
the rod of God is not upon them.
¹⁰Their bulls never fail to breed;
their cows calve and do not
miscarry.
¹¹They send forth their children as a
flock;
their little ones dance about.
¹²They sing to the music of tambourine
and harp;
they make merry to the sound of the
flute.
¹³They spend their years in prosperity
and go down to the grave^o in
peace.^p
¹⁴Yet they say to God, 'Leave us alone!
We have no desire to know your
ways.
¹⁵Who is the Almighty, that we should
serve him?
What would we gain by praying to
him?'
¹⁶But their prosperity is not in their own
hands,
so I stand aloof from the counsel of
the wicked.

¹⁷"Yet how often is the lamp of the
wicked snuffed out?
How often does calamity come upon
them,
the fate God allots in his anger?
¹⁸How often are they like straw before
the wind,
like chaff swept away by a gale?
¹⁹It is said,_」 'God stores up a man's
punishment for his sons.'
Let him repay the man himself, so
that he will know it!
²⁰Let his own eyes see his destruction;
let him drink of the wrath of the
Almighty.^q

²¹For what does he care about the
family he leaves behind
when his allotted months come to
an end?
²²"Can anyone teach knowledge to God,
since he judges even the highest?
²³One man dies in full vigor,
completely secure and at ease,
²⁴his body^r well nourished,
his bones rich with marrow.
²⁵Another man dies in bitterness of soul,
never having enjoyed anything
good.
²⁶Side by side they lie in the dust,
and worms cover them both.

²⁷"I know full well what you are
thinking,
the schemes by which you would
wrong me.
²⁸You say, 'Where now is the great
man's house,
the tents where wicked men lived?'
²⁹Have you never questioned those who
travel?
Have you paid no regard to their
accounts—
³⁰that the evil man is spared from the
day of calamity,
that he is delivered from^s the day
of wrath?
³¹Who denounces his conduct to his
face?
Who repays him for what he has
done?
³²He is carried to the grave,
and watch is kept over his tomb.
³³The soil in the valley is sweet to him;
all men follow after him,
and a countless throng goes^t before
him.
³⁴"So how can you console me with your
nonsense?
Nothing is left of your answers but
falsehood!"

^o13 Hebrew *Sheol*   ^p13 Or *in an instant*   ^q17-20 Verses 17 and 18 may be taken as exclamations and 19 and 20 as
declarations.   ^r24 The meaning of the Hebrew for this word is uncertain.   ^s30 Or *man is reserved for the day of calamity, /
that he is brought forth to*   ^t33 Or / *as a countless throng went*

MAY 24 □ DAY 145
JOB 22–24
Eliphaz Silenced (Third Debate)

OVERVIEW Job's self-appointed counselors have run out of arguments—but not out of words. In the final round of debates, Eliphaz and Bildad take turns accusing Job of being the "wicked man" they have been describing all along. Eliphaz, following his cause-and-effect view of sin and suffering, continues to search for a secret sin in Job's life. In a desperate plea for acquittal, Job turns his glance heavenward. He laments that God is hard to find (23:8–9), and yet acknowledges that God's purposes are single-minded, unchanging and beneficial for those who patiently wait upon him.

Chapter 22		Chapter 23	Chapter 24
"Don't Sin"	"Do Repent"	"Don't Hide from Me"	"Do Vindicate Me"
1 20	21 30		
Eliphaz to Job		Job to God	

YOUR DAILY WALK There is at least one thing Eliphaz and Job agreed upon—they both were appalled at the treatment received by the orphans.

We must learn to regard people less in the light of what they do or fail to do and more in the light of what they suffer.

Eliphaz stated in 22:9 that the wicked crushed the strength (literally, "arms") of the fatherless. The rightful privileges and means of support for orphans were taken away. Their boundary markers were moved; their flocks were driven off; they were left cold, hungry and at the mercy of the elements. But the God of all mercy had not forgotten them.

God has a special place in his heart for the fatherless and orphaned. Psalm 82:3 exhorts us to "defend the cause of the weak and the fatherless . . ." Do you know of a single-parent home in your neighborhood or a family that is destitute because of unemployment or illness? You can (and should) pray for them, but don't stop there. Carve out some time to spend with a fatherless youngster. Call up a needy neighbor and invite him or her over for dinner. Get involved in the lives of another family. If you have Christ, you have something to share!

INSIGHT Old Testament Cattle Rustling
Job 24:3 states that the wicked "drive away the orphan's donkey." Such an act would be damaging beyond repair. Orphan children would be unable to round up or recover the stolen livestock—a picture of utter helplessness and desperation. But such coldhearted acts are not hidden from the Lord.

CHAPTER 22
Then Eliphaz the Temanite replied:

2"Can a man be of benefit to God?
  Can even a wise man benefit him?
3What pleasure would it give the
     Almighty if you were
     righteous?
What would he gain if your ways
     were blameless?

4"Is it for your piety that he rebukes
     you
  and brings charges against you?
5Is not your wickedness great?
  Are not your sins endless?
6You demanded security from your
     brothers for no reason;
  you stripped men of their clothing,
     leaving them naked.
7You gave no water to the weary

and you withheld food from the
    hungry,
[8]though you were a powerful man,
    owning land—
    an honored man, living on it.
[9]And you sent widows away
    empty-handed
    and broke the strength of the
    fatherless.
[10]That is why snares are all around you,
    why sudden peril terrifies you,
[11]why it is so dark you cannot see,
    and why a flood of water covers
    you.

[12]"Is not God in the heights of heaven?
    And see how lofty are the highest
    stars!
[13]Yet you say, 'What does God know?
    Does he judge through such
    darkness?
[14]Thick clouds veil him, so he does not
    see us
    as he goes about in the vaulted
    heavens.'
[15]Will you keep to the old path
    that evil men have trod?
[16]They were carried off before their
    time,
    their foundations washed away by a
    flood.
[17]They said to God, 'Leave us alone!
    What can the Almighty do to us?'
[18]Yet it was he who filled their houses
    with good things,
    so I stand aloof from the counsel of
    the wicked.

[19]"The righteous see their ruin and
    rejoice;
    the innocent mock them, saying,
[20]'Surely our foes are destroyed,
    and fire devours their wealth.'

[21]"Submit to God and be at peace with
    him;
    in this way prosperity will come to
    you.
[22]Accept instruction from his mouth
    and lay up his words in your heart.
[23]If you return to the Almighty, you will
    be restored:
    If you remove wickedness far from
    your tent
[24]and assign your nuggets to the dust,
    your gold of Ophir to the rocks in
    the ravines,

[25]then the Almighty will be your gold,
    the choicest silver for you.
[26]Surely then you will find delight in
    the Almighty
    and will lift up your face to God.
[27]You will pray to him, and he will hear
    you,
    and you will fulfill your vows.
[28]What you decide on will be done,
    and light will shine on your ways.
[29]When men are brought low and you
    say, 'Lift them up!'
    then he will save the downcast.
[30]He will deliver even one who is not
    innocent,
    who will be delivered through the
    cleanness of your hands."

CHAPTER 23
Then Job replied:

[2]"Even today my complaint is bitter;
    his hand[u] is heavy in spite of[v] my
    groaning.
[3]If only I knew where to find him;
    if only I could go to his dwelling!
[4]I would state my case before him
    and fill my mouth with arguments.
[5]I would find out what he would
    answer me,
    and consider what he would say.
[6]Would he oppose me with great
    power?
    No, he would not press charges
    against me.
[7]There an upright man could present
    his case before him,
    and I would be delivered forever
    from my judge.

[8]"But if I go to the east, he is not there;
    if I go to the west, I do not find
    him.
[9]When he is at work in the north, I do
    not see him;
    when he turns to the south, I catch
    no glimpse of him.
[10]But he knows the way that I take;
    when he has tested me, I will come
    forth as gold.
[11]My feet have closely followed his
    steps;
    I have kept to his way without
    turning aside.
[12]I have not departed from the
    commands of his lips;

[u]2 Septuagint and Syriac; Hebrew / *the hand on me*   [v]2 Or *heavy on me in*

I have treasured the words of his
mouth more than my daily
bread.

¹³"But he stands alone, and who can
oppose him?
He does whatever he pleases.
¹⁴He carries out his decree against me,
and many such plans he still has in
store.
¹⁵That is why I am terrified before him;
when I think of all this, I fear him.
¹⁶God has made my heart faint;
the Almighty has terrified me.
¹⁷Yet I am not silenced by the darkness,
by the thick darkness that covers my
face.

CHAPTER 24

"Why does the Almighty not set times
for judgment?
Why must those who know him
look in vain for such days?
²Men move boundary stones;
they pasture flocks they have
stolen.
³They drive away the orphan's donkey
and take the widow's ox in pledge.
⁴They thrust the needy from the path
and force all the poor of the land
into hiding.
⁵Like wild donkeys in the desert,
the poor go about their labor of
foraging food;
the wasteland provides food for
their children.
⁶They gather fodder in the fields
and glean in the vineyards of the
wicked.
⁷Lacking clothes, they spend the night
naked;
they have nothing to cover
themselves in the cold.
⁸They are drenched by mountain rains
and hug the rocks for lack of
shelter.
⁹The fatherless child is snatched from
the breast;
the infant of the poor is seized for a
debt.
¹⁰Lacking clothes, they go about naked;
they carry the sheaves, but still go
hungry.
¹¹They crush olives among the
terracesʷ;

they tread the winepresses, yet
suffer thirst.
¹²The groans of the dying rise from the
city,
and the souls of the wounded cry
out for help.
But God charges no one with
wrongdoing.

¹³"There are those who rebel against the
light,
who do not know its ways
or stay in its paths.
¹⁴When daylight is gone, the murderer
rises up
and kills the poor and needy;
in the night he steals forth like a
thief.
¹⁵The eye of the adulterer watches for
dusk;
he thinks, 'No eye will see me,'
and he keeps his face concealed.
¹⁶In the dark, men break into houses,
but by day they shut themselves in;
they want nothing to do with the
light.
¹⁷For all of them, deep darkness is their
morningˣ;
they make friends with the terrors of
darkness.ʸ

¹⁸"Yet they are foam on the surface of
the water;
their portion of the land is cursed,
so that no one goes to the
vineyards.
¹⁹As heat and drought snatch away the
melted snow,
so the graveᶻ snatches away those
who have sinned.
²⁰The womb forgets them,
the worm feasts on them;
evil men are no longer remembered
but are broken like a tree.
²¹They prey on the barren and childless
woman,
and to the widow show no kindness.
²²But God drags away the mighty by his
power;
though they become established,
they have no assurance of life.
²³He may let them rest in a feeling of
security,
but his eyes are on their ways.
²⁴For a little while they are exalted, and
then they are gone;

ʷ11 Or olives between the millstones; the meaning of the Hebrew for this word is uncertain.   ˣ17 Or them, their morning is like
the shadow of death   ʸ17 Or of the shadow of death   ᶻ19 Hebrew Sheol

they are brought low and gathered
    up like all others;
they are cut off like heads of grain.

25"If this is not so, who can prove me
            false
    and reduce my words to nothing?"

MAY 25 □ DAY 146
JOB 25–28
Bildad and Zophar Silenced (Third Debate)

OVERVIEW The prosecution rests its case at last. All arguments have
been expended. In one final, angry, impatient outburst, Bildad repeats
his well-worn case. A person cannot be justified before a high and
holy God. Job, who agrees with Bildad's concept of a great God, contends that God is far bigger than even Bildad has yet shown. Insisting
upon his own innocence, Job describes God as the one who wisely
and justly rewards the righteous. Although humans have plumbed the
depths of the earth to find rich minerals, they have yet to find anything as valuable or precious as the wisdom of God.

Chapter 25	Chapter 26	Chapter 27	Chapter 28
"God Is Distant"	"God Is Powerful"	"God Is Just"	"God Is Wise"
Pessimism	Optimism		

YOUR DAILY WALK Here is a good thought from the book of Ecclesiastes to add to your Bible reading today: "Do not be quickly provoked in your spirit, for anger resides in the lap of fools" (Ecclesiastes 7:9).

The person who can suppress a moment's anger may prevent a day of sorrow.

When words have all been used up, tempers usually flare and fists
fly! Such was the case with Bildad. All his arguments had been refuted. There was nothing left to say. So he struck out in anger and
showed the shallowness of his own counsel.

Work on your "anger factor" today. If possible, carry a thermometer
with you in your coat pocket or purse. Or draw one on a note card
with the words of Ecclesiastes 7:9 on the back, and tuck it in your
pocket. Whenever you begin to boil about a problem today—a disagreement with your spouse, a traffic jam, a missed appointment, a
tedious assignment, an unexpected disappointment—pull out your
thermometer. Count the degree markings slowly ("96 . . . 97 . . . 98
. . ."). Then ask yourself these two questions: Is it worth making a fool
of myself? And, Is the God I serve big enough to handle it? Then deal
with your problem in God's way.

INSIGHT How Much Is Wisdom Really Worth?
Job stated that wisdom is more priceless than the earth's gold
(28:12–17). Just how valuable is that? One gold field in South Africa
alone has produced 49.4 million ounces. At an average price of $395
per ounce, that represents a "gold mine" of more than $19 billion!

CHAPTER 25

Then Bildad the Shuhite replied:

²"Dominion and awe belong to God;
    he establishes order in the heights of
        heaven.
³Can his forces be numbered?
    Upon whom does his light not rise?
⁴How then can a man be righteous
        before God?
    How can one born of woman be
        pure?
⁵If even the moon is not bright
    and the stars are not pure in his
        eyes,
⁶how much less man, who is but a
        maggot—
    a son of man, who is only a worm!"

CHAPTER 26

Then Job replied:

²"How you have helped the powerless!
    How you have saved the arm that is
        feeble!
³What advice you have offered to one
        without wisdom!
    And what great insight you have
        displayed!
⁴Who has helped you utter these
        words?
    And whose spirit spoke from your
        mouth?

⁵"The dead are in deep anguish,
    those beneath the waters and all that
        live in them.
⁶Death^a is naked before God;
    Destruction^b lies uncovered.
⁷He spreads out the northern ˻skies˼
        over empty space;
    he suspends the earth over nothing.
⁸He wraps up the waters in his clouds,
    yet the clouds do not burst under
        their weight.
⁹He covers the face of the full moon,
    spreading his clouds over it.
¹⁰He marks out the horizon on the face
        of the waters
    for a boundary between light and
        darkness.
¹¹The pillars of the heavens quake,
    aghast at his rebuke.
¹²By his power he churned up the sea;
    by his wisdom he cut Rahab to
        pieces.
¹³By his breath the skies became fair;

his hand pierced the gliding serpent.
¹⁴And these are but the outer fringe of
        his works;
    how faint the whisper we hear of
        him!
Who then can understand the
        thunder of his power?"

CHAPTER 27

And Job continued his discourse:

²"As surely as God lives, who has
        denied me justice,
    the Almighty, who has made me
        taste bitterness of soul,
³as long as I have life within me,
    the breath of God in my nostrils,
⁴my lips will not speak wickedness,
    and my tongue will utter no deceit.
⁵I will never admit you are in the right;
    till I die, I will not deny my
        integrity.
⁶I will maintain my righteousness and
        never let go of it;
    my conscience will not reproach me
        as long as I live.

⁷"May my enemies be like the wicked,
    my adversaries like the unjust!
⁸For what hope has the godless when
        he is cut off,
    when God takes away his life?
⁹Does God listen to his cry
    when distress comes upon him?
¹⁰Will he find delight in the Almighty?
    Will he call upon God at all times?

¹¹"I will teach you about the power of
        God;
    the ways of the Almighty I will not
        conceal.
¹²You have all seen this yourselves.
    Why then this meaningless talk?

¹³"Here is the fate God allots to the
        wicked,
    the heritage a ruthless man receives
        from the Almighty:
¹⁴However many his children, their fate
        is the sword;
    his offspring will never have enough
        to eat.
¹⁵The plague will bury those who
        survive him,
    and their widows will not weep for
        them.
¹⁶Though he heaps up silver like dust

^{a}6 Hebrew *Sheol* ^{b}6 Hebrew *Abaddon*

and clothes like piles of clay,
¹⁷what he lays up the righteous will
    wear,
    and the innocent will divide his
    silver.
¹⁸The house he builds is like a moth's
    cocoon,
    like a hut made by a watchman.
¹⁹He lies down wealthy, but will do so
    no more;
    when he opens his eyes, all is gone.
²⁰Terrors overtake him like a flood;
    a tempest snatches him away in the
    night.
²¹The east wind carries him off, and he
    is gone;
    it sweeps him out of his place.
²²It hurls itself against him without
    mercy
    as he flees headlong from its power.
²³It claps its hands in derision
    and hisses him out of his place.

CHAPTER 28
    "There is a mine for silver
    and a place where gold is refined.
²Iron is taken from the earth,
    and copper is smelted from ore.
³Man puts an end to the darkness;
    he searches the farthest recesses
    for ore in the blackest darkness.
⁴Far from where people dwell he cuts a
    shaft,
    in places forgotten by the foot of
    man;
    far from men he dangles and sways.
⁵The earth, from which food comes,
    is transformed below as by fire;
⁶sapphires^c come from its rocks,
    and its dust contains nuggets of
    gold.
⁷No bird of prey knows that hidden
    path,
    no falcon's eye has seen it.
⁸Proud beasts do not set foot on it,
    and no lion prowls there.
⁹Man's hand assaults the flinty rock
    and lays bare the roots of the
    mountains.
¹⁰He tunnels through the rock;
    his eyes see all its treasures.
¹¹He searches^d the sources of the rivers
    and brings hidden things to light.

¹²"But where can wisdom be found?
    Where does understanding dwell?
¹³Man does not comprehend its worth;
    it cannot be found in the land of the
    living.
¹⁴The deep says, 'It is not in me';
    the sea says, 'It is not with me.'
¹⁵It cannot be bought with the finest
    gold,
    nor can its price be weighed in
    silver.
¹⁶It cannot be bought with the gold of
    Ophir,
    with precious onyx or sapphires.
¹⁷Neither gold nor crystal can compare
    with it,
    nor can it be had for jewels of gold.
¹⁸Coral and jasper are not worthy of
    mention;
    the price of wisdom is beyond
    rubies.
¹⁹The topaz of Cush cannot compare
    with it;
    it cannot be bought with pure gold.

²⁰"Where then does wisdom come from?
    Where does understanding dwell?
²¹It is hidden from the eyes of every
    living thing,
    concealed even from the birds of the
    air.
²²Destruction^e and Death say,
    'Only a rumor of it has reached our
    ears.'
²³God understands the way to it
    and he alone knows where it dwells,
²⁴for he views the ends of the earth
    and sees everything under the
    heavens.
²⁵When he established the force of the
    wind
    and measured out the waters,
²⁶when he made a decree for the rain
    and a path for the thunderstorm,
²⁷then he looked at wisdom and
    appraised it;
    he confirmed it and tested it.
²⁸And he said to man,
    'The fear of the Lord—that is
    wisdom,
    and to shun evil is understanding.' "

^c6 Or lapis lazuli; also in verse 16   ^d11 Septuagint, Aquila and Vulgate; Hebrew He dams up   ^e22 Hebrew Abaddon

MAY 26 □ DAY 147
JOB 29–31
Job's Final Plea (Third Debate)

OVERVIEW Job's advisers have at last grown silent, but the problem of his suffering persists. Nearly overcome by depression, he longs for the good old days when he enjoyed his wealth and the presence of his children. In contrast to his former position of status and prestige, Job now experiences mockery from the young men of the city. And ever present is the excruciating pain of his loathsome disease. Job pauses. He thinks back over his life. Is there some area of sin he has overlooked? No. Has he manifested any bitter or negligent attitude toward his neighbors? No. Has he demonstrated an attitude of insensitivity toward God or others? No. And so with his personal and public life an open book before God, Job rests his case.

Chapter 29	Chapter 30	Chapter 31
The Good Old Days	The Bad New Days	A Personal Inventory
Job Remembers		Job Reexamines

YOUR DAILY WALK All good store managers periodically take stock of their inventory. They carefully examine their goods to see what they have on hand and what they don't, what they need to buy for their shelves and what they need to throw away. And they do this at regular intervals.

Suffering can produce great depths of character, mature understanding, warm compassion and rich spirituality.

That's precisely what Job did in chapter 31. He took stock of his life to see where his character, conduct and spiritual life were deficient. Although there was no grave area of sin, Job's attitude of confession prepared him for God's instruction later.

When was the last time you took personal inventory in your life? Right now, check up on your personal thought life, your behavior toward others and your walk with God. Confess your areas of sinful neglect, thank God for your areas of strength and map out a project today to begin "restocking the shelves" in places where you are weak.

INSIGHT Job's Moral Inventory
Notice the three areas of Job's self-examination: (1) *personal life* (31:1–12)—he checked for the sins of lust, lying and adultery; (2) *public life* (31:13–23)—he checked his treatment of servants, widows, fatherless and the needy; and (3) *spiritual life* (31:24–40)—he checked his use of money, worship of God, attitude toward revenge, use of hospitality and purity of motives.

CHAPTER 29
Job continued his discourse:

²"How I long for the months gone by,
    for the days when God watched over me,
³when his lamp shone upon my head
    and by his light I walked through darkness!
⁴Oh, for the days when I was in my prime,

when God's intimate friendship blessed my house,
⁵when the Almighty was still with me
    and my children were around me,
⁶when my path was drenched with cream
    and the rock poured out for me streams of olive oil.

⁷"When I went to the gate of the city
    and took my seat in the public square,

[8]the young men saw me and stepped
    aside
and the old men rose to their feet;
[9]the chief men refrained from speaking
    and covered their mouths with their
    hands;
[10]the voices of the nobles were hushed,
    and their tongues stuck to the roof
    of their mouths.
[11]Whoever heard me spoke well of me,
    and those who saw me commended
    me,
[12]because I rescued the poor who cried
    for help,
    and the fatherless who had none to
    assist him.
[13]The man who was dying blessed me;
    I made the widow's heart sing.
[14]I put on righteousness as my clothing;
    justice was my robe and my turban.
[15]I was eyes to the blind
    and feet to the lame.
[16]I was a father to the needy;
    I took up the case of the stranger.
[17]I broke the fangs of the wicked
    and snatched the victims from their
    teeth.

[18]"I thought, 'I will die in my own
    house,
    my days as numerous as the grains
    of sand.
[19]My roots will reach to the water,
    and the dew will lie all night on my
    branches.
[20]My glory will remain fresh in me,
    the bow ever new in my hand.'

[21]"Men listened to me expectantly,
    waiting in silence for my counsel.
[22]After I had spoken, they spoke no
    more;
    my words fell gently on their ears.
[23]They waited for me as for showers
    and drank in my words as the
    spring rain.
[24]When I smiled at them, they scarcely
    believed it;
    the light of my face was precious to
    them.[f]
[25]I chose the way for them and sat as
    their chief;
    I dwelt as a king among his troops;
    I was like one who comforts
    mourners.

CHAPTER 30

"But now they mock me,
    men younger than I,
    whose fathers I would have disdained
    to put with my sheep dogs.
[2]Of what use was the strength of their
    hands to me,
    since their vigor had gone from
    them?
[3]Haggard from want and hunger,
    they roamed[g] the parched land
    in desolate wastelands at night.
[4]In the brush they gathered salt herbs,
    and their food[h] was the root of the
    broom tree.
[5]They were banished from their fellow
    men,
    shouted at as if they were thieves.
[6]They were forced to live in the dry
    stream beds,
    among the rocks and in holes in the
    ground.
[7]They brayed among the bushes
    and huddled in the undergrowth.
[8]A base and nameless brood,
    they were driven out of the land.

[9]"And now their sons mock me in song;
    I have become a byword among
    them.
[10]They detest me and keep their
    distance;
    they do not hesitate to spit in my
    face.
[11]Now that God has unstrung my bow
    and afflicted me,
    they throw off restraint in my
    presence.
[12]On my right the tribe[i] attacks;
    they lay snares for my feet,
    they build their siege ramps against
    me.
[13]They break up my road;
    they succeed in destroying me—
    without anyone's helping them.[j]
[14]They advance as through a gaping
    breach;
    amid the ruins they come rolling in.
[15]Terrors overwhelm me;
    my dignity is driven away as by the
    wind,
    my safety vanishes like a cloud.

[16]"And now my life ebbs away;
    days of suffering grip me.
[17]Night pierces my bones;

---

[f]24 The meaning of the Hebrew for this clause is uncertain.   [g]3 Or gnawed   [h]4 Or fuel   [i]12 The meaning of the Hebrew
for this word is uncertain.   [j]13 Or me. / 'No one can help him,' they say.

my gnawing pains never rest.
¹⁸In his great power ⌊God⌋ becomes like
    clothing to me^k;
  he binds me like the neck of my
    garment.
¹⁹He throws me into the mud,
  and I am reduced to dust and ashes.

²⁰"I cry out to you, O God, but you do
    not answer;
  I stand up, but you merely look at
    me.
²¹You turn on me ruthlessly;
  with the might of your hand you
    attack me.
²²You snatch me up and drive me before
    the wind;
  you toss me about in the storm.
²³I know you will bring me down to
    death,
  to the place appointed for all the
    living.

²⁴"Surely no one lays a hand on a
    broken man
  when he cries for help in his
    distress.
²⁵Have I not wept for those in trouble?
  Has not my soul grieved for the
    poor?
²⁶Yet when I hoped for good, evil came;
  when I looked for light, then came
    darkness.
²⁷The churning inside me never stops;
  days of suffering confront me.
²⁸I go about blackened, but not by the
    sun;
  I stand up in the assembly and cry
    for help.
²⁹I have become a brother of jackals,
  a companion of owls.
³⁰My skin grows black and peels;
  my body burns with fever.
³¹My harp is tuned to mourning,
  and my flute to the sound of
    wailing.

CHAPTER 31
  "I made a covenant with my eyes
    not to look lustfully at a girl.
²For what is man's lot from God above,
  his heritage from the Almighty on
    high?
³Is it not ruin for the wicked,
  disaster for those who do wrong?

⁴Does he not see my ways
  and count my every step?

⁵"If I have walked in falsehood
  or my foot has hurried after deceit—
⁶let God weigh me in honest scales
  and he will know that I am
    blameless—
⁷if my steps have turned from the path,
  if my heart has been led by my eyes,
  or if my hands have been defiled,
⁸then may others eat what I have sown,
  and may my crops be uprooted.

⁹"If my heart has been enticed by a
    woman,
  or if I have lurked at my neighbor's
    door,
¹⁰then may my wife grind another
    man's grain,
  and may other men sleep with her.
¹¹For that would have been shameful,
  a sin to be judged.
¹²It is a fire that burns to Destruction^l;
  it would have uprooted my harvest.

¹³"If I have denied justice to my
    menservants and maidservants
  when they had a grievance against
    me,
¹⁴what will I do when God confronts
    me?
  What will I answer when called to
    account?
¹⁵Did not he who made me in the womb
    make them?
  Did not the same one form us both
    within our mothers?

¹⁶"If I have denied the desires of the
    poor
  or let the eyes of the widow grow
    weary,
¹⁷if I have kept my bread to myself,
  not sharing it with the fatherless—
¹⁸but from my youth I reared him as
    would a father,
  and from my birth I guided the
    widow—
¹⁹if I have seen anyone perishing for
    lack of clothing,
  or a needy man without a garment,
²⁰and his heart did not bless me
  for warming him with the fleece
    from my sheep,
²¹if I have raised my hand against the
    fatherless,

^k18 Hebrew; Septuagint ⌊God⌋ grasps my clothing   ^l12 Hebrew Abaddon

knowing that I had influence in
court,
²²then let my arm fall from the shoulder,
let it be broken off at the joint.
²³For I dreaded destruction from God,
and for fear of his splendor I could
not do such things.

²⁴"If I have put my trust in gold
or said to pure gold, 'You are my
security,'
²⁵if I have rejoiced over my great
wealth,
the fortune my hands had gained,
²⁶if I have regarded the sun in its
radiance
or the moon moving in splendor,
²⁷so that my heart was secretly enticed
and my hand offered them a kiss of
homage,
²⁸then these also would be sins to be
judged,
for I would have been unfaithful to
God on high.

²⁹"If I have rejoiced at my enemy's
misfortune
or gloated over the trouble that
came to him—
³⁰I have not allowed my mouth to sin
by invoking a curse against his life—
³¹if the men of my household have
never said,
'Who has not had his fill of Job's
meat?'—

ᵐ33 Or as Adam did

³²but no stranger had to spend the night
in the street,
for my door was always open to the
traveler—
³³if I have concealed my sin as men
do,ᵐ
by hiding my guilt in my heart
³⁴because I so feared the crowd
and so dreaded the contempt of the
clans
that I kept silent and would not go
outside

³⁵("Oh, that I had someone to hear me!
I sign now my defense—let the
Almighty answer me;
let my accuser put his indictment in
writing.
³⁶Surely I would wear it on my
shoulder,
I would put it on like a crown.
³⁷I would give him an account of my
every step;
like a prince I would approach
him.)—

³⁸"if my land cries out against me
and all its furrows are wet with
tears,
³⁹if I have devoured its yield without
payment
or broken the spirit of its tenants,
⁴⁰then let briers come up instead of
wheat
and weeds instead of barley."

The words of Job are ended.

MAY 27 ☐ DAY 148
JOB 32–34
Elihu and Job (Part One)

 OVERVIEW Job's three "comfortless counselors" fall silent at last, their
arguments exhausted, with Job no nearer a solution to his suffering.
Enter Elihu, a younger contemporary of Eliphaz, Bildad and Zophar, to
offer his counsel. He begins by analyzing Job's response to his suffering and his insistence that God provide answers to his questions. Elihu
points out that the Sovereign's actions are often educational, not
merely disciplinary, in the life of his subjects. Using many quotes from
Job's previous responses, Elihu gives a lengthy defense of God's dealings with humans. His conclusion: "It is unthinkable that God would
do wrong, that the Almighty would prevert justice" (34:12).

Chapter 32	Chapter 33	Chapter 34
"Both Sides, Listen to Me"	"God Is Greater than Man"	"Far Be It from God to Do Wickedness"
Elihu's Request	Elihu's Response	

YOUR DAILY WALK Can you think of three occupations from the world of government, business, medicine or sports that demand absolute impartiality if the job is to be done correctly? Write them in the space provided: _____

Most of our suspicions of others are aroused by our knowledge of ourselves.

Did you think of things like: Supreme Court judge, personnel manager, surgeon or umpire? These are all examples of jobs requiring impartiality in the workaday world. But what about in the Christian life? How impartial does God want *you* to be?

Have you ever given preferential treatment to a prominent guest at church? Have you ever made a special effort to avoid someone who obviously came from a different ethnic, financial or spiritual background than you? If so, you were exercising partiality. According to James 2:9, God looks on such respect of persons as sin.

Elihu realized that God is absolutely impartial (34:16–20) and expects his children to be the same! Check up on your own personal contacts in your neighborhood, office or church. What needs to change about your treatment of others so that James 2:1 is not true of you?

INSIGHT Words to Be Sampled and Savored
Elihu quoted a proverb, "For the ear tests words as the tongue tastes food" (34:3), in order to urge his listeners to test his words as carefully as a gourmet would taste his delicacies.

CHAPTER 32

So these three men stopped answering Job, because he was righteous in his own eyes. ²But Elihu son of Barakel the Buzite, of the family of Ram, became very angry with Job for justifying himself rather than God. ³He was also angry with the three friends, because they had found no way to refute Job, and yet had condemned him.ⁿ ⁴Now Elihu had waited before speaking to Job because they were older than he. ⁵But when he saw that the three men had nothing more to say, his anger was aroused.

⁶So Elihu son of Barakel the Buzite said:

"I am young in years,
    and you are old;
that is why I was fearful,
    not daring to tell you what I know.
⁷I thought, 'Age should speak;
    advanced years should teach
        wisdom.'

⁸But it is the spiritᵒ in a man,
    the breath of the Almighty, that
        gives him understanding.
⁹It is not only the oldᵖ who are wise,
    not only the aged who understand
        what is right.

¹⁰"Therefore I say: Listen to me;
    I too will tell you what I know.
¹¹I waited while you spoke,
    I listened to your reasoning;
while you were searching for words,
¹²   I gave you my full attention.
But not one of you has proved Job
        wrong;
    none of you has answered his
        arguments.
¹³Do not say, 'We have found wisdom;
    let God refute him, not man.'
¹⁴But Job has not marshaled his words
        against me,
    and I will not answer him with your
        arguments.

ⁿ3 Masoretic Text; an ancient Hebrew scribal tradition *Job, and so had condemned God*   ᵒ8 Or *Spirit*; also in verse 18   ᵖ9 Or *many*; or *great*

15"They are dismayed and have no more
to say;
words have failed them.
16Must I wait, now that they are silent,
now that they stand there with no
reply?
17I too will have my say;
I too will tell what I know.
18For I am full of words,
and the spirit within me compels
me;
19inside I am like bottled-up wine,
like new wineskins ready to burst.
20I must speak and find relief;
I must open my lips and reply.
21I will show partiality to no one,
nor will I flatter any man;
22for if I were skilled in flattery,
my Maker would soon take me
away.

CHAPTER 33

"But now, Job, listen to my words;
pay attention to everything I say.
2I am about to open my mouth;
my words are on the tip of my
tongue.
3My words come from an upright
heart;
my lips sincerely speak what I
know.
4The Spirit of God has made me;
the breath of the Almighty gives me
life.
5Answer me then, if you can;
prepare yourself and confront me.
6I am just like you before God;
I too have been taken from clay.
7No fear of me should alarm you,
nor should my hand be heavy upon
you.

8"But you have said in my hearing—
I heard the very words—
9'I am pure and without sin;
I am clean and free from guilt.
10Yet God has found fault with me;
he considers me his enemy.
11He fastens my feet in shackles;
he keeps close watch on all my
paths.'
12"But I tell you, in this you are not
right,
for God is greater than man.
13Why do you complain to him

that he answers none of man's
words⁹?
14For God does speak—now one way,
now another—
though man may not perceive it.
15In a dream, in a vision of the night,
when deep sleep falls on men
as they slumber in their beds,
16he may speak in their ears
and terrify them with warnings,
17to turn man from wrongdoing
and keep him from pride,
18to preserve his soul from the pit,ʳ
his life from perishing by the
sword.ˢ
19Or a man may be chastened on a bed
of pain
with constant distress in his bones,
20so that his very being finds food
repulsive
and his soul loathes the choicest
meal.
21His flesh wastes away to nothing,
and his bones, once hidden, now
stick out.
22His soul draws near to the pit,ᵗ
and his life to the messengers of
death.ᵘ
23"Yet if there is an angel on his side
as a mediator, one out of a
thousand,
to tell a man what is right for him,
24to be gracious to him and say,
'Spare him from going down to the
pitᵛ;
I have found a ransom for him'—
25then his flesh is renewed like a child's;
it is restored as in the days of his
youth.
26He prays to God and finds favor with
him,
he sees God's face and shouts for
joy;
he is restored by God to his
righteous state.
27Then he comes to men and says,
'I sinned, and perverted what was
right,
but I did not get what I deserved.
28He redeemed my soul from going
down to the pit,ʷ
and I will live to enjoy the light.'
29"God does all these things to a man—
twice, even three times—

³⁰to turn back his soul from the pit,ˣ
  that the light of life may shine on
  him.

³¹"Pay attention, Job, and listen to me;
  be silent, and I will speak.
³²If you have anything to say, answer
  me;
  speak up, for I want you to be
  cleared.
³³But if not, then listen to me;
  be silent, and I will teach you
  wisdom."

CHAPTER 34

Then Elihu said:

²"Hear my words, you wise men;
  listen to me, you men of learning.
³For the ear tests words
  as the tongue tastes food.
⁴Let us discern for ourselves what is
  right;
  let us learn together what is good.

⁵"Job says, 'I am innocent,
  but God denies me justice.
⁶Although I am right,
  I am considered a liar;
 although I am guiltless,
  his arrow inflicts an incurable
  wound.'
⁷What man is like Job,
  who drinks scorn like water?
⁸He keeps company with evildoers;
  he associates with wicked men.
⁹For he says, 'It profits a man nothing
  when he tries to please God.'

¹⁰"So listen to me, you men of
  understanding.
  Far be it from God to do evil,
  from the Almighty to do wrong.
¹¹He repays a man for what he has
  done;
  he brings upon him what his
  conduct deserves.
¹²It is unthinkable that God would do
  wrong,
  that the Almighty would pervert
  justice.
¹³Who appointed him over the earth?
  Who put him in charge of the whole
  world?
¹⁴If it were his intention
  and he withdrew his spiritʸ and
  breath,

¹⁵all mankind would perish together
  and man would return to the dust.

¹⁶"If you have understanding, hear this;
  listen to what I say.
¹⁷Can he who hates justice govern?
  Will you condemn the just and
  mighty One?
¹⁸Is he not the One who says to kings,
  'You are worthless,'
  and to nobles, 'You are wicked,'
¹⁹who shows no partiality to princes
  and does not favor the rich over the
  poor,
  for they are all the work of his
  hands?
²⁰They die in an instant, in the middle
  of the night;
  the people are shaken and they pass
  away;
  the mighty are removed without
  human hand.

²¹"His eyes are on the ways of men;
  he sees their every step.
²²There is no dark place, no deep
  shadow,
  where evildoers can hide.
²³God has no need to examine men
  further,
  that they should come before him
  for judgment.
²⁴Without inquiry he shatters the mighty
  and sets up others in their place.
²⁵Because he takes note of their deeds,
  he overthrows them in the night and
  they are crushed.
²⁶He punishes them for their wickedness
  where everyone can see them,
²⁷because they turned from following
  him
  and had no regard for any of his
  ways.
²⁸They caused the cry of the poor to
  come before him,
  so that he heard the cry of the
  needy.
²⁹But if he remains silent, who can
  condemn him?
  If he hides his face, who can see
  him?
  Yet he is over man and nation alike,
³⁰ to keep a godless man from ruling,
  from laying snares for the people.

³¹"Suppose a man says to God,
  'I am guilty but will offend no more.

ˣ30 Or turn him back from the grave   ʸ14 Or Spirit

³²Teach me what I cannot see;
   if I have done wrong, I will not do
      so again.'
³³Should God then reward you on your
      terms,
   when you refuse to repent?
You must decide, not I;
   so tell me what you know.

³⁴"Men of understanding declare,
   wise men who hear me say to me,

³⁵'Job speaks without knowledge;
   his words lack insight.'
³⁶Oh, that Job might be tested to the
      utmost
   for answering like a wicked
      man!
³⁷To his sin he adds rebellion;
   scornfully he claps his hands
      among us
   and multiplies his words against
      God."

MAY 28 ☐ DAY 149
Searching for Answers (in All the Wrong Places)

LOOK BACK Debates have a tendency of going round and round, back and forth. And Job's debate with his three persistent friends is no different, as the verbal Ping-Pong match continues chapter after chapter.

Eliphaz, Bildad and Zophar have taken turns attacking Job's credibility and affirming God's justice. From their vantage point, Job deserves what he is getting. With each round of debate, the arguments become more pointed and the atmosphere more charged. Diplomacy and tact give way to allegations and attack. The interaction produces plenty of heat but not much light, as Job struggles to defend himself before God and man and find a satisfying answer to the confusing circumstances that have befallen him.

When argument and accusation fail to produce a solution, anger takes over. The third and final round of "debate" demonstrates that there has been a noticeable "hardening of the attitudes" on the part of Job and his three self-appointed counselors. Job continues to maintain his integrity; his friends continue to insist God's ways and wisdom are unimpeachable. And the stalemate continues.

LOOK UP What do you know for sure—not hope, or wish, or think, or accept as conventional wisdom—but *know* with absolute certainty? Notice the strength of Job's assertions in chapter 27:

The fire of God in your heart will melt the lead in your feet.

"As surely as God lives . . ." (v. 2)
"As long as I have life within me . . ." (v. 3)
"As long as I live . . ." (v. 6)

These are not the hopeful musings of an incurable optimist, but the gut-wrenching convictions of an embattled saint. Job knows for sure that wickedness and deceit have no place in his response to unexplained suffering. And he knows with equal confidence that integrity and righteousness are always the God-honoring alternative. Regardless of how dark the night or bewildering the circumstances, it's always safe to trust the Lord.

LOOK AHEAD No one yearns to be crushed; no one welcomes the pain and pressure of adversity. Crushing is a painful, agonizing process—and the scars it leaves behind are real. But only through crushing can God release the full fragrance of his mercy in the life of the man or woman of God. If you are feeling the heat and pressure of painful circumstances today, then you are in good company! Place a copy of these triumphant words of Job in a prominent place and make them yours:

"I know that my Redeemer lives, and that in the end he will stand upon the earth. And after my skin has been destroyed, yet in my flesh I will see God; I myself will see him with my own eyes—I, and not another. How my heart yearns within me!" (19:25–27)

MAY 29 ☐ DAY 150
JOB 35–37
Elihu and Job (Part Two)

 OVERVIEW Elihu deals with two of Job's most persistent complaints: What profit is there for acting righteously when you end up suffering anyway (35:1–8), and why doesn't God listen to the cries of a broken heart (35:9–16)? In the first case, Elihu concludes that God's perfect justice is not determined or altered by human behavior. Concerning unanswered prayer, Elihu argues that the only prayers God ignores are those that are proud and empty (35:12–13). God is sovereign over history and nature. His character is awesome and his ways unsearchable. "The Almighty is beyond our reach and exalted in power" (37:23).

Chapter 35		Chapter 36	Chapter 37
"Man Is Not like God"			"God Is Not like Man"
His Conduct		His Pride	His Power
Elihu's Exhortation			Elihu's Explanation

 YOUR DAILY WALK Here are three of the most difficult words any Christian will ever have to utter: *I don't know.*

Somehow the notion has developed that being unable to explain God's actions and attributes is a sign of spiritual weakness or immaturity. Job repeatedly took God to task because of the seemingly unreasonable things God was doing in his life. Knowing that God was absolutely just and impartial, Job concluded that God owed him an explanation. But it took young Elihu to remind Job of another important truth about God: His ways are different from human ways. The LORD told the prophet Isaiah, "For my thoughts are not your thoughts, neither are your ways my ways" (Isaiah 55:8).

A Christian with absolutely no doubts or questions is overlooking something.

Just as you must trust the surgeon to do his skillful work even though you do not understand all his techniques, so God is asking you to trust him to accomplish his purposes in your life—even though it may involve "surgery" you will not understand this side of heaven.

 INSIGHT What's in a Name?
Many times Bible names characterize their bearers. In the case of Elihu, his name captures the major theme of his message on the sovereignty of God. *Elihu* means "He is my God!" Do you know the meaning of your name and those of your family members?

CHAPTER 35
Then Elihu said:

2"Do you think this is just?
   You say, 'I will be cleared by
      God.z'
3Yet you ask him, 'What profit is it to
      me,a
   and what do I gain by not sinning?'

4"I would like to reply to you
   and to your friends with you.
5Look up at the heavens and see;
   gaze at the clouds so high above
      you.
6If you sin, how does that affect him?
   If your sins are many, what does
      that do to him?
7If you are righteous, what do you give
      to him,
   or what does he receive from your
      hand?
8Your wickedness affects only a man
      like yourself,
   and your righteousness only the
      sons of men.

9"Men cry out under a load of
      oppression;
   they plead for relief from the arm of
      the powerful.
10But no one says, 'Where is God my
      Maker,
   who gives songs in the night,
11who teaches more to us than tob the
      beasts of the earth
   and makes us wiser thanc the birds
      of the air?'
12He does not answer when men cry out
   because of the arrogance of the
      wicked.
13Indeed, God does not listen to their
      empty plea;
   the Almighty pays no attention to it.
14How much less, then, will he listen
   when you say that you do not see
      him,
   that your case is before him
   and you must wait for him,
15and further, that his anger never
      punishes
   and he does not take the least notice
      of wickedness.d
16So Job opens his mouth with empty
      talk;

without knowledge he multiplies
   words."

CHAPTER 36
Elihu continued:

2"Bear with me a little longer and I will
      show you
   that there is more to be said in
      God's behalf.
3I get my knowledge from afar;
   I will ascribe justice to my Maker.
4Be assured that my words are not
      false;
   one perfect in knowledge is with
      you.

5"God is mighty, but does not despise
      men;
   he is mighty, and firm in his
      purpose.
6He does not keep the wicked alive
   but gives the afflicted their rights.
7He does not take his eyes off the
      righteous;
   he enthrones them with kings
   and exalts them forever.
8But if men are bound in chains,
   held fast by cords of affliction,
9he tells them what they have done—
   that they have sinned arrogantly.
10He makes them listen to correction
   and commands them to repent of
      their evil.
11If they obey and serve him,
   they will spend the rest of their days
      in prosperity
   and their years in contentment.
12But if they do not listen,
   they will perish by the sworde
   and die without knowledge.

13"The godless in heart harbor
      resentment;
   even when he fetters them, they do
      not cry for help.
14They die in their youth,
   among male prostitutes of the
      shrines.
15But those who suffer he delivers in
      their suffering;
   he speaks to them in their affliction.

16"He is wooing you from the jaws of
      distress
   to a spacious place free from
      restriction,

---

z2 Or *My righteousness is more than God's*   a3 Or *you*   b11 Or *teaches us by*   c11 Or *us wise by*   d15 Symmachus,
Theodotion and Vulgate; the meaning of the Hebrew for this word is uncertain.   e12 Or *will cross the River*

to the comfort of your table laden
  with choice food.
¹⁷But now you are laden with the
  judgment due the wicked;
  judgment and justice have taken
    hold of you.
¹⁸Be careful that no one entices you by
    riches;
  do not let a large bribe turn you
    aside.
¹⁹Would your wealth
  or even all your mighty efforts
  sustain you so you would not be in
    distress?
²⁰Do not long for the night,
  to drag people away from their
    homes.ᶠ
²¹Beware of turning to evil,
  which you seem to prefer to
    affliction.

²²"God is exalted in his power.
  Who is a teacher like him?
²³Who has prescribed his ways for him,
  or said to him, 'You have done
    wrong'?
²⁴Remember to extol his work,
  which men have praised in song.
²⁵All mankind has seen it;
  men gaze on it from afar.
²⁶How great is God—beyond our
    understanding!
  The number of his years is past
    finding out.

²⁷"He draws up the drops of water,
  which distill as rain to the streamsᵍ;
²⁸the clouds pour down their moisture
  and abundant showers fall on
    mankind.
²⁹Who can understand how he spreads
    out the clouds,
  how he thunders from his pavilion?
³⁰See how he scatters his lightning about
    him,
  bathing the depths of the sea.
³¹This is the way he governsʰ the
    nations
  and provides food in abundance.
³²He fills his hands with lightning
  and commands it to strike its mark.
³³His thunder announces the coming
    storm;
  even the cattle make known its
    approach.ⁱ

CHAPTER 37

"At this my heart pounds
  and leaps from its place.
²Listen! Listen to the roar of his voice,
  to the rumbling that comes from his
    mouth.
³He unleashes his lightning beneath the
    whole heaven
  and sends it to the ends of the earth.
⁴After that comes the sound of his roar;
  he thunders with his majestic voice.
When his voice resounds,
  he holds nothing back.
⁵God's voice thunders in marvelous
    ways;
  he does great things beyond our
    understanding.
⁶He says to the snow, 'Fall on the
    earth,'
  and to the rain shower, 'Be a mighty
    downpour.'
⁷So that all men he has made may
    know his work,
  he stops every man from his labor.ʲ
⁸The animals take cover;
  they remain in their dens.
⁹The tempest comes out from its
    chamber,
  the cold from the driving winds.
¹⁰The breath of God produces ice,
  and the broad waters become frozen.
¹¹He loads the clouds with moisture;
  he scatters his lightning through
    them.
¹²At his direction they swirl around
  over the face of the whole earth
  to do whatever he commands them.
¹³He brings the clouds to punish men,
  or to water his earthᵏ and show his
    love.

¹⁴"Listen to this, Job;
  stop and consider God's wonders.
¹⁵Do you know how God controls the
    clouds
  and makes his lightning flash?
¹⁶Do you know how the clouds hang
    poised,
  those wonders of him who is perfect
    in knowledge?
¹⁷You who swelter in your clothes
  when the land lies hushed under the
    south wind,

ᶠ20 The meaning of the Hebrew for verses 18-20 is uncertain.   ᵍ27 Or distill from the mist as rain   ʰ31 Or nourishes
ⁱ33 Or announces his coming— / the One zealous against evil   ʲ7 Or / he fills all men with fear by his power   ᵏ13 Or to favor them

¹⁸can you join him in spreading out the
    skies,
  hard as a mirror of cast bronze?

¹⁹"Tell us what we should say to him;
  we cannot draw up our case because
    of our darkness.
²⁰Should he be told that I want to
    speak?
  Would any man ask to be
    swallowed up?
²¹Now no one can look at the sun,
  bright as it is in the skies

after the wind has swept them
    clean.
²²Out of the north he comes in golden
    splendor;
  God comes in awesome majesty.
²³The Almighty is beyond our reach and
    exalted in power;
  in his justice and great
    righteousness, he does not
    oppress.
²⁴Therefore, men revere him,
  for does he not have regard for all
    the wise in heart?^l"

^l24 Or *for he does not have regard for any who think they are wise.*

MAY 30 □ DAY 151
JOB 38–39
Controversy between the Lord and Job

OVERVIEW Job does not answer Elihu. The sufferer awaits the words of the one he has sought for thirty-seven chapters! At last God speaks to Job out of a storm. But rather than answer Job's persistent questions, God ministers to the needs of Job's heart. He guides Job on a panoramic sweep of nature, showing Job the vastness of the mind and works of God and the insignificance of puny humans. Using a series of pointed questions, the infinite God challenges Job to answer: "Where were you when I laid the earth's foundation?" (38:4). "Have you comprehended the vast expanses of the earth?" (38:18). "Do you give the horse his strength?" (39:19). "Does the hawk take flight by your wisdom and spread his wings toward the south?" (39:26). Clearly, the answer to all of these is no. The God of creation rules the world. Though a God of justice and mercy, he is intimately acquainted with all his creatures.

Chapter 38	Chapter 39
The Vastness of God in the Physical World	The Variety of God in the Animal World
A Bigger Picture of Job's God	

YOUR DAILY WALK Nature is not God (as pantheism claims), but God is revealed by nature (Romans 1:18–21). You have read today how God's works in the world of nature demonstrate his power and glory.

The greatness of the Promiser enhances the greatness of the promises.

With this thought in mind, do an outdoor "daily walk" today. See how many characteristics or attributes of God you can find by observing the natural world around you. Then look for an application of each characteristic of God to your life today.

For example, observe the sun. It rises every day—same time, same place. This shows God is unchangeable. And if God is unchanging, then his promises aren't fickle. They can be relied on today and tomorrow and forever! Now see what else you can learn from nature about God's infinity (not limited by space), eternity (not limited by time), omnipresence (everywhere present) and omnipotence (unlimited power). Better yet, do this while you take a walk with a friend!

 INSIGHT A Challenge That Can Get You into Deep Trouble
Drop a heavy anchor into the Pacific Ocean over the Marianas Trench, and an hour later it still will not have touched bottom—nearly seven miles below! This sheds new light on God's challenge to Job in 38:16.

CHAPTER 38
Then the LORD answered Job out of the storm. He said:

2"Who is this that darkens my counsel
    with words without knowledge?
3Brace yourself like a man;
    I will question you,
    and you shall answer me.

4"Where were you when I laid the
        earth's foundation?
    Tell me, if you understand.
5Who marked off its dimensions?
        Surely you know!
    Who stretched a measuring line
        across it?
6On what were its footings set,
    or who laid its cornerstone—
7while the morning stars sang together
    and all the angels*m* shouted for joy?

8"Who shut up the sea behind doors
    when it burst forth from the womb,
9when I made the clouds its garment
    and wrapped it in thick darkness,
10when I fixed limits for it
    and set its doors and bars in place,
11when I said, 'This far you may come
        and no farther;
    here is where your proud waves
        halt'?

12"Have you ever given orders to the
        morning,
    or shown the dawn its place,
13that it might take the earth by the
        edges
    and shake the wicked out of it?
14The earth takes shape like clay under a
        seal;
    its features stand out like those of a
        garment.
15The wicked are denied their light,
    and their upraised arm is broken.

16"Have you journeyed to the springs of
        the sea
    or walked in the recesses of the
        deep?

17Have the gates of death been shown to
        you?
    Have you seen the gates of the
        shadow of death*n*?
18Have you comprehended the vast
        expanses of the earth?
    Tell me, if you know all this.

19"What is the way to the abode of light?
    And where does darkness reside?
20Can you take them to their places?
    Do you know the paths to their
        dwellings?
21Surely you know, for you were
        already born!
    You have lived so many years!

22"Have you entered the storehouses of
        the snow
    or seen the storehouses of the hail,
23which I reserve for times of trouble,
    for days of war and battle?
24What is the way to the place where
        the lightning is dispersed,
    or the place where the east winds
        are scattered over the earth?
25Who cuts a channel for the torrents of
        rain,
    and a path for the thunderstorm,
26to water a land where no man lives,
    a desert with no one in it,
27to satisfy a desolate wasteland
    and make it sprout with grass?
28Does the rain have a father?
    Who fathers the drops of dew?
29From whose womb comes the ice?
    Who gives birth to the frost from the
        heavens
30when the waters become hard as
        stone,
    when the surface of the deep is
        frozen?

31"Can you bind the beautiful*o*
        Pleiades?
    Can you loose the cords of Orion?

*m*7 Hebrew *the sons of God*   *n*17 Or *gates of deep shadows*   *o*31 Or *the twinkling;* or *the chains of the*

³²Can you bring forth the constellations
    in their seasonsᵖ
  or lead out the Bear�q with its cubs?
³³Do you know the laws of the heavens?
    Can you set up ˻God'sʳ˼ dominion
    over the earth?

³⁴"Can you raise your voice to the
    clouds
  and cover yourself with a flood of
    water?
³⁵Do you send the lightning bolts on
    their way?
  Do they report to you, 'Here we
    are'?
³⁶Who endowed the heartˢ with
    wisdom
  or gave understanding to the
    mindˢ?
³⁷Who has the wisdom to count the
    clouds?
  Who can tip over the water jars of
    the heavens
³⁸when the dust becomes hard
  and the clods of earth stick together?

³⁹"Do you hunt the prey for the lioness
  and satisfy the hunger of the lions
⁴⁰when they crouch in their dens
  or lie in wait in a thicket?
⁴¹Who provides food for the raven
  when its young cry out to God
  and wander about for lack of food?

CHAPTER 39

"Do you know when the mountain
    goats give birth?
  Do you watch when the doe bears
    her fawn?
²Do you count the months till they
    bear?
  Do you know the time they give
    birth?
³They crouch down and bring forth
    their young;
  their labor pains are ended.
⁴Their young thrive and grow strong in
    the wilds;
  they leave and do not return.

⁵"Who let the wild donkey go free?
  Who untied his ropes?
⁶I gave him the wasteland as his home,
  the salt flats as his habitat.
⁷He laughs at the commotion in the
    town;

he does not hear a driver's shout.
⁸He ranges the hills for his pasture
  and searches for any green thing.

⁹"Will the wild ox consent to serve you?
  Will he stay by your manger at
    night?
¹⁰Can you hold him to the furrow with
    a harness?
  Will he till the valleys behind you?
¹¹Will you rely on him for his great
    strength?
  Will you leave your heavy work to
    him?
¹²Can you trust him to bring in your
    grain
  and gather it to your threshing
    floor?

¹³"The wings of the ostrich flap joyfully,
  but they cannot compare with the
    pinions and feathers of the
    stork.
¹⁴She lays her eggs on the ground
  and lets them warm in the sand,
¹⁵unmindful that a foot may crush them,
  that some wild animal may trample
    them.
¹⁶She treats her young harshly, as if they
    were not hers;
  she cares not that her labor was in
    vain,
¹⁷for God did not endow her with
    wisdom
  or give her a share of good sense.
¹⁸Yet when she spreads her feathers to
    run,
  she laughs at horse and rider.

¹⁹"Do you give the horse his strength
  or clothe his neck with a flowing
    mane?
²⁰Do you make him leap like a locust,
  striking terror with his proud
    snorting?
²¹He paws fiercely, rejoicing in his
    strength,
  and charges into the fray.
²²He laughs at fear, afraid of nothing;
  he does not shy away from the
    sword.
²³The quiver rattles against his side,
  along with the flashing spear and
    lance.
²⁴In frenzied excitement he eats up the
    ground;

ᵖ32 Or *the morning star in its season*   q32 Or *out Leo*   ʳ33 Or *his; or their*   ˢ36 The meaning of the Hebrew for this word
is uncertain.

he cannot stand still when the
  trumpet sounds.
²⁵At the blast of the trumpet he snorts,
  'Aha!'
He catches the scent of battle from
  afar,
the shout of commanders and the
  battle cry.

²⁶"Does the hawk take flight by your
  wisdom

and spread his wings toward the
  south?
²⁷Does the eagle soar at your command
  and build his nest on high?
²⁸He dwells on a cliff and stays there at
  night;
  a rocky crag is his stronghold.
²⁹From there he seeks out his food;
  his eyes detect it from afar.
³⁰His young ones feast on blood,
  and where the slain are, there is he."

MAY 31 □ DAY 152
JOB 40–42
Job's Response and Reward

OVERVIEW Though Job is willing to acknowledge God's power and wisdom, there yet remains the question of God's judgment (40:8). Once again God challenges Job to a face-to-face confrontation, this time over the issue of God's justice. Through interrogation, invitation and illustration, God brings Job to the point of repentance for his presumptuous attitude. Now Job is willing to trust God completely, even though he doesn't completely understand his ways!

Chapters 40–41	Chapter 42	
God's Challenge to Job: "Can You Rule in My Place?"	Job's Response to God: Repentance	Job's Reward from God: Riches
1	6 7	17
The Sinfulness of Criticizing God		

Pray for a faith that will not shrink when washed in the waters of affliction.

YOUR DAILY WALK Nowhere in the book of Job does God answer any of the burning questions that caused so much debate between Job and his friends. He simply answers the needs of Job's heart. God does not explain each phase of the battle, but he makes Job more than conqueror in it. Job's knowledge of God before his trials was primarily secondhand, "My ears had heard of you" (42:5), perhaps from his parents, friends and acquaintances. But now, after passing through the fire of adversity, he sees God more clearly and gains faith and courage to trust him personally.

God doesn't put just any of his children through a Job-like experience. Remember chapter 1? It was because of Job's God-fearing lifestyle that God permitted him to be tested by Satan in order that his devotion might run even deeper. Are you facing a severe test of your faith today? View it not as a sign that God has left you but as a token of his desire to deepen and strengthen your commitment to him. Complete this sentence: "Though I do not understand why, God is asking me to show my trust in him by _____, and I will!"

INSIGHT Double for Your Trouble
As his reward for faithfulness under fire, Job received back from God twice as many sheep, camels, oxen and donkeys as he had had before, but not twice as many children (since he would one day see again the ones he had lost).

CHAPTER 40

The LORD said to Job:

2"Will the one who contends with the
    Almighty correct him?
  Let him who accuses God answer
    him!"

3Then Job answered the LORD:

4"I am unworthy—how can I reply to
    you?
  I put my hand over my mouth.
5I spoke once, but I have no answer—
  twice, but I will say no more."

6Then the LORD spoke to Job out of the
storm:

7"Brace yourself like a man;
  I will question you,
  and you shall answer me.

8"Would you discredit my justice?
  Would you condemn me to justify
    yourself?
9Do you have an arm like God's,
  and can your voice thunder like his?
10Then adorn yourself with glory and
    splendor,
  and clothe yourself in honor and
    majesty.
11Unleash the fury of your wrath,
  look at every proud man and bring
    him low,
12look at every proud man and humble
    him,
  crush the wicked where they stand.
13Bury them all in the dust together;
  shroud their faces in the grave.
14Then I myself will admit to you
  that your own right hand can save
    you.

15"Look at the behemoth,*t*
  which I made along with you
  and which feeds on grass like an ox.
16What strength he has in his loins,
  what power in the muscles of his
    belly!
17His tail*u* sways like a cedar;
  the sinews of his thighs are
    close-knit.
18His bones are tubes of bronze,
  his limbs like rods of iron.
19He ranks first among the works of
    God,
  yet his Maker can approach him
    with his sword.

20The hills bring him their produce,
  and all the wild animals play
    nearby.
21Under the lotus plants he lies,
  hidden among the reeds in the
    marsh.
22The lotuses conceal him in their
    shadow;
  the poplars by the stream surround
    him.
23When the river rages, he is not
    alarmed;
  he is secure, though the Jordan
    should surge against his mouth.
24Can anyone capture him by the eyes,*v*
  or trap him and pierce his nose?

CHAPTER 41

"Can you pull in the leviathan*w* with a
    fishhook
  or tie down his tongue with a rope?
2Can you put a cord through his nose
  or pierce his jaw with a hook?
3Will he keep begging you for mercy?
  Will he speak to you with gentle
    words?
4Will he make an agreement with you
  for you to take him as your slave for
    life?
5Can you make a pet of him like a bird
  or put him on a leash for your girls?
6Will traders barter for him?
  Will they divide him up among the
    merchants?
7Can you fill his hide with harpoons
  or his head with fishing spears?
8If you lay a hand on him,
  you will remember the struggle and
    never do it again!
9Any hope of subduing him is false;
  the mere sight of him is
    overpowering.
10No one is fierce enough to rouse him.
  Who then is able to stand against
    me?
11Who has a claim against me that I
    must pay?
  Everything under heaven belongs to
    me.

12"I will not fail to speak of his limbs,
  his strength and his graceful form.
13Who can strip off his outer coat?
  Who would approach him with a
    bridle?

t15 Possibly the hippopotamus or the elephant   *u17* Possibly trunk   *v24* Or *by a water hole*   *w1* Possibly the crocodile

¹⁴Who dares open the doors of his
        mouth,
    ringed about with his fearsome
        teeth?
¹⁵His back has^x rows of shields
    tightly sealed together;
¹⁶each is so close to the next
    that no air can pass between.
¹⁷They are joined fast to one another;
    they cling together and cannot be
        parted.
¹⁸His snorting throws out flashes of
        light;
    his eyes are like the rays of dawn.
¹⁹Firebrands stream from his mouth;
    sparks of fire shoot out.
²⁰Smoke pours from his nostrils
    as from a boiling pot over a fire of
        reeds.
²¹His breath sets coals ablaze,
    and flames dart from his mouth.
²²Strength resides in his neck;
    dismay goes before him.
²³The folds of his flesh are tightly
        joined;
    they are firm and immovable.
²⁴His chest is hard as rock,
    hard as a lower millstone.
²⁵When he rises up, the mighty are
        terrified;
    they retreat before his thrashing.
²⁶The sword that reaches him has no
        effect,
    nor does the spear or the dart or the
        javelin.
²⁷Iron he treats like straw
    and bronze like rotten wood.
²⁸Arrows do not make him flee;
    slingstones are like chaff to him.
²⁹A club seems to him but a piece of
        straw;
    he laughs at the rattling of the lance.
³⁰His undersides are jagged potsherds,
    leaving a trail in the mud like a
        threshing sledge.
³¹He makes the depths churn like a
        boiling caldron
    and stirs up the sea like a pot of
        ointment.
³²Behind him he leaves a glistening
        wake;
    one would think the deep had white
        hair.
³³Nothing on earth is his equal—
    a creature without fear.

³⁴He looks down on all that are
        haughty;
    he is king over all that are proud."

CHAPTER 42
Then Job replied to the LORD:

²"I know that you can do all things;
    no plan of yours can be thwarted.
³⌊You asked,⌋ 'Who is this that obscures
        my counsel without
        knowledge?'
    Surely I spoke of things I did not
        understand,
    things too wonderful for me to
        know.

⁴⌊"You said,⌋ 'Listen now, and I will
        speak;
    I will question you,
        and you shall answer me.'
⁵My ears had heard of you
    but now my eyes have seen you.
⁶Therefore I despise myself
    and repent in dust and ashes."

⁷After the LORD had said these things to
Job, he said to Eliphaz the Temanite, "I am
angry with you and your two friends, because you have not spoken of me what is
right, as my servant Job has. ⁸So now take
seven bulls and seven rams and go to my
servant Job and sacrifice a burnt offering
for yourselves. My servant Job will pray
for you, and I will accept his prayer and
not deal with you according to your folly.
You have not spoken of me what is right,
as my servant Job has." ⁹So Eliphaz the
Temanite, Bildad the Shuhite and Zophar
the Naamathite did what the LORD told
them; and the LORD accepted Job's prayer.

¹⁰After Job had prayed for his friends,
the LORD made him prosperous again and
gave him twice as much as he had before.
¹¹All his brothers and sisters and every-
one who had known him before came and
ate with him in his house. They comforted
and consoled him over all the trouble the
LORD had brought upon him, and each
one gave him a piece of silver^y and a
gold ring.

¹²The LORD blessed the latter part of
Job's life more than the first. He had
fourteen thousand sheep, six thousand
camels, a thousand yoke of oxen and a
thousand donkeys. ¹³And he also had
seven sons and three daughters. ¹⁴The first

^x15 Or *His pride is his*   ^y11 Hebrew *him a kesitah*; a kesitah was a unit of money of unknown weight and value.

daughter he named Jemimah, the second Keziah and the third Keren-Happuch. [15]Nowhere in all the land were there found women as beautiful as Job's daughters, and their father granted them an inheritance along with their brothers.

[16]After this, Job lived a hundred and forty years; he saw his children and their children to the fourth generation. [17]And so he died, old and full of years.

Psalms

WRITTEN by at least seven authors (of which David is the most notable), the book of Psalms spans one thousand years of Israel's rich history—from the time of Moses to the return from exile in Babylonia. The word *psalm* comes from a Greek word meaning "a song sung to the accompaniment of a plucked instrument." Used as the temple hymnbook, the Psalms express the diversity of human emotion—praise to God in good times, fear of enemies in bad times and an overriding confidence in God's goodness, majesty and power.

Section	Book 1 (1–41)	Book 2 (42–72)	Book 3 (73–89)	Book 4 (90–106)	Book 5 (107–150)
Chief Author	David	David/ Asaph	Asaph	Anony- mous	David
No. of Psalms	41	31	17	17	44
Summary of Content	Songs of Worship	Hymns of National Interest		Anthem of Praise	
Possible Compiler	David	Hezekiah/Josiah		Ezra/Nehemiah	
Dates of Compilation	c. 1020– 970 B.C.	c. 970–610 B.C.		Until c. 430 B.C.	
Topical Similarity to Pentateuch	Genesis: Mankind and Creation	Exodus: Delivered and Redeemed	Leviticus: Worship and Sanctuary	Numbers: Desert and Wandering	Deut: Scripture and Praise
Closing Doxology	41:13	72:18-19	89:52	106:48	150:1-6
Span of Authorship	About 1,000 Years (c. 1410–430 B.C.)				

JUNE 1 ☐ DAY 153
PSALMS 1–6
The Last Laugh

OVERVIEW The gateway to the book of Psalms is guarded by two major declarations concerning God's revelation of himself: He can be known through his Word, which brings blessing (Psalm 1), and he can be known in the person of his Son, who rules over creation (2). The servant of God can cling to him with confidence, knowing that God's help and consolation are assured in both good times and bad. No foe (3) nor failure (4), no frustration (5) nor cause for fainting (6) can change the fact that God is in control.

Psalm 1	Psalm 2	Psalm 3	Psalm 4	Psalm 5	Psalm 6
God's Word Prospers	God's Son Prevails	Foes	God's Servant Is Protected from		
			Failure	Frustration	Fainting
Proclamation		Petition			

YOUR DAILY WALK Laughter has been called the sensation of feeling good all over and showing it principally in one place. Everyone enjoys a good laugh . . . unless the laugh is at his or her expense. Then laughter can become a painful, rather than a pleasurable, experience.

The singing of a hymn should be a conversation between friends.

   Psalm 2 describes the world's rulers gathered together. With great fury and indignation, they shake their fists in the face of God and threaten to overthrow his rule (2:3). And what is God's response to their impressive show of power and independence?

   A cosmic guffaw, loud enough to shake the heavens (2:4), at the absurdity of the nations' rejecting the sovereign Creator who fashioned them! From God's perspective, it is a fool indeed who will not fall down and acknowledge his greatness. And those who put their trust in him are truly blessed.

   Find a copy of today's newspaper, and spend a few minutes scanning it for news of the nations. Over each frightening or discouraging headline, write the words *God is in control!* That's a truth no one—king or commoner—can avoid.

INSIGHT Something Old, Something New
These words summarize the relationship between the Old and New Testaments: *The New is in the Old contained; the Old is in the New explained.* This statement can be proved by noting how the New Testament writers quote and explain portions of Psalm 2 in Acts 4:25–26 (quoting Psalm 2:1–2) and in Acts 13:33 and Hebrews 5:5 (both quoting Psalm 2:7).

BOOK I
Psalms 1–41

PSALM 1

¹Blessed is the man
   who does not walk in the counsel of
      the wicked

or stand in the way of sinners
   or sit in the seat of mockers.
²But his delight is in the law of the LORD,
   and on his law he meditates day
      and night.
³He is like a tree planted by streams of
      water,

which yields its fruit in season
and whose leaf does not wither.
　Whatever he does prospers.

4Not so the wicked!
　They are like chaff
　that the wind blows away.
5Therefore the wicked will not stand in
　　the judgment,
　nor sinners in the assembly of the
　　righteous.

6For the LORD watches over the way of
　　the righteous,
　but the way of the wicked will
　　perish.

PSALM 2

1Why do the nations conspire[a]
　and the peoples plot in vain?
2The kings of the earth take their
　　stand
　and the rulers gather together
against the LORD
　and against his Anointed One.[b]
3"Let us break their chains," they say,
　"and throw off their fetters."

4The One enthroned in heaven laughs;
　the Lord scoffs at them.
5Then he rebukes them in his anger
　and terrifies them in his wrath,
　　saying,
6"I have installed my King[c]
　on Zion, my holy hill."

7I will proclaim the decree of the
　LORD:

He said to me, "You are my Son[d];
　today I have become your
　　Father.[e]
8Ask of me,
　and I will make the nations your
　　inheritance,
　the ends of the earth your
　　possession.
9You will rule them with an iron
　　scepter[f];
　you will dash them to pieces like
　　pottery."

10Therefore, you kings, be wise;
　be warned, you rulers of the
　　earth.
11Serve the LORD with fear
　and rejoice with trembling.
12Kiss the Son, lest he be angry
　and you be destroyed in your
　　way,
for his wrath can flare up in a
　　moment.
Blessed are all who take refuge in
　　him.

PSALM 3
A psalm of David. When he fled from
his son Absalom.

1O LORD, how many are my foes!
　How many rise up against me!
2Many are saying of me,
　"God will not deliver him."　Selah[g]

3But you are a shield around me,
　O LORD;
　you bestow glory on me and lift[h]
　　up my head.
4To the LORD I cry aloud,
　and he answers me from his holy
　　hill.　　　　　　　　　　Selah

5I lie down and sleep;
　I wake again, because the LORD
　　sustains me.
6I will not fear the tens of thousands
　drawn up against me on every
　　side.

7Arise, O LORD!
　Deliver me, O my God!
　Strike all my enemies on the jaw;
　break the teeth of the wicked.

8From the LORD comes deliverance.
　May your blessing be on your
　　people.　　　　　　　　Selah

PSALM 4
For the director of music. With stringed
instruments. A psalm of David.

1Answer me when I call to you,
　O my righteous God.
Give me relief from my distress;

---

a1 Hebrew; Septuagint *rage*　　b2 Or *anointed one*　　c6 Or *king*　　d7 Or *son*; also in verse 12　　e7 Or *have begotten you*
f9 Or *will break them with a rod of iron*　　g2 A word of uncertain meaning, occurring frequently in the Psalms; possibly a
musical term　　h3 Or LORD, / *my Glorious One, who lifts*

be merciful to me and hear my
   prayer.
²How long, O men, will you turn my
   glory into shame[i]?
   How long will you love delusions
      and seek false gods[j]?   *Selah*
³Know that the LORD has set apart the
   godly for himself;
   the LORD will hear when I call to
      him.

⁴In your anger do not sin;
   when you are on your beds,
   search your hearts and be silent.
                                    Selah

⁵Offer right sacrifices
   and trust in the LORD.

⁶Many are asking, "Who can show us
   any good?"
   Let the light of your face shine upon
      us, O LORD.
⁷You have filled my heart with greater
      joy
   than when their grain and new wine
      abound.
⁸I will lie down and sleep in peace,
   for you alone, O LORD,
   make me dwell in safety.

PSALM 5
For the director of music. For flutes.
A psalm of David.

¹Give ear to my words, O LORD,
   consider my sighing.
²Listen to my cry for help,
   my King and my God,
   for to you I pray.
³In the morning, O LORD, you hear my
      voice;
   in the morning I lay my requests
      before you
   and wait in expectation.

⁴You are not a God who takes pleasure
      in evil;
   with you the wicked cannot dwell.
⁵The arrogant cannot stand in your
      presence;
   you hate all who do wrong.
⁶You destroy those who tell lies;
   bloodthirsty and deceitful men
   the LORD abhors.

⁷But I, by your great mercy,
   will come into your house;

in reverence will I bow down
   toward your holy temple.
⁸Lead me, O LORD, in your
      righteousness
   because of my enemies—
   make straight your way before me.

⁹Not a word from their mouth can be
      trusted;
   their heart is filled with
      destruction.
   Their throat is an open grave;
   with their tongue they speak deceit.
¹⁰Declare them guilty, O God!
   Let their intrigues be their
      downfall.
   Banish them for their many sins,
   for they have rebelled against you.

¹¹But let all who take refuge in you be
      glad;
   let them ever sing for joy.
   Spread your protection over them,
   that those who love your name may
      rejoice in you.
¹²For surely, O LORD, you bless the
      righteous;
   you surround them with your favor
   as with a shield.

PSALM 6
For the director of music. With stringed
instruments. According to *sheminith.*[k]
A psalm of David.

¹O LORD, do not rebuke me in your
      anger
   or discipline me in your wrath.
²Be merciful to me, LORD, for I am
      faint;
   O LORD, heal me, for my bones are
      in agony.
³My soul is in anguish.
   How long, O LORD, how long?

⁴Turn, O LORD, and deliver me;
   save me because of your unfailing
      love.
⁵No one remembers you when he is
      dead.
   Who praises you from the grave[l]?

⁶I am worn out from groaning;
   all night long I flood my bed with
      weeping
   and drench my couch with tears.
⁷My eyes grow weak with sorrow;
   they fail because of all my foes.

---

[i]2 Or *you dishonor my Glorious One*   [j]2 Or *seek lies*   [k]Title: Probably a musical term   [l]5 Hebrew *Sheol*

⁸Away from me, all you who do evil,
    for the LORD has heard my weeping.
⁹The LORD has heard my cry for mercy;
    the LORD accepts my prayer.

¹⁰All my enemies will be ashamed and
    dismayed;
  they will turn back in sudden
    disgrace.

JUNE 2 ☐ DAY 154
PSALMS 7–12
Let's Just Praise the Lord

OVERVIEW The enemies of God's people are also the enemies of
God. Responding to these enemies is David's burden in each of the
psalms in today's reading. In the face of dangerous opposition, David
seeks God's justice (Psalm 7), protection (9–10) and deliverance
(11–12). The God who created people to rule over his creation is the
God who will one day silence and subdue his enemies (8).

Psalm 7	Psalm 8	Psalms 9–10	Psalms 11–12
Desire for Vindication	Delight in Creation	Defense against Enemies	Deliverance from the Wicked
The Righteous Look to God		God Looks after the Righteous	

One who is sincere is sincere in all places and at all times.

YOUR DAILY WALK A famous author once commented that "one of
the difficulties in language is that all our words have lost their edge
from loose usage." Sadly, the church is not immune to this phenome-
non. Christian clichés develop so quickly . . . so subtly. Almost before
you realize what's happening, words that once prompted heartfelt response have turned into empty shells, phrases spoken more from habit
than from the heart.

The exercise of praising God never became a well-worn routine for
David. Rather, it involved a deliberate, reasoned response to God. The
first two verses of Psalm 9 summarize David's pattern of praise. First,
he rejoices in God's person; then he publicly proclaims God's wondrous ways. Put them together, and you have meditation turned into
communication, inward delight turned into outward demonstration. In
a word, *praise.*

Try David's plan for praising the Lord. Take an aspect of God's
character that you discover while reading today's passage, and translate it into the language of praise to God by singing a hymn, composing a short poem of praise or reading aloud the words of Psalm 9.
Make this a habit, and you—like David—will become a person after
God's own heart!

INSIGHT The Psalm with the Split Personality
The absence of a title in Psalm 10 and the sequence of initial letters in
the Hebrew text (every other verse of Psalms 9–10 begins with a successive letter of the Hebrew alphabet, forming a handy and memorable acrostic) have led many commentators to conclude that Psalms
9–10 were originally one long song composed by David.

PSALM 7

A *shiggaion*[m] of David, which he sang to the LORD concerning Cush, a Benjamite.

[1]O LORD my God, I take refuge in you;
  save and deliver me from all who
    pursue me,
[2]or they will tear me like a lion
  and rip me to pieces with no one to
    rescue me.

[3]O LORD my God, if I have done this
  and there is guilt on my hands—
[4]if I have done evil to him who is at
    peace with me
  or without cause have robbed my
    foe—
[5]then let my enemy pursue and
    overtake me;
  let him trample my life to the
    ground
  and make me sleep in the dust. *Selah*

[6]Arise, O LORD, in your anger;
  rise up against the rage of my
    enemies.
  Awake, my God; decree justice.
[7]Let the assembled peoples gather
    around you.
  Rule over them from on high;
[8] let the LORD judge the peoples.
Judge me, O LORD, according to my
    righteousness,
  according to my integrity, O Most
    High.
[9]O righteous God,
  who searches minds and hearts,
bring to an end the violence of the
    wicked
  and make the righteous secure.

[10]My shield[n] is God Most High,
  who saves the upright in heart.
[11]God is a righteous judge,
  a God who expresses his wrath
    every day.
[12]If he does not relent,
  he[o] will sharpen his sword;
  he will bend and string his bow.
[13]He has prepared his deadly weapons;
  he makes ready his flaming arrows.

[14]He who is pregnant with evil
  and conceives trouble gives birth to
    disillusionment.
[15]He who digs a hole and scoops it out
  falls into the pit he has made.

[16]The trouble he causes recoils on
    himself;
  his violence comes down on his own
    head.

[17]I will give thanks to the LORD because
    of his righteousness
  and will sing praise to the name of
    the LORD Most High.

PSALM 8

For the director of music. According to
gittith.[p] A psalm of David.

[1]O LORD, our Lord,
  how majestic is your name in all the
    earth!

You have set your glory
  above the heavens.
[2]From the lips of children and infants
  you have ordained praise[q]
because of your enemies,
  to silence the foe and the avenger.

[3]When I consider your heavens,
  the work of your fingers,
the moon and the stars,
  which you have set in place,
[4]what is man that you are mindful of
    him,
  the son of man that you care for
    him?
[5]You made him a little lower than the
    heavenly beings[r]
  and crowned him with glory and
    honor.

[6]You made him ruler over the works of
    your hands;
  you put everything under his feet:
[7]all flocks and herds,
  and the beasts of the field,
[8]the birds of the air,
  and the fish of the sea,
  all that swim the paths of the seas.

[9]O LORD, our Lord,
  how majestic is your name in all the
    earth!

PSALM 9[s]

For the director of music. To ⌊the tune of⌋
"The Death of the Son." A psalm
of David.

[1]I will praise you, O LORD, with all my
    heart;

---

[m] Title: Probably a literary or musical term   [n] 10 Or *sovereign*   [o] 12 Or *If a man does not repent, / God*   [p] Title: Probably a musical term   [q] 2 Or *strength*   [r] 5 Or *than God*   [s] Psalms 9 and 10 may have been originally a single acrostic poem, the stanzas of which begin with the successive letters of the Hebrew alphabet. In the Septuagint they constitute one psalm.

I will tell of all your wonders.
²I will be glad and rejoice in you;
  I will sing praise to your name,
    O Most High.

³My enemies turn back;
  they stumble and perish before you.
⁴For you have upheld my right and my
    cause;
  you have sat on your throne,
    judging righteously.
⁵You have rebuked the nations and
    destroyed the wicked;
  you have blotted out their name for
    ever and ever.
⁶Endless ruin has overtaken the enemy,
  you have uprooted their cities;
  even the memory of them has
    perished.

⁷The LORD reigns forever;
  he has established his throne for
    judgment.
⁸He will judge the world in
    righteousness;
  he will govern the peoples with
    justice.
⁹The LORD is a refuge for the oppressed,
  a stronghold in times of trouble.
¹⁰Those who know your name will trust
    in you,
  for you, LORD, have never forsaken
    those who seek you.

¹¹Sing praises to the LORD, enthroned in
    Zion;
  proclaim among the nations what he
    has done.
¹²For he who avenges blood remembers;
  he does not ignore the cry of the
    afflicted.

¹³O LORD, see how my enemies persecute
    me!
  Have mercy and lift me up from the
    gates of death,
¹⁴that I may declare your praises
  in the gates of the Daughter of Zion
  and there rejoice in your salvation.
¹⁵The nations have fallen into the pit
    they have dug;
  their feet are caught in the net they
    have hidden.
¹⁶The LORD is known by his justice;

the wicked are ensnared by the
    work of their hands.   *Higgaion.*ᵗ
                              Selah
¹⁷The wicked return to the grave,ᵘ
  all the nations that forget God.
¹⁸But the needy will not always be
    forgotten,
  nor the hope of the afflicted ever
    perish.

¹⁹Arise, O LORD, let not man triumph;
  let the nations be judged in your
    presence.
²⁰Strike them with terror, O LORD;
  let the nations know they are but
    men.   Selah

PSALM 10ᵛ

¹Why, O LORD, do you stand far off?
  Why do you hide yourself in times
    of trouble?

²In his arrogance the wicked man hunts
    down the weak,
  who are caught in the schemes he
    devises.
³He boasts of the cravings of his heart;
  he blesses the greedy and reviles the
    LORD.
⁴In his pride the wicked does not seek
    him;
  in all his thoughts there is no room
    for God.
⁵His ways are always prosperous;
  he is haughty and your laws are far
    from him;
  he sneers at all his enemies.
⁶He says to himself, "Nothing will
    shake me;
  I'll always be happy and never have
    trouble."
⁷His mouth is full of curses and lies
    and threats;
  trouble and evil are under his
    tongue.
⁸He lies in wait near the villages;
  from ambush he murders the
    innocent,
  watching in secret for his victims.
⁹He lies in wait like a lion in cover;
  he lies in wait to catch the helpless;
  he catches the helpless and drags
    them off in his net.
¹⁰His victims are crushed, they collapse;
  they fall under his strength.

ᵗ16 Or *Meditation*; possibly a musical notation   ᵘ17 Hebrew *Sheol*   ᵛPsalms 9 and 10 may have been originally a single acrostic poem, the stanzas of which begin with the successive letters of the Hebrew alphabet. In the Septuagint they constitute one psalm.

¹¹He says to himself, "God has forgotten;
he covers his face and never sees."

¹²Arise, L<small>ORD</small>! Lift up your hand, O God.
Do not forget the helpless.
¹³Why does the wicked man revile God?
Why does he say to himself,
"He won't call me to account"?
¹⁴But you, O God, do see trouble and grief;
you consider it to take it in hand.
The victim commits himself to you;
you are the helper of the fatherless.
¹⁵Break the arm of the wicked and evil man;
call him to account for his wickedness
that would not be found out.

¹⁶The L<small>ORD</small> is King for ever and ever;
the nations will perish from his land.
¹⁷You hear, O L<small>ORD</small>, the desire of the afflicted;
you encourage them, and you listen to their cry,
¹⁸defending the fatherless and the oppressed,
in order that man, who is of the earth, may terrify no more.

PSALM 11
For the director of music. Of David.

¹In the L<small>ORD</small> I take refuge.
How then can you say to me:
"Flee like a bird to your mountain.
²For look, the wicked bend their bows;
they set their arrows against the strings
to shoot from the shadows
at the upright in heart.
³When the foundations are being destroyed,
what can the righteous do^w?"

⁴The L<small>ORD</small> is in his holy temple;
the L<small>ORD</small> is on his heavenly throne.

He observes the sons of men;
his eyes examine them.
⁵The L<small>ORD</small> examines the righteous,
but the wicked^x and those who love violence
his soul hates.
⁶On the wicked he will rain
fiery coals and burning sulfur;
a scorching wind will be their lot.

⁷For the L<small>ORD</small> is righteous,
he loves justice;
upright men will see his face.

PSALM 12
For the director of music. According to
sheminith.^y A psalm of David.

¹Help, L<small>ORD</small>, for the godly are no more;
the faithful have vanished from among men.
²Everyone lies to his neighbor;
their flattering lips speak with deception.

³May the L<small>ORD</small> cut off all flattering lips
and every boastful tongue
⁴that says, "We will triumph with our tongues;
we own our lips^z—who is our master?"

⁵"Because of the oppression of the weak
and the groaning of the needy,
I will now arise," says the L<small>ORD</small>.
"I will protect them from those who malign them."
⁶And the words of the L<small>ORD</small> are flawless,
like silver refined in a furnace of clay,
purified seven times.

⁷O L<small>ORD</small>, you will keep us safe
and protect us from such people forever.
⁸The wicked freely strut about
when what is vile is honored among men.

---

^w3 Or *what is the Righteous One doing*   ^x5 Or *The L<small>ORD</small>, the Righteous One, examines the wicked,* | ^yTitle: Probably a musical term   ^z4 Or */ our lips are our plowshares*

JUNE 3 □ DAY 155
PSALMS 13–18
No Fooling

OVERVIEW Today, as in David's day, believers in God face many challenges to their faith, both from their own fearful hearts (Psalm 13) and from those who foolishly deny God's existence (14). The answer? Walking in fellowship with God (15), being sustained by the promises of God (16) and drawing upon God's ever-available resources (17–18).

Psalm 13	Psalm 14	Psalms 15–16	Psalm 17	Psalm 18
Anxious Believers	Atheistic Fools	Promise of Life	Prayer for Protection	Praise for Preservation
Challenged Faith		Confident Faith		

YOUR DAILY WALK Webster defines an *atheist* as "one who denies the existence of God." But Webster stops short of answering the question "Why do atheists refuse to believe in God?" How would you answer that question? Is it because

If God gives himself to us in promises, we must give ourselves to him in duties.

• they cannot accept God rationally or intellectually?
• they are untaught and ignorant of the things of God?
• they are unwilling to repent of sin in their lives?

While each of those answers may, in fact, be true, Psalm 14 highlights the root problem. Atheism is the by-product of a proud unwillingness to acknowledge sin before a holy God. David's use of such descriptions as "corrupt . . . evil . . . wicked" shows that the basic issue is moral, not intellectual.

Understanding that will help you the next time you share your faith. Rather than trying to prove God's existence (a common approach), focus instead on forgiveness in Jesus Christ. Intellectual objections can—and should—be answered. But only the grace of God can remove the guilt and stain of sin. Though you may not have the answers to all of the questions, you can be confident you have the answer to the need of every human heart because you have Christ in *your* heart! And that truth will prompt you to join David in praising God: "But I trust in your unfailing love; my heart rejoices in your salvation. I will sing to the LORD, because he has been good to me" (13:5–6).

INSIGHT Haven't I Sung That Somewhere Before?
If the words of Psalm 18 seem familiar, it's probably because you read them before in 2 Samuel 22. Do you recall the occasion that prompted David to compose these verses?

PSALM 13
For the director of music. A psalm of David.

¹How long, O LORD? Will you forget me forever?
How long will you hide your face from me?
²How long must I wrestle with my thoughts
and every day have sorrow in my heart?

How long will my enemy triumph over me?

³Look on me and answer, O LORD my God.
Give light to my eyes, or I will sleep in death;
⁴my enemy will say, "I have overcome him,"
and my foes will rejoice when I fall.

⁵But I trust in your unfailing love;

my heart rejoices in your
    salvation.
[6]I will sing to the LORD,
    for he has been good to me.

PSALM 14
For the director of music. Of David.

[1]The fool[a] says in his heart,
    "There is no God."
They are corrupt, their deeds are
    vile;
    there is no one who does good.

[2]The LORD looks down from heaven
    on the sons of men
to see if there are any who
    understand,
    any who seek God.
[3]All have turned aside,
    they have together become
        corrupt;
there is no one who does good,
    not even one.

[4]Will evildoers never learn—
    those who devour my people as
        men eat bread
    and who do not call on the LORD?
[5]There they are, overwhelmed with
    dread,
    for God is present in the company
        of the righteous.
[6]You evildoers frustrate the plans of the
    poor,
    but the LORD is their refuge.

[7]Oh, that salvation for Israel would
    come out of Zion!
When the LORD restores the fortunes
    of his people,
    let Jacob rejoice and Israel be glad!

PSALM 15
A psalm of David.

[1]LORD, who may dwell in your
    sanctuary?
    Who may live on your holy hill?

[2]He whose walk is blameless
    and who does what is righteous,
who speaks the truth from his heart
[3]   and has no slander on his tongue,
who does his neighbor no wrong
    and casts no slur on his
        fellowman,

[4]who despises a vile man
    but honors those who fear the LORD,
who keeps his oath
    even when it hurts,
[5]who lends his money without usury
    and does not accept a bribe against
        the innocent.

He who does these things
    will never be shaken.

PSALM 16
A miktam[b] of David.

[1]Keep me safe, O God,
    for in you I take refuge.

[2]I said to the LORD, "You are my Lord;
    apart from you I have no good
        thing."
[3]As for the saints who are in the land,
    they are the glorious ones in whom
        is all my delight.[c]
[4]The sorrows of those will increase
    who run after other gods.
I will not pour out their libations of
    blood
    or take up their names on my lips.

[5]LORD, you have assigned me my
    portion and my cup;
    you have made my lot secure.
[6]The boundary lines have fallen for me
    in pleasant places;
    surely I have a delightful
        inheritance.

[7]I will praise the LORD, who counsels
    me;
    even at night my heart instructs me.
[8]I have set the LORD always before me.
    Because he is at my right hand,
    I will not be shaken.

[9]Therefore my heart is glad and my
    tongue rejoices;
    my body also will rest secure,
[10]because you will not abandon me to
    the grave,[d]
    nor will you let your Holy One[e] see
        decay.
[11]You have made[f] known to me the
    path of life;
    you will fill me with joy in your
        presence,
    with eternal pleasures at your right
        hand.

---

[a]1 The Hebrew words rendered fool in Psalms denote one who is morally deficient.   [b]Title: Probably a literary or musical
term   [c]3 Or As for the pagan priests who are in the land / and the nobles in whom all delight, I said: [d]10 Hebrew Sheol
[e]10 Or your faithful one   [f]11 Or You will make

PSALM 17
A prayer of David.

¹Hear, O Lᴏʀᴅ, my righteous plea;
  listen to my cry.
Give ear to my prayer—
  it does not rise from deceitful lips.
²May my vindication come from you;
  may your eyes see what is right.

³Though you probe my heart and
    examine me at night,
  though you test me, you will find
    nothing;
  I have resolved that my mouth will
    not sin.
⁴As for the deeds of men—
  by the word of your lips
I have kept myself
  from the ways of the violent.
⁵My steps have held to your paths;
  my feet have not slipped.

⁶I call on you, O God, for you will
    answer me;
  give ear to me and hear my prayer.
⁷Show the wonder of your great love,
  you who save by your right hand
  those who take refuge in you from
    their foes.
⁸Keep me as the apple of your eye;
  hide me in the shadow of your
    wings
⁹from the wicked who assail me,
  from my mortal enemies who
    surround me.

¹⁰They close up their callous hearts,
  and their mouths speak with
    arrogance.
¹¹They have tracked me down, they now
    surround me,
  with eyes alert, to throw me to the
    ground.
¹²They are like a lion hungry for prey,
  like a great lion crouching in cover.

¹³Rise up, O Lᴏʀᴅ, confront them, bring
    them down;
  rescue me from the wicked by your
    sword.
¹⁴O Lᴏʀᴅ, by your hand save me from
    such men,
  from men of this world whose
    reward is in this life.

You still the hunger of those you
    cherish;

their sons have plenty,
  and they store up wealth for their
    children.
¹⁵And I—in righteousness I will see your
    face;
  when I awake, I will be satisfied
    with seeing your likeness.

PSALM 18
For the director of music. Of David the
servant of the Lᴏʀᴅ. He sang to the Lᴏʀᴅ
the words of this song when the Lᴏʀᴅ
delivered him from the hand of all his
enemies and from the hand of Saul.
He said:

¹I love you, O Lᴏʀᴅ, my strength.

²The Lᴏʀᴅ is my rock, my fortress and
    my deliverer;
  my God is my rock, in whom I take
    refuge.
  He is my shield and the horn*ᵍ* of
    my salvation, my stronghold.
³I call to the Lᴏʀᴅ, who is worthy of
    praise,
  and I am saved from my enemies.

⁴The cords of death entangled me;
  the torrents of destruction
    overwhelmed me.
⁵The cords of the grave*ʰ* coiled around
    me;
  the snares of death confronted me.
⁶In my distress I called to the Lᴏʀᴅ;
  I cried to my God for help.
From his temple he heard my voice;
  my cry came before him, into his
    ears.

⁷The earth trembled and quaked,
  and the foundations of the
    mountains shook;
  they trembled because he was angry.
⁸Smoke rose from his nostrils;
  consuming fire came from his
    mouth,
  burning coals blazed out of it.
⁹He parted the heavens and came
    down;
  dark clouds were under his feet.
¹⁰He mounted the cherubim and flew;
  he soared on the wings of the wind.
¹¹He made darkness his covering, his
    canopy around him—
  the dark rain clouds of the sky.
¹²Out of the brightness of his presence
    clouds advanced,

---

*g*2 *Horn* here symbolizes strength.   *h*5 Hebrew *Sheol*

with hailstones and bolts of
    lightning.
¹³The LORD thundered from heaven;
    the voice of the Most High
    resounded.ⁱ
¹⁴He shot his arrows and scattered ˌthe
    enemiesˌ,
    great bolts of lightning and routed
    them.
¹⁵The valleys of the sea were exposed
    and the foundations of the earth laid
    bare
at your rebuke, O LORD,
    at the blast of breath from your
    nostrils.

¹⁶He reached down from on high and
    took hold of me;
    he drew me out of deep waters.
¹⁷He rescued me from my powerful
    enemy,
    from my foes, who were too strong
    for me.
¹⁸They confronted me in the day of my
    disaster,
    but the LORD was my support.
¹⁹He brought me out into a spacious
    place;
    he rescued me because he delighted
    in me.

²⁰The LORD has dealt with me according
    to my righteousness;
    according to the cleanness of my
    hands he has rewarded me.
²¹For I have kept the ways of the LORD;
    I have not done evil by turning from
    my God.
²²All his laws are before me;
    I have not turned away from his
    decrees.
²³I have been blameless before him
    and have kept myself from sin.
²⁴The LORD has rewarded me according
    to my righteousness,
    according to the cleanness of my
    hands in his sight.

²⁵To the faithful you show yourself
    faithful,
    to the blameless you show yourself
    blameless,
²⁶to the pure you show yourself pure,
    but to the crooked you show
    yourself shrewd.
²⁷You save the humble

but bring low those whose eyes are
    haughty.
²⁸You, O LORD, keep my lamp burning;
    my God turns my darkness into
    light.
²⁹With your help I can advance against
    a troopʲ;
    with my God I can scale a wall.

³⁰As for God, his way is perfect;
    the word of the LORD is flawless.
He is a shield
    for all who take refuge in him.
³¹For who is God besides the LORD?
    And who is the Rock except our
    God?
³²It is God who arms me with strength
    and makes my way perfect.
³³He makes my feet like the feet of a
    deer;
    he enables me to stand on the
    heights.
³⁴He trains my hands for battle;
    my arms can bend a bow of bronze.
³⁵You give me your shield of victory,
    and your right hand sustains me;
    you stoop down to make me great.
³⁶You broaden the path beneath me,
    so that my ankles do not turn.

³⁷I pursued my enemies and overtook
    them;
    I did not turn back till they were
    destroyed.
³⁸I crushed them so that they could not
    rise;
    they fell beneath my feet.
³⁹You armed me with strength for battle;
    you made my adversaries bow at
    my feet.
⁴⁰You made my enemies turn their
    backs in flight,
    and I destroyed my foes.
⁴¹They cried for help, but there was no
    one to save them—
    to the LORD, but he did not answer.
⁴²I beat them as fine as dust borne on
    the wind;
    I poured them out like mud in the
    streets.
⁴³You have delivered me from the
    attacks of the people;
    you have made me the head of
    nations;

ⁱ13 Some Hebrew manuscripts and Septuagint (see also 2 Samuel 22:14); most Hebrew manuscripts *resounded, / amid hailstones and bolts of lightning*   ʲ29 Or *can run through a barricade*

people I did not know are subject to
me.
⁴⁴As soon as they hear me, they obey
me;
foreigners cringe before me.
⁴⁵They all lose heart;
they come trembling from their
strongholds.

⁴⁶The LORD lives! Praise be to my Rock!
Exalted be God my Savior!
⁴⁷He is the God who avenges me,

who subdues nations under me,
⁴⁸ who saves me from my enemies.
You exalted me above my foes;
from violent men you rescued me.
⁴⁹Therefore I will praise you among the
nations, O LORD;
I will sing praises to your name.
⁵⁰He gives his king great victories;
he shows unfailing kindness to his
anointed,
to David and his descendants
forever.

JUNE 4 ☐ DAY 156
PSALMS 19–24
In God We Trust

OVERVIEW God's involvement in the lives of his people is the domi-
nant theme of the psalms in today's reading. God reveals himself in
the world and in the Word (Psalm 19); he gives enablement and victory to those who do battle for him (20–21); he sends his Messiah to
suffer on the cross (22), shepherd his people (23) and establish his
rule over the earth (24). Indeed, he is worthy to be trusted!

Psalm 19	Psalm 20	Psalm 21	Psalms 22–24
Works and Words	Prayer before Victory	Praise after Victory	Portraits of Messiah
Revelation	Reliance		Redeemer

YOUR DAILY WALK Question: What do retirement funds, college degrees and nuclear submarines have in common?

Answer: They are all designed to give you a sense of security. Security for your future, security for your vocation, security for your protection. But do they?

*They are well
kept whom
God keeps.*

Security in an increasingly insecure world is one of today's most
sought after—and elusive—commodities.

Nearly three thousand years ago, the ultimate military weapons
were the chariot and the horse. Armies that could field a cavalry or
chariot brigade were considered virtually invincible.

But Israel was to be different. God's law forbade her king to multiply horses (Deuteronomy 17:16). Rather than put her confidence in
strategic arms, Israel was to trust in the everlasting arms, for God had
promised to fight for his people. That is why David's affirmation of
trust in a delivering God (Psalm 20:7) is so appropriate. It's the answer
to the national security problem—both in his day and yours.

On scratch paper, list in pencil five things the world says will make
you secure. Then across the list, write in ink the words of Psalm 20:7:
"We trust in the name of the LORD our God." America's coins are
stamped "In God We Trust." What sentiment is stamped on your
heart?

INSIGHT And Speaking of Chariots . . .
Israel's security was often threatened by chariot-equipped armies.
What was the outcome of the skirmishes described in Exodus 14? in
Judges 4? in 2 Kings 6?

PSALM 19
For the director of music. A psalm
of David.

¹The heavens declare the glory of God;
    the skies proclaim the work of his
    hands.
²Day after day they pour forth speech;
    night after night they display
    knowledge.
³There is no speech or language
    where their voice is not heard.ᵏ
⁴Their voiceˡ goes out into all the
    earth,
    their words to the ends of the world.

In the heavens he has pitched a tent
    for the sun,
5   which is like a bridegroom coming
    forth from his pavilion,
    like a champion rejoicing to run his
    course.
⁶It rises at one end of the heavens
    and makes its circuit to the other;
    nothing is hidden from its heat.

⁷The law of the LORD is perfect,
    reviving the soul.
The statutes of the LORD are
    trustworthy,
    making wise the simple.
⁸The precepts of the LORD are right,
    giving joy to the heart.
The commands of the LORD are radiant,
    giving light to the eyes.
⁹The fear of the LORD is pure,
    enduring forever.
The ordinances of the LORD are sure
    and altogether righteous.
¹⁰They are more precious than gold,
    than much pure gold;
they are sweeter than honey,
    than honey from the comb.
¹¹By them is your servant warned;
    in keeping them there is great
    reward.

¹²Who can discern his errors?
    Forgive my hidden faults.
¹³Keep your servant also from willful
    sins;

may they not rule over me.
Then will I be blameless,
    innocent of great transgression.

¹⁴May the words of my mouth and the
    meditation of my heart
be pleasing in your sight,
    O LORD, my Rock and my Redeemer.

PSALM 20
For the director of music. A psalm
of David.

¹May the LORD answer you when you
    are in distress;
    may the name of the God of Jacob
    protect you.
²May he send you help from the
    sanctuary
    and grant you support from Zion.
³May he remember all your sacrifices
    and accept your burnt offerings.
                                    Selah
⁴May he give you the desire of your
    heart
    and make all your plans succeed.
⁵We will shout for joy when you are
    victorious
    and will lift up our banners in the
    name of our God.
May the LORD grant all your requests.

⁶Now I know that the LORD saves his
    anointed;
    he answers him from his holy
    heaven
    with the saving power of his right
    hand.
⁷Some trust in chariots and some in
    horses,
    but we trust in the name of the LORD
    our God.
⁸They are brought to their knees and
    fall,
    but we rise up and stand firm.

⁹O LORD, save the king!
    Answerᵐ us when we call!

ᵏ3 Or *They have no speech, there are no words; / no sound is heard from them*   ˡ4 Septuagint, Jerome and Syriac; Hebrew *line*
ᵐ9 Or *save! / O King, answer*

PSALM 21
For the director of music. A psalm
of David.

¹O LORD, the king rejoices in your
   strength.
   How great is his joy in the victories
   you give!
²You have granted him the desire of his
   heart
   and have not withheld the request
   of his lips.   *Selah*
³You welcomed him with rich
   blessings
   and placed a crown of pure gold on
   his head.
⁴He asked you for life, and you gave it
   to him—
   length of days, for ever and ever.
⁵Through the victories you gave, his
   glory is great;
   you have bestowed on him splendor
   and majesty.
⁶Surely you have granted him eternal
   blessings
   and made him glad with the joy of
   your presence.
⁷For the king trusts in the LORD;
   through the unfailing love of the
   Most High
   he will not be shaken.

⁸Your hand will lay hold on all your
   enemies;
   your right hand will seize your
   foes.
⁹At the time of your appearing
   you will make them like a fiery
   furnace.
In his wrath the LORD will swallow
   them up,
   and his fire will consume them.
¹⁰You will destroy their descendants
   from the earth,
   their posterity from mankind.
¹¹Though they plot evil against you
   and devise wicked schemes, they
   cannot succeed;
¹²for you will make them turn their
   backs
   when you aim at them with drawn
   bow.

¹³Be exalted, O LORD, in your strength;
   we will sing and praise your
   might.

PSALM 22
For the director of music. To ⌊the tune of⌋
"The Doe of the Morning." A psalm
of David.

¹My God, my God, why have you
   forsaken me?
   Why are you so far from saving me,
   so far from the words of my
   groaning?
²O my God, I cry out by day, but you
   do not answer,
   by night, and am not silent.

³Yet you are enthroned as the Holy
   One;
   you are the praise of Israel.ⁿ
⁴In you our fathers put their trust;
   they trusted and you delivered
   them.
⁵They cried to you and were saved;
   in you they trusted and were not
   disappointed.

⁶But I am a worm and not a man,
   scorned by men and despised by the
   people.
⁷All who see me mock me;
   they hurl insults, shaking their
   heads:
⁸"He trusts in the LORD;
   let the LORD rescue him.
Let him deliver him,
   since he delights in him."

⁹Yet you brought me out of the womb;
   you made me trust in you
   even at my mother's breast.
¹⁰From birth I was cast upon you;
   from my mother's womb you have
   been my God.
¹¹Do not be far from me,
   for trouble is near
   and there is no one to help.

¹²Many bulls surround me;
   strong bulls of Bashan encircle me.
¹³Roaring lions tearing their prey
   open their mouths wide against me.
¹⁴I am poured out like water,
   and all my bones are out of joint.
My heart has turned to wax;
   it has melted away within me.
¹⁵My strength is dried up like a
   potsherd,
   and my tongue sticks to the roof of
   my mouth;
   you lay meᵒ in the dust of death.

ⁿ3 Or *Yet you are holy, / enthroned on the praises of Israel*   ᵒ15 Or *I am laid*

16Dogs have surrounded me;
　　a band of evil men has encircled me,
　　they have pierced[p] my hands and
　　　　my feet.
17I can count all my bones;
　　people stare and gloat over me.
18They divide my garments among them
　　and cast lots for my clothing.

19But you, O LORD, be not far off;
　　O my Strength, come quickly to help
　　　　me.
20Deliver my life from the sword,
　　my precious life from the power of
　　　　the dogs.
21Rescue me from the mouth of the
　　　　lions;
　　save[q] me from the horns of the
　　　　wild oxen.

22I will declare your name to my
　　　　brothers;
　　in the congregation I will praise you.
23You who fear the LORD, praise him!
　　All you descendants of Jacob, honor
　　　　him!
　　Revere him, all you descendants of
　　　　Israel!
24For he has not despised or disdained
　　the suffering of the afflicted one;
　　he has not hidden his face from him
　　but has listened to his cry for help.

25From you comes the theme of my
　　　　praise in the great assembly;
　　before those who fear you[r] will I
　　　　fulfill my vows.
26The poor will eat and be satisfied;
　　they who seek the LORD will praise
　　　　him—
　　may your hearts live forever!
27All the ends of the earth
　　will remember and turn to the LORD,
　　and all the families of the nations
　　will bow down before him,
28for dominion belongs to the LORD
　　and he rules over the nations.

29All the rich of the earth will feast and
　　　　worship;
　　all who go down to the dust will
　　　　kneel before him—
　　those who cannot keep themselves
　　　　alive.
30Posterity will serve him;
　　future generations will be told about
　　　　the Lord.

31They will proclaim his righteousness
　　to a people yet unborn—
　　for he has done it.

PSALM 23
A psalm of David.

1The LORD is my shepherd, I shall not
　　be in want.
2　He makes me lie down in green
　　　　pastures,
he leads me beside quiet waters,
3　he restores my soul.
He guides me in paths of
　　　　righteousness
　　for his name's sake.
4Even though I walk
　　through the valley of the shadow of
　　　　death,[s]
I will fear no evil,
　　for you are with me;
your rod and your staff,
　　they comfort me.

5You prepare a table before me
　　in the presence of my enemies.
You anoint my head with oil;
　　my cup overflows.
6Surely goodness and love will follow
　　　　me
all the days of my life,
and I will dwell in the house of the
　　　　LORD
　　forever.

PSALM 24
Of David. A psalm.

1The earth is the LORD's, and everything
　　in it,
　　the world, and all who live in it;
2for he founded it upon the seas
　　and established it upon the waters.

3Who may ascend the hill of the LORD?
　　Who may stand in his holy place?
4He who has clean hands and a pure
　　　　heart,
　　who does not lift up his soul to an
　　　　idol
　　or swear by what is false.[t]
5He will receive blessing from the LORD
　　and vindication from God his
　　　　Savior.
6Such is the generation of those who
　　seek him,

---

p16 Some Hebrew manuscripts, Septuagint and Syriac; most Hebrew manuscripts / like the lion,   q21 Or / you have heard
r25 Hebrew him   s4 Or through the darkest valley   t4 Or swear falsely

who seek your face, O God of
   Jacob.ᵘ   *Selah*

⁷Lift up your heads, O you gates;
   be lifted up, you ancient doors,
   that the King of glory may come
      in.
⁸Who is this King of glory?

The LORD strong and mighty,
   the LORD mighty in battle.
⁹Lift up your heads, O you gates;
   lift them up, you ancient doors,
   that the King of glory may come in.
¹⁰Who is he, this King of glory?
   The LORD Almighty—
   he is the King of glory.   *Selah*

ᵘ6 Two Hebrew manuscripts and Syriac (see also Septuagint); most Hebrew manuscripts *face, Jacob*

JUNE 5 □ DAY 157
PSALMS 25–30
Praise and Thanks

OVERVIEW A growing relationship with God includes a growing understanding of what he can accomplish in your life as you trust in him.
He will guide you in his way (Psalm 25), vindicate you when you're
wronged (26) and protect you when you're in danger (27–28). David's response—and the response God desires from every true believer—is an outpouring of heartfelt praise (29) and thanksgiving (30).

Psalm 25	Psalm 26	Psalm 27	Psalm 28	Psalm 29	Psalm 30
Watching for God's		Waiting for God's		Worshiping God in	
Direction	Defense	Salvation	Strength	Person	Power
Petition					Praise

YOUR DAILY WALK *Praise* and *thanks.* Are those terms synonymous,
or is there a difference between them?

*God is still on
the throne,
we're still on
his footstool,
and there's
only a knee's
distance
between.*

Psalms 29 and 30 provide a helpful illustration of the difference.
Psalm 29, a paean of praise, focuses on God's glory as revealed in an
earthshaking thunderstorm. Psalm 30, a testimony of thanksgiving,
centers on David's experience of divine deliverance and his resulting
gratitude to God. Psalm 29 illustrates praise, which is God-centered,
focusing on God's glory as revealed in his mighty attributes and
works. Psalm 30 illustrates thanksgiving, which is more human-
centered, highlighting David's gratitude for God's involvement in his life.

Understanding the difference between the two can add a new
dimension to your prayer life! It's easy to develop the habit of me-
centered prayers in which your problems are central. And though petition
is an important part of prayer (Matthew 7:7–8), it is not the only part.
As you take time to pray today, begin instead with praise for God's
glory and character (you-centered prayer). Make it a pattern in your
praying that before you get caught up in your own concerns, you get
caught up in God's greatness. Then you, like the psalmist, will be both
praising and thanking the Lord!

INSIGHT The Praise-Packed Psalms
Praise and thanksgiving permeate the Psalms—a fact seen in the repetition of the terms *praise* (209 times), *thanks* (26 times) and *thanksgiving* (5 times). It's difficult to miss the psalmist's intent that you learn
to "praise the LORD" and "give thanks to him in song"!

PSALM 25[v]
Of David.

[1]To you, O Lord, I lift up my soul;
[2]   in you I trust, O my God.
Do not let me be put to shame,
   nor let my enemies triumph over
   me.
[3]No one whose hope is in you
   will ever be put to shame,
but they will be put to shame
   who are treacherous without excuse.

[4]Show me your ways, O Lord,
   teach me your paths;
[5]guide me in your truth and teach me,
   for you are God my Savior,
   and my hope is in you all day long.
[6]Remember, O Lord, your great mercy
   and love,
   for they are from of old.
[7]Remember not the sins of my youth
   and my rebellious ways;
   according to your love remember me,
   for you are good, O Lord.

[8]Good and upright is the Lord;
   therefore he instructs sinners in his
   ways.
[9]He guides the humble in what is right
   and teaches them his way.
[10]All the ways of the Lord are loving
   and faithful
   for those who keep the demands of
   his covenant.
[11]For the sake of your name, O Lord,
   forgive my iniquity, though it is
   great.
[12]Who, then, is the man that fears the
   Lord?
He will instruct him in the way
   chosen for him.
[13]He will spend his days in prosperity,
   and his descendants will inherit the
   land.
[14]The Lord confides in those who fear
   him;
   he makes his covenant known to
   them.
[15]My eyes are ever on the Lord,
   for only he will release my feet from
   the snare.

[16]Turn to me and be gracious to me,
   for I am lonely and afflicted.
[17]The troubles of my heart have
   multiplied;

free me from my anguish.
[18]Look upon my affliction and my
   distress
   and take away all my sins.
[19]See how my enemies have increased
   and how fiercely they hate me!
[20]Guard my life and rescue me;
   let me not be put to shame,
   for I take refuge in you.
[21]May integrity and uprightness protect
   me,
   because my hope is in you.

[22]Redeem Israel, O God,
   from all their troubles!

PSALM 26
Of David.

[1]Vindicate me, O Lord,
   for I have led a blameless life;
I have trusted in the Lord
   without wavering.
[2]Test me, O Lord, and try me,
   examine my heart and my mind;
[3]for your love is ever before me,
   and I walk continually in your truth.
[4]I do not sit with deceitful men,
   nor do I consort with hypocrites;
[5]I abhor the assembly of evildoers
   and refuse to sit with the wicked.
[6]I wash my hands in innocence,
   and go about your altar, O Lord,
[7]proclaiming aloud your praise
   and telling of all your wonderful
   deeds.
[8]I love the house where you live,
   O Lord,
   the place where your glory dwells.

[9]Do not take away my soul along with
   sinners,
   my life with bloodthirsty men,
[10]in whose hands are wicked schemes,
   whose right hands are full of bribes.
[11]But I lead a blameless life;
   redeem me and be merciful to me.

[12]My feet stand on level ground;
   in the great assembly I will praise
   the Lord.

PSALM 27
Of David.

[1]The Lord is my light and my
   salvation—
   whom shall I fear?

[v]This psalm is an acrostic poem, the verses of which begin with the successive letters of the Hebrew alphabet.

The LORD is the stronghold of my life—
    of whom shall I be afraid?
2When evil men advance against me
    to devour my flesh,*w*
when my enemies and my foes attack
        me,
    they will stumble and fall.
3Though an army besiege me,
    my heart will not fear;
though war break out against me,
    even then will I be confident.

4One thing I ask of the LORD,
    this is what I seek:
that I may dwell in the house of the
        LORD
    all the days of my life,
to gaze upon the beauty of the LORD
    and to seek him in his temple.
5For in the day of trouble
    he will keep me safe in his dwelling;
he will hide me in the shelter of his
        tabernacle
    and set me high upon a rock.
6Then my head will be exalted
    above the enemies who surround
        me;
at his tabernacle will I sacrifice with
        shouts of joy;
    I will sing and make music to the
        LORD.

7Hear my voice when I call, O LORD;
    be merciful to me and answer me.
8My heart says of you, "Seek his*x* face!"
    Your face, LORD, I will seek.
9Do not hide your face from me,
    do not turn your servant away in
        anger;
    you have been my helper.
Do not reject me or forsake me,
    O God my Savior.
10Though my father and mother forsake
        me,
    the LORD will receive me.
11Teach me your way, O LORD;
    lead me in a straight path
    because of my oppressors.
12Do not turn me over to the desire of
        my foes,
    for false witnesses rise up against
        me,
    breathing out violence.

13I am still confident of this:
    I will see the goodness of the LORD
    in the land of the living.

14Wait for the LORD;
    be strong and take heart
    and wait for the LORD.

PSALM 28
Of David.

1To you I call, O LORD my Rock;
    do not turn a deaf ear to me.
For if you remain silent,
    I will be like those who have gone
        down to the pit.
2Hear my cry for mercy
    as I call to you for help,
as I lift up my hands
    toward your Most Holy Place.

3Do not drag me away with the
        wicked,
    with those who do evil,
who speak cordially with their
        neighbors
    but harbor malice in their hearts.
4Repay them for their deeds
    and for their evil work;
repay them for what their hands have
        done
    and bring back upon them what
        they deserve.
5Since they show no regard for the
        works of the LORD
    and what his hands have done,
he will tear them down
    and never build them up again.

6Praise be to the LORD,
    for he has heard my cry for mercy.
7The LORD is my strength and my
        shield;
    my heart trusts in him, and I am
        helped.
My heart leaps for joy
    and I will give thanks to him in
        song.

8The LORD is the strength of his people,
    a fortress of salvation for his
        anointed one.
9Save your people and bless your
        inheritance;
    be their shepherd and carry them
        forever.

PSALM 29
A psalm of David.

1Ascribe to the LORD, O mighty ones,
    ascribe to the LORD glory and
        strength.

---

*w*2 Or *to slander me*   *x*8 Or *To you, O my heart, he has said, "Seek my*

²Ascribe to the LORD the glory due his
  name;
    worship the LORD in the splendor of
    his^y holiness.

³The voice of the LORD is over the
    waters;
    the God of glory thunders,
    the LORD thunders over the mighty
    waters.
⁴The voice of the LORD is powerful;
    the voice of the LORD is majestic.
⁵The voice of the LORD breaks the
    cedars;
    the LORD breaks in pieces the cedars
    of Lebanon.
⁶He makes Lebanon skip like a calf,
    Sirion^z like a young wild ox.
⁷The voice of the LORD strikes
    with flashes of lightning.
⁸The voice of the LORD shakes the
    desert;
    the LORD shakes the Desert of
    Kadesh.
⁹The voice of the LORD twists the oaks^a
    and strips the forests bare.
    And in his temple all cry, "Glory!"

¹⁰The LORD sits^b enthroned over the
    flood;
    the LORD is enthroned as King
    forever.
¹¹The LORD gives strength to his people;
    the LORD blesses his people with
    peace.

PSALM 30

A psalm. A song. For the dedication of
the temple.^c Of David.

¹I will exalt you, O LORD,
    for you lifted me out of the depths

and did not let my enemies gloat
    over me.
²O LORD my God, I called to you for
    help
    and you healed me.
³O LORD, you brought me up from the
    grave^d;
    you spared me from going down
    into the pit.

⁴Sing to the LORD, you saints of his;
    praise his holy name.
⁵For his anger lasts only a moment,
    but his favor lasts a lifetime;
    weeping may remain for a night,
    but rejoicing comes in the morning.

⁶When I felt secure, I said,
    "I will never be shaken."
⁷O LORD, when you favored me,
    you made my mountain^e stand
    firm;
    but when you hid your face,
    I was dismayed.

⁸To you, O LORD, I called;
    to the Lord I cried for mercy:
⁹"What gain is there in my
    destruction,^f
    in my going down into the pit?
    Will the dust praise you?
    Will it proclaim your faithfulness?
¹⁰Hear, O LORD, and be merciful to me;
    O LORD, be my help."

¹¹You turned my wailing into dancing;
    you removed my sackcloth and
    clothed me with joy,
¹²that my heart may sing to you and not
    be silent.
    O LORD my God, I will give you
    thanks forever.

---

^y2 Or LORD with the splendor of   ^z6 That is, Mount Hermon   ^a9 Or LORD makes the deer give birth   ^b10 Or sat   ^cTitle: Or
palace   ^d3 Hebrew Sheol   ^e7 Or hill country   ^f9 Or there if I am silenced

JUNE 6 □ DAY 158
PSALMS 31–35
A Musical Manifesto

OVERVIEW Think of today's reading as forming a pyramid. The outer two psalms (31 and 35) form the foundation and deal with believers' struggles against their enemies. In each case David finds his refuge from external foes in God alone. In the next level of the pyramid (32 and 34), David faces internal woes: unconfessed sin and secret fear. In each situation the psalmist learns from his failures in the past so that he (and all who read his words) might respond rightly to similar perils in the future. The peak of the pyramid is formed by a beautiful psalm of praise to God whose "plans . . . stand firm forever" (33:11).

Psalm 31	Psalm 32	Psalm 33	Psalms 34–35
Refuge for the Ravaged	Restoration for the Repentant	Rejoicing for the Righteous	Rescue for the Rejected
God's Care over His Children			

YOUR DAILY WALK A little boy who loved to listen to music was bitterly disappointed because he could neither play nor sing. But a kindly gentleman encouraged him with these words: "There are many ways of making music. What matters is the song in your heart." That little boy—Antonio Stradivari—took the man at his word and became the world's greatest violin maker.

Music strikes in me a profound contemplation of the First Composer.

Perhaps you have an equally low estimation of your own singing ability. If so, Psalm 33:1–3 will challenge you with the privilege and responsibility of singing joyfully to the Lord. As if anticipating excuses, the psalmist opens with the command to sing. This is not just a suggestion! The character of God makes musical expression an appropriate part of worship, including instrumental arrangements (v. 2), songs of your own creation and rousing expressions of praise (v. 3). Your sovereign Creator is worthy of them all.

It's time to sing! Find a hymnbook—and, if possible, a willing friend or two—for a time of musical rejoicing in the Lord.

INSIGHT Scripture Memory Old Testament Style
Psalm 34 is one of seven acrostics in the book of Psalms. Each verse begins with a different letter of the Hebrew alphabet, a definite memory aid. In this way the reader could trace and remember David's sequence of thought.

PSALM 31
For the director of music. A psalm of David.

¹In you, O LORD, I have taken refuge;
let me never be put to shame;
deliver me in your righteousness.
²Turn your ear to me,
come quickly to my rescue;
be my rock of refuge,
a strong fortress to save me.
³Since you are my rock and my fortress,

for the sake of your name lead and guide me.
⁴Free me from the trap that is set for me,
for you are my refuge.
⁵Into your hands I commit my spirit;
redeem me, O LORD, the God of truth.

⁶I hate those who cling to worthless idols;
I trust in the LORD.
⁷I will be glad and rejoice in your love,

for you saw my affliction
and knew the anguish of my soul.
[8]You have not handed me over to the
enemy
but have set my feet in a spacious
place.

[9]Be merciful to me, O Lord, for I am in
distress;
my eyes grow weak with sorrow,
my soul and my body with grief.
[10]My life is consumed by anguish
and my years by groaning;
my strength fails because of my
affliction,[g]
and my bones grow weak.
[11]Because of all my enemies,
I am the utter contempt of my
neighbors;
I am a dread to my friends—
those who see me on the street flee
from me.
[12]I am forgotten by them as though I
were dead;
I have become like broken pottery.
[13]For I hear the slander of many;
there is terror on every side;
they conspire against me
and plot to take my life.

[14]But I trust in you, O Lord;
I say, "You are my God."
[15]My times are in your hands;
deliver me from my enemies
and from those who pursue me.
[16]Let your face shine on your servant;
save me in your unfailing love.
[17]Let me not be put to shame, O Lord,
for I have cried out to you;
but let the wicked be put to shame
and lie silent in the grave.[h]
[18]Let their lying lips be silenced,
for with pride and contempt
they speak arrogantly against the
righteous.

[19]How great is your goodness,
which you have stored up for those
who fear you,
which you bestow in the sight of men
on those who take refuge in you.
[20]In the shelter of your presence you
hide them
from the intrigues of men;
in your dwelling you keep them safe
from accusing tongues.

[21]Praise be to the Lord,
for he showed his wonderful love to
me
when I was in a besieged city.
[22]In my alarm I said,
"I am cut off from your sight!"
Yet you heard my cry for mercy
when I called to you for help.

[23]Love the Lord, all his saints!
The Lord preserves the faithful,
but the proud he pays back in full.
[24]Be strong and take heart,
all you who hope in the Lord.

PSALM 32
Of David. A *maskil.*[i]

[1]Blessed is he
whose transgressions are forgiven,
whose sins are covered.
[2]Blessed is the man
whose sin the Lord does not count
against him
and in whose spirit is no deceit.

[3]When I kept silent,
my bones wasted away
through my groaning all day long.
[4]For day and night
your hand was heavy upon me;
my strength was sapped
as in the heat of summer.   *Selah*
[5]Then I acknowledged my sin to you
and did not cover up my iniquity.
I said, "I will confess
my transgressions to the Lord"—
and you forgave
the guilt of my sin.   *Selah*

[6]Therefore let everyone who is godly
pray to you
while you may be found;
surely when the mighty waters rise,
they will not reach him.
[7]You are my hiding place;
you will protect me from trouble
and surround me with songs of
deliverance.   *Selah*

[8]I will instruct you and teach you in
the way you should go;
I will counsel you and watch over
you.
[9]Do not be like the horse or the mule,
which have no understanding
but must be controlled by bit and
bridle

---

g 10 Or *guilt*   *h* 17 Hebrew *Sheol*   *i* Title: Probably a literary or musical term

or they will not come to you.
¹⁰Many are the woes of the wicked,
    but the LORD's unfailing love
    surrounds the man who trusts in
    him.

¹¹Rejoice in the LORD and be glad, you
    righteous;
    sing, all you who are upright in
    heart!

PSALM 33

¹Sing joyfully to the LORD, you
    righteous;
    it is fitting for the upright to praise
    him.
²Praise the LORD with the harp;
    make music to him on the
    ten-stringed lyre.
³Sing to him a new song;
    play skillfully, and shout for joy.

⁴For the word of the LORD is right and
    true;
    he is faithful in all he does.
⁵The LORD loves righteousness and
    justice;
    the earth is full of his unfailing love.

⁶By the word of the LORD were the
    heavens made,
    their starry host by the breath of his
    mouth.
⁷He gathers the waters of the sea into
    jars^j;
    he puts the deep into storehouses.
⁸Let all the earth fear the LORD;
    let all the people of the world revere
    him.
⁹For he spoke, and it came to be;
    he commanded, and it stood firm.
¹⁰The LORD foils the plans of the nations;
    he thwarts the purposes of the
    peoples.
¹¹But the plans of the LORD stand firm
    forever,
    the purposes of his heart through all
    generations.

¹²Blessed is the nation whose God is the
    LORD,
    the people he chose for his
    inheritance.
¹³From heaven the LORD looks down
    and sees all mankind;
¹⁴from his dwelling place he watches
    all who live on earth—

¹⁵he who forms the hearts of all,
    who considers everything they do.
¹⁶No king is saved by the size of his
    army;
    no warrior escapes by his great
    strength.
¹⁷A horse is a vain hope for deliverance;
    despite all its great strength it
    cannot save.
¹⁸But the eyes of the LORD are on those
    who fear him,
    on those whose hope is in his
    unfailing love,
¹⁹to deliver them from death
    and keep them alive in famine.

²⁰We wait in hope for the LORD;
    he is our help and our shield.
²¹In him our hearts rejoice,
    for we trust in his holy name.
²²May your unfailing love rest upon us,
    O LORD,
    even as we put our hope in you.

PSALM 34^k
Of David. When he pretended to be
insane before Abimelech, who drove him
away, and he left.

¹I will extol the LORD at all times;
    his praise will always be on my lips.
²My soul will boast in the LORD;
    let the afflicted hear and rejoice.
³Glorify the LORD with me;
    let us exalt his name together.

⁴I sought the LORD, and he answered
    me;
    he delivered me from all my fears.
⁵Those who look to him are radiant;
    their faces are never covered with
    shame.
⁶This poor man called, and the LORD
    heard him;
    he saved him out of all his troubles.
⁷The angel of the LORD encamps around
    those who fear him,
    and he delivers them.

⁸Taste and see that the LORD is good;
    blessed is the man who takes refuge
    in him.
⁹Fear the LORD, you his saints,
    for those who fear him lack nothing.
¹⁰The lions may grow weak and hungry,
    but those who seek the LORD lack no
    good thing.

---

^j7 Or *sea as into a heap*   ^kThis psalm is an acrostic poem, the verses of which begin with the successive letters of the Hebrew
alphabet.

¹¹Come, my children, listen to me;
  I will teach you the fear of the LORD.
¹²Whoever of you loves life
  and desires to see many good days,
¹³keep your tongue from evil
  and your lips from speaking lies.
¹⁴Turn from evil and do good;
  seek peace and pursue it.

¹⁵The eyes of the LORD are on the
    righteous
  and his ears are attentive to their
    cry;
¹⁶the face of the LORD is against those
    who do evil,
  to cut off the memory of them from
    the earth.

¹⁷The righteous cry out, and the LORD
    hears them;
  he delivers them from all their
    troubles.
¹⁸The LORD is close to the brokenhearted
  and saves those who are crushed in
    spirit.

¹⁹A righteous man may have many
    troubles,
  but the LORD delivers him from them
    all;
²⁰he protects all his bones,
  not one of them will be broken.

²¹Evil will slay the wicked;
  the foes of the righteous will be
    condemned.
²²The LORD redeems his servants;
  no one will be condemned who
    takes refuge in him.

PSALM 35
Of David.

¹Contend, O LORD, with those who
    contend with me;
  fight against those who fight against
    me.
²Take up shield and buckler;
  arise and come to my aid.
³Brandish spear and javelin^l
  against those who pursue me.
  Say to my soul,
  "I am your salvation."

⁴May those who seek my life
  be disgraced and put to shame;
  may those who plot my ruin
  be turned back in dismay.

⁵May they be like chaff before the
    wind,
  with the angel of the LORD driving
    them away;
⁶may their path be dark and slippery,
  with the angel of the LORD pursuing
    them.
⁷Since they hid their net for me without
    cause
  and without cause dug a pit for me,
⁸may ruin overtake them by surprise—
  may the net they hid entangle them,
  may they fall into the pit, to their
    ruin.
⁹Then my soul will rejoice in the LORD
  and delight in his salvation.
¹⁰My whole being will exclaim,
  "Who is like you, O LORD?
  You rescue the poor from those too
    strong for them,
  the poor and needy from those who
    rob them."

¹¹Ruthless witnesses come forward;
  they question me on things I know
    nothing about.
¹²They repay me evil for good
  and leave my soul forlorn.
¹³Yet when they were ill, I put on
    sackcloth
  and humbled myself with fasting.
  When my prayers returned to me
    unanswered,
¹⁴ I went about mourning
  as though for my friend or brother.
  I bowed my head in grief
  as though weeping for my mother.
¹⁵But when I stumbled, they gathered in
    glee;
  attackers gathered against me when
    I was unaware.
  They slandered me without ceasing.
¹⁶Like the ungodly they maliciously
    mocked^m;
  they gnashed their teeth at me.
¹⁷O Lord, how long will you look on?
  Rescue my life from their ravages,
  my precious life from these lions.
¹⁸I will give you thanks in the great
    assembly;
  among throngs of people I will
    praise you.

¹⁹Let not those gloat over me
  who are my enemies without cause;

^l3 Or *and block the way*   ^m16 Septuagint; Hebrew may mean *ungodly circle of mockers.*

let not those who hate me without
   reason
  maliciously wink the eye.
²⁰They do not speak peaceably,
  but devise false accusations
  against those who live quietly in the
     land.
²¹They gape at me and say, "Aha! Aha!
  With our own eyes we have seen it."

²²O LORD, you have seen this; be not
     silent.
  Do not be far from me, O Lord.
²³Awake, and rise to my defense!
  Contend for me, my God and Lord.
²⁴Vindicate me in your righteousness,
     O LORD my God;
  do not let them gloat over me.

²⁵Do not let them think, "Aha, just what
     we wanted!"
  or say, "We have swallowed him
     up."
²⁶May all who gloat over my distress
     be put to shame and confusion;
  may all who exalt themselves over me
     be clothed with shame and disgrace.
²⁷May those who delight in my
     vindication
  shout for joy and gladness;
  may they always say, "The LORD be
     exalted,
  who delights in the well-being of
     his servant."
²⁸My tongue will speak of your
     righteousness
  and of your praises all day long.

JUNE 7 ☐ DAY 159
Hitting the Prophetic Bull's-Eye

LOOK BACK The book of Job introduced you to the *sovereignty* of God. The book of Psalms will help you learn to *worship* God.

Psalms is the longest book in the Bible, and you'll need an entire month to read your way through it. But don't let the size of the book overwhelm you. Think of it as 150 "songs of the heart"—poems set to music by David, Asaph, Moses, Solomon and others as they walked with God and reflected on the many facets of his character.

You'll find a psalm for every mood: excitement and depression, gladness and gloom, expectation and exasperation. The human experiences behind the psalms bring the authors' words to life (don't miss the superscriptions at the beginning of many of the psalms—they give important historical information about the occasion on which the psalm was written). You may want to review what you have already read in 2 Samuel and 1 Chronicles as a backdrop for the psalms David wrote.

Psalms is more than a big book of meter and verse. Think of it as God's love letter to you. He wants you to get to know him better, for to know him is to love him as Shepherd, Guide, Provider, Protector and King.

LOOK UP The Psalms are more than a treasure chest of poetry and praise. They are also the source of many of the messianic prophecies in the Old Testament.

The humble Carpenter of Nazareth was also the mighty Architect of the Universe.

Hundreds of years before the birth of Christ, God used the pen of the psalmist to predict with remarkable precision the details concerning the birth, life, ministry, death and resurrection of Jesus of Nazareth. As you continue to read through the Old Testament, find a spiral notebook and begin a "Portfolio of Prophecies" about the Messiah. Here is a partial list from the Psalms to get you started:

A Messianic Prediction in the Psalms . . .	. . . Fulfilled in the New Testament
All things would be put under his feet (8:6).	Hebrews 2:8
He would be resurrected from the dead (16:10).	Mark 16:6–7

He would be forsaken by God (22:1).	Matthew 27:46
He would be scorned and mocked (22:7–8).	Luke 23:35
His hands and feet would be pierced (22:16).	John 20:25, 27
Soldiers would gamble for his clothes (22:18).	Matthew 27:35–36
Not one of his bones would be broken (34:20).	John 19:32–36
He would be hated without a cause (35:19).	John 15:25
Zeal for God's house would consume him (69:9).	John 2:17
He would be given vinegar/wine mixed with gall to drink (69:21).	Matthew 27:34

 LOOK AHEAD Imagine that you have been given the task of predicting the birth of a child eight hundred years from today. You must correctly predict his name, place of birth, time of birth, circumstances surrounding his birth, how he will live, how he will minister, how he will die and what his final words will be before he dies.

"Why, that's impossible!" you say. And you'd be quite right . . . unless, of course, you were declaring God's message with a prophet's unerring accuracy. Aren't you glad you serve a God like that? Don't you wish everyone did? Share what you have learned about the messianic prophecies of Jesus with one other person this week, and invite him or her to meet the Messiah in a personal, life-changing way.

JUNE 8 □ DAY 160
PSALMS 36–41
Looking Up from Down Under

 OVERVIEW Every honest believer admits to having ups and downs, and David is no exception. In the face of great wickedness, he takes comfort in God's loving care (Psalms 36–37). Despite inner conflict with guilt and discouragement, he finds strength in God's help (38–39). Out of the darkness of his circumstances, David proclaims a shining testimony of God's deliverance and mercy (40–41). No matter what life may bring, David knows that in God he has found a source of strength to rise above his circumstances rather than sink beneath them.

Psalms 36–37	Psalms 38–39	Psalms 40–41
Opposition from Without	Oppression from Within	Overcoming by God's Mercy
Trials	Turmoil	Testimony

 YOUR DAILY WALK Think about it: "Ninety-five percent of all adults surveyed readily admit to having occasional times of depression; the other 5 percent were too depressed to respond to the survey." Does that humorous thought depress you or encourage you?

A head hung in despair cannot scan the horizon of God's provision.

Discouragement, depression, personal loss, a sense of hopelessness—they're the universal experience of people. Psalm 40 describes one such moment in the life of King David—a time he likened to being in a "slimy pit." There he learned that the question is not, Will I find myself from time to time in the pits?—you will! Rather, the question is, What will I do once I find myself there?

David discovered a way to move from the mire (v. 2) to the choir (v. 3). Resisting the temptation to complain, get bitter, give up or grow angry, David cried out to God, waited for God to answer and carefully gave God the credit when it came!

Take time today to call up a friend you sense may be "in the pits," and share David's testimony from Psalm 40. As you reach out to someone in need, you'll be amazed how God will encourage you both!

INSIGHT Lend Me Your Ears for Life
Israel's law made provision for a servant who, having fulfilled his obligations of service, loved his master and wanted to devote the rest of his life to his lord's service. This commitment was signified and sealed by piercing the servant's ear, a practice alluded to in Psalm 40:6. Read about this picturesque symbol of total devotion in Deuteronomy 15:12–17.

PSALM 36
For the director of music. Of David the servant of the LORD.

[1]An oracle is within my heart
   concerning the sinfulness of the
      wicked:[n]
There is no fear of God
   before his eyes.
[2]For in his own eyes he flatters himself
   too much to detect or hate his sin.
[3]The words of his mouth are wicked
      and deceitful;
   he has ceased to be wise and to do
      good.
[4]Even on his bed he plots evil;
   he commits himself to a sinful
      course
   and does not reject what is wrong.

[5]Your love, O LORD, reaches to the
      heavens,
   your faithfulness to the skies.
[6]Your righteousness is like the mighty
      mountains,
   your justice like the great deep.
O LORD, you preserve both man and
      beast.
[7]   How priceless is your unfailing love!
Both high and low among men
   find[o] refuge in the shadow of your
      wings.
[8]They feast on the abundance of your
      house;
   you give them drink from your river
      of delights.
[9]For with you is the fountain of life;
   in your light we see light.

[10]Continue your love to those who
      know you,
   your righteousness to the upright in
      heart.
[11]May the foot of the proud not come
      against me,
   nor the hand of the wicked drive me
      away.
[12]See how the evildoers lie fallen—
   thrown down, not able to rise!

PSALM 37[p]
Of David.

[1]Do not fret because of evil men
   or be envious of those who do
      wrong;
[2]for like the grass they will soon
      wither,
   like green plants they will soon die
      away.

[3]Trust in the LORD and do good;
   dwell in the land and enjoy safe
      pasture.
[4]Delight yourself in the LORD
   and he will give you the desires of
      your heart.

[5]Commit your way to the LORD;
   trust in him and he will do this:
[6]He will make your righteousness shine
      like the dawn,
   the justice of your cause like the
      noonday sun.

[7]Be still before the LORD and wait
      patiently for him;
   do not fret when men succeed in
      their ways,

---

[n]1 Or *heart: | Sin proceeds from the wicked.*   [o]7 Or *love, O God! | Men find; or love! | Both heavenly beings and men | find*   [p]This psalm is an acrostic poem, the stanzas of which begin with the successive letters of the Hebrew alphabet.

when they carry out their wicked
  schemes.

8Refrain from anger and turn from
    wrath;
  do not fret—it leads only to evil.
9For evil men will be cut off,
  but those who hope in the LORD will
    inherit the land.

10A little while, and the wicked will be
    no more;
  though you look for them, they will
    not be found.
11But the meek will inherit the land
  and enjoy great peace.

12The wicked plot against the righteous
  and gnash their teeth at them;
13but the Lord laughs at the wicked,
  for he knows their day is coming.

14The wicked draw the sword
  and bend the bow
 to bring down the poor and needy,
  to slay those whose ways are
    upright.
15But their swords will pierce their own
    hearts,
  and their bows will be broken.

16Better the little that the righteous have
  than the wealth of many wicked;
17for the power of the wicked will be
    broken,
  but the LORD upholds the righteous.

18The days of the blameless are known
    to the LORD,
  and their inheritance will endure
    forever.
19In times of disaster they will not
    wither;
  in days of famine they will enjoy
    plenty.

20But the wicked will perish:
  The LORD's enemies will be like the
    beauty of the fields,
  they will vanish—vanish like smoke.

21The wicked borrow and do not repay,
  but the righteous give generously;
22those the LORD blesses will inherit the
    land,
  but those he curses will be cut off.

23If the LORD delights in a man's way,
  he makes his steps firm;
24though he stumble, he will not fall,

q37 Or there will be posterity   r38 Or posterity

for the LORD upholds him with his
    hand.

25I was young and now I am old,
  yet I have never seen the righteous
    forsaken
  or their children begging bread.
26They are always generous and lend
    freely;
  their children will be blessed.

27Turn from evil and do good;
  then you will dwell in the land
    forever.
28For the LORD loves the just
  and will not forsake his faithful
    ones.

 They will be protected forever,
  but the offspring of the wicked will
    be cut off;
29the righteous will inherit the land
  and dwell in it forever.

30The mouth of the righteous man utters
    wisdom,
  and his tongue speaks what is just.
31The law of his God is in his heart;
  his feet do not slip.

32The wicked lie in wait for the
    righteous,
  seeking their very lives;
33but the LORD will not leave them in
    their power
  or let them be condemned when
    brought to trial.

34Wait for the LORD
  and keep his way.
 He will exalt you to inherit the land;
  when the wicked are cut off, you
    will see it.

35I have seen a wicked and ruthless man
  flourishing like a green tree in its
    native soil,
36but he soon passed away and was no
    more;
  though I looked for him, he could
    not be found.

37Consider the blameless, observe the
    upright;
  there is a futureq for the man of
    peace.
38But all sinners will be destroyed;
  the futurer of the wicked will be
    cut off.

[39]The salvation of the righteous comes
from the LORD;
he is their stronghold in time of
trouble.
[40]The LORD helps them and delivers
them;
he delivers them from the wicked
and saves them,
because they take refuge in him.

PSALM 38
A psalm of David. A petition.

[1]O LORD, do not rebuke me in your
anger
or discipline me in your wrath.
[2]For your arrows have pierced me,
and your hand has come down
upon me.
[3]Because of your wrath there is no
health in my body;
my bones have no soundness
because of my sin.
[4]My guilt has overwhelmed me
like a burden too heavy to bear.

[5]My wounds fester and are loathsome
because of my sinful folly.
[6]I am bowed down and brought very
low;
all day long I go about mourning.
[7]My back is filled with searing pain;
there is no health in my body.
[8]I am feeble and utterly crushed;
I groan in anguish of heart.

[9]All my longings lie open before you,
O Lord;
my sighing is not hidden from you.
[10]My heart pounds, my strength fails
me;
even the light has gone from my
eyes.
[11]My friends and companions avoid me
because of my wounds;
my neighbors stay far away.
[12]Those who seek my life set their traps,
those who would harm me talk of
my ruin;
all day long they plot deception.

[13]I am like a deaf man, who cannot
hear,
like a mute, who cannot open his
mouth;
[14]I have become like a man who does
not hear,
whose mouth can offer no reply.
[15]I wait for you, O LORD;

you will answer, O Lord my God.
[16]For I said, "Do not let them gloat
or exalt themselves over me when
my foot slips."

[17]For I am about to fall,
and my pain is ever with me.
[18]I confess my iniquity;
I am troubled by my sin.
[19]Many are those who are my vigorous
enemies;
those who hate me without reason
are numerous.
[20]Those who repay my good with evil
slander me when I pursue what is
good.

[21]O LORD, do not forsake me;
be not far from me, O my God.
[22]Come quickly to help me,
O Lord my Savior.

PSALM 39
For the director of music. For Jeduthun.
A psalm of David.

[1]I said, "I will watch my ways
and keep my tongue from sin;
I will put a muzzle on my mouth
as long as the wicked are in my
presence."
[2]But when I was silent and still,
not even saying anything good,
my anguish increased.
[3]My heart grew hot within me,
and as I meditated, the fire burned;
then I spoke with my tongue:

[4]"Show me, O LORD, my life's end
and the number of my days;
let me know how fleeting is my life.
[5]You have made my days a mere
handbreadth;
the span of my years is as nothing
before you.
Each man's life is but a breath. *Selah*
[6]Man is a mere phantom as he goes to
and fro:
He bustles about, but only in vain;
he heaps up wealth, not knowing
who will get it.

[7]"But now, Lord, what do I look for?
My hope is in you.
[8]Save me from all my transgressions;
do not make me the scorn of fools.
[9]I was silent; I would not open my
mouth,

for you are the one who has done
    this.
[10]Remove your scourge from me;
    I am overcome by the blow of your
        hand.
[11]You rebuke and discipline men for
        their sin;
    you consume their wealth like a
        moth—
    each man is but a breath.   *Selah*

[12]"Hear my prayer, O LORD,
    listen to my cry for help;
    be not deaf to my weeping.
For I dwell with you as an alien,
    a stranger, as all my fathers were.
[13]Look away from me, that I may rejoice
        again
    before I depart and am no more."

PSALM 40

For the director of music. Of David.
A psalm.

[1]I waited patiently for the LORD;
    he turned to me and heard my cry.
[2]He lifted me out of the slimy pit,
    out of the mud and mire;
he set my feet on a rock
    and gave me a firm place to stand.
[3]He put a new song in my mouth,
    a hymn of praise to our God.
Many will see and fear
    and put their trust in the LORD.

[4]Blessed is the man
    who makes the LORD his trust,
who does not look to the proud,
    to those who turn aside to false
        gods.[s]
[5]Many, O LORD my God,
    are the wonders you have done.
The things you planned for us
    no one can recount to you;
were I to speak and tell of them,
    they would be too many to declare.

[6]Sacrifice and offering you did not
        desire,
    but my ears you have pierced[t,u];
burnt offerings and sin offerings
    you did not require.
[7]Then I said, "Here I am, I have come—
    it is written about me in the scroll.[v]
[8]I desire to do your will, O my God;
    your law is within my heart."

[9]I proclaim righteousness in the great
        assembly;
    I do not seal my lips,
    as you know, O LORD.
[10]I do not hide your righteousness in
        my heart;
    I speak of your faithfulness and
        salvation.
    I do not conceal your love and your
        truth
    from the great assembly.

[11]Do not withhold your mercy from me,
        O LORD;
    may your love and your truth
        always protect me.
[12]For troubles without number surround
        me;
    my sins have overtaken me, and I
        cannot see.
They are more than the hairs of my
        head,
    and my heart fails within me.

[13]Be pleased, O LORD, to save me;
    O LORD, come quickly to help me.
[14]May all who seek to take my life
    be put to shame and confusion;
may all who desire my ruin
    be turned back in disgrace.
[15]May those who say to me, "Aha! Aha!"
    be appalled at their own shame.
[16]But may all who seek you
    rejoice and be glad in you;
may those who love your salvation
        always say,
    "The LORD be exalted!"

[17]Yet I am poor and needy;
    may the Lord think of me.
You are my help and my deliverer;
    O my God, do not delay.

PSALM 41

For the director of music. A psalm
of David.

[1]Blessed is he who has regard for the
        weak;
    the LORD delivers him in times of
        trouble.
[2]The LORD will protect him and
        preserve his life;
    he will bless him in the land
    and not surrender him to the desire
        of his foes.

[s]4 Or *to falsehood*   [t]6 Hebrew; Septuagint *but a body you have prepared for me* (see also Symmachus and Theodotion)
[u]6 Or *opened*   [v]7 Or *come / with the scroll written for me*

³The LORD will sustain him on his
  sickbed
and restore him from his bed of
  illness.

⁴I said, "O LORD, have mercy on me;
  heal me, for I have sinned against
  you."
⁵My enemies say of me in malice,
  "When will he die and his name
  perish?"
⁶Whenever one comes to see me,
  he speaks falsely, while his heart
  gathers slander;
then he goes out and spreads it
  abroad.

⁷All my enemies whisper together
  against me;
they imagine the worst for me,
  saying,

⁸"A vile disease has beset him;
  he will never get up from the place
  where he lies."
⁹Even my close friend, whom I trusted,
  he who shared my bread,
  has lifted up his heel against me.

¹⁰But you, O LORD, have mercy on me;
  raise me up, that I may repay them.
¹¹I know that you are pleased with me,
  for my enemy does not triumph
  over me.
¹²In my integrity you uphold me
  and set me in your presence forever.

¹³Praise be to the LORD, the God of
  Israel,
from everlasting to everlasting.
  Amen and Amen.

JUNE 9 ☐ DAY 161
PSALMS 42–49
A Mighty Fortress

 OVERVIEW Book II of Psalms begins with a collection of psalms attributed to the Sons of Korah. The first two express the longing of the troubled soul for God (Psalms 42–43), followed by a prayer for victory in the midst of trouble (44). By contrast, Psalms 45–48 extol God's majesty (45), protection (46) and power (47–48). The section concludes with wise instruction concerning true riches (49).

Psalms 42–44	Psalms 45–48	Psalm 49
Appealing for God's Help	Acclaiming God's Greatness	Acknowledging God's Sufficiency
Yearning	Yielding	

 YOUR DAILY WALK Every tomorrow has two handles: the handle of anxiety and the handle of faith. Which will you use to get a "handle" on your day?

Anxiety never strengthens you for tomorrow; it only weakens you for today.

Second only to the fear of standing before a large audience is the widespread phobia known as "fear of the unknown." In a day when pressing problems greatly outnumber available solutions in matters of national and international concern, where do you turn for stability?

You turn to the same refuge the psalmist found.

In Psalm 46 the Sons of Korah portray the worst calamities imaginable upon earth: earthquakes, landslides and a raging sea (vv. 2–3). And when everything seems to be breaking loose, they proclaim that there remains an immovable Refuge: the God of Israel.

Before you close your Bible today, follow the instructions of verse 10. Remove as many distractions as possible, and take a few minutes to be silent before the Lord. Turn over to him any fears you may be harboring; then write down the words of Psalm 46:10 on a three-by-five-inch card and carry it with you throughout the day. When fear, like acid, begins to eat away at your peace of mind, pull out your reminder from the Sons of Korah and refresh your memory. Your Refuge "is the same yesterday and today and forever" (Hebrews 13:8).

 INSIGHT And Now a Word about the Authors
The sons of Korah were Levites, descendants of the man who died for his rebellion against Moses (Numbers 16). One part of the family became temple gatekeepers (1 Chronicles 9:19) and another the singers and musicians in the temple choir (1 Chronicles 6:31–47).

BOOK II
Psalms 42–72

P S A L M   4 2ʷ
For the director of music. A *maskil*ˣ of
the Sons of Korah.

¹As the deer pants for streams of
water,
  so my soul pants for you, O God.
²My soul thirsts for God, for the living
God.
  When can I go and meet with God?
³My tears have been my food
day and night,
while men say to me all day long,
  "Where is your God?"
⁴These things I remember
  as I pour out my soul:
how I used to go with the multitude,
  leading the procession to the house
    of God,
with shouts of joy and thanksgiving
among the festive throng.

⁵Why are you downcast, O my soul?
  Why so disturbed within me?
Put your hope in God,
  for I will yet praise him,
  my Savior and ⁶my God.

Myʸ soul is downcast within me;
  therefore I will remember you
from the land of the Jordan,
  the heights of Hermon—from Mount
    Mizar.
⁷Deep calls to deep
  in the roar of your waterfalls;
all your waves and breakers
  have swept over me.

⁸By day the Lᴏʀᴅ directs his love,
  at night his song is with me—
  a prayer to the God of my life.

⁹I say to God my Rock,
  "Why have you forgotten me?
Why must I go about mourning,
  oppressed by the enemy?"
¹⁰My bones suffer mortal agony
  as my foes taunt me,
saying to me all day long,
  "Where is your God?"

¹¹Why are you downcast, O my
soul?
  Why so disturbed within me?
Put your hope in God,
  for I will yet praise him,
  my Savior and my God.

P S A L M   4 3ʷ
¹Vindicate me, O God,
  and plead my cause against an
    ungodly nation;
  rescue me from deceitful and wicked
    men.
²You are God my stronghold.
  Why have you rejected me?
Why must I go about mourning,
  oppressed by the enemy?
³Send forth your light and your truth,
  let them guide me;
let them bring me to your holy
  mountain,
  to the place where you dwell.
⁴Then will I go to the altar of God,
  to God, my joy and my delight.
I will praise you with the harp,
  O God, my God.

⁵Why are you downcast, O my
soul?
  Why so disturbed within me?
Put your hope in God,
  for I will yet praise him,
  my Savior and my God.

ʷIn many Hebrew manuscripts Psalms 42 and 43 constitute one psalm.   ˣTitle: Probably a literary or musical term
ʸ5,6 A few Hebrew manuscripts, Septuagint and Syriac; most Hebrew manuscripts *praise him for his saving help.* / ⁶O my
God, my

PSALM 44

For the director of music. Of the Sons of
Korah. A *maskil*.[z]

[1]We have heard with our ears, O God;
  our fathers have told us
what you did in their days,
  in days long ago.
[2]With your hand you drove out the
    nations
  and planted our fathers;
you crushed the peoples
  and made our fathers flourish.
[3]It was not by their sword that they
    won the land,
  nor did their arm bring them
    victory;
it was your right hand, your arm,
  and the light of your face, for you
    loved them.

[4]You are my King and my God,
  who decrees[a] victories for Jacob.
[5]Through you we push back our
    enemies;
  through your name we trample our
    foes.
[6]I do not trust in my bow,
  my sword does not bring me
    victory;
[7]but you give us victory over our
    enemies,
  you put our adversaries to shame.
[8]In God we make our boast all day
    long,
  and we will praise your name
    forever.   *Selah*

[9]But now you have rejected and
    humbled us;
  you no longer go out with our
    armies.
[10]You made us retreat before the enemy,
  and our adversaries have plundered
    us.
[11]You gave us up to be devoured like
    sheep
  and have scattered us among the
    nations.
[12]You sold your people for a pittance,
  gaining nothing from their sale.

[13]You have made us a reproach to our
    neighbors,
  the scorn and derision of those
    around us.
[14]You have made us a byword among
    the nations;

the peoples shake their heads at us.
[15]My disgrace is before me all day long,
  and my face is covered with shame
[16]at the taunts of those who reproach
    and revile me,
  because of the enemy, who is bent
    on revenge.

[17]All this happened to us,
  though we had not forgotten you
  or been false to your covenant.
[18]Our hearts had not turned back;
  our feet had not strayed from your
    path.
[19]But you crushed us and made us a
    haunt for jackals
  and covered us over with deep
    darkness.

[20]If we had forgotten the name of our
    God
  or spread out our hands to a foreign
    god,
[21]would not God have discovered it,
  since he knows the secrets of the
    heart?
[22]Yet for your sake we face death all
    day long;
  we are considered as sheep to be
    slaughtered.

[23]Awake, O Lord! Why do you sleep?
  Rouse yourself! Do not reject us
    forever.
[24]Why do you hide your face
  and forget our misery and
    oppression?

[25]We are brought down to the dust;
  our bodies cling to the ground.
[26]Rise up and help us;
  redeem us because of your unfailing
    love.

PSALM 45

For the director of music. To ⌊the tune of⌋
"Lilies." Of the Sons of Korah. A *maskil*.[z]
A wedding song.

[1]My heart is stirred by a noble theme
  as I recite my verses for the king;
  my tongue is the pen of a skillful
    writer.

[2]You are the most excellent of men
  and your lips have been anointed
    with grace,
  since God has blessed you forever.

[z] Title: Probably a literary or musical term   [a] 4 Septuagint, Aquila and Syriac; Hebrew *King, O God; / command*

³Gird your sword upon your side,
    O mighty one;
clothe yourself with splendor and
    majesty.
⁴In your majesty ride forth victoriously
    in behalf of truth, humility and
    righteousness;
let your right hand display awesome
    deeds.
⁵Let your sharp arrows pierce the
      hearts of the king's enemies;
let the nations fall beneath your feet.
⁶Your throne, O God, will last for ever
    and ever;
a scepter of justice will be the
    scepter of your kingdom.
⁷You love righteousness and hate
    wickedness;
therefore God, your God, has set
    you above your companions
by anointing you with the oil of joy.
⁸All your robes are fragrant with myrrh
    and aloes and cassia;
from palaces adorned with ivory
    the music of the strings makes you
    glad.
⁹Daughters of kings are among your
    honored women;
at your right hand is the royal bride
    in gold of Ophir.

¹⁰Listen, O daughter, consider and give
    ear:
Forget your people and your father's
    house.
¹¹The king is enthralled by your beauty;
    honor him, for he is your lord.
¹²The Daughter of Tyre will come with a
    gift,ᵇ
men of wealth will seek your favor.

¹³All glorious is the princess within ˌher
    chamber⌟;
her gown is interwoven with gold.
¹⁴In embroidered garments she is led to
    the king;
her virgin companions follow her
    and are brought to you.
¹⁵They are led in with joy and gladness;
    they enter the palace of the king.

¹⁶Your sons will take the place of your
    fathers;
you will make them princes
    throughout the land.
¹⁷I will perpetuate your memory
    through all generations;

therefore the nations will praise you
    for ever and ever.

PSALM 46
For the director of music. Of the Sons of
Korah. According to *alamoth.*ᶜ A song.

¹God is our refuge and strength,
    an ever-present help in trouble.
²Therefore we will not fear, though the
    earth give way
and the mountains fall into the heart
    of the sea,
³though its waters roar and foam
    and the mountains quake with their
    surging.   *Selah*

⁴There is a river whose streams make
    glad the city of God,
the holy place where the Most High
    dwells.
⁵God is within her, she will not fall;
    God will help her at break of day.
⁶Nations are in uproar, kingdoms fall;
    he lifts his voice, the earth melts.

⁷The Lord Almighty is with us;
    the God of Jacob is our fortress.
                    Selah

⁸Come and see the works of the Lord,
    the desolations he has brought on
    the earth.
⁹He makes wars cease to the ends of
    the earth;
he breaks the bow and shatters the
    spear,
he burns the shieldsᵈ with fire.
¹⁰"Be still, and know that I am God;
    I will be exalted among the nations,
    I will be exalted in the earth."

¹¹The Lord Almighty is with us;
    the God of Jacob is our fortress.
                    Selah

PSALM 47
For the director of music. Of the Sons of
Korah. A psalm.

¹Clap your hands, all you nations;
    shout to God with cries of joy.
²How awesome is the Lord Most High,
    the great King over all the earth!
³He subdued nations under us,
    peoples under our feet.
⁴He chose our inheritance for us,
    the pride of Jacob, whom he loved.
                    Selah

ᵇ12 Or *A Tyrian robe is among the gifts*   ᶜTitle: Probably a musical term   ᵈ9 Or *chariots*

⁵God has ascended amid shouts of joy,
  the Lord amid the sounding of
    trumpets.
⁶Sing praises to God, sing praises;
  sing praises to our King, sing
    praises.

⁷For God is the King of all the earth;
  sing to him a psalm*e* of praise.
⁸God reigns over the nations;
  God is seated on his holy throne.
⁹The nobles of the nations assemble
  as the people of the God of
    Abraham,
for the kings*f* of the earth belong to
    God;
  he is greatly exalted.

PSALM 48
A song. A psalm of the Sons of Korah.

¹Great is the Lord, and most worthy of
    praise,
  in the city of our God, his holy
    mountain.
²It is beautiful in its loftiness,
  the joy of the whole earth.
Like the utmost heights of Zaphon*g* is
    Mount Zion,
  the*h* city of the Great King.
³God is in her citadels;
  he has shown himself to be her
    fortress.

⁴When the kings joined forces,
  when they advanced together,
⁵they saw ⌐her⌐ and were astounded;
  they fled in terror.
⁶Trembling seized them there,
  pain like that of a woman in labor.
⁷You destroyed them like ships of
    Tarshish
  shattered by an east wind.

⁸As we have heard,
  so have we seen
in the city of the Lord Almighty,
  in the city of our God:
God makes her secure forever.   *Selah*

⁹Within your temple, O God,
  we meditate on your unfailing love.
¹⁰Like your name, O God,
  your praise reaches to the ends of
    the earth;
  your right hand is filled with
    righteousness.

¹¹Mount Zion rejoices,
  the villages of Judah are glad
because of your judgments.

¹²Walk about Zion, go around her,
  count her towers,
¹³consider well her ramparts,
  view her citadels,
  that you may tell of them to the next
    generation.
¹⁴For this God is our God for ever and
    ever;
  he will be our guide even to the
    end.

PSALM 49
For the director of music. Of the Sons of
Korah. A psalm.

¹Hear this, all you peoples;
  listen, all who live in this world,
²both low and high,
  rich and poor alike:
³My mouth will speak words of
    wisdom;
  the utterance from my heart will
    give understanding.
⁴I will turn my ear to a proverb;
  with the harp I will expound my
    riddle:

⁵Why should I fear when evil days
    come,
  when wicked deceivers surround
    me—
⁶those who trust in their wealth
  and boast of their great riches?
⁷No man can redeem the life of another
  or give to God a ransom for him—
⁸the ransom for a life is costly,
  no payment is ever enough—
⁹that he should live on forever
  and not see decay.

¹⁰For all can see that wise men die;
  the foolish and the senseless alike
    perish
  and leave their wealth to others.
¹¹Their tombs will remain their houses*i*
    forever,
  their dwellings for endless
    generations,
  though they had*j* named lands
    after themselves.

---

*e*7 Or *a maskil* (probably a literary or musical term)   *f*9 Or *shields*   *g*2 *Zaphon* can refer to a sacred mountain or the
direction north.   *h*2 Or *earth, / Mount Zion, on the northern side / of the*   *i*11 Septuagint and Syriac; Hebrew *In their thoughts
their houses will remain*   *j*11 Or / *for they have*

¹²But man, despite his riches, does not endure;
he is[k] like the beasts that perish.

¹³This is the fate of those who trust in themselves,
and of their followers, who approve their sayings.   *Selah*

¹⁴Like sheep they are destined for the grave,[l]
and death will feed on them.
The upright will rule over them in the morning;
their forms will decay in the grave,[l]
far from their princely mansions.

¹⁵But God will redeem my life[m] from the grave;
he will surely take me to himself.   *Selah*

¹⁶Do not be overawed when a man grows rich,
when the splendor of his house increases;

¹⁷for he will take nothing with him when he dies,
his splendor will not descend with him.

¹⁸Though while he lived he counted himself blessed—
and men praise you when you prosper—

¹⁹he will join the generation of his fathers,
who will never see the light ⌊of life⌋.

²⁰A man who has riches without understanding
is like the beasts that perish.

[k]12 Hebrew; Septuagint and Syriac read verse 12 the same as verse 20.   [l]14 Hebrew *Sheol*; also in verse 15   [m]15 Or *soul*

JUNE 10 ☐ DAY 162
PSALMS 50–54
Betrayed but Triumphant

OVERVIEW God in his righteousness deals with sin in the lives of believers and unbelievers alike. For those who claim a false righteousness characterized by outward devotion but inward wickedness, there is warning and rebuke (Psalm 50). For those who acknowledge and turn from sin, there is forgiveness and restoration (51). The evil liar (52) and the foolish atheist (53) face destruction, but the righteous one who suffers at the hands of evil men can trust in God's ultimate victory (54).

Psalm 50	Psalm 51	Psalms 52–53	Psalm 54
Conviction of the Hypocrite	Confession of the Penitent	Condemnation of the Treacherous	Comfort for the Afflicted
God, the Righteous Judge			

You never so touch the ocean of God's love as when you forgive and love your enemies.

YOUR DAILY WALK Take it from David: There is something worse than being wounded by an enemy—and that is being wounded by a friend. And when a trusted associate or fellow worker has stabbed you in the back, how should you handle the natural feelings of resentment that come?

Answer: Handle them with prayer. When Doeg the Edomite reported David's whereabouts to King Saul, it must have come as no surprise to either Saul or David, for Doeg was a known ally of the king. But when the Ziphites—whose border town of Keilah David had personally rescued from a Philistine onslaught (1 Samuel 23:1–5)—betrayed their deliverer, the sting must have been intense.

Anger . . . bitterness . . . revenge . . . a desire to run. All are natural responses to betrayal. But none resolves the issue or helps the one betrayed. For that you must turn to God, who alone can heal the wound with a spirit of forgiveness and love. (See David's example in 52:8–9; 54:6–7; 55:22.)

Have you been wounded by a friend in recent days? Then finish this prayer: "Lord, you know I have every right to treat _____ as my enemy. Though I could respond naturally, help me in your strength to respond supernaturally."

 INSIGHT The Carbon Copy Psalm
If upon reading Psalm 53 you get the distinct impression you have read that material before, you're right! Psalms 14 and 53 are almost identical. The titles differ slightly, one verse is omitted (which one?) and the name *God* is substituted for *Lord* in three places in Psalm 53. Upon reflection, can you suggest a reason why the message of Psalm 14 might be important enough to repeat in Psalm 53?

PSALM 50
A psalm of Asaph.

¹The Mighty One, God, the Lord,
  speaks and summons the earth
  from the rising of the sun to the
    place where it sets.
²From Zion, perfect in beauty,
  God shines forth.
³Our God comes and will not be silent;
  a fire devours before him,
  and around him a tempest rages.
⁴He summons the heavens above,
  and the earth, that he may judge his
    people:
⁵"Gather to me my consecrated ones,
  who made a covenant with me by
    sacrifice."
⁶And the heavens proclaim his
    righteousness,
  for God himself is judge.   *Selah*

⁷"Hear, O my people, and I will speak,
  O Israel, and I will testify against
    you:
  I am God, your God.
⁸I do not rebuke you for your sacrifices
  or your burnt offerings, which are
    ever before me.
⁹I have no need of a bull from your
    stall
  or of goats from your pens,
¹⁰for every animal of the forest is mine,
  and the cattle on a thousand hills.
¹¹I know every bird in the mountains,
  and the creatures of the field are
    mine.
¹²If I were hungry I would not tell you,

for the world is mine, and all that is
  in it.
¹³Do I eat the flesh of bulls
  or drink the blood of goats?
¹⁴Sacrifice thank offerings to God,
  fulfill your vows to the Most High,
¹⁵and call upon me in the day of
    trouble;
  I will deliver you, and you will
    honor me."

¹⁶But to the wicked, God says:

"What right have you to recite my
    laws
  or take my covenant on your lips?
¹⁷You hate my instruction
  and cast my words behind you.
¹⁸When you see a thief, you join with
    him;
  you throw in your lot with
    adulterers.
¹⁹You use your mouth for evil
  and harness your tongue to deceit.
²⁰You speak continually against your
    brother
  and slander your own mother's son.
²¹These things you have done and I kept
    silent;
  you thought I was altogether[n] like
    you.
But I will rebuke you
  and accuse you to your face.
²²"Consider this, you who forget God,
  or I will tear you to pieces, with
    none to rescue:
²³He who sacrifices thank offerings
    honors me,
  and he prepares the way

n 21 Or thought the 'I am' was

so that I may show him*o* the
salvation of God."

PSALM 51

For the director of music. A psalm of
David. When the prophet Nathan came
to him after David had committed
adultery with Bathsheba.

¹Have mercy on me, O God,
    according to your unfailing love;
according to your great compassion
    blot out my transgressions.
²Wash away all my iniquity
    and cleanse me from my sin.

³For I know my transgressions,
    and my sin is always before me.
⁴Against you, you only, have I sinned
    and done what is evil in your sight,
so that you are proved right when you
        speak
    and justified when you judge.
⁵Surely I was sinful at birth,
    sinful from the time my mother
        conceived me.
⁶Surely you desire truth in the inner
        parts*p*;
    you teach*q* me wisdom in the
        inmost place.

⁷Cleanse me with hyssop, and I will be
        clean;
    wash me, and I will be whiter than
        snow.
⁸Let me hear joy and gladness;
    let the bones you have crushed
        rejoice.
⁹Hide your face from my sins
    and blot out all my iniquity.

¹⁰Create in me a pure heart, O God,
    and renew a steadfast spirit within
        me.
¹¹Do not cast me from your presence
    or take your Holy Spirit from me.
¹²Restore to me the joy of your salvation
    and grant me a willing spirit, to
        sustain me.

¹³Then I will teach transgressors your
        ways,
    and sinners will turn back to you.
¹⁴Save me from bloodguilt, O God,
    the God who saves me,
    and my tongue will sing of your
        righteousness.
¹⁵O Lord, open my lips,

and my mouth will declare your
        praise.
¹⁶You do not delight in sacrifice, or I
        would bring it;
    you do not take pleasure in burnt
        offerings.
¹⁷The sacrifices of God are*r* a broken
        spirit;
    a broken and contrite heart,
    O God, you will not despise.

¹⁸In your good pleasure make Zion
        prosper;
    build up the walls of Jerusalem.
¹⁹Then there will be righteous sacrifices,
    whole burnt offerings to delight you;
    then bulls will be offered on your
        altar.

PSALM 52

For the director of music. A *maskil*ˢ
of David. When Doeg the Edomite had
gone to Saul and told him: "David has
gone to the house of Ahimelech."

¹Why do you boast of evil, you mighty
        man?
    Why do you boast all day long,
    you who are a disgrace in the eyes
        of God?
²Your tongue plots destruction;
    it is like a sharpened razor,
    you who practice deceit.
³You love evil rather than good,
    falsehood rather than speaking the
        truth.   *Selah*
⁴You love every harmful word,
    O you deceitful tongue!

⁵Surely God will bring you down to
        everlasting ruin:
    He will snatch you up and tear you
        from your tent;
    he will uproot you from the land of
        the living.   *Selah*
⁶The righteous will see and fear;
    they will laugh at him, saying,
⁷"Here now is the man
    who did not make God his
        stronghold
but trusted in his great wealth
    and grew strong by destroying
        others!"

⁸But I am like an olive tree
    flourishing in the house of God;
I trust in God's unfailing love

*o*23 Or *and to him who considers his way | I will show*   *p*6 The meaning of the Hebrew for this phrase is uncertain.   *q*6 Or *you*
desired . . . ; | you taught   *r*17 Or *My sacrifice, O God, is*   *s*Title: Probably a literary or musical term

for ever and ever.
⁹I will praise you forever for what you
have done;
in your name I will hope, for your
name is good.
I will praise you in the presence of
your saints.

PSALM 53

For the director of music. According to
*mahalath.*ᵗ A *maskil*ᵘ of David.

¹The fool says in his heart,
"There is no God."
They are corrupt, and their ways are
vile;
there is no one who does good.

²God looks down from heaven
on the sons of men
to see if there are any who
understand,
any who seek God.
³Everyone has turned away,
they have together become corrupt;
there is no one who does good,
not even one.

⁴Will the evildoers never learn—
those who devour my people as
men eat bread
and who do not call on God?
⁵There they were, overwhelmed with
dread,
where there was nothing to dread.
God scattered the bones of those who
attacked you;

ᵗTitle: Probably a musical term   ᵘTitle: Probably a literary or musical term

you put them to shame, for God
despised them.

⁶Oh, that salvation for Israel would
come out of Zion!
When God restores the fortunes of
his people,
let Jacob rejoice and Israel be glad!

PSALM 54

For the director of music. With stringed
instruments. A *maskil*ᵘ of David. When
the Ziphites had gone to Saul and said,
"Is not David hiding among us?"

¹Save me, O God, by your name;
vindicate me by your might.
²Hear my prayer, O God;
listen to the words of my mouth.

³Strangers are attacking me;
ruthless men seek my life—
men without regard for God.   *Selah*

⁴Surely God is my help;
the Lord is the one who sustains me.

⁵Let evil recoil on those who slander
me;
in your faithfulness destroy them.

⁶I will sacrifice a freewill offering to
you;
I will praise your name, O LORD,
for it is good.
⁷For he has delivered me from all my
troubles,
and my eyes have looked in triumph
on my foes.

JUNE 11 □ DAY 163
PSALMS 55–59
The Link of Faith

 OVERVIEW Great peril can cause great discouragement; it can also disclose great faith in God. Although David cries out in anguish to God when faced with the betrayal of a friend (Psalm 55), the vicious pursuit of an enemy (56–57) and the hatred of violent judges (58), at the same time he demonstrates great confidence in God's ability to vindicate him at the proper time and in the proper way (59).

Psalm 55	Psalms 56–57	Psalm 58	Psalm 59
Deceitful Betrayers	Dangerous Enemies	Distorted Judge	Defiant Attacker
God, the Faithful Deliverer			

YOUR DAILY WALK When the forecast calls for storms, ships need a strong anchor; buildings, a sure foundation; trees, a deep root system. In each case, their very survival through the storm depends upon a strong link to that which cannot be moved.

The beginning of anxiety is the end of faith; the beginning of true faith is the end of anxiety.

David's anchor in stormy circumstances was an unshakable faith in an unchanging God. Each psalm in today's reading describes an unsettling, disrupting influence that swept into his life. David pictures these onslaughts as a storm (55:8), as ravenous beasts (57:4), as venomous snakes (58:4–5) and as snarling dogs (59:6). But rather than focus on the forces swirling around him, David concentrates on his link of faith to God (55:22; 56:10–11; 57:11; 58:11; 59:9). And since his anchor is fixed to an immovable Rock, David finds that he, too, is immovable.

Is there a storm on the horizon in your life? Are you facing fierce opposition because of your faith? Using David's expressions of trust as your model, compose in your own words a two- or three-sentence statement of your confidence in the God who never changes. Post your statement on a bulletin board or bathroom mirror, where it can remind you in coming days that you needn't fear the storms of life if you have a sure foundation—an anchor in the Lord.

INSIGHT Self-Portrait of a Traitor
Though the identity of the traitor described in Psalm 55:12–14 remains unknown to us, ironically David was painting a graphic picture of his own treachery toward Uriah the Hittite, one of David's staunchest allies and the victim of his murderous plot (2 Samuel 11).

PSALM 55
For the director of music. With stringed instruments. A *maskil*[v] of David.

¹Listen to my prayer, O God,
    do not ignore my plea;
²   hear me and answer me.
My thoughts trouble me and I am
        distraught
³   at the voice of the enemy,
    at the stares of the wicked;
for they bring down suffering upon
        me
    and revile me in their anger.

⁴My heart is in anguish within me;
    the terrors of death assail me.
⁵Fear and trembling have beset me;
    horror has overwhelmed me.
⁶I said, "Oh, that I had the wings of a
        dove!
    I would fly away and be at rest—
⁷I would flee far away
    and stay in the desert;   *Selah*

⁸I would hurry to my place of shelter,
    far from the tempest and storm."

⁹Confuse the wicked, O Lord, confound
        their speech,
    for I see violence and strife in the
        city.
¹⁰Day and night they prowl about on its
        walls;
    malice and abuse are within it.
¹¹Destructive forces are at work in the
        city;
    threats and lies never leave its
        streets.

¹²If an enemy were insulting me,
    I could endure it;
if a foe were raising himself against
        me,
    I could hide from him.
¹³But it is you, a man like myself,
    my companion, my close friend,

[v]Title: Probably a literary or musical term

[14]with whom I once enjoyed sweet
　　fellowship
　as we walked with the throng at the
　　house of God.

[15]Let death take my enemies by
　　surprise;
　let them go down alive to the
　　grave,[w]
　for evil finds lodging among them.

[16]But I call to God,
　and the LORD saves me.
[17]Evening, morning and noon
　I cry out in distress,
　and he hears my voice.
[18]He ransoms me unharmed
　from the battle waged against me,
　even though many oppose me.
[19]God, who is enthroned forever,
　will hear them and afflict them—
　　　　　　　　　　　　　　Selah
men who never change their ways
　and have no fear of God.

[20]My companion attacks his friends;
　he violates his covenant.
[21]His speech is smooth as butter,
　yet war is in his heart;
　his words are more soothing than oil,
　yet they are drawn swords.

[22]Cast your cares on the LORD
　and he will sustain you;
　he will never let the righteous fall.
[23]But you, O God, will bring down the
　　wicked
　into the pit of corruption;
　bloodthirsty and deceitful men
　will not live out half their days.

But as for me, I trust in you.

PSALM 56

For the director of music. To ⌊the tune of⌋
"A Dove on Distant Oaks." Of David. A
miktam.[x] When the Philistines had
seized him in Gath.

[1]Be merciful to me, O God, for men
　　hotly pursue me;
　all day long they press their attack.
[2]My slanderers pursue me all day long;
　many are attacking me in their
　　pride.
[3]When I am afraid,
　I will trust in you.
[4]In God, whose word I praise,

in God I trust; I will not be afraid.
　What can mortal man do to me?

[5]All day long they twist my words;
　they are always plotting to harm
　　me.
[6]They conspire, they lurk,
　they watch my steps,
　eager to take my life.
[7]On no account let them escape;
　in your anger, O God, bring down
　　the nations.
[8]Record my lament;
　list my tears on your scroll[y]—
　are they not in your record?
[9]Then my enemies will turn back
　when I call for help.
　By this I will know that God is for
　　me.
[10]In God, whose word I praise,
　in the LORD, whose word I praise—
[11]in God I trust; I will not be afraid.
　What can man do to me?

[12]I am under vows to you, O God;
　I will present my thank offerings to
　　you.
[13]For you have delivered me[z] from
　　death
　and my feet from stumbling,
that I may walk before God
　in the light of life.[a]

PSALM 57

For the director of music. ⌊To the tune of⌋
"Do Not Destroy." Of David. A miktam.[x]
When he had fled from Saul into the
cave.

[1]Have mercy on me, O God, have
　　mercy on me,
　for in you my soul takes refuge.
I will take refuge in the shadow of
　　your wings
　until the disaster has passed.

[2]I cry out to God Most High,
　to God, who fulfills ⌊his purpose⌋ for
　　me.
[3]He sends from heaven and saves me,
　rebuking those who hotly pursue
　　me;　　　　　　　　　　　Selah
　God sends his love and his
　　faithfulness.

[4]I am in the midst of lions;
　I lie among ravenous beasts—

---

[w]15 Hebrew Sheol　　[x]Title: Probably a literary or musical term　　[y]8 Or / put my tears in your wineskin　　[z]13 Or my soul
[a]13 Or the land of the living

men whose teeth are spears and
    arrows,
  whose tongues are sharp swords.

5Be exalted, O God, above the heavens;
  let your glory be over all the earth.

6They spread a net for my feet—
  I was bowed down in distress.
They dug a pit in my path—
  but they have fallen into it
    themselves.   *Selah*

7My heart is steadfast, O God,
  my heart is steadfast;
  I will sing and make music.
8Awake, my soul!
  Awake, harp and lyre!
  I will awaken the dawn.

9I will praise you, O Lord, among the
    nations;
  I will sing of you among the
    peoples.
10For great is your love, reaching to the
    heavens;
  your faithfulness reaches to the
    skies.

11Be exalted, O God, above the heavens;
  let your glory be over all the earth.

PSALM 58

For the director of music. ⌊To the tune of⌋
"Do Not Destroy." Of David. A *miktam.*[b]

1Do you rulers indeed speak justly?
  Do you judge uprightly among
    men?
2No, in your heart you devise injustice,
  and your hands mete out violence
    on the earth.
3Even from birth the wicked go astray;
  from the womb they are wayward
    and speak lies.
4Their venom is like the venom of a
    snake,
  like that of a cobra that has stopped
    its ears,
5that will not heed the tune of the
    charmer,
  however skillful the enchanter may
    be.

6Break the teeth in their mouths,
    O God;
  tear out, O Lord, the fangs of the
    lions!

7Let them vanish like water that flows
    away;
  when they draw the bow, let their
    arrows be blunted.
8Like a slug melting away as it moves
    along,
  like a stillborn child, may they not
    see the sun.

9Before your pots can feel ⌊the heat of⌋
    the thorns—
  whether they be green or dry—the
    wicked will be swept away.[c]
10The righteous will be glad when they
    are avenged,
  when they bathe their feet in the
    blood of the wicked.
11Then men will say,
  "Surely the righteous still are
    rewarded;
  surely there is a God who judges the
    earth."

PSALM 59

For the director of music. ⌊To the tune of⌋
"Do Not Destroy." Of David. A *miktam.*[b]
When Saul had sent men to watch
David's house in order to kill him.

1Deliver me from my enemies, O God;
  protect me from those who rise up
    against me.
2Deliver me from evildoers
  and save me from bloodthirsty men.

3See how they lie in wait for me!
  Fierce men conspire against me
  for no offense or sin of mine,
    O Lord.
4I have done no wrong, yet they are
    ready to attack me.
  Arise to help me; look on my plight!
5O Lord God Almighty, the God of
    Israel,
  rouse yourself to punish all the
    nations;
  show no mercy to wicked traitors.
                                    Selah

6They return at evening,
  snarling like dogs,
  and prowl about the city.
7See what they spew from their
    mouths—
  they spew out swords from their
    lips,
  and they say, "Who can hear us?"

b Title: Probably a literary or musical term   c 9 The meaning of the Hebrew for this verse is uncertain.

8But you, O LORD, laugh at them;
  you scoff at all those nations.

9O my Strength, I watch for you;
  you, O God, are my fortress, 10my
  loving God.

God will go before me
  and will let me gloat over those who
  slander me.
11But do not kill them, O Lord our
  shield,d
  or my people will forget.
In your might make them wander
  about,
  and bring them down.
12For the sins of their mouths,
  for the words of their lips,
  let them be caught in their pride.
For the curses and lies they utter,

d11 Or sovereign

13   consume them in wrath,
  consume them till they are no more.
Then it will be known to the ends of
  the earth
  that God rules over Jacob.   *Selah*

14They return at evening,
  snarling like dogs,
  and prowl about the city.
15They wander about for food
  and howl if not satisfied.
16But I will sing of your strength,
  in the morning I will sing of your
  love;
for you are my fortress,
  my refuge in times of trouble.

17O my Strength, I sing praise to you;
  you, O God, are my fortress, my
  loving God.

JUNE 12 ☐ DAY 164
PSALMS 60–66
Through the Night Watches

OVERVIEW The freedom to be transparent before God, to express to him exactly how you feel, is an important part of prayer. David's prayer life reveals the deepest emotions of his heart. The welfare of his nation (Psalm 60) and the duties of his office (61) weigh heavily upon him. He yearns for a growing relationship with God (62–64)—a relationship his enemies do not experience. He stands in awe of God's powerful creation (65) and revels in God's matchless salvation (66), inviting all who read his words to "come and see what God has done" (66:5).

Psalms 60–61	Psalms 62–64	Psalms 65–66
Prosperity for the Nation and King	Protection for the Seeking Soul	Praise for the God Who Provides
Supplication		Acclamation

No daily meal is complete without the bread of life.

YOUR DAILY WALK Psalm 63 was penned by David "when he was in the Desert of Judah," a desolate region where water is scarce, vegetation is almost nonexistent and the heat of the day makes every activity a burden.

These barren surroundings prompted David to write, "my soul thirsts for you, my body longs for you, in a dry and weary land" (v. 1). Soul and body, David longs to be in the presence of God.

David knows that the thirst and hunger he feels for God will be satisfied as he follows hard after him: "My soul will be satisfied as with the richest of foods" (v. 5). In seeking God early, David finds elements of God's character to reflect upon late into the night (v. 6). Because

God has helped him, David rejoices "in the shadow of [God's] wings" (v. 7). In cleaving to God, David finds God upholding him (v. 8).

Jesus told his followers, "Blessed are those who hunger and thirst for righteousness, for they will be filled" (Matthew 5:6). How is your spiritual appetite? Carve out some time to be alone with God today for fifteen minutes or so of "thirst quenching." Enjoy his presence; feast on his Word; let him satisfy the yearning of your heart.

 INSIGHT A Sleepless Night for a Thirsty Soul
In Bible times, the night was divided into three periods or "watches" for soldiers and shepherds: sunset to approximately 10:00 P.M., 10:00 P.M. to 2:00 A.M. and 2:00 A.M. to dawn. Now read Psalm 63:6 to discover a telltale sign of David's devotion to God!

PSALM 60

For the director of music. To ⌊the tune of⌋ "The Lily of the Covenant." A *miktam*[e] of David. For teaching. When he fought Aram Naharaim[f] and Aram Zobah,[g] and when Joab returned and struck down twelve thousand Edomites in the Valley of Salt.

¹You have rejected us, O God, and burst forth upon us;
   you have been angry—now restore us!
²You have shaken the land and torn it open;
   mend its fractures, for it is quaking.
³You have shown your people desperate times;
   you have given us wine that makes us stagger.

⁴But for those who fear you, you have raised a banner
   to be unfurled against the bow. *Selah*

⁵Save us and help us with your right hand,
   that those you love may be delivered.
⁶God has spoken from his sanctuary:
   "In triumph I will parcel out Shechem
   and measure off the Valley of Succoth.
⁷Gilead is mine, and Manasseh is mine;
   Ephraim is my helmet,
   Judah my scepter.
⁸Moab is my washbasin,
   upon Edom I toss my sandal;
   over Philistia I shout in triumph."

⁹Who will bring me to the fortified city?
   Who will lead me to Edom?

¹⁰Is it not you, O God, you who have rejected us
   and no longer go out with our armies?
¹¹Give us aid against the enemy,
   for the help of man is worthless.
¹²With God we will gain the victory,
   and he will trample down our enemies.

PSALM 61

For the director of music. With stringed instruments. Of David.

¹Hear my cry, O God;
   listen to my prayer.

²From the ends of the earth I call to you,
   I call as my heart grows faint;
   lead me to the rock that is higher than I.
³For you have been my refuge,
   a strong tower against the foe.

⁴I long to dwell in your tent forever
   and take refuge in the shelter of your wings. *Selah*
⁵For you have heard my vows, O God;
   you have given me the heritage of those who fear your name.

⁶Increase the days of the king's life,
   his years for many generations.
⁷May he be enthroned in God's presence forever;
   appoint your love and faithfulness to protect him.

⁸Then will I ever sing praise to your name
   and fulfill my vows day after day.

*e*Title: Probably a literary or musical term   *f*Title: That is, Arameans of Northwest Mesopotamia   *g*Title: That is, Arameans of central Syria

PSALM 62
For the director of music. For Jeduthun.
A psalm of David.

¹My soul finds rest in God alone;
my salvation comes from him.
²He alone is my rock and my salvation;
he is my fortress, I will never be
shaken.

³How long will you assault a man?
Would all of you throw him down—
this leaning wall, this tottering
fence?
⁴They fully intend to topple him
from his lofty place;
they take delight in lies.
With their mouths they bless,
but in their hearts they curse.   *Selah*

⁵Find rest, O my soul, in God alone;
my hope comes from him.
⁶He alone is my rock and my salvation;
he is my fortress, I will not be
shaken.
⁷My salvation and my honor depend
on God *h*;
he is my mighty rock, my refuge.
⁸Trust in him at all times, O people;
pour out your hearts to him,
for God is our refuge.   *Selah*

⁹Lowborn men are but a breath,
the highborn are but a lie;
if weighed on a balance, they are
nothing;
together they are only a breath.
¹⁰Do not trust in extortion
or take pride in stolen goods;
though your riches increase,
do not set your heart on them.

¹¹One thing God has spoken,
two things have I heard:
that you, O God, are strong,
¹² and that you, O Lord, are loving.
Surely you will reward each person
according to what he has done.

PSALM 63
A psalm of David. When he was in the
Desert of Judah.

¹O God, you are my God,
earnestly I seek you;
my soul thirsts for you,
my body longs for you,
in a dry and weary land
where there is no water.

²I have seen you in the sanctuary
and beheld your power and your
glory.
³Because your love is better than life,
my lips will glorify you.
⁴I will praise you as long as I live,
and in your name I will lift up my
hands.
⁵My soul will be satisfied as with the
richest of foods;
with singing lips my mouth will
praise you.

⁶On my bed I remember you;
I think of you through the watches
of the night.
⁷Because you are my help,
I sing in the shadow of your wings.
⁸My soul clings to you;
your right hand upholds me.

⁹They who seek my life will be
destroyed;
they will go down to the depths of
the earth.
¹⁰They will be given over to the sword
and become food for jackals.

¹¹But the king will rejoice in God;
all who swear by God's name will
praise him,
while the mouths of liars will be
silenced.

PSALM 64
For the director of music. A psalm
of David.

¹Hear me, O God, as I voice my
complaint;
protect my life from the threat of the
enemy.
²Hide me from the conspiracy of the
wicked,
from that noisy crowd of evildoers.

³They sharpen their tongues like
swords
and aim their words like deadly
arrows.
⁴They shoot from ambush at the
innocent man;
they shoot at him suddenly, without
fear.

⁵They encourage each other in evil
plans,
they talk about hiding their snares;
they say, "Who will see them *i*?"

h7 Or / God Most High is my salvation and my honor   i5 Or us

⁶They plot injustice and say,
  "We have devised a perfect plan!"
  Surely the mind and heart of man
    are cunning.

⁷But God will shoot them with arrows;
  suddenly they will be struck down.
⁸He will turn their own tongues against
    them
  and bring them to ruin;
  all who see them will shake their
    heads in scorn.

⁹All mankind will fear;
  they will proclaim the works of God
  and ponder what he has done.
¹⁰Let the righteous rejoice in the LORD
  and take refuge in him;
  let all the upright in heart praise
    him!

PSALM 65

For the director of music. A psalm
of David. A song.

¹Praise awaits*ʲ* you, O God, in Zion;
  to you our vows will be fulfilled.
²O you who hear prayer,
  to you all men will come.
³When we were overwhelmed by sins,
  you forgave*ᵏ* our transgressions.
⁴Blessed are those you choose
  and bring near to live in your
    courts!
We are filled with the good things of
    your house,
  of your holy temple.

⁵You answer us with awesome deeds of
    righteousness,
  O God our Savior,
the hope of all the ends of the earth
  and of the farthest seas,
⁶who formed the mountains by your
    power,
  having armed yourself with
    strength,
⁷who stilled the roaring of the seas,
  the roaring of their waves,
  and the turmoil of the nations.
⁸Those living far away fear your
    wonders;
  where morning dawns and evening
    fades
  you call forth songs of joy.

⁹You care for the land and water it;

you enrich it abundantly.
The streams of God are filled with
    water
  to provide the people with grain,
  for so you have ordained it.*ˡ*
¹⁰You drench its furrows
  and level its ridges;
you soften it with showers
  and bless its crops.
¹¹You crown the year with your
    bounty,
  and your carts overflow with
    abundance.
¹²The grasslands of the desert overflow;
  the hills are clothed with gladness.
¹³The meadows are covered with flocks
  and the valleys are mantled with
    grain;
  they shout for joy and sing.

PSALM 66

For the director of music. A song.
A psalm.

¹Shout with joy to God, all the earth!
² Sing the glory of his name;
  make his praise glorious!
³Say to God, "How awesome are your
    deeds!
  So great is your power
  that your enemies cringe before you.
⁴All the earth bows down to you;
  they sing praise to you,
  they sing praise to your name." *Selah*

⁵Come and see what God has done,
  how awesome his works in man's
    behalf!
⁶He turned the sea into dry land,
  they passed through the waters on
    foot—
  come, let us rejoice in him.
⁷He rules forever by his power,
  his eyes watch the nations—
  let not the rebellious rise up against
    him.   *Selah*

⁸Praise our God, O peoples,
  let the sound of his praise be heard;
⁹he has preserved our lives
  and kept our feet from slipping.
¹⁰For you, O God, tested us;
  you refined us like silver.
¹¹You brought us into prison
  and laid burdens on our backs.
¹²You let men ride over our heads;

ʲ1 Or *befits;* the meaning of the Hebrew for this word is uncertain.   *ᵏ3* Or *made atonement for*   *ˡ9* Or *for that is how you*
prepare the land

we went through fire and water,
but you brought us to a place of
abundance.

¹³I will come to your temple with burnt
offerings
and fulfill my vows to you—
¹⁴vows my lips promised and my mouth
spoke
when I was in trouble.
¹⁵I will sacrifice fat animals to you
and an offering of rams;
I will offer bulls and goats.   *Selah*

¹⁶Come and listen, all you who fear
God;
let me tell you what he has done for
me.
¹⁷I cried out to him with my mouth;
his praise was on my tongue.
¹⁸If I had cherished sin in my heart,
the Lord would not have listened;
¹⁹but God has surely listened
and heard my voice in prayer.
²⁰Praise be to God,
who has not rejected my prayer
or withheld his love from me!

JUNE 13 ☐ DAY 165
PSALMS 67–72
Your Burden Bearer

 OVERVIEW Book II of Psalms concludes with six proclamations showing that God is worthy of praise and trust. The nations acknowledge
God's righteous rule (Psalm 67), exulting in his care of the fatherless
and homeless (68). He hears the cry of the distressed (69), speedily
delivers the oppressed (70), strengthens the feeble (71) and exercises
dominion over kings and kingdoms (72). Truly "all kings will bow
down to him and all nations will serve him" (72:11).

Psalm 67	Psalm 68	Psalms 69–70	Psalm 71	Psalm 72
"Extol the Lord"	"Exalt the Lord"	"Don't Delay, Lord"	"Don't Desert Me, Lord"	"Bless the Lord"
Praise		Pleading		Prayer

 YOUR DAILY WALK It has been well said, "Our days are identical
suitcases—all the same size—but some people can pack more into
them than others."

In the midst of your busy schedule, never lose sight of the fact that
God is busy, too—on your behalf! After you read Psalm 68 today, see
if you can discover and jot down at least five things God has promised
to do for you today—and every day.

We have no power from God unless we live in the persuasion that we have none of our own.

In our computerized world where people are often reduced to face-
less records, it's encouraging to know there is someone to whom
you'll never be just a number. Someone who daily loads us with benefits. Someone who enters into your joys and sorrows, exchanging
your heavy burdens for his light ones (Matthew 11:28–30).

Five times, in Psalm 68, strength is mentioned—strength God longs
to demonstrate on behalf of his people. Have you drawn upon that
strength today, enabling you to do in his strength what you would be
powerless to do in your own? After all, "the God of Israel gives power
and strength to his people" (68:35).

 INSIGHT The Final Stop on a Four-Hundred-Year Journey
The exact occasion for which David composed Psalm 68 is not known,
but quite possibly it marked the bringing of the ark of the covenant
into Jerusalem (2 Samuel 6:12). This joyous event is the climax of a

journey begun centuries before at Mount Sinai. There the ark had been fashioned; from there it went before Israel into the promised land. Now the ark reaches the summit of Mount Zion, where it will reside as the symbol of God's abiding presence.

PSALM 67
For the director of music. With stringed instruments. A psalm. A song.

¹May God be gracious to us and bless us
and make his face shine upon us,
                                                    Selah
²that your ways may be known on earth,
your salvation among all nations.

³May the peoples praise you, O God;
may all the peoples praise you.
⁴May the nations be glad and sing for joy,
for you rule the peoples justly
and guide the nations of the earth.
                                                    Selah
⁵May the peoples praise you, O God;
may all the peoples praise you.

⁶Then the land will yield its harvest,
and God, our God, will bless us.
⁷God will bless us,
and all the ends of the earth will fear him.

PSALM 68
For the director of music. Of David. A psalm. A song.

¹May God arise, may his enemies be scattered;
may his foes flee before him.
²As smoke is blown away by the wind,
may you blow them away;
as wax melts before the fire,
may the wicked perish before God.
³But may the righteous be glad
and rejoice before God;
may they be happy and joyful.

⁴Sing to God, sing praise to his name,
extol him who rides on the clouds[m]—
his name is the LORD—
and rejoice before him.
⁵A father to the fatherless, a defender of widows,
is God in his holy dwelling.
⁶God sets the lonely in families,[n]

he leads forth the prisoners with singing;
but the rebellious live in a sun-scorched land.

⁷When you went out before your people, O God,
when you marched through the wasteland,   *Selah*
⁸the earth shook,
the heavens poured down rain,
before God, the One of Sinai,
before God, the God of Israel.
⁹You gave abundant showers, O God;
you refreshed your weary inheritance.
¹⁰Your people settled in it,
and from your bounty, O God, you provided for the poor.

¹¹The Lord announced the word,
and great was the company of those who proclaimed it:
¹²"Kings and armies flee in haste;
in the camps men divide the plunder.
¹³Even while you sleep among the campfires,[o]
the wings of ⌐my¬ dove are sheathed with silver,
its feathers with shining gold."
¹⁴When the Almighty[p] scattered the kings in the land,
it was like snow fallen on Zalmon.

¹⁵The mountains of Bashan are majestic mountains;
rugged are the mountains of Bashan.
¹⁶Why gaze in envy, O rugged mountains,
at the mountain where God chooses to reign,
where the LORD himself will dwell forever?
¹⁷The chariots of God are tens of thousands
and thousands of thousands;
the Lord ⌐has come¬ from Sinai into his sanctuary.
¹⁸When you ascended on high,
you led captives in your train;

---

[m]4 Or / prepare the way for him who rides through the deserts   [n]6 Or the desolate in a homeland   [o]13 Or saddlebags
[p]14 Hebrew Shaddai

you received gifts from men,
even from^q the rebellious—
   that you,^{r} O Lord God, might dwell
   there.

¹⁹Praise be to the Lord, to God our
   Savior,
   who daily bears our burdens.   *Selah*
²⁰Our God is a God who saves;
   from the Sovereign Lord comes
   escape from death.

²¹Surely God will crush the heads of his
   enemies,
   the hairy crowns of those who go on
   in their sins.
²²The Lord says, "I will bring them from
   Bashan;
   I will bring them from the depths of
   the sea,
²³that you may plunge your feet in the
   blood of your foes,
   while the tongues of your dogs have
   their share."

²⁴Your procession has come into view,
   O God,
   the procession of my God and King
   into the sanctuary.
²⁵In front are the singers, after them the
   musicians;
   with them are the maidens playing
   tambourines.
²⁶Praise God in the great congregation;
   praise the Lord in the assembly of
   Israel.
²⁷There is the little tribe of Benjamin,
   leading them,
   there the great throng of Judah's
   princes,
   and there the princes of Zebulun
   and of Naphtali.

²⁸Summon your power, O God^s;
   show us your strength, O God, as
   you have done before.
²⁹Because of your temple at Jerusalem
   kings will bring you gifts.
³⁰Rebuke the beast among the reeds,
   the herd of bulls among the calves
   of the nations.
   Humbled, may it bring bars of silver.
   Scatter the nations who delight in
   war.
³¹Envoys will come from Egypt;
   Cush^t will submit herself to God.

³²Sing to God, O kingdoms of the earth,
   sing praise to the Lord,   *Selah*
³³to him who rides the ancient skies
   above,
   who thunders with mighty voice.
³⁴Proclaim the power of God,
   whose majesty is over Israel,
   whose power is in the skies.
³⁵You are awesome, O God, in your
   sanctuary;
   the God of Israel gives power and
   strength to his people.

Praise be to God!

PSALM 69
For the director of music. To ⌊the tune of⌋
"Lilies." Of David.

¹Save me, O God,
   for the waters have come up to my
   neck.
²I sink in the miry depths,
   where there is no foothold.
   I have come into the deep waters;
   the floods engulf me.
³I am worn out calling for help;
   my throat is parched.
   My eyes fail,
   looking for my God.
⁴Those who hate me without reason
   outnumber the hairs of my head;
   many are my enemies without cause,
   those who seek to destroy me.
   I am forced to restore
   what I did not steal.

⁵You know my folly, O God;
   my guilt is not hidden from you.

⁶May those who hope in you
   not be disgraced because of me,
   O Lord, the Lord Almighty;
   may those who seek you
   not be put to shame because of me,
   O God of Israel.
⁷For I endure scorn for your sake,
   and shame covers my face.
⁸I am a stranger to my brothers,
   an alien to my own mother's sons;
⁹for zeal for your house consumes me,
   and the insults of those who insult
   you fall on me.
¹⁰When I weep and fast,
   I must endure scorn;
¹¹when I put on sackcloth,
   people make sport of me.

^{q}18 Or *gifts for men, / even* ^{r}18 Or *they* ^{s}28 Many Hebrew manuscripts, Septuagint and Syriac; most Hebrew manuscripts
Your God has summoned power for you ^{t}31 That is, the upper Nile region

¹²Those who sit at the gate mock me,
  and I am the song of the drunkards.

¹³But I pray to you, O LORD,
  in the time of your favor;
in your great love, O God,
  answer me with your sure salvation.
¹⁴Rescue me from the mire,
  do not let me sink;
deliver me from those who hate me,
  from the deep waters.
¹⁵Do not let the floodwaters engulf me
  or the depths swallow me up
  or the pit close its mouth over me.
¹⁶Answer me, O LORD, out of the
      goodness of your love;
  in your great mercy turn to me.
¹⁷Do not hide your face from your
      servant;
  answer me quickly, for I am in
      trouble.
¹⁸Come near and rescue me;
  redeem me because of my foes.

¹⁹You know how I am scorned,
      disgraced and shamed;
  all my enemies are before you.
²⁰Scorn has broken my heart
  and has left me helpless;
I looked for sympathy, but there was
      none,
  for comforters, but I found none.
²¹They put gall in my food
  and gave me vinegar for my thirst.

²²May the table set before them become
      a snare;
  may it become retribution and ᵘ a
      trap.
²³May their eyes be darkened so they
      cannot see,
  and their backs be bent forever.
²⁴Pour out your wrath on them;
  let your fierce anger overtake them.
²⁵May their place be deserted;
  let there be no one to dwell in their
      tents.
²⁶For they persecute those you wound
  and talk about the pain of those you
      hurt.
²⁷Charge them with crime upon crime;
  do not let them share in your
      salvation.
²⁸May they be blotted out of the book of
      life
  and not be listed with the righteous.

²⁹I am in pain and distress;
  may your salvation, O God, protect
      me.
³⁰I will praise God's name in song
  and glorify him with thanksgiving.
³¹This will please the LORD more than an
      ox,
  more than a bull with its horns and
      hoofs.
³²The poor will see and be glad—
  you who seek God, may your hearts
      live!
³³The LORD hears the needy
  and does not despise his captive
      people.
³⁴Let heaven and earth praise him,
  the seas and all that move in them,
³⁵for God will save Zion
  and rebuild the cities of Judah.
Then people will settle there and
      possess it;
³⁶ the children of his servants will
      inherit it,
  and those who love his name will
      dwell there.

PSALM 70
For the director of music. Of David.
A petition.

¹Hasten, O God, to save me;
  O LORD, come quickly to help me.
²May those who seek my life
  be put to shame and confusion;
may all who desire my ruin
  be turned back in disgrace.
³May those who say to me, "Aha! Aha!"
  turn back because of their shame.
⁴But may all who seek you
  rejoice and be glad in you;
may those who love your salvation
      always say,
  "Let God be exalted!"

⁵Yet I am poor and needy;
  come quickly to me, O God.
You are my help and my deliverer;
  O LORD, do not delay.

PSALM 71

¹In you, O LORD, I have taken refuge;
  let me never be put to shame.
²Rescue me and deliver me in your
      righteousness;
  turn your ear to me and save me.
³Be my rock of refuge,

ᵘ22 Or snare / and their fellowship become

to which I can always go;
give the command to save me,
    for you are my rock and my
        fortress.
⁴Deliver me, O my God, from the hand
    of the wicked,
    from the grasp of evil and cruel
        men.

⁵For you have been my hope,
    O Sovereign LORD,
my confidence since my youth.
⁶From birth I have relied on you;
    you brought me forth from my
        mother's womb.
I will ever praise you.
⁷I have become like a portent to many,
    but you are my strong refuge.
⁸My mouth is filled with your praise,
    declaring your splendor all day
        long.

⁹Do not cast me away when I am old;
    do not forsake me when my
        strength is gone.
¹⁰For my enemies speak against me;
    those who wait to kill me conspire
        together.
¹¹They say, "God has forsaken him;
    pursue him and seize him,
    for no one will rescue him."
¹²Be not far from me, O God;
    come quickly, O my God, to help
        me.
¹³May my accusers perish in shame;
    may those who want to harm me
    be covered with scorn and disgrace.

¹⁴But as for me, I will always have
        hope;
    I will praise you more and more.
¹⁵My mouth will tell of your
        righteousness,
    of your salvation all day long,
    though I know not its measure.
¹⁶I will come and proclaim your mighty
        acts, O Sovereign LORD;
    I will proclaim your righteousness,
        yours alone.
¹⁷Since my youth, O God, you have
        taught me,
    and to this day I declare your
        marvelous deeds.
¹⁸Even when I am old and gray,
    do not forsake me, O God,

till I declare your power to the next
        generation,
    your might to all who are to come.
¹⁹Your righteousness reaches to the
        skies, O God,
    you who have done great things.
    Who, O God, is like you?
²⁰Though you have made me see
        troubles, many and bitter,
    you will restore my life again;
from the depths of the earth
    you will again bring me up.
²¹You will increase my honor
    and comfort me once again.

²²I will praise you with the harp
    for your faithfulness, O my God;
I will sing praise to you with the lyre,
    O Holy One of Israel.
²³My lips will shout for joy
    when I sing praise to you—
    I, whom you have redeemed.
²⁴My tongue will tell of your righteous
        acts
    all day long,
for those who wanted to harm me
    have been put to shame and
        confusion.

PSALM 72
Of Solomon.

¹Endow the king with your justice,
    O God,
    the royal son with your
        righteousness.
²He will^v judge your people in
        righteousness,
    your afflicted ones with justice.
³The mountains will bring prosperity to
        the people,
    the hills the fruit of righteousness.
⁴He will defend the afflicted among the
        people
    and save the children of the needy;
    he will crush the oppressor.

⁵He will endure^w as long as the sun,
    as long as the moon, through all
        generations.
⁶He will be like rain falling on a mown
        field,
    like showers watering the earth.
⁷In his days the righteous will flourish;
    prosperity will abound till the moon
        is no more.

---

^{v}2 Or *May he*; similarly in verses 3-11 and 17 ^{w}5 Septuagint; Hebrew *You will be feared*

⁸He will rule from sea to sea
  and from the River^x to the ends of
    the earth.^y
⁹The desert tribes will bow before him
  and his enemies will lick the dust.
¹⁰The kings of Tarshish and of distant
    shores
  will bring tribute to him;
the kings of Sheba and Seba
  will present him gifts.
¹¹All kings will bow down to him
  and all nations will serve him.

¹²For he will deliver the needy who cry
    out,
  the afflicted who have no one to
    help.
¹³He will take pity on the weak and the
    needy
and save the needy from death.
¹⁴He will rescue them from oppression
    and violence,
  for precious is their blood in his
    sight.
¹⁵Long may he live!

^x8 That is, the Euphrates   ^y8 Or *the end of the land*

May gold from Sheba be given him.
May people ever pray for him
  and bless him all day long.
¹⁶Let grain abound throughout the land;
  on the tops of the hills may it sway.
Let its fruit flourish like Lebanon;
  let it thrive like the grass of the
    field.
¹⁷May his name endure forever;
  may it continue as long as the sun.

All nations will be blessed through
    him,
  and they will call him blessed.

¹⁸Praise be to the LORD God, the God of
    Israel,
  who alone does marvelous deeds.
¹⁹Praise be to his glorious name forever;
  may the whole earth be filled with
    his glory.
    Amen and Amen.

²⁰This concludes the prayers of David
    son of Jesse.

JUNE 14 ☐ DAY 166
It's All in the Call

 LOOK BACK As the psalmist spotlights the character of God, he finds himself adjusting his conduct accordingly. God's love reaches to the heavens; therefore, there is no need to fret. God is an ever-present help in trouble; therefore, there is no reason to be downcast. God's greatness is astounding; therefore, let his praises be known to all.

By contrast, humans are frail and finite, sinful and guilty. The psalmist's cry for mercy and forgiveness is met by God's promise of cleansing and comfort. Seeing God's greatness and grandeur puts the psalmist in line to draw upon God's strength and supply. It's a lesson each new generation must learn—and one of the best places to learn it is at the knee of silver-haired saints who have walked with God for a lifetime (71:18).

 LOOK UP Even a five-year-old child knows the significance of the telephone number 9–1–1. It's the magic number that unlocks incredible lifesaving resources in a matter of seconds. Those confronted with a life-threatening situation have only to call 9–1–1 to find help in time of need, comfort in the face of danger and protection from the forces that would seek to harm and destroy.

The melody of praise is best played with the notes of praise, adoration, confession and thanksgiving.

But stop for a moment and ask yourself this question: Why do people in trouble reach for the phone and dial 9–1–1? Is it because
  • they *think* someone might be on the other end of the line to hear their plea?
  • they *hope* there is help to be found somewhere?
  • they *wish* there were a solution to their dilemma? or

• they *know* that someone who is trained, ready, willing and able to help is poised to respond the instant their call arrives?

Think of Psalm 70 as the psalmist's 9-1-1 prayer:

"Hasten, O God, to save me; O LORD, come quickly to help me. . . . You are my help and my deliverer; O LORD, do not delay" (70:1, 5).

And why does the psalmist call upon the Lord? Not because he hopes or thinks or wishes or wonders if God will come to his rescue, but because "[God] *will* deliver the needy who cry out, . . . He *will* take pity on the weak and the needy . . . He *will* rescue them from oppression and violence" (Psalm 72:12-14, emphasis added). It's the same idea expressed by Jeremiah the prophet when he said, "This is what the LORD says, . . . 'Call to me and I will answer you and tell you great and unsearchable things you do not know' " (Jeremiah 33:2-3).

 LOOK AHEAD When life seems to be out of control and circumstances are as bewildering as a three-alarm fire, you have several options as to how you will respond. You can lean on your own strength and understanding, even though you've been warned not to (Proverbs 3:5). You can surround yourself with busyness or indulge yourself in pleasure, but that won't remove the feelings of fear and inadequacy. You can ignore your problems and hope they will go away, but chances are they won't.

Or you can call upon the Lord, the only one who has promised never to leave you or forsake you (Matthew 28:20; Hebrews 13:5). It may sound like a simple solution—and in some ways it is. But with a Tower of Strength and Mercy like that awaiting your call twenty-four hours a day, why would anyone look elsewhere for help?

JUNE 15 □ DAY 167
PSALMS 73-77
Peoples' Questions, God's Answers

 OVERVIEW Book III of Psalms begins with several selections by Asaph, a gifted musician appointed by David to direct the Levitical choirs. Asaph first probes the hard question, Why do the wicked flourish (Psalm 73) while Israel flounders (74)? By focusing on God's justice (75-76) and God's faithfulness to his people (77), Asaph discovers a solid foundation of hope, even as the wicked seem to get away with murder.

Psalm 73	Psalm 74	Psalms 75-76	Psalm 77
Prosperity of the Wicked	Plight of the Righteous	Praise for God's Justice	Promise of God's Favor
Questions		Answers	

 YOUR DAILY WALK A sheriff was asked by a local resident, "Do you think you will ever eliminate crime?"

The sheriff wisely replied, "I'm not naive enough to think that crime can ever be eliminated. There were prostitutes and pickpockets in the days of Christ. There was gambling and debauchery in the days of the prophets. There will always be some who submit to the soft, glittery

If you don't want the fruits of sin in your life, stay out of sin's orchard.

pleasures of the world, and it will always be for the spiritually strong to lead them back."

His words ring true in a day when, according to FBI statistics, one serious crime is committed in this country every 2 seconds . . . one robbery every 10 seconds . . . one murder every 5.8 minutes.

Asaph, in observing the criminal element in his day, was honest enough to ask God some searching questions: Is godliness really worth the struggle? Have I made the wrong choice? (73:13–14). Implied in those words is another protest: God, do you really care?

If you've asked the same questions, you need what Asaph found: perspective. As he drew close to the Lord (73:17), the psalmist saw that the wicked would be repaid for their sinfulness and the faithful would receive a great reward. All this will happen in God's perfect timing.

In the meantime, you need strength for today—strength to forgo the expedient and concentrate on the obedient.

 INSIGHT Asaph—No Second Fiddle When It Comes to Music
Asaph was one of the singers appointed by David to direct the choir of Levites (1 Chronicles 15:16, 19). Later, he was ranked with David as one of Israel's finest musicians (Nehemiah 12:46).

BOOK III
Psalms 73–89

PSALM 73
A psalm of Asaph.

¹Surely God is good to Israel,
  to those who are pure in heart.

²But as for me, my feet had almost
    slipped;
  I had nearly lost my foothold.
³For I envied the arrogant
  when I saw the prosperity of the
    wicked.

⁴They have no struggles;
  their bodies are healthy and
    strong.ᶻ
⁵They are free from the burdens
    common to man;
  they are not plagued by human ills.
⁶Therefore pride is their necklace;
  they clothe themselves with
    violence.
⁷From their callous hearts comes
    iniquityᵃ;
  the evil conceits of their minds
    know no limits.
⁸They scoff, and speak with malice;
  in their arrogance they threaten
    oppression.
⁹Their mouths lay claim to heaven,
  and their tongues take possession of
    the earth.

¹⁰Therefore their people turn to them
  and drink up waters in abundance.ᵇ
¹¹They say, "How can God know?
  Does the Most High have
    knowledge?"

¹²This is what the wicked are like—
  always carefree, they increase in
    wealth.

¹³Surely in vain have I kept my heart
    pure;
  in vain have I washed my hands in
    innocence.
¹⁴All day long I have been plagued;
  I have been punished every
    morning.

¹⁵If I had said, "I will speak thus,"
  I would have betrayed your
    children.
¹⁶When I tried to understand all this,
  it was oppressive to me
¹⁷till I entered the sanctuary of God;
  then I understood their final destiny.

¹⁸Surely you place them on slippery
    ground;
  you cast them down to ruin.
¹⁹How suddenly are they destroyed,
  completely swept away by terrors!
²⁰As a dream when one awakes,
  so when you arise, O Lord,
  you will despise them as fantasies.

²¹When my heart was grieved

ᶻ4 With a different word division of the Hebrew; Masoretic Text *struggles at their death; / their bodies are healthy*   ᵃ7 Syriac (see also Septuagint); Hebrew *Their eyes bulge with fat*   ᵇ10 The meaning of the Hebrew for this verse is uncertain.

and my spirit embittered,
22I was senseless and ignorant;
  I was a brute beast before you.

23Yet I am always with you;
  you hold me by my right hand.
24You guide me with your counsel,
  and afterward you will take me into
    glory.
25Whom have I in heaven but you?
  And earth has nothing I desire
    besides you.
26My flesh and my heart may fail,
  but God is the strength of my heart
  and my portion forever.

27Those who are far from you will
    perish;
  you destroy all who are unfaithful to
    you.
28But as for me, it is good to be near
    God.
  I have made the Sovereign LORD my
    refuge;
  I will tell of all your deeds.

PSALM 74
A *maskil*[c] of Asaph.

1Why have you rejected us forever,
    O God?
  Why does your anger smolder
    against the sheep of your
    pasture?
2Remember the people you purchased
    of old,
  the tribe of your inheritance, whom
    you redeemed—
  Mount Zion, where you dwelt.
3Turn your steps toward these
    everlasting ruins,
  all this destruction the enemy has
    brought on the sanctuary.

4Your foes roared in the place where
    you met with us;
  they set up their standards as signs.
5They behaved like men wielding axes
  to cut through a thicket of trees.
6They smashed all the carved paneling
  with their axes and hatchets.
7They burned your sanctuary to the
    ground;
  they defiled the dwelling place of
    your Name.
8They said in their hearts, "We will
    crush them completely!"

cTitle: Probably a literary or musical term

They burned every place where God
    was worshiped in the land.
9We are given no miraculous signs;
  no prophets are left,
  and none of us knows how long this
    will be.

10How long will the enemy mock you,
    O God?
  Will the foe revile your name
    forever?
11Why do you hold back your hand,
    your right hand?
  Take it from the folds of your
    garment and destroy them!

12But you, O God, are my king from of
    old;
  you bring salvation upon the earth.
13It was you who split open the sea by
    your power;
  you broke the heads of the monster
    in the waters.
14It was you who crushed the heads of
    Leviathan
  and gave him as food to the
    creatures of the desert.
15It was you who opened up springs
    and streams;
  you dried up the ever flowing
    rivers.
16The day is yours, and yours also the
    night;
  you established the sun and moon.
17It was you who set all the boundaries
    of the earth;
  you made both summer and winter.

18Remember how the enemy has
    mocked you, O LORD,
  how foolish people have reviled
    your name.
19Do not hand over the life of your dove
    to wild beasts;
  do not forget the lives of your
    afflicted people forever.
20Have regard for your covenant,
  because haunts of violence fill the
    dark places of the land.
21Do not let the oppressed retreat in
    disgrace;
  may the poor and needy praise your
    name.
22Rise up, O God, and defend your
    cause;

remember how fools mock you all
day long.
²³Do not ignore the clamor of your
adversaries,
the uproar of your enemies, which
rises continually.

PSALM 75
For the director of music. ⌊To the tune of⌋
"Do Not Destroy." A psalm of Asaph.
A song.

¹We give thanks to you, O God,
we give thanks, for your Name is
near;
men tell of your wonderful deeds.

²You say, "I choose the appointed time;
it is I who judge uprightly.
³When the earth and all its people
quake,
it is I who hold its pillars firm. *Selah*
⁴To the arrogant I say, 'Boast no more,'
and to the wicked, 'Do not lift up
your horns.
⁵Do not lift your horns against heaven;
do not speak with outstretched
neck.' "

⁶No one from the east or the west
or from the desert can exalt a man.
⁷But it is God who judges:
He brings one down, he exalts
another.
⁸In the hand of the LORD is a cup
full of foaming wine mixed with
spices;
he pours it out, and all the wicked of
the earth
drink it down to its very dregs.

⁹As for me, I will declare this forever;
I will sing praise to the God of
Jacob.
¹⁰I will cut off the horns of all the
wicked,
but the horns of the righteous will
be lifted up.

PSALM 76
For the director of music. With stringed
instruments. A psalm of Asaph. A song.

¹In Judah God is known;
his name is great in Israel.
²His tent is in Salem,
his dwelling place in Zion.
³There he broke the flashing arrows,

the shields and the swords, the
weapons of war.   *Selah*

⁴You are resplendent with light,
more majestic than mountains rich
with game.
⁵Valiant men lie plundered,
they sleep their last sleep;
not one of the warriors
can lift his hands.
⁶At your rebuke, O God of Jacob,
both horse and chariot lie still.
⁷You alone are to be feared.
Who can stand before you when you
are angry?
⁸From heaven you pronounced
judgment,
and the land feared and was quiet—
⁹when you, O God, rose up to judge,
to save all the afflicted of the land.
Selah
¹⁰Surely your wrath against men brings
you praise,
and the survivors of your wrath are
restrained.ᵈ

¹¹Make vows to the LORD your God and
fulfill them;
let all the neighboring lands
bring gifts to the One to be feared.
¹²He breaks the spirit of rulers;
he is feared by the kings of the
earth.

PSALM 77
For the director of music. For Jeduthun.
Of Asaph. A psalm.

¹I cried out to God for help;
I cried out to God to hear me.
²When I was in distress, I sought the
Lord;
at night I stretched out untiring
hands
and my soul refused to be
comforted.

³I remembered you, O God, and I
groaned;
I mused, and my spirit grew faint.
Selah
⁴You kept my eyes from closing;
I was too troubled to speak.
⁵I thought about the former days,
the years of long ago;
⁶I remembered my songs in the night.
My heart mused and my spirit
inquired:

ᵈ10 Or *Surely the wrath of men brings you praise, / and with the remainder of wrath you arm yourself*

⁷"Will the Lord reject forever?
  Will he never show his favor again?
⁸Has his unfailing love vanished
      forever?
  Has his promise failed for all time?
⁹Has God forgotten to be merciful?
  Has he in anger withheld his
      compassion?"   *Selah*

¹⁰Then I thought, "To this I will appeal:
  the years of the right hand of the
      Most High."
¹¹I will remember the deeds of the LORD;
  yes, I will remember your miracles
      of long ago.
¹²I will meditate on all your works
  and consider all your mighty deeds.

¹³Your ways, O God, are holy.
  What god is so great as our God?
¹⁴You are the God who performs
      miracles;
  you display your power among the
      peoples.

¹⁵With your mighty arm you redeemed
      your people,
  the descendants of Jacob and Joseph.
                                    Selah

¹⁶The waters saw you, O God,
  the waters saw you and writhed;
  the very depths were convulsed.
¹⁷The clouds poured down water,
  the skies resounded with thunder;
  your arrows flashed back and forth.
¹⁸Your thunder was heard in the
      whirlwind,
  your lightning lit up the world;
  the earth trembled and quaked.
¹⁹Your path led through the sea,
  your way through the mighty
      waters,
  though your footprints were not
      seen.
²⁰You led your people like a flock
  by the hand of Moses and Aaron.

JUNE 16 ☐ DAY 168
PSALMS 78–83
Warmth for Cold Hearts

 OVERVIEW Asaph's final contribution to the Psalter is found in today's reading. There he recounts Israel's history of disobedience (Psalm 78) and cries out to God to restore his people to the place of blessing (79–80). A lament over the nation's failure to obey God (81) is followed by an appeal for God's justice to prevail over Israel's oppressors (82–83).

Psalm 78	Psalms 79–80	Psalm 81	Psalms 82–83
Israel's Rebellion	Israel's Restoration	Israel's Stubbornness	Israel's Savior
Admission	Appeal	Admonition	Petition

 YOUR DAILY WALK A woman asked her physician, "Doctor, why am I seized with these restless longings for the glamorous and faraway?"

"My dear lady," he replied, "those are the usual symptoms of abundant comfort in the home and ingratitude in the heart."

The more we count the blessings we have, the less we crave the luxuries we haven't.

Three times in Psalm 78 Asaph points out how the nation Israel put God to the test by placing demands on God (v. 18), forgetting his past deliverance (v. 42) and disobeying his commands (v. 56). In each case, the problem was ingratitude—the subtle temptation first to grow accustomed to . . . then to expect . . . and finally to demand . . . the blessings of God.

Ingratitude in the face of God's gracious provision chipped away at the nation's relationship with God. Is ingratitude doing the same in your life? How do you relate to the blessings of God? Has abundance produced apathy or appreciation? Has your heart grown cold from the consistency of God's provision?

This gospel hymn is still a timely reminder:

"Count your blessings, name them one by one;
Count your many blessings, see what God hath done!"

Try it! In the next two minutes can you list twenty-five ways God has enriched your life—twenty-five blessings for which you want to tell him thanks? Remember, it is with gratitude that life becomes rich!

 INSIGHT A Millennium of God's Mercy
Psalm 78, the second longest psalm, might well be subtitled "From Zoan to Zion." In the space of just fifty-seven verses (vv. 12–68) Asaph traces Israel's history from bondage in Egypt to David's rule in Zion—a thousand-year record of God's faithfulness!

PSALM 78
A *maskil*ᵉ of Asaph.

¹O my people, hear my teaching;
  listen to the words of my mouth.
²I will open my mouth in parables,
  I will utter hidden things, things
    from of old—
³what we have heard and known,
  what our fathers have told us.
⁴We will not hide them from their
    children;
  we will tell the next generation
the praiseworthy deeds of the LORD,
  his power, and the wonders he has
    done.
⁵He decreed statutes for Jacob
  and established the law in Israel,
which he commanded our forefathers
  to teach their children,
⁶so the next generation would know
    them,
  even the children yet to be born,
  and they in turn would tell their
    children.
⁷Then they would put their trust in
    God
  and would not forget his deeds
  but would keep his commands.
⁸They would not be like their
    forefathers—
  a stubborn and rebellious
    generation,
whose hearts were not loyal to God,
  whose spirits were not faithful to
    him.
⁹The men of Ephraim, though armed
    with bows,
  turned back on the day of battle;
¹⁰they did not keep God's covenant

and refused to live by his law.
¹¹They forgot what he had done,
  the wonders he had shown them.
¹²He did miracles in the sight of their
    fathers
  in the land of Egypt, in the region of
    Zoan.
¹³He divided the sea and led them
    through;
  he made the water stand firm like a
    wall.
¹⁴He guided them with the cloud by day
  and with light from the fire all
    night.
¹⁵He split the rocks in the desert
  and gave them water as abundant as
    the seas;
¹⁶he brought streams out of a rocky crag
  and made water flow down like
    rivers.

¹⁷But they continued to sin against him,
  rebelling in the desert against the
    Most High.
¹⁸They willfully put God to the test
  by demanding the food they craved.
¹⁹They spoke against God, saying,
  "Can God spread a table in the
    desert?
²⁰When he struck the rock, water
    gushed out,
  and streams flowed abundantly.
But can he also give us food?
  Can he supply meat for his people?"
²¹When the LORD heard them, he was
    very angry;
  his fire broke out against Jacob,
  and his wrath rose against Israel,
²²for they did not believe in God
  or trust in his deliverance.

ᵉTitle: Probably a literary or musical term

²³Yet he gave a command to the skies
above
and opened the doors of the
heavens;
²⁴he rained down manna for the people
to eat,
he gave them the grain of heaven.
²⁵Men ate the bread of angels;
he sent them all the food they could
eat.
²⁶He let loose the east wind from the
heavens
and led forth the south wind by his
power.
²⁷He rained meat down on them like
dust,
flying birds like sand on the
seashore.
²⁸He made them come down inside their
camp,
all around their tents.
²⁹They ate till they had more than
enough,
for he had given them what they
craved.
³⁰But before they turned from the food
they craved,
even while it was still in their
mouths,
³¹God's anger rose against them;
he put to death the sturdiest among
them,
cutting down the young men of
Israel.

³²In spite of all this, they kept on
sinning;
in spite of his wonders, they did not
believe.
³³So he ended their days in futility
and their years in terror.
³⁴Whenever God slew them, they would
seek him;
they eagerly turned to him again.
³⁵They remembered that God was their
Rock,
that God Most High was their
Redeemer.
³⁶But then they would flatter him with
their mouths,
lying to him with their tongues;
³⁷their hearts were not loyal to him,
they were not faithful to his
covenant.
³⁸Yet he was merciful;
he forgave their iniquities
and did not destroy them.

Time after time he restrained his anger
and did not stir up his full wrath.
³⁹He remembered that they were but
flesh,
a passing breeze that does not
return.

⁴⁰How often they rebelled against him
in the desert
and grieved him in the wasteland!
⁴¹Again and again they put God to the
test;
they vexed the Holy One of Israel.
⁴²They did not remember his power—
the day he redeemed them from the
oppressor,
⁴³the day he displayed his miraculous
signs in Egypt,
his wonders in the region of Zoan.
⁴⁴He turned their rivers to blood;
they could not drink from their
streams.
⁴⁵He sent swarms of flies that devoured
them,
and frogs that devastated them.
⁴⁶He gave their crops to the
grasshopper,
their produce to the locust.
⁴⁷He destroyed their vines with hail
and their sycamore-figs with sleet.
⁴⁸He gave over their cattle to the hail,
their livestock to bolts of lightning.
⁴⁹He unleashed against them his hot
anger,
his wrath, indignation and
hostility—
a band of destroying angels.
⁵⁰He prepared a path for his anger;
he did not spare them from death
but gave them over to the plague.
⁵¹He struck down all the firstborn of
Egypt,
the firstfruits of manhood in the
tents of Ham.
⁵²But he brought his people out like a
flock;
he led them like sheep through the
desert.
⁵³He guided them safely, so they were
unafraid;
but the sea engulfed their enemies.
⁵⁴Thus he brought them to the border of
his holy land,
to the hill country his right hand
had taken.
⁵⁵He drove out nations before them

and allotted their lands to them as
    an inheritance;
he settled the tribes of Israel in their
    homes.

⁵⁶But they put God to the test
    and rebelled against the Most High;
    they did not keep his statutes.
⁵⁷Like their fathers they were disloyal
    and faithless,
    as unreliable as a faulty bow.
⁵⁸They angered him with their high
    places;
    they aroused his jealousy with their
    idols.
⁵⁹When God heard them, he was very
    angry;
he rejected Israel completely.
⁶⁰He abandoned the tabernacle of
    Shiloh,
    the tent he had set up among men.
⁶¹He sent ⌊the ark of⌋ his might into
    captivity,
    his splendor into the hands of the
    enemy.
⁶²He gave his people over to the sword;
    he was very angry with his
    inheritance.
⁶³Fire consumed their young men,
    and their maidens had no wedding
    songs;
⁶⁴their priests were put to the sword,
    and their widows could not weep.

⁶⁵Then the Lord awoke as from sleep,
    as a man wakes from the stupor of
    wine.
⁶⁶He beat back his enemies;
    he put them to everlasting shame.
⁶⁷Then he rejected the tents of Joseph,
    he did not choose the tribe of
    Ephraim;
⁶⁸but he chose the tribe of Judah,
    Mount Zion, which he loved.
⁶⁹He built his sanctuary like the heights,
    like the earth that he established
    forever.
⁷⁰He chose David his servant
    and took him from the sheep pens;
⁷¹from tending the sheep he brought
    him
    to be the shepherd of his people
    Jacob,
    of Israel his inheritance.
⁷²And David shepherded them with
    integrity of heart;
    with skillful hands he led them.

PSALM 79
A psalm of Asaph.

¹O God, the nations have invaded your
    inheritance;
    they have defiled your holy temple,
    they have reduced Jerusalem to
    rubble.
²They have given the dead bodies of
    your servants
    as food to the birds of the air,
    the flesh of your saints to the beasts
    of the earth.
³They have poured out blood like water
    all around Jerusalem,
    and there is no one to bury the
    dead.
⁴We are objects of reproach to our
    neighbors,
    of scorn and derision to those
    around us.

⁵How long, O LORD? Will you be angry
    forever?
    How long will your jealousy burn
    like fire?
⁶Pour out your wrath on the nations
    that do not acknowledge you,
  on the kingdoms
    that do not call on your name;
⁷for they have devoured Jacob
    and destroyed his homeland.
⁸Do not hold against us the sins of the
    fathers;
    may your mercy come quickly to
    meet us,
    for we are in desperate need.

⁹Help us, O God our Savior,
    for the glory of your name;
  deliver us and forgive our sins
    for your name's sake.
¹⁰Why should the nations say,
    "Where is their God?"
  Before our eyes, make known among
    the nations
    that you avenge the outpoured
    blood of your servants.
¹¹May the groans of the prisoners come
    before you;
    by the strength of your arm
    preserve those condemned to die.

¹²Pay back into the laps of our
    neighbors seven times
    the reproach they have hurled at
    you, O Lord.
¹³Then we your people, the sheep of
    your pasture,

will praise you forever;
from generation to generation
  we will recount your praise.

PSALM 80

For the director of music. To ¸the tune of¸
"The Lilies of the Covenant." Of Asaph.
A psalm.

[1]Hear us, O Shepherd of Israel,
  you who lead Joseph like a flock;
you who sit enthroned between the
    cherubim, shine forth
[2] before Ephraim, Benjamin and
    Manasseh.
  Awaken your might;
    come and save us.

[3]Restore us, O God;
  make your face shine upon us,
    that we may be saved.

[4]O LORD God Almighty,
  how long will your anger smolder
    against the prayers of your people?
[5]You have fed them with the bread of
    tears;
  you have made them drink tears by
    the bowlful.
[6]You have made us a source of
    contention to our neighbors,
  and our enemies mock us.

[7]Restore us, O God Almighty;
  make your face shine upon us,
    that we may be saved.

[8]You brought a vine out of Egypt;
  you drove out the nations and
    planted it.
[9]You cleared the ground for it,
  and it took root and filled the land.
[10]The mountains were covered with its
    shade,
  the mighty cedars with its branches.
[11]It sent out its boughs to the Sea,[f]
  its shoots as far as the River.[g]

[12]Why have you broken down its walls
  so that all who pass by pick its
    grapes?
[13]Boars from the forest ravage it
  and the creatures of the field feed on
    it.
[14]Return to us, O God Almighty!
  Look down from heaven and see!
  Watch over this vine,

[15] the root your right hand has
    planted,
  the son[h] you have raised up for
    yourself.
[16]Your vine is cut down, it is burned
    with fire;
  at your rebuke your people perish.
[17]Let your hand rest on the man at your
    right hand,
  the son of man you have raised up
    for yourself.
[18]Then we will not turn away from you;
  revive us, and we will call on your
    name.

[19]Restore us, O LORD God Almighty;
  make your face shine upon us,
    that we may be saved.

PSALM 81

For the director of music. According to
gittith.[i] Of Asaph.

[1]Sing for joy to God our strength;
  shout aloud to the God of Jacob!
[2]Begin the music, strike the tambourine,
  play the melodious harp and lyre.

[3]Sound the ram's horn at the New
    Moon,
  and when the moon is full, on the
    day of our Feast;
[4]this is a decree for Israel,
  an ordinance of the God of Jacob.
[5]He established it as a statute for
    Joseph
  when he went out against Egypt,
  where we heard a language we did
    not understand.[j]

[6]He says, "I removed the burden from
    their shoulders;
  their hands were set free from the
    basket.
[7]In your distress you called and I
    rescued you,
  I answered you out of a
    thundercloud;
  I tested you at the waters of
    Meribah.   *Selah*

[8]"Hear, O my people, and I will warn
    you—
  if you would but listen to me,
    O Israel!
[9]You shall have no foreign god among
    you;

---

[f]11 Probably the Mediterranean   [g]11 That is, the Euphrates   [h]15 Or *branch*   [i]Title: Probably a musical term   [j]5 Or /
and we heard a voice we had not known

you shall not bow down to an alien
    god.
¹⁰I am the LORD your God,
    who brought you up out of Egypt.
    Open wide your mouth and I will
        fill it.
¹¹"But my people would not listen to
        me;
    Israel would not submit to me.
¹²So I gave them over to their stubborn
        hearts
    to follow their own devices.

¹³"If my people would but listen to me,
    if Israel would follow my ways,
¹⁴how quickly would I subdue their
        enemies
    and turn my hand against their foes!
¹⁵Those who hate the LORD would cringe
        before him,
    and their punishment would last
        forever.
¹⁶But you would be fed with the finest
        of wheat;
    with honey from the rock I would
        satisfy you."

PSALM 82
A psalm of Asaph.

¹God presides in the great assembly;
    he gives judgment among the
        "gods":

²"How long will you ᵏ defend the
        unjust
    and show partiality to the wicked?
                                    Selah
³Defend the cause of the weak and
        fatherless;
    maintain the rights of the poor and
        oppressed.
⁴Rescue the weak and needy;
    deliver them from the hand of the
        wicked.

⁵"They know nothing, they understand
        nothing.
    They walk about in darkness;
    all the foundations of the earth are
        shaken.

⁶"I said, 'You are "gods";
    you are all sons of the Most High.'
⁷But you will die like mere men;
    you will fall like every other ruler."

⁸Rise up, O God, judge the earth,

for all the nations are your
        inheritance.

PSALM 83
A song. A psalm of Asaph.

¹O God, do not keep silent;
    be not quiet, O God, be not still.
²See how your enemies are astir,
    how your foes rear their heads.
³With cunning they conspire against
        your people;
    they plot against those you cherish.
⁴"Come," they say, "let us destroy them
        as a nation,
    that the name of Israel be
        remembered no more."

⁵With one mind they plot together;
    they form an alliance against you—
⁶the tents of Edom and the Ishmaelites,
    of Moab and the Hagrites,
⁷Gebal,ˡ Ammon and Amalek,
    Philistia, with the people of Tyre.
⁸Even Assyria has joined them
    to lend strength to the descendants
        of Lot.   Selah

⁹Do to them as you did to Midian,
    as you did to Sisera and Jabin at the
        river Kishon,
¹⁰who perished at Endor
    and became like refuse on the
        ground.
¹¹Make their nobles like Oreb and Zeeb,
    all their princes like Zebah and
        Zalmunna,
¹²who said, "Let us take possession
    of the pasturelands of God."

¹³Make them like tumbleweed, O my
        God,
    like chaff before the wind.
¹⁴As fire consumes the forest
    or a flame sets the mountains ablaze,
¹⁵so pursue them with your tempest
    and terrify them with your storm.
¹⁶Cover their faces with shame
    so that men will seek your name,
        O LORD.

¹⁷May they ever be ashamed and
        dismayed;
    may they perish in disgrace.
¹⁸Let them know that you, whose name
        is the LORD—
    that you alone are the Most High
        over all the earth.

ᵏ2 The Hebrew is plural.   ˡ7 That is, Byblos

JUNE 17 □ DAY 169
PSALMS 84–89
A Promise-Keeping God

OVERVIEW Several different authors are represented in the six psalms in today's reading. The Sons of Korah yearn to be in God's presence (Psalm 84) and to see the nation restored to fellowship with God (85). David seeks the great and merciful God amid opposition (86), while the Sons of Korah proclaim the greatness of the city of God (87). The final two laments record the mournful cry of Heman when he was afflicted (88) and the pleading of Ethan, who remembers God's words to Israel (89).

Psalms 84–85	Psalms 86–87	Psalms 88–89
Longing for God	Looking to God	Leaning on God
Desire	Dependence	Doxology

You cannot starve a person who is feeding on God's promises.

YOUR DAILY WALK If someone has made a promise to you and then circumstances change, making it seemingly impossible for that person to keep his or her word, you are faced with a choice: You can either let your problems cast a shadow on the promise or allow the promise to shed light on your problems. It all depends on the trustworthiness—and power—of the promise maker.

God made a promise to David (89:3–4). You'll find it recorded in 2 Samuel 7:13–16. God promised David an everlasting family line, throne and kingdom. On at least two occasions the "royal family" was reduced to only a single member (2 Chronicles 21:4; 22:8–12). Did that mean God's promise was in danger? Not at all! It only highlighted the importance of daily faith in the Promise Maker, for when the darkness is most severe, God's promises only shine more brightly.

To spark your faith in the God who keeps his word, find a sheet of paper and label one side "Promises God Made to People in the Bible but Never Kept"; the other, "Promises God Made—and Kept—to People in the Bible." Then do your own survey of Noah . . . Abraham . . . Jonah . . . and others. You'll find only one side of the paper filling up! What did these people discover about the promises of God? And does that cast a shadow or shed light on God's promises to you?

INSIGHT Unmasking a Maskil
Psalm 89 is a contemplation (Hebrew, *maskil*), a song of wisdom or insight designed to help you, the reader, reach your goal in life. Thirteen psalms are contemplations.

PSALM 84
For the director of music. According to *gittith.*ᵐ Of the Sons of Korah. A psalm.

¹How lovely is your dwelling place,
O LORD Almighty!
²My soul yearns, even faints,
for the courts of the LORD;
my heart and my flesh cry out
for the living God.

³Even the sparrow has found a home,
and the swallow a nest for herself,
where she may have her young—
a place near your altar,
O LORD Almighty, my King and my
God.
⁴Blessed are those who dwell in your
house;
they are ever praising you.   *Selah*

ᵐTitle: Probably a musical term

⁵Blessed are those whose strength is in
    you,
    who have set their hearts on
        pilgrimage.
⁶As they pass through the Valley of
    Baca,
    they make it a place of springs;
    the autumn rains also cover it with
        pools.ⁿ
⁷They go from strength to strength,
    till each appears before God in Zion.

⁸Hear my prayer, O LORD God
    Almighty;
    listen to me, O God of Jacob.   *Selah*
⁹Look upon our shield,ᵒ O God;
    look with favor on your anointed
        one.

¹⁰Better is one day in your courts
    than a thousand elsewhere;
    I would rather be a doorkeeper in the
        house of my God
    than dwell in the tents of the
        wicked.
¹¹For the LORD God is a sun and shield;
    the LORD bestows favor and honor;
    no good thing does he withhold
    from those whose walk is blameless.

¹²O LORD Almighty,
    blessed is the man who trusts in
        you.

PSALM 85

For the director of music. Of the Sons of
Korah. A psalm.

¹You showed favor to your land,
    O LORD;
    you restored the fortunes of Jacob.
²You forgave the iniquity of your
    people
    and covered all their sins.   *Selah*
³You set aside all your wrath
    and turned from your fierce anger.

⁴Restore us again, O God our Savior,
    and put away your displeasure
        toward us.
⁵Will you be angry with us forever?
    Will you prolong your anger
        through all generations?
⁶Will you not revive us again,
    that your people may rejoice in you?
⁷Show us your unfailing love, O LORD,
    and grant us your salvation.

⁸I will listen to what God the LORD will
    say;
    he promises peace to his people, his
        saints—
    but let them not return to folly.
⁹Surely his salvation is near those who
    fear him,
    that his glory may dwell in our
        land.

¹⁰Love and faithfulness meet together;
    righteousness and peace kiss each
        other.
¹¹Faithfulness springs forth from the
    earth,
    and righteousness looks down from
        heaven.
¹²The LORD will indeed give what is
    good,
    and our land will yield its harvest.
¹³Righteousness goes before him
    and prepares the way for his steps.

PSALM 86
A prayer of David.

¹Hear, O LORD, and answer me,
    for I am poor and needy.
²Guard my life, for I am devoted to
    you.
    You are my God; save your servant
    who trusts in you.
³Have mercy on me, O Lord,
    for I call to you all day long.
⁴Bring joy to your servant,
    for to you, O Lord,
    I lift up my soul.

⁵You are forgiving and good, O Lord,
    abounding in love to all who call to
        you.
⁶Hear my prayer, O LORD;
    listen to my cry for mercy.
⁷In the day of my trouble I will call to
    you,
    for you will answer me.

⁸Among the gods there is none like
    you, O Lord;
    no deeds can compare with yours.
⁹All the nations you have made
    will come and worship before you,
        O Lord;
    they will bring glory to your name.
¹⁰For you are great and do marvelous
    deeds;
    you alone are God.

ⁿ6 Or *blessings*   ᵒ9 Or *sovereign*

[11]Teach me your way, O LORD,
  and I will walk in your truth;
give me an undivided heart,
  that I may fear your name.
[12]I will praise you, O Lord my God,
  with all my heart;
I will glorify your name forever.
[13]For great is your love toward me;
  you have delivered me from the
    depths of the grave.[p]

[14]The arrogant are attacking me, O God;
  a band of ruthless men seeks my
    life—
  men without regard for you.
[15]But you, O Lord, are a compassionate
  and gracious God,
slow to anger, abounding in love
  and faithfulness.
[16]Turn to me and have mercy on me;
  grant your strength to your servant
and save the son of your
    maidservant.[q]
[17]Give me a sign of your goodness,
  that my enemies may see it and be
    put to shame,
for you, O LORD, have helped me
  and comforted me.

PSALM 87
Of the Sons of Korah. A psalm. A song.

[1]He has set his foundation on the holy
    mountain;
[2] the LORD loves the gates of Zion
  more than all the dwellings of Jacob.
[3]Glorious things are said of you,
  O city of God: *Selah*
[4]"I will record Rahab[r] and Babylon
  among those who acknowledge
    me—
Philistia too, and Tyre, along with
    Cush[s]—
and will say, 'This[t] one was born
  in Zion.' "

[5]Indeed, of Zion it will be said,
  "This one and that one were born in
    her,
and the Most High himself will
    establish her."
[6]The LORD will write in the register of
    the peoples:
  "This one was born in Zion."   *Selah*
[7]As they make music they will sing,
  "All my fountains are in you."

PSALM 88
A song. A psalm of the Sons of Korah.
For the director of music. According to
mahalath leannoth.[u] A *maskil*[v] of Heman
the Ezrahite.

[1]O LORD, the God who saves me,
  day and night I cry out before you.
[2]May my prayer come before you;
  turn your ear to my cry.

[3]For my soul is full of trouble
  and my life draws near the grave.[p]
[4]I am counted among those who go
    down to the pit;
  I am like a man without strength.
[5]I am set apart with the dead,
  like the slain who lie in the grave,
whom you remember no more,
  who are cut off from your care.

[6]You have put me in the lowest pit,
  in the darkest depths.
[7]Your wrath lies heavily upon me;
  you have overwhelmed me with all
    your waves.   *Selah*
[8]You have taken from me my closest
    friends
and have made me repulsive to
    them.
I am confined and cannot escape;
[9] my eyes are dim with grief.

I call to you, O LORD, every day;
  I spread out my hands to you.
[10]Do you show your wonders to the
    dead?
  Do those who are dead rise up and
    praise you?   *Selah*
[11]Is your love declared in the grave,
  your faithfulness in Destruction[w]?
[12]Are your wonders known in the place
  of darkness,
  or your righteous deeds in the land
    of oblivion?

[13]But I cry to you for help, O LORD;
  in the morning my prayer comes
    before you.
[14]Why, O LORD, do you reject me
  and hide your face from me?

[15]From my youth I have been afflicted
  and close to death;
  I have suffered your terrors and am
    in despair.
[16]Your wrath has swept over me;

---

[p]13,3 Hebrew *Sheol*   [q]16 Or *save your faithful son*   [r]4 A poetic name for Egypt   [s]4 That is, the upper Nile region
[t]4 Or "O Rahab and Babylon, / Philistia, Tyre and Cush, / I will record concerning those who acknowledge me: / 'This   [u]Title:
Possibly a tune, "The Suffering of Affliction"   [v]Title: Probably a literary or musical term   [w]11 Hebrew *Abaddon*

your terrors have destroyed me.
[17]All day long they surround me like a
     flood;
  they have completely engulfed me.
[18]You have taken my companions and
     loved ones from me;
  the darkness is my closest friend.

PSALM 89
A *maskil*[x] of Ethan the Ezrahite.

[1]I will sing of the LORD's great love
     forever;
  with my mouth I will make your
     faithfulness known through all
     generations.
[2]I will declare that your love stands
     firm forever,
  that you established your
     faithfulness in heaven itself.

[3]You said, "I have made a covenant
     with my chosen one,
  I have sworn to David my servant,
[4]'I will establish your line forever
  and make your throne firm through
     all generations.' "   *Selah*

[5]The heavens praise your wonders,
     O LORD,
  your faithfulness too, in the
     assembly of the holy ones.
[6]For who in the skies above can
     compare with the LORD?
  Who is like the LORD among the
     heavenly beings?
[7]In the council of the holy ones God is
     greatly feared;
  he is more awesome than all who
     surround him.
[8]O LORD God Almighty, who is like
     you?
  You are mighty, O LORD, and your
     faithfulness surrounds you.

[9]You rule over the surging sea;
  when its waves mount up, you still
     them.
[10]You crushed Rahab like one of the
     slain;
  with your strong arm you scattered
     your enemies.
[11]The heavens are yours, and yours also
     the earth;
  you founded the world and all that
     is in it.
[12]You created the north and the south;

Tabor and Hermon sing for joy at
     your name.
[13]Your arm is endued with power;
  your hand is strong, your right hand
     exalted.
[14]Righteousness and justice are the
     foundation of your throne;
  love and faithfulness go before you.
[15]Blessed are those who have learned to
     acclaim you,
  who walk in the light of your
     presence, O LORD.
[16]They rejoice in your name all day
     long;
  they exult in your righteousness.
[17]For you are their glory and strength,
  and by your favor you exalt our
     horn.[y]
[18]Indeed, our shield[z] belongs to the
     LORD,
  our king to the Holy One of Israel.

[19]Once you spoke in a vision,
  to your faithful people you said:
"I have bestowed strength on a
     warrior;
  I have exalted a young man from
     among the people.
[20]I have found David my servant;
  with my sacred oil I have anointed
     him.
[21]My hand will sustain him;
  surely my arm will strengthen him.
[22]No enemy will subject him to tribute;
  no wicked man will oppress him.
[23]I will crush his foes before him
  and strike down his adversaries.
[24]My faithful love will be with him,
  and through my name his horn[a]
     will be exalted.
[25]I will set his hand over the sea,
  his right hand over the rivers.
[26]He will call out to me, 'You are my
     Father,
  my God, the Rock my Savior.'
[27]I will also appoint him my firstborn,
  the most exalted of the kings of the
     earth.
[28]I will maintain my love to him forever,
  and my covenant with him will
     never fail.
[29]I will establish his line forever,
  his throne as long as the heavens
     endure.

[x] Title: Probably a literary or musical term   [y] 17 *Horn* here symbolizes strong one.   [z] 18 Or *sovereign*   [a] 24 *Horn* here symbolizes strength.

30"If his sons forsake my law
　and do not follow my statutes,
31if they violate my decrees
　and fail to keep my commands,
32I will punish their sin with the rod,
　their iniquity with flogging;
33but I will not take my love from him,
　nor will I ever betray my
　　faithfulness.
34I will not violate my covenant
　or alter what my lips have uttered.
35Once for all, I have sworn by my
　holiness—
　and I will not lie to David—
36that his line will continue forever
　and his throne endure before me
　　like the sun;
37it will be established forever like the
　moon,
　the faithful witness in the sky." *Selah*

38But you have rejected, you have
　spurned,
　you have been very angry with your
　　anointed one.
39You have renounced the covenant with
　your servant
　and have defiled his crown in the
　　dust.
40You have broken through all his walls
　and reduced his strongholds to
　　ruins.
41All who pass by have plundered him;
　he has become the scorn of his
　　neighbors.
42You have exalted the right hand of his
　foes;

b48 Hebrew *Sheol*　　*c50* Or *your servants have*

you have made all his enemies
　rejoice.
43You have turned back the edge of his
　sword
　and have not supported him in
　　battle.
44You have put an end to his splendor
　and cast his throne to the ground.
45You have cut short the days of his
　youth;
　you have covered him with a mantle
　　of shame.　　　　　*Selah*

46How long, O LORD? Will you hide
　yourself forever?
　How long will your wrath burn like
　　fire?
47Remember how fleeting is my life.
　For what futility you have created
　　all men!
48What man can live and not see death,
　or save himself from the power of
　　the grave*b*?　　　　*Selah*
49O Lord, where is your former great
　love,
　which in your faithfulness you
　　swore to David?
50Remember, Lord, how your servant
　has*c* been mocked,
　how I bear in my heart the taunts of
　　all the nations,
51the taunts with which your enemies
　have mocked, O LORD,
　with which they have mocked every
　　step of your anointed one.

52Praise be to the LORD forever!
　Amen and Amen.

JUNE 18 ☐ DAY 170
PSALMS 90–97
God's Seal of Approval

OVERVIEW Book IV opens with the oldest of the psalms, Moses' testimony of faith in an eternal God (Psalm 90). God's people find their refuge (91) and their joy (92) in the God who reigns over all (93) and avenges the wrongs done to his own (94). The invitation is extended for all to worship (95), sing praises (96) and gladly acknowledge the incomparable greatness of the God of Israel (97).

Psalms 90–92	Psalms 93–94	Psalms 95–97
God's People	God's Person	God's Praise
Mortal	Mighty	Majestic

The person who does good for God's glory seeks neither praise nor reward but is sure of both in the end.

YOUR DAILY WALK Because of its smallness, you seldom notice it unless you are looking for it. Yet thousands of items sold today display it proudly.

What is it? A seal of approval granted by a testing agency such as the Good Housekeeping Institute. For many shoppers, the presence— or absence—of such a recommendation has a significant impact on their decision to buy the product.

In Psalm 90 Moses speaks of another "seal of approval"—this one found, not on a product, but on a life; one issued, not by a testing agency, but by God himself. In contrast to the briefness of human life, God reserves his stamp of approval for endeavors of eternal significance. Earthly products soon rust or wear out, but God's seal of approval is the mark of eternity on a life. Whatever is done apart from God ends in death; whatever is accomplished for his glory lasts for eternity (Matthew 6:19–21).

Look for a seal of approval on a product or appliance you have around the house. Carefully remove the seal, and put it in a prominent place in your home or office to remind you throughout the day to live for God's approval—with eternity's values in view.

INSIGHT The Dark Background of Psalm 90
Verses 7–12 seem to indicate that Moses wrote Psalm 90 during the time of desert wandering—the forty-year period when six hundred thousand Israelite men (and their wives) died for unbelief (Numbers 14:21–23). What clearer reminder of Israel's mortality could there be (Psalm 90:9–10) than an average of *one funeral every twenty minutes, twenty-four hours a day, for forty years!*

BOOK IV
Psalms 90–106

PSALM 90
A prayer of Moses the man of God.

¹Lord, you have been our dwelling place
throughout all generations.
²Before the mountains were born
or you brought forth the earth and the world,
from everlasting to everlasting you are God.

³You turn men back to dust,
saying, "Return to dust, O sons of men."
⁴For a thousand years in your sight
are like a day that has just gone by,
or like a watch in the night.
⁵You sweep men away in the sleep of death;

they are like the new grass of the morning—
⁶though in the morning it springs up new,
by evening it is dry and withered.

⁷We are consumed by your anger
and terrified by your indignation.
⁸You have set our iniquities before you,
our secret sins in the light of your presence.
⁹All our days pass away under your wrath;
we finish our years with a moan.
¹⁰The length of our days is seventy years—
or eighty, if we have the strength;
yet their span^d is but trouble and sorrow,
for they quickly pass, and we fly away.
¹¹Who knows the power of your anger?

---
^{d}**10** Or *yet the best of them*

For your wrath is as great as the
    fear that is due you.
12Teach us to number our days aright,
    that we may gain a heart of wisdom.

13Relent, O LORD! How long will it be?
    Have compassion on your servants.
14Satisfy us in the morning with your
    unfailing love,
    that we may sing for joy and be
        glad all our days.
15Make us glad for as many days as you
    have afflicted us,
    for as many years as we have seen
        trouble.
16May your deeds be shown to your
    servants,
    your splendor to their children.

17May the favor*e* of the Lord our God
    rest upon us;
    establish the work of our hands for
        us—
    yes, establish the work of our hands.

PSALM 91

1He who dwells in the shelter of the
    Most High
    will rest in the shadow of the
        Almighty.*f*
2I will say*g* of the LORD, "He is my
    refuge and my fortress,
    my God, in whom I trust."

3Surely he will save you from the
    fowler's snare
    and from the deadly pestilence.
4He will cover you with his feathers,
    and under his wings you will find
        refuge;
    his faithfulness will be your shield
        and rampart.
5You will not fear the terror of night,
    nor the arrow that flies by day,
6nor the pestilence that stalks in the
    darkness,
    nor the plague that destroys at
        midday.
7A thousand may fall at your side,
    ten thousand at your right hand,
    but it will not come near you.
8You will only observe with your eyes
    and see the punishment of the
        wicked.
9If you make the Most High your
    dwelling—

even the LORD, who is my refuge—
10then no harm will befall you,
    no disaster will come near your tent.
11For he will command his angels
    concerning you
    to guard you in all your ways;
12they will lift you up in their hands,
    so that you will not strike your foot
        against a stone.
13You will tread upon the lion and the
    cobra;
    you will trample the great lion and
        the serpent.
14"Because he loves me," says the LORD,
    "I will rescue him;
    I will protect him, for he
        acknowledges my name.
15He will call upon me, and I will
    answer him;
    I will be with him in trouble,
    I will deliver him and honor him.
16With long life will I satisfy him
    and show him my salvation."

PSALM 92
A psalm. A song. For the Sabbath day.

1It is good to praise the LORD
    and make music to your name,
        O Most High,
2to proclaim your love in the morning
    and your faithfulness at night,
3to the music of the ten-stringed lyre
    and the melody of the harp.

4For you make me glad by your deeds,
    O LORD;
    I sing for joy at the works of your
        hands.
5How great are your works, O LORD,
    how profound your thoughts!
6The senseless man does not know,
    fools do not understand,
7that though the wicked spring up like
    grass
    and all evildoers flourish,
    they will be forever destroyed.

8But you, O LORD, are exalted forever.

9For surely your enemies, O LORD,
    surely your enemies will perish;
    all evildoers will be scattered.
10You have exalted my horn*h* like that
    of a wild ox;
    fine oils have been poured upon me.

*e*17 Or *beauty*   *f*1 Hebrew *Shaddai*   *g*2 Or *He says*   *h*10 *Horn* here symbolizes strength.

¹¹My eyes have seen the defeat of my
    adversaries;
  my ears have heard the rout of my
    wicked foes.

¹²The righteous will flourish like a palm
    tree,
  they will grow like a cedar of
    Lebanon;
¹³planted in the house of the LORD,
  they will flourish in the courts of
    our God.
¹⁴They will still bear fruit in old age,
  they will stay fresh and green,
¹⁵proclaiming, "The LORD is upright;
  he is my Rock, and there is no
    wickedness in him."

PSALM 93

¹The LORD reigns, he is robed in
    majesty;
  the LORD is robed in majesty
  and is armed with strength.
The world is firmly established;
  it cannot be moved.
²Your throne was established long ago;
  you are from all eternity.

³The seas have lifted up, O LORD,
  the seas have lifted up their voice;
  the seas have lifted up their
    pounding waves.
⁴Mightier than the thunder of the great
    waters,
  mightier than the breakers of the
    sea—
  the LORD on high is mighty.

⁵Your statutes stand firm;
  holiness adorns your house
  for endless days, O LORD.

PSALM 94

¹O LORD, the God who avenges,
  O God who avenges, shine forth.
²Rise up, O Judge of the earth;
  pay back to the proud what they
    deserve.
³How long will the wicked, O LORD,
  how long will the wicked be
    jubilant?

⁴They pour out arrogant words;
  all the evildoers are full of boasting.
⁵They crush your people, O LORD;
  they oppress your inheritance.
⁶They slay the widow and the alien;
  they murder the fatherless.

⁷They say, "The LORD does not see;
  the God of Jacob pays no heed."

⁸Take heed, you senseless ones among
    the people;
  you fools, when will you become
    wise?
⁹Does he who implanted the ear not
    hear?
  Does he who formed the eye not
    see?
¹⁰Does he who disciplines nations not
    punish?
  Does he who teaches man lack
    knowledge?
¹¹The LORD knows the thoughts of man;
  he knows that they are futile.

¹²Blessed is the man you discipline,
    O LORD,
  the man you teach from your law;
¹³you grant him relief from days of
    trouble,
  till a pit is dug for the wicked.
¹⁴For the LORD will not reject his people;
  he will never forsake his inheritance.
¹⁵Judgment will again be founded on
    righteousness,
  and all the upright in heart will
    follow it.

¹⁶Who will rise up for me against the
    wicked?
  Who will take a stand for me
    against evildoers?
¹⁷Unless the LORD had given me help,
  I would soon have dwelt in the
    silence of death.
¹⁸When I said, "My foot is slipping,"
  your love, O LORD, supported me.
¹⁹When anxiety was great within me,
  your consolation brought joy to my
    soul.

²⁰Can a corrupt throne be allied with
    you—
  one that brings on misery by its
    decrees?
²¹They band together against the
    righteous
  and condemn the innocent to death.
²²But the LORD has become my fortress,
  and my God the rock in whom I
    take refuge.
²³He will repay them for their sins
  and destroy them for their
    wickedness;
  the LORD our God will destroy them.

PSALM 95

¹Come, let us sing for joy to the LORD;
  let us shout aloud to the Rock of our
    salvation.
²Let us come before him with
    thanksgiving
  and extol him with music and song.

³For the LORD is the great God,
  the great King above all gods.
⁴In his hand are the depths of the earth,
  and the mountain peaks belong to
    him.
⁵The sea is his, for he made it,
  and his hands formed the dry land.

⁶Come, let us bow down in worship,
  let us kneel before the LORD our
    Maker;
⁷for he is our God
  and we are the people of his
    pasture,
  the flock under his care.

  Today, if you hear his voice,
⁸ do not harden your hearts as you
      did at Meribah,ⁱ
  as you did that day at Massahʲ in
    the desert,
⁹where your fathers tested and tried
    me,
  though they had seen what I did.
¹⁰For forty years I was angry with that
    generation;
  I said, "They are a people whose
    hearts go astray,
  and they have not known my ways."
¹¹So I declared on oath in my anger,
  "They shall never enter my rest."

PSALM 96

¹Sing to the LORD a new song;
  sing to the LORD, all the earth.
²Sing to the LORD, praise his name;
  proclaim his salvation day after day.
³Declare his glory among the nations,
  his marvelous deeds among all
    peoples.

⁴For great is the LORD and most worthy
    of praise;
  he is to be feared above all gods.
⁵For all the gods of the nations are
    idols,
  but the LORD made the heavens.
⁶Splendor and majesty are before him;

strength and glory are in his
  sanctuary.

⁷Ascribe to the LORD, O families of
    nations,
  ascribe to the LORD glory and
    strength.
⁸Ascribe to the LORD the glory due his
    name;
  bring an offering and come into his
    courts.
⁹Worship the LORD in the splendor of
    hisᵏ holiness;
  tremble before him, all the earth.

¹⁰Say among the nations, "The LORD
    reigns."
  The world is firmly established, it
    cannot be moved;
  he will judge the peoples with
    equity.
¹¹Let the heavens rejoice, let the earth be
    glad;
  let the sea resound, and all that is in
    it;
¹² let the fields be jubilant, and
      everything in them.
  Then all the trees of the forest will
    sing for joy;
¹³ they will sing before the LORD, for he
      comes,
  he comes to judge the earth.
  He will judge the world in
    righteousness
  and the peoples in his truth.

PSALM 97

¹The LORD reigns, let the earth be glad;
  let the distant shores rejoice.

²Clouds and thick darkness surround
    him;
  righteousness and justice are the
    foundation of his throne.
³Fire goes before him
  and consumes his foes on every
    side.
⁴His lightning lights up the world;
  the earth sees and trembles.
⁵The mountains melt like wax before
    the LORD,
  before the Lord of all the earth.
⁶The heavens proclaim his
    righteousness,
  and all the peoples see his glory.

ⁱ8 *Meribah* means *quarreling.*   ʲ8 *Massah* means *testing.*   ᵏ9 Or LORD *with the splendor of*

7All who worship images are put to
shame,
those who boast in idols—
worship him, all you gods!

8Zion hears and rejoices
and the villages of Judah are glad
because of your judgments, O LORD.
9For you, O LORD, are the Most High
over all the earth;
you are exalted far above all gods.

10Let those who love the LORD hate
evil,
for he guards the lives of his faithful
ones
and delivers them from the hand of
the wicked.
11Light is shed upon the righteous
and joy on the upright in heart.
12Rejoice in the LORD, you who are
righteous,
and praise his holy name.

JUNE 19 ☐ DAY 171
PSALMS 98–103
A Joyful Noise

OVERVIEW Perhaps no other six psalms picture God's praiseworthy
character as graphically as the ones in today's reading. God in his
righteousness (Psalm 98), in his exalted place of authority (99) and in
his everlasting mercy (100) demands and deserves admiration and
adoration by his people. In view of God's character, the psalmist
pledges his obedience (101), expresses his dependence (102) and acknowledges his gratitude for God's rich blessings (103).

Psalm 98	Psalm 99	Psalm 100	Psalms 101–103
Singing God's Justice	Speaking God's Forgiveness	Shouting God's Faithfulness	Living Life Gratefully
Reverence			Response

YOUR DAILY WALK You'll notice in Psalm 98:4 (and again in 100:1)
that you are not required to make beautiful music but only a joyful
shout to the Lord. Even monotones can vocalize their praise to the
Lord!

*Where the
benefits received
are infinite,
the praises
cannot be too
extravagant.*

The writer of Psalm 98 knew what rejoicing in the Lord meant. Have
you learned his secret? When God has done something wonderful in
your life, when you are bubbling over with appreciation for his mighty
deeds, how can you express your joy? How can you say thank you to
God in a way that befits his majesty and splendor?

Answer: You can sing! "Sing to the LORD a new song, . . . Shout for
joy to the LORD, . . . make music to the LORD with the harp, with the
harp and the sound of singing" (vv. 1, 4–5). One thing you can take
with you throughout the day is a song. Spend the next few minutes
singing some of your favorite hymns or choruses. Think about the
words as you sing them. You'll have a song in your heart all day!

INSIGHT Praise Expressed Full Circle
In Psalm 103, David constructs a "circle of praise" in which the entire
universe breaks forth in a doxology to God:
• Himself: "O my soul" (vv. 1–5)
• The people of Israel (vv. 6–18)
• The angels (vv. 19–22)
Finally, David ends where he began: "Praise the LORD, O my soul."

PSALM 98
A psalm.

[1]Sing to the LORD a new song,
  for he has done marvelous things;
his right hand and his holy arm
  have worked salvation for him.
[2]The LORD has made his salvation
    known
  and revealed his righteousness to
    the nations.
[3]He has remembered his love
  and his faithfulness to the house of
    Israel;
all the ends of the earth have seen
  the salvation of our God.

[4]Shout for joy to the LORD, all the earth,
  burst into jubilant song with music;
[5]make music to the LORD with the harp,
  with the harp and the sound of
    singing,
[6]with trumpets and the blast of the
    ram's horn—
  shout for joy before the LORD, the
    King.

[7]Let the sea resound, and everything in
    it,
  the world, and all who live in it.
[8]Let the rivers clap their hands,
  let the mountains sing together for
    joy;
[9]let them sing before the LORD,
  for he comes to judge the earth.
He will judge the world in
    righteousness
  and the peoples with equity.

PSALM 99

[1]The LORD reigns,
  let the nations tremble;
he sits enthroned between the
    cherubim,
  let the earth shake.
[2]Great is the LORD in Zion;
  he is exalted over all the nations.
[3]Let them praise your great and
    awesome name—
  he is holy.

[4]The King is mighty, he loves justice—
  you have established equity;
in Jacob you have done
  what is just and right.
[5]Exalt the LORD our God

and worship at his footstool;
  he is holy.

[6]Moses and Aaron were among his
    priests,
  Samuel was among those who called
    on his name;
they called on the LORD
  and he answered them.
[7]He spoke to them from the pillar of
    cloud;
  they kept his statutes and the
    decrees he gave them.

[8]O LORD our God,
  you answered them;
you were to Israel[l] a forgiving God,
  though you punished their
    misdeeds.[m]
[9]Exalt the LORD our God
  and worship at his holy mountain,
  for the LORD our God is holy.

PSALM 100
A psalm. For giving thanks.

[1]Shout for joy to the LORD, all the earth.
[2] Worship the LORD with gladness;
  come before him with joyful songs.
[3]Know that the LORD is God.
  It is he who made us, and we are
    his[n];
  we are his people, the sheep of his
    pasture.

[4]Enter his gates with thanksgiving
  and his courts with praise;
  give thanks to him and praise his
    name.
[5]For the LORD is good and his love
    endures forever;
  his faithfulness continues through all
    generations.

PSALM 101
Of David. A psalm.

[1]I will sing of your love and justice;
  to you, O LORD, I will sing praise.
[2]I will be careful to lead a blameless
    life—
  when will you come to me?

I will walk in my house
  with blameless heart.
[3]I will set before my eyes
  no vile thing.

The deeds of faithless men I hate;

---

[l]8 Hebrew *them*   [m]8 Or / *an avenger of the wrongs done to them*   [n]3 Or *and not we ourselves*

they will not cling to me.
⁴Men of perverse heart shall be far
     from me;
  I will have nothing to do with evil.

⁵Whoever slanders his neighbor in
     secret,
  him will I put to silence;
whoever has haughty eyes and a
     proud heart,
  him will I not endure.

⁶My eyes will be on the faithful in the
     land,
  that they may dwell with me;
he whose walk is blameless
  will minister to me.

⁷No one who practices deceit
  will dwell in my house;
no one who speaks falsely
  will stand in my presence.

⁸Every morning I will put to silence
  all the wicked in the land;
I will cut off every evildoer
  from the city of the LORD.

PSALM 102

A prayer of an afflicted man. When he is
faint and pours out his lament before the
LORD.

¹Hear my prayer, O LORD;
  let my cry for help come to you.
²Do not hide your face from me
  when I am in distress.
Turn your ear to me;
  when I call, answer me quickly.

³For my days vanish like smoke;
  my bones burn like glowing embers.
⁴My heart is blighted and withered like
     grass;
  I forget to eat my food.
⁵Because of my loud groaning
  I am reduced to skin and bones.
⁶I am like a desert owl,
  like an owl among the ruins.
⁷I lie awake; I have become
  like a bird alone on a roof.
⁸All day long my enemies taunt me;
  those who rail against me use my
     name as a curse.
⁹For I eat ashes as my food
  and mingle my drink with tears
¹⁰because of your great wrath,
  for you have taken me up and
     thrown me aside.

¹¹My days are like the evening shadow;
  I wither away like grass.

¹²But you, O LORD, sit enthroned forever;
  your renown endures through all
     generations.
¹³You will arise and have compassion
     on Zion,
  for it is time to show favor to her;
  the appointed time has come.
¹⁴For her stones are dear to your
     servants;
  her very dust moves them to pity.
¹⁵The nations will fear the name of the
     LORD,
  all the kings of the earth will revere
     your glory.
¹⁶For the LORD will rebuild Zion
  and appear in his glory.
¹⁷He will respond to the prayer of the
     destitute;
  he will not despise their plea.

¹⁸Let this be written for a future
     generation,
  that a people not yet created may
     praise the LORD:
¹⁹"The LORD looked down from his
     sanctuary on high,
  from heaven he viewed the earth,
²⁰to hear the groans of the prisoners
  and release those condemned to
     death."
²¹So the name of the LORD will be
     declared in Zion
  and his praise in Jerusalem
²²when the peoples and the kingdoms
  assemble to worship the LORD.

²³In the course of my lifeᵒ he broke my
     strength;
  he cut short my days.
²⁴So I said:
  "Do not take me away, O my God,
     in the midst of my days;
  your years go on through all
     generations.
²⁵In the beginning you laid the
     foundations of the earth,
  and the heavens are the work of
     your hands.
²⁶They will perish, but you remain;
  they will all wear out like a
     garment.
Like clothing you will change them
  and they will be discarded.
²⁷But you remain the same,

ᵒ23 Or By his power

and your years will never end.
²⁸The children of your servants will live
    in your presence;
    their descendants will be established
        before you."

PSALM 103
Of David.

¹Praise the LORD, O my soul;
    all my inmost being, praise his holy
        name.
²Praise the LORD, O my soul,
    and forget not all his benefits—
³who forgives all your sins
    and heals all your diseases,
⁴who redeems your life from the pit
    and crowns you with love and
        compassion,
⁵who satisfies your desires with good
        things
    so that your youth is renewed like
        the eagle's.

⁶The LORD works righteousness
    and justice for all the oppressed.

⁷He made known his ways to Moses,
    his deeds to the people of Israel:
⁸The LORD is compassionate and
        gracious,
    slow to anger, abounding in love.
⁹He will not always accuse,
    nor will he harbor his anger forever;
¹⁰he does not treat us as our sins
        deserve
    or repay us according to our
        iniquities.
¹¹For as high as the heavens are above
        the earth,

so great is his love for those who
    fear him;
¹²as far as the east is from the west,
    so far has he removed our
        transgressions from us.
¹³As a father has compassion on his
        children,
    so the LORD has compassion on those
        who fear him;
¹⁴for he knows how we are formed,
    he remembers that we are dust.
¹⁵As for man, his days are like grass,
    he flourishes like a flower of the
        field;
¹⁶the wind blows over it and it is gone,
    and its place remembers it no more.
¹⁷But from everlasting to everlasting
    the LORD's love is with those who
        fear him,
    and his righteousness with their
        children's children—
¹⁸with those who keep his covenant
    and remember to obey his precepts.

¹⁹The LORD has established his throne in
        heaven,
    and his kingdom rules over all.

²⁰Praise the LORD, you his angels,
    you mighty ones who do his
        bidding,
    who obey his word.
²¹Praise the LORD, all his heavenly hosts,
    you his servants who do his will.
²²Praise the LORD, all his works
    everywhere in his dominion.

Praise the LORD, O my soul.

JUNE 20 ☐ DAY 172
PSALMS 104–106
Growing or Groaning? (Psalm 106)

 OVERVIEW Book IV of Psalms closes with three majestic portraits of
God. He is the powerful God of creation (Psalm 104, a psalm that
closely parallels the creation account of Genesis 1); he is the faithful
God of the covenant, who formed a mighty nation out of people in
bondage (105); he is the long-suffering God, who patiently disciplines
but never deserts the objects of his love—a stiff-necked people (106).

Psalm 104	Psalm 105	Psalm 106
The Fullness of God's Creation	The Faithfulness of God to His People in Their Foundation	in Their Failures
God of Power	God of Patience	

YOUR DAILY WALK Memories, like fire, can both bless with warmth and burn with searing heat. As you look back over the first half of this year, do your memories give you more pleasure or pain?

Use the past as a springboard, not a sofa.

Probably you experienced a bit of both sensations. As the psalmist reviewed Israel's history, he delighted in the faithfulness of God, who never failed his people, and despaired over the faithlessness of Israel, who repeatedly disobeyed God. The nation's history speaks eloquently of the pain of waywardness and the persistence of God in guiding his people down the path of righteousness and blessing.

If you were asked to write *The History of My Life: Part I,* would it read like Psalm 106? Would it include pleasant memories of God's provision and painful memories of your rebellious moments? Have you thanked God for the former? Have you experienced God's forgiveness for the latter (1 John 1:9)? And have you learned a lesson in the process? Or are you—like the Israelites in Psalm 106—repeating your errors and forfeiting God's blessings?

Find a few minutes to take a quiet walk alone today, with just God and your thoughts for companions. Reminisce over the first six months of this year: the good times (thank him for them) and the bad (confess your rebellious moments to him). Ask God to help you grow wiser—not just older—for the rest of the year.

INSIGHT A Psalmist's Paraphrase of Genesis 1:1–2:3
Psalm 104 closely parallels the seven days of creation found in Genesis 1–2. Read through both passages side by side and notice how each section of the psalm acts as a free translation of the corresponding passage in Genesis. Can you match up all seven days of creation?

PSALM 104

¹Praise the LORD, O my soul.

O LORD my God, you are very great;
    you are clothed with splendor and
        majesty.
²He wraps himself in light as with a
        garment;
    he stretches out the heavens like a
        tent
³   and lays the beams of his upper
        chambers on their waters.
He makes the clouds his chariot
    and rides on the wings of the wind.
⁴He makes winds his messengers,ᵖ
    flames of fire his servants.

⁵He set the earth on its foundations;
    it can never be moved.
⁶You covered it with the deep as with a
        garment;
    the waters stood above the
        mountains.

⁷But at your rebuke the waters fled,
    at the sound of your thunder they
        took to flight;
⁸they flowed over the mountains,
    they went down into the valleys,
    to the place you assigned for them.
⁹You set a boundary they cannot cross;
    never again will they cover the
        earth.

¹⁰He makes springs pour water into the
        ravines;
    it flows between the mountains.
¹¹They give water to all the beasts of the
        field;
    the wild donkeys quench their thirst.
¹²The birds of the air nest by the waters;
    they sing among the branches.
¹³He waters the mountains from his
        upper chambers;
    the earth is satisfied by the fruit of
        his work.
¹⁴He makes grass grow for the cattle,

ᵖ4 Or *angels*

and plants for man to cultivate—
  bringing forth food from the earth:
¹⁵wine that gladdens the heart of man,
  oil to make his face shine,
  and bread that sustains his heart.
¹⁶The trees of the LORD are well watered,
  the cedars of Lebanon that he
    planted.
¹⁷There the birds make their nests;
  the stork has its home in the pine
    trees.
¹⁸The high mountains belong to the wild
    goats;
  the crags are a refuge for the
    coneys.�q

¹⁹The moon marks off the seasons,
  and the sun knows when to go
    down.
²⁰You bring darkness, it becomes night,
  and all the beasts of the forest
    prowl.
²¹The lions roar for their prey
  and seek their food from God.
²²The sun rises, and they steal away;
  they return and lie down in their
    dens.
²³Then man goes out to his work,
  to his labor until evening.

²⁴How many are your works, O LORD!
  In wisdom you made them all;
  the earth is full of your creatures.
²⁵There is the sea, vast and spacious,
  teeming with creatures beyond
    number—
  living things both large and small.
²⁶There the ships go to and fro,
  and the leviathan, which you formed
    to frolic there.

²⁷These all look to you
  to give them their food at the proper
    time.
²⁸When you give it to them,
  they gather it up;
  when you open your hand,
  they are satisfied with good things.
²⁹When you hide your face,
  they are terrified;
  when you take away their breath,
  they die and return to the dust.
³⁰When you send your Spirit,
  they are created,
  and you renew the face of the earth.

³¹May the glory of the LORD endure
    forever;
  may the LORD rejoice in his works—
³²he who looks at the earth, and it
    trembles,
  who touches the mountains, and
    they smoke.

³³I will sing to the LORD all my life;
  I will sing praise to my God as long
    as I live.
³⁴May my meditation be pleasing to
    him,
  as I rejoice in the LORD.
³⁵But may sinners vanish from the earth
  and the wicked be no more.

  Praise the LORD, O my soul.

  Praise the LORD.ʳ

PSALM 105

¹Give thanks to the LORD, call on his
    name;
  make known among the nations
    what he has done.
²Sing to him, sing praise to him;
  tell of all his wonderful acts.
³Glory in his holy name;
  let the hearts of those who seek the
    LORD rejoice.
⁴Look to the LORD and his strength;
  seek his face always.

⁵Remember the wonders he has done,
  his miracles, and the judgments he
    pronounced,
⁶O descendants of Abraham his
    servant,
  O sons of Jacob, his chosen ones.

⁷He is the LORD our God;
  his judgments are in all the earth.

⁸He remembers his covenant forever,
  the word he commanded, for a
    thousand generations,
⁹the covenant he made with Abraham,
  the oath he swore to Isaac.
¹⁰He confirmed it to Jacob as a decree,
  to Israel as an everlasting covenant:
¹¹"To you I will give the land of Canaan
  as the portion you will inherit."

¹²When they were but few in number,
  few indeed, and strangers in it,
¹³they wandered from nation to nation,
  from one kingdom to another.
¹⁴He allowed no one to oppress them;

q18 That is, the hyrax or rock badger   r35 Hebrew *Hallelu Yah*; in the Septuagint this line stands at the beginning of
Psalm 105.

for their sake he rebuked kings:
¹⁵"Do not touch my anointed ones;
    do my prophets no harm."

¹⁶He called down famine on the land
    and destroyed all their supplies of
        food;
¹⁷and he sent a man before them—
    Joseph, sold as a slave.
¹⁸They bruised his feet with shackles,
    his neck was put in irons,
¹⁹till what he foretold came to pass,
    till the word of the LORD proved him
        true.
²⁰The king sent and released him,
    the ruler of peoples set him free.
²¹He made him master of his household,
    ruler over all he possessed,
²²to instruct his princes as he pleased
    and teach his elders wisdom.

²³Then Israel entered Egypt;
    Jacob lived as an alien in the land of
        Ham.
²⁴The LORD made his people very
        fruitful;
    he made them too numerous for
        their foes,
²⁵whose hearts he turned to hate his
        people,
    to conspire against his servants.
²⁶He sent Moses his servant,
    and Aaron, whom he had chosen.
²⁷They performed his miraculous signs
        among them,
    his wonders in the land of Ham.
²⁸He sent darkness and made the land
        dark—
    for had they not rebelled against his
        words?
²⁹He turned their waters into blood,
    causing their fish to die.
³⁰Their land teemed with frogs,
    which went up into the bedrooms of
        their rulers.
³¹He spoke, and there came swarms of
        flies,
    and gnats throughout their country.
³²He turned their rain into hail,
    with lightning throughout their land;
³³he struck down their vines and fig
        trees
    and shattered the trees of their
        country.
³⁴He spoke, and the locusts came,
    grasshoppers without number;

³⁵they ate up every green thing in their
        land,
    ate up the produce of their soil.
³⁶Then he struck down all the firstborn
        in their land,
    the firstfruits of all their manhood.
³⁷He brought out Israel, laden with
        silver and gold,
    and from among their tribes no one
        faltered.
³⁸Egypt was glad when they left,
    because dread of Israel had fallen on
        them.
³⁹He spread out a cloud as a covering,
    and a fire to give light at night.
⁴⁰They asked, and he brought them
        quail
    and satisfied them with the bread of
        heaven.
⁴¹He opened the rock, and water gushed
        out;
    like a river it flowed in the desert.

⁴²For he remembered his holy promise
    given to his servant Abraham.
⁴³He brought out his people with
        rejoicing,
    his chosen ones with shouts of joy;
⁴⁴he gave them the lands of the nations,
    and they fell heir to what others had
        toiled for—
⁴⁵that they might keep his precepts
    and observe his laws.

    Praise the LORD.^s

PSALM 106

¹Praise the LORD.^t

Give thanks to the LORD, for he is
        good;
    his love endures forever.
²Who can proclaim the mighty acts of
        the LORD
    or fully declare his praise?
³Blessed are they who maintain justice,
    who constantly do what is right.
⁴Remember me, O LORD, when you
        show favor to your people,
    come to my aid when you save
        them,
⁵that I may enjoy the prosperity of your
        chosen ones,
    that I may share in the joy of your
        nation

^s45 Hebrew *Hallelu Yah*   ^t1 Hebrew *Hallelu Yah*; also in verse 48

and join your inheritance in giving
    praise.
⁶We have sinned, even as our fathers
    did;
  we have done wrong and acted
    wickedly.
⁷When our fathers were in Egypt,
  they gave no thought to your
    miracles;
  they did not remember your many
    kindnesses,
  and they rebelled by the sea, the
    Red Sea.ᵘ
⁸Yet he saved them for his name's sake,
  to make his mighty power known.
⁹He rebuked the Red Sea, and it dried
    up;
  he led them through the depths as
    through a desert.
¹⁰He saved them from the hand of the
    foe;
  from the hand of the enemy he
    redeemed them.
¹¹The waters covered their adversaries;
  not one of them survived.
¹²Then they believed his promises
  and sang his praise.

¹³But they soon forgot what he had
    done
  and did not wait for his counsel.
¹⁴In the desert they gave in to their
    craving;
  in the wasteland they put God to
    the test.
¹⁵So he gave them what they asked for,
  but sent a wasting disease upon
    them.

¹⁶In the camp they grew envious of
    Moses
  and of Aaron, who was consecrated
    to the LORD.
¹⁷The earth opened up and swallowed
    Dathan;
  it buried the company of Abiram.
¹⁸Fire blazed among their followers;
  a flame consumed the wicked.

¹⁹At Horeb they made a calf
  and worshiped an idol cast from
    metal.
²⁰They exchanged their Glory
  for an image of a bull, which eats
    grass.
²¹They forgot the God who saved them,

who had done great things in Egypt,
²²miracles in the land of Ham
  and awesome deeds by the Red Sea.
²³So he said he would destroy them—
  had not Moses, his chosen one,
  stood in the breach before him
  to keep his wrath from destroying
    them.

²⁴Then they despised the pleasant land;
  they did not believe his promise.
²⁵They grumbled in their tents
  and did not obey the LORD.
²⁶So he swore to them with uplifted
    hand
  that he would make them fall in the
    desert,
²⁷make their descendants fall among the
    nations
  and scatter them throughout the
    lands.

²⁸They yoked themselves to the Baal of
    Peor
  and ate sacrifices offered to lifeless
    gods;
²⁹they provoked the LORD to anger by
    their wicked deeds,
  and a plague broke out among
    them.
³⁰But Phinehas stood up and intervened,
  and the plague was checked.
³¹This was credited to him as
    righteousness
  for endless generations to come.

³²By the waters of Meribah they angered
    the LORD,
  and trouble came to Moses because
    of them;
³³for they rebelled against the Spirit of
    God,
  and rash words came from Moses'
    lips.ᵛ

³⁴They did not destroy the peoples
  as the LORD had commanded them,
³⁵but they mingled with the nations
  and adopted their customs.
³⁶They worshiped their idols,
  which became a snare to them.
³⁷They sacrificed their sons
  and their daughters to demons.
³⁸They shed innocent blood,
  the blood of their sons and
    daughters,

ᵘ7 Hebrew *Yam Suph*; that is, Sea of Reeds; also in verses 9 and 22   ᵛ33 Or *against his spirit, / and rash words came from his lips*

whom they sacrificed to the idols of
    Canaan,
and the land was desecrated by their
    blood.
39They defiled themselves by what they
    did;
    by their deeds they prostituted
        themselves.

40Therefore the LORD was angry with his
    people
    and abhorred his inheritance.
41He handed them over to the nations,
    and their foes ruled over them.
42Their enemies oppressed them
    and subjected them to their power.
43Many times he delivered them,
    but they were bent on rebellion
    and they wasted away in their sin.

44But he took note of their distress
    when he heard their cry;
45for their sake he remembered his
    covenant
    and out of his great love he
        relented.
46He caused them to be pitied
    by all who held them captive.

47Save us, O LORD our God,
    and gather us from the nations,
that we may give thanks to your holy
    name
    and glory in your praise.

48Praise be to the LORD, the God of
    Israel,
    from everlasting to everlasting.
Let all the people say, "Amen!"

Praise the LORD.

JUNE 21 ☐ DAY 173
Don't Forget to Remember!

 LOOK BACK The psalms you have read this past week ask and answer some of the intriguing *why* questions everyone is tempted to ask from time to time: Why do the wicked seem to get away with murder (Psalm 73)? Why has God seemingly rejected us (74, 77)? Why is God so patient with his people (78)? Why do the pagans question God's very existence (79)? Why does God judge his people (80)? Why does God sometimes seem to hide his face (88)?

The answers are as clear as the character of God. He is eternal (90), omnipotent (91), majestic (93), righteous (97), compassionate, gracious (103), creative (104) and promise-keeping (106). In short, "the LORD is God" (100:3), and to love him and fear him is to unlock many of the secrets of this life and the next (103).

The person who will not command his or her thoughts will soon lose command of his or her actions.

LOOK UP Try this pop quiz on important bits of trivia:
1. When is your spouse's (or mother's) birthday?
2. What is your social security number?
3. If you have a will, who is the executor?
4. If you have a safe-deposit box, what is its number?
5. When were the batteries last changed in your smoke detectors?

When it comes to important information, the best advice is also the simplest: Don't forget! Perhaps you are in the habit of writing down important birthdays or anniversaries on a master calendar . . . keeping important documents in a special place . . . changing the batteries in your smoke detectors whenever you change your clocks to (or from) daylight saving time.

The psalmist David has a similar reminder for you in Psalm 103. He wants you to remember who God is (his attributes) . . . what he has done (his activities) . . . how well he knows you (his omniscience) . . . how much he is in control (his sovereignty) . . . and how worthy he is to be praised. But none of that information will do you any good if you don't remember it!

LOOK AHEAD Think of Psalm 103 as a mother lode of golden truths about the God you serve. It takes only a few minutes of meditation and reflection to discover shimmering bits of insight about the greatness of your God. Try it! Take the next five minutes and see how many of these statements you can complete, using the words you have read in Psalm 103.

Don't forget . . . what God has done:

_____

Don't forget . . . what God is like:

_____

Don't forget . . . what God is *not* like:

_____

Don't forget . . . how much God loves you:

_____

Don't forget . . . how well God knows you:

_____

Don't forget . . . how much God is in control:

_____

Don't forget . . . how worthy God is to be praised:

_____

And lest you forget what you have just remembered, tie a string around your finger (or place a ribbon on the antenna of your car). Then when someone asks you what the string or ribbon is for (and they will), be ready to give an answer for the hope that is in you (1 Peter 3:15).

JUNE 22 □ DAY 174
PSALMS 107–110
Handling Slander (Psalm 109)

OVERVIEW Book V begins with a vibrant note of thanksgiving for God's deliverance from danger (Psalm 107). David voices praise for God's help against his enemies (108), then cries out for vindication against those who have slandered him (109). But whether his enemies prosper or suffer swift punishment, David knows the future lies securely in the hands of God's righteous Ruler who will triumph over all (110).

Psalm 107	Psalm 108	Psalm 109	Psalm 110
God's Redeemed	God's Remnant	God's Reproached	God's Ruler
Testifying	Trusting		Triumphant

YOUR DAILY WALK Character assassination. It's a malady you won't find in any medical text. And if it happens to you, chances are you won't end up in a hospital emergency room. But the pain is still acute, the damage severe, the recovery slow, the scars difficult to remove.

How do you react when you've been unjustly accused and maliciously slandered? David responded with some of the strongest words to be found in Scripture (109:6–20). In fact, these denunciations sound so uncharacteristic of the "sweet singer of Israel" that some

No greater injury can be inflicted upon someone than to wound his or her reputation. commentators have suggested David's accuser (rather than David) is the one being quoted.

But David was zealous to defend the righteousness of God wherever it was attacked. His harsh cries were his way of expressing hatred for sin.

But the question remains: How do you handle a slanderous attack? David's advice would be this: Seek God's help and let him vindicate you (Psalm 109:26–27); let your enemies bring shame upon their own heads, rather than trying to do it yourself (v. 29); continue to praise the Lord throughout the ordeal (v. 30).

 INSIGHT Psalms of Vengeance
Psalm 109 is just one of a number of "imprecatory" psalms in which the author asks God to judge his enemies (others include 7, 35, 55, 58, 59, 69, 79, 137, 139). In his indignation over sin, the psalmist cries out for God's swift and just punishment of evil.

BOOK V
Psalms 107–150

PSALM 107

¹Give thanks to the LORD, for he is
 good;
 his love endures forever.
²Let the redeemed of the LORD say
 this—
 those he redeemed from the hand of
 the foe,
³those he gathered from the lands,
 from east and west, from north and
 south.ʷ

⁴Some wandered in desert wastelands,
 finding no way to a city where they
 could settle.
⁵They were hungry and thirsty,
 and their lives ebbed away.
⁶Then they cried out to the LORD in
 their trouble,
 and he delivered them from their
 distress.
⁷He led them by a straight way
 to a city where they could settle.
⁸Let them give thanks to the LORD for
 his unfailing love
 and his wonderful deeds for men,
⁹for he satisfies the thirsty
 and fills the hungry with good
 things.

¹⁰Some sat in darkness and the deepest
 gloom,
 prisoners suffering in iron chains,
¹¹for they had rebelled against the
 words of God
 and despised the counsel of the
 Most High.

¹²So he subjected them to bitter labor;
 they stumbled, and there was no
 one to help.
¹³Then they cried to the LORD in their
 trouble,
 and he saved them from their
 distress.
¹⁴He brought them out of darkness and
 the deepest gloom
 and broke away their chains.
¹⁵Let them give thanks to the LORD for
 his unfailing love
 and his wonderful deeds for men,
¹⁶for he breaks down gates of bronze
 and cuts through bars of iron.

¹⁷Some became fools through their
 rebellious ways
 and suffered affliction because of
 their iniquities.
¹⁸They loathed all food
 and drew near the gates of death.
¹⁹Then they cried to the LORD in their
 trouble,
 and he saved them from their
 distress.
²⁰He sent forth his word and healed
 them;
 he rescued them from the grave.
²¹Let them give thanks to the LORD for
 his unfailing love
 and his wonderful deeds for men.
²²Let them sacrifice thank offerings
 and tell of his works with songs of
 joy.

²³Others went out on the sea in ships;
 they were merchants on the mighty
 waters.
²⁴They saw the works of the LORD,

ʷ3 Hebrew *north and the sea*

his wonderful deeds in the deep.
25For he spoke and stirred up a tempest
that lifted high the waves.
26They mounted up to the heavens and
went down to the depths;
in their peril their courage melted
away.
27They reeled and staggered like
drunken men;
they were at their wits' end.
28Then they cried out to the LORD in
their trouble,
and he brought them out of their
distress.
29He stilled the storm to a whisper;
the waves of the sea were hushed.
30They were glad when it grew calm,
and he guided them to their desired
haven.
31Let them give thanks to the LORD for
his unfailing love
and his wonderful deeds for men.
32Let them exalt him in the assembly of
the people
and praise him in the council of the
elders.

33He turned rivers into a desert,
flowing springs into thirsty ground,
34and fruitful land into a salt waste,
because of the wickedness of those
who lived there.
35He turned the desert into pools of
water
and the parched ground into
flowing springs;
36there he brought the hungry to live,
and they founded a city where they
could settle.
37They sowed fields and planted
vineyards
that yielded a fruitful harvest;
38he blessed them, and their numbers
greatly increased,
and he did not let their herds
diminish.

39Then their numbers decreased, and
they were humbled
by oppression, calamity and sorrow;
40he who pours contempt on nobles
made them wander in a trackless
waste.
41But he lifted the needy out of their
affliction
and increased their families like
flocks.
42The upright see and rejoice,

but all the wicked shut their
mouths.

43Whoever is wise, let him heed these
things
and consider the great love of the
LORD.

PSALM 108
A song. A psalm of David.

1My heart is steadfast, O God;
I will sing and make music with all
my soul.
2Awake, harp and lyre!
I will awaken the dawn.
3I will praise you, O LORD, among the
nations;
I will sing of you among the
peoples.
4For great is your love, higher than the
heavens;
your faithfulness reaches to the
skies.
5Be exalted, O God, above the heavens,
and let your glory be over all the
earth.

6Save us and help us with your right
hand,
that those you love may be
delivered.
7God has spoken from his sanctuary:
"In triumph I will parcel out
Shechem
and measure off the Valley of
Succoth.
8Gilead is mine, Manasseh is mine;
Ephraim is my helmet,
Judah my scepter.
9Moab is my washbasin,
upon Edom I toss my sandal;
over Philistia I shout in triumph."

10Who will bring me to the fortified
city?
Who will lead me to Edom?
11Is it not you, O God, you who have
rejected us
and no longer go out with our
armies?
12Give us aid against the enemy,
for the help of man is worthless.
13With God we will gain the victory,
and he will trample down our
enemies.

PSALM 109
For the director of music. Of David.
A psalm.

¹O God, whom I praise,
   do not remain silent,
²for wicked and deceitful men
   have opened their mouths against
      me;
   they have spoken against me with
      lying tongues.
³With words of hatred they surround
      me;
   they attack me without cause.
⁴In return for my friendship they
      accuse me,
   but I am a man of prayer.
⁵They repay me evil for good,
   and hatred for my friendship.

⁶Appoint ˣ an evil man ʸ to oppose
      him;
   let an accuser ᶻ stand at his right
      hand.
⁷When he is tried, let him be found
      guilty,
   and may his prayers condemn him.
⁸May his days be few;
   may another take his place of
      leadership.
⁹May his children be fatherless
   and his wife a widow.
¹⁰May his children be wandering
      beggars;
   may they be driven ᵃ from their
      ruined homes.
¹¹May a creditor seize all he has;
   may strangers plunder the fruits of
      his labor.
¹²May no one extend kindness to him
   or take pity on his fatherless
      children.
¹³May his descendants be cut off,
   their names blotted out from the
      next generation.
¹⁴May the iniquity of his fathers be
      remembered before the LORD;
   may the sin of his mother never be
      blotted out.
¹⁵May their sins always remain before
      the LORD,
   that he may cut off the memory of
      them from the earth.

¹⁶For he never thought of doing a
      kindness,

but hounded to death the poor
   and the needy and the
      brokenhearted.
¹⁷He loved to pronounce a curse—
   may it ᵇ come on him;
   he found no pleasure in blessing—
   may it be ᶜ far from him.
¹⁸He wore cursing as his garment;
   it entered into his body like water,
   into his bones like oil.
¹⁹May it be like a cloak wrapped about
      him,
   like a belt tied forever around him.
²⁰May this be the LORD's payment to my
      accusers,
   to those who speak evil of me.

²¹But you, O Sovereign LORD,
   deal well with me for your name's
      sake;
   out of the goodness of your love,
      deliver me.
²²For I am poor and needy,
   and my heart is wounded within
      me.
²³I fade away like an evening shadow;
   I am shaken off like a locust.
²⁴My knees give way from fasting;
   my body is thin and gaunt.
²⁵I am an object of scorn to my accusers;
   when they see me, they shake their
      heads.

²⁶Help me, O LORD my God;
   save me in accordance with your
      love.
²⁷Let them know that it is your hand,
   that you, O LORD, have done it.
²⁸They may curse, but you will bless;
   when they attack they will be put to
      shame,
   but your servant will rejoice.
²⁹My accusers will be clothed with
      disgrace
   and wrapped in shame as in a cloak.

³⁰With my mouth I will greatly extol the
      LORD;
   in the great throng I will praise him.
³¹For he stands at the right hand of the
      needy one,
   to save his life from those who
      condemn him.

ˣ6 Or They say: "Appoint (with quotation marks at the end of verse 19)   ʸ6 Or the Evil One   ᶻ6 Or let Satan
ᵃ10 Septuagint; Hebrew sought   ᵇ17 Or curse, / and it has   ᶜ17 Or blessing, / and it is

PSALM 110
Of David. A psalm.

[1]The LORD says to my Lord:
"Sit at my right hand
until I make your enemies
a footstool for your feet."

[2]The LORD will extend your mighty
scepter from Zion;
you will rule in the midst of your
enemies.
[3]Your troops will be willing
on your day of battle.
Arrayed in holy majesty,
from the womb of the dawn
you will receive the dew of your
youth.[d]

[4]The LORD has sworn
and will not change his mind:
"You are a priest forever,
in the order of Melchizedek."

[5]The Lord is at your right hand;
he will crush kings on the day of his
wrath.
[6]He will judge the nations, heaping up
the dead
and crushing the rulers of the whole
earth.
[7]He will drink from a brook beside the
way[e];
therefore he will lift up his
head.

[d]3 Or / your young men will come to you like the dew   [e]7 Or / The One who grants succession will set him in authority

JUNE 23 ☐ DAY 175
PSALMS 111–118
God Understands

OVERVIEW The reasons for praising God are innumerable, but today's psalms will give you a few to start with! You can praise him for his tender care (Psalm 111), his blessings for the upright (112), his remembrance of the poor (113), his watchfulness over Israel (114–115), his restoration of the sorrowing (116) and his enduring love (117–118).

Psalm 111	Psalm 112	Psalms 113–115	Psalms 116–118
Faithful Care	Fearing Child	Life, Love and Liberty	Death, Devotion and Destruction
God's Delight		God's Deeds	God's Deliverance

YOUR DAILY WALK "Judge a tree by its fruit; not by its leaves" (Euripides).

"Examine the contents, not the bottle" (Jewish Talmud).

"You can't judge a book by its cover" (Anonymous).

If people speak ill of you, live so that no one will believe them.

Three ways of saying the same thing: The only thing worse than making a surface judgment is being the victim of one!

What do you do when you suffer from superficial evaluations by your friends, superiors or coworkers? Where can you turn when your actions or motives are misunderstood?

Turn to the one who experienced being misunderstood himself— "the stone the builders rejected" who has today "become the capstone" (118:22). Christ knew what it meant to be rejected unjustly . . . condemned wrongfully . . . crucified unmercifully. He knows what you are going through. That's why you can come to him confidently to experience his presence (118:6), help (118:7) and protection (118:8–14) in times of misunderstanding.

Three times in the New Testament, Psalm 118:22 is quoted to show that human misunderstanding cannot thwart the good purposes of God (Matthew 21:42; Acts 4:11; 1 Peter 2:7). Put your initials next to one of those passages as your silent testimony of confidence in God's ability to do the same in your life today!

INSIGHT Psalm 118, the Palm Sunday Psalm
Just before Jesus quoted from Psalm 118 in Matthew 21, he had entered Jerusalem on the back of a colt to the acclamations of the multitude shouting the words of Psalm 118:26. (What are they? See Matthew 21:9.)

PSALM 111*f*

¹Praise the LORD.*g*

I will extol the LORD with all my heart
    in the council of the upright and in
        the assembly.

²Great are the works of the LORD;
    they are pondered by all who
        delight in them.
³Glorious and majestic are his deeds,
    and his righteousness endures
        forever.
⁴He has caused his wonders to be
        remembered;
    the LORD is gracious and
        compassionate.
⁵He provides food for those who fear
        him;
    he remembers his covenant forever.
⁶He has shown his people the power of
        his works,
    giving them the lands of other
        nations.
⁷The works of his hands are faithful
        and just;
    all his precepts are trustworthy.
⁸They are steadfast for ever and ever,
    done in faithfulness and uprightness.
⁹He provided redemption for his
        people;
    he ordained his covenant forever—
        holy and awesome is his name.

¹⁰The fear of the LORD is the beginning
        of wisdom;
    all who follow his precepts have
        good understanding.
    To him belongs eternal praise.

PSALM 112*f*

¹Praise the LORD.*g*

Blessed is the man who fears the LORD,

who finds great delight in his
        commands.
²His children will be mighty in the
        land;
    the generation of the upright will be
        blessed.
³Wealth and riches are in his house,
    and his righteousness endures
        forever.
⁴Even in darkness light dawns for the
        upright,
    for the gracious and compassionate
        and righteous man.*h*
⁵Good will come to him who is
        generous and lends freely,
    who conducts his affairs with justice.
⁶Surely he will never be shaken;
    a righteous man will be remembered
        forever.
⁷He will have no fear of bad news;
    his heart is steadfast, trusting in the
        LORD.
⁸His heart is secure, he will have no
        fear;
    in the end he will look in triumph
        on his foes.
⁹He has scattered abroad his gifts to the
        poor,
    his righteousness endures forever;
    his horn*i* will be lifted high in
        honor.

¹⁰The wicked man will see and be
        vexed,
    he will gnash his teeth and waste
        away;
    the longings of the wicked will come
        to nothing.

PSALM 113

¹Praise the LORD.*j*

Praise, O servants of the LORD,

---

*f*This psalm is an acrostic poem, the lines of which begin with the successive letters of the Hebrew alphabet.   *g*1 Hebrew *Hallelu Yah*   *h*4 Or / *for* ⸢the LORD⸣ *is gracious and compassionate and righteous*   *i*9 Horn here symbolizes dignity.   *j*1 Hebrew *Hallelu Yah*; also in verse 9

praise the name of the LORD.
²Let the name of the LORD be praised,
  both now and forevermore.
³From the rising of the sun to the place
    where it sets,
  the name of the LORD is to be
    praised.

⁴The LORD is exalted over all the
    nations,
  his glory above the heavens.
⁵Who is like the LORD our God,
  the One who sits enthroned on high,
⁶who stoops down to look
  on the heavens and the earth?

⁷He raises the poor from the dust
  and lifts the needy from the ash
    heap;
⁸he seats them with princes,
  with the princes of their people.
⁹He settles the barren woman in her
    home
  as a happy mother of children.

Praise the LORD.

PSALM 114

¹When Israel came out of Egypt,
  the house of Jacob from a people of
    foreign tongue,
²Judah became God's sanctuary,
  Israel his dominion.

³The sea looked and fled,
  the Jordan turned back;
⁴the mountains skipped like rams,
  the hills like lambs.

⁵Why was it, O sea, that you fled,
  O Jordan, that you turned back,
⁶you mountains, that you skipped like
    rams,
  you hills, like lambs?

⁷Tremble, O earth, at the presence of
    the Lord,
  at the presence of the God of Jacob,
⁸who turned the rock into a pool,
  the hard rock into springs of water.

PSALM 115

¹Not to us, O LORD, not to us
  but to your name be the glory,
  because of your love and
    faithfulness.

²Why do the nations say,
  "Where is their God?"

³Our God is in heaven;
  he does whatever pleases him.
⁴But their idols are silver and gold,
  made by the hands of men.
⁵They have mouths, but cannot speak,
  eyes, but they cannot see;
⁶they have ears, but cannot hear,
  noses, but they cannot smell;
⁷they have hands, but cannot feel,
  feet, but they cannot walk;
  nor can they utter a sound with
    their throats.
⁸Those who make them will be like
    them,
  and so will all who trust in them.

⁹O house of Israel, trust in the LORD—
  he is their help and shield.
¹⁰O house of Aaron, trust in the LORD—
  he is their help and shield.
¹¹You who fear him, trust in the LORD—
  he is their help and shield.

¹²The LORD remembers us and will bless
    us:
  He will bless the house of Israel,
  he will bless the house of Aaron,
¹³he will bless those who fear the LORD—
  small and great alike.

¹⁴May the LORD make you increase,
  both you and your children.
¹⁵May you be blessed by the LORD,
  the Maker of heaven and earth.

¹⁶The highest heavens belong to the
    LORD,
  but the earth he has given to man.
¹⁷It is not the dead who praise the LORD,
  those who go down to silence;
¹⁸it is we who extol the LORD,
  both now and forevermore.

Praise the LORD.ᵏ

PSALM 116

¹I love the LORD, for he heard my voice;
  he heard my cry for mercy.
²Because he turned his ear to me,
  I will call on him as long as I live.

³The cords of death entangled me,
  the anguish of the graveˡ came
    upon me;
  I was overcome by trouble and
    sorrow.
⁴Then I called on the name of the LORD:
  "O LORD, save me!"

ᵏ18 Hebrew *Hallelu Yah*   ˡ3 Hebrew *Sheol*

⁵The LORD is gracious and righteous;
  our God is full of compassion.
⁶The LORD protects the simplehearted;
  when I was in great need, he saved
    me.

⁷Be at rest once more, O my soul,
  for the LORD has been good to you.

⁸For you, O LORD, have delivered my
    soul from death,
  my eyes from tears,
  my feet from stumbling,
⁹that I may walk before the LORD
  in the land of the living.
¹⁰I believed; therefore[m] I said,
  "I am greatly afflicted."
¹¹And in my dismay I said,
  "All men are liars."

¹²How can I repay the LORD
  for all his goodness to me?
¹³I will lift up the cup of salvation
  and call on the name of the LORD.
¹⁴I will fulfill my vows to the LORD
  in the presence of all his people.

¹⁵Precious in the sight of the LORD
  is the death of his saints.
¹⁶O LORD, truly I am your servant;
  I am your servant, the son of your
    maidservant[n];
  you have freed me from my chains.

¹⁷I will sacrifice a thank offering to you
  and call on the name of the LORD.
¹⁸I will fulfill my vows to the LORD
  in the presence of all his people,
¹⁹in the courts of the house of the
    LORD—
  in your midst, O Jerusalem.

  Praise the LORD.[o]

PSALM 117

¹Praise the LORD, all you nations;
  extol him, all you peoples.
²For great is his love toward us,
  and the faithfulness of the LORD
    endures forever.

  Praise the LORD.[o]

PSALM 118

¹Give thanks to the LORD, for he is
    good;
  his love endures forever.

²Let Israel say:
  "His love endures forever."
³Let the house of Aaron say:
  "His love endures forever."
⁴Let those who fear the LORD say:
  "His love endures forever."

⁵In my anguish I cried to the LORD,
  and he answered by setting me free.
⁶The LORD is with me; I will not be
    afraid.
  What can man do to me?
⁷The LORD is with me; he is my helper.
  I will look in triumph on my
    enemies.

⁸It is better to take refuge in the LORD
  than to trust in man.
⁹It is better to take refuge in the LORD
  than to trust in princes.

¹⁰All the nations surrounded me,
  but in the name of the LORD I cut
    them off.
¹¹They surrounded me on every side,
  but in the name of the LORD I cut
    them off.
¹²They swarmed around me like bees,
  but they died out as quickly as
    burning thorns;
  in the name of the LORD I cut them
    off.
¹³I was pushed back and about to fall,
  but the LORD helped me.
¹⁴The LORD is my strength and my song;
  he has become my salvation.

¹⁵Shouts of joy and victory
  resound in the tents of the righteous:
  "The LORD's right hand has done
    mighty things!
¹⁶ The LORD's right hand is lifted high;
  the LORD's right hand has done
    mighty things!"

¹⁷I will not die but live,
  and will proclaim what the LORD has
    done.
¹⁸The LORD has chastened me severely,
  but he has not given me over to
    death.

¹⁹Open for me the gates of
    righteousness;
  I will enter and give thanks to the
    LORD.
²⁰This is the gate of the LORD

---

[m]10 Or *believed even when*   [n]16 Or *servant, your faithful son*   [o]19,2 Hebrew *Hallelu Yah*

through which the righteous may
    enter.
²¹I will give you thanks, for you
    answered me;
    you have become my salvation.

²²The stone the builders rejected
    has become the capstone;
²³the LORD has done this,
    and it is marvelous in our eyes.
²⁴This is the day the LORD has made;
    let us rejoice and be glad in it.

²⁵O LORD, save us;
    O LORD, grant us success.
²⁶Blessed is he who comes in the name
    of the LORD.

From the house of the LORD we bless
    you.ᴾ
²⁷The LORD is God,
    and he has made his light shine
    upon us.
With boughs in hand, join in the festal
    procession
    up�q to the horns of the altar.

²⁸You are my God, and I will give you
    thanks;
    you are my God, and I will exalt
    you.

²⁹Give thanks to the LORD, for he is
    good;
    his love endures forever.

ᴾ26 The Hebrew is plural.   �q27 Or Bind the festal sacrifice with ropes / and take it

JUNE 24 ☐ DAY 176
PSALM 119
The Riches of God's Revelation

 OVERVIEW The wonders of God's Word fill the 176 verses of Psalm 119—the longest song and the longest chapter in the Bible. Like a prism breaking a beam of light into colors, the psalmist holds aloft the Word of God to examine it from different angles. Six synonyms for Scripture dominate the psalm—each with a lesson:

- *Law*—God's Word reveals his will.
- *Statutes*—God's Word is faithful and true.
- *Precepts*—God's Word gives particular instructions.
- *Decrees*—God's Word has binding force and permanence.
- *Commands*—God's Word possesses authority.
- *Word*—God's Word contains truth in all its forms.

Psalm 119
The Riches of God's Revelation in 22 Stanzas
"Oh, how I love your law! I meditate on it all day long" (v. 97).

 YOUR DAILY WALK Why do you study God's Word? Could you list a dozen reasons for making God's inspired Word the focus of your daily meditation?

You could if you were the author of Psalm 119! The motivation for studying the Bible should never be solely a what's-in-it-for-me? mentality. An understanding of the benefits you will enjoy from a daily time in God's Word can only encourage you to spend more time mastering—and being mastered by—the book of books.

Martin Luther said, "I have done nothing; the Word has done and accomplished everything."

Psalm 119 resembles a treasure chest of benefits. For every eight verses, see if you can discover one benefit. For example, in verses 1–8, following God's Word spares the believer from shame; in verses 9–16, obedience to God's Word purifies the believer.

INSIGHT From *A* to *Z*
The psalmist uses each of the twenty-two letters of the Hebrew alphabet to begin eight verses in Psalm 119. From memory, can you think of Bible verses that begin with each of the twenty-six letters of the English alphabet? For example, *A:* "Ask and it will be given to you" (Matthew 7:7). Ten or fewer means your memory work needs dusting off!

PSALM 119ʳ

א   Aleph

¹Blessed are they whose ways are
    blameless,
  who walk according to the law of
    the LORD.
²Blessed are they who keep his statutes
  and seek him with all their heart.
³They do nothing wrong;
  they walk in his ways.
⁴You have laid down precepts
  that are to be fully obeyed.
⁵Oh, that my ways were steadfast
  in obeying your decrees!
⁶Then I would not be put to shame
  when I consider all your commands.
⁷I will praise you with an upright heart
  as I learn your righteous laws.
⁸I will obey your decrees;
  do not utterly forsake me.

ב   Beth

⁹How can a young man keep his way
    pure?
  By living according to your word.
¹⁰I seek you with all my heart;
  do not let me stray from your
    commands.
¹¹I have hidden your word in my heart
  that I might not sin against you.
¹²Praise be to you, O LORD;
  teach me your decrees.
¹³With my lips I recount
  all the laws that come from your
    mouth.
¹⁴I rejoice in following your statutes
  as one rejoices in great riches.
¹⁵I meditate on your precepts
  and consider your ways.
¹⁶I delight in your decrees;
  I will not neglect your word.

ג   Gimel

¹⁷Do good to your servant, and I will
    live;
  I will obey your word.

¹⁸Open my eyes that I may see
  wonderful things in your law.
¹⁹I am a stranger on earth;
  do not hide your commands from
    me.
²⁰My soul is consumed with longing
  for your laws at all times.
²¹You rebuke the arrogant, who are
    cursed
  and who stray from your
    commands.
²²Remove from me scorn and contempt,
  for I keep your statutes.
²³Though rulers sit together and slander
    me,
  your servant will meditate on your
    decrees.
²⁴Your statutes are my delight;
  they are my counselors.

ד   Daleth

²⁵I am laid low in the dust;
  preserve my life according to your
    word.
²⁶I recounted my ways and you
    answered me;
  teach me your decrees.
²⁷Let me understand the teaching of
    your precepts;
  then I will meditate on your
    wonders.
²⁸My soul is weary with sorrow;
  strengthen me according to your
    word.
²⁹Keep me from deceitful ways;
  be gracious to me through your law.
³⁰I have chosen the way of truth;
  I have set my heart on your laws.
³¹I hold fast to your statutes, O LORD;
  do not let me be put to shame.
³²I run in the path of your commands,
  for you have set my heart free.

ה   He

³³Teach me, O LORD, to follow your
    decrees;
  then I will keep them to the end.

ʳThis psalm is an acrostic poem; the verses of each stanza begin with the same letter of the Hebrew alphabet.

³⁴Give me understanding, and I will
   keep your law
   and obey it with all my heart.
³⁵Direct me in the path of your
   commands,
   for there I find delight.
³⁶Turn my heart toward your statutes
   and not toward selfish gain.
³⁷Turn my eyes away from worthless
   things;
   preserve my life according to your
   word.ˢ
³⁸Fulfill your promise to your servant,
   so that you may be feared.
³⁹Take away the disgrace I dread,
   for your laws are good.
⁴⁰How I long for your precepts!
   Preserve my life in your
   righteousness.

ז   Waw

⁴¹May your unfailing love come to me,
   O LORD,
   your salvation according to your
   promise;
⁴²then I will answer the one who taunts
   me,
   for I trust in your word.
⁴³Do not snatch the word of truth from
   my mouth,
   for I have put my hope in your
   laws.
⁴⁴I will always obey your law,
   for ever and ever.
⁴⁵I will walk about in freedom,
   for I have sought out your precepts.
⁴⁶I will speak of your statutes before
   kings
   and will not be put to shame,
⁴⁷for I delight in your commands
   because I love them.
⁴⁸I lift up my hands toᵗ your
   commands, which I love,
   and I meditate on your decrees.

ז   Zayin

⁴⁹Remember your word to your servant,
   for you have given me hope.
⁵⁰My comfort in my suffering is this:
   Your promise preserves my life.
⁵¹The arrogant mock me without
   restraint,
   but I do not turn from your law.
⁵²I remember your ancient laws, O LORD,
   and I find comfort in them.

⁵³Indignation grips me because of the
   wicked,
   who have forsaken your law.
⁵⁴Your decrees are the theme of my
   song
   wherever I lodge.
⁵⁵In the night I remember your name,
   O LORD,
   and I will keep your law.
⁵⁶This has been my practice:
   I obey your precepts.

ח   Heth

⁵⁷You are my portion, O LORD;
   I have promised to obey your
   words.
⁵⁸I have sought your face with all my
   heart;
   be gracious to me according to your
   promise.
⁵⁹I have considered my ways
   and have turned my steps to your
   statutes.
⁶⁰I will hasten and not delay
   to obey your commands.
⁶¹Though the wicked bind me with
   ropes,
   I will not forget your law.
⁶²At midnight I rise to give you thanks
   for your righteous laws.
⁶³I am a friend to all who fear you,
   to all who follow your precepts.
⁶⁴The earth is filled with your love,
   O LORD;
   teach me your decrees.

ט   Teth

⁶⁵Do good to your servant
   according to your word, O LORD.
⁶⁶Teach me knowledge and good
   judgment,
   for I believe in your commands.
⁶⁷Before I was afflicted I went astray,
   but now I obey your word.
⁶⁸You are good, and what you do is
   good;
   teach me your decrees.
⁶⁹Though the arrogant have smeared me
   with lies,
   I keep your precepts with all my
   heart.
⁷⁰Their hearts are callous and unfeeling,
   but I delight in your law.
⁷¹It was good for me to be afflicted
   so that I might learn your decrees.

ˢ37 Two manuscripts of the Masoretic Text and Dead Sea Scrolls; most manuscripts of the Masoretic Text *life in your way*
ᵗ48 Or *for*

⁷²The law from your mouth is more
    precious to me
  than thousands of pieces of silver
    and gold.

י Yodh

⁷³Your hands made me and formed me;
  give me understanding to learn your
    commands.
⁷⁴May those who fear you rejoice when
    they see me,
  for I have put my hope in your
    word.
⁷⁵I know, O LORD, that your laws are
    righteous,
  and in faithfulness you have
    afflicted me.
⁷⁶May your unfailing love be my
    comfort,
  according to your promise to your
    servant.
⁷⁷Let your compassion come to me that I
    may live,
  for your law is my delight.
⁷⁸May the arrogant be put to shame for
    wronging me without cause;
  but I will meditate on your precepts.
⁷⁹May those who fear you turn to me,
  those who understand your statutes.
⁸⁰May my heart be blameless toward
    your decrees,
  that I may not be put to shame.

כ Kaph

⁸¹My soul faints with longing for your
    salvation,
  but I have put my hope in your
    word.
⁸²My eyes fail, looking for your promise;
  I say, "When will you comfort me?"
⁸³Though I am like a wineskin in the
    smoke,
  I do not forget your decrees.
⁸⁴How long must your servant wait?
  When will you punish my
    persecutors?
⁸⁵The arrogant dig pitfalls for me,
  contrary to your law.
⁸⁶All your commands are trustworthy;
  help me, for men persecute me
    without cause.
⁸⁷They almost wiped me from the earth,
  but I have not forsaken your
    precepts.
⁸⁸Preserve my life according to your
    love,

and I will obey the statutes of your
  mouth.

ל Lamedh

⁸⁹Your word, O LORD, is eternal;
  it stands firm in the heavens.
⁹⁰Your faithfulness continues through all
    generations;
  you established the earth, and it
    endures.
⁹¹Your laws endure to this day,
  for all things serve you.
⁹²If your law had not been my delight,
  I would have perished in my
    affliction.
⁹³I will never forget your precepts,
  for by them you have preserved my
    life.
⁹⁴Save me, for I am yours;
  I have sought out your precepts.
⁹⁵The wicked are waiting to destroy me,
  but I will ponder your statutes.
⁹⁶To all perfection I see a limit;
  but your commands are boundless.

מ Mem

⁹⁷Oh, how I love your law!
  I meditate on it all day long.
⁹⁸Your commands make me wiser than
    my enemies,
  for they are ever with me.
⁹⁹I have more insight than all my
    teachers,
  for I meditate on your statutes.
¹⁰⁰I have more understanding than the
    elders,
  for I obey your precepts.
¹⁰¹I have kept my feet from every evil
    path
  so that I might obey your word.
¹⁰²I have not departed from your laws,
  for you yourself have taught me.
¹⁰³How sweet are your words to my
    taste,
  sweeter than honey to my mouth!
¹⁰⁴I gain understanding from your
    precepts;
  therefore I hate every wrong path.

נ Nun

¹⁰⁵Your word is a lamp to my feet
  and a light for my path.
¹⁰⁶I have taken an oath and confirmed it,
  that I will follow your righteous
    laws.
¹⁰⁷I have suffered much;

preserve my life, O Lᴏʀᴅ, according
    to your word.
¹⁰⁸Accept, O Lᴏʀᴅ, the willing praise of
    my mouth,
    and teach me your laws.
¹⁰⁹Though I constantly take my life in
    my hands,
    I will not forget your law.
¹¹⁰The wicked have set a snare for me,
    but I have not strayed from your
    precepts.
¹¹¹Your statutes are my heritage forever;
    they are the joy of my heart.
¹¹²My heart is set on keeping your
    decrees
    to the very end.

ם   Samekh

¹¹³I hate double-minded men,
    but I love your law.
¹¹⁴You are my refuge and my shield;
    I have put my hope in your word.
¹¹⁵Away from me, you evildoers,
    that I may keep the commands of
    my God!
¹¹⁶Sustain me according to your
    promise, and I will live;
    do not let my hopes be dashed.
¹¹⁷Uphold me, and I will be delivered;
    I will always have regard for your
    decrees.
¹¹⁸You reject all who stray from your
    decrees,
    for their deceitfulness is in vain.
¹¹⁹All the wicked of the earth you
    discard like dross;
    therefore I love your statutes.
¹²⁰My flesh trembles in fear of you;
    I stand in awe of your laws.

ע   Ayin

¹²¹I have done what is righteous and
    just;
    do not leave me to my oppressors.
¹²²Ensure your servant's well-being;
    let not the arrogant oppress me.
¹²³My eyes fail, looking for your
    salvation,
    looking for your righteous promise.
¹²⁴Deal with your servant according to
    your love
    and teach me your decrees.
¹²⁵I am your servant; give me
    discernment
    that I may understand your statutes.
¹²⁶It is time for you to act, O Lᴏʀᴅ;
    your law is being broken.

¹²⁷Because I love your commands
    more than gold, more than pure
    gold,
¹²⁸and because I consider all your
    precepts right,
    I hate every wrong path.

פ   Pe

¹²⁹Your statutes are wonderful;
    therefore I obey them.
¹³⁰The unfolding of your words gives
    light;
    it gives understanding to the simple.
¹³¹I open my mouth and pant,
    longing for your commands.
¹³²Turn to me and have mercy on me,
    as you always do to those who love
    your name.
¹³³Direct my footsteps according to your
    word;
    let no sin rule over me.
¹³⁴Redeem me from the oppression of
    men,
    that I may obey your precepts.
¹³⁵Make your face shine upon your
    servant
    and teach me your decrees.
¹³⁶Streams of tears flow from my eyes,
    for your law is not obeyed.

צ   Tsadhe

¹³⁷Righteous are you, O Lᴏʀᴅ,
    and your laws are right.
¹³⁸The statutes you have laid down are
    righteous;
    they are fully trustworthy.
¹³⁹My zeal wears me out,
    for my enemies ignore your words.
¹⁴⁰Your promises have been thoroughly
    tested,
    and your servant loves them.
¹⁴¹Though I am lowly and despised,
    I do not forget your precepts.
¹⁴²Your righteousness is everlasting
    and your law is true.
¹⁴³Trouble and distress have come
    upon me,
    but your commands are my delight.
¹⁴⁴Your statutes are forever right;
    give me understanding that I may
    live.

ק   Qoph

¹⁴⁵I call with all my heart; answer me,
    O Lᴏʀᴅ,
    and I will obey your decrees.
¹⁴⁶I call out to you; save me

and I will keep your statutes.

¹⁴⁷I rise before dawn and cry for help;
    I have put my hope in your word.
¹⁴⁸My eyes stay open through the
        watches of the night,
    that I may meditate on your
        promises.
¹⁴⁹Hear my voice in accordance with
        your love;
    preserve my life, O LORD, according
        to your laws.
¹⁵⁰Those who devise wicked schemes are
        near,
    but they are far from your law.
¹⁵¹Yet you are near, O LORD,
    and all your commands are true.
¹⁵²Long ago I learned from your statutes
    that you established them to last
        forever.

ר   Resh

¹⁵³Look upon my suffering and
        deliver me,
    for I have not forgotten your law.
¹⁵⁴Defend my cause and redeem me;
    preserve my life according to your
        promise.
¹⁵⁵Salvation is far from the wicked,
    for they do not seek out your
        decrees.
¹⁵⁶Your compassion is great, O LORD;
    preserve my life according to your
        laws.
¹⁵⁷Many are the foes who persecute me,
    but I have not turned from your
        statutes.
¹⁵⁸I look on the faithless with loathing,
    for they do not obey your word.
¹⁵⁹See how I love your precepts;
    preserve my life, O LORD, according
        to your love.
¹⁶⁰All your words are true;
    all your righteous laws are eternal.

ש   Sin and Shin

¹⁶¹Rulers persecute me without cause,
    but my heart trembles at your word.
¹⁶²I rejoice in your promise
    like one who finds great spoil.
¹⁶³I hate and abhor falsehood
    but I love your law.
¹⁶⁴Seven times a day I praise you
    for your righteous laws.
¹⁶⁵Great peace have they who love your
        law,
    and nothing can make them
        stumble.
¹⁶⁶I wait for your salvation, O LORD,
    and I follow your commands.
¹⁶⁷I obey your statutes,
    for I love them greatly.
¹⁶⁸I obey your precepts and your
        statutes,
    for all my ways are known to you.

ת   Taw

¹⁶⁹May my cry come before you, O LORD;
    give me understanding according to
        your word.
¹⁷⁰May my supplication come before
        you;
    deliver me according to your
        promise.
¹⁷¹May my lips overflow with praise,
    for you teach me your decrees.
¹⁷²May my tongue sing of your word,
    for all your commands are
        righteous.
¹⁷³May your hand be ready to help me,
    for I have chosen your precepts.
¹⁷⁴I long for your salvation, O LORD,
    and your law is my delight.
¹⁷⁵Let me live that I may praise you,
    and may your laws sustain me.
¹⁷⁶I have strayed like a lost sheep.
    Seek your servant,
    for I have not forgotten your
        commands.

JUNE 25 ☐ DAY 177
PSALMS 120–127
Hymn of the Highway

OVERVIEW Psalms 120–134, which each bear the title "A song of ascents," were orginally sung by Jewish worshipers on their thrice-yearly pilgrimages to Jerusalem for the Feast of the Passover, the Feast of Weeks and the Feast of Tabernacles. These travel tunes reflect the thoughts of a pilgrim away from home, longing for peace, protection and provision.

Psalm 120	Psalm 121	Psalms 122–123	Psalms 124–125	Psalms 126–127
Life among Liars	Trust of the Traveler	Joy in Jerusalem	Praise for Protection	Hope in God's Heritage
Pilgrimage			Provision	

When you pray, do you give God instructions, or do you report for duty?

YOUR DAILY WALK The world of the psalmist—of about 1000 B.C.—has given way to the global village of A.D. 2000. Advances in communication and transportation have radically altered the way people live. Distances that would have taken David days to traverse can now be covered by car in hours . . . by jet plane in minutes. Where once message delivery took weeks, you can now pick up the phone and speak with someone half a world away.

Thanks to technology, much has changed. But two things remain the same: the speed with which you can reach God in prayer (Psalm 120) and the need for safety as you travel (Psalm 121). Every time you buckle up your seat belt today, remind yourself that "the LORD will watch over your coming and going" (121:8). And every time you dial a phone number today, let the first ring remind you that "I call on the LORD in my distress, and he answers me" (120:1).

INSIGHT Smitten by the Moon . . . or Something More?
A common Hebrew figure of speech is the *merism,* which uses two extremes to speak of the totality of something. A few examples will illustrate the point (emphasis added):

"In the beginning God created *the heavens and the earth*" (and everything in between, a merism for *all of creation;* Genesis 1:1).

"O LORD, . . . You know when *I sit and when I rise*" (a merism for *my every movement throughout the day;* Psalm 139:1–2).

Now read Psalm 121:6. Using the principle of interpreting merisms as suggested by the examples above, how would you translate the psalmist's thought?

PSALM 120
A song of ascents.

¹I call on the LORD in my distress,
  and he answers me.
²Save me, O LORD, from lying lips
  and from deceitful tongues.

³What will he do to you,
  and what more besides, O deceitful
    tongue?

⁴He will punish you with a warrior's
    sharp arrows,
  with burning coals of the broom tree.

⁵Woe to me that I dwell in Meshech,
  that I live among the tents of Kedar!
⁶Too long have I lived
  among those who hate peace.
⁷I am a man of peace;
  but when I speak, they are for war.

PSALM 121
A song of ascents.

¹I lift up my eyes to the hills—
  where does my help come from?
²My help comes from the LORD,
  the Maker of heaven and earth.

³He will not let your foot slip—
  he who watches over you will not
    slumber;
⁴indeed, he who watches over Israel
  will neither slumber nor sleep.

⁵The LORD watches over you—
  the LORD is your shade at your right
    hand;
⁶the sun will not harm you by day,
  nor the moon by night.

⁷The LORD will keep you from all
    harm—
  he will watch over your life;
⁸the LORD will watch over your coming
    and going
  both now and forevermore.

PSALM 122
A song of ascents. Of David.

¹I rejoiced with those who said to me,
  "Let us go to the house of the LORD."
²Our feet are standing
  in your gates, O Jerusalem.

³Jerusalem is built like a city
  that is closely compacted together.
⁴That is where the tribes go up,
  the tribes of the LORD,
 to praise the name of the LORD
  according to the statute given to
    Israel.
⁵There the thrones for judgment stand,
  the thrones of the house of David.

⁶Pray for the peace of Jerusalem:
  "May those who love you be secure.
⁷May there be peace within your walls
  and security within your citadels."
⁸For the sake of my brothers and
    friends,
  I will say, "Peace be within you."
⁹For the sake of the house of the LORD
    our God,
  I will seek your prosperity.

PSALM 123
A song of ascents.

¹I lift up my eyes to you,
  to you whose throne is in heaven.

²As the eyes of slaves look to the hand
    of their master,
  as the eyes of a maid look to the
    hand of her mistress,
 so our eyes look to the LORD our God,
  till he shows us his mercy.

³Have mercy on us, O LORD, have
    mercy on us,
  for we have endured much
    contempt.
⁴We have endured much ridicule from
    the proud,
  much contempt from the arrogant.

PSALM 124
A song of ascents. Of David.

¹If the LORD had not been on our side—
  let Israel say—
²if the LORD had not been on our side
  when men attacked us,
³when their anger flared against us,
  they would have swallowed us
    alive;
⁴the flood would have engulfed us,
  the torrent would have swept over
    us,
⁵the raging waters
  would have swept us away.

⁶Praise be to the LORD,
  who has not let us be torn by their
    teeth.
⁷We have escaped like a bird
  out of the fowler's snare;
  the snare has been broken,
  and we have escaped.
⁸Our help is in the name of the LORD,
  the Maker of heaven and earth.

PSALM 125
A song of ascents.

¹Those who trust in the LORD are like
    Mount Zion,
  which cannot be shaken but endures
    forever.
²As the mountains surround Jerusalem,
  so the LORD surrounds his people
  both now and forevermore.

³The scepter of the wicked will not
    remain
  over the land allotted to the
    righteous,
  for then the righteous might use
    their hands to do evil.

⁴Do good, O LORD, to those who are
    good,
  to those who are upright in heart.
⁵But those who turn to crooked ways
    the LORD will banish with the
    evildoers.

Peace be upon Israel.

PSALM 126
A song of ascents.

¹When the LORD brought back the
    captives to ᵘ Zion,
  we were like men who dreamed.ᵛ
²Our mouths were filled with laughter,
  our tongues with songs of joy.
Then it was said among the nations,
    "The LORD has done great things for
    them."
³The LORD has done great things for us,
  and we are filled with joy.

⁴Restore our fortunes,ʷ O LORD,
  like streams in the Negev.
⁵Those who sow in tears
  will reap with songs of joy.
⁶He who goes out weeping,

carrying seed to sow,
  will return with songs of joy,
  carrying sheaves with him.

PSALM 127
A song of ascents. Of Solomon.

¹Unless the LORD builds the house,
  its builders labor in vain.
Unless the LORD watches over the city,
  the watchmen stand guard in vain.
²In vain you rise early
  and stay up late,
toiling for food to eat—
  for he grants sleep toˣ those he
    loves.

³Sons are a heritage from the LORD,
  children a reward from him.
⁴Like arrows in the hands of a warrior
  are sons born in one's youth.
⁵Blessed is the man
  whose quiver is full of them.
They will not be put to shame
  when they contend with their
    enemies in the gate.

ᵘ1 Or LORD *restored the fortunes of*   ᵛ1 Or *men restored to health*   ʷ4 Or *Bring back our captives*   ˣ2 Or *eat—/ for while they sleep he provides for*

JUNE 26 ☐ DAY 178
PSALMS 128–134
Portraits of Harmony

OVERVIEW The pilgrim, continuing his journey to Jerusalem, contem-
plates the blessings of God upon his family (Psalm 128), the deliverance by God from danger (129) and depression (130), the sufficiency
of God (131), the joy of serving God (132) and the unity of the
household of God (133). An outburst of praise concludes the pilgrim's
journey (134).

Psalm 128	Psalms 129–130	Psalm 131	Psalm 132	Psalms 133–134
Children from God	Crying Out to God	Contentment in God	Covenant of God	Communion with God's People
Satisfaction			Strength	

YOUR DAILY WALK Psalm 133 uses two Old Testament illustrations
to describe the beautiful harmony of God's people dwelling together
in unity (133:1). The first picture is of Aaron's anointing. When the
high priest was anointed (Exodus 29:7; 30:22–25, 30), the ceremony
involved the messy procedure of pouring special oil upon the priest's
head. But the costly fragrant lotion pictured the beauty of the priest's

*Too often
Christian
unity can be
illustrated by
two cold
porcupines
huddling
together—they
need each other,
but they needle
each other.*

spiritual role in bringing the nation to God. In the same way, unity in the brotherhood of believers is a pleasing fragrance to God and an attractive aroma to those in the world who find peace so elusive.

The second picture is of the dew on Mount Hermon. In an arid land where rainfall is scarce, the dew brings life-sustaining moisture to parched ground. Through the long, dry summers in Palestine, plants survive and blossom because of the dew. Unity in the brotherhood of believers is like that dew: a gift from God to bring blessing and fruitfulness in an otherwise barren world.

Have Christians today achieved this biblical ideal of unity? For the answer, first look at your own life. Read John 17:11, 21; then ask: Do my relationships in the body of Christ provide the fragrance of ointment and the refreshment of dew? What needs to change?

 INSIGHT Ascent to the Holy City
Jerusalem, also known as Mount Zion, is located on a hill rising 2,600 feet above sea level. Because of its elevation, pilgrims arriving from any direction must go "up to Jerusalem." The temple and walls rising above the surrounding terrain must have provided a breathtaking first glimpse for those marching to the holy city.

PSALM 128
A song of ascents.

¹Blessed are all who fear the LORD,
  who walk in his ways.
²You will eat the fruit of your labor;
  blessings and prosperity will be
    yours.
³Your wife will be like a fruitful vine
  within your house;
your sons will be like olive shoots
  around your table.
⁴Thus is the man blessed
  who fears the LORD.

⁵May the LORD bless you from Zion
  all the days of your life;
may you see the prosperity of
    Jerusalem,
6   and may you live to see your
    children's children.

Peace be upon Israel.

PSALM 129
A song of ascents.

¹They have greatly oppressed me from
    my youth—
  let Israel say—
²they have greatly oppressed me from
    my youth,
  but they have not gained the victory
    over me.
³Plowmen have plowed my back
  and made their furrows long.
⁴But the LORD is righteous;
  he has cut me free from the cords of
    the wicked.

⁵May all who hate Zion
  be turned back in shame.
⁶May they be like grass on the roof,
  which withers before it can grow;
⁷with it the reaper cannot fill his hands,
  nor the one who gathers fill his
    arms.
⁸May those who pass by not say,
  "The blessing of the LORD be upon
    you;
  we bless you in the name of the
    LORD."

PSALM 130
A song of ascents.

¹Out of the depths I cry to you, O LORD;
2   O Lord, hear my voice.
Let your ears be attentive
  to my cry for mercy.

³If you, O LORD, kept a record of sins,
  O Lord, who could stand?
⁴But with you there is forgiveness;
  therefore you are feared.

⁵I wait for the LORD, my soul waits,
  and in his word I put my hope.
⁶My soul waits for the Lord
  more than watchmen wait for the
    morning,
  more than watchmen wait for the
    morning.

⁷O Israel, put your hope in the LORD,
  for with the LORD is unfailing love
  and with him is full redemption.
⁸He himself will redeem Israel
  from all their sins.

PSALM 131
A song of ascents. Of David.

¹My heart is not proud, O LORD,
my eyes are not haughty;
I do not concern myself with great
matters
or things too wonderful for me.
²But I have stilled and quieted my soul;
like a weaned child with its mother,
like a weaned child is my soul
within me.

³O Israel, put your hope in the LORD
both now and forevermore.

PSALM 132
A song of ascents.

¹O LORD, remember David
and all the hardships he endured.

²He swore an oath to the LORD
and made a vow to the Mighty One
of Jacob:
³"I will not enter my house
or go to my bed—
⁴I will allow no sleep to my eyes,
no slumber to my eyelids,
⁵till I find a place for the LORD,
a dwelling for the Mighty One of
Jacob."

⁶We heard it in Ephrathah,
we came upon it in the fields of
Jaar*ʸ*: *ᶻ*
⁷"Let us go to his dwelling place;
let us worship at his footstool—
⁸arise, O LORD, and come to your
resting place,
you and the ark of your might.
⁹May your priests be clothed with
righteousness;
may your saints sing for joy."

¹⁰For the sake of David your servant,
do not reject your anointed one.

¹¹The LORD swore an oath to David,
a sure oath that he will not revoke:
"One of your own descendants
I will place on your throne—
¹²if your sons keep my covenant
and the statutes I teach them,

then their sons will sit
on your throne for ever and ever."

¹³For the LORD has chosen Zion,
he has desired it for his dwelling:
¹⁴"This is my resting place for ever and
ever;
here I will sit enthroned, for I have
desired it—
¹⁵I will bless her with abundant
provisions;
her poor will I satisfy with food.
¹⁶I will clothe her priests with salvation,
and her saints will ever sing for joy.

¹⁷"Here I will make a horn*ᵃ* grow for
David
and set up a lamp for my anointed
one.
¹⁸I will clothe his enemies with shame,
but the crown on his head will be
resplendent."

PSALM 133
A song of ascents. Of David.

¹How good and pleasant it is
when brothers live together in unity!
²It is like precious oil poured on the
head,
running down on the beard,
running down on Aaron's beard,
down upon the collar of his robes.
³It is as if the dew of Hermon
were falling on Mount Zion.
For there the LORD bestows his
blessing,
even life forevermore.

PSALM 134
A song of ascents.

¹Praise the LORD, all you servants of the
LORD
who minister by night in the house
of the LORD.
²Lift up your hands in the sanctuary
and praise the LORD.

³May the LORD, the Maker of heaven
and earth,
bless you from Zion.

---

*ʸ*6 That is, Kiriath Jearim   *ᶻ*6 Or *heard of it in Ephrathah, | we found it in the fields of Jaar.* (And no quotes around verses 7-9)
*ᵃ*17 *Horn* here symbolizes strong one, that is, king.

JUNE 27 □ DAY 179
PSALMS 135–139
The God Who Is There

OVERVIEW From the heights of joy to the depths of sorrow, today's reading spans a wide range of emotions. In recalling past dealings with God—both in creation and in the redemption of God's people—the psalmist breaks forth in glad songs of praise (Psalms 135–136). Reliving the desperate days of exile, the psalmist expresses deep sorrow (137). But even times of trouble can be met with acclamation (138) by remembering God's infinite knowledge and unceasing presence (139).

Psalms 135–136	Psalm 137	Psalms 138–139
Adoration for God's Mighty Acts	Agony of the Exile	Awe at God's Greatness
Worship	Weeping	Wonder

YOUR DAILY WALK Three of God's attributes are beautifully depicted in Psalm 139: his omniscience (he knows everything about you), his omnipresence (he goes everywhere with you) and his omnipotence (he is infinitely powerful, enough to meet your every need).

Prayer is a shield to the soul, a sacrifice to God and a scourge for Satan.

The question arises, If all that is true, then why should I pray? There are many good reasons to pray, but here are just three:

• Pray because God has commanded it (Jeremiah 33:3).
• Pray because God delights in giving good gifts to those who ask (Matthew 7:7–11).
• Pray because prayer changes things . . . but mostly, prayer changes people, and that means prayer changes *you!*

Notice in Psalm 139 how David's attitude changes. In the opening verses David is cautious, almost fearful, at the thought that his life is an open book before God. But by the end, he is humble and eager to please God—even in the secret compartments of his life. Do you need to pray David's prayer today (vv. 23–24)?

INSIGHT Mercy, Mercy, Mercy
Before you read Psalm 136, reflect on a few of the many ways in which translators have captured the refrain "His love endures forever" (repeated twenty-six times in the psalm):
• "His kindness never fails" (Moffatt).
• "His steadfast love endures for ever" (Revised Standard Version).
• "His mercy endures forever" (New King James Version).

PSALM 135
¹Praise the LORD.*b*

Praise the name of the LORD;
    praise him, you servants of the
        LORD,
²you who minister in the house of the
        LORD,
    in the courts of the house of our
        God.

³Praise the LORD, for the LORD is good;

sing praise to his name, for that is
    pleasant.
⁴For the LORD has chosen Jacob to be
    his own,
    Israel to be his treasured possession.

⁵I know that the LORD is great,
    that our Lord is greater than all
        gods.
⁶The LORD does whatever pleases him,
    in the heavens and on the earth,
    in the seas and all their depths.

*b*1 Hebrew *Hallelu Yah*; also in verses 3 and 21

⁷He makes clouds rise from the ends of
the earth;
he sends lightning with the rain
and brings out the wind from his
storehouses.

⁸He struck down the firstborn of Egypt,
the firstborn of men and animals.
⁹He sent his signs and wonders into
your midst, O Egypt,
against Pharaoh and all his servants.
¹⁰He struck down many nations
and killed mighty kings—
¹¹Sihon king of the Amorites,
Og king of Bashan
and all the kings of Canaan—
¹²and he gave their land as an
inheritance,
an inheritance to his people Israel.

¹³Your name, O LORD, endures forever,
your renown, O LORD, through all
generations.
¹⁴For the LORD will vindicate his people
and have compassion on his
servants.

¹⁵The idols of the nations are silver and
gold,
made by the hands of men.
¹⁶They have mouths, but cannot speak,
eyes, but they cannot see;
¹⁷they have ears, but cannot hear,
nor is there breath in their mouths.
¹⁸Those who make them will be like
them,
and so will all who trust in them.

¹⁹O house of Israel, praise the LORD;
O house of Aaron, praise the LORD;
²⁰O house of Levi, praise the LORD;
you who fear him, praise the LORD.
²¹Praise be to the LORD from Zion,
to him who dwells in Jerusalem.

Praise the LORD.

PSALM 136

¹Give thanks to the LORD, for he is
good.
His love endures forever.
²Give thanks to the God of gods.
His love endures forever.
³Give thanks to the Lord of lords:
His love endures forever.

⁴to him who alone does great wonders,
His love endures forever.

⁵who by his understanding made the
heavens,
His love endures forever.
⁶who spread out the earth upon the
waters,
His love endures forever.
⁷who made the great lights—
His love endures forever.
⁸the sun to govern the day,
His love endures forever.
⁹the moon and stars to govern the
night;
His love endures forever.

¹⁰to him who struck down the firstborn
of Egypt
His love endures forever.
¹¹and brought Israel out from among
them
His love endures forever.
¹²with a mighty hand and outstretched
arm;
His love endures forever.
¹³to him who divided the Red Sea*ᶜ*
asunder
His love endures forever.
¹⁴and brought Israel through the midst
of it,
His love endures forever.
¹⁵but swept Pharaoh and his army into
the Red Sea;
His love endures forever.
¹⁶to him who led his people through the
desert,
His love endures forever.
¹⁷who struck down great kings,
His love endures forever.
¹⁸and killed mighty kings—
His love endures forever.
¹⁹Sihon king of the Amorites
His love endures forever.
²⁰and Og king of Bashan—
His love endures forever.
²¹and gave their land as an inheritance,
His love endures forever.
²²an inheritance to his servant Israel;
His love endures forever.

²³to the One who remembered us in our
low estate
His love endures forever.
²⁴and freed us from our enemies,
His love endures forever.
²⁵and who gives food to every creature.
His love endures forever.

ᶜ13 Hebrew *Yam Suph;* that is, Sea of Reeds; also in verse 15

²⁶Give thanks to the God of heaven.
His love endures forever.

PSALM 137

¹By the rivers of Babylon we sat and
wept
when we remembered Zion.
²There on the poplars
we hung our harps,
³for there our captors asked us for
songs,
our tormentors demanded songs of
joy;
they said, "Sing us one of the songs
of Zion!"

⁴How can we sing the songs of the
LORD
while in a foreign land?
⁵If I forget you, O Jerusalem,
may my right hand forget ⌞its skill⌟.
⁶May my tongue cling to the roof of
my mouth
if I do not remember you,
if I do not consider Jerusalem
my highest joy.

⁷Remember, O LORD, what the Edomites
did
on the day Jerusalem fell.
"Tear it down," they cried,
"tear it down to its foundations!"

⁸O Daughter of Babylon, doomed to
destruction,
happy is he who repays you
for what you have done to us—
⁹he who seizes your infants
and dashes them against the rocks.

PSALM 138
Of David.

¹I will praise you, O LORD, with all my
heart;
before the "gods" I will sing your
praise.
²I will bow down toward your holy
temple
and will praise your name
for your love and your faithfulness,
for you have exalted above all things
your name and your word.
³When I called, you answered me;
you made me bold and stouthearted.

⁴May all the kings of the earth praise
you, O LORD,

when they hear the words of your
mouth.
⁵May they sing of the ways of the LORD,
for the glory of the LORD is great.

⁶Though the LORD is on high, he looks
upon the lowly,
but the proud he knows from afar.
⁷Though I walk in the midst of trouble,
you preserve my life;
you stretch out your hand against the
anger of my foes,
with your right hand you save me.
⁸The LORD will fulfill ⌞his purpose⌟ for
me;
your love, O LORD, endures forever—
do not abandon the works of your
hands.

PSALM 139
For the director of music. Of David.
A psalm.

¹O LORD, you have searched me
and you know me.
²You know when I sit and when I rise;
you perceive my thoughts from afar.
³You discern my going out and my
lying down;
you are familiar with all my ways.
⁴Before a word is on my tongue
you know it completely, O LORD.

⁵You hem me in—behind and before;
you have laid your hand upon me.
⁶Such knowledge is too wonderful for
me,
too lofty for me to attain.

⁷Where can I go from your Spirit?
Where can I flee from your
presence?
⁸If I go up to the heavens, you are
there;
if I make my bed in the depths,ᵈ
you are there.
⁹If I rise on the wings of the dawn,
if I settle on the far side of the sea,
¹⁰even there your hand will guide me,
your right hand will hold me fast.
¹¹If I say, "Surely the darkness will hide
me
and the light become night around
me,"
¹²even the darkness will not be dark to
you;

ᵈ8 Hebrew *Sheol*

the night will shine like the day,
   for darkness is as light to you.

13For you created my inmost being;
   you knit me together in my mother's
      womb.
14I praise you because I am fearfully and
      wonderfully made;
   your works are wonderful,
   I know that full well.
15My frame was not hidden from you
   when I was made in the secret place.
When I was woven together in the
      depths of the earth,
16 your eyes saw my unformed body.
All the days ordained for me
   were written in your book
   before one of them came to be.

17How precious to*e* me are your
      thoughts, O God!
   How vast is the sum of them!
18Were I to count them,
   they would outnumber the grains of
      sand.

e17 Or concerning

When I awake,
   I am still with you.

19If only you would slay the wicked,
      O God!
   Away from me, you bloodthirsty
      men!
20They speak of you with evil intent;
   your adversaries misuse your name.
21Do I not hate those who hate you,
      O LORD,
   and abhor those who rise up against
      you?
22I have nothing but hatred for them;
   I count them my enemies.

23Search me, O God, and know my
      heart;
   test me and know my anxious
      thoughts.
24See if there is any offensive way in
      me,
   and lead me in the way everlasting.

JUNE 28 □ DAY 180
Thanks, and Thanks Again

LOOK BACK Metaphors abound in the Psalms. Already you have discovered that God is your shepherd, light, salvation, rock, fortress, refuge, strength, defense, glory and judge. The list will continue to grow as you read further in this magnificent "diary of devotion." When you learn a new truth *about* God, don't forget to respond in worship *to* God. Psalms was not written for your information but for your transformation.

    For a change of pace, try reading a portion of the Psalms just before you go to bed at night. Or leave your Bible open to the Psalms, and make it your meditation the first thing in the morning. Stick a small copy of the Psalms in your pocket or purse, and "chew" on a psalm as you enjoy lunch. If you have access to the Bible on cassette tape, try listening to a portion of the book of Psalms as you drive back and forth to work. In the process you'll be taking to heart the first psalm: "Blessed is the man . . . [whose] delight is in the law of the LORD, and on his law he meditates day and night. He is like a tree planted by streams of water, which yields its fruit in season and whose leaf does not wither. Whatever he does prospers" (Psalm 1:1–3).

LOOK UP Find a dictionary and look up the word *refrain*. What definition does the author suggest?

    Now compare that definition with this one: "A refrain is the reverberation of the heart when touched by the greatness of God." It is a heartfelt exclamation that deserves to be repeated—and so it is! Refrains are what you have discovered in several of the psalms you read this past week. Think of them as divine "ditto marks" that highlight a

God's work of creation is done; our work of praising is just begun. particular facet of God's character or program. Repetition needn't be redundant if the motive behind it is to underscore something of great importance.

Can you find the *refrain* in each of the following psalms? (Hint: Look for the portion of the verse that is repeated virtually verbatim.)

- Psalm 107:6, 13, 19, 28
- Psalm 107:8, 15, 21, 31
- Psalm 136 (every verse!)

LOOK AHEAD Thanksgiving ought to be more than a holiday on the calendar. God intends it to be the attitude of your heart. How can you know for sure? He said so . . . twenty-six times!

In Psalm 136 the psalmist rehearses dozens of memorable moments from the history of God's people to stimulate an "attitude of gratitude." As you read the psalm, you begin to anticipate the refrain that concludes each and every verse: "His love endures forever." Can you find a reference in the historical books of the Old Testament (the first seventeen books, Genesis through Esther) to which the psalmist is referring in each verse? For example, verses 7–9 are a reminder of what God did in Genesis 1:14–19. How many others can you find? And if you feel like joining the psalmist in his heartfelt refrain, well, don't refrain!

JUNE 29 □ DAY 181
PSALMS 140–145
A Heart like God's

OVERVIEW The six psalms you will read today contain David's prayer for protection from those who would harm him (Psalms 140–141), as well as his testimony of trust in the one who is his refuge and portion (142–143). Because David has seen God's care over his life in the past (144), his faith is fortified to look for God's provision in the future (145).

Psalms 140–141	Psalms 142–143	Psalm 144	Psalm 145
Protection from Evil Men	Preservation from Enemies	Provision for Needs	Praise for God's Grace
Receiving from God			Responding to God

YOUR DAILY WALK Wanted: A Man after God's Own Heart.

The "position available"? The throne of Israel. The one involved in the "job search"? The God of Abraham, Isaac and Jacob.

David, the man after God's own heart, didn't do his devotions; he lived them. When God wanted a man to do his will (1 Samuel 13:14), he found what he was looking for in an obscure lad from the pasturelands of Judea. Notice some of the qualities of David's character that many of his later writings reveal:

- Confidence in God in time of danger (Psalm 140:1, 4, 7)
- Hunger for righteousness (141:3–4)
- Transparent honesty before God (142:1–2)
- A good memory for God's past dealings (143:5)
- A desire to see God's justice prevail (144:5–8)
- Overflowing praise to God (145:1–21)

God is looking for similar individuals today—people with a heart like David's; that is, people with a heart like God's (2 Chronicles 16:9). After studying David's heart as revealed in Psalms 140–145, are you interested in applying for the position? Tell God so!

INSIGHT The Case of the Missing Letter
David's last psalm (Psalm 145) is also the last of eight acrostic psalms based on the Hebrew alphabet. One letter of the alphabet, nun, was omitted from the Hebrew text, causing the Hebrew reader to "stumble" at verse 14 (much the same way you might if you were reading the sequence "J, K, L, M, O, P"). But wouldn't you agree that verse 14 is a good one to "catch" yourself on?

PSALM 140
For the director of music. A psalm of David.

¹Rescue me, O LORD, from evil men;
    protect me from men of violence,
²who devise evil plans in their hearts
    and stir up war every day.
³They make their tongues as sharp as a serpent's;
    the poison of vipers is on their lips.
                                    Selah

⁴Keep me, O LORD, from the hands of the wicked;
    protect me from men of violence
    who plan to trip my feet.
⁵Proud men have hidden a snare for me;
    they have spread out the cords of their net
    and have set traps for me along my path.   *Selah*

⁶O LORD, I say to you, "You are my God."
    Hear, O LORD, my cry for mercy.
⁷O Sovereign LORD, my strong deliverer,
    who shields my head in the day of battle—
⁸do not grant the wicked their desires, O LORD;
    do not let their plans succeed,
    or they will become proud.   *Selah*

⁹Let the heads of those who surround me
    be covered with the trouble their lips have caused.
¹⁰Let burning coals fall upon them;
    may they be thrown into the fire,
    into miry pits, never to rise.
¹¹Let slanderers not be established in the land;

may disaster hunt down men of violence.
¹²I know that the LORD secures justice for the poor
    and upholds the cause of the needy.
¹³Surely the righteous will praise your name
    and the upright will live before you.

PSALM 141
A psalm of David.

¹O LORD, I call to you; come quickly to me.
    Hear my voice when I call to you.
²May my prayer be set before you like incense;
    may the lifting up of my hands be like the evening sacrifice.

³Set a guard over my mouth, O LORD;
    keep watch over the door of my lips.
⁴Let not my heart be drawn to what is evil,
    to take part in wicked deeds
with men who are evildoers;
    let me not eat of their delicacies.

⁵Let a righteous man*ᶠ* strike me—it is a kindness;
    let him rebuke me—it is oil on my head.
    My head will not refuse it.

Yet my prayer is ever against the deeds of evildoers;
⁶ their rulers will be thrown down from the cliffs,
    and the wicked will learn that my words were well spoken.
⁷⌊They will say,⌋ "As one plows and breaks up the earth,

f5 Or Let the Righteous One

745

so our bones have been scattered at
    the mouth of the grave.*"*

⁸But my eyes are fixed on you,
    O Sovereign Lᴏʀᴅ;
in you I take refuge—do not give me
    over to death.
⁹Keep me from the snares they have
    laid for me,
from the traps set by evildoers.
¹⁰Let the wicked fall into their own nets,
    while I pass by in safety.

PSALM 142

A *maskil*ʰ of David. When he was in the
cave. A prayer.

¹I cry aloud to the Lᴏʀᴅ;
    I lift up my voice to the Lᴏʀᴅ for
    mercy.
²I pour out my complaint before him;
    before him I tell my trouble.

³When my spirit grows faint within me,
    it is you who know my way.
In the path where I walk
    men have hidden a snare for me.
⁴Look to my right and see;
    no one is concerned for me.
I have no refuge;
    no one cares for my life.

⁵I cry to you, O Lᴏʀᴅ;
    I say, "You are my refuge,
    my portion in the land of the living."
⁶Listen to my cry,
    for I am in desperate need;
rescue me from those who pursue me,
    for they are too strong for me.
⁷Set me free from my prison,
    that I may praise your name.

Then the righteous will gather about
    me
    because of your goodness to me.

PSALM 143

A psalm of David.

¹O Lᴏʀᴅ, hear my prayer,
    listen to my cry for mercy;
in your faithfulness and righteousness
    come to my relief.
²Do not bring your servant into
    judgment,
    for no one living is righteous before
    you.
³The enemy pursues me,

he crushes me to the ground;
he makes me dwell in darkness
    like those long dead.
⁴So my spirit grows faint within me;
    my heart within me is dismayed.

⁵I remember the days of long ago;
    I meditate on all your works
    and consider what your hands have
    done.
⁶I spread out my hands to you;
    my soul thirsts for you like a
    parched land.   *Selah*

⁷Answer me quickly, O Lᴏʀᴅ;
    my spirit fails.
Do not hide your face from me
    or I will be like those who go down
    to the pit.
⁸Let the morning bring me word of
    your unfailing love,
    for I have put my trust in you.
Show me the way I should go,
    for to you I lift up my soul.
⁹Rescue me from my enemies, O Lᴏʀᴅ,
    for I hide myself in you.
¹⁰Teach me to do your will,
    for you are my God;
may your good Spirit
    lead me on level ground.

¹¹For your name's sake, O Lᴏʀᴅ,
    preserve my life;
in your righteousness, bring me out
    of trouble.
¹²In your unfailing love, silence my
    enemies;
    destroy all my foes,
    for I am your servant.

PSALM 144

Of David.

¹Praise be to the Lᴏʀᴅ my Rock,
    who trains my hands for war,
    my fingers for battle.
²He is my loving God and my fortress,
    my stronghold and my deliverer,
my shield, in whom I take refuge,
    who subdues peoplesⁱ under me.

³O Lᴏʀᴅ, what is man that you care for
    him,
    the son of man that you think of
    him?
⁴Man is like a breath;
    his days are like a fleeting shadow.

*g*7 Hebrew *Sheol*   *ʰ*Title: Probably a literary or musical term   *ⁱ*2 Many manuscripts of the Masoretic Text, Dead Sea Scrolls,
Aquila, Jerome and Syriac; most manuscripts of the Masoretic Text *subdues my people*

⁵Part your heavens, O LORD, and come
    down;
  touch the mountains, so that they
    smoke.
⁶Send forth lightning and scatter ͺthe
    enemiesͺ;
  shoot your arrows and rout them.
⁷Reach down your hand from on
    high;
  deliver me and rescue me
from the mighty waters,
  from the hands of foreigners
⁸whose mouths are full of lies,
  whose right hands are deceitful.

⁹I will sing a new song to you, O God;
  on the ten-stringed lyre I will make
    music to you,
¹⁰to the One who gives victory to kings,
  who delivers his servant David from
    the deadly sword.

¹¹Deliver me and rescue me
  from the hands of foreigners
whose mouths are full of lies,
  whose right hands are deceitful.

¹²Then our sons in their youth
  will be like well-nurtured plants,
and our daughters will be like pillars
  carved to adorn a palace.
¹³Our barns will be filled
  with every kind of provision.
Our sheep will increase by thousands,
  by tens of thousands in our fields;
¹⁴ our oxen will draw heavy loads.ʲ
There will be no breaching of walls,
  no going into captivity,
  no cry of distress in our streets.

¹⁵Blessed are the people of whom this is
    true;
  blessed are the people whose God is
    the LORD.

PSALM 145ᵏ
A psalm of praise. Of David.

¹I will exalt you, my God the King;
  I will praise your name for ever and
    ever.
²Every day I will praise you
  and extol your name for ever and
    ever.

³Great is the LORD and most worthy of
    praise;
  his greatness no one can fathom.
⁴One generation will commend your
    works to another;
  they will tell of your mighty acts.
⁵They will speak of the glorious
    splendor of your majesty,
  and I will meditate on your
    wonderful works.ˡ
⁶They will tell of the power of your
    awesome works,
  and I will proclaim your great
    deeds.
⁷They will celebrate your abundant
    goodness
  and joyfully sing of your
    righteousness.

⁸The LORD is gracious and
    compassionate,
  slow to anger and rich in love.
⁹The LORD is good to all;
  he has compassion on all he has
    made.
¹⁰All you have made will praise you,
    O LORD;
  your saints will extol you.
¹¹They will tell of the glory of your
    kingdom
  and speak of your might,
¹²so that all men may know of your
    mighty acts
  and the glorious splendor of your
    kingdom.
¹³Your kingdom is an everlasting
    kingdom,
  and your dominion endures through
    all generations.

The LORD is faithful to all his promises
  and loving toward all he has
    made.ᵐ
¹⁴The LORD upholds all those who fall
  and lifts up all who are bowed
    down.
¹⁵The eyes of all look to you,
  and you give them their food at the
    proper time.
¹⁶You open your hand
  and satisfy the desires of every
    living thing.

ʲ14 Or *our chieftains will be firmly established*   ᵏThis psalm is an acrostic poem, the verses of which (including verse 13b) begin
with the successive letters of the Hebrew alphabet.   ˡ5 Dead Sea Scrolls and Syriac (see also Septuagint); Masoretic Text *On
the glorious splendor of your majesty / and on your wonderful works I will meditate*   ᵐ13 One manuscript of the Masoretic Text,
Dead Sea Scrolls and Syriac (see also Septuagint); most manuscripts of the Masoretic Text do not have the last two lines of
verse 13.

¹⁷The LORD is righteous in all his ways
    and loving toward all he has
    made.
¹⁸The LORD is near to all who call on
    him,
    to all who call on him in truth.
¹⁹He fulfills the desires of those who
    fear him;
    he hears their cry and saves them.

²⁰The LORD watches over all who love
    him,
    but all the wicked he will destroy.

²¹My mouth will speak in praise of the
    LORD.
    Let every creature praise his holy
    name
    for ever and ever.

JUNE 30 □ DAY 182
PSALMS 146–150
A Lifestyle of Praise

OVERVIEW It is appropriate in a book with the Hebrew title *tehillim*— which means "praises"—that the final five selections should be filled with precisely that. First, the individual believer voices praise for God's trustworthiness (Psalm 146); next, the nation of Israel praises God for his tender care (147); then all creation praises God for his power (148); God's choice servants join the chorus by extolling God for his love (149); finally, accompanied by a grand orchestra of instruments, all living things praise our matchless, mighty God (150).

Psalm 146	Psalm 147	Psalm 148	Psalm 149	Psalm 150
"Praise the LORD"				
My Soul	My Nation	Creation	His Saints	Everyone
"How good it is to sing praises to our God" (147:1).				

YOUR DAILY WALK Congratulations! Today you will finish reading the longest book of the Bible—the believer's handbook of worship.

While you are catching your breath and preparing to begin the book of Proverbs tomorrow, pause long enough to ask yourself one question: Is there anything different about my walk with God today for having spent the past month in the book of Psalms?

Psalm 147:1 gives three reasons for God's people to praise him: (1) It is good in God's eyes; (2) it is pleasant (delightful) to the one doing the praising; and (3) it is beautiful for all who share the praise experience.

Praise is like a bride's wedding ring. The bride's husband rejoices to see her wear it; she herself delights in it; and it testifies to others of the beauty of the couple's relationship. Tie a small piece of colored yarn around a ring you are wearing to remind you throughout the day that it's always in style to adorn your life with praise to God.

Praising and adoring God is the noblest part of the saint's work on earth, as it will be his chief employ in heaven.

INSIGHT Inspired Psalms, Inspiring Psalms

The Psalter has become the hymnbook of the ages. It is read, recited or sung virtually every day. And in the majestic strains of more recent hymns based on its verses (such as Martin Luther's "A Mighty Fortress Is Our God" and Isaac Watts's "O God, Our Help in Ages Past"), the message of the Psalter still rings around the world.

PSALM 146

[1]Praise the LORD.[n]

Praise the LORD, O my soul.
[2] I will praise the LORD all my life;
  I will sing praise to my God as long
    as I live.

[3]Do not put your trust in princes,
  in mortal men, who cannot save.
[4]When their spirit departs, they return
    to the ground;
  on that very day their plans come to
    nothing.

[5]Blessed is he whose help is the God of
    Jacob,
  whose hope is in the LORD his God,
[6]the Maker of heaven and earth,
  the sea, and everything in them—
  the LORD, who remains faithful
    forever.
[7]He upholds the cause of the oppressed
  and gives food to the hungry.
  The LORD sets prisoners free,
[8] the LORD gives sight to the blind,
  the LORD lifts up those who are bowed
    down,
  the LORD loves the righteous.
[9]The LORD watches over the alien
  and sustains the fatherless and the
    widow,
  but he frustrates the ways of the
    wicked.

[10]The LORD reigns forever,
  your God, O Zion, for all
    generations.

Praise the LORD.

PSALM 147

[1]Praise the LORD.[o]

How good it is to sing praises to our
    God,
  how pleasant and fitting to praise
    him!

[2]The LORD builds up Jerusalem;
  he gathers the exiles of Israel.
[3]He heals the brokenhearted
  and binds up their wounds.
[4]He determines the number of the stars
  and calls them each by name.
[5]Great is our Lord and mighty in
    power;
  his understanding has no limit.

[6]The LORD sustains the humble
  but casts the wicked to the ground.

[7]Sing to the LORD with thanksgiving;
  make music to our God on the harp.
[8]He covers the sky with clouds;
  he supplies the earth with rain
  and makes grass grow on the hills.
[9]He provides food for the cattle
  and for the young ravens when they
    call.

[10]His pleasure is not in the strength of
    the horse,
  nor his delight in the legs of a man;
[11]the LORD delights in those who fear
    him,
  who put their hope in his unfailing
    love.

[12]Extol the LORD, O Jerusalem;
  praise your God, O Zion,
[13]for he strengthens the bars of your
    gates
  and blesses your people within you.
[14]He grants peace to your borders
  and satisfies you with the finest of
    wheat.

[15]He sends his command to the earth;
  his word runs swiftly.
[16]He spreads the snow like wool
  and scatters the frost like ashes.
[17]He hurls down his hail like pebbles.
  Who can withstand his icy blast?
[18]He sends his word and melts them;
  he stirs up his breezes, and the
    waters flow.

[19]He has revealed his word to Jacob,
  his laws and decrees to Israel.
[20]He has done this for no other nation;
  they do not know his laws.

  Praise the LORD.

PSALM 148

[1]Praise the LORD.[p]

Praise the LORD from the heavens,
  praise him in the heights above.
[2]Praise him, all his angels,
  praise him, all his heavenly hosts.
[3]Praise him, sun and moon,
  praise him, all you shining stars.
[4]Praise him, you highest heavens
  and you waters above the skies.
[5]Let them praise the name of the LORD,

[n]1 Hebrew *Hallelu Yah*; also in verse 10   [o]1 Hebrew *Hallelu Yah*; also in verse 20   [p]1 Hebrew *Hallelu Yah*; also in verse 14

for he commanded and they were
   created.
⁶He set them in place for ever and ever;
   he gave a decree that will never
      pass away.

⁷Praise the LORD from the earth,
   you great sea creatures and all ocean
      depths,
⁸lightning and hail, snow and clouds,
   stormy winds that do his bidding,
⁹you mountains and all hills,
   fruit trees and all cedars,
¹⁰wild animals and all cattle,
   small creatures and flying birds,
¹¹kings of the earth and all nations,
   you princes and all rulers on earth,
¹²young men and maidens,
   old men and children.

¹³Let them praise the name of the LORD,
   for his name alone is exalted;
   his splendor is above the earth and
      the heavens.
¹⁴He has raised up for his people a
      horn,�q
   the praise of all his saints,
   of Israel, the people close to his
      heart.

Praise the LORD.

PSALM 149

¹Praise the LORD.ʳ

Sing to the LORD a new song,
   his praise in the assembly of the
      saints.

²Let Israel rejoice in their Maker;
   let the people of Zion be glad in
      their King.
³Let them praise his name with dancing
   and make music to him with
      tambourine and harp.

⁴For the LORD takes delight in his
      people;
   he crowns the humble with
      salvation.
⁵Let the saints rejoice in this honor
   and sing for joy on their beds.

⁶May the praise of God be in their
      mouths
   and a double-edged sword in their
      hands,
⁷to inflict vengeance on the nations
   and punishment on the peoples,
⁸to bind their kings with fetters,
   their nobles with shackles of iron,
⁹to carry out the sentence written
      against them.
   This is the glory of all his saints.

Praise the LORD.

PSALM 150

¹Praise the LORD.ˢ

Praise God in his sanctuary;
   praise him in his mighty heavens.
²Praise him for his acts of power;
   praise him for his surpassing
      greatness.
³Praise him with the sounding of the
      trumpet,
   praise him with the harp and lyre,
⁴praise him with tambourine and
      dancing,
   praise him with the strings and
      flute,
⁵praise him with the clash of cymbals,
   praise him with resounding cymbals.

⁶Let everything that has breath praise
      the LORD.

Praise the LORD.

---

q14 *Horn* here symbolizes strong one, that is, king.   r1 Hebrew *Hallelu Yah*; also in verse 9   s1 Hebrew *Hallelu Yah*; also in
verse 6

Proverbs

ONE of the most practical books in the Old Testament is Proverbs—timeless teaching for everyday living. A collection of approximately nine hundred inspired precepts, Proverbs provides godly counsel for virtually every facet of human relationships. These maxims deal with folly and wisdom, pride and humility, vengeance and justice, laziness and initiative, poverty and wealth, enemies and friends, lust and love, anger and anxiety, masters and servants, life and death.

Focus	Skillful Living in the Fear of the Lord					
Divisions	A Father's Words of Wisdom	Proverbs of Solomon (First Collection)	Words of Wisdom and Folly	Proverbs of Solomon (Second Collection)	Wisdom of Twos, Threes and Fours	Alphabet of a Noble Wife
	1 9	10 21	22 24	25 29	30	31
Topics	Solomon				Agur	Lemuel
	Commendation	Counsel			Comparison	
Place	Judah				Unknown	
Time	Written and Compiled about 950–700 B.C.					

JULY 1 ☐ DAY 183
PROVERBS 1–4
A Father's Words of Wisdom

OVERVIEW Proverbs is the book of heavenly wisdom for your earthly walk. Solomon states his purpose in the opening verses: "for attaining wisdom and discipline" (1:2). Wisdom in life begins with the fear of the Lord (1:7)—reverential respect for God and careful attention to the moral and ethical principles of his Word.

Chapter 1	Chapter 2	Chapter 3	Chapter 4
Beginning of Wisdom	Benefits of Wisdom	Searching for Wisdom	Supremacy of Wisdom
Fear God	Know God	Trust God	Hear God

YOUR DAILY WALK The young bank clerk was being promoted to vice president—a position of great responsibility and one for which he felt ill-equipped. Approaching the wise and aged bank president, he asked, "But, sir, what is the secret of success in my new position?"

A good learner is one whose ears get as much use as his or her mouth.

The president replied, "Right decisions."

"And what, sir, is the secret of making right decisions?"

Again the president was quick to respond: "Experience."

"And what, sir, is the secret of gaining experience?"

The president smiled as he replied, "Wrong decisions."

In life, as in banking, the goal is to make right decisions—decisions that honor God, promote growth, and bring blessing to others. Proverbs was written to help you make those kinds of decisions both in your personal and professional life.

But it is also a realistic book. Others have made foolish and naive decisions in the past—and you can learn from their mistakes. "To err is human . . . ," or so the saying goes. But to repeat those errors is both tragic and unnecessary.

As you begin to read Proverbs, do so with a notebook and pen in hand. Jot down your insights on "wise choices" and "foolish choices." Solomon's God-given wisdom and experience will steer you into right decisions . . . if you'll leave the driving to God!

INSIGHT A Structural Summary of Proverbs
Fatherly Proverbs—"my son" (1–9)
Antithetic Proverbs—"but" (10–15)
Synthetic Proverbs—"and" (16–22)
Extended Proverbs—more than one verse (23–31)

CHAPTER 1
The proverbs of Solomon son of David, king of Israel:

²for attaining wisdom and discipline;
  for understanding words of insight;
³for acquiring a disciplined and
  prudent life,

doing what is right and just and
  fair;
⁴for giving prudence to the
  simple,
knowledge and discretion to the
  young—
⁵let the wise listen and add to their
  learning,

and let the discerning get guidance—
⁶for understanding proverbs and
parables,
the sayings and riddles of the wise.

⁷The fear of the LORD is the beginning
of knowledge,
but fools^a despise wisdom and
discipline.

⁸Listen, my son, to your father's
instruction
and do not forsake your mother's
teaching.
⁹They will be a garland to grace your
head
and a chain to adorn your neck.

¹⁰My son, if sinners entice you,
do not give in to them.
¹¹If they say, "Come along with us;
let's lie in wait for someone's blood,
let's waylay some harmless soul;
¹²let's swallow them alive, like the
grave,^b
and whole, like those who go down
to the pit;
¹³we will get all sorts of valuable things
and fill our houses with plunder;
¹⁴throw in your lot with us,
and we will share a common
purse"—
¹⁵my son, do not go along with them,
do not set foot on their paths;
¹⁶for their feet rush into sin,
they are swift to shed blood.
¹⁷How useless to spread a net
in full view of all the birds!
¹⁸These men lie in wait for their own
blood;
they waylay only themselves!
¹⁹Such is the end of all who go after
ill-gotten gain;
it takes away the lives of those who
get it.

²⁰Wisdom calls aloud in the street,
she raises her voice in the public
squares;
²¹at the head of the noisy streets^c she
cries out,
in the gateways of the city she
makes her speech:

²²"How long will you simple ones^d love
your simple ways?

How long will mockers delight in
mockery
and fools hate knowledge?
²³If you had responded to my rebuke,
I would have poured out my heart
to you
and made my thoughts known to
you.
²⁴But since you rejected me when I
called
and no one gave heed when I
stretched out my hand,
²⁵since you ignored all my advice
and would not accept my rebuke,
²⁶I in turn will laugh at your disaster;
I will mock when calamity overtakes
you—
²⁷when calamity overtakes you like a
storm,
when disaster sweeps over you like
a whirlwind,
when distress and trouble
overwhelm you.

²⁸"Then they will call to me but I will
not answer;
they will look for me but will not
find me.
²⁹Since they hated knowledge
and did not choose to fear the LORD,
³⁰since they would not accept my advice
and spurned my rebuke,
³¹they will eat the fruit of their ways
and be filled with the fruit of their
schemes.
³²For the waywardness of the simple
will kill them,
and the complacency of fools will
destroy them;
³³but whoever listens to me will live in
safety
and be at ease, without fear of
harm."

CHAPTER 2

My son, if you accept my words
and store up my commands within
you,
²turning your ear to wisdom
and applying your heart to
understanding,
³and if you call out for insight
and cry aloud for understanding,
⁴and if you look for it as for silver

^a7 The Hebrew words rendered fool in Proverbs, and often elsewhere in the Old Testament, denote one who is morally
deficient.   ^b12 Hebrew Sheol   ^c21 Hebrew; Septuagint / on the tops of the walls   ^d22 The Hebrew word rendered simple in
Proverbs generally denotes one without moral direction and inclined to evil.

and search for it as for hidden
   treasure,
[5]then you will understand the fear of
   the LORD
   and find the knowledge of God.
[6]For the LORD gives wisdom,
   and from his mouth come
      knowledge and understanding.
[7]He holds victory in store for the
   upright,
   he is a shield to those whose walk is
      blameless,
[8]for he guards the course of the just
   and protects the way of his faithful
      ones.

[9]Then you will understand what is
   right and just
   and fair—every good path.
[10]For wisdom will enter your heart,
   and knowledge will be pleasant to
      your soul.
[11]Discretion will protect you,
   and understanding will guard you.

[12]Wisdom will save you from the ways
   of wicked men,
   from men whose words are
      perverse,
[13]who leave the straight paths
   to walk in dark ways,
[14]who delight in doing wrong
   and rejoice in the perverseness of
      evil,
[15]whose paths are crooked
   and who are devious in their ways.

[16]It will save you also from the
   adulteress,
   from the wayward wife with her
      seductive words,
[17]who has left the partner of her youth
   and ignored the covenant she made
      before God.[e]
[18]For her house leads down to death
   and her paths to the spirits of the
      dead.
[19]None who go to her return
   or attain the paths of life.

[20]Thus you will walk in the ways of
   good men
   and keep to the paths of the
      righteous.
[21]For the upright will live in the land,
   and the blameless will remain in it;

[22]but the wicked will be cut off from the
   land,
   and the unfaithful will be torn from
      it.

CHAPTER 3

My son, do not forget my teaching,
   but keep my commands in your
      heart,
[2]for they will prolong your life many
   years
   and bring you prosperity.

[3]Let love and faithfulness never leave
   you;
   bind them around your neck,
   write them on the tablet of your
      heart.
[4]Then you will win favor and a good
   name
   in the sight of God and man.

[5]Trust in the LORD with all your heart
   and lean not on your own
      understanding;
[6]in all your ways acknowledge him,
   and he will make your paths
      straight.[f]

[7]Do not be wise in your own eyes;
   fear the LORD and shun evil.
[8]This will bring health to your body
   and nourishment to your bones.

[9]Honor the LORD with your wealth,
   with the firstfruits of all your crops;
[10]then your barns will be filled to
   overflowing,
   and your vats will brim over with
      new wine.

[11]My son, do not despise the LORD's
   discipline
   and do not resent his rebuke,
[12]because the LORD disciplines those he
   loves,
   as a father[g] the son he delights in.

[13]Blessed is the man who finds wisdom,
   the man who gains understanding,
[14]for she is more profitable than silver
   and yields better returns than gold.
[15]She is more precious than rubies;
   nothing you desire can compare
      with her.
[16]Long life is in her right hand;
   in her left hand are riches and
      honor.

[e]17 Or covenant of her God   [f]6 Or will direct your paths   [g]12 Hebrew; Septuagint / and he punishes

¹⁷Her ways are pleasant ways,
  and all her paths are peace.
¹⁸She is a tree of life to those who
    embrace her;
  those who lay hold of her will be
    blessed.

¹⁹By wisdom the LORD laid the earth's
    foundations,
  by understanding he set the heavens
    in place;
²⁰by his knowledge the deeps were
    divided,
  and the clouds let drop the dew.

²¹My son, preserve sound judgment and
    discernment,
  do not let them out of your sight;
²²they will be life for you,
  an ornament to grace your neck.
²³Then you will go on your way in
    safety,
  and your foot will not stumble;
²⁴when you lie down, you will not be
    afraid;
  when you lie down, your sleep will
    be sweet.
²⁵Have no fear of sudden disaster
  or of the ruin that overtakes the
    wicked,
²⁶for the LORD will be your confidence
  and will keep your foot from being
    snared.

²⁷Do not withhold good from those who
    deserve it,
  when it is in your power to act.
²⁸Do not say to your neighbor,
  "Come back later; I'll give it
    tomorrow"—
  when you now have it with you.

²⁹Do not plot harm against your
    neighbor,
  who lives trustfully near you.
³⁰Do not accuse a man for no reason—
  when he has done you no harm.
³¹Do not envy a violent man
  or choose any of his ways,
³²for the LORD detests a perverse man
  but takes the upright into his
    confidence.
³³The LORD's curse is on the house of the
    wicked,
  but he blesses the home of the
    righteous.

³⁴He mocks proud mockers
  but gives grace to the humble.
³⁵The wise inherit honor,
  but fools he holds up to shame.

CHAPTER 4

Listen, my sons, to a father's
    instruction;
  pay attention and gain
    understanding.
²I give you sound learning,
  so do not forsake my teaching.
³When I was a boy in my father's
    house,
  still tender, and an only child of my
    mother,
⁴he taught me and said,
  "Lay hold of my words with all your
    heart;
  keep my commands and you will
    live.
⁵Get wisdom, get understanding;
  do not forget my words or swerve
    from them.
⁶Do not forsake wisdom, and she will
    protect you;
  love her, and she will watch over
    you.
⁷Wisdom is supreme; therefore get
    wisdom.
  Though it cost all you have,^h get
    understanding.
⁸Esteem her, and she will exalt you;
  embrace her, and she will honor
    you.
⁹She will set a garland of grace on your
    head
  and present you with a crown of
    splendor."

¹⁰Listen, my son, accept what I say,
  and the years of your life will be
    many.
¹¹I guide you in the way of wisdom
  and lead you along straight paths.
¹²When you walk, your steps will not be
    hampered;
  when you run, you will not stumble.
¹³Hold on to instruction, do not let it go;
  guard it well, for it is your life.
¹⁴Do not set foot on the path of the
    wicked
  or walk in the way of evil men.
¹⁵Avoid it, do not travel on it;
  turn from it and go on your way.
¹⁶For they cannot sleep till they do evil;

^h7 Or Whatever else you get

they are robbed of slumber till they
  make someone fall.
[17]They eat the bread of wickedness
  and drink the wine of violence.

[18]The path of the righteous is like the
  first gleam of dawn,
  shining ever brighter till the full
  light of day.
[19]But the way of the wicked is like deep
  darkness;
  they do not know what makes them
  stumble.

[20]My son, pay attention to what I say;
  listen closely to my words.

[21]Do not let them out of your sight,
  keep them within your heart;
[22]for they are life to those who find
  them
  and health to a man's whole body.
[23]Above all else, guard your heart,
  for it is the wellspring of life.
[24]Put away perversity from your mouth;
  keep corrupt talk far from your lips.
[25]Let your eyes look straight ahead,
  fix your gaze directly before you.
[26]Make level[i] paths for your feet
  and take only ways that are firm.
[27]Do not swerve to the right or the left;
  keep your foot from evil.

[i]26 Or Consider the

JULY 2 ☐ DAY 184
PROVERBS 5–9
A Father's Exhortation on Wisdom

OVERVIEW The word *wisdom* in Hebrew is a feminine noun. Thus, it is natural for Solomon to personify it as a woman—a virtuous woman—in contrast to the foolish and immoral ways of an adulteress. Both wisdom and folly beckon with similar invitations: "Come in here" (9:4, 16). But the invitation you choose to accept will determine whether you find virtue or vice. Solomon warns his son, and all those reading his words, to watch out for sin's clever disguise and wise up to the importance of following God's instructions.

Chapters 5–6	Chapter 7	Chapter 8	Chapter 9
Warning against		Appeal for	
Adultery	Adulteresses	Wisdom	Watchfulness
Watch Out!		Wise Up!	

YOUR DAILY WALK Few people plan to ruin their lives. Yet many a life ends in ruin. Why? Because someone else planned to ruin it for them.

Wisdom opens the eyes to both the glories of heaven and the hollowness of earth.

Satan is alive and well . . . and craftily cunning in his attempts to destroy the moral fiber of God's children. His alternate route to God's ordained pattern for love, sex, marriage and family is both attractive and inviting (7:10–23). The naive will play with fire—and get burned (6:28–29). The foolish will take the bait—and find that every kick offered by Satan also contains a kickback.

The path leading to adultery is broad and inviting. Tragically, it is a path many find irresistible. But though the trail is well worn, no one need follow its deadly course. Whether young or old, married or single, Solomon's message is aimed at the heart: Don't play with matches—especially if the match belongs to someone else! Carry a book of matches with you today to keep that warning fresh in your mind and heart.

INSIGHT Christ in the Proverbs
Notice the description of wisdom in chapter 8: It is divine (8:22–31); it is the source of life (8:35–36); it is righteous and moral (8:8–9); it is available to all (8:1–6, 32–35). This wisdom became incarnate in Christ—"in whom are hidden all the treasures of wisdom and knowledge" (Colossians 2:3) and "who has become for us wisdom from God (1 Corinthians 1:30). Do you know that wisdom firsthand?

CHAPTER 5

My son, pay attention to my wisdom,
  listen well to my words of insight,
²that you may maintain discretion
  and your lips may preserve
    knowledge.
³For the lips of an adulteress drip
    honey,
  and her speech is smoother than oil;
⁴but in the end she is bitter as gall,
  sharp as a double-edged sword.
⁵Her feet go down to death;
  her steps lead straight to the
    grave.ʲ
⁶She gives no thought to the way of
    life;
  her paths are crooked, but she
    knows it not.

⁷Now then, my sons, listen to me;
  do not turn aside from what I say.
⁸Keep to a path far from her,
  do not go near the door of her
    house,
⁹lest you give your best strength to
    others
  and your years to one who is cruel,
¹⁰lest strangers feast on your wealth
  and your toil enrich another man's
    house.
¹¹At the end of your life you will groan,
  when your flesh and body are spent.
¹²You will say, "How I hated discipline!
  How my heart spurned correction!
¹³I would not obey my teachers
  or listen to my instructors.
¹⁴I have come to the brink of utter ruin
  in the midst of the whole assembly."

¹⁵Drink water from your own cistern,
  running water from your own well.
¹⁶Should your springs overflow in the
    streets,
  your streams of water in the public
    squares?
¹⁷Let them be yours alone,
  never to be shared with strangers.
¹⁸May your fountain be blessed,

and may you rejoice in the wife of
    your youth.
¹⁹A loving doe, a graceful deer—
  may her breasts satisfy you always,
  may you ever be captivated by her
    love.
²⁰Why be captivated, my son, by an
    adulteress?
  Why embrace the bosom of another
    man's wife?

²¹For a man's ways are in full view of
    the LORD,
  and he examines all his paths.
²²The evil deeds of a wicked man
    ensnare him;
  the cords of his sin hold him fast.
²³He will die for lack of discipline,
  led astray by his own great folly.

CHAPTER 6

My son, if you have put up security
    for your neighbor,
  if you have struck hands in pledge
    for another,
²if you have been trapped by what you
    said,
  ensnared by the words of your
    mouth,
³then do this, my son, to free yourself,
  since you have fallen into your
    neighbor's hands:
  Go and humble yourself;
  press your plea with your neighbor!
⁴Allow no sleep to your eyes,
  no slumber to your eyelids.
⁵Free yourself, like a gazelle from the
    hand of the hunter,
  like a bird from the snare of the
    fowler.

⁶Go to the ant, you sluggard;
  consider its ways and be wise!
⁷It has no commander,
  no overseer or ruler,
⁸yet it stores its provisions in summer
  and gathers its food at harvest.

ʲ5 Hebrew *Sheol*

⁹How long will you lie there, you
　　sluggard?
　When will you get up from your
　　sleep?
¹⁰A little sleep, a little slumber,
　a little folding of the hands to rest—
¹¹and poverty will come on you like a
　　bandit
　and scarcity like an armed man.ᵏ

¹²A scoundrel and villain,
　who goes about with a corrupt
　　mouth,
¹³　who winks with his eye,
　signals with his feet
　and motions with his fingers,
¹⁴　who plots evil with deceit in his
　　heart—
　he always stirs up dissension.
¹⁵Therefore disaster will overtake him in
　　an instant;
　he will suddenly be destroyed—
　　without remedy.

¹⁶There are six things the LORD hates,
　seven that are detestable to him:
¹⁷　haughty eyes,
　a lying tongue,
　hands that shed innocent blood,
¹⁸　a heart that devises wicked
　　schemes,
　feet that are quick to rush into
　　evil,
¹⁹　a false witness who pours out lies
　and a man who stirs up
　　dissension among brothers.

²⁰My son, keep your father's commands
　and do not forsake your mother's
　　teaching.
²¹Bind them upon your heart forever;
　fasten them around your neck.
²²When you walk, they will guide you;
　when you sleep, they will watch
　　over you;
　when you awake, they will speak to
　　you.
²³For these commands are a lamp,
　this teaching is a light,
　and the corrections of discipline
　are the way to life,
²⁴keeping you from the immoral
　　woman,
　from the smooth tongue of the
　　wayward wife.
²⁵Do not lust in your heart after her
　　beauty

or let her captivate you with her
　　eyes,
²⁶for the prostitute reduces you to a loaf
　　of bread,
　and the adulteress preys upon your
　　very life.
²⁷Can a man scoop fire into his lap
　without his clothes being burned?
²⁸Can a man walk on hot coals
　without his feet being scorched?
²⁹So is he who sleeps with another
　　man's wife;
　no one who touches her will go
　　unpunished.

³⁰Men do not despise a thief if he steals
　to satisfy his hunger when he is
　　starving.
³¹Yet if he is caught, he must pay
　　sevenfold,
　though it costs him all the wealth of
　　his house.
³²But a man who commits adultery lacks
　　judgment;
　whoever does so destroys himself.
³³Blows and disgrace are his lot,
　and his shame will never be wiped
　　away;
³⁴for jealousy arouses a husband's fury,
　and he will show no mercy when he
　　takes revenge.
³⁵He will not accept any compensation;
　he will refuse the bribe, however
　　great it is.

CHAPTER 7
　My son, keep my words
　　and store up my commands within
　　　you.
　²Keep my commands and you will live;
　　guard my teachings as the apple of
　　　your eye.
　³Bind them on your fingers;
　　write them on the tablet of your
　　　heart.
　⁴Say to wisdom, "You are my sister,"
　　and call understanding your
　　　kinsman;
　⁵they will keep you from the
　　　adulteress,
　　from the wayward wife with her
　　　seductive words.

　⁶At the window of my house
　　I looked out through the lattice.
　⁷I saw among the simple,

ᵏ11 Or like a vagrant / and scarcity like a beggar

I noticed among the young men,
a youth who lacked judgment.
⁸He was going down the street near her
corner,
walking along in the direction of her
house
⁹at twilight, as the day was fading,
as the dark of night set in.

¹⁰Then out came a woman to meet him,
dressed like a prostitute and with
crafty intent.
¹¹(She is loud and defiant,
her feet never stay at home;
¹²now in the street, now in the squares,
at every corner she lurks.)
¹³She took hold of him and kissed him
and with a brazen face she said:

¹⁴"I have fellowship offeringsˡ at home;
today I fulfilled my vows.
¹⁵So I came out to meet you;
I looked for you and have found
you!
¹⁶I have covered my bed
with colored linens from Egypt.
¹⁷I have perfumed my bed
with myrrh, aloes and cinnamon.
¹⁸Come, let's drink deep of love till
morning;
let's enjoy ourselves with love!
¹⁹My husband is not at home;
he has gone on a long journey.
²⁰He took his purse filled with money
and will not be home till full moon."

²¹With persuasive words she led him
astray;
she seduced him with her smooth
talk.
²²All at once he followed her
like an ox going to the slaughter,
like a deerᵐ stepping into a nooseⁿ
²³ till an arrow pierces his liver,
like a bird darting into a snare,
little knowing it will cost him his
life.

²⁴Now then, my sons, listen to me;
pay attention to what I say.
²⁵Do not let your heart turn to her ways
or stray into her paths.
²⁶Many are the victims she has brought
down;
her slain are a mighty throng.
²⁷Her house is a highway to the grave,ᵒ

leading down to the chambers of
death.

CHAPTER 8
Does not wisdom call out?
Does not understanding raise her
voice?
²On the heights along the way,
where the paths meet, she takes her
stand;
³beside the gates leading into the city,
at the entrances, she cries aloud:
⁴"To you, O men, I call out;
I raise my voice to all mankind.
⁵You who are simple, gain prudence;
you who are foolish, gain
understanding.
⁶Listen, for I have worthy things to say;
I open my lips to speak what is
right.
⁷My mouth speaks what is true,
for my lips detest wickedness.
⁸All the words of my mouth are just;
none of them is crooked or perverse.
⁹To the discerning all of them are right;
they are faultless to those who have
knowledge.
¹⁰Choose my instruction instead of
silver,
knowledge rather than choice gold,
¹¹for wisdom is more precious than
rubies,
and nothing you desire can compare
with her.

¹²"I, wisdom, dwell together with
prudence;
I possess knowledge and discretion.
¹³To fear the LORD is to hate evil;
I hate pride and arrogance,
evil behavior and perverse speech.
¹⁴Counsel and sound judgment are
mine;
I have understanding and power.
¹⁵By me kings reign
and rulers make laws that are just;
¹⁶by me princes govern,
and all nobles who rule on earth.ᵖ
¹⁷I love those who love me,
and those who seek me find me.
¹⁸With me are riches and honor,
enduring wealth and prosperity.
¹⁹My fruit is better than fine gold;
what I yield surpasses choice silver.
²⁰I walk in the way of righteousness,

ˡ14 Traditionally *peace offerings*   ᵐ22 Syriac (see also Septuagint); Hebrew *fool*   ⁿ22 The meaning of the Hebrew for this
line is uncertain.   ᵒ27 Hebrew *Sheol*   ᵖ16 Many Hebrew manuscripts and Septuagint; most Hebrew manuscripts *and
nobles—all righteous rulers*

along the paths of justice,
²¹bestowing wealth on those who love
me
and making their treasuries full.

²²"The LORD brought me forth as the first
of his works,*q,r*
before his deeds of old;
²³I was appointed*s* from eternity,
from the beginning, before the world
began.
²⁴When there were no oceans, I was
given birth,
when there were no springs
abounding with water;
²⁵before the mountains were settled in
place,
before the hills, I was given birth,
²⁶before he made the earth or its fields
or any of the dust of the world.
²⁷I was there when he set the heavens in
place,
when he marked out the horizon on
the face of the deep,
²⁸when he established the clouds above
and fixed securely the fountains of
the deep,
²⁹when he gave the sea its boundary
so the waters would not overstep his
command,
and when he marked out the
foundations of the earth.
30   Then I was the craftsman at his
side.
I was filled with delight day after
day,
rejoicing always in his presence,
³¹rejoicing in his whole world
and delighting in mankind.
³²"Now then, my sons, listen to me;
blessed are those who keep my
ways.
³³Listen to my instruction and be
wise;
do not ignore it.
³⁴Blessed is the man who listens to me,
watching daily at my doors,
waiting at my doorway.
³⁵For whoever finds me finds life
and receives favor from the
LORD.
³⁶But whoever fails to find me harms
himself;
all who hate me love death."

CHAPTER 9

Wisdom has built her house;
she has hewn out its seven pillars.
²She has prepared her meat and mixed
her wine;
she has also set her table.
³She has sent out her maids, and she
calls
from the highest point of the city.
⁴"Let all who are simple come in
here!"
she says to those who lack
judgment.
⁵"Come, eat my food
and drink the wine I have mixed.
⁶Leave your simple ways and you will
live;
walk in the way of understanding.

⁷"Whoever corrects a mocker invites
insult;
whoever rebukes a wicked man
incurs abuse.
⁸Do not rebuke a mocker or he will
hate you;
rebuke a wise man and he will love
you.
⁹Instruct a wise man and he will be
wiser still;
teach a righteous man and he will
add to his learning.

¹⁰"The fear of the LORD is the beginning
of wisdom,
and knowledge of the Holy One is
understanding.
¹¹For through me your days will be
many,
and years will be added to your
life.
¹²If you are wise, your wisdom will
reward you;
if you are a mocker, you alone will
suffer."

¹³The woman Folly is loud;
she is undisciplined and without
knowledge.
¹⁴She sits at the door of her house,
on a seat at the highest point of the
city,
¹⁵calling out to those who pass by,
who go straight on their way.
¹⁶"Let all who are simple come in
here!"

---

*q*22 Or *way;* or *dominion*   *r*22 Or *The LORD possessed me at the beginning of his work;* or *The LORD brought me forth at the beginning of his work*   *s*23 Or *fashioned*

she says to those who lack
        judgment.
17"Stolen water is sweet;
    food eaten in secret is delicious!"

18But little do they know that the dead
        are there,
    that her guests are in the depths of
        the grave.[1]

JULY 3 □ DAY 185
PROVERBS 10–13
Wisdom vs. Folly

 OVERVIEW Proverbs is more than a book on how to be wise. If you choose, it can also be a book on how to be foolish. Every wise course of action to pursue is contrasted with a foolish course of action to avoid. These four chapters, and the verses extending through chapter 22, are mainly comprised of authentic proverbs—proverbs in which a contrast is introduced by the word *but*.

Chapter 10	Chapter 11	Chapter 12	Chapter 13
Lips and Labor	Riches and Reward	Snares and Sluggards	Prudence and Poverty
Faithfulness Contrasted with Folly			

 YOUR DAILY WALK A young child awakens and, for the next hour, resists all his parent's attempts to get him dressed, fed and on his way to school. If you were his parent, how would you feel?

The opposite of ignorance in the spiritual realm is not knowledge but obedience.

The same child awakens, goes to his closet, selects his clothes and dresses himself without being asked. The net result is the same: He is dressed. But how do you as his parent feel?

A wise son obeys his father willingly; a foolish son only does so grudgingly or under compulsion. Which characterizes your obedience to your heavenly Father? Read 10:1 thoughtfully. Then complete this sentence: Today I want to bring gladness (rather than heaviness) to the heart of God by gladly (rather than grudgingly) obeying him in the matter of _____. Now that's putting wisdom to work!

 INSIGHT The Fool's Self-Destruction
When people rebel against God, they end up destroying themselves. They fall by their own wickedness (11:5) and are snared by their own sin (29:6). Ponder the timelessness of God's wisdom as you consider the results of abortion, drug abuse, broken homes and homosexuality in our day.

CHAPTER 10
The proverbs of Solomon:

A wise son brings joy to his father,
    but a foolish son grief to his mother.

2Ill-gotten treasures are of no value,

but righteousness delivers from
        death.

3The LORD does not let the righteous go
        hungry
    but he thwarts the craving of the
        wicked.

[1]18 Hebrew *Sheol*

[4]Lazy hands make a man poor,
   but diligent hands bring wealth.

[5]He who gathers crops in summer is a
      wise son,
   but he who sleeps during harvest is
      a disgraceful son.

[6]Blessings crown the head of the
      righteous,
   but violence overwhelms the mouth
      of the wicked. [u]

[7]The memory of the righteous will be a
      blessing,
   but the name of the wicked will
      rot.

[8]The wise in heart accept commands,
   but a chattering fool comes to
      ruin.

[9]The man of integrity walks securely,
   but he who takes crooked paths will
      be found out.

[10]He who winks maliciously causes
      grief,
   and a chattering fool comes to
      ruin.

[11]The mouth of the righteous is a
      fountain of life,
   but violence overwhelms the mouth
      of the wicked.

[12]Hatred stirs up dissension,
   but love covers over all wrongs.

[13]Wisdom is found on the lips of the
      discerning,
   but a rod is for the back of him who
      lacks judgment.

[14]Wise men store up knowledge,
   but the mouth of a fool invites
      ruin.

[15]The wealth of the rich is their fortified
      city,
   but poverty is the ruin of the poor.

[16]The wages of the righteous bring them
      life,
   but the income of the wicked brings
      them punishment.

[u]6 Or *but the mouth of the wicked conceals violence*; also in verse 11

[17]He who heeds discipline shows the
      way to life,
   but whoever ignores correction leads
      others astray.

[18]He who conceals his hatred has lying
      lips,
   and whoever spreads slander is a
      fool.

[19]When words are many, sin is not
      absent,
   but he who holds his tongue is
      wise.

[20]The tongue of the righteous is choice
      silver,
   but the heart of the wicked is of
      little value.

[21]The lips of the righteous nourish
      many,
   but fools die for lack of judgment.

[22]The blessing of the LORD brings
      wealth,
   and he adds no trouble to it.

[23]A fool finds pleasure in evil conduct,
   but a man of understanding delights
      in wisdom.

[24]What the wicked dreads will overtake
      him;
   what the righteous desire will be
      granted.

[25]When the storm has swept by, the
      wicked are gone,
   but the righteous stand firm
      forever.

[26]As vinegar to the teeth and smoke to
      the eyes,
   so is a sluggard to those who send
      him.

[27]The fear of the LORD adds length to
      life,
   but the years of the wicked are cut
      short.

[28]The prospect of the righteous is joy,
   but the hopes of the wicked come to
      nothing.

[29]The way of the LORD is a refuge for the
      righteous,
   but it is the ruin of those who do
      evil.

³⁰The righteous will never be uprooted,
   but the wicked will not remain in
      the land.

³¹The mouth of the righteous brings
      forth wisdom,
   but a perverse tongue will be cut
      out.

³²The lips of the righteous know what is
      fitting,
   but the mouth of the wicked only
      what is perverse.

CHAPTER 11

The LORD abhors dishonest scales,
   but accurate weights are his delight.

²When pride comes, then comes
      disgrace,
   but with humility comes wisdom.

³The integrity of the upright guides
      them,
   but the unfaithful are destroyed by
      their duplicity.

⁴Wealth is worthless in the day of
      wrath,
   but righteousness delivers from
      death.

⁵The righteousness of the blameless
      makes a straight way for them,
   but the wicked are brought down by
      their own wickedness.

⁶The righteousness of the upright
      delivers them,
   but the unfaithful are trapped by
      evil desires.

⁷When a wicked man dies, his hope
      perishes;
   all he expected from his power
      comes to nothing.

⁸The righteous man is rescued from
      trouble,
   and it comes on the wicked instead.

⁹With his mouth the godless destroys
      his neighbor,
   but through knowledge the
      righteous escape.

¹⁰When the righteous prosper, the city
      rejoices;
   when the wicked perish, there are
      shouts of joy.

¹¹Through the blessing of the upright a
      city is exalted,

but by the mouth of the wicked it is
   destroyed.

¹²A man who lacks judgment derides his
      neighbor,
   but a man of understanding holds
      his tongue.

¹³A gossip betrays a confidence,
   but a trustworthy man keeps a
      secret.

¹⁴For lack of guidance a nation falls,
   but many advisers make victory
      sure.

¹⁵He who puts up security for another
      will surely suffer,
   but whoever refuses to strike hands
      in pledge is safe.

¹⁶A kindhearted woman gains respect,
   but ruthless men gain only wealth.

¹⁷A kind man benefits himself,
   but a cruel man brings trouble on
      himself.

¹⁸The wicked man earns deceptive
      wages,
   but he who sows righteousness
      reaps a sure reward.

¹⁹The truly righteous man attains life,
   but he who pursues evil goes to his
      death.

²⁰The LORD detests men of perverse heart
   but he delights in those whose ways
      are blameless.

²¹Be sure of this: The wicked will not go
      unpunished,
   but those who are righteous will go
      free.

²²Like a gold ring in a pig's snout
   is a beautiful woman who shows no
      discretion.

²³The desire of the righteous ends only
      in good,
   but the hope of the wicked only in
      wrath.

²⁴One man gives freely, yet gains even
      more;
   another withholds unduly, but
      comes to poverty.

²⁵A generous man will prosper;
   he who refreshes others will himself
      be refreshed.

²⁶People curse the man who hoards
    grain,
  but blessing crowns him who is
      willing to sell.

²⁷He who seeks good finds goodwill,
  but evil comes to him who searches
      for it.

²⁸Whoever trusts in his riches will fall,
  but the righteous will thrive like a
      green leaf.

²⁹He who brings trouble on his family
      will inherit only wind,
  and the fool will be servant to the
      wise.

³⁰The fruit of the righteous is a tree of
      life,
  and he who wins souls is wise.

³¹If the righteous receive their due on
      earth,
  how much more the ungodly and
      the sinner!

CHAPTER 12
  Whoever loves discipline loves
      knowledge,
  but he who hates correction is
      stupid.

²A good man obtains favor from the
      LORD,
  but the LORD condemns a crafty
      man.

³A man cannot be established through
      wickedness,
  but the righteous cannot be
      uprooted.

⁴A wife of noble character is her
      husband's crown,
  but a disgraceful wife is like decay
      in his bones.

⁵The plans of the righteous are just,
  but the advice of the wicked is
      deceitful.

⁶The words of the wicked lie in wait
      for blood,
  but the speech of the upright rescues
      them.

⁷Wicked men are overthrown and are
      no more,
  but the house of the righteous
      stands firm.

⁸A man is praised according to his
      wisdom,
  but men with warped minds are
      despised.

⁹Better to be a nobody and yet have a
      servant
  than pretend to be somebody and
      have no food.

¹⁰A righteous man cares for the needs of
      his animal,
  but the kindest acts of the wicked
      are cruel.

¹¹He who works his land will have
      abundant food,
  but he who chases fantasies lacks
      judgment.

¹²The wicked desire the plunder of evil
      men,
  but the root of the righteous
      flourishes.

¹³An evil man is trapped by his sinful
      talk,
  but a righteous man escapes trouble.

¹⁴From the fruit of his lips a man is
      filled with good things
  as surely as the work of his hands
      rewards him.

¹⁵The way of a fool seems right to him,
  but a wise man listens to advice.

¹⁶A fool shows his annoyance at once,
  but a prudent man overlooks an
      insult.

¹⁷A truthful witness gives honest
      testimony,
  but a false witness tells lies.

¹⁸Reckless words pierce like a sword,
  but the tongue of the wise brings
      healing.

¹⁹Truthful lips endure forever,
  but a lying tongue lasts only a
      moment.

²⁰There is deceit in the hearts of those
      who plot evil,
  but joy for those who promote
      peace.

²¹No harm befalls the righteous,
  but the wicked have their fill of
      trouble.

²²The LORD detests lying lips,

but he delights in men who are
   truthful.

²³A prudent man keeps his knowledge
   to himself,
but the heart of fools blurts out
   folly.

²⁴Diligent hands will rule,
but laziness ends in slave labor.

²⁵An anxious heart weighs a man down,
but a kind word cheers him up.

²⁶A righteous man is cautious in
   friendship,ᵛ
but the way of the wicked leads
   them astray.

²⁷The lazy man does not roastʷ his
   game,
but the diligent man prizes his
   possessions.

²⁸In the way of righteousness there is
   life;
along that path is immortality.

CHAPTER 13

A wise son heeds his father's
   instruction,
but a mocker does not listen to
   rebuke.

²From the fruit of his lips a man enjoys
   good things,
but the unfaithful have a craving for
   violence.

³He who guards his lips guards his life,
but he who speaks rashly will come
   to ruin.

⁴The sluggard craves and gets nothing,
but the desires of the diligent are
   fully satisfied.

⁵The righteous hate what is false,
but the wicked bring shame and
   disgrace.

⁶Righteousness guards the man of
   integrity,
but wickedness overthrows the
   sinner.

⁷One man pretends to be rich, yet has
   nothing;
another pretends to be poor, yet has
   great wealth.

⁸A man's riches may ransom his life,
but a poor man hears no threat.

⁹The light of the righteous shines
   brightly,
but the lamp of the wicked is
   snuffed out.

¹⁰Pride only breeds quarrels,
but wisdom is found in those who
   take advice.

¹¹Dishonest money dwindles away,
but he who gathers money little by
   little makes it grow.

¹²Hope deferred makes the heart sick,
but a longing fulfilled is a tree of
   life.

¹³He who scorns instruction will pay for
   it,
but he who respects a command is
   rewarded.

¹⁴The teaching of the wise is a fountain
   of life,
turning a man from the snares of
   death.

¹⁵Good understanding wins favor,
but the way of the unfaithful is
   hard.ˣ

¹⁶Every prudent man acts out of
   knowledge,
but a fool exposes his folly.

¹⁷A wicked messenger falls into trouble,
but a trustworthy envoy brings
   healing.

¹⁸He who ignores discipline comes to
   poverty and shame,
but whoever heeds correction is
   honored.

¹⁹A longing fulfilled is sweet to the soul,
but fools detest turning from evil.

²⁰He who walks with the wise grows
   wise,
but a companion of fools suffers
   harm.

²¹Misfortune pursues the sinner,
but prosperity is the reward of the
   righteous.

²²A good man leaves an inheritance for
   his children's children,

ᵛ26 Or *man is a guide to his neighbor*   ʷ27 The meaning of the Hebrew for this word is uncertain.   ˣ15 Or *unfaithful does not endure*

but a sinner's wealth is stored up for
the righteous.

²³A poor man's field may produce
abundant food,
but injustice sweeps it away.

²⁴He who spares the rod hates his son,

but he who loves him is careful to
discipline him.

²⁵The righteous eat to their hearts'
content,
but the stomach of the wicked goes
hungry.

JULY 4 □ DAY 186
PROVERBS 14–17
Wisdom in Daily Conduct

OVERVIEW For a quick overview of today's reading, notice the first verse of each chapter. Solomon offers God's perspective on the home (14:1; 17:1), the tongue (15:1) and the heart (16:1). If you are skillful in those three areas of life, you are well on your way to establishing harmony in your interpersonal relationships.

Chapter 14	Chapter 15	Chapter 16	Chapter 17
Cribs and Crowns	Herbs and Ears	Kings and Conduct	Peacemakers and Troublemakers
Fear the Lord		Follow the Lord	

YOUR DAILY WALK As you read through today's passage, look for the word *Lord,* and circle it every time it appears.

God writes with a pen that never blots, speaks with a tongue that never slips and acts with a hand that never fails.

The frequent repetition of *Lord* acts as a constant reminder that Proverbs is not just a collection of secular maxims or a Farmer's Almanac of wit and wisdom. The counsel it contains is not recorded primarily for society as a whole but rather to instruct the people of God on how to live godly lives in an ungodly world.

The name *Lord* appears eighty-seven times in the book, and twenty-four times in today's reading alone. (How many times can you find it in chapter 16?) As one commentator has remarked, "It is good to be reminded over and over again that the Lord is the key to all righteous living, as its author, standard, inspirer, empowerer, judge, and rewarder."

Write the word *Lord* on an index card, and place it in a conspicuous place where you will see it often during the day (your refrigerator, car dashboard, bathroom mirror). Let it be a constant reminder to you today that the Lord is the answer, regardless of what the question might be! Then try to think of one way in which God has shown himself to be your Author, Standard, Inspirer, Empowerer, Judge and Rewarder.

INSIGHT The Lord Is Here, but God Is Strangely Absent
The word translated "God" appears only seven times in Proverbs, compared to eighty-seven times for the *Lord.* *Lord* is the title God uses most frequently when dealing with his chosen people; *God* is a less intimate term, used mostly in his dealings with mankind as a whole. Thus, Proverbs was written primarily for the family of God—which explains why its precepts don't always make sense to the world.

CHAPTER 14

The wise woman builds her house,
but with her own hands the foolish
one tears hers down.

²He whose walk is upright fears the
LORD,
but he whose ways are devious
despises him.

³A fool's talk brings a rod to his back,
but the lips of the wise protect them.

⁴Where there are no oxen, the manger
is empty,
but from the strength of an ox
comes an abundant harvest.

⁵A truthful witness does not deceive,
but a false witness pours out lies.

⁶The mocker seeks wisdom and finds
none,
but knowledge comes easily to the
discerning.

⁷Stay away from a foolish man,
for you will not find knowledge on
his lips.

⁸The wisdom of the prudent is to give
thought to their ways,
but the folly of fools is deception.

⁹Fools mock at making amends for sin,
but goodwill is found among the
upright.

¹⁰Each heart knows its own bitterness,
and no one else can share its joy.

¹¹The house of the wicked will be
destroyed,
but the tent of the upright will
flourish.

¹²There is a way that seems right to a
man,
but in the end it leads to death.

¹³Even in laughter the heart may ache,
and joy may end in grief.

¹⁴The faithless will be fully repaid for
their ways,
and the good man rewarded for his.

¹⁵A simple man believes anything,
but a prudent man gives thought to
his steps.

¹⁶A wise man fears the LORD and shuns
evil,
but a fool is hotheaded and reckless.

¹⁷A quick-tempered man does foolish
things,
and a crafty man is hated.

¹⁸The simple inherit folly,
but the prudent are crowned with
knowledge.

¹⁹Evil men will bow down in the
presence of the good,
and the wicked at the gates of the
righteous.

²⁰The poor are shunned even by their
neighbors,
but the rich have many friends.

²¹He who despises his neighbor sins,
but blessed is he who is kind to the
needy.

²²Do not those who plot evil go astray?
But those who plan what is good
find ʸ love and faithfulness.

²³All hard work brings a profit,
but mere talk leads only to poverty.

²⁴The wealth of the wise is their crown,
but the folly of fools yields folly.

²⁵A truthful witness saves lives,
but a false witness is deceitful.

²⁶He who fears the LORD has a secure
fortress,
and for his children it will be a
refuge.

²⁷The fear of the LORD is a fountain of
life,
turning a man from the snares of
death.

²⁸A large population is a king's glory,
but without subjects a prince is
ruined.

²⁹A patient man has great
understanding,
but a quick-tempered man displays
folly.

³⁰A heart at peace gives life to the body,
but envy rots the bones.

³¹He who oppresses the poor shows
contempt for their Maker,

ʸ22 Or show

but whoever is kind to the needy
   honors God.

³²When calamity comes, the wicked are
   brought down,
   but even in death the righteous have
    a refuge.

³³Wisdom reposes in the heart of the
   discerning
   and even among fools she lets
    herself be known. ^z

³⁴Righteousness exalts a nation,
   but sin is a disgrace to any people.

³⁵A king delights in a wise servant,
   but a shameful servant incurs his
    wrath.

CHAPTER 15

A gentle answer turns away wrath,
   but a harsh word stirs up anger.

²The tongue of the wise commends
   knowledge,
   but the mouth of the fool gushes
    folly.

³The eyes of the LORD are everywhere,
   keeping watch on the wicked and
    the good.

⁴The tongue that brings healing is a
   tree of life,
   but a deceitful tongue crushes the
    spirit.

⁵A fool spurns his father's discipline,
   but whoever heeds correction shows
    prudence.

⁶The house of the righteous contains
   great treasure,
   but the income of the wicked brings
    them trouble.

⁷The lips of the wise spread knowledge;
   not so the hearts of fools.

⁸The LORD detests the sacrifice of the
   wicked,
   but the prayer of the upright pleases
    him.

⁹The LORD detests the way of the
   wicked
   but he loves those who pursue
    righteousness.

¹⁰Stern discipline awaits him who leaves
   the path;
   he who hates correction will die.

¹¹Death and Destruction^a lie open
   before the LORD—
   how much more the hearts of men!

¹²A mocker resents correction;
   he will not consult the wise.

¹³A happy heart makes the face cheerful,
   but heartache crushes the spirit.

¹⁴The discerning heart seeks knowledge,
   but the mouth of a fool feeds on
    folly.

¹⁵All the days of the oppressed are
   wretched,
   but the cheerful heart has a
    continual feast.

¹⁶Better a little with the fear of the LORD
   than great wealth with turmoil.

¹⁷Better a meal of vegetables where
   there is love
   than a fattened calf with hatred.

¹⁸A hot-tempered man stirs up
   dissension,
   but a patient man calms a quarrel.

¹⁹The way of the sluggard is blocked
   with thorns,
   but the path of the upright is a
    highway.

²⁰A wise son brings joy to his father,
   but a foolish man despises his
    mother.

²¹Folly delights a man who lacks
   judgment,
   but a man of understanding keeps a
    straight course.

²²Plans fail for lack of counsel,
   but with many advisers they
    succeed.

²³A man finds joy in giving an apt
   reply—
   and how good is a timely word!

²⁴The path of life leads upward for the
   wise
   to keep him from going down to the
    grave.^b

---

^z33 Hebrew; Septuagint and Syriac / *but in the heart of fools she is not known*   ^a11 Hebrew *Sheol and Abaddon*
^b24 Hebrew *Sheol*

²⁵The LORD tears down the proud man's
house
but he keeps the widow's
boundaries intact.

²⁶The LORD detests the thoughts of the
wicked,
but those of the pure are pleasing to
him.

²⁷A greedy man brings trouble to his
family,
but he who hates bribes will live.

²⁸The heart of the righteous weighs its
answers,
but the mouth of the wicked gushes
evil.

²⁹The LORD is far from the wicked
but he hears the prayer of the
righteous.

³⁰A cheerful look brings joy to the heart,
and good news gives health to the
bones.

³¹He who listens to a life-giving rebuke
will be at home among the wise.

³²He who ignores discipline despises
himself,
but whoever heeds correction gains
understanding.

³³The fear of the LORD teaches a man
wisdom,ᶜ
and humility comes before honor.

CHAPTER 16
To man belong the plans of the heart,
but from the LORD comes the reply
of the tongue.

²All a man's ways seem innocent to
him,
but motives are weighed by the
LORD.

³Commit to the LORD whatever you do,
and your plans will succeed.

⁴The LORD works out everything for his
own ends—
even the wicked for a day of
disaster.

⁵The LORD detests all the proud of
heart.
Be sure of this: They will not go
unpunished.

⁶Through love and faithfulness sin is
atoned for;
through the fear of the LORD a man
avoids evil.

⁷When a man's ways are pleasing to
the LORD,
he makes even his enemies live at
peace with him.

⁸Better a little with righteousness
than much gain with injustice.

⁹In his heart a man plans his course,
but the LORD determines his steps.

¹⁰The lips of a king speak as an oracle,
and his mouth should not betray
justice.

¹¹Honest scales and balances are from
the LORD;
all the weights in the bag are of his
making.

¹²Kings detest wrongdoing,
for a throne is established through
righteousness.

¹³Kings take pleasure in honest lips;
they value a man who speaks the
truth.

¹⁴A king's wrath is a messenger of
death,
but a wise man will appease it.

¹⁵When a king's face brightens, it means
life;
his favor is like a rain cloud in
spring.

¹⁶How much better to get wisdom than
gold,
to choose understanding rather than
silver!

¹⁷The highway of the upright avoids
evil;
he who guards his way guards his
life.

¹⁸Pride goes before destruction,
a haughty spirit before a fall.

¹⁹Better to be lowly in spirit and among
the oppressed
than to share plunder with the
proud.

²⁰Whoever gives heed to instruction
prospers,

ᶜ33 Or Wisdom teaches the fear of the LORD

and blessed is he who trusts in the
  LORD.

²¹The wise in heart are called discerning,
  and pleasant words promote
    instruction.ᵈ

²²Understanding is a fountain of life to
    those who have it,
  but folly brings punishment to fools.

²³A wise man's heart guides his mouth,
  and his lips promote instruction.ᵉ

²⁴Pleasant words are a honeycomb,
  sweet to the soul and healing to the
    bones.

²⁵There is a way that seems right to a
    man,
  but in the end it leads to death.

²⁶The laborer's appetite works for him;
  his hunger drives him on.

²⁷A scoundrel plots evil,
  and his speech is like a scorching
    fire.

²⁸A perverse man stirs up dissension,
  and a gossip separates close friends.

²⁹A violent man entices his neighbor
  and leads him down a path that is
    not good.

³⁰He who winks with his eye is plotting
    perversity;
  he who purses his lips is bent on
    evil.

³¹Gray hair is a crown of splendor;
  it is attained by a righteous life.

³²Better a patient man than a warrior,
  a man who controls his temper than
    one who takes a city.

³³The lot is cast into the lap,
  but its every decision is from the
    LORD.

CHAPTER 17
  Better a dry crust with peace and quiet
    than a house full of feasting,ᶠ with
      strife.

²A wise servant will rule over a
    disgraceful son,
  and will share the inheritance as one
    of the brothers.

³The crucible for silver and the furnace
    for gold,
  but the LORD tests the heart.

⁴A wicked man listens to evil lips;
  a liar pays attention to a malicious
    tongue.

⁵He who mocks the poor shows
    contempt for their Maker;
  whoever gloats over disaster will not
    go unpunished.

⁶Children's children are a crown to the
    aged,
  and parents are the pride of their
    children.

⁷Arrogantᵍ lips are unsuited to a fool—
  how much worse lying lips to a
    ruler!

⁸A bribe is a charm to the one who
    gives it;
  wherever he turns, he succeeds.

⁹He who covers over an offense
    promotes love,
  but whoever repeats the matter
    separates close friends.

¹⁰A rebuke impresses a man of
    discernment
  more than a hundred lashes a fool.

¹¹An evil man is bent only on rebellion;
  a merciless official will be sent
    against him.

¹²Better to meet a bear robbed of her
    cubs
  than a fool in his folly.

¹³If a man pays back evil for good,
  evil will never leave his house.

¹⁴Starting a quarrel is like breaching a
    dam;
  so drop the matter before a dispute
    breaks out.

¹⁵Acquitting the guilty and condemning
    the innocent—
  the LORD detests them both.

¹⁶Of what use is money in the hand of a
    fool,
  since he has no desire to get
    wisdom?

¹⁷A friend loves at all times,
  and a brother is born for adversity.

ᵈ21 Or words make a man persuasive   ᵉ23 Or mouth / and makes his lips persuasive   ᶠ1 Hebrew sacrifices   ᵍ7 Or Eloquent

¹⁸A man lacking in judgment strikes
    hands in pledge
and puts up security for his
    neighbor.

¹⁹He who loves a quarrel loves sin;
he who builds a high gate invites
    destruction.

²⁰A man of perverse heart does not
    prosper;
he whose tongue is deceitful falls
    into trouble.

²¹To have a fool for a son brings grief;
there is no joy for the father of a
    fool.

²²A cheerful heart is good medicine,
but a crushed spirit dries up the
    bones.

²³A wicked man accepts a bribe in secret
to pervert the course of justice.

²⁴A discerning man keeps wisdom in
    view,
but a fool's eyes wander to the ends
    of the earth.

²⁵A foolish son brings grief to his father
and bitterness to the one who bore
    him.

²⁶It is not good to punish an innocent
    man,
or to flog officials for their integrity.

²⁷A man of knowledge uses words with
    restraint,
and a man of understanding is
    even-tempered.

²⁸Even a fool is thought wise if he keeps
    silent,
and discerning if he holds his
    tongue.

JULY 5 □ DAY 187
PROVERBS 18–21
Wisdom in Daily Choices

OVERVIEW Had all the proverbs composed by Solomon during his lifetime been a part of the inspired book of Proverbs, it would have stretched to more than three thousand verses (1 Kings 4:32)—making it by far the longest book in the Bible! But the nine hundred or so inspired maxims actually contained in Proverbs will provide a lifetime of challenge on the daily issues of life: speech, conduct, money, avoiding evil, maintaining proper motives and walking in integrity.

Chapter 18	Chapter 19	Chapter 20	Chapter 21
Noble Neighbors	Sons and Sluggards	Mockers and Mothers	Haughtiness and Heartache
Responding to People			Responding to God

Child training is chiefly a matter of knowing which end of the child to pat—and when.

YOUR DAILY WALK A teacher sent home this note pinned to the coat of an unruly student: "Dear Mrs. Jones: I regret to inform you that your son Robert is disruptive. He needs a good spanking, and I strongly urge you to give him one." The next day this reply came back pinned to Bobby's jacket: "Dear Mrs. Smith: Spank him yourself; he hasn't disobeyed me!"

The right discipline tailored to the right person in the right situation—that's the challenge of anyone entrusted with leadership authority. But beware! There is something potentially as dangerous as exercising *no* discipline—that is, exercising the same discipline in every situation.

According to 19:25, there are three kinds of temperament and three kinds of discipline, one appropriate to each temperament. How would Solomon tell you to discipline the following?

The mocker: _____

The simple: _____

The discerning man: _____

Now ask the Lord, "In whose life do you desire me to be a discerning disciplinarian?"

INSIGHT How's Your Heart?

Open-heart surgery is not a twentieth-century invention as you might have thought. It's as old as the book of Proverbs. As you read through the book, you'll discover the word *heart* used seventy times, showing it is through the heart—and a proper heart attitude—that you find and apply God's wisdom for your Christian walk.

CHAPTER 18

An unfriendly man pursues selfish ends;
  he defies all sound judgment.

2A fool finds no pleasure in understanding
  but delights in airing his own opinions.

3When wickedness comes, so does contempt,
  and with shame comes disgrace.

4The words of a man's mouth are deep waters,
  but the fountain of wisdom is a bubbling brook.

5It is not good to be partial to the wicked
  or to deprive the innocent of justice.

6A fool's lips bring him strife,
  and his mouth invites a beating.

7A fool's mouth is his undoing,
  and his lips are a snare to his soul.

8The words of a gossip are like choice morsels;
  they go down to a man's inmost parts.

9One who is slack in his work
  is brother to one who destroys.

10The name of the LORD is a strong tower;
  the righteous run to it and are safe.

11The wealth of the rich is their fortified city;
  they imagine it an unscalable wall.

12Before his downfall a man's heart is proud,
  but humility comes before honor.

13He who answers before listening—
  that is his folly and his shame.

14A man's spirit sustains him in sickness,
  but a crushed spirit who can bear?

15The heart of the discerning acquires knowledge;
  the ears of the wise seek it out.

16A gift opens the way for the giver
  and ushers him into the presence of the great.

17The first to present his case seems right,
  till another comes forward and questions him.

18Casting the lot settles disputes
  and keeps strong opponents apart.

19An offended brother is more unyielding than a fortified city,
  and disputes are like the barred gates of a citadel.

20From the fruit of his mouth a man's stomach is filled;
  with the harvest from his lips he is satisfied.

21The tongue has the power of life and death,
  and those who love it will eat its fruit.

22He who finds a wife finds what is good
  and receives favor from the LORD.

²³A poor man pleads for mercy,
but a rich man answers harshly.

²⁴A man of many companions may
come to ruin,
but there is a friend who sticks
closer than a brother.

CHAPTER 19

Better a poor man whose walk is
blameless
than a fool whose lips are perverse.

²It is not good to have zeal without
knowledge,
nor to be hasty and miss the way.

³A man's own folly ruins his life,
yet his heart rages against the LORD.

⁴Wealth brings many friends,
but a poor man's friend deserts him.

⁵A false witness will not go
unpunished,
and he who pours out lies will not
go free.

⁶Many curry favor with a ruler,
and everyone is the friend of a man
who gives gifts.

⁷A poor man is shunned by all his
relatives—
how much more do his friends
avoid him!
Though he pursues them with
pleading,
they are nowhere to be found.ʰ

⁸He who gets wisdom loves his own
soul;
he who cherishes understanding
prospers.

⁹A false witness will not go
unpunished,
and he who pours out lies will
perish.

¹⁰It is not fitting for a fool to live in
luxury—
how much worse for a slave to rule
over princes!

¹¹A man's wisdom gives him patience;
it is to his glory to overlook an
offense.

¹²A king's rage is like the roar of a lion,
but his favor is like dew on the
grass.

¹³A foolish son is his father's ruin,
and a quarrelsome wife is like a
constant dripping.

¹⁴Houses and wealth are inherited from
parents,
but a prudent wife is from the LORD.

¹⁵Laziness brings on deep sleep,
and the shiftless man goes hungry.

¹⁶He who obeys instructions guards his
life,
but he who is contemptuous of his
ways will die.

¹⁷He who is kind to the poor lends to
the LORD,
and he will reward him for what he
has done.

¹⁸Discipline your son, for in that there is
hope;
do not be a willing party to his
death.

¹⁹A hot-tempered man must pay the
penalty;
if you rescue him, you will have to
do it again.

²⁰Listen to advice and accept instruction,
and in the end you will be wise.

²¹Many are the plans in a man's heart,
but it is the LORD's purpose that
prevails.

²²What a man desires is unfailing loveⁱ;
better to be poor than a liar.

²³The fear of the LORD leads to life:
Then one rests content, untouched
by trouble.

²⁴The sluggard buries his hand in the
dish;
he will not even bring it back to his
mouth!

²⁵Flog a mocker, and the simple will
learn prudence;
rebuke a discerning man, and he
will gain knowledge.

²⁶He who robs his father and drives out
his mother
is a son who brings shame and
disgrace.

ʰ7 The meaning of the Hebrew for this sentence is uncertain.   ⁱ22 Or *A man's greed is his shame*

²⁷Stop listening to instruction, my son,
  and you will stray from the words
    of knowledge.

²⁸A corrupt witness mocks at justice,
  and the mouth of the wicked gulps
    down evil.

²⁹Penalties are prepared for mockers,
  and beatings for the backs of fools.

CHAPTER 20

Wine is a mocker and beer a brawler;
  whoever is led astray by them is not
    wise.

²A king's wrath is like the roar of a
    lion;
  he who angers him forfeits his life.

³It is to a man's honor to avoid strife,
  but every fool is quick to quarrel.

⁴A sluggard does not plow in season;
  so at harvest time he looks but finds
    nothing.

⁵The purposes of a man's heart are
    deep waters,
  but a man of understanding draws
    them out.

⁶Many a man claims to have unfailing
    love,
  but a faithful man who can find?

⁷The righteous man leads a blameless
    life;
  blessed are his children after him.

⁸When a king sits on his throne to
    judge,
  he winnows out all evil with his
    eyes.

⁹Who can say, "I have kept my heart
    pure;
  I am clean and without sin"?

¹⁰Differing weights and differing
    measures—
  the LORD detests them both.

¹¹Even a child is known by his actions,
  by whether his conduct is pure and
    right.

¹²Ears that hear and eyes that see—
  the LORD has made them both.

¹³Do not love sleep or you will grow
    poor;

stay awake and you will have food
    to spare.

¹⁴"It's no good, it's no good!" says the
    buyer;
  then off he goes and boasts about
    his purchase.

¹⁵Gold there is, and rubies in
    abundance,
  but lips that speak knowledge are a
    rare jewel.

¹⁶Take the garment of one who puts up
    security for a stranger;
  hold it in pledge if he does it for a
    wayward woman.

¹⁷Food gained by fraud tastes sweet to a
    man,
  but he ends up with a mouth full of
    gravel.

¹⁸Make plans by seeking advice;
  if you wage war, obtain guidance.

¹⁹A gossip betrays a confidence;
  so avoid a man who talks too much.

²⁰If a man curses his father or mother,
  his lamp will be snuffed out in pitch
    darkness.

²¹An inheritance quickly gained at the
    beginning
  will not be blessed at the end.

²²Do not say, "I'll pay you back for this
    wrong!"
  Wait for the LORD, and he will
    deliver you.

²³The LORD detests differing weights,
  and dishonest scales do not please
    him.

²⁴A man's steps are directed by the
    LORD.
  How then can anyone understand
    his own way?

²⁵It is a trap for a man to dedicate
    something rashly
  and only later to consider his vows.

²⁶A wise king winnows out the wicked;
  he drives the threshing wheel over
    them.

²⁷The lamp of the LORD searches the
    spirit of a manʲ;
  it searches out his inmost being.

ʲ27 Or The spirit of man is the LORD's lamp

²⁸Love and faithfulness keep a king safe;
through love his throne is made
secure.

²⁹The glory of young men is their
strength,
gray hair the splendor of the old.

³⁰Blows and wounds cleanse away evil,
and beatings purge the inmost
being.

CHAPTER 21

The king's heart is in the hand of the
LORD;
he directs it like a watercourse
wherever he pleases.

²All a man's ways seem right to him,
but the LORD weighs the heart.

³To do what is right and just
is more acceptable to the LORD than
sacrifice.

⁴Haughty eyes and a proud heart,
the lamp of the wicked, are sin!

⁵The plans of the diligent lead to profit
as surely as haste leads to poverty.

⁶A fortune made by a lying tongue
is a fleeting vapor and a deadly
snare.ᵏ

⁷The violence of the wicked will drag
them away,
for they refuse to do what is right.

⁸The way of the guilty is devious,
but the conduct of the innocent is
upright.

⁹Better to live on a corner of the roof
than share a house with a
quarrelsome wife.

¹⁰The wicked man craves evil;
his neighbor gets no mercy from
him.

¹¹When a mocker is punished, the
simple gain wisdom;
when a wise man is instructed, he
gets knowledge.

¹²The Righteous Oneˡ takes note of the
house of the wicked
and brings the wicked to ruin.

¹³If a man shuts his ears to the cry of
the poor,

he too will cry out and not be
answered.

¹⁴A gift given in secret soothes anger,
and a bribe concealed in the cloak
pacifies great wrath.

¹⁵When justice is done, it brings joy to
the righteous
but terror to evildoers.

¹⁶A man who strays from the path of
understanding
comes to rest in the company of the
dead.

¹⁷He who loves pleasure will become
poor;
whoever loves wine and oil will
never be rich.

¹⁸The wicked become a ransom for the
righteous,
and the unfaithful for the upright.

¹⁹Better to live in a desert
than with a quarrelsome and
ill-tempered wife.

²⁰In the house of the wise are stores of
choice food and oil,
but a foolish man devours all he
has.

²¹He who pursues righteousness and
love
finds life, prosperityᵐ and honor.

²²A wise man attacks the city of the
mighty
and pulls down the stronghold in
which they trust.

²³He who guards his mouth and his
tongue
keeps himself from calamity.

²⁴The proud and arrogant man—
"Mocker" is his name;
he behaves with overweening
pride.

²⁵The sluggard's craving will be the
death of him,
because his hands refuse to
work.

²⁶All day long he craves for more,
but the righteous give without
sparing.

ᵏ6 Some Hebrew manuscripts, Septuagint and Vulgate; most Hebrew manuscripts *vapor for those who seek death*   ˡ12 Or *The
righteous man*   ᵐ21 Or *righteousness*

²⁷The sacrifice of the wicked is
    detestable—
  how much more so when brought
    with evil intent!

²⁸A false witness will perish,
  and whoever listens to him will be
    destroyed forever.ⁿ

²⁹A wicked man puts up a bold front,

ⁿ28 Or / but the words of an obedient man will live on

but an upright man gives thought to
  his ways.

³⁰There is no wisdom, no insight, no
    plan
  that can succeed against the LORD.

³¹The horse is made ready for the day of
    battle,
  but victory rests with the LORD.

JULY 6 ☐ DAY 188
PROVERBS 22–24
Words of Wise Men

 OVERVIEW No one needs wisdom more than those in positions of
authority and responsibility. Parents, teachers, civic leaders, pastors—
the need is the same: skill in making moral, ethical and spiritual decisions consistent with God's Word and will. Why? Because their choices
impact not only their lives but also the lives of those they are attempting to lead into righteous paths of conduct and character.

Chapter 22	Chapter 23	Chapter 24
The King's Humility	The King's Habits	The King's House
Character	Conduct	Consistency

 YOUR DAILY WALK Motto on a procrastinator's desk: Never put off
till tomorrow what you can put off till the day after tomorrow!

*Those who
expect to repent
tomorrow
usually die
today.*

Laziness is nothing new. The apostle Paul wrestled with the problem
in the church at Thessalonica (2 Thessalonians 3:10–11). And the
book of Proverbs paints a graphic picture of the danger of laziness
(24:30–34). The lazy person can expect his endeavors and possessions
to crumble and fall apart—not from doing *wrong*, but from doing
nothing. The end result: an impoverished person whose destruction
has come suddenly . . . a day at a time.

What has been left undone in your life? Have you been putting off
reading a good Christian book, beginning an exercise program, writing some overdue letters, visiting a shut-in or relative?

Go outside right now, and pull a weed or two from the nearest
patch of grass. Then bring your "object lesson" indoors, take out a
sheet of paper and write down five neglected tasks you need to complete by the end of the month. Arrange them in order of priority, and
put a date by each, showing when you intend to complete them.
Then tackle "Project " today. You'll be amazed how fast your list—and
the weeds it represents—will start to disappear!

 INSIGHT Good . . . and Good for You!
Complete these three verses from today's section to discover some
"good" news!
  "A good *NAME* is more desirable than great riches" (22:1).
  "Eat _____, . . . for it is good" (24:13).
  "But it will _____ with those who convict the guilty" (24:25).

CHAPTER 22

A good name is more desirable than
    great riches;
  to be esteemed is better than silver
    or gold.

2Rich and poor have this in common:
  The LORD is the Maker of them all.

3A prudent man sees danger and takes
    refuge,
  but the simple keep going and suffer
    for it.

4Humility and the fear of the LORD
  bring wealth and honor and life.

5In the paths of the wicked lie thorns
    and snares,
  but he who guards his soul stays far
    from them.

6Train*o* a child in the way he should
    go,
  and when he is old he will not turn
    from it.

7The rich rule over the poor,
  and the borrower is servant to the
    lender.

8He who sows wickedness reaps
    trouble,
  and the rod of his fury will be
    destroyed.

9A generous man will himself be
    blessed,
  for he shares his food with the poor.

10Drive out the mocker, and out goes
    strife;
  quarrels and insults are ended.

11He who loves a pure heart and whose
    speech is gracious
  will have the king for his friend.

12The eyes of the LORD keep watch over
    knowledge,
  but he frustrates the words of the
    unfaithful.

13The sluggard says, "There is a lion
    outside!"
  or, "I will be murdered in the
    streets!"

14The mouth of an adulteress is a deep
    pit;
  he who is under the LORD's wrath
    will fall into it.

15Folly is bound up in the heart of a
    child,
  but the rod of discipline will drive it
    far from him.

16He who oppresses the poor to increase
    his wealth
  and he who gives gifts to the rich—
    both come to poverty.

17Pay attention and listen to the sayings
    of the wise;
  apply your heart to what I teach,
18for it is pleasing when you keep them
    in your heart
  and have all of them ready on your
    lips.
19So that your trust may be in the LORD,
  I teach you today, even you.
20Have I not written thirty*p* sayings for
    you,
  sayings of counsel and knowledge,
21teaching you true and reliable words,
  so that you can give sound answers
    to him who sent you?

22Do not exploit the poor because they
    are poor
  and do not crush the needy in court,
23for the LORD will take up their case
  and will plunder those who plunder
    them.

24Do not make friends with a
    hot-tempered man,
  do not associate with one easily
    angered,
25or you may learn his ways
  and get yourself ensnared.

26Do not be a man who strikes hands in
    pledge
  or puts up security for debts;
27if you lack the means to pay,
  your very bed will be snatched from
    under you.

28Do not move an ancient boundary
    stone
  set up by your forefathers.

29Do you see a man skilled in his work?
  He will serve before kings;
  he will not serve before obscure
    men.

CHAPTER 23

When you sit to dine with a ruler,
  note well what*q* is before you,

*o*6 Or *Start*   *p*20 Or *not formerly written; or not written excellent*   *q*1 Or *who*

²and put a knife to your throat
  if you are given to gluttony.
³Do not crave his delicacies,
  for that food is deceptive.

⁴Do not wear yourself out to get rich;
  have the wisdom to show restraint.
⁵Cast but a glance at riches, and they
    are gone,
  for they will surely sprout wings
  and fly off to the sky like an eagle.

⁶Do not eat the food of a stingy man,
  do not crave his delicacies;
⁷for he is the kind of man
  who is always thinking about the
    cost.ʳ
  "Eat and drink," he says to you,
  but his heart is not with you.
⁸You will vomit up the little you have
    eaten
  and will have wasted your
    compliments.

⁹Do not speak to a fool,
  for he will scorn the wisdom of your
    words.

¹⁰Do not move an ancient boundary
    stone
  or encroach on the fields of the
    fatherless,
¹¹for their Defender is strong;
  he will take up their case against
    you.

¹²Apply your heart to instruction
  and your ears to words of
    knowledge.

¹³Do not withhold discipline from a
    child;
  if you punish him with the rod, he
    will not die.
¹⁴Punish him with the rod
  and save his soul from death.ˢ

¹⁵My son, if your heart is wise,
  then my heart will be glad;
¹⁶my inmost being will rejoice
  when your lips speak what is right.

¹⁷Do not let your heart envy sinners,
  but always be zealous for the fear of
    the LORD.
¹⁸There is surely a future hope for you,
  and your hope will not be cut off.

¹⁹Listen, my son, and be wise,

and keep your heart on the right
    path.
²⁰Do not join those who drink too much
    wine
  or gorge themselves on meat,
²¹for drunkards and gluttons become
    poor,
  and drowsiness clothes them in rags.

²²Listen to your father, who gave you
    life,
  and do not despise your mother
    when she is old.
²³Buy the truth and do not sell it;
  get wisdom, discipline and
    understanding.
²⁴The father of a righteous man has
    great joy;
  he who has a wise son delights in
    him.
²⁵May your father and mother be glad;
  may she who gave you birth rejoice!

²⁶My son, give me your heart
  and let your eyes keep to my ways,
²⁷for a prostitute is a deep pit
  and a wayward wife is a narrow
    well.
²⁸Like a bandit she lies in wait,
  and multiplies the unfaithful among
    men.

²⁹Who has woe? Who has sorrow?
  Who has strife? Who has
    complaints?
  Who has needless bruises? Who has
    bloodshot eyes?
³⁰Those who linger over wine,
  who go to sample bowls of mixed
    wine.
³¹Do not gaze at wine when it is red,
  when it sparkles in the cup,
  when it goes down smoothly!
³²In the end it bites like a snake
  and poisons like a viper.
³³Your eyes will see strange sights
  and your mind imagine confusing
    things.
³⁴You will be like one sleeping on the
    high seas,
  lying on top of the rigging.
³⁵"They hit me," you will say, "but I'm
    not hurt!
  They beat me, but I don't feel it!
  When will I wake up
  so I can find another drink?"

ʳ7 Or for as he thinks within himself, / so he is; or for as he puts on a feast, / so he is   ˢ14 Hebrew Sheol

CHAPTER 24

Do not envy wicked men,
  do not desire their company;
2for their hearts plot violence,
  and their lips talk about making
    trouble.

3By wisdom a house is built,
  and through understanding it is
    established;
4through knowledge its rooms are
    filled
  with rare and beautiful treasures.

5A wise man has great power,
  and a man of knowledge increases
    strength;
6for waging war you need guidance,
  and for victory many advisers.

7Wisdom is too high for a fool;
  in the assembly at the gate he has
    nothing to say.

8He who plots evil
  will be known as a schemer.
9The schemes of folly are sin,
  and men detest a mocker.

10If you falter in times of trouble,
  how small is your strength!

11Rescue those being led away to
    death;
  hold back those staggering toward
    slaughter.
12If you say, "But we knew nothing
    about this,"
  does not he who weighs the heart
    perceive it?
  Does not he who guards your life
    know it?
  Will he not repay each person
    according to what he has done?

13Eat honey, my son, for it is good;
  honey from the comb is sweet to
    your taste.
14Know also that wisdom is sweet to
    your soul;
  if you find it, there is a future hope
    for you,
  and your hope will not be cut off.

15Do not lie in wait like an outlaw
    against a righteous man's
    house,
  do not raid his dwelling place;
16for though a righteous man falls seven
    times, he rises again,

but the wicked are brought down by
  calamity.

17Do not gloat when your enemy falls;
  when he stumbles, do not let your
    heart rejoice,
18or the LORD will see and disapprove
  and turn his wrath away from him.

19Do not fret because of evil men
  or be envious of the wicked,
20for the evil man has no future hope,
  and the lamp of the wicked will be
    snuffed out.

21Fear the LORD and the king, my son,
  and do not join with the rebellious,
22for those two will send sudden
    destruction upon them,
  and who knows what calamities
    they can bring?

23These also are sayings of the wise:

To show partiality in judging is not
    good:
24Whoever says to the guilty, "You are
    innocent"—
  peoples will curse him and nations
    denounce him.
25But it will go well with those who
    convict the guilty,
  and rich blessing will come upon
    them.

26An honest answer
  is like a kiss on the lips.

27Finish your outdoor work
  and get your fields ready;
  after that, build your house.

28Do not testify against your neighbor
    without cause,
  or use your lips to deceive.
29Do not say, "I'll do to him as he has
    done to me;
  I'll pay that man back for what he
    did."

30I went past the field of the sluggard,
  past the vineyard of the man who
    lacks judgment;
31thorns had come up everywhere,
  the ground was covered with weeds,
  and the stone wall was in ruins.
32I applied my heart to what I observed
  and learned a lesson from what I
    saw:

³³A little sleep, a little slumber,   ³⁴and poverty will come on you like a
  a little folding of the hands to   bandit
       rest—   and scarcity like an armed man.ᶦ

ᶦ34 Or like a vagrant / and scarcity like a beggar

JULY 7 □ DAY 189
Learning the Skill of Living

 LOOK BACK The closer you find yourself to the end of the book of
Psalms, the greater becomes the crescendo of praise. Psalms 144–146
encourage you to praise God personally; Psalms 147–150 exhort you
to praise God corporately. But whether you are alone or in a crowd,
the result is the same: God, who is worthy of our highest adoration,
receives from his creation the glory he so richly deserves.

Worshiping the Lord includes a healthy reverence for the Lord, for
"the fear of the LORD is the beginning of wisdom" (Proverbs 9:10). In
more than nine hundred nuggets of common (and uncommon) sense,
Solomon challenges the reader of Proverbs to hunt for, embrace and
employ heavenly wisdom for each earthly decision.

Making something beautiful out of the raw materials of life is God's
plan and purpose for each of his children. But whether you choose the
life of wisdom or the life of a fool, the choice is up to you!

 LOOK UP Proverbs is such a treasure chest of insight that you'll want
to read it more than once. In fact, you may want to begin the habit of
reading one chapter from Proverbs each day of the month (e.g., on
the twenty-fourth day of the month, read Proverbs 24). As you read,
notice the different kinds of proverbs and the lessons to be learned
from each:

A wise person will desire no more than he or she may get justly, use soberly, distribute cheerfully and leave contentedly.

Contrasting proverbs use the word *but* to set up a comparison. "The
wise inherit honor, but fools he holds up to shame" (3:35).

Cause/effect proverbs use the words *then* or *for* to show the cause-
and-effect relationship of actions and reactions. "Honor the LORD with
your wealth . . . then your barns will be filled to overflowing"
(3:9–10).

Numerical proverbs make a statement, then itemize a list. "There are
six things the LORD hates—, seven that are detestable to him: haughty
eyes, a lying tongue, . . ." (6:16–19).

Comparative proverbs use the word *better* to suggest something . . .
better! "Better a little with the fear of the LORD than great wealth with
turmoil" (15:16).

 LOOK AHEAD If a carpenter can take a block of wood and turn it
into a beautiful piece of furniture, we say that that person is a gifted
craftsman.

If a conductor can shape the myriad skills of an entire orchestra to
produce the sounds of a symphony, we say that that person is a musical genius.

And if a man or woman, boy or girl, can take the raw materials of
life and shape them skillfully according to the blueprint God has provided in his Word, we say that that person is wise. It has nothing to
do with IQ and everything to do with obedience! You can be wise
with an IQ of 70; you can be a fool with an IQ of 170. The choice is
up to you.

Whether you are a parent struggling to discipline a child . . . a teenager wrestling with peer pressure . . . or a rising executive tempted to follow the crowd in an unethical choice, you'll find Proverbs brimming with insight for living. Pick a topic you are eager to study from God's perspective, and retrace your steps through the book of Proverbs. Don't be surprised if God provides some heavenly (un)common sense!

JULY 8 ☐ DAY 190
PROVERBS 25–29
Wise Words from the King

OVERVIEW Today's section contains proverbs written by Solomon but compiled and arranged by King Hezekiah perhaps 250 years later. They represent a timeless treasure from a sovereign to his subjects: warnings against spiritual erosion and instructions regarding godly lifestyles. Solomon touches on many personalities and walks of life: the rich and the poor, false witnesses and friends, the lazy and the diligent, the deceitful and the dependable. In each case there is a right response and a proper perspective for the upright of heart.

Chapter 25	Chapter 26	Chapter 27	Chapter 28	Chapter 29
Gold and Good News	Whips and Lips	Kisses and Curses	Laws and Lions	Flattery and Fools
Wise Words for All Walks of Life				

YOUR DAILY WALK

Truth is always narrow, but error goes off in all directions.

Many verses in Proverbs could be called homilies in similes, sermons in the form of a comparison using the words *like* or *as*. In fact, the Hebrew word for *proverb* comes from a root meaning "to be like." Can you match up each statement with the thing it is "like," according to Proverbs?

___1. "As charcoal to embers and as wood to fire . . ."

a. "is one who sings songs to a heavy heart" (25:20).

___2. "Like a roaring lion or a charging bear . . ."

b. "so is a quarrelsome man for kindling strife" (26:21).

___3. "As iron sharpens iron . . ."

c. "is a wicked man ruling over a helpless people" (28:15).

___4. "Like one who takes away a garment on a cold day, . . ."

d. "so one man sharpens another" (27:17).

Can you explain each comparison? More important, can you think of a way to exemplify the truth of one of these proverbs today?

INSIGHT Counsel by Comparison in Chapter 25

As you read chapter 25, see if you can locate at least one helpful piece of counsel regarding these everyday situations:
- Receiving honor
- Answering a quarrelsome person
- Ministering to a depressed friend
- Eating sweets
- Staying with a friend

CHAPTER 25

These are more proverbs of Solomon, copied by the men of Hezekiah king of Judah:

² It is the glory of God to conceal a matter;
 to search out a matter is the glory of kings.

³ As the heavens are high and the earth is deep,
 so the hearts of kings are unsearchable.

⁴ Remove the dross from the silver,
 and out comes material for[u] the silversmith;
⁵ remove the wicked from the king's presence,
 and his throne will be established through righteousness.

⁶ Do not exalt yourself in the king's presence,
 and do not claim a place among great men;
⁷ it is better for him to say to you, "Come up here,"
 than for him to humiliate you before a nobleman.

 What you have seen with your eyes
⁸ do not bring[v] hastily to court,
 for what will you do in the end
 if your neighbor puts you to shame?

⁹ If you argue your case with a neighbor,
 do not betray another man's confidence,
¹⁰ or he who hears it may shame you
 and you will never lose your bad reputation.

¹¹ A word aptly spoken
 is like apples of gold in settings of silver.

¹² Like an earring of gold or an ornament of fine gold
 is a wise man's rebuke to a listening ear.

¹³ Like the coolness of snow at harvest time
 is a trustworthy messenger to those who send him;
 he refreshes the spirit of his masters.

¹⁴ Like clouds and wi...
 is a man who boas...
 not give.

¹⁵ Through patience a rule...
 persuaded,
 and a gentle tongue can...
 bone.

¹⁶ If you find honey, eat just en...
 too much of it, and you wil...
¹⁷ Seldom set foot in your neighb...
 house—
 too much of you, and he will h...
 you.

¹⁸ Like a club or a sword or a sharp arrow
 is the man who gives false testimony against his neighbor.

¹⁹ Like a bad tooth or a lame foot
 is reliance on the unfaithful in times of trouble.

²⁰ Like one who takes away a garment on a cold day,
 or like vinegar poured on soda,
 is one who sings songs to a heavy heart.

²¹ If your enemy is hungry, give him food to eat;
 if he is thirsty, give him water to drink.
²² In doing this, you will heap burning coals on his head,
 and the LORD will reward you.

²³ As a north wind brings rain,
 so a sly tongue brings angry looks.

²⁴ Better to live on a corner of the roof
 than share a house with a quarrelsome wife.

²⁵ Like cold water to a weary soul
 is good news from a distant land.

²⁶ Like a muddied spring or a polluted well
 is a righteous man who gives way to the wicked.

²⁷ It is not good to eat too much honey,
 nor is it honorable to seek one's own honor.

²⁸ Like a city whose walls are broken down
 is a man who lacks self-control.

JULY 8 /
CHA
Li

in

ol.

a darting

s not come

alter for the

of fools!

cording to his

him yourself.

cording to his folly,
e wise in his own eyes.

ing off one's feet or drinking
violence
is the sending of a message by the
hand of a fool.

⁷Like a lame man's legs that hang limp
is a proverb in the mouth of a fool.

⁸Like tying a stone in a sling
is the giving of honor to a fool.

⁹Like a thornbush in a drunkard's hand
is a proverb in the mouth of a fool.

¹⁰Like an archer who wounds at random
is he who hires a fool or any
passer-by.

¹¹As a dog returns to its vomit,
so a fool repeats his folly.

¹²Do you see a man wise in his own
eyes?
There is more hope for a fool than
for him.

¹³The sluggard says, "There is a lion in
the road,
a fierce lion roaming the streets!"

¹⁴As a door turns on its hinges,
so a sluggard turns on his bed.

¹⁵The sluggard buries his hand in the
dish;
he is too lazy to bring it back to his
mouth.

¹⁶The sluggard is wiser in his own eyes
than seven men who answer
discreetly.

¹⁷Like one who seizes a dog by the ears
is a passer-by who meddles in a
quarrel not his own.

¹⁸Like a madman shooting
firebrands or deadly arrows
¹⁹is a man who deceives his neighbor
and says, "I was only joking!"

²⁰Without wood a fire goes out;
without gossip a quarrel dies down.

²¹As charcoal to embers and as wood to
fire,
so is a quarrelsome man for kindling
strife.

²²The words of a gossip are like choice
morsels;
they go down to a man's inmost
parts.

²³Like a coating of glaze^w over
earthenware
are fervent lips with an evil heart.

²⁴A malicious man disguises himself
with his lips,
but in his heart he harbors deceit.
²⁵Though his speech is charming, do not
believe him,
for seven abominations fill his heart.
²⁶His malice may be concealed by
deception,
but his wickedness will be exposed
in the assembly.

²⁷If a man digs a pit, he will fall into it;
if a man rolls a stone, it will roll
back on him.

²⁸A lying tongue hates those it hurts,
and a flattering mouth works ruin.

CHAPTER 27

Do not boast about tomorrow,
for you do not know what a day
may bring forth.

²Let another praise you, and not your
own mouth;
someone else, and not your own
lips.

³Stone is heavy and sand a burden,
but provocation by a fool is heavier
than both.

⁴Anger is cruel and fury overwhelming,
but who can stand before jealousy?

^{w}23 With a different word division of the Hebrew; Masoretic Text *of silver dross*

5Better is open rebuke
  than hidden love.

6Wounds from a friend can be trusted,
  but an enemy multiplies kisses.

7He who is full loathes honey,
  but to the hungry even what is
    bitter tastes sweet.

8Like a bird that strays from its nest
  is a man who strays from his home.

9Perfume and incense bring joy to the
    heart,
  and the pleasantness of one's friend
    springs from his earnest
    counsel.

10Do not forsake your friend and the
    friend of your father,
  and do not go to your brother's
    house when disaster strikes
    you—
  better a neighbor nearby than a
    brother far away.

11Be wise, my son, and bring joy to my
    heart;
  then I can answer anyone who treats
    me with contempt.

12The prudent see danger and take
    refuge,
  but the simple keep going and suffer
    for it.

13Take the garment of one who puts up
    security for a stranger;
  hold it in pledge if he does it for a
    wayward woman.

14If a man loudly blesses his neighbor
    early in the morning,
  it will be taken as a curse.

15A quarrelsome wife is like
  a constant dripping on a rainy day;
16restraining her is like restraining the
    wind
  or grasping oil with the hand.

17As iron sharpens iron,
  so one man sharpens another.

18He who tends a fig tree will eat its
    fruit,
  and he who looks after his master
    will be honored.

19As water reflects a face,
  so a man's heart reflects the man.

20Death and Destruc[tion are never]
    satisfied,
  and neither are th[e eyes of man.]

21The crucible for silv[er and the furnace]
    for gold,
  but man is tested [by the praise he]
    receives.

22Though you grind a [fool in] a mortar,
  grinding him like grain with a
    pestle,
  you will not remove his folly from
    him.

23Be sure you know the condition of
    your flocks,
  give careful attention to your herds;
24for riches do not endure forever,
  and a crown is not secure for all
    generations.
25When the hay is removed and new
    growth appears
  and the grass from the hills is
    gathered in,
26the lambs will provide you with
    clothing,
  and the goats with the price of a
    field.
27You will have plenty of goats' milk
  to feed you and your family
  and to nourish your servant girls.

CHAPTER 28
  The wicked man flees though no one
    pursues,
  but the righteous are as bold as a
    lion.

2When a country is rebellious, it has
    many rulers,
  but a man of understanding and
    knowledge maintains order.

3A rulery who oppresses the poor
  is like a driving rain that leaves no
    crops.

4Those who forsake the law praise the
    wicked,
  but those who keep the law resist
    them.

5Evil men do not understand justice,
  but those who seek the LORD
    understand it fully.

6Better a poor man whose walk is
    blameless

x20 Hebrew *Sheol and Abaddon*   y3 Or *A poor man*

rich man whose ways are
 perverse.

He who keeps the law is a discerning
 son,
 but a companion of gluttons
 disgraces his father.

⁸He who increases his wealth by
 exorbitant interest
 amasses it for another, who will be
 kind to the poor.

⁹If anyone turns a deaf ear to the law,
 even his prayers are detestable.

¹⁰He who leads the upright along an
 evil path
 will fall into his own trap,
 but the blameless will receive a
 good inheritance.

¹¹A rich man may be wise in his own
 eyes,
 but a poor man who has
 discernment sees through him.

¹²When the righteous triumph, there is
 great elation;
 but when the wicked rise to power,
 men go into hiding.

¹³He who conceals his sins does not
 prosper,
 but whoever confesses and
 renounces them finds mercy.

¹⁴Blessed is the man who always fears
 the LORD,
 but he who hardens his heart falls
 into trouble.

¹⁵Like a roaring lion or a charging bear
 is a wicked man ruling over a
 helpless people.

¹⁶A tyrannical ruler lacks judgment,
 but he who hates ill-gotten gain
 will enjoy a long life.

¹⁷A man tormented by the guilt of
 murder
 will be a fugitive till death;
 let no one support him.

¹⁸He whose walk is blameless is kept
 safe,
 but he whose ways are perverse will
 suddenly fall.

¹⁹He who works his land will have
 abundant food,

but the one who chases fantasies
 will have his fill of poverty.

²⁰A faithful man will be richly blessed,
 but one eager to get rich will not go
 unpunished.

²¹To show partiality is not good—
 yet a man will do wrong for a piece
 of bread.

²²A stingy man is eager to get rich
 and is unaware that poverty awaits
 him.

²³He who rebukes a man will in the end
 gain more favor
 than he who has a flattering tongue.

²⁴He who robs his father or mother
 and says, "It's not wrong"—
 he is partner to him who destroys.

²⁵A greedy man stirs up dissension,
 but he who trusts in the LORD will
 prosper.

²⁶He who trusts in himself is a fool,
 but he who walks in wisdom is kept
 safe.

²⁷He who gives to the poor will lack
 nothing,
 but he who closes his eyes to them
 receives many curses.

²⁸When the wicked rise to power,
 people go into hiding;
 but when the wicked perish, the
 righteous thrive.

CHAPTER 29
 A man who remains stiff-necked after
 many rebukes
 will suddenly be destroyed—without
 remedy.

²When the righteous thrive, the people
 rejoice;
 when the wicked rule, the people
 groan.

³A man who loves wisdom brings joy
 to his father,
 but a companion of prostitutes
 squanders his wealth.

⁴By justice a king gives a country
 stability,
 but one who is greedy for bribes
 tears it down.

[5]Whoever flatters his neighbor
is spreading a net for his feet.

[6]An evil man is snared by his own sin,
but a righteous one can sing and be
glad.

[7]The righteous care about justice for the
poor,
but the wicked have no such
concern.

[8]Mockers stir up a city,
but wise men turn away anger.

[9]If a wise man goes to court with a
fool,
the fool rages and scoffs, and there
is no peace.

[10]Bloodthirsty men hate a man of
integrity
and seek to kill the upright.

[11]A fool gives full vent to his anger,
but a wise man keeps himself under
control.

[12]If a ruler listens to lies,
all his officials become wicked.

[13]The poor man and the oppressor have
this in common:
The Lord gives sight to the eyes of
both.

[14]If a king judges the poor with fairness,
his throne will always be secure.

[15]The rod of correction imparts wisdom,
but a child left to himself disgraces
his mother.

[16]When the wicked thrive, so does sin,
but the righteous will see their
downfall.

[z]21 The meaning of the Hebrew for this word is uncertain.

[17]Discipline your son, and he will give
you peace;
he will bring delight to your soul.

[18]Where there is no revelation, the
people cast off restraint;
but blessed is he who keeps the law.

[19]A servant cannot be corrected by mere
words;
though he understands, he will not
respond.

[20]Do you see a man who speaks in
haste?
There is more hope for a fool than
for him.

[21]If a man pampers his servant from
youth,
he will bring grief[z] in the end.

[22]An angry man stirs up dissension,
and a hot-tempered one commits
many sins.

[23]A man's pride brings him low,
but a man of lowly spirit gains
honor.

[24]The accomplice of a thief is his own
enemy;
he is put under oath and dare not
testify.

[25]Fear of man will prove to be a snare,
but whoever trusts in the Lord is
kept safe.

[26]Many seek an audience with a ruler,
but it is from the Lord that man gets
justice.

[27]The righteous detest the dishonest;
the wicked detest the upright.

JULY 9 ☐ DAY 191
PROVERBS 30–31
Alphabet of a Noble Wife

OVERVIEW Proverbs closes with the wise counsel of two godly men:
Agur and Lemuel. Using numerical proverbs and pictures from the
natural world, Agur summarizes many of the themes that have been
woven throughout the book: wisdom and folly, greed and gluttony,
adultery and hypocrisy. Then in a beautiful acrostic poem—one in

which each verse begins with a succeeding letter of the Hebrew alphabet—Lemuel extols the noble wife and mother.

Chapter 30	Chapter 31	
Wisdom in Twos, Threes and Fours	Wisdom from a Godly Mother	Wisdom for a Godly Wife
1	9 10	31
Advice from Agur	Lectures from Lemuel	

YOUR DAILY WALK Nothing is as contemporary as the question of women's rights and roles—both inside and outside the home. And nothing generates more heat and less light than debating the issue without first consulting God's Word on the subject.

Virtue has more admirers than followers.

In Proverbs 31:10–31 Lemuel profiles a woman who is godly, industrious, creative, sensitive, multitalented . . . and a wife and mother! She wears many different hats: seamstress (v. 13), merchant (v. 14), cook (v. 15), real estate agent (v. 16), gardener (v. 16), physical fitness enthusiast (v. 17), community volunteer (v. 20). But her energies are directed primarily toward the home. "She watches over the affairs of her household" (v. 27) and is a blessing to her family.

Wives, God has placed you in the home, not to stifle your creativity, but to stimulate it! Think of your home as a laboratory and Proverbs 31 as your lab manual. Pick one verse and make it your "Experiment in Fulfilled Womanhood" today.

And if you're not a wife, consider how your life has been enriched by a "Mrs. Far-above-Rubies"—and let her know today how much you appreciate her!

INSIGHT Where Has All the Time Gone?
Home weaving looms of Bible times were often inefficient and time consuming. No wonder this noble woman's candle didn't go out at night. She spent much of her time making beautiful clothing from scratch for the family and the family business.

CHAPTER 30
The sayings of Agur son of Jakeh—an oracle[a]:

This man declared to Ithiel,
  to Ithiel and to Ucal:[b]

2"I am the most ignorant of men;
  I do not have a man's
    understanding.
3I have not learned wisdom,
  nor have I knowledge of the Holy
    One.
4Who has gone up to heaven and come
    down?
  Who has gathered up the wind in
    the hollow of his hands?
  Who has wrapped up the waters in his
    cloak?
  Who has established all the ends of
    the earth?

What is his name, and the name of his
    son?
  Tell me if you know!

5"Every word of God is flawless;
  he is a shield to those who take
    refuge in him.
6Do not add to his words,
  or he will rebuke you and prove
    you a liar.

7"Two things I ask of you, O LORD;
  do not refuse me before I die:
8Keep falsehood and lies far from me;
  give me neither poverty nor riches,
  but give me only my daily bread.
9Otherwise, I may have too much and
    disown you
  and say, 'Who is the LORD?'
  Or I may become poor and steal,
  and so dishonor the name of my
    God.

a1 Or *Jakeh of Massa*   *b1* Masoretic Text; with a different word division of the Hebrew *declared,* "I am weary, O God; / I am weary, O God, and faint.

¹⁰"Do not slander a servant to his
        master,
    or he will curse you, and you will
        pay for it.

¹¹"There are those who curse their
        fathers
    and do not bless their mothers;
¹²those who are pure in their own eyes
    and yet are not cleansed of their
        filth;
¹³those whose eyes are ever so haughty,
    whose glances are so disdainful;
¹⁴those whose teeth are swords
    and whose jaws are set with knives
to devour the poor from the earth,
    the needy from among mankind.

¹⁵"The leech has two daughters.
    'Give! Give!' they cry.

"There are three things that are never
        satisfied,
    four that never say, 'Enough!':
¹⁶the grave,ᶜ the barren womb,
    land, which is never satisfied with
        water,
    and fire, which never says,
        'Enough!'

¹⁷"The eye that mocks a father,
    that scorns obedience to a mother,
will be pecked out by the ravens of
        the valley,
    will be eaten by the vultures.

¹⁸"There are three things that are too
        amazing for me,
    four that I do not understand:
¹⁹the way of an eagle in the sky,
    the way of a snake on a rock,
the way of a ship on the high seas,
    and the way of a man with a
        maiden.

²⁰"This is the way of an adulteress:
    She eats and wipes her mouth
    and says, 'I've done nothing wrong.'

²¹"Under three things the earth trembles,
    under four it cannot bear up:
²²a servant who becomes king,
    a fool who is full of food,
²³an unloved woman who is married,
    and a maidservant who displaces
        her mistress.

²⁴"Four things on earth are small,
    yet they are extremely wise:

²⁵Ants are creatures of little strength,
    yet they store up their food in the
        summer;
²⁶coneysᵈ are creatures of little power,
    yet they make their home in the
        crags;
²⁷locusts have no king,
    yet they advance together in ranks;
²⁸a lizard can be caught with the hand,
    yet it is found in kings' palaces.

²⁹"There are three things that are stately
        in their stride,
    four that move with stately bearing:
³⁰a lion, mighty among beasts,
    who retreats before nothing;
³¹a strutting rooster, a he-goat,
    and a king with his army around
        him.ᵉ

³²"If you have played the fool and
        exalted yourself,
    or if you have planned evil,
    clap your hand over your mouth!
³³For as churning the milk produces
        butter,
    and as twisting the nose produces
        blood,
    so stirring up anger produces strife."

CHAPTER 31
The sayings of King Lemuel—an oracleᶠ
his mother taught him:

²"O my son, O son of my womb,
    O son of my vows,ᵍ
³do not spend your strength on women,
    your vigor on those who ruin kings.

⁴"It is not for kings, O Lemuel—
    not for kings to drink wine,
    not for rulers to crave beer,
⁵lest they drink and forget what the
        law decrees,
    and deprive all the oppressed of
        their rights.
⁶Give beer to those who are perishing,
    wine to those who are in anguish;
⁷let them drink and forget their poverty
    and remember their misery no more.

⁸"Speak up for those who cannot speak
        for themselves,
    for the rights of all who are
        destitute.
⁹Speak up and judge fairly;

ᶜ16 Hebrew *Sheol*   ᵈ26 That is, the hyrax or rock badger   ᵉ31 Or *king secure against revolt*   ᶠ1 Or *of Lemuel king of Massa,*
which   ᵍ2 Or / *the answer to my prayers*

defend the rights of the poor and
needy."

[10][h]A wife of noble character who can
find?
She is worth far more than rubies.
[11]Her husband has full confidence in her
and lacks nothing of value.
[12]She brings him good, not harm,
all the days of her life.
[13]She selects wool and flax
and works with eager hands.
[14]She is like the merchant ships,
bringing her food from afar.
[15]She gets up while it is still dark;
she provides food for her family
and portions for her servant girls.
[16]She considers a field and buys it;
out of her earnings she plants a
vineyard.
[17]She sets about her work vigorously;
her arms are strong for her tasks.
[18]She sees that her trading is profitable,
and her lamp does not go out at
night.
[19]In her hand she holds the distaff
and grasps the spindle with her
fingers.
[20]She opens her arms to the poor
and extends her hands to the needy.
[21]When it snows, she has no fear for her
household;
for all of them are clothed in scarlet.

[22]She makes coverings for her bed;
she is clothed in fine linen and
purple.
[23]Her husband is respected at the city
gate,
where he takes his seat among the
elders of the land.
[24]She makes linen garments and sells
them,
and supplies the merchants with
sashes.
[25]She is clothed with strength and
dignity;
she can laugh at the days to come.
[26]She speaks with wisdom,
and faithful instruction is on her
tongue.
[27]She watches over the affairs of her
household
and does not eat the bread of
idleness.
[28]Her children arise and call her blessed;
her husband also, and he praises
her:
[29]"Many women do noble things,
but you surpass them all."
[30]Charm is deceptive, and beauty is
fleeting;
but a woman who fears the LORD is
to be praised.
[31]Give her the reward she has earned,
and let her works bring her praise at
the city gate.

[h]10 Verses 10-31 are an acrostic, each verse beginning with a successive letter of the Hebrew alphabet.

Ecclesiastes

THE AUTHOR of Ecclesiastes (traditionally thought to be Solomon) enjoyed power, wealth and access to all of life's pursuits and pleasures. After experiencing a full measure of life "under the sun," he declares it all to be futile and unsatisfying. Only as he lives "above the sun"—with an eye toward God—does life become meaningful and fulfilling. Ultimate satisfaction comes not from the good things of life but from the Giver of life, the one we are to fear, honor and obey.

Focus	Exploration				Exhortation		
Divisions	All Is Meaningless	Doing Is Meaningless	Having Is Meaningless		Being Is Meaningless	Using Life Well	Source of True Living
	1	2 4	5 6		7 9	10 11	12
Topics	Exploring Life's Inconsistencies				Explaining Life's Inconsistencies		
	Fickleness of Life vs. Fear of the Lord						
Place	Under the Sun						
Time	Decades of Searching (in the Days of King Solomon)						

JULY 10 ☐ DAY 192
ECCLESIASTES 1–6
Exploring Life's Inconsistencies

 OVERVIEW Truly life is an enigma . . . a riddle . . . a puzzle. From the perspective of those who do not know God, there can only be one word for it: *meaningless*. That's the word the Teacher uses in 1:2—and thirty-four other times in the book—to describe the futility of life apart from God. And he ought to know! Every earthly prescription for happiness has been tried . . . and found wanting. Only when life is viewed as a precious gift "from the hand of God" (2:24) does it begin to come into sharp focus—a focus only possible *above* the sun, so to speak.

Chapter 1	Chapters 2–4	Chapters 5–6
The Meaninglessness of Everything	The Meaninglessness of Toil	The Meaninglessness of Riches
Premise	Proof	

 YOUR DAILY WALK What would you think if your life began at the age of eighty and gradually approached eighteen? Would you live it differently?

Life asks no questions that faith cannot answer.

The Teacher has no illusions about life. He has learned from first-hand experience that nothing under the sun will bring lasting satisfaction. But even in the midst of his voyage into meaninglessness, the Teacher grows wiser, for he discovers the hand of God at work (2:24; 9:1). God is the Giver of "wisdom, knowledge and happiness" (2:26). He enables a person to "eat and drink, and find satisfaction in all his toil" (3:13).

Why not plan a "praise party" for this evening? With family or friends, fix a special meal specifically for the purpose of thanking God publicly for his good gifts. You'll find that it is habit-forming!

 INSIGHT The Teacher: Solomon or Someone Else?
Compare the description of the Teacher in Ecclesiastes with the corresponding description of Solomon in 1 Kings.

Who Is the Teacher? (Ecclesiastes)   *Who Is Solomon?* (1 Kings)
- son of David (1:1)   _____(2:1)
- king in Jerusalem (1:1)   _____(8:1)
- searcher of wisdom (1:13)   _____(3:12)
- builder and gardener (2:4–6) _____(7:1–12)
- collector of treasure (2:7–10) _____(10:14–29)

Decide for yourself: Is "the Teacher" Solomon . . . or someone else?

CHAPTER 1

The words of the Teacher,*ᵃ* son of David, king in Jerusalem:

²"Meaningless! Meaningless!"
  says the Teacher.

"Utterly meaningless!
  Everything is meaningless."

³What does man gain from all his labor
  at which he toils under the sun?
⁴Generations come and generations go,

ᵃ1 Or leader of the assembly; also in verses 2 and 12

but the earth remains forever.
⁵The sun rises and the sun sets,
    and hurries back to where it rises.
⁶The wind blows to the south
    and turns to the north;
round and round it goes,
    ever returning on its course.
⁷All streams flow into the sea,
    yet the sea is never full.
To the place the streams come from,
    there they return again.
⁸All things are wearisome,
    more than one can say.
The eye never has enough of seeing,
    nor the ear its fill of hearing.
⁹What has been will be again,
    what has been done will be done
        again;
    there is nothing new under the sun.
¹⁰Is there anything of which one can
        say,
    "Look! This is something new"?
It was here already, long ago;
    it was here before our time.
¹¹There is no remembrance of men of
        old,
    and even those who are yet to come
will not be remembered
    by those who follow.

¹²I, the Teacher, was king over Israel in Jerusalem. ¹³I devoted myself to study and to explore by wisdom all that is done under heaven. What a heavy burden God has laid on men! ¹⁴I have seen all the things that are done under the sun; all of them are meaningless, a chasing after the wind.

¹⁵What is twisted cannot be
        straightened;
    what is lacking cannot be counted.

¹⁶I thought to myself, "Look, I have grown and increased in wisdom more than anyone who has ruled over Jerusalem before me; I have experienced much of wisdom and knowledge." ¹⁷Then I applied myself to the understanding of wisdom, and also of madness and folly, but I learned that this, too, is a chasing after the wind.

¹⁸For with much wisdom comes much
        sorrow;
    the more knowledge, the more grief.

ᵇ8 The meaning of the Hebrew for this phrase is uncertain.

CHAPTER 2

I thought in my heart, "Come now, I will test you with pleasure to find out what is good." But that also proved to be meaningless. ²"Laughter," I said, "is foolish. And what does pleasure accomplish?" ³I tried cheering myself with wine, and embracing folly—my mind still guiding me with wisdom. I wanted to see what was worthwhile for men to do under heaven during the few days of their lives.

⁴I undertook great projects: I built houses for myself and planted vineyards. ⁵I made gardens and parks and planted all kinds of fruit trees in them. ⁶I made reservoirs to water groves of flourishing trees. ⁷I bought male and female slaves and had other slaves who were born in my house. I also owned more herds and flocks than anyone in Jerusalem before me. ⁸I amassed silver and gold for myself, and the treasure of kings and provinces. I acquired men and women singers, and a haremᵇ as well—the delights of the heart of man. ⁹I became greater by far than anyone in Jerusalem before me. In all this my wisdom stayed with me.

¹⁰I denied myself nothing my eyes
        desired;
    I refused my heart no pleasure.
My heart took delight in all my work,
    and this was the reward for all my
        labor.
¹¹Yet when I surveyed all that my hands
        had done
    and what I had toiled to achieve,
everything was meaningless, a chasing
        after the wind;
    nothing was gained under the sun.

¹²Then I turned my thoughts to consider
        wisdom,
    and also madness and folly.
What more can the king's successor do
    than what has already been done?
¹³I saw that wisdom is better than folly,
    just as light is better than darkness.
¹⁴The wise man has eyes in his head,
    while the fool walks in the darkness;
but I came to realize
    that the same fate overtakes them
        both.

¹⁵Then I thought in my heart,

"The fate of the fool will overtake me
  also.
What then do I gain by being wise?"
I said in my heart,
"This too is meaningless."
[16]For the wise man, like the fool, will
  not be long remembered;
  in days to come both will be
    forgotten.
Like the fool, the wise man too must
    die!

[17]So I hated life, because the work that is done under the sun was grievous to me. All of it is meaningless, a chasing after the wind. [18]I hated all the things I had toiled for under the sun, because I must leave them to the one who comes after me. [19]And who knows whether he will be a wise man or a fool? Yet he will have control over all the work into which I have poured my effort and skill under the sun. This too is meaningless. [20]So my heart began to despair over all my toilsome labor under the sun. [21]For a man may do his work with wisdom, knowledge and skill, and then he must leave all he owns to someone who has not worked for it. This too is meaningless and a great misfortune. [22]What does a man get for all the toil and anxious striving with which he labors under the sun? [23]All his days his work is pain and grief; even at night his mind does not rest. This too is meaningless.

[24]A man can do nothing better than to eat and drink and find satisfaction in his work. This too, I see, is from the hand of God, [25]for without him, who can eat or find enjoyment? [26]To the man who pleases him, God gives wisdom, knowledge and happiness, but to the sinner he gives the task of gathering and storing up wealth to hand it over to the one who pleases God. This too is meaningless, a chasing after the wind.

CHAPTER 3

There is a time for everything,
  and a season for every activity
    under heaven:

[2] a time to be born and a time to die,
  a time to plant and a time to uproot,
[3] a time to kill and a time to heal,
  a time to tear down and a time to
    build,

[4] a time to weep and a time to laugh,
  a time to mourn and a time to
    dance,
[5] a time to scatter stones and a time to
    gather them,
  a time to embrace and a time to
    refrain,
[6] a time to search and a time to give
    up,
  a time to keep and a time to throw
    away,
[7] a time to tear and a time to mend,
  a time to be silent and a time to
    speak,
[8] a time to love and a time to hate,
  a time for war and a time for peace.

[9]What does the worker gain from his toil? [10]I have seen the burden God has laid on men. [11]He has made everything beautiful in its time. He has also set eternity in the hearts of men; yet they cannot fathom what God has done from beginning to end. [12]I know that there is nothing better for men than to be happy and do good while they live. [13]That everyone may eat and drink, and find satisfaction in all his toil—this is the gift of God. [14]I know that everything God does will endure forever; nothing can be added to it and nothing taken from it. God does it so that men will revere him.

[15]Whatever is has already been,
  and what will be has been before;
  and God will call the past to
    account.[c]

[16]And I saw something else under the sun:

In the place of judgment—wickedness
    was there,
  in the place of justice—wickedness
    was there.

[17]I thought in my heart,

"God will bring to judgment
  both the righteous and the wicked,
for there will be a time for every
    activity,
  a time for every deed."

[18]I also thought, "As for men, God tests them so that they may see that they are like the animals. [19]Man's fate is like that of the animals; the same fate awaits them both: As one dies, so dies the other. All

---

[c]15 Or *God calls back the past*

have the same breath[d]; man has no advantage over the animal. Everything is meaningless. [20]All go to the same place; all come from dust, and to dust all return. [21]Who knows if the spirit of man rises upward and if the spirit of the animal[e] goes down into the earth?"

[22]So I saw that there is nothing better for a man than to enjoy his work, because that is his lot. For who can bring him to see what will happen after him?

CHAPTER 4

Again I looked and saw all the oppression that was taking place under the sun:

I saw the tears of the oppressed—
    and they have no comforter;
power was on the side of their
        oppressors—
    and they have no comforter.
[2]And I declared that the dead,
    who had already died,
are happier than the living,
    who are still alive.
[3]But better than both
    is he who has not yet been,
who has not seen the evil
    that is done under the sun.

[4]And I saw that all labor and all achievement spring from man's envy of his neighbor. This too is meaningless, a chasing after the wind.

[5]The fool folds his hands
    and ruins himself.
[6]Better one handful with tranquillity
    than two handfuls with toil
    and chasing after the wind.

[7]Again I saw something meaningless under the sun:

[8]There was a man all alone;
    he had neither son nor brother.
There was no end to his toil,
    yet his eyes were not content with
        his wealth.
"For whom am I toiling," he asked,
    "and why am I depriving myself of
        enjoyment?"
This too is meaningless—
    a miserable business!

[9]Two are better than one,
    because they have a good return for
        their work:

[10]If one falls down,
    his friend can help him up.
But pity the man who falls
    and has no one to help him up!
[11]Also, if two lie down together, they
        will keep warm.
But how can one keep warm alone?
[12]Though one may be overpowered,
    two can defend themselves.
A cord of three strands is not quickly
        broken.

[13]Better a poor but wise youth than an old but foolish king who no longer knows how to take warning. [14]The youth may have come from prison to the kingship, or he may have been born in poverty within his kingdom. [15]I saw that all who lived and walked under the sun followed the youth, the king's successor. [16]There was no end to all the people who were before them. But those who came later were not pleased with the successor. This too is meaningless, a chasing after the wind.

CHAPTER 5

Guard your steps when you go to the house of God. Go near to listen rather than to offer the sacrifice of fools, who do not know that they do wrong.

[2]Do not be quick with your mouth,
    do not be hasty in your heart
    to utter anything before God.
God is in heaven
    and you are on earth,
    so let your words be few.
[3]As a dream comes when there are
        many cares,
    so the speech of a fool when there
        are many words.

[4]When you make a vow to God, do not delay in fulfilling it. He has no pleasure in fools; fulfill your vow. [5]It is better not to vow than to make a vow and not fulfill it. [6]Do not let your mouth lead you into sin. And do not protest to the ⌊temple⌋ messenger, "My vow was a mistake." Why should God be angry at what you say and destroy the work of your hands? [7]Much dreaming and many words are meaningless. Therefore stand in awe of God.

[8]If you see the poor oppressed in a district, and justice and rights denied, do not be surprised at such things; for one official is eyed by a higher one, and over

---

[d]19 Or spirit   [e]21 Or Who knows the spirit of man, which rises upward, or the spirit of the animal, which

them both are others higher still. ⁹The increase from the land is taken by all; the king himself profits from the fields.

¹⁰Whoever loves money never has
      money enough;
   whoever loves wealth is never
      satisfied with his income.
   This too is meaningless.

¹¹As goods increase,
   so do those who consume them.
   And what benefit are they to the
      owner
   except to feast his eyes on them?

¹²The sleep of a laborer is sweet,
   whether he eats little or much,
but the abundance of a rich man
   permits him no sleep.

¹³I have seen a grievous evil under the
sun:

   wealth hoarded to the harm of its
      owner,
¹⁴   or wealth lost through some
      misfortune,
   so that when he has a son
      there is nothing left for him.
¹⁵Naked a man comes from his mother's
      womb,
   and as he comes, so he departs.
   He takes nothing from his labor
      that he can carry in his hand.

¹⁶This too is a grievous evil:

   As a man comes, so he departs,
      and what does he gain,
      since he toils for the wind?
¹⁷All his days he eats in darkness,
   with great frustration, affliction and
      anger.

¹⁸Then I realized that it is good and proper for a man to eat and drink, and to find satisfaction in his toilsome labor under the sun during the few days of life God has given him—for this is his lot. ¹⁹Moreover, when God gives any man wealth and possessions, and enables him to enjoy them, to accept his lot and be happy in his work—this is a gift of God. ²⁰He seldom reflects on the days of his

life, because God keeps him occupied with gladness of heart.

CHAPTER 6

I have seen another evil under the sun, and it weighs heavily on men: ²God gives a man wealth, possessions and honor, so that he lacks nothing his heart desires, but God does not enable him to enjoy them, and a stranger enjoys them instead. This is meaningless, a grievous evil.

³A man may have a hundred children and live many years; yet no matter how long he lives, if he cannot enjoy his prosperity and does not receive proper burial, I say that a stillborn child is better off than he. ⁴It comes without meaning, it departs in darkness, and in darkness its name is shrouded. ⁵Though it never saw the sun or knew anything, it has more rest than does that man— ⁶even if he lives a thousand years twice over but fails to enjoy his prosperity. Do not all go to the same place?

⁷All man's efforts are for his mouth,
   yet his appetite is never satisfied.
⁸What advantage has a wise man
      over a fool?
   What does a poor man gain
      by knowing how to conduct himself
         before others?
⁹Better what the eye sees
      than the roving of the appetite.
   This too is meaningless,
      a chasing after the wind.

¹⁰Whatever exists has already been
      named,
   and what man is has been known;
   no man can contend
      with one who is stronger than he.
¹¹The more the words,
      the less the meaning,
      and how does that profit anyone?

¹²For who knows what is good for a man in life, during the few and meaningless days he passes through like a shadow? Who can tell him what will happen under the sun after he is gone?

JULY 11 ☐ DAY 193
ECCLESIASTES 7–12
Explaining Life's Inconsistencies

OVERVIEW Not only is there meaninglessness in what you do and in what you have, but apart from God there is meaninglessness in what you are. Righteous people are treated as if they were wicked (8:14). One sinner can destroy the work of many good men (9:18). Even moral, upright character seems to profit nothing. But once again, God's perspective turns futility into purpose. "Although a wicked man commits a hundred crimes and still lives a long time, I know that it will go better with God-fearing men, who are reverent before God" (8:12). "Be happy, young man, while you are young, and let your heart give you joy in the days of your youth. Follow the ways of your heart and whatever your eyes see, but know that for all these things God will bring you to judgment" (11:9).

Chapters 7–10	Chapters 11–12
The Meaninglessness of Being (Wise, Good, Mortal)	The Solution to Life's Meaninglessness: "Fear God and Keep His Commandments"
Life under the Sun	Life above the Sun

YOUR DAILY WALK Every blessing from God carries with it a corresponding responsibility.

Are you young (11:9–10)? Then God holds you accountable for the way you use your strength and vitality.

A useless life is only an early death.

Are you a member of the Geritol generation (12:1–7)? Don't use that as an alibi! God holds you equally accountable for the years of experience you have accumulated.

In the final two verses of Ecclesiastes, the Teacher summarizes his thoughts. Life at any age apart from God is meaningless, regardless of how wise, wealthy or industrious you are. Things can never fill the void that God desires to fill in your life. Therefore, "fear God and keep his commandments" (12:13).

Analyze your life according to what you do, what you have and what you are. Is God the focus of your activities? Is God more important than your possessions? Is God the center of your being? If not, what changes do you need to make today?

INSIGHT An Allegory of Old Age

As you read Ecclesiastes 12:3, did you note the literal elements of old age that are pictured in allegorical form? For example, "keepers of the house" refers to hands and arms; "strong men" to legs; "grinders" to teeth; "those looking through the windows" to eyes.

CHAPTER 7

A good name is better than fine perfume,
and the day of death better than the day of birth.
2It is better to go to a house of mourning
than to go to a house of feasting,
for death is the destiny of every man;
the living should take this to heart.

3Sorrow is better than laughter,
because a sad face is good for the heart.
4The heart of the wise is in the house of mourning,
but the heart of fools is in the house of pleasure.
5It is better to heed a wise man's rebuke
than to listen to the song of fools.

⁶Like the crackling of thorns under the
     pot,
   so is the laughter of fools.
   This too is meaningless.

⁷Extortion turns a wise man into a fool,
   and a bribe corrupts the heart.

⁸The end of a matter is better than its
     beginning,
   and patience is better than pride.
⁹Do not be quickly provoked in your
     spirit,
   for anger resides in the lap of fools.

¹⁰Do not say, "Why were the old days
     better than these?"
   For it is not wise to ask such
     questions.

¹¹Wisdom, like an inheritance, is a good
     thing
   and benefits those who see the sun.
¹²Wisdom is a shelter
   as money is a shelter,
   but the advantage of knowledge is
     this:
     that wisdom preserves the life of its
       possessor.

¹³Consider what God has done:

   Who can straighten
     what he has made crooked?
¹⁴When times are good, be happy;
     but when times are bad, consider:
   God has made the one
     as well as the other.
   Therefore, a man cannot discover
     anything about his future.

¹⁵In this meaningless life of mine I have
   seen both of these:

   a righteous man perishing in his
     righteousness,
   and a wicked man living long in his
     wickedness.
¹⁶Do not be overrighteous,
     neither be overwise—
   why destroy yourself?
¹⁷Do not be overwicked,
     and do not be a fool—
   why die before your time?
¹⁸It is good to grasp the one
     and not let go of the other.
   The man who fears God will avoid
     all ⌊extremes⌋.ᶠ

¹⁹Wisdom makes one wise man more
     powerful
   than ten rulers in a city.

²⁰There is not a righteous man on earth
   who does what is right and never
     sins.

²¹Do not pay attention to every word
     people say,
   or you may hear your servant
     cursing you—
²²for you know in your heart
   that many times you yourself have
     cursed others.

²³All this I tested by wisdom and I said,

   "I am determined to be wise"—
     but this was beyond me.
²⁴Whatever wisdom may be,
   it is far off and most profound—
     who can discover it?
²⁵So I turned my mind to understand,
   to investigate and to search out
     wisdom and the scheme of
       things
   and to understand the stupidity of
     wickedness
   and the madness of folly.

²⁶I find more bitter than death
   the woman who is a snare,
   whose heart is a trap
   and whose hands are chains.
   The man who pleases God will escape
     her,
   but the sinner she will ensnare.

²⁷"Look," says the Teacher,ᵍ "this is
   what I have discovered:

   "Adding one thing to another to
       discover the scheme of things—
²⁸   while I was still searching
     but not finding—
   I found one ⌊upright⌋ man among a
       thousand,
   but not one ⌊upright⌋ woman among
       them all.
²⁹This only have I found:
   God made mankind upright,
   but men have gone in search of
     many schemes."

CHAPTER 8
   Who is like the wise man?
     Who knows the explanation of
       things?

ᶠ18 Or will follow them both   ᵍ27 Or leader of the assembly

Wisdom brightens a man's face
     and changes its hard appearance.

²Obey the king's command, I say, because you took an oath before God. ³Do not be in a hurry to leave the king's presence. Do not stand up for a bad cause, for he will do whatever he pleases. ⁴Since a king's word is supreme, who can say to him, "What are you doing?"

⁵Whoever obeys his command will
          come to no harm,
     and the wise heart will know the
          proper time and procedure.
⁶For there is a proper time and
          procedure for every matter,
     though a man's misery weighs
          heavily upon him.

⁷Since no man knows the future,
     who can tell him what is to come?
⁸No man has power over the wind to
          contain it ʰ;
     so no one has power over the day of
          his death.
As no one is discharged in time of
          war,
     so wickedness will not release those
          who practice it.

⁹All this I saw, as I applied my mind to everything done under the sun. There is a time when a man lords it over others to his own ⁱ hurt. ¹⁰Then too, I saw the wicked buried—those who used to come and go from the holy place and receive praise ʲ in the city where they did this. This too is meaningless. ¹¹When the sentence for a crime is not quickly carried out, the hearts of the people are filled with schemes to do wrong. ¹²Although a wicked man commits a hundred crimes and still lives a long time, I know that it will go better with God-fearing men, who are reverent before God. ¹³Yet because the wicked do not fear God, it will not go well with them, and their days will not lengthen like a shadow. ¹⁴There is something else meaningless that occurs on earth: righteous men who get what the wicked deserve, and wicked men who get what the righteous deserve. This too, I say, is meaningless. ¹⁵So I commend the enjoyment of life, because nothing is better for a man under the sun than to eat and drink and be glad. Then joy will accompany him in his work all the days of the life God has given him under the sun.

¹⁶When I applied my mind to know wisdom and to observe man's labor on earth—his eyes not seeing sleep day or night— ¹⁷then I saw all that God has done. No one can comprehend what goes on under the sun. Despite all his efforts to search it out, man cannot discover its meaning. Even if a wise man claims he knows, he cannot really comprehend it.

CHAPTER 9
So I reflected on all this and concluded that the righteous and the wise and what they do are in God's hands, but no man knows whether love or hate awaits him. ²All share a common destiny—the righteous and the wicked, the good and the bad, ᵏ the clean and the unclean, those who offer sacrifices and those who do not.

As it is with the good man,
     so with the sinner;
as it is with those who take oaths,
     so with those who are afraid to take
          them.

³This is the evil in everything that happens under the sun: The same destiny overtakes all. The hearts of men, moreover, are full of evil and there is madness in their hearts while they live, and afterward they join the dead. ⁴Anyone who is among the living has hope ˡ—even a live dog is better off than a dead lion!

⁵For the living know that they will die,
     but the dead know nothing;
they have no further reward,
     and even the memory of them is
          forgotten.
⁶Their love, their hate
     and their jealousy have long since
          vanished;
never again will they have a part
     in anything that happens under the
          sun.

⁷Go, eat your food with gladness, and drink your wine with a joyful heart, for it is now that God favors what you do. ⁸Always be clothed in white, and always

ʰ8 Or over his spirit to retain it   ⁱ9 Or to their   ʲ10 Some Hebrew manuscripts and Septuagint (Aquila); most Hebrew manuscripts and are forgotten   ᵏ2 Septuagint (Aquila), Vulgate and Syriac; Hebrew does not have and the bad.   ˡ4 Or What then is to be chosen? With all who live, there is hope anoint your head with oil. [9]Enjoy life with your wife, whom you love, all the days of this meaningless life that God has given you under the sun— all your meaningless days. For this is your lot in life and in your toilsome labor under the sun. [10]Whatever your hand finds to do, do it with all your might, for in the grave,[m] where you are going, there is neither working nor planning nor knowledge nor wisdom.

[11]I have seen something else under the sun:

The race is not to the swift
    or the battle to the strong,
nor does food come to the wise
    or wealth to the brilliant
    or favor to the learned;
but time and chance happen to them
    all.

[12]Moreover, no man knows when his hour will come:

As fish are caught in a cruel net,
    or birds are taken in a snare,
so men are trapped by evil times
    that fall unexpectedly upon them.

[13]I also saw under the sun this example of wisdom that greatly impressed me: [14]There was once a small city with only a few people in it. And a powerful king came against it, surrounded it and built huge siegeworks against it. [15]Now there lived in that city a man poor but wise, and he saved the city by his wisdom. But nobody remembered that poor man. [16]So I said, "Wisdom is better than strength." But the poor man's wisdom is despised, and his words are no longer heeded.

[17]The quiet words of the wise are more
    to be heeded
    than the shouts of a ruler of fools.
[18]Wisdom is better than weapons of
    war,
    but one sinner destroys much good.

CHAPTER 10
As dead flies give perfume a bad
    smell,
    so a little folly outweighs wisdom
    and honor.
[2]The heart of the wise inclines to the
    right,

but the heart of the fool to the left.
[3]Even as he walks along the road,
    the fool lacks sense
    and shows everyone how stupid he
    is.
[4]If a ruler's anger rises against you,
    do not leave your post;
    calmness can lay great errors to rest.

[5]There is an evil I have seen under the
    sun,
    the sort of error that arises from a
    ruler:
[6]Fools are put in many high positions,
    while the rich occupy the low ones.
[7]I have seen slaves on horseback,
    while princes go on foot like slaves.

[8]Whoever digs a pit may fall into it;
    whoever breaks through a wall may
    be bitten by a snake.
[9]Whoever quarries stones may be
    injured by them;
    whoever splits logs may be
    endangered by them.

[10]If the ax is dull
    and its edge unsharpened,
more strength is needed
    but skill will bring success.

[11]If a snake bites before it is charmed,
    there is no profit for the charmer.

[12]Words from a wise man's mouth are
    gracious,
    but a fool is consumed by his own
    lips.
[13]At the beginning his words are folly;
    at the end they are wicked
    madness—
[14]   and the fool multiplies words.

No one knows what is coming—
    who can tell him what will happen
    after him?

[15]A fool's work wearies him;
    he does not know the way to town.

[16]Woe to you, O land whose king was a
    servant[n]
    and whose princes feast in the
    morning.
[17]Blessed are you, O land whose king is
    of noble birth
    and whose princes eat at a proper
    time—

[m]10 Hebrew Sheol   [n]16 Or king is a child

for strength and not for drunkenness.

¹⁸If a man is lazy, the rafters sag;
   if his hands are idle, the house leaks.

¹⁹A feast is made for laughter,
   and wine makes life merry,
   but money is the answer for everything.

²⁰Do not revile the king even in your thoughts,
   or curse the rich in your bedroom,
   because a bird of the air may carry your words,
   and a bird on the wing may report what you say.

CHAPTER 11

Cast your bread upon the waters,
   for after many days you will find it again.
²Give portions to seven, yes to eight,
   for you do not know what disaster may come upon the land.

³If clouds are full of water,
   they pour rain upon the earth.
Whether a tree falls to the south or to the north,
   in the place where it falls, there will it lie.
⁴Whoever watches the wind will not plant;
   whoever looks at the clouds will not reap.

⁵As you do not know the path of the wind,
   or how the body is formed° in a mother's womb,
   so you cannot understand the work of God,
   the Maker of all things.

⁶Sow your seed in the morning,
   and at evening let not your hands be idle,
   for you do not know which will succeed,
   whether this or that,
   or whether both will do equally well.

⁷Light is sweet,
   and it pleases the eyes to see the sun.

⁸However many years a man may live,
   let him enjoy them all.
But let him remember the days of darkness,
   for they will be many.
Everything to come is meaningless.

⁹Be happy, young man, while you are young,
   and let your heart give you joy in the days of your youth.
Follow the ways of your heart
   and whatever your eyes see,
but know that for all these things
   God will bring you to judgment.
¹⁰So then, banish anxiety from your heart
   and cast off the troubles of your body,
   for youth and vigor are meaningless.

CHAPTER 12

Remember your Creator
   in the days of your youth,
before the days of trouble come
   and the years approach when you will say,
   "I find no pleasure in them"—
²before the sun and the light
   and the moon and the stars grow dark,
   and the clouds return after the rain;
³when the keepers of the house tremble,
   and the strong men stoop,
when the grinders cease because they are few,
   and those looking through the windows grow dim;
⁴when the doors to the street are closed
   and the sound of grinding fades;
when men rise up at the sound of birds,
   but all their songs grow faint;
⁵when men are afraid of heights
   and of dangers in the streets;
when the almond tree blossoms
   and the grasshopper drags himself along
   and desire no longer is stirred.
Then man goes to his eternal home
   and mourners go about the streets.

⁶Remember him—before the silver cord is severed,
   or the golden bowl is broken;

°5 Or *know how life* (or *the spirit*) / *enters the body being formed*

before the pitcher is shattered at the
        spring,
    or the wheel broken at the well,
⁷and the dust returns to the ground it
        came from,
    and the spirit returns to God who
        gave it.

⁸"Meaningless! Meaningless!" says the
        Teacher.ᵖ
    "Everything is meaningless!"

⁹Not only was the Teacher wise, but
also he imparted knowledge to the people. He pondered and searched out and
set in order many proverbs. ¹⁰The Teacher
searched to find just the right words, and
what he wrote was upright and true.

ᵖ8 Or *the leader of the assembly*; also in verses 9 and 10

¹¹The words of the wise are like goads,
their collected sayings like firmly embed-
ded nails—given by one Shepherd. ¹²Be
warned, my son, of anything in addition
to them.

Of making many books there is no end,
and much study wearies the body.

¹³Now all has been heard;
    here is the conclusion of the matter:
Fear God and keep his
        commandments,
    for this is the whole ⌐duty⌐ of man.
¹⁴For God will bring every deed into
        judgment,
    including every hidden thing,
        whether it is good or evil.

Song of Songs

KING SOLOMON, who wrote over a thousand songs, calls this his "song of songs." Full of oriental imagery, the Song of Songs recounts his marrying a country maiden. While it extols the bliss of married love and the burning devotion of spouses to one another, it also speaks of the heartaches of marriage. Though some interpreters consider it a fictional drama and others view it as a literal event of Solomon's life, all have caught an intimate glimpse of God's fervent love for his people within these lyrics.

Focus	Fostering of Love			Faithfulness of Love		
Divisions	Adoration of Lover		Joined to Lover	Separated from Lover		Devoted to Lover
	1:1 3:5		3:6 5:1	5:2 7:9		7:10 8:14
Topics	Courtship	Consummation		Conflict		Cultivation
	Love Growing	Love Fulfilled		Love Tried		Love Enduring
Place	Israel, in the Country and the Palace					
Time	Perhaps 1 Year					

JULY 12 □ DAY 194
SONG OF SONGS 1–8
Extolling Marital Love

OVERVIEW Song of Songs is a love song written by Solomon that abounds in metaphor and oriental imagery. Historically, it depicts the wooing and wedding of a shepherdess by King Solomon and the joys and heartaches of their love for each other. Many have seen in the book a majestic picture of God's love for his people, Israel, and of Christ's love for his bride, the church. As human love finds its highest fulfillment in the love of husband and wife, so spiritual love finds its highest fulfillment in the love of the Creator for his creation.

Chapters 1–3	Chapter 4	Chapters 5–6	Chapters 7–8
Falling in Love	United in Love	Divided in Love	Devoted in Love
Fostering of Love		Faithfulness of Love	

Nothing in this lost world bears the imprint of the Son of God so surely as forgiveness.

YOUR DAILY WALK True or False: Love means never having to say you're sorry.

Modern-day balladeers seem to imply by that statement that apologizing is out of vogue when true love exists. Nothing could be further from the truth. If the young woman had followed that ill-guided advice instead of seeking her lover's forgiveness, she might still be in the locked bedroom!

But on the other side of the coin, Solomon's response to his lover's request for forgiveness is equally noteworthy. It would have been easy for him to take advantage of the apologizing partner and make her suffer through a series of *I told you so's*. But look at Solomon's response in 6:4–10. He compliments her beauty and dignity, praises her hair and bright smile and sets her apart as the one and only woman for him. In short, he reassures her of his forgiveness and continuing love.

What a pattern for forgiving and being forgiven in family disputes! Have you wronged your mate . . . or parent . . . or child through something you have said or done? Then take the initiative in asking for forgiveness. Remember, "Love means *wanting* to say you're sorry . . . and in God's strength *doing* it!"

INSIGHT Potent Lessons from a Moving Love Story
Apart from its historical significance, the Song of Songs pictures for the reader the strength of Christ's love (8:7), his delight in hearing and answering prayer (8:13) and the danger of failing to respond immediately to his knocking (5:2–6).

CHAPTER 1
Solomon's Song of Songs.

²Let him kiss me with the kisses of his mouth—

for your love is more delightful than wine.

³Pleasing is the fragrance of your perfumes;

your name is like perfume poured
out.
No wonder the maidens love you!
⁴Take me away with you—let us hurry!
Let the king bring me into his
chambers.
We rejoice and delight in you*[a];
we will praise your love more than
wine.
How right they are to adore you!

⁵Dark am I, yet lovely,
O daughters of Jerusalem,
dark like the tents of Kedar,
like the tent curtains of Solomon.[b]
⁶Do not stare at me because I am dark,
because I am darkened by the sun.
My mother's sons were angry with me
and made me take care of the
vineyards;
my own vineyard I have neglected.
⁷Tell me, you whom I love, where you
graze your flock
and where you rest your sheep at
midday.
Why should I be like a veiled woman
beside the flocks of your friends?
⁸If you do not know, most beautiful of
women,
follow the tracks of the sheep
and graze your young goats
by the tents of the shepherds.
⁹I liken you, my darling, to a mare
harnessed to one of the chariots of
Pharaoh.
¹⁰Your cheeks are beautiful with
earrings,
your neck with strings of jewels.
¹¹We will make you earrings of gold,
studded with silver.
¹²While the king was at his table,
my perfume spread its fragrance.
¹³My lover is to me a sachet of myrrh
resting between my breasts.
¹⁴My lover is to me a cluster of henna
blossoms
from the vineyards of En Gedi.
¹⁵How beautiful you are, my darling!
Oh, how beautiful!
Your eyes are doves.
¹⁶How handsome you are, my lover!
Oh, how charming!
And our bed is verdant.
¹⁷The beams of our house are cedars;
our rafters are firs.

CHAPTER 2

I am a rose[c] of Sharon,
a lily of the valleys.
²Like a lily among thorns
is my darling among the maidens.
³Like an apple tree among the trees of
the forest
is my lover among the young men.
I delight to sit in his shade,
and his fruit is sweet to my taste.
⁴He has taken me to the banquet hall,
and his banner over me is love.
⁵Strengthen me with raisins,
refresh me with apples,
for I am faint with love.
⁶His left arm is under my head,
and his right arm embraces me.
⁷Daughters of Jerusalem, I charge you
by the gazelles and by the does of
the field:
Do not arouse or awaken love
until it so desires.

⁸Listen! My lover!
Look! Here he comes,
leaping across the mountains,
bounding over the hills.
⁹My lover is like a gazelle or a young
stag.
Look! There he stands behind our
wall,
gazing through the windows,
peering through the lattice.
¹⁰My lover spoke and said to me,
"Arise, my darling,
my beautiful one, and come with
me.
¹¹See! The winter is past;
the rains are over and gone.
¹²Flowers appear on the earth;
the season of singing has come,
the cooing of doves
is heard in our land.
¹³The fig tree forms its early fruit;
the blossoming vines spread their
fragrance.
Arise, come, my darling;
my beautiful one, come with me."
¹⁴My dove in the clefts of the rock,
in the hiding places on the
mountainside,
show me your face,
let me hear your voice;
for your voice is sweet,
and your face is lovely.
¹⁵Catch for us the foxes,

*a*4 The Hebrew is masculine singular.   *b*5 Or *Salma*   *c*1 Possibly a member of the crocus family

the little foxes
that ruin the vineyards,
our vineyards that are in bloom.
¹⁶My lover is mine and I am his;
he browses among the lilies.
¹⁷Until the day breaks
and the shadows flee,
turn, my lover,
and be like a gazelle
or like a young stag
on the rugged hills.*d*

CHAPTER 3
All night long on my bed
I looked for the one my heart loves;
I looked for him but did not find
him.
²I will get up now and go about the
city,
through its streets and squares;
I will search for the one my heart
loves.
So I looked for him but did not find
him.
³The watchmen found me
as they made their rounds in the
city.
"Have you seen the one my heart
loves?"
⁴Scarcely had I passed them
when I found the one my heart
loves.
I held him and would not let him go
till I had brought him to my
mother's house,
to the room of the one who
conceived me.
⁵Daughters of Jerusalem, I charge you
by the gazelles and by the does of
the field:
Do not arouse or awaken love
until it so desires.

⁶Who is this coming up from the desert
like a column of smoke,
perfumed with myrrh and incense
made from all the spices of the
merchant?
⁷Look! It is Solomon's carriage,
escorted by sixty warriors,
the noblest of Israel,
⁸all of them wearing the sword,
all experienced in battle,
each with his sword at his side,
prepared for the terrors of the night.

⁹King Solomon made for himself the
carriage;
he made it of wood from Lebanon.
¹⁰Its posts he made of silver,
its base of gold.
Its seat was upholstered with purple,
its interior lovingly inlaid
by*e* the daughters of Jerusalem.
¹¹Come out, you daughters of Zion,
and look at King Solomon wearing
the crown,
the crown with which his mother
crowned him
on the day of his wedding,
the day his heart rejoiced.

CHAPTER 4
How beautiful you are, my darling!
Oh, how beautiful!
Your eyes behind your veil are
doves.
Your hair is like a flock of goats
descending from Mount Gilead.
²Your teeth are like a flock of sheep
just shorn,
coming up from the washing.
Each has its twin;
not one of them is alone.
³Your lips are like a scarlet ribbon;
your mouth is lovely.
Your temples behind your veil
are like the halves of a pomegranate.
⁴Your neck is like the tower of David,
built with elegance*f*;
on it hang a thousand shields,
all of them shields of warriors.
⁵Your two breasts are like two fawns,
like twin fawns of a gazelle
that browse among the lilies.
⁶Until the day breaks
and the shadows flee,
I will go to the mountain of myrrh
and to the hill of incense.
⁷All beautiful you are, my darling;
there is no flaw in you.

⁸Come with me from Lebanon, my
bride,
come with me from Lebanon.
Descend from the crest of Amana,
from the top of Senir, the summit of
Hermon,
from the lions' dens
and the mountain haunts of the
leopards.

*d*17 Or *the hills of Bether*   *e*10 Or *its inlaid interior a gift of love | from*   *f*4 The meaning of the Hebrew for this word is
uncertain.

⁹You have stolen my heart, my sister,
     my bride;
  you have stolen my heart
  with one glance of your eyes,
     with one jewel of your necklace.
¹⁰How delightful is your love, my sister,
     my bride!
  How much more pleasing is your
     love than wine,
     and the fragrance of your perfume
        than any spice!
¹¹Your lips drop sweetness as the
        honeycomb, my bride;
  milk and honey are under your
        tongue.
  The fragrance of your garments is
     like that of Lebanon.
¹²You are a garden locked up, my sister,
     my bride;
  you are a spring enclosed, a sealed
     fountain.
¹³Your plants are an orchard of
        pomegranates
     with choice fruits,
     with henna and nard,
¹⁴   nard and saffron,
     calamus and cinnamon,
     with every kind of incense tree,
     with myrrh and aloes
     and all the finest spices.
¹⁵You are⁸ a garden fountain,
     a well of flowing water
     streaming down from Lebanon.
¹⁶Awake, north wind,
     and come, south wind!
  Blow on my garden,
     that its fragrance may spread
        abroad.
  Let my lover come into his garden
     and taste its choice fruits.

CHAPTER 5
  I have come into my garden, my sister,
     my bride;
  I have gathered my myrrh with my
     spice.
  I have eaten my honeycomb and my
     honey;
  I have drunk my wine and my milk.
  Eat, O friends, and drink;
     drink your fill, O lovers.
²I slept but my heart was awake.
  Listen! My lover is knocking:
  "Open to me, my sister, my darling,
     my dove, my flawless one.

My head is drenched with dew,
  my hair with the dampness of the
     night."
³I have taken off my robe—
  must I put it on again?
  I have washed my feet—
  must I soil them again?
⁴My lover thrust his hand through the
     latch-opening;
  my heart began to pound for him.
⁵I arose to open for my lover,
  and my hands dripped with myrrh,
  my fingers with flowing myrrh,
  on the handles of the lock.
⁶I opened for my lover,
  but my lover had left; he was gone.
  My heart sank at his departure.ʰ
  I looked for him but did not find him.
  I called him but he did not answer.
⁷The watchmen found me
  as they made their rounds in the
     city.
  They beat me, they bruised me;
  they took away my cloak,
  those watchmen of the walls!
⁸O daughters of Jerusalem, I charge
     you—
  if you find my lover,
  what will you tell him?
  Tell him I am faint with love.
⁹How is your beloved better than
     others,
  most beautiful of women?
  How is your beloved better than
     others,
  that you charge us so?
¹⁰My lover is radiant and ruddy,
  outstanding among ten thousand.
¹¹His head is purest gold;
  his hair is wavy
  and black as a raven.
¹²His eyes are like doves
  by the water streams,
  washed in milk,
  mounted like jewels.
¹³His cheeks are like beds of spice
  yielding perfume.
  His lips are like lilies
  dripping with myrrh.
¹⁴His arms are rods of gold
  set with chrysolite.
  His body is like polished ivory
  decorated with sapphires.ⁱ
¹⁵His legs are pillars of marble
  set on bases of pure gold.

⁸15 Or *I am* (spoken by the *Beloved*)   ʰ6 Or *heart had gone out to him when he spoke*   ⁱ14 Or *lapis lazuli*

His appearance is like Lebanon,
  choice as its cedars.
[16]His mouth is sweetness itself;
  he is altogether lovely.
This is my lover, this my friend,
  O daughters of Jerusalem.

CHAPTER 6
Where has your lover gone,
  most beautiful of women?
Which way did your lover turn,
  that we may look for him with you?
[2]My lover has gone down to his
    garden,
  to the beds of spices,
to browse in the gardens
  and to gather lilies.
[3]I am my lover's and my lover is mine;
  he browses among the lilies.
[4]You are beautiful, my darling, as
    Tirzah,
  lovely as Jerusalem,
  majestic as troops with banners.
[5]Turn your eyes from me;
  they overwhelm me.
Your hair is like a flock of goats
  descending from Gilead.
[6]Your teeth are like a flock of sheep
  coming up from the washing.
Each has its twin,
  not one of them is alone.
[7]Your temples behind your veil
  are like the halves of a pomegranate.
[8]Sixty queens there may be,
  and eighty concubines,
  and virgins beyond number;
[9]but my dove, my perfect one, is
    unique,
  the only daughter of her mother,
  the favorite of the one who bore her.
The maidens saw her and called her
    blessed;
  the queens and concubines praised
    her.
[10]Who is this that appears like the
    dawn,
  fair as the moon, bright as the sun,
  majestic as the stars in procession?
[11]I went down to the grove of nut trees
  to look at the new growth in the
    valley,
to see if the vines had budded
  or the pomegranates were in bloom.
[12]Before I realized it,

my desire set me among the royal
  chariots of my people.[j]
[13]Come back, come back, O Shulammite;
  come back, come back, that we may
    gaze on you!
Why would you gaze on the
    Shulammite
  as on the dance of Mahanaim?

CHAPTER 7
How beautiful your sandaled feet,
  O prince's daughter!
Your graceful legs are like jewels,
  the work of a craftsman's hands.
[2]Your navel is a rounded goblet
  that never lacks blended wine.
Your waist is a mound of wheat
  encircled by lilies.
[3]Your breasts are like two fawns,
  twins of a gazelle.
[4]Your neck is like an ivory tower.
Your eyes are the pools of Heshbon
  by the gate of Bath Rabbim.
Your nose is like the tower of Lebanon
  looking toward Damascus.
[5]Your head crowns you like Mount
    Carmel.
Your hair is like royal tapestry;
  the king is held captive by its
    tresses.
[6]How beautiful you are and how
    pleasing,
  O love, with your delights!
[7]Your stature is like that of the palm,
  and your breasts like clusters of
    fruit.
[8]I said, "I will climb the palm tree;
  I will take hold of its fruit."
May your breasts be like the clusters
    of the vine,
  the fragrance of your breath like
    apples,
[9] and your mouth like the best wine.
May the wine go straight to my lover,
  flowing gently over lips and teeth.[k]
[10]I belong to my lover,
  and his desire is for me.
[11]Come, my lover, let us go to the
    countryside,
  let us spend the night in the
    villages.[l]
[12]Let us go early to the vineyards
  to see if the vines have budded,
  if their blossoms have opened,

---

[j]12 Or among the chariots of Amminadab; or among the chariots of the people of the prince   [k]9 Septuagint, Aquila, Vulgate and
Syriac; Hebrew lips of sleepers   [l]11 Or henna bushes

and if the pomegranates are in
　　bloom—
　there I will give you my love.
¹³The mandrakes send out their
　　fragrance,
　and at our door is every delicacy,
both new and old,
　that I have stored up for you, my
　　lover.

CHAPTER 8

If only you were to me like a brother,
　who was nursed at my mother's
　　breasts!
　Then, if I found you outside,
　I would kiss you,
　and no one would despise me.
²I would lead you
　and bring you to my mother's
　　house—
　she who has taught me.
I would give you spiced wine to drink,
　the nectar of my pomegranates.
³His left arm is under my head
　and his right arm embraces me.
⁴Daughters of Jerusalem, I charge you:
　Do not arouse or awaken love
　until it so desires.
⁵Who is this coming up from the desert
　leaning on her lover?
Under the apple tree I roused you;
　there your mother conceived you,
　there she who was in labor gave you
　　birth.
⁶Place me like a seal over your heart,
　like a seal on your arm;
for love is as strong as death,
　its jealousy[m] unyielding as the
　　grave.[n]

It burns like blazing fire,
　like a mighty flame.[o]
⁷Many waters cannot quench love;
　rivers cannot wash it away.
If one were to give
　all the wealth of his house for love,
　it[p] would be utterly scorned.
⁸We have a young sister,
　and her breasts are not yet grown.
What shall we do for our sister
　for the day she is spoken for?
⁹If she is a wall,
　we will build towers of silver on
　　her.
If she is a door,
　we will enclose her with panels of
　　cedar.
¹⁰I am a wall,
　and my breasts are like towers.
Thus I have become in his eyes
　like one bringing contentment.
¹¹Solomon had a vineyard in Baal
　　Hamon;
　he let out his vineyard to tenants.
Each was to bring for its fruit
　a thousand shekels[q] of silver.
¹²But my own vineyard is mine to give;
　the thousand shekels are for you,
　　O Solomon,
　and two hundred[r] are for those
　　who tend its fruit.
¹³You who dwell in the gardens
　with friends in attendance,
　let me hear your voice!
¹⁴Come away, my lover,
　and be like a gazelle
or like a young stag
　on the spice-laden mountains.

---

[m]6 Or *ardor*　　[n]6 Hebrew *Sheol*　　[o]6 Or / *like the very flame of the* LORD　　[p]7 Or *he*　　[q]11 That is, about 25 pounds (about 11.5 kilograms); also in verse 12　　[r]12 That is, about 5 pounds (about 2.3 kilograms)

Isaiah

THE BOOK of Isaiah, the mother lode of Hebrew prophecy, sets forth a lifetime of preaching by the statesman and prophet for whom it is named. In the first thirty-nine chapters, the prophet stresses righteousness, holiness and the justice of God, announcing God's terrible judgment upon a world stained scarlet with sin (1:18). But the last twenty-seven chapters portray God's glory and compassion and the undeserved favor he bestows. Messiah will come as a Savior to bear a cross and as a Sovereign to wear a crown.

Focus	Condemnation			Interlude	Consolation		
Divisions	Judgment Is Coming upon . . . Judah (1–12)	the Nations (13–27)	the World (28–35)	Judah's Day of Judgment	God's Sovereignty	God's Salvation	God's Restoration
	1 35			36 39	40 48	49 57	58 66
Topics	Horror			History	Hope		
	Groaning under God's Judgment (1:4)				Glorying in God's Salvation (40:1-2)		
Place	Judah and Her Neighbors				Israel and the World		
Time	About 40 Years (722–681 B.C.)				Thousands of Years		

JULY 13 ☐ DAY 195
ISAIAH 1–4
Judah's Shallow Religion

OVERVIEW *The date:* About 740 B.C. *The setting:* Judah, the southern kingdom. Judah faces extinction at the hands of the cruel Assyrians. In this crucial hour of national emergency, God sends Isaiah—a unique man with an unpleasant message. The nation of Judah is rotten to the core and ripe for judgment. Her habitual sins of idolatry, hypocrisy, injustice and corruption have not escaped the notice of her holy God. His righteous wrath will soon fall upon king and commoner alike, that all might learn that the Lord Almighty cannot and will not be mocked.

Chapter 1	Chapter 2	Chapter 3	Chapter 4
A Nation Denounced	A House Cleansed	A People Humbled	A Prince Announced
Iniquity		Indignation	"In That Day"

People used to argue as to whether the world was square or round—but the Bible says it is crooked!

YOUR DAILY WALK The truth hurts.

No one minds looking into a mirror, provided the image reflected back is flattering to the viewer. But allow that mirror to reflect a painful truth about a person's appearance, and you just might end up with a broken mirror—and some hurt feelings!

Isaiah held up the mirror of God's Word before the people of Judah to show how stained with sin the nation had become. And when he did, neither the prophet nor the people liked what they saw! Yet in spite of the bleak reflection, there was hope if only the people would respond to God's invitation.

Find a piece of white cotton material (a cotton ball will do nicely), and stain it with a few drops of red food coloring. Now try to wash it as clean and white as it was originally.

Give up? Isaiah 1:18 will show you how to enjoy cleansing from even the most stubborn stain of sin. Have you been washed as "white as snow" by the blood of Christ?

INSIGHT Pattern of a Prophet's Pronouncements

When broadly outlined, many of Isaiah's messages are strikingly similar: (1) accusation, (2) threat of judgment, (3) exhortation to repentance and (4) promise of blessing. See if you can apply this general outline to Isaiah's first message in chapter 1. (Hint: Divide the chapter at verses 10, 18 and 21.)

CHAPTER 1

The vision concerning Judah and Jerusalem that Isaiah son of Amoz saw during the reigns of Uzziah, Jotham, Ahaz and Hezekiah, kings of Judah.

²Hear, O heavens! Listen, O earth!
   For the LORD has spoken:

"I reared children and brought them
      up,
   but they have rebelled against
      me.
³The ox knows his master,
      the donkey his owner's manger,
but Israel does not know,
   my people do not understand."

4Ah, sinful nation,
    a people loaded with guilt,
a brood of evildoers,
    children given to corruption!
They have forsaken the LORD;
    they have spurned the Holy One of
        Israel
    and turned their backs on him.

5Why should you be beaten anymore?
    Why do you persist in rebellion?
Your whole head is injured,
    your whole heart afflicted.
6From the sole of your foot to the top
        of your head
    there is no soundness—
only wounds and welts
    and open sores,
not cleansed or bandaged
    or soothed with oil.

7Your country is desolate,
    your cities burned with fire;
your fields are being stripped by
        foreigners
    right before you,
    laid waste as when overthrown by
        strangers.
8The Daughter of Zion is left
    like a shelter in a vineyard,
like a hut in a field of melons,
    like a city under siege.
9Unless the LORD Almighty
    had left us some survivors,
we would have become like Sodom,
    we would have been like Gomorrah.

10Hear the word of the LORD,
    you rulers of Sodom;
listen to the law of our God,
    you people of Gomorrah!
11"The multitude of your sacrifices—
    what are they to me?" says the LORD.
"I have more than enough of burnt
        offerings,
    of rams and the fat of fattened
        animals;
I have no pleasure
    in the blood of bulls and lambs and
        goats.
12When you come to appear before me,
    who has asked this of you,
    this trampling of my courts?
13Stop bringing meaningless offerings!
    Your incense is detestable to me.
New Moons, Sabbaths and
        convocations—

I cannot bear your evil assemblies.
14Your New Moon festivals and your
        appointed feasts
    my soul hates.
They have become a burden to me;
    I am weary of bearing them.
15When you spread out your hands in
        prayer,
    I will hide my eyes from you;
even if you offer many prayers,
    I will not listen.
Your hands are full of blood;
16   wash and make yourselves clean.
Take your evil deeds
    out of my sight!
Stop doing wrong,
17   learn to do right!
Seek justice,
    encourage the oppressed.ᵃ
Defend the cause of the fatherless,
    plead the case of the widow.

18"Come now, let us reason together,"
    says the LORD.
"Though your sins are like scarlet,
    they shall be as white as snow;
though they are red as crimson,
    they shall be like wool.
19If you are willing and obedient,
    you will eat the best from the land;
20but if you resist and rebel,
    you will be devoured by the sword."
        For the mouth of the LORD
            has spoken.

21See how the faithful city
    has become a harlot!
She once was full of justice;
    righteousness used to dwell in her—
    but now murderers!
22Your silver has become dross,
    your choice wine is diluted with
        water.
23Your rulers are rebels,
    companions of thieves;
they all love bribes
    and chase after gifts.
They do not defend the cause of the
        fatherless;
    the widow's case does not come
        before them.
24Therefore the Lord, the LORD Almighty,
    the Mighty One of Israel, declares:
"Ah, I will get relief from my foes
    and avenge myself on my enemies.
25I will turn my hand against you;

ᵃ17 Or / rebuke the oppressor

I will thoroughly purge away your
  dross
  and remove all your impurities.
26I will restore your judges as in days of
  old,
  your counselors as at the beginning.
Afterward you will be called
  the City of Righteousness,
  the Faithful City."

27Zion will be redeemed with justice,
  her penitent ones with
    righteousness.
28But rebels and sinners will both be
  broken,
  and those who forsake the LORD will
    perish.

29"You will be ashamed because of the
    sacred oaks
  in which you have delighted;
you will be disgraced because of the
    gardens
  that you have chosen.
30You will be like an oak with fading
  leaves,
  like a garden without water.
31The mighty man will become tinder
  and his work a spark;
both will burn together,
  with no one to quench the fire."

CHAPTER 2
This is what Isaiah son of Amoz saw concerning Judah and Jerusalem:

  2In the last days

  the mountain of the LORD's temple will
    be established
    as chief among the mountains;
  it will be raised above the hills,
    and all nations will stream to it.

  3Many peoples will come and say,

  "Come, let us go up to the mountain of
    the LORD,
    to the house of the God of Jacob.
  He will teach us his ways,
    so that we may walk in his paths."
  The law will go out from Zion,
    the word of the LORD from
      Jerusalem.
  4He will judge between the nations
    and will settle disputes for many
      peoples.

They will beat their swords into
  plowshares
  and their spears into pruning hooks.
Nation will not take up sword against
    nation,
  nor will they train for war anymore.

5Come, O house of Jacob,
  let us walk in the light of the LORD.

6You have abandoned your people,
  the house of Jacob.
They are full of superstitions from the
    East;
  they practice divination like the
    Philistines
  and clasp hands with pagans.
7Their land is full of silver and gold;
  there is no end to their treasures.
Their land is full of horses;
  there is no end to their chariots.
8Their land is full of idols;
  they bow down to the work of their
    hands,
  to what their fingers have made.
9So man will be brought low
  and mankind humbled—
  do not forgive them.b

10Go into the rocks,
  hide in the ground
from dread of the LORD
  and the splendor of his majesty!
11The eyes of the arrogant man will be
    humbled
  and the pride of men brought low;
the LORD alone will be exalted in that
    day.

12The LORD Almighty has a day in store
  for all the proud and lofty,
  for all that is exalted
  (and they will be humbled),
13for all the cedars of Lebanon, tall and
    lofty,
  and all the oaks of Bashan,
14for all the towering mountains
  and all the high hills,
15for every lofty tower
  and every fortified wall,
16for every trading shipc
  and every stately vessel.
17The arrogance of man will be brought
    low
  and the pride of men humbled;

b9 Or not raise them up   c16 Hebrew every ship of Tarshish

the LORD alone will be exalted in that
day,
18 and the idols will totally disappear.

19Men will flee to caves in the rocks
and to holes in the ground
from dread of the LORD
and the splendor of his majesty,
when he rises to shake the earth.
20In that day men will throw away
to the rodents and bats
their idols of silver and idols of gold,
which they made to worship.
21They will flee to caverns in the rocks
and to the overhanging crags
from dread of the LORD
and the splendor of his majesty,
when he rises to shake the earth.

22Stop trusting in man,
who has but a breath in his nostrils.
Of what account is he?

CHAPTER 3
See now, the Lord,
the LORD Almighty,
is about to take from Jerusalem and
Judah
both supply and support:
all supplies of food and all supplies of
water,
2 the hero and warrior,
the judge and prophet,
the soothsayer and elder,
3the captain of fifty and man of rank,
the counselor, skilled craftsman and
clever enchanter.

4I will make boys their officials;
mere children will govern them.
5People will oppress each other—
man against man, neighbor against
neighbor.
The young will rise up against the old,
the base against the honorable.

6A man will seize one of his brothers
at his father's home, and say,
"You have a cloak, you be our leader;
take charge of this heap of ruins!"
7But in that day he will cry out,
"I have no remedy.
I have no food or clothing in my
house;
do not make me the leader of the
people."

8Jerusalem staggers,
Judah is falling;

their words and deeds are against the
LORD,
defying his glorious presence.
9The look on their faces testifies against
them;
they parade their sin like Sodom;
they do not hide it.
Woe to them!
They have brought disaster upon
themselves.

10Tell the righteous it will be well with
them,
for they will enjoy the fruit of their
deeds.
11Woe to the wicked! Disaster is upon
them!
They will be paid back for what their
hands have done.

12Youths oppress my people,
women rule over them.
O my people, your guides lead you
astray;
they turn you from the path.

13The LORD takes his place in court;
he rises to judge the people.
14The LORD enters into judgment
against the elders and leaders of his
people:
"It is you who have ruined my
vineyard;
the plunder from the poor is in your
houses.
15What do you mean by crushing my
people
and grinding the faces of the poor?"
declares the Lord,
the LORD Almighty.

16The LORD says,
"The women of Zion are haughty,
walking along with outstretched necks,
flirting with their eyes,
tripping along with mincing steps,
with ornaments jingling on their
ankles.
17Therefore the Lord will bring sores on
the heads of the women of
Zion;
the LORD will make their scalps
bald."

18In that day the Lord will snatch away
their finery: the bangles and headbands
and crescent necklaces, 19the earrings and
bracelets and veils, 20the headdresses and
ankle chains and sashes, the perfume bot-

tles and charms, ²¹the signet rings and nose rings, ²²the fine robes and the capes and cloaks, the purses ²³and mirrors, and the linen garments and tiaras and shawls.

²⁴Instead of fragrance there will be a stench;
  instead of a sash, a rope;
  instead of well-dressed hair, baldness;
  instead of fine clothing, sackcloth;
  instead of beauty, branding.
²⁵Your men will fall by the sword,
  your warriors in battle.
²⁶The gates of Zion will lament and mourn;
  destitute, she will sit on the ground.

CHAPTER 4
In that day seven women
  will take hold of one man
and say, "We will eat our own food
  and provide our own clothes;

^d4 Or the Spirit

only let us be called by your name.
  Take away our disgrace!"

²In that day the Branch of the LORD will be beautiful and glorious, and the fruit of the land will be the pride and glory of the survivors in Israel. ³Those who are left in Zion, who remain in Jerusalem, will be called holy, all who are recorded among the living in Jerusalem. ⁴The Lord will wash away the filth of the women of Zion; he will cleanse the bloodstains from Jerusalem by a spirit^d of judgment and a spirit^d of fire. ⁵Then the LORD will create over all of Mount Zion and over those who assemble there a cloud of smoke by day and a glow of flaming fire by night; over all the glory will be a canopy. ⁶It will be a shelter and shade from the heat of the day, and a refuge and hiding place from the storm and rain.

JULY 14 □ DAY 196
Search for Significance

LOOK BACK Proverbs, Ecclesiastes, Song of Songs—three books historically attributed to King Solomon, the wisest man who ever lived. But notice how these books parallel the downward spiral of his life: Song of Songs (when Solomon early in life was full of youthful passion and fervor); Proverbs (when Solomon in his midlife had learned much about the importance of choices, good and bad); and finally, Ecclesiastes (when Solomon in later life had discovered the bitterness of empty pursuits, and the high price of chasing the wind and reaping the whirlwind).

By contrast, Isaiah sets his compass on the commission he receives from the Lord and follows it with the determination of a laser beam. For more than fifty years, spanning the administrations of four kings of Judah, Isaiah stays true to his calling—delivering a ringing indictment upon God's disobedient people.

LOOK UP One of Satan's most effective tools to distract, disable and ultimately destroy God's people is the phrase "If only . . ."

Most people don't know what they want, but it is something different from what they have.

"If only I could get a high school or college degree, then I'd be on my way."

"If only I could find a good job, then I'd have status and worth."

"If only I could get married and have a family, then I'd be truly happy."

"If only I could win the lottery, then I'd be set for life."

"If only I could write a best-selling book, then I'd be someone important."

"If only [you complete the sentence now!]."

Take it from Solomon, the wisest . . . richest . . . most accomplished

. . . most published . . . most married . . . most you-name-it individual in the Bible. If you are looking for significance and satisfaction in the pursuits of life, you are in for a rude disappointment. Purpose and meaning can never be found there; they are found only in the Giver of life himself. That's why at the end of his twelve-chapter odyssey, Solomon concludes with these words: "Fear God and keep his commandments, for this is the whole duty of man" (Ecclesiastes 12:13). The hymn writer put it this way:

"Trust and obey, for there's no other way,
To be happy in Jesus, but to trust and obey."

LOOK AHEAD
Take a few moments to thoughtfully complete this "Significance Survey." It just might change the way you look at your "net worth" and accomplishments.

1. I have $_____ in the bank right now, but my real riches are what I have because I am in Christ (Ephesians 1:3).

2. I have earned a _____ degree, but I realize that all I can boast about is my relationship with God (Jeremiah 9:23–24).

3. I am respected in my community because of _____, but whatever has been to my profit I consider loss for the sake of Christ (Philippians 3:7).

4. I have written _____ books and articles, but in the final analysis, all that matters is what I have done with the Book, God's Word.

Society today is marked by an obsession with significance. It's a pursuit as old as the days of Solomon—and just as fruitless unless God is the center and circumference of the search. Let your search end with him, and you will never be disappointed.

JULY 15 ☐ DAY 197
ISAIAH 5–8
Judah's Untamed Wickedness

OVERVIEW No sooner does Isaiah complete his scathing indictment upon Judah than he turns to share a comforting word of encouragement. God's displeasure with the unrighteous harvest of the vineyard he has planted (Israel and Judah) causes him to commission his prophet (Isaiah) to deliver a declaration of doom. But after the prophet's message of heartache comes a balm of hope. The Messiah will be born of a virgin, hostilities will cease and Judah's enemies will be brought low. Isaiah's response in the face of such unusual announcements? "I will wait for the LORD . . . I will put my trust in him" (8:17).

Chapter 5	Chapter 6	Chapter 7	Chapter 8
Wasted Grapes	Woeful Prophet	Prediction of an Infant	Prediction of an Invasion
Israel	Isaiah	Immanuel	Assyria

YOUR DAILY WALK You cannot impart what you do not possess. In Isaiah's case, before he could be used by God to call the people back to holy living, he himself had to be cleansed and prepared for holy service.

Seeing God for who he is will open your eyes to who you are.

It was important for Isaiah to have an indelible vision of the Lord in all his holiness, for Isaiah's mission would be to preach to a people of unclean lips and hardened hearts. Before he could confront kings and princes, he needed a firsthand glimpse of the King of the universe sitting "on a throne, high and exalted" (6:1). Only then was Isaiah ready to exchange his sinful inadequacy ("Woe to me") for God's holy adequacy ("Go and tell").

Cleansing . . . calling . . . commitment. That pattern is still valid today. God is looking for men and women who will respond to his holiness by volunteering for holy service.

"Woe . . . Go . . ." Put those two words in your pocket—and on your heart—for they are the key to fulfilling your God-given calling today and every day.

 INSIGHT The Six-Decade Servant of God
According to 6:1, Isaiah's long ministry began in the year of King Uzziah's death (about 740 B.C.). It would, according to 1:1, continue through the reigns of Jotham (739–731), Ahaz (731–715) and Hezekiah (715–685)—a period of nearly sixty years!

CHAPTER 5

I will sing for the one I love
　a song about his vineyard:
My loved one had a vineyard
　on a fertile hillside.
²He dug it up and cleared it of stones
　and planted it with the choicest
　　vines.
He built a watchtower in it
　and cut out a winepress as well.
Then he looked for a crop of good
　　grapes,
　but it yielded only bad fruit.

³"Now you dwellers in Jerusalem and
　　men of Judah,
　judge between me and my vineyard.
⁴What more could have been done for
　　my vineyard
　than I have done for it?
When I looked for good grapes,
　why did it yield only bad?
⁵Now I will tell you
　what I am going to do to my
　　vineyard:
I will take away its hedge,
　and it will be destroyed;
I will break down its wall,
　and it will be trampled.
⁶I will make it a wasteland,
　neither pruned nor cultivated,
　and briers and thorns will grow
　　there.
I will command the clouds
　not to rain on it."

⁷The vineyard of the LORD Almighty
　is the house of Israel,
and the men of Judah
　are the garden of his delight.
And he looked for justice, but saw
　　bloodshed;
for righteousness, but heard cries of
　　distress.

⁸Woe to you who add house to house
　and join field to field
till no space is left
　and you live alone in the land.

⁹The LORD Almighty has declared in my hearing:

"Surely the great houses will become
　　desolate,
　the fine mansions left without
　　occupants.
¹⁰A ten-acre*ᵉ* vineyard will produce
　　only a bath*ᶠ* of wine,
　a homer*ᵍ* of seed only an ephah*ʰ*
　　of grain."

¹¹Woe to those who rise early in the
　　morning
　to run after their drinks,
who stay up late at night
　till they are inflamed with wine.
¹²They have harps and lyres at their
　　banquets,
　tambourines and flutes and wine,
but they have no regard for the deeds
　　of the LORD,
　no respect for the work of his hands.

ᵉ10 Hebrew *ten-yoke,* that is, the land plowed by 10 yoke of oxen in one day　*ᶠ10* That is, probably about 6 gallons (about 22 liters)　*ᵍ10* That is, probably about 6 bushels (about 220 liters)　*ʰ10* That is, probably about 3/5 bushel (about 22 liters)

¹³Therefore my people will go into exile
for lack of understanding;
their men of rank will die of hunger
and their masses will be parched
with thirst.
¹⁴Therefore the grave^{*i*} enlarges its
appetite
and opens its mouth without limit;
into it will descend their nobles and
masses
with all their brawlers and revelers.
¹⁵So man will be brought low
and mankind humbled,
the eyes of the arrogant humbled.
¹⁶But the LORD Almighty will be exalted
by his justice,
and the holy God will show himself
holy by his righteousness.
¹⁷Then sheep will graze as in their own
pasture;
lambs will feed^{*j*} among the ruins of
the rich.

¹⁸Woe to those who draw sin along with
cords of deceit,
and wickedness as with cart ropes,
¹⁹to those who say, "Let God hurry,
let him hasten his work
so we may see it.
Let it approach,
let the plan of the Holy One of
Israel come,
so we may know it."

²⁰Woe to those who call evil good
and good evil,
who put darkness for light
and light for darkness,
who put bitter for sweet
and sweet for bitter.

²¹Woe to those who are wise in their
own eyes
and clever in their own sight.

²²Woe to those who are heroes at
drinking wine
and champions at mixing drinks,
²³who acquit the guilty for a bribe,
but deny justice to the innocent.
²⁴Therefore, as tongues of fire lick up
straw
and as dry grass sinks down in the
flames,
so their roots will decay
and their flowers blow away like
dust;

for they have rejected the law of the
LORD Almighty
and spurned the word of the Holy
One of Israel.
²⁵Therefore the LORD's anger burns
against his people;
his hand is raised and he strikes
them down.
The mountains shake,
and the dead bodies are like refuse
in the streets.

Yet for all this, his anger is not turned
away,
his hand is still upraised.

²⁶He lifts up a banner for the distant
nations,
he whistles for those at the ends of
the earth.
Here they come,
swiftly and speedily!
²⁷Not one of them grows tired or
stumbles,
not one slumbers or sleeps;
not a belt is loosened at the waist,
not a sandal thong is broken.
²⁸Their arrows are sharp,
all their bows are strung;
their horses' hoofs seem like flint,
their chariot wheels like a
whirlwind.
²⁹Their roar is like that of the lion,
they roar like young lions;
they growl as they seize their prey
and carry it off with no one to
rescue.
³⁰In that day they will roar over it
like the roaring of the sea.
And if one looks at the land,
he will see darkness and distress;
even the light will be darkened by
the clouds.

CHAPTER 6

In the year that King Uzziah died, I saw
the Lord seated on a throne, high and exalted, and the train of his robe filled the
temple. ²Above him were seraphs, each
with six wings: With two wings they covered their faces, with two they covered
their feet, and with two they were flying.
³And they were calling to one another:

"Holy, holy, holy is the LORD Almighty;
the whole earth is full of his glory."

^{*i*}14 Hebrew *Sheol*   ^{*j*}17 Septuagint; Hebrew / *strangers will eat*

[4]At the sound of their voices the door-posts and thresholds shook and the temple was filled with smoke.

[5]"Woe to me!" I cried. "I am ruined! For I am a man of unclean lips, and I live among a people of unclean lips, and my eyes have seen the King, the LORD Almighty."

[6]Then one of the seraphs flew to me with a live coal in his hand, which he had taken with tongs from the altar. [7]With it he touched my mouth and said, "See, this has touched your lips; your guilt is taken away and your sin atoned for."

[8]Then I heard the voice of the Lord saying, "Whom shall I send? And who will go for us?"

And I said, "Here am I. Send me!"

[9]He said, "Go and tell this people:

" 'Be ever hearing, but never
     understanding;
  be ever seeing, but never
     perceiving.'
[10]Make the heart of this people
     calloused;
  make their ears dull
  and close their eyes.[k]
Otherwise they might see with their
     eyes,
  hear with their ears,
  understand with their hearts,
and turn and be healed."

[11]Then I said, "For how long, O Lord?" And he answered:

"Until the cities lie ruined
  and without inhabitant,
until the houses are left deserted
  and the fields ruined and ravaged,
[12]until the LORD has sent everyone far
     away
  and the land is utterly forsaken.
[13]And though a tenth remains in the
     land,
  it will again be laid waste.
But as the terebinth and oak
  leave stumps when they are cut
     down,
  so the holy seed will be the stump
     in the land."

CHAPTER 7

When Ahaz son of Jotham, the son of Uzziah, was king of Judah, King Rezin of Aram and Pekah son of Remaliah king of Israel marched up to fight against Jerusalem, but they could not overpower it.

[2]Now the house of David was told, "Aram has allied itself with[l] Ephraim"; so the hearts of Ahaz and his people were shaken, as the trees of the forest are shaken by the wind.

[3]Then the LORD said to Isaiah, "Go out, you and your son Shear-Jashub,[m] to meet Ahaz at the end of the aqueduct of the Upper Pool, on the road to the Washerman's Field. [4]Say to him, 'Be careful, keep calm and don't be afraid. Do not lose heart because of these two smoldering stubs of firewood—because of the fierce anger of Rezin and Aram and of the son of Remaliah. [5]Aram, Ephraim and Remaliah's son have plotted your ruin, saying, [6]"Let us invade Judah; let us tear it apart and divide it among ourselves, and make the son of Tabeel king over it." [7]Yet this is what the Sovereign LORD says:

" 'It will not take place,
  it will not happen,
[8]for the head of Aram is Damascus,
  and the head of Damascus is only
     Rezin.
Within sixty-five years
  Ephraim will be too shattered to be
     a people.
[9]The head of Ephraim is Samaria,
  and the head of Samaria is only
     Remaliah's son.
If you do not stand firm in your faith,
  you will not stand at all.' "

[10]Again the LORD spoke to Ahaz, [11]"Ask the LORD your God for a sign, whether in the deepest depths or in the highest heights."

[12]But Ahaz said, "I will not ask; I will not put the LORD to the test."

[13]Then Isaiah said, "Hear now, you house of David! Is it not enough to try the patience of men? Will you try the patience of my God also? [14]Therefore the Lord himself will give you[n] a sign: The virgin will be with child and will give birth to a son, and[o] will call him Immanuel.[p] [15]He

[k]9,10 Hebrew; Septuagint 'You will be ever hearing, but never understanding; / you will be ever seeing, but never perceiving.' / [10]This people's heart has become calloused; / they hardly hear with their ears, / and they have closed their eyes   [l]2 Or has set up camp in   [m]3 Shear-Jashub means a remnant will return.   [n]14 The Hebrew is plural.   [o]14 Masoretic Text; Dead Sea Scrolls and he or and they   [p]14 Immanuel means God with us.

will eat curds and honey when he knows enough to reject the wrong and choose the right. ¹⁶But before the boy knows enough to reject the wrong and choose the right, the land of the two kings you dread will be laid waste. ¹⁷The LORD will bring on you and on your people and on the house of your father a time unlike any since Ephraim broke away from Judah—he will bring the king of Assyria."

¹⁸In that day the LORD will whistle for flies from the distant streams of Egypt and for bees from the land of Assyria. ¹⁹They will all come and settle in the steep ravines and in the crevices in the rocks, on all the thornbushes and at all the water holes. ²⁰In that day the Lord will use a razor hired from beyond the River^q—the king of Assyria—to shave your head and the hair of your legs, and to take off your beards also. ²¹In that day, a man will keep alive a young cow and two goats. ²²And because of the abundance of the milk they give, he will have curds to eat. All who remain in the land will eat curds and honey. ²³In that day, in every place where there were a thousand vines worth a thousand silver shekels,^r there will be only briers and thorns. ²⁴Men will go there with bow and arrow, for the land will be covered with briers and thorns. ²⁵As for all the hills once cultivated by the hoe, you will no longer go there for fear of the briers and thorns; they will become places where cattle are turned loose and where sheep run.

CHAPTER 8

The LORD said to me, "Take a large scroll and write on it with an ordinary pen: Maher-Shalal-Hash-Baz.^s ²And I will call in Uriah the priest and Zechariah son of Jeberekiah as reliable witnesses for me."

³Then I went to the prophetess, and she conceived and gave birth to a son. And the LORD said to me, "Name him Maher-Shalal-Hash-Baz. ⁴Before the boy knows how to say 'My father' or 'My mother,' the wealth of Damascus and the plunder of Samaria will be carried off by the king of Assyria."

⁵The LORD spoke to me again:

⁶"Because this people has rejected
    the gently flowing waters of Shiloah

and rejoices over Rezin
    and the son of Remaliah,
⁷therefore the Lord is about to bring
        against them
    the mighty floodwaters of the
        River^q—
    the king of Assyria with all his
        pomp.
It will overflow all its channels,
    run over all its banks
⁸and sweep on into Judah, swirling
        over it,
    passing through it and reaching up
        to the neck.
Its outspread wings will cover the
        breadth of your land,
    O Immanuel^t!"

⁹Raise the war cry,^u you nations, and
        be shattered!
    Listen, all you distant lands.
Prepare for battle, and be shattered!
Prepare for battle, and be shattered!
¹⁰Devise your strategy, but it will be
        thwarted;
    propose your plan, but it will not
        stand,
    for God is with us.^v

¹¹The LORD spoke to me with his strong hand upon me, warning me not to follow the way of this people. He said:

¹²"Do not call conspiracy
    everything that these people call
        conspiracy^w;
do not fear what they fear,
    and do not dread it.
¹³The LORD Almighty is the one you are
        to regard as holy,
he is the one you are to fear,
    he is the one you are to dread,
¹⁴and he will be a sanctuary;
    but for both houses of Israel he will
        be
a stone that causes men to stumble
    and a rock that makes them fall.
And for the people of Jerusalem he
        will be
a trap and a snare.
¹⁵Many of them will stumble;
    they will fall and be broken,
    they will be snared and captured."

¹⁶Bind up the testimony

and seal up the law among my
    disciples.
17I will wait for the LORD,
    who is hiding his face from the
        house of Jacob.
I will put my trust in him.

18Here am I, and the children the LORD
has given me. We are signs and symbols
in Israel from the LORD Almighty, who
dwells on Mount Zion.
19When men tell you to consult mediums and spiritists, who whisper and
mutter, should not a people inquire of
their God? Why consult the dead on behalf of the living? 20To the law and to the
testimony! If they do not speak according
to this word, they have no light of dawn.
21Distressed and hungry, they will roam
through the land; when they are famished, they will become enraged and,
looking upward, will curse their king and
their God. 22Then they will look toward
the earth and see only distress and darkness and fearful gloom, and they will be
thrust into utter darkness.

JULY 16 ☐ DAY 198
ISAIAH 9–12
Judah's Darkness and Dawn

OVERVIEW Chapters 9–12 (along with 7 and 8, which you read yesterday) have been called "The Book of Immanuel" because of the
many prophecies and allusions regarding Messiah:
    He would be born of a virgin (7:14).
    He would be given the name *Immanuel*, "God with us" (7:14).
    He would be a stone that causes Israel to stumble (8:14).
    He would be a great light to the nations (9:2).
    He would be a ruler, counselor and prince (9:6).
    He would come from the line of David (11:1).
Is it any wonder the redeemed gather together for a grand chorus
of praise and worship at the thought of their Immanuel?

Chapter 9	Chapter 10	Chapter 11	Chapter 12
Prince of Peace	Promise of Punishment	Promise of Peace	Postlude of Praise
Exhortation	Explanation		Exaltation

YOUR DAILY WALK Titles can be deceiving.
    A young executive was describing with evident pride his recent pro-
motion to the position of vice president. "Aw, that's nothing," responded a friend. "Vice presidents are a dime a dozen. Why, I'll bet
there's even a vice president of peanuts at the supermarket."

The more you think about Christ, the more you think of him.

    "You're on!" exclaimed the executive, as he dialed the store on the
phone. "May I speak to the vice president of peanuts, please?"
    The reply came back, "Packaged or bulk?"
    By contrast, the titles you will find attributed to Christ are highly
significant! His name will be called "Wonderful Counselor"—and God
alone is "wonderful in counsel and magnificent in wisdom" (28:29). He
is the "Mighty God"—the same term used to describe "the LORD, the
Holy One of Israel" (10:20). Thus, his titles underscore his deity.
    Share with a person today the significance of one of the names of
Jesus. Ask God to open a door of witness through it!

INSIGHT First to Feel the Groan, First to See the Glory
The land of Zebulun and Naphtali—the first region to succumb to the
Assyrian onslaught within months of Isaiah's meeting with Ahaz
(7:1–9)—would also be the first to see the glory of the Lord (9:1–2)
. . . a striking prophecy that went unheeded when the Messiah came
(John 1:46; 7:52).

CHAPTER 9

Nevertheless, there will be no more gloom for those who were in distress. In the past he humbled the land of Zebulun and the land of Naphtali, but in the future he will honor Galilee of the Gentiles, by the way of the sea, along the Jordan—

²The people walking in darkness
　have seen a great light;
on those living in the land of the
　　shadow of death*
　a light has dawned.
³You have enlarged the nation
　and increased their joy;
they rejoice before you
　as people rejoice at the harvest,
as men rejoice
　when dividing the plunder.
⁴For as in the day of Midian's defeat,
　you have shattered
the yoke that burdens them,
　the bar across their shoulders,
　the rod of their oppressor.
⁵Every warrior's boot used in battle
　and every garment rolled in blood
will be destined for burning,
　will be fuel for the fire.
⁶For to us a child is born,
　to us a son is given,
and the government will be on his
　　shoulders.
And he will be called
　Wonderful Counselor,ʸ Mighty
　　God,
　Everlasting Father, Prince of Peace.
⁷Of the increase of his government and
　　peace
there will be no end.
He will reign on David's throne
　and over his kingdom,
establishing and upholding it
　with justice and righteousness
　from that time on and forever.
The zeal of the LORD Almighty
　will accomplish this.

⁸The Lord has sent a message against
　Jacob;
　it will fall on Israel.
⁹All the people will know it—
　Ephraim and the inhabitants of
　　Samaria—
who say with pride
　and arrogance of heart,
¹⁰"The bricks have fallen down,
　but we will rebuild with dressed
　　stone;
the fig trees have been felled,
　but we will replace them with
　　cedars."
¹¹But the LORD has strengthened Rezin's
　　foes against them
　and has spurred their enemies on.
¹²Arameans from the east and Philistines
　　from the west
have devoured Israel with open
　　mouth.

Yet for all this, his anger is not turned
　　away,
　his hand is still upraised.

¹³But the people have not returned to
　　him who struck them,
　nor have they sought the LORD
　　Almighty.
¹⁴So the LORD will cut off from Israel
　　both head and tail,
　both palm branch and reed in a
　　single day;
¹⁵the elders and prominent men are the
　　head,
　the prophets who teach lies are the
　　tail.
¹⁶Those who guide this people mislead
　　them,
　and those who are guided are led
　　astray.
¹⁷Therefore the Lord will take no
　　pleasure in the young men,
　nor will he pity the fatherless and
　　widows,
for everyone is ungodly and wicked,
　every mouth speaks vileness.

Yet for all this, his anger is not turned
　　away,
　his hand is still upraised.

*2 Or *land of darkness*　ʸ6 Or *Wonderful, Counselor*

[18]Surely wickedness burns like a fire;
it consumes briers and thorns,
it sets the forest thickets ablaze,
so that it rolls upward in a column
of smoke.
[19]By the wrath of the LORD Almighty
the land will be scorched
and the people will be fuel for the fire;
no one will spare his brother.
[20]On the right they will devour,
but still be hungry;
on the left they will eat,
but not be satisfied.
Each will feed on the flesh of his own
offspring[z]:
[21] Manasseh will feed on Ephraim, and
Ephraim on Manasseh;
together they will turn against
Judah.

Yet for all this, his anger is not turned
away,
his hand is still upraised.

CHAPTER 10
Woe to those who make unjust laws,
to those who issue oppressive
decrees,
[2]to deprive the poor of their rights
and withhold justice from the
oppressed of my people,
making widows their prey
and robbing the fatherless.
[3]What will you do on the day of
reckoning,
when disaster comes from afar?
To whom will you run for help?
Where will you leave your riches?
[4]Nothing will remain but to cringe
among the captives
or fall among the slain.

Yet for all this, his anger is not turned
away,
his hand is still upraised.

[5]"Woe to the Assyrian, the rod of my
anger,
in whose hand is the club of my
wrath!
[6]I send him against a godless nation,
I dispatch him against a people who
anger me,
to seize loot and snatch plunder,
and to trample them down like mud
in the streets.
[7]But this is not what he intends,

this is not what he has in mind;
his purpose is to destroy,
to put an end to many nations.
[8]'Are not my commanders all kings?'
he says.
[9] 'Has not Calno fared like
Carchemish?
Is not Hamath like Arpad,
and Samaria like Damascus?
[10]As my hand seized the kingdoms of
the idols,
kingdoms whose images excelled
those of Jerusalem and
Samaria—
[11]shall I not deal with Jerusalem and her
images
as I dealt with Samaria and her
idols?' "

[12]When the Lord has finished all his
work against Mount Zion and Jerusalem,
he will say, "I will punish the king of Assyria for the willful pride of his heart and
the haughty look in his eyes. [13]For he
says:

" 'By the strength of my hand I have
done this,
and by my wisdom, because I have
understanding.
I removed the boundaries of nations,
I plundered their treasures;
like a mighty one I subdued[a] their
kings.
[14]As one reaches into a nest,
so my hand reached for the wealth
of the nations;
as men gather abandoned eggs,
so I gathered all the countries;
not one flapped a wing,
or opened its mouth to chirp.' "

[15]Does the ax raise itself above him who
swings it,
or the saw boast against him who
uses it?
As if a rod were to wield him who
lifts it up,
or a club brandish him who is not
wood!
[16]Therefore, the Lord, the LORD
Almighty,
will send a wasting disease upon his
sturdy warriors;
under his pomp a fire will be kindled
like a blazing flame.
[17]The Light of Israel will become a fire,

[z]20 Or arm   [a]13 Or / I subdued the mighty,

their Holy One a flame;
in a single day it will burn and
consume
his thorns and his briers.
[18]The splendor of his forests and fertile
fields
it will completely destroy,
as when a sick man wastes away.
[19]And the remaining trees of his forests
will be so few
that a child could write them down.

[20]In that day the remnant of Israel,
the survivors of the house of Jacob,
will no longer rely on him
who struck them down
but will truly rely on the LORD,
the Holy One of Israel.
[21]A remnant will return,[b] a remnant of
Jacob
will return to the Mighty God.
[22]Though your people, O Israel, be like
the sand by the sea,
only a remnant will return.
Destruction has been decreed,
overwhelming and righteous.
[23]The Lord, the LORD Almighty, will
carry out
the destruction decreed upon the
whole land.

[24]Therefore, this is what the Lord, the
LORD Almighty, says:

"O my people who live in Zion,
do not be afraid of the Assyrians,
who beat you with a rod
and lift up a club against you, as
Egypt did.
[25]Very soon my anger against you will
end
and my wrath will be directed to
their destruction."

[26]The LORD Almighty will lash them
with a whip,
as when he struck down Midian at
the rock of Oreb;
and he will raise his staff over the
waters,
as he did in Egypt.
[27]In that day their burden will be lifted
from your shoulders,
their yoke from your neck;
the yoke will be broken
because you have grown so fat.[c]

[28]They enter Aiath;

they pass through Migron;
they store supplies at Micmash.
[29]They go over the pass, and say,
"We will camp overnight at Geba."
Ramah trembles;
Gibeah of Saul flees.
[30]Cry out, O Daughter of Gallim!
Listen, O Laishah!
Poor Anathoth!
[31]Madmenah is in flight;
the people of Gebim take cover.
[32]This day they will halt at Nob;
they will shake their fist
at the mount of the Daughter of Zion,
at the hill of Jerusalem.

[33]See, the Lord, the LORD Almighty,
will lop off the boughs with great
power.
The lofty trees will be felled,
the tall ones will be brought low.
[34]He will cut down the forest thickets
with an ax;
Lebanon will fall before the Mighty
One.

CHAPTER 11
A shoot will come up from the stump
of Jesse;
from his roots a Branch will bear
fruit.
[2]The Spirit of the LORD will rest on
him—
the Spirit of wisdom and of
understanding,
the Spirit of counsel and of power,
the Spirit of knowledge and of the
fear of the LORD—
[3]and he will delight in the fear of the
LORD.

He will not judge by what he sees
with his eyes,
or decide by what he hears with his
ears;
[4]but with righteousness he will judge
the needy,
with justice he will give decisions
for the poor of the earth.
He will strike the earth with the rod of
his mouth;
with the breath of his lips he will
slay the wicked.
[5]Righteousness will be his belt
and faithfulness the sash around his
waist.

[b]21 Hebrew *shear-jashub*; also in verse 22   [c]27 Hebrew; Septuagint *broken* / *from your shoulders*

6The wolf will live with the lamb,
　　the leopard will lie down with the
　　　goat,
　the calf and the lion and the yearling[d]
　　together;
　and a little child will lead them.
7The cow will feed with the bear,
　　their young will lie down together,
　　and the lion will eat straw like the
　　　ox.
8The infant will play near the hole of
　　the cobra,
　　and the young child put his hand
　　　into the viper's nest.
9They will neither harm nor destroy
　on all my holy mountain,
　for the earth will be full of the
　　knowledge of the LORD
　　　as the waters cover the sea.

10In that day the Root of Jesse will stand
as a banner for the peoples; the nations
will rally to him, and his place of rest will
be glorious. 11In that day the Lord will
reach out his hand a second time to re-
claim the remnant that is left of his people
from Assyria, from Lower Egypt, from
Upper Egypt,[e] from Cush,[f] from Elam,
from Babylonia,[g] from Hamath and from
the islands of the sea.

12He will raise a banner for the nations
　　and gather the exiles of Israel;
　he will assemble the scattered people
　　of Judah
　from the four quarters of the earth.
13Ephraim's jealousy will vanish,
　　and Judah's enemies[h] will be cut
　　　off;
　Ephraim will not be jealous of Judah,
　　nor Judah hostile toward Ephraim.
14They will swoop down on the slopes
　　of Philistia to the west;
　together they will plunder the
　　people to the east.
　They will lay hands on Edom and
　　Moab,

and the Ammonites will be subject
　to them.
15The LORD will dry up
　　the gulf of the Egyptian sea;
　with a scorching wind he will sweep
　　his hand
　　over the Euphrates River.[i]
　He will break it up into seven streams
　　so that men can cross over in
　　　sandals.
16There will be a highway for the
　　remnant of his people
　　that is left from Assyria,
　as there was for Israel
　　when they came up from Egypt.

CHAPTER 12

In that day you will say:

　"I will praise you, O LORD.
　　Although you were angry with me,
　your anger has turned away
　　and you have comforted me.
2Surely God is my salvation;
　　I will trust and not be afraid.
　The LORD, the LORD, is my strength and
　　my song;
　　he has become my salvation."
3With joy you will draw water
　　from the wells of salvation.

4In that day you will say:

　"Give thanks to the LORD, call on his
　　name;
　make known among the nations
　　what he has done,
　　and proclaim that his name is
　　　exalted.
5Sing to the LORD, for he has done
　　glorious things;
　　let this be known to all the world.
6Shout aloud and sing for joy, people of
　　Zion,
　　for great is the Holy One of Israel
　　among you."

d6 Hebrew; Septuagint lion will feed   e11 Hebrew from Pathros   f11 That is, the upper Nile region   g11 Hebrew Shinar
h13 Or hostility   i15 Hebrew the River

JULY 17 ☐ DAY 199
ISAIAH 13–16
Woes on Babylon and Moab

 OVERVIEW God is sovereign over his nation; he is also sovereign over all nations. No empire or tribe on earth is exempt from the judgment of God when wickedness replaces righteousness. Isaiah now turns his verbal missiles upon the Gentile nations, which will melt away before the furnace of God's wrath for their opposition to his people and plan. Babylon is faced with the gloomy prospect of being dominated by the Medes (it happened in 539 B.C.). The cities of Moab can look forward to being sacked (it happened in 701 B.C.). Clearly, wicked kings and kingdoms are no match for the justice and holiness of God.

Chapter 13	Chapter 14	Chapter 15	Chapter 16
The Downfall of Babylon		The Desolation of Moab	
Predicted	Praised	Prophesied	Publicized
Gloom		Doom	

 YOUR DAILY WALK There's something deliciously satisfying about seeing "the other guy" get his just deserts . . . or watching the speeding car ahead of you get pulled over . . . or learning that your obnoxious next-door neighbor is being audited . . . or reading about a corrupt politician landing in jail.

Knowledge humbles great people, astonishes common people and puffs up little people.

But wait! Smugness in the face of another's calamity diminishes when you remember your own shortcomings and imperfections. God in his Word has included the bad with the good, the *condemnation* of nations as well as their *commendation,* that you might profit from their example. The fact that nations such as Babylon and Moab no longer exist should warn you that when God promises punishment for persistent sin, it is no idle threat.

Think of a recent calamity that has befallen someone you know because of his or her inattention to God's Word. How can you save yourself some grief by learning from that example?

 INSIGHT Tomorrow's Headlines Prophesied Today
The gist of Isaiah's prophecy regarding Babylon is this: Media would supersede Babylon (13:17); and Babylon would disappear forever (13:19–22). Historically, Babylon conquered Assyria in 607 B.C. and fell to Medo-Persian armies in 538 B.C.

CHAPTER 13

An oracle concerning Babylon that Isaiah son of Amoz saw:

²Raise a banner on a bare hilltop,
shout to them;
beckon to them
to enter the gates of the nobles.
³I have commanded my holy ones;
I have summoned my warriors to
carry out my wrath—
those who rejoice in my triumph.

⁴Listen, a noise on the mountains,
like that of a great multitude!
Listen, an uproar among the
kingdoms,
like nations massing together!
The LORD Almighty is mustering
an army for war.
⁵They come from faraway lands,
from the ends of the heavens—
the LORD and the weapons of his
wrath—
to destroy the whole country.

⁶Wail, for the day of the LORD is
near;

it will come like destruction from
the Almighty.*ʲ*

⁷Because of this, all hands will go limp,
every man's heart will melt.

⁸Terror will seize them,
pain and anguish will grip them;
they will writhe like a woman in
labor.
They will look aghast at each other,
their faces aflame.

⁹See, the day of the LORD is coming
—a cruel day, with wrath and fierce
anger—
to make the land desolate
and destroy the sinners within it.

¹⁰The stars of heaven and their
constellations
will not show their light.
The rising sun will be darkened
and the moon will not give its light.

¹¹I will punish the world for its evil,
the wicked for their sins.
I will put an end to the arrogance of
the haughty
and will humble the pride of the
ruthless.

¹²I will make man scarcer than pure
gold,
more rare than the gold of Ophir.

¹³Therefore I will make the heavens
tremble;
and the earth will shake from its
place
at the wrath of the LORD Almighty,
in the day of his burning anger.

¹⁴Like a hunted gazelle,
like sheep without a shepherd,
each will return to his own people,
each will flee to his native land.

¹⁵Whoever is captured will be thrust
through;
all who are caught will fall by the
sword.

¹⁶Their infants will be dashed to pieces
before their eyes;
their houses will be looted and their
wives ravished.

¹⁷See, I will stir up against them the
Medes,
who do not care for silver
and have no delight in gold.

¹⁸Their bows will strike down the young
men;

they will have no mercy on infants
nor will they look with compassion
on children.

¹⁹Babylon, the jewel of kingdoms,
the glory of the Babylonians'*ᵏ*
pride,
will be overthrown by God
like Sodom and Gomorrah.

²⁰She will never be inhabited
or lived in through all generations;
no Arab will pitch his tent there,
no shepherd will rest his flocks
there.

²¹But desert creatures will lie there,
jackals will fill her houses;
there the owls will dwell,
and there the wild goats will leap
about.

²²Hyenas will howl in her strongholds,
jackals in her luxurious palaces.
Her time is at hand,
and her days will not be prolonged.

CHAPTER 14

The LORD will have compassion on
Jacob;
once again he will choose Israel
and will settle them in their own
land.
Aliens will join them
and unite with the house of Jacob.

²Nations will take them
and bring them to their own place.
And the house of Israel will possess
the nations
as menservants and maidservants in
the LORD's land.
They will make captives of their
captors
and rule over their oppressors.

³On the day the LORD gives you relief
from suffering and turmoil and cruel
bondage, ⁴you will take up this taunt
against the king of Babylon:

How the oppressor has come to an
end!
How his fury*ˡ* has ended!

⁵The LORD has broken the rod of the
wicked,
the scepter of the rulers,

⁶which in anger struck down peoples
with unceasing blows,
and in fury subdued nations
with relentless aggression.

ʲ6 Hebrew *Shaddai*   *ᵏ19* Or *Chaldeans'*   *ˡ4* Dead Sea Scrolls, Septuagint and Syriac; the meaning of the word in the
Masoretic Text is uncertain.

⁷All the lands are at rest and at peace;
  they break into singing.
⁸Even the pine trees and the cedars of
    Lebanon
  exult over you and say,
  "Now that you have been laid low,
  no woodsman comes to cut us
    down."

⁹The grave*ᵐ* below is all astir
  to meet you at your coming;
it rouses the spirits of the departed to
    greet you—
  all those who were leaders in the
    world;
it makes them rise from their thrones—
  all those who were kings over the
    nations.
¹⁰They will all respond,
  they will say to you,
  "You also have become weak, as we
    are;
  you have become like us."
¹¹All your pomp has been brought
    down to the grave,
  along with the noise of your harps;
maggots are spread out beneath you
  and worms cover you.

¹²How you have fallen from heaven,
  O morning star, son of the dawn!
You have been cast down to the earth,
  you who once laid low the nations!
¹³You said in your heart,
  "I will ascend to heaven;
I will raise my throne
  above the stars of God;
I will sit enthroned on the mount of
    assembly,
  on the utmost heights of the sacred
    mountain.*ⁿ*
¹⁴I will ascend above the tops of the
    clouds;
  I will make myself like the Most
    High."
¹⁵But you are brought down to the
    grave,
  to the depths of the pit.

¹⁶Those who see you stare at you,
  they ponder your fate:
  "Is this the man who shook the earth
  and made kingdoms tremble,
¹⁷the man who made the world a desert,
  who overthrew its cities
  and would not let his captives go
    home?"

¹⁸All the kings of the nations lie in state,
  each in his own tomb.
¹⁹But you are cast out of your tomb
  like a rejected branch;
you are covered with the slain,
  with those pierced by the sword,
  those who descend to the stones of
    the pit.
Like a corpse trampled underfoot,
²⁰ you will not join them in burial,
for you have destroyed your land
  and killed your people.

The offspring of the wicked
  will never be mentioned again.
²¹Prepare a place to slaughter his sons
  for the sins of their forefathers;
they are not to rise to inherit the land
  and cover the earth with their cities.

²²"I will rise up against them,"
  declares the LORD Almighty.
"I will cut off from Babylon her name
    and survivors,
  her offspring and descendants,"
                   declares the LORD.
²³"I will turn her into a place for owls
    and into swampland;
I will sweep her with the broom of
    destruction,"
  declares the LORD Almighty.

²⁴The LORD Almighty has sworn,

"Surely, as I have planned, so it will
    be,
  and as I have purposed, so it will
    stand.
²⁵I will crush the Assyrian in my land;
  on my mountains I will trample him
    down.
His yoke will be taken from my
    people,
  and his burden removed from their
    shoulders."
²⁶This is the plan determined for the
    whole world;
  this is the hand stretched out over
    all nations.
²⁷For the LORD Almighty has purposed,
    and who can thwart him?
  His hand is stretched out, and who
    can turn it back?

²⁸This oracle came in the year King
Ahaz died:

²⁹Do not rejoice, all you Philistines,

ᵐ9 Hebrew *Sheol*; also in verses 11 and 15   *ⁿ13* Or *the north*; Hebrew *Zaphon*

that the rod that struck you is
broken;
from the root of that snake will spring
up a viper,
its fruit will be a darting, venomous
serpent.
30The poorest of the poor will find
pasture,
and the needy will lie down in
safety.
But your root I will destroy by famine;
it will slay your survivors.

31Wail, O gate! Howl, O city!
Melt away, all you Philistines!
A cloud of smoke comes from the
north,
and there is not a straggler in its
ranks.
32What answer shall be given
to the envoys of that nation?
"The LORD has established Zion,
and in her his afflicted people will
find refuge."

CHAPTER 15

An oracle concerning Moab:

Ar in Moab is ruined,
destroyed in a night!
Kir in Moab is ruined,
destroyed in a night!
2Dibon goes up to its temple,
to its high places to weep;
Moab wails over Nebo and Medeba.
Every head is shaved
and every beard cut off.
3In the streets they wear sackcloth;
on the roofs and in the public
squares
they all wail,
prostrate with weeping.
4Heshbon and Elealeh cry out,
their voices are heard all the way to
Jahaz.
Therefore the armed men of Moab cry
out,
and their hearts are faint.

5My heart cries out over Moab;
her fugitives flee as far as Zoar,
as far as Eglath Shelishiyah.
They go up the way to Luhith,
weeping as they go;
on the road to Horonaim
they lament their destruction.
6The waters of Nimrim are dried up

and the grass is withered;
the vegetation is gone
and nothing green is left.
7So the wealth they have acquired and
stored up
they carry away over the Ravine of
the Poplars.
8Their outcry echoes along the border
of Moab;
their wailing reaches as far as
Eglaim,
their lamentation as far as Beer Elim.
9Dimon's[o] waters are full of blood,
but I will bring still more upon
Dimon[o]—
a lion upon the fugitives of Moab
and upon those who remain in the
land.

CHAPTER 16

Send lambs as tribute
to the ruler of the land,
from Sela, across the desert,
to the mount of the Daughter of
Zion.
2Like fluttering birds
pushed from the nest,
so are the women of Moab
at the fords of the Arnon.

3"Give us counsel,
render a decision.
Make your shadow like night—
at high noon.
Hide the fugitives,
do not betray the refugees.
4Let the Moabite fugitives stay with
you;
be their shelter from the destroyer."

The oppressor will come to an end,
and destruction will cease;
the aggressor will vanish from the
land.
5In love a throne will be established;
in faithfulness a man will sit on it—
one from the house[p] of David—
one who in judging seeks justice
and speeds the cause of
righteousness.

6We have heard of Moab's pride—
her overweening pride and conceit,
her pride and her insolence—
but her boasts are empty.
7Therefore the Moabites wail,
they wail together for Moab.

o9 Masoretic Text; Dead Sea Scrolls, some Septuagint manuscripts and Vulgate Dibon   p5 Hebrew tent

Lament and grieve
for the men⁹ of Kir Hareseth.
⁸The fields of Heshbon wither,
the vines of Sibmah also.
The rulers of the nations
have trampled down the choicest
vines,
which once reached Jazer
and spread toward the desert.
Their shoots spread out
and went as far as the sea.
⁹So I weep, as Jazer weeps,
for the vines of Sibmah.
O Heshbon, O Elealeh,
I drench you with tears!
The shouts of joy over your ripened
fruit
and over your harvests have been
stilled.
¹⁰Joy and gladness are taken away from
the orchards;

⁹7 Or *"raisin cakes,"* a wordplay

no one sings or shouts in the
vineyards;
no one treads out wine at the presses,
for I have put an end to the
shouting.
¹¹My heart laments for Moab like a
harp,
my inmost being for Kir Hareseth.
¹²When Moab appears at her high
place,
she only wears herself out;
when she goes to her shrine to pray,
it is to no avail.

¹³This is the word the LORD has already
spoken concerning Moab. ¹⁴But now the
LORD says: "Within three years, as a servant bound by contract would count
them, Moab's splendor and all her many
people will be despised, and her survivors will be very few and feeble."

JULY 18 □ DAY 200
ISAIAH 17–20
Collapse from Corruption

OVERVIEW Damascus, Cush and Egypt are next to feel the hot blast
of Isaiah's burdens of judgment. The glory of Damascus would be removed, leaving behind leanness of body and soul. But a handful
would repent and—like the gleanings from an olive tree—provide hope
for a future harvest. Cush, though tall in stature and smooth of skin,
would be pruned away like branches and one day return to Zion to
pay homage to God and acknowledge him as her Sovereign. Egypt
would experience civil war, economic ruin and spiritual poverty,
showing the bankruptcy of Egypt's false gods. But one day the Lord
Almighty would declare, "Blessed be Egypt my people" (19:25).

Chapter 17	Chapter 18	Chapter 19	Chapter 20
Doom for Damascus	Cutting Off Cush	Infamy for Egypt	Enemies for Egypt
Removal		Reproof	

YOUR DAILY WALK The courtroom scene unfolds as it has countless
times before.
The case is presented; the jury recesses; a verdict is reached: Guilty!
But then the trial takes an unexpected twist. The presiding judge also
happens to be the father of the convicted criminal. And just before his
son reaches the bar, where the fine is to be assessed, the judge steps
down from his seat, takes off his robe and approaches the bar to pay
the fine for his guilty son. Justice . . . and mercy!

Mercy without justice becomes unmerciful; justice without mercy, unjust.

That story illustrates a divine truth. The judge would not have been just if he had allowed his son to go free. But his love caused him to take his son's place in paying the fine. The same is true about God. He would not be just if he ignored the sins committed against him. At the same time, his great love shines forth in the gift of his Son to pay the price for humanity's sins.

Isaiah 14:1–8 is a message of mercy inserted between many dark chapters of judgment. God is just, but he is also loving toward all who trust him. In his love he has provided the answer to humanity's sin problem (11:10)—a Savior. What is your answer to him today?

 INSIGHT Old Testament POWs

As part of his judgment on Egypt, God instructed Isaiah to dress like a prisoner of war—unclothed and barefoot—for three years as a sign of the calamity God was going to bring on Egypt (20:1–4).

CHAPTER 17

An oracle concerning Damascus:

"See, Damascus will no longer be a city
but will become a heap of ruins.
²The cities of Aroer will be deserted
and left to flocks, which will lie down,
with no one to make them afraid.
³The fortified city will disappear from Ephraim,
and royal power from Damascus;
the remnant of Aram will be
like the glory of the Israelites,"
declares the LORD Almighty.

⁴"In that day the glory of Jacob will fade;
the fat of his body will waste away.
⁵It will be as when a reaper gathers the standing grain
and harvests the grain with his arm—
as when a man gleans heads of grain
in the Valley of Rephaim.
⁶Yet some gleanings will remain,
as when an olive tree is beaten,
leaving two or three olives on the topmost branches,
four or five on the fruitful boughs,"
declares the LORD, the God of Israel.

⁷In that day men will look to their Maker
and turn their eyes to the Holy One of Israel.
⁸They will not look to the altars,
the work of their hands,

and they will have no regard for the Asherah poles ʳ
and the incense altars their fingers have made.

⁹In that day their strong cities, which they left because of the Israelites, will be like places abandoned to thickets and undergrowth. And all will be desolation.

¹⁰You have forgotten God your Savior;
you have not remembered the Rock, your fortress.
Therefore, though you set out the finest plants
and plant imported vines,
¹¹though on the day you set them out, you make them grow,
and on the morning when you plant them, you bring them to bud,
yet the harvest will be as nothing
in the day of disease and incurable pain.

¹²Oh, the raging of many nations—
they rage like the raging sea!
Oh, the uproar of the peoples—
they roar like the roaring of great waters!
¹³Although the peoples roar like the roar of surging waters,
when he rebukes them they flee far away,
driven before the wind like chaff on the hills,
like tumbleweed before a gale.
¹⁴In the evening, sudden terror!
Before the morning, they are gone!
This is the portion of those who loot us,
the lot of those who plunder us.

ʳ8 That is, symbols of the goddess Asherah

CHAPTER 18

Woe to the land of whirring wings[s]
  along the rivers of Cush,[t]
[2]which sends envoys by sea
  in papyrus boats over the water.

Go, swift messengers,
  to a people tall and smooth-skinned,
  to a people feared far and wide,
an aggressive nation of strange speech,
  whose land is divided by rivers.

[3]All you people of the world,
  you who live on the earth,
when a banner is raised on the
      mountains,
  you will see it,
and when a trumpet sounds,
  you will hear it.
[4]This is what the LORD says to me:
  "I will remain quiet and will look on
      from my dwelling place,
like shimmering heat in the sunshine,
  like a cloud of dew in the heat of
      harvest."
[5]For, before the harvest, when the
      blossom is gone
  and the flower becomes a ripening
      grape,
he will cut off the shoots with pruning
      knives,
  and cut down and take away the
      spreading branches.
[6]They will all be left to the mountain
      birds of prey
  and to the wild animals;
the birds will feed on them all
      summer,
  the wild animals all winter.

[7]At that time gifts will be brought to the
LORD Almighty

from a people tall and
      smooth-skinned,
  from a people feared far and wide,
an aggressive nation of strange speech,
  whose land is divided by rivers—

the gifts will be brought to Mount Zion,
the place of the Name of the LORD Almighty.

CHAPTER 19

An oracle concerning Egypt:

See, the LORD rides on a swift cloud
  and is coming to Egypt.

The idols of Egypt tremble before him,
  and the hearts of the Egyptians melt
      within them.
[2]"I will stir up Egyptian against
      Egyptian—
  brother will fight against brother,
  neighbor against neighbor,
  city against city,
  kingdom against kingdom.
[3]The Egyptians will lose heart,
  and I will bring their plans to
      nothing;
they will consult the idols and the
      spirits of the dead,
  the mediums and the spiritists.
[4]I will hand the Egyptians over
  to the power of a cruel master,
and a fierce king will rule over them,"
  declares the Lord, the LORD
      Almighty.

[5]The waters of the river will dry up,
  and the riverbed will be parched
      and dry.
[6]The canals will stink;
  the streams of Egypt will dwindle
      and dry up.
The reeds and rushes will wither,
[7] also the plants along the Nile,
  at the mouth of the river.
Every sown field along the Nile
  will become parched, will blow
      away and be no more.
[8]The fishermen will groan and lament,
  all who cast hooks into the Nile;
those who throw nets on the water
  will pine away.
[9]Those who work with combed flax
      will despair,
  the weavers of fine linen will lose
      hope.
[10]The workers in cloth will be dejected,
  and all the wage earners will be sick
      at heart.

[11]The officials of Zoan are nothing but
      fools;
  the wise counselors of Pharaoh give
      senseless advice.
How can you say to Pharaoh,
  "I am one of the wise men,
  a disciple of the ancient kings"?

[12]Where are your wise men now?
  Let them show you and make
      known

---

[s]1 Or of locusts   [t]1 That is, the upper Nile region

what the LORD Almighty
has planned against Egypt.
¹³The officials of Zoan have become
fools,
the leaders of Memphis ᵘ are
deceived;
the cornerstones of her peoples
have led Egypt astray.
¹⁴The LORD has poured into them
a spirit of dizziness;
they make Egypt stagger in all that she
does,
as a drunkard staggers around in his
vomit.
¹⁵There is nothing Egypt can do—
head or tail, palm branch or reed.

¹⁶In that day the Egyptians will be like
women. They will shudder with fear at
the uplifted hand that the LORD Almighty
raises against them. ¹⁷And the land of Judah will bring terror to the Egyptians; everyone to whom Judah is mentioned will
be terrified, because of what the LORD Almighty is planning against them.

¹⁸In that day five cities in Egypt will
speak the language of Canaan and swear
allegiance to the LORD Almighty. One of
them will be called the City of Destruc-
tion.ᵛ

¹⁹In that day there will be an altar to the
LORD in the heart of Egypt, and a monument to the LORD at its border. ²⁰It will be
a sign and witness to the LORD Almighty
in the land of Egypt. When they cry out to
the LORD because of their oppressors, he
will send them a savior and defender, and
he will rescue them. ²¹So the LORD will
make himself known to the Egyptians,
and in that day they will acknowledge the
LORD. They will worship with sacrifices
and grain offerings; they will make vows

to the LORD and keep them. ²²The LORD
will strike Egypt with a plague; he will
strike them and heal them. They will turn
to the LORD, and he will respond to their
pleas and heal them.

²³In that day there will be a highway
from Egypt to Assyria. The Assyrians will
go to Egypt and the Egyptians to Assyria.
The Egyptians and Assyrians will worship together. ²⁴In that day Israel will be
the third, along with Egypt and Assyria,
a blessing on the earth. ²⁵The LORD Almighty will bless them, saying, "Blessed
be Egypt my people, Assyria my handi-
work, and Israel my inheritance."

CHAPTER 20
In the year that the supreme commander,
sent by Sargon king of Assyria, came to
Ashdod and attacked and captured it—
²at that time the LORD spoke through Isaiah son of Amoz. He said to him, "Take off
the sackcloth from your body and the
sandals from your feet." And he did so,
going around stripped and barefoot.

³Then the LORD said, "Just as my servant
Isaiah has gone stripped and barefoot for
three years, as a sign and portent against
Egypt and Cush,ʷ ⁴so the king of Assyria
will lead away stripped and barefoot the
Egyptian captives and Cushite exiles,
young and old, with buttocks bared—to
Egypt's shame. ⁵Those who trusted in
Cush and boasted in Egypt will be afraid
and put to shame. ⁶In that day the people
who live on this coast will say, 'See what
has happened to those we relied on, those
we fled to for help and deliverance from
the king of Assyria! How then can we escape?'"

ᵘ13 Hebrew *Noph*   ᵛ18 Most manuscripts of the Masoretic Text; some manuscripts of the Masoretic Text, Dead Sea Scrolls
and Vulgate *City of the Sun* (that is, Heliopolis)   ʷ3 That is, the upper Nile region; also in verse 5

JULY 19 □ DAY 201
ISAIAH 21–23
Judgment Near and Far

OVERVIEW Isaiah is not finished yet with his woes for Judah's foes. In
today's reading he mentions two more neighboring powers that are in
line for God's chastening hand: Arabia and Tyre. But in the midst of
his list of "endangered nations," Isaiah shocks his countrymen by

including Jerusalem with the rest. Because of the careless indulgence of its inhabitants, the city would suffer siege and destruction.

Chapter 21	Chapter 22	Chapter 23
Down with Idolatry	Down with Insensitivity	Down with Pride
Arabia	Jerusalem	Tyre

YOUR DAILY WALK Have you ever wondered why you can feel so convicted *after* you sin but remain so indifferent *before* you sin? If there were only a way for you to reverse these conditions—to feel as remorseful before as you do after you disobey God—temptation would surely be easier to resist.

Sin is the womb of our sorrows and the grave of our comforts.

Well, God's verbal warnings are designed to do precisely that! He sent his prophets to paint in grim, unmistakable tones the calamity awaiting his people if they continued in their wicked ways. Pestilence, plague, defeat in battle, destruction of home and family—all these and more would be the wages they would richly deserve for their sin. Harsh prophecies of national catastrophe were designed by God to deter his people's mad dash for power and prestige at the expense of righteousness and justice. The pain of hearing about these promised calamities was God's way of breaking down indifference and bringing his people to the point of repentance.

If the specific wages of specific sins were revealed to you ahead of time, would you be as eager to earn them? Find a canceled payroll statement and on it write these words: "Is sin worth the pain it brings?" Leave those words in your billfold or purse as a reminder of the high price of unholy living—wages you can't afford to earn!

INSIGHT A Nickname That Makes Sense
The "Valley of Vision" (22:1) refers to Jerusalem, an apt description because the hill on which Jerusalem is situated is surrounded by valleys, with higher hills beyond. In addition, the temple in Jerusalem was the place where God was "visible" to his people.

CHAPTER 21

An oracle concerning the Desert by the Sea:

Like whirlwinds sweeping through the
southland,
an invader comes from the desert,
from a land of terror.

²A dire vision has been shown to me:
The traitor betrays, the looter takes
loot.
Elam, attack! Media, lay siege!
I will bring to an end all the
groaning she caused.

³At this my body is racked with pain,
pangs seize me, like those of a
woman in labor;
I am staggered by what I hear,
I am bewildered by what I see.
⁴My heart falters,

fear makes me tremble;
the twilight I longed for
has become a horror to me.

⁵They set the tables,
they spread the rugs,
they eat, they drink!
Get up, you officers,
oil the shields!

⁶This is what the Lord says to me:

"Go, post a lookout
and have him report what he sees.
⁷When he sees chariots
with teams of horses,
riders on donkeys
or riders on camels,
let him be alert,
fully alert."

⁸And the lookoutˣ shouted,

ˣ8 Dead Sea Scrolls and Syriac; Masoretic Text *A lion*

"Day after day, my lord, I stand on the
watchtower;
every night I stay at my post.
⁹Look, here comes a man in a chariot
with a team of horses.
And he gives back the answer:
'Babylon has fallen, has fallen!
All the images of its gods
lie shattered on the ground!' "

¹⁰O my people, crushed on the threshing
floor,
I tell you what I have heard
from the LORD Almighty,
from the God of Israel.

¹¹An oracle concerning Dumahʸ:

Someone calls to me from Seir,
"Watchman, what is left of the
night?
Watchman, what is left of the
night?"
¹²The watchman replies,
"Morning is coming, but also the
night.
If you would ask, then ask;
and come back yet again."

¹³An oracle concerning Arabia:

You caravans of Dedanites,
who camp in the thickets of Arabia,
14   bring water for the thirsty;
you who live in Tema,
bring food for the fugitives.
¹⁵They flee from the sword,
from the drawn sword,
from the bent bow
and from the heat of battle.

¹⁶This is what the Lord says to me:
"Within one year, as a servant bound by
contract would count it, all the pomp of
Kedar will come to an end. ¹⁷The survivors of the bowmen, the warriors of Kedar, will be few." The LORD, the God of
Israel, has spoken.

CHAPTER 22
An oracle concerning the Valley of Vision:

What troubles you now,
that you have all gone up on the
roofs,
²O town full of commotion,
O city of tumult and revelry?
Your slain were not killed by the
sword,

nor did they die in battle.
³All your leaders have fled together;
they have been captured without
using the bow.
All you who were caught were taken
prisoner together,
having fled while the enemy was
still far away.
⁴Therefore I said, "Turn away from me;
let me weep bitterly.
Do not try to console me
over the destruction of my people."

⁵The Lord, the LORD Almighty, has a
day
of tumult and trampling and terror
in the Valley of Vision,
a day of battering down walls
and of crying out to the mountains.
⁶Elam takes up the quiver,
with her charioteers and horses;
Kir uncovers the shield.
⁷Your choicest valleys are full of
chariots,
and horsemen are posted at the city
gates;
8   the defenses of Judah are stripped
away.

And you looked in that day
to the weapons in the Palace of the
Forest;
⁹you saw that the City of David
had many breaches in its defenses;
you stored up water
in the Lower Pool.
¹⁰You counted the buildings in
Jerusalem
and tore down houses to strengthen
the wall.
¹¹You built a reservoir between the two
walls
for the water of the Old Pool,
but you did not look to the One who
made it,
or have regard for the One who
planned it long ago.

¹²The Lord, the LORD Almighty,
called you on that day
to weep and to wail,
to tear out your hair and put on
sackcloth.
¹³But see, there is joy and revelry,
slaughtering of cattle and killing of
sheep,
eating of meat and drinking of wine!

ʸ11 Dumah means *silence* or *stillness*, a wordplay on *Edom*.

"Let us eat and drink," you say,
"for tomorrow we die!"

[14]The LORD Almighty has revealed this in my hearing: "Till your dying day this sin will not be atoned for," says the Lord, the LORD Almighty.

[15]This is what the Lord, the LORD Almighty, says:

"Go, say to this steward,
  to Shebna, who is in charge of the
    palace:
[16]What are you doing here and who
    gave you permission
  to cut out a grave for yourself here,
hewing your grave on the height
  and chiseling your resting place in
    the rock?

[17]"Beware, the LORD is about to take firm
    hold of you
  and hurl you away, O you mighty
    man.
[18]He will roll you up tightly like a ball
  and throw you into a large country.
There you will die
  and there your splendid chariots
    will remain—
  you disgrace to your master's house!
[19]I will depose you from your office,
  and you will be ousted from your
    position.

[20]"In that day I will summon my servant, Eliakim son of Hilkiah. [21]I will clothe him with your robe and fasten your sash around him and hand your authority over to him. He will be a father to those who live in Jerusalem and to the house of Judah. [22]I will place on his shoulder the key to the house of David; what he opens no one can shut, and what he shuts no one can open. [23]I will drive him like a peg into a firm place; he will be a seat[z] of honor for the house of his father. [24]All the glory of his family will hang on him: its offspring and offshoots—all its lesser vessels, from the bowls to all the jars.

[25]"In that day," declares the LORD Almighty, "the peg driven into the firm place will give way; it will be sheared off and will fall, and the load hanging on it will be cut down." The LORD has spoken.

CHAPTER 23
An oracle concerning Tyre:

Wail, O ships of Tarshish!
  For Tyre is destroyed
  and left without house or harbor.
From the land of Cyprus[a]
  word has come to them.

[2]Be silent, you people of the island
  and you merchants of Sidon,
  whom the seafarers have enriched.
[3]On the great waters
  came the grain of the Shihor;
the harvest of the Nile[b] was the
    revenue of Tyre,
  and she became the marketplace of
    the nations.

[4]Be ashamed, O Sidon, and you,
    O fortress of the sea,
  for the sea has spoken:
"I have neither been in labor nor given
    birth;
  I have neither reared sons nor
    brought up daughters."
[5]When word comes to Egypt,
  they will be in anguish at the report
    from Tyre.

[6]Cross over to Tarshish;
  wail, you people of the island.
[7]Is this your city of revelry,
  the old, old city,
whose feet have taken her
  to settle in far-off lands?
[8]Who planned this against Tyre,
  the bestower of crowns,
whose merchants are princes,
  whose traders are renowned in the
    earth?
[9]The LORD Almighty planned it,
  to bring low the pride of all glory
  and to humble all who are
    renowned on the earth.

[10]Till[c] your land as along the Nile,
    O Daughter of Tarshish,
  for you no longer have a harbor.
[11]The LORD has stretched out his hand
    over the sea
  and made its kingdoms tremble.
He has given an order concerning
    Phoenicia[d]
  that her fortresses be destroyed.
[12]He said, "No more of your reveling,

---

[z]23 Or *throne*   [a]1 Hebrew *Kittim*   [b]2,3 Masoretic Text; one Dead Sea Scroll *Sidon, / who cross over the sea; / your envoys* [3]*are on the great waters. / The grain of the Shihor, / the harvest of the Nile,*   [c]10 Dead Sea Scrolls and some Septuagint manuscripts; Masoretic Text *Go through*   [d]11 Hebrew *Canaan*

O Virgin Daughter of Sidon, now
  crushed!

"Up, cross over to Cyprus*;*
  even there you will find no rest."
¹³Look at the land of the Babylonians,*ᶠ*
  this people that is now of no
    account!
The Assyrians have made it
  a place for desert creatures;
they raised up their siege towers,
  they stripped its fortresses bare
  and turned it into a ruin.

¹⁴Wail, you ships of Tarshish;
  your fortress is destroyed!

¹⁵At that time Tyre will be forgotten for
seventy years, the span of a king's life.
But at the end of these seventy years, it

e12 Hebrew Kittim   f13 Or Chaldeans

will happen to Tyre as in the song of the
prostitute:

¹⁶"Take up a harp, walk through the
    city,
  O prostitute forgotten;
play the harp well, sing many a song,
  so that you will be remembered."

¹⁷At the end of seventy years, the LORD
will deal with Tyre. She will return to her
hire as a prostitute and will ply her trade
with all the kingdoms on the face of the
earth. ¹⁸Yet her profit and her earnings
will be set apart for the LORD; they will not
be stored up or hoarded. Her profits will
go to those who live before the LORD, for
abundant food and fine clothes.

JULY 20 ☐ DAY 202
ISAIAH 24–27
Judgment and Jubilation

OVERVIEW After eleven chapters of pronouncements upon specific
nations, Isaiah's focus changes. There is coming a day when the entire
earth will reel in judgment, its inhabitants quaking in terror and dismay. But the redeemed of the Lord will welcome that day and sing
hymns of praise to the God of their salvation. "Surely this is our God;
we trusted in him, and he saved us. This is the LORD, we trusted in
him; let us rejoice and be glad in his salvation" (25:9). While the nations of the world writhe in judgment, Israel enjoys the benefits of
peace and prosperity.

Chapter 24	Chapter 25	Chapter 26	Chapter 27
Day of the Lord	Devotion to the Lord	Delight in the Lord	Deliverance from the Lord
Reeling	Rejoicing	Singing	Saving

YOUR DAILY WALK During a violent thunderstorm, a mother tiptoed
upstairs to her young son's bedroom, assuming he would need comfort from his fears. She found him kneeling by his bed talking to
God—not in fear but in excitement. With each new flash of lightning,
the mother heard her son exclaim, "Do it again, God! Do it again!"

You cannot have a holy country until you first have holy citizens.

In the midst of God's prophecy of a "thunderstorm" of judgment
upon Israel and the surrounding nations, Isaiah pauses to praise God
for his promise to overthrow the wicked ("Do it again, God!"). Isaiah
knew it was meaningless to speak of judgment for sin on a national
scale and ignore the fact that nations are made up of individuals, for
to have a holy country, you must first have holy citizens.

Spend a few extra minutes today pondering chapter 26, Isaiah's hymn of praise for God's power "to punish the people of the earth for their sins" (26:21). And if you feel an uncomfortable pinching sensation as you read, maybe God is trying to speak to you!

INSIGHT There's Coming a Day
Isaiah 24–27 has been called "Isaiah's Apocalypse" because of the similarity of these chapters to the New Testament book of Revelation. One way Isaiah indicates he is prophesying is by using the phrase *in that day*. It occurs forty-two times in the book as a whole; how many times can you find it in today's section? (Hint: Begin with the first verses of Isaiah 26 and 27.)

CHAPTER 24

See, the LORD is going to lay waste the
  earth
  and devastate it;
he will ruin its face
  and scatter its inhabitants—
²it will be the same
  for priest as for people,
  for master as for servant,
  for mistress as for maid,
  for seller as for buyer,
  for borrower as for lender,
  for debtor as for creditor.
³The earth will be completely laid
  waste
  and totally plundered.
    The LORD has spoken this word.

⁴The earth dries up and withers,
  the world languishes and withers,
  the exalted of the earth languish.
⁵The earth is defiled by its people;
  they have disobeyed the laws,
violated the statutes
  and broken the everlasting covenant.
⁶Therefore a curse consumes the earth;
  its people must bear their guilt.
Therefore earth's inhabitants are
  burned up,
  and very few are left.
⁷The new wine dries up and the vine
  withers;
  all the merrymakers groan.
⁸The gaiety of the tambourines is
  stilled,
  the noise of the revelers has
  stopped,
  the joyful harp is silent.
⁹No longer do they drink wine with a
  song;
  the beer is bitter to its drinkers.
¹⁰The ruined city lies desolate;
  the entrance to every house is
  barred.
¹¹In the streets they cry out for wine;

all joy turns to gloom,
  all gaiety is banished from the earth.
¹²The city is left in ruins,
  its gate is battered to pieces.
¹³So will it be on the earth
  and among the nations,
  as when an olive tree is beaten,
  or as when gleanings are left after
    the grape harvest.

¹⁴They raise their voices, they shout for
  joy;
  from the west they acclaim the
    LORD's majesty.
¹⁵Therefore in the east give glory to the
  LORD;
  exalt the name of the LORD, the God
    of Israel,
  in the islands of the sea.
¹⁶From the ends of the earth we hear
  singing:
  "Glory to the Righteous One."

But I said, "I waste away, I waste
  away!
  Woe to me!
The treacherous betray!
  With treachery the treacherous
    betray!"
¹⁷Terror and pit and snare await you,
  O people of the earth.
¹⁸Whoever flees at the sound of terror
  will fall into a pit;
  whoever climbs out of the pit
  will be caught in a snare.

The floodgates of the heavens are
  opened,
  the foundations of the earth shake.
¹⁹The earth is broken up,
  the earth is split asunder,
  the earth is thoroughly shaken.
²⁰The earth reels like a drunkard,
  it sways like a hut in the wind;

so heavy upon it is the guilt of its
  rebellion
    that it falls—never to rise again.

²¹In that day the LORD will punish
  the powers in the heavens above
  and the kings on the earth below.
²²They will be herded together
  like prisoners bound in a dungeon;
  they will be shut up in prison
  and be punished⁸ after many days.
²³The moon will be abashed, the sun
    ashamed;
  for the LORD Almighty will reign
  on Mount Zion and in Jerusalem,
    and before its elders, gloriously.

CHAPTER 25
  O LORD, you are my God;
  I will exalt you and praise your
    name,
  for in perfect faithfulness
    you have done marvelous things,
    things planned long ago.
²You have made the city a heap of
    rubble,
  the fortified town a ruin,
  the foreigners' stronghold a city no
    more;
  it will never be rebuilt.
³Therefore strong peoples will honor
    you;
  cities of ruthless nations will revere
    you.
⁴You have been a refuge for the poor,
  a refuge for the needy in his
    distress,
  a shelter from the storm
  and a shade from the heat.
For the breath of the ruthless
  is like a storm driving against a wall
⁵ and like the heat of the desert.
  You silence the uproar of foreigners;
  as heat is reduced by the shadow of
    a cloud,
  so the song of the ruthless is stilled.

⁶On this mountain the LORD Almighty
    will prepare
  a feast of rich food for all peoples,
  a banquet of aged wine—
    the best of meats and the finest of
    wines.
⁷On this mountain he will destroy
  the shroud that enfolds all peoples,
  the sheet that covers all nations;

⁸ he will swallow up death forever.
The Sovereign LORD will wipe away
    the tears
  from all faces;
he will remove the disgrace of his
    people
  from all the earth.
                    The LORD has spoken.

⁹In that day they will say,

"Surely this is our God;
  we trusted in him, and he saved us.
This is the LORD, we trusted in him;
  let us rejoice and be glad in his
    salvation."

¹⁰The hand of the LORD will rest on this
    mountain;
  but Moab will be trampled under
    him
  as straw is trampled down in the
    manure.
¹¹They will spread out their hands in it,
  as a swimmer spreads out his hands
    to swim.
God will bring down their pride
  despite the cleverness^h of their
    hands.
¹²He will bring down your high fortified
    walls
  and lay them low;
he will bring them down to the
    ground,
  to the very dust.

CHAPTER 26
In that day this song will be sung in the
land of Judah:

We have a strong city;
  God makes salvation
    its walls and ramparts.
²Open the gates
  that the righteous nation may enter,
  the nation that keeps faith.
³You will keep in perfect peace
  him whose mind is steadfast,
  because he trusts in you.
⁴Trust in the LORD forever,
  for the LORD, the LORD, is the Rock
    eternal.
⁵He humbles those who dwell on high,
  he lays the lofty city low;
he levels it to the ground
  and casts it down to the dust.
⁶Feet trample it down—

the feet of the oppressed,
the footsteps of the poor.

⁷The path of the righteous is level;
O upright One, you make the way
of the righteous smooth.
⁸Yes, LORD, walking in the way of your
laws,ⁱ
we wait for you;
your name and renown
are the desire of our hearts.
⁹My soul yearns for you in the night;
in the morning my spirit longs for
you.
When your judgments come upon the
earth,
the people of the world learn
righteousness.
¹⁰Though grace is shown to the wicked,
they do not learn righteousness;
even in a land of uprightness they go
on doing evil
and regard not the majesty of the
LORD.
¹¹O LORD, your hand is lifted high,
but they do not see it.
Let them see your zeal for your people
and be put to shame;
let the fire reserved for your
enemies consume them.

¹²LORD, you establish peace for us;
all that we have accomplished you
have done for us.
¹³O LORD, our God, other lords besides
you have ruled over us,
but your name alone do we honor.
¹⁴They are now dead, they live no more;
those departed spirits do not rise.
You punished them and brought them
to ruin;
you wiped out all memory of them.
¹⁵You have enlarged the nation, O LORD;
you have enlarged the nation.
You have gained glory for yourself;
you have extended all the borders of
the land.

¹⁶LORD, they came to you in their
distress;
when you disciplined them,
they could barely whisper a
prayer.^j
¹⁷As a woman with child and about to
give birth
writhes and cries out in her pain,

so were we in your presence,
O LORD.
¹⁸We were with child, we writhed in
pain,
but we gave birth to wind.
We have not brought salvation to the
earth;
we have not given birth to people of
the world.

¹⁹But your dead will live;
their bodies will rise.
You who dwell in the dust,
wake up and shout for joy.
Your dew is like the dew of the
morning;
the earth will give birth to her dead.

²⁰Go, my people, enter your rooms
and shut the doors behind you;
hide yourselves for a little while
until his wrath has passed by.
²¹See, the LORD is coming out of his
dwelling
to punish the people of the earth for
their sins.
The earth will disclose the blood shed
upon her;
she will conceal her slain no longer.

CHAPTER 27
In that day,

the LORD will punish with his sword,
his fierce, great and powerful sword,
Leviathan the gliding serpent,
Leviathan the coiling serpent;
he will slay the monster of the sea.

²In that day—

"Sing about a fruitful vineyard:
³ I, the LORD, watch over it;
I water it continually.
I guard it day and night
so that no one may harm it.
⁴ I am not angry.
If only there were briers and thorns
confronting me!
I would march against them in
battle;
I would set them all on fire.
⁵Or else let them come to me for
refuge;
let them make peace with me,
yes, let them make peace with me."

⁶In days to come Jacob will take root,

ⁱ8 Or *judgments*   ^j16 The meaning of the Hebrew for this clause is uncertain.

Israel will bud and blossom
   and fill all the world with fruit.

⁷Has ⌊the LORD⌋ struck her
   as he struck down those who struck
      her?
Has she been killed
   as those were killed who killed
      her?
⁸By warfareᵏ and exile you contend
      with her—
   with his fierce blast he drives her
      out,
   as on a day the east wind blows.
⁹By this, then, will Jacob's guilt be
      atoned for,
   and this will be the full fruitage of
      the removal of his sin:
When he makes all the altar
      stones
   to be like chalk stones crushed to
      pieces,
no Asherah polesˡ or incense altars
   will be left standing.
¹⁰The fortified city stands desolate,

an abandoned settlement, forsaken
      like the desert;
there the calves graze,
   there they lie down;
   they strip its branches bare.
¹¹When its twigs are dry, they are
      broken off
   and women come and make fires
      with them.
For this is a people without
      understanding;
   so their Maker has no compassion
      on them,
   and their Creator shows them no
      favor.

¹²In that day the LORD will thresh from
the flowing Euphratesᵐ to the Wadi of
Egypt, and you, O Israelites, will be gathered up one by one. ¹³And in that day a
great trumpet will sound. Those who
were perishing in Assyria and those who
were exiled in Egypt will come and worship the LORD on the holy mountain in Jerusalem.

ᵏ8 See Septuagint; the meaning of the Hebrew for this word is uncertain.   ˡ9 That is, symbols of the goddess Asherah
ᵐ12 Hebrew *River*

JULY 21 □ DAY 203
As Good As Done

 LOOK BACK It's hard to read Isaiah 5–27 without the aid of a good Bible atlas. Some of the nations and cities mentioned should be famil-iar because they still exist today (Damascus, Ethiopia, Egypt, Tyre, Arabia). Others have long since disappeared from the pages of history (Assyria, Babylon, Moab). Still others have names that will take a little sleuthing to understand. The "Desert by the Sea" is a synonym for Babylon; the "Valley of Vision" (21:1) is identified for you in 22:9–10. Like a mighty threshing machine, the judgment of God falls upon small and great alike "in that day," punishing the arrogant, rewarding the faithful and leading all humanity to worship the one who opens what no one can shut and shuts what no one can open (22:22).

 LOOK UP Do you remember where you were and what you were doing when you heard the news that the space shuttle *Challenger* had exploded?

Every loss leaves a space that can be filled by God's presence.

For those of you over forty, do you remember where you were and what you were doing when you heard the news that President Kennedy had been assassinated?

Of course you do. Both events touched the heart and soul of the nation. In a moment frozen in time, the nation held its breath, hop-ing, praying that the headlines were a mistake.

Now read Isaiah 6:1: "In the year that King Uzziah died . . ." One of the most beloved monarchs in Judah's history, a man who had ruled for more than half a century, was dead. The only ruler many in Judah had ever known had died a tragic death, leaving an enormous leadership vacuum in the nation. No doubt many questions filled the air: How will we get along without good king Uzziah? What will happen to us and our nation? What will the future hold? Everything seemed so uncertain, so frightening, so fragile.

But then Isaiah saw something more. He saw the Lord, "seated on a throne, high and exalted" (6:1). Suddenly his fears melted away and his questions seemed unimportant. Who was in control? *God was in control.* Even though the king of Judah had passed from the scene, the King of the universe would continue to rule forever.

 LOOK AHEAD One wag has commented, "If you can keep your wits about you when everyone else around you is losing theirs, you obviously don't understand the situation." Perhaps. But it's equally possible you have a source of comfort and confidence that others around you haven't experienced. And that comforting Presence can give you a peace that defies human explanation, even in the face of tragedy (Philippians 4:6-7).

At a time when the nation of Judah was traumatized by front-page news, Isaiah was focusing on his holy, awesome, almighty God. The result was a quiet confidence that would fortify Isaiah for a lifetime of ministry to a hostile audience. How about you? Instead of reading a paper today, allow Isaiah's pen to be your eyes and ears as you look upon and listen to your mighty God. And don't be surprised if "peace like a river" is the result.

JULY 22 ☐ DAY 204
ISAIAH 28–30
A Painful Example

 OVERVIEW Isaiah now declares a series of specific woes upon Israel and Judah. Targeting his messages for the capital cities of Samaria and Jerusalem (much like a modern reporter would speak of Washington, D.C., or Moscow), Isaiah declares that destruction is imminent. For "Ephraim's [Israel] drunkards," it is too late to repent; judgment is inescapable. But Jerusalem can still learn from the fate of her sister nation. Lulled into a false sense of security by empty ritualism, Jerusalem must awake from spiritual stupor. Otherwise, it will follow Israel's fatal error of substituting foolish alliances for faith in God.

Chapter 28	Chapter 29	Chapter 30
No Time for Israel	Woe to Jerusalem	Warning to Judah
"Too Late!"	"Shape Up!"	"Trust God!"

 YOUR DAILY WALK When was the last time you tried to help God solve one of your problems? *After all,* you probably reasoned, *God must not know how desperate my situation really is! If he did, he would come to my rescue. But since I don't see him working, I'd better get in there and give him a helping hand. Right?*

Wrong! That was precisely the mistake Judah made. To prevent the onslaught of Assyria, Judah looked to her pagan neighbors for alliances

Walking by faith means being prepared to trust where we are not permitted to see. to offset Assyria's mighty armies. Look at 29:15–16 and you'll see that Judah thought she was doing this without God's knowledge. But God compares Judah's self-help program to a lump of clay trying to aid the potter who is shaping it!

Carry a shoestring with you today as a constant reminder of the danger of pulling yourself up by your own bootstraps. Rather, "in quietness and trust is your strength" (30:15).

INSIGHT A Fitting Title for Judah's Capital
Ariel (29:1), literally "altar," refers to Jerusalem. It can also be translated "hearth," an apt description of the city where the ark of God's presence resided and where all too soon the fire of God's judgment would fall with devastating fury.

CHAPTER 28

Woe to that wreath, the pride of
    Ephraim's drunkards,
  to the fading flower, his glorious
    beauty,
set on the head of a fertile valley—
  to that city, the pride of those laid
    low by wine!
²See, the Lord has one who is powerful
    and strong.
  Like a hailstorm and a destructive
    wind,
like a driving rain and a flooding
    downpour,
  he will throw it forcefully to the
    ground.
³That wreath, the pride of Ephraim's
    drunkards,
  will be trampled underfoot.
⁴That fading flower, his glorious
    beauty,
  set on the head of a fertile valley,
will be like a fig ripe before harvest—
  as soon as someone sees it and takes
    it in his hand,
  he swallows it.

⁵In that day the LORD Almighty
  will be a glorious crown,
a beautiful wreath
  for the remnant of his people.
⁶He will be a spirit of justice
  to him who sits in judgment,
a source of strength
  to those who turn back the battle at
    the gate.

⁷And these also stagger from wine
  and reel from beer:
Priests and prophets stagger from beer
  and are befuddled with wine;
they reel from beer,

they stagger when seeing visions,
  they stumble when rendering
    decisions.
⁸All the tables are covered with vomit
  and there is not a spot without filth.

⁹"Who is it he is trying to teach?
  To whom is he explaining his
    message?
To children weaned from their milk,
  to those just taken from the breast?
¹⁰For it is:
  Do and do, do and do,
  rule on rule, rule on rule[n];
  a little here, a little there."

¹¹Very well then, with foreign lips and
    strange tongues
  God will speak to this people,
¹²to whom he said,
  "This is the resting place, let the
    weary rest";
and, "This is the place of repose"—
  but they would not listen.
¹³So then, the word of the LORD to them
    will become:
  Do and do, do and do,
  rule on rule, rule on rule;
  a little here, a little there—
so that they will go and fall backward,
  be injured and snared and captured.

¹⁴Therefore hear the word of the LORD,
    you scoffers
  who rule this people in Jerusalem.
¹⁵You boast, "We have entered into a
    covenant with death,
  with the grave[o] we have made an
    agreement.
When an overwhelming scourge
    sweeps by,
  it cannot touch us,

n10 Hebrew / *sav lasav sav lasav* / *kav lakav kav lakav* (possibly meaningless sounds; perhaps a mimicking of the prophet's words); also in verse 13   o15 Hebrew *Sheol*; also in verse 18

for we have made a lie our refuge
  and falsehood^p our hiding place."

^{16}So this is what the Sovereign LORD
says:

"See, I lay a stone in Zion,
  a tested stone,
a precious cornerstone for a sure
    foundation;
  the one who trusts will never be
    dismayed.
^{17}I will make justice the measuring line
  and righteousness the plumb line;
hail will sweep away your refuge, the
    lie,
  and water will overflow your hiding
    place.
^{18}Your covenant with death will be
    annulled;
  your agreement with the grave will
    not stand.
When the overwhelming scourge
    sweeps by,
  you will be beaten down by it.
^{19}As often as it comes it will carry you
    away;
  morning after morning, by day and
    by night,
  it will sweep through."

The understanding of this message
  will bring sheer terror.
^{20}The bed is too short to stretch out on,
  the blanket too narrow to wrap
    around you.
^{21}The LORD will rise up as he did at
    Mount Perazim,
  he will rouse himself as in the
    Valley of Gibeon—
to do his work, his strange work,
  and perform his task, his alien task.
^{22}Now stop your mocking,
  or your chains will become heavier;
the Lord, the LORD Almighty, has told
    me
  of the destruction decreed against
    the whole land.

^{23}Listen and hear my voice;
  pay attention and hear what I say.
^{24}When a farmer plows for planting,
  does he plow continually?
  Does he keep on breaking up and
    harrowing the soil?
^{25}When he has leveled the surface,

does he not sow caraway and scatter
    cummin?
Does he not plant wheat in its place,^{q}
  barley in its plot,^{q}
  and spelt in its field?
^{26}His God instructs him
  and teaches him the right way.

^{27}Caraway is not threshed with a sledge,
  nor is a cartwheel rolled over
    cummin;
caraway is beaten out with a rod,
  and cummin with a stick.
^{28}Grain must be ground to make bread;
  so one does not go on threshing it
    forever.
Though he drives the wheels of his
    threshing cart over it,
  his horses do not grind it.
^{29}All this also comes from the LORD
    Almighty,
  wonderful in counsel and
    magnificent in wisdom.

CHAPTER 29
Woe to you, Ariel, Ariel,
  the city where David settled!
Add year to year
  and let your cycle of festivals go on.
^{2}Yet I will besiege Ariel;
  she will mourn and lament,
  she will be to me like an altar
    hearth.^{r}
^{3}I will encamp against you all around;
  I will encircle you with towers
  and set up my siege works against
    you.
^{4}Brought low, you will speak from the
    ground;
  your speech will mumble out of the
    dust.
Your voice will come ghostlike from
    the earth;
  out of the dust your speech will
    whisper.

^{5}But your many enemies will become
    like fine dust,
  the ruthless hordes like blown chaff.
Suddenly, in an instant,
^{6} the LORD Almighty will come
with thunder and earthquake and
    great noise,
  with windstorm and tempest and
    flames of a devouring fire.

^{p}15 Or *false gods* ^{q}25 The meaning of the Hebrew for this word is uncertain. ^{r}2 The Hebrew for *altar hearth* sounds
like the Hebrew for *Ariel*.

7Then the hordes of all the nations that
   fight against Ariel,
   that attack her and her fortress and
      besiege her,
will be as it is with a dream,
   with a vision in the night—
8as when a hungry man dreams that he
      is eating,
   but he awakens, and his hunger
      remains;
as when a thirsty man dreams that he
   is drinking,
   but he awakens faint, with his thirst
      unquenched.
So will it be with the hordes of all the
      nations
   that fight against Mount Zion.

9Be stunned and amazed,
   blind yourselves and be sightless;
be drunk, but not from wine,
   stagger, but not from beer.
10The LORD has brought over you a deep
      sleep:
   He has sealed your eyes (the
      prophets);
   he has covered your heads (the
      seers).

11For you this whole vision is nothing
but words sealed in a scroll. And if you
give the scroll to someone who can read,
and say to him, "Read this, please," he will
answer, "I can't; it is sealed." 12Or if you
give the scroll to someone who cannot
read, and say, "Read this, please," he will
answer, "I don't know how to read."

13The Lord says:

"These people come near to me with
      their mouth
   and honor me with their lips,
   but their hearts are far from me.
Their worship of me
   is made up only of rules taught by
      men.s
14Therefore once more I will astound
      these people
   with wonder upon wonder;
the wisdom of the wise will perish,
   the intelligence of the intelligent will
      vanish."
15Woe to those who go to great depths
   to hide their plans from the LORD,
who do their work in darkness and
      think,

"Who sees us? Who will know?"
16You turn things upside down,
   as if the potter were thought to be
      like the clay!
Shall what is formed say to him who
      formed it,
   "He did not make me"?
Can the pot say of the potter,
   "He knows nothing"?

17In a very short time, will not Lebanon
      be turned into a fertile field
   and the fertile field seem like a
      forest?
18In that day the deaf will hear the
      words of the scroll,
   and out of gloom and darkness
   the eyes of the blind will see.
19Once more the humble will rejoice in
      the LORD;
   the needy will rejoice in the Holy
      One of Israel.
20The ruthless will vanish,
   the mockers will disappear,
   and all who have an eye for evil will
      be cut down—
21those who with a word make a man
      out to be guilty,
   who ensnare the defender in court
   and with false testimony deprive the
      innocent of justice.

22Therefore this is what the LORD, who
redeemed Abraham, says to the house of
Jacob:

"No longer will Jacob be ashamed;
   no longer will their faces grow pale.
23When they see among them their
      children,
   the work of my hands,
they will keep my name holy;
   they will acknowledge the holiness
      of the Holy One of Jacob,
   and will stand in awe of the God of
      Israel.
24Those who are wayward in spirit will
      gain understanding;
   those who complain will accept
      instruction."

CHAPTER 30
"Woe to the obstinate children,"
   declares the LORD,
"to those who carry out plans that are
      not mine,

s13 Hebrew; Septuagint *They worship me in vain; / their teachings are but rules taught by men*

forming an alliance, but not by my
  Spirit,
heaping sin upon sin;
²who go down to Egypt
  without consulting me;
who look for help to Pharaoh's
  protection,
to Egypt's shade for refuge.
³But Pharaoh's protection will be to
  your shame,
Egypt's shade will bring you
  disgrace.
⁴Though they have officials in Zoan
  and their envoys have arrived in
    Hanes,
⁵everyone will be put to shame
  because of a people useless to them,
who bring neither help nor advantage,
  but only shame and disgrace."

⁶An oracle concerning the animals of
the Negev:

Through a land of hardship and
  distress,
  of lions and lionesses,
  of adders and darting snakes,
the envoys carry their riches on
  donkeys' backs,
  their treasures on the humps of
    camels,
to that unprofitable nation,
⁷ to Egypt, whose help is utterly
    useless.
Therefore I call her
  Rahab the Do-Nothing.

⁸Go now, write it on a tablet for them,
  inscribe it on a scroll,
that for the days to come
  it may be an everlasting witness.
⁹These are rebellious people, deceitful
  children,
  children unwilling to listen to the
    LORD's instruction.
¹⁰They say to the seers,
  "See no more visions!"
and to the prophets,
  "Give us no more visions of what is
    right!
Tell us pleasant things,
  prophesy illusions.
¹¹Leave this way,
  get off this path,
and stop confronting us
  with the Holy One of Israel!"

¹²Therefore, this is what the Holy One
of Israel says:

"Because you have rejected this
  message,
relied on oppression
  and depended on deceit,
¹³this sin will become for you
  like a high wall, cracked and
    bulging,
  that collapses suddenly, in an
    instant.
¹⁴It will break in pieces like pottery,
  shattered so mercilessly
that among its pieces not a fragment
  will be found
  for taking coals from a hearth
  or scooping water out of a cistern."

¹⁵This is what the Sovereign LORD, the
Holy One of Israel, says:

"In repentance and rest is your
  salvation,
in quietness and trust is your
  strength,
  but you would have none of it.
¹⁶You said, 'No, we will flee on horses.'
  Therefore you will flee!
You said, 'We will ride off on swift
  horses.'
  Therefore your pursuers will be
    swift!
¹⁷A thousand will flee
  at the threat of one;
at the threat of five
  you will all flee away,
till you are left
  like a flagstaff on a mountaintop,
  like a banner on a hill."

¹⁸Yet the LORD longs to be gracious to
  you;
  he rises to show you compassion.
For the LORD is a God of justice.
  Blessed are all who wait for him!

¹⁹O people of Zion, who live in Jerusalem, you will weep no more. How gracious he will be when you cry for help!
As soon as he hears, he will answer you.
²⁰Although the Lord gives you the bread
of adversity and the water of affliction,
your teachers will be hidden no more;
with your own eyes you will see them.
²¹Whether you turn to the right or to the
left, your ears will hear a voice behind
you, saying, "This is the way; walk in it."
²²Then you will defile your idols overlaid
with silver and your images covered with
gold; you will throw them away like a

menstrual cloth and say to them, "Away with you!"

²³He will also send you rain for the seed you sow in the ground, and the food that comes from the land will be rich and plentiful. In that day your cattle will graze in broad meadows. ²⁴The oxen and donkeys that work the soil will eat fodder and mash, spread out with fork and shovel. ²⁵In the day of great slaughter, when the towers fall, streams of water will flow on every high mountain and every lofty hill. ²⁶The moon will shine like the sun, and the sunlight will be seven times brighter, like the light of seven full days, when the LORD binds up the bruises of his people and heals the wounds he inflicted.

²⁷See, the Name of the LORD comes from afar,
    with burning anger and dense clouds of smoke;
his lips are full of wrath,
    and his tongue is a consuming fire.
²⁸His breath is like a rushing torrent,
    rising up to the neck.
He shakes the nations in the sieve of destruction;
    he places in the jaws of the peoples a bit that leads them astray.
²⁹And you will sing

as on the night you celebrate a holy festival;
your hearts will rejoice
    as when people go up with flutes
to the mountain of the LORD,
    to the Rock of Israel.
³⁰The LORD will cause men to hear his majestic voice
    and will make them see his arm coming down
with raging anger and consuming fire,
    with cloudburst, thunderstorm and hail.
³¹The voice of the LORD will shatter Assyria;
    with his scepter he will strike them down.
³²Every stroke the LORD lays on them with his punishing rod
will be to the music of tambourines and harps,
    as he fights them in battle with the blows of his arm.
³³Topheth has long been prepared;
    it has been made ready for the king.
Its fire pit has been made deep and wide,
    with an abundance of fire and wood;
the breath of the LORD,
    like a stream of burning sulfur,
    sets it ablaze.

JULY 23 □ DAY 205
ISAIAH 31–35
Coming Destruction, Coming King

 OVERVIEW As Isaiah ponders the joyous prophecy of Israel's deliverance from Assyria, his thoughts naturally turn to the arrival of the much-prophesied future King whose rule and righteousness would be worldwide. In the light of this glorious future, Isaiah urges the people of Judah to remain strong in their trust of God, even though the gathering storm clouds of Assyrian invasion can be seen on the horizon. With faith in God they can wait expectantly for the promised era of restored prosperity when "sorrow and sighing will flee away" (35:10).

Chapter 31	Chapter 32	Chapters 33–34	Chapter 35
Coming Calamity	Coming King	Sword of the Lord	The Nation Restored
Egypt	Messiah	Assyria	Redeemed

YOUR DAILY WALK When your heart is disturbed by fear or worry, where do you turn to find peace and provision?

Faith is dead to doubt, dumb to discouragement, blind to impossibilities.

The story is told of an all-church meeting called to discuss an urgent matter. There were insufficient funds on hand to pay an important bill. Worried expressions furrowed many a brow. Where could the church turn? Suddenly, a wealthy businessman stood to his feet and offered to underwrite the full amount. Sighs of relief were heard throughout the room—until one older Christian reminded the members that God had promised to underwrite his work all along.

By nature it is easier for people to trust limited human resources than God's inexhaustible supply. Judah looked to the military might of Egypt for security, forgetting that the God of Israel had shown once before how fragile that "might" might prove (Exodus 14)!

What need is uppermost in your life right now? Are the resources of God enough to put your mind at ease, or are you seeking relief from another source? You wouldn't ask a child to do what only an adult is capable of doing. But are you trusting others to do what only God can—and will—do on your behalf? Talk to him about it.

 INSIGHT No Smooth Path to Peace
The pampered women of 32:9 provide only one example of the self-indulgent society of Israel's day (see also 22:13; 28:15). But God cannot bring peace to a self-indulgent people. The ground must be cleared and resown with righteousness, of which peace is the fruit (32:16–17).

CHAPTER 31

Woe to those who go down to Egypt
    for help,
who rely on horses,
who trust in the multitude of their
        chariots
    and in the great strength of their
        horsemen,
but do not look to the Holy One of
        Israel,
    or seek help from the LORD.
²Yet he too is wise and can bring
        disaster;
    he does not take back his words.
He will rise up against the house of
        the wicked,
    against those who help evildoers.
³But the Egyptians are men and not
        God;
    their horses are flesh and not spirit.
When the LORD stretches out his hand,
    he who helps will stumble,
    he who is helped will fall;
    both will perish together.

⁴This is what the LORD says to me:

"As a lion growls,
    a great lion over his prey—
and though a whole band of
        shepherds
    is called together against him,
he is not frightened by their shouts

or disturbed by their clamor—
so the LORD Almighty will come down
    to do battle on Mount Zion and on
        its heights.
⁵Like birds hovering overhead,
    the LORD Almighty will shield
        Jerusalem;
he will shield it and deliver it,
    he will 'pass over' it and will rescue
        it."

⁶Return to him you have so greatly revolted against, O Israelites. ⁷For in that day every one of you will reject the idols of silver and gold your sinful hands have made.

⁸"Assyria will fall by a sword that is
        not of man;
    a sword, not of mortals, will devour
        them.
They will flee before the sword
    and their young men will be put to
        forced labor.
⁹Their stronghold will fall because of
        terror;
    at sight of the battle standard their
        commanders will panic,"
declares the LORD,
    whose fire is in Zion,
    whose furnace is in Jerusalem.

CHAPTER 32

See, a king will reign in righteousness
    and rulers will rule with justice.
²Each man will be like a shelter from
        the wind
    and a refuge from the storm,
like streams of water in the desert
    and the shadow of a great rock in a
        thirsty land.

³Then the eyes of those who see will no
        longer be closed,
    and the ears of those who hear will
        listen.
⁴The mind of the rash will know and
        understand,
    and the stammering tongue will be
        fluent and clear.
⁵No longer will the fool be called noble
    nor the scoundrel be highly
        respected.
⁶For the fool speaks folly,
    his mind is busy with evil:
He practices ungodliness
    and spreads error concerning the
        LORD;
    the hungry he leaves empty
    and from the thirsty he withholds
        water.
⁷The scoundrel's methods are wicked,
    he makes up evil schemes
to destroy the poor with lies,
    even when the plea of the needy is
        just.
⁸But the noble man makes noble plans,
    and by noble deeds he stands.

⁹You women who are so complacent,
    rise up and listen to me;
you daughters who feel secure,
    hear what I have to say!
¹⁰In little more than a year
    you who feel secure will tremble;
the grape harvest will fail,
    and the harvest of fruit will not
        come.
¹¹Tremble, you complacent women;
    shudder, you daughters who feel
        secure!
Strip off your clothes,
    put sackcloth around your waists.
¹²Beat your breasts for the pleasant
        fields,
    for the fruitful vines
¹³and for the land of my people,
    a land overgrown with thorns and
        briers—
yes, mourn for all houses of merriment

and for this city of revelry.
¹⁴The fortress will be abandoned,
    the noisy city deserted;
citadel and watchtower will become a
        wasteland forever,
    the delight of donkeys, a pasture for
        flocks,
¹⁵till the Spirit is poured upon us from
        on high,
    and the desert becomes a fertile
        field,
    and the fertile field seems like a
        forest.
¹⁶Justice will dwell in the desert
    and righteousness live in the fertile
        field.
¹⁷The fruit of righteousness will be
        peace;
    the effect of righteousness will be
        quietness and confidence
        forever.
¹⁸My people will live in peaceful
        dwelling places,
    in secure homes,
    in undisturbed places of rest.
¹⁹Though hail flattens the forest
    and the city is leveled completely,
²⁰how blessed you will be,
    sowing your seed by every stream,
    and letting your cattle and donkeys
        range free.

CHAPTER 33

Woe to you, O destroyer,
    you who have not been destroyed!
Woe to you, O traitor,
    you who have not been betrayed!
When you stop destroying,
    you will be destroyed;
when you stop betraying,
    you will be betrayed.

²O LORD, be gracious to us;
    we long for you.
Be our strength every morning,
    our salvation in time of distress.
³At the thunder of your voice, the
        peoples flee;
    when you rise up, the nations
        scatter.
⁴Your plunder, O nations, is harvested
        as by young locusts;
    like a swarm of locusts men pounce
        on it.

⁵The LORD is exalted, for he dwells on
        high;

he will fill Zion with justice and
  righteousness.
[6]He will be the sure foundation for
    your times,
  a rich store of salvation and wisdom
    and knowledge;
  the fear of the LORD is the key to this
    treasure.[f]

[7]Look, their brave men cry aloud in the
    streets;
  the envoys of peace weep bitterly.
[8]The highways are deserted,
  no travelers are on the roads.
  The treaty is broken,
    its witnesses[u] are despised,
  no one is respected.
[9]The land mourns[v] and wastes away,
  Lebanon is ashamed and withers;
  Sharon is like the Arabah,
    and Bashan and Carmel drop their
      leaves.

[10]"Now will I arise," says the LORD.
  "Now will I be exalted;
  now will I be lifted up.
[11]You conceive chaff,
    you give birth to straw;
  your breath is a fire that consumes
    you.
[12]The peoples will be burned as if to
    lime;
  like cut thornbushes they will be set
    ablaze."

[13]You who are far away, hear what I
    have done;
  you who are near, acknowledge my
    power!
[14]The sinners in Zion are terrified;
  trembling grips the godless:
  "Who of us can dwell with the
    consuming fire?
  Who of us can dwell with
    everlasting burning?"
[15]He who walks righteously
    and speaks what is right,
  who rejects gain from extortion
    and keeps his hand from accepting
      bribes,
  who stops his ears against plots of
    murder
    and shuts his eyes against
      contemplating evil—
[16]this is the man who will dwell on the
    heights,

whose refuge will be the mountain
    fortress.
  His bread will be supplied,
    and water will not fail him.

[17]Your eyes will see the king in his
    beauty
  and view a land that stretches afar.
[18]In your thoughts you will ponder the
    former terror:
  "Where is that chief officer?
  Where is the one who took the
    revenue?
  Where is the officer in charge of the
    towers?"
[19]You will see those arrogant people no
    more,
  those people of an obscure speech,
  with their strange, incomprehensible
    tongue.

[20]Look upon Zion, the city of our
    festivals;
  your eyes will see Jerusalem,
  a peaceful abode, a tent that will not
    be moved;
  its stakes will never be pulled up,
    nor any of its ropes broken.
[21]There the LORD will be our Mighty
    One.
  It will be like a place of broad rivers
    and streams.
  No galley with oars will ride them,
    no mighty ship will sail them.
[22]For the LORD is our judge,
    the LORD is our lawgiver,
  the LORD is our king;
    it is he who will save us.

[23]Your rigging hangs loose:
  The mast is not held secure,
    the sail is not spread.
  Then an abundance of spoils will be
    divided
    and even the lame will carry off
      plunder.
[24]No one living in Zion will say, "I am
    ill";
  and the sins of those who dwell
    there will be forgiven.

CHAPTER 34
Come near, you nations, and listen;
    pay attention, you peoples!
  Let the earth hear, and all that is in it,
    the world, and all that comes out of
      it!

²The Lord is angry with all nations;
  his wrath is upon all their armies.
He will totally destroyʷ them,
  he will give them over to slaughter.
³Their slain will be thrown out,
  their dead bodies will send up a
    stench;
  the mountains will be soaked with
    their blood.
⁴All the stars of the heavens will be
    dissolved
  and the sky rolled up like a scroll;
all the starry host will fall
  like withered leaves from the vine,
  like shriveled figs from the fig tree.

⁵My sword has drunk its fill in the
    heavens;
  see, it descends in judgment on
    Edom,
  the people I have totally destroyed.
⁶The sword of the Lord is bathed in
    blood,
  it is covered with fat—
the blood of lambs and goats,
  fat from the kidneys of rams.
For the Lord has a sacrifice in Bozrah
  and a great slaughter in Edom.
⁷And the wild oxen will fall with them,
  the bull calves and the great bulls.
Their land will be drenched with
    blood,
  and the dust will be soaked with fat.

⁸For the Lord has a day of vengeance,
  a year of retribution, to uphold
    Zion's cause.
⁹Edom's streams will be turned into
    pitch,
  her dust into burning sulfur;
  her land will become blazing pitch!
¹⁰It will not be quenched night and day;
  its smoke will rise forever.
From generation to generation it will
    lie desolate;
  no one will ever pass through it
    again.
¹¹The desert owlˣ and screech owlˣ
    will possess it;
  the great owlˣ and the raven will
    nest there.
God will stretch out over Edom
  the measuring line of chaos
  and the plumb line of desolation.
¹²Her nobles will have nothing there to
    be called a kingdom,

all her princes will vanish away.
¹³Thorns will overrun her citadels,
  nettles and brambles her
    strongholds.
She will become a haunt for jackals,
  a home for owls.
¹⁴Desert creatures will meet with
    hyenas,
  and wild goats will bleat to each
    other;
there the night creatures will also
    repose
  and find for themselves places of
    rest.
¹⁵The owl will nest there and lay eggs,
  she will hatch them, and care for her
    young under the shadow of her
    wings;
there also the falcons will gather,
  each with its mate.

¹⁶Look in the scroll of the Lord and
read:

None of these will be missing,
  not one will lack her mate.
For it is his mouth that has given the
    order,
  and his Spirit will gather them
    together.
¹⁷He allots their portions;
  his hand distributes them by
    measure.
They will possess it forever
  and dwell there from generation to
    generation.

CHAPTER 35

The desert and the parched land will
    be glad;
  the wilderness will rejoice and
    blossom.
Like the crocus, ²it will burst into
    bloom;
  it will rejoice greatly and shout for
    joy.
The glory of Lebanon will be given to
    it,
  the splendor of Carmel and Sharon;
they will see the glory of the Lord,
  the splendor of our God.

³Strengthen the feeble hands,
  steady the knees that give way;
⁴say to those with fearful hearts,
  "Be strong, do not fear;

your God will come,
he will come with vengeance;
with divine retribution
he will come to save you."

⁵Then will the eyes of the blind be
opened
and the ears of the deaf unstopped.
⁶Then will the lame leap like a deer,
and the mute tongue shout for joy.
Water will gush forth in the
wilderness
and streams in the desert.
⁷The burning sand will become a pool,
the thirsty ground bubbling springs.
In the haunts where jackals once lay,
grass and reeds and papyrus will
grow.
⁸And a highway will be there;

y8 Or / the simple will not stray from it

it will be called the Way of Holiness.
The unclean will not journey on it;
it will be for those who walk in that
Way;
wicked fools will not go about on
it.ʸ
⁹No lion will be there,
nor will any ferocious beast get up
on it;
they will not be found there.
But only the redeemed will walk there,
10   and the ransomed of the LORD will
return.
They will enter Zion with singing;
everlasting joy will crown their
heads.
Gladness and joy will overtake them,
and sorrow and sighing will flee
away.

JULY 24 ☐ DAY 206
ISAIAH 36–39
Judah's Day of Judgment

OVERVIEW Today's reading represents a four-chapter interlude in Isaiah's prophecy—a historical parenthesis that shows the fulfillment of some of Isaiah's early prophecies and sets the stage for many of his later ones. The focus throughout is on godly king Hezekiah, perhaps the premier reformer of Judah. A man of prayer and principle, Hezekiah sees God destroy 185,000 Assyrian invaders and extend his own life by fifteen years. But by responding in foolish pride to Babylonian envoys, Hezekiah seals the fate of his nation.

Chapter 36	Chapter 37	Chapter 38	Chapter 39
Arrogant Assyria	Divine Deliverance	A Mortal Illness	A Fatal Error
Hezekiah's Faithfulness		Hezekiah's Failure	

YOUR DAILY WALK Something happened (on the average) every twenty seconds last year. It affected the lives of 1.5 million Americans. Can you guess what it was? (Hint: It had nothing to do with Ronald McDonald!)

No one ever repented of being a Christian on his or her deathbed.

Answer: Every twenty seconds, someone in the United States suffered a heart attack . . . and suddenly came to realize that death was only a heartbeat away. And for six hundred thousand Americans that realization became a reality.

Death. It's a universally distasteful subject. But the fact remains that one out of one dies! For King Hezekiah—as with many people—the approach of death brought tears (38:1–3)—tears of regret . . . tears of remorse. So many good intentions . . . so many half-finished projects. God gave Hezekiah a gift of fifteen additional years—but that doesn't always happen. When it's time for you to die, will you be ready—or regretful—to see the Lord face-to-face? Find the obituary column in your newspaper, and pretend for a moment that your name is there (you may even want to write it in, just to emphasize the point). Now talk to God about how you want to spend the rest of your days!

INSIGHT A Historic Spot Revisited
King Sennacherib's field commander "stopped at the aqueduct of the Upper Pool, on the road to the Washerman's field" when he shouted his arrogant threats (36:2). Twenty-three years earlier, God had told a man to stand in the same spot and declare his message. Do you remember who? (If you're stumped, check 7:3–9.)

CHAPTER 36

In the fourteenth year of King Hezekiah's reign, Sennacherib king of Assyria attacked all the fortified cities of Judah and captured them. ²Then the king of Assyria sent his field commander with a large army from Lachish to King Hezekiah at Jerusalem. When the commander stopped at the aqueduct of the Upper Pool, on the road to the Washerman's Field, ³Eliakim son of Hilkiah the palace administrator, Shebna the secretary, and Joah son of Asaph the recorder went out to him.

⁴The field commander said to them, "Tell Hezekiah,

" 'This is what the great king, the king of Assyria, says: On what are you basing this confidence of yours? ⁵You say you have strategy and military strength—but you speak only empty words. On whom are you depending, that you rebel against me? ⁶Look now, you are depending on Egypt, that splintered reed of a staff, which pierces a man's hand and wounds him if he leans on it! Such is Pharaoh king of Egypt to all who depend on him. ⁷And if you say to me, "We are depending on the LORD our God"—isn't he the one whose high places and altars Hezekiah removed, saying to Judah and Jerusalem, "You must worship before this altar"?

⁸" 'Come now, make a bargain with my master, the king of Assyria: I will give you two thousand horses—if you can put riders on them! ⁹How then can you repulse one officer of the least of my master's officials, even though you are depending on Egypt for chariots and horsemen? ¹⁰Furthermore, have I come to attack and destroy this land without the LORD? The LORD himself told me to march against this country and destroy it.' "

¹¹Then Eliakim, Shebna and Joah said to the field commander, "Please speak to your servants in Aramaic, since we understand it. Don't speak to us in Hebrew in the hearing of the people on the wall."

¹²But the commander replied, "Was it only to your master and you that my master sent me to say these things, and not to the men sitting on the wall—who, like you, will have to eat their own filth and drink their own urine?"

¹³Then the commander stood and called out in Hebrew, "Hear the words of the great king, the king of Assyria! ¹⁴This is what the king says: Do not let Hezekiah deceive you. He cannot deliver you! ¹⁵Do not let Hezekiah persuade you to trust in the LORD when he says, 'The LORD will surely deliver us; this city will not be given into the hand of the king of Assyria.'

¹⁶"Do not listen to Hezekiah. This is what the king of Assyria says: Make peace with me and come out to me. Then every one of you will eat from his own vine and fig tree and drink water from his own cistern, ¹⁷until I come and take you to a land like your own—a land of grain and new wine, a land of bread and vineyards.

¹⁸"Do not let Hezekiah mislead you when he says, 'The LORD will deliver us.' Has the god of any nation ever delivered his land from the hand of the king of Assyria? ¹⁹Where are the gods of Hamath and Arpad? Where are the gods of Sepharvaim? Have they rescued Samaria from my hand? ²⁰Who of all the gods of these countries has been able to save his land from me? How then can the LORD deliver Jerusalem from my hand?"

²¹But the people remained silent and

said nothing in reply, because the king had commanded, "Do not answer him."

²²Then Eliakim son of Hilkiah the palace administrator, Shebna the secretary, and Joah son of Asaph the recorder went to Hezekiah, with their clothes torn, and told him what the field commander had said.

CHAPTER 37

When King Hezekiah heard this, he tore his clothes and put on sackcloth and went into the temple of the LORD. ²He sent Eliakim the palace administrator, Shebna the secretary, and the leading priests, all wearing sackcloth, to the prophet Isaiah son of Amoz. ³They told him, "This is what Hezekiah says: This day is a day of distress and rebuke and disgrace, as when children come to the point of birth and there is no strength to deliver them. ⁴It may be that the LORD your God will hear the words of the field commander, whom his master, the king of Assyria, has sent to ridicule the living God, and that he will rebuke him for the words the LORD your God has heard. Therefore pray for the remnant that still survives."

⁵When King Hezekiah's officials came to Isaiah, ⁶Isaiah said to them, "Tell your master, 'This is what the LORD says: Do not be afraid of what you have heard— those words with which the underlings of the king of Assyria have blasphemed me. ⁷Listen! I am going to put a spirit in him so that when he hears a certain report, he will return to his own country, and there I will have him cut down with the sword.' "

⁸When the field commander heard that the king of Assyria had left Lachish, he withdrew and found the king fighting against Libnah.

⁹Now Sennacherib received a report that Tirhakah, the Cushite^z king of Egypt, was marching out to fight against him. When he heard it, he sent messengers to Hezekiah with this word: ¹⁰"Say to Hezekiah king of Judah: Do not let the god you depend on deceive you when he says, 'Jerusalem will not be handed over to the king of Assyria.' ¹¹Surely you have heard what the kings of Assyria have done to all the countries, destroying them completely. And will you be delivered?

¹²Did the gods of the nations that were destroyed by my forefathers deliver them—the gods of Gozan, Haran, Rezeph and the people of Eden who were in Tel Assar? ¹³Where is the king of Hamath, the king of Arpad, the king of the city of Sepharvaim, or of Hena or Ivvah?"

¹⁴Hezekiah received the letter from the messengers and read it. Then he went up to the temple of the LORD and spread it out before the LORD. ¹⁵And Hezekiah prayed to the LORD: ¹⁶"O LORD Almighty, God of Israel, enthroned between the cherubim, you alone are God over all the kingdoms of the earth. You have made heaven and earth. ¹⁷Give ear, O LORD, and hear; open your eyes, O LORD, and see; listen to all the words Sennacherib has sent to insult the living God.

¹⁸"It is true, O LORD, that the Assyrian kings have laid waste all these peoples and their lands. ¹⁹They have thrown their gods into the fire and destroyed them, for they were not gods but only wood and stone, fashioned by human hands. ²⁰Now, O LORD our God, deliver us from his hand, so that all kingdoms on earth may know that you alone, O LORD, are God.^{a}"

²¹Then Isaiah son of Amoz sent a message to Hezekiah: "This is what the LORD, the God of Israel, says: Because you have prayed to me concerning Sennacherib king of Assyria, ²²this is the word the LORD has spoken against him:

"The Virgin Daughter of Zion
   despises and mocks you.
The Daughter of Jerusalem
   tosses her head as you flee.
²³Who is it you have insulted and
      blasphemed?
   Against whom have you raised your
      voice
and lifted your eyes in pride?
   Against the Holy One of Israel!
²⁴By your messengers
   you have heaped insults on the
      Lord.
And you have said,
   'With my many chariots
I have ascended the heights of the
      mountains,
   the utmost heights of Lebanon.
I have cut down its tallest cedars,
   the choicest of its pines.
I have reached its remotest heights,

---

^{z}9 That is, from the upper Nile region ^{a}20 Dead Sea Scrolls (see also 2 Kings 19:19); Masoretic Text *alone are the* LORD

the finest of its forests.
25I have dug wells in foreign lands*b*
   and drunk the water there.
With the soles of my feet
   I have dried up all the streams of
      Egypt.'

26"Have you not heard?
   Long ago I ordained it.
In days of old I planned it;
   now I have brought it to pass,
that you have turned fortified cities
   into piles of stone.
27Their people, drained of power,
   are dismayed and put to shame.
They are like plants in the field,
   like tender green shoots,
like grass sprouting on the roof,
   scorched*c* before it grows up.

28"But I know where you stay
   and when you come and go
   and how you rage against me.
29Because you rage against me
   and because your insolence has
      reached my ears,
I will put my hook in your nose
   and my bit in your mouth,
and I will make you return
   by the way you came.

30"This will be the sign for you,
O Hezekiah:

"This year you will eat what grows by
   itself,
   and the second year what springs
      from that.
But in the third year sow and reap,
   plant vineyards and eat their fruit.
31Once more a remnant of the house of
      Judah
   will take root below and bear fruit
      above.
32For out of Jerusalem will come a
      remnant,
   and out of Mount Zion a band of
      survivors.
The zeal of the LORD Almighty
   will accomplish this.

33"Therefore this is what the LORD says
concerning the king of Assyria:

"He will not enter this city
   or shoot an arrow here.
He will not come before it with shield

or build a siege ramp against it.
34By the way that he came he will
      return;
   he will not enter this city,"
                              declares the LORD.
35"I will defend this city and save it,
   for my sake and for the sake of
      David my servant!"

36Then the angel of the LORD went out
and put to death a hundred and eighty-
five thousand men in the Assyrian camp.
When the people got up the next morning—there were all the dead bodies! 37So
Sennacherib king of Assyria broke camp
and withdrew. He returned to Nineveh
and stayed there.

38One day, while he was worshiping in
the temple of his god Nisroch, his sons
Adrammelech and Sharezer cut him
down with the sword, and they escaped
to the land of Ararat. And Esarhaddon his
son succeeded him as king.

CHAPTER 38

In those days Hezekiah became ill and
was at the point of death. The prophet
Isaiah son of Amoz went to him and said,
"This is what the LORD says: Put your
house in order, because you are going to
die; you will not recover."

2Hezekiah turned his face to the wall
and prayed to the LORD, 3"Remember,
O LORD, how I have walked before you
faithfully and with wholehearted devotion and have done what is good in your
eyes." And Hezekiah wept bitterly.

4Then the word of the LORD came to
Isaiah: 5"Go and tell Hezekiah, 'This is
what the LORD, the God of your father
David, says: I have heard your prayer and
seen your tears; I will add fifteen years to
your life. 6And I will deliver you and this
city from the hand of the king of Assyria.
I will defend this city.

7" 'This is the LORD's sign to you that the
LORD will do what he has promised: 8I will
make the shadow cast by the sun go back
the ten steps it has gone down on the
stairway of Ahaz.' " So the sunlight went
back the ten steps it had gone down.

9A writing of Hezekiah king of Judah
after his illness and recovery:

10I said, "In the prime of my life

*b*25 Dead Sea Scrolls (see also 2 Kings 19:24); Masoretic Text does not have *in foreign lands*.   *c*27 Some manuscripts of the
Masoretic Text, Dead Sea Scrolls and some Septuagint manuscripts (see also 2 Kings 19:26); most manuscripts of the Masoretic
Text *roof | and terraced fields*

must I go through the gates of
  death[d]
and be robbed of the rest of my
  years?"
[11]I said, "I will not again see the LORD,
  the LORD, in the land of the living;
no longer will I look on mankind,
  or be with those who now dwell in
  this world.[e]
[12]Like a shepherd's tent my house
  has been pulled down and taken
  from me.
Like a weaver I have rolled up my life,
  and he has cut me off from the
  loom;
  day and night you made an end of
  me.
[13]I waited patiently till dawn,
  but like a lion he broke all my
  bones;
  day and night you made an end of
  me.
[14]I cried like a swift or thrush,
  I moaned like a mourning dove.
My eyes grew weak as I looked to the
  heavens.
  I am troubled; O Lord, come to my
  aid!"

[15]But what can I say?
  He has spoken to me, and he
  himself has done this.
I will walk humbly all my years
  because of this anguish of my soul.
[16]Lord, by such things men live;
  and my spirit finds life in them too.
You restored me to health
  and let me live.
[17]Surely it was for my benefit
  that I suffered such anguish.
In your love you kept me
  from the pit of destruction;
you have put all my sins
  behind your back.
[18]For the grave[d] cannot praise you,
  death cannot sing your praise;
those who go down to the pit
  cannot hope for your faithfulness.
[19]The living, the living—they praise you,
  as I am doing today;
fathers tell their children
  about your faithfulness.

[20]The LORD will save me,
  and we will sing with stringed
  instruments
all the days of our lives
  in the temple of the LORD.

[21]Isaiah had said, "Prepare a poultice of
figs and apply it to the boil, and he will
recover."
[22]Hezekiah had asked, "What will be
the sign that I will go up to the temple of
the LORD?"

CHAPTER 39

At that time Merodach-Baladan son of
Baladan king of Babylon sent Hezekiah
letters and a gift, because he had heard of
his illness and recovery. [2]Hezekiah received the envoys gladly and showed
them what was in his storehouses—the
silver, the gold, the spices, the fine oil, his
entire armory and everything found
among his treasures. There was nothing
in his palace or in all his kingdom that
Hezekiah did not show them.

[3]Then Isaiah the prophet went to King
Hezekiah and asked, "What did those
men say, and where did they come from?"

"From a distant land," Hezekiah replied.
"They came to me from Babylon."

[4]The prophet asked, "What did they see
in your palace?"

"They saw everything in my palace,"
Hezekiah said. "There is nothing among
my treasures that I did not show them."

[5]Then Isaiah said to Hezekiah, "Hear
the word of the LORD Almighty: [6]The time
will surely come when everything in your
palace, and all that your fathers have
stored up until this day, will be carried off
to Babylon. Nothing will be left, says the
LORD. [7]And some of your descendants,
your own flesh and blood who will be
born to you, will be taken away, and they
will become eunuchs in the palace of the
king of Babylon."

[8]"The word of the LORD you have spoken is good," Hezekiah replied. For he
thought, "There will be peace and security
in my lifetime."

[d]10,18 Hebrew Sheol   [e]11 A few Hebrew manuscripts; most Hebrew manuscripts in the place of cessation

JULY 25 ☐ DAY 207
ISAIAH 40–43
Mighty Lord vs. Idle Idols

OVERVIEW Beginning with chapter 40, Isaiah changes the focus of his message. For thirty-nine chapters (much like the thirty-nine books of the Old Testament), his major message has been the condemnation resulting from the waywardness and wickedness of God's people. But now comes a heartwarming message of hope and comfort. Like the twenty-seven books of the New Testament, the next twenty-seven chapters declare the coming salvation of the Lord. He is sovereign over creation; he is sovereign in the selection and protection of his nation Israel. And thus there can be certainty that he will comfort and deliver his people.

Chapter 40	Chapter 41	Chapter 42	Chapter 43
God's Comfort for Israel	God's Case against Idols	God's Perfect Servant: Messiah	God's Wayward Servant: Israel
Consolation	Confrontation	Revelation	Restoration

YOUR DAILY WALK Today, rather than looking for a practical project in which to put God's truth to work, spend some quiet moments contemplating the greatness of the God who made you and whose you are. Here are some thoughts to prepare your mind for worship and reflection:

God is not made greater when you worship him, but you are made greater when you serve him.

The oceans of the world contain more than 340 quintillion gallons of water; yet God holds them in the hollow of his hand (40:12).

The earth weighs 6 sextillion metric tons; yet to God it represents but dust on the scale (40:12, 15).

The known universe stretches more than 30 billion light years (200 sextillion miles); yet to God that great expanse represents a hand breadth (40:12).

That same universe contains at least 100 billion galaxies, each made up of approximately 100 billion stars—yet God knows them all by name (40:26).

Now do you see why it is absurd to offer the God of heaven your *advice* rather than your *worship?* Even so, he says to you: "Fear not, for I have redeemed you; . . . you are mine" (43:1)!

INSIGHT A Key Verse for Isaiah 40–66
One verse (40:2) previews all of chapters 40–66: (1) "her hard service has been completed" describes the *deliverance* of 40–48; (2) "her sin has been paid for" describes the *deliverer* of 49–57; (3) "she has received" describes the the *delivered captives* of 58–66.

CHAPTER 40
Comfort, comfort my people,
   says your God.
²Speak tenderly to Jerusalem,
   and proclaim to her
that her hard service has been
   completed,
that her sin has been paid
   for,

that she has received from the LORD's
   hand
double for all her sins.

³A voice of one calling:
"In the desert prepare
   the way for the LORD*f*;
make straight in the wilderness
   a highway for our God.*g*

*f*3 Or *A voice of one calling in the desert:* / *"Prepare the way for the* LORD   *g*3 Hebrew; Septuagint *make straight the paths of our God*

⁴Every valley shall be raised up,
  every mountain and hill made low;
the rough ground shall become level,
  the rugged places a plain.
⁵And the glory of the LORD will be
    revealed,
  and all mankind together will see it.
      For the mouth of the LORD
          has spoken."

⁶A voice says, "Cry out."
  And I said, "What shall I cry?"

"All men are like grass,
  and all their glory is like the flowers
    of the field.
⁷The grass withers and the flowers fall,
  because the breath of the LORD blows
    on them.
  Surely the people are grass.
⁸The grass withers and the flowers fall,
  but the word of our God stands
    forever."

⁹You who bring good tidings to Zion,
  go up on a high mountain.
You who bring good tidings to
    Jerusalem,^h
  lift up your voice with a shout,
lift it up, do not be afraid;
  say to the towns of Judah,
  "Here is your God!"
¹⁰See, the Sovereign LORD comes with
    power,
  and his arm rules for him.
See, his reward is with him,
  and his recompense accompanies
    him.
¹¹He tends his flock like a shepherd:
  He gathers the lambs in his arms
and carries them close to his heart;
  he gently leads those that have
    young.

¹²Who has measured the waters in the
    hollow of his hand,
  or with the breadth of his hand
    marked off the heavens?
Who has held the dust of the earth in
    a basket,
  or weighed the mountains on the
    scales
and the hills in a balance?
¹³Who has understood the mindⁱ of the
    LORD,
  or instructed him as his counselor?

¹⁴Whom did the LORD consult to
    enlighten him,
  and who taught him the right way?
Who was it that taught him
    knowledge
  or showed him the path of
    understanding?

¹⁵Surely the nations are like a drop in a
    bucket;
  they are regarded as dust on the
    scales;
  he weighs the islands as though
    they were fine dust.
¹⁶Lebanon is not sufficient for altar fires,
  nor its animals enough for burnt
    offerings.
¹⁷Before him all the nations are as
    nothing;
  they are regarded by him as
    worthless
  and less than nothing.

¹⁸To whom, then, will you compare
    God?
  What image will you compare him
    to?
¹⁹As for an idol, a craftsman casts it,
  and a goldsmith overlays it with
    gold
  and fashions silver chains for it.
²⁰A man too poor to present such an
    offering
  selects wood that will not rot.
He looks for a skilled craftsman
  to set up an idol that will not
    topple.

²¹Do you not know?
  Have you not heard?
Has it not been told you from the
    beginning?
  Have you not understood since the
    earth was founded?
²²He sits enthroned above the circle of
    the earth,
  and its people are like grasshoppers.
He stretches out the heavens like a
    canopy,
  and spreads them out like a tent to
    live in.
²³He brings princes to naught
  and reduces the rulers of this world
    to nothing.
²⁴No sooner are they planted,
  no sooner are they sown,

^h9 Or O Zion, bringer of good tidings, / go up on a high mountain. / O Jerusalem, bringer of good tidings   ⁱ13 Or Spirit; or spirit

no sooner do they take root in the
    ground,
than he blows on them and they
    wither,
    and a whirlwind sweeps them away
        like chaff.

25"To whom will you compare me?
    Or who is my equal?" says the Holy
        One.
26Lift your eyes and look to the heavens:
    Who created all these?
He who brings out the starry host one
        by one,
    and calls them each by name.
Because of his great power and mighty
        strength,
    not one of them is missing.

27Why do you say, O Jacob,
    and complain, O Israel,
"My way is hidden from the LORD;
    my cause is disregarded by my
        God"?
28Do you not know?
    Have you not heard?
The LORD is the everlasting God,
    the Creator of the ends of the earth.
He will not grow tired or weary,
    and his understanding no one can
        fathom.
29He gives strength to the weary
    and increases the power of the
        weak.
30Even youths grow tired and weary,
    and young men stumble and fall;
31but those who hope in the LORD
    will renew their strength.
They will soar on wings like eagles;
    they will run and not grow weary,
    they will walk and not be faint.

CHAPTER 41
"Be silent before me, you islands!
    Let the nations renew their strength!
Let them come forward and speak;
    let us meet together at the place of
        judgment.

2"Who has stirred up one from the east,
    calling him in righteousness to his
        service[j]?
He hands nations over to him
    and subdues kings before him.
He turns them to dust with his sword,
    to windblown chaff with his bow.

3He pursues them and moves on
    unscathed,
    by a path his feet have not traveled
        before.
4Who has done this and carried it
        through,
    calling forth the generations from
        the beginning?
I, the LORD—with the first of them
    and with the last—I am he."

5The islands have seen it and fear;
    the ends of the earth tremble.
They approach and come forward;
6   each helps the other
    and says to his brother, "Be strong!"
7The craftsman encourages the
        goldsmith,
    and he who smooths with the
        hammer
    spurs on him who strikes the anvil.
He says of the welding, "It is good."
    He nails down the idol so it will not
        topple.

8"But you, O Israel, my servant,
    Jacob, whom I have chosen,
    you descendants of Abraham my
        friend,
9I took you from the ends of the earth,
    from its farthest corners I called you.
I said, 'You are my servant';
    I have chosen you and have not
        rejected you.
10So do not fear, for I am with you;
    do not be dismayed, for I am your
        God.
I will strengthen you and help you;
    I will uphold you with my righteous
        right hand.

11"All who rage against you
    will surely be ashamed and
        disgraced;
those who oppose you
    will be as nothing and perish.
12Though you search for your enemies,
    you will not find them.
Those who wage war against you
    will be as nothing at all.
13For I am the LORD, your God,
    who takes hold of your right hand
and says to you, Do not fear;
    I will help you.
14Do not be afraid, O worm Jacob,
    O little Israel,

j2 Or / whom victory meets at every step

for I myself will help you," declares
  the LORD,
  your Redeemer, the Holy One of
    Israel.
¹⁵"See, I will make you into a threshing
    sledge,
  new and sharp, with many teeth.
You will thresh the mountains and
    crush them,
  and reduce the hills to chaff.
¹⁶You will winnow them, the wind will
    pick them up,
  and a gale will blow them away.
But you will rejoice in the LORD
  and glory in the Holy One of Israel.

¹⁷"The poor and needy search for water,
  but there is none;
  their tongues are parched with
    thirst.
But I the LORD will answer them;
  I, the God of Israel, will not forsake
    them.
¹⁸I will make rivers flow on barren
    heights,
  and springs within the valleys.
I will turn the desert into pools of
    water,
  and the parched ground into
    springs.
¹⁹I will put in the desert
  the cedar and the acacia, the myrtle
    and the olive.
I will set pines in the wasteland,
  the fir and the cypress together,
²⁰so that people may see and know,
  may consider and understand,
that the hand of the LORD has done
    this,
  that the Holy One of Israel has
    created it.

²¹"Present your case," says the LORD.
  "Set forth your arguments," says
    Jacob's King.
²²"Bring in ⌊your idols⌋ to tell us
  what is going to happen.
Tell us what the former things were,
  so that we may consider them
  and know their final outcome.
Or declare to us the things to come,
²³ tell us what the future holds,
  so we may know that you are gods.
Do something, whether good or bad,
  so that we will be dismayed and
    filled with fear.
²⁴But you are less than nothing

and your works are utterly
    worthless;
  he who chooses you is detestable.

²⁵"I have stirred up one from the north,
    and he comes—
  one from the rising sun who calls on
    my name.
He treads on rulers as if they were
    mortar,
  as if he were a potter treading the
    clay.
²⁶Who told of this from the beginning,
    so we could know,
  or beforehand, so we could say, 'He
    was right'?
No one told of this,
  no one foretold it,
  no one heard any words from you.
²⁷I was the first to tell Zion, 'Look, here
    they are!'
  I gave to Jerusalem a messenger of
    good tidings.
²⁸I look but there is no one—
  no one among them to give counsel,
  no one to give answer when I ask
    them.
²⁹See, they are all false!
  Their deeds amount to nothing;
  their images are but wind and
    confusion.

CHAPTER 42

"Here is my servant, whom I uphold,
  my chosen one in whom I delight;
I will put my Spirit on him
  and he will bring justice to the
    nations.
²He will not shout or cry out,
  or raise his voice in the streets.
³A bruised reed he will not break,
  and a smoldering wick he will not
    snuff out.
In faithfulness he will bring forth
    justice;
⁴ he will not falter or be discouraged
till he establishes justice on earth.
  In his law the islands will put their
    hope."

⁵This is what God the LORD says—
  he who created the heavens and
    stretched them out,
  who spread out the earth and all
    that comes out of it,
who gives breath to its people,
  and life to those who walk on it:

⁶"I, the LORD, have called you in
   righteousness;
   I will take hold of your hand.
I will keep you and will make you
   to be a covenant for the people
   and a light for the Gentiles,
⁷to open eyes that are blind,
   to free captives from prison
   and to release from the dungeon
      those who sit in darkness.

⁸"I am the LORD; that is my name!
   I will not give my glory to another
   or my praise to idols.
⁹See, the former things have taken
      place,
   and new things I declare;
before they spring into being
   I announce them to you."

¹⁰Sing to the LORD a new song,
   his praise from the ends of the earth,
you who go down to the sea, and all
      that is in it,
   you islands, and all who live in
      them.
¹¹Let the desert and its towns raise their
      voices;
   let the settlements where Kedar lives
      rejoice.
Let the people of Sela sing for joy;
   let them shout from the
      mountaintops.
¹²Let them give glory to the LORD
   and proclaim his praise in the
      islands.
¹³The LORD will march out like a mighty
      man,
   like a warrior he will stir up his
      zeal;
with a shout he will raise the battle
      cry
   and will triumph over his enemies.

¹⁴"For a long time I have kept silent,
   I have been quiet and held myself
      back.
But now, like a woman in childbirth,
   I cry out, I gasp and pant.
¹⁵I will lay waste the mountains and
      hills
   and dry up all their vegetation;
I will turn rivers into islands
   and dry up the pools.
¹⁶I will lead the blind by ways they
      have not known,
   along unfamiliar paths I will guide
      them;

I will turn the darkness into light
      before them
   and make the rough places smooth.
These are the things I will do;
   I will not forsake them.
¹⁷But those who trust in idols,
   who say to images, 'You are our
      gods,'
   will be turned back in utter shame.

¹⁸"Hear, you deaf;
   look, you blind, and see!
¹⁹Who is blind but my servant,
   and deaf like the messenger I send?
Who is blind like the one committed
      to me,
   blind like the servant of the LORD?
²⁰You have seen many things, but have
      paid no attention;
   your ears are open, but you hear
      nothing."
²¹It pleased the LORD
   for the sake of his righteousness
   to make his law great and glorious.
²²But this is a people plundered and
      looted,
   all of them trapped in pits
   or hidden away in prisons.
They have become plunder,
   with no one to rescue them;
they have been made loot,
   with no one to say, "Send them
      back."

²³Which of you will listen to this
   or pay close attention in time to
      come?
²⁴Who handed Jacob over to become
      loot,
   and Israel to the plunderers?
Was it not the LORD,
   against whom we have sinned?
For they would not follow his ways;
   they did not obey his law.
²⁵So he poured out on them his burning
      anger,
   the violence of war.
It enveloped them in flames, yet they
      did not understand;
   it consumed them, but they did not
      take it to heart.

CHAPTER 43
But now, this is what the LORD says—
   he who created you, O Jacob,
   he who formed you, O Israel:
"Fear not, for I have redeemed you;

I have summoned you by name; you
    are mine.
²When you pass through the waters,
    I will be with you;
and when you pass through the rivers,
    they will not sweep over you.
When you walk through the fire,
    you will not be burned;
    the flames will not set you ablaze.
³For I am the LORD, your God,
    the Holy One of Israel, your Savior;
I give Egypt for your ransom,
    Cush[k] and Seba in your stead.
⁴Since you are precious and honored in
    my sight,
    and because I love you,
I will give men in exchange for you,
    and people in exchange for your life.
⁵Do not be afraid, for I am with you;
    I will bring your children from the
        east
    and gather you from the west.
⁶I will say to the north, 'Give them up!'
    and to the south, 'Do not hold them
        back.'
Bring my sons from afar
    and my daughters from the ends of
        the earth—
⁷everyone who is called by my name,
    whom I created for my glory,
    whom I formed and made."

⁸Lead out those who have eyes but are
    blind,
    who have ears but are deaf.
⁹All the nations gather together
    and the peoples assemble.
Which of them foretold this
    and proclaimed to us the former
        things?
Let them bring in their witnesses to
    prove they were right,
    so that others may hear and say, "It
        is true."
¹⁰"You are my witnesses," declares the
    LORD,
    "and my servant whom I have
        chosen,
so that you may know and believe me
    and understand that I am he.
Before me no god was formed,
    nor will there be one after me.
¹¹I, even I, am the LORD,
    and apart from me there is no
        savior.

¹²I have revealed and saved and
    proclaimed—
    I, and not some foreign god among
        you.
You are my witnesses," declares the
    LORD, "that I am God.
¹³   Yes, and from ancient days I am he.
No one can deliver out of my hand.
    When I act, who can reverse it?"

¹⁴This is what the LORD says—
    your Redeemer, the Holy One of
        Israel:
"For your sake I will send to Babylon
    and bring down as fugitives all the
        Babylonians,[l]
    in the ships in which they took
        pride.
¹⁵I am the LORD, your Holy One,
    Israel's Creator, your King."

¹⁶This is what the LORD says—
    he who made a way through the
        sea,
    a path through the mighty waters,
¹⁷who drew out the chariots and horses,
    the army and reinforcements
        together,
and they lay there, never to rise again,
    extinguished, snuffed out like a
        wick:
¹⁸"Forget the former things;
    do not dwell on the past.
¹⁹See, I am doing a new thing!
    Now it springs up; do you not
        perceive it?
I am making a way in the desert
    and streams in the wasteland.
²⁰The wild animals honor me,
    the jackals and the owls,
because I provide water in the desert
    and streams in the wasteland,
to give drink to my people, my
    chosen,
²¹   the people I formed for myself
    that they may proclaim my praise.

²²"Yet you have not called upon me,
    O Jacob,
    you have not wearied yourselves for
        me, O Israel.
²³You have not brought me sheep for
    burnt offerings,
    nor honored me with your sacrifices.
I have not burdened you with grain
    offerings

k3 That is, the upper Nile region   l14 Or Chaldeans

nor wearied you with demands for
   incense.
²⁴You have not bought any fragrant
   calamus for me,
   or lavished on me the fat of your
   sacrifices.
But you have burdened me with your
   sins
and wearied me with your offenses.

²⁵"I, even I, am he who blots out
   your transgressions, for my own
   sake,

and remembers your sins no
   more.
²⁶Review the past for me,
   let us argue the matter together;
   state the case for your innocence.
²⁷Your first father sinned;
   your spokesmen rebelled against
   me.
²⁸So I will disgrace the dignitaries of
   your temple,
   and I will consign Jacob to
   destruction^m
   and Israel to scorn.

---

^m28 The Hebrew term refers to the irrevocable giving over of things or persons to the LORD, often by totally destroying them.

JULY 26 □ DAY 208
ISAIAH 44–48
God's Choice and Babylon's Fall

OVERVIEW Isaiah next contrasts the impotence of idols with the omnipotence of Israel's God. From the same piece of wood a workman
fashions gods to be worshiped and logs to be burned. By contrast, the
God of creation predicts centuries in advance the agent of his comfort
(Cyrus, king of Persia) and the means he will employ to deliver his
oppressed people. Is it any wonder God calls forth judgment upon
idolatrous Babylon, which would dare to substitute trees and rocks for
the Lord Almighty, the Holy One of Israel?

Chapter 44	Chapter 45	Chapters 46–47	Chapter 48
The People's Choice	The Lord's Choice	Babylon's Calamity	Judah's Caution
Impotent Idols		Omnipotent God	

YOUR DAILY WALK Have you ever wondered about the unusual way
God uses people and events to accomplish his purposes on earth?
   God used a wet piece of "wool" to call Gideon into his service
(Judges 6:36–38). He used a talking donkey to rebuke Balaam (Numbers 22:28). He used a hungry fish to turn Jonah around (Jonah 1:17).
He swept his spiritually dirty nation clean by using an even dirtier
"broom"—the brutal Babylonians. And he raised up a heathen king to
free his people from exile and rebuild his holy house of worship (Isaiah
45:1, 4)!
   Can you see God's purpose linked with personal events in your life
or with international developments in the life of your nation? Go back
through chapter 45, and circle the phrases *I have, I am,* and *I will* every time you find them. Then make three columns on a sheet of paper
describing God's activities in the past ("I have . . ."), the present ("I am
. . .") and the future ("I will . . ."). When you're finished, you'll have a
wonderful prayer and praise prompter: *Father, as I see your trustworthiness in the past, build my confidence in you to accomplish your purposes in the present and future as well!*

*God can do
more in a
moment than
man in a
millennium.*

INSIGHT Predicting the Rebuilding of a House Not Yet Toppled
Cyrus, who ruled Medo-Persia from 546 to 530 b.c.—more than 150
years after Isaiah's specific prophecies concerning him—is announced
as the one to command the rebuilding of the Jerusalem temple, *which
in Isaiah's day had not yet been destroyed* (44:28)!

CHAPTER 44

"But now listen, O Jacob, my servant,
    Israel, whom I have chosen.
²This is what the Lord says—
    he who made you, who formed you
        in the womb,
    and who will help you:
Do not be afraid, O Jacob, my servant,
    Jeshurun, whom I have chosen.
³For I will pour water on the thirsty
        land,
    and streams on the dry ground;
I will pour out my Spirit on your
        offspring,
    and my blessing on your
        descendants.
⁴They will spring up like grass in a
        meadow,
    like poplar trees by flowing streams.
⁵One will say, 'I belong to the Lord';
    another will call himself by the
        name of Jacob;
still another will write on his hand,
    'The Lord's,'
    and will take the name Israel.

⁶"This is what the Lord says—
    Israel's King and Redeemer, the
        Lord Almighty:
I am the first and I am the last;
    apart from me there is no God.
⁷Who then is like me? Let him proclaim
        it.
    Let him declare and lay out before
        me
what has happened since I established
        my ancient people,
    and what is yet to come—
    yes, let him foretell what will come.
⁸Do not tremble, do not be afraid.
    Did I not proclaim this and foretell
        it long ago?
You are my witnesses. Is there any
        God besides me?
    No, there is no other Rock; I know
        not one."

⁹All who make idols are nothing,
    and the things they treasure are
        worthless.

Those who would speak up for them
        are blind;
    they are ignorant, to their own
        shame.
¹⁰Who shapes a god and casts an idol,
    which can profit him nothing?
¹¹He and his kind will be put to shame;
    craftsmen are nothing but men.
Let them all come together and take
        their stand;
    they will be brought down to terror
        and infamy.

¹²The blacksmith takes a tool
    and works with it in the coals;
he shapes an idol with hammers,
    he forges it with the might of his
        arm.
He gets hungry and loses his strength;
    he drinks no water and grows faint.
¹³The carpenter measures with a line
    and makes an outline with a marker;
he roughs it out with chisels
    and marks it with compasses.
He shapes it in the form of man,
    of man in all his glory,
    that it may dwell in a shrine.
¹⁴He cut down cedars,
    or perhaps took a cypress or oak.
He let it grow among the trees of the
        forest,
    or planted a pine, and the rain made
        it grow.
¹⁵It is man's fuel for burning;
    some of it he takes and warms
        himself,
he kindles a fire and bakes bread.
But he also fashions a god and
        worships it;
    he makes an idol and bows down to
        it.
¹⁶Half of the wood he burns in the fire;
    over it he prepares his meal,
    he roasts his meat and eats his fill.
He also warms himself and says,
    "Ah! I am warm; I see the fire."
¹⁷From the rest he makes a god, his idol;
    he bows down to it and worships.
He prays to it and says,
    "Save me; you are my god."

[18]They know nothing, they understand
    nothing;
  their eyes are plastered over so they
    cannot see,
  and their minds closed so they
    cannot understand.
[19]No one stops to think,
  no one has the knowledge or
    understanding to say,
  "Half of it I used for fuel;
  I even baked bread over its coals,
  I roasted meat and I ate.
  Shall I make a detestable thing from
    what is left?
  Shall I bow down to a block of
    wood?"
[20]He feeds on ashes, a deluded heart
    misleads him;
  he cannot save himself, or say,
  "Is not this thing in my right hand a
    lie?"

[21]"Remember these things, O Jacob,
  for you are my servant, O Israel.
  I have made you, you are my servant;
  O Israel, I will not forget you.
[22]I have swept away your offenses like a
    cloud,
  your sins like the morning mist.
  Return to me,
  for I have redeemed you."

[23]Sing for joy, O heavens, for the LORD
    has done this;
  shout aloud, O earth beneath.
  Burst into song, you mountains,
  you forests and all your trees,
  for the LORD has redeemed Jacob,
  he displays his glory in Israel.

[24]"This is what the LORD says—
  your Redeemer, who formed you in
    the womb:

  I am the LORD,
  who has made all things,
  who alone stretched out the heavens,
  who spread out the earth by myself,

[25]who foils the signs of false prophets
  and makes fools of diviners,
  who overthrows the learning of the
    wise
  and turns it into nonsense,
[26]who carries out the words of his
    servants
  and fulfills the predictions of his
    messengers,

who says of Jerusalem, 'It shall be
    inhabited,'
  of the towns of Judah, 'They shall be
    built,'
  and of their ruins, 'I will restore
    them,'
[27]who says to the watery deep, 'Be dry,
  and I will dry up your streams,'
[28]who says of Cyrus, 'He is my
    shepherd
  and will accomplish all that I please;
  he will say of Jerusalem, "Let it be
    rebuilt,"
  and of the temple, "Let its
    foundations be laid." '

CHAPTER 45
  "This is what the LORD says to his
    anointed,
  to Cyrus, whose right hand I take
    hold of
  to subdue nations before him
  and to strip kings of their armor,
  to open doors before him
  so that gates will not be shut:
[2]I will go before you
  and will level the mountains[n];
  I will break down gates of bronze
  and cut through bars of iron.
[3]I will give you the treasures of
    darkness,
  riches stored in secret places,
  so that you may know that I am the
    LORD,
  the God of Israel, who summons
    you by name.
[4]For the sake of Jacob my servant,
  of Israel my chosen,
  I summon you by name
  and bestow on you a title of honor,
  though you do not acknowledge me.
[5]I am the LORD, and there is no other;
  apart from me there is no God.
  I will strengthen you,
  though you have not acknowledged
    me,
[6]so that from the rising of the sun
  to the place of its setting
  men may know there is none besides
    me.
  I am the LORD, and there is no other.
[7]I form the light and create darkness,
  I bring prosperity and create
    disaster;
  I, the LORD, do all these things.

[n]2 Dead Sea Scrolls and Septuagint; the meaning of the word in the Masoretic Text is uncertain.

8"You heavens above, rain down
        righteousness;
    let the clouds shower it down.
Let the earth open wide,
    let salvation spring up,
let righteousness grow with it;
    I, the LORD, have created it.

9"Woe to him who quarrels with his
        Maker,
    to him who is but a potsherd among
        the potsherds on the ground.
Does the clay say to the potter,
    'What are you making?'
Does your work say,
    'He has no hands'?
10Woe to him who says to his father,
    'What have you begotten?'
or to his mother,
    'What have you brought to birth?'

11"This is what the LORD says—
    the Holy One of Israel, and its
        Maker:
Concerning things to come,
    do you question me about my
        children,
    or give me orders about the work of
        my hands?
12It is I who made the earth
    and created mankind upon it.
My own hands stretched out the
        heavens;
    I marshaled their starry hosts.
13I will raise up Cyrus⁰ in my
        righteousness:
    I will make all his ways straight.
He will rebuild my city
    and set my exiles free,
but not for a price or reward,
    says the LORD Almighty."

14This is what the LORD says:

"The products of Egypt and the
        merchandise of Cush,ᵖ
    and those tall Sabeans—
they will come over to you
    and will be yours;
they will trudge behind you,
    coming over to you in chains.
They will bow down before you
    and plead with you, saying,
    'Surely God is with you, and there is
        no other;
    there is no other god.' "

15Truly you are a God who hides
        himself,
    O God and Savior of Israel.
16All the makers of idols will be put to
        shame and disgraced;
    they will go off into disgrace
        together.
17But Israel will be saved by the LORD
    with an everlasting salvation;
you will never be put to shame or
        disgraced,
    to ages everlasting.

18For this is what the LORD says—
    he who created the heavens,
        he is God;
he who fashioned and made the earth,
        he founded it;
he did not create it to be empty,
    but formed it to be inhabited—
he says:
    "I am the LORD,
    and there is no other.
19I have not spoken in secret,
    from somewhere in a land of
        darkness;
I have not said to Jacob's descendants,
    'Seek me in vain.'
I, the LORD, speak the truth;
    I declare what is right.

20"Gather together and come;
    assemble, you fugitives from the
        nations.
Ignorant are those who carry about
        idols of wood,
    who pray to gods that cannot save.
21Declare what is to be, present it—
    let them take counsel together.
Who foretold this long ago,
    who declared it from the distant
        past?
Was it not I, the LORD?
    And there is no God apart from me,
a righteous God and a Savior;
    there is none but me.

22"Turn to me and be saved,
    all you ends of the earth;
    for I am God, and there is no other.
23By myself I have sworn,
    my mouth has uttered in all
        integrity
    a word that will not be revoked:
Before me every knee will bow;
    by me every tongue will swear.
24They will say of me, 'In the LORD alone

⁰13 Hebrew him   ᵖ14 That is, the upper Nile region

are righteousness and strength.' "
All who have raged against him
   will come to him and be put to
     shame.
²⁵But in the LORD all the descendants of
   Israel
   will be found righteous and will
     exult.

CHAPTER 46

Bel bows down, Nebo stoops low;
   their idols are borne by beasts of
     burden.�q
The images that are carried about are
     burdensome,
   a burden for the weary.
²They stoop and bow down together;
   unable to rescue the burden,
   they themselves go off into captivity.

³"Listen to me, O house of Jacob,
   all you who remain of the house of
     Israel,
you whom I have upheld since you
     were conceived,
   and have carried since your birth.
⁴Even to your old age and gray hairs
   I am he, I am he who will sustain
     you.
I have made you and I will carry you;
   I will sustain you and I will rescue
     you.

⁵"To whom will you compare me or
     count me equal?
   To whom will you liken me that we
     may be compared?
⁶Some pour out gold from their bags
   and weigh out silver on the scales;
they hire a goldsmith to make it into a
     god,
   and they bow down and worship it.
⁷They lift it to their shoulders and carry
     it;
   they set it up in its place, and there
     it stands.
From that spot it cannot move.
Though one cries out to it, it does not
     answer;
   it cannot save him from his troubles.

⁸"Remember this, fix it in mind,
   take it to heart, you rebels.
⁹Remember the former things, those of
     long ago;
   I am God, and there is no other;
   I am God, and there is none like me.

¹⁰I make known the end from the
     beginning,
   from ancient times, what is still to
     come.
I say: My purpose will stand,
   and I will do all that I please.
¹¹From the east I summon a bird of
     prey;
   from a far-off land, a man to fulfill
     my purpose.
What I have said, that will I bring
     about;
   what I have planned, that will I do.
¹²Listen to me, you stubborn-hearted,
   you who are far from righteousness.
¹³I am bringing my righteousness near,
   it is not far away;
   and my salvation will not be
     delayed.
I will grant salvation to Zion,
   my splendor to Israel.

CHAPTER 47

"Go down, sit in the dust,
   Virgin Daughter of Babylon;
sit on the ground without a throne,
   Daughter of the Babylonians.ʳ
No more will you be called
   tender or delicate.
²Take millstones and grind flour;
   take off your veil.
Lift up your skirts, bare your legs,
   and wade through the streams.
³Your nakedness will be exposed
   and your shame uncovered.
I will take vengeance;
   I will spare no one."

⁴Our Redeemer—the LORD Almighty is
     his name—
   is the Holy One of Israel.

⁵"Sit in silence, go into darkness,
   Daughter of the Babylonians;
no more will you be called
   queen of kingdoms.
⁶I was angry with my people
   and desecrated my inheritance;
I gave them into your hand,
   and you showed them no mercy.
Even on the aged
   you laid a very heavy yoke.
⁷You said, 'I will continue forever—
   the eternal queen!'
But you did not consider these things
   or reflect on what might happen.

�q1 Or *are but beasts and cattle*   ʳ1 Or *Chaldeans*; also in verse 5

8"Now then, listen, you wanton
creature,
  lounging in your security
and saying to yourself,
  'I am, and there is none besides
  me.
I will never be a widow
  or suffer the loss of children.'
9Both of these will overtake you
  in a moment, on a single day:
  loss of children and widowhood.
They will come upon you in full
  measure,
  in spite of your many sorceries
  and all your potent spells.
10You have trusted in your wickedness
  and have said, 'No one sees me.'
Your wisdom and knowledge mislead
  you
  when you say to yourself,
  'I am, and there is none besides
  me.'
11Disaster will come upon you,
  and you will not know how to
  conjure it away.
A calamity will fall upon you
  that you cannot ward off with a
  ransom;
  a catastrophe you cannot foresee
  will suddenly come upon you.

12"Keep on, then, with your magic
  spells
  and with your many sorceries,
  which you have labored at since
  childhood.
Perhaps you will succeed,
  perhaps you will cause terror.
13All the counsel you have received has
  only worn you out!
Let your astrologers come forward,
  those stargazers who make predictions
  month by month,
  let them save you from what is
  coming upon you.
14Surely they are like stubble;
  the fire will burn them up.
They cannot even save themselves
  from the power of the flame.
Here are no coals to warm anyone;
  here is no fire to sit by.
15That is all they can do for you—
  these you have labored with
  and trafficked with since
  childhood.
Each of them goes on in his error;
  there is not one that can save you.

CHAPTER 48

"Listen to this, O house of Jacob,
  you who are called by the name of
  Israel
  and come from the line of Judah,
you who take oaths in the name of the
  LORD
  and invoke the God of Israel—
  but not in truth or righteousness—
2you who call yourselves citizens of the
  holy city
  and rely on the God of Israel—
  the LORD Almighty is his name:
3I foretold the former things long ago,
  my mouth announced them and I
  made them known;
  then suddenly I acted, and they
  came to pass.
4For I knew how stubborn you were;
  the sinews of your neck were iron,
  your forehead was bronze.
5Therefore I told you these things long
  ago;
  before they happened I announced
  them to you
so that you could not say,
  'My idols did them;
  my wooden image and metal god
  ordained them.'
6You have heard these things; look at
  them all.
Will you not admit them?

"From now on I will tell you of new
  things,
  of hidden things unknown to you.
7They are created now, and not long
  ago;
  you have not heard of them before
  today.
So you cannot say,
  'Yes, I knew of them.'
8You have neither heard nor
  understood;
  from of old your ear has not been
  open.
Well do I know how treacherous you
  are;
  you were called a rebel from birth.
9For my own name's sake I delay my
  wrath;
  for the sake of my praise I hold it
  back from you,
  so as not to cut you off.
10See, I have refined you, though not as
  silver;

I have tested you in the furnace of
    affliction.
[11]For my own sake, for my own sake, I
    do this.
How can I let myself be defamed?
I will not yield my glory to another.

[12]"Listen to me, O Jacob,
    Israel, whom I have called:
I am he;
I am the first and I am the last.
[13]My own hand laid the foundations of
    the earth,
    and my right hand spread out the
      heavens;
when I summon them,
    they all stand up together.

[14]"Come together, all of you, and listen:
    Which of ⌊the idols⌋ has foretold
      these things?
The LORD's chosen ally
    will carry out his purpose against
      Babylon;
    his arm will be against the
      Babylonians.ˢ
[15]I, even I, have spoken;
    yes, I have called him.
I will bring him,
    and he will succeed in his mission.

[16]"Come near me and listen to this:

"From the first announcement I have
    not spoken in secret;
    at the time it happens, I am there."

And now the Sovereign LORD has sent
    me,
    with his Spirit.

ˢ14 Or *Chaldeans*; also in verse 20

[17]This is what the LORD says—
    your Redeemer, the Holy One of
      Israel:
"I am the LORD your God,
    who teaches you what is best for
      you,
    who directs you in the way you
      should go.
[18]If only you had paid attention to my
    commands,
    your peace would have been like a
      river,
    your righteousness like the waves of
      the sea.
[19]Your descendants would have been
    like the sand,
    your children like its numberless
      grains;
their name would never be cut off
    nor destroyed from before me."

[20]Leave Babylon,
    flee from the Babylonians!
Announce this with shouts of joy
    and proclaim it.
Send it out to the ends of the earth;
    say, "The LORD has redeemed his
      servant Jacob."
[21]They did not thirst when he led them
    through the deserts;
    he made water flow for them from
      the rock;
he split the rock
    and water gushed out.

[22]"There is no peace," says the LORD, "for
    the wicked."

JULY 27 ☐ DAY 209
ISAIAH 49–51
The Prince of Peace

 OVERVIEW The first nine chapters of Isaiah's message of comfort
have centered on God's deliverance of his people through Cyrus. Now
Isaiah focuses on the one who will bring deliverance through his suffering and death (Isaiah 49–55). He would come as a Servant to his
people and a Light to the surrounding nations, providing strength for
the weary and compassion for the downcast. And as the crowning act
of servanthood, he would offer himself as a sacrifice for sin.

Chapter 49	Chapter 50	Chapter 51
Call of the Servant	Commitment of the Servant	Consolation from the Servant
Salvation	Suffering	Solace

YOUR DAILY WALK Definition: A free country is a place where people can say whatever they think—provided they aren't overheard by a spouse, neighbor, minister or boss.

Freedom is a two-sided coin: On one side is privilege; on the other, responsibility.

Independence—the freedom to speak, write, assemble and worship without fear of a tyrant's intervention—is a prized possession. But never forget as you enjoy your *independence* that you were also created to enjoy *dependence* under the lordship of Jesus Christ.

A violin string, when totally "independent" of the violin for which it was created, is "free" to twist and turn—but not to do what a violin string is designed to do: produce music. By the same token, you are "free" when your life is uncommitted—but not free to be what God intended you to be.

Real freedom is not freedom *from* God, but freedom *with* God through the salvation that is in Jesus Christ (51:5–6, 8). In your travels today, look for a quiet place marked Free Parking, where you can pause and thank God for your independence as a citizen of earth—and your dependence as a citizen of heaven.

INSIGHT Isaiah, the Evangelical Prophet
Perhaps the most remarkable feature of Isaiah's lengthy book is the detailed way in which he describes Jesus Christ—more than seven centuries before his birth! Here are just a few of the dozens of "Snapshots of the Savior" you will find in the book: 7:14; 9:2, 6–7; 11:1–2; 35:4–6; 40:10–11; 42:1–4, 6–7; 50:6; 52:13–53:12; 61:1–2. Spend a few minutes looking them up and marking them. They may be just the key you need to open a door of witness to a Jewish friend or relative for whom you have been praying.

CHAPTER 49
Listen to me, you islands;
   hear this, you distant nations:
Before I was born the LORD called me;
   from my birth he has made mention
      of my name.
²He made my mouth like a sharpened
      sword,
   in the shadow of his hand he hid
      me;
he made me into a polished arrow
   and concealed me in his quiver.
³He said to me, "You are my servant,
   Israel, in whom I will display my
      splendor."
⁴But I said, "I have labored to no
      purpose;
I have spent my strength in vain
   and for nothing.
Yet what is due me is in the LORD's
      hand,
   and my reward is with my God."
⁵And now the LORD says—

he who formed me in the womb to
      be his servant
to bring Jacob back to him
   and gather Israel to himself,
for I am honored in the eyes of the
      LORD
   and my God has been my strength—
⁶he says:
"It is too small a thing for you to be
      my servant
to restore the tribes of Jacob
   and bring back those of Israel I have
      kept.
I will also make you a light for the
      Gentiles,
   that you may bring my salvation to
      the ends of the earth."

⁷This is what the LORD says—
   the Redeemer and Holy One of
      Israel—
to him who was despised and
      abhorred by the nation,
   to the servant of rulers:

"Kings will see you and rise up,
    princes will see and bow down,
because of the LORD, who is faithful,
    the Holy One of Israel, who has
        chosen you."

⁸This is what the LORD says:

"In the time of my favor I will answer
        you,
    and in the day of salvation I will
        help you;
I will keep you and will make you
    to be a covenant for the people,
to restore the land
    and to reassign its desolate
        inheritances,
⁹to say to the captives, 'Come out,'
    and to those in darkness, 'Be free!'

"They will feed beside the roads
    and find pasture on every barren
        hill.
¹⁰They will neither hunger nor thirst,
    nor will the desert heat or the sun
        beat upon them.
He who has compassion on them will
        guide them
    and lead them beside springs of
        water.
¹¹I will turn all my mountains into
        roads,
    and my highways will be raised up.
¹²See, they will come from afar—
    some from the north, some from the
        west,
    some from the region of Aswan.ᵗ"

¹³Shout for joy, O heavens;
    rejoice, O earth;
    burst into song, O mountains!
For the LORD comforts his people
    and will have compassion on his
        afflicted ones.

¹⁴But Zion said, "The LORD has forsaken
        me,
    the Lord has forgotten me."

¹⁵"Can a mother forget the baby at her
        breast
    and have no compassion on the
        child she has borne?
Though she may forget,
    I will not forget you!
¹⁶See, I have engraved you on the palms
        of my hands;
    your walls are ever before me.

¹⁷Your sons hasten back,
    and those who laid you waste
        depart from you.
¹⁸Lift up your eyes and look around;
    all your sons gather and come to
        you.
As surely as I live," declares the LORD,
    "you will wear them all as
        ornaments;
    you will put them on, like a bride.

¹⁹"Though you were ruined and made
        desolate
    and your land laid waste,
now you will be too small for your
        people,
    and those who devoured you will be
        far away.
²⁰The children born during your
        bereavement
    will yet say in your hearing,
'This place is too small for us;
    give us more space to live in.'
²¹Then you will say in your heart,
    'Who bore me these?
I was bereaved and barren;
    I was exiled and rejected.
Who brought these up?
I was left all alone,
    but these—where have they come
        from?' "

²²This is what the Sovereign LORD says:

"See, I will beckon to the Gentiles,
    I will lift up my banner to the
        peoples;
they will bring your sons in their arms
    and carry your daughters on their
        shoulders.
²³Kings will be your foster fathers,
    and their queens your nursing
        mothers.
They will bow down before you with
        their faces to the ground;
    they will lick the dust at your feet.
Then you will know that I am the
        LORD;
    those who hope in me will not be
        disappointed."

²⁴Can plunder be taken from warriors,
    or captives rescued from the
        fierceᵘ?

²⁵But this is what the LORD says:

"Yes, captives will be taken from
   warriors,
   and plunder retrieved from the
      fierce;
I will contend with those who contend
   with you,
   and your children I will save.
²⁶I will make your oppressors eat their
   own flesh;
   they will be drunk on their own
      blood, as with wine.
Then all mankind will know
   that I, the LORD, am your Savior,
   your Redeemer, the Mighty One of
      Jacob."

CHAPTER 50
This is what the LORD says:

"Where is your mother's certificate of
   divorce
   with which I sent her away?
Or to which of my creditors
   did I sell you?
Because of your sins you were sold;
   because of your transgressions your
      mother was sent away.
²When I came, why was there no one?
   When I called, why was there no
      one to answer?
Was my arm too short to ransom you?
   Do I lack the strength to rescue you?
By a mere rebuke I dry up the sea,
   I turn rivers into a desert;
their fish rot for lack of water
   and die of thirst.
³I clothe the sky with darkness
   and make sackcloth its covering."

⁴The Sovereign LORD has given me an
   instructed tongue,
   to know the word that sustains the
      weary.
He wakens me morning by morning,
   wakens my ear to listen like one
      being taught.
⁵The Sovereign LORD has opened my
   ears,
   and I have not been rebellious;
   I have not drawn back.
⁶I offered my back to those who beat
   me,
   my cheeks to those who pulled out
      my beard;
I did not hide my face
   from mocking and spitting.
⁷Because the Sovereign LORD helps me,
   I will not be disgraced.

Therefore have I set my face like flint,
   and I know I will not be put to
      shame.
⁸He who vindicates me is near.
   Who then will bring charges against
      me?
   Let us face each other!
Who is my accuser?
   Let him confront me!
⁹It is the Sovereign LORD who helps me.
   Who is he that will condemn me?
They will all wear out like a garment;
   the moths will eat them up.

¹⁰Who among you fears the LORD
   and obeys the word of his servant?
Let him who walks in the dark,
   who has no light,
trust in the name of the LORD
   and rely on his God.
¹¹But now, all you who light fires
   and provide yourselves with flaming
      torches,
go, walk in the light of your fires
   and of the torches you have set
      ablaze.
This is what you shall receive from my
   hand:
   You will lie down in torment.

CHAPTER 51
"Listen to me, you who pursue
   righteousness
   and who seek the LORD:
Look to the rock from which you were
   cut
   and to the quarry from which you
      were hewn;
²look to Abraham, your father,
   and to Sarah, who gave you birth.
When I called him he was but one,
   and I blessed him and made him
      many.
³The LORD will surely comfort Zion
   and will look with compassion on
      all her ruins;
he will make her deserts like Eden,
   her wastelands like the garden of
      the LORD.
Joy and gladness will be found in her,
   thanksgiving and the sound of
      singing.

⁴"Listen to me, my people;
   hear me, my nation:
The law will go out from me;
   my justice will become a light to the
      nations.

⁵My righteousness draws near speedily,
　　my salvation is on the way,
　　and my arm will bring justice to the
　　　nations.
　The islands will look to me
　　and wait in hope for my arm.
⁶Lift up your eyes to the heavens,
　　look at the earth beneath;
　the heavens will vanish like smoke,
　　the earth will wear out like a
　　　garment
　　and its inhabitants die like flies.
　But my salvation will last forever,
　　my righteousness will never fail.

⁷"Hear me, you who know what is
　　right,
　　you people who have my law in
　　　your hearts:
　Do not fear the reproach of men
　　or be terrified by their insults.
⁸For the moth will eat them up like a
　　garment;
　　the worm will devour them like
　　　wool.
　But my righteousness will last forever,
　　my salvation through all
　　　generations."

⁹Awake, awake! Clothe yourself with
　　strength,
　O arm of the LORD;
　awake, as in days gone by,
　　as in generations of old.
　Was it not you who cut Rahab to
　　pieces,
　　who pierced that monster through?
¹⁰Was it not you who dried up the sea,
　　the waters of the great deep,
　who made a road in the depths of the
　　sea
　so that the redeemed might cross
　　over?
¹¹The ransomed of the LORD will return.
　They will enter Zion with singing;
　　everlasting joy will crown their
　　　heads.
　Gladness and joy will overtake them,
　　and sorrow and sighing will flee
　　　away.

¹²"I, even I, am he who comforts you.
　Who are you that you fear mortal
　　men,
　　the sons of men, who are but grass,
¹³that you forget the LORD your Maker,
　who stretched out the heavens

and laid the foundations of the
　　earth,
that you live in constant terror every
　　day
because of the wrath of the
　　oppressor,
who is bent on destruction?
For where is the wrath of the
　　oppressor?
¹⁴　The cowering prisoners will soon be
　　set free;
they will not die in their dungeon,
　　nor will they lack bread.
¹⁵For I am the LORD your God,
　who churns up the sea so that its
　　waves roar—
　the LORD Almighty is his name.
¹⁶I have put my words in your mouth
　and covered you with the shadow of
　　my hand—
I who set the heavens in place,
　who laid the foundations of the
　　earth,
　and who say to Zion, 'You are my
　　people.' "

¹⁷Awake, awake!
　Rise up, O Jerusalem,
you who have drunk from the hand of
　　the LORD
　the cup of his wrath,
you who have drained to its dregs
　　the goblet that makes men stagger.
¹⁸Of all the sons she bore
　　there was none to guide her;
of all the sons she reared
　　there was none to take her by the
　　　hand.
¹⁹These double calamities have come
　　upon you—
　who can comfort you?—
ruin and destruction, famine and
　　sword—
　who can*ᵛ* console you?
²⁰Your sons have fainted;
　they lie at the head of every street,
　like antelope caught in a net.
They are filled with the wrath of the
　　LORD
　and the rebuke of your God.

²¹Therefore hear this, you afflicted one,
　made drunk, but not with wine.
²²This is what your Sovereign LORD says,
　your God, who defends his people:
"See, I have taken out of your hand

ᵛ19 Dead Sea Scrolls, Septuagint, Vulgate and Syriac; Masoretic Text / *how can I*

the cup that made you stagger;
from that cup, the goblet of my
    wrath,
you will never drink again.
²³I will put it into the hands of your
    tormentors,

who said to you,
  'Fall prostrate that we may walk
    over you.'
And you made your back like the
    ground,
  like a street to be walked over."

JULY 28 □ DAY 210
Walking in the Light

LOOK BACK Disciplining an obstinate child is painful, both for the child and for the parent. God's loyal love for his people is tempered by his heartache over the pain they are inflicting upon themselves because of their disobedience. They say the right words, but their lives betray their true allegiance. They substitute man-made rules for wholehearted worship. They know full well whom to trust and where to turn, but have willfully chosen not to do either. They look to foreign alliances for deliverance, rather than to the Lord Almighty.

Shining like a bright light in a dark room is righteous king Hezekiah. Faced with a tidal wave of Assyrian soldiers, Hezekiah turns to the one true Lifeguard—the living God. Faced with a life-threatening illness, Hezekiah turns to the Great Physician. In each case, the answer that comes can only have one explanation (God did it) and one outcome ("so that all kingdoms on earth may know that you alone, O LORD, are God" 37:20). Indeed, comfort, instruction and guidance are near at hand for all who look to the Holy One of Israel.

LOOK UP How do you walk with a holy God? If he is truly a consuming fire (Hebrews 12:29), how do you stay in step with him, enjoying his company without being consumed by his glory? How do you talk with him? fellowship with him? please him? serve him?

A person should give a lot of thought to a sudden decision.

The answer is as close as Isaiah 33:15–16. Those who aspire to walk with God cannot be casual or indifferent about their conduct and conversation. The ones who long to please God in everything are the ones

- who are honest and fair;
- who reject making a profit by extortion;
- who stay far away from bribes; and
- who refuse to listen to those who plot murder, who shut their eyes against contemplating evil.

And what reward awaits those willing to pay the high price for holy living?

- "[They] . . . will dwell on the heights" (heaven will be their home).
- "[Their] bread will be supplied, and water will not fail [them]" (God will supply their physical needs, Philippians 4:19).
- "[Their] refuge will be the mountain fortress" (God will protect and defend them from their enemies).

LOOK AHEAD It's not easy taking a stand for what's *right* when everyone around you is running after what's *wrong*. It's not fun swimming against the current of public opinion or walking against the wind of selfish pursuits. If the truth were known, it's hard work. But don't be quick to go with the flow. After all, it was Jesus who warned us that "small is the gate and narrow the road that leads to life, and only a few find it" (Matthew 7:14).

Even if you are the only one in your office or school who refuses to cheat and cut corners, *tell the truth*. Even if you are the only one in your dorm or class who has committed yourself to sexual abstinence until marriage, *be willing to wait*. Standing alone may not be popular, but it is always profitable for the man or woman who chooses to walk with God.

JULY 29 ☐ DAY 211
ISAIAH 52–57
The Suffering Servant

 OVERVIEW Isaiah the prophet—Isaac Watts the hymnist. More than twenty-four centuries separate their lives. And yet the words you will read today about the selfless sacrifice of the Suffering Servant bear a striking similarity to these familiar, yet ever-moving stanzas:

> When I survey the wondrous cross,
> On which the Prince of glory died,
> My richest gain I count but loss,
> And pour contempt on all my pride.

> See, from His head, His hands, His feet,
> Sorrow and love flow mingled down;
> Did e'er such love and sorrow meet,
> Or thorns compose so rich a crown?

Chapters 52–53	Chapters 54–56	Chapter 57
Redemption Accomplished	Redemption Applied	Redemption Rejected
Results	Response	

 YOUR DAILY WALK Consider Christopher Columbus writing a book about space traveler George Washington predicting the outcome of the 1996 presidential election.

Christ's blood is heaven's key.

Absurd? Of course! No one can predict events like those centuries in advance. No one, that is, except a prophet of God.

As you read chapters 52 and 53 of Isaiah's prophecy, the details appear so vivid as to make you think Isaiah is standing at the foot of the cross. In his mind the events are so clear that he narrates them in the past tense, as if Christ's death had already taken place. Yet Isaiah penned his prophecies fully seven centuries before!

Spend some thoughtful minutes meditating on today's reading.

Put yourself into the passage in Isaiah 53: "But he was pierced for *my* transgressions, he was crushed for *my* iniquities; the punishment that brought *me* peace was upon him, and by his wounds *I* [was] healed." Then close your daily walk by giving God a heartfelt thank-you for sending his Son to die on the cross—for *you*.

 INSIGHT The Bull's-Eye of Comfort
In Isaiah's prophecies of comfort (40–66), locate the middle chapter and the middle verse. Wouldn't you agree that that's a good "central passage" on comfort? (In case you can't find it, it's 53:6!)

CHAPTER 52

Awake, awake, O Zion,
    clothe yourself with strength.
Put on your garments of splendor,
    O Jerusalem, the holy city.
The uncircumcised and defiled
    will not enter you again.
²Shake off your dust;
    rise up, sit enthroned, O Jerusalem.
Free yourself from the chains on your
    neck,
    O captive Daughter of Zion.

³For this is what the LORD says:

"You were sold for nothing,
    and without money you will be
    redeemed."

⁴For this is what the Sovereign LORD
says:

"At first my people went down to
    Egypt to live;
lately, Assyria has oppressed them.

⁵"And now what do I have here?" declares the LORD.

"For my people have been taken away
    for nothing,
and those who rule them mock,ʷ"
                   declares the LORD.

"And all day long
    my name is constantly blasphemed.
⁶Therefore my people will know my
    name;
    therefore in that day they will know
that it is I who foretold it.
    Yes, it is I."

⁷How beautiful on the mountains
    are the feet of those who bring good
    news,
who proclaim peace,
    who bring good tidings,
    who proclaim salvation,
who say to Zion,
    "Your God reigns!"
⁸Listen! Your watchmen lift up their
    voices;
    together they shout for joy.
When the LORD returns to Zion,
    they will see it with their own eyes.
⁹Burst into songs of joy together,
    you ruins of Jerusalem,
for the LORD has comforted his people,
    he has redeemed Jerusalem.

¹⁰The LORD will lay bare his holy arm
    in the sight of all the nations,
and all the ends of the earth will see
    the salvation of our God.

¹¹Depart, depart, go out from there!
    Touch no unclean thing!
Come out from it and be pure,
    you who carry the vessels of the
    LORD.
¹²But you will not leave in haste
    or go in flight;
for the LORD will go before you,
    the God of Israel will be your rear
    guard.

¹³See, my servant will act wisely*ˣ*;
    he will be raised and lifted up and
    highly exalted.
¹⁴Just as there were many who were
    appalled at himʸ—
his appearance was so disfigured
    beyond that of any man
and his form marred beyond human
    likeness—
¹⁵so will he sprinkle many nations,ᶻ
    and kings will shut their mouths
    because of him.
For what they were not told, they will
    see,
and what they have not heard, they
    will understand.

CHAPTER 53

Who has believed our message
    and to whom has the arm of the
    LORD been revealed?
²He grew up before him like a tender
    shoot,
    and like a root out of dry ground.
He had no beauty or majesty to attract
    us to him,
nothing in his appearance that we
    should desire him.
³He was despised and rejected by men,
    a man of sorrows, and familiar with
    suffering.
Like one from whom men hide their
    faces
he was despised, and we esteemed
    him not.

⁴Surely he took up our infirmities
    and carried our sorrows,
yet we considered him stricken by
    God,

ʷ5 Dead Sea Scrolls and Vulgate; Masoretic Text *wail*   ˣ13 Or *will prosper*   ʸ14 Hebrew *you*   ᶻ15 Hebrew; Septuagint *so will many nations marvel at him*

smitten by him, and afflicted.
⁵But he was pierced for our
   transgressions,
   he was crushed for our iniquities;
the punishment that brought us peace
   was upon him,
   and by his wounds we are healed.
⁶We all, like sheep, have gone astray,
   each of us has turned to his own
      way;
and the LORD has laid on him
   the iniquity of us all.

⁷He was oppressed and afflicted,
   yet he did not open his mouth;
he was led like a lamb to the
      slaughter,
   and as a sheep before her shearers is
      silent,
   so he did not open his mouth.
⁸By oppressionᵃ and judgment he was
      taken away.
   And who can speak of his
      descendants?
For he was cut off from the land of the
      living;
   for the transgression of my people
      he was stricken.ᵇ
⁹He was assigned a grave with the
      wicked,
   and with the rich in his death,
though he had done no violence,
   nor was any deceit in his mouth.

¹⁰Yet it was the LORD's will to crush him
   and cause him to suffer,
   and though the LORD makesᶜ his life
      a guilt offering,
he will see his offspring and prolong
      his days,
   and the will of the LORD will prosper
      in his hand.
¹¹After the suffering of his soul,
   he will see the light ₒf lifeᵈ and be
      satisfiedᵉ;
by his knowledgeᶠ my righteous
      servant will justify many,
   and he will bear their iniquities.
¹²Therefore I will give him a portion
      among the great,ᵍ
   and he will divide the spoils with
      the strong,ʰ
because he poured out his life unto
      death,

and was numbered with the
      transgressors.
For he bore the sin of many,
   and made intercession for the
      transgressors.

CHAPTER 54
"Sing, O barren woman,
   you who never bore a child;
burst into song, shout for joy,
   you who were never in labor;
because more are the children of the
      desolate woman
   than of her who has a husband,"
                              says the LORD.
²"Enlarge the place of your tent,
   stretch your tent curtains wide,
   do not hold back;
lengthen your cords,
   strengthen your stakes.
³For you will spread out to the right
      and to the left;
   your descendants will dispossess
      nations
   and settle in their desolate cities.

⁴"Do not be afraid; you will not suffer
      shame.
   Do not fear disgrace; you will not be
      humiliated.
You will forget the shame of your
      youth
   and remember no more the reproach
      of your widowhood.
⁵For your Maker is your husband—
   the LORD Almighty is his name—
the Holy One of Israel is your
      Redeemer;
   he is called the God of all the earth.
⁶The LORD will call you back
   as if you were a wife deserted and
      distressed in spirit—
a wife who married young,
   only to be rejected," says your God.
⁷"For a brief moment I abandoned you,
   but with deep compassion I will
      bring you back.
⁸In a surge of anger
   I hid my face from you for a
      moment,
but with everlasting kindness
   I will have compassion on you,"
says the LORD your Redeemer.

ᵃ8 Or From arrest   ᵇ8 Or away. / Yet who of his generation considered / that he was cut off from the land of the living / for the transgression of my people, / to whom the blow was due?   ᶜ10 Hebrew though you make   ᵈ11 Dead Sea Scrolls (see also Septuagint); Masoretic Text does not have the light ₒf life.   ᵉ11 Or (with Masoretic Text) ¹¹He will see the result of the suffering of his soul / and be satisfied   ᶠ11 Or by knowledge of him   ᵍ12 Or many   ʰ12 Or numerous

⁹"To me this is like the days of Noah,
  when I swore that the waters of
      Noah would never again cover
      the earth.
So now I have sworn not to be angry
      with you,
  never to rebuke you again.
¹⁰Though the mountains be shaken
  and the hills be removed,
yet my unfailing love for you will not
      be shaken
  nor my covenant of peace be
      removed,"
  says the LORD, who has compassion
      on you.

¹¹"O afflicted city, lashed by storms and
      not comforted,
  I will build you with stones of
      turquoise,ⁱ
  your foundations with sapphires.ʲ
¹²I will make your battlements of rubies,
  your gates of sparkling jewels,
  and all your walls of precious
      stones.
¹³All your sons will be taught by the
      LORD,
  and great will be your children's
      peace.
¹⁴In righteousness you will be
      established:
Tyranny will be far from you;
  you will have nothing to fear.
Terror will be far removed;
  it will not come near you.
¹⁵If anyone does attack you, it will not
      be my doing;
  whoever attacks you will surrender
      to you.

¹⁶"See, it is I who created the blacksmith
  who fans the coals into flame
  and forges a weapon fit for its work.
And it is I who have created the
      destroyer to work havoc;
¹⁷   no weapon forged against you will
      prevail,
  and you will refute every tongue
      that accuses you.
This is the heritage of the servants of
      the LORD,
  and this is their vindication from
      me,"
                    declares the LORD.

CHAPTER 55

"Come, all you who are thirsty,
  come to the waters;
and you who have no money,
  come, buy and eat!
Come, buy wine and milk
  without money and without cost.
²Why spend money on what is not
      bread,
  and your labor on what does not
      satisfy?
Listen, listen to me, and eat what is
      good,
  and your soul will delight in the
      richest of fare.
³Give ear and come to me;
  hear me, that your soul may live.
I will make an everlasting covenant
      with you,
  my faithful love promised to David.
⁴See, I have made him a witness to the
      peoples,
  a leader and commander of the
      peoples.
⁵Surely you will summon nations you
      know not,
  and nations that do not know you
      will hasten to you,
because of the LORD your God,
  the Holy One of Israel,
  for he has endowed you with
      splendor."

⁶Seek the LORD while he may be found;
  call on him while he is near.
⁷Let the wicked forsake his way
  and the evil man his thoughts.
Let him turn to the LORD, and he will
      have mercy on him,
  and to our God, for he will freely
      pardon.

⁸"For my thoughts are not your
      thoughts,
  neither are your ways my ways,"
                    declares the LORD.
⁹"As the heavens are higher than the
      earth,
  so are my ways higher than your
      ways
  and my thoughts than your
      thoughts.
¹⁰As the rain and the snow
  come down from heaven,
and do not return to it
  without watering the earth

ⁱ11 The meaning of the Hebrew for this word is uncertain.   ʲ11 Or *lapis lazuli*

and making it bud and flourish,
    so that it yields seed for the sower
        and bread for the eater,
[11]so is my word that goes out from my
      mouth:
    It will not return to me empty,
but will accomplish what I desire
    and achieve the purpose for which I
      sent it.
[12]You will go out in joy
    and be led forth in peace;
the mountains and hills
    will burst into song before you,
and all the trees of the field
    will clap their hands.
[13]Instead of the thornbush will grow the
      pine tree,
    and instead of briers the myrtle will
      grow.
This will be for the LORD's renown,
    for an everlasting sign,
    which will not be destroyed."

CHAPTER 56

This is what the LORD says:

"Maintain justice
    and do what is right,
for my salvation is close at hand
    and my righteousness will soon be
      revealed.
[2]Blessed is the man who does this,
    the man who holds it fast,
who keeps the Sabbath without
      desecrating it,
    and keeps his hand from doing any
      evil."

[3]Let no foreigner who has bound
      himself to the LORD say,
    "The LORD will surely exclude me
      from his people."
And let not any eunuch complain,
    "I am only a dry tree."

[4]For this is what the LORD says:

"To the eunuchs who keep my
      Sabbaths,
    who choose what pleases me
    and hold fast to my covenant—
[5]to them I will give within my temple
      and its walls
    a memorial and a name
    better than sons and daughters;
I will give them an everlasting name
    that will not be cut off.
[6]And foreigners who bind themselves
      to the LORD

to serve him,
to love the name of the LORD,
    and to worship him,
all who keep the Sabbath without
      desecrating it
    and who hold fast to my covenant—
[7]these I will bring to my holy mountain
    and give them joy in my house of
      prayer.
Their burnt offerings and sacrifices
    will be accepted on my altar;
for my house will be called
    a house of prayer for all nations."
[8]The Sovereign LORD declares—
    he who gathers the exiles of Israel:
"I will gather still others to them
    besides those already gathered."

[9]Come, all you beasts of the field,
    come and devour, all you beasts of
      the forest!
[10]Israel's watchmen are blind,
    they all lack knowledge;
they are all mute dogs,
    they cannot bark;
they lie around and dream,
    they love to sleep.
[11]They are dogs with mighty appetites;
    they never have enough.
They are shepherds who lack
      understanding;
    they all turn to their own way,
    each seeks his own gain.
[12]"Come," each one cries, "let me get
      wine!
    Let us drink our fill of beer!
And tomorrow will be like today,
    or even far better."

CHAPTER 57

The righteous perish,
    and no one ponders it in his heart;
devout men are taken away,
    and no one understands
that the righteous are taken away
    to be spared from evil.
[2]Those who walk uprightly
    enter into peace;
    they find rest as they lie in death.

[3]"But you—come here, you sons of a
      sorceress,
    you offspring of adulterers and
      prostitutes!
[4]Whom are you mocking?
    At whom do you sneer
    and stick out your tongue?
Are you not a brood of rebels,

the offspring of liars?
⁵You burn with lust among the oaks
    and under every spreading tree;
you sacrifice your children in the
    ravines
    and under the overhanging crags.
⁶⌊The idols⌋ among the smooth stones
    of the ravines are your portion;
    they, they are your lot.
Yes, to them you have poured out
    drink offerings
    and offered grain offerings.
In the light of these things, should I
    relent?
⁷You have made your bed on a high
    and lofty hill;
    there you went up to offer your
    sacrifices.
⁸Behind your doors and your doorposts
    you have put your pagan symbols.
Forsaking me, you uncovered your
    bed,
    you climbed into it and opened it
    wide;
you made a pact with those whose
    beds you love,
    and you looked on their nakedness.
⁹You went to Molech ᵏ with olive oil
    and increased your perfumes.
You sent your ambassadors ˡ far
    away;
    you descended to the grave ᵐ itself!
¹⁰You were wearied by all your ways,
    but you would not say, 'It is
    hopeless.'
You found renewal of your strength,
    and so you did not faint.

¹¹"Whom have you so dreaded and
    feared
    that you have been false to me,
and have neither remembered me
    nor pondered this in your hearts?
Is it not because I have long been
    silent
    that you do not fear me?
¹²I will expose your righteousness and
    your works,
    and they will not benefit you.

ᵏ9 Or *to the king*   ˡ9 Or *idols*   ᵐ9 Hebrew *Sheol*

¹³When you cry out for help,
    let your collection ⌊of idols⌋ save
    you!
The wind will carry all of them off,
    a mere breath will blow them away.
But the man who makes me his refuge
    will inherit the land
    and possess my holy mountain."

¹⁴And it will be said:

"Build up, build up, prepare the road!
    Remove the obstacles out of the way
    of my people."
¹⁵For this is what the high and lofty One
    says—
    he who lives forever, whose name is
    holy:
"I live in a high and holy place,
    but also with him who is contrite
    and lowly in spirit,
to revive the spirit of the lowly
    and to revive the heart of the
    contrite.
¹⁶I will not accuse forever,
    nor will I always be angry,
for then the spirit of man would grow
    faint before me—
    the breath of man that I have
    created.
¹⁷I was enraged by his sinful greed;
    I punished him, and hid my face in
    anger,
    yet he kept on in his willful ways.
¹⁸I have seen his ways, but I will heal
    him;
    I will guide him and restore comfort
    to him,
¹⁹ creating praise on the lips of the
    mourners in Israel.
Peace, peace, to those far and near,"
    says the LORD. "And I will heal
    them."
²⁰But the wicked are like the tossing sea,
    which cannot rest,
    whose waves cast up mire and mud.
²¹"There is no peace," says my God, "for
    the wicked."

JULY 30 □ DAY 212
ISAIAH 58–62
Consummation of Judgment

OVERVIEW Comfort is coming in the form of a deliverer (Cyrus, 40–48); comfort is coming in the form of a Suffering Servant (Messiah, 49–57); and finally, comfort is coming in the form of a delivered people (Judah, 58–66). Obedience to God's commands has always been the path to individual and corporate blessing. And the future of God's people is bright indeed! When the Messiah, the light of Jerusalem, comes, then righteousness and salvation will shine forth to the nations of the world (60:1; 62:1), and Jerusalem will be "the praise of the earth" (62:7).

Chapter 58	Chapter 59	Chapter 60	Chapter 61
Ungodly Worship	Ungodly Ways	A New Wealth	A New Name
Judah's Groan		Judah's Glory	

YOUR DAILY WALK Some people are so indecisive, their favorite color is plaid. For instance, when a lady was asked, "Do you always have trouble making up your mind?" she replied, "Well, yes and no."

But there comes a time when changing your mind is not only desirable, it is imperative—and that is when God tells you to!

Repentance may be old-fashioned, but as long as there is sin, it will never be outdated.

Chapter 58 describes a nation of people who needed to change their minds about God, themselves and the wickedness that characterized their lives. In a word, they needed to repent. Their worship was full of shallow formalism; their outward piety was not matched by inward purity; they fasted for public recognition while ignoring the needs of others all around them.

Whenever an improper attitude or action has crept into your life, it's time for a change. Do these three words describe your lifestyle before God today? *Pure . . . undefiled . . . unspotted.* If not, let James 1:27 point the way to an *outward* religion that is consistent with your *inward* relationship with Jesus Christ.

INSIGHT A New Name Promised and Provided
In 62:2 the Lord promises the ransomed community of Zion "a new name." Keep reading and you'll discover not one new name but four, all contained in the same verse (62:12). What are they?

CHAPTER 58
"Shout it aloud, do not hold back.
    Raise your voice like a trumpet.
Declare to my people their rebellion
    and to the house of Jacob their sins.
²For day after day they seek me out;
    they seem eager to know my ways,
as if they were a nation that does what
        is right
    and has not forsaken the commands
        of its God.
They ask me for just decisions
    and seem eager for God to come
        near them.

³'Why have we fasted,' they say,
    'and you have not seen it?
Why have we humbled
        ourselves,
    and you have not noticed?'

"Yet on the day of your fasting, you
        do as you please
    and exploit all your workers.
⁴Your fasting ends in quarreling and
        strife,
    and in striking each other with
        wicked fists.
You cannot fast as you do today

and expect your voice to be heard
    on high.
⁵Is this the kind of fast I have chosen,
    only a day for a man to humble
        himself?
Is it only for bowing one's head like a
        reed
    and for lying on sackcloth and
        ashes?
Is that what you call a fast,
    a day acceptable to the LORD?

⁶"Is not this the kind of fasting I have
        chosen:
to loose the chains of injustice
    and untie the cords of the yoke,
to set the oppressed free
    and break every yoke?
⁷Is it not to share your food with the
        hungry
    and to provide the poor wanderer
        with shelter—
when you see the naked, to clothe
        him,
    and not to turn away from your
        own flesh and blood?
⁸Then your light will break forth like
        the dawn,
    and your healing will quickly
        appear;
then your righteousnessⁿ will go
        before you,
    and the glory of the LORD will be
        your rear guard.
⁹Then you will call, and the LORD will
        answer;
    you will cry for help, and he will
        say: Here am I.

"If you do away with the yoke of
        oppression,
    with the pointing finger and
        malicious talk,
¹⁰and if you spend yourselves in behalf
        of the hungry
    and satisfy the needs of the
        oppressed,
then your light will rise in the
        darkness,
    and your night will become like the
        noonday.
¹¹The LORD will guide you always;
    he will satisfy your needs in a
        sun-scorched land
    and will strengthen your frame.

You will be like a well-watered
        garden,
    like a spring whose waters never
        fail.
¹²Your people will rebuild the ancient
        ruins
    and will raise up the age-old
        foundations;
you will be called Repairer of Broken
        Walls,
    Restorer of Streets with Dwellings.

¹³"If you keep your feet from breaking
        the Sabbath
    and from doing as you please on my
        holy day,
if you call the Sabbath a delight
    and the LORD's holy day honorable,
and if you honor it by not going your
        own way
    and not doing as you please or
        speaking idle words,
¹⁴then you will find your joy in the
        LORD,
    and I will cause you to ride on the
        heights of the land
    and to feast on the inheritance of
        your father Jacob."
        The mouth of the LORD
            has spoken.

CHAPTER 59

Surely the arm of the LORD is not too
        short to save,
    nor his ear too dull to hear.
²But your iniquities have separated
    you from your God;
your sins have hidden his face from
        you,
    so that he will not hear.
³For your hands are stained with blood,
    your fingers with guilt.
Your lips have spoken lies,
    and your tongue mutters wicked
        things.
⁴No one calls for justice;
    no one pleads his case with
        integrity.
They rely on empty arguments and
        speak lies;
    they conceive trouble and give birth
        to evil.
⁵They hatch the eggs of vipers
    and spin a spider's web.
Whoever eats their eggs will die,

ⁿ8 Or your righteous One

and when one is broken, an adder is
    hatched.
⁶Their cobwebs are useless for clothing;
    they cannot cover themselves with
    what they make.
Their deeds are evil deeds,
    and acts of violence are in their
    hands.
⁷Their feet rush into sin;
    they are swift to shed innocent
    blood.
Their thoughts are evil thoughts;
    ruin and destruction mark their
    ways.
⁸The way of peace they do not know;
    there is no justice in their paths.
They have turned them into crooked
    roads;
    no one who walks in them will
    know peace.

⁹So justice is far from us,
    and righteousness does not reach us.
We look for light, but all is darkness;
    for brightness, but we walk in deep
    shadows.
¹⁰Like the blind we grope along the
    wall,
    feeling our way like men without
    eyes.
At midday we stumble as if it were
    twilight;
    among the strong, we are like the
    dead.
¹¹We all growl like bears;
    we moan mournfully like doves.
We look for justice, but find none;
    for deliverance, but it is far away.

¹²For our offenses are many in your
    sight,
    and our sins testify against us.
Our offenses are ever with us,
    and we acknowledge our iniquities:
¹³rebellion and treachery against the
    Lord,
turning our backs on our God,
fomenting oppression and revolt,
    uttering lies our hearts have
    conceived.
¹⁴So justice is driven back,
    and righteousness stands at a
    distance;
truth has stumbled in the streets,
    honesty cannot enter.
¹⁵Truth is nowhere to be found,

and whoever shuns evil becomes a
    prey.

The Lord looked and was displeased
    that there was no justice.
¹⁶He saw that there was no one,
    he was appalled that there was no
    one to intervene;
so his own arm worked salvation for
    him,
    and his own righteousness sustained
    him.
¹⁷He put on righteousness as his
    breastplate,
    and the helmet of salvation on his
    head;
he put on the garments of vengeance
    and wrapped himself in zeal as in a
    cloak.
¹⁸According to what they have done,
    so will he repay
wrath to his enemies
    and retribution to his foes;
    he will repay the islands their due.
¹⁹From the west, men will fear the name
    of the Lord,
    and from the rising of the sun, they
    will revere his glory.
For he will come like a pent-up flood
    that the breath of the Lord drives
    along.ᵒ
²⁰"The Redeemer will come to Zion,
    to those in Jacob who repent of their
    sins,"
                    declares the Lord.

²¹"As for me, this is my covenant with
them," says the Lord. "My Spirit, who is
on you, and my words that I have put in
your mouth will not depart from your
mouth, or from the mouths of your children, or from the mouths of their descendants from this time on and forever," says
the Lord.

CHAPTER 60
"Arise, shine, for your light has come,
    and the glory of the Lord rises upon
    you.
²See, darkness covers the earth
    and thick darkness is over the
    peoples,
but the Lord rises upon you
    and his glory appears over you.
³Nations will come to your light,

ᵒ19 Or When the enemy comes in like a flood, / the Spirit of the Lord will put him to flight

and kings to the brightness of your
    dawn.

[4]"Lift up your eyes and look about you:
    All assemble and come to you;
your sons come from afar,
    and your daughters are carried on
        the arm.
[5]Then you will look and be radiant,
    your heart will throb and swell with
        joy;
the wealth on the seas will be brought
        to you,
    to you the riches of the nations will
        come.
[6]Herds of camels will cover your land,
    young camels of Midian and Ephah.
And all from Sheba will come,
    bearing gold and incense
    and proclaiming the praise of the
        LORD.
[7]All Kedar's flocks will be gathered to
        you,
    the rams of Nebaioth will serve you;
they will be accepted as offerings on
        my altar,
    and I will adorn my glorious temple.

[8]"Who are these that fly along like
        clouds,
    like doves to their nests?
[9]Surely the islands look to me;
    in the lead are the ships of
        Tarshish,[p]
bringing your sons from afar,
    with their silver and gold,
to the honor of the LORD your God,
    the Holy One of Israel,
for he has endowed you with
        splendor.

[10]"Foreigners will rebuild your walls,
    and their kings will serve you.
Though in anger I struck you,
    in favor I will show you
        compassion.
[11]Your gates will always stand open,
    they will never be shut, day or
        night,
so that men may bring you the wealth
        of the nations—
    their kings led in triumphal
        procession.
[12]For the nation or kingdom that will
        not serve you will perish;
    it will be utterly ruined.

[13]"The glory of Lebanon will come to
        you,
    the pine, the fir and the cypress
        together,
to adorn the place of my sanctuary;
    and I will glorify the place of my
        feet.
[14]The sons of your oppressors will come
        bowing before you;
    all who despise you will bow down
        at your feet
and will call you the City of the LORD,
    Zion of the Holy One of Israel.

[15]"Although you have been forsaken and
        hated,
    with no one traveling through,
I will make you the everlasting pride
    and the joy of all generations.
[16]You will drink the milk of nations
    and be nursed at royal breasts.
Then you will know that I, the LORD,
        am your Savior,
    your Redeemer, the Mighty One of
        Jacob.
[17]Instead of bronze I will bring you
        gold,
    and silver in place of iron.
Instead of wood I will bring you
        bronze,
    and iron in place of stones.
I will make peace your governor
    and righteousness your ruler.
[18]No longer will violence be heard in
        your land,
    nor ruin or destruction within your
        borders,
but you will call your walls Salvation
    and your gates Praise.
[19]The sun will no more be your light by
        day,
    nor will the brightness of the moon
        shine on you,
for the LORD will be your everlasting
        light,
    and your God will be your glory.
[20]Your sun will never set again,
    and your moon will wane no more;
the LORD will be your everlasting light,
    and your days of sorrow will end.
[21]Then will all your people be righteous
    and they will possess the land
        forever.
They are the shoot I have planted,
    the work of my hands,
    for the display of my splendor.

[p] 9 Or the trading ships

²²The least of you will become a
      thousand,
   the smallest a mighty nation.
I am the LORD;
   in its time I will do this swiftly."

C H A P T E R   6 1

The Spirit of the Sovereign LORD is on
      me,
   because the LORD has anointed me
   to preach good news to the poor.
He has sent me to bind up the
      brokenhearted,
   to proclaim freedom for the captives
   and release from darkness for the
      prisoners,^q
²to proclaim the year of the LORD's
      favor
   and the day of vengeance of our
      God,
   to comfort all who mourn,
³   and provide for those who grieve in
      Zion—
   to bestow on them a crown of beauty
      instead of ashes,
   the oil of gladness
      instead of mourning,
   and a garment of praise
      instead of a spirit of despair.
They will be called oaks of
      righteousness,
   a planting of the LORD
   for the display of his splendor.

⁴They will rebuild the ancient ruins
   and restore the places long
      devastated;
   they will renew the ruined cities
   that have been devastated for
      generations.
⁵Aliens will shepherd your flocks;
   foreigners will work your fields and
      vineyards.
⁶And you will be called priests of the
      LORD,
   you will be named ministers of our
      God.
You will feed on the wealth of nations,
   and in their riches you will boast.

⁷Instead of their shame
   my people will receive a double
      portion,
   and instead of disgrace
   they will rejoice in their inheritance;

and so they will inherit a double
      portion in their land,
   and everlasting joy will be theirs.

⁸"For I, the LORD, love justice;
   I hate robbery and iniquity.
In my faithfulness I will reward them
   and make an everlasting covenant
      with them.
⁹Their descendants will be known
      among the nations
   and their offspring among the
      peoples.
All who see them will acknowledge
   that they are a people the LORD has
      blessed."

¹⁰I delight greatly in the LORD;
   my soul rejoices in my God.
For he has clothed me with garments
      of salvation
   and arrayed me in a robe of
      righteousness,
as a bridegroom adorns his head like a
      priest,
   and as a bride adorns herself with
      her jewels.
¹¹For as the soil makes the sprout come
      up
   and a garden causes seeds to grow,
so the Sovereign LORD will make
      righteousness and praise
   spring up before all nations.

C H A P T E R   6 2

For Zion's sake I will not keep silent,
   for Jerusalem's sake I will not
      remain quiet,
   till her righteousness shines out like
      the dawn,
   her salvation like a blazing torch.
²The nations will see your
      righteousness,
   and all kings your glory;
you will be called by a new name
   that the mouth of the LORD will
      bestow.
³You will be a crown of splendor in the
      LORD's hand,
   a royal diadem in the hand of your
      God.
⁴No longer will they call you Deserted,
   or name your land Desolate.
But you will be called Hephzibah,^r
   and your land Beulah^s;
   for the LORD will take delight in you,

^q1 Hebrew; Septuagint *the blind*   ^r4 *Hephzibah* means *my delight is in her.*   ^s4 *Beulah* means *married.*

and your land will be married.

⁵As a young man marries a maiden,
  so will your sons^t marry you;
as a bridegroom rejoices over his
    bride,
  so will your God rejoice over you.

⁶I have posted watchmen on your
    walls, O Jerusalem;
  they will never be silent day or
    night.
You who call on the LORD,
  give yourselves no rest,
⁷and give him no rest till he establishes
    Jerusalem
  and makes her the praise of the
    earth.

⁸The LORD has sworn by his right hand
    and by his mighty arm:
"Never again will I give your grain
  as food for your enemies,
and never again will foreigners drink
  the new wine

^t5 Or Builder

for which you have toiled;
⁹but those who harvest it will eat it
  and praise the LORD,
and those who gather the grapes will
    drink it
  in the courts of my sanctuary."

¹⁰Pass through, pass through the gates!
  Prepare the way for the people.
Build up, build up the highway!
  Remove the stones.
Raise a banner for the nations.

¹¹The LORD has made proclamation
  to the ends of the earth:
"Say to the Daughter of Zion,
  'See, your Savior comes!
See, his reward is with him,
  and his recompense accompanies
    him.' "
¹²They will be called the Holy People,
  the Redeemed of the LORD;
and you will be called Sought After,
  the City No Longer Deserted.

JULY 31 ☐ DAY 213
ISAIAH 63–66
Isaiah's Prayer and the Lord's Reply

 OVERVIEW Isaiah closes his great prophetic work with a stirring prayer of intercession for the house of Israel. While acknowledging their waywardness and frequent rebellions, he nevertheless claims God's promises on their behalf to redeem them and to refashion them into a people for his glory. God's response is both stern and comforting. The rebels will be punished for ignoring God's frequent invitations. Idolatry, covetousness, rebellion and disobedience will be rooted out of his people. In addition, a rich store of glory and blessing awaits God's faithful ones: a new heaven and earth, no more tears, no premature death, no want of food and no violence in nature. Isaiah concludes by summarizing the major themes of his book: God exalts the humble and contrite; the Messiah is coming to avenge his enemies; all nations will see God's glory; and all flesh will one day worship the Lord.

Chapter 63	Chapter 64	Chapter 65	Chapter 66
"Redeem Your People"	"Remake Your People"	"I Will Restore My People"	"I Will Refashion My Creation"
Isaiah's Prayer for Redemption		The Lord's Powerful Reply	

 YOUR DAILY WALK The book of Isaiah is a sobering reminder of the painful consequences of
  • taking God lightly;

Those who live in the Lord never see each other for the last time.

- ignoring his promises (and thereby forfeiting his blessing);
- ignoring his warnings (and thereby incurring judgment); and
- ignoring his invitations (and thereby missing the joy of a personal family relationship with God).

Isaiah's prophecy is long. It contains more chapters than any other Old Testament prophetic book. But his message is simple and concise—judgment and comfort: judgment for those who fail to heed God's voice and comfort for those who do.

Give yourself a spiritual hearing test right now. Are you tuned in to hear God's voice? Do you answer when he calls (6:8), or is your line constantly busy? There will come a day when the phone quits ringing forever. Spend the next few minutes telling God what you have learned from the book of Isaiah.

 INSIGHT An Old Testament "News" Paper
Notice how much "news" there is in chapters 65–66: new nations brought into the fold, a new name for God's people, a new heaven and earth for their inheritance and a new order of worship!

CHAPTER 63

Who is this coming from Edom,
    from Bozrah, with his garments
        stained crimson?
Who is this, robed in splendor,
    striding forward in the greatness of
        his strength?

"It is I, speaking in righteousness,
    mighty to save."

²Why are your garments red,
    like those of one treading the
        winepress?

³"I have trodden the winepress alone;
    from the nations no one was with
        me.
I trampled them in my anger
    and trod them down in my wrath;
their blood spattered my garments,
    and I stained all my clothing.
⁴For the day of vengeance was in my
        heart,
    and the year of my redemption has
        come.
⁵I looked, but there was no one to help,
    I was appalled that no one gave
        support;
so my own arm worked salvation for
        me,
    and my own wrath sustained me.
⁶I trampled the nations in my anger;
    in my wrath I made them drunk
    and poured their blood on the
        ground."

⁷I will tell of the kindnesses of the
        LORD,
    the deeds for which he is to be
        praised,
    according to all the LORD has done
        for us—
yes, the many good things he has done
        for the house of Israel,
    according to his compassion and
        many kindnesses.
⁸He said, "Surely they are my people,
    sons who will not be false to me";
    and so he became their Savior.
⁹In all their distress he too was
        distressed,
    and the angel of his presence saved
        them.
In his love and mercy he redeemed
        them;
    he lifted them up and carried them
    all the days of old.
¹⁰Yet they rebelled
    and grieved his Holy Spirit.
So he turned and became their enemy
    and he himself fought against them.

¹¹Then his people recalled ᵘ the days of
        old,
    the days of Moses and his people—
where is he who brought them
        through the sea,
    with the shepherd of his flock?
Where is he who set
    his Holy Spirit among them,
¹²who sent his glorious arm of power
    to be at Moses' right hand,
who divided the waters before them,

ᵘ **11** Or *But may he recall*

to gain for himself everlasting
   renown,
[13]who led them through the depths?
   Like a horse in open country,
     they did not stumble;
[14]like cattle that go down to the plain,
   they were given rest by the Spirit of
     the LORD.
   This is how you guided your people
     to make for yourself a glorious
     name.

[15]Look down from heaven and see
   from your lofty throne, holy and
     glorious.
   Where are your zeal and your might?
   Your tenderness and compassion are
     withheld from us.
[16]But you are our Father,
   though Abraham does not know us
   or Israel acknowledge us;
   you, O LORD, are our Father,
     our Redeemer from of old is your
     name.
[17]Why, O LORD, do you make us wander
   from your ways
   and harden our hearts so we do not
     revere you?
   Return for the sake of your servants,
     the tribes that are your inheritance.
[18]For a little while your people
   possessed your holy place,
   but now our enemies have trampled
     down your sanctuary.
[19]We are yours from of old;
   but you have not ruled over them,
   they have not been called by your
     name.[v]

CHAPTER 64
   Oh, that you would rend the heavens
     and come down,
   that the mountains would tremble
     before you!
[2]As when fire sets twigs ablaze
   and causes water to boil,
come down to make your name
   known to your enemies
and cause the nations to quake
   before you!
[3]For when you did awesome things
   that we did not expect,
   you came down, and the mountains
     trembled before you.
[4]Since ancient times no one has heard,
   no ear has perceived,

no eye has seen any God besides you,
   who acts on behalf of those who
     wait for him.
[5]You come to the help of those who
   gladly do right,
   who remember your ways.
   But when we continued to sin against
     them,
   you were angry.
   How then can we be saved?
[6]All of us have become like one who is
   unclean,
   and all our righteous acts are like
     filthy rags;
we all shrivel up like a leaf,
   and like the wind our sins sweep us
     away.
[7]No one calls on your name
   or strives to lay hold of you;
for you have hidden your face from us
   and made us waste away because of
     our sins.

[8]Yet, O LORD, you are our Father.
   We are the clay, you are the potter;
   we are all the work of your hand.
[9]Do not be angry beyond measure,
   O LORD;
   do not remember our sins forever.
   Oh, look upon us, we pray,
     for we are all your people.
[10]Your sacred cities have become a
   desert;
   even Zion is a desert, Jerusalem a
     desolation.
[11]Our holy and glorious temple, where
   our fathers praised you,
   has been burned with fire,
   and all that we treasured lies in
     ruins.
[12]After all this, O LORD, will you hold
   yourself back?
   Will you keep silent and punish us
     beyond measure?

CHAPTER 65
   "I revealed myself to those who did
     not ask for me;
   I was found by those who did not
     seek me.
   To a nation that did not call on my
     name,
   I said, 'Here am I, here am I.'
[2]All day long I have held out my hands
   to an obstinate people,
   who walk in ways not good,

[v]19 Or We are like those you have never ruled, / like those never called by your name

pursuing their own imaginations—
³a people who continually provoke me
to my very face,
offering sacrifices in gardens
and burning incense on altars of
brick;
⁴who sit among the graves
and spend their nights keeping
secret vigil;
who eat the flesh of pigs,
and whose pots hold broth of
unclean meat;
⁵who say, 'Keep away; don't come near
me,
for I am too sacred for you!'
Such people are smoke in my nostrils,
a fire that keeps burning all day.

⁶"See, it stands written before me:
I will not keep silent but will pay
back in full;
I will pay it back into their laps—
⁷both your sins and the sins of your
fathers,"
says the LORD.
"Because they burned sacrifices on the
mountains
and defied me on the hills,
I will measure into their laps
the full payment for their former
deeds."

⁸This is what the LORD says:

"As when juice is still found in a
cluster of grapes
and men say, 'Don't destroy it,
there is yet some good in it,'
so will I do in behalf of my servants;
I will not destroy them all.
⁹I will bring forth descendants from
Jacob,
and from Judah those who will
possess my mountains;
my chosen people will inherit them,
and there will my servants live.
¹⁰Sharon will become a pasture for
flocks,
and the Valley of Achor a resting
place for herds,
for my people who seek me.

¹¹"But as for you who forsake the LORD
and forget my holy mountain,
who spread a table for Fortune
and fill bowls of mixed wine for
Destiny,
¹²I will destine you for the sword,

and you will all bend down for the
slaughter;
for I called but you did not answer,
I spoke but you did not listen.
You did evil in my sight
and chose what displeases me."

¹³Therefore this is what the Sovereign
LORD says:

"My servants will eat,
but you will go hungry;
my servants will drink,
but you will go thirsty;
my servants will rejoice,
but you will be put to shame.
¹⁴My servants will sing
out of the joy of their hearts,
but you will cry out
from anguish of heart
and wail in brokenness of spirit.
¹⁵You will leave your name
to my chosen ones as a curse;
the Sovereign LORD will put you to
death,
but to his servants he will give
another name.
¹⁶Whoever invokes a blessing in the
land
will do so by the God of truth;
he who takes an oath in the land
will swear by the God of truth.
For the past troubles will be forgotten
and hidden from my eyes.

¹⁷"Behold, I will create
new heavens and a new earth.
The former things will not be
remembered,
nor will they come to mind.
¹⁸But be glad and rejoice forever
in what I will create,
for I will create Jerusalem to be a
delight
and its people a joy.
¹⁹I will rejoice over Jerusalem
and take delight in my people;
the sound of weeping and of crying
will be heard in it no more.

²⁰"Never again will there be in it
an infant who lives but a few days,
or an old man who does not live out
his years;
he who dies at a hundred
will be thought a mere youth;

he who fails to reach[w] a hundred
will be considered accursed.
²¹They will build houses and dwell in
them;
they will plant vineyards and eat
their fruit.
²²No longer will they build houses and
others live in them,
or plant and others eat.
For as the days of a tree,
so will be the days of my people;
my chosen ones will long enjoy
the works of their hands.
²³They will not toil in vain
or bear children doomed to
misfortune;
for they will be a people blessed by
the LORD,
they and their descendants with
them.
²⁴Before they call I will answer;
while they are still speaking I will
hear.
²⁵The wolf and the lamb will feed
together,
and the lion will eat straw like the
ox,
but dust will be the serpent's food.
They will neither harm nor destroy
on all my holy mountain,"
says the LORD.

CHAPTER 66

This is what the LORD says:

"Heaven is my throne,
and the earth is my footstool.
Where is the house you will build for
me?
Where will my resting place be?
²Has not my hand made all these
things,
and so they came into being?"
declares the LORD.

"This is the one I esteem:
he who is humble and contrite in
spirit,
and trembles at my word.
³But whoever sacrifices a bull
is like one who kills a man,
and whoever offers a lamb,
like one who breaks a dog's neck;
whoever makes a grain offering
is like one who presents pig's blood,
and whoever burns memorial incense,

like one who worships an idol.
They have chosen their own ways,
and their souls delight in their
abominations;
⁴so I also will choose harsh treatment
for them
and will bring upon them what they
dread.
For when I called, no one answered,
when I spoke, no one listened.
They did evil in my sight
and chose what displeases me."

⁵Hear the word of the LORD,
you who tremble at his word:
"Your brothers who hate you,
and exclude you because of my
name, have said,
'Let the LORD be glorified,
that we may see your joy!'
Yet they will be put to shame.
⁶Hear that uproar from the city,
hear that noise from the temple!
It is the sound of the LORD
repaying his enemies all they
deserve.

⁷"Before she goes into labor,
she gives birth;
before the pains come upon her,
she delivers a son.
⁸Who has ever heard of such a thing?
Who has ever seen such things?
Can a country be born in a day
or a nation be brought forth in a
moment?
Yet no sooner is Zion in labor
than she gives birth to her children.
⁹Do I bring to the moment of birth
and not give delivery?" says the
LORD.
"Do I close up the womb
when I bring to delivery?" says your
God.
¹⁰"Rejoice with Jerusalem and be glad
for her,
all you who love her;
rejoice greatly with her,
all you who mourn over her.
¹¹For you will nurse and be satisfied
at her comforting breasts;
you will drink deeply
and delight in her overflowing
abundance."

¹²For this is what the LORD says:

---

[w]20 Or / the sinner who reaches

"I will extend peace to her like a river,
and the wealth of nations like a
flooding stream;
you will nurse and be carried on her
arm
and dandled on her knees.
¹³As a mother comforts her child,
so will I comfort you;
and you will be comforted over
Jerusalem."

¹⁴When you see this, your heart will
rejoice
and you will flourish like grass;
the hand of the LORD will be made
known to his servants,
but his fury will be shown to his
foes.
¹⁵See, the LORD is coming with fire,
and his chariots are like a
whirlwind;
he will bring down his anger with
fury,
and his rebuke with flames of fire.
¹⁶For with fire and with his sword
the LORD will execute judgment upon
all men,
and many will be those slain by the
LORD.

¹⁷"Those who consecrate and purify
themselves to go into the gardens, following the one in the midst of ˣ those
who eat the flesh of pigs and rats and
other abominable things—they will meet
their end together," declares the LORD.

¹⁸"And I, because of their actions and
their imaginations, am about to come ʸ
and gather all nations and tongues, and
they will come and see my glory.

¹⁹"I will set a sign among them, and I
will send some of those who survive to
the nations—to Tarshish, to the Libyans ᶻ
and Lydians (famous as archers), to Tubal
and Greece, and to the distant islands that
have not heard of my fame or seen my
glory. They will proclaim my glory
among the nations. ²⁰And they will bring
all your brothers, from all the nations, to
my holy mountain in Jerusalem as an offering to the LORD—on horses, in chariots
and wagons, and on mules and camels,"
says the LORD. "They will bring them, as
the Israelites bring their grain offerings, to
the temple of the LORD in ceremonially
clean vessels. ²¹And I will select some of
them also to be priests and Levites," says
the LORD.

²²"As the new heavens and the new
earth that I make will endure before me,"
declares the LORD, "so will your name and
descendants endure. ²³From one New
Moon to another and from one Sabbath to
another, all mankind will come and bow
down before me," says the LORD. ²⁴"And
they will go out and look upon the dead
bodies of those who rebelled against me;
their worm will not die, nor will their fire
be quenched, and they will be loathsome
to all mankind."

ˣ17 Or gardens behind one of your temples, and   ʸ18 The meaning of the Hebrew for this clause is uncertain.   ᶻ19 Some
Septuagint manuscripts Put (Libyans); Hebrew Pul

Jeremiah

THE BOOK of Jeremiah presents the life and ministry of one of Judah's greatest prophets as he preaches to his once-mighty nation now teetering on the brink of disaster. For more than forty years Jeremiah proclaims an unpopular message: Repent or perish. His sermons go unheeded by his headstrong countrymen, who do their best to silence Jeremiah once and for all. Opposed, hated and imprisoned, the heartbroken prophet lives to see the cruel Babylonians carry away Judah's citizens.

Focus	Jeremiah's Sermons						Jeremiah's Experiences					
Divisions	Judah in Jeopardy	Judah in Idolatry	Judah in Rebellion	Judah in the Potter's Hand	Judah in a Leadership Crisis	Judah in Opposition	Hope amidst Judgment	Before the Fall	During the Fall	After the Fall	Gentiles in Judgment	Fall of Jerusalem
	1 6	7 10	11 15	16 20	21 25	26 29	30 33	34 36	37 39	40 45	46 51	52
Topics	Judgment						Hope	Judgment				
	Preaching							Portrayal			Prophecy	
Place	Judah											Bab-ylonia
Time	About 42 Years (627–585 B.C.)											

AUGUST 1 ☐ DAY 214
JEREMIAH 1–6
Judah in Jeopardy of Judgment

OVERVIEW God has patiently sent warning after warning through his prophetic spokesmen in an attempt to turn Judah from her hard-hearted ways. Now for the last time, God sends an ultimatum through a tender man of steel: Jeremiah. The prophet from Anathoth tells the people exactly what they need to hear, but through tear-filled eyes: God can bear with the sins of the nation no longer. Even now, the gathering clouds of Babylonian conquest can be viewed on the horizon by those having eyes to see and hearts to repent.

Chapter 1	Chapters 2–3	Chapters 4–6
Messenger of Judgment	Message of Judgment	Means of Judgment
Jeremiah's Call	Jeremiah's Cry	Judah's Conqueror

YOUR DAILY WALK Working with people is not so difficult. All you need is inexhaustible patience, unfailing insight, unshakable stability and a tremendous amount of experience!

There are no trivial assignments in the work of the Lord. God could have chosen to do his work another way, but he didn't. He chose to use people. People like Moses . . . and Isaiah . . . and Jeremiah . . . and you! God asked Moses to walk boldly into the court of Pharaoh and announce, "Let my people go!" God asked Isaiah to volunteer for an important mission. God asked Jeremiah to prophesy to a rebellious nation. Moses said, "I won't." Isaiah said, "Woe to me!" Jeremiah said, "I can't." Yet God supplied a tailor-made program of training and encouragement to prepare each messenger to deliver his message.

What message is God asking you to deliver for him today? What is your response to his assignment? Have you answered, "I can't" . . . or "I won't" . . . or "I will"? As you begin your study of Jeremiah's life and ministry, take one of your "can'ts" or "won'ts" and turn it into a "will." In the last five minutes of your quiet time today, write a short note to God expressing your desire to be used by him. Then watch him work *in* you and *through* you.

INSIGHT Deaf Ears in the Palace
Jeremiah's ministry spanned the reigns of five kings in Judah: Josiah, Jehoahaz, Jehoiakim, Jehoiachin and Zedekiah. All but Josiah were wicked kings who opposed or ignored the prophet's words.

CHAPTER 1

The words of Jeremiah son of Hilkiah, one of the priests at Anathoth in the territory of Benjamin. ²The word of the LORD came to him in the thirteenth year of the reign of Josiah son of Amon king of Judah, ³and through the reign of Jehoiakim son of Jo-siah king of Judah, down to the fifth month of the eleventh year of Zedekiah son of Josiah king of Judah, when the people of Jerusalem went into exile.

⁴The word of the LORD came to me, saying,

5"Before I formed you in the womb I
  knew[a] you,
 before you were born I set you
  apart;
 I appointed you as a prophet to the
  nations."

6"Ah, Sovereign LORD," I said, "I do not
know how to speak; I am only a child."

7But the LORD said to me, "Do not say, 'I
am only a child.' You must go to everyone
I send you to and say whatever I command you. 8Do not be afraid of them, for
I am with you and will rescue you," declares the LORD.

9Then the LORD reached out his hand
and touched my mouth and said to me,
"Now, I have put my words in your
mouth. 10See, today I appoint you over
nations and kingdoms to uproot and tear
down, to destroy and overthrow, to build
and to plant."

11The word of the LORD came to me:
"What do you see, Jeremiah?"

"I see the branch of an almond tree," I
replied.

12The LORD said to me, "You have seen
correctly, for I am watching[b] to see that
my word is fulfilled."

13The word of the LORD came to me
again: "What do you see?"

"I see a boiling pot, tilting away from
the north," I answered.

14The LORD said to me, "From the north
disaster will be poured out on all who live
in the land. 15I am about to summon all
the peoples of the northern kingdoms,"
declares the LORD.

"Their kings will come and set up their
  thrones
 in the entrance of the gates of
  Jerusalem;
they will come against all her
  surrounding walls
 and against all the towns of Judah.
16I will pronounce my judgments on my
  people
 because of their wickedness in
  forsaking me,
 in burning incense to other gods
 and in worshiping what their hands
  have made.

17"Get yourself ready! Stand up and say
to them whatever I command you. Do not
be terrified by them, or I will terrify you

before them. 18Today I have made you a
fortified city, an iron pillar and a bronze
wall to stand against the whole land—
against the kings of Judah, its officials, its
priests and the people of the land. 19They
will fight against you but will not overcome you, for I am with you and will rescue you," declares the LORD.

CHAPTER 2

The word of the LORD came to me: 2"Go
and proclaim in the hearing of Jerusalem:

" 'I remember the devotion of your
  youth,
 how as a bride you loved me
 and followed me through the desert,
  through a land not sown.
3Israel was holy to the LORD,
  the firstfruits of his harvest;
all who devoured her were held
  guilty,
 and disaster overtook them,' "
                    declares the LORD.

4Hear the word of the LORD, O house of
  Jacob,
 all you clans of the house of Israel.

5This is what the LORD says:

"What fault did your fathers find in
  me,
 that they strayed so far from me?
They followed worthless idols
 and became worthless themselves.
6They did not ask, 'Where is the LORD,
 who brought us up out of Egypt
and led us through the barren
  wilderness,
 through a land of deserts and rifts,
a land of drought and darkness,[c]
 a land where no one travels and no
  one lives?'
7I brought you into a fertile land
 to eat its fruit and rich produce.
But you came and defiled my land
 and made my inheritance detestable.
8The priests did not ask,
 'Where is the LORD?'
Those who deal with the law did not
  know me;
 the leaders rebelled against me.
The prophets prophesied by Baal,
 following worthless idols.

---

[a]5 Or chose   [b]12 The Hebrew for *watching* sounds like the Hebrew for *almond tree*.   [c]6 Or *and the shadow of death*

9"Therefore I bring charges against you
      again,"
                              declares the LORD.
"And I will bring charges against
      your children's children.
10Cross over to the coasts of Kittim*d*
      and look,
   send to Kedar*e* and observe closely;
   see if there has ever been anything
      like this:
11Has a nation ever changed its gods?
      (Yet they are not gods at all.)
   But my people have exchanged their*f*
      Glory
   for worthless idols.
12Be appalled at this, O heavens,
   and shudder with great horror,"
                              declares the LORD.
13"My people have committed two sins:
   They have forsaken me,
      the spring of living water,
   and have dug their own cisterns,
      broken cisterns that cannot hold
         water.
14Is Israel a servant, a slave by birth?
   Why then has he become plunder?
15Lions have roared;
   they have growled at him.
   They have laid waste his land;
      his towns are burned and deserted.
16Also, the men of Memphis*g* and
      Tahpanhes
   have shaved the crown of your
      head.*h*
17Have you not brought this on
      yourselves
   by forsaking the LORD your God
      when he led you in the way?
18Now why go to Egypt
   to drink water from the Shihor*i*?
   And why go to Assyria
   to drink water from the River*j*?
19Your wickedness will punish you;
   your backsliding will rebuke you.
   Consider then and realize
      how evil and bitter it is for you
   when you forsake the LORD your God
      and have no awe of me,"
                              declares the Lord,
                              the LORD Almighty.

20"Long ago you broke off your yoke
      and tore off your bonds;
   you said, 'I will not serve you!'

Indeed, on every high hill
   and under every spreading tree
      you lay down as a prostitute.
21I had planted you like a choice vine
      of sound and reliable stock.
   How then did you turn against me
      into a corrupt, wild vine?
22Although you wash yourself with soda
      and use an abundance of soap,
   the stain of your guilt is still before
      me,"
                  declares the Sovereign LORD.
23"How can you say, 'I am not defiled;
      I have not run after the Baals'?
   See how you behaved in the valley;
      consider what you have done.
   You are a swift she-camel
      running here and there,
24a wild donkey accustomed to the
         desert,
      sniffing the wind in her craving—
   in her heat who can restrain her?
   Any males that pursue her need not
         tire themselves;
      at mating time they will find her.
25Do not run until your feet are bare
      and your throat is dry.
   But you said, 'It's no use!
      I love foreign gods,
      and I must go after them.'

26"As a thief is disgraced when he is
         caught,
   so the house of Israel is disgraced—
      they, their kings and their officials,
      their priests and their prophets.
27They say to wood, 'You are my father,'
      and to stone, 'You gave me birth.'
   They have turned their backs to me
      and not their faces;
   yet when they are in trouble, they say,
      'Come and save us!'
28Where then are the gods you made for
         yourselves?
   Let them come if they can save you
      when you are in trouble!
   For you have as many gods
      as you have towns, O Judah.

29"Why do you bring charges against
         me?
   You have all rebelled against me,"
                              declares the LORD.
30"In vain I punished your people;
   they did not respond to correction.

---

*d*10 That is, Cyprus and western coastlands   *e*10 The home of Bedouin tribes in the Syro-Arabian desert   *f*11 Masoretic
Text; an ancient Hebrew scribal tradition *my*   *g*16 Hebrew *Noph*   *h*16 Or *have cracked your skull*   *i*18 That is, a branch of
the Nile   *j*18 That is, the Euphrates

Your sword has devoured your
    prophets
    like a ravening lion.

31"You of this generation, consider the
word of the LORD:

"Have I been a desert to Israel
    or a land of great darkness?
Why do my people say, 'We are free
    to roam;
    we will come to you no more'?
32Does a maiden forget her jewelry,
    a bride her wedding ornaments?
Yet my people have forgotten me,
    days without number.
33How skilled you are at pursuing love!
    Even the worst of women can learn
        from your ways.
34On your clothes men find
    the lifeblood of the innocent poor,
    though you did not catch them
        breaking in.
Yet in spite of all this
35   you say, 'I am innocent;
    he is not angry with me.'
But I will pass judgment on you
    because you say, 'I have not sinned.'
36Why do you go about so much,
    changing your ways?
You will be disappointed by Egypt
    as you were by Assyria.
37You will also leave that place
    with your hands on your head,
for the LORD has rejected those you
        trust;
    you will not be helped by them.

CHAPTER 3
"If a man divorces his wife
    and she leaves him and marries
        another man,
should he return to her again?
    Would not the land be completely
        defiled?
But you have lived as a prostitute with
    many lovers—
    would you now return to me?"
              declares the LORD.
2"Look up to the barren heights and
    see.
Is there any place where you have
    not been ravished?
By the roadside you sat waiting for
    lovers,
    sat like a nomad*k* in the desert.

You have defiled the land
    with your prostitution and
        wickedness.
3Therefore the showers have been
    withheld,
    and no spring rains have fallen.
Yet you have the brazen look of a
    prostitute;
    you refuse to blush with shame.
4Have you not just called to me:
    'My Father, my friend from my
        youth,
5will you always be angry?
    Will your wrath continue forever?'
This is how you talk,
    but you do all the evil you can."

6During the reign of King Josiah, the
LORD said to me, "Have you seen what
faithless Israel has done? She has gone up
on every high hill and under every
spreading tree and has committed adultery there. 7I thought that after she had
done all this she would return to me but
she did not, and her unfaithful sister Judah saw it. 8I gave faithless Israel her certificate of divorce and sent her away
because of all her adulteries. Yet I saw that
her unfaithful sister Judah had no fear;
she also went out and committed adultery. 9Because Israel's immorality mat-
tered so little to her, she defiled the land
and committed adultery with stone and
wood. 10In spite of all this, her unfaithful
sister Judah did not return to me with all
her heart, but only in pretense," declares
the LORD.

11The LORD said to me, "Faithless Israel
is more righteous than unfaithful Judah.
12Go, proclaim this message toward the
north:

" 'Return, faithless Israel,' declares the
    LORD,
    'I will frown on you no longer,
for I am merciful,' declares the LORD,
    'I will not be angry forever.
13Only acknowledge your guilt—
    you have rebelled against the LORD
        your God,
you have scattered your favors to
        foreign gods
    under every spreading tree,
    and have not obeyed me,' "
              declares the LORD.

14"Return, faithless people," declares the

*k*2 Or *an Arab*

LORD, "for I am your husband. I will choose you—one from a town and two from a clan—and bring you to Zion. ¹⁵Then I will give you shepherds after my own heart, who will lead you with knowledge and understanding. ¹⁶In those days, when your numbers have increased greatly in the land," declares the LORD, "men will no longer say, 'The ark of the covenant of the LORD.' It will never enter their minds or be remembered; it will not be missed, nor will another one be made. ¹⁷At that time they will call Jerusalem The Throne of the LORD, and all nations will gather in Jerusalem to honor the name of the LORD. No longer will they follow the stubbornness of their evil hearts. ¹⁸In those days the house of Judah will join the house of Israel, and together they will come from a northern land to the land I gave your forefathers as an inheritance.

¹⁹"I myself said,

" 'How gladly would I treat you like
      sons
   and give you a desirable land,
   the most beautiful inheritance of any
      nation.'
I thought you would call me 'Father'
   and not turn away from following
      me.
²⁰But like a woman unfaithful to her
      husband,
   so you have been unfaithful to me,
      O house of Israel,"
                        declares the LORD.

²¹A cry is heard on the barren heights,
   the weeping and pleading of the
      people of Israel,
because they have perverted their
      ways
   and have forgotten the LORD their
      God.

²²"Return, faithless people;
   I will cure you of backsliding."

"Yes, we will come to you,
   for you are the LORD our God.
²³Surely the ⌊idolatrous⌋ commotion on
      the hills
   and mountains is a deception;
surely in the LORD our God
   is the salvation of Israel.
²⁴From our youth shameful gods have
      consumed
   the fruits of our fathers' labor—
      their flocks and herds,

their sons and daughters.
²⁵Let us lie down in our shame,
   and let our disgrace cover us.
We have sinned against the LORD our
      God,
   both we and our fathers;
from our youth till this day
   we have not obeyed the LORD our
      God."

CHAPTER 4

"If you will return, O Israel,
   return to me,"
                        declares the LORD.
"If you put your detestable idols out of
      my sight
   and no longer go astray,
²and if in a truthful, just and righteous
      way
   you swear, 'As surely as the LORD
      lives,'
then the nations will be blessed by
      him
   and in him they will glory."

³This is what the LORD says to the men of Judah and to Jerusalem:

"Break up your unplowed ground
   and do not sow among thorns.
⁴Circumcise yourselves to the LORD,
   circumcise your hearts,
   you men of Judah and people of
      Jerusalem,
or my wrath will break out and burn
      like fire
   because of the evil you have done—
   burn with no one to quench it.

⁵"Announce in Judah and proclaim in
      Jerusalem and say:
   'Sound the trumpet throughout the
      land!'
Cry aloud and say:
   'Gather together!
   Let us flee to the fortified cities!'
⁶Raise the signal to go to Zion!
   Flee for safety without delay!
For I am bringing disaster from the
      north,
   even terrible destruction."

⁷A lion has come out of his lair;
   a destroyer of nations has set out.
He has left his place
   to lay waste your land.
Your towns will lie in ruins
   without inhabitant.
⁸So put on sackcloth,

lament and wail,
for the fierce anger of the LORD
has not turned away from us.

⁹"In that day," declares the LORD,
"the king and the officials will lose
heart,
the priests will be horrified,
and the prophets will be appalled."

¹⁰Then I said, "Ah, Sovereign LORD, how completely you have deceived this people and Jerusalem by saying, 'You will have peace,' when the sword is at our throats."
¹¹At that time this people and Jerusalem will be told, "A scorching wind from the barren heights in the desert blows toward my people, but not to winnow or cleanse; ¹²a wind too strong for that comes from me.¹ Now I pronounce my judgments against them."

¹³Look! He advances like the clouds,
his chariots come like a whirlwind,
his horses are swifter than eagles.
Woe to us! We are ruined!
¹⁴O Jerusalem, wash the evil from your
heart and be saved.
How long will you harbor wicked
thoughts?
¹⁵A voice is announcing from Dan,
proclaiming disaster from the hills of
Ephraim.
¹⁶"Tell this to the nations,
proclaim it to Jerusalem:
'A besieging army is coming from a
distant land,
raising a war cry against the cities of
Judah.
¹⁷They surround her like men guarding
a field,
because she has rebelled against
me,' "
declares the LORD.
¹⁸"Your own conduct and actions
have brought this upon you.
This is your punishment.
How bitter it is!
How it pierces to the heart!"

¹⁹Oh, my anguish, my anguish!
I writhe in pain.
Oh, the agony of my heart!
My heart pounds within me,
I cannot keep silent.
For I have heard the sound of the
trumpet;

¹ 12 Or *comes at my command*

I have heard the battle cry.
²⁰Disaster follows disaster;
the whole land lies in ruins.
In an instant my tents are destroyed,
my shelter in a moment.
²¹How long must I see the battle
standard
and hear the sound of the trumpet?

²²"My people are fools;
they do not know me.
They are senseless children;
they have no understanding.
They are skilled in doing evil;
they know not how to do good."

²³I looked at the earth,
and it was formless and empty;
and at the heavens,
and their light was gone.
²⁴I looked at the mountains,
and they were quaking;
all the hills were swaying.
²⁵I looked, and there were no people;
every bird in the sky had flown
away.
²⁶I looked, and the fruitful land was a
desert;
all its towns lay in ruins
before the LORD, before his fierce
anger.

²⁷This is what the LORD says:

"The whole land will be ruined,
though I will not destroy it
completely.
²⁸Therefore the earth will mourn
and the heavens above grow dark,
because I have spoken and will not
relent,
I have decided and will not turn
back."

²⁹At the sound of horsemen and archers
every town takes to flight.
Some go into the thickets;
some climb up among the rocks.
All the towns are deserted;
no one lives in them.

³⁰What are you doing, O devastated
one?
Why dress yourself in scarlet
and put on jewels of gold?
Why shade your eyes with paint?
You adorn yourself in vain.

Your lovers despise you;
   they seek your life.

³¹I hear a cry as of a woman in labor,
   a groan as of one bearing her first
       child—
the cry of the Daughter of Zion
   gasping for breath,
   stretching out her hands and saying,
"Alas! I am fainting;
   my life is given over to murderers."

CHAPTER 5

"Go up and down the streets of
   Jerusalem,
   look around and consider,
   search through her squares.
If you can find but one person
   who deals honestly and seeks the
      truth,
   I will forgive this city.
²Although they say, 'As surely as the
   LORD lives,'
   still they are swearing falsely."

³O LORD, do not your eyes look for
   truth?
   You struck them, but they felt no
      pain;
   you crushed them, but they refused
      correction.
They made their faces harder than
      stone
   and refused to repent.
⁴I thought, "These are only the poor;
   they are foolish,
for they do not know the way of the
   LORD,
   the requirements of their God.
⁵So I will go to the leaders
   and speak to them;
surely they know the way of the LORD,
   the requirements of their God."
But with one accord they too had
      broken off the yoke
   and torn off the bonds.
⁶Therefore a lion from the forest will
      attack them,
   a wolf from the desert will ravage
      them,
a leopard will lie in wait near their
      towns
   to tear to pieces any who venture
      out,
for their rebellion is great
   and their backslidings many.

⁷"Why should I forgive you?

Your children have forsaken me
   and sworn by gods that are not
      gods.
I supplied all their needs,
   yet they committed adultery
   and thronged to the houses of
      prostitutes.
⁸They are well-fed, lusty stallions,
   each neighing for another man's
      wife.
⁹Should I not punish them for this?"
   declares the LORD.
"Should I not avenge myself
   on such a nation as this?

¹⁰"Go through her vineyards and ravage
      them,
   but do not destroy them completely.
Strip off her branches,
   for these people do not belong to
      the LORD.
¹¹The house of Israel and the house of
   Judah
   have been utterly unfaithful to me,"
             declares the LORD.

¹²They have lied about the LORD;
   they said, "He will do nothing!
No harm will come to us;
   we will never see sword or famine.
¹³The prophets are but wind
   and the word is not in them;
   so let what they say be done to
      them."

¹⁴Therefore this is what the LORD God
Almighty says:

"Because the people have spoken these
      words,
   I will make my words in your
      mouth a fire
   and these people the wood it
      consumes.
¹⁵O house of Israel," declares the LORD,
   "I am bringing a distant nation
      against you—
an ancient and enduring nation,
   a people whose language you do not
      know,
   whose speech you do not
      understand.
¹⁶Their quivers are like an open grave;
   all of them are mighty warriors.
¹⁷They will devour your harvests and
      food,
   devour your sons and daughters;
they will devour your flocks and
      herds,

devour your vines and fig trees.
With the sword they will destroy
   the fortified cities in which you
      trust.

18"Yet even in those days," declares the LORD, "I will not destroy you completely. 19And when the people ask, 'Why has the LORD our God done all this to us?' you will tell them, 'As you have forsaken me and served foreign gods in your own land, so now you will serve foreigners in a land not your own.'

20"Announce this to the house of Jacob
   and proclaim it in Judah:
21Hear this, you foolish and senseless
      people,
   who have eyes but do not see,
   who have ears but do not hear:
22Should you not fear me?" declares the
   LORD.
   "Should you not tremble in my
      presence?
I made the sand a boundary for the
   sea,
   an everlasting barrier it cannot cross.
The waves may roll, but they cannot
   prevail;
   they may roar, but they cannot cross
      it.
23But these people have stubborn and
      rebellious hearts;
   they have turned aside and gone
      away.
24They do not say to themselves,
   'Let us fear the LORD our God,
who gives autumn and spring rains in
   season,
   who assures us of the regular weeks
      of harvest.'
25Your wrongdoings have kept these
      away;
   your sins have deprived you of
      good.

26"Among my people are wicked men
   who lie in wait like men who snare
      birds
   and like those who set traps to catch
      men.
27Like cages full of birds,
   their houses are full of deceit;
they have become rich and powerful
28   and have grown fat and sleek.
   Their evil deeds have no limit;
   they do not plead the case of the
      fatherless to win it,

they do not defend the rights of the
   poor.
29Should I not punish them for this?"
   declares the LORD.
   "Should I not avenge myself
      on such a nation as this?

30"A horrible and shocking thing
   has happened in the land:
31The prophets prophesy lies,
   the priests rule by their own
      authority,
and my people love it this way.
   But what will you do in the end?

CHAPTER 6

"Flee for safety, people of Benjamin!
   Flee from Jerusalem!
Sound the trumpet in Tekoa!
   Raise the signal over Beth
      Hakkerem!
For disaster looms out of the north,
   even terrible destruction.
2I will destroy the Daughter of Zion,
   so beautiful and delicate.
3Shepherds with their flocks will come
      against her;
   they will pitch their tents around
      her,
   each tending his own portion."

4"Prepare for battle against her!
   Arise, let us attack at noon!
But, alas, the daylight is fading,
   and the shadows of evening grow
      long.
5So arise, let us attack at night
   and destroy her fortresses!"

6This is what the LORD Almighty says:

"Cut down the trees
   and build siege ramps against
      Jerusalem.
This city must be punished;
   it is filled with oppression.
7As a well pours out its water,
   so she pours out her wickedness.
Violence and destruction resound in
      her;
   her sickness and wounds are ever
      before me.
8Take warning, O Jerusalem,
   or I will turn away from you
and make your land desolate
   so no one can live in it."

9This is what the LORD Almighty says:

"Let them glean the remnant of Israel

as thoroughly as a vine;
pass your hand over the branches
    again,
like one gathering grapes."

¹⁰To whom can I speak and give
    warning?
Who will listen to me?
Their ears are closed^m
    so they cannot hear.
The word of the LORD is offensive to
    them;
they find no pleasure in it.
¹¹But I am full of the wrath of the LORD,
    and I cannot hold it in.

"Pour it out on the children in the
    street
    and on the young men gathered
        together;
both husband and wife will be caught
    in it,
and the old, those weighed down
    with years.
¹²Their houses will be turned over to
    others,
    together with their fields and their
        wives,
when I stretch out my hand
    against those who live in the land,"
                    declares the LORD.
¹³"From the least to the greatest,
    all are greedy for gain;
prophets and priests alike,
    all practice deceit.
¹⁴They dress the wound of my people
    as though it were not serious.
'Peace, peace,' they say,
    when there is no peace.
¹⁵Are they ashamed of their loathsome
    conduct?
No, they have no shame at all;
    they do not even know how to
        blush.
So they will fall among the fallen;
    they will be brought down when I
        punish them,"
                    says the LORD.

¹⁶This is what the LORD says:

"Stand at the crossroads and look;
    ask for the ancient paths,
ask where the good way is, and walk
    in it,
    and you will find rest for your
        souls.

^m**10** Hebrew *uncircumcised*

But you said, 'We will not walk in
    it.'
¹⁷I appointed watchmen over you and
    said,
    'Listen to the sound of the trumpet!'
But you said, 'We will not listen.'
¹⁸Therefore hear, O nations;
    observe, O witnesses,
    what will happen to them.
¹⁹Hear, O earth:
I am bringing disaster on this people,
    the fruit of their schemes,
because they have not listened to my
    words
    and have rejected my law.
²⁰What do I care about incense from
    Sheba
    or sweet calamus from a distant
        land?
Your burnt offerings are not
    acceptable;
    your sacrifices do not please me."

²¹Therefore this is what the LORD says:

"I will put obstacles before this people.
Fathers and sons alike will stumble
    over them;
    neighbors and friends will perish."

²²This is what the LORD says:

"Look, an army is coming
    from the land of the north;
a great nation is being stirred up
    from the ends of the earth.
²³They are armed with bow and spear;
    they are cruel and show no mercy.
They sound like the roaring sea
    as they ride on their horses;
they come like men in battle formation
    to attack you, O Daughter of Zion."

²⁴We have heard reports about them,
    and our hands hang limp.
Anguish has gripped us,
    pain like that of a woman in labor.
²⁵Do not go out to the fields
    or walk on the roads,
for the enemy has a sword,
    and there is terror on every side.
²⁶O my people, put on sackcloth
    and roll in ashes;
mourn with bitter wailing
    as for an only son,
for suddenly the destroyer
    will come upon us.

²⁷"I have made you a tester of metals
   and my people the ore,
that you may observe
   and test their ways.
²⁸They are all hardened rebels,
   going about to slander.
They are bronze and iron;

   they all act corruptly.
²⁹The bellows blow fiercely
   to burn away the lead with fire,
but the refining goes on in vain;
   the wicked are not purged out.
³⁰They are called rejected silver,
   because the LORD has rejected them."

AUGUST 2 ☐ DAY 215
JEREMIAH 7–10
Judah in Idolatry

OVERVIEW The malignancy of idolatry and hypocrisy has permeated every segment of Judah's national life: families (7:18), the wise (counselors, 8:9), shepherds (leaders, 10:21) and even prophets and priests (8:10). Thinking that their privileged position as God's chosen people will ensure their immunity from God's wrath, they continue in a pattern of worthless worship. Because of their rebellion and indifference, their homeland will one day be reduced to a heap of ruins—a thought that reduces Jeremiah to a river of tears.

Chapter 7	Chapter 8	Chapter 9	Chapter 10
A Last Appeal	A Leaderless People	A Desolate Land	A Sovereign Lord
Judah's Shame			God's Glory

As a neglected garden tends toward weeds, so the faithless life tends toward ungodly chaos.

YOUR DAILY WALK Make a list of some of the things you have reason to take pride in (e.g., your financial success, physical strength, education, family, national heritage). Which item on your list gives you the greatest sense of satisfaction? Why?

Do you know there is something in which God wants you to glory? to "pop your buttons" over with pride? to derive an "ego boost" from every time you think about it? There is! But it isn't your bank account, your muscles or your mind. It's your relationship with him.

"This is what the LORD says: 'Let not the wise man boast of his wisdom or the strong man boast of his strength or the rich man boast of his riches, but let him who boasts boast about this: that he understands and knows me, that I am the LORD, who exercises kindness, justice and righteousness on earth, for in these I delight,' declares the LORD" (9:23–24).

Your personal relationship with the God of creation should be your source of greatest pride. But before you can enjoy that kind of relationship, you must first experience it through personal faith in his Son, Jesus. Turn to John 5:24 and read about the relationship that you can glory in today and every day.

INSIGHT Shiloh's Demise Recorded in the Digs
Shiloh (present-day Seilun), mentioned in 7:12, was the place where the ark resided in the days of Joshua (Joshua 18:1; 1 Samuel 1:3). It was abandoned by God (Psalm 78:60) and destroyed by the Philistines in approximately 1050 B.C., probably after the battle of Ebenezer (1 Samuel 4:10–11).

CHAPTER 7

This is the word that came to Jeremiah from the LORD: [2]"Stand at the gate of the LORD's house and there proclaim this message:

" 'Hear the word of the LORD, all you people of Judah who come through these gates to worship the LORD. [3]This is what the LORD Almighty, the God of Israel, says: Reform your ways and your actions, and I will let you live in this place. [4]Do not trust in deceptive words and say, "This is the temple of the LORD, the temple of the LORD, the temple of the LORD!" [5]If you really change your ways and your actions and deal with each other justly, [6]if you do not oppress the alien, the fatherless or the widow and do not shed innocent blood in this place, and if you do not follow other gods to your own harm, [7]then I will let you live in this place, in the land I gave your forefathers for ever and ever. [8]But look, you are trusting in deceptive words that are worthless.

[9]" 'Will you steal and murder, commit adultery and perjury,[n] burn incense to Baal and follow other gods you have not known, [10]and then come and stand before me in this house, which bears my Name, and say, "We are safe"—safe to do all these detestable things? [11]Has this house, which bears my Name, become a den of robbers to you? But I have been watching! declares the LORD.

[12]" 'Go now to the place in Shiloh where I first made a dwelling for my Name, and see what I did to it because of the wickedness of my people Israel. [13]While you were doing all these things, declares the LORD, I spoke to you again and again, but you did not listen; I called you, but you did not answer. [14]Therefore, what I did to Shiloh I will now do to the house that bears my Name, the temple you trust in, the place I gave to you and your fathers. [15]I will thrust you from my presence, just as I did all your brothers, the people of Ephraim.'

[16]"So do not pray for this people nor offer any plea or petition for them; do not plead with me, for I will not listen to you. [17]Do you not see what they are doing in the towns of Judah and in the streets of Jerusalem? [18]The children gather wood, the fathers light the fire, and the women knead the dough and make cakes of bread for the Queen of Heaven. They pour out drink offerings to other gods to provoke me to anger. [19]But am I the one they are provoking? declares the LORD. Are they not rather harming themselves, to their own shame?

[20]" 'Therefore this is what the Sovereign LORD says: My anger and my wrath will be poured out on this place, on man and beast, on the trees of the field and on the fruit of the ground, and it will burn and not be quenched.

[21]" 'This is what the LORD Almighty, the God of Israel, says: Go ahead, add your burnt offerings to your other sacrifices and eat the meat yourselves! [22]For when I brought your forefathers out of Egypt and spoke to them, I did not just give them commands about burnt offerings and sacrifices, [23]but I gave them this command: Obey me, and I will be your God and you will be my people. Walk in all the ways I command you, that it may go well with you. [24]But they did not listen or pay attention; instead, they followed the stubborn inclinations of their evil hearts. They went backward and not forward. [25]From the time your forefathers left Egypt until now, day after day, again and again I sent you my servants the prophets. [26]But they did not listen to me or pay attention. They were stiff-necked and did more evil than their forefathers.'

[27]"When you tell them all this, they will not listen to you; when you call to them, they will not answer. [28]Therefore say to them, 'This is the nation that has not obeyed the LORD its God or responded to correction. Truth has perished; it has vanished from their lips. [29]Cut off your hair and throw it away; take up a lament on the barren heights, for the LORD has rejected and abandoned this generation that is under his wrath.

[30]" 'The people of Judah have done evil in my eyes, declares the LORD. They have set up their detestable idols in the house that bears my Name and have defiled it. [31]They have built the high places of Topheth in the Valley of Ben Hinnom to burn their sons and daughters in the fire—something I did not command, nor did it enter my mind. [32]So beware, the days are coming, declares the LORD, when people

[n]9 Or and swear by false gods

will no longer call it Topheth or the Valley of Ben Hinnom, but the Valley of Slaughter, for they will bury the dead in Topheth until there is no more room. ³³Then the carcasses of this people will become food for the birds of the air and the beasts of the earth, and there will be no one to frighten them away. ³⁴I will bring an end to the sounds of joy and gladness and to the voices of bride and bridegroom in the towns of Judah and the streets of Jerusalem, for the land will become desolate.

CHAPTER 8

" 'At that time, declares the LORD, the bones of the kings and officials of Judah, the bones of the priests and prophets, and the bones of the people of Jerusalem will be removed from their graves. ²They will be exposed to the sun and the moon and all the stars of the heavens, which they have loved and served and which they have followed and consulted and worshiped. They will not be gathered up or buried, but will be like refuse lying on the ground. ³Wherever I banish them, all the survivors of this evil nation will prefer death to life, declares the LORD Almighty.'

⁴"Say to them, 'This is what the LORD says:

" 'When men fall down, do they not
    get up?
When a man turns away, does he
    not return?
⁵Why then have these people turned
    away?
Why does Jerusalem always turn
    away?
They cling to deceit;
    they refuse to return.
⁶I have listened attentively,
    but they do not say what is right.
No one repents of his wickedness,
    saying, "What have I done?"
Each pursues his own course
    like a horse charging into battle.
⁷Even the stork in the sky
    knows her appointed seasons,
and the dove, the swift and the thrush
    observe the time of their migration.
But my people do not know
    the requirements of the LORD.

⁸" 'How can you say, "We are wise,
    for we have the law of the LORD,"

when actually the lying pen of the
    scribes
    has handled it falsely?
⁹The wise will be put to shame;
    they will be dismayed and trapped.
Since they have rejected the word of
    the LORD,
    what kind of wisdom do they have?
¹⁰Therefore I will give their wives to
    other men
    and their fields to new owners.
From the least to the greatest,
    all are greedy for gain;
prophets and priests alike,
    all practice deceit.
¹¹They dress the wound of my people
    as though it were not serious.
"Peace, peace," they say,
    when there is no peace.
¹²Are they ashamed of their loathsome
    conduct?
No, they have no shame at all;
    they do not even know how to
    blush.
So they will fall among the fallen;
    they will be brought down when
    they are punished,
                        says the LORD.

¹³" 'I will take away their harvest,
                        declares the LORD.
There will be no grapes on the vine.
There will be no figs on the tree,
    and their leaves will wither.
What I have given them
    will be taken from them.ᵒ' "

¹⁴"Why are we sitting here?
    Gather together!
Let us flee to the fortified cities
    and perish there!
For the LORD our God has doomed us
    to perish
    and given us poisoned water to
    drink,
    because we have sinned against him.
¹⁵We hoped for peace
    but no good has come,
for a time of healing
    but there was only terror.
¹⁶The snorting of the enemy's horses
    is heard from Dan;
at the neighing of their stallions
    the whole land trembles.
They have come to devour

ᵒ13 The meaning of the Hebrew for this sentence is uncertain.

the land and everything in it,
the city and all who live there."

17"See, I will send venomous snakes
among you,
vipers that cannot be charmed,
and they will bite you,"
declares the LORD.

18O my Comforter[p] in sorrow,
my heart is faint within me.
19Listen to the cry of my people
from a land far away:
"Is the LORD not in Zion?
Is her King no longer there?"

"Why have they provoked me to anger
with their images,
with their worthless foreign idols?"

20"The harvest is past,
the summer has ended,
and we are not saved."

21Since my people are crushed, I am
crushed;
I mourn, and horror grips me.
22Is there no balm in Gilead?
Is there no physician there?
Why then is there no healing
for the wound of my people?

CHAPTER 9
1Oh, that my head were a spring of
water
and my eyes a fountain of tears!
I would weep day and night
for the slain of my people.
2Oh, that I had in the desert
a lodging place for travelers,
so that I might leave my people
and go away from them;
for they are all adulterers,
a crowd of unfaithful people.

3"They make ready their tongue
like a bow, to shoot lies;
it is not by truth
that they triumph[q] in the land.
They go from one sin to another;
they do not acknowledge me,"
declares the LORD.
4"Beware of your friends;
do not trust your brothers.
For every brother is a deceiver,[r]
and every friend a slanderer.
5Friend deceives friend,
and no one speaks the truth.
They have taught their tongues to lie;

they weary themselves with sinning.
6You[s] live in the midst of deception;
in their deceit they refuse to
acknowledge me,"
declares the LORD.

7Therefore this is what the LORD Almighty says:

"See, I will refine and test them,
for what else can I do
because of the sin of my people?
8Their tongue is a deadly arrow;
it speaks with deceit.
With his mouth each speaks cordially
to his neighbor,
but in his heart he sets a trap for
him.
9Should I not punish them for this?"
declares the LORD.
"Should I not avenge myself
on such a nation as this?"

10I will weep and wail for the
mountains
and take up a lament concerning the
desert pastures.
They are desolate and untraveled,
and the lowing of cattle is not heard.
The birds of the air have fled
and the animals are gone.

11"I will make Jerusalem a heap of ruins,
a haunt of jackals;
and I will lay waste the towns of
Judah
so no one can live there."

12What man is wise enough to understand this? Who has been instructed by the LORD and can explain it? Why has the land been ruined and laid waste like a desert that no one can cross?

13The LORD said, "It is because they have forsaken my law, which I set before them; they have not obeyed me or followed my law. 14Instead, they have followed the stubbornness of their hearts; they have followed the Baals, as their fathers taught them." 15Therefore, this is what the LORD Almighty, the God of Israel, says: "See, I will make this people eat bitter food and drink poisoned water. 16I will scatter them among nations that neither they nor their fathers have known, and I will pursue them with the sword until I have destroyed them."

---

p18 The meaning of the Hebrew for this word is uncertain.   q3 Or lies; / they are not valiant for truth   r4 Or a deceiving Jacob
s6 That is, Jeremiah (the Hebrew is singular)

¹⁷This is what the LORD Almighty says:

"Consider now! Call for the wailing
    women to come;
  send for the most skillful of them.
¹⁸Let them come quickly
  and wail over us
till our eyes overflow with tears
  and water streams from our eyelids.
¹⁹The sound of wailing is heard from
    Zion:
  'How ruined we are!
  How great is our shame!
We must leave our land
  because our houses are in ruins.' "

²⁰Now, O women, hear the word of the
    LORD;
  open your ears to the words of his
    mouth.
Teach your daughters how to wail;
  teach one another a lament.
²¹Death has climbed in through our
    windows
  and has entered our fortresses;
it has cut off the children from the
    streets
  and the young men from the public
    squares.

²²Say, "This is what the LORD declares:

" 'The dead bodies of men will lie
  like refuse on the open field,
like cut grain behind the reaper,
  with no one to gather them.' "

²³This is what the LORD says:

"Let not the wise man boast of his
    wisdom
  or the strong man boast of his
    strength
  or the rich man boast of his riches,
²⁴but let him who boasts boast about
    this:
  that he understands and knows me,
that I am the LORD, who exercises
    kindness,
  justice and righteousness on earth,
  for in these I delight,"
                declares the LORD.

²⁵"The days are coming," declares the
LORD, "when I will punish all who are circumcised only in the flesh— ²⁶Egypt, Judah, Edom, Ammon, Moab and all who
live in the desert in distant places.^t For
all these nations are really uncircumcised,
and even the whole house of Israel is uncircumcised in heart."

CHAPTER 10

Hear what the LORD says to you, O house
of Israel. ²This is what the LORD says:

"Do not learn the ways of the nations
  or be terrified by signs in the sky,
  though the nations are terrified by
    them.
³For the customs of the peoples are
    worthless;
  they cut a tree out of the forest,
  and a craftsman shapes it with his
    chisel.
⁴They adorn it with silver and gold;
  they fasten it with hammer and nails
  so it will not totter.
⁵Like a scarecrow in a melon patch,
  their idols cannot speak;
they must be carried
  because they cannot walk.
Do not fear them;
  they can do no harm
  nor can they do any good."

⁶No one is like you, O LORD;
  you are great,
  and your name is mighty in power.
⁷Who should not revere you,
  O King of the nations?
  This is your due.
Among all the wise men of the nations
  and in all their kingdoms,
  there is no one like you.
⁸They are all senseless and foolish;
  they are taught by worthless
    wooden idols.
⁹Hammered silver is brought from
    Tarshish
  and gold from Uphaz.
What the craftsman and goldsmith
    have made
  is then dressed in blue and purple—
  all made by skilled workers.
¹⁰But the LORD is the true God;
  he is the living God, the eternal
    King.
When he is angry, the earth trembles;
  the nations cannot endure his wrath.

¹¹"Tell them this: 'These gods, who did
not make the heavens and the earth, will
perish from the earth and from under the
heavens.' "^u

---

^t26 Or *desert and who clip the hair by their foreheads*   ^u11 The text of this verse is in Aramaic.

¹²But God made the earth by his power;
   he founded the world by his
      wisdom
   and stretched out the heavens by his
      understanding.
¹³When he thunders, the waters in the
      heavens roar;
   he makes clouds rise from the ends
      of the earth.
He sends lightning with the rain
   and brings out the wind from his
      storehouses.

¹⁴Everyone is senseless and without
      knowledge;
   every goldsmith is shamed by his
      idols.
His images are a fraud;
   they have no breath in them.
¹⁵They are worthless, the objects of
      mockery;
   when their judgment comes, they
      will perish.
¹⁶He who is the Portion of Jacob is not
      like these,
   for he is the Maker of all things,
including Israel, the tribe of his
      inheritance—
   the LORD Almighty is his name.

¹⁷Gather up your belongings to leave the
      land,
   you who live under siege.
¹⁸For this is what the LORD says:
   "At this time I will hurl out
   those who live in this land;
I will bring distress on them
   so that they may be captured."

¹⁹Woe to me because of my injury!
   My wound is incurable!
Yet I said to myself,
   "This is my sickness, and I must
      endure it."
²⁰My tent is destroyed;
   all its ropes are snapped.
My sons are gone from me and are no
      more;
   no one is left now to pitch my tent
   or to set up my shelter.
²¹The shepherds are senseless
   and do not inquire of the LORD;
so they do not prosper
   and all their flock is scattered.
²²Listen! The report is coming—
   a great commotion from the land of
      the north!
It will make the towns of Judah
      desolate,
   a haunt of jackals.

²³I know, O LORD, that a man's life is not
      his own;
   it is not for man to direct his steps.
²⁴Correct me, LORD, but only with
      justice—
   not in your anger,
   lest you reduce me to nothing.
²⁵Pour out your wrath on the nations
   that do not acknowledge you,
   on the peoples who do not call on
      your name.
For they have devoured Jacob;
   they have devoured him completely
   and destroyed his homeland.

AUGUST 3 ☐ DAY 216
JEREMIAH 11–15
Judah in Rebellion

 OVERVIEW Through the prophet Jeremiah, God brings a stern accusation against his people: "They . . . have broken the covenant I made
with their forefathers" (11:10). To shock the nation into realizing the
seriousness of their sin, God commands Jeremiah to provide them with
two object lessons: a rotten linen belt and full wineskins. God's judgment will be swift and severe, involving drought, invasion and exile.
As Jeremiah laments over the fate of his nation, God promises him
personal strength and protection as he carries out his prophetic ministry of doom.

Chapters 11–12	Chapter 13	Chapters 14–15
Disregarding the Covenant	Demonstrating Judah's Sinfulness	Detailing God's Judgment
Accusation	Application	Anticipation

YOUR DAILY WALK Make a list of the five people who, in your opinion, are the most popular personalities in the world today. Then ask yourself: How did they get where they are today? By being righteous? . . . serving God? . . . working hard? . . . getting the breaks? . . . keeping the law? . . . breaking the law?

Unless the heart is full, even a rich person is poor.

Now read Jeremiah's complaint to God in 12:1: "Why does the way of the wicked prosper? Why do all the faithless live at ease?" In other words, why do the ungodly prosper while the righteous are persecuted?

Long before Jeremiah's day, Job raised the same question. So did Asaph (Psalm 73). So did Habakkuk. And God's answer to each of them was basically the same: Consider the fate of the wicked. Granted, their lifestyle today and their seeming prosperity are attractive. But in the light of their eternal destiny, are you willing to trade places?

Never forget the sure outcome of those outside Christ. Make a list of five blessings you are experiencing as a child of God that those who do not belong to Christ know nothing about. Now thank God for the true riches you enjoy.

INSIGHT A Ruined Homecoming in Anathoth
Jeremiah's rude reception in his hometown is a grim reminder that "only in his hometown and in his own house is a prophet without honor" (Matthew 13:57)—the same kind of treatment that Christ received (John 1:11).

CHAPTER 11

This is the word that came to Jeremiah from the LORD: 2 "Listen to the terms of this covenant and tell them to the people of Judah and to those who live in Jerusalem. 3 Tell them that this is what the LORD, the God of Israel, says: 'Cursed is the man who does not obey the terms of this covenant— 4 the terms I commanded your forefathers when I brought them out of Egypt, out of the iron-smelting furnace.' I said, 'Obey me and do everything I command you, and you will be my people, and I will be your God. 5 Then I will fulfill the oath I swore to your forefathers, to give them a land flowing with milk and honey'—the land you possess today."

I answered, "Amen, LORD."

6 The LORD said to me, "Proclaim all these words in the towns of Judah and in the streets of Jerusalem: 'Listen to the terms of this covenant and follow them. 7 From the time I brought your forefathers up from Egypt until today, I warned them again and again, saying, "Obey me." 8 But they did not listen or pay attention; instead, they followed the stubbornness of their evil hearts. So I brought on them all the curses of the covenant I had commanded them to follow but that they did not keep.' "

9 Then the LORD said to me, "There is a conspiracy among the people of Judah and those who live in Jerusalem. 10 They have returned to the sins of their forefathers, who refused to listen to my words. They have followed other gods to serve them. Both the house of Israel and the house of Judah have broken the covenant I made with their forefathers. 11 Therefore this is what the LORD says: 'I will bring on them a disaster they cannot escape. Although they cry out to me, I will not listen to them. 12 The towns of Judah and the people of Jerusalem will go and cry out to the gods to whom they burn incense, but they will not help them at all when disaster strikes. 13 You have as many gods as you have towns, O Judah; and the altars you have set up to burn incense to that

shameful god Baal are as many as the streets of Jerusalem.'

¹⁴"Do not pray for this people nor offer any plea or petition for them, because I will not listen when they call to me in the time of their distress.

¹⁵"What is my beloved doing in my
    temple
  as she works out her evil schemes
    with many?
  Can consecrated meat avert ⌐your
    punishment⌐?
  When you engage in your wickedness,
    then you rejoice.ᵛ"

¹⁶The LORD called you a thriving olive
    tree
  with fruit beautiful in form.
  But with the roar of a mighty storm
    he will set it on fire,
    and its branches will be broken.

¹⁷The LORD Almighty, who planted you, has decreed disaster for you, because the house of Israel and the house of Judah have done evil and provoked me to anger by burning incense to Baal.

¹⁸Because the LORD revealed their plot to me, I knew it, for at that time he showed me what they were doing. ¹⁹I had been like a gentle lamb led to the slaughter; I did not realize that they had plotted against me, saying,

  "Let us destroy the tree and its fruit;
    let us cut him off from the land of
    the living,
    that his name be remembered no
      more."
²⁰But, O LORD Almighty, you who judge
    righteously
  and test the heart and mind,
  let me see your vengeance upon them,
    for to you I have committed my
      cause.

²¹"Therefore this is what the LORD says about the men of Anathoth who are seeking your life and saying, 'Do not prophesy in the name of the LORD or you will die by our hands'— ²²therefore this is what the LORD Almighty says: 'I will punish them. Their young men will die by the sword, their sons and daughters by famine. ²³Not even a remnant will be left to them, because I will bring disaster on the men of Anathoth in the year of their punishment.' "

CHAPTER 12

  You are always righteous, O LORD,
    when I bring a case before you.
  Yet I would speak with you about
    your justice:
  Why does the way of the wicked
    prosper?
  Why do all the faithless live at ease?
²You have planted them, and they have
    taken root;
  they grow and bear fruit.
  You are always on their lips
    but far from their hearts.
³Yet you know me, O LORD;
  you see me and test my thoughts
    about you.
  Drag them off like sheep to be
    butchered!
  Set them apart for the day of
    slaughter!
⁴How long will the land lie parchedʷ
  and the grass in every field be
    withered?
  Because those who live in it are
    wicked,
  the animals and birds have perished.
  Moreover, the people are saying,
    "He will not see what happens to
      us."

⁵"If you have raced with men on foot
    and they have worn you out,
  how can you compete with horses?
  If you stumble in safe country,ˣ
    how will you manage in the thickets
      byʸ the Jordan?
⁶Your brothers, your own family—
    even they have betrayed you;
  they have raised a loud cry against
      you.
  Do not trust them,
    though they speak well of you.

⁷"I will forsake my house,
    abandon my inheritance;
  I will give the one I love
    into the hands of her enemies.
⁸My inheritance has become to me
    like a lion in the forest.
  She roars at me;
    therefore I hate her.
⁹Has not my inheritance become to me
    like a speckled bird of prey

ᵛ15 Or Could consecrated meat avert your punishment? / Then you would rejoice   ʷ4 Or land mourn   ˣ5 Or If you put your trust
in a land of safety   ʸ5 Or the flooding of

that other birds of prey surround
and attack?
Go and gather all the wild beasts;
bring them to devour.
¹⁰Many shepherds will ruin my
vineyard
and trample down my field;
they will turn my pleasant field
into a desolate wasteland.
¹¹It will be made a wasteland,
parched and desolate before me;
the whole land will be laid waste
because there is no one who cares.
¹²Over all the barren heights in the
desert
destroyers will swarm,
for the sword of the LORD will devour
from one end of the land to the
other;
no one will be safe.
¹³They will sow wheat but reap thorns;
they will wear themselves out but
gain nothing.
So bear the shame of your harvest
because of the LORD's fierce anger."

¹⁴This is what the LORD says: "As for all
my wicked neighbors who seize the inheritance I gave my people Israel, I will
uproot them from their lands and I will
uproot the house of Judah from among
them. ¹⁵But after I uproot them, I will
again have compassion and will bring
each of them back to his own inheritance
and his own country. ¹⁶And if they learn
well the ways of my people and swear by
my name, saying, 'As surely as the LORD
lives'—even as they once taught my people to swear by Baal—then they will be
established among my people. ¹⁷But if
any nation does not listen, I will completely uproot and destroy it," declares
the LORD.

CHAPTER 13
This is what the LORD said to me: "Go and
buy a linen belt and put it around your
waist, but do not let it touch water." ²So I
bought a belt, as the LORD directed, and
put it around my waist.

³Then the word of the LORD came to me
a second time: ⁴"Take the belt you bought
and are wearing around your waist, and
go now to Perath �180 and hide it there in a
crevice in the rocks." ⁵So I went and hid it
at Perath, as the LORD told me.

⁶Many days later the LORD said to me,
"Go now to Perath and get the belt I told
you to hide there." ⁷So I went to Perath
and dug up the belt and took it from the
place where I had hidden it, but now it
was ruined and completely useless.

⁸Then the word of the LORD came to me:
⁹"This is what the LORD says: 'In the same
way I will ruin the pride of Judah and the
great pride of Jerusalem. ¹⁰These wicked
people, who refuse to listen to my words,
who follow the stubbornness of their
hearts and go after other gods to serve
and worship them, will be like this belt—
completely useless! ¹¹For as a belt is
bound around a man's waist, so I bound
the whole house of Israel and the whole
house of Judah to me,' declares the LORD,
'to be my people for my renown and
praise and honor. But they have not listened.'

¹²"Say to them: 'This is what the LORD,
the God of Israel, says: Every wineskin
should be filled with wine.' And if they
say to you, 'Don't we know that every
wineskin should be filled with wine?'
¹³then tell them, 'This is what the LORD
says: I am going to fill with drunkenness
all who live in this land, including the
kings who sit on David's throne, the
priests, the prophets and all those living
in Jerusalem. ¹⁴I will smash them one
against the other, fathers and sons alike,
declares the LORD. I will allow no pity or
mercy or compassion to keep me from
destroying them.' "

¹⁵Hear and pay attention,
do not be arrogant,
for the LORD has spoken.
¹⁶Give glory to the LORD your God
before he brings the darkness,
before your feet stumble
on the darkening hills.
You hope for light,
but he will turn it to thick darkness
and change it to deep gloom.
¹⁷But if you do not listen,
I will weep in secret
because of your pride;
my eyes will weep bitterly,
overflowing with tears,
because the LORD's flock will be
taken captive.

ͦ4 Or possibly the Euphrates; also in verses 5-7

¹⁸Say to the king and to the queen
    mother,
  "Come down from your thrones,
  for your glorious crowns
    will fall from your heads."
¹⁹The cities in the Negev will be shut
    up,
  and there will be no one to open
    them.
  All Judah will be carried into exile,
    carried completely away.

²⁰Lift up your eyes and see
    those who are coming from the
      north.
  Where is the flock that was entrusted
      to you,
    the sheep of which you boasted?
²¹What will you say when ˻the LORD˼
    sets over you
    those you cultivated as your special
      allies?
  Will not pain grip you
    like that of a woman in labor?
²²And if you ask yourself,
    "Why has this happened to me?"—
  it is because of your many sins
    that your skirts have been torn off
    and your body mistreated.
²³Can the Ethiopian[a] change his skin
    or the leopard its spots?
  Neither can you do good
    who are accustomed to doing evil.

²⁴"I will scatter you like chaff
    driven by the desert wind.
²⁵This is your lot,
    the portion I have decreed for you,"
                declares the LORD,
  "because you have forgotten me
    and trusted in false gods.
²⁶I will pull up your skirts over your
      face
    that your shame may be seen—
²⁷your adulteries and lustful neighings,
    your shameless prostitution!
  I have seen your detestable acts
    on the hills and in the fields.
  Woe to you, O Jerusalem!
    How long will you be unclean?"

CHAPTER 14
This is the word of the LORD to Jeremiah
concerning the drought:

²"Judah mourns,
  her cities languish;

a23 Hebrew *Cushite* (probably a person from the upper Nile region)

  they wail for the land,
    and a cry goes up from Jerusalem.
³The nobles send their servants for
      water;
  they go to the cisterns
    but find no water.
  They return with their jars unfilled;
    dismayed and despairing,
    they cover their heads.
⁴The ground is cracked
  because there is no rain in the land;
  the farmers are dismayed
    and cover their heads.
⁵Even the doe in the field
  deserts her newborn fawn
    because there is no grass.
⁶Wild donkeys stand on the barren
      heights
  and pant like jackals;
    their eyesight fails
    for lack of pasture."

⁷Although our sins testify against us,
  O LORD, do something for the sake
      of your name.
  For our backsliding is great;
    we have sinned against you.
⁸O Hope of Israel,
  its Savior in times of distress,
  why are you like a stranger in the
      land,
  like a traveler who stays only a
      night?
⁹Why are you like a man taken by
      surprise,
  like a warrior powerless to save?
  You are among us, O LORD,
    and we bear your name;
    do not forsake us!

¹⁰This is what the LORD says about this
people:

  "They greatly love to wander;
    they do not restrain their feet.
  So the LORD does not accept them;
    he will now remember their
      wickedness
    and punish them for their sins."

¹¹Then the LORD said to me, "Do not
pray for the well-being of this people.
¹²Although they fast, I will not listen to
their cry; though they offer burnt offerings and grain offerings, I will not accept
them. Instead, I will destroy them with
the sword, famine and plague."

¹³But I said, "Ah, Sovereign LORD, the prophets keep telling them, 'You will not see the sword or suffer famine. Indeed, I will give you lasting peace in this place.' "

¹⁴Then the LORD said to me, "The prophets are prophesying lies in my name. I have not sent them or appointed them or spoken to them. They are prophesying to you false visions, divinations, idolatries[b] and the delusions of their own minds. ¹⁵Therefore, this is what the LORD says about the prophets who are prophesying in my name: I did not send them, yet they are saying, 'No sword or famine will touch this land.' Those same prophets will perish by sword and famine. ¹⁶And the people they are prophesying to will be thrown out into the streets of Jerusalem because of the famine and sword. There will be no one to bury them or their wives, their sons or their daughters. I will pour out on them the calamity they deserve.

¹⁷"Speak this word to them:

" 'Let my eyes overflow with tears
    night and day without ceasing;
for my virgin daughter—my people—
    has suffered a grievous wound,
    a crushing blow.
¹⁸If I go into the country,
    I see those slain by the sword;
if I go into the city,
    I see the ravages of famine.
Both prophet and priest
    have gone to a land they know
    not.' "

¹⁹Have you rejected Judah completely?
    Do you despise Zion?
Why have you afflicted us
    so that we cannot be healed?
We hoped for peace
    but no good has come,
for a time of healing
    but there is only terror.
²⁰O LORD, we acknowledge our
    wickedness
    and the guilt of our fathers;
    we have indeed sinned against you.
²¹For the sake of your name do not
    despise us;
    do not dishonor your glorious
    throne.
Remember your covenant with us
    and do not break it.

²²Do any of the worthless idols of the
    nations bring rain?
    Do the skies themselves send down
    showers?
No, it is you, O LORD our God.
    Therefore our hope is in you,
    for you are the one who does all
    this.

CHAPTER 15

Then the LORD said to me: "Even if Moses and Samuel were to stand before me, my heart would not go out to this people. Send them away from my presence! Let them go! ²And if they ask you, 'Where shall we go?' tell them, 'This is what the LORD says:

" 'Those destined for death, to death;
    those for the sword, to the sword;
    those for starvation, to starvation;
    those for captivity, to captivity.'

³"I will send four kinds of destroyers against them," declares the LORD, "the sword to kill and the dogs to drag away and the birds of the air and the beasts of the earth to devour and destroy. ⁴I will make them abhorrent to all the kingdoms of the earth because of what Manasseh son of Hezekiah king of Judah did in Jerusalem.

⁵"Who will have pity on you,
    O Jerusalem?
    Who will mourn for you?
    Who will stop to ask how you are?
⁶You have rejected me," declares the
    LORD.
    "You keep on backsliding.
So I will lay hands on you and destroy
    you;
    I can no longer show compassion.
⁷I will winnow them with a winnowing
    fork
    at the city gates of the land.
I will bring bereavement and
    destruction on my people,
    for they have not changed their
    ways.
⁸I will make their widows more
    numerous
    than the sand of the sea.
At midday I will bring a destroyer
    against the mothers of their young
    men;
    suddenly I will bring down on them

---

b14 Or visions, worthless divinations

anguish and terror.
[9]The mother of seven will grow faint
    and breathe her last.
Her sun will set while it is still day;
    she will be disgraced and
        humiliated.
I will put the survivors to the sword
    before their enemies,"
                    declares the LORD.

[10]Alas, my mother, that you gave me
        birth,
    a man with whom the whole land
        strives and contends!
I have neither lent nor borrowed,
    yet everyone curses me.

[11]The LORD said,

"Surely I will deliver you for a good
        purpose;
    surely I will make your enemies
        plead with you
    in times of disaster and times of
        distress.

[12]"Can a man break iron—
    iron from the north—or bronze?
[13]Your wealth and your treasures
    I will give as plunder, without
        charge,
because of all your sins
    throughout your country.
[14]I will enslave you to your enemies
    in[c] a land you do not know,
for my anger will kindle a fire
    that will burn against you."

[15]You understand, O LORD;
    remember me and care for me.
    Avenge me on my persecutors.
You are long-suffering—do not take
    me away;

think of how I suffer reproach for
    your sake.
[16]When your words came, I ate them;
    they were my joy and my heart's
        delight,
for I bear your name,
    O LORD God Almighty.
[17]I never sat in the company of revelers,
    never made merry with them;
I sat alone because your hand was on
        me
and you had filled me with
        indignation.
[18]Why is my pain unending
    and my wound grievous and
        incurable?
Will you be to me like a deceptive
        brook,
    like a spring that fails?

[19]Therefore this is what the LORD says:

"If you repent, I will restore you
    that you may serve me;
if you utter worthy, not worthless,
        words,
    you will be my spokesman.
Let this people turn to you,
    but you must not turn to them.
[20]I will make you a wall to this people,
    a fortified wall of bronze;
they will fight against you
    but will not overcome you,
for I am with you
    to rescue and save you,"
                    declares the LORD.
[21]"I will save you from the hands of the
        wicked
    and redeem you from the grasp of
        the cruel."

[c]14 Some Hebrew manuscripts, Septuagint and Syriac (see also Jer. 17:4); most Hebrew manuscripts *I will cause your enemies to bring you* / *into*

AUGUST 4 □ DAY 217
JEREMIAH 16–20
Judah in the Potter's Hand

 OVERVIEW Frequently God asked his prophets to do unusual things to illustrate the message they were bringing. It was all part of being God's mouthpiece to a wayward people. In today's section Jeremiah is not allowed to marry or to attend funerals or feasts. Visually, Jeremiah is showing the people that they will lose their personal freedoms when the day of judgment finally arrives. Attempting to emphasize the coming calamity, the prophet smashes a clay pot at the feet of the leaders. But the response Jeremiah receives is discouragingly predictable. In place of the repentance he seeks, there is only rejection on the part of the people—a sure sign that judgment is near.

Chapter 16	Chapters 17–18	Chapter 19	Chapter 20
Hope in the Lord	Heart of the Matter	Hand of the Potter	Hurt of the Prophet
Consolation	Controversy	Clay Pot	Complaint

YOUR DAILY WALK Though few homemakers would enjoy the prospects of a dirt floor in their kitchen, there is one thing to be said in favor of a dirt floor: You don't worry about it getting dirty. However, it is equally true that no matter how much you clean it, your floor will always be just as dirty as the day it was "installed." That is the nature of dirt floors.

The heart is a triangle that only the Trinity can fill.

What is true of dirt floors is equally true of the human heart. The more you "scrub" it, the worse it becomes. Jeremiah delivers the bad news: "The heart is deceitful above all things and beyond cure. Who can understand it?" (17:9).

But there is good news as well. The Lord is a heart specialist (17:10). He is in the business, not simply of repairing hearts, but of replacing them with new hearts that desire to know him, love him and serve him. Have you experienced a spiritual heart transplant? If not, the Master Surgeon stands waiting to give you new life, hope and a real purpose for living. Talk to him right now. Tell him you want to "believe in your heart . . . [and] be saved" (Romans 10:9). On the basis of his Word, that is exactly what will happen!

INSIGHT Now You Know . . . and Wish You Didn't
Today's reading mentions for the first time where Judah would spend its years of exile and who would lead the nation there. Can you find it? (Hint: Look in chapter 20.)

CHAPTER 16

Then the word of the LORD came to me: 2"You must not marry and have sons or daughters in this place." 3For this is what the LORD says about the sons and daughters born in this land and about the women who are their mothers and the men who are their fathers: 4"They will die of deadly diseases. They will not be mourned or buried but will be like refuse lying on the ground. They will perish by sword and famine, and their dead bodies will become food for the birds of the air and the beasts of the earth."

5For this is what the LORD says: "Do not enter a house where there is a funeral meal; do not go to mourn or show sympathy, because I have withdrawn my blessing, my love and my pity from this people," declares the LORD. 6"Both high and low will die in this land. They will

not be buried or mourned, and no one will cut himself or shave his head for them. 7No one will offer food to comfort those who mourn for the dead—not even for a father or a mother—nor will anyone give them a drink to console them.

8"And do not enter a house where there is feasting and sit down to eat and drink. 9For this is what the LORD Almighty, the God of Israel, says: Before your eyes and in your days I will bring an end to the sounds of joy and gladness and to the voices of bride and bridegroom in this place.

10"When you tell these people all this and they ask you, 'Why has the LORD decreed such a great disaster against us? What wrong have we done? What sin have we committed against the LORD our God?' 11then say to them, 'It is because your fathers forsook me,' declares the

LORD, 'and followed other gods and served and worshiped them. They forsook me and did not keep my law. ¹²But you have behaved more wickedly than your fathers. See how each of you is following the stubbornness of his evil heart instead of obeying me. ¹³So I will throw you out of this land into a land neither you nor your fathers have known, and there you will serve other gods day and night, for I will show you no favor.'

¹⁴"However, the days are coming," declares the LORD, "when men will no longer say, 'As surely as the LORD lives, who brought the Israelites up out of Egypt,' ¹⁵but they will say, 'As surely as the LORD lives, who brought the Israelites up out of the land of the north and out of all the countries where he had banished them.' For I will restore them to the land I gave their forefathers.

¹⁶"But now I will send for many fishermen," declares the LORD, "and they will catch them. After that I will send for many hunters, and they will hunt them down on every mountain and hill and from the crevices of the rocks. ¹⁷My eyes are on all their ways; they are not hidden from me, nor is their sin concealed from my eyes. ¹⁸I will repay them double for their wickedness and their sin, because they have defiled my land with the lifeless forms of their vile images and have filled my inheritance with their detestable idols."

¹⁹O LORD, my strength and my fortress,
    my refuge in time of distress,
to you the nations will come
    from the ends of the earth and say,
"Our fathers possessed nothing but
        false gods,
    worthless idols that did them no
        good.
²⁰Do men make their own gods?
    Yes, but they are not gods!"

²¹"Therefore I will teach them—
    this time I will teach them
    my power and might.
Then they will know
    that my name is the LORD.

CHAPTER 17

"Judah's sin is engraved with an iron
        tool,

inscribed with a flint point,
    on the tablets of their hearts
    and on the horns of their altars.
²Even their children remember
    their altars and Asherah poles[d]
beside the spreading trees
    and on the high hills.
³My mountain in the land
    and your[e] wealth and all your
        treasures
I will give away as plunder,
    together with your high places,
    because of sin throughout your
        country.
⁴Through your own fault you will lose
    the inheritance I gave you.
I will enslave you to your enemies
    in a land you do not know,
for you have kindled my anger,
    and it will burn forever."

⁵This is what the LORD says:

"Cursed is the one who trusts in man,
    who depends on flesh for his
        strength
    and whose heart turns away from
        the LORD.
⁶He will be like a bush in the
        wastelands;
    he will not see prosperity when it
        comes.
He will dwell in the parched places of
        the desert,
    in a salt land where no one lives.

⁷"But blessed is the man who trusts in
        the LORD,
    whose confidence is in him.
⁸He will be like a tree planted by the
        water
    that sends out its roots by the
        stream.
It does not fear when heat comes;
    its leaves are always green.
It has no worries in a year of drought
    and never fails to bear fruit."

⁹The heart is deceitful above all things
    and beyond cure.
    Who can understand it?

¹⁰"I the LORD search the heart
    and examine the mind,
to reward a man according to his
        conduct,
    according to what his deeds
        deserve."

---

d2 That is, symbols of the goddess Asherah   e2,3 Or hills / ³and the mountains of the land. / Your

¹¹Like a partridge that hatches eggs it
    did not lay
  is the man who gains riches by
    unjust means.
  When his life is half gone, they will
    desert him,
  and in the end he will prove to be a
    fool.

¹²A glorious throne, exalted from the
    beginning,
  is the place of our sanctuary.
¹³O LORD, the hope of Israel,
  all who forsake you will be put to
    shame.
  Those who turn away from you will
    be written in the dust
  because they have forsaken the LORD,
  the spring of living water.

¹⁴Heal me, O LORD, and I will be healed;
  save me and I will be saved,
  for you are the one I praise.
¹⁵They keep saying to me,
  "Where is the word of the LORD?
  Let it now be fulfilled!"
¹⁶I have not run away from being your
    shepherd;
  you know I have not desired the
    day of despair.
  What passes my lips is open before
    you.
¹⁷Do not be a terror to me;
  you are my refuge in the day of
    disaster.
¹⁸Let my persecutors be put to shame,
  but keep me from shame;
  let them be terrified,
  but keep me from terror.
  Bring on them the day of disaster;
  destroy them with double
    destruction.

¹⁹This is what the LORD said to me: "Go
and stand at the gate of the people,
through which the kings of Judah go in
and out; stand also at all the other gates of
Jerusalem. ²⁰Say to them, 'Hear the word
of the LORD, O kings of Judah and all people of Judah and everyone living in Jerusalem who come through these gates.
²¹This is what the LORD says: Be careful
not to carry a load on the Sabbath day or
bring it through the gates of Jerusalem.
²²Do not bring a load out of your houses
or do any work on the Sabbath, but keep
the Sabbath day holy, as I commanded
your forefathers. ²³Yet they did not listen

or pay attention; they were stiff-necked
and would not listen or respond to discipline. ²⁴But if you are careful to obey me,
declares the LORD, and bring no load
through the gates of this city on the Sabbath, but keep the Sabbath day holy by
not doing any work on it, ²⁵then kings
who sit on David's throne will come
through the gates of this city with their
officials. They and their officials will come
riding in chariots and on horses, accompanied by the men of Judah and those
living in Jerusalem, and this city will be
inhabited forever. ²⁶People will come
from the towns of Judah and the villages
around Jerusalem, from the territory of
Benjamin and the western foothills, from
the hill country and the Negev, bringing
burnt offerings and sacrifices, grain offerings, incense and thank offerings to the
house of the LORD. ²⁷But if you do not
obey me to keep the Sabbath day holy by
not carrying any load as you come
through the gates of Jerusalem on the
Sabbath day, then I will kindle an unquenchable fire in the gates of Jerusalem
that will consume her fortresses.' "

CHAPTER 18

This is the word that came to Jeremiah
from the LORD: ²"Go down to the potter's
house, and there I will give you my message." ³So I went down to the potter's
house, and I saw him working at the
wheel. ⁴But the pot he was shaping from
the clay was marred in his hands; so the
potter formed it into another pot, shaping
it as seemed best to him.

⁵Then the word of the LORD came to me:
⁶"O house of Israel, can I not do with you
as this potter does?" declares the LORD.
"Like clay in the hand of the potter, so are
you in my hand, O house of Israel. ⁷If at
any time I announce that a nation or
kingdom is to be uprooted, torn down
and destroyed, ⁸and if that nation I
warned repents of its evil, then I will relent and not inflict on it the disaster I had
planned. ⁹And if at another time I announce that a nation or kingdom is to be
built up and planted, ¹⁰and if it does evil
in my sight and does not obey me, then I
will reconsider the good I had intended to
do for it.

¹¹"Now therefore say to the people of
Judah and those living in Jerusalem, 'This
is what the LORD says: Look! I am prepar-

ing a disaster for you and devising a plan against you. So turn from your evil ways, each one of you, and reform your ways and your actions.' ¹²But they will reply, 'It's no use. We will continue with our own plans; each of us will follow the stubbornness of his evil heart.' "

¹³Therefore this is what the LORD says:

"Inquire among the nations:
    Who has ever heard anything like
        this?
A most horrible thing has been done
    by Virgin Israel.
¹⁴Does the snow of Lebanon
    ever vanish from its rocky slopes?
Do its cool waters from distant sources
    ever cease to flow?ᶠ
¹⁵Yet my people have forgotten me;
    they burn incense to worthless idols,
    which made them stumble in their
        ways
    and in the ancient paths.
They made them walk in bypaths
    and on roads not built up.
¹⁶Their land will be laid waste,
    an object of lasting scorn;
all who pass by will be appalled
    and will shake their heads.
¹⁷Like a wind from the east,
    I will scatter them before their
        enemies;
I will show them my back and not my
        face
    in the day of their disaster."

¹⁸They said, "Come, let's make plans against Jeremiah; for the teaching of the law by the priest will not be lost, nor will counsel from the wise, nor the word from the prophets. So come, let's attack him with our tongues and pay no attention to anything he says."

¹⁹Listen to me, O LORD;
    hear what my accusers are saying!
²⁰Should good be repaid with evil?
    Yet they have dug a pit for me.
Remember that I stood before you
    and spoke in their behalf
    to turn your wrath away from them.
²¹So give their children over to famine;
    hand them over to the power of the
        sword.
Let their wives be made childless and
        widows;

let their men be put to death,
    their young men slain by the sword
        in battle.
²²Let a cry be heard from their houses
    when you suddenly bring invaders
        against them,
for they have dug a pit to capture me
    and have hidden snares for my feet.
²³But you know, O LORD,
    all their plots to kill me.
Do not forgive their crimes
    or blot out their sins from your
        sight.
Let them be overthrown before you;
    deal with them in the time of your
        anger.

CHAPTER 19

This is what the LORD says: "Go and buy a clay jar from a potter. Take along some of the elders of the people and of the priests ²and go out to the Valley of Ben Hinnom, near the entrance of the Potsherd Gate. There proclaim the words I tell you, ³and say, 'Hear the word of the LORD, O kings of Judah and people of Jerusalem. This is what the LORD Almighty, the God of Israel, says: Listen! I am going to bring a disaster on this place that will make the ears of everyone who hears of it tingle. ⁴For they have forsaken me and made this a place of foreign gods; they have burned sacrifices in it to gods that neither they nor their fathers nor the kings of Judah ever knew, and they have filled this place with the blood of the innocent. ⁵They have built the high places of Baal to burn their sons in the fire as offerings to Baal— something I did not command or mention, nor did it enter my mind. ⁶So beware, the days are coming, declares the LORD, when people will no longer call this place Topheth or the Valley of Ben Hinnom, but the Valley of Slaughter.

⁷" 'In this place I will ruinᵍ the plans of Judah and Jerusalem. I will make them fall by the sword before their enemies, at the hands of those who seek their lives, and I will give their carcasses as food to the birds of the air and the beasts of the earth. ⁸I will devastate this city and make it an object of scorn; all who pass by will be appalled and will scoff because of all its wounds. ⁹I will make them eat the flesh of their sons and daughters, and

ᶠ14 The meaning of the Hebrew for this sentence is uncertain. verses 1 and 10).   ᵍ7 The Hebrew for ruin sounds like the Hebrew for jar (see they will eat one another's flesh during the stress of the siege imposed on them by the enemies who seek their lives.'

¹⁰"Then break the jar while those who go with you are watching, ¹¹and say to them, 'This is what the LORD Almighty says: I will smash this nation and this city just as this potter's jar is smashed and cannot be repaired. They will bury the dead in Topheth until there is no more room. ¹²This is what I will do to this place and to those who live here, declares the LORD. I will make this city like Topheth. ¹³The houses in Jerusalem and those of the kings of Judah will be defiled like this place, Topheth—all the houses where they burned incense on the roofs to all the starry hosts and poured out drink offerings to other gods.'"

¹⁴Jeremiah then returned from Topheth, where the LORD had sent him to prophesy, and stood in the court of the LORD's temple and said to all the people, ¹⁵"This is what the LORD Almighty, the God of Israel, says: 'Listen! I am going to bring on this city and the villages around it every disaster I pronounced against them, because they were stiff-necked and would not listen to my words.'"

CHAPTER 20

When the priest Pashhur son of Immer, the chief officer in the temple of the LORD, heard Jeremiah prophesying these things, ²he had Jeremiah the prophet beaten and put in the stocks at the Upper Gate of Benjamin at the LORD's temple. ³The next day, when Pashhur released him from the stocks, Jeremiah said to him, "The LORD's name for you is not Pashhur, but Magor-Missabib.ʰ ⁴For this is what the LORD says: 'I will make you a terror to yourself and to all your friends; with your own eyes you will see them fall by the sword of their enemies. I will hand all Judah over to the king of Babylon, who will carry them away to Babylon or put them to the sword. ⁵I will hand over to their enemies all the wealth of this city—all its products, all its valuables and all the treasures of the kings of Judah. They will take it away as plunder and carry it off to Babylon. ⁶And you, Pashhur, and all who live in your house will go into exile to Babylon. There you will die and be bur-

ied, you and all your friends to whom you have prophesied lies.'"

⁷O LORD, you deceivedⁱ me, and I was deceivedⁱ;
    you overpowered me and prevailed.
I am ridiculed all day long;
    everyone mocks me.
⁸Whenever I speak, I cry out
    proclaiming violence and destruction.
So the word of the LORD has brought me
    insult and reproach all day long.
⁹But if I say, "I will not mention him
    or speak any more in his name,"
his word is in my heart like a fire,
    a fire shut up in my bones.
I am weary of holding it in;
    indeed, I cannot.
¹⁰I hear many whispering,
    "Terror on every side!
    Report him! Let's report him!"
All my friends
    are waiting for me to slip, saying,
"Perhaps he will be deceived;
    then we will prevail over him
    and take our revenge on him."

¹¹But the LORD is with me like a mighty warrior;
    so my persecutors will stumble and not prevail.
They will fail and be thoroughly disgraced;
    their dishonor will never be forgotten.
¹²O LORD Almighty, you who examine the righteous
    and probe the heart and mind,
let me see your vengeance upon them,
    for to you I have committed my cause.

¹³Sing to the LORD!
    Give praise to the LORD!
He rescues the life of the needy
    from the hands of the wicked.

¹⁴Cursed be the day I was born!
    May the day my mother bore me not be blessed!
¹⁵Cursed be the man who brought my father the news,
    who made him very glad, saying,
    "A child is born to you—a son!"
¹⁶May that man be like the towns

ʰ3 *Magor-Missabib* means *terror on every side*.   ⁱ7 Or *persuaded*

the LORD overthrew without pity.
May he hear wailing in the morning,
   a battle cry at noon.
¹⁷For he did not kill me in the womb,
   with my mother as my grave,

her womb enlarged forever.
¹⁸Why did I ever come out of the
   womb
to see trouble and sorrow
   and to end my days in shame?

AUGUST 5 □ DAY 218
JEREMIAH 21–25
Judah in a Leadership Crisis

 OVERVIEW Judah's downfall can ultimately be traced to the failure of its leadership—those wicked shepherds who plundered rather than protected the flock. In the midst of Jeremiah's dirge of doom upon the nation's false kings and prophets, he prophesies the coming of the Messiah, who will restore justice and righteousness. Exile is inevitable, but there is hope. In seventy years the deported will return to Judah, while their captors will feel God's wrath.

Chapters 21–22	Chapter 23	Chapter 24	Chapter 25
False Kings	False Prophets	Captive Nation	Condemned Nations
National Judgment		International Judgment	

 YOUR DAILY WALK Turn on your radio or TV, and almost any day of the week (especially on Sunday) chances are good that you will find someone claiming, "God told me this" or "The Lord said to me that . . . ." Perhaps you have been offered literature lately by someone claiming to have audibly heard from God and who therefore had an authoritative "word from God." With the ever-growing number of cults and "-isms," how can you be certain who is truly speaking for God?

The most dangerous of all false doctrines is that seasoned with a little truth.

In Jeremiah's day the people were plagued with false prophets, who claimed to know God's mind. Though these deceivers didn't have TV or radio to help propagate their statements, they still managed to lull the nation into complacency.

Jeremiah's warnings concerning false prophets are timely indeed! The next time you encounter someone who claims, "God told me . . . ," apply this twofold test: (1) Does his life match his words? (23:13); (2) does the Bible back up his statements? (23:21–22). If not, watch out! Read and remember 1 John 4:1–6. Don't just accept what someone says; learn to "test the spirits" and develop a discerning mind that won't be deceived.

 INSIGHT No Secret about the Seventy
The duration of the Babylonian exile (25:11–12) was a matter of public record. In fact, Daniel, as the result of reading Jeremiah's prophecy of the seventy years, began to pray specifically that God would restore the people to the land (Daniel 9:1–3). God knows the end from the beginning!

CHAPTER 21

The word came to Jeremiah from the LORD when King Zedekiah sent to him Pashhur son of Malkijah and the priest Zephaniah son of Maaseiah. They said: ²"Inquire now of the LORD for us because Nebuchadnezzar[j] king of Babylon is attacking us. Perhaps the LORD will perform wonders for us as in times past so that he will withdraw from us."

³But Jeremiah answered them, "Tell Zedekiah, ⁴'This is what the LORD, the God of Israel, says: I am about to turn against you the weapons of war that are in your hands, which you are using to fight the king of Babylon and the Babylonians[k] who are outside the wall besieging you. And I will gather them inside this city. ⁵I myself will fight against you with an outstretched hand and a mighty arm in anger and fury and great wrath. ⁶I will strike down those who live in this city—both men and animals—and they will die of a terrible plague. ⁷After that, declares the LORD, I will hand over Zedekiah king of Judah, his officials and the people in this city who survive the plague, sword and famine, to Nebuchadnezzar king of Babylon and to their enemies who seek their lives. He will put them to the sword; he will show them no mercy or pity or compassion.'

⁸"Furthermore, tell the people, 'This is what the LORD says: See, I am setting before you the way of life and the way of death. ⁹Whoever stays in this city will die by the sword, famine or plague. But whoever goes out and surrenders to the Babylonians who are besieging you will live; he will escape with his life. ¹⁰I have determined to do this city harm and not good, declares the LORD. It will be given into the hands of the king of Babylon, and he will destroy it with fire.'

¹¹"Moreover, say to the royal house of Judah, 'Hear the word of the LORD; ¹²O house of David, this is what the LORD says:

" 'Administer justice every morning;
    rescue from the hand of his
        oppressor
the one who has been robbed,
or my wrath will break out and burn
    like fire

because of the evil you have done—
    burn with no one to quench it.
¹³I am against you, ⌞Jerusalem,⌟
    you who live above this valley
    on the rocky plateau,
            declares the LORD—
you who say, "Who can come against
        us?
Who can enter our refuge?"
¹⁴I will punish you as your deeds
        deserve,
            declares the LORD.
I will kindle a fire in your forests
    that will consume everything around
        you.' "

CHAPTER 22

This is what the LORD says: "Go down to the palace of the king of Judah and proclaim this message there: ²'Hear the word of the LORD, O king of Judah, you who sit on David's throne—you, your officials and your people who come through these gates. ³This is what the LORD says: Do what is just and right. Rescue from the hand of his oppressor the one who has been robbed. Do no wrong or violence to the alien, the fatherless or the widow, and do not shed innocent blood in this place. ⁴For if you are careful to carry out these commands, then kings who sit on David's throne will come through the gates of this palace, riding in chariots and on horses, accompanied by their officials and their people. ⁵But if you do not obey these commands, declares the LORD, I swear by myself that this palace will become a ruin.' "

⁶For this is what the LORD says about the palace of the king of Judah:

"Though you are like Gilead to me,
    like the summit of Lebanon,
I will surely make you like a desert,
    like towns not inhabited.
⁷I will send destroyers against you,
    each man with his weapons,
and they will cut up your fine cedar
        beams
    and throw them into the fire.

⁸"People from many nations will pass by this city and will ask one another, 'Why has the LORD done such a thing to this great city?' ⁹And the answer will be: 'Because they have forsaken the covenant

---

of the LORD their God and have worshiped and served other gods.' "

[10]Do not weep for the dead ⌊king⌋ or
        mourn his loss;
    rather, weep bitterly for him who is
        exiled,
because he will never return
    nor see his native land again.

[11]For this is what the LORD says about Shallum[l] son of Josiah, who succeeded his father as king of Judah but has gone from this place: "He will never return. [12]He will die in the place where they have led him captive; he will not see this land again."

[13]"Woe to him who builds his palace by
        unrighteousness,
    his upper rooms by injustice,
making his countrymen work for
        nothing,
    not paying them for their labor.
[14]He says, 'I will build myself a great
        palace
    with spacious upper rooms.'
So he makes large windows in it,
    panels it with cedar
    and decorates it in red.

[15]"Does it make you a king
    to have more and more cedar?
Did not your father have food and
        drink?
    He did what was right and just,
        so all went well with him.
[16]He defended the cause of the poor and
        needy,
    and so all went well.
Is that not what it means to know
        me?"
        declares the LORD.
[17]"But your eyes and your heart
    are set only on dishonest gain,
on shedding innocent blood
    and on oppression and extortion."

[18]Therefore this is what the LORD says about Jehoiakim son of Josiah king of Judah:

"They will not mourn for him:
    'Alas, my brother! Alas, my sister!'
They will not mourn for him:
    'Alas, my master! Alas, his
        splendor!'
[19]He will have the burial of a donkey—

dragged away and thrown
    outside the gates of Jerusalem."

[20]"Go up to Lebanon and cry out,
    let your voice be heard in Bashan,
cry out from Abarim,
    for all your allies are crushed.
[21]I warned you when you felt secure,
    but you said, 'I will not listen!'
This has been your way from your
        youth;
    you have not obeyed me.
[22]The wind will drive all your
        shepherds away,
    and your allies will go into exile.
Then you will be ashamed and
        disgraced
    because of all your wickedness.
[23]You who live in 'Lebanon,[m]'
    who are nestled in cedar buildings,
how you will groan when pangs come
        upon you,
    pain like that of a woman in labor!

[24]"As surely as I live," declares the LORD, "even if you, Jehoiachin[n] son of Jehoiakim king of Judah, were a signet ring on my right hand, I would still pull you off. [25]I will hand you over to those who seek your life, those you fear—to Nebuchadnezzar king of Babylon and to the Babylonians.[o] [26]I will hurl you and the mother who gave you birth into another country, where neither of you was born, and there you both will die. [27]You will never come back to the land you long to return to."

[28]Is this man Jehoiachin a despised,
        broken pot,
    an object no one wants?
Why will he and his children be
        hurled out,
    cast into a land they do not know?
[29]O land, land, land,
    hear the word of the LORD!
[30]This is what the LORD says:
"Record this man as if childless,
    a man who will not prosper in his
        lifetime,
for none of his offspring will prosper,
    none will sit on the throne of David
    or rule anymore in Judah."

---

[l]11 Also called *Jehoahaz*   [m]23 That is, the palace in Jerusalem (see 1 Kings 7:2)   [n]24 Hebrew *Coniah*, a variant of *Jehoiachin*; also in verse 28   [o]25 Or *Chaldeans*

CHAPTER 23

"Woe to the shepherds who are destroying and scattering the sheep of my pasture!" declares the LORD. ²Therefore this is what the LORD, the God of Israel, says to the shepherds who tend my people: "Because you have scattered my flock and driven them away and have not bestowed care on them, I will bestow punishment on you for the evil you have done," declares the LORD. ³"I myself will gather the remnant of my flock out of all the countries where I have driven them and will bring them back to their pasture, where they will be fruitful and increase in number. ⁴I will place shepherds over them who will tend them, and they will no longer be afraid or terrified, nor will any be missing," declares the LORD.

⁵"The days are coming," declares the
    LORD,
    "when I will raise up to David^p a
        righteous Branch,
    a King who will reign wisely
        and do what is just and right in the
            land.
⁶In his days Judah will be saved
        and Israel will live in safety.
This is the name by which he will be
        called:
    The LORD Our Righteousness.

⁷"So then, the days are coming," declares the LORD, "when people will no longer say, 'As surely as the LORD lives, who brought the Israelites up out of Egypt,' ⁸but they will say, 'As surely as the LORD lives, who brought the descendants of Israel up out of the land of the north and out of all the countries where he had banished them.' Then they will live in their own land."

⁹Concerning the prophets:

My heart is broken within me;
        all my bones tremble.
I am like a drunken man,
        like a man overcome by wine,
because of the LORD
        and his holy words.
¹⁰The land is full of adulterers;
        because of the curse^q the land lies
            parched^r
        and the pastures in the desert are
            withered.

The ∟prophets⌐ follow an evil course
    and use their power unjustly.
¹¹"Both prophet and priest are godless;
    even in my temple I find their
        wickedness,"
                        declares the LORD.
¹²"Therefore their path will become
        slippery;
    they will be banished to darkness
        and there they will fall.
I will bring disaster on them
    in the year they are punished,"
                        declares the LORD.

¹³"Among the prophets of Samaria
        I saw this repulsive thing:
They prophesied by Baal
        and led my people Israel astray.
¹⁴And among the prophets of Jerusalem
        I have seen something horrible:
    They commit adultery and live a lie.
They strengthen the hands of
        evildoers,
    so that no one turns from his
        wickedness.
They are all like Sodom to me;
    the people of Jerusalem are like
        Gomorrah."

¹⁵Therefore, this is what the LORD Almighty says concerning the prophets:

"I will make them eat bitter food
    and drink poisoned water,
because from the prophets of
        Jerusalem
    ungodliness has spread throughout
        the land."

¹⁶This is what the LORD Almighty says:

"Do not listen to what the prophets are
        prophesying to you;
    they fill you with false hopes.
They speak visions from their own
        minds,
    not from the mouth of the LORD.
¹⁷They keep saying to those who despise
        me,
    'The LORD says: You will have
        peace.'
And to all who follow the
        stubbornness of their hearts
    they say, 'No harm will come to
        you.'
¹⁸But which of them has stood in the
        council of the LORD

P5 Or up from David's line   q10 Or because of these things   r10 Or land mourns

to see or to hear his word?
Who has listened and heard his
    word?
[19]See, the storm of the LORD
will burst out in wrath,
a whirlwind swirling down
on the heads of the wicked.
[20]The anger of the LORD will not turn
    back
until he fully accomplishes
    the purposes of his heart.
In days to come
you will understand it clearly.
[21]I did not send these prophets,
yet they have run with their
    message;
I did not speak to them,
yet they have prophesied.
[22]But if they had stood in my council,
they would have proclaimed my
    words to my people
and would have turned them from
    their evil ways
and from their evil deeds.

[23]"Am I only a God nearby,"
                    declares the LORD,
"and not a God far away?
[24]Can anyone hide in secret places
so that I cannot see him?"
                    declares the LORD.
"Do not I fill heaven and earth?"
                    declares the LORD.

[25]"I have heard what the prophets say
who prophesy lies in my name. They say,
'I had a dream! I had a dream!' [26]How
long will this continue in the hearts of
these lying prophets, who prophesy the
delusions of their own minds? [27]They
think the dreams they tell one another
will make my people forget my name, just
as their fathers forgot my name through
Baal worship. [28]Let the prophet who has a
dream tell his dream, but let the one who
has my word speak it faithfully. For what
has straw to do with grain?" declares the
LORD. [29]"Is not my word like fire," declares
the LORD, "and like a hammer that breaks
a rock in pieces?

[30]"Therefore," declares the LORD, "I am
against the prophets who steal from one
another words supposedly from me.
[31]Yes," declares the LORD, "I am against the
prophets who wag their own tongues and
yet declare, 'The LORD declares.' [32]Indeed,

I am against those who prophesy false
dreams," declares the LORD. "They tell
them and lead my people astray with
their reckless lies, yet I did not send or
appoint them. They do not benefit these
people in the least," declares the LORD.
[33]"When these people, or a prophet or a
priest, ask you, 'What is the oracle[s] of
the LORD?' say to them, 'What oracle?[t] I
will forsake you, declares the LORD.' [34]If a
prophet or a priest or anyone else claims,
'This is the oracle of the LORD,' I will punish that man and his household. [35]This is
what each of you keeps on saying to his
friend or relative: 'What is the LORD's answer?' or 'What has the LORD spoken?'
[36]But you must not mention 'the oracle of
the LORD' again, because every man's own
word becomes his oracle and so you distort the words of the living God, the LORD
Almighty, our God. [37]This is what you
keep saying to a prophet: 'What is the
LORD's answer to you?' or 'What has the
LORD spoken?' [38]Although you claim,
'This is the oracle of the LORD,' this is what
the LORD says: You used the words, 'This
is the oracle of the LORD,' even though I
told you that you must not claim, 'This is
the oracle of the LORD.' [39]Therefore, I will
surely forget you and cast you out of my
presence along with the city I gave to you
and your fathers. [40]I will bring upon you
everlasting disgrace—everlasting shame
that will not be forgotten."

CHAPTER 24

After Jehoiachin[u] son of Jehoiakim king
of Judah and the officials, the craftsmen
and the artisans of Judah were carried
into exile from Jerusalem to Babylon by
Nebuchadnezzar king of Babylon, the
LORD showed me two baskets of figs
placed in front of the temple of the LORD.
[2]One basket had very good figs, like those
that ripen early; the other basket had very
poor figs, so bad they could not be eaten.

[3]Then the LORD asked me, "What do you
see, Jeremiah?"

"Figs," I answered. "The good ones are
very good, but the poor ones are so bad
they cannot be eaten."

[4]Then the word of the LORD came to me:
[5]"This is what the LORD, the God of Israel,
says: 'Like these good figs, I regard as
good the exiles from Judah, whom I sent

away from this place to the land of the Babylonians.[v] [6]My eyes will watch over them for their good, and I will bring them back to this land. I will build them up and not tear them down; I will plant them and not uproot them. [7]I will give them a heart to know me, that I am the LORD. They will be my people, and I will be their God, for they will return to me with all their heart.

[8]" 'But like the poor figs, which are so bad they cannot be eaten,' says the LORD, 'so will I deal with Zedekiah king of Judah, his officials and the survivors from Jerusalem, whether they remain in this land or live in Egypt. [9]I will make them abhorrent and an offense to all the kingdoms of the earth, a reproach and a byword, an object of ridicule and cursing, wherever I banish them. [10]I will send the sword, famine and plague against them until they are destroyed from the land I gave to them and their fathers.' "

CHAPTER 25

The word came to Jeremiah concerning all the people of Judah in the fourth year of Jehoiakim son of Josiah king of Judah, which was the first year of Nebuchadnezzar king of Babylon. [2]So Jeremiah the prophet said to all the people of Judah and to all those living in Jerusalem: [3]For twenty-three years—from the thirteenth year of Josiah son of Amon king of Judah until this very day—the word of the LORD has come to me and I have spoken to you again and again, but you have not listened.

[4]And though the LORD has sent all his servants the prophets to you again and again, you have not listened or paid any attention. [5]They said, "Turn now, each of you, from your evil ways and your evil practices, and you can stay in the land the LORD gave to you and your fathers for ever and ever. [6]Do not follow other gods to serve and worship them; do not provoke me to anger with what your hands have made. Then I will not harm you."

[7]"But you did not listen to me," declares the LORD, "and you have provoked me with what your hands have made, and you have brought harm to yourselves."

[8]Therefore the LORD Almighty says this: "Because you have not listened to my words, [9]I will summon all the peoples of the north and my servant Nebuchadnezzar king of Babylon," declares the LORD, "and I will bring them against this land and its inhabitants and against all the surrounding nations. I will completely destroy[w] them and make them an object of horror and scorn, and an everlasting ruin. [10]I will banish from them the sounds of joy and gladness, the voices of bride and bridegroom, the sound of millstones and the light of the lamp. [11]This whole country will become a desolate wasteland, and these nations will serve the king of Babylon seventy years.

[12]"But when the seventy years are fulfilled, I will punish the king of Babylon and his nation, the land of the Babylonians,[v] for their guilt," declares the LORD, "and will make it desolate forever. [13]I will bring upon that land all the things I have spoken against it, all that are written in this book and prophesied by Jeremiah against all the nations. [14]They themselves will be enslaved by many nations and great kings; I will repay them according to their deeds and the work of their hands."

[15]This is what the LORD, the God of Israel, said to me: "Take from my hand this cup filled with the wine of my wrath and make all the nations to whom I send you drink it. [16]When they drink it, they will stagger and go mad because of the sword I will send among them."

[17]So I took the cup from the LORD's hand and made all the nations to whom he sent me drink it: [18]Jerusalem and the towns of Judah, its kings and officials, to make them a ruin and an object of horror and scorn and cursing, as they are today; [19]Pharaoh king of Egypt, his attendants, his officials and all his people, [20]and all the foreign people there; all the kings of Uz; all the kings of the Philistines (those of Ashkelon, Gaza, Ekron, and the people left at Ashdod); [21]Edom, Moab and Ammon; [22]all the kings of Tyre and Sidon; the kings of the coastlands across the sea; [23]Dedan, Tema, Buz and all who are in distant places[x]; [24]all the kings of Arabia and all the kings of the foreign people who live in the desert; [25]all the kings of Zimri, Elam and Media; [26]and all the kings of the north, near and far, one after the other—all the kingdoms on the face of

[v]5,12 Or *Chaldeans*   [w]9 The Hebrew term refers to the irrevocable giving over of things or persons to the LORD, often by totally destroying them.   [x]23 Or *who clip the hair by their foreheads*

the earth. And after all of them, the king of Sheshach[y] will drink it too.

27"Then tell them, 'This is what the LORD Almighty, the God of Israel, says: Drink, get drunk and vomit, and fall to rise no more because of the sword I will send among you.' 28But if they refuse to take the cup from your hand and drink, tell them, 'This is what the LORD Almighty says: You must drink it! 29See, I am beginning to bring disaster on the city that bears my Name, and will you indeed go unpunished? You will not go unpunished, for I am calling down a sword upon all who live on the earth, declares the LORD Almighty.'

30"Now prophesy all these words against them and say to them:

" 'The LORD will roar from on high;
    he will thunder from his holy
        dwelling
    and roar mightily against his land.
He will shout like those who tread the
        grapes,
    shout against all who live on the
        earth.
31The tumult will resound to the ends of
        the earth,
    for the LORD will bring charges
        against the nations;
he will bring judgment on all mankind
    and put the wicked to the sword,' "
                    declares the LORD.

32This is what the LORD Almighty says:

"Look! Disaster is spreading

from nation to nation;
a mighty storm is rising
    from the ends of the earth."

33At that time those slain by the LORD will be everywhere—from one end of the earth to the other. They will not be mourned or gathered up or buried, but will be like refuse lying on the ground.

34Weep and wail, you shepherds;
    roll in the dust, you leaders of the
        flock.
For your time to be slaughtered has
        come;
    you will fall and be shattered like
        fine pottery.
35The shepherds will have nowhere to
        flee,
    the leaders of the flock no place to
        escape.
36Hear the cry of the shepherds,
    the wailing of the leaders of the
        flock,
    for the LORD is destroying their
        pasture.
37The peaceful meadows will be laid
        waste
    because of the fierce anger of the
        LORD.
38Like a lion he will leave his lair,
    and their land will become desolate
because of the sword[z] of the
        oppressor
    and because of the LORD's fierce
        anger.

---

y26 Sheshach is a cryptogram for Babylon.   z38 Some Hebrew manuscripts and Septuagint (see also Jer. 46:16 and 50:16); most Hebrew manuscripts anger

AUGUST 6 ☐ DAY 219
JEREMIAH 26–29
Judah in Opposition to Jeremiah

OVERVIEW Preachers usually hope for some kind of response after delivering their message, and Jeremiah is no different. But in his case the audience's response is breathtaking—literally! After hearing his appeal for repentance, they rise up in unison and declare, "This man should be sentenced to death!" (26:11). Jeremiah is arrested and tried by a murderous crowd; his life hangs in the balance until he is vindicated. But the message must go forth. Wearing an ox yoke, Jeremiah stresses the importance of Judah and her neighbors' surrendering to (rather than revolting against) Babylon, for to do otherwise is to court certain death. Discredited by Hananiah, a prophet of false hope,

Jeremiah pens a letter to the recent deportees urging them to settle down in Babylon.

Chapter 26	Chapter 27	Chapter 28	Chapter 29
A Plot against the Prophet	A Yoke upon the Prophet	A Prophecy against the Prophet	A Letter from the Prophet
Extermination	Exile	Hananiah	Hope

YOUR DAILY WALK "I have learned to be content whatever the circumstances" (Philippians 4:11). Do you recognize those words? They aren't the declaration of a plaster saint or the meaningless small talk of featherbed royalty. Rather, they are the carefully reasoned words of Paul—a man who had been beaten, stoned, shipwrecked, imperiled and impoverished. He had learned the secret of being content, regardless of the circumstances swirling around him.

Those who truly aspire to be Christlike should not be surprised when the mob comes to crucify them.

Jeremiah was much like Paul. On trial for his life, slandered by a fellow prophet, faced with a howling mob demanding his blood, Jeremiah calmly went about delivering his God-given message of judgment and doom. He lived above his circumstances, not under them, in his walk with God.

Write the following words on a slip of paper, carry them with you today, and read them often: "Sometimes the Lord calms the storm; more often he lets the storm rage and calms the child." Now relax in the Lord.

INSIGHT The Babylonian Exile—Slavery or Something Else?
The Hebrew exiles in Babylon were not slaves but deportees who were free to live as they pleased (29:4–9). Some became wealthy merchants, and others attained high places in court.

CHAPTER 26
Early in the reign of Jehoiakim son of Josiah king of Judah, this word came from the LORD: ²"This is what the LORD says: Stand in the courtyard of the LORD's house and speak to all the people of the towns of Judah who come to worship in the house of the LORD. Tell them everything I command you; do not omit a word. ³Perhaps they will listen and each will turn from his evil way. Then I will relent and not bring on them the disaster I was planning because of the evil they have done. ⁴Say to them, 'This is what the LORD says: If you do not listen to me and follow my law, which I have set before you, ⁵and if you do not listen to the words of my servants the prophets, whom I have sent to you again and again (though you have not listened), ⁶then I will make this house like Shiloh and this city an object of cursing among all the nations of the earth.' "

⁷The priests, the prophets and all the people heard Jeremiah speak these words in the house of the LORD. ⁸But as soon as Jeremiah finished telling all the people everything the LORD had commanded him to say, the priests, the prophets and all the people seized him and said, "You must die! ⁹Why do you prophesy in the LORD's name that this house will be like Shiloh and this city will be desolate and deserted?" And all the people crowded around Jeremiah in the house of the LORD.

¹⁰When the officials of Judah heard about these things, they went up from the royal palace to the house of the LORD and took their places at the entrance of the New Gate of the LORD's house. ¹¹Then the priests and the prophets said to the officials and all the people, "This man should be sentenced to death because he has prophesied against this city. You have heard it with your own ears!"

¹²Then Jeremiah said to all the officials and all the people: "The LORD sent me to prophesy against this house and this city all the things you have heard. ¹³Now reform your ways and your actions and obey the LORD your God. Then the LORD will relent and not bring the disaster he has pronounced against you. ¹⁴As for me,

I am in your hands; do with me whatever you think is good and right. ¹⁵Be assured, however, that if you put me to death, you will bring the guilt of innocent blood on yourselves and on this city and on those who live in it, for in truth the LORD has sent me to you to speak all these words in your hearing."

¹⁶Then the officials and all the people said to the priests and the prophets, "This man should not be sentenced to death! He has spoken to us in the name of the LORD our God."

¹⁷Some of the elders of the land stepped forward and said to the entire assembly of people, ¹⁸"Micah of Moresheth prophesied in the days of Hezekiah king of Judah. He told all the people of Judah, 'This is what the LORD Almighty says:

" 'Zion will be plowed like a field,
    Jerusalem will become a heap of
        rubble,
    the temple hill a mound overgrown
        with thickets.'ᵃ

¹⁹"Did Hezekiah king of Judah or anyone else in Judah put him to death? Did not Hezekiah fear the LORD and seek his favor? And did not the LORD relent, so that he did not bring the disaster he pronounced against them? We are about to bring a terrible disaster on ourselves!"

²⁰(Now Uriah son of Shemaiah from Kiriath Jearim was another man who prophesied in the name of the LORD; he prophesied the same things against this city and this land as Jeremiah did. ²¹When King Jehoiakim and all his officers and officials heard his words, the king sought to put him to death. But Uriah heard of it and fled in fear to Egypt. ²²King Jehoiakim, however, sent Elnathan son of Acbor to Egypt, along with some other men. ²³They brought Uriah out of Egypt and took him to King Jehoiakim, who had him struck down with a sword and his body thrown into the burial place of the common people.)

²⁴Furthermore, Ahikam son of Shaphan supported Jeremiah, and so he was not handed over to the people to be put to death.

CHAPTER 27
Early in the reign of Zedekiahᵇ son of Josiah king of Judah, this word came to Jeremiah from the LORD: ²This is what the LORD said to me: "Make a yoke out of straps and crossbars and put it on your neck. ³Then send word to the kings of Edom, Moab, Ammon, Tyre and Sidon through the envoys who have come to Jerusalem to Zedekiah king of Judah. ⁴Give them a message for their masters and say, 'This is what the LORD Almighty, the God of Israel, says: "Tell this to your masters: ⁵With my great power and outstretched arm I made the earth and its people and the animals that are on it, and I give it to anyone I please. ⁶Now I will hand all your countries over to my servant Nebuchadnezzar king of Babylon; I will make even the wild animals subject to him. ⁷All nations will serve him and his son and his grandson until the time for his land comes; then many nations and great kings will subjugate him.

⁸" ' "If, however, any nation or kingdom will not serve Nebuchadnezzar king of Babylon or bow its neck under his yoke, I will punish that nation with the sword, famine and plague, declares the LORD, until I destroy it by his hand. ⁹So do not listen to your prophets, your diviners, your interpreters of dreams, your mediums or your sorcerers who tell you, 'You will not serve the king of Babylon.' ¹⁰They prophesy lies to you that will only serve to remove you far from your lands; I will banish you and you will perish. ¹¹But if any nation will bow its neck under the yoke of the king of Babylon and serve him, I will let that nation remain in its own land to till it and to live there, declares the LORD." ' "

¹²I gave the same message to Zedekiah king of Judah. I said, "Bow your neck under the yoke of the king of Babylon; serve him and his people, and you will live. ¹³Why will you and your people die by the sword, famine and plague with which the LORD has threatened any nation that will not serve the king of Babylon? ¹⁴Do not listen to the words of the prophets who say to you, 'You will not serve the king of Babylon,' for they are prophesying lies to you. ¹⁵'I have not sent them,' declares the LORD. 'They are prophesying

ᵃ18 Micah 3:12   ᵇ1 A few Hebrew manuscripts and Syriac (see also Jer. 27:3, 12 and 28:1); most Hebrew manuscripts Jehoiakim (Most Septuagint manuscripts do not have this verse.)

lies in my name. Therefore, I will banish you and you will perish, both you and the prophets who prophesy to you.' "

[16]Then I said to the priests and all these people, "This is what the LORD says: Do not listen to the prophets who say, 'Very soon now the articles from the LORD's house will be brought back from Babylon.' They are prophesying lies to you. [17]Do not listen to them. Serve the king of Babylon, and you will live. Why should this city become a ruin? [18]If they are prophets and have the word of the LORD, let them plead with the LORD Almighty that the furnishings remaining in the house of the LORD and in the palace of the king of Judah and in Jerusalem not be taken to Babylon. [19]For this is what the LORD Almighty says about the pillars, the Sea, the movable stands and the other furnishings that are left in this city, [20]which Nebuchadnezzar king of Babylon did not take away when he carried Jehoiachin[c] son of Jehoiakim king of Judah into exile from Jerusalem to Babylon, along with all the nobles of Judah and Jerusalem— [21]yes, this is what the LORD Almighty, the God of Israel, says about the things that are left in the house of the LORD and in the palace of the king of Judah and in Jerusalem: [22]'They will be taken to Babylon and there they will remain until the day I come for them,' declares the LORD. 'Then I will bring them back and restore them to this place.' "

CHAPTER 28

In the fifth month of that same year, the fourth year, early in the reign of Zedekiah king of Judah, the prophet Hananiah son of Azzur, who was from Gibeon, said to me in the house of the LORD in the presence of the priests and all the people: [2]"This is what the LORD Almighty, the God of Israel, says: 'I will break the yoke of the king of Babylon. [3]Within two years I will bring back to this place all the articles of the LORD's house that Nebuchadnezzar king of Babylon removed from here and took to Babylon. [4]I will also bring back to this place Jehoiachin[c] son of Jehoiakim king of Judah and all the other exiles from Judah who went to Babylon,' declares the LORD, 'for I will break the yoke of the king of Babylon.' "

[5]Then the prophet Jeremiah replied to the prophet Hananiah before the priests and all the people who were standing in the house of the LORD. [6]He said, "Amen! May the LORD do so! May the LORD fulfill the words you have prophesied by bringing the articles of the LORD's house and all the exiles back to this place from Babylon. [7]Nevertheless, listen to what I have to say in your hearing and in the hearing of all the people: [8]From early times the prophets who preceded you and me have prophesied war, disaster and plague against many countries and great kingdoms. [9]But the prophet who prophesies peace will be recognized as one truly sent by the LORD only if his prediction comes true."

[10]Then the prophet Hananiah took the yoke off the neck of the prophet Jeremiah and broke it, [11]and he said before all the people, "This is what the LORD says: 'In the same way will I break the yoke of Nebuchadnezzar king of Babylon off the neck of all the nations within two years.' " At this, the prophet Jeremiah went on his way.

[12]Shortly after the prophet Hananiah had broken the yoke off the neck of the prophet Jeremiah, the word of the LORD came to Jeremiah: [13]"Go and tell Hananiah, 'This is what the LORD says: You have broken a wooden yoke, but in its place you will get a yoke of iron. [14]This is what the LORD Almighty, the God of Israel, says: I will put an iron yoke on the necks of all these nations to make them serve Nebuchadnezzar king of Babylon, and they will serve him. I will even give him control over the wild animals.' "

[15]Then the prophet Jeremiah said to Hananiah the prophet, "Listen, Hananiah! The LORD has not sent you, yet you have persuaded this nation to trust in lies. [16]Therefore, this is what the LORD says: 'I am about to remove you from the face of the earth. This very year you are going to die, because you have preached rebellion against the LORD.' "

[17]In the seventh month of that same year, Hananiah the prophet died.

CHAPTER 29

This is the text of the letter that the prophet Jeremiah sent from Jerusalem to

[c]20,4 Hebrew *Jeconiah*, a variant of *Jehoiachin*

the surviving elders among the exiles and to the priests, the prophets and all the other people Nebuchadnezzar had carried into exile from Jerusalem to Babylon. ²(This was after King Jehoiachin[d] and the queen mother, the court officials and the leaders of Judah and Jerusalem, the craftsmen and the artisans had gone into exile from Jerusalem.) ³He entrusted the letter to Elasah son of Shaphan and to Gemariah son of Hilkiah, whom Zedekiah king of Judah sent to King Nebuchadnezzar in Babylon. It said:

⁴This is what the LORD Almighty, the God of Israel, says to all those I carried into exile from Jerusalem to Babylon: ⁵"Build houses and settle down; plant gardens and eat what they produce. ⁶Marry and have sons and daughters; find wives for your sons and give your daughters in marriage, so that they too may have sons and daughters. Increase in number there; do not decrease. ⁷Also, seek the peace and prosperity of the city to which I have carried you into exile. Pray to the LORD for it, because if it prospers, you too will prosper." ⁸Yes, this is what the LORD Almighty, the God of Israel, says: "Do not let the prophets and diviners among you deceive you. Do not listen to the dreams you encourage them to have. ⁹They are prophesying lies to you in my name. I have not sent them," declares the LORD.

¹⁰This is what the LORD says: "When seventy years are completed for Babylon, I will come to you and fulfill my gracious promise to bring you back to this place. ¹¹For I know the plans I have for you," declares the LORD, "plans to prosper you and not to harm you, plans to give you hope and a future. ¹²Then you will call upon me and come and pray to me, and I will listen to you. ¹³You will seek me and find me when you seek me with all your heart. ¹⁴I will be found by you," declares the LORD, "and will bring you back from captivity.[e] I will gather you from all the nations and places where I have banished you," declares the LORD, "and

will bring you back to the place from which I carried you into exile."

¹⁵You may say, "The LORD has raised up prophets for us in Babylon," ¹⁶but this is what the LORD says about the king who sits on David's throne and all the people who remain in this city, your countrymen who did not go with you into exile— ¹⁷yes, this is what the LORD Almighty says: "I will send the sword, famine and plague against them and I will make them like poor figs that are so bad they cannot be eaten. ¹⁸I will pursue them with the sword, famine and plague and will make them abhorrent to all the kingdoms of the earth and an object of cursing and horror, of scorn and reproach, among all the nations where I drive them. ¹⁹For they have not listened to my words," declares the LORD, "words that I sent to them again and again by my servants the prophets. And you exiles have not listened either," declares the LORD.

²⁰Therefore, hear the word of the LORD, all you exiles whom I have sent away from Jerusalem to Babylon. ²¹This is what the LORD Almighty, the God of Israel, says about Ahab son of Kolaiah and Zedekiah son of Maaseiah, who are prophesying lies to you in my name: "I will hand them over to Nebuchadnezzar king of Babylon, and he will put them to death before your very eyes. ²²Because of them, all the exiles from Judah who are in Babylon will use this curse: 'The LORD treat you like Zedekiah and Ahab, whom the king of Babylon burned in the fire.' ²³For they have done outrageous things in Israel; they have committed adultery with their neighbors' wives and in my name have spoken lies, which I did not tell them to do. I know it and am a witness to it," declares the LORD.

²⁴Tell Shemaiah the Nehelamite, ²⁵"This is what the LORD Almighty, the God of Israel, says: You sent letters in your own name to all the people in Jerusalem, to Zephaniah son of Maaseiah the priest, and to all the other priests. You said to Zephaniah, ²⁶'The LORD has appointed

---

[d]2 Hebrew Jeconiah, a variant of Jehoiachin   [e]14 Or will restore your fortunes

you priest in place of Jehoiada to be in charge of the house of the LORD; you should put any madman who acts like a prophet into the stocks and neck-irons. [27]So why have you not reprimanded Jeremiah from Anathoth, who poses as a prophet among you? [28]He has sent this message to us in Babylon: It will be a long time. Therefore build houses and settle down; plant gardens and eat what they produce.' "

[29]Zephaniah the priest, however, read the letter to Jeremiah the prophet. [30]Then the word of the LORD came to Jeremiah: [31]"Send this message to all the exiles: 'This is what the LORD says about Shemaiah the Nehelamite: Because Shemaiah has prophesied to you, even though I did not send him, and has led you to believe a lie, [32]this is what the LORD says: I will surely punish Shemaiah the Nehelamite and his descendants. He will have no one left among this people, nor will he see the good things I will do for my people, declares the LORD, because he has preached rebellion against me.' "

AUGUST 7 □ DAY 220
The Death That Brings Life

LOOK BACK Ironically, the good news that brings peace begins with bad news that brings brutality. The word picture you read in Isaiah 53 includes a graphic depiction of the Suffering Servant and his violent death at the hands of wicked men. He was "despised . . . rejected . . . stricken . . . crushed . . . oppressed . . . led like a lamb to the slaughter" (53:3–8). But far from being a tragic accident of history, his death "was the LORD's will" (53:10) because he "bore the sin of many, and made intercession for the transgressors" (53:12). Like water to a thirsty pilgrim and healing to a broken heart, this glorious news needs to be made known to the nations, and that's where the people of God come in!

But often, God's people feel totally inadequate for the assignment—like Jeremiah, whose tender spirit and frequent tears make him an unlikely candidate for the demanding role of prophet and proclaimer. For every excuse Jeremiah can raise ("Ah, Sovereign LORD"), God has a faith-building vision of what can happen through an obedient servant, even in the face of false accusations and death threats.

LOOK UP Have you discovered the liberating truth of God's patient promises?

As early as Genesis 3:15, God promised that one day the offspring of the woman would crush the head of the serpent—Messiah would come to deal Satan a crushing blow and provide the bridge between sinful humanity and holy God. The promise was sure, but the wait would last thousands of years!

Isaiah painted a prophetic portrait of the Suffering Servant hundreds of years before the birth of Christ. Crucifixion was unknown in Isaiah's day, yet he described the brutal procedure in minute detail. With unerring accuracy, Isaiah foretold details of Jesus' death as if he were at Calvary gazing upon the very scene.

Centuries later—right on schedule—it all came true just as Isaiah had predicted. With each passing year, the promise moved closer and closer to fulfillment, until at long last, "when the time had fully come, God sent his Son" (Galatians 4:4).

Patience is a tree whose root is bitter but whose fruit is very sweet.

LOOK AHEAD Waiting for the fulfillment of a promise can be as exasperating as waiting for Christmas to come. Time can seem to "stand still" when something you long for is long awaited. But those with the patient endurance to keep their eyes on the prize will one day discover it was all well worth the wait.

When you read "this is what the LORD says" in the pages of his Word, mark it down—it will come to pass! And when the time is right, you won't have to wonder or wait. Pick a promise from the list below, and lay it alongside Isaiah 60:22: "I am the LORD; in its time I will do this swiftly." Then wait with patient expectation, for in due season you will reap if you don't faint!

- "I am going there to prepare a place for you. . . . I will come back and take you to be with me" (John 14:2–3).
- "I will not leave you as orphans; I will come to you" (John 14:18).
- "God will bring with Jesus those who have fallen asleep in him. . . . Therefore encourage each other with these words" (1 Thessalonians 4:14, 18).

AUGUST 8 ☐ DAY 221
JEREMIAH 30–33
Hope amidst Judgment

 OVERVIEW It's always darkest just before the dawn, and Jeremiah's prophecy is no exception. The opening lines of chapter 30 paint the blackest picture yet of Israel's coming calamity. The pinnacle of the nation's age-long sufferings will be a unique period of tribulation. But the bleakness of judgment will give way to the glory of restoration and blessing. The people will be replanted in their homeland (31:4–6, 8), their mourning will be turned to joy (31:13) and God will make a new covenant with them (31:31–34). As a sign of his confidence in the promises of God, Jeremiah buys a field—knowing full well it will soon fall into Babylonian hands.

Chapter 30	Chapter 31	Chapter 32	Chapter 33
Judah's Protection	Judah's Promotion	Jeremiah's Purchase	The Lord's Promise
Calamity	Covenant	Confidence	

 YOUR DAILY WALK Are you building your life on God's promises or merely building a file full of them? One ambitious soul has counted all the promises contained in the Bible. How many do you suppose he found?

The possibilities of prayer run parallel with the promises of God.

There are, in fact, more than seven thousand promises buried in the Bible, most of which are targeted for you! But once you find a promise, don't just write it down, memorize it or file it away. Claim it. Act upon it. Let it change your life.

Jeremiah received a promise from God. His nation, though faced with the prospect of being swept away by a Babylonian tidal wave, would not be annihilated. God would bring them back. So Jeremiah bought real estate at a rock-bottom price as if to declare to his nation, "I'm standing on the promises of God! He will restore us!"

Pick a promise from God that you may have read, filed away and maybe even memorized—but never claimed. Now act upon it!

INSIGHT A Mother's Tears
Rachel, the mother of Joseph and Benjamin, is pictured weeping for her sons, signifying the attempt that was made to destroy the messianic line (31:15). Many years later other women of Ramah would weep as Herod slaughtered their children in an attempt to kill the promised Messiah (Matthew 2:16–18), a fulfillment of Jeremiah's prophecy.

CHAPTER 30

This is the word that came to Jeremiah from the LORD: 2"This is what the LORD, the God of Israel, says: 'Write in a book all the words I have spoken to you. 3The days are coming,' declares the LORD, 'when I will bring my people Israel and Judah back from captivity*f* and restore them to the land I gave their forefathers to possess,' says the LORD."

4These are the words the LORD spoke concerning Israel and Judah: 5"This is what the LORD says:

" 'Cries of fear are heard—
terror, not peace.
6Ask and see:
Can a man bear children?
Then why do I see every strong man
with his hands on his stomach like a
woman in labor,
every face turned deathly pale?
7How awful that day will be!
None will be like it.
It will be a time of trouble for Jacob,
but he will be saved out of it.

8" 'In that day,' declares the LORD
Almighty,
'I will break the yoke off their necks
and will tear off their bonds;
no longer will foreigners enslave
them.
9Instead, they will serve the LORD their
God
and David their king,
whom I will raise up for them.

10" 'So do not fear, O Jacob my servant;
do not be dismayed, O Israel,'
declares the LORD.
'I will surely save you out of a distant
place,
your descendants from the land of
their exile.
Jacob will again have peace and
security,
and no one will make him afraid.
11I am with you and will save you,'

declares the LORD.
'Though I completely destroy all the
nations
among which I scatter you,
I will not completely destroy you.
I will discipline you but only with
justice;
I will not let you go entirely
unpunished.'

12"This is what the LORD says:

" 'Your wound is incurable,
your injury beyond healing.
13There is no one to plead your cause,
no remedy for your sore,
no healing for you.
14All your allies have forgotten you;
they care nothing for you.
I have struck you as an enemy would
and punished you as would the
cruel,
because your guilt is so great
and your sins so many.
15Why do you cry out over your wound,
your pain that has no cure?
Because of your great guilt and many
sins
I have done these things to you.

16" 'But all who devour you will be
devoured;
all your enemies will go into exile.
Those who plunder you will be
plundered;
all who make spoil of you I will
despoil.
17But I will restore you to health
and heal your wounds,'
declares the LORD,
'because you are called an outcast,
Zion for whom no one cares.'

18"This is what the LORD says:

" 'I will restore the fortunes of Jacob's
tents
and have compassion on his
dwellings;
the city will be rebuilt on her ruins,

f3 Or will restore the fortunes of my people Israel and Judah

and the palace will stand in its
    proper place.
[19]From them will come songs of
    thanksgiving
and the sound of rejoicing.
I will add to their numbers,
    and they will not be decreased;
I will bring them honor,
    and they will not be disdained.
[20]Their children will be as in days of
    old,
and their community will be
    established before me;
I will punish all who oppress them.
[21]Their leader will be one of their own;
    their ruler will arise from among
    them.
I will bring him near and he will come
    close to me,
for who is he who will devote
    himself
to be close to me?'
                    declares the LORD.
[22]" 'So you will be my people,
    and I will be your God.' "

[23]See, the storm of the LORD
    will burst out in wrath,
a driving wind swirling down
    on the heads of the wicked.
[24]The fierce anger of the LORD will not
    turn back
until he fully accomplishes
    the purposes of his heart.
In days to come
    you will understand this.

CHAPTER 31
"At that time," declares the LORD, "I will be
the God of all the clans of Israel, and they
will be my people."
    [2]This is what the LORD says:

"The people who survive the sword
    will find favor in the desert;
I will come to give rest to Israel."

[3]The LORD appeared to us in the past,[g]
saying:

"I have loved you with an everlasting
    love;
I have drawn you with
    loving-kindness.
[4]I will build you up again
    and you will be rebuilt, O Virgin
    Israel.

Again you will take up your
    tambourines
and go out to dance with the joyful.
[5]Again you will plant vineyards
    on the hills of Samaria;
the farmers will plant them
    and enjoy their fruit.
[6]There will be a day when watchmen
    cry out
on the hills of Ephraim,
'Come, let us go up to Zion,
    to the LORD our God.' "

[7]This is what the LORD says:

"Sing with joy for Jacob;
    shout for the foremost of the
    nations.
Make your praises heard, and say,
    'O LORD, save your people,
    the remnant of Israel.'
[8]See, I will bring them from the land of
    the north
and gather them from the ends of
    the earth.
Among them will be the blind and the
    lame,
expectant mothers and women in
    labor;
a great throng will return.
[9]They will come with weeping;
    they will pray as I bring them back.
I will lead them beside streams of
    water
on a level path where they will not
    stumble,
because I am Israel's father,
    and Ephraim is my firstborn son.

[10]"Hear the word of the LORD, O nations;
    proclaim it in distant coastlands:
'He who scattered Israel will gather
    them
and will watch over his flock like a
    shepherd.'
[11]For the LORD will ransom Jacob
    and redeem them from the hand of
    those stronger than they.
[12]They will come and shout for joy on
    the heights of Zion;
they will rejoice in the bounty of the
    LORD—
the grain, the new wine and the oil,
    the young of the flocks and herds.
They will be like a well-watered
    garden,
and they will sorrow no more.

[g]3 Or LORD has appeared to us from afar

¹³Then maidens will dance and be glad,
    young men and old as well.
I will turn their mourning into
        gladness;
    I will give them comfort and joy
        instead of sorrow.
¹⁴I will satisfy the priests with
        abundance,
    and my people will be filled with
        my bounty,"
                    declares the LORD.

¹⁵This is what the LORD says:

"A voice is heard in Ramah,
    mourning and great weeping,
Rachel weeping for her children
    and refusing to be comforted,
    because her children are no more."

¹⁶This is what the LORD says:

"Restrain your voice from weeping
    and your eyes from tears,
for your work will be rewarded,"
                    declares the LORD.
    "They will return from the land of
        the enemy.
¹⁷So there is hope for your future,"
                    declares the LORD.
    "Your children will return to their
        own land.

¹⁸"I have surely heard Ephraim's
        moaning:
    'You disciplined me like an unruly
        calf,
    and I have been disciplined.
Restore me, and I will return,
    because you are the LORD my God.
¹⁹After I strayed,
    I repented;
after I came to understand,
    I beat my breast.
I was ashamed and humiliated
    because I bore the disgrace of my
        youth.'
²⁰Is not Ephraim my dear son,
    the child in whom I delight?
Though I often speak against him,
    I still remember him.
Therefore my heart yearns for him;
    I have great compassion for him,"
                    declares the LORD.

²¹"Set up road signs;
    put up guideposts.
Take note of the highway,

the road that you take.
Return, O Virgin Israel,
    return to your towns.
²²How long will you wander,
    O unfaithful daughter?
The LORD will create a new thing on
        earth—
    a woman will surround^h a man."

²³This is what the LORD Almighty, the
God of Israel, says: "When I bring them
back from captivity,^{i} the people in the
land of Judah and in its towns will once
again use these words: 'The LORD bless
you, O righteous dwelling, O sacred
mountain.' ²⁴People will live together in
Judah and all its towns—farmers and
those who move about with their flocks.
²⁵I will refresh the weary and satisfy the
faint."

²⁶At this I awoke and looked around.
My sleep had been pleasant to me.

²⁷"The days are coming," declares the
LORD, "when I will plant the house of Israel and the house of Judah with the offspring of men and of animals. ²⁸Just as I
watched over them to uproot and tear
down, and to overthrow, destroy and
bring disaster, so I will watch over them
to build and to plant," declares the LORD.
²⁹"In those days people will no longer say,

'The fathers have eaten sour grapes,
    and the children's teeth are set on
        edge.'

³⁰Instead, everyone will die for his own
sin; whoever eats sour grapes—his own
teeth will be set on edge.

³¹"The time is coming," declares the
        LORD,
    "when I will make a new covenant
with the house of Israel
    and with the house of Judah.
³²It will not be like the covenant
    I made with their forefathers
when I took them by the hand
    to lead them out of Egypt,
because they broke my covenant,
    though I was a husband to^j
        them,^{k}"
                    declares the LORD.
³³"This is the covenant I will make with
        the house of Israel
    after that time," declares the LORD.
"I will put my law in their minds

^{h}22 Or will go about ¸seeking¸; or will protect ^{i}23 Or I restore their fortunes ^{j}32 Hebrew; Septuagint and Syriac / and I turned
away from ^{k}32 Or was their master

and write it on their hearts.
I will be their God,
    and they will be my people.
[34]No longer will a man teach his
        neighbor,
    or a man his brother, saying, 'Know
        the LORD,'
because they will all know me,
    from the least of them to the
        greatest,"
                    declares the LORD.
"For I will forgive their wickedness
    and will remember their sins no
        more."

[35]This is what the LORD says,

he who appoints the sun
    to shine by day,
who decrees the moon and stars
    to shine by night,
who stirs up the sea
    so that its waves roar—
    the LORD Almighty is his name:
[36]"Only if these decrees vanish from my
        sight,"
    declares the LORD,
"will the descendants of Israel ever
        cease
    to be a nation before me."

[37]This is what the LORD says:

"Only if the heavens above can be
        measured
    and the foundations of the earth
        below be searched out
will I reject all the descendants of
        Israel
    because of all they have done,"
                    declares the LORD.

[38]"The days are coming," declares the
LORD, "when this city will be rebuilt for me
from the Tower of Hananel to the Corner
Gate. [39]The measuring line will stretch
from there straight to the hill of Gareb
and then turn to Goah. [40]The whole valley
where dead bodies and ashes are thrown,
and all the terraces out to the Kidron Valley on the east as far as the corner of the
Horse Gate, will be holy to the LORD. The
city will never again be uprooted or demolished."

CHAPTER 32
This is the word that came to Jeremiah
from the LORD in the tenth year of Zede-

kiah king of Judah, which was the eighteenth year of Nebuchadnezzar. [2]The
army of the king of Babylon was then besieging Jerusalem, and Jeremiah the
prophet was confined in the courtyard of
the guard in the royal palace of Judah.

[3]Now Zedekiah king of Judah had imprisoned him there, saying, "Why do you
prophesy as you do? You say, 'This is
what the LORD says: I am about to hand
this city over to the king of Babylon, and
he will capture it. [4]Zedekiah king of Judah will not escape out of the hands of
the Babylonians[l] but will certainly be
handed over to the king of Babylon, and
will speak with him face to face and see
him with his own eyes. [5]He will take
Zedekiah to Babylon, where he will remain until I deal with him, declares the
LORD. If you fight against the Babylonians,
you will not succeed.' "

[6]Jeremiah said, "The word of the LORD
came to me: [7]Hanamel son of Shallum
your uncle is going to come to you and
say, 'Buy my field at Anathoth, because as
nearest relative it is your right and duty
to buy it.'

[8]"Then, just as the LORD had said, my
cousin Hanamel came to me in the courtyard of the guard and said, 'Buy my field
at Anathoth in the territory of Benjamin.
Since it is your right to redeem it and
possess it, buy it for yourself.'

"I knew that this was the word of the
LORD; [9]so I bought the field at Anathoth
from my cousin Hanamel and weighed
out for him seventeen shekels[m] of silver.
[10]I signed and sealed the deed, had it witnessed, and weighed out the silver on the
scales. [11]I took the deed of purchase—the
sealed copy containing the terms and
conditions, as well as the unsealed copy—
[12]and I gave this deed to Baruch son of
Neriah, the son of Mahseiah, in the presence of my cousin Hanamel and of the
witnesses who had signed the deed and
of all the Jews sitting in the courtyard of
the guard.

[13]"In their presence I gave Baruch these
instructions: [14]'This is what the LORD Almighty, the God of Israel, says: Take these
documents, both the sealed and unsealed
copies of the deed of purchase, and put
them in a clay jar so they will last a
long time. [15]For this is what the LORD

---

[l]4 Or Chaldeans; also in verses 5, 24, 25, 28, 29 and 43   [m]9 That is, about 7 ounces (about 200 grams)

Almighty, the God of Israel, says: Houses, fields and vineyards will again be bought in this land.'

¹⁶"After I had given the deed of purchase to Baruch son of Neriah, I prayed to the LORD:

¹⁷"Ah, Sovereign LORD, you have made the heavens and the earth by your great power and outstretched arm. Nothing is too hard for you. ¹⁸You show love to thousands but bring the punishment for the fathers' sins into the laps of their children after them. O great and powerful God, whose name is the LORD Almighty, ¹⁹great are your purposes and mighty are your deeds. Your eyes are open to all the ways of men; you reward everyone according to his conduct and as his deeds deserve. ²⁰You performed miraculous signs and wonders in Egypt and have continued them to this day, both in Israel and among all mankind, and have gained the renown that is still yours. ²¹You brought your people Israel out of Egypt with signs and wonders, by a mighty hand and an outstretched arm and with great terror. ²²You gave them this land you had sworn to give their forefathers, a land flowing with milk and honey. ²³They came in and took possession of it, but they did not obey you or follow your law; they did not do what you commanded them to do. So you brought all this disaster upon them.

²⁴"See how the siege ramps are built up to take the city. Because of the sword, famine and plague, the city will be handed over to the Babylonians who are attacking it. What you said has happened, as you now see. ²⁵And though the city will be handed over to the Babylonians, you, O Sovereign LORD, say to me, 'Buy the field with silver and have the transaction witnessed.' "

²⁶Then the word of the LORD came to Jeremiah: ²⁷"I am the LORD, the God of all mankind. Is anything too hard for me? ²⁸Therefore, this is what the LORD says: I am about to hand this city over to the Babylonians and to Nebuchadnezzar king

of Babylon, who will capture it. ²⁹The Babylonians who are attacking this city will come in and set it on fire; they will burn it down, along with the houses where the people provoked me to anger by burning incense on the roofs to Baal and by pouring out drink offerings to other gods.

³⁰"The people of Israel and Judah have done nothing but evil in my sight from their youth; indeed, the people of Israel have done nothing but provoke me with what their hands have made, declares the LORD. ³¹From the day it was built until now, this city has so aroused my anger and wrath that I must remove it from my sight. ³²The people of Israel and Judah have provoked me by all the evil they have done—they, their kings and officials, their priests and prophets, the men of Judah and the people of Jerusalem. ³³They turned their backs to me and not their faces; though I taught them again and again, they would not listen or respond to discipline. ³⁴They set up their abominable idols in the house that bears my Name and defiled it. ³⁵They built high places for Baal in the Valley of Ben Hinnom to sacrifice their sons and daughters" to Molech, though I never commanded, nor did it enter my mind, that they should do such a detestable thing and so make Judah sin.

³⁶"You are saying about this city, 'By the sword, famine and plague it will be handed over to the king of Babylon'; but this is what the LORD, the God of Israel, says: ³⁷I will surely gather them from all the lands where I banish them in my furious anger and great wrath; I will bring them back to this place and let them live in safety. ³⁸They will be my people, and I will be their God. ³⁹I will give them singleness of heart and action, so that they will always fear me for their own good and the good of their children after them. ⁴⁰I will make an everlasting covenant with them: I will never stop doing good to them, and I will inspire them to fear me, so that they will never turn away from me. ⁴¹I will rejoice in doing them good and will assuredly plant them in this land with all my heart and soul.

⁴²"This is what the LORD says: As I have brought all this great calamity on this

" 35 Or to make their sons and daughters pass through the fire, people, so I will give them all the prosperity I have promised them. ⁴³Once more fields will be bought in this land of which you say, 'It is a desolate waste, without men or animals, for it has been handed over to the Babylonians.' ⁴⁴Fields will be bought for silver, and deeds will be signed, sealed and witnessed in the territory of Benjamin, in the villages around Jerusalem, in the towns of Judah and in the towns of the hill country, of the western foothills and of the Negev, because I will restore their fortunes,ᵒ declares the LORD."

CHAPTER 33

While Jeremiah was still confined in the courtyard of the guard, the word of the LORD came to him a second time: ²"This is what the LORD says, he who made the earth, the LORD who formed it and established it—the LORD is his name: ³'Call to me and I will answer you and tell you great and unsearchable things you do not know.' ⁴For this is what the LORD, the God of Israel, says about the houses in this city and the royal palaces of Judah that have been torn down to be used against the siege ramps and the sword ⁵in the fight with the Babyloniansᵖ: 'They will be filled with the dead bodies of the men I will slay in my anger and wrath. I will hide my face from this city because of all its wickedness.

⁶" 'Nevertheless, I will bring health and healing to it; I will heal my people and will let them enjoy abundant peace and security. ⁷I will bring Judah and Israel back from captivity�q and will rebuild them as they were before. ⁸I will cleanse them from all the sin they have committed against me and will forgive all their sins of rebellion against me. ⁹Then this city will bring me renown, joy, praise and honor before all nations on earth that hear of all the good things I do for it; and they will be in awe and will tremble at the abundant prosperity and peace I provide for it.'

¹⁰"This is what the LORD says: 'You say about this place, "It is a desolate waste, without men or animals." Yet in the towns of Judah and the streets of Jerusalem that are deserted, inhabited by neither men nor animals, there will be heard once

more ¹¹the sounds of joy and gladness, the voices of bride and bridegroom, and the voices of those who bring thank offerings to the house of the LORD, saying,

"Give thanks to the LORD Almighty,
    for the LORD is good;
    his love endures forever."

For I will restore the fortunes of the land as they were before,' says the LORD.

¹²"This is what the LORD Almighty says: 'In this place, desolate and without men or animals—in all its towns there will again be pastures for shepherds to rest their flocks. ¹³In the towns of the hill country, of the western foothills and of the Negev, in the territory of Benjamin, in the villages around Jerusalem and in the towns of Judah, flocks will again pass under the hand of the one who counts them,' says the LORD.

¹⁴" 'The days are coming,' declares the LORD, 'when I will fulfill the gracious promise I made to the house of Israel and to the house of Judah.

¹⁵" 'In those days and at that time
    I will make a righteous Branch
        sprout from David's line;
    he will do what is just and right in
        the land.
¹⁶In those days Judah will be saved
    and Jerusalem will live in safety.
This is the name by which itʳ will be
        called:
    The LORD Our Righteousness.'

¹⁷For this is what the LORD says: 'David will never fail to have a man to sit on the throne of the house of Israel, ¹⁸nor will the priests, who are Levites, ever fail to have a man to stand before me continually to offer burnt offerings, to burn grain offerings and to present sacrifices.' "

¹⁹The word of the LORD came to Jeremiah: ²⁰"This is what the LORD says: 'If you can break my covenant with the day and my covenant with the night, so that day and night no longer come at their appointed time, ²¹then my covenant with David my servant—and my covenant with the Levites who are priests ministering before me—can be broken and David will no longer have a descendant to reign on his throne. ²²I will make the descendants of David my servant and the

Levites who minister before me as count-less as the stars of the sky and as mea-sureless as the sand on the seashore.' "

²³The word of the LORD came to Jere-miah: ²⁴"Have you not noticed that these people are saying, 'The LORD has rejected the two kingdomsˢ he chose'? So they despise my people and no longer regard them as a nation. ²⁵This is what the LORD

says: 'If I have not established my cov-enant with day and night and the fixed laws of heaven and earth, ²⁶then I will re-ject the descendants of Jacob and David my servant and will not choose one of his sons to rule over the descendants of Abraham, Isaac and Jacob. For I will re-store their fortunes ᵗ and have compas-sion on them.' "

ˢ24 Or families   ᵗ26 Or will bring them back from captivity

AUGUST 9 ☐ DAY 222
JEREMIAH 34–36
Before the Fall of Jerusalem

 OVERVIEW With the close of chapter 33, Jeremiah completes the written account of his preaching ministry to the rebellious nation. Throughout the rest of the book, the prophet emphasizes his personal experiences during the nation's last days. Three events point out the advanced state of Judah's decline: the broken covenant under Zede-kiah, the contrasting faithfulness of the Recabite family and the utter rebellion of Jehoiakim in burning the scroll of the Lord.

Chapter 34	Chapter 35	Chapter 36
A Nation's Treachery	A Family's Testimony	A King's Tyranny
Rebuke	Righteousness	Rebellion

 YOUR DAILY WALK The next time you read your Bible, try this exer-cise. Whenever you come to a passage that points out your sin or tells you what you ought to do, tear out that page and burn it!

Ridiculous? Of course. No one today would do to God's Word what Jehoiakim did to Jeremiah's scroll . . . or would they?

If your study of God's Word does not change the way you live, either you are already perfect or not studying correctly.

Have you ever read a command in God's Word you didn't like and just ignored it and kept on reading? That's a sure way to save on ex-pensive Bibles—while accomplishing the same spiritual damage as the knife-wielding king Jehoiakim.

How should you read the Bible? The key is a responsive heart. God wants his Word to change your life as it convicts you of sin and in-structs you in righteousness. Ignoring God's commands is dangerous business. In fact, it would be better not to know them at all than to know them and then not obey.

Is there a specific command from Scripture you have been avoiding? Jehoiakim learned the hard way that you cannot alter God's truth by ignoring it. Confess your sin of omission to God (James 4:17), and like the servants in John 2:5, make a fresh commitment to obedience. "Do whatever he tells you."

 INSIGHT God's Commendation of a Nonconformist Family
The Recabites made the nomadic way of life and abstinence from drink a religious obligation (Jeremiah 35). God commended them, not for their rules, but for their faithfulness to those rules—a striking con-trast to Judah's infidelity.

CHAPTER 34

While Nebuchadnezzar king of Babylon and all his army and all the kingdoms and peoples in the empire he ruled were fighting against Jerusalem and all its surrounding towns, this word came to Jeremiah from the LORD: ²"This is what the LORD, the God of Israel, says: Go to Zedekiah king of Judah and tell him, 'This is what the LORD says: I am about to hand this city over to the king of Babylon, and he will burn it down. ³You will not escape from his grasp but will surely be captured and handed over to him. You will see the king of Babylon with your own eyes, and he will speak with you face to face. And you will go to Babylon.

⁴" 'Yet hear the promise of the LORD, O Zedekiah king of Judah. This is what the LORD says concerning you: You will not die by the sword; ⁵you will die peacefully. As people made a funeral fire in honor of your fathers, the former kings who preceded you, so they will make a fire in your honor and lament, "Alas, O master!" I myself make this promise, declares the LORD.' "

⁶Then Jeremiah the prophet told all this to Zedekiah king of Judah, in Jerusalem, ⁷while the army of the king of Babylon was fighting against Jerusalem and the other cities of Judah that were still holding out—Lachish and Azekah. These were the only fortified cities left in Judah.

⁸The word came to Jeremiah from the LORD after King Zedekiah had made a covenant with all the people in Jerusalem to proclaim freedom for the slaves. ⁹Everyone was to free his Hebrew slaves, both male and female; no one was to hold a fellow Jew in bondage. ¹⁰So all the officials and people who entered into this covenant agreed that they would free their male and female slaves and no longer hold them in bondage. They agreed, and set them free. ¹¹But afterward they changed their minds and took back the slaves they had freed and enslaved them again.

¹²Then the word of the LORD came to Jeremiah: ¹³"This is what the LORD, the God of Israel, says: I made a covenant with your forefathers when I brought them out of Egypt, out of the land of slavery. I said, ¹⁴'Every seventh year each of you must free any fellow Hebrew who has sold himself to you. After he has served you six years, you must let him go free.'ᵘ Your fathers, however, did not listen to me or pay attention to me. ¹⁵Recently you repented and did what is right in my sight: Each of you proclaimed freedom to his countrymen. You even made a covenant before me in the house that bears my Name. ¹⁶But now you have turned around and profaned my name; each of you has taken back the male and female slaves you had set free to go where they wished. You have forced them to become your slaves again.

¹⁷"Therefore, this is what the LORD says: You have not obeyed me; you have not proclaimed freedom for your fellow countrymen. So I now proclaim 'freedom' for you, declares the LORD—'freedom' to fall by the sword, plague and famine. I will make you abhorrent to all the kingdoms of the earth. ¹⁸The men who have violated my covenant and have not fulfilled the terms of the covenant they made before me, I will treat like the calf they cut in two and then walked between its pieces. ¹⁹The leaders of Judah and Jerusalem, the court officials, the priests and all the people of the land who walked between the pieces of the calf, ²⁰I will hand over to their enemies who seek their lives. Their dead bodies will become food for the birds of the air and the beasts of the earth.

²¹"I will hand Zedekiah king of Judah and his officials over to their enemies who seek their lives, to the army of the king of Babylon, which has withdrawn from you. ²²I am going to give the order, declares the LORD, and I will bring them back to this city. They will fight against it, take it and burn it down. And I will lay waste the towns of Judah so no one can live there."

CHAPTER 35

This is the word that came to Jeremiah from the LORD during the reign of Jehoiakim son of Josiah king of Judah: ²"Go to the Recabite family and invite them to come to one of the side rooms of the house of the LORD and give them wine to drink."

³So I went to get Jaazaniah son of

ᵘ14 Deut. 15:12

Jeremiah, the son of Habazziniah, and his brothers and all his sons—the whole family of the Recabites. ⁴I brought them into the house of the LORD, into the room of the sons of Hanan son of Igdaliah the man of God. It was next to the room of the officials, which was over that of Maaseiah son of Shallum the doorkeeper. ⁵Then I set bowls full of wine and some cups before the men of the Recabite family and said to them, "Drink some wine."

⁶But they replied, "We do not drink wine, because our forefather Jonadab son of Recab gave us this command: 'Neither you nor your descendants must ever drink wine. ⁷Also you must never build houses, sow seed or plant vineyards; you must never have any of these things, but must always live in tents. Then you will live a long time in the land where you are nomads.' ⁸We have obeyed everything our forefather Jonadab son of Recab commanded us. Neither we nor our wives nor our sons and daughters have ever drunk wine ⁹or built houses to live in or had vineyards, fields or crops. ¹⁰We have lived in tents and have fully obeyed everything our forefather Jonadab commanded us. ¹¹But when Nebuchadnezzar king of Babylon invaded this land, we said, 'Come, we must go to Jerusalem to escape the Babylonianᵛ and Aramean armies.' So we have remained in Jerusalem."

¹²Then the word of the LORD came to Jeremiah, saying: ¹³"This is what the LORD Almighty, the God of Israel, says: Go and tell the men of Judah and the people of Jerusalem, 'Will you not learn a lesson and obey my words?' declares the LORD. ¹⁴'Jonadab son of Recab ordered his sons not to drink wine and this command has been kept. To this day they do not drink wine, because they obey their forefather's command. But I have spoken to you again and again, yet you have not obeyed me. ¹⁵Again and again I sent all my servants the prophets to you. They said, "Each of you must turn from your wicked ways and reform your actions; do not follow other gods to serve them. Then you will live in the land I have given to you and your fathers." But you have not paid attention or listened to me. ¹⁶The descendants of Jonadab son of Recab have car-

ried out the command their forefather gave them, but these people have not obeyed me.'

¹⁷"Therefore, this is what the LORD God Almighty, the God of Israel, says: 'Listen! I am going to bring on Judah and on everyone living in Jerusalem every disaster I pronounced against them. I spoke to them, but they did not listen; I called to them, but they did not answer.' "

¹⁸Then Jeremiah said to the family of the Recabites, "This is what the LORD Almighty, the God of Israel, says: 'You have obeyed the command of your forefather Jonadab and have followed all his instructions and have done everything he ordered.' ¹⁹Therefore, this is what the LORD Almighty, the God of Israel, says: 'Jonadab son of Recab will never fail to have a man to serve me.' "

CHAPTER 36

In the fourth year of Jehoiakim son of Josiah king of Judah, this word came to Jeremiah from the LORD: ²"Take a scroll and write on it all the words I have spoken to you concerning Israel, Judah and all the other nations from the time I began speaking to you in the reign of Josiah till now. ³Perhaps when the people of Judah hear about every disaster I plan to inflict on them, each of them will turn from his wicked way; then I will forgive their wickedness and their sin."

⁴So Jeremiah called Baruch son of Neriah, and while Jeremiah dictated all the words the LORD had spoken to him, Baruch wrote them on the scroll. ⁵Then Jeremiah told Baruch, "I am restricted; I cannot go to the LORD's temple. ⁶So you go to the house of the LORD on a day of fasting and read to the people from the scroll the words of the LORD that you wrote as I dictated. Read them to all the people of Judah who come in from their towns. ⁷Perhaps they will bring their petition before the LORD, and each will turn from his wicked ways, for the anger and wrath pronounced against this people by the LORD are great."

⁸Baruch son of Neriah did everything Jeremiah the prophet told him to do; at the LORD's temple he read the words of the LORD from the scroll. ⁹In the ninth month of the fifth year of Jehoiakim son

ᵛ11 Or Chaldean

of Josiah king of Judah, a time of fasting before the LORD was proclaimed for all the people in Jerusalem and those who had come from the towns of Judah. [10]From the room of Gemariah son of Shaphan the secretary, which was in the upper courtyard at the entrance of the New Gate of the temple, Baruch read to all the people at the LORD's temple the words of Jeremiah from the scroll.

[11]When Micaiah son of Gemariah, the son of Shaphan, heard all the words of the LORD from the scroll, [12]he went down to the secretary's room in the royal palace, where all the officials were sitting: Elishama the secretary, Delaiah son of Shemaiah, Elnathan son of Acbor, Gemariah son of Shaphan, Zedekiah son of Hananiah, and all the other officials. [13]After Micaiah told them everything he had heard Baruch read to the people from the scroll, [14]all the officials sent Jehudi son of Nethaniah, the son of Shelemiah, the son of Cushi, to say to Baruch, "Bring the scroll from which you have read to the people and come." So Baruch son of Neriah went to them with the scroll in his hand. [15]They said to him, "Sit down, please, and read it to us."

So Baruch read it to them. [16]When they heard all these words, they looked at each other in fear and said to Baruch, "We must report all these words to the king." [17]Then they asked Baruch, "Tell us, how did you come to write all this? Did Jeremiah dictate it?"

[18]"Yes," Baruch replied, "he dictated all these words to me, and I wrote them in ink on the scroll."

[19]Then the officials said to Baruch, "You and Jeremiah, go and hide. Don't let anyone know where you are."

[20]After they put the scroll in the room of Elishama the secretary, they went to the king in the courtyard and reported everything to him. [21]The king sent Jehudi to get the scroll, and Jehudi brought it from the room of Elishama the secretary and read it to the king and all the officials standing beside him. [22]It was the ninth month and the king was sitting in the winter apartment, with a fire burning in the firepot in front of him. [23]Whenever Jehudi had read three or four columns of the scroll, the king cut them off with a scribe's knife and threw them into the firepot, until the entire scroll was burned in the fire. [24]The king and all his attendants who heard all these words showed no fear, nor did they tear their clothes. [25]Even though Elnathan, Delaiah and Gemariah urged the king not to burn the scroll, he would not listen to them. [26]Instead, the king commanded Jerahmeel, a son of the king, Seraiah son of Azriel and Shelemiah son of Abdeel to arrest Baruch the scribe and Jeremiah the prophet. But the LORD had hidden them.

[27]After the king burned the scroll containing the words that Baruch had written at Jeremiah's dictation, the word of the LORD came to Jeremiah: [28]"Take another scroll and write on it all the words that were on the first scroll, which Jehoiakim king of Judah burned up. [29]Also tell Jehoiakim king of Judah, 'This is what the LORD says: You burned that scroll and said, "Why did you write on it that the king of Babylon would certainly come and destroy this land and cut off both men and animals from it?" [30]Therefore, this is what the LORD says about Jehoiakim king of Judah: He will have no one to sit on the throne of David; his body will be thrown out and exposed to the heat by day and the frost by night. [31]I will punish him and his children and his attendants for their wickedness; I will bring on them and those living in Jerusalem and the people of Judah every disaster I pronounced against them, because they have not listened.' "

[32]So Jeremiah took another scroll and gave it to the scribe Baruch son of Neriah, and as Jeremiah dictated, Baruch wrote on it all the words of the scroll that Jehoiakim king of Judah had burned in the fire. And many similar words were added to them.

AUGUST 10 □ DAY 223
JEREMIAH 37–39
During the Fall of Jerusalem

OVERVIEW Jeremiah endures his worst persecution during the nation's last desperate days in the Babylonian siege. First, he is arrested on suspicion of treason. Next, his enemies conspire to throw him into a muddy cistern to die. Rescued at the last minute by order of King Zedekiah, Jeremiah offers yet again his familiar advice: "Surrender!" The king refuses, sealing the destruction of Jerusalem. All the horrors Jeremiah has so long predicted are now fully carried out by the merciless Babylonians, but Jeremiah himself is spared.

Chapter 37	Chapter 38	Chapter 39
Jeremiah's Arrest	Jeremiah's Abandonment	Judah's Annihilation
The King's Fearfulness		The King's Fate

Faith, like a muscle, grows by stretching.

YOUR DAILY WALK Have you ever received the pessimistic advice, "Cheer up, things could be worse"? So you cheered up, and sure enough, things got worse! Jeremiah could identify with your experience. No sooner had he left the prison court of King Zedekiah than he was thrown into the dungeon pit—from the frying pan into the mire, so to speak. He no doubt prayed things would get better, but instead they got "badder." Yet Jeremiah never wavered in his commitment to God or in his calling to preach an unpopular message. How was that possible?

Jeremiah's faith never wavered because his focus never wandered. Imprisonment and intimidation could not take his eyes off his Sovereign. With his gaze firmly fixed on God, Jeremiah could fearlessly proclaim God's message, trusting him to take care of the consequences.

In the midst of trials and discouragements, it's more important than ever to check your focus. Are you looking at your problem or your Problem Solver? Read Romans 8:37 right now, and underline the word *through*. Remember, it's not above or around all things, but *through* all things that we are more than conquerors through him who loved us.

INSIGHT The Obscure Man Who Made a Difference
It was not a Jew but a Cushite eunuch who persuaded the king to rescue Jeremiah from sure death in the cistern. For his faithfulness, Ebed-Melech was promised personal safety during Jerusalem's fall and received an eternal memorial in God's Word (38:7–13).

CHAPTER 37

Zedekiah son of Josiah was made king of Judah by Nebuchadnezzar king of Babylon; he reigned in place of Jehoiachin[w] son of Jehoiakim. ²Neither he nor his attendants nor the people of the land paid any attention to the words the LORD had spoken through Jeremiah the prophet.

³King Zedekiah, however, sent Jehucal son of Shelemiah with the priest Zephaniah son of Maaseiah to Jeremiah the prophet with this message: "Please pray to the LORD our God for us."

⁴Now Jeremiah was free to come and go among the people, for he had not yet been put in prison. ⁵Pharaoh's army had marched out of Egypt, and when the Babylonians[x] who were besieging Jerusalem heard the report about them, they withdrew from Jerusalem.

⁶Then the word of the LORD came to Jeremiah the prophet: ⁷"This is what the

w1 Hebrew Coniah, a variant of Jehoiachin   x5 Or Chaldeans; also in verses 8, 9, 13 and 14

LORD, the God of Israel, says: Tell the king of Judah, who sent you to inquire of me, 'Pharaoh's army, which has marched out to support you, will go back to its own land, to Egypt. [8]Then the Babylonians will return and attack this city; they will capture it and burn it down.'

[9]"This is what the LORD says: Do not deceive yourselves, thinking, 'The Babylonians will surely leave us.' They will not! [10]Even if you were to defeat the entire Babylonian[y] army that is attacking you and only wounded men were left in their tents, they would come out and burn this city down."

[11]After the Babylonian army had withdrawn from Jerusalem because of Pharaoh's army, [12]Jeremiah started to leave the city to go to the territory of Benjamin to get his share of the property among the people there. [13]But when he reached the Benjamin Gate, the captain of the guard, whose name was Irijah son of Shelemiah, the son of Hananiah, arrested him and said, "You are deserting to the Babylonians!"

[14]"That's not true!" Jeremiah said. "I am not deserting to the Babylonians." But Irijah would not listen to him; instead, he arrested Jeremiah and brought him to the officials. [15]They were angry with Jeremiah and had him beaten and imprisoned in the house of Jonathan the secretary, which they had made into a prison.

[16]Jeremiah was put into a vaulted cell in a dungeon, where he remained a long time. [17]Then King Zedekiah sent for him and had him brought to the palace, where he asked him privately, "Is there any word from the LORD?"

"Yes," Jeremiah replied, "you will be handed over to the king of Babylon."

[18]Then Jeremiah said to King Zedekiah, "What crime have I committed against you or your officials or this people, that you have put me in prison? [19]Where are your prophets who prophesied to you, 'The king of Babylon will not attack you or this land'? [20]But now, my lord the king, please listen. Let me bring my petition before you: Do not send me back to the house of Jonathan the secretary, or I will die there."

[21]King Zedekiah then gave orders for Jeremiah to be placed in the courtyard of the guard and given bread from the street of the bakers each day until all the bread in the city was gone. So Jeremiah remained in the courtyard of the guard.

CHAPTER 38

Shephatiah son of Mattan, Gedaliah son of Pashhur, Jehucal[z] son of Shelemiah, and Pashhur son of Malkijah heard what Jeremiah was telling all the people when he said, [2]"This is what the LORD says: 'Whoever stays in this city will die by the sword, famine or plague, but whoever goes over to the Babylonians[a] will live. He will escape with his life; he will live.' [3]And this is what the LORD says: 'This city will certainly be handed over to the army of the king of Babylon, who will capture it.' "

[4]Then the officials said to the king, "This man should be put to death. He is discouraging the soldiers who are left in this city, as well as all the people, by the things he is saying to them. This man is not seeking the good of these people but their ruin."

[5]"He is in your hands," King Zedekiah answered. "The king can do nothing to oppose you."

[6]So they took Jeremiah and put him into the cistern of Malkijah, the king's son, which was in the courtyard of the guard. They lowered Jeremiah by ropes into the cistern; it had no water in it, only mud, and Jeremiah sank down into the mud.

[7]But Ebed-Melech, a Cushite,[b] an official[c] in the royal palace, heard that they had put Jeremiah into the cistern. While the king was sitting in the Benjamin Gate, [8]Ebed-Melech went out of the palace and said to him, [9]"My lord the king, these men have acted wickedly in all they have done to Jeremiah the prophet. They have thrown him into a cistern, where he will starve to death when there is no longer any bread in the city."

[10]Then the king commanded Ebed-Melech the Cushite, "Take thirty men from here with you and lift Jeremiah the prophet out of the cistern before he dies."

[11]So Ebed-Melech took the men with him and went to a room under the treasury in the palace. He took some old rags and worn-out clothes from there and let them down with ropes to Jeremiah in the

---

[y]10 Or *Chaldean;* also in verse 11   [z]1 Hebrew *Jucal,* a variant of *Jehucal*   [a]2 Or *Chaldeans;* also in verses 18, 19 and 23
[b]7 Probably from the upper Nile region   [c]7 Or *a eunuch*

cistern. [12]Ebed-Melech the Cushite said to Jeremiah, "Put these old rags and worn-out clothes under your arms to pad the ropes." Jeremiah did so, [13]and they pulled him up with the ropes and lifted him out of the cistern. And Jeremiah remained in the courtyard of the guard.

[14]Then King Zedekiah sent for Jeremiah the prophet and had him brought to the third entrance to the temple of the LORD. "I am going to ask you something," the king said to Jeremiah. "Do not hide anything from me."

[15]Jeremiah said to Zedekiah, "If I give you an answer, will you not kill me? Even if I did give you counsel, you would not listen to me."

[16]But King Zedekiah swore this oath secretly to Jeremiah: "As surely as the LORD lives, who has given us breath, I will neither kill you nor hand you over to those who are seeking your life."

[17]Then Jeremiah said to Zedekiah, "This is what the LORD God Almighty, the God of Israel, says: 'If you surrender to the officers of the king of Babylon, your life will be spared and this city will not be burned down; you and your family will live. [18]But if you will not surrender to the officers of the king of Babylon, this city will be handed over to the Babylonians and they will burn it down; you yourself will not escape from their hands.' "

[19]King Zedekiah said to Jeremiah, "I am afraid of the Jews who have gone over to the Babylonians, for the Babylonians may hand me over to them and they will mistreat me."

[20]"They will not hand you over," Jeremiah replied. "Obey the LORD by doing what I tell you. Then it will go well with you, and your life will be spared. [21]But if you refuse to surrender, this is what the LORD has revealed to me: [22]All the women left in the palace of the king of Judah will be brought out to the officials of the king of Babylon. Those women will say to you:

" 'They misled you and overcame
        you—
    those trusted friends of yours.
Your feet are sunk in the mud;
    your friends have deserted you.'

[23]"All your wives and children will be brought out to the Babylonians. You

yourself will not escape from their hands but will be captured by the king of Babylon; and this city will[d] be burned down."

[24]Then Zedekiah said to Jeremiah, "Do not let anyone know about this conversation, or you may die. [25]If the officials hear that I talked with you, and they come to you and say, 'Tell us what you said to the king and what the king said to you; do not hide it from us or we will kill you,' [26]then tell them, 'I was pleading with the king not to send me back to Jonathan's house to die there.' "

[27]All the officials did come to Jeremiah and question him, and he told them everything the king had ordered him to say. So they said no more to him, for no one had heard his conversation with the king.

[28]And Jeremiah remained in the courtyard of the guard until the day Jerusalem was captured.

This is how Jerusalem was taken: CHAPTER 39 [1]In the ninth year of Zedekiah king of Judah, in the tenth month, Nebuchadnezzar king of Babylon marched against Jerusalem with his whole army and laid siege to it. [2]And on the ninth day of the fourth month of Zedekiah's eleventh year, the city wall was broken through. [3]Then all the officials of the king of Babylon came and took seats in the Middle Gate: Nergal-Sharezer of Samgar, Nebo-Sarsekim[e] a chief officer, Nergal-Sharezer a high official and all the other officials of the king of Babylon. [4]When Zedekiah king of Judah and all the soldiers saw them, they fled; they left the city at night by way of the king's garden, through the gate between the two walls, and headed toward the Arabah.[f]

[5]But the Babylonian[g] army pursued them and overtook Zedekiah in the plains of Jericho. They captured him and took him to Nebuchadnezzar king of Babylon at Riblah in the land of Hamath, where he pronounced sentence on him. [6]There at Riblah the king of Babylon slaughtered the sons of Zedekiah before his eyes and also killed all the nobles of Judah. [7]Then he put out Zedekiah's eyes and bound him with bronze shackles to take him to Babylon.

[d]23 Or and you will cause this city to   [e]3 Or Nergal-Sharezer, Samgar-Nebo, Sarsekim   [f]4 Or the Jordan Valley   [g]5 Or Chaldean

[8]The Babylonians[h] set fire to the royal palace and the houses of the people and broke down the walls of Jerusalem. [9]Nebuzaradan commander of the imperial guard carried into exile to Babylon the people who remained in the city, along with those who had gone over to him, and the rest of the people. [10]But Nebuzaradan the commander of the guard left behind in the land of Judah some of the poor people, who owned nothing; and at that time he gave them vineyards and fields.

[11]Now Nebuchadnezzar king of Babylon had given these orders about Jeremiah through Nebuzaradan commander of the imperial guard: [12]"Take him and look after him; don't harm him but do for him whatever he asks." [13]So Nebuzaradan the commander of the guard, Nebushazban a chief officer, Nergal-Sharezer a high official and all the other officers of the king of Babylon [14]sent and had Jeremiah taken out of the courtyard of the guard. They turned him over to Gedaliah son of Ahikam, the son of Shaphan, to take him back to his home. So he remained among his own people.

[15]While Jeremiah had been confined in the courtyard of the guard, the word of the LORD came to him: [16]"Go and tell Ebed-Melech the Cushite, 'This is what the LORD Almighty, the God of Israel, says: I am about to fulfill my words against this city through disaster, not prosperity. At that time they will be fulfilled before your eyes. [17]But I will rescue you on that day, declares the LORD; you will not be handed over to those you fear. [18]I will save you; you will not fall by the sword but will escape with your life, because you trust in me, declares the LORD.' "

[h] 8 Or Chaldeans

AUGUST 11 □ DAY 224
JEREMIAH 40–45
After the Fall of Jerusalem

OVERVIEW Jeremiah's ministry does not end with the fall of Jerusalem. Given carte blanche by the Babylonian king Nebuchadnezzar, he chooses to cast his lot with Gedaliah, the governor appointed to oversee Jerusalem. But after Gedaliah's brutal assassination by Ishmael, the Jewish remnant disregards God's specific command and flees into Egypt, taking Jeremiah along. This prompts Jeremiah to predict Egypt's destruction and the Jews' discipline at the hands of the Lord.

Chapters 40–41	Chapter 42	Chapter 43	Chapters 44–45
Gathering around Gedaliah	The Plan	Escaping into Egypt The Execution	The Aftermath
Safety in the City	Disaster through Disobedience		

There is no more difficult prayer to pray aright than "Thy will be done."

YOUR DAILY WALK Are you a "coin-collector Christian"? It is a common practice today for coin and stamp collectors (numismatists and philatelists, if you want to be proper!) to buy merchandise "on approval." That is, the company will send samples of coins or stamps through the mail. The buyer looks them over, keeps the ones he or she wants to buy and returns the rest. If the buyer doesn't like what is sent, he or she just sends it all back.

Some Christians view God's will that way! They pray, "Lord, show me what you want me to do." And when he does, they decide whether they want to do it *all* of it, *part* of it or *none* of it!

After the fall of Jerusalem, the survivors came to Jeremiah and asked him to pray for them. They wanted to know God's will "on approval."

They were looking for God to rubber-stamp what they had already decided to do: flee to Egypt! And when the answer came back *no!* they went anyway—with disastrous results.

Examine a decision you're wrestling with in prayer. Are you seeking God's will "on approval," or are you willing to go wherever he guides? Read Proverbs 3:5–6; then you decide.

INSIGHT The Word of the Lord Came . . . in Tahpanhes Tahpanhes (43:8–13) has been linked with a site about ten miles west of the Suez Canal. In 1886 Sir Flinders Petrie uncovered the ruins of a large castle, in front of which was a great open platform of brickwork. According to Petrie, it is likely Jeremiah hid the stones there that he referred to in his prophecy of Egypt's downfall!

CHAPTER 40

The word came to Jeremiah from the LORD after Nebuzaradan commander of the imperial guard had released him at Ramah. He had found Jeremiah bound in chains among all the captives from Jerusalem and Judah who were being carried into exile to Babylon. ²When the commander of the guard found Jeremiah, he said to him, "The LORD your God decreed this disaster for this place. ³And now the LORD has brought it about; he has done just as he said he would. All this happened because you people sinned against the LORD and did not obey him. ⁴But today I am freeing you from the chains on your wrists. Come with me to Babylon, if you like, and I will look after you; but if you do not want to, then don't come. Look, the whole country lies before you; go wherever you please." ⁵However, before Jeremiah turned to go,ⁱ Nebuzaradan added, "Go back to Gedaliah son of Ahikam, the son of Shaphan, whom the king of Babylon has appointed over the towns of Judah, and live with him among the people, or go anywhere else you please."

Then the commander gave him provisions and a present and let him go. ⁶So Jeremiah went to Gedaliah son of Ahikam at Mizpah and stayed with him among the people who were left behind in the land.

⁷When all the army officers and their men who were still in the open country heard that the king of Babylon had appointed Gedaliah son of Ahikam as governor over the land and had put him in charge of the men, women and children who were the poorest in the land and who had not been carried into exile to Babylon, ⁸they came to Gedaliah at Miz-

pah—Ishmael son of Nethaniah, Johanan and Jonathan the sons of Kareah, Seraiah son of Tanhumeth, the sons of Ephai the Netophathite, and Jaazaniahʲ the son of the Maacathite, and their men. ⁹Gedaliah son of Ahikam, the son of Shaphan, took an oath to reassure them and their men. "Do not be afraid to serve the Babylonians,ᵏ" he said. "Settle down in the land and serve the king of Babylon, and it will go well with you. ¹⁰I myself will stay at Mizpah to represent you before the Babylonians who come to us, but you are to harvest the wine, summer fruit and oil, and put them in your storage jars, and live in the towns you have taken over."

¹¹When all the Jews in Moab, Ammon, Edom and all the other countries heard that the king of Babylon had left a remnant in Judah and had appointed Gedaliah son of Ahikam, the son of Shaphan, as governor over them, ¹²they all came back to the land of Judah, to Gedaliah at Mizpah, from all the countries where they had been scattered. And they harvested an abundance of wine and summer fruit.

¹³Johanan son of Kareah and all the army officers still in the open country came to Gedaliah at Mizpah ¹⁴and said to him, "Don't you know that Baalis king of the Ammonites has sent Ishmael son of Nethaniah to take your life?" But Gedaliah son of Ahikam did not believe them.

¹⁵Then Johanan son of Kareah said privately to Gedaliah in Mizpah, "Let me go and kill Ishmael son of Nethaniah, and no one will know it. Why should he take your life and cause all the Jews who are gathered around you to be scattered and the remnant of Judah to perish?"

¹⁶But Gedaliah son of Ahikam said to Johanan son of Kareah, "Don't do such a

---

ⁱ5 Or *Jeremiah answered*   ʲ8 Hebrew *Jezaniah,* a variant of *Jaazaniah*   ᵏ9 Or *Chaldeans*; also in verse 10 thing! What you are saying about Ishmael is not true."

CHAPTER 41

In the seventh month Ishmael son of Nethaniah, the son of Elishama, who was of royal blood and had been one of the king's officers, came with ten men to Gedaliah son of Ahikam at Mizpah. While they were eating together there, ²Ishmael son of Nethaniah and the ten men who were with him got up and struck down Gedaliah son of Ahikam, the son of Shaphan, with the sword, killing the one whom the king of Babylon had appointed as governor over the land. ³Ishmael also killed all the Jews who were with Gedaliah at Mizpah, as well as the Babylonian¹ soldiers who were there.

⁴The day after Gedaliah's assassination, before anyone knew about it, ⁵eighty men who had shaved off their beards, torn their clothes and cut themselves came from Shechem, Shiloh and Samaria, bringing grain offerings and incense with them to the house of the LORD. ⁶Ishmael son of Nethaniah went out from Mizpah to meet them, weeping as he went. When he met them, he said, "Come to Gedaliah son of Ahikam." ⁷When they went into the city, Ishmael son of Nethaniah and the men who were with him slaughtered them and threw them into a cistern. ⁸But ten of them said to Ishmael, "Don't kill us! We have wheat and barley, oil and honey, hidden in a field." So he let them alone and did not kill them with the others. ⁹Now the cistern where he threw all the bodies of the men he had killed along with Gedaliah was the one King Asa had made as part of his defense against Baasha king of Israel. Ishmael son of Nethaniah filled it with the dead.

¹⁰Ishmael made captives of all the rest of the people who were in Mizpah—the king's daughters along with all the others who were left there, over whom Nebuzaradan commander of the imperial guard had appointed Gedaliah son of Ahikam. Ishmael son of Nethaniah took them captive and set out to cross over to the Ammonites.

¹¹When Johanan son of Kareah and all the army officers who were with him heard about all the crimes Ishmael son of

Nethaniah had committed, ¹²they took all their men and went to fight Ishmael son of Nethaniah. They caught up with him near the great pool in Gibeon. ¹³When all the people Ishmael had with him saw Johanan son of Kareah and the army officers who were with him, they were glad. ¹⁴All the people Ishmael had taken captive at Mizpah turned and went over to Johanan son of Kareah. ¹⁵But Ishmael son of Nethaniah and eight of his men escaped from Johanan and fled to the Ammonites.

¹⁶Then Johanan son of Kareah and all the army officers who were with him led away all the survivors from Mizpah whom he had recovered from Ishmael son of Nethaniah after he had assassinated Gedaliah son of Ahikam: the soldiers, women, children and court officials he had brought from Gibeon. ¹⁷And they went on, stopping at Geruth Kimham near Bethlehem on their way to Egypt ¹⁸to escape the Babylonians.ᵐ They were afraid of them because Ishmael son of Nethaniah had killed Gedaliah son of Ahikam, whom the king of Babylon had appointed as governor over the land.

CHAPTER 42

Then all the army officers, including Johanan son of Kareah and Jezaniahⁿ son of Hoshaiah, and all the people from the least to the greatest approached ²Jeremiah the prophet and said to him, "Please hear our petition and pray to the LORD your God for this entire remnant. For as you now see, though we were once many, now only a few are left. ³Pray that the LORD your God will tell us where we should go and what we should do."

⁴"I have heard you," replied Jeremiah the prophet. "I will certainly pray to the LORD your God as you have requested; I will tell you everything the LORD says and will keep nothing back from you."

⁵Then they said to Jeremiah, "May the LORD be a true and faithful witness against us if we do not act in accordance with everything the LORD your God sends you to tell us. ⁶Whether it is favorable or unfavorable, we will obey the LORD our God, to whom we are sending you, so that it will go well with us, for we will obey the LORD our God."

⁷Ten days later the word of the Lord came to Jeremiah. ⁸So he called together Johanan son of Kareah and all the army officers who were with him and all the people from the least to the greatest. ⁹He said to them, "This is what the Lord, the God of Israel, to whom you sent me to present your petition, says: ¹⁰'If you stay in this land, I will build you up and not tear you down; I will plant you and not uproot you, for I am grieved over the disaster I have inflicted on you. ¹¹Do not be afraid of the king of Babylon, whom you now fear. Do not be afraid of him, declares the Lord, for I am with you and will save you and deliver you from his hands. ¹²I will show you compassion so that he will have compassion on you and restore you to your land.'

¹³"However, if you say, 'We will not stay in this land,' and so disobey the Lord your God, ¹⁴and if you say, 'No, we will go and live in Egypt, where we will not see war or hear the trumpet or be hungry for bread,' ¹⁵then hear the word of the Lord, O remnant of Judah. This is what the Lord Almighty, the God of Israel, says: 'If you are determined to go to Egypt and you do go to settle there, ¹⁶then the sword you fear will overtake you there, and the famine you dread will follow you into Egypt, and there you will die. ¹⁷Indeed, all who are determined to go to Egypt to settle there will die by the sword, famine and plague; not one of them will survive or escape the disaster I will bring on them.' ¹⁸This is what the Lord Almighty, the God of Israel, says: 'As my anger and wrath have been poured out on those who lived in Jerusalem, so will my wrath be poured out on you when you go to Egypt. You will be an object of cursing and horror, of condemnation and reproach; you will never see this place again.'

¹⁹"O remnant of Judah, the Lord has told you, 'Do not go to Egypt.' Be sure of this: I warn you today ²⁰that you made a fatal mistake*ᵒ* when you sent me to the Lord your God and said, 'Pray to the Lord our God for us; tell us everything he says and we will do it.' ²¹I have told you today, but you still have not obeyed the Lord your God in all he sent me to tell you. ²²So now, be sure of this: You will die by the sword, famine and plague in the place where you want to go to settle."

CHAPTER 43

When Jeremiah finished telling the people all the words of the Lord their God—everything the Lord had sent him to tell them— ²Azariah son of Hoshaiah and Johanan son of Kareah and all the arrogant men said to Jeremiah, "You are lying! The Lord our God has not sent you to say, 'You must not go to Egypt to settle there.' ³But Baruch son of Neriah is inciting you against us to hand us over to the Babylonians,*ᵖ* so they may kill us or carry us into exile to Babylon."

⁴So Johanan son of Kareah and all the army officers and all the people disobeyed the Lord's command to stay in the land of Judah. ⁵Instead, Johanan son of Kareah and all the army officers led away all the remnant of Judah who had come back to live in the land of Judah from all the nations where they had been scattered. ⁶They also led away all the men, women and children and the king's daughters whom Nebuzaradan commander of the imperial guard had left with Gedaliah son of Ahikam, the son of Shaphan, and Jeremiah the prophet and Baruch son of Neriah. ⁷So they entered Egypt in disobedience to the Lord and went as far as Tahpanhes.

⁸In Tahpanhes the word of the Lord came to Jeremiah: ⁹"While the Jews are watching, take some large stones with you and bury them in clay in the brick pavement at the entrance to Pharaoh's palace in Tahpanhes. ¹⁰Then say to them, 'This is what the Lord Almighty, the God of Israel, says: I will send for my servant Nebuchadnezzar king of Babylon, and I will set his throne over these stones I have buried here; he will spread his royal canopy above them. ¹¹He will come and attack Egypt, bringing death to those destined for death, captivity to those destined for captivity, and the sword to those destined for the sword. ¹²He*q* will set fire to the temples of the gods of Egypt; he will burn their temples and take their gods captive. As a shepherd wraps his garment around him, so will he wrap Egypt around himself and depart from there unscathed. ¹³There in the temple of

ᵒ20 Or *you erred in your hearts*   *ᵖ3* Or *Chaldeans*   *q12* Or *I* the sun[r] in Egypt he will demolish the sacred pillars and will burn down the temples of the gods of Egypt.' "

CHAPTER 44

This word came to Jeremiah concerning all the Jews living in Lower Egypt—in Migdol, Tahpanhes and Memphis[s]—and in Upper Egypt[t]: [2]"This is what the LORD Almighty, the God of Israel, says: You saw the great disaster I brought on Jerusalem and on all the towns of Judah. Today they lie deserted and in ruins [3]because of the evil they have done. They provoked me to anger by burning incense and by worshiping other gods that neither they nor you nor your fathers ever knew. [4]Again and again I sent my servants the prophets, who said, 'Do not do this detestable thing that I hate!' [5]But they did not listen or pay attention; they did not turn from their wickedness or stop burning incense to other gods. [6]Therefore, my fierce anger was poured out; it raged against the towns of Judah and the streets of Jerusalem and made them the desolate ruins they are today.

[7]"Now this is what the LORD God Almighty, the God of Israel, says: Why bring such great disaster on yourselves by cutting off from Judah the men and women, the children and infants, and so leave yourselves without a remnant? [8]Why provoke me to anger with what your hands have made, burning incense to other gods in Egypt, where you have come to live? You will destroy yourselves and make yourselves an object of cursing and reproach among all the nations on earth. [9]Have you forgotten the wickedness committed by your fathers and by the kings and queens of Judah and the wickedness committed by you and your wives in the land of Judah and the streets of Jerusalem? [10]To this day they have not humbled themselves or shown reverence, nor have they followed my law and the decrees I set before you and your fathers.

[11]"Therefore, this is what the LORD Almighty, the God of Israel, says: I am determined to bring disaster on you and to destroy all Judah. [12]I will take away the remnant of Judah who were determined to go to Egypt to settle there. They will all perish in Egypt; they will fall by the sword or die from famine. From the least to the greatest, they will die by sword or famine. They will become an object of cursing and horror, of condemnation and reproach. [13]I will punish those who live in Egypt with the sword, famine and plague, as I punished Jerusalem. [14]None of the remnant of Judah who have gone to live in Egypt will escape or survive to return to the land of Judah, to which they long to return and live; none will return except a few fugitives."

[15]Then all the men who knew that their wives were burning incense to other gods, along with all the women who were present—a large assembly—and all the people living in Lower and Upper Egypt,[u] said to Jeremiah, [16]"We will not listen to the message you have spoken to us in the name of the LORD! [17]We will certainly do everything we said we would: We will burn incense to the Queen of Heaven and will pour out drink offerings to her just as we and our fathers, our kings and our officials did in the towns of Judah and in the streets of Jerusalem. At that time we had plenty of food and were well off and suffered no harm. [18]But ever since we stopped burning incense to the Queen of Heaven and pouring out drink offerings to her, we have had nothing and have been perishing by sword and famine."

[19]The women added, "When we burned incense to the Queen of Heaven and poured out drink offerings to her, did not our husbands know that we were making cakes like her image and pouring out drink offerings to her?"

[20]Then Jeremiah said to all the people, both men and women, who were answering him, [21]"Did not the LORD remember and think about the incense burned in the towns of Judah and the streets of Jerusalem by you and your fathers, your kings and your officials and the people of the land? [22]When the LORD could no longer endure your wicked actions and the detestable things you did, your land became an object of cursing and a desolate waste without inhabitants, as it is today. [23]Because you have burned incense and have sinned against the LORD and have not obeyed him or followed his law or his

---

[r]13 Or *in Heliopolis*   [s]1 Hebrew *Noph*   [t]1 Hebrew *in Pathros*   [u]15 Hebrew *in Egypt and Pathros*

decrees or his stipulations, this disaster has come upon you, as you now see."

²⁴Then Jeremiah said to all the people, including the women, "Hear the word of the LORD, all you people of Judah in Egypt. ²⁵This is what the LORD Almighty, the God of Israel, says: You and your wives have shown by your actions what you promised when you said, 'We will certainly carry out the vows we made to burn incense and pour out drink offerings to the Queen of Heaven.'

"Go ahead then, do what you promised! Keep your vows! ²⁶But hear the word of the LORD, all Jews living in Egypt: 'I swear by my great name,' says the LORD, 'that no one from Judah living anywhere in Egypt will ever again invoke my name or swear, "As surely as the Sovereign LORD lives." ²⁷For I am watching over them for harm, not for good; the Jews in Egypt will perish by sword and famine until they are all destroyed. ²⁸Those who escape the sword and return to the land of Judah from Egypt will be very few. Then the whole remnant of Judah who came to live in Egypt will know whose word will stand— mine or theirs.

²⁹" 'This will be the sign to you that I will punish you in this place,' declares the LORD, 'so that you will know that my threats of harm against you will surely stand.' ³⁰This is what the LORD says: 'I am going to hand Pharaoh Hophra king of Egypt over to his enemies who seek his life, just as I handed Zedekiah king of Judah over to Nebuchadnezzar king of Babylon, the enemy who was seeking his life.' "

CHAPTER 45

This is what Jeremiah the prophet told Baruch son of Neriah in the fourth year of Jehoiakim son of Josiah king of Judah, after Baruch had written on a scroll the words Jeremiah was then dictating: ²"This is what the LORD, the God of Israel, says to you, Baruch: ³You said, 'Woe to me! The LORD has added sorrow to my pain; I am worn out with groaning and find no rest.' "

⁴The LORD said, "Say this to him: 'This is what the LORD says: I will overthrow what I have built and uproot what I have planted, throughout the land. ⁵Should you then seek great things for yourself? Seek them not. For I will bring disaster on all people, declares the LORD, but wherever you go I will let you escape with your life.' "

AUGUST 12 □ DAY 225
JEREMIAH 46–52
The Fall of Jerusalem

 OVERVIEW With a last, far-reaching sweep of his prophetic pen, Jeremiah outlines the judgments to come on many of the ungodly nations of the world: Egypt, Philistia, Moab, Ammon and Babylon. All will feel the sting of God's chastening hand. Even Babylon, the mighty conqueror of God's people, will eventually fall. The final chapter of the book, like the final brush strokes of a dark and dreary painting, portrays the fall of Jerusalem in all its stark horror. But the book closes on a significant note of hope as the heir to Judah's throne enjoys kindly treatment at the hands of his Babylonian captors.

Chapter 46	Chapter 47	Chapter 48	Chapter 49	Chs. 50–51	Chapter 52
Discipline of God upon					
Egypt	Philistia	Moab	Ammon	Babylon	Jerusalem
Judah's Foes					Judah's Fall

 YOUR DAILY WALK Immunity to disease is a wonderful thing. But there are some immunities you would be better off without.
One such immunity is typically—and tragically—found among those

The recognition of sin is only the beginning of salvation. who regularly sit under the teaching of God's Word. Sunday by Sunday in church, conviction comes as God's truth "hits home" in your life. You promise to change—but don't. Conviction returns, and again you know what needs to happen—but somehow you never get around to doing it. After a time, you begin to see conviction as an end in itself. "Immunity" has set in.

Think back over the way God has spoken to you through the life of Jeremiah this month. Then ask yourself this question: How many of the areas of my life about which I've been convicted have I actually attempted to change? Choose one neglected area to work on today. Don't allow spiritual immunity to rob you of spiritual vitality.

INSIGHT Nations Then and Now
With your Bible and a world map before you, notice these Old Testament designations for modern-day regions: Philistia (Gaza); Moab, Ammon, Edom and Kedar (Jordan); Damascus (Syria); Elam and Babylon (Iraq/Iran). Of all the nations mentioned in chapters 46–49, Egypt is the only one to maintain its identity and name today!

CHAPTER 46

This is the word of the LORD that came to Jeremiah the prophet concerning the nations:

²Concerning Egypt:

This is the message against the army of Pharaoh Neco king of Egypt, which was defeated at Carchemish on the Euphrates River by Nebuchadnezzar king of Babylon in the fourth year of Jehoiakim son of Josiah king of Judah:

³"Prepare your shields, both large and small,
    and march out for battle!
⁴Harness the horses,
    mount the steeds!
Take your positions
    with helmets on!
Polish your spears,
    put on your armor!
⁵What do I see?
    They are terrified,
they are retreating,
    their warriors are defeated.
They flee in haste
    without looking back,
    and there is terror on every side,"
                declares the LORD.
⁶"The swift cannot flee
    nor the strong escape.
In the north by the River Euphrates
    they stumble and fall.

⁷"Who is this that rises like the Nile,
    like rivers of surging waters?

⁸Egypt rises like the Nile,
    like rivers of surging waters.
She says, 'I will rise and cover the
        earth;
    I will destroy cities and their
        people.'
⁹Charge, O horses!
    Drive furiously, O charioteers!
March on, O warriors—
    men of Cushᵛ and Put who carry
        shields,
    men of Lydia who draw the bow.
¹⁰But that day belongs to the Lord, the
        LORD Almighty—
    a day of vengeance, for vengeance
        on his foes.
The sword will devour till it is
        satisfied,
    till it has quenched its thirst with
        blood.
For the Lord, the LORD Almighty, will
        offer sacrifice
    in the land of the north by the River
        Euphrates.

¹¹"Go up to Gilead and get balm,
    O Virgin Daughter of Egypt.
But you multiply remedies in vain;
    there is no healing for you.
¹²The nations will hear of your shame;
    your cries will fill the earth.
One warrior will stumble over another;
    both will fall down together."

¹³This is the message the LORD spoke to Jeremiah the prophet about the coming of

ᵛ9 That is, the upper Nile region

Nebuchadnezzar king of Babylon to attack Egypt:

¹⁴"Announce this in Egypt, and proclaim
it in Migdol;
proclaim it also in Memphis^w and
Tahpanhes:
'Take your positions and get ready,
for the sword devours those around
you.'
¹⁵Why will your warriors be laid low?
They cannot stand, for the LORD will
push them down.
¹⁶They will stumble repeatedly;
they will fall over each other.
They will say, 'Get up, let us go back
to our own people and our native
lands,
away from the sword of the
oppressor.'
¹⁷There they will exclaim,
'Pharaoh king of Egypt is only a
loud noise;
he has missed his opportunity.'

¹⁸"As surely as I live," declares the King,
whose name is the LORD Almighty,
"one will come who is like Tabor
among the mountains,
like Carmel by the sea.
¹⁹Pack your belongings for exile,
you who live in Egypt,
for Memphis will be laid waste
and lie in ruins without inhabitant.

²⁰"Egypt is a beautiful heifer,
but a gadfly is coming
against her from the north.
²¹The mercenaries in her ranks
are like fattened calves.
They too will turn and flee together,
they will not stand their ground,
for the day of disaster is coming upon
them,
the time for them to be punished.
²²Egypt will hiss like a fleeing serpent
as the enemy advances in force;
they will come against her with axes,
like men who cut down trees.
²³They will chop down her forest,"
declares the LORD,
"dense though it be.
They are more numerous than locusts,
they cannot be counted.
²⁴The Daughter of Egypt will be put to
shame,

handed over to the people of the
north."

²⁵The LORD Almighty, the God of Israel,
says: "I am about to bring punishment on
Amon god of Thebes,^x on Pharaoh, on
Egypt and her gods and her kings, and
on those who rely on Pharaoh. ²⁶I will
hand them over to those who seek their
lives, to Nebuchadnezzar king of Babylon
and his officers. Later, however, Egypt
will be inhabited as in times past," declares the LORD.

²⁷"Do not fear, O Jacob my servant;
do not be dismayed, O Israel.
I will surely save you out of a distant
place,
your descendants from the land of
their exile.
Jacob will again have peace and
security,
and no one will make him afraid.
²⁸Do not fear, O Jacob my servant,
for I am with you," declares the
LORD.
"Though I completely destroy all the
nations
among which I scatter you,
I will not completely destroy you.
I will discipline you but only with
justice;
I will not let you go entirely
unpunished."

CHAPTER 47

This is the word of the LORD that came to
Jeremiah the prophet concerning the Philistines before Pharaoh attacked Gaza:

²This is what the LORD says:

"See how the waters are rising in the
north;
they will become an overflowing
torrent.
They will overflow the land and
everything in it,
the towns and those who live in
them.
The people will cry out;
all who dwell in the land will wail
³at the sound of the hoofs of galloping
steeds,
at the noise of enemy chariots
and the rumble of their wheels.

^w14 Hebrew *Noph*; also in verse 19   ^x25 Hebrew *No*

Fathers will not turn to help their
    children;
  their hands will hang limp.
4For the day has come
    to destroy all the Philistines
and to cut off all survivors
    who could help Tyre and Sidon.
The LORD is about to destroy the
    Philistines,
  the remnant from the coasts of
    Caphtor.y
5Gaza will shave her head in mourning;
  Ashkelon will be silenced.
O remnant on the plain,
  how long will you cut yourselves?

6" 'Ah, sword of the LORD,' ⌐you cry,⌐
    'how long till you rest?
Return to your scabbard;
  cease and be still.'
7But how can it rest
    when the LORD has commanded it,
when he has ordered it
    to attack Ashkelon and the coast?"

CHAPTER 48
Concerning Moab:

  This is what the LORD Almighty, the
God of Israel, says:

  "Woe to Nebo, for it will be ruined.
    Kiriathaim will be disgraced and
      captured;
    the strongholdz will be disgraced
      and shattered.
2Moab will be praised no more;
  in Heshbona men will plot her
      downfall:
    'Come, let us put an end to that
      nation.'
You too, O Madmen,b will be
      silenced;
  the sword will pursue you.
3Listen to the cries from Horonaim,
  cries of great havoc and destruction.
4Moab will be broken;
  her little ones will cry out.c
5They go up the way to Luhith,
  weeping bitterly as they go;
on the road down to Horonaim
  anguished cries over the destruction
    are heard.
6Flee! Run for your lives;
  become like a bushd in the desert.

7Since you trust in your deeds and
    riches,
  you too will be taken captive,
and Chemosh will go into exile,
  together with his priests and
      officials.
8The destroyer will come against every
    town,
  and not a town will escape.
The valley will be ruined
  and the plateau destroyed,
because the LORD has spoken.
9Put salt on Moab,
  for she will be laid wastee;
her towns will become desolate,
  with no one to live in them.

10"A curse on him who is lax in doing
    the LORD's work!
  A curse on him who keeps his
    sword from bloodshed!

11"Moab has been at rest from youth,
  like wine left on its dregs,
not poured from one jar to another—
  she has not gone into exile.
So she tastes as she did,
  and her aroma is unchanged.
12But days are coming,"
    declares the LORD,
  "when I will send men who pour from
    jars,
  and they will pour her out;
they will empty her jars
  and smash her jugs.
13Then Moab will be ashamed of
    Chemosh,
  as the house of Israel was ashamed
    when they trusted in Bethel.

14"How can you say, 'We are warriors,
    men valiant in battle'?
15Moab will be destroyed and her towns
    invaded;
  her finest young men will go down
    in the slaughter,"
    declares the King, whose name is
      the LORD Almighty.
16"The fall of Moab is at hand;
  her calamity will come quickly.
17Mourn for her, all who live around
    her,
  all who know her fame;

y4 That is, Crete　z1 Or / Misgab　a2 The Hebrew for Heshbon sounds like the Hebrew for plot.　b2 The name of the Moabite town Madmen sounds like the Hebrew for be silenced.　c4 Hebrew; Septuagint / proclaim it to Zoar　d6 Or like Aroer　e9 Or Give wings to Moab, / for she will fly away

say, 'How broken is the mighty
    scepter,
  how broken the glorious staff!'

¹⁸"Come down from your glory
  and sit on the parched ground,
  O inhabitants of the Daughter of
    Dibon,
for he who destroys Moab
  will come up against you
  and ruin your fortified cities.
¹⁹Stand by the road and watch,
  you who live in Aroer.
Ask the man fleeing and the woman
    escaping,
  ask them, 'What has happened?'
²⁰Moab is disgraced, for she is shattered.
  Wail and cry out!
Announce by the Arnon
  that Moab is destroyed.
²¹Judgment has come to the plateau—
  to Holon, Jahzah and Mephaath,
²² to Dibon, Nebo and Beth
    Diblathaim,
²³ to Kiriathaim, Beth Gamul and Beth
    Meon,
²⁴ to Kerioth and Bozrah—
  to all the towns of Moab, far and
    near.
²⁵Moab's horn^f is cut off;
  her arm is broken,"
                              declares the LORD.

²⁶"Make her drunk,
  for she has defied the LORD.
Let Moab wallow in her vomit;
  let her be an object of ridicule.
²⁷Was not Israel the object of your
    ridicule?
  Was she caught among thieves,
that you shake your head in scorn
  whenever you speak of her?
²⁸Abandon your towns and dwell
    among the rocks,
  you who live in Moab.
Be like a dove that makes its nest
  at the mouth of a cave.

²⁹"We have heard of Moab's pride—
  her overweening pride and conceit,
her pride and arrogance
  and the haughtiness of her heart.
³⁰I know her insolence but it is futile,"
                              declares the LORD,
  "and her boasts accomplish nothing.
³¹Therefore I wail over Moab,
  for all Moab I cry out,

I moan for the men of Kir Hareseth.
³²I weep for you, as Jazer weeps,
  O vines of Sibmah.
Your branches spread as far as the sea;
  they reached as far as the sea of
    Jazer.
The destroyer has fallen
  on your ripened fruit and grapes.
³³Joy and gladness are gone
  from the orchards and fields of
    Moab.
I have stopped the flow of wine from
    the presses;
  no one treads them with shouts of
    joy.
Although there are shouts,
  they are not shouts of joy.

³⁴"The sound of their cry rises
  from Heshbon to Elealeh and Jahaz,
from Zoar as far as Horonaim and
    Eglath Shelishiyah,
  for even the waters of Nimrim are
    dried up.
³⁵In Moab I will put an end
  to those who make offerings on the
    high places
  and burn incense to their gods,"
                              declares the LORD.
³⁶"So my heart laments for Moab like a
    flute;
  it laments like a flute for the men of
    Kir Hareseth.
The wealth they acquired is gone.
³⁷Every head is shaved
  and every beard cut off;
every hand is slashed
  and every waist is covered with
    sackcloth.
³⁸On all the roofs in Moab
  and in the public squares
there is nothing but mourning,
  for I have broken Moab
  like a jar that no one wants,"
                              declares the LORD.
³⁹"How shattered she is! How they wail!
  How Moab turns her back in shame!
Moab has become an object of ridicule,
  an object of horror to all those
    around her."

⁴⁰This is what the LORD says:

"Look! An eagle is swooping down,
  spreading its wings over Moab.
⁴¹Kerioth^g will be captured
  and the strongholds taken.

^f25 Horn here symbolizes strength.   ^g41 Or The cities

In that day the hearts of Moab's
    warriors
  will be like the heart of a woman in
    labor.
⁴²Moab will be destroyed as a nation
  because she defied the LORD.
⁴³Terror and pit and snare await you,
  O people of Moab,"
                  declares the LORD.
⁴⁴"Whoever flees from the terror
  will fall into a pit,
whoever climbs out of the pit
  will be caught in a snare;
for I will bring upon Moab
  the year of her punishment,"
                  declares the LORD.

⁴⁵"In the shadow of Heshbon
  the fugitives stand helpless,
for a fire has gone out from Heshbon,
  a blaze from the midst of Sihon;
it burns the foreheads of Moab,
  the skulls of the noisy boasters.
⁴⁶Woe to you, O Moab!
  The people of Chemosh are
    destroyed;
your sons are taken into exile
  and your daughters into captivity.

⁴⁷"Yet I will restore the fortunes of Moab
  in days to come,"
                  declares the LORD.

Here ends the judgment on Moab.

CHAPTER 49
Concerning the Ammonites:

This is what the LORD says:

"Has Israel no sons?
  Has she no heirs?
Why then has Molech*ʰ* taken
    possession of Gad?
Why do his people live in its towns?
²But the days are coming,"
  declares the LORD,
"when I will sound the battle cry
  against Rabbah of the Ammonites;
it will become a mound of ruins,
  and its surrounding villages will be
    set on fire.
Then Israel will drive out
  those who drove her out,"
                 says the LORD.
³"Wail, O Heshbon, for Ai is destroyed!
  Cry out, O inhabitants of Rabbah!
Put on sackcloth and mourn;

ʰ1 Or *their king;* Hebrew *malcam;* also in verse 3

rush here and there inside the walls,
for Molech will go into exile,
  together with his priests and
    officials.
⁴Why do you boast of your valleys,
  boast of your valleys so fruitful?
O unfaithful daughter,
  you trust in your riches and say,
  'Who will attack me?'
⁵I will bring terror on you
  from all those around you,"
               declares the Lord,
              the LORD Almighty.
"Every one of you will be driven
    away,
  and no one will gather the fugitives.

⁶"Yet afterward, I will restore the
    fortunes of the Ammonites,"
               declares the LORD.

⁷Concerning Edom:

This is what the LORD Almighty says:

"Is there no longer wisdom in Teman?
  Has counsel perished from the
    prudent?
  Has their wisdom decayed?
⁸Turn and flee, hide in deep caves,
  you who live in Dedan,
for I will bring disaster on Esau
  at the time I punish him.
⁹If grape pickers came to you,
  would they not leave a few grapes?
If thieves came during the night,
  would they not steal only as much
    as they wanted?
¹⁰But I will strip Esau bare;
  I will uncover his hiding places,
  so that he cannot conceal himself.
His children, relatives and neighbors
    will perish,
  and he will be no more.
¹¹Leave your orphans; I will protect
    their lives.
  Your widows too can trust in me."

¹²This is what the LORD says: "If those
who do not deserve to drink the cup must
drink it, why should you go unpunished?
You will not go unpunished, but must
drink it. ¹³I swear by myself," declares the
LORD, "that Bozrah will become a ruin and
an object of horror, of reproach and of
cursing; and all its towns will be in ruins
forever."

¹⁴I have heard a message from the LORD:
    An envoy was sent to the nations to
      say,
"Assemble yourselves to attack it!
    Rise up for battle!"

¹⁵"Now I will make you small among
    the nations,
    despised among men.
¹⁶The terror you inspire
    and the pride of your heart have
      deceived you,
you who live in the clefts of the rocks,
    who occupy the heights of the hill.
Though you build your nest as high as
    the eagle's,
    from there I will bring you down,"
                 declares the LORD.
¹⁷"Edom will become an object of horror;
    all who pass by will be appalled and
      will scoff
because of all its wounds.
¹⁸As Sodom and Gomorrah were
    overthrown,
    along with their neighboring towns,"
                 says the LORD,
"so no one will live there;
    no man will dwell in it.

¹⁹"Like a lion coming up from Jordan's
    thickets
    to a rich pastureland,
I will chase Edom from its land in an
    instant.
    Who is the chosen one I will appoint
      for this?
Who is like me and who can challenge
    me?
    And what shepherd can stand
      against me?"
²⁰Therefore, hear what the LORD has
    planned against Edom,
what he has purposed against those
    who live in Teman:
The young of the flock will be dragged
    away;
    he will completely destroy their
      pasture because of them.
²¹At the sound of their fall the earth will
    tremble;
    their cry will resound to the Red
      Sea.ⁱ
²²Look! An eagle will soar and swoop
    down,
    spreading its wings over Bozrah.

In that day the hearts of Edom's
    warriors
    will be like the heart of a woman in
      labor.

²³Concerning Damascus:

"Hamath and Arpad are dismayed,
    for they have heard bad news.
They are disheartened,
    troubled likeʲ the restless sea.
²⁴Damascus has become feeble,
    she has turned to flee
    and panic has gripped her;
anguish and pain have seized her,
    pain like that of a woman in labor.
²⁵Why has the city of renown not been
    abandoned,
    the town in which I delight?
²⁶Surely, her young men will fall in the
    streets;
    all her soldiers will be silenced in
      that day,"
             declares the LORD Almighty.
²⁷"I will set fire to the walls of
    Damascus;
    it will consume the fortresses of
      Ben-Hadad."

²⁸Concerning Kedar and the kingdoms
of Hazor, which Nebuchadnezzar king of
Babylon attacked:

This is what the LORD says:

"Arise, and attack Kedar
    and destroy the people of the East.
²⁹Their tents and their flocks will be
    taken;
    their shelters will be carried off
    with all their goods and camels.
Men will shout to them,
    'Terror on every side!'

³⁰"Flee quickly away!
    Stay in deep caves, you who live in
      Hazor,"
                declares the LORD.
"Nebuchadnezzar king of Babylon has
    plotted against you;
    he has devised a plan against you.

³¹"Arise and attack a nation at ease,
    which lives in confidence,"
               declares the LORD,
"a nation that has neither gates nor
    bars;
    its people live alone.
³²Their camels will become plunder,

ⁱ21 Hebrew *Yam Suph*; that is, Sea of Reeds   ʲ23 Hebrew *on* or *by*

and their large herds will be booty.
I will scatter to the winds those who
    are in distant places[k]
and will bring disaster on them from
    every side,"
        declares the LORD.
[33]"Hazor will become a haunt of jackals,
    a desolate place forever.
No one will live there;
    no man will dwell in it."

[34]This is the word of the LORD that came
to Jeremiah the prophet concerning Elam,
early in the reign of Zedekiah king of Judah:

[35]This is what the LORD Almighty says:

"See, I will break the bow of Elam,
    the mainstay of their might.
[36]I will bring against Elam the four
    winds
    from the four quarters of the
        heavens;
I will scatter them to the four winds,
    and there will not be a nation
    where Elam's exiles do not go.
[37]I will shatter Elam before their foes,
    before those who seek their lives;
I will bring disaster upon them,
    even my fierce anger,"
        declares the LORD.
"I will pursue them with the sword
    until I have made an end of them.
[38]I will set my throne in Elam
    and destroy her king and officials,"
        declares the LORD.

[39]"Yet I will restore the fortunes of Elam
    in days to come,"
        declares the LORD.

CHAPTER 50

This is the word the LORD spoke through
Jeremiah the prophet concerning Babylon
and the land of the Babylonians[l]:

[2]"Announce and proclaim among the
    nations,
lift up a banner and proclaim it;
    keep nothing back, but say,
'Babylon will be captured;
    Bel will be put to shame,
    Marduk filled with terror.
Her images will be put to shame
    and her idols filled with terror.'
[3]A nation from the north will attack her
    and lay waste her land.

No one will live in it;
    both men and animals will flee
        away.

[4]"In those days, at that time,"
    declares the LORD,
"the people of Israel and the people of
    Judah together
    will go in tears to seek the LORD
        their God.
[5]They will ask the way to Zion
    and turn their faces toward it.
They will come and bind themselves
    to the LORD
    in an everlasting covenant
    that will not be forgotten.

[6]"My people have been lost sheep;
    their shepherds have led them astray
    and caused them to roam on the
        mountains.
They wandered over mountain and
    hill
    and forgot their own resting place.
[7]Whoever found them devoured them;
    their enemies said, 'We are not
        guilty,
for they sinned against the LORD, their
    true pasture,
    the LORD, the hope of their fathers.'

[8]"Flee out of Babylon;
    leave the land of the Babylonians,
    and be like the goats that lead the
        flock.
[9]For I will stir up and bring against
    Babylon
    an alliance of great nations from the
        land of the north.
They will take up their positions
    against her,
    and from the north she will be
        captured.
Their arrows will be like skilled
    warriors
    who do not return empty-handed.
[10]So Babylonia[m] will be plundered;
    all who plunder her will have their
        fill,"
        declares the LORD.

[11]"Because you rejoice and are glad,
    you who pillage my inheritance,
because you frolic like a heifer
    threshing grain
    and neigh like stallions,
[12]your mother will be greatly ashamed;

---

[k]32 Or *who clip the hair by their foreheads*   [l]1 Or *Chaldeans*; also in verses 8, 25, 35 and 45   [m]10 Or *Chaldea*

she who gave you birth will be
    disgraced.
She will be the least of the nations—
    a wilderness, a dry land, a desert.
[13]Because of the LORD's anger she will
        not be inhabited
    but will be completely desolate.
All who pass Babylon will be horrified
        and scoff
    because of all her wounds.

[14]"Take up your positions around
        Babylon,
    all you who draw the bow.
Shoot at her! Spare no arrows,
    for she has sinned against the LORD.
[15]Shout against her on every side!
    She surrenders, her towers fall,
        her walls are torn down.
Since this is the vengeance of the LORD,
        take vengeance on her;
    do to her as she has done to others.
[16]Cut off from Babylon the sower,
    and the reaper with his sickle at
        harvest.
Because of the sword of the oppressor
    let everyone return to his own
        people,
    let everyone flee to his own land.

[17]"Israel is a scattered flock
    that lions have chased away.
The first to devour him
    was the king of Assyria;
the last to crush his bones
    was Nebuchadnezzar king of
        Babylon."

[18]Therefore this is what the LORD Almighty, the God of Israel, says:

"I will punish the king of Babylon and
        his land
    as I punished the king of Assyria.
[19]But I will bring Israel back to his own
        pasture
    and he will graze on Carmel and
        Bashan;
his appetite will be satisfied
    on the hills of Ephraim and Gilead.
[20]In those days, at that time,"
            declares the LORD,
"search will be made for Israel's guilt,
    but there will be none,
and for the sins of Judah,
    but none will be found,

for I will forgive the remnant I
    spare.

[21]"Attack the land of Merathaim
    and those who live in Pekod.
Pursue, kill and completely destroy[n]
    them,"
            declares the LORD.
    "Do everything I have commanded
        you.
[22]The noise of battle is in the land,
    the noise of great destruction!
[23]How broken and shattered
    is the hammer of the whole earth!
How desolate is Babylon
    among the nations!
[24]I set a trap for you, O Babylon,
    and you were caught before you
        knew it;
you were found and captured
    because you opposed the LORD.
[25]The LORD has opened his arsenal
    and brought out the weapons of his
        wrath,
for the Sovereign LORD Almighty has
        work to do
    in the land of the Babylonians.
[26]Come against her from afar.
    Break open her granaries;
    pile her up like heaps of grain.
Completely destroy her
    and leave her no remnant.
[27]Kill all her young bulls;
    let them go down to the slaughter!
Woe to them! For their day has come,
    the time for them to be punished.
[28]Listen to the fugitives and refugees
        from Babylon
    declaring in Zion
how the LORD our God has taken
        vengeance,
    vengeance for his temple.

[29]"Summon archers against Babylon,
    all those who draw the bow.
Encamp all around her;
    let no one escape.
Repay her for her deeds;
    do to her as she has done.
For she has defied the LORD,
    the Holy One of Israel.
[30]Therefore, her young men will fall in
        the streets;
    all her soldiers will be silenced in
        that day,"
            declares the LORD.

[n]21 The Hebrew term refers to the irrevocable giving over of things or persons to the LORD, often by totally destroying them;
also in verse 26.

31"See, I am against you, O arrogant
          one,"
     declares the Lord, the LORD
          Almighty,
  "for your day has come,
     the time for you to be punished.
32The arrogant one will stumble and fall
     and no one will help her up;
  I will kindle a fire in her towns
     that will consume all who are
          around her."

33This is what the LORD Almighty says:

"The people of Israel are oppressed,
     and the people of Judah as well.
  All their captors hold them fast,
     refusing to let them go.
34Yet their Redeemer is strong;
     the LORD Almighty is his name.
  He will vigorously defend their cause
     so that he may bring rest to their
          land,
     but unrest to those who live in
          Babylon.

35"A sword against the Babylonians!"
     declares the LORD—
  "against those who live in Babylon
     and against her officials and wise
          men!
36A sword against her false prophets!
     They will become fools.
  A sword against her warriors!
     They will be filled with terror.
37A sword against her horses and
          chariots
     and all the foreigners in her ranks!
     They will become women.
  A sword against her treasures!
     They will be plundered.
38A drought on° her waters!
     They will dry up.
  For it is a land of idols,
     idols that will go mad with terror.

39"So desert creatures and hyenas will
          live there,
     and there the owl will dwell.
  It will never again be inhabited
     or lived in from generation to
          generation.
40As God overthrew Sodom and
          Gomorrah
     along with their neighboring towns,"
          declares the LORD,

"so no one will live there;
     no man will dwell in it.

41"Look! An army is coming from the
          north;
     a great nation and many kings
     are being stirred up from the ends
          of the earth.
42They are armed with bows and spears;
     they are cruel and without mercy.
  They sound like the roaring sea
     as they ride on their horses;
  they come like men in battle formation
     to attack you, O Daughter of
          Babylon.
43The king of Babylon has heard reports
          about them,
     and his hands hang limp.
  Anguish has gripped him,
     pain like that of a woman in labor.
44Like a lion coming up from Jordan's
          thickets
     to a rich pastureland,
  I will chase Babylon from its land in
          an instant.
  Who is the chosen one I will appoint
          for this?
  Who is like me and who can challenge
          me?
     And what shepherd can stand
          against me?"
45Therefore, hear what the LORD has
          planned against Babylon,
     what he has purposed against the
          land of the Babylonians:
  The young of the flock will be dragged
          away;
     he will completely destroy their
          pasture because of them.
46At the sound of Babylon's capture the
          earth will tremble;
     its cry will resound among the
          nations.

CHAPTER 51

This is what the LORD says:

"See, I will stir up the spirit of a
          destroyer
     against Babylon and the people of
          Leb Kamai.P
2I will send foreigners to Babylon
     to winnow her and to devastate her
          land;
  they will oppose her on every side
     in the day of her disaster.

°38 Or A sword against   P1 Leb Kamai is a cryptogram for Chaldea, that is, Babylonia.

³Let not the archer string his bow,
  nor let him put on his armor.
Do not spare her young men;
  completely destroyq her army.
⁴They will fall down slain in Babylon,r
  fatally wounded in her streets.
⁵For Israel and Judah have not been
    forsaken
  by their God, the LORD Almighty,
though their lands is full of guilt
  before the Holy One of Israel.

⁶"Flee from Babylon!
  Run for your lives!
  Do not be destroyed because of her
    sins.
It is time for the LORD's vengeance;
  he will pay her what she deserves.
⁷Babylon was a gold cup in the LORD's
    hand;
  she made the whole earth drunk.
The nations drank her wine;
  therefore they have now gone mad.
⁸Babylon will suddenly fall and be
    broken.
  Wail over her!
Get balm for her pain;
  perhaps she can be healed.

⁹" 'We would have healed Babylon,
  but she cannot be healed;
let us leave her and each go to his
    own land,
  for her judgment reaches to the
    skies,
  it rises as high as the clouds.'

¹⁰" 'The LORD has vindicated us;
  come, let us tell in Zion
  what the LORD our God has done.'

¹¹"Sharpen the arrows,
  take up the shields!
The LORD has stirred up the kings of
    the Medes,
  because his purpose is to destroy
    Babylon.
The LORD will take vengeance,
  vengeance for his temple.
¹²Lift up a banner against the walls of
    Babylon!
Reinforce the guard,
station the watchmen,
  prepare an ambush!
The LORD will carry out his purpose,
  his decree against the people of
    Babylon.

¹³You who live by many waters
  and are rich in treasures,
your end has come,
  the time for you to be cut off.
¹⁴The LORD Almighty has sworn by
    himself:
  I will surely fill you with men, as
    with a swarm of locusts,
  and they will shout in triumph over
    you.

¹⁵"He made the earth by his power;
  he founded the world by his
    wisdom
  and stretched out the heavens by his
    understanding.
¹⁶When he thunders, the waters in the
    heavens roar;
  he makes clouds rise from the ends
    of the earth.
He sends lightning with the rain
  and brings out the wind from his
    storehouses.

¹⁷"Every man is senseless and without
    knowledge;
  every goldsmith is shamed by his
    idols.
His images are a fraud;
  they have no breath in them.
¹⁸They are worthless, the objects of
    mockery;
  when their judgment comes, they
    will perish.
¹⁹He who is the Portion of Jacob is not
    like these,
  for he is the Maker of all things,
including the tribe of his inheritance—
  the LORD Almighty is his name.

²⁰"You are my war club,
  my weapon for battle—
with you I shatter nations,
  with you I destroy kingdoms,
²¹with you I shatter horse and rider,
  with you I shatter chariot and
    driver,
²²with you I shatter man and woman,
  with you I shatter old man and
    youth,
  with you I shatter young man and
    maiden,
²³with you I shatter shepherd and flock,
  with you I shatter farmer and oxen,
  with you I shatter governors and
    officials.

q3 The Hebrew term refers to the irrevocable giving over of things or persons to the LORD, often by totally destroying them.
r4 Or *Chaldea*   s5 Or / *and the land of the Babylonians*

²⁴"Before your eyes I will repay Babylon and all who live in Babylonia^t for all the wrong they have done in Zion," declares the LORD.

²⁵"I am against you, O destroying mountain,
you who destroy the whole earth,"
declares the LORD.
"I will stretch out my hand against you,
roll you off the cliffs,
and make you a burned-out mountain.
²⁶No rock will be taken from you for a cornerstone,
nor any stone for a foundation,
for you will be desolate forever,"
declares the LORD.

²⁷"Lift up a banner in the land!
Blow the trumpet among the nations!
Prepare the nations for battle against her;
summon against her these kingdoms:
Ararat, Minni and Ashkenaz.
Appoint a commander against her;
send up horses like a swarm of locusts.
²⁸Prepare the nations for battle against her—
the kings of the Medes,
their governors and all their officials,
and all the countries they rule.
²⁹The land trembles and writhes,
for the LORD's purposes against Babylon stand—
to lay waste the land of Babylon
so that no one will live there.
³⁰Babylon's warriors have stopped fighting;
they remain in their strongholds.
Their strength is exhausted;
they have become like women.
Her dwellings are set on fire;
the bars of her gates are broken.
³¹One courier follows another
and messenger follows messenger
to announce to the king of Babylon
that his entire city is captured,
³²the river crossings seized,
the marshes set on fire,
and the soldiers terrified."

³³This is what the LORD Almighty, the God of Israel, says:

"The Daughter of Babylon is like a threshing floor
at the time it is trampled;
the time to harvest her will soon come."

³⁴"Nebuchadnezzar king of Babylon has devoured us,
he has thrown us into confusion,
he has made us an empty jar.
Like a serpent he has swallowed us
and filled his stomach with our delicacies,
and then has spewed us out.
³⁵May the violence done to our flesh^u
be upon Babylon,"
say the inhabitants of Zion.
"May our blood be on those who live in Babylonia,"
says Jerusalem.

³⁶Therefore, this is what the LORD says:

"See, I will defend your cause
and avenge you;
I will dry up her sea
and make her springs dry.
³⁷Babylon will be a heap of ruins,
a haunt of jackals,
an object of horror and scorn,
a place where no one lives.
³⁸Her people all roar like young lions,
they growl like lion cubs.
³⁹But while they are aroused,
I will set out a feast for them
and make them drunk,
so that they shout with laughter—
then sleep forever and not awake,"
declares the LORD.
⁴⁰"I will bring them down
like lambs to the slaughter,
like rams and goats.

⁴¹"How Sheshach^v will be captured,
the boast of the whole earth seized!
What a horror Babylon will be
among the nations!
⁴²The sea will rise over Babylon;
its roaring waves will cover her.
⁴³Her towns will be desolate,
a dry and desert land,
a land where no one lives,
through which no man travels.
⁴⁴I will punish Bel in Babylon

^t24 Or *Chaldea;* also in verse 35   ^u35 Or *done to us and to our children*   ^v41 *Sheshach* is a cryptogram for Babylon.

and make him spew out what he
    has swallowed.
The nations will no longer stream to
    him.
And the wall of Babylon will fall.

45"Come out of her, my people!
    Run for your lives!
    Run from the fierce anger of the
        LORD.
46Do not lose heart or be afraid
    when rumors are heard in the land;
one rumor comes this year, another
        the next,
    rumors of violence in the land
    and of ruler against ruler.
47For the time will surely come
    when I will punish the idols of
        Babylon;
her whole land will be disgraced
    and her slain will all lie fallen
        within her.
48Then heaven and earth and all that is
    in them
    will shout for joy over Babylon,
for out of the north
    destroyers will attack her,"
           declares the LORD.

49"Babylon must fall because of Israel's
    slain,
    just as the slain in all the earth
    have fallen because of Babylon.
50You who have escaped the sword,
    leave and do not linger!
Remember the LORD in a distant land,
    and think on Jerusalem."

51"We are disgraced,
    for we have been insulted
    and shame covers our faces,
because foreigners have entered
    the holy places of the LORD's house."

52"But days are coming," declares the
    LORD,
    "when I will punish her idols,
and throughout her land
    the wounded will groan.
53Even if Babylon reaches the sky
    and fortifies her lofty stronghold,
I will send destroyers against her,"
           declares the LORD.
54"The sound of a cry comes from
    Babylon,
    the sound of great destruction
    from the land of the Babylonians.w

w54 Or Chaldeans

55The LORD will destroy Babylon;
    he will silence her noisy din.
Waves ⌊of enemies⌋ will rage like great
    waters;
    the roar of their voices will resound.
56A destroyer will come against Babylon;
    her warriors will be captured,
    and their bows will be broken.
For the LORD is a God of retribution;
    he will repay in full.
57I will make her officials and wise men
    drunk,
    her governors, officers and warriors
    as well;
they will sleep forever and not awake,"
    declares the King, whose name is
    the LORD Almighty.

58This is what the LORD Almighty says:

"Babylon's thick wall will be leveled
    and her high gates set on fire;
the peoples exhaust themselves for
    nothing,
    the nations' labor is only fuel for the
    flames."

59This is the message Jeremiah gave to
the staff officer Seraiah son of Neriah, the
son of Mahseiah, when he went to Babylon with Zedekiah king of Judah in the
fourth year of his reign. 60Jeremiah had
written on a scroll about all the disasters
that would come upon Babylon—all that
had been recorded concerning Babylon.
61He said to Seraiah, "When you get to
Babylon, see that you read all these words
aloud. 62Then say, 'O LORD, you have said
you will destroy this place, so that neither
man nor animal will live in it; it will be
desolate forever.' 63When you finish
reading this scroll, tie a stone to it and
throw it into the Euphrates. 64Then say,
'So will Babylon sink to rise no more because of the disaster I will bring upon her.
And her people will fall.' "

The words of Jeremiah end here.

CHAPTER 52

Zedekiah was twenty-one years old
when he became king, and he reigned in
Jerusalem eleven years. His mother's
name was Hamutal daughter of Jeremiah;
she was from Libnah. 2He did evil in the
eyes of the LORD, just as Jehoiakim had
done. 3It was because of the LORD's anger

that all this happened to Jerusalem and Judah, and in the end he thrust them from his presence.

Now Zedekiah rebelled against the king of Babylon.

⁴So in the ninth year of Zedekiah's reign, on the tenth day of the tenth month, Nebuchadnezzar king of Babylon marched against Jerusalem with his whole army. They camped outside the city and built siege works all around it. ⁵The city was kept under siege until the eleventh year of King Zedekiah.

⁶By the ninth day of the fourth month the famine in the city had become so severe that there was no food for the people to eat. ⁷Then the city wall was broken through, and the whole army fled. They left the city at night through the gate between the two walls near the king's garden, though the Babylonians˟ were surrounding the city. They fled toward the Arabah,ʸ ⁸but the Babylonianᶻ army pursued King Zedekiah and overtook him in the plains of Jericho. All his soldiers were separated from him and scattered, ⁹and he was captured.

He was taken to the king of Babylon at Riblah in the land of Hamath, where he pronounced sentence on him. ¹⁰There at Riblah the king of Babylon slaughtered the sons of Zedekiah before his eyes; he also killed all the officials of Judah. ¹¹Then he put out Zedekiah's eyes, bound him with bronze shackles and took him to Babylon, where he put him in prison till the day of his death.

¹²On the tenth day of the fifth month, in the nineteenth year of Nebuchadnezzar king of Babylon, Nebuzaradan commander of the imperial guard, who served the king of Babylon, came to Jerusalem. ¹³He set fire to the temple of the LORD, the royal palace and all the houses of Jerusalem. Every important building he burned down. ¹⁴The whole Babylonian army under the commander of the imperial guard broke down all the walls around Jerusalem. ¹⁵Nebuzaradan the commander of the guard carried into exile some of the poorest people and those who remained in the city, along with the rest of the craftsmenᵃ and those who had gone over to the king of Babylon. ¹⁶But Nebu-

zaradan left behind the rest of the poorest people of the land to work the vineyards and fields.

¹⁷The Babylonians broke up the bronze pillars, the movable stands and the bronze Sea that were at the temple of the LORD and they carried all the bronze to Babylon. ¹⁸They also took away the pots, shovels, wick trimmers, sprinkling bowls, dishes and all the bronze articles used in the temple service. ¹⁹The commander of the imperial guard took away the basins, censers, sprinkling bowls, pots, lampstands, dishes and bowls used for drink offerings—all that were made of pure gold or silver.

²⁰The bronze from the two pillars, the Sea and the twelve bronze bulls under it, and the movable stands, which King Solomon had made for the temple of the LORD, was more than could be weighed. ²¹Each of the pillars was eighteen cubits high and twelve cubits in circumferenceᵇ; each was four fingers thick, and hollow. ²²The bronze capital on top of the one pillar was five cubitsᶜ high and was decorated with a network and pomegranates of bronze all around. The other pillar, with its pomegranates, was similar. ²³There were ninety-six pomegranates on the sides; the total number of pomegranates above the surrounding network was a hundred.

²⁴The commander of the guard took as prisoners Seraiah the chief priest, Zephaniah the priest next in rank and the three doorkeepers. ²⁵Of those still in the city, he took the officer in charge of the fighting men, and seven royal advisers. He also took the secretary who was chief officer in charge of conscripting the people of the land and sixty of his men who were found in the city. ²⁶Nebuzaradan the commander took them all and brought them to the king of Babylon at Riblah. ²⁷There at Riblah, in the land of Hamath, the king had them executed.

So Judah went into captivity, away from her land. ²⁸This is the number of the people Nebuchadnezzar carried into exile:

in the seventh year, 3,023 Jews;

˟7 Or *Chaldeans*; also in verse 17   ʸ7 Or *the Jordan Valley*   ᶻ8 Or *Chaldean*; also in verse 14   ᵃ15 Or *populace*   ᵇ21 That is, about 27 feet (about 8.1 meters) high and 18 feet (about 5.4 meters) in circumference   ᶜ22 That is, about 7 1/2 feet (about 2.3 meters)

[29]in Nebuchadnezzar's eighteenth
  year,
    832 people from Jerusalem;
[30]in his twenty-third year,
    745 Jews taken into exile by Neb-
      uzaradan the commander of the
      imperial guard.
    There were 4,600 people in all.

[31]In the thirty-seventh year of the exile
of Jehoiachin king of Judah, in the year
Evil-Merodach[d] became king of Bab-

[d]31 Also called *Amel-Marduk*

ylon, he released Jehoiachin king of Judah
and freed him from prison on the
twenty-fifth day of the twelfth month.
[32]He spoke kindly to him and gave him
a seat of honor higher than those of the
other kings who were with him in Babylon. [33]So Jehoiachin put aside his prison
clothes and for the rest of his life ate regularly at the king's table. [34]Day by day the
king of Babylon gave Jehoiachin a regular
allowance as long as he lived, till the day
of his death.

Lamentations

JEREMIAH the prophet had warned the people of Judah for years of their impending doom if they would not repent. When his prophecies were fulfilled and Jerusalem was destroyed by the Babylonians, Jeremiah wrote Lamentations, a funeral dirge for the city. Written in five poems, this is probably the saddest book of the Bible. However, Jeremiah saw ultimate reason and hope beyond the ruins of his city. God is sovereign—after all, he had described this judgment years before—and he is gracious. In his faithful mercy Jerusalem will be restored.

Focus	God's Chastening and Control				God's Character
Divisions	Destroyed City	Crushed Population	Lamenting Prophet	Lost Glory	Repentant Kingdom
	1:1 1:22	2:1 2:22	3:1 3:66	4:1 4:22	5:1 5:22
Topics	The Sorrow	The Reason	The Hope	The Contrast	The Plea
Place	Jerusalem				
Time	Approximately 586 B.C.				

AUGUST 13 □ DAY 226
LAMENTATIONS 1–5
Wailing without a Wall

OVERVIEW Lamentations describes the funeral of a city. It is a tear-stained portrait of once-proud Jerusalem, now reduced to a pile of rubble by the invading Babylonian hordes. In a five-poem dirge, Jeremiah lays bare his emotions. A death has occurred; Jerusalem lies barren. Jeremiah, traditionally acclaimed as the author of Lamentations, writes his lament in acrostic or alphabetical fashion. In the midst of this terrible holocaust, Jeremiah triumphantly cries out, "Great is [the Lord's] faithfulness" (3:23)! In the face of death and destruction, with life seeming to come apart at the seams, Jeremiah turns tragedy into a triumph of faith. God has never failed him in the past. God has promised to remain faithful in the future. In the light of the God he knows and loves, Jeremiah finds hope and comfort.

Chapter 1	Chapter 2	Chapter 3	Chapter 4	Chapter 5
Jerusalem Deserted	Jerusalem Destroyed	Triumphant Hope	Jerusalem Defeated	Jerusalem Distressed
Defeat		Victory	Defeat	

YOUR DAILY WALK It's a strange paradox that while the pages of Scripture are soaked with the tears of Jeremiah, David, Hezekiah, the Lord Jesus and a host of others, crying today is often looked upon as a sign of weakness.

The Christian should show more concern for people than for creeds.

Psalm 56:8 tells us that God puts our tears in a bottle and keeps track of them in a book. Stoic insensitivity is nothing to be proud of. A man or woman with God's heart for people can't help but get emotionally involved. If you've never done so, ask God to break your heart for people—to give you the kind of compassion that caused Jeremiah and Jesus to cry over the city of Jerusalem.

INSIGHT Jeremiah's Two Glimpses of Jerusalem's Fall

Book of Jeremiah	*Book of Lamentations*
Looking ahead to the fall of Jerusalem (Warning)	Looking back at the fall of Jerusalem (Mourning)

CHAPTER 1*ᵃ*

How deserted lies the city,
 once so full of people!
How like a widow is she,
 who once was great among the
 nations!
She who was queen among the
 provinces
 has now become a slave.

²Bitterly she weeps at night,

tears are upon her cheeks.
Among all her lovers
 there is none to comfort her.
All her friends have betrayed
 her;
 they have become her enemies.

³After affliction and harsh labor,
 Judah has gone into exile.
She dwells among the nations;

---

*ᵃ*This chapter is an acrostic poem, the verses of which begin with the successive letters of the Hebrew alphabet.

she finds no resting place.
All who pursue her have overtaken
her
in the midst of her distress.

⁴The roads to Zion mourn,
for no one comes to her appointed
feasts.
All her gateways are desolate,
her priests groan,
her maidens grieve,
and she is in bitter anguish.

⁵Her foes have become her masters;
her enemies are at ease.
The LORD has brought her grief
because of her many sins.
Her children have gone into exile,
captive before the foe.

⁶All the splendor has departed
from the Daughter of Zion.
Her princes are like deer
that find no pasture;
in weakness they have fled
before the pursuer.

⁷In the days of her affliction and
wandering
Jerusalem remembers all the
treasures
that were hers in days of old.
When her people fell into enemy
hands,
there was no one to help her.
Her enemies looked at her
and laughed at her destruction.

⁸Jerusalem has sinned greatly
and so has become unclean.
All who honored her despise her,
for they have seen her nakedness;
she herself groans
and turns away.

⁹Her filthiness clung to her skirts;
she did not consider her future.
Her fall was astounding;
there was none to comfort her.
"Look, O LORD, on my affliction,
for the enemy has triumphed."

¹⁰The enemy laid hands
on all her treasures;
she saw pagan nations
enter her sanctuary—
those you had forbidden
to enter your assembly.

¹¹All her people groan
as they search for bread;
they barter their treasures for food
to keep themselves alive.
"Look, O LORD, and consider,
for I am despised."

¹²"Is it nothing to you, all you who pass
by?
Look around and see.
Is any suffering like my suffering
that was inflicted on me,
that the LORD brought on me
in the day of his fierce anger?

¹³"From on high he sent fire,
sent it down into my bones.
He spread a net for my feet
and turned me back.
He made me desolate,
faint all the day long.

¹⁴"My sins have been bound into a
yoke[b];
by his hands they were woven
together.
They have come upon my neck
and the Lord has sapped my
strength.
He has handed me over
to those I cannot withstand.

¹⁵"The Lord has rejected
all the warriors in my midst;
he has summoned an army against me
to[c] crush my young men.
In his winepress the Lord has
trampled
the Virgin Daughter of Judah.

¹⁶"This is why I weep
and my eyes overflow with tears.
No one is near to comfort me,
no one to restore my spirit.
My children are destitute
because the enemy has prevailed."

¹⁷Zion stretches out her hands,
but there is no one to comfort her.
The LORD has decreed for Jacob
that his neighbors become his foes;
Jerusalem has become
an unclean thing among them.

¹⁸"The LORD is righteous,
yet I rebelled against his command.
Listen, all you peoples;
look upon my suffering.

---

[b]14 Most Hebrew manuscripts; Septuagint *He kept watch over my sins*   [c]15 Or *has set a time for me / when he will*

My young men and maidens
  have gone into exile.

19"I called to my allies
  but they betrayed me.
My priests and my elders
  perished in the city
while they searched for food
  to keep themselves alive.

20"See, O LORD, how distressed I am!
  I am in torment within,
and in my heart I am disturbed,
  for I have been most rebellious.
Outside, the sword bereaves;
  inside, there is only death.

21"People have heard my groaning,
  but there is no one to comfort me.
All my enemies have heard of my
    distress;
  they rejoice at what you have done.
May you bring the day you have
    announced
  so they may become like me.

22"Let all their wickedness come before
    you;
  deal with them
as you have dealt with me
  because of all my sins.
My groans are many
  and my heart is faint."

CHAPTER 2ᵈ
How the Lord has covered the
    Daughter of Zion
  with the cloud of his angerᵉ!
He has hurled down the splendor of
    Israel
  from heaven to earth;
he has not remembered his footstool
  in the day of his anger.

²Without pity the Lord has swallowed
    up
  all the dwellings of Jacob;
in his wrath he has torn down
  the strongholds of the Daughter of
    Judah.
He has brought her kingdom and its
    princes
  down to the ground in dishonor.

³In fierce anger he has cut off
  every hornᶠ of Israel.
He has withdrawn his right hand

at the approach of the enemy.
He has burned in Jacob like a flaming
    fire
  that consumes everything around it.

⁴Like an enemy he has strung his bow;
  his right hand is ready.
Like a foe he has slain
  all who were pleasing to the eye;
he has poured out his wrath like fire
  on the tent of the Daughter of Zion.

⁵The Lord is like an enemy;
  he has swallowed up Israel.
He has swallowed up all her palaces
  and destroyed her strongholds.
He has multiplied mourning and
    lamentation
  for the Daughter of Judah.

⁶He has laid waste his dwelling like a
    garden;
  he has destroyed his place of
    meeting.
The LORD has made Zion forget
  her appointed feasts and her
    Sabbaths;
in his fierce anger he has spurned
  both king and priest.

⁷The Lord has rejected his altar
  and abandoned his sanctuary.
He has handed over to the enemy
  the walls of her palaces;
they have raised a shout in the house
    of the LORD
  as on the day of an appointed feast.

⁸The LORD determined to tear down
  the wall around the Daughter of
    Zion.
He stretched out a measuring line
  and did not withhold his hand from
    destroying.
He made ramparts and walls lament;
  together they wasted away.

⁹Her gates have sunk into the ground;
  their bars he has broken and
    destroyed.
Her king and her princes are exiled
    among the nations,
  the law is no more,
and her prophets no longer find
  visions from the LORD.

¹⁰The elders of the Daughter of Zion

ᵈThis chapter is an acrostic poem, the verses of which begin with the successive letters of the Hebrew alphabet.   ᵉ1 Or How the Lord in his anger / has treated the Daughter of Zion with contempt   ᶠ3 Or / all the strength; or every king; horn here symbolizes strength.

sit on the ground in silence;
they have sprinkled dust on their
heads
and put on sackcloth.
The young women of Jerusalem
have bowed their heads to the
ground.

11My eyes fail from weeping,
I am in torment within,
my heart is poured out on the ground
because my people are destroyed,
because children and infants faint
in the streets of the city.

12They say to their mothers,
"Where is bread and wine?"
as they faint like wounded men
in the streets of the city,
as their lives ebb away
in their mothers' arms.

13What can I say for you?
With what can I compare you,
O Daughter of Jerusalem?
To what can I liken you,
that I may comfort you,
O Virgin Daughter of Zion?
Your wound is as deep as the sea.
Who can heal you?

14The visions of your prophets
were false and worthless;
they did not expose your sin
to ward off your captivity.
The oracles they gave you
were false and misleading.

15All who pass your way
clap their hands at you;
they scoff and shake their heads
at the Daughter of Jerusalem:
"Is this the city that was called
the perfection of beauty,
the joy of the whole earth?"

16All your enemies open their mouths
wide against you;
they scoff and gnash their teeth
and say, "We have swallowed her
up.
This is the day we have waited for;
we have lived to see it."

17The LORD has done what he planned;
he has fulfilled his word,
which he decreed long ago.
He has overthrown you without pity,

he has let the enemy gloat over you,
he has exalted the horn*g* of your
foes.

18The hearts of the people
cry out to the Lord.
O wall of the Daughter of Zion,
let your tears flow like a river
day and night;
give yourself no relief,
your eyes no rest.

19Arise, cry out in the night,
as the watches of the night begin;
pour out your heart like water
in the presence of the Lord.
Lift up your hands to him
for the lives of your children,
who faint from hunger
at the head of every street.

20"Look, O LORD, and consider:
Whom have you ever treated like
this?
Should women eat their offspring,
the children they have cared for?
Should priest and prophet be killed
in the sanctuary of the Lord?

21"Young and old lie together
in the dust of the streets;
my young men and maidens
have fallen by the sword.
You have slain them in the day of
your anger;
you have slaughtered them without
pity.

22"As you summon to a feast day,
so you summoned against me
terrors on every side.
In the day of the LORD's anger
no one escaped or survived;
those I cared for and reared,
my enemy has destroyed."

CHAPTER 3*h*
I am the man who has seen affliction
by the rod of his wrath.
2He has driven me away and made me
walk
in darkness rather than light;
3indeed, he has turned his hand against
me
again and again, all day long.

4He has made my skin and my flesh
grow old

---

g 17 *Horn* here symbolizes strength.   *h* This chapter is an acrostic poem; the verses of each stanza begin with the successive letters of the Hebrew alphabet, and the verses within each stanza begin with the same letter.

and has broken my bones.
⁵He has besieged me and surrounded
    me
  with bitterness and hardship.
⁶He has made me dwell in darkness
  like those long dead.

⁷He has walled me in so I cannot
    escape;
  he has weighed me down with
    chains.
⁸Even when I call out or cry for help,
  he shuts out my prayer.
⁹He has barred my way with blocks of
    stone;
  he has made my paths crooked.

¹⁰Like a bear lying in wait,
  like a lion in hiding,
¹¹he dragged me from the path and
    mangled me
  and left me without help.
¹²He drew his bow
  and made me the target for his
    arrows.

¹³He pierced my heart
  with arrows from his quiver.
¹⁴I became the laughingstock of all my
    people;
  they mock me in song all day long.
¹⁵He has filled me with bitter herbs
  and sated me with gall.

¹⁶He has broken my teeth with gravel;
  he has trampled me in the dust.
¹⁷I have been deprived of peace;
  I have forgotten what prosperity is.
¹⁸So I say, "My splendor is gone
  and all that I had hoped from the
    LORD."

¹⁹I remember my affliction and my
    wandering,
  the bitterness and the gall.
²⁰I well remember them,
  and my soul is downcast within me.
²¹Yet this I call to mind
  and therefore I have hope:

²²Because of the LORD's great love we are
    not consumed,
  for his compassions never fail.
²³They are new every morning;
  great is your faithfulness.
²⁴I say to myself, "The LORD is my
    portion;
  therefore I will wait for him."

²⁵The LORD is good to those whose hope
    is in him,
  to the one who seeks him;
²⁶it is good to wait quietly
  for the salvation of the LORD.
²⁷It is good for a man to bear the yoke
  while he is young.

²⁸Let him sit alone in silence,
  for the LORD has laid it on him.
²⁹Let him bury his face in the dust—
  there may yet be hope.
³⁰Let him offer his cheek to one who
    would strike him,
  and let him be filled with disgrace.

³¹For men are not cast off
  by the Lord forever.
³²Though he brings grief, he will show
    compassion,
  so great is his unfailing love.
³³For he does not willingly bring
    affliction
  or grief to the children of men.

³⁴To crush underfoot
  all prisoners in the land,
³⁵to deny a man his rights
  before the Most High,
³⁶to deprive a man of justice—
  would not the Lord see such things?

³⁷Who can speak and have it happen
  if the Lord has not decreed it?
³⁸Is it not from the mouth of the Most
    High
  that both calamities and good things
    come?
³⁹Why should any living man complain
  when punished for his sins?

⁴⁰Let us examine our ways and test
    them,
  and let us return to the LORD.
⁴¹Let us lift up our hearts and our hands
  to God in heaven, and say:
⁴²"We have sinned and rebelled
  and you have not forgiven.

⁴³"You have covered yourself with anger
    and pursued us;
  you have slain without pity.
⁴⁴You have covered yourself with a
    cloud
  so that no prayer can get through.
⁴⁵You have made us scum and refuse
  among the nations.
⁴⁶"All our enemies have opened their
    mouths

wide against us.
⁴⁷We have suffered terror and pitfalls,
   ruin and destruction."
⁴⁸Streams of tears flow from my eyes
   because my people are destroyed.

⁴⁹My eyes will flow unceasingly,
   without relief,
⁵⁰until the LORD looks down
   from heaven and sees.
⁵¹What I see brings grief to my soul
   because of all the women of my city.

⁵²Those who were my enemies without
      cause
   hunted me like a bird.
⁵³They tried to end my life in a pit
   and threw stones at me;
⁵⁴the waters closed over my head,
   and I thought I was about to be cut
      off.

⁵⁵I called on your name, O LORD,
   from the depths of the pit.
⁵⁶You heard my plea: "Do not close your
      ears
   to my cry for relief."
⁵⁷You came near when I called you,
   and you said, "Do not fear."

⁵⁸O Lord, you took up my case;
   you redeemed my life.
⁵⁹You have seen, O LORD, the wrong
      done to me.
   Uphold my cause!
⁶⁰You have seen the depth of their
      vengeance,
   all their plots against me.

⁶¹O LORD, you have heard their insults,
   all their plots against me—
⁶²what my enemies whisper and mutter
   against me all day long.
⁶³Look at them! Sitting or standing,
   they mock me in their songs.

⁶⁴Pay them back what they deserve,
      O LORD,
   for what their hands have done.
⁶⁵Put a veil over their hearts,
   and may your curse be on them!
⁶⁶Pursue them in anger and destroy
      them
   from under the heavens of the LORD.

CHAPTER 4ⁱ

How the gold has lost its luster,
   the fine gold become dull!

The sacred gems are scattered
   at the head of every street.

²How the precious sons of Zion,
   once worth their weight in gold,
are now considered as pots of clay,
   the work of a potter's hands!

³Even jackals offer their breasts
   to nurse their young,
but my people have become heartless
   like ostriches in the desert.

⁴Because of thirst the infant's tongue
   sticks to the roof of its mouth;
the children beg for bread,
   but no one gives it to them.

⁵Those who once ate delicacies
   are destitute in the streets.
Those nurtured in purple
   now lie on ash heaps.

⁶The punishment of my people
   is greater than that of Sodom,
which was overthrown in a moment
   without a hand turned to help her.

⁷Their princes were brighter than snow
   and whiter than milk,
their bodies more ruddy than rubies,
   their appearance like sapphires.ʲ

⁸But now they are blacker than soot;
   they are not recognized in the
      streets.
Their skin has shriveled on their
      bones;
   it has become as dry as a stick.

⁹Those killed by the sword are better
      off
   than those who die of famine;
racked with hunger, they waste away
   for lack of food from the field.

¹⁰With their own hands compassionate
      women
   have cooked their own children,
who became their food
   when my people were destroyed.

¹¹The LORD has given full vent to his
      wrath;
   he has poured out his fierce anger.
He kindled a fire in Zion
   that consumed her foundations.

¹²The kings of the earth did not believe,
   nor did any of the world's people,

ⁱThis chapter is an acrostic poem, the verses of which begin with the successive letters of the Hebrew alphabet.   ʲ7 Or *lapis lazuli*

that enemies and foes could enter
   the gates of Jerusalem.

¹³But it happened because of the sins of
   her prophets
   and the iniquities of her priests,
who shed within her
   the blood of the righteous.

¹⁴Now they grope through the streets
   like men who are blind.
They are so defiled with blood
   that no one dares to touch their
   garments.

¹⁵"Go away! You are unclean!" men cry
   to them.
   "Away! Away! Don't touch us!"
When they flee and wander about,
   people among the nations say,
   "They can stay here no longer."

¹⁶The LORD himself has scattered them;
   he no longer watches over them.
The priests are shown no honor,
   the elders no favor.

¹⁷Moreover, our eyes failed,
   looking in vain for help;
from our towers we watched
   for a nation that could not save us.

¹⁸Men stalked us at every step,
   so we could not walk in our
   streets.
Our end was near, our days were
   numbered,
   for our end had come.

¹⁹Our pursuers were swifter
   than eagles in the sky;
they chased us over the mountains
   and lay in wait for us in the
   desert.

²⁰The LORD's anointed, our very life
   breath,
   was caught in their traps.
We thought that under his shadow
   we would live among the nations.

²¹Rejoice and be glad, O Daughter of
   Edom,
   you who live in the land of Uz.
But to you also the cup will be
   passed;
   you will be drunk and stripped
   naked.

²²O Daughter of Zion, your punishment
   will end;
   he will not prolong your exile.

But, O Daughter of Edom, he will
   punish your sin
   and expose your wickedness.

CHAPTER 5

Remember, O LORD, what has
   happened to us;
   look, and see our disgrace.
²Our inheritance has been turned over
   to aliens,
   our homes to foreigners.
³We have become orphans and
   fatherless,
   our mothers like widows.
⁴We must buy the water we drink;
   our wood can be had only at a
   price.
⁵Those who pursue us are at our
   heels;
   we are weary and find no rest.
⁶We submitted to Egypt and Assyria
   to get enough bread.
⁷Our fathers sinned and are no more,
   and we bear their punishment.
⁸Slaves rule over us,
   and there is none to free us from
   their hands.
⁹We get our bread at the risk of our
   lives
   because of the sword in the desert.
¹⁰Our skin is hot as an oven,
   feverish from hunger.
¹¹Women have been ravished in Zion,
   and virgins in the towns of Judah.
¹²Princes have been hung up by their
   hands;
   elders are shown no respect.
¹³Young men toil at the millstones;
   boys stagger under loads of wood.
¹⁴The elders are gone from the city
   gate;
   the young men have stopped their
   music.
¹⁵Joy is gone from our hearts;
   our dancing has turned to
   mourning.
¹⁶The crown has fallen from our head.
   Woe to us, for we have sinned!
¹⁷Because of this our hearts are faint,
   because of these things our eyes
   grow dim
¹⁸for Mount Zion, which lies desolate,
   with jackals prowling over it.

¹⁹You, O LORD, reign forever;
   your throne endures from generation
   to generation.

971   **AUGUST 14 / LAMENTATIONS 5**

²⁰Why do you always forget us?
    Why do you forsake us so long?
²¹Restore us to yourself, O LORD, that we
    may return;

renew our days as of old
²²unless you have utterly rejected us
    and are angry with us beyond
    measure.

AUGUST 14 ☐ DAY 227
Light in the Darkest Hour

 LOOK BACK Sometimes through sermons, sometimes through silence and symbolic object lessons, Jeremiah confronts the people of Judah with the deadly consequences of their disobedience. His sermons are ignored by some and burned by others. His character is smeared and his motives questioned. Finally, Jeremiah is thrown into a muddy cistern, where he sinks to an all-time low (literally and figuratively). But through it all, God is at work in and through his choice messenger. When Jerusalem falls to the Babylonian onslaught, Jeremiah is freed and carried to Egypt. There he declares the future fortunes and misfortunes of Judah and her pagan neighbors. Though the present is grim, the future brims with hope if you know where to look (Jeremiah 52:31–34).

Lamentations is Jeremiah's "diary of disaster," penned as he watches calamity befall his beloved Jerusalem. You can almost wring out the pages, so soaked are they with Jeremiah's tears. But in the midst of Jeremiah's grief (Lamentations 3:22–23), he proclaims a truth so powerful, it has become the theme of one of the best-loved hymns of all time: "Great Is Thy Faithfulness." Governments rise and fall; economies crumble; even spiritual leaders disappoint us. But the Lord's mercies never fail!

 LOOK UP Have you ever experienced total darkness? You know, the kind you can *feel* as well as *see?*

Try it! Find an interior room, attic or closet in your house where there is little or no natural light. Put a blindfold over your eyes and
Life is filled with shadows, but it is Sonshine that makes them all.
close your eyes tightly. What you have is absolute darkness—the absence of any glimmer of light.

Metaphorically, the people of God were experiencing total darkness in Jeremiah 52 as they faced the Babylonian onslaught. After all, consider this:
- There was not a crust of bread left in the city (v. 6).
- The city's defenses were in shambles (v. 7).
- The army had all gone AWOL (v. 7).
- The king's family was slaughtered before his eyes. Then his eyes were gouged out, and he was deported in chains to a distant prison (vv. 10–11).
- The temple, city walls and chief buildings were burned down (vv. 13–14).
- The king's entire "cabinet" was taken prisoner and executed (vv. 24–27).
- Thousands of Jews were taken captive to a distant land (vv. 27–30).

Dark days for the people of God, to be sure. But don't miss the final four verses, for there you'll discover light in the darkness—hope in the midst of horror. Though Evil-Merodach had no earthly reason to do so, the king of Babylon showed kindness and courtesy to the exiled king of Judah. Why? Because *God was not finished with his people.* He knew that they needed hope and a future.

 LOOK AHEAD When your health is frail, when your financial prospects are bleak, when your family and friends are far away, when your job is uncertain, when tomorrow looks no brighter than today, it's easy to be overwhelmed by the darkness. But the light of one match can illuminate an entire room!

Take a moment to bask in the light of Psalm 27:1. There you'll discover that darkness is no match for the Light of your life, the one in whom there is no darkness at all (1 John 1:5).

> The LORD is my light and my salvation—
>   whom shall I fear?
> The LORD is the stronghold of my life—
>   of whom shall I be afraid?

Ezekiel

EZEKIEL'S ministry among the Jewish exiles in Babylonia during the last days of Judah's decline is similar to that of Jeremiah. But while Jeremiah delivers a chilling message of destruction, Ezekiel offers a warning message of reconstruction. Jeremiah is a man of tears; Ezekiel, a man of vision. And those visions stretch all the way from horrible condemnation of Judah's faithless leaders and godless enemies to hopeful consolation regarding Judah's future restoration.

Focus	Judah's End					Judah's Enemies		Judah's Future			
Divisions	Ezekiel's Call	Sins and Sorrows	Signs and Sermons	Parables of Judgment	Swords and Signposts	Judgment East & West	Judgment on Egypt	Watchman on the Wall	Gog and Magog	New Temple for Israel	New Worship for Israel
	1 6	7 11	12 15	16 19	20 23	24 28	29 32	33 36	37 39	40 43	44 48
Topics	Before the Fall (592–587 B.C.)					During the Fall (586 B.C.)		After the Fall (585–570 B.C.)			
	Prophecies of Judgment							Promises of Restoration			
Place	Babylonia										
Time	About 22 Years										

AUGUST 15 □ DAY 228
EZEKIEL 1–6
Ezekiel's Vision and Call

 OVERVIEW Six hundred miles from Jerusalem lives Ezekiel, another of God's handpicked mouthpieces. Ezekiel is called by God to preach both judgment and hope to the first Judean exiles in Babylonia. Because his prophetic assignment is so challenging, God first gives Ezekiel a most unusual vision of his greatness and glory. Fortified with a fresh glimpse of his great God, Ezekiel launches into his difficult task: explaining to the exiles why Jerusalem will fall and why the nation will spend the next seven decades in Babylonia.

Chapter 1	Chapters 2–3	Chapters 4–5	Chapter 6
Ezekiel's Vision	Ezekiel's Call	Judgment Visualized	Judgment Explained
The Prophet		The Prophecy	

 YOUR DAILY WALK How many times a day do you put into practice a "this is what the Sovereign LORD says" principle? You know the kinds of situations: You're tempted to gossip . . . you feel yourself losing control of your temper . . . you're confronted by a close friend who is caught in the quicksand of a deep personal problem . . . you feel like telling a half-truth (which, in reality, is a whole untruth).

Life without purpose inevitably falls prey to the perverted ways of the uncommitted life.

How do you tackle these and countless other sticky situations? Do you just ignore them and hope they'll go away? Do you share your own thoughts and wisdom on the subject? Or do you do what God told Ezekiel to do: "Go now to your countrymen in exile and speak to them. Say to them, 'This is what the Sovereign LORD says' " (3:11)?

This devotional guide can help you walk through the Bible, but how much of the *Bible* are you allowing to walk through *you* . . . in your thoughts, habits, speech and conduct? Put these words on an index card for quick reference: "God said it, I believe it, I will do it, and that settles it." Then today, with God's help, translate a "this is what the Sovereign LORD says" into a "this is what my life says."

 INSIGHT Repetition Is the Mother of Learning
Ezekiel's style of instruction might be summarized this way: "If a point is worth making, it is worth making at least four times!" It might be easy to miss the prophet's point if stated only once, but it is nearly impossible to miss when stated four times in one chapter (6:7, 10, 13–14)! Find it and state it in your own words.

CHAPTER 1

In the*ᵃ* thirtieth year, in the fourth month on the fifth day, while I was among the exiles by the Kebar River, the heavens were opened and I saw visions of God.

²On the fifth of the month—it was the fifth year of the exile of King Jehoiachin—³the word of the LORD came to Ezekiel the priest, the son of Buzi,*ᵇ* by the Kebar River in the land of the Babylonians.*ᶜ* There the hand of the LORD was upon him.

⁴I looked, and I saw a windstorm com-

ᵃ1 Or ₐmyₐ   ᵇ3 Or Ezekiel son of Buzi the priest   ᶜ3 Or Chaldeans ing out of the north—an immense cloud with flashing lightning and surrounded by brilliant light. The center of the fire looked like glowing metal, 5and in the fire was what looked like four living creatures. In appearance their form was that of a man, 6but each of them had four faces and four wings. 7Their legs were straight; their feet were like those of a calf and gleamed like burnished bronze. 8Under their wings on their four sides they had the hands of a man. All four of them had faces and wings, 9and their wings touched one another. Each one went straight ahead; they did not turn as they moved.

10Their faces looked like this: Each of the four had the face of a man, and on the right side each had the face of a lion, and on the left the face of an ox; each also had the face of an eagle. 11Such were their faces. Their wings were spread out upward; each had two wings, one touching the wing of another creature on either side, and two wings covering its body. 12Each one went straight ahead. Wherever the spirit would go, they would go, without turning as they went. 13The appearance of the living creatures was like burning coals of fire or like torches. Fire moved back and forth among the creatures; it was bright, and lightning flashed out of it. 14The creatures sped back and forth like flashes of lightning.

15As I looked at the living creatures, I saw a wheel on the ground beside each creature with its four faces. 16This was the appearance and structure of the wheels: They sparkled like chrysolite, and all four looked alike. Each appeared to be made like a wheel intersecting a wheel. 17As they moved, they would go in any one of the four directions the creatures faced; the wheels did not turn about*d* as the creatures went. 18Their rims were high and awesome, and all four rims were full of eyes all around.

19When the living creatures moved, the wheels beside them moved; and when the living creatures rose from the ground, the wheels also rose. 20Wherever the spirit would go, they would go, and the wheels would rise along with them, because the spirit of the living creatures was in the wheels. 21When the creatures moved, they

also moved; when the creatures stood still, they also stood still; and when the creatures rose from the ground, the wheels rose along with them, because the spirit of the living creatures was in the wheels.

22Spread out above the heads of the living creatures was what looked like an expanse, sparkling like ice, and awesome. 23Under the expanse their wings were stretched out one toward the other, and each had two wings covering its body. 24When the creatures moved, I heard the sound of their wings, like the roar of rushing waters, like the voice of the Almighty,*e* like the tumult of an army. When they stood still, they lowered their wings.

25Then there came a voice from above the expanse over their heads as they stood with lowered wings. 26Above the expanse over their heads was what looked like a throne of sapphire,*f* and high above on the throne was a figure like that of a man. 27I saw that from what appeared to be his waist up he looked like glowing metal, as if full of fire, and that from there down he looked like fire; and brilliant light surrounded him. 28Like the appearance of a rainbow in the clouds on a rainy day, so was the radiance around him.

This was the appearance of the likeness of the glory of the LORD. When I saw it, I fell facedown, and I heard the voice of one speaking.

CHAPTER 2

He said to me, "Son of man, stand up on your feet and I will speak to you." 2As he spoke, the Spirit came into me and raised me to my feet, and I heard him speaking to me.

3He said: "Son of man, I am sending you to the Israelites, to a rebellious nation that has rebelled against me; they and their fathers have been in revolt against me to this very day. 4The people to whom I am sending you are obstinate and stubborn. Say to them, 'This is what the Sovereign LORD says.' 5And whether they listen or fail to listen—for they are a rebellious house—they will know that a prophet has been among them. 6And you, son of man, do not be afraid of them or their words. Do not be afraid, though

*d*17 Or *aside*   *e*24 Hebrew *Shaddai*   *f*26 Or *lapis lazuli* briers and thorns are all around you and you live among scorpions. Do not be afraid of what they say or terrified by them, though they are a rebellious house. ⁷You must speak my words to them, whether they listen or fail to listen, for they are rebellious. ⁸But you, son of man, listen to what I say to you. Do not rebel like that rebellious house; open your mouth and eat what I give you."

⁹Then I looked, and I saw a hand stretched out to me. In it was a scroll, ¹⁰which he unrolled before me. On both sides of it were written words of lament and mourning and woe.

CHAPTER 3

And he said to me, "Son of man, eat what is before you, eat this scroll; then go and speak to the house of Israel." ²So I opened my mouth, and he gave me the scroll to eat.

³Then he said to me, "Son of man, eat this scroll I am giving you and fill your stomach with it." So I ate it, and it tasted as sweet as honey in my mouth.

⁴He then said to me: "Son of man, go now to the house of Israel and speak my words to them. ⁵You are not being sent to a people of obscure speech and difficult language, but to the house of Israel— ⁶not to many peoples of obscure speech and difficult language, whose words you cannot understand. Surely if I had sent you to them, they would have listened to you. ⁷But the house of Israel is not willing to listen to you because they are not willing to listen to me, for the whole house of Israel is hardened and obstinate. ⁸But I will make you as unyielding and hardened as they are. ⁹I will make your forehead like the hardest stone, harder than flint. Do not be afraid of them or terrified by them, though they are a rebellious house."

¹⁰And he said to me, "Son of man, listen carefully and take to heart all the words I speak to you. ¹¹Go now to your countrymen in exile and speak to them. Say to them, 'This is what the Sovereign LORD says,' whether they listen or fail to listen."

¹²Then the Spirit lifted me up, and I heard behind me a loud rumbling sound—May the glory of the LORD be praised in his dwelling place!— ¹³the

sound of the wings of the living creatures brushing against each other and the sound of the wheels beside them, a loud rumbling sound. ¹⁴The Spirit then lifted me up and took me away, and I went in bitterness and in the anger of my spirit, with the strong hand of the LORD upon me. ¹⁵I came to the exiles who lived at Tel Abib near the Kebar River. And there, where they were living, I sat among them for seven days—overwhelmed.

¹⁶At the end of seven days the word of the LORD came to me: ¹⁷"Son of man, I have made you a watchman for the house of Israel; so hear the word I speak and give them warning from me. ¹⁸When I say to a wicked man, 'You will surely die,' and you do not warn him or speak out to dissuade him from his evil ways in order to save his life, that wicked man will die for*g* his sin, and I will hold you accountable for his blood. ¹⁹But if you do warn the wicked man and he does not turn from his wickedness or from his evil ways, he will die for his sin; but you will have saved yourself.

²⁰"Again, when a righteous man turns from his righteousness and does evil, and I put a stumbling block before him, he will die. Since you did not warn him, he will die for his sin. The righteous things he did will not be remembered, and I will hold you accountable for his blood. ²¹But if you do warn the righteous man not to sin and he does not sin, he will surely live because he took warning, and you will have saved yourself."

²²The hand of the LORD was upon me there, and he said to me, "Get up and go out to the plain, and there I will speak to you." ²³So I got up and went out to the plain. And the glory of the LORD was standing there, like the glory I had seen by the Kebar River, and I fell facedown.

²⁴Then the Spirit came into me and raised me to my feet. He spoke to me and said: "Go, shut yourself inside your house. ²⁵And you, son of man, they will tie with ropes; you will be bound so that you cannot go out among the people. ²⁶I will make your tongue stick to the roof of your mouth so that you will be silent and unable to rebuke them, though they are a rebellious house. ²⁷But when I speak to you, I will open your mouth and you shall

g 18 Or *in*; also in verses 19 and 20

say to them, 'This is what the Sovereign LORD says.' Whoever will listen let him listen, and whoever will refuse let him refuse; for they are a rebellious house.

CHAPTER 4

"Now, son of man, take a clay tablet, put it in front of you and draw the city of Jerusalem on it. ²Then lay siege to it: Erect siege works against it, build a ramp up to it, set up camps against it and put battering rams around it. ³Then take an iron pan, place it as an iron wall between you and the city and turn your face toward it. It will be under siege, and you shall besiege it. This will be a sign to the house of Israel.

⁴"Then lie on your left side and put the sin of the house of Israel upon yourself.ʰ You are to bear their sin for the number of days you lie on your side. ⁵I have assigned you the same number of days as the years of their sin. So for 390 days you will bear the sin of the house of Israel.

⁶"After you have finished this, lie down again, this time on your right side, and bear the sin of the house of Judah. I have assigned you 40 days, a day for each year. ⁷Turn your face toward the siege of Jerusalem and with bared arm prophesy against her. ⁸I will tie you up with ropes so that you cannot turn from one side to the other until you have finished the days of your siege.

⁹"Take wheat and barley, beans and lentils, millet and spelt; put them in a storage jar and use them to make bread for yourself. You are to eat it during the 390 days you lie on your side. ¹⁰Weigh out twenty shekelsⁱ of food to eat each day and eat it at set times. ¹¹Also measure out a sixth of a hinʲ of water and drink it at set times. ¹²Eat the food as you would a barley cake; bake it in the sight of the people, using human excrement for fuel."
¹³The LORD said, "In this way the people of Israel will eat defiled food among the nations where I will drive them."

¹⁴Then I said, "Not so, Sovereign LORD! I have never defiled myself. From my youth until now I have never eaten anything found dead or torn by wild animals. No unclean meat has ever entered my mouth."

¹⁵"Very well," he said, "I will let you bake your bread over cow manure instead of human excrement."

¹⁶He then said to me: "Son of man, I will cut off the supply of food in Jerusalem. The people will eat rationed food in anxiety and drink rationed water in despair, ¹⁷for food and water will be scarce. They will be appalled at the sight of each other and will waste away because ofᵏ their sin.

CHAPTER 5

"Now, son of man, take a sharp sword and use it as a barber's razor to shave your head and your beard. Then take a set of scales and divide up the hair. ²When the days of your siege come to an end, burn a third of the hair with fire inside the city. Take a third and strike it with the sword all around the city. And scatter a third to the wind. For I will pursue them with drawn sword. ³But take a few strands of hair and tuck them away in the folds of your garment. ⁴Again, take a few of these and throw them into the fire and burn them up. A fire will spread from there to the whole house of Israel.

⁵"This is what the Sovereign LORD says: This is Jerusalem, which I have set in the center of the nations, with countries all around her. ⁶Yet in her wickedness she has rebelled against my laws and decrees more than the nations and countries around her. She has rejected my laws and has not followed my decrees.

⁷"Therefore this is what the Sovereign LORD says: You have been more unruly than the nations around you and have not followed my decrees or kept my laws. You have not evenˡ conformed to the standards of the nations around you.

⁸"Therefore this is what the Sovereign LORD says: I myself am against you, Jerusalem, and I will inflict punishment on you in the sight of the nations. ⁹Because of all your detestable idols, I will do to you what I have never done before and will never do again. ¹⁰Therefore in your midst fathers will eat their children, and children will eat their fathers. I will inflict punishment on you and will scatter all your survivors to the winds. ¹¹Therefore as surely as I live, declares the Sovereign

ʰ4 Or *your side*   ⁱ10 That is, about 8 ounces (about 0.2 kilogram)   ʲ11 That is, about 2/3 quart (about 0.6 liter)
ᵏ17 Or *away in*   ˡ7 Most Hebrew manuscripts; some Hebrew manuscripts and Syriac *You have*

LORD, because you have defiled my sanctuary with all your vile images and detestable practices, I myself will withdraw my favor; I will not look on you with pity or spare you. [12]A third of your people will die of the plague or perish by famine inside you; a third will fall by the sword outside your walls; and a third I will scatter to the winds and pursue with drawn sword.

[13]"Then my anger will cease and my wrath against them will subside, and I will be avenged. And when I have spent my wrath upon them, they will know that I the LORD have spoken in my zeal.

[14]"I will make you a ruin and a reproach among the nations around you, in the sight of all who pass by. [15]You will be a reproach and a taunt, a warning and an object of horror to the nations around you when I inflict punishment on you in anger and in wrath and with stinging rebuke. I the LORD have spoken. [16]When I shoot at you with my deadly and destructive arrows of famine, I will shoot to destroy you. I will bring more and more famine upon you and cut off your supply of food. [17]I will send famine and wild beasts against you, and they will leave you childless. Plague and bloodshed will sweep through you, and I will bring the sword against you. I the LORD have spoken."

CHAPTER 6

The word of the LORD came to me: [2]"Son of man, set your face against the mountains of Israel; prophesy against them [3]and say: 'O mountains of Israel, hear the word of the Sovereign LORD. This is what the Sovereign LORD says to the mountains and hills, to the ravines and valleys: I am about to bring a sword against you, and I will destroy your high places. [4]Your altars will be demolished and your incense altars will be smashed; and I will slay your people in front of your idols. [5]I will lay

the dead bodies of the Israelites in front of their idols, and I will scatter your bones around your altars. [6]Wherever you live, the towns will be laid waste and the high places demolished, so that your altars will be laid waste and devastated, your idols smashed and ruined, your incense altars broken down, and what you have made wiped out. [7]Your people will fall slain among you, and you will know that I am the LORD.

[8]" 'But I will spare some, for some of you will escape the sword when you are scattered among the lands and nations. [9]Then in the nations where they have been carried captive, those who escape will remember me—how I have been grieved by their adulterous hearts, which have turned away from me, and by their eyes, which have lusted after their idols. They will loathe themselves for the evil they have done and for all their detestable practices. [10]And they will know that I am the LORD; I did not threaten in vain to bring this calamity on them.

[11]" 'This is what the Sovereign LORD says: Strike your hands together and stamp your feet and cry out "Alas!" because of all the wicked and detestable practices of the house of Israel, for they will fall by the sword, famine and plague. [12]He that is far away will die of the plague, and he that is near will fall by the sword, and he that survives and is spared will die of famine. So will I spend my wrath upon them. [13]And they will know that I am the LORD, when their people lie slain among their idols around their altars, on every high hill and on all the mountaintops, under every spreading tree and every leafy oak—places where they offered fragrant incense to all their idols. [14]And I will stretch out my hand against them and make the land a desolate waste from the desert to Diblah[m]— wherever they live. Then they will know that I am the LORD.' "

[m14] Most Hebrew manuscripts; a few Hebrew manuscripts *Riblah*

AUGUST 16 □ DAY 229

EZEKIEL 7–11
Sins and Sorrows

OVERVIEW For wayward Judah, the end has come. Past sins now give way to crushing horrors as the city of Jerusalem falls in the midst of confusion and brutality. The temple, God's abode among his people, no longer houses the glory of the Lord. Judah's leaders—blind leading the blind—watch helplessly as their beloved Jerusalem turns into a seething cauldron of death. Even the prophet Ezekiel wonders how any can survive such an onslaught. But the Word of the Lord returns in warming comfort: "I will gather you from the nations . . . and I will give you back the land of Israel again" (11:17).

Chapters 7–8	Chapter 9	Chapter 10	Chapter 11
Doom for Jerusalem	Death for the Guilty	Departure of God's Glory	Downfall of God's Leaders
Condemnation of Idolatry		Consequences of Idolatry	

YOUR DAILY WALK What is the longest distance you have ever walked or jogged without stopping? (If your answer is, "The distance from the couch to the refrigerator," read 1 Corinthians 9:27 . . . fast!)

To get through the hardest journey, take only one step at a time, but in God's strength keep on stepping.

There is a vast difference between training for a *sprint* (like the hundred-yard dash) and training for a *marathon* (which covers more than twenty-six miles). It means very little to a marathon runner if he covers the first hundred yards in ten seconds. A burst of speed is good, but in the long run it is the ability to stick with it mile after mile that counts. *Steadfastness,* not simply short-term *fastness,* determines the winner.

God told the prophet Ezekiel in advance that he was running a marathon (3:4, 7–9), not a sprint. His audience would be calloused, hard of hearing and indifferent to his message. Ezekiel would need strength for the long run.

What about you today? Your race is described in Hebrews 12:1–2. Put on your sneakers for a few minutes' walk as you ponder the marathon God has set before you and the resources he has provided in his Son—strength for each step of the way!

INSIGHT A Strong Name for a Demanding Assignment
Ezekiel's name literally means "God strengthens" or "strengthened by God." And his name becomes the testimony of his life (3:8–9), for who but God could strengthen a man to deliver the crushing message of chapters 7–11 week after week . . . for more than twenty years!

CHAPTER 7

The word of the Lord came to me: 2"Son of man, this is what the Sovereign Lord says to the land of Israel: The end! The end has come upon the four corners of the land. 3The end is now upon you and I will unleash my anger against you. I will judge you according to your conduct and repay you for all your detestable practices. 4I will not look on you with pity or spare

you; I will surely repay you for your conduct and the detestable practices among you. Then you will know that I am the Lord.

5"This is what the Sovereign Lord says: Disaster! An unheard-of[n] disaster is coming. 6The end has come! The end has come! It has roused itself against you. It has come! 7Doom has come upon you— you who dwell in the land. The time has

---

[n]5 Most Hebrew manuscripts; some Hebrew manuscripts and Syriac *Disaster after*

come, the day is near; there is panic, not joy, upon the mountains. [8]I am about to pour out my wrath on you and spend my anger against you; I will judge you according to your conduct and repay you for all your detestable practices. [9]I will not look on you with pity or spare you; I will repay you in accordance with your conduct and the detestable practices among you. Then you will know that it is I the LORD who strikes the blow.

[10]"The day is here! It has come! Doom has burst forth, the rod has budded, arrogance has blossomed! [11]Violence has grown into[o] a rod to punish wickedness; none of the people will be left, none of that crowd—no wealth, nothing of value. [12]The time has come, the day has arrived. Let not the buyer rejoice nor the seller grieve, for wrath is upon the whole crowd. [13]The seller will not recover the land he has sold as long as both of them live, for the vision concerning the whole crowd will not be reversed. Because of their sins, not one of them will preserve his life. [14]Though they blow the trumpet and get everything ready, no one will go into battle, for my wrath is upon the whole crowd.

[15]"Outside is the sword, inside are plague and famine; those in the country will die by the sword, and those in the city will be devoured by famine and plague. [16]All who survive and escape will be in the mountains, moaning like doves of the valleys, each because of his sins. [17]Every hand will go limp, and every knee will become as weak as water. [18]They will put on sackcloth and be clothed with terror. Their faces will be covered with shame and their heads will be shaved. [19]They will throw their silver into the streets, and their gold will be an unclean thing. Their silver and gold will not be able to save them in the day of the LORD's wrath. They will not satisfy their hunger or fill their stomachs with it, for it has made them stumble into sin. [20]They were proud of their beautiful jewelry and used it to make their detestable idols and vile images. Therefore I will turn these into an unclean thing for them. [21]I will hand it all over as plunder to foreigners and as loot to the wicked of the earth, and they will defile it. [22]I will turn my face

away from them, and they will desecrate my treasured place; robbers will enter it and desecrate it.

[23]"Prepare chains, because the land is full of bloodshed and the city is full of violence. [24]I will bring the most wicked of the nations to take possession of their houses; I will put an end to the pride of the mighty, and their sanctuaries will be desecrated. [25]When terror comes, they will seek peace, but there will be none. [26]Calamity upon calamity will come, and rumor upon rumor. They will try to get a vision from the prophet; the teaching of the law by the priest will be lost, as will the counsel of the elders. [27]The king will mourn, the prince will be clothed with despair, and the hands of the people of the land will tremble. I will deal with them according to their conduct, and by their own standards I will judge them. Then they will know that I am the LORD."

CHAPTER 8

In the sixth year, in the sixth month on the fifth day, while I was sitting in my house and the elders of Judah were sitting before me, the hand of the Sovereign LORD came upon me there. [2]I looked, and I saw a figure like that of a man.[p] From what appeared to be his waist down he was like fire, and from there up his appearance was as bright as glowing metal. [3]He stretched out what looked like a hand and took me by the hair of my head. The Spirit lifted me up between earth and heaven and in visions of God he took me to Jerusalem, to the entrance to the north gate of the inner court, where the idol that provokes to jealousy stood. [4]And there before me was the glory of the God of Israel, as in the vision I had seen in the plain.

[5]Then he said to me, "Son of man, look toward the north." So I looked, and in the entrance north of the gate of the altar I saw this idol of jealousy.

[6]And he said to me, "Son of man, do you see what they are doing—the utterly detestable things the house of Israel is doing here, things that will drive me far from my sanctuary? But you will see things that are even more detestable."

[7]Then he brought me to the entrance to the court. I looked, and I saw a hole in the wall. [8]He said to me, "Son of man, now

o 11 Or The violent one has become   p 2 Or saw a fiery figure dig into the wall." So I dug into the wall and saw a doorway there.

⁹And he said to me, "Go in and see the wicked and detestable things they are doing here." ¹⁰So I went in and looked, and I saw portrayed all over the walls all kinds of crawling things and detestable animals and all the idols of the house of Israel. ¹¹In front of them stood seventy elders of the house of Israel, and Jaazaniah son of Shaphan was standing among them. Each had a censer in his hand, and a fragrant cloud of incense was rising.

¹²He said to me, "Son of man, have you seen what the elders of the house of Israel are doing in the darkness, each at the shrine of his own idol? They say, 'The LORD does not see us; the LORD has forsaken the land.'" ¹³Again, he said, "You will see them doing things that are even more detestable."

¹⁴Then he brought me to the entrance to the north gate of the house of the LORD, and I saw women sitting there, mourning for Tammuz. ¹⁵He said to me, "Do you see this, son of man? You will see things that are even more detestable than this."

¹⁶He then brought me into the inner court of the house of the LORD, and there at the entrance to the temple, between the portico and the altar, were about twenty-five men. With their backs toward the temple of the LORD and their faces toward the east, they were bowing down to the sun in the east.

¹⁷He said to me, "Have you seen this, son of man? Is it a trivial matter for the house of Judah to do the detestable things they are doing here? Must they also fill the land with violence and continually provoke me to anger? Look at them putting the branch to their nose! ¹⁸Therefore I will deal with them in anger; I will not look on them with pity or spare them. Although they shout in my ears, I will not listen to them."

CHAPTER 9

Then I heard him call out in a loud voice, "Bring the guards of the city here, each with a weapon in his hand." ²And I saw six men coming from the direction of the upper gate, which faces north, each with a deadly weapon in his hand. With them was a man clothed in linen who had a writing kit at his side. They came in and stood beside the bronze altar.

³Now the glory of the God of Israel went up from above the cherubim, where it had been, and moved to the threshold of the temple. Then the LORD called to the man clothed in linen who had the writing kit at his side ⁴and said to him, "Go throughout the city of Jerusalem and put a mark on the foreheads of those who grieve and lament over all the detestable things that are done in it."

⁵As I listened, he said to the others, "Follow him through the city and kill, without showing pity or compassion. ⁶Slaughter old men, young men and maidens, women and children, but do not touch anyone who has the mark. Begin at my sanctuary." So they began with the elders who were in front of the temple.

⁷Then he said to them, "Defile the temple and fill the courts with the slain. Go!" So they went out and began killing throughout the city. ⁸While they were killing and I was left alone, I fell facedown, crying out, "Ah, Sovereign LORD! Are you going to destroy the entire remnant of Israel in this outpouring of your wrath on Jerusalem?"

⁹He answered me, "The sin of the house of Israel and Judah is exceedingly great; the land is full of bloodshed and the city is full of injustice. They say, 'The LORD has forsaken the land; the LORD does not see.' ¹⁰So I will not look on them with pity or spare them, but I will bring down on their own heads what they have done."

¹¹Then the man in linen with the writing kit at his side brought back word, saying, "I have done as you commanded."

CHAPTER 10

I looked, and I saw the likeness of a throne of sapphire�q above the expanse that was over the heads of the cherubim. ²The LORD said to the man clothed in linen, "Go in among the wheels beneath the cherubim. Fill your hands with burning coals from among the cherubim and scatter them over the city." And as I watched, he went in.

³Now the cherubim were standing on the south side of the temple when the man went in, and a cloud filled the inner court. ⁴Then the glory of the LORD rose

q1 Or lapis lazuli

from above the cherubim and moved to the threshold of the temple. The cloud filled the temple, and the court was full of the radiance of the glory of the LORD. ⁵The sound of the wings of the cherubim could be heard as far away as the outer court, like the voice of God Almighty*ʳ* when he speaks.

⁶When the LORD commanded the man in linen, "Take fire from among the wheels, from among the cherubim," the man went in and stood beside a wheel. ⁷Then one of the cherubim reached out his hand to the fire that was among them. He took up some of it and put it into the hands of the man in linen, who took it and went out. ⁸(Under the wings of the cherubim could be seen what looked like the hands of a man.)

⁹I looked, and I saw beside the cherubim four wheels, one beside each of the cherubim; the wheels sparkled like chrysolite. ¹⁰As for their appearance, the four of them looked alike; each was like a wheel intersecting a wheel. ¹¹As they moved, they would go in any one of the four directions the cherubim faced; the wheels did not turn about*ˢ* as the cherubim went. The cherubim went in whatever direction the head faced, without turning as they went. ¹²Their entire bodies, including their backs, their hands and their wings, were completely full of eyes, as were their four wheels. ¹³I heard the wheels being called "the whirling wheels." ¹⁴Each of the cherubim had four faces: One face was that of a cherub, the second the face of a man, the third the face of a lion, and the fourth the face of an eagle.

¹⁵Then the cherubim rose upward. These were the living creatures I had seen by the Kebar River. ¹⁶When the cherubim moved, the wheels beside them moved; and when the cherubim spread their wings to rise from the ground, the wheels did not leave their side. ¹⁷When the cherubim stood still, they also stood still; and when the cherubim rose, they rose with them, because the spirit of the living creatures was in them.

¹⁸Then the glory of the LORD departed from over the threshold of the temple and stopped above the cherubim. ¹⁹While I watched, the cherubim spread their wings and rose from the ground, and as they went, the wheels went with them. They stopped at the entrance to the east gate of the LORD's house, and the glory of the God of Israel was above them.

²⁰These were the living creatures I had seen beneath the God of Israel by the Kebar River, and I realized that they were cherubim. ²¹Each had four faces and four wings, and under their wings was what looked like the hands of a man. ²²Their faces had the same appearance as those I had seen by the Kebar River. Each one went straight ahead.

CHAPTER 11

Then the Spirit lifted me up and brought me to the gate of the house of the LORD that faces east. There at the entrance to the gate were twenty-five men, and I saw among them Jaazaniah son of Azzur and Pelatiah son of Benaiah, leaders of the people. ²The LORD said to me, "Son of man, these are the men who are plotting evil and giving wicked advice in this city. ³They say, 'Will it not soon be time to build houses?*ᵗ* This city is a cooking pot, and we are the meat.' ⁴Therefore prophesy against them; prophesy, son of man."

⁵Then the Spirit of the LORD came upon me, and he told me to say: "This is what the LORD says: That is what you are saying, O house of Israel, but I know what is going through your mind. ⁶You have killed many people in this city and filled its streets with the dead.

⁷"Therefore this is what the Sovereign LORD says: The bodies you have thrown there are the meat and this city is the pot, but I will drive you out of it. ⁸You fear the sword, and the sword is what I will bring against you, declares the Sovereign LORD. ⁹I will drive you out of the city and hand you over to foreigners and inflict punishment on you. ¹⁰You will fall by the sword, and I will execute judgment on you at the borders of Israel. Then you will know that I am the LORD. ¹¹This city will not be a pot for you, nor will you be the meat in it; I will execute judgment on you at the borders of Israel. ¹²And you will know that I am the LORD, for you have not followed my decrees or kept my laws but have conformed to the standards of the nations around you."

*ʳ*5 Hebrew *El-Shaddai*   *ˢ*11 Or *aside*   *ᵗ*3 Or *This is not the time to build houses.*

¹³Now as I was prophesying, Pelatiah son of Benaiah died. Then I fell facedown and cried out in a loud voice, "Ah, Sovereign LORD! Will you completely destroy the remnant of Israel?"

¹⁴The word of the LORD came to me: ¹⁵"Son of man, your brothers—your brothers who are your blood relatives ᵘ and the whole house of Israel—are those of whom the people of Jerusalem have said, 'They are ᵛ far away from the LORD; this land was given to us as our possession.'

¹⁶"Therefore say: 'This is what the Sovereign LORD says: Although I sent them far away among the nations and scattered them among the countries, yet for a little while I have been a sanctuary for them in the countries where they have gone.'

¹⁷"Therefore say: 'This is what the Sovereign LORD says: I will gather you from the nations and bring you back from the countries where you have been scattered, and I will give you back the land of Israel again.'

¹⁸"They will return to it and remove all its vile images and detestable idols. ¹⁹I will give them an undivided heart and put a new spirit in them; I will remove from them their heart of stone and give them a heart of flesh. ²⁰Then they will follow my decrees and be careful to keep my laws. They will be my people, and I will be their God. ²¹But as for those whose hearts are devoted to their vile images and detestable idols, I will bring down on their own heads what they have done, declares the Sovereign LORD."

²²Then the cherubim, with the wheels beside them, spread their wings, and the glory of the God of Israel was above them. ²³The glory of the LORD went up from within the city and stopped above the mountain east of it. ²⁴The Spirit lifted me up and brought me to the exiles in Babylonia ʷ in the vision given by the Spirit of God.

Then the vision I had seen went up from me, ²⁵and I told the exiles everything the LORD had shown me.

ᵘ15 Or *are in exile with you* (see Septuagint and Syriac)   ᵛ15 Or *those to whom the people of Jerusalem have said, 'Stay*
ʷ24 Or *Chaldea*

AUGUST 17 □ DAY 230
EZEKIEL 12–15
Signs and Sermons

OVERVIEW Jeremiah used object lessons extensively in his prophetic ministry. Ezekiel uses dramatic portrayals—divine charades designed to arouse the curiosity of the people and rivet their attention on the events soon to transpire in Jerusalem. Packing up his household belongings, Ezekiel heads for the city wall, where he digs a hole and climbs through—a picture of the soon-coming deportation of the people and the loss of all they called home.

Chapter 12	Chapter 13	Chapter 14	Chapter 15
Symbols of Exile	Sins Leading to Exile Involving		
	Prophets	Priests	People
Destruction	Disobedience		

YOUR DAILY WALK Look around your house and see if you can find at least five things that are virtually useless: burned-out light bulbs, broken shoestrings, pens with no ink, husbands watching baseball games, etc.

In chapter 15 Ezekiel likens Jerusalem to a useless vine. Vines are excellent for growing fruit, but when you stop and think about it, they are good for little else. You can't make furniture out of them, build a

People's character and their gardens both reflect the amount of weeding that was done during the growing season. good fire with them, or turn them into anything particularly useful. In fact, a vine that is fruitless is practically worthless.

The inhabitants of Jerusalem were worthless to God because of their wickedness and idolatry. Planted in the land to be a testimony to his name, they failed to produce the fruit God expected from them. There was nothing left to do but remove them—a painful but necessary way for God to get across the message, "I am the LORD."

Check up on your UQ (Usefulness Quotient) today. Does God have free rein to produce the fruit of the Spirit in your life (Galatians 5:22–23)? Press a leaf between the pages of your Bible as a reminder that fruitbearing is not just a good idea. It is one of the reasons God has placed you on this planet (John 15:1–6)!

 INSIGHT Famous Names in Unfamiliar Places
In Jeremiah you learned that even if _____ and _____ had prayed on Judah's behalf, God would not have listened (Jeremiah 15:1). Now in Ezekiel you will learn that even if _____, _____ and _____ had lived in Jerusalem, their presence would not have saved the city (Ezekiel 14:14, 18, 20).

CHAPTER 12

The word of the LORD came to me: ²"Son of man, you are living among a rebellious people. They have eyes to see but do not see and ears to hear but do not hear, for they are a rebellious people.

³"Therefore, son of man, pack your belongings for exile and in the daytime, as they watch, set out and go from where you are to another place. Perhaps they will understand, though they are a rebellious house. ⁴During the daytime, while they watch, bring out your belongings packed for exile. Then in the evening, while they are watching, go out like those who go into exile. ⁵While they watch, dig through the wall and take your belongings out through it. ⁶Put them on your shoulder as they are watching and carry them out at dusk. Cover your face so that you cannot see the land, for I have made you a sign to the house of Israel."

⁷So I did as I was commanded. During the day I brought out my things packed for exile. Then in the evening I dug through the wall with my hands. I took my belongings out at dusk, carrying them on my shoulders while they watched.

⁸In the morning the word of the LORD came to me: ⁹"Son of man, did not that rebellious house of Israel ask you, 'What are you doing?'

¹⁰"Say to them, 'This is what the Sovereign LORD says: This oracle concerns the prince in Jerusalem and the whole house of Israel who are there.' ¹¹Say to them, 'I am a sign to you.'

"As I have done, so it will be done to them. They will go into exile as captives.

¹²"The prince among them will put his things on his shoulder at dusk and leave, and a hole will be dug in the wall for him to go through. He will cover his face so that he cannot see the land. ¹³I will spread my net for him, and he will be caught in my snare; I will bring him to Babylonia, the land of the Chaldeans, but he will not see it, and there he will die. ¹⁴I will scatter to the winds all those around him—his staff and all his troops—and I will pursue them with drawn sword.

¹⁵"They will know that I am the LORD, when I disperse them among the nations and scatter them through the countries. ¹⁶But I will spare a few of them from the sword, famine and plague, so that in the nations where they go they may acknowledge all their detestable practices. Then they will know that I am the LORD."

¹⁷The word of the LORD came to me: ¹⁸"Son of man, tremble as you eat your food, and shudder in fear as you drink your water. ¹⁹Say to the people of the land: 'This is what the Sovereign LORD says about those living in Jerusalem and in the land of Israel: They will eat their food in anxiety and drink their water in despair, for their land will be stripped of everything in it because of the violence of all who live there. ²⁰The inhabited towns will be laid waste and the land will be desolate. Then you will know that I am the LORD.' "

²¹The word of the LORD came to me: ²²"Son of man, what is this proverb you have in the land of Israel: 'The days go by and every vision comes to nothing'? ²³Say to them, 'This is what the Sovereign LORD says: I am going to put an end to this proverb, and they will no longer quote it in Israel.' Say to them, 'The days are near when every vision will be fulfilled. ²⁴For there will be no more false visions or flattering divinations among the people of Israel. ²⁵But I the LORD will speak what I will, and it shall be fulfilled without delay. For in your days, you rebellious house, I will fulfill whatever I say, declares the Sovereign LORD.' "

²⁶The word of the LORD came to me: ²⁷"Son of man, the house of Israel is saying, 'The vision he sees is for many years from now, and he prophesies about the distant future.'

²⁸"Therefore say to them, 'This is what the Sovereign LORD says: None of my words will be delayed any longer; whatever I say will be fulfilled, declares the Sovereign LORD.' "

CHAPTER 13

The word of the LORD came to me: ²"Son of man, prophesy against the prophets of Israel who are now prophesying. Say to those who prophesy out of their own imagination: 'Hear the word of the LORD! ³This is what the Sovereign LORD says: Woe to the foolishˣ prophets who follow their own spirit and have seen nothing! ⁴Your prophets, O Israel, are like jackals among ruins. ⁵You have not gone up to the breaks in the wall to repair it for the house of Israel so that it will stand firm in the battle on the day of the LORD. ⁶Their visions are false and their divinations a lie. They say, "The LORD declares," when the LORD has not sent them; yet they expect their words to be fulfilled. ⁷Have you not seen false visions and uttered lying divinations when you say, "The LORD declares," though I have not spoken?

⁸" 'Therefore this is what the Sovereign LORD says: Because of your false words and lying visions, I am against you, declares the Sovereign LORD. ⁹My hand will be against the prophets who see false visions and utter lying divinations. They

will not belong to the council of my people or be listed in the records of the house of Israel, nor will they enter the land of Israel. Then you will know that I am the Sovereign LORD.

¹⁰" 'Because they lead my people astray, saying, "Peace," when there is no peace, and because, when a flimsy wall is built, they cover it with whitewash, ¹¹therefore tell those who cover it with whitewash that it is going to fall. Rain will come in torrents, and I will send hailstones hurtling down, and violent winds will burst forth. ¹²When the wall collapses, will people not ask you, "Where is the whitewash you covered it with?"

¹³" 'Therefore this is what the Sovereign LORD says: In my wrath I will unleash a violent wind, and in my anger hailstones and torrents of rain will fall with destructive fury. ¹⁴I will tear down the wall you have covered with whitewash and will level it to the ground so that its foundation will be laid bare. When itʸ falls, you will be destroyed in it; and you will know that I am the LORD. ¹⁵So I will spend my wrath against the wall and against those who covered it with whitewash. I will say to you, "The wall is gone and so are those who whitewashed it, ¹⁶those prophets of Israel who prophesied to Jerusalem and saw visions of peace for her when there was no peace, declares the Sovereign LORD." '

¹⁷"Now, son of man, set your face against the daughters of your people who prophesy out of their own imagination. Prophesy against them ¹⁸and say, 'This is what the Sovereign LORD says: Woe to the women who sew magic charms on all their wrists and make veils of various lengths for their heads in order to ensnare people. Will you ensnare the lives of my people but preserve your own? ¹⁹You have profaned me among my people for a few handfuls of barley and scraps of bread. By lying to my people, who listen to lies, you have killed those who should not have died and have spared those who should not live.

²⁰" 'Therefore this is what the Sovereign LORD says: I am against your magic charms with which you ensnare people like birds and I will tear them from your arms; I will set free the people that you

ensnare like birds. ²¹I will tear off your veils and save my people from your hands, and they will no longer fall prey to your power. Then you will know that I am the LORD. ²²Because you disheartened the righteous with your lies, when I had brought them no grief, and because you encouraged the wicked not to turn from their evil ways and so save their lives, ²³therefore you will no longer see false visions or practice divination. I will save my people from your hands. And then you will know that I am the LORD.' "

CHAPTER 14

Some of the elders of Israel came to me and sat down in front of me. ²Then the word of the LORD came to me: ³"Son of man, these men have set up idols in their hearts and put wicked stumbling blocks before their faces. Should I let them inquire of me at all? ⁴Therefore speak to them and tell them, 'This is what the Sovereign LORD says: When any Israelite sets up idols in his heart and puts a wicked stumbling block before his face and then goes to a prophet, I the LORD will answer him myself in keeping with his great idolatry. ⁵I will do this to recapture the hearts of the people of Israel, who have all deserted me for their idols.'

⁶"Therefore say to the house of Israel, 'This is what the Sovereign LORD says: Repent! Turn from your idols and renounce all your detestable practices!

⁷" 'When any Israelite or any alien living in Israel separates himself from me and sets up idols in his heart and puts a wicked stumbling block before his face and then goes to a prophet to inquire of me, I the LORD will answer him myself. ⁸I will set my face against that man and make him an example and a byword. I will cut him off from my people. Then you will know that I am the LORD.

⁹" 'And if the prophet is enticed to utter a prophecy, I the LORD have enticed that prophet, and I will stretch out my hand against him and destroy him from among my people Israel. ¹⁰They will bear their guilt—the prophet will be as guilty as the one who consults him. ¹¹Then the people of Israel will no longer stray from me, nor will they defile themselves anymore with

all their sins. They will be my people, and I will be their God, declares the Sovereign LORD.' "

¹²The word of the LORD came to me: ¹³"Son of man, if a country sins against me by being unfaithful and I stretch out my hand against it to cut off its food supply and send famine upon it and kill its men and their animals, ¹⁴even if these three men—Noah, Daniel ᶻ and Job—were in it, they could save only themselves by their righteousness, declares the Sovereign LORD.

¹⁵"Or if I send wild beasts through that country and they leave it childless and it becomes desolate so that no one can pass through it because of the beasts, ¹⁶as surely as I live, declares the Sovereign LORD, even if these three men were in it, they could not save their own sons or daughters. They alone would be saved, but the land would be desolate.

¹⁷"Or if I bring a sword against that country and say, 'Let the sword pass throughout the land,' and I kill its men and their animals, ¹⁸as surely as I live, declares the Sovereign LORD, even if these three men were in it, they could not save their own sons or daughters. They alone would be saved.

¹⁹"Or if I send a plague into that land and pour out my wrath upon it through bloodshed, killing its men and their animals, ²⁰as surely as I live, declares the Sovereign LORD, even if Noah, Daniel and Job were in it, they could save neither son nor daughter. They would save only themselves by their righteousness.

²¹"For this is what the Sovereign LORD says: How much worse will it be when I send against Jerusalem my four dreadful judgments—sword and famine and wild beasts and plague—to kill its men and their animals! ²²Yet there will be some survivors—sons and daughters who will be brought out of it. They will come to you, and when you see their conduct and their actions, you will be consoled regarding the disaster I have brought upon Jerusalem—every disaster I have brought upon it. ²³You will be consoled when you see their conduct and their actions, for you will know that I have done nothing in it without cause, declares the Sovereign LORD."

ᶻ14 Or *Danel*; the Hebrew spelling may suggest a person other than the prophet Daniel; also in verse 20.

C H A P T E R   15

The word of the LORD came to me: 2"Son of man, how is the wood of a vine better than that of a branch on any of the trees in the forest? 3Is wood ever taken from it to make anything useful? Do they make pegs from it to hang things on? 4And after it is thrown on the fire as fuel and the fire burns both ends and chars the middle, is it then useful for anything? 5If it was not useful for anything when it was whole, how much less can it be made into something useful when the fire has burned it and it is charred?

6"Therefore this is what the Sovereign LORD says: As I have given the wood of the vine among the trees of the forest as fuel for the fire, so will I treat the people living in Jerusalem. 7I will set my face against them. Although they have come out of the fire, the fire will yet consume them. And when I set my face against them, you will know that I am the LORD. 8I will make the land desolate because they have been unfaithful, declares the Sovereign LORD."

AUGUST 18 ☐ DAY 231
EZEKIEL 16–19
Parables of Judgment for Judah

 OVERVIEW Using a picturesque series of allegories and parables, Ezekiel continues his dual message of horror and hope. Like an unfaithful wife, God's people have gone after other gods. They have committed spiritual adultery and prostituted their privileged position. But God's love remains ever faithful for the objects of his delight. Using illustrations drawn from nature, the prophet portrays the reasons for God's coming discipline and gives the sobering reminder: "The soul who sins is the one who will die" (18:20).

Chapter 16	Chapter 17	Chapter 18	Chapter 19
Parable of the Adulterous Wife	Parable of the Eagles	Proverb of the Sour Grapes	Picture of the Lioness
Graphic Lessons			Grim Lament

 YOUR DAILY WALK Perhaps God's providence is nowhere more evident than in the fact that he gives parents twelve years to develop a love for their children before he turns them into teenagers!

The best way to keep teens at home is to make home pleasant—and let the air out of the tires.

Chapter 18 contains some sobering words for teens . . . and for God's children of all ages. It's a reminder of personal accountability—of the fact that we cannot and dare not attempt to pin the blame for today's problems on yesterday's generation.

Are you the product of godly parents? Then thank God, but don't think he will condone your willful rebellion (18:5–13). Are you the child of rebellious or backslidden parents? Don't think you can use that as an excuse for avoiding the clear and insistent commands of God's Word (18:20).

Make an appointment to take a parent or child out for a special meal this week. (Or call a family member who is out of town.) If there is a root of bitterness between you, confess it. If there has been indifference or a lack of accountability in your relationship, forsake it.

 INSIGHT The Madness of Israel's Unfaithfulness

You've heard the maxim: "Dog bites man, that's not news; man bites dog, that's news." A prostitute who is paid for her wickedness isn't newsworthy because she isn't unusual. On the other hand, a prostitute who pays those who come to her will definitely attract attention. In Ezekiel's day, Israel had become front-page material. She had committed such mad, willful idolatry that God likened her to a prostitute who paid her customers (16:33–34)!

CHAPTER 16

The word of the LORD came to me: ²"Son of man, confront Jerusalem with her detestable practices ³and say, 'This is what the Sovereign LORD says to Jerusalem: Your ancestry and birth were in the land of the Canaanites; your father was an Amorite and your mother a Hittite. ⁴On the day you were born your cord was not cut, nor were you washed with water to make you clean, nor were you rubbed with salt or wrapped in cloths. ⁵No one looked on you with pity or had compassion enough to do any of these things for you. Rather, you were thrown out into the open field, for on the day you were born you were despised.

⁶" 'Then I passed by and saw you kicking about in your blood, and as you lay there in your blood I said to you, "Live!"ᵃ ⁷I made you grow like a plant of the field. You grew up and developed and became the most beautiful of jewels.ᵇ Your breasts were formed and your hair grew, you who were naked and bare.

⁸" 'Later I passed by, and when I looked at you and saw that you were old enough for love, I spread the corner of my garment over you and covered your nakedness. I gave you my solemn oath and entered into a covenant with you, declares the Sovereign LORD, and you became mine.

⁹" 'I bathedᶜ you with water and washed the blood from you and put ointments on you. ¹⁰I clothed you with an embroidered dress and put leather sandals on you. I dressed you in fine linen and covered you with costly garments. ¹¹I adorned you with jewelry: I put bracelets on your arms and a necklace around your neck, ¹²and I put a ring on your nose, earrings on your ears and a beautiful crown on your head. ¹³So you were adorned with gold and silver; your clothes were of fine linen and costly fabric and embroidered cloth. Your food was fine flour, honey and olive oil. You became very

beautiful and rose to be a queen. ¹⁴And your fame spread among the nations on account of your beauty, because the splendor I had given you made your beauty perfect, declares the Sovereign LORD.

¹⁵" 'But you trusted in your beauty and used your fame to become a prostitute. You lavished your favors on anyone who passed by and your beauty became his.ᵈ ¹⁶You took some of your garments to make gaudy high places, where you carried on your prostitution. Such things should not happen, nor should they ever occur. ¹⁷You also took the fine jewelry I gave you, the jewelry made of my gold and silver, and you made for yourself male idols and engaged in prostitution with them. ¹⁸And you took your embroidered clothes to put on them, and you offered my oil and incense before them. ¹⁹Also the food I provided for you—the fine flour, olive oil and honey I gave you to eat—you offered as fragrant incense before them. That is what happened, declares the Sovereign LORD.

²⁰" 'And you took your sons and daughters whom you bore to me and sacrificed them as food to the idols. Was your prostitution not enough? ²¹You slaughtered my children and sacrificed themᵉ to the idols. ²²In all your detestable practices and your prostitution you did not remember the days of your youth, when you were naked and bare, kicking about in your blood.

²³" 'Woe! Woe to you, declares the Sovereign LORD. In addition to all your other wickedness, ²⁴you built a mound for yourself and made a lofty shrine in every public square. ²⁵At the head of every street you built your lofty shrines and degraded your beauty, offering your body with increasing promiscuity to anyone who passed by. ²⁶You engaged in prostitution with the Egyptians, your lustful neighbors, and provoked me to anger with your increasing promiscuity. ²⁷So I

ᵃ6 A few Hebrew manuscripts, Septuagint and Syriac; most Hebrew manuscripts *"Live!" And as you lay there in your blood I said to you, "Live!"* ᵇ7 Or *became mature* ᶜ9 Or *I had bathed* ᵈ15 Most Hebrew manuscripts; one Hebrew manuscript (see some Septuagint manuscripts) *by. Such a thing should not happen* ᵉ21 Or *and made them pass through the fire* stretched out my hand against you and reduced your territory; I gave you over to the greed of your enemies, the daughters of the Philistines, who were shocked by your lewd conduct. [28]You engaged in prostitution with the Assyrians too, because you were insatiable; and even after that, you still were not satisfied. [29]Then you increased your promiscuity to include Babylonia,[f] a land of merchants, but even with this you were not satisfied.

[30]" 'How weak-willed you are, declares the Sovereign LORD, when you do all these things, acting like a brazen prostitute! [31]When you built your mounds at the head of every street and made your lofty shrines in every public square, you were unlike a prostitute, because you scorned payment.

[32] 'You adulterous wife! You prefer strangers to your own husband! [33]Every prostitute receives a fee, but you give gifts to all your lovers, bribing them to come to you from everywhere for your illicit favors. [34]So in your prostitution you are the opposite of others; no one runs after you for your favors. You are the very opposite, for you give payment and none is given to you.

[35]" 'Therefore, you prostitute, hear the word of the LORD! [36]This is what the Sovereign LORD says: Because you poured out your wealth[g] and exposed your nakedness in your promiscuity with your lovers, and because of all your detestable idols, and because you gave them your children's blood, [37]therefore I am going to gather all your lovers, with whom you found pleasure, those you loved as well as those you hated. I will gather them against you from all around and will strip you in front of them, and they will see all your nakedness. [38]I will sentence you to the punishment of women who commit adultery and who shed blood; I will bring upon you the blood vengeance of my wrath and jealous anger. [39]Then I will hand you over to your lovers, and they will tear down your mounds and destroy your lofty shrines. They will strip you of your clothes and take your fine jewelry and leave you naked and bare. [40]They will bring a mob against you, who will stone you and hack you to pieces with their swords. [41]They will burn down your

houses and inflict punishment on you in the sight of many women. I will put a stop to your prostitution, and you will no longer pay your lovers. [42]Then my wrath against you will subside and my jealous anger will turn away from you; I will be calm and no longer angry.

[43]" 'Because you did not remember the days of your youth but enraged me with all these things, I will surely bring down on your head what you have done, declares the Sovereign LORD. Did you not add lewdness to all your other detestable practices?

[44]" 'Everyone who quotes proverbs will quote this proverb about you: "Like mother, like daughter." [45]You are a true daughter of your mother, who despised her husband and her children; and you are a true sister of your sisters, who despised their husbands and their children. Your mother was a Hittite and your father an Amorite. [46]Your older sister was Samaria, who lived to the north of you with her daughters; and your younger sister, who lived to the south of you with her daughters, was Sodom. [47]You not only walked in their ways and copied their detestable practices, but in all your ways you soon became more depraved than they. [48]As surely as I live, declares the Sovereign LORD, your sister Sodom and her daughters never did what you and your daughters have done.

[49]" 'Now this was the sin of your sister Sodom: She and her daughters were arrogant, overfed and unconcerned; they did not help the poor and needy. [50]They were haughty and did detestable things before me. Therefore I did away with them as you have seen. [51]Samaria did not commit half the sins you did. You have done more detestable things than they, and have made your sisters seem righteous by all these things you have done. [52]Bear your disgrace, for you have furnished some justification for your sisters. Because your sins were more vile than theirs, they appear more righteous than you. So then, be ashamed and bear your disgrace, for you have made your sisters appear righteous.

[53]" 'However, I will restore the fortunes of Sodom and her daughters and of Samaria and her daughters, and your fortunes along with them, [54]so that you may

bear your disgrace and be ashamed of all you have done in giving them comfort. [55]And your sisters, Sodom with her daughters and Samaria with her daughters, will return to what they were before; and you and your daughters will return to what you were before. [56]You would not even mention your sister Sodom in the day of your pride, [57]before your wickedness was uncovered. Even so, you are now scorned by the daughters of Edom[h] and all her neighbors and the daughters of the Philistines—all those around you who despise you. [58]You will bear the consequences of your lewdness and your detestable practices, declares the LORD.

[59]" 'This is what the Sovereign LORD says: I will deal with you as you deserve, because you have despised my oath by breaking the covenant. [60]Yet I will remember the covenant I made with you in the days of your youth, and I will establish an everlasting covenant with you. [61]Then you will remember your ways and be ashamed when you receive your sisters, both those who are older than you and those who are younger. I will give them to you as daughters, but not on the basis of my covenant with you. [62]So I will establish my covenant with you, and you will know that I am the LORD. [63]Then, when I make atonement for you for all you have done, you will remember and be ashamed and never again open your mouth because of your humiliation, declares the Sovereign LORD.' "

CHAPTER 17

The word of the LORD came to me: [2]"Son of man, set forth an allegory and tell the house of Israel a parable. [3]Say to them, 'This is what the Sovereign LORD says: A great eagle with powerful wings, long feathers and full plumage of varied colors came to Lebanon. Taking hold of the top of a cedar, [4]he broke off its topmost shoot and carried it away to a land of merchants, where he planted it in a city of traders.

[5]" 'He took some of the seed of your land and put it in fertile soil. He planted it like a willow by abundant water, [6]and it sprouted and became a low, spreading vine. Its branches turned toward him, but its roots remained under it. So it became a vine and produced branches and put out leafy boughs.

[7]" 'But there was another great eagle with powerful wings and full plumage. The vine now sent out its roots toward him from the plot where it was planted and stretched out its branches to him for water. [8]It had been planted in good soil by abundant water so that it would produce branches, bear fruit and become a splendid vine.'

[9]"Say to them, 'This is what the Sovereign LORD says: Will it thrive? Will it not be uprooted and stripped of its fruit so that it withers? All its new growth will wither. It will not take a strong arm or many people to pull it up by the roots. [10]Even if it is transplanted, will it thrive? Will it not wither completely when the east wind strikes it—wither away in the plot where it grew?' "

[11]Then the word of the LORD came to me: [12]"Say to this rebellious house, 'Do you not know what these things mean?' Say to them: 'The king of Babylon went to Jerusalem and carried off her king and her nobles, bringing them back with him to Babylon. [13]Then he took a member of the royal family and made a treaty with him, putting him under oath. He also carried away the leading men of the land, [14]so that the kingdom would be brought low, unable to rise again, surviving only by keeping his treaty. [15]But the king rebelled against him by sending his envoys to Egypt to get horses and a large army. Will he succeed? Will he who does such things escape? Will he break the treaty and yet escape?

[16]" 'As surely as I live, declares the Sovereign LORD, he shall die in Babylon, in the land of the king who put him on the throne, whose oath he despised and whose treaty he broke. [17]Pharaoh with his mighty army and great horde will be of no help to him in war, when ramps are built and siege works erected to destroy many lives. [18]He despised the oath by breaking the covenant. Because he had given his hand in pledge and yet did all these things, he shall not escape.

[19]" 'Therefore this is what the Sovereign LORD says: As surely as I live, I will bring down on his head my oath that he despised and my covenant that he broke. [20]I

[h]57 Many Hebrew manuscripts and Syriac; most Hebrew manuscripts, Septuagint and Vulgate *Aram*

will spread my net for him, and he will be caught in my snare. I will bring him to Babylon and execute judgment upon him there because he was unfaithful to me. ²¹All his fleeing troops will fall by the sword, and the survivors will be scattered to the winds. Then you will know that I the Lord have spoken.

²²" 'This is what the Sovereign Lord says: I myself will take a shoot from the very top of a cedar and plant it; I will break off a tender sprig from its topmost shoots and plant it on a high and lofty mountain. ²³On the mountain heights of Israel I will plant it; it will produce branches and bear fruit and become a splendid cedar. Birds of every kind will nest in it; they will find shelter in the shade of its branches. ²⁴All the trees of the field will know that I the Lord bring down the tall tree and make the low tree grow tall. I dry up the green tree and make the dry tree flourish.

" 'I the Lord have spoken, and I will do it.' "

CHAPTER 18

The word of the Lord came to me: ²"What do you people mean by quoting this proverb about the land of Israel:

" 'The fathers eat sour grapes,
  and the children's teeth are set on
    edge'?

³"As surely as I live, declares the Sovereign Lord, you will no longer quote this proverb in Israel. ⁴For every living soul belongs to me, the father as well as the son—both alike belong to me. The soul who sins is the one who will die.

⁵"Suppose there is a righteous man
  who does what is just and right.
⁶He does not eat at the mountain
    shrines
  or look to the idols of the house of
    Israel.
He does not defile his neighbor's wife
  or lie with a woman during her
    period.
⁷He does not oppress anyone,
  but returns what he took in pledge
    for a loan.
He does not commit robbery
  but gives his food to the hungry

and provides clothing for the naked.
⁸He does not lend at usury
  or take excessive interest.ⁱ
He withholds his hand from doing
    wrong
  and judges fairly between man and
    man.
⁹He follows my decrees
  and faithfully keeps my laws.
That man is righteous;
  he will surely live,
        declares the Sovereign Lord.

¹⁰"Suppose he has a violent son, who sheds blood or does any of these other thingsʲ ¹¹(though the father has done none of them):

"He eats at the mountain shrines.
He defiles his neighbor's wife.
¹²He oppresses the poor and needy.
He commits robbery.
He does not return what he took in
    pledge.
He looks to the idols.
He does detestable things.
¹³He lends at usury and takes excessive
    interest.

Will such a man live? He will not! Because he has done all these detestable things, he will surely be put to death and his blood will be on his own head.

¹⁴"But suppose this son has a son who sees all the sins his father commits, and though he sees them, he does not do such things:

¹⁵"He does not eat at the mountain
    shrines
  or look to the idols of the house of
    Israel.
He does not defile his neighbor's wife.
¹⁶He does not oppress anyone
  or require a pledge for a loan.
He does not commit robbery
  but gives his food to the hungry
  and provides clothing for the naked.
¹⁷He withholds his hand from sinᵏ
  and takes no usury or excessive
    interest.
He keeps my laws and follows my
    decrees.

He will not die for his father's sin; he will surely live. ¹⁸But his father will die for his own sin, because he practiced extortion,

---

ⁱ8 Or *take interest*; similarly in verses 13 and 17   ʲ10 Or *things to a brother*   ᵏ17 Septuagint (see also verse 8); Hebrew *from the poor* robbed his brother and did what was wrong among his people.

¹⁹"Yet you ask, 'Why does the son not share the guilt of his father?' Since the son has done what is just and right and has been careful to keep all my decrees, he will surely live. ²⁰The soul who sins is the one who will die. The son will not share the guilt of the father, nor will the father share the guilt of the son. The righteousness of the righteous man will be credited to him, and the wickedness of the wicked will be charged against him.

²¹"But if a wicked man turns away from all the sins he has committed and keeps all my decrees and does what is just and right, he will surely live; he will not die. ²²None of the offenses he has committed will be remembered against him. Because of the righteous things he has done, he will live. ²³Do I take any pleasure in the death of the wicked? declares the Sovereign LORD. Rather, am I not pleased when they turn from their ways and live?

²⁴"But if a righteous man turns from his righteousness and commits sin and does the same detestable things the wicked man does, will he live? None of the righteous things he has done will be remembered. Because of the unfaithfulness he is guilty of and because of the sins he has committed, he will die.

²⁵"Yet you say, 'The way of the Lord is not just.' Hear, O house of Israel: Is my way unjust? Is it not your ways that are unjust? ²⁶If a righteous man turns from his righteousness and commits sin, he will die for it; because of the sin he has committed he will die. ²⁷But if a wicked man turns away from the wickedness he has committed and does what is just and right, he will save his life. ²⁸Because he considers all the offenses he has committed and turns away from them, he will surely live; he will not die. ²⁹Yet the house of Israel says, 'The way of the Lord is not just.' Are my ways unjust, O house of Israel? Is it not your ways that are unjust?

³⁰"Therefore, O house of Israel, I will judge you, each one according to his ways, declares the Sovereign LORD. Repent! Turn away from all your offenses; then sin will not be your downfall. ³¹Rid yourselves of all the offenses you have committed, and get a new heart and a new spirit. Why will you die, O house of Israel? ³²For I take no pleasure in the death of anyone, declares the Sovereign LORD. Repent and live!

CHAPTER 19

"Take up a lament concerning the princes of Israel ²and say:

" 'What a lioness was your mother
    among the lions!
She lay down among the young lions
    and reared her cubs.
³She brought up one of her cubs,
    and he became a strong lion.
He learned to tear the prey
    and he devoured men.
⁴The nations heard about him,
    and he was trapped in their pit.
They led him with hooks
    to the land of Egypt.

⁵" 'When she saw her hope unfulfilled,
    her expectation gone,
she took another of her cubs
    and made him a strong lion.
⁶He prowled among the lions,
    for he was now a strong lion.
He learned to tear the prey
    and he devoured men.
⁷He broke down¹ their strongholds
    and devastated their towns.
The land and all who were in it
    were terrified by his roaring.
⁸Then the nations came against him,
    those from regions round about.
They spread their net for him,
    and he was trapped in their pit.
⁹With hooks they pulled him into a
        cage
    and brought him to the king of
        Babylon.
They put him in prison,
    so his roar was heard no longer
    on the mountains of Israel.

¹⁰" 'Your mother was like a vine in your
        vineyard ᵐ
    planted by the water;
it was fruitful and full of branches
    because of abundant water.
¹¹Its branches were strong,
    fit for a ruler's scepter.
It towered high
    above the thick foliage,
conspicuous for its height
    and for its many branches.

¹⁷ Targum (see Septuagint); Hebrew *He knew*   ᵐ¹⁰ Two Hebrew manuscripts; most Hebrew manuscripts *your blood*

¹²But it was uprooted in fury
  and thrown to the ground.
The east wind made it shrivel,
  it was stripped of its fruit;
its strong branches withered
  and fire consumed them.
¹³Now it is planted in the desert,
  in a dry and thirsty land.

ⁿ14 Or *from under its*

¹⁴Fire spread from one of its main ⁿ
  branches
  and consumed its fruit.
No strong branch is left on it
  fit for a ruler's scepter.'

This is a lament and is to be used as a lament."

AUGUST 19 □ DAY 232
EZEKIEL 20–23
Swords and Signposts

OVERVIEW Ezekiel the prophet often becomes Ezekiel the playwright as he uses a number of symbolic actions to dramatize the coming despair for Jerusalem. God's smelting furnace of wrath will refine the nation of Judah, burning away like dross her violence, immorality and idolatry. Like an adulterous woman she has followed the lewd example of her sister, Israel. As a result, Babylon—God's sword of punishment—is posed to strike. God declares, "Then all people will know that I the LORD have drawn my sword from its scabbard; it will not return again" (21:5).

Chapter 20	Chapter 21	Chapter 22	Chapter 23
Reviewing Judah's Sins	Removing Judah's King	Parable of the Silver	Parable of the Sisters
Swords		Signposts	

YOUR DAILY WALK When do you know that punishment has accomplished its intention?
  a. When the person being punished begins to cry
  b. When the person being punished responds, "Ouch!"
  c. When the person being punished changes his or her mind about repeating a course of action

Repentance may be old-fashioned, but it is not outdated so long as there is sin.

Punishment is always *painful*. But whether or not it is *profitable* depends on the response of the offender. Repeatedly Ezekiel has tried—through pictures, parables and illustrations—to visualize the agony of God's punishing hand. It is a sword, a furnace, a cooking pot. But God's underlying purpose is not to inflict pain; he is looking for repentance—a change of mind, heart and direction regarding a sinful action. Are you being prodded, refined or simmered today?

INSIGHT Sign Language for Exiles
God told Ezekiel, "I have made you a sign to the house of Israel" (12:6). See if you can complete the chart below that lists Ezekiel's ten signs designed to teach the nation ten divine truths:

Reference	Sign
4:1–3	
4:4–8	
4:9–17	
5:1–17	
12:1–7	

CHAPTER 20

In the seventh year, in the fifth month on the tenth day, some of the elders of Israel came to inquire of the LORD, and they sat down in front of me.

²Then the word of the LORD came to me: ³"Son of man, speak to the elders of Israel and say to them, 'This is what the Sovereign LORD says: Have you come to inquire of me? As surely as I live, I will not let you inquire of me, declares the Sovereign LORD.'

⁴"Will you judge them? Will you judge them, son of man? Then confront them with the detestable practices of their fathers ⁵and say to them: 'This is what the Sovereign LORD says: On the day I chose Israel, I swore with uplifted hand to the descendants of the house of Jacob and revealed myself to them in Egypt. With uplifted hand I said to them, "I am the LORD your God." ⁶On that day I swore to them that I would bring them out of Egypt into a land I had searched out for them, a land flowing with milk and honey, the most beautiful of all lands. ⁷And I said to them, "Each of you, get rid of the vile images you have set your eyes on, and do not defile yourselves with the idols of Egypt. I am the LORD your God."

⁸" 'But they rebelled against me and would not listen to me; they did not get rid of the vile images they had set their eyes on, nor did they forsake the idols of Egypt. So I said I would pour out my wrath on them and spend my anger against them in Egypt. ⁹But for the sake of my name I did what would keep it from being profaned in the eyes of the nations they lived among and in whose sight I had revealed myself to the Israelites by bringing them out of Egypt. ¹⁰Therefore I led them out of Egypt and brought them into the desert. ¹¹I gave them my decrees and made known to them my laws, for the man who obeys them will live by them. ¹²Also I gave them my Sabbaths as a sign between us, so they would know that I the LORD made them holy.

¹³" 'Yet the people of Israel rebelled against me in the desert. They did not follow my decrees but rejected my laws—although the man who obeys them will live by them—and they utterly desecrated my Sabbaths. So I said I would pour out my wrath on them and destroy them in the desert. ¹⁴But for the sake of my name I did what would keep it from being profaned in the eyes of the nations in whose sight I had brought them out. ¹⁵Also with uplifted hand I swore to them in the desert that I would not bring them into the land I had given them—a land flowing with milk and honey, most beautiful of all lands— ¹⁶because they rejected my laws and did not follow my decrees and desecrated my Sabbaths. For their hearts were devoted to their idols. ¹⁷Yet I looked on them with pity and did not destroy them or put an end to them in the desert. ¹⁸I said to their children in the desert, "Do not follow the statutes of your fathers or keep their laws or defile yourselves with their idols. ¹⁹I am the LORD your God; follow my decrees and be careful to keep my laws. ²⁰Keep my Sabbaths holy, that they may be a sign between us. Then you will know that I am the LORD your God."

²¹" 'But the children rebelled against me: They did not follow my decrees, they were not careful to keep my laws—although the man who obeys them will live by them—and they desecrated my Sabbaths. So I said I would pour out my wrath on them and spend my anger against them in the desert. ²²But I withheld my hand, and for the sake of my name I did what would keep it from being profaned in the eyes of the nations in whose sight I had brought them out. ²³Also with uplifted hand I swore to them in the desert that I would disperse them among the nations and scatter them through the countries, ²⁴because they had not obeyed my laws but had rejected my decrees and desecrated my Sabbaths, and their eyes ⌊lusted⌋ after their fathers' idols. ²⁵I also gave them over to statutes that were not good and laws they could not live by; ²⁶I let them become

defiled through their gifts—the sacrifice of every firstborn[o]—that I might fill them with horror so they would know that I am the LORD.'

[27]"Therefore, son of man, speak to the people of Israel and say to them, 'This is what the Sovereign LORD says: In this also your fathers blasphemed me by forsaking me: [28]When I brought them into the land I had sworn to give them and they saw any high hill or any leafy tree, there they offered their sacrifices, made offerings that provoked me to anger, presented their fragrant incense and poured out their drink offerings. [29]Then I said to them: What is this high place you go to?' " (It is called Bamah[p] to this day.)

[30]"Therefore say to the house of Israel: 'This is what the Sovereign LORD says: Will you defile yourselves the way your fathers did and lust after their vile images? [31]When you offer your gifts—the sacrifice of your sons in[q] the fire—you continue to defile yourselves with all your idols to this day. Am I to let you inquire of me, O house of Israel? As surely as I live, declares the Sovereign LORD, I will not let you inquire of me.

[32]" 'You say, "We want to be like the nations, like the peoples of the world, who serve wood and stone." But what you have in mind will never happen. [33]As surely as I live, declares the Sovereign LORD, I will rule over you with a mighty hand and an outstretched arm and with outpoured wrath. [34]I will bring you from the nations and gather you from the countries where you have been scattered—with a mighty hand and an outstretched arm and with outpoured wrath. [35]I will bring you into the desert of the nations and there, face to face, I will execute judgment upon you. [36]As I judged your fathers in the desert of the land of Egypt, so I will judge you, declares the Sovereign LORD. [37]I will take note of you as you pass under my rod, and I will bring you into the bond of the covenant. [38]I will purge you of those who revolt and rebel against me. Although I will bring them out of the land where they are living, yet they will not enter the land of Israel. Then you will know that I am the LORD.

[39]" 'As for you, O house of Israel, this is what the Sovereign LORD says: Go and serve your idols, every one of you! But afterward you will surely listen to me and no longer profane my holy name with your gifts and idols. [40]For on my holy mountain, the high mountain of Israel, declares the Sovereign LORD, there in the land the entire house of Israel will serve me, and there I will accept them. There I will require your offerings and your choice gifts,[r] along with all your holy sacrifices. [41]I will accept you as fragrant incense when I bring you out from the nations and gather you from the countries where you have been scattered, and I will show myself holy among you in the sight of the nations. [42]Then you will know that I am the LORD, when I bring you into the land of Israel, the land I had sworn with uplifted hand to give to your fathers. [43]There you will remember your conduct and all the actions by which you have defiled yourselves, and you will loathe yourselves for all the evil you have done. [44]You will know that I am the LORD, when I deal with you for my name's sake and not according to your evil ways and your corrupt practices, O house of Israel, declares the Sovereign LORD.' "

[45]The word of the LORD came to me: [46]"Son of man, set your face toward the south; preach against the south and prophesy against the forest of the southland. [47]Say to the southern forest: 'Hear the word of the LORD. This is what the Sovereign LORD says: I am about to set fire to you, and it will consume all your trees, both green and dry. The blazing flame will not be quenched, and every face from south to north will be scorched by it. [48]Everyone will see that I the LORD have kindled it; it will not be quenched.' "

[49]Then I said, "Ah, Sovereign LORD! They are saying of me, 'Isn't he just telling parables?' "

CHAPTER 21

The word of the LORD came to me: [2]"Son of man, set your face against Jerusalem and preach against the sanctuary. Prophesy against the land of Israel [3]and say to her: 'This is what the LORD says: I am against you. I will draw my sword from its scabbard and cut off from you both the righteous and the wicked. [4]Because I am

---

[o]26 Or —making every firstborn pass through the fire   [p]29 Bamah means high place.   [q]31 Or —making your sons pass through
[r]40 Or and the gifts of your firstfruits

going to cut off the righteous and the wicked, my sword will be unsheathed against everyone from south to north. ⁵Then all people will know that I the LORD have drawn my sword from its scabbard; it will not return again.'

⁶"Therefore groan, son of man! Groan before them with broken heart and bitter grief. ⁷And when they ask you, 'Why are you groaning?' you shall say, 'Because of the news that is coming. Every heart will melt and every hand go limp; every spirit will become faint and every knee become as weak as water.' It is coming! It will surely take place, declares the Sovereign LORD."

⁸The word of the LORD came to me: ⁹"Son of man, prophesy and say, 'This is what the Lord says:

" 'A sword, a sword,
    sharpened and polished—
¹⁰sharpened for the slaughter,
    polished to flash like lightning!

" 'Shall we rejoice in the scepter of my son ⌊Judah⌋? The sword despises every such stick.

¹¹" 'The sword is appointed to be
        polished,
    to be grasped with the hand;
    it is sharpened and polished,
    made ready for the hand of the
        slayer.
¹²Cry out and wail, son of man,
    for it is against my people;
    it is against all the princes of Israel.
They are thrown to the sword
    along with my people.
Therefore beat your breast.

¹³" 'Testing will surely come. And what if the scepter ⌊of Judah⌋, which the sword despises, does not continue? declares the Sovereign LORD.'

¹⁴"So then, son of man, prophesy
    and strike your hands together.
Let the sword strike twice,
    even three times.
It is a sword for slaughter—
    a sword for great slaughter,
    closing in on them from every side.
¹⁵So that hearts may melt
    and the fallen be many,
I have stationed the sword for
    slaughterˢ

at all their gates.
Oh! It is made to flash like lightning,
    it is grasped for slaughter.
¹⁶O sword, slash to the right,
    then to the left,
    wherever your blade is turned.
¹⁷I too will strike my hands together,
    and my wrath will subside.
I the LORD have spoken."

¹⁸The word of the LORD came to me: ¹⁹"Son of man, mark out two roads for the sword of the king of Babylon to take, both starting from the same country. Make a signpost where the road branches off to the city. ²⁰Mark out one road for the sword to come against Rabbah of the Ammonites and another against Judah and fortified Jerusalem. ²¹For the king of Babylon will stop at the fork in the road, at the junction of the two roads, to seek an omen: He will cast lots with arrows, he will consult his idols, he will examine the liver. ²²Into his right hand will come the lot for Jerusalem, where he is to set up battering rams, to give the command to slaughter, to sound the battle cry, to set battering rams against the gates, to build a ramp and to erect siege works. ²³It will seem like a false omen to those who have sworn allegiance to him, but he will remind them of their guilt and take them captive.

²⁴"Therefore this is what the Sovereign LORD says: 'Because you people have brought to mind your guilt by your open rebellion, revealing your sins in all that you do—because you have done this, you will be taken captive.

²⁵" 'O profane and wicked prince of Israel, whose day has come, whose time of punishment has reached its climax, ²⁶this is what the Sovereign LORD says: Take off the turban, remove the crown. It will not be as it was: The lowly will be exalted and the exalted will be brought low. ²⁷A ruin! A ruin! I will make it a ruin! It will not be restored until he comes to whom it rightfully belongs; to him I will give it.'

²⁸"And you, son of man, prophesy and say, 'This is what the Sovereign LORD says about the Ammonites and their insults:

" 'A sword, a sword,
    drawn for the slaughter,
    polished to consume

ˢ15 Septuagint; the meaning of the Hebrew for this word is uncertain.

and to flash like lightning!
²⁹Despite false visions concerning you
and lying divinations about you,
it will be laid on the necks
of the wicked who are to be slain,
whose day has come,
whose time of punishment has
reached its climax.
³⁰Return the sword to its scabbard.
In the place where you were created,
in the land of your ancestry,
I will judge you.
³¹I will pour out my wrath upon you
and breathe out my fiery anger
against you;
I will hand you over to brutal men,
men skilled in destruction.
³²You will be fuel for the fire,
your blood will be shed in your
land,
you will be remembered no more;
for I the LORD have spoken.' "

CHAPTER 22
The word of the LORD came to me: ²"Son of man, will you judge her? Will you judge this city of bloodshed? Then confront her with all her detestable practices ³and say: 'This is what the Sovereign LORD says: O city that brings on herself doom by shedding blood in her midst and defiles herself by making idols, ⁴you have become guilty because of the blood you have shed and have become defiled by the idols you have made. You have brought your days to a close, and the end of your years has come. Therefore I will make you an object of scorn to the nations and a laughingstock to all the countries. ⁵Those who are near and those who are far away will mock you, O infamous city, full of turmoil.

⁶" 'See how each of the princes of Israel who are in you uses his power to shed blood. ⁷In you they have treated father and mother with contempt; in you they have oppressed the alien and mistreated the fatherless and the widow. ⁸You have despised my holy things and desecrated my Sabbaths. ⁹In you are slanderous men bent on shedding blood; in you are those who eat at the mountain shrines and commit lewd acts. ¹⁰In you are those who dishonor their fathers' bed; in you are those who violate women during their

period, when they are ceremonially unclean. ¹¹In you one man commits a detestable offense with his neighbor's wife, another shamefully defiles his daughter-in-law, and another violates his sister, his own father's daughter. ¹²In you men accept bribes to shed blood; you take usury and excessive interest[t] and make unjust gain from your neighbors by extortion. And you have forgotten me, declares the Sovereign LORD.

¹³" 'I will surely strike my hands together at the unjust gain you have made and at the blood you have shed in your midst. ¹⁴Will your courage endure or your hands be strong in the day I deal with you? I the LORD have spoken, and I will do it. ¹⁵I will disperse you among the nations and scatter you through the countries; and I will put an end to your uncleanness. ¹⁶When you have been defiled[u] in the eyes of the nations, you will know that I am the LORD.' "

¹⁷Then the word of the LORD came to me: ¹⁸"Son of man, the house of Israel has become dross to me; all of them are the copper, tin, iron and lead left inside a furnace. They are but the dross of silver. ¹⁹Therefore this is what the Sovereign LORD says: 'Because you have all become dross, I will gather you into Jerusalem. ²⁰As men gather silver, copper, iron, lead and tin into a furnace to melt it with a fiery blast, so will I gather you in my anger and my wrath and put you inside the city and melt you. ²¹I will gather you and I will blow on you with my fiery wrath, and you will be melted inside her. ²²As silver is melted in a furnace, so you will be melted inside her, and you will know that I the LORD have poured out my wrath upon you.' "

²³Again the word of the LORD came to me: ²⁴"Son of man, say to the land, 'You are a land that has had no rain or showers[v] in the day of wrath.' ²⁵There is a conspiracy of her princes[w] within her like a roaring lion tearing its prey; they devour people, take treasures and precious things and make many widows within her. ²⁶Her priests do violence to my law and profane my holy things; they do not distinguish between the holy and the common; they teach that there is no difference between the unclean and the

clean; and they shut their eyes to the keeping of my Sabbaths, so that I am profaned among them. 27Her officials within her are like wolves tearing their prey; they shed blood and kill people to make unjust gain. 28Her prophets whitewash these deeds for them by false visions and lying divinations. They say, 'This is what the Sovereign Lord says'—when the Lord has not spoken. 29The people of the land practice extortion and commit robbery; they oppress the poor and needy and mistreat the alien, denying them justice.

30"I looked for a man among them who would build up the wall and stand before me in the gap on behalf of the land so I would not have to destroy it, but I found none. 31So I will pour out my wrath on them and consume them with my fiery anger, bringing down on their own heads all they have done, declares the Sovereign Lord."

CHAPTER 23

The word of the Lord came to me: 2"Son of man, there were two women, daughters of the same mother. 3They became prostitutes in Egypt, engaging in prostitution from their youth. In that land their breasts were fondled and their virgin bosoms caressed. 4The older was named Oholah, and her sister was Oholibah. They were mine and gave birth to sons and daughters. Oholah is Samaria, and Oholibah is Jerusalem.

5"Oholah engaged in prostitution while she was still mine; and she lusted after her lovers, the Assyrians—warriors 6clothed in blue, governors and commanders, all of them handsome young men, and mounted horsemen. 7She gave herself as a prostitute to all the elite of the Assyrians and defiled herself with all the idols of everyone she lusted after. 8She did not give up the prostitution she began in Egypt, when during her youth men slept with her, caressed her virgin bosom and poured out their lust upon her.

9"Therefore I handed her over to her lovers, the Assyrians, for whom she lusted. 10They stripped her naked, took away her sons and daughters and killed her with the sword. She became a byword among women, and punishment was inflicted on her.

11"Her sister Oholibah saw this, yet in her lust and prostitution she was more depraved than her sister. 12She too lusted after the Assyrians—governors and commanders, warriors in full dress, mounted horsemen, all handsome young men. 13I saw that she too defiled herself; both of them went the same way.

14"But she carried her prostitution still further. She saw men portrayed on a wall, figures of Chaldeans˟ portrayed in red, 15with belts around their waists and flowing turbans on their heads; all of them looked like Babylonian chariot officers, natives of Chaldea.ʸ 16As soon as she saw them, she lusted after them and sent messengers to them in Chaldea. 17Then the Babylonians came to her, to the bed of love, and in their lust they defiled her. After she had been defiled by them, she turned away from them in disgust. 18When she carried on her prostitution openly and exposed her nakedness, I turned away from her in disgust, just as I had turned away from her sister. 19Yet she became more and more promiscuous as she recalled the days of her youth, when she was a prostitute in Egypt. 20There she lusted after her lovers, whose genitals were like those of donkeys and whose emission was like that of horses. 21So you longed for the lewdness of your youth, when in Egypt your bosom was caressed and your young breasts fondled.ᶻ

22"Therefore, Oholibah, this is what the Sovereign Lord says: I will stir up your lovers against you, those you turned away from in disgust, and I will bring them against you from every side— 23the Babylonians and all the Chaldeans, the men of Pekod and Shoa and Koa, and all the Assyrians with them, handsome young men, all of them governors and commanders, chariot officers and men of high rank, all mounted on horses. 24They will come against you with weapons,ᵃ chariots and wagons and with a throng of people; they will take up positions against you on every side with large and small shields and with helmets. I will turn you over to them for punishment, and they will punish you according to their standards. 25I will direct my jealous anger against you, and they will deal with you in fury. They will cut off your noses and

---

˟14 Or Babylonians   ʸ15 Or Babylonia; also in verse 16   ᶻ21 Syriac (see also verse 3); Hebrew *caressed because of your young breasts*   ᵃ24 The meaning of the Hebrew for this word is uncertain.

your ears, and those of you who are left will fall by the sword. They will take away your sons and daughters, and those of you who are left will be consumed by fire. ²⁶They will also strip you of your clothes and take your fine jewelry. ²⁷So I will put a stop to the lewdness and prostitution you began in Egypt. You will not look on these things with longing or remember Egypt anymore.

²⁸"For this is what the Sovereign LORD says: I am about to hand you over to those you hate, to those you turned away from in disgust. ²⁹They will deal with you in hatred and take away everything you have worked for. They will leave you naked and bare, and the shame of your prostitution will be exposed. Your lewdness and promiscuity ³⁰have brought this upon you, because you lusted after the nations and defiled yourself with their idols. ³¹You have gone the way of your sister; so I will put her cup into your hand.

³²"This is what the Sovereign LORD says:

"You will drink your sister's cup,
    a cup large and deep;
it will bring scorn and derision,
    for it holds so much.
³³You will be filled with drunkenness
        and sorrow,
    the cup of ruin and desolation,
    the cup of your sister Samaria.
³⁴You will drink it and drain it dry;
    you will dash it to pieces
    and tear your breasts.

I have spoken, declares the Sovereign LORD.

³⁵"Therefore this is what the Sovereign LORD says: Since you have forgotten me and thrust me behind your back, you must bear the consequences of your lewdness and prostitution."

³⁶The LORD said to me: "Son of man, will you judge Oholah and Oholibah? Then confront them with their detestable practices, ³⁷for they have committed adultery

and blood is on their hands. They committed adultery with their idols; they even sacrificed their children, whom they bore to me,ᵇ as food for them. ³⁸They have also done this to me: At that same time they defiled my sanctuary and desecrated my Sabbaths. ³⁹On the very day they sacrificed their children to their idols, they entered my sanctuary and desecrated it. That is what they did in my house.

⁴⁰"They even sent messengers for men who came from far away, and when they arrived you bathed yourself for them, painted your eyes and put on your jewelry. ⁴¹You sat on an elegant couch, with a table spread before it on which you had placed the incense and oil that belonged to me.

⁴²"The noise of a carefree crowd was around her; Sabeansᶜ were brought from the desert along with men from the rabble, and they put bracelets on the arms of the woman and her sister and beautiful crowns on their heads. ⁴³Then I said about the one worn out by adultery, 'Now let them use her as a prostitute, for that is all she is.' ⁴⁴And they slept with her. As men sleep with a prostitute, so they slept with those lewd women, Oholah and Oholibah. ⁴⁵But righteous men will sentence them to the punishment of women who commit adultery and shed blood, because they are adulterous and blood is on their hands.

⁴⁶"This is what the Sovereign LORD says: Bring a mob against them and give them over to terror and plunder. ⁴⁷The mob will stone them and cut them down with their swords; they will kill their sons and daughters and burn down their houses.

⁴⁸"So I will put an end to lewdness in the land, that all women may take warning and not imitate you. ⁴⁹You will suffer the penalty for your lewdness and bear the consequences of your sins of idolatry. Then you will know that I am the Sovereign LORD."

ᵇ37 Or even made the children they bore to me pass through ⌊the fire⌋   ᶜ42 Or drunkards

AUGUST 20 ☐ DAY 233
EZEKIEL 24–28
Judgment East and West

OVERVIEW Gloating over the fate of another is one sure way to share that fate! Judah's neighbors, smug in their arrogance, stand next in line for Ezekiel's declaration of doom. Ammon, Moab, Edom, Philistia, Tyre—none will escape God's wrath according to Ezekiel's vision of doom. Age-old adversaries and great commercial empires alike will topple to show the world that God's justice cannot be thwarted.

Chapter 24	Chapter 25	Chapters 26–27	Chapter 28
Tears for Ezekiel	Terror for Ammon, Moab, Edom, Philistia	Toppling of Tyre's Pride	King
Dead Wife	Deadly Warfare	Deadly "Wisdom"	

YOUR DAILY WALK Do you have a problem with pride? If you answered no, are you proud of that fact?

Consider for a moment these insightful words on the subject of pride—a problem not limited to Ezekiel's day.

Humility is the embarrassment we feel when we tell others how wonderful we are.

Pride is a vice not limited to the emperors of far-flung realms. Almost anyone, by comparing him or herself with those who have less talent, less success, less popularity, can emerge with a feeling of satisfaction that is the very opposite of humility.

What is the remedy for pride? You'll find the prescription in 1 Corinthians 4:7. It's the daily realization that all you are and have is a gift from God. The king of Tyre got into "pride problems" by forgetting that fact. Ezekiel 28:12–19 shows numerous ways in which pride tripped up the king of Tyre. Are you in danger of being tripped as well? Then spend a few minutes reviewing these potent proverbs about pride and its pitfalls: Proverbs 8:13; 11:2; 13:10; 14:3; 16:18; 29:23.

INSIGHT When Ezekiel Talks, People Listen!

Tyre, located sixty miles northwest of Nazareth, was actually a split city—half on an island and half on the mainland with a channel in between. At the zenith of its power, Tyre controlled virtually all commerce on the Mediterranean and boasted colonies in Africa, Spain and Britain. After the Babylonian siege, however, it never regained its former glory. Today, the once-proud city is nothing more than a bare rock where fishermen spread their nets (26:4–5, 14)—a remarkable fulfillment of Ezekiel's prophecy (26:14, 21; 27:36).

CHAPTER 24

In the ninth year, in the tenth month on the tenth day, the word of the LORD came to me: ²"Son of man, record this date, this very date, because the king of Babylon has laid siege to Jerusalem this very day. ³Tell this rebellious house a parable and say to them: 'This is what the Sovereign LORD says:

" 'Put on the cooking pot; put it on

and pour water into it.
⁴Put into it the pieces of meat,
    all the choice pieces—the leg and the
        shoulder.
Fill it with the best of these bones;
⁵   take the pick of the flock.
Pile wood beneath it for the bones;
    bring it to a boil
    and cook the bones in it.

⁶" 'For this is what the Sovereign LORD says:

" 'Woe to the city of bloodshed,
   to the pot now encrusted,
   whose deposit will not go away!
 Empty it piece by piece
   without casting lots for them.

7" 'For the blood she shed is in her
      midst:
   She poured it on the bare rock;
 she did not pour it on the ground,
   where the dust would cover it.
8To stir up wrath and take revenge
   I put her blood on the bare rock,
   so that it would not be covered.

9" 'Therefore this is what the Sovereign
Lord says:

 " 'Woe to the city of bloodshed!
   I, too, will pile the wood high.
10So heap on the wood
   and kindle the fire.
 Cook the meat well,
   mixing in the spices;
   and let the bones be charred.
11Then set the empty pot on the coals
   till it becomes hot and its copper
      glows
 so its impurities may be melted
   and its deposit burned away.
12It has frustrated all efforts;
   its heavy deposit has not been
      removed,
   not even by fire.

13" 'Now your impurity is lewdness. Because I tried to cleanse you but you would not be cleansed from your impurity, you will not be clean again until my wrath against you has subsided.

14" 'I the Lord have spoken. The time has come for me to act. I will not hold back; I will not have pity, nor will I relent. You will be judged according to your conduct and your actions, declares the Sovereign Lord.' "

15The word of the Lord came to me: 16"Son of man, with one blow I am about to take away from you the delight of your eyes. Yet do not lament or weep or shed any tears. 17Groan quietly; do not mourn for the dead. Keep your turban fastened and your sandals on your feet; do not cover the lower part of your face or eat the customary food ˌof mournersˌ."

18So I spoke to the people in the morning, and in the evening my wife died. The next morning I did as I had been commanded.

19Then the people asked me, "Won't you tell us what these things have to do with us?"

20So I said to them, "The word of the Lord came to me: 21Say to the house of Israel, 'This is what the Sovereign Lord says: I am about to desecrate my sanctuary—the stronghold in which you take pride, the delight of your eyes, the object of your affection. The sons and daughters you left behind will fall by the sword. 22And you will do as I have done. You will not cover the lower part of your face or eat the customary food ˌof mournersˌ. 23You will keep your turbans on your heads and your sandals on your feet. You will not mourn or weep but will waste away because of[d] your sins and groan among yourselves. 24Ezekiel will be a sign to you; you will do just as he has done. When this happens, you will know that I am the Sovereign Lord.'

25"And you, son of man, on the day I take away their stronghold, their joy and glory, the delight of their eyes, their heart's desire, and their sons and daughters as well— 26on that day a fugitive will come to tell you the news. 27At that time your mouth will be opened; you will speak with him and will no longer be silent. So you will be a sign to them, and they will know that I am the Lord."

CHAPTER 25
The word of the Lord came to me: 2"Son of man, set your face against the Ammonites and prophesy against them. 3Say to them, 'Hear the word of the Sovereign Lord. This is what the Sovereign Lord says: Because you said "Aha!" over my sanctuary when it was desecrated and over the land of Israel when it was laid waste and over the people of Judah when they went into exile, 4therefore I am going to give you to the people of the East as a possession. They will set up their camps and pitch their tents among you; they will eat your fruit and drink your milk. 5I will turn Rabbah into a pasture for camels and Ammon into a resting place for sheep. Then you will know that I am the Lord.

d 23 Or away in

⁶For this is what the Sovereign LORD says: Because you have clapped your hands and stamped your feet, rejoicing with all the malice of your heart against the land of Israel, ⁷therefore I will stretch out my hand against you and give you as plunder to the nations. I will cut you off from the nations and exterminate you from the countries. I will destroy you, and you will know that I am the LORD.' "

⁸"This is what the Sovereign LORD says: 'Because Moab and Seir said, "Look, the house of Judah has become like all the other nations," ⁹therefore I will expose the flank of Moab, beginning at its frontier towns—Beth Jeshimoth, Baal Meon and Kiriathaim—the glory of that land. ¹⁰I will give Moab along with the Ammonites to the people of the East as a possession, so that the Ammonites will not be remembered among the nations; ¹¹and I will inflict punishment on Moab. Then they will know that I am the LORD.' "

¹²"This is what the Sovereign LORD says: 'Because Edom took revenge on the house of Judah and became very guilty by doing so, ¹³therefore this is what the Sovereign LORD says: I will stretch out my hand against Edom and kill its men and their animals. I will lay it waste, and from Teman to Dedan they will fall by the sword. ¹⁴I will take vengeance on Edom by the hand of my people Israel, and they will deal with Edom in accordance with my anger and my wrath; they will know my vengeance, declares the Sovereign LORD.' "

¹⁵"This is what the Sovereign LORD says: 'Because the Philistines acted in vengeance and took revenge with malice in their hearts, and with ancient hostility sought to destroy Judah, ¹⁶therefore this is what the Sovereign LORD says: I am about to stretch out my hand against the Philistines, and I will cut off the Kerethites and destroy those remaining along the coast. ¹⁷I will carry out great vengeance on them and punish them in my wrath. Then they will know that I am the LORD, when I take vengeance on them.' "

CHAPTER 26

In the eleventh year, on the first day of the month, the word of the LORD came to me:

²"Son of man, because Tyre has said of Jerusalem, 'Aha! The gate to the nations is broken, and its doors have swung open to me; now that she lies in ruins I will prosper,' ³therefore this is what the Sovereign LORD says: I am against you, O Tyre, and I will bring many nations against you, like the sea casting up its waves. ⁴They will destroy the walls of Tyre and pull down her towers; I will scrape away her rubble and make her a bare rock. ⁵Out in the sea she will become a place to spread fishnets, for I have spoken, declares the Sovereign LORD. She will become plunder for the nations, ⁶and her settlements on the mainland will be ravaged by the sword. Then they will know that I am the LORD.

⁷"For this is what the Sovereign LORD says: From the north I am going to bring against Tyre Nebuchadnezzarᵉ king of Babylon, king of kings, with horses and chariots, with horsemen and a great army. ⁸He will ravage your settlements on the mainland with the sword; he will set up siege works against you, build a ramp up to your walls and raise his shields against you. ⁹He will direct the blows of his battering rams against your walls and demolish your towers with his weapons. ¹⁰His horses will be so many that they will cover you with dust. Your walls will tremble at the noise of the war horses, wagons and chariots when he enters your gates as men enter a city whose walls have been broken through. ¹¹The hoofs of his horses will trample all your streets; he will kill your people with the sword, and your strong pillars will fall to the ground. ¹²They will plunder your wealth and loot your merchandise; they will break down your walls and demolish your fine houses and throw your stones, timber and rubble into the sea. ¹³I will put an end to your noisy songs, and the music of your harps will be heard no more. ¹⁴I will make you a bare rock, and you will become a place to spread fishnets. You will never be rebuilt, for I the LORD have spoken, declares the Sovereign LORD.

¹⁵"This is what the Sovereign LORD says to Tyre: Will not the coastlands tremble at the sound of your fall, when the wounded groan and the slaughter takes place in you? ¹⁶Then all the princes of the coast will step down from their thrones and lay

ᵉ7 Hebrew *Nebuchadrezzar*, of which *Nebuchadnezzar* is a variant; here and often in Ezekiel and Jeremiah aside their robes and take off their embroidered garments. Clothed with terror, they will sit on the ground, trembling every moment, appalled at you. [17]Then they will take up a lament concerning you and say to you:

" 'How you are destroyed, O city of
      renown,
   peopled by men of the sea!
You were a power on the seas,
   you and your citizens;
you put your terror
   on all who lived there.
[18]Now the coastlands tremble
   on the day of your fall;
the islands in the sea
   are terrified at your collapse.'

[19]"This is what the Sovereign LORD says: When I make you a desolate city, like cities no longer inhabited, and when I bring the ocean depths over you and its vast waters cover you, [20]then I will bring you down with those who go down to the pit, to the people of long ago. I will make you dwell in the earth below, as in ancient ruins, with those who go down to the pit, and you will not return or take your place[f] in the land of the living. [21]I will bring you to a horrible end and you will be no more. You will be sought, but you will never again be found, declares the Sovereign LORD."

CHAPTER 27
The word of the LORD came to me: [2]"Son of man, take up a lament concerning Tyre. [3]Say to Tyre, situated at the gateway to the sea, merchant of peoples on many coasts, 'This is what the Sovereign LORD says:

" 'You say, O Tyre,
   "I am perfect in beauty."
[4]Your domain was on the high seas;
   your builders brought your beauty
      to perfection.
[5]They made all your timbers
   of pine trees from Senir[g];
they took a cedar from Lebanon
   to make a mast for you.
[6]Of oaks from Bashan
   they made your oars;
of cypress wood[h] from the coasts of
      Cyprus[i]

they made your deck, inlaid with
      ivory.
[7]Fine embroidered linen from Egypt
   was your sail
   and served as your banner;
your awnings were of blue and purple
   from the coasts of Elishah.
[8]Men of Sidon and Arvad were your
      oarsmen;
   your skilled men, O Tyre, were
      aboard as your seamen.
[9]Veteran craftsmen of Gebal[j] were on
      board
   as shipwrights to caulk your seams.
All the ships of the sea and their
      sailors
   came alongside to trade for your
      wares.

[10]" 'Men of Persia, Lydia and Put
   served as soldiers in your army.
They hung their shields and helmets
   on your walls,
   bringing you splendor.
[11]Men of Arvad and Helech
   manned your walls on every side;
men of Gammad
   were in your towers.
They hung their shields around your
      walls;
   they brought your beauty to
      perfection.

[12]" 'Tarshish did business with you because of your great wealth of goods; they exchanged silver, iron, tin and lead for your merchandise.
[13]" 'Greece, Tubal and Meshech traded with you; they exchanged slaves and articles of bronze for your wares.
[14]" 'Men of Beth Togarmah exchanged work horses, war horses and mules for your merchandise.
[15]" 'The men of Rhodes[k] traded with you, and many coastlands were your customers; they paid you with ivory tusks and ebony.
[16]" 'Aram[l] did business with you because of your many products; they exchanged turquoise, purple fabric, embroidered work, fine linen, coral and rubies for your merchandise.
[17]" 'Judah and Israel traded with you; they exchanged wheat from Minnith and

confections,^m honey, oil and balm for your wares.

18" 'Damascus, because of your many products and great wealth of goods, did business with you in wine from Helbon and wool from Zahar.

19" 'Danites and Greeks from Uzal bought your merchandise; they exchanged wrought iron, cassia and calamus for your wares.

20" 'Dedan traded in saddle blankets with you.

21" 'Arabia and all the princes of Kedar were your customers; they did business with you in lambs, rams and goats.

22" 'The merchants of Sheba and Raamah traded with you; for your merchandise they exchanged the finest of all kinds of spices and precious stones, and gold.

23" 'Haran, Canneh and Eden and merchants of Sheba, Asshur and Kilmad traded with you. 24In your marketplace they traded with you beautiful garments, blue fabric, embroidered work and multicolored rugs with cords twisted and tightly knotted.

25" 'The ships of Tarshish serve
as carriers for your wares.
You are filled with heavy cargo
in the heart of the sea.
26Your oarsmen take you
out to the high seas.
But the east wind will break you to
pieces
in the heart of the sea.
27Your wealth, merchandise and wares,
your mariners, seamen and
shipwrights,
your merchants and all your soldiers,
and everyone else on board
will sink into the heart of the sea
on the day of your shipwreck.
28The shorelands will quake
when your seamen cry out.
29All who handle the oars
will abandon their ships;
the mariners and all the seamen
will stand on the shore.
30They will raise their voice
and cry bitterly over you;
they will sprinkle dust on their heads
and roll in ashes.
31They will shave their heads because of
you

and will put on sackcloth.
They will weep over you with anguish
of soul
and with bitter mourning.
32As they wail and mourn over you,
they will take up a lament
concerning you:
"Who was ever silenced like Tyre,
surrounded by the sea?"
33When your merchandise went out on
the seas,
you satisfied many nations;
with your great wealth and your
wares
you enriched the kings of the earth.
34Now you are shattered by the sea
in the depths of the waters;
your wares and all your company
have gone down with you.
35All who live in the coastlands
are appalled at you;
their kings shudder with horror
and their faces are distorted with
fear.
36The merchants among the nations hiss
at you;
you have come to a horrible end
and will be no more.' "

CHAPTER 28
The word of the LORD came to me: 2"Son of man, say to the ruler of Tyre, 'This is what the Sovereign LORD says:

" 'In the pride of your heart
you say, "I am a god;
I sit on the throne of a god
in the heart of the seas."
But you are a man and not a god,
though you think you are as wise as
a god.
3Are you wiser than Daniel^n?
Is no secret hidden from you?
4By your wisdom and understanding
you have gained wealth for yourself
and amassed gold and silver
in your treasuries.
5By your great skill in trading
you have increased your wealth,
and because of your wealth
your heart has grown proud.

6" 'Therefore this is what the Sovereign LORD says:

" 'Because you think you are wise,

---

^m17 The meaning of the Hebrew for this word is uncertain. ^n3 Or Danel; the Hebrew spelling may suggest a person other than the prophet Daniel.

as wise as a god,
⁷I am going to bring foreigners against
    you,
  the most ruthless of nations;
they will draw their swords against
    your beauty and wisdom
  and pierce your shining splendor.
⁸They will bring you down to the pit,
  and you will die a violent death
    in the heart of the seas.
⁹Will you then say, "I am a god,"
    in the presence of those who kill
      you?
  You will be but a man, not a god,
    in the hands of those who slay you.
¹⁰You will die the death of the
      uncircumcised
    at the hands of foreigners.

I have spoken, declares the Sovereign
LORD.' "

¹¹The word of the LORD came to me:
¹²"Son of man, take up a lament concerning the king of Tyre and say to him: 'This
is what the Sovereign LORD says:

  " 'You were the model of perfection,
    full of wisdom and perfect in
      beauty.
¹³You were in Eden,
    the garden of God;
  every precious stone adorned you:
    ruby, topaz and emerald,
    chrysolite, onyx and jasper,
    sapphire,ᵒ turquoise and beryl.ᵖ
  Your settings and mountings�q were
      made of gold;
    on the day you were created they
      were prepared.
¹⁴You were anointed as a guardian
      cherub,
    for so I ordained you.
  You were on the holy mount of God;
    you walked among the fiery stones.
¹⁵You were blameless in your ways
    from the day you were created
    till wickedness was found in you.
¹⁶Through your widespread trade
    you were filled with violence,
    and you sinned.
  So I drove you in disgrace from the
      mount of God,
    and I expelled you, O guardian
      cherub,
    from among the fiery stones.

¹⁷Your heart became proud
    on account of your beauty,
  and you corrupted your wisdom
    because of your splendor.
  So I threw you to the earth;
    I made a spectacle of you before
      kings.
¹⁸By your many sins and dishonest trade
    you have desecrated your
      sanctuaries.
  So I made a fire come out from you,
    and it consumed you,
  and I reduced you to ashes on the
      ground
    in the sight of all who were
      watching.
¹⁹All the nations who knew you
    are appalled at you;
  you have come to a horrible end
    and will be no more.' "

²⁰The word of the LORD came to me:
²¹"Son of man, set your face against Sidon;
prophesy against her ²²and say: 'This is
what the Sovereign LORD says:

  " 'I am against you, O Sidon,
    and I will gain glory within you.
  They will know that I am the LORD,
    when I inflict punishment on her
    and show myself holy within her.
²³I will send a plague upon her
    and make blood flow in her streets.
  The slain will fall within her,
    with the sword against her on every
      side.
  Then they will know that I am the
      LORD.

²⁴" 'No longer will the people of Israel
have malicious neighbors who are painful
briers and sharp thorns. Then they will
know that I am the Sovereign LORD.
²⁵" 'This is what the Sovereign LORD
says: When I gather the people of Israel
from the nations where they have been
scattered, I will show myself holy among
them in the sight of the nations. Then they
will live in their own land, which I gave
to my servant Jacob. ²⁶They will live there
in safety and will build houses and plant
vineyards; they will live in safety when I
inflict punishment on all their neighbors
who maligned them. Then they will know
that I am the LORD their God.' "

ᵒ13 Or *lapis lazuli*   ᵖ13 The precise identification of some of these precious stones is uncertain.   q13 The meaning of the
Hebrew for this phrase is uncertain.

AUGUST 21 ☐ DAY 234
Then You Will Know

LOOK BACK Isaiah, Jeremiah, Ezekiel—each shares a common experience. Early in their prophetic ministries, they experience a vision from God that shapes the entire course of their lives. Ezekiel discovers that the person God can use is awed by the glory of God . . . available to the Spirit of God . . . and acting on the Word of God. In signs and symbols, Ezekiel dramatizes the fate awaiting his countrymen: siege, enslavement and a "very close shave"! Indeed, the end is near, and God is going out of his way to be sure the world knows who is behind it all—the sovereign Lord.

As the glory departs from the temple, it is clear that judgment and exile for Judah's leaders cannot be far behind, for as go the leaders, so go the people. Jerusalem has been unfaithful and fruitless, but God has shown loyal love in the face of her spiritual prostitution. Lamenting loudly and repenting of her wicked ways are the only appropriate responses to God's undying love. They are responses that Judah and its pagan neighboring nations desperately need to learn.

LOOK UP *Specialization* has been defined as "the art of learning more and more about less and less." Wisdom comes more from living than from studying, and indeed, it is better to know some of the answers than all of the questions.

Draw a circle and get inside, then pray God will send revival within the circle.

There are many things God wants you to know, but perhaps the most important is the truth repeated dozens of times in the book of Ezekiel: "You will know that I am the LORD" (6:7). Whatever else you learn in life will be meaningless unless and until you discover that God exists and rewards those who diligently seek him (Hebrews 11:6).

Scan back through the chapters you have read this past week, and catalog a few of the things that should have led the people of God to the inescapable conclusion that there is a God and he is not silent. (All the references are in Ezekiel.)

5:13 _____
6:7 _____
7:4 _____
12:15 _____
13:14 _____
15:7 _____
16:62 _____
17:21 _____
20:20 _____
24:24 _____
28:24 _____

LOOK AHEAD God is sovereignly in control of what happens in your life, your family and your nation. Did you know that? If so, what difference does it make?

God is holy—totally apart from sin—and totally committed to helping you find power over every sinful habit that still clings to your life. Did you know that? If so, what is his will for you today?

God knows all about you and still loves you unconditionally. Did you know that? If so, there's nothing he would rather hear than "I love you, Lord," flowing from your heart to his. Have you told him that today? If not, there's no time like the present.

AUGUST 22 □ DAY 235
EZEKIEL 29–32
Judgment on Egypt

 OVERVIEW Ezekiel's concluding words to Judah's neighbors are addressed specifically to Egypt. The perennial enemy of God's people, Egypt would not be totally destroyed (as Ammon, Moab, Edom, Philistia and Tyre would be). Instead, it would be reduced to insignificance after a time of dispersion and regathering. Never again would the glory of the pharaohs shine. Egypt's wealth would be given to the Babylonians as a "reward" for carrying out God's will.

Chapter 29	Chapter 30	Chapter 31	Chapter 32
Egypt's Downfall	Egypt's Lament	Pharaoh's Downfall	Pharaoh's Lament
Judgment on Egypt			

 YOUR DAILY WALK God has always been in the business of working with the remnant, not the majority. Do you feel you're in the minority as a Christian? The next time you're tempted to say, "I'm a nobody . . . the church has so little influence . . . I'm insignificant," think about little Israel. Like Ezekiel, get your eyes off yourself and fix your focus on God. It will do wonders for your perspective!

 INSIGHT Tiny Nation, Great God

If you don't climb the mountain, you can't see the view.

The prophet has devoted a large section, fully one-sixth of his prophecy, to a denunciation of Israel's neighbors. It may seem strange to you that so much attention should be given to pagan countries in a book written to bring encouragement to God's people in exile.

Consider the relationship of Israel to the world around it. Compared to its neighbors, Israel was a tiny nation only a few thousand square miles in size. But by being located on the primary Near Eastern trade routes, Israel became significant to the foreign affairs of Assyria, Babylonia, Egypt and Persia.

Ezekiel's message to these great world powers is the same message God would proclaim to the nations today. The destiny of humankind does not rest in the control of kings and queens but in God alone. Secular historians may consider Israel of little consequence when compared with Babylonia and Egypt, the Soviet Union or the United States. But Ezekiel saw these world powers from God's perspective. Like specks of dust on the prophetic page, they would disappear from view, while God's program for his people lived on!

CHAPTER 29

In the tenth year, in the tenth month on the twelfth day, the word of the LORD came to me: ²"Son of man, set your face against Pharaoh king of Egypt and prophesy against him and against all Egypt. ³Speak to him and say: 'This is what the Sovereign LORD says:

" 'I am against you, Pharaoh king of
    Egypt,

you great monster lying among your
    streams.
You say, "The Nile is mine;
    I made it for myself."
⁴But I will put hooks in your jaws
    and make the fish of your streams
        stick to your scales.
I will pull you out from among your
    streams,
    with all the fish sticking to your
        scales.

⁵I will leave you in the desert,
 you and all the fish of your
  streams.
You will fall on the open field
 and not be gathered or picked up.
I will give you as food
 to the beasts of the earth and the
  birds of the air.

⁶Then all who live in Egypt will know that I am the LORD.

" 'You have been a staff of reed for the house of Israel. ⁷When they grasped you with their hands, you splintered and you tore open their shoulders; when they leaned on you, you broke and their backs were wrenched.ʳ

⁸" 'Therefore this is what the Sovereign LORD says: I will bring a sword against you and kill your men and their animals. ⁹Egypt will become a desolate wasteland. Then they will know that I am the LORD.

" 'Because you said, "The Nile is mine; I made it," ¹⁰therefore I am against you and against your streams, and I will make the land of Egypt a ruin and a desolate waste from Migdol to Aswan, as far as the border of Cush.ˢ ¹¹No foot of man or animal will pass through it; no one will live there for forty years. ¹²I will make the land of Egypt desolate among devastated lands, and her cities will lie desolate forty years among ruined cities. And I will disperse the Egyptians among the nations and scatter them through the countries.

¹³" 'Yet this is what the Sovereign LORD says: At the end of forty years I will gather the Egyptians from the nations where they were scattered. ¹⁴I will bring them back from captivity and return them to Upper Egypt,ᵗ the land of their ancestry. There they will be a lowly kingdom. ¹⁵It will be the lowliest of kingdoms and will never again exalt itself above the other nations. I will make it so weak that it will never again rule over the nations. ¹⁶Egypt will no longer be a source of confidence for the people of Israel but will be a reminder of their sin in turning to her for help. Then they will know that I am the Sovereign LORD.' "

¹⁷In the twenty-seventh year, in the first month on the first day, the word of the LORD came to me: ¹⁸"Son of man, Nebuchadnezzar king of Babylon drove his army in a hard campaign against Tyre; every head was rubbed bare and every shoulder made raw. Yet he and his army got no reward from the campaign he led against Tyre. ¹⁹Therefore this is what the Sovereign LORD says: I am going to give Egypt to Nebuchadnezzar king of Babylon, and he will carry off its wealth. He will loot and plunder the land as pay for his army. ²⁰I have given him Egypt as a reward for his efforts because he and his army did it for me, declares the Sovereign LORD. ²¹On that day I will make a hornᵘ grow for the house of Israel, and I will open your mouth among them. Then they will know that I am the LORD."

CHAPTER 30

The word of the LORD came to me: ²"Son of man, prophesy and say: 'This is what the Sovereign LORD says:

" 'Wail and say,
 "Alas for that day!"
³For the day is near,
 the day of the LORD is near—
a day of clouds,
 a time of doom for the nations.
⁴A sword will come against Egypt,
 and anguish will come upon
  Cush.ᵛ
When the slain fall in Egypt,
 her wealth will be carried away
 and her foundations torn down.

⁵Cush and Put, Lydia and all Arabia, Libyaʷ and the people of the covenant land will fall by the sword along with Egypt.

⁶" 'This is what the LORD says:

" 'The allies of Egypt will fall
 and her proud strength will fail.
From Migdol to Aswan
 they will fall by the sword within
  her,
    declares the Sovereign LORD.
⁷" 'They will be desolate
 among desolate lands,

ʳ7 Syriac (see also Septuagint and Vulgate); Hebrew *and you caused their backs to stand*   ˢ10 That is, the upper Nile region
ᵗ14 Hebrew *to Pathros*   ᵘ21 *Horn* here symbolizes strength.   ᵛ4 That is, the upper Nile region; also in verses 5 and 9
ʷ5 Hebrew *Cub*

and their cities will lie
    among ruined cities.
[8]Then they will know that I am the
    LORD,
    when I set fire to Egypt
    and all her helpers are crushed.

[9]" 'On that day messengers will go out
from me in ships to frighten Cush out of
her complacency. Anguish will take hold
of them on the day of Egypt's doom, for it
is sure to come.

[10]" 'This is what the Sovereign LORD
says:

" 'I will put an end to the hordes of
    Egypt
    by the hand of Nebuchadnezzar
    king of Babylon.
[11]He and his army—the most ruthless of
    nations—
    will be brought in to destroy the
    land.
They will draw their swords against
    Egypt
    and fill the land with the slain.
[12]I will dry up the streams of the Nile
    and sell the land to evil men;
    by the hand of foreigners
    I will lay waste the land and
    everything in it.

I the LORD have spoken.

[13]" 'This is what the Sovereign LORD
says:

" 'I will destroy the idols
    and put an end to the images in
    Memphis.[x]
No longer will there be a prince in
    Egypt,
    and I will spread fear throughout
    the land.
[14]I will lay waste Upper Egypt,[y]
    set fire to Zoan
    and inflict punishment on
    Thebes.[z]
[15]I will pour out my wrath on
    Pelusium,[a]
    the stronghold of Egypt,
    and cut off the hordes of
    Thebes.

[16]I will set fire to Egypt;
    Pelusium will writhe in agony.
Thebes will be taken by storm;
    Memphis will be in constant
    distress.
[17]The young men of Heliopolis[b] and
    Bubastis[c]
    will fall by the sword,
    and the cities themselves will go
    into captivity.
[18]Dark will be the day at Tahpanhes
    when I break the yoke of Egypt;
    there her proud strength will come
    to an end.
She will be covered with clouds,
    and her villages will go into
    captivity.
[19]So I will inflict punishment on
    Egypt,
    and they will know that I am the
    LORD.' "

[20]In the eleventh year, in the first month
on the seventh day, the word of the LORD
came to me: [21]"Son of man, I have broken
the arm of Pharaoh king of Egypt. It has
not been bound up for healing or put in a
splint so as to become strong enough to
hold a sword. [22]Therefore this is what the
Sovereign LORD says: I am against Pharaoh king of Egypt. I will break both his
arms, the good arm as well as the broken
one, and make the sword fall from his
hand. [23]I will disperse the Egyptians
among the nations and scatter them
through the countries. [24]I will strengthen
the arms of the king of Babylon and put
my sword in his hand, but I will break the
arms of Pharaoh, and he will groan before
him like a mortally wounded man. [25]I will
strengthen the arms of the king of Babylon, but the arms of Pharaoh will fall
limp. Then they will know that I am the
LORD, when I put my sword into the hand
of the king of Babylon and he brandishes
it against Egypt. [26]I will disperse the
Egyptians among the nations and scatter
them through the countries. Then they
will know that I am the LORD."

CHAPTER 31
In the eleventh year, in the third month
on the first day, the word of the LORD
came to me: [2]"Son of man, say to Pharaoh
king of Egypt and to his hordes:

---

[x]13 Hebrew *Noph*; also in verse 16   [y]14 Hebrew *waste Pathros*   [z]14 Hebrew *No*; also in verses 15 and 16   [a]15 Hebrew *Sin*;
also in verse 16   [b]17 Hebrew *Awen* (or *On*)   [c]17 Hebrew *Pi Beseth*

" 'Who can be compared with you in
    majesty?
³Consider Assyria, once a cedar in
    Lebanon,
  with beautiful branches
    overshadowing the forest;
  it towered on high,
    its top above the thick foliage.
⁴The waters nourished it,
    deep springs made it grow tall;
  their streams flowed
    all around its base
  and sent their channels
    to all the trees of the field.
⁵So it towered higher
    than all the trees of the field;
  its boughs increased
    and its branches grew long,
    spreading because of abundant
      waters.
⁶All the birds of the air
    nested in its boughs,
  all the beasts of the field
    gave birth under its branches;
  all the great nations
    lived in its shade.
⁷It was majestic in beauty,
    with its spreading boughs,
  for its roots went down
    to abundant waters.
⁸The cedars in the garden of God
    could not rival it,
  nor could the pine trees
    equal its boughs,
  nor could the plane trees
    compare with its branches—
  no tree in the garden of God
    could match its beauty.
⁹I made it beautiful
    with abundant branches,
  the envy of all the trees of Eden
    in the garden of God.

¹⁰" 'Therefore this is what the Sovereign
LORD says: Because it towered on high,
lifting its top above the thick foliage, and
because it was proud of its height, ¹¹I
handed it over to the ruler of the nations,
for him to deal with according to its
wickedness. I cast it aside, ¹²and the most
ruthless of foreign nations cut it down
and left it. Its boughs fell on the mountains and in all the valleys; its branches
lay broken in all the ravines of the land.
All the nations of the earth came out from

under its shade and left it. ¹³All the birds
of the air settled on the fallen tree, and
all the beasts of the field were among its
branches. ¹⁴Therefore no other trees by
the waters are ever to tower proudly on
high, lifting their tops above the thick foliage. No other trees so well-watered are
ever to reach such a height; they are all
destined for death, for the earth below,
among mortal men, with those who go
down to the pit.

¹⁵" 'This is what the Sovereign LORD
says: On the day it was brought down to
the grave^d I covered the deep springs
with mourning for it; I held back its
streams, and its abundant waters were
restrained. Because of it I clothed Lebanon with gloom, and all the trees of the
field withered away. ¹⁶I made the nations
tremble at the sound of its fall when I
brought it down to the grave with those
who go down to the pit. Then all the trees
of Eden, the choicest and best of Lebanon,
all the trees that were well-watered, were
consoled in the earth below. ¹⁷Those who
lived in its shade, its allies among the nations, had also gone down to the grave
with it, joining those killed by the
sword.

¹⁸" 'Which of the trees of Eden can be
compared with you in splendor and majesty? Yet you, too, will be brought down
with the trees of Eden to the earth below;
you will lie among the uncircumcised,
with those killed by the sword.

" 'This is Pharaoh and all his hordes,
declares the Sovereign LORD.' "

CHAPTER 32

In the twelfth year, in the twelfth month
on the first day, the word of the LORD
came to me: ²"Son of man, take up a lament concerning Pharaoh king of Egypt
and say to him:

" 'You are like a lion among the
    nations;
  you are like a monster in the
    seas
thrashing about in your streams,
  churning the water with your
    feet
  and muddying the streams.

³" 'This is what the Sovereign LORD says:

^d15 Hebrew *Sheol*; also in verses 16 and 17

" 'With a great throng of people
  I will cast my net over you,
  and they will haul you up in my
     net.
⁴I will throw you on the land
  and hurl you on the open field.
I will let all the birds of the air settle
     on you
  and all the beasts of the earth gorge
     themselves on you.
⁵I will spread your flesh on the
     mountains
  and fill the valleys with your
     remains.
⁶I will drench the land with your
     flowing blood
  all the way to the mountains,
  and the ravines will be filled with
     your flesh.
⁷When I snuff you out, I will cover the
     heavens
  and darken their stars;
I will cover the sun with a cloud,
  and the moon will not give its
     light.
⁸All the shining lights in the heavens
  I will darken over you;
  I will bring darkness over your land,
     declares the Sovereign LORD.
⁹I will trouble the hearts of many
     peoples
  when I bring about your destruction
     among the nations,
  among^e lands you have not known.
¹⁰I will cause many peoples to be
     appalled at you,
  and their kings will shudder with
     horror because of you
  when I brandish my sword before
     them.
On the day of your downfall
  each of them will tremble
  every moment for his life.

¹¹" 'For this is what the Sovereign LORD
says:

" 'The sword of the king of Babylon
  will come against you.
¹²I will cause your hordes to fall
  by the swords of mighty men—
  the most ruthless of all nations.
They will shatter the pride of Egypt,
  and all her hordes will be
     overthrown.

¹³I will destroy all her cattle
  from beside abundant waters
  no longer to be stirred by the foot of
     man
  or muddied by the hoofs of cattle.
¹⁴Then I will let her waters settle
  and make her streams flow like oil,
     declares the Sovereign LORD.
¹⁵When I make Egypt desolate
  and strip the land of everything in
     it,
  when I strike down all who live
     there,
  then they will know that I am the
     LORD.'

¹⁶"This is the lament they will chant for her. The daughters of the nations will chant it; for Egypt and all her hordes they will chant it, declares the Sovereign LORD."

¹⁷In the twelfth year, on the fifteenth day of the month, the word of the LORD came to me: ¹⁸"Son of man, wail for the hordes of Egypt and consign to the earth below both her and the daughters of mighty nations, with those who go down to the pit. ¹⁹Say to them, 'Are you more favored than others? Go down and be laid among the uncircumcised.' ²⁰They will fall among those killed by the sword. The sword is drawn; let her be dragged off with all her hordes. ²¹From within the grave^f the mighty leaders will say of Egypt and her allies, 'They have come down and they lie with the uncircumcised, with those killed by the sword.'

²²"Assyria is there with her whole army; she is surrounded by the graves of all her slain, all who have fallen by the sword. ²³Their graves are in the depths of the pit and her army lies around her grave. All who had spread terror in the land of the living are slain, fallen by the sword.

²⁴"Elam is there, with all her hordes around her grave. All of them are slain, fallen by the sword. All who had spread terror in the land of the living went down uncircumcised to the earth below. They bear their shame with those who go down to the pit. ²⁵A bed is made for her among the slain, with all her hordes around her grave. All of them are uncircumcised,

---

^e9 Hebrew; Septuagint *bring you into captivity among the nations,* / *to*   ^f21 Hebrew *Sheol*; also in verse 27 killed by the sword. Because their terror had spread in the land of the living, they bear their shame with those who go down to the pit; they are laid among the slain.

²⁶"Meshech and Tubal are there, with all their hordes around their graves. All of them are uncircumcised, killed by the sword because they spread their terror in the land of the living. ²⁷Do they not lie with the other uncircumcised warriors who have fallen, who went down to the grave with their weapons of war, whose swords were placed under their heads? The punishment for their sins rested on their bones, though the terror of these warriors had stalked through the land of the living.

²⁸"You too, O Pharaoh, will be broken and will lie among the uncircumcised, with those killed by the sword.

²⁹"Edom is there, her kings and all her princes; despite their power, they are laid with those killed by the sword. They lie with the uncircumcised, with those who go down to the pit.

³⁰"All the princes of the north and all the Sidonians are there; they went down with the slain in disgrace despite the terror caused by their power. They lie uncircumcised with those killed by the sword and bear their shame with those who go down to the pit.

³¹"Pharaoh—he and all his army—will see them and he will be consoled for all his hordes that were killed by the sword, declares the Sovereign LORD. ³²Although I had him spread terror in the land of the living, Pharaoh and all his hordes will be laid among the uncircumcised, with those killed by the sword, declares the Sovereign LORD."

AUGUST 23 □ DAY 236
EZEKIEL 33–36
Watchman on the Wall

 OVERVIEW The fall of Jerusalem brings a significant shift in the focus of the prophet's message. Up to this point Ezekiel has declared coming calamity for Jerusalem's citizens (Ezekiel 1–32). But now he looks ahead to the day of coming comfort for Babylon's captives (Ezekiel 33–48). God is preparing a time of consolation—a time when he will regather, restore and refresh his covenant people. Though the nation is presently experiencing groaning, there is coming a day of glory when even the mountains and hills, rivers and valleys will declare the greatness of the God of Israel.

Chapter 33	Chapter 34	Chapter 35	Chapter 36
Watchman on the Wall	Shepherds and Sheep	Edom's Doom	Israel's Delight
Duty	Denunciation	Calamity	Cleansing

 YOUR DAILY WALK Can you think of a promise you made to someone during the past month and then failed to keep?

Can you think of a promise someone made to you and then went back on?

One thing you can give and still keep is your word.

Can you think of a promise God made to you and then forgot about or failed to fulfill?

There is a wonderful *promise about promises* stated in Numbers 23:19 and illustrated in Ezekiel 33–36. "God is not a man, that he should lie." God is not fickle or vacillating in keeping his Word. When he states, "This is what the Sovereign LORD says," you can stake your life on it—every time!

Are you ready to become a prospector for the promises of God? Then here are some nuggets of gold to get you started. But be careful. Collecting and claiming God's promises can be contagious!

Matthew 6:14; 7:7–8   Philippians 1:6; 4:6–7, 13
Luke 6:38   James 1:12; 4:7–8; 5:16
John 14:2–3

 INSIGHT Where There's a "Will," There's a Promise!
At least twenty-one times in chapter 36 God declares, "I will [do something]" on behalf of his covenant people. Take two minutes and see how many of the twenty-one you can discover for yourself.

CHAPTER 33

The word of the LORD came to me: ²"Son of man, speak to your countrymen and say to them: 'When I bring the sword against a land, and the people of the land choose one of their men and make him their watchman, ³and he sees the sword coming against the land and blows the trumpet to warn the people, ⁴then if anyone hears the trumpet but does not take warning and the sword comes and takes his life, his blood will be on his own head. ⁵Since he heard the sound of the trumpet but did not take warning, his blood will be on his own head. If he had taken warning, he would have saved himself. ⁶But if the watchman sees the sword coming and does not blow the trumpet to warn the people and the sword comes and takes the life of one of them, that man will be taken away because of his sin, but I will hold the watchman accountable for his blood.'

⁷"Son of man, I have made you a watchman for the house of Israel; so hear the word I speak and give them warning from me. ⁸When I say to the wicked, 'O wicked man, you will surely die,' and you do not speak out to dissuade him from his ways, that wicked man will die for⁸ his sin, and I will hold you accountable for his blood. ⁹But if you do warn the wicked man to turn from his ways and he does not do so, he will die for his sin, but you will have saved yourself.

¹⁰"Son of man, say to the house of Israel, 'This is what you are saying: "Our offenses and sins weigh us down, and we are wasting away because of ʰ them. How then can we live?" ' ¹¹Say to them, 'As surely as I live, declares the Sovereign LORD, I take no pleasure in the death of the wicked, but rather that they turn from their ways and live. Turn! Turn from your evil ways! Why will you die, O house of Israel?'

¹²"Therefore, son of man, say to your countrymen, 'The righteousness of the righteous man will not save him when he disobeys, and the wickedness of the wicked man will not cause him to fall when he turns from it. The righteous man, if he sins, will not be allowed to live because of his former righteousness.' ¹³If I tell the righteous man that he will surely live, but then he trusts in his righteousness and does evil, none of the righteous things he has done will be remembered; he will die for the evil he has done. ¹⁴And if I say to the wicked man, 'You will surely die,' but he then turns away from his sin and does what is just and right— ¹⁵if he gives back what he took in pledge for a loan, returns what he has stolen, follows the decrees that give life, and does no evil, he will surely live; he will not die. ¹⁶None of the sins he has committed will be remembered against him. He has done what is just and right; he will surely live.

¹⁷"Yet your countrymen say, 'The way of the Lord is not just.' But it is their way that is not just. ¹⁸If a righteous man turns from his righteousness and does evil, he will die for it. ¹⁹And if a wicked man turns away from his wickedness and does what is just and right, he will live by doing so. ²⁰Yet, O house of Israel, you say, 'The way of the Lord is not just.' But I will judge each of you according to his own ways."

²¹In the twelfth year of our exile, in the tenth month on the fifth day, a man who had escaped from Jerusalem came to me and said, "The city has fallen!" ²²Now the evening before the man arrived, the hand of the LORD was upon me, and he opened

⁸8 Or *in;* also in verse 9   ʰ10 Or *away in*

my mouth before the man came to me in the morning. So my mouth was opened and I was no longer silent.

23Then the word of the LORD came to me: 24"Son of man, the people living in those ruins in the land of Israel are saying, 'Abraham was only one man, yet he possessed the land. But we are many; surely the land has been given to us as our possession.' 25Therefore say to them, 'This is what the Sovereign LORD says: Since you eat meat with the blood still in it and look to your idols and shed blood, should you then possess the land? 26You rely on your sword, you do detestable things, and each of you defiles his neighbor's wife. Should you then possess the land?'

27"Say this to them: 'This is what the Sovereign LORD says: As surely as I live, those who are left in the ruins will fall by the sword, those out in the country I will give to the wild animals to be devoured, and those in strongholds and caves will die of a plague. 28I will make the land a desolate waste, and her proud strength will come to an end, and the mountains of Israel will become desolate so that no one will cross them. 29Then they will know that I am the LORD, when I have made the land a desolate waste because of all the detestable things they have done.'

30"As for you, son of man, your countrymen are talking together about you by the walls and at the doors of the houses, saying to each other, 'Come and hear the message that has come from the LORD.' 31My people come to you, as they usually do, and sit before you to listen to your words, but they do not put them into practice. With their mouths they express devotion, but their hearts are greedy for unjust gain. 32Indeed, to them you are nothing more than one who sings love songs with a beautiful voice and plays an instrument well, for they hear your words but do not put them into practice.

33"When all this comes true—and it surely will—then they will know that a prophet has been among them."

CHAPTER 34

The word of the LORD came to me: 2"Son of man, prophesy against the shepherds of Israel; prophesy and say to them: 'This is what the Sovereign LORD says: Woe to the shepherds of Israel who only take care of themselves! Should not shepherds take

care of the flock? 3You eat the curds, clothe yourselves with the wool and slaughter the choice animals, but you do not take care of the flock. 4You have not strengthened the weak or healed the sick or bound up the injured. You have not brought back the strays or searched for the lost. You have ruled them harshly and brutally. 5So they were scattered because there was no shepherd, and when they were scattered they became food for all the wild animals. 6My sheep wandered over all the mountains and on every high hill. They were scattered over the whole earth, and no one searched or looked for them.

7" 'Therefore, you shepherds, hear the word of the LORD: 8As surely as I live, declares the Sovereign LORD, because my flock lacks a shepherd and so has been plundered and has become food for all the wild animals, and because my shepherds did not search for my flock but cared for themselves rather than for my flock, 9therefore, O shepherds, hear the word of the LORD: 10This is what the Sovereign LORD says: I am against the shepherds and will hold them accountable for my flock. I will remove them from tending the flock so that the shepherds can no longer feed themselves. I will rescue my flock from their mouths, and it will no longer be food for them.

11" 'For this is what the Sovereign LORD says: I myself will search for my sheep and look after them. 12As a shepherd looks after his scattered flock when he is with them, so will I look after my sheep. I will rescue them from all the places where they were scattered on a day of clouds and darkness. 13I will bring them out from the nations and gather them from the countries, and I will bring them into their own land. I will pasture them on the mountains of Israel, in the ravines and in all the settlements in the land. 14I will tend them in a good pasture, and the mountain heights of Israel will be their grazing land. There they will lie down in good grazing land, and there they will feed in a rich pasture on the mountains of Israel. 15I myself will tend my sheep and have them lie down, declares the Sovereign LORD. 16I will search for the lost and bring back the strays. I will bind up the injured and strengthen the weak, but the sleek and the strong I will destroy. I will shepherd the flock with justice.

17" 'As for you, my flock, this is what the Sovereign LORD says: I will judge between one sheep and another, and between rams and goats. 18Is it not enough for you to feed on the good pasture? Must you also trample the rest of your pasture with your feet? Is it not enough for you to drink clear water? Must you also muddy the rest with your feet? 19Must my flock feed on what you have trampled and drink what you have muddied with your feet?

20" 'Therefore this is what the Sovereign LORD says to them: See, I myself will judge between the fat sheep and the lean sheep. 21Because you shove with flank and shoulder, butting all the weak sheep with your horns until you have driven them away, 22I will save my flock, and they will no longer be plundered. I will judge between one sheep and another. 23I will place over them one shepherd, my servant David, and he will tend them; he will tend them and be their shepherd. 24I the LORD will be their God, and my servant David will be prince among them. I the LORD have spoken.

25" 'I will make a covenant of peace with them and rid the land of wild beasts so that they may live in the desert and sleep in the forests in safety. 26I will bless them and the places surrounding my hill.*i* I will send down showers in season; there will be showers of blessing. 27The trees of the field will yield their fruit and the ground will yield its crops; the people will be secure in their land. They will know that I am the LORD, when I break the bars of their yoke and rescue them from the hands of those who enslaved them. 28They will no longer be plundered by the nations, nor will wild animals devour them. They will live in safety, and no one will make them afraid. 29I will provide for them a land renowned for its crops, and they will no longer be victims of famine in the land or bear the scorn of the nations. 30Then they will know that I, the LORD their God, am with them and that they, the house of Israel, are my people, declares the Sovereign LORD. 31You my sheep, the sheep of my pasture, are peo-

ple, and I am your God, declares the Sovereign LORD.' "

CHAPTER 35

The word of the LORD came to me: 2"Son of man, set your face against Mount Seir; prophesy against it 3and say: 'This is what the Sovereign LORD says: I am against you, Mount Seir, and I will stretch out my hand against you and make you a desolate waste. 4I will turn your towns into ruins and you will be desolate. Then you will know that I am the LORD.

5" 'Because you harbored an ancient hostility and delivered the Israelites over to the sword at the time of their calamity, the time their punishment reached its climax, 6therefore as surely as I live, declares the Sovereign LORD, I will give you over to bloodshed and it will pursue you. Since you did not hate bloodshed, bloodshed will pursue you. 7I will make Mount Seir a desolate waste and cut off from it all who come and go. 8I will fill your mountains with the slain; those killed by the sword will fall on your hills and in your valleys and in all your ravines. 9I will make you desolate forever; your towns will not be inhabited. Then you will know that I am the LORD.

10" 'Because you have said, "These two nations and countries will be ours and we will take possession of them," even though I the LORD was there, 11therefore as surely as I live, declares the Sovereign LORD, I will treat you in accordance with the anger and jealousy you showed in your hatred of them and I will make myself known among them when I judge you. 12Then you will know that I the LORD have heard all the contemptible things you have said against the mountains of Israel. You said, "They have been laid waste and have been given over to us to devour." 13You boasted against me and spoke against me without restraint, and I heard it. 14This is what the Sovereign LORD says: While the whole earth rejoices, I will make you desolate. 15Because you rejoiced when the inheritance of the house of Israel became desolate, that is how I will treat you. You will be desolate, O Mount Seir, you and all of Edom. Then they will know that I am the LORD.' "

---

*i*26 Or *I will make them and the places surrounding my hill a blessing*

CHAPTER 36

"Son of man, prophesy to the mountains of Israel and say, 'O mountains of Israel, hear the word of the LORD. ²This is what the Sovereign LORD says: The enemy said of you, "Aha! The ancient heights have become our possession." ' ³Therefore prophesy and say, 'This is what the Sovereign LORD says: Because they ravaged and hounded you from every side so that you became the possession of the rest of the nations and the object of people's malicious talk and slander, ⁴therefore, O mountains of Israel, hear the word of the Sovereign LORD: This is what the Sovereign LORD says to the mountains and hills, to the ravines and valleys, to the desolate ruins and the deserted towns that have been plundered and ridiculed by the rest of the nations around you— ⁵this is what the Sovereign LORD says: In my burning zeal I have spoken against the rest of the nations, and against all Edom, for with glee and with malice in their hearts they made my land their own possession so that they might plunder its pastureland.' ⁶Therefore prophesy concerning the land of Israel and say to the mountains and hills, to the ravines and valleys: 'This is what the Sovereign LORD says: I speak in my jealous wrath because you have suffered the scorn of the nations. ⁷Therefore this is what the Sovereign LORD says: I swear with uplifted hand that the nations around you will also suffer scorn.

⁸" 'But you, O mountains of Israel, will produce branches and fruit for my people Israel, for they will soon come home. ⁹I am concerned for you and will look on you with favor; you will be plowed and sown, ¹⁰and I will multiply the number of people upon you, even the whole house of Israel. The towns will be inhabited and the ruins rebuilt. ¹¹I will increase the number of men and animals upon you, and they will be fruitful and become numerous. I will settle people on you as in the past and will make you prosper more than before. Then you will know that I am the LORD. ¹²I will cause people, my people Israel, to walk upon you. They will possess you, and you will be their inheritance; you will never again deprive them of their children.

¹³" 'This is what the Sovereign LORD says: Because people say to you, "You devour men and deprive your nation of its children," ¹⁴therefore you will no longer devour men or make your nation childless, declares the Sovereign LORD. ¹⁵No longer will I make you hear the taunts of the nations, and no longer will you suffer the scorn of the peoples or cause your nation to fall, declares the Sovereign LORD.' "

¹⁶Again the word of the LORD came to me: ¹⁷"Son of man, when the people of Israel were living in their own land, they defiled it by their conduct and their actions. Their conduct was like a woman's monthly uncleanness in my sight. ¹⁸So I poured out my wrath on them because they had shed blood in the land and because they had defiled it with their idols. ¹⁹I dispersed them among the nations, and they were scattered through the countries; I judged them according to their conduct and their actions. ²⁰And wherever they went among the nations they profaned my holy name, for it was said of them, 'These are the LORD's people, and yet they had to leave his land.' ²¹I had concern for my holy name, which the house of Israel profaned among the nations where they had gone.

²²"Therefore say to the house of Israel, 'This is what the Sovereign LORD says: It is not for your sake, O house of Israel, that I am going to do these things, but for the sake of my holy name, which you have profaned among the nations where you have gone. ²³I will show the holiness of my great name, which has been profaned among the nations, the name you have profaned among them. Then the nations will know that I am the LORD, declares the Sovereign LORD, when I show myself holy through you before their eyes.

²⁴" 'For I will take you out of the nations; I will gather you from all the countries and bring you back into your own land. ²⁵I will sprinkle clean water on you, and you will be clean; I will cleanse you from all your impurities and from all your idols. ²⁶I will give you a new heart and put a new spirit in you; I will remove from you your heart of stone and give you a heart of flesh. ²⁷And I will put my Spirit in you and move you to follow my decrees and be careful to keep my laws. ²⁸You will live in the land I gave your forefathers; you will be my people, and I will be your God. ²⁹I will save you from all your uncleanness. I will call for the

grain and make it plentiful and will not bring famine upon you. [30]I will increase the fruit of the trees and the crops of the field, so that you will no longer suffer disgrace among the nations because of famine. [31]Then you will remember your evil ways and wicked deeds, and you will loathe yourselves for your sins and detestable practices. [32]I want you to know that I am not doing this for your sake, declares the Sovereign LORD. Be ashamed and disgraced for your conduct, O house of Israel!

[33]" 'This is what the Sovereign LORD says: On the day I cleanse you from all your sins, I will resettle your towns, and the ruins will be rebuilt. [34]The desolate land will be cultivated instead of lying desolate in the sight of all who pass through it. [35]They will say, "This land that was laid waste has become like the garden of Eden; the cities that were lying in ruins, desolate and destroyed, are now fortified and inhabited." [36]Then the nations around you that remain will know that I the LORD have rebuilt what was destroyed and have replanted what was desolate. I the LORD have spoken, and I will do it.'

[37]"This is what the Sovereign LORD says: Once again I will yield to the plea of the house of Israel and do this for them: I will make their people as numerous as sheep, [38]as numerous as the flocks for offerings at Jerusalem during her appointed feasts. So will the ruined cities be filled with flocks of people. Then they will know that I am the LORD."

AUGUST 24 ☐ DAY 237
EZEKIEL 37–39
Gog and Magog

OVERVIEW Even if you have never read it, you have probably sung about it: "The foot bone's connected to the ankle bone; the ankle bone's connected to the leg bone . . ." Today you will read about Ezekiel's well-known vision of the valley of dry bones in chapter 37. This vision summarizes the entire message of the book. The dry bones symbolize the spiritual condition of the nation as the people languish in captivity. But even in the bleak valley of judgment, there is hope. As Ezekiel looks on, the bones begin to join themselves together, a picture of the future restoration of the nation. God will again breathe life into his people. Their present deadness because of sin and judgment will give way to future life as the nation is regathered.

Chapter 37	Chapter 38	Chapter 39
Valley of Dry Bones	Victory over Gog	
	The Attack	The Annihilation
Restoration	Rescue	

YOUR DAILY WALK Have you ever composed a spiritual autobiography? There was a time when you, like those dead, dry bones in Ezekiel's vision, had no life, no hope, no purpose for living. But if you know Christ, there was a point at which he picked you up, put the pieces of your life together again, clothed you with his righteousness and breathed into you the breath of spiritual life. From that day forward you have been a different person. You have been spiritually alive—a person with limitless hope for the future.

Many problems, like storms, never arrive in spite of threatening skies.

Take time today to write out a three-minute testimony of your spiritual pilgrimage: your life before you met Christ, the way in which you met Christ and your life since you met Christ. Then share your "literary masterpiece" with your Sunday school class, your pastor or a close Christian friend. You'll be surprised at how encouraged others will be upon reading your spiritual autobiography! (For an added challenge, share it with an unsaved friend or neighbor and watch what happens!)

If you can't yet write a spiritual autobiography, ask a Christian friend to share his or hers with you . . . and to help you take the first step in creating one of your own.

 INSIGHT Magog and a Cast of Thousands
Ezekiel describes an alliance between Magog (a great power from the north, 38:15) and Persia (Iran), Ethiopia, Libya, Gomer (Ukraine) and Beth-togarmah (southeast of the Black Sea). See Genesis 10 for the historical roots of these different nations.

CHAPTER 37

The hand of the LORD was upon me, and he brought me out by the Spirit of the LORD and set me in the middle of a valley; it was full of bones. ²He led me back and forth among them, and I saw a great many bones on the floor of the valley, bones that were very dry. ³He asked me, "Son of man, can these bones live?"

I said, "O Sovereign LORD, you alone know."

⁴Then he said to me, "Prophesy to these bones and say to them, 'Dry bones, hear the word of the LORD! ⁵This is what the Sovereign LORD says to these bones: I will make breathʲ enter you, and you will come to life. ⁶I will attach tendons to you and make flesh come upon you and cover you with skin; I will put breath in you, and you will come to life. Then you will know that I am the LORD.' "

⁷So I prophesied as I was commanded. And as I was prophesying, there was a noise, a rattling sound, and the bones came together, bone to bone. ⁸I looked, and tendons and flesh appeared on them and skin covered them, but there was no breath in them.

⁹Then he said to me, "Prophesy to the breath; prophesy, son of man, and say to it, 'This is what the Sovereign LORD says: Come from the four winds, O breath, and breathe into these slain, that they may live.' " ¹⁰So I prophesied as he commanded me, and breath entered them; they came to life and stood up on their feet—a vast army.

¹¹Then he said to me: "Son of man, these bones are the whole house of Israel. They say, 'Our bones are dried up and our hope is gone; we are cut off.' ¹²Therefore

prophesy and say to them: 'This is what the Sovereign LORD says: O my people, I am going to open your graves and bring you up from them; I will bring you back to the land of Israel. ¹³Then you, my people, will know that I am the LORD, when I open your graves and bring you up from them. ¹⁴I will put my Spirit in you and you will live, and I will settle you in your own land. Then you will know that I the LORD have spoken, and I have done it, declares the LORD.' "

¹⁵The word of the LORD came to me: ¹⁶"Son of man, take a stick of wood and write on it, 'Belonging to Judah and the Israelites associated with him.' Then take another stick of wood, and write on it, 'Ephraim's stick, belonging to Joseph and all the house of Israel associated with him.' ¹⁷Join them together into one stick so that they will become one in your hand.

¹⁸"When your countrymen ask you, 'Won't you tell us what you mean by this?' ¹⁹say to them, 'This is what the Sovereign LORD says: I am going to take the stick of Joseph—which is in Ephraim's hand—and of the Israelite tribes associated with him, and join it to Judah's stick, making them a single stick of wood, and they will become one in my hand.' ²⁰Hold before their eyes the sticks you have written on ²¹and say to them, 'This is what the Sovereign LORD says: I will take the Israelites out of the nations where they have gone. I will gather them from all around and bring them back into their own land. ²²I will make them one nation in the land, on the mountains of Israel. There will be one king over all of them and they will never again be two nations or be divided

ʲ5 The Hebrew for this word can also mean *wind* or *spirit* (see verses 6-14).

into two kingdoms. [23]They will no longer defile themselves with their idols and vile images or with any of their offenses, for I will save them from all their sinful backsliding,[k] and I will cleanse them. They will be my people, and I will be their God. [24]" 'My servant David will be king over them, and they will all have one shepherd. They will follow my laws and be careful to keep my decrees. [25]They will live in the land I gave to my servant Jacob, the land where your fathers lived. They and their children and their children's children will live there forever, and David my servant will be their prince forever. [26]I will make a covenant of peace with them; it will be an everlasting covenant. I will establish them and increase their numbers, and I will put my sanctuary among them forever. [27]My dwelling place will be with them; I will be their God, and they will be my people. [28]Then the nations will know that I the LORD make Israel holy, when my sanctuary is among them forever.' "

CHAPTER 38

The word of the LORD came to me: [2]"Son of man, set your face against Gog, of the land of Magog, the chief prince of[l] Meshech and Tubal; prophesy against him [3]and say: 'This is what the Sovereign LORD says: I am against you, O Gog, chief prince of[m] Meshech and Tubal. [4]I will turn you around, put hooks in your jaws and bring you out with your whole army—your horses, your horsemen fully armed, and a great horde with large and small shields, all of them brandishing their swords. [5]Persia, Cush[n] and Put will be with them, all with shields and helmets, [6]also Gomer with all its troops, and Beth Togarmah from the far north with all its troops—the many nations with you.

[7]" 'Get ready; be prepared, you and all the hordes gathered about you, and take command of them. [8]After many days you will be called to arms. In future years you will invade a land that has recovered from war, whose people were gathered from many nations to the mountains of Israel, which had long been desolate. They had been brought out from the nations, and now all of them live in safety. [9]You and all your troops and the many

nations with you will go up, advancing like a storm; you will be like a cloud covering the land.

[10]" 'This is what the Sovereign LORD says: On that day thoughts will come into your mind and you will devise an evil scheme. [11]You will say, "I will invade a land of unwalled villages; I will attack a peaceful and unsuspecting people—all of them living without walls and without gates and bars. [12]I will plunder and loot and turn my hand against the resettled ruins and the people gathered from the nations, rich in livestock and goods, living at the center of the land." [13]Sheba and Dedan and the merchants of Tarshish and all her villages[o] will say to you, "Have you come to plunder? Have you gathered your hordes to loot, to carry off silver and gold, to take away livestock and goods and to seize much plunder?" '

[14]"Therefore, son of man, prophesy and say to Gog: 'This is what the Sovereign LORD says: In that day, when my people Israel are living in safety, will you not take notice of it? [15]You will come from your place in the far north, you and many nations with you, all of them riding on horses, a great horde, a mighty army. [16]You will advance against my people Israel like a cloud that covers the land. In days to come, O Gog, I will bring you against my land, so that the nations may know me when I show myself holy through you before their eyes.

[17]" 'This is what the Sovereign LORD says: Are you not the one I spoke of in former days by my servants the prophets of Israel? At that time they prophesied for years that I would bring you against them. [18]This is what will happen in that day: When Gog attacks the land of Israel, my hot anger will be aroused, declares the Sovereign LORD. [19]In my zeal and fiery wrath I declare that at that time there shall be a great earthquake in the land of Israel. [20]The fish of the sea, the birds of the air, the beasts of the field, every creature that moves along the ground, and all the people on the face of the earth will tremble at my presence. The mountains will be overturned, the cliffs will crumble and every wall will fall to the ground. [21]I will summon a sword against Gog on all my mountains, declares the Sovereign

---

[k]23 Many Hebrew manuscripts (see also Septuagint); most Hebrew manuscripts *all their dwelling places where they sinned* [l]2 Or *the prince of Rosh,* [m]3 Or *Gog, prince of Rosh,* [n]5 That is, the upper Nile region [o]13 Or *her strong lions*

LORD. Every man's sword will be against his brother. [22]I will execute judgment upon him with plague and bloodshed; I will pour down torrents of rain, hailstones and burning sulfur on him and on his troops and on the many nations with him. [23]And so I will show my greatness and my holiness, and I will make myself known in the sight of many nations. Then they will know that I am the LORD.'

CHAPTER 39

"Son of man, prophesy against Gog and say: 'This is what the Sovereign LORD says: I am against you, O Gog, chief prince of[p] Meshech and Tubal. [2]I will turn you around and drag you along. I will bring you from the far north and send you against the mountains of Israel. [3]Then I will strike your bow from your left hand and make your arrows drop from your right hand. [4]On the mountains of Israel you will fall, you and all your troops and the nations with you. I will give you as food to all kinds of carrion birds and to the wild animals. [5]You will fall in the open field, for I have spoken, declares the Sovereign LORD. [6]I will send fire on Magog and on those who live in safety in the coastlands, and they will know that I am the LORD.

[7]" 'I will make known my holy name among my people Israel. I will no longer let my holy name be profaned, and the nations will know that I the LORD am the Holy One in Israel. [8]It is coming! It will surely take place, declares the Sovereign LORD. This is the day I have spoken of.

[9]" 'Then those who live in the towns of Israel will go out and use the weapons for fuel and burn them up—the small and large shields, the bows and arrows, the war clubs and spears. For seven years they will use them for fuel. [10]They will not need to gather wood from the fields or cut it from the forests, because they will use the weapons for fuel. And they will plunder those who plundered them and loot those who looted them, declares the Sovereign LORD.

[11]" 'On that day I will give Gog a burial place in Israel, in the valley of those who travel east toward[q] the Sea.[r] It will block the way of travelers, because Gog and all his hordes will be buried there.

So it will be called the Valley of Hamon Gog.[s]

[12]" 'For seven months the house of Israel will be burying them in order to cleanse the land. [13]All the people of the land will bury them, and the day I am glorified will be a memorable day for them, declares the Sovereign LORD.

[14]" 'Men will be regularly employed to cleanse the land. Some will go throughout the land and, in addition to them, others will bury those that remain on the ground. At the end of the seven months they will begin their search. [15]As they go through the land and one of them sees a human bone, he will set up a marker beside it until the gravediggers have buried it in the Valley of Hamon Gog. [16](Also a town called Hamonah[t] will be there.) And so they will cleanse the land.'

[17]"Son of man, this is what the Sovereign LORD says: Call out to every kind of bird and all the wild animals: 'Assemble and come together from all around to the sacrifice I am preparing for you, the great sacrifice on the mountains of Israel. There you will eat flesh and drink blood. [18]You will eat the flesh of mighty men and drink the blood of the princes of the earth as if they were rams and lambs, goats and bulls—all of them fattened animals from Bashan. [19]At the sacrifice I am preparing for you, you will eat fat till you are glutted and drink blood till you are drunk. [20]At my table you will eat your fill of horses and riders, mighty men and soldiers of every kind,' declares the Sovereign LORD.

[21]"I will display my glory among the nations, and all the nations will see the punishment I inflict and the hand I lay upon them. [22]From that day forward the house of Israel will know that I am the LORD their God. [23]And the nations will know that the people of Israel went into exile for their sin, because they were unfaithful to me. So I hid my face from them and handed them over to their enemies, and they all fell by the sword. [24]I dealt with them according to their uncleanness and their offenses, and I hid my face from them.

[25]"Therefore this is what the Sovereign LORD says: I will now bring Jacob back from captivity[u] and will have compas-

sion on all the people of Israel, and I will be zealous for my holy name. ²⁶They will forget their shame and all the unfaithfulness they showed toward me when they lived in safety in their land with no one to make them afraid. ²⁷When I have brought them back from the nations and have gathered them from the countries of their enemies, I will show myself holy through them in the sight of many nations. ²⁸Then they will know that I am the LORD their God, for though I sent them into exile among the nations, I will gather them to their own land, not leaving any behind. ²⁹I will no longer hide my face from them, for I will pour out my Spirit on the house of Israel, declares the Sovereign LORD."

AUGUST 25 ☐ DAY 238
EZEKIEL 40–43
New Temple for Israel

OVERVIEW Twenty years earlier, Ezekiel had been transported to Jerusalem in a vision to pronounce its doom (8:1–3). He now returns in a vision to the destroyed city to proclaim its reconstruction. Like a precise architect, Ezekiel carefully measures and records the dimensions and details. But his joy over the thought of a rebuilt temple pales in comparison with the thrill of seeing the glory of God, long since departed (11:23), now return to take up residence in the temple's Most Holy Place.

Chapters 40–41	Chapter 42	Chapter 43
Temple Courts and Gates	Temple Rooms	Temple Consecration
Blueprint for Ezekiel's Temple		Glory in Ezekiel's Temple

YOUR DAILY WALK God has always desired to dwell in the midst of his people. Prove that to yourself!

In the Garden of Eden, what was God doing in the cool of the day (Genesis 3:8)?

It's when we rub shoulders with someone that we discover what that person has up his or her sleeve.

When the tabernacle was completed, what happened to show that God was there (Exodus 40:34–35)?

When Solomon's temple was finished, where was God to be found (2 Chronicles 7:1–3)?

And what does 1 Corinthians 6:19–20 say about the temple (tabernacle, abode) of God today?

God's presence is once again abiding in the midst of his people. In the Old Testament tabernacle and temple it was plain for all to see. Could that be said of your life as well? As you read the blueprint of Ezekiel's temple, map out another blueprint. You could call this one "The blueprint for making a part of my life a showcase for God's glory today." Your tongue, temper, work habits, leisure time—each can show forth God's glory.

INSIGHT The Significance of Mountains
Ezekiel's vision was on a mountain. The giving of the Law to Moses, the Sermon on the Mount, the transfiguration and the Great Commission all occurred on mountains. These and other events point us toward the time when Jesus will reign and the mountain of the Lord's house will be supreme (Isaiah 2:2). Can you think of at least two other

mountains mentioned in the Bible that are associated with significant events?

CHAPTER 40

In the twenty-fifth year of our exile, at the beginning of the year, on the tenth of the month, in the fourteenth year after the fall of the city—on that very day the hand of the LORD was upon me and he took me there. [2]In visions of God he took me to the land of Israel and set me on a very high mountain, on whose south side were some buildings that looked like a city. [3]He took me there, and I saw a man whose appearance was like bronze; he was standing in the gateway with a linen cord and a measuring rod in his hand. [4]The man said to me, "Son of man, look with your eyes and hear with your ears and pay attention to everything I am going to show you, for that is why you have been brought here. Tell the house of Israel everything you see."

[5]I saw a wall completely surrounding the temple area. The length of the measuring rod in the man's hand was six long cubits, each of which was a cubit[v] and a handbreadth.[w] He measured the wall; it was one measuring rod thick and one rod high.

[6]Then he went to the gate facing east. He climbed its steps and measured the threshold of the gate; it was one rod deep.[x] [7]The alcoves for the guards were one rod long and one rod wide, and the projecting walls between the alcoves were five cubits thick. And the threshold of the gate next to the portico facing the temple was one rod deep.

[8]Then he measured the portico of the gateway; [9]it[y] was eight cubits deep and its jambs were two cubits thick. The portico of the gateway faced the temple.

[10]Inside the east gate were three alcoves on each side; the three had the same measurements, and the faces of the projecting walls on each side had the same measurements. [11]Then he measured the width of the entrance to the gateway; it was ten cubits and its length was thirteen cubits. [12]In front of each alcove was a wall one cubit high, and the alcoves were six cubits square. [13]Then he measured the gateway from the top of the rear wall of one alcove to the top of the opposite one; the distance was twenty-five cubits from one parapet opening to the opposite one. [14]He measured along the faces of the projecting walls all around the inside of the gateway—sixty cubits. The measurement was up to the portico[z] facing the courtyard.[a] [15]The distance from the entrance of the gateway to the far end of its portico was fifty cubits. [16]The alcoves and the projecting walls inside the gateway were surmounted by narrow parapet openings all around, as was the portico; the openings all around faced inward. The faces of the projecting walls were decorated with palm trees.

[17]Then he brought me into the outer court. There I saw some rooms and a pavement that had been constructed all around the court; there were thirty rooms along the pavement. [18]It abutted the sides of the gateways and was as wide as they were long; this was the lower pavement. [19]Then he measured the distance from the inside of the lower gateway to the outside of the inner court; it was a hundred cubits on the east side as well as on the north.

[20]Then he measured the length and width of the gate facing north, leading into the outer court. [21]Its alcoves—three on each side—its projecting walls and its portico had the same measurements as those of the first gateway. It was fifty cubits long and twenty-five cubits wide. [22]Its openings, its portico and its palm tree decorations had the same measurements as those of the gate facing east. Seven steps led up to it, with its portico opposite them. [23]There was a gate to the inner court facing the north gate, just as there was on the east. He measured from one gate to the opposite one; it was a hundred cubits.

[24]Then he led me to the south side and I saw a gate facing south. He measured its jambs and its portico, and they had the same measurements as the others. [25]The gateway and its portico had narrow openings all around, like the openings of

[v]5 The common cubit was about 1 1/2 feet (about 0.5 meter).   [w]5 That is, about 3 inches (about 8 centimeters)
[x]6 Septuagint; Hebrew *deep, the first threshold, one rod deep*   [y]8,9 Many Hebrew manuscripts, Septuagint, Vulgate and Syriac;
most Hebrew manuscripts *gateway facing the temple; it was one rod deep.* [9]*Then he measured the portico of the gateway; it*
[z]14 Septuagint; Hebrew *projecting wall*   [a]14 The meaning of the Hebrew for this verse is uncertain.

the others. It was fifty cubits long and twenty-five cubits wide. ²⁶Seven steps led up to it, with its portico opposite them; it had palm tree decorations on the faces of the projecting walls on each side. ²⁷The inner court also had a gate facing south, and he measured from this gate to the outer gate on the south side; it was a hundred cubits.

²⁸Then he brought me into the inner court through the south gate, and he measured the south gate; it had the same measurements as the others. ²⁹Its alcoves, its projecting walls and its portico had the same measurements as the others. The gateway and its portico had openings all around. It was fifty cubits long and twenty-five cubits wide. ³⁰(The porticoes of the gateways around the inner court were twenty-five cubits wide and five cubits deep.) ³¹Its portico faced the outer court; palm trees decorated its jambs, and eight steps led up to it.

³²Then he brought me to the inner court on the east side, and he measured the gateway; it had the same measurements as the others. ³³Its alcoves, its projecting walls and its portico had the same measurements as the others. The gateway and its portico had openings all around. It was fifty cubits long and twenty-five cubits wide. ³⁴Its portico faced the outer court; palm trees decorated the jambs on either side, and eight steps led up to it.

³⁵Then he brought me to the north gate and measured it. It had the same measurements as the others, ³⁶as did its alcoves, its projecting walls and its portico, and it had openings all around. It was fifty cubits long and twenty-five cubits wide. ³⁷Its portico*b* faced the outer court; palm trees decorated the jambs on either side, and eight steps led up to it.

³⁸A room with a doorway was by the portico in each of the inner gateways, where the burnt offerings were washed. ³⁹In the portico of the gateway were two tables on each side, on which the burnt offerings, sin offerings and guilt offerings were slaughtered. ⁴⁰By the outside wall of the portico of the gateway, near the steps at the entrance to the north gateway were two tables, and on the other side of the steps were two tables. ⁴¹So there were four tables on one side of the gateway and four on the other—eight tables in all—on which the sacrifices were slaughtered. ⁴²There were also four tables of dressed stone for the burnt offerings, each a cubit and a half long, a cubit and a half wide and a cubit high. On them were placed the utensils for slaughtering the burnt offerings and the other sacrifices. ⁴³And double-pronged hooks, each a handbreadth long, were attached to the wall all around. The tables were for the flesh of the offerings.

⁴⁴Outside the inner gate, within the inner court, were two rooms, one*c* at the side of the north gate and facing south, and another at the side of the south*d* gate and facing north. ⁴⁵He said to me, "The room facing south is for the priests who have charge of the temple, ⁴⁶and the room facing north is for the priests who have charge of the altar. These are the sons of Zadok, who are the only Levites who may draw near to the Lord to minister before him."

⁴⁷Then he measured the court: It was square—a hundred cubits long and a hundred cubits wide. And the altar was in front of the temple.

⁴⁸He brought me to the portico of the temple and measured the jambs of the portico; they were five cubits wide on either side. The width of the entrance was fourteen cubits and its projecting walls were*e* three cubits wide on either side. ⁴⁹The portico was twenty cubits wide, and twelve*f* cubits from front to back. It was reached by a flight of stairs,*g* and there were pillars on each side of the jambs.

CHAPTER 41

Then the man brought me to the outer sanctuary and measured the jambs; the width of the jambs was six cubits*h* on each side.*i* ²The entrance was ten cubits wide, and the projecting walls on each side of it were five cubits wide. He also measured the outer sanctuary; it was forty cubits long and twenty cubits wide.

³Then he went into the inner sanctuary and measured the jambs of the entrance; each was two cubits wide. The entrance

---

b37 Septuagint (see also verses 31 and 34); Hebrew *jambs*   *c44* Septuagint; Hebrew *were rooms for singers, which were*   *d44* Septuagint; Hebrew *east*   *e48* Septuagint; Hebrew *entrance was*   *f49* Septuagint; Hebrew *eleven*   *g49* Hebrew; Septuagint *Ten steps led up to it*   *h1* The common cubit was about 1 1/2 feet (about 0.5 meter).   *i1* One Hebrew manuscript and Septuagint; most Hebrew manuscripts *side, the width of the tent* was six cubits wide, and the projecting walls on each side of it were seven cubits wide. ⁴And he measured the length of the inner sanctuary; it was twenty cubits, and its width was twenty cubits across the end of the outer sanctuary. He said to me, "This is the Most Holy Place."

⁵Then he measured the wall of the temple; it was six cubits thick, and each side room around the temple was four cubits wide. ⁶The side rooms were on three levels, one above another, thirty on each level. There were ledges all around the wall of the temple to serve as supports for the side rooms, so that the supports were not inserted into the wall of the temple. ⁷The side rooms all around the temple were wider at each successive level. The structure surrounding the temple was built in ascending stages, so that the rooms widened as one went upward. A stairway went up from the lowest floor to the top floor through the middle floor.

⁸I saw that the temple had a raised base all around it, forming the foundation of the side rooms. It was the length of the rod, six long cubits. ⁹The outer wall of the side rooms was five cubits thick. The open area between the side rooms of the temple ¹⁰and the ⌊priests'⌋ rooms was twenty cubits wide all around the temple. ¹¹There were entrances to the side rooms from the open area, one on the north and another on the south; and the base adjoining the open area was five cubits wide all around.

¹²The building facing the temple courtyard on the west side was seventy cubits wide. The wall of the building was five cubits thick all around, and its length was ninety cubits.

¹³Then he measured the temple; it was a hundred cubits long, and the temple courtyard and the building with its walls were also a hundred cubits long. ¹⁴The width of the temple courtyard on the east, including the front of the temple, was a hundred cubits.

¹⁵Then he measured the length of the building facing the courtyard at the rear of the temple, including its galleries on each side; it was a hundred cubits.

The outer sanctuary, the inner sanctuary and the portico facing the court, ¹⁶as well as the thresholds and the narrow

windows and galleries around the three of them—everything beyond and including the threshold was covered with wood. The floor, the wall up to the windows, and the windows were covered. ¹⁷In the space above the outside of the entrance to the inner sanctuary and on the walls at regular intervals all around the inner and outer sanctuary ¹⁸were carved cherubim and palm trees. Palm trees alternated with cherubim. Each cherub had two faces: ¹⁹the face of a man toward the palm tree on one side and the face of a lion toward the palm tree on the other. They were carved all around the whole temple. ²⁰From the floor to the area above the entrance, cherubim and palm trees were carved on the wall of the outer sanctuary.

²¹The outer sanctuary had a rectangular doorframe, and the one at the front of the Most Holy Place was similar. ²²There was a wooden altar three cubits high and two cubits square*ʲ*; its corners, its base*ᵏ* and its sides were of wood. The man said to me, "This is the table that is before the LORD." ²³Both the outer sanctuary and the Most Holy Place had double doors. ²⁴Each door had two leaves—two hinged leaves for each door. ²⁵And on the doors of the outer sanctuary were carved cherubim and palm trees like those carved on the walls, and there was a wooden overhang on the front of the portico. ²⁶On the sidewalls of the portico were narrow windows with palm trees carved on each side. The side rooms of the temple also had overhangs.

C H A P T E R   4 2

Then the man led me northward into the outer court and brought me to the rooms opposite the temple courtyard and opposite the outer wall on the north side. ²The building whose door faced north was a hundred cubits*ˡ* long and fifty cubits wide. ³Both in the section twenty cubits from the inner court and in the section opposite the pavement of the outer court, gallery faced gallery at the three levels. ⁴In front of the rooms was an inner passageway ten cubits wide and a hundred cubits*ᵐ* long. Their doors were on the north. ⁵Now the upper rooms were narrower, for the galleries took more space from them than from the rooms on the lower and middle floors of the building. [6]The rooms on the third floor had no pillars, as the courts had; so they were smaller in floor space than those on the lower and middle floors. [7]There was an outer wall parallel to the rooms and the outer court; it extended in front of the rooms for fifty cubits. [8]While the row of rooms on the side next to the outer court was fifty cubits long, the row on the side nearest the sanctuary was a hundred cubits long. [9]The lower rooms had an entrance on the east side as one enters them from the outer court.

[10]On the south side[n] along the length of the wall of the outer court, adjoining the temple courtyard and opposite the outer wall, were rooms [11]with a passageway in front of them. These were like the rooms on the north; they had the same length and width, with similar exits and dimensions. Similar to the doorways on the north [12]were the doorways of the rooms on the south. There was a doorway at the beginning of the passageway that was parallel to the corresponding wall extending eastward, by which one enters the rooms.

[13]Then he said to me, "The north and south rooms facing the temple courtyard are the priests' rooms, where the priests who approach the LORD will eat the most holy offerings. There they will put the most holy offerings—the grain offerings, the sin offerings and the guilt offerings—for the place is holy. [14]Once the priests enter the holy precincts, they are not to go into the outer court until they leave behind the garments in which they minister, for these are holy. They are to put on other clothes before they go near the places that are for the people."

[15]When he had finished measuring what was inside the temple area, he led me out by the east gate and measured the area all around: [16]He measured the east side with the measuring rod; it was five hundred cubits.[o] [17]He measured the north side; it was five hundred cubits[p] by the measuring rod. [18]He measured the south side; it was five hundred cubits by the measuring rod. [19]Then he turned to the west side and measured; it was five hundred cubits by the measuring rod. [20]So he measured the area on all four sides. It had a wall around it, five hundred cubits long and five hundred cubits wide, to separate the holy from the common.

CHAPTER 43

Then the man brought me to the gate facing east, [2]and I saw the glory of the God of Israel coming from the east. His voice was like the roar of rushing waters, and the land was radiant with his glory. [3]The vision I saw was like the vision I had seen when he[q] came to destroy the city and like the visions I had seen by the Kebar River, and I fell facedown. [4]The glory of the LORD entered the temple through the gate facing east. [5]Then the Spirit lifted me up and brought me into the inner court, and the glory of the LORD filled the temple.

[6]While the man was standing beside me, I heard someone speaking to me from inside the temple. [7]He said: "Son of man, this is the place of my throne and the place for the soles of my feet. This is where I will live among the Israelites forever. The house of Israel will never again defile my holy name—neither they nor their kings—by their prostitution[r] and the lifeless idols[s] of their kings at their high places. [8]When they placed their threshold next to my threshold and their doorposts beside my doorposts, with only a wall between me and them, they defiled my holy name by their detestable practices. So I destroyed them in my anger. [9]Now let them put away from me their prostitution and the lifeless idols of their kings, and I will live among them forever.

[10]"Son of man, describe the temple to the people of Israel, that they may be ashamed of their sins. Let them consider the plan, [11]and if they are ashamed of all they have done, make known to them the design of the temple—its arrangement, its exits and entrances—its whole design and all its regulations[t] and laws. Write these down before them so that they may be faithful to its design and follow all its regulations.

¹²"This is the law of the temple: All the surrounding area on top of the mountain will be most holy. Such is the law of the temple.

¹³"These are the measurements of the altar in long cubits, that cubit being a cubit*ᵘ* and a handbreadth*ᵛ*: Its gutter is a cubit deep and a cubit wide, with a rim of one span*ʷ* around the edge. And this is the height of the altar: ¹⁴From the gutter on the ground up to the lower ledge it is two cubits high and a cubit wide, and from the smaller ledge up to the larger ledge it is four cubits high and a cubit wide. ¹⁵The altar hearth is four cubits high, and four horns project upward from the hearth. ¹⁶The altar hearth is square, twelve cubits long and twelve cubits wide. ¹⁷The upper ledge also is square, fourteen cubits long and fourteen cubits wide, with a rim of half a cubit and a gutter of a cubit all around. The steps of the altar face east."

¹⁸Then he said to me, "Son of man, this is what the Sovereign LORD says: These will be the regulations for sacrificing burnt offerings and sprinkling blood upon the altar when it is built: ¹⁹You are to give a young bull as a sin offering to the priests, who are Levites, of the family of Zadok, who come near to minister before me, declares the Sovereign LORD.

²⁰You are to take some of its blood and put it on the four horns of the altar and on the four corners of the upper ledge and all around the rim, and so purify the altar and make atonement for it. ²¹You are to take the bull for the sin offering and burn it in the designated part of the temple area outside the sanctuary.

²²"On the second day you are to offer a male goat without defect for a sin offering, and the altar is to be purified as it was purified with the bull. ²³When you have finished purifying it, you are to offer a young bull and a ram from the flock, both without defect. ²⁴You are to offer them before the LORD, and the priests are to sprinkle salt on them and sacrifice them as a burnt offering to the LORD.

²⁵"For seven days you are to provide a male goat daily for a sin offering; you are also to provide a young bull and a ram from the flock, both without defect. ²⁶For seven days they are to make atonement for the altar and cleanse it; thus they will dedicate it. ²⁷At the end of these days, from the eighth day on, the priests are to present your burnt offerings and fellowship offerings*ˣ* on the altar. Then I will accept you, declares the Sovereign LORD."

ᵘ13 The common cubit was about 1 1/2 feet (about 0.5 meter).   *ᵛ13* That is, about 3 inches (about 8 centimeters)   *ʷ13* That is, about 9 inches (about 22 centimeters)   *ˣ27* Traditionally *peace offerings*

AUGUST 26 □ DAY 239
EZEKIEL 44–48
New Worship for Israel

 OVERVIEW The new temple Ezekiel envisions is more than a religious shrine; it is the hub of activity in the rebuilt nation! The new order of worship, much like the worship in the days of Solomon, will involve priests, Levites, sacrifices, offerings, feasts and designated portions and places for the priesthood. In that day the nation will occupy all the territory originally promised to Israel in the covenant God made with Abraham (Genesis 15:18–21; 17:8). And over the city will hang the name, "The LORD Is There"—a reminder of the burden Ezekiel has carried throughout his life and ministry, that men and women everywhere might see and acknowledge God as the Lord.

Chapter 44	Chapter 45	Chapter 46	Chapter 47	Chapter 48
Priestly Service	Priestly Supplies	Priestly Sacrifices	Boundaries of the Nation	Boundaries of the Tribes
United in Service			Divided Inheritance	

YOUR DAILY WALK Using a measuring tape (or with the help of a floor plan), spend a few minutes reviewing the dimensions of your home: the length and width of your house; the size of your yard; the location of the doors, windows, sidewalks and driveways. When you have finished, you will probably be the only human being who knows (or cares to know) those details.

God loves each of us as if there were only one of us.

But there is someone else who knows. He's the God who never loses track of the hairs on your head or the days of your life (Matthew 10:30; Job 14:5). He's waiting to share your hurts and carry your burdens. As Ezekiel learned, God cares about the smallest details of life. Share one of your "little hurts" with him now!

INSIGHT The Lord Is Here . . . There . . . Everywhere
The concluding statement of Ezekiel, "The LORD Is There" (48:35), becomes the recurring theme of John in the book of Revelation. God's abiding presence becomes the chief joy of those in the new heaven and new earth (Revelation 21:3–4, 7, 22–23; 22:3–5).

CHAPTER 44
Then the man brought me back to the outer gate of the sanctuary, the one facing east, and it was shut. ²The LORD said to me, "This gate is to remain shut. It must not be opened; no one may enter through it. It is to remain shut because the LORD, the God of Israel, has entered through it. ³The prince himself is the only one who may sit inside the gateway to eat in the presence of the LORD. He is to enter by way of the portico of the gateway and go out the same way."

⁴Then the man brought me by way of the north gate to the front of the temple. I looked and saw the glory of the LORD filling the temple of the LORD, and I fell facedown.

⁵The LORD said to me, "Son of man, look carefully, listen closely and give attention to everything I tell you concerning all the regulations regarding the temple of the LORD. Give attention to the entrance of the temple and all the exits of the sanctuary. ⁶Say to the rebellious house of Israel, 'This is what the Sovereign LORD says: Enough of your detestable practices, O house of Israel! ⁷In addition to all your other detestable practices, you brought foreigners uncircumcised in heart and flesh into my sanctuary, desecrating my temple while you offered me food, fat and

blood, and you broke my covenant. ⁸Instead of carrying out your duty in regard to my holy things, you put others in charge of my sanctuary. ⁹This is what the Sovereign LORD says: No foreigner uncircumcised in heart and flesh is to enter my sanctuary, not even the foreigners who live among the Israelites.

¹⁰" 'The Levites who went far from me when Israel went astray and who wandered from me after their idols must bear the consequences of their sin. ¹¹They may serve in my sanctuary, having charge of the gates of the temple and serving in it; they may slaughter the burnt offerings and sacrifices for the people and stand before the people and serve them. ¹²But because they served them in the presence of their idols and made the house of Israel fall into sin, therefore I have sworn with uplifted hand that they must bear the consequences of their sin, declares the Sovereign LORD. ¹³They are not to come near to serve me as priests or come near any of my holy things or my most holy offerings; they must bear the shame of their detestable practices. ¹⁴Yet I will put them in charge of the duties of the temple and all the work that is to be done in it.

¹⁵" 'But the priests, who are Levites and descendants of Zadok and who faithfully carried out the duties of my sanctuary

when the Israelites went astray from me, are to come near to minister before me; they are to stand before me to offer sacrifices of fat and blood, declares the Sovereign LORD. [16]They alone are to enter my sanctuary; they alone are to come near my table to minister before me and perform my service.

[17]" 'When they enter the gates of the inner court, they are to wear linen clothes; they must not wear any woolen garment while ministering at the gates of the inner court or inside the temple. [18]They are to wear linen turbans on their heads and linen undergarments around their waists. They must not wear anything that makes them perspire. [19]When they go out into the outer court where the people are, they are to take off the clothes they have been ministering in and are to leave them in the sacred rooms, and put on other clothes, so that they do not consecrate the people by means of their garments.

[20]" 'They must not shave their heads or let their hair grow long, but they are to keep the hair of their heads trimmed. [21]No priest is to drink wine when he enters the inner court. [22]They must not marry widows or divorced women; they may marry only virgins of Israelite descent or widows of priests. [23]They are to teach my people the difference between the holy and the common and show them how to distinguish between the unclean and the clean.

[24]" 'In any dispute, the priests are to serve as judges and decide it according to my ordinances. They are to keep my laws and my decrees for all my appointed feasts, and they are to keep my Sabbaths holy.

[25]" 'A priest must not defile himself by going near a dead person; however, if the dead person was his father or mother, son or daughter, brother or unmarried sister, then he may defile himself. [26]After he is cleansed, he must wait seven days. [27]On the day he goes into the inner court of the sanctuary to minister in the sanctuary, he is to offer a sin offering for himself, declares the Sovereign LORD.

[28]" 'I am to be the only inheritance the priests have. You are to give them no possession in Israel; I will be their posses-

sion. [29]They will eat the grain offerings, the sin offerings and the guilt offerings; and everything in Israel devoted[y] to the LORD will belong to them. [30]The best of all the firstfruits and of all your special gifts will belong to the priests. You are to give them the first portion of your ground meal so that a blessing may rest on your household. [31]The priests must not eat anything, bird or animal, found dead or torn by wild animals.

CHAPTER 45

" 'When you allot the land as an inheritance, you are to present to the LORD a portion of the land as a sacred district, 25,000 cubits long and 20,000[z] cubits wide; the entire area will be holy. [2]Of this, a section 500 cubits square is to be for the sanctuary, with 50 cubits around it for open land. [3]In the sacred district, measure off a section 25,000 cubits[a] long and 10,000 cubits[b] wide. In it will be the sanctuary, the Most Holy Place. [4]It will be the sacred portion of the land for the priests, who minister in the sanctuary and who draw near to minister before the LORD. It will be a place for their houses as well as a holy place for the sanctuary. [5]An area 25,000 cubits long and 10,000 cubits wide will belong to the Levites, who serve in the temple, as their possession for towns to live in.[c]

[6]" 'You are to give the city as its property an area 5,000 cubits wide and 25,000 cubits long, adjoining the sacred portion; it will belong to the whole house of Israel.

[7]" 'The prince will have the land bordering each side of the area formed by the sacred district and the property of the city. It will extend westward from the west side and eastward from the east side, running lengthwise from the western to the eastern border parallel to one of the tribal portions. [8]This land will be his possession in Israel. And my princes will no longer oppress my people but will allow the house of Israel to possess the land according to their tribes.

[9]" 'This is what the Sovereign LORD says: You have gone far enough, O princes of Israel! Give up your violence and oppression and do what is just and right. Stop dispossessing my people, declares the

Sovereign LORD. [10]You are to use accurate scales, an accurate ephah[d] and an accurate bath.[e] [11]The ephah and the bath are to be the same size, the bath containing a tenth of a homer[f] and the ephah a tenth of a homer; the homer is to be the standard measure for both. [12]The shekel[g] is to consist of twenty gerahs. Twenty shekels plus twenty-five shekels plus fifteen shekels equal one mina.[h]

[13]" 'This is the special gift you are to offer: a sixth of an ephah from each homer of wheat and a sixth of an ephah from each homer of barley. [14]The prescribed portion of oil, measured by the bath, is a tenth of a bath from each cor (which consists of ten baths or one homer, for ten baths are equivalent to a homer). [15]Also one sheep is to be taken from every flock of two hundred from the well-watered pastures of Israel. These will be used for the grain offerings, burnt offerings and fellowship offerings[i] to make atonement for the people, declares the Sovereign LORD. [16]All the people of the land will participate in this special gift for the use of the prince in Israel. [17]It will be the duty of the prince to provide the burnt offerings, grain offerings and drink offerings at the festivals, the New Moons and the Sabbaths—at all the appointed feasts of the house of Israel. He will provide the sin offerings, grain offerings, burnt offerings and fellowship offerings to make atonement for the house of Israel.

[18]" 'This is what the Sovereign LORD says: In the first month on the first day you are to take a young bull without defect and purify the sanctuary. [19]The priest is to take some of the blood of the sin offering and put it on the doorposts of the temple, on the four corners of the upper ledge of the altar and on the gateposts of the inner court. [20]You are to do the same on the seventh day of the month for anyone who sins unintentionally or through ignorance; so you are to make atonement for the temple.

[21]" 'In the first month on the fourteenth day you are to observe the Passover, a feast lasting seven days, during which you shall eat bread made without yeast. [22]On that day the prince is to provide a

bull as a sin offering for himself and for all the people of the land. [23]Every day during the seven days of the Feast he is to provide seven bulls and seven rams without defect as a burnt offering to the LORD, and a male goat for a sin offering. [24]He is to provide as a grain offering an ephah for each bull and an ephah for each ram, along with a hin[j] of oil for each ephah.

[25]" 'During the seven days of the Feast, which begins in the seventh month on the fifteenth day, he is to make the same provision for sin offerings, burnt offerings, grain offerings and oil.

CHAPTER 46

" 'This is what the Sovereign LORD says: The gate of the inner court facing east is to be shut on the six working days, but on the Sabbath day and on the day of the New Moon it is to be opened. [2]The prince is to enter from the outside through the portico of the gateway and stand by the gatepost. The priests are to sacrifice his burnt offering and his fellowship offerings.[k] He is to worship at the threshold of the gateway and then go out, but the gate will not be shut until evening. [3]On the Sabbaths and New Moons the people of the land are to worship in the presence of the LORD at the entrance to that gateway. [4]The burnt offering the prince brings to the LORD on the Sabbath day is to be six male lambs and a ram, all without defect. [5]The grain offering given with the ram is to be an ephah,[l] and the grain offering with the lambs is to be as much as he pleases, along with a hin[j] of oil for each ephah. [6]On the day of the New Moon he is to offer a young bull, six lambs and a ram, all without defect. [7]He is to provide as a grain offering one ephah with the bull, one ephah with the ram, and with the lambs as much as he wants to give, along with a hin of oil with each ephah. [8]When the prince enters, he is to go in through the portico of the gateway, and he is to come out the same way.

[9]" 'When the people of the land come before the LORD at the appointed feasts, whoever enters by the north gate to worship is to go out the south gate; and

[d]10 An ephah was a dry measure.   [e] A bath was a liquid measure.   [f]11 A homer was a dry measure.   [g]12 A shekel weighed about 2/5 ounce (about 11.5 grams).   [h]12 That is, 60 shekels; the common mina was 50 shekels.   [i]15 Traditionally *peace offerings*; also in verse 17   [j]24,5 That is, probably about 4 quarts (about 4 liters)   [k]2 Traditionally *peace offerings*; also in verse 12   [l]5 That is, probably about 3/5 bushel (about 22 liters)

whoever enters by the south gate is to go out the north gate. No one is to return through the gate by which he entered, but each is to go out the opposite gate. ¹⁰The prince is to be among them, going in when they go in and going out when they go out.

¹¹" 'At the festivals and the appointed feasts, the grain offering is to be an ephah with a bull, an ephah with a ram, and with the lambs as much as one pleases, along with a hin of oil for each ephah. ¹²When the prince provides a freewill offering to the LORD—whether a burnt offering or fellowship offerings—the gate facing east is to be opened for him. He shall offer his burnt offering or his fellowship offerings as he does on the Sabbath day. Then he shall go out, and after he has gone out, the gate will be shut.

¹³" 'Every day you are to provide a year-old lamb without defect for a burnt offering to the LORD; morning by morning you shall provide it. ¹⁴You are also to provide with it morning by morning a grain offering, consisting of a sixth of an ephah with a third of a hin of oil to moisten the flour. The presenting of this grain offering to the LORD is a lasting ordinance. ¹⁵So the lamb and the grain offering and the oil shall be provided morning by morning for a regular burnt offering.

¹⁶" 'This is what the Sovereign LORD says: If the prince makes a gift from his inheritance to one of his sons, it will also belong to his descendants; it is to be their property by inheritance. ¹⁷If, however, he makes a gift from his inheritance to one of his servants, the servant may keep it until the year of freedom; then it will revert to the prince. His inheritance belongs to his sons only; it is theirs. ¹⁸The prince must not take any of the inheritance of the people, driving them off their property. He is to give his sons their inheritance out of his own property, so that none of my people will be separated from his property.' "

¹⁹Then the man brought me through the entrance at the side of the gate to the sacred rooms facing north, which belonged to the priests, and showed me a place at the western end. ²⁰He said to me, "This is the place where the priests will cook the guilt offering and the sin offering and

bake the grain offering, to avoid bringing them into the outer court and consecrating the people."

²¹He then brought me to the outer court and led me around to its four corners, and I saw in each corner another court. ²²In the four corners of the outer court were enclosed[m] courts, forty cubits long and thirty cubits wide; each of the courts in the four corners was the same size. ²³Around the inside of each of the four courts was a ledge of stone, with places for fire built all around under the ledge. ²⁴He said to me, "These are the kitchens where those who minister at the temple will cook the sacrifices of the people."

CHAPTER 47

The man brought me back to the entrance of the temple, and I saw water coming out from under the threshold of the temple toward the east (for the temple faced east). The water was coming down from under the south side of the temple, south of the altar. ²He then brought me out through the north gate and led me around the outside to the outer gate facing east, and the water was flowing from the south side.

³As the man went eastward with a measuring line in his hand, he measured off a thousand cubits[n] and then led me through water that was ankle-deep. ⁴He measured off another thousand cubits and led me through water that was knee-deep. He measured off another thousand and led me through water that was up to the waist. ⁵He measured off another thousand, but now it was a river that I could not cross, because the water had risen and was deep enough to swim in—a river that no one could cross. ⁶He asked me, "Son of man, do you see this?"

Then he led me back to the bank of the river. ⁷When I arrived there, I saw a great number of trees on each side of the river. ⁸He said to me, "This water flows toward the eastern region and goes down into the Arabah,[o] where it enters the Sea.[p] When it empties into the Sea,[p] the water there becomes fresh. ⁹Swarms of living creatures will live wherever the river flows. There will be large numbers of fish, because this water flows there and makes the salt water fresh; so where the river

---

m22 The meaning of the Hebrew for this word is uncertain.   n3 That is, about 1,500 feet (about 450 meters)   o8 Or the Jordan Valley   p8 That is, the Dead Sea flows everything will live. [10]Fishermen will stand along the shore; from En Gedi to En Eglaim there will be places for spreading nets. The fish will be of many kinds—like the fish of the Great Sea.[q] [11]But the swamps and marshes will not become fresh; they will be left for salt. [12]Fruit trees of all kinds will grow on both banks of the river. Their leaves will not wither, nor will their fruit fail. Every month they will bear, because the water from the sanctuary flows to them. Their fruit will serve for food and their leaves for healing."

[13]This is what the Sovereign LORD says: "These are the boundaries by which you are to divide the land for an inheritance among the twelve tribes of Israel, with two portions for Joseph. [14]You are to divide it equally among them. Because I swore with uplifted hand to give it to your forefathers, this land will become your inheritance.

[15]"This is to be the boundary of the land:

"On the north side it will run from the Great Sea by the Hethlon road past Lebo[r] Hamath to Zedad, [16]Berothah[s] and Sibraim (which lies on the border between Damascus and Hamath), as far as Hazer Hatticon, which is on the border of Hauran. [17]The boundary will extend from the sea to Hazar Enan,[t] along the northern border of Damascus, with the border of Hamath to the north. This will be the north boundary.

[18]"On the east side the boundary will run between Hauran and Damascus, along the Jordan between Gilead and the land of Israel, to the eastern sea and as far as Tamar.[u] This will be the east boundary.

[19]"On the south side it will run from Tamar as far as the waters of Meribah Kadesh, then along the Wadi ⌞of Egypt⌟ to the Great Sea. This will be the south boundary.

[20]"On the west side, the Great Sea will be the boundary to a point opposite Lebo[v] Hamath. This will be the west boundary.

[21]"You are to distribute this land among yourselves according to the tribes of Israel. [22]You are to allot it as an inheritance for yourselves and for the aliens who have settled among you and who have children. You are to consider them as native-born Israelites; along with you they are to be allotted an inheritance among the tribes of Israel. [23]In whatever tribe the alien settles, there you are to give him his inheritance," declares the Sovereign LORD.

C H A P T E R   4 8

"These are the tribes, listed by name: At the northern frontier, Dan will have one portion; it will follow the Hethlon road to Lebo[w] Hamath; Hazar Enan and the northern border of Damascus next to Hamath will be part of its border from the east side to the west side.

[2]"Asher will have one portion; it will border the territory of Dan from east to west.

[3]"Naphtali will have one portion; it will border the territory of Asher from east to west.

[4]"Manasseh will have one portion; it will border the territory of Naphtali from east to west.

[5]"Ephraim will have one portion; it will border the territory of Manasseh from east to west.

[6]"Reuben will have one portion; it will border the territory of Ephraim from east to west.

[7]"Judah will have one portion; it will border the territory of Reuben from east to west.

[8]"Bordering the territory of Judah from east to west will be the portion you are to present as a special gift. It will be 25,000 cubits[x] wide, and its length from east to west will equal one of the tribal portions; the sanctuary will be in the center of it.

[9]"The special portion you are to offer to the LORD will be 25,000 cubits long and 10,000 cubits[y] wide. [10]This will be the sacred portion for the priests. It will be 25,000 cubits long on the north side, 10,000 cubits wide on the west side, 10,000 cubits wide on the east side and 25,000 cubits long on the south side. In the center of it will be the sanctuary of the

---

[q]10 That is, the Mediterranean; also in verses 15, 19 and 20   [r]15 Or past the entrance to   [s]15,16 See Septuagint and Ezekiel 48:1; Hebrew road to go into Zedad, [16]Hamath, Berothah   [t]17 Hebrew Enon, a variant of Enan   [u]18 Septuagint and Syriac; Hebrew Israel. You will measure to the eastern sea   [v]20 Or opposite the entrance to   [w]1 Or to the entrance to   [x]8 That is, about 7 miles (about 12 kilometers)   [y]9 That is, about 3 miles (about 5 kilometers)

LORD. [11]This will be for the consecrated priests, the Zadokites, who were faithful in serving me and did not go astray as the Levites did when the Israelites went astray. [12]It will be a special gift to them from the sacred portion of the land, a most holy portion, bordering the territory of the Levites.

[13]"Alongside the territory of the priests, the Levites will have an allotment 25,000 cubits long and 10,000 cubits wide. Its total length will be 25,000 cubits and its width 10,000 cubits. [14]They must not sell or exchange any of it. This is the best of the land and must not pass into other hands, because it is holy to the LORD.

[15]"The remaining area, 5,000 cubits wide and 25,000 cubits long, will be for the common use of the city, for houses and for pastureland. The city will be in the center of it [16]and will have these measurements: the north side 4,500 cubits, the south side 4,500 cubits, the east side 4,500 cubits, and the west side 4,500 cubits. [17]The pastureland for the city will be 250 cubits on the north, 250 cubits on the south, 250 cubits on the east, and 250 cubits on the west. [18]What remains of the area, bordering on the sacred portion and running the length of it, will be 10,000 cubits on the east side and 10,000 cubits on the west side. Its produce will supply food for the workers of the city. [19]The workers from the city who farm it will come from all the tribes of Israel. [20]The entire portion will be a square, 25,000 cubits on each side. As a special gift you will set aside the sacred portion, along with the property of the city.

[21]"What remains on both sides of the area formed by the sacred portion and the city property will belong to the prince. It will extend eastward from the 25,000 cubits of the sacred portion to the eastern border, and westward from the 25,000 cubits to the western border. Both these areas running the length of the tribal portions will belong to the prince, and the sacred portion with the temple sanctuary will be in the center of them. [22]So the property of the Levites and the property of the city will lie in the center of the area

that belongs to the prince. The area belonging to the prince will lie between the border of Judah and the border of Benjamin.

[23]"As for the rest of the tribes: Benjamin will have one portion; it will extend from the east side to the west side.

[24]"Simeon will have one portion; it will border the territory of Benjamin from east to west.

[25]"Issachar will have one portion; it will border the territory of Simeon from east to west.

[26]"Zebulun will have one portion; it will border the territory of Issachar from east to west.

[27]"Gad will have one portion; it will border the territory of Zebulun from east to west.

[28]"The southern boundary of Gad will run south from Tamar to the waters of Meribah Kadesh, then along the Wadi ⌊of Egypt⌋ to the Great Sea.[z]

[29]"This is the land you are to allot as an inheritance to the tribes of Israel, and these will be their portions," declares the Sovereign LORD.

[30]"These will be the exits of the city: Beginning on the north side, which is 4,500 cubits long, [31]the gates of the city will be named after the tribes of Israel. The three gates on the north side will be the gate of Reuben, the gate of Judah and the gate of Levi.

[32]"On the east side, which is 4,500 cubits long, will be three gates: the gate of Joseph, the gate of Benjamin and the gate of Dan.

[33]"On the south side, which measures 4,500 cubits, will be three gates: the gate of Simeon, the gate of Issachar and the gate of Zebulun.

[34]"On the west side, which is 4,500 cubits long, will be three gates: the gate of Gad, the gate of Asher and the gate of Naphtali.

[35]"The distance all around will be 18,000 cubits.

"And the name of the city from that time on will be:

THE LORD IS THERE."

[z]28 That is, the Mediterranean

³Then the king ordered Ashpenaz, chief of his court officials, to bring in some of the Israelites from the royal family and the nobility— ⁴young men without any physical defect, handsome, showing aptitude for every kind of learning, well informed, quick to understand, and qualified to serve in the king's palace. He was to teach them the language and literature of the Babylonians.ᵇ ⁵The king assigned them a daily amount of food and wine from the king's table. They were to be trained for three years, and after that they were to enter the king's service.

⁶Among these were some from Judah: Daniel, Hananiah, Mishael and Azariah. ⁷The chief official gave them new names: to Daniel, the name Belteshazzar; to Hananiah, Shadrach; to Mishael, Meshach; and to Azariah, Abednego.

⁸But Daniel resolved not to defile himself with the royal food and wine, and he asked the chief official for permission not to defile himself this way. ⁹Now God had caused the official to show favor and sympathy to Daniel, ¹⁰but the official told Daniel, "I am afraid of my lord the king, who has assigned yourᶜ food and drink. Why should he see you looking worse than the other young men your age? The king would then have my head because of you."

¹¹Daniel then said to the guard whom the chief official had appointed over Daniel, Hananiah, Mishael and Azariah, ¹²"Please test your servants for ten days: Give us nothing but vegetables to eat and water to drink. ¹³Then compare our appearance with that of the young men who eat the royal food, and treat your servants in accordance with what you see." ¹⁴So he agreed to this and tested them for ten days.

¹⁵At the end of the ten days they looked healthier and better nourished than any of the young men who ate the royal food. ¹⁶So the guard took away their choice food and the wine they were to drink and gave them vegetables instead.

¹⁷To these four young men God gave knowledge and understanding of all kinds of literature and learning. And Daniel could understand visions and dreams of all kinds.

¹⁸At the end of the time set by the king to bring them in, the chief official presented them to Nebuchadnezzar. ¹⁹The king talked with them, and he found none equal to Daniel, Hananiah, Mishael and Azariah; so they entered the king's service. ²⁰In every matter of wisdom and understanding about which the king questioned them, he found them ten times better than all the magicians and enchanters in his whole kingdom.

²¹And Daniel remained there until the first year of King Cyrus.

CHAPTER 2

In the second year of his reign, Nebuchadnezzar had dreams; his mind was troubled and he could not sleep. ²So the king summoned the magicians, enchanters, sorcerers and astrologersᵈ to tell him what he had dreamed. When they came in and stood before the king, ³he said to them, "I have had a dream that troubles me and I want to know what it means.ᵉ"

⁴Then the astrologers answered the king in Aramaic,ᶠ "O king, live forever! Tell your servants the dream, and we will interpret it."

⁵The king replied to the astrologers, "This is what I have firmly decided: If you do not tell me what my dream was and interpret it, I will have you cut into pieces and your houses turned into piles of rubble. ⁶But if you tell me the dream and explain it, you will receive from me gifts and rewards and great honor. So tell me the dream and interpret it for me."

⁷Once more they replied, "Let the king tell his servants the dream, and we will interpret it."

⁸Then the king answered, "I am certain that you are trying to gain time, because you realize that this is what I have firmly decided: ⁹If you do not tell me the dream, there is just one penalty for you. You have conspired to tell me misleading and wicked things, hoping the situation will change. So then, tell me the dream, and I will know that you can interpret it for me."

¹⁰The astrologers answered the king, "There is not a man on earth who can do what the king asks! No king, however great and mighty, has ever asked such a thing of any magician or enchanter or astrologer. ¹¹What the king asks is too

ᵇ4 Or Chaldeans   ᶜ10 The Hebrew for your and you in this verse is plural.   ᵈ2 Or Chaldeans; also in verses 4, 5 and 10
ᵉ3 Or was   ᶠ4 The text from here through chapter 7 is in Aramaic.

difficult. No one can reveal it to the king except the gods, and they do not live among men."

[12] This made the king so angry and furious that he ordered the execution of all the wise men of Babylon. [13] So the decree was issued to put the wise men to death, and men were sent to look for Daniel and his friends to put them to death.

[14] When Arioch, the commander of the king's guard, had gone out to put to death the wise men of Babylon, Daniel spoke to him with wisdom and tact. [15] He asked the king's officer, "Why did the king issue such a harsh decree?" Arioch then explained the matter to Daniel. [16] At this, Daniel went in to the king and asked for time, so that he might interpret the dream for him.

[17] Then Daniel returned to his house and explained the matter to his friends Hananiah, Mishael and Azariah. [18] He urged them to plead for mercy from the God of heaven concerning this mystery, so that he and his friends might not be executed with the rest of the wise men of Babylon. [19] During the night the mystery was revealed to Daniel in a vision. Then Daniel praised the God of heaven [20] and said:

"Praise be to the name of God for ever and ever;
    wisdom and power are his.
[21] He changes times and seasons;
    he sets up kings and deposes them.
He gives wisdom to the wise
    and knowledge to the discerning.
[22] He reveals deep and hidden things;
    he knows what lies in darkness,
    and light dwells with him.
[23] I thank and praise you, O God of my fathers:
    You have given me wisdom and power,
    you have made known to me what we asked of you,
    you have made known to us the dream of the king."

[24] Then Daniel went to Arioch, whom the king had appointed to execute the wise men of Babylon, and said to him, "Do not execute the wise men of Babylon. Take me to the king, and I will interpret his dream for him."

[25] Arioch took Daniel to the king at once and said, "I have found a man among the exiles from Judah who can tell the king what his dream means."

[26] The king asked Daniel (also called Belteshazzar), "Are you able to tell me what I saw in my dream and interpret it?"

[27] Daniel replied, "No wise man, enchanter, magician or diviner can explain to the king the mystery he has asked about, [28] but there is a God in heaven who reveals mysteries. He has shown King Nebuchadnezzar what will happen in days to come. Your dream and the visions that passed through your mind as you lay on your bed are these:

[29] "As you were lying there, O king, your mind turned to things to come, and the revealer of mysteries showed you what is going to happen. [30] As for me, this mystery has been revealed to me, not because I have greater wisdom than other living men, but so that you, O king, may know the interpretation and that you may understand what went through your mind.

[31] "You looked, O king, and there before you stood a large statue—an enormous, dazzling statue, awesome in appearance. [32] The head of the statue was made of pure gold, its chest and arms of silver, its belly and thighs of bronze, [33] its legs of iron, its feet partly of iron and partly of baked clay. [34] While you were watching, a rock was cut out, but not by human hands. It struck the statue on its feet of iron and clay and smashed them. [35] Then the iron, the clay, the bronze, the silver and the gold were broken to pieces at the same time and became like chaff on a threshing floor in the summer. The wind swept them away without leaving a trace. But the rock that struck the statue became a huge mountain and filled the whole earth.

[36] "This was the dream, and now we will interpret it to the king. [37] You, O king, are the king of kings. The God of heaven has given you dominion and power and might and glory; [38] in your hands he has placed mankind and the beasts of the field and the birds of the air. Wherever they live, he has made you ruler over them all. You are that head of gold.

[39] "After you, another kingdom will rise, inferior to yours. Next, a third kingdom, one of bronze, will rule over the whole earth. [40] Finally, there will be a fourth kingdom, strong as iron—for iron breaks and smashes everything—and as iron

breaks things to pieces, so it will crush and break all the others. ⁴¹Just as you saw that the feet and toes were partly of baked clay and partly of iron, so this will be a divided kingdom; yet it will have some of the strength of iron in it, even as you saw iron mixed with clay. ⁴²As the toes were partly iron and partly clay, so this kingdom will be partly strong and partly brittle. ⁴³And just as you saw the iron mixed with baked clay, so the people will be a mixture and will not remain united, any more than iron mixes with clay.

⁴⁴"In the time of those kings, the God of heaven will set up a kingdom that will never be destroyed, nor will it be left to another people. It will crush all those kingdoms and bring them to an end, but it will itself endure forever. ⁴⁵This is the meaning of the vision of the rock cut out of a mountain, but not by human hands— a rock that broke the iron, the bronze, the clay, the silver and the gold to pieces.

"The great God has shown the king what will take place in the future. The dream is true and the interpretation is trustworthy."

⁴⁶Then King Nebuchadnezzar fell prostrate before Daniel and paid him honor and ordered that an offering and incense be presented to him. ⁴⁷The king said to Daniel, "Surely your God is the God of gods and the Lord of kings and a revealer of mysteries, for you were able to reveal this mystery."

⁴⁸Then the king placed Daniel in a high position and lavished many gifts on him. He made him ruler over the entire province of Babylon and placed him in charge of all its wise men. ⁴⁹Moreover, at Daniel's request the king appointed Shadrach, Meshach and Abednego administrators over the province of Babylon, while Daniel himself remained at the royal court.

CHAPTER 3
King Nebuchadnezzar made an image of gold, ninety feet high and nine feetᵍ wide, and set it up on the plain of Dura in the province of Babylon. ²He then summoned the satraps, prefects, governors, advisers, treasurers, judges, magistrates and all the other provincial officials to come to the dedication of the image he had set up. ³So the satraps, prefects, gov-

ernors, advisers, treasurers, judges, magistrates and all the other provincial officials assembled for the dedication of the image that King Nebuchadnezzar had set up, and they stood before it.

⁴Then the herald loudly proclaimed, "This is what you are commanded to do, O peoples, nations and men of every language: ⁵As soon as you hear the sound of the horn, flute, zither, lyre, harp, pipes and all kinds of music, you must fall down and worship the image of gold that King Nebuchadnezzar has set up. ⁶Whoever does not fall down and worship will immediately be thrown into a blazing furnace."

⁷Therefore, as soon as they heard the sound of the horn, flute, zither, lyre, harp and all kinds of music, all the peoples, nations and men of every language fell down and worshiped the image of gold that King Nebuchadnezzar had set up.

⁸At this time some astrologersʰ came forward and denounced the Jews. ⁹They said to King Nebuchadnezzar, "O king, live forever! ¹⁰You have issued a decree, O king, that everyone who hears the sound of the horn, flute, zither, lyre, harp, pipes and all kinds of music must fall down and worship the image of gold, ¹¹and that whoever does not fall down and worship will be thrown into a blazing furnace. ¹²But there are some Jews whom you have set over the affairs of the province of Babylon—Shadrach, Meshach and Abednego—who pay no attention to you, O king. They neither serve your gods nor worship the image of gold you have set up."

¹³Furious with rage, Nebuchadnezzar summoned Shadrach, Meshach and Abednego. So these men were brought before the king, ¹⁴and Nebuchadnezzar said to them, "Is it true, Shadrach, Meshach and Abednego, that you do not serve my gods or worship the image of gold I have set up? ¹⁵Now when you hear the sound of the horn, flute, zither, lyre, harp, pipes and all kinds of music, if you are ready to fall down and worship the image I made, very good. But if you do not worship it, you will be thrown immediately into a blazing furnace. Then what god will be able to rescue you from my hand?"

ᵍ1 Aramaic *sixty cubits high and six cubits wide* (about 27 meters high and 2.7 meters wide)   ʰ8 Or *Chaldeans*

¹⁶Shadrach, Meshach and Abednego replied to the king, "O Nebuchadnezzar, we do not need to defend ourselves before you in this matter. ¹⁷If we are thrown into the blazing furnace, the God we serve is able to save us from it, and he will rescue us from your hand, O king. ¹⁸But even if he does not, we want you to know, O king, that we will not serve your gods or worship the image of gold you have set up."

¹⁹Then Nebuchadnezzar was furious with Shadrach, Meshach and Abednego, and his attitude toward them changed. He ordered the furnace heated seven times hotter than usual ²⁰and commanded some of the strongest soldiers in his army to tie up Shadrach, Meshach and Abednego and throw them into the blazing furnace. ²¹So these men, wearing their robes, trousers, turbans and other clothes, were bound and thrown into the blazing furnace. ²²The king's command was so urgent and the furnace so hot that the flames of the fire killed the soldiers who took up Shadrach, Meshach and Abednego, ²³and these three men, firmly tied, fell into the blazing furnace.

²⁴Then King Nebuchadnezzar leaped to his feet in amazement and asked his advisers, "Weren't there three men that we tied up and threw into the fire?"

They replied, "Certainly, O king."

²⁵He said, "Look! I see four men walking around in the fire, unbound and unharmed, and the fourth looks like a son of the gods."

²⁶Nebuchadnezzar then approached the opening of the blazing furnace and shouted, "Shadrach, Meshach and Abednego, servants of the Most High God, come out! Come here!"

So Shadrach, Meshach and Abednego came out of the fire, ²⁷and the satraps, prefects, governors and royal advisers crowded around them. They saw that the fire had not harmed their bodies, nor was a hair of their heads singed; their robes were not scorched, and there was no smell of fire on them.

²⁸Then Nebuchadnezzar said, "Praise be to the God of Shadrach, Meshach and Abednego, who has sent his angel and rescued his servants! They trusted in him and defied the king's command and were willing to give up their lives rather than serve or worship any god except their own God. ²⁹Therefore I decree that the people of any nation or language who say anything against the God of Shadrach, Meshach and Abednego be cut into pieces and their houses be turned into piles of rubble, for no other god can save in this way."

³⁰Then the king promoted Shadrach, Meshach and Abednego in the province of Babylon.

AUGUST 28 ☐ DAY 241
Watching and Waiting

 LOOK BACK This past week you have seen Judah herself receive the full brunt of Ezekiel's assault. Like a diligent watchman, Ezekiel guards the house of Israel by warning of impending judgment. He calls and calls, but no one is listening. And finally the end has come, for "the city has fallen" (Ezekiel 33:21). They are curious to hear the word of the Lord but do not put it into practice.

Knowing what to do must be translated into doing what you know. Like sheep without a shepherd, like dry, lifeless, disconnected bones, the nation lies plundered and devoured by its pagan neighbors. But even in defeat, God's purposes shine through, for he wants the nations to know that God alone is the Lord. The book ends with a glorious display demonstrating that God is not finished with his people or their temple.

By contrast, Daniel is torn from his beloved Jerusalem to begin a three-year "resident program" in Babylonian studies. In his diet and his dreams, Daniel demonstrates to his captors that "there is a God in heaven" (Daniel 2:28), who interprets the world's most difficult dreams and protects his exiled people far from home.

A well-worn path is not necessarily the right one.

LOOK UP Life has been described as "a series of crises cleverly connected by the mundane of the everyday." In Daniel's young existence, the mundane of life in Jerusalem gave way almost overnight to the crisis of living out his faith in a foreign land.

Captured as a prisoner of war, Daniel was soon confronted with numerous choices: Should I eat what they feed me? Should I accept the name they give me? Should I take the credit for being able to interpret dreams? Should I bow down to an idol of gold, at the risk of my life if I don't?

Daniel's parents could not possibly have anticipated the perils their son would encounter in Babylonia—but they would have been proud of his wise response in translating his faith into daily decisions. Little wonder that Daniel's reputation grew and grew. No longer merely a transplanted teenager, Daniel was growing into a man of God whose wisdom and tact were legendary.

LOOK AHEAD Though you never read of Daniel preaching a sermon, that's precisely what he did with his life—in the choices he made, the wisdom he demonstrated, the priority that he gave to prayer and the diligence he demonstrated toward every task set before him.

"Dare to Be a Daniel" is more than a gospel song. It is a timeless challenge for each new generation intent on being God's "change agents" wherever he might send them. You may never see the inside of a kingly castle (or lions' den), but you can be sure your life will be full of excitement and challenge.

Daniel demonstrated by his dietary habits that his body was the temple of God. Your body is the only vehicle God will give you to do his will this side of heaven. Are you taking good care of it—eating a nourishing diet, getting adequate rest and exercise and avoiding harmful substances? If not, study Daniel's example carefully, and then "dare to be a Daniel."

AUGUST 29 □ DAY 242
DANIEL 4–6
Daniel's Faith in the Lions' Den

OVERVIEW Today's section shows the sovereignty of the God of Israel in the affairs of people and nations. Because of Nebuchadnezzar's great pride, he is "put out to pasture" to live like the cattle of the field. When his reason returns to him, he voices a testimony of praise to the one who is God of heaven and earth. His grandson Belshazzar sees the hand of God (literally!) in a different way. In the midst of a drunken feast, God's finger appears to write Belshazzar's death sentence on the palace wall. That very night, Darius conquers Belshazzar, and the kingdom of Babylonia falls. During the reign of Darius, God displays his power of protection in Daniel's life by shutting the lions' mouths.

Chapter 4	Chapter 5	Chapter 6
Disciplined in the Pasture	Weighed on the Scales	Protected in the Lions' Den
Nebuchadnezzar	Belshazzar	Daniel

God grants with each burden the strength to bear it— seldom more, never less.

YOUR DAILY WALK The little girl was only weeks old when she contracted an eye disease. Her parents took her to a physician, and in the process of treatment the doctor accidentally prescribed the wrong medication. As a result, the girl became permanently blind. And yet, in spite of her blindness, she composed more than eight thousand hymns during her lifetime.

Toward the end of Fanny Crosby's life a friend asked her, "Do you ever feel any bitterness toward the doctor?" She replied, "No, you see, it may have been a mistake on the doctor's part, but not on God's part." Fanny Crosby's God was the God of Daniel—the God in perfect control of all things in heaven and earth.

Is Daniel's God your God? Do you have that same confidence in a sovereign Lord that sustained Fanny Crosby? Find a hymnal, turn to the author index, and select two or three hymns written by Fanny Crosby. Then prayerfully read some of the stanzas penned by a woman of God whose faith was unshakable. Does this testimony of praise express what is on your heart?

INSIGHT Not a Seal of Approval

Darius and his nobles sealed the lions' pit, which was to have been Daniel's tomb, to prevent outside interference. Hundreds of years later Pilate also sealed a tomb to prevent human interference with Jesus' body. But a mere king's seal cannot stop the power of God.

CHAPTER 4
King Nebuchadnezzar,

To the peoples, nations and men of every language, who live in all the world:

May you prosper greatly!

[2]It is my pleasure to tell you about the miraculous signs and wonders that the Most High God has performed for me.

[3]How great are his signs,
    how mighty his wonders!
His kingdom is an eternal
    kingdom;
his dominion endures from
    generation to generation.

[4]I, Nebuchadnezzar, was at home in my palace, contented and prosperous. [5]I had a dream that made me afraid. As I was lying in my bed, the images and visions that passed through my mind terrified me. [6]So I commanded that all the wise men of

Babylon be brought before me to interpret the dream for me. [7]When the magicians, enchanters, astrologers[i] and diviners came, I told them the dream, but they could not interpret it for me. [8]Finally, Daniel came into my presence and I told him the dream. (He is called Belteshazzar, after the name of my god, and the spirit of the holy gods is in him.)

[9]I said, "Belteshazzar, chief of the magicians, I know that the spirit of the holy gods is in you, and no mystery is too difficult for you. Here is my dream; interpret it for me. [10]These are the visions I saw while lying in my bed: I looked, and there before me stood a tree in the middle of the land. Its height was enormous. [11]The tree grew large and strong and its top touched the sky; it was visible to the ends of the earth. [12]Its leaves were beautiful, its fruit abundant, and on it was food for all. Under it the beasts of the field found shelter, and the birds of the air lived in its

[i]7 Or *Chaldeans*

branches; from it every creature was fed.

¹³"In the visions I saw while lying in my bed, I looked, and there before me was a messenger,ʲ a holy one, coming down from heaven. ¹⁴He called in a loud voice: 'Cut down the tree and trim off its branches; strip off its leaves and scatter its fruit. Let the animals flee from under it and the birds from its branches. ¹⁵But let the stump and its roots, bound with iron and bronze, remain in the ground, in the grass of the field.

" 'Let him be drenched with the dew of heaven, and let him live with the animals among the plants of the earth. ¹⁶Let his mind be changed from that of a man and let him be given the mind of an animal, till seven timesᵏ pass by for him.

¹⁷" 'The decision is announced by messengers, the holy ones declare the verdict, so that the living may know that the Most High is sovereign over the kingdoms of men and gives them to anyone he wishes and sets over them the lowliest of men.'

¹⁸"This is the dream that I, King Nebuchadnezzar, had. Now, Belteshazzar, tell me what it means, for none of the wise men in my kingdom can interpret it for me. But you can, because the spirit of the holy gods is in you."

¹⁹Then Daniel (also called Belteshazzar) was greatly perplexed for a time, and his thoughts terrified him. So the king said, "Belteshazzar, do not let the dream or its meaning alarm you."

Belteshazzar answered, "My lord, if only the dream applied to your enemies and its meaning to your adversaries! ²⁰The tree you saw, which grew large and strong, with its top touching the sky, visible to the whole earth, ²¹with beautiful leaves and abundant fruit, providing food for all, giving shelter to the beasts of the field, and having nesting places in its branches for the birds of the air— ²²you, O king, are that tree! You have become great and strong; your greatness has grown until it reaches the

sky, and your dominion extends to distant parts of the earth.

²³"You, O king, saw a messenger, a holy one, coming down from heaven and saying, 'Cut down the tree and destroy it, but leave the stump, bound with iron and bronze, in the grass of the field, while its roots remain in the ground. Let him be drenched with the dew of heaven; let him live like the wild animals, until seven times pass by for him.'

²⁴"This is the interpretation, O king, and this is the decree the Most High has issued against my lord the king: ²⁵You will be driven away from people and will live with the wild animals; you will eat grass like cattle and be drenched with the dew of heaven. Seven times will pass by for you until you acknowledge that the Most High is sovereign over the kingdoms of men and gives them to anyone he wishes. ²⁶The command to leave the stump of the tree with its roots means that your kingdom will be restored to you when you acknowledge that Heaven rules. ²⁷Therefore, O king, be pleased to accept my advice: Renounce your sins by doing what is right, and your wickedness by being kind to the oppressed. It may be that then your prosperity will continue."

²⁸All this happened to King Nebuchadnezzar. ²⁹Twelve months later, as the king was walking on the roof of the royal palace of Babylon, ³⁰he said, "Is not this the great Babylon I have built as the royal residence, by my mighty power and for the glory of my majesty?"

³¹The words were still on his lips when a voice came from heaven, "This is what is decreed for you, King Nebuchadnezzar: Your royal authority has been taken from you. ³²You will be driven away from people and will live with the wild animals; you will eat grass like cattle. Seven times will pass by for you until you acknowledge that the Most High is sovereign over the kingdoms of men and gives them to anyone he wishes."

³³Immediately what had been said

ʲ13 Or *watchman*; also in verses 17 and 23   ᵏ16 Or *years*; also in verses 23, 25 and 32 about Nebuchadnezzar was fulfilled. He was driven away from people and ate grass like cattle. His body was drenched with the dew of heaven until his hair grew like the feathers of an eagle and his nails like the claws of a bird.

³⁴At the end of that time, I, Nebuchadnezzar, raised my eyes toward heaven, and my sanity was restored. Then I praised the Most High; I honored and glorified him who lives forever.

His dominion is an eternal dominion;
　his kingdom endures from
　　generation to generation.
³⁵All the peoples of the earth
　are regarded as nothing.
He does as he pleases
　with the powers of heaven
　and the peoples of the earth.
No one can hold back his hand
　or say to him: "What have you
　　done?"

³⁶At the same time that my sanity was restored, my honor and splendor were returned to me for the glory of my kingdom. My advisers and nobles sought me out, and I was restored to my throne and became even greater than before. ³⁷Now I, Nebuchadnezzar, praise and exalt and glorify the King of heaven, because everything he does is right and all his ways are just. And those who walk in pride he is able to humble.

CHAPTER 5

King Belshazzar gave a great banquet for a thousand of his nobles and drank wine with them. ²While Belshazzar was drinking his wine, he gave orders to bring in the gold and silver goblets that Nebuchadnezzar his father*l* had taken from the temple in Jerusalem, so that the king and his nobles, his wives and his concubines might drink from them. ³So they brought in the gold goblets that had been taken from the temple of God in Jerusalem, and the king and his nobles, his wives and his concubines drank from them. ⁴As they drank the wine, they praised the gods of gold and silver, of bronze, iron, wood and stone.

⁵Suddenly the fingers of a human hand appeared and wrote on the plaster of the wall, near the lampstand in the royal palace. The king watched the hand as it wrote. ⁶His face turned pale and he was so frightened that his knees knocked together and his legs gave way.

⁷The king called out for the enchanters, astrologers*m* and diviners to be brought and said to these wise men of Babylon, "Whoever reads this writing and tells me what it means will be clothed in purple and have a gold chain placed around his neck, and he will be made the third highest ruler in the kingdom."

⁸Then all the king's wise men came in, but they could not read the writing or tell the king what it meant. ⁹So King Belshazzar became even more terrified and his face grew more pale. His nobles were baffled.

¹⁰The queen,*n* hearing the voices of the king and his nobles, came into the banquet hall. "O king, live forever!" she said. "Don't be alarmed! Don't look so pale! ¹¹There is a man in your kingdom who has the spirit of the holy gods in him. In the time of your father he was found to have insight and intelligence and wisdom like that of the gods. King Nebuchadnezzar your father—your father the king, I say—appointed him chief of the magicians, enchanters, astrologers and diviners. ¹²This man Daniel, whom the king called Belteshazzar, was found to have a keen mind and knowledge and understanding, and also the ability to interpret dreams, explain riddles and solve difficult problems. Call for Daniel, and he will tell you what the writing means."

¹³So Daniel was brought before the king, and the king said to him, "Are you Daniel, one of the exiles my father the king brought from Judah? ¹⁴I have heard that the spirit of the gods is in you and that you have insight, intelligence and outstanding wisdom. ¹⁵The wise men and enchanters were brought before me to read this writing and tell me what it means, but they could not explain it. ¹⁶Now I have heard that you are able to give interpretations and to solve difficult problems. If you can read this writing and tell me what it means, you will be clothed in purple and have a gold chain placed

---

l 2 Or ancestor; or predecessor; also in verses 11, 13 and 18   m 7 Or Chaldeans; also in verse 11   n 10 Or queen mother around your neck, and you will be made the third highest ruler in the kingdom."

17Then Daniel answered the king, "You may keep your gifts for yourself and give your rewards to someone else. Nevertheless, I will read the writing for the king and tell him what it means.

18"O king, the Most High God gave your father Nebuchadnezzar sovereignty and greatness and glory and splendor. 19Because of the high position he gave him, all the peoples and nations and men of every language dreaded and feared him. Those the king wanted to put to death, he put to death; those he wanted to spare, he spared; those he wanted to promote, he promoted; and those he wanted to humble, he humbled. 20But when his heart became arrogant and hardened with pride, he was deposed from his royal throne and stripped of his glory. 21He was driven away from people and given the mind of an animal; he lived with the wild donkeys and ate grass like cattle; and his body was drenched with the dew of heaven, until he acknowledged that the Most High God is sovereign over the kingdoms of men and sets over them anyone he wishes.

22"But you his son,o O Belshazzar, have not humbled yourself, though you knew all this. 23Instead, you have set yourself up against the Lord of heaven. You had the goblets from his temple brought to you, and you and your nobles, your wives and your concubines drank wine from them. You praised the gods of silver and gold, of bronze, iron, wood and stone, which cannot see or hear or understand. But you did not honor the God who holds in his hand your life and all your ways. 24Therefore he sent the hand that wrote the inscription.

25"This is the inscription that was written:

MENE, MENE, TEKEL, PARSINp

26"This is what these words mean:

Meneq: God has numbered the days of your reign and brought it to an end.
27Tekelr: You have been weighed

on the scales and found wanting.
28Peress: Your kingdom is divided and given to the Medes and Persians."

29Then at Belshazzar's command, Daniel was clothed in purple, a gold chain was placed around his neck, and he was proclaimed the third highest ruler in the kingdom.

30That very night Belshazzar, king of the Babylonians,t was slain, 31and Darius the Mede took over the kingdom, at the age of sixty-two.

CHAPTER 6

It pleased Darius to appoint 120 satraps to rule throughout the kingdom, 2with three administrators over them, one of whom was Daniel. The satraps were made accountable to them so that the king might not suffer loss. 3Now Daniel so distinguished himself among the administrators and the satraps by his exceptional qualities that the king planned to set him over the whole kingdom. 4At this, the administrators and the satraps tried to find grounds for charges against Daniel in his conduct of government affairs, but they were unable to do so. They could find no corruption in him, because he was trustworthy and neither corrupt nor negligent. 5Finally these men said, "We will never find any basis for charges against this man Daniel unless it has something to do with the law of his God."

6So the administrators and the satraps went as a group to the king and said: "O King Darius, live forever! 7The royal administrators, prefects, satraps, advisers and governors have all agreed that the king should issue an edict and enforce the decree that anyone who prays to any god or man during the next thirty days, except to you, O king, shall be thrown into the lions' den. 8Now, O king, issue the decree and put it in writing so that it cannot be altered—in accordance with the laws of the Medes and Persians, which cannot be repealed." 9So King Darius put the decree in writing.

10Now when Daniel learned that the decree had been published, he went home to his upstairs room where the windows opened toward Jerusalem. Three times a day he got down on his knees and prayed, giving thanks to his God, just as he had done before. [11]Then these men went as a group and found Daniel praying and asking God for help. [12]So they went to the king and spoke to him about his royal decree: "Did you not publish a decree that during the next thirty days anyone who prays to any god or man except to you, O king, would be thrown into the lions' den?"

The king answered, "The decree stands—in accordance with the laws of the Medes and Persians, which cannot be repealed."

[13]Then they said to the king, "Daniel, who is one of the exiles from Judah, pays no attention to you, O king, or to the decree you put in writing. He still prays three times a day." [14]When the king heard this, he was greatly distressed; he was determined to rescue Daniel and made every effort until sundown to save him.

[15]Then the men went as a group to the king and said to him, "Remember, O king, that according to the law of the Medes and Persians no decree or edict that the king issues can be changed."

[16]So the king gave the order, and they brought Daniel and threw him into the lions' den. The king said to Daniel, "May your God, whom you serve continually, rescue you!"

[17]A stone was brought and placed over the mouth of the den, and the king sealed it with his own signet ring and with the rings of his nobles, so that Daniel's situation might not be changed. [18]Then the king returned to his palace and spent the night without eating and without any entertainment being brought to him. And he could not sleep.

[19]At the first light of dawn, the king got up and hurried to the lions' den. [20]When

u 28 Or Darius, that is, the reign of Cyrus

he came near the den, he called to Daniel in an anguished voice, "Daniel, servant of the living God, has your God, whom you serve continually, been able to rescue you from the lions?"

[21]Daniel answered, "O king, live forever! [22]My God sent his angel, and he shut the mouths of the lions. They have not hurt me, because I was found innocent in his sight. Nor have I ever done any wrong before you, O king."

[23]The king was overjoyed and gave orders to lift Daniel out of the den. And when Daniel was lifted from the den, no wound was found on him, because he had trusted in his God.

[24]At the king's command, the men who had falsely accused Daniel were brought in and thrown into the lions' den, along with their wives and children. And before they reached the floor of the den, the lions overpowered them and crushed all their bones.

[25]Then King Darius wrote to all the peoples, nations and men of every language throughout the land:

"May you prosper greatly!

[26]"I issue a decree that in every part of my kingdom people must fear and reverence the God of Daniel.

"For he is the living God
and he endures forever;
his kingdom will not be destroyed,
his dominion will never end.
[27]He rescues and he saves;
he performs signs and wonders
in the heavens and on the earth.
He has rescued Daniel
from the power of the lions."

[28]So Daniel prospered during the reign of Darius and the reign of Cyrus[u] the Persian.

AUGUST 30 □ DAY 243
DANIEL 7–9
Beasts, Kings and Seventy Weeks

 OVERVIEW Today's section contains prophecies of breathtaking scope. Interestingly, much of what Daniel prophesied is explained right in the passage. Watch for keys to the interpretation of the various beasts and animals as you read through these chapters. Chapter 9 is a record of Daniel's prayer for himself and his countrymen based on the truth he encountered while reading the prophecy of Jeremiah. In response to Daniel's prayer, God sends the angel Gabriel to give Daniel added insight into coming events.

Chapter 7	Chapter 8	Chapter 9
The Lion, Bear, Leopard and Beast	The Ram, Goat and Little Horn	The Prayer, Angel and Explanation
Daniel's Visions: History Foretold		

 YOUR DAILY WALK One night a soldier was caught creeping back to his quarters from the nearby woods. Taken before his commanding officer, the soldier was charged with communicating with the enemy. The man pleaded that he had gone into the woods to pray alone.

Does your life affirm the reality of your God or refute it? "Then you'd better start praying now!" roared the officer. "You never needed it so much!" Expecting certain death, the soldier knelt and poured out his soul in eloquent prayer. "You may go," said the officer when the soldier had finished. "I believe your story. If you hadn't drilled so often, you wouldn't be doing so well under fire."

How well do you pray "on the spot"? Have you learned through practice and persistence to communicate often and long with your heavenly Father? Standing side by side with Daniel's confidence in God was his communication with God. The two are inseparable, for to trust God is to talk to him, and to talk to God is to trust him all the more.

How often have you talked to God in the last twenty-four hours? If the answer discourages you, then try this. Tape the words *Pray Now* to the face of your wristwatch. Then, as often as you are reminded, talk to your heavenly Father. You'll find your love for him and your trust in him growing with each passing hour.

 INSIGHT Correlating the Creatures of Daniel
It may help you in your reading of chapters 7–8 to remember that both the leopard and the male goat represent Greece, while both the bear and the ram represent Medo-Persia.

CHAPTER 7
In the first year of Belshazzar king of Babylon, Daniel had a dream, and visions passed through his mind as he was lying on his bed. He wrote down the substance of his dream.

²Daniel said: "In my vision at night I looked, and there before me were the four winds of heaven churning up the great sea. ³Four great beasts, each different from the others, came up out of the sea.

⁴"The first was like a lion, and it had the wings of an eagle. I watched until its wings were torn off and it was lifted from the ground so that it stood on two feet like a man, and the heart of a man was given to it.

⁵"And there before me was a second beast, which looked like a bear. It was raised up on one of its sides, and it had three ribs in its mouth between its teeth. It was told, 'Get up and eat your fill of flesh!'

⁶"After that, I looked, and there before me was another beast, one that looked like a leopard. And on its back it had four wings like those of a bird. This beast had four heads, and it was given authority to rule.

⁷"After that, in my vision at night I looked, and there before me was a fourth beast—terrifying and frightening and very powerful. It had large iron teeth; it crushed and devoured its victims and trampled underfoot whatever was left. It was different from all the former beasts, and it had ten horns.

⁸"While I was thinking about the horns, there before me was another horn, a little one, which came up among them; and three of the first horns were uprooted before it. This horn had eyes like the eyes of a man and a mouth that spoke boastfully.

⁹"As I looked,

"thrones were set in place,
    and the Ancient of Days took his
        seat.
His clothing was as white as snow;
    the hair of his head was white like
        wool.
His throne was flaming with fire,
    and its wheels were all ablaze.
¹⁰A river of fire was flowing,
    coming out from before him.
Thousands upon thousands attended
    him;
    ten thousand times ten thousand
        stood before him.
The court was seated,
    and the books were opened.

¹¹"Then I continued to watch because of the boastful words the horn was speaking. I kept looking until the beast was slain and its body destroyed and thrown into the blazing fire. ¹²(The other beasts had been stripped of their authority, but were allowed to live for a period of time.)

¹³"In my vision at night I looked, and there before me was one like a son of man, coming with the clouds of heaven. He approached the Ancient of Days and was led into his presence. ¹⁴He was given authority, glory and sovereign power; all peoples, nations and men of every language worshiped him. His dominion is an

everlasting dominion that will not pass away, and his kingdom is one that will never be destroyed.

¹⁵"I, Daniel, was troubled in spirit, and the visions that passed through my mind disturbed me. ¹⁶I approached one of those standing there and asked him the true meaning of all this.

"So he told me and gave me the interpretation of these things: ¹⁷'The four great beasts are four kingdoms that will rise from the earth. ¹⁸But the saints of the Most High will receive the kingdom and will possess it forever—yes, for ever and ever.'

¹⁹"Then I wanted to know the true meaning of the fourth beast, which was different from all the others and most terrifying, with its iron teeth and bronze claws—the beast that crushed and devoured its victims and trampled underfoot whatever was left. ²⁰I also wanted to know about the ten horns on its head and about the other horn that came up, before which three of them fell—the horn that looked more imposing than the others and that had eyes and a mouth that spoke boastfully. ²¹As I watched, this horn was waging war against the saints and defeating them, ²²until the Ancient of Days came and pronounced judgment in favor of the saints of the Most High, and the time came when they possessed the kingdom.

²³"He gave me this explanation: 'The fourth beast is a fourth kingdom that will appear on earth. It will be different from all the other kingdoms and will devour the whole earth, trampling it down and crushing it. ²⁴The ten horns are ten kings who will come from this kingdom. After them another king will arise, different from the earlier ones; he will subdue three kings. ²⁵He will speak against the Most High and oppress his saints and try to change the set times and the laws. The saints will be handed over to him for a time, times and half a time.ᵛ

²⁶" 'But the court will sit, and his power will be taken away and completely destroyed forever. ²⁷Then the sovereignty, power and greatness of the kingdoms under the whole heaven will be handed over to the saints, the people of the Most High. His kingdom will be an everlasting king-

ᵛ25 Or for a year, two years and half a year

dom, and all rulers will worship and obey him.'

²⁸"This is the end of the matter. I, Daniel, was deeply troubled by my thoughts, and my face turned pale, but I kept the matter to myself."

CHAPTER 8

In the third year of King Belshazzar's reign, I, Daniel, had a vision, after the one that had already appeared to me. ²In my vision I saw myself in the citadel of Susa in the province of Elam; in the vision I was beside the Ulai Canal. ³I looked up, and there before me was a ram with two horns, standing beside the canal, and the horns were long. One of the horns was longer than the other but grew up later. ⁴I watched the ram as he charged toward the west and the north and the south. No animal could stand against him, and none could rescue from his power. He did as he pleased and became great.

⁵As I was thinking about this, suddenly a goat with a prominent horn between his eyes came from the west, crossing the whole earth without touching the ground. ⁶He came toward the two-horned ram I had seen standing beside the canal and charged at him in great rage. ⁷I saw him attack the ram furiously, striking the ram and shattering his two horns. The ram was powerless to stand against him; the goat knocked him to the ground and trampled on him, and none could rescue the ram from his power. ⁸The goat became very great, but at the height of his power his large horn was broken off, and in its place four prominent horns grew up toward the four winds of heaven.

⁹Out of one of them came another horn, which started small but grew in power to the south and to the east and toward the Beautiful Land. ¹⁰It grew until it reached the host of the heavens, and it threw some of the starry host down to the earth and trampled on them. ¹¹It set itself up to be as great as the Prince of the host; it took away the daily sacrifice from him, and the place of his sanctuary was brought low. ¹²Because of rebellion, the host ˻of the saints˼ʷ and the daily sacrifice were given over to it. It prospered in everything it did, and truth was thrown to the ground.

¹³Then I heard a holy one speaking, and another holy one said to him, "How long will it take for the vision to be fulfilled—the vision concerning the daily sacrifice, the rebellion that causes desolation, and the surrender of the sanctuary and of the host that will be trampled underfoot?"

¹⁴He said to me, "It will take 2,300 evenings and mornings; then the sanctuary will be reconsecrated."

¹⁵While I, Daniel, was watching the vision and trying to understand it, there before me stood one who looked like a man. ¹⁶And I heard a man's voice from the Ulai calling, "Gabriel, tell this man the meaning of the vision."

¹⁷As he came near the place where I was standing, I was terrified and fell prostrate. "Son of man," he said to me, "understand that the vision concerns the time of the end."

¹⁸While he was speaking to me, I was in a deep sleep, with my face to the ground. Then he touched me and raised me to my feet.

¹⁹He said: "I am going to tell you what will happen later in the time of wrath, because the vision concerns the appointed time of the end.ˣ ²⁰The two-horned ram that you saw represents the kings of Media and Persia. ²¹The shaggy goat is the king of Greece, and the large horn between his eyes is the first king. ²²The four horns that replaced the one that was broken off represent four kingdoms that will emerge from his nation but will not have the same power.

²³"In the latter part of their reign, when rebels have become completely wicked, a stern-faced king, a master of intrigue, will arise. ²⁴He will become very strong, but not by his own power. He will cause astounding devastation and will succeed in whatever he does. He will destroy the mighty men and the holy people. ²⁵He will cause deceit to prosper, and he will consider himself superior. When they feel secure, he will destroy many and take his stand against the Prince of princes. Yet he will be destroyed, but not by human power.

²⁶"The vision of the evenings and mornings that has been given you is true, but seal up the vision, for it concerns the distant future."

ʷ**12** Or *rebellion, the armies*   ˣ**19** Or *because the end will be at the appointed time*

²⁷I, Daniel, was exhausted and lay ill for several days. Then I got up and went about the king's business. I was appalled by the vision; it was beyond understanding.

CHAPTER 9

In the first year of Darius son of Xerxes*y* (a Mede by descent), who was made ruler over the Babylonian*z* kingdom— ²in the first year of his reign, I, Daniel, understood from the Scriptures, according to the word of the LORD given to Jeremiah the prophet, that the desolation of Jerusalem would last seventy years. ³So I turned to the Lord God and pleaded with him in prayer and petition, in fasting, and in sackcloth and ashes.

⁴I prayed to the LORD my God and confessed:

"O Lord, the great and awesome God, who keeps his covenant of love with all who love him and obey his commands, ⁵we have sinned and done wrong. We have been wicked and have rebelled; we have turned away from your commands and laws. ⁶We have not listened to your servants the prophets, who spoke in your name to our kings, our princes and our fathers, and to all the people of the land.

⁷"Lord, you are righteous, but this day we are covered with shame—the men of Judah and people of Jerusalem and all Israel, both near and far, in all the countries where you have scattered us because of our unfaithfulness to you. ⁸O LORD, we and our kings, our princes and our fathers are covered with shame because we have sinned against you. ⁹The Lord our God is merciful and forgiving, even though we have rebelled against him; ¹⁰we have not obeyed the LORD our God or kept the laws he gave us through his servants the prophets. ¹¹All Israel has transgressed your law and turned away, refusing to obey you.

"Therefore the curses and sworn judgments written in the Law of Moses, the servant of God, have been poured out on us, because we have sinned against you. ¹²You have ful-

filled the words spoken against us and against our rulers by bringing upon us great disaster. Under the whole heaven nothing has ever been done like what has been done to Jerusalem. ¹³Just as it is written in the Law of Moses, all this disaster has come upon us, yet we have not sought the favor of the LORD our God by turning from our sins and giving attention to your truth. ¹⁴The LORD did not hesitate to bring the disaster upon us, for the LORD our God is righteous in everything he does; yet we have not obeyed him.

¹⁵"Now, O Lord our God, who brought your people out of Egypt with a mighty hand and who made for yourself a name that endures to this day, we have sinned, we have done wrong. ¹⁶O Lord, in keeping with all your righteous acts, turn away your anger and your wrath from Jerusalem, your city, your holy hill. Our sins and the iniquities of our fathers have made Jerusalem and your people an object of scorn to all those around us.

¹⁷"Now, our God, hear the prayers and petitions of your servant. For your sake, O Lord, look with favor on your desolate sanctuary. ¹⁸Give ear, O God, and hear; open your eyes and see the desolation of the city that bears your Name. We do not make requests of you because we are righteous, but because of your great mercy. ¹⁹O Lord, listen! O Lord, forgive! O Lord, hear and act! For your sake, O my God, do not delay, because your city and your people bear your Name."

²⁰While I was speaking and praying, confessing my sin and the sin of my people Israel and making my request to the LORD my God for his holy hill— ²¹while I was still in prayer, Gabriel, the man I had seen in the earlier vision, came to me in swift flight about the time of the evening sacrifice. ²²He instructed me and said to me, "Daniel, I have now come to give you insight and understanding. ²³As soon as you began to pray, an answer was given, which I have come to tell you, for you are

---

y1 Hebrew *Ahasuerus*   *z1* Or *Chaldean*

highly esteemed. Therefore, consider the message and understand the vision:

[24]"Seventy 'sevens'[a] are decreed for your people and your holy city to finish[b] transgression, to put an end to sin, to atone for wickedness, to bring in everlasting righteousness, to seal up vision and prophecy and to anoint the most holy.[c]

[25]"Know and understand this: From the issuing of the decree[d] to restore and rebuild Jerusalem until the Anointed One,[e] the ruler, comes, there will be seven 'sevens,' and sixty-two 'sevens.' It will be rebuilt with streets and a trench, but in times of trouble. [26]After the sixty-two 'sevens,' the Anointed One will be cut off and will have nothing.[f] The people of the ruler who will come will destroy the city and the sanctuary. The end will come like a flood: War will continue until the end, and desolations have been decreed. [27]He will confirm a covenant with many for one 'seven.'[g] In the middle of the 'seven'[g] he will put an end to sacrifice and offering. And on a wing ˻of the temple˼ he will set up an abomination that causes desolation, until the end that is decreed is poured out on him.[h]" [i]

[a]24 Or 'weeks'; also in verses 25 and 26   [b]24 Or restrain   [c]24 Or Most Holy Place; or most holy One   [d]25 Or word
[e]25 Or an anointed one; also in verse 26   [f]26 Or off and will have no one; or off, but not for himself   [g]27 Or 'week'   [h]27 Or it
[i]27 Or And one who causes desolation will come upon the pinnacle of the abominable ˻temple˼, until the end that is decreed is poured out on the desolated ˻city˼

AUGUST 31 □ DAY 244
DANIEL 10–12
Previews of Israel's Future

OVERVIEW You may find comfort in knowing that even Daniel didn't understand everything that was revealed to him in his visions (12:8). (While you're at it, glance at 2 Peter 3:15–16, and notice that Peter had the same trouble with some of Paul's writings!) Don't be overly concerned about the parts of today's reading you don't understand. Instead, like Daniel, worry about the parts you do! In Daniel's final visions he sees a titanic struggle between kings from the south and north vying for control of "the Beautiful Land" (11:41) in a climactic "time of distress" (12:1). Though the final chapter of world history is not revealed to Daniel (12:9), the outcome is sure: purifying judgment.

Chapter 10	Chapter 11	Chapter 12
Daniel's Prayer and an Angel's Visit	Persia and Greece in Israel's Future	Punishment and Reward in Israel's Future
Preparation	Prophecy	Preview

YOUR DAILY WALK It does seem strange, but Daniel—God's great prophetic mouthpiece during the exile—probably knew less about his prophetic visions than you do.

Looking back over the course of history as it has transpired, with the great world powers all carefully documented by secular historians and archaeologists, you can match leaders and nations with parts of Daniel's visions in a way that Daniel never dreamed possible. Babylonia . . . Medo-Persia . . . Greece . . . Rome—much of their history was foretold centuries before from the mouth of a godly government servant in Babylon! Add to that the additional insight of the New Testament, and you have a sharper picture of the future course of this

No Bible subject matter holds more practical implications than prophecy.

world than did any Old Testament prophet! What a privilege—what a responsibility.

Set aside some extra time to study a particularly difficult passage from the book of Daniel. Your pastor or local Christian bookstore can suggest a good commentary or two to make your time even more profitable.

 INSIGHT Final Score: Daniel—100, Critics—0
Chapter 11 alone contains more than one hundred specific prophecies of historical events that literally came true! It is little wonder that some critics attempt to place Daniel two hundred years later in order to undermine the miraculous character of his prophecies.

CHAPTER 10

In the third year of Cyrus king of Persia, a revelation was given to Daniel (who was called Belteshazzar). Its message was true and it concerned a great war.[j] The understanding of the message came to him in a vision.

[2]At that time I, Daniel, mourned for three weeks. [3]I ate no choice food; no meat or wine touched my lips; and I used no lotions at all until the three weeks were over.

[4]On the twenty-fourth day of the first month, as I was standing on the bank of the great river, the Tigris, [5]I looked up and there before me was a man dressed in linen, with a belt of the finest gold around his waist. [6]His body was like chrysolite, his face like lightning, his eyes like flaming torches, his arms and legs like the gleam of burnished bronze, and his voice like the sound of a multitude.

[7]I, Daniel, was the only one who saw the vision; the men with me did not see it, but such terror overwhelmed them that they fled and hid themselves. [8]So I was left alone, gazing at this great vision; I had no strength left, my face turned deathly pale and I was helpless. [9]Then I heard him speaking, and as I listened to him, I fell into a deep sleep, my face to the ground.

[10]A hand touched me and set me trembling on my hands and knees. [11]He said, "Daniel, you who are highly esteemed, consider carefully the words I am about to speak to you, and stand up, for I have now been sent to you." And when he said this to me, I stood up trembling.

[12]Then he continued, "Do not be afraid, Daniel. Since the first day that you set your mind to gain understanding and to humble yourself before your God, your words were heard, and I have come in response to them. [13]But the prince of the Persian kingdom resisted me twenty-one days. Then Michael, one of the chief princes, came to help me, because I was detained there with the king of Persia. [14]Now I have come to explain to you what will happen to your people in the future, for the vision concerns a time yet to come."

[15]While he was saying this to me, I bowed with my face toward the ground and was speechless. [16]Then one who looked like a man[k] touched my lips, and I opened my mouth and began to speak. I said to the one standing before me, "I am overcome with anguish because of the vision, my lord, and I am helpless. [17]How can I, your servant, talk with you, my lord? My strength is gone and I can hardly breathe."

[18]Again the one who looked like a man touched me and gave me strength. [19]"Do not be afraid, O man highly esteemed," he said. "Peace! Be strong now; be strong."

When he spoke to me, I was strengthened and said, "Speak, my lord, since you have given me strength."

[20]So he said, "Do you know why I have come to you? Soon I will return to fight against the prince of Persia, and when I go, the prince of Greece will come; [21]but first I will tell you what is written in the Book of Truth. (No one supports me against them except Michael, your CHAPTER 11 prince. [1]And in the first year of Darius the Mede, I took my stand to support and protect him.)

[2]"Now then, I tell you the truth: Three more kings will appear in Persia, and then a fourth, who will be far richer than all

[j]1 Or *true and burdensome*   [k]16 Most manuscripts of the Masoretic Text; one manuscript of the Masoretic Text, Dead Sea Scrolls and Septuagint *Then something that looked like a man's hand*

the others. When he has gained power by his wealth, he will stir up everyone against the kingdom of Greece. [3]Then a mighty king will appear, who will rule with great power and do as he pleases. [4]After he has appeared, his empire will be broken up and parceled out toward the four winds of heaven. It will not go to his descendants, nor will it have the power he exercised, because his empire will be uprooted and given to others.

[5]"The king of the South will become strong, but one of his commanders will become even stronger than he and will rule his own kingdom with great power. [6]After some years, they will become allies. The daughter of the king of the South will go to the king of the North to make an alliance, but she will not retain her power, and he and his power[l] will not last. In those days she will be handed over, together with her royal escort and her father[m] and the one who supported her.

[7]"One from her family line will arise to take her place. He will attack the forces of the king of the North and enter his fortress; he will fight against them and be victorious. [8]He will also seize their gods, their metal images and their valuable articles of silver and gold and carry them off to Egypt. For some years he will leave the king of the North alone. [9]Then the king of the North will invade the realm of the king of the South but will retreat to his own country. [10]His sons will prepare for war and assemble a great army, which will sweep on like an irresistible flood and carry the battle as far as his fortress.

[11]"Then the king of the South will march out in a rage and fight against the king of the North, who will raise a large army, but it will be defeated. [12]When the army is carried off, the king of the South will be filled with pride and will slaughter many thousands, yet he will not remain triumphant. [13]For the king of the North will muster another army, larger than the first; and after several years, he will advance with a huge army fully equipped.

[14]"In those times many will rise against the king of the South. The violent men among your own people will rebel in fulfillment of the vision, but without success. [15]Then the king of the North will come and build up siege ramps and will capture a fortified city. The forces of the South will be powerless to resist; even their best troops will not have the strength to stand. [16]The invader will do as he pleases; no one will be able to stand against him. He will establish himself in the Beautiful Land and will have the power to destroy it. [17]He will determine to come with the might of his entire kingdom and will make an alliance with the king of the South. And he will give him a daughter in marriage in order to overthrow the kingdom, but his plans[n] will not succeed or help him. [18]Then he will turn his attention to the coastlands and will take many of them, but a commander will put an end to his insolence and will turn his insolence back upon him. [19]After this, he will turn back toward the fortresses of his own country but will stumble and fall, to be seen no more.

[20]"His successor will send out a tax collector to maintain the royal splendor. In a few years, however, he will be destroyed, yet not in anger or in battle.

[21]"He will be succeeded by a contemptible person who has not been given the honor of royalty. He will invade the kingdom when its people feel secure, and he will seize it through intrigue. [22]Then an overwhelming army will be swept away before him; both it and a prince of the covenant will be destroyed. [23]After coming to an agreement with him, he will act deceitfully, and with only a few people he will rise to power. [24]When the richest provinces feel secure, he will invade them and will achieve what neither his fathers nor his forefathers did. He will distribute plunder, loot and wealth among his followers. He will plot the overthrow of fortresses—but only for a time.

[25]"With a large army he will stir up his strength and courage against the king of the South. The king of the South will wage war with a large and very powerful army, but he will not be able to stand because of the plots devised against him. [26]Those who eat from the king's provisions will try to destroy him; his army will be swept away, and many will fall in battle. [27]The two kings, with their hearts bent on evil, will sit at the same table and lie to each other, but to no avail, because an end will still come at the appointed

[l]6 Or *offspring*   [m]6 Or *child* (see Vulgate and Syriac)   [n]17 Or *but she*

time. ²⁸The king of the North will return to his own country with great wealth, but his heart will be set against the holy covenant. He will take action against it and then return to his own country.

²⁹"At the appointed time he will invade the South again, but this time the outcome will be different from what it was before. ³⁰Ships of the western coastlands⁰ will oppose him, and he will lose heart. Then he will turn back and vent his fury against the holy covenant. He will return and show favor to those who forsake the holy covenant.

³¹"His armed forces will rise up to desecrate the temple fortress and will abolish the daily sacrifice. Then they will set up the abomination that causes desolation. ³²With flattery he will corrupt those who have violated the covenant, but the people who know their God will firmly resist him.

³³"Those who are wise will instruct many, though for a time they will fall by the sword or be burned or captured or plundered. ³⁴When they fall, they will receive a little help, and many who are not sincere will join them. ³⁵Some of the wise will stumble, so that they may be refined, purified and made spotless until the time of the end, for it will still come at the appointed time.

³⁶"The king will do as he pleases. He will exalt and magnify himself above every god and will say unheard-of things against the God of gods. He will be successful until the time of wrath is completed, for what has been determined must take place. ³⁷He will show no regard for the gods of his fathers or for the one desired by women, nor will he regard any god, but will exalt himself above them all. ³⁸Instead of them, he will honor a god of fortresses; a god unknown to his fathers he will honor with gold and silver, with precious stones and costly gifts. ³⁹He will attack the mightiest fortresses with the help of a foreign god and will greatly honor those who acknowledge him. He will make them rulers over many people and will distribute the land at a price.ᵖ

⁴⁰"At the time of the end the king of the South will engage him in battle, and the king of the North will storm out against him with chariots and cavalry and a great

fleet of ships. He will invade many countries and sweep through them like a flood. ⁴¹He will also invade the Beautiful Land. Many countries will fall, but Edom, Moab and the leaders of Ammon will be delivered from his hand. ⁴²He will extend his power over many countries; Egypt will not escape. ⁴³He will gain control of the treasures of gold and silver and all the riches of Egypt, with the Libyans and Nubians in submission. ⁴⁴But reports from the east and the north will alarm him, and he will set out in a great rage to destroy and annihilate many. ⁴⁵He will pitch his royal tents between the seas at�q the beautiful holy mountain. Yet he will come to his end, and no one will help him.

CHAPTER 12

"At that time Michael, the great prince who protects your people, will arise. There will be a time of distress such as has not happened from the beginning of nations until then. But at that time your people—everyone whose name is found written in the book—will be delivered. ²Multitudes who sleep in the dust of the earth will awake: some to everlasting life, others to shame and everlasting contempt. ³Those who are wiseʳ will shine like the brightness of the heavens, and those who lead many to righteousness, like the stars for ever and ever. ⁴But you, Daniel, close up and seal the words of the scroll until the time of the end. Many will go here and there to increase knowledge."

⁵Then I, Daniel, looked, and there before me stood two others, one on this bank of the river and one on the opposite bank. ⁶One of them said to the man clothed in linen, who was above the waters of the river, "How long will it be before these astonishing things are fulfilled?"

⁷The man clothed in linen, who was above the waters of the river, lifted his right hand and his left hand toward heaven, and I heard him swear by him who lives forever, saying, "It will be for a time, times and half a time.ˢ When the power of the holy people has been finally broken, all these things will be completed."

⁰30 Hebrew of Kittim   ᵖ39 Or land for a reward   q45 Or the sea and   ʳ3 Or who impart wisdom   ˢ7 Or a year, two years and half a year

⁸I heard, but I did not understand. So I asked, "My lord, what will the outcome of all this be?"

⁹He replied, "Go your way, Daniel, because the words are closed up and sealed until the time of the end. ¹⁰Many will be purified, made spotless and refined, but the wicked will continue to be wicked. None of the wicked will understand, but those who are wise will understand.

¹¹"From the time that the daily sacrifice is abolished and the abomination that causes desolation is set up, there will be 1,290 days. ¹²Blessed is the one who waits for and reaches the end of the 1,335 days.

¹³"As for you, go your way till the end. You will rest, and then at the end of the days you will rise to receive your allotted inheritance."

Hosea

HOSEA'S book is a bittersweet story of unfaithfulness and undying love. It involves two similar relationships: the prophet Hosea to his adulterous wife, Gomer, and God to his faithless covenant people. Gomer abandons Hosea for other lovers; Israel abandons God by going after pagan idols. But perfect love keeps on loving even after being spurned. In Hosea's case, that means buying back his wayward wife from her lovers; for Israel, purifying punishment will be followed by restoration.

Focus	Harlotry and Hope in Hosea's Day				
Divisions	Moral Sins of Gomer	National Sins of Israel	International Sins of Israel	Promise of Israel's Ruin	Promise of Israel's Renewal
	1 3	4 6:11a	6:11b 8	9 11:11	11:12 14
Topics	Physical Adultery	Spiritual Adultery			
	Personal Tragedy	National Transgression			
Place	Northern Kingdom of Israel				
Time	About 45 Years (755–710 B.C.)				

SEPTEMBER 1 □ DAY 245
HOSEA 1–3
Moral Sins of Gomer

OVERVIEW Hosea's family life becomes a painful but accurate picture of the problems within his nation. He marries a woman named Gomer, who bears him three children appropriately named by God as signs to Israel: Jezreel, "God plants"; Lo-Ruhamah, "not loved"; and Lo-Ammi, "not my people." All too soon, Hosea's home is shattered by Gomer's unfaithfulness. She leaves her prophet-husband in search of other lovers and sinks to such depths that Hosea must redeem her from her lovers. Hosea's steadfast love in the face of such unfaithfulness parallels God's love for his people in the midst of their idolatry.

Chapter 1	Chapter 2	Chapter 3
Marriage of Hosea and Gomer	Unfaithfulness of Gomer	Undying Love of Hosea
Faithless Wife		Forgiving Husband

Like a delicate seismograph, Hosea's sensitive soul recorded the hidden and secret rumblings of divine judgment.

YOUR DAILY WALK What do the following have in common: a conversation with a brick wall . . . a telephone call answered by a recorded voice . . . and a debate with a corpse?

Answer: They all represent one-sided conversations. Try as you might, you will never get the brick wall, answering machine or corpse to respond to you. Why? Because there is no life in them.

There is something pathetic about a one-sided relationship, the kind in which one partner remains faithful and committed, while the other fails to respond to that love. Does that describe God's relationship with you? Romans 5:8 states: "But God demonstrates his own love for us in this: While we were still sinners, Christ died for us." God has demonstrated his love for you; have you responded to that love in kind? If *one-sided* describes God's relationship with you (as it did Hosea's relationship with Gomer and God's relationship with Israel), then why not respond today? By putting your faith in the fact of Christ's love and sacrificial death, you can become a child of God right now. A love like that is just too good to ignore (1 John 4:10)!

INSIGHT The Prophet Who Outlived His Audience

According to 1:1, Hosea ministered during the reigns of four kings in Judah (southern kingdom). Hosea's long career, therefore, spanned the reigns of the last six kings of Israel (northern kingdom), making him one of the few "ten-king prophets" in the Bible.

CHAPTER 1

The word of the LORD that came to Hosea son of Beeri during the reigns of Uzziah, Jotham, Ahaz and Hezekiah, kings of Judah, and during the reign of Jeroboam son of Jehoash[a] king of Israel:

[a]1 Hebrew *Joash*, a variant of *Jehoash*

²When the LORD began to speak through Hosea, the LORD said to him, "Go, take to yourself an adulterous wife and children of unfaithfulness, because the land is guilty of the vilest adultery in departing from the LORD." ³So he married Gomer

daughter of Diblaim, and she conceived and bore him a son.

⁴Then the LORD said to Hosea, "Call him Jezreel, because I will soon punish the house of Jehu for the massacre at Jezreel, and I will put an end to the kingdom of Israel. ⁵In that day I will break Israel's bow in the Valley of Jezreel."

⁶Gomer conceived again and gave birth to a daughter. Then the LORD said to Hosea, "Call her Lo-Ruhamah,ᵇ for I will no longer show love to the house of Israel, that I should at all forgive them. ⁷Yet I will show love to the house of Judah; and I will save them—not by bow, sword or battle, or by horses and horsemen, but by the LORD their God."

⁸After she had weaned Lo-Ruhamah, Gomer had another son. ⁹Then the LORD said, "Call him Lo-Ammi,ᶜ for you are not my people, and I am not your God.

¹⁰"Yet the Israelites will be like the sand on the seashore, which cannot be measured or counted. In the place where it was said to them, 'You are not my people,' they will be called 'sons of the living God.' ¹¹The people of Judah and the people of Israel will be reunited, and they will appoint one leader and will come up out of the land, for great will be the day of Jezreel.

CHAPTER 2

"Say of your brothers, 'My people,' and of your sisters, 'My loved one.'

²"Rebuke your mother, rebuke her,
  for she is not my wife,
  and I am not her husband.
Let her remove the adulterous look
    from her face
  and the unfaithfulness from between
    her breasts.
³Otherwise I will strip her naked
  and make her as bare as on the day
    she was born;
I will make her like a desert,
  turn her into a parched land,
  and slay her with thirst.
⁴I will not show my love to her
    children,
  because they are the children of
    adultery.
⁵Their mother has been unfaithful
  and has conceived them in disgrace.
She said, 'I will go after my lovers,

who give me my food and my
    water,
  my wool and my linen, my oil and
    my drink.'
⁶Therefore I will block her path with
    thornbushes;
  I will wall her in so that she cannot
    find her way.
⁷She will chase after her lovers but not
    catch them;
  she will look for them but not find
    them.
Then she will say,
  'I will go back to my husband as at
    first,
  for then I was better off than now.'
⁸She has not acknowledged that I was
    the one
  who gave her the grain, the new
    wine and oil,
who lavished on her the silver and
    gold—
  which they used for Baal.

⁹"Therefore I will take away my grain
    when it ripens,
  and my new wine when it is ready.
I will take back my wool and my
    linen,
  intended to cover her nakedness.
¹⁰So now I will expose her lewdness
  before the eyes of her lovers;
  no one will take her out of my
    hands.
¹¹I will stop all her celebrations:
  her yearly festivals, her New Moons,
  her Sabbath days—all her appointed
    feasts.
¹²I will ruin her vines and her fig trees,
  which she said were her pay from
    her lovers;
I will make them a thicket,
  and wild animals will devour them.
¹³I will punish her for the days
  she burned incense to the Baals;
she decked herself with rings and
    jewelry,
  and went after her lovers,
  but me she forgot,"
                    declares the LORD.

¹⁴"Therefore I am now going to allure
    her;
  I will lead her into the desert
  and speak tenderly to her.

ᵇ6 Lo-Ruhamah means not loved.   ᶜ9 Lo-Ammi means not my people.

15There I will give her back her
    vineyards,
    and will make the Valley of Achor[d]
    a door of hope.
There she will sing[e] as in the days of
    her youth,
    as in the day she came up out of
    Egypt.

16"In that day," declares the LORD,
    "you will call me 'my husband';
    you will no longer call me 'my
    master.'[f]
17I will remove the names of the Baals
    from her lips;
    no longer will their names be
    invoked.
18In that day I will make a covenant for
    them
    with the beasts of the field and the
    birds of the air
    and the creatures that move along
    the ground.
Bow and sword and battle
    I will abolish from the land,
    so that all may lie down in safety.
19I will betroth you to me forever;
    I will betroth you in[g] righteousness
    and justice,
    in[h] love and compassion.
20I will betroth you in faithfulness,
    and you will acknowledge the
    LORD.

21"In that day I will respond,"
    declares the LORD—

"I will respond to the skies,
    and they will respond to the earth;
22and the earth will respond to the
    grain,
    the new wine and oil,
    and they will respond to Jezreel.[i]
23I will plant her for myself in the
    land;
    I will show my love to the one I
    called 'Not my loved one.'[j]
I will say to those called 'Not my
    people,[k]' 'You are my people';
    and they will say, 'You are my
    God.'"

CHAPTER 3
The LORD said to me, "Go, show your love
to your wife again, though she is loved by
another and is an adulteress. Love her as
the LORD loves the Israelites, though they
turn to other gods and love the sacred
raisin cakes."

2So I bought her for fifteen shekels[l] of
silver and about a homer and a lethek[m] of
barley. 3Then I told her, "You are to live
with[n] me many days; you must not be a
prostitute or be intimate with any man,
and I will live with[n] you."

4For the Israelites will live many days
without king or prince, without sacrifice
or sacred stones, without ephod or idol.
5Afterward the Israelites will return and
seek the LORD their God and David their
king. They will come trembling to the
LORD and to his blessings in the last
days.

d15 Achor means trouble.   e15 Or respond   f16 Hebrew baal   g19 Or with; also in verse 20   h19 Or with   i22 Jezreel
means God plants.   j23 Hebrew Lo-Ruhamah   k23 Hebrew Lo-Ammi   l2 That is, about 6 ounces (about 170 grams)
m2 That is, probably about 10 bushels (about 330 liters)   n3 Or wait for

SEPTEMBER 2 □ DAY 246
HOSEA 4–6:11a
National Sins of Israel

OVERVIEW Because of his own painful experiences, Hosea is able to
identify with the sorrow of God over the sinfulness of Israel. Hosea's
loyal love for Gomer pictures God's undying love for his people. But
Israel's sin-hardened populace refuses to respond to God's last gracious appeal. The people stand guilty and defenseless before God's
accusations. Even now God is willing to heal and redeem them, but in
their arrogance and idolatry they refuse to return.

Chapter 4	Chapter 5	Chapter 6
Guilty People and Priests	Rebellious Priests and Princes	Merciful God of Goodness
God's Indictment	God's Displeasure	God's Demands

YOUR DAILY WALK Complete this sentence at least five different ways: "I know for certain that . . ."

The knowledge of God is far from the love of him.

Now examine the responses you gave. Is the level of your "knowledge" the same in all cases, or does it vary? Perhaps you said, "I know for certain that my name is Norman (or Norma) Christian." That is knowledge from firsthand experience. But is that the same kind of knowledge as represented in the statements "I know the world is round" and "I know my car will start tomorrow morning"?

Death and destruction were coming upon the people of Israel. Why? In God's own words: "My people are destroyed from lack of knowledge" (4:6). In a nation founded by God, built upon godly principles and centered around the temple of God, it seems incredible to think there was no knowledge of God. But the issue was not facts *about* God; the issue was firsthand experience *with* God.

Might the shocking statement of Hosea 4:6 be true of your nation as well? Godly foundations and an abundance of churches are no guarantee of the knowledge of God. Remember, if the knowledge of God is to permeate your country, it first must be the experience of your life.

INSIGHT The Tattered Ten Commandments

Chapters 4–6 show how the nation has broken each of the Ten Commandments (Exodus 20:1–17). Can you find at least one statement corresponding to each broken command?

CHAPTER 4

Hear the word of the LORD, you
    Israelites,
  because the LORD has a charge to
      bring
    against you who live in the land:
"There is no faithfulness, no love,
    no acknowledgment of God in the
      land.
²There is only cursing,ᵒ lying and
      murder,
    stealing and adultery;
  they break all bounds,
    and bloodshed follows bloodshed.
³Because of this the land mourns,ᵖ
    and all who live in it waste away;
  the beasts of the field and the birds of
      the air
    and the fish of the sea are dying.

⁴"But let no man bring a charge,
    let no man accuse another,
  for your people are like those
    who bring charges against a priest.

⁵You stumble day and night,
    and the prophets stumble with you.
  So I will destroy your mother—
⁶   my people are destroyed from lack
      of knowledge.

"Because you have rejected knowledge,
    I also reject you as my priests;
  because you have ignored the law of
      your God,
    I also will ignore your children.
⁷The more the priests increased,
    the more they sinned against me;
  they exchangedᑫ theirʳ Glory for
      something disgraceful.
⁸They feed on the sins of my people
    and relish their wickedness.
⁹And it will be: Like people, like
      priests.
  I will punish both of them for their
      ways
    and repay them for their deeds.
¹⁰"They will eat but not have enough;

ᵒ2 That is, to pronounce a curse upon   ᵖ3 Or *dries up*   ᑫ7 Syriac and an ancient Hebrew scribal tradition; Masoretic Text *I will exchange*   ʳ7 Masoretic Text; an ancient Hebrew scribal tradition *my*

they will engage in prostitution but
    not increase,
because they have deserted the LORD
    to give themselves ¹¹to prostitution,
to old wine and new,
    which take away the understanding
       ¹²of my people.
They consult a wooden idol
    and are answered by a stick of
       wood.
A spirit of prostitution leads them
    astray;
    they are unfaithful to their God.
¹³They sacrifice on the mountaintops
    and burn offerings on the hills,
under oak, poplar and terebinth,
    where the shade is pleasant.
Therefore your daughters turn to
    prostitution
and your daughters-in-law to
    adultery.

¹⁴"I will not punish your daughters
    when they turn to prostitution,
nor your daughters-in-law
    when they commit adultery,
because the men themselves consort
    with harlots
    and sacrifice with shrine
       prostitutes—
    a people without understanding will
       come to ruin!

¹⁵"Though you commit adultery,
    O Israel,
    let not Judah become guilty.

    "Do not go to Gilgal;
    do not go up to Beth Aven.ˢ
    And do not swear, 'As surely as the
       LORD lives!'
¹⁶The Israelites are stubborn,
    like a stubborn heifer.
How then can the LORD pasture them
    like lambs in a meadow?
¹⁷Ephraim is joined to idols;
    leave him alone!
¹⁸Even when their drinks are gone,
    they continue their prostitution;
    their rulers dearly love shameful
       ways.
¹⁹A whirlwind will sweep them away,
    and their sacrifices will bring them
       shame.

CHAPTER 5

"Hear this, you priests!
    Pay attention, you Israelites!
Listen, O royal house!
    This judgment is against you:
You have been a snare at Mizpah,
    a net spread out on Tabor.
²The rebels are deep in slaughter.
    I will discipline all of them.
³I know all about Ephraim;
    Israel is not hidden from me.
Ephraim, you have now turned to
    prostitution;
    Israel is corrupt.

⁴"Their deeds do not permit them
    to return to their God.
A spirit of prostitution is in their
    heart;
    they do not acknowledge the LORD.
⁵Israel's arrogance testifies against
    them;
    the Israelites, even Ephraim, stumble
       in their sin;
    Judah also stumbles with them.
⁶When they go with their flocks and
    herds
    to seek the LORD,
they will not find him;
    he has withdrawn himself from
       them.
⁷They are unfaithful to the LORD;
    they give birth to illegitimate
       children.
Now their New Moon festivals
    will devour them and their fields.

⁸"Sound the trumpet in Gibeah,
    the horn in Ramah.
Raise the battle cry in Beth Avenˢ;
    lead on, O Benjamin.
⁹Ephraim will be laid waste
    on the day of reckoning.
Among the tribes of Israel
    I proclaim what is certain.
¹⁰Judah's leaders are like those
    who move boundary stones.
I will pour out my wrath on them
    like a flood of water.
¹¹Ephraim is oppressed,
    trampled in judgment,
    intent on pursuing idols.ᵗ
¹²I am like a moth to Ephraim,
    like rot to the people of Judah.

¹³"When Ephraim saw his sickness,

ˢ15,8 Beth Aven means house of wickedness (a name for Bethel, which means house of God).   ᵗ11 The meaning of the Hebrew for this word is uncertain.

and Judah his sores,
then Ephraim turned to Assyria,
and sent to the great king for help.
But he is not able to cure you,
not able to heal your sores.
¹⁴For I will be like a lion to Ephraim,
like a great lion to Judah.
I will tear them to pieces and go away;
I will carry them off, with no one to
rescue them.
¹⁵Then I will go back to my place
until they admit their guilt.
And they will seek my face;
in their misery they will earnestly
seek me."

C H A P T E R 6

"Come, let us return to the LORD.
He has torn us to pieces
but he will heal us;
he has injured us
but he will bind up our wounds.
²After two days he will revive us;
on the third day he will restore us,
that we may live in his presence.
³Let us acknowledge the LORD;
let us press on to acknowledge him.
As surely as the sun rises,
he will appear;
he will come to us like the winter
rains,

ᵘ7 Or As at Adam; or Like men

like the spring rains that water the
earth."
⁴"What can I do with you, Ephraim?
What can I do with you, Judah?
Your love is like the morning mist,
like the early dew that disappears.
⁵Therefore I cut you in pieces with my
prophets,
I killed you with the words of my
mouth;
my judgments flashed like lightning
upon you.
⁶For I desire mercy, not sacrifice,
and acknowledgment of God rather
than burnt offerings.
⁷Like Adam,ᵘ they have broken the
covenant—
they were unfaithful to me there.
⁸Gilead is a city of wicked men,
stained with footprints of blood.
⁹As marauders lie in ambush for a
man,
so do bands of priests;
they murder on the road to Shechem,
committing shameful crimes.
¹⁰I have seen a horrible thing
in the house of Israel.
There Ephraim is given to prostitution
and Israel is defiled.

¹¹"Also for you, Judah,
a harvest is appointed.

SEPTEMBER 3 ☐ DAY 247
HOSEA 6:11b–8
International Sins of Israel

OVERVIEW Israel's sin remains the focus of Hosea's prophecy. The nation's iniquity is like a raging fire. Her rebellion has weakened her to the point of spiritual stupor. She is beyond realizing who God is or what he has done for her. For this idolatrous, sin-riddled nation there can be only one verdict: exile.

Chapters 6–7		Chapter 8	
Burning Sin	Betraying God	Blight of Idolatry	Banishment from the Land
6:11b 7:10	11 16	1 7	8 14
Sowing the Wind		Reaping the Whirlwind	

YOUR DAILY WALK A bird lies fluttering on the ground, obviously injured. You respond to this pitiful sight by reaching out your hand to try and help. Instead of recognizing your intent, the bird jerks free in a frantic effort to escape. You are the only one who can help, and yet the bird refuses your assistance—perhaps at the cost of its life.

By chastening, the Lord separates the sin that he hates from the sinner whom he loves.

"How foolish! How wasteful!" you say. And yet that is precisely how God's people responded to God's overtures. "I would heal Israel," cried the Lord, but Israel refused (7:1). Blinded by sin and devoured by wickedness, the people rejected God's gracious offers. And the heart of God grieved. Instead of compassion, he was forced to extend a hand of chastening—punishment in place of pardon, exile rather than encouragement.

Are you grieving the Lord today by your stubborn refusal to respond to his grace? Pinpoint a bad habit, an unchecked passion, a persistent sin that is saddening your Lord. Then remember the illustration of the injured bird. The choice is up to you. Yield to God's love before you feel his hand of discipline.

INSIGHT Will They Never Learn?
The golden calf, which nearly cost Aaron his life and resulted in the deaths of three thousand Israelites, was later destroyed (Exodus 32). But the idea lived on during the reign of Jeroboam, first king of the northern kingdom. He ordered similar golden calves to be erected at Dan (in the north) and Bethel (in the south). For years these calves were the focus of Israel's idolatrous worship (1 Kings 12:26–33). And perhaps it was in the very shadow of these same calves that Hosea stood as he prophesied destruction for idol and idolater alike (8:5–7).

"Whenever I would restore the
        fortunes of my people,
CHAPTER 7
1   whenever I would heal Israel,
the sins of Ephraim are exposed
        and the crimes of Samaria revealed.
They practice deceit,
        thieves break into houses,
        bandits rob in the streets;
2but they do not realize
        that I remember all their evil deeds.
Their sins engulf them;
        they are always before me.

3"They delight the king with their
        wickedness,
        the princes with their lies.
4They are all adulterers,
        burning like an oven
whose fire the baker need not stir
        from the kneading of the dough till
        it rises.
5On the day of the festival of our king
        the princes become inflamed with
        wine,
        and he joins hands with the
        mockers.
6Their hearts are like an oven;
        they approach him with intrigue.
Their passion smolders all night;

in the morning it blazes like a
        flaming fire.
7All of them are hot as an oven;
        they devour their rulers.
All their kings fall,
        and none of them calls on me.

8"Ephraim mixes with the nations;
        Ephraim is a flat cake not turned
        over.
9Foreigners sap his strength,
        but he does not realize it.
His hair is sprinkled with gray,
        but he does not notice.
10Israel's arrogance testifies against him,
        but despite all this
he does not return to the LORD his God
        or search for him.

11"Ephraim is like a dove,
        easily deceived and senseless—
now calling to Egypt,
        now turning to Assyria.
12When they go, I will throw my net
        over them;
        I will pull them down like birds of
        the air.
When I hear them flocking together,
        I will catch them.
13Woe to them,
        because they have strayed from me!

Destruction to them,
  because they have rebelled against
    me!
I long to redeem them
  but they speak lies against me.
¹⁴They do not cry out to me from their
    hearts
  but wail upon their beds.
They gather togetherᵛ for grain and
    new wine
  but turn away from me.
¹⁵I trained them and strengthened them,
  but they plot evil against me.
¹⁶They do not turn to the Most High;
  they are like a faulty bow.
Their leaders will fall by the sword
  because of their insolent words.
For this they will be ridiculed
  in the land of Egypt.

CHAPTER 8

"Put the trumpet to your lips!
  An eagle is over the house of the
    LORD
because the people have broken my
    covenant
  and rebelled against my law.
²Israel cries out to me,
  'O our God, we acknowledge you!'
³But Israel has rejected what is good;
  an enemy will pursue him.
⁴They set up kings without my consent;
  they choose princes without my
    approval.
With their silver and gold
  they make idols for themselves
  to their own destruction.
⁵Throw out your calf-idol, O Samaria!
  My anger burns against them.
How long will they be incapable of
    purity?
⁶ They are from Israel!
This calf—a craftsman has made it;

it is not God.
It will be broken in pieces,
  that calf of Samaria.

⁷"They sow the wind
  and reap the whirlwind.
The stalk has no head;
  it will produce no flour.
Were it to yield grain,
  foreigners would swallow it up.
⁸Israel is swallowed up;
  now she is among the nations
  like a worthless thing.
⁹For they have gone up to Assyria
  like a wild donkey wandering alone.
Ephraim has sold herself to lovers.
¹⁰Although they have sold themselves
    among the nations,
  I will now gather them together.
They will begin to waste away
  under the oppression of the mighty
    king.

¹¹"Though Ephraim built many altars for
    sin offerings,
  these have become altars for sinning.
¹²I wrote for them the many things of
    my law,
  but they regarded them as
    something alien.
¹³They offer sacrifices given to me
  and they eat the meat,
  but the LORD is not pleased with
    them.
Now he will remember their
    wickedness
  and punish their sins:
  They will return to Egypt.
¹⁴Israel has forgotten his Maker
  and built palaces;
  Judah has fortified many towns.
But I will send fire upon their cities
  that will consume their fortresses."

ᵛ14 Most Hebrew manuscripts; some Hebrew manuscripts and Septuagint *They slash themselves*

SEPTEMBER 4 □ DAY 248
HOSEA 9–11:11
Promise of Israel's Ruin

 OVERVIEW Like the pounding of a hammer, Hosea's indictment of Israel continues. Worship has no meaning for God when offered by
people with idolatrous hearts. The nation has been wasted by unchecked sin. Once a fruitful vine, Israel now lies spiritually barren and

fruitless. Yet God remains loyal to his people. His love will not permit him to leave sin unpunished—just as a loving father must discipline his erring children. But in the midst of that painful process, God's promise shines brightly. Restoration and blessing await his people when the painful punishment is over.

Chapter 9	Chapter 10	Chapter 11
God's Hatred for Israel's Barrenness	God's Promise of Israel's Bondage	God's Heart for Israel's Blessing
	1	11
Punishment Coming		Restoration Coming

YOUR DAILY WALK Contrast these two statements from today's reading: "I hated them [Israel] there" (9:15). "My heart is changed within me; all my compassion is aroused [for Israel]" (11:8). How can you reconcile these verses? Is God contradicting himself?

A prophet deserves honor, not because he foresees the coming event, but because he sees the meaning within the current event.

The answer can be found in the ageless maxim "God hates the sin but loves the sinner." A holy God can never excuse or condone sin. Yet God never blurs the distinction between the sinner and his or her sin. His love for the sinner never ends, nor does his hatred for the sin.

How do you view those around you who have fallen into gross sin? Have you been so offended by their actions that you now shun them? Remember, "God demonstrates his own love for us in this: While we were still sinners, Christ died for us" (Romans 5:8). Pick someone whose lifestyle would normally cause you to avoid him or her, and plan an activity to demonstrate God's love toward that person. Ask the Holy Spirit to cause the individual to see in your love the extended hand of a loving God, whose compassions never end!

INSIGHT Determined Declaration of Love
The concluding five verses of chapter 11 have been called "the finest presentation in the Old Testament of the tension between the love and justice of God." The final resolution of this tension is seen at the cross, for it is there that God becomes both "just and the one who justifies" (Romans 3:26).

CHAPTER 9

Do not rejoice, O Israel;
    do not be jubilant like the other
        nations.
For you have been unfaithful to your
        God;
    you love the wages of a prostitute
    at every threshing floor.
²Threshing floors and winepresses will
        not feed the people;
    the new wine will fail them.
³They will not remain in the LORD's
        land;
    Ephraim will return to Egypt
    and eat unclean*ʷ* food in Assyria.
⁴They will not pour out wine offerings
        to the LORD,
    nor will their sacrifices please him.
Such sacrifices will be to them like the
        bread of mourners;

all who eat them will be unclean.
This food will be for themselves;
    it will not come into the temple of
        the LORD.

⁵What will you do on the day of your
        appointed feasts,
    on the festival days of the LORD?
⁶Even if they escape from destruction,
    Egypt will gather them,
    and Memphis will bury them.
Their treasures of silver will be taken
        over by briers,
    and thorns will overrun their tents.
⁷The days of punishment are coming,
    the days of reckoning are at hand.
    Let Israel know this.
Because your sins are so many
    and your hostility so great,
the prophet is considered a fool,
    the inspired man a maniac.

ʷ3 That is, ceremonially unclean

8The prophet, along with my God,
   is the watchman over Ephraim,[x]
yet snares await him on all his paths,
   and hostility in the house of his
      God.
9They have sunk deep into corruption,
   as in the days of Gibeah.
God will remember their wickedness
   and punish them for their sins.

10"When I found Israel,
   it was like finding grapes in the
      desert;
when I saw your fathers,
   it was like seeing the early fruit on
      the fig tree.
But when they came to Baal Peor,
   they consecrated themselves to that
      shameful idol
   and became as vile as the thing they
      loved.
11Ephraim's glory will fly away like a
      bird—
no birth, no pregnancy, no
      conception.
12Even if they rear children,
   I will bereave them of every one.
Woe to them
   when I turn away from them!
13I have seen Ephraim, like Tyre,
   planted in a pleasant place.
But Ephraim will bring out
   their children to the slayer."

14Give them, O LORD—
   what will you give them?
Give them wombs that miscarry
   and breasts that are dry.
15"Because of all their wickedness in
      Gilgal,
   I hated them there.
Because of their sinful deeds,
   I will drive them out of my house.
I will no longer love them;
   all their leaders are rebellious.
16Ephraim is blighted,
   their root is withered,
   they yield no fruit.
Even if they bear children,
   I will slay their cherished offspring."

17My God will reject them
   because they have not obeyed him;
they will be wanderers among the
      nations.

CHAPTER 10

Israel was a spreading vine;
   he brought forth fruit for himself.
As his fruit increased,
   he built more altars;
as his land prospered,
   he adorned his sacred stones.
2Their heart is deceitful,
   and now they must bear their guilt.
The LORD will demolish their altars
   and destroy their sacred stones.

3Then they will say, "We have no king
   because we did not revere the LORD.
But even if we had a king,
   what could he do for us?"
4They make many promises,
   take false oaths
   and make agreements;
therefore lawsuits spring up
   like poisonous weeds in a plowed
      field.
5The people who live in Samaria fear
   for the calf-idol of Beth Aven.[y]
Its people will mourn over it,
   and so will its idolatrous priests,
those who had rejoiced over its
      splendor,
because it is taken from them into
      exile.
6It will be carried to Assyria
   as tribute for the great king.
Ephraim will be disgraced;
   Israel will be ashamed of its wooden
      idols.[z]
7Samaria and its king will float away
   like a twig on the surface of the
      waters.
8The high places of wickedness[a] will
      be destroyed—
   it is the sin of Israel.
Thorns and thistles will grow up
   and cover their altars.
Then they will say to the mountains,
      "Cover us!"
   and to the hills, "Fall on us!"

9"Since the days of Gibeah, you have
      sinned, O Israel,
   and there you have remained.[b]
Did not war overtake
   the evildoers in Gibeah?
10When I please, I will punish them;
   nations will be gathered against
      them

---

x8 Or *The prophet is the watchman over Ephraim, | the people of my God*   y5 *Beth Aven* means *house of wickedness* (a name for Bethel, which means *house of God*).   z6 Or *its counsel*   a8 Hebrew *aven,* a reference to Beth Aven (a derogatory name for Bethel)   b9 Or *there a stand was taken*

to put them in bonds for their
double sin.
11Ephraim is a trained heifer
that loves to thresh;
so I will put a yoke
on her fair neck.
I will drive Ephraim,
Judah must plow,
and Jacob must break up the
ground.
12Sow for yourselves righteousness,
reap the fruit of unfailing love,
and break up your unplowed ground;
for it is time to seek the LORD,
until he comes
and showers righteousness on you.
13But you have planted wickedness,
you have reaped evil,
you have eaten the fruit of
deception.
Because you have depended on your
own strength
and on your many warriors,
14the roar of battle will rise against your
people,
so that all your fortresses will be
devastated—
as Shalman devastated Beth Arbel on
the day of battle,
when mothers were dashed to the
ground with their children.
15Thus will it happen to you, O Bethel,
because your wickedness is great.
When that day dawns,
the king of Israel will be completely
destroyed.

CHAPTER 11
"When Israel was a child, I loved him,
and out of Egypt I called my son.
2But the more Ic called Israel,
the further they went from me.d
They sacrificed to the Baals
and they burned incense to images.

3It was I who taught Ephraim to walk,
taking them by the arms;
but they did not realize
it was I who healed them.
4I led them with cords of human
kindness,
with ties of love;
I lifted the yoke from their neck
and bent down to feed them.
5"Will they not return to Egypt
and will not Assyria rule over them
because they refuse to repent?
6Swords will flash in their cities,
will destroy the bars of their gates
and put an end to their plans.
7My people are determined to turn
from me.
Even if they call to the Most High,
he will by no means exalt them.
8"How can I give you up, Ephraim?
How can I hand you over, Israel?
How can I treat you like Admah?
How can I make you like Zeboiim?
My heart is changed within me;
all my compassion is aroused.
9I will not carry out my fierce anger,
nor will I turn and devastate
Ephraim.
For I am God, and not man—
the Holy One among you.
I will not come in wrath.e
10They will follow the LORD;
he will roar like a lion.
When he roars,
his children will come trembling
from the west.
11They will come trembling
like birds from Egypt,
like doves from Assyria.
I will settle them in their homes,"
declares the LORD.

c2 Some Septuagint manuscripts; Hebrew they   d2 Septuagint; Hebrew them   e9 Or come against any city

SEPTEMBER 5 □ DAY 249
HOSEA 11:12–14
Promise of Israel's Renewal

OVERVIEW Hosea ends his book the same way he began it—by driving home his three-part theme: Israel's past is stained with disobedience and rebellion; Israel's future holds the ominous threat of calamity; and Israel's present demands an immediate and complete change of heart if that calamity is to be averted. Hosea's heart has already been broken by the adultery and shame of his wife, Gomer. Now he pleads one last time with his countrymen that they not duplicate Gomer's folly: "Return, O Israel, to the LORD your God" (14:1).

Chapters 11–12		Chapter 13	Chapter 14
11:12	Israel's Past Recounted 12:14	Israel's Future Previewed	Israel's Present Responsibility
Rebellion		Removal	Repentance

YOUR DAILY WALK Few sentences in the English language are more difficult to say than the little two-word phrase *I'm sorry*. You've sinned; you've failed miserably. How do you tell God about it? How do you make it right with him so you can enjoy fellowship once again?

As long as we live we should more and more be turning from all that is evil and to all that is good.

Hosea 14 has been called by some the backslider's chapter. It describes the steps necessary for God's erring people to be restored to fellowship with him:

1. Return to the Lord (14:1). Remember, if God seems distant from you, it must mean *you* have moved!
2. Confess your sins to the Lord (14:2). Agree with him that what you have done is wrong and needs to be forsaken.
3. Put your confidence in the Lord (14:3). Trusting your own strength or understanding can only bring disappointment. Instead, lean on the Rock that can never be moved.

Are you, like Israel in Hosea's day, estranged from your God? Restoration is only a prayer away. Read chapter 14 twice. Then do business with God. He's waiting for you, and his door is always open.

INSIGHT Great Truths in Tiny Capsules
Think through these fragments of thought from Hosea's pen. What great truths about God do they teach you?
"I desire mercy, not sacrifice" (6:6).
"How can I give you up?" (11:8).
"I will heal their waywardness" (14:4).

¹²Ephraim has surrounded me with
    lies,
  the house of Israel with deceit.
And Judah is unruly against God,
  even against the faithful Holy One.
CHAPTER 12
¹Ephraim feeds on the wind;
  he pursues the east wind all day
  and multiplies lies and violence.
He makes a treaty with Assyria

and sends olive oil to Egypt.
²The LORD has a charge to bring against
    Judah;
  he will punish Jacobᶠ according to
    his ways
  and repay him according to his
    deeds.
³In the womb he grasped his brother's
    heel;
  as a man he struggled with God.

ƒ2 *Jacob* means *he grasps the heel* (figuratively, *he deceives*).

⁴He struggled with the angel and
    overcame him;
  he wept and begged for his favor.
He found him at Bethel
  and talked with him there—
⁵the Lord God Almighty,
  the Lord is his name of renown!
⁶But you must return to your God;
  maintain love and justice,
  and wait for your God always.

⁷The merchant uses dishonest scales;
  he loves to defraud.
⁸Ephraim boasts,
  "I am very rich; I have become
    wealthy.
With all my wealth they will not find
    in me
  any iniquity or sin."

⁹"I am the Lord your God,
  ⌊who brought you⌋ out of⁸ Egypt;
I will make you live in tents again,
  as in the days of your appointed
    feasts.
¹⁰I spoke to the prophets,
  gave them many visions
  and told parables through them."

¹¹Is Gilead wicked?
  Its people are worthless!
Do they sacrifice bulls in Gilgal?
  Their altars will be like piles of
    stones
  on a plowed field.
¹²Jacob fled to the country of Aramʰ;
  Israel served to get a wife,
  and to pay for her he tended sheep.
¹³The Lord used a prophet to bring
    Israel up from Egypt,
  by a prophet he cared for him.
¹⁴But Ephraim has bitterly provoked
    him to anger;
  his Lord will leave upon him the
    guilt of his bloodshed
  and will repay him for his contempt.

CHAPTER 13

When Ephraim spoke, men trembled;
  he was exalted in Israel.
But he became guilty of Baal
    worship and died.
²Now they sin more and more;
  they make idols for themselves from
    their silver,
  cleverly fashioned images,

all of them the work of craftsmen.
It is said of these people,
  "They offer human sacrifice
  and kissⁱ the calf-idols."
³Therefore they will be like the
    morning mist,
  like the early dew that disappears,
  like chaff swirling from a threshing
    floor,
  like smoke escaping through a
    window.

⁴"But I am the Lord your God,
  ⌊who brought you⌋ out of⁸ Egypt.
You shall acknowledge no God but
    me,
  no Savior except me.
⁵I cared for you in the desert,
  in the land of burning heat.
⁶When I fed them, they were satisfied;
  when they were satisfied, they
    became proud;
  then they forgot me.
⁷So I will come upon them like a lion,
  like a leopard I will lurk by the
    path.
⁸Like a bear robbed of her cubs,
  I will attack them and rip them
    open.
Like a lion I will devour them;
  a wild animal will tear them apart.

⁹"You are destroyed, O Israel,
  because you are against me, against
    your helper.
¹⁰Where is your king, that he may save
    you?
  Where are your rulers in all your
    towns,
of whom you said,
  'Give me a king and princes'?
¹¹So in my anger I gave you a king,
  and in my wrath I took him away.
¹²The guilt of Ephraim is stored up,
  his sins are kept on record.
¹³Pains as of a woman in childbirth
    come to him,
  but he is a child without wisdom;
when the time arrives,
  he does not come to the opening of
    the womb.

¹⁴"I will ransom them from the power of
    the graveʲ;
  I will redeem them from death.
Where, O death, are your plagues?

---

⁸9,4 Or *God | ever since you were in*   ʰ12 That is, Northwest Mesopotamia   ⁱ2 Or *"Men who sacrifice | kiss*   ʲ14 Hebrew
Sheol

Where, O grave,[k] is your
destruction?

"I will have no compassion,
15 even though he thrives among his
brothers.
An east wind from the LORD will come,
blowing in from the desert;
his spring will fail
and his well dry up.
His storehouse will be plundered
of all its treasures.
16The people of Samaria must bear their
guilt,
because they have rebelled against
their God.
They will fall by the sword;
their little ones will be dashed to the
ground,
their pregnant women ripped open."

C H A P T E R 1 4
Return, O Israel, to the LORD your God.
Your sins have been your downfall!
2Take words with you
and return to the LORD.
Say to him:
"Forgive all our sins
and receive us graciously,
that we may offer the fruit of our
lips.[l]
3Assyria cannot save us;
we will not mount war-horses.
We will never again say 'Our gods'

to what our own hands have made,
for in you the fatherless find
compassion."

4"I will heal their waywardness
and love them freely,
for my anger has turned away from
them.
5I will be like the dew to Israel;
he will blossom like a lily.
Like a cedar of Lebanon
he will send down his roots;
6 his young shoots will grow.
His splendor will be like an olive tree,
his fragrance like a cedar of
Lebanon.
7Men will dwell again in his shade.
He will flourish like the grain.
He will blossom like a vine,
and his fame will be like the wine
from Lebanon.
8O Ephraim, what more have I[m] to do
with idols?
I will answer him and care for him.
I am like a green pine tree;
your fruitfulness comes from me."

9Who is wise? He will realize these
things.
Who is discerning? He will
understand them.
The ways of the LORD are right;
the righteous walk in them,
but the rebellious stumble in them.

[k]14 Hebrew Sheol   [l]2 Or offer our lips as sacrifices of bulls   [m]8 Or What more has Ephraim

Joel

THE LOCUSTS have come. And suddenly every green thing is gone. God's spokesman Joel uses this national disaster to bring a dire warning of a far worse catastrophe. Not locusts, but an army from the north will attack Judah. The only hope of escape in this day of the Lord is to repent: "Rend your heart and not your garments" (2:13). If his people will repent, God will send unparalleled blessing instead of devastating judgment. He will judge the nations that hurt his people and bring peace to Zion.

Focus	Past Judgment of God's People	Future Judgment and Restoration of God's People	
Divisions	Devastation of the Locusts	Day of the Lord	Doom of the Nations
	1:1 1:20	2:1 2:32	3:1 3:21
Topics	Israel's Review	Israel's Future	Gentiles' Future
	Historical Invasion	Prophetic Invasions	
Place	Southern Kingdom of Judah		
Time	Approximately 835 B.C.		

SEPTEMBER 6 □ DAY 250
JOEL 1–3
Locusts and the Day of the Lord

OVERVIEW Disaster struck the southern kingdom of Judah without warning. An ominous black cloud descended upon the land—the dreaded locusts. In a matter of hours, every green living thing had been stripped bare. Joel, God's spokesman during the reign of Joash (835–796 B.C.), seizes the occasion to proclaim God's message. The locust plague has been a terrible judgment for sin. Yet God's future judgments during the day of the Lord will make that plague pale by comparison. In that day God will destroy his enemies but bring unparalleled blessing to those who faithfully obey him.

Chapter 1	Chapter 2	Chapter 3
Devastation of the Locusts	Day of the Lord	Doom of the Nations
Israel's Present	Israel's Future	Gentiles' Future

The judgment of God shall turn topsy-turvy the judgments of people.

YOUR DAILY WALK After reading Joel's little three-chapter book, see if you can summarize its description of God in a single word: _____.

The book of Joel reads like the screenplay from a disaster movie: locust swarms, drought, famine, raging brush fires, invading armies, astronomical catastrophes. But why all these "fireworks"? Why this display of calamitous events? One reason becomes apparent at the end of the book: "Then you will know that I, the LORD your God, dwell in Zion, my holy hill" (3:17). You can't read Joel without coming to grips with the almighty God who sovereignly controls the course of history.

Not only is God big enough to move mountains, he is concerned enough to be "a refuge for his people, a stronghold for the people of Israel" (3:16). That means he is your refuge, your stronghold, your fortress (all good words to choose for your one-word summary). Pick up a small rock and carry it with you today. Let it remind you that your rock and fortress is big enough to rule this mighty universe (and your own personal locust plagues), yet small enough to live within your heart.

INSIGHT Joel in the Old, Peter in the New
Peter, preaching on the day of Pentecost (Acts 2), referred to Joel 2:28–32 to explain to the multitudes the miracle they were witnessing. Although the complete fulfillment of this prophecy would not occur until later, Joel's message showed that Pentecost was the work of God's Holy Spirit, not of alcoholic spirits.

CHAPTER 1
The word of the LORD that came to Joel son of Pethuel.

²Hear this, you elders;
  listen, all who live in the land.
Has anything like this ever happened
    in your days
  or in the days of your forefathers?
³Tell it to your children,
  and let your children tell it to their
    children,

and their children to the next
    generation.
⁴What the locust swarm has left
    the great locusts have eaten;
what the great locusts have left
    the young locusts have eaten;
what the young locusts have left
    other locusts*ᵃ* have eaten.

⁵Wake up, you drunkards, and
    weep!
  Wail, all you drinkers of wine;
wail because of the new wine,
    for it has been snatched from your
    lips.
⁶A nation has invaded my land,
    powerful and without number;
it has the teeth of a lion,
    the fangs of a lioness.
⁷It has laid waste my vines
    and ruined my fig trees.
It has stripped off their bark
    and thrown it away,
    leaving their branches white.

⁸Mourn like a virgin*ᵇ* in sackcloth
    grieving for the husband*ᶜ* of her
    youth.
⁹Grain offerings and drink offerings
    are cut off from the house of the
    LORD.
The priests are in mourning,
    those who minister before the
    LORD.
¹⁰The fields are ruined,
    the ground is dried up*ᵈ*;
the grain is destroyed,
    the new wine is dried up,
    the oil fails.
¹¹Despair, you farmers,
    wail, you vine growers;
grieve for the wheat and the barley,
    because the harvest of the field is
    destroyed.
¹²The vine is dried up
    and the fig tree is withered;
the pomegranate, the palm and the
    apple tree—
    all the trees of the field—are dried
    up.
Surely the joy of mankind
    is withered away.

¹³Put on sackcloth, O priests, and
    mourn;
wail, you who minister before the
    altar.
Come, spend the night in sackcloth,
    you who minister before my God;
for the grain offerings and drink
    offerings
    are withheld from the house of your
    God.
¹⁴Declare a holy fast;
    call a sacred assembly.
Summon the elders
    and all who live in the land
to the house of the LORD your God,
    and cry out to the LORD.

¹⁵Alas for that day!
    For the day of the LORD is near;
    it will come like destruction from
    the Almighty.*ᵉ*

¹⁶Has not the food been cut off
    before our very eyes—
joy and gladness
    from the house of our God?
¹⁷The seeds are shriveled
    beneath the clods.*ᶠ*
The storehouses are in ruins,
    the granaries have been broken
    down,
    for the grain has dried up.
¹⁸How the cattle moan!
    The herds mill about
because they have no pasture;
    even the flocks of sheep are
    suffering.

¹⁹To you, O LORD, I call,
    for fire has devoured the open
    pastures
    and flames have burned up all the
    trees of the field.
²⁰Even the wild animals pant for you;
    the streams of water have dried up
    and fire has devoured the open
    pastures.

CHAPTER 2

Blow the trumpet in Zion;
    sound the alarm on my holy hill.
Let all who live in the land tremble,
    for the day of the LORD is coming.
It is close at hand—
²   a day of darkness and gloom,
    a day of clouds and blackness.
Like dawn spreading across the
    mountains

ᵃ4 The precise meaning of the four Hebrew words used here for locusts is uncertain.   *ᵇ8* Or *young woman*   *ᶜ8* Or *betrothed*
ᵈ10 Or *ground mourns*   *ᵉ15* Hebrew *Shaddai*   *ᶠ17* The meaning of the Hebrew for this word is uncertain.

a large and mighty army comes,
  such as never was of old
    nor ever will be in ages to come.

[3]Before them fire devours,
  behind them a flame blazes.
Before them the land is like the garden
    of Eden,
behind them, a desert waste—
  nothing escapes them.
[4]They have the appearance of horses;
  they gallop along like cavalry.
[5]With a noise like that of chariots
  they leap over the mountaintops,
like a crackling fire consuming stubble,
  like a mighty army drawn up for
    battle.

[6]At the sight of them, nations are in
    anguish;
  every face turns pale.
[7]They charge like warriors;
  they scale walls like soldiers.
They all march in line,
  not swerving from their course.
[8]They do not jostle each other;
  each marches straight ahead.
They plunge through defenses
  without breaking ranks.
[9]They rush upon the city;
  they run along the wall.
They climb into the houses;
  like thieves they enter through the
    windows.

[10]Before them the earth shakes,
  the sky trembles,
the sun and moon are darkened,
  and the stars no longer shine.
[11]The LORD thunders
  at the head of his army;
his forces are beyond number,
  and mighty are those who obey his
    command.
The day of the LORD is great;
  it is dreadful.
  Who can endure it?

[12]"Even now," declares the LORD,
  "return to me with all your heart,
  with fasting and weeping and
    mourning."

[13]Rend your heart
  and not your garments.
Return to the LORD your God,

for he is gracious and
    compassionate,
slow to anger and abounding in love,
  and he relents from sending
    calamity.
[14]Who knows? He may turn and have
    pity
  and leave behind a blessing—
grain offerings and drink offerings
  for the LORD your God.

[15]Blow the trumpet in Zion,
  declare a holy fast,
  call a sacred assembly.
[16]Gather the people,
  consecrate the assembly;
bring together the elders,
  gather the children,
  those nursing at the breast.
Let the bridegroom leave his room
  and the bride her chamber.
[17]Let the priests, who minister before
    the LORD,
  weep between the temple porch and
    the altar.
Let them say, "Spare your people,
    O LORD.
Do not make your inheritance an
    object of scorn,
  a byword among the nations.
Why should they say among the
    peoples,
  'Where is their God?' "

[18]Then the LORD will be jealous for his
    land
  and take pity on his people.
[19]The LORD will reply[g] to them:

"I am sending you grain, new wine
    and oil,
  enough to satisfy you fully;
never again will I make you
  an object of scorn to the nations.

[20]"I will drive the northern army far
    from you,
  pushing it into a parched and barren
    land,
with its front columns going into the
    eastern sea[h]
  and those in the rear into the
    western sea.[i]
And its stench will go up;
  its smell will rise."

Surely he has done great things.[j]

[g]18,19 Or LORD was jealous . . . / and took pity . . . / [19]The LORD replied [h]20 That is, the Dead Sea [i]20 That is, the
Mediterranean [j]20 Or rise. / Surely it has done great things."

²¹ Be not afraid, O land;
   be glad and rejoice.
Surely the LORD has done great things.
²² Be not afraid, O wild animals,
   for the open pastures are becoming
      green.
The trees are bearing their fruit;
   the fig tree and the vine yield their
      riches.
²³Be glad, O people of Zion,
   rejoice in the LORD your God,
for he has given you
   the autumn rains in righteousness.ᵏ
He sends you abundant showers,
   both autumn and spring rains, as
      before.
²⁴The threshing floors will be filled with
      grain;
   the vats will overflow with new
      wine and oil.

²⁵"I will repay you for the years the
      locusts have eaten—
   the great locust and the young
      locust,
   the other locusts and the locust
      swarmˡ—
my great army that I sent among you.
²⁶You will have plenty to eat, until you
      are full,
   and you will praise the name of the
      LORD your God,
   who has worked wonders for you;
never again will my people be
      shamed.
²⁷Then you will know that I am in
      Israel,
   that I am the LORD your God,
   and that there is no other;
never again will my people be
      shamed.

²⁸"And afterward,
   I will pour out my Spirit on all
      people.
Your sons and daughters will
      prophesy,
   your old men will dream dreams,
   your young men will see visions.
²⁹Even on my servants, both men and
      women,
   I will pour out my Spirit in those
      days.
³⁰I will show wonders in the heavens
      and on the earth,
   blood and fire and billows of smoke.

³¹The sun will be turned to darkness
   and the moon to blood
   before the coming of the great and
      dreadful day of the LORD.
³²And everyone who calls
   on the name of the LORD will be
      saved;
for on Mount Zion and in Jerusalem
   there will be deliverance,
   as the LORD has said,
among the survivors
   whom the LORD calls.

C H A P T E R   3
"In those days and at that time,
   when I restore the fortunes of Judah
      and Jerusalem,
²I will gather all nations
   and bring them down to the Valley
      of Jehoshaphat.ᵐ
There I will enter into judgment
      against them
   concerning my inheritance, my
      people Israel,
for they scattered my people among
      the nations
   and divided up my land.
³They cast lots for my people
   and traded boys for prostitutes;
they sold girls for wine
   that they might drink.

⁴"Now what have you against me,
O Tyre and Sidon and all you regions of
Philistia? Are you repaying me for something I have done? If you are paying me
back, I will swiftly and speedily return on
your own heads what you have done.
⁵For you took my silver and my gold and
carried off my finest treasures to your
temples. ⁶You sold the people of Judah
and Jerusalem to the Greeks, that you
might send them far from their homeland.
⁷"See, I am going to rouse them out of
the places to which you sold them, and I
will return on your own heads what you
have done. ⁸I will sell your sons and
daughters to the people of Judah, and
they will sell them to the Sabeans, a nation far away." The LORD has spoken.

⁹Proclaim this among the nations:
   Prepare for war!
Rouse the warriors!
   Let all the fighting men draw near
      and attack.

ᵏ23 Or / the teacher for righteousness: ˡ25 The precise meaning of the four Hebrew words used here for locusts is uncertain.
ᵐ2 Jehoshaphat means the LORD judges; also in verse 12.

10Beat your plowshares into swords
   and your pruning hooks into spears.
Let the weakling say,
   "I am strong!"
11Come quickly, all you nations from
    every side,
   and assemble there.

Bring down your warriors, O LORD!

12"Let the nations be roused;
   let them advance into the Valley of
    Jehoshaphat,
for there I will sit
   to judge all the nations on every
    side.
13Swing the sickle,
   for the harvest is ripe.
Come, trample the grapes,
   for the winepress is full
   and the vats overflow—
so great is their wickedness!"

14Multitudes, multitudes
   in the valley of decision!
For the day of the LORD is near
   in the valley of decision.
15The sun and moon will be darkened,
   and the stars no longer shine.
16The LORD will roar from Zion
   and thunder from Jerusalem;
   the earth and the sky will tremble.

ⁿ18 Or Valley of Shittim

But the LORD will be a refuge for his
   people,
   a stronghold for the people of Israel.
17"Then you will know that I, the LORD
   your God,
   dwell in Zion, my holy hill.
Jerusalem will be holy;
   never again will foreigners invade
   her.

18"In that day the mountains will drip
   new wine,
   and the hills will flow with milk;
   all the ravines of Judah will run
   with water.
A fountain will flow out of the LORD's
   house
   and will water the valley of
   acacias.ⁿ
19But Egypt will be desolate,
   Edom a desert waste,
because of violence done to the people
   of Judah,
   in whose land they shed innocent
   blood.
20Judah will be inhabited forever
   and Jerusalem through all
   generations.
21Their bloodguilt, which I have not
   pardoned,
   I will pardon."

The LORD dwells in Zion!

SEPTEMBER 7 ☐ DAY 251
Faithfulness through the Years

LOOK BACK Daniel first appeared in the book that bears his name as a transplanted teenager. By chapter 4, he was probably about seventy-six years old. And by the end of the book, he was a spry ninety-three!

Again and again Daniel demonstrated the *power* of God in the life of the *child* of God, enabling him to read writing on the banquet room wall . . . untangle beastly visions . . . decipher dreams involving seventies and sevens.

Daniel's life of singleness and single-minded devotion contrasts with Hosea's life as father of three and husband of an unfaithful wife. Hosea's fractured home became the backdrop for preaching to a fractured and faithless nation. God would heal, God would restore—if only Judah were interested in being cured. But her unrelenting disobedience and indifference left room for only one conclusion: "God will reject them because they have not obeyed him" (Hosea 9:17).

In the wake of a devastating locust plague, Joel wrote his message of comfort and caution to the southern kingdom of Judah. Joy and gladness had evaporated from the house of the Lord, and the day of his vengeance is near. But the solution has always been the same, in Joel's generation and in yours: "Everyone who calls on the name of the LORD will be saved" (Joel 2:32).

LOOK UP What's in a name? If you're a character in the pages of Scripture, the likely answer is "Plenty!" Here is a cast of characters from the book of Hosea and a suggested meaning for each name. Can you retell the story of the book of Hosea and his family experience just by using the names of his family members? Try it!

Love is a fabric that doesn't fade when washed in the water of adversity and grief.

    Hosea means "salvation."
    Gomer (his wife) means "completion."
    Jezreel (his son) means "God plants."
    Lo-Ruhamah (his daughter) means "not loved."
    Lo-Ammi (his other son) means "not my people."

LOOK AHEAD There are no perfect families in the Bible because there are no perfect people. Regardless of your family background, you'll find something to identify with in the pages of the Bible.

Did you come from a home filled with jealousy and backbiting? You're in good company. So did the shepherd boy David and the eleventh of twelve brothers, Joseph.

Were your parents perhaps unfaithful to one another? Join the ranks with Jephthah, whose mother was a prostitute (Judges 11:1).

Has one of your parents been married more than once? Welcome to the club. The Samaritan woman whom Jesus met one day by a well in Sychar had been married and divorced *five times* and at the time was living with a sixth man (John 4:16–18).

The Bible does not condone this behavior, but neither does it seek to conceal the real family situation. And the point is clear: Regardless of the family situation from which you have come, God has a wonderful family in mind for your future—the family of God. His unconditional, undying love for you is modeled in Hosea's love for his unfaithful wife. It's a love that doesn't know when to quit! Do the members of your earthly family know about God's love yet? They can, you know, even without your saying a word (1 Peter 3:1).

Amos

TIMES were good in Israel. The nation basked in peace, prosperity, strength and security. Then came Amos, breaking through the facade of respectability and exposing the rotten core of immorality, injustice, false optimism and shallow piety. To those who had grown soft and lax in luxurious living, Amos declares God's terrible warning and issues God's last call to repentance. But the people fail to respond, and Amos announces God's unwelcome but necessary discipline.

Focus	Judgment Is Sure		Judgment Is Soon	
Divisions	Funnel of Fire	Fallen Family	Woes and Warnings	Rejection and Restoration
	1　　　　　　　2	3　　　　　　　5	6　　　　　　　7	8　　　　　　　9
Topics	Vengeance	Vindication	Visions	Victory
	Pronouncements		Pictures	
Place	Neighboring Nations	Northern Kingdom of Israel		
Time	About 10 Years (760–750 B.C.)			

SEPTEMBER 8 □ DAY 252
AMOS 1–2
The Funnel of Fire

OVERVIEW Amos, a southern shepherd sent north with God's awful message for Israel, begins with a series of stinging judgments on Israel's neighbors. In characteristically prophetic fashion, he harshly condemns the transgressions of the seven nations that surround Israel, and then he gradually "zeros in" on Israel itself. Each of his eight oracles in today's two chapters begins with the words, "For three sins . . . even for four," which add up to seven, the biblical number of fulness. Each nation is full of sin. Therefore each nation receives the same sentence of doom: "I will send fire" (1:4, 7, 10, 12, 14; 2:2, 5).

Chapter 1					Chapter 2		
Fiery Judgment on the Nations of							
Damascus	Gaza	Tyre	Edom	Ammon	Moab	Judah	Israel
1 5	6 8	9 10	11 12	13 15	1 3	4 5	6 16
Gentiles					Jews		

YOUR DAILY WALK Imagine Amos standing on your street corner loudly condemning the sins of your neighbors. He names your friends house by house, moving steadily around the block: "the Hoovers . . . the Kirks . . . the Wallaces . . . the Holmeses . . ." And then, horrified, you hear him name . . . you!

There is no such thing as a little sin because there is no such person as a little God to sin against.

What would Amos say about you? Mentally list those shortcomings, failures and excesses that would embarrass you the most if announced from your street corner. Announce them yourself right now to God! There's no need to wait for fire to fall—or a prophet to knock—before you tend to an area of your life overdue for change!

INSIGHT Amos's Funnel of Fire
God is concerned for all nations, and they all must answer to his justice and judgment. Amos begins his "Rogues Gallery" with Israel's neighbors on all sides, then spirals inward, leaving the judgment of Israel for last. Can you sense the expectation building as Amos moves ever closer to the principal target of his sermon?

CHAPTER 1
The words of Amos, one of the shepherds of Tekoa—what he saw concerning Israel two years before the earthquake, when Uzziah was king of Judah and Jeroboam son of Jehoash[a] was king of Israel. ²He said:

"The LORD roars from Zion
    and thunders from Jerusalem;
the pastures of the shepherds dry
    up,[b]

and the top of Carmel
    withers."

³This is what the LORD says:

"For three sins of Damascus,
    even for four, I will not turn back
    ⌞my wrath⌟.
Because she threshed Gilead
    with sledges having iron teeth,
⁴I will send fire upon the house of
    Hazael

---

*a*1 Hebrew *Joash,* a variant of *Jehoash*   *b*2 Or *shepherds mourn*

that will consume the fortresses of
Ben-Hadad.
[5]I will break down the gate of
Damascus;
I will destroy the king who is in[c]
the Valley of Aven[d]
and the one who holds the scepter in
Beth Eden.
The people of Aram will go into
exile to Kir,"
                          says the LORD.

[6]This is what the LORD says:

"For three sins of Gaza,
even for four, I will not turn back
⌊my wrath⌋.
Because she took captive whole
communities
and sold them to Edom,
[7]I will send fire upon the walls of Gaza
that will consume her fortresses.
[8]I will destroy the king[e] of Ashdod
and the one who holds the scepter
in Ashkelon.
I will turn my hand against Ekron,
till the last of the Philistines is
dead,"
                says the Sovereign LORD.

[9]This is what the LORD says:

"For three sins of Tyre,
even for four, I will not turn back
⌊my wrath⌋.
Because she sold whole communities
of captives to Edom,
disregarding a treaty of brotherhood,
[10]I will send fire upon the walls of Tyre
that will consume her fortresses."

[11]This is what the LORD says:

"For three sins of Edom,
even for four, I will not turn back
⌊my wrath⌋.
Because he pursued his brother with a
sword,
stifling all compassion,[f]
because his anger raged continually
and his fury flamed unchecked,
[12]I will send fire upon Teman
that will consume the fortresses of
Bozrah."

[13]This is what the LORD says:

"For three sins of Ammon,

even for four, I will not turn back
⌊my wrath⌋.
Because he ripped open the pregnant
women of Gilead
in order to extend his borders,
[14]I will set fire to the walls of Rabbah
that will consume her fortresses
amid war cries on the day of battle,
amid violent winds on a stormy day.
[15]Her king[g] will go into exile,
he and his officials together,"
                          says the LORD.

CHAPTER 2
This is what the LORD says:

"For three sins of Moab,
even for four, I will not turn back
⌊my wrath⌋.
Because he burned, as if to lime,
the bones of Edom's king,
[2]I will send fire upon Moab
that will consume the fortresses of
Kerioth.[h]
Moab will go down in great tumult
amid war cries and the blast of the
trumpet.
[3]I will destroy her ruler
and kill all her officials with him,"
                          says the LORD.

[4]This is what the LORD says:

"For three sins of Judah,
even for four, I will not turn back
⌊my wrath⌋.
Because they have rejected the law of
the LORD
and have not kept his decrees,
because they have been led astray by
false gods,[i]
the gods[j] their ancestors followed,
[5]I will send fire upon Judah
that will consume the fortresses of
Jerusalem."

[6]This is what the LORD says:

"For three sins of Israel,
even for four, I will not turn back
⌊my wrath⌋.
They sell the righteous for silver,
and the needy for a pair of sandals.
[7]They trample on the heads of the poor
as upon the dust of the ground
and deny justice to the oppressed.
Father and son use the same girl

---

[c]5 Or the inhabitants of   [d]5 Aven means wickedness.   [e]8 Or inhabitants   [f]11 Or sword / and destroyed his allies   [g]15 Or /
Molech; Hebrew malcam   [h]2 Or of her cities   [i]4 Or by lies   [j]4 Or lies

and so profane my holy name.
⁸They lie down beside every altar
on garments taken in pledge.
In the house of their god
they drink wine taken as fines.

⁹"I destroyed the Amorite before them,
though he was tall as the cedars
and strong as the oaks.
I destroyed his fruit above
and his roots below.

¹⁰"I brought you up out of Egypt,
and I led you forty years in the
desert
to give you the land of the
Amorites.
¹¹I also raised up prophets from among
your sons
and Nazirites from among your
young men.
Is this not true, people of Israel?"
declares the LORD.

¹²"But you made the Nazirites drink
wine
and commanded the prophets not to
prophesy.

¹³"Now then, I will crush you
as a cart crushes when loaded with
grain.
¹⁴The swift will not escape,
the strong will not muster their
strength,
and the warrior will not save his
life.
¹⁵The archer will not stand his ground,
the fleet-footed soldier will not get
away,
and the horseman will not save his
life.
¹⁶Even the bravest warriors
will flee naked on that day,"
declares the LORD.

SEPTEMBER 9 ☐ DAY 253
AMOS 3–5
A Fallen Family

OVERVIEW Many times over God has tried to bring the self-satisfied family of Israel to repentance. Famine, pestilence, drought, blight, death, defeat—and still the people of God cling to their sin. Violence and injustice, drunkenness and greed remain the hallmarks of their decadent way of life. The prophet has only one message left: "Prepare to meet your God, O Israel!" (4:12).

Chapter 3	Chapter 4	Chapter 5
Israel's Rebellion	God's Rejection	Resulting Retribution
Guilty	Judged	Sentenced

YOUR DAILY WALK Your car stalls repeatedly, so you go to a mechanic. He takes it for a test drive, and sure enough, while ascending a hill, the engine dies. Stepping on the brakes, he turns and announces to you cheerily, "Well, it's not so bad. After all, you could be rolling backwards!"

Do all the good you can, in all the ways you can, to all the people you can, as long as you can.

How would you evaluate that "mechanic"?

After reading today's section dealing with the sins of the fallen family of Israel, you may be tempted to conclude, "Well, at least I'm not that bad!" And you may be right. But are you "stalled" on the upward road of righteousness, your brakes firmly set—not really running after wickedness, but not actively pursuing godliness either?

Amos proposed to the people that they "seek good, . . . that [they] may live" (5:14). It is not enough, Amos declared, to avoid evil; you

must also actively "seek good." And that never happens by accident!
Across the top of the next five daily readings, write the name of one
person you'll see each day. Then think of an "active good" you can do
in the life of that individual: Offer a helping hand, a sincere compliment, a free lunch, an expression of friendship. Now let off those
brakes and start again, confident that the Lord will be with you as you
"train yourself to be godly" (1 Timothy 4:7).

 INSIGHT The Hand That Rocks the Cradle Steadies the Nation
A comment by J. E. McFayden is cogent, and Amos 4:1–3 provides a
case in point: "All the Hebrew prophets knew that for the temper and
quality of a civilization, the women are greatly responsible. A country
is largely what its women make it; if they are careless or unwomanly,
the country is on the road to ruin." Think about that!

CHAPTER 3

Hear this word the Lord has spoken
against you, O people of Israel—against
the whole family I brought up out of
Egypt:

²"You only have I chosen
of all the families of the earth;
therefore I will punish you
for all your sins."

³Do two walk together
unless they have agreed to do so?
⁴Does a lion roar in the thicket
when he has no prey?
Does he growl in his den
when he has caught nothing?
⁵Does a bird fall into a trap on the
ground
where no snare has been set?
Does a trap spring up from the earth
when there is nothing to catch?
⁶When a trumpet sounds in a city,
do not the people tremble?
When disaster comes to a city,
has not the Lord caused it?

⁷Surely the Sovereign Lord does
nothing
without revealing his plan
to his servants the prophets.

⁸The lion has roared—
who will not fear?
The Sovereign Lord has spoken—
who can but prophesy?

⁹Proclaim to the fortresses of Ashdod
and to the fortresses of Egypt:
"Assemble yourselves on the
mountains of Samaria;
see the great unrest within her

and the oppression among her
people."

¹⁰"They do not know how to do right,"
declares the Lord,
"who hoard plunder and loot in
their fortresses."

¹¹Therefore this is what the Sovereign
Lord says:

"An enemy will overrun the land;
he will pull down your strongholds
and plunder your fortresses."

¹²This is what the Lord says:

"As a shepherd saves from the lion's
mouth
only two leg bones or a piece of an
ear,
so will the Israelites be saved,
those who sit in Samaria
on the edge of their beds
and in Damascus on their
couches.ᵏ"

¹³"Hear this and testify against the
house of Jacob," declares the Lord, the
Lord God Almighty.

¹⁴"On the day I punish Israel for her
sins,
I will destroy the altars of Bethel;
the horns of the altar will be cut off
and fall to the ground.
¹⁵I will tear down the winter house
along with the summer house;
the houses adorned with ivory will be
destroyed
and the mansions will be
demolished,"
declares the Lord.

ᵏ12 The meaning of the Hebrew for this line is uncertain.

CHAPTER 4

Hear this word, you cows of Bashan
    on Mount Samaria,
you women who oppress the poor
    and crush the needy
and say to your husbands, "Bring us
    some drinks!"
²The Sovereign LORD has sworn by his
    holiness:
"The time will surely come
when you will be taken away with
    hooks,
    the last of you with fishhooks.
³You will each go straight out
    through breaks in the wall,
and you will be cast out toward
    Harmon,¹"
                        declares the LORD.
⁴"Go to Bethel and sin;
    go to Gilgal and sin yet more.
Bring your sacrifices every morning,
    your tithes every three years.ᵐ
⁵Burn leavened bread as a thank
    offering
and brag about your freewill
    offerings—
boast about them, you Israelites,
    for this is what you love to do,"
                declares the Sovereign LORD.

⁶"I gave you empty stomachsⁿ in every
    city
and lack of bread in every town,
    yet you have not returned to me,"
                        declares the LORD.

⁷"I also withheld rain from you
    when the harvest was still three
        months away.
I sent rain on one town,
    but withheld it from another.
One field had rain;
    another had none and dried up.
⁸People staggered from town to town
    for water
but did not get enough to drink,
    yet you have not returned to me,"
                        declares the LORD.

⁹"Many times I struck your gardens and
    vineyards,
    I struck them with blight and
        mildew.
Locusts devoured your fig and olive
    trees,

    yet you have not returned to me,"
                        declares the LORD.

¹⁰"I sent plagues among you
    as I did to Egypt.
I killed your young men with the
    sword,
    along with your captured horses.
I filled your nostrils with the stench of
    your camps,
    yet you have not returned to me,"
                        declares the LORD.

¹¹"I overthrew some of you
    as Iº overthrew Sodom and
        Gomorrah.
You were like a burning stick snatched
    from the fire,
    yet you have not returned to me,"
                        declares the LORD.

¹²"Therefore this is what I will do to
        you, Israel,
and because I will do this to you,
    prepare to meet your God, O Israel."

¹³He who forms the mountains,
    creates the wind,
    and reveals his thoughts to man,
he who turns dawn to darkness,
    and treads the high places of the
        earth—
    the LORD God Almighty is his name.

CHAPTER 5

Hear this word, O house of Israel, this lament I take up concerning you:

²"Fallen is Virgin Israel,
    never to rise again,
deserted in her own land,
    with no one to lift her up."

³This is what the Sovereign LORD says:

"The city that marches out a thousand
        strong for Israel
    will have only a hundred left;
the town that marches out a hundred
        strong
    will have only ten left."

⁴This is what the LORD says to the house
of Israel:

"Seek me and live;
⁵   do not seek Bethel,
do not go to Gilgal,
    do not journey to Beersheba.

�l3 Masoretic Text; with a different word division of the Hebrew (see Septuagint) *out, O mountain of oppression*   ᵐ4 Or *tithes
on the third day*   ⁿ6 Hebrew *you cleanness of teeth*   º11 Hebrew *God*

For Gilgal will surely go into exile,
   and Bethel will be reduced to
      nothing.*p"*
⁶Seek the LORD and live,
   or he will sweep through the house
      of Joseph like a fire;
   it will devour,
   and Bethel will have no one to
      quench it.

⁷You who turn justice into bitterness
   and cast righteousness to the
      ground
⁸(he who made the Pleiades and Orion,
   who turns blackness into dawn
   and darkens day into night,
who calls for the waters of the sea
   and pours them out over the face of
      the land—
   the LORD is his name—
⁹he flashes destruction on the
      stronghold
   and brings the fortified city to
      ruin),
¹⁰you hate the one who reproves in
      court
   and despise him who tells the truth.

¹¹You trample on the poor
   and force him to give you grain.
Therefore, though you have built stone
      mansions,
   you will not live in them;
though you have planted lush
      vineyards,
   you will not drink their wine.
¹²For I know how many are your
      offenses
   and how great your sins.

You oppress the righteous and take
      bribes
   and you deprive the poor of justice
      in the courts.
¹³Therefore the prudent man keeps quiet
      in such times,
   for the times are evil.

¹⁴Seek good, not evil,
   that you may live.
Then the LORD God Almighty will be
      with you,
   just as you say he is.
¹⁵Hate evil, love good;
   maintain justice in the courts.

Perhaps the LORD God Almighty will
      have mercy
   on the remnant of Joseph.

¹⁶Therefore this is what the Lord, the
LORD God Almighty, says:

"There will be wailing in all the streets
   and cries of anguish in every public
      square.
The farmers will be summoned to
      weep
   and the mourners to wail.
¹⁷There will be wailing in all the
      vineyards,
   for I will pass through your midst,"
                 says the LORD.

¹⁸Woe to you who long
   for the day of the LORD!
Why do you long for the day of the
      LORD?
   That day will be darkness, not light.
¹⁹It will be as though a man fled from a
      lion
   only to meet a bear,
as though he entered his house
   and rested his hand on the wall
   only to have a snake bite him.
²⁰Will not the day of the LORD be
      darkness, not light—
   pitch-dark, without a ray of
      brightness?

²¹"I hate, I despise your religious feasts;
   I cannot stand your assemblies.
²²Even though you bring me burnt
      offerings and grain offerings,
   I will not accept them.
Though you bring choice fellowship
      offerings,*q*
   I will have no regard for them.
²³Away with the noise of your songs!
   I will not listen to the music of your
      harps.
²⁴But let justice roll on like a river,
   righteousness like a never-failing
      stream!

²⁵"Did you bring me sacrifices and
      offerings
   forty years in the desert, O house of
      Israel?
²⁶You have lifted up the shrine of your
      king,

*p5 Or grief; or wickedness; Hebrew aven, a reference to Beth Aven (a derogatory name for Bethel)   q22 Traditionally peace
offerings*

the pedestal of your idols,
the star of your god[r]—
which you made for
yourselves.

²⁷Therefore I will send you into exile
beyond Damascus,"
says the LORD, whose name is God
Almighty.

[r] 26 Or *lifted up Sakkuth your king | and Kaiwan your idols, | your star-gods;* Septuagint *lifted up the shrine of Molech | and the star of your god Rephan, | their idols*

SEPTEMBER 10 □ DAY 254
AMOS 6–7
Woes and Warnings

 OVERVIEW Israel has grown fat, apathetic and proud, choking on its own luxury. God's verdict is fitting: "Therefore, you will be among the first to go into exile; your feasting and lounging will end" (6:7). The prophet relates a series of visions in which God stays his hand of punishment repeatedly—but no more. The plumb line of his righteousness shows how far out of line the people have drifted, prompting Amos to report God's new resolve: "I will spare them no longer" (7:8).

Chapter 6		Chapter 7
Woe to the Complacent	Woe to the Proud	Three Warnings of Doom
1 7	8 14	
Violations of God's Law		Visions of God's Wrath

 YOUR DAILY WALK A wife and mother looks for employment in order to help pay for the family's second car—a car purchased so that she would have good transportation to and from her new job! A man works double shifts and weekends so that his overtime income will cover the payments on his new camper and boat. But when vacation time comes, he's too exhausted to drive to the lake.

Close your eyes and you will see everything you actually possess.

A wealthy executive relates how, as a young man, he recklessly spent his health to make millions—and now, later in life, he finds himself spending the millions he earned to regain the health he lost.

Each of these stories illustrates the subtle effects of materialism—a sickness characterized by an overwhelming desire to own things that all too often turn around and begin to "own" you!

Luxury-loving Israel was so "owned" by its possessions and materialistic lifestyle that God had become the "previous owner." Enjoying *things* from God had replaced enjoying *God himself.*

You may proudly think of your house, your car, your boat, your (whatever) as being "owned by me," but never forget it is also "loaned by God"! Wouldn't now be a good time to consider a "transfer of ownership"?

 INSIGHT Wine by the Bowlful
For the gluttonous people of God, an ordinary cup was not large enough (6:6), so they used enormous vessels customarily reserved for sacrificial purposes (Exodus 38:3; Zechariah 14:20).

CHAPTER 6

Woe to you who are complacent in
      Zion,
   and to you who feel secure on
      Mount Samaria,
   you notable men of the foremost
      nation,
   to whom the people of Israel come!
²Go to Calneh and look at it;
   go from there to great Hamath,
   and then go down to Gath in
      Philistia.
   Are they better off than your two
      kingdoms?
   Is their land larger than yours?
³You put off the evil day
   and bring near a reign of terror.
⁴You lie on beds inlaid with ivory
   and lounge on your couches.
You dine on choice lambs
   and fattened calves.
⁵You strum away on your harps like
      David
   and improvise on musical
      instruments.
⁶You drink wine by the bowlful
   and use the finest lotions,
   but you do not grieve over the ruin
      of Joseph.
⁷Therefore you will be among the first
      to go into exile;
   your feasting and lounging will end.

⁸The Sovereign LORD has sworn by
himself—the LORD God Almighty declares:

   "I abhor the pride of Jacob
      and detest his fortresses;
   I will deliver up the city
      and everything in it."

⁹If ten men are left in one house, they
too will die. ¹⁰And if a relative who is to
burn the bodies comes to carry them out
of the house and asks anyone still hiding
there, "Is anyone with you?" and he says,
"No," then he will say, "Hush! We must
not mention the name of the LORD."

¹¹For the LORD has given the command,
   and he will smash the great house
      into pieces
   and the small house into bits.

¹²Do horses run on the rocky crags?
   Does one plow there with oxen?
But you have turned justice into
      poison

and the fruit of righteousness into
      bitterness—
¹³you who rejoice in the conquest of Lo
      Debarˢ
   and say, "Did we not take Karnaimᵗ
      by our own strength?"

¹⁴For the LORD God Almighty declares,
   "I will stir up a nation against you,
      O house of Israel,
   that will oppress you all the way
      from Leboᵘ Hamath to the valley of
         the Arabah."

CHAPTER 7

This is what the Sovereign LORD showed
me: He was preparing swarms of locusts
after the king's share had been harvested
and just as the second crop was coming
up. ²When they had stripped the land
clean, I cried out, "Sovereign LORD, forgive! How can Jacob survive? He is so
small!"
³So the LORD relented.
"This will not happen," the LORD said.
⁴This is what the Sovereign LORD
showed me: The Sovereign LORD was calling for judgment by fire; it dried up the
great deep and devoured the land. ⁵Then
I cried out, "Sovereign LORD, I beg you,
stop! How can Jacob survive? He is so
small!"
⁶So the LORD relented.
"This will not happen either," the Sovereign LORD said.

⁷This is what he showed me: The Lord
was standing by a wall that had been built
true to plumb, with a plumb line in his
hand. ⁸And the LORD asked me, "What do
you see, Amos?"
"A plumb line," I replied.
Then the Lord said, "Look, I am setting
a plumb line among my people Israel; I
will spare them no longer.

⁹"The high places of Isaac will be
      destroyed
   and the sanctuaries of Israel will be
      ruined;
   with my sword I will rise against
      the house of Jeroboam."

¹⁰Then Amaziah the priest of Bethel
sent a message to Jeroboam king of Israel:
"Amos is raising a conspiracy against you
in the very heart of Israel. The land cannot

ˢ13 Lo Debar means *nothing.*   ᵗ13 Karnaim means *horns; horn* here symbolizes strength.   ᵘ14 Or *from the entrance to* bear all his words. ¹¹For this is what Amos is saying:

" 'Jeroboam will die by the sword,
    and Israel will surely go into exile,
    away from their native land.' "

¹²Then Amaziah said to Amos, "Get out, you seer! Go back to the land of Judah. Earn your bread there and do your prophesying there. ¹³Don't prophesy anymore at Bethel, because this is the king's sanctuary and the temple of the kingdom."

¹⁴Amos answered Amaziah, "I was neither a prophet nor a prophet's son, but I was a shepherd, and I also took care of sycamore-fig trees. ¹⁵But the LORD took me from tending the flock and said to me,

ᵛ17 Hebrew *an unclean*

'Go, prophesy to my people Israel.' ¹⁶Now then, hear the word of the LORD. You say,

" 'Do not prophesy against Israel,
    and stop preaching against the
        house of Isaac.'

¹⁷"Therefore this is what the LORD says:

" 'Your wife will become a prostitute
    in the city,
    and your sons and daughters will
        fall by the sword.
Your land will be measured and
    divided up,
    and you yourself will die in a
        paganᵛ country.
And Israel will certainly go into exile,
    away from their native land.' "

SEPTEMBER 11 □ DAY 255
AMOS 8–9
Visions of Horror and Hope

OVERVIEW Amos's series of visions concludes with a picture of the people's irreversible corruption (basket of ripe fruit) and a sign of God's inescapable judgment (the Lord on the altar). Disaster will come like a flood, leaving the people in helpless despair. And yet, through the present darkness comes a prophetic glimmer of hope: " 'In that day I will restore Daivd's fallen tent. . . . I will bring back my exiled people Israel; . . . I will plant Israel in their own land, never again to be uprooted from the land I have given them,' says the LORD your God" (9:11, 14–15).

Chapter 8		Chapter 9	
Judgment Is Ripe		The Lord Is Right	Israel Is Restored
	1	10	11 15
No Escape		No Partiality	New Prosperity

YOUR DAILY WALK God pursues. His love causes him to pursue us in order to show his mercy. And when we reject his gracious overtures, his holiness causes him to pursue us in order to show his justice.

This is the fundamental thing, the most serious thing of all, that we are always in the presence of God.

How do you run away from the God who is everywhere? "Though they dig down to the depths of the grave, from there my hand will take them. Though they climb up to the heavens, from there I will bring them down" (9:2). Climb the highest mountain or plunge the deepest depth, and even there you will find the pursuing God.

Have you been seeking to elude God? Amos's message is clear: Run to him, not *from* him. He stands ready to restore, to forgive, to cleanse—if you will just let him. The nation of Israel refused to acknowledge God's pursuit, and the rest is sordid history. Talk to God now about what you want the outcome of his pursuit to be in your life.

INSIGHT Law Enforcement God's Way
The first six verses of chapter 9 paint the darkest picture yet of Israel's coming captivity. There will be total destruction and death—no possible way of escape, no spiritual refuge or earthly security. God's people will learn—the hard way—that the God who is big enough to declare such threats in advance is also powerful enough to put his threats into effect!

CHAPTER 8

This is what the Sovereign LORD showed me: a basket of ripe fruit. ²"What do you see, Amos?" he asked.

"A basket of ripe fruit," I answered.

Then the LORD said to me, "The time is ripe for my people Israel; I will spare them no longer.

³"In that day," declares the Sovereign LORD, "the songs in the temple will turn to wailing.ʷ Many, many bodies—flung everywhere! Silence!"

⁴Hear this, you who trample the needy
and do away with the poor of the
land,

⁵saying,

"When will the New Moon be over
that we may sell grain,
and the Sabbath be ended
that we may market wheat?"—
skimping the measure,
boosting the price
and cheating with dishonest scales,
⁶buying the poor with silver
and the needy for a pair of sandals,
selling even the sweepings with the
wheat.

⁷The LORD has sworn by the Pride of Jacob: "I will never forget anything they have done.

⁸"Will not the land tremble for this,
and all who live in it mourn?
The whole land will rise like the Nile;
it will be stirred up and then sink
like the river of Egypt.

⁹"In that day," declares the Sovereign LORD,

"I will make the sun go down at noon
and darken the earth in broad
daylight.

¹⁰I will turn your religious feasts into
mourning
and all your singing into weeping.
I will make all of you wear sackcloth
and shave your heads.
I will make that time like mourning
for an only son
and the end of it like a bitter day.

¹¹"The days are coming," declares the
Sovereign LORD,
"when I will send a famine through
the land—
not a famine of food or a thirst for
water,
but a famine of hearing the words of
the LORD.
¹²Men will stagger from sea to sea
and wander from north to east,
searching for the word of the LORD,
but they will not find it.

¹³"In that day

"the lovely young women and strong
young men
will faint because of thirst.
¹⁴They who swear by the shameˣ of
Samaria,
or say, 'As surely as your god lives,
O Dan,'
or, 'As surely as the godʸ of
Beersheba lives'—
they will fall,
never to rise again."

CHAPTER 9

I saw the Lord standing by the altar, and he said:

"Strike the tops of the pillars
so that the thresholds shake.
Bring them down on the heads of all
the people;
those who are left I will kill with the
sword.
Not one will get away,

ʷ3 Or "the temple singers will wail   ˣ14 Or by Ashima; or by the idol   ʸ14 Or power

none will escape.
²Though they dig down to the depths
    of the grave,^z
from there my hand will take them.
Though they climb up to the heavens,
    from there I will bring them down.
³Though they hide themselves on the
    top of Carmel,
there I will hunt them down and
    seize them.
Though they hide from me at the
    bottom of the sea,
there I will command the serpent to
    bite them.
⁴Though they are driven into exile by
    their enemies,
there I will command the sword to
    slay them.
I will fix my eyes upon them
    for evil and not for good."

⁵The Lord, the LORD Almighty,
    he who touches the earth and it
      melts,
and all who live in it mourn—
the whole land rises like the Nile,
    then sinks like the river of Egypt—
⁶he who builds his lofty palace^a in the
    heavens
and sets its foundation^b on the
    earth,
who calls for the waters of the sea
    and pours them out over the face of
      the land—
    the LORD is his name.

⁷"Are not you Israelites
    the same to me as the Cushites^c?"
                declares the LORD.
"Did I not bring Israel up from Egypt,
    the Philistines from Caphtor^d
    and the Arameans from Kir?

⁸"Surely the eyes of the Sovereign LORD
    are on the sinful kingdom.
I will destroy it
    from the face of the earth—
yet I will not totally destroy

the house of Jacob,"
                declares the LORD.
⁹"For I will give the command,
    and I will shake the house of
    Israel
among all the nations
as grain is shaken in a sieve,
    and not a pebble will reach the
      ground.
¹⁰All the sinners among my people
    will die by the sword,
all those who say,
    'Disaster will not overtake or meet
      us.'

¹¹"In that day I will restore
    David's fallen tent.
I will repair its broken places,
    restore its ruins,
    and build it as it used to be,
¹²so that they may possess the remnant
    of Edom
and all the nations that bear my
    name,^e"
                declares the LORD,
            who will do these things.

¹³"The days are coming," declares the
LORD,

"when the reaper will be overtaken by
    the plowman
    and the planter by the one treading
      grapes.
New wine will drip from the
    mountains
    and flow from all the hills.
¹⁴I will bring back my exiled^f people
    Israel;
they will rebuild the ruined cities
    and live in them.
They will plant vineyards and drink
    their wine;
they will make gardens and eat their
    fruit.
¹⁵I will plant Israel in their own land,
    never again to be uprooted
    from the land I have given them,"
           says the LORD your God.

---

^z2 Hebrew *to Sheol*   ^a6 The meaning of the Hebrew for this phrase is uncertain.   ^b6 The meaning of the Hebrew for this word is uncertain.   ^c7 That is, people from the upper Nile region   ^d7 That is, Crete   ^e12 Hebrew; Septuagint *so that the remnant of men / and all the nations that bear my name may seek the Lord*   ^f14 Or *will restore the fortunes of my*

Obadiah

EDOM and Israel should have existed in brotherly harmony as neighbors. After all, they are in the same family: Edom is descended from Esau and Israel from Jacob. But in a moment of urgent need, with Israel's enemies knocking at the gates of Jerusalem, the Edomites rush in to help . . . the enemy! As a result, God sends his prophet Obadiah to predict extinction for the haughty Edomites. In contrast, God promises that his people will ultimately destroy their enemies and live in peace.

Focus	Destruction of Edom		Success of Israel	
Divisions	Destruction Predicted	Destruction Explained	Judgment on Nations	Restoration of Israel
	1:1 1:9	1:10 1:14	1:15 1:16	1:17 1:21
Topics	Edom's Arrogance	Edom's Antagonism	Edom's Annihilation	
	Defeat of Israel		Victory of Israel	
Place	Edom and Israel			
Time	Approximately 840 B.C.			

SEPTEMBER 12 ☐ DAY 256
OBADIAH
An Ancient Family Feud

OVERVIEW A struggle that began in the womb between twin brothers, Esau and Jacob, grows into a struggle between their respective descendants, the Edomites and the Israelites. Obadiah soundly condemns the Edomites for their stubborn refusal to aid Israel, first during the time of desert wandering (Numbers 20:14–21) and later during a time of invasion. This little-known prophet describes the Edomites' crimes, tries their case and pronounces their judgment: total destruction. Did the prophet's prediction of doom come true? To find out, you need only look at a map of the world today.

Verses 1-9	Verses 10-14	Verses 15-21
Edom's Arrogance	Edom's Antagonism	Edom's Annihilation
Condemnation	Charge	Consummation

YOUR DAILY WALK *Family Feud* (definition #1): a TV game show that pits two families against each other. The goal: huge sums of prize money. Ratings: high. Future prospects: syndicated reruns.

Family Feud (definition #2): an ancient struggle between two brother nations. The goal: preserving personal pride. Ratings: low (audience of one—God himself!). Future prospects: soon to be canceled (v. 10).

Hating others is like burning down your house to get rid of a rat.

What a tragedy that the strife between Esau and Jacob, a contention settled in their own lifetimes (Genesis 32–33), should reappear in the form of bitter jealousy and hatred between their respective nations. Esau's offspring maintained their enmity toward Israel for more than a thousand years!

How are things in your immediate family? Is there someone—brother, sister, parent, child, in-law—with whom you are holding a family feud? Let Psalm 133:1 show you a time-tested way to resolve that conflict. Learn from the doom of Edom.

INSIGHT A Major Distinction for a Minor Prophet
Evidence indicates that Obadiah's message against Edom was probably delivered in response to the Edomites' opposition to Israel (and collaboration with the Philistines in a raid on Jerusalem) during Jehoram's reign about 845 B.C. (See 2 Chronicles 21:8–10, 16–17.) If so, this would make Obadiah the earliest of the minor prophets.

¹The vision of Obadiah.

This is what the Sovereign LORD says about Edom—

We have heard a message from the LORD:
An envoy was sent to the nations to say,

"Rise, and let us go against her for battle"—

²"See, I will make you small among the nations;
you will be utterly despised.
³The pride of your heart has deceived you,

you who live in the clefts of the
    rocks[a]
and make your home on the heights,
you who say to yourself,
    'Who can bring me down to the
       ground?'
[4]Though you soar like the eagle
    and make your nest among the
       stars,
from there I will bring you down,"
                declares the LORD.
[5]"If thieves came to you,
    if robbers in the night—
Oh, what a disaster awaits you—
    would they not steal only as much
       as they wanted?
If grape pickers came to you,
    would they not leave a few grapes?
[6]But how Esau will be ransacked,
    his hidden treasures pillaged!
[7]All your allies will force you to the
       border;
    your friends will deceive and
       overpower you;
those who eat your bread will set a
       trap for you,[b]
    but you will not detect it.

[8]"In that day," declares the LORD,
    "will I not destroy the wise men of
       Edom,
    men of understanding in the
       mountains of Esau?
[9]Your warriors, O Teman, will be
       terrified,
    and everyone in Esau's mountains
    will be cut down in the slaughter.
[10]Because of the violence against your
       brother Jacob,
    you will be covered with shame;
    you will be destroyed forever.
[11]On the day you stood aloof
    while strangers carried off his
       wealth
and foreigners entered his gates
    and cast lots for Jerusalem,
    you were like one of them.
[12]You should not look down on your
       brother
    in the day of his misfortune,
nor rejoice over the people of Judah
    in the day of their destruction,
nor boast so much
    in the day of their trouble.

[13]You should not march through the
    gates of my people
    in the day of their disaster,
nor look down on them in their
    calamity
    in the day of their disaster,
nor seize their wealth
    in the day of their disaster.
[14]You should not wait at the crossroads
    to cut down their fugitives,
nor hand over their survivors
    in the day of their trouble.

[15]"The day of the LORD is near
    for all nations.
As you have done, it will be done to
    you;
    your deeds will return upon your
       own head.
[16]Just as you drank on my holy hill,
    so all the nations will drink
       continually;
    they will drink and drink
    and be as if they had never been.
[17]But on Mount Zion will be
    deliverance;
    it will be holy,
    and the house of Jacob
    will possess its inheritance.
[18]The house of Jacob will be a fire
    and the house of Joseph a flame;
the house of Esau will be stubble,
    and they will set it on fire and
       consume it.
There will be no survivors
    from the house of Esau."
                The LORD has spoken.

[19]People from the Negev will occupy
    the mountains of Esau,
and people from the foothills will
    possess
    the land of the Philistines.
They will occupy the fields of Ephraim
    and Samaria,
    and Benjamin will possess Gilead.
[20]This company of Israelite exiles who
    are in Canaan
will possess ₗthe landₗ as far as
    Zarephath;
the exiles from Jerusalem who are in
    Sepharad
    will possess the towns of the Negev.
[21]Deliverers will go up on[c] Mount Zion
    to govern the mountains of Esau.
And the kingdom will be the LORD's.

[a]3 Or of Sela   [b]7 The meaning of the Hebrew for this clause is uncertain.   [c]21 Or from

Jonah

JONAH despised the brutal Assyrian city of Nineveh. So when God tells him to go warn them of their impending destruction, Jonah sets sail in the opposite direction. God sends a storm to fetch him back, and at his own request Jonah is tossed overboard. A great fish swallows God's prophet and deposits him on dry land. Result: Jonah goes straight to Nineveh. When the people repent, God mercifully withholds punishment. God then teaches the resentful Jonah firsthand of his compassion.

Focus	Revival for a Prophet				Revival for a Pagan City			
Divisions	Prophet's Disobedience	Prophet's Danger	Prophet's Prayer	Prophet's Deliverance	Prophet's Obedience	Pagan's Repentance	Prophet's Complaint	Prophet's Rebuke
	1:1 1:3	1:4 1:17	2:1 2:9	2:10	3:1 3:4	3:5 3:10	4:1 4:5	4:6 4:11
Topics	Mercy on Jonah				Mercy on Nineveh			
	Jonah in the Ship		Jonah in the Fish		Jonah in the City		Jonah in the Suburbs	
Place	The Sea				The City			
Time	Approximately 760 B.C.							

SEPTEMBER 13 □ DAY 257
JONAH 1–4
God's Reaching Mercy

OVERVIEW When God assigns Jonah to preach a revival in Nineveh, the reluctant prophet ships out instead for Tarshish—precisely in the opposite direction! But God pursues him. He uses a fierce wind and a hungry fish to deposit Jonah on shore once again, ready now to respond to God's directive. Using a divinely given one-sentence sermon, Jonah watches in amazement as one of the greatest revivals in history takes place—"from the greatest to the least" of the inhabitants of Nineveh (3:5). But rather than rejoice at Nineveh's spiritual awakening, Jonah is disappointed that Israel's archenemy now will not be destroyed. God must teach his pouting prophet a lesson on divine mercy.

Chapter 1	Chapter 2	Chapter 3	Chapter 4
Jonah's Disobedience	Jonah's Distress	Jonah's Declaration	Jonah's Displeasure
In the Ship	In the Fish	In the City	In the Sunlight

YOUR DAILY WALK God has a marvelous way of bringing his children great opportunities brilliantly disguised as impossible situations!

Mercy imitates God and disappoints Satan.

Consider Jonah. Summoned by God on short notice to preach to Israel's cruelest foe, Jonah hits the panic button and runs for cover. Finally turned around by God and sent by "special delivery" to Nineveh, Jonah reluctantly preaches his message of repentance. Once again, God does the unexpected by bringing sweeping revival to the city. But instead of rejoicing over the salvation of lost souls, Jonah withdraws to grumble at God.

Are you prepared to handle a "mission impossible" today? a shift in plans? an unexpected interruption? an opportunity cleverly disguised as an imposition? Today, the first time something unexpected happens (and it will!), resist the urge to hit the panic button. Instead, look for the door of opportunity God is opening to you, and take it. Let others experience God's mercy through you!

INSIGHT Jonah's Story—*Did* It Happen? *Could* It Happen?
There are at least two documented cases of men who were swallowed by sharks or whales and lived to tell about it. In answer to the question, Did it happen? check Matthew 12:38–41 for confirmation from an irrefutable source!

CHAPTER 1

The word of the LORD came to Jonah son of Amittai: ²"Go to the great city of Nineveh and preach against it, because its wickedness has come up before me."

³But Jonah ran away from the LORD and headed for Tarshish. He went down to Joppa, where he found a ship bound for that port. After paying the fare, he went aboard and sailed for Tarshish to flee from the LORD.

⁴Then the LORD sent a great wind on the sea, and such a violent storm arose that the ship threatened to break up. ⁵All the

sailors were afraid and each cried out to his own god. And they threw the cargo into the sea to lighten the ship.

But Jonah had gone below deck, where he lay down and fell into a deep sleep. ⁶The captain went to him and said, "How can you sleep? Get up and call on your god! Maybe he will take notice of us, and we will not perish."

⁷Then the sailors said to each other, "Come, let us cast lots to find out who is responsible for this calamity." They cast lots and the lot fell on Jonah.

⁸So they asked him, "Tell us, who is responsible for making all this trouble for us? What do you do? Where do you come from? What is your country? From what people are you?"

⁹He answered, "I am a Hebrew and I worship the LORD, the God of heaven, who made the sea and the land."

¹⁰This terrified them and they asked, "What have you done?" (They knew he was running away from the LORD, because he had already told them so.)

¹¹The sea was getting rougher and rougher. So they asked him, "What should we do to you to make the sea calm down for us?"

¹²"Pick me up and throw me into the sea," he replied, "and it will become calm. I know that it is my fault that this great storm has come upon you."

¹³Instead, the men did their best to row back to land. But they could not, for the sea grew even wilder than before. ¹⁴Then they cried to the LORD, "O LORD, please do not let us die for taking this man's life. Do not hold us accountable for killing an innocent man, for you, O LORD, have done as you pleased." ¹⁵Then they took Jonah and threw him overboard, and the raging sea grew calm. ¹⁶At this the men greatly feared the LORD, and they offered a sacrifice to the LORD and made vows to him.

¹⁷But the LORD provided a great fish to swallow Jonah, and Jonah was inside the fish three days and three nights.

CHAPTER 2

From inside the fish Jonah prayed to the LORD his God. ²He said:

"In my distress I called to the LORD,
    and he answered me.

From the depths of the grave^a I called
        for help,
    and you listened to my cry.
³You hurled me into the deep,
    into the very heart of the seas,
    and the currents swirled about me;
all your waves and breakers
    swept over me.
⁴I said, 'I have been banished
    from your sight;
yet I will look again
    toward your holy temple.'
⁵The engulfing waters threatened me,^b
    the deep surrounded me;
    seaweed was wrapped around my
        head.
⁶To the roots of the mountains I sank
        down;
    the earth beneath barred me in
        forever.
But you brought my life up from the
        pit,
    O LORD my God.

⁷"When my life was ebbing away,
    I remembered you, LORD,
and my prayer rose to you,
    to your holy temple.

⁸"Those who cling to worthless idols
    forfeit the grace that could be theirs.
⁹But I, with a song of thanksgiving,
    will sacrifice to you.
What I have vowed I will make good.
    Salvation comes from the LORD."

¹⁰And the LORD commanded the fish, and it vomited Jonah onto dry land.

CHAPTER 3

Then the word of the LORD came to Jonah a second time: ²"Go to the great city of Nineveh and proclaim to it the message I give you."

³Jonah obeyed the word of the LORD and went to Nineveh. Now Nineveh was a very important city—a visit required three days. ⁴On the first day, Jonah started into the city. He proclaimed: "Forty more days and Nineveh will be overturned." ⁵The Ninevites believed God. They declared a fast, and all of them, from the greatest to the least, put on sackcloth.

⁶When the news reached the king of Nineveh, he rose from his throne, took off his royal robes, covered himself with

^a2 Hebrew *Sheol*   ^b5 Or *waters were at my throat*

sackcloth and sat down in the dust. ⁷Then he issued a proclamation in Nineveh:

"By the decree of the king and his nobles:

Do not let any man or beast, herd or flock, taste anything; do not let them eat or drink. ⁸But let man and beast be covered with sackcloth. Let everyone call urgently on God. Let them give up their evil ways and their violence. ⁹Who knows? God may yet relent and with compassion turn from his fierce anger so that we will not perish."

¹⁰When God saw what they did and how they turned from their evil ways, he had compassion and did not bring upon them the destruction he had threatened.

CHAPTER 4
But Jonah was greatly displeased and became angry. ²He prayed to the LORD, "O LORD, is this not what I said when I was still at home? That is why I was so quick to flee to Tarshish. I knew that you are a gracious and compassionate God, slow to anger and abounding in love, a God who relents from sending calamity.

³Now, O LORD, take away my life, for it is better for me to die than to live."

⁴But the LORD replied, "Have you any right to be angry?"

⁵Jonah went out and sat down at a place east of the city. There he made himself a shelter, sat in its shade and waited to see what would happen to the city. ⁶Then the LORD God provided a vine and made it grow up over Jonah to give shade for his head to ease his discomfort, and Jonah was very happy about the vine. ⁷But at dawn the next day God provided a worm, which chewed the vine so that it withered. ⁸When the sun rose, God provided a scorching east wind, and the sun blazed on Jonah's head so that he grew faint. He wanted to die, and said, "It would be better for me to die than to live."

⁹But God said to Jonah, "Do you have a right to be angry about the vine?"

"I do," he said. "I am angry enough to die."

¹⁰But the LORD said, "You have been concerned about this vine, though you did not tend it or make it grow. It sprang up overnight and died overnight. ¹¹But Nineveh has more than a hundred and twenty thousand people who cannot tell their right hand from their left, and many cattle as well. Should I not be concerned about that great city?"

SEPTEMBER 14 ☐ DAY 258
Loving Others as Only God Can

 LOOK BACK Amos, Obadiah and Jonah were three minor prophets with a message of major importance. Amos (whose name means "burden bearer") leaves his country roots as a shepherd and a caretaker of sycamore-fig trees to bring a fiery message of judgment upon the northern kingdom of Israel. Obadiah ("servant of the Lord") declares a scathing indictment upon the Edomites for their cruelty toward their brother nation Israel; and Jonah ("dove") takes a boat ride and a "whale" of a thrill ride before he arrives in Nineveh to announce a forty-day countdown to calamity for the mighty nation of Assyria.

Amos uses three sermons and five visions to portray in graphic detail Israel's unavoidable judgment. Obadiah, though the shortest book in the Old Testament, carries one of the strongest messages of judgment, offering Edom no plea to return and no promise of avoiding national calamity. Jonah, the only Old Testament prophetic book that revolves exclusively around a Gentile nation, shows it is possible for the audience (Nineveh) to repent, even though the preacher (Jonah) is hesitant to preach!

LOOK UP "The world would be a better place if only God would destroy _____ .

God invites us to burden him with what burdens us.

Few of us are bold enough to *utter* those words, but most of us have *considered* that thought at one time or another. If only God would get rid of the world powers that threaten the safety of our nation . . . the criminals who kill without conscience . . . the doctors who terminate life rather than protect it . . . the political and social zealots who murder for their cause . . . the parents who abuse and even murder their children.

The book of Jonah addresses our desire for revenge and retribution upon evildoers. The Assyrians were the most brutal, bloodthirsty power on earth in Jonah's day. Given the chance, Jonah would have asked God to destroy them—and felt good about his request! But God had other ideas. He wanted Jonah to see the Ninevites as God saw them: lost, desperate, without hope, spiritually naive, in need of mercy and worthy of saving.

Jonah's prejudice toward the Assyrians ran deep. His hatred was intense, and he longed to see God's mercy withheld from his enemies. For four chapters, God patiently worked with his stubborn prophet. When the book closes, the issue is still in doubt. What do you think? Do you suppose Jonah ever got on God's "wavelength" regarding the Ninevites?

LOOK AHEAD Don't allow an individual or a group of people who are objects of God's love to become objects of your hatred or revenge. That doesn't mean condoning conduct that God condemns. But it does mean releasing any bitterness or unforgiveness you may be harboring toward those whom God loves. Regardless of the *reason* for your hatred, the *response* should be the same: seeing others as God sees them and loving others as God loves them.

The psalmist David prayed this way: "Search me, O God, and know my heart; test me and know my anxious thoughts. See if there is any offensive way in me, and lead me in the way everlasting" (Psalm 139:23–24). Don't allow Jonah's "hardening of the attitudes" to poison your heart as well. Life is too short to spend it hating the very people God longs to love and save.

Micah

THE MESSAGE of Micah, like that of prophets before him, is neither pleasant nor popular: God knows the sins of his people, and terrible judgment is close at hand. For continued social injustice, oppression, exploitation and the self-serving interests of leaders and false prophets, the nation will experience destruction and a generation of captivity. But in the midst of this, Micah offers a word of hope. A divine Deliverer is coming, and when he does, righteousness and justice will prevail.

Focus	Violence	Victory	Vindication
Divisions	Judah's Day of Judgment	Judah's Day of Triumph	Judah's Day in Court
	1 2	3 5	6 7
Topics	Condemnation	Consolation	Conflict
	Punishment for Injustice	Promise of a Justice Bringer	Preservation of Justice
Place	Judah and Israel		
Time	About 25 Years (735–710 B.C.)		

SEPTEMBER 15 □ DAY 259
MICAH 1–2
Judah's Day of Judgment

 OVERVIEW The southern kingdom has begun the final "countdown to captivity." In the face of anarchy from within and annihilation from without, Micah emerges with a message from the Lord. God's day of judgment upon his complacent people is fast approaching, and woe to the one upon whom the judgment falls. It is too late to turn over a new leaf, too late to repent. Judah's wound is incurable, and only divine surgery can remove the malignancy of sin.

Chapter 1		Chapter 2	
Incurable Wounds	Inescapable Wrath	Indicted Princes	Ingathered People
1 7	8 16	1 11	12 13
Rebellion	Rebuke		Reward

 YOUR DAILY WALK What do you think about when you're not thinking about anything? Where does your mind wander during the moments before you fall asleep? What is the first thing that crosses your mind when you awaken in the morning? Answer those questions honestly, and you will discover the greatest passion in your life.

We lose the peace of years when we hunt after the rapture of moments.

What was it that consumed David's thoughts morning and evening? (See Psalm 63:1; 139:17–18.)

Where did the thoughts of Judah's leaders turn throughout the day? (See Micah 2:1–2.)

And where does your mind focus when you wake up . . . when you pause from the frantic pace of your day . . . when you lie down to rest at night? Paul urged Timothy, his son in the faith, to "have nothing to do with godless myths and old wives' tales; rather train yourself to be godly" (1 Timothy 4:7). And to the Colossians he wrote, "Set your minds on things above" (Colossians 3:2). Filling your mind with the things of God takes a deliberate act of the will; it won't happen by accident! Take a brisk walk sometime today, and as you exercise your body, exercise your mind as well with Bible verses, hymns and thoughts of God. It's habit-forming.

 INSIGHT Don't Fool Around with the Farms
Israel was primarily an agrarian society in which each family owned a portion of land. Only under extreme conditions was a family to give up its land. Micah condemns those who exploited the poor by acquiring their land (2:1–2), thus creating an impoverished, landless class that would be a burden on society. See Leviticus 25:25–28.

CHAPTER 1
The word of the LORD that came to Micah of Moresheth during the reigns of Jotham, Ahaz and Hezekiah, kings of Judah—the vision he saw concerning Samaria and Jerusalem.

²Hear, O peoples, all of you,
    listen, O earth and all who are in
      it,
that the Sovereign LORD may witness
    against you,
    the Lord from his holy temple.

³Look! The LORD is coming from his
   dwelling place;
he comes down and treads the high
   places of the earth.
⁴The mountains melt beneath him
   and the valleys split apart,
like wax before the fire,
   like water rushing down a slope.
⁵All this is because of Jacob's
   transgression,
because of the sins of the house of
   Israel.
What is Jacob's transgression?
   Is it not Samaria?
What is Judah's high place?
   Is it not Jerusalem?

⁶"Therefore I will make Samaria a heap
   of rubble,
a place for planting vineyards.
I will pour her stones into the valley
   and lay bare her foundations.
⁷All her idols will be broken to pieces;
   all her temple gifts will be burned
     with fire;
   I will destroy all her images.
Since she gathered her gifts from the
   wages of prostitutes,
as the wages of prostitutes they will
   again be used."

⁸Because of this I will weep and wail;
   I will go about barefoot and naked.
I will howl like a jackal
   and moan like an owl.
⁹For her wound is incurable;
   it has come to Judah.
Itᵃ has reached the very gate of my
   people,
even to Jerusalem itself.
¹⁰Tell it not in Gathᵇ;
   weep not at all.ᶜ
In Beth Ophrahᵈ
   roll in the dust.
¹¹Pass on in nakedness and shame,
   you who live in Shaphir.ᵉ
Those who live in Zaananᶠ
   will not come out.
Beth Ezel is in mourning;
   its protection is taken from you.
¹²Those who live in Marothᵍ writhe in
   pain,
waiting for relief,

because disaster has come from the
   LORD,
even to the gate of Jerusalem.
¹³You who live in Lachish,ʰ
   harness the team to the chariot.
You were the beginning of sin
   to the Daughter of Zion,
for the transgressions of Israel
   were found in you.
¹⁴Therefore you will give parting gifts
   to Moresheth Gath.
The town of Aczibⁱ will prove
   deceptive
to the kings of Israel.
¹⁵I will bring a conqueror against you
   who live in Mareshah.ʲ
He who is the glory of Israel
   will come to Adullam.
¹⁶Shave your heads in mourning
   for the children in whom you
     delight;
make yourselves as bald as the
   vulture,
for they will go from you into exile.

CHAPTER 2

Woe to those who plan iniquity,
   to those who plot evil on their beds!
At morning's light they carry it out
   because it is in their power to do it.
²They covet fields and seize them,
   and houses, and take them.
They defraud a man of his home,
   a fellowman of his inheritance.

³Therefore, the LORD says:

"I am planning disaster against this
   people,
from which you cannot save
   yourselves.
You will no longer walk proudly,
   for it will be a time of calamity.
⁴In that day men will ridicule you;
   they will taunt you with this
     mournful song:
'We are utterly ruined;
   my people's possession is divided
     up.
He takes it from me!
   He assigns our fields to traitors.' "

⁵Therefore you will have no one in the
   assembly of the LORD
to divide the land by lot.

ᵃ9 Or He   ᵇ10 Gath sounds like the Hebrew for tell.   ᶜ10 Hebrew; Septuagint may suggest not in Acco. The Hebrew for in
Acco sounds like the Hebrew for weep.   ᵈ10 Beth Ophrah means house of dust.   ᵉ11 Shaphir means pleasant.   ᶠ11 Zaanan
sounds like the Hebrew for come out.   ᵍ12 Maroth sounds like the Hebrew for bitter.   ʰ13 Lachish sounds like the Hebrew
for team.   ⁱ14 Aczib means deception.   ʲ15 Mareshah sounds like the Hebrew for conqueror.

6"Do not prophesy," their prophets say.
"Do not prophesy about these things;
  disgrace will not overtake us."
7Should it be said, O house of Jacob:
"Is the Spirit of the LORD angry?
Does he do such things?"

"Do not my words do good
  to him whose ways are upright?
8Lately my people have risen up
  like an enemy.
You strip off the rich robe
  from those who pass by without a
    care,
  like men returning from battle.
9You drive the women of my people
  from their pleasant homes.
You take away my blessing
  from their children forever.
10Get up, go away!
For this is not your resting place,
  because it is defiled,

it is ruined, beyond all remedy.
11If a liar and deceiver comes and says,
'I will prophesy for you plenty of
  wine and beer,'
he would be just the prophet for this
  people!

12"I will surely gather all of you,
  O Jacob;
I will surely bring together the
  remnant of Israel.
I will bring them together like sheep
  in a pen,
  like a flock in its pasture;
  the place will throng with people.
13One who breaks open the way will go
  up before them;
they will break through the gate and
  go out.
Their king will pass through before
  them,
  the LORD at their head."

SEPTEMBER 16 ☐ DAY 260
MICAH 3–5
Judah's Day of Triumph

OVERVIEW Like princes, like people. Micah knows that the nation's morals can be no stronger than the nation's leaders. But prince and priest alike pervert justice, oppress the helpless and minister for bribes. For their greed and injustice, Micah declares their judgment will be swift and severe. By contrast, in the last days righteousness will be a way of life, and the afflicted will be the objects of God's special attention. Messiah will emerge from the obscurity of Bethlehem to be "ruler over Israel" (5:2) and executor of vengeance upon the nations (5:15).

Chapter 3	Chapter 4	Chapter 5
Rebuking False Prophets	Restoring True Religion	Ruling Jacob's Remnant
False Peace	Kingdom of Peace	Prince of Peace

Good leaders take more than their share of blame and less than their share of credit.

YOUR DAILY WALK A good leader is someone who
• balances sensitivity with responsibility;
• has earned the confidence of others through integrity;
• facilitates development in others through being a servant;
• takes more than his share of the blame and less than his share of the credit; and
• keeps hope alive in others.
Using that list of definitions, spend a few extra minutes evaluating Judah's leaders. Where did they fail in their God-given assignment and why? Now add to the list of definitions one more: A leader is someone who is willing to learn from those who won't.

Take a hard look at one of your personal leadership roles: in the home, at the office, in the dorm, at the church. Can you spot one error, committed centuries ago by Judah's leaders, that you are in danger of duplicating today? If your ability to lead as God intended depends on your willingness to learn from the mistakes of others, then what will you do with that insight, beginning right now?

 INSIGHT Prophet of Birth, Prophet of Death
Micah and Isaiah ministered at the same time (and perhaps, on occasion, side by side) to the nation of Judah. While their books are similar in style and content, Micah is best known for his prophecies regarding the birth of Christ (5:2), Isaiah for his prophecies describing the death of Christ (Isaiah 52:13–53:12).

CHAPTER 3

Then I said,

"Listen, you leaders of Jacob,
  you rulers of the house of Israel.
Should you not know justice,
2 you who hate good and love evil;
who tear the skin from my people
  and the flesh from their bones;
3who eat my people's flesh,
  strip off their skin
  and break their bones in pieces;
who chop them up like meat for the
    pan,
  like flesh for the pot?"

4Then they will cry out to the LORD,
  but he will not answer them.
At that time he will hide his face from
    them
  because of the evil they have done.

5This is what the LORD says:

"As for the prophets
  who lead my people astray,
if one feeds them,
  they proclaim 'peace';
if he does not,
  they prepare to wage war against
    him.
6Therefore night will come over you,
    without visions,
  and darkness, without divination.
The sun will set for the prophets,
  and the day will go dark for them.
7The seers will be ashamed
  and the diviners disgraced.
They will all cover their faces
  because there is no answer from
    God."

8But as for me, I am filled with power,
  with the Spirit of the LORD,
  and with justice and might,
to declare to Jacob his transgression,
  to Israel his sin.
9Hear this, you leaders of the house of
    Jacob,
  you rulers of the house of Israel,
who despise justice
  and distort all that is right;
10who build Zion with bloodshed,
  and Jerusalem with wickedness.
11Her leaders judge for a bribe,
  her priests teach for a price,
  and her prophets tell fortunes for
    money.
Yet they lean upon the LORD and say,
  "Is not the LORD among us?
  No disaster will come upon us."
12Therefore because of you,
  Zion will be plowed like a field,
Jerusalem will become a heap of
    rubble,
  the temple hill a mound overgrown
    with thickets.

CHAPTER 4

In the last days

the mountain of the LORD's temple will
    be established
  as chief among the mountains;
it will be raised above the hills,
  and peoples will stream to it.

2Many nations will come and say,

"Come, let us go up to the mountain of
    the LORD,
  to the house of the God of Jacob.
He will teach us his ways,
  so that we may walk in his paths."
The law will go out from Zion,
  the word of the LORD from
    Jerusalem.
3He will judge between many peoples
  and will settle disputes for strong
    nations far and wide.

They will beat their swords into
    plowshares
and their spears into pruning hooks.
Nation will not take up sword against
    nation,
nor will they train for war anymore.
⁴Every man will sit under his own vine
    and under his own fig tree,
and no one will make them afraid,
    for the LORD Almighty has spoken.
⁵All the nations may walk
    in the name of their gods;
we will walk in the name of the LORD
    our God for ever and ever.

⁶"In that day," declares the LORD,

"I will gather the lame;
    I will assemble the exiles
    and those I have brought to grief.
⁷I will make the lame a remnant,
    those driven away a strong nation.
The LORD will rule over them in Mount
    Zion
from that day and forever.
⁸As for you, O watchtower of the flock,
    O stronghold ᵏ of the Daughter of
        Zion,
the former dominion will be restored
    to you;
    kingship will come to the Daughter
        of Jerusalem."

⁹Why do you now cry aloud—
    have you no king?
Has your counselor perished,
    that pain seizes you like that of a
        woman in labor?
¹⁰Writhe in agony, O Daughter of Zion,
    like a woman in labor,
for now you must leave the city
    to camp in the open field.
You will go to Babylon;
    there you will be rescued.
There the LORD will redeem you
    out of the hand of your enemies.

¹¹But now many nations
    are gathered against you.
They say, "Let her be defiled,
    let our eyes gloat over Zion!"
¹²But they do not know
    the thoughts of the LORD;
they do not understand his plan,
    he who gathers them like sheaves to
        the threshing floor.

¹³"Rise and thresh, O Daughter of Zion,
    for I will give you horns of iron;
I will give you hoofs of bronze
    and you will break to pieces many
        nations."

You will devote their ill-gotten gains
    to the LORD,
    their wealth to the Lord of all the
        earth.

CHAPTER 5
Marshal your troops, O city of
    troops,ˡ
    for a siege is laid against us.
They will strike Israel's ruler
    on the cheek with a rod.

²"But you, Bethlehem Ephrathah,
    though you are small among the
        clansᵐ of Judah,
out of you will come for me
    one who will be ruler over Israel,
whose originsⁿ are from of old,
    from ancient times.ᵒ"

³Therefore Israel will be abandoned
    until the time when she who is in
        labor gives birth
and the rest of his brothers return
    to join the Israelites.

⁴He will stand and shepherd his flock
    in the strength of the LORD,
    in the majesty of the name of the
        LORD his God.
And they will live securely, for then
        his greatness
    will reach to the ends of the earth.
⁵   And he will be their peace.

When the Assyrian invades our land
    and marches through our fortresses,
we will raise against him seven
        shepherds,
    even eight leaders of men.
⁶They will ruleᵖ the land of Assyria
    with the sword,
    the land of Nimrod with drawn
        sword.�q
He will deliver us from the Assyrian
    when he invades our land
    and marches into our borders.

⁷The remnant of Jacob will be
    in the midst of many peoples
like dew from the LORD,
    like showers on the grass,

ᵏ8 Or hill   ˡ1 Or Strengthen your walls, O walled city   ᵐ2 Or rulers   ⁿ2 Hebrew goings out   ᵒ2 Or from days of eternity
ᵖ6 Or crush   q6 Or Nimrod in its gates

which do not wait for man
    or linger for mankind.
[8]The remnant of Jacob will be among
        the nations,
    in the midst of many peoples,
    like a lion among the beasts of the
        forest,
    like a young lion among flocks of
        sheep,
    which mauls and mangles as it goes,
        and no one can rescue.
[9]Your hand will be lifted up in triumph
        over your enemies,
    and all your foes will be destroyed.

[10]"In that day," declares the LORD,

"I will destroy your horses from
    among you

[r]14 That is, symbols of the goddess Asherah

    and demolish your chariots.
[11]I will destroy the cities of your land
    and tear down all your
        strongholds.
[12]I will destroy your witchcraft
    and you will no longer cast spells.
[13]I will destroy your carved images
    and your sacred stones from among
        you;
    you will no longer bow down
        to the work of your hands.
[14]I will uproot from among you your
        Asherah poles[r]
    and demolish your cities.
[15]I will take vengeance in anger and
        wrath
    upon the nations that have not
        obeyed me."

SEPTEMBER 17 □ DAY 261
MICAH 6–7
Judah's Day in Court

 OVERVIEW Micah's prophecy closes with a courtroom scene. God has a controversy with his people, and he calls the mountains and hills together to sit in judgment on the case. The people have replaced wholehearted worship with halfhearted ritual. They have divorced God's righteous standards from their daily business transactions in order to justify their greed and corruption. In short, they have failed to understand what God requires of his covenant people.

Chapter 6		Chapter 7	
Judah's Ingratitude	Judah's Injustice	The Lord's Verdict	Judah's Victory
1 8	9 16	1 7	8 20
God's Justice		God's Mercy	

 YOUR DAILY WALK Picture this scene. You are sharing with another person the deepest burden of your heart. Suddenly, for no apparent reason, the hearer turns away and puts his fingers in his ears. What do you conclude? And would that dampen your enthusiasm to share again?

What a person believes, he or she will die for. What a person merely thinks, he or she will change his mind about.

Micah prophesied to Judah during the reigns of three kings over a period of at least twenty-five years (1:1). Like his contemporary Isaiah, he saw little fruit from his ministry. Most of his hearers turned away in unbelief (2:6) or indifference (3:11). But Micah firmly believed his task was a divine mandate, not simply a hobby or religious activity. Fortified with that conviction, Micah could stand for God even when no one was willing to listen and take his message to heart.

Micah's confidence is reflected in his prayer: "But as for me, I watch in hope for the LORD, I wait for God my Savior; my God will hear me" (7:7). Use his example as a motivation to start (or an encouragement to continue) sharing the claims of Christ with an unsaved friend, neighbor or relative.

INSIGHT John 3:16 of the Old Testament
In the New Testament, John 3:16 answers the question, How can sinful man and holy God be restored to fellowship with one another? In the Old Testament, Micah 6:8 answers the same question for God's covenant people.

CHAPTER 6
Listen to what the LORD says:

"Stand up, plead your case before the
    mountains;
  let the hills hear what you have to
    say.
²Hear, O mountains, the LORD's
    accusation;
  listen, you everlasting foundations of
    the earth.
For the LORD has a case against his
    people;
  he is lodging a charge against Israel.

³"My people, what have I done to you?
  How have I burdened you? Answer
    me.
⁴I brought you up out of Egypt
  and redeemed you from the land of
    slavery.
I sent Moses to lead you,
  also Aaron and Miriam.
⁵My people, remember
  what Balak king of Moab counseled
  and what Balaam son of Beor
    answered.
Remember ∟your journey⌐ from
    Shittim to Gilgal,
  that you may know the righteous
    acts of the LORD."

⁶With what shall I come before the
    LORD
  and bow down before the exalted
    God?
Shall I come before him with burnt
    offerings,
  with calves a year old?
⁷Will the LORD be pleased with
    thousands of rams,
  with ten thousand rivers of oil?
Shall I offer my firstborn for my
    transgression,
  the fruit of my body for the sin of
    my soul?

⁸He has showed you, O man, what is
    good.
  And what does the LORD require of
    you?
To act justly and to love mercy
  and to walk humbly with your
    God.

⁹Listen! The LORD is calling to the
    city—
  and to fear your name is wisdom—
  "Heed the rod and the One who
    appointed it.ˢ
¹⁰Am I still to forget, O wicked house,
  your ill-gotten treasures
  and the short ephah,ᵗ which is
    accursed?
¹¹Shall I acquit a man with dishonest
    scales,
  with a bag of false weights?
¹²Her rich men are violent;
  her people are liars
  and their tongues speak deceitfully.
¹³Therefore, I have begun to destroy
    you,
  to ruin you because of your sins.
¹⁴You will eat but not be satisfied;
  your stomach will still be empty.ᵘ
You will store up but save nothing,
  because what you save I will give to
    the sword.
¹⁵You will plant but not harvest;
  you will press olives but not use the
    oil on yourselves,
  you will crush grapes but not drink
    the wine.
¹⁶You have observed the statutes of
    Omri
  and all the practices of Ahab's
    house,
  and you have followed their
    traditions.
Therefore I will give you over to ruin
  and your people to derision;
  you will bear the scorn of the
    nations.ᵛ"

ˢ9 The meaning of the Hebrew for this line is uncertain.   ᵗ10 An ephah was a dry measure.   ᵘ14 The meaning of the Hebrew for this word is uncertain.   ᵛ16 Septuagint; Hebrew *scorn due my people*

C H A P T E R 7

What misery is mine!
I am like one who gathers summer
        fruit
    at the gleaning of the vineyard;
there is no cluster of grapes to eat,
    none of the early figs that I crave.
²The godly have been swept from the
        land;
    not one upright man remains.
All men lie in wait to shed blood;
    each hunts his brother with a net.
³Both hands are skilled in doing evil;
    the ruler demands gifts,
the judge accepts bribes,
    the powerful dictate what they
        desire—
    they all conspire together.
⁴The best of them is like a brier,
    the most upright worse than a thorn
        hedge.
The day of your watchmen has come,
    the day God visits you.
Now is the time of their confusion.
⁵Do not trust a neighbor;
    put no confidence in a friend.
Even with her who lies in your
        embrace
    be careful of your words.
⁶For a son dishonors his father,
    a daughter rises up against her
        mother,
a daughter-in-law against her
        mother-in-law—
    a man's enemies are the members of
        his own household.

⁷But as for me, I watch in hope for the
        LORD,
    I wait for God my Savior;
    my God will hear me.

⁸Do not gloat over me, my enemy!
    Though I have fallen, I will rise.
Though I sit in darkness,
    the LORD will be my light.
⁹Because I have sinned against him,
    I will bear the LORD's wrath,
until he pleads my case
    and establishes my right.
He will bring me out into the light;
    I will see his righteousness.
¹⁰Then my enemy will see it
    and will be covered with shame,
she who said to me,
    "Where is the LORD your God?"

w 14 Or *in the middle of Carmel*

My eyes will see her downfall;
    even now she will be trampled
        underfoot
    like mire in the streets.
¹¹The day for building your walls will
        come,
    the day for extending your
        boundaries.
¹²In that day people will come to you
    from Assyria and the cities of Egypt,
even from Egypt to the Euphrates
    and from sea to sea
    and from mountain to mountain.
¹³The earth will become desolate
    because of its inhabitants,
    as the result of their deeds.

¹⁴Shepherd your people with your staff,
    the flock of your inheritance,
which lives by itself in a forest,
    in fertile pasturelands.ʷ
Let them feed in Bashan and Gilead
    as in days long ago.

¹⁵"As in the days when you came out of
        Egypt,
    I will show them my wonders."

¹⁶Nations will see and be ashamed,
    deprived of all their power.
They will lay their hands on their
        mouths
    and their ears will become deaf.
¹⁷They will lick dust like a snake,
    like creatures that crawl on the
        ground.
They will come trembling out of their
        dens;
    they will turn in fear to the LORD our
        God
    and will be afraid of you.
¹⁸Who is a God like you,
    who pardons sin and forgives the
        transgression
    of the remnant of his inheritance?
You do not stay angry forever
    but delight to show mercy.
¹⁹You will again have compassion on us;
    you will tread our sins underfoot
    and hurl all our iniquities into the
        depths of the sea.
²⁰You will be true to Jacob,
    and show mercy to Abraham,
as you pledged on oath to our fathers
    in days long ago.

Nahum

IT HAS been about a century since Nineveh had repented under the preaching of Jonah, and Nineveh is as wicked a city as it has ever been. The inhabitants fear no judgment; after all, the walls are wide and high, and they are surrounded by a deep moat. But God speaks of Nineveh's destruction through Nahum—and his message is not a warning of doom that could be averted like Jonah's, but a description of certain coming death. God's prophecy comes true to the letter, and Nineveh's grave is so effectively dug that it will lie undiscovered for twenty-five hundred years.

Focus	God's Displeasure Proclaimed		Nineveh's Doom Predicted		Nineveh's Downfall Portrayed	
Divisions	Praise for God's Justice	Joy for Nineveh's Destruction	Destruction of Nineveh	Contrast with Former Glory	Sins of Nineveh	Inevitability of Destruction
	1:1 1:7	1:8 1:15	2:1 2:10	2:11 2:13	3:1 3:4	3:5 3:19
Topics	Sentence of Judgment		Sight of Judgment		Sense of Judgment	
	Psalm of Justice		Description of Justice		Reason for Justice	
Place	In Judah against Nineveh, capital of Assyria					
Time	Approximately 660 B.C.					

SEPTEMBER 18 □ DAY 262
NAHUM 1–3
A Flood of Judgment on Nineveh

OVERVIEW More than a century has passed since Jonah preached his way through the streets of Nineveh. Though revival came in Jonah's day, the repentance was short-lived. At last God's patience runs out, and he sends another prophet—Nahum (whose name means "burden")—to deliver an ominous decree. Nineveh's end will come in "an overwhelming flood" (1:8).

Chapter 1	Chapter 2	Chapter 3
Wrath against Nineveh	Warning to Nineveh	Woe to Nineveh
Destruction	Dirge	Doom

YOUR DAILY WALK The book of Nahum provides God's evaluation of the widely held view that "might makes right." If ever there was a nation that deserved the title "Most Likely to Survive," Assyria was it! Its vast armies and fortified defenses made it virtually impregnable—from a human point of view. But because the Assyrians boasted in their might and would not acknowledge their pride and brutality, from God's point of view the nation's fall was inevitable. One good rainstorm, and the mightiest military power on earth was conquered and demolished.

Trusting God is not faith without evidence; it is commitment without reservation.

If the great Assyrian Empire couldn't shake its fist in the face of God and get away with it, what does that suggest about your chances of doing the same today? Rebellion in God's eyes is as abominable as witchcraft, and stubbornness as intolerable as idolatry (1 Samuel 15:23). But those who put their trust in him find him a faithful and forgiving refuge (Nahum 1:7). What are you relying on: your *might,* or your *Mighty One?* It's easy to tell, for the former will fail you often, while the latter remains forever faithful!

INSIGHT A Literal and Figurative Flood
The prophecy of Nahum 1:8—that Nineveh's end would come in "an overwhelming flood"—literally came true. In 612 B.C. heavy rains caused the Tigris to overflow its banks and destroy a portion of the city wall, allowing both the river and the invading Babylonians to sweep in like floods. Truly "the LORD is slow to anger and great in power" (1:3).

CHAPTER 1

An oracle concerning Nineveh. The book of the vision of Nahum the Elkoshite.

²The LORD is a jealous and avenging God;
the LORD takes vengeance and is filled with wrath.
The LORD takes vengeance on his foes and maintains his wrath against his enemies.
³The LORD is slow to anger and great in power;
the LORD will not leave the guilty unpunished.
His way is in the whirlwind and the storm,
and clouds are the dust of his feet.

4He rebukes the sea and dries it up;
    he makes all the rivers run dry.
Bashan and Carmel wither
    and the blossoms of Lebanon
        fade.
5The mountains quake before him
    and the hills melt away.
The earth trembles at his presence,
    the world and all who live in it.
6Who can withstand his indignation?
    Who can endure his fierce anger?
His wrath is poured out like fire;
    the rocks are shattered before him.

7The LORD is good,
    a refuge in times of trouble.
He cares for those who trust in him,
8 but with an overwhelming flood
he will make an end of ⌊Nineveh⌋;
    he will pursue his foes into
        darkness.

9Whatever they plot against the LORD
    he*a* will bring to an end;
    trouble will not come a second
        time.
10They will be entangled among thorns
    and drunk from their wine;
    they will be consumed like dry
        stubble.*b*
11From you, ⌊O Nineveh,⌋ has one come
        forth
    who plots evil against the LORD
    and counsels wickedness.

12This is what the LORD says:

"Although they have allies and are
        numerous,
    they will be cut off and pass away.
Although I have afflicted you,
    ⌊O Judah,⌋
    I will afflict you no more.
13Now I will break their yoke from your
        neck
    and tear your shackles away."

14The LORD has given a command
        concerning you, ⌊Nineveh⌋:
    "You will have no descendants to
        bear your name.
I will destroy the carved images and
        cast idols
    that are in the temple of your gods.
I will prepare your grave,
    for you are vile."

15Look, there on the mountains,
    the feet of one who brings good
        news,
    who proclaims peace!
Celebrate your festivals, O Judah,
    and fulfill your vows.
No more will the wicked invade you;
    they will be completely destroyed.

CHAPTER 2
An attacker advances against you,
    ⌊Nineveh⌋.
    Guard the fortress,
    watch the road,
    brace yourselves,
    marshal all your strength!

2The LORD will restore the splendor of
        Jacob
    like the splendor of Israel,
though destroyers have laid them
        waste
    and have ruined their vines.

3The shields of his soldiers are red;
    the warriors are clad in scarlet.
The metal on the chariots flashes
    on the day they are made ready;
    the spears of pine are brandished.*c*
4The chariots storm through the
        streets,
    rushing back and forth through the
        squares.
They look like flaming torches;
    they dart about like lightning.

5He summons his picked troops,
    yet they stumble on their way.
They dash to the city wall;
    the protective shield is put in place.
6The river gates are thrown open
    and the palace collapses.
7It is decreed*d* that ⌊the city⌋
    be exiled and carried away.
Its slave girls moan like doves
    and beat upon their breasts.
8Nineveh is like a pool,
    and its water is draining away.
"Stop! Stop!" they cry,
    but no one turns back.
9Plunder the silver!
    Plunder the gold!
The supply is endless,
    the wealth from all its treasures!
10She is pillaged, plundered, stripped!
    Hearts melt, knees give way,

*a***9** Or *What do you foes plot against the LORD? | He*   *b***10** The meaning of the Hebrew for this verse is uncertain.   *c***3** Hebrew;
Septuagint and Syriac / *the horsemen rush to and fro*   *d***7** The meaning of the Hebrew for this word is uncertain.

bodies tremble, every face grows
    pale.
¹¹Where now is the lions' den,
    the place where they fed their
        young,
where the lion and lioness went,
    and the cubs, with nothing to fear?
¹²The lion killed enough for his cubs
    and strangled the prey for his mate,
filling his lairs with the kill
    and his dens with the prey.

¹³"I am against you,"
    declares the LORD Almighty.
"I will burn up your chariots in smoke,
    and the sword will devour your
        young lions.
I will leave you no prey on the
    earth.
The voices of your messengers
    will no longer be heard."

CHAPTER 3

Woe to the city of blood,
    full of lies,
full of plunder,
    never without victims!
²The crack of whips,
    the clatter of wheels,
galloping horses
    and jolting chariots!
³Charging cavalry,
    flashing swords
    and glittering spears!
Many casualties,
    piles of dead,
bodies without number,
    people stumbling over the
        corpses—
⁴all because of the wanton lust of a
    harlot,
alluring, the mistress of sorceries,
who enslaved nations by her
    prostitution
    and peoples by her witchcraft.

⁵"I am against you," declares the LORD
    Almighty.
"I will lift your skirts over your
    face.
I will show the nations your
    nakedness
    and the kingdoms your shame.
⁶I will pelt you with filth,
    I will treat you with contempt

and make you a spectacle.
⁷All who see you will flee from you
    and say,
'Nineveh is in ruins—who will
    mourn for her?'
Where can I find anyone to comfort
    you?"

⁸Are you better than Thebes,^e
    situated on the Nile,
    with water around her?
The river was her defense,
    the waters her wall.
⁹Cush^f and Egypt were her boundless
    strength;
Put and Libya were among her
    allies.
¹⁰Yet she was taken captive
    and went into exile.
Her infants were dashed to pieces
    at the head of every street.
Lots were cast for her nobles,
    and all her great men were put in
        chains.
¹¹You too will become drunk;
    you will go into hiding
    and seek refuge from the enemy.

¹²All your fortresses are like fig trees
    with their first ripe fruit;
when they are shaken,
    the figs fall into the mouth of the
        eater.
¹³Look at your troops—
    they are all women!
The gates of your land
    are wide open to your enemies;
    fire has consumed their bars.

¹⁴Draw water for the siege,
    strengthen your defenses!
Work the clay,
    tread the mortar,
    repair the brickwork!
¹⁵There the fire will devour you;
    the sword will cut you down
    and, like grasshoppers, consume
        you.
Multiply like grasshoppers,
    multiply like locusts!
¹⁶You have increased the number of
    your merchants
till they are more than the stars of
    the sky,
but like locusts they strip the land
    and then fly away.
¹⁷Your guards are like locusts,

^e8 Hebrew No Amon   ^f9 That is, the upper Nile region

your officials like swarms of locusts
that settle in the walls on a cold
    day—
but when the sun appears they fly
    away,
and no one knows where.

[18]O king of Assyria, your shepherds[g]
    slumber;
your nobles lie down to rest.

Your people are scattered on the
    mountains
with no one to gather them.
[19]Nothing can heal your wound;
    your injury is fatal.
Everyone who hears the news about
    you
claps his hands at your fall,
for who has not felt
    your endless cruelty?

g18 Or *rulers*

Habakkuk

HABAKKUK ministers during Judah's death throes. Though repeatedly called to repentance, the nation stubbornly refuses to change its sinful ways. Habakkuk, knowing the hardheartedness of his countrymen, asks God how long this intolerable condition can be tolerated. God replies that the Babylonians will be his chastening rod upon the nation—an announcement that sends the prophet to his knees, where he acknowledges that the just in any generation will live by faith, not by sight.

Focus	Habakkuk's Perplexity				Habakkuk's Prayer
Divisions	First Question: Israel's Sin	First Response: Babylonian Invasion	Second Question: Babylon's Sin	Second Response: Babylon's Destruction	Prayer and Praise
	1:1 1:4	1:5 1:11	1:12 2:1	2:2 2:20	3:1 3:19
Topics	Sweeping a Dirty Nation Clean . . .	Using an Even Dirtier Broom . . .			As Only God Can Do!
	Questions and Answers				Wonder and Worship
Place	Judah				
Time	Approximately 607 B.C.				

SEPTEMBER 19 ☐ DAY 263
HABAKKUK 1–3
Living by Faith in Hard Times

OVERVIEW Habakkuk prophesies in Judah just before its final destruction at the hands of the Babylonians. Like Job, he honestly raises the perplexing issue of why a just God is silent, and why the cries of the faithful seem to go unheard (1:2) "while the wicked swallow up those more righteous than themselves" (1:13). In reply, God declares to his prophet a timeless principle of trust in his sovereignty. The wicked will be dealt with—in God's own way, in God's own time. But in the meantime, "the righteous will live by his faith" (2:4).

Chapter 1	Chapter 2	Chapter 3
Questions and Answers	Woes and Warnings	Wonder and Worship
Dialogue	Monologue	Devotion

Faith is reason at rest with God.

YOUR DAILY WALK A swimmer far from shore flails helplessly in the water. A lifeguard rushes to his aid—and is greeted with this surprising retort: "Why don't you mind your own business?" Of course, the correct response from the lifeguard would be: "I *am* minding my own business—and you're part of it! You may not fully understand what I am doing, but just trust me to bring you to shore."

Life is filled with occasions when you are called upon to put your trust in a *person* even though you may not fully understand the *process.* A surgeon's scalpel, a pilot's skill, a doctor's prescription—these are all things you have learned to trust. Doesn't it make sense, therefore, to trust God when it comes to the "business" he specializes in?

Habakkuk was distraught at seeing the wicked get away with murder. But the prophet's focus sharpened when he saw that he was trying to mind God's business instead of the business God had entrusted to him—the business of walking by faith!

"Mind your own business." It may sound harsh, but perhaps it's just the reminder you need today to stay on target in your walk with God!

INSIGHT May I Quote You, Mr. Habakkuk?
The last half of 2:4 is so significant that it's quoted three times in the New Testament: twice by Paul (Romans 1:17; Galatians 3:11) and once by the writer to the Hebrews (Hebrews 10:38).

CHAPTER 1
The oracle that Habakkuk the prophet received.

²How long, O Lᴏʀᴅ, must I call for
    help,
  but you do not listen?
Or cry out to you, "Violence!"
  but you do not save?

³Why do you make me look at
    injustice?
Why do you tolerate wrong?
Destruction and violence are before
    me;
  there is strife, and conflict
    abounds.
⁴Therefore the law is paralyzed,
  and justice never prevails.

The wicked hem in the righteous,
    so that justice is perverted.

5"Look at the nations and watch—
    and be utterly amazed.
For I am going to do something in
      your days
    that you would not believe,
    even if you were told.
6I am raising up the Babylonians,*a*
    that ruthless and impetuous people,
who sweep across the whole earth
    to seize dwelling places not their
      own.
7They are a feared and dreaded people;
    they are a law to themselves
    and promote their own honor.
8Their horses are swifter than leopards,
    fiercer than wolves at dusk.
Their cavalry gallops headlong;
    their horsemen come from afar.
They fly like a vulture swooping to
      devour;
9   they all come bent on violence.
Their hordes*b* advance like a desert
      wind
    and gather prisoners like sand.
10They deride kings
    and scoff at rulers.
They laugh at all fortified cities;
    they build earthen ramps and
      capture them.
11Then they sweep past like the wind
    and go on—
    guilty men, whose own strength is
      their god."

12O LORD, are you not from everlasting?
    My God, my Holy One, we will not
      die.
O LORD, you have appointed them to
      execute judgment;
    O Rock, you have ordained them to
      punish.
13Your eyes are too pure to look on evil;
    you cannot tolerate wrong.
Why then do you tolerate the
      treacherous?
Why are you silent while the wicked
swallow up those more righteous
    than themselves?
14You have made men like fish in the
      sea,
    like sea creatures that have no ruler.

15The wicked foe pulls all of them up
      with hooks,
    he catches them in his net,
he gathers them up in his dragnet;
    and so he rejoices and is glad.
16Therefore he sacrifices to his net
    and burns incense to his dragnet,
for by his net he lives in luxury
    and enjoys the choicest food.
17Is he to keep on emptying his net,
    destroying nations without mercy?

CHAPTER 2
I will stand at my watch
    and station myself on the ramparts;
I will look to see what he will say to
      me,
    and what answer I am to give to
      this complaint.*c*

2Then the LORD replied:

"Write down the revelation
    and make it plain on tablets
    so that a herald*d* may run with it.
3For the revelation awaits an appointed
      time;
    it speaks of the end
    and will not prove false.
Though it linger, wait for it;
    it*e* will certainly come and will not
      delay.

4"See, he is puffed up;
    his desires are not upright—
    but the righteous will live by his
      faith*f*—
5indeed, wine betrays him;
    he is arrogant and never at rest.
Because he is as greedy as the grave*g*
    and like death is never satisfied,
he gathers to himself all the nations
    and takes captive all the peoples.

6"Will not all of them taunt him with
ridicule and scorn, saying,

  " 'Woe to him who piles up stolen
      goods
    and makes himself wealthy by
      extortion!
    How long must this go on?'
7Will not your debtors*h* suddenly
      arise?
    Will they not wake up and make
      you tremble?
    Then you will become their victim.

*a*6 Or *Chaldeans*   *b*9 The meaning of the Hebrew for this word is uncertain.   *c*1 Or *and what to answer when I am rebuked*
*d*2 Or *so that whoever reads it*   *e*3 Or *Though he linger, wait for him; | he*   *f*4 Or *faithfulness*   *g*5 Hebrew *Sheol*
*h*7 Or *creditors*

⁸Because you have plundered many
    nations,
  the peoples who are left will
    plunder you.
For you have shed man's blood;
  you have destroyed lands and cities
    and everyone in them.

⁹"Woe to him who builds his realm by
    unjust gain
  to set his nest on high,
  to escape the clutches of ruin!
¹⁰You have plotted the ruin of many
    peoples,
  shaming your own house and
    forfeiting your life.
¹¹The stones of the wall will cry out,
  and the beams of the woodwork will
    echo it.

¹²"Woe to him who builds a city with
    bloodshed
  and establishes a town by crime!
¹³Has not the LORD Almighty determined
  that the people's labor is only fuel
    for the fire,
  that the nations exhaust themselves
    for nothing?
¹⁴For the earth will be filled with the
    knowledge of the glory of the
    LORD,
  as the waters cover the sea.

¹⁵"Woe to him who gives drink to his
    neighbors,
  pouring it from the wineskin till
    they are drunk,
  so that he can gaze on their naked
    bodies.
¹⁶You will be filled with shame instead
    of glory.
  Now it is your turn! Drink and be
    exposed[i]!
The cup from the LORD's right hand is
    coming around to you,
  and disgrace will cover your glory.
¹⁷The violence you have done to
    Lebanon will overwhelm you,
  and your destruction of animals will
    terrify you.
For you have shed man's blood;
  you have destroyed lands and cities
    and everyone in them.

¹⁸"Of what value is an idol, since a man
    has carved it?
  Or an image that teaches lies?

For he who makes it trusts in his own
    creation;
  he makes idols that cannot speak.
¹⁹Woe to him who says to wood, 'Come
    to life!'
  Or to lifeless stone, 'Wake up!'
Can it give guidance?
  It is covered with gold and silver;
    there is no breath in it.
²⁰But the LORD is in his holy temple;
  let all the earth be silent before him."

CHAPTER 3

A prayer of Habakkuk the prophet. On
shigionoth.[j]

²LORD, I have heard of your fame;
  I stand in awe of your deeds,
    O LORD.
Renew them in our day,
  in our time make them known;
  in wrath remember mercy.

³God came from Teman,
  the Holy One from Mount Paran.
                              Selah[k]
His glory covered the heavens
  and his praise filled the earth.
⁴His splendor was like the sunrise;
  rays flashed from his hand,
  where his power was hidden.
⁵Plague went before him;
  pestilence followed his steps.
⁶He stood, and shook the earth;
  he looked, and made the nations
    tremble.
The ancient mountains crumbled
  and the age-old hills collapsed.
  His ways are eternal.
⁷I saw the tents of Cushan in distress,
  the dwellings of Midian in anguish.

⁸Were you angry with the rivers,
    O LORD?
  Was your wrath against the streams?
Did you rage against the sea
  when you rode with your horses
  and your victorious chariots?
⁹You uncovered your bow,
  you called for many arrows.   *Selah*
You split the earth with rivers;
¹⁰ the mountains saw you and writhed.
Torrents of water swept by;
  the deep roared
  and lifted its waves on high.

---

[i]**16** Masoretic Text; Dead Sea Scrolls, Aquila, Vulgate and Syriac (see also Septuagint) *and stagger*   [j]**1** Probably a literary or
musical term   [k]**3** A word of uncertain meaning; possibly a musical term; also in verses 9 and 13

¹¹Sun and moon stood still in the
    heavens
  at the glint of your flying arrows,
  at the lightning of your flashing
    spear.
¹²In wrath you strode through the earth
  and in anger you threshed the
    nations.
¹³You came out to deliver your people,
  to save your anointed one.
  You crushed the leader of the land of
    wickedness,
    you stripped him from head to foot.
                                    Selah
¹⁴With his own spear you pierced his
    head
  when his warriors stormed out to
    scatter us,
  gloating as though about to devour
  the wretched who were in hiding.
¹⁵You trampled the sea with your
    horses,
  churning the great waters.

¹⁶I heard and my heart pounded,
  my lips quivered at the sound;
  decay crept into my bones,
  and my legs trembled.
  Yet I will wait patiently for the day of
    calamity
  to come on the nation invading us.
¹⁷Though the fig tree does not bud
  and there are no grapes on the
    vines,
  though the olive crop fails
  and the fields produce no food,
  though there are no sheep in the pen
  and no cattle in the stalls,
¹⁸yet I will rejoice in the LORD,
  I will be joyful in God my Savior.

¹⁹The Sovereign LORD is my strength;
  he makes my feet like the feet of a
    deer,
  he enables me to go on the heights.

For the director of music. On my
    stringed instruments.

Zephaniah

ZEPHANIAH is possessed by one passion, motivated by one concern: the impending day of the Lord. That day signifies God's final judgment of the earth and the ensuing time of blessing and peace. He shudders at Judah's flouting God, moving away from him instead of moving toward him. Judah will be punished. But beyond that cloud brightness blazes: God will purify his people; he will restore their fortunes; he will rejoice over them with shouts of joy; he will make them great; he will be in their midst. Beyond judgment there is joy.

Focus	The Judgment of the Day of the Lord			The Salvation of the Day of the Lord		
Divisions	Judgment of the Whole Earth	Judgment of Judah	Judgment of the Nations	Need of Salvation	Promise of Salvation	Promise of Restoration
	1:1 1:3	1:4 2:3	2:4 2:15	3:1 3:8	3:9 3:13	3:14 3:20
Topics	God's Wrath on Judah		God's Woes on the Nations	God's Will for the Remnant		
	Retribution and Judgment			Restoration and Joy		
Place	Judah and the Nations					
Time	Approximately 630 B.C.					

SEPTEMBER 20 ☐ DAY 264
ZEPHANIAH 1–3
Judgment Day Is Coming

OVERVIEW During Judah's hectic political and religious history, reform would come from time to time. Zephaniah's forceful prophecy may have been a factor in the reform that occurred during Josiah's reign—a "revival" that produced outward change but could not remove the inward heart of corruption that characterized the leadership of the nation. Zephaniah hammers home his message repeatedly that the day of the Lord—Judgment Day—is coming when the malignancy of sin will be dealt with. Israel and her Gentile neighbors will soon experience the crushing hand of God's wrath. But after the chastening process is complete, blessing will come in the person of the Messiah, who will be the cause for praise and singing.

Chapter 1	Chapter 2	Chapter 3
God's Wrath on Judah	God's Woes on the Nations	God's Will for the Remnant
Judgment		Joy

The calm that puts us to sleep may be more deadly than a storm that keeps us wide awake.

YOUR DAILY WALK When it comes to responding to spiritual truth, there are three "temperatures" of individuals: hot (responsive), cold (rebellious) and lukewarm (indifferent). God rewards the hot, reaches out to the cold but rejects the lukewarm (Revelation 3:14–16)!

The people of Jerusalem during Zephaniah's day had become lukewarm—indifferent toward the Lord (1:12). Their problem was not a lack of *knowledge* about God's will, but rather a lack of *willingness* to do what they knew to be right.

What would Zephaniah have to say about your "spiritual temperature"? Have you reached a plateau, a leveling off, a point of complacency in your spiritual life? Are you stimulated by God's Word or stagnant toward it? Complete this sentence: "If I knew I had to face my God and Judge tomorrow and account for my life, I would spend my time today [doing what?]." There's no time like the present to leave lukewarmness behind!

INSIGHT Hidden Meaning in a Hidden Name
Zephaniah's name, which means "the Lord hides," had great significance for his message. In the midst of a graphic description of divine judgment "on that day," Zephaniah inserts a note of hope for the righteous remnant. Read about it in 2:3!

CHAPTER 1

The word of the LORD that came to Zephaniah son of Cushi, the son of Gedaliah, the son of Amariah, the son of Hezekiah, during the reign of Josiah son of Amon king of Judah:

²"I will sweep away everything
    from the face of the earth,"
                    declares the LORD.
³"I will sweep away both men and
    animals;
    I will sweep away the birds of the air

and the fish of the sea.
The wicked will have only heaps of
    rubble[a]
when I cut off man from the face of
    the earth,"
                        declares the LORD.

⁴"I will stretch out my hand against
    Judah
and against all who live in
    Jerusalem.
I will cut off from this place every
    remnant of Baal,
the names of the pagan and the
    idolatrous priests—
⁵those who bow down on the roofs
    to worship the starry host,
those who bow down and swear by
    the LORD
and who also swear by Molech,[b]
⁶those who turn back from following
    the LORD
and neither seek the LORD nor
    inquire of him.
⁷Be silent before the Sovereign LORD,
    for the day of the LORD is near.
The LORD has prepared a sacrifice;
    he has consecrated those he has
        invited.
⁸On the day of the LORD's sacrifice
    I will punish the princes
    and the king's sons
and all those clad
    in foreign clothes.
⁹On that day I will punish
    all who avoid stepping on the
        threshold,[c]
who fill the temple of their gods
    with violence and deceit.

¹⁰"On that day," declares the LORD,
    "a cry will go up from the Fish Gate,
    wailing from the New Quarter,
    and a loud crash from the hills.
¹¹Wail, you who live in the market
        district[d];
    all your merchants will be wiped
        out,
    all who trade with[e] silver will be
        ruined.
¹²At that time I will search Jerusalem
        with lamps
    and punish those who are
        complacent,
    who are like wine left on its dregs,
    who think, 'The LORD will do nothing,

either good or bad.'
¹³Their wealth will be plundered,
    their houses demolished.
They will build houses
    but not live in them;
they will plant vineyards
    but not drink the wine.

¹⁴"The great day of the LORD is near—
    near and coming quickly.
Listen! The cry on the day of the LORD
    will be bitter,
    the shouting of the warrior there.
¹⁵That day will be a day of wrath,
    a day of distress and anguish,
a day of trouble and ruin,
    a day of darkness and gloom,
    a day of clouds and blackness,
¹⁶a day of trumpet and battle cry
    against the fortified cities
    and against the corner towers.
¹⁷I will bring distress on the people
    and they will walk like blind men,
    because they have sinned against the
        LORD.
Their blood will be poured out like dust
    and their entrails like filth.
¹⁸Neither their silver nor their gold
    will be able to save them
    on the day of the LORD's wrath.
In the fire of his jealousy
    the whole world will be consumed,
for he will make a sudden end
    of all who live in the earth."

C H A P T E R   2
Gather together, gather together,
    O shameful nation,
²before the appointed time arrives
    and that day sweeps on like chaff,
before the fierce anger of the LORD
        comes upon you,
    before the day of the LORD's wrath
        comes upon you.
³Seek the LORD, all you humble of the
        land,
    you who do what he commands.
Seek righteousness, seek humility;
    perhaps you will be sheltered
    on the day of the LORD's anger.

⁴Gaza will be abandoned
    and Ashkelon left in ruins.
At midday Ashdod will be emptied
    and Ekron uprooted.
⁵Woe to you who live by the sea,

---

[a]3 The meaning of the Hebrew for this line is uncertain.   [b]5 Hebrew *Malcam*, that is, Milcom   [c]9 See 1 Samuel 5:5.
[d]11 Or *the Mortar*   [e]11 Or *in*

O Kerethite people;
the word of the LORD is against you,
O Canaan, land of the Philistines.

"I will destroy you,
and none will be left."

6The land by the sea, where the
Kerethites*f* dwell,
will be a place for shepherds and
sheep pens.
7It will belong to the remnant of the
house of Judah;
there they will find pasture.
In the evening they will lie down
in the houses of Ashkelon.
The LORD their God will care for them;
he will restore their fortunes.*g*

8"I have heard the insults of Moab
and the taunts of the Ammonites,
who insulted my people
and made threats against their land.
9Therefore, as surely as I live,"
declares the LORD Almighty, the God
of Israel,
"surely Moab will become like Sodom,
the Ammonites like Gomorrah—
a place of weeds and salt pits,
a wasteland forever.
The remnant of my people will
plunder them;
the survivors of my nation will
inherit their land."

10This is what they will get in return for
their pride,
for insulting and mocking the
people of the LORD Almighty.
11The LORD will be awesome to them
when he destroys all the gods of the
land.
The nations on every shore will
worship him,
every one in its own land.

12"You too, O Cushites,*h*
will be slain by my sword."

13He will stretch out his hand against
the north
and destroy Assyria,
leaving Nineveh utterly desolate
and dry as the desert.
14Flocks and herds will lie down there,
creatures of every kind.
The desert owl and the screech owl
will roost on her columns.

Their calls will echo through the
windows,
rubble will be in the doorways,
the beams of cedar will be exposed.
15This is the carefree city
that lived in safety.
She said to herself,
"I am, and there is none besides me."
What a ruin she has become,
a lair for wild beasts!
All who pass by her scoff
and shake their fists.

CHAPTER 3

Woe to the city of oppressors,
rebellious and defiled!
2She obeys no one,
she accepts no correction.
She does not trust in the LORD,
she does not draw near to her God.
3Her officials are roaring lions,
her rulers are evening wolves,
who leave nothing for the morning.
4Her prophets are arrogant;
they are treacherous men.
Her priests profane the sanctuary
and do violence to the law.
5The LORD within her is righteous;
he does no wrong.
Morning by morning he dispenses his
justice,
and every new day he does not fail,
yet the unrighteous know no shame.

6"I have cut off nations;
their strongholds are demolished.
I have left their streets deserted,
with no one passing through.
Their cities are destroyed;
no one will be left—no one at all.
7I said to the city,
'Surely you will fear me
and accept correction!'
Then her dwelling would not be cut
off,
nor all my punishments come upon
her.
But they were still eager
to act corruptly in all they did.
8Therefore wait for me," declares the
LORD,
"for the day I will stand up to
testify.*i*
I have decided to assemble the nations,
to gather the kingdoms

*f6 The meaning of the Hebrew for this word is uncertain.   g7 Or will bring back their captives   h12 That is, people from the
upper Nile region   i8 Septuagint and Syriac; Hebrew will rise up to plunder*

and to pour out my wrath on them—
    all my fierce anger.
The whole world will be consumed
    by the fire of my jealous anger.

9"Then will I purify the lips of the
        peoples,
    that all of them may call on the
        name of the LORD
    and serve him shoulder to shoulder.
10From beyond the rivers of Cush[j]
    my worshipers, my scattered people,
    will bring me offerings.
11On that day you will not be put to
        shame
    for all the wrongs you have done to
        me,
because I will remove from this city
    those who rejoice in their pride.
Never again will you be haughty
    on my holy hill.
12But I will leave within you
    the meek and humble,
    who trust in the name of the LORD.
13The remnant of Israel will do no
        wrong;
    they will speak no lies,
    nor will deceit be found in their
        mouths.
They will eat and lie down
    and no one will make them afraid."

14Sing, O Daughter of Zion;
    shout aloud, O Israel!
Be glad and rejoice with all your heart,
    O Daughter of Jerusalem!

15The LORD has taken away your
        punishment,
    he has turned back your enemy.
The LORD, the King of Israel, is with
        you;
    never again will you fear any harm.
16On that day they will say to Jerusalem,
    "Do not fear, O Zion;
    do not let your hands hang limp.
17The LORD your God is with you,
    he is mighty to save.
He will take great delight in you,
    he will quiet you with his love,
    he will rejoice over you with
        singing."

18"The sorrows for the appointed feasts
    I will remove from you;
    they are a burden and a reproach to
        you.[k]
19At that time I will deal
    with all who oppressed you;
I will rescue the lame
    and gather those who have been
        scattered.
I will give them praise and honor
    in every land where they were put
        to shame.
20At that time I will gather you;
    at that time I will bring you home.
I will give you honor and praise
    among all the peoples of the earth
when I restore your fortunes[l]
    before your very eyes,"
                        says the LORD.

[j]10 That is, the upper Nile region   [k]18 Or "I will gather you who mourn for the appointed feasts; / your reproach is a burden to you
[l]20 Or I bring back your captives

SEPTEMBER 21 ☐ DAY 265
Mercy and Justice for All

 LOOK BACK Micah (whose name means "who is like the Lord?") has been called the prophet for the exploited and downtrodden. Corrupt kings, false prophets, bribed judges and pilfering priests all become targets of Micah's prophetic barbs. Every level of Judah's society has been taken captive by greed and opportunism.

Nahum ("burden") concludes the saga begun more than a century earlier in the book of Jonah. The Ninevites, who have experienced a short-lived repentance, now face a tidal wave of judgment. Total destruction is sure, and escape is impossible.

Habakkuk ("embrace") is not afraid to wrestle with tough issues that test his faith. His questions of "Why?" and "How long?" are met by comforting descriptions of the person and program of God. The more Habakkuk knows about the plan of God, the more he can relax in the loving arms of the Planner, for indeed, "the righteous will live by his faith" (Habakkuk 2:4).

Zephaniah ("the Lord hides") paints a grim picture of death, destruction and darkness for wayward Judah. He looks in all four directions before focusing on Jerusalem, the focus of God's chastening and the object of God's love.

LOOK UP Last week you read the book of Jonah and discovered that God delights to show his love to even the most wicked.

Those who see God's hand in everything can best leave everything in God's hand.

Perhaps it surprised you to read this week that the city of Nineveh, which was the object of God's love in the book of Jonah, became the object of his wrath and judgment in the book of Nahum. How can this be? Is God fickle in his feelings? How could God be angry with Jonah for failing to show mercy to the Ninevites, then turn around and act precisely the same way himself?

The key is found back in Exodus 34:6–7. There you will learn how the mercy of God and the justice of God blend together perfectly: "The LORD, the LORD, the compassionate and gracious God, slow to anger, abounding in love and faithfulness, maintaining love to thousands, and forgiving wickedness, rebellion and sin. Yet he does not leave the guilty unpunished; he punishes the children and their children for the sin of the fathers to the third and fourth generation [just like the book of Nahum presents him]."

LOOK AHEAD How can so many people get away with murder today?

Because it is "today." The time is coming when God will settle all accounts equitably, when it will be too late for mercy, and in its place justice will prevail. For the Ninevites, that "day of reckoning" came approximately 150 years after Jonah's memorable visit. The Assyrians' change of heart in the days of Jonah became "business as usual" within a handful of years. God's patience is great, but it is not endless. And while he may be *long-suffering* today, you can be sure there is coming a day when others will be doing the *suffering* if they have not gotten right with him!

On a three-by-five-inch card, make a list of any grievances you are carrying against others that, from your perspective, are as yet unsettled. Now take your list of "unrighted wrongs," commit each to the Lord in prayer and then tear up the list. Practice showing mercy; leave justice to God.

Haggai

HAVING just returned from exile in Babylonia, the people are confronted by a heartbreaking sight. Nebuchadnezzar had made a shambles of their city, including the glorious structure that was once Solomon's temple. Work progresses on a new temple until opposition arises. For sixteen years the Jews ignore the unfinished temple to pursue personal prosperity. Onto the scene steps Haggai, an aged, straight-talking prophet of God, who minces no words in his call to "finish what you have begun," for future blessing is promised to the obedient.

Focus	Finishing God's House		Finding God's Blessing	
Divisions	A Call to Build	A Promise of Glory	A Problem with Defilement	A Promise to a Servant
	1:1 1:15	2:1 2:9	2:10 2:19	2:20 2:23
Topics	Wrong Priorities	Wrong Perspectives	Incomplete Purity	Encouraging Promises
	". . . build the house, so that I may take pleasure in it and be honored." (1:8)			
Place	Jerusalem			
Time	September 1, 520 B.C.	October 21, 520 B.C.	December 24, 520 B.C.	

SEPTEMBER 22 ☐ DAY 266
HAGGAI 1–2
Don't Throw in the Trowel!

OVERVIEW The final three Old Testament books are known as the post-exilic prophets because their messages are addressed to the returnees in Jerusalem following the Babylonian exile. The people waste no time beginning to restore their beloved temple. But delays and distractions soon undermine the work, setting the stage for Haggai to appear with a new word from the Lord. In four brief but powerful messages, Haggai exhorts the people to put first things first. With renewed courage and commitment, the citizens respond by completing the temple—and clearing a place for God in their hearts.

Chapter 1		Chapter 2	
Wrong Priorities	Wrong Perspectives	Incomplete Purity	Encouraging Promises
1	9	10 19	20 23
"Build the house, so that I may . . . be honored" (1:8).			

YOUR DAILY WALK It has been well said, "If you aim at nothing, you will hit it every time." You will often accomplish what you set out to do, but you will rarely (if ever) accomplish that which you never even intended to do.

Some people dream of worthy accomplishments, while others stay awake and do them.

Every person has exactly the same number of hours in a week: 168. Why is it that some people accomplish so much more with those same hours than others do?

Answer: *Priorities!* Achievers determine in advance what they want to do, then tackle their tasks in the order of importance.

Haggai's contemporaries built a temple in the midst of stiff opposition because that was their number one priority. Now transfer that concept to your spiritual life. What do you want to be able to look back on when you reach the age of forty? . . . fifty-five? . . . seventy? A deep familiarity with the Bible? A consistent prayer life? A family that is walking with God? If someone were to determine your priorities by looking at the way you spent the last 168 hours, what would they decide? And what will be your priorities as you spend the next 168?

INSIGHT Words That Carry Clout
Four times Haggai introduces his words with the phrase "the word of the Lord came through the prophet"; five times he uses "this is what the Lord Almighty says" and twelve times "declares the Lord." Mark these twenty-one phrases in your Bible, for they give the key to the prophet's power. He was speaking for none other than the Lord Almighty.

CHAPTER 1

In the second year of King Darius, on the first day of the sixth month, the word of the Lord came through the prophet Haggai to Zerubbabel son of Shealtiel, governor of Judah, and to Joshua[a] son of Jehozadak, the high priest:

²This is what the Lord Almighty says:

a1 A variant of Jeshua; here and elsewhere in Haggai

"These people say, 'The time has not yet come for the LORD's house to be built.'"

³Then the word of the LORD came through the prophet Haggai: ⁴"Is it a time for you yourselves to be living in your paneled houses, while this house remains a ruin?"

⁵Now this is what the LORD Almighty says: "Give careful thought to your ways. ⁶You have planted much, but have harvested little. You eat, but never have enough. You drink, but never have your fill. You put on clothes, but are not warm. You earn wages, only to put them in a purse with holes in it."

⁷This is what the LORD Almighty says: "Give careful thought to your ways. ⁸Go up into the mountains and bring down timber and build the house, so that I may take pleasure in it and be honored," says the LORD. ⁹"You expected much, but see, it turned out to be little. What you brought home, I blew away. Why?" declares the LORD Almighty. "Because of my house, which remains a ruin, while each of you is busy with his own house. ¹⁰Therefore, because of you the heavens have withheld their dew and the earth its crops. ¹¹I called for a drought on the fields and the mountains, on the grain, the new wine, the oil and whatever the ground produces, on men and cattle, and on the labor of your hands."

¹²Then Zerubbabel son of Shealtiel, Joshua son of Jehozadak, the high priest, and the whole remnant of the people obeyed the voice of the LORD their God and the message of the prophet Haggai, because the LORD their God had sent him. And the people feared the LORD.

¹³Then Haggai, the LORD's messenger, gave this message of the LORD to the people: "I am with you," declares the LORD. ¹⁴So the LORD stirred up the spirit of Zerubbabel son of Shealtiel, governor of Judah, and the spirit of Joshua son of Jehozadak, the high priest, and the spirit of the whole remnant of the people. They came and began to work on the house of the LORD Almighty, their God, ¹⁵on the twenty-fourth day of the sixth month in the second year of King Darius.

CHAPTER 2

On the twenty-first day of the seventh month, the word of the LORD came through the prophet Haggai: ²"Speak to Zerubbabel son of Shealtiel, governor of Judah, to Joshua son of Jehozadak, the high priest, and to the remnant of the people. Ask them, ³'Who of you is left who saw this house in its former glory? How does it look to you now? Does it not seem to you like nothing? ⁴But now be strong, O Zerubbabel,' declares the LORD. 'Be strong, O Joshua son of Jehozadak, the high priest. Be strong, all you people of the land,' declares the LORD, 'and work. For I am with you,' declares the LORD Almighty. ⁵'This is what I covenanted with you when you came out of Egypt. And my Spirit remains among you. Do not fear.'

⁶"This is what the LORD Almighty says: 'In a little while I will once more shake the heavens and the earth, the sea and the dry land. ⁷I will shake all nations, and the desired of all nations will come, and I will fill this house with glory,' says the LORD Almighty. ⁸'The silver is mine and the gold is mine,' declares the LORD Almighty. ⁹'The glory of this present house will be greater than the glory of the former house,' says the LORD Almighty. 'And in this place I will grant peace,' declares the LORD Almighty."

¹⁰On the twenty-fourth day of the ninth month, in the second year of Darius, the word of the LORD came to the prophet Haggai: ¹¹"This is what the LORD Almighty says: 'Ask the priests what the law says: ¹²If a person carries consecrated meat in the fold of his garment, and that fold touches some bread or stew, some wine, oil or other food, does it become consecrated?'"

The priests answered, "No."

¹³Then Haggai said, "If a person defiled by contact with a dead body touches one of these things, does it become defiled?"

"Yes," the priests replied, "it becomes defiled."

¹⁴Then Haggai said, "'So it is with this people and this nation in my sight,' declares the LORD. 'Whatever they do and whatever they offer there is defiled.

¹⁵"'Now give careful thought to this from this day onᵇ—consider how things

ᵇ15 Or to the days past

were before one stone was laid on another in the LORD's temple. ¹⁶When anyone came to a heap of twenty measures, there were only ten. When anyone went to a wine vat to draw fifty measures, there were only twenty. ¹⁷I struck all the work of your hands with blight, mildew and hail, yet you did not turn to me,' declares the LORD. ¹⁸'From this day on, from this twenty-fourth day of the ninth month, give careful thought to the day when the foundation of the LORD's temple was laid. Give careful thought: ¹⁹Is there yet any seed left in the barn? Until now, the vine and the fig tree, the pomegranate and the olive tree have not borne fruit.

" 'From this day on I will bless you.' "

²⁰The word of the LORD came to Haggai a second time on the twenty-fourth day of the month: ²¹"Tell Zerubbabel governor of Judah that I will shake the heavens and the earth. ²²I will overturn royal thrones and shatter the power of the foreign kingdoms. I will overthrow chariots and their drivers; horses and their riders will fall, each by the sword of his brother.

²³" 'On that day,' declares the LORD Almighty, 'I will take you, my servant Zerubbabel son of Shealtiel,' declares the LORD, 'and I will make you like my signet ring, for I have chosen you,' declares the LORD Almighty."

Zechariah

THE TEMPLE rebuilding had begun amid great excitement in 536 B.C. But the early enthusiasm had waned, and sixteen years later the only movement in the unfinished building was the stirring of the wind. Enter Zechariah, commissioned by God to join Haggai in motivating the workers to finish what they had begun. His message is one of consolation: The temple will be no ordinary building, but will house Messiah himself. All hands to the task, for "see, your king comes to you" (9:9).

Focus	Corrections				Directions	
Divisions	Visions of Horses and Horns	Visions of Scrolls and Chariots		To Fast or Not to Fast	Israel's Coming King and Shepherd	Israel's Coming Consolation
	1	2 3	6	7 8	9 11 12	14
Topics	Eight Visions			Four Sermons	Two Burdens	
	Present Problems				Future Promises	
Place	Jerusalem					
Time	While Rebuilding the Temple (520–518 B.C.)				After Rebuilding the Temple (480–410 B.C.)	

SEPTEMBER 23 ☐ DAY 267
ZECHARIAH 1-2
Visions of Horses and Horns

OVERVIEW Zechariah, the longest of the minor prophets, contains a message of encouragement to the temple builders after the exile. A younger contemporary of Haggai, Zechariah delivers a similar message in a strikingly different manner. Haggai used sermons; Zechariah uses visions. Haggai was an exhorter; Zechariah is an encourager. Haggai proclaimed a strong message of rebuke; Zechariah brings a soothing message of restoration. Haggai was concerned with the present: "Take part and finish the temple!" Zechariah is concerned with the future: "Take heart. Messiah is coming." The first six chapters of Zechariah's prophecy contain night visions describing Israel's fortunes and future both in Zechariah's day and the days to come.

Chapter 1		Chapter 2	
Vision of the Horses	Vision of the Horns	Vision of the Surveyor	Survey of the Visions
1 17	18 21	1 5	6 13
Israel's Fortunes and Future			

YOUR DAILY WALK On a scale of 1 to 10 (1= hopeless; 10= excellent), how would you rate your managerial skills in the following areas?

Buoyant and zealous, Zechariah had the soul of an artist and the eyes of a seer.

_____ Getting your family to help around the house
_____ Supervising your subordinates at work
_____ Motivating committee members to do their jobs
_____ Encouraging members of your Sunday school class

Not all of these situations may apply to you, but here is one that does: challenging others to follow the Lord. Zechariah's task, in a nutshell, was to encourage his countrymen not to "throw in the trowel" in their walk with God. You can do the same!

Look for a small but significant (and sincere) compliment you can pay to each person you encounter today. Watch how attitudes change as others see you seeking to build them up, rather than trying to tear them down. After all, we are put on this earth, not to *see through* one another, but to *see* one another *through*—and encouragement helps!

INSIGHT Zechariah, Alias Smith and Jones
With the aid of a Bible concordance or Bible dictionary, do some "Scripture sleuthing" to see how many different people you can find in the Bible named Zechariah. The answer will surprise you. (Hint: When you get to twenty, you've only just begun.)

CHAPTER 1
In the eighth month of the second year of Darius, the word of the LORD came to the prophet Zechariah son of Berekiah, the son of Iddo:

²"The LORD was very angry with your forefathers. ³Therefore tell the people: This is what the LORD Almighty says: 'Return to me,' declares the LORD Almighty, 'and I will return to you,' says the LORD Almighty. ⁴Do not be like your forefathers, to whom the earlier prophets pro-

claimed: This is what the LORD Almighty says: 'Turn from your evil ways and your evil practices.' But they would not listen or pay attention to me, declares the LORD. ⁵Where are your forefathers now? And the prophets, do they live forever? ⁶But did not my words and my decrees, which I commanded my servants the prophets, overtake your forefathers?

"Then they repented and said, 'The LORD Almighty has done to us what our ways and practices deserve, just as he determined to do.' "

⁷On the twenty-fourth day of the eleventh month, the month of Shebat, in the second year of Darius, the word of the LORD came to the prophet Zechariah son of Berekiah, the son of Iddo.

⁸During the night I had a vision—and there before me was a man riding a red horse! He was standing among the myrtle trees in a ravine. Behind him were red, brown and white horses.

⁹I asked, "What are these, my lord?"

The angel who was talking with me answered, "I will show you what they are."

¹⁰Then the man standing among the myrtle trees explained, "They are the ones the LORD has sent to go throughout the earth."

¹¹And they reported to the angel of the LORD, who was standing among the myrtle trees, "We have gone throughout the earth and found the whole world at rest and in peace."

¹²Then the angel of the LORD said, "LORD Almighty, how long will you withhold mercy from Jerusalem and from the towns of Judah, which you have been angry with these seventy years?" ¹³So the LORD spoke kind and comforting words to the angel who talked with me.

¹⁴Then the angel who was speaking to me said, "Proclaim this word: This is what the LORD Almighty says: 'I am very jealous for Jerusalem and Zion, ¹⁵but I am very angry with the nations that feel secure. I was only a little angry, but they added to the calamity.'

¹⁶"Therefore, this is what the LORD says: 'I will return to Jerusalem with mercy, and there my house will be rebuilt. And the measuring line will be stretched out

over Jerusalem,' declares the LORD Almighty.

¹⁷"Proclaim further: This is what the LORD Almighty says: 'My towns will again overflow with prosperity, and the LORD will again comfort Zion and choose Jerusalem.' "

¹⁸Then I looked up—and there before me were four horns! ¹⁹I asked the angel who was speaking to me, "What are these?"

He answered me, "These are the horns that scattered Judah, Israel and Jerusalem."

²⁰Then the LORD showed me four craftsmen. ²¹I asked, "What are these coming to do?"

He answered, "These are the horns that scattered Judah so that no one could raise his head, but the craftsmen have come to terrify them and throw down these horns of the nations who lifted up their horns against the land of Judah to scatter its people."

CHAPTER 2

Then I looked up—and there before me was a man with a measuring line in his hand! ²I asked, "Where are you going?"

He answered me, "To measure Jerusalem, to find out how wide and how long it is."

³Then the angel who was speaking to me left, and another angel came to meet him ⁴and said to him: "Run, tell that young man, 'Jerusalem will be a city without walls because of the great number of men and livestock in it. ⁵And I myself will be a wall of fire around it,' declares the LORD, 'and I will be its glory within.'

⁶"Come! Come! Flee from the land of the north," declares the LORD, "for I have scattered you to the four winds of heaven," declares the LORD.

⁷"Come, O Zion! Escape, you who live in the Daughter of Babylon!" ⁸For this is what the LORD Almighty says: "After he has honored me and has sent me against the nations that have plundered you—for whoever touches you touches the apple of his eye— ⁹I will surely raise my hand against them so that their slaves will plunder them.ᵃ Then you will know that the LORD Almighty has sent me.

ᵃ8,9 Or *says after . . . eye:* 9"*I . . . plunder them.*"

¹⁰"Shout and be glad, O Daughter of Zion. For I am coming, and I will live among you," declares the LORD. ¹¹"Many nations will be joined with the LORD in that day and will become my people. I will live among you and you will know that the LORD Almighty has sent me to you. ¹²The LORD will inherit Judah as his portion in the holy land and will again choose Jerusalem. ¹³Be still before the LORD, all mankind, because he has roused himself from his holy dwelling."

SEPTEMBER 24 □ DAY 268
ZECHARIAH 3–4
Visions of Priests and Olive Trees

 OVERVIEW In his eight-part series that might be titled "Visions to Revitalize a Nation," Zechariah uses an assortment of symbols and signs to portray the future of his people. Certain themes emerge repeatedly: the need for cleansing, the certainty of judgment, the sovereignty of God over sinful men and women. Like a candlestick in a darkened room, Israel will bear light to a darkened world, " 'not by might nor by power, but by my Spirit,' says the LORD Almighty" (4:6).

Chapter 3	Chapter 4
Vision of the High Priest	Vision of the Gold Lampstand and Olive Trees
Zechariah's Night Visions	

 YOUR DAILY WALK Becoming a Christian has been likened to taking a step into the unknown . . . and landing on a Rock. There are many things about the Bible you may not fully understand. You may have many questions about points of theology. But the all-important issue you must face is simply this: Is Jesus Christ who he claimed to be? Either you will accept his claim as Messiah (as amply supported by the many specific prophecies in Zechariah), or you will reject it. But you cannot straddle the fence. What will you do with Jesus today?

The person who insists upon seeing with perfect clearness before he or she decides never decides.

 INSIGHT The Messiah in Zechariah
With the exception of Isaiah, no other Old Testament book contains more specific prophecies regarding the coming Messiah than Zechariah does. You may want to mark the following passages for quick reference:

Reference in Zechariah	Picture of Messiah
3:8	Servant (Mark 10:45)
6:13	Priest (Hebrews 6:20–7:1)
6:13; 9:9–10	King (Matthew 21:4–5)
11:12–13	Betrayed (Matthew 27:5–10)
12:10	Pierced (John 19:34, 37)
13:1	Fountain (Revelation 21:6)
13:7	Shepherd (John 10:11)
13:7–9	God (John 1:1)
14:9	King over the Whole Earth (Revelation 11:15)

CHAPTER 3

Then he showed me Joshua[b] the high priest standing before the angel of the Lord, and Satan[c] standing at his right side to accuse him. [2]The Lord said to Satan, "The Lord rebuke you, Satan! The Lord, who has chosen Jerusalem, rebuke you! Is not this man a burning stick snatched from the fire?"

[3]Now Joshua was dressed in filthy clothes as he stood before the angel. [4]The angel said to those who were standing before him, "Take off his filthy clothes."

Then he said to Joshua, "See, I have taken away your sin, and I will put rich garments on you."

[5]Then I said, "Put a clean turban on his head." So they put a clean turban on his head and clothed him, while the angel of the Lord stood by.

[6]The angel of the Lord gave this charge to Joshua: [7]"This is what the Lord Almighty says: 'If you will walk in my ways and keep my requirements, then you will govern my house and have charge of my courts, and I will give you a place among these standing here.

[8]" 'Listen, O high priest Joshua and your associates seated before you, who are men symbolic of things to come: I am going to bring my servant, the Branch. [9]See, the stone I have set in front of Joshua! There are seven eyes[d] on that one stone, and I will engrave an inscription on it,' says the Lord Almighty, 'and I will remove the sin of this land in a single day.

[10]" 'In that day each of you will invite his neighbor to sit under his vine and fig tree,' declares the Lord Almighty."

CHAPTER 4

Then the angel who talked with me returned and wakened me, as a man is wakened from his sleep. [2]He asked me, "What do you see?"

I answered, "I see a solid gold lampstand with a bowl at the top and seven lights on it, with seven channels to the lights. [3]Also there are two olive trees by it, one on the right of the bowl and the other on its left."

[4]I asked the angel who talked with me, "What are these, my lord?"

[5]He answered, "Do you not know what these are?"

"No, my lord," I replied.

[6]So he said to me, "This is the word of the Lord to Zerubbabel: 'Not by might nor by power, but by my Spirit,' says the Lord Almighty.

[7]"What[e] are you, O mighty mountain? Before Zerubbabel you will become level ground. Then he will bring out the capstone to shouts of 'God bless it! God bless it!' "

[8]Then the word of the Lord came to me: [9]"The hands of Zerubbabel have laid the foundation of this temple; his hands will also complete it. Then you will know that the Lord Almighty has sent me to you.

[10]"Who despises the day of small things? Men will rejoice when they see the plumb line in the hand of Zerubbabel.

"(These seven are the eyes of the Lord, which range throughout the earth.)"

[11]Then I asked the angel, "What are these two olive trees on the right and the left of the lampstand?"

[12]Again I asked him, "What are these two olive branches beside the two gold pipes that pour out golden oil?"

[13]He replied, "Do you not know what these are?"

"No, my lord," I said.

[14]So he said, "These are the two who are anointed to[f] serve the Lord of all the earth."

---

[b]1 A variant of Jeshua; here and elsewhere in Zechariah   [c]1 Satan means accuser.   [d]9 Or facets   [e]7 Or Who   [f]14 Or two who bring oil and

SEPTEMBER 25 □ DAY 269
ZECHARIAH 5-6
Visions of Scrolls and Chariots

OVERVIEW You'll notice a distinct change in emphasis in today's section. All of Zechariah's visions so far have revolved around the nation of Israel: its temple, its future, its Messiah. But now the focus shifts to include all the earth. God's program is not limited merely to his chosen people. He is the Sovereign of *all* nations. The balance of Zechariah's book represents a concentrated package of messianic prophecies designed to encourage and motivate God's people to complete the task of erecting the temple.

Chapter 5		Chapter 6	
Vision of the Flying Scroll	Vision of the Woman	Vision of the Chariots	Parable of the Crowns
1 4	5 11	1 8	9 15
Zechariah's Night Visions (cont.)			

YOUR DAILY WALK Often in the pages of Scripture you will find God preparing a worker for a particular task by displaying a dramatic picture of himself. Think back over the experiences of Isaiah (Isaiah 6:1–7), Ezekiel (Ezekiel 1:1–2:1) and Moses (Exodus 3:1–8). Throughout history God has prepared the workers before he turned them loose to do the work. Armed with a fresh, clear understanding of the great God they served, his men and women then confidently marched forth to perform the task for which God had selected and equipped them.

Today's preparation determines tomorrow's achievement.

If your fervor and commitment for God's work have been waning, chances are you need to stop and refocus on the wonderful character of God. Before you tackle your Sunday school lesson, Bible study, sermon notes or other ministry preparation this week, set aside some quiet moments alone with your Lord. Read from his Word, talk to him openly and honestly about your fears and frustrations, and fall in love with him all over again.

INSIGHT Behold the Man . . .
The crowning of Joshua (6:9–14) prefigures the dual role of the coming man "whose name is the Branch." He will be both priest and king, and peace will result from the union of the kingly and priestly functions in the one person.

CHAPTER 5

I looked again—and there before me was a flying scroll!

2He asked me, "What do you see?"

I answered, "I see a flying scroll, thirty feet long and fifteen feet wide.*g*"

3And he said to me, "This is the curse that is going out over the whole land; for according to what it says on one side, every thief will be banished, and according to what it says on the other, everyone who swears falsely will be banished. 4The

Lord Almighty declares, 'I will send it out, and it will enter the house of the thief and the house of him who swears falsely by my name. It will remain in his house and destroy it, both its timbers and its stones.' "

5Then the angel who was speaking to me came forward and said to me, "Look up and see what this is that is appearing."

6I asked, "What is it?"

He replied, "It is a measuring basket.*h*"

*g*2 Hebrew *twenty cubits long and ten cubits wide* (about 9 meters long and 4.5 meters wide)   *h*6 Hebrew *an ephah*; also in verses 7-11

And he added, "This is the iniquity[i] of the people throughout the land."

[7]Then the cover of lead was raised, and there in the basket sat a woman! [8]He said, "This is wickedness," and he pushed her back into the basket and pushed the lead cover down over its mouth.

[9]Then I looked up—and there before me were two women, with the wind in their wings! They had wings like those of a stork, and they lifted up the basket between heaven and earth.

[10]"Where are they taking the basket?" I asked the angel who was speaking to me.

[11]He replied, "To the country of Babylonia[j] to build a house for it. When it is ready, the basket will be set there in its place."

CHAPTER 6

I looked up again—and there before me were four chariots coming out from between two mountains—mountains of bronze! [2]The first chariot had red horses, the second black, [3]the third white, and the fourth dappled—all of them powerful. [4]I asked the angel who was speaking to me, "What are these, my lord?"

[5]The angel answered me, "These are the four spirits[k] of heaven, going out from standing in the presence of the Lord of the whole world. [6]The one with the black horses is going toward the north country, the one with the white horses toward the west,[l] and the one with the dappled horses toward the south."

[7]When the powerful horses went out, they were straining to go throughout the earth. And he said, "Go throughout the earth!" So they went throughout the earth.

[8]Then he called to me, "Look, those going toward the north country have given my Spirit[m] rest in the land of the north."

[9]The word of the LORD came to me: [10]"Take ˌsilver and goldˌ from the exiles Heldai, Tobijah and Jedaiah, who have arrived from Babylon. Go the same day to the house of Josiah son of Zephaniah. [11]Take the silver and gold and make a crown, and set it on the head of the high priest, Joshua son of Jehozadak. [12]Tell him this is what the LORD Almighty says: 'Here is the man whose name is the Branch, and he will branch out from his place and build the temple of the LORD. [13]It is he who will build the temple of the LORD, and he will be clothed with majesty and will sit and rule on his throne. And he will be a priest on his throne. And there will be harmony between the two.' [14]The crown will be given to Heldai,[n] Tobijah, Jedaiah and Hen[o] son of Zephaniah as a memorial in the temple of the LORD. [15]Those who are far away will come and help to build the temple of the LORD, and you will know that the LORD Almighty has sent me to you. This will happen if you diligently obey the LORD your God."

[i]6 Or *appearance*   [j]11 Hebrew *Shinar*   [k]5 Or *winds*   [l]6 Or *horses after them*   [m]8 Or *spirit*   [n]14 Syriac; Hebrew *Helem*
[o]14 Or *and the gracious one, the*

SEPTEMBER 26 ☐ DAY 270
ZECHARIAH 7–8
To Fast or Not to Fast

 OVERVIEW Two years after his night visions, Zechariah is commanded by God to deliver four messages to his people on the subject of fasting. The people are fasting in the fourth, fifth, seventh and tenth months to commemorate events surrounding the siege and destruction of Jerusalem. Now that they have returned to the land and rebuilt the city, the question naturally arises, "Should we continue to observe the fasts as before?" God's reply through Zechariah is both sobering and comforting. The object of fasting is the key (7:5–7). The way you *live* is more important than the way you *fast* (7:8–14). God's blessing falls on those who exercise truth and love—not empty rituals (8:1–17). True fasting can take place even during feasting (8:18–23)!

Chapter 7		Chapter 8	
Insincere Fasts	Incomplete Obedience	Complete Restoration	Complete Righteousness
1　　　　　　7	8　　　　　14	1　　　　　17	18　　　　　23
Present Problems		Future Problems	

YOUR DAILY WALK Have you ever been so captivated by the Lord's presence, so absorbed by his Word or engrossed in talking with him, that you skipped a meal? Then whether you knew it or not, you were fasting!

The prophets of God were fearless men who believed that one plus God was always a majority.

Today's section gives God's commentary on fasting. At its heart, fasting is more an *attitude* than an *action*. You can go days without food and never be fasting if your motive is wrong (remember the hypocrites in Matthew 6:16–18?). Conversely, you can be in an attitude of true fasting even as you enjoy a banquet!

Using a good concordance, take an expedition through the Bible to discover what else it has to say about fasting. (You'll discover that David, Hezekiah, Ezra, Nehemiah, Esther, Jesus and many others fasted.) Notice especially *why* these individuals fasted. Then ask God what the role of fasting should be in your life.

INSIGHT Giving Credit (or Placing Blame) Where It's Due
Here is a tricky question with a significant answer: Who was responsible for scattering the nation of Israel in judgment? According to Zechariah 7:8–14, there is a three-part answer: God initiated the judgment (7:14); God's enemies executed the judgment (7:14); and God's people are charged with the ultimate responsibility for the judgment because their sins were the underlying cause (7:11–13).

CHAPTER 7

In the fourth year of King Darius, the word of the LORD came to Zechariah on the fourth day of the ninth month, the month of Kislev. ²The people of Bethel had sent Sharezer and Regem-Melech, together with their men, to entreat the LORD ³by asking the priests of the house of the LORD Almighty and the prophets, "Should I mourn and fast in the fifth month, as I have done for so many years?"

⁴Then the word of the LORD Almighty came to me: ⁵"Ask all the people of the land and the priests, 'When you fasted and mourned in the fifth and seventh months for the past seventy years, was it really for me that you fasted? ⁶And when you were eating and drinking, were you not just feasting for yourselves? ⁷Are these not the words the LORD proclaimed through the earlier prophets when Jerusalem and its surrounding towns were at rest and prosperous, and the Negev and the western foothills were settled?' "

⁸And the word of the LORD came again to Zechariah: ⁹"This is what the LORD Almighty says: 'Administer true justice;

show mercy and compassion to one another. ¹⁰Do not oppress the widow or the fatherless, the alien or the poor. In your hearts do not think evil of each other.'

¹¹"But they refused to pay attention; stubbornly they turned their backs and stopped up their ears. ¹²They made their hearts as hard as flint and would not listen to the law or to the words that the LORD Almighty had sent by his Spirit through the earlier prophets. So the LORD Almighty was very angry.

¹³" 'When I called, they did not listen; so when they called, I would not listen,' says the LORD Almighty. ¹⁴'I scattered them with a whirlwind among all the nations, where they were strangers. The land was left so desolate behind them that no one could come or go. This is how they made the pleasant land desolate.' "

CHAPTER 8

Again the word of the LORD Almighty came to me. ²This is what the LORD Almighty says: "I am very jealous for Zion; I am burning with jealousy for her."

³This is what the LORD says: "I will return to Zion and dwell in Jerusalem. Then

Jerusalem will be called the City of Truth, and the mountain of the LORD Almighty will be called the Holy Mountain."

⁴This is what the LORD Almighty says: "Once again men and women of ripe old age will sit in the streets of Jerusalem, each with cane in hand because of his age. ⁵The city streets will be filled with boys and girls playing there."

⁶This is what the LORD Almighty says: "It may seem marvelous to the remnant of this people at that time, but will it seem marvelous to me?" declares the LORD Almighty.

⁷This is what the LORD Almighty says: "I will save my people from the countries of the east and the west. ⁸I will bring them back to live in Jerusalem; they will be my people, and I will be faithful and righteous to them as their God."

⁹This is what the LORD Almighty says: "You who now hear these words spoken by the prophets who were there when the foundation was laid for the house of the LORD Almighty, let your hands be strong so that the temple may be built. ¹⁰Before that time there were no wages for man or beast. No one could go about his business safely because of his enemy, for I had turned every man against his neighbor. ¹¹But now I will not deal with the remnant of this people as I did in the past," declares the LORD Almighty.

¹²"The seed will grow well, the vine will yield its fruit, the ground will produce its crops, and the heavens will drop their dew. I will give all these things as an inheritance to the remnant of this people. ¹³As you have been an object of cursing among the nations, O Judah and Israel, so will I save you, and you will be a blessing. Do not be afraid, but let your hands be strong."

¹⁴This is what the LORD Almighty says: "Just as I had determined to bring disaster upon you and showed no pity when your fathers angered me," says the LORD Almighty, ¹⁵"so now I have determined to do good again to Jerusalem and Judah. Do not be afraid. ¹⁶These are the things you are to do: Speak the truth to each other, and render true and sound judgment in your courts; ¹⁷do not plot evil against your neighbor, and do not love to swear falsely. I hate all this," declares the LORD.

¹⁸Again the word of the LORD Almighty came to me. ¹⁹This is what the LORD Almighty says: "The fasts of the fourth, fifth, seventh and tenth months will become joyful and glad occasions and happy festivals for Judah. Therefore love truth and peace."

²⁰This is what the LORD Almighty says: "Many peoples and the inhabitants of many cities will yet come, ²¹and the inhabitants of one city will go to another and say, 'Let us go at once to entreat the LORD and seek the LORD Almighty. I myself am going.' ²²And many peoples and powerful nations will come to Jerusalem to seek the LORD Almighty and to entreat him."

²³This is what the LORD Almighty says: "In those days ten men from all languages and nations will take firm hold of one Jew by the hem of his robe and say, 'Let us go with you, because we have heard that God is with you.' "

SEPTEMBER 27 ☐ DAY 271
ZECHARIAH 9–11
Israel's Coming King and Shepherd

OVERVIEW In an amazingly specific series of prophecies, Zechariah foretells Israel's immediate future. Israel's neighbors would be defeated by an invading force, while Israel would be preserved to the day of the coming Messiah. He would arrive on the colt of a donkey, coming to defend his people and defeat his enemies, as he had promised. Tragically, he would be rejected by the people and betrayed for thirty pieces of silver. In his place false shepherds would emerge to scatter the flock and lead his people astray.

Chapter 9		Chapter 10	Chapter 11
Coming Calamity	Coming King	Messiah's Redemption	Messiah's Rejection
1 8	9 17		
Judgment and Justice		Salvation and Suffering	

YOUR DAILY WALK Does God have limitations? Is there anything God cannot do? A seminary student, wrestling with those difficult questions, posed the problem to his professor in the form of a riddle: "Professor, can God make a rock so big that he cannot pick it up?" To which the teacher wisely responded, "Yes . . . and then he would pick it up anyway!"

The prophets laid bare the moral and spiritual condition of the nation.

God is infinite, all-powerful, all-knowing, almighty. But he does have limitations: He cannot act contrary to his promises; he will never contradict his written Word; and he will not release individuals from the consequences of (and responsibility for) their personal choices in life.

This explains why Jesus, the fulfillment of prophecy, God's only Son, the Messiah, could be rejected by Israel. God would not force the nation to accept him if it chose instead to reject him. But though the people were free to make the choice, they were powerless to escape the consequences of that choice.

Where in your life has God made his will clear to you through his Word, parental or pastoral counsel or prayer—and yet you are resisting it? Zechariah would be the first to tell you that it is dangerous to say no to God.

INSIGHT Greece, a Sticky Problem for the Critics
Like Daniel (Daniel 8:21; 10:20; 11:2), Zechariah mentions a nation's rise to power (Greece, in 9:13) long before it occurred. And like Daniel, he receives the critics' doubts for this supernatural insight!

An Oracle

CHAPTER 9
The word of the LORD is against the
    land of Hadrach
and will rest upon Damascus—
for the eyes of men and all the tribes
    of Israel
are on the LORD—ᴾ
²and upon Hamath too, which borders
    on it,
and upon Tyre and Sidon, though
    they are very skillful.
³Tyre has built herself a stronghold;
she has heaped up silver like dust,
and gold like the dirt of the streets.
⁴But the Lord will take away her
    possessions
and destroy her power on the sea,
and she will be consumed by fire.
⁵Ashkelon will see it and fear;
Gaza will writhe in agony,
and Ekron too, for her hope will
    wither.

Gaza will lose her king
    and Ashkelon will be deserted.
⁶Foreigners will occupy Ashdod,
    and I will cut off the pride of the
        Philistines.
⁷I will take the blood from their
    mouths,
    the forbidden food from between
        their teeth.
Those who are left will belong to our
    God
    and become leaders in Judah,
    and Ekron will be like the Jebusites.
⁸But I will defend my house
    against marauding forces.
Never again will an oppressor overrun
    my people,
    for now I am keeping watch.

⁹Rejoice greatly, O Daughter of Zion!
    Shout, Daughter of Jerusalem!
See, your king�q comes to you,
    righteous and having salvation,
    gentle and riding on a donkey,

ᴾ1 Or *Damascus. / For the eye of the* LORD *is on all mankind, / as well as on the tribes of Israel,*   q9 Or *King*

on a colt, the foal of a donkey.
¹⁰I will take away the chariots from
            Ephraim
    and the war-horses from Jerusalem,
    and the battle bow will be broken.
He will proclaim peace to the nations.
    His rule will extend from sea to sea
    and from the River^r to the ends of
            the earth.^s
¹¹As for you, because of the blood of my
            covenant with you,
    I will free your prisoners from the
            waterless pit.
¹²Return to your fortress, O prisoners of
            hope;
    even now I announce that I will
            restore twice as much to you.
¹³I will bend Judah as I bend my bow
    and fill it with Ephraim.
    I will rouse your sons, O Zion,
            against your sons, O Greece,
    and make you like a warrior's
            sword.

¹⁴Then the LORD will appear over them;
    his arrow will flash like lightning.
The Sovereign LORD will sound the
            trumpet;
    he will march in the storms of the
            south,
¹⁵   and the LORD Almighty will shield
            them.
    They will destroy
    and overcome with slingstones.
    They will drink and roar as with wine;
    they will be full like a bowl
    used for sprinkling^t the corners of
            the altar.
¹⁶The LORD their God will save them on
            that day
    as the flock of his people.
    They will sparkle in his land
    like jewels in a crown.
¹⁷How attractive and beautiful they will
            be!
    Grain will make the young men
            thrive,
    and new wine the young women.

CHAPTER 10
Ask the LORD for rain in the
            springtime;
    it is the LORD who makes the storm
            clouds.
He gives showers of rain to men,
    and plants of the field to everyone.

²The idols speak deceit,
    diviners see visions that lie;
    they tell dreams that are false,
    they give comfort in vain.
Therefore the people wander like
            sheep
    oppressed for lack of a shepherd.

³"My anger burns against the
            shepherds,
    and I will punish the leaders;
for the LORD Almighty will care
    for his flock, the house of Judah,
    and make them like a proud horse
            in battle.
⁴From Judah will come the cornerstone,
    from him the tent peg,
    from him the battle bow,
    from him every ruler.
⁵Together they^u will be like mighty
            men
    trampling the muddy streets in
            battle.
Because the LORD is with them,
    they will fight and overthrow the
            horsemen.

⁶"I will strengthen the house of Judah
    and save the house of Joseph.
I will restore them
    because I have compassion on them.
They will be as though
    I had not rejected them,
for I am the LORD their God
    and I will answer them.
⁷The Ephraimites will become like
            mighty men,
    and their hearts will be glad as with
            wine.
Their children will see it and be joyful;
    their hearts will rejoice in the LORD.
⁸I will signal for them
    and gather them in.
Surely I will redeem them;
    they will be as numerous as before.
⁹Though I scatter them among the
            peoples,
    yet in distant lands they will
            remember me.
They and their children will survive,
    and they will return.
¹⁰I will bring them back from Egypt
    and gather them from Assyria.
I will bring them to Gilead and
            Lebanon,

^r10 That is, the Euphrates   ^s10 Or the end of the land   ^t15 Or bowl, / like   ^u4,5 Or ruler, all of them together. / 5They

and there will not be room enough
for them.
[11]They will pass through the sea of
trouble;
the surging sea will be subdued
and all the depths of the Nile will
dry up.
Assyria's pride will be brought down
and Egypt's scepter will pass away.
[12]I will strengthen them in the LORD
and in his name they will walk,"
declares the LORD.

CHAPTER 11

Open your doors, O Lebanon,
so that fire may devour your cedars!
[2]Wail, O pine tree, for the cedar has
fallen;
the stately trees are ruined!
Wail, oaks of Bashan;
the dense forest has been cut down!
[3]Listen to the wail of the shepherds;
their rich pastures are destroyed!
Listen to the roar of the lions;
the lush thicket of the Jordan is
ruined!

[4]This is what the LORD my God says:
"Pasture the flock marked for slaughter.
[5]Their buyers slaughter them and go unpunished. Those who sell them say,
'Praise the LORD, I am rich!' Their own
shepherds do not spare them. [6]For I will
no longer have pity on the people of the
land," declares the LORD. "I will hand everyone over to his neighbor and his king.
They will oppress the land, and I will not
rescue them from their hands."

[7]So I pastured the flock marked for
slaughter, particularly the oppressed of
the flock. Then I took two staffs and called
one Favor and the other Union, and I
pastured the flock. [8]In one month I got rid
of the three shepherds.

The flock detested me, and I grew
weary of them [9]and said, "I will not be
your shepherd. Let the dying die, and the
perishing perish. Let those who are left
eat one another's flesh."

[10]Then I took my staff called Favor and
broke it, revoking the covenant I had
made with all the nations. [11]It was revoked on that day, and so the afflicted of
the flock who were watching me knew it
was the word of the LORD.

[12]I told them, "If you think it best, give
me my pay; but if not, keep it." So they
paid me thirty pieces of silver.

[13]And the LORD said to me, "Throw it to
the potter"—the handsome price at which
they priced me! So I took the thirty pieces
of silver and threw them into the house of
the LORD to the potter.

[14]Then I broke my second staff called
Union, breaking the brotherhood between
Judah and Israel.

[15]Then the LORD said to me, "Take again
the equipment of a foolish shepherd. [16]For
I am going to raise up a shepherd over the
land who will not care for the lost, or seek
the young, or heal the injured, or feed the
healthy, but will eat the meat of the choice
sheep, tearing off their hoofs.

[17]"Woe to the worthless shepherd,
who deserts the flock!
May the sword strike his arm and his
right eye!
May his arm be completely
withered,
his right eye totally blinded!"

SEPTEMBER 28 ☐ DAY 272
Finishing Touches

 LOOK BACK Haggai (whose name means "festive") and Zechariah
("the Lord remembers") are prophetic contemporaries with contrasting
styles and messages. Haggai delivers a powerful call to arms, urging
the people of Judah to *take part* and complete the rebuilding of the
temple. Zechariah, by contrast, uses a series of visions, messages and
burdens to gently urge the people of Judah to *take heart,* regain courage and see the future as bright with the promises of God. Haggai
exhorts the people to action with strong words of rebuke; Zechariah

urges the people to action with gentle reminders of the future importance of the temple.

Haggai, the second shortest book in the Old Testament, jars the nation out of its complacency and preoccupation. Because of Judah's misplaced priorities, the temple that should have been finished years earlier still stands half-completed and useless. By contrast, Zechariah reminds the nation of God's covenant faithfulness. When times are tough and the future is uncertain, it's always safe to trust the Lord. Together, these prophets urge God's people to rise up and complete the rebuilding of the temple. And, indeed, that is precisely what they did!

LOOK UP Here is a simple three-question quiz with a profound point to it:

- How long does it take to cook a one-minute steak? _____
- How long does it take to complete a four-year bachelor's degree? _____

To do nothing is tiresome because you cannot stop and take a rest.

- How long does it take to read the Bible all the way through with the help of a through-the-Bible-in-a-year devotional program? _____

The answer to each question is the same: No one knows for sure! It all depends on your attentiveness and persistence.

A one-minute steak *should* take about a minute . . . unless the cook gets distracted or interrupted, in which case the steak might cook indefinitely (with predictable results).

A four-year degree program *ought* to be completed in about four years, but many who start with the best of intentions find themselves mired in a half-completed program after more than a decade.

A through-the-Bible-in-a-year reading plan *can* be completed in a year, if it remains a daily priority with the reader! But allow the goal to grow fuzzy or other priorities to compete for the necessary twenty minutes a day, and the goal may prove elusive indeed.

LOOK AHEAD Even a goal as worthy as rebuilding the temple has a way of becoming slippery and elusive when other priorities are allowed to compete. As the project dragged on year after year, the homes and comforts of God's people became more important than the temple and glory of God. And the result? Sixteen years after Cyrus had issued the proclamation launching the project, there were *weeds* instead of *walls* growing from the foundation.

Haggai and Zechariah held their countrymen accountable to finish what they had begun. Haggai (with exhortation) and Zechariah (with encouragement) both urged the builders not to "throw in the trowel." If you're having trouble completing a long-term project you began more than a year ago, why not enlist the help of a friend or family member? A weekly time of accountability and progress reporting might be just the thing you need to stay on target and bring to completion a worthy endeavor.

SEPTEMBER 29 ☐ DAY 273
ZECHARIAH 12–14
Israel's Coming Consolation

OVERVIEW Consolation is coming for the people of God, and Zechariah closes his prophecy with a stirring portrayal of what will happen "on that day." God will destroy Jerusalem's enemies; the nation will be cleansed of idols and false prophets; mountains will move; hard hearts will melt; and the Lord will be king over all the earth (14:9). What began as a vision of horror in chapters 1 and 2 ends as a vision of hope.

Chapter 12	Chapter 13	Chapter 14
"Jerusalem Will Be Strong"	"The LORD Is Our God"	"The LORD Will Be King"
Deliverance	Delight	Dominion

YOUR DAILY WALK If you had to select the three strongest men in the Bible, whom would you pick?

Let us pray not for lighter burdens but for stronger backs.

Chances are the names you listed are examples of physical strength. Perhaps you chose men like Samson . . . or David . . . or Joshua—men of might, men of warfare, men of the outdoors. But did you ever stop to think that some of the strongest men in the Bible were, from a physical point of view, some of the weakest? Daniel (whose greatest claim to fame was sitting quietly in the corner of a lions' den); Jeremiah (who turned into a fountain of tears at the thought of his exiled people, yet preached with fire and faithfulness for forty years); Timothy (who stood toe-to-toe with heretics in spite of his young age, poor health and timid temperament).

As Zechariah looks ahead on the prophetic calendar, he predicts, "The feeblest among them will be like David" (12:8). Their strength will come, not from physical, material or military superiority, but from their relationship to God. Is that true of you today? Regardless of your physical stamina or financial condition, you can be strong in the Lord. Place these words next to your medicine cabinet: *My strength is in the Lord Almighty.* Then every time you reach for a pill or prescription, you'll be reminded of the strength that's available in limitless supply!

INSIGHT Jerusalem in the Forefront
In chapter 14 you will find at least eight specific references to the city of Jerusalem—an important clue to the original intent of Zechariah's visions and to God's program "on that day."

An Oracle

CHAPTER 12

This is the word of the LORD concerning Israel. The LORD, who stretches out the heavens, who lays the foundation of the earth, and who forms the spirit of man within him, declares: ²"I am going to make Jerusalem a cup that sends all the surrounding peoples reeling. Judah will be besieged as well as Jerusalem. ³On that day, when all the nations of the earth are gathered against her, I will make Jerusa-lem an immovable rock for all the nations. All who try to move it will injure themselves. ⁴On that day I will strike every horse with panic and its rider with madness," declares the LORD. "I will keep a watchful eye over the house of Judah, but I will blind all the horses of the nations. ⁵Then the leaders of Judah will say in their hearts, 'The people of Jerusalem are strong, because the LORD Almighty is their God.'

⁶"On that day I will make the leaders of Judah like a firepot in a woodpile, like a

flaming torch among sheaves. They will consume right and left all the surrounding peoples, but Jerusalem will remain intact in her place.

7"The LORD will save the dwellings of Judah first, so that the honor of the house of David and of Jerusalem's inhabitants may not be greater than that of Judah. 8On that day the LORD will shield those who live in Jerusalem, so that the feeblest among them will be like David, and the house of David will be like God, like the Angel of the LORD going before them. 9On that day I will set out to destroy all the nations that attack Jerusalem.

10"And I will pour out on the house of David and the inhabitants of Jerusalem a spirit^v of grace and supplication. They will look on^w me, the one they have pierced, and they will mourn for him as one mourns for an only child, and grieve bitterly for him as one grieves for a first-born son. 11On that day the weeping in Jerusalem will be great, like the weeping of Hadad Rimmon in the plain of Megiddo. 12The land will mourn, each clan by itself, with their wives by themselves: the clan of the house of David and their wives, the clan of the house of Nathan and their wives, 13the clan of the house of Levi and their wives, the clan of Shimei and their wives, 14and all the rest of the clans and their wives.

CHAPTER 13
"On that day a fountain will be opened to the house of David and the inhabitants of Jerusalem, to cleanse them from sin and impurity.

2"On that day, I will banish the names of the idols from the land, and they will be remembered no more," declares the LORD Almighty. "I will remove both the prophets and the spirit of impurity from the land. 3And if anyone still prophesies, his father and mother, to whom he was born, will say to him, 'You must die, because you have told lies in the LORD's name.' When he prophesies, his own parents will stab him.

4"On that day every prophet will be ashamed of his prophetic vision. He will not put on a prophet's garment of hair in order to deceive. 5He will say, 'I am not a prophet. I am a farmer; the land has been

my livelihood since my youth.^{x}' 6If someone asks him, 'What are these wounds on your body^y?' he will answer, 'The wounds I was given at the house of my friends.'

7"Awake, O sword, against my
    shepherd,
  against the man who is close to me!"
  declares the LORD Almighty.
"Strike the shepherd,
  and the sheep will be scattered,
  and I will turn my hand against the
    little ones.
8In the whole land," declares the LORD,
  "two-thirds will be struck down
    and perish;
  yet one-third will be left in it.
9This third I will bring into the fire;
  I will refine them like silver
  and test them like gold.
They will call on my name
  and I will answer them;
I will say, 'They are my people,'
  and they will say, 'The LORD is our
    God.'"

CHAPTER 14
A day of the LORD is coming when your plunder will be divided among you.

2I will gather all the nations to Jerusalem to fight against it; the city will be captured, the houses ransacked, and the women raped. Half of the city will go into exile, but the rest of the people will not be taken from the city.

3Then the LORD will go out and fight against those nations, as he fights in the day of battle. 4On that day his feet will stand on the Mount of Olives, east of Jerusalem, and the Mount of Olives will be split in two from east to west, forming a great valley, with half of the mountain moving north and half moving south. 5You will flee by my mountain valley, for it will extend to Azel. You will flee as you fled from the earthquake^z in the days of Uzziah king of Judah. Then the LORD my God will come, and all the holy ones with him.

6On that day there will be no light, no cold or frost. 7It will be a unique day, without daytime or nighttime—a day known to the LORD. When evening comes, there will be light.

^{v}10 Or the Spirit ^{w}10 Or to ^{x}5 Or farmer; a man sold me in my youth ^{y}6 Or wounds between your hands ^{z}5 Or 5My mountain valley will be blocked and will extend to Azel. It will be blocked as it was blocked because of the earthquake

⁸On that day living water will flow out from Jerusalem, half to the eastern sea*ᵃ* and half to the western sea;*ᵇ* in summer and in winter.

⁹The LORD will be king over the whole earth. On that day there will be one LORD, and his name the only name.

¹⁰The whole land, from Geba to Rimmon, south of Jerusalem, will become like the Arabah. But Jerusalem will be raised up and remain in its place, from the Benjamin Gate to the site of the First Gate, to the Corner Gate, and from the Tower of Hananel to the royal winepresses. ¹¹It will be inhabited; never again will it be destroyed. Jerusalem will be secure.

¹²This is the plague with which the LORD will strike all the nations that fought against Jerusalem: Their flesh will rot while they are still standing on their feet, their eyes will rot in their sockets, and their tongues will rot in their mouths. ¹³On that day men will be stricken by the LORD with great panic. Each man will seize the hand of another, and they will attack each other. ¹⁴Judah too will fight at Jerusalem. The wealth of all the surrounding nations will be collected—great quantities of gold and silver and clothing.

¹⁵A similar plague will strike the horses and mules, the camels and donkeys, and all the animals in those camps.

¹⁶Then the survivors from all the nations that have attacked Jerusalem will go up year after year to worship the King, the LORD Almighty, and to celebrate the Feast of Tabernacles. ¹⁷If any of the peoples of the earth do not go up to Jerusalem to worship the King, the LORD Almighty, they will have no rain. ¹⁸If the Egyptian people do not go up and take part, they will have no rain. The LORD*ᶜ* will bring on them the plague he inflicts on the nations that do not go up to celebrate the Feast of Tabernacles. ¹⁹This will be the punishment of Egypt and the punishment of all the nations that do not go up to celebrate the Feast of Tabernacles.

²⁰On that day HOLY TO THE LORD will be inscribed on the bells of the horses, and the cooking pots in the LORD's house will be like the sacred bowls in front of the altar. ²¹Every pot in Jerusalem and Judah will be holy to the LORD Almighty, and all who come to sacrifice will take some of the pots and cook in them. And on that day there will no longer be a Canaanite*ᵈ* in the house of the LORD Almighty.

ᵃ8 That is, the Dead Sea   *ᵇ8* That is, the Mediterranean   *ᶜ18* Or part, then the LORD   *ᵈ21* Or merchant

Malachi

IT HAS been years since God restored his people to their land. But they have lapsed into the very sins that brought about their captivity. God sends Malachi to remind his people that he loves them, but they have not returned his love. The priests have dishonored him and led his people astray. The men have married heathen women. And all have hardened their hearts to persist in their sins. Malachi gives them a final warning of the purifying day of the Lord, after which God's people would hear no more from him for four hundred years.

Focus	God's Love		God's Rebuke		God's Promise		
Divisions	God's Love for the People	Rebuke of the Priests	Rebuke of the People	Righteous Remembered	Wicked Destroyed	Elijah Coming
	1:1 1:5	1:6 2:9	2:10 3:15	3:16 3:18	4:1 4:3	4:4 4:6
	Past	Present		Future		
Topics	Questions and Answers			Invitation and Warning		
Place	Jerusalem						
Time	Approximately 432–425 B.C.						

SEPTEMBER 30 ☐ DAY 274
MALACHI 1–4
Hard Words for Hearts of Stone

OVERVIEW Malachi marks the sunset of Old Testament prophecy. Malachi the prophet and Nehemiah the builder were contemporaries, and the situations Nehemiah faced—corrupt priests, mixed marriages, neglected tithes—formed the basis for Malachi's sermons. The book is constructed around a three-part pattern involving accusation, interrogation and refutation. For example:

Accusation: "Judah has broken faith" (2:11).
Interrogation: "You ask, 'Why?' " (2:14).
Refutation: "It is because the LORD is acting as the witness between you and the wife of your youth, because you have broken faith with her" (2:14). Can you find more examples in the book?

Arrogant insensitivity shows that the nation has hit rock bottom spiritually. The people have become so sin-hardened that God's proddings no longer prick their conscience. With his intense, convicting words, Malachi ushers in four hundred years of silence, which will be broken at last when John the Baptist emerges to proclaim, "Look, the Lamb of God, who takes away the sin of the world!" (John 1:29).

Chapter 1	Chapter 2	Chapter 3	Chapter 4
Sins of the Priests	Sins of the People	Payday for the People	Coming Day of the Lord
Questions and Answers			Invitation and Warning

YOUR DAILY WALK It is fitting that the last word of the Old Testament should be *curse*. A curse is something to be avoided—the result of a neglected command or disobedient action. Malachi brings down the curtain on the Old Testament with a final reminder that sin must be dealt with. When the New Testament opens, the scene will be set for the one who alone can cure humanity's sin sickness: Jesus the Messiah.

Malachi's prophecy, like a morning dawn, brings with it the promise of a new and more glorious day.

Close your study of Malachi with a time of prayer. If you know Christ as Savior, tell him how much he means to you. If you don't, wouldn't now be a perfect time to put your trust in him?

INSIGHT Will the Real Elijah Please Stand Up?
John the Baptist was the fulfillment of Malachi's prophecy that Elijah would come as Messiah's forerunner (4:5; Matthew 17:12). And according to Malachi, another Elijah-like forerunner will precede Christ's second coming as well (4:6; Matthew 17:11)!

CHAPTER 1

An oracle: The word of the LORD to Israel through Malachi.*a*

²"I have loved you," says the LORD.
"But you ask, 'How have you loved us?'

"Was not Esau Jacob's brother?" the LORD says. "Yet I have loved Jacob, ³but Esau I have hated, and I have turned his mountains into a wasteland and left his inheritance to the desert jackals."

a1 Malachi means my messenger.

[4]Edom may say, "Though we have been crushed, we will rebuild the ruins."

But this is what the LORD Almighty says: "They may build, but I will demolish. They will be called the Wicked Land, a people always under the wrath of the LORD. [5]You will see it with your own eyes and say, 'Great is the LORD—even beyond the borders of Israel!'

[6]"A son honors his father, and a servant his master. If I am a father, where is the honor due me? If I am a master, where is the respect due me?" says the LORD Almighty. "It is you, O priests, who show contempt for my name.

"But you ask, 'How have we shown contempt for your name?'

[7]"You place defiled food on my altar.

"But you ask, 'How have we defiled you?'

"By saying that the LORD's table is contemptible. [8]When you bring blind animals for sacrifice, is that not wrong? When you sacrifice crippled or diseased animals, is that not wrong? Try offering them to your governor! Would he be pleased with you? Would he accept you?" says the LORD Almighty.

[9]"Now implore God to be gracious to us. With such offerings from your hands, will he accept you?"—says the LORD Almighty.

[10]"Oh, that one of you would shut the temple doors, so that you would not light useless fires on my altar! I am not pleased with you," says the LORD Almighty, "and I will accept no offering from your hands. [11]My name will be great among the nations, from the rising to the setting of the sun. In every place incense and pure offerings will be brought to my name, because my name will be great among the nations," says the LORD Almighty.

[12]"But you profane it by saying of the Lord's table, 'It is defiled,' and of its food, 'It is contemptible.' [13]And you say, 'What a burden!' and you sniff at it contemptuously," says the LORD Almighty.

"When you bring injured, crippled or diseased animals and offer them as sacrifices, should I accept them from your hands?" says the LORD. [14]"Cursed is the cheat who has an acceptable male in his flock and vows to give it, but then sacrifices a blemished animal to the Lord. For I am a great king," says the LORD Almighty, "and my name is to be feared among the nations.

CHAPTER 2

"And now this admonition is for you, O priests. [2]If you do not listen, and if you do not set your heart to honor my name," says the LORD Almighty, "I will send a curse upon you, and I will curse your blessings. Yes, I have already cursed them, because you have not set your heart to honor me.

[3]"Because of you I will rebuke[b] your descendants[c]; I will spread on your faces the offal from your festival sacrifices, and you will be carried off with it. [4]And you will know that I have sent you this admonition so that my covenant with Levi may continue," says the LORD Almighty. [5]"My covenant was with him, a covenant of life and peace, and I gave them to him; this called for reverence and he revered me and stood in awe of my name. [6]True instruction was in his mouth and nothing false was found on his lips. He walked with me in peace and uprightness, and turned many from sin.

[7]"For the lips of a priest ought to preserve knowledge, and from his mouth men should seek instruction—because he is the messenger of the LORD Almighty. [8]But you have turned from the way and by your teaching have caused many to stumble; you have violated the covenant with Levi," says the LORD Almighty. [9]"So I have caused you to be despised and humiliated before all the people, because you have not followed my ways but have shown partiality in matters of the law."

[10]Have we not all one Father[d]? Did not one God create us? Why do we profane the covenant of our fathers by breaking faith with one another?

[11]Judah has broken faith. A detestable thing has been committed in Israel and in Jerusalem: Judah has desecrated the sanctuary the LORD loves, by marrying the daughter of a foreign god. [12]As for the man who does this, whoever he may be, may the LORD cut him off from the tents of Jacob[e]—even though he brings offerings to the LORD Almighty.

[13]Another thing you do: You flood the LORD's altar with tears. You weep and

[b]3 Or cut off (see Septuagint)   [c]3 Or will blight your grain   [d]10 Or father   [e]12 Or [12]May the LORD cut off from the tents of Jacob anyone who gives testimony in behalf of the man who does this

wail because he no longer pays attention to your offerings or accepts them with pleasure from your hands. ¹⁴You ask, "Why?" It is because the LORD is acting as the witness between you and the wife of your youth, because you have broken faith with her, though she is your partner, the wife of your marriage covenant.

¹⁵Has not ⌊the LORD⌋ made them one? In flesh and spirit they are his. And why one? Because he was seeking godly offspring.ᶠ So guard yourself in your spirit, and do not break faith with the wife of your youth.

¹⁶"I hate divorce," says the LORD God of Israel, "and I hate a man's covering himselfᵍ with violence as well as with his garment," says the LORD Almighty.

So guard yourself in your spirit, and do not break faith.

¹⁷You have wearied the LORD with your words.

"How have we wearied him?" you ask.

By saying, "All who do evil are good in the eyes of the LORD, and he is pleased with them" or "Where is the God of justice?"

CHAPTER 3
"See, I will send my messenger, who will prepare the way before me. Then suddenly the Lord you are seeking will come to his temple; the messenger of the covenant, whom you desire, will come," says the LORD Almighty.

²But who can endure the day of his coming? Who can stand when he appears? For he will be like a refiner's fire or a launderer's soap. ³He will sit as a refiner and purifier of silver; he will purify the Levites and refine them like gold and silver. Then the LORD will have men who will bring offerings in righteousness, ⁴and the offerings of Judah and Jerusalem will be acceptable to the LORD, as in days gone by, as in former years.

⁵"So I will come near to you for judgment. I will be quick to testify against sorcerers, adulterers and perjurers, against those who defraud laborers of their wages, who oppress the widows and the fatherless, and deprive aliens of justice, but do not fear me," says the LORD Almighty.

⁶"I the LORD do not change. So you,

O descendants of Jacob, are not destroyed. ⁷Ever since the time of your forefathers you have turned away from my decrees and have not kept them. Return to me, and I will return to you," says the LORD Almighty.

"But you ask, 'How are we to return?'

⁸"Will a man rob God? Yet you rob me.

"But you ask, 'How do we rob you?'

"In tithes and offerings. ⁹You are under a curse—the whole nation of you—because you are robbing me. ¹⁰Bring the whole tithe into the storehouse, that there may be food in my house. Test me in this," says the LORD Almighty, "and see if I will not throw open the floodgates of heaven and pour out so much blessing that you will not have room enough for it. ¹¹I will prevent pests from devouring your crops, and the vines in your fields will not cast their fruit," says the LORD Almighty. ¹²"Then all the nations will call you blessed, for yours will be a delightful land," says the LORD Almighty.

¹³"You have said harsh things against me," says the LORD.

"Yet you ask, 'What have we said against you?'

¹⁴"You have said, 'It is futile to serve God. What did we gain by carrying out his requirements and going about like mourners before the LORD Almighty? ¹⁵But now we call the arrogant blessed. Certainly the evildoers prosper, and even those who challenge God escape.' "

¹⁶Then those who feared the LORD talked with each other, and the LORD listened and heard. A scroll of remembrance was written in his presence concerning those who feared the LORD and honored his name.

¹⁷"They will be mine," says the LORD Almighty, "in the day when I make up my treasured possession.ʰ I will spare them, just as in compassion a man spares his son who serves him. ¹⁸And you will again see the distinction between the righteous and the wicked, between those who serve God and those who do not.

CHAPTER 4
"Surely the day is coming; it will burn like a furnace. All the arrogant and every evildoer will be stubble, and that day that is coming will set them on fire," says the

---

ᶠ15 Or ¹⁵But the one ⌊who is our father⌋ did not do this, not as long as life remained in him. And what was he seeking? An offspring from God   ᵍ16 Or his wife   ʰ17 Or Almighty, "my treasured possession, in the day when I act

LORD Almighty. "Not a root or a branch will be left to them. ²But for you who revere my name, the sun of righteousness will rise with healing in its wings. And you will go out and leap like calves released from the stall. ³Then you will trample down the wicked; they will be ashes under the soles of your feet on the day when I do these things," says the LORD Almighty.

⁴"Remember the law of my servant Moses, the decrees and laws I gave him at Horeb for all Israel.

⁵"See, I will send you the prophet Elijah before that great and dreadful day of the LORD comes. ⁶He will turn the hearts of the fathers to their children, and the hearts of the children to their fathers; or else I will come and strike the land with a curse."

Matthew

THE FIRST verse of the Gospel of Matthew announces the event predicted by Old Testament prophets and long awaited by Israel: the coming of the Anointed One, "Jesus Christ the son of David, the son of Abraham." Under the Spirit's guidance, Matthew carefully documents Christ's claim to be the Messiah: He possesses the credentials of the Messiah and ministers in the predicted pattern of the Messiah. He preaches messages only the Messiah could deliver and finally dies the death only the Messiah could die.

Focus	Preparation	Pattern			Proclamation		Passion
Divisions	Pedigree of the King	Preaching of the King	Power of the King	Parables of the King	Principles of the King	Predictions of the King	Passion of the King
	1 4	5 7	8 11	12 15	16 19	20 25	26 28
Topics	Teaching the Throngs				Teaching the Twelve		
	Growing Reception				Growing Rejection		
Place	Bethlehem and Nazareth	Galilee				Jerusalem	
Time	4 B.C.–A.D. 33						

OCTOBER 1 □ DAY 275
MATTHEW 1–4
Pedigree of the King

OVERVIEW What was *anticipated* in the last book of the Old Testament (Malachi) now *arrives* in the first book of the New Testament (Matthew): the Messiah of God. He must come from the kingly line—and Jesus does. He must bear the name of royalty—and Jesus' name means "the Lord saves." He must be worthy of worship—and wise men from the east travel great distances to pay homage to him. He must be a light to the Gentiles, be announced by a forerunner and demonstrate power over Satan, demons, disease and death—and Jesus does all this and more. The Messiah has come!

Chapter 1	Chapter 2	Chapter 3	Chapter 4
Pedigree of the King	Presentation of the King	Proclamation of the King	Power of the King
Joseph	Magi	John	Satan

YOUR DAILY WALK How well do you know your Old Testament?

That may seem like an unusual question to ask as you begin reading the New Testament. But you'll quickly discover that the key to unlocking the *New* is a foundational knowledge of the *Old!* In order to persuade his fellow Jews to believe in Jesus as their long-awaited King and Messiah, Matthew used the Old Testament as proof. When Jesus faced the triple temptation by Satan in the desert, he used Scripture from the fifth book of the Old Testament (Deuteronomy) as his basis of defense.

You can never starve the person who feeds on God's promises.

Underline each Old Testament quotation you find in today's reading. (Hint: Watch for such phrases as "to fulfill what was said through the prophet.") Then spend a few extra minutes looking up those Old Testament prophecies that became New Testament realities. Wouldn't it be fitting to close your time in God's Word today by thanking God that his centuries-old promises are trustworthy? Do that right now!

INSIGHT Great Expectations . . . Unfulfilled!

The Jewish world of Jesus' day longed for a deliverer from the iron heel of Roman oppression. But many thought the Messiah would not arrive until they were good enough to "deserve" him. One commonly held notion was that the Messiah would only come when the nation had kept the Sabbath for *four consecutive weeks*. There was just one problem. No one could keep all the Mosaic laws for even *one* day! God sent the Savior as a gift for the godless—not as a reward for the righteous.

CHAPTER 1

A record of the genealogy of Jesus Christ the son of David, the son of Abraham:

²Abraham was the father of Isaac,

Isaac the father of Jacob,
Jacob the father of Judah and his brothers,
³Judah the father of Perez and Zerah, whose mother was Tamar,

Perez the father of Hezron,
Hezron the father of Ram,
4Ram the father of Amminadab,
Amminadab the father of Nahshon,
Nahshon the father of Salmon,
5Salmon the father of Boaz, whose
mother was Rahab,
Boaz the father of Obed, whose
mother was Ruth,
Obed the father of Jesse,
6and Jesse the father of King David.

David was the father of Solomon,
whose mother had been Uriah's
wife,
7Solomon the father of Rehoboam,
Rehoboam the father of Abijah,
Abijah the father of Asa,
8Asa the father of Jehoshaphat,
Jehoshaphat the father of Jehoram,
Jehoram the father of Uzziah,
9Uzziah the father of Jotham,
Jotham the father of Ahaz,
Ahaz the father of Hezekiah,
10Hezekiah the father of Manasseh,
Manasseh the father of Amon,
Amon the father of Josiah,
11and Josiah the father of Jeconiah*a*
and his brothers at the time of
the exile to Babylon.

12After the exile to Babylon:
Jeconiah was the father of Shealtiel,
Shealtiel the father of Zerubbabel,
13Zerubbabel the father of Abiud,
Abiud the father of Eliakim,
Eliakim the father of Azor,
14Azor the father of Zadok,
Zadok the father of Akim,
Akim the father of Eliud,
15Eliud the father of Eleazar,
Eleazar the father of Matthan,
Matthan the father of Jacob,
16and Jacob the father of Joseph,
the husband of Mary, of whom
was born Jesus, who is called
Christ.

17Thus there were fourteen generations
in all from Abraham to David, fourteen
from David to the exile to Babylon, and
fourteen from the exile to the Christ.*b*
18This is how the birth of Jesus Christ
came about: His mother Mary was

pledged to be married to Joseph, but before they came together, she was found
to be with child through the Holy Spirit.
19Because Joseph her husband was a righteous man and did not want to expose her
to public disgrace, he had in mind to divorce her quietly.

20But after he had considered this, an
angel of the Lord appeared to him in a
dream and said, "Joseph son of David, do
not be afraid to take Mary home as your
wife, because what is conceived in her is
from the Holy Spirit. 21She will give birth
to a son, and you are to give him the
name Jesus,*c* because he will save his
people from their sins."

22All this took place to fulfill what
the Lord had said through the prophet:
23"The virgin will be with child and will
give birth to a son, and they will call
him Immanuel"*d*—which means, "God
with us."

24When Joseph woke up, he did what
the angel of the Lord had commanded
him and took Mary home as his wife.
25But he had no union with her until she
gave birth to a son. And he gave him the
name Jesus.

CHAPTER 2
After Jesus was born in Bethlehem in Judea, during the time of King Herod,
Magi*e* from the east came to Jerusalem
2and asked, "Where is the one who has
been born king of the Jews? We saw his
star in the east*f* and have come to worship him."

3When King Herod heard this he was
disturbed, and all Jerusalem with him.
4When he had called together all the people's chief priests and teachers of the law,
he asked them where the Christ*g* was to
be born. 5"In Bethlehem in Judea," they
replied, "for this is what the prophet has
written:

6" 'But you, Bethlehem, in the land of
Judah,
are by no means least among the
rulers of Judah;
for out of you will come a ruler
who will be the shepherd of my
people Israel.'*h* "

7Then Herod called the Magi secretly

*a*11 That is, Jehoiachin; also in verse 12   *b*17 Or *Messiah*. "The Christ" (Greek) and "the Messiah" (Hebrew) both mean "the
Anointed One."   *c*21 *Jesus* is the Greek form of *Joshua*, which means *the LORD saves*.   *d*23 Isaiah 7:14   *e*1 Traditionally *Wise
Men*   *f*2 Or *star when it rose*   *g*4 Or *Messiah*   *h*6 Micah 5:2

and found out from them the exact time the star had appeared. [8]He sent them to Bethlehem and said, "Go and make a careful search for the child. As soon as you find him, report to me, so that I too may go and worship him."

[9]After they had heard the king, they went on their way, and the star they had seen in the east[i] went ahead of them until it stopped over the place where the child was. [10]When they saw the star, they were overjoyed. [11]On coming to the house, they saw the child with his mother Mary, and they bowed down and worshiped him. Then they opened their treasures and presented him with gifts of gold and of incense and of myrrh. [12]And having been warned in a dream not to go back to Herod, they returned to their country by another route.

[13]When they had gone, an angel of the Lord appeared to Joseph in a dream. "Get up," he said, "take the child and his mother and escape to Egypt. Stay there until I tell you, for Herod is going to search for the child to kill him."

[14]So he got up, took the child and his mother during the night and left for Egypt, [15]where he stayed until the death of Herod. And so was fulfilled what the Lord had said through the prophet: "Out of Egypt I called my son."[j]

[16]When Herod realized that he had been outwitted by the Magi, he was furious, and he gave orders to kill all the boys in Bethlehem and its vicinity who were two years old and under, in accordance with the time he had learned from the Magi. [17]Then what was said through the prophet Jeremiah was fulfilled:

[18]"A voice is heard in Ramah,
    weeping and great mourning,
Rachel weeping for her children
    and refusing to be comforted,
because they are no more."[k]

[19]After Herod died, an angel of the Lord appeared in a dream to Joseph in Egypt [20]and said, "Get up, take the child and his mother and go to the land of Israel, for those who were trying to take the child's life are dead."

[21]So he got up, took the child and his mother and went to the land of Israel. [22]But when he heard that Archelaus was reigning in Judea in place of his father Herod, he was afraid to go there. Having been warned in a dream, he withdrew to the district of Galilee, [23]and he went and lived in a town called Nazareth. So was fulfilled what was said through the prophets: "He will be called a Nazarene."

CHAPTER 3

In those days John the Baptist came, preaching in the Desert of Judea [2]and saying, "Repent, for the kingdom of heaven is near." [3]This is he who was spoken of through the prophet Isaiah:

"A voice of one calling in the desert,
'Prepare the way for the Lord,
    make straight paths for him.' "[l]

[4]John's clothes were made of camel's hair, and he had a leather belt around his waist. His food was locusts and wild honey. [5]People went out to him from Jerusalem and all Judea and the whole region of the Jordan. [6]Confessing their sins, they were baptized by him in the Jordan River.

[7]But when he saw many of the Pharisees and Sadducees coming to where he was baptizing, he said to them: "You brood of vipers! Who warned you to flee from the coming wrath? [8]Produce fruit in keeping with repentance. [9]And do not think you can say to yourselves, 'We have Abraham as our father.' I tell you that out of these stones God can raise up children for Abraham. [10]The ax is already at the root of the trees, and every tree that does not produce good fruit will be cut down and thrown into the fire.

[11]"I baptize you with[m] water for repentance. But after me will come one who is more powerful than I, whose sandals I am not fit to carry. He will baptize you with the Holy Spirit and with fire. [12]His winnowing fork is in his hand, and he will clear his threshing floor, gathering his wheat into the barn and burning up the chaff with unquenchable fire."

[13]Then Jesus came from Galilee to the Jordan to be baptized by John. [14]But John tried to deter him, saying, "I need to be baptized by you, and do you come to me?"

[15]Jesus replied, "Let it be so now; it is

---

[i]9 Or seen when it rose   [j]15 Hosea 11:1   [k]18 Jer. 31:15   [l]3 Isaiah 40:3   [m]11 Or in

proper for us to do this to fulfill all righteousness." Then John consented.

[16]As soon as Jesus was baptized, he went up out of the water. At that moment heaven was opened, and he saw the Spirit of God descending like a dove and lighting on him. [17]And a voice from heaven said, "This is my Son, whom I love; with him I am well pleased."

CHAPTER 4

Then Jesus was led by the Spirit into the desert to be tempted by the devil. [2]After fasting forty days and forty nights, he was hungry. [3]The tempter came to him and said, "If you are the Son of God, tell these stones to become bread."

[4]Jesus answered, "It is written: 'Man does not live on bread alone, but on every word that comes from the mouth of God.'[n]"

[5]Then the devil took him to the holy city and had him stand on the highest point of the temple. [6]"If you are the Son of God," he said, "throw yourself down. For it is written:

" 'He will command his angels
        concerning you,
    and they will lift you up in their
        hands,
so that you will not strike your foot
        against a stone.'[o]"

[7]Jesus answered him, "It is also written: 'Do not put the Lord your God to the test.'[p]"

[8]Again, the devil took him to a very high mountain and showed him all the kingdoms of the world and their splendor. [9]"All this I will give you," he said, "if you will bow down and worship me."

[10]Jesus said to him, "Away from me, Satan! For it is written: 'Worship the Lord your God, and serve him only.'[q]"

[11]Then the devil left him, and angels came and attended him.

[12]When Jesus heard that John had been put in prison, he returned to Galilee. [13]Leaving Nazareth, he went and lived in Capernaum, which was by the lake in the area of Zebulun and Naphtali— [14]to fulfill what was said through the prophet Isaiah:

[15]"Land of Zebulun and land of
        Naphtali,
    the way to the sea, along the Jordan,
        Galilee of the Gentiles—
[16]the people living in darkness
    have seen a great light;
on those living in the land of the
        shadow of death
    a light has dawned."[r]

[17]From that time on Jesus began to preach, "Repent, for the kingdom of heaven is near."

[18]As Jesus was walking beside the Sea of Galilee, he saw two brothers, Simon called Peter and his brother Andrew. They were casting a net into the lake, for they were fishermen. [19]"Come, follow me," Jesus said, "and I will make you fishers of men." [20]At once they left their nets and followed him.

[21]Going on from there, he saw two other brothers, James son of Zebedee and his brother John. They were in a boat with their father Zebedee, preparing their nets. Jesus called them, [22]and immediately they left the boat and their father and followed him.

[23]Jesus went throughout Galilee, teaching in their synagogues, preaching the good news of the kingdom, and healing every disease and sickness among the people. [24]News about him spread all over Syria, and people brought to him all who were ill with various diseases, those suffering severe pain, the demon-possessed, those having seizures, and the paralyzed, and he healed them. [25]Large crowds from Galilee, the Decapolis,[s] Jerusalem, Judea and the region across the Jordan followed him.

---

[n]4 Deut. 8:3   [o]6 Psalm 91:11,12   [p]7 Deut. 6:16   [q]10 Deut. 6:13   [r]16 Isaiah 9:1,2   [s]25 That is, the Ten Cities

OCTOBER 2 ☐ DAY 276
MATTHEW 5–7
Preaching of the King

OVERVIEW Matthew's Gospel is not primarily chronological in its arrangement but topical, alternating between Jesus' deeds and his discourses, between his miracles and his messages. Today's reading, traditionally called the Sermon on the Mount, is really ten "sermonettes" in one and was preached on a mountainside overlooking the Sea of Galilee (5:1).

Chapter 5	Chapter 6	Chapter 7
How We Stand before the Law	How We Stand before the World	How We Stand before God
Holy Actions	Holy Attitudes	Holy Judgment

YOUR DAILY WALK Try this quiz on attitudes and actions:

1. True or False: It is possible to do the right thing for the wrong reason.

2. True or False: It is possible to do the wrong thing for the right reason.

Although disciples are to be seen doing good works, they must not do good works in order to be seen.

If spirituality were measured in units of activity, surely the Pharisees of Jesus' day were candidates for spiritual greatness! They gave a tithe of all they possessed, right down to the spices on their shelves (Luke 11:42), and they fasted twice weekly (Luke 18:12). Judging from the externals, they were models of holy zeal. But inwardly, where only God can see, they were like "whitewashed tombs . . . full of dead men's bones" (Matthew 23:27).

That's why Jesus said, "Unless your righteousness surpasses that of the Pharisees and the teachers of the law, you will certainly not enter the kingdom of heaven" (Matthew 5:20).

It's not that we need to do more than the Pharisees or discard what they did in favor of something better (Luke 11:42), but we must couple their outer zeal with an inner heart for God's love and justice—the kind of heart portrayed in the Beatitudes of Matthew 5:3–11. Think of these as "Be Attitudes"—attitudes God wants you to demonstrate in your life and service for him. Pick one (there are eight to choose from), write it in your own words and with God's help make it your holy "exercise project" for today.

INSIGHT Open Mouth, Open Heart

Matthew introduces Jesus' sermon by saying, "He began to teach them, saying" (5:2)—a phrase in Greek that refers to an utterance from deep within the heart and soul of a person.

CHAPTER 5

Now when he saw the crowds, he went up on a mountainside and sat down. His disciples came to him, ²and he began to teach them, saying:

³"Blessed are the poor in spirit,
for theirs is the kingdom of heaven.
⁴Blessed are those who mourn,
for they will be comforted.

⁵Blessed are the meek,
for they will inherit the earth.
⁶Blessed are those who hunger and
thirst for righteousness,
for they will be filled.
⁷Blessed are the merciful,
for they will be shown mercy.
⁸Blessed are the pure in heart,
for they will see God.
⁹Blessed are the peacemakers,

for they will be called sons of God. [10]Blessed are those who are persecuted because of righteousness, for theirs is the kingdom of heaven.

[11]"Blessed are you when people insult you, persecute you and falsely say all kinds of evil against you because of me. [12]Rejoice and be glad, because great is your reward in heaven, for in the same way they persecuted the prophets who were before you.

[13]"You are the salt of the earth. But if the salt loses its saltiness, how can it be made salty again? It is no longer good for anything, except to be thrown out and trampled by men.

[14]"You are the light of the world. A city on a hill cannot be hidden. [15]Neither do people light a lamp and put it under a bowl. Instead they put it on its stand, and it gives light to everyone in the house. [16]In the same way, let your light shine before men, that they may see your good deeds and praise your Father in heaven.

[17]"Do not think that I have come to abolish the Law or the Prophets; I have not come to abolish them but to fulfill them. [18]I tell you the truth, until heaven and earth disappear, not the smallest letter, not the least stroke of a pen, will by any means disappear from the Law until everything is accomplished. [19]Anyone who breaks one of the least of these commandments and teaches others to do the same will be called least in the kingdom of heaven, but whoever practices and teaches these commands will be called great in the kingdom of heaven. [20]For I tell you that unless your righteousness surpasses that of the Pharisees and the teachers of the law, you will certainly not enter the kingdom of heaven.

[21]"You have heard that it was said to the people long ago, 'Do not murder,[t] and anyone who murders will be subject to judgment.' [22]But I tell you that anyone who is angry with his brother[u] will be subject to judgment. Again, anyone who says to his brother, 'Raca,[v]' is answerable to the Sanhedrin. But anyone who says, 'You fool!' will be in danger of the fire of hell.

[23]"Therefore, if you are offering your gift at the altar and there remember that your brother has something against you, [24]leave your gift there in front of the altar. First go and be reconciled to your brother; then come and offer your gift.

[25]"Settle matters quickly with your adversary who is taking you to court. Do it while you are still with him on the way, or he may hand you over to the judge, and the judge may hand you over to the officer, and you may be thrown into prison. [26]I tell you the truth, you will not get out until you have paid the last penny.[w]

[27]"You have heard that it was said, 'Do not commit adultery.'[x] [28]But I tell you that anyone who looks at a woman lustfully has already committed adultery with her in his heart. [29]If your right eye causes you to sin, gouge it out and throw it away. It is better for you to lose one part of your body than for your whole body to be thrown into hell. [30]And if your right hand causes you to sin, cut it off and throw it away. It is better for you to lose one part of your body than for your whole body to go into hell.

[31]"It has been said, 'Anyone who divorces his wife must give her a certificate of divorce.'[y] [32]But I tell you that anyone who divorces his wife, except for marital unfaithfulness, causes her to become an adulteress, and anyone who marries the divorced woman commits adultery.

[33]"Again, you have heard that it was said to the people long ago, 'Do not break your oath, but keep the oaths you have made to the Lord.' [34]But I tell you, Do not swear at all: either by heaven, for it is God's throne; [35]or by the earth, for it is his footstool; or by Jerusalem, for it is the city of the Great King. [36]And do not swear by your head, for you cannot make even one hair white or black. [37]Simply let your 'Yes' be 'Yes,' and your 'No,' 'No'; anything beyond this comes from the evil one.

[38]"You have heard that it was said, 'Eye for eye, and tooth for tooth.'[z] [39]But I tell you, Do not resist an evil person. If someone strikes you on the right cheek, turn to him the other also. [40]And if someone wants to sue you and take your tunic, let him have your cloak as well. [41]If someone forces you to go one mile, go with him two miles. [42]Give to the one who asks

---

[t]21 Exodus 20:13   [u]22 Some manuscripts *brother without cause*   [v]22 An Aramaic term of contempt   [w]26 Greek *kodrantes*
[x]27 Exodus 20:14   [y]31 Deut. 24:1   [z]38 Exodus 21:24; Lev. 24:20; Deut. 19:21

you, and do not turn away from the one who wants to borrow from you.

[43]"You have heard that it was said, 'Love your neighbor[a] and hate your enemy.' [44]But I tell you: Love your enemies[b] and pray for those who persecute you, [45]that you may be sons of your Father in heaven. He causes his sun to rise on the evil and the good, and sends rain on the righteous and the unrighteous. [46]If you love those who love you, what reward will you get? Are not even the tax collectors doing that? [47]And if you greet only your brothers, what are you doing more than others? Do not even pagans do that? [48]Be perfect, therefore, as your heavenly Father is perfect.

CHAPTER 6

"Be careful not to do your 'acts of righteousness' before men, to be seen by them. If you do, you will have no reward from your Father in heaven.

[2]"So when you give to the needy, do not announce it with trumpets, as the hypocrites do in the synagogues and on the streets, to be honored by men. I tell you the truth, they have received their reward in full. [3]But when you give to the needy, do not let your left hand know what your right hand is doing, [4]so that your giving may be in secret. Then your Father, who sees what is done in secret, will reward you.

[5]"And when you pray, do not be like the hypocrites, for they love to pray standing in the synagogues and on the street corners to be seen by men. I tell you the truth, they have received their reward in full. [6]But when you pray, go into your room, close the door and pray to your Father, who is unseen. Then your Father, who sees what is done in secret, will reward you. [7]And when you pray, do not keep on babbling like pagans, for they think they will be heard because of their many words. [8]Do not be like them, for your Father knows what you need before you ask him.

[9]"This, then, is how you should pray:

" 'Our Father in heaven,
    hallowed be your name,
[10]your kingdom come,
    your will be done

on earth as it is in heaven.
[11]Give us today our daily bread.
[12]Forgive us our debts,
    as we also have forgiven our
        debtors.
[13]And lead us not into temptation,
    but deliver us from the evil one.[c]'

[14]For if you forgive men when they sin against you, your heavenly Father will also forgive you. [15]But if you do not forgive men their sins, your Father will not forgive your sins.

[16]"When you fast, do not look somber as the hypocrites do, for they disfigure their faces to show men they are fasting. I tell you the truth, they have received their reward in full. [17]But when you fast, put oil on your head and wash your face, [18]so that it will not be obvious to men that you are fasting, but only to your Father, who is unseen; and your Father, who sees what is done in secret, will reward you.

[19]"Do not store up for yourselves treasures on earth, where moth and rust destroy, and where thieves break in and steal. [20]But store up for yourselves treasures in heaven, where moth and rust do not destroy, and where thieves do not break in and steal. [21]For where your treasure is, there your heart will be also.

[22]"The eye is the lamp of the body. If your eyes are good, your whole body will be full of light. [23]But if your eyes are bad, your whole body will be full of darkness. If then the light within you is darkness, how great is that darkness!

[24]"No one can serve two masters. Either he will hate the one and love the other, or he will be devoted to the one and despise the other. You cannot serve both God and Money.

[25]"Therefore I tell you, do not worry about your life, what you will eat or drink; or about your body, what you will wear. Is not life more important than food, and the body more important than clothes? [26]Look at the birds of the air; they do not sow or reap or store away in barns, and yet your heavenly Father feeds them. Are you not much more valuable than they? [27]Who of you by worrying can add a single hour to his life[d]?

[28]"And why do you worry about clothes? See how the lilies of the field

---

[a]43 Lev. 19:18   [b]44 Some late manuscripts *enemies, bless those who curse you, do good to those who hate you*   [c]13 Or *from evil*;
some late manuscripts *one, / for yours is the kingdom and the power and the glory forever. Amen.*   [d]27 Or *single cubit to his height*

grow. They do not labor or spin. ²⁹Yet I tell you that not even Solomon in all his splendor was dressed like one of these. ³⁰If that is how God clothes the grass of the field, which is here today and tomorrow is thrown into the fire, will he not much more clothe you, O you of little faith? ³¹So do not worry, saying, 'What shall we eat?' or 'What shall we drink?' or 'What shall we wear?' ³²For the pagans run after all these things, and your heavenly Father knows that you need them. ³³But seek first his kingdom and his righteousness, and all these things will be given to you as well. ³⁴Therefore do not worry about tomorrow, for tomorrow will worry about itself. Each day has enough trouble of its own.

CHAPTER 7

"Do not judge, or you too will be judged. ²For in the same way you judge others, you will be judged, and with the measure you use, it will be measured to you.

³"Why do you look at the speck of sawdust in your brother's eye and pay no attention to the plank in your own eye? ⁴How can you say to your brother, 'Let me take the speck out of your eye,' when all the time there is a plank in your own eye? ⁵You hypocrite, first take the plank out of your own eye, and then you will see clearly to remove the speck from your brother's eye.

⁶"Do not give dogs what is sacred; do not throw your pearls to pigs. If you do, they may trample them under their feet, and then turn and tear you to pieces.

⁷"Ask and it will be given to you; seek and you will find; knock and the door will be opened to you. ⁸For everyone who asks receives; he who seeks finds; and to him who knocks, the door will be opened.

⁹"Which of you, if his son asks for bread, will give him a stone? ¹⁰Or if he asks for a fish, will give him a snake? ¹¹If you, then, though you are evil, know how to give good gifts to your children, how much more will your Father in heaven give good gifts to those who ask him! ¹²So in everything, do to others what you

would have them do to you, for this sums up the Law and the Prophets.

¹³"Enter through the narrow gate. For wide is the gate and broad is the road that leads to destruction, and many enter through it. ¹⁴But small is the gate and narrow the road that leads to life, and only a few find it.

¹⁵"Watch out for false prophets. They come to you in sheep's clothing, but inwardly they are ferocious wolves. ¹⁶By their fruit you will recognize them. Do people pick grapes from thornbushes, or figs from thistles? ¹⁷Likewise every good tree bears good fruit, but a bad tree bears bad fruit. ¹⁸A good tree cannot bear bad fruit, and a bad tree cannot bear good fruit. ¹⁹Every tree that does not bear good fruit is cut down and thrown into the fire. ²⁰Thus, by their fruit you will recognize them.

²¹"Not everyone who says to me, 'Lord, Lord,' will enter the kingdom of heaven, but only he who does the will of my Father who is in heaven. ²²Many will say to me on that day, 'Lord, Lord, did we not prophesy in your name, and in your name drive out demons and perform many miracles?' ²³Then I will tell them plainly, 'I never knew you. Away from me, you evildoers!'

²⁴"Therefore everyone who hears these words of mine and puts them into practice is like a wise man who built his house on the rock. ²⁵The rain came down, the streams rose, and the winds blew and beat against that house; yet it did not fall, because it had its foundation on the rock. ²⁶But everyone who hears these words of mine and does not put them into practice is like a foolish man who built his house on sand. ²⁷The rain came down, the streams rose, and the winds blew and beat against that house, and it fell with a great crash."

²⁸When Jesus had finished saying these things, the crowds were amazed at his teaching, ²⁹because he taught as one who had authority, and not as their teachers of the law.

OCTOBER 3 ☐ DAY 277
MATTHEW 8–11
Power of the King

OVERVIEW It is one thing for a preacher to proclaim the words contained in the Sermon on the Mount; it is something else to be able to back up those words with power—power that could only come from God. Jesus' miracles serve at least two vital functions: (1) They demonstrate his authority over sin, sickness, demons and nature; and (2) they show his heart of compassion toward the objects of his love. An incurable leper . . . a disillusioned woman who was subject to bleeding . . . a timid band of disciples on the raging Sea of Galilee—each receives comfort and consolation from the powerful words of the Savior.

Chapter 8	Chapter 9	Chapter 10	Chapter 11
Christ Supreme over Nature	Christ Supreme over Death	Christ Multiplied in His Men	Christ Justified in His Deeds
Jesus Shows His Love		Jesus Sends His Disciples	

A religion without wonders is false. A theology without wonders is heretical.

YOUR DAILY WALK Put yourself in the sandals of one of Jesus' disciples for a moment. You have just been informed by the Master, "All authority in heaven and on earth has been given to me" (as he will tell them in 28:18).

Taken in isolation, that statement might seem like the proud boast of an egotist. But in this case, it has been preceded by no fewer than nine miracles! You have watched hopeless medical cases healed, violent storms silenced, even dead people raised to life. *Now* how do you react to Christ's words?

Seeing is believing. One of the strongest encouragements for trusting God today is seeing God's power in the past. Below are spaces for you to record the nine miracles found in today's reading plus a tenth from the hand of God in your own life over the past week. If you can't think of one, then ask him to make your life a miracle today!

1. _____ 4. _____ 7. _____
2. _____ 5. _____ 8. _____
3. _____ 6. _____ 9. _____
And in my life . . . 10. _____

INSIGHT "Anyone Who Does Not Take His Cross"
The Cross casts its terrible shadow across all four Gospels. In Matthew it's mentioned numerous times, as in 10:38, for example. Jesus knew he would die by crucifixion when he spoke these words, but only much later would his disciples see the deep significance of his statement.

CHAPTER 8
When he came down from the mountainside, large crowds followed him. ²A man with leprosy*ᵉ* came and knelt before him and said, "Lord, if you are willing, you can make me clean."

³Jesus reached out his hand and touched the man. "I am willing," he said. "Be clean!" Immediately he was cured*ᶠ* of his leprosy. ⁴Then Jesus said to him, "See that you don't tell anyone. But go, show yourself to the priest and offer the gift Moses commanded, as a testimony to them."

ᵉ2 The Greek word was used for various diseases affecting the skin—not necessarily leprosy.   ᶠ3 Greek made clean

⁵When Jesus had entered Capernaum, a centurion came to him, asking for help. ⁶"Lord," he said, "my servant lies at home paralyzed and in terrible suffering."

⁷Jesus said to him, "I will go and heal him."

⁸The centurion replied, "Lord, I do not deserve to have you come under my roof. But just say the word, and my servant will be healed. ⁹For I myself am a man under authority, with soldiers under me. I tell this one, 'Go,' and he goes; and that one, 'Come,' and he comes. I say to my servant, 'Do this,' and he does it."

¹⁰When Jesus heard this, he was astonished and said to those following him, "I tell you the truth, I have not found anyone in Israel with such great faith. ¹¹I say to you that many will come from the east and the west, and will take their places at the feast with Abraham, Isaac and Jacob in the kingdom of heaven. ¹²But the subjects of the kingdom will be thrown outside, into the darkness, where there will be weeping and gnashing of teeth."

¹³Then Jesus said to the centurion, "Go! It will be done just as you believed it would." And his servant was healed at that very hour.

¹⁴When Jesus came into Peter's house, he saw Peter's mother-in-law lying in bed with a fever. ¹⁵He touched her hand and the fever left her, and she got up and began to wait on him.

¹⁶When evening came, many who were demon-possessed were brought to him, and he drove out the spirits with a word and healed all the sick. ¹⁷This was to fulfill what was spoken through the prophet Isaiah:

"He took up our infirmities
   and carried our diseases."ᵍ

¹⁸When Jesus saw the crowd around him, he gave orders to cross to the other side of the lake. ¹⁹Then a teacher of the law came to him and said, "Teacher, I will follow you wherever you go."

²⁰Jesus replied, "Foxes have holes and birds of the air have nests, but the Son of Man has no place to lay his head."

²¹Another disciple said to him, "Lord, first let me go and bury my father."

²²But Jesus told him, "Follow me, and let the dead bury their own dead."

²³Then he got into the boat and his disciples followed him. ²⁴Without warning, a furious storm came up on the lake, so that the waves swept over the boat. But Jesus was sleeping. ²⁵The disciples went and woke him, saying, "Lord, save us! We're going to drown!"

²⁶He replied, "You of little faith, why are you so afraid?" Then he got up and rebuked the winds and the waves, and it was completely calm.

²⁷The men were amazed and asked, "What kind of man is this? Even the winds and the waves obey him!"

²⁸When he arrived at the other side in the region of the Gadarenes,ʰ two demon-possessed men coming from the tombs met him. They were so violent that no one could pass that way. ²⁹"What do you want with us, Son of God?" they shouted. "Have you come here to torture us before the appointed time?"

³⁰Some distance from them a large herd of pigs was feeding. ³¹The demons begged Jesus, "If you drive us out, send us into the herd of pigs."

³²He said to them, "Go!" So they came out and went into the pigs, and the whole herd rushed down the steep bank into the lake and died in the water. ³³Those tending the pigs ran off, went into the town and reported all this, including what had happened to the demon-possessed men. ³⁴Then the whole town went out to meet Jesus. And when they saw him, they pleaded with him to leave their region.

CHAPTER 9

Jesus stepped into a boat, crossed over and came to his own town. ²Some men brought to him a paralytic, lying on a mat. When Jesus saw their faith, he said to the paralytic, "Take heart, son; your sins are forgiven."

³At this, some of the teachers of the law said to themselves, "This fellow is blaspheming!"

⁴Knowing their thoughts, Jesus said, "Why do you entertain evil thoughts in

ᵍ17 Isaiah 53:4   ʰ28 Some manuscripts Gergesenes; others Gerasenes your hearts? [5]Which is easier: to say, 'Your sins are forgiven,' or to say, 'Get up and walk'? [6]But so that you may know that the Son of Man has authority on earth to forgive sins . . ." Then he said to the paralytic, "Get up, take your mat and go home." [7]And the man got up and went home. [8]When the crowd saw this, they were filled with awe; and they praised God, who had given such authority to men.

[9]As Jesus went on from there, he saw a man named Matthew sitting at the tax collector's booth. "Follow me," he told him, and Matthew got up and followed him.

[10]While Jesus was having dinner at Matthew's house, many tax collectors and "sinners" came and ate with him and his disciples. [11]When the Pharisees saw this, they asked his disciples, "Why does your teacher eat with tax collectors and 'sinners'?"

[12]On hearing this, Jesus said, "It is not the healthy who need a doctor, but the sick. [13]But go and learn what this means: 'I desire mercy, not sacrifice.'[i] For I have not come to call the righteous, but sinners."

[14]Then John's disciples came and asked him, "How is it that we and the Pharisees fast, but your disciples do not fast?"

[15]Jesus answered, "How can the guests of the bridegroom mourn while he is with them? The time will come when the bridegroom will be taken from them; then they will fast.

[16]"No one sews a patch of unshrunk cloth on an old garment, for the patch will pull away from the garment, making the tear worse. [17]Neither do men pour new wine into old wineskins. If they do, the skins will burst, the wine will run out and the wineskins will be ruined. No, they pour new wine into new wineskins, and both are preserved."

[18]While he was saying this, a ruler came and knelt before him and said, "My daughter has just died. But come and put your hand on her, and she will live." [19]Jesus got up and went with him, and so did his disciples.

[20]Just then a woman who had been subject to bleeding for twelve years came up behind him and touched the edge of his cloak. [21]She said to herself, "If I only touch his cloak, I will be healed."

[22]Jesus turned and saw her. "Take heart, daughter," he said, "your faith has healed you." And the woman was healed from that moment.

[23]When Jesus entered the ruler's house and saw the flute players and the noisy crowd, [24]he said, "Go away. The girl is not dead but asleep." But they laughed at him. [25]After the crowd had been put outside, he went in and took the girl by the hand, and she got up. [26]News of this spread through all that region.

[27]As Jesus went on from there, two blind men followed him, calling out, "Have mercy on us, Son of David!"

[28]When he had gone indoors, the blind men came to him, and he asked them, "Do you believe that I am able to do this?"

"Yes, Lord," they replied.

[29]Then he touched their eyes and said, "According to your faith will it be done to you"; [30]and their sight was restored. Jesus warned them sternly, "See that no one knows about this." [31]But they went out and spread the news about him all over that region.

[32]While they were going out, a man who was demon-possessed and could not talk was brought to Jesus. [33]And when the demon was driven out, the man who had been mute spoke. The crowd was amazed and said, "Nothing like this has ever been seen in Israel."

[34]But the Pharisees said, "It is by the prince of demons that he drives out demons."

[35]Jesus went through all the towns and villages, teaching in their synagogues, preaching the good news of the kingdom and healing every disease and sickness. [36]When he saw the crowds, he had compassion on them, because they were harassed and helpless, like sheep without a shepherd. [37]Then he said to his disciples, "The harvest is plentiful but the workers are few. [38]Ask the Lord of the harvest, therefore, to send out workers into his harvest field."

CHAPTER 10

He called his twelve disciples to him and gave them authority to drive out evil[j]

[i]13 Hosea 6:6   [j]1 Greek unclean

spirits and to heal every disease and sickness.

²These are the names of the twelve apostles: first, Simon (who is called Peter) and his brother Andrew; James son of Zebedee, and his brother John; ³Philip and Bartholomew; Thomas and Matthew the tax collector; James son of Alphaeus, and Thaddaeus; ⁴Simon the Zealot and Judas Iscariot, who betrayed him.

⁵These twelve Jesus sent out with the following instructions: "Do not go among the Gentiles or enter any town of the Samaritans. ⁶Go rather to the lost sheep of Israel. ⁷As you go, preach this message: 'The kingdom of heaven is near.' ⁸Heal the sick, raise the dead, cleanse those who have leprosy,ᵏ drive out demons. Freely you have received, freely give. ⁹Do not take along any gold or silver or copper in your belts; ¹⁰take no bag for the journey, or extra tunic, or sandals or a staff; for the worker is worth his keep.

¹¹"Whatever town or village you enter, search for some worthy person there and stay at his house until you leave. ¹²As you enter the home, give it your greeting. ¹³If the home is deserving, let your peace rest on it; if it is not, let your peace return to you. ¹⁴If anyone will not welcome you or listen to your words, shake the dust off your feet when you leave that home or town. ¹⁵I tell you the truth, it will be more bearable for Sodom and Gomorrah on the day of judgment than for that town. ¹⁶I am sending you out like sheep among wolves. Therefore be as shrewd as snakes and as innocent as doves.

¹⁷"Be on your guard against men; they will hand you over to the local councils and flog you in their synagogues. ¹⁸On my account you will be brought before governors and kings as witnesses to them and to the Gentiles. ¹⁹But when they arrest you, do not worry about what to say or how to say it. At that time you will be given what to say, ²⁰for it will not be you speaking, but the Spirit of your Father speaking through you.

²¹"Brother will betray brother to death, and a father his child; children will rebel against their parents and have them put to death. ²²All men will hate you because of me, but he who stands firm to the end will be saved. ²³When you are persecuted

in one place, flee to another. I tell you the truth, you will not finish going through the cities of Israel before the Son of Man comes.

²⁴"A student is not above his teacher, nor a servant above his master. ²⁵It is enough for the student to be like his teacher, and the servant like his master. If the head of the house has been called Beelzebub,ˡ how much more the members of his household!

²⁶"So do not be afraid of them. There is nothing concealed that will not be disclosed, or hidden that will not be made known. ²⁷What I tell you in the dark, speak in the daylight; what is whispered in your ear, proclaim from the roofs. ²⁸Do not be afraid of those who kill the body but cannot kill the soul. Rather, be afraid of the One who can destroy both soul and body in hell. ²⁹Are not two sparrows sold for a penny ᵐ? Yet not one of them will fall to the ground apart from the will of your Father. ³⁰And even the very hairs of your head are all numbered. ³¹So don't be afraid; you are worth more than many sparrows.

³²"Whoever acknowledges me before men, I will also acknowledge him before my Father in heaven. ³³But whoever disowns me before men, I will disown him before my Father in heaven.

³⁴"Do not suppose that I have come to bring peace to the earth. I did not come to bring peace, but a sword. ³⁵For I have come to turn

" 'a man against his father,
  a daughter against her mother,
a daughter-in-law against her
        mother-in-law—
³⁶ a man's enemies will be the
        members of his own
        household.'ⁿ

³⁷"Anyone who loves his father or mother more than me is not worthy of me; anyone who loves his son or daughter more than me is not worthy of me; ³⁸and anyone who does not take his cross and follow me is not worthy of me. ³⁹Whoever finds his life will lose it, and whoever loses his life for my sake will find it.

⁴⁰"He who receives you receives me, and he who receives me receives the one who sent me. ⁴¹Anyone who receives a

---

ᵏ8 The Greek word was used for various diseases affecting the skin—not necessarily leprosy.   ˡ25 Greek *Beezeboul* or *Beelzeboul*   ᵐ29 Greek *an assarion*   ⁿ36 Micah 7:6

prophet because he is a prophet will receive a prophet's reward, and anyone who receives a righteous man because he is a righteous man will receive a righteous man's reward. ⁴²And if anyone gives even a cup of cold water to one of these little ones because he is my disciple, I tell you the truth, he will certainly not lose his reward."

CHAPTER 11

After Jesus had finished instructing his twelve disciples, he went on from there to teach and preach in the towns of Galilee.ᵒ ²When John heard in prison what Christ was doing, he sent his disciples ³to ask him, "Are you the one who was to come, or should we expect someone else?"

⁴Jesus replied, "Go back and report to John what you hear and see: ⁵The blind receive sight, the lame walk, those who have leprosyᵖ are cured, the deaf hear, the dead are raised, and the good news is preached to the poor. ⁶Blessed is the man who does not fall away on account of me."

⁷As John's disciples were leaving, Jesus began to speak to the crowd about John: "What did you go out into the desert to see? A reed swayed by the wind? ⁸If not, what did you go out to see? A man dressed in fine clothes? No, those who wear fine clothes are in kings' palaces. ⁹Then what did you go out to see? A prophet? Yes, I tell you, and more than a prophet. ¹⁰This is the one about whom it is written:

" 'I will send my messenger ahead of
    you,
 who will prepare your way before
    you.'�q

¹¹I tell you the truth: Among those born of women there has not risen anyone greater than John the Baptist; yet he who is least in the kingdom of heaven is greater than he. ¹²From the days of John the Baptist until now, the kingdom of heaven has been forcefully advancing, and forceful men lay hold of it. ¹³For all the Prophets and the Law prophesied until John. ¹⁴And if you are willing to accept it, he is the Elijah who was to come. ¹⁵He who has ears, let him hear.

¹⁶"To what can I compare this generation? They are like children sitting in the marketplaces and calling out to others:

¹⁷" 'We played the flute for you,
    and you did not dance;
 we sang a dirge,
    and you did not mourn.'

¹⁸For John came neither eating nor drinking, and they say, 'He has a demon.' ¹⁹The Son of Man came eating and drinking, and they say, 'Here is a glutton and a drunkard, a friend of tax collectors and "sinners." ' But wisdom is proved right by her actions."

²⁰Then Jesus began to denounce the cities in which most of his miracles had been performed, because they did not repent. ²¹"Woe to you, Korazin! Woe to you, Bethsaida! If the miracles that were performed in you had been performed in Tyre and Sidon, they would have repented long ago in sackcloth and ashes. ²²But I tell you, it will be more bearable for Tyre and Sidon on the day of judgment than for you. ²³And you, Capernaum, will you be lifted up to the skies? No, you will go down to the depths.ʳ If the miracles that were performed in you had been performed in Sodom, it would have remained to this day. ²⁴But I tell you that it will be more bearable for Sodom on the day of judgment than for you."

²⁵At that time Jesus said, "I praise you, Father, Lord of heaven and earth, because you have hidden these things from the wise and learned, and revealed them to little children. ²⁶Yes, Father, for this was your good pleasure.

²⁷"All things have been committed to me by my Father. No one knows the Son except the Father, and no one knows the Father except the Son and those to whom the Son chooses to reveal him.

²⁸"Come to me, all you who are weary and burdened, and I will give you rest. ²⁹Take my yoke upon you and learn from me, for I am gentle and humble in heart, and you will find rest for your souls. ³⁰For my yoke is easy and my burden is light."

ᵒ1 Greek *in their towns*   ᵖ5 The Greek word was used for various diseases affecting the skin—not necessarily leprosy.
�q10 Mal. 3:1   ʳ23 Greek *Hades*

OCTOBER 4 □ DAY 278
MATTHEW 12–15
Parables of the King

OVERVIEW Even as the multitudes press around Jesus to experience his healing touch, the religious leaders are plotting his downfall and ultimate destruction. Those who refuse to acknowledge the clear evidence of his miracles have no choice but to attribute his power to Satan. To them, Jesus responds with warnings of judgment and condemnation. But to all who will accept his claims, he offers rest and forgiveness. In the midst of this drama involving both growing reception and growing rejection, Jesus portrays his kingdom program in seven parables—earthly stories portraying heavenly realities.

Chapter 12	Chapter 13	Chapter 14	Chapter 15
Suppressors of the Truth	Expressions of the Truth	Feeding the 5,000	Feeling Compassion
Pharisees	Parables	Miracles	

YOUR DAILY WALK "There are none so blind as those who will not see."

It's one thing to have a legitimate question for which you are seeking an answer. Jesus welcomed seekers and questioners (7:7), promising to teach them, take their burdens and grant them rest. But it's quite another thing to demand a sign and refuse to be convinced when the evidence is ample (12:38–42).

Faith is to believe what we do not see, and the reward of this faith is to see what we believe.

Think about your own relationship with God. In what ways are you honestly and sincerely seeking answers from God with a humble disposition to obey? In what areas are you demanding that God conform to your will, with an attitude that says, "My mind is made up, God, so don't confuse me with your plan for my life"?

A number of groups are portrayed in the passage you are reading today—and each responded with a different heart attitude.

The scribes demanded, "We want to see a miraculous sign" (12:38).
The Nazarenes asked, "Isn't this the carpenter's son?" (13:55).
The apostle Peter exclaimed, "Tell me to come to you" (14:28).
Which "seeker" found what he sought? Which one will you seek to emulate today as you walk humbly with God?

INSIGHT Teaching Techniques from the Master Teacher
Notice in Jesus' parables how his teaching was characterized by simplicity, informality and specificity. His goal was to communicate truth, not to impress his audience. Is that your goal in teaching?

CHAPTER 12

At that time Jesus went through the grainfields on the Sabbath. His disciples were hungry and began to pick some heads of grain and eat them. ²When the Pharisees saw this, they said to him, "Look! Your disciples are doing what is unlawful on the Sabbath."

³He answered, "Haven't you read what David did when he and his companions were hungry? ⁴He entered the house of God, and he and his companions ate the consecrated bread—which was not lawful for them to do, but only for the priests. ⁵Or haven't you read in the Law that on the Sabbath the priests in the temple desecrate the day and yet are innocent? ⁶I tell you that one⁵ greater than the temple is here. ⁷If you had known what these words mean, 'I desire mercy, not sacri-

ˢ6 Or *something*; also in verses 41 and 42

fice,'[t] you would not have condemned the innocent. [8]For the Son of Man is Lord of the Sabbath."

[9]Going on from that place, he went into their synagogue, [10]and a man with a shriveled hand was there. Looking for a reason to accuse Jesus, they asked him, "Is it lawful to heal on the Sabbath?"

[11]He said to them, "If any of you has a sheep and it falls into a pit on the Sabbath, will you not take hold of it and lift it out? [12]How much more valuable is a man than a sheep! Therefore it is lawful to do good on the Sabbath."

[13]Then he said to the man, "Stretch out your hand." So he stretched it out and it was completely restored, just as sound as the other. [14]But the Pharisees went out and plotted how they might kill Jesus.

[15]Aware of this, Jesus withdrew from that place. Many followed him, and he healed all their sick, [16]warning them not to tell who he was. [17]This was to fulfill what was spoken through the prophet Isaiah:

[18]"Here is my servant whom I have
        chosen,
    the one I love, in whom I delight;
  I will put my Spirit on him,
    and he will proclaim justice to the
        nations.
[19]He will not quarrel or cry out;
    no one will hear his voice in the
        streets.
[20]A bruised reed he will not break,
    and a smoldering wick he will not
        snuff out,
  till he leads justice to victory.
[21] In his name the nations will put
        their hope."[u]

[22]Then they brought him a demon-possessed man who was blind and mute, and Jesus healed him, so that he could both talk and see. [23]All the people were astonished and said, "Could this be the Son of David?"

[24]But when the Pharisees heard this, they said, "It is only by Beelzebub,[v] the prince of demons, that this fellow drives out demons."

[25]Jesus knew their thoughts and said to them, "Every kingdom divided against itself will be ruined, and every city or household divided against itself will not stand. [26]If Satan drives out Satan, he is divided against himself. How then can his kingdom stand? [27]And if I drive out demons by Beelzebub, by whom do your people drive them out? So then, they will be your judges. [28]But if I drive out demons by the Spirit of God, then the kingdom of God has come upon you.

[29]"Or again, how can anyone enter a strong man's house and carry off his possessions unless he first ties up the strong man? Then he can rob his house.

[30]"He who is not with me is against me, and he who does not gather with me scatters. [31]And so I tell you, every sin and blasphemy will be forgiven men, but the blasphemy against the Spirit will not be forgiven. [32]Anyone who speaks a word against the Son of Man will be forgiven, but anyone who speaks against the Holy Spirit will not be forgiven, either in this age or in the age to come.

[33]"Make a tree good and its fruit will be good, or make a tree bad and its fruit will be bad, for a tree is recognized by its fruit. [34]You brood of vipers, how can you who are evil say anything good? For out of the overflow of the heart the mouth speaks. [35]The good man brings good things out of the good stored up in him, and the evil man brings evil things out of the evil stored up in him. [36]But I tell you that men will have to give account on the day of judgment for every careless word they have spoken. [37]For by your words you will be acquitted, and by your words you will be condemned."

[38]Then some of the Pharisees and teachers of the law said to him, "Teacher, we want to see a miraculous sign from you."

[39]He answered, "A wicked and adulterous generation asks for a miraculous sign! But none will be given it except the sign of the prophet Jonah. [40]For as Jonah was three days and three nights in the belly of a huge fish, so the Son of Man will be three days and three nights in the heart of the earth. [41]The men of Nineveh will stand up at the judgment with this generation and condemn it; for they repented at the preaching of Jonah, and now one[w] greater than Jonah is here. [42]The Queen of the South will rise at the judgment with this generation and condemn it; for she

---

[t]7 Hosea 6:6   [u]21 Isaiah 42:1-4   [v]24 Greek *Beezeboul* or *Beelzeboul*; also in verse 27   [w]41 Or *something*; also in verse 42

came from the ends of the earth to listen to Solomon's wisdom, and now one greater than Solomon is here.

43"When an evil[x] spirit comes out of a man, it goes through arid places seeking rest and does not find it. 44Then it says, 'I will return to the house I left.' When it arrives, it finds the house unoccupied, swept clean and put in order. 45Then it goes and takes with it seven other spirits more wicked than itself, and they go in and live there. And the final condition of that man is worse than the first. That is how it will be with this wicked generation."

46While Jesus was still talking to the crowd, his mother and brothers stood outside, wanting to speak to him. 47Someone told him, "Your mother and brothers are standing outside, wanting to speak to you."[y]

48He replied to him, "Who is my mother, and who are my brothers?" 49Pointing to his disciples, he said, "Here are my mother and my brothers. 50For whoever does the will of my Father in heaven is my brother and sister and mother."

CHAPTER 13

That same day Jesus went out of the house and sat by the lake. 2Such large crowds gathered around him that he got into a boat and sat in it, while all the people stood on the shore. 3Then he told them many things in parables, saying: "A farmer went out to sow his seed. 4As he was scattering the seed, some fell along the path, and the birds came and ate it up. 5Some fell on rocky places, where it did not have much soil. It sprang up quickly, because the soil was shallow. 6But when the sun came up, the plants were scorched, and they withered because they had no root. 7Other seed fell among thorns, which grew up and choked the plants. 8Still other seed fell on good soil, where it produced a crop—a hundred, sixty or thirty times what was sown. 9He who has ears, let him hear."

10The disciples came to him and asked, "Why do you speak to the people in parables?"

11He replied, "The knowledge of the secrets of the kingdom of heaven has been given to you, but not to them. 12Whoever has will be given more, and he will have an abundance. Whoever does not have, even what he has will be taken from him. 13This is why I speak to them in parables:

"Though seeing, they do not see;
    though hearing, they do not hear or
    understand.

14In them is fulfilled the prophecy of Isaiah:

" 'You will be ever hearing but never
    understanding;
    you will be ever seeing but never
    perceiving.
15For this people's heart has become
    calloused;
    they hardly hear with their ears,
    and they have closed their eyes.
Otherwise they might see with their
    eyes,
    hear with their ears,
    understand with their hearts
and turn, and I would heal them.'[z]

16But blessed are your eyes because they see, and your ears because they hear. 17For I tell you the truth, many prophets and righteous men longed to see what you see but did not see it, and to hear what you hear but did not hear it.

18"Listen then to what the parable of the sower means: 19When anyone hears the message about the kingdom and does not understand it, the evil one comes and snatches away what was sown in his heart. This is the seed sown along the path. 20The one who received the seed that fell on rocky places is the man who hears the word and at once receives it with joy. 21But since he has no root, he lasts only a short time. When trouble or persecution comes because of the word, he quickly falls away. 22The one who received the seed that fell among the thorns is the man who hears the word, but the worries of this life and the deceitfulness of wealth choke it, making it unfruitful. 23But the one who received the seed that fell on good soil is the man who hears the word and understands it. He produces a crop, yielding a hundred, sixty or thirty times what was sown."

24Jesus told them another parable: "The kingdom of heaven is like a man who

---

x43 Greek unclean   y47 Some manuscripts do not have verse 47.   z15 Isaiah 6:9,10 sowed good seed in his field. ²⁵But while everyone was sleeping, his enemy came and sowed weeds among the wheat, and went away. ²⁶When the wheat sprouted and formed heads, then the weeds also appeared.

²⁷"The owner's servants came to him and said, 'Sir, didn't you sow good seed in your field? Where then did the weeds come from?'

²⁸" 'An enemy did this,' he replied.

"The servants asked him, 'Do you want us to go and pull them up?'

²⁹" 'No,' he answered, 'because while you are pulling the weeds, you may root up the wheat with them. ³⁰Let both grow together until the harvest. At that time I will tell the harvesters: First collect the weeds and tie them in bundles to be burned; then gather the wheat and bring it into my barn.' "

³¹He told them another parable: "The kingdom of heaven is like a mustard seed, which a man took and planted in his field. ³²Though it is the smallest of all your seeds, yet when it grows, it is the largest of garden plants and becomes a tree, so that the birds of the air come and perch in its branches."

³³He told them still another parable: "The kingdom of heaven is like yeast that a woman took and mixed into a large amount*a* of flour until it worked all through the dough."

³⁴Jesus spoke all these things to the crowd in parables; he did not say anything to them without using a parable. ³⁵So was fulfilled what was spoken through the prophet:

"I will open my mouth in parables,
    I will utter things hidden since the
        creation of the world."*b*

³⁶Then he left the crowd and went into the house. His disciples came to him and said, "Explain to us the parable of the weeds in the field."

³⁷He answered, "The one who sowed the good seed is the Son of Man. ³⁸The field is the world, and the good seed stands for the sons of the kingdom. The weeds are the sons of the evil one, ³⁹and the enemy who sows them is the devil. The harvest is the end of the age, and the harvesters are angels.

⁴⁰"As the weeds are pulled up and burned in the fire, so it will be at the end of the age. ⁴¹The Son of Man will send out his angels, and they will weed out of his kingdom everything that causes sin and all who do evil. ⁴²They will throw them into the fiery furnace, where there will be weeping and gnashing of teeth. ⁴³Then the righteous will shine like the sun in the kingdom of their Father. He who has ears, let him hear.

⁴⁴"The kingdom of heaven is like treasure hidden in a field. When a man found it, he hid it again, and then in his joy went and sold all he had and bought that field.

⁴⁵"Again, the kingdom of heaven is like a merchant looking for fine pearls. ⁴⁶When he found one of great value, he went away and sold everything he had and bought it.

⁴⁷"Once again, the kingdom of heaven is like a net that was let down into the lake and caught all kinds of fish. ⁴⁸When it was full, the fishermen pulled it up on the shore. Then they sat down and collected the good fish in baskets, but threw the bad away. ⁴⁹This is how it will be at the end of the age. The angels will come and separate the wicked from the righteous ⁵⁰and throw them into the fiery furnace, where there will be weeping and gnashing of teeth.

⁵¹"Have you understood all these things?" Jesus asked.

"Yes," they replied.

⁵²He said to them, "Therefore every teacher of the law who has been instructed about the kingdom of heaven is like the owner of a house who brings out of his storeroom new treasures as well as old."

⁵³When Jesus had finished these parables, he moved on from there. ⁵⁴Coming to his hometown, he began teaching the people in their synagogue, and they were amazed. "Where did this man get this wisdom and these miraculous powers?" they asked. ⁵⁵"Isn't this the carpenter's son? Isn't his mother's name Mary, and aren't his brothers James, Joseph, Simon and Judas? ⁵⁶Aren't all his sisters with us? Where then did this man get all these things?" ⁵⁷And they took offense at him.

But Jesus said to them, "Only in his

a33 Greek *three satas* (probably about 1/2 bushel or 22 liters)   *b35* Psalm 78:2

hometown and in his own house is a prophet without honor."

[58]And he did not do many miracles there because of their lack of faith.

CHAPTER 14

At that time Herod the tetrarch heard the reports about Jesus, [2]and he said to his attendants, "This is John the Baptist; he has risen from the dead! That is why miraculous powers are at work in him."

[3]Now Herod had arrested John and bound him and put him in prison because of Herodias, his brother Philip's wife, [4]for John had been saying to him: "It is not lawful for you to have her." [5]Herod wanted to kill John, but he was afraid of the people, because they considered him a prophet.

[6]On Herod's birthday the daughter of Herodias danced for them and pleased Herod so much [7]that he promised with an oath to give her whatever she asked. [8]Prompted by her mother, she said, "Give me here on a platter the head of John the Baptist." [9]The king was distressed, but because of his oaths and his dinner guests, he ordered that her request be granted [10]and had John beheaded in the prison. [11]His head was brought in on a platter and given to the girl, who carried it to her mother. [12]John's disciples came and took his body and buried it. Then they went and told Jesus.

[13]When Jesus heard what had happened, he withdrew by boat privately to a solitary place. Hearing of this, the crowds followed him on foot from the towns. [14]When Jesus landed and saw a large crowd, he had compassion on them and healed their sick.

[15]As evening approached, the disciples came to him and said, "This is a remote place, and it's already getting late. Send the crowds away, so they can go to the villages and buy themselves some food."

[16]Jesus replied, "They do not need to go away. You give them something to eat."

[17]"We have here only five loaves of bread and two fish," they answered.

[18]"Bring them here to me," he said. [19]And he directed the people to sit down on the grass. Taking the five loaves and the two fish and looking up to heaven, he gave thanks and broke the loaves. Then he gave them to the disciples, and the disciples gave them to the people. [20]They all ate and were satisfied, and the disciples picked up twelve basketfuls of broken pieces that were left over. [21]The number of those who ate was about five thousand men, besides women and children.

[22]Immediately Jesus made the disciples get into the boat and go on ahead of him to the other side, while he dismissed the crowd. [23]After he had dismissed them, he went up on a mountainside by himself to pray. When evening came, he was there alone, [24]but the boat was already a considerable distance[c] from land, buffeted by the waves because the wind was against it.

[25]During the fourth watch of the night Jesus went out to them, walking on the lake. [26]When the disciples saw him walking on the lake, they were terrified. "It's a ghost," they said, and cried out in fear.

[27]But Jesus immediately said to them: "Take courage! It is I. Don't be afraid."

[28]"Lord, if it's you," Peter replied, "tell me to come to you on the water."

[29]"Come," he said.

Then Peter got down out of the boat, walked on the water and came toward Jesus. [30]But when he saw the wind, he was afraid and, beginning to sink, cried out, "Lord, save me!"

[31]Immediately Jesus reached out his hand and caught him. "You of little faith," he said, "why did you doubt?"

[32]And when they climbed into the boat, the wind died down. [33]Then those who were in the boat worshiped him, saying, "Truly you are the Son of God."

[34]When they had crossed over, they landed at Gennesaret. [35]And when the men of that place recognized Jesus, they sent word to all the surrounding country. People brought all their sick to him [36]and begged him to let the sick just touch the edge of his cloak, and all who touched him were healed.

CHAPTER 15

Then some Pharisees and teachers of the law came to Jesus from Jerusalem and asked, [2]"Why do your disciples break the tradition of the elders? They don't wash their hands before they eat!"

[c]24 Greek *many stadia*

³Jesus replied, "And why do you break the command of God for the sake of your tradition? ⁴For God said, 'Honor your father and mother'*d* and 'Anyone who curses his father or mother must be put to death.'*e* ⁵But you say that if a man says to his father or mother, 'Whatever help you might otherwise have received from me is a gift devoted to God,' ⁶he is not to 'honor his father*f*' with it. Thus you nullify the word of God for the sake of your tradition. ⁷You hypocrites! Isaiah was right when he prophesied about you:

⁸" 'These people honor me with their lips,
　　but their hearts are far from me.
⁹They worship me in vain;
　　their teachings are but rules taught by men.'*g*"

¹⁰Jesus called the crowd to him and said, "Listen and understand. ¹¹What goes into a man's mouth does not make him 'unclean,' but what comes out of his mouth, that is what makes him 'unclean.' "

¹²Then the disciples came to him and asked, "Do you know that the Pharisees were offended when they heard this?"

¹³He replied, "Every plant that my heavenly Father has not planted will be pulled up by the roots. ¹⁴Leave them; they are blind guides.*h* If a blind man leads a blind man, both will fall into a pit."

¹⁵Peter said, "Explain the parable to us."

¹⁶"Are you still so dull?" Jesus asked them. ¹⁷"Don't you see that whatever enters the mouth goes into the stomach and then out of the body? ¹⁸But the things that come out of the mouth come from the heart, and these make a man 'unclean.' ¹⁹For out of the heart come evil thoughts, murder, adultery, sexual immorality, theft, false testimony, slander. ²⁰These are what make a man 'unclean'; but eating with unwashed hands does not make him 'unclean.' "

²¹Leaving that place, Jesus withdrew to the region of Tyre and Sidon. ²²A Canaanite woman from that vicinity came to him, crying out, "Lord, Son of David, have mercy on me! My daughter is suffering terribly from demon-possession."

²³Jesus did not answer a word. So his disciples came to him and urged him, "Send her away, for she keeps crying out after us."

²⁴He answered, "I was sent only to the lost sheep of Israel."

²⁵The woman came and knelt before him. "Lord, help me!" she said.

²⁶He replied, "It is not right to take the children's bread and toss it to their dogs."

²⁷"Yes, Lord," she said, "but even the dogs eat the crumbs that fall from their masters' table."

²⁸Then Jesus answered, "Woman, you have great faith! Your request is granted." And her daughter was healed from that very hour.

²⁹Jesus left there and went along the Sea of Galilee. Then he went up on a mountainside and sat down. ³⁰Great crowds came to him, bringing the lame, the blind, the crippled, the mute and many others, and laid them at his feet; and he healed them. ³¹The people were amazed when they saw the mute speaking, the crippled made well, the lame walking and the blind seeing. And they praised the God of Israel.

³²Jesus called his disciples to him and said, "I have compassion for these people; they have already been with me three days and have nothing to eat. I do not want to send them away hungry, or they may collapse on the way."

³³His disciples answered, "Where could we get enough bread in this remote place to feed such a crowd?"

³⁴"How many loaves do you have?" Jesus asked.

"Seven," they replied, "and a few small fish."

³⁵He told the crowd to sit down on the ground. ³⁶Then he took the seven loaves and the fish, and when he had given thanks, he broke them and gave them to the disciples, and they in turn to the people. ³⁷They all ate and were satisfied. Afterward the disciples picked up seven basketfuls of broken pieces that were left over. ³⁸The number of those who ate was four thousand, besides women and children. ³⁹After Jesus had sent the crowd away, he got into the boat and went to the vicinity of Magadan.

---

d **4** Exodus 20:12; Deut. 5:16   *e* **4** Exodus 21:17; Lev. 20:9   *f* **6** Some manuscripts *father or his mother*   *g* **9** Isaiah 29:13
h **14** Some manuscripts *guides of the blind*

OCTOBER 5 □ DAY 279
MATTHEW 16–19
Principles of the King

OVERVIEW Though Jesus takes time to minister to hungry crowds, confront the increasingly hostile Pharisees and comfort the believing Canaanite woman, it is clear that his primary concern is for the disciples—those he will soon leave behind to continue the work he has begun. His miracles and parables, healings and discourses all focus on his faithful followers to prepare them for difficult days just ahead.

Chapter 16	Chapter 17	Chapter 18	Chapter 19
Accusation of the King	Affirmation of the King	Instruction on the Kingdom	Correction for Kingdom Dwellers
Test	Transfiguration	Devotion	Divorce

YOUR DAILY WALK Think of the book of Matthew as a mountain with the action rising to a peak and then subsiding. Some commentators have suggested you'll find the "peak," the pivotal climax of the book, in the dramatic confession of Peter in chapter 16.

Christ is the meeting point between the Trinity and the sinner's soul.

    Up to this point Jesus has been seeking to prove his claim of messiahship through words and deeds. Now it is time to see if the lesson has been learned.

    Jesus gives his disciples a "public opinion" survey: "Who do people say the Son of Man is?" (16:13). The disciples report that public opinion is divided. Some say he's John, others Elijah or one of the prophets. Then Jesus cuts to the heart of the matter: "Who do you say I am?" And suddenly the disciples have no public opinion to hide behind. They must make an intelligent personal choice based on Christ's miracles and messages.

    On the basis of what you have read in the first half of Matthew's Gospel, what would be your response to Jesus' penetrating question: "Who do you say I am?"

    Now check 16:16 to find the correct answer to the question. Take a few moments to memorize it—and make it your own answer!

INSIGHT An Inspired Commentary on the Transfiguration
What does the transfiguration of Jesus mean (17:1–9)? Peter, one of the observers, gives the inspired explanation in 2 Peter 1:17–18. It was the unveiling of the glory of Jesus, a "sneak preview" of what heaven will be like!

CHAPTER 16

The Pharisees and Sadducees came to Jesus and tested him by asking him to show them a sign from heaven.

²He replied,[i] "When evening comes, you say, 'It will be fair weather, for the sky is red,' ³and in the morning, 'Today it will be stormy, for the sky is red and overcast.' You know how to interpret the appearance of the sky, but you cannot interpret the signs of the times. ⁴A wicked and adulterous generation looks for a miraculous sign, but none will be given it except the sign of Jonah." Jesus then left them and went away.

⁵When they went across the lake, the disciples forgot to take bread. ⁶"Be careful," Jesus said to them. "Be on your guard against the yeast of the Pharisees and Sadducees."

i2 Some early manuscripts do not have the rest of verse 2 and all of verse 3.

⁷They discussed this among themselves and said, "It is because we didn't bring any bread."

⁸Aware of their discussion, Jesus asked, "You of little faith, why are you talking among yourselves about having no bread? ⁹Do you still not understand? Don't you remember the five loaves for the five thousand, and how many basketfuls you gathered? ¹⁰Or the seven loaves for the four thousand, and how many basketfuls you gathered? ¹¹How is it you don't understand that I was not talking to you about bread? But be on your guard against the yeast of the Pharisees and Sadducees." ¹²Then they understood that he was not telling them to guard against the yeast used in bread, but against the teaching of the Pharisees and Sadducees.

¹³When Jesus came to the region of Caesarea Philippi, he asked his disciples, "Who do people say the Son of Man is?"

¹⁴They replied, "Some say John the Baptist; others say Elijah; and still others, Jeremiah or one of the prophets."

¹⁵"But what about you?" he asked. "Who do you say I am?"

¹⁶Simon Peter answered, "You are the Christ,ʲ the Son of the living God."

¹⁷Jesus replied, "Blessed are you, Simon son of Jonah, for this was not revealed to you by man, but by my Father in heaven. ¹⁸And I tell you that you are Peter,ᵏ and on this rock I will build my church, and the gates of Hadesˡ will not overcome it.ᵐ ¹⁹I will give you the keys of the kingdom of heaven; whatever you bind on earth will beⁿ bound in heaven, and whatever you loose on earth will beⁿ loosed in heaven." ²⁰Then he warned his disciples not to tell anyone that he was the Christ.

²¹From that time on Jesus began to explain to his disciples that he must go to Jerusalem and suffer many things at the hands of the elders, chief priests and teachers of the law, and that he must be killed and on the third day be raised to life.

²²Peter took him aside and began to rebuke him. "Never, Lord!" he said. "This shall never happen to you!"

²³Jesus turned and said to Peter, "Get behind me, Satan! You are a stumbling block to me; you do not have in mind the things of God, but the things of men."

²⁴Then Jesus said to his disciples, "If anyone would come after me, he must deny himself and take up his cross and follow me. ²⁵For whoever wants to save his lifeᵒ will lose it, but whoever loses his life for me will find it. ²⁶What good will it be for a man if he gains the whole world, yet forfeits his soul? Or what can a man give in exchange for his soul? ²⁷For the Son of Man is going to come in his Father's glory with his angels, and then he will reward each person according to what he has done. ²⁸I tell you the truth, some who are standing here will not taste death before they see the Son of Man coming in his kingdom."

CHAPTER 17

After six days Jesus took with him Peter, James and John the brother of James, and led them up a high mountain by themselves. ²There he was transfigured before them. His face shone like the sun, and his clothes became as white as the light. ³Just then there appeared before them Moses and Elijah, talking with Jesus.

⁴Peter said to Jesus, "Lord, it is good for us to be here. If you wish, I will put up three shelters—one for you, one for Moses and one for Elijah."

⁵While he was still speaking, a bright cloud enveloped them, and a voice from the cloud said, "This is my Son, whom I love; with him I am well pleased. Listen to him!"

⁶When the disciples heard this, they fell facedown to the ground, terrified. ⁷But Jesus came and touched them. "Get up," he said. "Don't be afraid." ⁸When they looked up, they saw no one except Jesus.

⁹As they were coming down the mountain, Jesus instructed them, "Don't tell anyone what you have seen, until the Son of Man has been raised from the dead."

¹⁰The disciples asked him, "Why then do the teachers of the law say that Elijah must come first?"

¹¹Jesus replied, "To be sure, Elijah comes and will restore all things. ¹²But I tell you, Elijah has already come, and they did not recognize him, but have done to

ʲ16 Or *Messiah*; also in verse 20   ᵏ18 *Peter* means *rock*.   ˡ18 Or *hell*   ᵐ18 Or *not prove stronger than it*   ⁿ19 Or *have been*
ᵒ25 The Greek word means either *life* or *soul*; also in verse 26.

him everything they wished. In the same way the Son of Man is going to suffer at their hands." [13]Then the disciples understood that he was talking to them about John the Baptist.

[14]When they came to the crowd, a man approached Jesus and knelt before him. [15]"Lord, have mercy on my son," he said. "He has seizures and is suffering greatly. He often falls into the fire or into the water. [16]I brought him to your disciples, but they could not heal him."

[17]"O unbelieving and perverse generation," Jesus replied, "how long shall I stay with you? How long shall I put up with you? Bring the boy here to me." [18]Jesus rebuked the demon, and it came out of the boy, and he was healed from that moment.

[19]Then the disciples came to Jesus in private and asked, "Why couldn't we drive it out?"

[20]He replied, "Because you have so little faith. I tell you the truth, if you have faith as small as a mustard seed, you can say to this mountain, 'Move from here to there' and it will move. Nothing will be impossible for you.[p]"

[22]When they came together in Galilee, he said to them, "The Son of Man is going to be betrayed into the hands of men. [23]They will kill him, and on the third day he will be raised to life." And the disciples were filled with grief.

[24]After Jesus and his disciples arrived in Capernaum, the collectors of the two-drachma tax came to Peter and asked, "Doesn't your teacher pay the temple tax[q]?"

[25]"Yes, he does," he replied.

When Peter came into the house, Jesus was the first to speak. "What do you think, Simon?" he asked. "From whom do the kings of the earth collect duty and taxes—from their own sons or from others?"

[26]"From others," Peter answered.

"Then the sons are exempt," Jesus said to him. [27]"But so that we may not offend them, go to the lake and throw out your line. Take the first fish you catch; open its mouth and you will find a four-drachma coin. Take it and give it to them for my tax and yours."

CHAPTER 18

At that time the disciples came to Jesus and asked, "Who is the greatest in the kingdom of heaven?"

[2]He called a little child and had him stand among them. [3]And he said: "I tell you the truth, unless you change and become like little children, you will never enter the kingdom of heaven. [4]Therefore, whoever humbles himself like this child is the greatest in the kingdom of heaven.

[5]"And whoever welcomes a little child like this in my name welcomes me. [6]But if anyone causes one of these little ones who believe in me to sin, it would be better for him to have a large millstone hung around his neck and to be drowned in the depths of the sea.

[7]"Woe to the world because of the things that cause people to sin! Such things must come, but woe to the man through whom they come! [8]If your hand or your foot causes you to sin, cut it off and throw it away. It is better for you to enter life maimed or crippled than to have two hands or two feet and be thrown into eternal fire. [9]And if your eye causes you to sin, gouge it out and throw it away. It is better for you to enter life with one eye than to have two eyes and be thrown into the fire of hell.

[10]"See that you do not look down on one of these little ones. For I tell you that their angels in heaven always see the face of my Father in heaven.[r]

[12]"What do you think? If a man owns a hundred sheep, and one of them wanders away, will he not leave the ninety-nine on the hills and go to look for the one that wandered off? [13]And if he finds it, I tell you the truth, he is happier about that one sheep than about the ninety-nine that did not wander off. [14]In the same way your Father in heaven is not willing that any of these little ones should be lost.

[15]"If your brother sins against you,[s] go and show him his fault, just between the two of you. If he listens to you, you have won your brother over. [16]But if he will not listen, take one or two others along, so that 'every matter may be established by the testimony of two or three witnesses.'[t] [17]If he refuses to listen to them, tell it to the church; and if he refuses to listen even

---

[p]20 Some manuscripts you. [21]But this kind does not go out except by prayer and fasting.   [q]24 Greek the two drachmas   [r]10 Some manuscripts heaven. [11]The Son of Man came to save what was lost.   [s]15 Some manuscripts do not have against you.
[t]16 Deut. 19:15

to the church, treat him as you would a pagan or a tax collector.

[18]"I tell you the truth, whatever you bind on earth will be[u] bound in heaven, and whatever you loose on earth will be[u] loosed in heaven.

[19]"Again, I tell you that if two of you on earth agree about anything you ask for, it will be done for you by my Father in heaven. [20]For where two or three come together in my name, there am I with them."

[21]Then Peter came to Jesus and asked, "Lord, how many times shall I forgive my brother when he sins against me? Up to seven times?"

[22]Jesus answered, "I tell you, not seven times, but seventy-seven times.[v]

[23]"Therefore, the kingdom of heaven is like a king who wanted to settle accounts with his servants. [24]As he began the settlement, a man who owed him ten thousand talents[w] was brought to him. [25]Since he was not able to pay, the master ordered that he and his wife and his children and all that he had be sold to repay the debt.

[26]"The servant fell on his knees before him. 'Be patient with me,' he begged, 'and I will pay back everything.' [27]The servant's master took pity on him, canceled the debt and let him go.

[28]"But when that servant went out, he found one of his fellow servants who owed him a hundred denarii.[x] He grabbed him and began to choke him. 'Pay back what you owe me!' he demanded.

[29]"His fellow servant fell to his knees and begged him, 'Be patient with me, and I will pay you back.'

[30]"But he refused. Instead, he went off and had the man thrown into prison until he could pay the debt. [31]When the other servants saw what had happened, they were greatly distressed and went and told their master everything that had happened.

[32]"Then the master called the servant in. 'You wicked servant,' he said, 'I canceled all that debt of yours because you begged me to. [33]Shouldn't you have had mercy on your fellow servant just as I had on you?' [34]In anger his master turned him over to

the jailers to be tortured, until he should pay back all he owed.

[35]"This is how my heavenly Father will treat each of you unless you forgive your brother from your heart."

CHAPTER 19

When Jesus had finished saying these things, he left Galilee and went into the region of Judea to the other side of the Jordan. [2]Large crowds followed him, and he healed them there.

[3]Some Pharisees came to him to test him. They asked, "Is it lawful for a man to divorce his wife for any and every reason?"

[4]"Haven't you read," he replied, "that at the beginning the Creator 'made them male and female,'[y] [5]and said, 'For this reason a man will leave his father and mother and be united to his wife, and the two will become one flesh'[z]? [6]So they are no longer two, but one. Therefore what God has joined together, let man not separate."

[7]"Why then," they asked, "did Moses command that a man give his wife a certificate of divorce and send her away?"

[8]Jesus replied, "Moses permitted you to divorce your wives because your hearts were hard. But it was not this way from the beginning. [9]I tell you that anyone who divorces his wife, except for marital unfaithfulness, and marries another woman commits adultery."

[10]The disciples said to him, "If this is the situation between a husband and wife, it is better not to marry."

[11]Jesus replied, "Not everyone can accept this word, but only those to whom it has been given. [12]For some are eunuchs because they were born that way; others were made that way by men; and others have renounced marriage[a] because of the kingdom of heaven. The one who can accept this should accept it."

[13]Then little children were brought to Jesus for him to place his hands on them and pray for them. But the disciples rebuked those who brought them.

[14]Jesus said, "Let the little children come to me, and do not hinder them, for the kingdom of heaven belongs to such as these." [15]When he had placed his hands on them, he went on from there.

---

[u]18 Or have been　　[v]22 Or seventy times seven　　[w]24 That is, millions of dollars　　[x]28 That is, a few dollars　　[y]4 Gen. 1:27
[z]5 Gen. 2:24　　[a]12 Or have made themselves eunuchs

¹⁶Now a man came up to Jesus and asked, "Teacher, what good thing must I do to get eternal life?"

¹⁷"Why do you ask me about what is good?" Jesus replied. "There is only One who is good. If you want to enter life, obey the commandments."

¹⁸"Which ones?" the man inquired.

Jesus replied, " 'Do not murder, do not commit adultery, do not steal, do not give false testimony, ¹⁹honor your father and mother,'^b and 'love your neighbor as yourself.'^c"

²⁰"All these I have kept," the young man said. "What do I still lack?"

²¹Jesus answered, "If you want to be perfect, go, sell your possessions and give to the poor, and you will have treasure in heaven. Then come, follow me."

²²When the young man heard this, he went away sad, because he had great wealth.

²³Then Jesus said to his disciples, "I tell you the truth, it is hard for a rich man to enter the kingdom of heaven. ²⁴Again I tell you, it is easier for a camel to go through the eye of a needle than for a rich man to enter the kingdom of God."

²⁵When the disciples heard this, they were greatly astonished and asked, "Who then can be saved?"

²⁶Jesus looked at them and said, "With man this is impossible, but with God all things are possible."

²⁷Peter answered him, "We have left everything to follow you! What then will there be for us?"

²⁸Jesus said to them, "I tell you the truth, at the renewal of all things, when the Son of Man sits on his glorious throne, you who have followed me will also sit on twelve thrones, judging the twelve tribes of Israel. ²⁹And everyone who has left houses or brothers or sisters or father or mother^d or children or fields for my sake will receive a hundred times as much and will inherit eternal life. ³⁰But many who are first will be last, and many who are last will be first.

^b19 Exodus 20:12-16; Deut. 5:16-20   ^c19 Lev. 19:18   ^d29 Some manuscripts *mother or wife*

OCTOBER 6 ☐ DAY 280
MATTHEW 20–23
More Parables of the King

OVERVIEW Though public opinion regarding Jesus is divided, there can be no mistaking the murderous intent of the scribes and Pharisees. Jesus repeatedly warns his men of the soon coming dark days of his suffering and death (16:21; 20:18–19). Arriving in Jerusalem to a hero's welcome, Jesus is hailed as King while making his entrance into the city. But even in the midst of this joyful reception, he mourns over the fickleness and fate of his countrymen.

Chapter 20	Chapter 21	Chapter 22	Chapter 23
Privilege before the King	Presentation of the King	Tricky Questions from Opponents	Harsh Words for Hypocrites
Haughtiness	Humility	Interrogation	Condemnation

YOUR DAILY WALK A voice of authority (a teacher, parent, boss, church leader) speaks . . . and one of three things happens: (1) Because of *inattention* you fail to hear and heed the leader's words; (2) because of *irritation* you refuse to obey; or (3) because of *conviction* you respond obediently. Which response(s) do you see modeled in the parable of the vineyard (20:1–16)? the parable of the two sons (21:28–32)? the parable of the tenants (21:33–46)?

The more your heart is washed, the more you'll sense its remaining defilement.

God's Word has a way of being irritatingly convicting. You wish you could ignore its truth, but there it is—persistent, penetrating, uncompromising. And until you respond in obedience, you will feel uncomfortable and without peace. Like the Pharisees whom Christ called "blind guides," "hypocrites" and "whitewashed tombs," you will either find a way to silence the Preacher . . . or submit your life to the truth of his sermon!

Is there a burr under your spiritual saddle today? Don't ignore it; God has placed it there for a purpose—to make it too painful *not* to change! So how will you respond?

 INSIGHT Condemned by Jews, Crucified by Gentiles
Jesus' declaration of his coming death (20:18–19) was accurate in every detail. The crime of which Jesus was accused by the Jews—blasphemy—was punishable by death. But since only the Roman civil authorities could execute such a sentence, Jesus was taken before Pilate and Herod—Roman rulers of his day—to gain the necessary permission for his crucifixion.

CHAPTER 20

"For the kingdom of heaven is like a landowner who went out early in the morning to hire men to work in his vineyard. ²He agreed to pay them a denarius for the day and sent them into his vineyard.

³"About the third hour he went out and saw others standing in the marketplace doing nothing. ⁴He told them, 'You also go and work in my vineyard, and I will pay you whatever is right.' ⁵So they went.

"He went out again about the sixth hour and the ninth hour and did the same thing. ⁶About the eleventh hour he went out and found still others standing around. He asked them, 'Why have you been standing here all day long doing nothing?'

⁷" 'Because no one has hired us,' they answered.

"He said to them, 'You also go and work in my vineyard.'

⁸"When evening came, the owner of the vineyard said to his foreman, 'Call the workers and pay them their wages, beginning with the last ones hired and going on to the first.'

⁹"The workers who were hired about the eleventh hour came and each received a denarius. ¹⁰So when those came who were hired first, they expected to receive more. But each one of them also received a denarius. ¹¹When they received it, they began to grumble against the landowner.

¹²'These men who were hired last worked only one hour,' they said, 'and you have made them equal to us who have borne the burden of the work and the heat of the day.'

¹³"But he answered one of them, 'Friend, I am not being unfair to you. Didn't you agree to work for a denarius? ¹⁴Take your pay and go. I want to give the man who was hired last the same as I gave you. ¹⁵Don't I have the right to do what I want with my own money? Or are you envious because I am generous?'

¹⁶"So the last will be first, and the first will be last."

¹⁷Now as Jesus was going up to Jerusalem, he took the twelve disciples aside and said to them, ¹⁸"We are going up to Jerusalem, and the Son of Man will be betrayed to the chief priests and the teachers of the law. They will condemn him to death ¹⁹and will turn him over to the Gentiles to be mocked and flogged and crucified. On the third day he will be raised to life!"

²⁰Then the mother of Zebedee's sons came to Jesus with her sons and, kneeling down, asked a favor of him.

²¹"What is it you want?" he asked.

She said, "Grant that one of these two sons of mine may sit at your right and the other at your left in your kingdom."

²²"You don't know what you are asking," Jesus said to them. "Can you drink the cup I am going to drink?"

"We can," they answered.

²³Jesus said to them, "You will indeed drink from my cup, but to sit at my right or left is not for me to grant. These places

belong to those for whom they have been prepared by my Father."

24When the ten heard about this, they were indignant with the two brothers. 25Jesus called them together and said, "You know that the rulers of the Gentiles lord it over them, and their high officials exercise authority over them. 26Not so with you. Instead, whoever wants to become great among you must be your servant, 27and whoever wants to be first must be your slave— 28just as the Son of Man did not come to be served, but to serve, and to give his life as a ransom for many."

29As Jesus and his disciples were leaving Jericho, a large crowd followed him. 30Two blind men were sitting by the roadside, and when they heard that Jesus was going by, they shouted, "Lord, Son of David, have mercy on us!"

31The crowd rebuked them and told them to be quiet, but they shouted all the louder, "Lord, Son of David, have mercy on us!"

32Jesus stopped and called them. "What do you want me to do for you?" he asked.

33"Lord," they answered, "we want our sight."

34Jesus had compassion on them and touched their eyes. Immediately they received their sight and followed him.

CHAPTER 21
As they approached Jerusalem and came to Bethphage on the Mount of Olives, Jesus sent two disciples, 2saying to them, "Go to the village ahead of you, and at once you will find a donkey tied there, with her colt by her. Untie them and bring them to me. 3If anyone says anything to you, tell him that the Lord needs them, and he will send them right away."

4This took place to fulfill what was spoken through the prophet:

5"Say to the Daughter of Zion,
    'See, your king comes to you,
 gentle and riding on a donkey,
    on a colt, the foal of a donkey.' "e

6The disciples went and did as Jesus had instructed them. 7They brought the donkey and the colt, placed their cloaks on them, and Jesus sat on them. 8A very large crowd spread their cloaks on the road, while others cut branches from the trees and spread them on the road. 9The crowds that went ahead of him and those that followed shouted,

"Hosannaf to the Son of David!"

"Blessed is he who comes in the name
    of the Lord!"g

"Hosannaf in the highest!"

10When Jesus entered Jerusalem, the whole city was stirred and asked, "Who is this?"

11The crowds answered, "This is Jesus, the prophet from Nazareth in Galilee."

12Jesus entered the temple area and drove out all who were buying and selling there. He overturned the tables of the money changers and the benches of those selling doves. 13"It is written," he said to them, " 'My house will be called a house of prayer,'h but you are making it a 'den of robbers.'i"

14The blind and the lame came to him at the temple, and he healed them. 15But when the chief priests and the teachers of the law saw the wonderful things he did and the children shouting in the temple area, "Hosanna to the Son of David," they were indignant.

16"Do you hear what these children are saying?" they asked him.

"Yes," replied Jesus, "have you never read,

" 'From the lips of children and infants
    you have ordained praise'j?"

17And he left them and went out of the city to Bethany, where he spent the night.

18Early in the morning, as he was on his way back to the city, he was hungry. 19Seeing a fig tree by the road, he went up to it but found nothing on it except leaves. Then he said to it, "May you never bear fruit again!" Immediately the tree withered.

20When the disciples saw this, they were amazed. "How did the fig tree wither so quickly?" they asked.

21Jesus replied, "I tell you the truth, if you have faith and do not doubt, not only can you do what was done to the fig tree, but also you can say to this mountain, 'Go, throw yourself into the sea,' and it

e5 Zech. 9:9   f9 A Hebrew expression meaning "Save!" which became an exclamation of praise; also in verse 15
g9 Psalm 118:26   h13 Isaiah 56:7   i13 Jer. 7:11   j16 Psalm 8:2

will be done. ²²If you believe, you will receive whatever you ask for in prayer."

²³Jesus entered the temple courts, and, while he was teaching, the chief priests and the elders of the people came to him. "By what authority are you doing these things?" they asked. "And who gave you this authority?"

²⁴Jesus replied, "I will also ask you one question. If you answer me, I will tell you by what authority I am doing these things. ²⁵John's baptism—where did it come from? Was it from heaven, or from men?"

They discussed it among themselves and said, "If we say, 'From heaven,' he will ask, 'Then why didn't you believe him?' ²⁶But if we say, 'From men'—we are afraid of the people, for they all hold that John was a prophet."

²⁷So they answered Jesus, "We don't know."

Then he said, "Neither will I tell you by what authority I am doing these things.

²⁸"What do you think? There was a man who had two sons. He went to the first and said, 'Son, go and work today in the vineyard.'

²⁹" 'I will not,' he answered, but later he changed his mind and went.

³⁰"Then the father went to the other son and said the same thing. He answered, 'I will, sir,' but he did not go.

³¹"Which of the two did what his father wanted?"

"The first," they answered.

Jesus said to them, "I tell you the truth, the tax collectors and the prostitutes are entering the kingdom of God ahead of you. ³²For John came to you to show you the way of righteousness, and you did not believe him, but the tax collectors and the prostitutes did. And even after you saw this, you did not repent and believe him.

³³"Listen to another parable: There was a landowner who planted a vineyard. He put a wall around it, dug a winepress in it and built a watchtower. Then he rented the vineyard to some farmers and went away on a journey. ³⁴When the harvest time approached, he sent his servants to the tenants to collect his fruit.

³⁵"The tenants seized his servants; they beat one, killed another, and stoned a third. ³⁶Then he sent other servants to them, more than the first time, and the tenants treated them the same way. ³⁷Last of all, he sent his son to them. 'They will respect my son,' he said.

³⁸"But when the tenants saw the son, they said to each other, 'This is the heir. Come, let's kill him and take his inheritance.' ³⁹So they took him and threw him out of the vineyard and killed him.

⁴⁰"Therefore, when the owner of the vineyard comes, what will he do to those tenants?"

⁴¹"He will bring those wretches to a wretched end," they replied, "and he will rent the vineyard to other tenants, who will give him his share of the crop at harvest time."

⁴²Jesus said to them, "Have you never read in the Scriptures:

" 'The stone the builders rejected
   has become the capstone*ᵏ*;
the Lord has done this,
   and it is marvelous in our eyes'*ˡ*?

⁴³"Therefore I tell you that the kingdom of God will be taken away from you and given to a people who will produce its fruit. ⁴⁴He who falls on this stone will be broken to pieces, but he on whom it falls will be crushed." *ᵐ*

⁴⁵When the chief priests and the Pharisees heard Jesus' parables, they knew he was talking about them. ⁴⁶They looked for a way to arrest him, but they were afraid of the crowd because the people held that he was a prophet.

CHAPTER 22
Jesus spoke to them again in parables, saying: ²"The kingdom of heaven is like a king who prepared a wedding banquet for his son. ³He sent his servants to those who had been invited to the banquet to tell them to come, but they refused to come.

⁴"Then he sent some more servants and said, 'Tell those who have been invited that I have prepared my dinner: My oxen and fattened cattle have been butchered, and everything is ready. Come to the wedding banquet.'

⁵"But they paid no attention and went

ᵏ42 Or *cornerstone*   ˡ42 Psalm 118:22,23   ᵐ44 Some manuscripts do not have verse 44.

off—one to his field, another to his business. ⁶The rest seized his servants, mistreated them and killed them. ⁷The king was enraged. He sent his army and destroyed those murderers and burned their city.

⁸"Then he said to his servants, 'The wedding banquet is ready, but those I invited did not deserve to come. ⁹Go to the street corners and invite to the banquet anyone you find.' ¹⁰So the servants went out into the streets and gathered all the people they could find, both good and bad, and the wedding hall was filled with guests.

¹¹"But when the king came in to see the guests, he noticed a man there who was not wearing wedding clothes. ¹²'Friend,' he asked, 'how did you get in here without wedding clothes?' The man was speechless.

¹³"Then the king told the attendants, 'Tie him hand and foot, and throw him outside, into the darkness, where there will be weeping and gnashing of teeth.'

¹⁴"For many are invited, but few are chosen."

¹⁵Then the Pharisees went out and laid plans to trap him in his words. ¹⁶They sent their disciples to him along with the Herodians. "Teacher," they said, "we know you are a man of integrity and that you teach the way of God in accordance with the truth. You aren't swayed by men, because you pay no attention to who they are. ¹⁷Tell us then, what is your opinion? Is it right to pay taxes to Caesar or not?"

¹⁸But Jesus, knowing their evil intent, said, "You hypocrites, why are you trying to trap me? ¹⁹Show me the coin used for paying the tax." They brought him a denarius, ²⁰and he asked them, "Whose portrait is this? And whose inscription?"

²¹"Caesar's," they replied.

Then he said to them, "Give to Caesar what is Caesar's, and to God what is God's."

²²When they heard this, they were amazed. So they left him and went away.

²³That same day the Sadducees, who say there is no resurrection, came to him with a question. ²⁴"Teacher," they said, "Moses told us that if a man dies without having children, his brother must marry the widow and have children for him.

²⁵Now there were seven brothers among us. The first one married and died, and since he had no children, he left his wife to his brother. ²⁶The same thing happened to the second and third brother, right on down to the seventh. ²⁷Finally, the woman died. ²⁸Now then, at the resurrection, whose wife will she be of the seven, since all of them were married to her?"

²⁹Jesus replied, "You are in error because you do not know the Scriptures or the power of God. ³⁰At the resurrection people will neither marry nor be given in marriage; they will be like the angels in heaven. ³¹But about the resurrection of the dead—have you not read what God said to you, ³²'I am the God of Abraham, the God of Isaac, and the God of Jacob'ⁿ? He is not the God of the dead but of the living."

³³When the crowds heard this, they were astonished at his teaching.

³⁴Hearing that Jesus had silenced the Sadducees, the Pharisees got together. ³⁵One of them, an expert in the law, tested him with this question: ³⁶"Teacher, which is the greatest commandment in the Law?"

³⁷Jesus replied: " 'Love the Lord your God with all your heart and with all your soul and with all your mind.'ᵒ ³⁸This is the first and greatest commandment. ³⁹And the second is like it: 'Love your neighbor as yourself.'ᵖ ⁴⁰All the Law and the Prophets hang on these two commandments."

⁴¹While the Pharisees were gathered together, Jesus asked them, ⁴²"What do you think about the Christ۹? Whose son is he?"

"The son of David," they replied.

⁴³He said to them, "How is it then that David, speaking by the Spirit, calls him 'Lord'? For he says,

⁴⁴" 'The Lord said to my Lord:
    "Sit at my right hand
until I put your enemies
    under your feet." 'ʳ

⁴⁵If then David calls him 'Lord,' how can he be his son?" ⁴⁶No one could say a word in reply, and from that day on no one dared to ask him any more questions.

ⁿ32 Exodus 3:6   ᵒ37 Deut. 6:5   ᵖ39 Lev. 19:18   ۹42 Or *Messiah*   ʳ44 Psalm 110:1

CHAPTER 23

Then Jesus said to the crowds and to his disciples: 2"The teachers of the law and the Pharisees sit in Moses' seat. 3So you must obey them and do everything they tell you. But do not do what they do, for they do not practice what they preach. 4They tie up heavy loads and put them on men's shoulders, but they themselves are not willing to lift a finger to move them.

5"Everything they do is done for men to see: They make their phylacteries[s] wide and the tassels on their garments long; 6they love the place of honor at banquets and the most important seats in the synagogues; 7they love to be greeted in the marketplaces and to have men call them 'Rabbi.'

8"But you are not to be called 'Rabbi,' for you have only one Master and you are all brothers. 9And do not call anyone on earth 'father,' for you have one Father, and he is in heaven. 10Nor are you to be called 'teacher,' for you have one Teacher, the Christ.[t] 11The greatest among you will be your servant. 12For whoever exalts himself will be humbled, and whoever humbles himself will be exalted.

13"Woe to you, teachers of the law and Pharisees, you hypocrites! You shut the kingdom of heaven in men's faces. You yourselves do not enter, nor will you let those enter who are trying to.[u]

15"Woe to you, teachers of the law and Pharisees, you hypocrites! You travel over land and sea to win a single convert, and when he becomes one, you make him twice as much a son of hell as you are.

16"Woe to you, blind guides! You say, 'If anyone swears by the temple, it means nothing; but if anyone swears by the gold of the temple, he is bound by his oath.' 17You blind fools! Which is greater: the gold, or the temple that makes the gold sacred? 18You also say, 'If anyone swears by the altar, it means nothing; but if anyone swears by the gift on it, he is bound by his oath.' 19You blind men! Which is greater: the gift, or the altar that makes the gift sacred? 20Therefore, he who swears by the altar swears by it and by

everything on it. 21And he who swears by the temple swears by it and by the one who dwells in it. 22And he who swears by heaven swears by God's throne and by the one who sits on it.

23"Woe to you, teachers of the law and Pharisees, you hypocrites! You give a tenth of your spices—mint, dill and cummin. But you have neglected the more important matters of the law—justice, mercy and faithfulness. You should have practiced the latter, without neglecting the former. 24You blind guides! You strain out a gnat but swallow a camel.

25"Woe to you, teachers of the law and Pharisees, you hypocrites! You clean the outside of the cup and dish, but inside they are full of greed and self-indulgence. 26Blind Pharisee! First clean the inside of the cup and dish, and then the outside also will be clean.

27"Woe to you, teachers of the law and Pharisees, you hypocrites! You are like whitewashed tombs, which look beautiful on the outside but on the inside are full of dead men's bones and everything unclean. 28In the same way, on the outside you appear to people as righteous but on the inside you are full of hypocrisy and wickedness.

29"Woe to you, teachers of the law and Pharisees, you hypocrites! You build tombs for the prophets and decorate the graves of the righteous. 30And you say, 'If we had lived in the days of our forefathers, we would not have taken part with them in shedding the blood of the prophets.' 31So you testify against yourselves that you are the descendants of those who murdered the prophets. 32Fill up, then, the measure of the sin of your forefathers!

33"You snakes! You brood of vipers! How will you escape being condemned to hell? 34Therefore I am sending you prophets and wise men and teachers. Some of them you will kill and crucify; others you will flog in your synagogues and pursue from town to town. 35And so upon you will come all the righteous blood that has been shed on earth, from the blood of righteous Abel to the blood of Zechariah son of Berekiah, whom you

---

[s] 5 That is, boxes containing Scripture verses, worn on forehead and arm   [t] 10 Or Messiah   [u] 13 Some manuscripts to. 14Woe to you, teachers of the law and Pharisees, you hypocrites! You devour widows' houses and for a show make lengthy prayers. Therefore you will be punished more severely.

murdered between the temple and the altar. ³⁶I tell you the truth, all this will come upon this generation.

³⁷"O Jerusalem, Jerusalem, you who kill the prophets and stone those sent to you, how often I have longed to gather your children together, as a hen gathers her chicks under her wings, but you were not willing. ³⁸Look, your house is left to you desolate. ³⁹For I tell you, you will not see me again until you say, 'Blessed is he who comes in the name of the Lord.'ᵛ"

ᵛ39 Psalm 118:26

OCTOBER 7 ☐ DAY 281
Something Old, Something New

LOOK BACK "The Old is in the New revealed; the New is in the Old concealed." With those words, one poet has attempted to explain the relationship between the two halves of the Bible. The Old Testament prophets provided hundreds of details about the coming Messiah: where he would be born, how he would be born, how he would live, how he would die and what would be accomplished by his death. Now as you read the book of Matthew, you will see predictions that were *concealed* in the Old Testament and *revealed* in the New Testament.

Matthew, a Jewish tax collector, writes to a Jewish audience presenting Jesus as the promised King of the Jews. As with any king, his genealogy, upbringing and demeanor come under intense scrutiny to determine whether he has the qualifications to be king. By word and deed, by public miracle and private message, Jesus validates his credentials, setting the stage for the dramatic conclusion of his earthly life and mission.

We are never alone when we are alone with Jesus.

LOOK UP Find the last verse in the Old Testament. Write the reference to it here: _____

Now find the first verse in the New Testament. Write the reference to it here: _____

How far apart are those two verses in your Bible? In terms of inches, the answer may be as short as the thickness of one or two sheets of paper. But in terms of time, between Malachi 4:6 and Matthew 1:1 there is an "intermission" of no less than four hundred years! Four long centuries come and go before the silence that begins with the last verse of Malachi is broken by the first verse of Matthew.

Galatians 4:4 tells us why the long intermission was necessary between the close of the Old Testament and the opening of the New Testament. "But when the time had fully come, God sent his Son. . . ." Like a pregnant woman awaiting the precise moment when her child is due to enter the world, so God was awaiting the precise moment when the world was uniquely prepared for the coming of his Son.

If the good news of his coming was to spread quickly around the world, there had to be a language common to all. And there was! It was called Koine Greek.

If the good news of his coming was to be carried to the farthest corners of the known world, there had to be an extensive network of roads. And there was! The Roman legions had seen to that.

LOOK AHEAD If Jesus were walking the earth in bodily form today instead of in the first century A.D., just think what a stir his presence would create! Imagine how many television cameras would follow his every move . . . how many talk shows would clamor for interviews . . . the crowds that would shadow his every step.

But God knew that the perfect moment for his Son to enter human history was not the twentieth (or twenty-first!) century but the first. As you continue to read about Jesus' encounters with men and women, boys and girls, don't overlook the fact that today he longs to welcome all who will come to him in childlike faith (Matthew 19:14). His arms are open . . . to you!

OCTOBER 8 ☐ DAY 282
MATTHEW 24–25
Predictions of the King

 OVERVIEW Prominent in Jesus' day was the magnificent temple of Herod. The disciples, duly impressed with its immense splendor, are stunned by Jesus' words that it will one day lie in rubble. This naturally raises questions in their minds regarding how and when such destruction will occur—an occasion Jesus seizes upon to teach them about events even more significant than the conquest of Jerusalem. He goes on to instruct them about his future second coming to earth and the unmistakable signs preceding it.

Chapter 24		Chapter 25
Predictions of Coming Calamity	Preparation for Coming Calamity	Parables of the Kingdom of Heaven
"Beware!"	"Be Watchful!"	"Be Working!"

 YOUR DAILY WALK It has been well said, "A person can live forty days without food, seven days without water, and a few minutes without air; but he cannot live one second without hope."

There is no medicine like hope—the expectation that tomorrow will be better than today. And for the Christian, that hope is no idle dream. Your future can brim with expectation because of Jesus' promise, "I will come back" (John 14:3). But in the meantime, you need the daily reminder and encouragement that your waiting is not in vain. In Jesus' response to his disciples' questions, he offers several principles to help them—and you—pass the time until his return:

"Hope" is biblical shorthand for "unconditional certainty."

1. Don't get sidetracked (24:4). False christs will abound, but there will be no doubt when Jesus returns (24:24–31).

2. Don't become a date-setter (24:36). Only God himself knows when that great event will happen.

3. Do be a wise steward of your time and opportunities (24:14, 45–46). God wants you to sow seed, not scan the horizon!

On your appointment calendar, pick a date later in October and add this memo line: "It's later than it's ever been before. Am I more prepared than I've ever been before?"

 INSIGHT Something Old, Something New
Chapters 20–23 employ at least eleven quotations from the Old Testament. All together, Matthew contains about seventy-four such quotations and allusions—more than any other New Testament book.

CHAPTER 24

Jesus left the temple and was walking away when his disciples came up to him to call his attention to its buildings. 2"Do you see all these things?" he asked. "I tell you the truth, not one stone here will be left on another; every one will be thrown down."

3As Jesus was sitting on the Mount of Olives, the disciples came to him privately. "Tell us," they said, "when will this happen, and what will be the sign of your coming and of the end of the age?"

4Jesus answered: "Watch out that no one deceives you. 5For many will come in my name, claiming, 'I am the Christ,ʷ' and will deceive many. 6You will hear of wars and rumors of wars, but see to it that you are not alarmed. Such things must happen, but the end is still to come. 7Nation will rise against nation, and kingdom against kingdom. There will be famines and earthquakes in various places. 8All these are the beginning of birth pains.

9"Then you will be handed over to be persecuted and put to death, and you will be hated by all nations because of me. 10At that time many will turn away from the faith and will betray and hate each other, 11and many false prophets will appear and deceive many people. 12Because of the increase of wickedness, the love of most will grow cold, 13but he who stands firm to the end will be saved. 14And this gospel of the kingdom will be preached in the whole world as a testimony to all nations, and then the end will come.

15"So when you see standing in the holy place 'the abomination that causes desolation,'ˣ spoken of through the prophet Daniel—let the reader understand—16then let those who are in Judea flee to the mountains. 17Let no one on the roof of his house go down to take anything out of the house. 18Let no one in the field go back to get his cloak. 19How dreadful it will be in those days for pregnant women and nursing mothers! 20Pray that your flight will not take place in winter or on the Sabbath. 21For then there will be great distress, unequaled from the beginning of the world until now—and never to be equaled again. 22If those days had not been cut short, no one would survive, but for the sake of the elect those days will be

shortened. 23At that time if anyone says to you, 'Look, here is the Christ!' or, 'There he is!' do not believe it. 24For false Christs and false prophets will appear and perform great signs and miracles to deceive even the elect—if that were possible. 25See, I have told you ahead of time.

26"So if anyone tells you, 'There he is, out in the desert,' do not go out; or, 'Here he is, in the inner rooms,' do not believe it. 27For as lightning that comes from the east is visible even in the west, so will be the coming of the Son of Man. 28Wherever there is a carcass, there the vultures will gather.

29"Immediately after the distress of those days

" 'the sun will be darkened,
    and the moon will not give its light;
the stars will fall from the sky,
    and the heavenly bodies will be
        shaken.'ʸ

30"At that time the sign of the Son of Man will appear in the sky, and all the nations of the earth will mourn. They will see the Son of Man coming on the clouds of the sky, with power and great glory. 31And he will send his angels with a loud trumpet call, and they will gather his elect from the four winds, from one end of the heavens to the other.

32"Now learn this lesson from the fig tree: As soon as its twigs get tender and its leaves come out, you know that summer is near. 33Even so, when you see all these things, you know that itᶻ is near, right at the door. 34I tell you the truth, this generationᵃ will certainly not pass away until all these things have happened. 35Heaven and earth will pass away, but my words will never pass away.

36"No one knows about that day or hour, not even the angels in heaven, nor the Son,ᵇ but only the Father. 37As it was in the days of Noah, so it will be at the coming of the Son of Man. 38For in the days before the flood, people were eating and drinking, marrying and giving in marriage, up to the day Noah entered the ark; 39and they knew nothing about what would happen until the flood came and took them all away. That is how it will be at the coming of the Son of Man. 40Two men will be in the field; one will be taken and the other left. ⁴¹Two women will be grinding with a hand mill; one will be taken and the other left.

⁴²"Therefore keep watch, because you do not know on what day your Lord will come. ⁴³But understand this: If the owner of the house had known at what time of night the thief was coming, he would have kept watch and would not have let his house be broken into. ⁴⁴So you also must be ready, because the Son of Man will come at an hour when you do not expect him.

⁴⁵"Who then is the faithful and wise servant, whom the master has put in charge of the servants in his household to give them their food at the proper time? ⁴⁶It will be good for that servant whose master finds him doing so when he returns. ⁴⁷I tell you the truth, he will put him in charge of all his possessions. ⁴⁸But suppose that servant is wicked and says to himself, 'My master is staying away a long time,' ⁴⁹and he then begins to beat his fellow servants and to eat and drink with drunkards. ⁵⁰The master of that servant will come on a day when he does not expect him and at an hour he is not aware of. ⁵¹He will cut him to pieces and assign him a place with the hypocrites, where there will be weeping and gnashing of teeth.

CHAPTER 25

"At that time the kingdom of heaven will be like ten virgins who took their lamps and went out to meet the bridegroom. ²Five of them were foolish and five were wise. ³The foolish ones took their lamps but did not take any oil with them. ⁴The wise, however, took oil in jars along with their lamps. ⁵The bridegroom was a long time in coming, and they all became drowsy and fell asleep.

⁶"At midnight the cry rang out: 'Here's the bridegroom! Come out to meet him!'

⁷"Then all the virgins woke up and trimmed their lamps. ⁸The foolish ones said to the wise, 'Give us some of your oil; our lamps are going out.'

⁹" 'No,' they replied, 'there may not be enough for both us and you. Instead, go to those who sell oil and buy some for yourselves.'

¹⁰"But while they were on their way to buy the oil, the bridegroom arrived. The virgins who were ready went in with him to the wedding banquet. And the door was shut.

¹¹"Later the others also came. 'Sir! Sir!' they said. 'Open the door for us!'

¹²"But he replied, 'I tell you the truth, I don't know you.'

¹³"Therefore keep watch, because you do not know the day or the hour.

¹⁴"Again, it will be like a man going on a journey, who called his servants and entrusted his property to them. ¹⁵To one he gave five talents^c of money, to another two talents, and to another one talent, each according to his ability. Then he went on his journey. ¹⁶The man who had received the five talents went at once and put his money to work and gained five more. ¹⁷So also, the one with the two talents gained two more. ¹⁸But the man who had received the one talent went off, dug a hole in the ground and hid his master's money.

¹⁹"After a long time the master of those servants returned and settled accounts with them. ²⁰The man who had received the five talents brought the other five. 'Master,' he said, 'you entrusted me with five talents. See, I have gained five more.'

²¹"His master replied, 'Well done, good and faithful servant! You have been faithful with a few things; I will put you in charge of many things. Come and share your master's happiness!'

²²"The man with the two talents also came. 'Master,' he said, 'you entrusted me with two talents; see, I have gained two more.'

²³"His master replied, 'Well done, good and faithful servant! You have been faithful with a few things; I will put you in charge of many things. Come and share your master's happiness!'

²⁴"Then the man who had received the one talent came. 'Master,' he said, 'I knew that you are a hard man, harvesting where you have not sown and gathering where you have not scattered seed. ²⁵So I was afraid and went out and hid your talent in the ground. See, here is what belongs to you.'

²⁶"His master replied, 'You wicked, lazy servant! So you knew that I harvest where I have not sown and gather where I have

^{c}15 A talent was worth more than a thousand dollars.

not scattered seed? ²⁷Well then, you should have put my money on deposit with the bankers, so that when I returned I would have received it back with interest.

²⁸" 'Take the talent from him and give it to the one who has the ten talents. ²⁹For everyone who has will be given more, and he will have an abundance. Whoever does not have, even what he has will be taken from him. ³⁰And throw that worthless servant outside, into the darkness, where there will be weeping and gnashing of teeth.'

³¹"When the Son of Man comes in his glory, and all the angels with him, he will sit on his throne in heavenly glory. ³²All the nations will be gathered before him, and he will separate the people one from another as a shepherd separates the sheep from the goats. ³³He will put the sheep on his right and the goats on his left.

³⁴"Then the King will say to those on his right, 'Come, you who are blessed by my Father; take your inheritance, the kingdom prepared for you since the creation of the world. ³⁵For I was hungry and you gave me something to eat, I was thirsty and you gave me something to drink, I was a stranger and you invited me in, ³⁶I needed clothes and you clothed me, I was sick and you looked after me, I was in prison and you came to visit me.'

³⁷"Then the righteous will answer him, 'Lord, when did we see you hungry and feed you, or thirsty and give you something to drink? ³⁸When did we see you a stranger and invite you in, or needing clothes and clothe you? ³⁹When did we see you sick or in prison and go to visit you?'

⁴⁰"The King will reply, 'I tell you the truth, whatever you did for one of the least of these brothers of mine, you did for me.'

⁴¹"Then he will say to those on his left, 'Depart from me, you who are cursed, into the eternal fire prepared for the devil and his angels. ⁴²For I was hungry and you gave me nothing to eat, I was thirsty and you gave me nothing to drink, ⁴³I was a stranger and you did not invite me in, I needed clothes and you did not clothe me, I was sick and in prison and you did not look after me.'

⁴⁴"They also will answer, 'Lord, when did we see you hungry or thirsty or a stranger or needing clothes or sick or in prison, and did not help you?'

⁴⁵"He will reply, 'I tell you the truth, whatever you did not do for one of the least of these, you did not do for me.'

⁴⁶"Then they will go away to eternal punishment, but the righteous to eternal life."

OCTOBER 9 ☐ DAY 283
MATTHEW 26–28
Passion of the King

 OVERVIEW The one who only days before was hailed as King now experiences arrest, scourging, ridicule and crucifixion as "criminal." His royal title hangs in mockery from the top of his rugged cross. And in his death, he fulfills more Old Testament prophecies than he did in his lifetime. Not one of his bones is broken, as befitting the Passover lamb. And at the moment of his death, the veil in the temple is split from top to bottom, indicating free and unlimited access to God through him. Buried in haste in a borrowed tomb and mourned by his followers for three dark days, he rises in victory at dawn on that first Easter morning, later commissioning all who have put their saving trust in him to go and teach all nations (28:19–20).

Chapter 26	Chapter 27	Chapter 28
The King's Last Supper	The King's Crucifixion	The King's Resurrection
Passover	Passion	Proclamation

YOUR DAILY WALK Perhaps the worst time to celebrate Christmas is at Christmas!

Why? Because the truth of that great event all too often gets lost in the tinsel and trappings.

Death died when Christ arose.

Similarly, the worst time to celebrate Easter is when the bunnies, baskets and bonnets are in abundance! Which means right now would be a wonderful time to celebrate the resurrection!

Don't hurry through today's reading. The story of Jesus' crucifixion is one of the most graphic depictions of love ever penned. Ask the Holy Spirit to take the familiar phrases of the Calvary story and infuse them with fresh meaning and life for you. If you can, read the three chapters in today's section straight through at a single sitting. Then, with your Bible open and your heart brimming with gratitude, offer God a sacrifice of praise for the Savior, whose suffering and death made it all possible. "He has risen from the dead" (28:7), so rejoice!

INSIGHT Taunting the King with the Truth

Over the head of every victim of Roman crucifixion was inscribed his crime. In Jesus' case the indictment was made in mockery: "THIS IS JESUS, THE KING OF THE JEWS" (27:37). How little did the unbelieving soldiers realize the truth of their taunt!

C H A P T E R   2 6

When Jesus had finished saying all these things, he said to his disciples, 2"As you know, the Passover is two days away—and the Son of Man will be handed over to be crucified."

3Then the chief priests and the elders of the people assembled in the palace of the high priest, whose name was Caiaphas, 4and they plotted to arrest Jesus in some sly way and kill him. 5"But not during the Feast," they said, "or there may be a riot among the people."

6While Jesus was in Bethany in the home of a man known as Simon the Leper, 7a woman came to him with an alabaster jar of very expensive perfume, which she poured on his head as he was reclining at the table.

8When the disciples saw this, they were indignant. "Why this waste?" they asked. 9"This perfume could have been sold at a high price and the money given to the poor."

10Aware of this, Jesus said to them, "Why are you bothering this woman? She has done a beautiful thing to me. 11The poor you will always have with you, but

you will not always have me. 12When she poured this perfume on my body, she did it to prepare me for burial. 13I tell you the truth, wherever this gospel is preached throughout the world, what she has done will also be told, in memory of her."

14Then one of the Twelve—the one called Judas Iscariot—went to the chief priests 15and asked, "What are you willing to give me if I hand him over to you?" So they counted out for him thirty silver coins. 16From then on Judas watched for an opportunity to hand him over.

17On the first day of the Feast of Unleavened Bread, the disciples came to Jesus and asked, "Where do you want us to make preparations for you to eat the Passover?"

18He replied, "Go into the city to a certain man and tell him, 'The Teacher says: My appointed time is near. I am going to celebrate the Passover with my disciples at your house.' " 19So the disciples did as Jesus had directed them and prepared the Passover.

20When evening came, Jesus was reclining at the table with the Twelve. 21And while they were eating, he said, "I tell you the truth, one of you will betray me."

²²They were very sad and began to say to him one after the other, "Surely not I, Lord?"

²³Jesus replied, "The one who has dipped his hand into the bowl with me will betray me. ²⁴The Son of Man will go just as it is written about him. But woe to that man who betrays the Son of Man! It would be better for him if he had not been born."

²⁵Then Judas, the one who would betray him, said, "Surely not I, Rabbi?"

Jesus answered, "Yes, it is you."ᵈ

²⁶While they were eating, Jesus took bread, gave thanks and broke it, and gave it to his disciples, saying, "Take and eat; this is my body."

²⁷Then he took the cup, gave thanks and offered it to them, saying, "Drink from it, all of you. ²⁸This is my blood of theᵉ covenant, which is poured out for many for the forgiveness of sins. ²⁹I tell you, I will not drink of this fruit of the vine from now on until that day when I drink it anew with you in my Father's kingdom."

³⁰When they had sung a hymn, they went out to the Mount of Olives.

³¹Then Jesus told them, "This very night you will all fall away on account of me, for it is written:

" 'I will strike the shepherd,
    and the sheep of the flock will be
        scattered.'ᶠ

³²But after I have risen, I will go ahead of you into Galilee."

³³Peter replied, "Even if all fall away on account of you, I never will."

³⁴"I tell you the truth," Jesus answered, "this very night, before the rooster crows, you will disown me three times."

³⁵But Peter declared, "Even if I have to die with you, I will never disown you." And all the other disciples said the same.

³⁶Then Jesus went with his disciples to a place called Gethsemane, and he said to them, "Sit here while I go over there and pray." ³⁷He took Peter and the two sons of Zebedee along with him, and he began to be sorrowful and troubled. ³⁸Then he said to them, "My soul is overwhelmed with sorrow to the point of death. Stay here and keep watch with me."

³⁹Going a little farther, he fell with his face to the ground and prayed, "My Father, if it is possible, may this cup be taken from me. Yet not as I will, but as you will."

⁴⁰Then he returned to his disciples and found them sleeping. "Could you men not keep watch with me for one hour?" he asked Peter. ⁴¹"Watch and pray so that you will not fall into temptation. The spirit is willing, but the body is weak."

⁴²He went away a second time and prayed, "My Father, if it is not possible for this cup to be taken away unless I drink it, may your will be done."

⁴³When he came back, he again found them sleeping, because their eyes were heavy. ⁴⁴So he left them and went away once more and prayed the third time, saying the same thing.

⁴⁵Then he returned to the disciples and said to them, "Are you still sleeping and resting? Look, the hour is near, and the Son of Man is betrayed into the hands of sinners. ⁴⁶Rise, let us go! Here comes my betrayer!"

⁴⁷While he was still speaking, Judas, one of the Twelve, arrived. With him was a large crowd armed with swords and clubs, sent from the chief priests and the elders of the people. ⁴⁸Now the betrayer had arranged a signal with them: "The one I kiss is the man; arrest him." ⁴⁹Going at once to Jesus, Judas said, "Greetings, Rabbi!" and kissed him.

⁵⁰Jesus replied, "Friend, do what you came for."ᵍ

Then the men stepped forward, seized Jesus and arrested him. ⁵¹With that, one of Jesus' companions reached for his sword, drew it out and struck the servant of the high priest, cutting off his ear.

⁵²"Put your sword back in its place," Jesus said to him, "for all who draw the sword will die by the sword. ⁵³Do you think I cannot call on my Father, and he will at once put at my disposal more than twelve legions of angels? ⁵⁴But how then would the Scriptures be fulfilled that say it must happen in this way?"

⁵⁵At that time Jesus said to the crowd, "Am I leading a rebellion, that you have come out with swords and clubs to cap-

ᵈ25 Or "You yourself have said it"   ᵉ28 Some manuscripts the new   ᶠ31 Zech. 13:7   ᵍ50 Or "Friend, why have you come?"

ture me? Every day I sat in the temple courts teaching, and you did not arrest me. ⁵⁶But this has all taken place that the writings of the prophets might be fulfilled." Then all the disciples deserted him and fled.

⁵⁷Those who had arrested Jesus took him to Caiaphas, the high priest, where the teachers of the law and the elders had assembled. ⁵⁸But Peter followed him at a distance, right up to the courtyard of the high priest. He entered and sat down with the guards to see the outcome.

⁵⁹The chief priests and the whole Sanhedrin were looking for false evidence against Jesus so that they could put him to death. ⁶⁰But they did not find any, though many false witnesses came forward.

Finally two came forward ⁶¹and declared, "This fellow said, 'I am able to destroy the temple of God and rebuild it in three days.'"

⁶²Then the high priest stood up and said to Jesus, "Are you not going to answer? What is this testimony that these men are bringing against you?" ⁶³But Jesus remained silent.

The high priest said to him, "I charge you under oath by the living God: Tell us if you are the Christ,ʰ the Son of God."

⁶⁴"Yes, it is as you say," Jesus replied. "But I say to all of you: In the future you will see the Son of Man sitting at the right hand of the Mighty One and coming on the clouds of heaven."

⁶⁵Then the high priest tore his clothes and said, "He has spoken blasphemy! Why do we need any more witnesses? Look, now you have heard the blasphemy. ⁶⁶What do you think?"

"He is worthy of death," they answered.

⁶⁷Then they spit in his face and struck him with their fists. Others slapped him ⁶⁸and said, "Prophesy to us, Christ. Who hit you?"

⁶⁹Now Peter was sitting out in the courtyard, and a servant girl came to him. "You also were with Jesus of Galilee," she said.

⁷⁰But he denied it before them all. "I don't know what you're talking about," he said.

⁷¹Then he went out to the gateway, where another girl saw him and said to the people there, "This fellow was with Jesus of Nazareth."

⁷²He denied it again, with an oath: "I don't know the man!"

⁷³After a little while, those standing there went up to Peter and said, "Surely you are one of them, for your accent gives you away."

⁷⁴Then he began to call down curses on himself and he swore to them, "I don't know the man!"

Immediately a rooster crowed. ⁷⁵Then Peter remembered the word Jesus had spoken: "Before the rooster crows, you will disown me three times." And he went outside and wept bitterly.

CHAPTER 27

Early in the morning, all the chief priests and the elders of the people came to the decision to put Jesus to death. ²They bound him, led him away and handed him over to Pilate, the governor.

³When Judas, who had betrayed him, saw that Jesus was condemned, he was seized with remorse and returned the thirty silver coins to the chief priests and the elders. ⁴"I have sinned," he said, "for I have betrayed innocent blood."

"What is that to us?" they replied. "That's your responsibility."

⁵So Judas threw the money into the temple and left. Then he went away and hanged himself.

⁶The chief priests picked up the coins and said, "It is against the law to put this into the treasury, since it is blood money." ⁷So they decided to use the money to buy the potter's field as a burial place for foreigners. ⁸That is why it has been called the Field of Blood to this day. ⁹Then what was spoken by Jeremiah the prophet was fulfilled: "They took the thirty silver coins, the price set on him by the people of Israel, ¹⁰and they used them to buy the potter's field, as the Lord commanded me."ⁱ

¹¹Meanwhile Jesus stood before the governor, and the governor asked him, "Are you the king of the Jews?"

"Yes, it is as you say," Jesus replied.

¹²When he was accused by the chief priests and the elders, he gave no answer. ¹³Then Pilate asked him, "Don't you hear the testimony they are bringing against you?" ¹⁴But Jesus made no reply, not even

ʰ63 Or Messiah; also in verse 68   ⁱ10 See Zech. 11:12,13; Jer. 19:1-13; 32:6-9.

to a single charge—to the great amazement of the governor.

¹⁵Now it was the governor's custom at the Feast to release a prisoner chosen by the crowd. ¹⁶At that time they had a notorious prisoner, called Barabbas. ¹⁷So when the crowd had gathered, Pilate asked them, "Which one do you want me to release to you: Barabbas, or Jesus who is called Christ?" ¹⁸For he knew it was out of envy that they had handed Jesus over to him.

¹⁹While Pilate was sitting on the judge's seat, his wife sent him this message: "Don't have anything to do with that innocent man, for I have suffered a great deal today in a dream because of him."

²⁰But the chief priests and the elders persuaded the crowd to ask for Barabbas and to have Jesus executed.

²¹"Which of the two do you want me to release to you?" asked the governor.

"Barabbas," they answered.

²²"What shall I do, then, with Jesus who is called Christ?" Pilate asked.

They all answered, "Crucify him!"

²³"Why? What crime has he committed?" asked Pilate.

But they shouted all the louder, "Crucify him!"

²⁴When Pilate saw that he was getting nowhere, but that instead an uproar was starting, he took water and washed his hands in front of the crowd. "I am innocent of this man's blood," he said. "It is your responsibility!"

²⁵All the people answered, "Let his blood be on us and on our children!"

²⁶Then he released Barabbas to them. But he had Jesus flogged, and handed him over to be crucified.

²⁷Then the governor's soldiers took Jesus into the Praetorium and gathered the whole company of soldiers around him. ²⁸They stripped him and put a scarlet robe on him, ²⁹and then twisted together a crown of thorns and set it on his head. They put a staff in his right hand and knelt in front of him and mocked him. "Hail, king of the Jews!" they said. ³⁰They spit on him, and took the staff and struck him on the head again and again. ³¹After they had mocked him, they took off the robe and put his own clothes on

him. Then they led him away to crucify him.

³²As they were going out, they met a man from Cyrene, named Simon, and they forced him to carry the cross. ³³They came to a place called Golgotha (which means The Place of the Skull). ³⁴There they offered Jesus wine to drink, mixed with gall; but after tasting it, he refused to drink it. ³⁵When they had crucified him, they divided up his clothes by casting lots.ʲ ³⁶And sitting down, they kept watch over him there. ³⁷Above his head they placed the written charge against him: THIS IS JESUS, THE KING OF THE JEWS. ³⁸Two robbers were crucified with him, one on his right and one on his left. ³⁹Those who passed by hurled insults at him, shaking their heads ⁴⁰and saying, "You who are going to destroy the temple and build it in three days, save yourself! Come down from the cross, if you are the Son of God!"

⁴¹In the same way the chief priests, the teachers of the law and the elders mocked him. ⁴²"He saved others," they said, "but he can't save himself! He's the King of Israel! Let him come down now from the cross, and we will believe in him. ⁴³He trusts in God. Let God rescue him now if he wants him, for he said, 'I am the Son of God.' " ⁴⁴In the same way the robbers who were crucified with him also heaped insults on him.

⁴⁵From the sixth hour until the ninth hour darkness came over all the land. ⁴⁶About the ninth hour Jesus cried out in a loud voice, "Eloi, Eloi,ᵏ lama sabachthani?"—which means, "My God, my God, why have you forsaken me?"ˡ

⁴⁷When some of those standing there heard this, they said, "He's calling Elijah."

⁴⁸Immediately one of them ran and got a sponge. He filled it with wine vinegar, put it on a stick, and offered it to Jesus to drink. ⁴⁹The rest said, "Now leave him alone. Let's see if Elijah comes to save him."

⁵⁰And when Jesus had cried out again in a loud voice, he gave up his spirit.

⁵¹At that moment the curtain of the temple was torn in two from top to bottom. The earth shook and the rocks split. ⁵²The tombs broke open and the bodies of many holy people who had died were raised to life. ⁵³They came out of the

ʲ35 A few late manuscripts lots that the word spoken by the prophet might be fulfilled: "They divided my garments among themselves and cast lots for my clothing" (Psalm 22:18)   ᵏ46 Some manuscripts Eli, Eli   ˡ46 Psalm 22:1

tombs, and after Jesus' resurrection they went into the holy city and appeared to many people.

⁵⁴When the centurion and those with him who were guarding Jesus saw the earthquake and all that had happened, they were terrified, and exclaimed, "Surely he was the Son*m* of God!"

⁵⁵Many women were there, watching from a distance. They had followed Jesus from Galilee to care for his needs. ⁵⁶Among them were Mary Magdalene, Mary the mother of James and Joses, and the mother of Zebedee's sons.

⁵⁷As evening approached, there came a rich man from Arimathea, named Joseph, who had himself become a disciple of Jesus. ⁵⁸Going to Pilate, he asked for Jesus' body, and Pilate ordered that it be given to him. ⁵⁹Joseph took the body, wrapped it in a clean linen cloth, ⁶⁰and placed it in his own new tomb that he had cut out of the rock. He rolled a big stone in front of the entrance to the tomb and went away. ⁶¹Mary Magdalene and the other Mary were sitting there opposite the tomb.

⁶²The next day, the one after Preparation Day, the chief priests and the Pharisees went to Pilate. ⁶³"Sir," they said, "we remember that while he was still alive that deceiver said, 'After three days I will rise again.' ⁶⁴So give the order for the tomb to be made secure until the third day. Otherwise, his disciples may come and steal the body and tell the people that he has been raised from the dead. This last deception will be worse than the first."

⁶⁵"Take a guard," Pilate answered. "Go, make the tomb as secure as you know how." ⁶⁶So they went and made the tomb secure by putting a seal on the stone and posting the guard.

CHAPTER 28

After the Sabbath, at dawn on the first day of the week, Mary Magdalene and the other Mary went to look at the tomb.

²There was a violent earthquake, for an angel of the Lord came down from heaven and, going to the tomb, rolled back the stone and sat on it. ³His appearance was like lightning, and his clothes were white as snow. ⁴The guards were so afraid of him that they shook and became like dead men.

⁵The angel said to the women, "Do not be afraid, for I know that you are looking for Jesus, who was crucified. ⁶He is not here; he has risen, just as he said. Come and see the place where he lay. ⁷Then go quickly and tell his disciples: 'He has risen from the dead and is going ahead of you into Galilee. There you will see him.' Now I have told you."

⁸So the women hurried away from the tomb, afraid yet filled with joy, and ran to tell his disciples. ⁹Suddenly Jesus met them. "Greetings," he said. They came to him, clasped his feet and worshiped him. ¹⁰Then Jesus said to them, "Do not be afraid. Go and tell my brothers to go to Galilee; there they will see me."

¹¹While the women were on their way, some of the guards went into the city and reported to the chief priests everything that had happened. ¹²When the chief priests had met with the elders and devised a plan, they gave the soldiers a large sum of money, ¹³telling them, "You are to say, 'His disciples came during the night and stole him away while we were asleep.' ¹⁴If this report gets to the governor, we will satisfy him and keep you out of trouble." ¹⁵So the soldiers took the money and did as they were instructed. And this story has been widely circulated among the Jews to this very day.

¹⁶Then the eleven disciples went to Galilee, to the mountain where Jesus had told them to go. ¹⁷When they saw him, they worshiped him; but some doubted. ¹⁸Then Jesus came to them and said, "All authority in heaven and on earth has been given to me. ¹⁹Therefore go and make disciples of all nations, baptizing them in*n* the name of the Father and of the Son and of the Holy Spirit, ²⁰and teaching them to obey everything I have commanded you. And surely I am with you always, to the very end of the age."

m 54 Or *a son*   *n 19* Or *into*; see Acts 8:16; 19:5; Romans 6:3; 1 Cor. 1:13; 10:2 and Gal. 3:27.

Mark

WRITING in the present tense, Mark involves his readers in the dramatic immediacy of Christ's life. He sets forth in convincing style the credentials of Jesus of Nazareth, the Servant of God. In pithy statements and brief paragraphs, Mark captures the ministry of Jesus but focuses more on what Jesus does than on what he says. The theme of Mark's Gospel is that Jesus' service and sacrifice provide the pattern of living for his followers (16:20).

Focus	Proclamation		Rejection		Exaltation
Divisions	Power of the Servant	Compassion of the Servant	Teaching of the Servant	Signs of the Servant	Suffering of the Servant
	1 3	4 7	8 10	11 13	14 16
Topics	Servant to the Multitudes		Servant to the Disciples	Sacrifice for the World	
	Ministry to Individuals				Ministry to Mankind
Place	Galilee and Perea			Jerusalem	
Time	A.D. 29–33				

OCTOBER 10 □ DAY 284
MARK 1–3
Power of the Servant

OVERVIEW Mark's unadorned opening to his account ("The beginning of the gospel about Jesus Christ, the Son of God") introduces the character of his entire book: brisk, vivid and to the point—just like the character and conduct of an active servant. For this is the biography of Jesus Christ, the Perfect Servant. Over and over, Mark uses the word *immediately* to accelerate the pace of events in the book. He omits details of Christ's genealogy and childhood (of what relevance is that for a servant?) and plunges immediately into Christ's public ministry in the region of Galilee.

Chapter 1	Chapter 2	Chapter 3
Preparation of the Servant	Power and Preaching of the Servant	Opposition to the Servant
"Son Whom I Love"	"Son of Man"	"Son of God"

I have a great need for Christ; I have a great Christ for my need.

YOUR DAILY WALK Do you have a balanced view of Jesus Christ? Down through the centuries, Christians have wrestled with the incarnation of Jesus Christ, trying to describe adequately that unique blend of perfect humanity and undiminished deity that he possessed as he walked the face of the earth. Some Christians emphasize his deity, focusing on the attributes and actions that could only belong to God and forgetting that Jesus ate, slept and wept like other men. Others focus on his humanity, neglecting the many things Jesus did that only God could do.

Today's reading portrays both attributes of Jesus: his *deity* (e.g., healing the sick and casting out demons, 1:11, 29–34) and his *humanity* (e.g., rising early the next morning to pray, 1:35). Mark alerts his readers at the very beginning of the book to the power behind Jesus' ministry.

What about you? Are you engaged in a busy schedule of ministry for God? Are you taking the necessary time in prayer and preparation first? If Jesus needed to pray, how can we expect to minister effectively without prayer? Have your own fifteen-minute prayer retreat right now.

INSIGHT Mark, a Gospel of Actions, Not Words
Of the seventy parables the gospel writers recorded, only eighteen are contained in Mark, and many are only one sentence in length. However, of Jesus' thirty-five recorded miracles, Mark gives an account of more than half.

CHAPTER 1
The beginning of the gospel about Jesus Christ, the Son of God.*

²It is written in Isaiah the prophet:

"I will send my messenger ahead of you,
who will prepare your way"*—
³"a voice of one calling in the desert,

*1 Some manuscripts do not have *the Son of God*.   *2 Mal. 3:1

'Prepare the way for the Lord,
    make straight paths for him.' "^c

⁴And so John came, baptizing in the desert region and preaching a baptism of repentance for the forgiveness of sins. ⁵The whole Judean countryside and all the people of Jerusalem went out to him. Confessing their sins, they were baptized by him in the Jordan River. ⁶John wore clothing made of camel's hair, with a leather belt around his waist, and he ate locusts and wild honey. ⁷And this was his message: "After me will come one more powerful than I, the thongs of whose sandals I am not worthy to stoop down and untie. ⁸I baptize you with^d water, but he will baptize you with the Holy Spirit."

⁹At that time Jesus came from Nazareth in Galilee and was baptized by John in the Jordan. ¹⁰As Jesus was coming up out of the water, he saw heaven being torn open and the Spirit descending on him like a dove. ¹¹And a voice came from heaven: "You are my Son, whom I love; with you I am well pleased."

¹²At once the Spirit sent him out into the desert, ¹³and he was in the desert forty days, being tempted by Satan. He was with the wild animals, and angels attended him.

¹⁴After John was put in prison, Jesus went into Galilee, proclaiming the good news of God. ¹⁵"The time has come," he said. "The kingdom of God is near. Repent and believe the good news!"

¹⁶As Jesus walked beside the Sea of Galilee, he saw Simon and his brother Andrew casting a net into the lake, for they were fishermen. ¹⁷"Come, follow me," Jesus said, "and I will make you fishers of men." ¹⁸At once they left their nets and followed him.

¹⁹When he had gone a little farther, he saw James son of Zebedee and his brother John in a boat, preparing their nets. ²⁰Without delay he called them, and they left their father Zebedee in the boat with the hired men and followed him.

²¹They went to Capernaum, and when the Sabbath came, Jesus went into the synagogue and began to teach. ²²The people were amazed at his teaching, because he taught them as one who had authority, not as the teachers of the law.

²³Just then a man in their synagogue who was possessed by an evil^e spirit cried out, ²⁴"What do you want with us, Jesus of Nazareth? Have you come to destroy us? I know who you are—the Holy One of God!"

²⁵"Be quiet!" said Jesus sternly. "Come out of him!" ²⁶The evil spirit shook the man violently and came out of him with a shriek.

²⁷The people were all so amazed that they asked each other, "What is this? A new teaching—and with authority! He even gives orders to evil spirits and they obey him." ²⁸News about him spread quickly over the whole region of Galilee.

²⁹As soon as they left the synagogue, they went with James and John to the home of Simon and Andrew. ³⁰Simon's mother-in-law was in bed with a fever, and they told Jesus about her. ³¹So he went to her, took her hand and helped her up. The fever left her and she began to wait on them.

³²That evening after sunset the people brought to Jesus all the sick and demon-possessed. ³³The whole town gathered at the door, ³⁴and Jesus healed many who had various diseases. He also drove out many demons, but he would not let the demons speak because they knew who he was.

³⁵Very early in the morning, while it was still dark, Jesus got up, left the house and went off to a solitary place, where he prayed. ³⁶Simon and his companions went to look for him, ³⁷and when they found him, they exclaimed: "Everyone is looking for you!"

³⁸Jesus replied, "Let us go somewhere else—to the nearby villages—so I can preach there also. That is why I have come." ³⁹So he traveled throughout Galilee, preaching in their synagogues and driving out demons.

⁴⁰A man with leprosy^f came to him and begged him on his knees, "If you are willing, you can make me clean."

⁴¹Filled with compassion, Jesus reached out his hand and touched the man. "I am willing," he said. "Be clean!" ⁴²Immediately the leprosy left him and he was cured.

⁴³Jesus sent him away at once with a strong warning: ⁴⁴"See that you don't tell

^c3 Isaiah 40:3   ^d8 Or in   ^e23 Greek unclean; also in verses 26 and 27   ^f40 The Greek word was used for various diseases affecting the skin—not necessarily leprosy.

this to anyone. But go, show yourself to the priest and offer the sacrifices that Moses commanded for your cleansing, as a testimony to them." ⁴⁵Instead he went out and began to talk freely, spreading the news. As a result, Jesus could no longer enter a town openly but stayed outside in lonely places. Yet the people still came to him from everywhere.

CHAPTER 2

A few days later, when Jesus again entered Capernaum, the people heard that he had come home. ²So many gathered that there was no room left, not even outside the door, and he preached the word to them. ³Some men came, bringing to him a paralytic, carried by four of them. ⁴Since they could not get him to Jesus because of the crowd, they made an opening in the roof above Jesus and, after digging through it, lowered the mat the paralyzed man was lying on. ⁵When Jesus saw their faith, he said to the paralytic, "Son, your sins are forgiven."

⁶Now some teachers of the law were sitting there, thinking to themselves, ⁷"Why does this fellow talk like that? He's blaspheming! Who can forgive sins but God alone?"

⁸Immediately Jesus knew in his spirit that this was what they were thinking in their hearts, and he said to them, "Why are you thinking these things? ⁹Which is easier: to say to the paralytic, 'Your sins are forgiven,' or to say, 'Get up, take your mat and walk'? ¹⁰But that you may know that the Son of Man has authority on earth to forgive sins . . ." He said to the paralytic, ¹¹"I tell you, get up, take your mat and go home." ¹²He got up, took his mat and walked out in full view of them all. This amazed everyone and they praised God, saying, "We have never seen anything like this!"

¹³Once again Jesus went out beside the lake. A large crowd came to him, and he began to teach them. ¹⁴As he walked along, he saw Levi son of Alphaeus sitting at the tax collector's booth. "Follow me," Jesus told him, and Levi got up and followed him.

¹⁵While Jesus was having dinner at Levi's house, many tax collectors and "sinners" were eating with him and his disciples, for there were many who followed him. ¹⁶When the teachers of the law who were Pharisees saw him eating with the "sinners" and tax collectors, they asked his disciples: "Why does he eat with tax collectors and 'sinners'?"

¹⁷On hearing this, Jesus said to them, "It is not the healthy who need a doctor, but the sick. I have not come to call the righteous, but sinners."

¹⁸Now John's disciples and the Pharisees were fasting. Some people came and asked Jesus, "How is it that John's disciples and the disciples of the Pharisees are fasting, but yours are not?"

¹⁹Jesus answered, "How can the guests of the bridegroom fast while he is with them? They cannot, so long as they have him with them. ²⁰But the time will come when the bridegroom will be taken from them, and on that day they will fast.

²¹"No one sews a patch of unshrunk cloth on an old garment. If he does, the new piece will pull away from the old, making the tear worse. ²²And no one pours new wine into old wineskins. If he does, the wine will burst the skins, and both the wine and the wineskins will be ruined. No, he pours new wine into new wineskins."

²³One Sabbath Jesus was going through the grainfields, and as his disciples walked along, they began to pick some heads of grain. ²⁴The Pharisees said to him, "Look, why are they doing what is unlawful on the Sabbath?"

²⁵He answered, "Have you never read what David did when he and his companions were hungry and in need? ²⁶In the days of Abiathar the high priest, he entered the house of God and ate the consecrated bread, which is lawful only for priests to eat. And he also gave some to his companions."

²⁷Then he said to them, "The Sabbath was made for man, not man for the Sabbath. ²⁸So the Son of Man is Lord even of the Sabbath."

CHAPTER 3

Another time he went into the synagogue, and a man with a shriveled hand was there. ²Some of them were looking for a reason to accuse Jesus, so they watched him closely to see if he would heal him on the Sabbath. ³Jesus said to the man with the shriveled hand, "Stand up in front of everyone."

⁴Then Jesus asked them, "Which is

lawful on the Sabbath: to do good or to do evil, to save life or to kill?" But they remained silent.

⁵He looked around at them in anger and, deeply distressed at their stubborn hearts, said to the man, "Stretch out your hand." He stretched it out, and his hand was completely restored. ⁶Then the Pharisees went out and began to plot with the Herodians how they might kill Jesus.

⁷Jesus withdrew with his disciples to the lake, and a large crowd from Galilee followed. ⁸When they heard all he was doing, many people came to him from Judea, Jerusalem, Idumea, and the regions across the Jordan and around Tyre and Sidon. ⁹Because of the crowd he told his disciples to have a small boat ready for him, to keep the people from crowding him. ¹⁰For he had healed many, so that those with diseases were pushing forward to touch him. ¹¹Whenever the evilᵍ spirits saw him, they fell down before him and cried out, "You are the Son of God." ¹²But he gave them strict orders not to tell who he was.

¹³Jesus went up on a mountainside and called to him those he wanted, and they came to him. ¹⁴He appointed twelve—designating them apostlesʰ—that they might be with him and that he might send them out to preach ¹⁵and to have authority to drive out demons. ¹⁶These are the twelve he appointed: Simon (to whom he gave the name Peter); ¹⁷James son of Zebedee and his brother John (to them he gave the name Boanerges, which means Sons of Thunder); ¹⁸Andrew, Philip, Bartholomew, Matthew, Thomas, James son of Alphaeus, Thaddaeus, Simon the Zealot ¹⁹and Judas Iscariot, who betrayed him.

²⁰Then Jesus entered a house, and again a crowd gathered, so that he and his disciples were not even able to eat. ²¹When his family heard about this, they went to take charge of him, for they said, "He is out of his mind."

²²And the teachers of the law who came down from Jerusalem said, "He is possessed by Beelzebubⁱ! By the prince of demons he is driving out demons."

²³So Jesus called them and spoke to them in parables: "How can Satan drive out Satan? ²⁴If a kingdom is divided against itself, that kingdom cannot stand. ²⁵If a house is divided against itself, that house cannot stand. ²⁶And if Satan opposes himself and is divided, he cannot stand; his end has come. ²⁷In fact, no one can enter a strong man's house and carry off his possessions unless he first ties up the strong man. Then he can rob his house. ²⁸I tell you the truth, all the sins and blasphemies of men will be forgiven them. ²⁹But whoever blasphemes against the Holy Spirit will never be forgiven; he is guilty of an eternal sin."

³⁰He said this because they were saying, "He has an evil spirit."

³¹Then Jesus' mother and brothers arrived. Standing outside, they sent someone in to call him. ³²A crowd was sitting around him, and they told him, "Your mother and brothers are outside looking for you."

³³"Who are my mother and my brothers?" he asked.

³⁴Then he looked at those seated in a circle around him and said, "Here are my mother and my brothers! ³⁵Whoever does God's will is my brother and sister and mother."

ᵍ11 Greek *unclean*; also in verse 30   ʰ14 Some manuscripts do not have *designating them apostles*.   ⁱ22 Greek *Beezeboul* or *Beelzeboul*

OCTOBER 11 ☐ DAY 285
MARK 4–7
Compassion of the Servant

OVERVIEW Beginning with chapter 4, Mark pauses in his rapid portrayal of Jesus' life and ministry to focus briefly on his teaching concerning the kingdom of God. Returning to his action-packed narrative, Mark then relates four miracles that reveal Jesus' power over nature, demons, disease and death. After a brief (and discouraging) visit to his hometown of Nazareth, Jesus multiplies his ministry by sending out the twelve disciples to teach and to heal. Upon their return, Jesus performs a different kind of ministry of multiplication as he takes a boy's lunch and increases it to feed a multitude of hungry seekers.

Chapter 4	Chapter 5	Chapter 6	Chapter 7
Ministry of Teaching	Ministry of Healing	Ministry of Multiplying	Ministry of Diagnosing
Parables	Miracles		Debates

No trial troubles the child of God who knows God has a reason for allowing it.

YOUR DAILY WALK The Sea of Galilee is fifteen miles long by seven miles wide, cradled between hills that tower more than two thousand feet above the shore. Usually calm and tranquil, it can become treacherous when violent storms spring up without warning. The Sea of Galilee is like life itself: beautiful and tranquil at times, stormy and threatening at others.

At the end of a long day of instruction on the shores of Galilee, Jesus and his disciples got into a boat (4:35–36). After pushing away from the shore, Jesus fell asleep . . . just as a storm exploded in full fury. Twelve frightened men rushed to the Savior and exclaimed in unison, "Teacher, don't you care if we drown?" (4:38). Now go back and reread verse 35. What was it Christ had said to his disciples just before entering the boat? "Let us go to the middle of the lake and drown"? Of course not! "Let us go over to the other side."

What stormy, unexpected event in your life has you feeling panicked and fretful? Remember, Christ intends to take you to the other side safe and secure and not let you drown. Invite him into your "boat" right now, and let him calm your anxieties and still your storms of doubt.

INSIGHT The Tower of Peace

The command Jesus gives to the storm in today's reading is the same command (in Greek) that he uses to heal the tortured soul in Mark 1:25. Is it any wonder Paul identifies this powerful peace as that "which transcends all understanding" (Philippians 4:7)?

CHAPTER 4

Again Jesus began to teach by the lake. The crowd that gathered around him was so large that he got into a boat and sat in it out on the lake, while all the people were along the shore at the water's edge. ²He taught them many things by parables, and in his teaching said: ³"Listen! A farmer went out to sow his seed. ⁴As he was scattering the seed, some fell along the path, and the birds came and ate it up. ⁵Some fell on rocky places, where it did not have much soil. It sprang up quickly, because the soil was shallow. ⁶But when the sun came up, the plants were scorched, and they withered because they had no root. ⁷Other seed fell among thorns, which grew up and choked the plants, so that they did not bear grain. ⁸Still other seed fell on good soil. It came up, grew and produced a crop, multiplying thirty, sixty, or even a hundred times."

⁹Then Jesus said, "He who has ears to hear, let him hear."

¹⁰When he was alone, the Twelve and the others around him asked him about the parables. ¹¹He told them, "The secret of the kingdom of God has been given to you. But to those on the outside everything is said in parables ¹²so that,

" 'they may be ever seeing but never
      perceiving,
   and ever hearing but never
      understanding;

otherwise they might turn and be forgiven!'*j*"

[13]Then Jesus said to them, "Don't you understand this parable? How then will you understand any parable? [14]The farmer sows the word. [15]Some people are like seed along the path, where the word is sown. As soon as they hear it, Satan comes and takes away the word that was sown in them. [16]Others, like seed sown on rocky places, hear the word and at once receive it with joy. [17]But since they have no root, they last only a short time. When trouble or persecution comes because of the word, they quickly fall away. [18]Still others, like seed sown among thorns, hear the word; [19]but the worries of this life, the deceitfulness of wealth and the desires for other things come in and choke the word, making it unfruitful. [20]Others, like seed sown on good soil, hear the word, accept it, and produce a crop—thirty, sixty or even a hundred times what was sown."

[21]He said to them, "Do you bring in a lamp to put it under a bowl or a bed? Instead, don't you put it on its stand? [22]For whatever is hidden is meant to be disclosed, and whatever is concealed is meant to be brought out into the open. [23]If anyone has ears to hear, let him hear."

[24]"Consider carefully what you hear," he continued. "With the measure you use, it will be measured to you—and even more. [25]Whoever has will be given more; whoever does not have, even what he has will be taken from him."

[26]He also said, "This is what the kingdom of God is like. A man scatters seed on the ground. [27]Night and day, whether he sleeps or gets up, the seed sprouts and grows, though he does not know how. [28]All by itself the soil produces grain—first the stalk, then the head, then the full kernel in the head. [29]As soon as the grain is ripe, he puts the sickle to it, because the harvest has come."

[30]Again he said, "What shall we say the kingdom of God is like, or what parable shall we use to describe it? [31]It is like a mustard seed, which is the smallest seed you plant in the ground. [32]Yet when planted, it grows and becomes the largest of all garden plants, with such big branches that the birds of the air can perch in its shade."

[33]With many similar parables Jesus spoke the word to them, as much as they could understand. [34]He did not say anything to them without using a parable. But when he was alone with his own disciples, he explained everything.

[35]That day when evening came, he said to his disciples, "Let us go over to the other side." [36]Leaving the crowd behind, they took him along, just as he was, in the boat. There were also other boats with him. [37]A furious squall came up, and the waves broke over the boat, so that it was nearly swamped. [38]Jesus was in the stern, sleeping on a cushion. The disciples woke him and said to him, "Teacher, don't you care if we drown?"

[39]He got up, rebuked the wind and said to the waves, "Quiet! Be still!" Then the wind died down and it was completely calm.

[40]He said to his disciples, "Why are you so afraid? Do you still have no faith?"

[41]They were terrified and asked each other, "Who is this? Even the wind and the waves obey him!"

CHAPTER 5

They went across the lake to the region of the Gerasenes.*k* [2]When Jesus got out of the boat, a man with an evil*l* spirit came from the tombs to meet him. [3]This man lived in the tombs, and no one could bind him any more, not even with a chain. [4]For he had often been chained hand and foot, but he tore the chains apart and broke the irons on his feet. No one was strong enough to subdue him. [5]Night and day among the tombs and in the hills he would cry out and cut himself with stones.

[6]When he saw Jesus from a distance, he ran and fell on his knees in front of him. [7]He shouted at the top of his voice, "What do you want with me, Jesus, Son of the Most High God? Swear to God that you won't torture me!" [8]For Jesus had said to him, "Come out of this man, you evil spirit!"

[9]Then Jesus asked him, "What is your name?"

"My name is Legion," he replied, "for we are many." [10]And he begged Jesus again and again not to send them out of the area.

---

*j*12 Isaiah 6:9,10   *k*1 Some manuscripts *Gadarenes*; other manuscripts *Gergesenes*   *l*2 Greek *unclean*; also in verses 8 and 13

[11]A large herd of pigs was feeding on the nearby hillside. [12]The demons begged Jesus, "Send us among the pigs; allow us to go into them." [13]He gave them permission, and the evil spirits came out and went into the pigs. The herd, about two thousand in number, rushed down the steep bank into the lake and were drowned.

[14]Those tending the pigs ran off and reported this in the town and countryside, and the people went out to see what had happened. [15]When they came to Jesus, they saw the man who had been possessed by the legion of demons, sitting there, dressed and in his right mind; and they were afraid. [16]Those who had seen it told the people what had happened to the demon-possessed man—and told about the pigs as well. [17]Then the people began to plead with Jesus to leave their region.

[18]As Jesus was getting into the boat, the man who had been demon-possessed begged to go with him. [19]Jesus did not let him, but said, "Go home to your family and tell them how much the Lord has done for you, and how he has had mercy on you." [20]So the man went away and began to tell in the Decapolis[m] how much Jesus had done for him. And all the people were amazed.

[21]When Jesus had again crossed over by boat to the other side of the lake, a large crowd gathered around him while he was by the lake. [22]Then one of the synagogue rulers, named Jairus, came there. Seeing Jesus, he fell at his feet [23]and pleaded earnestly with him, "My little daughter is dying. Please come and put your hands on her so that she will be healed and live." [24]So Jesus went with him.

A large crowd followed and pressed around him. [25]And a woman was there who had been subject to bleeding for twelve years. [26]She had suffered a great deal under the care of many doctors and had spent all she had, yet instead of getting better she grew worse. [27]When she heard about Jesus, she came up behind him in the crowd and touched his cloak, [28]because she thought, "If I just touch his clothes, I will be healed." [29]Immediately her bleeding stopped and she felt in her body that she was freed from her suffering.

[30]At once Jesus realized that power had gone out from him. He turned around in the crowd and asked, "Who touched my clothes?"

[31]"You see the people crowding against you," his disciples answered, "and yet you can ask, 'Who touched me?' "

[32]But Jesus kept looking around to see who had done it. [33]Then the woman, knowing what had happened to her, came and fell at his feet and, trembling with fear, told him the whole truth. [34]He said to her, "Daughter, your faith has healed you. Go in peace and be freed from your suffering."

[35]While Jesus was still speaking, some men came from the house of Jairus, the synagogue ruler. "Your daughter is dead," they said. "Why bother the teacher any more?"

[36]Ignoring what they said, Jesus told the synagogue ruler, "Don't be afraid; just believe."

[37]He did not let anyone follow him except Peter, James and John the brother of James. [38]When they came to the home of the synagogue ruler, Jesus saw a commotion, with people crying and wailing loudly. [39]He went in and said to them, "Why all this commotion and wailing? The child is not dead but asleep." [40]But they laughed at him.

After he put them all out, he took the child's father and mother and the disciples who were with him, and went in where the child was. [41]He took her by the hand and said to her, *"Talitha koum!"* (which means, "Little girl, I say to you, get up!"). [42]Immediately the girl stood up and walked around (she was twelve years old). At this they were completely astonished. [43]He gave strict orders not to let anyone know about this, and told them to give her something to eat.

CHAPTER 6

Jesus left there and went to his hometown, accompanied by his disciples. [2]When the Sabbath came, he began to teach in the synagogue, and many who heard him were amazed.

"Where did this man get these things?" they asked. "What's this wisdom that has been given him, that he even does miracles! [3]Isn't this the carpenter? Isn't this

[m]20 That is, the Ten Cities

Mary's son and the brother of James, Joseph,[n] Judas and Simon? Aren't his sisters here with us?" And they took offense at him.

[4]Jesus said to them, "Only in his hometown, among his relatives and in his own house is a prophet without honor." [5]He could not do any miracles there, except lay his hands on a few sick people and heal them. [6]And he was amazed at their lack of faith.

Then Jesus went around teaching from village to village. [7]Calling the Twelve to him, he sent them out two by two and gave them authority over evil[o] spirits.

[8]These were his instructions: "Take nothing for the journey except a staff—no bread, no bag, no money in your belts. [9]Wear sandals but not an extra tunic. [10]Whenever you enter a house, stay there until you leave that town. [11]And if any place will not welcome you or listen to you, shake the dust off your feet when you leave, as a testimony against them."

[12]They went out and preached that people should repent. [13]They drove out many demons and anointed many sick people with oil and healed them.

[14]King Herod heard about this, for Jesus' name had become well known. Some were saying,[p] "John the Baptist has been raised from the dead, and that is why miraculous powers are at work in him."

[15]Others said, "He is Elijah."

And still others claimed, "He is a prophet, like one of the prophets of long ago."

[16]But when Herod heard this, he said, "John, the man I beheaded, has been raised from the dead!"

[17]For Herod himself had given orders to have John arrested, and he had him bound and put in prison. He did this because of Herodias, his brother Philip's wife, whom he had married. [18]For John had been saying to Herod, "It is not lawful for you to have your brother's wife." [19]So Herodias nursed a grudge against John and wanted to kill him. But she was not able to, [20]because Herod feared John and protected him, knowing him to be a righteous and holy man. When Herod heard John, he was greatly puzzled[q]; yet he liked to listen to him.

[21]Finally the opportune time came. On his birthday Herod gave a banquet for his high officials and military commanders and the leading men of Galilee. [22]When the daughter of Herodias came in and danced, she pleased Herod and his dinner guests.

The king said to the girl, "Ask me for anything you want, and I'll give it to you." [23]And he promised her with an oath, "Whatever you ask I will give you, up to half my kingdom."

[24]She went out and said to her mother, "What shall I ask for?"

"The head of John the Baptist," she answered.

[25]At once the girl hurried in to the king with the request: "I want you to give me right now the head of John the Baptist on a platter."

[26]The king was greatly distressed, but because of his oaths and his dinner guests, he did not want to refuse her. [27]So he immediately sent an executioner with orders to bring John's head. The man went, beheaded John in the prison, [28]and brought back his head on a platter. He presented it to the girl, and she gave it to her mother. [29]On hearing of this, John's disciples came and took his body and laid it in a tomb.

[30]The apostles gathered around Jesus and reported to him all they had done and taught. [31]Then, because so many people were coming and going that they did not even have a chance to eat, he said to them, "Come with me by yourselves to a quiet place and get some rest."

[32]So they went away by themselves in a boat to a solitary place. [33]But many who saw them leaving recognized them and ran on foot from all the towns and got there ahead of them. [34]When Jesus landed and saw a large crowd, he had compassion on them, because they were like sheep without a shepherd. So he began teaching them many things.

[35]By this time it was late in the day, so his disciples came to him. "This is a remote place," they said, "and it's already very late. [36]Send the people away so they can go to the surrounding countryside and villages and buy themselves something to eat."

[n]3 Greek *Joses*, a variant of *Joseph*   [o]7 Greek *unclean*   [p]14 Some early manuscripts *He was saying*   [q]20 Some early manuscripts *he did many things*

[37]But he answered, "You give them something to eat."

They said to him, "That would take eight months of a man's wages[r]! Are we to go and spend that much on bread and give it to them to eat?"

[38]"How many loaves do you have?" he asked. "Go and see."

When they found out, they said, "Five—and two fish."

[39]Then Jesus directed them to have all the people sit down in groups on the green grass. [40]So they sat down in groups of hundreds and fifties. [41]Taking the five loaves and the two fish and looking up to heaven, he gave thanks and broke the loaves. Then he gave them to his disciples to set before the people. He also divided the two fish among them all. [42]They all ate and were satisfied, [43]and the disciples picked up twelve basketfuls of broken pieces of bread and fish. [44]The number of the men who had eaten was five thousand.

[45]Immediately Jesus made his disciples get into the boat and go on ahead of him to Bethsaida, while he dismissed the crowd. [46]After leaving them, he went up on a mountainside to pray.

[47]When evening came, the boat was in the middle of the lake, and he was alone on land. [48]He saw the disciples straining at the oars, because the wind was against them. About the fourth watch of the night he went out to them, walking on the lake. He was about to pass by them, [49]but when they saw him walking on the lake, they thought he was a ghost. They cried out, [50]because they all saw him and were terrified.

Immediately he spoke to them and said, "Take courage! It is I. Don't be afraid." [51]Then he climbed into the boat with them, and the wind died down. They were completely amazed, [52]for they had not understood about the loaves; their hearts were hardened.

[53]When they had crossed over, they landed at Gennesaret and anchored there. [54]As soon as they got out of the boat, people recognized Jesus. [55]They ran throughout that whole region and carried the sick on mats to wherever they heard he was. [56]And wherever he went—into villages, towns or countryside—they placed the sick in the marketplaces. They begged him to let them touch even the edge of his cloak, and all who touched him were healed.

CHAPTER 7

The Pharisees and some of the teachers of the law who had come from Jerusalem gathered around Jesus and [2]saw some of his disciples eating food with hands that were "unclean," that is, unwashed. [3](The Pharisees and all the Jews do not eat unless they give their hands a ceremonial washing, holding to the tradition of the elders. [4]When they come from the marketplace they do not eat unless they wash. And they observe many other traditions, such as the washing of cups, pitchers and kettles.[s])

[5]So the Pharisees and teachers of the law asked Jesus, "Why don't your disciples live according to the tradition of the elders instead of eating their food with 'unclean' hands?"

[6]He replied, "Isaiah was right when he prophesied about you hypocrites; as it is written:

" 'These people honor me with their
       lips,
   but their hearts are far from me.
[7]They worship me in vain;
   their teachings are but rules taught
       by men.'[t]

[8]You have let go of the commands of God and are holding on to the traditions of men."

[9]And he said to them: "You have a fine way of setting aside the commands of God in order to observe[u] your own traditions! [10]For Moses said, 'Honor your father and your mother,'[v] and, 'Anyone who curses his father or mother must be put to death.'[w] [11]But you say that if a man says to his father or mother: 'Whatever help you might otherwise have received from me is Corban' (that is, a gift devoted to God), [12]then you no longer let him do anything for his father or mother. [13]Thus you nullify the word of God by your tradition that you have handed down. And you do many things like that."

---

[r]37 Greek *take two hundred denarii*   [s]4 Some early manuscripts *pitchers, kettles and dining couches*   [t]6,7 Isaiah 29:13
[u]9 Some manuscripts *set up*   [v]10 Exodus 20:12; Deut. 5:16   [w]10 Exodus 21:17; Lev. 20:9

¹⁴Again Jesus called the crowd to him and said, "Listen to me, everyone, and understand this. ¹⁵Nothing outside a man can make him 'unclean' by going into him. Rather, it is what comes out of a man that makes him 'unclean.'ˣ"

¹⁷After he had left the crowd and entered the house, his disciples asked him about this parable. ¹⁸"Are you so dull?" he asked. "Don't you see that nothing that enters a man from the outside can make him 'unclean'? ¹⁹For it doesn't go into his heart but into his stomach, and then out of his body." (In saying this, Jesus declared all foods "clean.")

²⁰He went on: "What comes out of a man is what makes him 'unclean.' ²¹For from within, out of men's hearts, come evil thoughts, sexual immorality, theft, murder, adultery, ²²greed, malice, deceit, lewdness, envy, slander, arrogance and folly. ²³All these evils come from inside and make a man 'unclean.'"

²⁴Jesus left that place and went to the vicinity of Tyre.ʸ He entered a house and did not want anyone to know it; yet he could not keep his presence secret. ²⁵In fact, as soon as she heard about him, a woman whose little daughter was possessed by an evilᶻ spirit came and fell at his feet. ²⁶The woman was a Greek, born in Syrian Phoenicia. She begged Jesus to drive the demon out of her daughter.

²⁷"First let the children eat all they want," he told her, "for it is not right to take the children's bread and toss it to their dogs."

²⁸"Yes, Lord," she replied, "but even the dogs under the table eat the children's crumbs."

²⁹Then he told her, "For such a reply, you may go; the demon has left your daughter."

³⁰She went home and found her child lying on the bed, and the demon gone.

³¹Then Jesus left the vicinity of Tyre and went through Sidon, down to the Sea of Galilee and into the region of the Decapolis.ᵃ ³²There some people brought to him a man who was deaf and could hardly talk, and they begged him to place his hand on the man.

³³After he took him aside, away from the crowd, Jesus put his fingers into the man's ears. Then he spit and touched the man's tongue. ³⁴He looked up to heaven and with a deep sigh said to him, "*Eph-phatha!*" (which means, "Be opened!"). ³⁵At this, the man's ears were opened, his tongue was loosened and he began to speak plainly.

³⁶Jesus commanded them not to tell anyone. But the more he did so, the more they kept talking about it. ³⁷People were overwhelmed with amazement. "He has done everything well," they said. "He even makes the deaf hear and the mute speak."

ˣ15 Some early manuscripts *'unclean.'* ¹⁶*If anyone has ears to hear, let him hear.*   ʸ24 Many early manuscripts *Tyre and Sidon*
ᶻ25 Greek *unclean*   ᵃ31 That is, the Ten Cities

OCTOBER 12 □ DAY 286
MARK 8–10
Teaching of the Servant

 OVERVIEW Many of Christ's sayings and sermons are uttered in response to the questions and attacks of the Pharisees. The same is true of his discussions with the disciples—conversations that lead to important teachings on such subjects as discipleship, humility, stumbling blocks and proper priorities. But even as he teaches, Jesus is constantly on the move, traveling across the Sea of Galilee to Caesarea Philippi and finally through Perea to Jerusalem.

Chapter 8	Chapter 9	Chapter 10
Lessons from the Loaves	Lessons on Prayer and Pride	Lessons on Servanthood
"Be Careful!"	"Be Prayerful!"	"Be Available!"

YOUR DAILY WALK Ask a truck driver, a senior citizen and a teenager how to get from point A to point B, and you will probably get three different answers. The truck driver may suggest, "Take the freeway"; the senior citizen, "Take the bus"; and the teenager, "You can't get there from here!" Same goal, but different paths to achieve it.

If someone's sense of security depends on having all people speak well of him or her, he or she can never be secure following Christ.

In today's section you will read two accounts of Jesus healing blind men (8:22–26; 10:46–52). In the case of the blind man of Bethsaida, Jesus led the man out of town, spit on his eyes and placed his hands on the man's face twice before his sight was fully restored. With Bartimaeus of Jericho, full healing came with but the speaking of a word.

So it is with spiritual lessons God wants to teach us. God may teach your friend to depend on him through financial problems; you learn the same lesson through illness. Another Christian learns to walk by faith in affluence; you learn it in poverty. One person learns patience through being single; another learns it through having a spouse . . . and little spouslings! In each case, it is dangerous to compare—rather than commit to—God's perfect curriculum. Every time you see an Under Construction sign next to a building or highway this month, let it remind you that God is not finished with you yet!

INSIGHT The Toughest of the Ten
The rich young man (10:17–22) gloried in his observance of the Ten Commandments, but he had never really gotten past the first one (Exodus 20:3). His possessions had become his god . . . his idol . . . the focus of his affections. Read 1 John 5:21 and restate it in your own words.

CHAPTER 8
During those days another large crowd gathered. Since they had nothing to eat, Jesus called his disciples to him and said, ²"I have compassion for these people; they have already been with me three days and have nothing to eat. ³If I send them home hungry, they will collapse on the way, because some of them have come a long distance."

⁴His disciples answered, "But where in this remote place can anyone get enough bread to feed them?"

⁵"How many loaves do you have?" Jesus asked.

"Seven," they replied.

⁶He told the crowd to sit down on the ground. When he had taken the seven loaves and given thanks, he broke them and gave them to his disciples to set before the people, and they did so. ⁷They had a few small fish as well; he gave thanks for them also and told the disciples to distribute them. ⁸The people ate and

were satisfied. Afterward the disciples picked up seven basketfuls of broken pieces that were left over. ⁹About four thousand men were present. And having sent them away, ¹⁰he got into the boat with his disciples and went to the region of Dalmanutha.

¹¹The Pharisees came and began to question Jesus. To test him, they asked him for a sign from heaven. ¹²He sighed deeply and said, "Why does this generation ask for a miraculous sign? I tell you the truth, no sign will be given to it." ¹³Then he left them, got back into the boat and crossed to the other side.

¹⁴The disciples had forgotten to bring bread, except for one loaf they had with them in the boat. ¹⁵"Be careful," Jesus warned them. "Watch out for the yeast of the Pharisees and that of Herod."

¹⁶They discussed this with one another and said, "It is because we have no bread."

¹⁷Aware of their discussion, Jesus asked them: "Why are you talking about having

no bread? Do you still not see or understand? Are your hearts hardened? [18]Do you have eyes but fail to see, and ears but fail to hear? And don't you remember? [19]When I broke the five loaves for the five thousand, how many basketfuls of pieces did you pick up?"

"Twelve," they replied.

[20]"And when I broke the seven loaves for the four thousand, how many basketfuls of pieces did you pick up?"

They answered, "Seven."

[21]He said to them, "Do you still not understand?"

[22]They came to Bethsaida, and some people brought a blind man and begged Jesus to touch him. [23]He took the blind man by the hand and led him outside the village. When he had spit on the man's eyes and put his hands on him, Jesus asked, "Do you see anything?"

[24]He looked up and said, "I see people; they look like trees walking around."

[25]Once more Jesus put his hands on the man's eyes. Then his eyes were opened, his sight was restored, and he saw everything clearly. [26]Jesus sent him home, saying, "Don't go into the village.[b]"

[27]Jesus and his disciples went on to the villages around Caesarea Philippi. On the way he asked them, "Who do people say I am?"

[28]They replied, "Some say John the Baptist; others say Elijah; and still others, one of the prophets."

[29]"But what about you?" he asked. "Who do you say I am?"

Peter answered, "You are the Christ.[c]"

[30]Jesus warned them not to tell anyone about him.

[31]He then began to teach them that the Son of Man must suffer many things and be rejected by the elders, chief priests and teachers of the law, and that he must be killed and after three days rise again. [32]He spoke plainly about this, and Peter took him aside and began to rebuke him.

[33]But when Jesus turned and looked at his disciples, he rebuked Peter. "Get behind me, Satan!" he said. "You do not have in mind the things of God, but the things of men."

[34]Then he called the crowd to him along with his disciples and said: "If anyone would come after me, he must deny himself and take up his cross and follow me. [35]For whoever wants to save his life[d] will lose it, but whoever loses his life for me and for the gospel will save it. [36]What good is it for a man to gain the whole world, yet forfeit his soul? [37]Or what can a man give in exchange for his soul? [38]If anyone is ashamed of me and my words in this adulterous and sinful generation, the Son of Man will be ashamed of him when he comes in his Father's glory with the holy angels."

CHAPTER 9

And he said to them, "I tell you the truth, some who are standing here will not taste death before they see the kingdom of God come with power."

[2]After six days Jesus took Peter, James and John with him and led them up a high mountain, where they were all alone. There he was transfigured before them. [3]His clothes became dazzling white, whiter than anyone in the world could bleach them. [4]And there appeared before them Elijah and Moses, who were talking with Jesus.

[5]Peter said to Jesus, "Rabbi, it is good for us to be here. Let us put up three shelters—one for you, one for Moses and one for Elijah." [6](He did not know what to say, they were so frightened.)

[7]Then a cloud appeared and enveloped them, and a voice came from the cloud: "This is my Son, whom I love. Listen to him!"

[8]Suddenly, when they looked around, they no longer saw anyone with them except Jesus.

[9]As they were coming down the mountain, Jesus gave them orders not to tell anyone what they had seen until the Son of Man had risen from the dead. [10]They kept the matter to themselves, discussing what "rising from the dead" meant.

[11]And they asked him, "Why do the teachers of the law say that Elijah must come first?"

[12]Jesus replied, "To be sure, Elijah does come first, and restores all things. Why then is it written that the Son of Man must suffer much and be rejected? [13]But I tell you, Elijah has come, and they have done

[b]26 Some manuscripts *Don't go and tell anyone in the village*   [c]29 Or *Messiah.* "The Christ" (Greek) and "the Messiah" (Hebrew) both mean "the Anointed One."   [d]35 The Greek word means either *life* or *soul*; also in verse 36.

to him everything they wished, just as it is written about him."

¹⁴When they came to the other disciples, they saw a large crowd around them and the teachers of the law arguing with them. ¹⁵As soon as all the people saw Jesus, they were overwhelmed with wonder and ran to greet him.

¹⁶"What are you arguing with them about?" he asked.

¹⁷A man in the crowd answered, "Teacher, I brought you my son, who is possessed by a spirit that has robbed him of speech. ¹⁸Whenever it seizes him, it throws him to the ground. He foams at the mouth, gnashes his teeth and becomes rigid. I asked your disciples to drive out the spirit, but they could not."

¹⁹"O unbelieving generation," Jesus replied, "how long shall I stay with you? How long shall I put up with you? Bring the boy to me."

²⁰So they brought him. When the spirit saw Jesus, it immediately threw the boy into a convulsion. He fell to the ground and rolled around, foaming at the mouth.

²¹Jesus asked the boy's father, "How long has he been like this?"

"From childhood," he answered. ²²"It has often thrown him into fire or water to kill him. But if you can do anything, take pity on us and help us."

²³" 'If you can'?" said Jesus. "Everything is possible for him who believes."

²⁴Immediately the boy's father exclaimed, "I do believe; help me overcome my unbelief!"

²⁵When Jesus saw that a crowd was running to the scene, he rebuked the evil*ᵉ* spirit. "You deaf and mute spirit," he said, "I command you, come out of him and never enter him again."

²⁶The spirit shrieked, convulsed him violently and came out. The boy looked so much like a corpse that many said, "He's dead." ²⁷But Jesus took him by the hand and lifted him to his feet, and he stood up.

²⁸After Jesus had gone indoors, his disciples asked him privately, "Why couldn't we drive it out?"

²⁹He replied, "This kind can come out only by prayer.*ᶠ*"

³⁰They left that place and passed through Galilee. Jesus did not want anyone to know where they were, ³¹because he was teaching his disciples. He said to them, "The Son of Man is going to be betrayed into the hands of men. They will kill him, and after three days he will rise." ³²But they did not understand what he meant and were afraid to ask him about it.

³³They came to Capernaum. When he was in the house, he asked them, "What were you arguing about on the road?" ³⁴But they kept quiet because on the way they had argued about who was the greatest.

³⁵Sitting down, Jesus called the Twelve and said, "If anyone wants to be first, he must be the very last, and the servant of all."

³⁶He took a little child and had him stand among them. Taking him in his arms, he said to them, ³⁷"Whoever welcomes one of these little children in my name welcomes me; and whoever welcomes me does not welcome me but the one who sent me."

³⁸"Teacher," said John, "we saw a man driving out demons in your name and we told him to stop, because he was not one of us."

³⁹"Do not stop him," Jesus said. "No one who does a miracle in my name can in the next moment say anything bad about me, ⁴⁰for whoever is not against us is for us. ⁴¹I tell you the truth, anyone who gives you a cup of water in my name because you belong to Christ will certainly not lose his reward.

⁴²"And if anyone causes one of these little ones who believe in me to sin, it would be better for him to be thrown into the sea with a large millstone tied around his neck. ⁴³If your hand causes you to sin, cut it off. It is better for you to enter life maimed than with two hands to go into hell, where the fire never goes out.*ᵍ* ⁴⁵And if your foot causes you to sin, cut it off. It is better for you to enter life crippled than to have two feet and be thrown into hell.*ʰ* ⁴⁷And if your eye causes you to sin, pluck it out. It is better for you to enter the kingdom of God with one eye than to have two eyes and be thrown into hell, ⁴⁸where

---

*ᵉ*25 Greek *unclean*   *ᶠ*29 Some manuscripts *prayer and fasting*   *ᵍ*43 Some manuscripts *out,* ⁴⁴*where |* " *'their worm does not die, |*
and the fire is not quenched.'   *ʰ*45 Some manuscripts *hell,* ⁴⁶*where |* " *'their worm does not die, | and the fire is not quenched.'*

" 'their worm does not die,
    and the fire is not quenched.'[i]

[49]Everyone will be salted with fire.

[50]"Salt is good, but if it loses its saltiness, how can you make it salty again? Have salt in yourselves, and be at peace with each other."

CHAPTER 10

Jesus then left that place and went into the region of Judea and across the Jordan. Again crowds of people came to him, and as was his custom, he taught them.

[2]Some Pharisees came and tested him by asking, "Is it lawful for a man to divorce his wife?"

[3]"What did Moses command you?" he replied.

[4]They said, "Moses permitted a man to write a certificate of divorce and send her away."

[5]"It was because your hearts were hard that Moses wrote you this law," Jesus replied. [6]"But at the beginning of creation God 'made them male and female.'[j] [7]'For this reason a man will leave his father and mother and be united to his wife,[k] [8]and the two will become one flesh.'[l] So they are no longer two, but one. [9]Therefore what God has joined together, let man not separate."

[10]When they were in the house again, the disciples asked Jesus about this. [11]He answered, "Anyone who divorces his wife and marries another woman commits adultery against her. [12]And if she divorces her husband and marries another man, she commits adultery."

[13]People were bringing little children to Jesus to have him touch them, but the disciples rebuked them. [14]When Jesus saw this, he was indignant. He said to them, "Let the little children come to me, and do not hinder them, for the kingdom of God belongs to such as these. [15]I tell you the truth, anyone who will not receive the kingdom of God like a little child will never enter it." [16]And he took the children in his arms, put his hands on them and blessed them.

[17]As Jesus started on his way, a man ran up to him and fell on his knees before him. "Good teacher," he asked, "what must I do to inherit eternal life?"

[18]"Why do you call me good?" Jesus answered. "No one is good—except God alone. [19]You know the commandments: 'Do not murder, do not commit adultery, do not steal, do not give false testimony, do not defraud, honor your father and mother.'[m]"

[20]"Teacher," he declared, "all these I have kept since I was a boy."

[21]Jesus looked at him and loved him. "One thing you lack," he said. "Go, sell everything you have and give to the poor, and you will have treasure in heaven. Then come, follow me."

[22]At this the man's face fell. He went away sad, because he had great wealth.

[23]Jesus looked around and said to his disciples, "How hard it is for the rich to enter the kingdom of God!"

[24]The disciples were amazed at his words. But Jesus said again, "Children, how hard it is[n] to enter the kingdom of God! [25]It is easier for a camel to go through the eye of a needle than for a rich man to enter the kingdom of God."

[26]The disciples were even more amazed, and said to each other, "Who then can be saved?"

[27]Jesus looked at them and said, "With man this is impossible, but not with God; all things are possible with God."

[28]Peter said to him, "We have left everything to follow you!"

[29]"I tell you the truth," Jesus replied, "no one who has left home or brothers or sisters or mother or father or children or fields for me and the gospel [30]will fail to receive a hundred times as much in this present age (homes, brothers, sisters, mothers, children and fields—and with them, persecutions) and in the age to come, eternal life. [31]But many who are first will be last, and the last first."

[32]They were on their way up to Jerusalem, with Jesus leading the way, and the disciples were astonished, while those who followed were afraid. Again he took the Twelve aside and told them what was going to happen to him. [33]"We are going up to Jerusalem," he said, "and the Son of Man will be betrayed to the chief priests and teachers of the law. They will condemn him to death and will hand him over to the Gentiles, [34]who will mock him

---

[i]48 Isaiah 66:24   [j]6 Gen. 1:27   [k]7 Some early manuscripts do not have *and be united to his wife.*   [l]8 Gen. 2:24
[m]19 Exodus 20:12-16; Deut. 5:16-20   [n]24 Some manuscripts *is for those who trust in riches*

and spit on him, flog him and kill him. Three days later he will rise."

³⁵Then James and John, the sons of Zebedee, came to him. "Teacher," they said, "we want you to do for us whatever we ask."

³⁶"What do you want me to do for you?" he asked.

³⁷They replied, "Let one of us sit at your right and the other at your left in your glory."

³⁸"You don't know what you are asking," Jesus said. "Can you drink the cup I drink or be baptized with the baptism I am baptized with?"

³⁹"We can," they answered.

Jesus said to them, "You will drink the cup I drink and be baptized with the baptism I am baptized with, ⁴⁰but to sit at my right or left is not for me to grant. These places belong to those for whom they have been prepared."

⁴¹When the ten heard about this, they became indignant with James and John. ⁴²Jesus called them together and said, "You know that those who are regarded as rulers of the Gentiles lord it over them, and their high officials exercise authority over them. ⁴³Not so with you. Instead,

whoever wants to become great among you must be your servant, ⁴⁴and whoever wants to be first must be slave of all. ⁴⁵For even the Son of Man did not come to be served, but to serve, and to give his life as a ransom for many."

⁴⁶Then they came to Jericho. As Jesus and his disciples, together with a large crowd, were leaving the city, a blind man, Bartimaeus (that is, the Son of Timaeus), was sitting by the roadside begging. ⁴⁷When he heard that it was Jesus of Nazareth, he began to shout, "Jesus, Son of David, have mercy on me!"

⁴⁸Many rebuked him and told him to be quiet, but he shouted all the more, "Son of David, have mercy on me!"

⁴⁹Jesus stopped and said, "Call him."

So they called to the blind man, "Cheer up! On your feet! He's calling you." ⁵⁰Throwing his cloak aside, he jumped to his feet and came to Jesus.

⁵¹"What do you want me to do for you?" Jesus asked him.

The blind man said, "Rabbi, I want to see."

⁵²"Go," said Jesus, "your faith has healed you." Immediately he received his sight and followed Jesus along the road.

OCTOBER 13 □ DAY 287
MARK 11–13
Signs of the Servant

 OVERVIEW Mark, who has written seven chapters covering the first three years of Jesus' active ministry and three chapters describing the next six months, now devotes six chapters—fully 40 percent of his book—to the final eight days! Throughout this last week Jesus' activities revolve around the temple as he confronts chief priests, scribes, elders, Pharisees, Herodians and Sadducees with his irrefutable claims. Though the adoring cries of "Hosanna" announce his arrival in Jerusalem, only a few days later he will hear the frenzied cry "Crucify him!" Jesus is now taking his final steps to the cross.

Chapter 11	Chapter 12	Chapter 13
Arrival in Jerusalem	Antagonism from the Jews	Anticipation of the Future
Triumph	Turmoil	Tribulation

YOUR DAILY WALK Sometimes it's difficult to remember that the people living in Jesus' day did not have the New Testament to read. They knew no John 3:16 to declare the good news of the gospel . . . no Romans 3:23–24 to explain the significance of the cross . . . no Ephesians 2:1–7 to describe the miracle of new life in Jesus Christ. All they had to help them anticipate and understand the events of their day was the Old Testament: the Law of Moses . . . the predictions of the prophets . . . the word pictures contained in the Psalms.

Jesus Christ is God's everything for everyone's total need.

Mark draws heavily on that vital material to show the significance of events during Christ's final days on earth. Put yourself in the sandals of a first-century Jew. See if you can walk your way through today's section by reading these Old Testament passages in sequence: Psalm 118:25–26; Isaiah 56:7; Jeremiah 7:11; Isaiah 5:1–7; Psalm 118:22–23; Deuteronomy 6:4–5; Leviticus 19:18; Psalm 110:1; Daniel 9:27; 11:31; 12:11; Isaiah 13:10.

INSIGHT The Unridden Donkey
In Old Testament times an object to be consecrated to God—that is, set apart for special service—could never have been used previously for common purposes (Numbers 19:2; 1 Samuel 6:7). This may explain why Christ selected a young colt that had never been ridden (Mark 11:2) and why he would later be buried in a new tomb that had never been occupied (Luke 23:53).

CHAPTER 11

As they approached Jerusalem and came to Bethphage and Bethany at the Mount of Olives, Jesus sent two of his disciples, ²saying to them, "Go to the village ahead of you, and just as you enter it, you will find a colt tied there, which no one has ever ridden. Untie it and bring it here. ³If anyone asks you, 'Why are you doing this?' tell him, 'The Lord needs it and will send it back here shortly.' "

⁴They went and found a colt outside in the street, tied at a doorway. As they untied it, ⁵some people standing there asked, "What are you doing, untying that colt?" ⁶They answered as Jesus had told them to, and the people let them go. ⁷When they brought the colt to Jesus and threw their cloaks over it, he sat on it. ⁸Many people spread their cloaks on the road, while others spread branches they had cut in the fields. ⁹Those who went ahead and those who followed shouted,

"Hosanna!*ᵒ*"

"Blessed is he who comes in the name of the Lord!"*ᵖ*

¹⁰"Blessed is the coming kingdom of our father David!"

"Hosanna in the highest!"

¹¹Jesus entered Jerusalem and went to the temple. He looked around at everything, but since it was already late, he went out to Bethany with the Twelve.

¹²The next day as they were leaving Bethany, Jesus was hungry. ¹³Seeing in the distance a fig tree in leaf, he went to find out if it had any fruit. When he reached it, he found nothing but leaves, because it was not the season for figs. ¹⁴Then he said to the tree, "May no one ever eat fruit from you again." And his disciples heard him say it.

¹⁵On reaching Jerusalem, Jesus entered the temple area and began driving out those who were buying and selling there. He overturned the tables of the money changers and the benches of those selling doves, ¹⁶and would not allow anyone to carry merchandise through the temple courts. ¹⁷And as he taught them, he said, "Is it not written:

" 'My house will be called
    a house of prayer for all nations'*q*?

But you have made it 'a den of robbers.'*r*"

¹⁸The chief priests and the teachers of the law heard this and began looking for a way to kill him, for they feared him, because the whole crowd was amazed at his teaching.

ᵒ9 A Hebrew expression meaning "Save!" which became an exclamation of praise; also in verse 10   *ᵖ9* Psalm 118:25,26
q17 Isaiah 56:7   *r17* Jer. 7:11

[19]When evening came, they[s] went out of the city.

[20]In the morning, as they went along, they saw the fig tree withered from the roots. [21]Peter remembered and said to Jesus, "Rabbi, look! The fig tree you cursed has withered!"

[22]"Have[t] faith in God," Jesus answered. [23]"I tell you the truth, if anyone says to this mountain, 'Go, throw yourself into the sea,' and does not doubt in his heart but believes that what he says will happen, it will be done for him. [24]Therefore I tell you, whatever you ask for in prayer, believe that you have received it, and it will be yours. [25]And when you stand praying, if you hold anything against anyone, forgive him, so that your Father in heaven may forgive you your sins.[u]"

[27]They arrived again in Jerusalem, and while Jesus was walking in the temple courts, the chief priests, the teachers of the law and the elders came to him. [28]"By what authority are you doing these things?" they asked. "And who gave you authority to do this?"

[29]Jesus replied, "I will ask you one question. Answer me, and I will tell you by what authority I am doing these things. [30]John's baptism—was it from heaven, or from men? Tell me!"

[31]They discussed it among themselves and said, "If we say, 'From heaven,' he will ask, 'Then why didn't you believe him?' [32]But if we say, 'From men' . . . ." (They feared the people, for everyone held that John really was a prophet.)

[33]So they answered Jesus, "We don't know."

Jesus said, "Neither will I tell you by what authority I am doing these things."

CHAPTER 12

He then began to speak to them in parables: "A man planted a vineyard. He put a wall around it, dug a pit for the winepress and built a watchtower. Then he rented the vineyard to some farmers and went away on a journey. [2]At harvest time he sent a servant to the tenants to collect from them some of the fruit of the vineyard. [3]But they seized him, beat him and sent him away empty-handed. [4]Then he sent another servant to them; they struck this man on the head and treated him

shamefully. [5]He sent still another, and that one they killed. He sent many others; some of them they beat, others they killed.

[6]"He had one left to send, a son, whom he loved. He sent him last of all, saying, 'They will respect my son.'

[7]"But the tenants said to one another, 'This is the heir. Come, let's kill him, and the inheritance will be ours.' [8]So they took him and killed him, and threw him out of the vineyard.

[9]"What then will the owner of the vineyard do? He will come and kill those tenants and give the vineyard to others. [10]Haven't you read this scripture:

" 'The stone the builders rejected
　　has become the capstone[v];
[11]the Lord has done this,
　　and it is marvelous in our eyes'[w]?"

[12]Then they looked for a way to arrest him because they knew he had spoken the parable against them. But they were afraid of the crowd; so they left him and went away.

[13]Later they sent some of the Pharisees and Herodians to Jesus to catch him in his words. [14]They came to him and said, "Teacher, we know you are a man of integrity. You aren't swayed by men, because you pay no attention to who they are; but you teach the way of God in accordance with the truth. Is it right to pay taxes to Caesar or not? [15]Should we pay or shouldn't we?"

But Jesus knew their hypocrisy. "Why are you trying to trap me?" he asked. "Bring me a denarius and let me look at it." [16]They brought the coin, and he asked them, "Whose portrait is this? And whose inscription?"

"Caesar's," they replied.

[17]Then Jesus said to them, "Give to Caesar what is Caesar's and to God what is God's."

And they were amazed at him.

[18]Then the Sadducees, who say there is no resurrection, came to him with a question. [19]"Teacher," they said, "Moses wrote for us that if a man's brother dies and leaves a wife but no children, the man must marry the widow and have children for his brother. [20]Now there were seven brothers. The first one married and died

without leaving any children. ²¹The second one married the widow, but he also died, leaving no child. It was the same with the third. ²²In fact, none of the seven left any children. Last of all, the woman died too. ²³At the resurrection^x whose wife will she be, since the seven were married to her?"

²⁴Jesus replied, "Are you not in error because you do not know the Scriptures or the power of God? ²⁵When the dead rise, they will neither marry nor be given in marriage; they will be like the angels in heaven. ²⁶Now about the dead rising—have you not read in the book of Moses, in the account of the bush, how God said to him, 'I am the God of Abraham, the God of Isaac, and the God of Jacob'^y? ²⁷He is not the God of the dead, but of the living. You are badly mistaken!"

²⁸One of the teachers of the law came and heard them debating. Noticing that Jesus had given them a good answer, he asked him, "Of all the commandments, which is the most important?"

²⁹"The most important one," answered Jesus, "is this: 'Hear, O Israel, the Lord our God, the Lord is one.^z ³⁰Love the Lord your God with all your heart and with all your soul and with all your mind and with all your strength.'^a ³¹The second is this: 'Love your neighbor as yourself.'^b There is no commandment greater than these."

³²"Well said, teacher," the man replied. "You are right in saying that God is one and there is no other but him. ³³To love him with all your heart, with all your understanding and with all your strength, and to love your neighbor as yourself is more important than all burnt offerings and sacrifices."

³⁴When Jesus saw that he had answered wisely, he said to him, "You are not far from the kingdom of God." And from then on no one dared ask him any more questions.

³⁵While Jesus was teaching in the temple courts, he asked, "How is it that the teachers of the law say that the Christ^c is the son of David? ³⁶David himself, speaking by the Holy Spirit, declared:

" 'The Lord said to my Lord:
   "Sit at my right hand

until I put your enemies
   under your feet." '^d

³⁷David himself calls him 'Lord.' How then can he be his son?"

The large crowd listened to him with delight.

³⁸As he taught, Jesus said, "Watch out for the teachers of the law. They like to walk around in flowing robes and be greeted in the marketplaces, ³⁹and have the most important seats in the synagogues and the places of honor at banquets. ⁴⁰They devour widows' houses and for a show make lengthy prayers. Such men will be punished most severely."

⁴¹Jesus sat down opposite the place where the offerings were put and watched the crowd putting their money into the temple treasury. Many rich people threw in large amounts. ⁴²But a poor widow came and put in two very small copper coins,^e worth only a fraction of a penny.^f

⁴³Calling his disciples to him, Jesus said, "I tell you the truth, this poor widow has put more into the treasury than all the others. ⁴⁴They all gave out of their wealth; but she, out of her poverty, put in everything—all she had to live on."

CHAPTER 13

As he was leaving the temple, one of his disciples said to him, "Look, Teacher! What massive stones! What magnificent buildings!"

²"Do you see all these great buildings?" replied Jesus. "Not one stone here will be left on another; every one will be thrown down."

³As Jesus was sitting on the Mount of Olives opposite the temple, Peter, James, John and Andrew asked him privately, ⁴"Tell us, when will these things happen? And what will be the sign that they are all about to be fulfilled?"

⁵Jesus said to them: "Watch out that no one deceives you. ⁶Many will come in my name, claiming, 'I am he,' and will deceive many. ⁷When you hear of wars and rumors of wars, do not be alarmed. Such things must happen, but the end is still to come. ⁸Nation will rise against nation, and kingdom against kingdom. There will be earthquakes in various places, and

^x23 Some manuscripts *resurrection, when men rise from the dead,*   ^y26 Exodus 3:6   ^z29 Or *the Lord our God is one Lord*   ^a30 Deut. 6:4,5   ^b31 Lev. 19:18   ^c35 Or *Messiah*   ^d36 Psalm 110:1   ^e42 Greek *two lepta*   ^f42 Greek *kodrantes*

famines. These are the beginning of birth pains.

⁹"You must be on your guard. You will be handed over to the local councils and flogged in the synagogues. On account of me you will stand before governors and kings as witnesses to them. ¹⁰And the gospel must first be preached to all nations. ¹¹Whenever you are arrested and brought to trial, do not worry beforehand about what to say. Just say whatever is given you at the time, for it is not you speaking, but the Holy Spirit.

¹²"Brother will betray brother to death, and a father his child. Children will rebel against their parents and have them put to death. ¹³All men will hate you because of me, but he who stands firm to the end will be saved.

¹⁴"When you see 'the abomination that causes desolation'ᵍ standing where itʰ does not belong—let the reader understand—then let those who are in Judea flee to the mountains. ¹⁵Let no one on the roof of his house go down or enter the house to take anything out. ¹⁶Let no one in the field go back to get his cloak. ¹⁷How dreadful it will be in those days for pregnant women and nursing mothers! ¹⁸Pray that this will not take place in winter, ¹⁹because those will be days of distress unequaled from the beginning, when God created the world, until now—and never to be equaled again. ²⁰If the Lord had not cut short those days, no one would survive. But for the sake of the elect, whom he has chosen, he has shortened them. ²¹At that time if anyone says to you, 'Look, here is the Christⁱ!' or, 'Look, there he is!' do not believe it. ²²For false Christs and false prophets will appear and perform signs and miracles to deceive the elect—if that were possible. ²³So be on

your guard; I have told you everything ahead of time.

²⁴"But in those days, following that distress,

" 'the sun will be darkened,
    and the moon will not give its light;
²⁵the stars will fall from the sky,
    and the heavenly bodies will be
        shaken.'ʲ

²⁶"At that time men will see the Son of Man coming in clouds with great power and glory. ²⁷And he will send his angels and gather his elect from the four winds, from the ends of the earth to the ends of the heavens.

²⁸"Now learn this lesson from the fig tree: As soon as its twigs get tender and its leaves come out, you know that summer is near. ²⁹Even so, when you see these things happening, you know that it is near, right at the door. ³⁰I tell you the truth, this generationᵏ will certainly not pass away until all these things have happened. ³¹Heaven and earth will pass away, but my words will never pass away.

³²"No one knows about that day or hour, not even the angels in heaven, nor the Son, but only the Father. ³³Be on guard! Be alertˡ! You do not know when that time will come. ³⁴It's like a man going away: He leaves his house and puts his servants in charge, each with his assigned task, and tells the one at the door to keep watch.

³⁵"Therefore keep watch because you do not know when the owner of the house will come back—whether in the evening, or at midnight, or when the rooster crows, or at dawn. ³⁶If he comes suddenly, do not let him find you sleeping. ³⁷What I say to you, I say to everyone: 'Watch!' "

ᵍ14 Daniel 9:27; 11:31; 12:11   ʰ14 Or he; also in verse 29   ⁱ21 Or Messiah   ʲ25 Isaiah 13:10; 34:4   ᵏ30 Or race   ˡ33 Some manuscripts alert and pray

OCTOBER 14 □ DAY 288
Committed to the Task

 LOOK BACK The final week of Jesus' life is so important, fully 40 percent of the verses in the four gospel accounts focus on the "week that changed the world." This past week you have read Matthew's account, and tomorrow you will read Mark's (and in the next three weeks you'll come to Luke's and John's). Notice which elements are repeated, which are omitted and which are elaborated upon by the different gospel writers. In each case, the author's intent is not to confuse you but to convince you that Jesus is indeed
- the King of the Jews (Matthew)
- the Selfless Servant (Mark)
- the Son of Man (Luke)
- the Son of God (John)

As you see the final days of Jesus' life through the eyes of a tax collector (Matthew), a missionary (Mark), a physician (Luke) and a fisherman (John), don't be surprised if your vision is sharpened to see his purpose in coming and his purpose for leaving you here on earth until his return.

 LOOK UP *Last* words have a tendency to be *lasting* words. And the final utterances of Jesus are no different.

Those on the road to heaven will not be content to go there alone.

The *Great Commission* is the name given to the final marching orders Jesus delivered to his disciples just before his death. You'll find the Great Commission in each of the four gospel accounts and (for good measure) in the book of Acts. Take a few moments to look up each of the following verses, and write down in your own words what Jesus told his disciples to do while he was away preparing an eternal home for them:

- Matthew 28:19–20 _____

- Mark 16:15 _____

- Luke 24:47 _____

- John 20:21 _____

- Acts 1:8 _____

 LOOK AHEAD Coca-Cola . . . General Motors . . . IBM . . . Why is it that a cola or car or computer can become a household word in places most people can hardly find on a map, while the good news of Jesus Christ remains a mystery to millions nearly twenty centuries after the news first broke?

Is it because their "product" has a better name than ours? Not likely. After all, we're introducing people to the one whose name is majestic in all the earth (Psalm 8:1).

Is it because their "product" is better for you than ours? Hardly. We have the privilege of introducing people to the bread of life and the water of life.

Is it because their budget is bigger than ours? Maybe. And yet, more than $2 billion is invested in world missions every year.

Or is it perhaps because they are simply more committed to *their* commission than we as Christians are committed to *ours*? It's well worth pondering and praying over.

OCTOBER 15 □ DAY 289
MARK 14–16
Suffering of the Servant

OVERVIEW While the devout Jews prepare for a feast, the chief priests prepare for an execution. The target of their conspiracy: Jesus of Nazareth, the Passover lamb of God. Judas's treachery and Jesus' last meal with his disciples set the stage for his arrest, trial, denial, scourging, crucifixion, burial and resurrection. But the story is not finished, for now his disciples are commissioned to bear the glad tidings worldwide—the Lord working with them (16:20)—servants in partnership with the Master Servant.

Chapter 14		Chapter 15	Chapter 16	
Servant's Anointing	Servant's Arrest	Servant's Abuse	Servant's Arising	Servant's Appearing
1 9	10 72	1	8	9 20
Preparation		Crucifixion	Resurrection	

Jesus Christ changed sunset into sunrise.

YOUR DAILY WALK What if . . . ? Pretend for a moment that the book of Mark ended at 15:37, rather than 16:20. Would that change the way you face life today?

The apostle Paul wrote an entire chapter probing the question "What if Jesus had died . . . and that was all?" See if you agree with his conclusions (1 Corinthians 15:12–19):

• Faith in Christ would be useless (v. 14).
• Christians would be false witnesses (v. 15).
• Christians would still be lost in their sins (v. 17).
• Deceased Christians would be hopelessly lost (v. 18).
• Christians would be the most pitiful people alive (v. 19).

Now read Paul's triumphant declaration in verse 20 (the same message Mark declares in 15:38–16:20). The heart of Christianity is Christ's resurrection. In the margin jot down three life-changing implications of that truth from 1 Corinthians 15:20–28. The message of Easter is not "what if . . . ?" but "because he lives!"

INSIGHT A Passover Population Bulge
Why did the chief priests want to wait till after the Passover to apprehend Jesus? Perhaps because Jerusalem's population skyrocketed from about fifty thousand to several hundred thousand each year during the Passover and the Feast of Unleavened Bread. With pilgrims from different districts and tribes mixing with Jews who had traveled in from other regions, any disturbances could have caused a large-scale riot.

CHAPTER 14
Now the Passover and the Feast of Unleavened Bread were only two days away, and the chief priests and the teachers of the law were looking for some sly way to arrest Jesus and kill him. ²"But not during the Feast," they said, "or the people may riot."

³While he was in Bethany, reclining at the table in the home of a man known as Simon the Leper, a woman came with an alabaster jar of very expensive perfume, made of pure nard. She broke the jar and poured the perfume on his head.

⁴Some of those present were saying indignantly to one another, "Why this waste of perfume? ⁵It could have been sold for more than a year's wages^m and the money given to the poor." And they rebuked her harshly.

^m 5 Greek *than three hundred denarii*

[6]"Leave her alone," said Jesus. "Why are you bothering her? She has done a beautiful thing to me. [7]The poor you will always have with you, and you can help them any time you want. But you will not always have me. [8]She did what she could. She poured perfume on my body beforehand to prepare for my burial. [9]I tell you the truth, wherever the gospel is preached throughout the world, what she has done will also be told, in memory of her."

[10]Then Judas Iscariot, one of the Twelve, went to the chief priests to betray Jesus to them. [11]They were delighted to hear this and promised to give him money. So he watched for an opportunity to hand him over.

[12]On the first day of the Feast of Unleavened Bread, when it was customary to sacrifice the Passover lamb, Jesus' disciples asked him, "Where do you want us to go and make preparations for you to eat the Passover?"

[13]So he sent two of his disciples, telling them, "Go into the city, and a man carrying a jar of water will meet you. Follow him. [14]Say to the owner of the house he enters, 'The Teacher asks: Where is my guest room, where I may eat the Passover with my disciples?' [15]He will show you a large upper room, furnished and ready. Make preparations for us there."

[16]The disciples left, went into the city and found things just as Jesus had told them. So they prepared the Passover.

[17]When evening came, Jesus arrived with the Twelve. [18]While they were reclining at the table eating, he said, "I tell you the truth, one of you will betray me—one who is eating with me."

[19]They were saddened, and one by one they said to him, "Surely not I?"

[20]"It is one of the Twelve," he replied, "one who dips bread into the bowl with me. [21]The Son of Man will go just as it is written about him. But woe to that man who betrays the Son of Man! It would be better for him if he had not been born."

[22]While they were eating, Jesus took bread, gave thanks and broke it, and gave it to his disciples, saying, "Take it; this is my body."

[23]Then he took the cup, gave thanks and offered it to them, and they all drank from it.

[24]"This is my blood of the[n] covenant, which is poured out for many," he said to them. [25]"I tell you the truth, I will not drink again of the fruit of the vine until that day when I drink it anew in the kingdom of God."

[26]When they had sung a hymn, they went out to the Mount of Olives.

[27]"You will all fall away," Jesus told them, "for it is written:

" 'I will strike the shepherd,
    and the sheep will be scattered.'[o]

[28]But after I have risen, I will go ahead of you into Galilee."

[29]Peter declared, "Even if all fall away, I will not."

[30]"I tell you the truth," Jesus answered, "today—yes, tonight—before the rooster crows twice[p] you yourself will disown me three times."

[31]But Peter insisted emphatically, "Even if I have to die with you, I will never disown you." And all the others said the same.

[32]They went to a place called Gethsemane, and Jesus said to his disciples, "Sit here while I pray." [33]He took Peter, James and John along with him, and he began to be deeply distressed and troubled. [34]"My soul is overwhelmed with sorrow to the point of death," he said to them. "Stay here and keep watch."

[35]Going a little farther, he fell to the ground and prayed that if possible the hour might pass from him. [36]"Abba,[q] Father," he said, "everything is possible for you. Take this cup from me. Yet not what I will, but what you will."

[37]Then he returned to his disciples and found them sleeping. "Simon," he said to Peter, "are you asleep? Could you not keep watch for one hour? [38]Watch and pray so that you will not fall into temptation. The spirit is willing, but the body is weak."

[39]Once more he went away and prayed the same thing. [40]When he came back, he again found them sleeping, because their eyes were heavy. They did not know what to say to him.

[41]Returning the third time, he said to them, "Are you still sleeping and resting? Enough! The hour has come. Look, the Son of Man is betrayed into the hands of

---

[n]24 Some manuscripts *the new*   [o]27 Zech. 13:7   [p]30 Some early manuscripts do not have *twice.*   [q]36 Aramaic for *Father*

sinners. [42]Rise! Let us go! Here comes my betrayer!"

[43]Just as he was speaking, Judas, one of the Twelve, appeared. With him was a crowd armed with swords and clubs, sent from the chief priests, the teachers of the law, and the elders.

[44]Now the betrayer had arranged a signal with them: "The one I kiss is the man; arrest him and lead him away under guard." [45]Going at once to Jesus, Judas said, "Rabbi!" and kissed him. [46]The men seized Jesus and arrested him. [47]Then one of those standing near drew his sword and struck the servant of the high priest, cutting off his ear.

[48]"Am I leading a rebellion," said Jesus, "that you have come out with swords and clubs to capture me? [49]Every day I was with you, teaching in the temple courts, and you did not arrest me. But the Scriptures must be fulfilled." [50]Then everyone deserted him and fled.

[51]A young man, wearing nothing but a linen garment, was following Jesus. When they seized him, [52]he fled naked, leaving his garment behind.

[53]They took Jesus to the high priest, and all the chief priests, elders and teachers of the law came together. [54]Peter followed him at a distance, right into the courtyard of the high priest. There he sat with the guards and warmed himself at the fire.

[55]The chief priests and the whole Sanhedrin were looking for evidence against Jesus so that they could put him to death, but they did not find any. [56]Many testified falsely against him, but their statements did not agree.

[57]Then some stood up and gave this false testimony against him: [58]"We heard him say, 'I will destroy this man-made temple and in three days will build another, not made by man.' " [59]Yet even then their testimony did not agree.

[60]Then the high priest stood up before them and asked Jesus, "Are you not going to answer? What is this testimony that these men are bringing against you?" [61]But Jesus remained silent and gave no answer.

Again the high priest asked him, "Are you the Christ,[r] the Son of the Blessed One?"

[62]"I am," said Jesus. "And you will see the Son of Man sitting at the right hand of the Mighty One and coming on the clouds of heaven."

[63]The high priest tore his clothes. "Why do we need any more witnesses?" he asked. [64]"You have heard the blasphemy. What do you think?"

They all condemned him as worthy of death. [65]Then some began to spit at him; they blindfolded him, struck him with their fists, and said, "Prophesy!" And the guards took him and beat him.

[66]While Peter was below in the courtyard, one of the servant girls of the high priest came by. [67]When she saw Peter warming himself, she looked closely at him.

"You also were with that Nazarene, Jesus," she said.

[68]But he denied it. "I don't know or understand what you're talking about," he said, and went out into the entryway.[s]

[69]When the servant girl saw him there, she said again to those standing around, "This fellow is one of them." [70]Again he denied it.

After a little while, those standing near said to Peter, "Surely you are one of them, for you are a Galilean."

[71]He began to call down curses on himself, and he swore to them, "I don't know this man you're talking about."

[72]Immediately the rooster crowed the second time.[t] Then Peter remembered the word Jesus had spoken to him: "Before the rooster crows twice[u] you will disown me three times." And he broke down and wept.

CHAPTER 15

Very early in the morning, the chief priests, with the elders, the teachers of the law and the whole Sanhedrin, reached a decision. They bound Jesus, led him away and handed him over to Pilate.

[2]"Are you the king of the Jews?" asked Pilate.

"Yes, it is as you say," Jesus replied.

[3]The chief priests accused him of many things. [4]So again Pilate asked him, "Aren't you going to answer? See how many things they are accusing you of."

[5]But Jesus still made no reply, and Pilate was amazed.

[6]Now it was the custom at the Feast to

---

[r]61 Or Messiah   [s]68 Some early manuscripts entryway and the rooster crowed   [t]72 Some early manuscripts do not have the second time.   [u]72 Some early manuscripts do not have twice.

release a prisoner whom the people requested. [7]A man called Barabbas was in prison with the insurrectionists who had committed murder in the uprising. [8]The crowd came up and asked Pilate to do for them what he usually did.

[9]"Do you want me to release to you the king of the Jews?" asked Pilate, [10]knowing it was out of envy that the chief priests had handed Jesus over to him. [11]But the chief priests stirred up the crowd to have Pilate release Barabbas instead.

[12]"What shall I do, then, with the one you call the king of the Jews?" Pilate asked them.

[13]"Crucify him!" they shouted.

[14]"Why? What crime has he committed?" asked Pilate.

But they shouted all the louder, "Crucify him!"

[15]Wanting to satisfy the crowd, Pilate released Barabbas to them. He had Jesus flogged, and handed him over to be crucified.

[16]The soldiers led Jesus away into the palace (that is, the Praetorium) and called together the whole company of soldiers. [17]They put a purple robe on him, then twisted together a crown of thorns and set it on him. [18]And they began to call out to him, "Hail, king of the Jews!" [19]Again and again they struck him on the head with a staff and spit on him. Falling on their knees, they paid homage to him. [20]And when they had mocked him, they took off the purple robe and put his own clothes on him. Then they led him out to crucify him.

[21]A certain man from Cyrene, Simon, the father of Alexander and Rufus, was passing by on his way in from the country, and they forced him to carry the cross. [22]They brought Jesus to the place called Golgotha (which means The Place of the Skull). [23]Then they offered him wine mixed with myrrh, but he did not take it. [24]And they crucified him. Dividing up his clothes, they cast lots to see what each would get.

[25]It was the third hour when they crucified him. [26]The written notice of the charge against him read: THE KING OF THE JEWS. [27]They crucified two robbers with him, one on his right and one on his left.[v] [29]Those who passed by hurled insults at him, shaking their heads and saying, "So! You who are going to destroy the temple and build it in three days, [30]come down from the cross and save yourself!"

[31]In the same way the chief priests and the teachers of the law mocked him among themselves. "He saved others," they said, "but he can't save himself! [32]Let this Christ,[w] this King of Israel, come down now from the cross, that we may see and believe." Those crucified with him also heaped insults on him.

[33]At the sixth hour darkness came over the whole land until the ninth hour. [34]And at the ninth hour Jesus cried out in a loud voice, "Eloi, Eloi, lama sabachthani?"—which means, "My God, my God, why have you forsaken me?"[x]

[35]When some of those standing near heard this, they said, "Listen, he's calling Elijah."

[36]One man ran, filled a sponge with wine vinegar, put it on a stick, and offered it to Jesus to drink. "Now leave him alone. Let's see if Elijah comes to take him down," he said.

[37]With a loud cry, Jesus breathed his last.

[38]The curtain of the temple was torn in two from top to bottom. [39]And when the centurion, who stood there in front of Jesus, heard his cry and[y] saw how he died, he said, "Surely this man was the Son[z] of God!"

[40]Some women were watching from a distance. Among them were Mary Magdalene, Mary the mother of James the younger and of Joses, and Salome. [41]In Galilee these women had followed him and cared for his needs. Many other women who had come up with him to Jerusalem were also there.

[42]It was Preparation Day (that is, the day before the Sabbath). So as evening approached, [43]Joseph of Arimathea, a prominent member of the Council, who was himself waiting for the kingdom of God, went boldly to Pilate and asked for Jesus' body. [44]Pilate was surprised to hear that he was already dead. Summoning the centurion, he asked him if Jesus had already died. [45]When he learned from the centurion that it was so, he gave the body to Joseph. [46]So Joseph bought some linen cloth, took down the body, wrapped it in

---

[v]27 Some manuscripts left, [28]and the scripture was fulfilled which says, "He was counted with the lawless ones" (Isaiah 53:12)   [w]32 Or Messiah   [x]34 Psalm 22:1   [y]39 Some manuscripts do not have heard his cry and   [z]39 Or a son

the linen, and placed it in a tomb cut out of rock. Then he rolled a stone against the entrance of the tomb. ⁴⁷Mary Magdalene and Mary the mother of Joses saw where he was laid.

CHAPTER 16

When the Sabbath was over, Mary Magdalene, Mary the mother of James, and Salome bought spices so that they might go to anoint Jesus' body. ²Very early on the first day of the week, just after sunrise, they were on their way to the tomb ³and they asked each other, "Who will roll the stone away from the entrance of the tomb?"

⁴But when they looked up, they saw that the stone, which was very large, had been rolled away. ⁵As they entered the tomb, they saw a young man dressed in a white robe sitting on the right side, and they were alarmed.

⁶"Don't be alarmed," he said. "You are looking for Jesus the Nazarene, who was crucified. He has risen! He is not here. See the place where they laid him. ⁷But go, tell his disciples and Peter, 'He is going ahead of you into Galilee. There you will see him, just as he told you.' "

⁸Trembling and bewildered, the women went out and fled from the tomb. They said nothing to anyone, because they were afraid.

[The earliest manuscripts and some other ancient witnesses do not have Mark 16:9–20.]

⁹When Jesus rose early on the first day of the week, he appeared first to Mary Magdalene, out of whom he had driven seven demons. ¹⁰She went and told those who had been with him and who were mourning and weeping. ¹¹When they heard that Jesus was alive and that she had seen him, they did not believe it.

¹²Afterward Jesus appeared in a different form to two of them while they were walking in the country. ¹³These returned and reported it to the rest; but they did not believe them either.

¹⁴Later Jesus appeared to the Eleven as they were eating; he rebuked them for their lack of faith and their stubborn refusal to believe those who had seen him after he had risen.

¹⁵He said to them, "Go into all the world and preach the good news to all creation. ¹⁶Whoever believes and is baptized will be saved, but whoever does not believe will be condemned. ¹⁷And these signs will accompany those who believe: In my name they will drive out demons; they will speak in new tongues; ¹⁸they will pick up snakes with their hands; and when they drink deadly poison, it will not hurt them at all; they will place their hands on sick people, and they will get well."

¹⁹After the Lord Jesus had spoken to them, he was taken up into heaven and he sat at the right hand of God. ²⁰Then the disciples went out and preached everywhere, and the Lord worked with them and confirmed his word by the signs that accompanied it.

Luke

LUKE, a Greek physician and missionary companion of the apostle Paul, intends his Gospel—along with the book of Acts—to be a primer for a new Christian named Theophilus. Luke stresses the humanity of Jesus as the one who understands people's weaknesses and cares for their needs. Luke's interest in historical accuracy leads him under divine inspiration to research and record the details of Jesus' life, including his family tree, social contacts and inner life of prayer and compassion.

Focus	Presentation			Exhortation					Resur-rection
Divisions	Advent of the Son of Man	Authority of the Son of Man	Activities of the Son of Man	Antagonism toward the Son of Man	Parables of the Son of Man (Part 1)	Parables of the Son of Man (Part 2)	Praise for the Son of Man		Passion of the Son of Man
	1 2	3 6	7 9	10 12	13 15	16 18	19 21		22 24
Topics	Miracles Prominent			Parables Prominent					
	Early Years		Earthly Ministry						Last Days
Place	Judea			Samaria and Perea					Jerusalem
Time	5 B.C–A.D. 33								

OCTOBER 16 ☐ DAY 290
LUKE 1–2
Advent of the Son of Man

OVERVIEW A careful historian, Luke seeks to relate the story of Christ's life in chronological order. He begins with the angelic announcements of two miraculous births: John the forerunner, who would prepare the way for Messiah, and Jesus the Christ, who would be born of a virgin. The arrival of the Christ child is described in meticulous detail, as you would expect from a physician. Angelic hosts and humble shepherds proclaim his arrival. The law is fulfilled in the infant Jesus' circumcision. Simeon and Anna, representatives of Israel's godly remnant, proclaim his identity. The silent years of growth in Nazareth are broken only by the incident in the temple at age twelve, an event that foreshadows the ministry of the Perfect Man.

	Chapter 1			Chapter 2
A Son for a Priest		A Son for a Virgin	A Prophet Named John	A Savior Named Jesus
1 25	26	56	57 80	
Angelic Announcements			Miraculous Births	

When you pray, make sure your will is in neutral so God can shift it.

YOUR DAILY WALK How abandoned are you to the will of God? How much of your life is available for God to direct—or redirect? Have you given him your finances? . . . your dating life? . . . your career plans? . . . your family?

Consider the case of a young Jewish maiden named Mary. God-fearing, virtuous, engaged and no doubt full of cherished dreams for the future, Mary was confronted by the angel Gabriel who announced she was God's choice to conceive and bear the Messiah. What must have gone through her mind at that point? *Who will believe I have conceived as a virgin? How will Joseph react to the news? What will happen to our wedding plans? What will my parents and friends think?* In spite of her questions, Mary's response was faith inspired. "I am the Lord's servant . . . May it be to me as you have said" (1:38).

God will never ask of you what he did of Mary, but he desires the same attitude from you: abandonment . . . availability . . . allegiance. Now go back and reread the questions in the first paragraph.

INSIGHT Know Your Angels by Name
Three angels are named in the Bible: Gabriel, the revealing angel (Daniel 8:16; 9:21; Luke 1:19, 26); Lucifer, the fallen angel (Isaiah 14:12); and Michael, the archangel (Daniel 10:13, 21; 12:1; Jude 9; Revelation 12:7).

CHAPTER 1
Many have undertaken to draw up an account of the things that have been fulfilled[a] among us, 2just as they were handed down to us by those who from the first were eyewitnesses and servants of the word. 3Therefore, since I myself have carefully investigated everything from the beginning, it seemed good also to me to write an orderly account for you,

[a]1 Or *been surely believed*

most excellent Theophilus, ⁴so that you may know the certainty of the things you have been taught.

⁵In the time of Herod king of Judea there was a priest named Zechariah, who belonged to the priestly division of Abijah; his wife Elizabeth was also a descendant of Aaron. ⁶Both of them were upright in the sight of God, observing all the Lord's commandments and regulations blamelessly. ⁷But they had no children, because Elizabeth was barren; and they were both well along in years.

⁸Once when Zechariah's division was on duty and he was serving as priest before God, ⁹he was chosen by lot, according to the custom of the priesthood, to go into the temple of the Lord and burn incense. ¹⁰And when the time for the burning of incense came, all the assembled worshipers were praying outside.

¹¹Then an angel of the Lord appeared to him, standing at the right side of the altar of incense. ¹²When Zechariah saw him, he was startled and was gripped with fear. ¹³But the angel said to him: "Do not be afraid, Zechariah; your prayer has been heard. Your wife Elizabeth will bear you a son, and you are to give him the name John. ¹⁴He will be a joy and delight to you, and many will rejoice because of his birth, ¹⁵for he will be great in the sight of the Lord. He is never to take wine or other fermented drink, and he will be filled with the Holy Spirit even from birth.ᵇ ¹⁶Many of the people of Israel will he bring back to the Lord their God. ¹⁷And he will go on before the Lord, in the spirit and power of Elijah, to turn the hearts of the fathers to their children and the disobedient to the wisdom of the righteous—to make ready a people prepared for the Lord."

¹⁸Zechariah asked the angel, "How can I be sure of this? I am an old man and my wife is well along in years."

¹⁹The angel answered, "I am Gabriel. I stand in the presence of God, and I have been sent to speak to you and to tell you this good news. ²⁰And now you will be silent and not able to speak until the day this happens, because you did not believe my words, which will come true at their proper time."

²¹Meanwhile, the people were waiting for Zechariah and wondering why he stayed so long in the temple. ²²When he came out, he could not speak to them. They realized he had seen a vision in the temple, for he kept making signs to them but remained unable to speak.

²³When his time of service was completed, he returned home. ²⁴After this his wife Elizabeth became pregnant and for five months remained in seclusion. ²⁵"The Lord has done this for me," she said. "In these days he has shown his favor and taken away my disgrace among the people."

²⁶In the sixth month, God sent the angel Gabriel to Nazareth, a town in Galilee, ²⁷to a virgin pledged to be married to a man named Joseph, a descendant of David. The virgin's name was Mary. ²⁸The angel went to her and said, "Greetings, you who are highly favored! The Lord is with you."

²⁹Mary was greatly troubled at his words and wondered what kind of greeting this might be. ³⁰But the angel said to her, "Do not be afraid, Mary, you have found favor with God. ³¹You will be with child and give birth to a son, and you are to give him the name Jesus. ³²He will be great and will be called the Son of the Most High. The Lord God will give him the throne of his father David, ³³and he will reign over the house of Jacob forever; his kingdom will never end."

³⁴"How will this be," Mary asked the angel, "since I am a virgin?"

³⁵The angel answered, "The Holy Spirit will come upon you, and the power of the Most High will overshadow you. So the holy one to be born will be calledᶜ the Son of God. ³⁶Even Elizabeth your relative is going to have a child in her old age, and she who was said to be barren is in her sixth month. ³⁷For nothing is impossible with God."

³⁸"I am the Lord's servant," Mary answered. "May it be to me as you have said." Then the angel left her.

³⁹At that time Mary got ready and hurried to a town in the hill country of Judea, ⁴⁰where she entered Zechariah's home and greeted Elizabeth. ⁴¹When Elizabeth heard Mary's greeting, the baby leaped in her womb, and Elizabeth was filled with the Holy Spirit. ⁴²In a loud voice she ex-

ᵇ15 Or from his mother's womb   ᶜ35 Or So the child to be born will be called holy, claimed: "Blessed are you among women, and blessed is the child you will bear! ⁴³But why am I so favored, that the mother of my Lord should come to me? ⁴⁴As soon as the sound of your greeting reached my ears, the baby in my womb leaped for joy. ⁴⁵Blessed is she who has believed that what the Lord has said to her will be accomplished!"

⁴⁶And Mary said:

"My soul glorifies the Lord
⁴⁷   and my spirit rejoices in God my
         Savior,
⁴⁸for he has been mindful
    of the humble state of his servant.
From now on all generations will call
    me blessed,
⁴⁹   for the Mighty One has done great
         things for me—
    holy is his name.
⁵⁰His mercy extends to those who fear
    him,
    from generation to generation.
⁵¹He has performed mighty deeds with
    his arm;
    he has scattered those who are
         proud in their inmost thoughts.
⁵²He has brought down rulers from their
         thrones
    but has lifted up the humble.
⁵³He has filled the hungry with good
         things
    but has sent the rich away empty.
⁵⁴He has helped his servant Israel,
    remembering to be merciful
⁵⁵to Abraham and his descendants
         forever,
    even as he said to our fathers."

⁵⁶Mary stayed with Elizabeth for about three months and then returned home.

⁵⁷When it was time for Elizabeth to have her baby, she gave birth to a son. ⁵⁸Her neighbors and relatives heard that the Lord had shown her great mercy, and they shared her joy.

⁵⁹On the eighth day they came to circumcise the child, and they were going to name him after his father Zechariah, ⁶⁰but his mother spoke up and said, "No! He is to be called John."

⁶¹They said to her, "There is no one among your relatives who has that name."

⁶²Then they made signs to his father, to find out what he would like to name the child. ⁶³He asked for a writing tablet, and to everyone's astonishment he wrote, "His name is John." ⁶⁴Immediately his mouth was opened and his tongue was loosed, and he began to speak, praising God. ⁶⁵The neighbors were all filled with awe, and throughout the hill country of Judea people were talking about all these things. ⁶⁶Everyone who heard this wondered about it, asking, "What then is this child going to be?" For the Lord's hand was with him.

⁶⁷His father Zechariah was filled with the Holy Spirit and prophesied:

⁶⁸"Praise be to the Lord, the God of
         Israel,
    because he has come and has
         redeemed his people.
⁶⁹He has raised up a horn*d* of salvation
         for us
    in the house of his servant David
⁷⁰(as he said through his holy prophets
         of long ago),
⁷¹salvation from our enemies
    and from the hand of all who hate
         us—
⁷²to show mercy to our fathers
    and to remember his holy covenant,
⁷³   the oath he swore to our father
         Abraham:
⁷⁴to rescue us from the hand of our
         enemies,
    and to enable us to serve him
         without fear
⁷⁵   in holiness and righteousness before
         him all our days.

⁷⁶And you, my child, will be called a
         prophet of the Most High;
    for you will go on before the Lord
         to prepare the way for him,
⁷⁷to give his people the knowledge of
         salvation
    through the forgiveness of their sins,
⁷⁸because of the tender mercy of our
         God,
    by which the rising sun will come to
         us from heaven
⁷⁹to shine on those living in darkness
    and in the shadow of death,
    to guide our feet into the path of
         peace."

⁸⁰And the child grew and became strong in spirit; and he lived in the desert until he appeared publicly to Israel.

d 69 Horn here symbolizes strength.

CHAPTER 2

In those days Caesar Augustus issued a decree that a census should be taken of the entire Roman world. ²(This was the first census that took place while Quirinius was governor of Syria.) ³And everyone went to his own town to register.

⁴So Joseph also went up from the town of Nazareth in Galilee to Judea, to Bethlehem the town of David, because he belonged to the house and line of David. ⁵He went there to register with Mary, who was pledged to be married to him and was expecting a child. ⁶While they were there, the time came for the baby to be born, ⁷and she gave birth to her firstborn, a son. She wrapped him in cloths and placed him in a manger, because there was no room for them in the inn.

⁸And there were shepherds living out in the fields nearby, keeping watch over their flocks at night. ⁹An angel of the Lord appeared to them, and the glory of the Lord shone around them, and they were terrified. ¹⁰But the angel said to them, "Do not be afraid. I bring you good news of great joy that will be for all the people. ¹¹Today in the town of David a Savior has been born to you; he is Christ[e] the Lord. ¹²This will be a sign to you: You will find a baby wrapped in cloths and lying in a manger."

¹³Suddenly a great company of the heavenly host appeared with the angel, praising God and saying,

¹⁴"Glory to God in the highest,
    and on earth peace to men on whom
        his favor rests."

¹⁵When the angels had left them and gone into heaven, the shepherds said to one another, "Let's go to Bethlehem and see this thing that has happened, which the Lord has told us about."

¹⁶So they hurried off and found Mary and Joseph, and the baby, who was lying in the manger. ¹⁷When they had seen him, they spread the word concerning what had been told them about this child, ¹⁸and all who heard it were amazed at what the shepherds said to them. ¹⁹But Mary treasured up all these things and pondered them in her heart. ²⁰The shepherds returned, glorifying and praising God for all the things they had heard and seen, which were just as they had been told.

²¹On the eighth day, when it was time to circumcise him, he was named Jesus, the name the angel had given him before he had been conceived.

²²When the time of their purification according to the Law of Moses had been completed, Joseph and Mary took him to Jerusalem to present him to the Lord ²³(as it is written in the Law of the Lord, "Every firstborn male is to be consecrated to the Lord"[f]), ²⁴and to offer a sacrifice in keeping with what is said in the Law of the Lord: "a pair of doves or two young pigeons."[g]

²⁵Now there was a man in Jerusalem called Simeon, who was righteous and devout. He was waiting for the consolation of Israel, and the Holy Spirit was upon him. ²⁶It had been revealed to him by the Holy Spirit that he would not die before he had seen the Lord's Christ. ²⁷Moved by the Spirit, he went into the temple courts. When the parents brought in the child Jesus to do for him what the custom of the Law required, ²⁸Simeon took him in his arms and praised God, saying:

²⁹"Sovereign Lord, as you have
        promised,
    you now dismiss[h] your servant in
        peace.
³⁰For my eyes have seen your salvation,
³¹   which you have prepared in the
        sight of all people,
³²a light for revelation to the Gentiles
    and for glory to your people Israel."

³³The child's father and mother marveled at what was said about him. ³⁴Then Simeon blessed them and said to Mary, his mother: "This child is destined to cause the falling and rising of many in Israel, and to be a sign that will be spoken against, ³⁵so that the thoughts of many hearts will be revealed. And a sword will pierce your own soul too."

³⁶There was also a prophetess, Anna, the daughter of Phanuel, of the tribe of Asher. She was very old; she had lived with her husband seven years after her marriage, ³⁷and then was a widow until she was eighty-four.[i] She never left the temple but worshiped night and day,

e 11 Or Messiah. "The Christ" (Greek) and "the Messiah" (Hebrew) both mean "the Anointed One"; also in verse 26.
f 23 Exodus 13:2,12   g 24 Lev. 12:8   h 29 Or promised, / now dismiss   i 37 Or widow for eighty-four years

fasting and praying. [38]Coming up to them at that very moment, she gave thanks to God and spoke about the child to all who were looking forward to the redemption of Jerusalem.

[39]When Joseph and Mary had done everything required by the Law of the Lord, they returned to Galilee to their own town of Nazareth. [40]And the child grew and became strong; he was filled with wisdom, and the grace of God was upon him.

[41]Every year his parents went to Jerusalem for the Feast of the Passover. [42]When he was twelve years old, they went up to the Feast, according to the custom. [43]After the Feast was over, while his parents were returning home, the boy Jesus stayed behind in Jerusalem, but they were unaware of it. [44]Thinking he was in their company, they traveled on for a day. Then they began looking for him among their relatives and friends. [45]When they did not find him, they went back to Jerusalem to look for him. [46]After three days they found him in the temple courts, sitting among the teachers, listening to them and asking them questions. [47]Everyone who heard him was amazed at his understanding and his answers. [48]When his parents saw him, they were astonished. His mother said to him, "Son, why have you treated us like this? Your father and I have been anxiously searching for you."

[49]"Why were you searching for me?" he asked. "Didn't you know I had to be in my Father's house?" [50]But they did not understand what he was saying to them.

[51]Then he went down to Nazareth with them and was obedient to them. But his mother treasured all these things in her heart. [52]And Jesus grew in wisdom and stature, and in favor with God and men.

OCTOBER 17 ☐ DAY 291
LUKE 3–6
Authority of the Son of Man

 OVERVIEW Before Jesus can begin his public ministry, he undertakes a period of preparation to show that he is worthy to minister. John, the promised forerunner, baptizes Jesus in the Jordan—an occasion marked by an audible voice from heaven declaring God's approval of his beloved Son. The character and obedience of Christ are tested through a series of temptations by Satan in the desert. Again Jesus emerges victorious. Returning "to Galilee in the power of the Spirit" (4:14), Jesus is ready to begin his earthly ministry as the obedient, approved Savior sent from God.

Chapter 3		Chapter 4	Chapter 5	Chapter 6
Preaching of John	Baptism of Jesus	Temptation of Jesus	Miracles of Jesus	Teaching of Jesus
1 20	21 38			
Preparation			Practice	

 YOUR DAILY WALK How important is Scripture memory in your personal schedule? Is it something you do hit-or-miss? (Usually that will result in missing more than you hit!)

Study carefully Christ's defense against the attacks of Satan (4:1–13). He did not preach; he did not argue; he merely quoted Scripture passages from the Old Testament. Three times Christ responded, "It is written" (4:4, 8, 12). Even more surprising, he quoted from a book of the Old Testament that most Christians have trouble spelling, much less explaining. (What is it?)

Apply yourself wholly to the Scriptures and the Scriptures wholly to yourself.

How well stocked are you with scriptural ammunition to counter the attacks of Satan? One good source of ammunition is a supply of memorized verses. Stop by your local Christian bookstore, or ask your pastor to recommend a plan. Also consider asking a friend or family member to listen as you recite your verses from time to time. Begin with a single verse and learn it well. You might want to start with one of the three verses that Christ found to be valuable in his own personal struggles with Satan: Deuteronomy 6:13, 16; 8:3. Memorizing Scripture takes time, but it's a habit worth developing.

 INSIGHT Significant Preparation for a Significant Decision
What steps of preparation do you take before making a major decision in your life? Notice what Jesus did the night before he selected the twelve disciples: "One of those days Jesus went out to a mountainside to pray, and spent the night praying to God" (6:12).

CHAPTER 3

In the fifteenth year of the reign of Tiberius Caesar—when Pontius Pilate was governor of Judea, Herod tetrarch of Galilee, his brother Philip tetrarch of Iturea and Traconitis, and Lysanias tetrarch of Abilene— ²during the high priesthood of Annas and Caiaphas, the word of God came to John son of Zechariah in the desert. ³He went into all the country around the Jordan, preaching a baptism of repentance for the forgiveness of sins. ⁴As is written in the book of the words of Isaiah the prophet:

"A voice of one calling in the desert,
'Prepare the way for the Lord,
    make straight paths for him.
⁵Every valley shall be filled in,
    every mountain and hill made low.
The crooked roads shall become
        straight,
    the rough ways smooth.
⁶And all mankind will see God's
        salvation.' " ʲ

⁷John said to the crowds coming out to be baptized by him, "You brood of vipers! Who warned you to flee from the coming wrath? ⁸Produce fruit in keeping with repentance. And do not begin to say to yourselves, 'We have Abraham as our father.' For I tell you that out of these stones God can raise up children for Abraham. ⁹The ax is already at the root of the trees, and every tree that does not produce good fruit will be cut down and thrown into the fire."

¹⁰"What should we do then?" the crowd asked.

¹¹John answered, "The man with two tunics should share with him who has

none, and the one who has food should do the same."

¹²Tax collectors also came to be baptized. "Teacher," they asked, "what should we do?"

¹³"Don't collect any more than you are required to," he told them.

¹⁴Then some soldiers asked him, "And what should we do?"

He replied, "Don't extort money and don't accuse people falsely—be content with your pay."

¹⁵The people were waiting expectantly and were all wondering in their hearts if John might possibly be the Christ.ᵏ ¹⁶John answered them all, "I baptize you withˡ water. But one more powerful than I will come, the thongs of whose sandals I am not worthy to untie. He will baptize you with the Holy Spirit and with fire. ¹⁷His winnowing fork is in his hand to clear his threshing floor and to gather the wheat into his barn, but he will burn up the chaff with unquenchable fire." ¹⁸And with many other words John exhorted the people and preached the good news to them.

¹⁹But when John rebuked Herod the tetrarch because of Herodias, his brother's wife, and all the other evil things he had done, ²⁰Herod added this to them all: He locked John up in prison.

²¹When all the people were being baptized, Jesus was baptized too. And as he was praying, heaven was opened ²²and the Holy Spirit descended on him in bodily form like a dove. And a voice came from heaven: "You are my Son, whom I love; with you I am well pleased."

²³Now Jesus himself was about thirty years old when he began his ministry. He was the son, so it was thought, of Joseph,

ʲ6 Isaiah 40:3-5   ᵏ15 Or Messiah   ˡ16 Or in

the son of Heli, [24]the son of Matthat,
the son of Levi, the son of Melki,
the son of Jannai, the son of Joseph,
[25]the son of Mattathias, the son of
   Amos,
the son of Nahum, the son of Esli,
the son of Naggai, [26]the son of Ma-
   ath,
the son of Mattathias, the son of
   Semein,
the son of Josech, the son of Joda,
[27]the son of Joanan, the son of Rhesa,
the son of Zerubbabel, the son of
   Shealtiel,
the son of Neri, [28]the son of Melki,
the son of Addi, the son of Cosam,
the son of Elmadam, the son of Er,
[29]the son of Joshua, the son of Eliezer,
the son of Jorim, the son of Matthat,
the son of Levi, [30]the son of Simeon,
the son of Judah, the son of Joseph,
the son of Jonam, the son of Eliakim,
[31]the son of Melea, the son of Menna,
the son of Mattatha, the son of Nathan,
the son of David, [32]the son of Jesse,
the son of Obed, the son of Boaz,
the son of Salmon,[m] the son of Nahshon,
[33]the son of Amminadab, the son of
   Ram,[n]
the son of Hezron, the son of Perez,
the son of Judah, [34]the son of Jacob,
the son of Isaac, the son of Abraham,
the son of Terah, the son of Nahor,
[35]the son of Serug, the son of Reu,
the son of Peleg, the son of Eber,
the son of Shelah, [36]the son of Cainan,
the son of Arphaxad, the son of
   Shem,
the son of Noah, the son of Lamech,
[37]the son of Methuselah, the son of
   Enoch,
the son of Jared, the son of Mahalalel,
the son of Kenan, [38]the son of Enosh,
the son of Seth, the son of Adam,
the son of God.

CHAPTER 4

Jesus, full of the Holy Spirit, returned
from the Jordan and was led by the Spirit
in the desert, [2]where for forty days he was
tempted by the devil. He ate nothing dur-

ing those days, and at the end of them he
was hungry.

[3]The devil said to him, "If you are the
Son of God, tell this stone to become
bread."

[4]Jesus answered, "It is written: 'Man
does not live on bread alone.'[o]"

[5]The devil led him up to a high place
and showed him in an instant all the
kingdoms of the world. [6]And he said to
him, "I will give you all their authority
and splendor, for it has been given to me,
and I can give it to anyone I want to. [7]So
if you worship me, it will all be yours."

[8]Jesus answered, "It is written: 'Worship
the Lord your God and serve him
only.'[p]"

[9]The devil led him to Jerusalem and
had him stand on the highest point of the
temple. "If you are the Son of God," he
said, "throw yourself down from here.
[10]For it is written:

" 'He will command his angels
      concerning you
   to guard you carefully;
[11]they will lift you up in their hands,
   so that you will not strike your foot
      against a stone.'[q]"

[12]Jesus answered, "It says: 'Do not put
the Lord your God to the test.'[r]"

[13]When the devil had finished all this
tempting, he left him until an opportune
time.

[14]Jesus returned to Galilee in the power
of the Spirit, and news about him spread
through the whole countryside. [15]He
taught in their synagogues, and everyone
praised him.

[16]He went to Nazareth, where he had
been brought up, and on the Sabbath day
he went into the synagogue, as was his
custom. And he stood up to read. [17]The
scroll of the prophet Isaiah was handed
to him. Unrolling it, he found the place
where it is written:

[18]"The Spirit of the Lord is on me,
   because he has anointed me
   to preach good news to the poor.
He has sent me to proclaim freedom
   for the prisoners
   and recovery of sight for the blind,
to release the oppressed,

---

m32 Some early manuscripts *Sala*   n33 Some manuscripts *Amminadab, the son of Admin, the son of Arni*; other manuscripts
vary widely.   o4 Deut. 8:3   p8 Deut. 6:13   q11 Psalm 91:11,12   r12 Deut. 6:16

[19] to proclaim the year of the Lord's favor."[s]

[20]Then he rolled up the scroll, gave it back to the attendant and sat down. The eyes of everyone in the synagogue were fastened on him, [21]and he began by saying to them, "Today this scripture is fulfilled in your hearing."

[22]All spoke well of him and were amazed at the gracious words that came from his lips. "Isn't this Joseph's son?" they asked.

[23]Jesus said to them, "Surely you will quote this proverb to me: 'Physician, heal yourself! Do here in your hometown what we have heard that you did in Capernaum.'"

[24]"I tell you the truth," he continued, "no prophet is accepted in his hometown. [25]I assure you that there were many widows in Israel in Elijah's time, when the sky was shut for three and a half years and there was a severe famine throughout the land. [26]Yet Elijah was not sent to any of them, but to a widow in Zarephath in the region of Sidon. [27]And there were many in Israel with leprosy[t] in the time of Elisha the prophet, yet not one of them was cleansed—only Naaman the Syrian."

[28]All the people in the synagogue were furious when they heard this. [29]They got up, drove him out of the town, and took him to the brow of the hill on which the town was built, in order to throw him down the cliff. [30]But he walked right through the crowd and went on his way.

[31]Then he went down to Capernaum, a town in Galilee, and on the Sabbath began to teach the people. [32]They were amazed at his teaching, because his message had authority.

[33]In the synagogue there was a man possessed by a demon, an evil[u] spirit. He cried out at the top of his voice, [34]"Ha! What do you want with us, Jesus of Nazareth? Have you come to destroy us? I know who you are—the Holy One of God!"

[35]"Be quiet!" Jesus said sternly. "Come out of him!" Then the demon threw the man down before them all and came out without injuring him.

[36]All the people were amazed and said to each other, "What is this teaching? With authority and power he gives orders to evil spirits and they come out!" [37]And the news about him spread throughout the surrounding area.

[38]Jesus left the synagogue and went to the home of Simon. Now Simon's mother-in-law was suffering from a high fever, and they asked Jesus to help her. [39]So he bent over her and rebuked the fever, and it left her. She got up at once and began to wait on them.

[40]When the sun was setting, the people brought to Jesus all who had various kinds of sickness, and laying his hands on each one, he healed them. [41]Moreover, demons came out of many people, shouting, "You are the Son of God!" But he rebuked them and would not allow them to speak, because they knew he was the Christ.[v]

[42]At daybreak Jesus went out to a solitary place. The people were looking for him and when they came to where he was, they tried to keep him from leaving them. [43]But he said, "I must preach the good news of the kingdom of God to the other towns also, because that is why I was sent." [44]And he kept on preaching in the synagogues of Judea.[w]

CHAPTER 5

One day as Jesus was standing by the Lake of Gennesaret,[x] with the people crowding around him and listening to the word of God, [2]he saw at the water's edge two boats, left there by the fishermen, who were washing their nets. [3]He got into one of the boats, the one belonging to Simon, and asked him to put out a little from shore. Then he sat down and taught the people from the boat.

[4]When he had finished speaking, he said to Simon, "Put out into deep water, and let down[y] the nets for a catch."

[5]Simon answered, "Master, we've worked hard all night and haven't caught anything. But because you say so, I will let down the nets."

[6]When they had done so, they caught such a large number of fish that their nets began to break. [7]So they signaled their partners in the other boat to come and

[s]19 Isaiah 61:1,2   [t]27 The Greek word was used for various diseases affecting the skin—not necessarily leprosy.   [u]33 Greek unclean; also in verse 36   [v]41 Or Messiah   [w]44 Or the land of the Jews; some manuscripts Galilee   [x]1 That is, Sea of Galilee [y]4 The Greek verb is plural.

help them, and they came and filled both boats so full that they began to sink.

⁸When Simon Peter saw this, he fell at Jesus' knees and said, "Go away from me, Lord; I am a sinful man!" ⁹For he and all his companions were astonished at the catch of fish they had taken, ¹⁰and so were James and John, the sons of Zebedee, Simon's partners.

Then Jesus said to Simon, "Don't be afraid; from now on you will catch men." ¹¹So they pulled their boats up on shore, left everything and followed him.

¹²While Jesus was in one of the towns, a man came along who was covered with leprosy.ᶻ When he saw Jesus, he fell with his face to the ground and begged him, "Lord, if you are willing, you can make me clean."

¹³Jesus reached out his hand and touched the man. "I am willing," he said. "Be clean!" And immediately the leprosy left him.

¹⁴Then Jesus ordered him, "Don't tell anyone, but go, show yourself to the priest and offer the sacrifices that Moses commanded for your cleansing, as a testimony to them."

¹⁵Yet the news about him spread all the more, so that crowds of people came to hear him and to be healed of their sicknesses. ¹⁶But Jesus often withdrew to lonely places and prayed.

¹⁷One day as he was teaching, Pharisees and teachers of the law, who had come from every village of Galilee and from Judea and Jerusalem, were sitting there. And the power of the Lord was present for him to heal the sick. ¹⁸Some men came carrying a paralytic on a mat and tried to take him into the house to lay him before Jesus. ¹⁹When they could not find a way to do this because of the crowd, they went up on the roof and lowered him on his mat through the tiles into the middle of the crowd, right in front of Jesus.

²⁰When Jesus saw their faith, he said, "Friend, your sins are forgiven."

²¹The Pharisees and the teachers of the law began thinking to themselves, "Who is this fellow who speaks blasphemy? Who can forgive sins but God alone?"

²²Jesus knew what they were thinking and asked, "Why are you thinking these things in your hearts? ²³Which is easier: to say, 'Your sins are forgiven,' or to say, 'Get up and walk'? ²⁴But that you may know that the Son of Man has authority on earth to forgive sins . . ." He said to the paralyzed man, "I tell you, get up, take your mat and go home." ²⁵Immediately he stood up in front of them, took what he had been lying on and went home praising God. ²⁶Everyone was amazed and gave praise to God. They were filled with awe and said, "We have seen remarkable things today."

²⁷After this, Jesus went out and saw a tax collector by the name of Levi sitting at his tax booth. "Follow me," Jesus said to him, ²⁸and Levi got up, left everything and followed him.

²⁹Then Levi held a great banquet for Jesus at his house, and a large crowd of tax collectors and others were eating with them. ³⁰But the Pharisees and the teachers of the law who belonged to their sect complained to his disciples, "Why do you eat and drink with tax collectors and 'sinners'?"

³¹Jesus answered them, "It is not the healthy who need a doctor, but the sick. ³²I have not come to call the righteous, but sinners to repentance."

³³They said to him, "John's disciples often fast and pray, and so do the disciples of the Pharisees, but yours go on eating and drinking."

³⁴Jesus answered, "Can you make the guests of the bridegroom fast while he is with them? ³⁵But the time will come when the bridegroom will be taken from them; in those days they will fast."

³⁶He told them this parable: "No one tears a patch from a new garment and sews it on an old one. If he does, he will have torn the new garment, and the patch from the new will not match the old. ³⁷And no one pours new wine into old wineskins. If he does, the new wine will burst the skins, the wine will run out and the wineskins will be ruined. ³⁸No, new wine must be poured into new wineskins. ³⁹And no one after drinking old wine wants the new, for he says, 'The old is better.'"

CHAPTER 6
One Sabbath Jesus was going through the grainfields, and his disciples began to

ᶻ12 The Greek word was used for various diseases affecting the skin—not necessarily leprosy.

pick some heads of grain, rub them in their hands and eat the kernels. ²Some of the Pharisees asked, "Why are you doing what is unlawful on the Sabbath?"

³Jesus answered them, "Have you never read what David did when he and his companions were hungry? ⁴He entered the house of God, and taking the consecrated bread, he ate what is lawful only for priests to eat. And he also gave some to his companions." ⁵Then Jesus said to them, "The Son of Man is Lord of the Sabbath."

⁶On another Sabbath he went into the synagogue and was teaching, and a man was there whose right hand was shriveled. ⁷The Pharisees and the teachers of the law were looking for a reason to accuse Jesus, so they watched him closely to see if he would heal on the Sabbath. ⁸But Jesus knew what they were thinking and said to the man with the shriveled hand, "Get up and stand in front of everyone." So he got up and stood there.

⁹Then Jesus said to them, "I ask you, which is lawful on the Sabbath: to do good or to do evil, to save life or to destroy it?"

¹⁰He looked around at them all, and then said to the man, "Stretch out your hand." He did so, and his hand was completely restored. ¹¹But they were furious and began to discuss with one another what they might do to Jesus.

¹²One of those days Jesus went out to a mountainside to pray, and spent the night praying to God. ¹³When morning came, he called his disciples to him and chose twelve of them, whom he also designated apostles: ¹⁴Simon (whom he named Peter), his brother Andrew, James, John, Philip, Bartholomew, ¹⁵Matthew, Thomas, James son of Alphaeus, Simon who was called the Zealot, ¹⁶Judas son of James, and Judas Iscariot, who became a traitor.

¹⁷He went down with them and stood on a level place. A large crowd of his disciples was there and a great number of people from all over Judea, from Jerusalem, and from the coast of Tyre and Sidon, ¹⁸who had come to hear him and to be healed of their diseases. Those troubled by evil*ᵃ* spirits were cured, ¹⁹and the people all tried to touch him, because

power was coming from him and healing them all.

²⁰Looking at his disciples, he said:

"Blessed are you who are poor,
     for yours is the kingdom of God.
²¹Blessed are you who hunger now,
     for you will be satisfied.
Blessed are you who weep now,
     for you will laugh.
²²Blessed are you when men hate you,
     when they exclude you and insult
          you
     and reject your name as evil,
          because of the Son of Man.

²³"Rejoice in that day and leap for joy, because great is your reward in heaven. For that is how their fathers treated the prophets.

²⁴"But woe to you who are rich,
     for you have already received your
          comfort.
²⁵Woe to you who are well fed now,
     for you will go hungry.
Woe to you who laugh now,
     for you will mourn and weep.
²⁶Woe to you when all men speak well
          of you,
     for that is how their fathers treated
          the false prophets.

²⁷"But I tell you who hear me: Love your enemies, do good to those who hate you, ²⁸bless those who curse you, pray for those who mistreat you. ²⁹If someone strikes you on one cheek, turn to him the other also. If someone takes your cloak, do not stop him from taking your tunic. ³⁰Give to everyone who asks you, and if anyone takes what belongs to you, do not demand it back. ³¹Do to others as you would have them do to you.

³²"If you love those who love you, what credit is that to you? Even 'sinners' love those who love them. ³³And if you do good to those who are good to you, what credit is that to you? Even 'sinners' do that. ³⁴And if you lend to those from whom you expect repayment, what credit is that to you? Even 'sinners' lend to 'sinners,' expecting to be repaid in full. ³⁵But love your enemies, do good to them, and lend to them without expecting to get anything back. Then your reward will be great, and you will be sons of the Most

ᵃ18 Greek *unclean*

High, because he is kind to the ungrateful and wicked. ³⁶Be merciful, just as your Father is merciful.

³⁷"Do not judge, and you will not be judged. Do not condemn, and you will not be condemned. Forgive, and you will be forgiven. ³⁸Give, and it will be given to you. A good measure, pressed down, shaken together and running over, will be poured into your lap. For with the measure you use, it will be measured to you."

³⁹He also told them this parable: "Can a blind man lead a blind man? Will they not both fall into a pit? ⁴⁰A student is not above his teacher, but everyone who is fully trained will be like his teacher.

⁴¹"Why do you look at the speck of sawdust in your brother's eye and pay no attention to the plank in your own eye? ⁴²How can you say to your brother, 'Brother, let me take the speck out of your eye,' when you yourself fail to see the plank in your own eye? You hypocrite, first take the plank out of your eye, and then you will see clearly to remove the speck from your brother's eye.

⁴³"No good tree bears bad fruit, nor does a bad tree bear good fruit. ⁴⁴Each tree is recognized by its own fruit. People do not pick figs from thornbushes, or grapes from briers. ⁴⁵The good man brings good things out of the good stored up in his heart, and the evil man brings evil things out of the evil stored up in his heart. For out of the overflow of his heart his mouth speaks.

⁴⁶"Why do you call me, 'Lord, Lord,' and do not do what I say? ⁴⁷I will show you what he is like who comes to me and hears my words and puts them into practice. ⁴⁸He is like a man building a house, who dug down deep and laid the foundation on rock. When a flood came, the torrent struck that house but could not shake it, because it was well built. ⁴⁹But the one who hears my words and does not put them into practice is like a man who built a house on the ground without a foundation. The moment the torrent struck that house, it collapsed and its destruction was complete."

OCTOBER 18 □ DAY 292
LUKE 7–9
Activities of the Son of Man

 OVERVIEW Today's reading may leave you just a little breathless. In the space of these three chapters Jesus travels from the region of Galilee to the surrounding provinces east of the Sea of Galilee, north to Caesarea Philippi and finally south through Samaria. As he travels, the demands on him increase. He is busily engaged in healing the sick, raising the dead, teaching through parables, calming storms and casting out demons. But Jesus knows his days on earth will be short. So he choses twelve men—disciples—to whom he delegates his power and authority to minister. This is no halfhearted call to discipleship, for the terms of commitment are drastic indeed (9:23–26, 57–62).

Chapter 7	Chapter 8	Chapter 9
The Testimony of Healing	The Testimony of Teaching	The Testimony of Training
The Son of Man Did Not Come to Destroy Men's Lives, but to Save Them.		

 YOUR DAILY WALK What would be different about your life if you were a "drastic disciple" of Jesus Christ?

The lessons for disciples and tests of discipleship that are contained in chapter 9 do not make for easy reading. They are painfully pointed, calling for commitment in matters of allegiance, lifestyle and goals.

God deserves the same place in your heart that he holds in the universe. Christ made the terms of discipleship unmistakably clear. Read the following verses prayerfully, asking yourself, How do I need to change if my Christian life is to reflect that kind of commitment?

"If anyone would come after me, he must deny himself and take up his cross daily and follow me" (9:23).

"If anyone is ashamed of me and my words, the Son of Man will be ashamed of him" (9:26).

"No one who puts his hand to the plow and looks back is fit for service in the kingdom of God" (9:62).

 INSIGHT The Messiah of Many Names
Look for the variety of names and titles ascribed to Jesus in these chapters. Can you find the two times he is identified as the Son of God? How about the six occurrences of Jesus' favorite name for himself, *Son of Man?* How many times does *Lord* occur? There is only one use of the word *Christ* ("the Anointed One") in these chapters. Can you find it? What other names and titles can you find?

CHAPTER 7

When Jesus had finished saying all this in the hearing of the people, he entered Capernaum. ²There a centurion's servant, whom his master valued highly, was sick and about to die. ³The centurion heard of Jesus and sent some elders of the Jews to him, asking him to come and heal his servant. ⁴When they came to Jesus, they pleaded earnestly with him, "This man deserves to have you do this, ⁵because he loves our nation and has built our synagogue." ⁶So Jesus went with them.

He was not far from the house when the centurion sent friends to say to him: "Lord, don't trouble yourself, for I do not deserve to have you come under my roof. ⁷That is why I did not even consider myself worthy to come to you. But say the word, and my servant will be healed. ⁸For I myself am a man under authority, with soldiers under me. I tell this one, 'Go,' and he goes; and that one, 'Come,' and he comes. I say to my servant, 'Do this,' and he does it."

⁹When Jesus heard this, he was amazed at him, and turning to the crowd following him, he said, "I tell you, I have not found such great faith even in Israel." ¹⁰Then the men who had been sent returned to the house and found the servant well.

¹¹Soon afterward, Jesus went to a town called Nain, and his disciples and a large crowd went along with him. ¹²As he approached the town gate, a dead person was being carried out—the only son of his mother, and she was a widow. And a large crowd from the town was with her. ¹³When the Lord saw her, his heart went out to her and he said, "Don't cry."

¹⁴Then he went up and touched the coffin, and those carrying it stood still. He said, "Young man, I say to you, get up!" ¹⁵The dead man sat up and began to talk, and Jesus gave him back to his mother.

¹⁶They were all filled with awe and praised God. "A great prophet has appeared among us," they said. "God has come to help his people." ¹⁷This news about Jesus spread throughout Judea^b and the surrounding country.

¹⁸John's disciples told him about all these things. Calling two of them, ¹⁹he sent them to the Lord to ask, "Are you the one who was to come, or should we expect someone else?"

²⁰When the men came to Jesus, they said, "John the Baptist sent us to you to ask, 'Are you the one who was to come, or should we expect someone else?' "

²¹At that very time Jesus cured many who had diseases, sicknesses and evil spirits, and gave sight to many who were blind. ²²So he replied to the messengers, "Go back and report to John what you have seen and heard: The blind receive sight, the lame walk, those who have leprosy^c are cured, the deaf hear, the dead are raised, and the good news is preached to the poor. ²³Blessed is the man who does not fall away on account of me."

²⁴After John's messengers left, Jesus began to speak to the crowd about John: "What did you go out into the desert to see? A reed swayed by the wind? ²⁵If not,

^b17 Or *the land of the Jews*   ^c22 The Greek word was used for various diseases affecting the skin—not necessarily leprosy.

what did you go out to see? A man dressed in fine clothes? No, those who wear expensive clothes and indulge in luxury are in palaces. ²⁶But what did you go out to see? A prophet? Yes, I tell you, and more than a prophet. ²⁷This is the one about whom it is written:

" 'I will send my messenger ahead of
    you,
  who will prepare your way before
    you.'ᵈ

²⁸I tell you, among those born of women there is no one greater than John; yet the one who is least in the kingdom of God is greater than he."

²⁹(All the people, even the tax collectors, when they heard Jesus' words, acknowledged that God's way was right, because they had been baptized by John. ³⁰But the Pharisees and experts in the law rejected God's purpose for themselves, because they had not been baptized by John.)

³¹"To what, then, can I compare the people of this generation? What are they like? ³²They are like children sitting in the marketplace and calling out to each other:

" 'We played the flute for you,
    and you did not dance;
  we sang a dirge,
    and you did not cry.'

³³For John the Baptist came neither eating bread nor drinking wine, and you say, 'He has a demon.' ³⁴The Son of Man came eating and drinking, and you say, 'Here is a glutton and a drunkard, a friend of tax collectors and "sinners." ' ³⁵But wisdom is proved right by all her children."

³⁶Now one of the Pharisees invited Jesus to have dinner with him, so he went to the Pharisee's house and reclined at the table. ³⁷When a woman who had lived a sinful life in that town learned that Jesus was eating at the Pharisee's house, she brought an alabaster jar of perfume, ³⁸and as she stood behind him at his feet weeping, she began to wet his feet with her tears. Then she wiped them with her hair, kissed them and poured perfume on them.

³⁹When the Pharisee who had invited him saw this, he said to himself, "If this man were a prophet, he would know who is touching him and what kind of woman she is—that she is a sinner."

⁴⁰Jesus answered him, "Simon, I have something to tell you."

"Tell me, teacher," he said.

⁴¹"Two men owed money to a certain moneylender. One owed him five hundred denarii,ᵉ and the other fifty. ⁴²Neither of them had the money to pay him back, so he canceled the debts of both. Now which of them will love him more?"

⁴³Simon replied, "I suppose the one who had the bigger debt canceled."

"You have judged correctly," Jesus said.

⁴⁴Then he turned toward the woman and said to Simon, "Do you see this woman? I came into your house. You did not give me any water for my feet, but she wet my feet with her tears and wiped them with her hair. ⁴⁵You did not give me a kiss, but this woman, from the time I entered, has not stopped kissing my feet. ⁴⁶You did not put oil on my head, but she has poured perfume on my feet. ⁴⁷Therefore, I tell you, her many sins have been forgiven—for she loved much. But he who has been forgiven little loves little."

⁴⁸Then Jesus said to her, "Your sins are forgiven."

⁴⁹The other guests began to say among themselves, "Who is this who even forgives sins?"

⁵⁰Jesus said to the woman, "Your faith has saved you; go in peace."

CHAPTER 8

After this, Jesus traveled about from one town and village to another, proclaiming the good news of the kingdom of God. The Twelve were with him, ²and also some women who had been cured of evil spirits and diseases: Mary (called Magdalene) from whom seven demons had come out; ³Joanna the wife of Cuza, the manager of Herod's household; Susanna; and many others. These women were helping to support them out of their own means.

⁴While a large crowd was gathering and people were coming to Jesus from town after town, he told this parable: ⁵"A farmer went out to sow his seed. As he was scattering the seed, some fell along the path; it was trampled on, and the birds of the air ate it up. ⁶Some fell on

ᵈ27 Mal. 3:1　ᵉ41 A denarius was a coin worth about a day's wages.

rock, and when it came up, the plants withered because they had no moisture. [7]Other seed fell among thorns, which grew up with it and choked the plants. [8]Still other seed fell on good soil. It came up and yielded a crop, a hundred times more than was sown."

When he said this, he called out, "He who has ears to hear, let him hear."

[9]His disciples asked him what this parable meant. [10]He said, "The knowledge of the secrets of the kingdom of God has been given to you, but to others I speak in parables, so that,

" 'though seeing, they may not see;
    though hearing, they may not
        understand.'[f]

[11]"This is the meaning of the parable: The seed is the word of God. [12]Those along the path are the ones who hear, and then the devil comes and takes away the word from their hearts, so that they may not believe and be saved. [13]Those on the rock are the ones who receive the word with joy when they hear it, but they have no root. They believe for a while, but in the time of testing they fall away. [14]The seed that fell among thorns stands for those who hear, but as they go on their way they are choked by life's worries, riches and pleasures, and they do not mature. [15]But the seed on good soil stands for those with a noble and good heart, who hear the word, retain it, and by persevering produce a crop.

[16]"No one lights a lamp and hides it in a jar or puts it under a bed. Instead, he puts it on a stand, so that those who come in can see the light. [17]For there is nothing hidden that will not be disclosed, and nothing concealed that will not be known or brought out into the open. [18]Therefore consider carefully how you listen. Whoever has will be given more; whoever does not have, even what he thinks he has will be taken from him."

[19]Now Jesus' mother and brothers came to see him, but they were not able to get near him because of the crowd. [20]Someone told him, "Your mother and brothers are standing outside, wanting to see you."

[21]He replied, "My mother and brothers are those who hear God's word and put it into practice."

[22]One day Jesus said to his disciples, "Let's go over to the other side of the lake." So they got into a boat and set out. [23]As they sailed, he fell asleep. A squall came down on the lake, so that the boat was being swamped, and they were in great danger.

[24]The disciples went and woke him, saying, "Master, Master, we're going to drown!"

He got up and rebuked the wind and the raging waters; the storm subsided, and all was calm. [25]"Where is your faith?" he asked his disciples.

In fear and amazement they asked one another, "Who is this? He commands even the winds and the water, and they obey him."

[26]They sailed to the region of the Gerasenes,[g] which is across the lake from Galilee. [27]When Jesus stepped ashore, he was met by a demon-possessed man from the town. For a long time this man had not worn clothes or lived in a house, but had lived in the tombs. [28]When he saw Jesus, he cried out and fell at his feet, shouting at the top of his voice, "What do you want with me, Jesus, Son of the Most High God? I beg you, don't torture me!" [29]For Jesus had commanded the evil[h] spirit to come out of the man. Many times it had seized him, and though he was chained hand and foot and kept under guard, he had broken his chains and had been driven by the demon into solitary places.

[30]Jesus asked him, "What is your name?"

"Legion," he replied, because many demons had gone into him. [31]And they begged him repeatedly not to order them to go into the Abyss.

[32]A large herd of pigs was feeding there on the hillside. The demons begged Jesus to let them go into them, and he gave them permission. [33]When the demons came out of the man, they went into the pigs, and the herd rushed down the steep bank into the lake and was drowned.

[34]When those tending the pigs saw what had happened, they ran off and reported this in the town and countryside, [35]and the people went out to see what had happened. When they came to Jesus, they found the man from whom the demons

[f]10 Isaiah 6:9   [g]26 Some manuscripts *Gadarenes*; other manuscripts *Gergesenes*; also in verse 37   [h]29 Greek *unclean*

had gone out, sitting at Jesus' feet, dressed and in his right mind; and they were afraid. 36Those who had seen it told the people how the demon-possessed man had been cured. 37Then all the people of the region of the Gerasenes asked Jesus to leave them, because they were overcome with fear. So he got into the boat and left.

38The man from whom the demons had gone out begged to go with him, but Jesus sent him away, saying, 39"Return home and tell how much God has done for you." So the man went away and told all over town how much Jesus had done for him.

40Now when Jesus returned, a crowd welcomed him, for they were all expecting him. 41Then a man named Jairus, a ruler of the synagogue, came and fell at Jesus' feet, pleading with him to come to his house 42because his only daughter, a girl of about twelve, was dying.

As Jesus was on his way, the crowds almost crushed him. 43And a woman was there who had been subject to bleeding for twelve years,*i* but no one could heal her. 44She came up behind him and touched the edge of his cloak, and immediately her bleeding stopped.

45"Who touched me?" Jesus asked.

When they all denied it, Peter said, "Master, the people are crowding and pressing against you."

46But Jesus said, "Someone touched me; I know that power has gone out from me."

47Then the woman, seeing that she could not go unnoticed, came trembling and fell at his feet. In the presence of all the people, she told why she had touched him and how she had been instantly healed. 48Then he said to her, "Daughter, your faith has healed you. Go in peace."

49While Jesus was still speaking, someone came from the house of Jairus, the synagogue ruler. "Your daughter is dead," he said. "Don't bother the teacher any more."

50Hearing this, Jesus said to Jairus, "Don't be afraid; just believe, and she will be healed."

51When he arrived at the house of Jairus, he did not let anyone go in with him except Peter, John and James, and the child's father and mother. 52Meanwhile, all the people were wailing and mourning for her. "Stop wailing," Jesus said. "She is not dead but asleep."

53They laughed at him, knowing that she was dead. 54But he took her by the hand and said, "My child, get up!" 55Her spirit returned, and at once she stood up. Then Jesus told them to give her something to eat. 56Her parents were astonished, but he ordered them not to tell anyone what had happened.

CHAPTER 9

When Jesus had called the Twelve together, he gave them power and authority to drive out all demons and to cure diseases, 2and he sent them out to preach the kingdom of God and to heal the sick. 3He told them: "Take nothing for the journey— no staff, no bag, no bread, no money, no extra tunic. 4Whatever house you enter, stay there until you leave that town. 5If people do not welcome you, shake the dust off your feet when you leave their town, as a testimony against them." 6So they set out and went from village to village, preaching the gospel and healing people everywhere.

7Now Herod the tetrarch heard about all that was going on. And he was perplexed, because some were saying that John had been raised from the dead, 8others that Elijah had appeared, and still others that one of the prophets of long ago had come back to life. 9But Herod said, "I beheaded John. Who, then, is this I hear such things about?" And he tried to see him.

10When the apostles returned, they reported to Jesus what they had done. Then he took them with him and they withdrew by themselves to a town called Bethsaida, 11but the crowds learned about it and followed him. He welcomed them and spoke to them about the kingdom of God, and healed those who needed healing.

12Late in the afternoon the Twelve came to him and said, "Send the crowd away so they can go to the surrounding villages and countryside and find food and lodging, because we are in a remote place here."

i43 Many manuscripts *years, and she had spent all she had on doctors*

¹³He replied, "You give them something to eat."

They answered, "We have only five loaves of bread and two fish—unless we go and buy food for all this crowd." ¹⁴(About five thousand men were there.)

But he said to his disciples, "Have them sit down in groups of about fifty each." ¹⁵The disciples did so, and everybody sat down. ¹⁶Taking the five loaves and the two fish and looking up to heaven, he gave thanks and broke them. Then he gave them to the disciples to set before the people. ¹⁷They all ate and were satisfied, and the disciples picked up twelve basketfuls of broken pieces that were left over.

¹⁸Once when Jesus was praying in private and his disciples were with him, he asked them, "Who do the crowds say I am?"

¹⁹They replied, "Some say John the Baptist; others say Elijah; and still others, that one of the prophets of long ago has come back to life."

²⁰"But what about you?" he asked. "Who do you say I am?"

Peter answered, "The Christʲ of God."

²¹Jesus strictly warned them not to tell this to anyone. ²²And he said, "The Son of Man must suffer many things and be rejected by the elders, chief priests and teachers of the law, and he must be killed and on the third day be raised to life."

²³Then he said to them all: "If anyone would come after me, he must deny himself and take up his cross daily and follow me. ²⁴For whoever wants to save his life will lose it, but whoever loses his life for me will save it. ²⁵What good is it for a man to gain the whole world, and yet lose or forfeit his very self? ²⁶If anyone is ashamed of me and my words, the Son of Man will be ashamed of him when he comes in his glory and in the glory of the Father and of the holy angels. ²⁷I tell you the truth, some who are standing here will not taste death before they see the kingdom of God."

²⁸About eight days after Jesus said this, he took Peter, John and James with him and went up onto a mountain to pray. ²⁹As he was praying, the appearance of his face changed, and his clothes became as bright as a flash of lightning. ³⁰Two

men, Moses and Elijah, ³¹appeared in glorious splendor, talking with Jesus. They spoke about his departure, which he was about to bring to fulfillment at Jerusalem. ³²Peter and his companions were very sleepy, but when they became fully awake, they saw his glory and the two men standing with him. ³³As the men were leaving Jesus, Peter said to him, "Master, it is good for us to be here. Let us put up three shelters—one for you, one for Moses and one for Elijah." (He did not know what he was saying.)

³⁴While he was speaking, a cloud appeared and enveloped them, and they were afraid as they entered the cloud. ³⁵A voice came from the cloud, saying, "This is my Son, whom I have chosen; listen to him." ³⁶When the voice had spoken, they found that Jesus was alone. The disciples kept this to themselves, and told no one at that time what they had seen.

³⁷The next day, when they came down from the mountain, a large crowd met him. ³⁸A man in the crowd called out, "Teacher, I beg you to look at my son, for he is my only child. ³⁹A spirit seizes him and he suddenly screams; it throws him into convulsions so that he foams at the mouth. It scarcely ever leaves him and is destroying him. ⁴⁰I begged your disciples to drive it out, but they could not."

⁴¹"O unbelieving and perverse generation," Jesus replied, "how long shall I stay with you and put up with you? Bring your son here."

⁴²Even while the boy was coming, the demon threw him to the ground in a convulsion. But Jesus rebuked the evilᵏ spirit, healed the boy and gave him back to his father. ⁴³And they were all amazed at the greatness of God.

While everyone was marveling at all that Jesus did, he said to his disciples, ⁴⁴"Listen carefully to what I am about to tell you: The Son of Man is going to be betrayed into the hands of men." ⁴⁵But they did not understand what this meant. It was hidden from them, so that they did not grasp it, and they were afraid to ask him about it.

⁴⁶An argument started among the disciples as to which of them would be the greatest. ⁴⁷Jesus, knowing their thoughts, took a little child and had him stand be-

ʲ20 Or Messiah   ᵏ42 Greek unclean

side him. 48Then he said to them, "Whoever welcomes this little child in my name welcomes me; and whoever welcomes me welcomes the one who sent me. For he who is least among you all—he is the greatest."

49"Master," said John, "we saw a man driving out demons in your name and we tried to stop him, because he is not one of us."

50"Do not stop him," Jesus said, "for whoever is not against you is for you."

51As the time approached for him to be taken up to heaven, Jesus resolutely set out for Jerusalem. 52And he sent messengers on ahead, who went into a Samaritan village to get things ready for him; 53but the people there did not welcome him, because he was heading for Jerusalem. 54When the disciples James and John saw this, they asked, "Lord, do you want us to call fire down from heaven to destroy them*?" 55But Jesus turned and rebuked them, 56and*m* they went to another village.

57As they were walking along the road, a man said to him, "I will follow you wherever you go."

58Jesus replied, "Foxes have holes and birds of the air have nests, but the Son of Man has no place to lay his head."

59He said to another man, "Follow me."

But the man replied, "Lord, first let me go and bury my father."

60Jesus said to him, "Let the dead bury their own dead, but you go and proclaim the kingdom of God."

61Still another said, "I will follow you, Lord; but first let me go back and say good-by to my family."

62Jesus replied, "No one who puts his hand to the plow and looks back is fit for service in the kingdom of God."

l54 Some manuscripts *them, even as Elijah did*   *m55,56* Some manuscripts *them. And he said, "You do not know what kind of spirit you are of, for the Son of Man did not come to destroy men's lives, but to save them."* 56And

OCTOBER 19 ☐ DAY 293
LUKE 10–12
Antagonism toward the Son of Man

OVERVIEW The corps of disciples expands as Jesus sends out thirty-five pairs of ministers to prepare the way before him. As the opportunities for ministry increase, so too does the opposition. Open rejection by the Pharisees leads Christ to pronounce woes on the hypocritical religious leaders and to warn his disciples of the Pharisees' damaging influence. This leads to a series of parables and warnings concerning the future judgment of God on those who are indifferent or unfaithful in their service for God.

Chapter 10	Chapter 11	Chapter 12
Denouncing the Unresponsive	Denouncing the Insincere	Denouncing the Unfaithful
Capernaum	Pharisees	Parables

YOUR DAILY WALK What do sparrows, hairs, ravens, lilies and you have in common?

Answer: They are all objects of God's special care.

Go to the nearest window and watch for a bird. Then ponder this: God has the welfare of that tiny creature on his mind (12:6).

Pull out your comb or hair brush, run it through your hair several times and notice the hairs that were pulled out. Then ponder this: God knows exactly how many hairs you have left (12:7).

Faith never knows where it is being led, but it loves and knows the one who is leading.

Take a walk on your lunch hour today to enjoy the beauties of nature around you. Then ponder this: God is making sure that the flowers have rain and the birds have food (12:24, 27–28).

Now stand in front of a mirror to see one of God's creations about which he cares infinitely more than the flowers and birds: *you!* If God expends such energy and tender attention on the less important parts of his creation, how much more must he be interested in your welfare and happiness?

Spend a few extra minutes meditating on 12:22–31 until your "little faith" is rekindled in the constant loving care of your heavenly Father.

 INSIGHT Something's Fishy about This Sign
Luke records Jesus' words comparing himself with the prophet Jonah and speaking of the "sign of Jonah" (11:29–30). But what is the sign of Jonah? Luke doesn't say. Check Matthew 12:38–40. Could you explain it to a non-Christian friend? Try it.

CHAPTER 10

After this the Lord appointed seventy-two[n] others and sent them two by two ahead of him to every town and place where he was about to go. ²He told them, "The harvest is plentiful, but the workers are few. Ask the Lord of the harvest, therefore, to send out workers into his harvest field. ³Go! I am sending you out like lambs among wolves. ⁴Do not take a purse or bag or sandals; and do not greet anyone on the road.

⁵"When you enter a house, first say, 'Peace to this house.' ⁶If a man of peace is there, your peace will rest on him; if not, it will return to you. ⁷Stay in that house, eating and drinking whatever they give you, for the worker deserves his wages. Do not move around from house to house.

⁸"When you enter a town and are welcomed, eat what is set before you. ⁹Heal the sick who are there and tell them, 'The kingdom of God is near you.' ¹⁰But when you enter a town and are not welcomed, go into its streets and say, ¹¹'Even the dust of your town that sticks to our feet we wipe off against you. Yet be sure of this: The kingdom of God is near.' ¹²I tell you, it will be more bearable on that day for Sodom than for that town.

¹³"Woe to you, Korazin! Woe to you, Bethsaida! For if the miracles that were performed in you had been performed in Tyre and Sidon, they would have repented long ago, sitting in sackcloth and ashes. ¹⁴But it will be more bearable for Tyre and Sidon at the judgment than for

you. ¹⁵And you, Capernaum, will you be lifted up to the skies? No, you will go down to the depths.[o]

¹⁶"He who listens to you listens to me; he who rejects you rejects me; but he who rejects me rejects him who sent me."

¹⁷The seventy-two returned with joy and said, "Lord, even the demons submit to us in your name."

¹⁸He replied, "I saw Satan fall like lightning from heaven. ¹⁹I have given you authority to trample on snakes and scorpions and to overcome all the power of the enemy; nothing will harm you. ²⁰However, do not rejoice that the spirits submit to you, but rejoice that your names are written in heaven."

²¹At that time Jesus, full of joy through the Holy Spirit, said, "I praise you, Father, Lord of heaven and earth, because you have hidden these things from the wise and learned, and revealed them to little children. Yes, Father, for this was your good pleasure.

²²"All things have been committed to me by my Father. No one knows who the Son is except the Father, and no one knows who the Father is except the Son and those to whom the Son chooses to reveal him."

²³Then he turned to his disciples and said privately, "Blessed are the eyes that see what you see. ²⁴For I tell you that many prophets and kings wanted to see what you see but did not see it, and to hear what you hear but did not hear it."

²⁵On one occasion an expert in the law stood up to test Jesus. "Teacher," he asked, "what must I do to inherit eternal life?"

---

n1 Some manuscripts seventy; also in verse 17   o15 Greek Hades

26"What is written in the Law?" he replied. "How do you read it?"

27He answered: " 'Love the Lord your God with all your heart and with all your soul and with all your strength and with all your mind' *p*; and, 'Love your neighbor as yourself.' *q*"

28"You have answered correctly," Jesus replied. "Do this and you will live."

29But he wanted to justify himself, so he asked Jesus, "And who is my neighbor?"

30In reply Jesus said: "A man was going down from Jerusalem to Jericho, when he fell into the hands of robbers. They stripped him of his clothes, beat him and went away, leaving him half dead. 31A priest happened to be going down the same road, and when he saw the man, he passed by on the other side. 32So too, a Levite, when he came to the place and saw him, passed by on the other side. 33But a Samaritan, as he traveled, came where the man was; and when he saw him, he took pity on him. 34He went to him and bandaged his wounds, pouring on oil and wine. Then he put the man on his own donkey, took him to an inn and took care of him. 35The next day he took out two silver coins *r* and gave them to the innkeeper. 'Look after him,' he said, 'and when I return, I will reimburse you for any extra expense you may have.'

36"Which of these three do you think was a neighbor to the man who fell into the hands of robbers?"

37The expert in the law replied, "The one who had mercy on him."

Jesus told him, "Go and do likewise."

38As Jesus and his disciples were on their way, he came to a village where a woman named Martha opened her home to him. 39She had a sister called Mary, who sat at the Lord's feet listening to what he said. 40But Martha was distracted by all the preparations that had to be made. She came to him and asked, "Lord, don't you care that my sister has left me to do the work by myself? Tell her to help me!"

41"Martha, Martha," the Lord answered, "you are worried and upset about many things, 42but only one thing is needed. *s*

Mary has chosen what is better, and it will not be taken away from her."

CHAPTER 11

One day Jesus was praying in a certain place. When he finished, one of his disciples said to him, "Lord, teach us to pray, just as John taught his disciples."

2He said to them, "When you pray, say:

" 'Father, *t*
hallowed be your name,
your kingdom come. *u*
3Give us each day our daily bread.
4Forgive us our sins,
    for we also forgive everyone who
        sins against us. *v*
And lead us not into temptation. *w* ' "

5Then he said to them, "Suppose one of you has a friend, and he goes to him at midnight and says, 'Friend, lend me three loaves of bread, 6because a friend of mine on a journey has come to me, and I have nothing to set before him.'

7"Then the one inside answers, 'Don't bother me. The door is already locked, and my children are with me in bed. I can't get up and give you anything.' 8I tell you, though he will not get up and give him the bread because he is his friend, yet because of the man's boldness *x* he will get up and give him as much as he needs.

9"So I say to you: Ask and it will be given to you; seek and you will find; knock and the door will be opened to you. 10For everyone who asks receives; he who seeks finds; and to him who knocks, the door will be opened.

11"Which of you fathers, if your son asks for *y* a fish, will give him a snake instead? 12Or if he asks for an egg, will give him a scorpion? 13If you then, though you are evil, know how to give good gifts to your children, how much more will your Father in heaven give the Holy Spirit to those who ask him!"

14Jesus was driving out a demon that was mute. When the demon left, the man who had been mute spoke, and the crowd was amazed. 15But some of them said, "By Beelzebub, *z* the prince of demons, he is driving out demons." 16Others tested him by asking for a sign from heaven.

---

*p*27 Deut. 6:5   *q*27 Lev. 19:18   *r*35 Greek *two denarii*   *s*42 Some manuscripts *but few things are needed—or only one*
*t*2 Some manuscripts *Our Father in heaven*   *u*2 Some manuscripts *come. May your will be done on earth as it is in heaven.*
*v*4 Greek *everyone who is indebted to us*   *w*4 Some manuscripts *temptation but deliver us from the evil one*   *x*8 Or *persistence*
*y*11 Some manuscripts *for bread, will give him a stone; or if he asks for*   *z*15 Greek *Beezeboul* or *Beelzeboul*; also in verses 18 and 19

¹⁷Jesus knew their thoughts and said to them: "Any kingdom divided against itself will be ruined, and a house divided against itself will fall. ¹⁸If Satan is divided against himself, how can his kingdom stand? I say this because you claim that I drive out demons by Beelzebub. ¹⁹Now if I drive out demons by Beelzebub, by whom do your followers drive them out? So then, they will be your judges. ²⁰But if I drive out demons by the finger of God, then the kingdom of God has come to you.

²¹"When a strong man, fully armed, guards his own house, his possessions are safe. ²²But when someone stronger attacks and overpowers him, he takes away the armor in which the man trusted and divides up the spoils.

²³"He who is not with me is against me, and he who does not gather with me, scatters.

²⁴"When an evil*a* spirit comes out of a man, it goes through arid places seeking rest and does not find it. Then it says, 'I will return to the house I left.' ²⁵When it arrives, it finds the house swept clean and put in order. ²⁶Then it goes and takes seven other spirits more wicked than itself, and they go in and live there. And the final condition of that man is worse than the first."

²⁷As Jesus was saying these things, a woman in the crowd called out, "Blessed is the mother who gave you birth and nursed you."

²⁸He replied, "Blessed rather are those who hear the word of God and obey it."

²⁹As the crowds increased, Jesus said, "This is a wicked generation. It asks for a miraculous sign, but none will be given it except the sign of Jonah. ³⁰For as Jonah was a sign to the Ninevites, so also will the Son of Man be to this generation. ³¹The Queen of the South will rise at the judgment with the men of this generation and condemn them; for she came from the ends of the earth to listen to Solomon's wisdom, and now one*b* greater than Solomon is here. ³²The men of Nineveh will stand up at the judgment with this generation and condemn it; for they repented at the preaching of Jonah, and now one greater than Jonah is here.

³³"No one lights a lamp and puts it in a place where it will be hidden, or under a bowl. Instead he puts it on its stand, so that those who come in may see the light. ³⁴Your eye is the lamp of your body. When your eyes are good, your whole body also is full of light. But when they are bad, your body also is full of darkness. ³⁵See to it, then, that the light within you is not darkness. ³⁶Therefore, if your whole body is full of light, and no part of it dark, it will be completely lighted, as when the light of a lamp shines on you."

³⁷When Jesus had finished speaking, a Pharisee invited him to eat with him; so he went in and reclined at the table. ³⁸But the Pharisee, noticing that Jesus did not first wash before the meal, was surprised.

³⁹Then the Lord said to him, "Now then, you Pharisees clean the outside of the cup and dish, but inside you are full of greed and wickedness. ⁴⁰You foolish people! Did not the one who made the outside make the inside also? ⁴¹But give what is inside ⸢the dish⸣*c* to the poor, and everything will be clean for you.

⁴²"Woe to you Pharisees, because you give God a tenth of your mint, rue and all other kinds of garden herbs, but you neglect justice and the love of God. You should have practiced the latter without leaving the former undone.

⁴³"Woe to you Pharisees, because you love the most important seats in the synagogues and greetings in the marketplaces.

⁴⁴"Woe to you, because you are like unmarked graves, which men walk over without knowing it."

⁴⁵One of the experts in the law answered him, "Teacher, when you say these things, you insult us also."

⁴⁶Jesus replied, "And you experts in the law, woe to you, because you load people down with burdens they can hardly carry, and you yourselves will not lift one finger to help them.

⁴⁷"Woe to you, because you build tombs for the prophets, and it was your forefathers who killed them. ⁴⁸So you testify that you approve of what your forefathers did; they killed the prophets, and you build their tombs. ⁴⁹Because of this, God in his wisdom said, 'I will send them prophets and apostles, some of whom they will kill and others they will persecute.' ⁵⁰Therefore this generation will be

---

a **24** Greek *unclean*   *b* **31** Or *something*; also in verse 32   *c* **41** Or *what you have* held responsible for the blood of all the prophets that has been shed since the beginning of the world, [51]from the blood of Abel to the blood of Zechariah, who was killed between the altar and the sanctuary. Yes, I tell you, this generation will be held responsible for it all.

[52]"Woe to you experts in the law, because you have taken away the key to knowledge. You yourselves have not entered, and you have hindered those who were entering."

[53]When Jesus left there, the Pharisees and the teachers of the law began to oppose him fiercely and to besiege him with questions, [54]waiting to catch him in something he might say.

CHAPTER 12

Meanwhile, when a crowd of many thousands had gathered, so that they were trampling on one another, Jesus began to speak first to his disciples, saying: "Be on your guard against the yeast of the Pharisees, which is hypocrisy. [2]There is nothing concealed that will not be disclosed, or hidden that will not be made known. [3]What you have said in the dark will be heard in the daylight, and what you have whispered in the ear in the inner rooms will be proclaimed from the roofs.

[4]"I tell you, my friends, do not be afraid of those who kill the body and after that can do no more. [5]But I will show you whom you should fear: Fear him who, after the killing of the body, has power to throw you into hell. Yes, I tell you, fear him. [6]Are not five sparrows sold for two pennies[d]? Yet not one of them is forgotten by God. [7]Indeed, the very hairs of your head are all numbered. Don't be afraid; you are worth more than many sparrows.

[8]"I tell you, whoever acknowledges me before men, the Son of Man will also acknowledge him before the angels of God. [9]But he who disowns me before men will be disowned before the angels of God. [10]And everyone who speaks a word against the Son of Man will be forgiven, but anyone who blasphemes against the Holy Spirit will not be forgiven.

[11]"When you are brought before synagogues, rulers and authorities, do not worry about how you will defend your-

selves or what you will say, [12]for the Holy Spirit will teach you at that time what you should say."

[13]Someone in the crowd said to him, "Teacher, tell my brother to divide the inheritance with me."

[14]Jesus replied, "Man, who appointed me a judge or an arbiter between you?" [15]Then he said to them, "Watch out! Be on your guard against all kinds of greed; a man's life does not consist in the abundance of his possessions."

[16]And he told them this parable: "The ground of a certain rich man produced a good crop. [17]He thought to himself, 'What shall I do? I have no place to store my crops.'

[18]"Then he said, 'This is what I'll do. I will tear down my barns and build bigger ones, and there I will store all my grain and my goods. [19]And I'll say to myself, "You have plenty of good things laid up for many years. Take life easy; eat, drink and be merry." '

[20]"But God said to him, 'You fool! This very night your life will be demanded from you. Then who will get what you have prepared for yourself?'

[21]"This is how it will be with anyone who stores up things for himself but is not rich toward God."

[22]Then Jesus said to his disciples: "Therefore I tell you, do not worry about your life, what you will eat; or about your body, what you will wear. [23]Life is more than food, and the body more than clothes. [24]Consider the ravens: They do not sow or reap, they have no storeroom or barn; yet God feeds them. And how much more valuable you are than birds! [25]Who of you by worrying can add a single hour to his life[e]? [26]Since you cannot do this very little thing, why do you worry about the rest?

[27]"Consider how the lilies grow. They do not labor or spin. Yet I tell you, not even Solomon in all his splendor was dressed like one of these. [28]If that is how God clothes the grass of the field, which is here today, and tomorrow is thrown into the fire, how much more will he clothe you, O you of little faith! [29]And do not set your heart on what you will eat or drink; do not worry about it. [30]For the pagan world runs after all such things, and your

---

[d]6 Greek *two assaria*   [e]25 Or *single cubit to his height*

Father knows that you need them. ³¹But seek his kingdom, and these things will be given to you as well.

³²"Do not be afraid, little flock, for your Father has been pleased to give you the kingdom. ³³Sell your possessions and give to the poor. Provide purses for yourselves that will not wear out, a treasure in heaven that will not be exhausted, where no thief comes near and no moth destroys. ³⁴For where your treasure is, there your heart will be also.

³⁵"Be dressed ready for service and keep your lamps burning, ³⁶like men waiting for their master to return from a wedding banquet, so that when he comes and knocks they can immediately open the door for him. ³⁷It will be good for those servants whose master finds them watching when he comes. I tell you the truth, he will dress himself to serve, will have them recline at the table and will come and wait on them. ³⁸It will be good for those servants whose master finds them ready, even if he comes in the second or third watch of the night. ³⁹But understand this: If the owner of the house had known at what hour the thief was coming, he would not have let his house be broken into. ⁴⁰You also must be ready, because the Son of Man will come at an hour when you do not expect him."

⁴¹Peter asked, "Lord, are you telling this parable to us, or to everyone?"

⁴²The Lord answered, "Who then is the faithful and wise manager, whom the master puts in charge of his servants to give them their food allowance at the proper time? ⁴³It will be good for that servant whom the master finds doing so when he returns. ⁴⁴I tell you the truth, he will put him in charge of all his possessions. ⁴⁵But suppose the servant says to himself, 'My master is taking a long time in coming,' and he then begins to beat the menservants and maidservants and to eat and drink and get drunk. ⁴⁶The master of that servant will come on a day when he does not expect him and at an hour he is not aware of. He will cut him to pieces and assign him a place with the unbelievers.

⁴⁷"That servant who knows his master's will and does not get ready or does not do what his master wants will be beaten with many blows. ⁴⁸But the one who does not know and does things deserving punishment will be beaten with few blows. From everyone who has been given much, much will be demanded; and from the one who has been entrusted with much, much more will be asked.

⁴⁹"I have come to bring fire on the earth, and how I wish it were already kindled! ⁵⁰But I have a baptism to undergo, and how distressed I am until it is completed! ⁵¹Do you think I came to bring peace on earth? No, I tell you, but division. ⁵²From now on there will be five in one family divided against each other, three against two and two against three. ⁵³They will be divided, father against son and son against father, mother against daughter and daughter against mother, mother-in-law against daughter-in-law and daughter-in-law against mother-in-law."

⁵⁴He said to the crowd: "When you see a cloud rising in the west, immediately you say, 'It's going to rain,' and it does. ⁵⁵And when the south wind blows, you say, 'It's going to be hot,' and it is. ⁵⁶Hypocrites! You know how to interpret the appearance of the earth and the sky. How is it that you don't know how to interpret this present time?

⁵⁷"Why don't you judge for yourselves what is right? ⁵⁸As you are going with your adversary to the magistrate, try hard to be reconciled to him on the way, or he may drag you off to the judge, and the judge turn you over to the officer, and the officer throw you into prison. ⁵⁹I tell you, you will not get out until you have paid the last penny.ᶠ"

ᶠ59 Greek lepton

OCTOBER 20 ☐ DAY 294
LUKE 13–15
Parables of the Son of Man (Part 1)

 OVERVIEW Jesus uses a recent report of Pilate's slaughter of some Galileans to emphasize the need for repentance. God is patient, but his sense of justice is perfect. Though it may sometimes seem overdue, justice will indeed come—a truth that brings tears to the Savior's eyes as he gazes at the hard-hearted city of Jerusalem. Jesus knows that, just as the people have spurned his message, so, too, they will treat his disciples with contempt. Discipleship will be costly for those who take up their cross to follow him. But in God's sight, every lost sinner is a cause for seeking, and every converted sinner a cause for heavenly rejoicing.

Chapter 13	Chapter 14	Chapter 15
The Need for Repentance	The Price of Discipleship	The Value of the Individual
Counting the Cost		Seeking the Lost

 YOUR DAILY WALK In military operations the machinery, equipment, supplies and even personnel are commonly considered "expendable" for the sake of the battle in order to insure the ultimate victory.

You can give without loving, but you cannot love without giving.

Contrast that with spiritual warfare in which each human being is infinitely valuable. In spiritual conflict only one person was deemed "expendable"—the Lord Jesus Christ—and even his seeming defeat on the cross was turned to victory three days later.

How great is God's love for lost men? "God demonstrates his own love for us in this: While we were still sinners, Christ died for us" (Romans 5:8).

How can you help to send this good news of sins forgiven to an unsaved friend across the street . . . or halfway around the world? Why not send a special gift to the mission agency of your choice today and take a baked treat (and a word of witness) to a neighbor, so that sinners far and near might learn of God's love firsthand? After all, what if you had been considered "expendable" by the one who shared the gospel with you?

 INSIGHT More than Mere Gifts
The lost son's father had more in mind than simply providing for his son's needs when he gave him a robe, a ring and sandals. The gifts symbolized how he again accepted him as a son: A robe signified honor; a ring, power; and sandals set him apart from the barefooted servants.

CHAPTER 13
Now there were some present at that time who told Jesus about the Galileans whose blood Pilate had mixed with their sacrifices. ²Jesus answered, "Do you think that these Galileans were worse sinners than all the other Galileans because they suffered this way? ³I tell you, no! But unless you repent, you too will all perish. ⁴Or those eighteen who died when the tower

in Siloam fell on them—do you think they were more guilty than all the others living in Jerusalem? ⁵I tell you, no! But unless you repent, you too will all perish."

⁶Then he told this parable: "A man had a fig tree, planted in his vineyard, and he went to look for fruit on it, but did not find any. ⁷So he said to the man who took care of the vineyard, 'For three years now I've been coming to look for fruit on this

fig tree and haven't found any. Cut it down! Why should it use up the soil?'

8" 'Sir,' the man replied, 'leave it alone for one more year, and I'll dig around it and fertilize it. 9If it bears fruit next year, fine! If not, then cut it down.' "

10On a Sabbath Jesus was teaching in one of the synagogues, 11and a woman was there who had been crippled by a spirit for eighteen years. She was bent over and could not straighten up at all. 12When Jesus saw her, he called her forward and said to her, "Woman, you are set free from your infirmity." 13Then he put his hands on her, and immediately she straightened up and praised God.

14Indignant because Jesus had healed on the Sabbath, the synagogue ruler said to the people, "There are six days for work. So come and be healed on those days, not on the Sabbath."

15The Lord answered him, "You hypocrites! Doesn't each of you on the Sabbath untie his ox or donkey from the stall and lead it out to give it water? 16Then should not this woman, a daughter of Abraham, whom Satan has kept bound for eighteen long years, be set free on the Sabbath day from what bound her?"

17When he said this, all his opponents were humiliated, but the people were delighted with all the wonderful things he was doing.

18Then Jesus asked, "What is the kingdom of God like? What shall I compare it to? 19It is like a mustard seed, which a man took and planted in his garden. It grew and became a tree, and the birds of the air perched in its branches."

20Again he asked, "What shall I compare the kingdom of God to? 21It is like yeast that a woman took and mixed into a large amount$g$ of flour until it worked all through the dough."

22Then Jesus went through the towns and villages, teaching as he made his way to Jerusalem. 23Someone asked him, "Lord, are only a few people going to be saved?"

He said to them, 24"Make every effort to enter through the narrow door, because many, I tell you, will try to enter and will not be able to. 25Once the owner of the house gets up and closes the door, you will stand outside knocking and pleading, 'Sir, open the door for us.'

"But he will answer, 'I don't know you or where you come from.'

26"Then you will say, 'We ate and drank with you, and you taught in our streets.'

27"But he will reply, 'I don't know you or where you come from. Away from me, all you evildoers!'

28"There will be weeping there, and gnashing of teeth, when you see Abraham, Isaac and Jacob and all the prophets in the kingdom of God, but you yourselves thrown out. 29People will come from east and west and north and south, and will take their places at the feast in the kingdom of God. 30Indeed there are those who are last who will be first, and first who will be last."

31At that time some Pharisees came to Jesus and said to him, "Leave this place and go somewhere else. Herod wants to kill you."

32He replied, "Go tell that fox, 'I will drive out demons and heal people today and tomorrow, and on the third day I will reach my goal.' 33In any case, I must keep going today and tomorrow and the next day—for surely no prophet can die outside Jerusalem!

34"O Jerusalem, Jerusalem, you who kill the prophets and stone those sent to you, how often I have longed to gather your children together, as a hen gathers her chicks under her wings, but you were not willing! 35Look, your house is left to you desolate. I tell you, you will not see me again until you say, 'Blessed is he who comes in the name of the Lord.'h "

CHAPTER 14

One Sabbath, when Jesus went to eat in the house of a prominent Pharisee, he was being carefully watched. 2There in front of him was a man suffering from dropsy. 3Jesus asked the Pharisees and experts in the law, "Is it lawful to heal on the Sabbath or not?" 4But they remained silent. So taking hold of the man, he healed him and sent him away.

5Then he asked them, "If one of you has a son$i$ or an ox that falls into a well on the Sabbath day, will you not immediately pull him out?" 6And they had nothing to say.

g21 Greek three satas (probably about 1/2 bushel or 22 liters) h35 Psalm 118:26 i5 Some manuscripts donkey

7When he noticed how the guests picked the places of honor at the table, he told them this parable: 8"When someone invites you to a wedding feast, do not take the place of honor, for a person more distinguished than you may have been invited. 9If so, the host who invited both of you will come and say to you, 'Give this man your seat.' Then, humiliated, you will have to take the least important place. 10But when you are invited, take the lowest place, so that when your host comes, he will say to you, 'Friend, move up to a better place.' Then you will be honored in the presence of all your fellow guests. 11For everyone who exalts himself will be humbled, and he who humbles himself will be exalted."

12Then Jesus said to his host, "When you give a luncheon or dinner, do not invite your friends, your brothers or relatives, or your rich neighbors; if you do, they may invite you back and so you will be repaid. 13But when you give a banquet, invite the poor, the crippled, the lame, the blind, 14and you will be blessed. Although they cannot repay you, you will be repaid at the resurrection of the righteous."

15When one of those at the table with him heard this, he said to Jesus, "Blessed is the man who will eat at the feast in the kingdom of God."

16Jesus replied: "A certain man was preparing a great banquet and invited many guests. 17At the time of the banquet he sent his servant to tell those who had been invited, 'Come, for everything is now ready.'

18"But they all alike began to make excuses. The first said, 'I have just bought a field, and I must go and see it. Please excuse me.'

19"Another said, 'I have just bought five yoke of oxen, and I'm on my way to try them out. Please excuse me.'

20"Still another said, 'I just got married, so I can't come.'

21"The servant came back and reported this to his master. Then the owner of the house became angry and ordered his servant, 'Go out quickly into the streets and alleys of the town and bring in the poor, the crippled, the blind and the lame.'

22" 'Sir,' the servant said, 'what you ordered has been done, but there is still room.'

23"Then the master told his servant, 'Go out to the roads and country lanes and make them come in, so that my house will be full. 24I tell you, not one of those men who were invited will get a taste of my banquet.' "

25Large crowds were traveling with Jesus, and turning to them he said: 26"If anyone comes to me and does not hate his father and mother, his wife and children, his brothers and sisters—yes, even his own life—he cannot be my disciple. 27And anyone who does not carry his cross and follow me cannot be my disciple.

28"Suppose one of you wants to build a tower. Will he not first sit down and estimate the cost to see if he has enough money to complete it? 29For if he lays the foundation and is not able to finish it, everyone who sees it will ridicule him, 30saying, 'This fellow began to build and was not able to finish.'

31"Or suppose a king is about to go to war against another king. Will he not first sit down and consider whether he is able with ten thousand men to oppose the one coming against him with twenty thousand? 32If he is not able, he will send a delegation while the other is still a long way off and will ask for terms of peace. 33In the same way, any of you who does not give up everything he has cannot be my disciple.

34"Salt is good, but if it loses its saltiness, how can it be made salty again? 35It is fit neither for the soil nor for the manure pile; it is thrown out.

"He who has ears to hear, let him hear."

CHAPTER 15

Now the tax collectors and "sinners" were all gathering around to hear him. 2But the Pharisees and the teachers of the law muttered, "This man welcomes sinners and eats with them."

3Then Jesus told them this parable: 4"Suppose one of you has a hundred sheep and loses one of them. Does he not leave the ninety-nine in the open country and go after the lost sheep until he finds it? 5And when he finds it, he joyfully puts it on his shoulders 6and goes home. Then he calls his friends and neighbors together and says, 'Rejoice with me; I have found my lost sheep.' 7I tell you that in the same way there will be more rejoicing in heaven over one sinner who repents than over ninety-nine righteous persons who do not need to repent.

⁸"Or suppose a woman has ten silver coins^j and loses one. Does she not light a lamp, sweep the house and search carefully until she finds it? ⁹And when she finds it, she calls her friends and neighbors together and says, 'Rejoice with me; I have found my lost coin.' ¹⁰In the same way, I tell you, there is rejoicing in the presence of the angels of God over one sinner who repents."

¹¹Jesus continued: "There was a man who had two sons. ¹²The younger one said to his father, 'Father, give me my share of the estate.' So he divided his property between them.

¹³"Not long after that, the younger son got together all he had, set off for a distant country and there squandered his wealth in wild living. ¹⁴After he had spent everything, there was a severe famine in that whole country, and he began to be in need. ¹⁵So he went and hired himself out to a citizen of that country, who sent him to his fields to feed pigs. ¹⁶He longed to fill his stomach with the pods that the pigs were eating, but no one gave him anything.

¹⁷"When he came to his senses, he said, 'How many of my father's hired men have food to spare, and here I am starving to death! ¹⁸I will set out and go back to my father and say to him: Father, I have sinned against heaven and against you. ¹⁹I am no longer worthy to be called your son; make me like one of your hired men.' ²⁰So he got up and went to his father.

"But while he was still a long way off, his father saw him and was filled with compassion for him; he ran to his son, threw his arms around him and kissed him.

²¹"The son said to him, 'Father, I have sinned against heaven and against you. I am no longer worthy to be called your son.$^{k'}$

²²"But the father said to his servants, 'Quick! Bring the best robe and put it on him. Put a ring on his finger and sandals on his feet. ²³Bring the fattened calf and kill it. Let's have a feast and celebrate. ²⁴For this son of mine was dead and is alive again; he was lost and is found.' So they began to celebrate.

²⁵"Meanwhile, the older son was in the field. When he came near the house, he heard music and dancing. ²⁶So he called one of the servants and asked him what was going on. ²⁷'Your brother has come,' he replied, 'and your father has killed the fattened calf because he has him back safe and sound.'

²⁸"The older brother became angry and refused to go in. So his father went out and pleaded with him. ²⁹But he answered his father, 'Look! All these years I've been slaving for you and never disobeyed your orders. Yet you never gave me even a young goat so I could celebrate with my friends. ³⁰But when this son of yours who has squandered your property with prostitutes comes home, you kill the fattened calf for him!'

³¹" 'My son,' the father said, 'you are always with me, and everything I have is yours. ³²But we had to celebrate and be glad, because this brother of yours was dead and is alive again; he was lost and is found.' "

---

^{j}8 Greek *ten drachmas*, each worth about a day's wages ^{k}21 Some early manuscripts *son. Make me like one of your hired men.*

OCTOBER 21 □ DAY 295
Going with the Gospel

 LOOK BACK Mark presents Jesus as the Selfless Servant, instantly obedient to the will of his Father. (The word *immediately* appears nearly a dozen times in the book.) "For even the Son of Man did not come to be served, but to serve, and to give his life as a ransom for many" (Mark 10:45).

Luke presents Jesus as the Perfect Man, keenly interested in the human condition. (The phrase *Son of Man* occurs twenty-five times in the book.) "For the Son of Man came to seek and to save what was lost" (Luke 19:10).

Mark and Luke are two of the "synoptic Gospels" (Matthew being the third), so called because they recount many of the same events from the life and ministry of Jesus and as such can be profitably studied side by side (*synoptic* comes from the root idea "to see side by side").

It is good to be a Christian and know it; it is better to be a Christian and show it.

LOOK UP Be careful where you get your information, for your facts will be no more reliable than your source.

After reading the Christmas accounts in the Gospels, try this Christmas Story Trivia Quiz. It may surprise you to learn how many of the "facts" you thought you knew are merely the stuff of Christmas cards and carols!

_____ 1. How did Joseph and Mary travel to Bethlehem? *(a)* by donkey, *(b)* by camel, *(c)* on foot, *(d)* the Bible doesn't say.

_____ 2. Which animals were present at Jesus' birth? *(a)* cows, sheep, goats, *(b)* cows, donkeys, sheep, *(c)* sheep and goats, *(d)* the Bible doesn't say.

_____ 3. What did the angels sing? *(a)* "Joy to the World," *(b)* "Alleluia," *(c)* "For unto Us a Child Is Born," *(d)* "Glory to God in the Highest," *(e)* none of the above.

_____ 4. How many wise men came to see Jesus? *(a)* three, *(b)* more than three, *(c)* less than three, *(d)* the Bible doesn't say.

_____ 5. Where did the wise men find Jesus? *(a)* in the manger, *(b)* in a stable, *(c)* in a house, *(d)* in an inn.

_____ 6. What is frankincense? *(a)* a precious metal, *(b)* a precious fabric, *(c)* a precious perfume, *(d)* an Eastern monster.

_____ 7. Where do we find the Christmas story in order to check up on all these facts? *(a)* Matthew; *(b)* Mark; *(c)* Luke; *(d)* John; *(e)* all of these; *(f)* only *a* and *b*; *(g)* only *a* and *c*; *(h)* only *a, b* and *c*; *(i)* none of the above.

Answers: 1. *(d)*, 2. *(d)*, 3. *(e)* (the Bible doesn't say they sang), 4. *(d)*, 5. *(c)*, 6. *(c)*, 7. *(g)*

LOOK AHEAD Good news deserves to be shared. As you continue to read through the Gospels, notice how Jesus engages in conversations with those who need to know God's love firsthand. Some individuals come to him with questions and needs (Luke 8:4; 10:25); other times, Jesus initiates the conversation (Luke 9:1–5).

Today, you will likely experience both kinds of encounters: those you initiate (such as shopping at a store or filling your tank at a gas station) and those initiated by others (such as delivering your mail or keeping an appointment at your office). In both cases, follow the advice of 1 Peter 3:15. "Always be prepared to give an answer to everyone who asks you to give the reason for the hope that you have. But do this with gentleness and respect." After all, the first two letters in the word *gospel* spell GO!

OCTOBER 22 □ DAY 296
LUKE 16–18
Parables of the Son of Man (Part 2)

OVERVIEW Christ continues his "School of Discipleship" with an assortment of parables designed to teach his men stewardship of money, time and talents; the importance of forgiveness and faith; and the primacy of prayer in a disciple's life. The curriculum is concentrated because time is short. Just beyond Jericho lies the city of Jerusalem, where the final dramatic events in the life of the Son of Man will soon be played out.

Chapter 16	Chapter 17	Chapter 18
Serving Two Masters	Waiting for the Son of Man	Praying with Persistence
"You Can't!"	"Be Ready!"	"Don't Forget!"

YOUR DAILY WALK Select the proper response to complete this verse (1 Corinthians 4:2): "Now it is required that those who have been given a trust must prove . . ." *(a)* gifted, *(b)* dynamic, *(c)* faithful, *(d)* famous, *(e)* educated, *(f)* wealthy.

Give according to your income lest God make your income according to your giving.

The correct answer, of course, is *(c)* faithful; in other words, trustworthy, dependable.

But how do you know if you are faithful, the kind of steward God is looking for? Luke 16 will help you. There you'll find the threefold test of a faithful man or woman, boy or girl. Take this "trustworthiness check-up" for yourself; then enlist the aid of your spouse, child or friend in helping you work on an area that is weak. They'll be delighted to help.

- Are you faithful in little things (v. 10)? little promises? small amounts of time, talent and responsibility?
- Are you faithful with money (v. 11)? God's Word has much to say on money matters.
- Are you faithful in the affairs of others (v. 12)? Are you as careful with their possessions and reputations as you are with your own?

INSIGHT The Big "Little Horn" of the Scriptures
The "least stroke" (Greek *keraian*, "little horn," 16:17) is a small projection or "hook" that distinguishes one Hebrew letter from another. Jesus was saying that, even down to the smallest detail, God's Word will maintain its reliability "until heaven and earth disappear" (Matthew 5:18).

CHAPTER 16
Jesus told his disciples: "There was a rich man whose manager was accused of wasting his possessions. ²So he called him in and asked him, 'What is this I hear about you? Give an account of your management, because you cannot be manager any longer.'

³"The manager said to himself, 'What shall I do now? My master is taking away my job. I'm not strong enough to dig, and I'm ashamed to beg— ⁴I know what I'll do so that, when I lose my job here, people will welcome me into their houses.'

⁵"So he called in each one of his master's debtors. He asked the first, 'How much do you owe my master?'

⁶" 'Eight hundred gallons¹ of olive oil,' he replied.

"The manager told him, 'Take your bill, sit down quickly, and make it four hundred.'

¹6 Greek *one hundred batous* (probably about 3 kiloliters)

7"Then he asked the second, 'And how much do you owe?'

" 'A thousand bushels^m of wheat,' he replied.

"He told him, 'Take your bill and make it eight hundred.'

8"The master commended the dishonest manager because he had acted shrewdly. For the people of this world are more shrewd in dealing with their own kind than are the people of the light. 9I tell you, use worldly wealth to gain friends for yourselves, so that when it is gone, you will be welcomed into eternal dwellings.

10"Whoever can be trusted with very little can also be trusted with much, and whoever is dishonest with very little will also be dishonest with much. 11So if you have not been trustworthy in handling worldly wealth, who will trust you with true riches? 12And if you have not been trustworthy with someone else's property, who will give you property of your own?

13"No servant can serve two masters. Either he will hate the one and love the other, or he will be devoted to the one and despise the other. You cannot serve both God and Money."

14The Pharisees, who loved money, heard all this and were sneering at Jesus. 15He said to them, "You are the ones who justify yourselves in the eyes of men, but God knows your hearts. What is highly valued among men is detestable in God's sight.

16"The Law and the Prophets were proclaimed until John. Since that time, the good news of the kingdom of God is being preached, and everyone is forcing his way into it. 17It is easier for heaven and earth to disappear than for the least stroke of a pen to drop out of the Law.

18"Anyone who divorces his wife and marries another woman commits adultery, and the man who marries a divorced woman commits adultery.

19"There was a rich man who was dressed in purple and fine linen and lived in luxury every day. 20At his gate was laid a beggar named Lazarus, covered with sores 21and longing to eat what fell from the rich man's table. Even the dogs came and licked his sores.

22"The time came when the beggar died and the angels carried him to Abraham's side. The rich man also died and was buried. 23In hell,^{n} where he was in torment, he looked up and saw Abraham far away, with Lazarus by his side. 24So he called to him, 'Father Abraham, have pity on me and send Lazarus to dip the tip of his finger in water and cool my tongue, because I am in agony in this fire.'

25"But Abraham replied, 'Son, remember that in your lifetime you received your good things, while Lazarus received bad things, but now he is comforted here and you are in agony. 26And besides all this, between us and you a great chasm has been fixed, so that those who want to go from here to you cannot, nor can anyone cross over from there to us.'

27"He answered, 'Then I beg you, father, send Lazarus to my father's house, 28for I have five brothers. Let him warn them, so that they will not also come to this place of torment.'

29"Abraham replied, 'They have Moses and the Prophets; let them listen to them.'

30" 'No, father Abraham,' he said, 'but if someone from the dead goes to them, they will repent.'

31"He said to him, 'If they do not listen to Moses and the Prophets, they will not be convinced even if someone rises from the dead.' "

CHAPTER 17
Jesus said to his disciples: "Things that cause people to sin are bound to come, but woe to that person through whom they come. 2It would be better for him to be thrown into the sea with a millstone tied around his neck than for him to cause one of these little ones to sin. 3So watch yourselves.

"If your brother sins, rebuke him, and if he repents, forgive him. 4If he sins against you seven times in a day, and seven times comes back to you and says, 'I repent,' forgive him."

5The apostles said to the Lord, "Increase our faith!"

6He replied, "If you have faith as small as a mustard seed, you can say to this mulberry tree, 'Be uprooted and planted in the sea,' and it will obey you.

7"Suppose one of you had a servant plowing or looking after the sheep.

^{m}7 Greek one hundred korous (probably about 35 kiloliters) ^{n}23 Greek Hades

Would he say to the servant when he comes in from the field, 'Come along now and sit down to eat'? [8]Would he not rather say, 'Prepare my supper, get yourself ready and wait on me while I eat and drink; after that you may eat and drink'? [9]Would he thank the servant because he did what he was told to do? [10]So you also, when you have done everything you were told to do, should say, 'We are unworthy servants; we have only done our duty.' "

[11]Now on his way to Jerusalem, Jesus traveled along the border between Samaria and Galilee. [12]As he was going into a village, ten men who had leprosy[o] met him. They stood at a distance [13]and called out in a loud voice, "Jesus, Master, have pity on us!"

[14]When he saw them, he said, "Go, show yourselves to the priests." And as they went, they were cleansed.

[15]One of them, when he saw he was healed, came back, praising God in a loud voice. [16]He threw himself at Jesus' feet and thanked him—and he was a Samaritan.

[17]Jesus asked, "Were not all ten cleansed? Where are the other nine? [18]Was no one found to return and give praise to God except this foreigner?" [19]Then he said to him, "Rise and go; your faith has made you well."

[20]Once, having been asked by the Pharisees when the kingdom of God would come, Jesus replied, "The kingdom of God does not come with your careful observation, [21]nor will people say, 'Here it is,' or 'There it is,' because the kingdom of God is within[p] you."

[22]Then he said to his disciples, "The time is coming when you will long to see one of the days of the Son of Man, but you will not see it. [23]Men will tell you, 'There he is!' or 'Here he is!' Do not go running off after them. [24]For the Son of Man in his day[q] will be like the lightning, which flashes and lights up the sky from one end to the other. [25]But first he must suffer many things and be rejected by this generation.

[26]"Just as it was in the days of Noah, so also will it be in the days of the Son of Man. [27]People were eating, drinking, marrying and being given in marriage up to the day Noah entered the ark. Then the flood came and destroyed them all.

[28]"It was the same in the days of Lot. People were eating and drinking, buying and selling, planting and building. [29]But the day Lot left Sodom, fire and sulfur rained down from heaven and destroyed them all.

[30]"It will be just like this on the day the Son of Man is revealed. [31]On that day no one who is on the roof of his house, with his goods inside, should go down to get them. Likewise, no one in the field should go back for anything. [32]Remember Lot's wife! [33]Whoever tries to keep his life will lose it, and whoever loses his life will preserve it. [34]I tell you, on that night two people will be in one bed; one will be taken and the other left. [35]Two women will be grinding grain together; one will be taken and the other left.[r]"

[37]"Where, Lord?" they asked.

He replied, "Where there is a dead body, there the vultures will gather."

CHAPTER 18

Then Jesus told his disciples a parable to show them that they should always pray and not give up. [2]He said: "In a certain town there was a judge who neither feared God nor cared about men. [3]And there was a widow in that town who kept coming to him with the plea, 'Grant me justice against my adversary.'

[4]"For some time he refused. But finally he said to himself, 'Even though I don't fear God or care about men, [5]yet because this widow keeps bothering me, I will see that she gets justice, so that she won't eventually wear me out with her coming!' "

[6]And the Lord said, "Listen to what the unjust judge says. [7]And will not God bring about justice for his chosen ones, who cry out to him day and night? Will he keep putting them off? [8]I tell you, he will see that they get justice, and quickly. However, when the Son of Man comes, will he find faith on the earth?"

[9]To some who were confident of their own righteousness and looked down on everybody else, Jesus told this parable: [10]"Two men went up to the temple to

---

[o]12 The Greek word was used for various diseases affecting the skin—not necessarily leprosy.   [p]21 Or *among*   [q]24 Some manuscripts do not have *in his day.*   [r]35 Some manuscripts *left.* [36]*Two men will be in the field; one will be taken and the other left.*

pray, one a Pharisee and the other a tax collector. [11]The Pharisee stood up and prayed about[s] himself: 'God, I thank you that I am not like other men—robbers, evildoers, adulterers—or even like this tax collector. [12]I fast twice a week and give a tenth of all I get.'

[13]"But the tax collector stood at a distance. He would not even look up to heaven, but beat his breast and said, 'God, have mercy on me, a sinner.'

[14]"I tell you that this man, rather than the other, went home justified before God. For everyone who exalts himself will be humbled, and he who humbles himself will be exalted."

[15]People were also bringing babies to Jesus to have him touch them. When the disciples saw this, they rebuked them. [16]But Jesus called the children to him and said, "Let the little children come to me, and do not hinder them, for the kingdom of God belongs to such as these. [17]I tell you the truth, anyone who will not receive the kingdom of God like a little child will never enter it."

[18]A certain ruler asked him, "Good teacher, what must I do to inherit eternal life?"

[19]"Why do you call me good?" Jesus answered. "No one is good—except God alone. [20]You know the commandments: 'Do not commit adultery, do not murder, do not steal, do not give false testimony, honor your father and mother.'[t]"

[21]"All these I have kept since I was a boy," he said.

[22]When Jesus heard this, he said to him, "You still lack one thing. Sell everything you have and give to the poor, and you will have treasure in heaven. Then come, follow me."

[23]When he heard this, he became very sad, because he was a man of great wealth. [24]Jesus looked at him and said, "How hard it is for the rich to enter the kingdom of God! [25]Indeed, it is easier for a camel to go through the eye of a needle

than for a rich man to enter the kingdom of God."

[26]Those who heard this asked, "Who then can be saved?"

[27]Jesus replied, "What is impossible with men is possible with God."

[28]Peter said to him, "We have left all we had to follow you!"

[29]"I tell you the truth," Jesus said to them, "no one who has left home or wife or brothers or parents or children for the sake of the kingdom of God [30]will fail to receive many times as much in this age and, in the age to come, eternal life."

[31]Jesus took the Twelve aside and told them, "We are going up to Jerusalem, and everything that is written by the prophets about the Son of Man will be fulfilled. [32]He will be handed over to the Gentiles. They will mock him, insult him, spit on him, flog him and kill him. [33]On the third day he will rise again."

[34]The disciples did not understand any of this. Its meaning was hidden from them, and they did not know what he was talking about.

[35]As Jesus approached Jericho, a blind man was sitting by the roadside begging. [36]When he heard the crowd going by, he asked what was happening. [37]They told him, "Jesus of Nazareth is passing by."

[38]He called out, "Jesus, Son of David, have mercy on me!"

[39]Those who led the way rebuked him and told him to be quiet, but he shouted all the more, "Son of David, have mercy on me!"

[40]Jesus stopped and ordered the man to be brought to him. When he came near, Jesus asked him, [41]"What do you want me to do for you?"

"Lord, I want to see," he replied.

[42]Jesus said to him, "Receive your sight; your faith has healed you." [43]Immediately he received his sight and followed Jesus, praising God. When all the people saw it, they also praised God.

[s]11 Or to   [t]20 Exodus 20:12-16; Deut. 5:16-20

OCTOBER 23 ☐ DAY 297
LUKE 19–21
Praise for the Son of Man

OVERVIEW People don't just "peacefully coexist" with the Son of Man. They either embrace his claims and call him Messiah or reject his claims and become his enemy. A Jewish tax collector named Zacchaeus finds new life in Jesus . . . while the Jewish religious leaders plot to destroy him. The disciples of Christ flock to the streets to welcome their Teacher . . . while his enemies question his authority at every turn. In less than a week, the Triumphal Entry will turn into a tragic exit as the Son of Man becomes the sacrifice for sin.

Chapter 19	Chapter 20	Chapter 21
Acclamation for the Son of Man	Authority of the Son of Man	Appearing of the Son of Man
Triumphal Entry	Testing Questions	Timely Signs

Money alone has never yet made anyone rich.

YOUR DAILY WALK Today's section might well be titled "Money—Its Use and Abuse." Notice how prominent earthly wealth becomes in the final days of Jesus' ministry: Zacchaeus's use of money becomes a testimony of his new faith in Christ (19:8–10); the parable of the ten servants teaches the disciples to use it (for God's glory) or lose it (19:11–27); Jesus cleanses the temple of those who have turned his Father's house into a supermarket of animals and moneychangers (19:45–48); paying taxes to Caesar becomes a test of Christ's authority (20:20–26); and the widow's two, copper coin offering becomes an object lesson of sacrificial giving—the kind God is pleased with (21:1–4).

Why is your use of money such a good barometer of your walk with God? Because "where your treasure is, there your heart will be also" (Matthew 6:21). Type a verse dealing with money from today's section on an index card (you might want to use 20:25 or 21:3–4), but instead of striking the *s* key, strike the dollar sign ($). Let that card remind you throughout the day of God'$ principle$ regarding the u$e . . . and abu$e . . . of hi$ material ble$$ing$.

INSIGHT The Clearest Cloudy Day on Record
Jesus predicted that he would come back to earth "in a cloud with power and great glory" (21:27). The cloud would not obscure the event but rather make it unmistakably clear (Acts 1:9–11; Revelation 1:7). Do you remember another occasion in Luke's Gospel when a cloud highlighted, rather than hid, Jesus' identity? (See Luke 9:28–36.)

CHAPTER 19
Jesus entered Jericho and was passing through. ²A man was there by the name of Zacchaeus; he was a chief tax collector and was wealthy. ³He wanted to see who Jesus was, but being a short man he could not, because of the crowd. ⁴So he ran ahead and climbed a sycamore-fig tree to see him, since Jesus was coming that way.

⁵When Jesus reached the spot, he looked up and said to him, "Zacchaeus, come down immediately. I must stay at your house today." ⁶So he came down at once and welcomed him gladly.

⁷All the people saw this and began to mutter, "He has gone to be the guest of a 'sinner.' "

⁸But Zacchaeus stood up and said to the Lord, "Look, Lord! Here and now I give half of my possessions to the poor, and if I have cheated anybody out of anything, I will pay back four times the amount."

[9]Jesus said to him, "Today salvation has come to this house, because this man, too, is a son of Abraham. [10]For the Son of Man came to seek and to save what was lost."

[11]While they were listening to this, he went on to tell them a parable, because he was near Jerusalem and the people thought that the kingdom of God was going to appear at once. [12]He said: "A man of noble birth went to a distant country to have himself appointed king and then to return. [13]So he called ten of his servants and gave them ten minas.[u] 'Put this money to work,' he said, 'until I come back.'

[14]"But his subjects hated him and sent a delegation after him to say, 'We don't want this man to be our king.'

[15]"He was made king, however, and returned home. Then he sent for the servants to whom he had given the money, in order to find out what they had gained with it.

[16]"The first one came and said, 'Sir, your mina has earned ten more.'

[17]" 'Well done, my good servant!' his master replied. 'Because you have been trustworthy in a very small matter, take charge of ten cities.'

[18]"The second came and said, 'Sir, your mina has earned five more.'

[19]"His master answered, 'You take charge of five cities.'

[20]"Then another servant came and said, 'Sir, here is your mina; I have kept it laid away in a piece of cloth. [21]I was afraid of you, because you are a hard man. You take out what you did not put in and reap what you did not sow.'

[22]"His master replied, 'I will judge you by your own words, you wicked servant! You knew, did you, that I am a hard man, taking out what I did not put in, and reaping what I did not sow? [23]Why then didn't you put my money on deposit, so that when I came back, I could have collected it with interest?'

[24]"Then he said to those standing by, 'Take his mina away from him and give it to the one who has ten minas.'

[25]" 'Sir,' they said, 'he already has ten!'

[26]"He replied, 'I tell you that to everyone who has, more will be given, but as for the one who has nothing, even what he has will be taken away. [27]But those enemies of mine who did not want me to be king over them—bring them here and kill them in front of me.' "

[28]After Jesus had said this, he went on ahead, going up to Jerusalem. [29]As he approached Bethphage and Bethany at the hill called the Mount of Olives, he sent two of his disciples, saying to them, [30]"Go to the village ahead of you, and as you enter it, you will find a colt tied there, which no one has ever ridden. Untie it and bring it here. [31]If anyone asks you, 'Why are you untying it?' tell him, 'The Lord needs it.' "

[32]Those who were sent ahead went and found it just as he had told them. [33]As they were untying the colt, its owners asked them, "Why are you untying the colt?"

[34]They replied, "The Lord needs it."

[35]They brought it to Jesus, threw their cloaks on the colt and put Jesus on it. [36]As he went along, people spread their cloaks on the road.

[37]When he came near the place where the road goes down the Mount of Olives, the whole crowd of disciples began joyfully to praise God in loud voices for all the miracles they had seen:

[38]"Blessed is the king who comes in the
    name of the Lord!"[v]

"Peace in heaven and glory in the
    highest!"

[39]Some of the Pharisees in the crowd said to Jesus, "Teacher, rebuke your disciples!"

[40]"I tell you," he replied, "if they keep quiet, the stones will cry out."

[41]As he approached Jerusalem and saw the city, he wept over it [42]and said, "If you, even you, had only known on this day what would bring you peace—but now it is hidden from your eyes. [43]The days will come upon you when your enemies will build an embankment against you and encircle you and hem you in on every side. [44]They will dash you to the ground, you and the children within your walls. They will not leave one stone on another, because you did not recognize the time of God's coming to you."

[45]Then he entered the temple area and began driving out those who were selling. [46]"It is written," he said to them, " 'My

---

[u]13 A mina was about three months' wages.   [v]38 Psalm 118:26

house will be a house of prayer'ʷ; but you have made it 'a den of robbers.'ˣ"

⁴⁷Every day he was teaching at the temple. But the chief priests, the teachers of the law and the leaders among the people were trying to kill him. ⁴⁸Yet they could not find any way to do it, because all the people hung on his words.

CHAPTER 20

One day as he was teaching the people in the temple courts and preaching the gospel, the chief priests and the teachers of the law, together with the elders, came up to him. ²"Tell us by what authority you are doing these things," they said. "Who gave you this authority?"

³He replied, "I will also ask you a question. Tell me, ⁴John's baptism—was it from heaven, or from men?"

⁵They discussed it among themselves and said, "If we say, 'From heaven,' he will ask, 'Why didn't you believe him?' ⁶But if we say, 'From men,' all the people will stone us, because they are persuaded that John was a prophet."

⁷So they answered, "We don't know where it was from."

⁸Jesus said, "Neither will I tell you by what authority I am doing these things."

⁹He went on to tell the people this parable: "A man planted a vineyard, rented it to some farmers and went away for a long time. ¹⁰At harvest time he sent a servant to the tenants so they would give him some of the fruit of the vineyard. But the tenants beat him and sent him away empty-handed. ¹¹He sent another servant, but that one also they beat and treated shamefully and sent away empty-handed. ¹²He sent still a third, and they wounded him and threw him out.

¹³"Then the owner of the vineyard said, 'What shall I do? I will send my son, whom I love; perhaps they will respect him.'

¹⁴"But when the tenants saw him, they talked the matter over. 'This is the heir,' they said. 'Let's kill him, and the inheritance will be ours.' ¹⁵So they threw him out of the vineyard and killed him.

"What then will the owner of the vineyard do to them? ¹⁶He will come and kill those tenants and give the vineyard to others."

When the people heard this, they said, "May this never be!"

¹⁷Jesus looked directly at them and asked, "Then what is the meaning of that which is written:

" 'The stone the builders rejected
    has become the capstoneʸ'ᶻ?

¹⁸Everyone who falls on that stone will be broken to pieces, but he on whom it falls will be crushed."

¹⁹The teachers of the law and the chief priests looked for a way to arrest him immediately, because they knew he had spoken this parable against them. But they were afraid of the people.

²⁰Keeping a close watch on him, they sent spies, who pretended to be honest. They hoped to catch Jesus in something he said so that they might hand him over to the power and authority of the governor. ²¹So the spies questioned him: "Teacher, we know that you speak and teach what is right, and that you do not show partiality but teach the way of God in accordance with the truth. ²²Is it right for us to pay taxes to Caesar or not?"

²³He saw through their duplicity and said to them, ²⁴"Show me a denarius. Whose portrait and inscription are on it?"

²⁵"Caesar's," they replied.

He said to them, "Then give to Caesar what is Caesar's, and to God what is God's."

²⁶They were unable to trap him in what he had said there in public. And astonished by his answer, they became silent.

²⁷Some of the Sadducees, who say there is no resurrection, came to Jesus with a question. ²⁸"Teacher," they said, "Moses wrote for us that if a man's brother dies and leaves a wife but no children, the man must marry the widow and have children for his brother. ²⁹Now there were seven brothers. The first one married a woman and died childless. ³⁰The second ³¹and then the third married her, and in the same way the seven died, leaving no children. ³²Finally, the woman died too. ³³Now then, at the resurrection whose wife will she be, since the seven were married to her?"

³⁴Jesus replied, "The people of this age marry and are given in marriage. ³⁵But those who are considered worthy of tak-

ʷ46 Isaiah 56:7   ˣ46 Jer. 7:11   ʸ17 Or cornerstone   ᶻ17 Psalm 118:22

ing part in that age and in the resurrection from the dead will neither marry nor be given in marriage, 36and they can no longer die; for they are like the angels. They are God's children, since they are children of the resurrection. 37But in the account of the bush, even Moses showed that the dead rise, for he calls the Lord 'the God of Abraham, and the God of Isaac, and the God of Jacob.'*a* 38He is not the God of the dead, but of the living, for to him all are alive."

39Some of the teachers of the law responded, "Well said, teacher!" 40And no one dared to ask him any more questions.

41Then Jesus said to them, "How is it that they say the Christ*b* is the Son of David? 42David himself declares in the Book of Psalms:

" 'The Lord said to my Lord:
    "Sit at my right hand
43until I make your enemies
    a footstool for your feet." '*c*

44David calls him 'Lord.' How then can he be his son?"

45While all the people were listening, Jesus said to his disciples, 46"Beware of the teachers of the law. They like to walk around in flowing robes and love to be greeted in the marketplaces and have the most important seats in the synagogues and the places of honor at banquets. 47They devour widows' houses and for a show make lengthy prayers. Such men will be punished most severely."

CHAPTER 21
As he looked up, Jesus saw the rich putting their gifts into the temple treasury. 2He also saw a poor widow put in two very small copper coins.*d* 3"I tell you the truth," he said, "this poor widow has put in more than all the others. 4All these people gave their gifts out of their wealth; but she out of her poverty put in all she had to live on."

5Some of his disciples were remarking about how the temple was adorned with beautiful stones and with gifts dedicated to God. But Jesus said, 6"As for what you see here, the time will come when not one stone will be left on another; every one of them will be thrown down."

7"Teacher," they asked, "when will these things happen? And what will be the sign that they are about to take place?"

8He replied: "Watch out that you are not deceived. For many will come in my name, claiming, 'I am he,' and, 'The time is near.' Do not follow them. 9When you hear of wars and revolutions, do not be frightened. These things must happen first, but the end will not come right away."

10Then he said to them: "Nation will rise against nation, and kingdom against kingdom. 11There will be great earthquakes, famines and pestilences in various places, and fearful events and great signs from heaven.

12"But before all this, they will lay hands on you and persecute you. They will deliver you to synagogues and prisons, and you will be brought before kings and governors, and all on account of my name. 13This will result in your being witnesses to them. 14But make up your mind not to worry beforehand how you will defend yourselves. 15For I will give you words and wisdom that none of your adversaries will be able to resist or contradict. 16You will be betrayed even by parents, brothers, relatives and friends, and they will put some of you to death. 17All men will hate you because of me. 18But not a hair of your head will perish. 19By standing firm you will gain life.

20"When you see Jerusalem being surrounded by armies, you will know that its desolation is near. 21Then let those who are in Judea flee to the mountains, let those in the city get out, and let those in the country not enter the city. 22For this is the time of punishment in fulfillment of all that has been written. 23How dreadful it will be in those days for pregnant women and nursing mothers! There will be great distress in the land and wrath against this people. 24They will fall by the sword and will be taken as prisoners to all the nations. Jerusalem will be trampled on by the Gentiles until the times of the Gentiles are fulfilled.

25"There will be signs in the sun, moon and stars. On the earth, nations will be in anguish and perplexity at the roaring and tossing of the sea. 26Men will faint from

a37 Exodus 3:6   *b41* Or *Messiah*   *c43* Psalm 110:1   *d2* Greek *two lepta* terror, apprehensive of what is coming on the world, for the heavenly bodies will be shaken. ²⁷At that time they will see the Son of Man coming in a cloud with power and great glory. ²⁸When these things begin to take place, stand up and lift up your heads, because your redemption is drawing near."

²⁹He told them this parable: "Look at the fig tree and all the trees. ³⁰When they sprout leaves, you can see for yourselves and know that summer is near. ³¹Even so, when you see these things happening, you know that the kingdom of God is near.

³²"I tell you the truth, this generation*ᵉ* will certainly not pass away until all these things have happened. ³³Heaven and earth will pass away, but my words will never pass away.

³⁴"Be careful, or your hearts will be weighed down with dissipation, drunkenness and the anxieties of life, and that day will close on you unexpectedly like a trap. ³⁵For it will come upon all those who live on the face of the whole earth. ³⁶Be always on the watch, and pray that you may be able to escape all that is about to happen, and that you may be able to stand before the Son of Man."

³⁷Each day Jesus was teaching at the temple, and each evening he went out to spend the night on the hill called the Mount of Olives, ³⁸and all the people came early in the morning to hear him at the temple.

ᵉ32 Or race

OCTOBER 24 ☐ DAY 298
LUKE 22–24
Passion of the Son of Man

 In his account of the closing days of Jesus' earthly ministry, Luke includes a number of details not given by the other gospel writers. Only Luke records the verbal strife among the disciples as they jostle for positions of honor in the kingdom of God. Only Luke records Jesus' warning to Peter of Satan's desire to use him. Only Luke records the healing of the high priest's servant. Only Luke provides the details of Jesus' trial before Herod Antipas. Only Luke reveals the repentance of one of the two thieves crucified with Jesus. And only Luke presents the resurrection day appearance to the two disciples on the road to Emmaus.

Chapter 22	Chapter 23	Chapter 24
Condemnation by the Jews	Execution by the Romans	Exaltation by the God of Heaven
Passover Lamb	King of the Jews	Risen Redeemer

 YOUR DAILY WALK Do you have difficulty from time to time understanding the Word of God as you read it in this devotional Bible? You're not alone! The two on the road to Emmaus were called "foolish . . . and how slow of heart to believe" (24:25) by none other than Jesus Christ, who had to explain to them the things concerning himself (24:27). The Ethiopian eunuch confessed to Philip that he did not understand what he read from the book of Isaiah (Acts 8:30–31). Even the apostle Peter admitted that some of the letters written by Paul were weighty and difficult to understand (2 Peter 3:15–16)!

When you don't feel like reading your Bible, that's the time to read it.

Two elements are necessary if you are to understand the Word of God. On your part there must be a diligent reading and study of the Scriptures. (This may include the use of tools like Bible concordances, reference works and commentaries penned by godly Bible scholars.) On God's part there will be the illuminating work of the Holy Spirit, providing spiritual insight and understanding (John 16:13–15). God has promised to do his part; are you doing yours? Today would be a good day to drop by your church library or local Christian bookstore to find a tool that will help you in your daily study and application of God's Word.

INSIGHT   End of Volume I, Beginning of Volume II
Luke closes his Gospel of the incarnate Son of God with a report of Jesus' ascension to heaven (24:51), exactly the same event he will use to open his continuing account of the Acts of the Apostles (Acts 1:1–2).

CHAPTER 22

Now the Feast of Unleavened Bread, called the Passover, was approaching, 2and the chief priests and the teachers of the law were looking for some way to get rid of Jesus, for they were afraid of the people. 3Then Satan entered Judas, called Iscariot, one of the Twelve. 4And Judas went to the chief priests and the officers of the temple guard and discussed with them how he might betray Jesus. 5They were delighted and agreed to give him money. 6He consented, and watched for an opportunity to hand Jesus over to them when no crowd was present.

7Then came the day of Unleavened Bread on which the Passover lamb had to be sacrificed. 8Jesus sent Peter and John, saying, "Go and make preparations for us to eat the Passover."

9"Where do you want us to prepare for it?" they asked.

10He replied, "As you enter the city, a man carrying a jar of water will meet you. Follow him to the house that he enters, 11and say to the owner of the house, 'The Teacher asks: Where is the guest room, where I may eat the Passover with my disciples?' 12He will show you a large upper room, all furnished. Make preparations there."

13They left and found things just as Jesus had told them. So they prepared the Passover.

14When the hour came, Jesus and his apostles reclined at the table. 15And he said to them, "I have eagerly desired to eat this Passover with you before I suffer. 16For I tell you, I will not eat it again until it finds fulfillment in the kingdom of God."

17After taking the cup, he gave thanks and said, "Take this and divide it among you. 18For I tell you I will not drink again of the fruit of the vine until the kingdom of God comes."

19And he took bread, gave thanks and broke it, and gave it to them, saying, "This is my body given for you; do this in remembrance of me."

20In the same way, after the supper he took the cup, saying, "This cup is the new covenant in my blood, which is poured out for you. 21But the hand of him who is going to betray me is with mine on the table. 22The Son of Man will go as it has been decreed, but woe to that man who betrays him." 23They began to question among themselves which of them it might be who would do this.

24Also a dispute arose among them as to which of them was considered to be greatest. 25Jesus said to them, "The kings of the Gentiles lord it over them; and those who exercise authority over them call themselves Benefactors. 26But you are not to be like that. Instead, the greatest among you should be like the youngest, and the one who rules like the one who serves. 27For who is greater, the one who is at the table or the one who serves? Is it not the one who is at the table? But I am among you as one who serves. 28You are those who have stood by me in my trials. 29And I confer on you a kingdom, just as my Father conferred one on me, 30so that you may eat and drink at my table in my kingdom and sit on thrones, judging the twelve tribes of Israel.

31"Simon, Simon, Satan has asked to sift you*f* as wheat. 32But I have prayed for you, Simon, that your faith may not fail. And when you have turned back, strengthen your brothers."

f31 The Greek is plural.

[33]But he replied, "Lord, I am ready to go with you to prison and to death."

[34]Jesus answered, "I tell you, Peter, before the rooster crows today, you will deny three times that you know me."

[35]Then Jesus asked them, "When I sent you without purse, bag or sandals, did you lack anything?"

"Nothing," they answered.

[36]He said to them, "But now if you have a purse, take it, and also a bag; and if you don't have a sword, sell your cloak and buy one. [37]It is written: 'And he was numbered with the transgressors'[g]; and I tell you that this must be fulfilled in me. Yes, what is written about me is reaching its fulfillment."

[38]The disciples said, "See, Lord, here are two swords."

"That is enough," he replied.

[39]Jesus went out as usual to the Mount of Olives, and his disciples followed him. [40]On reaching the place, he said to them, "Pray that you will not fall into temptation." [41]He withdrew about a stone's throw beyond them, knelt down and prayed, [42]"Father, if you are willing, take this cup from me; yet not my will, but yours be done." [43]An angel from heaven appeared to him and strengthened him. [44]And being in anguish, he prayed more earnestly, and his sweat was like drops of blood falling to the ground.[h]

[45]When he rose from prayer and went back to the disciples, he found them asleep, exhausted from sorrow. [46]"Why are you sleeping?" he asked them. "Get up and pray so that you will not fall into temptation."

[47]While he was still speaking a crowd came up, and the man who was called Judas, one of the Twelve, was leading them. He approached Jesus to kiss him, [48]but Jesus asked him, "Judas, are you betraying the Son of Man with a kiss?"

[49]When Jesus' followers saw what was going to happen, they said, "Lord, should we strike with our swords?" [50]And one of them struck the servant of the high priest, cutting off his right ear.

[51]But Jesus answered, "No more of this!" And he touched the man's ear and healed him.

[52]Then Jesus said to the chief priests, the officers of the temple guard, and the elders, who had come for him, "Am I leading a rebellion, that you have come with swords and clubs? [53]Every day I was with you in the temple courts, and you did not lay a hand on me. But this is your hour—when darkness reigns."

[54]Then seizing him, they led him away and took him into the house of the high priest. Peter followed at a distance. [55]But when they had kindled a fire in the middle of the courtyard and had sat down together, Peter sat down with them. [56]A servant girl saw him seated there in the firelight. She looked closely at him and said, "This man was with him."

[57]But he denied it. "Woman, I don't know him," he said.

[58]A little later someone else saw him and said, "You also are one of them."

"Man, I am not!" Peter replied.

[59]About an hour later another asserted, "Certainly this fellow was with him, for he is a Galilean."

[60]Peter replied, "Man, I don't know what you're talking about!" Just as he was speaking, the rooster crowed. [61]The Lord turned and looked straight at Peter. Then Peter remembered the word the Lord had spoken to him: "Before the rooster crows today, you will disown me three times." [62]And he went outside and wept bitterly.

[63]The men who were guarding Jesus began mocking and beating him. [64]They blindfolded him and demanded, "Prophesy! Who hit you?" [65]And they said many other insulting things to him.

[66]At daybreak the council of the elders of the people, both the chief priests and teachers of the law, met together, and Jesus was led before them. [67]"If you are the Christ,[i]" they said, "tell us."

Jesus answered, "If I tell you, you will not believe me, [68]and if I asked you, you would not answer. [69]But from now on, the Son of Man will be seated at the right hand of the mighty God."

[70]They all asked, "Are you then the Son of God?"

He replied, "You are right in saying I am."

[71]Then they said, "Why do we need any more testimony? We have heard it from his own lips."

[g]37 Isaiah 53:12   [h]44 Some early manuscripts do not have verses 43 and 44.   [i]67 Or *Messiah*

CHAPTER 23

Then the whole assembly rose and led him off to Pilate. ²And they began to accuse him, saying, "We have found this man subverting our nation. He opposes payment of taxes to Caesar and claims to be Christ,ʲ a king."

³So Pilate asked Jesus, "Are you the king of the Jews?"

"Yes, it is as you say," Jesus replied.

⁴Then Pilate announced to the chief priests and the crowd, "I find no basis for a charge against this man."

⁵But they insisted, "He stirs up the people all over Judeaᵏ by his teaching. He started in Galilee and has come all the way here."

⁶On hearing this, Pilate asked if the man was a Galilean. ⁷When he learned that Jesus was under Herod's jurisdiction, he sent him to Herod, who was also in Jerusalem at that time.

⁸When Herod saw Jesus, he was greatly pleased, because for a long time he had been wanting to see him. From what he had heard about him, he hoped to see him perform some miracle. ⁹He plied him with many questions, but Jesus gave him no answer. ¹⁰The chief priests and the teachers of the law were standing there, vehemently accusing him. ¹¹Then Herod and his soldiers ridiculed and mocked him. Dressing him in an elegant robe, they sent him back to Pilate. ¹²That day Herod and Pilate became friends—before this they had been enemies.

¹³Pilate called together the chief priests, the rulers and the people, ¹⁴and said to them, "You brought me this man as one who was inciting the people to rebellion. I have examined him in your presence and have found no basis for your charges against him. ¹⁵Neither has Herod, for he sent him back to us; as you can see, he has done nothing to deserve death. ¹⁶Therefore, I will punish him and then release him.ˡ"

¹⁸With one voice they cried out, "Away with this man! Release Barabbas to us!" ¹⁹(Barabbas had been thrown into prison for an insurrection in the city, and for murder.)

²⁰Wanting to release Jesus, Pilate appealed to them again. ²¹But they kept shouting, "Crucify him! Crucify him!"

²²For the third time he spoke to them: "Why? What crime has this man committed? I have found in him no grounds for the death penalty. Therefore I will have him punished and then release him."

²³But with loud shouts they insistently demanded that he be crucified, and their shouts prevailed. ²⁴So Pilate decided to grant their demand. ²⁵He released the man who had been thrown into prison for insurrection and murder, the one they asked for, and surrendered Jesus to their will.

²⁶As they led him away, they seized Simon from Cyrene, who was on his way in from the country, and put the cross on him and made him carry it behind Jesus. ²⁷A large number of people followed him, including women who mourned and wailed for him. ²⁸Jesus turned and said to them, "Daughters of Jerusalem, do not weep for me; weep for yourselves and for your children. ²⁹For the time will come when you will say, 'Blessed are the barren women, the wombs that never bore and the breasts that never nursed!' ³⁰Then

" 'they will say to the mountains, "Fall
    on us!"
and to the hills, "Cover us!" 'ᵐ

³¹For if men do these things when the tree is green, what will happen when it is dry?"

³²Two other men, both criminals, were also led out with him to be executed. ³³When they came to the place called the Skull, there they crucified him, along with the criminals—one on his right, the other on his left. ³⁴Jesus said, "Father, forgive them, for they do not know what they are doing."ⁿ And they divided up his clothes by casting lots.

³⁵The people stood watching, and the rulers even sneered at him. They said, "He saved others; let him save himself if he is the Christ of God, the Chosen One."

³⁶The soldiers also came up and mocked him. They offered him wine vinegar ³⁷and said, "If you are the king of the Jews, save yourself."

³⁸There was a written notice above him, which read: THIS IS THE KING OF THE JEWS.

³⁹One of the criminals who hung there hurled insults at him: "Aren't you the Christ? Save yourself and us!"

ʲ2 Or Messiah; also in verses 35 and 39   ᵏ5 Or over the land of the Jews   ˡ16 Some manuscripts him." ¹⁷Now he was obliged to release one man to them at the Feast.   ᵐ30 Hosea 10:8   ⁿ34 Some early manuscripts do not have this sentence.

[40]But the other criminal rebuked him. "Don't you fear God," he said, "since you are under the same sentence? [41]We are punished justly, for we are getting what our deeds deserve. But this man has done nothing wrong."

[42]Then he said, "Jesus, remember me when you come into your kingdom.[o]"

[43]Jesus answered him, "I tell you the truth, today you will be with me in paradise."

[44]It was now about the sixth hour, and darkness came over the whole land until the ninth hour, [45]for the sun stopped shining. And the curtain of the temple was torn in two. [46]Jesus called out with a loud voice, "Father, into your hands I commit my spirit." When he had said this, he breathed his last.

[47]The centurion, seeing what had happened, praised God and said, "Surely this was a righteous man." [48]When all the people who had gathered to witness this sight saw what took place, they beat their breasts and went away. [49]But all those who knew him, including the women who had followed him from Galilee, stood at a distance, watching these things.

[50]Now there was a man named Joseph, a member of the Council, a good and upright man, [51]who had not consented to their decision and action. He came from the Judean town of Arimathea and he was waiting for the kingdom of God. [52]Going to Pilate, he asked for Jesus' body. [53]Then he took it down, wrapped it in linen cloth and placed it in a tomb cut in the rock, one in which no one had yet been laid. [54]It was Preparation Day, and the Sabbath was about to begin.

[55]The women who had come with Jesus from Galilee followed Joseph and saw the tomb and how his body was laid in it. [56]Then they went home and prepared spices and perfumes. But they rested on the Sabbath in obedience to the commandment.

CHAPTER 24

On the first day of the week, very early in the morning, the women took the spices they had prepared and went to the tomb. [2]They found the stone rolled away from the tomb, [3]but when they entered, they did not find the body of the Lord Jesus.

[4]While they were wondering about this, suddenly two men in clothes that gleamed like lightning stood beside them. [5]In their fright the women bowed down with their faces to the ground, but the men said to them, "Why do you look for the living among the dead? [6]He is not here; he has risen! Remember how he told you, while he was still with you in Galilee: [7]'The Son of Man must be delivered into the hands of sinful men, be crucified and on the third day be raised again.'" [8]Then they remembered his words.

[9]When they came back from the tomb, they told all these things to the Eleven and to all the others. [10]It was Mary Magdalene, Joanna, Mary the mother of James, and the others with them who told this to the apostles. [11]But they did not believe the women, because their words seemed to them like nonsense. [12]Peter, however, got up and ran to the tomb. Bending over, he saw the strips of linen lying by themselves, and he went away, wondering to himself what had happened.

[13]Now that same day two of them were going to a village called Emmaus, about seven miles[p] from Jerusalem. [14]They were talking with each other about everything that had happened. [15]As they talked and discussed these things with each other, Jesus himself came up and walked along with them; [16]but they were kept from recognizing him.

[17]He asked them, "What are you discussing together as you walk along?"

They stood still, their faces downcast. [18]One of them, named Cleopas, asked him, "Are you only a visitor to Jerusalem and do not know the things that have happened there in these days?"

[19]"What things?" he asked.

"About Jesus of Nazareth," they replied. "He was a prophet, powerful in word and deed before God and all the people. [20]The chief priests and our rulers handed him over to be sentenced to death, and they crucified him; [21]but we had hoped that he was the one who was going to redeem Israel. And what is more, it is the third day since all this took place. [22]In addition, some of our women amazed us. They went to the tomb early this morning [23]but didn't find his body. They came and told

[o]42 Some manuscripts *come with your kingly power*   [p]13 Greek *sixty stadia* (about 11 kilometers)

us that they had seen a vision of angels, who said he was alive. ²⁴Then some of our companions went to the tomb and found it just as the women had said, but him they did not see."

²⁵He said to them, "How foolish you are, and how slow of heart to believe all that the prophets have spoken! ²⁶Did not the Christ⁹ have to suffer these things and then enter his glory?" ²⁷And beginning with Moses and all the Prophets, he explained to them what was said in all the Scriptures concerning himself.

²⁸As they approached the village to which they were going, Jesus acted as if he were going farther. ²⁹But they urged him strongly, "Stay with us, for it is nearly evening; the day is almost over." So he went in to stay with them.

³⁰When he was at the table with them, he took bread, gave thanks, broke it and began to give it to them. ³¹Then their eyes were opened and they recognized him, and he disappeared from their sight. ³²They asked each other, "Were not our hearts burning within us while he talked with us on the road and opened the Scriptures to us?"

³³They got up and returned at once to Jerusalem. There they found the Eleven and those with them, assembled together ³⁴and saying, "It is true! The Lord has risen and has appeared to Simon." ³⁵Then the two told what had happened on the way, and how Jesus was recognized by them when he broke the bread.

³⁶While they were still talking about this, Jesus himself stood among them and said to them, "Peace be with you."

⁹26 Or *Messiah*; also in verse 46

³⁷They were startled and frightened, thinking they saw a ghost. ³⁸He said to them, "Why are you troubled, and why do doubts rise in your minds? ³⁹Look at my hands and my feet. It is I myself! Touch me and see; a ghost does not have flesh and bones, as you see I have."

⁴⁰When he had said this, he showed them his hands and feet. ⁴¹And while they still did not believe it because of joy and amazement, he asked them, "Do you have anything here to eat?" ⁴²They gave him a piece of broiled fish, ⁴³and he took it and ate it in their presence.

⁴⁴He said to them, "This is what I told you while I was still with you: Everything must be fulfilled that is written about me in the Law of Moses, the Prophets and the Psalms."

⁴⁵Then he opened their minds so they could understand the Scriptures. ⁴⁶He told them, "This is what is written: The Christ will suffer and rise from the dead on the third day, ⁴⁷and repentance and forgiveness of sins will be preached in his name to all nations, beginning at Jerusalem. ⁴⁸You are witnesses of these things. ⁴⁹I am going to send you what my Father has promised; but stay in the city until you have been clothed with power from on high."

⁵⁰When he had led them out to the vicinity of Bethany, he lifted up his hands and blessed them. ⁵¹While he was blessing them, he left them and was taken up into heaven. ⁵²Then they worshiped him and returned to Jerusalem with great joy. ⁵³And they stayed continually at the temple, praising God.

John

EVEN though the book of John covers the same basic outline of Jesus' life as the other three Gospels, it displays marked differences in content and viewpoint. John highlights many encounters with the Son of God that are found nowhere else: the miracle at Cana, the visit by Nicodemus, the Samaritan woman at the well, an invalid man at the pool of Bethesda, the man born blind, the beloved Lazarus. Why this selectivity? "These are written that you may believe that Jesus is the Christ" (20:31).

Focus	Ministry to Many				Ministry to Few	
Divisions	Manifestation of the Son of God	Ministry to Individuals by God's Son	Ministry to the Multitudes by God's Son	Mounting Anger toward God's Son	Ministry to the Disciples by God's Son	The Resurrected Son of God
	1 2	3 5	6 8	9 12	13 17	18 21
Topics	Signs				Sermons	Sacrifice
	Public Ministry				Private Ministry	Paschal Ministry
Place	Galilee and Judea				Jerusalem	
Time	About 3½ Years				Only a Few Days	

OCTOBER 25 □ DAY 299
JOHN 1-2
Manifestation of the Son of God

OVERVIEW The opening of John's Gospel makes it clear he is giving a different perspective on the life and ministry of Jesus Christ than did the other three Gospel writers. John begins with the preexistence and deity of the Word, the one who became flesh to show God to mankind and to fulfill God's promises of a Messiah to Israel. Proclaiming the identity of Jesus as the Word is the ministry of John the Baptist, who directs his disciples to become Jesus' first followers. At a wedding in Cana, Jesus demonstrates his miraculous power for the first time. Later in Jerusalem, his zeal for his Father's house causes him to challenge the status quo, an act which forces an early confrontation over his claims.

	Chapter 1		Chapter 2
The Identity of the Son of God			The Authority of the Son of God
Affirmed 1 18	Proclaimed 19 34	Acknowledged 35 51	
By God	By John	By Disciples	Over Nature

The object in witnessing is not to win arguments but to win disciples.

YOUR DAILY WALK Turn to Acts 1:13. There you will find the names of eleven of the twelve disciples of Jesus. Glance down the list, and see if you can recall one significant fact about each man. (For example, Peter—walked on the water, etc.) Which disciples come up "anonymous" in your mind?

Chances are, Andrew fits that category. Although he was one of the twelve apostles, he lived his life in the shadow of his brother, Peter. Outside of John's Gospel he is mentioned only in the lists of the apostles. He was an ordinary and little-known person. And yet Andrew was distinctive in at least one way: He was constantly bringing people to Jesus. First his brother (John 1:40–42) and later a little boy (6:8–9) came to the Savior because of Andrew's invitation.

Witnessing for Christ may sound like a scary assignment. But could you "invite" another person to meet a Friend who has changed your life? This week invite a neighbor to go to church with you. You'll both be glad you did!

INSIGHT A Handy Outline in a Handy Place

Prologue	Description	Expanded in . . .
1:1–4	Revelation of the Son of God	1:19–6:71
1:5–11	Rejection of the Son of God	7:1–12:50
1:12–18	Acceptance of the Son of God	13:1–21:25

CHAPTER 1

In the beginning was the Word, and the Word was with God, and the Word was God. ²He was with God in the beginning. ³Through him all things were made; without him nothing was made that has been made. ⁴In him was life, and that life was the light of men. ⁵The light shines in the darkness, but the darkness has not understood[a] it.

---

a5 Or darkness, and the darkness has not overcome

⁶There came a man who was sent from God; his name was John. ⁷He came as a witness to testify concerning that light, so that through him all men might believe. ⁸He himself was not the light; he came only as a witness to the light. ⁹The true light that gives light to every man was coming into the world.ᵇ

¹⁰He was in the world, and though the world was made through him, the world did not recognize him. ¹¹He came to that which was his own, but his own did not receive him. ¹²Yet to all who received him, to those who believed in his name, he gave the right to become children of God— ¹³children born not of natural descent,ᶜ nor of human decision or a husband's will, but born of God.

¹⁴The Word became flesh and made his dwelling among us. We have seen his glory, the glory of the One and Only,ᵈ who came from the Father, full of grace and truth.

¹⁵John testifies concerning him. He cries out, saying, "This was he of whom I said, 'He who comes after me has surpassed me because he was before me.' " ¹⁶From the fullness of his grace we have all received one blessing after another. ¹⁷For the law was given through Moses; grace and truth came through Jesus Christ. ¹⁸No one has ever seen God, but God the One and Only,ᵈ,ᵉ who is at the Father's side, has made him known.

¹⁹Now this was John's testimony when the Jews of Jerusalem sent priests and Levites to ask him who he was. ²⁰He did not fail to confess, but confessed freely, "I am not the Christ.ᶠ"

²¹They asked him, "Then who are you? Are you Elijah?"

He said, "I am not."

"Are you the Prophet?"

He answered, "No."

²²Finally they said, "Who are you? Give us an answer to take back to those who sent us. What do you say about yourself?"

²³John replied in the words of Isaiah the prophet, "I am the voice of one calling in the desert, 'Make straight the way for the Lord.' "ᵍ

²⁴Now some Pharisees who had been sent ²⁵questioned him, "Why then do you baptize if you are not the Christ, nor Elijah, nor the Prophet?"

²⁶"I baptize withʰ water," John replied, "but among you stands one you do not know. ²⁷He is the one who comes after me, the thongs of whose sandals I am not worthy to untie."

²⁸This all happened at Bethany on the other side of the Jordan, where John was baptizing.

²⁹The next day John saw Jesus coming toward him and said, "Look, the Lamb of God, who takes away the sin of the world! ³⁰This is the one I meant when I said, 'A man who comes after me has surpassed me because he was before me.' ³¹I myself did not know him, but the reason I came baptizing with water was that he might be revealed to Israel."

³²Then John gave this testimony: "I saw the Spirit come down from heaven as a dove and remain on him. ³³I would not have known him, except that the one who sent me to baptize with water told me, 'The man on whom you see the Spirit come down and remain is he who will baptize with the Holy Spirit.' ³⁴I have seen and I testify that this is the Son of God."

³⁵The next day John was there again with two of his disciples. ³⁶When he saw Jesus passing by, he said, "Look, the Lamb of God!"

³⁷When the two disciples heard him say this, they followed Jesus. ³⁸Turning around, Jesus saw them following and asked, "What do you want?"

They said, "Rabbi" (which means Teacher), "where are you staying?"

³⁹"Come," he replied, "and you will see."

So they went and saw where he was staying, and spent that day with him. It was about the tenth hour.

⁴⁰Andrew, Simon Peter's brother, was one of the two who heard what John had said and who had followed Jesus. ⁴¹The first thing Andrew did was to find his brother Simon and tell him, "We have found the Messiah" (that is, the Christ). ⁴²And he brought him to Jesus.

Jesus looked at him and said, "You are

ᵇ9 Or *This was the true light that gives light to every man who comes into the world*   ᶜ13 Greek *of bloods*   ᵈ14,18 Or *the Only Begotten*   ᵉ18 Some manuscripts *but the only (or only begotten) Son*   ᶠ20 Or *Messiah*. "The Christ" (Greek) and "the Messiah" (Hebrew) both mean "the Anointed One"; also in verse 25.   ᵍ23 Isaiah 40:3   ʰ26 Or *in*; also in verses 31 and 33

Simon son of John. You will be called Cephas" (which, when translated, is Peter[i]).

⁴³The next day Jesus decided to leave for Galilee. Finding Philip, he said to him, "Follow me."

⁴⁴Philip, like Andrew and Peter, was from the town of Bethsaida. ⁴⁵Philip found Nathanael and told him, "We have found the one Moses wrote about in the Law, and about whom the prophets also wrote—Jesus of Nazareth, the son of Joseph."

⁴⁶"Nazareth! Can anything good come from there?" Nathanael asked.

"Come and see," said Philip.

⁴⁷When Jesus saw Nathanael approaching, he said of him, "Here is a true Israelite, in whom there is nothing false."

⁴⁸"How do you know me?" Nathanael asked.

Jesus answered, "I saw you while you were still under the fig tree before Philip called you."

⁴⁹Then Nathanael declared, "Rabbi, you are the Son of God; you are the King of Israel."

⁵⁰Jesus said, "You believe[j] because I told you I saw you under the fig tree. You shall see greater things than that." ⁵¹He then added, "I tell you[k] the truth, you[k] shall see heaven open, and the angels of God ascending and descending on the Son of Man."

CHAPTER 2

On the third day a wedding took place at Cana in Galilee. Jesus' mother was there, ²and Jesus and his disciples had also been invited to the wedding. ³When the wine was gone, Jesus' mother said to him, "They have no more wine."

⁴"Dear woman, why do you involve me?" Jesus replied. "My time has not yet come."

⁵His mother said to the servants, "Do whatever he tells you."

⁶Nearby stood six stone water jars, the kind used by the Jews for ceremonial washing, each holding from twenty to thirty gallons.[l]

⁷Jesus said to the servants, "Fill the jars with water"; so they filled them to the brim.

⁸Then he told them, "Now draw some out and take it to the master of the banquet."

They did so, ⁹and the master of the banquet tasted the water that had been turned into wine. He did not realize where it had come from, though the servants who had drawn the water knew. Then he called the bridegroom aside ¹⁰and said, "Everyone brings out the choice wine first and then the cheaper wine after the guests have had too much to drink; but you have saved the best till now."

¹¹This, the first of his miraculous signs, Jesus performed at Cana in Galilee. He thus revealed his glory, and his disciples put their faith in him.

¹²After this he went down to Capernaum with his mother and brothers and his disciples. There they stayed for a few days.

¹³When it was almost time for the Jewish Passover, Jesus went up to Jerusalem. ¹⁴In the temple courts he found men selling cattle, sheep and doves, and others sitting at tables exchanging money. ¹⁵So he made a whip out of cords, and drove all from the temple area, both sheep and cattle; he scattered the coins of the money changers and overturned their tables. ¹⁶To those who sold doves he said, "Get these out of here! How dare you turn my Father's house into a market!"

¹⁷His disciples remembered that it is written: "Zeal for your house will consume me."[m]

¹⁸Then the Jews demanded of him, "What miraculous sign can you show us to prove your authority to do all this?"

¹⁹Jesus answered them, "Destroy this temple, and I will raise it again in three days."

²⁰The Jews replied, "It has taken forty-six years to build this temple, and you are going to raise it in three days?" ²¹But the temple he had spoken of was his body. ²²After he was raised from the dead, his disciples recalled what he had said. Then they believed the Scripture and the words that Jesus had spoken.

---

i42 Both *Cephas* (Aramaic) and *Peter* (Greek) mean *rock*.　 j50 Or *Do you believe . . . ?*　 k51 The Greek is plural.　 l6 Greek *two to three metretes* (probably about 75 to 115 liters)　 m17 Psalm 69:9

23Now while he was in Jerusalem at the Passover Feast, many people saw the miraculous signs he was doing and believed in his name.ⁿ 24But Jesus would not entrust himself to them, for he knew all men. 25He did not need man's testimony about man, for he knew what was in a man.

ⁿ23 Or and believed in him

OCTOBER 26 □ DAY 300
JOHN 3–5
Ministry to Individuals by God's Son

OVERVIEW Today's section centers around Jesus' encounters with three individuals: Nicodemus, the Samaritan woman at the well, and the invalid man at the pool of Bethesda. In each instance, Christ's dealings with the individual have a far-reaching impact on others as well. His contact with the Samaritan woman (John 4) leads to the evangelization of the town of Sychar. The healing of the invalid man (John 5) produces an angry confrontation with Jews intent on killing Jesus. Christ's night visit from Nicodemus (John 3) provides the context for one of the most beloved verses in all of Scripture: John 3:16—"For God so loved the world that he gave his one and only Son. . . ."

Chapter 3	Chapter 4	Chapter 5
Life for the Seeker	Cleansing for the Sinner	Healing for the Sick
Nicodemus	Samaritan Woman	Paralyzed Man

YOUR DAILY WALK Have you ever used a freeway on-ramp? (If you've tried to enter a freeway at rush hour, you perhaps have felt like you *lived* on an on-ramp!) Though the on-ramp is not technically part of the freeway itself, without it the freeway would be virtually useless. On-ramps get you onto the freeway. They provide access to the highway itself.

"You are a teacher who has come from God," said Nicodemus of Jesus. Jesus was more—he was God come to teach.

Now think of the gospel of Jesus Christ as a freeway. How are you at finding "on-ramps" to share that Good News with others? In each of the three chapters you will read today, Jesus uses an on-ramp to open a door of opportunity for his listener to hear and receive the gospel. Can you discover the on-ramps Jesus used? And can you suggest one you might use with a friend or fellow worker today?

INSIGHT Tracing the Roots of the Samaritans
The Samaritans were a mixed race of people, resulting from the intermarriage of Jews with the pagan colonists the Assyrians used to repopulate the northern kingdom after its dispersal in 722 B.C. Racial hatred ensued, causing the Samaritans to form their own national and religious identity, complete with their own holy mountain and sacred writings. Though Samaria was considered off-limits to devout Jews, Jesus and his disciples passed through it in order to keep a divine appointment (4:4).

CHAPTER 3

Now there was a man of the Pharisees named Nicodemus, a member of the Jewish ruling council. ²He came to Jesus at night and said, "Rabbi, we know you are a teacher who has come from God. For no one could perform the miraculous signs you are doing if God were not with him."

³In reply Jesus declared, "I tell you the truth, no one can see the kingdom of God unless he is born again.ᵒ"

⁴"How can a man be born when he is old?" Nicodemus asked. "Surely he cannot enter a second time into his mother's womb to be born!"

⁵Jesus answered, "I tell you the truth, no one can enter the kingdom of God unless he is born of water and the Spirit. ⁶Flesh gives birth to flesh, but the Spiritᵖ gives birth to spirit. ⁷You should not be surprised at my saying, 'You�q must be born again.' ⁸The wind blows wherever it pleases. You hear its sound, but you cannot tell where it comes from or where it is going. So it is with everyone born of the Spirit."

⁹"How can this be?" Nicodemus asked.

¹⁰"You are Israel's teacher," said Jesus, "and do you not understand these things? ¹¹I tell you the truth, we speak of what we know, and we testify to what we have seen, but still you people do not accept our testimony. ¹²I have spoken to you of earthly things and you do not believe; how then will you believe if I speak of heavenly things? ¹³No one has ever gone into heaven except the one who came from heaven—the Son of Man.ʳ ¹⁴Just as Moses lifted up the snake in the desert, so the Son of Man must be lifted up, ¹⁵that everyone who believes in him may have eternal life.ˢ

¹⁶"For God so loved the world that he gave his one and only Son,ᵗ that whoever believes in him shall not perish but have eternal life. ¹⁷For God did not send his Son into the world to condemn the world, but to save the world through him. ¹⁸Whoever believes in him is not condemned, but whoever does not believe stands condemned already because he has not believed in the name of God's one and only Son.ᵘ ¹⁹This is the verdict: Light has come into the world, but men loved darkness instead of light because their deeds were evil. ²⁰Everyone who does evil hates the light, and will not come into the light for fear that his deeds will be exposed. ²¹But whoever lives by the truth comes into the light, so that it may be seen plainly that what he has done has been done through God."ᵛ

²²After this, Jesus and his disciples went out into the Judean countryside, where he spent some time with them, and baptized. ²³Now John also was baptizing at Aenon near Salim, because there was plenty of water, and people were constantly coming to be baptized. ²⁴(This was before John was put in prison.) ²⁵An argument developed between some of John's disciples and a certain Jewʷ over the matter of ceremonial washing. ²⁶They came to John and said to him, "Rabbi, that man who was with you on the other side of the Jordan—the one you testified about—well, he is baptizing, and everyone is going to him."

²⁷To this John replied, "A man can receive only what is given him from heaven. ²⁸You yourselves can testify that I said, 'I am not the Christˣ but am sent ahead of him.' ²⁹The bride belongs to the bridegroom. The friend who attends the bridegroom waits and listens for him, and is full of joy when he hears the bridegroom's voice. That joy is mine, and it is now complete. ³⁰He must become greater; I must become less.

³¹"The one who comes from above is above all; the one who is from the earth belongs to the earth, and speaks as one from the earth. The one who comes from heaven is above all. ³²He testifies to what he has seen and heard, but no one accepts his testimony. ³³The man who has accepted it has certified that God is truthful. ³⁴For the one whom God has sent speaks the words of God, for Godʸ gives the Spirit without limit. ³⁵The Father loves the Son and has placed everything in his hands. ³⁶Whoever believes in the Son has eternal life, but whoever rejects the Son will not see life, for God's wrath remains on him."ᶻ

ᵒ3 Or born from above; also in verse 7   ᵖ6 Or but spirit   �q7 The Greek is plural.   ʳ13 Some manuscripts Man, who is in heaven   ˢ15 Or believes may have eternal life in him   ᵗ16 Or his only begotten Son   ᵘ18 Or God's only begotten Son   ᵛ21 Some interpreters end the quotation after verse 15.   ʷ25 Some manuscripts and certain Jews   ˣ28 Or Messiah   ʸ34 Greek he   ᶻ36 Some interpreters end the quotation after verse 30.

CHAPTER 4

The Pharisees heard that Jesus was gaining and baptizing more disciples than John, [2]although in fact it was not Jesus who baptized, but his disciples. [3]When the Lord learned of this, he left Judea and went back once more to Galilee.

[4]Now he had to go through Samaria. [5]So he came to a town in Samaria called Sychar, near the plot of ground Jacob had given to his son Joseph. [6]Jacob's well was there, and Jesus, tired as he was from the journey, sat down by the well. It was about the sixth hour.

[7]When a Samaritan woman came to draw water, Jesus said to her, "Will you give me a drink?" [8](His disciples had gone into the town to buy food.)

[9]The Samaritan woman said to him, "You are a Jew and I am a Samaritan woman. How can you ask me for a drink?" (For Jews do not associate with Samaritans.[a])

[10]Jesus answered her, "If you knew the gift of God and who it is that asks you for a drink, you would have asked him and he would have given you living water."

[11]"Sir," the woman said, "you have nothing to draw with and the well is deep. Where can you get this living water? [12]Are you greater than our father Jacob, who gave us the well and drank from it himself, as did also his sons and his flocks and herds?"

[13]Jesus answered, "Everyone who drinks this water will be thirsty again, [14]but whoever drinks the water I give him will never thirst. Indeed, the water I give him will become in him a spring of water welling up to eternal life."

[15]The woman said to him, "Sir, give me this water so that I won't get thirsty and have to keep coming here to draw water."

[16]He told her, "Go, call your husband and come back."

[17]"I have no husband," she replied.

Jesus said to her, "You are right when you say you have no husband. [18]The fact is, you have had five husbands, and the man you now have is not your husband. What you have just said is quite true."

[19]"Sir," the woman said, "I can see that you are a prophet. [20]Our fathers worshiped on this mountain, but you Jews claim that the place where we must worship is in Jerusalem."

[21]Jesus declared, "Believe me, woman, a time is coming when you will worship the Father neither on this mountain nor in Jerusalem. [22]You Samaritans worship what you do not know; we worship what we do know, for salvation is from the Jews. [23]Yet a time is coming and has now come when the true worshipers will worship the Father in spirit and truth, for they are the kind of worshipers the Father seeks. [24]God is spirit, and his worshipers must worship in spirit and in truth."

[25]The woman said, "I know that Messiah" (called Christ) "is coming. When he comes, he will explain everything to us."

[26]Then Jesus declared, "I who speak to you am he."

[27]Just then his disciples returned and were surprised to find him talking with a woman. But no one asked, "What do you want?" or "Why are you talking with her?"

[28]Then, leaving her water jar, the woman went back to the town and said to the people, [29]"Come, see a man who told me everything I ever did. Could this be the Christ[b]?" [30]They came out of the town and made their way toward him.

[31]Meanwhile his disciples urged him, "Rabbi, eat something."

[32]But he said to them, "I have food to eat that you know nothing about."

[33]Then his disciples said to each other, "Could someone have brought him food?"

[34]"My food," said Jesus, "is to do the will of him who sent me and to finish his work. [35]Do you not say, 'Four months more and then the harvest'? I tell you, open your eyes and look at the fields! They are ripe for harvest. [36]Even now the reaper draws his wages, even now he harvests the crop for eternal life, so that the sower and the reaper may be glad together. [37]Thus the saying 'One sows and another reaps' is true. [38]I sent you to reap what you have not worked for. Others have done the hard work, and you have reaped the benefits of their labor."

[39]Many of the Samaritans from that town believed in him because of the woman's testimony, "He told me everything I ever did." [40]So when the Samaritans came to him, they urged him to stay with them, and he stayed two days. [41]And

[a]9 Or do not use dishes Samaritans have used   [b]29 Or Messiah

because of his words many more became believers.

⁴²They said to the woman, "We no longer believe just because of what you said; now we have heard for ourselves, and we know that this man really is the Savior of the world."

⁴³After the two days he left for Galilee. ⁴⁴(Now Jesus himself had pointed out that a prophet has no honor in his own country.) ⁴⁵When he arrived in Galilee, the Galileans welcomed him. They had seen all that he had done in Jerusalem at the Passover Feast, for they also had been there.

⁴⁶Once more he visited Cana in Galilee, where he had turned the water into wine. And there was a certain royal official whose son lay sick at Capernaum. ⁴⁷When this man heard that Jesus had arrived in Galilee from Judea, he went to him and begged him to come and heal his son, who was close to death.

⁴⁸"Unless you people see miraculous signs and wonders," Jesus told him, "you will never believe."

⁴⁹The royal official said, "Sir, come down before my child dies."

⁵⁰Jesus replied, "You may go. Your son will live."

The man took Jesus at his word and departed. ⁵¹While he was still on the way, his servants met him with the news that his boy was living. ⁵²When he inquired as to the time when his son got better, they said to him, "The fever left him yesterday at the seventh hour."

⁵³Then the father realized that this was the exact time at which Jesus had said to him, "Your son will live." So he and all his household believed.

⁵⁴This was the second miraculous sign that Jesus performed, having come from Judea to Galilee.

CHAPTER 5

Some time later, Jesus went up to Jerusalem for a feast of the Jews. ²Now there is in Jerusalem near the Sheep Gate a pool, which in Aramaic is called Bethesda*c* and which is surrounded by five covered colonnades. ³Here a great number of disabled people used to lie—the blind, the lame, the paralyzed.*d* ⁵One who was

there had been an invalid for thirty-eight years. ⁶When Jesus saw him lying there and learned that he had been in this condition for a long time, he asked him, "Do you want to get well?"

⁷"Sir," the invalid replied, "I have no one to help me into the pool when the water is stirred. While I am trying to get in, someone else goes down ahead of me."

⁸Then Jesus said to him, "Get up! Pick up your mat and walk." ⁹At once the man was cured; he picked up his mat and walked.

The day on which this took place was a Sabbath, ¹⁰and so the Jews said to the man who had been healed, "It is the Sabbath; the law forbids you to carry your mat."

¹¹But he replied, "The man who made me well said to me, 'Pick up your mat and walk.' "

¹²So they asked him, "Who is this fellow who told you to pick it up and walk?"

¹³The man who was healed had no idea who it was, for Jesus had slipped away into the crowd that was there.

¹⁴Later Jesus found him at the temple and said to him, "See, you are well again. Stop sinning or something worse may happen to you." ¹⁵The man went away and told the Jews that it was Jesus who had made him well.

¹⁶So, because Jesus was doing these things on the Sabbath, the Jews persecuted him. ¹⁷Jesus said to them, "My Father is always at his work to this very day, and I, too, am working." ¹⁸For this reason the Jews tried all the harder to kill him; not only was he breaking the Sabbath, but he was even calling God his own Father, making himself equal with God.

¹⁹Jesus gave them this answer: "I tell you the truth, the Son can do nothing by himself; he can do only what he sees his Father doing, because whatever the Father does the Son also does. ²⁰For the Father loves the Son and shows him all he does. Yes, to your amazement he will show him even greater things than these. ²¹For just as the Father raises the dead and gives them life, even so the Son gives life to whom he is pleased to give it. ²²Moreover, the Father judges no one, but has entrusted all judgment to the Son, ²³that all may honor the Son just as they

---

*c*2 Some manuscripts *Bethzatha*; other manuscripts *Bethsaida*   *d*3 Some less important manuscripts *paralyzed—and they waited for the moving of the waters.* ⁴*From time to time an angel of the Lord would come down and stir up the waters. The first one into the pool after each such disturbance would be cured of whatever disease he had.*

honor the Father. He who does not honor the Son does not honor the Father, who sent him.

²⁴"I tell you the truth, whoever hears my word and believes him who sent me has eternal life and will not be condemned; he has crossed over from death to life. ²⁵I tell you the truth, a time is coming and has now come when the dead will hear the voice of the Son of God and those who hear will live. ²⁶For as the Father has life in himself, so he has granted the Son to have life in himself. ²⁷And he has given him authority to judge because he is the Son of Man.

²⁸"Do not be amazed at this, for a time is coming when all who are in their graves will hear his voice ²⁹and come out—those who have done good will rise to live, and those who have done evil will rise to be condemned. ³⁰By myself I can do nothing; I judge only as I hear, and my judgment is just, for I seek not to please myself but him who sent me.

³¹"If I testify about myself, my testimony is not valid. ³²There is another who testifies in my favor, and I know that his testimony about me is valid.

³³"You have sent to John and he has testified to the truth. ³⁴Not that I accept human testimony; but I mention it that you may be saved. ³⁵John was a lamp that burned and gave light, and you chose for a time to enjoy his light.

³⁶"I have testimony weightier than that of John. For the very work that the Father has given me to finish, and which I am doing, testifies that the Father has sent me. ³⁷And the Father who sent me has himself testified concerning me. You have never heard his voice nor seen his form, ³⁸nor does his word dwell in you, for you do not believe the one he sent. ³⁹You diligently study*ᵉ* the Scriptures because you think that by them you possess eternal life. These are the Scriptures that testify about me, ⁴⁰yet you refuse to come to me to have life.

⁴¹"I do not accept praise from men, ⁴²but I know you. I know that you do not have the love of God in your hearts. ⁴³I have come in my Father's name, and you do not accept me; but if someone else comes in his own name, you will accept him. ⁴⁴How can you believe if you accept praise from one another, yet make no effort to obtain the praise that comes from the only God*ᶠ*?

⁴⁵"But do not think I will accuse you before the Father. Your accuser is Moses, on whom your hopes are set. ⁴⁶If you believed Moses, you would believe me, for he wrote about me. ⁴⁷But since you do not believe what he wrote, how are you going to believe what I say?"

ᵉ39 Or *Study diligently* (the imperative)   *ᶠ44* Some early manuscripts *the Only One*

OCTOBER 27 ☐ DAY 301

JOHN 6–8
Ministry to the Multitudes by God's Son

 OVERVIEW John relates his record of Jesus' life and ministry to the major feasts of the Jews. The feeding of the five thousand and Jesus' discourse on the true bread of life take place during the Passover (6:4). The discourses of chapters 7 and 8 are given during Jesus' visit to Jerusalem for the Feast of Tabernacles (7:2, 10). Though in both cases it is a time for feasting, clearly the temperament of the Jewish leaders is more akin to murder than to merriment as they take up rocks to stone Christ (8:59).

Chapter 6	Chapter 7	Chapter 8
The Bread of Life	The Water of Life	The Light of the World
Feast of Passover	Feast of Tabernacles	

YOUR DAILY WALK Do you stand alone in your family circle as a Christian? And do you find your home environment hard on your spiritual life and growth? Then take heart. The Lord Jesus faced the same discouraging problem in his earthly family (7:5). His mother, Mary, of course, knew her Son's true identity. But none of his brothers believed he was the Messiah until after his resurrection. Not only were they unbelieving, but they made fun of his claims and ministry.

Wherever you see persecution, there is more than a probability that truth is on the persecuted side.

The way Jesus dealt with unbelief and sarcasm in his family will work for you, too. First, he ignored their taunts. Do not respond to scoffing, either in anger or in rebuttal. Response is what the scoffers want. It only feeds the fires of antagonism. Second, Jesus quietly and consistently continued his ministry for God. Do not be intimidated by unbelieving family members. Ask God to enable you to be faithful to him and to live a consistent, vibrant Christian life before them as a witness. Remember, you may be the only "Bible" your unsaved family will ever read. Third, Jesus drew strength and encouragement from other believers (Matthew 12:46–50). Can you hope to grow spiritually without doing the same? Schedule a time of prayer with one of your brothers or sisters in Christ. You need it—and so do they!

INSIGHT "I AM" in the Old, "I AM" in the New
In Exodus 3:14 God reveals his name to Moses as "I AM," the self-existent, all-sufficient God. The claims of Jesus in today's section (6:35, 48; 8:12) make it clear he is identifying himself as the same person—a claim the Jewish leaders understand all too clearly.

CHAPTER 6
Some time after this, Jesus crossed to the far shore of the Sea of Galilee (that is, the Sea of Tiberias), ²and a great crowd of people followed him because they saw the miraculous signs he had performed on the sick. ³Then Jesus went up on a mountainside and sat down with his disciples. ⁴The Jewish Passover Feast was near.

⁵When Jesus looked up and saw a great crowd coming toward him, he said to Philip, "Where shall we buy bread for these people to eat?" ⁶He asked this only to test him, for he already had in mind what he was going to do.

⁷Philip answered him, "Eight months' wages⁸ would not buy enough bread for each one to have a bite!"

⁸Another of his disciples, Andrew, Simon Peter's brother, spoke up, ⁹"Here is a boy with five small barley loaves and two small fish, but how far will they go among so many?"

¹⁰Jesus said, "Have the people sit down." There was plenty of grass in that place, and the men sat down, about five thousand of them. ¹¹Jesus then took the loaves, gave thanks, and distributed to those who were seated as much as they wanted. He did the same with the fish.

¹²When they had all had enough to eat, he said to his disciples, "Gather the pieces that are left over. Let nothing be wasted." ¹³So they gathered them and filled twelve baskets with the pieces of the five barley loaves left over by those who had eaten.

¹⁴After the people saw the miraculous sign that Jesus did, they began to say, "Surely this is the Prophet who is to come into the world." ¹⁵Jesus, knowing that they intended to come and make him king by force, withdrew again to a mountain by himself.

¹⁶When evening came, his disciples

8 7 Greek two hundred denarii

went down to the lake, [17]where they got into a boat and set off across the lake for Capernaum. By now it was dark, and Jesus had not yet joined them. [18]A strong wind was blowing and the waters grew rough. [19]When they had rowed three or three and a half miles,[h] they saw Jesus approaching the boat, walking on the water; and they were terrified. [20]But he said to them, "It is I; don't be afraid." [21]Then they were willing to take him into the boat, and immediately the boat reached the shore where they were heading.

[22]The next day the crowd that had stayed on the opposite shore of the lake realized that only one boat had been there, and that Jesus had not entered it with his disciples, but that they had gone away alone. [23]Then some boats from Tiberias landed near the place where the people had eaten the bread after the Lord had given thanks. [24]Once the crowd realized that neither Jesus nor his disciples were there, they got into the boats and went to Capernaum in search of Jesus.

[25]When they found him on the other side of the lake, they asked him, "Rabbi, when did you get here?"

[26]Jesus answered, "I tell you the truth, you are looking for me, not because you saw miraculous signs but because you ate the loaves and had your fill. [27]Do not work for food that spoils, but for food that endures to eternal life, which the Son of Man will give you. On him God the Father has placed his seal of approval."

[28]Then they asked him, "What must we do to do the works God requires?"

[29]Jesus answered, "The work of God is this: to believe in the one he has sent."

[30]So they asked him, "What miraculous sign then will you give that we may see it and believe you? What will you do? [31]Our forefathers ate the manna in the desert; as it is written: 'He gave them bread from heaven to eat.'[i]"

[32]Jesus said to them, "I tell you the truth, it is not Moses who has given you the bread from heaven, but it is my Father who gives you the true bread from heaven. [33]For the bread of God is he who comes down from heaven and gives life to the world."

[34]"Sir," they said, "from now on give us this bread."

[35]Then Jesus declared, "I am the bread of life. He who comes to me will never go hungry, and he who believes in me will never be thirsty. [36]But as I told you, you have seen me and still you do not believe. [37]All that the Father gives me will come to me, and whoever comes to me I will never drive away. [38]For I have come down from heaven not to do my will but to do the will of him who sent me. [39]And this is the will of him who sent me, that I shall lose none of all that he has given me, but raise them up at the last day. [40]For my Father's will is that everyone who looks to the Son and believes in him shall have eternal life, and I will raise him up at the last day."

[41]At this the Jews began to grumble about him because he said, "I am the bread that came down from heaven." [42]They said, "Is this not Jesus, the son of Joseph, whose father and mother we know? How can he now say, 'I came down from heaven'?"

[43]"Stop grumbling among yourselves," Jesus answered. [44]"No one can come to me unless the Father who sent me draws him, and I will raise him up at the last day. [45]It is written in the Prophets: 'They will all be taught by God.'[j] Everyone who listens to the Father and learns from him comes to me. [46]No one has seen the Father except the one who is from God; only he has seen the Father. [47]I tell you the truth, he who believes has everlasting life. [48]I am the bread of life. [49]Your forefathers ate the manna in the desert, yet they died. [50]But here is the bread that comes down from heaven, which a man may eat and not die. [51]I am the living bread that came down from heaven. If anyone eats of this bread, he will live forever. This bread is my flesh, which I will give for the life of the world."

[52]Then the Jews began to argue sharply among themselves, "How can this man give us his flesh to eat?"

[53]Jesus said to them, "I tell you the truth, unless you eat the flesh of the Son of Man and drink his blood, you have no life in you. [54]Whoever eats my flesh and drinks my blood has eternal life, and I will raise him up at the last day. [55]For my flesh is real food and my blood is real drink. [56]Whoever eats my flesh and drinks my blood remains in me, and I in

[h]19 Greek rowed twenty-five or thirty stadia (about 5 or 6 kilometers)   [i]31 Exodus 16:4; Neh. 9:15; Psalm 78:24,25
[j]45 Isaiah 54:13

him. ⁵⁷Just as the living Father sent me and I live because of the Father, so the one who feeds on me will live because of me. ⁵⁸This is the bread that came down from heaven. Your forefathers ate manna and died, but he who feeds on this bread will live forever." ⁵⁹He said this while teaching in the synagogue in Capernaum.

⁶⁰On hearing it, many of his disciples said, "This is a hard teaching. Who can accept it?"

⁶¹Aware that his disciples were grumbling about this, Jesus said to them, "Does this offend you? ⁶²What if you see the Son of Man ascend to where he was before! ⁶³The Spirit gives life; the flesh counts for nothing. The words I have spoken to you are spirit^k and they are life. ⁶⁴Yet there are some of you who do not believe." For Jesus had known from the beginning which of them did not believe and who would betray him. ⁶⁵He went on to say, "This is why I told you that no one can come to me unless the Father has enabled him."

⁶⁶From this time many of his disciples turned back and no longer followed him.

⁶⁷"You do not want to leave too, do you?" Jesus asked the Twelve.

⁶⁸Simon Peter answered him, "Lord, to whom shall we go? You have the words of eternal life. ⁶⁹We believe and know that you are the Holy One of God."

⁷⁰Then Jesus replied, "Have I not chosen you, the Twelve? Yet one of you is a devil!" ⁷¹(He meant Judas, the son of Simon Iscariot, who, though one of the Twelve, was later to betray him.)

CHAPTER 7

After this, Jesus went around in Galilee, purposely staying away from Judea because the Jews there were waiting to take his life. ²But when the Jewish Feast of Tabernacles was near, ³Jesus' brothers said to him, "You ought to leave here and go to Judea, so that your disciples may see the miracles you do. ⁴No one who wants to become a public figure acts in secret. Since you are doing these things, show yourself to the world." ⁵For even his own brothers did not believe in him.

⁶Therefore Jesus told them, "The right time for me has not yet come; for you any time is right. ⁷The world cannot hate you,

but it hates me because I testify that what it does is evil. ⁸You go to the Feast. I am not yet^l going up to this Feast, because for me the right time has not yet come." ⁹Having said this, he stayed in Galilee.

¹⁰However, after his brothers had left for the Feast, he went also, not publicly, but in secret. ¹¹Now at the Feast the Jews were watching for him and asking, "Where is that man?"

¹²Among the crowds there was widespread whispering about him. Some said, "He is a good man."

Others replied, "No, he deceives the people." ¹³But no one would say anything publicly about him for fear of the Jews.

¹⁴Not until halfway through the Feast did Jesus go up to the temple courts and begin to teach. ¹⁵The Jews were amazed and asked, "How did this man get such learning without having studied?"

¹⁶Jesus answered, "My teaching is not my own. It comes from him who sent me. ¹⁷If anyone chooses to do God's will, he will find out whether my teaching comes from God or whether I speak on my own. ¹⁸He who speaks on his own does so to gain honor for himself, but he who works for the honor of the one who sent him is a man of truth; there is nothing false about him. ¹⁹Has not Moses given you the law? Yet not one of you keeps the law. Why are you trying to kill me?"

²⁰"You are demon-possessed," the crowd answered. "Who is trying to kill you?"

²¹Jesus said to them, "I did one miracle, and you are all astonished. ²²Yet, because Moses gave you circumcision (though actually it did not come from Moses, but from the patriarchs), you circumcise a child on the Sabbath. ²³Now if a child can be circumcised on the Sabbath so that the law of Moses may not be broken, why are you angry with me for healing the whole man on the Sabbath? ²⁴Stop judging by mere appearances, and make a right judgment."

²⁵At that point some of the people of Jerusalem began to ask, "Isn't this the man they are trying to kill? ²⁶Here he is, speaking publicly, and they are not saying a word to him. Have the authorities really concluded that he is the Christ^m? ²⁷But we know where this man is from;

*k*63 Or *Spirit*   *l*8 Some early manuscripts do not have *yet.*   *m*26 Or *Messiah*; also in verses 27, 31, 41 and 42 when the Christ comes, no one will know where he is from."

[28] Then Jesus, still teaching in the temple courts, cried out, "Yes, you know me, and you know where I am from. I am not here on my own, but he who sent me is true. You do not know him, [29] but I know him because I am from him and he sent me."

[30] At this they tried to seize him, but no one laid a hand on him, because his time had not yet come. [31] Still, many in the crowd put their faith in him. They said, "When the Christ comes, will he do more miraculous signs than this man?"

[32] The Pharisees heard the crowd whispering such things about him. Then the chief priests and the Pharisees sent temple guards to arrest him.

[33] Jesus said, "I am with you for only a short time, and then I go to the one who sent me. [34] You will look for me, but you will not find me; and where I am, you cannot come."

[35] The Jews said to one another, "Where does this man intend to go that we cannot find him? Will he go where our people live scattered among the Greeks, and teach the Greeks? [36] What did he mean when he said, 'You will look for me, but you will not find me,' and 'Where I am, you cannot come'?"

[37] On the last and greatest day of the Feast, Jesus stood and said in a loud voice, "If anyone is thirsty, let him come to me and drink. [38] Whoever believes in me, as [n] the Scripture has said, streams of living water will flow from within him." [39] By this he meant the Spirit, whom those who believed in him were later to receive. Up to that time the Spirit had not been given, since Jesus had not yet been glorified.

[40] On hearing his words, some of the people said, "Surely this man is the Prophet."

[41] Others said, "He is the Christ."

Still others asked, "How can the Christ come from Galilee? [42] Does not the Scripture say that the Christ will come from David's family [o] and from Bethlehem, the town where David lived?" [43] Thus the people were divided because of Jesus. [44] Some wanted to seize him, but no one laid a hand on him.

[45] Finally the temple guards went back to the chief priests and Pharisees, who asked them, "Why didn't you bring him in?"

[46] "No one ever spoke the way this man does," the guards declared.

[47] "You mean he has deceived you also?" the Pharisees retorted. [48] "Has any of the rulers or of the Pharisees believed in him? [49] No! But this mob that knows nothing of the law—there is a curse on them."

[50] Nicodemus, who had gone to Jesus earlier and who was one of their own number, asked, [51] "Does our law condemn anyone without first hearing him to find out what he is doing?"

[52] They replied, "Are you from Galilee, too? Look into it, and you will find that a prophet [p] does not come out of Galilee."

[The earliest manuscripts and many other ancient witnesses do not have John 7:53–8:11.]

[53] Then each went to his own home.

CHAPTER 8

But Jesus went to the Mount of Olives. [2] At dawn he appeared again in the temple courts, where all the people gathered around him, and he sat down to teach them. [3] The teachers of the law and the Pharisees brought in a woman caught in adultery. They made her stand before the group [4] and said to Jesus, "Teacher, this woman was caught in the act of adultery. [5] In the Law Moses commanded us to stone such women. Now what do you say?" [6] They were using this question as a trap, in order to have a basis for accusing him.

But Jesus bent down and started to write on the ground with his finger. [7] When they kept on questioning him, he straightened up and said to them, "If any one of you is without sin, let him be the first to throw a stone at her." [8] Again he stooped down and wrote on the ground.

[9] At this, those who heard began to go away one at a time, the older ones first, until only Jesus was left, with the woman still standing there. [10] Jesus straightened up and asked her, "Woman, where are they? Has no one condemned you?"

[11] "No one, sir," she said.

[n] 37,38 Or / If anyone is thirsty, let him come to me. / And let him drink, 38who believes in me. / As   [o] 42 Greek seed
[p] 52 Two early manuscripts the Prophet

"Then neither do I condemn you," Jesus declared. "Go now and leave your life of sin."

12When Jesus spoke again to the people, he said, "I am the light of the world. Whoever follows me will never walk in darkness, but will have the light of life."

13The Pharisees challenged him, "Here you are, appearing as your own witness; your testimony is not valid."

14Jesus answered, "Even if I testify on my own behalf, my testimony is valid, for I know where I came from and where I am going. But you have no idea where I come from or where I am going. 15You judge by human standards; I pass judgment on no one. 16But if I do judge, my decisions are right, because I am not alone. I stand with the Father, who sent me. 17In your own Law it is written that the testimony of two men is valid. 18I am one who testifies for myself; my other witness is the Father, who sent me."

19Then they asked him, "Where is your father?"

"You do not know me or my Father," Jesus replied. "If you knew me, you would know my Father also." 20He spoke these words while teaching in the temple area near the place where the offerings were put. Yet no one seized him, because his time had not yet come.

21Once more Jesus said to them, "I am going away, and you will look for me, and you will die in your sin. Where I go, you cannot come."

22This made the Jews ask, "Will he kill himself? Is that why he says, 'Where I go, you cannot come'?"

23But he continued, "You are from below; I am from above. You are of this world; I am not of this world. 24I told you that you would die in your sins; if you do not believe that I am ⌊the one I claim to be⌋,q you will indeed die in your sins."

25"Who are you?" they asked.

"Just what I have been claiming all along," Jesus replied. 26"I have much to say in judgment of you. But he who sent me is reliable, and what I have heard from him I tell the world."

27They did not understand that he was telling them about his Father. 28So Jesus said, "When you have lifted up the Son of Man, then you will know that I am ⌊the one I claim to be⌋ and that I do nothing on my own but speak just what the Father has taught me. 29The one who sent me is with me; he has not left me alone, for I always do what pleases him." 30Even as he spoke, many put their faith in him.

31To the Jews who had believed him, Jesus said, "If you hold to my teaching, you are really my disciples. 32Then you will know the truth, and the truth will set you free."

33They answered him, "We are Abraham's descendants r and have never been slaves of anyone. How can you say that we shall be set free?"

34Jesus replied, "I tell you the truth, everyone who sins is a slave to sin. 35Now a slave has no permanent place in the family, but a son belongs to it forever. 36So if the Son sets you free, you will be free indeed. 37I know you are Abraham's descendants. Yet you are ready to kill me, because you have no room for my word. 38I am telling you what I have seen in the Father's presence, and you do what you have heard from your father.s"

39"Abraham is our father," they answered.

"If you were Abraham's children," said Jesus, "then you would t do the things Abraham did. 40As it is, you are determined to kill me, a man who has told you the truth that I heard from God. Abraham did not do such things. 41You are doing the things your own father does."

"We are not illegitimate children," they protested. "The only Father we have is God himself."

42Jesus said to them, "If God were your Father, you would love me, for I came from God and now am here. I have not come on my own; but he sent me. 43Why is my language not clear to you? Because you are unable to hear what I say. 44You belong to your father, the devil, and you want to carry out your father's desire. He was a murderer from the beginning, not holding to the truth, for there is no truth in him. When he lies, he speaks his native language, for he is a liar and the father of lies. 45Yet because I tell the truth, you do not believe me! 46Can any of you prove me guilty of sin? If I am telling the truth,

---

q24 Or I am he; also in verse 28   r33 Greek seed; also in verse 37   s38 Or presence. Therefore do what you have heard from the Father.   t39 Some early manuscripts "If you are Abraham's children," said Jesus, "then" why don't you believe me? [47]He who belongs to God hears what God says. The reason you do not hear is that you do not belong to God."

[48]The Jews answered him, "Aren't we right in saying that you are a Samaritan and demon-possessed?"

[49]"I am not possessed by a demon," said Jesus, "but I honor my Father and you dishonor me. [50]I am not seeking glory for myself; but there is one who seeks it, and he is the judge. [51]I tell you the truth, if anyone keeps my word, he will never see death."

[52]At this the Jews exclaimed, "Now we know that you are demon-possessed! Abraham died and so did the prophets, yet you say that if anyone keeps your word, he will never taste death. [53]Are you greater than our father Abraham? He

died, and so did the prophets. Who do you think you are?"

[54]Jesus replied, "If I glorify myself, my glory means nothing. My Father, whom you claim as your God, is the one who glorifies me. [55]Though you do not know him, I know him. If I said I did not, I would be a liar like you, but I do know him and keep his word. [56]Your father Abraham rejoiced at the thought of seeing my day; he saw it and was glad."

[57]"You are not yet fifty years old," the Jews said to him, "and you have seen Abraham!"

[58]"I tell you the truth," Jesus answered, "before Abraham was born, I am!" [59]At this, they picked up stones to stone him, but Jesus hid himself, slipping away from the temple grounds.

OCTOBER 28 □ DAY 302
Ready with an Answer

 LOOK BACK In contrast to the synoptic Gospels (Matthew, Mark and Luke), John's Gospel might well be called the *supplemental* Gospel, for about 93 percent of John's account is found nowhere else in the gospel records. Such favorite characters as the woman at the well, Nicodemus, Jesus' dear friend Lazarus and the nameless Good Samaritan are found in John's Gospel alone.

Luke writes with the precision of a careful historian as he documents the life and times of Jesus, for that is his purpose: "to write an orderly account for you . . . that you may know the certainty of the things you have been taught" (Luke 1:3–4). By contrast, John focuses on the miraculous signs Jesus performed (seven in the first twelve chapters alone) "that you may believe that Jesus is the Christ, the Son of God, and that by believing you may have life in his name" (John 20:30–31).

Many verses you have read this past week would make excellent memory work projects. Why not hide a bit of God's Word in your heart this next week, beginning with one of the following verses: Luke 16:13; 18:16; 19:10; 20:25; John 1:12, 14; 3:16, 36; 5:24; 8:32.

 LOOK UP There is a knock at your door. It is late, and visitors at night are rare. But this visitor turns out to be your minister or religious leader. After a few minutes of polite conversation, the discussion takes a serious turn. He asks you, "How can I know I am a Christian?"

Your mission field is the next unsaved person you meet. Would you be surprised? Of course you would! After all, ministers and religious leaders are supposed to know the answers to spiritual questions. But here is a man asking the very questions he should have been prepared to answer.

In John 3 you've read a true account that in many ways parallels the fictitious story about your minister. Nicodemus was a Pharisee, a religious man. Trained in the Mosaic Law, he was an expert in the Old Testament Scriptures. Quite likely he taught children in the synagogue school. But here he was asking Jesus the very question he should have been prepared to answer himself: "How can a man be born when he is old?" (John 3:4). In other words, how can a person experience the second birth and be born again?

Jesus' answer has become the most familiar verse in the entire Bible—John 3:16. There you will find the best piece of good news ever broadcast to the world. Do you know what it is?

LOOK AHEAD Here is a handy way to remember what Jesus told Nicodemus during that evening encounter. By writing down the letters in the word *gospel*, you are not only ready to discover the Good News for yourself, but to share it with anyone who will listen to you for two minutes!

G _____ so loved the world that he gave his

O _____ and only

S _____, that whoever believes in him shall not

P _____ but have

E _____

L _____

If you have put your confident trust in Jesus as your Sin Bearer, it means that you, like Nicodemus, have experienced the second birth. Eternal life is God's gift to all who acknowledge their need of a Savior and turn to Jesus in believing faith. Have you heard the Good News? Good! Now pass it on to someone else who has yet to hear.

OCTOBER 29 ☐ DAY 303
JOHN 9–12
Mounting Anger toward God's Son

OVERVIEW Continuing his ministry in Jerusalem following the Feast of Tabernacles, Jesus first gives physical sight to a blind man, then opens spiritual eyes as well. This leads to a discussion with the Jews about "the blind leading the blind" and the importance of a Shepherd who both guides and guards his sheep. Jesus' seventh and climactic miracle takes place in Bethany, where he raises Lazarus from the dead. Though Bethany is astir with wonderment and belief, from this point on Jesus is a marked man (11:53), his every step leading closer to the cross.

Chapter 9	Chapter 10	Chapter 11	Chapter 12
"I Am the Light"	"I Am the Gate"	"I Am the Resurrection"	"Blessed Is the King of Israel"
Blind Man	Lost Sheep	Lazarus	Last Week

We must not only give what we have; we must also give what we are.

YOUR DAILY WALK Mary of Bethany is a woman every Christian should emulate. She is mentioned three separate times in the Gospels, and each time she is described as being at the feet of Jesus (Luke 10:39; John 11:32; 12:3). In this position she worshiped him, received instruction from him and experienced his comfort in the midst of sorrow. You cannot literally take the position of Mary, but in attitude you can. It is the position of submission and dependence.

Mary also was willing to sacrifice her most precious and costly possession in an act of devotion to Jesus. The pint of pure nard oil was worth hundreds of dollars by today's standards. It may well have been her dowry in anticipation of a wedding proposal. Yet she poured it over the feet of Jesus in an offering of love.

Perhaps you are wondering, *What do I have that I can give to Jesus as an act of worship?* The most precious thing you possess is yourself. If you have never done so before, assume the posture of Mary as you prayerfully read Romans 12:1, and give yourself as an offering today. It's an act of worship God never grows tired of receiving.

 INSIGHT The Door-less Door of the Sheep
In ancient times the sheepfold was a circular stone corral with a single narrow opening. After the sheep were inside, the shepherd would lie down across the opening, using his own body to form the gate or "door" of the sheepfold. Nothing could enter or leave the fold without the shepherd knowing about it. Keep that image in mind as you read Jesus' words in 10:7.

CHAPTER 9

As he went along, he saw a man blind from birth. ²His disciples asked him, "Rabbi, who sinned, this man or his parents, that he was born blind?"

³"Neither this man nor his parents sinned," said Jesus, "but this happened so that the work of God might be displayed in his life. ⁴As long as it is day, we must do the work of him who sent me. Night is coming, when no one can work. ⁵While I am in the world, I am the light of the world."

⁶Having said this, he spit on the ground, made some mud with the saliva, and put it on the man's eyes. ⁷"Go," he told him, "wash in the Pool of Siloam" (this word means Sent). So the man went and washed, and came home seeing.

⁸His neighbors and those who had formerly seen him begging asked, "Isn't this the same man who used to sit and beg?" ⁹Some claimed that he was.

Others said, "No, he only looks like him."

But he himself insisted, "I am the man."

¹⁰"How then were your eyes opened?" they demanded.

¹¹He replied, "The man they call Jesus made some mud and put it on my eyes. He told me to go to Siloam and wash. So I went and washed, and then I could see."

¹²"Where is this man?" they asked him.

"I don't know," he said.

¹³They brought to the Pharisees the man who had been blind. ¹⁴Now the day on which Jesus had made the mud and opened the man's eyes was a Sabbath.

¹⁵Therefore the Pharisees also asked him how he had received his sight. "He put mud on my eyes," the man replied, "and I washed, and now I see."

¹⁶Some of the Pharisees said, "This man is not from God, for he does not keep the Sabbath."

But others asked, "How can a sinner do such miraculous signs?" So they were divided.

¹⁷Finally they turned again to the blind man, "What have you to say about him? It was your eyes he opened."

The man replied, "He is a prophet."

¹⁸The Jews still did not believe that he had been blind and had received his sight until they sent for the man's parents. ¹⁹"Is this your son?" they asked. "Is this the one you say was born blind? How is it that now he can see?"

²⁰"We know he is our son," the parents answered, "and we know he was born blind. ²¹But how he can see now, or who opened his eyes, we don't know. Ask him. He is of age; he will speak for himself." ²²His parents said this because they were afraid of the Jews, for already the Jews had decided that anyone who acknowledged that Jesus was the Christ*ᵘ* would be put out of the synagogue. ²³That was why his parents said, "He is of age; ask him."

²⁴A second time they summoned the man who had been blind. "Give glory to God,*ᵛ*" they said. "We know this man is a sinner."

²⁵He replied, "Whether he is a sinner or not, I don't know. One thing I do know. I was blind but now I see!"

*ᵘ*22 Or *Messiah*   *ᵛ*24 A solemn charge to tell the truth (see Joshua 7:19)

26Then they asked him, "What did he do to you? How did he open your eyes?"

27He answered, "I have told you already and you did not listen. Why do you want to hear it again? Do you want to become his disciples, too?"

28Then they hurled insults at him and said, "You are this fellow's disciple! We are disciples of Moses! 29We know that God spoke to Moses, but as for this fellow, we don't even know where he comes from."

30The man answered, "Now that is remarkable! You don't know where he comes from, yet he opened my eyes. 31We know that God does not listen to sinners. He listens to the godly man who does his will. 32Nobody has ever heard of opening the eyes of a man born blind. 33If this man were not from God, he could do nothing."

34To this they replied, "You were steeped in sin at birth; how dare you lecture us!" And they threw him out.

35Jesus heard that they had thrown him out, and when he found him, he said, "Do you believe in the Son of Man?"

36"Who is he, sir?" the man asked. "Tell me so that I may believe in him."

37Jesus said, "You have now seen him; in fact, he is the one speaking with you."

38Then the man said, "Lord, I believe," and he worshiped him.

39Jesus said, "For judgment I have come into this world, so that the blind will see and those who see will become blind."

40Some Pharisees who were with him heard him say this and asked, "What? Are we blind too?"

41Jesus said, "If you were blind, you would not be guilty of sin; but now that you claim you can see, your guilt remains.

CHAPTER 10

"I tell you the truth, the man who does not enter the sheep pen by the gate, but climbs in by some other way, is a thief and a robber. 2The man who enters by the gate is the shepherd of his sheep. 3The watchman opens the gate for him, and the sheep listen to his voice. He calls his own sheep by name and leads them out. 4When he has brought out all his own, he goes on ahead of them, and his sheep follow him because they know his voice. 5But they will never follow a stranger; in fact, they will run away from him because they do not recognize a stranger's voice." 6Jesus used this figure of speech, but they did not understand what he was telling them.

7Therefore Jesus said again, "I tell you the truth, I am the gate for the sheep. 8All who ever came before me were thieves and robbers, but the sheep did not listen to them. 9I am the gate; whoever enters through me will be saved.w He will come in and go out, and find pasture. 10The thief comes only to steal and kill and destroy; I have come that they may have life, and have it to the full.

11"I am the good shepherd. The good shepherd lays down his life for the sheep. 12The hired hand is not the shepherd who owns the sheep. So when he sees the wolf coming, he abandons the sheep and runs away. Then the wolf attacks the flock and scatters it. 13The man runs away because he is a hired hand and cares nothing for the sheep.

14"I am the good shepherd; I know my sheep and my sheep know me— 15just as the Father knows me and I know the Father—and I lay down my life for the sheep. 16I have other sheep that are not of this sheep pen. I must bring them also. They too will listen to my voice, and there shall be one flock and one shepherd. 17The reason my Father loves me is that I lay down my life—only to take it up again. 18No one takes it from me, but I lay it down of my own accord. I have authority to lay it down and authority to take it up again. This command I received from my Father."

19At these words the Jews were again divided. 20Many of them said, "He is demon-possessed and raving mad. Why listen to him?"

21But others said, "These are not the sayings of a man possessed by a demon. Can a demon open the eyes of the blind?"

22Then came the Feast of Dedicationx at Jerusalem. It was winter, 23and Jesus was in the temple area walking in Solomon's Colonnade. 24The Jews gathered around him, saying, "How long will you keep us in suspense? If you are the Christ,y tell us plainly."

25Jesus answered, "I did tell you, but you do not believe. The miracles I do in

w9 Or kept safe   x22 That is, Hanukkah   y24 Or Messiah

my Father's name speak for me, [26]but you do not believe because you are not my sheep. [27]My sheep listen to my voice; I know them, and they follow me. [28]I give them eternal life, and they shall never perish; no one can snatch them out of my hand. [29]My Father, who has given them to me, is greater than all[z]; no one can snatch them out of my Father's hand. [30]I and the Father are one."

[31]Again the Jews picked up stones to stone him, [32]but Jesus said to them, "I have shown you many great miracles from the Father. For which of these do you stone me?"

[33]"We are not stoning you for any of these," replied the Jews, "but for blasphemy, because you, a mere man, claim to be God."

[34]Jesus answered them, "Is it not written in your Law, 'I have said you are gods'[a]? [35]If he called them 'gods,' to whom the word of God came—and the Scripture cannot be broken— [36]what about the one whom the Father set apart as his very own and sent into the world? Why then do you accuse me of blasphemy because I said, 'I am God's Son'? [37]Do not believe me unless I do what my Father does. [38]But if I do it, even though you do not believe me, believe the miracles, that you may know and understand that the Father is in me, and I in the Father." [39]Again they tried to seize him, but he escaped their grasp.

[40]Then Jesus went back across the Jordan to the place where John had been baptizing in the early days. Here he stayed [41]and many people came to him. They said, "Though John never performed a miraculous sign, all that John said about this man was true." [42]And in that place many believed in Jesus.

CHAPTER 11

Now a man named Lazarus was sick. He was from Bethany, the village of Mary and her sister Martha. [2]This Mary, whose brother Lazarus now lay sick, was the same one who poured perfume on the Lord and wiped his feet with her hair. [3]So the sisters sent word to Jesus, "Lord, the one you love is sick."

[4]When he heard this, Jesus said, "This sickness will not end in death. No, it is for God's glory so that God's Son may be glorified through it." [5]Jesus loved Martha and her sister and Lazarus. [6]Yet when he heard that Lazarus was sick, he stayed where he was two more days.

[7]Then he said to his disciples, "Let us go back to Judea."

[8]"But Rabbi," they said, "a short while ago the Jews tried to stone you, and yet you are going back there?"

[9]Jesus answered, "Are there not twelve hours of daylight? A man who walks by day will not stumble, for he sees by this world's light. [10]It is when he walks by night that he stumbles, for he has no light."

[11]After he had said this, he went on to tell them, "Our friend Lazarus has fallen asleep; but I am going there to wake him up."

[12]His disciples replied, "Lord, if he sleeps, he will get better." [13]Jesus had been speaking of his death, but his disciples thought he meant natural sleep.

[14]So then he told them plainly, "Lazarus is dead, [15]and for your sake I am glad I was not there, so that you may believe. But let us go to him."

[16]Then Thomas (called Didymus) said to the rest of the disciples, "Let us also go, that we may die with him."

[17]On his arrival, Jesus found that Lazarus had already been in the tomb for four days. [18]Bethany was less than two miles[b] from Jerusalem, [19]and many Jews had come to Martha and Mary to comfort them in the loss of their brother. [20]When Martha heard that Jesus was coming, she went out to meet him, but Mary stayed at home.

[21]"Lord," Martha said to Jesus, "if you had been here, my brother would not have died. [22]But I know that even now God will give you whatever you ask."

[23]Jesus said to her, "Your brother will rise again."

[24]Martha answered, "I know he will rise again in the resurrection at the last day."

[25]Jesus said to her, "I am the resurrection and the life. He who believes in me will live, even though he dies; [26]and whoever lives and believes in me will never die. Do you believe this?"

[27]"Yes, Lord," she told him, "I believe

---

[z]**29** Many early manuscripts *What my Father has given me is greater than all*   [a]**34** Psalm 82:6   [b]**18** Greek *fifteen stadia* (about 3 kilometers)

that you are the Christ,^{c} the Son of God, who was to come into the world."

²⁸And after she had said this, she went back and called her sister Mary aside. "The Teacher is here," she said, "and is asking for you." ²⁹When Mary heard this, she got up quickly and went to him. ³⁰Now Jesus had not yet entered the village, but was still at the place where Martha had met him. ³¹When the Jews who had been with Mary in the house, comforting her, noticed how quickly she got up and went out, they followed her, supposing she was going to the tomb to mourn there.

³²When Mary reached the place where Jesus was and saw him, she fell at his feet and said, "Lord, if you had been here, my brother would not have died."

³³When Jesus saw her weeping, and the Jews who had come along with her also weeping, he was deeply moved in spirit and troubled. ³⁴"Where have you laid him?" he asked.

"Come and see, Lord," they replied.

³⁵Jesus wept.

³⁶Then the Jews said, "See how he loved him!"

³⁷But some of them said, "Could not he who opened the eyes of the blind man have kept this man from dying?"

³⁸Jesus, once more deeply moved, came to the tomb. It was a cave with a stone laid across the entrance. ³⁹"Take away the stone," he said.

"But, Lord," said Martha, the sister of the dead man, "by this time there is a bad odor, for he has been there four days."

⁴⁰Then Jesus said, "Did I not tell you that if you believed, you would see the glory of God?"

⁴¹So they took away the stone. Then Jesus looked up and said, "Father, I thank you that you have heard me. ⁴²I knew that you always hear me, but I said this for the benefit of the people standing here, that they may believe that you sent me."

⁴³When he had said this, Jesus called in a loud voice, "Lazarus, come out!" ⁴⁴The dead man came out, his hands and feet wrapped with strips of linen, and a cloth around his face.

Jesus said to them, "Take off the grave clothes and let him go."

⁴⁵Therefore many of the Jews who had come to visit Mary, and had seen what Jesus did, put their faith in him. ⁴⁶But some of them went to the Pharisees and told them what Jesus had done. ⁴⁷Then the chief priests and the Pharisees called a meeting of the Sanhedrin.

"What are we accomplishing?" they asked. "Here is this man performing many miraculous signs. ⁴⁸If we let him go on like this, everyone will believe in him, and then the Romans will come and take away both our place^d and our nation."

⁴⁹Then one of them, named Caiaphas, who was high priest that year, spoke up, "You know nothing at all! ⁵⁰You do not realize that it is better for you that one man die for the people than that the whole nation perish."

⁵¹He did not say this on his own, but as high priest that year he prophesied that Jesus would die for the Jewish nation, ⁵²and not only for that nation but also for the scattered children of God, to bring them together and make them one. ⁵³So from that day on they plotted to take his life.

⁵⁴Therefore Jesus no longer moved about publicly among the Jews. Instead he withdrew to a region near the desert, to a village called Ephraim, where he stayed with his disciples.

⁵⁵When it was almost time for the Jewish Passover, many went up from the country to Jerusalem for their ceremonial cleansing before the Passover. ⁵⁶They kept looking for Jesus, and as they stood in the temple area they asked one another, "What do you think? Isn't he coming to the Feast at all?" ⁵⁷But the chief priests and Pharisees had given orders that if anyone found out where Jesus was, he should report it so that they might arrest him.

CHAPTER 12

Six days before the Passover, Jesus arrived at Bethany, where Lazarus lived, whom Jesus had raised from the dead. ²Here a dinner was given in Jesus' honor. Martha served, while Lazarus was among those reclining at the table with him. ³Then Mary took about a pint^e of pure nard, an expensive perfume; she poured it on Jesus' feet and wiped his feet with her

^{c}27 Or Messiah ^{d}48 Or temple ^{e}3 Greek a litra (probably about 0.5 liter)

hair. And the house was filled with the fragrance of the perfume.

⁴But one of his disciples, Judas Iscariot, who was later to betray him, objected, ⁵"Why wasn't this perfume sold and the money given to the poor? It was worth a year's wages.ᶠ" ⁶He did not say this because he cared about the poor but because he was a thief; as keeper of the money bag, he used to help himself to what was put into it.

⁷"Leave her alone," Jesus replied. "⌊It was intended⌋ that she should save this perfume for the day of my burial. ⁸You will always have the poor among you, but you will not always have me."

⁹Meanwhile a large crowd of Jews found out that Jesus was there and came, not only because of him but also to see Lazarus, whom he had raised from the dead. ¹⁰So the chief priests made plans to kill Lazarus as well, ¹¹for on account of him many of the Jews were going over to Jesus and putting their faith in him.

¹²The next day the great crowd that had come for the Feast heard that Jesus was on his way to Jerusalem. ¹³They took palm branches and went out to meet him, shouting,

"Hosanna!ᵍ"

"Blessed is he who comes in the name
        of the Lord!"ʰ

"Blessed is the King of Israel!"

¹⁴Jesus found a young donkey and sat upon it, as it is written,

¹⁵"Do not be afraid, O Daughter of Zion;
    see, your king is coming,
    seated on a donkey's colt."ⁱ

¹⁶At first his disciples did not understand all this. Only after Jesus was glorified did they realize that these things had been written about him and that they had done these things to him.

¹⁷Now the crowd that was with him when he called Lazarus from the tomb and raised him from the dead continued to spread the word. ¹⁸Many people, because they had heard that he had given this miraculous sign, went out to meet him. ¹⁹So the Pharisees said to one another, "See, this is getting us nowhere.

Look how the whole world has gone after him!"

²⁰Now there were some Greeks among those who went up to worship at the Feast. ²¹They came to Philip, who was from Bethsaida in Galilee, with a request. "Sir," they said, "we would like to see Jesus." ²²Philip went to tell Andrew; Andrew and Philip in turn told Jesus.

²³Jesus replied, "The hour has come for the Son of Man to be glorified. ²⁴I tell you the truth, unless a kernel of wheat falls to the ground and dies, it remains only a single seed. But if it dies, it produces many seeds. ²⁵The man who loves his life will lose it, while the man who hates his life in this world will keep it for eternal life. ²⁶Whoever serves me must follow me; and where I am, my servant also will be. My Father will honor the one who serves me.

²⁷"Now my heart is troubled, and what shall I say? 'Father, save me from this hour'? No, it was for this very reason I came to this hour. ²⁸Father, glorify your name!"

Then a voice came from heaven, "I have glorified it, and will glorify it again." ²⁹The crowd that was there and heard it said it had thundered; others said an angel had spoken to him.

³⁰Jesus said, "This voice was for your benefit, not mine. ³¹Now is the time for judgment on this world; now the prince of this world will be driven out. ³²But I, when I am lifted up from the earth, will draw all men to myself." ³³He said this to show the kind of death he was going to die.

³⁴The crowd spoke up, "We have heard from the Law that the Christʲ will remain forever, so how can you say, 'The Son of Man must be lifted up'? Who is this 'Son of Man'?"

³⁵Then Jesus told them, "You are going to have the light just a little while longer. Walk while you have the light, before darkness overtakes you. The man who walks in the dark does not know where he is going. ³⁶Put your trust in the light while you have it, so that you may become sons of light." When he had finished speaking, Jesus left and hid himself from them.

³⁷Even after Jesus had done all these

ᶠ5 Greek *three hundred denarii*   ᵍ13 A Hebrew expression meaning "Save!" which became an exclamation of praise
ʰ13 Psalm 118:25, 26   ⁱ15 Zech. 9:9   ʲ34 Or *Messiah*

miraculous signs in their presence, they still would not believe in him. [38]This was to fulfill the word of Isaiah the prophet:

"Lord, who has believed our message
    and to whom has the arm of the
        Lord been revealed?"[k]

[39]For this reason they could not believe, because, as Isaiah says elsewhere:

[40]"He has blinded their eyes
    and deadened their hearts,
so they can neither see with their eyes,
    nor understand with their hearts,
    nor turn—and I would heal them."[l]

[41]Isaiah said this because he saw Jesus' glory and spoke about him.

[42]Yet at the same time many even among the leaders believed in him. But because of the Pharisees they would not confess their faith for fear they would be put out of the synagogue; [43]for they loved praise from men more than praise from God.

[44]Then Jesus cried out, "When a man believes in me, he does not believe in me only, but in the one who sent me. [45]When he looks at me, he sees the one who sent me. [46]I have come into the world as a light, so that no one who believes in me should stay in darkness.

[47]"As for the person who hears my words but does not keep them, I do not judge him. For I did not come to judge the world, but to save it. [48]There is a judge for the one who rejects me and does not accept my words; that very word which I spoke will condemn him at the last day. [49]For I did not speak of my own accord, but the Father who sent me commanded me what to say and how to say it. [50]I know that his command leads to eternal life. So whatever I say is just what the Father has told me to say."

k[38] Isaiah 53:1   l[40] Isaiah 6:10

OCTOBER 30 ☐ DAY 304
JOHN 13–17
Ministry to the Disciples by God's Son

 OVERVIEW Today's section, traditionally called the Upper Room Discourse, actually takes place partly in an upper room (John 13–14) and partly in an unspecified location (John 15–17; see 14:31). These verses constitute Jesus' final instructions to his disciples before his death. In them you will read of the importance of a servant's heart, the necessity of Christ's return to heaven and the provision of the Holy Spirit in Christ's absence. There are many spiritual insights yet to be grasped by the disciples—a realization that drives Christ to his knees as he prays for his followers both present and future.

Chapter 13	Chapters 14–15	Chapter 16	Chapter 17
	Instructions to the Disciples Regarding		Intercession for the Disciples
Foot Washing	Fruit Bearing	Future Events	
	Talking to the Disciples		Talking to God

 YOUR DAILY WALK Reflect upon this thought-provoking statement by Robert Murray McCheyne: "If I could hear Christ praying for me in the next room, I would not fear a million enemies. Yet distance makes no difference. He is praying for me."

In John 17, Jesus Christ prayed fervently and specifically for his disciples—those he would leave behind to continue the work in his absence. And that means he was praying for you. Read the chapter that way, inserting your name in the appropriate places beginning with verse 6: I have revealed you to _____ whom you gave me out of the world. _____ was yours; you gave _____ to me. . . . I pray for _____. I am not praying for the world, but for _____ whom you have given me, for _____ is yours. . . . I will remain in the world no longer, but _____ is still in the world. . . . My prayer is not that you take _____ out of the world but that you protect _____ from the evil one.

INSIGHT Mission Accomplished . . . Cross Yet to Come
In his prayer to God the Father, Jesus reported, "I have brought you glory on earth by completing the work you gave me to do" (17:4). Though Jesus' death was still a day away, victory was certain as the Savior bathed each step to the cross in prayer. You can face today with confidence, too!

CHAPTER 13

It was just before the Passover Feast. Jesus knew that the time had come for him to leave this world and go to the Father. Having loved his own who were in the world, he now showed them the full extent of his love.[m]

[2]The evening meal was being served, and the devil had already prompted Judas Iscariot, son of Simon, to betray Jesus. [3]Jesus knew that the Father had put all things under his power, and that he had come from God and was returning to God; [4]so he got up from the meal, took off his outer clothing, and wrapped a towel around his waist. [5]After that, he poured water into a basin and began to wash his disciples' feet, drying them with the towel that was wrapped around him.

[6]He came to Simon Peter, who said to him, "Lord, are you going to wash my feet?"

[7]Jesus replied, "You do not realize now what I am doing, but later you will understand."

[8]"No," said Peter, "you shall never wash my feet."

Jesus answered, "Unless I wash you, you have no part with me."

[9]"Then, Lord," Simon Peter replied, "not just my feet but my hands and my head as well!"

[10]Jesus answered, "A person who has had a bath needs only to wash his feet; his whole body is clean. And you are clean, though not every one of you." [11]For he knew who was going to betray him, and that was why he said not every one was clean.

[12]When he had finished washing their feet, he put on his clothes and returned to his place. "Do you understand what I have done for you?" he asked them. [13]"You call me 'Teacher' and 'Lord,' and rightly so, for that is what I am. [14]Now that I, your Lord and Teacher, have washed your feet, you also should wash one another's feet. [15]I have set you an example that you should do as I have done for you. [16]I tell you the truth, no servant is greater than his master, nor is a messenger greater than the one who sent him. [17]Now that you know these things, you will be blessed if you do them.

[18]"I am not referring to all of you; I know those I have chosen. But this is to fulfill the scripture: 'He who shares my bread has lifted up his heel against me.'[n]

[19]"I am telling you now before it happens, so that when it does happen you will believe that I am He. [20]I tell you the truth, whoever accepts anyone I send accepts me; and whoever accepts me accepts the one who sent me."

[21]After he had said this, Jesus was troubled in spirit and testified, "I tell you the truth, one of you is going to betray me."

[22]His disciples stared at one another, at a loss to know which of them he meant. [23]One of them, the disciple whom Jesus loved, was reclining next to him. [24]Simon Peter motioned to this disciple and said, "Ask him which one he means."

[25]Leaning back against Jesus, he asked him, "Lord, who is it?"

[26]Jesus answered, "It is the one to whom I will give this piece of bread when I have dipped it in the dish." Then, dipping the piece of bread, he gave it to Judas Iscariot, son of Simon. [27]As soon as Judas took the bread, Satan entered into him.

"What you are about to do, do quickly,"

[m]1 Or *he loved them to the last*   [n]18 Psalm 41:9

Jesus told him, 28but no one at the meal understood why Jesus said this to him. 29Since Judas had charge of the money, some thought Jesus was telling him to buy what was needed for the Feast, or to give something to the poor. 30As soon as Judas had taken the bread, he went out. And it was night.

31When he was gone, Jesus said, "Now is the Son of Man glorified and God is glorified in him. 32If God is glorified in him,*o* God will glorify the Son in himself, and will glorify him at once.

33"My children, I will be with you only a little longer. You will look for me, and just as I told the Jews, so I tell you now: Where I am going, you cannot come.

34"A new command I give you: Love one another. As I have loved you, so you must love one another. 35By this all men will know that you are my disciples, if you love one another."

36Simon Peter asked him, "Lord, where are you going?"

Jesus replied, "Where I am going, you cannot follow now, but you will follow later."

37Peter asked, "Lord, why can't I follow you now? I will lay down my life for you."

38Then Jesus answered, "Will you really lay down your life for me? I tell you the truth, before the rooster crows, you will disown me three times!

CHAPTER 14

"Do not let your hearts be troubled. Trust in God*p*; trust also in me. 2In my Father's house are many rooms; if it were not so, I would have told you. I am going there to prepare a place for you. 3And if I go and prepare a place for you, I will come back and take you to be with me that you also may be where I am. 4You know the way to the place where I am going."

5Thomas said to him, "Lord, we don't know where you are going, so how can we know the way?"

6Jesus answered, "I am the way and the truth and the life. No one comes to the Father except through me. 7If you really knew me, you would know*q* my Father as well. From now on, you do know him and have seen him."

8Philip said, "Lord, show us the Father and that will be enough for us."

9Jesus answered: "Don't you know me, Philip, even after I have been among you such a long time? Anyone who has seen me has seen the Father. How can you say, 'Show us the Father'? 10Don't you believe that I am in the Father, and that the Father is in me? The words I say to you are not just my own. Rather, it is the Father, living in me, who is doing his work. 11Believe me when I say that I am in the Father and the Father is in me; or at least believe on the evidence of the miracles themselves. 12I tell you the truth, anyone who has faith in me will do what I have been doing. He will do even greater things than these, because I am going to the Father. 13And I will do whatever you ask in my name, so that the Son may bring glory to the Father. 14You may ask me for anything in my name, and I will do it.

15"If you love me, you will obey what I command. 16And I will ask the Father, and he will give you another Counselor to be with you forever— 17the Spirit of truth. The world cannot accept him, because it neither sees him nor knows him. But you know him, for he lives with you and will be*r* in you. 18I will not leave you as orphans; I will come to you. 19Before long, the world will not see me anymore, but you will see me. Because I live, you also will live. 20On that day you will realize that I am in my Father, and you are in me, and I am in you. 21Whoever has my commands and obeys them, he is the one who loves me. He who loves me will be loved by my Father, and I too will love him and show myself to him."

22Then Judas (not Judas Iscariot) said, "But, Lord, why do you intend to show yourself to us and not to the world?"

23Jesus replied, "If anyone loves me, he will obey my teaching. My Father will love him, and we will come to him and make our home with him. 24He who does not love me will not obey my teaching. These words you hear are not my own; they belong to the Father who sent me.

25"All this I have spoken while still with you. 26But the Counselor, the Holy Spirit, whom the Father will send in my name, will teach you all things and will remind you of everything I have said to you. 27Peace I leave with you; my peace I give you. I do not give to you as the world gives. Do not let your hearts be troubled and do not be afraid.

[28]"You heard me say, 'I am going away and I am coming back to you.' If you loved me, you would be glad that I am going to the Father, for the Father is greater than I. [29]I have told you now before it happens, so that when it does happen you will believe. [30]I will not speak with you much longer, for the prince of this world is coming. He has no hold on me, [31]but the world must learn that I love the Father and that I do exactly what my Father has commanded me.

"Come now; let us leave.

CHAPTER 15

"I am the true vine, and my Father is the gardener. [2]He cuts off every branch in me that bears no fruit, while every branch that does bear fruit he prunes[s] so that it will be even more fruitful. [3]You are already clean because of the word I have spoken to you. [4]Remain in me, and I will remain in you. No branch can bear fruit by itself; it must remain in the vine. Neither can you bear fruit unless you remain in me.

[5]"I am the vine; you are the branches. If a man remains in me and I in him, he will bear much fruit; apart from me you can do nothing. [6]If anyone does not remain in me, he is like a branch that is thrown away and withers; such branches are picked up, thrown into the fire and burned. [7]If you remain in me and my words remain in you, ask whatever you wish, and it will be given you. [8]This is to my Father's glory, that you bear much fruit, showing yourselves to be my disciples.

[9]"As the Father has loved me, so have I loved you. Now remain in my love. [10]If you obey my commands, you will remain in my love, just as I have obeyed my Father's commands and remain in his love. [11]I have told you this so that my joy may be in you and that your joy may be complete. [12]My command is this: Love each other as I have loved you. [13]Greater love has no one than this, that he lay down his life for his friends. [14]You are my friends if you do what I command. [15]I no longer call you servants, because a servant does not

know his master's business. Instead, I have called you friends, for everything that I learned from my Father I have made known to you. [16]You did not choose me, but I chose you and appointed you to go and bear fruit—fruit that will last. Then the Father will give you whatever you ask in my name. [17]This is my command: Love each other.

[18]"If the world hates you, keep in mind that it hated me first. [19]If you belonged to the world, it would love you as its own. As it is, you do not belong to the world, but I have chosen you out of the world. That is why the world hates you. [20]Remember the words I spoke to you: 'No servant is greater than his master.'[t] If they persecuted me, they will persecute you also. If they obeyed my teaching, they will obey yours also. [21]They will treat you this way because of my name, for they do not know the One who sent me. [22]If I had not come and spoken to them, they would not be guilty of sin. Now, however, they have no excuse for their sin. [23]He who hates me hates my Father as well. [24]If I had not done among them what no one else did, they would not be guilty of sin. But now they have seen these miracles, and yet they have hated both me and my Father. [25]But this is to fulfill what is written in their Law: 'They hated me without reason.'[u]

[26]"When the Counselor comes, whom I will send to you from the Father, the Spirit of truth who goes out from the Father, he will testify about me. [27]And you also must testify, for you have been with me from the beginning.

CHAPTER 16

"All this I have told you so that you will not go astray. [2]They will put you out of the synagogue; in fact, a time is coming when anyone who kills you will think he is offering a service to God. [3]They will do such things because they have not known the Father or me. [4]I have told you this, so that when the time comes you will remember that I warned you. I did not tell you this at first because I was with you.

[5]"Now I am going to him who sent me, yet none of you asks me, 'Where are you going?' [6]Because I have said these things, you are filled with grief. [7]But I tell you the

[s]2 The Greek for *prunes* also means *cleans*.   [t]20 John 13:16   [u]25 Psalms 35:19; 69:4

truth: It is for your good that I am going away. Unless I go away, the Counselor will not come to you; but if I go, I will send him to you. [8]When he comes, he will convict the world of guilt[v] in regard to sin and righteousness and judgment: [9]in regard to sin, because men do not believe in me; [10]in regard to righteousness, because I am going to the Father, where you can see me no longer; [11]and in regard to judgment, because the prince of this world now stands condemned.

[12]"I have much more to say to you, more than you can now bear. [13]But when he, the Spirit of truth, comes, he will guide you into all truth. He will not speak on his own; he will speak only what he hears, and he will tell you what is yet to come. [14]He will bring glory to me by taking from what is mine and making it known to you. [15]All that belongs to the Father is mine. That is why I said the Spirit will take from what is mine and make it known to you.

[16]"In a little while you will see me no more, and then after a little while you will see me."

[17]Some of his disciples said to one another, "What does he mean by saying, 'In a little while you will see me no more, and then after a little while you will see me,' and 'Because I am going to the Father'?" [18]They kept asking, "What does he mean by 'a little while'? We don't understand what he is saying."

[19]Jesus saw that they wanted to ask him about this, so he said to them, "Are you asking one another what I meant when I said, 'In a little while you will see me no more, and then after a little while you will see me'? [20]I tell you the truth, you will weep and mourn while the world rejoices. You will grieve, but your grief will turn to joy. [21]A woman giving birth to a child has pain because her time has come; but when her baby is born she forgets the anguish because of her joy that a child is born into the world. [22]So with you: Now is your time of grief, but I will see you again and you will rejoice, and no one will take away your joy. [23]In that day you will no longer ask me anything. I tell you the truth, my Father will give you whatever you ask in my name. [24]Until now you have not asked for anything in my name.

Ask and you will receive, and your joy will be complete.

[25]"Though I have been speaking figuratively, a time is coming when I will no longer use this kind of language but will tell you plainly about my Father. [26]In that day you will ask in my name. I am not saying that I will ask the Father on your behalf. [27]No, the Father himself loves you because you have loved me and have believed that I came from God. [28]I came from the Father and entered the world; now I am leaving the world and going back to the Father."

[29]Then Jesus' disciples said, "Now you are speaking clearly and without figures of speech. [30]Now we can see that you know all things and that you do not even need to have anyone ask you questions. This makes us believe that you came from God."

[31]"You believe at last!"[w] Jesus answered. [32]"But a time is coming, and has come, when you will be scattered, each to his own home. You will leave me all alone. Yet I am not alone, for my Father is with me.

[33]"I have told you these things, so that in me you may have peace. In this world you will have trouble. But take heart! I have overcome the world."

CHAPTER 17

After Jesus said this, he looked toward heaven and prayed:

"Father, the time has come. Glorify your Son, that your Son may glorify you. [2]For you granted him authority over all people that he might give eternal life to all those you have given him. [3]Now this is eternal life: that they may know you, the only true God, and Jesus Christ, whom you have sent. [4]I have brought you glory on earth by completing the work you gave me to do. [5]And now, Father, glorify me in your presence with the glory I had with you before the world began.

[6]"I have revealed you[x] to those whom you gave me out of the world. They were yours; you gave them to me and they have obeyed your word. [7]Now they know that everything you have given me comes from you. [8]For

---

[v]8 Or *will expose the guilt of the world*   [w]31 Or *"Do you now believe?"*   [x]6 Greek *your name*; also in verse 26

I gave them the words you gave me and they accepted them. They knew with certainty that I came from you, and they believed that you sent me. [9]I pray for them. I am not praying for the world, but for those you have given me, for they are yours. [10]All I have is yours, and all you have is mine. And glory has come to me through them. [11]I will remain in the world no longer, but they are still in the world, and I am coming to you. Holy Father, protect them by the power of your name—the name you gave me—so that they may be one as we are one. [12]While I was with them, I protected them and kept them safe by that name you gave me. None has been lost except the one doomed to destruction so that Scripture would be fulfilled.

[13]"I am coming to you now, but I say these things while I am still in the world, so that they may have the full measure of my joy within them. [14]I have given them your word and the world has hated them, for they are not of the world any more than I am of the world. [15]My prayer is not that you take them out of the world but that you protect them from the evil one. [16]They are not of the world, even as I am not of it. [17]Sanctify[y] them by the truth; your word is truth. [18]As you sent me into the world, I have sent them into the world. [19]For them I sanctify myself, that they too may be truly sanctified.

[20]"My prayer is not for them alone. I pray also for those who will believe in me through their message, [21]that all of them may be one, Father, just as you are in me and I am in you. May they also be in us so that the world may believe that you have sent me. [22]I have given them the glory that you gave me, that they may be one as we are one: [23]I in them and you in me. May they be brought to complete unity to let the world know that you sent me and have loved them even as you have loved me.

[24]"Father, I want those you have given me to be with me where I am, and to see my glory, the glory you have given me because you loved me before the creation of the world.

[25]"Righteous Father, though the world does not know you, I know you, and they know that you have sent me. [26]I have made you known to them, and will continue to make you known in order that the love you have for me may be in them and that I myself may be in them."

[y]17 Greek *hagiazo* (set apart for sacred use or make holy); also in verse 19

OCTOBER 31 ☐ DAY 305
JOHN 18–21
The Resurrected Son of God

 OVERVIEW After reading the closing events of Christ's life in each of the other three Gospels, you may be tempted to skim John's account. But don't! Put yourself in the sandals of the key individuals in the narrative, and feel the emotions as the crucifixion unfolds: Judas's disillusionment . . . Peter's denial . . . Pilate's concession . . . the crowd's frenzied screams . . . the rugged cross . . . the nail-pierced hands . . . the bleeding side . . . the hurried burial. Experience with the women the shock of finding the tomb empty. Follow Thomas's transformation from a doubting disciple to a devoted believer. Listen as Peter receives his marching orders—to feed God's flock until the Shepherd returns.

Chapter 18	Chapter 19	Chapters 20–21	
Arrest and Trials	Crucifixion and Burial	Disappearance of the Corpse 20:1 20:10	Appearance of the Christ 20:11 21:25
The Crucified King		The Risen Savior	

YOUR DAILY WALK Read John 20:30–31 carefully to refresh your memory regarding John's purpose in writing. He is not merely trying to satisfy your curiosity about the historical person of Christ or fill your head with little-known facts about him or teach you all the events *If ever a man* from Bethlehem to Calvary in chronological order. Rather, John is *was God, or* seeking to move you to a point of commitment. Unless Jesus Christ *God man, Jesus* has invaded your life, you are lost in your sins: without God, without *was both.* life, without hope of heaven.

Becoming a Christian is not simply joining a church, signing a card or walking an aisle—though these can certainly be valid expressions of your desire to become a Christian. But true faith comes as the result of believing on Jesus Christ, God's Son, to solve your sin problem. It is trusting him to do something for you that you cannot do yourself. Have you done that? If not, what better way to close your reading of the Gospels than by opening your heart to the Savior of whom those Gospels speak: Jesus Christ.

INSIGHT Evidence Enough for John

John records that he saw the graveclothes and head cloth lying undisturbed in Jesus' tomb with a space between them. For him this was clear and convincing evidence that Jesus' body had passed through them and that Jesus was alive. John saw and believed!

CHAPTER 18

When he had finished praying, Jesus left with his disciples and crossed the Kidron Valley. On the other side there was an olive grove, and he and his disciples went into it.

²Now Judas, who betrayed him, knew the place, because Jesus had often met there with his disciples. ³So Judas came to the grove, guiding a detachment of soldiers and some officials from the chief priests and Pharisees. They were carrying torches, lanterns and weapons.

⁴Jesus, knowing all that was going to happen to him, went out and asked them, "Who is it you want?"

⁵"Jesus of Nazareth," they replied.

"I am he," Jesus said. (And Judas the traitor was standing there with them.) ⁶When Jesus said, "I am he," they drew back and fell to the ground.

⁷Again he asked them, "Who is it you want?"

And they said, "Jesus of Nazareth."

⁸"I told you that I am he," Jesus answered. "If you are looking for me, then

let these men go." ⁹This happened so that the words he had spoken would be fulfilled: "I have not lost one of those you gave me."ᶻ

¹⁰Then Simon Peter, who had a sword, drew it and struck the high priest's servant, cutting off his right ear. (The servant's name was Malchus.)

¹¹Jesus commanded Peter, "Put your sword away! Shall I not drink the cup the Father has given me?"

¹²Then the detachment of soldiers with its commander and the Jewish officials arrested Jesus. They bound him ¹³and brought him first to Annas, who was the father-in-law of Caiaphas, the high priest that year. ¹⁴Caiaphas was the one who had advised the Jews that it would be good if one man died for the people.

¹⁵Simon Peter and another disciple were following Jesus. Because this disciple was known to the high priest, he went with Jesus into the high priest's courtyard, ¹⁶but Peter had to wait outside at the door. The other disciple, who was known to the high priest, came back,

ᶻ**9** John 6:39

spoke to the girl on duty there and brought Peter in.

[17]"You are not one of his disciples, are you?" the girl at the door asked Peter.

He replied, "I am not."

[18]It was cold, and the servants and officials stood around a fire they had made to keep warm. Peter also was standing with them, warming himself.

[19]Meanwhile, the high priest questioned Jesus about his disciples and his teaching.

[20]"I have spoken openly to the world," Jesus replied. "I always taught in synagogues or at the temple, where all the Jews come together. I said nothing in secret. [21]Why question me? Ask those who heard me. Surely they know what I said."

[22]When Jesus said this, one of the officials nearby struck him in the face. "Is this the way you answer the high priest?" he demanded.

[23]"If I said something wrong," Jesus replied, "testify as to what is wrong. But if I spoke the truth, why did you strike me?" [24]Then Annas sent him, still bound, to Caiaphas the high priest.[a]

[25]As Simon Peter stood warming himself, he was asked, "You are not one of his disciples, are you?"

He denied it, saying, "I am not."

[26]One of the high priest's servants, a relative of the man whose ear Peter had cut off, challenged him, "Didn't I see you with him in the olive grove?" [27]Again Peter denied it, and at that moment a rooster began to crow.

[28]Then the Jews led Jesus from Caiaphas to the palace of the Roman governor. By now it was early morning, and to avoid ceremonial uncleanness the Jews did not enter the palace; they wanted to be able to eat the Passover. [29]So Pilate came out to them and asked, "What charges are you bringing against this man?"

[30]"If he were not a criminal," they replied, "we would not have handed him over to you."

[31]Pilate said, "Take him yourselves and judge him by your own law."

"But we have no right to execute anyone," the Jews objected. [32]This happened so that the words Jesus had spoken indi-

cating the kind of death he was going to die would be fulfilled.

[33]Pilate then went back inside the palace, summoned Jesus and asked him, "Are you the king of the Jews?"

[34]"Is that your own idea," Jesus asked, "or did others talk to you about me?"

[35]"Am I a Jew?" Pilate replied. "It was your people and your chief priests who handed you over to me. What is it you have done?"

[36]Jesus said, "My kingdom is not of this world. If it were, my servants would fight to prevent my arrest by the Jews. But now my kingdom is from another place."

[37]"You are a king, then!" said Pilate.

Jesus answered, "You are right in saying I am a king. In fact, for this reason I was born, and for this I came into the world, to testify to the truth. Everyone on the side of truth listens to me."

[38]"What is truth?" Pilate asked. With this he went out again to the Jews and said, "I find no basis for a charge against him. [39]But it is your custom for me to release to you one prisoner at the time of the Passover. Do you want me to release 'the king of the Jews'?"

[40]They shouted back, "No, not him! Give us Barabbas!" Now Barabbas had taken part in a rebellion.

CHAPTER 19

Then Pilate took Jesus and had him flogged. [2]The soldiers twisted together a crown of thorns and put it on his head. They clothed him in a purple robe [3]and went up to him again and again, saying, "Hail, king of the Jews!" And they struck him in the face.

[4]Once more Pilate came out and said to the Jews, "Look, I am bringing him out to you to let you know that I find no basis for a charge against him." [5]When Jesus came out wearing the crown of thorns and the purple robe, Pilate said to them, "Here is the man!"

[6]As soon as the chief priests and their officials saw him, they shouted, "Crucify! Crucify!"

But Pilate answered, "You take him and crucify him. As for me, I find no basis for a charge against him."

[7]The Jews insisted, "We have a law, and

[a] 24 Or (Now Annas had sent him, still bound, to Caiaphas the high priest.)

according to that law he must die, because he claimed to be the Son of God."

[8]When Pilate heard this, he was even more afraid, [9]and he went back inside the palace. "Where do you come from?" he asked Jesus, but Jesus gave him no answer. [10]"Do you refuse to speak to me?" Pilate said. "Don't you realize I have power either to free you or to crucify you?"

[11]Jesus answered, "You would have no power over me if it were not given to you from above. Therefore the one who handed me over to you is guilty of a greater sin."

[12]From then on, Pilate tried to set Jesus free, but the Jews kept shouting, "If you let this man go, you are no friend of Caesar. Anyone who claims to be a king opposes Caesar."

[13]When Pilate heard this, he brought Jesus out and sat down on the judge's seat at a place known as the Stone Pavement (which in Aramaic is Gabbatha). [14]It was the day of Preparation of Passover Week, about the sixth hour.

"Here is your king," Pilate said to the Jews.

[15]But they shouted, "Take him away! Take him away! Crucify him!"

"Shall I crucify your king?" Pilate asked.

"We have no king but Caesar," the chief priests answered.

[16]Finally Pilate handed him over to them to be crucified.

So the soldiers took charge of Jesus. [17]Carrying his own cross, he went out to the place of the Skull (which in Aramaic is called Golgotha). [18]Here they crucified him, and with him two others—one on each side and Jesus in the middle.

[19]Pilate had a notice prepared and fastened to the cross. It read: JESUS OF NAZARETH, THE KING OF THE JEWS. [20]Many of the Jews read this sign, for the place where Jesus was crucified was near the city, and the sign was written in Aramaic, Latin and Greek. [21]The chief priests of the Jews protested to Pilate, "Do not write 'The King of the Jews,' but that this man claimed to be king of the Jews."

[22]Pilate answered, "What I have written, I have written."

[23]When the soldiers crucified Jesus, they took his clothes, dividing them into four shares, one for each of them, with the undergarment remaining. This garment was seamless, woven in one piece from top to bottom.

[24]"Let's not tear it," they said to one another. "Let's decide by lot who will get it."

This happened that the scripture might be fulfilled which said,

"They divided my garments among
　　them
　　and cast lots for my clothing."[b]

So this is what the soldiers did.

[25]Near the cross of Jesus stood his mother, his mother's sister, Mary the wife of Clopas, and Mary Magdalene. [26]When Jesus saw his mother there, and the disciple whom he loved standing nearby, he said to his mother, "Dear woman, here is your son," [27]and to the disciple, "Here is your mother." From that time on, this disciple took her into his home.

[28]Later, knowing that all was now completed, and so that the Scripture would be fulfilled, Jesus said, "I am thirsty." [29]A jar of wine vinegar was there, so they soaked a sponge in it, put the sponge on a stalk of the hyssop plant, and lifted it to Jesus' lips. [30]When he had received the drink, Jesus said, "It is finished." With that, he bowed his head and gave up his spirit.

[31]Now it was the day of Preparation, and the next day was to be a special Sabbath. Because the Jews did not want the bodies left on the crosses during the Sabbath, they asked Pilate to have the legs broken and the bodies taken down. [32]The soldiers therefore came and broke the legs of the first man who had been crucified with Jesus, and then those of the other. [33]But when they came to Jesus and found that he was already dead, they did not break his legs. [34]Instead, one of the soldiers pierced Jesus' side with a spear, bringing a sudden flow of blood and water. [35]The man who saw it has given testimony, and his testimony is true. He knows that he tells the truth, and he testifies so that you also may believe. [36]These things happened so that the scripture would be fulfilled: "Not one of his bones will be broken,"[c] [37]and, as another scripture says, "They will look on the one they have pierced."[d]

[38]Later, Joseph of Arimathea asked

[b]24 Psalm 22:18　　[c]36 Exodus 12:46; Num. 9:12; Psalm 34:20　　[d]37 Zech. 12:10

Pilate for the body of Jesus. Now Joseph was a disciple of Jesus, but secretly because he feared the Jews. With Pilate's permission, he came and took the body away. [39]He was accompanied by Nicodemus, the man who earlier had visited Jesus at night. Nicodemus brought a mixture of myrrh and aloes, about seventy-five pounds.[e] [40]Taking Jesus' body, the two of them wrapped it, with the spices, in strips of linen. This was in accordance with Jewish burial customs. [41]At the place where Jesus was crucified, there was a garden, and in the garden a new tomb, in which no one had ever been laid. [42]Because it was the Jewish day of Preparation and since the tomb was nearby, they laid Jesus there.

CHAPTER 20

Early on the first day of the week, while it was still dark, Mary Magdalene went to the tomb and saw that the stone had been removed from the entrance. [2]So she came running to Simon Peter and the other disciple, the one Jesus loved, and said, "They have taken the Lord out of the tomb, and we don't know where they have put him!"

[3]So Peter and the other disciple started for the tomb. [4]Both were running, but the other disciple outran Peter and reached the tomb first. [5]He bent over and looked in at the strips of linen lying there but did not go in. [6]Then Simon Peter, who was behind him, arrived and went into the tomb. He saw the strips of linen lying there, [7]as well as the burial cloth that had been around Jesus' head. The cloth was folded up by itself, separate from the linen. [8]Finally the other disciple, who had reached the tomb first, also went inside. He saw and believed. [9](They still did not understand from Scripture that Jesus had to rise from the dead.)

[10]Then the disciples went back to their homes, [11]but Mary stood outside the tomb crying. As she wept, she bent over to look into the tomb [12]and saw two angels in white, seated where Jesus' body had been, one at the head and the other at the foot.

[13]They asked her, "Woman, why are you crying?"

"They have taken my Lord away," she said, "and I don't know where they have put him." [14]At this, she turned around and saw Jesus standing there, but she did not realize that it was Jesus.

[15]"Woman," he said, "why are you crying? Who is it you are looking for?"

Thinking he was the gardener, she said, "Sir, if you have carried him away, tell me where you have put him, and I will get him."

[16]Jesus said to her, "Mary."

She turned toward him and cried out in Aramaic, "Rabboni!" (which means Teacher).

[17]Jesus said, "Do not hold on to me, for I have not yet returned to the Father. Go instead to my brothers and tell them, 'I am returning to my Father and your Father, to my God and your God.' "

[18]Mary Magdalene went to the disciples with the news: "I have seen the Lord!" And she told them that he had said these things to her.

[19]On the evening of that first day of the week, when the disciples were together, with the doors locked for fear of the Jews, Jesus came and stood among them and said, "Peace be with you!" [20]After he said this, he showed them his hands and side. The disciples were overjoyed when they saw the Lord.

[21]Again Jesus said, "Peace be with you! As the Father has sent me, I am sending you." [22]And with that he breathed on them and said, "Receive the Holy Spirit. [23]If you forgive anyone his sins, they are forgiven; if you do not forgive them, they are not forgiven."

[24]Now Thomas (called Didymus), one of the Twelve, was not with the disciples when Jesus came. [25]So the other disciples told him, "We have seen the Lord!"

But he said to them, "Unless I see the nail marks in his hands and put my finger where the nails were, and put my hand into his side, I will not believe it."

[26]A week later his disciples were in the house again, and Thomas was with them. Though the doors were locked, Jesus came and stood among them and said, "Peace be with you!" [27]Then he said to Thomas, "Put your finger here; see my hands. Reach out your hand and put it into my side. Stop doubting and believe."

[28]Thomas said to him, "My Lord and my God!"

[29]Then Jesus told him, "Because you

[e]39 Greek *a hundred litrai* (about 34 kilograms)

have seen me, you have believed; blessed are those who have not seen and yet have believed."

³⁰Jesus did many other miraculous signs in the presence of his disciples, which are not recorded in this book. ³¹But these are written that you may*f* believe that Jesus is the Christ, the Son of God, and that by believing you may have life in his name.

CHAPTER 21

Afterward Jesus appeared again to his disciples, by the Sea of Tiberias.*g* It happened this way: ²Simon Peter, Thomas (called Didymus), Nathanael from Cana in Galilee, the sons of Zebedee, and two other disciples were together. ³"I'm going out to fish," Simon Peter told them, and they said, "We'll go with you." So they went out and got into the boat, but that night they caught nothing.

⁴Early in the morning, Jesus stood on the shore, but the disciples did not realize that it was Jesus.

⁵He called out to them, "Friends, haven't you any fish?"

"No," they answered.

⁶He said, "Throw your net on the right side of the boat and you will find some." When they did, they were unable to haul the net in because of the large number of fish.

⁷Then the disciple whom Jesus loved said to Peter, "It is the Lord!" As soon as Simon Peter heard him say, "It is the Lord," he wrapped his outer garment around him (for he had taken it off) and jumped into the water. ⁸The other disciples followed in the boat, towing the net full of fish, for they were not far from shore, about a hundred yards.*h* ⁹When they landed, they saw a fire of burning coals there with fish on it, and some bread.

¹⁰Jesus said to them, "Bring some of the fish you have just caught."

¹¹Simon Peter climbed aboard and dragged the net ashore. It was full of large fish, 153, but even with so many the net was not torn. ¹²Jesus said to them, "Come and have breakfast." None of the disciples dared ask him, "Who are you?" They knew it was the Lord. ¹³Jesus came, took the bread and gave it to them, and did the same with the fish. ¹⁴This was now the third time Jesus appeared to his disciples after he was raised from the dead.

¹⁵When they had finished eating, Jesus said to Simon Peter, "Simon son of John, do you truly love me more than these?"

"Yes, Lord," he said, "you know that I love you."

Jesus said, "Feed my lambs."

¹⁶Again Jesus said, "Simon son of John, do you truly love me?"

He answered, "Yes, Lord, you know that I love you."

Jesus said, "Take care of my sheep."

¹⁷The third time he said to him, "Simon son of John, do you love me?"

Peter was hurt because Jesus asked him the third time, "Do you love me?" He said, "Lord, you know all things; you know that I love you."

Jesus said, "Feed my sheep. ¹⁸I tell you the truth, when you were younger you dressed yourself and went where you wanted; but when you are old you will stretch out your hands, and someone else will dress you and lead you where you do not want to go." ¹⁹Jesus said this to indicate the kind of death by which Peter would glorify God. Then he said to him, "Follow me!"

²⁰Peter turned and saw that the disciple whom Jesus loved was following them. (This was the one who had leaned back against Jesus at the supper and had said, "Lord, who is going to betray you?") ²¹When Peter saw him, he asked, "Lord, what about him?"

²²Jesus answered, "If I want him to remain alive until I return, what is that to you? You must follow me." ²³Because of this, the rumor spread among the brothers that this disciple would not die. But Jesus did not say that he would not die; he only said, "If I want him to remain alive until I return, what is that to you?"

²⁴This is the disciple who testifies to these things and who wrote them down. We know that his testimony is true.

²⁵Jesus did many other things as well. If every one of them were written down, I suppose that even the whole world would not have room for the books that would be written.

f31 Some manuscripts *may continue to*   *g1* That is, Sea of Galilee   *h8* Greek *about two hundred cubits* (about 90 meters)

Acts

WITH the coming of the Holy Spirit at Pentecost, Jesus' small band of disciples is empowered and emboldened to take the Good News of the risen Savior to Jerusalem, Judea, Samaria and "to the ends of the earth" (1:8). Paul, apostle to the Gentiles, spearheads the gospel advance on three far-reaching missionary journeys. The book of Acts ends in Rome with Paul's imprisonment. Paul's ministry is drawing to a close, but an unstoppable message is just beginning.

Focus	Peter		Philip		Paul					
Divisions	Power of the Church	Progress of the Church	Persecution of the Church	Propagation of the Church	Paul's First Journey	Paul's Second Journey	Paul's Third Journey	Paul's Arrest	Paul's Three Trials	Paul's Trip to Rome
	1 4	5 7	8 9	10 12	13 15	16 18	19 20	21 23	24 26	27 28
Topics	History of the Church				History of a Church Planter					
	Establish-ment		Extension		Expansion		Explanation			
Place	Jerusalem		Judea and Samaria		Ends of the Earth					
Time	2 Years (A.D. 33–35)		13 Years (A.D. 35–48)		14 Years (A.D. 48–62)					

NOVEMBER 1 □ DAY 306
ACTS 1–4
Power of the Church

OVERVIEW Luke's two books, the Gospel of Luke and the book of Acts, might well be called a two-volume "History of the New Testament Church"—Volume 1: *The History of the Founder of the Church;* Volume 2: *The History of the Followers of the Church.* With the ascension of Jesus Christ into heaven, the disciples are left in Jerusalem with good news to share and a command to obey: "Wait for the gift my Father promised" (1:4). True to Christ's word, on the day of Pentecost the Holy Spirit arrives, accompanied by dramatic signs. With the Spirit's empowerment, the disciples move out to proclaim the glad tidings.

Chapter 1	Chapter 2	Chapter 3	Chapter 4
Waiting for Power	Witnessing Power	Powerful Cure	Powerful Appeal
Holy Spirit		Holy Boldness	

YOUR DAILY WALK Is your life a wonder to those around you? Is there anything about your lifestyle—the way you use your time . . . spend your money . . . treat your family . . . love your neighbors—that causes others to sit up and take notice?

Without God, we are inadequate; with him, we are invincible.

There was no ignoring the powerful witness of those first-century Christians. "Everyone was filled with awe" when they saw the "many wonders and miraculous signs" the apostles did in their midst (2:43). One such sign in chapter 3 involved a crippled beggar—a man who begged for alms but who received legs instead! As others looked at his changed life, they responded in "wonder and amazement" (3:10). Peter's preaching turned that casual encounter by the Beautiful Gate into a wonderful revival with hundreds responding to the good news of a risen Savior. But it all began with one changed life.

It's never too late for revival to break in your family or neighborhood. All God needs is one life to use as a showcase for his transforming power. Are you willing to let that revival begin with you? Then write God a note in the margin and tell him so.

INSIGHT A Bit of Arithmetic in Acts
In 1:15 the band of disciples consisted of 120. In 2:41, their number had swelled to more than three thousand. By 4:4 that total had increased by several thousand more. At first, disciples were *added* daily (2:47). But soon the believers were *multiplying* rapidly (6:7)!

CHAPTER 1
In my former book, Theophilus, I wrote about all that Jesus began to do and to teach ²until the day he was taken up to heaven, after giving instructions through the Holy Spirit to the apostles he had chosen. ³After his suffering, he showed himself to these men and gave many convincing proofs that he was alive. He appeared to them over a period of forty days and spoke about the kingdom of God. ⁴On one occasion, while he was eating

with them, he gave them this command: "Do not leave Jerusalem, but wait for the gift my Father promised, which you have heard me speak about. 5For John baptized with[a] water, but in a few days you will be baptized with the Holy Spirit."

6So when they met together, they asked him, "Lord, are you at this time going to restore the kingdom to Israel?"

7He said to them: "It is not for you to know the times or dates the Father has set by his own authority. 8But you will receive power when the Holy Spirit comes on you; and you will be my witnesses in Jerusalem, and in all Judea and Samaria, and to the ends of the earth."

9After he said this, he was taken up before their very eyes, and a cloud hid him from their sight.

10They were looking intently up into the sky as he was going, when suddenly two men dressed in white stood beside them. 11"Men of Galilee," they said, "why do you stand here looking into the sky? This same Jesus, who has been taken from you into heaven, will come back in the same way you have seen him go into heaven."

12Then they returned to Jerusalem from the hill called the Mount of Olives, a Sabbath day's walk[b] from the city. 13When they arrived, they went upstairs to the room where they were staying. Those present were Peter, John, James and Andrew; Philip and Thomas, Bartholomew and Matthew; James son of Alphaeus and Simon the Zealot, and Judas son of James. 14They all joined together constantly in prayer, along with the women and Mary the mother of Jesus, and with his brothers.

15In those days Peter stood up among the believers[c] (a group numbering about a hundred and twenty) 16and said, "Brothers, the Scripture had to be fulfilled which the Holy Spirit spoke long ago through the mouth of David concerning Judas, who served as guide for those who arrested Jesus— 17he was one of our number and shared in this ministry."

18(With the reward he got for his wickedness, Judas bought a field; there he fell headlong, his body burst open and all his intestines spilled out. 19Everyone in Jerusalem heard about this, so they called that field in their language Akeldama, that is, Field of Blood.)

20"For," said Peter, "it is written in the book of Psalms,

" 'May his place be deserted;
   let there be no one to dwell in it,'[d]

and,

" 'May another take his place of
      leadership.'[e]

21Therefore it is necessary to choose one of the men who have been with us the whole time the Lord Jesus went in and out among us, 22beginning from John's baptism to the time when Jesus was taken up from us. For one of these must become a witness with us of his resurrection."

23So they proposed two men: Joseph called Barsabbas (also known as Justus) and Matthias. 24Then they prayed, "Lord, you know everyone's heart. Show us which of these two you have chosen 25to take over this apostolic ministry, which Judas left to go where he belongs." 26Then they cast lots, and the lot fell to Matthias; so he was added to the eleven apostles.

CHAPTER 2

When the day of Pentecost came, they were all together in one place. 2Suddenly a sound like the blowing of a violent wind came from heaven and filled the whole house where they were sitting. 3They saw what seemed to be tongues of fire that separated and came to rest on each of them. 4All of them were filled with the Holy Spirit and began to speak in other tongues[f] as the Spirit enabled them.

5Now there were staying in Jerusalem God-fearing Jews from every nation under heaven. 6When they heard this sound, a crowd came together in bewilderment, because each one heard them speaking in his own language. 7Utterly amazed, they asked: "Are not all these men who are speaking Galileans? 8Then how is it that each of us hears them in his own native language? 9Parthians, Medes and Elamites; residents of Mesopotamia, Judea and Cappadocia, Pontus and Asia, 10Phrygia and Pamphylia, Egypt and the parts of Libya near Cyrene; visitors from Rome 11(both Jews and converts to Judaism); Cretans and Arabs—we hear them declaring the wonders of God in our own tongues!" 12Amazed and perplexed, they

a5 Or in   b12 That is, about 3/4 mile (about 1,100 meters)   c15 Greek brothers   d20 Psalm 69:25   e20 Psalm 109:8
f4 Or languages; also in verse 11

asked one another, "What does this mean?"

[13]Some, however, made fun of them and said, "They have had too much wine.[8]"

[14]Then Peter stood up with the Eleven, raised his voice and addressed the crowd: "Fellow Jews and all of you who live in Jerusalem, let me explain this to you; listen carefully to what I say. [15]These men are not drunk, as you suppose. It's only nine in the morning! [16]No, this is what was spoken by the prophet Joel:

[17]" 'In the last days, God says,
    I will pour out my Spirit on all
        people.
Your sons and daughters will
        prophesy,
    your young men will see visions,
    your old men will dream dreams.
[18]Even on my servants, both men and
        women,
    I will pour out my Spirit in those
        days,
    and they will prophesy.
[19]I will show wonders in the heaven
        above
    and signs on the earth below,
    blood and fire and billows of smoke.
[20]The sun will be turned to darkness
    and the moon to blood
    before the coming of the great and
        glorious day of the Lord.
[21]And everyone who calls
    on the name of the Lord will be
        saved.'[h]

[22]"Men of Israel, listen to this: Jesus of Nazareth was a man accredited by God to you by miracles, wonders and signs, which God did among you through him, as you yourselves know. [23]This man was handed over to you by God's set purpose and foreknowledge; and you, with the help of wicked men,[i] put him to death by nailing him to the cross. [24]But God raised him from the dead, freeing him from the agony of death, because it was impossible for death to keep its hold on him. [25]David said about him:

" 'I saw the Lord always before me.
    Because he is at my right hand,
    I will not be shaken.

[26]Therefore my heart is glad and my
        tongue rejoices;
    my body also will live in hope,
[27]because you will not abandon me to
        the grave,
    nor will you let your Holy One see
        decay.
[28]You have made known to me the
        paths of life;
    you will fill me with joy in your
        presence.'[j]

[29]"Brothers, I can tell you confidently that the patriarch David died and was buried, and his tomb is here to this day. [30]But he was a prophet and knew that God had promised him on oath that he would place one of his descendants on his throne. [31]Seeing what was ahead, he spoke of the resurrection of the Christ,[k] that he was not abandoned to the grave, nor did his body see decay. [32]God has raised this Jesus to life, and we are all witnesses of the fact. [33]Exalted to the right hand of God, he has received from the Father the promised Holy Spirit and has poured out what you now see and hear. [34]For David did not ascend to heaven, and yet he said,

" 'The Lord said to my Lord:
    "Sit at my right hand
[35]until I make your enemies
    a footstool for your feet." '[l]

[36]"Therefore let all Israel be assured of this: God has made this Jesus, whom you crucified, both Lord and Christ."

[37]When the people heard this, they were cut to the heart and said to Peter and the other apostles, "Brothers, what shall we do?"

[38]Peter replied, "Repent and be baptized, every one of you, in the name of Jesus Christ for the forgiveness of your sins. And you will receive the gift of the Holy Spirit. [39]The promise is for you and your children and for all who are far off— for all whom the Lord our God will call."

[40]With many other words he warned them; and he pleaded with them, "Save yourselves from this corrupt generation." [41]Those who accepted his message were baptized, and about three thousand were added to their number that day.

[8]13 Or *sweet wine*   [h]21 Joel 2:28-32   [i]23 Or *of those not having the law* (that is, Gentiles)   [j]28 Psalm 16:8-11
[k]31 Or *Messiah*. "The Christ" (Greek) and "the Messiah" (Hebrew) both mean "the Anointed One"; also in verse 36.
[l]35 Psalm 110:1

42They devoted themselves to the apostles' teaching and to the fellowship, to the breaking of bread and to prayer. 43Everyone was filled with awe, and many wonders and miraculous signs were done by the apostles. 44All the believers were together and had everything in common. 45Selling their possessions and goods, they gave to anyone as he had need. 46Every day they continued to meet together in the temple courts. They broke bread in their homes and ate together with glad and sincere hearts, 47praising God and enjoying the favor of all the people. And the Lord added to their number daily those who were being saved.

CHAPTER 3

One day Peter and John were going up to the temple at the time of prayer—at three in the afternoon. 2Now a man crippled from birth was being carried to the temple gate called Beautiful, where he was put every day to beg from those going into the temple courts. 3When he saw Peter and John about to enter, he asked them for money. 4Peter looked straight at him, as did John. Then Peter said, "Look at us!" 5So the man gave them his attention, expecting to get something from them.

6Then Peter said, "Silver or gold I do not have, but what I have I give you. In the name of Jesus Christ of Nazareth, walk." 7Taking him by the right hand, he helped him up, and instantly the man's feet and ankles became strong. 8He jumped to his feet and began to walk. Then he went with them into the temple courts, walking and jumping, and praising God. 9When all the people saw him walking and praising God, 10they recognized him as the same man who used to sit begging at the temple gate called Beautiful, and they were filled with wonder and amazement at what had happened to him.

11While the beggar held on to Peter and John, all the people were astonished and came running to them in the place called Solomon's Colonnade. 12When Peter saw this, he said to them: "Men of Israel, why does this surprise you? Why do you stare at us as if by our own power or godliness

we had made this man walk? 13The God of Abraham, Isaac and Jacob, the God of our fathers, has glorified his servant Jesus. You handed him over to be killed, and you disowned him before Pilate, though he had decided to let him go. 14You disowned the Holy and Righteous One and asked that a murderer be released to you. 15You killed the author of life, but God raised him from the dead. We are witnesses of this. 16By faith in the name of Jesus, this man whom you see and know was made strong. It is Jesus' name and the faith that comes through him that has given this complete healing to him, as you can all see.

17"Now, brothers, I know that you acted in ignorance, as did your leaders. 18But this is how God fulfilled what he had foretold through all the prophets, saying that his Christ[m] would suffer. 19Repent, then, and turn to God, so that your sins may be wiped out, that times of refreshing may come from the Lord, 20and that he may send the Christ, who has been appointed for you—even Jesus. 21He must remain in heaven until the time comes for God to restore everything, as he promised long ago through his holy prophets. 22For Moses said, 'The Lord your God will raise up for you a prophet like me from among your own people; you must listen to everything he tells you. 23Anyone who does not listen to him will be completely cut off from among his people.'[n]

24"Indeed, all the prophets from Samuel on, as many as have spoken, have foretold these days. 25And you are heirs of the prophets and of the covenant God made with your fathers. He said to Abraham, 'Through your offspring all peoples on earth will be blessed.'[o] 26When God raised up his servant, he sent him first to you to bless you by turning each of you from your wicked ways."

CHAPTER 4

The priests and the captain of the temple guard and the Sadducees came up to Peter and John while they were speaking to the people. 2They were greatly disturbed because the apostles were teaching the people and proclaiming in Jesus the resurrection of the dead. 3They seized Peter

m18 Or Messiah; also in verse 20   n23 Deut. 18:15,18,19   o25 Gen. 22:18; 26:4

and John, and because it was evening, they put them in jail until the next day. [4]But many who heard the message believed, and the number of men grew to about five thousand.

[5]The next day the rulers, elders and teachers of the law met in Jerusalem. [6]Annas the high priest was there, and so were Caiaphas, John, Alexander and the other men of the high priest's family. [7]They had Peter and John brought before them and began to question them: "By what power or what name did you do this?"

[8]Then Peter, filled with the Holy Spirit, said to them: "Rulers and elders of the people! [9]If we are being called to account today for an act of kindness shown to a cripple and are asked how he was healed, [10]then know this, you and all the people of Israel: It is by the name of Jesus Christ of Nazareth, whom you crucified but whom God raised from the dead, that this man stands before you healed. [11]He is

" 'the stone you builders rejected,
    which has become the capstone.[p][q]

[12]Salvation is found in no one else, for there is no other name under heaven given to men by which we must be saved."

[13]When they saw the courage of Peter and John and realized that they were unschooled, ordinary men, they were astonished and they took note that these men had been with Jesus. [14]But since they could see the man who had been healed standing there with them, there was nothing they could say. [15]So they ordered them to withdraw from the Sanhedrin and then conferred together. [16]"What are we going to do with these men?" they asked. "Everybody living in Jerusalem knows they have done an outstanding miracle, and we cannot deny it. [17]But to stop this thing from spreading any further among the people, we must warn these men to speak no longer to anyone in this name."

[18]Then they called them in again and commanded them not to speak or teach at all in the name of Jesus. [19]But Peter and

John replied, "Judge for yourselves whether it is right in God's sight to obey you rather than God. [20]For we cannot help speaking about what we have seen and heard."

[21]After further threats they let them go. They could not decide how to punish them, because all the people were praising God for what had happened. [22]For the man who was miraculously healed was over forty years old.

[23]On their release, Peter and John went back to their own people and reported all that the chief priests and elders had said to them. [24]When they heard this, they raised their voices together in prayer to God. "Sovereign Lord," they said, "you made the heaven and the earth and the sea, and everything in them. [25]You spoke by the Holy Spirit through the mouth of your servant, our father David:

" 'Why do the nations rage
    and the peoples plot in vain?
[26]The kings of the earth take their stand
    and the rulers gather together
  against the Lord
    and against his Anointed One.[r][s]

[27]Indeed Herod and Pontius Pilate met together with the Gentiles and the people[t] of Israel in this city to conspire against your holy servant Jesus, whom you anointed. [28]They did what your power and will had decided beforehand should happen. [29]Now, Lord, consider their threats and enable your servants to speak your word with great boldness. [30]Stretch out your hand to heal and perform miraculous signs and wonders through the name of your holy servant Jesus."

[31]After they prayed, the place where they were meeting was shaken. And they were all filled with the Holy Spirit and spoke the word of God boldly.

[32]All the believers were one in heart and mind. No one claimed that any of his possessions was his own, but they shared everything they had. [33]With great power the apostles continued to testify to the resurrection of the Lord Jesus, and much grace was upon them all. [34]There were no needy persons among them. For from time to time

p11 Or *cornerstone*   q11 Psalm 118:22   r26 That is, Christ or Messiah   s26 Psalm 2:1,2   t27 The Greek is plural.

those who owned lands or houses sold them, brought the money from the sales [35]and put it at the apostles' feet, and it was distributed to anyone as he had need.

[36]Joseph, a Levite from Cyprus, whom the apostles called Barnabas (which means Son of Encouragement), [37]sold a field he owned and brought the money and put it at the apostles' feet.

NOVEMBER 2 □ DAY 307
ACTS 5–8:1a
Progress of the Church

 OVERVIEW Every church has its problems, and the newly organized church in Jerusalem is no exception. On the heels of Peter's miraculous healing of a crippled beggar, several waves of trouble arrive: scandal in the church involving Ananias and Sapphira, sharp dissension between Jews and Greeks over the provision for widows in the church and the brutal martyrdom of Stephen after his eloquent and convicting address before the Sanhedrin. But even in the face of such strong adversity, God is at work. One of the witnesses of Stephen's death is Saul, the Jewish persecutor who would soon become one of the chief figures in the expanding church!

Chapter 5	Chapter 6	Chapters 7–8
Embezzlement in the Church	Overlooked Needs in the Church	Opposition outside the Church 7:1 8:1a
Discipline	Deacons	Death

 YOUR DAILY WALK Two pastors were exchanging the latest news. Said one, "Did you hear about the revival we had at our church?" "No," replied the other, "how many new members did you add?" "None," responded the first, "but we had some very helpful subtrac-

Revival is nothing more than a new beginning of obedience to God.

tions!"

The early chapters of Acts are marked by both kinds of "revival." There was dramatic growth by *addition:* at first three thousand, then five thousand more were added. But don't overlook the growth by *subtraction.* Ananias and Sapphira felt God's disciplining hand, and "more and more men and women believed in the Lord and were added to their number" (5:14). Stephen, the church's spokesman, died a terrible death by stoning, and consequently "those who had been scattered preached the word wherever they went" (8:4).

Start a revival in your own life today by either *adding* something that is sorely missing (like making time to read good Christian books) or *subtracting* something that is hindering your walk with God (like too much television or too many late-night activities).

 INSIGHT Stephen's Sermon—The Old Testament in a Nugget
With the help of this Bible, "walk" your way through the Old Testament with Stephen, marking in Acts 7 where each Old Testament book begins and ends. For example, Genesis begins with verse 2 and ends with verse 16. See how many more you can find. Have fun!

CHAPTER 5

Now a man named Ananias, together with his wife Sapphira, also sold a piece of property. [2]With his wife's full knowledge he kept back part of the money for himself, but brought the rest and put it at the apostles' feet.

[3]Then Peter said, "Ananias, how is it that Satan has so filled your heart that you have lied to the Holy Spirit and have kept for yourself some of the money you received for the land? [4]Didn't it belong to you before it was sold? And after it was sold, wasn't the money at your disposal? What made you think of doing such a thing? You have not lied to men but to God."

[5]When Ananias heard this, he fell down and died. And great fear seized all who heard what had happened. [6]Then the young men came forward, wrapped up his body, and carried him out and buried him.

[7]About three hours later his wife came in, not knowing what had happened. [8]Peter asked her, "Tell me, is this the price you and Ananias got for the land?"

"Yes," she said, "that is the price."

[9]Peter said to her, "How could you agree to test the Spirit of the Lord? Look! The feet of the men who buried your husband are at the door, and they will carry you out also."

[10]At that moment she fell down at his feet and died. Then the young men came in and, finding her dead, carried her out and buried her beside her husband. [11]Great fear seized the whole church and all who heard about these events.

[12]The apostles performed many miraculous signs and wonders among the people. And all the believers used to meet together in Solomon's Colonnade. [13]No one else dared join them, even though they were highly regarded by the people. [14]Nevertheless, more and more men and women believed in the Lord and were added to their number. [15]As a result, people brought the sick into the streets and laid them on beds and mats so that at least Peter's shadow might fall on some of them as he passed by. [16]Crowds gathered also from the towns around Jerusalem, bringing their sick and those tormented by evil[u] spirits, and all of them were healed.

[17]Then the high priest and all his associates, who were members of the party of the Sadducees, were filled with jealousy. [18]They arrested the apostles and put them in the public jail. [19]But during the night an angel of the Lord opened the doors of the jail and brought them out. [20]"Go, stand in the temple courts," he said, "and tell the people the full message of this new life."

[21]At daybreak they entered the temple courts, as they had been told, and began to teach the people.

When the high priest and his associates arrived, they called together the Sanhedrin—the full assembly of the elders of Israel—and sent to the jail for the apostles. [22]But on arriving at the jail, the officers did not find them there. So they went back and reported, [23]"We found the jail securely locked, with the guards standing at the doors; but when we opened them, we found no one inside." [24]On hearing this report, the captain of the temple guard and the chief priests were puzzled, wondering what would come of this.

[25]Then someone came and said, "Look! The men you put in jail are standing in the temple courts teaching the people." [26]At that, the captain went with his officers and brought the apostles. They did not use force, because they feared that the people would stone them.

[27]Having brought the apostles, they made them appear before the Sanhedrin to be questioned by the high priest. [28]"We gave you strict orders not to teach in this name," he said. "Yet you have filled Jerusalem with your teaching and are determined to make us guilty of this man's blood."

[29]Peter and the other apostles replied: "We must obey God rather than men! [30]The God of our fathers raised Jesus from the dead—whom you had killed by hanging him on a tree. [31]God exalted him to his own right hand as Prince and Savior that he might give repentance and forgiveness of sins to Israel. [32]We are witnesses of these things, and so is the Holy Spirit, whom God has given to those who obey him."

[33]When they heard this, they were furious and wanted to put them to death.

[u]16 Greek unclean

³⁴But a Pharisee named Gamaliel, a teacher of the law, who was honored by all the people, stood up in the Sanhedrin and ordered that the men be put outside for a little while. ³⁵Then he addressed them: "Men of Israel, consider carefully what you intend to do to these men. ³⁶Some time ago Theudas appeared, claiming to be somebody, and about four hundred men rallied to him. He was killed, all his followers were dispersed, and it all came to nothing. ³⁷After him, Judas the Galilean appeared in the days of the census and led a band of people in revolt. He too was killed, and all his followers were scattered. ³⁸Therefore, in the present case I advise you: Leave these men alone! Let them go! For if their purpose or activity is of human origin, it will fail. ³⁹But if it is from God, you will not be able to stop these men; you will only find yourselves fighting against God."

⁴⁰His speech persuaded them. They called the apostles in and had them flogged. Then they ordered them not to speak in the name of Jesus, and let them go.

⁴¹The apostles left the Sanhedrin, rejoicing because they had been counted worthy of suffering disgrace for the Name. ⁴²Day after day, in the temple courts and from house to house, they never stopped teaching and proclaiming the good news that Jesus is the Christ.ᵛ

CHAPTER 6

In those days when the number of disciples was increasing, the Grecian Jews among them complained against the Hebraic Jews because their widows were being overlooked in the daily distribution of food. ²So the Twelve gathered all the disciples together and said, "It would not be right for us to neglect the ministry of the word of God in order to wait on tables. ³Brothers, choose seven men from among you who are known to be full of the Spirit and wisdom. We will turn this responsibility over to them ⁴and will give our attention to prayer and the ministry of the word."

⁵This proposal pleased the whole group. They chose Stephen, a man full of faith and of the Holy Spirit; also Philip, Procorus, Nicanor, Timon, Parmenas, and Nicolas from Antioch, a convert to Judaism. ⁶They presented these men to the apostles, who prayed and laid their hands on them.

⁷So the word of God spread. The number of disciples in Jerusalem increased rapidly, and a large number of priests became obedient to the faith.

⁸Now Stephen, a man full of God's grace and power, did great wonders and miraculous signs among the people. ⁹Opposition arose, however, from members of the Synagogue of the Freedmen (as it was called)—Jews of Cyrene and Alexandria as well as the provinces of Cilicia and Asia. These men began to argue with Stephen, ¹⁰but they could not stand up against his wisdom or the Spirit by whom he spoke.

¹¹Then they secretly persuaded some men to say, "We have heard Stephen speak words of blasphemy against Moses and against God."

¹²So they stirred up the people and the elders and the teachers of the law. They seized Stephen and brought him before the Sanhedrin. ¹³They produced false witnesses, who testified, "This fellow never stops speaking against this holy place and against the law. ¹⁴For we have heard him say that this Jesus of Nazareth will destroy this place and change the customs Moses handed down to us."

¹⁵All who were sitting in the Sanhedrin looked intently at Stephen, and they saw that his face was like the face of an angel.

CHAPTER 7

Then the high priest asked him, "Are these charges true?"

²To this he replied: "Brothers and fathers, listen to me! The God of glory appeared to our father Abraham while he was still in Mesopotamia, before he lived in Haran. ³'Leave your country and your people,' God said, 'and go to the land I will show you.'ʷ

⁴"So he left the land of the Chaldeans and settled in Haran. After the death of his father, God sent him to this land where you are now living. ⁵He gave him no inheritance here, not even a foot of ground. But God promised him that he and his descendants after him would possess the land, even though at that time

ᵛ42 Or Messiah   ʷ3 Gen. 12:1

Abraham had no child. [6]God spoke to him in this way: 'Your descendants will be strangers in a country not their own, and they will be enslaved and mistreated four hundred years. [7]But I will punish the nation they serve as slaves,' God said, 'and afterward they will come out of that country and worship me in this place.'[x] [8]Then he gave Abraham the covenant of circumcision. And Abraham became the father of Isaac and circumcised him eight days after his birth. Later Isaac became the father of Jacob, and Jacob became the father of the twelve patriarchs.

[9]"Because the patriarchs were jealous of Joseph, they sold him as a slave into Egypt. But God was with him [10]and rescued him from all his troubles. He gave Joseph wisdom and enabled him to gain the goodwill of Pharaoh king of Egypt; so he made him ruler over Egypt and all his palace.

[11]"Then a famine struck all Egypt and Canaan, bringing great suffering, and our fathers could not find food. [12]When Jacob heard that there was grain in Egypt, he sent our fathers on their first visit. [13]On their second visit, Joseph told his brothers who he was, and Pharaoh learned about Joseph's family. [14]After this, Joseph sent for his father Jacob and his whole family, seventy-five in all. [15]Then Jacob went down to Egypt, where he and our fathers died. [16]Their bodies were brought back to Shechem and placed in the tomb that Abraham had bought from the sons of Hamor at Shechem for a certain sum of money.

[17]"As the time drew near for God to fulfill his promise to Abraham, the number of our people in Egypt greatly increased. [18]Then another king, who knew nothing about Joseph, became ruler of Egypt. [19]He dealt treacherously with our people and oppressed our forefathers by forcing them to throw out their newborn babies so that they would die.

[20]"At that time Moses was born, and he was no ordinary child.[y] For three months he was cared for in his father's house. [21]When he was placed outside, Pharaoh's daughter took him and brought him up as her own son. [22]Moses was educated in all the wisdom of the Egyptians and was powerful in speech and action.

[23]"When Moses was forty years old, he decided to visit his fellow Israelites. [24]He saw one of them being mistreated by an Egyptian, so he went to his defense and avenged him by killing the Egyptian. [25]Moses thought that his own people would realize that God was using him to rescue them, but they did not. [26]The next day Moses came upon two Israelites who were fighting. He tried to reconcile them by saying, 'Men, you are brothers; why do you want to hurt each other?'

[27]"But the man who was mistreating the other pushed Moses aside and said, 'Who made you ruler and judge over us? [28]Do you want to kill me as you killed the Egyptian yesterday?'[z] [29]When Moses heard this, he fled to Midian, where he settled as a foreigner and had two sons.

[30]"After forty years had passed, an angel appeared to Moses in the flames of a burning bush in the desert near Mount Sinai. [31]When he saw this, he was amazed at the sight. As he went over to look more closely, he heard the Lord's voice: [32]'I am the God of your fathers, the God of Abraham, Isaac and Jacob.'[a] Moses trembled with fear and did not dare to look.

[33]"Then the Lord said to him, 'Take off your sandals; the place where you are standing is holy ground. [34]I have indeed seen the oppression of my people in Egypt. I have heard their groaning and have come down to set them free. Now come, I will send you back to Egypt.'[b]

[35]"This is the same Moses whom they had rejected with the words, 'Who made you ruler and judge?' He was sent to be their ruler and deliverer by God himself, through the angel who appeared to him in the bush. [36]He led them out of Egypt and did wonders and miraculous signs in Egypt, at the Red Sea[c] and for forty years in the desert.

[37]"This is that Moses who told the Israelites, 'God will send you a prophet like me from your own people.'[d] [38]He was in the assembly in the desert, with the angel who spoke to him on Mount Sinai, and with our fathers; and he received living words to pass on to us.

[39]"But our fathers refused to obey him. Instead, they rejected him and in their hearts turned back to Egypt. [40]They told Aaron, 'Make us gods who will go before

---

[x]7 Gen. 15:13,14   [y]20 Or was fair in the sight of God   [z]28 Exodus 2:14   [a]32 Exodus 3:6   [b]34 Exodus 3:5,7,8,10   [c]36 That is, Sea of Reeds   [d]37 Deut. 18:15

us. As for this fellow Moses who led us out of Egypt—we don't know what has happened to him!'*e* 41That was the time they made an idol in the form of a calf. They brought sacrifices to it and held a celebration in honor of what their hands had made. 42But God turned away and gave them over to the worship of the heavenly bodies. This agrees with what is written in the book of the prophets:

" 'Did you bring me sacrifices and
     offerings
   forty years in the desert, O house of
     Israel?
43You have lifted up the shrine of
     Molech
   and the star of your god Rephan,
     the idols you made to worship.
Therefore I will send you into exile'*f*
     beyond Babylon.

44"Our forefathers had the tabernacle of the Testimony with them in the desert. It had been made as God directed Moses, according to the pattern he had seen. 45Having received the tabernacle, our fathers under Joshua brought it with them when they took the land from the nations God drove out before them. It remained in the land until the time of David, 46who enjoyed God's favor and asked that he might provide a dwelling place for the God of Jacob.*g* 47But it was Solomon who built the house for him.

48"However, the Most High does not live in houses made by men. As the prophet says:

49" 'Heaven is my throne,
     and the earth is my footstool.

What kind of house will you build for
     me?
                                    says the Lord.
   Or where will my resting place be?
50Has not my hand made all these
     things?'*h*

51"You stiff-necked people, with uncircumcised hearts and ears! You are just like your fathers: You always resist the Holy Spirit! 52Was there ever a prophet your fathers did not persecute? They even killed those who predicted the coming of the Righteous One. And now you have betrayed and murdered him— 53you who have received the law that was put into effect through angels but have not obeyed it."

54When they heard this, they were furious and gnashed their teeth at him. 55But Stephen, full of the Holy Spirit, looked up to heaven and saw the glory of God, and Jesus standing at the right hand of God. 56"Look," he said, "I see heaven open and the Son of Man standing at the right hand of God."

57At this they covered their ears and, yelling at the top of their voices, they all rushed at him, 58dragged him out of the city and began to stone him. Meanwhile, the witnesses laid their clothes at the feet of a young man named Saul.

59While they were stoning him, Stephen prayed, "Lord Jesus, receive my spirit." 60Then he fell on his knees and cried out, "Lord, do not hold this sin against them." When he had said this, he fell asleep.

CHAPTER 8
And Saul was there, giving approval to his death.

e40 Exodus 32:1   *f43* Amos 5:25-27   *g46* Some early manuscripts *the house of Jacob*   *h50* Isaiah 66:1,2

NOVEMBER 3 □ DAY 308
ACTS 8:1b–9
Persecution of the Church

OVERVIEW Saul's intense persecution against the Christians in Jerusalem forces them to scatter to the regions of Judea and Samaria—exactly as Christ had predicted in 1:8. Philip the evangelist becomes God's instrument to lead many to faith in the city of Samaria, and later he shares the Good News with an Ethiopian official on the road to Gaza. But the most strategic conversion takes place more than a hundred miles to the north, where Saul comes face-to-face with the very Lord whose servants he has persecuted.

Chapter 8		Chapter 9	
Evangelism in Samaria	Evangelism in the Desert	Encounter near Damascus	Escape in a Basket
1b 25	26 40	1 19a	19b 43
Philip's Preaching		Saul's Conversion	

YOUR DAILY WALK What does the Second Law of Thermodynamics ("the greater the heat, the greater the expansion") have to do with the book of Acts?

To know God is to know that he should be obeyed.

Answer: It is an accurate description of the process by which the gospel message expanded beyond the city of Jerusalem.

Two years after Jesus spoke the words recorded in Acts 1:8, the disciples resided only in Jerusalem . . . and so the Good News they were commissioned to share stayed within the city walls. But that meant that only phase one of the Great Commission was being accomplished. So God allowed a little "heat" in the form of persecution to encourage the expansion of the gospel into the regions of Judea and Samaria.

Postponed obedience to the command of God is disobedience. And God has many loving (but often painful) ways to encourage you to obey. The choice is yours: You can "beat the heat" by doing his bidding or "feel the heat" of his chastening hand. At least five times in today's passage an individual is commanded to "go" and do something. Locate and circle the response in each case, and let that guide your response the next time you receive a similar command!

INSIGHT Why Down Is Up in Palestine
We read in 8:5 that "Philip went down to a city in Samaria," even though Samaria is *north* of Jerusalem. This makes sense when we realize that Israel's capital city is located atop a hill, and Samaria lies in a low plain. Moreover, we draw our maps with the top facing north, but the Palestinians drew them with the top facing east, looking inland from the Mediterranean.

On that day a great persecution broke out against the church at Jerusalem, and all except the apostles were scattered throughout Judea and Samaria. ²Godly men buried Stephen and mourned deeply for him. ³But Saul began to destroy the church. Going from house to house, he dragged off men and women and put them in prison.

⁴Those who had been scattered preached the word wherever they went. ⁵Philip went down to a city in Samaria and proclaimed the Christ*ⁱ* there. ⁶When the crowds heard Philip and saw the miraculous signs he did, they all paid close attention to what he said. ⁷With shrieks, evil*ʲ* spirits came out of many, and many paralytics and cripples were healed. ⁸So there was great joy in that city.

⁹Now for some time a man named Simon had practiced sorcery in the city and amazed all the people of Samaria. He boasted that he was someone great, ¹⁰and all the people, both high and low, gave him their attention and exclaimed, "This man is the divine power known as the Great Power." ¹¹They followed him because he had amazed them for a long time with his magic. ¹²But when they believed Philip as he preached the good news of the kingdom of God and the name of Jesus Christ, they were baptized, both men and women. ¹³Simon himself believed and was baptized. And he followed Philip everywhere, astonished by the great signs and miracles he saw.

¹⁴When the apostles in Jerusalem heard that Samaria had accepted the word of

ⁱ5 Or Messiah   ʲ7 Greek unclean

God, they sent Peter and John to them. [15]When they arrived, they prayed for them that they might receive the Holy Spirit, [16]because the Holy Spirit had not yet come upon any of them; they had simply been baptized into[k] the name of the Lord Jesus. [17]Then Peter and John placed their hands on them, and they received the Holy Spirit.

[18]When Simon saw that the Spirit was given at the laying on of the apostles' hands, he offered them money [19]and said, "Give me also this ability so that everyone on whom I lay my hands may receive the Holy Spirit."

[20]Peter answered: "May your money perish with you, because you thought you could buy the gift of God with money! [21]You have no part or share in this ministry, because your heart is not right before God. [22]Repent of this wickedness and pray to the Lord. Perhaps he will forgive you for having such a thought in your heart. [23]For I see that you are full of bitterness and captive to sin."

[24]Then Simon answered, "Pray to the Lord for me so that nothing you have said may happen to me."

[25]When they had testified and proclaimed the word of the Lord, Peter and John returned to Jerusalem, preaching the gospel in many Samaritan villages.

[26]Now an angel of the Lord said to Philip, "Go south to the road—the desert road—that goes down from Jerusalem to Gaza." [27]So he started out, and on his way he met an Ethiopian[l] eunuch, an important official in charge of all the treasury of Candace, queen of the Ethiopians. This man had gone to Jerusalem to worship, [28]and on his way home was sitting in his chariot reading the book of Isaiah the prophet. [29]The Spirit told Philip, "Go to that chariot and stay near it."

[30]Then Philip ran up to the chariot and heard the man reading Isaiah the prophet. "Do you understand what you are reading?" Philip asked.

[31]"How can I," he said, "unless someone explains it to me?" So he invited Philip to come up and sit with him.

[32]The eunuch was reading this passage of Scripture:

"He was led like a sheep to the
   slaughter,
and as a lamb before the shearer is
   silent,
so he did not open his mouth.
[33]In his humiliation he was deprived of
   justice.
Who can speak of his descendants?
For his life was taken from the
   earth."[m]

[34]The eunuch asked Philip, "Tell me, please, who is the prophet talking about, himself or someone else?" [35]Then Philip began with that very passage of Scripture and told him the good news about Jesus.

[36]As they traveled along the road, they came to some water and the eunuch said, "Look, here is water. Why shouldn't I be baptized?"[n] [38]And he gave orders to stop the chariot. Then both Philip and the eunuch went down into the water and Philip baptized him. [39]When they came up out of the water, the Spirit of the Lord suddenly took Philip away, and the eunuch did not see him again, but went on his way rejoicing. [40]Philip, however, appeared at Azotus and traveled about, preaching the gospel in all the towns until he reached Caesarea.

CHAPTER 9
Meanwhile, Saul was still breathing out murderous threats against the Lord's disciples. He went to the high priest [2]and asked him for letters to the synagogues in Damascus, so that if he found any there who belonged to the Way, whether men or women, he might take them as prisoners to Jerusalem. [3]As he neared Damascus on his journey, suddenly a light from heaven flashed around him. [4]He fell to the ground and heard a voice say to him, "Saul, Saul, why do you persecute me?"

[5]"Who are you, Lord?" Saul asked.

"I am Jesus, whom you are persecuting," he replied. [6]"Now get up and go into the city, and you will be told what you must do."

[7]The men traveling with Saul stood there speechless; they heard the sound but did not see anyone. [8]Saul got up from the ground, but when he opened his eyes

[k]16 Or in [l]27 That is, from the upper Nile region [m]33 Isaiah 53:7,8 [n]36 Some late manuscripts baptized?" [37]Philip said, "If you believe with all your heart, you may." The eunuch answered, "I believe that Jesus Christ is the Son of God."

he could see nothing. So they led him by the hand into Damascus. ⁹For three days he was blind, and did not eat or drink anything.

¹⁰In Damascus there was a disciple named Ananias. The Lord called to him in a vision, "Ananias!"

"Yes, Lord," he answered.

¹¹The Lord told him, "Go to the house of Judas on Straight Street and ask for a man from Tarsus named Saul, for he is praying. ¹²In a vision he has seen a man named Ananias come and place his hands on him to restore his sight."

¹³"Lord," Ananias answered, "I have heard many reports about this man and all the harm he has done to your saints in Jerusalem. ¹⁴And he has come here with authority from the chief priests to arrest all who call on your name."

¹⁵But the Lord said to Ananias, "Go! This man is my chosen instrument to carry my name before the Gentiles and their kings and before the people of Israel. ¹⁶I will show him how much he must suffer for my name."

¹⁷Then Ananias went to the house and entered it. Placing his hands on Saul, he said, "Brother Saul, the Lord—Jesus, who appeared to you on the road as you were coming here—has sent me so that you may see again and be filled with the Holy Spirit." ¹⁸Immediately, something like scales fell from Saul's eyes, and he could see again. He got up and was baptized, ¹⁹and after taking some food, he regained his strength.

Saul spent several days with the disciples in Damascus. ²⁰At once he began to preach in the synagogues that Jesus is the Son of God. ²¹All those who heard him were astonished and asked, "Isn't he the man who raised havoc in Jerusalem among those who call on this name? And hasn't he come here to take them as prisoners to the chief priests?" ²²Yet Saul grew more and more powerful and baffled the Jews living in Damascus by proving that Jesus is the Christ.ᵒ

²³After many days had gone by, the Jews conspired to kill him, ²⁴but Saul learned of their plan. Day and night they kept close watch on the city gates in order to kill him. ²⁵But his followers took him

by night and lowered him in a basket through an opening in the wall.

²⁶When he came to Jerusalem, he tried to join the disciples, but they were all afraid of him, not believing that he really was a disciple. ²⁷But Barnabas took him and brought him to the apostles. He told them how Saul on his journey had seen the Lord and that the Lord had spoken to him, and how in Damascus he had preached fearlessly in the name of Jesus. ²⁸So Saul stayed with them and moved about freely in Jerusalem, speaking boldly in the name of the Lord. ²⁹He talked and debated with the Grecian Jews, but they tried to kill him. ³⁰When the brothers learned of this, they took him down to Caesarea and sent him off to Tarsus.

³¹Then the church throughout Judea, Galilee and Samaria enjoyed a time of peace. It was strengthened; and encouraged by the Holy Spirit, it grew in numbers, living in the fear of the Lord.

³²As Peter traveled about the country, he went to visit the saints in Lydda. ³³There he found a man named Aeneas, a paralytic who had been bedridden for eight years. ³⁴"Aeneas," Peter said to him, "Jesus Christ heals you. Get up and take care of your mat." Immediately Aeneas got up. ³⁵All those who lived in Lydda and Sharon saw him and turned to the Lord.

³⁶In Joppa there was a disciple named Tabitha (which, when translated, is Dorcasᵖ), who was always doing good and helping the poor. ³⁷About that time she became sick and died, and her body was washed and placed in an upstairs room. ³⁸Lydda was near Joppa; so when the disciples heard that Peter was in Lydda, they sent two men to him and urged him, "Please come at once!"

³⁹Peter went with them, and when he arrived he was taken upstairs to the room. All the widows stood around him, crying and showing him the robes and other clothing that Dorcas had made while she was still with them.

⁴⁰Peter sent them all out of the room; then he got down on his knees and prayed. Turning toward the dead woman, he said, "Tabitha, get up." She opened her

ᵒ22 Or Messiah   ᵖ36 Both Tabitha (Aramaic) and Dorcas (Greek) mean gazelle.

eyes, and seeing Peter she sat up. [41]He took her by the hand and helped her to her feet. Then he called the believers and the widows and presented her to them alive. [42]This became known all over Joppa, and many people believed in the Lord. [43]Peter stayed in Joppa for some time with a tanner named Simon.

NOVEMBER 4 □ DAY 309
ACTS 10–12
Propagation of the Church

OVERVIEW After his encounter with the Ethiopian, Philip the evangelist leaves for Caesarea and is not mentioned again until chapter 21. Another resident of Caesarea—a Gentile centurion named Cornelius—becomes the first non-Jewish convert to Christianity. God gives Peter a thrice-repeated vision to break down centuries of deep-seated prejudice between Jew and Gentile, setting the stage for the third and most expansive phase of the gospel advance—this time to the remotest corners of the known world.

Chapter 10	Chapter 11	Chapter 12
Peter's Revelation	Peter's Explanation	Peter's Incarceration
Vision	Vindication	Vast Expansion

YOUR DAILY WALK Using a dictionary (or better yet, a medical dictionary), look up the following words: *spleen, pancreas, kidney, pituitary gland, hypothalamus.*

What do they all have in common? Here are two suggestions:
1. They are hidden from view.
2. They are essential to the proper functioning of the body.

We find it easier to go to church than to be the church.

It's easy to be aware of the visible parts of an organism—whether it's a human body or the body of Christ. But just as vital—and perhaps more so—are those parts you never see and seldom think about.

A diabetic may look perfectly healthy at a casual glance. But deep within this person's body a single organ has ceased to make its essential contribution, and, as a result, the entire body suffers. In the church at Antioch, Barnabas and Saul taught (11:26), but countless others exercised the gifts of giving, helps, mercy and prayer to undergird their ministry (11:29; 12:5). One without the other would have left the church anemic and ineffective. Have you discovered the role God wants you to play in your local church? If not, your minister or church leader would be delighted to help you find it . . . and fill it!

INSIGHT The Third Time's a Charm
For Peter, almost every major lesson had to be repeated three times before he got the message. Three times he denied the Lord (Matthew 26:69–75); three times he was commanded by Christ to feed God's sheep (John 21:15–17); and three times the sheet rose and fell before Peter saw the significance of it (Acts 10:9–16).

CHAPTER 10

At Caesarea there was a man named Cornelius, a centurion in what was known as the Italian Regiment. [2]He and all his family were devout and God-fearing; he gave generously to those in need and prayed to God regularly. [3]One day at about three in the afternoon he had a vision. He distinctly saw an angel of God, who came to him and said, "Cornelius!"

[4]Cornelius stared at him in fear. "What is it, Lord?" he asked.

The angel answered, "Your prayers and gifts to the poor have come up as a memorial offering before God. [5]Now send men to Joppa to bring back a man named Simon who is called Peter. [6]He is staying with Simon the tanner, whose house is by the sea."

[7]When the angel who spoke to him had gone, Cornelius called two of his servants and a devout soldier who was one of his attendants. [8]He told them everything that had happened and sent them to Joppa.

[9]About noon the following day as they were on their journey and approaching the city, Peter went up on the roof to pray. [10]He became hungry and wanted something to eat, and while the meal was being prepared, he fell into a trance. [11]He saw heaven opened and something like a large sheet being let down to earth by its four corners. [12]It contained all kinds of four-footed animals, as well as reptiles of the earth and birds of the air. [13]Then a voice told him, "Get up, Peter. Kill and eat."

[14]"Surely not, Lord!" Peter replied. "I have never eaten anything impure or unclean."

[15]The voice spoke to him a second time, "Do not call anything impure that God has made clean."

[16]This happened three times, and immediately the sheet was taken back to heaven.

[17]While Peter was wondering about the meaning of the vision, the men sent by Cornelius found out where Simon's house was and stopped at the gate. [18]They called out, asking if Simon who was known as Peter was staying there.

[19]While Peter was still thinking about the vision, the Spirit said to him, "Simon, three[q] men are looking for you. [20]So get up and go downstairs. Do not hesitate to go with them, for I have sent them."

[21]Peter went down and said to the men, "I'm the one you're looking for. Why have you come?"

[22]The men replied, "We have come from Cornelius the centurion. He is a righteous and God-fearing man, who is respected by all the Jewish people. A holy angel told him to have you come to his house so that he could hear what you have to say." [23]Then Peter invited the men into the house to be his guests.

The next day Peter started out with them, and some of the brothers from Joppa went along. [24]The following day he arrived in Caesarea. Cornelius was expecting them and had called together his relatives and close friends. [25]As Peter entered the house, Cornelius met him and fell at his feet in reverence. [26]But Peter made him get up. "Stand up," he said, "I am only a man myself."

[27]Talking with him, Peter went inside and found a large gathering of people. [28]He said to them: "You are well aware that it is against our law for a Jew to associate with a Gentile or visit him. But God has shown me that I should not call any man impure or unclean. [29]So when I was sent for, I came without raising any objection. May I ask why you sent for me?"

[30]Cornelius answered: "Four days ago I was in my house praying at this hour, at three in the afternoon. Suddenly a man in shining clothes stood before me [31]and said, 'Cornelius, God has heard your prayer and remembered your gifts to the poor. [32]Send to Joppa for Simon who is called Peter. He is a guest in the home of Simon the tanner, who lives by the sea.' [33]So I sent for you immediately, and it was good of you to come. Now we are all here in the presence of God to listen to everything the Lord has commanded you to tell us."

[34]Then Peter began to speak: "I now realize how true it is that God does not show favoritism [35]but accepts men from every nation who fear him and do what is right. [36]You know the message God sent to the people of Israel, telling the good news of peace through Jesus Christ, who is Lord of all. [37]You know what has happened throughout Judea, beginning in

---

q19 One early manuscript *two*; other manuscripts do not have the number.

Galilee after the baptism that John preached— [38]how God anointed Jesus of Nazareth with the Holy Spirit and power, and how he went around doing good and healing all who were under the power of the devil, because God was with him.

[39]"We are witnesses of everything he did in the country of the Jews and in Jerusalem. They killed him by hanging him on a tree, [40]but God raised him from the dead on the third day and caused him to be seen. [41]He was not seen by all the people, but by witnesses whom God had already chosen—by us who ate and drank with him after he rose from the dead. [42]He commanded us to preach to the people and to testify that he is the one whom God appointed as judge of the living and the dead. [43]All the prophets testify about him that everyone who believes in him receives forgiveness of sins through his name."

[44]While Peter was still speaking these words, the Holy Spirit came on all who heard the message. [45]The circumcised believers who had come with Peter were astonished that the gift of the Holy Spirit had been poured out even on the Gentiles. [46]For they heard them speaking in tongues[r] and praising God.

Then Peter said, [47]"Can anyone keep these people from being baptized with water? They have received the Holy Spirit just as we have." [48]So he ordered that they be baptized in the name of Jesus Christ. Then they asked Peter to stay with them for a few days.

CHAPTER 11

The apostles and the brothers throughout Judea heard that the Gentiles also had received the word of God. [2]So when Peter went up to Jerusalem, the circumcised believers criticized him [3]and said, "You went into the house of uncircumcised men and ate with them."

[4]Peter began and explained everything to them precisely as it had happened: [5]"I was in the city of Joppa praying, and in a trance I saw a vision. I saw something like a large sheet being let down from heaven by its four corners, and it came down to

where I was. [6]I looked into it and saw four-footed animals of the earth, wild beasts, reptiles, and birds of the air. [7]Then I heard a voice telling me, 'Get up, Peter. Kill and eat.'

[8]"I replied, 'Surely not, Lord! Nothing impure or unclean has ever entered my mouth.'

[9]"The voice spoke from heaven a second time, 'Do not call anything impure that God has made clean.' [10]This happened three times, and then it was all pulled up to heaven again.

[11]"Right then three men who had been sent to me from Caesarea stopped at the house where I was staying. [12]The Spirit told me to have no hesitation about going with them. These six brothers also went with me, and we entered the man's house. [13]He told us how he had seen an angel appear in his house and say, 'Send to Joppa for Simon who is called Peter. [14]He will bring you a message through which you and all your household will be saved.'

[15]"As I began to speak, the Holy Spirit came on them as he had come on us at the beginning. [16]Then I remembered what the Lord had said: 'John baptized with[s] water, but you will be baptized with the Holy Spirit.' [17]So if God gave them the same gift as he gave us, who believed in the Lord Jesus Christ, who was I to think that I could oppose God?"

[18]When they heard this, they had no further objections and praised God, saying, "So then, God has granted even the Gentiles repentance unto life."

[19]Now those who had been scattered by the persecution in connection with Stephen traveled as far as Phoenicia, Cyprus and Antioch, telling the message only to Jews. [20]Some of them, however, men from Cyprus and Cyrene, went to Antioch and began to speak to Greeks also, telling them the good news about the Lord Jesus. [21]The Lord's hand was with them, and a great number of people believed and turned to the Lord.

[22]News of this reached the ears of the church at Jerusalem, and they sent Barnabas to Antioch. [23]When he arrived and saw the evidence of the grace of God, he was glad and encouraged them all to remain true to the Lord with all their hearts.

[r]46 Or other languages   [s]16 Or in

²⁴He was a good man, full of the Holy Spirit and faith, and a great number of people were brought to the Lord.

²⁵Then Barnabas went to Tarsus to look for Saul, ²⁶and when he found him, he brought him to Antioch. So for a whole year Barnabas and Saul met with the church and taught great numbers of people. The disciples were called Christians first at Antioch.

²⁷During this time some prophets came down from Jerusalem to Antioch. ²⁸One of them, named Agabus, stood up and through the Spirit predicted that a severe famine would spread over the entire Roman world. (This happened during the reign of Claudius.) ²⁹The disciples, each according to his ability, decided to provide help for the brothers living in Judea. ³⁰This they did, sending their gift to the elders by Barnabas and Saul.

CHAPTER 12

It was about this time that King Herod arrested some who belonged to the church, intending to persecute them. ²He had James, the brother of John, put to death with the sword. ³When he saw that this pleased the Jews, he proceeded to seize Peter also. This happened during the Feast of Unleavened Bread. ⁴After arresting him, he put him in prison, handing him over to be guarded by four squads of four soldiers each. Herod intended to bring him out for public trial after the Passover.

⁵So Peter was kept in prison, but the church was earnestly praying to God for him.

⁶The night before Herod was to bring him to trial, Peter was sleeping between two soldiers, bound with two chains, and sentries stood guard at the entrance. ⁷Suddenly an angel of the Lord appeared and a light shone in the cell. He struck Peter on the side and woke him up. "Quick, get up!" he said, and the chains fell off Peter's wrists.

⁸Then the angel said to him, "Put on your clothes and sandals." And Peter did so. "Wrap your cloak around you and follow me," the angel told him. ⁹Peter followed him out of the prison, but he had no idea that what the angel was doing

was really happening; he thought he was seeing a vision. ¹⁰They passed the first and second guards and came to the iron gate leading to the city. It opened for them by itself, and they went through it. When they had walked the length of one street, suddenly the angel left him.

¹¹Then Peter came to himself and said, "Now I know without a doubt that the Lord sent his angel and rescued me from Herod's clutches and from everything the Jewish people were anticipating."

¹²When this had dawned on him, he went to the house of Mary the mother of John, also called Mark, where many people had gathered and were praying. ¹³Peter knocked at the outer entrance, and a servant girl named Rhoda came to answer the door. ¹⁴When she recognized Peter's voice, she was so overjoyed she ran back without opening it and exclaimed, "Peter is at the door!"

¹⁵"You're out of your mind," they told her. When she kept insisting that it was so, they said, "It must be his angel."

¹⁶But Peter kept on knocking, and when they opened the door and saw him, they were astonished. ¹⁷Peter motioned with his hand for them to be quiet and described how the Lord had brought him out of prison. "Tell James and the brothers about this," he said, and then he left for another place.

¹⁸In the morning, there was no small commotion among the soldiers as to what had become of Peter. ¹⁹After Herod had a thorough search made for him and did not find him, he cross-examined the guards and ordered that they be executed.

Then Herod went from Judea to Caesarea and stayed there a while. ²⁰He had been quarreling with the people of Tyre and Sidon; they now joined together and sought an audience with him. Having secured the support of Blastus, a trusted personal servant of the king, they asked for peace, because they depended on the king's country for their food supply.

²¹On the appointed day Herod, wearing his royal robes, sat on his throne and delivered a public address to the

people. ²²They shouted, "This is the voice of a god, not of a man." ²³Immediately, because Herod did not give praise to God, an angel of the Lord struck him down, and he was eaten by worms and died.

²⁵ Some manuscripts to

²⁴But the word of God continued to increase and spread.

²⁵When Barnabas and Saul had finished their mission, they returned from¹ Jerusalem, taking with them John, also called Mark.

NOVEMBER 5 □ DAY 310
ACTS 13–15
Paul's First Journey

OVERVIEW Beginning with chapter 13, Syrian Antioch replaces Jerusalem as the missionary headquarters of the church. While five men are ministering in the church at Antioch, the Holy Spirit selects two to spearhead phase three of the gospel advance, this time "to the ends of the earth" (1:8). Paul and Barnabas leave for Cyprus, making stops in Antioch, Iconium, Lystra and Derbe before returning home to Jerusalem. There they find that their success in making Gentile converts has caused a major dispute among Jewish believers, prompting an all-church council to settle the matter.

Chapter 13	Chapter 14	Chapter 15
Commission of Saul and Barnabas	Mission to Iconium, Lystra and Derbe	Circumcision in Question
First Missionary Journey		First Church Council

YOUR DAILY WALK Ask ten Christians, "Who is the greatest missionary in the New Testament apart from Jesus Christ?" and chances are at least nine will answer without hesitation, "The apostle Paul!"

But did you ever stop to consider that missionaries today face even greater challenges than Paul did in his day? For example:

The more we know the mind of Christ, the more missionary-minded we become.

Paul did not need to learn a foreign language. Every part of the known world spoke the same universal language—Greek.

Paul did not need to adjust to a foreign culture. Rome ruled the known world, providing the same rights and privileges for Roman citizens worldwide. A little bit of Rome awaited Paul everywhere he went. Not so for today's overseas missionaries!

Repeatedly in his letters, Paul asked for prayer as he traveled and ministered (see Colossians 4:3 and 1 Thessalonians 5:25, for example). Don't your missionaries today deserve the same? Locate a picture of a missionary family you or your church supports, and place it in a prominent place at your home or office. Then make Philippians 1:3–4 your daily discipline in prayer on their behalf!

INSIGHT A Preview of Paul's Travels

Journey	Length	Locale	Personnel
#1	2 years	Galatia	Paul and Barnabas
#2	3 years	Macedonia/ Achaia	Paul and Silas
#3	4 years	Asia Minor	Paul and others

CHAPTER 13

In the church at Antioch there were prophets and teachers: Barnabas, Simeon called Niger, Lucius of Cyrene, Manaen (who had been brought up with Herod the tetrarch) and Saul. [2]While they were worshiping the Lord and fasting, the Holy Spirit said, "Set apart for me Barnabas and Saul for the work to which I have called them." [3]So after they had fasted and prayed, they placed their hands on them and sent them off.

[4]The two of them, sent on their way by the Holy Spirit, went down to Seleucia and sailed from there to Cyprus. [5]When they arrived at Salamis, they proclaimed the word of God in the Jewish synagogues. John was with them as their helper.

[6]They traveled through the whole island until they came to Paphos. There they met a Jewish sorcerer and false prophet named Bar-Jesus, [7]who was an attendant of the proconsul, Sergius Paulus. The proconsul, an intelligent man, sent for Barnabas and Saul because he wanted to hear the word of God. [8]But Elymas the sorcerer (for that is what his name means) opposed them and tried to turn the proconsul from the faith. [9]Then Saul, who was also called Paul, filled with the Holy Spirit, looked straight at Elymas and said, [10]"You are a child of the devil and an enemy of everything that is right! You are full of all kinds of deceit and trickery. Will you never stop perverting the right ways of the Lord? [11]Now the hand of the Lord is against you. You are going to be blind, and for a time you will be unable to see the light of the sun."

Immediately mist and darkness came over him, and he groped about, seeking someone to lead him by the hand. [12]When the proconsul saw what had happened, he believed, for he was amazed at the teaching about the Lord.

[13]From Paphos, Paul and his companions sailed to Perga in Pamphylia, where John left them to return to Jerusalem. [14]From Perga they went on to Pisidian Antioch. On the Sabbath they entered the synagogue and sat down. [15]After the reading from the Law and the Prophets, the synagogue rulers sent word to them, saying, "Brothers, if you have a message of encouragement for the people, please speak."

[16]Standing up, Paul motioned with his hand and said: "Men of Israel and you Gentiles who worship God, listen to me! [17]The God of the people of Israel chose our fathers; he made the people prosper during their stay in Egypt, with mighty power he led them out of that country, [18]he endured their conduct[u] for about forty years in the desert, [19]he overthrew seven nations in Canaan and gave their land to his people as their inheritance. [20]All this took about 450 years.

"After this, God gave them judges until the time of Samuel the prophet. [21]Then the people asked for a king, and he gave them Saul son of Kish, of the tribe of Benjamin, who ruled forty years. [22]After removing Saul, he made David their king. He testified concerning him: 'I have found David son of Jesse a man after my own heart; he will do everything I want him to do.'

[23]"From this man's descendants God has brought to Israel the Savior Jesus, as he promised. [24]Before the coming of Jesus, John preached repentance and baptism to all the people of Israel. [25]As John was completing his work, he said: 'Who do you think I am? I am not that one. No, but he is coming after me, whose sandals I am not worthy to untie.'

[26]"Brothers, children of Abraham, and you God-fearing Gentiles, it is to us that this message of salvation has been sent. [27]The people of Jerusalem and their rulers did not recognize Jesus, yet in condemning him they fulfilled the words of the prophets that are read every Sabbath. [28]Though they found no proper ground for a death sentence, they asked Pilate to have him executed. [29]When they had carried out all that was written about him, they took him down from the tree and laid him in a tomb. [30]But God raised him from the dead, [31]and for many days he was seen by those who had traveled with him from Galilee to Jerusalem. They are now his witnesses to our people.

[32]"We tell you the good news: What God promised our fathers [33]he has fulfilled for us, their children, by raising up Jesus. As it is written in the second Psalm:

" 'You are my Son;

---

[u]18 Some manuscripts *and cared for them*

today I have become your
Father.*v' w*

34The fact that God raised him from the
dead, never to decay, is stated in these
words:

" 'I will give you the holy and sure
    blessings promised to David.'*x*

35So it is stated elsewhere:

" 'You will not let your Holy One see
    decay.'*y*

36"For when David had served God's
purpose in his own generation, he fell
asleep; he was buried with his fathers and
his body decayed. 37But the one whom
God raised from the dead did not see decay.

38"Therefore, my brothers, I want you to
know that through Jesus the forgiveness
of sins is proclaimed to you. 39Through
him everyone who believes is justified
from everything you could not be justified from by the law of Moses. 40Take care
that what the prophets have said does not
happen to you:

41" 'Look, you scoffers,
    wonder and perish,
for I am going to do something in
        your days
    that you would never believe,
    even if someone told you.'*z*"

42As Paul and Barnabas were leaving
the synagogue, the people invited them to
speak further about these things on the
next Sabbath. 43When the congregation
was dismissed, many of the Jews and devout converts to Judaism followed Paul
and Barnabas, who talked with them and
urged them to continue in the grace of
God.

44On the next Sabbath almost the whole
city gathered to hear the word of the
Lord. 45When the Jews saw the crowds,
they were filled with jealousy and talked
abusively against what Paul was saying.

46Then Paul and Barnabas answered
them boldly: "We had to speak the word
of God to you first. Since you reject it and
do not consider yourselves worthy of
eternal life, we now turn to the Gentiles.
47For this is what the Lord has commanded us:

" 'I have made you*a* a light for the
    Gentiles,
that you*a* may bring salvation to
    the ends of the earth.'*b*"

48When the Gentiles heard this, they
were glad and honored the word of the
Lord; and all who were appointed for
eternal life believed.

49The word of the Lord spread through
the whole region. 50But the Jews incited
the God-fearing women of high standing
and the leading men of the city. They
stirred up persecution against Paul and
Barnabas, and expelled them from their
region. 51So they shook the dust from
their feet in protest against them and
went to Iconium. 52And the disciples were
filled with joy and with the Holy Spirit.

CHAPTER 14
At Iconium Paul and Barnabas went as
usual into the Jewish synagogue. There
they spoke so effectively that a great
number of Jews and Gentiles believed.
2But the Jews who refused to believe
stirred up the Gentiles and poisoned their
minds against the brothers. 3So Paul and
Barnabas spent considerable time there,
speaking boldly for the Lord, who confirmed the message of his grace by enabling them to do miraculous signs and
wonders. 4The people of the city were divided; some sided with the Jews, others
with the apostles. 5There was a plot afoot
among the Gentiles and Jews, together
with their leaders, to mistreat them and
stone them. 6But they found out about it
and fled to the Lycaonian cities of Lystra
and Derbe and to the surrounding country, 7where they continued to preach the
good news.

8In Lystra there sat a man crippled in
his feet, who was lame from birth and had
never walked. 9He listened to Paul as he
was speaking. Paul looked directly at
him, saw that he had faith to be healed
10and called out, "Stand up on your feet!"
At that, the man jumped up and began to
walk.

11When the crowd saw what Paul had
done, they shouted in the Lycaonian language, "The gods have come down to us
in human form!" 12Barnabas they called
Zeus, and Paul they called Hermes be-

v 33 Or have begotten you   w 33 Psalm 2:7   x 34 Isaiah 55:3   y 35 Psalm 16:10   z 41 Hab. 1:5   a 47 The Greek is singular.
b 47 Isaiah 49:6

cause he was the chief speaker. [13]The priest of Zeus, whose temple was just outside the city, brought bulls and wreaths to the city gates because he and the crowd wanted to offer sacrifices to them.

[14]But when the apostles Barnabas and Paul heard of this, they tore their clothes and rushed out into the crowd, shouting: [15]"Men, why are you doing this? We too are only men, human like you. We are bringing you good news, telling you to turn from these worthless things to the living God, who made heaven and earth and sea and everything in them. [16]In the past, he let all nations go their own way. [17]Yet he has not left himself without testimony: He has shown kindness by giving you rain from heaven and crops in their seasons; he provides you with plenty of food and fills your hearts with joy." [18]Even with these words, they had difficulty keeping the crowd from sacrificing to them.

[19]Then some Jews came from Antioch and Iconium and won the crowd over. They stoned Paul and dragged him outside the city, thinking he was dead. [20]But after the disciples had gathered around him, he got up and went back into the city. The next day he and Barnabas left for Derbe.

[21]They preached the good news in that city and won a large number of disciples. Then they returned to Lystra, Iconium and Antioch, [22]strengthening the disciples and encouraging them to remain true to the faith. "We must go through many hardships to enter the kingdom of God," they said. [23]Paul and Barnabas appointed elders[c] for them in each church and, with prayer and fasting, committed them to the Lord, in whom they had put their trust. [24]After going through Pisidia, they came into Pamphylia, [25]and when they had preached the word in Perga, they went down to Attalia.

[26]From Attalia they sailed back to Antioch, where they had been committed to the grace of God for the work they had now completed. [27]On arriving there, they gathered the church together and reported all that God had done through them and how he had opened the door of faith to the Gentiles. [28]And they stayed there a long time with the disciples.

CHAPTER 15

Some men came down from Judea to Antioch and were teaching the brothers: "Unless you are circumcised, according to the custom taught by Moses, you cannot be saved." [2]This brought Paul and Barnabas into sharp dispute and debate with them. So Paul and Barnabas were appointed, along with some other believers, to go up to Jerusalem to see the apostles and elders about this question. [3]The church sent them on their way, and as they traveled through Phoenicia and Samaria, they told how the Gentiles had been converted. This news made all the brothers very glad. [4]When they came to Jerusalem, they were welcomed by the church and the apostles and elders, to whom they reported everything God had done through them.

[5]Then some of the believers who belonged to the party of the Pharisees stood up and said, "The Gentiles must be circumcised and required to obey the law of Moses."

[6]The apostles and elders met to consider this question. [7]After much discussion, Peter got up and addressed them: "Brothers, you know that some time ago God made a choice among you that the Gentiles might hear from my lips the message of the gospel and believe. [8]God, who knows the heart, showed that he accepted them by giving the Holy Spirit to them, just as he did to us. [9]He made no distinction between us and them, for he purified their hearts by faith. [10]Now then, why do you try to test God by putting on the necks of the disciples a yoke that neither we nor our fathers have been able to bear? [11]No! We believe it is through the grace of our Lord Jesus that we are saved, just as they are."

[12]The whole assembly became silent as they listened to Barnabas and Paul telling about the miraculous signs and wonders God had done among the Gentiles through them. [13]When they finished, James spoke up: "Brothers, listen to me. [14]Simon[d] has described to us how God at first showed his concern by taking from the Gentiles a people for himself. [15]The

---

[c]23 Or Barnabas ordained elders; or Barnabas had elders elected   [d]14 Greek Simeon, a variant of Simon; that is, Peter

words of the prophets are in agreement with this, as it is written:

16" 'After this I will return
    and rebuild David's fallen tent.
Its ruins I will rebuild,
    and I will restore it,
17that the remnant of men may seek the
        Lord,
    and all the Gentiles who bear my
        name,
says the Lord, who does these
        things'ᵉ
18   that have been known for ages.ᶠ

19"It is my judgment, therefore, that we should not make it difficult for the Gentiles who are turning to God. 20Instead we should write to them, telling them to abstain from food polluted by idols, from sexual immorality, from the meat of strangled animals and from blood. 21For Moses has been preached in every city from the earliest times and is read in the synagogues on every Sabbath."

22Then the apostles and elders, with the whole church, decided to choose some of their own men and send them to Antioch with Paul and Barnabas. They chose Judas (called Barsabbas) and Silas, two men who were leaders among the brothers. 23With them they sent the following letter:

The apostles and elders, your brothers,

To the Gentile believers in Antioch, Syria and Cilicia:

Greetings.

24We have heard that some went out from us without our authorization and disturbed you, troubling your minds by what they said. 25So we all agreed to choose some men and send them to you with our dear friends Barnabas and Paul— 26men

who have risked their lives for the name of our Lord Jesus Christ. 27Therefore we are sending Judas and Silas to confirm by word of mouth what we are writing. 28It seemed good to the Holy Spirit and to us not to burden you with anything beyond the following requirements: 29You are to abstain from food sacrificed to idols, from blood, from the meat of strangled animals and from sexual immorality. You will do well to avoid these things.

Farewell.

30The men were sent off and went down to Antioch, where they gathered the church together and delivered the letter. 31The people read it and were glad for its encouraging message. 32Judas and Silas, who themselves were prophets, said much to encourage and strengthen the brothers. 33After spending some time there, they were sent off by the brothers with the blessing of peace to return to those who had sent them.ᵍ 35But Paul and Barnabas remained in Antioch, where they and many others taught and preached the word of the Lord.

36Some time later Paul said to Barnabas, "Let us go back and visit the brothers in all the towns where we preached the word of the Lord and see how they are doing." 37Barnabas wanted to take John, also called Mark, with them, 38but Paul did not think it wise to take him, because he had deserted them in Pamphylia and had not continued with them in the work. 39They had such a sharp disagreement that they parted company. Barnabas took Mark and sailed for Cyprus, 40but Paul chose Silas and left, commended by the brothers to the grace of the Lord. 41He went through Syria and Cilicia, strengthening the churches.

ᵉ17 Amos 9:11,12   ᶠ17,18 Some manuscripts things'— / ¹⁸known to the Lord for ages is his work   ᵍ33 Some manuscripts them, ³⁴but Silas decided to remain there

NOVEMBER 6 □ DAY 311
ACTS 16–18
Paul's Second Journey

OVERVIEW John Mark, Barnabas's cousin and a traveling companion for part of the first journey, becomes the focus of a sharp dispute between Paul and Barnabas. As a result, the two veteran missionaries part company. Barnabas stays with Mark and sails for Cyprus. Paul, accompanied by Silas and Timothy, travels more than three thousand miles, planting and building up churches in Macedonia, Achaia and Greece.

Chapter 16	Chapter 17	Chapter 18
Entrance to Europe	Trouble in Thessalonica	Co-laborers in Corinth
Paul's Second Missionary Journey		

YOUR DAILY WALK Disagreements in the church are nothing new. Even Paul and Barnabas had a falling-out! But we can learn much from the way they wisely resolved their conflict.

Force may subdue, but love gains; and he that forgives first wins the laurel.

The reason for their sharp disagreement was John Mark, who had left the team midway through the first journey. Barnabas (whose name means "son of encouragement") was concerned primarily for the *worker* and wanted to give his cousin a second chance. Paul, on the other hand, was more concerned about the *work*, not wanting to lose the momentum of the first journey through another desertion. In the end they parted company to form two gospel teams instead of one. The impact of Paul's second journey is well documented in today's section. And in Colossians 4:10 and 2 Timothy 4:11, Paul himself warmly notes John Mark's contribution to his ministry.

Being reconciled does not always mean holding the same view. Sometimes it can mean agreeing to disagree in a spirit of love and humility. Are you having a disagreement today? Take the first step toward reconciling it by assuring the other person, "I accept you as you are; let's support one another as we labor for God's glory."

INSIGHT Called by a Man, Confronted by a Woman
In his vision Paul saw a "man of Macedonia" (16:9) pleading with him to come to Europe with the message of Good News. But when Paul arrived in Philippi, there were no God-fearing men to be found. Undaunted, Paul began working instead with women. Result: The first Macedonian convert to Christianity was not a man at all! (Can you find her name in today's section?)

CHAPTER 16

He came to Derbe and then to Lystra, where a disciple named Timothy lived, whose mother was a Jewess and a believer, but whose father was a Greek. ²The brothers at Lystra and Iconium spoke well of him. ³Paul wanted to take him along on the journey, so he circumcised him because of the Jews who lived in that area, for they all knew that his father was a Greek. ⁴As they traveled from town to town, they delivered the decisions reached by the apostles and elders in Jerusalem for the people to obey. ⁵So the churches were strengthened in the faith and grew daily in numbers.

⁶Paul and his companions traveled throughout the region of Phrygia and Galatia, having been kept by the Holy Spirit from preaching the word in the province of Asia. ⁷When they came to the border of Mysia, they tried to enter Bithynia, but

the Spirit of Jesus would not allow them to. [8]So they passed by Mysia and went down to Troas. [9]During the night Paul had a vision of a man of Macedonia standing and begging him, "Come over to Macedonia and help us." [10]After Paul had seen the vision, we got ready at once to leave for Macedonia, concluding that God had called us to preach the gospel to them.

[11]From Troas we put out to sea and sailed straight for Samothrace, and the next day on to Neapolis. [12]From there we traveled to Philippi, a Roman colony and the leading city of that district of Macedonia. And we stayed there several days.

[13]On the Sabbath we went outside the city gate to the river, where we expected to find a place of prayer. We sat down and began to speak to the women who had gathered there. [14]One of those listening was a woman named Lydia, a dealer in purple cloth from the city of Thyatira, who was a worshiper of God. The Lord opened her heart to respond to Paul's message. [15]When she and the members of her household were baptized, she invited us to her home. "If you consider me a believer in the Lord," she said, "come and stay at my house." And she persuaded us.

[16]Once when we were going to the place of prayer, we were met by a slave girl who had a spirit by which she predicted the future. She earned a great deal of money for her owners by fortune-telling. [17]This girl followed Paul and the rest of us, shouting, "These men are servants of the Most High God, who are telling you the way to be saved." [18]She kept this up for many days. Finally Paul became so troubled that he turned around and said to the spirit, "In the name of Jesus Christ I command you to come out of her!" At that moment the spirit left her.

[19]When the owners of the slave girl realized that their hope of making money was gone, they seized Paul and Silas and dragged them into the marketplace to face the authorities. [20]They brought them before the magistrates and said, "These men are Jews, and are throwing our city into an uproar [21]by advocating customs unlawful for us Romans to accept or practice."

[22]The crowd joined in the attack against Paul and Silas, and the magistrates ordered them to be stripped and beaten.

[23]After they had been severely flogged, they were thrown into prison, and the jailer was commanded to guard them carefully. [24]Upon receiving such orders, he put them in the inner cell and fastened their feet in the stocks.

[25]About midnight Paul and Silas were praying and singing hymns to God, and the other prisoners were listening to them. [26]Suddenly there was such a violent earthquake that the foundations of the prison were shaken. At once all the prison doors flew open, and everybody's chains came loose. [27]The jailer woke up, and when he saw the prison doors open, he drew his sword and was about to kill himself because he thought the prisoners had escaped. [28]But Paul shouted, "Don't harm yourself! We are all here!"

[29]The jailer called for lights, rushed in and fell trembling before Paul and Silas. [30]He then brought them out and asked, "Sirs, what must I do to be saved?"

[31]They replied, "Believe in the Lord Jesus, and you will be saved—you and your household." [32]Then they spoke the word of the Lord to him and to all the others in his house. [33]At that hour of the night the jailer took them and washed their wounds; then immediately he and all his family were baptized. [34]The jailer brought them into his house and set a meal before them; he was filled with joy because he had come to believe in God—he and his whole family.

[35]When it was daylight, the magistrates sent their officers to the jailer with the order: "Release those men." [36]The jailer told Paul, "The magistrates have ordered that you and Silas be released. Now you can leave. Go in peace."

[37]But Paul said to the officers: "They beat us publicly without a trial, even though we are Roman citizens, and threw us into prison. And now do they want to get rid of us quietly? No! Let them come themselves and escort us out."

[38]The officers reported this to the magistrates, and when they heard that Paul and Silas were Roman citizens, they were alarmed. [39]They came to appease them and escorted them from the prison, requesting them to leave the city. [40]After Paul and Silas came out of the prison, they went to Lydia's house, where they met with the brothers and encouraged them. Then they left.

CHAPTER 17

When they had passed through Amphipolis and Apollonia, they came to Thessalonica, where there was a Jewish synagogue. [2]As his custom was, Paul went into the synagogue, and on three Sabbath days he reasoned with them from the Scriptures, [3]explaining and proving that the Christ[h] had to suffer and rise from the dead. "This Jesus I am proclaiming to you is the Christ,[h]" he said. [4]Some of the Jews were persuaded and joined Paul and Silas, as did a large number of God-fearing Greeks and not a few prominent women.

[5]But the Jews were jealous; so they rounded up some bad characters from the marketplace, formed a mob and started a riot in the city. They rushed to Jason's house in search of Paul and Silas in order to bring them out to the crowd.[i] [6]But when they did not find them, they dragged Jason and some other brothers before the city officials, shouting: "These men who have caused trouble all over the world have now come here, [7]and Jason has welcomed them into his house. They are all defying Caesar's decrees, saying that there is another king, one called Jesus." [8]When they heard this, the crowd and the city officials were thrown into turmoil. [9]Then they made Jason and the others post bond and let them go.

[10]As soon as it was night, the brothers sent Paul and Silas away to Berea. On arriving there, they went to the Jewish synagogue. [11]Now the Bereans were of more noble character than the Thessalonians, for they received the message with great eagerness and examined the Scriptures every day to see if what Paul said was true. [12]Many of the Jews believed, as did also a number of prominent Greek women and many Greek men.

[13]When the Jews in Thessalonica learned that Paul was preaching the word of God at Berea, they went there too, agitating the crowds and stirring them up. [14]The brothers immediately sent Paul to the coast, but Silas and Timothy stayed at Berea. [15]The men who escorted Paul brought him to Athens and then left with instructions for Silas and Timothy to join him as soon as possible.

[16]While Paul was waiting for them in Athens, he was greatly distressed to see that the city was full of idols. [17]So he reasoned in the synagogue with the Jews and the God-fearing Greeks, as well as in the marketplace day by day with those who happened to be there. [18]A group of Epicurean and Stoic philosophers began to dispute with him. Some of them asked, "What is this babbler trying to say?" Others remarked, "He seems to be advocating foreign gods." They said this because Paul was preaching the good news about Jesus and the resurrection. [19]Then they took him and brought him to a meeting of the Areopagus, where they said to him, "May we know what this new teaching is that you are presenting? [20]You are bringing some strange ideas to our ears, and we want to know what they mean." [21](All the Athenians and the foreigners who lived there spent their time doing nothing but talking about and listening to the latest ideas.)

[22]Paul then stood up in the meeting of the Areopagus and said: "Men of Athens! I see that in every way you are very religious. [23]For as I walked around and looked carefully at your objects of worship, I even found an altar with this inscription: TO AN UNKNOWN GOD. Now what you worship as something unknown I am going to proclaim to you.

[24]"The God who made the world and everything in it is the Lord of heaven and earth and does not live in temples built by hands. [25]And he is not served by human hands, as if he needed anything, because he himself gives all men life and breath and everything else. [26]From one man he made every nation of men, that they should inhabit the whole earth; and he determined the times set for them and the exact places where they should live. [27]God did this so that men would seek him and perhaps reach out for him and find him, though he is not far from each one of us. [28]'For in him we live and move and have our being.' As some of your own poets have said, 'We are his offspring.'

[29]"Therefore since we are God's offspring, we should not think that the divine being is like gold or silver or stone—an image made by man's design and skill.

[h]3 Or *Messiah*   [i]5 Or *the assembly of the people*

³⁰In the past God overlooked such ignorance, but now he commands all people everywhere to repent. ³¹For he has set a day when he will judge the world with justice by the man he has appointed. He has given proof of this to all men by raising him from the dead."

³²When they heard about the resurrection of the dead, some of them sneered, but others said, "We want to hear you again on this subject." ³³At that, Paul left the Council. ³⁴A few men became followers of Paul and believed. Among them was Dionysius, a member of the Areopagus, also a woman named Damaris, and a number of others.

CHAPTER 18

After this, Paul left Athens and went to Corinth. ²There he met a Jew named Aquila, a native of Pontus, who had recently come from Italy with his wife Priscilla, because Claudius had ordered all the Jews to leave Rome. Paul went to see them, ³and because he was a tentmaker as they were, he stayed and worked with them. ⁴Every Sabbath he reasoned in the synagogue, trying to persuade Jews and Greeks.

⁵When Silas and Timothy came from Macedonia, Paul devoted himself exclusively to preaching, testifying to the Jews that Jesus was the Christ.ʲ ⁶But when the Jews opposed Paul and became abusive, he shook out his clothes in protest and said to them, "Your blood be on your own heads! I am clear of my responsibility. From now on I will go to the Gentiles."

⁷Then Paul left the synagogue and went next door to the house of Titius Justus, a worshiper of God. ⁸Crispus, the synagogue ruler, and his entire household believed in the Lord; and many of the Corinthians who heard him believed and were baptized.

⁹One night the Lord spoke to Paul in a vision: "Do not be afraid; keep on speaking, do not be silent. ¹⁰For I am with you, and no one is going to attack and harm you, because I have many people in this city." ¹¹So Paul stayed for a year and a half, teaching them the word of God.

¹²While Gallio was proconsul of Achaia, the Jews made a united attack on Paul and brought him into court. ¹³"This man," they charged, "is persuading the people to worship God in ways contrary to the law."

¹⁴Just as Paul was about to speak, Gallio said to the Jews, "If you Jews were making a complaint about some misdemeanor or serious crime, it would be reasonable for me to listen to you. ¹⁵But since it involves questions about words and names and your own law—settle the matter yourselves. I will not be a judge of such things." ¹⁶So he had them ejected from the court. ¹⁷Then they all turned on Sosthenes the synagogue ruler and beat him in front of the court. But Gallio showed no concern whatever.

¹⁸Paul stayed on in Corinth for some time. Then he left the brothers and sailed for Syria, accompanied by Priscilla and Aquila. Before he sailed, he had his hair cut off at Cenchrea because of a vow he had taken. ¹⁹They arrived at Ephesus, where Paul left Priscilla and Aquila. He himself went into the synagogue and reasoned with the Jews. ²⁰When they asked him to spend more time with them, he declined. ²¹But as he left, he promised, "I will come back if it is God's will." Then he set sail from Ephesus. ²²When he landed at Caesarea, he went up and greeted the church and then went down to Antioch.

²³After spending some time in Antioch, Paul set out from there and traveled from place to place throughout the region of Galatia and Phrygia, strengthening all the disciples.

²⁴Meanwhile a Jew named Apollos, a native of Alexandria, came to Ephesus. He was a learned man, with a thorough knowledge of the Scriptures. ²⁵He had been instructed in the way of the Lord, and he spoke with great fervorᵏ and taught about Jesus accurately, though he knew only the baptism of John. ²⁶He began to speak boldly in the synagogue. When Priscilla and Aquila heard him, they invited him to their home and explained to him the way of God more adequately.

ʲ5 Or *Messiah*; also in verse 28   ᵏ25 Or *with fervor in the Spirit*

²⁷When Apollos wanted to go to Achaia, the brothers encouraged him and wrote to the disciples there to welcome him. On arriving, he was a great help to those who by grace had believed. ²⁸For he vigorously refuted the Jews in public debate, proving from the Scriptures that Jesus was the Christ.

NOVEMBER 7 ☐ DAY 312
Seeing and Hearing Is Believing

LOOK BACK Jesus' *miracles* were designed to validate his *message*. When he said, "I am the resurrection and the life" (John 11:25), he meant it! And to validate his claim that he was the source of life, he raised Lazarus from the grave.

John's account of the death, burial and resurrection of Jesus is poignant and personal, as befitting the one who was nicknamed the disciple "whom Jesus loved" (John 13:23). The final chapter of John's Gospel tells of a breakfast meeting between Jesus and seven of his disciples. They came to that encounter discouraged and ready to quit; they left fortified with courage to follow their Lord even unto death.

The book of Acts continues the story of Jesus' followers as they go forth in the power of the Spirit to broadcast the news about their risen Leader and Lord. First in Jerusalem, then in Judea and Samaria and finally to the farthest corners of the known world, the New Testament church carries out its marching orders in spite of persecution from without and problems from within.

LOOK UP Two cars collide in the intersection in front of you. From the safety of your own car, you see the entire drama unfold. Now answer the following questions:

Do not expect God to use you as a lighthouse somewhere else if God cannot use you as a candle right where you are.

1. Are you a witness to the accident?
2. If yes, why are you a witness?
3. What did you have to do to become a witness?
4. How sure are you that you are a witness?
5. Would you know what to say if called to the witness stand?
6. And what would that be?

Being a witness for your Lord is no different. Only those who have seen and heard something firsthand about Jesus Christ are eligible to be his witnesses. "That which . . . we have seen with our eyes, which we have looked at and our hands have touched—this we proclaim concerning the Word of life. . . . We proclaim to you what we have seen and heard" (1 John 1:1, 3). If you have seen the miracle of new birth in your own life, then you are a candidate to be a witness for your Lord.

LOOK AHEAD The book of Acts is the exciting account of men and women who bore testimony of the truth they had experienced firsthand. Most of them were not trained preachers or educated philosophers. They were simple people whose lives had been simply touched and transformed for eternity!

After they met Jesus in a life-changing way, he told them to "go and tell." And so, they went and told. And everywhere they went, the power of God was evident. They testified as much by the quality of their lives as by the testimony of their lips.

It's the same today. People all around you may never visit a church or tune in to a Christian radio or television program. But they will listen to the gospel according to you—in your office . . . your home . . .

your neighborhood . . . your school. Why? Because they know you, and they can see with their own eyes and hear with their own ears the difference Jesus has made in your life. They've seen the difference; now they need to know what (or rather, who) has made the difference.

Well, what do you say, witness?

NOVEMBER 8 ☐ DAY 313
ACTS 19–20
Paul's Third Journey

OVERVIEW Turn back to Acts 18:23 to pick up the beginning of Paul's third journey—an expedition that takes him throughout the province of Asia, where he visits churches founded on previous trips. The church at Ephesus hosts Paul for nearly three years, while he conducts a ministry so successful that "all the Jews and Greeks who lived in the province of Asia heard the word of the Lord" (19:10). Leaving Ephesus, Paul visits churches in Macedonia and Achaia before setting sail for Jerusalem and an uncertain future.

Chapter 19		Chapter 20	
Persuasion at Ephesus	Persecution at Ephesus	Travels to Greece	Testimonial to Ephesians
1 22	23 41	1 16	17 38
Paul's Third Missionary Journey			

YOUR DAILY WALK Put yourself in the following situation. You have just received word that an adult bookstore is opening next door to your house or apartment. What is your response? Are you indifferent or indignant? What action would you take?

Our sense of sin is in proportion to our nearness to God.

Paul was surrounded by sinful influences and corrupting pressures during his public ministry. Corinth was notorious for its immorality, Ephesus for its idolatry, Athens for its polytheism. And yet, through the power of the Holy Spirit, Paul was able to move among sinful people, making an impact on their lives for Jesus Christ. In Corinth and Ephesus he left behind growing young churches.

What impact is your life making on sinful people and sinful situations around you? Is your influence for God being felt? Make a list of three or four corrupting influences in your neighborhood that you would like to see changed. Select one item from your list, and make it the focus of your prayer time. Then write your mayor, city council member or congressional representative, and tell him or her about your concern.

INSIGHT Standing Room Only in Ephesus
The Grand Theatre in Ephesus, site of the famous "pro-Artemis, anti-Paul rally," was a large outdoor amphitheater that seated more than twenty-five thousand people—all of whom screamed for two hours, "Great is Artemis of the Ephesians!" (19:34). The site still stands today near Selcuk, Turkey.

CHAPTER 19

While Apollos was at Corinth, Paul took the road through the interior and arrived at Ephesus. There he found some disciples [2]and asked them, "Did you receive the Holy Spirit when[1] you believed?"

They answered, "No, we have not even heard that there is a Holy Spirit."

[3]So Paul asked, "Then what baptism did you receive?"

"John's baptism," they replied.

[4]Paul said, "John's baptism was a baptism of repentance. He told the people to believe in the one coming after him, that is, in Jesus." [5]On hearing this, they were baptized into[m] the name of the Lord Jesus. [6]When Paul placed his hands on them, the Holy Spirit came on them, and they spoke in tongues[n] and prophesied. [7]There were about twelve men in all.

[8]Paul entered the synagogue and spoke boldly there for three months, arguing persuasively about the kingdom of God. [9]But some of them became obstinate; they refused to believe and publicly maligned the Way. So Paul left them. He took the disciples with him and had discussions daily in the lecture hall of Tyrannus. [10]This went on for two years, so that all the Jews and Greeks who lived in the province of Asia heard the word of the Lord.

[11]God did extraordinary miracles through Paul, [12]so that even handkerchiefs and aprons that had touched him were taken to the sick, and their illnesses were cured and the evil spirits left them. [13]Some Jews who went around driving out evil spirits tried to invoke the name of the Lord Jesus over those who were demon-possessed. They would say, "In the name of Jesus, whom Paul preaches, I command you to come out." [14]Seven sons of Sceva, a Jewish chief priest, were doing this. [15]One day, the evil spirit answered them, "Jesus I know, and I know about Paul, but who are you?" [16]Then the man who had the evil spirit jumped on them and overpowered them all. He gave them such a beating that they ran out of the house naked and bleeding.

[17]When this became known to the Jews and Greeks living in Ephesus, they were all seized with fear, and the name of the Lord Jesus was held in high honor. [18]Many of those who believed now came and openly confessed their evil deeds. [19]A number who had practiced sorcery brought their scrolls together and burned them publicly. When they calculated the value of the scrolls, the total came to fifty thousand drachmas.[o] [20]In this way the word of the Lord spread widely and grew in power.

[21]After all this had happened, Paul decided to go to Jerusalem, passing through Macedonia and Achaia. "After I have been there," he said, "I must visit Rome also." [22]He sent two of his helpers, Timothy and Erastus, to Macedonia, while he stayed in the province of Asia a little longer.

[23]About that time there arose a great disturbance about the Way. [24]A silversmith named Demetrius, who made silver shrines of Artemis, brought in no little business for the craftsmen. [25]He called them together, along with the workmen in related trades, and said: "Men, you know we receive a good income from this business. [26]And you see and hear how this fellow Paul has convinced and led astray large numbers of people here in Ephesus and in practically the whole province of Asia. He says that man-made gods are no gods at all. [27]There is danger not only that our trade will lose its good name, but also that the temple of the great goddess Artemis will be discredited, and the goddess herself, who is worshiped throughout the province of Asia and the world, will be robbed of her divine majesty."

[28]When they heard this, they were furious and began shouting: "Great is Artemis of the Ephesians!" [29]Soon the whole city was in an uproar. The people seized Gaius and Aristarchus, Paul's traveling companions from Macedonia, and rushed as one man into the theater. [30]Paul wanted to appear before the crowd, but the disciples would not let him. [31]Even some of the officials of the province, friends of Paul, sent him a message begging him not to venture into the theater.

[32]The assembly was in confusion: Some were shouting one thing, some another. Most of the people did not even know why they were there. [33]The Jews pushed Alexander to the front, and some of the crowd shouted instructions to him. He

[1]2 Or after   [m]5 Or in   [n]6 Or other languages   [o]19 A drachma was a silver coin worth about a day's wages.

motioned for silence in order to make a defense before the people. ³⁴But when they realized he was a Jew, they all shouted in unison for about two hours: "Great is Artemis of the Ephesians!"

³⁵The city clerk quieted the crowd and said: "Men of Ephesus, doesn't all the world know that the city of Ephesus is the guardian of the temple of the great Artemis and of her image, which fell from heaven? ³⁶Therefore, since these facts are undeniable, you ought to be quiet and not do anything rash. ³⁷You have brought these men here, though they have neither robbed temples nor blasphemed our goddess. ³⁸If, then, Demetrius and his fellow craftsmen have a grievance against anybody, the courts are open and there are proconsuls. They can press charges. ³⁹If there is anything further you want to bring up, it must be settled in a legal assembly. ⁴⁰As it is, we are in danger of being charged with rioting because of today's events. In that case we would not be able to account for this commotion, since there is no reason for it." ⁴¹After he had said this, he dismissed the assembly.

CHAPTER 20

When the uproar had ended, Paul sent for the disciples and, after encouraging them, said good-by and set out for Macedonia. ²He traveled through that area, speaking many words of encouragement to the people, and finally arrived in Greece, ³where he stayed three months. Because the Jews made a plot against him just as he was about to sail for Syria, he decided to go back through Macedonia. ⁴He was accompanied by Sopater son of Pyrrhus from Berea, Aristarchus and Secundus from Thessalonica, Gaius from Derbe, Timothy also, and Tychicus and Trophimus from the province of Asia. ⁵These men went on ahead and waited for us at Troas. ⁶But we sailed from Philippi after the Feast of Unleavened Bread, and five days later joined the others at Troas, where we stayed seven days.

⁷On the first day of the week we came together to break bread. Paul spoke to the people and, because he intended to leave the next day, kept on talking until midnight. ⁸There were many lamps in the upstairs room where we were meeting. ⁹Seated in a window was a young man named Eutychus, who was sinking into a deep sleep as Paul talked on and on. When he was sound asleep, he fell to the ground from the third story and was picked up dead. ¹⁰Paul went down, threw himself on the young man and put his arms around him. "Don't be alarmed," he said. "He's alive!" ¹¹Then he went upstairs again and broke bread and ate. After talking until daylight, he left. ¹²The people took the young man home alive and were greatly comforted.

¹³We went on ahead to the ship and sailed for Assos, where we were going to take Paul aboard. He had made this arrangement because he was going there on foot. ¹⁴When he met us at Assos, we took him aboard and went on to Mitylene. ¹⁵The next day we set sail from there and arrived off Kios. The day after that we crossed over to Samos, and on the following day arrived at Miletus. ¹⁶Paul had decided to sail past Ephesus to avoid spending time in the province of Asia, for he was in a hurry to reach Jerusalem, if possible, by the day of Pentecost.

¹⁷From Miletus, Paul sent to Ephesus for the elders of the church. ¹⁸When they arrived, he said to them: "You know how I lived the whole time I was with you, from the first day I came into the province of Asia. ¹⁹I served the Lord with great humility and with tears, although I was severely tested by the plots of the Jews. ²⁰You know that I have not hesitated to preach anything that would be helpful to you but have taught you publicly and from house to house. ²¹I have declared to both Jews and Greeks that they must turn to God in repentance and have faith in our Lord Jesus.

²²"And now, compelled by the Spirit, I am going to Jerusalem, not knowing what will happen to me there. ²³I only know that in every city the Holy Spirit warns me that prison and hardships are facing me. ²⁴However, I consider my life worth nothing to me, if only I may finish the race and complete the task the Lord Jesus has given me—the task of testifying to the gospel of God's grace.

²⁵"Now I know that none of you among whom I have gone about preaching the kingdom will ever see me again. ²⁶Therefore, I declare to you today that I am innocent of the blood of all men. ²⁷For I have not hesitated to proclaim to you the whole will of God. ²⁸Keep watch over

yourselves and all the flock of which the Holy Spirit has made you overseers.ᵖ Be shepherds of the church of God,�q which he bought with his own blood. ²⁹I know that after I leave, savage wolves will come in among you and will not spare the flock. ³⁰Even from your own number men will arise and distort the truth in order to draw away disciples after them. ³¹So be on your guard! Remember that for three years I never stopped warning each of you night and day with tears.

³²"Now I commit you to God and to the word of his grace, which can build you up and give you an inheritance among all those who are sanctified. ³³I have not

p28 Traditionally bishops   q28 Many manuscripts of the Lord

coveted anyone's silver or gold or clothing. ³⁴You yourselves know that these hands of mine have supplied my own needs and the needs of my companions. ³⁵In everything I did, I showed you that by this kind of hard work we must help the weak, remembering the words the Lord Jesus himself said: 'It is more blessed to give than to receive.' "

³⁶When he had said this, he knelt down with all of them and prayed. ³⁷They all wept as they embraced him and kissed him. ³⁸What grieved them most was his statement that they would never see his face again. Then they accompanied him to the ship.

NOVEMBER 9 □ DAY 314
ACTS 21–23
Paul's Arrest

OVERVIEW Ominous signs accompany Paul's third missionary journey. A prophet named Agabus binds himself with Paul's belt, demonstrating the fate awaiting Paul in Jerusalem. True to the prophet's word, Paul's arrival sparks angry opposition and false accusations. Once before the crowd and again before the Sanhedrin, Paul attempts to defend himself. But after narrowly averting an assassination plot, he finds himself in prison, awaiting the opportunity to declare the gospel before governors, kings and Caesar himself.

Chapter 21	Chapter 22	Chapter 23
Paul's Arrest	Paul's Accusers	Paul's Attempted Assassination
Jerusalem	Jews	Jeopardy

People like not only to be loved but also to be told they are loved; the realm of silence is large enough beyond the grave.

YOUR DAILY WALK "A word aptly spoken is like apples of gold in settings of silver" (Proverbs 25:11). That verse would provide a fitting title for Acts 21–28—chapters in which Paul speaks before many different audiences: mobs and councils, governors and kings, prisoners and sailors. In each case his speech is appropriate to the occasion: gracious praise for those in authority, terse commands to those on the ship and courteous apology to the high priest.

Paul knew that words are easy to cast but difficult to reel in! Munch on an apple, and think about how you have been communicating with those around you lately. Have your words been golden apples or crab apples? List below a "word aptly spoken" that you can share this week with your

- boss or coworker: _____
- parent or teacher: _____
- pastor or minister: _____
- spouse or friend: _____
- unsaved neighbor: _____

 INSIGHT Tale of Two Journeys
A striking series of parallels can be drawn between the last journeys to Jerusalem of Paul and Jesus. The outcomes of both journeys were predicted in advance (21:10–11; Mark 10:33). Both men were bound by the Jews and delivered to the Gentiles. And both desired above all else that the will of God be done (21:14; Luke 22:42).

CHAPTER 21

After we had torn ourselves away from them, we put out to sea and sailed straight to Cos. The next day we went to Rhodes and from there to Patara. ²We found a ship crossing over to Phoenicia, went on board and set sail. ³After sighting Cyprus and passing to the south of it, we sailed on to Syria. We landed at Tyre, where our ship was to unload its cargo. ⁴Finding the disciples there, we stayed with them seven days. Through the Spirit they urged Paul not to go on to Jerusalem. ⁵But when our time was up, we left and continued on our way. All the disciples and their wives and children accompanied us out of the city, and there on the beach we knelt to pray. ⁶After saying good-by to each other, we went aboard the ship, and they returned home.

⁷We continued our voyage from Tyre and landed at Ptolemais, where we greeted the brothers and stayed with them for a day. ⁸Leaving the next day, we reached Caesarea and stayed at the house of Philip the evangelist, one of the Seven. ⁹He had four unmarried daughters who prophesied.

¹⁰After we had been there a number of days, a prophet named Agabus came down from Judea. ¹¹Coming over to us, he took Paul's belt, tied his own hands and feet with it and said, "The Holy Spirit says, 'In this way the Jews of Jerusalem will bind the owner of this belt and will hand him over to the Gentiles.' "

¹²When we heard this, we and the people there pleaded with Paul not to go up to Jerusalem. ¹³Then Paul answered, "Why are you weeping and breaking my heart? I am ready not only to be bound, but also to die in Jerusalem for the name of the Lord Jesus." ¹⁴When he would not

be dissuaded, we gave up and said, "The Lord's will be done."

¹⁵After this, we got ready and went up to Jerusalem. ¹⁶Some of the disciples from Caesarea accompanied us and brought us to the home of Mnason, where we were to stay. He was a man from Cyprus and one of the early disciples.

¹⁷When we arrived at Jerusalem, the brothers received us warmly. ¹⁸The next day Paul and the rest of us went to see James, and all the elders were present. ¹⁹Paul greeted them and reported in detail what God had done among the Gentiles through his ministry.

²⁰When they heard this, they praised God. Then they said to Paul: "You see, brother, how many thousands of Jews have believed, and all of them are zealous for the law. ²¹They have been informed that you teach all the Jews who live among the Gentiles to turn away from Moses, telling them not to circumcise their children or live according to our customs. ²²What shall we do? They will certainly hear that you have come, ²³so do what we tell you. There are four men with us who have made a vow. ²⁴Take these men, join in their purification rites and pay their expenses, so that they can have their heads shaved. Then everybody will know there is no truth in these reports about you, but that you yourself are living in obedience to the law. ²⁵As for the Gentile believers, we have written to them our decision that they should abstain from food sacrificed to idols, from blood, from the meat of strangled animals and from sexual immorality."

²⁶The next day Paul took the men and purified himself along with them. Then he went to the temple to give notice of the date when the days of purification would

end and the offering would be made for each of them.

27When the seven days were nearly over, some Jews from the province of Asia saw Paul at the temple. They stirred up the whole crowd and seized him, 28shouting, "Men of Israel, help us! This is the man who teaches all men everywhere against our people and our law and this place. And besides, he has brought Greeks into the temple area and defiled this holy place." 29(They had previously seen Trophimus the Ephesian in the city with Paul and assumed that Paul had brought him into the temple area.)

30The whole city was aroused, and the people came running from all directions. Seizing Paul, they dragged him from the temple, and immediately the gates were shut. 31While they were trying to kill him, news reached the commander of the Roman troops that the whole city of Jerusalem was in an uproar. 32He at once took some officers and soldiers and ran down to the crowd. When the rioters saw the commander and his soldiers, they stopped beating Paul.

33The commander came up and arrested him and ordered him to be bound with two chains. Then he asked who he was and what he had done. 34Some in the crowd shouted one thing and some another, and since the commander could not get at the truth because of the uproar, he ordered that Paul be taken into the barracks. 35When Paul reached the steps, the violence of the mob was so great he had to be carried by the soldiers. 36The crowd that followed kept shouting, "Away with him!"

37As the soldiers were about to take Paul into the barracks, he asked the commander, "May I say something to you?"

"Do you speak Greek?" he replied. 38"Aren't you the Egyptian who started a revolt and led four thousand terrorists out into the desert some time ago?"

39Paul answered, "I am a Jew, from Tarsus in Cilicia, a citizen of no ordinary city. Please let me speak to the people."

40Having received the commander's permission, Paul stood on the steps and motioned to the crowd. When they were all silent, he said to them in

CHAPTER 22 Aramaic*r*: 1"Brothers and fathers, listen now to my defense."

2When they heard him speak to them in Aramaic, they became very quiet.

Then Paul said: 3"I am a Jew, born in Tarsus of Cilicia, but brought up in this city. Under Gamaliel I was thoroughly trained in the law of our fathers and was just as zealous for God as any of you are today. 4I persecuted the followers of this Way to their death, arresting both men and women and throwing them into prison, 5as also the high priest and all the Council can testify. I even obtained letters from them to their brothers in Damascus, and went there to bring these people as prisoners to Jerusalem to be punished.

6"About noon as I came near Damascus, suddenly a bright light from heaven flashed around me. 7I fell to the ground and heard a voice say to me, 'Saul! Saul! Why do you persecute me?'

8" 'Who are you, Lord?' I asked.

" 'I am Jesus of Nazareth, whom you are persecuting,' he replied. 9My companions saw the light, but they did not understand the voice of him who was speaking to me.

10" 'What shall I do, Lord?' I asked.

" 'Get up,' the Lord said, 'and go into Damascus. There you will be told all that you have been assigned to do.' 11My companions led me by the hand into Damascus, because the brilliance of the light had blinded me.

12"A man named Ananias came to see me. He was a devout observer of the law and highly respected by all the Jews living there. 13He stood beside me and said, 'Brother Saul, receive your sight!' And at that very moment I was able to see him.

14"Then he said: 'The God of our fathers has chosen you to know his will and to see the Righteous One and to hear words from his mouth. 15You will be his witness to all men of what you have seen and heard. 16And now what are you waiting for? Get up, be baptized and wash your sins away, calling on his name.'

17"When I returned to Jerusalem and was praying at the temple, I fell into a trance 18and saw the Lord speaking. 'Quick!' he said to me. 'Leave Jerusalem immediately, because they will not accept your testimony about me.'

r40 Or possibly Hebrew; also in 22:2

[19]" 'Lord,' I replied, 'these men know that I went from one synagogue to another to imprison and beat those who believe in you. [20]And when the blood of your martyr[s] Stephen was shed, I stood there giving my approval and guarding the clothes of those who were killing him.'

[21]"Then the Lord said to me, 'Go; I will send you far away to the Gentiles.' "

[22]The crowd listened to Paul until he said this. Then they raised their voices and shouted, "Rid the earth of him! He's not fit to live!"

[23]As they were shouting and throwing off their cloaks and flinging dust into the air, [24]the commander ordered Paul to be taken into the barracks. He directed that he be flogged and questioned in order to find out why the people were shouting at him like this. [25]As they stretched him out to flog him, Paul said to the centurion standing there, "Is it legal for you to flog a Roman citizen who hasn't even been found guilty?"

[26]When the centurion heard this, he went to the commander and reported it. "What are you going to do?" he asked. "This man is a Roman citizen."

[27]The commander went to Paul and asked, "Tell me, are you a Roman citizen?"

"Yes, I am," he answered.

[28]Then the commander said, "I had to pay a big price for my citizenship."

"But I was born a citizen," Paul replied.

[29]Those who were about to question him withdrew immediately. The commander himself was alarmed when he realized that he had put Paul, a Roman citizen, in chains.

[30]The next day, since the commander wanted to find out exactly why Paul was being accused by the Jews, he released him and ordered the chief priests and all the Sanhedrin to assemble. Then he brought Paul and had him stand before them.

CHAPTER 23

Paul looked straight at the Sanhedrin and said, "My brothers, I have fulfilled my duty to God in all good conscience to this day." [2]At this the high priest Ananias ordered those standing near Paul to strike him on the mouth. [3]Then Paul said to

him, "God will strike you, you whitewashed wall! You sit there to judge me according to the law, yet you yourself violate the law by commanding that I be struck!"

[4]Those who were standing near Paul said, "You dare to insult God's high priest?"

[5]Paul replied, "Brothers, I did not realize that he was the high priest; for it is written: 'Do not speak evil about the ruler of your people.'[t]"

[6]Then Paul, knowing that some of them were Sadducees and the others Pharisees, called out in the Sanhedrin, "My brothers, I am a Pharisee, the son of a Pharisee. I stand on trial because of my hope in the resurrection of the dead." [7]When he said this, a dispute broke out between the Pharisees and the Sadducees, and the assembly was divided. [8](The Sadducees say that there is no resurrection, and that there are neither angels nor spirits, but the Pharisees acknowledge them all.)

[9]There was a great uproar, and some of the teachers of the law who were Pharisees stood up and argued vigorously. "We find nothing wrong with this man," they said. "What if a spirit or an angel has spoken to him?" [10]The dispute became so violent that the commander was afraid Paul would be torn to pieces by them. He ordered the troops to go down and take him away from them by force and bring him into the barracks.

[11]The following night the Lord stood near Paul and said, "Take courage! As you have testified about me in Jerusalem, so you must also testify in Rome."

[12]The next morning the Jews formed a conspiracy and bound themselves with an oath not to eat or drink until they had killed Paul. [13]More than forty men were involved in this plot. [14]They went to the chief priests and elders and said, "We have taken a solemn oath not to eat anything until we have killed Paul. [15]Now then, you and the Sanhedrin petition the commander to bring him before you on the pretext of wanting more accurate information about his case. We are ready to kill him before he gets here."

[16]But when the son of Paul's sister heard of this plot, he went into the barracks and told Paul.

[s]20 Or witness   [t]5 Exodus 22:28

¹⁷Then Paul called one of the centurions and said, "Take this young man to the commander; he has something to tell him." ¹⁸So he took him to the commander.

The centurion said, "Paul, the prisoner, sent for me and asked me to bring this young man to you because he has something to tell you."

¹⁹The commander took the young man by the hand, drew him aside and asked, "What is it you want to tell me?"

²⁰He said: "The Jews have agreed to ask you to bring Paul before the Sanhedrin tomorrow on the pretext of wanting more accurate information about him. ²¹Don't give in to them, because more than forty of them are waiting in ambush for him. They have taken an oath not to eat or drink until they have killed him. They are ready now, waiting for your consent to their request."

²²The commander dismissed the young man and cautioned him, "Don't tell anyone that you have reported this to me."

²³Then he called two of his centurions and ordered them, "Get ready a detachment of two hundred soldiers, seventy horsemen and two hundred spearmen" to go to Caesarea at nine tonight. ²⁴Provide mounts for Paul so that he may be taken safely to Governor Felix."

²⁵He wrote a letter as follows:

²⁶Claudius Lysias,

ᵘ23 The meaning of the Greek for this word is uncertain.

To His Excellency, Governor Felix:

Greetings.

²⁷This man was seized by the Jews and they were about to kill him, but I came with my troops and rescued him, for I had learned that he is a Roman citizen. ²⁸I wanted to know why they were accusing him, so I brought him to their Sanhedrin. ²⁹I found that the accusation had to do with questions about their law, but there was no charge against him that deserved death or imprisonment. ³⁰When I was informed of a plot to be carried out against the man, I sent him to you at once. I also ordered his accusers to present to you their case against him.

³¹So the soldiers, carrying out their orders, took Paul with them during the night and brought him as far as Antipatris. ³²The next day they let the cavalry go on with him, while they returned to the barracks. ³³When the cavalry arrived in Caesarea, they delivered the letter to the governor and handed Paul over to him. ³⁴The governor read the letter and asked what province he was from. Learning that he was from Cilicia, ³⁵he said, "I will hear your case when your accusers get here." Then he ordered that Paul be kept under guard in Herod's palace.

NOVEMBER 10 □ DAY 315
ACTS 24–26
Paul's Three Trials

 OVERVIEW Two years pass before Paul's case reaches the courtroom. But political pressure keeps two governors, Felix and Festus, from resolving the issue. When Festus suggests the case be sent back to Jerusalem—an almost certain death sentence—there can be only one response from Paul: "I appeal to Caesar" (25:11). While preparations are being made for the two-thousand-mile journey to Rome, King Agrippa arrives, giving Paul yet another opportunity to defend the gospel.

Chapter 24	Chapter 25	Chapter 26
Trial before Governor Felix	Trial before Governor Festus	Trial before King Agrippa
Almost Released	Almost Murdered	Almost Persuaded

YOUR DAILY WALK Doctor to parent: "And how is your little boy doing at controlling his behavior this week?"

> Parent: "He's trying, doctor."
> Doctor: "Good, I'm glad to hear it."
> Parent: "Yes, Doc, he's very, *very* trying!"

Only the willingness to suffer can conquer suffering.

Trials. They come in all shapes and sizes. But the bottom line is the same: God wants you to rise above them, persevere through them and emerge stronger from them. Peter puts it this way: "These have come so that your faith—of greater worth than gold, which perishes even though refined by fire—may be proved geniune and may result in praise, glory and honor when Jesus Christ is revealed" (1 Peter 1:7).

Paul could have viewed his three trials as a bother. Instead, he welcomed them as a blessing—not because they were pleasant, but because he knew they were purposeful. Developing a faith like gold requires the fiery heat of refining situations. If you have a fireplace, build a fire there this evening as you consider this question: "Is God finding that I am trying to cooperate with him . . . or that I'm just plain *trying?*"

INSIGHT: "The Power of a King with the Mind of a Slave"

The historian Tacitus made the above statement about Felix, and Felix's treatment of Paul in 24:24–27 seems to bear out this character analysis. He often met with Paul, not to wrestle with the issues that Paul raised, but to give Paul an opportunity to bribe him. Paul, of course, did not oblige and thus had to sit in prison for two years.

CHAPTER 24

Five days later the high priest Ananias went down to Caesarea with some of the elders and a lawyer named Tertullus, and they brought their charges against Paul before the governor. ²When Paul was called in, Tertullus presented his case before Felix: "We have enjoyed a long period of peace under you, and your foresight has brought about reforms in this nation. ³Everywhere and in every way, most excellent Felix, we acknowledge this with profound gratitude. ⁴But in order not to weary you further, I would request that you be kind enough to hear us briefly.

⁵"We have found this man to be a troublemaker, stirring up riots among the Jews all over the world. He is a ringleader of the Nazarene sect ⁶and even tried to desecrate the temple; so we seized him. ⁸Byᵛ examining him yourself you will be able to learn the truth about all these charges we are bringing against him."

⁹The Jews joined in the accusation, asserting that these things were true.

¹⁰When the governor motioned for him to speak, Paul replied: "I know that for a number of years you have been a judge over this nation; so I gladly make my defense. ¹¹You can easily verify that no more than twelve days ago I went up to Jerusalem to worship. ¹²My accusers did not find me arguing with anyone at the temple, or stirring up a crowd in the synagogues or anywhere else in the city. ¹³And they cannot prove to you the charges they are now making against me. ¹⁴However, I admit that I worship the God of our fathers as a follower of the Way, which they call a sect. I believe everything that agrees with the Law and that is written in the Prophets, ¹⁵and I have the same hope in God as these men,

ᵛ 6-8 Some manuscripts *him and wanted to judge him according to our law.* ⁷*But the commander, Lysias, came and with the use of much force snatched him from our hands* ⁸*and ordered his accusers to come before you. By* that there will be a resurrection of both the righteous and the wicked. ¹⁶So I strive always to keep my conscience clear before God and man.

¹⁷"After an absence of several years, I came to Jerusalem to bring my people gifts for the poor and to present offerings. ¹⁸I was ceremonially clean when they found me in the temple courts doing this. There was no crowd with me, nor was I involved in any disturbance. ¹⁹But there are some Jews from the province of Asia, who ought to be here before you and bring charges if they have anything against me. ²⁰Or these who are here should state what crime they found in me when I stood before the Sanhedrin— ²¹unless it was this one thing I shouted as I stood in their presence: 'It is concerning the resurrection of the dead that I am on trial before you today.' "

²²Then Felix, who was well acquainted with the Way, adjourned the proceedings. "When Lysias the commander comes," he said, "I will decide your case." ²³He ordered the centurion to keep Paul under guard but to give him some freedom and permit his friends to take care of his needs.

²⁴Several days later Felix came with his wife Drusilla, who was a Jewess. He sent for Paul and listened to him as he spoke about faith in Christ Jesus. ²⁵As Paul discoursed on righteousness, self-control and the judgment to come, Felix was afraid and said, "That's enough for now! You may leave. When I find it convenient, I will send for you." ²⁶At the same time he was hoping that Paul would offer him a bribe, so he sent for him frequently and talked with him.

²⁷When two years had passed, Felix was succeeded by Porcius Festus, but because Felix wanted to grant a favor to the Jews, he left Paul in prison.

CHAPTER 25

Three days after arriving in the province, Festus went up from Caesarea to Jerusalem, ²where the chief priests and Jewish leaders appeared before him and presented the charges against Paul. ³They urgently requested Festus, as a favor to them, to have Paul transferred to Jerusalem, for they were preparing an ambush to kill him along the way. ⁴Festus answered, "Paul is being held at Caesarea,

and I myself am going there soon. ⁵Let some of your leaders come with me and press charges against the man there, if he has done anything wrong."

⁶After spending eight or ten days with them, he went down to Caesarea, and the next day he convened the court and ordered that Paul be brought before him. ⁷When Paul appeared, the Jews who had come down from Jerusalem stood around him, bringing many serious charges against him, which they could not prove.

⁸Then Paul made his defense: "I have done nothing wrong against the law of the Jews or against the temple or against Caesar."

⁹Festus, wishing to do the Jews a favor, said to Paul, "Are you willing to go up to Jerusalem and stand trial before me there on these charges?"

¹⁰Paul answered: "I am now standing before Caesar's court, where I ought to be tried. I have not done any wrong to the Jews, as you yourself know very well. ¹¹If, however, I am guilty of doing anything deserving death, I do not refuse to die. But if the charges brought against me by these Jews are not true, no one has the right to hand me over to them. I appeal to Caesar!"

¹²After Festus had conferred with his council, he declared: "You have appealed to Caesar. To Caesar you will go!"

¹³A few days later King Agrippa and Bernice arrived at Caesarea to pay their respects to Festus. ¹⁴Since they were spending many days there, Festus discussed Paul's case with the king. He said: "There is a man here whom Felix left as a prisoner. ¹⁵When I went to Jerusalem, the chief priests and elders of the Jews brought charges against him and asked that he be condemned.

¹⁶"I told them that it is not the Roman custom to hand over any man before he has faced his accusers and has had an opportunity to defend himself against their charges. ¹⁷When they came here with me, I did not delay the case, but convened the court the next day and ordered the man to be brought in. ¹⁸When his accusers got up to speak, they did not charge him with any of the crimes I had expected. ¹⁹Instead, they had some points of dispute with him about their own religion and about a dead man named Jesus who Paul claimed was alive. ²⁰I was at a loss how to

investigate such matters; so I asked if he would be willing to go to Jerusalem and stand trial there on these charges. [21]When Paul made his appeal to be held over for the Emperor's decision, I ordered him held until I could send him to Caesar."

[22]Then Agrippa said to Festus, "I would like to hear this man myself."

He replied, "Tomorrow you will hear him."

[23]The next day Agrippa and Bernice came with great pomp and entered the audience room with the high ranking officers and the leading men of the city. At the command of Festus, Paul was brought in. [24]Festus said: "King Agrippa, and all who are present with us, you see this man! The whole Jewish community has petitioned me about him in Jerusalem and here in Caesarea, shouting that he ought not to live any longer. [25]I found he had done nothing deserving of death, but because he made his appeal to the Emperor I decided to send him to Rome. [26]But I have nothing definite to write to His Majesty about him. Therefore I have brought him before all of you, and especially before you, King Agrippa, so that as a result of this investigation I may have something to write. [27]For I think it is unreasonable to send on a prisoner without specifying the charges against him."

CHAPTER 26
Then Agrippa said to Paul, "You have permission to speak for yourself."

So Paul motioned with his hand and began his defense: [2]"King Agrippa, I consider myself fortunate to stand before you today as I make my defense against all the accusations of the Jews, [3]and especially so because you are well acquainted with all the Jewish customs and controversies. Therefore, I beg you to listen to me patiently.

[4]"The Jews all know the way I have lived ever since I was a child, from the beginning of my life in my own country, and also in Jerusalem. [5]They have known me for a long time and can testify, if they are willing, that according to the strictest sect of our religion, I lived as a Pharisee. [6]And now it is because of my hope in what God has promised our fathers that I am on trial today. [7]This is the promise our

twelve tribes are hoping to see fulfilled as they earnestly serve God day and night. O king, it is because of this hope that the Jews are accusing me. [8]Why should any of you consider it incredible that God raises the dead?

[9]"I too was convinced that I ought to do all that was possible to oppose the name of Jesus of Nazareth. [10]And that is just what I did in Jerusalem. On the authority of the chief priests I put many of the saints in prison, and when they were put to death, I cast my vote against them. [11]Many a time I went from one synagogue to another to have them punished, and I tried to force them to blaspheme. In my obsession against them, I even went to foreign cities to persecute them.

[12]"On one of these journeys I was going to Damascus with the authority and commission of the chief priests. [13]About noon, O king, as I was on the road, I saw a light from heaven, brighter than the sun, blazing around me and my companions. [14]We all fell to the ground, and I heard a voice saying to me in Aramaic,[w] 'Saul, Saul, why do you persecute me? It is hard for you to kick against the goads.'

[15]"Then I asked, 'Who are you, Lord?'

" 'I am Jesus, whom you are persecuting,' the Lord replied. [16]'Now get up and stand on your feet. I have appeared to you to appoint you as a servant and as a witness of what you have seen of me and what I will show you. [17]I will rescue you from your own people and from the Gentiles. I am sending you to them [18]to open their eyes and turn them from darkness to light, and from the power of Satan to God, so that they may receive forgiveness of sins and a place among those who are sanctified by faith in me.'

[19]"So then, King Agrippa, I was not disobedient to the vision from heaven. [20]First to those in Damascus, then to those in Jerusalem and in all Judea, and to the Gentiles also, I preached that they should repent and turn to God and prove their repentance by their deeds. [21]That is why the Jews seized me in the temple courts and tried to kill me. [22]But I have had God's help to this very day, and so I stand here and testify to small and great alike. I am saying nothing beyond what the prophets and Moses said would happen—

w14 Or Hebrew

²³that the Christˣ would suffer and, as the first to rise from the dead, would proclaim light to his own people and to the Gentiles."

²⁴At this point Festus interrupted Paul's defense. "You are out of your mind, Paul!" he shouted. "Your great learning is driving you insane."

²⁵"I am not insane, most excellent Festus," Paul replied. "What I am saying is true and reasonable. ²⁶The king is familiar with these things, and I can speak freely to him. I am convinced that none of this has escaped his notice, because it was not done in a corner. ²⁷King Agrippa, do you believe the prophets? I know you do."

ˣ23 Or *Messiah*

²⁸Then Agrippa said to Paul, "Do you think that in such a short time you can persuade me to be a Christian?"

²⁹Paul replied, "Short time or long—I pray God that not only you but all who are listening to me today may become what I am, except for these chains."

³⁰The king rose, and with him the governor and Bernice and those sitting with them. ³¹They left the room, and while talking with one another, they said, "This man is not doing anything that deserves death or imprisonment."

³²Agrippa said to Festus, "This man could have been set free if he had not appealed to Caesar."

NOVEMBER 11 ☐ DAY 316
ACTS 27–28
Paul's Trip to Rome

OVERVIEW During the perilous voyage by sea to Rome, God assures Paul in a dream that he will stand before Caesar to bear witness to the gospel. What God does not tell Paul is that before he arrives in Rome, he will experience a shipwreck and a snakebite! The account closes with Paul under house arrest for two years, "[preaching] the kingdom of God and [teaching] about the Lord Jesus Christ" (28:31).

Chapters 27–28			
Sailing for Rome	Shipwrecked on Malta	Reception in Rome	House Arrest in Rome
27:1 27:26	27:27 28:10	28:11 28:16	28:17 28:31
Peril in the Water		Peril on the Land	

YOUR DAILY WALK Even the best seeds germinate only in the proper soil.

Acts 28:24 is a summary of the response to Paul's "seed sowing" in the city of Rome: "Some were convinced by what he said, but others would not believe." It's a reminder that even the apostle Paul couldn't persuade a person into heaven if that individual was not willing to "see . . . hear . . . understand . . . and turn" (28:27).

We conquer not in any brilliant fashion—we conquer by continuing.

You can expect the same response as you venture forth with the words of life! Some will believe, for God has promised that his Word will not return empty (Isaiah 55:11). And some will not believe—not because the message is deficient, but because they are unwilling to repent. Don't be discouraged at the latter; and don't be surprised at the former! Like Paul, keep praying, sharing and looking up.

INSIGHT Acts beyond the Book of Acts

Chapter 28 concludes Luke's account, but significant events continued to transpire in the life of Paul and the New Testament church. The following is a suggested chronology:

CHAPTER 27

When it was decided that we would sail for Italy, Paul and some other prisoners were handed over to a centurion named Julius, who belonged to the Imperial Regiment. [2]We boarded a ship from Adramyttium about to sail for ports along the coast of the province of Asia, and we put out to sea. Aristarchus, a Macedonian from Thessalonica, was with us.

[3]The next day we landed at Sidon; and Julius, in kindness to Paul, allowed him to go to his friends so they might provide for his needs. [4]From there we put out to sea again and passed to the lee of Cyprus because the winds were against us. [5]When we had sailed across the open sea off the coast of Cilicia and Pamphylia, we landed at Myra in Lycia. [6]There the centurion found an Alexandrian ship sailing for Italy and put us on board. [7]We made slow headway for many days and had difficulty arriving off Cnidus. When the wind did not allow us to hold our course, we sailed to the lee of Crete, opposite Salmone. [8]We moved along the coast with difficulty and came to a place called Fair Havens, near the town of Lasea.

[9]Much time had been lost, and sailing had already become dangerous because by now it was after the Fast.*y* So Paul warned them, [10]"Men, I can see that our voyage is going to be disastrous and bring great loss to ship and cargo, and to our own lives also." [11]But the centurion, instead of listening to what Paul said, followed the advice of the pilot and of the owner of the ship. [12]Since the harbor was unsuitable to winter in, the majority decided that we should sail on, hoping to reach Phoenix and winter there. This was a harbor in Crete, facing both southwest and northwest.

[13]When a gentle south wind began to blow, they thought they had obtained what they wanted; so they weighed anchor and sailed along the shore of Crete. [14]Before very long, a wind of hurricane force, called the "northeaster," swept down from the island. [15]The ship was caught by the storm and could not head into the wind; so we gave way to it and were driven along. [16]As we passed to the lee of a small island called Cauda, we were hardly able to make the lifeboat secure. [17]When the men had hoisted it aboard, they passed ropes under the ship itself to hold it together. Fearing that they would run aground on the sandbars of Syrtis, they lowered the sea anchor and let the ship be driven along. [18]We took such a violent battering from the storm that the next day they began to throw the cargo overboard. [19]On the third day, they threw the ship's tackle overboard with their own hands. [20]When neither sun nor stars appeared for many days and the storm continued raging, we finally gave up all hope of being saved.

[21]After the men had gone a long time without food, Paul stood up before them and said: "Men, you should have taken my advice not to sail from Crete; then you would have spared yourselves this damage and loss. [22]But now I urge you to keep up your courage, because not one of you will be lost; only the ship will be destroyed. [23]Last night an angel of the God whose I am and whom I serve stood beside me [24]and said, 'Do not be afraid, Paul. You must stand trial before Caesar; and God has graciously given you the lives of all who sail with you.' [25]So keep up your courage, men, for I have faith in God that it will happen just as he told me. [26]Nevertheless, we must run aground on some island."

[27]On the fourteenth night we were still

---

y 9 That is, the Day of Atonement (Yom Kippur)

being driven across the Adriatic[z] Sea, when about midnight the sailors sensed they were approaching land. 28They took soundings and found that the water was a hundred and twenty feet[a] deep. A short time later they took soundings again and found it was ninety feet[b] deep. 29Fearing that we would be dashed against the rocks, they dropped four anchors from the stern and prayed for daylight. 30In an attempt to escape from the ship, the sailors let the lifeboat down into the sea, pretending they were going to lower some anchors from the bow. 31Then Paul said to the centurion and the soldiers, "Unless these men stay with the ship, you cannot be saved." 32So the soldiers cut the ropes that held the lifeboat and let it fall away.

33Just before dawn Paul urged them all to eat. "For the last fourteen days," he said, "you have been in constant suspense and have gone without food—you haven't eaten anything. 34Now I urge you to take some food. You need it to survive. Not one of you will lose a single hair from his head." 35After he said this, he took some bread and gave thanks to God in front of them all. Then he broke it and began to eat. 36They were all encouraged and ate some food themselves. 37Altogether there were 276 of us on board. 38When they had eaten as much as they wanted, they lightened the ship by throwing the grain into the sea.

39When daylight came, they did not recognize the land, but they saw a bay with a sandy beach, where they decided to run the ship aground if they could. 40Cutting loose the anchors, they left them in the sea and at the same time untied the ropes that held the rudders. Then they hoisted the foresail to the wind and made for the beach. 41But the ship struck a sandbar and ran aground. The bow stuck fast and would not move, and the stern was broken to pieces by the pounding of the surf.

42The soldiers planned to kill the prisoners to prevent any of them from swimming away and escaping. 43But the centurion wanted to spare Paul's life and kept them from carrying out their plan. He ordered those who could swim to jump overboard first and get to land. 44The rest were to get there on planks or on pieces of the ship. In this way everyone reached land in safety.

CHAPTER 28

Once safely on shore, we found out that the island was called Malta. 2The islanders showed us unusual kindness. They built a fire and welcomed us all because it was raining and cold. 3Paul gathered a pile of brushwood and, as he put it on the fire, a viper, driven out by the heat, fastened itself on his hand. 4When the islanders saw the snake hanging from his hand, they said to each other, "This man must be a murderer; for though he escaped from the sea, Justice has not allowed him to live." 5But Paul shook the snake off into the fire and suffered no ill effects. 6The people expected him to swell up or suddenly fall dead, but after waiting a long time and seeing nothing unusual happen to him, they changed their minds and said he was a god.

7There was an estate nearby that belonged to Publius, the chief official of the island. He welcomed us to his home and for three days entertained us hospitably. 8His father was sick in bed, suffering from fever and dysentery. Paul went in to see him and, after prayer, placed his hands on him and healed him. 9When this had happened, the rest of the sick on the island came and were cured. 10They honored us in many ways and when we were ready to sail, they furnished us with the supplies we needed.

11After three months we put out to sea in a ship that had wintered in the island. It was an Alexandrian ship with the figurehead of the twin gods Castor and Pollux. 12We put in at Syracuse and stayed there three days. 13From there we set sail and arrived at Rhegium. The next day the south wind came up, and on the following day we reached Puteoli. 14There we found some brothers who invited us to spend a week with them. And so we came to Rome. 15The brothers there had heard that we were coming, and they traveled as far as the Forum of Appius and the Three Taverns to meet us. At the sight of these men Paul thanked God and was encouraged. 16When we got to Rome, Paul was allowed to live by himself, with a soldier to guard him.

z27 In ancient times the name referred to an area extending well south of Italy.   a28 Greek twenty orguias (about 37 meters)
b28 Greek fifteen orguias (about 27 meters)

[17]Three days later he called together the leaders of the Jews. When they had assembled, Paul said to them: "My brothers, although I have done nothing against our people or against the customs of our ancestors, I was arrested in Jerusalem and handed over to the Romans. [18]They examined me and wanted to release me, because I was not guilty of any crime deserving death. [19]But when the Jews objected, I was compelled to appeal to Caesar—not that I had any charge to bring against my own people. [20]For this reason I have asked to see you and talk with you. It is because of the hope of Israel that I am bound with this chain."

[21]They replied, "We have not received any letters from Judea concerning you, and none of the brothers who have come from there has reported or said anything bad about you. [22]But we want to hear what your views are, for we know that people everywhere are talking against this sect."

[23]They arranged to meet Paul on a certain day, and came in even larger numbers to the place where he was staying. From morning till evening he explained and declared to them the kingdom of God and tried to convince them about Jesus from the Law of Moses and from the Prophets. [24]Some were convinced by what he said, but others would not believe. [25]They disagreed among themselves and began to leave after Paul had made this final statement: "The Holy Spirit spoke the truth to your forefathers when he said through Isaiah the prophet:

[26]" 'Go to this people and say,
"You will be ever hearing but never understanding;
you will be ever seeing but never perceiving."
[27]For this people's heart has become calloused;
they hardly hear with their ears,
and they have closed their eyes.
Otherwise they might see with their eyes,
hear with their ears,
understand with their hearts
and turn, and I would heal them.'[c]

[28]"Therefore I want you to know that God's salvation has been sent to the Gentiles, and they will listen!"[d]

[30]For two whole years Paul stayed there in his own rented house and welcomed all who came to see him. [31]Boldly and without hindrance he preached the kingdom of God and taught about the Lord Jesus Christ.

[c]27 Isaiah 6:9,10   [d]28 Some manuscripts *listen!" 29After he said this, the Jews left, arguing vigorously among themselves.*

Romans

WHILE the four Gospels recount the life of Jesus Christ, the book of Romans explores the significance of his sacrificial death. As such, it has been called "the gospel according to Paul." In a question and answer format, Romans is the most systematic presentation of doctrine in the Bible. But the Good News is more than a theology to be pondered; it is a life to be lived—a life of righteousness befitting one whom God declares "justified freely by his grace through the redemption that came by Christ Jesus" (3:24).

Focus	Sin	Salvation	Struggle	Sovereignty	Service
Divisions	Everyone's Need of Righteousness	God's Provision of Righteousness	God's Power for Righteous Living	God's Plan of Righteousness	Practical Outworking of Righteousness
	1 3	4 5	6 8	9 11	12 16
Topics	Basis of the Gospel			Behavior of the Gospel	
	Condemnation	Justification	Sanctification	Vindication	Application
Place	Probably Corinth				
Time	A.D. 57				

NOVEMBER 12 □ DAY 317
ROMANS 1–3
Everyone's Need of Righteousness

OVERVIEW Unlike most of Paul's letters, Romans is addressed to believers Paul has never met. Resembling a doctrinal treatise more than a personal letter, it explores in carefully worded phrases the need, provision and outworking of God's grace. Paul begins with God's wrath upon sinful humanity. Without exception, all have sinned and face the condemnation of God. But there is hope in the person of Jesus Christ, by whom God provides righteousness to all who believe (3:22).

Chapter 1		Chapter 2	Chapter 3
Nature of the Gospel	Need for the Gospel	Objects of the Gospel	Outcome of the Gospel
1 17	18 32		
Judgment			Grace

YOUR DAILY WALK Webster defines the verb *to earn* this way: "To receive as return for work done or services rendered." With that in mind, go on an expedition through the Scriptures to discover what God says about unsaved peoples' good works.

All the sorrows of faith put together do not equal in bitterness one drop of the sorrows of sin.

Their righteous acts are like _____ (Isaiah 64:6).

Their sins are like _____ and are red as _____ (Isaiah 1:18).

Their hearts are _____ above all things and beyond _____ (Jeremiah 17:9).

In short, the verdict of Paul the apostle, echoing the words of David the psalmist, is this: "There is no one who does good, not even one" (Romans 3:12; see also Psalms 14:3; 53:3). And what are the wages that that sinful, unrighteous condition earns? (See Romans 6:23.)

Now do you understand why it is so important to view your sinfulness the way God views it? Not as a character weakness . . . or an unfortunate setback . . . but as a terminal condition.

The prognosis is grim—unless Jesus is your Savior. Is he? If not, new life is only a prayer away. Take him at his word right now. All you have to lose is a hopeless eternity (John 3:16–18).

INSIGHT Glad Tidings Oft Told
Romans has been called "the gospel according to Paul" with good reason. Twelve times in the book you'll find the word *gospel*, compared to only nine times in the four Gospels combined!

CHAPTER 1

Paul, a servant of Christ Jesus, called to be an apostle and set apart for the gospel of God— [2]the gospel he promised beforehand through his prophets in the Holy Scriptures [3]regarding his Son, who as to his human nature was a descendant of David, [4]and who through the Spirit[a] of holiness was declared with power to be the Son of God[b] by his resurrection from the dead: Jesus Christ our Lord. [5]Through him and for his name's sake, we received grace and apostleship to call people from among all the Gentiles to the obedience

[a]4 Or *who as to his spirit*   [b]4 Or *was appointed to be the Son of God with power*

that comes from faith. [6]And you also are among those who are called to belong to Jesus Christ.

[7]To all in Rome who are loved by God and called to be saints:

Grace and peace to you from God our Father and from the Lord Jesus Christ.

[8]First, I thank my God through Jesus Christ for all of you, because your faith is being reported all over the world. [9]God, whom I serve with my whole heart in preaching the gospel of his Son, is my witness how constantly I remember you [10]in my prayers at all times; and I pray that now at last by God's will the way may be opened for me to come to you.

[11]I long to see you so that I may impart to you some spiritual gift to make you strong— [12]that is, that you and I may be mutually encouraged by each other's faith. [13]I do not want you to be unaware, brothers, that I planned many times to come to you (but have been prevented from doing so until now) in order that I might have a harvest among you, just as I have had among the other Gentiles.

[14]I am obligated both to Greeks and non-Greeks, both to the wise and the foolish. [15]That is why I am so eager to preach the gospel also to you who are at Rome.

[16]I am not ashamed of the gospel, because it is the power of God for the salvation of everyone who believes: first for the Jew, then for the Gentile. [17]For in the gospel a righteousness from God is revealed, a righteousness that is by faith from first to last,[c] just as it is written: "The righteous will live by faith."[d]

[18]The wrath of God is being revealed from heaven against all the godlessness and wickedness of men who suppress the truth by their wickedness, [19]since what may be known about God is plain to them, because God has made it plain to them. [20]For since the creation of the world God's invisible qualities—his eternal power and divine nature—have been clearly seen, being understood from what has been made, so that men are without excuse.

[21]For although they knew God, they neither glorified him as God nor gave thanks to him, but their thinking became

futile and their foolish hearts were darkened. [22]Although they claimed to be wise, they became fools [23]and exchanged the glory of the immortal God for images made to look like mortal man and birds and animals and reptiles.

[24]Therefore God gave them over in the sinful desires of their hearts to sexual impurity for the degrading of their bodies with one another. [25]They exchanged the truth of God for a lie, and worshiped and served created things rather than the Creator—who is forever praised. Amen.

[26]Because of this, God gave them over to shameful lusts. Even their women exchanged natural relations for unnatural ones. [27]In the same way the men also abandoned natural relations with women and were inflamed with lust for one another. Men committed indecent acts with other men, and received in themselves the due penalty for their perversion.

[28]Furthermore, since they did not think it worthwhile to retain the knowledge of God, he gave them over to a depraved mind, to do what ought not to be done. [29]They have become filled with every kind of wickedness, evil, greed and depravity. They are full of envy, murder, strife, deceit and malice. They are gossips, [30]slanderers, God-haters, insolent, arrogant and boastful; they invent ways of doing evil; they disobey their parents; [31]they are senseless, faithless, heartless, ruthless. [32]Although they know God's righteous decree that those who do such things deserve death, they not only continue to do these very things but also approve of those who practice them.

CHAPTER 2

You, therefore, have no excuse, you who pass judgment on someone else, for at whatever point you judge the other, you are condemning yourself, because you who pass judgment do the same things. [2]Now we know that God's judgment against those who do such things is based on truth. [3]So when you, a mere man, pass judgment on them and yet do the same things, do you think you will escape God's judgment? [4]Or do you show contempt for the riches of his kindness, tolerance and patience, not realizing that

c17 Or is from faith to faith   d17 Hab. 2:4

God's kindness leads you toward repentance?

⁵But because of your stubbornness and your unrepentant heart, you are storing up wrath against yourself for the day of God's wrath, when his righteous judgment will be revealed. ⁶God "will give to each person according to what he has done."ᵉ ⁷To those who by persistence in doing good seek glory, honor and immortality, he will give eternal life. ⁸But for those who are self-seeking and who reject the truth and follow evil, there will be wrath and anger. ⁹There will be trouble and distress for every human being who does evil: first for the Jew, then for the Gentile; ¹⁰but glory, honor and peace for everyone who does good: first for the Jew, then for the Gentile. ¹¹For God does not show favoritism.

¹²All who sin apart from the law will also perish apart from the law, and all who sin under the law will be judged by the law. ¹³For it is not those who hear the law who are righteous in God's sight, but it is those who obey the law who will be declared righteous. ¹⁴(Indeed, when Gentiles, who do not have the law, do by nature things required by the law, they are a law for themselves, even though they do not have the law, ¹⁵since they show that the requirements of the law are written on their hearts, their consciences also bearing witness, and their thoughts now accusing, now even defending them.) ¹⁶This will take place on the day when God will judge men's secrets through Jesus Christ, as my gospel declares.

¹⁷Now you, if you call yourself a Jew; if you rely on the law and brag about your relationship to God; ¹⁸if you know his will and approve of what is superior because you are instructed by the law; ¹⁹if you are convinced that you are a guide for the blind, a light for those who are in the dark, ²⁰an instructor of the foolish, a teacher of infants, because you have in the law the embodiment of knowledge and truth— ²¹you, then, who teach others, do you not teach yourself? You who preach against stealing, do you steal? ²²You who say that people should not commit adultery, do you commit adultery? You who abhor idols, do you rob temples? ²³You who brag about the law, do you dishonor God by breaking the law? ²⁴As it is written: "God's name is blasphemed among the Gentiles because of you."ᶠ

²⁵Circumcision has value if you observe the law, but if you break the law, you have become as though you had not been circumcised. ²⁶If those who are not circumcised keep the law's requirements, will they not be regarded as though they were circumcised? ²⁷The one who is not circumcised physically and yet obeys the law will condemn you who, even though you have theᵍ written code and circumcision, are a lawbreaker.

²⁸A man is not a Jew if he is only one outwardly, nor is circumcision merely outward and physical. ²⁹No, a man is a Jew if he is one inwardly; and circumcision is circumcision of the heart, by the Spirit, not by the written code. Such a man's praise is not from men, but from God.

CHAPTER 3
What advantage, then, is there in being a Jew, or what value is there in circumcision? ²Much in every way! First of all, they have been entrusted with the very words of God.

³What if some did not have faith? Will their lack of faith nullify God's faithfulness? ⁴Not at all! Let God be true, and every man a liar. As it is written:

"So that you may be proved right
    when you speak
and prevail when you judge."ʰ

⁵But if our unrighteousness brings out God's righteousness more clearly, what shall we say? That God is unjust in bringing his wrath on us? (I am using a human argument.) ⁶Certainly not! If that were so, how could God judge the world? ⁷Someone might argue, "If my falsehood enhances God's truthfulness and so increases his glory, why am I still condemned as a sinner?" ⁸Why not say— as we are being slanderously reported as saying and as some claim that we say— "Let us do evil that good may result"? Their condemnation is deserved.

⁹What shall we conclude then? Are we any betterⁱ? Not at all! We have already made the charge that Jews and Gentiles alike are all under sin. ¹⁰As it is written:

"There is no one righteous, not even
  one;
11 there is no one who understands,
     no one who seeks God.
12All have turned away,
     they have together become
        worthless;
there is no one who does good,
     not even one."^{j}
13"Their throats are open graves;
     their tongues practice deceit."^{k}
"The poison of vipers is on their
     lips."^{l}
14 "Their mouths are full of cursing
     and bitterness."^{m}
15"Their feet are swift to shed blood;
16 ruin and misery mark their ways,
17and the way of peace they do not
     know."^{n}
18 "There is no fear of God before their
     eyes."^{o}

19Now we know that whatever the law
says, it says to those who are under the
law, so that every mouth may be silenced
and the whole world held accountable to
God. 20Therefore no one will be declared
righteous in his sight by observing the
law; rather, through the law we become
conscious of sin.

21But now a righteousness from God,

apart from law, has been made known, to
which the Law and the Prophets testify.
22This righteousness from God comes
through faith in Jesus Christ to all who
believe. There is no difference, 23for all
have sinned and fall short of the glory of
God, 24and are justified freely by his grace
through the redemption that came by
Christ Jesus. 25God presented him as a
sacrifice of atonement,^{p} through faith in
his blood. He did this to demonstrate his
justice, because in his forbearance he had
left the sins committed beforehand unpunished— 26he did it to demonstrate his
justice at the present time, so as to be just
and the one who justifies those who have
faith in Jesus.

27Where, then, is boasting? It is excluded. On what principle? On that of
observing the law? No, but on that of
faith. 28For we maintain that a man is justified by faith apart from observing the
law. 29Is God the God of Jews only? Is he
not the God of Gentiles too? Yes, of Gentiles too, 30since there is only one God,
who will justify the circumcised by faith
and the uncircumcised through that same
faith. 31Do we, then, nullify the law by
this faith? Not at all! Rather, we uphold
the law.

^{j}12 Psalms 14:1-3; 53:1-3; Eccles. 7:20 ^{k}13 Psalm 5:9 ^{l}13 Psalm 140:3 ^{m}14 Psalm 10:7 ^{n}17 Isaiah 59:7,8
^{o}18 Psalm 36:1 ^{p}25 Or as the one who would turn aside his wrath, taking away sin

NOVEMBER 13 ☐ DAY 318
ROMANS 4–5
God's Provision of Righteousness

 OVERVIEW In today's reading, Paul illustrates the doctrine of justification by citing Abraham as one who "believed God, and it was credited to him as righteousness" (4:3). Abraham's faith points to two
changeless truths: (1) Since the beginning of time, God's method of
salvation has been justification by faith. (2) Justification results in peace
between God and humans. Paul discusses that peace in chapter 5,
then contrasts the disobedience of Adam with the obedience of Christ.
Adam's sin caused humans to be alienated from God; Christ's death
provided a way for humans to be reconciled to God.

Chapter 4	Chapter 5	
Justifying Faith Illustrated	Justifying Faith Demonstrated	Justifying Faith Contrasted
1	11 12	21
Abraham	All Believers	Adam

YOUR DAILY WALK "Only forty shopping days till Christmas!" Though Christmas is still more than a month away, perhaps you have already begun your Christmas shopping. Who is on your Christmas list this year? your immediate family members? close relatives? intimate friends? Those are the obvious choices. But what about the person at work who rubs you the wrong way? the neighbor next door who has a questionable lifestyle? the relative who holds a grudge against you? Are they high on your gift list? Probably not, for gift giving is usually directed to those you love.

We make a living by what we get; we make a life by what we give.

But God's gift to mankind—salvation—was provided "while we were still sinners" (5:8) . . . when there was nothing lovely about us at all! Paul describes those for whom Christ died as sinners and enemies of God (5:8, 10).

With God's love as a model, make a "Christmas list" of five people you know who need to receive God's free gift of salvation. By the end of the day, try to share God's plan of salvation with one of the five. Make it your goal to share the Good News of Christ with everyone on your list by Christmas Day!

INSIGHT All Roads Lead to Rome
Romans is one of the few epistles written by Paul to a church he had not previously visited, and yet in chapter 16 he includes a long list of personal greetings—twenty-six in all!

CHAPTER 4

What then shall we say that Abraham, our forefather, discovered in this matter? [2]If, in fact, Abraham was justified by works, he had something to boast about—but not before God. [3]What does the Scripture say? "Abraham believed God, and it was credited to him as righteousness."[q]

[4]Now when a man works, his wages are not credited to him as a gift, but as an obligation. [5]However, to the man who does not work but trusts God who justifies the wicked, his faith is credited as righteousness. [6]David says the same thing when he speaks of the blessedness of the man to whom God credits righteousness apart from works:

[7]"Blessed are they
  whose transgressions are forgiven,
  whose sins are covered.
[8]Blessed is the man
  whose sin the Lord will never count
    against him."[r]

[9]Is this blessedness only for the circumcised, or also for the uncircumcised? We have been saying that Abraham's faith was credited to him as righteousness. [10]Under what circumstances was it credited? Was it after he was circumcised, or before? It was not after, but before! [11]And

he received the sign of circumcision, a seal of the righteousness that he had by faith while he was still uncircumcised. So then, he is the father of all who believe but have not been circumcised, in order that righteousness might be credited to them. [12]And he is also the father of the circumcised who not only are circumcised but who also walk in the footsteps of the faith that our father Abraham had before he was circumcised.

[13]It was not through law that Abraham and his offspring received the promise that he would be heir of the world, but through the righteousness that comes by faith. [14]For if those who live by law are heirs, faith has no value and the promise is worthless, [15]because law brings wrath. And where there is no law there is no transgression.

[16]Therefore, the promise comes by faith, so that it may be by grace and may be guaranteed to all Abraham's offspring—not only to those who are of the law but also to those who are of the faith of Abraham. He is the father of us all. [17]As it is written: "I have made you a father of many nations."[s] He is our father in the sight of God, in whom he believed—the God who gives life to the dead and calls things that are not as though they were.

*q*3 Gen. 15:6; also in verse 22   *r*8 Psalm 32:1,2   *s*17 Gen. 17:5

[18]Against all hope, Abraham in hope believed and so became the father of many nations, just as it had been said to him, "So shall your offspring be."[t] [19]Without weakening in his faith, he faced the fact that his body was as good as dead—since he was about a hundred years old—and that Sarah's womb was also dead. [20]Yet he did not waver through unbelief regarding the promise of God, but was strengthened in his faith and gave glory to God, [21]being fully persuaded that God had power to do what he had promised. [22]This is why "it was credited to him as righteousness." [23]The words "it was credited to him" were written not for him alone, [24]but also for us, to whom God will credit righteousness—for us who believe in him who raised Jesus our Lord from the dead. [25]He was delivered over to death for our sins and was raised to life for our justification.

CHAPTER 5

Therefore, since we have been justified through faith, we[u] have peace with God through our Lord Jesus Christ, [2]through whom we have gained access by faith into this grace in which we now stand. And we[u] rejoice in the hope of the glory of God. [3]Not only so, but we[u] also rejoice in our sufferings, because we know that suffering produces perseverance; [4]perseverance, character; and character, hope. [5]And hope does not disappoint us, because God has poured out his love into our hearts by the Holy Spirit, whom he has given us.

[6]You see, at just the right time, when we were still powerless, Christ died for the ungodly. [7]Very rarely will anyone die for a righteous man, though for a good man someone might possibly dare to die. [8]But God demonstrates his own love for us in this: While we were still sinners, Christ died for us.

[9]Since we have now been justified by his blood, how much more shall we be saved from God's wrath through him! [10]For if, when we were God's enemies, we were reconciled to him through the death of his Son, how much more, having been reconciled, shall we be saved through his life! [11]Not only is this so, but we also rejoice in God through our Lord Jesus Christ, through whom we have now received reconciliation.

[12]Therefore, just as sin entered the world through one man, and death through sin, and in this way death came to all men, because all sinned— [13]for before the law was given, sin was in the world. But sin is not taken into account when there is no law. [14]Nevertheless, death reigned from the time of Adam to the time of Moses, even over those who did not sin by breaking a command, as did Adam, who was a pattern of the one to come.

[15]But the gift is not like the trespass. For if the many died by the trespass of the one man, how much more did God's grace and the gift that came by the grace of the one man, Jesus Christ, overflow to the many! [16]Again, the gift of God is not like the result of the one man's sin: The judgment followed one sin and brought condemnation, but the gift followed many trespasses and brought justification. [17]For if, by the trespass of the one man, death reigned through that one man, how much more will those who receive God's abundant provision of grace and of the gift of righteousness reign in life through the one man, Jesus Christ.

[18]Consequently, just as the result of one trespass was condemnation for all men, so also the result of one act of righteousness was justification that brings life for all men. [19]For just as through the disobedience of the one man the many were made sinners, so also through the obedience of the one man the many will be made righteous.

[20]The law was added so that the trespass might increase. But where sin increased, grace increased all the more, [21]so that, just as sin reigned in death, so also grace might reign through righteousness to bring eternal life through Jesus Christ our Lord.

[t]18 Gen. 15:5   [u]1,2,3 Or let us

NOVEMBER 14 ☐ DAY 319
Unreservedly Available

 LOOK BACK Saul the persecutor becomes Paul the apostle to the Gentiles. His "travel diary" reads like a modern-day adventure novel as he faces mobs and magistrates, stonings and shipwreck for the privilege of spreading the Good News from Antioch to Rome.

Paul's missionary journeys cover thousands of miles and more than a decade of his life. Following his trips to such areas as Galatia, Macedonia and Asia, Paul is arrested in Jerusalem and faces a series of trials at the hands of Felix, Festus and Agrippa. Failing to find justice in the courts, Paul declares, "I appeal to Caesar" (Acts 25:11), and to Rome he goes! The journey by land and sea is fraught with peril, but at last Paul arrives to await trial. During his imprisonment in Rome, he is not free to travel but is able to meet with his spiritual children and prepare them for the ministry that will soon be passed on to them.

The *epistles* (letters) of Paul correspond to the *expeditions* of Paul. On his first journey, he writes the book of Galatians. On his second journey, he writes the books of 1 and 2 Thessalonians. On his third journey, he writes the books of Romans and 1 and 2 Corinthians. As you read these epistles in the coming weeks, turn back to the corresponding chapter in Acts to establish the setting for the letter.

 LOOK UP Imagine that you are part of a military unit stationed on the edge of enemy territory. To make matters worse, the enemy is headed your way—fast.

True greatness is to serve unnoticed and to work unseen.

You await orders to retreat, but instead you hear your commanding officer give these orders: "Men, you are to stay right where you are and fight as hard as you can, as long as you can, until you are killed or captured." (Incidentally, a situation very similar to this actually happened during World War II. You'll find it documented in the book and movie entitled *They Were Expendable*.)

How would you feel about such an assignment? It's definitely not a role for the fainthearted. But those willing to look death in the face and become "walking dead men" can wreak havoc on the enemy. Why? Because death holds no sway over them. They are fearless and focused. They have nothing to lose and everything to gain. They have already counted the cost of service. In short, they are a dangerous foe because they are expendable.

 LOOK AHEAD The apostles and disciples in the book of Acts saw themselves as expendable in the service of their Lord. Self-preservation was the last thought on their minds. They were totally, unreservedly available to their Lord. You can see that attitude in a number of verses from Paul's letters:

"I have been crucified with Christ and I no longer live, but Christ lives in me. The life I live in the body, I live by faith in the Son of God, who loved me and gave himself for me" (Galatians 2:20).

"For to me, to live is Christ and to die is gain" (Philippians 1:21).

If self-promotion or self-preservation is your goal in life, you have yet to discover the liberating power of expendability. But once you see your time, talents and treasure as 100 percent available in the service of your Lord, then you'll be able to say with Paul: "However, I consider my life worth nothing to me, if only I may finish the race and complete the task the Lord Jesus has given me—the task of testifying to the gospel of God's grace" (Acts 20:24).

NOVEMBER 15 □ DAY 320
ROMANS 6–8
God's Power for Righteous Living

OVERVIEW Paul, the gifted debater, anticipates the logical questions that will follow his explanation of justification by faith: Since grace abounds, may I continue to sin? Can I sin because I am no longer under the law, but under grace? Is the law sinful? After answering these and other questions, Paul moves on to discuss the constant struggle between the two natures: the flesh and the spirit. He concludes his arguments by revealing two liberating facts: There is no condemnation for those who are in Christ (8:1); and nothing on earth or in heaven can separate us from the love of God (8:39).

Chapter 6	Chapter 7	Chapter 8
The Potential for Holy Living	The Problem with Holy Living	The Power for Holy Living
Perfect Christ	Wretched Man	Ministering Spirit

If sin rules us, it will inevitably ruin us.

YOUR DAILY WALK In the margin, write down the name of a former employer, someone you *used* to work for. Now suppose you were to walk into your former employer's office and he told you, "All right, don't just stand there. Get to work!" What would you do?

Probably you'd do absolutely nothing . . . except walk out of the building. Why? Because you no longer work for your former employer. When you were under his authority, you did whatever he told you to do. But now that you work for someone else, he has lost that position of authority. You answer to another boss now!

Now read 6:16–18. Do you see the parallel? Formerly you were a servant to sin. Sin was your master, your employer. But now in Christ you have been set free from that bondage in order to become a "slave" to righteousness. Christ is your new Employer, and your responsibility is to answer to him!

Are you still taking orders from your old employer, sin, as if it had ultimate control over you? Write out the words of 6:13, put them in a prominent place and make them your "marching orders" for today. You might even share them with your boss at work!

INSIGHT The Winning Team for Nearly 2,000 Years
The words *we are more than conquerors* (8:37) literally mean "we are in the process of winning." Let your actions today demonstrate the confidence you gain from being on the winning team!

CHAPTER 6
What shall we say, then? Shall we go on sinning so that grace may increase? ²By no means! We died to sin; how can we live in it any longer? ³Or don't you know that all of us who were baptized into Christ Jesus were baptized into his death? ⁴We were therefore buried with him through baptism into death in order that, just as Christ was raised from the dead through the glory

of the Father, we too may live a new life.

⁵If we have been united with him like this in his death, we will certainly also be united with him in his resurrection. ⁶For we know that our old self was crucified with him so that the body of sin might be done away with,ᵛ that we should no longer be slaves to sin— ⁷because anyone who has died has been freed from sin.

⁸Now if we died with Christ, we believe

ᵛ6 Or be rendered powerless

that we will also live with him. ⁹For we know that since Christ was raised from the dead, he cannot die again; death no longer has mastery over him. ¹⁰The death he died, he died to sin once for all; but the life he lives, he lives to God.

¹¹In the same way, count yourselves dead to sin but alive to God in Christ Jesus. ¹²Therefore do not let sin reign in your mortal body so that you obey its evil desires. ¹³Do not offer the parts of your body to sin, as instruments of wickedness, but rather offer yourselves to God, as those who have been brought from death to life; and offer the parts of your body to him as instruments of righteousness. ¹⁴For sin shall not be your master, because you are not under law, but under grace.

¹⁵What then? Shall we sin because we are not under law but under grace? By no means! ¹⁶Don't you know that when you offer yourselves to someone to obey him as slaves, you are slaves to the one whom you obey—whether you are slaves to sin, which leads to death, or to obedience, which leads to righteousness? ¹⁷But thanks be to God that, though you used to be slaves to sin, you wholeheartedly obeyed the form of teaching to which you were entrusted. ¹⁸You have been set free from sin and have become slaves to righteousness.

¹⁹I put this in human terms because you are weak in your natural selves. Just as you used to offer the parts of your body in slavery to impurity and to ever-increasing wickedness, so now offer them in slavery to righteousness leading to holiness. ²⁰When you were slaves to sin, you were free from the control of righteousness. ²¹What benefit did you reap at that time from the things you are now ashamed of? Those things result in death! ²²But now that you have been set free from sin and have become slaves to God, the benefit you reap leads to holiness, and the result is eternal life. ²³For the wages of sin is death, but the gift of God is eternal life in^w Christ Jesus our Lord.

CHAPTER 7

Do you not know, brothers—for I am speaking to men who know the law—that the law has authority over a man only as long as he lives? ²For example, by law a married woman is bound to her husband as long as he is alive, but if her husband dies, she is released from the law of marriage. ³So then, if she marries another man while her husband is still alive, she is called an adulteress. But if her husband dies, she is released from that law and is not an adulteress, even though she marries another man.

⁴So, my brothers, you also died to the law through the body of Christ, that you might belong to another, to him who was raised from the dead, in order that we might bear fruit to God. ⁵For when we were controlled by the sinful nature,^{x} the sinful passions aroused by the law were at work in our bodies, so that we bore fruit for death. ⁶But now, by dying to what once bound us, we have been released from the law so that we serve in the new way of the Spirit, and not in the old way of the written code.

⁷What shall we say, then? Is the law sin? Certainly not! Indeed I would not have known what sin was except through the law. For I would not have known what coveting really was if the law had not said, "Do not covet."^{y} ⁸But sin, seizing the opportunity afforded by the commandment, produced in me every kind of covetous desire. For apart from law, sin is dead. ⁹Once I was alive apart from law; but when the commandment came, sin sprang to life and I died. ¹⁰I found that the very commandment that was intended to bring life actually brought death. ¹¹For sin, seizing the opportunity afforded by the commandment, deceived me, and through the commandment put me to death. ¹²So then, the law is holy, and the commandment is holy, righteous and good.

¹³Did that which is good, then, become death to me? By no means! But in order that sin might be recognized as sin, it produced death in me through what was good, so that through the commandment sin might become utterly sinful.

¹⁴We know that the law is spiritual; but I am unspiritual, sold as a slave to sin. ¹⁵I do not understand what I do. For what I want to do I do not do, but what I hate I do. ¹⁶And if I do what I do not want to do, I agree that the law is good. ¹⁷As it is, it is no longer I myself who do it, but it

^{w}23 Or *through* ^{x}5 Or *the flesh*; also in verse 25 ^{y}7 Exodus 20:17; Deut. 5:21

is sin living in me. [18]I know that nothing good lives in me, that is, in my sinful nature.[z] For I have the desire to do what is good, but I cannot carry it out. [19]For what I do is not the good I want to do; no, the evil I do not want to do—this I keep on doing. [20]Now if I do what I do not want to do, it is no longer I who do it, but it is sin living in me that does it.

[21]So I find this law at work: When I want to do good, evil is right there with me. [22]For in my inner being I delight in God's law; [23]but I see another law at work in the members of my body, waging war against the law of my mind and making me a prisoner of the law of sin at work within my members. [24]What a wretched man I am! Who will rescue me from this body of death? [25]Thanks be to God— through Jesus Christ our Lord!

So then, I myself in my mind am a slave to God's law, but in the sinful nature a slave to the law of sin.

CHAPTER 8

Therefore, there is now no condemnation for those who are in Christ Jesus,[a] [2]because through Christ Jesus the law of the Spirit of life set me free from the law of sin and death. [3]For what the law was powerless to do in that it was weakened by the sinful nature,[b] God did by sending his own Son in the likeness of sinful man to be a sin offering.[c] And so he condemned sin in sinful man,[d] [4]in order that the righteous requirements of the law might be fully met in us, who do not live according to the sinful nature but according to the Spirit.

[5]Those who live according to the sinful nature have their minds set on what that nature desires; but those who live in accordance with the Spirit have their minds set on what the Spirit desires. [6]The mind of sinful man[e] is death, but the mind controlled by the Spirit is life and peace; [7]the sinful mind[f] is hostile to God. It does not submit to God's law, nor can it do so. [8]Those controlled by the sinful nature cannot please God.

[9]You, however, are controlled not by the sinful nature but by the Spirit, if the Spirit of God lives in you. And if anyone does not have the Spirit of Christ, he does not belong to Christ. [10]But if Christ is in you, your body is dead because of sin, yet your spirit is alive because of righteousness. [11]And if the Spirit of him who raised Jesus from the dead is living in you, he who raised Christ from the dead will also give life to your mortal bodies through his Spirit, who lives in you.

[12]Therefore, brothers, we have an obligation—but it is not to the sinful nature, to live according to it. [13]For if you live according to the sinful nature, you will die; but if by the Spirit you put to death the misdeeds of the body, you will live, [14]because those who are led by the Spirit of God are sons of God. [15]For you did not receive a spirit that makes you a slave again to fear, but you received the Spirit of sonship.[g] And by him we cry, "Abba,[h] Father." [16]The Spirit himself testifies with our spirit that we are God's children. [17]Now if we are children, then we are heirs—heirs of God and co-heirs with Christ, if indeed we share in his sufferings in order that we may also share in his glory.

[18]I consider that our present sufferings are not worth comparing with the glory that will be revealed in us. [19]The creation waits in eager expectation for the sons of God to be revealed. [20]For the creation was subjected to frustration, not by its own choice, but by the will of the one who subjected it, in hope [21]that[i] the creation itself will be liberated from its bondage to decay and brought into the glorious freedom of the children of God.

[22]We know that the whole creation has been groaning as in the pains of childbirth right up to the present time. [23]Not only so, but we ourselves, who have the firstfruits of the Spirit, groan inwardly as we wait eagerly for our adoption as sons, the redemption of our bodies. [24]For in this hope we were saved. But hope that is seen is no hope at all. Who hopes for what he already has? [25]But if we hope for what we do not yet have, we wait for it patiently.

[26]In the same way, the Spirit helps us in our weakness. We do not know what we ought to pray for, but the Spirit himself intercedes for us with groans that words cannot express. [27]And he who searches our hearts knows the mind of the Spirit,

[z]18 Or my flesh　[a]1 Some later manuscripts Jesus, who do not live according to the sinful nature but according to the Spirit,
[b]3 Or the flesh; also in verses 4, 5, 8, 9, 12 and 13　[c]3 Or man, for sin　[d]3 Or in the flesh　[e]6 Or mind set on the flesh
[f]7 Or the mind set on the flesh　[g]15 Or adoption　[h]15 Aramaic for Father　[i]20,21 Or subjected it in hope. 21For

because the Spirit intercedes for the saints in accordance with God's will.

²⁸And we know that in all things God works for the good of those who love him,ʲ whoᵏ have been called according to his purpose. ²⁹For those God foreknew he also predestined to be conformed to the likeness of his Son, that he might be the firstborn among many brothers. ³⁰And those he predestined, he also called; those he called, he also justified; those he justified, he also glorified.

³¹What, then, shall we say in response to this? If God is for us, who can be against us? ³²He who did not spare his own Son, but gave him up for us all—how will he not also, along with him, graciously give us all things? ³³Who will bring any charge against those whom God has chosen? It is God who justifies. ³⁴Who is he that condemns? Christ Jesus, who died—more than that, who was raised to life—is at the right hand of God and is also interceding for us. ³⁵Who shall separate us from the love of Christ? Shall trouble or hardship or persecution or famine or nakedness or danger or sword? ³⁶As it is written:

"For your sake we face death all day
        long;
    we are considered as sheep to be
        slaughtered."ˡ

³⁷No, in all these things we are more than conquerors through him who loved us. ³⁸For I am convinced that neither death nor life, neither angels nor demons,ᵐ neither the present nor the future, nor any powers, ³⁹neither height nor depth, nor anything else in all creation, will be able to separate us from the love of God that is in Christ Jesus our Lord.

ʲ28 Some manuscripts *And we know that all things work together for good to those who love God*   ᵏ28 Or *works together with those who love him to bring about what is good—with those who*   ˡ36 Psalm 44:22   ᵐ38 Or *nor heavenly rulers*

NOVEMBER 16 ☐ DAY 321
ROMANS 9–11
God's Plan of Righteousness

OVERVIEW In one sense Romans 9–11 resembles a parenthesis because of the way chapters 8 and 12 flow together. (Read 8:39 and 12:1). Even so, these chapters are essential to Paul's argument and are strategically placed in the epistle. Paul has said that salvation is by grace—God's undeserved favor from start to finish! This raises the question: If God's people (the Jews) have rejected his grace, then hasn't God also discarded his people? Paul answers with three observations:
1. God chose the Jews by sovereign selection.
2. The Jews turned away from God by willful rejection.
3. God's rejection of his people is both incomplete (there is a remnant) and temporary (they will be restored).

Paul then concludes the section with praise to God for his incomprehensible ways—an appropriate response!

Chapter 9	Chapter 10	Chapter 11
Israel's Past	Israel's Present	Israel's Future
Election	Rejection	Restoration

YOUR DAILY WALK It hurts to see someone reject the gospel. It hurts even more when that "someone" is part of your family. But it hurts most when that "someone" who rejects the gospel prides him or herself on being religious!

The authority for faith is the revelation of God. Paul lamented that his own people, the Jews, had rejected the gospel. Though their religious zeal was exemplary, it was based on something other than Christ. It was a zeal without knowledge—activity without reality—which only led to self-deception and false pride. No one could doubt the sincerity of their beliefs and actions. But they were sincerely wrong . . . and so they died in their sins.

The best way to combat such misplaced confidence is by a clear proclamation of the gospel. Using 10:13–15 as your model, look for one sincere—but sincerely wrong—individual to whom you can bring "good news" today!

INSIGHT Paul, the Old Testament Whiz
In the space of these three chapters, Paul demonstrates his thorough knowledge of the Old Testament Scriptures by quoting from ten different books. How many can you identify? Have fun!

CHAPTER 9

I speak the truth in Christ—I am not lying, my conscience confirms it in the Holy Spirit— ²I have great sorrow and unceasing anguish in my heart. ³For I could wish that I myself were cursed and cut off from Christ for the sake of my brothers, those of my own race, ⁴the people of Israel. Theirs is the adoption as sons; theirs the divine glory, the covenants, the receiving of the law, the temple worship and the promises. ⁵Theirs are the patriarchs, and from them is traced the human ancestry of Christ, who is God over all, forever praised!ⁿ Amen.

⁶It is not as though God's word had failed. For not all who are descended from Israel are Israel. ⁷Nor because they are his descendants are they all Abraham's children. On the contrary, "It is through Isaac that your offspring will be reckoned."ᵒ ⁸In other words, it is not the natural children who are God's children, but it is the children of the promise who are regarded as Abraham's offspring. ⁹For this was how the promise was stated: "At the appointed time I will return, and Sarah will have a son."ᵖ

¹⁰Not only that, but Rebekah's children had one and the same father, our father Isaac. ¹¹Yet, before the twins were born or had done anything good or bad—in order that God's purpose in election might stand: ¹²not by works but by him who calls—she was told, "The older will serve the younger."�q ¹³Just as it is written: "Jacob I loved, but Esau I hated."ʳ

¹⁴What then shall we say? Is God unjust? Not at all! ¹⁵For he says to Moses,

"I will have mercy on whom I have
    mercy,
  and I will have compassion on
    whom I have compassion."ˢ

¹⁶It does not, therefore, depend on man's desire or effort, but on God's mercy. ¹⁷For the Scripture says to Pharaoh: "I raised you up for this very purpose, that I might display my power in you and that my name might be proclaimed in all the earth."ᵗ ¹⁸Therefore God has mercy on whom he wants to have mercy, and he hardens whom he wants to harden.

¹⁹One of you will say to me: "Then why does God still blame us? For who resists his will?" ²⁰But who are you, O man, to talk back to God? "Shall what is formed say to him who formed it, 'Why did you make me like this?' "ᵘ ²¹Does not the potter have the right to make out of the same lump of clay some pottery for noble purposes and some for common use?

²²What if God, choosing to show his wrath and make his power known, bore with great patience the objects of his wrath—prepared for destruction? ²³What if he did this to make the riches of his glory known to the objects of his mercy, whom he prepared in advance for glory— ²⁴even us, whom he also called, not only from the Jews but also from the Gentiles? ²⁵As he says in Hosea:

"I will call them 'my people' who are
    not my people;
  and I will call her 'my loved one'
    who is not my loved one,"ᵛ

²⁶and,

ⁿ5 Or *Christ, who is over all. God be forever praised!* Or *Christ. God who is over all be forever praised!*   ᵒ7 Gen. 21:12
ᵖ9 Gen. 18:10,14   �q12 Gen. 25:23   ʳ13 Mal. 1:2,3   ˢ15 Exodus 33:19   ᵗ17 Exodus 9:16   ᵘ20 Isaiah 29:16; 45:9
ᵛ25 Hosea 2:23

"It will happen that in the very place
    where it was said to them,
    'You are not my people,'
they will be called 'sons of the living
    God.' "w

27Isaiah cries out concerning Israel:

"Though the number of the Israelites
    be like the sand by the sea,
    only the remnant will be saved.
28For the Lord will carry out
    his sentence on earth with speed
    and finality."x

29It is just as Isaiah said previously:

"Unless the Lord Almighty
    had left us descendants,
we would have become like Sodom,
we would have been like
    Gomorrah."y

30What then shall we say? That the
Gentiles, who did not pursue righteousness, have obtained it, a righteousness
that is by faith; 31but Israel, who pursued
a law of righteousness, has not attained it.
32Why not? Because they pursued it not
by faith but as if it were by works. They
stumbled over the "stumbling stone." 33As
it is written:

"See, I lay in Zion a stone that causes
    men to stumble
    and a rock that makes them fall,
and the one who trusts in him will
    never be put to shame."z

CHAPTER 10
Brothers, my heart's desire and prayer to
God for the Israelites is that they may be
saved. 2For I can testify about them that
they are zealous for God, but their zeal is
not based on knowledge. 3Since they did
not know the righteousness that comes
from God and sought to establish their
own, they did not submit to God's righteousness. 4Christ is the end of the law so
that there may be righteousness for everyone who believes.
    5Moses describes in this way the righ-
teousness that is by the law: "The man
who does these things will live by
them."a 6But the righteousness that is by
faith says: "Do not say in your heart, 'Who
will ascend into heaven?'b" (that is, to

bring Christ down) 7"or 'Who will descend into the deep?'c" (that is, to bring
Christ up from the dead). 8But what does
it say? "The word is near you; it is in your
mouth and in your heart,"d that is, the
word of faith we are proclaiming: 9That
if you confess with your mouth, "Jesus is
Lord," and believe in your heart that God
raised him from the dead, you will be
saved. 10For it is with your heart that you
believe and are justified, and it is with
your mouth that you confess and are
saved. 11As the Scripture says, "Anyone
who trusts in him will never be put to
shame."e 12For there is no difference between Jew and Gentile—the same Lord is
Lord of all and richly blesses all who call
on him, 13for, "Everyone who calls on the
name of the Lord will be saved."f
    14How, then, can they call on the one
they have not believed in? And how can
they believe in the one of whom they have
not heard? And how can they hear without someone preaching to them? 15And
how can they preach unless they are sent?
As it is written, "How beautiful are the
feet of those who bring good news!"g
    16But not all the Israelites accepted the
good news. For Isaiah says, "Lord, who
has believed our message?"h 17Conse-
quently, faith comes from hearing the
message, and the message is heard
through the word of Christ. 18But I ask:
Did they not hear? Of course they did:

"Their voice has gone out into all the
    earth,
    their words to the ends of the
    world."i

19Again I ask: Did Israel not understand?
First, Moses says,

"I will make you envious by those who
    are not a nation;
I will make you angry by a nation
    that has no understanding."j

20And Isaiah boldly says,

"I was found by those who did not
    seek me;
I revealed myself to those who did
    not ask for me."k

21But concerning Israel he says,

w26 Hosea 1:10   x28 Isaiah 10:22,23   y29 Isaiah 1:9   z33 Isaiah 8:14; 28:16   a5 Lev. 18:5   b6 Deut. 30:12
c7 Deut. 30:13   d8 Deut. 30:14   e11 Isaiah 28:16   f13 Joel 2:32   g15 Isaiah 52:7   h16 Isaiah 53:1   i18 Psalm 19:4
j19 Deut. 32:21   k20 Isaiah 65:1

"All day long I have held out my
      hands
   to a disobedient and obstinate
      people."[l]

CHAPTER 11

I ask then: Did God reject his people? By
no means! I am an Israelite myself, a
descendant of Abraham, from the tribe of
Benjamin. [2]God did not reject his people,
whom he foreknew. Don't you know
what the Scripture says in the passage
about Elijah—how he appealed to God
against Israel: [3]"Lord, they have killed
your prophets and torn down your altars;
I am the only one left, and they are trying
to kill me"[m]? [4]And what was God's answer to him? "I have reserved for myself
seven thousand who have not bowed the
knee to Baal."[n] [5]So too, at the present
time there is a remnant chosen by grace.
[6]And if by grace, then it is no longer by
works; if it were, grace would no longer
be grace.[o]

[7]What then? What Israel sought so earnestly it did not obtain, but the elect did.
The others were hardened, [8]as it is written:

"God gave them a spirit of stupor,
   eyes so that they could not see
   and ears so that they could not hear,
to this very day."[p]

[9]And David says:

"May their table become a snare and a
      trap,
   a stumbling block and a retribution
      for them.
[10]May their eyes be darkened so they
      cannot see,
   and their backs be bent forever."[q]

[11]Again I ask: Did they stumble so as to
fall beyond recovery? Not at all! Rather,
because of their transgression, salvation
has come to the Gentiles to make Israel
envious. [12]But if their transgression
means riches for the world, and their loss
means riches for the Gentiles, how much
greater riches will their fullness bring!

[13]I am talking to you Gentiles. Inas-
much as I am the apostle to the Gentiles, I
make much of my ministry [14]in the hope
that I may somehow arouse my own peo-

ple to envy and save some of them. [15]For
if their rejection is the reconciliation of the
world, what will their acceptance be but
life from the dead? [16]If the part of the
dough offered as firstfruits is holy, then
the whole batch is holy; if the root is holy,
so are the branches.

[17]If some of the branches have been
broken off, and you, though a wild olive
shoot, have been grafted in among the
others and now share in the nourishing
sap from the olive root, [18]do not boast
over those branches. If you do, consider
this: You do not support the root, but the
root supports you. [19]You will say then,
"Branches were broken off so that I could
be grafted in." [20]Granted. But they were
broken off because of unbelief, and you
stand by faith. Do not be arrogant, but be
afraid. [21]For if God did not spare the natural branches, he will not spare you either.

[22]Consider therefore the kindness and
sternness of God: sternness to those who
fell, but kindness to you, provided that
you continue in his kindness. Otherwise,
you also will be cut off. [23]And if they do
not persist in unbelief, they will be
grafted in, for God is able to graft them in
again. [24]After all, if you were cut out of an
olive tree that is wild by nature, and contrary to nature were grafted into a cultivated olive tree, how much more readily
will these, the natural branches, be
grafted into their own olive tree!

[25]I do not want you to be ignorant of
this mystery, brothers, so that you may
not be conceited: Israel has experienced a
hardening in part until the full number of
the Gentiles has come in. [26]And so all Israel will be saved, as it is written:

"The deliverer will come from Zion;
   he will turn godlessness away from
      Jacob.
[27]And this is[r] my covenant with them
   when I take away their sins."[s]

[28]As far as the gospel is concerned, they
are enemies on your account; but as far as
election is concerned, they are loved on
account of the patriarchs, [29]for God's gifts
and his call are irrevocable. [30]Just as you
who were at one time disobedient to God
have now received mercy as a result of

---

[l]21 Isaiah 65:2   [m]3 1 Kings 19:10,14   [n]4 1 Kings 19:18   [o]6 Some manuscripts *by grace. But if by works, then it is no longer
grace; if it were, work would no longer be work.*   [p]8 Deut. 29:4; Isaiah 29:10   [q]10 Psalm 69:22,23   [r]27 Or *will be*
[s]27 Isaiah 59:20,21; 27:9; Jer. 31:33,34

their disobedience, [31]so they too have now become disobedient in order that they too may now[t] receive mercy as a result of God's mercy to you. [32]For God has bound all men over to disobedience so that he may have mercy on them all.

[33]Oh, the depth of the riches of the wisdom and[u] knowledge of God!

How unsearchable his judgments, and his paths beyond tracing out!
[34]"Who has known the mind of the Lord?
Or who has been his counselor?"[v]
[35]"Who has ever given to God, that God should repay him?"[w]
[36]For from him and through him and to him are all things.
To him be the glory forever! Amen.

[t]31 Some manuscripts do not have *now*.   [u]33 Or *riches and the wisdom and the*   [v]34 Isaiah 40:13   [w]35 Job 41:11

NOVEMBER 17 □ DAY 322
ROMANS 12–16
Practical Outworking of Righteousness

OVERVIEW In the first eleven chapters, Paul has discussed the key doctrines of the Christian faith. But Christian living requires more than theory; it demands attention to duty as well, the daily outworking of applied doctrine. To Paul, what you believe and how you behave are inseparable. Doctrine dictates that love must control a believer's conduct both inside and outside the church (Romans 12), that a Christian must be a good citizen (Romans 13) and that a Christian must make proper ethical choices in consideration of weaker believers (Romans 14). Paul concludes his letter with a summary of his travel plans, a list of personal greetings and a warning against false teachers.

Chapter 12	Chapter 13	Chapters 14–15	Chapter 16
Serve One Another	Submit to Authority	Support the Weak	Salute the Saints
Practical Appeals			Personal Postscripts

YOUR DAILY WALK "WANTED: DEAD AND ALIVE!" Do you detect anything peculiar about a "wanted" poster like this?

God wants you dead (to sin and self), but he also wants you alive (for service). In the Old Testament, animals were offered for sacrifices, and they had no say-so in the matter! But now, based on God's abundant mercies on your behalf, he is calling you to become a voluntary living sacrifice as a reasonable expression of your gratitude for all he has done for you and through you.

Sacrifice is the ecstasy of giving the best we have to the one we love the most.

The trouble with being a living sacrifice is that, when the heat's on, the tendency is to crawl off the altar! If you have trouble volunteering for such an assignment, chances are you need to review God's mercies in your life. Thumb back through the pages of Romans, and see if you can discover at least six of those mercies . . . but don't stop there!

1. _____ (3:24) 4. _____ ( )
2. _____ (5:1)   5. _____ ( )
3. _____ (8:1)   6. _____ ( )

INSIGHT A Doxology of Doxologies
The word *doxology* comes from a Greek word meaning "brightness, radiance, splendor, glory." Notice how frequently Paul breaks forth in a spontaneous doxology (11:33–36; 15:9–13; 16:25–27) and whose glory is in view!

CHAPTER 12

Therefore, I urge you, brothers, in view of God's mercy, to offer your bodies as living sacrifices, holy and pleasing to God— this is your spiritual[x] act of worship. [2]Do not conform any longer to the pattern of this world, but be transformed by the renewing of your mind. Then you will be able to test and approve what God's will is—his good, pleasing and perfect will.

[3]For by the grace given me I say to every one of you: Do not think of yourself more highly than you ought, but rather think of yourself with sober judgment, in accordance with the measure of faith God has given you. [4]Just as each of us has one body with many members, and these members do not all have the same function, [5]so in Christ we who are many form one body, and each member belongs to all the others. [6]We have different gifts, according to the grace given us. If a man's gift is prophesying, let him use it in proportion to his[y] faith. [7]If it is serving, let him serve; if it is teaching, let him teach; [8]if it is encouraging, let him encourage; if it is contributing to the needs of others, let him give generously; if it is leadership, let him govern diligently; if it is showing mercy, let him do it cheerfully.

[9]Love must be sincere. Hate what is evil; cling to what is good. [10]Be devoted to one another in brotherly love. Honor one another above yourselves. [11]Never be lacking in zeal, but keep your spiritual fervor, serving the Lord. [12]Be joyful in hope, patient in affliction, faithful in prayer. [13]Share with God's people who are in need. Practice hospitality.

[14]Bless those who persecute you; bless and do not curse. [15]Rejoice with those who rejoice; mourn with those who mourn. [16]Live in harmony with one another. Do not be proud, but be willing to associate with people of low position.[z] Do not be conceited.

[17]Do not repay anyone evil for evil. Be careful to do what is right in the eyes of everybody. [18]If it is possible, as far as it depends on you, live at peace with everyone. [19]Do not take revenge, my friends, but leave room for God's wrath, for it is written: "It is mine to avenge; I will repay,"[a] says the Lord. [20]On the contrary:

"If your enemy is hungry, feed him;
    if he is thirsty, give him something
        to drink.
In doing this, you will heap burning
    coals on his head."[b]

[21]Do not be overcome by evil, but overcome evil with good.

CHAPTER 13

Everyone must submit himself to the governing authorities, for there is no authority except that which God has established. The authorities that exist have been established by God. [2]Consequently, he who rebels against the authority is rebelling against what God has instituted, and those who do so will bring judgment on themselves. [3]For rulers hold no terror for those who do right, but for those who do wrong. Do you want to be free from fear of the one in authority? Then do what is right and he will commend you. [4]For he is God's servant to do you good. But if you do wrong, be afraid, for he does not bear the sword for nothing. He is God's servant, an agent of wrath to bring punishment on the wrongdoer. [5]Therefore, it is necessary to submit to the authorities, not only because of possible punishment but also because of conscience.

[6]This is also why you pay taxes, for the authorities are God's servants, who give their full time to governing. [7]Give everyone what you owe him: If you owe taxes, pay taxes; if revenue, then revenue; if respect, then respect; if honor, then honor.

[8]Let no debt remain outstanding, except the continuing debt to love one another, for he who loves his fellowman has fulfilled the law. [9]The commandments, "Do not commit adultery," "Do not murder," "Do not steal," "Do not covet,"[c] and

---

[x]1 Or *reasonable*   [y]6 Or *in agreement with the*   [z]16 Or *willing to do menial work*   [a]19 Deut. 32:35   [b]20 Prov. 25:21,22
[c]9 Exodus 20:13-15,17; Deut. 5:17-19,21

whatever other commandment there may be, are summed up in this one rule: "Love your neighbor as yourself."[d] [10]Love does no harm to its neighbor. Therefore love is the fulfillment of the law.

[11]And do this, understanding the present time. The hour has come for you to wake up from your slumber, because our salvation is nearer now than when we first believed. [12]The night is nearly over; the day is almost here. So let us put aside the deeds of darkness and put on the armor of light. [13]Let us behave decently, as in the daytime, not in orgies and drunkenness, not in sexual immorality and debauchery, not in dissension and jealousy. [14]Rather, clothe yourselves with the Lord Jesus Christ, and do not think about how to gratify the desires of the sinful nature.[e]

CHAPTER 14

Accept him whose faith is weak, without passing judgment on disputable matters. [2]One man's faith allows him to eat everything, but another man, whose faith is weak, eats only vegetables. [3]The man who eats everything must not look down on him who does not, and the man who does not eat everything must not condemn the man who does, for God has accepted him. [4]Who are you to judge someone else's servant? To his own master he stands or falls. And he will stand, for the Lord is able to make him stand.

[5]One man considers one day more sacred than another; another man considers every day alike. Each one should be fully convinced in his own mind. [6]He who regards one day as special, does so to the Lord. He who eats meat, eats to the Lord, for he gives thanks to God; and he who abstains, does so to the Lord and gives thanks to God. [7]For none of us lives to himself alone and none of us dies to himself alone. [8]If we live, we live to the Lord; and if we die, we die to the Lord. So, whether we live or die, we belong to the Lord.

[9]For this very reason, Christ died and returned to life so that he might be the Lord of both the dead and the living. [10]You, then, why do you judge your brother? Or why do you look down on your brother? For we will all stand before God's judgment seat. [11]It is written:

" 'As surely as I live,' says the Lord,
'every knee will bow before me;
    every tongue will confess to
        God.' "[f]

[12]So then, each of us will give an account of himself to God.

[13]Therefore let us stop passing judgment on one another. Instead, make up your mind not to put any stumbling block or obstacle in your brother's way. [14]As one who is in the Lord Jesus, I am fully convinced that no food[g] is unclean in itself. But if anyone regards something as unclean, then for him it is unclean. [15]If your brother is distressed because of what you eat, you are no longer acting in love. Do not by your eating destroy your brother for whom Christ died. [16]Do not allow what you consider good to be spoken of as evil. [17]For the kingdom of God is not a matter of eating and drinking, but of righteousness, peace and joy in the Holy Spirit, [18]because anyone who serves Christ in this way is pleasing to God and approved by men.

[19]Let us therefore make every effort to do what leads to peace and to mutual edification. [20]Do not destroy the work of God for the sake of food. All food is clean, but it is wrong for a man to eat anything that causes someone else to stumble. [21]It is better not to eat meat or drink wine or to do anything else that will cause your brother to fall.

[22]So whatever you believe about these things keep between yourself and God. Blessed is the man who does not condemn himself by what he approves. [23]But the man who has doubts is condemned if he eats, because his eating is not from faith; and everything that does not come from faith is sin.

CHAPTER 15

We who are strong ought to bear with the failings of the weak and not to please ourselves. [2]Each of us should please his neighbor for his good, to build him up. [3]For even Christ did not please himself but, as it is written: "The insults of those who insult you have fallen on me."[h] [4]For everything that was written in the past

---

[d]9 Lev. 19:18   [e]14 Or *the flesh*   [f]11 Isaiah 45:23   [g]14 Or *that nothing*   [h]3 Psalm 69:9

was written to teach us, so that through endurance and the encouragement of the Scriptures we might have hope.

[5]May the God who gives endurance and encouragement give you a spirit of unity among yourselves as you follow Christ Jesus, [6]so that with one heart and mouth you may glorify the God and Father of our Lord Jesus Christ.

[7]Accept one another, then, just as Christ accepted you, in order to bring praise to God. [8]For I tell you that Christ has become a servant of the Jews[i] on behalf of God's truth, to confirm the promises made to the patriarchs [9]so that the Gentiles may glorify God for his mercy, as it is written:

"Therefore I will praise you among the
    Gentiles;
  I will sing hymns to your name."[j]

[10]Again, it says,

"Rejoice, O Gentiles, with his
    people."[k]

[11]And again,

"Praise the Lord, all you Gentiles,
  and sing praises to him, all you
    peoples."[l]

[12]And again, Isaiah says,

"The Root of Jesse will spring up,
  one who will arise to rule over the
    nations;
  the Gentiles will hope in him."[m]

[13]May the God of hope fill you with all joy and peace as you trust in him, so that you may overflow with hope by the power of the Holy Spirit.

[14]I myself am convinced, my brothers, that you yourselves are full of goodness, complete in knowledge and competent to instruct one another. [15]I have written you quite boldly on some points, as if to remind you of them again, because of the grace God gave me [16]to be a minister of Christ Jesus to the Gentiles with the priestly duty of proclaiming the gospel of God, so that the Gentiles might become an offering acceptable to God, sanctified by the Holy Spirit.

[17]Therefore I glory in Christ Jesus in my service to God. [18]I will not venture to speak of anything except what Christ has accomplished through me in leading the Gentiles to obey God by what I have said and done— [19]by the power of signs and miracles, through the power of the Spirit. So from Jerusalem all the way around to Illyricum, I have fully proclaimed the gospel of Christ. [20]It has always been my ambition to preach the gospel where Christ was not known, so that I would not be building on someone else's foundation. [21]Rather, as it is written:

"Those who were not told about him
    will see,
  and those who have not heard will
    understand."[n]

[22]This is why I have often been hindered from coming to you.

[23]But now that there is no more place for me to work in these regions, and since I have been longing for many years to see you, [24]I plan to do so when I go to Spain. I hope to visit you while passing through and to have you assist me on my journey there, after I have enjoyed your company for a while. [25]Now, however, I am on my way to Jerusalem in the service of the saints there. [26]For Macedonia and Achaia were pleased to make a contribution for the poor among the saints in Jerusalem. [27]They were pleased to do it, and indeed they owe it to them. For if the Gentiles have shared in the Jews' spiritual blessings, they owe it to the Jews to share with them their material blessings. [28]So after I have completed this task and have made sure that they have received this fruit, I will go to Spain and visit you on the way. [29]I know that when I come to you, I will come in the full measure of the blessing of Christ.

[30]I urge you, brothers, by our Lord Jesus Christ and by the love of the Spirit, to join me in my struggle by praying to God for me. [31]Pray that I may be rescued from the unbelievers in Judea and that my service in Jerusalem may be acceptable to the saints there, [32]so that by God's will I may come to you with joy and together with you be refreshed. [33]The God of peace be with you all. Amen.

CHAPTER 16
I commend to you our sister Phoebe, a servant[o] of the church in Cenchrea. [2]I ask

[i]8 Greek *circumcision*   [j]9 2 Samuel 22:50; Psalm 18:49   [k]10 Deut. 32:43   [l]11 Psalm 117:1   [m]12 Isaiah 11:10
[n]21 Isaiah 52:15   [o]1 Or *deaconess*

you to receive her in the Lord in a way worthy of the saints and to give her any help she may need from you, for she has been a great help to many people, including me.

³Greet Priscilla*p* and Aquila, my fellow workers in Christ Jesus. ⁴They risked their lives for me. Not only I but all the churches of the Gentiles are grateful to them. ⁵Greet also the church that meets at their house.

Greet my dear friend Epenetus, who was the first convert to Christ in the province of Asia.

⁶Greet Mary, who worked very hard for you.

⁷Greet Andronicus and Junias, my relatives who have been in prison with me. They are outstanding among the apostles, and they were in Christ before I was.

⁸Greet Ampliatus, whom I love in the Lord.

⁹Greet Urbanus, our fellow worker in Christ, and my dear friend Stachys.

¹⁰Greet Apelles, tested and approved in Christ.

Greet those who belong to the household of Aristobulus.

¹¹Greet Herodion, my relative.

Greet those in the household of Narcissus who are in the Lord.

¹²Greet Tryphena and Tryphosa, those women who work hard in the Lord.

Greet my dear friend Persis, another woman who has worked very hard in the Lord.

¹³Greet Rufus, chosen in the Lord, and his mother, who has been a mother to me, too.

¹⁴Greet Asyncritus, Phlegon, Hermes, Patrobas, Hermas and the brothers with them.

¹⁵Greet Philologus, Julia, Nereus and his sister, and Olympas and all the saints with them.

¹⁶Greet one another with a holy kiss.

All the churches of Christ send greetings.

¹⁷I urge you, brothers, to watch out for those who cause divisions and put obstacles in your way that are contrary to the teaching you have learned. Keep away from them. ¹⁸For such people are not serving our Lord Christ, but their own appetites. By smooth talk and flattery they deceive the minds of naive people. ¹⁹Everyone has heard about your obedience, so I am full of joy over you; but I want you to be wise about what is good, and innocent about what is evil.

²⁰The God of peace will soon crush Satan under your feet.

The grace of our Lord Jesus be with you.

²¹Timothy, my fellow worker, sends his greetings to you, as do Lucius, Jason and Sosipater, my relatives.

²²I, Tertius, who wrote down this letter, greet you in the Lord.

²³Gaius, whose hospitality I and the whole church here enjoy, sends you his greetings.

Erastus, who is the city's director of public works, and our brother Quartus send you their greetings.*q*

²⁵Now to him who is able to establish you by my gospel and the proclamation of Jesus Christ, according to the revelation of the mystery hidden for long ages past, ²⁶but now revealed and made known through the prophetic writings by the command of the eternal God, so that all nations might believe and obey him— ²⁷to the only wise God be glory forever through Jesus Christ! Amen.

---

p 3 Greek *Prisca*, a variant of *Priscilla*   *q 23* Some manuscripts *their greetings. 24May the grace of our Lord Jesus Christ be with all of you. Amen.*

1 Corinthians

FAMOUS as a commercial center, Corinth was also infamous for immorality and paganism. But despite great obstacles, Paul planted a Christian church there in his second missionary journey (Acts 18:1-17). Though gifted and growing, the church was plagued with problems—moral and ethical, doctrinal and practical, corporate and private. Paul writes this letter to deal with some of the disorders and to answer questions the Christians at Corinth had raised.

Focus	Disruptions		Debates		Doubts	
Divisions	Problems with Divisions	Problems with Immorality	Problems with Marriage	Problems with Food and Idols	Problems with Worship and Gifts	Problems with Doctrinal Error
	1 4	5 6	7	8 10	11 14	15 16
Topics	In the Body		In the Home		In the Church	
	Responding to Reports			Answering Questions		
Place	Written in Ephesus					
Time	About A.D. 56					

NOVEMBER 18 □ DAY 323
1 CORINTHIANS 1–6
Problems with Divisions

OVERVIEW Despite all the problems in the church at Corinth, the believers there had received God's grace (1:4) and were "sanctified in Christ Jesus" (1:2). The existence of factions in the church was caused by exalting human leaders and embracing human wisdom. This practice, Paul points out, opposes the wisdom of God. Human leaders are only instruments to accomplish God's work. They are his stewards, and their faithfulness will one day be judged by him. But factions are not the only problem in the Corinthian fellowship. Gross immorality and lawsuits between believers are also causing disunity in the church—a condition Paul finds intolerable.

Chapters 1–2	Chapters 3–4	Chapter 5	Chapter 6
Worldly Wisdom	Carnal Co-laborers	Moral Misconduct	Unjust Judges
Divisions in the Church		Disorders in the Church	

YOUR DAILY WALK There are three kinds of people in the business world: those who make things happen, those who watch things happen and those who ask, "What happened?" Which kind are you?

No one is living at his or her best who is not living at his or her best spiritually.

There are three kinds of people in the spiritual world: those who are spiritually dead (without the Spirit, 2:14), those who are spiritually immature (worldly, 3:1) and those who are spiritually discerning (spiritual man, 2:15–16). Which kind are you?

The *natural* person does not have the Spirit of God and cannot understand or apply spiritual truth. The *carnal* person is a Christian who is acting like a natural person (3:3). This person's growth in Christ is stunted. He or she is still feeding on spiritual "milk" when he or she should be eating "meat." The *spiritual* person has "the mind of the Lord" (2:16) and is able to take the truths of God's Word and translate them into obedient action. In the margin of your Bible place your name next to the verse that most accurately describes your life today. Then talk to God about what needs to change before you could be described as "he [or she] who is spiritual."

INSIGHT Apollos Would Have Been Appalled!
The "Apollos party" (3:4–5) claimed allegiance to Apollos, an Alexandrian Jew who was a gifted orator. Apollos had known the message of John the Baptist and had been instructed more fully in the truth of Jesus Christ by Aquila and Priscilla (Acts 18:24—19:1).

CHAPTER 1

Paul, called to be an apostle of Christ Jesus by the will of God, and our brother Sosthenes,

²To the church of God in Corinth, to those sanctified in Christ Jesus and called to be holy, together with all those everywhere who call on the name of our Lord Jesus Christ—their Lord and ours:

³Grace and peace to you from God our Father and the Lord Jesus Christ.

[4]I always thank God for you because of his grace given you in Christ Jesus. [5]For in him you have been enriched in every way—in all your speaking and in all your knowledge— [6]because our testimony about Christ was confirmed in you. [7]Therefore you do not lack any spiritual gift as you eagerly wait for our Lord Jesus Christ to be revealed. [8]He will keep you strong to the end, so that you will be blameless on the day of our Lord Jesus Christ. [9]God, who has called you into fellowship with his Son Jesus Christ our Lord, is faithful.

[10]I appeal to you, brothers, in the name of our Lord Jesus Christ, that all of you agree with one another so that there may be no divisions among you and that you may be perfectly united in mind and thought. [11]My brothers, some from Chloe's household have informed me that there are quarrels among you. [12]What I mean is this: One of you says, "I follow Paul"; another, "I follow Apollos"; another, "I follow Cephas[a]"; still another, "I follow Christ."

[13]Is Christ divided? Was Paul crucified for you? Were you baptized into[b] the name of Paul? [14]I am thankful that I did not baptize any of you except Crispus and Gaius, [15]so no one can say that you were baptized into my name. [16](Yes, I also baptized the household of Stephanas; beyond that, I don't remember if I baptized anyone else.) [17]For Christ did not send me to baptize, but to preach the gospel—not with words of human wisdom, lest the cross of Christ be emptied of its power.

[18]For the message of the cross is foolishness to those who are perishing, but to us who are being saved it is the power of God. [19]For it is written:

> "I will destroy the wisdom of the wise;
> the intelligence of the intelligent I
> will frustrate."[c]

[20]Where is the wise man? Where is the scholar? Where is the philosopher of this age? Has not God made foolish the wisdom of the world? [21]For since in the wisdom of God the world through its wisdom did not know him, God was pleased through the foolishness of what was preached to save those who believe. [22]Jews demand miraculous signs and Greeks look for wisdom, [23]but we preach Christ crucified: a stumbling block to Jews and foolishness to Gentiles, [24]but to those whom God has called, both Jews and Greeks, Christ the power of God and the wisdom of God. [25]For the foolishness of God is wiser than man's wisdom, and the weakness of God is stronger than man's strength.

[26]Brothers, think of what you were when you were called. Not many of you were wise by human standards; not many were influential; not many were of noble birth. [27]But God chose the foolish things of the world to shame the wise; God chose the weak things of the world to shame the strong. [28]He chose the lowly things of this world and the despised things—and the things that are not—to nullify the things that are, [29]so that no one may boast before him. [30]It is because of him that you are in Christ Jesus, who has become for us wisdom from God—that is, our righteousness, holiness and redemption. [31]Therefore, as it is written: "Let him who boasts boast in the Lord."[d]

CHAPTER 2

When I came to you, brothers, I did not come with eloquence or superior wisdom as I proclaimed to you the testimony about God.[e] [2]For I resolved to know nothing while I was with you except Jesus Christ and him crucified. [3]I came to you in weakness and fear, and with much trembling. [4]My message and my preaching were not with wise and persuasive words, but with a demonstration of the Spirit's power, [5]so that your faith might not rest on men's wisdom, but on God's power.

[6]We do, however, speak a message of wisdom among the mature, but not the wisdom of this age or of the rulers of this age, who are coming to nothing. [7]No, we speak of God's secret wisdom, a wisdom that has been hidden and that God destined for our glory before time began. [8]None of the rulers of this age understood it, for if they had, they would not have crucified the Lord of glory. [9]However, as it is written:

> "No eye has seen,
> no ear has heard,

no mind has conceived
　　what God has prepared for those
　　　who love him"*f*—

[10]but God has revealed it to us by his Spirit.

The Spirit searches all things, even the deep things of God. [11]For who among men knows the thoughts of a man except the man's spirit within him? In the same way no one knows the thoughts of God except the Spirit of God. [12]We have not received the spirit of the world but the Spirit who is from God, that we may understand what God has freely given us. [13]This is what we speak, not in words taught us by human wisdom but in words taught by the Spirit, expressing spiritual truths in spiritual words.*g* [14]The man without the Spirit does not accept the things that come from the Spirit of God, for they are foolishness to him, and he cannot understand them, because they are spiritually discerned. [15]The spiritual man makes judgments about all things, but he himself is not subject to any man's judgment:

[16]"For who has known the mind of the
　　　Lord
　　that he may instruct him?"*h*

But we have the mind of Christ.

CHAPTER 3

Brothers, I could not address you as spiritual but as worldly—mere infants in Christ. [2]I gave you milk, not solid food, for you were not yet ready for it. Indeed, you are still not ready. [3]You are still worldly. For since there is jealousy and quarreling among you, are you not worldly? Are you not acting like mere men? [4]For when one says, "I follow Paul," and another, "I follow Apollos," are you not mere men?

[5]What, after all, is Apollos? And what is Paul? Only servants, through whom you came to believe—as the Lord has assigned to each his task. [6]I planted the seed, Apollos watered it, but God made it grow. [7]So neither he who plants nor he who waters is anything, but only God, who makes things grow. [8]The man who plants and the man who waters have one purpose, and each will be rewarded according to his own labor. [9]For we are God's fellow workers; you are God's field, God's building.

[10]By the grace God has given me, I laid a foundation as an expert builder, and someone else is building on it. But each one should be careful how he builds. [11]For no one can lay any foundation other than the one already laid, which is Jesus Christ. [12]If any man builds on this foundation using gold, silver, costly stones, wood, hay or straw, [13]his work will be shown for what it is, because the Day will bring it to light. It will be revealed with fire, and the fire will test the quality of each man's work. [14]If what he has built survives, he will receive his reward. [15]If it is burned up, he will suffer loss; he himself will be saved, but only as one escaping through the flames.

[16]Don't you know that you yourselves are God's temple and that God's Spirit lives in you? [17]If anyone destroys God's temple, God will destroy him; for God's temple is sacred, and you are that temple.

[18]Do not deceive yourselves. If any one of you thinks he is wise by the standards of this age, he should become a "fool" so that he may become wise. [19]For the wisdom of this world is foolishness in God's sight. As it is written: "He catches the wise in their craftiness"*i*; [20]and again, "The Lord knows that the thoughts of the wise are futile."*j* [21]So then, no more boasting about men! All things are yours, [22]whether Paul or Apollos or Cephas*k* or the world or life or death or the present or the future—all are yours, [23]and you are of Christ, and Christ is of God.

CHAPTER 4

So then, men ought to regard us as servants of Christ and as those entrusted with the secret things of God. [2]Now it is required that those who have been given a trust must prove faithful. [3]I care very little if I am judged by you or by any human court; indeed, I do not even judge myself. [4]My conscience is clear, but that does not make me innocent. It is the Lord who judges me. [5]Therefore judge nothing before the appointed time; wait till the Lord comes. He will bring to light what is hidden in darkness and will expose the

---

f9 Isaiah 64:4　　*g13* Or *Spirit, interpreting spiritual truths to spiritual men*　　*h16* Isaiah 40:13　　*i19* Job 5:13　　*j20* Psalm 94:11
k22 That is, Peter

motives of men's hearts. At that time each will receive his praise from God.

[6]Now, brothers, I have applied these things to myself and Apollos for your benefit, so that you may learn from us the meaning of the saying, "Do not go beyond what is written." Then you will not take pride in one man over against another. [7]For who makes you different from anyone else? What do you have that you did not receive? And if you did receive it, why do you boast as though you did not?

[8]Already you have all you want! Already you have become rich! You have become kings—and that without us! How I wish that you really had become kings so that we might be kings with you! [9]For it seems to me that God has put us apostles on display at the end of the procession, like men condemned to die in the arena. We have been made a spectacle to the whole universe, to angels as well as to men. [10]We are fools for Christ, but you are so wise in Christ! We are weak, but you are strong! You are honored, we are dishonored! [11]To this very hour we go hungry and thirsty, we are in rags, we are brutally treated, we are homeless. [12]We work hard with our own hands. When we are cursed, we bless; when we are persecuted, we endure it; [13]when we are slandered, we answer kindly. Up to this moment we have become the scum of the earth, the refuse of the world.

[14]I am not writing this to shame you, but to warn you, as my dear children. [15]Even though you have ten thousand guardians in Christ, you do not have many fathers, for in Christ Jesus I became your father through the gospel. [16]Therefore I urge you to imitate me. [17]For this reason I am sending to you Timothy, my son whom I love, who is faithful in the Lord. He will remind you of my way of life in Christ Jesus, which agrees with what I teach everywhere in every church.

[18]Some of you have become arrogant, as if I were not coming to you. [19]But I will come to you very soon, if the Lord is willing, and then I will find out not only how these arrogant people are talking, but what power they have. [20]For the kingdom of God is not a matter of talk but of power. [21]What do you prefer? Shall I

come to you with a whip, or in love and with a gentle spirit?

CHAPTER 5

It is actually reported that there is sexual immorality among you, and of a kind that does not occur even among pagans: A man has his father's wife. [2]And you are proud! Shouldn't you rather have been filled with grief and have put out of your fellowship the man who did this? [3]Even though I am not physically present, I am with you in spirit. And I have already passed judgment on the one who did this, just as if I were present. [4]When you are assembled in the name of our Lord Jesus and I am with you in spirit, and the power of our Lord Jesus is present, [5]hand this man over to Satan, so that the sinful nature[l] may be destroyed and his spirit saved on the day of the Lord.

[6]Your boasting is not good. Don't you know that a little yeast works through the whole batch of dough? [7]Get rid of the old yeast that you may be a new batch without yeast—as you really are. For Christ, our Passover lamb, has been sacrificed. [8]Therefore let us keep the Festival, not with the old yeast, the yeast of malice and wickedness, but with bread without yeast, the bread of sincerity and truth.

[9]I have written you in my letter not to associate with sexually immoral people—[10]not at all meaning the people of this world who are immoral, or the greedy and swindlers, or idolaters. In that case you would have to leave this world. [11]But now I am writing you that you must not associate with anyone who calls himself a brother but is sexually immoral or greedy, an idolater or a slanderer, a drunkard or a swindler. With such a man do not even eat.

[12]What business is it of mine to judge those outside the church? Are you not to judge those inside? [13]God will judge those outside. "Expel the wicked man from among you."[m]

CHAPTER 6

If any of you has a dispute with another, dare he take it before the ungodly for judgment instead of before the saints? [2]Do you not know that the saints will judge the world? And if you are to judge the world, are you not competent to judge

[l]5 Or that his body; or that the flesh   [m]13 Deut. 17:7; 19:19; 21:21; 22:21,24; 24:7

trivial cases? ³Do you not know that we will judge angels? How much more the things of this life! ⁴Therefore, if you have disputes about such matters, appoint as judges even men of little account in the church!ⁿ ⁵I say this to shame you. Is it possible that there is nobody among you wise enough to judge a dispute between believers? ⁶But instead, one brother goes to law against another—and this in front of unbelievers!

⁷The very fact that you have lawsuits among you means you have been completely defeated already. Why not rather be wronged? Why not rather be cheated? ⁸Instead, you yourselves cheat and do wrong, and you do this to your brothers.

⁹Do you not know that the wicked will not inherit the kingdom of God? Do not be deceived: Neither the sexually immoral nor idolaters nor adulterers nor male prostitutes nor homosexual offenders ¹⁰nor thieves nor the greedy nor drunkards nor slanderers nor swindlers will inherit the kingdom of God. ¹¹And that is what some of you were. But you were washed, you were sanctified, you were justified in the name of the Lord Jesus Christ and by the Spirit of our God.

¹²"Everything is permissible for me"—but not everything is beneficial. "Everything is permissible for me"—but I will not be mastered by anything. ¹³"Food for the stomach and the stomach for food"—but God will destroy them both. The body is not meant for sexual immorality, but for the Lord, and the Lord for the body. ¹⁴By his power God raised the Lord from the dead, and he will raise us also. ¹⁵Do you not know that your bodies are members of Christ himself? Shall I then take the members of Christ and unite them with a prostitute? Never! ¹⁶Do you not know that he who unites himself with a prostitute is one with her in body? For it is said, "The two will become one flesh."ᵒ ¹⁷But he who unites himself with the Lord is one with him in spirit.

¹⁸Flee from sexual immorality. All other sins a man commits are outside his body, but he who sins sexually sins against his own body. ¹⁹Do you not know that your body is a temple of the Holy Spirit, who is in you, whom you have received from God? You are not your own; ²⁰you were bought at a price. Therefore honor God with your body.

ⁿ4 *Or matters, do you appoint as judges men of little account in the church?* ᵒ16 Gen. 2:24

NOVEMBER 19 □ DAY 324
1 CORINTHIANS 7–11:1
Problems with Daily Life

OVERVIEW Beginning with chapter 7, Paul answers a series of questions raised by the believers at Corinth that neither the Old Testament nor the words of Christ resolve: Is celibacy better than marriage? Is it permissible for Christians to eat meat offered to idols? Is it proper for a minister of the gospel to derive his living from the gospel? If an action is lawful, is it therefore permissible? Paul draws upon Old Testament passages, the teaching of Christ and his own apostolic authority to set forth principles for the proper use of Christian liberty.

Chapter 7	Chapter 8	Chapter 9	Chapters 10–11
Counsel and Commands Regarding			
Marriage	Meat	Ministers	Muttering 10:1 11:1
It Is a Gift	Be Careful	Share with Them	Learn from the Past

YOUR DAILY WALK There are several God-ordained institutions in the pages of Scripture, but perhaps the two most important are the *church* and the *home*. So it is no coincidence that they are interrelated. Leadership ability in the home is a prerequisite for leadership in the church (1 Timothy 3:4–5); love and submission in the home are to be patterned after the relationship between Christ and the church.

If the young could be old for a day, they would neither fear so much growing old, nor foolishly squander the days of their youth.

Chapter 7 is an important passage on marriage. Regardless of your marital status (single, married, divorced, widowed, remarried), you'll find helpful counsel for dealing with the stresses and decisions of marriage. Set aside a few extra minutes today to concentrate on these forty verses. You might want to divide a sheet of paper into five columns and label them: Marriage, Celibacy, Mixed Marriage, Divorce, Remarriage. Now catalog what Paul has to say about each topic, paying careful attention to the column you are in . . . or plan to join! Then prayerfully apply your study to a decision you may be facing.

INSIGHT Where Did Paul Get His Advice on Marriage?
Notice in 7:6, 10, 12, 25, 40 the origin of Paul's counsel. On certain matters he had no written or oral command from Christ (such as in Matthew 19:6, used in 7:10). In such cases, however, he made it clear that his "judgment" (opinion) was Spirit-guided (7:25, 40) and therefore authoritative. This is not merely a first-century "Dear Abby" column but rather inspired Scripture and fully authoritative for your life!

CHAPTER 7

Now for the matters you wrote about: It is good for a man not to marry.*ᵖ* ²But since there is so much immorality, each man should have his own wife, and each woman her own husband. ³The husband should fulfill his marital duty to his wife, and likewise the wife to her husband. ⁴The wife's body does not belong to her alone but also to her husband. In the same way, the husband's body does not belong to him alone but also to his wife. ⁵Do not deprive each other except by mutual consent and for a time, so that you may devote yourselves to prayer. Then come together again so that Satan will not tempt you because of your lack of self-control. ⁶I say this as a concession, not as a command. ⁷I wish that all men were as I am. But each man has his own gift from God; one has this gift, another has that.

⁸Now to the unmarried and the widows I say: It is good for them to stay unmarried, as I am. ⁹But if they cannot control themselves, they should marry, for it is better to marry than to burn with passion.

¹⁰To the married I give this command (not I, but the Lord): A wife must not separate from her husband. ¹¹But if she does, she must remain unmarried or else be reconciled to her husband. And a husband must not divorce his wife.

¹²To the rest I say this (I, not the Lord): If any brother has a wife who is not a believer and she is willing to live with him, he must not divorce her. ¹³And if a woman has a husband who is not a believer and he is willing to live with her, she must not divorce him. ¹⁴For the unbelieving husband has been sanctified through his wife, and the unbelieving wife has been sanctified through her believing husband. Otherwise your children would be unclean, but as it is, they are holy.

¹⁵But if the unbeliever leaves, let him do so. A believing man or woman is not bound in such circumstances; God has called us to live in peace. ¹⁶How do you know, wife, whether you will save your husband? Or, how do you know, husband, whether you will save your wife?

¹⁷Nevertheless, each one should retain the place in life that the Lord assigned to him and to which God has called him. This is the rule I lay down in all the churches. ¹⁸Was a man already circumcised when he was called? He should not become uncircumcised. Was a man uncircumcised when he was called? He should not be circumcised. ¹⁹Circumcision is nothing and uncircumcision is nothing. Keeping God's commands is what counts. ²⁰Each one should remain in the situation

ᵖ1 Or "It is good for a man not to have sexual relations with a woman."

which he was in when God called him. [21]Were you a slave when you were called? Don't let it trouble you—although if you can gain your freedom, do so. [22]For he who was a slave when he was called by the Lord is the Lord's freedman; similarly, he who was a free man when he was called is Christ's slave. [23]You were bought at a price; do not become slaves of men. [24]Brothers, each man, as responsible to God, should remain in the situation God called him to.

[25]Now about virgins: I have no command from the Lord, but I give a judgment as one who by the Lord's mercy is trustworthy. [26]Because of the present crisis, I think that it is good for you to remain as you are. [27]Are you married? Do not seek a divorce. Are you unmarried? Do not look for a wife. [28]But if you do marry, you have not sinned; and if a virgin marries, she has not sinned. But those who marry will face many troubles in this life, and I want to spare you this.

[29]What I mean, brothers, is that the time is short. From now on those who have wives should live as if they had none; [30]those who mourn, as if they did not; those who are happy, as if they were not; those who buy something, as if it were not theirs to keep; [31]those who use the things of the world, as if not engrossed in them. For this world in its present form is passing away.

[32]I would like you to be free from concern. An unmarried man is concerned about the Lord's affairs—how he can please the Lord. [33]But a married man is concerned about the affairs of this world—how he can please his wife— [34]and his interests are divided. An unmarried woman or virgin is concerned about the Lord's affairs: Her aim is to be devoted to the Lord in both body and spirit. But a married woman is concerned about the affairs of this world—how she can please her husband. [35]I am saying this for your own good, not to restrict you, but that you may live in a right way in undivided devotion to the Lord.

[36]If anyone thinks he is acting improperly toward the virgin he is engaged to, and if she is getting along in years and he

feels he ought to marry, he should do as he wants. He is not sinning. They should get married. [37]But the man who has settled the matter in his own mind, who is under no compulsion but has control over his own will, and who has made up his mind not to marry the virgin—this man also does the right thing. [38]So then, he who marries the virgin does right, but he who does not marry her does even better.[q]

[39]A woman is bound to her husband as long as he lives. But if her husband dies, she is free to marry anyone she wishes, but he must belong to the Lord. [40]In my judgment, she is happier if she stays as she is—and I think that I too have the Spirit of God.

CHAPTER 8

Now about food sacrificed to idols: We know that we all possess knowledge.[r] Knowledge puffs up, but love builds up. [2]The man who thinks he knows something does not yet know as he ought to know. [3]But the man who loves God is known by God.

[4]So then, about eating food sacrificed to idols: We know that an idol is nothing at all in the world and that there is no God but one. [5]For even if there are so-called gods, whether in heaven or on earth (as indeed there are many "gods" and many "lords"), [6]yet for us there is but one God, the Father, from whom all things came and for whom we live; and there is but one Lord, Jesus Christ, through whom all things came and through whom we live.

[7]But not everyone knows this. Some people are still so accustomed to idols that when they eat such food they think of it as having been sacrificed to an idol, and since their conscience is weak, it is defiled. [8]But food does not bring us near to God; we are no worse if we do not eat, and no better if we do.

[9]Be careful, however, that the exercise of your freedom does not become a stumbling block to the weak. [10]For if anyone with a weak conscience sees you who have this knowledge eating in an idol's temple, won't he be emboldened to eat what has been sacrificed to idols? [11]So this

---

[q]36-38 Or [36]If anyone thinks he is not treating his daughter properly, and if she is getting along in years, and he feels she ought to marry, he should do as he wants. He is not sinning. He should let her get married. [37]But the man who has settled the matter in his own mind, who is under no compulsion but has control over his own will, and who has made up his mind to keep the virgin unmarried—this man also does the right thing. [38]So then, he who gives his virgin in marriage does right, but he who does not give her in marriage does even better.   [r]1 Or "We all possess knowledge," as you say

weak brother, for whom Christ died, is destroyed by your knowledge. [12]When you sin against your brothers in this way and wound their weak conscience, you sin against Christ. [13]Therefore, if what I eat causes my brother to fall into sin, I will never eat meat again, so that I will not cause him to fall.

CHAPTER 9

Am I not free? Am I not an apostle? Have I not seen Jesus our Lord? Are you not the result of my work in the Lord? [2]Even though I may not be an apostle to others, surely I am to you! For you are the seal of my apostleship in the Lord.

[3]This is my defense to those who sit in judgment on me. [4]Don't we have the right to food and drink? [5]Don't we have the right to take a believing wife along with us, as do the other apostles and the Lord's brothers and Cephas[s]? [6]Or is it only I and Barnabas who must work for a living?

[7]Who serves as a soldier at his own expense? Who plants a vineyard and does not eat of its grapes? Who tends a flock and does not drink of the milk? [8]Do I say this merely from a human point of view? Doesn't the Law say the same thing? [9]For it is written in the Law of Moses: "Do not muzzle an ox while it is treading out the grain."[t] Is it about oxen that God is concerned? [10]Surely he says this for us, doesn't he? Yes, this was written for us, because when the plowman plows and the thresher threshes, they ought to do so in the hope of sharing in the harvest. [11]If we have sown spiritual seed among you, is it too much if we reap a material harvest from you? [12]If others have this right of support from you, shouldn't we have it all the more?

But we did not use this right. On the contrary, we put up with anything rather than hinder the gospel of Christ. [13]Don't you know that those who work in the temple get their food from the temple, and those who serve at the altar share in what is offered on the altar? [14]In the same way, the Lord has commanded that those who preach the gospel should receive their living from the gospel.

[15]But I have not used any of these rights. And I am not writing this in the hope that you will do such things for me. I would rather die than have anyone deprive me of this boast. [16]Yet when I preach the gospel, I cannot boast, for I am compelled to preach. Woe to me if I do not preach the gospel! [17]If I preach voluntarily, I have a reward; if not voluntarily, I am simply discharging the trust committed to me. [18]What then is my reward? Just this: that in preaching the gospel I may offer it free of charge, and so not make use of my rights in preaching it.

[19]Though I am free and belong to no man, I make myself a slave to everyone, to win as many as possible. [20]To the Jews I became like a Jew, to win the Jews. To those under the law I became like one under the law (though I myself am not under the law), so as to win those under the law. [21]To those not having the law I became like one not having the law (though I am not free from God's law but am under Christ's law), so as to win those not having the law. [22]To the weak I became weak, to win the weak. I have become all things to all men so that by all possible means I might save some. [23]I do all this for the sake of the gospel, that I may share in its blessings.

[24]Do you not know that in a race all the runners run, but only one gets the prize? Run in such a way as to get the prize. [25]Everyone who competes in the games goes into strict training. They do it to get a crown that will not last; but we do it to get a crown that will last forever. [26]Therefore I do not run like a man running aimlessly; I do not fight like a man beating the air. [27]No, I beat my body and make it my slave so that after I have preached to others, I myself will not be disqualified for the prize.

CHAPTER 10

For I do not want you to be ignorant of the fact, brothers, that our forefathers were all under the cloud and that they all passed through the sea. [2]They were all baptized into Moses in the cloud and in the sea. [3]They all ate the same spiritual food [4]and drank the same spiritual drink; for they drank from the spiritual rock that accompanied them, and that rock was Christ. [5]Nevertheless, God was not pleased with most of them; their bodies were scattered over the desert.

⁶Now these things occurred as examples" to keep us from setting our hearts on evil things as they did. ⁷Do not be idolaters, as some of them were; as it is written: "The people sat down to eat and drink and got up to indulge in pagan revelry."ᵛ ⁸We should not commit sexual immorality, as some of them did—and in one day twenty-three thousand of them died. ⁹We should not test the Lord, as some of them did—and were killed by snakes. ¹⁰And do not grumble, as some of them did—and were killed by the destroying angel.

¹¹These things happened to them as examples and were written down as warnings for us, on whom the fulfillment of the ages has come. ¹²So, if you think you are standing firm, be careful that you don't fall! ¹³No temptation has seized you except what is common to man. And God is faithful; he will not let you be tempted beyond what you can bear. But when you are tempted, he will also provide a way out so that you can stand up under it.

¹⁴Therefore, my dear friends, flee from idolatry. ¹⁵I speak to sensible people; judge for yourselves what I say. ¹⁶Is not the cup of thanksgiving for which we give thanks a participation in the blood of Christ? And is not the bread that we break a participation in the body of Christ? ¹⁷Because there is one loaf, we, who are many, are one body, for we all partake of the one loaf.

¹⁸Consider the people of Israel: Do not those who eat the sacrifices participate in the altar? ¹⁹Do I mean then that a sacrifice offered to an idol is anything, or that an idol is anything? ²⁰No, but the sacrifices

of pagans are offered to demons, not to God, and I do not want you to be participants with demons. ²¹You cannot drink the cup of the Lord and the cup of demons too; you cannot have a part in both the Lord's table and the table of demons. ²²Are we trying to arouse the Lord's jealousy? Are we stronger than he?

²³"Everything is permissible"—but not everything is beneficial. "Everything is permissible"—but not everything is constructive. ²⁴Nobody should seek his own good, but the good of others.

²⁵Eat anything sold in the meat market without raising questions of conscience, ²⁶for, "The earth is the Lord's, and everything in it."ʷ

²⁷If some unbeliever invites you to a meal and you want to go, eat whatever is put before you without raising questions of conscience. ²⁸But if anyone says to you, "This has been offered in sacrifice," then do not eat it, both for the sake of the man who told you and for conscience' sakeˣ— ²⁹the other man's conscience, I mean, not yours. For why should my freedom be judged by another's conscience? ³⁰If I take part in the meal with thankfulness, why am I denounced because of something I thank God for?

³¹So whether you eat or drink or whatever you do, do it all for the glory of God. ³²Do not cause anyone to stumble, whether Jews, Greeks or the church of God— ³³even as I try to please everybody in every way. For I am not seeking my own good but the good of many, so that they may be C H A P T E R   1 1 saved. ¹Follow my example, as I follow the example of Christ.

ᵘ6 Or *types*; also in verse 11   ᵛ7 Exodus 32:6   ʷ26 Psalm 24:1   ˣ28 Some manuscripts *conscience' sake, for "the earth is the Lord's and everything in it"*

NOVEMBER 20 ☐ DAY 325
1 CORINTHIANS 11:2–14
Problems with Worship and Gifts

 OVERVIEW In previous chapters Paul has dealt with the Corinthians' personal problems. Now he turns his attention to problems of a public nature, specifically, disorders in the church's worship. In chapter 11 he answers questions regarding the role of women in the church, then gives a sharp rebuke for the Corinthians' misconduct during the Lord's Supper. In chapters 12–14 Paul addresses the issue of spiritual gifts in the church, emphasizing the diversity of gifts and the fundamental test of love in the exercise of spiritual gifts. Orderliness should characterize all Christian worship (14:40).

Chapter 11		Chapter 12	Chapter 13	Chapter 14
The Role of Women 2 16	The Sanctity of Communion 17 34	The Use of Spiritual Gifts		
		in Question	in Love	in Church
Submission	Examination	Participation		

YOUR DAILY WALK Imagine that you have given your best friend a gift for his or her birthday. The big day arrives, and you call to find out how your gift was received. To your surprise, the reply comes, "Oh, I don't know, I haven't opened it yet. I decided to keep it wrapped up." Encouraging your friend to open it, you wait another day or two and call again, this time to ask if your gift (a clock radio) was being put to good use. Instead, you hear these discouraging words: "Oh, I opened it all right, but I decided to leave it in the closet."

God's gift to you is often God's gift to others through you.

God doesn't give spiritual gifts (1 Corinthians 12–14) merely to have them left undiscovered or unused. Just as he has given you eyes, ears and feet to be used in your physical body, so, too, he has given you gifts to be employed in the spiritual body, his church. In which areas of ministry has God gifted you? Is your local church profiting from the use of those gifts, or are your gifts still unwrapped and unused? Talk to your pastor, Sunday school teacher or a close friend about the way you can begin to put your gifts to work this week.

INSIGHT Does Your Gift Lack the Key Ingredient?
Paul lists four classes of spiritual gifts: ecstatic (tongues), instructive (prophecy), wonder-working (faith) and helps (giving). But without love, the results of such gifts are futile: I communicate nothing (13:1); I am nothing (13:2); I gain nothing (13:3).

²I praise you for remembering me in everything and for holding to the teachings,ʸ just as I passed them on to you.

³Now I want you to realize that the head of every man is Christ, and the head of the woman is man, and the head of Christ is God. ⁴Every man who prays or prophesies with his head covered dishonors his head. ⁵And every woman who prays or prophesies with her head uncovered dishonors her head—it is just as though her head were shaved. ⁶If a woman does not cover her head, she should have her hair cut off; and if it is a disgrace for a woman to have her hair cut or shaved off, she should cover her head. ⁷A man ought not to cover his head,ᶻ since he is the image and glory of God;

but the woman is the glory of man. ⁸For man did not come from woman, but woman from man; ⁹neither was man created for woman, but woman for man. ¹⁰For this reason, and because of the angels, the woman ought to have a sign of authority on her head.

¹¹In the Lord, however, woman is not independent of man, nor is man independent of woman. ¹²For as woman came from man, so also man is born of woman. But everything comes from God. ¹³Judge for yourselves: Is it proper for a woman to pray to God with her head uncovered? ¹⁴Does not the very nature of things teach you that if a man has long hair, it is a disgrace to him, ¹⁵but that if a woman has long hair, it is her glory? For long hair

---

ʸ2 Or *traditions*   ᶻ4-7 Or ⁴*Every man who prays or prophesies with long hair dishonors his head.* ⁵*And every woman who prays or prophesies with no covering of hair on her head dishonors her head—she is just like one of the "shorn women."* ⁶*If a woman has no covering, let her be for now with short hair, but since it is a disgrace for a woman to have her hair shorn or shaved, she should grow it again.* ⁷*A man ought not to have long hair* is given to her as a covering. [16]If anyone wants to be contentious about this, we have no other practice—nor do the churches of God.

[17]In the following directives I have no praise for you, for your meetings do more harm than good. [18]In the first place, I hear that when you come together as a church, there are divisions among you, and to some extent I believe it. [19]No doubt there have to be differences among you to show which of you have God's approval. [20]When you come together, it is not the Lord's Supper you eat, [21]for as you eat, each of you goes ahead without waiting for anybody else. One remains hungry, another gets drunk. [22]Don't you have homes to eat and drink in? Or do you despise the church of God and humiliate those who have nothing? What shall I say to you? Shall I praise you for this? Certainly not!

[23]For I received from the Lord what I also passed on to you: The Lord Jesus, on the night he was betrayed, took bread, [24]and when he had given thanks, he broke it and said, "This is my body, which is for you; do this in remembrance of me." [25]In the same way, after supper he took the cup, saying, "This cup is the new covenant in my blood; do this, whenever you drink it, in remembrance of me." [26]For whenever you eat this bread and drink this cup, you proclaim the Lord's death until he comes.

[27]Therefore, whoever eats the bread or drinks the cup of the Lord in an unworthy manner will be guilty of sinning against the body and blood of the Lord. [28]A man ought to examine himself before he eats of the bread and drinks of the cup. [29]For anyone who eats and drinks without recognizing the body of the Lord eats and drinks judgment on himself. [30]That is why many among you are weak and sick, and a number of you have fallen asleep. [31]But if we judged ourselves, we would not come under judgment. [32]When we are judged by the Lord, we are being disciplined so that we will not be condemned with the world.

[33]So then, my brothers, when you come together to eat, wait for each other. [34]If anyone is hungry, he should eat at home,

so that when you meet together it may not result in judgment.

And when I come I will give further directions.

CHAPTER 12

Now about spiritual gifts, brothers, I do not want you to be ignorant. [2]You know that when you were pagans, somehow or other you were influenced and led astray to mute idols. [3]Therefore I tell you that no one who is speaking by the Spirit of God says, "Jesus be cursed," and no one can say, "Jesus is Lord," except by the Holy Spirit.

[4]There are different kinds of gifts, but the same Spirit. [5]There are different kinds of service, but the same Lord. [6]There are different kinds of working, but the same God works all of them in all men.

[7]Now to each one the manifestation of the Spirit is given for the common good. [8]To one there is given through the Spirit the message of wisdom, to another the message of knowledge by means of the same Spirit, [9]to another faith by the same Spirit, to another gifts of healing by that one Spirit, [10]to another miraculous powers, to another prophecy, to another distinguishing between spirits, to another speaking in different kinds of tongues,[a] and to still another the interpretation of tongues.[a] [11]All these are the work of one and the same Spirit, and he gives them to each one, just as he determines.

[12]The body is a unit, though it is made up of many parts; and though all its parts are many, they form one body. So it is with Christ. [13]For we were all baptized by[b] one Spirit into one body—whether Jews or Greeks, slave or free—and we were all given the one Spirit to drink.

[14]Now the body is not made up of one part but of many. [15]If the foot should say, "Because I am not a hand, I do not belong to the body," it would not for that reason cease to be part of the body. [16]And if the ear should say, "Because I am not an eye, I do not belong to the body," it would not for that reason cease to be part of the body. [17]If the whole body were an eye, where would the sense of hearing be? If the whole body were an ear, where would the sense of smell be? [18]But in fact God has arranged the parts in the body, every

---

[a] 10 Or languages; also in verse 28   [b] 13 Or with; or in

one of them, just as he wanted them to be. ¹⁹If they were all one part, where would the body be? ²⁰As it is, there are many parts, but one body.

²¹The eye cannot say to the hand, "I don't need you!" And the head cannot say to the feet, "I don't need you!" ²²On the contrary, those parts of the body that seem to be weaker are indispensable, ²³and the parts that we think are less honorable we treat with special honor. And the parts that are unpresentable are treated with special modesty, ²⁴while our presentable parts need no special treatment. But God has combined the members of the body and has given greater honor to the parts that lacked it, ²⁵so that there should be no division in the body, but that its parts should have equal concern for each other. ²⁶If one part suffers, every part suffers with it; if one part is honored, every part rejoices with it.

²⁷Now you are the body of Christ, and each one of you is a part of it. ²⁸And in the church God has appointed first of all apostles, second prophets, third teachers, then workers of miracles, also those having gifts of healing, those able to help others, those with gifts of administration, and those speaking in different kinds of tongues. ²⁹Are all apostles? Are all prophets? Are all teachers? Do all work miracles? ³⁰Do all have gifts of healing? Do all speak in tongues*c*? Do all interpret? ³¹But eagerly desire*d* the greater gifts.

And now I will show you the most excellent way.

CHAPTER 13

If I speak in the tongues*e* of men and of angels, but have not love, I am only a resounding gong or a clanging cymbal. ²If I have the gift of prophecy and can fathom all mysteries and all knowledge, and if I have a faith that can move mountains, but have not love, I am nothing. ³If I give all I possess to the poor and surrender my body to the flames,*f* but have not love, I gain nothing.

⁴Love is patient, love is kind. It does not envy, it does not boast, it is not proud. ⁵It is not rude, it is not self-seeking, it is not easily angered, it keeps no record of wrongs. ⁶Love does not delight in evil but rejoices with the truth. ⁷It always protects, always trusts, always hopes, always perseveres.

⁸Love never fails. But where there are prophecies, they will cease; where there are tongues, they will be stilled; where there is knowledge, it will pass away. ⁹For we know in part and we prophesy in part, ¹⁰but when perfection comes, the imperfect disappears. ¹¹When I was a child, I talked like a child, I thought like a child, I reasoned like a child. When I became a man, I put childish ways behind me. ¹²Now we see but a poor reflection as in a mirror; then we shall see face to face. Now I know in part; then I shall know fully, even as I am fully known.

¹³And now these three remain: faith, hope and love. But the greatest of these is love.

CHAPTER 14

Follow the way of love and eagerly desire spiritual gifts, especially the gift of prophecy. ²For anyone who speaks in a tongue*g* does not speak to men but to God. Indeed, no one understands him; he utters mysteries with his spirit.*h* ³But everyone who prophesies speaks to men for their strengthening, encouragement and comfort. ⁴He who speaks in a tongue edifies himself, but he who prophesies edifies the church. ⁵I would like every one of you to speak in tongues,*i* but I would rather have you prophesy. He who prophesies is greater than one who speaks in tongues,*i* unless he interprets, so that the church may be edified.

⁶Now, brothers, if I come to you and speak in tongues, what good will I be to you, unless I bring you some revelation or knowledge or prophecy or word of instruction? ⁷Even in the case of lifeless things that make sounds, such as the flute or harp, how will anyone know what tune is being played unless there is a distinction in the notes? ⁸Again, if the trumpet does not sound a clear call, who will get ready for battle? ⁹So it is with you. Unless you speak intelligible words with your tongue, how will anyone know what you are saying? You will just be speaking into the air. ¹⁰Undoubtedly there are all sorts

---

*c*30 Or *other languages*   *d*31 Or *But you are eagerly desiring*   *e*1 Or *languages*   *f*3 Some early manuscripts *body that I may boast*   *g*2 Or *another language*; also in verses 4, 13, 14, 19, 26 and 27   *h*2 Or *by the Spirit*   *i*5 Or *other languages*; also in verses 6, 18, 22, 23 and 39 of languages in the world, yet none of them is without meaning. [11] If then I do not grasp the meaning of what someone is saying, I am a foreigner to the speaker, and he is a foreigner to me. [12] So it is with you. Since you are eager to have spiritual gifts, try to excel in gifts that build up the church.

[13] For this reason anyone who speaks in a tongue should pray that he may interpret what he says. [14] For if I pray in a tongue, my spirit prays, but my mind is unfruitful. [15] So what shall I do? I will pray with my spirit, but I will also pray with my mind; I will sing with my spirit, but I will also sing with my mind. [16] If you are praising God with your spirit, how can one who finds himself among those who do not understand[j] say "Amen" to your thanksgiving, since he does not know what you are saying? [17] You may be giving thanks well enough, but the other man is not edified.

[18] I thank God that I speak in tongues more than all of you. [19] But in the church I would rather speak five intelligible words to instruct others than ten thousand words in a tongue.

[20] Brothers, stop thinking like children. In regard to evil be infants, but in your thinking be adults. [21] In the Law it is written:

"Through men of strange tongues
    and through the lips of foreigners
I will speak to this people,
    but even then they will not listen to
        me,"[k]
says the Lord.

[22] Tongues, then, are a sign, not for believers but for unbelievers; prophecy, however, is for believers, not for unbelievers. [23] So if the whole church comes together and everyone speaks in tongues, and some who do not understand[l] or some unbelievers come in, will they not say that you are out of your mind? [24] But if an unbeliever or someone who does not

understand[m] comes in while everybody is prophesying, he will be convinced by all that he is a sinner and will be judged by all, [25] and the secrets of his heart will be laid bare. So he will fall down and worship God, exclaiming, "God is really among you!"

[26] What then shall we say, brothers? When you come together, everyone has a hymn, or a word of instruction, a revelation, a tongue or an interpretation. All of these must be done for the strengthening of the church. [27] If anyone speaks in a tongue, two—or at the most three—should speak, one at a time, and someone must interpret. [28] If there is no interpreter, the speaker should keep quiet in the church and speak to himself and God.

[29] Two or three prophets should speak, and the others should weigh carefully what is said. [30] And if a revelation comes to someone who is sitting down, the first speaker should stop. [31] For you can all prophesy in turn so that everyone may be instructed and encouraged. [32] The spirits of prophets are subject to the control of prophets. [33] For God is not a God of disorder but of peace.

As in all the congregations of the saints, [34] women should remain silent in the churches. They are not allowed to speak, but must be in submission, as the Law says. [35] If they want to inquire about something, they should ask their own husbands at home; for it is disgraceful for a woman to speak in the church.

[36] Did the word of God originate with you? Or are you the only people it has reached? [37] If anybody thinks he is a prophet or spiritually gifted, let him acknowledge that what I am writing to you is the Lord's command. [38] If he ignores this, he himself will be ignored.[n]

[39] Therefore, my brothers, be eager to prophesy, and do not forbid speaking in tongues. [40] But everything should be done in a fitting and orderly way.

[j]16 Or *among the inquirers*   [k]21 Isaiah 28:11,12   [l]23 Or *some inquirers*   [m]24 Or *or some inquirer*   [n]38 Some manuscripts *If he is ignorant of this, let him be ignorant*

NOVEMBER 21 □ DAY 326
Questions and Answers

LOOK BACK Romans has been called "the gospel according to Paul." Writing like a trained lawyer, Paul probes the significance of Jesus' death and resurrection. All people stand condemned before a holy God. Jew and Gentile alike are without excuse.

But what the human race was powerless to do for itself, God did in the person of his Son, Jesus. Through his sinless life and sacrificial death we are declared "not guilty" before God—not because of anything we have done, but because of his love and grace. We had a debt we could not pay; Jesus paid a debt he did not owe. And the result? Sin's power has been broken, freeing us to live a new life in him.

But that new life is not a problem-free life, as you'll learn by reading Paul's letter to the Corinthians. Here, a church that was "sanctified in Christ Jesus, and called to be holy" (1 Corinthians 1:2) was, nonetheless, beset by a myriad of sins and excesses that needed Paul's discipline and direction. Clearly, the *wealth* of the believer must be translated into a *worthy walk* for the believer.

Every day holds the possibility of miracles.

LOOK UP What is one of the most effective teaching methods? *Answer:* The use of question and answer.

Romans 8 is one of the richest "mother lodes" in the Bible. There you'll discover nugget after nugget of truth for the Christian: the limitless boundaries of God's love, the proven way to be an overcomer in any circumstance, the role of the Holy Spirit in the life of the Christian.

There you'll also find the answers to several important questions. According to Romans 8:31–39,

- if God is for us, who can be against us?
- who will bring any charge against those whom God has chosen?
- who shall separate us from the love of Christ?

In case you had trouble with the above exercise, the answer to all three questions is the same: *no one!*

LOOK AHEAD The challenge is often to take what we know about God from the pages of his Word and apply it to real-life situations that have us baffled and anxious. For example:

- Who is seemingly against you and out to get you today? (Answer: my boss, my spouse, my rebellious teenager, the IRS, my business competitors—in short, *everyone!*)
- But in reality, if God is for you, who can be against you?
- Who is accusing you falsely today of things you never did or said?
- But in reality, who can bring any charge against God's chosen, and make it stick?
- Who or what is trying to drive a wedge between you and your Lord today?
- But in reality, who or what can separate you from the love of Christ?

NOVEMBER 22 ☐ DAY 327
1 CORINTHIANS 15–16
Problems with Doctrinal Error

OVERVIEW Two final matters attract Paul's attention as he closes his letter: the problem of disbelief in the resurrection and of distribution to the needs of the saints at Jerusalem. Paul relates a string of consequences that will result like a row of falling dominoes if, in fact, there is no resurrection of the dead: If Christ did not rise from the dead, preaching about him is meaningless, your faith is empty, you are still in your sins, those who have died believing in Christ are without hope and you are to be pitied for your delusion. Then with one gentle nudge, Paul refutes the first fallen domino ("But Christ has indeed been raised from the dead") and watches the rest of his conclusions fall over as well! Our hope in Christ is as secure as the historical foundation of our faith.

Chapter 15			Chapter 16	
Prominence of Resurrection	Proofs of Resurrection	Power of Resurrection	Liberal Giving	Loving Greetings
1　　　　4	5　　　　19	20　　　　58	1　　　　4	5　　　　24
Errors concerning the Gospel			Errors concerning Money	

YOUR DAILY WALK No doubt you are aware that God has a future program for your soul (salvation). But did you know he has a program for your body as well (resurrection)? Chapter 15 describes the future body God has in store for you—and it is exciting to consider!

Our friends take us to the grave and leave us there, but God will not.

• It will be imperishable (15:42) and won't wrinkle, age, wear out or fall apart.
• It will be glorious and powerful (15:43), eternally beautiful and supernaturally strong.
• It will be a spiritual body (15:44), not limited by flesh and blood, time or space.
• It will be a body over which death and sin have no power (15:54–57).
• And best of all, you will be fitted with it "in a flash, in the twinkling of an eye" (15:52), with no waiting in line!

Do you know a Christian who is physically limited by age, illness or injury? Why not invite that person over for a meal—and encourage him or her with God's promise of a resurrected body!

INSIGHT Living Today in the Light of Tomorrow's Promises
In 1 Corinthians 15:58 you'll find a call to *action* and a call to *immobility*. Why are both appropriate responses to Paul's appeal?

CHAPTER 15

Now, brothers, I want to remind you of the gospel I preached to you, which you received and on which you have taken your stand. ²By this gospel you are saved, if you hold firmly to the word I preached to you. Otherwise, you have believed in vain.

³For what I received I passed on to you as of first importanceᵒ: that Christ died for our sins according to the Scriptures, ⁴that he was buried, that he was raised on the third day according to the Scriptures, ⁵and that he appeared to Peter,ᵖ and then to the Twelve. ⁶After that, he appeared to more than five hundred of the brothers at the same time, most of whom are still living, though some have fallen asleep. ⁷Then he appeared to James, then to all the apostles, ⁸and last of all he ap-

ᵒ3 Or *you at the first*　ᵖ5 Greek *Cephas*

peared to me also, as to one abnormally born.

[9]For I am the least of the apostles and do not even deserve to be called an apostle, because I persecuted the church of God. [10]But by the grace of God I am what I am, and his grace to me was not without effect. No, I worked harder than all of them—yet not I, but the grace of God that was with me. [11]Whether, then, it was I or they, this is what we preach, and this is what you believed.

[12]But if it is preached that Christ has been raised from the dead, how can some of you say that there is no resurrection of the dead? [13]If there is no resurrection of the dead, then not even Christ has been raised. [14]And if Christ has not been raised, our preaching is useless and so is your faith. [15]More than that, we are then found to be false witnesses about God, for we have testified about God that he raised Christ from the dead. But he did not raise him if in fact the dead are not raised. [16]For if the dead are not raised, then Christ has not been raised either. [17]And if Christ has not been raised, your faith is futile; you are still in your sins. [18]Then those also who have fallen asleep in Christ are lost. [19]If only for this life we have hope in Christ, we are to be pitied more than all men.

[20]But Christ has indeed been raised from the dead, the firstfruits of those who have fallen asleep. [21]For since death came through a man, the resurrection of the dead comes also through a man. [22]For as in Adam all die, so in Christ all will be made alive. [23]But each in his own turn: Christ, the firstfruits; then, when he comes, those who belong to him. [24]Then the end will come, when he hands over the kingdom to God the Father after he has destroyed all dominion, authority and power. [25]For he must reign until he has put all his enemies under his feet. [26]The last enemy to be destroyed is death. [27]For he "has put everything under his feet."[q] Now when it says that "everything" has been put under him, it is clear that this does not include God himself, who put everything under Christ. [28]When he has done this, then the Son himself will be made subject to him who put everything under him, so that God may be all in all.

[29]Now if there is no resurrection, what will those do who are baptized for the dead? If the dead are not raised at all, why are people baptized for them? [30]And as for us, why do we endanger ourselves every hour? [31]I die every day—I mean that, brothers—just as surely as I glory over you in Christ Jesus our Lord. [32]If I fought wild beasts in Ephesus for merely human reasons, what have I gained? If the dead are not raised,

"Let us eat and drink,
    for tomorrow we die."[r]

[33]Do not be misled: "Bad company corrupts good character." [34]Come back to your senses as you ought, and stop sinning; for there are some who are ignorant of God—I say this to your shame.

[35]But someone may ask, "How are the dead raised? With what kind of body will they come?" [36]How foolish! What you sow does not come to life unless it dies. [37]When you sow, you do not plant the body that will be, but just a seed, perhaps of wheat or of something else. [38]But God gives it a body as he has determined, and to each kind of seed he gives its own body. [39]All flesh is not the same: Men have one kind of flesh, animals have another, birds another and fish another. [40]There are also heavenly bodies and there are earthly bodies; but the splendor of the heavenly bodies is one kind, and the splendor of the earthly bodies is another. [41]The sun has one kind of splendor, the moon another and the stars another; and star differs from star in splendor.

[42]So will it be with the resurrection of the dead. The body that is sown is perishable, it is raised imperishable; [43]it is sown in dishonor, it is raised in glory; it is sown in weakness, it is raised in power; [44]it is sown a natural body, it is raised a spiritual body.

If there is a natural body, there is also a spiritual body. [45]So it is written: "The first man Adam became a living being"[s]; the last Adam, a life-giving spirit. [46]The spiritual did not come first, but the natural, and after that the spiritual. [47]The first man was of the dust of the earth, the second man from heaven. [48]As was the earthly man, so are those who are of the earth; and as is the man from heaven, so

[q]27 Psalm 8:6   [r]32 Isaiah 22:13   [s]45 Gen. 2:7

also are those who are of heaven. [49]And just as we have borne the likeness of the earthly man, so shall we[t] bear the likeness of the man from heaven.

[50]I declare to you, brothers, that flesh and blood cannot inherit the kingdom of God, nor does the perishable inherit the imperishable. [51]Listen, I tell you a mystery: We will not all sleep, but we will all be changed— [52]in a flash, in the twinkling of an eye, at the last trumpet. For the trumpet will sound, the dead will be raised imperishable, and we will be changed. [53]For the perishable must clothe itself with the imperishable, and the mortal with immortality. [54]When the perishable has been clothed with the imperishable, and the mortal with immortality, then the saying that is written will come true: "Death has been swallowed up in victory."[u]

[55]"Where, O death, is your victory?
    Where, O death, is your sting?"[v]

[56]The sting of death is sin, and the power of sin is the law. [57]But thanks be to God! He gives us the victory through our Lord Jesus Christ.

[58]Therefore, my dear brothers, stand firm. Let nothing move you. Always give yourselves fully to the work of the Lord, because you know that your labor in the Lord is not in vain.

CHAPTER 16
Now about the collection for God's people: Do what I told the Galatian churches to do. [2]On the first day of every week, each one of you should set aside a sum of money in keeping with his income, saving it up, so that when I come no collections will have to be made. [3]Then, when I arrive, I will give letters of introduction to the men you approve and send them with your gift to Jerusalem. [4]If it seems advisable for me to go also, they will accompany me.

[5]After I go through Macedonia, I will come to you—for I will be going through Macedonia. [6]Perhaps I will stay with you awhile, or even spend the winter, so that

you can help me on my journey, wherever I go. [7]I do not want to see you now and make only a passing visit; I hope to spend some time with you, if the Lord permits. [8]But I will stay on at Ephesus until Pentecost, [9]because a great door for effective work has opened to me, and there are many who oppose me.

[10]If Timothy comes, see to it that he has nothing to fear while he is with you, for he is carrying on the work of the Lord, just as I am. [11]No one, then, should refuse to accept him. Send him on his way in peace so that he may return to me. I am expecting him along with the brothers.

[12]Now about our brother Apollos: I strongly urged him to go to you with the brothers. He was quite unwilling to go now, but he will go when he has the opportunity.

[13]Be on your guard; stand firm in the faith; be men of courage; be strong. [14]Do everything in love.

[15]You know that the household of Stephanas were the first converts in Achaia, and they have devoted themselves to the service of the saints. I urge you, brothers, [16]to submit to such as these and to everyone who joins in the work, and labors at it. [17]I was glad when Stephanas, Fortunatus and Achaicus arrived, because they have supplied what was lacking from you. [18]For they refreshed my spirit and yours also. Such men deserve recognition.

[19]The churches in the province of Asia send you greetings. Aquila and Priscilla[w] greet you warmly in the Lord, and so does the church that meets at their house. [20]All the brothers here send you greetings. Greet one another with a holy kiss.

[21]I, Paul, write this greeting in my own hand.

[22]If anyone does not love the Lord—a curse be on him. Come, O Lord[x]!

[23]The grace of the Lord Jesus be with you.

[24]My love to all of you in Christ Jesus. Amen.[y]

---

[t]49 Some early manuscripts *so let us*　　[u]54 Isaiah 25:8　　[v]55 Hosea 13:14　　[w]19 Greek *Prisca*, a variant of *Priscilla*
[x]22 In Aramaic the expression *Come, O Lord* is *Marana tha*.　　[y]24 Some manuscripts do not have *Amen*.

2 Corinthians

FALSE teachers in Corinth—angered by Paul's first letter—swayed the people against him. They claimed Paul was fickle, proud, unimpressive in appearance and speech, dishonest and unqualified as an apostle. After Paul sent Titus to deal with the situation, he rejoiced to hear of the Corinthians' change of heart. Paul wrote this letter to thank the repentant majority for their support and to appeal to the rebellious minority to accept his authority, as he defends his conduct, character and calling.

Focus	Ministry of the Gospel		Minister of the Gospel
Divisions	Paul's Attitudes in Ministry	Paul's Motivation and Model in Ministry	Paul's Authority in Ministry
	1 5	6 9	10 13
Topics	Character	Commitment	Credentials
	Explanation	Exhortation	Vindication
Place	Written in Macedonia		
Time	About A.D. 56		

NOVEMBER 23 □ DAY 328
2 CORINTHIANS 1–5
Paul's Attitude in Ministry

 OVERVIEW The numerous problems in the church at Corinth, coupled with Paul's personal conflicts with certain individuals, were weighing heavily upon him. Nevertheless, God had comforted him so that he in turn could comfort others. Despite the most trying circumstances, the faithful minister of God can enjoy daily strength and victory—not that he might be comfortable, but that he might be a comforter. The gospel ministry is a ministry of glory that seeks to exalt Jesus Christ in all things. Motivated by Christ's example of love, and living daily in the fear of the Lord, the faithful minister can rejoice in his role as an ambassador for Christ—proclaiming reconciliation and restoration for estranged sinners.

Chapters 1–2	Chapters 3–4	Chapter 5
A Ministry of Comfort	A Ministry of Glory	A Ministry of Reconciliation
Triumph in Christ	Temple of Christ	

 YOUR DAILY WALK Your best friend's marriage is in trouble. The husband moves out; the couple seeks professional help. Then you hear the welcome news: They have been *reconciled.* What does that mean?

It takes two sides to make a lasting peace, but it only takes one to make the first step.

A union goes on strike for higher wages and shorter hours. The management refuses to meet the union's demands. The two sides sit down to negotiate. At last an announcement is made: They *reconciled* their differences. What does that mean?

An estranged sinner has gone his own way (Isaiah 53:6), wandering far from the God who made him. You as an ambassador of Jesus Christ come to share with him the good news that a bridge has been provided to restore fellowship between sinful humanity and holy God (5:19). You extend the invitation, "Will you be *reconciled* to God?" What are you asking the person to do?

Yours is the precious privilege of inviting others to be *reconciled* to God. Have you reported for work yet today?

 INSIGHT They Didn't Even Like His Looks!
Paul's need to write 2 Corinthians becomes clear when you note the severity of the charges against him: fickleness (1:17–23), pride (3:1), weakness (10:10), rude speech (11:6), meanness (7:8–10), dishonesty (12:16–19) and mental instability (5:13).

CHAPTER 1

Paul, an apostle of Christ Jesus by the will of God, and Timothy our brother,

To the church of God in Corinth, together with all the saints throughout Achaia:

[2] Grace and peace to you from God our Father and the Lord Jesus Christ.

[3] Praise be to the God and Father of our Lord Jesus Christ, the Father of compassion and the God of all comfort, [4] who comforts us in all our troubles, so that we

can comfort those in any trouble with the comfort we ourselves have received from God. [5]For just as the sufferings of Christ flow over into our lives, so also through Christ our comfort overflows. [6]If we are distressed, it is for your comfort and salvation; if we are comforted, it is for your comfort, which produces in you patient endurance of the same sufferings we suffer. [7]And our hope for you is firm, because we know that just as you share in our sufferings, so also you share in our comfort.

[8]We do not want you to be uninformed, brothers, about the hardships we suffered in the province of Asia. We were under great pressure, far beyond our ability to endure, so that we despaired even of life. [9]Indeed, in our hearts we felt the sentence of death. But this happened that we might not rely on ourselves but on God, who raises the dead. [10]He has delivered us from such a deadly peril, and he will deliver us. On him we have set our hope that he will continue to deliver us, [11]as you help us by your prayers. Then many will give thanks on our[a] behalf for the gracious favor granted us in answer to the prayers of many.

[12]Now this is our boast: Our conscience testifies that we have conducted ourselves in the world, and especially in our relations with you, in the holiness and sincerity that are from God. We have done so not according to worldly wisdom but according to God's grace. [13]For we do not write you anything you cannot read or understand. And I hope that, [14]as you have understood us in part, you will come to understand fully that you can boast of us just as we will boast of you in the day of the Lord Jesus.

[15]Because I was confident of this, I planned to visit you first so that you might benefit twice. [16]I planned to visit you on my way to Macedonia and to come back to you from Macedonia, and then to have you send me on my way to Judea. [17]When I planned this, did I do it lightly? Or do I make my plans in a worldly manner so that in the same breath I say, "Yes, yes" and "No, no"?

[18]But as surely as God is faithful, our message to you is not "Yes" and "No." [19]For the Son of God, Jesus Christ, who was preached among you by me and Silas[b] and Timothy, was not "Yes" and "No," but in him it has always been "Yes." [20]For no matter how many promises God has made, they are "Yes" in Christ. And so through him the "Amen" is spoken by us to the glory of God. [21]Now it is God who makes both us and you stand firm in Christ. He anointed us, [22]set his seal of ownership on us, and put his Spirit in our hearts as a deposit, guaranteeing what is to come.

[23]I call God as my witness that it was in order to spare you that I did not return to Corinth. [24]Not that we lord it over your faith, but we work with you for your joy, because it is by faith you stand C H A P T E R 2 firm. [1]So I made up my mind that I would not make another painful visit to you. [2]For if I grieve you, who is left to make me glad but you whom I have grieved? [3]I wrote as I did so that when I came I should not be distressed by those who ought to make me rejoice. I had confidence in all of you, that you would all share my joy. [4]For I wrote you out of great distress and anguish of heart and with many tears, not to grieve you but to let you know the depth of my love for you.

[5]If anyone has caused grief, he has not so much grieved me as he has grieved all of you, to some extent—not to put it too severely. [6]The punishment inflicted on him by the majority is sufficient for him. [7]Now instead, you ought to forgive and comfort him, so that he will not be overwhelmed by excessive sorrow. [8]I urge you, therefore, to reaffirm your love for him. [9]The reason I wrote you was to see if you would stand the test and be obedient in everything. [10]If you forgive anyone, I also forgive him. And what I have forgiven—if there was anything to forgive—I have forgiven in the sight of Christ for your sake, [11]in order that Satan might not outwit us. For we are not unaware of his schemes.

[12]Now when I went to Troas to preach the gospel of Christ and found that the Lord had opened a door for me, [13]I still had no peace of mind, because I did not find my brother Titus there. So I said good-by to them and went on to Macedonia.

[14]But thanks be to God, who always leads us in triumphal procession in Christ and through us spreads everywhere the fragrance of the knowledge of him. [15]For we are to God the aroma of Christ among those who are being saved and those who are perishing. [16]To the one we are the smell of death; to the other, the fragrance of life. And who is equal to such a task? [17]Unlike so many, we do not peddle the word of God for profit. On the contrary, in Christ we speak before God with sincerity, like men sent from God.

CHAPTER 3

Are we beginning to commend ourselves again? Or do we need, like some people, letters of recommendation to you or from you? [2]You yourselves are our letter, written on our hearts, known and read by everybody. [3]You show that you are a letter from Christ, the result of our ministry, written not with ink but with the Spirit of the living God, not on tablets of stone but on tablets of human hearts.

[4]Such confidence as this is ours through Christ before God. [5]Not that we are competent in ourselves to claim anything for ourselves, but our competence comes from God. [6]He has made us competent as ministers of a new covenant—not of the letter but of the Spirit; for the letter kills, but the Spirit gives life.

[7]Now if the ministry that brought death, which was engraved in letters on stone, came with glory, so that the Israelites could not look steadily at the face of Moses because of its glory, fading though it was, [8]will not the ministry of the Spirit be even more glorious? [9]If the ministry that condemns men is glorious, how much more glorious is the ministry that brings righteousness! [10]For what was glorious has no glory now in comparison with the surpassing glory. [11]And if what was fading away came with glory, how much greater is the glory of that which lasts!

[12]Therefore, since we have such a hope, we are very bold. [13]We are not like Moses, who would put a veil over his face to keep the Israelites from gazing at it while the radiance was fading away. [14]But their minds were made dull, for to this day the same veil remains when the old covenant is read. It has not been removed, because only in Christ is it taken away. [15]Even to this day when Moses is read, a veil covers their hearts. [16]But whenever anyone turns to the Lord, the veil is taken away. [17]Now the Lord is the Spirit, and where the Spirit of the Lord is, there is freedom. [18]And we, who with unveiled faces all reflect[c] the Lord's glory, are being transformed into his likeness with ever-increasing glory, which comes from the Lord, who is the Spirit.

CHAPTER 4

Therefore, since through God's mercy we have this ministry, we do not lose heart. [2]Rather, we have renounced secret and shameful ways; we do not use deception, nor do we distort the word of God. On the contrary, by setting forth the truth plainly we commend ourselves to every man's conscience in the sight of God. [3]And even if our gospel is veiled, it is veiled to those who are perishing. [4]The god of this age has blinded the minds of unbelievers, so that they cannot see the light of the gospel of the glory of Christ, who is the image of God. [5]For we do not preach ourselves, but Jesus Christ as Lord, and ourselves as your servants for Jesus' sake. [6]For God, who said, "Let light shine out of darkness,"[d] made his light shine in our hearts to give us the light of the knowledge of the glory of God in the face of Christ.

[7]But we have this treasure in jars of clay to show that this all-surpassing power is from God and not from us. [8]We are hard pressed on every side, but not crushed; perplexed, but not in despair; [9]persecuted, but not abandoned; struck down, but not destroyed. [10]We always carry around in our body the death of Jesus, so that the life of Jesus may also be revealed in our body. [11]For we who are alive are always being given over to death for Jesus' sake, so that his life may be revealed in our mortal body. [12]So then, death is at work in us, but life is at work in you.

[13]It is written: "I believed; therefore I have spoken."[e] With that same spirit of faith we also believe and therefore speak, [14]because we know that the one who raised the Lord Jesus from the dead will also raise us with Jesus and present us

---

[c]18 Or contemplate   [d]6 Gen. 1:3   [e]13 Psalm 116:10

with you in his presence. [15]All this is for your benefit, so that the grace that is reaching more and more people may cause thanksgiving to overflow to the glory of God.

[16]Therefore we do not lose heart. Though outwardly we are wasting away, yet inwardly we are being renewed day by day. [17]For our light and momentary troubles are achieving for us an eternal glory that far outweighs them all. [18]So we fix our eyes not on what is seen, but on what is unseen. For what is seen is temporary, but what is unseen is eternal.

CHAPTER 5

Now we know that if the earthly tent we live in is destroyed, we have a building from God, an eternal house in heaven, not built by human hands. [2]Meanwhile we groan, longing to be clothed with our heavenly dwelling, [3]because when we are clothed, we will not be found naked. [4]For while we are in this tent, we groan and are burdened, because we do not wish to be unclothed but to be clothed with our heavenly dwelling, so that what is mortal may be swallowed up by life. [5]Now it is God who has made us for this very purpose and has given us the Spirit as a deposit, guaranteeing what is to come.

[6]Therefore we are always confident and know that as long as we are at home in the body we are away from the Lord. [7]We live by faith, not by sight. [8]We are confident, I say, and would prefer to be away from the body and at home with the Lord. [9]So we make it our goal to please him, whether we are at home in the body or away from it. [10]For we must all appear before the judgment seat of Christ, that each one may receive what is due him for the things done while in the body, whether good or bad.

[11]Since, then, we know what it is to fear the Lord, we try to persuade men. What we are is plain to God, and I hope it is also plain to your conscience. [12]We are not trying to commend ourselves to you again, but are giving you an opportunity to take pride in us, so that you can answer those who take pride in what is seen rather than in what is in the heart. [13]If we are out of our mind, it is for the sake of God; if we are in our right mind, it is for you. [14]For Christ's love compels us, because we are convinced that one died for all, and therefore all died. [15]And he died for all, that those who live should no longer live for themselves but for him who died for them and was raised again.

[16]So from now on we regard no one from a worldly point of view. Though we once regarded Christ in this way, we do so no longer. [17]Therefore, if anyone is in Christ, he is a new creation; the old has gone, the new has come! [18]All this is from God, who reconciled us to himself through Christ and gave us the ministry of reconciliation: [19]that God was reconciling the world to himself in Christ, not counting men's sins against them. And he has committed to us the message of reconciliation. [20]We are therefore Christ's ambassadors, as though God were making his appeal through us. We implore you on Christ's behalf: Be reconciled to God. [21]God made him who had no sin to be sin[f] for us, so that in him we might become the righteousness of God.

f21 Or be a sin offering

NOVEMBER 24 □ DAY 329
2 CORINTHIANS 6–9
Paul's Motivation and Model

 OVERVIEW Being a partner in the gospel means, first and foremost, allowing the gospel to have its life-changing effect on you. As their fellow worker in the gospel ministry, Paul exhorts the Corinthians not to receive the grace of God in an empty, purposeless way. Fellowship with darkness, filthiness of the flesh and insensitivity to financial needs around you are all inconsistent with the grace of God. Those truly motivated by the gospel will seek to exercise generosity toward those in need.

Chapter 6	Chapter 7	Chapter 8	Chapter 9
A Ministry of Purity	A Message of Praise	A Ministry of Giving	A Method of Giving
Separation		Stewardship	

YOUR DAILY WALK A man complained to his pastor, "It's getting to be just one continuous 'give, give, give.' "

To which the pastor replied, "Say, that's one of the best descriptions of Christianity I've ever heard!"

All we can hold in our cold, dead hands is what we have given away.

Here are some sermons-in-a-sentence on the subject of giving:
- Only by giving of oneself is enough taken away to make room for receiving more.
- Discontentment makes rich men poor; contentment makes poor men rich.
- Two telltale marks of a Christian are giving and forgiving, for the world knows little about either.

The average American churchgoer gives 3 percent of his or her income to church and charity. If 2 Corinthians 8:1–2 were being written about you and your church—rather than the churches of Macedonia—what would Paul say? And would you be pleased or pained to know others were reading about your model of giving? Write the words of 2 Corinthians 9:7 inside your checkbook. Let them remind you that cheerful giving comes from the heart, not just the checkbook!

INSIGHT Grace: The Gift That Keeps On Giving
In chapters 8 and 9 the word *grace* appears six times. Since grace is an undeserved gift, you should not be surprised to discover it is a key word in a passage dealing with money!

CHAPTER 6

As God's fellow workers we urge you not to receive God's grace in vain. ²For he says,

"In the time of my favor I heard you,
    and in the day of salvation I helped
    you."⁸

I tell you, now is the time of God's favor, now is the day of salvation.

³We put no stumbling block in anyone's path, so that our ministry will not be discredited. ⁴Rather, as servants of God we commend ourselves in every way: in great endurance; in troubles, hardships and distresses; ⁵in beatings, imprisonments and riots; in hard work, sleepless nights and hunger; ⁶in purity, understanding, patience and kindness; in the Holy Spirit and in sincere love; ⁷in truthful speech and in the power of God; with weapons of righteousness in the right hand and in the left; ⁸through glory and

dishonor, bad report and good report; genuine, yet regarded as impostors; ⁹known, yet regarded as unknown; dying, and yet we live on; beaten, and yet not killed; ¹⁰sorrowful, yet always rejoicing; poor, yet making many rich; having nothing, and yet possessing everything.

¹¹We have spoken freely to you, Corinthians, and opened wide our hearts to you. ¹²We are not withholding our affection from you, but you are withholding yours from us. ¹³As a fair exchange—I speak as to my children—open wide your hearts also.

¹⁴Do not be yoked together with unbelievers. For what do righteousness and wickedness have in common? Or what fellowship can light have with darkness? ¹⁵What harmony is there between Christ and Belial⁸? What does a believer have in common with an unbeliever? ¹⁶What agreement is there between the temple of God and idols? For we are the temple of

⁸2 Isaiah 49:8   ʰ15 Greek *Beliar*, a variant of *Belial*

the living God. As God has said: "I will live with them and walk among them, and I will be their God, and they will be my people."[i]

[17]"Therefore come out from them
    and be separate,
                        says the Lord.
Touch no unclean thing,
    and I will receive you."[j]
[18]"I will be a Father to you,
    and you will be my sons and
        daughters,
                says the Lord Almighty."[k]

CHAPTER 7

Since we have these promises, dear friends, let us purify ourselves from everything that contaminates body and spirit, perfecting holiness out of reverence for God.

[2]Make room for us in your hearts. We have wronged no one, we have corrupted no one, we have exploited no one. [3]I do not say this to condemn you; I have said before that you have such a place in our hearts that we would live or die with you. [4]I have great confidence in you; I take great pride in you. I am greatly encouraged; in all our troubles my joy knows no bounds.

[5]For when we came into Macedonia, this body of ours had no rest, but we were harassed at every turn—conflicts on the outside, fears within. [6]But God, who comforts the downcast, comforted us by the coming of Titus, [7]and not only by his coming but also by the comfort you had given him. He told us about your longing for me, your deep sorrow, your ardent concern for me, so that my joy was greater than ever.

[8]Even if I caused you sorrow by my letter, I do not regret it. Though I did regret it—I see that my letter hurt you, but only for a little while— [9]yet now I am happy, not because you were made sorry, but because your sorrow led you to repentance. For you became sorrowful as God intended and so were not harmed in any way by us. [10]Godly sorrow brings repentance that leads to salvation and leaves no regret, but worldly sorrow brings death. [11]See what this godly sorrow has produced in you: what earnestness, what ea-

gerness to clear yourselves, what indignation, what alarm, what longing, what concern, what readiness to see justice done. At every point you have proved yourselves to be innocent in this matter. [12]So even though I wrote to you, it was not on account of the one who did the wrong or of the injured party, but rather that before God you could see for yourselves how devoted to us you are. [13]By all this we are encouraged.

In addition to our own encouragement, we were especially delighted to see how happy Titus was, because his spirit has been refreshed by all of you. [14]I had boasted to him about you, and you have not embarrassed me. But just as everything we said to you was true, so our boasting about you to Titus has proved to be true as well. [15]And his affection for you is all the greater when he remembers that you were all obedient, receiving him with fear and trembling. [16]I am glad I can have complete confidence in you.

CHAPTER 8

And now, brothers, we want you to know about the grace that God has given the Macedonian churches. [2]Out of the most severe trial, their overflowing joy and their extreme poverty welled up in rich generosity. [3]For I testify that they gave as much as they were able, and even beyond their ability. Entirely on their own, [4]they urgently pleaded with us for the privilege of sharing in this service to the saints. [5]And they did not do as we expected, but they gave themselves first to the Lord and then to us in keeping with God's will. [6]So we urged Titus, since he had earlier made a beginning, to bring also to completion this act of grace on your part. [7]But just as you excel in everything—in faith, in speech, in knowledge, in complete earnestness and in your love for us[l]—see that you also excel in this grace of giving.

[8]I am not commanding you, but I want to test the sincerity of your love by comparing it with the earnestness of others. [9]For you know the grace of our Lord Jesus Christ, that though he was rich, yet for your sakes he became poor, so that you through his poverty might become rich.

[10]And here is my advice about what is best for you in this matter: Last year you

[i]16 Lev. 26:12; Jer. 32:38; Ezek. 37:27   [j]17 Isaiah 52:11; Ezek. 20:34,41   [k]18 2 Samuel 7:14; 7:8   [l]7 Some manuscripts in our love for you

were the first not only to give but also to have the desire to do so. [11]Now finish the work, so that your eager willingness to do it may be matched by your completion of it, according to your means. [12]For if the willingness is there, the gift is acceptable according to what one has, not according to what he does not have.

[13]Our desire is not that others might be relieved while you are hard pressed, but that there might be equality. [14]At the present time your plenty will supply what they need, so that in turn their plenty will supply what you need. Then there will be equality, [15]as it is written: "He who gathered much did not have too much, and he who gathered little did not have too little." [m]

[16]I thank God, who put into the heart of Titus the same concern I have for you. [17]For Titus not only welcomed our appeal, but he is coming to you with much enthusiasm and on his own initiative. [18]And we are sending along with him the brother who is praised by all the churches for his service to the gospel. [19]What is more, he was chosen by the churches to accompany us as we carry the offering, which we administer in order to honor the Lord himself and to show our eagerness to help. [20]We want to avoid any criticism of the way we administer this liberal gift. [21]For we are taking pains to do what is right, not only in the eyes of the Lord but also in the eyes of men.

[22]In addition, we are sending with them our brother who has often proved to us in many ways that he is zealous, and now even more so because of his great confidence in you. [23]As for Titus, he is my partner and fellow worker among you; as for our brothers, they are representatives of the churches and an honor to Christ. [24]Therefore show these men the proof of your love and the reason for our pride in you, so that the churches can see it.

CHAPTER 9

There is no need for me to write to you about this service to the saints. [2]For I know your eagerness to help, and I have been boasting about it to the Macedonians, telling them that since last year you

in Achaia were ready to give; and your enthusiasm has stirred most of them to action. [3]But I am sending the brothers in order that our boasting about you in this matter should not prove hollow, but that you may be ready, as I said you would be. [4]For if any Macedonians come with me and find you unprepared, we—not to say anything about you—would be ashamed of having been so confident. [5]So I thought it necessary to urge the brothers to visit you in advance and finish the arrangements for the generous gift you had promised. Then it will be ready as a generous gift, not as one grudgingly given.

[6]Remember this: Whoever sows sparingly will also reap sparingly, and whoever sows generously will also reap generously. [7]Each man should give what he has decided in his heart to give, not reluctantly or under compulsion, for God loves a cheerful giver. [8]And God is able to make all grace abound to you, so that in all things at all times, having all that you need, you will abound in every good work. [9]As it is written:

"He has scattered abroad his gifts to
    the poor;
  his righteousness endures forever." [n]

[10]Now he who supplies seed to the sower and bread for food will also supply and increase your store of seed and will enlarge the harvest of your righteousness. [11]You will be made rich in every way so that you can be generous on every occasion, and through us your generosity will result in thanksgiving to God.

[12]This service that you perform is not only supplying the needs of God's people but is also overflowing in many expressions of thanks to God. [13]Because of the service by which you have proved yourselves, men will praise God for the obedience that accompanies your confession of the gospel of Christ, and for your generosity in sharing with them and with everyone else. [14]And in their prayers for you their hearts will go out to you, because of the surpassing grace God has given you. [15]Thanks be to God for his indescribable gift!

[m]15 Exodus 16:18   [n]9 Psalm 112:9

NOVEMBER 25 □ DAY 330
2 CORINTHIANS 10–13
Paul's Authority in Ministry

OVERVIEW Discipline is never pleasant, but the task becomes doubly difficult when the authority of the disciplinarian is under attack. In order to defend his authority as an apostle of Jesus Christ, Paul relates certain events from his background, including his heavenly visions and thorn in the flesh. His letter closes with a warning that he will soon make his third visit to Corinth, and so he urges the believers there to take his exhortations to heart.

Chapter 10	Chapter 11	Chapter 12	Chapter 13
Authority Declared	Authority Defended	Authority Dramatized	A Visit Described
Paul, the Minister		Paul, the Messenger	

YOUR DAILY WALK How are splinters, thorns and chewing gum alike?

Answer: It's easier to get attached to them than to get rid of them! Paul's thorn in the flesh has been the subject of much speculation.

Those who would have nothing to do with thorns must never attempt to gather flowers.

Though the biblical account is brief, this much is clear:
- God allowed it for a purpose—to promote humility in Paul's life and keep him from exalting himself above measure (12:7).
- It was of satanic origin—similar to Job's loss of wealth, health, family and status (12:7; Job 1–2).
- No amount of prayer would remove it (12:8)—regardless of how fervent or frequent the petition.
- It was used to show the sufficiency of God in the face of human weakness (12:9–10).

The exact nature of Paul's thorn is unclear—perhaps so you can learn a lesson from your own "thorny" situation. A lingering illness, a physical handicap, a speech impediment—God is adequate for them all. Carry a stick of gum today to remind you that God's strength is a promise that will "stick" with you. Now that's a thought worth chewing on!

INSIGHT What's in a Thorn?

The list of suggestions regarding Paul's thorn in the flesh reads like a medical dictionary. Ideas include epilepsy, eye disease, malaria, leprosy, migraine headaches, depression and stammering.

CHAPTER 10

By the meekness and gentleness of Christ, I appeal to you—I, Paul, who am "timid" when face to face with you, but "bold" when away! ²I beg you that when I come I may not have to be as bold as I expect to be toward some people who think that we live by the standards of this world. ³For though we live in the world, we do not wage war as the world does. ⁴The weapons we fight with are not the weapons of the world. On the contrary, they have divine power to demolish strongholds. ⁵We demolish arguments and every pretension that sets itself up against the knowledge of God, and we take captive every thought to make it obedient to Christ. ⁶And we will be ready to punish every act of disobedience, once your obedience is complete.

⁷You are looking only on the surface of things.ᵒ If anyone is confident that he

ᵒ7 Or Look at the obvious facts

belongs to Christ, he should consider again that we belong to Christ just as much as he. [8]For even if I boast somewhat freely about the authority the Lord gave us for building you up rather than pulling you down, I will not be ashamed of it. [9]I do not want to seem to be trying to frighten you with my letters. [10]For some say, "His letters are weighty and forceful, but in person he is unimpressive and his speaking amounts to nothing." [11]Such people should realize that what we are in our letters when we are absent, we will be in our actions when we are present.

[12]We do not dare to classify or compare ourselves with some who commend themselves. When they measure themselves by themselves and compare themselves with themselves, they are not wise. [13]We, however, will not boast beyond proper limits, but will confine our boasting to the field God has assigned to us, a field that reaches even to you. [14]We are not going too far in our boasting, as would be the case if we had not come to you, for we did get as far as you with the gospel of Christ. [15]Neither do we go beyond our limits by boasting of work done by others.[p] Our hope is that, as your faith continues to grow, our area of activity among you will greatly expand, [16]so that we can preach the gospel in the regions beyond you. For we do not want to boast about work already done in another man's territory. [17]But, "Let him who boasts boast in the Lord."[q] [18]For it is not the one who commends himself who is approved, but the one whom the Lord commends.

CHAPTER 11

I hope you will put up with a little of my foolishness; but you are already doing that. [2]I am jealous for you with a godly jealousy. I promised you to one husband, to Christ, so that I might present you as a pure virgin to him. [3]But I am afraid that just as Eve was deceived by the serpent's cunning, your minds may somehow be led astray from your sincere and pure devotion to Christ. [4]For if someone comes to you and preaches a Jesus other than the Jesus we preached, or if you receive a different spirit from the one you received, or a different gospel from the one you accepted, you put up with it easily enough. [5]But I do not think I am in the least inferior to those "super-apostles." [6]I may not be a trained speaker, but I do have knowledge. We have made this perfectly clear to you in every way.

[7]Was it a sin for me to lower myself in order to elevate you by preaching the gospel of God to you free of charge? [8]I robbed other churches by receiving support from them so as to serve you. [9]And when I was with you and needed something, I was not a burden to anyone, for the brothers who came from Macedonia supplied what I needed. I have kept myself from being a burden to you in any way, and will continue to do so. [10]As surely as the truth of Christ is in me, nobody in the regions of Achaia will stop this boasting of mine. [11]Why? Because I do not love you? God knows I do! [12]And I will keep on doing what I am doing in order to cut the ground from under those who want an opportunity to be considered equal with us in the things they boast about.

[13]For such men are false apostles, deceitful workmen, masquerading as apostles of Christ. [14]And no wonder, for Satan himself masquerades as an angel of light. [15]It is not surprising, then, if his servants masquerade as servants of righteousness. Their end will be what their actions deserve.

[16]I repeat: Let no one take me for a fool. But if you do, then receive me just as you would a fool, so that I may do a little boasting. [17]In this self-confident boasting I am not talking as the Lord would, but as a fool. [18]Since many are boasting in the way the world does, I too will boast. [19]You gladly put up with fools since you are so wise! [20]In fact, you even put up with anyone who enslaves you or exploits you or takes advantage of you or pushes himself forward or slaps you in the face. [21]To my shame I admit that we were too weak for that!

What anyone else dares to boast about—I am speaking as a fool—I also dare to boast about. [22]Are they Hebrews? So am I. Are they Israelites? So am I. Are they Abraham's descendants? So am I.

[p] 13-15 Or [13]We, however, will not boast about things that cannot be measured, but we will boast according to the standard of measurement that the God of measure has assigned us—a measurement that relates even to you. [14] . . . . [15]Neither do we boast about things that cannot be measured in regard to the work done by others.   [q] 17 Jer. 9:24

23 Are they servants of Christ? (I am out of my mind to talk like this.) I am more. I have worked much harder, been in prison more frequently, been flogged more severely, and been exposed to death again and again. 24 Five times I received from the Jews the forty lashes minus one. 25 Three times I was beaten with rods, once I was stoned, three times I was shipwrecked, I spent a night and a day in the open sea, 26 I have been constantly on the move. I have been in danger from rivers, in danger from bandits, in danger from my own countrymen, in danger from Gentiles; in danger in the city, in danger in the country, in danger at sea; and in danger from false brothers. 27 I have labored and toiled and have often gone without sleep; I have known hunger and thirst and have often gone without food; I have been cold and naked. 28 Besides everything else, I face daily the pressure of my concern for all the churches. 29 Who is weak, and I do not feel weak? Who is led into sin, and I do not inwardly burn?

30 If I must boast, I will boast of the things that show my weakness. 31 The God and Father of the Lord Jesus, who is to be praised forever, knows that I am not lying. 32 In Damascus the governor under King Aretas had the city of the Damascenes guarded in order to arrest me. 33 But I was lowered in a basket from a window in the wall and slipped through his hands.

CHAPTER 12

I must go on boasting. Although there is nothing to be gained, I will go on to visions and revelations from the Lord. 2 I know a man in Christ who fourteen years ago was caught up to the third heaven. Whether it was in the body or out of the body I do not know—God knows. 3 And I know that this man—whether in the body or apart from the body I do not know, but God knows— 4 was caught up to paradise. He heard inexpressible things, things that man is not permitted to tell. 5 I will boast about a man like that, but I will not boast about myself, except about my weaknesses. 6 Even if I should choose to boast, I would not be a fool, because I would be speaking the truth. But I refrain, so no one will think more of me than is warranted by what I do or say.

7 To keep me from becoming conceited because of these surpassingly great revelations, there was given me a thorn in my flesh, a messenger of Satan, to torment me. 8 Three times I pleaded with the Lord to take it away from me. 9 But he said to me, "My grace is sufficient for you, for my power is made perfect in weakness." Therefore I will boast all the more gladly about my weaknesses, so that Christ's power may rest on me. 10 That is why, for Christ's sake, I delight in weaknesses, in insults, in hardships, in persecutions, in difficulties. For when I am weak, then I am strong.

11 I have made a fool of myself, but you drove me to it. I ought to have been commended by you, for I am not in the least inferior to the "super-apostles," even though I am nothing. 12 The things that mark an apostle—signs, wonders and miracles—were done among you with great perseverance. 13 How were you inferior to the other churches, except that I was never a burden to you? Forgive me this wrong!

14 Now I am ready to visit you for the third time, and I will not be a burden to you, because what I want is not your possessions but you. After all, children should not have to save up for their parents, but parents for their children. 15 So I will very gladly spend for you everything I have and expend myself as well. If I love you more, will you love me less? 16 Be that as it may, I have not been a burden to you. Yet, crafty fellow that I am, I caught you by trickery! 17 Did I exploit you through any of the men I sent you? 18 I urged Titus to go to you and I sent our brother with him. Titus did not exploit you, did he? Did we not act in the same spirit and follow the same course?

19 Have you been thinking all along that we have been defending ourselves to you? We have been speaking in the sight of God as those in Christ; and everything we do, dear friends, is for your strengthening. 20 For I am afraid that when I come I may not find you as I want you to be, and you may not find me as you want me to be. I fear that there may be quarreling, jealousy, outbursts of anger, factions, slander, gossip, arrogance and disorder. 21 I am afraid that when I come again my God will humble me before you, and I will be grieved over many who have sinned earlier and have not repented of

the impurity, sexual sin and debauchery in which they have indulged.

CHAPTER 13

This will be my third visit to you. "Every matter must be established by the testimony of two or three witnesses."r 2I already gave you a warning when I was with you the second time. I now repeat it while absent: On my return I will not spare those who sinned earlier or any of the others, 3since you are demanding proof that Christ is speaking through me. He is not weak in dealing with you, but is powerful among you. 4For to be sure, he was crucified in weakness, yet he lives by God's power. Likewise, we are weak in him, yet by God's power we will live with him to serve you.

5Examine yourselves to see whether you are in the faith; test yourselves. Do you not realize that Christ Jesus is in you—unless, of course, you fail the test? 6And I trust that you will discover that we have not failed the test. 7Now we pray to God that you will not do anything wrong. Not that people will see that we have stood the test but that you will do what is right even though we may seem to have failed. 8For we cannot do anything against the truth, but only for the truth. 9We are glad whenever we are weak but you are strong; and our prayer is for your perfection. 10This is why I write these things when I am absent, that when I come I may not have to be harsh in my use of authority—the authority the Lord gave me for building you up, not for tearing you down.

11Finally, brothers, good-by. Aim for perfection, listen to my appeal, be of one mind, live in peace. And the God of love and peace will be with you.

12Greet one another with a holy kiss. 13All the saints send their greetings.

14May the grace of the Lord Jesus Christ, and the love of God, and the fellowship of the Holy Spirit be with you all.

r1 Deut. 19:15

Galatians

PAUL'S epistle to the Galatians is an attempt to avert disaster. Having launched their Christian experience by faith, the Galatians now seem willing to leave their faith voyage and chart a new and misguided course based on works. Paul blends boldness with benevolence as he repudiates the bondage the Galatians have imposed on themselves. After reminding them that it is through grace, not the law, that heaven is obtained, Paul goes on to show that it is in the Spirit, not the flesh, that the Christian life is successfully lived. Freedom in Christ means freedom to produce the fruits of righteousness through a Spirit-led lifestyle.

Focus	Defending the Gospel's Minister		Defending the Gospel's Message		Demonstrating the Gospel's Might	
Divisions	Perverters' Renunciation	Paul's Apostleship	Law Cannot Set Free	Grace Sets Free	Peril to Freedom	Practice in Freedom
	1:1 1:10	1:11 2:21	3:1 4:20	4:21 4:31	5:1 5:12	5:13 6:18
Topics	Autobiography		Authority		Application	
	Authority, Not Opinion		Freedom, Not Bondage		Spirit, Not Flesh	
Place	South Galatian Theory: Syrian Antioch North Galatian Theory: Ephesus or Macedonia					
Time	South Galatian Theory: A.D. 49 North Galatian Theory: A.D. 53–56					

NOVEMBER 26 □ DAY 331
GALATIANS 1–6
Unshackled in Christ

OVERVIEW After Paul's first missionary journey, the Jerusalem council (Acts 15) reached a landmark decision in which it acknowledged that a person does not first have to become a Jew in order to become a Christian. However, the apostle Paul continued to struggle with those who would add the requirement of Jewish law to the simple message of salvation. It is not through keeping the Mosaic Law that the Christian faith is either begun or continued. The law enslaves; faith in Jesus Christ liberates. But liberty is not license to sin.

Chapters 1–2	Chapters 3–4	Chapters 5–6
Defending the Gospel Minister	Defending the Gospel Message	Demonstrating the Gospel's Might
Autobiography	Authority	Application

Legalism is bound to produce pride of heart.

YOUR DAILY WALK Imagine for a moment that you have been invited to witness a most unusual wedding ceremony. The bride and groom are there in all their finery. But before the ceremony begins, each hands the other a contract detailing the rules of their new relationship and life together. The husband-to-be reads, "You must help with the dishes each evening; you must cut the lawn each Saturday; you must not soil the carpets with your muddy fishing boots." And conversely, the wife-to-be reads with shock and dismay, "You must cook the meals; you must keep a clean house; you must make the beds. . . ." What's the problem here? They are trying to legislate what love would cause them to do willingly in the first place!

Now carry that illustration over into the spiritual realm. A Spirit-controlled person needs no law to make him or her live a righteous life. Why? Because the motivation to do so comes from within.

Take a hard look at your walk with God. Is it characterized by a growing list of *rules* or a growing love *relationship?* Remember, without the fruit of the Spirit you are just a religious noise (1 Corinthians 13:1)! Pick one characteristic listed in 5:22–23 to cultivate today.

INSIGHT Galatians: The Large-Print Edition
Verses such as 6:11 seem to indicate that Paul suffered from poor eyesight. As a result he usually dictated his letters (Romans 16:22), adding a handwritten greeting (1 Corinthians 16:21). This evidence leads some commentators to believe that Paul's "thorn in the flesh" may have been an eye disease.

CHAPTER 1

Paul, an apostle—sent not from men nor by man, but by Jesus Christ and God the Father, who raised him from the dead—²and all the brothers with me,

To the churches in Galatia:

³Grace and peace to you from God our Father and the Lord Jesus Christ, ⁴who gave himself for our sins to rescue us from the present evil age, according to the will of our God and Father, ⁵to whom be glory for ever and ever. Amen.

⁶I am astonished that you are so quickly deserting the one who called you by the grace of Christ and are turning to a different gospel— ⁷which is really no gospel at all. Evidently some people are throwing you into confusion and are trying to pervert the gospel of Christ. ⁸But even if we or an angel from heaven should preach a gospel other than the one we preached to you, let him be eternally condemned! ⁹As we have already said, so now I say again: If anybody is preaching to you a gospel other than what you accepted, let him be eternally condemned!

¹⁰Am I now trying to win the approval of men, or of God? Or am I trying to please men? If I were still trying to please men, I would not be a servant of Christ.

¹¹I want you to know, brothers, that the gospel I preached is not something that man made up. ¹²I did not receive it from any man, nor was I taught it; rather, I received it by revelation from Jesus Christ.

¹³For you have heard of my previous way of life in Judaism, how intensely I persecuted the church of God and tried to destroy it. ¹⁴I was advancing in Judaism beyond many Jews of my own age and was extremely zealous for the traditions of my fathers. ¹⁵But when God, who set me apart from birth*ᵃ* and called me by his grace, was pleased ¹⁶to reveal his Son in me so that I might preach him among the Gentiles, I did not consult any man, ¹⁷nor did I go up to Jerusalem to see those who were apostles before I was, but I went immediately into Arabia and later returned to Damascus.

¹⁸Then after three years, I went up to Jerusalem to get acquainted with Peter*ᵇ* and stayed with him fifteen days. ¹⁹I saw none of the other apostles—only James, the Lord's brother. ²⁰I assure you before God that what I am writing you is no lie. ²¹Later I went to Syria and Cilicia. ²²I was personally unknown to the churches of Judea that are in Christ. ²³They only heard the report: "The man who formerly persecuted us is now preaching the faith he once tried to destroy." ²⁴And they praised God because of me.

CHAPTER 2
Fourteen years later I went up again to Jerusalem, this time with Barnabas. I took Titus along also. ²I went in response to a revelation and set before them the gospel that I preach among the Gentiles. But I did this privately to those who seemed to be leaders, for fear that I was running or had run my race in vain. ³Yet not even Titus, who was with me, was compelled to be circumcised, even though he was a Greek. ⁴This matter arose₎ because some false brothers had infiltrated our ranks to spy on the freedom we have in Christ Jesus and to make us slaves. ⁵We did not give in to them for a moment, so that the truth of the gospel might remain with you.

⁶As for those who seemed to be important—whatever they were makes no difference to me; God does not judge by external appearance—those men added nothing to my message. ⁷On the contrary, they saw that I had been entrusted with the task of preaching the gospel to the Gentiles,*ᶜ* just as Peter had been to the Jews.*ᵈ* ⁸For God, who was at work in the ministry of Peter as an apostle to the Jews, was also at work in my ministry as an apostle to the Gentiles. ⁹James, Peter*ᵉ* and John, those reputed to be pillars, gave me and Barnabas the right hand of fellowship when they recognized the grace given to me. They agreed that we should go to the Gentiles, and they to the Jews. ¹⁰All they asked was that we should continue to remember the poor, the very thing I was eager to do.

¹¹When Peter came to Antioch, I opposed him to his face, because he was clearly in the wrong. ¹²Before certain men came from James, he used to eat with the Gentiles. But when they arrived, he began to draw back and separate himself from the Gentiles because he was afraid of those who belonged to the circumcision group. ¹³The other Jews joined him in his hypocrisy, so that by their hypocrisy even Barnabas was led astray.

¹⁴When I saw that they were not acting in line with the truth of the gospel, I said to Peter in front of them all, "You are a Jew, yet you live like a Gentile and not like a Jew. How is it, then, that you force Gentiles to follow Jewish customs?

¹⁵"We who are Jews by birth and not 'Gentile sinners' ¹⁶know that a man is not justified by observing the law, but by faith

ᵃ15 Or *from my mother's womb*   *ᵇ18* Greek *Cephas*   *ᶜ7* Greek *uncircumcised*   *ᵈ7* Greek *circumcised*; also in verses 8 and 9
ᵉ9 Greek *Cephas*; also in verses 11 and 14

in Jesus Christ. So we, too, have put our faith in Christ Jesus that we may be justified by faith in Christ and not by observing the law, because by observing the law no one will be justified.

[17]"If, while we seek to be justified in Christ, it becomes evident that we ourselves are sinners, does that mean that Christ promotes sin? Absolutely not! [18]If I rebuild what I destroyed, I prove that I am a lawbreaker. [19]For through the law I died to the law so that I might live for God. [20]I have been crucified with Christ and I no longer live, but Christ lives in me. The life I live in the body, I live by faith in the Son of God, who loved me and gave himself for me. [21]I do not set aside the grace of God, for if righteousness could be gained through the law, Christ died for nothing!"[f]

CHAPTER 3

You foolish Galatians! Who has bewitched you? Before your very eyes Jesus Christ was clearly portrayed as crucified. [2]I would like to learn just one thing from you: Did you receive the Spirit by observing the law, or by believing what you heard? [3]Are you so foolish? After beginning with the Spirit, are you now trying to attain your goal by human effort? [4]Have you suffered so much for nothing—if it really was for nothing? [5]Does God give you his Spirit and work miracles among you because you observe the law, or because you believe what you heard?

[6]Consider Abraham: "He believed God, and it was credited to him as righteousness."[g] [7]Understand, then, that those who believe are children of Abraham. [8]The Scripture foresaw that God would justify the Gentiles by faith, and announced the gospel in advance to Abraham: "All nations will be blessed through you."[h] [9]So those who have faith are blessed along with Abraham, the man of faith.

[10]All who rely on observing the law are under a curse, for it is written: "Cursed is everyone who does not continue to do everything written in the Book of the Law."[i] [11]Clearly no one is justified before God by the law, because, "The righteous will live by faith."[j] [12]The law is not based on faith; on the contrary, "The man who

does these things will live by them."[k] [13]Christ redeemed us from the curse of the law by becoming a curse for us, for it is written: "Cursed is everyone who is hung on a tree."[l] [14]He redeemed us in order that the blessing given to Abraham might come to the Gentiles through Christ Jesus, so that by faith we might receive the promise of the Spirit.

[15]Brothers, let me take an example from everyday life. Just as no one can set aside or add to a human covenant that has been duly established, so it is in this case. [16]The promises were spoken to Abraham and to his seed. The Scripture does not say "and to seeds," meaning many people, but "and to your seed,"[m] meaning one person, who is Christ. [17]What I mean is this: The law, introduced 430 years later, does not set aside the covenant previously established by God and thus do away with the promise. [18]For if the inheritance depends on the law, then it no longer depends on a promise; but God in his grace gave it to Abraham through a promise.

[19]What, then, was the purpose of the law? It was added because of transgressions until the Seed to whom the promise referred had come. The law was put into effect through angels by a mediator. [20]A mediator, however, does not represent just one party; but God is one.

[21]Is the law, therefore, opposed to the promises of God? Absolutely not! For if a law had been given that could impart life, then righteousness would certainly have come by the law. [22]But the Scripture declares that the whole world is a prisoner of sin, so that what was promised, being given through faith in Jesus Christ, might be given to those who believe.

[23]Before this faith came, we were held prisoners by the law, locked up until faith should be revealed. [24]So the law was put in charge to lead us to Christ[n] that we might be justified by faith. [25]Now that faith has come, we are no longer under the supervision of the law.

[26]You are all sons of God through faith in Christ Jesus, [27]for all of you who were baptized into Christ have clothed yourselves with Christ. [28]There is neither Jew nor Greek, slave nor free, male nor female, for you are all one in Christ Jesus. [29]If you belong to Christ, then you are

f21 Some interpreters end the quotation after verse 14.   *g6* Gen. 15:6   *h8* Gen. 12:3; 18:18; 22:18   *i10* Deut. 27:26
j11 Hab. 2:4   *k12* Lev. 18:5   *l13* Deut. 21:23   *m16* Gen. 12:7; 13:15; 24:7   *n24* Or *charge until Christ came*

Abraham's seed, and heirs according to the promise.

CHAPTER 4

What I am saying is that as long as the heir is a child, he is no different from a slave, although he owns the whole estate. ²He is subject to guardians and trustees until the time set by his father. ³So also, when we were children, we were in slavery under the basic principles of the world. ⁴But when the time had fully come, God sent his Son, born of a woman, born under law, ⁵to redeem those under law, that we might receive the full rights of sons. ⁶Because you are sons, God sent the Spirit of his Son into our hearts, the Spirit who calls out, *"Abba,ᵒ* Father." ⁷So you are no longer a slave, but a son; and since you are a son, God has made you also an heir.

⁸Formerly, when you did not know God, you were slaves to those who by nature are not gods. ⁹But now that you know God—or rather are known by God—how is it that you are turning back to those weak and miserable principles? Do you wish to be enslaved by them all over again? ¹⁰You are observing special days and months and seasons and years! ¹¹I fear for you, that somehow I have wasted my efforts on you.

¹²I plead with you, brothers, become like me, for I became like you. You have done me no wrong. ¹³As you know, it was because of an illness that I first preached the gospel to you. ¹⁴Even though my illness was a trial to you, you did not treat me with contempt or scorn. Instead, you welcomed me as if I were an angel of God, as if I were Christ Jesus himself. ¹⁵What has happened to all your joy? I can testify that, if you could have done so, you would have torn out your eyes and given them to me. ¹⁶Have I now become your enemy by telling you the truth?

¹⁷Those people are zealous to win you over, but for no good. What they want is to alienate you ⌊from us⌋, so that you may be zealous for them. ¹⁸It is fine to be zealous, provided the purpose is good, and to be so always and not just when I am with you. ¹⁹My dear children, for whom I am again in the pains of childbirth until Christ is formed in you, ²⁰how I wish I

could be with you now and change my tone, because I am perplexed about you!

²¹Tell me, you who want to be under the law, are you not aware of what the law says? ²²For it is written that Abraham had two sons, one by the slave woman and the other by the free woman. ²³His son by the slave woman was born in the ordinary way; but his son by the free woman was born as the result of a promise.

²⁴These things may be taken figuratively, for the women represent two covenants. One covenant is from Mount Sinai and bears children who are to be slaves: This is Hagar. ²⁵Now Hagar stands for Mount Sinai in Arabia and corresponds to the present city of Jerusalem, because she is in slavery with her children. ²⁶But the Jerusalem that is above is free, and she is our mother. ²⁷For it is written:

> "Be glad, O barren woman,
>   who bears no children;
> break forth and cry aloud,
>   you who have no labor pains;
> because more are the children of the
>   desolate woman
>   than of her who has a husband."ᵖ

²⁸Now you, brothers, like Isaac, are children of promise. ²⁹At that time the son born in the ordinary way persecuted the son born by the power of the Spirit. It is the same now. ³⁰But what does the Scripture say? "Get rid of the slave woman and her son, for the slave woman's son will never share in the inheritance with the free woman's son."�q ³¹Therefore, brothers, we are not children of the slave woman, but of the free woman.

CHAPTER 5

It is for freedom that Christ has set us free. Stand firm, then, and do not let yourselves be burdened again by a yoke of slavery.

²Mark my words! I, Paul, tell you that if you let yourselves be circumcised, Christ will be of no value to you at all. ³Again I declare to every man who lets himself be circumcised that he is obligated to obey the whole law. ⁴You who are trying to be justified by law have been alienated from Christ; you have fallen away from grace. ⁵But by faith we eagerly await through

---

ᵒ6 Aramaic for *Father*   ᵖ27 Isaiah 54:1   q30 Gen. 21:10

the Spirit the righteousness for which we hope. [6]For in Christ Jesus neither circumcision nor uncircumcision has any value. The only thing that counts is faith expressing itself through love.

[7]You were running a good race. Who cut in on you and kept you from obeying the truth? [8]That kind of persuasion does not come from the one who calls you. [9]"A little yeast works through the whole batch of dough." [10]I am confident in the Lord that you will take no other view. The one who is throwing you into confusion will pay the penalty, whoever he may be. [11]Brothers, if I am still preaching circumcision, why am I still being persecuted? In that case the offense of the cross has been abolished. [12]As for those agitators, I wish they would go the whole way and emasculate themselves!

[13]You, my brothers, were called to be free. But do not use your freedom to indulge the sinful nature[r]; rather, serve one another in love. [14]The entire law is summed up in a single command: "Love your neighbor as yourself."[s] [15]If you keep on biting and devouring each other, watch out or you will be destroyed by each other.

[16]So I say, live by the Spirit, and you will not gratify the desires of the sinful nature. [17]For the sinful nature desires what is contrary to the Spirit, and the Spirit what is contrary to the sinful nature. They are in conflict with each other, so that you do not do what you want. [18]But if you are led by the Spirit, you are not under law.

[19]The acts of the sinful nature are obvious: sexual immorality, impurity and debauchery; [20]idolatry and witchcraft; hatred, discord, jealousy, fits of rage, selfish ambition, dissensions, factions [21]and envy; drunkenness, orgies, and the like. I warn you, as I did before, that those who live like this will not inherit the kingdom of God.

[22]But the fruit of the Spirit is love, joy, peace, patience, kindness, goodness, faithfulness, [23]gentleness and self-control. Against such things there is no law. [24]Those who belong to Christ Jesus have crucified the sinful nature with its passions and desires. [25]Since we live by the Spirit, let us keep in step with the Spirit. [26]Let us not become conceited, provoking and envying each other.

CHAPTER 6

Brothers, if someone is caught in a sin, you who are spiritual should restore him gently. But watch yourself, or you also may be tempted. [2]Carry each other's burdens, and in this way you will fulfill the law of Christ. [3]If anyone thinks he is something when he is nothing, he deceives himself. [4]Each one should test his own actions. Then he can take pride in himself, without comparing himself to somebody else, [5]for each one should carry his own load.

[6]Anyone who receives instruction in the word must share all good things with his instructor.

[7]Do not be deceived: God cannot be mocked. A man reaps what he sows. [8]The one who sows to please his sinful nature, from that nature[t] will reap destruction; the one who sows to please the Spirit, from the Spirit will reap eternal life. [9]Let us not become weary in doing good, for at the proper time we will reap a harvest if we do not give up. [10]Therefore, as we have opportunity, let us do good to all people, especially to those who belong to the family of believers.

[11]See what large letters I use as I write to you with my own hand!

[12]Those who want to make a good impression outwardly are trying to compel you to be circumcised. The only reason they do this is to avoid being persecuted for the cross of Christ. [13]Not even those who are circumcised obey the law, yet they want you to be circumcised that they may boast about your flesh. [14]May I never boast except in the cross of our Lord Jesus Christ, through which[u] the world has been crucified to me, and I to the world. [15]Neither circumcision nor uncircumcision means anything; what counts is a new creation. [16]Peace and mercy to all who follow this rule, even to the Israel of God.

[17]Finally, let no one cause me trouble, for I bear on my body the marks of Jesus.

[18]The grace of our Lord Jesus Christ be with your spirit, brothers. Amen.

[r]13 Or the flesh; also in verses 16, 17, 19 and 24   [s]14 Lev. 19:18   [t]8 Or his flesh, from the flesh   [u]14 Or whom

Ephesians

ALL who have trusted in Christ possess the priceless bounty of "every spiritual blessing in Christ" (1:3). Yet many continue to live like spiritual paupers. Paul writes this epistle to make Christians more aware of their heavenly wealth in Christ and to motivate them to draw upon those resources in their earthly walk. Chapters 1–3 outline the believer's heavenly possessions: adoption, redemption, inheritance, power, life, citizenship. Chapters 4–6 urge the children of God to conduct themselves according to their calling.

Focus	The Christian's Wealth			The Christian's Walk			
Divisions	Thanksgiving for Wealth	Wealth of Salvation	Wealth of the Church	Walk at Church	Walk in Holiness	Walk at Home and Work	Walk in Warfare
	1:1 1:23	2:1 2:22	3:1 3:21	4:1 4:16	4:17 5:21	5:22 6:9	6:10 6:24
Topics	Calling			Conduct			
	Privileges			Practicalities			
Place	Rome						
Time	A.D. 60–61						

NOVEMBER 27 □ DAY 332
EPHESIANS 1–6
Unity in Christ

OVERVIEW There once was an old farmer who became a millionaire overnight when oil was discovered beneath his land. The wealth had always been there, but the farmer never knew it. So, too, the Ephesians possessed a wealth of spiritual blessings but had never recognized their own abundance. Their spiritual condition prompts Paul to write a letter in which he describes the believer's incredible wealth in Christ. The doctrinal truths of chapters 1–3 are followed by practical applications of those truths in chapters 4–6.

Chapter 1	Chapter 2	Chapter 3	Chapter 4	Chapter 5	Chapter 6
Blessings in Christ	Oneness in Christ	Mission for Christ	Unity in Diversity	Holiness in Life	Preparation for War
Belief			Behavior		

YOUR DAILY WALK Have you ever tried to hammer a nail with your shoe? or tighten a screw with your fingernail file? or shield yourself from a rainstorm with just a newspaper? When you need a hammer or a screwdriver or an umbrella, nothing else will quite do. Are you living your spiritual life that way, using shoes for hammers and newspapers for umbrellas? God has provided the implements necessary for successful Christian living, but perhaps you have tried to make do by substituting your own tools and plans.

Why is it we spend so much time focusing on the concerns of the world we'll soon leave and so little time on the eternity we're headed for?

Even though Ephesians 6:10–20 may be familiar to you, read it with a new sense of urgency today. As Paul comes to each implement for successful Christian living, write it on a sheet of paper. Then think of a "shoe" or "hammer" you may have been substituting for God's spiritual weapons. A shoelace or nail carried with you today will remind you of the importance of using your spiritual wealth the way God intended it to be used.

INSIGHT The Watermark of Paul's Style
As you read Ephesians, watch for the phrase *in Christ Jesus* and its equivalents. If you are a careful reader, you will note its occurrence more than thirty times. The phrase implies not only personal identification of Paul with Christ, but in some contexts it indicates the body of Christ (see 1 Corinthians 12:12).

CHAPTER 1

Paul, an apostle of Christ Jesus by the will of God,

To the saints in Ephesus,*a* the faithful*b* in Christ Jesus:

²Grace and peace to you from God our Father and the Lord Jesus Christ.

³Praise be to the God and Father of our Lord Jesus Christ, who has blessed us in the heavenly realms with every spiritual blessing in Christ. ⁴For he chose us in him before the creation of the world to be holy and blameless in his sight. In love ⁵he*c* predestined us to be adopted as his sons through Jesus Christ, in accordance with

a1 Some early manuscripts do not have in Ephesus.   b1 Or believers who are   c4,5 Or sight in love. 5He his pleasure and will— [6]to the praise of his glorious grace, which he has freely given us in the One he loves. [7]In him we have redemption through his blood, the forgiveness of sins, in accordance with the riches of God's grace [8]that he lavished on us with all wisdom and understanding. [9]And he[d] made known to us the mystery of his will according to his good pleasure, which he purposed in Christ, [10]to be put into effect when the times will have reached their fulfillment—to bring all things in heaven and on earth together under one head, even Christ.

[11]In him we were also chosen,[e] having been predestined according to the plan of him who works out everything in conformity with the purpose of his will, [12]in order that we, who were the first to hope in Christ, might be for the praise of his glory. [13]And you also were included in Christ when you heard the word of truth, the gospel of your salvation. Having believed, you were marked in him with a seal, the promised Holy Spirit, [14]who is a deposit guaranteeing our inheritance until the redemption of those who are God's possession—to the praise of his glory.

[15]For this reason, ever since I heard about your faith in the Lord Jesus and your love for all the saints, [16]I have not stopped giving thanks for you, remembering you in my prayers. [17]I keep asking that the God of our Lord Jesus Christ, the glorious Father, may give you the Spirit[f] of wisdom and revelation, so that you may know him better. [18]I pray also that the eyes of your heart may be enlightened in order that you may know the hope to which he has called you, the riches of his glorious inheritance in the saints, [19]and his incomparably great power for us who believe. That power is like the working of his mighty strength, [20]which he exerted in Christ when he raised him from the dead and seated him at his right hand in the heavenly realms, [21]far above all rule and authority, power and dominion, and every title that can be given, not only in the present age but also in the one to come. [22]And God placed all things under his feet and appointed him to be head over everything for the church, [23]which is his body, the fullness of him who fills everything in every way.

CHAPTER 2

As for you, you were dead in your transgressions and sins, [2]in which you used to live when you followed the ways of this world and of the ruler of the kingdom of the air, the spirit who is now at work in those who are disobedient. [3]All of us also lived among them at one time, gratifying the cravings of our sinful nature[g] and following its desires and thoughts. Like the rest, we were by nature objects of wrath. [4]But because of his great love for us, God, who is rich in mercy, [5]made us alive with Christ even when we were dead in transgressions—it is by grace you have been saved. [6]And God raised us up with Christ and seated us with him in the heavenly realms in Christ Jesus, [7]in order that in the coming ages he might show the incomparable riches of his grace, expressed in his kindness to us in Christ Jesus. [8]For it is by grace you have been saved, through faith—and this not from yourselves, it is the gift of God— [9]not by works, so that no one can boast. [10]For we are God's workmanship, created in Christ Jesus to do good works, which God prepared in advance for us to do.

[11]Therefore, remember that formerly you who are Gentiles by birth and called "uncircumcised" by those who call themselves "the circumcision" (that done in the body by the hands of men)— [12]remember that at that time you were separate from Christ, excluded from citizenship in Israel and foreigners to the covenants of the promise, without hope and without God in the world. [13]But now in Christ Jesus you who once were far away have been brought near through the blood of Christ.

[14]For he himself is our peace, who has made the two one and has destroyed the barrier, the dividing wall of hostility, [15]by abolishing in his flesh the law with its commandments and regulations. His purpose was to create in himself one new man out of the two, thus making peace, [16]and in this one body to reconcile both of them to God through the cross, by which he put to death their hostility. [17]He came and preached peace to you who were far away and peace to those who were near. [18]For through him we both have access to the Father by one Spirit.

[19]Consequently, you are no longer

---

[d]8,9 Or us. With all wisdom and understanding, [9]he   [e]11 Or were made heirs   [f]17 Or a spirit   [g]3 Or our flesh

foreigners and aliens, but fellow citizens with God's people and members of God's household, ²⁰built on the foundation of the apostles and prophets, with Christ Jesus himself as the chief cornerstone. ²¹In him the whole building is joined together and rises to become a holy temple in the Lord. ²²And in him you too are being built together to become a dwelling in which God lives by his Spirit.

CHAPTER 3

For this reason I, Paul, the prisoner of Christ Jesus for the sake of you Gentiles—

²Surely you have heard about the administration of God's grace that was given to me for you, ³that is, the mystery made known to me by revelation, as I have already written briefly. ⁴In reading this, then, you will be able to understand my insight into the mystery of Christ, ⁵which was not made known to men in other generations as it has now been revealed by the Spirit to God's holy apostles and prophets. ⁶This mystery is that through the gospel the Gentiles are heirs together with Israel, members together of one body, and sharers together in the promise in Christ Jesus.

⁷I became a servant of this gospel by the gift of God's grace given me through the working of his power. ⁸Although I am less than the least of all God's people, this grace was given me: to preach to the Gentiles the unsearchable riches of Christ, ⁹and to make plain to everyone the administration of this mystery, which for ages past was kept hidden in God, who created all things. ¹⁰His intent was that now, through the church, the manifold wisdom of God should be made known to the rulers and authorities in the heavenly realms, ¹¹according to his eternal purpose which he accomplished in Christ Jesus our Lord. ¹²In him and through faith in him we may approach God with freedom and confidence. ¹³I ask you, therefore, not to be discouraged because of my sufferings for you, which are your glory.

¹⁴For this reason I kneel before the Father, ¹⁵from whom his whole family^h in heaven and on earth derives its name. ¹⁶I pray that out of his glorious riches he may strengthen you with power through his

Spirit in your inner being, ¹⁷so that Christ may dwell in your hearts through faith. And I pray that you, being rooted and established in love, ¹⁸may have power, together with all the saints, to grasp how wide and long and high and deep is the love of Christ, ¹⁹and to know this love that surpasses knowledge—that you may be filled to the measure of all the fullness of God.

²⁰Now to him who is able to do immeasurably more than all we ask or imagine, according to his power that is at work within us, ²¹to him be glory in the church and in Christ Jesus throughout all generations, for ever and ever! Amen.

CHAPTER 4

As a prisoner for the Lord, then, I urge you to live a life worthy of the calling you have received. ²Be completely humble and gentle; be patient, bearing with one another in love. ³Make every effort to keep the unity of the Spirit through the bond of peace. ⁴There is one body and one Spirit— just as you were called to one hope when you were called— ⁵one Lord, one faith, one baptism; ⁶one God and Father of all, who is over all and through all and in all.

⁷But to each one of us grace has been given as Christ apportioned it. ⁸This is why it^i says:

"When he ascended on high,
    he led captives in his train
    and gave gifts to men."^j

⁹(What does "he ascended" mean except that he also descended to the lower, earthly regions^k? ¹⁰He who descended is the very one who ascended higher than all the heavens, in order to fill the whole universe.) ¹¹It was he who gave some to be apostles, some to be prophets, some to be evangelists, and some to be pastors and teachers, ¹²to prepare God's people for works of service, so that the body of Christ may be built up ¹³until we all reach unity in the faith and in the knowledge of the Son of God and become mature, attaining to the whole measure of the fullness of Christ.

¹⁴Then we will no longer be infants, tossed back and forth by the waves, and blown here and there by every wind of

teaching and by the cunning and craftiness of men in their deceitful scheming. [15]Instead, speaking the truth in love, we will in all things grow up into him who is the Head, that is, Christ. [16]From him the whole body, joined and held together by every supporting ligament, grows and builds itself up in love, as each part does its work.

[17]So I tell you this, and insist on it in the Lord, that you must no longer live as the Gentiles do, in the futility of their thinking. [18]They are darkened in their understanding and separated from the life of God because of the ignorance that is in them due to the hardening of their hearts. [19]Having lost all sensitivity, they have given themselves over to sensuality so as to indulge in every kind of impurity, with a continual lust for more.

[20]You, however, did not come to know Christ that way. [21]Surely you heard of him and were taught in him in accordance with the truth that is in Jesus. [22]You were taught, with regard to your former way of life, to put off your old self, which is being corrupted by its deceitful desires; [23]to be made new in the attitude of your minds; [24]and to put on the new self, created to be like God in true righteousness and holiness.

[25]Therefore each of you must put off falsehood and speak truthfully to his neighbor, for we are all members of one body. [26]"In your anger do not sin"[l]: Do not let the sun go down while you are still angry, [27]and do not give the devil a foothold. [28]He who has been stealing must steal no longer, but must work, doing something useful with his own hands, that he may have something to share with those in need.

[29]Do not let any unwholesome talk come out of your mouths, but only what is helpful for building others up according to their needs, that it may benefit those who listen. [30]And do not grieve the Holy Spirit of God, with whom you were sealed for the day of redemption. [31]Get rid of all bitterness, rage and anger, brawling and slander, along with every form of malice. [32]Be kind and compassionate to one another, forgiving each other, just as in Christ God forgave you.

CHAPTER 5

Be imitators of God, therefore, as dearly loved children [2]and live a life of love, just as Christ loved us and gave himself up for us as a fragrant offering and sacrifice to God.

[3]But among you there must not be even a hint of sexual immorality, or of any kind of impurity, or of greed, because these are improper for God's holy people. [4]Nor should there be obscenity, foolish talk or coarse joking, which are out of place, but rather thanksgiving. [5]For of this you can be sure: No immoral, impure or greedy person—such a man is an idolater—has any inheritance in the kingdom of Christ and of God.[m] [6]Let no one deceive you with empty words, for because of such things God's wrath comes on those who are disobedient. [7]Therefore do not be partners with them.

[8]For you were once darkness, but now you are light in the Lord. Live as children of light [9](for the fruit of the light consists in all goodness, righteousness and truth) [10]and find out what pleases the Lord. [11]Have nothing to do with the fruitless deeds of darkness, but rather expose them. [12]For it is shameful even to mention what the disobedient do in secret. [13]But everything exposed by the light becomes visible, [14]for it is light that makes everything visible. This is why it is said:

"Wake up, O sleeper,
   rise from the dead,
and Christ will shine on you."

[15]Be very careful, then, how you live—not as unwise but as wise, [16]making the most of every opportunity, because the days are evil. [17]Therefore do not be foolish, but understand what the Lord's will is. [18]Do not get drunk on wine, which leads to debauchery. Instead, be filled with the Spirit. [19]Speak to one another with psalms, hymns and spiritual songs. Sing and make music in your heart to the Lord, [20]always giving thanks to God the Father for everything, in the name of our Lord Jesus Christ.

[21]Submit to one another out of reverence for Christ.

[22]Wives, submit to your husbands as to the Lord. [23]For the husband is the head of the wife as Christ is the head of the

[l]26 Psalm 4:4   [m]5 Or *kingdom of the Christ and God*

church, his body, of which he is the Savior. [24]Now as the church submits to Christ, so also wives should submit to their husbands in everything.

[25]Husbands, love your wives, just as Christ loved the church and gave himself up for her [26]to make her holy, cleansing[n] her by the washing with water through the word, [27]and to present her to himself as a radiant church, without stain or wrinkle or any other blemish, but holy and blameless. [28]In this same way, husbands ought to love their wives as their own bodies. He who loves his wife loves himself. [29]After all, no one ever hated his own body, but he feeds and cares for it, just as Christ does the church— [30]for we are members of his body. [31]"For this reason a man will leave his father and mother and be united to his wife, and the two will become one flesh."[o] [32]This is a profound mystery—but I am talking about Christ and the church. [33]However, each one of you also must love his wife as he loves himself, and the wife must respect her husband.

CHAPTER 6
Children, obey your parents in the Lord, for this is right. [2]"Honor your father and mother"—which is the first commandment with a promise— [3]"that it may go well with you and that you may enjoy long life on the earth."[p]

[4]Fathers, do not exasperate your children; instead, bring them up in the training and instruction of the Lord.

[5]Slaves, obey your earthly masters with respect and fear, and with sincerity of heart, just as you would obey Christ. [6]Obey them not only to win their favor when their eye is on you, but like slaves of Christ, doing the will of God from your heart. [7]Serve wholeheartedly, as if you were serving the Lord, not men, [8]because you know that the Lord will reward everyone for whatever good he does, whether he is slave or free.

[9]And masters, treat your slaves in the same way. Do not threaten them, since you know that he who is both their Master and yours is in heaven, and there is no favoritism with him.

[10]Finally, be strong in the Lord and in his mighty power. [11]Put on the full armor of God so that you can take your stand against the devil's schemes. [12]For our struggle is not against flesh and blood, but against the rulers, against the authorities, against the powers of this dark world and against the spiritual forces of evil in the heavenly realms. [13]Therefore put on the full armor of God, so that when the day of evil comes, you may be able to stand your ground, and after you have done everything, to stand. [14]Stand firm then, with the belt of truth buckled around your waist, with the breastplate of righteousness in place, [15]and with your feet fitted with the readiness that comes from the gospel of peace. [16]In addition to all this, take up the shield of faith, with which you can extinguish all the flaming arrows of the evil one. [17]Take the helmet of salvation and the sword of the Spirit, which is the word of God. [18]And pray in the Spirit on all occasions with all kinds of prayers and requests. With this in mind, be alert and always keep on praying for all the saints.

[19]Pray also for me, that whenever I open my mouth, words may be given me so that I will fearlessly make known the mystery of the gospel, [20]for which I am an ambassador in chains. Pray that I may declare it fearlessly, as I should.

[21]Tychicus, the dear brother and faithful servant in the Lord, will tell you everything, so that you also may know how I am and what I am doing. [22]I am sending him to you for this very purpose, that you may know how we are, and that he may encourage you.

[23]Peace to the brothers, and love with faith from God the Father and the Lord Jesus Christ. [24]Grace to all who love our Lord Jesus Christ with an undying love.

[n]26 Or *having cleansed*   [o]31 Gen. 2:24   [p]3 Deut. 5:16

NOVEMBER 28 ☐ DAY 333
Eternal Riches

 LOOK BACK Everything you have read this past week was from the potent pen of the apostle Paul, the most prolific of the New Testament writers. At least thirteen letters (epistles) were written by Paul during the course of his three missionary journeys and numerous imprisonments.

In 1 Corinthians, Paul is confronting the saints at Corinth about their lifestyle of disobedience. Divisions, disorders and difficulties abound in the Corinthian church. The reaction to Paul's first letter prompts him to write yet another (2 Corinthians) in which he sets forth the "anatomy of an apostle," explaining the authority by which he wrote his earlier letter.

Galatians has been called the Christian's "emancipation proclamation." There Paul explains the liberty that comes through the redemption that is in Christ Jesus. We are neither saved nor sanctified by embracing the false gospel of works—a message directed to anyone willing to give up his or her freedom in Christ for bondage to the law.

In Christ Jesus we are "unshackled" from the law (Galatians) and indescribably rich in the family of God (Ephesians). Our heavenly inheritance includes adoption and redemption, power and position, citizenship in heaven and spiritual resources on earth to live out the love of Christ in our daily lives.

 LOOK UP How rich are you *in dollars and cents?* (That's what is often called your "net worth"—how much you *own* less how much you *owe*.)

How rich are you *in family and friends?* (That's the circle of lives you have touched that would otherwise be impoverished for not having known you. It's the theme developed in the timeless movie *It's a Wonderful Life*.)

A Christian is one who does not have to consult a bank book to see how wealthy he or she really is.

How rich are you *in Christ?* (That's your spiritual inheritance as part of God's family of faith. Through faith in Christ you are a child of God and a fellow heir with Christ. Think of it—all the fullness of Christ is yours because you are in him.)

All the wealth in the world will not buy you a cup of coffee unless you *know* you are rich and know how to *appropriate* that wealth. Take it from a man in east Texas who died in abject poverty . . . and lived till his dying day in a house that sat just a few feet above the largest undiscovered oil reserve in the world! Wealthy, yet living like a pauper. It's the sad condition of many a Christian as well.

 LOOK AHEAD Take a few minutes to review the book of Ephesians and inventory all that you are and have because you are "in Christ." It's as simple as reviewing all the occurrences of the little phrase *in Christ* or *in him,* which you located yesterday. Use what you have discovered to complete this sentence: "Because I am in Christ, I have _____, and to show it, today with God's help I will _____. (Example from Ephesians 1:7— "Because I am in Christ, I have forgiveness of sins, and to show it, today with God's help I will forgive someone else who doesn't deserve my forgiveness but needs it nonetheless.")

If you can find five "nuggets" in Ephesians, you are doing well; six to ten nuggets, you are a first-class prospector; eleven to fifteen nuggets, you are a super sleuth; more than fifteen, you deserve a gold medal!

Philippians

PHILIPPIANS is a letter of joy written by Paul from a Roman prison to a church he founded on his second missionary journey (Acts 16). In spite of his circumstances, he encourages the believers in the midst of persecution to "rejoice in the Lord always" (4:4). After all, Paul has much to be thankful for: their financial assistance, the hope of visiting them soon, their steadfast testimony for the gospel. Though that testimony is threatened by divisions, Paul is confident their unity will be restored as they imitate the humble servanthood of Christ.

Focus	Rejoice in God's Will				Relax in God's Peace		
Divisions	Paul and Philippians	Paul and Prison	Christ and Living	Timothy and Epaphroditus	Philippians and Errors	Philippians and Holiness	Paul and a Gift
	1:1 1:11	1:12 1:26	1:27 2:18	2:19 2:30	3:1 4:1	4:2 4:9	4:10 4:23
Topics	Information	Appeal	Plans	Warning	Exhortation		Thanks
	Rejoicing in Affliction	Rejoicing in Ministry		Rejoicing in Jesus	Rejoicing in Blessings		
Place	Rome						
Time	Approximately A.D. 62						

NOVEMBER 29 □ DAY 334
PHILIPPIANS 1–4
Joy in Christ

OVERVIEW Philippians is unique among Paul's Epistles for at least two reasons: (1) It is virtually "problem-free," lacking the usual disciplinary tone of Paul's letters. (2) It is filled with joyful statements, even though Paul is chained in prison! Paul has learned that joy comes, not as the result of external conditions, but from internal confidence that God is in control. Being a good teacher, Paul not only exhorts the Philippians to rejoice always, but he also exemplifies the very principle he is preaching.

Chapter 1		Chapter 2		Chapter 3	Chapter 4
Paul's Prayer	Paul's Plea	Christ's Pattern	Paul's Plan	Paul's Example	Paul's Exhortation
1 11	12 30	1 18	19 30		
Rejoice in God's Will				Relax in God's Peace	

YOUR DAILY WALK A lady walks into a downtown department store, seeks out the customer service counter and announces, "I don't want this item."

Worry and worship are mutually exclusive.

"Fine," responds the clerk. "If you'll just give it to me, I'll be happy to help you find something else you do like."

"No," answers the lady, "I don't want to give this up."

Perhaps you're as confused as the salesclerk by now! But did you know that is how many Christians pray? "Lord, I have a problem that I'm worried about."

"Fine," responds the Lord. "Exchange those worries for my matchless peace."

"Oh no, I'd rather keep worrying!"

Philippians 4:6–7 makes it clear that you and God can't "worry" about the same problem at the same time. Either *you* will (and forfeit his peace in the process), or *he* will (leaving you free to relax in his strong arms). That's a good reason for you to make a "worry list" of the anxieties you're nursing right now and turn it into a prayer list! Then you, too, can enjoy the "peace of God" (4:7), which is only possible by knowing the "God of peace" (4:9).

INSIGHT It's All in Your Head!

You will find the word *rejoice* repeated in every chapter of Philippians. To rejoice, one needs to be filled with joy. But joy is not simply a smile on the lips; it is peace in the heart as a result of our mind being continually kept on Christ. And that's peace no circumstance can shatter!

CHAPTER 1
Paul and Timothy, servants of Christ Jesus,

To all the saints in Christ Jesus at Phi-lippi, together with the overseers[a] and deacons:

²Grace and peace to you from God our Father and the Lord Jesus Christ.

a1 Traditionally bishops

[3]I thank my God every time I remember you. [4]In all my prayers for all of you, I always pray with joy [5]because of your partnership in the gospel from the first day until now, [6]being confident of this, that he who began a good work in you will carry it on to completion until the day of Christ Jesus.

[7]It is right for me to feel this way about all of you, since I have you in my heart; for whether I am in chains or defending and confirming the gospel, all of you share in God's grace with me. [8]God can testify how I long for all of you with the affection of Christ Jesus.

[9]And this is my prayer: that your love may abound more and more in knowledge and depth of insight, [10]so that you may be able to discern what is best and may be pure and blameless until the day of Christ, [11]filled with the fruit of righteousness that comes through Jesus Christ—to the glory and praise of God.

[12]Now I want you to know, brothers, that what has happened to me has really served to advance the gospel. [13]As a result, it has become clear throughout the whole palace guard[b] and to everyone else that I am in chains for Christ. [14]Because of my chains, most of the brothers in the Lord have been encouraged to speak the word of God more courageously and fearlessly.

[15]It is true that some preach Christ out of envy and rivalry, but others out of goodwill. [16]The latter do so in love, knowing that I am put here for the defense of the gospel. [17]The former preach Christ out of selfish ambition, not sincerely, supposing that they can stir up trouble for me while I am in chains.[c] [18]But what does it matter? The important thing is that in every way, whether from false motives or true, Christ is preached. And because of this I rejoice.

Yes, and I will continue to rejoice, [19]for I know that through your prayers and the help given by the Spirit of Jesus Christ, what has happened to me will turn out for my deliverance.[d] [20]I eagerly expect and hope that I will in no way be ashamed, but will have sufficient courage so that now as always Christ will be exalted in my body, whether by life or by death. [21]For to me, to live is Christ and to die is gain. [22]If I am to go on living in the body, this will mean fruitful labor for me. Yet what shall I choose? I do not know! [23]I am torn between the two: I desire to depart and be with Christ, which is better by far; [24]but it is more necessary for you that I remain in the body. [25]Convinced of this, I know that I will remain, and I will continue with all of you for your progress and joy in the faith, [26]so that through my being with you again your joy in Christ Jesus will overflow on account of me.

[27]Whatever happens, conduct yourselves in a manner worthy of the gospel of Christ. Then, whether I come and see you or only hear about you in my absence, I will know that you stand firm in one spirit, contending as one man for the faith of the gospel [28]without being frightened in any way by those who oppose you. This is a sign to them that they will be destroyed, but that you will be saved—and that by God. [29]For it has been granted to you on behalf of Christ not only to believe on him, but also to suffer for him, [30]since you are going through the same struggle you saw I had, and now hear that I still have.

CHAPTER 2

If you have any encouragement from being united with Christ, if any comfort from his love, if any fellowship with the Spirit, if any tenderness and compassion, [2]then make my joy complete by being like-minded, having the same love, being one in spirit and purpose. [3]Do nothing out of selfish ambition or vain conceit, but in humility consider others better than yourselves. [4]Each of you should look not only to your own interests, but also to the interests of others.

[5]Your attitude should be the same as that of Christ Jesus:

[6]Who, being in very nature[e] God,
    did not consider equality with God
        something to be grasped,
[7]but made himself nothing,
    taking the very nature[f] of a
        servant,
    being made in human likeness.
[8]And being found in appearance as a
        man,
    he humbled himself

and became obedient to death—
   even death on a cross!
9Therefore God exalted him to the
   highest place
and gave him the name that is
   above every name,
10that at the name of Jesus every knee
   should bow,
   in heaven and on earth and under
    the earth,
11and every tongue confess that Jesus
   Christ is Lord,
   to the glory of God the Father.

12Therefore, my dear friends, as you have always obeyed—not only in my presence, but now much more in my absence—continue to work out your salvation with fear and trembling, 13for it is God who works in you to will and to act according to his good purpose.

14Do everything without complaining or arguing, 15so that you may become blameless and pure, children of God without fault in a crooked and depraved generation, in which you shine like stars in the universe 16as you hold outg the word of life—in order that I may boast on the day of Christ that I did not run or labor for nothing. 17But even if I am being poured out like a drink offering on the sacrifice and service coming from your faith, I am glad and rejoice with all of you. 18So you too should be glad and rejoice with me.

19I hope in the Lord Jesus to send Timothy to you soon, that I also may be cheered when I receive news about you. 20I have no one else like him, who takes a genuine interest in your welfare. 21For everyone looks out for his own interests, not those of Jesus Christ. 22But you know that Timothy has proved himself, because as a son with his father he has served with me in the work of the gospel. 23I hope, therefore, to send him as soon as I see how things go with me. 24And I am confident in the Lord that I myself will come soon.

25But I think it is necessary to send back to you Epaphroditus, my brother, fellow worker and fellow soldier, who is also your messenger, whom you sent to take care of my needs. 26For he longs for all of you and is distressed because you heard he was ill. 27Indeed he was ill, and almost

died. But God had mercy on him, and not on him only but also on me, to spare me sorrow upon sorrow. 28Therefore I am all the more eager to send him, so that when you see him again you may be glad and I may have less anxiety. 29Welcome him in the Lord with great joy, and honor men like him, 30because he almost died for the work of Christ, risking his life to make up for the help you could not give me.

CHAPTER 3
Finally, my brothers, rejoice in the Lord! It is no trouble for me to write the same things to you again, and it is a safeguard for you.

2Watch out for those dogs, those men who do evil, those mutilators of the flesh. 3For it is we who are the circumcision, we who worship by the Spirit of God, who glory in Christ Jesus, and who put no confidence in the flesh— 4though I myself have reasons for such confidence.

If anyone else thinks he has reasons to put confidence in the flesh, I have more: 5circumcised on the eighth day, of the people of Israel, of the tribe of Benjamin, a Hebrew of Hebrews; in regard to the law, a Pharisee; 6as for zeal, persecuting the church; as for legalistic righteousness, faultless.

7But whatever was to my profit I now consider loss for the sake of Christ. 8What is more, I consider everything a loss compared to the surpassing greatness of knowing Christ Jesus my Lord, for whose sake I have lost all things. I consider them rubbish, that I may gain Christ 9and be found in him, not having a righteousness of my own that comes from the law, but that which is through faith in Christ—the righteousness that comes from God and is by faith. 10I want to know Christ and the power of his resurrection and the fellowship of sharing in his sufferings, becoming like him in his death, 11and so, somehow, to attain to the resurrection from the dead.

12Not that I have already obtained all this, or have already been made perfect, but I press on to take hold of that for which Christ Jesus took hold of me. 13Brothers, I do not consider myself yet to have taken hold of it. But one thing I do: Forgetting what is behind and straining

g16 Or hold on to

toward what is ahead, [14]I press on toward the goal to win the prize for which God has called me heavenward in Christ Jesus.

[15]All of us who are mature should take such a view of things. And if on some point you think differently, that too God will make clear to you. [16]Only let us live up to what we have already attained.

[17]Join with others in following my example, brothers, and take note of those who live according to the pattern we gave you. [18]For, as I have often told you before and now say again even with tears, many live as enemies of the cross of Christ. [19]Their destiny is destruction, their god is their stomach, and their glory is in their shame. Their mind is on earthly things. [20]But our citizenship is in heaven. And we eagerly await a Savior from there, the Lord Jesus Christ, [21]who, by the power that enables him to bring everything under his control, will transform our lowly bodies so that they will be like his glorious body.

CHAPTER 4

Therefore, my brothers, you whom I love and long for, my joy and crown, that is how you should stand firm in the Lord, dear friends!

[2]I plead with Euodia and I plead with Syntyche to agree with each other in the Lord. [3]Yes, and I ask you, loyal yokefellow,[h] help these women who have contended at my side in the cause of the gospel, along with Clement and the rest of my fellow workers, whose names are in the book of life.

[4]Rejoice in the Lord always. I will say it again: Rejoice! [5]Let your gentleness be evident to all. The Lord is near. [6]Do not be anxious about anything, but in everything, by prayer and petition, with thanksgiving, present your requests to God. [7]And the peace of God, which transcends all understanding, will guard your hearts and your minds in Christ Jesus.

[8]Finally, brothers, whatever is true, whatever is noble, whatever is right, whatever is pure, whatever is lovely, whatever is admirable—if anything is excellent or praiseworthy—think about such things. [9]Whatever you have learned or received or heard from me, or seen in me—put it into practice. And the God of peace will be with you.

[10]I rejoice greatly in the Lord that at last you have renewed your concern for me. Indeed, you have been concerned, but you had no opportunity to show it. [11]I am not saying this because I am in need, for I have learned to be content whatever the circumstances. [12]I know what it is to be in need, and I know what it is to have plenty. I have learned the secret of being content in any and every situation, whether well fed or hungry, whether living in plenty or in want. [13]I can do everything through him who gives me strength.

[14]Yet it was good of you to share in my troubles. [15]Moreover, as you Philippians know, in the early days of your acquaintance with the gospel, when I set out from Macedonia, not one church shared with me in the matter of giving and receiving, except you only; [16]for even when I was in Thessalonica, you sent me aid again and again when I was in need. [17]Not that I am looking for a gift, but I am looking for what may be credited to your account. [18]I have received full payment and even more; I am amply supplied, now that I have received from Epaphroditus the gifts you sent. They are a fragrant offering, an acceptable sacrifice, pleasing to God. [19]And my God will meet all your needs according to his glorious riches in Christ Jesus.

[20]To our God and Father be glory for ever and ever. Amen.

[21]Greet all the saints in Christ Jesus. The brothers who are with me send greetings. [22]All the saints send you greetings, especially those who belong to Caesar's household.

[23]The grace of the Lord Jesus Christ be with your spirit. Amen.[i]

h3 Or loyal Syzygus   i23 Some manuscripts do not have Amen.

Colossians

ALL is not well in Colosse. A heresy is growing that promotes empty ritual, useless asceticism and false mysticism. In order to encourage the Colossians to hold on to the truth, Paul refutes the heresy in a positive way—he shows them who Christ is. Christ as Lord of all gives complete salvation, and he is sufficient for every need. And if Christ is all and in all, then he ought to be in all we say, do and think. So Paul encourages the Colossians to pursue a godly lifestyle befitting those who "have been raised with Christ" (3:1).

Focus	Christ, the Lord of the Universe				Christ, the Lord of Life			
Divisions	Prayer to Father of Christ	Supremacy of Christ	Sufficiency of Christ		New Life	Home Life	Christian Life	Conclusion
	1:1　　1:12	1:13　　2:3	2:4　　2:23		3:1　3:17	3:18　4:1	4:2　4:6	4:7　4:18
Topics	Transforming Relationship				Transformed Relationships			
	Consistent Doctrine				Consistent Life			
Place	Rome							
Time	A.D. 60–61							

NOVEMBER 30 □ DAY 335
COLOSSIANS 1–4
Christ, the Head of the Body

OVERVIEW If Ephesians can be labeled as portraying the "church of Christ," then Colossians must surely portray the "Christ of the church." Ephesians focuses on the body; Colossians, on the Head. Like Ephesians, the little book of Colossians divides neatly in half, with the first portion being doctrinal (Colossians 1–2) and the second, practical (Colossians 3–4). Paul's purpose is to show that Christ is supreme—first and foremost in everything—and the Christian's life should reflect that priority. Because believers are rooted in him, built up in him, dead in him, risen with him, alive with him, hidden in him and complete in him, it is utterly inconsistent for them to live without him. Clothed in his love, with his peace ruling in their hearts, they are equipped to make Christ supreme in every walk of life.

Chapter 1	Chapter 2	Chapters 3–4
Christ, the Head of the Body	Christ, the Lord of the Universe	Christ, the Head of the Home
Christ . . . Supreme in All Things		

YOUR DAILY WALK Here are seven words to think about today: "Christ is all, and is in all" (3:11).

Notice how Paul expands that thought throughout his letter. In the space of a single paragraph (1:15–18), he lists at least eight evidences of Christ's supremacy: He created you, set you free and forgave you; he is the image of God and the firstborn of all creation; he preceded all things, designed all things and holds all things together. In short, he is all . . . and is in all!

In Christ we see God's purpose in making the world and in making us.

And that means he wants to be in all you say, do, or think. Concentrate on your thought life today. Each time you finish a phone call, recite quietly to yourself a favorite Bible verse or stanza of a hymn about Christ.

INSIGHT Being a Friend Means Being Informed
"Tychicus will tell you all the news about me. . . . I am sending him to you for the express purpose that you may know about our circumstances . . . They [Tychicus and Onesimus] will tell you everything that is happening here" (4:7–9). Friendship demands communication. Is a letter or phone call to a friend overdue? Invest a few minutes now!

CHAPTER 1

Paul, an apostle of Christ Jesus by the will of God, and Timothy our brother,

²To the holy and faithful*ᵃ* brothers in Christ at Colosse:

Grace and peace to you from God our Father.*ᵇ*

³We always thank God, the Father of our Lord Jesus Christ, when we pray for you, ⁴because we have heard of your faith

ᵃ2 Or believing   ᵇ2 Some manuscripts Father and the Lord Jesus Christ in Christ Jesus and of the love you have for all the saints— [5]the faith and love that spring from the hope that is stored up for you in heaven and that you have already heard about in the word of truth, the gospel [6]that has come to you. All over the world this gospel is bearing fruit and growing, just as it has been doing among you since the day you heard it and understood God's grace in all its truth. [7]You learned it from Epaphras, our dear fellow servant, who is a faithful minister of Christ on our[c] behalf, [8]and who also told us of your love in the Spirit.

[9]For this reason, since the day we heard about you, we have not stopped praying for you and asking God to fill you with the knowledge of his will through all spiritual wisdom and understanding. [10]And we pray this in order that you may live a life worthy of the Lord and may please him in every way: bearing fruit in every good work, growing in the knowledge of God, [11]being strengthened with all power according to his glorious might so that you may have great endurance and patience, and joyfully [12]giving thanks to the Father, who has qualified you[d] to share in the inheritance of the saints in the kingdom of light. [13]For he has rescued us from the dominion of darkness and brought us into the kingdom of the Son he loves, [14]in whom we have redemption,[e] the forgiveness of sins.

[15]He is the image of the invisible God, the firstborn over all creation. [16]For by him all things were created: things in heaven and on earth, visible and invisible, whether thrones or powers or rulers or authorities; all things were created by him and for him. [17]He is before all things, and in him all things hold together. [18]And he is the head of the body, the church; he is the beginning and the firstborn from among the dead, so that in everything he might have the supremacy. [19]For God was pleased to have all his fullness dwell in him, [20]and through him to reconcile to himself all things, whether things on earth or things in heaven, by making peace through his blood, shed on the cross.

[21]Once you were alienated from God and were enemies in your minds because

off[f] your evil behavior. [22]But now he has reconciled you by Christ's physical body through death to present you holy in his sight, without blemish and free from accusation— [23]if you continue in your faith, established and firm, not moved from the hope held out in the gospel. This is the gospel that you heard and that has been proclaimed to every creature under heaven, and of which I, Paul, have become a servant.

[24]Now I rejoice in what was suffered for you, and I fill up in my flesh what is still lacking in regard to Christ's afflictions, for the sake of his body, which is the church. [25]I have become its servant by the commission God gave me to present to you the word of God in its fullness— [26]the mystery that has been kept hidden for ages and generations, but is now disclosed to the saints. [27]To them God has chosen to make known among the Gentiles the glorious riches of this mystery, which is Christ in you, the hope of glory.

[28]We proclaim him, admonishing and teaching everyone with all wisdom, so that we may present everyone perfect in Christ. [29]To this end I labor, struggling with all his energy, which so powerfully works in me.

CHAPTER 2

I want you to know how much I am struggling for you and for those at Laodicea, and for all who have not met me personally. [2]My purpose is that they may be encouraged in heart and united in love, so that they may have the full riches of complete understanding, in order that they may know the mystery of God, namely, Christ, [3]in whom are hidden all the treasures of wisdom and knowledge. [4]I tell you this so that no one may deceive you by fine-sounding arguments. [5]For though I am absent from you in body, I am present with you in spirit and delight to see how orderly you are and how firm your faith in Christ is.

[6]So then, just as you received Christ Jesus as Lord, continue to live in him, [7]rooted and built up in him, strengthened in the faith as you were taught, and overflowing with thankfulness.

c7 Some manuscripts your　d12 Some manuscripts us　e14 A few late manuscripts redemption through his blood
f21 Or minds, as shown by

⁸See to it that no one takes you captive through hollow and deceptive philosophy, which depends on human tradition and the basic principles of this world rather than on Christ.

⁹For in Christ all the fullness of the Deity lives in bodily form, ¹⁰and you have been given fullness in Christ, who is the head over every power and authority. ¹¹In him you were also circumcised, in the putting off of the sinful nature,ᵍ not with a circumcision done by the hands of men but with the circumcision done by Christ, ¹²having been buried with him in baptism and raised with him through your faith in the power of God, who raised him from the dead.

¹³When you were dead in your sins and in the uncircumcision of your sinful nature,ʰ God made youⁱ alive with Christ. He forgave us all our sins, ¹⁴having canceled the written code, with its regulations, that was against us and that stood opposed to us; he took it away, nailing it to the cross. ¹⁵And having disarmed the powers and authorities, he made a public spectacle of them, triumphing over them by the cross.ʲ

¹⁶Therefore do not let anyone judge you by what you eat or drink, or with regard to a religious festival, a New Moon celebration or a Sabbath day. ¹⁷These are a shadow of the things that were to come; the reality, however, is found in Christ. ¹⁸Do not let anyone who delights in false humility and the worship of angels disqualify you for the prize. Such a person goes into great detail about what he has seen, and his unspiritual mind puffs him up with idle notions. ¹⁹He has lost connection with the Head, from whom the whole body, supported and held together by its ligaments and sinews, grows as God causes it to grow.

²⁰Since you died with Christ to the basic principles of this world, why, as though you still belonged to it, do you submit to its rules: ²¹"Do not handle! Do not taste! Do not touch!"? ²²These are all destined to perish with use, because they are based on human commands and teachings. ²³Such regulations indeed have an appearance of wisdom, with their self-imposed worship, their false humility

and their harsh treatment of the body, but they lack any value in restraining sensual indulgence.

CHAPTER 3
Since, then, you have been raised with Christ, set your hearts on things above, where Christ is seated at the right hand of God. ²Set your minds on things above, not on earthly things. ³For you died, and your life is now hidden with Christ in God. ⁴When Christ, who is yourᵏ life, appears, then you also will appear with him in glory.

⁵Put to death, therefore, whatever belongs to your earthly nature: sexual immorality, impurity, lust, evil desires and greed, which is idolatry. ⁶Because of these, the wrath of God is coming.ˡ ⁷You used to walk in these ways, in the life you once lived. ⁸But now you must rid yourselves of all such things as these: anger, rage, malice, slander, and filthy language from your lips. ⁹Do not lie to each other, since you have taken off your old self with its practices ¹⁰and have put on the new self, which is being renewed in knowledge in the image of its Creator. ¹¹Here there is no Greek or Jew, circumcised or uncircumcised, barbarian, Scythian, slave or free, but Christ is all, and is in all.

¹²Therefore, as God's chosen people, holy and dearly loved, clothe yourselves with compassion, kindness, humility, gentleness and patience. ¹³Bear with each other and forgive whatever grievances you may have against one another. Forgive as the Lord forgave you. ¹⁴And over all these virtues put on love, which binds them all together in perfect unity.

¹⁵Let the peace of Christ rule in your hearts, since as members of one body you were called to peace. And be thankful. ¹⁶Let the word of Christ dwell in you richly as you teach and admonish one another with all wisdom, and as you sing psalms, hymns and spiritual songs with gratitude in your hearts to God. ¹⁷And whatever you do, whether in word or deed, do it all in the name of the Lord Jesus, giving thanks to God the Father through him.

¹⁸Wives, submit to your husbands, as is fitting in the Lord.

ᵍ11 Or the flesh ʰ13 Or your flesh ⁱ13 Some manuscripts us ʲ15 Or them in him ᵏ4 Some manuscripts our ˡ6 Some
early manuscripts coming on those who are disobedient

[19]Husbands, love your wives and do not be harsh with them.

[20]Children, obey your parents in everything, for this pleases the Lord.

[21]Fathers, do not embitter your children, or they will become discouraged.

[22]Slaves, obey your earthly masters in everything; and do it, not only when their eye is on you and to win their favor, but with sincerity of heart and reverence for the Lord. [23]Whatever you do, work at it with all your heart, as working for the Lord, not for men, [24]since you know that you will receive an inheritance from the Lord as a reward. It is the Lord Christ you are serving. [25]Anyone who does wrong will be repaid for his wrong, and there is no favoritism.

CHAPTER 4

Masters, provide your slaves with what is right and fair, because you know that you also have a Master in heaven.

[2]Devote yourselves to prayer, being watchful and thankful. [3]And pray for us, too, that God may open a door for our message, so that we may proclaim the mystery of Christ, for which I am in chains. [4]Pray that I may proclaim it clearly, as I should. [5]Be wise in the way you act toward outsiders; make the most of every opportunity. [6]Let your conversation be always full of grace, seasoned with salt, so that you may know how to answer everyone.

[7]Tychicus will tell you all the news about me. He is a dear brother, a faithful minister and fellow servant in the Lord. [8]I

am sending him to you for the express purpose that you may know about our[m] circumstances and that he may encourage your hearts. [9]He is coming with Onesimus, our faithful and dear brother, who is one of you. They will tell you everything that is happening here.

[10]My fellow prisoner Aristarchus sends you his greetings, as does Mark, the cousin of Barnabas. (You have received instructions about him; if he comes to you, welcome him.) [11]Jesus, who is called Justus, also sends greetings. These are the only Jews among my fellow workers for the kingdom of God, and they have proved a comfort to me. [12]Epaphras, who is one of you and a servant of Christ Jesus, sends greetings. He is always wrestling in prayer for you, that you may stand firm in all the will of God, mature and fully assured. [13]I vouch for him that he is working hard for you and for those at Laodicea and Hierapolis. [14]Our dear friend Luke, the doctor, and Demas send greetings. [15]Give my greetings to the brothers at Laodicea, and to Nympha and the church in her house.

[16]After this letter has been read to you, see that it is also read in the church of the Laodiceans and that you in turn read the letter from Laodicea.

[17]Tell Archippus: "See to it that you complete the work you have received in the Lord."

[18]I, Paul, write this greeting in my own hand. Remember my chains. Grace be with you.

---

[m]8 Some manuscripts *that he may know about your*

1 Thessalonians

PROSPEROUS, prominent and thoroughly pagan, the seaport city of Thessalonica first heard the gospel on Paul's second missionary journey. A dynamic fellowship developed there, becoming a continual joy to Paul. He writes 1 Thessalonians to encourage them. They were being persecuted; he urges them to persevere. They have heard slander about Paul; he refutes it. Their city is full of sensual temptation; he exhorts them to hold to Christian standards. Finally, he corrects some misunderstandings about the return of Christ.

Focus	Personal Relations to the Thessalonians		Practical Instructions to the Thessalonians		
Divisions	Paul's Memories	Paul's Methods	Paul's Directions	Christ's Return	Paul's Reminders
	1:1 1:10	2:1 3:13	4:1 4:12	4:13 5:11	5:12 5:28
Topics	Personal	Parental		Prophetic	Practical
	A Saving Hope	A Purifying Hope		A Comforting Hope	
Place	Corinth				
Time	Approximately A.D. 51				

DECEMBER 1 □ DAY 336
1 THESSALONIANS 1–5
Stay on Target

 OVERVIEW The church at Thessalonica was in many ways a model church. Paul had many things to commend the believers for: their exemplary faith, diligent service, patient steadfastness and overflowing joy. But in the midst of his commendation, Paul voices a word of caution. Abounding in the work of the Lord is only one step removed from abandoning the work of the Lord through complacency. Thus, Paul exhorts the Thessalonians to excel in their faith, to increase in their love for one another and to give thanks for all things. At the same time, to know Christ must always be their primary goal. In short, Paul encourages them to "stay on target" as they labor for the Lord.

Chapter 1	Chapters 2–3	Chapter 4	Chapter 5
Paul's Memories	Paul's Methods	Christ's Return	Paul's Reminders
Personal	Parental	Prophetic	Practical

 YOUR DAILY WALK Do you *believe* Jesus Christ is coming again? Do you *behave* as if Jesus Christ is coming again?

The first question is straightforward and simple to answer. Either you do or you don't. But the second is more difficult because it involves looking for practical, everyday ways to translate your belief into behavior and then making those activities and attitudes a priority in your daily Christian life.

If your behavior does not reflect your beliefs, then your beliefs are of no value.

Each of the five chapters of 1 Thessalonians ends with an exhortation based on the fact that Jesus Christ is coming again. Read the indicated verses prayerfully; then write out a step of *behavior* you can begin today to put your *beliefs* to work!

- 1:9–10   I will look for someone to serve as I wait for God's Son.
- 2:19–20 _____.
- 3:11–13 _____.
- 4:13–18 I will comfort someone today with the thought of his coming.
- 5:23–24 _____.

 INSIGHT Graduate Course for Kindergarten Christians
Prophecy is often considered a weighty subject that is reserved for mature, well-taught Christians and seminary graduates. But Paul spent considerable time teaching prophecy to new converts (5:1–2). How knowledgeable are you of God's blueprint for future events?

CHAPTER 1
Paul, Silas[a] and Timothy,

To the church of the Thessalonians in God the Father and the Lord Jesus Christ:

Grace and peace to you.[b]

²We always thank God for all of you, mentioning you in our prayers. ³We continually remember before our God and

---

[a]1 Greek *Silvanus*, a variant of *Silas*   [b]1 Some early manuscripts *you from God our Father and the Lord Jesus Christ*

Father your work produced by faith, your labor prompted by love, and your endurance inspired by hope in our Lord Jesus Christ.

[4]For we know, brothers loved by God, that he has chosen you, [5]because our gospel came to you not simply with words, but also with power, with the Holy Spirit and with deep conviction. You know how we lived among you for your sake. [6]You became imitators of us and of the Lord; in spite of severe suffering, you welcomed the message with the joy given by the Holy Spirit. [7]And so you became a model to all the believers in Macedonia and Achaia. [8]The Lord's message rang out from you not only in Macedonia and Achaia—your faith in God has become known everywhere. Therefore we do not need to say anything about it, [9]for they themselves report what kind of reception you gave us. They tell how you turned to God from idols to serve the living and true God, [10]and to wait for his Son from heaven, whom he raised from the dead—Jesus, who rescues us from the coming wrath.

CHAPTER 2

You know, brothers, that our visit to you was not a failure. [2]We had previously suffered and been insulted in Philippi, as you know, but with the help of our God we dared to tell you his gospel in spite of strong opposition. [3]For the appeal we make does not spring from error or impure motives, nor are we trying to trick you. [4]On the contrary, we speak as men approved by God to be entrusted with the gospel. We are not trying to please men but God, who tests our hearts. [5]You know we never used flattery, nor did we put on a mask to cover up greed—God is our witness. [6]We were not looking for praise from men, not from you or anyone else.

As apostles of Christ we could have been a burden to you, [7]but we were gentle among you, like a mother caring for her little children. [8]We loved you so much that we were delighted to share with you not only the gospel of God but our lives as well, because you had become so dear to us. [9]Surely you remember, brothers, our toil and hardship; we worked night and day in order not to be a burden to anyone while we preached the gospel of God to you.

[10]You are witnesses, and so is God, of how holy, righteous and blameless we were among you who believed. [11]For you know that we dealt with each of you as a father deals with his own children, [12]encouraging, comforting and urging you to live lives worthy of God, who calls you into his kingdom and glory.

[13]And we also thank God continually because, when you received the word of God, which you heard from us, you accepted it not as the word of men, but as it actually is, the word of God, which is at work in you who believe. [14]For you, brothers, became imitators of God's churches in Judea, which are in Christ Jesus: You suffered from your own countrymen the same things those churches suffered from the Jews, [15]who killed the Lord Jesus and the prophets and also drove us out. They displease God and are hostile to all men [16]in their effort to keep us from speaking to the Gentiles so that they may be saved. In this way they always heap up their sins to the limit. The wrath of God has come upon them at last.[c]

[17]But, brothers, when we were torn away from you for a short time (in person, not in thought), out of our intense longing we made every effort to see you. [18]For we wanted to come to you—certainly I, Paul, did, again and again—but Satan stopped us. [19]For what is our hope, our joy, or the crown in which we will glory in the presence of our Lord Jesus when he comes? Is it not you? [20]Indeed, you are our glory and joy.

CHAPTER 3

So when we could stand it no longer, we thought it best to be left by ourselves in Athens. [2]We sent Timothy, who is our brother and God's fellow worker[d] in spreading the gospel of Christ, to strengthen and encourage you in your faith, [3]so that no one would be unsettled by these trials. You know quite well that we were destined for them. [4]In fact, when we were with you, we kept telling you that we would be persecuted. And it turned out that way, as you

[c]16 Or *them fully*   [d]2 Some manuscripts *brother and fellow worker*; other manuscripts *brother and God's servant*

well know. ⁵For this reason, when I could stand it no longer, I sent to find out about your faith. I was afraid that in some way the tempter might have tempted you and our efforts might have been useless.

⁶But Timothy has just now come to us from you and has brought good news about your faith and love. He has told us that you always have pleasant memories of us and that you long to see us, just as we also long to see you. ⁷Therefore, brothers, in all our distress and persecution we were encouraged about you because of your faith. ⁸For now we really live, since you are standing firm in the Lord. ⁹How can we thank God enough for you in return for all the joy we have in the presence of our God because of you? ¹⁰Night and day we pray most earnestly that we may see you again and supply what is lacking in your faith.

¹¹Now may our God and Father himself and our Lord Jesus clear the way for us to come to you. ¹²May the Lord make your love increase and overflow for each other and for everyone else, just as ours does for you. ¹³May he strengthen your hearts so that you will be blameless and holy in the presence of our God and Father when our Lord Jesus comes with all his holy ones.

CHAPTER 4

Finally, brothers, we instructed you how to live in order to please God, as in fact you are living. Now we ask you and urge you in the Lord Jesus to do this more and more. ²For you know what instructions we gave you by the authority of the Lord Jesus.

³It is God's will that you should be sanctified: that you should avoid sexual immorality; ⁴that each of you should learn to control his own body^e in a way that is holy and honorable, ⁵not in passionate lust like the heathen, who do not know God; ⁶and that in this matter no one should wrong his brother or take advantage of him. The Lord will punish men for all such sins, as we have already told you and warned you. ⁷For God did not call us to be impure, but to live a holy life. ⁸Therefore, he who rejects this instruction

does not reject man but God, who gives you his Holy Spirit.

⁹Now about brotherly love we do not need to write to you, for you yourselves have been taught by God to love each other. ¹⁰And in fact, you do love all the brothers throughout Macedonia. Yet we urge you, brothers, to do so more and more.

¹¹Make it your ambition to lead a quiet life, to mind your own business and to work with your hands, just as we told you, ¹²so that your daily life may win the respect of outsiders and so that you will not be dependent on anybody.

¹³Brothers, we do not want you to be ignorant about those who fall asleep, or to grieve like the rest of men, who have no hope. ¹⁴We believe that Jesus died and rose again and so we believe that God will bring with Jesus those who have fallen asleep in him. ¹⁵According to the Lord's own word, we tell you that we who are still alive, who are left till the coming of the Lord, will certainly not precede those who have fallen asleep. ¹⁶For the Lord himself will come down from heaven, with a loud command, with the voice of the archangel and with the trumpet call of God, and the dead in Christ will rise first. ¹⁷After that, we who are still alive and are left will be caught up together with them in the clouds to meet the Lord in the air. And so we will be with the Lord forever. ¹⁸Therefore encourage each other with these words.

CHAPTER 5

Now, brothers, about times and dates we do not need to write to you, ²for you know very well that the day of the Lord will come like a thief in the night. ³While people are saying, "Peace and safety," destruction will come on them suddenly, as labor pains on a pregnant woman, and they will not escape.

⁴But you, brothers, are not in darkness so that this day should surprise you like a thief. ⁵You are all sons of the light and sons of the day. We do not belong to the night or to the darkness. ⁶So then, let us not be like others, who are asleep, but let us be alert and self-controlled. ⁷For those who sleep, sleep at night, and those who

^e4 Or *learn to live with his own wife; or learn to acquire a wife*

get drunk, get drunk at night. [8]But since we belong to the day, let us be self-controlled, putting on faith and love as a breastplate, and the hope of salvation as a helmet. [9]For God did not appoint us to suffer wrath but to receive salvation through our Lord Jesus Christ. [10]He died for us so that, whether we are awake or asleep, we may live together with him. [11]Therefore encourage one another and build each other up, just as in fact you are doing.

[12]Now we ask you, brothers, to respect those who work hard among you, who are over you in the Lord and who admonish you. [13]Hold them in the highest regard in love because of their work. Live in peace with each other. [14]And we urge you, brothers, warn those who are idle, encourage the timid, help the weak, be patient with everyone. [15]Make sure that nobody pays back wrong for wrong, but always try to be kind to each other and to everyone else.

[16]Be joyful always; [17]pray continually; [18]give thanks in all circumstances, for this is God's will for you in Christ Jesus.

[19]Do not put out the Spirit's fire; [20]do not treat prophecies with contempt. [21]Test everything. Hold on to the good. [22]Avoid every kind of evil.

[23]May God himself, the God of peace, sanctify you through and through. May your whole spirit, soul and body be kept blameless at the coming of our Lord Jesus Christ. [24]The one who calls you is faithful and he will do it.

[25]Brothers, pray for us. [26]Greet all the brothers with a holy kiss. [27]I charge you before the Lord to have this letter read to all the brothers.

[28]The grace of our Lord Jesus Christ be with you.

2 Thessalonians

PAUL opens this letter by encouraging the Thessalonians in the midst of their persecution that God's judgment would more than even the score. However, because some had been teaching that the day of the Lord had already arrived, many were quitting their jobs and interfering with those who continued to work. Paul instructs them about the future and exhorts them not to sit back and wait for Christ's coming but to take advantage of the limited time available now.

Focus	Commendation	Instruction	Correction
Divisions	Return of Christ	Revelation of Antichrist	Return to Work
	1:1 1:12	2:1 2:17	3:1 3:18
Topics	Strengthening the Stressful	Confirming the Confused	Disciplining the Disorderly
	Encouragement	Explanation	Exhortation
Place	Corinth		
Time	Approximately A.D. 51		

DECEMBER 2 □ DAY 337
2 THESSALONIANS 1–3
Work While You Wait

OVERVIEW The Thessalonians were waiting expectantly for Christ's return, and that was good. But in addition, some were waiting unproductively, and that was bad. False teachers had been claiming that the "day of the Lord" had already arrived. Paul refutes their teaching by reminding the Thessalonians of the events that must precede the coming of the Lord. But how should they respond in the light of that joyful expectation? Not with lazy resignation, but with renewed labor for the Lord. Therefore, Paul urges them to "never tire of doing what is right" (3:13).

Chapter 1	Chapter 2	Chapter 3
Strengthening the Stressed	Comforting the Confused	Disciplining the Disorderly
Commendation	Instruction	Correction

Live every moment as if expecting him at any moment.

YOUR DAILY WALK Is there at least one other person you pray for every day? Is there at least one time every day (apart from mealtimes) when you regularly pray? Is there at least one person you regularly pray with about mutually shared problems and praise items?

Paul entreated the Thessalonian Christians, "Pray for us" (3:1). He also asked for prayer in 1 Thessalonians (5:25), in Colossians (4:3–4) and in Ephesians (6:18–20). The apostle Paul was acutely aware of his need for prayer support to undergird his ministry for Jesus Christ. And he labored daily for the Lord, knowing that dozens of people in congregations scattered throughout the Roman Empire were praying for him by name.

Do you pray regularly for your spouse? for your children? for your roommate? for your pastor and church staff? for the leaders of strategic Christian schools and organizations? They need your prayers just as badly as Paul needed the prayers of the Thessalonians. Take your calendar for December, and write the name of one person you will pray for on each day of the month.

INSIGHT The Mark of Authenticity
Although Paul sometimes dictated his letters to a secretary (or *amanuensis* such as Tertius, Romans 16:22), he always added a handwritten salutation and signature in order to identify his letters as genuine (3:17; compare 1 Corinthians 16:21 and Colossians 4:18).

CHAPTER 1
Paul, Silas[a] and Timothy,

To the church of the Thessalonians in God our Father and the Lord Jesus Christ:

²Grace and peace to you from God the Father and the Lord Jesus Christ.

³We ought always to thank God for you, brothers, and rightly so, because your faith is growing more and more, and

[a]1 Greek *Silvanus*, a variant of *Silas*

the love every one of you has for each other is increasing. ⁴Therefore, among God's churches we boast about your perseverance and faith in all the persecutions and trials you are enduring.

⁵All this is evidence that God's judgment is right, and as a result you will be counted worthy of the kingdom of God, for which you are suffering. ⁶God is just: He will pay back trouble to those who trouble you ⁷and give relief to you who are troubled, and to us as well. This will happen when the Lord Jesus is revealed from heaven in blazing fire with his powerful angels. ⁸He will punish those who do not know God and do not obey the gospel of our Lord Jesus. ⁹They will be punished with everlasting destruction and shut out from the presence of the Lord and from the majesty of his power ¹⁰on the day he comes to be glorified in his holy people and to be marveled at among all those who have believed. This includes you, because you believed our testimony to you.

¹¹With this in mind, we constantly pray for you, that our God may count you worthy of his calling, and that by his power he may fulfill every good purpose of yours and every act prompted by your faith. ¹²We pray this so that the name of our Lord Jesus may be glorified in you, and you in him, according to the grace of our God and the Lord Jesus Christ.ᵇ

CHAPTER 2

Concerning the coming of our Lord Jesus Christ and our being gathered to him, we ask you, brothers, ²not to become easily unsettled or alarmed by some prophecy, report or letter supposed to have come from us, saying that the day of the Lord has already come. ³Don't let anyone deceive you in any way, for ⌊that day will not come⌋ until the rebellion occurs and the man of lawlessnessᶜ is revealed, the man doomed to destruction. ⁴He will oppose and will exalt himself over everything that is called God or is worshiped, so that he sets himself up in God's temple, proclaiming himself to be God.

⁵Don't you remember that when I was with you I used to tell you these things? ⁶And now you know what is holding him back, so that he may be revealed at the

proper time. ⁷For the secret power of lawlessness is already at work; but the one who now holds it back will continue to do so till he is taken out of the way. ⁸And then the lawless one will be revealed, whom the Lord Jesus will overthrow with the breath of his mouth and destroy by the splendor of his coming. ⁹The coming of the lawless one will be in accordance with the work of Satan displayed in all kinds of counterfeit miracles, signs and wonders, ¹⁰and in every sort of evil that deceives those who are perishing. They perish because they refused to love the truth and so be saved. ¹¹For this reason God sends them a powerful delusion so that they will believe the lie ¹²and so that all will be condemned who have not believed the truth but have delighted in wickedness.

¹³But we ought always to thank God for you, brothers loved by the Lord, because from the beginning God chose youᵈ to be saved through the sanctifying work of the Spirit and through belief in the truth. ¹⁴He called you to this through our gospel, that you might share in the glory of our Lord Jesus Christ. ¹⁵So then, brothers, stand firm and hold to the teachingsᵉ we passed on to you, whether by word of mouth or by letter.

¹⁶May our Lord Jesus Christ himself and God our Father, who loved us and by his grace gave us eternal encouragement and good hope, ¹⁷encourage your hearts and strengthen you in every good deed and word.

CHAPTER 3

Finally, brothers, pray for us that the message of the Lord may spread rapidly and be honored, just as it was with you. ²And pray that we may be delivered from wicked and evil men, for not everyone has faith. ³But the Lord is faithful, and he will strengthen and protect you from the evil one. ⁴We have confidence in the Lord that you are doing and will continue to do the things we command. ⁵May the Lord direct your hearts into God's love and Christ's perseverance.

⁶In the name of the Lord Jesus Christ, we command you, brothers, to keep away from every brother who is idle and does not live according to the teachingᶠ you

---

ᵇ12 Or God and Lord, Jesus Christ   ᶜ3 Some manuscripts sin   ᵈ13 Some manuscripts because God chose you as his firstfruits
ᵉ15 Or traditions   ᶠ6 Or tradition

received from us. [7]For you yourselves know how you ought to follow our example. We were not idle when we were with you, [8]nor did we eat anyone's food without paying for it. On the contrary, we worked night and day, laboring and toiling so that we would not be a burden to any of you. [9]We did this, not because we do not have the right to such help, but in order to make ourselves a model for you to follow. [10]For even when we were with you, we gave you this rule: "If a man will not work, he shall not eat."

[11]We hear that some among you are idle. They are not busy; they are busybodies. [12]Such people we command and urge in the Lord Jesus Christ to settle down and earn the bread they eat. [13]And as for you, brothers, never tire of doing what is right.

[14]If anyone does not obey our instruction in this letter, take special note of him. Do not associate with him, in order that he may feel ashamed. [15]Yet do not regard him as an enemy, but warn him as a brother.

[16]Now may the Lord of peace himself give you peace at all times and in every way. The Lord be with all of you.

[17]I, Paul, write this greeting in my own hand, which is the distinguishing mark in all my letters. This is how I write.

[18]The grace of our Lord Jesus Christ be with you all.

1 Timothy

TIMOTHY, a young disciple discovered by Paul on his second missionary journey (Acts 16:1), enjoyed a unique relationship with the apostle. Referred to by Paul as "my true son in the faith," Timothy ministered side by side with Paul as a missionary and later received the challenging assignment of pastoring the church at Ephesus. Paul's first letter to him resembles a manual for building church leadership. But more generally, it is a rich mine of principles for anyone who wishes to have a spiritual impact in the lives of others.

Focus	Organization in the Church			Operation of the Church		
Divisions	Law and Grace	Worship and Women	Overseers and Deacons	False Teaching in the Church	Age Groups in the Church	Areas of Conflict in the Church
	1:1　　1:20	2:1　　2:15	3:1　　3:16	4:1　　4:16	5:1　　5:25	6:1　　6:21
Topics	Life of the Church	Leaders of the Church	Apostasy of the Church	Groups in the Church	Example to the Church	
	Plans			Problems		
Place	Macedonia					
Time	Approximately A.D. 62–63					

DECEMBER 3 ☐ DAY 338
1 TIMOTHY 1–3
The Pastor and Church Government

OVERVIEW Timothy, Paul's son in the faith, was facing a heavy burden of responsibility in the church at Ephesus. False doctrine and numerous disorders required his prayerful attention. But Timothy was facing an even greater challenge in selecting and developing leadership in the church. Paul's first letter to Timothy is, in many ways, a "leadership manual" describing the qualifications of leaders in the household of God. Family life and finances, attitudes and habits, reputation both inside and outside the church—all provide evidence of a person's readiness to serve as a leader in the church of Jesus Christ.

Chapter 1	Chapter 2	Chapter 3
Law and Grace	Worship and Women	Overseers and Deacons
"How people ought to conduct themselves in God's household" (3:15).		

Our God has a big eraser.

YOUR DAILY WALK If you had to select a candidate for the title "The Worst Sinner Who Ever Lived," who would you choose and why?

Now consider this. The man who penned more books of the Bible than any other person . . . the man considered by many to be the greatest church leader who ever lived . . . the man who, during his lifetime, carried the gospel to the farthest reaches of the known world, by his own estimation deserved the title "World's Worst Sinner." Listen to these remarkable words from Paul: "Christ Jesus came into the world to save sinners—of whom I am the worst" (1:15).

The tendency is to focus on what Paul *became in Christ* while overlooking the horrible background from which Paul *came to Christ*: "a blasphemer and a persecutor and a violent man" (1:13). Regardless of your background or past sins, Jesus stands ready to save you, a sinner like Paul, if you will only accept his invitation. Will you come to Christ today—just as you are? You'll find a Savior eager to forgive you, even if you are the "World's Worst Sinner."

INSIGHT Who's Who among Overseers and Deacons
Though later separated into two levels of responsibility in the history of the church, the terms *overseer* and *deacon* originally referred to the same position in the early church. (Compare 1 Timothy 3:1; Acts 20:17, 28; Titus 1:5, 7.) The same role was alternately referred to as *elder*.

CHAPTER 1

Paul, an apostle of Christ Jesus by the command of God our Savior and of Christ Jesus our hope,

²To Timothy my true son in the faith:

Grace, mercy and peace from God the Father and Christ Jesus our Lord.

³As I urged you when I went into Macedonia, stay there in Ephesus so that you may command certain men not to teach

false doctrines any longer [4]nor to devote themselves to myths and endless genealogies. These promote controversies rather than God's work—which is by faith. [5]The goal of this command is love, which comes from a pure heart and a good conscience and a sincere faith. [6]Some have wandered away from these and turned to meaningless talk. [7]They want to be teachers of the law, but they do not know what they are talking about or what they so confidently affirm.

[8]We know that the law is good if one uses it properly. [9]We also know that law[a] is made not for the righteous but for lawbreakers and rebels, the ungodly and sinful, the unholy and irreligious; for those who kill their fathers or mothers, for murderers, [10]for adulterers and perverts, for slave traders and liars and perjurers— and for whatever else is contrary to the sound doctrine [11]that conforms to the glorious gospel of the blessed God, which he entrusted to me.

[12]I thank Christ Jesus our Lord, who has given me strength, that he considered me faithful, appointing me to his service. [13]Even though I was once a blasphemer and a persecutor and a violent man, I was shown mercy because I acted in ignorance and unbelief. [14]The grace of our Lord was poured out on me abundantly, along with the faith and love that are in Christ Jesus.

[15]Here is a trustworthy saying that deserves full acceptance: Christ Jesus came into the world to save sinners—of whom I am the worst. [16]But for that very reason I was shown mercy so that in me, the worst of sinners, Christ Jesus might display his unlimited patience as an example for those who would believe on him and receive eternal life. [17]Now to the King eternal, immortal, invisible, the only God, be honor and glory for ever and ever. Amen.

[18]Timothy, my son, I give you this instruction in keeping with the prophecies once made about you, so that by following them you may fight the good fight, [19]holding on to faith and a good conscience. Some have rejected these and so have shipwrecked their faith. [20]Among them are Hymenaeus and Alexander, whom I have handed over to Satan to be taught not to blaspheme.

CHAPTER 2

I urge, then, first of all, that requests, prayers, intercession and thanksgiving be made for everyone— [2]for kings and all those in authority, that we may live peaceful and quiet lives in all godliness and holiness. [3]This is good, and pleases God our Savior, [4]who wants all men to be saved and to come to a knowledge of the truth. [5]For there is one God and one mediator between God and men, the man Christ Jesus, [6]who gave himself as a ransom for all men—the testimony given in its proper time. [7]And for this purpose I was appointed a herald and an apostle—I am telling the truth, I am not lying—and a teacher of the true faith to the Gentiles.

[8]I want men everywhere to lift up holy hands in prayer, without anger or disputing.

[9]I also want women to dress modestly, with decency and propriety, not with braided hair or gold or pearls or expensive clothes, [10]but with good deeds, appropriate for women who profess to worship God.

[11]A woman should learn in quietness and full submission. [12]I do not permit a woman to teach or to have authority over a man; she must be silent. [13]For Adam was formed first, then Eve. [14]And Adam was not the one deceived; it was the woman who was deceived and became a sinner. [15]But women[b] will be saved[c] through childbearing—if they continue in faith, love and holiness with propriety.

CHAPTER 3

Here is a trustworthy saying: If anyone sets his heart on being an overseer,[d] he desires a noble task. [2]Now the overseer must be above reproach, the husband of but one wife, temperate, self-controlled, respectable, hospitable, able to teach, [3]not given to drunkenness, not violent but gentle, not quarrelsome, not a lover of money. [4]He must manage his own family well and see that his children obey him with proper respect. [5](If anyone does not know how to manage his own family, how can he take care of God's church?) [6]He must not be a recent convert, or he may become conceited and fall under the same judgment as the devil. [7]He must

---

[a]9 Or *that the law*   [b]15 Greek *she*   [c]15 Or *restored*   [d]1 Traditionally *bishop*; also in verse 2

also have a good reputation with outsiders, so that he will not fall into disgrace and into the devil's trap.

[8]Deacons, likewise, are to be men worthy of respect, sincere, not indulging in much wine, and not pursuing dishonest gain. [9]They must keep hold of the deep truths of the faith with a clear conscience. [10]They must first be tested; and then if there is nothing against them, let them serve as deacons.

[11]In the same way, their wives[e] are to be women worthy of respect, not malicious talkers but temperate and trustworthy in everything.

[12]A deacon must be the husband of but one wife and must manage his children and his household well. [13]Those who have served well gain an excellent standing and great assurance in their faith in Christ Jesus.

[14]Although I hope to come to you soon, I am writing you these instructions so that, [15]if I am delayed, you will know how people ought to conduct themselves in God's household, which is the church of the living God, the pillar and foundation of the truth. [16]Beyond all question, the mystery of godliness is great:

> He[f] appeared in a body,[g]
>   was vindicated by the Spirit,
> was seen by angels,
>   was preached among the nations,
> was believed on in the world,
>   was taken up in glory.

[e]11 Or way, deaconesses   [f]16 Some manuscripts God   [g]16 Or in the flesh

DECEMBER 4 ☐ DAY 339
1 TIMOTHY 4–6
The Pastor and Personal Progress

OVERVIEW No single letter (even one from the apostle Paul) could hope to cover all the potential problem areas in a church congregation. But Paul does the next best thing. He warns Timothy of some of the major dangers he is sure to face in the "later times" (4:1)—a period filled with obstacles and opportunities. False teaching, frivolous speculation, improper conduct, inconsistent example and greedy motives must be dealt with decisively. There are certain things from which Timothy and his congregation must flee, and there are others they must pursue if they are to "fight the good fight of the faith" (6:12).

Chapter 4	Chapter 5	Chapter 6
False Teaching in the Church	Age Groups in the Church	Areas of Conflict in the Church
"Set an example for the believers" (4:12).		

YOUR DAILY WALK Do you have a written (or unwritten) code of conduct at your house, a set of rules each family member is expected to know and abide by? Here is one family's "Five Commandments for Household Survival":

The best form of spiritual exercise is to touch the floor regularly with your knees.

1. Eat a little of whatever is cooked.
2. No dessert until Rule 1 is observed.
3. Sleeping with the dog is forbidden.
4. Telephone calls limited to 5 minutes' duration.
5. If you got it dirty, you get it clean!

In the same way, the church—the household of God—needs guidelines if its conduct is to bring glory to God (3:15). Read today's section with pencil in hand, and circle each command that Paul delivers to Timothy. Pick one that speaks to a specific need in your local congregation, and ask God what he would have you do to promote harmony and growth in the family of God. And don't forget to check up on your own conduct first. You can't be part of the solution if you are part of the problem.

INSIGHT A Majestic Doxology to Your Majestic Lord
The mere mention of the second coming of Jesus (6:14) immediately catapults Paul into one of the most majestic doxologies to be found anywhere in the Scriptures. Its theme is the incomparable glory of God. Worship this King over all kings and Lord over all lords by reading verses 15 and 16 aloud—"To him be honor and might forever. Amen."

CHAPTER 4

The Spirit clearly says that in later times some will abandon the faith and follow deceiving spirits and things taught by demons. ²Such teachings come through hypocritical liars, whose consciences have been seared as with a hot iron. ³They forbid people to marry and order them to abstain from certain foods, which God created to be received with thanksgiving by those who believe and who know the truth. ⁴For everything God created is good, and nothing is to be rejected if it is received with thanksgiving, ⁵because it is consecrated by the word of God and prayer.

⁶If you point these things out to the brothers, you will be a good minister of Christ Jesus, brought up in the truths of the faith and of the good teaching that you have followed. ⁷Have nothing to do with godless myths and old wives' tales; rather, train yourself to be godly. ⁸For physical training is of some value, but godliness has value for all things, holding promise for both the present life and the life to come.

⁹This is a trustworthy saying that deserves full acceptance ¹⁰(and for this we labor and strive), that we have put our hope in the living God, who is the Savior of all men, and especially of those who believe.

¹¹Command and teach these things. ¹²Don't let anyone look down on you because you are young, but set an example for the believers in speech, in life, in love, in faith and in purity. ¹³Until I come, devote yourself to the public reading of Scripture, to preaching and to teaching. ¹⁴Do not neglect your gift, which was given you through a prophetic message when the body of elders laid their hands on you.

¹⁵Be diligent in these matters; give yourself wholly to them, so that everyone may see your progress. ¹⁶Watch your life and doctrine closely. Persevere in them, because if you do, you will save both yourself and your hearers.

CHAPTER 5

Do not rebuke an older man harshly, but exhort him as if he were your father. Treat younger men as brothers, ²older women as mothers, and younger women as sisters, with absolute purity.

³Give proper recognition to those widows who are really in need. ⁴But if a widow has children or grandchildren, these should learn first of all to put their religion into practice by caring for their own family and so repaying their parents and grandparents, for this is pleasing to God. ⁵The widow who is really in need and left all alone puts her hope in God and continues night and day to pray and to ask God for help. ⁶But the widow who lives for pleasure is dead even while she lives. ⁷Give the people these instructions, too, so that no one may be open to blame. ⁸If anyone does not provide for his relatives, and especially for his immediate family, he has denied the faith and is worse than an unbeliever.

⁹No widow may be put on the list of widows unless she is over sixty, has been faithful to her husband,ʰ ¹⁰and is well known for her good deeds, such as bringing up children, showing hospitality, washing the feet of the saints, helping those in trouble and devoting herself to all kinds of good deeds.

¹¹As for younger widows, do not put

ʰ9 Or *has had but one husband*

them on such a list. For when their sensual desires overcome their dedication to Christ, they want to marry. [12]Thus they bring judgment on themselves, because they have broken their first pledge. [13]Besides, they get into the habit of being idle and going about from house to house. And not only do they become idlers, but also gossips and busybodies, saying things they ought not to. [14]So I counsel younger widows to marry, to have children, to manage their homes and to give the enemy no opportunity for slander. [15]Some have in fact already turned away to follow Satan.

[16]If any woman who is a believer has widows in her family, she should help them and not let the church be burdened with them, so that the church can help those widows who are really in need.

[17]The elders who direct the affairs of the church well are worthy of double honor, especially those whose work is preaching and teaching. [18]For the Scripture says, "Do not muzzle the ox while it is treading out the grain,"[i] and "The worker deserves his wages."[j] [19]Do not entertain an accusation against an elder unless it is brought by two or three witnesses. [20]Those who sin are to be rebuked publicly, so that the others may take warning.

[21]I charge you, in the sight of God and Christ Jesus and the elect angels, to keep these instructions without partiality, and to do nothing out of favoritism.

[22]Do not be hasty in the laying on of hands, and do not share in the sins of others. Keep yourself pure.

[23]Stop drinking only water, and use a little wine because of your stomach and your frequent illnesses.

[24]The sins of some men are obvious, reaching the place of judgment ahead of them; the sins of others trail behind them. [25]In the same way, good deeds are obvious, and even those that are not cannot be hidden.

CHAPTER 6

All who are under the yoke of slavery should consider their masters worthy of full respect, so that God's name and our teaching may not be slandered. [2]Those who have believing masters are not to show less respect for them because they

are brothers. Instead, they are to serve them even better, because those who benefit from their service are believers, and dear to them. These are the things you are to teach and urge on them.

[3]If anyone teaches false doctrines and does not agree to the sound instruction of our Lord Jesus Christ and to godly teaching, [4]he is conceited and understands nothing. He has an unhealthy interest in controversies and quarrels about words that result in envy, strife, malicious talk, evil suspicions [5]and constant friction between men of corrupt mind, who have been robbed of the truth and who think that godliness is a means to financial gain.

[6]But godliness with contentment is great gain. [7]For we brought nothing into the world, and we can take nothing out of it. [8]But if we have food and clothing, we will be content with that. [9]People who want to get rich fall into temptation and a trap and into many foolish and harmful desires that plunge men into ruin and destruction. [10]For the love of money is a root of all kinds of evil. Some people, eager for money, have wandered from the faith and pierced themselves with many griefs.

[11]But you, man of God, flee from all this, and pursue righteousness, godliness, faith, love, endurance and gentleness. [12]Fight the good fight of the faith. Take hold of the eternal life to which you were called when you made your good confession in the presence of many witnesses. [13]In the sight of God, who gives life to everything, and of Christ Jesus, who while testifying before Pontius Pilate made the good confession, I charge you [14]to keep this command without spot or blame until the appearing of our Lord Jesus Christ, [15]which God will bring about in his own time—God, the blessed and only Ruler, the King of kings and Lord of lords, [16]who alone is immortal and who lives in unapproachable light, whom no one has seen or can see. To him be honor and might forever. Amen.

[17]Command those who are rich in this present world not to be arrogant nor to put their hope in wealth, which is so uncertain, but to put their hope in God, who richly provides us with everything for our enjoyment. [18]Command them to do good, to be rich in good deeds, and to be gener-

i18 Deut. 25:4   *j18* Luke 10:7

ous and willing to share. ¹⁹In this way they will lay up treasure for themselves as a firm foundation for the coming age, so that they may take hold of the life that is truly life.

²⁰Timothy, guard what has been en-trusted to your care. Turn away from godless chatter and the opposing ideas of what is falsely called knowledge, ²¹which some have professed and in so doing have wandered from the faith.

Grace be with you.

2 Timothy

SECOND Timothy is the dying appeal of Paul to his young coworker. Underlying each theme is the importance of God's Word. Paul encourages Timothy, naturally timid and facing persecution, to find in Scripture all he needs to persevere. In the same pages he would find what he needs to preach and to practice. Lonely in his death-row cell, Paul asks Timothy to visit as soon as possible—and to bring him a copy of the Word. He offers a stirring testimony of how God has used his life to spread that Word—and of the reward awaiting him.

Focus	Be Faithful in Your Ministry			Be Faithful in Your Doctrine		
Divisions	Thanksgiving for Timothy	Exhortation to Timothy	Duties of Timothy	False Teachers and Timothy	Charge to Timothy	Death of Timothy's Friend
	1:1 1:5	1:6 1:18	2:1 2:13	2:14 3:17	4:1 4:5	4:6 4:22
Topics	Guard the Gospel		Pass on the Gospel	Protect the Gospel	Preach the Gospel	
	Foundation		Faithfulness	Foes	Fearlessness	
Place	Roman Prison					
Time	Approximately A.D. 67					

DECEMBER 5 □ DAY 340
2 TIMOTHY 1–4
Paul's Combat Manual

OVERVIEW Chronologically, 2 Timothy is Paul's final epistle. Written from a Roman prison cell, it contains words of wisdom and encouragement for Timothy, who is laboring in the midst of hardship and opposition in Ephesus. Paul stresses the importance of godly living, consistent biblical preaching and adequate preparation for difficult days yet to come. Underlying all that Paul says is the importance of God's Word—the only foundation strong enough to stand upon in perilous times.

Chapter 1	Chapter 2	Chapter 3	Chapter 4
Power of the Truth	Practice of the Truth	Persecution of the Truth	Preaching of the Truth
Foundation	Faithfulness	Foes	Fearlessness

YOUR DAILY WALK "'Tis the season to be jolly," exclaims the Christmas chorus.

Football season . . . holiday season . . . planting season . . . harvesting season . . . there's a time and season for everything (Ecclesiastes 3:1). Everything, that is, except sharing the Good News of Jesus Christ; that important task is *always* "in season."

Paul exhorts young Timothy, "Preach the Word; be prepared in season and out of season" (4:2). There will be occasions when you have virtually all the time you need to prepare what you want to say about Jesus Christ. A Sunday school lesson, sermon manuscript, magazine article, study group devotional—each represents an opportunity to "preach the Word . . . *in season.*" But what about those times when you are suddenly called upon to speak for your Lord—and there isn't a Bible in sight? Paul's counsel to you is the same: "Preach the Word; be prepared . . . *out of season.*" In short, be prepared to share the Good News whenever and wherever the occasion might arise!

Get a head start on that assignment by writing out your personal testimony today as you would want to share it with another person. You may find the opportunity to do precisely that!

You do not choose to be in the business of bringing others to Christ; you choose Christ and you are at once in the business.

INSIGHT A Warm Coat for a Cold Apostle

Writing in the fall, Paul was naturally concerned about staying warm during the coming winter. His unheated underground cell, believed to be in the Mamertine Prison, probably measured only ten by nineteen feet and was six feet high. It was accessible through only a hole in the ceiling. Now reread 4:9–13 . . . with feeling!

CHAPTER 1

Paul, an apostle of Christ Jesus by the will of God, according to the promise of life that is in Christ Jesus,

²To Timothy, my dear son:

Grace, mercy and peace from God the Father and Christ Jesus our Lord.

³I thank God, whom I serve, as my forefathers did, with a clear conscience, as night and day I constantly remember you

in my prayers. [4]Recalling your tears, I long to see you, so that I may be filled with joy. [5]I have been reminded of your sincere faith, which first lived in your grandmother Lois and in your mother Eunice and, I am persuaded, now lives in you also. [6]For this reason I remind you to fan into flame the gift of God, which is in you through the laying on of my hands. [7]For God did not give us a spirit of timidity, but a spirit of power, of love and of self-discipline.

[8]So do not be ashamed to testify about our Lord, or ashamed of me his prisoner. But join with me in suffering for the gospel, by the power of God, [9]who has saved us and called us to a holy life—not because of anything we have done but because of his own purpose and grace. This grace was given us in Christ Jesus before the beginning of time, [10]but it has now been revealed through the appearing of our Savior, Christ Jesus, who has destroyed death and has brought life and immortality to light through the gospel. [11]And of this gospel I was appointed a herald and an apostle and a teacher. [12]That is why I am suffering as I am. Yet I am not ashamed, because I know whom I have believed, and am convinced that he is able to guard what I have entrusted to him for that day.

[13]What you heard from me, keep as the pattern of sound teaching, with faith and love in Christ Jesus. [14]Guard the good deposit that was entrusted to you—guard it with the help of the Holy Spirit who lives in us.

[15]You know that everyone in the province of Asia has deserted me, including Phygelus and Hermogenes.

[16]May the Lord show mercy to the household of Onesiphorus, because he often refreshed me and was not ashamed of my chains. [17]On the contrary, when he was in Rome, he searched hard for me until he found me. [18]May the Lord grant that he will find mercy from the Lord on that day! You know very well in how many ways he helped me in Ephesus.

CHAPTER 2

You then, my son, be strong in the grace that is in Christ Jesus. [2]And the things you have heard me say in the presence of many witnesses entrust to reliable men who will also be qualified to teach others. [3]Endure hardship with us like a good soldier of Christ Jesus. [4]No one serving as a soldier gets involved in civilian affairs— he wants to please his commanding officer. [5]Similarly, if anyone competes as an athlete, he does not receive the victor's crown unless he competes according to the rules. [6]The hardworking farmer should be the first to receive a share of the crops. [7]Reflect on what I am saying, for the Lord will give you insight into all this.

[8]Remember Jesus Christ, raised from the dead, descended from David. This is my gospel, [9]for which I am suffering even to the point of being chained like a criminal. But God's word is not chained. [10]Therefore I endure everything for the sake of the elect, that they too may obtain the salvation that is in Christ Jesus, with eternal glory.

[11]Here is a trustworthy saying:

If we died with him,
　we will also live with him;
[12]if we endure,
　we will also reign with him.
If we disown him,
　he will also disown us;
[13]if we are faithless,
　he will remain faithful,
　for he cannot disown himself.

[14]Keep reminding them of these things. Warn them before God against quarreling about words; it is of no value, and only ruins those who listen. [15]Do your best to present yourself to God as one approved, a workman who does not need to be ashamed and who correctly handles the word of truth. [16]Avoid godless chatter, because those who indulge in it will become more and more ungodly. [17]Their teaching will spread like gangrene. Among them are Hymenaeus and Philetus, [18]who have wandered away from the truth. They say that the resurrection has already taken place, and they destroy the faith of some. [19]Nevertheless, God's solid foundation stands firm, sealed with this inscription: "The Lord knows those who are his,"[a] and, "Everyone who confesses the name of the Lord must turn away from wickedness."

[20]In a large house there are articles not

---

[a]19 Num. 16:5 (see Septuagint)

only of gold and silver, but also of wood and clay; some are for noble purposes and some for ignoble. 21If a man cleanses himself from the latter, he will be an instrument for noble purposes, made holy, useful to the Master and prepared to do any good work.

22Flee the evil desires of youth, and pursue righteousness, faith, love and peace, along with those who call on the Lord out of a pure heart. 23Don't have anything to do with foolish and stupid arguments, because you know they produce quarrels. 24And the Lord's servant must not quarrel; instead, he must be kind to everyone, able to teach, not resentful. 25Those who oppose him he must gently instruct, in the hope that God will grant them repentance leading them to a knowledge of the truth, 26and that they will come to their senses and escape from the trap of the devil, who has taken them captive to do his will.

C H A P T E R   3
But mark this: There will be terrible times in the last days. 2People will be lovers of themselves, lovers of money, boastful, proud, abusive, disobedient to their parents, ungrateful, unholy, 3without love, unforgiving, slanderous, without self-control, brutal, not lovers of the good, 4treacherous, rash, conceited, lovers of pleasure rather than lovers of God— 5having a form of godliness but denying its power. Have nothing to do with them. 6They are the kind who worm their way into homes and gain control over weak-willed women, who are loaded down with sins and are swayed by all kinds of evil desires, 7always learning but never able to acknowledge the truth. 8Just as Jannes and Jambres opposed Moses, so also these men oppose the truth—men of depraved minds, who, as far as the faith is concerned, are rejected. 9But they will not get very far because, as in the case of those men, their folly will be clear to everyone.

10You, however, know all about my teaching, my way of life, my purpose, faith, patience, love, endurance, 11persecutions, sufferings—what kinds of things happened to me in Antioch, Iconium and Lystra, the persecutions I endured. Yet the Lord rescued me from all of them. 12In fact, everyone who wants to live a godly life in Christ Jesus will be persecuted, 13while evil men and impostors will go from bad to worse, deceiving and being deceived. 14But as for you, continue in what you have learned and have become convinced of, because you know those from whom you learned it, 15and how from infancy you have known the holy Scriptures, which are able to make you wise for salvation through faith in Christ Jesus. 16All Scripture is God-breathed and is useful for teaching, rebuking, correcting and training in righteousness, 17so that the man of God may be thoroughly equipped for every good work.

C H A P T E R   4
In the presence of God and of Christ Jesus, who will judge the living and the dead, and in view of his appearing and his kingdom, I give you this charge: 2Preach the Word; be prepared in season and out of season; correct, rebuke and encourage—with great patience and careful instruction. 3For the time will come when men will not put up with sound doctrine. Instead, to suit their own desires, they will gather around them a great number of teachers to say what their itching ears want to hear. 4They will turn their ears away from the truth and turn aside to myths. 5But you, keep your head in all situations, endure hardship, do the work of an evangelist, discharge all the duties of your ministry.

6For I am already being poured out like a drink offering, and the time has come for my departure. 7I have fought the good fight, I have finished the race, I have kept the faith. 8Now there is in store for me the crown of righteousness, which the Lord, the righteous Judge, will award to me on that day—and not only to me, but also to all who have longed for his appearing.

9Do your best to come to me quickly, 10for Demas, because he loved this world, has deserted me and has gone to Thessalonica. Crescens has gone to Galatia, and Titus to Dalmatia. 11Only Luke is with me. Get Mark and bring him with you, because he is helpful to me in my ministry. 12I sent Tychicus to Ephesus. 13When you come, bring the cloak that I left with Carpus at Troas, and my scrolls, especially the parchments.

14Alexander the metalworker did me a great deal of harm. The Lord will repay him for what he has done. [15]You too should be on your guard against him, because he strongly opposed our message.

[16]At my first defense, no one came to my support, but everyone deserted me. May it not be held against them. [17]But the Lord stood at my side and gave me strength, so that through me the message might be fully proclaimed and all the Gentiles might hear it. And I was delivered from the lion's mouth. [18]The Lord will rescue me from every evil attack and will bring me safely to his heavenly kingdom. To him be glory for ever and ever. Amen.

[19]Greet Priscilla[b] and Aquila and the household of Onesiphorus. [20]Erastus stayed in Corinth, and I left Trophimus sick in Miletus. [21]Do your best to get here before winter. Eubulus greets you, and so do Pudens, Linus, Claudia and all the brothers.

[22]The Lord be with your spirit. Grace be with you.

[b]19 Greek *Prisca*, a variant of *Priscilla*

Titus

TITUS lived among a people who had one of the worst reputations in the world. He was organizing and shepherding the new believers on Crete, the largest island in the Mediterranean. Paul writes to authorize him for this work and instruct him in it. Titus was to appoint spiritual leaders as elders and to promote sound teaching. False teachers should be quickly detected and removed, and all must be encouraged to live worthy of the gospel. The epistle to Titus is known for its summary of Christian doctrine and its emphasis on holy living.

Focus	Duties of Church Leaders		Duties of Church Members	
Divisions	Elders Designated	Heresy Described	Good Works Demanded	Heretics Denounced
	1:1 1:9	1:10 1:16	2:1 2:15	3:1 3:15
Topics	Servants		Service	Salvation
	Preservation of Truth		Use of Truth	
Place	Probably Written in Corinth			
Time	Approximately A.D. 63			

DECEMBER 6 □ DAY 341
TITUS 1–3
Practicing the Faith

 OVERVIEW Titus, a young minister, is left on the Mediterranean island of Crete by Paul to begin the challenging task of organizing new
converts into local churches. In this letter, Paul shares with Titus some
practical wisdom regarding church organization and administration.
For example: Leaders must be chosen on the basis of proven character
and conduct; false teachers must be quickly detected and removed;
church members of all ages must be encouraged to live in a way that
is worthy of the gospel they claim to believe. Young and old, leader
and laity, all must demonstrate the reality of their faith by being
"careful to devote themselves to doing what is good" (3:8).

Chapter 1		Chapter 2	Chapter 3
Elders Designated	Heresy Described	Good Works Demanded	Heretics Denounced
1 9	10 16		
The Church Organized		The Church in Operation	

 YOUR DAILY WALK True or False: Good works cannot save you.
True or False: Good works for the Christian are unimportant.
True or False: Good works come naturally for a child of God.

*To keep the
faith we must
teach the faith.*
Perhaps you found the first questions easy (the first is true, 3:5, and
the second, false, 3:8). But the third one may have been more difficult! In 2 Corinthians 5:17 Paul makes it clear that a new Christian is a
new creation, with new desires, ambitions and enablement to live for
God. But just as children need guidance and training by their parents
if they are to develop normally, so spiritual children must be taught
"sound doctrine" (2:1). New believers of all ages in the church at
Crete needed instruction in proper Christian conduct.

Paul has some timely words for you as well, regardless of your age,
gender or level of maturity as a Christian. As you read, watch for his
exhortations aimed straight at you and your peers. Write them in a
notebook or on a sheet of paper. If possible, find another daily walker
and discuss together what you have learned.

 INSIGHT Parallel Epistles with Parallel Emphases

	1 Timothy	Titus
False Teachers	1:6–11, 19–20; 6:3–5	1:10–16; 3:9–11
Faithful Leaders	3:1–13	1:6–9
Faithful Believers	5:1—6:2	2:1–15

CHAPTER 1

Paul, a servant of God and an apostle of
Jesus Christ for the faith of God's elect
and the knowledge of the truth that leads
to godliness— ²a faith and knowledge
resting on the hope of eternal life, which
God, who does not lie, promised before
the beginning of time, ³and at his appointed season he brought his word to
light through the preaching entrusted to
me by the command of God our Savior,

⁴To Titus, my true son in our common
faith:

Grace and peace from God the Father and Christ Jesus our Savior.

5The reason I left you in Crete was that you might straighten out what was left unfinished and appointᵃ elders in every town, as I directed you. 6An elder must be blameless, the husband of but one wife, a man whose children believe and are not open to the charge of being wild and disobedient. 7Since an overseerᵇ is entrusted with God's work, he must be blameless—not overbearing, not quick-tempered, not given to drunkenness, not violent, not pursuing dishonest gain. 8Rather he must be hospitable, one who loves what is good, who is self-controlled, upright, holy and disciplined. 9He must hold firmly to the trustworthy message as it has been taught, so that he can encourage others by sound doctrine and refute those who oppose it.

10For there are many rebellious people, mere talkers and deceivers, especially those of the circumcision group. 11They must be silenced, because they are ruining whole households by teaching things they ought not to teach—and that for the sake of dishonest gain. 12Even one of their own prophets has said, "Cretans are always liars, evil brutes, lazy gluttons." 13This testimony is true. Therefore, rebuke them sharply, so that they will be sound in the faith 14and will pay no attention to Jewish myths or to the commands of those who reject the truth. 15To the pure, all things are pure, but to those who are corrupted and do not believe, nothing is pure. In fact, both their minds and consciences are corrupted. 16They claim to know God, but by their actions they deny him. They are detestable, disobedient and unfit for doing anything good.

CHAPTER 2

You must teach what is in accord with sound doctrine. 2Teach the older men to be temperate, worthy of respect, self-controlled, and sound in faith, in love and in endurance.

3Likewise, teach the older women to be reverent in the way they live, not to be slanderers or addicted to much wine, but to teach what is good. 4Then they can train the younger women to love their husbands and children, 5to be self-controlled and pure, to be busy at home, to be kind, and to be subject to their husbands, so that no one will malign the word of God.

6Similarly, encourage the young men to be self-controlled. 7In everything set them an example by doing what is good. In your teaching show integrity, seriousness 8and soundness of speech that cannot be condemned, so that those who oppose you may be ashamed because they have nothing bad to say about us.

9Teach slaves to be subject to their masters in everything, to try to please them, not to talk back to them, 10and not to steal from them, but to show that they can be fully trusted, so that in every way they will make the teaching about God our Savior attractive.

11For the grace of God that brings salvation has appeared to all men. 12It teaches us to say "No" to ungodliness and worldly passions, and to live self-controlled, upright and godly lives in this present age, 13while we wait for the blessed hope—the glorious appearing of our great God and Savior, Jesus Christ, 14who gave himself for us to redeem us from all wickedness and to purify for himself a people that are his very own, eager to do what is good.

15These, then, are the things you should teach. Encourage and rebuke with all authority. Do not let anyone despise you.

CHAPTER 3

Remind the people to be subject to rulers and authorities, to be obedient, to be ready to do whatever is good, 2to slander no one, to be peaceable and considerate, and to show true humility toward all men.

3At one time we too were foolish, disobedient, deceived and enslaved by all kinds of passions and pleasures. We lived in malice and envy, being hated and hating one another. 4But when the kindness and love of God our Savior appeared, 5he saved us, not because of righteous things we had done, but because of his mercy. He saved us through the washing of rebirth and renewal by the Holy Spirit, 6whom he poured out on us generously through Jesus Christ our Savior, 7so that,

ᵃ5 Or ordain   ᵇ7 Traditionally bishop

having been justified by his grace, we might become heirs having the hope of eternal life. [8]This is a trustworthy saying. And I want you to stress these things, so that those who have trusted in God may be careful to devote themselves to doing what is good. These things are excellent and profitable for everyone.

[9]But avoid foolish controversies and genealogies and arguments and quarrels about the law, because these are unprofitable and useless. [10]Warn a divisive person once, and then warn him a second time. After that, have nothing to do with him. [11]You may be sure that such a man is warped and sinful; he is self-condemned.

[12]As soon as I send Artemas or Tychicus to you, do your best to come to me at Nicopolis, because I have decided to winter there. [13]Do everything you can to help Zenas the lawyer and Apollos on their way and see that they have everything they need. [14]Our people must learn to devote themselves to doing what is good, in order that they may provide for daily necessities and not live unproductive lives.

[15]Everyone with me sends you greetings. Greet those who love us in the faith.

Grace be with you all.

DECEMBER 7 □ DAY 342
Happily Humble

 LOOK BACK The Pauline Epistles have been the focus of your reading over the past couple of weeks. Here's a "key" to help you unlock and remember each book:

Philippians: "Happily Humble" (The path of true happiness for the Christian is the path of genuine humility modeled by Jesus Christ.)

Colossians: "Commander in Chief" (Jesus is supreme in everything and deserves first place in your life.)

1 Thessalonians: "Stay on Target" (Don't become distracted or discouraged as you seek to make faith, hope and love the hallmarks of your faith.)

2 Thessalonians: "Work While You Wait" (There is work to be done in the harvest fields of the Lord as you await his return.)

1 Timothy: "Leadership Manual" (How to know when you are ready to assume leadership responsibility in the household of faith)

2 Timothy: "Combat Manual" (How to do battle with the enemy as you live for Jesus)

Titus: "Conduct Manual" (How to behave in the household of faith)

 LOOK UP Find two glasses of differing shapes, and fill one with water. Now pour the full glass into the empty glass. What you now have is all of the water from the first glass contained in a new "form."

To grow tall spiritually, a Christian must first learn to kneel.

In a crude way, that illustrates what happened when Jesus Christ, the Second Person of the Godhead, took upon himself human form and became a man. Without in any way ceasing to be *divine* (his original nature), he took upon himself a new form (*flesh*, human nature). And the result? When Jesus walked the earth, in reality he was all of God in a human body—"the incarnation." He was God come in the flesh, total divinity combined with perfect humanity. Jesus "emptied" himself of the use of many of his divine attributes (such as omnipotence and omnipresence) in order to dwell among the objects of his love: men and women, boys and girls (John 1:14).

And the result? A series of glorious ironies! The Christ of creation (John 1:3) was laid in a manger made from one of the trees he created. The Carpenter from Nazareth is busy today preparing our eternal "condominium" (John 14:1–4).

LOOK AHEAD Philippians 2:5–11 describes Christ's example of humility as he emptied himself of his divine rights and privileges (remember our illustration with the glasses?) and made himself of no reputation. By rights, Jesus could have demanded that every knee bow to his authority. Instead, he suffered and died at the hands of wicked men in order that our response to him would be out of love, not coercion. He was willing to renounce his heavenly citizenship for an earthly one. Now he asks his followers to do just the opposite!

What price are you willing to pay today to follow in his footsteps? Are you willing to be inconvenienced by someone who calls or drops by unannounced with a need for your time and attention? Are you willing to rearrange your priorities in order to serve the needs of someone else? Are you willing to use money you were saving for a personal purchase to meet someone else's need?

Taking the form of a servant may not earn you any applause or fanfare, but it will demonstrate that you are serious about having the mind of Christ (Philippians 2:5). And after you read verse 9, perhaps you will agree that that's definitely the mind to have!

Philemon

ONESIMUS is a desperate slave who has wronged his master, Philemon. Slaves were crucified for lesser offenses than his! He had run away to Rome, where he found—through Paul—a glorious new slavery: to Jesus Christ. In gratefulness, Onesimus serves Paul. He repents, but he has not made restitution. Paul sends him back to his master with this letter, asking Philemon to forgive and accept him as a fellow brother in the Lord. This "postcard" provides a glimpse of Paul's affectionate heart and reminds us of our forgiveness in Christ.

Focus	Praise for Philemon		Plea for Onesimus		Preparation for Paul
Divisions	Paul's Preface	Paul's Commendation	Paul's Intercession	Paul's Promise	Paul's Messages
	1 3	4 7	8 16	17 21	22 25
Topics	Greetings	Gratitude	Grace		Good Words
	Courtesy	Compliment	Counsel		Conclusion
Place	Rome				
Time	Approximately A.D. 60–61				

DECEMBER 8 ☐ DAY 343
PHILEMON
Forgiveness in the Church

OVERVIEW Philemon is the shortest and one of the most personal of Paul's letters. Paul has befriended Onesimus, a runaway slave and new convert to Christianity. Now Onesimus must deal with his obligations to his former master, Philemon, who is also a Christian. Paul sends Onesimus back with a brief note in which Paul appeals for leniency based on love: Philemon's love for Paul and God's love for Philemon. Knowing the reality of Philemon's faith, Paul is confident that brotherly love will carry the day.

Verses 1-3	Verses 4-7	Verses 8-21	Verses 22-25
Paul's Courtesy	Paul's Compliment	Paul's Counsel	Paul's Conclusion
Salutation	Commendation	Intercession	Anticipation

Those who profess repentance must practice it.

YOUR DAILY WALK Place a check next to each item for which you have received an "overdue notice" in the past year:
- Library book
- Loan repayment
- Charge account
- Debt of restitution

Were you puzzled by the last item? Allow the life of Onesimus to demonstrate what restitution is and why it is so important.

When the runaway slave was confronted with the claims of Christ and responded in believing faith, many things changed. His sins were forgiven by God; he became a part of the family of God (with many new brothers and sisters in Christ, including Paul and Philemon); he received a whole new motivation for living! But some things did not change. He was still Philemon's servant—and a runaway servant at that. He was still a thief, with a debt to repay to his master. There were "overdue" accounts to settle involving restitution, repentance and a return to Philemon's authority.

Is there an overdue account from your "B.C." (before Christ) days? Take a moment to honor the Christ who settled your heavenly debt by settling an earthly one today!

INSIGHT The Man Who Lived Up to His Name
Onesimus literally means "useful," which explains Paul's play on words in verse 11. What was formerly "useless" to Philemon is now "useful" to both Philemon and Paul!

¹Paul, a prisoner of Christ Jesus, and Timothy our brother,

To Philemon our dear friend and fellow worker, ²to Apphia our sister, to Archippus our fellow soldier and to the church that meets in your home:

³Grace to you and peace from God our Father and the Lord Jesus Christ.

⁴I always thank my God as I remember you in my prayers, ⁵because I hear about your faith in the Lord Jesus and your love for all the saints. ⁶I pray that you may be

active in sharing your faith, so that you will have a full understanding of every good thing we have in Christ. [7]Your love has given me great joy and encouragement, because you, brother, have refreshed the hearts of the saints.

[8]Therefore, although in Christ I could be bold and order you to do what you ought to do, [9]yet I appeal to you on the basis of love. I then, as Paul—an old man and now also a prisoner of Christ Jesus— [10]I appeal to you for my son Onesimus,[a] who became my son while I was in chains. [11]Formerly he was useless to you, but now he has become useful both to you and to me.

[12]I am sending him—who is my very heart—back to you. [13]I would have liked to keep him with me so that he could take your place in helping me while I am in chains for the gospel. [14]But I did not want to do anything without your consent, so that any favor you do will be spontaneous and not forced. [15]Perhaps the reason he was separated from you for a little while was that you might have him back for

a 10 *Onesimus* means *useful.*

good— [16]no longer as a slave, but better than a slave, as a dear brother. He is very dear to me but even dearer to you, both as a man and as a brother in the Lord.

[17]So if you consider me a partner, welcome him as you would welcome me. [18]If he has done you any wrong or owes you anything, charge it to me. [19]I, Paul, am writing this with my own hand. I will pay it back—not to mention that you owe me your very self. [20]I do wish, brother, that I may have some benefit from you in the Lord; refresh my heart in Christ. [21]Confident of your obedience, I write to you, knowing that you will do even more than I ask.

[22]And one thing more: Prepare a guest room for me, because I hope to be restored to you in answer to your prayers.

[23]Epaphras, my fellow prisoner in Christ Jesus, sends you greetings. [24]And so do Mark, Aristarchus, Demas and Luke, my fellow workers.

[25]The grace of the Lord Jesus Christ be with your spirit.

Hebrews

THE ANONYMOUS first-century writer of Hebrews sent this letter of exhortation to professing Jewish Christians suffering persecution for their faith in Christ. Many, in fact, were considering renouncing their profession in order to return to the safety of Judaism (10:38–39). The writer exhorts them to hold fast to their faith and press on to spiritual maturity. The Christian faith is the true worship and service of the living God. Jesus Christ, as both the sacrifice and high priest of the new covenant, is superior in every way to the Mosaic Law.

Focus	"Jesus [is] the author and perfecter of our faith" (12:2).				
Divisions	Christ, Superior to the Angels	Christ, Superior to Moses and Joshua	Christ, Superior to Aaron's Priesthood	Christ, Superior to the Mosaic Law	Christ, the Secret of a Superior Lifestyle
	1 2	3 4	5 7	8 10	11 13
Topics	Revelation	Leader	Priest	Sacrifice	Example
	A Better Way				A Living Way
Place	Written to Scattered Jewish Christians				
Time	About A.D. 64–68				

DECEMBER 9 ☐ DAY 344
HEBREWS 1–2
Christ, Superior to Angels

OVERVIEW God has revealed himself and his plans in many ways through long centuries of Old Testament history, but now he has provided the climactic chapter in the person of his Son. Angels have frequently been involved in God's program, but none of them could claim to be a royal Son of the King or suffer and die as the Savior of humankind. Only Jesus Christ could do that! Though made a little lower than the angels for a time, he provided the way to lift both Jews and Gentiles into the family of God through his sacrificial death.

Chapter 1		Chapter 2	
Christ, the Superior			
Message	Messenger	Savior	Sufferer
1　　　　　3	4　　　　14	1　　　　8	9　　　　18
Better than the Angels		A Little Lower than the Angels	

YOUR DAILY WALK Can you complete this comparison chart from the first two verses of the book of Hebrews?

God spoke

In the creation, the Lord made humans like himself; but in the redemption he made himself like humans.

in the past . . .　　　　　　in these last days . . .

to our forefathers　　_____

through the prophets _____

What God has said in the past is important, but what he is saying *today* through his Son is even more important! As you read today's passage, look for statements describing who Christ is and what he has accomplished. You might want to share the results of your study with a friend who is seriously considering the claims of Christ. It might be just the evidence that person needs to find new life in the one before whom even angels bow!

INSIGHT "Let Me Express It This Way. . . ."
The Greek word translated "exact representation" (1:3) is the root of the English term *character* and means "a stamp or impress, as on a coin or seal." The exact representation is therefore an exact reproduction, a truthful and complete picture in every detail of the original object. Do you want to know what the character of the invisible God is like? Just study the character of his Son, who came in the flesh.

CHAPTER 1

In the past God spoke to our forefathers through the prophets at many times and in various ways, ²but in these last days he has spoken to us by his Son, whom he appointed heir of all things, and through whom he made the universe. ³The Son is the radiance of God's glory and the exact representation of his being, sustaining all things by his powerful word.

After he had provided purification for sins, he sat down at the right hand of the Majesty in heaven. ⁴So he became as much superior to the angels as the name he has inherited is superior to theirs.

⁵For to which of the angels did God ever say,

"You are my Son;

today I have become your
Father[a]"[b]?

Or again,

"I will be his Father,
and he will be my Son"[c]?

[6]And again, when God brings his first-born into the world, he says,

"Let all God's angels worship him."[d]

[7]In speaking of the angels he says,

"He makes his angels winds,
his servants flames of fire."[e]

[8]But about the Son he says,

"Your throne, O God, will last for ever
and ever,
and righteousness will be the scepter
of your kingdom.
[9]You have loved righteousness and
hated wickedness;
therefore God, your God, has set
you above your companions
by anointing you with the oil of
joy."[f]

[10]He also says,

"In the beginning, O Lord, you laid the
foundations of the earth,
and the heavens are the work of
your hands.
[11]They will perish, but you remain;
they will all wear out like a
garment.
[12]You will roll them up like a robe;
like a garment they will be changed.
But you remain the same,
and your years will never end."[g]

[13]To which of the angels did God ever say,

"Sit at my right hand
until I make your enemies
a footstool for your feet"[h]?

[14]Are not all angels ministering spirits sent to serve those who will inherit salvation?

CHAPTER 2

We must pay more careful attention, therefore, to what we have heard, so that we do not drift away. [2]For if the message spoken by angels was binding, and every violation and disobedience received its just punishment, [3]how shall we escape if we ignore such a great salvation? This salvation, which was first announced by the Lord, was confirmed to us by those who heard him. [4]God also testified to it by signs, wonders and various miracles, and gifts of the Holy Spirit distributed according to his will.

[5]It is not to angels that he has subjected the world to come, about which we are speaking. [6]But there is a place where someone has testified:

"What is man that you are mindful of
him,
the son of man that you care for
him?
[7]You made him a little[i] lower than the
angels;
you crowned him with glory and
honor
[8]   and put everything under his feet."[j]

In putting everything under him, God left nothing that is not subject to him. Yet at present we do not see everything subject to him. [9]But we see Jesus, who was made a little lower than the angels, now crowned with glory and honor because he suffered death, so that by the grace of God he might taste death for everyone.

[10]In bringing many sons to glory, it was fitting that God, for whom and through whom everything exists, should make the author of their salvation perfect through suffering. [11]Both the one who makes men holy and those who are made holy are of the same family. So Jesus is not ashamed to call them brothers. [12]He says,

"I will declare your name to my
brothers;
in the presence of the congregation I
will sing your praises."[k]

[13]And again,

"I will put my trust in him."[l]

And again he says,

"Here am I, and the children God has
given me."[m]

[14]Since the children have flesh and blood, he too shared in their humanity so that by his death he might destroy him who holds the power of death—that is, the

[a]5 Or have begotten you   [b]5 Psalm 2:7   [c]5 2 Samuel 7:14; 1 Chron. 17:13   [d]6 Deut. 32:43 (see Dead Sea Scrolls and Septuagint)   [e]7 Psalm 104:4   [f]9 Psalm 45:6,7   [g]12 Psalm 102:25-27   [h]13 Psalm 110:1   [i]7 Or him for a little while; also in verse 9   [j]8 Psalm 8:4-6   [k]12 Psalm 22:22   [l]13 Isaiah 8:17   [m]13 Isaiah 8:18

devil— [15]and free those who all their lives were held in slavery by their fear of death. [16]For surely it is not angels he helps, but Abraham's descendants. [17]For this reason he had to be made like his brothers in every way, in order that he

might become a merciful and faithful high priest in service to God, and that he might make atonement for[n] the sins of the people. [18]Because he himself suffered when he was tempted, he is able to help those who are being tempted.

[n]17 Or and that he might turn aside God's wrath, taking away

DECEMBER 10 ☐ DAY 345
HEBREWS 3–4
Christ, Superior to Moses and Joshua

OVERVIEW Humanly speaking, Israel's two greatest leaders during its establishment as a nation were Moses and Joshua. Moses was the great deliverer from Egyptian bondage—Israel's savior from slavery. Joshua was Israel's commander in chief during the conquest of Canaan—Israel's provider of peace. But both were merely servants and ministers of God in caring for his people. By contrast, Jesus is the Son of God who formed the people in the first place! Through the nation's unbelief, Moses and Joshua were unable to provide the ultimate peace and rest that the people sought. Today "there remains, then, a Sabbath-rest for the people of God" (4:9)—a rest found only in Jesus Christ.

Chapter 3	Chapter 4
Christ, Superior Because	
He Is the Son, Not the Servant	He Passes the "Rest-Test"
Better than Moses	Better than Joshua

A field that has rested gives a bountiful crop.

YOUR DAILY WALK Sit down in a comfortable chair, grab a pencil or pen and in the margin of this page note all the ways you can think of in which you are resting today. (For example, "Resting my tired feet, resting in my faith in Christ, resting in the confidence that God never rests . . .")

The writer to the Hebrews declares, "There remains . . . a Sabbath-rest for the people of God" (4:9). This relates first to the individual's ceasing from all his or her efforts to *earn* salvation (an impossible task) and appropriating with restful faith the finished work of Jesus Christ. Is that a rest you are enjoying today?

But for the people of God, there is a second rest—a rest the wandering Israelites never experienced because they never learned to be content. It is the rest of walking day by day in God's strength rather than your own. Philippians 4:13 says it all: "I can do everything through [and rest confidently in] him who gives me strength." Is that a rest you know firsthand?

INSIGHT The Results of Christ's Priestly Work
In Old Testament times only the priests were able to approach God in worshipful service. But because Jesus suffered and knows what we are going through, we now can "approach the throne of grace with confidence" (4:16). The right of priestly approach is extended to all Christians. Are you taking full advantage of this marvelous privilege?

CHAPTER 3

Therefore, holy brothers, who share in the heavenly calling, fix your thoughts on Jesus, the apostle and high priest whom we confess. ²He was faithful to the one who appointed him, just as Moses was faithful in all God's house. ³Jesus has been found worthy of greater honor than Moses, just as the builder of a house has greater honor than the house itself. ⁴For every house is built by someone, but God is the builder of everything. ⁵Moses was faithful as a servant in all God's house, testifying to what would be said in the future. ⁶But Christ is faithful as a son over God's house. And we are his house, if we hold on to our courage and the hope of which we boast.

⁷So, as the Holy Spirit says:

"Today, if you hear his voice,
⁸ do not harden your hearts
as you did in the rebellion,
    during the time of testing in the
        desert,
⁹where your fathers tested and tried me
    and for forty years saw what I did.
¹⁰That is why I was angry with that
        generation,
    and I said, 'Their hearts are always
        going astray,
    and they have not known my ways.'
¹¹So I declared on oath in my anger,
    'They shall never enter my rest.' "ᵒ

¹²See to it, brothers, that none of you has a sinful, unbelieving heart that turns away from the living God. ¹³But encourage one another daily, as long as it is called Today, so that none of you may be hardened by sin's deceitfulness. ¹⁴We have come to share in Christ if we hold firmly till the end the confidence we had at first. ¹⁵As has just been said:

"Today, if you hear his voice,
    do not harden your hearts
    as you did in the rebellion."ᵖ

¹⁶Who were they who heard and rebelled? Were they not all those Moses led out of Egypt? ¹⁷And with whom was he angry for forty years? Was it not with those who sinned, whose bodies fell in the desert? ¹⁸And to whom did God swear that they would never enter his rest if not to those who disobeyed𐞥? ¹⁹So we see that they were not able to enter, because of their unbelief.

CHAPTER 4

Therefore, since the promise of entering his rest still stands, let us be careful that none of you be found to have fallen short of it. ²For we also have had the gospel preached to us, just as they did; but the message they heard was of no value to them, because those who heard did not combine it with faith.ʳ ³Now we who have believed enter that rest, just as God has said,

"So I declared on oath in my anger,
    'They shall never enter my rest.' "ˢ

And yet his work has been finished since the creation of the world. ⁴For somewhere he has spoken about the seventh day in these words: "And on the seventh day God rested from all his work."ᵗ ⁵And again in the passage above he says, "They shall never enter my rest."

⁶It still remains that some will enter that rest, and those who formerly had the gospel preached to them did not go in, because of their disobedience. ⁷Therefore God again set a certain day, calling it Today, when a long time later he spoke through David, as was said before:

"Today, if you hear his voice,
    do not harden your hearts."ᵖ

⁸For if Joshua had given them rest, God would not have spoken later about another day. ⁹There remains, then, a Sabbath-rest for the people of God; ¹⁰for anyone who enters God's rest also rests from his own work, just as God did from his. ¹¹Let us, therefore, make every effort to enter that rest, so that no one will fall by following their example of disobedience.

¹²For the word of God is living and active. Sharper than any double-edged sword, it penetrates even to dividing soul and spirit, joints and marrow; it judges the thoughts and attitudes of the heart. ¹³Nothing in all creation is hidden from God's sight. Everything is uncovered and laid bare before the eyes of him to whom we must give account.

ᵒ11 Psalm 95:7-11   ᵖ15,7 Psalm 95:7,8   𐞥18 Or *disbelieved*   ʳ2 Many manuscripts *because they did not share in the faith of*
those who obeyed   ˢ3 Psalm 95:11; also in verse 5   ᵗ4 Gen. 2:2

¹⁴Therefore, since we have a great high priest who has gone through the heavens,ᵘ Jesus the Son of God, let us hold firmly to the faith we profess. ¹⁵For we do not have a high priest who is unable to sympathize with our weaknesses, but we have one who has been tempted in every way, just as we are—yet was without sin. ¹⁶Let us then approach the throne of grace with confidence, so that we may receive mercy and find grace to help us in our time of need.

ᵘ14 Or gone into heaven

DECEMBER 11 ☐ DAY 346
HEBREWS 5–7
Christ, Superior to Aaron's Priesthood

 OVERVIEW At the center of Israel's life was its worship in the tabernacle and later in the temple. Crucial to that worship was the priesthood, beginning with the high priest, Aaron, and his sons. But the Lord Jesus Christ is a superior priest because he belongs to a superior order: the order of Melchizedek, the king-priest (Genesis 14:18–20). Why? Because Melchizedek came before Aaron, and his priesthood was a timeless one without beginning or end. In the same way, Christ is an eternal priest, who died once for all time as the eternal sacrifice for sin. These difficult truths, the writer of Hebrews admits, require maturity to grasp but are life-changing in their impact.

Chapter 5	Chapter 6	Chapter 7
Christ, the High Priest	"Grow Up in Christ!"	Christ, the Eternal Priest
A Better Priest	A Better Response	A Better Priesthood

 YOUR DAILY WALK Complete the following sentences:
- The priest's job was to . . .
- The priest's job was never finished because . . .
- The priest acted as a bridge builder between holy God and sinful humanity by . . .

The true meaning of the gospel is not what a person says about it, but what he or she does with it.

One of the doctrines recaptured and reemphasized in the Reformation was the priesthood of the believer. Each Christian, as a member of the body of Christ, is given the role of a priest (1 Peter 2:9), serving under Jesus Christ, the great high priest, by praying for others (1 Timothy 2:1) and showing others what true worship is all about (1 Peter 2:9).

Now put your name in place of "the priest" in the three statements above, and complete them again:
- My job is to . . .
- My job is never finished because . . .
- I am to act as a bridge builder between holy God and sinful humanity by . . .

 INSIGHT High Marks for a High Priest
The writer to the Hebrews lists these identifying marks for the high priest: (1) He was a man chosen by God. (2) He represented humankind to God. (3) He offered gifts and sacrifices to God on behalf of humankind. (4) He exercised compassion in his ministry for God.

CHAPTER 5

Every high priest is selected from among men and is appointed to represent them in matters related to God, to offer gifts and sacrifices for sins. ²He is able to deal gently with those who are ignorant and are going astray, since he himself is subject to weakness. ³This is why he has to offer sacrifices for his own sins, as well as for the sins of the people.

⁴No one takes this honor upon himself; he must be called by God, just as Aaron was. ⁵So Christ also did not take upon himself the glory of becoming a high priest. But God said to him,

"You are my Son;
     today I have become your
         Father.ᵛ"ʷ

⁶And he says in another place,

"You are a priest forever,
     in the order of Melchizedek."ˣ

⁷During the days of Jesus' life on earth, he offered up prayers and petitions with loud cries and tears to the one who could save him from death, and he was heard because of his reverent submission. ⁸Although he was a son, he learned obedience from what he suffered ⁹and, once made perfect, he became the source of eternal salvation for all who obey him ¹⁰and was designated by God to be high priest in the order of Melchizedek.

¹¹We have much to say about this, but it is hard to explain because you are slow to learn. ¹²In fact, though by this time you ought to be teachers, you need someone to teach you the elementary truths of God's word all over again. You need milk, not solid food! ¹³Anyone who lives on milk, being still an infant, is not acquainted with the teaching about righteousness. ¹⁴But solid food is for the mature, who by constant use have trained themselves to distinguish good from evil.

CHAPTER 6

Therefore let us leave the elementary teachings about Christ and go on to maturity, not laying again the foundation of repentance from acts that lead to death,ʸ and of faith in God, ²instruction about baptisms, the laying on of hands, the resurrection of the dead, and eternal judg-ment. ³And God permitting, we will do so.

⁴It is impossible for those who have once been enlightened, who have tasted the heavenly gift, who have shared in the Holy Spirit, ⁵who have tasted the goodness of the word of God and the powers of the coming age, ⁶if they fall away, to be brought back to repentance, becauseᶻ to their loss they are crucifying the Son of God all over again and subjecting him to public disgrace.

⁷Land that drinks in the rain often falling on it and that produces a crop useful to those for whom it is farmed receives the blessing of God. ⁸But land that produces thorns and thistles is worthless and is in danger of being cursed. In the end it will be burned.

⁹Even though we speak like this, dear friends, we are confident of better things in your case—things that accompany salvation. ¹⁰God is not unjust; he will not forget your work and the love you have shown him as you have helped his people and continue to help them. ¹¹We want each of you to show this same diligence to the very end, in order to make your hope sure. ¹²We do not want you to become lazy, but to imitate those who through faith and patience inherit what has been promised.

¹³When God made his promise to Abraham, since there was no one greater for him to swear by, he swore by himself, ¹⁴saying, "I will surely bless you and give you many descendants."ᵃ ¹⁵And so after waiting patiently, Abraham received what was promised.

¹⁶Men swear by someone greater than themselves, and the oath confirms what is said and puts an end to all argument. ¹⁷Because God wanted to make the unchanging nature of his purpose very clear to the heirs of what was promised, he confirmed it with an oath. ¹⁸God did this so that, by two unchangeable things in which it is impossible for God to lie, we who have fled to take hold of the hope offered to us may be greatly encouraged. ¹⁹We have this hope as an anchor for the soul, firm and secure. It enters the inner sanctuary behind the curtain, ²⁰where Jesus, who went before us, has entered on

---

ᵛ*5* Or *have begotten you*   ʷ*5* Psalm 2:7   ˣ*6* Psalm 110:4   ʸ*1* Or *from useless rituals*   ᶻ*6* Or *repentance while*   ᵃ*14* Gen. 22:17

our behalf. He has become a high priest forever, in the order of Melchizedek.

CHAPTER 7

This Melchizedek was king of Salem and priest of God Most High. He met Abraham returning from the defeat of the kings and blessed him, ²and Abraham gave him a tenth of everything. First, his name means "king of righteousness"; then also, "king of Salem" means "king of peace." ³Without father or mother, without genealogy, without beginning of days or end of life, like the Son of God he remains a priest forever.

⁴Just think how great he was: Even the patriarch Abraham gave him a tenth of the plunder! ⁵Now the law requires the descendants of Levi who become priests to collect a tenth from the people—that is, their brothers—even though their brothers are descended from Abraham. ⁶This man, however, did not trace his descent from Levi, yet he collected a tenth from Abraham and blessed him who had the promises. ⁷And without doubt the lesser person is blessed by the greater. ⁸In the one case, the tenth is collected by men who die; but in the other case, by him who is declared to be living. ⁹One might even say that Levi, who collects the tenth, paid the tenth through Abraham, ¹⁰because when Melchizedek met Abraham, Levi was still in the body of his ancestor.

¹¹If perfection could have been attained through the Levitical priesthood (for on the basis of it the law was given to the people), why was there still need for another priest to come—one in the order of Melchizedek, not in the order of Aaron? ¹²For when there is a change of the priesthood, there must also be a change of the law. ¹³He of whom these things are said belonged to a different tribe, and no one from that tribe has ever served at the altar. ¹⁴For it is clear that our Lord descended from Judah, and in regard to that tribe Moses said nothing about priests. ¹⁵And what we have said is even more clear if another priest like Melchizedek appears, ¹⁶one who has become a priest not on the basis of a regulation as to his ancestry but on the basis of the power of an indestructible life. ¹⁷For it is declared:

"You are a priest forever,
   in the order of Melchizedek."ᵇ

¹⁸The former regulation is set aside because it was weak and useless ¹⁹(for the law made nothing perfect), and a better hope is introduced, by which we draw near to God.

²⁰And it was not without an oath! Others became priests without any oath, ²¹but he became a priest with an oath when God said to him:

"The Lord has sworn
   and will not change his mind:
'You are a priest forever.' "ᵇ

²²Because of this oath, Jesus has become the guarantee of a better covenant.

²³Now there have been many of those priests, since death prevented them from continuing in office; ²⁴but because Jesus lives forever, he has a permanent priesthood. ²⁵Therefore he is able to save completelyᶜ those who come to God through him, because he always lives to intercede for them.

²⁶Such a high priest meets our need—one who is holy, blameless, pure, set apart from sinners, exalted above the heavens. ²⁷Unlike the other high priests, he does not need to offer sacrifices day after day, first for his own sins, and then for the sins of the people. He sacrificed for their sins once for all when he offered himself. ²⁸For the law appoints as high priests men who are weak; but the oath, which came after the law, appointed the Son, who has been made perfect forever.

ᵇ17,21 Psalm 110:4   ᶜ25 Or forever

DECEMBER 12 □ DAY 347
HEBREWS 8–10
Christ, Superior to the Mosaic Law

OVERVIEW Aaron and his sons ministered in a tabernacle built according to the specifications God gave to Moses. They offered animal and grain sacrifices in accordance with divine regulations. All of this was part of the Mosaic Law that God established as a covenant with his people on Mount Sinai. Consequently, if Jesus Christ is superior to both Moses and Aaron, it follows that God has established with him a superior covenant based upon a superior sacrifice. Even the Old Testament bore witness that the Mosaic system was temporary and would be replaced by a new covenant—a covenant made with the Messiah and based upon the once-for-all-time sacrifice of his life.

Chapter 8	Chapter 9	Chapter 10
A Better Covenant	A Better Tabernacle	A Better Sacrifice
Christ	Better than the Old Covenant	

The faintest whisper of encouragement uttered to a Christian brother or sister is heard in heaven.

YOUR DAILY WALK Hebrews 10 has been described as the "lettuce" chapter. Three times in the space of three verses (22–24) you'll find the phrase "Let us . . ." And whenever you do, you can be sure the author has provided ample reason to do precisely that! "Therefore, brothers, since we have confidence to enter . . . by the blood of Jesus, . . . and since we have a great priest over the house of God, let us draw near . . . Let us hold unswervingly . . . And let us consider how we may spur one another on toward love and good deeds" (10:19–24). The two elements—exhortation and explanation—are inseparable, for without the second, there is no motivation to do the first. Duty in the Christian life flows naturally from doctrine.

Notice in each case the author uses the word *us*. There is a mutual responsibility for Christians to consider one another . . . be accountable to one another . . . encourage one another. Ask someone to help you with your memory work or a personal-growth project this week by checking up on your progress each day. You'll both be glad you did!

INSIGHT The Timely, Superior New Covenant
God's covenant with Jesus Christ is obviously *new* in point of time; but the Greek word translated "new" also emphasizes its newness "in respect to form or quality" and, therefore, its superiority to the old covenant, which it supersedes.

CHAPTER 8

The point of what we are saying is this: We do have such a high priest, who sat down at the right hand of the throne of the Majesty in heaven, ²and who serves in the sanctuary, the true tabernacle set up by the Lord, not by man.

³Every high priest is appointed to offer both gifts and sacrifices, and so it was necessary for this one also to have some-

thing to offer. ⁴If he were on earth, he would not be a priest, for there are already men who offer the gifts prescribed by the law. ⁵They serve at a sanctuary that is a copy and shadow of what is in heaven. This is why Moses was warned when he was about to build the tabernacle: "See to it that you make everything according to the pattern shown you on the mountain."*d* ⁶But the ministry Jesus

*d*5 Exodus 25:40

has received is as superior to theirs as the covenant of which he is mediator is superior to the old one, and it is founded on better promises.

⁷For if there had been nothing wrong with that first covenant, no place would have been sought for another. ⁸But God found fault with the people and said⁴:

"The time is coming, declares the Lord,
  when I will make a new covenant
with the house of Israel
  and with the house of Judah.
⁹It will not be like the covenant
  I made with their forefathers
when I took them by the hand
  to lead them out of Egypt,
because they did not remain faithful to
    my covenant,
  and I turned away from them,
                          declares the Lord.
¹⁰This is the covenant I will make with
    the house of Israel
  after that time, declares the Lord.
I will put my laws in their minds
  and write them on their hearts.
I will be their God,
  and they will be my people.
¹¹No longer will a man teach his
    neighbor,
  or a man his brother, saying, 'Know
    the Lord,'
because they will all know me,
  from the least of them to the
    greatest.
¹²For I will forgive their wickedness
  and will remember their sins no
    more."ᶠ

¹³By calling this covenant "new," he has made the first one obsolete; and what is obsolete and aging will soon disappear.

CHAPTER 9
Now the first covenant had regulations for worship and also an earthly sanctuary. ²A tabernacle was set up. In its first room were the lampstand, the table and the consecrated bread; this was called the Holy Place. ³Behind the second curtain was a room called the Most Holy Place, ⁴which had the golden altar of incense and the gold-covered ark of the covenant. This ark contained the gold jar of manna, Aaron's staff that had budded, and the stone tablets of the covenant.

⁵Above the ark were the cherubim of the Glory, overshadowing the atonement cover.ᵍ But we cannot discuss these things in detail now.

⁶When everything had been arranged like this, the priests entered regularly into the outer room to carry on their ministry. ⁷But only the high priest entered the inner room, and that only once a year, and never without blood, which he offered for himself and for the sins the people had committed in ignorance. ⁸The Holy Spirit was showing by this that the way into the Most Holy Place had not yet been disclosed as long as the first tabernacle was still standing. ⁹This is an illustration for the present time, indicating that the gifts and sacrifices being offered were not able to clear the conscience of the worshiper. ¹⁰They are only a matter of food and drink and various ceremonial washings— external regulations applying until the time of the new order.

¹¹When Christ came as high priest of the good things that are already here,ʰ he went through the greater and more perfect tabernacle that is not man-made, that is to say, not a part of this creation. ¹²He did not enter by means of the blood of goats and calves; but he entered the Most Holy Place once for all by his own blood, having obtained eternal redemption. ¹³The blood of goats and bulls and the ashes of a heifer sprinkled on those who are ceremonially unclean sanctify them so that they are outwardly clean. ¹⁴How much more, then, will the blood of Christ, who through the eternal Spirit offered himself unblemished to God, cleanse our consciences from acts that lead to death,ⁱ so that we may serve the living God!

¹⁵For this reason Christ is the mediator of a new covenant, that those who are called may receive the promised eternal inheritance—now that he has died as a ransom to set them free from the sins committed under the first covenant.

¹⁶In the case of a will,ʲ it is necessary to prove the death of the one who made it, ¹⁷because a will is in force only when somebody has died; it never takes effect while the one who made it is living. ¹⁸This is why even the first covenant was not put into effect without blood. ¹⁹When Moses had proclaimed every commandment of

---

ᵉ8 Some manuscripts may be translated *fault and said to the people.*   ᶠ12 Jer. 31:31-34   ᵍ5 Traditionally *the mercy seat*
ʰ11 Some early manuscripts *are to come*   ⁱ14 Or *from useless rituals*   ʲ16 Same Greek word as *covenant*; also in verse 17

the law to all the people, he took the blood of calves, together with water, scarlet wool and branches of hyssop, and sprinkled the scroll and all the people. [20]He said, "This is the blood of the covenant, which God has commanded you to keep."[k] [21]In the same way, he sprinkled with the blood both the tabernacle and everything used in its ceremonies. [22]In fact, the law requires that nearly everything be cleansed with blood, and without the shedding of blood there is no forgiveness.

[23]It was necessary, then, for the copies of the heavenly things to be purified with these sacrifices, but the heavenly things themselves with better sacrifices than these. [24]For Christ did not enter a man-made sanctuary that was only a copy of the true one; he entered heaven itself, now to appear for us in God's presence. [25]Nor did he enter heaven to offer himself again and again, the way the high priest enters the Most Holy Place every year with blood that is not his own. [26]Then Christ would have had to suffer many times since the creation of the world. But now he has appeared once for all at the end of the ages to do away with sin by the sacrifice of himself. [27]Just as man is destined to die once, and after that to face judgment, [28]so Christ was sacrificed once to take away the sins of many people; and he will appear a second time, not to bear sin, but to bring salvation to those who are waiting for him.

CHAPTER 10
The law is only a shadow of the good things that are coming—not the realities themselves. For this reason it can never, by the same sacrifices repeated endlessly year after year, make perfect those who draw near to worship. [2]If it could, would they not have stopped being offered? For the worshipers would have been cleansed once for all, and would no longer have felt guilty for their sins. [3]But those sacrifices are an annual reminder of sins, [4]because it is impossible for the blood of bulls and goats to take away sins.

[5]Therefore, when Christ came into the world, he said:

"Sacrifice and offering you did not
    desire,

but a body you prepared for me;
[6]with burnt offerings and sin offerings
    you were not pleased.
[7]Then I said, 'Here I am—it is written
    about me in the scroll—
I have come to do your will,
    O God.' "[l]

[8]First he said, "Sacrifices and offerings, burnt offerings and sin offerings you did not desire, nor were you pleased with them" (although the law required them to be made). [9]Then he said, "Here I am, I have come to do your will." He sets aside the first to establish the second. [10]And by that will, we have been made holy through the sacrifice of the body of Jesus Christ once for all.

[11]Day after day every priest stands and performs his religious duties; again and again he offers the same sacrifices, which can never take away sins. [12]But when this priest had offered for all time one sacrifice for sins, he sat down at the right hand of God. [13]Since that time he waits for his enemies to be made his footstool, [14]because by one sacrifice he has made perfect forever those who are being made holy.

[15]The Holy Spirit also testifies to us about this. First he says:

[16]"This is the covenant I will make with
    them
    after that time, says the Lord.
I will put my laws in their hearts,
    and I will write them on their
        minds."[m]

[17]Then he adds:

"Their sins and lawless acts
    I will remember no more."[n]

[18]And where these have been forgiven, there is no longer any sacrifice for sin.

[19]Therefore, brothers, since we have confidence to enter the Most Holy Place by the blood of Jesus, [20]by a new and living way opened for us through the curtain, that is, his body, [21]and since we have a great priest over the house of God, [22]let us draw near to God with a sincere heart in full assurance of faith, having our hearts sprinkled to cleanse us from a guilty conscience and having our bodies washed with pure water. [23]Let us hold unswervingly to the hope we profess, for he who promised is faithful. [24]And let us

consider how we may spur one another on toward love and good deeds. ²⁵Let us not give up meeting together, as some are in the habit of doing, but let us encourage one another—and all the more as you see the Day approaching.

²⁶If we deliberately keep on sinning after we have received the knowledge of the truth, no sacrifice for sins is left, ²⁷but only a fearful expectation of judgment and of raging fire that will consume the enemies of God. ²⁸Anyone who rejected the law of Moses died without mercy on the testimony of two or three witnesses. ²⁹How much more severely do you think a man deserves to be punished who has trampled the Son of God under foot, who has treated as an unholy thing the blood of the covenant that sanctified him, and who has insulted the Spirit of grace? ³⁰For we know him who said, "It is mine to avenge; I will repay,"ᵒ and again, "The Lord will judge his people."ᵖ ³¹It is a dreadful thing to fall into the hands of the living God.

³²Remember those earlier days after you had received the light, when you stood your ground in a great contest in the face of suffering. ³³Sometimes you were publicly exposed to insult and persecution; at other times you stood side by side with those who were so treated. ³⁴You sympathized with those in prison and joyfully accepted the confiscation of your property, because you knew that you yourselves had better and lasting possessions.

³⁵So do not throw away your confidence; it will be richly rewarded. ³⁶You need to persevere so that when you have done the will of God, you will receive what he has promised. ³⁷For in just a very little while,

"He who is coming will come and will not delay.
³⁸   But my righteous one�q will live by faith.
And if he shrinks back,
    I will not be pleased with him."ʳ

³⁹But we are not of those who shrink back and are destroyed, but of those who believe and are saved.

ᵒ30 Deut. 32:35   ᵖ30 Deut. 32:36; Psalm 135:14   �q38 One early manuscript *But the righteous*   ʳ38 Hab. 2:3,4

DECEMBER 13 □ DAY 348
HEBREWS 11–13
Christ, Supreme Example of Faith

OVERVIEW The letter to the Hebrews closes with an appeal to leave behind the obsolete order of the old covenant and to approach God by the new and living way Jesus made possible through his death. Through steadfast hope and faith it is possible to have a firm assurance of those eternal truths that are invisible to the outward eye. Such forward-looking faith characterized the Old Testament saints who gained God's approval. They lived their lives on the basis of God's promises—promises whose fulfillment came centuries later—and it is their example and Christ's you are called to follow.

Chapter 11	Chapter 12	Chapter 13
Live by Faith	Run the Race	Keep on Loving
Examples	Children	Others

YOUR DAILY WALK In Cooperstown, New York, stands a monument to the great men who have excelled at the game of baseball. They are all there—Ruth . . . DiMaggio . . . Cobb—men who helped make base-

Live your life in such a way that it would not make sense if God did not exist. ball a household word, filling the Baseball Hall of Fame and providing encouragement for those who would seek to follow in their steps. If you have any doubts that it is humanly possible to hit sixty home runs in a year or bat safely in fifty-six consecutive games, you have only to visit Cooperstown to remove your doubts. It can be done. They did it!

Are you discouraged in your walk with God? Have you almost concluded that the Christian life is a hopeless assignment, that walking by faith in a godless society is impossible? Then spend some long moments in the Believers' Hall of Fame—Hebrews 11. There you'll find those who excelled at the life of faith: Enoch . . . Abraham . . . Joseph . . . and many others. If you have any doubts that it is spiritually possible to walk by faith, just study their lives!

Then join their ranks by writing a short paragraph about yourself as you'd want it to appear in Hebrews 11: "By faith [who?] walked with God by obediently [doing what?]."

INSIGHT Faith at Work in a Workaday World
Hebrews 11 describes the faith-inspired steps of a shepherd, prophet, shipbuilder, itinerant rancher and prince-turned-deliverer. Try to match up each profession with the right person.

CHAPTER 11

Now faith is being sure of what we hope for and certain of what we do not see. ²This is what the ancients were commended for.

³By faith we understand that the universe was formed at God's command, so that what is seen was not made out of what was visible.

⁴By faith Abel offered God a better sacrifice than Cain did. By faith he was commended as a righteous man, when God spoke well of his offerings. And by faith he still speaks, even though he is dead.

⁵By faith Enoch was taken from this life, so that he did not experience death; he could not be found, because God had taken him away. For before he was taken, he was commended as one who pleased God. ⁶And without faith it is impossible to please God, because anyone who comes to him must believe that he exists and that he rewards those who earnestly seek him.

⁷By faith Noah, when warned about things not yet seen, in holy fear built an ark to save his family. By his faith he condemned the world and became heir of the righteousness that comes by faith.

⁸By faith Abraham, when called to go to a place he would later receive as his inheritance, obeyed and went, even though he did not know where he was going. ⁹By faith he made his home in the promised land like a stranger in a foreign country;

he lived in tents, as did Isaac and Jacob, who were heirs with him of the same promise. ¹⁰For he was looking forward to the city with foundations, whose architect and builder is God.

¹¹By faith Abraham, even though he was past age—and Sarah herself was barren—was enabled to become a father because heˢ considered him faithful who had made the promise. ¹²And so from this one man, and he as good as dead, came descendants as numerous as the stars in the sky and as countless as the sand on the seashore.

¹³All these people were still living by faith when they died. They did not receive the things promised; they only saw them and welcomed them from a distance. And they admitted that they were aliens and strangers on earth. ¹⁴People who say such things show that they are looking for a country of their own. ¹⁵If they had been thinking of the country they had left, they would have had opportunity to return. ¹⁶Instead, they were longing for a better country—a heavenly one. Therefore God is not ashamed to be called their God, for he has prepared a city for them.

¹⁷By faith Abraham, when God tested him, offered Isaac as a sacrifice. He who had received the promises was about to sacrifice his one and only son, ¹⁸even though God had said to him, "It is through Isaac that your offspringᵗ will

---

ˢ11 Or *By faith even Sarah, who was past age, was enabled to bear children because she*   ᵗ18 Greek *seed* be reckoned."ᵘ ¹⁹Abraham reasoned that God could raise the dead, and figuratively speaking, he did receive Isaac back from death.

²⁰By faith Isaac blessed Jacob and Esau in regard to their future.

²¹By faith Jacob, when he was dying, blessed each of Joseph's sons, and worshiped as he leaned on the top of his staff.

²²By faith Joseph, when his end was near, spoke about the exodus of the Israelites from Egypt and gave instructions about his bones.

²³By faith Moses' parents hid him for three months after he was born, because they saw he was no ordinary child, and they were not afraid of the king's edict.

²⁴By faith Moses, when he had grown up, refused to be known as the son of Pharaoh's daughter. ²⁵He chose to be mistreated along with the people of God rather than to enjoy the pleasures of sin for a short time. ²⁶He regarded disgrace for the sake of Christ as of greater value than the treasures of Egypt, because he was looking ahead to his reward. ²⁷By faith he left Egypt, not fearing the king's anger; he persevered because he saw him who is invisible. ²⁸By faith he kept the Passover and the sprinkling of blood, so that the destroyer of the firstborn would not touch the firstborn of Israel.

²⁹By faith the people passed through the Red Seaᵛ as on dry land; but when the Egyptians tried to do so, they were drowned.

³⁰By faith the walls of Jericho fell, after the people had marched around them for seven days.

³¹By faith the prostitute Rahab, because she welcomed the spies, was not killed with those who were disobedient.ʷ

³²And what more shall I say? I do not have time to tell about Gideon, Barak, Samson, Jephthah, David, Samuel and the prophets, ³³who through faith conquered kingdoms, administered justice, and gained what was promised; who shut the mouths of lions, ³⁴quenched the fury of the flames, and escaped the edge of the sword; whose weakness was turned to strength; and who became powerful in battle and routed foreign armies. ³⁵Women received back their dead, raised to life again. Others were tortured and re-

fused to be released, so that they might gain a better resurrection. ³⁶Some faced jeers and flogging, while still others were chained and put in prison. ³⁷They were stonedˣ; they were sawed in two; they were put to death by the sword. They went about in sheepskins and goatskins, destitute, persecuted and mistreated— ³⁸the world was not worthy of them. They wandered in deserts and mountains, and in caves and holes in the ground.

³⁹These were all commended for their faith, yet none of them received what had been promised. ⁴⁰God had planned something better for us so that only together with us would they be made perfect.

CHAPTER 12

Therefore, since we are surrounded by such a great cloud of witnesses, let us throw off everything that hinders and the sin that so easily entangles, and let us run with perseverance the race marked out for us. ²Let us fix our eyes on Jesus, the author and perfecter of our faith, who for the joy set before him endured the cross, scorning its shame, and sat down at the right hand of the throne of God. ³Consider him who endured such opposition from sinful men, so that you will not grow weary and lose heart.

⁴In your struggle against sin, you have not yet resisted to the point of shedding your blood. ⁵And you have forgotten that word of encouragement that addresses you as sons:

"My son, do not make light of the
    Lord's discipline,
  and do not lose heart when he
    rebukes you,
⁶because the Lord disciplines those he
    loves,
  and he punishes everyone he accepts
    as a son."ʸ

⁷Endure hardship as discipline; God is treating you as sons. For what son is not disciplined by his father? ⁸If you are not disciplined (and everyone undergoes discipline), then you are illegitimate children and not true sons. ⁹Moreover, we have all had human fathers who disciplined us and we respected them for it. How much more should we submit to the Father of

ᵘ18 Gen. 21:12   ᵛ29 That is, Sea of Reeds   ʷ31 Or unbelieving
ʸ6 Prov. 3:11,12   ˣ37 Some early manuscripts stoned; they were put to the test;

our spirits and live! [10]Our fathers disciplined us for a little while as they thought best; but God disciplines us for our good, that we may share in his holiness. [11]No discipline seems pleasant at the time, but painful. Later on, however, it produces a harvest of righteousness and peace for those who have been trained by it.

[12]Therefore, strengthen your feeble arms and weak knees. [13]"Make level paths for your feet,"[z] so that the lame may not be disabled, but rather healed.

[14]Make every effort to live in peace with all men and to be holy; without holiness no one will see the Lord. [15]See to it that no one misses the grace of God and that no bitter root grows up to cause trouble and defile many. [16]See that no one is sexually immoral, or is godless like Esau, who for a single meal sold his inheritance rights as the oldest son. [17]Afterward, as you know, when he wanted to inherit this blessing, he was rejected. He could bring about no change of mind, though he sought the blessing with tears.

[18]You have not come to a mountain that can be touched and that is burning with fire; to darkness, gloom and storm; [19]to a trumpet blast or to such a voice speaking words that those who heard it begged that no further word be spoken to them, [20]because they could not bear what was commanded: "If even an animal touches the mountain, it must be stoned."[a] [21]The sight was so terrifying that Moses said, "I am trembling with fear."[b]

[22]But you have come to Mount Zion, to the heavenly Jerusalem, the city of the living God. You have come to thousands upon thousands of angels in joyful assembly, [23]to the church of the firstborn, whose names are written in heaven. You have come to God, the judge of all men, to the spirits of righteous men made perfect, [24]to Jesus the mediator of a new covenant, and to the sprinkled blood that speaks a better word than the blood of Abel.

[25]See to it that you do not refuse him who speaks. If they did not escape when they refused him who warned them on earth, how much less will we, if we turn away from him who warns us from heaven? [26]At that time his voice shook the earth, but now he has promised, "Once

more I will shake not only the earth but also the heavens."[c] [27]The words "once more" indicate the removing of what can be shaken—that is, created things—so that what cannot be shaken may remain.

[28]Therefore, since we are receiving a kingdom that cannot be shaken, let us be thankful, and so worship God acceptably with reverence and awe, [29]for our "God is a consuming fire."[d]

CHAPTER 13

Keep on loving each other as brothers. [2]Do not forget to entertain strangers, for by so doing some people have entertained angels without knowing it. [3]Remember those in prison as if you were their fellow prisoners, and those who are mistreated as if you yourselves were suffering.

[4]Marriage should be honored by all, and the marriage bed kept pure, for God will judge the adulterer and all the sexually immoral. [5]Keep your lives free from the love of money and be content with what you have, because God has said,

"Never will I leave you;
    never will I forsake you."[e]

[6]So we say with confidence,

"The Lord is my helper; I will not be
    afraid.
What can man do to me?"[f]

[7]Remember your leaders, who spoke the word of God to you. Consider the outcome of their way of life and imitate their faith. [8]Jesus Christ is the same yesterday and today and forever.

[9]Do not be carried away by all kinds of strange teachings. It is good for our hearts to be strengthened by grace, not by ceremonial foods, which are of no value to those who eat them. [10]We have an altar from which those who minister at the tabernacle have no right to eat.

[11]The high priest carries the blood of animals into the Most Holy Place as a sin offering, but the bodies are burned outside the camp. [12]And so Jesus also suffered outside the city gate to make the people holy through his own blood. [13]Let us, then, go to him outside the camp, bearing the disgrace he bore. [14]For here we do not have an enduring city, but we are looking for the city that is to come.

¹⁵Through Jesus, therefore, let us continually offer to God a sacrifice of praise—the fruit of lips that confess his name. ¹⁶And do not forget to do good and to share with others, for with such sacrifices God is pleased.

¹⁷Obey your leaders and submit to their authority. They keep watch over you as men who must give an account. Obey them so that their work will be a joy, not a burden, for that would be of no advantage to you.

¹⁸Pray for us. We are sure that we have a clear conscience and desire to live honorably in every way. ¹⁹I particularly urge you to pray so that I may be restored to you soon.

²⁰May the God of peace, who through the blood of the eternal covenant brought back from the dead our Lord Jesus, that great Shepherd of the sheep, ²¹equip you with everything good for doing his will, and may he work in us what is pleasing to him, through Jesus Christ, to whom be glory for ever and ever. Amen.

²²Brothers, I urge you to bear with my word of exhortation, for I have written you only a short letter.

²³I want you to know that our brother Timothy has been released. If he arrives soon, I will come with him to see you.

²⁴Greet all your leaders and all God's people. Those from Italy send you their greetings.

²⁵Grace be with you all.

DECEMBER 14 □ DAY 349
Enduring Faith

 LOOK BACK Though the authorship of Hebrews remains a mystery, the thrust of its message could not be clearer. Spiritual birth is only the beginning. It is imperative that Christians go on to maturity and develop a grown-up and growing relationship with Jesus Christ. Don't be tempted to return to your pre-Christian past, for the path of Jesus is better in every way. Jesus is better than the angels . . . better than Moses . . . better than Joshua . . . better than the prophets. He offers a better way . . . a better sacrifice . . . a better work . . . a better rest. And because of that, the author is "confident of better things" (6:9) for his readers as they press on to maturity in Christ.

The path is well trod by Old Testament martyrs and models, whose faith and perseverance can become a constant source of encouragement. In them we discover the liberating truth that "anyone who comes to him [God] must believe that he exists and that he rewards those who earnestly seek him" (11:6).

 LOOK UP What is the longest distance you have ever run without stopping? And how did you feel when the run was finally over?

Chances are, your answer was something less than a marathon (26.2 miles). And even if you have run a marathon sometime in your life, when it was over you probably had no desire to repeat the experience anytime soon!

Faith is the daring of the soul to go farther than it can see.

The Christian life would be a breeze if it were only a sprint—a hundred-yard dash of endurance, a quarter mile of patience, half a lap of steadfastness. Unfortunately, that's just not the case. The Christian life is more like a marathon. For Moses, it turned out to be a 120-year "hike" from Egypt to Midian, back to Egypt and on to Moab. For Noah, it involved a century-long shipbuilding project under God's watchful eye. For Abraham, it meant a wait of twenty-five years for a promised son. No sprint, to be sure, but an exercise in endurance. And it was their enduring faith over the long haul that provided these heroes of the Old Testament with an enduring testimony that continues right up to the present.

LOOK AHEAD When you think of models of enduring faith from your own generation, who comes to mind? Here are some suggestions of worthy candidates:

- a minister who has faithfully preached the gospel for forty years
- a couple who has stayed married and worked through their problems, rather than allowing those problems to drive them apart
- a missionary who has labored in a harvest field of the world for thirty years
- the Sunday school teacher who has faithfully taught class after class of fifth graders (including the fifth-grade children of those who once upon a time were his or her fifth graders!)

Why not honor their faithfulness today with a special phone call or note of appreciation? Their lives are living examples of Hebrews 12:1–2 in action. And it would no doubt make their day to know that you are following in their footsteps.

James

FAITH without works isn't really faith. It is dead, and a dead faith is worse than no faith at all. Faith must work; it must produce; it must be visible. Verbal faith is not enough; mental faith is insufficient. Faith must move into action. Throughout his epistle to Jewish believers, James integrates true faith and everyday practical experience by stressing that true faith "works" because it produces doers of the Word.

Focus	Tests of Faith							
Divisions	Trials and Temptations	Test of Attitude toward the Bible	Test of Social Distinctions	Test of Works	Test of Self-Control	Test of Reactions to World	Test of Prayer	
	1:1 1:18	1:19 1:27	2:1 2:13	2:14 2:26	3:1 3:18	4:1 5:12	5:13 5:20	
Topics	Wisdom		Works		Words	Walk	Wait	
	Faith Tested		Faith Displayed		Faith Proved	Faith Con-trasted	Faith Re-warded	
Place	Probably Jerusalem							
Time	A.D. 46–49							

DECEMBER 15 □ DAY 350
JAMES 1–5
Doers of the Word

OVERVIEW James recognizes there can be a dangerous false conclusion from the simple equation "salvation = faith + nothing." One may conclude, "As long as I have faith, it doesn't matter how I act." But James responds with ringing clarity that a faith that produces no change in attitude is really no faith at all. Partiality, neglect of the poor, quarreling, a bitter tongue, a proud attitude—all are inconsistent with the royal law of love that Christ proclaimed.

Chapter 1	Chapter 2	Chapter 3	Chapter 4	Chapter 5
Trials of Faith	Works of Faith	Words of Faith	Walk of Faith	Waiting Faith
"Do not merely listen to the word. . . . Do what it says" (1:22).				

More can be learned from life's trials than from its triumphs.

YOUR DAILY WALK In the Chinese picture-letter alphabet, the symbol for *crisis* is a combination of two characters—one meaning "danger" and the other "opportunity." You can look at it either way.

The same can be said of trials in the Christian life. A crisis that appears to one Christian as a calamity may be viewed by another as an opportunity. You can see your problems as purposeful and joyful if you see them from God's perspective. Tested faith produces patience (1:3), maturity (1:4) and God's rich reward (1:12).

As you read through the book of James, how would you catalog the various tests of faith you discover? Do you find some of the same crises you are presently facing?

Next to the ones on your list that look painfully familiar, put a check mark. Then ponder this question: If God intends these problems as *opportunities* for me to grow rather than *dangers* for me to fear, how can I cooperate with him to make the most of these faith-stretching trials? Then close your time with God by telling him what you intend to do about your new perspective on your problems.

INSIGHT Was James Eavesdropping on the Mount?
Four verses in the book of James correspond to passages from Jesus' famous Sermon on the Mount. Read Matthew 5:10–12, 34–37; 7:16–20, 24, 26. Can you find the four corresponding allusions in today's reading?

CHAPTER 1
James, a servant of God and of the Lord Jesus Christ,

To the twelve tribes scattered among the nations:

Greetings.

²Consider it pure joy, my brothers, whenever you face trials of many kinds,

³because you know that the testing of your faith develops perseverance. ⁴Perseverance must finish its work so that you may be mature and complete, not lacking anything. ⁵If any of you lacks wisdom, he should ask God, who gives generously to all without finding fault, and it will be given to him. ⁶But when he asks, he must believe and not doubt, because he who doubts is like a wave of the sea, blown

and tossed by the wind. [7]That man should not think he will receive anything from the Lord; [8]he is a double-minded man, unstable in all he does.

[9]The brother in humble circumstances ought to take pride in his high position. [10]But the one who is rich should take pride in his low position, because he will pass away like a wild flower. [11]For the sun rises with scorching heat and withers the plant; its blossom falls and its beauty is destroyed. In the same way, the rich man will fade away even while he goes about his business.

[12]Blessed is the man who perseveres under trial, because when he has stood the test, he will receive the crown of life that God has promised to those who love him.

[13]When tempted, no one should say, "God is tempting me." For God cannot be tempted by evil, nor does he tempt anyone; [14]but each one is tempted when, by his own evil desire, he is dragged away and enticed. [15]Then, after desire has conceived, it gives birth to sin; and sin, when it is full-grown, gives birth to death.

[16]Don't be deceived, my dear brothers. [17]Every good and perfect gift is from above, coming down from the Father of the heavenly lights, who does not change like shifting shadows. [18]He chose to give us birth through the word of truth, that we might be a kind of firstfruits of all he created.

[19]My dear brothers, take note of this: Everyone should be quick to listen, slow to speak and slow to become angry, [20]for man's anger does not bring about the righteous life that God desires. [21]Therefore, get rid of all moral filth and the evil that is so prevalent and humbly accept the word planted in you, which can save you.

[22]Do not merely listen to the word, and so deceive yourselves. Do what it says. [23]Anyone who listens to the word but does not do what it says is like a man who looks at his face in a mirror [24]and, after looking at himself, goes away and immediately forgets what he looks like. [25]But the man who looks intently into the perfect law that gives freedom, and continues to do this, not forgetting what he has heard, but doing it—he will be blessed in what he does.

[26]If anyone considers himself religious and yet does not keep a tight rein on his tongue, he deceives himself and his religion is worthless. [27]Religion that God our Father accepts as pure and faultless is this: to look after orphans and widows in their distress and to keep oneself from being polluted by the world.

CHAPTER 2

My brothers, as believers in our glorious Lord Jesus Christ, don't show favoritism. [2]Suppose a man comes into your meeting wearing a gold ring and fine clothes, and a poor man in shabby clothes also comes in. [3]If you show special attention to the man wearing fine clothes and say, "Here's a good seat for you," but say to the poor man, "You stand there" or "Sit on the floor by my feet," [4]have you not discriminated among yourselves and become judges with evil thoughts?

[5]Listen, my dear brothers: Has not God chosen those who are poor in the eyes of the world to be rich in faith and to inherit the kingdom he promised those who love him? [6]But you have insulted the poor. Is it not the rich who are exploiting you? Are they not the ones who are dragging you into court? [7]Are they not the ones who are slandering the noble name of him to whom you belong?

[8]If you really keep the royal law found in Scripture, "Love your neighbor as yourself,"[a] you are doing right. [9]But if you show favoritism, you sin and are convicted by the law as lawbreakers. [10]For whoever keeps the whole law and yet stumbles at just one point is guilty of breaking all of it. [11]For he who said, "Do not commit adultery,"[b] also said, "Do not murder."[c] If you do not commit adultery but do commit murder, you have become a lawbreaker.

[12]Speak and act as those who are going to be judged by the law that gives freedom, [13]because judgment without mercy will be shown to anyone who has not been merciful. Mercy triumphs over judgment!

[14]What good is it, my brothers, if a man claims to have faith but has no deeds? Can such faith save him? [15]Suppose a

[a]8 Lev. 19:18   [b]11 Exodus 20:14; Deut. 5:18   [c]11 Exodus 20:13; Deut. 5:17

brother or sister is without clothes and daily food. [16]If one of you says to him, "Go, I wish you well; keep warm and well fed," but does nothing about his physical needs, what good is it? [17]In the same way, faith by itself, if it is not accompanied by action, is dead.

[18]But someone will say, "You have faith; I have deeds."

Show me your faith without deeds, and I will show you my faith by what I do. [19]You believe that there is one God. Good! Even the demons believe that—and shudder.

[20]You foolish man, do you want evidence that faith without deeds is useless[d]? [21]Was not our ancestor Abraham considered righteous for what he did when he offered his son Isaac on the altar? [22]You see that his faith and his actions were working together, and his faith was made complete by what he did. [23]And the scripture was fulfilled that says, "Abraham believed God, and it was credited to him as righteousness,"[e] and he was called God's friend. [24]You see that a person is justified by what he does and not by faith alone.

[25]In the same way, was not even Rahab the prostitute considered righteous for what she did when she gave lodging to the spies and sent them off in a different direction? [26]As the body without the spirit is dead, so faith without deeds is dead.

CHAPTER 3

Not many of you should presume to be teachers, my brothers, because you know that we who teach will be judged more strictly. [2]We all stumble in many ways. If anyone is never at fault in what he says, he is a perfect man, able to keep his whole body in check.

[3]When we put bits into the mouths of horses to make them obey us, we can turn the whole animal. [4]Or take ships as an example. Although they are so large and are driven by strong winds, they are steered by a very small rudder wherever the pilot wants to go. [5]Likewise the tongue is a small part of the body, but it makes great boasts. Consider what a great forest is set on fire by a small spark. [6]The tongue also is a fire, a world of evil among the parts of the body. It corrupts

the whole person, sets the whole course of his life on fire, and is itself set on fire by hell.

[7]All kinds of animals, birds, reptiles and creatures of the sea are being tamed and have been tamed by man, [8]but no man can tame the tongue. It is a restless evil, full of deadly poison.

[9]With the tongue we praise our Lord and Father, and with it we curse men, who have been made in God's likeness. [10]Out of the same mouth come praise and cursing. My brothers, this should not be. [11]Can both fresh water and salt[f] water flow from the same spring? [12]My brothers, can a fig tree bear olives, or a grapevine bear figs? Neither can a salt spring produce fresh water.

[13]Who is wise and understanding among you? Let him show it by his good life, by deeds done in the humility that comes from wisdom. [14]But if you harbor bitter envy and selfish ambition in your hearts, do not boast about it or deny the truth. [15]Such "wisdom" does not come down from heaven but is earthly, unspiritual, of the devil. [16]For where you have envy and selfish ambition, there you find disorder and every evil practice.

[17]But the wisdom that comes from heaven is first of all pure; then peace-loving, considerate, submissive, full of mercy and good fruit, impartial and sincere. [18]Peacemakers who sow in peace raise a harvest of righteousness.

CHAPTER 4

What causes fights and quarrels among you? Don't they come from your desires that battle within you? [2]You want something but don't get it. You kill and covet, but you cannot have what you want. You quarrel and fight. You do not have, because you do not ask God. [3]When you ask, you do not receive, because you ask with wrong motives, that you may spend what you get on your pleasures.

[4]You adulterous people, don't you know that friendship with the world is hatred toward God? Anyone who chooses to be a friend of the world becomes an enemy of God. [5]Or do you think Scripture says without reason that the spirit he caused to live in us envies intensely?[g]

---

[d]20 Some early manuscripts *dead*   [e]23 Gen. 15:6   [f]11 Greek *bitter* (see also verse 14)   [g]5 Or *that God jealously longs for the spirit that he made to live in us; or that the Spirit he caused to live in us longs jealously*

[6]But he gives us more grace. That is why Scripture says:

"God opposes the proud
    but gives grace to the humble."[h]

[7]Submit yourselves, then, to God. Resist the devil, and he will flee from you. [8]Come near to God and he will come near to you. Wash your hands, you sinners, and purify your hearts, you double-minded. [9]Grieve, mourn and wail. Change your laughter to mourning and your joy to gloom. [10]Humble yourselves before the Lord, and he will lift you up.

[11]Brothers, do not slander one another. Anyone who speaks against his brother or judges him speaks against the law and judges it. When you judge the law, you are not keeping it, but sitting in judgment on it. [12]There is only one Lawgiver and Judge, the one who is able to save and destroy. But you—who are you to judge your neighbor?

[13]Now listen, you who say, "Today or tomorrow we will go to this or that city, spend a year there, carry on business and make money." [14]Why, you do not even know what will happen tomorrow. What is your life? You are a mist that appears for a little while and then vanishes. [15]Instead, you ought to say, "If it is the Lord's will, we will live and do this or that." [16]As it is, you boast and brag. All such boasting is evil. [17]Anyone, then, who knows the good he ought to do and doesn't do it, sins.

CHAPTER 5

Now listen, you rich people, weep and wail because of the misery that is coming upon you. [2]Your wealth has rotted, and moths have eaten your clothes. [3]Your gold and silver are corroded. Their corrosion will testify against you and eat your flesh like fire. You have hoarded wealth in the last days. [4]Look! The wages you failed to pay the workmen who mowed your fields are crying out against you. The cries of the harvesters have reached the ears of the Lord Almighty. [5]You have lived on earth in luxury and self-indulgence. You have fattened yourselves in the day of slaughter.[i] [6]You have condemned and murdered innocent men, who were not opposing you.

[7]Be patient, then, brothers, until the Lord's coming. See how the farmer waits for the land to yield its valuable crop and how patient he is for the autumn and spring rains. [8]You too, be patient and stand firm, because the Lord's coming is near. [9]Don't grumble against each other, brothers, or you will be judged. The Judge is standing at the door!

[10]Brothers, as an example of patience in the face of suffering, take the prophets who spoke in the name of the Lord. [11]As you know, we consider blessed those who have persevered. You have heard of Job's perseverance and have seen what the Lord finally brought about. The Lord is full of compassion and mercy.

[12]Above all, my brothers, do not swear—not by heaven or by earth or by anything else. Let your "Yes" be yes, and your "No," no, or you will be condemned.

[13]Is any one of you in trouble? He should pray. Is anyone happy? Let him sing songs of praise. [14]Is any one of you sick? He should call the elders of the church to pray over him and anoint him with oil in the name of the Lord. [15]And the prayer offered in faith will make the sick person well; the Lord will raise him up. If he has sinned, he will be forgiven. [16]Therefore confess your sins to each other and pray for each other so that you may be healed. The prayer of a righteous man is powerful and effective.

[17]Elijah was a man just like us. He prayed earnestly that it would not rain, and it did not rain on the land for three and a half years. [18]Again he prayed, and the heavens gave rain, and the earth produced its crops.

[19]My brothers, if one of you should wander from the truth and someone should bring him back, [20]remember this: Whoever turns a sinner from the error of his way will save him from death and cover over a multitude of sins.

[h]6 Prov. 3:34   [i]5 Or yourselves as in a day of feasting

1 Peter

THE APOSTLE PETER writes to scattered Jewish Christians, who are undergoing intense persecution for their faith. He reminds his readers that God has given them the privilege of being born again. Therefore, they shouldn't be surprised when suffering comes their way; they should expect it, prepare for it and respond to it correctly. He also encourages them to imitate Christ through a submissive spirit toward one another. If they do, God will richly reward them when the trials of life are over.

Focus	Christian Salvation		Christian Relationships				Christian Suffering			Christian Discipline	
Divisions	Salvation	Sanctification	World	State	Home	Church	Blessings	Example	Encouragement	Church	Individual
	1:1 1:12	1:13 2:10	2:11 2:12	2:13 2:17	2:18 3:7	3:8 3:12	3:13 3:17	3:18 3:22	4:1 4:19	5:1 5:6	5:7 5:14
Topics	New Birth		New Building				Necessary Bulwark				
	Salvation		Submission				Suffering				
Place	Rome or Babylon										
Time	Approximately A.D. 63–64										

DECEMBER 16 □ DAY 351
1 PETER 1–5
Courage in Suffering

OVERVIEW Persecution can cause you either to grow or to grumble in the Christian life. It all depends on your response! In writing to Jewish believers struggling in the midst of persecution, Peter reminds them of their "roots." They have been born again to a living hope, and therefore both their character and conduct should be above reproach as they imitate the Holy One who called them. Since they are God's special people, their lives should be marked by submission to others, producing law-abiding citizens, obedient employees, submissive wives and understanding husbands.

Chapter 1	Chapters 2–3	Chapters 4–5
Called to Salvation	Called to Submission	Called to Suffering
Belief	Behavior	Buffeting

Getting into hot water occasionally has a way of keeping a person clean.

YOUR DAILY WALK The book of 1 Peter might well be titled "A Survival Manual for Suffering Saints." It presents God's time-tested strategy for holding up, rather than folding up, in the midst of difficulties.

If you want to get in shape physically, there are some helpful steps you can take: Eat properly, get adequate sleep, take a multi-vitamin capsule every day. But in the final analysis, there is no substitute for exercise—working against a resistance. The same is true in the Christian life. Proper nourishment from the Word is essential, but so is "exercise"—in God's strength, facing and conquering trials and difficulties. God—the perfect Coach—knows exactly what kind of "workout" you need in order to turn an area of weakness into an area of Christlikeness.

Before you go to bed this evening, write out the words of 1 Peter 1:7, and place them in one of the shoes you'll wear tomorrow. When you awake, let that note remind you that God wants to "tone up" your faith today—and trials may well be part of the workout!

INSIGHT The All-Important Cornerstone
Peter makes an obvious allusion to Christ when he quotes Isaiah 28:16: "See, I lay a stone in Zion, a chosen and precious cornerstone" (2:6). In biblical times a stone was put where two walls met. More than just a foundation, the cornerstone helped align the building horizontally and vertically and held it together. Thus, Christ is the all-important one on whom we, as "living stones," are built into a spiritual house.

CHAPTER 1

Peter, an apostle of Jesus Christ,

To God's elect, strangers in the world, scattered throughout Pontus, Galatia, Cappadocia, Asia and Bithynia, ²who have been chosen according to the foreknowledge of God the Father, through the sanctifying work of the Spirit, for obedience to Jesus Christ and sprinkling by his blood:

Grace and peace be yours in abundance.

[3]Praise be to the God and Father of our Lord Jesus Christ! In his great mercy he has given us new birth into a living hope through the resurrection of Jesus Christ from the dead, [4]and into an inheritance that can never perish, spoil or fade—kept in heaven for you, [5]who through faith are shielded by God's power until the coming of the salvation that is ready to be revealed in the last time. [6]In this you greatly rejoice, though now for a little while you may have had to suffer grief in all kinds of trials. [7]These have come so that your faith—of greater worth than gold, which perishes even though refined by fire—may be proved genuine and may result in praise, glory and honor when Jesus Christ is revealed. [8]Though you have not seen him, you love him; and even though you do not see him now, you believe in him and are filled with an inexpressible and glorious joy, [9]for you are receiving the goal of your faith, the salvation of your souls.

[10]Concerning this salvation, the prophets, who spoke of the grace that was to come to you, searched intently and with the greatest care, [11]trying to find out the time and circumstances to which the Spirit of Christ in them was pointing when he predicted the sufferings of Christ and the glories that would follow. [12]It was revealed to them that they were not serving themselves but you, when they spoke of the things that have now been told you by those who have preached the gospel to you by the Holy Spirit sent from heaven. Even angels long to look into these things.

[13]Therefore, prepare your minds for action; be self-controlled; set your hope fully on the grace to be given you when Jesus Christ is revealed. [14]As obedient children, do not conform to the evil desires you had when you lived in ignorance. [15]But just as he who called you is holy, so be holy in all you do; [16]for it is written: "Be holy, because I am holy."[a]

[17]Since you call on a Father who judges each man's work impartially, live your lives as strangers here in reverent fear. [18]For you know that it was not with perishable things such as silver or gold that you were redeemed from the empty way of life handed down to you from your forefathers, [19]but with the precious blood of Christ, a lamb without blemish or defect. [20]He was chosen before the creation of the world, but was revealed in these last times for your sake. [21]Through him you believe in God, who raised him from the dead and glorified him, and so your faith and hope are in God.

[22]Now that you have purified yourselves by obeying the truth so that you have sincere love for your brothers, love one another deeply, from the heart.[b] [23]For you have been born again, not of perishable seed, but of imperishable, through the living and enduring word of God. [24]For,

"All men are like grass,
    and all their glory is like the flowers
        of the field;
the grass withers and the flowers fall,
[25]   but the word of the Lord stands
        forever."[c]

And this is the word that was preached to you.

CHAPTER 2

Therefore, rid yourselves of all malice and all deceit, hypocrisy, envy, and slander of every kind. [2]Like newborn babies, crave pure spiritual milk, so that by it you may grow up in your salvation, [3]now that you have tasted that the Lord is good.

[4]As you come to him, the living Stone—rejected by men but chosen by God and precious to him— [5]you also, like living stones, are being built into a spiritual house to be a holy priesthood, offering spiritual sacrifices acceptable to God through Jesus Christ. [6]For in Scripture it says:

"See, I lay a stone in Zion,
    a chosen and precious cornerstone,
and the one who trusts in him
    will never be put to shame."[d]

[7]Now to you who believe, this stone is precious. But to those who do not believe,

"The stone the builders rejected
    has become the capstone,[e]"[f]

[8]and,

[a]16 Lev. 11:44,45; 19:2; 20:7   [b]22 Some early manuscripts *from a pure heart*   [c]25 Isaiah 40:6-8   [d]6 Isaiah 28:16
[e]7 Or *cornerstone*   [f]7 Psalm 118:22

"A stone that causes men to stumble
and a rock that makes them fall."⁸

They stumble because they disobey the message—which is also what they were destined for.

⁹But you are a chosen people, a royal priesthood, a holy nation, a people belonging to God, that you may declare the praises of him who called you out of darkness into his wonderful light. ¹⁰Once you were not a people, but now you are the people of God; once you had not received mercy, but now you have received mercy.

¹¹Dear friends, I urge you, as aliens and strangers in the world, to abstain from sinful desires, which war against your soul. ¹²Live such good lives among the pagans that, though they accuse you of doing wrong, they may see your good deeds and glorify God on the day he visits us.

¹³Submit yourselves for the Lord's sake to every authority instituted among men: whether to the king, as the supreme authority, ¹⁴or to governors, who are sent by him to punish those who do wrong and to commend those who do right. ¹⁵For it is God's will that by doing good you should silence the ignorant talk of foolish men. ¹⁶Live as free men, but do not use your freedom as a cover-up for evil; live as servants of God. ¹⁷Show proper respect to everyone: Love the brotherhood of believers, fear God, honor the king.

¹⁸Slaves, submit yourselves to your masters with all respect, not only to those who are good and considerate, but also to those who are harsh. ¹⁹For it is commendable if a man bears up under the pain of unjust suffering because he is conscious of God. ²⁰But how is it to your credit if you receive a beating for doing wrong and endure it? But if you suffer for doing good and you endure it, this is commendable before God. ²¹To this you were called, because Christ suffered for you, leaving you an example, that you should follow in his steps.

²²"He committed no sin,
and no deceit was found in his
mouth."ʰ

²³When they hurled their insults at him, he did not retaliate; when he suffered, he made no threats. Instead, he entrusted himself to him who judges justly. ²⁴He himself bore our sins in his body on the tree, so that we might die to sins and live for righteousness; by his wounds you have been healed. ²⁵For you were like sheep going astray, but now you have returned to the Shepherd and Overseer of your souls.

CHAPTER 3

Wives, in the same way be submissive to your husbands so that, if any of them do not believe the word, they may be won over without words by the behavior of their wives, ²when they see the purity and reverence of your lives. ³Your beauty should not come from outward adornment, such as braided hair and the wearing of gold jewelry and fine clothes. ⁴Instead, it should be that of your inner self, the unfading beauty of a gentle and quiet spirit, which is of great worth in God's sight. ⁵For this is the way the holy women of the past who put their hope in God used to make themselves beautiful. They were submissive to their own husbands, ⁶like Sarah, who obeyed Abraham and called him her master. You are her daughters if you do what is right and do not give way to fear.

⁷Husbands, in the same way be considerate as you live with your wives, and treat them with respect as the weaker partner and as heirs with you of the gracious gift of life, so that nothing will hinder your prayers.

⁸Finally, all of you, live in harmony with one another; be sympathetic, love as brothers, be compassionate and humble. ⁹Do not repay evil with evil or insult with insult, but with blessing, because to this you were called so that you may inherit a blessing. ¹⁰For,

"Whoever would love life
and see good days
must keep his tongue from evil
and his lips from deceitful speech.
¹¹He must turn from evil and do good;
he must seek peace and pursue it.
¹²For the eyes of the Lord are on the
righteous
and his ears are attentive to their
prayer,

⁸8 Isaiah 8:14   ʰ22 Isaiah 53:9

but the face of the Lord is against
those who do evil."[i]

[13]Who is going to harm you if you are eager to do good? [14]But even if you should suffer for what is right, you are blessed. "Do not fear what they fear[j]; do not be frightened."[k] [15]But in your hearts set apart Christ as Lord. Always be prepared to give an answer to everyone who asks you to give the reason for the hope that you have. But do this with gentleness and respect, [16]keeping a clear conscience, so that those who speak maliciously against your good behavior in Christ may be ashamed of their slander. [17]It is better, if it is God's will, to suffer for doing good than for doing evil. [18]For Christ died for sins once for all, the righteous for the unrighteous, to bring you to God. He was put to death in the body but made alive by the Spirit, [19]through whom[l] also he went and preached to the spirits in prison [20]who disobeyed long ago when God waited patiently in the days of Noah while the ark was being built. In it only a few people, eight in all, were saved through water, [21]and this water symbolizes baptism that now saves you also—not the removal of dirt from the body but the pledge[m] of a good conscience toward God. It saves you by the resurrection of Jesus Christ, [22]who has gone into heaven and is at God's right hand—with angels, authorities and powers in submission to him.

CHAPTER 4

Therefore, since Christ suffered in his body, arm yourselves also with the same attitude, because he who has suffered in his body is done with sin. [2]As a result, he does not live the rest of his earthly life for evil human desires, but rather for the will of God. [3]For you have spent enough time in the past doing what pagans choose to do—living in debauchery, lust, drunkenness, orgies, carousing and detestable idolatry. [4]They think it strange that you do not plunge with them into the same flood of dissipation, and they heap abuse on you. [5]But they will have to give account to him who is ready to judge the living and the dead. [6]For this is the reason

the gospel was preached even to those who are now dead, so that they might be judged according to men in regard to the body, but live according to God in regard to the spirit.

[7]The end of all things is near. Therefore be clear minded and self-controlled so that you can pray. [8]Above all, love each other deeply, because love covers over a multitude of sins. [9]Offer hospitality to one another without grumbling. [10]Each one should use whatever gift he has received to serve others, faithfully administering God's grace in its various forms. [11]If anyone speaks, he should do it as one speaking the very words of God. If anyone serves, he should do it with the strength God provides, so that in all things God may be praised through Jesus Christ. To him be the glory and the power for ever and ever. Amen.

[12]Dear friends, do not be surprised at the painful trial you are suffering, as though something strange were happening to you. [13]But rejoice that you participate in the sufferings of Christ, so that you may be overjoyed when his glory is revealed. [14]If you are insulted because of the name of Christ, you are blessed, for the Spirit of glory and of God rests on you. [15]If you suffer, it should not be as a murderer or thief or any other kind of criminal, or even as a meddler. [16]However, if you suffer as a Christian, do not be ashamed, but praise God that you bear that name. [17]For it is time for judgment to begin with the family of God; and if it begins with us, what will the outcome be for those who do not obey the gospel of God? [18]And,

"If it is hard for the righteous to be
　　saved,
　what will become of the ungodly
　　and the sinner?"[n]

[19]So then, those who suffer according to God's will should commit themselves to their faithful Creator and continue to do good.

CHAPTER 5

To the elders among you, I appeal as a fellow elder, a witness of Christ's sufferings and one who also will share in the glory to be revealed: [2]Be

---

[i]12 Psalm 34:12-16　　[j]14 Or not fear their threats　　[k]14 Isaiah 8:12　　[l]18,19 Or alive in the spirit, [19]through which
[m]21 Or response　　[n]18 Prov. 11:31

shepherds of God's flock that is under your care, serving as overseers—not because you must, but because you are willing, as God wants you to be; not greedy for money, but eager to serve; ³not lording it over those entrusted to you, but being examples to the flock. ⁴And when the Chief Shepherd appears, you will receive the crown of glory that will never fade away.

⁵Young men, in the same way be submissive to those who are older. All of you, clothe yourselves with humility toward one another, because,

> "God opposes the proud
> but gives grace to the humble."ᵒ

⁶Humble yourselves, therefore, under God's mighty hand, that he may lift you up in due time. ⁷Cast all your anxiety on him because he cares for you.

⁸Be self-controlled and alert. Your enemy the devil prowls around like a roaring lion looking for someone to devour. ⁹Resist him, standing firm in the faith, because you know that your brothers throughout the world are undergoing the same kind of sufferings.

¹⁰And the God of all grace, who called you to his eternal glory in Christ, after you have suffered a little while, will himself restore you and make you strong, firm and steadfast. ¹¹To him be the power for ever and ever. Amen.

¹²With the help of Silas,ᵖ whom I regard as a faithful brother, I have written to you briefly, encouraging you and testifying that this is the true grace of God. Stand fast in it.

¹³She who is in Babylon, chosen together with you, sends you her greetings, and so does my son Mark. ¹⁴Greet one another with a kiss of love.

Peace to all of you who are in Christ.

ᵒ5 Prov. 3:34   ᵖ12 Greek *Silvanus*, a variant of *Silas*

2 Peter

IN HIS first letter Peter taught his readers to endure external enemies with hope; 2 Peter teaches the same audience to oppose internal enemies with knowledge of the truth. Apostasy within the church can be much more devastating than persecution against the church. Peter warns against the moral perversions and denial of Christ's return that false teachers propagate, then exhorts his readers to resist errors by growing in grace and knowledge. Knowledge is the prominent theme of this letter and the best antidote for heresies.

Focus	True Knowledge			False Knowledge			Challenge		
Divisions	Salutation	Growth in Knowledge	Source of Knowledge	Fear of False Teachers	Fate of False Teachers	Facts about False Teachers	Denial of Return	Truth of Return	Application of Return
	1:1 1:2	1:3 1:11	1:12 1:21	2:1 2:3	2:4 2:9	2:10 2:22	3:1 3:7	3:8 3:10	3:11 3:18
Topics	Growing in Grace			Growing in Knowledge			Growing in Expectation		
	"Grow Up!"			"Watch Out!"			"Look Up!"		
Place	Probably Rome								
Time	Approximately A.D. 64–66								

DECEMBER 17 ☐ DAY 352
2 PETER 1–3
Poison in the Pew

OVERVIEW Peter's second letter warns against the heretical teachers who are making inroads in the church by preaching false doctrine and practicing immorality. To refute these "peddlers of poison," Peter affirms the true knowledge of the Christian faith. Those who are growing in their knowledge and love of God will not fall prey to doctrinal error. But woe to those who attempt to introduce such destructive ways! Their punishment will be swift and severe, like that of Sodom and Gomorrah. What is the Christian's responsibility in the face of such danger? "Be on your guard" (3:17).

Chapter 1	Chapter 2	Chapter 3
Faith Considered	Faith Contradicted	Faith Consummated
"Add to It!"	"Guard It!"	"Watch for It!"

There is a world of difference between activity and progress.

YOUR DAILY WALK How are your mathematical skills? If the third of your three R's—reading, (w)riting and (a)rithmetic—has grown a little dusty from lack of use, 2 Peter 1 will give you a chance to dust it off. In the space of that single chapter you'll discover . . .

• *Multiplication* ("Grace and peace be yours in abundance," v. 2)
• *Addition* ("Add to your faith goodness," v. 5)
• *Subtraction* ("He has been cleansed from his past sins," v. 9)

Peter reminds you that the Christian life is largely a matter of addition. Verses 5–7 list seven characteristics that God wants you to add to your life, building upon the foundation of your faith in Jesus Christ. Why? Because growth in grace is the surest way to avoid error and prepare for the Lord's return.

It's not enough to ask for godly character (like the person who prayed, "God, give me patience, and give it to me NOW!"). Rather, it demands daily attention in your Christian life. Pick a virtue from Peter's list, and add one activity to your "Must Do" list for today that will help you cultivate that Christlike quality.

INSIGHT Last Letters from Peter and Paul

Second Peter is the "swan song" of Peter, just as 2 Timothy is that of Paul. Both warn of apostasy, both speak in a joyful manner of approaching death, and both anchor the church to the immovable rock of Scripture as the only sure defense against false doctrine.

CHAPTER 1

Simon Peter, a servant and apostle of Jesus Christ,

To those who through the righteousness of our God and Savior Jesus Christ have received a faith as precious as ours:

²Grace and peace be yours in abundance through the knowledge of God and of Jesus our Lord.

³His divine power has given us everything we need for life and godliness through our knowledge of him who called us by his own glory and goodness.

⁴Through these he has given us his very great and precious promises, so that through them you may participate in the divine nature and escape the corruption in the world caused by evil desires.

⁵For this very reason, make every effort to add to your faith goodness; and to goodness, knowledge; ⁶and to knowledge, self-control; and to self-control, perseverance; and to perseverance, godliness; ⁷and to godliness, brotherly kindness; and to brotherly kindness, love. ⁸For if you possess these qualities in increasing measure, they will keep you from being ineffective and unproductive in your knowledge of our Lord Jesus Christ. ⁹But if anyone does not have them, he is nearsighted and blind, and has forgotten that he has been cleansed from his past sins.

¹⁰Therefore, my brothers, be all the more eager to make your calling and election sure. For if you do these things, you will never fall, ¹¹and you will receive a rich welcome into the eternal kingdom of our Lord and Savior Jesus Christ.

¹²So I will always remind you of these things, even though you know them and are firmly established in the truth you now have. ¹³I think it is right to refresh your memory as long as I live in the tent of this body, ¹⁴because I know that I will soon put it aside, as our Lord Jesus Christ has made clear to me. ¹⁵And I will make every effort to see that after my departure you will always be able to remember these things.

¹⁶We did not follow cleverly invented stories when we told you about the power and coming of our Lord Jesus Christ, but we were eyewitnesses of his majesty. ¹⁷For he received honor and glory from God the Father when the voice came to him from the Majestic Glory, saying, "This is my Son, whom I love; with him I am well pleased."ᵃ ¹⁸We ourselves heard this voice that came from heaven when we were with him on the sacred mountain.

¹⁹And we have the word of the prophets made more certain, and you will do well to pay attention to it, as to a light shining in a dark place, until the day dawns and the morning star rises in your hearts. ²⁰Above all, you must understand that no prophecy of Scripture came about by the prophet's own interpretation. ²¹For

prophecy never had its origin in the will of man, but men spoke from God as they were carried along by the Holy Spirit.

CHAPTER 2

But there were also false prophets among the people, just as there will be false teachers among you. They will secretly introduce destructive heresies, even denying the sovereign Lord who bought them—bringing swift destruction on themselves. ²Many will follow their shameful ways and will bring the way of truth into disrepute. ³In their greed these teachers will exploit you with stories they have made up. Their condemnation has long been hanging over them, and their destruction has not been sleeping.

⁴For if God did not spare angels when they sinned, but sent them to hell,ᵇ putting them into gloomy dungeonsᶜ to be held for judgment; ⁵if he did not spare the ancient world when he brought the flood on its ungodly people, but protected Noah, a preacher of righteousness, and seven others; ⁶if he condemned the cities of Sodom and Gomorrah by burning them to ashes, and made them an example of what is going to happen to the ungodly; ⁷and if he rescued Lot, a righteous man, who was distressed by the filthy lives of lawless men ⁸(for that righteous man, living among them day after day, was tormented in his righteous soul by the lawless deeds he saw and heard)— ⁹if this is so, then the Lord knows how to rescue godly men from trials and to hold the unrighteous for the day of judgment, while continuing their punishment.ᵈ ¹⁰This is especially true of those who follow the corrupt desire of the sinful natureᵉ and despise authority.

Bold and arrogant, these men are not afraid to slander celestial beings; ¹¹yet even angels, although they are stronger and more powerful, do not bring slanderous accusations against such beings in the presence of the Lord. ¹²But these men blaspheme in matters they do not understand. They are like brute beasts, creatures of instinct, born only to be caught and destroyed, and like beasts they too will perish.

¹³They will be paid back with harm for the harm they have done. Their idea of

---

ᵃ17 Matt. 17:5; Mark 9:7; Luke 9:35   ᵇ4 Greek *Tartarus*   ᶜ4 Some manuscripts *into chains of darkness*   ᵈ9 Or *unrighteous for punishment until the day of judgment*   ᵉ10 Or *the flesh* pleasure is to carouse in broad daylight. They are blots and blemishes, reveling in their pleasures while they feast with you./ ¹⁴With eyes full of adultery, they never stop sinning; they seduce the unstable; they are experts in greed—an accursed brood! ¹⁵They have left the straight way and wandered off to follow the way of Balaam son of Beor, who loved the wages of wickedness. ¹⁶But he was rebuked for his wrongdoing by a donkey—a beast without speech—who spoke with a man's voice and restrained the prophet's madness.

¹⁷These men are springs without water and mists driven by a storm. Blackest darkness is reserved for them. ¹⁸For they mouth empty, boastful words and, by appealing to the lustful desires of sinful human nature, they entice people who are just escaping from those who live in error. ¹⁹They promise them freedom, while they themselves are slaves of depravity—for a man is a slave to whatever has mastered him. ²⁰If they have escaped the corruption of the world by knowing our Lord and Savior Jesus Christ and are again entangled in it and overcome, they are worse off at the end than they were at the beginning. ²¹It would have been better for them not to have known the way of righteousness, than to have known it and then to turn their backs on the sacred command that was passed on to them. ²²Of them the proverbs are true: "A dog returns to its vomit,"⁸ and, "A sow that is washed goes back to her wallowing in the mud."

CHAPTER 3

Dear friends, this is now my second letter to you. I have written both of them as reminders to stimulate you to wholesome thinking. ²I want you to recall the words spoken in the past by the holy prophets and the command given by our Lord and Savior through your apostles.

³First of all, you must understand that in the last days scoffers will come, scoffing and following their own evil desires. ⁴They will say, "Where is this 'coming' he promised? Ever since our fathers died, everything goes on as it has since the beginning of creation." ⁵But they deliberately forget that long ago by God's word

the heavens existed and the earth was formed out of water and by water. ⁶By these waters also the world of that time was deluged and destroyed. ⁷By the same word the present heavens and earth are reserved for fire, being kept for the day of judgment and destruction of ungodly men.

⁸But do not forget this one thing, dear friends: With the Lord a day is like a thousand years, and a thousand years are like a day. ⁹The Lord is not slow in keeping his promise, as some understand slowness. He is patient with you, not wanting anyone to perish, but everyone to come to repentance.

¹⁰But the day of the Lord will come like a thief. The heavens will disappear with a roar; the elements will be destroyed by fire, and the earth and everything in it will be laid bare.ʰ

¹¹Since everything will be destroyed in this way, what kind of people ought you to be? You ought to live holy and godly lives ¹²as you look forward to the day of God and speed its coming.ⁱ That day will bring about the destruction of the heavens by fire, and the elements will melt in the heat. ¹³But in keeping with his promise we are looking forward to a new heaven and a new earth, the home of righteousness.

¹⁴So then, dear friends, since you are looking forward to this, make every effort to be found spotless, blameless and at peace with him. ¹⁵Bear in mind that our Lord's patience means salvation, just as our dear brother Paul also wrote you with the wisdom that God gave him. ¹⁶He writes the same way in all his letters, speaking in them of these matters. His letters contain some things that are hard to understand, which ignorant and unstable people distort, as they do the other Scriptures, to their own destruction.

¹⁷Therefore, dear friends, since you already know this, be on your guard so that you may not be carried away by the error of lawless men and fall from your secure position. ¹⁸But grow in the grace and knowledge of our Lord and Savior Jesus Christ. To him be glory both now and forever! Amen.

/13 Some manuscripts in their love feasts   ⁸22 Prov. 26:11   ʰ10 Some manuscripts be burned up   ⁱ12 Or as you wait eagerly for the day of God to come

1 John

JOHN, "the disciple whom Jesus loved," had long known and enjoyed fellowship with the Lord. He writes 1 John to help his spiritual brothers and sisters in their walk with the God who is light, love and life. He wants them to be grounded in the assurance of their salvation, experiencing victory over sin and the full joys of the Christian life. He reminds them that all these gems can be dimmed by false teaching and that belief should be based on the facts about Christ's incarnation and accompanied by the responsibility to walk like Christ.

Focus	Assurance through Fellowship		Assurance through Conflict			Assurance through Love		Assurance through the Spirit	
Divisions	Basis of Fellowship	Obedience of Fellowship	Truth vs. Error	Purity vs. Impurity	Fact vs. Falsehood	God's Love	Our Love	External Witness	Internal Witness
	1:1 2:2	2:3 2:17	2:18 2:28	2:29 3:24	4:1 4:6	4:7 4:16	4:17 5:5	5:6 5:9	5:10 5:21
Topics	Walking		Warring			Wooing		Witnessing	
	Abiding in Christ		Abiding in Truth			Abiding in Love		Abiding Assurance	
Place	Ephesus								
Time	Approximately A.D. 90								

DECEMBER 18 □ DAY 353
1 JOHN 1–5
Fellowship Barometer

OVERVIEW John, the beloved apostle with a pastor's heart, writes to his "dear children" (2:1, 18, 28; 3:7, 18; 5:21) and "dear friends" in the faith (3:2, 21; 4:1, 7, 11). His letter has at least five stated purposes: to promote fellowship (1:3), to produce joy (1:4), to protect holiness (2:1), to prevent heresy (2:26) and to provide hope (5:13). Fellowship with God is not a vague, nebulous experience. It can be an objective, daily reality. John sets forth three tests that can act as a "fellowship barometer" for his spiritual children in their walk with God: (1) Have I confessed all known sins to God (1:9)? (2) Am I walking in obedience to the light of God's Word (2:4–5)? (3) Am I demonstrating a love for the brethren (2:9–10)?

Chapter 1	Chapters 2–3	Chapters 4–5
Requirement for Fellowship	Pattern for Fellowship	Proof of Fellowship
Confession	Christ	Conduct

The Son of God became the Son of Man so that sons of men might become sons of God.

YOUR DAILY WALK Here is a reminder you could probably do without: Christmas is less than a week away! No doubt you have pondered and puzzled over *who* should get *what* as you celebrate the birth of the Savior. Here is a gift-giving suggestion you may have overlooked: Why not offer an unsaved friend or family member the gift of eternal life?

At perhaps no other time during the year will your loved ones' thoughts turn more readily to spiritual things than at Christmas. Perhaps all that is keeping them from coming to faith in Jesus Christ is a clear, convincing presentation of who he is and why he came to earth—a presentation you could share via a letter . . . over the phone . . . or just sitting around the Christmas tree. Begin to pray right now that Christmas Day will mark more than the birth of the Savior; pray that it will mark the spiritual birth of someone you love.

INSIGHT Contrasting John's Gospel with His First Epistle

The Gospel of John
• Written to spark belief (20:31)
• Emphasizes miracles
• Historical
• Addressed to "whoever" (3:16)

The Epistle of 1 John
• Written to promote joy (1:4)
• Emphasizes love
• Experiential
• Addressed to "my dear children" (2:1, 18, 28)

CHAPTER 1

That which was from the beginning, which we have heard, which we have seen with our eyes, which we have looked at and our hands have touched—this we proclaim concerning the Word of life.

²The life appeared; we have seen it and testify to it, and we proclaim to you the eternal life, which was with the Father and has appeared to us. ³We proclaim to you what we have seen and heard, so that you also may have fellowship with us.

And our fellowship is with the Father and with his Son, Jesus Christ. [4]We write this to make our[a] joy complete.

[5]This is the message we have heard from him and declare to you: God is light; in him there is no darkness at all. [6]If we claim to have fellowship with him yet walk in the darkness, we lie and do not live by the truth. [7]But if we walk in the light, as he is in the light, we have fellowship with one another, and the blood of Jesus, his Son, purifies us from all[b] sin.

[8]If we claim to be without sin, we deceive ourselves and the truth is not in us. [9]If we confess our sins, he is faithful and just and will forgive us our sins and purify us from all unrighteousness. [10]If we claim we have not sinned, we make him out to be a liar and his word has no place in our lives.

CHAPTER 2

My dear children, I write this to you so that you will not sin. But if anybody does sin, we have one who speaks to the Father in our defense—Jesus Christ, the Righteous One. [2]He is the atoning sacrifice for our sins, and not only for ours but also for[c] the sins of the whole world.

[3]We know that we have come to know him if we obey his commands. [4]The man who says, "I know him," but does not do what he commands is a liar, and the truth is not in him. [5]But if anyone obeys his word, God's love[d] is truly made complete in him. This is how we know we are in him: [6]Whoever claims to live in him must walk as Jesus did.

[7]Dear friends, I am not writing you a new command but an old one, which you have had since the beginning. This old command is the message you have heard. [8]Yet I am writing you a new command; its truth is seen in him and you, because the darkness is passing and the true light is already shining.

[9]Anyone who claims to be in the light but hates his brother is still in the darkness. [10]Whoever loves his brother lives in the light, and there is nothing in him[e] to make him stumble. [11]But whoever hates his brother is in the darkness and walks around in the darkness; he does not know where he is going, because the darkness has blinded him.

[12]I write to you, dear children,
because your sins have been
forgiven on account of his
name.
[13]I write to you, fathers,
because you have known him who
is from the beginning.
I write to you, young men,
because you have overcome the evil
one.
I write to you, dear children,
because you have known the Father.
[14]I write to you, fathers,
because you have known him who
is from the beginning.
I write to you, young men,
because you are strong,
and the word of God lives in you,
and you have overcome the evil one.

[15]Do not love the world or anything in the world. If anyone loves the world, the love of the Father is not in him. [16]For everything in the world—the cravings of sinful man, the lust of his eyes and the boasting of what he has and does—comes not from the Father but from the world. [17]The world and its desires pass away, but the man who does the will of God lives forever.

[18]Dear children, this is the last hour; and as you have heard that the antichrist is coming, even now many antichrists have come. This is how we know it is the last hour. [19]They went out from us, but they did not really belong to us. For if they had belonged to us, they would have remained with us; but their going showed that none of them belonged to us.

[20]But you have an anointing from the Holy One, and all of you know the truth.[f] [21]I do not write to you because you do not know the truth, but because you do know it and because no lie comes from the truth. [22]Who is the liar? It is the man who denies that Jesus is the Christ. Such a man is the antichrist—he denies the Father and the Son. [23]No one who denies the Son has the Father; whoever acknowledges the Son has the Father also.

[24]See that what you have heard from the beginning remains in you. If it does, you also will remain in the Son and in the

---

[a]4 Some manuscripts *your*   [b]7 Or *every*   [c]2 Or *He is the one who turns aside God's wrath, taking away our sins, and not only ours but also*   [d]5 Or *word, love for God*   [e]10 Or *it*   [f]20 Some manuscripts *and you know all things*

Father. ²⁵And this is what he promised us—even eternal life.

²⁶I am writing these things to you about those who are trying to lead you astray. ²⁷As for you, the anointing you received from him remains in you, and you do not need anyone to teach you. But as his anointing teaches you about all things and as that anointing is real, not counterfeit—just as it has taught you, remain in him.

²⁸And now, dear children, continue in him, so that when he appears we may be confident and unashamed before him at his coming.

²⁹If you know that he is righteous, you know that everyone who does what is right has been born of him.

CHAPTER 3
How great is the love the Father has lavished on us, that we should be called children of God! And that is what we are! The reason the world does not know us is that it did not know him. ²Dear friends, now we are children of God, and what we will be has not yet been made known. But we know that when he appears,⁸ we shall be like him, for we shall see him as he is. ³Everyone who has this hope in him purifies himself, just as he is pure.

⁴Everyone who sins breaks the law; in fact, sin is lawlessness. ⁵But you know that he appeared so that he might take away our sins. And in him is no sin. ⁶No one who lives in him keeps on sinning. No one who continues to sin has either seen him or known him.

⁷Dear children, do not let anyone lead you astray. He who does what is right is righteous, just as he is righteous. ⁸He who does what is sinful is of the devil, because the devil has been sinning from the beginning. The reason the Son of God appeared was to destroy the devil's work. ⁹No one who is born of God will continue to sin, because God's seed remains in him; he cannot go on sinning, because he has been born of God. ¹⁰This is how we know who the children of God are and who the children of the devil are: Anyone who does not do what is right is not a child of God; nor is anyone who does not love his brother.

¹¹This is the message you heard from

the beginning: We should love one another. ¹²Do not be like Cain, who belonged to the evil one and murdered his brother. And why did he murder him? Because his own actions were evil and his brother's were righteous. ¹³Do not be surprised, my brothers, if the world hates you. ¹⁴We know that we have passed from death to life, because we love our brothers. Anyone who does not love remains in death. ¹⁵Anyone who hates his brother is a murderer, and you know that no murderer has eternal life in him.

¹⁶This is how we know what love is: Jesus Christ laid down his life for us. And we ought to lay down our lives for our brothers. ¹⁷If anyone has material possessions and sees his brother in need but has no pity on him, how can the love of God be in him? ¹⁸Dear children, let us not love with words or tongue but with actions and in truth. ¹⁹This then is how we know that we belong to the truth, and how we set our hearts at rest in his presence ²⁰whenever our hearts condemn us. For God is greater than our hearts, and he knows everything.

²¹Dear friends, if our hearts do not condemn us, we have confidence before God ²²and receive from him anything we ask, because we obey his commands and do what pleases him. ²³And this is his command: to believe in the name of his Son, Jesus Christ, and to love one another as he commanded us. ²⁴Those who obey his commands live in him, and he in them. And this is how we know that he lives in us: We know it by the Spirit he gave us.

CHAPTER 4
Dear friends, do not believe every spirit, but test the spirits to see whether they are from God, because many false prophets have gone out into the world. ²This is how you can recognize the Spirit of God: Every spirit that acknowledges that Jesus Christ has come in the flesh is from God, ³but every spirit that does not acknowledge Jesus is not from God. This is the spirit of the antichrist, which you have heard is coming and even now is already in the world.

⁴You, dear children, are from God and have overcome them, because the one who is in you is greater than the one who

⁸2 Or *when it is made known*

is in the world. [5]They are from the world and therefore speak from the viewpoint of the world, and the world listens to them. [6]We are from God, and whoever knows God listens to us; but whoever is not from God does not listen to us. This is how we recognize the Spirit[h] of truth and the spirit of falsehood.

[7]Dear friends, let us love one another, for love comes from God. Everyone who loves has been born of God and knows God. [8]Whoever does not love does not know God, because God is love. [9]This is how God showed his love among us: He sent his one and only Son[i] into the world that we might live through him. [10]This is love: not that we loved God, but that he loved us and sent his Son as an atoning sacrifice for[j] our sins. [11]Dear friends, since God so loved us, we also ought to love one another. [12]No one has ever seen God; but if we love one another, God lives in us and his love is made complete in us.

[13]We know that we live in him and he in us, because he has given us of his Spirit. [14]And we have seen and testify that the Father has sent his Son to be the Savior of the world. [15]If anyone acknowledges that Jesus is the Son of God, God lives in him and he in God. [16]And so we know and rely on the love God has for us.

God is love. Whoever lives in love lives in God, and God in him. [17]In this way, love is made complete among us so that we will have confidence on the day of judgment, because in this world we are like him. [18]There is no fear in love. But perfect love drives out fear, because fear has to do with punishment. The one who fears is not made perfect in love.

[19]We love because he first loved us. [20]If anyone says, "I love God," yet hates his brother, he is a liar. For anyone who does not love his brother, whom he has seen, cannot love God, whom he has not seen. [21]And he has given us this command: Whoever loves God must also love his brother.

CHAPTER 5

Everyone who believes that Jesus is the Christ is born of God, and everyone who loves the father loves his child as well. [2]This is how we know that we love the children of God: by loving God and carrying out his commands. [3]This is love for God: to obey his commands. And his commands are not burdensome, [4]for everyone born of God overcomes the world. This is the victory that has overcome the world, even our faith. [5]Who is it that overcomes the world? Only he who believes that Jesus is the Son of God.

[6]This is the one who came by water and blood—Jesus Christ. He did not come by water only, but by water and blood. And it is the Spirit who testifies, because the Spirit is the truth. [7]For there are three that testify: [8]the[k] Spirit, the water and the blood; and the three are in agreement. [9]We accept man's testimony, but God's testimony is greater because it is the testimony of God, which he has given about his Son. [10]Anyone who believes in the Son of God has this testimony in his heart. Anyone who does not believe God has made him out to be a liar, because he has not believed the testimony God has given about his Son. [11]And this is the testimony: God has given us eternal life, and this life is in his Son. [12]He who has the Son has life; he who does not have the Son of God does not have life.

[13]I write these things to you who believe in the name of the Son of God so that you may know that you have eternal life. [14]This is the confidence we have in approaching God: that if we ask anything according to his will, he hears us. [15]And if we know that he hears us—whatever we ask—we know that we have what we asked of him.

[16]If anyone sees his brother commit a sin that does not lead to death, he should pray and God will give him life. I refer to those whose sin does not lead to death. There is a sin that leads to death. I am not saying that he should pray about that. [17]All wrongdoing is sin, and there is sin that does not lead to death.

[18]We know that anyone born of God does not continue to sin; the one who was born of God keeps him safe, and the evil one cannot harm him. [19]We know that we are children of God, and that the whole world is under the control of the evil one.

[h]6 Or spirit   [i]9 Or his only begotten Son   [j]10 Or as the one who would turn aside his wrath, taking away   [k]7,8 Late manuscripts of the Vulgate testify in heaven: the Father, the Word and the Holy Spirit, and these three are one. [8]And there are three that testify on earth: the (not found in any Greek manuscript before the sixteenth century)

[20]We know also that the Son of God has come and has given us understanding, so that we may know him who is true. And we are in him who is true—even in his Son Jesus Christ. He is the true God and eternal life.

[21]Dear children, keep yourselves from idols.

2 John

"IF YOU think you are standing firm, be careful that you don't fall!" These words of Paul (1 Corinthians 10:12) could be a subtitle for 2 John, a brief letter from the apostle John that stresses the importance of balance. The readers, a "chosen lady" and "her children," are walking in the truth, and John commends them for it. But he warns them not to aid false teachers who deny the true humanity of Christ. John exhorts the readers to love God and one another and to obey God's commandments but warns them not to encourage false teachers in any way, whereby they would open the door to false teaching and share in their evil work.

Focus	Practicing the Truth		Protecting the Truth		
Divisions	Greeting	Exhortation	Wrong Doctrine	Right Response	Conclusion
	1	3 4	6 7	9 10	11 12 13
Topics	Living in Truth and Love		Learning to Detect False Teaching		Looking for John's Coming
	Important Command		Timely Caution		Tender Conclusion
Place	Ephesus				
Time	Approximately A.D. 90				

DECEMBER 19 □ DAY 354
2 JOHN
Fellowship with Enemies

OVERVIEW John's first epistle was written to a group of believers in danger of following false teachers. His second letter is addressed to a "chosen lady and her children" who are undergoing similar temptations. John wastes no words in making his point: "If anyone comes to you and does not bring this teaching, do not take him into your house or welcome him" (v. 10). Though John commends love as a necessary ingredient of the Christian life, it must not sentimentally embrace those who willfully seek to destroy the truth. To do so is to diminish the proper love that Christians must have for one another. John's warning is stern, but he knows a letter is not the best place to elaborate. He promises to deal more fully with the problem when he makes a personal visit.

Verses 1-6	Verses 7-11	Verses 12-13
Living in Truth and Love	Learning to Detect False Teaching	Looking for John's Coming
"This is love:	that we walk in obedience to his commands" (v. 6).	

YOUR DAILY WALK The point of John's second epistle is that love must be discerning. Love cannot be divorced from truth. God's love is not blind sentiment; it is just, truthful, demanding. God's love motivated him to send his Son to Calvary; but those who do not believe are condemned. Calvary and condemnation are both aspects of love. The one represents love extended; the other signifies love rejected.

The fruit of our righteousness is obedience to God and love toward others.

How wise and discerning has your love been lately? Are you being too easy on yourself or other Christians in the name of love and acceptance? Are you silently condoning error because you have been unwilling to "speak the truth in love"?

Check up on your love relationships today, and make sure they're truly biblical, not merely sentimental.

INSIGHT "Dear You-Know-Who . . ."
One possible reason why the recipient's name is not given in 2 John has to do with the persecution suffered by the church at the time. If the letter had fallen into the wrong hands, those who were to receive it might have been ill-treated. By not identifying the recipient, John reduced that possibility.

¹The elder,

To the chosen lady and her children, whom I love in the truth—and not I only, but also all who know the truth— ²because of the truth, which lives in us and will be with us forever:

³Grace, mercy and peace from God the Father and from Jesus Christ, the Father's Son, will be with us in truth and love.

⁴It has given me great joy to find some of your children walking in the truth, just as the Father commanded us. ⁵And now, dear lady, I am not writing you a new command but one we have had from the beginning. I ask that we love one another.

[6]And this is love: that we walk in obedience to his commands. As you have heard from the beginning, his command is that you walk in love.

[7]Many deceivers, who do not acknowledge Jesus Christ as coming in the flesh, have gone out into the world. Any such person is the deceiver and the antichrist. [8]Watch out that you do not lose what you have worked for, but that you may be rewarded fully. [9]Anyone who runs ahead and does not continue in the teaching of Christ does not have God; whoever continues in the teaching has both the Father and the Son. [10]If anyone comes to you and does not bring this teaching, do not take him into your house or welcome him. [11]Anyone who welcomes him shares in his wicked work.

[12]I have much to write to you, but I do not want to use paper and ink. Instead, I hope to visit you and talk with you face to face, so that our joy may be complete.

[13]The children of your chosen sister send their greetings.

3 John

THE SHORTEST of John's Epistles begins with the expressed desire for Gaius's prosperity (v. 2) and ends with a longing for Gaius's presence (v. 14). In between, John commends him and Demetrius for their faithful witness and good testimony and makes note of one disruptive individual. John concludes his letter by promising that when he makes a personal visit, he will speak face-to-face with them about the things he could not cover in writing.

Focus	Hospitality		Haughtiness	Holiness	
Divisions	Greeting	Commendation	Censuring	Compliment	Close
	1	2 8	9 10	11 12	13 14
Topics	Commendation of Gaius		Censuring of Diotrephes	Compliment of Demetrius	
	Helping through Hospitality		Harming through Haughtiness	Honoring Holiness	
Place	Ephesus				
Time	Approximately A.D. 90				

DECEMBER 20 ☐ DAY 355
3 JOHN
Open the Door in the Name of the Lord

OVERVIEW Far from being problem-free, the church of John's day had its share of shortcomings, contentious saints and false teachers. In his third epistle, John makes a special note of one such disruptive individual named Diotrephes, a gossiper "who loves to be first" (v. 9). But there are two shining examples of commendable saints in 3 John. Gaius is a constant source of joy to John because he walks in the truth (v. 3), and Demetrius is a faithful servant in the church, one who has been a good testimony to everyone (v. 12). John concludes his letter by promising that the things he could not cover in writing, he will deal with face-to-face.

Verses 1-8	Verses 9-10	Verses 11-14
Helping through Hospitality	Harming through Haughtiness	Honoring Holiness
Gaius	Diotrephes	Demetrius

Hospitals should not have a monopoly on hospitality.

YOUR DAILY WALK Hospitality speaks volumes about a person's Christianity. A Christian who practices hospitality is saying in effect, "My house or apartment may not be a candidate for *Better Homes and Gardens,* but I care enough about you to share it with you." Hospitality is other-oriented, for it seeks to benefit others who are in need. To help you practice hospitality, sit down with your calendar, and select one date in the next few weeks when you will share your home with others. Reserve that date, telephone someone you've been meaning to invite and plan your own "Operation Gaius."

INSIGHT "If I've Said It Once, I've Said It a Dozen Times!"
Notice the repetition of three themes in John's writings:

John	1 John	2 John	3 John
Love 13:34–35	2:7–11; 3:10–14; 4:7—5:3	5–6	1
Truth 1:17; 3:21; 14:6, 17	1:6–7; 2:4, 21, 27; 4:6	1–4	3, 8, 12
Joy 16:24; 17:13	1:4		12

¹The elder,

To my dear friend Gaius, whom I love in the truth.

²Dear friend, I pray that you may enjoy good health and that all may go well with you, even as your soul is getting along well. ³It gave me great joy to have some brothers come and tell about your faithfulness to the truth and how you continue to walk in the truth. ⁴I have no greater joy than to hear that my children are walking in the truth.

⁵Dear friend, you are faithful in what you are doing for the brothers, even though they are strangers to you. ⁶They have told the church about your love. You will do well to send them on their way in a manner worthy of God. ⁷It was for the sake of the Name that they went out, receiving no help from the pagans. ⁸We ought therefore to show hospitality to such men so that we may work together for the truth.

⁹I wrote to the church, but Diotrephes, who loves to be first, will have nothing to

do with us. [10]So if I come, I will call attention to what he is doing, gossiping maliciously about us. Not satisfied with that, he refuses to welcome the brothers. He also stops those who want to do so and puts them out of the church.

[11]Dear friend, do not imitate what is evil but what is good. Anyone who does what is good is from God. Anyone who does what is evil has not seen God. [12]Demetrius is well spoken of by everyone—

and even by the truth itself. We also speak well of him, and you know that our testimony is true.

[13]I have much to write you, but I do not want to do so with pen and ink. [14]I hope to see you soon, and we will talk face to face.

Peace to you. The friends here send their greetings. Greet the friends there by name.

DECEMBER 21 ☐ DAY 356
Unscrambling the Truth

 LOOK BACK This week's selection of readings is from the "General Epistles," so called because the letters are typically addressed to scattered Christians generally, rather than to a specific individual or church. In contrast to Paul's letters, where the name of the book tells you the *recipient* of the letter, these books have names that indicate the *writer* of the letter: James, Peter, John. Here are six keys to help you unlock each book and remember its theme:

James: "Faith Gauge" (How to know if you have a living, breathing faith in God)

1 Peter: "Pain with a Purpose" (How to face painful circumstances that invade your life)

2 Peter: "Poison in the Pew" (How to deal with false teaching and false teachers that arise from within your church)

1 John: "Fellowship Barometer" (How to know if you are walking in fellowship with God, and what to do if you aren't)

2 John: "Bolt the Door" (How to be discerning and wise about false teachers)

3 John: "Open the Door" (How to be hospitable and supportive toward genuine teachers)

 LOOK UP Try your hand at a little word quiz. Rearrange the letters in each word or phrase to form the name of a book of the Bible. You have one minute. Go!

We should have regular checkups to avoid truth-decay.

- CATS = the book of ___ ___ ___ ___.
- MT. WHEAT is no mountain at all but the book of

  ___ ___ ___ ___ ___ ___ ___.
- LAMPSS is a bright idea for the book of ___ ___ ___ ___ ___ ___.
- NEUTER MOODY is a funny way to mix up the book of

  ___ ___ ___ ___ ___ ___ ___ ___ ___ ___ ___.
- SEE SING is not the name of a new prison but the book of

  ___ ___ ___ ___ ___ ___ ___.
- AH HAZE PIN is a sharp idea for scrambling the book of

  ___ ___ ___ ___ ___ ___ ___ ___ ___.

Now that you've got the idea, why not try your hand at a few others? It's a fun way to help a friend or family member learn the books of the Bible. (Be sure there is a copy of the Table of Contents to the Bible handy for ready reference!)

(*Answers:* Acts, Matthew, Psalms, Deuteronomy, Genesis, Zephaniah)

LOOK AHEAD The epistles you have read this past week at first may seem to have confusing and even contradictory messages.

"After all," you might ask, "am I supposed to 'Bolt the Door' (2 John) or 'Open the Door' (3 John)? Am I supposed to give thanks for painful circumstances (1 Peter) or avoid the source of that pain (2 Peter)? If good works can't save me (James), then what are good works really good for anyway?" The key is in the context.

You should bolt the door if someone is selling you poison (and certainly, false teaching is every bit as lethal as poison), but you should open the door to faithful teachers and preachers of the truth.

You should give thanks for circumstances you *cannot* change, but you should work hard to change things you *can* change—such as the presence of false teachers in your church.

You should remember that good works cannot save you, but you are saved for the purpose of good works.

Take a letter you have read this past week, and make it your marching orders for the coming week. Don't just traffic in the truth—be a doer of it!

Jude

JUDE writes a fiery letter about the war the church must fight against destroyers in its own ranks. These corrupt teachers have a perverted view of God's grace and liberty, using salvation as an opportunity to sin with safety. Because they prefer their own ideas to God's truths, their beliefs result in shocking immorality. Jude reminds his readers of God's severe judgment on such hypocrites. He tells true believers to do two things: keep themselves from such sin and rescue others stumbling toward it.

Focus	Emergency	Examples	Exhortations
Divisions	Announcement of Falling Away 1　　　　4	Anatomy of Falling Away 5　　　　16	Antidote for Falling Away 17　　　　25
Topics	Why Contend for the Faith		How to Contend for the Faith
	Contention	Condemnation	Caution
Place	Unknown		
Time	Approximately A.D. 66–80		

DECEMBER 22 ☐ DAY 357

JUDE
Contending for the Faith

OVERVIEW When the truth of God is under attack, it is time to enter the spiritual battle and fight for the faith. But beware! Only believers who are spiritually "in shape" will be ready to answer the summons. Jude begins a letter about the mutual mercy, peace and love shared by all believers. But instead he feels compelled to challenge them to contend for the faith. The danger is real: False teachers have crept into the church, turning God's grace into license to do as they please. Jude reminds such people of God's past dealings with faithless Israel, disobedient angels and wicked Sodom. In the face of such warnings, Christians have no excuse to be caught off guard.

Verses 1-4	Verses 5-16	Verses 17-25
Announcement of Falling Away	Anatomy of Falling Away	Antidote for Falling Away
Emergency	Examples	Exhortations

Lay hold of the Bible until the Bible lays hold of you.

YOUR DAILY WALK Arrange a postage stamp, a sheet of paper, an envelope and a pen before you. Then prayerfully read the following:

"If Christ comes to rule the hearts of men, it will be because we take him with us on the tractor, behind the desk, when we're making a sale to a customer, or when we're driving on the road."—Alexander Nunn

"The deathless Book has survived three great dangers: the negligence of its friends; the false systems built upon it; and the warfare of those who have hated it."—Isaac Taylor

"I have a very simple thing to ask of you. I ask every man and woman that from this day on they will realize that part of the destiny of America lies in their daily perusal of this great Book."—Woodrow Wilson

Is the "faith of our fathers" worth proclaiming? Take ten minutes right now . . . and write someone a letter about it!

INSIGHT Triads of Trouble
Jude illustrates his message in threes: three examples of judgment (Egypt, angels, Sodom); three declarations of woe (Cain, Balaam, Korah); and three exhortations to caution (what are they?).

¹Jude, a servant of Jesus Christ and a brother of James,

To those who have been called, who are loved by God the Father and kept by*ᵃ* Jesus Christ:

²Mercy, peace and love be yours in abundance.

³Dear friends, although I was very eager to write to you about the salvation we share, I felt I had to write and urge you to contend for the faith that was once for all entrusted to the saints. ⁴For certain men whose condemnation was written about*ᵇ* long ago have secretly slipped in among you. They are godless men, who change

ᵃ1 Or for; or in   ᵇ4 Or men who were marked out for condemnation the grace of our God into a license for immorality and deny Jesus Christ our only Sovereign and Lord.

[5]Though you already know all this, I want to remind you that the Lord[c] delivered his people out of Egypt, but later destroyed those who did not believe. [6]And the angels who did not keep their positions of authority but abandoned their own home—these he has kept in darkness, bound with everlasting chains for judgment on the great Day. [7]In a similar way, Sodom and Gomorrah and the surrounding towns gave themselves up to sexual immorality and perversion. They serve as an example of those who suffer the punishment of eternal fire.

[8]In the very same way, these dreamers pollute their own bodies, reject authority and slander celestial beings. [9]But even the archangel Michael, when he was disputing with the devil about the body of Moses, did not dare to bring a slanderous accusation against him, but said, "The Lord rebuke you!" [10]Yet these men speak abusively against whatever they do not understand; and what things they do understand by instinct, like unreasoning animals—these are the very things that destroy them.

[11]Woe to them! They have taken the way of Cain; they have rushed for profit into Balaam's error; they have been destroyed in Korah's rebellion.

[12]These men are blemishes at your love feasts, eating with you without the slightest qualm—shepherds who feed only themselves. They are clouds without rain, blown along by the wind; autumn trees, without fruit and uprooted—twice dead. [13]They are wild waves of the sea, foaming up their shame; wandering stars, for whom blackest darkness has been reserved forever.

[14]Enoch, the seventh from Adam, prophesied about these men: "See, the Lord is coming with thousands upon thousands of his holy ones [15]to judge everyone, and to convict all the ungodly of all the ungodly acts they have done in the ungodly way, and of all the harsh words ungodly sinners have spoken against him." [16]These men are grumblers and faultfinders; they follow their own evil desires; they boast about themselves and flatter others for their own advantage.

[17]But, dear friends, remember what the apostles of our Lord Jesus Christ foretold. [18]They said to you, "In the last times there will be scoffers who will follow their own ungodly desires." [19]These are the men who divide you, who follow mere natural instincts and do not have the Spirit.

[20]But you, dear friends, build yourselves up in your most holy faith and pray in the Holy Spirit. [21]Keep yourselves in God's love as you wait for the mercy of our Lord Jesus Christ to bring you to eternal life.

[22]Be merciful to those who doubt; [23]snatch others from the fire and save them; to others show mercy, mixed with fear—hating even the clothing stained by corrupted flesh.

[24]To him who is able to keep you from falling and to present you before his glorious presence without fault and with great joy— [25]to the only God our Savior be glory, majesty, power and authority, through Jesus Christ our Lord, before all ages, now and forevermore! Amen.

[c]5 Some early manuscripts Jesus

Revelation

JOHN, while exiled on the island of Patmos, receives the visions contained in the book of Revelation. As the first verse states, through a dramatic series of pictures, signs and symbols, Jesus Christ reveals to John—and to all subsequent readers—what will happen at the end of time. John depicts cataclysmic judgment upon the earth, the final destruction of satanic forces and the beginning of a new heaven and new earth.

Focus	Heaven	Earth					New Heaven and Earth
Divisions	Letters to Seven Churches	Opening the Seven Seals	Blowing the Seven Trumpets	Describing the Seven Signs	Pouring Out the Seven Bowls	Destroying God's Enemies	Making All Things New
	1 3	4 6	7 9	10 13	14 16	17 19	20 22
Topics	Coming King	Coming Calamity					Coming Kingdom
	Judge	Judgment					Joy
Place		Aegean Island of Patmos					
Time		About A.D. 95–96					

DECEMBER 23 ☐ DAY 358
REVELATION 1–3
Letters to Seven Churches

 OVERVIEW John's opening words provide the theme for the book. This is "The Revelation of Jesus Christ" in all his power and holiness, majesty and justice. John is commanded to write seven letters, each containing a message of reproof, rebuke or reassurance, to seven first-century churches in Asia Minor. The Lord of the church knows the condition of the church. Like a skilled physician, he diagnoses the sin that must be dealt with if each congregation is to overcome, rather than be overcome, in the evil day.

Chapter 1	Chapters 2–3
Standing among the Churches	Speaking to the Churches: Ephesus, Smyrna, Pergamum, Thyatira, Sardis, Philadelphia, Laodicea
Seven Lampstands	Seven Letters

 YOUR DAILY WALK If someone were to evaluate your Christian life today, which of the seven churches addressed in Revelation 2–3 would they say it most closely resembles?

When your work speaks for itself, don't interrupt.

• Ephesus (where love for Christ had grown cold)?
• Sardis (where the church was like a morgue)?
• Laodicea (where Christians were yawning and self-satisfied)?

Once you've thought about the *diagnosis* of your spiritual life, don't stop there! Read on to discover the specific *cure* Christ recommends for that spiritual ill. Then, with God's help, put that cure to work today so that your light can burn brightly for the Savior.

 INSIGHT The Five Books of John
The apostle John wrote about the message of life in three different kinds of Scripture: the *Gospel* of John (biography), which speaks of eternal life; the *Epistles* of John (letters), which speak of the Christian life; and the *prophecies* of Revelation (visions), which speak of victorious life now and for eternity.

CHAPTER 1

The revelation of Jesus Christ, which God gave him to show his servants what must soon take place. He made it known by sending his angel to his servant John, ²who testifies to everything he saw—that is, the word of God and the testimony of Jesus Christ. ³Blessed is the one who reads the words of this prophecy, and blessed are those that hear it and take to heart what is written in it, because the time is near.

⁴John,

To the seven churches in the province of Asia:

Grace and peace to you from him who is, and who was, and who is to come, and from the seven spirits*a* before his throne, ⁵and from Jesus Christ, who is the faithful witness, the firstborn from the dead, and the ruler of the kings of the earth.

To him who loves us and has freed us from our sins by his blood, ⁶and has made

a4 Or *the sevenfold Spirit*

us to be a kingdom and priests to serve his God and Father—to him be glory and power for ever and ever! Amen.

⁷Look, he is coming with the clouds,
  and every eye will see him,
even those who pierced him;
  and all the peoples of the earth will
    mourn because of him.
          So shall it be! Amen.

⁸"I am the Alpha and the Omega," says the Lord God, "who is, and who was, and who is to come, the Almighty."

⁹I, John, your brother and companion in the suffering and kingdom and patient endurance that are ours in Jesus, was on the island of Patmos because of the word of God and the testimony of Jesus. ¹⁰On the Lord's Day I was in the Spirit, and I heard behind me a loud voice like a trumpet, ¹¹which said: "Write on a scroll what you see and send it to the seven churches: to Ephesus, Smyrna, Pergamum, Thyatira, Sardis, Philadelphia and Laodicea."

¹²I turned around to see the voice that was speaking to me. And when I turned I saw seven golden lampstands, ¹³and among the lampstands was someone "like a son of man,"^b dressed in a robe reaching down to his feet and with a golden sash around his chest. ¹⁴His head and hair were white like wool, as white as snow, and his eyes were like blazing fire. ¹⁵His feet were like bronze glowing in a furnace, and his voice was like the sound of rushing waters. ¹⁶In his right hand he held seven stars, and out of his mouth came a sharp double-edged sword. His face was like the sun shining in all its brilliance.

¹⁷When I saw him, I fell at his feet as though dead. Then he placed his right hand on me and said: "Do not be afraid. I am the First and the Last. ¹⁸I am the Living One; I was dead, and behold I am alive for ever and ever! And I hold the keys of death and Hades.

¹⁹"Write, therefore, what you have seen, what is now and what will take place later. ²⁰The mystery of the seven stars that you saw in my right hand and of the seven golden lampstands is this: The seven stars are the angels^c of the seven churches, and the seven lampstands are the seven churches.

CHAPTER 2

"To the angel^d of the church in Ephesus write:

These are the words of him who holds the seven stars in his right hand and walks among the seven golden lampstands: ²I know your deeds, your hard work and your perseverance. I know that you cannot tolerate wicked men, that you have tested those who claim to be apostles but are not, and have found them false. ³You have persevered and have endured hardships for my name, and have not grown weary.

⁴Yet I hold this against you: You have forsaken your first love. ⁵Remember the height from which you have fallen! Repent and do the things you did at first. If you do not repent, I will come to you and remove your lampstand from its place. ⁶But you have this in your favor: You hate the practices of the Nicolaitans, which I also hate.

⁷He who has an ear, let him hear what the Spirit says to the churches. To him who overcomes, I will give the right to eat from the tree of life, which is in the paradise of God.

⁸"To the angel of the church in Smyrna write:

These are the words of him who is the First and the Last, who died and came to life again. ⁹I know your afflictions and your poverty—yet you are rich! I know the slander of those who say they are Jews and are not, but are a synagogue of Satan. ¹⁰Do not be afraid of what you are about to suffer. I tell you, the devil will put some of you in prison to test you, and you will suffer persecution for ten days. Be faithful, even to the point of death, and I will give you the crown of life.

¹¹He who has an ear, let him hear what the Spirit says to the churches. He who overcomes will not be hurt at all by the second death.

^b13 Daniel 7:13   ^c20 Or messengers   ^d1 Or messenger; also in verses 8, 12 and 18

¹²"To the angel of the church in Perga-
mum write:

These are the words of him who
has the sharp, double-edged sword.
¹³I know where you live—where Satan has his throne. Yet you remain
true to my name. You did not renounce your faith in me, even in the
days of Antipas, my faithful witness,
who was put to death in your city—
where Satan lives.

¹⁴Nevertheless, I have a few things
against you: You have people there
who hold to the teaching of Balaam,
who taught Balak to entice the Israelites to sin by eating food sacrificed to
idols and by committing sexual immorality. ¹⁵Likewise you also have
those who hold to the teaching of the
Nicolaitans. ¹⁶Repent therefore! Otherwise, I will soon come to you and
will fight against them with the
sword of my mouth.

¹⁷He who has an ear, let him hear
what the Spirit says to the churches.
To him who overcomes, I will give
some of the hidden manna. I will also
give him a white stone with a new
name written on it, known only to
him who receives it.

¹⁸"To the angel of the church in Thyatira
write:

These are the words of the Son of
God, whose eyes are like blazing fire
and whose feet are like burnished
bronze. ¹⁹I know your deeds, your
love and faith, your service and perseverance, and that you are now doing more than you did at first.

²⁰Nevertheless, I have this against
you: You tolerate that woman Jezebel, who calls herself a prophetess.
By her teaching she misleads my servants into sexual immorality and the
eating of food sacrificed to idols. ²¹I
have given her time to repent of her
immorality, but she is unwilling. ²²So
I will cast her on a bed of suffering,
and I will make those who commit
adultery with her suffer intensely,
unless they repent of her ways. ²³I
will strike her children dead. Then all

the churches will know that I am he
who searches hearts and minds, and I
will repay each of you according to
your deeds. ²⁴Now I say to the rest of
you in Thyatira, to you who do not
hold to her teaching and have not
learned Satan's so-called deep secrets (I will not impose any other
burden on you): ²⁵Only hold on to
what you have until I come.

²⁶To him who overcomes and does
my will to the end, I will give authority over the nations—

²⁷'He will rule them with an iron
      scepter;
    he will dash them to pieces
      like pottery'ᵉ—

just as I have received authority from
my Father. ²⁸I will also give him the
morning star. ²⁹He who has an ear,
let him hear what the Spirit says to
the churches.

CHAPTER 3
"To the angelᶠ of the church in Sardis
write:

These are the words of him who
holds the seven spiritsᵍ of God and
the seven stars. I know your deeds;
you have a reputation of being alive,
but you are dead. ²Wake up!
Strengthen what remains and is
about to die, for I have not found
your deeds complete in the sight of
my God. ³Remember, therefore, what
you have received and heard; obey it,
and repent. But if you do not wake
up, I will come like a thief, and you
will not know at what time I will
come to you.

⁴Yet you have a few people in Sardis who have not soiled their clothes.
They will walk with me, dressed in
white, for they are worthy. ⁵He who
overcomes will, like them, be dressed
in white. I will never blot out his
name from the book of life, but will
acknowledge his name before my
Father and his angels. ⁶He who has
an ear, let him hear what the Spirit
says to the churches.

⁷"To the angel of the church in Philadel-
phia write:

ᵉ27 Psalm 2:9   ᶠ1 Or *messenger*; also in verses 7 and 14   ᵍ1 Or *the sevenfold Spirit*

These are the words of him who is holy and true, who holds the key of David. What he opens no one can shut, and what he shuts no one can open. [8]I know your deeds. See, I have placed before you an open door that no one can shut. I know that you have little strength, yet you have kept my word and have not denied my name. [9]I will make those who are of the synagogue of Satan, who claim to be Jews though they are not, but are liars—I will make them come and fall down at your feet and acknowledge that I have loved you. [10]Since you have kept my command to endure patiently, I will also keep you from the hour of trial that is going to come upon the whole world to test those who live on the earth.

[11]I am coming soon. Hold on to what you have, so that no one will take your crown. [12]Him who overcomes I will make a pillar in the temple of my God. Never again will he leave it. I will write on him the name of my God and the name of the city of my God, the new Jerusalem, which is coming down out of heaven from my God; and I will also write on him my new name. [13]He who has an ear, let him hear what the Spirit says to the churches.

[14]"To the angel of the church in Laodicea write:

These are the words of the Amen, the faithful and true witness, the ruler of God's creation. [15]I know your deeds, that you are neither cold nor hot. I wish you were either one or the other! [16]So, because you are lukewarm—neither hot nor cold—I am about to spit you out of my mouth. [17]You say, 'I am rich; I have acquired wealth and do not need a thing.' But you do not realize that you are wretched, pitiful, poor, blind and naked. [18]I counsel you to buy from me gold refined in the fire, so you can become rich; and white clothes to wear, so you can cover your shameful nakedness; and salve to put on your eyes, so you can see.

[19]Those whom I love I rebuke and discipline. So be earnest, and repent. [20]Here I am! I stand at the door and knock. If anyone hears my voice and opens the door, I will come in and eat with him, and he with me.

[21]To him who overcomes, I will give the right to sit with me on my throne, just as I overcame and sat down with my Father on his throne. [22]He who has an ear, let him hear what the Spirit says to the churches."

DECEMBER 24 ☐ DAY 359
REVELATION 4–6
Opening the Seven Seals

 OVERVIEW Beginning with chapter 4, John is invited to "come up here" in order to see "what must take place after this" (4:1). Transported in the spirit, John first sees a "technicolor" vision of the sovereign God upon his heavenly throne, holding a scroll in which are written his judgments for the earth. No one is qualified to open the seals of the scroll and execute God's judgments except the Lamb, "the Lion of the tribe of Judah" (5:5). One by one he breaks the seals, and horrible judgments fall upon the earth and its inhabitants.

Chapter 4	Chapter 5	Chapter 6
The One Who Sits on the Throne	The Lamb Who Opens the Scroll	The Plagues of the Seven Seals
Majestic	Worthy	Devastating

YOUR DAILY WALK Here is a thought worthy of your consideration: The elders who surround the throne of God proclaim, "You are worthy, our Lord" (4:11). Later they say to the Lamb, "You are worthy" (5:9), and still later all the hosts of heaven exclaim, "Worthy is the Lamb!" (5:12). What makes the God of heaven and the Lamb of God so worthy of receiving worship and adoration?

We are not Christ's lawyers; we are his witnesses.

First, God is worthy because of who he is—the God of infinite perfection and holiness. Second, God is worthy because of what he has done—the Father in creation, and his Son, the Lamb, in redemption and salvation.

The question to ponder is this: How can I show in my daily walk that I serve a worthy God? Is my speech worthy of him? Is my conduct worthy of my privileged position in the family of God? Do I talk about him often? worship him wholeheartedly? seek to please him daily?

Tape the words of Revelation 4:11 to your dashboard or mirror to remind you frequently that God is deserving of your greatest devotion and act of service. Indeed, he is worthy.

INSIGHT The Invisible God Made Visible
The Bible describes God as "invisible" (Colossians 1:15), reminding us that "no one has ever seen God" (John 1:18). Thus, John's awesome and majestic description of God the Father upon the throne (Revelation 4:2–3) is perhaps as much of God as humans will ever see this side of heaven.

CHAPTER 4

After this I looked, and there before me was a door standing open in heaven. And the voice I had first heard speaking to me like a trumpet said, "Come up here, and I will show you what must take place after this." ²At once I was in the Spirit, and there before me was a throne in heaven with someone sitting on it. ³And the one who sat there had the appearance of jasper and carnelian. A rainbow, resembling an emerald, encircled the throne. ⁴Surrounding the throne were twenty-four other thrones, and seated on them were twenty-four elders. They were dressed in white and had crowns of gold on their heads. ⁵From the throne came flashes of lightning, rumblings and peals of thunder. Before the throne, seven lamps were blazing. These are the seven spirits[h] of God. ⁶Also before the throne there was what looked like a sea of glass, clear as crystal.

In the center, around the throne, were four living creatures, and they were covered with eyes, in front and in back. ⁷The first living creature was like a lion, the second was like an ox, the third had a face like a man, the fourth was like a flying eagle. ⁸Each of the four living creatures had six wings and was covered with eyes all around, even under his wings. Day and night they never stop saying:

"Holy, holy, holy
is the Lord God Almighty,
who was, and is, and is to come."

⁹Whenever the living creatures give glory, honor and thanks to him who sits on the throne and who lives for ever and ever, ¹⁰the twenty-four elders fall down before him who sits on the throne, and worship him who lives for ever and ever. They lay their crowns before the throne and say:

¹¹"You are worthy, our Lord and God,
to receive glory and honor and
power,
for you created all things,
and by your will they were created
and have their being."

CHAPTER 5

Then I saw in the right hand of him who sat on the throne a scroll with writing on both sides and sealed with seven seals. ²And I saw a mighty angel proclaiming in a loud voice, "Who is worthy to break the seals and open the scroll?" ³But no one in heaven or on earth or under the earth could open the scroll or even look inside

h5 Or the sevenfold Spirit

it. ⁴I wept and wept because no one was found who was worthy to open the scroll or look inside. ⁵Then one of the elders said to me, "Do not weep! See, the Lion of the tribe of Judah, the Root of David, has triumphed. He is able to open the scroll and its seven seals."

⁶Then I saw a Lamb, looking as if it had been slain, standing in the center of the throne, encircled by the four living creatures and the elders. He had seven horns and seven eyes, which are the seven spirits[i] of God sent out into all the earth. ⁷He came and took the scroll from the right hand of him who sat on the throne. ⁸And when he had taken it, the four living creatures and the twenty-four elders fell down before the Lamb. Each one had a harp and they were holding golden bowls full of incense, which are the prayers of the saints. ⁹And they sang a new song:

"You are worthy to take the scroll
   and to open its seals,
because you were slain,
   and with your blood you purchased
      men for God
   from every tribe and language and
      people and nation.
¹⁰You have made them to be a kingdom
    and priests to serve our God,
   and they will reign on the earth."

¹¹Then I looked and heard the voice of many angels, numbering thousands upon thousands, and ten thousand times ten thousand. They encircled the throne and the living creatures and the elders. ¹²In a loud voice they sang:

"Worthy is the Lamb, who was slain,
to receive power and wealth and
     wisdom and strength
and honor and glory and praise!"

¹³Then I heard every creature in heaven and on earth and under the earth and on the sea, and all that is in them, singing:

"To him who sits on the throne and to
   the Lamb
be praise and honor and glory and
   power,
      for ever and ever!"

¹⁴The four living creatures said, "Amen," and the elders fell down and worshiped.

CHAPTER 6

I watched as the Lamb opened the first of the seven seals. Then I heard one of the four living creatures say in a voice like thunder, "Come!" ²I looked, and there before me was a white horse! Its rider held a bow, and he was given a crown, and he rode out as a conqueror bent on conquest.

³When the Lamb opened the second seal, I heard the second living creature say, "Come!" ⁴Then another horse came out, a fiery red one. Its rider was given power to take peace from the earth and to make men slay each other. To him was given a large sword.

⁵When the Lamb opened the third seal, I heard the third living creature say, "Come!" I looked, and there before me was a black horse! Its rider was holding a pair of scales in his hand. ⁶Then I heard what sounded like a voice among the four living creatures, saying, "A quart[j] of wheat for a day's wages,[k] and three quarts of barley for a day's wages,[k] and do not damage the oil and the wine!"

⁷When the Lamb opened the fourth seal, I heard the voice of the fourth living creature say, "Come!" ⁸I looked, and there before me was a pale horse! Its rider was named Death, and Hades was following close behind him. They were given power over a fourth of the earth to kill by sword, famine and plague, and by the wild beasts of the earth.

⁹When he opened the fifth seal, I saw under the altar the souls of those who had been slain because of the word of God and the testimony they had maintained. ¹⁰They called out in a loud voice, "How long, Sovereign Lord, holy and true, until you judge the inhabitants of the earth and avenge our blood?" ¹¹Then each of them was given a white robe, and they were told to wait a little longer, until the number of their fellow servants and brothers who were to be killed as they had been was completed.

¹²I watched as he opened the sixth seal. There was a great earthquake. The sun turned black like sackcloth made of goat hair, the whole moon turned blood red, ¹³and the stars in the sky fell to earth, as late figs drop from a fig tree when shaken by a strong wind. ¹⁴The sky receded like a

---

i 6 Or the sevenfold Spirit   j 6 Greek a choinix (probably about a liter)   k 6 Greek a denarius scroll, rolling up, and every mountain and island was removed from its place.

¹⁵Then the kings of the earth, the princes, the generals, the rich, the mighty, and every slave and every free man hid in caves and among the rocks of the moun-

tains. ¹⁶They called to the mountains and the rocks, "Fall on us and hide us from the face of him who sits on the throne and from the wrath of the Lamb! ¹⁷For the great day of their wrath has come, and who can stand?"

DECEMBER 25 ☐ DAY 360
MATTHEW 1:18—2:12; LUKE 2:1–10
The Original Christmas Present

 OVERVIEW On this most important of birthdays, we interrupt our normal Bible reading schedule to reflect on the two Gospel accounts of our Lord's birth.

In Matthew we see him as a King to be worshiped. Tracing his genealogy back to Abraham shows that Jesus is indeed in line to be King of the Jews. His miraculous conception fulfills the prophecy made by Isaiah that he would be born of a virgin. His name, *Immanuel* ("God with us"), reminds us of his divine mission. The place of his birth (Bethlehem) fulfills Micah's prediction. His flight to Egypt to escape the death threat of crazed King Herod fulfills Hosea's word and Jeremiah's heartrending lament.

In Luke we see Jesus as a Babe lying in a manger. Caesar's census causes his earthly parents to return to the city of David to register. There, with no "emergency room" but a stable and no "attendants" but barn animals, God becomes a man . . . a Savior . . . Christ the Lord.

The angels greet his birth by saying, "Glory to God in the highest"; the shepherds announce his arrival by "glorifying and praising God for all the things they had heard and seen." How will you respond to the joyous news that a Savior has come into the world?

 YOUR DAILY WALK Who, in your opinion, is Jesus of Nazareth? How would you describe him to a person who had never met him? And if he came knocking at the door of your heart this Christmas season, would he find room in the inn . . . or a No Vacancy sign prominently displayed?

Jesus is God spelling himself out in language the world can understand.

Singing and reciting the songs of the season are marvelous ways to tune your heart for Christmas. Before you close your quiet time today, find a hymnbook and a quiet place where you can be alone. Read out loud (or sing softly) a verse or two of the following Christmas favorites. Let the words remind you of the "reason for the season"—the matchless Savior who is Jesus.

- "Thou Didst Leave Thy Throne"
- "Silent Night, Holy Night"
- "O Little Town of Bethlehem"
- "While Shepherds Watched Their Flocks"
- "Away in a Manger"
- "The First Noel the Angel Did Say"

 INSIGHT Who Do You Say That He Is?
Down through the centuries, the miraculous account of Jesus' birth and life has prompted men and women to respond in praise and worship. Listen to what the sons of men have said about the Son of God:

"If Shakespeare should come into this room, we would all rise; but if Jesus Christ should come in, we would all kneel."—Charles Lamb

"I know men; and I tell you that Jesus Christ is no mere man. Between him and every other person in the world there is no possible term of comparison."—Napoléon

"Man's ultimate destiny depends not on whether he can learn new lessons or make new discoveries and conquests, but on his acceptance of the lesson taught him close upon two thousand years ago."—Inscription at the eastern entrance of Rockefeller Center, New York City

MATTHEW 1:18 — 2:12

18This is how the birth of Jesus Christ came about: His mother Mary was pledged to be married to Joseph, but before they came together, she was found to be with child through the Holy Spirit. 19Because Joseph her husband was a righteous man and did not want to expose her to public disgrace, he had in mind to divorce her quietly.

20But after he had considered this, an angel of the Lord appeared to him in a dream and said, "Joseph son of David, do not be afraid to take Mary home as your wife, because what is conceived in her is from the Holy Spirit. 21She will give birth to a son, and you are to give him the name Jesus,*l* because he will save his people from their sins."

22All this took place to fulfill what the Lord had said through the prophet: 23"The virgin will be with child and will give birth to a son, and they will call him Immanuel"*m*—which means, "God with us."

24When Joseph woke up, he did what the angel of the Lord had commanded him and took Mary home as his wife. 25But he had no union with her until she gave birth to a son. And he gave him the name Jesus.

CHAPTER 2

After Jesus was born in Bethlehem in Judea, during the time of King Herod, Magi*n* from the east came to Jerusalem 2and asked, "Where is the one who has been born king of the Jews? We saw his star in the east*o* and have come to worship him."

3When King Herod heard this he was disturbed, and all Jerusalem with him. 4When he had called together all the people's chief priests and teachers of the law, he asked them where the Christ*p* was to be born. 5"In Bethlehem in Judea," they

replied, "for this is what the prophet has written:

6" 'But you, Bethlehem, in the land of Judah,
   are by no means least among the rulers of Judah;
for out of you will come a ruler
   who will be the shepherd of my people Israel.'*q* "

7Then Herod called the Magi secretly and found out from them the exact time the star had appeared. 8He sent them to Bethlehem and said, "Go and make a careful search for the child. As soon as you find him, report to me, so that I too may go and worship him."

9After they had heard the king, they went on their way, and the star they had seen in the east*r* went ahead of them until it stopped over the place where the child was. 10When they saw the star, they were overjoyed. 11On coming to the house, they saw the child with his mother Mary, and they bowed down and worshiped him. Then they opened their treasures and presented him with gifts of gold and of incense and of myrrh. 12And having been warned in a dream not to go back to Herod, they returned to their country by another route.

LUKE 2:1-10

In those days Caesar Augustus issued a decree that a census should be taken of the entire Roman world. 2(This was the first census that took place while Quirinius was governor of Syria.) 3And everyone went to his own town to register.

4So Joseph also went up from the town of Nazareth in Galilee to Judea, to Bethlehem the town of David, because he belonged to the house and line of David. 5He went there to register with Mary, who was pledged to be married to him

---

l21 Jesus is the Greek form of *Joshua,* which means *the* LORD *saves.*   *m23* Isaiah 7:14   *n1* Traditionally *Wise Men*   *o2* Or *star when it rose*   *p4* Or *Messiah*   *q6* Micah 5:2   *r9* Or *seen when it rose* and was expecting a child. 6While they were there, the time came for the baby to be born, 7and she gave birth to her first-born, a son. She wrapped him in cloths and placed him in a manger, because there was no room for them in the inn.

8And there were shepherds living out in the fields nearby, keeping watch over their flocks at night. 9An angel of the Lord appeared to them, and the glory of the Lord shone around them, and they were terrified. 10But the angel said to them, "Do not be afraid. I bring you good news of great joy that will be for all the people.

DECEMBER 26 □ DAY 361
REVELATION 7–9
Blowing the Seven Trumpets

OVERVIEW The book of Revelation is organized around a series of cycles interrupted by parenthetical sections. Three cycles of judgments (seals, trumpets and bowls) emerge like three sections of a telescope, each more severe and far-reaching than the previous cycle. Before the seventh seal is opened, John sees four angels place a seal upon 144,000 "servants of . . . God," 12,000 from each of the twelve tribes of Israel (7:3–4). In contrast to this, John next sees a vast, innumerable host of martyrs "who have come out of the great tribulation" (7:14) for the cause of Christ. At last, the breaking of the seventh seal releases seven trumpets of judgment, which bring death and darkness, tears and torment upon humanity.

Chapter 7		Chapters 8–9	
Numbering a Multitude	A Numberless Multitude	The Seventh Seal	The Seven Trumpets
1 8	9 17	8:1 8:5	8:6 9:21
Sealed	Saved	Silence	Woes

YOUR DAILY WALK How many "purposes for prayer" can you think of? In the margin, see if you can list at least ten before reading on.

There are prayers of praise, thanksgiving, worship and rejoicing. There are prayers of confession and repentance. There are prayers for

Prayer is listening to what God might want to say to you.

personal needs, such as food, health, strength, wisdom and forgiveness. There are prayers of intercession for the needs of others, for the salvation of unsaved loved ones and for the ministry of local churches, missionaries and schools.

Your prayers are a sweet fragrance to God (8:4) as you admit your own inadequacy and lean upon God's promises of provision and power. If you have not already done so, make prayer an indispensable part of your daily time with God. Five minutes on a daily basis represents more than thirty hours in a year . . . and, by any standard, that's a lot of praise, thanksgiving, worship and rejoicing! Begin today, and every day, with prayer.

INSIGHT Seventh Seal—Seven Angels and Seven Trumpets
Seven was a sacred number to the ancient Hebrew people. It often symbolized perfection, fullness, abundance, rest and completion. The number seven also had a ritual importance to the Hebrews. Since the number seven is so symbolic in nature, it is no coincidence that it appears frequently in Revelation, a book noted for its rich symbolism and imagery.

CHAPTER 7

After this I saw four angels standing at the four corners of the earth, holding back the four winds of the earth to prevent any wind from blowing on the land or on the sea or on any tree. ²Then I saw another angel coming up from the east, having the seal of the living God. He called out in a loud voice to the four angels who had been given power to harm the land and the sea: ³"Do not harm the land or the sea or the trees until we put a seal on the foreheads of the servants of our God." ⁴Then I heard the number of those who were sealed: 144,000 from all the tribes of Israel.

⁵From the tribe of Judah 12,000 were
    sealed,
  from the tribe of Reuben 12,000,
  from the tribe of Gad 12,000,
⁶from the tribe of Asher 12,000,
  from the tribe of Naphtali 12,000,
  from the tribe of Manasseh 12,000,
⁷from the tribe of Simeon 12,000,
  from the tribe of Levi 12,000,
  from the tribe of Issachar 12,000,
⁸from the tribe of Zebulun 12,000,
  from the tribe of Joseph 12,000,
  from the tribe of Benjamin 12,000.

⁹After this I looked and there before me was a great multitude that no one could count, from every nation, tribe, people and language, standing before the throne and in front of the Lamb. They were wearing white robes and were holding palm branches in their hands. ¹⁰And they cried out in a loud voice:

"Salvation belongs to our God,
who sits on the throne,
and to the Lamb."

¹¹All the angels were standing around the throne and around the elders and the four living creatures. They fell down on their faces before the throne and worshiped God, ¹²saying:

"Amen!
Praise and glory
and wisdom and thanks and honor
and power and strength
be to our God for ever and ever.
Amen!"

¹³Then one of the elders asked me, "These in white robes—who are they, and where did they come from?"

¹⁴I answered, "Sir, you know."

And he said, "These are they who have come out of the great tribulation; they have washed their robes and made them white in the blood of the Lamb. ¹⁵Therefore,

"they are before the throne of God
  and serve him day and night in his
    temple;
and he who sits on the throne will
    spread his tent over them.
¹⁶Never again will they hunger;
  never again will they thirst.
The sun will not beat upon them,
  nor any scorching heat.
¹⁷For the Lamb at the center of the
    throne will be their shepherd;
  he will lead them to springs of
    living water.
And God will wipe away every tear
    from their eyes."

CHAPTER 8

When he opened the seventh seal, there was silence in heaven for about half an hour.

²And I saw the seven angels who stand before God, and to them were given seven trumpets.

³Another angel, who had a golden censer, came and stood at the altar. He was given much incense to offer, with the prayers of all the saints, on the golden altar before the throne. ⁴The smoke of the incense, together with the prayers of the saints, went up before God from the angel's hand. ⁵Then the angel took the censer, filled it with fire from the altar, and hurled it on the earth; and there came peals of thunder, rumblings, flashes of lightning and an earthquake.

⁶Then the seven angels who had the seven trumpets prepared to sound them.

⁷The first angel sounded his trumpet, and there came hail and fire mixed with blood, and it was hurled down upon the earth. A third of the earth was burned up, a third of the trees were burned up, and all the green grass was burned up.

⁸The second angel sounded his trumpet, and something like a huge mountain, all ablaze, was thrown into the sea. A third of the sea turned into blood, ⁹a third of the living creatures in the sea died, and a third of the ships were destroyed.

¹⁰The third angel sounded his trumpet,

and a great star, blazing like a torch, fell from the sky on a third of the rivers and on the springs of water— [11]the name of the star is Wormwood.[s] A third of the waters turned bitter, and many people died from the waters that had become bitter.

[12]The fourth angel sounded his trumpet, and a third of the sun was struck, a third of the moon, and a third of the stars, so that a third of them turned dark. A third of the day was without light, and also a third of the night.

[13]As I watched, I heard an eagle that was flying in midair call out in a loud voice: "Woe! Woe! Woe to the inhabitants of the earth, because of the trumpet blasts about to be sounded by the other three angels!"

CHAPTER 9

The fifth angel sounded his trumpet, and I saw a star that had fallen from the sky to the earth. The star was given the key to the shaft of the Abyss. [2]When he opened the Abyss, smoke rose from it like the smoke from a gigantic furnace. The sun and sky were darkened by the smoke from the Abyss. [3]And out of the smoke locusts came down upon the earth and were given power like that of scorpions of the earth. [4]They were told not to harm the grass of the earth or any plant or tree, but only those people who did not have the seal of God on their foreheads. [5]They were not given power to kill them, but only to torture them for five months. And the agony they suffered was like that of the sting of a scorpion when it strikes a man. [6]During those days men will seek death, but will not find it; they will long to die, but death will elude them.

[7]The locusts looked like horses prepared for battle. On their heads they wore something like crowns of gold, and their faces resembled human faces. [8]Their hair was like women's hair, and their teeth were like lions' teeth. [9]They had breastplates like breastplates of iron, and the sound of their wings was like the thundering of many horses and chariots rushing into battle. [10]They had tails and stings like scorpions, and in their tails they had power to torment people for five months. [11]They had as king over them the angel of the Abyss, whose name in Hebrew is Abaddon, and in Greek, Apollyon.[t]

[12]The first woe is past; two other woes are yet to come.

[13]The sixth angel sounded his trumpet, and I heard a voice coming from the horns[u] of the golden altar that is before God. [14]It said to the sixth angel who had the trumpet, "Release the four angels who are bound at the great river Euphrates." [15]And the four angels who had been kept ready for this very hour and day and month and year were released to kill a third of mankind. [16]The number of the mounted troops was two hundred million. I heard their number.

[17]The horses and riders I saw in my vision looked like this: Their breastplates were fiery red, dark blue, and yellow as sulfur. The heads of the horses resembled the heads of lions, and out of their mouths came fire, smoke and sulfur. [18]A third of mankind was killed by the three plagues of fire, smoke and sulfur that came out of their mouths. [19]The power of the horses was in their mouths and in their tails; for their tails were like snakes, having heads with which they inflict injury.

[20]The rest of mankind that were not killed by these plagues still did not repent of the work of their hands; they did not stop worshiping demons, and idols of gold, silver, bronze, stone and wood— idols that cannot see or hear or walk. [21]Nor did they repent of their murders, their magic arts, their sexual immorality or their thefts.

[s]11 That is, Bitterness   [t]11 *Abaddon* and *Apollyon* mean *Destroyer*.   [u]13 That is, projections

DECEMBER 27 □ DAY 362
REVELATION 10–13
Describing the Seven Signs

OVERVIEW Before the seventh trumpet sounds, John sees a vision of a mighty angel and a little scroll. John is instructed to eat the book, which proves sweet to the taste but sour in the stomach. Next, John sees two witnesses who have an astonishing ministry on earth for 1,260 days but then are martyred for their testimony. The sounding of the seventh trumpet is followed by a description of seven persons in chapters 12 and 13. The first four (a sun-clothed woman, a dragon, a male child and the angel Michael) are all engaged in a struggle that begins in heaven and ends on earth, where the dragon displays his wrath against the fifth, the "rest of [the woman's] offspring" (12:17). John then sees the final two figures in the drama: the beast from the sea (13:1–10) and the second beast from the earth (13:11–18).

Chapter 10	Chapter 11	Chapter 12	Chapter 13
The Little Scroll	The Two Witnesses	The Terrible Conflict	The Two Beasts
Bitterness	Boldness	Birth	Blasphemies

Seek neither more nor less than God's will for you.

YOUR DAILY WALK Here is a thought worth clipping and pondering: You are indestructible until God's purpose for your life is completed.

Nowhere is that statement more eloquently illustrated than in the lives of the two witnesses John describes in 11:3–12. Though they face a seeming "suicide mission," they are divinely protected until they "finished their testimony" (11:7). Only then are the forces of evil permitted to "overpower them and kill them." But no power on earth can hold them in the grave! At the appointed time, they ascend to heaven to receive God's commendation: Mission accomplished!

You are under this same umbrella of God's protection today. He has a purpose for your life on this earth; and no matter what the obstacles, *he will preserve you until your mission is accomplished.* Let that assurance of God's hand on your life give you added boldness as you testify for him today. But remember, time is short. There is no guarantee that you, like the two witnesses, have 1,260 days to finish your God-given mission!

INSIGHT Revelation, a Beastly Book
Of the forty occurrences of the word *beast* in the New Testament, thirty-nine of them are found in the book of Revelation!

CHAPTER 10
Then I saw another mighty angel coming down from heaven. He was robed in a cloud, with a rainbow above his head; his face was like the sun, and his legs were like fiery pillars. ²He was holding a little scroll, which lay open in his hand. He planted his right foot on the sea and his left foot on the land, ³and he gave a loud shout like the roar of a lion. When he shouted, the voices of the seven thunders spoke. ⁴And when the seven thunders

spoke, I was about to write; but I heard a voice from heaven say, "Seal up what the seven thunders have said and do not write it down."

⁵Then the angel I had seen standing on the sea and on the land raised his right hand to heaven. ⁶And he swore by him who lives for ever and ever, who created the heavens and all that is in them, the earth and all that is in it, and the sea and all that is in it, and said, "There will be no more delay! ⁷But in the days when the

seventh angel is about to sound his trumpet, the mystery of God will be accomplished, just as he announced to his servants the prophets."

[8]Then the voice that I had heard from heaven spoke to me once more: "Go, take the scroll that lies open in the hand of the angel who is standing on the sea and on the land."

[9]So I went to the angel and asked him to give me the little scroll. He said to me, "Take it and eat it. It will turn your stomach sour, but in your mouth it will be as sweet as honey." [10]I took the little scroll from the angel's hand and ate it. It tasted as sweet as honey in my mouth, but when I had eaten it, my stomach turned sour. [11]Then I was told, "You must prophesy again about many peoples, nations, languages and kings."

CHAPTER 11

I was given a reed like a measuring rod and was told, "Go and measure the temple of God and the altar, and count the worshipers there. [2]But exclude the outer court; do not measure it, because it has been given to the Gentiles. They will trample on the holy city for 42 months. [3]And I will give power to my two witnesses, and they will prophesy for 1,260 days, clothed in sackcloth." [4]These are the two olive trees and the two lampstands that stand before the Lord of the earth. [5]If anyone tries to harm them, fire comes from their mouths and devours their enemies. This is how anyone who wants to harm them must die. [6]These men have power to shut up the sky so that it will not rain during the time they are prophesying; and they have power to turn the waters into blood and to strike the earth with every kind of plague as often as they want.

[7]Now when they have finished their testimony, the beast that comes up from the Abyss will attack them, and overpower and kill them. [8]Their bodies will lie in the street of the great city, which is figuratively called Sodom and Egypt, where also their Lord was crucified. [9]For three and a half days men from every people, tribe, language and nation will gaze on their bodies and refuse them burial. [10]The inhabitants of the earth will gloat over them and will celebrate by sending each other gifts, because these two prophets

had tormented those who live on the earth.

[11]But after the three and a half days a breath of life from God entered them, and they stood on their feet, and terror struck those who saw them. [12]Then they heard a loud voice from heaven saying to them, "Come up here." And they went up to heaven in a cloud, while their enemies looked on.

[13]At that very hour there was a severe earthquake and a tenth of the city collapsed. Seven thousand people were killed in the earthquake, and the survivors were terrified and gave glory to the God of heaven.

[14]The second woe has passed; the third woe is coming soon.

[15]The seventh angel sounded his trumpet, and there were loud voices in heaven, which said:

> "The kingdom of the world has
>   become the kingdom of our
>   Lord and of his Christ,
>   and he will reign for ever and ever."

[16]And the twenty-four elders, who were seated on their thrones before God, fell on their faces and worshiped God, [17]saying:

> "We give thanks to you, Lord God
>   Almighty,
>   the One who is and who was,
> because you have taken your great
>   power
>   and have begun to reign.
> [18]The nations were angry;
>   and your wrath has come.
> The time has come for judging the
>   dead,
>   and for rewarding your servants the
>   prophets
> and your saints and those who
>   reverence your name,
>   both small and great—
> and for destroying those who destroy
>   the earth."

[19]Then God's temple in heaven was opened, and within his temple was seen the ark of his covenant. And there came flashes of lightning, rumblings, peals of thunder, an earthquake and a great hailstorm.

CHAPTER 12

A great and wondrous sign appeared in heaven: a woman clothed with the sun, with the moon under her feet and a crown of twelve stars on her head. ²She was pregnant and cried out in pain as she was about to give birth. ³Then another sign appeared in heaven: an enormous red dragon with seven heads and ten horns and seven crowns on his heads. ⁴His tail swept a third of the stars out of the sky and flung them to the earth. The dragon stood in front of the woman who was about to give birth, so that he might devour her child the moment it was born. ⁵She gave birth to a son, a male child, who will rule all the nations with an iron scepter. And her child was snatched up to God and to his throne. ⁶The woman fled into the desert to a place prepared for her by God, where she might be taken care of for 1,260 days.

⁷And there was war in heaven. Michael and his angels fought against the dragon, and the dragon and his angels fought back. ⁸But he was not strong enough, and they lost their place in heaven. ⁹The great dragon was hurled down—that ancient serpent called the devil, or Satan, who leads the whole world astray. He was hurled to the earth, and his angels with him.

¹⁰Then I heard a loud voice in heaven say:

"Now have come the salvation and the
        power and the kingdom of our
        God,
    and the authority of his Christ.
For the accuser of our brothers,
    who accuses them before our God
        day and night,
    has been hurled down.
¹¹They overcame him
    by the blood of the Lamb
    and by the word of their testimony;
they did not love their lives so much
    as to shrink from death.
¹²Therefore rejoice, you heavens
    and you who dwell in them!
But woe to the earth and the sea,
    because the devil has gone down to
        you!
He is filled with fury,
    because he knows that his time is
        short."

¹³When the dragon saw that he had been hurled to the earth, he pursued the woman who had given birth to the male child. ¹⁴The woman was given the two wings of a great eagle, so that she might fly to the place prepared for her in the desert, where she would be taken care of for a time, times and half a time, out of the serpent's reach. ¹⁵Then from his mouth the serpent spewed water like a river, to overtake the woman and sweep her away with the torrent. ¹⁶But the earth helped the woman by opening its mouth and swallowing the river that the dragon had spewed out of his mouth. ¹⁷Then the dragon was enraged at the woman and went off to make war against the rest of her offspring—those who obey God's commandments and hold to the testimony CHAPTER 13 of Jesus. ¹And the dragon* stood on the shore of the sea.

And I saw a beast coming out of the sea. He had ten horns and seven heads, with ten crowns on his horns, and on each head a blasphemous name. ²The beast I saw resembled a leopard, but had feet like those of a bear and a mouth like that of a lion. The dragon gave the beast his power and his throne and great authority. ³One of the heads of the beast seemed to have had a fatal wound, but the fatal wound had been healed. The whole world was astonished and followed the beast. ⁴Men worshiped the dragon because he had given authority to the beast, and they also worshiped the beast and asked, "Who is like the beast? Who can make war against him?"

⁵The beast was given a mouth to utter proud words and blasphemies and to exercise his authority for forty-two months. ⁶He opened his mouth to blaspheme God, and to slander his name and his dwelling place and those who live in heaven. ⁷He was given power to make war against the saints and to conquer them. And he was given authority over every tribe, people, language and nation. ⁸All inhabitants of the earth will worship the beast—all whose names have not been written in the book of life belonging to the Lamb that was slain from the creation of the world.*

⁹He who has an ear, let him hear.

¹⁰If anyone is to go into captivity,
    into captivity he will go.

v1 Some late manuscripts And I   w8 Or written from the creation of the world in the book of life belonging to the Lamb that was slain

If anyone is to be killed^x with the
    sword,
  with the sword he will be killed.

This calls for patient endurance and
faithfulness on the part of the saints.
[11]Then I saw another beast, coming out
of the earth. He had two horns like a
lamb, but he spoke like a dragon. [12]He
exercised all the authority of the first
beast on his behalf, and made the earth
and its inhabitants worship the first beast,
whose fatal wound had been healed.
[13]And he performed great and miraculous
signs, even causing fire to come down
from heaven to earth in full view of men.
[14]Because of the signs he was given power
to do on behalf of the first beast, he de-

ceived the inhabitants of the earth. He ordered them to set up an image in honor of
the beast who was wounded by the sword
and yet lived. [15]He was given power to
give breath to the image of the first beast,
so that it could speak and cause all who
refused to worship the image to be killed.
[16]He also forced everyone, small and
great, rich and poor, free and slave, to receive a mark on his right hand or on his
forehead, [17]so that no one could buy or
sell unless he had the mark, which is the
name of the beast or the number of his
name.

[18]This calls for wisdom. If anyone has
insight, let him calculate the number of
the beast, for it is man's number. His
number is 666.

^x10 Some manuscripts *anyone kills*

DECEMBER 28 ☐ DAY 363
Alpha and Omega

LOOK BACK The final two books of the New Testament are the "long
and the short of it"—the powerful little book of Jude and the awe-
inspiring book of Revelation. Jude challenges his readers to "fight for the
faith" because it is a faith worth fighting for. False teachers prowl like
ravaging wolves, looking for the weak and unprepared. Christians dare
not be naive about the danger, for the Old Testament shows clearly
what happened to the fallen angels and the wicked cities of Sodom
and Gomorrah.

One of God's titles is "the Alpha and the Omega" (Revelation 1:8).
What began in the book of Genesis now comes to completion in the
book of Revelation. John the "beloved apostle" (the same man who
wrote the Gospel of John and the three Epistles of John) writes from
his island exile, unveiling "the things which you have seen [Revelation
1], and the things which are [Revelation 2–3] and the things which
will take place after this [Revelation 4–22]." Highlights of the book include seven letters to seven churches and three cycles of judgment
upon the earth.

Revelation concludes with a final glimpse of God's grandeur, an invitation to the reader and a warning to all who would attempt to add
to, or delete from, the message of the book. Though the story of the
Bible has stretched over sixty-six books, one day the curtain on human history will drop and "The End" will come. "Amen! Come, Lord
Jesus!" (Revelation 22:20).

LOOK UP Earlier in your journey through the New Testament, you
read these words from the apostle Paul: "Being confident of this, that
he who began a good work in you will carry it on to completion until
the day of Christ Jesus" (Philippians 1:6).

In a word, God finishes what he starts. To see that more clearly, notice this startling series of contrasts between the first three chapters of
the Bible (Genesis 1–3) and the final three chapters (Revelation
20–22):

In Genesis We Read . . .	In Revelation We Read . . .
"In the beginning God created the heavens and the earth" (1:1)	"I saw a new heaven and a new earth" (21:1)
"The darkness he called 'night'" (1:5)	"No more night" (22:5)
"God made two great lights [sun and moon]" (1:16)	"The city does not need the sun or the moon" (21:23)
"You will surely die" (2:17)	"No more death" (21:4)
"I will greatly increase your pains" (3:16)	"No more . . . pain" (21:4)
"Cursed is the ground because of you" (3:17)	"No longer will there be any curse" (22:3)
"He drove the man out" (3:24)	"They will see his face" (22:4)

LOOK AHEAD Over the past year, you've developed a new habit of holiness—the habit of consistently reading and obeying God's Word. Congratulations! As the New Year begins, why not retrace your steps through the sixty-six books of the Bible? This time have a question in mind as you read: What does the Bible say about managing my money? being a godly spouse and parent? making wise decisions? praying prayers God delights to answer?

Keep a journal of your discoveries, and expect God to meet you each day along your *daily walk*.

DECEMBER 29 □ DAY 364
REVELATION 14–16
Pouring Out the Seven Bowls

OVERVIEW Accompanied by the singing of the 144,000, the final outpouring of God's wrath begins. The earth is ripe in its wickedness and richly deserving of the calamities that are about to befall it. Seven angels arrive with seven bowls full of plagues, pestilence, disease and death. As the bowls of God's wrath are poured out—judgments that are "true and just" (16:7)—people refuse to acknowledge the Creator, but instead curse "the God of heaven because of their pains and their sores" (16:11). Following the seventh bowl, a loud voice from heaven declares, "It is done!" (16:17).

Chapter 14	Chapter 15	Chapter 16
The Judge Is Coming	Judgment Is Coming	Judgment Is Here
Lamb of God	Wrath of God	Bowls of God's Wrath

YOUR DAILY WALK When was the last time your spouse was angry with you? Do you recall the circumstances? How about the last time your boss was mad at you? What was the outcome?

Anger can be a fearful emotion, whether expressed by a spouse or child, friend or foe. Now imagine that it is not another human being who is angry with you, but the God of the universe . . . the God who created you from dust . . . the God who will one day destroy "the

Sinners may oppose God's ways, but not his wrath. elements . . . in . . . heat" (2 Peter 3:10, 12). How would you face that kind of anger? Where would you go to escape it? The answer, of course, is *nowhere!*

Today God offers his love and mercy, but there is coming a day when his wrath and judgment will pour down upon all who have ignored his invitation. That means *you* if you have spurned his offer of salvation in Jesus Christ. That means your unsaved family members and friends. And that means there is no better time than *now* to warn those you love of the peril they face by continuing in their unbelief. Can you afford to wait?

 INSIGHT Armageddon—the Big Little Mountain
Apart from its significance in Bible times, during which it witnessed two great victories (Judges 4:15; 7:1–25) and two stunning defeats (1 Samuel 31:4–10; 2 Kings 23:29–30), the hill of Meggido has been the site of battles involving Pompey, Napoléon, Alexander the Great and (more recently) Lord Allenby in 1917.

CHAPTER 14

Then I looked, and there before me was the Lamb, standing on Mount Zion, and with him 144,000 who had his name and his Father's name written on their foreheads. ²And I heard a sound from heaven like the roar of rushing waters and like a loud peal of thunder. The sound I heard was like that of harpists playing their harps. ³And they sang a new song before the throne and before the four living creatures and the elders. No one could learn the song except the 144,000 who had been redeemed from the earth. ⁴These are those who did not defile themselves with women, for they kept themselves pure. They follow the Lamb wherever he goes. They were purchased from among men and offered as firstfruits to God and the Lamb. ⁵No lie was found in their mouths; they are blameless.

⁶Then I saw another angel flying in midair, and he had the eternal gospel to proclaim to those who live on the earth—to every nation, tribe, language and people. ⁷He said in a loud voice, "Fear God and give him glory, because the hour of his judgment has come. Worship him who made the heavens, the earth, the sea and the springs of water."

⁸A second angel followed and said, "Fallen! Fallen is Babylon the Great, which made all the nations drink the maddening wine of her adulteries."

⁹A third angel followed them and said in a loud voice: "If anyone worships the beast and his image and receives his mark on the forehead or on the hand, ¹⁰he, too, will drink of the wine of God's fury, which has been poured full strength into the cup of his wrath. He will be tormented with burning sulfur in the presence of the holy angels and of the Lamb. ¹¹And the smoke of their torment rises for ever and ever. There is no rest day or night for those who worship the beast and his image, or for anyone who receives the mark of his name." ¹²This calls for patient endurance on the part of the saints who obey God's commandments and remain faithful to Jesus.

¹³Then I heard a voice from heaven say, "Write: Blessed are the dead who die in the Lord from now on."

"Yes," says the Spirit, "they will rest from their labor, for their deeds will follow them."

¹⁴I looked, and there before me was a white cloud, and seated on the cloud was one "like a son of man"ʸ with a crown of gold on his head and a sharp sickle in his hand. ¹⁵Then another angel came out of the temple and called in a loud voice to him who was sitting on the cloud, "Take your sickle and reap, because the time to reap has come, for the harvest of the earth is ripe." ¹⁶So he who was seated on the cloud swung his sickle over the earth, and the earth was harvested.

¹⁷Another angel came out of the temple in heaven, and he too had a sharp sickle. ¹⁸Still another angel, who had charge of the fire, came from the altar and called in a loud voice to him who had the sharp sickle, "Take your sharp sickle and gather the clusters of grapes from the earth's

ʸ14 Daniel 7:13

vine, because its grapes are ripe." [19]The angel swung his sickle on the earth, gathered its grapes and threw them into the great winepress of God's wrath. [20]They were trampled in the winepress outside the city, and blood flowed out of the press, rising as high as the horses' bridles for a distance of 1,600 stadia.[z]

CHAPTER 15

I saw in heaven another great and marvelous sign: seven angels with the seven last plagues—last, because with them God's wrath is completed. [2]And I saw what looked like a sea of glass mixed with fire and, standing beside the sea, those who had been victorious over the beast and his image and over the number of his name. They held harps given them by God [3]and sang the song of Moses the servant of God and the song of the Lamb:

"Great and marvelous are your deeds,
　Lord God Almighty.
Just and true are your ways,
　King of the ages.
[4]Who will not fear you, O Lord,
　and bring glory to your name?
For you alone are holy.
All nations will come
　and worship before you,
for your righteous acts have been
　revealed."

[5]After this I looked and in heaven the temple, that is, the tabernacle of the Testimony, was opened. [6]Out of the temple came the seven angels with the seven plagues. They were dressed in clean, shining linen and wore golden sashes around their chests. [7]Then one of the four living creatures gave to the seven angels seven golden bowls filled with the wrath of God, who lives for ever and ever. [8]And the temple was filled with smoke from the glory of God and from his power, and no one could enter the temple until the seven plagues of the seven angels were completed.

CHAPTER 16

Then I heard a loud voice from the temple saying to the seven angels, "Go, pour out the seven bowls of God's wrath on the earth."

[2]The first angel went and poured out his bowl on the land, and ugly and painful sores broke out on the people who had the mark of the beast and worshiped his image.

[3]The second angel poured out his bowl on the sea, and it turned into blood like that of a dead man, and every living thing in the sea died.

[4]The third angel poured out his bowl on the rivers and springs of water, and they became blood. [5]Then I heard the angel in charge of the waters say:

"You are just in these judgments,
　you who are and who were, the
　　Holy One,
because you have so judged;
[6]for they have shed the blood of your
　saints and prophets,
　and you have given them blood to
　　drink as they deserve."

[7]And I heard the altar respond:

"Yes, Lord God Almighty,
　true and just are your judgments."

[8]The fourth angel poured out his bowl on the sun, and the sun was given power to scorch people with fire. [9]They were seared by the intense heat and they cursed the name of God, who had control over these plagues, but they refused to repent and glorify him.

[10]The fifth angel poured out his bowl on the throne of the beast, and his kingdom was plunged into darkness. Men gnawed their tongues in agony [11]and cursed the God of heaven because of their pains and their sores, but they refused to repent of what they had done.

[12]The sixth angel poured out his bowl on the great river Euphrates, and its water was dried up to prepare the way for the kings from the East. [13]Then I saw three evil[a] spirits that looked like frogs; they came out of the mouth of the dragon, out of the mouth of the beast and out of the mouth of the false prophet. [14]They are spirits of demons performing miraculous signs, and they go out to the kings of the whole world, to gather them for the battle on the great day of God Almighty.

[15]"Behold, I come like a thief! Blessed is he who stays awake and keeps his clothes with him, so that he may not go naked and be shamefully exposed."

[z]20 That is, about 180 miles (about 300 kilometers)　　[a]13 Greek *unclean*

¹⁶Then they gathered the kings together to the place that in Hebrew is called Armageddon.

¹⁷The seventh angel poured out his bowl into the air, and out of the temple came a loud voice from the throne, saying, "It is done!" ¹⁸Then there came flashes of lightning, rumblings, peals of thunder and a severe earthquake. No earthquake like it has ever occurred since man has been on earth, so tremendous was the quake. ¹⁹The great city split into three parts, and the cities of the nations collapsed. God remembered Babylon the Great and gave her the cup filled with the wine of the fury of his wrath. ²⁰Every island fled away and the mountains could not be found. ²¹From the sky huge hailstones of about a hundred pounds each fell upon men. And they cursed God on account of the plague of hail, because the plague was so terrible.

DECEMBER 30 ☐ DAY 365
REVELATION 17–19
Destroying God's Enemies

 OVERVIEW John sees God's judgment poured out on more than just the physical universe. Babylon, headquarters of religious and civil authority, is warned by an angelic messenger of its approaching doom. The city's destruction—complete and irrevocable—is mourned by kings and merchants alike who profited from her rich trade and false religion. By contrast, heaven rejoices in the demise of the wicked city. After the wedding supper of the Lamb in heaven, the scene shifts back to the earth, where the King of kings comes to judge and destroy his human enemies.

Chapter 17	Chapter 18	Chapter 19	
Babylon's Description	Babylon's Destruction	Salvation from the Lord	A Supper for the Lamb
		1 5	6 21
Climax of Punishment		Commencement of Praise	

 YOUR DAILY WALK In the cast of characters in the unfolding drama of God's plan of the ages, the leading role is played by the Lord Jesus Christ: the promised Messiah in the Old Testament, the Lamb of God in the New Testament and the returning King of kings and Lord of lords (19:16). This is the significance of the angel's statement to John: "The testimony of Jesus is the spirit of prophecy" (19:10). The totality of Scripture as the prophetic message of God to humankind centers on the person and ministry of the Lord Jesus Christ. Therefore, Jesus should be "visible" in every page of your Bible.

Time has no power over the name and deeds and words of Jesus Christ.

Try it! Thumb back through the books of the Bible you have studied this year, and see if you can suggest the way Jesus is pictured in each. For example, Genesis: the one who will crush Satan's head (3:15); Exodus: the Redeemer from bondage to sin; Leviticus: the Holy One of God, etc. Have fun!

 INSIGHT The Supremely Appropriate Title
The woman dressed in purple "who sits on many waters" (17:1) is given the title "Mystery, Babylon the Great" (17:5)—a most appropriate caption for this mysterious person who has prompted commentators to suggest a wide variety of different identities, including: (1) the actual rebuilt city on the site of ancient Babylon; (2) an actual city, but

different from Babylon; (3) a false religious system; (4) an atheistic political system.

CHAPTER 17

One of the seven angels who had the seven bowls came and said to me, "Come, I will show you the punishment of the great prostitute, who sits on many waters. ²With her the kings of the earth committed adultery and the inhabitants of the earth were intoxicated with the wine of her adulteries."

³Then the angel carried me away in the Spirit into a desert. There I saw a woman sitting on a scarlet beast that was covered with blasphemous names and had seven heads and ten horns. ⁴The woman was dressed in purple and scarlet, and was glittering with gold, precious stones and pearls. She held a golden cup in her hand, filled with abominable things and the filth of her adulteries. ⁵This title was written on her forehead:

MYSTERY

BABYLON THE GREAT

THE MOTHER OF PROSTITUTES

AND OF THE ABOMINATIONS OF THE EARTH.

⁶I saw that the woman was drunk with the blood of the saints, the blood of those who bore testimony to Jesus.

When I saw her, I was greatly astonished. ⁷Then the angel said to me: "Why are you astonished? I will explain to you the mystery of the woman and of the beast she rides, which has the seven heads and ten horns. ⁸The beast, which you saw, once was, now is not, and will come up out of the Abyss and go to his destruction. The inhabitants of the earth whose names have not been written in the book of life from the creation of the world will be astonished when they see the beast, because he once was, now is not, and yet will come.

⁹"This calls for a mind with wisdom. The seven heads are seven hills on which the woman sits. ¹⁰They are also seven kings. Five have fallen, one is, the other has not yet come; but when he does come, he must remain for a little while. ¹¹The beast who once was, and now is not, is an eighth king. He belongs to the seven and is going to his destruction.

¹²"The ten horns you saw are ten kings who have not yet received a kingdom, but who for one hour will receive authority as kings along with the beast. ¹³They have one purpose and will give their power and authority to the beast. ¹⁴They will make war against the Lamb, but the Lamb will overcome them because he is Lord of lords and King of kings—and with him will be his called, chosen and faithful followers."

¹⁵Then the angel said to me, "The waters you saw, where the prostitute sits, are peoples, multitudes, nations and languages. ¹⁶The beast and the ten horns you saw will hate the prostitute. They will bring her to ruin and leave her naked; they will eat her flesh and burn her with fire. ¹⁷For God has put it into their hearts to accomplish his purpose by agreeing to give the beast their power to rule, until God's words are fulfilled. ¹⁸The woman you saw is the great city that rules over the kings of the earth."

CHAPTER 18

After this I saw another angel coming down from heaven. He had great authority, and the earth was illuminated by his splendor. ²With a mighty voice he shouted:

"Fallen! Fallen is Babylon the Great!
    She has become a home for demons
and a haunt for every evil*ᵇ* spirit,
    a haunt for every unclean and
        detestable bird.
³For all the nations have drunk
    the maddening wine of her
        adulteries.
The kings of the earth committed
        adultery with her,
    and the merchants of the earth grew
        rich from her excessive
        luxuries."

⁴Then I heard another voice from heaven say:

"Come out of her, my people,
    so that you will not share in her
        sins,
    so that you will not receive any of
        her plagues;
⁵for her sins are piled up to heaven,

ᵇ2 Greek unclean

and God has remembered her
crimes.
[6]Give back to her as she has given;
pay her back double for what she
has done.
Mix her a double portion from her
own cup.
[7]Give her as much torture and grief
as the glory and luxury she gave
herself.
In her heart she boasts,
'I sit as queen; I am not a widow,
and I will never mourn.'
[8]Therefore in one day her plagues will
overtake her:
death, mourning and famine.
She will be consumed by fire,
for mighty is the Lord God who
judges her.

[9]"When the kings of the earth who
committed adultery with her and shared
her luxury see the smoke of her burning,
they will weep and mourn over her.
[10]Terrified at her torment, they will stand
far off and cry:

" 'Woe! Woe, O great city,
O Babylon, city of power!
In one hour your doom has come!'

[11]"The merchants of the earth will weep
and mourn over her because no one buys
their cargoes any more— [12]cargoes of
gold, silver, precious stones and pearls;
fine linen, purple, silk and scarlet cloth;
every sort of citron wood, and articles of
every kind made of ivory, costly wood,
bronze, iron and marble; [13]cargoes of cinnamon and spice, of incense, myrrh and
frankincense, of wine and olive oil, of fine
flour and wheat; cattle and sheep; horses
and carriages; and bodies and souls of
men.
[14]"They will say, 'The fruit you longed
for is gone from you. All your riches and
splendor have vanished, never to be recovered.' [15]The merchants who sold these
things and gained their wealth from her
will stand far off, terrified at her torment.
They will weep and mourn [16]and cry out:

" 'Woe! Woe, O great city,
dressed in fine linen, purple and
scarlet,
and glittering with gold, precious
stones and pearls!
[17]In one hour such great wealth has
been brought to ruin!'

"Every sea captain, and all who travel
by ship, the sailors, and all who earn their
living from the sea, will stand far off.
[18]When they see the smoke of her burning, they will exclaim, 'Was there ever a
city like this great city?' [19]They will throw
dust on their heads, and with weeping
and mourning cry out:

" 'Woe! Woe, O great city,
where all who had ships on the sea
became rich through her wealth!
In one hour she has been brought to
ruin!
[20]Rejoice over her, O heaven!
Rejoice, saints and apostles and
prophets!
God has judged her for the way she
treated you.' "

[21]Then a mighty angel picked up a
boulder the size of a large millstone and
threw it into the sea, and said:

"With such violence
the great city of Babylon will be
thrown down,
never to be found again.
[22]The music of harpists and musicians,
flute players and trumpeters,
will never be heard in you again.
No workman of any trade
will ever be found in you again.
The sound of a millstone
will never be heard in you again.
[23]The light of a lamp
will never shine in you again.
The voice of bridegroom and bride
will never be heard in you again.
Your merchants were the world's great
men.
By your magic spell all the nations
were led astray.
[24]In her was found the blood of
prophets and of the saints,
and of all who have been killed on
the earth."

CHAPTER 19
After this I heard what sounded like the
roar of a great multitude in heaven
shouting:

"Hallelujah!
Salvation and glory and power belong
to our God,
[2]　for true and just are his judgments.
He has condemned the great prostitute

who corrupted the earth by her
adulteries.
He has avenged on her the blood of
his servants."

[3]And again they shouted:

"Hallelujah!
The smoke from her goes up for ever
and ever."

[4]The twenty-four elders and the four
living creatures fell down and worshiped
God, who was seated on the throne. And
they cried:

"Amen, Hallelujah!"

[5]Then a voice came from the throne,
saying:

"Praise our God,
all you his servants,
you who fear him,
both small and great!"

[6]Then I heard what sounded like a great
multitude, like the roar of rushing waters
and like loud peals of thunder, shouting:

"Hallelujah!
For our Lord God Almighty reigns.
[7]Let us rejoice and be glad
and give him glory!
For the wedding of the Lamb has
come,
and his bride has made herself
ready.
[8]Fine linen, bright and clean,
was given her to wear."
(Fine linen stands for the righteous acts of
the saints.)

[9]Then the angel said to me, "Write:
'Blessed are those who are invited to the
wedding supper of the Lamb!' " And he
added, "These are the true words of God."

[10]At this I fell at his feet to worship him.
But he said to me, "Do not do it! I am a
fellow servant with you and with your
brothers who hold to the testimony of

[c]15 Psalm 2:9

Jesus. Worship God! For the testimony of
Jesus is the spirit of prophecy."

[11]I saw heaven standing open and there
before me was a white horse, whose rider
is called Faithful and True. With justice he
judges and makes war. [12]His eyes are like
blazing fire, and on his head are many
crowns. He has a name written on him
that no one knows but he himself. [13]He is
dressed in a robe dipped in blood, and his
name is the Word of God. [14]The armies
of heaven were following him, riding on
white horses and dressed in fine linen,
white and clean. [15]Out of his mouth
comes a sharp sword with which to strike
down the nations. "He will rule them with
an iron scepter."[c] He treads the winepress of the fury of the wrath of God Almighty. [16]On his robe and on his thigh he
has this name written:

KING OF KINGS AND LORD OF LORDS.

[17]And I saw an angel standing in the
sun, who cried in a loud voice to all the
birds flying in midair, "Come, gather together for the great supper of God, [18]so
that you may eat the flesh of kings, generals, and mighty men, of horses and their
riders, and the flesh of all people, free and
slave, small and great."

[19]Then I saw the beast and the kings of
the earth and their armies gathered together to make war against the rider on
the horse and his army. [20]But the beast
was captured, and with him the false
prophet who had performed the miraculous signs on his behalf. With these signs
he had deluded those who had received
the mark of the beast and worshiped his
image. The two of them were thrown
alive into the fiery lake of burning sulfur.
[21]The rest of them were killed with the
sword that came out of the mouth of the
rider on the horse, and all the birds
gorged themselves on their flesh.

DECEMBER 31 ☐ DAY 366
REVELATION 20–22
Making All Things New

OVERVIEW The consummation of God's judgment includes the doom of two other enemies of humankind: the devil and death. Their being cast into the lake of fire (20:10, 14) paves the way for the introduction of a new heaven and earth where there is no night . . . no tears . . . no pain . . . no sun . . . no moon; a place where "nothing impure will ever enter it" (21:27). Once again, God and his people live in perfect, unbroken fellowship. John's book ends with the people of God assembled in the presence of God, worshiping him in holiness and reigning together over all he has created, much like Adam and Eve in the garden many centuries before. John, whose heart yearns for that day, is moved to write—even as millions have been moved to pray—"Amen! Come, Lord Jesus!" (22:20).

Chapter 20	Chapter 21	Chapter 22
The End of the Devil and Death	The Beginning of a New Heaven and Earth	A Final Warning "I Am Coming Soon"
Punishment	Pictures	Promises

YOUR DAILY WALK Congratulations! If you began reading through the Bible last January (and have stayed on schedule), today you will finish reading the 31,173 verses in the New International Version of the Bible.

We are not at our best perched at the summit; we are climbers, at our best when the way is steep.

Perhaps occasionally, as you found yourself swimming through Psalms or jumping through Jeremiah, you were tempted to breathe the prayer that was on John's lips as he concluded writing down the lengthy book of Revelation: "Amen! Come, Lord Jesus" (22:20). But if Jesus tarries, the coming year will bring the exciting challenge of new steps of growth.

INSIGHT Sadness in the Old, Gladness in the New
Perhaps the saddest words in the entire Old Testament are these: "The LORD God banished [man] from the Garden of Eden. . . . he drove the man out" (Genesis 3:23–24). By contrast, some of the gladdest words in all the New Testament are found in today's section: "They will see his face" (Revelation 22:4). As one commentator put it, "Sin drove man from one garden. Grace brings man to an eternal Paradise." Are you ready for that day of gladness and joy?

CHAPTER 20

And I saw an angel coming down out of heaven, having the key to the Abyss and holding in his hand a great chain. ²He seized the dragon, that ancient serpent, who is the devil, or Satan, and bound him for a thousand years. ³He threw him into the Abyss, and locked and sealed it over him, to keep him from deceiving the nations anymore until the thousand years were ended. After that, he must be set free for a short time.

⁴I saw thrones on which were seated those who had been given authority to judge. And I saw the souls of those who had been beheaded because of their testimony for Jesus and because of the word of God. They had not worshiped the beast or his image and had not received his mark on their foreheads or their hands. They came to life and reigned with Christ a thousand years. ⁵(The rest of the dead did not come to life until the thousand years were ended.) This is the first resurrection. ⁶Blessed and holy are those who have part in the first resurrection. The

second death has no power over them, but they will be priests of God and of Christ and will reign with him for a thousand years.

[7]When the thousand years are over, Satan will be released from his prison [8]and will go out to deceive the nations in the four corners of the earth—Gog and Magog—to gather them for battle. In number they are like the sand on the seashore. [9]They marched across the breadth of the earth and surrounded the camp of God's people, the city he loves. But fire came down from heaven and devoured them. [10]And the devil, who deceived them, was thrown into the lake of burning sulfur, where the beast and the false prophet had been thrown. They will be tormented day and night for ever and ever.

[11]Then I saw a great white throne and him who was seated on it. Earth and sky fled from his presence, and there was no place for them. [12]And I saw the dead, great and small, standing before the throne, and books were opened. Another book was opened, which is the book of life. The dead were judged according to what they had done as recorded in the books. [13]The sea gave up the dead that were in it, and death and Hades gave up the dead that were in them, and each person was judged according to what he had done. [14]Then death and Hades were thrown into the lake of fire. The lake of fire is the second death. [15]If anyone's name was not found written in the book of life, he was thrown into the lake of fire.

CHAPTER 21

Then I saw a new heaven and a new earth, for the first heaven and the first earth had passed away, and there was no longer any sea. [2]I saw the Holy City, the new Jerusalem, coming down out of heaven from God, prepared as a bride beautifully dressed for her husband. [3]And I heard a loud voice from the throne saying, "Now the dwelling of God is with men, and he will live with them. They will be his people, and God himself will be with them and be their God. [4]He will wipe every tear from their eyes. There will be no more death or mourning or crying or pain, for the old order of things has passed away."

[5]He who was seated on the throne said, "I am making everything new!" Then he said, "Write this down, for these words are trustworthy and true."

[6]He said to me: "It is done. I am the Alpha and the Omega, the Beginning and the End. To him who is thirsty I will give to drink without cost from the spring of the water of life. [7]He who overcomes will inherit all this, and I will be his God and he will be my son. [8]But the cowardly, the unbelieving, the vile, the murderers, the sexually immoral, those who practice magic arts, the idolaters and all liars—their place will be in the fiery lake of burning sulfur. This is the second death."

[9]One of the seven angels who had the seven bowls full of the seven last plagues came and said to me, "Come, I will show you the bride, the wife of the Lamb." [10]And he carried me away in the Spirit to a mountain great and high, and showed me the Holy City, Jerusalem, coming down out of heaven from God. [11]It shone with the glory of God, and its brilliance was like that of a very precious jewel, like a jasper, clear as crystal. [12]It had a great, high wall with twelve gates, and with twelve angels at the gates. On the gates were written the names of the twelve tribes of Israel. [13]There were three gates on the east, three on the north, three on the south and three on the west. [14]The wall of the city had twelve foundations, and on them were the names of the twelve apostles of the Lamb.

[15]The angel who talked with me had a measuring rod of gold to measure the city, its gates and its walls. [16]The city was laid out like a square, as long as it was wide. He measured the city with the rod and found it to be 12,000 stadia[d] in length, and as wide and high as it is long. [17]He measured its wall and it was 144 cubits[e] thick,[f] by man's measurement, which the angel was using. [18]The wall was made of jasper, and the city of pure gold, as pure as glass. [19]The foundations of the city walls were decorated with every kind of precious stone. The first foundation was jasper, the second sapphire, the third chalcedony, the fourth emerald, [20]the fifth sardonyx, the sixth carnelian, the seventh chrysolite, the eighth beryl, the ninth topaz, the tenth chrysoprase, the

---

[d]16 That is, about 1,400 miles (about 2,200 kilometers)   [e]17 That is, about 200 feet (about 65 meters)   [f]17 Or high

eleventh jacinth, and the twelfth amethyst.^{g} ^{21}The twelve gates were twelve pearls, each gate made of a single pearl. The great street of the city was of pure gold, like transparent glass.

^{22}I did not see a temple in the city, because the Lord God Almighty and the Lamb are its temple. ^{23}The city does not need the sun or the moon to shine on it, for the glory of God gives it light, and the Lamb is its lamp. ^{24}The nations will walk by its light, and the kings of the earth will bring their splendor into it. ^{25}On no day will its gates ever be shut, for there will be no night there. ^{26}The glory and honor of the nations will be brought into it. ^{27}Nothing impure will ever enter it, nor will anyone who does what is shameful or deceitful, but only those whose names are written in the Lamb's book of life.

CHAPTER 22
Then the angel showed me the river of the water of life, as clear as crystal, flowing from the throne of God and of the Lamb ^{2}down the middle of the great street of the city. On each side of the river stood the tree of life, bearing twelve crops of fruit, yielding its fruit every month. And the leaves of the tree are for the healing of the nations. ^{3}No longer will there be any curse. The throne of God and of the Lamb will be in the city, and his servants will serve him. ^{4}They will see his face, and his name will be on their foreheads. ^{5}There will be no more night. They will not need the light of a lamp or the light of the sun, for the Lord God will give them light. And they will reign for ever and ever.

^{6}The angel said to me, "These words are trustworthy and true. The Lord, the God of the spirits of the prophets, sent his angel to show his servants the things that must soon take place."

^{7}"Behold, I am coming soon! Blessed is he who keeps the words of the prophecy in this book."

^{8}I, John, am the one who heard and saw these things. And when I had heard and seen them, I fell down to worship at the feet of the angel who had been showing

them to me. ^{9}But he said to me, "Do not do it! I am a fellow servant with you and with your brothers the prophets and of all who keep the words of this book. Worship God!"

^{10}Then he told me, "Do not seal up the words of the prophecy of this book, because the time is near. ^{11}Let him who does wrong continue to do wrong; let him who is vile continue to be vile; let him who does right continue to do right; and let him who is holy continue to be holy."

^{12}"Behold, I am coming soon! My reward is with me, and I will give to everyone according to what he has done. ^{13}I am the Alpha and the Omega, the First and the Last, the Beginning and the End.

^{14}"Blessed are those who wash their robes, that they may have the right to the tree of life and may go through the gates into the city. ^{15}Outside are the dogs, those who practice magic arts, the sexually immoral, the murderers, the idolaters and everyone who loves and practices falsehood.

^{16}"I, Jesus, have sent my angel to give you^h this testimony for the churches. I am the Root and the Offspring of David, and the bright Morning Star."

^{17}The Spirit and the bride say, "Come!" And let him who hears say, "Come!" Whoever is thirsty, let him come; and whoever wishes, let him take the free gift of the water of life.

^{18}I warn everyone who hears the words of the prophecy of this book: If anyone adds anything to them, God will add to him the plagues described in this book. ^{19}And if anyone takes words away from this book of prophecy, God will take away from him his share in the tree of life and in the holy city, which are described in this book.

^{20}He who testifies to these things says, "Yes, I am coming soon."

Amen. Come, Lord Jesus.

^{21}The grace of the Lord Jesus be with God's people. Amen.

---

g 20 The precise identification of some of these precious stones is uncertain. h 16 The Greek is plural.